THE OXFORD TEXTBOOK ON CRIMINOLOGY

THE OXFORD TEXTBOOK ON CRIMINOLOGY

SECOND EDITION

CASE • JOHNSON • MANLOW • SMITH • WILLIAMS

Chapters 7 and 12 contributed by **Angus Nurse**

Chapter 8 contributed by **Angus Nurse** and **Mark Walters**

Chapter 10 contributed by **Neena Samota**

Chapter 11 contributed by **Pamela Ugwudike**

Chapters 13 and 14 contributed by **Sacha Darke**

Great Clarendon Street, Oxford, OX2 6DP,
United Kingdom

Oxford University Press is a department of the University of Oxford.
It furthers the University's objective of excellence in research, scholarship,
and education by publishing worldwide. Oxford is a registered trade mark of
Oxford University Press in the UK and in certain other countries

© Oxford University Press 2021

The moral rights of the authors have been asserted

First Edition 2017

Impression: 1

All rights reserved. No part of this publication may be reproduced, stored in
a retrieval system, or transmitted, in any form or by any means, without the
prior permission in writing of Oxford University Press, or as expressly permitted
by law, by licence or under terms agreed with the appropriate reprographics
rights organization. Enquiries concerning reproduction outside the scope of the
above should be sent to the Rights Department, Oxford University Press, at the
address above

You must not circulate this work in any other form
and you must impose this same condition on any acquirer

Public sector information reproduced under Open Government Licence v3.0
(http://www.nationalarchives.gov.uk/doc/open-government-licence/open-government-licence.htm)

Published in the United States of America by Oxford University Press
198 Madison Avenue, New York, NY 10016, United States of America

British Library Cataloguing in Publication Data

Data available

Library of Congress Control Number: 2021930844

ISBN 978-0-19-883583-7

Printed in Great Britain by
Bell & Bain Ltd., Glasgow

Links to third party websites are provided by Oxford in good faith and
for information only. Oxford disclaims any responsibility for the materials
contained in any third party website referenced in this work.

BRIEF TABLE OF CONTENTS

PART 1
JOURNEYING INTO CRIMINOLOGY — 3
1. Studying criminology — 5

PART 2
EXPLORING CRIME — 25
2. What is 'crime'? — 27
3. What is 'justice'? — 55
4. How criminology produces knowledge — 95
5. Crime statistics — 123
6. Crime and the media — 147
7. Victimology — 187
8. Hate crime — 211
9. Youth offending and youth justice — 237
10. Race, ethnicities, and the criminal justice system — 273
11. Gender and feminist criminology — 309
12. Green criminology — 345
13. Global criminology 1: Comparative criminology — 375
14. Global criminology 2: Transnational criminology — 409

PART 3
EXPLAINING CRIME — 441
15. Free will, classicism, and rational choice — 443
16. Biological and psychological positivism — 475
17. Sociological positivism — 515
18. Critical criminology — 561
19. Social harm — 591
20. Right and left realism — 619
21. Integrated theories of crime — 647
22. Searching for the causes of crime — 669

PART 4
RESPONDING TO CRIME — 691
23. Criminal justice principles — 693
24. Criminal justice institutions — 719
25. Criminal justice policies and practices — 743
26. Crime prevention — 769
27. Crime control — 803
28. Punishment — 837
29. Rehabilitation of offenders — 863
30. Alternatives to punishment — 895
31. Critical perspectives on punishment — 929

PART 5
RESEARCH AND CAREERS IN CRIMINOLOGY — 957
32. Conducting criminological research — 959
33. Employability and careers — 1001

DETAILED TABLE OF CONTENTS

Preface	x
New to this edition	xi
Acknowledgements	xii
About the authors	xiii
Guide to using this textbook	xiv
Resources for lecturers	xvii

PART 1
JOURNEYING INTO CRIMINOLOGY — 3

1. Studying criminology — 5
- 1.1 Introduction — 6
- 1.2 What is criminology? — 6
- 1.3 Studying criminology — 10
- 1.4 Getting the most from your studies — 17
- 1.5 Conclusion — 22

PART 2
EXPLORING CRIME — 25

2. What is 'crime'? — 27
- 2.1 Introduction — 28
- 2.2 Crime as a social construct — 28
- 2.3 Crime and deviance — 32
- 2.4 Defining 'crime': the harm principle — 36
- 2.5 Other ways to decide whether an action should be a crime — 44
- 2.6 Do we need the criminal law? — 48
- 2.7 Conclusion — 50

3. What is 'justice'? — 55
- 3.1 Introduction — 56
- 3.2 Defining justice — 56
- 3.3 Criminal justice models — 64
- 3.4 Philosophical ideas of justice — 74
- 3.5 Systems of criminal justice — 83
- 3.6 Drawing ideas together — 87
- 3.7 Conclusion — 90

4. How criminology produces knowledge — 95
- 4.1 Introduction — 96
- 4.2 Producing criminological knowledge — 97
- 4.3 The evolution of criminological theories — 99
- 4.4 Subjectivity — 100
- 4.5 Supposition — 105
- 4.6 Study — 107
- 4.7 Conclusion — 119

5. Crime statistics — 123
- 5.1 Introduction — 124
- 5.2 How to approach crime statistics — 124
- 5.3 The development of national crime statistics — 127
- 5.4 Police recorded crime statistics — 130
- 5.5 The Crime Survey for England and Wales — 136
- 5.6 Conclusion — 142

6. Crime and the media — 147
- 6.1 Introduction — 148
- 6.2 Criminological studies of the media — 149
- 6.3 Media representation of crime — 153
- 6.4 Media effects on crime — 173
- 6.5 Conclusion — 180

7. Victimology — 187
- 7.1 Introduction — 188
- 7.2 Defining victims — 188
- 7.3 Theories, concepts, and debates in victimology — 192
- 7.4 Measuring victimisation — 198
- 7.5 Victims and the criminal justice process — 205
- 7.6 Conclusion — 206

8. Hate crime — 211
- 8.1 Introduction — 212
- 8.2 Understanding hate crime — 212
- 8.3 Disablist hate crime — 219
- 8.4 LGBT+ hate crime — 223
- 8.5 Racially motivated hate crime — 226
- 8.6 Religiously motivated hate crime — 229
- 8.7 Conclusion — 231

9.	**Youth offending and youth justice**	**237**
9.1	Introduction	238
9.2	What do we mean by 'childhood'?	238
9.3	Individualised explanations for youth offending	244
9.4	Contextual explanations for youth offending	250
9.5	Mainstream responses to youth offending	259
9.6	Progressive approaches to youth offending	264
9.7	Conclusion	267
10.	**Race, ethnicities, and the criminal justice system**	**273**
10.1	Introduction	274
10.2	Understanding racial inequality in the UK	275
10.3	How do we 'know' about race, ethnicity, and crime?	279
10.4	Victimisation, offending, and ethnicity	281
10.5	Race, ethnicity, and the criminal justice system	284
10.6	Addressing racial inequality in crime and the criminal justice system	294
10.7	Theorising race, ethnicities, and the CJS: critical race theory	299
10.8	Conclusion	304
11.	**Gender and feminist criminology**	**309**
11.1	Introduction	310
11.2	Gender and criminology: an overview	310
11.3	Feminist criminology	324
11.4	Theoretical traditions of feminist criminology	327
11.5	Feminist epistemologies	334
11.6	Newer perspectives in feminist criminology	337
11.7	Conclusion	340
12.	**Green criminology**	**345**
12.1	Introduction	346
12.2	What is green criminology?	346
12.3	Green criminology and the 'market society'	352
12.4	Key concepts in green criminology	357
12.5	Green crimes or green harms?	362
12.6	Policing green crimes	366
12.7	Conclusion	370
13.	**Global criminology 1: Comparative criminology**	**375**
13.1	Introduction	376
13.2	Globalisation, crime, and justice	376
13.3	Comparative criminology	381
13.4	Global convergences: the positivist approach	384
13.5	Global divergences: the interpretivist approach	393
13.6	Conclusion	403
14.	**Global criminology 2: Transnational criminology**	**409**
14.1	Introduction	410
14.2	What is transnational criminology?	411
14.3	Key areas of concern for transnational criminology	419
14.4	Critical issues in transnational criminology	435
14.5	Conclusion	437

PART 3
EXPLAINING CRIME 441

15.	**Free will, classicism, and rational choice**	**443**
15.1	Introduction	444
15.2	Understanding theory	444
15.3	Criminological theory	451
15.4	Classical criminology	453
15.5	Conclusion	469
16.	**Biological and psychological positivism**	**475**
16.1	Introduction	476
16.2	Positivism and positivist criminology	476
16.3	Causation and correlation	477
16.4	Positivism, punishment, and rehabilitation	478
16.5	Early positivism	480
16.6	Biological theories	485
16.7	Psychological theories	494
16.8	Learning theories	500
16.9	Conclusion	509
17.	**Sociological positivism**	**515**
17.1	Introduction	516
17.2	Sociological theories	517
17.3	Key concepts in sociology	518
17.4	Social process/interaction theories	523
17.5	Social structural theories: social strain and social disorganisation theories	527
17.6	Social structural theories: culture and subcultural theories	539
17.7	Conclusion	555
18.	**Critical criminology**	**561**
18.1	Introduction	562
18.2	What is critical about critical criminology?	563
18.3	Social construction and power	564
18.4	Labelling perspectives	566
18.5	Marxist-inspired critical theories	572
18.6	Examples of the diversity of critical criminological theories	576
18.7	Conclusion	586

19. Social harm — 591
- 19.1 Introduction — 592
- 19.2 What is social harm? — 592
- 19.3 How social harm theorists critique criminology — 595
- 19.4 How the social harm approach works — 602
- 19.5 The production and reduction of social harm — 609
- 19.6 Critique of the social harm approach — 612
- 19.7 Conclusion — 614

20. Right and left realism — 619
- 20.1 Introduction — 620
- 20.2 The rise of realism in context — 620
- 20.3 Right realism: key ideas — 623
- 20.4 Right realism: policy implications — 624
- 20.5 Evaluating right realism — 630
- 20.6 Left realism: key ideas — 631
- 20.7 Left realism: policy implications — 634
- 20.8 Evaluating left realism — 637
- 20.9 Beyond 'left' and 'right' realism? — 639
- 20.10 Conclusion — 642

21. Integrated theories of crime — 647
- 21.1 Introduction — 648
- 21.2 Integrated theories in context — 648
- 21.3 Integrated positivist theories — 650
- 21.4 Integrated risk factor theories — 655
- 21.5 Conclusion — 664

22. Searching for the causes of crime — 669
- 22.1 Introduction — 670
- 22.2 Thinking about and defining causes of crime — 671
- 22.3 Exploring the causes of crime in research — 674
- 22.4 Explaining crime by identifying causes — 679
- 22.5 Responding to crime — 680
- 22.6 Chaos theory — 686
- 22.7 Conclusion — 687

PART 4
RESPONDING TO CRIME — 691

23. Criminal justice principles — 693
- 23.1 Introduction — 694
- 23.2 The rule of law: an overview — 695
- 23.3 The rule of law: an independent judiciary — 697
- 23.4 The rule of law: due process — 701
- 23.5 The rule of law: human rights — 707
- 23.6 Adversarial justice — 710
- 23.7 Restorative justice — 713
- 23.8 Conclusion — 715

24. Criminal justice institutions — 719
- 24.1 Introduction — 720
- 24.2 The police — 720
- 24.3 The Crown Prosecution Service — 724
- 24.4 The courts — 729
- 24.5 Probation services and community sanctions — 732
- 24.6 Prisons — 735
- 24.7 Conclusion — 739

25. Criminal justice policies and practices — 743
- 25.1 Introduction — 744
- 25.2 Criminal justice policies — 744
- 25.3 Criminal justice practices — 754
- 25.4 People in criminal justice — 761
- 25.5 Conclusion — 763

26. Crime prevention — 769
- 26.1 Introduction — 770
- 26.2 What is crime prevention? — 770
- 26.3 Perspectives on crime prevention — 776
- 26.4 Frameworks for policy and practice — 779
- 26.5 Implementing crime prevention measures — 790
- 26.6 What does prevention achieve? — 792
- 26.7 Consequences of crime prevention — 794
- 26.8 Reviewing the limitations of crime prevention — 797
- 26.9 Conclusion — 799

27. Crime control — 803
- 27.1 Introduction — 804
- 27.2 What is crime control? — 804
- 27.3 Objectives of crime control — 808
- 27.4 The role of the police in crime control — 811
- 27.5 The role of other agencies and interests in crime control — 816
- 27.6 The objects and technologies of crime control — 820
- 27.7 What does crime control achieve? — 822
- 27.8 Does crime control 'work'? — 828
- 27.9 The limitations of crime control — 831
- 27.10 Conclusion — 833

28. Punishment — 837
- 28.1 Introduction — 838
- 28.2 What is punishment? — 838
- 28.3 What is punishment intended to achieve? — 840
- 28.4 How punishments are imposed — 844
- 28.5 The objects of punishment — 849
- 28.6 Punishment: policies, practices, and consequences — 852

28.7	What are the effects of punishment?	855
28.8	Punishment, justice, and the public	858
28.9	Conclusion	859

29. Rehabilitation of offenders — 863

29.1	Introduction	864
29.2	What is rehabilitation?	864
29.3	What is rehabilitation for?	867
29.4	How has rehabilitation developed?	870
29.5	The objects of rehabilitation	873
29.6	Models and practices in the delivery of rehabilitative services	876
29.7	How do we judge whether rehabilitation is successful?	880
29.8	What is the impact of rehabilitation?	884
29.9	The limitations of rehabilitation	886
29.10	Conclusion	891

30. Alternatives to punishment — 895

30.1	Introduction	896
30.2	Alternative responses to crime: an overview	896
30.3	Restorative justice and diversion	901
30.4	Delivering alternatives to punishment	906
30.5	The meaning and impact of alternatives to punishment	917
30.6	Conclusion	925

31. Critical perspectives on punishment — 929

31.1	Introduction	930
31.2	What are critical perspectives on punishment?	930
31.3	Unjust punishment	933
31.4	Social control theory, punishment, and legitimacy	936
31.5	Crimes of the privileged and powerful	938
31.6	What is to be done about crime?	942
31.7	Limitations of critical perspectives on punishment	951
31.8	Conclusion	954

PART 5
RESEARCH AND CAREERS IN CRIMINOLOGY — 957

32. Conducting criminological research — 959

32.1	Introduction	960
32.2	Why research?	960
32.3	What makes a good student research project?	962
32.4	Choosing your research topic	965
32.5	Reviewing academic literature	969
32.6	Choosing your research strategy	971
32.7	Collecting data	975
32.8	Analysing data	977
32.9	Writing up your research	980
32.10	Planning your research project	987
32.11	Ethics and legality in research	989
32.12	Conclusion	996

33. Employability and careers — 1001

33.1	Introduction	1002
33.2	Reflective learning and employability	1002
33.3	What employers are looking for	1004
33.4	How to boost your employability	1007
33.5	Producing your 'RARE' employability framework	1010
33.6	Can people 'HEAR' your successes?	1011
33.7	Journeying into careers	1011
33.8	Criminology-related careers	1013
33.9	'Joining the DOTS' in your career plans	1019
33.10	Conclusion	1020

Glossary	1023
Bibliography	1037
Index	1083

PREFACE

Developed in close partnership with lecturers and students across the UK, *The Oxford Textbook on Criminology* aims to be the most stimulating, critical, and applied textbook available in this subject area.

The book has been written for undergraduate criminology students with the intention of encouraging student engagement, facilitating effective study, and exploring the use of criminology in the real world. Our approach is informed by broad experience of undergraduate teaching, curriculum design, student engagement, and applied criminological research.

The overarching goal is to provide the foundational knowledge and a powerful framework for engaging with criminology as an academic subject and as an applied field of research, policy, practice, and employment. As such, we speak directly to the reader throughout, with the aim of challenging and motivating them to be an active participant in their own learning journey. This aim is reflected in the book's five-part structure: journeying into criminology; exploring crime; explaining crime; responding to crime; and research and careers in criminology.

Every chapter's core discussion is complemented by a series of carefully developed pedagogical features and digital resources (please see the 'Guide to using this textbook' for further details) that are designed to promote and enable close, critical student engagement with topics and debates.

This book is intended to support readers through the whole undergraduate degree, providing the grounding and springboard for further reading. We hope that it will help readers become active criminologists who carry their knowledge, enthusiasm, and newly honed skills through their studies and into practice, research, policy, and/or other employment.

Steve Case
Phil Johnson
David Manlow
Roger Smith
Kate Williams

NEW TO THIS EDITION

- Thoroughly updated to provide full coverage of today's most pressing criminological issues. The text includes new chapters on global criminology (covering issues such as organised crime, cybercrime, human trafficking, and terrorism, and highlighting the importance of perspectives from the Global South), social harm, and green criminology. Other content has been expanded, including that on victimology, hate crime, and the workings of the criminal justice system.
- The text includes discussion of the impact of the Covid-19 pandemic on society, crime, and justice, as well as fuller coverage of issues of racial inequality in society and the criminal justice system. At numerous points throughout the book, the reader is encouraged to reflect on the short- and longer-term implications of both the pandemic and the Black Lives Matter movement.
- The introductory and concluding parts have been streamlined to provide even more practical, focused coverage of beginning criminological studies and applying criminological knowledge to research, careers, and further study.
- In addition to being thoroughly updated to reflect the latest developments, every chapter's content has been refined to ensure that explanations, pedagogical features, and chapter structures are as clear and effective as possible.
- Brand new boxed features throughout include additional 'Conversations' with a wide range of people connected to criminology, crime, and the criminal justice system, including lecturers, students, NGOs, lawyers, victims, former convicts, campaigners, and both leaders and participants of the graduate schemes offered by key criminal justice institutions.
- The updated and expanded online resources include additional multiple-choice questions and notes on answers to end-of-chapter questions for students, plus teaching packs which provide ideas for group activities and help lecturers to make use of the book's content in class. The second edition is also available as an e-book enhanced with self-assessment activities and multi-media content to offer a fully immersive experience and extra learning support.

ACKNOWLEDGEMENTS

The idea for an engaging, accessible, and student-friendly textbook came from our interactions with students over many years, so it is to these honest, forthright, and dedicated criminologists that we offer our thanks for raising the issues that brought our book to fruition.

We are grateful to Angus Nurse, Mark Walters, Neena Samota, Pamela Ugwudike, and Sacha Darke for contributing valuable chapters to the book. Further thanks must go to Anita Lavorgna for her assistance with the cybercrime material within Chapter 14, and to our diligent body of expert reviewers, both lecturers and students, whose invaluable feedback has significantly enhanced the accessibility, quality, and scope of the work. We offer these reviewers our profound appreciation for giving up their time and energies to comment on the material, for constantly motivating us to improve, and for giving us confidence that our book is worthwhile.

We also owe a huge debt of gratitude to the talented staff at Oxford University Press. Without their expertise, support, and boundless enthusiasm, our project may have drifted aimlessly onto the rocks. However, they never lost faith, never stopped pushing, and never ceased encouraging. Particular thanks must go to our editorial team of Livy Watson and Helen Swann (for this second edition) and Nicola Hartley and Tom Young (for the first edition)—a nicer, more professional and talented group of editors you could not hope to be given.

Steve would like to personally thank Livy, Helen, Nicola and Tom for their ceaseless support in this exciting endeavour. Steve would also like to thank Professor Kevin Haines, who has always been a great mentor and friend.

Phil would like to particularly thank Belinda Child for all her assistance and support throughout his career—her constant advice and encouragement has inspired many of his new approaches to teaching and learning in higher education. Phil would also like to thank his UCBC colleagues Ian Ashworth, Gillian Dickinson, Dr Tass Hussain, and Mark Thistlethwaite for being major sources of help and expertise.

David would like to thank his many academic friends and colleagues, particularly those who contributed such excellent pieces for the feature boxes in his chapters. He would like to extend special thanks to Anita Hobson, Mick Fleming, Maggie Sumner, and Jax Freedman for their support and encouragement, and particularly to Zoe: without her unhealthy knowledge of crime fiction and storehouse of obscure facts, his chapters for this book would undoubtedly have been shorter and duller.

Roger would like to add his thanks to Nigel Hinks, Mike Payne, and all the other unsung heroes who have continued to try and ensure that criminal justice has a human face.

Kate would like to thank LJ, ME, AJ, SH, and DJ (they know who they are). Importantly, she also wants to thank all her students both for their interest and the questions they ask, each of which has helped to shape this work.

Steve Case
Phil Johnson
David Manlow
Roger Smith
Kate Williams

The publishers would like to acknowledge everybody who kindly granted us permission to reproduce images, figures, and quotations throughout this text. Every effort was made to trace copyright holders, but we would be pleased to make suitable arrangements to clear permission for material reproduced in this book with any copyright holders whom it has not been possible to contact.

ABOUT THE AUTHORS

Professor Steve Case

I am a Professor of Criminology and Director of Studies in the Department of Social Sciences at Loughborough University, teaching modules on research methods and youth justice (this is the focus of my research and writing—good teaching is informed by research). In 2012, I led the team at Swansea University that won the British Society of Criminology's National Award for Excellence in Teaching Criminology for designing an undergraduate criminology degree programme that really engaged with students, linking its different elements together logically and effectively. I have conducted large-scale funded research projects for the Home Office, the Youth Justice Board, the National Institute for Health and Social Care, and the Welsh Government.

Dr Phil Johnson

I am the Academic Subject Leader for Criminology at the University Centre at Blackburn College and my main teaching and research interests are criminal justice, visual criminology, and employability. In 2014 I was appointed Senior Fellow of the Higher Education Academy in recognition of my work embedding both alternative approaches to employability and visual assessment methods into a range of undergraduate courses in the social sciences. I gained my PhD in Applied Social Science (Lancaster) in 2009 and have continued to research various aspects of community sentencing, policy, and practice.

David Manlow

I am Principal Lecturer in Criminology at the University of Westminster in London, where I also lead the BA Criminology programme. My main teaching and research interests are in the fields of youth justice, crime in the media, and critical criminological theory. I am currently researching the portrayal of crime in post-war British film and television, together with work on developing new forms of accessible and diverse pedagogy for undergraduate students. In 2016, I was proud to be the first individual to be awarded the British Society of Criminology's National Award for Excellence in Teaching Criminology.

Professor Roger Smith

I began my career in the probation service, and went on to work in an important diversion project with young offenders in Northamptonshire in the 1980s. After that, I worked for The Children's Society as Head of Policy, where I held a brief for promoting children's rights and challenging inequality. My horizontal career continued with a move into academia in 2000: I am currently Professor of Social Work at Durham University, where I teach, write, and research extensively at the interface between social work and youth justice. I have a particular interest in participatory research methods and I am still committed to children's rights.

Professor Kate Williams

I am both a Professor of Criminology at the University of South Wales and Director of the Welsh Centre for Crime and Social Justice. My teaching is informed by research which keeps it fresh, interesting, and relevant, and I enjoy students' questions which often push me to think of things in different ways. Much of my recent research involves the treatment of women and young people who offend, consideration of the work of the voluntary sector in re-settlement of offenders, and is always linked to human rights and social justice. I sit on the Youth Justice Board (YJB) Academic Advisory Panel, the YJB Cymru's Practice Development Panel (Hwb Doeth), and have advised the Welsh and Westminster Governments on various subjects. I have conducted large-scale research projects funded by the Home Office, Ministry of Justice, Welsh Government, Leverhulme, and Government Research Councils.

GUIDE TO USING THIS TEXTBOOK

The Oxford Textbook on Criminology provides a rich learning experience in which the subject is brought to life and set in a real world context, and in which readers are guided and supported to become active, critical thinkers. Outlined here are the key features and resources included in the book and its **online resources** to ensure that you not only understand each topic but also can apply, interrogate, and build on this knowledge.

www.oup.com/uk/case2e

Understand and contextualize the topic at hand

Key issues listed at the start of each chapter outline the themes to be covered and the skills you will develop. They reappear at the end of each chapter as a **Summary**, accompanied by notes on the important ideas in relation to each issue. Chapter **Introductions** set each topic into the context of criminology as a discipline, as well as into a wider societal context, helping you appreciate their practical relevance.

Apply theory to practice through real-world experiences and examples

Academic concepts and theories are set into a practical, real-world context throughout the text. **Conversations** boxes bring in the voices of a wide range of people connected to criminology and criminal justice (including ex-convicts, victims, criminal justice system practitioners, researchers, students, and graduate employers), and **Controversy and debate** boxes describe real world examples that have divided opinion.

Reflect and critique to take an active role in your studies

The importance of adopting an ABC ('Always Be Critical') mindset is explained in Chapter 1 and reinforced throughout the text, most notably through **What do you think?** boxes. These features use questions and hypothetical scenarios to help you interrogate criminological knowledge, uncover and challenge assumptions (both yours and other people's), and develop your own views on the issues.

Extend your exploration through independent reading and research

New frontiers boxes outline new and emerging developments; the **Conclusion** to each chapter reflects on the salient issues for the topic, and its likely future directions; and annotated **Further reading** lists recommend key on- and offline sources for each topic. Together, these features provide numerous ideas and starting points for additional reading and independent research.

Test and revise your knowledge of key terms and concepts

Over 330 **self-test questions** online provide instant feedback to help you check your understanding of each section. These are supplemented by end-of-chapter **review questions**, for which answer guidance is provided online. Throughout the text, **glossary terms** are emboldened with colour, allowing you to test your recall of key criminological words and phrases using the glossary at the end of the book.

Enhance your studies with additional resources

Checklists, templates, and resources on making sense of academic writing, principles of research ethics, and assessing your employability are available online, together with **additional chapters** on the criminal justice systems of Wales, Scotland, and Northern Ireland.

RESOURCES FOR LECTURERS

The Oxford Textbook on Criminology offers a complete package of information and resources to support your undergraduate teaching of this subject. It is packed with real-world examples and reflective, interactive activities that will engage and inspire your students, as well as thought-provoking questions and extensive further reading suggestions to challenge and stretch them.

Adopting lecturers can visit the book's **online resources** to access:

- A teaching pack for each chapter, featuring advice on how to use the book's content in lectures, seminars, and tutorials and links to additional useful resources such as freely available video content
- A customisable PowerPoint presentation for each chapter
- Downloadable versions of every figure included in the book, for use in your teaching
- A bank of exam and essay questions for use in, or as starting points for, your assessments

www.oup.com/uk/case2e

PART OUTLINE

1. Studying criminology

In this opening part of the book we introduce you to the journey that is studying criminology at university. We have kept this part brief and focused so that you can move quickly on to the 'meat' of the subject, but we urge you to take the time to read its single, concise chapter (**Chapter 1**) as it will help you get the most out of your studies. In the chapter we look at the nature of criminology as an academic subject; how you will be expected to study it; and the resources you will need to call on and skills you will need to develop in order to become an effective, engaged, and employable student of criminology. We present the route to becoming this kind of student as a reflective journey that you should embark upon in an informed, active, and critical way.

In this part we introduce the idea of the 'triad of criminology'; a way of understanding how criminology fits together and the framework around which we have structured this book. The three elements of the triad are exploring and *defining* crime (**Part 2**), *explaining* criminal behaviour (**Part 3**), and *responding* to crime and criminal behaviour (**Part 4**). In the final part, **Part 5**, we revisit Part 1 as we look at how you can employ the skills, knowledge, and understanding you gain in order to become a researcher and producer of criminological knowledge (**Chapter 32**) and to succeed in your chosen career (**Chapter 33**).

PART 1

JOURNEYING INTO CRIMINOLOGY

CHAPTER OUTLINE

1.1	Introduction	6
1.2	What is criminology?	6
1.3	Studying criminology	10
1.4	Getting the most from your studies	17
1.5	Conclusion	22

1

Studying criminology

KEY ISSUES

After reading this chapter, you should be able to:

- appreciate what criminology looks like as an academic subject;
- begin to cultivate the mindset and skills that will ensure you make the most of your studies in criminology.

1.1 Introduction

Welcome to criminology, the academic subject. This is your first step on a personal and educational journey that will hopefully continue long after you graduate. Whatever your current level of criminological studies and whatever your current life stage (for example, fresh out of school, a mature student returning to education), we hope that you will consider this book your guide and a key companion to help you to find your way through the complexities of studying criminology.

The 'journey' metaphor can be overused in education and culture more widely, but we think it is the most accurate depiction of criminological study—that is, a continuous process of learning and exploration. Even seasoned academics are still on this journey, continually reassessing the way they move through and work within criminology in response to new information and understandings. We have therefore grouped the chapters of this book into parts which reflect what we see as the main stages of the criminological journey, and which are shown diagrammatically in **Figure 1.1**: preparation and 'reconnaissance' (fact-finding), represented by this chapter; proactively defining and *exploring* crime (**Part 2**); attempting to *explain* crime (**Part 3**); considering how we could *respond* to crime (**Part 4**); and conducting *research* to gather more information about crime (**Part 5**), which brings us back to the first exploration stage again—remember that there is no final destination in criminological learning.

Doing some preparation for a big journey makes it all the more fulfilling and enjoyable, so we recommend that before you leap straight into exploring crime, you take some time to read this short chapter. It will give you a sense of the route and ground to be covered in your learning journey, the skills and mindset you'll need, what you are aiming to

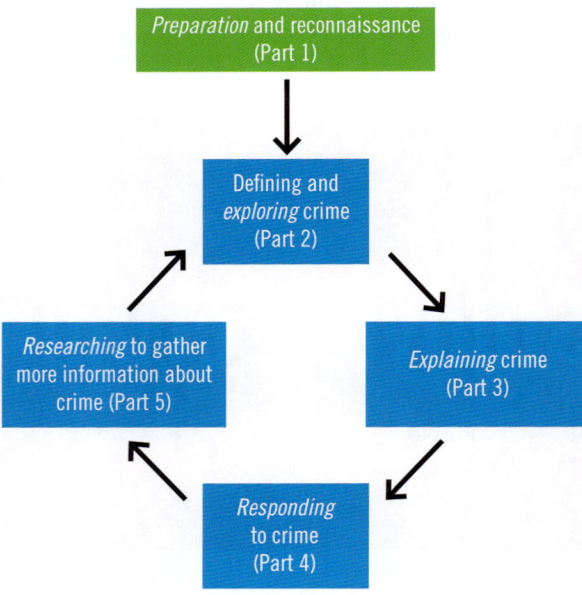

Figure 1.1 The stages of the criminological journey to understanding 'crime'

achieve (and how this textbook can facilitate these goals), and will make sure that you are fully aware of the people and resources you can call on for help, and to enhance your university experience. We have written this chapter so that it is useful to all our readers, whether new students or midway through their studies, so if you are new to higher education we would strongly suggest that you first read any information and guidance about university life and how it differs from school that your course leader has supplied.

1.2 What is criminology?

In this section, we examine what the academic subject of criminology actually is. We discuss the idea that it is the scientific study of crime, and what this means in terms of its aims and focuses, and the idea that it is an interdisciplinary meeting point, shaped by both academic and non-academic influences. See **What do you think? 1.1**.

WHAT DO YOU THINK? 1.1

What is criminology?

It will help you begin or continue in your studies with a clear sense of purpose if you give careful consideration to the following important questions:

- Why do/did you want to study criminology?
- What do/did you expect your studies to look like?
- What do you hope to gain from them?
- What do you expect yourself to look like as a learner, a potential employee, and an individual at the end of your studies?

You might like to write down your responses to these questions in a notebook or save them in a Word document so that you can refer back to them during and at the end of your degree.

The scientific study of crime

Criminology is the scientific study of crime. This apparently simple statement, however, is complex and contested, much like criminology itself. Indeed, you could spend hours scouring criminology textbooks without finding an agreed or unproblematic definition of 'criminology'. Using our definition, for example, it depends on what is meant by 'scientific', what is meant by 'study', and in particular what is meant by 'crime'. This use of inverted commas indicates that, as is common in criminology, concepts are ambiguous (can have different meanings) and debatable, so please bear this in mind as we move forward. Understanding the meaning of crime is central to criminology and is a debate that is specifically discussed in **Chapter 2**, but one with which we will engage throughout this book. Criminology is an academic subject in that it produces knowledge and understanding through:

- **teaching and learning**—typically in educational institutions;
- **scholarship**—experts writing and arguing about the subject;
- **research**—for example, observation, testing, asking, analysing;
- **debate**—for example, the presentation, comparison, and contrast of reasoned and supported arguments;
- **critique**—for example, the structured analysis and evaluation of academic scholarship, research, debate, and non-academic arguments, such as those presented by politicians, policymakers, and, especially, the media.

'Criminologists' are generally considered to be the lecturers, scholars, and researchers who create and impart criminological knowledge and understanding to inform the development of academic theories and arguments, and also of policies and practice relating to crime and people who come into conflict with the law (such as offenders, victims, families). Students of criminology are rarely considered criminologists in this sense, but they could be and they should be. From the moment you begin to study criminology, you should consider yourself a criminologist.

The study of criminology can be divided into the three interconnected areas that form the three core parts of this book and that each contribute to our understanding and knowledge of crime: defining and exploring crime, explaining crime, and responding to crime.

Defining crime

Defining crime includes exploring, describing, and debating issues such as:

- what crime is, and who decides what is considered crime;
- how much crime is committed, recorded, or reported (the extent of crime);
- which different types of crime are committed, recorded, or reported (the nature of crime), being aware that some crime is not noticed or recorded in reports and statistics (so-called 'dark figure' crime, discussed in **Chapter 5**);
- who commits crime and is labelled as an offender (such as what is the age of criminal responsibility and the official difference between a young and adult offender? See also **Chapter 9**);
- when and where crime is committed, recorded, or reported
- how the criminal law is enforced (for instance, the extent and nature of activity in the criminal justice system—arrest, sentencing, and punishment)

Defining and exploring crime is often closely linked to discussions of what (criminal) justice is (discussed in **Chapter 3**) and what methods are used to better understand crime and justice.

We cover these issues in **Part 2** of the book.

Explaining crime

We *explain* crime by producing theories and arguments about what predicts, affects (increases or reduces), and prevents crime and associated behaviours (for example, antisocial behaviour, substance use, social harm) of different types by different groups and individuals in different places at different times. As with defining crime, explanations incorporate the study of who is doing the explaining, an evaluation of the methods they employ to arrive at their explanations, and discussions of the historical and ongoing debates between different explanations and theorists.

We cover these issues in **Part 3** of the book on explaining crime.

Responding to crime

Responding to crime involves discussing how we respond to and should respond to crime and those who commit crime through policies (courses of action) and practices. Included in these are lawmaking, law enforcement, criminal justice measures (for example, sentencing and punishment), restorative justice, surveillance, control, treatment, rehabilitation, intervention, crime reduction and crime prevention programmes, service provision, relationship building, study, and research. There is often a focus on key criminal justice stakeholder organisations and staff, such as police, courts, prison, probation, and victim services. We cover these issues in detail in **Part 4** of the book in relation to responding to crime.

The triad of criminology

We can depict these three elements as not only a journey which leads on to research, but also as a *triad of criminology* (see **Figure 1.2**). You can see from the two-way arrows in **Figure 1.2** that the three concepts in the triad of criminology are interrelated. They are what criminologists might call reciprocal, in that they are mutually dependent and mutually reinforcing.

To take an example, how we define crime (in a particular country or culture at a given point in history) shapes and influences how we try to explain it, because the definition determines what type of behaviour or concept we are trying to explain as 'crime'. Consequently, how we explain crime determines or influences how we choose to respond to it (or at least should) because how we choose to understand the behaviour or concept of crime shapes our views of how it should be addressed—if we explain certain crimes as having been caused or provoked by injustice in society, this might affect whether, or how severely, we want to punish those who commit them. This alignment can work the other way around too. How we explain crime can influence how we choose to define it and redefine it in the future based on our new understandings, information and evidence, technological advances, social changes, and so on. How we respond to crime may also bring us new evidence and insights that affect our subsequent explanations and definitions of crime as a behaviour or concept.

Although these three elements *can* all influence one another through the new knowledge and understandings that they create, whether they always *do* influence each other in reality is debatable as there are so many other influences on criminological knowledge construction. Definitions of, explanation of, and responses to crime are dynamic or *socially constructed* concepts—the constantly changing and evolving products of human understandings (Williams, 2012). These understandings are the creations of criminologists and others and consistently change what we view as crime. The social construction of crime is a theme that runs throughout this book.

An interdisciplinary meeting point

Criminology is often seen as a 'social science' because it uses scientific methods (that is, similar to those used in the natural sciences of physics, chemistry, and biology) and quasi (approximating) scientific methods, particularly **empirical** research (see **Chapter 4**), to create knowledge and progress understanding relating to crime as an individual and social issue. David Downes called criminology 'a rendezvous subject' (2008, in Millie, 2016) as it is a point at which several other subjects meet and overlap, and the discipline is shaped by both academic and non-academic influences.

Academic influences

Criminology is a hybrid (interdisciplinary) academic subject in that it has developed by adopting, adapting, and applying (using real-life situations; see, for example, **Figure 1.4**) ideas and approaches from other academic subjects, many of which are hybrid in nature themselves. As illustrated in **Figure 1.3** (see also Young, 2003), these include:

- **sociology**—the study of the behaviour of human beings, organisations, and institutions in social settings (such as the study of crime and deviance);
- **psychology**—the study of the mind and individual human behaviour (such as the influence of psychological characteristics and illness on criminal behaviour);

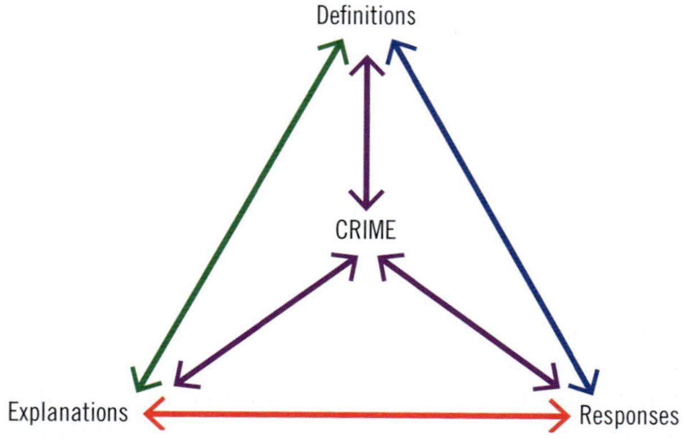

Figure 1.2 The triad of criminology

Figure 1.3 The interrelationships between criminology and other subject areas

 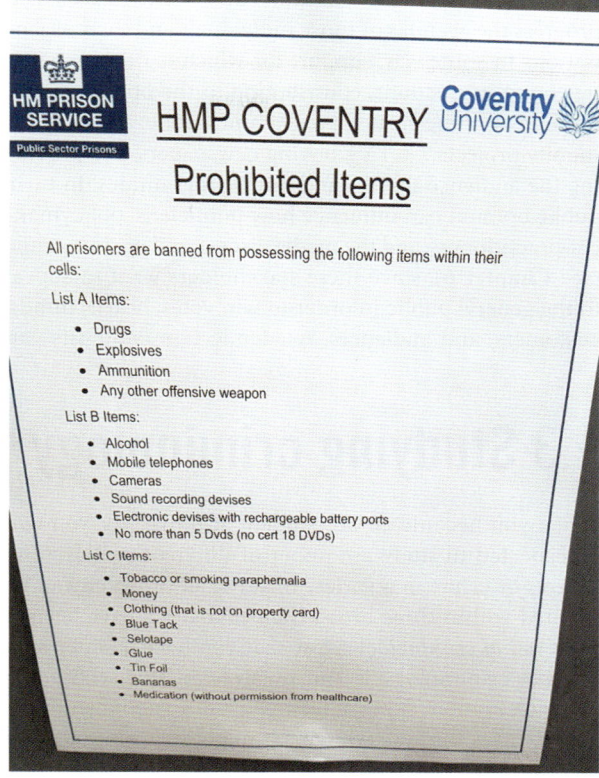

Figure 1.4 Coventry University uses mock prison cells as part of its criminology teaching, to help students better understand the lived experiences of prisoners
Source: Photos by Oxford University Press, 2018

- **law**—the study of lawmaking, legal systems, and legal processes and practices (such as the criminal justice process);
- **social policy**—the study of human well-being and needs, problems (such as poverty), and the political/governmental responses to them (such as the role of welfare systems and services in responding to crime);
- **anthropology**—the study of human beings, societies, and cultures in the past and present (such as how the law, criminal definitions, and legal systems have developed).

Criminology's interrelationships with other more humanities-orientated subjects have also been noted, for example by Millie (2016). These include politics, history, philosophy, international relations, cultural studies, and human geography.

As a consequence of the hybrid nature of our subject, criminologists are interested in the sociological, psychological, legal, policy, and anthropological influences on defining, explaining, and responding to crime. They may also look at historical, political, economic, and geographical influences.

Non-academic influences

We have seen that criminology is an academic subject in that it produces knowledge and understanding through teaching and learning, scholarship, research, debate, and critique (see the discussion of the academic study of crime earlier in this section), but many of these elements also involve non-academic players and arguments, and academic knowledge is not the only kind produced within criminology. Criminological knowledge and understandings can be created, informed, and critiqued by a variety of non-academic stakeholders (people with an interest in or concern about a certain organisation or area), including politicians (for instance, the Prime Minister), policymakers (for instance, civil servants working in the Ministry of Justice) and practitioners (for instance, judges, prison and police officers, the media).

The public also play a key role in the production of criminological knowledge. The criminological knowledge and understanding produced by these non-academic stakeholders is typically intended to influence the general public's perception of crime (Jones 2013)—in other words, their views of the most appropriate definitions, explanations, and responses to crime—to the benefit of the stakeholders' agendas. This influence is often exerted to progress the agendas of those individuals and their organisations in some way, support for which is demonstrated by voting in elections, contributing to the operation and funding of crime-related programmes (for example, community projects, CCTV), buying newspapers, and providing the audience for TV and radio programmes. In turn, public opinion can influence how politicians, policymakers, practitioners, and the media discuss and portray crime (see **Chapter 6**), since these stakeholders want to appeal to the general public in order to win votes, hearts, minds, customers, and audiences. Academic criminologists can also influence public opinion, but rarely to the same extent. The power of public opinion can lead individuals outside academia, especially politicians and those in the media, to give the public what they think they want to see and hear in relation to crime. This may result in the circulation of a certain amount of half-truths and misinformation, rather than representations of crime that are valid (a term that we will explore in **Chapter 4**). The relationship between public opinion of crime and non-academic representations of crime is therefore another pairing within criminology which, like the elements of the triad, is reciprocal and mutually reinforcing.

1.3 Studying criminology

When you become an HE student at university, you will be expected to study a number of different and exciting aspects of crime in a variety of ways, all of which can be situated within three broad themes that we have termed the *triad of criminology*. Now that you have a better idea of what criminology is and involves, in this section we will look in more depth at how you will go about studying it: the lenses through which you might be encouraged to view the subject, the methods through which you'll study it, and how your learning might be assessed.

Unpacking criminology

The typical content of an undergraduate criminology degree programme focuses on specific areas that help you to unpack the complexities of the subject into smaller and more manageable chunks. The broad headline areas in criminology can, as we have seen, be seen as definitions, explanations, and responses, but these areas can be further broken down into categories of crime, theories of crime and justice, and the people, organisations, and systems who work with crime and the people who commit crime.

Whether you are a new student seeking to understand the structure and focuses of criminology or an existing student reflecting critically on how the nature of criminology can inform your developing learning (see the discussion of E3 students in **section 1.4**), it is useful to analyse the component parts of our subject as we do in the following sections. If you are not already familiar with the overall structure of your course and the compulsory and optional modules available to you in each year, now would be a good time to look this up online or in your programme handbook. Doing this in the light of the information in the following sections will enable you to gain a better understanding of how your programme leaders have chosen to unpack criminology.

Categories

It is common for criminology courses to be broken down into modules and topics based around different types or categories of crime, reflected by the general content of this book. Courses can be divided into anything from general crime categories, such as serious, violent, property, youth, female, and ethnic, to more specific crime categories, such as drug- and alcohol-related, cyber, corporate/**white-collar crime**, environmental, hate, organised, terrorism, sexual, **homicide**, political, economic, and animal crime, along with victimology (the study of crime victims) and **zemiology** (the study of social harms), all of which can be studied by learning about and applying *criminological research methods* (see **Part 5** of this book).

Theories

The different frameworks for understanding the **aetiology** (origins, causes) and effects (for example, on victims) of crime (Jones, 2013) are central to any undergraduate criminology programme. These theories include **classical** and **rational choice** approaches (crime is a product of choice); **biological**, **psychological**, and **sociological positivism/determinism** (crime is influenced by factors within the individual or their immediate environment); **critical and radical theories** (crime is a creation or label of the powerful that is imposed on the powerless); and **realism** (crime is a real phenomenon with real, damaging effects). We will cover each of these theoretical frameworks in detail in this book. Theoretical debates also consider why and how organisations and systems should respond to crime (such as penology—the theory of why and how we should punish, sentence, and treat criminal behaviour) and the philosophies, principles, and ethical considerations of studying and working with crime and the people who commit crime (see Williams, 2012).

People, organisations, and systems

Criminology involves studying the work of the staff/practitioners, policymakers, and decision-makers in organisations relevant to criminology more broadly (for example, universities, governments, research institutions, pressure groups, charities, support groups), as well as key stakeholders who work within criminal justice specifically (for example, police, courts, probation, prisons, local authorities). Criminologists may also study how these people, organisations, and systems work together (or do not, as the case may be) as part of the systems and structures seeking to understand and respond to crime (for example, criminal justice systems, youth/juvenile justice systems, multi-agency partnerships, cross-national and international agencies). University modules can also focus on the different groups of people who are affected by crime, such as victims, women and girls, black and ethnic minorities, young people, disabled people, and the systems (for example, communities, cultures, countries) that these people contribute to and live within.

Themes and issues

A series of critical concepts influence the extent and nature of understanding we can have about the categories, theories and people, organisations, and systems that form the focus of our definitions, explanations, and responses to crime. Across all undergraduate criminology modules at all levels of study, you are likely to examine themes and issues such as cross-cultural comparisons and differences between and within countries; differences between the extent and nature of crime at the local, national, and global levels; differences related to age, gender, ethnicity, and class and so on (see Hale et al., 2013). These crucial themes and issues have been woven into discussions across several of the chapters in this book.

You are also likely to study the growing influence of the media on our understandings and knowledge of crime, along with the increasing importance of social harm—a broader topic that studies damaging behaviours and actions that have not been labelled as crime through traditional, restricted definitions of it. A common critical theme is the social construction (creation, manipulation, exaggeration) of crime by powerful social groups (for instance, men, white people, the wealthy, adults, the western world) over the history of criminology; in particular, the ways in which criminological study and knowledge is:

- androcentric—gender-biased—dominated by men, conducted by men on men for men; and
- ethnocentric—culturally biased—dominated by white people (typically men) from the white westernised world; namely Europe, North America, and Australasia.

The critical theme of social construction is often compared and contrasted with the concept/theme of realism—a perspective that crime is a real-life, actual, measurable phenomenon with real consequences for real people, as opposed to an inflated creation or social construction by powerful groups.

The multitude of ways in which criminology can be unpacked and studied contribute to making it such a dynamic, stimulating, frustrating, and engaging subject. With this in mind, let us consider *how* you might be expected to study on a typical undergraduate criminology degree programme. Again, we would suggest that current students of criminology engage with this information as a means of consolidating their existing knowledge and learning, but if you feel familiar with and confident about these methods (skim the following sections first to check), you may prefer to jump ahead to **section 1.4**.

Learning and teaching methods

Throughout your criminology degree studies at university, you will be exposed to a variety of learning experiences and teaching and assessment methods, generally falling into the categories of direct, face-to-face teaching, such as lectures, and indirect teaching, such as distance-learning and independent study. We will consider each in turn here. As noted earlier, if you are new to higher education you can find more detailed and general (not criminology-specific) information about the different learning and assessment methods in Finch and Fafinski, 2019.

Direct teaching methods

If you are reading this book having already started your course, you will be familiar with the fact that direct teaching for criminology is mainly delivered via the following three methods:

- **Lectures:** Traditionally an academic delivering a talk on a certain topic from the front of a classroom or lecture theatre, perhaps using some audiovisual aids (for example, PowerPoint slides or a handout) and writing on a board or flip-chart, but increasingly involving interactive individual and group activities—shown in **Figure 1.5**. Typically, the lecture is an introduction to a particular topic that aims to give the student a flavour of the area to stimulate further study.
- **Seminars or workshops:** Smaller and more interactive versions of lectures, for which attendance is often monitored, which aim to help students explore topics in more detail and to hear the views of others

Figure 1.5 In less interactive lectures it is particularly important to be an active learner
Source: Syda Productions/Shutterstock

on their course via discussion and presentations—shown in **Figure 1.6**. Seminars can be hosted online, as webinars, or in extended formats as half-day or all-day workshops, sometimes involving field work (outside the classroom).

- **Tutorials:** Meetings with your personal tutor to discuss your academic progress, any pastoral care issues you experience, and to help you work on your employability.

Although these direct methods may feel similar in some ways to school or college teaching, the trick to making the most of this face-to-face support is to be an 'active' learner of criminology (an individual who takes ownership of their learning process through participation, involvement, interactions, analysis, and other proactive methods, rather than passively receiving knowledge), thinking carefully about how your lectures and lecturers are helping you to understand course content and ultimately to produce new

knowledge of your own. We will discuss the topic of getting the most from your studies in **section 1.4**.

Indirect teaching methods

Indirect teaching methods may be less familiar to you from previous educational experiences and you may have certain preconceptions/worries about this element of university teaching. Try not to be anxious. These methods can be extremely supportive and enjoyable if you can engage with them fully, which will happen as you gain confidence and experience as a criminology student. They include:

- **Virtual and/or distance learning:** Online methods such as guided discussions and the posting of course-related content on websites, social media sites (see '**About the authors**' at the start of this book for the details of our authors' social media accounts), online discussion boards, video chat programmes (such as Zoom, FaceTime), instant messaging, and a university's Virtual Learning Environment (such as Moodle, Blackboard).

- **Distance learning:** Modules and courses with limited or no face-to-face teaching contact. Students receive study schedules and course materials online or (less so nowadays) in printed form, along with recommended criminological readings that can be accessed through the university's library.

- **Work-based learning**: Employability-enhancing **placements** in criminological and criminal justice organisations. These placements can take the form of work shadowing (watching someone do the job), work experience (you conduct tasks related to the role), or research **internships** (you complete a small piece of job-related research for the organisation). They may be formally assessed as a module or part of a module or be conducted outside official contact hours, or on a year abroad.

- **Independent learning:** Unlike lower levels of the education system, in HE the majority of learning takes place informally and independently, outside timetabled contact hours. Direct teaching is intended to give you the foundational knowledge for a topic and to motivate and excite you to investigate it in more depth in your own time. Independent study need not be entirely independent or solitary—you can do it with classmates, and your teaching staff should provide you with or guide you towards useful materials (module handbooks and guidance documents as well as academic works), and will be available to help support you as you develop the essential skill of self-directed studying.

Figure 1.6 If you feel comfortable enough to actively participate in seminar group discussions, you will get the most out of these learning opportunities
Source: © Monkey Business Images/Shutterstock

How your learning will be assessed

Your understanding of what you have learned and been taught, along with your ability to apply it to original questions and to manipulate it to support arguments, will be regularly tested and measured through a variety of types of assessment.

These assessments will either be formative (informal, part-way through a module or course) and summative (formal, final), with summative grades counting towards your module grades and, usually only in the second and third years of your degree, towards your final degree grade. They will take various different forms: written, spoken/oral; practical; visual with accompanying discussion. Each form of assessment is intended to measure your knowledge and understanding of criminological topics, concepts, themes, and issues and will be closely linked to your course and module content, learning objectives, and learning and teaching methods. Here, we summarise the various assessment methods you might experience.

Written assessments

Assessments in HE, particularly in social science subjects like criminology, have been traditionally based on written forms of assessment. As we will see, other methods of assessment are emerging as understandings of student learning styles and employers' requirements from graduates shift and develop, but most criminology courses include (although don't necessarily prioritise) written methods, including:

- **Essay coursework:** A written or word-processed response to a stimulus (prompting) question, statement, quote, or instruction, provided within a set word limit and submitted by a set deadline. (See **What do you think? 1.2** for some examples of essay stimuli.)
- **Reviews:** These include the literature review, which is an overview of a topic area, such as a summary of the key debates, issues, theories, research findings, policies, and authors, and the book/chapter/article review, where you are asked to conduct a discussion or critical review of the content, structure, style, and value of a criminological text. They can differ from essays in that they may be more contextualised and descriptive (although not necessarily) and focused on setting the context for and describing an area, rather than writing a detailed evaluation or critique in response to a stimulus question or statement (Redman and Maples, 2011).
- **Dissertations:** An extended independent essay (often between 8,000 and 10,000 words) supervised by a staff member that is usually completed in your final year and focused on a topic of your choosing. They have chapters (unlike essays) and can be either desk-based critical literature reviews of criminological topics or research-based critical discussions of a piece of empirical research in criminology (that is, based on a controlled study, observation, experiment, experience).
- **Exams:** These can occasionally be practical, but they are usually essays completed under timed conditions. Exams can be 'seen' or 'unseen', depending on whether the stimuli are given in advance, and in 'open book' exams you may be allowed to take course materials into the exam with you. Multiple-choice question exams are becoming increasingly popular.

A further written method of assessment that is gaining popularity is the blog—teaching staff may ask you to demonstrate your understanding and knowledge of a criminological topic by summarising it and discussing it

WHAT DO YOU THINK? 1.2

Tackling essay questions in criminology

Here are some examples of differently worded essay stimuli requiring equivalent responses, based on the topic of female offenders:

- **Question:** What is the most effective way to respond to females who commit crimes?
- **Statement:** Females should be treated differently to males by the criminal justice system. Discuss.
- **Quote:** According to the former UK Government Home Secretary Michael Howard, 'prison works'. Assess this claim in relation to females who commit crime.
- **Instruction:** Explore the argument that we should treat females differently when they enter the criminal justice system.

What are your views on these essay stimuli? How would you respond to the stimuli? What issues and themes would you introduce and explore in order to provide a detailed response and why?

concisely (in about 500–1,000 words), using informal language, and in a way that would be easy for a non-expert audience to follow. Writing a blog uses similar skills to those required for an essay; it is just presented in a different way, and encourages you to be flexible in the ways you communicate. Writing in this way can also help you to develop important skills that will help you to use academic, 'scientific' literature more effectively in your studies; in particular, by encouraging you to think critically about your course materials. In the words of Dr Andrew Whiting of Birmingham City University, in his blog guidance to first year criminology students:

> There is no better way of demonstrating that you understand a concept or theory than being able to explain it to your house mate, parents or grandparents.
>
> (Whiting, 2018)

Presentations

The traditional preference for written assessments in criminology is being challenged by the increasing popularity of the oral presentation, which involves preparing and delivering a formal presentation or talk on a topic. The format of this exercise varies between universities and modules in terms of whether they are prepared and delivered individually or as part of a group, whether you choose the topic or it is given to you, whether the presentation needs to follow a formal structure, whether there is a time limit, how it is assessed, and whether it counts towards a module. Some students feel nervous and even scared about the idea of presenting (see **Conversations 1.1** for two students' perspectives) but we would advise you to seize any opportunities you have to overcome any nerves and develop this key skill.

CONVERSATIONS 1.1

The criminology student's view of presentations

with **Emma Hurren** and **Amy Rowe**

Emma Hurren, a criminology graduate from Swansea University, says, 'So you are stood there, the room full of people ready to listen to you and to see your presentation. Thinking about this filled me with dread and the majority of us found it very stressful. What if I say something wrong? What if they think I am stupid? Many of us let our anxieties take over and we worry about the idea of giving a presentation and forget about the reality. However, remember that presentations are often part of group work, so you have support, reassurance, and confidence from those around you. Also, remember who you are delivering the presentation to. Often it's your course mates, who will be giving a presentation too, so you are in the same boat. This takes off a lot of pressure.

'It is really important to remember how valuable presentations can be—it is an extremely beneficial tool for the learning process. Yes, you learn from writing essays, but having to freely discuss and explain a concept to others gives you a whole new understanding of the subject and increases your confidence in that understanding. This is an extremely useful skill to take into the working world once you've graduated. Some jobs require presentations as part of the interview process. With the experience of giving presentations in university, you can go to interview knowing you can talk with conviction and confidence. Presentations actually increase your self-esteem—it's such an achievement to overcome anxieties and do something you are truly proud of. Who knows, you might even find some enjoyment in it!'

Emma's course mate, Amy Rowe, adds, 'I am not naturally confident talking to groups of people, particularly when there is the added pressure of being graded on various aspects including content and presentation. The prospect of group presentations was really daunting for me. Whilst I was as reluctant to speak as the rest of my group, I decided that the best way to deal with my nerves was to face them, so I volunteered to share the speaking role in the knowledge that doing this would leave me better equipped for future presentations. This gave me experience and confidence, so my next presentation went much more smoothly than the first and I actually quite enjoyed it in the end!

'The transferable skills I gained from presentations have been useful in so many ways. I am more confident to speak to large groups of people, such as when a friend asked me to propose her for a position within the Students Union to a group of 100+ people. Most importantly, I found the experience invaluable when I was asked to give a presentation as part of an interview for a job. I felt confident that I knew how to present information effectively and argue my case in a clear and persuasive way. It might be tempting to take a back seat in a group presentation and allow others to take on the speaking roles, but ultimately you will benefit much more from involving yourself as much as possible.'

Emma Hurren (pictured left) and Amy Rowe (pictured right), BA Criminology graduates, Swansea University

The experiencing of preparing and delivering presentations can be constructive, rewarding, and enjoyable. Compared to other forms of assessment, presentations may be shorter, may require less preparatory work (especially if you are part of a larger group—which brings with it group working skills), and can have less demanding expectations in terms of detail, content, structure, and referencing. Better still, the assessment criteria for presentations can be more achievable, so you should be less anxious about them. Not only that, but the skills you develop and the experiences that you gain will look better and more relevant on your CV than anything you will get from essays and exams.

Research-based assessment

An increasing number of criminology degree programmes are integrating criminological research methods and evidence (see **Chapter 4**) with their learning, teaching, and assessment, helping students to develop valuable (and transferable—that is, applicable in other settings beyond university, and even beyond criminology) research skills that will benefit both their immediate learning and their future employability. These research skills include team working, conducting critical literature reviews, understanding research methodologies, data analysis, and sharing research in presentations and reports (see Clark et al., 2021). Research-based assessments include:

- **The research report:** Requires you (individually or in a group) to describe, discuss, and evaluate a research project that you have conducted, focusing on the background literature and research in that area, choice of question, the methods used, the results obtained and what these mean, and how you will disseminate (share, publicise) your study.

- **The research proposal:** Either individually or in a group, you provide a report/plan explaining how and why you intend to conduct a piece of criminological research in the future. The research proposal basically has the same structure as the research report, except that it reports and discusses what you *will* do (it is *prospective*), rather than what you *have* done (which would be *retrospective*).

- **The research poster:** This method is growing in popularity. It is efficient and it enhances transferable skills and employability because along with presentations, posters are the most common way for academic researchers to disseminate their research to others at conferences. The poster involves the individual or group presenting their study details visually on a large poster-sized board or sheet of paper (see Clark et al., 2021) using a mixture of narrative and graphics (see **Figure 1.7**).

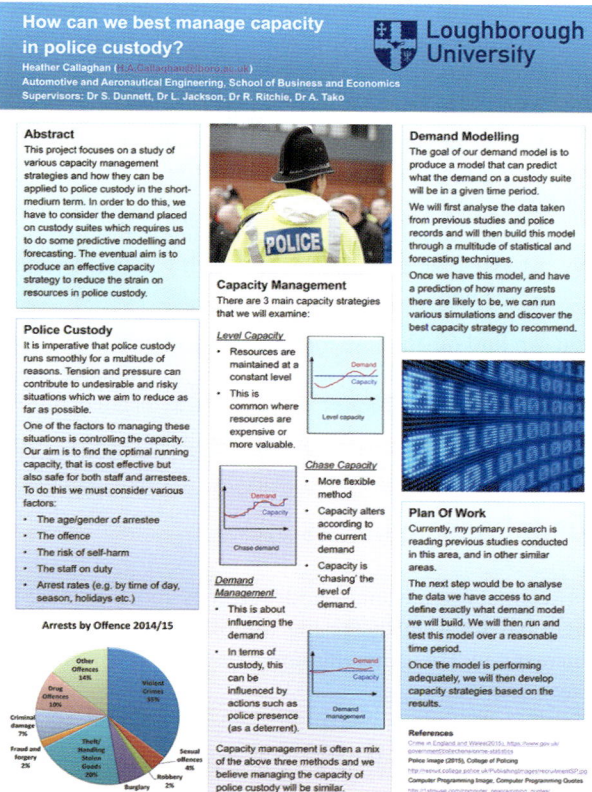

Figure 1.7 Posters, which involve a mixture of narrative and graphics displayed on a large board or sheet, are one of the main ways that researchers disseminate their findings to others at conferences

Source: Heather Callaghan, Loughborough University

You may also find that you will be given specific assessments focused on the individual elements of a research project, for example you may be asked to complete a critical literature review as a formative or summative assessment, or to produce a methodology report or to conduct a piece of data analysis related to your proposal or completed research project.

Work-based assessment

The growing emphasis on employability as part of undergraduate criminology degree programmes has meant that an appropriate range of work-based assessments have been developed to measure the associated learning. These usually involve one or all of the following:

- **Workplace observations:** Staff members (from the university, from the workplace organisation) assess the student's performance against a set of assessment criteria.

- **Self- and/or staff-assessed reflection:** This might involve the completion of a reflective blog, diary,

or journal, possibly in conjunction with other assessments such as essays, research reports, and presentations.
- **The curriculum vitae (CV):** This can form a major part of careers-based modules, and its beauty is that it is both formative and summative—it can be updated and enhanced throughout your studies, far beyond the duration of the module for which it is assessed; plus, you can take it with you when you've graduated.

You can find much more information and guidance about criminology-related careers and how to enhance your employability in **Chapter 33** and its associated online resources.

Visual assessments

As technology advances and becomes more accessible, there has been an increasing use of visual forms of assessment in HE generally and criminology specifically.

A typical format is the use of photos or videos to illustrate a topic (for example, based on a statement, question, instruction), supplemented by a narrative that is either written or spoken. So, for example, Phil Johnson, one of our authors, asks his students at the University Centre at Blackburn College to choose five photos to illustrate a topic (for example, 'The Environment and Corporate Crime') and to accompany each with a 250-word (written) description of how, when, and why the photo was taken, an explanation of what it represents about the topic, and a justification of why it is appropriate as an illustration of the issues raised by the topic. Other universities, such as Coventry University, ask students to reflect on their experiences in their placement year or year abroad through an Instagram story.

You can read about Phil's experience of these forms of assessment in **New frontiers 1.1**. Each university teaches and assesses criminology in its own way, and is likely to have chosen its assessment methods for good reason, but if your university doesn't offer non-written means of assessment and you think it should, this might be something you want to raise via a student feedback forum or society.

NEW FRONTIERS 1.1

Using photos as assessment in criminology

with author **Phil Johnson**

I have long been questioning the suitability of assessment methods in today's HE context and the sheer number of written words required from undergraduates over the course of a three-year degree. There are other concerns over our current assessment practices, such as the perceived lack of relevance of writing skills in the world of work, regardless of how valid (or not) this perception may be. Traditional essays may also discourage individual thought—the very thing HE is supposed to promote. Writing 'I think . . .' can be so strongly disapproved of, in favour of more conservative approaches and formulaic essay structures. Consequently, the critically enthusiastic voices so often heard in seminars and workshops are replaced by answers that 'do the right thing' but do not reflect what a student actually thinks.

Many years ago, I was inspired to try a new approach. Kings College London advertised an unusual photography competition called 'Harm . . . Crime . . . Injustice . . . What does it look like to you?' I adapted its requirements into a formal assessment and got validation from Lancaster University to use it as an alternative method. In my proposal to the university, I did not use the 'a picture is worth a thousand words' cliché, although for the purposes of word limits for modules, that is exactly what it can become. The general interest in crime photography meant that when I first ran this assessment method, there was a chance the students' assignments would end up on the front page of the national newspaper sponsoring the competition. My use of assignments has since moved online; this move has resulted in extra opportunities for e-learning as the assessment method can now include the students producing videos of their visual images hosted on an open access YouTube channel; this results in an audience far in excess of traditional assessment approaches, which generally only involves a student and a lecturer.

The number of words a photo is deemed equivalent to varies with the detail in the assignment question and it can also be accompanied by tasks requiring written or verbal justifications for the taken images. So instead of writing *another* 2,500-word essay, students can choose *how* they present their work. A visual approach to assessing undergraduate criminology encourages the 'reading' of photos; this can be done by paying close attention to all of the detail that is both *in* and *out* of this frame. This involves appreciating their connotations (what they suggest) and denotations (what they actually show)—this learning can result in the students' creation of photos that express themselves in ways that may not have been possible through the conventional written word. The reading of photos can be an effective way for using your ABC approach (see **section 1.4**), as 'the source of the source' of photos, like anything else (see **Chapter 4**), is fundamental to what they show. In addition to considering the possible truth in photos, this type of learning can also enhance ethical and legal awareness as by taking the role of a photographer in society, you are placed directly in a situation where these dilemmas occur.

Chapter 32 offers more information on visual ways of presenting your findings when you come to produce research of your own.

1.4 Getting the most from your studies

Criminology is a vast and fascinating subject, and in this book we try to explain it in an accessible, practical, and student-focused way, to bring it to life, and to support you on your academic learning journey. But we do not just want to impart information in an engaging way. Through the main text and the boxed learning features (the purposes of which are described in the '**Guide to using this textbook**' at the start of this book), we aim to equip you with the techniques and strategies that will allow you to maximise your experience of studying criminology by taking ownership of it, learning in an active and dynamic way, and ultimately evolving from a consumer of knowledge into a *producer* of knowledge (see **Figure 1.8**). This will not only benefit your marks, but your whole experience—criminology is much more enjoyable when you engage with it in this way.

The keys to making this transformation are clear goals and expectations, the mindset and skills to be an active learner, and being aware of—and willing to make use of—the many forms of support available to you at university. These ideas reappear throughout the book but are summarised in this section, so that you can bear them in mind as you get to grips with the subject.

The goal: becoming an E3 student

To maximise your student experience, you should maintain the clear goal of becoming what we think of as an 'E3' student: a student who is effective, engaged, and employable (see **Figure 1.9**). This goal applies whatever type of student you are—undergraduate, postgraduate taught, postgraduate research, distance learner, international,

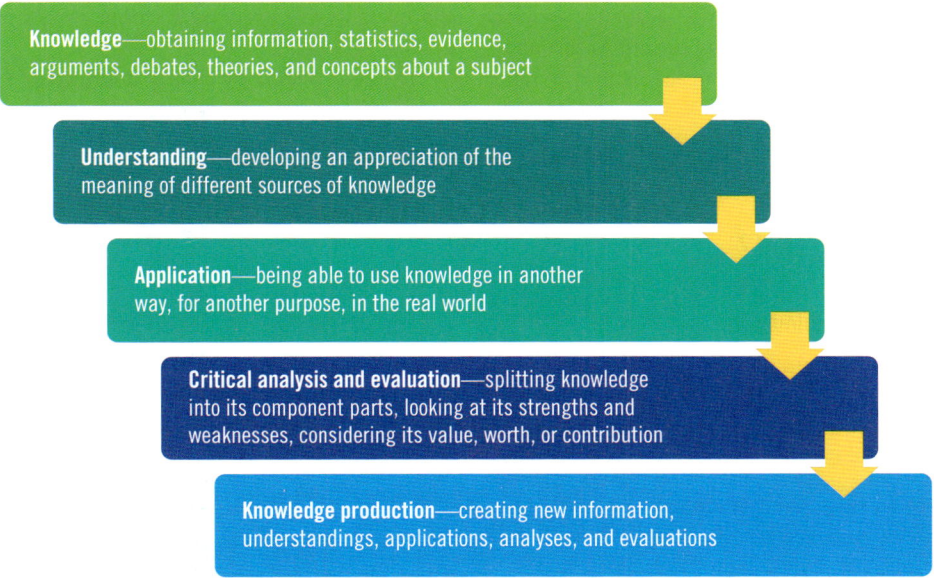

Figure 1.8 The evolution of student knowledge production

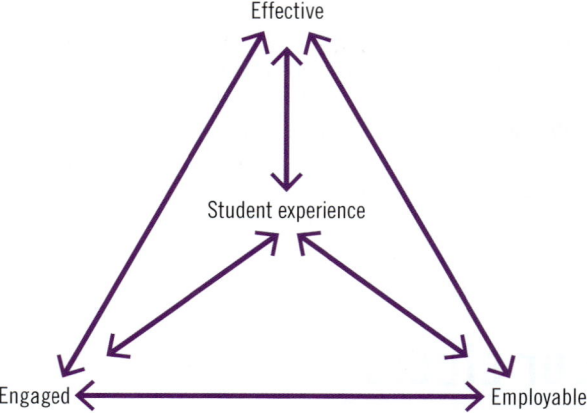

Figure 1.9 The E3 student

mature; whatever subject you are studying and wherever in the world you are studying. Let's unpack the three Es.

1. **Effective:** This means being fully informed and aware of what you need to do, and what and who you need to know, to help you to succeed to the best of your abilities, academically. It means being motivated, proactive, strategic, constructive, and critical in everything you do, with an understanding of *how* to study well (see Finch and Fafinski, 2019) and an awareness of *why* you are doing what you are doing. It is not limited to high grades; it could also apply, for example, to working productively with others and making the most of your university experience.

2. **Engaged:** Being engaged means being willing and committed to maximising your student experience through full and active participation in, and dedication to, both academic and non-academic (social, extra-curricular, work-based) opportunities throughout your time at university. Engagement is a state of mind, an attitude, and a physical involvement in activities and opportunities. It is a key tool for fulfilling your potential and enhancing your student experience.

3. **Employable:** This means developing the skills and mindset to ensure that you are as attractive to potential employers as possible so that you can get the job that you want after university. Enhancing your employability involves building your CV, gaining work experience, and developing **personal transferable skills** through your degree programme and extracurricular activities. There is an increasing focus on working constructively at university to become employable throughout and by the end of your studies.

In summary, striving to be an E3 student means making the most of your limited and busy time at university. You are an adult expending much time, effort, and money on enjoying the student experience in the short-term and on studying to give yourself a better life in the long-term (see **What do you think? 1.3**). As authors, we sincerely hope that this chapter (and the rest of the book) goes a long way to helping you to do just that.

The mindset: The ABC approach

As you may by now have gathered, this is *not* a textbook that simply gives you facts, information, and arguments to remember and regurgitate later. What we *will* do is to help and challenge you to be an *active learner*, to think, to critique, and to generate knowledge of your own. Having this experience will not only benefit your studies in criminology, but also what you do after you have completed your course. This is where the guiding principle of this chapter and the book as a whole comes in—*Always Be Critical* or ABC.

We need to start by clearly defining or **operationalising** our central concept so that we know what we are working

---

WHAT DO YOU THINK? 1.3

Effective, engaged, employable

How can you become more effective, engaged, and employable? Advice on these points is included throughout the book and its online resources, but you could start by considering the following questions:

- What factors increase/have increased your ability to be effective and engaged whilst at university and to become employable by the time you leave?

- What differences do/did you anticipate experiencing between college or sixth form (further education) and university (higher education) study? How do you plan to manage them?

- Who and what can help you to become effective, engaged, and employable?

- How can you help yourself? What exactly do you need to do?

with going forwards. The key term is 'critical'. This does not mean that you should criticise or reject everything that you see, hear, read, and do. Being critical is not an unconstructive exercise in negativity, it is a constructive exercise in being focused, deliberate, and analytical to enable you to move your learning and understanding forwards. ABC is not just a mindset but a way of travel.

You should strive to ensure that the information and support you gain along your learning journey complements the type of learner that *you* are, the E3 student that you want to become, and the student experience that you desire. Make sure that everything that you do academically moves you forward as a learner. Think critically about the quality and personal utility (usefulness to you) of the information and services you are receiving, the decisions that you are making, and the work (for instance, study, assessment, employability-based) that you are doing—all of which are related to one another. *Always be critical* about whether you are making the most effective study choices. Ask yourself, are you:

- choosing the most suitable modules and research/dissertation topics (for example, to match your interests, skills, knowledge base, career plans)?
- engaging with the most useful learning materials and attending the most appropriate learning sessions (for example, every formal lecture, seminar, workshop and tutorial, extracurricular talks, and presentations)?
- taking the right study notes about the right content in the right way; planning, preparing, and executing your assessments in a painless, focused, strategic way?
- asking for support from the right people at the right times?
- always looking for opportunities to enhance your personal transferable skills and employability?
- organising your student experience (study, work placements, extracurricular activities, socialising) in a balanced and strategic way?

Try to adopt and apply a consistent ABC mindset about the hows and whys: how could I enhance my student experience and maximise my potential to succeed; why have I chosen this approach to what I am doing?

ABC means that you choose to evolve from a passive recipient and *re*producer of information (a sponge who sits and soaks up knowledge) to an active learner, a proactive *producer* of knowledge. ABC means challenging yourself.

This mindset should be your constant travel partner as you journey through the following chapters of our book, where we will discuss how criminologists explore, explain, and respond to crime and criminals, before concluding with a reflection on you as an original researcher of criminology and producer of knowledge (**Chapter 33**). Use ABC and the 'What do you think?' feature boxes to engage with the content of these chapters, to ask yourself whether you understand or agree with it, to judge the quality and completeness of the information, to decide how it can help you in your studies and in your career. ABC is a positive, constructive mindset to drive your learning forwards and to enhance your student experience.

The support: choosing and using your 'travel partners'

As we have discussed, independent learning is crucial at university and *you* are ultimately responsible for the quality of your academic and student experience, but do remember that you are not alone on your criminology learning journey: plenty of 'travel partners' are available to you at both a university and degree programme level, as well as a host of academic and non-academic textual resources.

You may benefit from using some of these travel partners throughout your degree, from an early stage, whereas others you may need only if you experience unforeseen difficulties and problems (welfare, accommodation, finance, crime, gender-specific issues, and so on), but it is very important that you are aware of what support is available and can proactively seek out help when you need it.

In this section, we will just list and briefly explain the types of support that are likely to be available to you at your university and on your programme, since this varies from course to course. We intend this information to act as starting points for you to explore further, and to see what form each takes at your own university. (You can even start this process before you officially begin at your chosen university and you may have done so already.)

University travel partners

The following travel partners are likely to be available to you at a university level:

- **Disability and additional learning support:** Your university's Disability Office and Learning Support Office can provide support and advice about your circumstances and what they may be able to offer you. If you have a disability or additional learning need, do consider paying them a visit. This is not asking for special treatment or an unfair advantage, it simply levels the playing field so that you have the same opportunities as other students.

- **Mental health support:** Most universities offer support to students experiencing mental health (also known as 'well-being') issues as part of a wider package of student support that is often located within the student union. Mental health issues can include (but are not limited to) difficulties associated with the *transition* into university, student finances, learning and assessment-related stress, coping with student life, and existing physical or mental health issues. If you are unsure of the support available, please ask your department or personal tutor as it is their job to guide you towards appropriate services.

- **International student support:** Many universities offer support to help international students living and studying away from home to acclimatise to the country in which they are living, to improve their language skills, and to help them with accommodation, finances, and welfare. They can also put you in contact with other international students and point you towards relevant societies.

- **Employability services:** You can find employability-related guidance in **Chapter 33** and our online resources, but your university (and possibly your department too) will have a careers service or employability service, whether this be a physical office or an online portal or website. Engage with your careers service as early as possible in your studies to discuss your options and learn how you can boost your employability—do not wait until you are about to graduate.

- **Library and computing services:** Your university library is home to the majority of the learning material/resources, both hard copy and digital, that you will draw upon when studying. A good way to find out what support and facilities are available is to attend any advertised library induction or familiarisation tours and talks in the opening weeks of the new academic year. Do this even if you are in your second or third year—what have you got to lose?

- **Academic writing clinics:** In some universities, this kind of support is offered as part of the library services, whereas in others it is a separate provision. We offer some guidance on academic writing in **Chapter 32**, in the context of writing up your research, and you will find many helpful tips in Finch and Fafinski (2019—see **Further Reading** at the end of this chapter), but we strongly recommend investigating what support is on offer at your university. However it is delivered, this service can offer invaluable help with all kinds

Figure 1.10 University libraries can help you develop your academic writing skills, including through writing workshops or one-to-one clinics
Source: Photo by Christina Morillo from Pexels

of academic writing, with staff working with students on a one-to-one basis, advising on how to improve the style, content, or structure of written work (see **Figure 1.10**).

- **Student societies:** These can be academic (a criminology society, or societies for related subjects like psychology) or non-academic (for example, sports, music, drama societies), but can offer a whole range of benefits for you personally and for your learning journey and employability. Student societies are often coordinated by a Students' Union (SU), so this is a good place to start exploring your options.

Programme travel partners

Your social sciences or criminology department and criminology degree programme will have a variety of staff, structures, strategies, and course materials (learning resources) in place to support you as travel partners on your voyage of discovery in criminology. We have outlined them here as it is really important to familiarise yourself with the whats, whos, and hows of these sources of departmental and programme support.

- **Staff:** Productive working relationships with teaching staff (including lecturers, module leaders, programme directors, and personal tutors) as well as with administration staff will be invaluable throughout your degree—they can give you direct assistance and point you towards the relevant people and services.

- **Fellow students and student–staff committees:** Don't forget to call upon and work with your fellow students throughout your studies, especially those who are involved in a student–staff committee (or a similarly named group), which is a forum in which students can communicate their programme-based experiences and feedback to staff.

- **Programme handbook:** You will have been given access to a handbook of information about your programme and modules at the start of your course. You should, of course, read it carefully when you begin studying, but do not forget to keep referring back to it—it will contain invaluable information about teaching methods, assessments, module objectives, timetables, and sources of learning support.
- **VLE:** Your university's Virtual Learning Environment, such as Moodle or Blackboard, will house a huge number of important documents and links relating to your course, and may also facilitate chat rooms and discussion groups for your course.

Criminological learning resources

There are many types of learning resources available to students of criminology, and it is important to understand what each aims to do so that you can use them effectively over the course of your studies, and when directed to do so by your lecturers. We have summarised below the main types of resources you will (or should!) come across. Within our online resources you will find guidance on how to read material that is written in a more academic tone than most textbooks (including this one), and might at first seem intimidating: look for the 'Academic writing demystified' documents.

The main resources used in criminological studies are as follows:

- **Textbooks:** Textbooks, like this one, are your starting point in criminology and will give you a broad, mainly objective (unbiased), overview of the subject and its sub-topics. Your textbooks will act as reliable companions for your degree, but as they mainly contain secondary information (reporting the ideas of others) it is essential that you also explore relevant primary sources (original opinion and research) for each topic if you want to fulfil your potential in criminology.
- **Monographs (research-based books):** These books are specialist pieces of writing about an area of criminology, usually by a single author. They are often based on the author's research and scholarship, so can be classed as a primary source.
- **Critical analysis texts:** These are primary sources of original scholarship that take a topic area and subject it to detailed and intensive critical analysis using evidence, (secondary) research data, and the author's academic opinions. The information in these books may be more subjective than that in textbooks, which aim to be more objective and descriptive.
- **Edited texts:** Some books on criminology or specific topic areas within it have an editor, or a few editors, who have an overview of the book and have brought the material together, but consist of chapters written separately (that is, without collaborating with others) by multiple authors.
- **Academic journals:** Criminology has a wide range of specialist academic journals, which are collections of (largely) journal articles—these can be research-based and critical analysis essays, reports, or position pieces/statements. Journals may also feature book reviews. These articles will give you a more in-depth understanding of a specific topic or argument in criminology.
- **Reports:** These are descriptions, discussions, and evaluations of information and data processes (quantitative and qualitative) in a particular area of criminology or criminal justice. They are usually held up as being more objective than other types of academic learning materials, but as you will come to see as you read this book, everyone has an agenda and a particular way of looking at an issue which can influence their findings or argument.
- **Alternative learning materials:** These might include blogs, vlogs, social media (including our authors' Twitter accounts, through which they share useful materials and articles), podcasts, newspapers, films, and TV programmes. You may use many of these formats and sources for information and entertainment in your personal life, but they can also host really engaging and up-to-date information relating to your studies, and many of the people and organisations we mention throughout this book post regular updates on social media.

At various points in your studies you will also need to refer to legislation and government-issued guidance (for example, on how regional criminal justice agencies should implement certain policies). As with all the resources we have discussed, these documents should be approached with an ABC mindset, but it is also important to remember that they are regularly updated and replaced. As such, when you come across them it is always worth looking up the original source to check that you are referring to the most recent version. The same point applies to crime statistics (see **Chapter 5**) and some types of official reports.

1.5 Conclusion

At this early stage in your journey, hopefully you now have a better understanding of what criminology looks like, what it means to study criminology at university, and what you can expect during your studies. We've set out the essential learning mechanisms (for example, teaching methods) and learning resources (for example, travel partners, course materials) that you will experience and draw upon throughout your criminology programme. However, the most important lesson to take from this chapter regards the importance of the ABC mindset and how it can push you towards becoming an effective, engaged, and employable (E3) student—so maximising your university experience. You are now equipped to take this foundational learning forward into the next phase of your journey—exploring criminology. Remember that the ABC mindset is your friend and your guide—it is a way of travel, not a destination!

SUMMARY

After reading this chapter and working your way through its features you should now be able to:

- **Appreciate what criminology looks like as an academic subject**

Criminology can be most simply defined as the academic study of crime, but this is a much more complex definition than it might seem as the key terms are ambiguous and widely debated. Criminology is a hybrid subject influenced by a range of other social science, humanities, and other subjects and by different academic and non-academic 'stakeholders'. Criminology is usually studied at university by breaking it down into smaller, manageable chunks, viewing it through the lenses of categories, theories, people, organisations and systems, and themes and issues. Criminology is learnt and taught through a wide variety of methods (lectures, seminars, tutorials, work-based, virtual, and distance learning, independent study), and the same goes for its assessment formats (formative, summative, written, spoken/oral, practical, visual).

- **Begin to cultivate the mindset and skills that will ensure you make the most of your studies in criminology**

To make the most of your studies in criminology, you need to have clear goals—becoming an 'E3' (effective, engaged, and employable) student; to maintain an 'ABC' (*Always Be Critical*) approach to your studies; and be aware of and prepared to call on the many kinds of support offered by your university, programme, and learning resources, considering them key travel partners in your criminological journey.

 Test your understanding of the chapter's key points by attempting the self-test questions on the **online resources** at www.oup.com/he/case2e

REVIEW QUESTIONS

1. Now that you have read this chapter, how would you respond to the original question of 'What is criminology?' Has your understanding changed since beginning this book?
2. What is the 'triad of criminology'?
3. What are the academic and non-academic influences on what criminology looks like?

4. What learning and teaching methods can you expect to experience when studying criminology?

5. What is meant by the term 'travel partners' in the context of studying criminology?

 Access the **online resources** at www.oup.com/he/case2e to check your answers to the review questions.

FURTHER READING

Finch, E. and Fafinski, S. (2019) *Criminology Skills* **(3rd edn). Oxford: Oxford University Press.**
Before you move on to Chapter 2, delving fully into the more 'academic' content of this book, it will be worth your time to consult Part II of *Criminology Skills*. Aimed specifically at criminology students, this skills book elaborates on writing skills, essay writing, presentations, and many other skills you will need to complete your degree.

Millie, A. (2016) *Philosophical Criminology.* **Bristol: Policy Press.**
This asks big questions based on six philosophical ideas concerning our relations with others: values, morality, aesthetics, order, rules, and respect. Building on the author's theoretical and empirical research, the book considers the boundaries of criminology and the scope for greater exchange between criminology and philosophy.

Steve Case, 'Studying criminology: why and how?': www.youtube.com/watch?v=RIs883hZ468
In this YouTube video Steve Case, a member of our author team, discusses what makes criminology such a fascinating subject to study and explains how students should approach their learning You should find this a useful summary of the themes we have covered in this chapter.

 Access the **online resources** to view a wealth of extra information relating to your study of criminology, including self-test questions, answers to review questions, and links to other resources that will help you enjoy and fulfil your potential within your studies.
www.oup.com/he/case2e

PART OUTLINE

2. What is 'crime'?
3. What is 'justice'?
4. How criminology produces knowledge
5. Crime statistics
6. Crime and the media
7. Victimology
8. Hate crime
9. Youth offending and youth justice
10. Race, ethnicities, and the criminal justice system
11. Gender and feminist criminology
12. Green criminology
13. Global criminology 1: Comparative criminology
14. Global criminology 2: Transnational criminology

Welcome to **Part 2**, where we embark on our first critical explorations of crime.

In the first chapter, we discussed the nature of a criminology degree and focused on foundational issues with which all criminologists critically engage at the start of their criminological journeys; now we take things a stage further. By questioning the common-sense ideas that 'crime' is simply law violation, or that 'justice' amounts to little more than 'criminal justice', these chapters form the starting points for the ABC (*Always Be Critical*) approach that runs through this book.

We then reflect on two questions: firstly, what do we actually know about crime and, secondly, how do we know this? We go on to consider how criminologists can interpret statistics and official knowledge claims, unearthing relevant issues that should be considered in policymaking, before exploring the relationship between media and crime—from more traditional concerns of how media represent criminality, and the resulting impact on crime and justice, to a consideration of newer forms of media as a site of crime. Next, we consider the causes and impact of victimisation, moving on to discuss hate crime, and the various forms it can take.

Bringing together insights from previous chapters, we then focus on young people, race, and gender, and how these categories are interrelated. We conclude Part 2 by examining some aspects of criminology that have been emerging and becoming central issues in the last ten years. Here, we focus on green criminology, comparative criminology, and transnational criminology.

PART 2
EXPLORING CRIME

CHAPTER OUTLINE

2.1	Introduction	28
2.2	Crime as a social construct	28
2.3	Crime and deviance	32
2.4	Defining 'crime': the harm principle	36
2.5	Other ways to decide whether an action should be a crime	44
2.6	Do we need the criminal law?	48
2.7	Conclusion	50

2

What is 'crime'?

KEY ISSUES

After studying this chapter, you should be able to:

- identify what the criminal law is and what it is for;
- understand why the criminal law can be seen as a social construct that changes over time;
- consider the reasons why some actions are criminalised, and assess how well these reasons are applied;
- evaluate whether we need the criminal law in order to hold people to account and punish them.

2.1 Introduction

This chapter is entitled 'What is "crime"?', but before we consider what crime is, it's worth considering why we need to describe and define it at all. Why do we need to term certain behaviours and actions 'criminal'?

The need to regulate human behaviour stems from the fact that there is an unavoidable conflict between two key aspects of human life: our desire for autonomy (the ability to express our individuality through choosing how we live, free of external control) and our preference for living with others, in communities and societies. It is in our best interests to live with others as they can help us to meet some of our needs, both physical (food, etc.) and emotional (happiness and well-being), but social living limits our autonomy because, in a community, our completely free choices may interfere with the free choices of another. Imagine, for example, that Amy has acquired an iPhone that Beth wants. Beth decides to try and take it. Amy and Beth fight over the iPhone and the strongest, or maybe the most cunning, wins. If nothing in the community stops Beth challenging and fighting (or sneakily stealing) each time she wants something, then every member of that society will give up free choice. Such a society would be less healthy (because it would be more unfair) and less safe, because the weak would not be protected: its social harmony would be threatened because the strong would prosper at the expense of the weak.

We can see that marking some conduct out as unacceptable behaviour—in other words, as 'crime'—is necessary. But how to define this concept? At one level, the question 'what is crime?' is easy to answer by merely saying what a crime is in legal terms. You could say: crime is any act or omission that a state at this time says is criminal, and to which the state attaches criminal consequences. That means that agents of the state such as the police and prosecutors can bring the person they believe is responsible to court to be prosecuted, to answer for their action or omission. If it is considered a crime and they are found guilty then the court may decide they should be punished by the state, so their money (if they are fined), their liberty (if they are imprisoned), their freedom to chose what to do (if they are required to do unpaid work or to turn up to **probation** meetings), and in some states even their life (if there is the death penalty) may be at risk. In theory, criminal law is supposed to deliver justice and fairness into the community to level the playing field.

To simplify it, in law a crime is:

- a norm or set of **norms** (rules);
- backed up by the threat of societal sanctions.

We now know what crime is in legal, technical terms, but this definition does not get criminologists very far. For example, it does not tell us why societies criminalise some activities but not others, nor does it tell us what types of activities might be considered crimes. There are some activities, such as murder, rape, and theft, that are prohibited in almost all societies. However, other activities are less universally considered criminal, for example fox hunting with dogs, smoking in enclosed public places, using certain drugs, dropping litter, swearing in public, not wearing a seat belt, etc. Even with serious, violent crimes like murder and rape there is disagreement about exactly what should be banned, so how does society decide exactly which activities should be classed as crimes?

In this chapter, we will look in some detail at what sorts of activities are criminalised and why; what the criminal law may tell us about our society and what matters to it; and what we can learn about those who choose to break the rules and whether it matters what type of rule they break.

2.2 Crime as a social construct

No matter how universally its ideas and regulations are accepted, it is important to understand and not lose sight of the fact that crime is a **social construct**. Particular behaviours become controlled through the criminal law because a society (or those who hold power in that society) decides that it wants to control them to achieve certain aims. Society often labels a certain behaviour 'criminal' because of the social response it produces: overall, and at that time, society considers this behaviour to be undesirable. There is nothing in acts or behaviours *themselves* that intrinsically means they have to be prohibited; prohibition is always a societal choice (a social construct).

Because crime is socially constructed, ideas of unacceptable and criminal behaviour alter across cultures, for example, in some largely Arab states, such as Bangladesh, drinking alcohol is a criminal offence, whereas other substances such as cannabis may be legal, but in the UK (and many other western states) it is the other way around. What is criminal also alters over time; every year the UK Parliament alters the criminal law to ensure it continues

Figure 2.1 The legalisation of gay marriage in some states shows that what is considered a crime can change over time, and can depend on societal perspectives
Source: Q Wang/Shutterstock

serving the needs of our society—adding some activities as new offences and removing others;, that is, legalising them—so the list of prohibited activities is constantly changing. For example, s. 33 of the Criminal Justice and Courts Act 2015 made 'disclosing private sexual photographs and films with intent to cause distress' (**revenge porn**) a criminal offence; and, since the beginning of November 2018, the medical use of cannabis (prescribed through the NHS) is now legal in certain situations. Also, until the Sexual Offences Act 1967 legalised homosexuality, it was a criminal offence in England and Wales and homosexuals were prosecuted. Since then, society has altered so much that gay couples can now be legally married—see **Figure 2.1**—although it is important to note that legalising a behaviour doesn't make it instantly acceptable in society: some people are still prejudiced against homosexuality.

Crime is socially constructed (and continually reconstructed) by both the general public and by the powers who lead them—hopefully working together, with the state reflecting and protecting the values of the people, but sometimes in conflict (perhaps you noticed the use of 'and/or' in the first paragraph of this section). Let's consider the state and the public's influence on what constitutes crime.

The state

Although (theoretically) the state acts on behalf of and reflects a society, it is the state that ultimately solidifies the social constructs of crime. Its leaders have the power to choose which activities to criminalise and how—or how vigorously—to pursue those who offend, so the shape that laws take depends on the priorities of the lawmakers, who are often very powerful people in society. The criminal law is quite malleable, which is positive in that it can evolve to keep pace with societal change, but also means that the powerful within a state may use the law to protect their own interests (cultural, political, and economic) or those of other powerful groups at the expense of ordinary people, the powerless, or minorities (see **Chapter 18**).

To take an example, one of the activities most feared in our society is terrorism: 'the unlawful use of violence and intimidation, especially against civilians, in the pursuit of political aims' (*Oxford Dictionary*). Most states have laws that prohibit both acts that cause terror (such as murder) and specialist terrorist activities, so it is reasonable to conclude that governments try their best to keep their citizens safe from terrorism. Yet throughout history, most of the very worst acts of terrorism have been carried out by people working for the state. State-sanctioned terror is rarely illegal within a state. Examples are the persecution and murder of Jews in Nazi Germany; the Cambodian genocide (often called the 'killing fields', where more than a million people were killed by Pol Pot's Khmer Rouge regime between 1975 and 1979); the many human rights violations including killings committed by the state in Myanmar (Burma) since the 1960s, including the ongoing **victimisation** of the Rohingyas, many of whom have been slaughtered and raped, others have fled to Bangladesh; the mass killing of Tutsis by the Hutus in the Rwandan genocide of 1994, and then the expulsion of Hutus by the Tutsis when they regained power about 100 days later. None of these acts were considered criminal within the states at the time; the perpetrators were often following state orders. For a fuller consideration of state terrorism, see Jackson, Murphy, and Poynting (2009) and Coleman et al. (2009).

Is there a limit to the power of the state? Although states have a great deal of control, international standards called human rights aim to prevent them from interfering in individual freedoms. A particular community or society may set standards of behaviour they find acceptable, but in doing this they should respect the human rights of individuals. These form the limits of what the international community believes a state should be permitted to do; they set the standards states or societies should uphold. When states breach these standards, they are sometimes called to account (for example, the Nuremberg trials of 1945–6 and the International Criminal Tribunal for Rwanda (ICTR), 1994), however, often the international community does not intervene because the acts of terror are considered an internal state matter (for example, the cases of Myanmar and Cambodia above). Therefore, although the international community sets standards, such as of human rights, that states are expected to uphold and respect, they do not always punish states who fail to comply.

This demonstrates that what is defined as a crime by a state is socially constructed and serves those in power at the time, sometimes at the expense of the powerless

(Tombs and Whyte, 2003). This means that not only is crime a social construct, but it is shaped to fit the interests (cultural, political, and economic) of those in power. Very often their interests coincide with those of the wider population, and the areas controlled by the criminal law can be seen as acceptable to the broader population, but this is not always the case.

The public

Outside important state interests, what becomes a crime often turns on what the public wants—or more usually on what a strong or powerful social movement wants—to be prohibited or controlled (for example, smoking in public, see the change in the depiction of smoking over time in **Figure 2.2**). The criminalisation of many activities by the state is often supported by most of the wider public, who disapprove of the people who participate in such activities. Over time, the public talk negatively about the behaviour as being 'criminal', and this marks it out as being significantly worse than behaviour that is merely naughty or unpleasant—the switch to negative connotations can happen before a state criminalises the behaviour. Those who participate in prohibited activities are termed criminals and are often excluded from 'good' society; they are stigmatised and considered to be unacceptable as friends and colleagues.

This exclusion often arises when the activity has a clear victim, such as violence or theft, especially if that victim is another individual. In most societies, including the UK, there is a deeply ingrained ethos—a sort of common-sense feeling—that one should not harm other people. This idea is often discussed in the context of the **harm principle** for criminal laws, which suggests that activities should only be crimes if they harm other people—see **section 2.4**. However, someone may be excluded due to engaging in criminal activity where there is no clear victim, but the activity has become ingrained in society as being unacceptable. For example, the use of illegal substances which, although no one is directly harmed (apart from the user), might be seen as immoral or as requiring criminalisation to protect the individual from harming themselves (this is known as **paternalism**, see Hart, 1963: 30–4). People can even be excluded owing to a perceived association with unacceptability, for example parents trying to stop their children playing with a child whose parents are criminals, the child is thought of as 'bad' even though they have done nothing wrong.

Whilst the public generally considers crime to be wrong and unacceptable, there are varying degrees of unacceptability (see **What do you think? 2.1**). For example, if a worker steals pens and paper from their employer most people would not vilify them in the same way as if they had done the same thing from a shop or an individual's home. Somehow, we talk about theft from employers as a 'perk of the job' or as 'fiddling' or 'pilfering', and this bending of the language allows us to refrain from thinking of people who do this—including ourselves—as criminals and therefore from considering them 'bad' and excluding them from society (see Ditton, 1977). Another example of this flexibility over what is acceptable is that many would view lying on a tax form and so cheating HM Revenue and Customs (HMRC) or bringing in more duty-free goods than permitted from abroad (cheating HMRC) as less bad than 'proper' theft. For example, we talk about the MPs' 'expenses scandal' of 2009 rather than MPs' theft (even the eight who were convicted are rarely described as thieves). Similarly, many of us tell ourselves that everybody drives a little too fast sometimes, so it is excusable, even if a little unacceptable (while we know that it is actually illegal).

Generally, people who do these things are not excluded until someone is harmed, for instance in a traffic accident caused by excess speed. Even when someone is injured in a driving accident and the speeding driver is at fault, quite often friends and family will not exclude the driver—they

Figure 2.2 Changing perceptions of smoking—from sophisticated to frowned upon—illustrate how ideas of acceptable behaviour can shift over time

Source: Keystone Press/Alamy Stock Photo (left); Shutterstock (right)

WHAT DO YOU THINK? 2.1

Are some unlawful activities more acceptable than others?

Can you think of any unlawful activities (such as the example given earlier—see the discussion of the state earlier in this section—of stealing pens from a company) that are considered to be more acceptable than others? Would you, for example, think differently about someone who 'borrowed' a glass from a pub because she had not finished her drink and another person who took a glass from a shop because she liked it?

Think about your own actions and behaviour; have you ever done something that, even if seemingly minor and the norm amongst your friends, is technically against the law? If so:

- How did you justify this?
- If that same activity was looked down upon by your immediate community or peers, would this be more of a deterrent against committing the act again than the fact it is illegal?
- If you knew that your parents would find out, would that prevent you from participating in the activity?

Listed below are a variety of different excuses for crimes. Consider these reasons and the language used. Do you recognise these excuses, and do you think that we should give them any credibility?

- Clare, a CEO, denies her own responsibility and blames her 'crime' on the negligence of those working beneath her.
- Debbie claims she did not intend to hurt anyone, she was just showing off her knife-throwing skills to friends.
- Ehab says that shoplifting is not a real crime because the shop is always insured.
- Fred says that hitting his wife is a 'private matter', and in any case she deserved it because she nagged him.
- Garit says that his victim started the fight so 'deserved' what he got.
- Ian insists that he did not rape Jane; she was flirting with him and he could not be expected to be able to stop once fully aroused.
- Keith claims that he should not be tried for burglary because all police and judges are hypocrites or corrupt; they have all offended as well but no one holds them to account, and 'look how they let off all those MPs who stole loads more than me in their expenses'.
- Lateef is convicted for assault and says that he does not care what society thinks because his friends think he was right to hit his girlfriend when she disrespected him.

---

may remember the times they have exceeded the speed limit and consider the driver unfortunate. The crime of death by dangerous (or reckless) driving was only introduced in the Road Traffic Act 1956 because juries were reluctant to convict a fellow driver of manslaughter. By 1991, this law was focused almost entirely on the nature of the driving rather than the intent to cause harm, again increasing the likelihood that a jury would convict. Over time, these ways in which we 'neutralise' criminal acts can alter, for example drunk driving used to be socially acceptable, now it is often recognised as a criminal act. There are many examples of these offences that people turn a blind eye to, what Karstedt and Farrell (2006) refer to as the 'crimes of the everyday', see also Ditton (1977) and Henry (1978).

We have so far noted that the concept of crime can vary according to culture, the suggestion being that each state or society has a set of agreed standards. However, societies are more complex than that. Different groups in a society may have different standards or ideas of what is criminal or unacceptable. So, a group of young people may applaud one of their members for defacing someone's property with graffiti, whereas the owners of the property and others in the neighbourhood may want that person prosecuted and punished, and see them as bad people who should be excluded from society. In fact, the owner and others in the neighbourhood may well wish to exclude not just the person who actually drew the graffiti but also those who applauded them, they may consider the whole group to be undesirables, the media may join in and write about the individual and the group in very negative ways. Even if no crime is committed by anyone in the group—if they sit on a street corner or hang around a park, being a little noisy and calling out to people but not doing anything 'wrong'—adults may still consider them 'bad', because they feel intimidated by them or feel they spoil the look and feel of the neighbourhood. We therefore also need to look at the intersection of groups within a society. See Becker's (1963) seminal discussion of how certain groups get treated as 'outsiders' and Quinney's

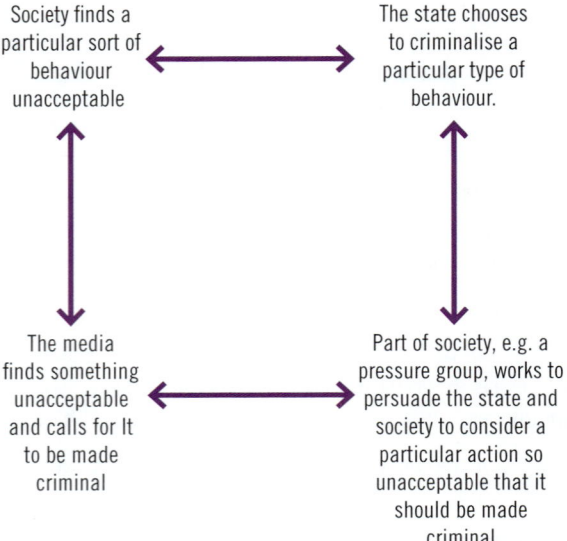

Figure 2.3 The interrelating factors that lead to an action becoming criminalised

(1977) critical Marxist discussion of criminal law and criminal justice which shows us how we can question the conventional ideas which we have been brought up to consider to be 'right'.

It will be becoming clear that whilst only the state can make an act criminal, the route to behaviour being criminalised is complex. It might start with society, the state, a pressure group, or the media, and the ways in which these four elements interact affect both whether the activity is made criminal and how society views those who take part in the behaviour. The two-way relationships between these elements are shown diagrammatically in **Figure 2.3**.

We have seen that what makes up the criminal law (the motivations and perceptions that help to shape it) and how those who break the law are treated are both very complicated areas of discussion. Each depends on the society you are considering and the period of history you are looking at. For most of the rest of this chapter we will focus on England and Wales today, in the early 2020s, looking at:

- the difference between crime and 'deviance';
- how a society may decide which actions to criminalise;
- some of the legal requirements of criminalisation; and
- whether we should have criminal laws at all—does criminalising activity cause more harm than it solves?

2.3 Crime and deviance

Many criminologists discuss 'deviance' rather than crime. They construct **theories** that explain why people may be deviant rather than why they offend. Are deviance and crime different and, if so, how? Deviance is almost always a wider concept than crime. It includes behaviour that is different, out of the ordinary, or not accepted but is not legally controlled (Downes et al., 2016: 21–6). In general usage, to say that behaviour is deviant simply means that it is odd or unacceptable and, in sociology, deviant behaviour is outside the acceptable standards of behaviour in a society, particularly social or sexual standards of behaviour. Breaking social rules (being deviant) can also involve breaking legal rules (committing a crime), but not necessarily (for a fuller discussion see Goode, 2016; Erikson, 1966). Deviance could be stealing a chocolate bar or carrying out a murder (both of which are also crimes) but it might also include picking your nose or scratching your private parts in public, and is very much based on the cultural standards in a society, or even the cultural expectations of part of a society.

In the case of deviance, it is often difficult to work out exactly how certain acts get classified as deviant or how one that used to be deviant becomes acceptable, if there is no criminalisation the state does not need to be involved. It is possible for the movement to come from normal people, especially if they use the internet to garner support. However, those in power (or famous film and sports stars) are still more influential both online and on social media where their tweets or ideas may be circulated more widely and agreed with or 'liked' more frequently. More normally, even today, apart from local ideas of deviance, the actions to be thought of as deviant or acceptable are still very much influenced by powerful organisations such as the church (and other religious bodies), the media, education, and even the state.

Adhering to social rules and norms

Most societies have an unwritten, though largely accepted, set of norms (rules, standards, or values) that members of that society are expected to live by. These are social rules and not legally enforceable. The norms or rules are specific to each culture; what is deviant in one society may not be deviant in another. In some Islamic societies (or parts of societies), women may be expected to wear the hijab or the burqa and failure to dress correctly would be considered deviant. Whereas in some societies wearing the hijab or burqa may be considered deviant, in France to wear a burqa in public is a *crime*. It is often not the behaviour that is deviant, but the behaviour *in that context*. For example, it is perfectly acceptable to tackle someone and take their legs from under them in a rugby match, but to do that to someone on the street would be both deviant and a crime; to shout at a rugby match might be acceptable, but to do so at an orchestral concert is generally not (it is deviant); to have sexual intercourse in the privacy of your own home is acceptable, but to do so on the central reservation of a motorway would be deviant, maybe even criminal.

Even the acts at the centre of the most serious crimes are sometimes allowed, and even called for by a society in certain situations. For example, killing is generally considered to be a very serious crime (murder or manslaughter), but governments condone (accept) killing in some circumstances, such as to defend yourself (you can use appropriate force to defend yourself, even if that results in the death of another person) or where it is accidental (a failed operation to try to help the patient), and even call on people to kill others in the act of war (see **Controversy and debate 2.1**). The social and cultural rules governing each society are complex, never written down, and are finely balanced, often difficult for an outsider to understand and live by. The way in which the rules are applied is often perplexing. For example, the actions of many heroes might just as easily be defined as deviant. Some criminal acts are not thought of as deviant: driving over 60 mph on the open road in England and Wales is a crime but is often thought of as normal rather than deviant behaviour.

Societies and parts of societies (often referred to as 'subcultures' in criminological writing) use positive and negative reinforcements (encouragements or **punishments**) to try to encourage people to conform to their group or subcultural social norms. This is called **social control**. So, a child will be praised for saying please and thank you in the right places; or a child will be told off and may have to stay late at school if they fail to do their homework. Similarly, an adult who does as an employer asks or expects at work may get promotion, whereas one who is constantly late or fails to perform tasks correctly may lose their employment. None of these things is criminal but such incentives and punishments are used to enforce criminal laws. So, individuals and society might praise someone for good behaviour and for recognising (and reporting) criminal behaviour in others through, for example, honours (such as the Queen's Honours List, published biannually) and positive stories about them in the media. However, if a person is violent to another they may be punished by the state (imprisonment) and on release they may also be 'punished', in a sense, by society through a display of disapproval, for example rejection by employers or exclusion from certain groups or activities. The media may also publicly humiliate them in some way.

Deviance as healthy: Durkheim's view

Émile Durkheim (1858–1917) was a famous French sociologist who saw deviance as a normal and necessary part of people living together in social groups; he saw a certain level of deviance as an indication of a healthy society (Durkheim, 1895). Durkheim suggested that all groups of people had to set out certain agreed standards or values by which they should live, and these boundaries allowed people to learn what was acceptable. In every group there is always someone who is prepared to intentionally break the expected standards, to offend or be a deviant, often for their own gain. Durkheim also argued that the group is not entirely homogeneous (the same): each person would interpret the boundaries as being in a slightly different place, so one person might believe they are acting within the boundaries set by the group whereas in fact other members believe they have overstepped the boundaries. In this case, they are deviant. We have seen this very clearly in recent years in the **#MeToo** campaign, where some of the men who have been accused clearly do not feel that they did anything wrong (for example, touching a woman on the knee without asking, as Adam Sandler did on the Graham Norton Show in October 2017), whereas society considers their acts deviant and judges them in that light. For Durkheim, the fact that someone breaks the norm gives the rule a purpose: to try to prevent others from following suit and to allow the group to show what should happen in such circumstances, to show their idea of justice. It also allows the group to mark the deviant person out as different and as someone who should not be copied.

The frequency with which deviant acts are committed can affect how society perceives the deviant person. If lots of people break a particular rule, then the breach starts to become normal and the society may decide to change the rule: this deviance can lead to social change and renewal. For example, the use of marijuana used to be a criminal offence which was heavily punished and considered very deviant by most people in society. Today it remains a crime, but those who are found to have a small amount of the drug for personal use are often not prosecuted (this is called decriminalisation because it is still technically illegal but not usually prosecuted). This movement towards cannabis being more widely accepted in the UK came into clear focus when the prescription and use of cannabis to treat certain well-defined medical problems was legalised in October 2018. Since this development, there has been a lot of discussion about whether

CONTROVERSY AND DEBATE 2.1

Attitudes towards killing

Killing is a complex issue and there is a lot of disagreement about its nature; how it is viewed depends on the perspective of the individual and the society. These two famous quotes give a flavour of some of the disagreements:

> To my mind, to kill in war is not a whit better than to commit ordinary murder.
>
> (Albert Einstein)

> Kill a man, and you are an assassin. Kill millions of men, and you are a conqueror. Kill everyone, and you are a god.
>
> (Jean Rostand, famous French botanist)

Intentionally killing another person leads to many difficult questions about where we should draw the line concerning what should be considered illegal killing (murder or manslaughter), and what should be condoned, or even glorified. The drawing of this line was the issue in these two real-life controversies.

Kay Gilderdale

In 2010, a judge criticised the Crown Prosecution Service for pursuing a case of attempted murder against a loving mother, Kay Gilderdale, who helped her seriously ill adult daughter to die after the daughter failed in a suicide attempt. The judge praised the jury for taking only two hours to clear Ms Gilderdale.

This is a controversial case because when a jury acquits a person who has clearly committed a criminal act, they are saying that they believe that it would be unjust or immoral to punish in this particular case; they are saying the law is wrong. Although it was clear that they did not want the law to be applied in this case, it is difficult to interpret exactly what they thought the law *should* be. Did they think that assisted dying should be legalised, or just that the law on it should not apply in this particular case? It is also impossible to know whether that jury was representative of society as a whole, in other words whether the rest of society would support the legalisation of assisted dying in certain cases.

Read more about this case online (try this article, BBC News Magazine, 'Why I helped my daughter to die', 1 February 2010) and consider the following questions:

- What do you think should have happened?
- Would your answer change if the daughter was a child?
- If you think the jury made the right decision, how can we ensure that relatives are not killed because they are a burden, rather than because they are terminally ill and want to die?

Nicolas Bonnemaison

In 2014, a French doctor, Nicolas Bonnemaison, was acquitted of killing seven of his vulnerable and terminally ill patients over a 14-month period. Again, strictly speaking, the doctor had committed murder under French law. He admitted giving injections but claimed to be relieving pain not intending to kill, though he knew that the dose was likely to cause the patient to die. He was acquitted, though he was struck off the medical register so that he could no longer practise as a doctor.

This decision was controversial because doctors are supposed to save lives, not take them. In France, the decision of whether someone is guilty or innocent is taken by judges, so it is difficult to gauge from the decision alone whether it would be generally supported, but those in the courtroom applauded when the doctor was acquitted and the case was positively reported in the media.

- Do you agree with the decision in this case? Should a doctor be able to kill, or assist their patients to die?
- If so, under what circumstances? Should it be only when patients ask them to or, if patients are incapable, should their relatives be able to make such a request?
- Should all doctors be expected to help their patients to die, or should it be possible for doctors and nurses to say it contravenes their beliefs and they do not want to assist anyone to die?

(Note: a year later, the appeal court upheld the acquittal of six of the cases but convicted on one, they sentenced him leniently, a two-year suspended sentence, a punishment that is not enforced unless the person commits another offence within that period.)

These two cases reveal some of the many issues around the idea of illegal killing (murder and manslaughter), and when it should be condoned or permitted. You need to be able to consider these kinds of cases from all angles and build your own arguments as to what you believe should be permitted and why.

---

the production, sale, and use of cannabis should be fully legalised, as this would allow it to be regulated and provided in safe doses.

On the other hand, Durkheim recognised that if in a particular community an act which might be legal becomes thought of as deviant by society, with those who participate increasingly excluded, then it will be committed less and less frequently. It might even be criminalised, or if it is already criminal, the sentencing might become increasingly harsh. An example of these changing views of deviance is society's attitudes to smoking. In the 1950s and 1960s, smoking was widespread and was glamorised in films, but slowly the view of this activity has altered. Today it is illegal to smoke in confined public spaces and smokers are often looked down upon or negatively judged; they often apologise for their habit and are expected to ask permission before lighting up when other people are present. This type of social change can happen in pockets of society, for example in many low crime areas people are concerned for very low-level offences, or actions which are not even crimes, and will exclude people who fail to act in what they consider to be acceptable ways. For example, some communities are very intolerant of anyone who drops litter, whereas in other communities the dropping of litter is almost the norm.

At this point, it might be helpful to briefly summarise what deviance is:

- Deviance is any violation of social norms, values, or expectations.
- It changes over time and is different in different cultures or societies. It may even be different in different parts of a society, for example youth culture can accept acts which older people find deviant.
- People who break societal expectations are often called deviant.
- People who make the rules and decide who is deviant and how they should be treated have social power and can control others in the society.

Possibly the most important thing to recognise and remember about deviance is that unlike crime (breaches of the criminal law), it is in the eye of the beholder—what one person classes as deviant another will not and so, as with crime, deviance is socially constructed (Downes et al., 2016: 21–6). It is very important to remember this because many of the theories in this book try to explain why some people take part in deviant behaviour and try to find the causes of deviance. If we cannot agree on what behaviour is deviant, it becomes more difficult to explain or find causes for that behaviour (see **What do you think? 2.2**).

WHAT DO YOU THINK? 2.2

What kinds of behaviour should be considered deviant?

Consider which, if any, of the following acts are deviant.

- Smoking.
- Writing a special scientific theory and winning a Nobel prize. (This person is clearly out of the ordinary, but are they deviant?)
- Drinking alcohol. (Alcohol is very common in our society—it is offered at almost all social functions and is used to symbolise celebration of success on many greetings cards. In such a society, is the deviant person the alcoholic or the teetotaller; that is, someone who does not drink?)
- Living as a hermit.
- Cheating at cards. (What about cheating when playing Patience, a card game against yourself?)
- Being rude to people.
- Failing to pick up after your dog if it fouls:
  - on the pavement,
  - in the park,
  - in the woods or the open countryside.

  (In light of environmental concern about our use of plastics, is it now *more* deviant to pick up the dog mess with a plastic bag or to leave it where it is?)
- Becoming an eco-warrior.

The final point is a particularly interesting one, given how quickly societal views are changing about the environment, and what is and is not acceptable. Do you think it is acceptable or deviant to:

- discuss your views on the need to protect the environment with friends or make TV programmes about the dangers plastic poses for sea life;
- try to make friends and other people feel uncomfortable if they buy or use lots of plastic;
- go out on marches to call on government to change the laws to support the environment;
- physically attack people or companies (by attacking their premises) for their failure to protect the environment;
- use your fame to try to influence others to protect the environment, and make public verbal attacks on individuals and corporations for doing things which are damaging to the environment (verbal attacks)?

We have seen that although deviance is an important concept for criminologists, crime is more than deviance. This means that to attempt to define crime, we need to try to isolate the factor or factors that mark it out as different to 'just' non-criminal, deviant acts—what makes criminal behaviour worthy of criminalising? This is an important question because—as we have discussed—those in positions of influence need to have limits placed on their power. If members of a government could each choose things they merely did not like and have them criminalised then that would clearly be unacceptable. For example, burping might be criminalised and punishable with imprisonment, but most people would think that was absurd and unfair. Some dictators have passed some odd laws, for example in Romania in the 1980s, Ceaușescu made it a criminal offence to own a typewriter without a government licence, and in the 1990s the President of Turkmenistan, Saparmurat Niyazov, banned dogs in the capital city and closed all libraries and hospitals outside it. What if the government decided to criminalise crossing the road, talking with your mouth full, showering or bathing, or even breathing on Mondays? Need we go on? Without limits, without some guiding principles to decide whether an activity should be criminalised, justice would be left to chance.

2.4 Defining 'crime': the harm principle

Many suggest that what is known as the 'harm principle' might be the best standard by which we should decide whether an activity should be criminal. By this principle, set out by John Stuart Mill (1806–73), an English philosopher, any conduct or activity should be legal unless it harms other people. Mill stated that:

> the only purpose for which power can be rightfully exercised over any member of a civilised community against his will is to prevent harm to others. His own good, either physical or moral, is not sufficient warrant. He cannot rightfully be compelled to do or forebear because in the opinion of others to do so would be wise or even right.
>
> (Mill, 1859: 6)

What constitutes 'harm'?

This principle holds that if conduct is not harmful to others it should not be criminal, even if others strongly dislike it. For example, picking your nose may be considered disgusting and unpleasant but it does not harm others; therefore it should not be criminal. Another example could be being naked in public (see **Controversy and debate 2.2**). Taking your clothes off does not harm anyone else. The most complete discussion of the harm principle and where its limits lie was by Joel Feinberg (1984–8), who in four large volumes considered the issues in detail. Here we will only look briefly at some of the concerns and areas where there is still a lot of debate.

With any discussion of the harm principle there is always discussion about what constitutes harm. Does it need to be physical harm or will emotional or psychological harm count? And, if we include psychological harm, then what about actions which disgust us or offend our sensibilities (are disagreeable to us, hurt our feelings or our sense of dignity)? Each person who writes about harm disagrees about its limits (Mill, 1859; Feinberg, 1985). Is public nudity harmful or is it merely a moral issue? Does harm include acts of omission? If you fail to jump into a lake to save a drowning child or fail to stop to help someone injured in a car accident have you harmed them and, if so, should your failures be criminal? If you are a match as a donor, should failure to donate a kidney be an offence?

These are very difficult questions which have concerned criminologists, lawyers, and philosophers for a long time. Sometimes, understanding why the harm principle is important can help us to find answers to these questions. Many argue that applying the harm principle as the test for criminalising activities is the best way of protecting our autonomy. All of us should be able to choose to do lots of silly things. For example, you may choose to never step on the cracks when you walk along the pavement, or to talk to yourself all the time, to watch television for 15 hours a day, to only eat toast during term time, to listen to advertising jingles, to only communicate through tweets: these choices may be a little strange to others but they are not harming anyone, so others should respect your right to make them. This is a sort of 'live and let live' policy; in any society there needs to be tolerance of others even if we find them a little odd. Finding something odd or disliking it does not mean that it causes us any harm.

As well as protecting our freedom of choice, the harm principle also ensures that we are each protected from the actions of others when they might harm us or diminish our freedom of choice. As Isiah Berlin (1958) wrote, 'Freedom for the pike is death for the minnows' (at page 4, Berlin attributes the quote to Tawney though most people attribute it to Berlin); in other words, the liberty of some must depend on the restraint of others, usually those who are less powerful. For example, if you choose to save up money to travel to London and someone steals the money,

CONTROVERSY AND DEBATE 2.2

Legal moralism: debates about public nudity

A good example of a moral issue that is the subject of much debate is that of public nudity. Consider the following example.

On a warm sunny day, Meryl and Ned are enjoying a picnic in the local park and decide to remove their clothes, to feel free. Other park visitors have different reactions: some find it amusing; others find it odd but are willing to tolerate it; many are offended, even outraged by their behaviour. Meryl and Ned argue that they enjoy the feeling of freedom they get from not wearing clothes, that it does not harm anyone, and that they should not be judged by the moral standards of others. Those who are offended want them to put their clothes back on, and some are so upset that they will feel excluded from using the park unless such behaviour is prohibited, limiting their freedom to use this amenity.

What do you think should happen in this situation?

- Should Meryl and Ned be free to go nude in the park?
- Should society make nudity unacceptable and deviant so that nudists are treated less favourably?
- Should nudity be made criminal? At the moment it is not illegal to be nude in public unless you expose your genitals intending to cause 'alarm or distress', see s. 66 of the Sexual Offences Act 2003.

This is a difficult case to decide. To force Meryl and Ned to wear clothes because others are offended is to criminalise the activity on largely moral grounds, because it offends some people and this goes against the harm principle. It interferes with Meryl and Ned's autonomy and does not harm others. Mill would argue that an individual 'cannot rightfully be compelled to do or forebear because in the opinion of others to do so would be wise or even right' (1859: 6). However, to fail to prevent nudity may lead those offended to feel their experience and feelings are less important, they may feel unable to visit places where people are nude.

A real-life example which, though it may seem silly, has brought up similar issues and proved very expensive for the state, is that of Stephen Gough, also known as the 'naked rambler'. Gough is an advocate for public nudity and, as a political statement, he refuses to wear clothes—see **Figure 2.4**. Gough has spent over nine years in prison simply for refusing to cover his private parts. As we have noted, nudity in public is not a criminal offence unless you intend to cause alarm or distress, but under the Crime and Disorder Act 1998, any person who acts in a way that has 'caused or is likely to cause harassment alarm or distress to one or more persons' can be required, through a civil Anti-Social Behaviour Order (ASBO), to refrain from acting in that way. Mr Gough, an ex-soldier, was given an ASBO that requires him to cover his genitals and buttocks when he is in public (note: now these laws are largely found in the Anti-Social Behaviour, Crime and Policing Act 2014). He refuses to wear anything except his rucksack, so breaches the order and is then imprisoned for that breach. At the time of writing, Gough has spent longer in prison than most rapists would, as long as those who rape a young child, and his case has probably cost the state about £465,000 already—the imprisonment alone is expensive but there is also the cost of the police and court time (he has been to the Court of Appeal).

All of this has happened despite the fact that in 2001 a jury refused to convict another nudist, Vincent Bethell, because they did not think that merely being naked on the streets necessarily caused harm and distress. Therefore, the debate we considered earlier in relation to the hypothetical example of Meryl and Ned is, in fact, very real. The 'naked rambler' is not a sexual predator, he is not violent or a threat to anyone, he commits no crime, he only breaches his ASBO (something designed specifically to control him). Is anyone harmed from his actions? Is it just to imprison him for this lifestyle choice? Is this a breach of his human rights?

Figure 2.4 The 'naked rambler' on a 'from fear to freedom' protest walk in London

Source: Tom Pilston/The Independent/Shutterstock

they not only steal the money itself but also your freedom to choose to spend it as you like and, in this instance, your freedom to travel to London. Society hopes that having a law against theft of this sort will make people less likely to steal from one another, so the law is intended to protect us all, to protect our autonomy.

Before we move on to discuss other aspects of the harm principle, it is important to note that whilst this principle may allow a society to make a harm-producing act criminal and to punish those who transgress, it does not require the society to make *all* harmful activities criminal. It is therefore a *necessary* (only things which are harmful should be crimes) but not a *sufficient* test (not all things which are harmful must be made into crimes) (see Duff, 2007). For example, if a parent goes out every week and spends all their wages on gambling and alcohol, clearly the family suffers or is harmed, but should the society make gambling and drinking alcohol illegal?

It is clear that the harm principle as a basis for understanding why actions are made crimes is attractive, and few people reject it entirely, but it has been argued to be too vague to use as a hard-and-fast test as to whether to *make* an act into a criminal offence. We therefore need to consider the limits of the idea in more detail. In this section, we will consider whether and how the harm principle applies to the following:

- moral issues, including offence and anxiety;
- harm to the self;
- indirect harm.

We will conclude our consideration of the harm principle by summing up its limitations.

Acts causing offence and anxiety: moral issues

We have seen that the harm principle does *not* permit criminalising something just because it is immoral, because it breaks the general norms of behaviour, or because others dislike it or find it offensive. Criminalisation on moral grounds is usually referred to as **legal moralism** and it involves prohibiting acts merely because they are offensive to the majority in that society, or because it is believed that if one fails to prohibit them they might destroy the very fabric of a society. In the past, many acts were criminalised because they broke some of our moral codes, usually because they went against Christian principles and performance of these acts was thought to harm that religion or question the divine authority, for example blasphemy, suicide, and many sexual practices.

However, as society in the UK has become more secular (non-religious), as well as more multicultural and multifaith, it has moved away from the idea that morals in our society are fixed and never alter, and must be protected from change. One of the most famous arguments given for this kind of protection against change was a pamphlet written by Lord Justice Devlin in 1965. At this time, Parliament in England and Wales was considering legalising homosexual acts between adults (aged 21 or over, at that time) in private, and Devlin argued that it was important to retain homosexuality as illegal in order to 'protect the moral fibre' of our society. For Devlin, the moral fibre of a society (its essential ideas about morality) was essential to its existence, so failing to protect society against seriously immoral behaviour would lead to social disintegration and therefore prove harmful. Whilst this is a moral argument, it could also be seen as citing the harm principle by claiming that the moral standing of a society is linked to its health. Whilst few would now align themselves with Devlin, we retain many criminal laws which might be seen as part of legal moralism; laws such as the use of illegal substances, laws against common prostitution or against brothels, and laws that prohibit sadomasochism among consenting adults (this arose from *R* v *Brown* [1994] 1 AC 212) are just a few examples. Many would wish to retain these as crimes, but it is very difficult to argue for their retention on anything other than moral (or maybe paternal) grounds. Take a look at **Controversy and debate 2.2**.

The simple harm principle offers little in the way of resolving the issue put forward in **Controversy and debate 2.2**, but there are some possible solutions. Feinberg (1985: Ch. 8) suggested that where something might cause serious offence then it is harmful and could be prohibited. He describes 'serious offence' as being more than causing squeamishness, disgust, or being unpleasant. To qualify, the activity should cause a psychological reaction or emotional trauma (shock, maybe) in someone of a normal disposition (not overly susceptible to offence), and to test for this one should consider the intensity, duration, and extent of the feeling.

An offence becomes more serious if a large proportion of the population find it more than just unpleasant. This is not really measurable and therefore Feinberg also suggests that even if there is such a reaction, if individuals can reasonably avoid the behaviour which causes them to feel that way it should not be criminal. People can avoid the park where Meryl and Ned are naked (but is it reasonable to expect them to do that, especially if it is the only park in their area), whereas, in the example of the naked rambler, people cannot avoid his behaviour. If a sufficient number of people are seriously offended by public nudity and it is not something they can reasonably and easily avoid, then Feinberg argues that it should be criminalised. He seems to argue for this outcome because serious offence is akin to harm. For Feinberg, there is a two-pronged test: is the activity seriously offensive; can it be reasonably avoided? Now try applying this test to **Controversy and debate 2.2** (is there an argument for setting aside part of a public park for nudity, or for making simple nudity in public a criminal offence?) and to the other crimes noted earlier: the use of illegal substances; laws against common prostitution or against brothels; laws that prohibit sadomasochism among consenting adults.

Take a look at another example, set out in **What do you think? 2.3**. If that situation happened 80 years ago, the number of people of Ola's race in the society may have been small, and the majority might not have been concerned about this kind of incident. Today, however, UK society is multicultural, so many would strongly argue that this kind of speech should not be legal (does this indicate a more or less tolerant society?—see Waldron, 2012). This suggests that if only a few people are offended, everything is acceptable, and the activity should not be criminalised, but if many people are offended then the state should criminalise the activity. Does this make sense? Should this decision depend on the number of people offended or on something more? Does hate speech (such as racial hatred) differ from insulting speech or behaviour? In some ways, it does not differ as both racial hatred and other insulting speech is usually aimed at someone and is intentionally used to offend them and hurt their feelings. However, many would argue that hate speech goes further than other forms of verbal abuse, such as insulting someone for something they have done: it hurts or harms a whole race (or other group) so although there is or may be a particular victim, there is also a whole race (or other group) which is attacked. The perpetrator(s) of such speech choose the victim because of what that person represents—here a racial group, but it might also be religion, sexual orientation, etc., or what the perpetrator thinks they represent and what they disapprove of or hate. The harm is intentional, or at least done knowing it is likely to offend, and the victim or immediate target (as arguably the whole group is victimised) is chosen because of something they cannot change—their race or sexual orientation—or could only change by denying a core part of who they are—their religion—so they cannot really escape vulnerability.

These factors mark racial hatred out as different from other insults and actions that may cause offence. Feinberg (1985: Ch. 8) allows for this eventuality by calling on a society to take into account the personal importance of the behaviour to the actor themselves (for instance, if they are trying to make a political point) and whether it serves any social value. Racial hatred may be important to the person espousing it—they may believe in the truth of what they say and wish to enjoy freedom of speech to express themselves—but the social value of such speech is low, if not negative. Feinberg also calls on society to take account of two other things:

1. Where and when the conduct took place—could the freedom to express these views have been enjoyed somewhere else or at a different time?
2. The extent to which there was a spiteful intention.

These two considerations would often permit an inference against normal freedom of speech towards that of racial hatred, as the latter is most inflammatory when it takes

WHAT DO YOU THINK? 2.3

What constitutes hate speech and should it be legal?

A young woman, Ola, visits a local 24-hour shop late in the evening to pick up some small items for her family for the next morning. Just outside the shop, she is verbally attacked by two young men, Peter and Quinn, that she has never seen before and who have never seen her before. They are shouting racial hatred at her. She is very shaken by the events but was not physically attacked and no one in the shop thought twice about it, they see it as a bit insulting but nothing more.

- What do you think would or should happen in this type of case?
- What would be the outcome of applying Feinberg's rule to the situation?

See **Figure 2.5** and the associated press release, 'Government launches new national hate crime awareness campaign' (https://www.gov.uk/government/news/government-launches-new-national-hate-crime-awareness-campaign).

Figure 2.5 An advert from the 2018 government campaign aimed at increasing awareness of hate crime

Source: HM Government/Crown copyright

place in public or is directed at those most likely to be offended.

What do you think? 2.4 provides examples of activities in which it is assumed that if there is consent there should be no crime. Without consent, the first would be rape and the second actual or grievous bodily harm (ABH or GBH depending on the extent of the injuries)—they would be crimes because they would harm the non-consenting participants. However, if there is true consent there is no harm (except that consented to and welcomed), so it would seem that the only reason to criminalise is the protection of morals. Dempsey (2005) would disagree and argues that in the first example there is potential harm which is so great that we need to protect against it by criminalising all sales of sexual favours. She argues that when someone pays for sex they cannot be sure that the sex worker is willingly consenting. The sex worker may appear willing but may (a) have been trafficked, (b) have been forced into this by a pimp, or (c) be too young to consent. In (a) or (b), the central crime is by another person (in our example, the trafficker or the pimp, not Steve), but in all three, without consent Steve would be guilty of a sexual offence. The situation could be viewed as similar in the case of the sadomasochists, as a third party may traffic or otherwise pressurise someone to participate to provide sexual gratification. Where, for example, Tom and Una have been trafficked (clearly that is a crime but the activities later may not be) and are being paid to inflict pain on Vicky and Wahib, there may be no harm to Tom and Una (who might be happy to inflict pain) and the harm to Vicky and Wahib is consensual (paid for, even) so still there should be no crime.

Under the harm principle, a crime has only been committed if someone does not fully consent. To criminalise without direct harm and in case there is a harm (such as people trafficked for prostitution) is known as controlling due to remote harm. The decision in *R v Brown* [1994] 1 AC 212 at 246 (this case was discussed earlier in this section) opened up another type of remote harm; the judges were concerned that others, particularly children, might be tempted to imitate and so participate in sadomasochistic acts. Many would argue that remote harm takes harm too far (see, for example, Baker, 2007) and the law should seek to prosecute the direct wrongdoers (the trafficker and the pimp) rather than the person who buys the sexual favour. Husak (2007), for example, would suggest that no one should face criminal charges because of a remote harm unless:

> they have some degree of culpability for the ultimate harm risked. It is not enough that the performance of the proscribed conduct just happens to make the occurrence of the ultimate harm more likely.
>
> (Husak, 2007: 174)

Therefore, in our examples (**What do you think 2.4**), Steve's buying of sexual favours should not be criminalised unless his actions make the trafficking more likely. Some might argue that they do. However, in this sort of example remote harm is hiding a moral wrong—here maybe not the sexual morals but the exploitation of certain groups, particularly women (see the discussion in **Chapters 13** and **14**). In some instances, people are trafficked to work on farms or to clean people's homes (where they may work as slaves,

---

WHAT DO YOU THINK? 2.4

Should consensual harm be criminal?

Example 1: Rachel is 20 and a sex worker. Steve regularly visits her to pay for sex.

- Is there any crime in this scenario?
- Should it be possible to prosecute Steve for his behaviour?
- Is Steve's behaviour harmful?

Note: If Rachel willingly consents then arguably there is no harm—it is a victimless activity so should it be a crime at all? Many might argue that morals provide the only reason for this being a crime, do you agree and, if so, should it be criminalised at all?

Example 2: Tom, Una, Vicky, and Wahib are all adults and good friends. They are also sadomasochists who meet regularly to participate in sadomasochism for sexual gratification. They all consent to the behaviour and each of them enjoys it equally, no one is being exploited.
This behaviour is criminal.

- Should it be?
- Is it harmful?

Note: If they all consent and no one is exploited, is there any harm apart from harm to self (as assessed by others) and, in that case, should the activities be legal? Should these actions be criminalised merely because some people are morally appalled that anyone should find this behaviour sexually gratifying?

These are both examples of activities which might be criminalised merely because some people find them immoral. Is that acceptable?

unpaid, and unable to leave). Does that mean that we should outlaw the hiring of farm labourers or domestic cleaners? Is the suggestion to criminalise the buying of sexual favours made in relation to prostitution partly on moral grounds and partly to protect a vulnerable group—women—from being exploited? Dempsey (2005) would recognise that where there is genuine consent buying sex involves no direct harm, but would find that potentially there is a very serious harm (rape). There is no social gain in selling sex, so she would argue that Steve's activity should be criminalised. This is not the same in the case of farm labourers and domestic cleaners who provide what others see as a positive benefit to society, to get food on the table or have a clean house. This appears to ignore the moral dilemma until one asks why there is no social gain for selling sexual favours—surely it is because we consider it to have less worth (morally or ethically) than other occupations, though arguably it fulfils a sexual need (particularly for those who cannot get sexual gratification elsewhere). Why is this less valuable than a need for a clean house? For a more in-depth discussion of moral issues, see Millie (2016: Ch. 3).

Harm to self

Where behaviour harms someone else it clearly falls within the harm principle and is activity which may be criminalised. However, what about behaviour that only harms one person? The harm principle does not normally protect people from themselves. Rock climbing may be dangerous and to do it without proper equipment may not be in a person's best interests, but it should not be a crime and people should be allowed to take part in rock climbing even if it is not very sensible, as long as it does not harm other people. Here, the argument is that harm (or potential harm) to one person should not be sufficient; this certainly falls in line with Mill's principle (1859) which refers to 'harm to others' and specifically states that 'His own good, either physical or moral, is not sufficient warrant' (1859: 6).

Taking actions for the good of an adult (to protect their life, health, or safety) when they do not choose to be protected is called **paternalism** (you might have heard the phrase 'nanny state' used in the media to suggest that the state is trying to exert too much control over individuals' choices and lifestyles for societal good; for example, the introduction of the sugar tax to try to limit childhood obesity). Generally, the fact that an action could result in an individual harming themselves should not be sufficient to make it criminal, but there are examples of paternalism in our criminal laws, such as requiring people to wear seat belts in cars or helmets on motorbikes. Each of these is paternalistic, so would be difficult to justify under the harm principle. They do limit individual autonomy, but having to wear a seat belt or helmet is a small infringement on our freedom and does not impinge our life choices so maybe we should tolerate laws like these, particularly if they produce positive benefits for society, such as fewer injuries as a result of traffic accidents. Furthermore, wearing seat belts and helmets prevents greater reliance on the (already struggling) health service, saving all taxpayers money. Supporters of these laws also say that if one suggested seat belts and helmets to rational people and explained all the reasons for using them, they would choose to use them.

All these arguments may be true, but they do not make the requirement to wear a seat belt/helmet (or face a criminal penalty) any less paternalistic. Some other examples that may interfere more with real-life choices or which rational people might well reject are listed in **What do you think? 2.5**.

In all three of the examples described in **What do you think 2.5**, some people might argue that each individual is being harmed by the substance. However, others might suggest that they are being more seriously harmed by the criminalisation of the behaviour. Feinberg, 1988: introduction to Vol. 4, *Harmless Wrongdoing*), noted that the concept of harm is both vague and unclear and may be linked to wrongdoing; harm is therefore difficult to tie down and this is particularly the case when the person harmed is oneself. Clearly, this also shows that 'harm' is a constructed idea, meaning different things to different people and in different contexts. An interesting issue to examine in the context of relative harm to self, and the efforts to control this, is drug use: see **Table 2.1** for a discussion about this issue (note: legalising substance possession and use would still leave dealing through illegitimate means as a serious crime). We can see that whilst many substances (some of which are already legal) are harmful to individual users, a lot of the harm from substances comes from their misuse and some of this is exacerbated due to criminalisation. Many academics and some police officers also argue that there is little proof that criminalisation performs useful functions and advocate legalisation, or at least a more harm-based approach to the resolution of issues caused by substance misuse (Brunstrom, 2007; see more generally the websites for the Drug Equality Alliance (www.drugequality.org/reading.htm) and the Film Exchange on Alcohol and Drugs (www.fead.org.uk/)).

Indirect harm and harm to non-humans

At a number of points in this chapter, harm has been mentioned as something which does not directly hurt an individual but is more indirect, for example not wearing

WHAT DO YOU THINK? 2.5

Criminalising harm to the self

Xavia, Yara, and Zach are all 18 and each of them uses illegal substances.

Xavia smokes cannabis regularly as he enjoys how mellow it makes him feel (see **Figure 2.6**). He does not drink alcohol as he believes this is more harmful. When his friends drink, he notices that they become aggressive and attack other people and he does not want this to happen to him. Cannabis never makes him feel aggressive. He sometimes thinks about the law and about the feeling of unease he gets from the people he meets to buy his drugs.

Yara uses party drugs and sometimes some cocaine or similar substances. She is studying to be a lawyer and when she unwinds she likes the feeling drugs give her of losing herself and letting go of all her tensions. But Yara is very worried that if she is caught using illegal drugs she will lose her chance of becoming a lawyer. She used to try to stay ahead of the law and to use 'legal highs', though she worried a lot about how dangerous these might be as their effects were still unknown. She knows that there is now no such thing as legal highs but she continues to buy her drugs online as she feels safer sourcing them that way. Now she worries both about what the chemicals are doing and that just by possessing the drugs she is breaking the law.

Zach is addicted to heroin. He would like to give it up, but all his friends use and he cannot see a life beyond using. He craves the drug's effect but hates what it is doing to him.

- Should their drug use be criminal? Is it harmful?
- Is the harm caused by using the substance or by the fact that the substance is illegal?

Figure 2.6 Cannabis is a Class B illegal drug
Source: Ryan Lange/Unsplash

a seat belt means more people will suffer serious injuries due to accidents (direct harm) and the cost to the National Health Service, and therefore also the taxpayer, will rise (indirect harm). There are many other examples too, such as non-payment of taxes or erroneous applications for benefits. There may also be cases where there is the capacity to do harm, but no harm may arise; examples include breaches of health and safety, carrying weapons such as knives or guns, acts preparatory to an offence (planning a robbery and starting to collect the items necessary to carrying it out), or acts leading to terrorism.

These are an eclectic collection of crimes that are awkward to explain under the harm principle as there is no clear 'other' who is harmed. Von Hirsch (1996) argues that the harm principle can be extended to encompass at least some of these remote or indirect harms if there is a strong public interest which has been or might be breached. For example, it is harmful to us all if too much money is spent on car accidents or too little collected via taxation, or if our streets are made potentially more dangerous because people take potentially harmful items out with them and do not intend to do anything useful with those items. The last example is interesting, a car is potentially dangerous but serves the purpose of moving people and things around, whereas a gun is dangerous but carrying it on the street rarely serves any useful purpose. It is therefore possible to explain these offences using the harm principle, but this needs great care as the argument could permit the state to interfere in our lives in many and surprising ways by claiming its actions are for the public good. Certainly, Ashworth and Zedner (2008) have suggested that the way in which the criminal law is being used now is too broad; they argue that it is used to manage social order, for easy governance and control, rather than to protect the public.

Another area of indirect harm that is presently causing a lot of controversy is environmental or ecological harm—an idea we consider further in **Chapter 12**. This does not harm people directly, but it harms other species or the environment. Furthermore, the harm is not generally suffered by one individual or group, but causes a problem for everyone within and outside a nation's borders. Whilst increasingly people are arguing that this should be regulated through the criminal law (some even argue for an international crime of ecocide, see Mehta and Merz,

2.4 DEFINING 'CRIME': THE HARM PRINCIPLE

Harms caused by non-medical use of drugs	Death or health problems as a result of taking drugs	Addiction and side effects as a result of taking drugs	Accidents involving drug users and others which occur as a result of performing activities (such as driving) while under the influence of drugs.
Current solution	**Criminalisation of drug use.**		
Harms at least partially caused by current solution—caused by criminalisation of substance use	• The emergence of an illegal, unregulated 'black market' in which many dealers add substances to the drugs to 'pad them out'. These substances can be toxic or 'safe', but both cause harm: – the toxic substances cause many deaths; – the 'safe' substances mean that users do not know what dose of the drug they are using, leading to some accidental overdoses. • **Drugs are more expensive and more addictive** as dealers try to ensure they have a market. This drives users into poverty and addiction, and leading to people committing theft to 'feed their habit'. • **It is difficult for users to request help**, whether to combat addiction or because they are experiencing negative side effects, if they are using illegal substances. • **Users have to connect with criminals** to obtain drugs. Being seen to befriend criminals may lead to them being socially excluded, meaning they will socialise mainly with other users and find it more difficult to break their habit. • **People who are otherwise upstanding and law-abiding are criminalised** for using certain substances. This costs the justice system time and money and if the criminalised person—or others—consider the criminalisation unjust, this could reduce their respect for and dedication to the law.		
Alternative solutions—consider decriminalisation and addressing harms in other ways	• Medical and then social interventions. • Legalising and selling by licence, meaning that: – the content of each substance would be controlled and they would be carefully labelled, so unknown substances would not be added (the substances would be safer); – the user would know what dose they were taking so reducing the likelihood of overdosing (certainly unintentional overdosing would reduce); – fewer people would be criminalised, saving time and money. The justice system could focus on other offences and taxes could help pay for the healthcare needed by drug users; – prices may drop or at least stop rising, reducing the likelihood of people committing other crimes (theft and burglary) to 'feed their habit'. Addicts might also be able to get some substances free as part of their health treatment; – legalising and selling by licence would prevent people moving to ever stronger and more addictive substances—there would be no dealers to tempt or persuade them; – legalising and selling by licence might reduce the need for and size of the black market so might help to reduce serious and organised crime. • Testing for substances (and offering healthcare) to deter people from performing tasks under the influence of drugs and identify and address drug use before accidents happen.		

Note: Even if possession and use were legalised, dealing and smuggling would remain serious offences.

Table 2.1 Harms caused by the use and control of the use of drugs

Figure 2.7 Insect decline is an example of one of the consequences of ecological harm
Source: Kathy Servian/Unsplash

to illustrate the complexity of the concept of harm and who and what it should protect (see **Figure 2.7**).

The limits of the harm principle

We have seen that the harm principle has many limitations: just because something is harmful does not mean that it should be criminalised (Duff, 2007). If you go to work with a cold, you may be contagious and cause harm to your colleagues, but that should not be a criminal act. So, it is not logical to say 'actions should be criminalised if they are harmful to others'. You can say: 'the state should not criminalise activities which are not harmful to others'; or 'if an action is harmful then the state may be sensible to consider whether it should be criminalised'. In other words, 'harm to others' acts as a gatekeeper. It should be necessary to show that an activity harms others before you criminalise it, but that alone should not be sufficient grounds to say an activity *should* be criminalised. As Gardner states:

> [t]he harm principle says that the law should not be used to restrict or punish harmless activities. . . . it adds that the law should not restrict or punish harmful activities in ways which are disproportionate to the harm. But beyond this, it says nothing about how, or even when, harmful activities should be dealt with by the law.
>
> (Gardner, 1994: 213–14)

2015), would this argument stand on the harm principle or on some other basis? Most of the discussion seems based on indirect harm, similar to that of economic harms but would this bring it into conflict with Ashworth and Zedner's (2008) overcriminalisation thesis?

The final area of harm to be briefly mentioned here is that done to non-human sentient species, and would include animal cruelty. This is particularly difficult to fit within the harm principle as it is so focused on harms to humans, and yet increasingly it is an area of behaviour that people want controlled at both a national and international level (see Maher et al., 2017). Our cruelty to and protection of animals has had a complex history, and religion, rights, and moral and ethical arguments have all been used to both protect the right of humans to use animals as we choose and to protect animals against our abusive acts. The debate will not be opened here and is mentioned only

In conclusion, the harm principle is sometimes useful to test which activities should *not* be criminalised but is not very useful in deciding which activities *should* be criminalised. For a clear discussion of all of these issues, see Herring (2015), Williams (2012), and, for a rather different perspective, Dorling et al. (2008).

2.5 Other ways to decide whether an action should be a crime

If we return to our starting point, setting out the need for criminal law as an arbiter (solver of a dispute) between individual freedoms and harmonious social living, including social interactions, then this provides both the impetus towards criminalising certain acts, but also the reason for limiting the types of actions which attract a criminal sanction. Criminalisation, especially when backed up with punishment, is harmful: it imposes extreme restrictions on a person's freedom via, for example, imprisonment, which can cause some offenders psychological harm or lead to social exclusion or removal of funds (fines), which may mean that the individual and their family have less money to spend. Acts should therefore only be criminalised and punished if there is a very good reason for this. If a state interferes with the rights and freedoms of an individual in cases where there is no harm to others or no acceptable reason for the intervention, then it is an abuse of power (Henry and Milivanovic, 1996; Quinney, 1977). However, some state interference is necessary to protect citizens from the abuse of power or rights by some people, so many argue that some criminal law is necessary.

In this section we recognise that whilst in many cases the harm principle is central to deciding whether an act should be criminal, it is not useful in all cases. It is often suggested that when deciding whether an act should be a crime we should also take account of values (such as human rights or protecting groups of people) and the need to protect people through regulating potentially dangerous acts, or the use of potentially dangerous objects. In this section we will examine issues which may be taken into consideration alongside or instead of the harm principle when deciding whether and how to criminalise certain behaviours:

- Deciding on crimes using values and regulations: whether the group interest is sometimes more important than the individual interest, and how regulations can be used to provide order or safety, with breach of the regulation being a criminal offence.
- How rights can form the basis for and act as limits to criminal laws.

Deciding on 'crimes' using values and regulations

We briefly touched on the idea that the criminal law can be used to protect group interests when discussing the example of Ola given in **What do you think? 2.3**. Cane had this to say about the issue of individual freedom and group interests:

> individual freedom would have little or no value in the absence of external constraints. In this light, it seems hard to justify giving the individual's interest in freedom of choice lexical priority over the interest in social cooperation and coordination.

(Cane, 2006: 23)

Few would dispute that without criminal law the freedoms of many might be reduced, but is Cane right to suggest that the group be prioritised over the individual? The question here is whether we should use the criminal law to protect the group interest when this will lead to individuals being convicted and punished if they break the law. In some situations where the group interests are strong, this might be the correct way forward. In the context of the example of Ola, we considered the case for making racial hatred a crime where other verbal abuse should escape and there we noted that where the group was disadvantaged and there was no social gain to the abuse, more harm might be done by permitting the speech (because a whole group would be harmed) than prohibiting it. This illustrates that, in some cases, the community or group interest must be considered. Furthermore, Marshall and Duff (1998) suggest that a community may need to protect its values because some of these:

> are so central to a community's identity and self-understanding, to its conception of its members' good, that actions which attack or flout those values are not merely individual matters . . . but attacks on the community.

(Marshall and Duff, 1998: 21–2)

They do not indicate which values fall into this category but in modern Britain racism may breach our societal value to respect each person equally. The question still arises as to whether this should attract a *criminal* level of control by that community; is the community permitted to harm the perpetrator because they breach that value? Presumably, we only need to criminalise actions which are so dangerous to society as to necessitate the use of punishment if someone breaches the value, but Marshall and Duff were silent on which values should be protected in that way. However, they argued that it was an inquiry that should be made, and they wanted to place community values at the centre of the process of deciding which actions should be criminalised (presumably to replace or rival the harm principle).

The question here, therefore, is whether there are any actions which are so abhorrent to our values that they should be controlled through the criminal law; whether in the absence of harm (or only minimal harm) to an individual there should still be an offence (see the sadomasochist case of Tom, Una, Vicky, and Wahib in **What do you think? 2.4**). See also the discussion on rights-based systems in the following section.

The second area to discuss is the regulation of certain actions in order to prevent harm. As we have seen, many of our criminal laws permit punishment despite the absence of direct harms: dangerous driving, attempted robbery (attempting almost any crime), selling firearms, selling or dealing in drugs or any other illicit substance, selling infected meat, controls to protect public hygiene, firing a gun (not on a firing range or at a gun club), almost all driving offences (speeding, no lights, on the wrong side of the road), health and safety at work, rules governing some professions (such as training for a doctor).

You might also include Rachel and Steve's case in **What do you think? 2.4** (visiting the sex worker who may have been trafficked). None of these necessarily or directly involves any harm so presumably they are prohibited because they increase the possibility or risk of harm occurring. For example, driving offences may increase danger on the road even if the driver is careful to only speed (or break other rules) when there is no problem ahead, when it will cause no harm. However, whether the driver is careful or not, whether they only intend to hurry and not to harm anyone, the risk is still there. Road travel is, in many cases, a public good which needs to be facilitated but people also need to be protected from unnecessary harms or dangers, so regulation is used to deliver a safe mode of transport; regulation lowers the risk. For example, we need to specify which side of the road cars should travel on. There is nothing automatically safe about driving on the left and dangerous about driving on the right or vice versa; it is just that each state needs to specify which side it will use because if the decision was left to individuals, the dangers of road travel would be immense. Similarly, the sale of firearms does not cause harm unless and until the purchaser shoots someone, but there is no other use for a firearm other than for shooting so the seller needs to ensure that the gun is only to be used for sporting purposes. On the other hand, crowbars are often used in burglary but their sale is not similarly restricted as they have legitimate uses in the building trade. Potentially dangerous actions and objects need to be regulated for the smooth running of a society and sometimes this may require use of the criminal law.

A more recent example of the use of restriction in order to control potential harm were the restrictions enforced on individuals and businesses in the UK during the Covid-19 pandemic in 2020. The freedom of movement, religious worship, and rights to family and to freedom of association (to meet with people when you would like) were all severely restricted in order to try to protect the community (and particularly some vulnerable individuals within the community) from the disease. The desire was to protect the group and the group ideal of safety by restricting individual freedoms. It is important to consider whether the restrictions on individual freedoms were acceptable, whether the end of containing the virus and reducing deaths was worth the loss of liberty. Furthermore, we should consider whether some in the community had their freedoms interfered with more seriously than others in order to deliver safety, and whether this was fair. Here we will not answer these questions, but we hope you understand how important it is to ask them. In this case, it might be argued that two group values—individual rights and individual and group safety—were set against each other and the latter were found more compelling. You need to consider whether the rules were fair and whether they were fairly applied—see, for example, how MPs and others in the public light were not prosecuted despite breaking the rules (for example, Dominic Cummings, a senior adviser to the Prime Minister who broke lockdown rules in March 2020, see BBC News, 26 May 2020). In some cases, MPs were not even required to resign from their positions, whilst others in our communities faced fines and convictions for breaking the restrictions. It might be asked whether there was justice in how these restrictions were applied, and whether the lapses mean that the activities should never have been regulated by the criminal law, or do they show the necessity for activities to be criminally restricted?

We (criminologists, lawmakers, and members of the public) have to look carefully at our criminal laws to decide whether each and every one of them should remain criminal or whether they could be dealt with through other processes. Most people would use the harm principle as the core of this test; some might use values and some might use regulation. In some cases, all three considerations (the harm principle, values, and regulation) may come together, but none sufficient alone to argue for criminalisation. For example, what should happen about pollution by an industry? There may be some *harm* from each factory or other working unit, though the pollution by each alone may not be sufficient to harm anyone; however, when others in the industry behave in a similar manner, the cumulative effect may be very large, such as the cumulative effect of substances farmers have put on their fields being washed into rivers or of plastic packaging being dumped in the environment (see also **Chapter 12**). There may be a need to *regulate* the use or disposal of certain substances by all in certain industries in order to prevent this cumulative problem of pollution, which might adversely affect the health of many people. This might also affect a *value* of a community, that of respect for the environment. Should individuals then be criminalised if they dispose of their rubbish in a way which might be harmful, for example dropping litter in the street or failing to recycle rubbish, and if they breach societal expectations should they face conviction and punishment under the criminal law?

If we permit these ideas of protection from harm, the need for regulation, and protection of values to be used together, are we allowing too much power to those who make the criminal laws? Might they use and abuse that power to restrict our freedoms in an illegitimate way—see **Figure 2.8**? We touched on this idea earlier, and later chapters will explore the ways in which power can be used to protect certain parts of a society—often at the expense of other parts. Arguably, actions of the powerful (for instance, tax evasion) are treated less severely than those of the powerless (for instance, benefit fraud) for this reason. Some see this unfairness as necessarily underlying all criminal laws since it is always those in power who set the rules (if, for example, following a revolution the revolutionaries win, then the acts of the previous government are often criminalised and vice versa). Therefore, whilst academics may try to rationalise the extent and content of the criminal law, it may be power and the protection of vested interests that finally decides it. This is problematic because if we thoughtlessly apply the harm or value principles, it may be the harms to and values of the powerful (but proportionately small) elite that are protected (Vold, Bernard, and Snipes, 2002; Alvesto and Tombs, 2002; Tombs and Whyte, 2003; Green and Ward, 2004). This need not always be true; some groups may manage to be heard by those in power and may achieve protection for some vulnerable sections of society. For example, some feminists fought hard for the legal definition of domestic violence to be broadened to encompass domestic abuse; others to ensure that the laws protecting against sexual violence remained largely gendered (Jones, 2004: 62). There is no justice in the way that some vulnerable groups are heard whilst others are not, and it might still be considered an abuse of power (see **Chapter 18**), but

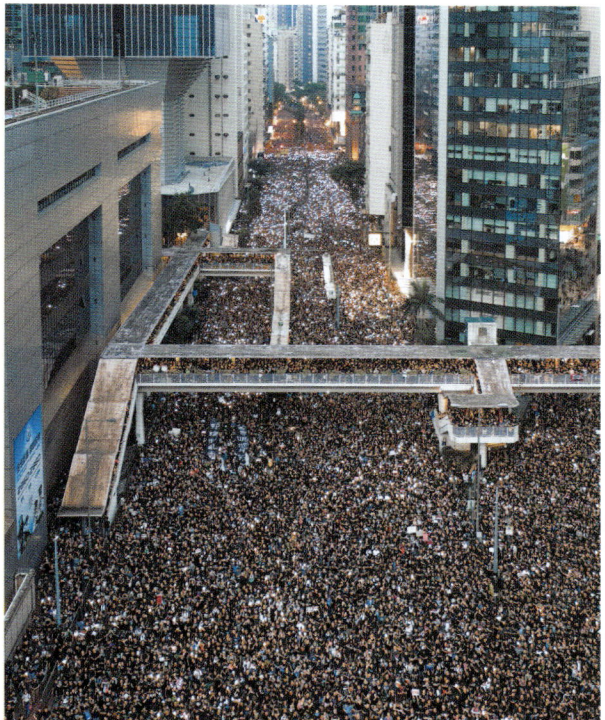

Figure 2.8 Hong Kong citizens began large-scale protests in 2019 against proposed laws seen as infringing civil liberties
Source: Manson Yim/Unsplash

between 1997 and 2010, leaving things to politicians and the elite led to over 3,000 new criminal offences being created (Law Commission, 2010). Not all can possibly pass the standards set out here, so why were they passed and whose interests did they serve?

Rights-based systems

To minimise the risk of our becoming subject to laws that are potentially shaped and created to benefit the powerful, some have argued that we should rely on a widely accepted standard such as human rights; a framework that we touched upon earlier (see the discussion of the state in **section 2.1**). This is a system based on individual rights and autonomy (as claimed by the harm principle) but which recognises that certain rights should always be protected.

The European Convention on Human Rights (ECHR)

International human rights conventions suggest that states must protect their citizens against some conduct and, at the time of writing, the UK is subject to the ECHR. It is important to remember that the ECHR is completely separate from the European Union (EU). The former regulates our rights, whereas the latter was concerned with many other areas of our lives until, in June 2016, the British people voted to leave the EU. Even after Brexit, the UK will still be a member of the ECHR, and will still be bound to respect human rights.

The ECHR requires, under Art. 3, that states protect their citizens from torture and inhuman and degrading treatment. Not only are states required to refrain from torture or from using inhuman and degrading treatment, but they are also expected to ensure that no one in their country is subjected to such treatment at the hands of anyone else. In a case from Germany, the European Court of Human Rights decided that police officers who threatened the applicant with imminent (though brief) pain in order to get information they hoped would save the life of his victim (a child; unfortunately it transpired that he had already killed the child), were breaching the article because this was 'inhuman treatment' (*Gäfgen v Germany* (2011) 52 EHRR 1; see also **Controversy and debate 2.1**). In a decision involving the UK, the same court decided that Parliament had failed to protect children because the level of chastisement parents are allowed to use to control their children—under UK law—permitted 'inhuman treatment' (*A v United Kingdom* (1999) 27 EHRR 611). In such situations, the state is obligated, under international law, to ensure that individuals are protected, and one of the most sure ways of fulfilling that obligation is to criminalise the activity, especially as any breaches in the case of Art. 3 of the ECHR are likely to harm the individual as well as break the values of European nations that no individual should ever face torture or inhuman treatment at the hands of the state or any other person or group. Other aspects of the ECHR are similarly protected. There is a general expectation that individuals feel sufficiently secure to enjoy the freedoms guaranteed under the Convention such as, under Art. 8, a family life, meaning that if the state fails to protect citizens against something like racial hatred, this might make people feel so insecure as to undermine their Art. 8 rights, and offences of racial hatred might legitimately be criminalised.

This reliance on human rights brings an important difference: a system based on rights recognises that states themselves (or those acting for them, such as presidents) can be perpetrators of criminal wrongs. Human rights put responsibilities on states to ensure the rights of their citizens. Here, therefore, those acting on behalf of states can offend; this is important and was at the core of human rights conventions and declarations post-Second World War. It underlies the United Nations conventions and the ECHR and the idea can be seen most clearly in the International Criminal Court (set up in 2002 to try people accused of serious international violations such as genocide, war crimes, and crimes against humanity). For an academic discussion of rights or the protection of dignity as the basis for crime, see Schwendinger and Schwendinger (1970).

Broader, non-legal rights

The discussion of a rights-based system has, so far, been based on the rights guaranteed under the ECHR or other international conventions, but some authors suggest they need not be bound to such legal documents. For example, Von Hirsch and Jareborg (1991) have a broader scheme, intended to protect four types of interests: physical integrity, privacy, autonomy, and freedom from humiliation or degrading treatment. Schwendinger and Schwendinger (1970) would go further, claiming that all violations of basic human rights should be considered as criminal violations, whether included in the criminal law or not. In many instances it would be state actors who would be the perpetrators, so the powerful in the state would be called to account when they breached either internationally recognised standards of human rights or activities which undermine physical integrity, privacy, or autonomy or that humiliate or degrade individuals, and this would mean the criminal law would be a tool of rights rather than of state control.

The Schwendinger approach is a criminal law system based on rights violations and, like that based on harm, it might go too far; it might criminalise minor instances, leading to an abuse of power under the criminal law in punishing when no punishment is warranted. It may perhaps be better to control some rights violations through other means, for example education or civil law.

2.6 Do we need the criminal law?

One question we have not yet addressed is whether we need the criminal law at all. We discussed in **section 2.1**, and have mentioned at other points, the need to regulate human behaviour in some way, owing to the conflict between individual freedoms and social living, but many critical criminologists have questioned whether several aspects of the criminal law are really needed, and even whether we require a criminal law at all. Those who fall into the latter category are often known as **zemiologists** (see also the discussion in **Chapter 19**). Zemiologists focus on harm rather than crime. Having just spent much of this chapter considering the harm principle and its place in the criminalisation of activities, this may sound strange and you may think 'So what, what is the difference?' The difference is enormous.

The criminal law is only interested in some harms, generally those where an individual (the perpetrator) can be blamed. It assumes that intentional acts are more deserving of punishment than acts of indifference, but this is questioned by Box (1983) and Pemberton (2004). If Adam intentionally kills Bob, is it worse than Chopak, acting as part of a company, choosing to make and sell a dangerous baby float, knowing that the straps tend to break, allowing the baby to slip through and drown, so it will likely kill some babies, but not caring about this or taking steps to prevent it? (A company called Aqua-Leisure actually did this and 31 babies died before the product was recalled. The recall was for at least 4 million floats. The company was fined $650,000—a regulatory fine, but no director or employee was charged with a crime.) And is an intentional act worse than Dean, a dictator, choosing to spend state money on sending a rocket to space, knowing that many who could have been saved from starvation in his country will now die because the money was spent on the space race rather than on food? In the first example, a clearly criminal case, one person dies so there is a clear victim. In both the others, more than one person will die (or does die); however, they may not be considered at all by the criminal law and are unlikely to be considered victims in the same way. A further example of this is explored in **Controversy and debate 2.3**.

Many critical criminologists and zemiologists often view criminal harms as less serious than other major forms of harm (see Boulki and Kotzé, 2018; Hillyard and Tombs, 2004). The criminal law, they argue, ignores many of the more serious **social harms** people suffer, not all of which are crimes, for example poverty, inadequate housing, poor diet, poor education, inadequate healthcare, unemployment, pollution, inequalities of treatment, inequality of opportunity, inequality of outcome, unsafe working conditions, unsafe environments, and so on (Hillyard and Tombs, 2004). They ask us to consider all harms suffered by individuals, families, groups, or communities, however caused, and whether the harm be physical, psychological, cultural (especially cultural safety), or economic (Hillyard and Tombs, 2004). They question the prioritising of criminal harms (some of which are minor) over other harms (some of which are serious) and suggest that we should have more sympathy for those who suffer other harms and be angrier about the causes of these harms. Consequently, they argue that we should strive to both redress harm (however caused) and prevent further harm (from whatever source). More money and energy should be spent on resolving harms such as poverty, rather than just focusing on blaming and calling criminals to account.

Many of the examples already considered in this chapter, including poverty, may be considered to be outcomes of the capitalist economic model prevalent in western societies, but there are also social harms caused by other types of system, such as communism (especially the

! CONTROVERSY AND DEBATE 2.3

The limitations of the criminal law

Consider the opening scenes of the film *Fight Club* (see **Figure 2.9**), when there is a conversation about how a fictional major car company makes decisions around recalling cars.

Narrator: A new car built by my company leaves somewhere travelling at 60 mph. The rear differential locks up. The car crashes and burns with everyone trapped inside. Now, should we initiate a recall? Take the number of vehicles in the field, A, multiply by the probable rate of failure, B, multiply by the average out-of-court settlement, C. A times B times C equals X. If X is less than the cost of a recall, we don't do one.

Woman on plane: Are there a lot of these kinds of accidents?

Narrator: You wouldn't believe.

Woman on plane: Which car company do you work for?

Narrator: A major one.

Do you think the narrator committed a crime, if so what is it? Has he acted in a deviant way? Has the company committed a crime, if so what is it? Can a company or a state commit a crime? We can't imprison a company so how can we punish them?

Controversially, financial considerations like this can supersede the potential of harm in decisions made by large companies.

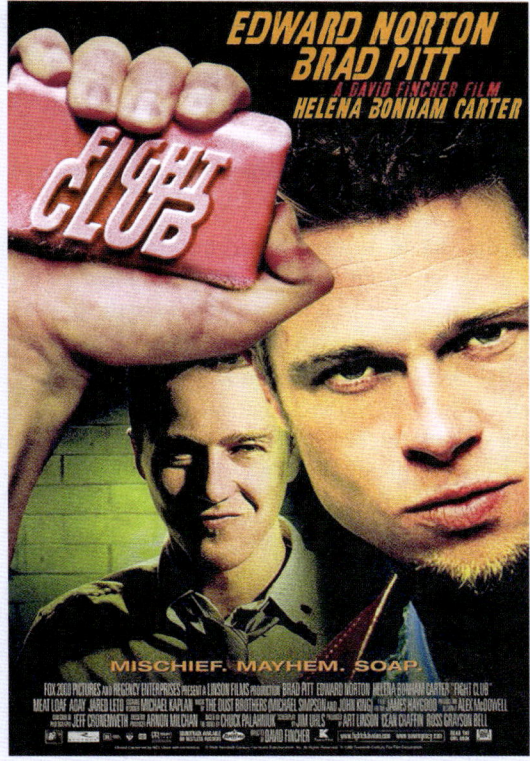

Figure 2.9 Has the narrator of the film *Fight Club*—or the company he works for—committed a crime?

Source: 20th Century Fox/The Kobal Collection

---

limiting of autonomy, see Dorling et al., 2008). Thinking of harms in a broader sense may serve to question the way in which some of our criminal laws are framed (see the discussion of harm to self in **section 2.4**). It may also make us think more carefully about what is important and how to make our society safer (see the earlier examples of Bob, Chopak, and Dean). Who are the true victims: only direct victims of crime or also others who suffer? What is harm and what is harmful to either an individual or a community is not self-evident and needs to be carefully discussed. Who takes responsibility, how, and to what extent also needs to be teased out. These last questions are immensely problematic. For example, the responsibility issue is important. Clearly, we do not wish to criminalise all activities that cause all forms of harm but if we are to address the problem and change things for the better, we need to understand what needs to be altered and how making these changes will reduce overall harm (Reiman, 2006; Pemberton, 2004). Put simply, most critical criminologists recognise that life will always involve problematic and potentially harmful situations. Problematic situations and harm are a natural part of social living. These theorists recognise that some harms may be intended but that calling this 'crime' and punishing those who harm others does not improve our society. They argue that the ideal is to influence society, its structures, and the individuals who live in our communities to reduce those situations as far as possible and that this will not be achieved through criminalising behaviours but rather through civilising people and supporting and respecting all those who are harmed. It is also important to remember that some situations:

- are seen as problematic for all those directly concerned (all those facing a gunman are likely to feel fear at the prospect that they may be killed);
- are problematic for some of those directly involved (if the gunman only threatens those with blonde hair the others may feel relieved and their fear may dissipate);

- may not be considered problematic by any of those directly involved but people viewing things from the outside may consider them problematic (if the gunman tells them all it is a toy gun then it is only a problem for those not directly involved).

In each of these situations, the problem may arise from different sources. Hulsman (1986) calls these frames of reference and suggests that for each frame of reference the action and need may differ. Hulsman takes the example of a collision on the road where one driver, Eve, is injured:

- This may be an accident—a natural part of life—if, say, a tyre blows out or there is black ice and then the community needs to do all it can to help the injured party to heal.
- The incident may result from a structural problem, such as the way traffic is managed in that spot (in other cases it might be a problem with the community), it will still be called an accident and we should work to change the social/structural problem so as to prevent future harms.
- If one person, Faye, is to blame then the other, Eve, may want compensation or for the 'perpetrator' to be punished. If the 'victim', Eve, is willing to forgive, then should the compensation/punishment be reduced? If the injured party, Eve, is the one to blame then should the compensation/punishment reflect the injury they've already suffered? Why/why not? If the injured party, Eve, is also the perpetrator should we prosecute? Why/why not?

Hulsman goes through a number of examples but the core of his message is that addressing the harm is the most important aspect and that this is rarely achieved through punishment, and therefore rarely through criminal law.

This perspective calls into question the need for criminal law and, by implication, the need for the study of criminology. Whilst this is an interesting way of thinking, it is not one shared by everyone, and therefore we will continue for the rest of this book to assume that most societies feel the need to censure and to ban certain activities and so states will continue to choose to call some behaviours criminal. In this situation, some people will choose both to deviate from accepted ways of behaving and to commit offences, either because they do not think the activities should be criminal or because they choose to break the law.

2.7 Conclusion

In this chapter we have considered the question 'What is "crime"?' From our discussion, it is clear that criminal laws are set by the state, they are not a natural set of laws that are accepted at all times and in all places, rather they change over time and each state sets its own criminal laws. This quality means that crime is clearly socially constructed—there is nothing about particular acts that of themselves means that they are always crimes, each state decides what should be prohibited at any particular time. Whilst it is true that a state (through its government or its courts) dictates what the law should be, what is defined as a crime is often led by society and what society seems to think and want at that time. At various times there may be social movements calling for something to be criminalised or decriminalised, and so some activities that many people in a society disapprove of might become criminal laws. However, many things that a society may disapprove of are never criminalised, they are just seen as deviant and are controlled in other ways (see **Figure 2.10**).

In a democracy, the willingness to follow the calls of a group in society may be seen as a strength—a government listening to its people. However, it might also be used by a powerful group (such as a racial majority or the rich) in order to control a less powerful group (a minority, racial or other, or powerless group such as the poor). This means that although the criminal law is intended to protect a community and its people from crime, it may in fact prove to be unfair and actually harm some people. At times, the criminal law may not be ethical and might not even live up to human rights standards.

Much of our discussion in this chapter considered how a state might best decide what should be criminalised. Generally, harm is an important factor in the decision—if an activity is harmful, it should be considered to see whether it should be criminalised. However, as we have learned, harm is a complex concept that might not be restricted to physical harm, but should take into account other aspects, possibly even (in some circumstances) moral upset. There is debate as to whether we should prevent people from harming themselves (participating in dangerous sports or using some substances such as tobacco or alcohol) or harming those who consent to or maybe even enjoy the harm (sadomasochists). However we define harm, we need to be careful—just because an activity is harmful, we do not always need to criminalise it to control the behaviour (Duff, 2007). Harm—at least harm to others—should necessarily be identified as a consequence of a behaviour before it can be prohibited, but this consequence should not *require* the behaviour to be made illegal. The harm principle may, in fact, be a more

Figure 2.10 Ways through which a state or society can control and regulate behaviour

useful test as to which activities should *not* be criminalised but is not very useful in deciding which activities *should* be criminalised.

Some criminal laws are not based on the harm principle. Some may arise because those in power take advantage and protect against behaviours they do not agree with, while others arise because many in a society want to protect the moral interests of the group even if there is no actual harm. From this, it is clear that the harm principle is something that is not always followed and that no one rule can explain how a state chooses which activities to criminalise. Despite the fact that the harm principle is important in deciding what to criminalise, other things also need to be considered. For example, if something is potentially harmful, such as driving or smoking, it might be sensible to regulate how or where the behaviour occurs so as to reduce its harmful effects, even if it only harms the participants. This regulation may be done through the criminal law or in other ways (see **Figure 2.10**). In any use of the criminal law, it is important to ask whether the criminalisation is justified. An interesting test situation arises out of the use of the criminal law to control some of our most basic freedoms, such as freedom of movement, association, and the right to a family life in order to protect society from Covid-19. Are these restrictions acceptable and necessary in a modern society? Should the control have occurred in other ways—through social criticism, seeing those who endangered us all as social deviants rather than criminals (such as the MPs who were not prosecuted for breaking Covid-19 restrictions, but were vilified by the press). Is the use of the criminal law justified if it delivers a safer society—should the ends justify the means or not?

Overall, the message has to be that crime is a social construct, each society chooses what to criminalise and how to punish those who transgress.

SUMMARY

- Identify what the criminal law is and what it is for

Basically, the criminal law is a set of rules backed up by sanctions designed to prevent behaviour that a state (or community) wants to control. Criminal laws are generally used to prevent actions that harm other people or harm the community/state. Therefore, crime is socially constructed—each state decides what should be prohibited, and there is no one act or behaviour that is always considered a crime.

- Understand why the criminal law can be seen as a social construct that changes over time

As the criminal law is a social construct, social movements such as calls to legalise assisted suicide or to criminalise smoking in public often shape the criminal law—the law bends to the conventions that society most wants. This allows the criminal law to represent people's views of what is acceptable behaviour. However, it may allow the criminal law to protect one (powerful) group at the expense of another, less powerful (or minority) group. Therefore, social construction may not be fair, and it may not protect people; it is not required to follow any particular ethical or human rights standards.

- Consider the reasons why some actions are criminalised, and assess how well these reasons are applied

Most activities are only criminalised if they are harmful to other people—known as the harm principle. Not all harmful acts must be criminalised, but people should be allowed to do things that are not harmful to others. Some criminal laws are not based on the harm principle, as those in power may use their position to prevent activities they dislike or may refuse to criminalise harmful behaviour if it is useful to them. Many criminal laws seem to protect moral interests rather than prevent harm to others, while some criminal laws regulate potentially dangerous activities (for example, driving) before any harm arises. So, the harm principle is not always followed, and no single rule can explain how a state chooses which activities to criminalise.

- Evaluate whether we need the criminal law in order to hold people to account and punish them

The criminal law deals with problems by blaming individuals and punishing them. Punishment may be considered the best way of persuading most of us not to participate in crime. However, if you ask most people why they do not offend, few will answer that they do not want to be punished. Most people either believe criminal acts to be 'wrong' or they do not want to disappoint loved ones by participating in activities they know are unacceptable to most people. Behaviour control is therefore part of our general upbringing and education that may be very effective at preventing crime. If the criminal law does not deliver safer societies then some thinkers, zemiologists, argue that we should stop blaming people and instead spend money on supporting victims, those who suffer harm, however that harm arises.

 Test your understanding of the chapter's key points by attempting the self-test questions on the **online resources** at www.oup.com/he/case2e

REVIEW QUESTIONS

1. What is the criminal law?
2. What can the criminal law be used for?

3. In what ways can the criminal law be considered a social construct?

4. What is the harm principle?

5. What are the main differences between crime and deviance?

6. Can you identify three reasons why certain actions may be criminalised?

7. What are the main differences between crime and social harm?

 Access the **online resources** at www.oup.com/he/case2e to check your answers to the review questions.

FURTHER READING

Dorling, D. et al. (2008) *Criminal obsessions: Why harm matters more than crime* (2nd edn). London: Centre for Crime and Justice Studies. Especially Ch. 5, pp. 70–90.
A discussion of harm has been central to this chapter. For a clear and novel consideration of how to differentiate harm and crime, it would be sensible to consult this book.

Herring, J. (2012) *Great Debates: Criminal Law*. Basingstoke: Palgrave Macmillan. Ch. 1.
A useful, clear, and easily understood discussion of the subject. It is a brilliant place to start your extra reading and introduces the debates in an easily readable manner.

Lacey, N. and Zedner, L. (2017) 'Criminalization: Historical, Legal, and Criminological Perspectives' in A. Liebling, S. Maruna, and L. McAra (eds) *The Oxford Handbook of Criminology* (6th edn). Oxford: Oxford University Press.
A particularly incisive and analytical discussion. This book gives a more detailed consideration of the legal and contextual construction of crime. It introduces some of the more complex legal and criminological theories and guides the reader through the ways in which they might be analysed.

Williams, K. S. (2012) *Textbook on Criminology* (8th edn). Oxford: Oxford University Press. Ch. 2, especially pp. 20–39.
There are many textbooks which consider where we should set the limits of the criminal law. Most criminal law books have a brief section set aside to discuss these issues though many of these are overly legalistic for your use. However, this book (and the last) is particularly helpful and approachable.

Steve Case discussing the question 'What is crime?': www.youtube.com/watch?v=a2IIcZPW6oU
In this YouTube video, Steve Case, one of this book's authors, reflects on the difficulties of trying to define 'crime'.

 Access the **online resources** to view a wealth of extra information relating to your study of criminology, including self-test questions, answers to review questions, and links to other resources that will help you enjoy and fulfil your potential within your studies.

www.oup.com/he/case2e

CHAPTER OUTLINE

3.1	Introduction	56
3.2	Defining justice	56
3.3	Criminal justice models	64
3.4	Philosophical ideas of justice	74
3.5	Systems of criminal justice	83
3.6	Drawing ideas together	87
3.7	Conclusion	90

3

What is 'justice'?

KEY ISSUES

After studying this chapter, you should be able to:

- explain and appreciate why justice is so important;
- critically consider the criminal justice approaches to justice and evaluate how these help our understanding of the concept and its outcomes;
- describe the six criminal justice models and be able to critically assess each one;
- outline and evaluate the four philosophical approaches to justice that take a broad view of the concept and allow you to see how justice and injustice can impact on society, crime, security, and well-being;
- explain and critically compare the two main systems of criminal justice.

3.1 Introduction

'Crime' is the word that most people would associate with studying criminology but in fact 'justice' is equally central. Justice essentially describes or assesses how well and fairly people (including organisations and nations) behave towards others. It comes up in all areas of our lives, from personal relationships to sports games, and it concerns things like equality, fair access to resources, and the ability and freedom to live well. Yet despite its importance, the term justice is often used very loosely or imprecisely. It is an abstract, fluid concept—an idea that most understand but few can explain. We know injustice when we experience it—we recognise it when we feel aggrieved—and we assume other people think about justice in the same way we do, but this is often not the case.

In this chapter, we consider justice in an absolute sense, but also justice in the context of the criminal justice system—the system of rules and practices under which government institutions and agencies (police, courts, lawyers, probation, prison, etc.) act in order to prevent or control crime, deal with those who break the law, and support victims. When we talk about justice in the context of criminal justice, we are therefore discussing the extent to which the system aims to prevent or reduce offending; ensures that those who are accused, convicted, and sentenced are treated fairly (justly); and works to support victims and communities. Justice is (or, rather, should be) guaranteed by the laws, especially the criminal laws, in any state and it should be clearly present in all decisions on crime and social issues made by those working for the state. Justice is core to almost every aspect of the criminal justice system. It is instrumental in decisions about:

- when and how an investigation should be conducted—what sort of rights suspects should enjoy, how and when police should be permitted to question them;
- what rights the accused should enjoy in court and how victims and witnesses should be protected.
- whether we should take the interests of victims into account and, if so, when;
- how much to punish people;
- how punishment should be administered and how prisoners should be treated whilst they are incarcerated;
- whether community punishments are justly administered;
- whether there is injustice in society. If so, whether societal injustice impacts on criminal behaviour and whether punishing such behaviour is therefore just.

In this chapter, we will not reach any definitive answers as to where justice lies—there is no final answer to that question—but we will challenge our ideas of justice and consider what a just criminal justice system might look like, exploring both theoretical ideas about the concept and its practical applications. This will involve looking at broad definitions of justice, frameworks called criminal justice models on which we can anchor our understanding of justice within the criminal justice system, philosophical ideas about the concept, and the main systems used to bring about criminal justice. We will discuss the types of questions you might ask in order to decide what might be just, both in a particular case and more generally, and these will help you evaluate what a state does at each point in the system.

Getting a firm grip on what justice means can feel a little like trying to catch a bar of soap, but it is important that you give this tricky concept careful consideration. By the end of this chapter, you should have a nuanced understanding of the concept, be confident in explaining or writing about the various schools of thought concerning it, and be able to use justice to test other aspects of your criminological studies.

3.2 Defining justice

We saw in **Chapter 2** (**section 2.4**), that absolute autonomy (freedom of choice) is incompatible with the human need to live in societies because we cannot all exercise freedom—one person's free choices will limit the choices available to another. For this reason, we consider some behaviour, such as theft, unacceptable and label it 'criminal'. In a similar way, we need to have a common idea of justice so that all members of society feel that they are being treated fairly and granted equal amounts of freedom, with their interests protected.

In this section, we consider some important definitions of justice. We look at a basic definition of the core concept, then the legal definition, then at other ideas that we need to take into account when defining justice. Finally, we critically reflect on and challenge these definitions. Before you begin with this section, take a moment to consider your own ideas about justice, and how they have been formed, by reading **What do you think? 3.1**.

WHAT DO YOU THINK? 3.1

Your ideas about 'justice'

The term 'justice' is used in many different ways by different people but, as we will see in **Chapter 6**, both news and entertainment media have a significant influence on our ideas of what it means, and how justice should be served. Read the following media quotes and headlines relating to the idea of justice (though not all of them use this specific word) then consider the questions that follow.

> They watched George Floyd call out for his mother as his life ebbed away and they watched the US president trample over the pain that followed. They saw the cheapness of a black life—and they began to realise that all the excuses they had made in the past for not seeing it would no longer hold. . . . [C]omplaints of racial injustice have always been invalidated . . . turned into matters of opinion, removed from the realm of moral justice and placed in the realm of competing cultural values. This is how movements for racial equality are easily framed as unprovoked assaults on our cherished culture.
>
> (*The Guardian* online, 21 June 2020)

> Bereaved families seek 'justice' for UK victims of coronavirus.
>
> (*The Guardian*, 11 May 2020)

> Grenfell survivors begin journey towards justice.
>
> (*Al Jazeera*, 30 October 2019)

> My dad died at Hillsborough. I will never stop fighting for justice.
>
> (*The Independent*, 29 June 2018)

> Legal aid cuts have created a 'two-tier justice system' benefiting the wealthy. Since 2010, the Conservatives have implemented unprecedented cuts to legal aid—putting justice beyond the reach of thousands.
>
> (*The Independent*, 25 November 2016)

> Dogs' innate sense of fairness being eroded by humans, study suggests.
>
> (*The Independent*, 8 June 2017)

> There's a troubling inequality at the heart of our justice system—We are supposed to be held equal before the law. But if we're clever, white, and have great prospects, could it be that some of us are more equal than others?
>
> (James Moore, *The Independent*, 17 May 2017)

> Should crime victims have the right to meet the perpetrator? 'Restorative Justice' provides the chance for victims and offenders to meet or communicate, but would it really help to reduce offending rates?
>
> (*The Independent*, 5 September 2016)

> Former Nazi guard goes on trial over deaths of 170,000 people at Auschwitz. Former camp inmate Erna de Vries: 'I am not hateful, but it somehow feels like justice to see this man, who was working there when my mother died, on trial.'
>
> (*The Independent*, 11 February 2016)

> Rapists and other violent criminals let off with a 'slap on the wrist'
>
> (*The Telegraph*, 6 January 2013)

1. What conclusions do you draw from the quotes above? How do they make you think about justice? Also, think about any other media crime stories you have come across recently that might be about 'justice' or which made you think about whether something was 'just'.

2. What synonyms (alternative words) could you use for justice as presented by the media? Which is most useful to you when you think about these issues?

3. Think about where your ideas of justice come from. Are they from the media, family, friends, or elsewhere? Also, think carefully about the similarities and differences in the ideas of justice from these different sources and how you decide which is most acceptable to you. In doing this, you may want to consider how your family and friends would react to the issues above and consider why their reactions might differ.

4. What are the practical implications of individual people's ideas of justice—however they are formed—for criminal justice?

A basic definition of justice

We have noted that justice in its fullest form can be hard to pin down, but it is possible to formally define the core concept: justice can be said to have been served *when the rules are applied*, and injustice arises if the rules are either not applied or are misapplied. This definition is too narrow and oversimplifies the issues, but it is a useful starting point if we are to use the term to help us think about criminology.

The 'rules' that must be applied will differ depending on the situation. For example, if you are playing netball it is the rules (usually international rules) of that sport; if you are visiting France it will be the laws or legal rules of that country.

In order to be just, the law (state rules) must be applied fairly, objectively, and correctly. In criminal law this happens when the guilty are convicted and punished, and when the innocent are acquitted (found not guilty).

This may all sound very logical. So why is it too narrow a definition? First, the rules may not be fair or just. For example, they may prioritise one group over another. Secondly, the human experience is too complex for us to be able to apply a set of rules in a consistent, mechanical way and hope to get a just result every time. To take a sentencing example (a sentence is the punishment imposed on someone who is found guilty of a crime—we consider this aspect of justice in **What do you think? 3.2**), we might think that if two drivers are driving at 40 mph through the same 30 mph speed-restricted area, we should apply the same rule(s) to both cases to determine how they should be punished. But what if one of the drivers was trying to get someone to hospital in order to save the life of a passenger, or one of the drivers is very rich and the other very poor, struggling to feed their family—is it still fair to apply the rules in the same way and impose on both a £100 fine? Would this represent justice?

Most simple definitions therefore call for consideration from a number of perspectives. For example, justice may be what a society regards as fair when it takes a rational assessment of ethics, law, religion/morals, dignity, equality, equity, and fairness. This is very broad and needs to be refined.

Legal definitions of justice

There is another way we can think about justice: its strict legal definition. In England and Wales, justice has a visual depiction in the form of the statue of Lady Justice which sits prominently above the Old Bailey, the Central Criminal Court of London (see **Figure 3.1**). The figure holds a sword in one hand and the scales of justice in the other.

This statue aims to symbolise that justice will be dispensed in the courts and that law without justice is wrong, or unfair. The scales are supposed to convey that in law, especially criminal law, there are two sides, two arguments, but this is another idea that is too simplistic.

First, there may be more than two sides. In criminal law there may be the state, the accused, and the victim. Each of these might have a very different idea of where justice would lie. Members of the public and the communities in which the victim and offender live may also each have their own ideas of justice. So although only the state and the accused are represented in a criminal case—that is, only they have a voice (see **Chapter 7** for more on the marginalisation of the victim)—they may not represent the only ideas which should be considered. The scales are too simple.

Figure 3.1 The scales of justice above the Old Bailey in London symbolise a common conception of justice—but is it accurate?
Source: BasPhoto/Shutterstock

Secondly, the scales suggest that if they tip the right way justice is served, but it may not be. Even if justice is done (that is, the side that wins has the most just case), the *reason* for the decision may be unjust.

Key considerations when defining justice

You may now be beginning to appreciate the difficulties involved in defining and discussing justice. In order to explore justice further and use it as a tool to test claims and real-life situations, we need to factor in some broader considerations. They are:

- the importance of just reasoning;
- the distinction between injustice and bad luck;
- the concept of social justice—and its implications for criminal justice;
- the idea of justice as a social construct.

The importance of just reasoning

Despite what the statue of Lady Justice above the Old Bailey (**Figure 3.1**) might suggest, definitions and discussions of justice cannot focus solely on outcomes; they must also take account of *why* a decision is made. In the 18th century, Lord Mansfield (a very famous judge) advised a colonial governor not to explain his decisions, saying:

> consider what you think justice requires and decide accordingly. But never give your reasons; for your judgement will probably be right, but your reasons will certainly be wrong.
>
> (Lord Mansfield, quoted in Sen, 2010: 4)

Whilst failing to explain decisions protects the decision-maker from attack or question, it prevents others from knowing whether decisions are based on acceptable reasoning. You might feel that the reasons do not matter so long as the outcome is just, but imagine that a football referee decides that the handball rule is too difficult to implement, so she gives a penalty on every alternate occurrence; last time she saw a handball incident she awarded a penalty, so this time she does not. Sometimes the decision may be correct, but the reasoning is clearly unjust. To take a criminological example, an innocent person may be acquitted, which sounds like a just result, but if the reason for acquittal is that the magistrates were impressed not by the evidence but by the **defendant**'s overall appearance and demeanour then we could question whether justice was done.

Therefore, justice is not only about the outcome, but also about how you reach that outcome. It is important that the values—generally moral values—that you apply to arrive at a decision are 'just' and 'fair', not only that the outcome is correct. This assumes that in order to 'live well' there are moral values about how we should treat others (what we should do and not do to others) and how we should make decisions that affect others. This takes into account that we are mutually dependent (human beings live in close proximity to each other) which means we need to respect and treat others with dignity.

Injustice or bad luck?

Another idea to consider is where the line lies between injustice and bad luck. If we continue with the handball example, is it unjust if the offence is committed but the player is not awarded a penalty because the referee and linesmen were looking the other way? Presumably the referee and linesmen did everything possible to watch the game carefully; it may be unlucky if they miss this one, but is it really unjust? It would be if the referee deliberately looked away or was not paying due care and attention to the game (maybe using their phone), but if not, the fact that they did not see the incident is probably not a reason to claim that the decision is unjust. Similarly, it is not unjust if lots of people are killed in an earthquake, although it is certainly very distressing and a major disaster. It is only unjust if something could and should have been done to prevent the deaths, for example if it was known that it was about to happen and nothing was done to evacuate people.

In criminal justice terms, states cannot prevent all crime but, just as with natural disasters, when agencies are aware of a possible major crime event, like terrorism, they should warn individuals. To ensure that justice is served, the state should also take reasonable precautions to try to prevent such attacks (see **Figure 3.2**), and potentially also to prevent other crimes, for example using toughened glass to protect bank tellers, as well as providing advice on how to behave if certain events occur, like asking people to report unattended bags or to 'Run, Hide and Tell' (the slogan used by the National Police Chiefs' Council) if caught in a terrorist attack. Justice might also involve working with potential offenders to reduce their likelihood of offending. This approach has been used to try to prevent terrorism but could be applied to help prevent other crimes, for example by running an educational campaign in which the police are involved, and encouraging those who are worried that they are behaving—or are tempted to behave—in a harmful or criminal way, such as committing a sexual offence, to come forward and request help. If people seek and are not given help then go on to offend, who should be blamed—the state, the individual, or both? And should this alter the punishment for the individual's behaviour?

Social justice

As well as being essential when discussing law and rules, justice is also an issue in deciding who should have what within a society: **social justice**. This idea involves considering the way in which all benefits and burdens are

Figure 3.2 Anti-terror precautions, such as these barriers installed in Edinburgh to prevent vehicles being driven into crowds at the city's arts festivals, are one way in which the state tries to prevent injustice
Source: Kay Roxby/Alamy Stock Photo

distributed and asking how this distribution came about. How and why are some rich, others reasonably well off, while some live in poverty? Is this situation fair? And how and why are some people rewarded with almost limitless choices whilst others enjoy only some choices, and some are penalised, controlled, punished, and maybe even put to death or allowed to die? A just situation does not necessarily mean that everything must be equally distributed; it will often require an understanding of why the situation has arisen. For example, poverty will be unjust if it is the result of exploitation or of arbitrary factors such as race, but we may feel differently if it is potentially caused by an individual's criminal behaviour. Justice asks whether the situation can be seen as just when full and proper account has been taken of all relevant issues. It also means considering whether the law and social rules are being manipulated (intentionally or not) to ensure that the interests of some groups are always protected.

Social justice issues can affect whether justice is achieved or experienced in a criminal justice context. We can explore this by looking at the criminal justice outcomes from different perspectives (different types of groups). There is a lot of evidence (Skogan, 2006; Macpherson, 1999) that different groups of people have very different experiences of the criminal justice system. People might be treated differently depending on their age; ethnicity; gender; religion; sexuality; the community they live in; whether they have or lack money, influence, or power etc. To take ethnicity as an example (one that we consider in depth in **Chapter 10**), black people or those of Afro-Caribbean origin appear more frequently at all levels of the criminal justice system (are arrested, cautioned, convicted, punished harshly, etc.) than might be expected from their numbers in the population. At one time, it was assumed that people in these ethnic groups simply offended more frequently than others, but this assumption has been heavily questioned (Skogan, 2006; Macpherson, 1999) and the system has been accused of operating unjustly, most notably by the Stephen Lawrence Inquiry.

This was an inquiry led by William Macpherson, a former High Court judge, into the handling of the death of Stephen Lawrence, a black teenager from south-east London, portrayed in **Figure 3.3**. Lawrence was killed in 1993 in an unprovoked racist knife attack by white youths but no one was prosecuted and many accused the police of not conducting a fair investigation. Macpherson's inquiry identified a wider social justice issue of 'institutional racism' which went beyond racist views held by individual officers (Macpherson, 1999). He defined this term as:

> The collective failure of an organisation to provide an appropriate and professional service to people because of their colour, culture, or ethnic origin. It can be seen or detected in processes, attitudes and behaviour which amount to discrimination through unwitting prejudice, ignorance, thoughtlessness and racist stereotyping which disadvantage minority ethnic people.
>
> (Macpherson, 1999: para. 6.34)

Macpherson was claiming that the criminal justice system worked against certain racial groups and was therefore unjust in its operation. It is important to note that Macpherson was not necessarily saying that the *system* was unjust, and that the rules were wrong (though there were and are examples of this). He was suggesting that those applying the rules, the people working in the criminal justice system—from the bottom all the way to the top in all criminal justice organisations—tended to make decisions which were likely to go against certain racial groups and that this was unjust and needed to be tackled. They made racist decisions because such racism was ingrained in society and in the decision-making of the criminal justice agencies along with educational and social agencies.

Figure 3.3 The Lawrence Inquiry, prompted by the murder of teenager Stephen Lawrence, produced the phrase 'institutional racism'

Source: Photo News Service/Shutterstock

CONTROVERSY AND DEBATE 3.1

Social injustice and offending: the causes of the 2011 riots

In August 2011, there were a series of riots in cities and towns across England in which there was mass looting (taking things from shops) and arson, and armed police were deployed. Five people died.

The riots were prompted by the fatal shooting by police of a 29-year-old black man named Mark Duggan, but rioters noted various injustices (generally social injustice, though some also claimed injustice at the hands of the police) that they had experienced, illustrating how broad social injustices can underlie why some people feel they are entitled to offend.

The quotes below are taken from a piece of research into the causes of the riots. They have been selected to help us consider how participants explained their actions and they are not intended to excuse the activities or the suffering of the victims of the riots (see **Figure 3.4**), it is simply used to illustrate the importance of broad social injustices as they may underlie why some people feel they are free to offend.

> These young people are coming out to prove they have an existence, to prove that if you don't listen to them and you don't take into account our views, potentially this is a destructive force.
>
> (Man, mid-20s, north London: p. 13)

> You see the rioting yeah? Everything the police have done to us, did to us, was in our heads. That's what gave everyone their adrenaline to want to fight the police . . . It was because of the way they treated us.
>
> (Man, 20, from London: p. 18)

> The government needed someone to blame and [put] everything together under 'gangs'. I don't believe there was much planned gangland activity. I believe there was a lot of angry, very working-class, disillusioned young men that realised 'hang on a minute, it's going off'.
>
> (Man, 21, Salford: p. 22)

> When I left my house . . . it wasn't anything to do with the police . . . I literally went there to say, 'All right then, well, everyone's getting free stuff, I'm joining in', like, 'cos, it's fucking my area. These fucking shops, like, I've given them a hundred CVs . . . not one job. That's why I left my house. It's not like I haven't got GCSEs . . . but I see people with no GCSEs nothing like that, and they're working in places. Like somewhere like Tesco. I'm not being funny like, I don't need any GCSEs to work in Tesco. But I've got them. So here's my CV. I don't need A-levels, but you know, here's my CV. Why haven't I even got [an] interview? . . . I feel like I haven't [been] given the same opportunities and chances as other people . . . If I had a job . . . I honestly wouldn't have stolen nothing . . . Like you could work in Tesco but . . . Tesco could make you feel like you're a valuable worker, and you could be on £5 an hour. But it doesn't matter, yeah, cos you feel you're worth something you would never jeopardise that. Because that feeling's better than making £10 an hour. Do you see what I'm saying? And that's what I feel like: people are not worth anything in this area.
>
> (Man, 22, from south London: p. 26)

Source: The Guardian and LSE (2012) Reading the Riots: Investigating England's summer of disorder. London: The Guardian and LSE (http://eprints.lse.ac.uk/46297/1/Reading%20the%20riots(published).pdf)

Figure 3.4 The social injustices cited by those involved in the 2011 riots illustrate how this can fuel criminal behaviour

Source: PA Images/Alamy Stock Photo (left); Neil Hall/Shutterstock (right)

The examples of 'institutional racism' that led to the injustices associated with Stephen Lawrence's death and the 'injustices' which the rioters (see **Controversy and debate 3.1**) felt were the background to their behaviour illustrates how powerful justice is as a construct. They show how injustices can free people to offend against others, victimise them in unjust and unacceptable ways. It also shows how justice—or injustice—can be used to force organisations and the state to recognise when they need to change their behaviour or their systems. It can be used to improve the criminal justice system, to make it fairer.

So has the system become fairer since 1999? Unfortunately, whilst things have certainly improved (see Home Office, 2009) there are still major problems, especially in areas such as stop and search (see **section 3.6**). We can see these problems in the 2020 worldwide protests in the 'Black Lives Matter' movement, which followed the killing of George Floyd by a police officer in Minnesota, US (see also **New frontiers 8.1**). The killing was videoed and went viral allowing people to see a police officer killing a black man while onlookers protested. The protesters argued that this devalued and dehumanised black people and was evidence of the inequalities, inhumanities, and injustices they suffer every day. It once again highlighted the injustice that many black citizens face, sparking similar protests internationally, including in the UK. The protestors feel that the state can and should act to prevent injustices, particularly those caused by agents of the state or by government policy, yet they do nothing, or very little. The protesters were calling for the government to act but, even if they do, change is likely to be slow. Macpherson pointed out institutional racism in the UK over 20 years ago (Macpherson, 1999), and yet in general, black people are concentrated in the poorest communities in the UK and suffer multiple injustices including racial prejudice and poverty; racial injustice is still part of the established order. Over the years since 1999, there have been racial issues in many other cases of social injustice. For example:

- In 2011, there were riots following the killing of a young man called Mark Duggan. While these were largely about a disillusioned and unjustly treated poor, young population, there was a racial undercurrent in that many of the people involved were from racial minorities (see **Controversy and debate 3.1**);
- In 2017, a large number of the 72 deaths caused by the Grenfell Tower fire were from racial minorities (see **section 19.4**); and
- In 2020, it was found that black people were more than four times more likely to die from Covid-19 than white people (R. Booth and G. Barr, 'Black People Four Times More Likely to Die from Covid-19, ONS finds', *The Guardian*, 7 May 2020).

Justice as a social construct

In **Chapter 2** we discussed that the activities a society chooses to label as crimes depend on both the cultural ideals of the society (what is crime in England and Wales may not be in Australia or India) and the time period you are studying (what is defined as crime alters along with the society). Many academics, like Scottish philosopher David Hume (1711–76), have argued that the idea of justice is constructed in a similar way: that it is a socially constructed concept.

Hume argued that justice is important as it has social utility and can be adjusted as communities and societies progress. For Hume, justice is therefore a set of standards used in a particular culture or society at a particular time to help to decide where one person's self-interest should be controlled to protect others (controls can be through moral or other social expectations, not just in relation to crime, and can include societal or community interference with self-interest, for example taxation). Whilst a number of the theorists whose views we discuss in this chapter might disagree with this idea, particularly in relation to social justice, there is certainly an element of **social construction** where criminal justice is concerned.

Criminal justice does not necessarily embrace all the elements of social justice or what might be seen as an absolute idea of justice. A criminal justice system is not fixed and is—as we will see in **Part 4, Chapters 23 to 31**—continually being adjusted in response to societal views. For example, today many people in England and Wales (though not necessarily a majority) consider the death penalty to be an unjust punishment whereas 300 years ago few people would have held that view. Ideas about what is just and unjust for states to do within a criminal justice arena can therefore be seen as socially constructed (see Degoey, 2000).

Challenging definitions of justice

The definitions we have explored in this section try to pin down justice by simplifying and reducing it. Happily (or frustratingly, depending on how you see it), justice is more complex than a simple set of scales, or a mechanical act of applying certain rules. These ideas are a very narrow, legalistic, and contained view of justice. If the law decreed that all people with blue eyes should be put to death by the state (or, as was the case in Nazi Germany, that all Jews should be put into concentration camps with many killed; or, as it was in South Africa, that all black people should be disadvantaged) then most would agree that putting those laws into operation could not be seen as justice. In that case, the law itself would be unjust, so applying it could only lead to unjust outcomes.

The simplified, legalistic concept of justice misses the wider and more important point that should be considered in order to test for justice: whether the law itself is fair or good. This is an evaluative test—we are trying to test or evaluate whether one law would be fairer or lead to more justice than another. At this point, ethical issues enter the equation and we are testing what the outcome *ought* to be, and therefore what the law should be in order to deliver that outcome.

Much of our discussion in **Chapter 2** questioned what sorts of behaviour should be considered criminal; decisions on this question and others like it should always take account of what would be just. Many theorists begin with the assumption that the rules in our society are just and simply try to explain why some people obey or break those rules and discuss what should be done to punish them. Other theorists question or attack the very foundations of the way in which the criminal law is formed (what actions should be criminal) or operates (what a state can legitimately do to enforce those rules), questioning some of the core principles on which our society builds its ideas of justice (see Waldron, 2001).

Recognising that justice is at the core of many discussions in criminology, criminal justice and law opens up important issues. Those theorists who assume that the law is just and try to explain why some breach it (or obey it) can be questioned on their implicit acceptance of the status quo. Those who question the law should be called to account in terms of their understanding of justice; how would their proposed change be an improvement? It is important to recognise that ideas about justice vary from person to person and justice in any situation is experienced differently depending on perspective—as demonstrated in **What do you think? 3.2**. The culture in which the event(s) occur may be important, but so is the culture/sub-culture (part of society) in which the people (especially the victim and offender) are brought up. The expectations and understanding of justice may

WHAT DO YOU THINK? 3.2

Does justice depend on context?

Let's consider what might constitute 'justice' in two scenarios:

1. Amy has stolen food from Ben.
2. Colin has stolen a similar amount of food from Deepak.

Society may call for each person to be punished equally. This might sound very logical, but do your views on what would constitute justice in these scenarios change when you know more about the situations, motivations, and views of the people involved?

In Scenario 1:

- Ben wants to see Amy suffer and be punished, but he also wants an apology; a recognition that Amy has done him harm and regrets it. He would like to receive compensation or reparation to make up for his **victimisation** in some small way.

- Amy is poor and close to starving, and feels that she deserves the food more than Ben, who is rich. For this reason, she feels that any punishment would be unjust, though she is willing to apologise for her actions.

Whereas in Scenario 2:

- Deepak is forgiving. She takes the view that it is only food and she should be willing to share food. She hopes for an apology from Colin but does not want to see him punished for such a small breach.

- Colin is not poor and stole the food for fun—just because he wanted to and could. He does not regret his actions—he feels that the theft was minor and resents the fact that it has been reported as a crime at all—and is not willing to apologise.

Now that you are equipped with this additional information, consider the following questions in the context of the two scenarios:

1. What do you think would be the most just outcome in each scenario and why?

2. Should we take an objective societal view of wrongdoing and punish all similar offences in the same way, or should this vary depending on the victim's view or the situation and motivation of the offender?

3. Given that justice is a matter of perspective, and your classmates are likely to give a different answer to Question 3 to you, how can we decide whose idea of justice should be given legal backing and be imposed on others?

These are, of course, very difficult questions, and often impossible to answer with certainty one way or another, but it is important that you consider them carefully and begin to form views on the answers.

differ. In such a complex and uncertain world, how can we decide whether something is just/fair or unjust/unfair?

For example, why is it 'just' to punish? Society often says that if someone commits a crime the state not only *can* punish that person but has an *obligation* to punish them. The argument is that the perpetrator has disturbed justice in that society and therefore must be punished. They should not be allowed to gain by doing wrong. The crime is an affront to everyone in that society and needs to be marked out as such (see Hudson, 2003: Ch. 2). For example, we all own things that we do not want others to take, so when the state punishes for stealing it is protecting the interests of everyone who owns something.

In short, when we discuss and attempt to define justice, we need to consider and respect a variety of standpoints.

3.3 Criminal justice models

To deepen our discussion of justice, we need to be familiar with some theoretical and philosophical ideas about justice and criminal justice systems.

In 1981, criminological theorist Michael King wanted to understand the principles and characteristics of the criminal justice system, things which might be seen to underpin the 'justice' of the system. In doing so, he identified six models (frameworks) of criminal justice (King, 1981: 13), which can be divided into two categories, with three defined as **descriptive** and three as **normative**. These models—and the philosophical ideas of justice that follow—represent some of the most famous ideas related to justice, and they are not intended to be directly political (that is, related to a particular political standpoint). You will come across other ideas of justice in later chapters, many of which (for example, feminist, critical, or radical criminological theories) will not be represented as justice theories but do still centre on issues of justice. At their core, these approaches argue that something in our society is unfair or unjust and that the behaviour of individuals and the state cannot be properly appreciated or judged without an understanding and consideration of that issue.

As we will see, it would be difficult or impossible to implement some of these theoretical and philosophical ideas in practice, especially in their full forms, so the ideas we discuss here may at first seem a little abstract. However, they are in fact relevant to most of what you will study in criminology and, as you delve more deeply into the criminal justice system and look at specific issues or cases, you will find that they can be very useful in helping you consider whether the system or a decision is just, and how things might be improved. Their relevance and uses in your studies will become clearer in **section 3.6**. In this section, we will briefly look at some of these descriptive and normative criminal justice models, but also widen the consideration out to some others which King does not include (for an overview, see **Tables 3.1** and **3.2**).

Descriptive models

The descriptive models King identified describe what researchers found when they studied the systems; no claim was made as to whether this was a just or unjust way of setting up the system. They are:

- the bureaucratic model;
- the **stigmatisation** or status passage model;
- the power model.

Each of these models simply describes and questions what they find, though in some cases the description has later been put forward as something a system should aspire to and in others it is a negative evaluation. The last, the power model (propounded by radical and critical theorists), goes further than the former two; theorists use this model to attack the system for being a tool of domination (see **Chapters 18** and **19**). We will briefly consider these three descriptive models in turn.

Weber: the bureaucratic model

The bureaucratic model comes from the work of the German sociologist and philosopher Max Weber (1864–1920) and is linked to what is often called **Weberian sociology**. Observing the systems in use at that time, Weber suggested that criminal justice systems (such as rules of evidence) operated on standardised procedures, and adhering to these was considered to be good practice. There are four elements to this model:

1. Adherence to procedures, rights, and powers.
2. Recording of information.
3. Resolution of cases as efficiently as possible.
4. Limitation of costs.

The first element of the model is that in every criminal case there were procedures to follow to prevent arbitrary decisions. The procedures were there not to guarantee fairness, but because they limited discretion (an individual's ability to use their own judgement to decide on the right action), and so delivered consistency and prevented political interference in cases. The procedures set out the rights and powers of the state and its citizens (for instance, the power to stop and search), and a central part of this was to ensure that each person was treated equally without political bias, favouritism, or discrimination. An example of an attempt to set out such rules can be found in the Police and Criminal Evidence Act 1984 and the codes of practice to which it gave rise. These documents set limits to police powers and how they should be used.

The second element was to record all information. A criminal case then consisted of what was officially recorded, the court read the contents of the file to decide where the truth lay and on guilt or innocence. In this type of system, written evidence is prioritised over oral evidence (spoken testimony)—this aspect is more relevant in continental systems and we will look at it later in the chapter when we consider inquisitorial systems. Thirdly, these systems expected cases to be resolved as quickly as possible—justice should be swift and the result of efficient systems. Finally, these systems prioritised cost limitation, using **cost–benefit analysis** (an analysis of whether the costs outweigh the benefits in deciding whether a particular course of action is sensible or better than others) to decide whether something was worth doing.

The linking of cost limitation and swift justice meant that these systems prioritised diversion from costly trials by full use of guilty pleas. Weber was not advocating this as an ideal way of delivering justice, but rather noting that complex organisations have a tendency to become bureaucratic. However, in modern systems some of these elements are suggested as being something to which we should aspire. This approach can be seen clearly in England and Wales, starting with the Royal Commission on Criminal Justice 1993 (the Runciman Commission) and running through many policies up to today where consistent systems, speed, and cost-effectiveness are seen as positive. (See, for example, policies such as managing the risks of known offenders.)

A central element of the bureaucratic model is that cases should be tried and sentenced (or acquitted) quickly and efficiently (such a system is more cost-effective). A system may achieve these ends but using this model it is difficult to tell whether the system or any particular outcome is fair or just. We can apply cost-effectiveness to decide whether pursuing an issue is financially viable, but it offers little help in deciding issues themselves or identifying justice. Indeed, whilst efficiency may call for a quick decision from reading what is in the file, justice may require the case to be tried and, if the accused is innocent, justice requires an acquittal whereas the bureaucratic model sees acquittals (at least, a large number of acquittals) as a problem because of the perceived waste of court time and taxpayers' money.

Durkheim: the stigmatisation or status passage model

Émile Durkheim (1858–1917), a French sociologist and philosopher, noted that **stigmatisation** helped to reinforce social cohesion, making a society stronger; he saw this as being used by states to build stronger societies (Durkheim, 1895). Stigmatising offenders (and maybe even defendants, on the basis that there is no smoke without fire) sets them apart from law-abiding members of the community. It makes the law-abiding feel good about themselves and appreciate the same goodness in others. Spreading information about offending behaviour is valuable as it allows the whole society to denounce the behaviour of the offenders, and often to denounce or reject the offenders themselves as being bad.

Durkheim saw states and communities using the broad dissemination of information about trial and punishment of criminals as positive, as helping to unite the good against the bad. Historically, this information would have been conveyed by enacting punishments in public (such as public hanging or public flogging); more recently it is done through the media and online (see **Chapter 6**). Reporting of the trial and punishment expresses society's disapproval of criminal activity. Durkheim understood that any state, with any political bent, could use this to build social cohesion; it can therefore be used to uphold some very unjust regimes. Strong feelings of belonging to the mainstream and stigmatising others are used in many dystopian novels such as Orwell's *Nineteen Eighty-Four* and Atwood's *The Handmaid's Tale* where characters are expected to report 'unacceptable' behaviour to prove they are 'good'. A system which has stigmatisation and denunciation at its centre may not be just, it may make the victim feel their plight is taken seriously and so deliver *part* of a just outcome, but it does little to ensure a fully just outcome.

Power models

As we will see in **Chapter 18**, radical and critical theorists describe (and attack) the criminal justice system as something which maintains the domination of one group over another. Power models are based on this dynamic. Domination may arise from a number of factors: it might be class, social grouping, religion, gender, race, etc. or a combination of these. They analyse and assess the whole of the criminal justice system (from decisions about which activities are criminalised through to how to punish). Their analysis generally accuses criminal justice systems of allowing a powerful group to subjugate a less powerful group—and therefore not being about social cohesion but about control. They often emphasise the historical role of the criminal justice system in maintaining political, social, cultural, and economic domination.

Domination may be achieved by having rules which are directed more at one group than another, for example by more closely policing certain areas. When done most effectively, power theorists (such as Quinney, 1970) remark that the powerless group accepts the perspective of the dominant group and may even ask for greater domination to resolve social problems they suffer. These theorists challenge systems of dominance, for instance **patriarchy**, class systems, and colonialism, and see the punishment of offenders as proof of the domination, pointing to an over-representation of the dominated group among those being punished.

These descriptive models, summarised in **Table 3.1**, are useful to ensure that in looking for justice we are aware of the way in which laws can be abused; they remind us to question and search for justice. However, whilst in describing them the theorists are not generally setting out to be directly political (except in the case of the critical/radical models), they are, in reality, describing very politicised systems, and so do not necessarily help us to ensure or even evaluate just outcomes.

Normative models

Whereas the descriptive models we have considered mainly describe and question what they observe to be the case in existing systems, the next collection of models King identified, the normative models, are presented as just and moral ways to run a criminal justice system. Aspects of them are visible within current systems, but the 'pure' forms are ideals, rather than practical realities. King suggested the following models:

- the crime control model;
- the due process model;
- the medical model.

The first two, crime control and due process, are traditionally linked to the criminal justice system and each claims to be delivering justice. They were most famously compared by Herbert Packer (1968) in his work *The Limits of the Criminal Sanction*. The third is a more limited idea, largely focused on **rehabilitation** of the offender.

In this section, we will also discuss two more normative models that King did not highlight:

- the rights model;
- the victims' rights model.

The first of these is linked to international and theoretical ideals of human rights and the second, as the name suggests, focuses on victims.

We will consider each normative model in turn.

Crime control model

Crime control, which we discuss in depth in **Chapter 27**, is often associated with ideas of **utilitarianism** (greatest good for the greatest number), a system which tries to ensure that most people are looked after. In terms of criminal justice, this means that offenders and maybe even suspects should be repressed and controlled to protect the good. This should happen through an efficient and accurate quest for truth, allowing society to express disgust and generally denunciate criminals and criminal activities. Crime control wants to repress crime by apprehending, convicting, and punishing offenders swiftly and efficiently.

	Bureaucratic model	Stigmatisation or status passage model	Power model
Characteristics	Procedures, recording information, efficiency, cost-limitation measures	Societal	Accuses the law, especially criminal law, of allowing the domination of one group over another
Benefits	This model has the potential to save time and money. It involves the management of crime and criminals	Society gains strength through social cohesion	Opens our eyes to the injustices that may be in our legal systems
Limitations	The rules do not need to be fair or just	Does not always deliver a just outcome	Often it simply describes and questions what it sees the criminal justice system as doing without suggesting or building alternatives

Table 3.1 Outline characteristics of the three descriptive models of criminal justice

The denunciation aspect of crime control helps to strengthen moral standards and pulls law-abiding people together (it is therefore related to the status passage model advocated by Durkheim), but it ensures that individuals are not tempted to take matters into their own hands. Crime control requires a strong criminal justice system, one which relies on professional judgement (judgement of police, prosecutors, judges, correctional officers) and does not put too many limitations on the ability of these professionals to make decisions—it permits a lot of professional discretion, a cycle shown in **Figure 3.5**. Ideally, most of those who are tried should be found guilty (to show that the professionals are doing their jobs properly) and then be swiftly and harshly punished. A few acquittals can be explained due to technical problems in the evidence or the jury misunderstanding something, but if there are a significant number this could be seen as a failure of the system.

The crime control model calls on people to trust the professionals so that if both the police and prosecutor think this person is guilty, they probably are (a presumption of guilt). A strong and harsh system, one which efficiently catches, convicts, and punishes people, is thought to deter the person being punished, and also to deter other people from choosing to offend. If this deterrence is real, it would deliver something positive. It also makes people feel as if crime is being controlled, so law-abiding citizens feel free to enjoy their lives (and if it really does reduce crime then they can also do so safely).

Crime control aims to guarantee social freedom to those who do not offend. The model sees legal controls to protect the defendant (suspect) as something which can be bent or broken in order to ensure a swift conviction and to protect the innocent. Those acquitted are often thought to 'have got away with it', rather than being innocent. Here, the presumption of innocence only really rules the way in which the court process is conducted; the presumption of guilt is the factor which predicts the most common and expected outcome. The central element is the control of crime, which requires a high rate of apprehension and conviction of criminals, and results must be seen to be met very quickly. If occasionally some innocent individuals are sacrificed by being wrongly punished, this may be a necessary evil in order to ensure that the guilty are

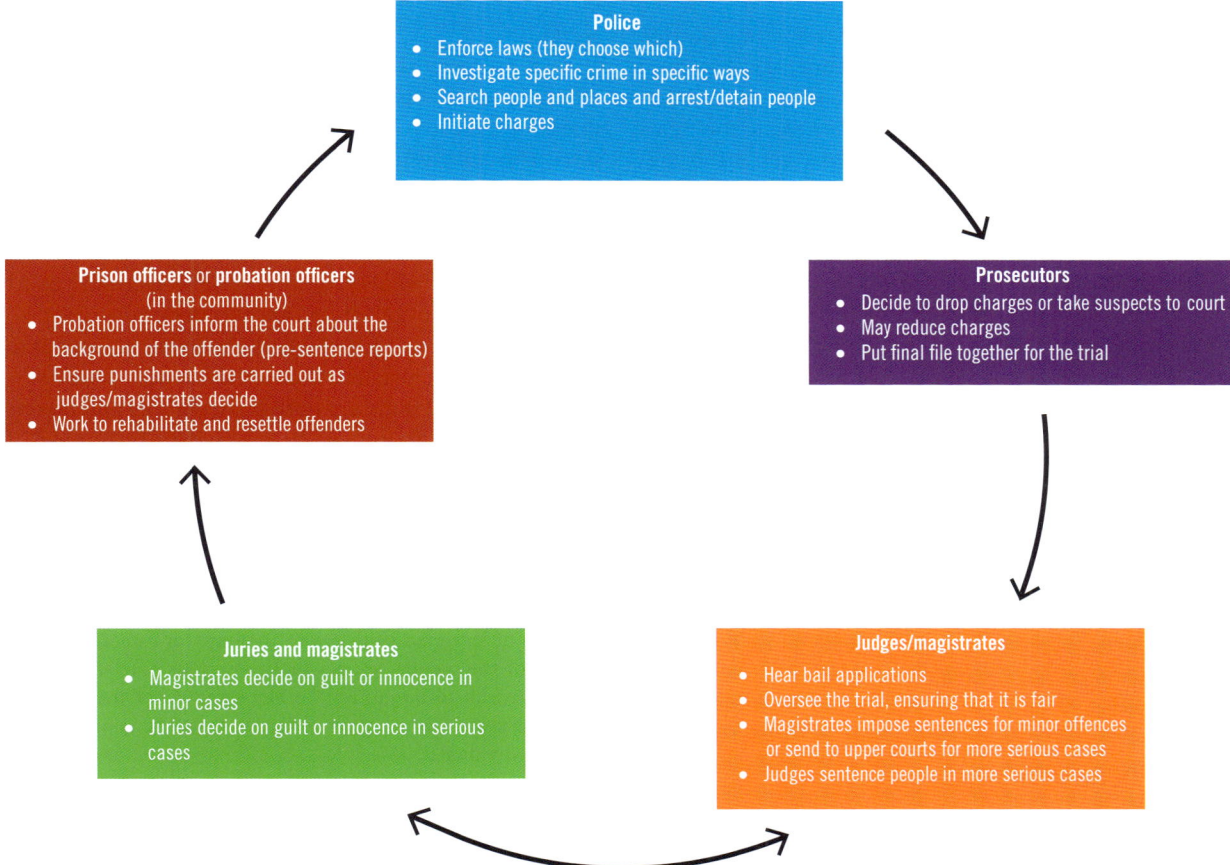

Figure 3.5 The cycle of professional discretion and decision-making within the crime control model

punished and that crime is controlled. This model asserts the rights of victims and society over those of suspects and defendants. The bottom line is that society's reaction should be swift, punitive, and proportional to ensure that it is clearly linked to the offending and allows law-abiding people to see justice done; the offender should be seen to be punished. It is also intended to demonstrate that crime does not pay—if you offend you are likely to be caught and punished.

Formal procedures are kept to an absolute minimum and their breach should never lead to the exclusion of evidence which is otherwise thought reliable; the guilty should never be acquitted on a technicality. This type of model would encourage the police to pursue someone they know to be guilty to ensure they are convicted and to bend or break rules, such as the need for a search warrant, in order to secure proof of guilt. Here, the end of crime control—punishing the guilty—always justifies the means. Police collecting evidence with little respect for the rights of suspects (a crime control-type of action) has led to police procedures being more carefully set out in rules such as those contained in the Police and Criminal Evidence Act 1984 and all its codes of practice that try to instruct the police on what is and is not acceptable.

To take an example, Reiner et al. (2001) discuss the ways in which the police, and their roles in crime control, are portrayed in films over time and how these cultural representations may indicate our changing ideas of policing. From 1945 until about 1964, they argue that films depict the police as sticking within the rules and bringing criminals to justice but since 1965 they argue that films portray the police as taking the law into their own hands, often by killing the offender rather than bringing them before a court and breaking rules designed to limit police powers in order to ensure that the 'bad' guys do not win. This can be seen in many films, for example the *Dirty Harry* films in which Clint Eastwood is the cop who breaks all the rules but delivers justice, whereas his 'weak' colleagues who stay within the rules fail to stop the 'bad' guys. Similar scenarios play out in films such as the *Beverly Hills Cop* series or *LA Confidential* (see also detailed discussion by Gustafson, 2007) and the chilling depictions of the very real dangers of a system based on crime control such as the documentary films *The Paradise Lost* trilogy, *Capturing the Friedman's*, and *Kids of Cash*.

The crime control model can be juxtaposed to the next model—the **due process model**.

Due process model

Both crime control and due process argue that the state has a duty to protect the community from crime and criminals; they both expect the state to punish the guilty. However, due process places greater responsibility on the state to prove the guilt of the defendant *beyond reasonable doubt*. Many films, TV series, and books refer to due process or aspects of it as being necessary to ensure fair treatment in the criminal justice system—examples include Lee's *To Kill a Mockingbird* (later made into a film), the film *A Few Good Men*, and many crime scene or forensic-related police dramas such as *CSI* and *Silent Witness*. Some depict the horror when due process fails to deliver justice (see, for example, *Reversal of Fortune*).

Some of the ideas of due process theorists might be seen as being embedded in the theories of Beccaria, which we discuss in **Chapter 15**. To punish an innocent person is seen as a double injustice; first, the guilty person goes free and, secondly, an innocent person is wrongly punished, their rights are violated by the state. To prevent this, due process requires a fair balance between the power of the state and the ability of individuals to defend themselves. When a crime occurs the state generally enjoys a lot of legal power to investigate and try a case; a suspect or the accused lacks power. Due process theorists set up rules to limit the power of the state (often the police) and ensure that the power balance is more equal between the individual and the state, resulting in suspects being more fairly treated.

Due process theorists recognise that the police may have an honest belief that a suspect is guilty, but they might be mistaken or may be misled by witnesses or victims who are mistaken or lying to the police. Suspects may also confess because they feel under pressure: for that reason, due process theorists argue that formal rules and processes need to protect individuals from excessive use of power and the whole process should be tested in a court case, re-trials, and appeals in case of other errors. The processes are important to protect the individual. Central to this model is the presumption of innocence—every suspect is presumed innocent until proven guilty and no one should have to incriminate themselves. In this model, if breaking the rules leads to evidence, even irrefutable evidence, it should not be used to prove guilt. Allowing such evidence:

> would I believe encourage serious wrongdoing from some police officers who might be tempted to exert force or fabricate or suppress evidence in the hope of establishing the guilt of the suspect, especially in a serious case where they believe him to be guilty. . . . The integrity of the criminal justice system is a higher objective than the conviction of any individual.
>
> (Zander, Runciman Report (Cm 2263), 1993: 234–5)

If, within the process rules, the state proves a person guilty they can punish them. Of course, there may still be an error and the person may not actually be guilty, but at least the state has done everything it can to ensure that the process and trial is fair (just). In ensuring that no or very few innocent people are convicted, due process theorists recognise and accept that some guilty people will go free. They see this as being fairer or more just than convicting the innocent.

To be truly aligned with the due process model, a system would need not just to follow the rules but to ensure that the intentions underlying them are not ignored and that the ethical intentions are preserved—this ideal is clear in the quote from Michael Zander. This is **procedural justice**—it follows procedures and if the procedures are fair, the outcome should be fair and just. By focusing on protection of suspects, however, there is a tendency to ignore the rights and interests of victims and of communities. It is important to note that the due process model does not *guarantee* a just outcome, it merely sets up procedures to ensure that the criminal process is fair to the suspect and to prevent the state using its power unjustly, even if that state action would be popular.

Medical model

This model calls on the criminal justice system to adopt a therapeutic approach to dealing with offenders. Here, criminal offenders are 'treated' as if they were 'ill'; probation officers and other criminal justice system workers are expected to work with them to address the causes of their criminal behaviour and thereby rehabilitate the offender and make society safer. This model came to prominence in the 1950s and 1960s as being a more humane way of dealing with offenders. Basically, the model argues that there is something 'wrong', often a mental issue, with offenders which can be 'corrected' via close, medicalised one-to-one work. The medical model was often embraced by the state in part, at least, because as with punishment, it focuses on the individual offender as the problem rather than seeing structural problems as underlying criminality; it assumes the root cause is individual dysfunction rather than social ills and injustices such as poverty, inequality, or unemployment.

In practice, rehabilitation rarely had anything to do with a medical problem but probation officers worked to support offenders, often supporting them to overcome or cope with socio-structural problems (homelessness, unemployment, etc). This one-to-one rehabilitative working style was undermined by Martinson (1974), whose work gave rise to the idea that 'nothing works'. This idea argued that the causes of criminality are structural and therefore there was nothing to be gained in working one-to-one with offenders. 'Nothing works' led to a loss of confidence in most criminological learning about offender behaviour, as proponents did not believe it 'worked' to alter behaviour and make offenders more law abiding. However, slowly a more positive agenda has been allowed to come to the fore through the 'what works' movement (Cullen and Gendreau, 2001) and ideas such as **desistance** theory (Weaver, 2019; Farall et al., 2010; Maruna, 2001), all of which show how a professionalised and evidence-based probation service can have a positive effect on offending behaviour (see also **Chapter 29**). This is not really a move back to the medical model (which is no longer a central idea in criminology), but rather a criminal justice-focused way of tackling behaviour that is used once someone admits guilt or has been convicted.

Rights model

The rights model takes the procedural restraints set out in the due process model, chooses those that are most fundamental to the freedom of the individual, and terms them rights. Once protections are recognised internationally as rights, they should be respected even if they interfere with the criminal justice system or make it more difficult to get a conviction (see **section 2.5**). A model based on rights is designed to ensure that the state and its representatives do not use their powers arbitrarily to unacceptably interfere with the democratic freedoms that they are supposed to protect: things like immunity from arbitrary arrest, detention, and exile; right to a fair trial; freedom of speech, demonstration, and association. However, poor policing or a deficient criminal justice system can quickly undermine freedom and be used to repress people or parts of communities.

Rights set out standards below which no state should ever fall. They are generally basic standards and states are supposed to improve on them in their liberties and due process. Their real value lies in the fact that they are standards which sit above states; they can be used to test the actions of a state, to test the laws and the use of force (see the example of Edward in the discussion of applying the normative models later in this section). Each state can set its due processes or civil liberties, but rights standards can only be altered by agreement of many states. This is important because even where a state is under extreme threat (for example, a threatened terror attack) it is important that it does not resort to human rights violations such as torture. At these times, rights set standards and limits to the use of power to try to ensure that a state does not overreach acceptable power in order to deal with a terrorist threat. There are some things that we have an *absolute* right to, such as not being found guilty of a crime if the activity was not criminal when you participated. The rules can be altered for those who follow you but should not be altered for you.

Victims' interests/rights model

Whilst there are some early studies that focus on victims, and they have always been an important source of evidence in court, victims only really began to become central to criminal justice in the 1970s (see **Chapter 7**). Once victims' interests/rights began to become a focus (of the system, academics, and politicians), their needs and interests began to come to the fore in criminal justice. Slowly, the 'victims' movement' evolved and the need to consider victims as central to criminal justice became accepted. The victims' movement and victims' interests/rights began to emerge. There are two aspects to this model: the punitive and non-punitive models of victims' interests/rights.

The punitive model calls for victims' rights and interests to be core at every stage of the criminal justice system, from investigation through court case to sentencing and punishment, even release of offenders. At each of these stages, the expectation is that the interests, rights, and needs of victims will be taken into account alongside those of offenders and the community/state. Here the victim is not just a witness but also a central player. Focusing on victims has reduced understanding and support for offenders and has increased calls to blame them, call them to account, and punish them more harshly. This is a natural result of taking victims more into consideration in the system; any changes are likely to have a negative knock-on effect for offenders. Similarly, any increase in rights for defendants and offenders is often seen as diminishing the interests of victims. We can see the rise of the importance of victims in the criminal justice system in many films and TV dramas, for example *The Accused* and *Three Billboards Outside Ebbing, Missouri*.

In contrast, the non-punitive interests/rights model focuses on crime prevention and community building, often through restorative justice. For more detail, see the discussion of radical communitarianism in **section 3.4**.

Applying the normative models

As we noted at the start of this section, it can sometimes be difficult to see the relevance—both in practice and for your studies—of theoretical ideas like these. To make this clearer, let's take one realistic example and apply it to each of the normative models we have discussed. Imagine that we know that an individual, Edward, has vital information about a bombing which is to take place in the near future. How would each normative model apply in this situation?

- Under the crime control model, the ideal is to protect the people; this might permit Edward to be tortured to get the information.

- Under due process, the state is not normally permitted to torture but some states may permit the police to *threaten* torture, hoping that Edward will tell them something. If there is time then under the due process model Parliament might choose to pass a law permitting extreme measures (maybe even torture) in certain very limited circumstances (with lots of checks and balances to its use), and again torture may be threatened and possibly even permitted.

- The medical model would not be relevant to this question.

- Under a rights model, torture is absolutely prohibited and under no circumstances can the state or any of its agents conduct or threaten torture, even if it means that they might not uncover an active bomb threat.

- The victims' interest/rights model means focusing on the prevention of victimisation. In the punitive model, this might have a similar outcome to the crime control model, whereas in the non-punitive model the focus on prevention of victimisation might involve community-based activities instead of or as well as focusing on questioning Edward.

The example of Edward is loosely based on a real case, that of *Ireland v United Kingdom* (App. no. 5310/71) [1978] ECHR 1. In the early 1970s, there had been acts of terrorism committed by members of the Irish Republican Army (IRA). The authorities arrested and detained several members of the IRA. They were interrogated for hours at a time using tactics that included wall-standing, hooding, and deprivation of food and sleep. The European Court of Human Rights decided that the techniques did not quite amount to torture but were examples of 'inhuman and degrading' treatment which violated Art. 3 of the European Convention on Human Rights (ECHR). The rights set out in Art. 3 are protected absolutely: they can never be breached by any state which is party to the Human Rights Convention. It was unacceptable for any state to use either torture or cruel and inhuman treatment even if it thought that the tactics might give it information which would prevent an act of terrorism; some activities are never permissible. For discussion of another example, see **Controversy and debate 3.2**.

Let's take another example that might be relevant in more cases: it used to be the case that if a suspect remained silent or refused to comment no one could assume that they were guilty, even if most people thought that an innocent person would answer the question(s). How would each model consider this view?

A crime control model is focused on conviction of the guilty. This model would always have permitted a judge or jury to infer guilt from silence in the belief that an

CONTROVERSY AND DEBATE 3.2

Breaching rights in the interests of justice: the *Gäfgen* case

A young boy is abducted. His parents are asked for a ransom, which they then pay, but the child is not returned. The police arrest a man and all the evidence points to his having abducted the child; he even admits that this is what happened. The man refuses to tell the police where the child is. Should police officers be permitted to threaten to torture the suspect if they believe this may save the life of an innocent child?

These basic facts are from an actual case. The situation arose in Germany in 2002 and the police did threaten the suspect with considerable violence and suffering if he did not disclose the whereabouts of the child. The police believed the child was still alive and were worried he might die if they did not find him soon. The suspect, Magnus Gäfgen (now known as Thomas David Lukas Olsen, pictured in **Figure 3.6**), confessed to abducting and killing the boy and directed the police to where they could find his body. The court decided that the German police could not, under any circumstances, either torture or threaten to torture a suspect (as this was inhuman treatment). They did, however, permit the court to use the finding of the boy's body and evidence found with the body to be used to convict the suspect (see *Gäfgen* v *Germany* (App. no. 22978/05) (2011) 52 EHRR 1).

Part of the reasoning against the use or threat of torture is that we can never be certain that the suspect has the information. In this case, the police threatened Gäfgen because they believed the child was alive and wanted to save him. But they were wrong; nothing could save the boy, he was already dead. This is proof that the authorities may get things wrong and to allow certain breaches of rights should never be condoned, it would be unjust.

However, would the threat or use of torture ever be justified if (using this case) the boy *were* in fact still alive?

Figure 3.6 Magnus Gäfgen, now known as Thomas David Lukas Olsen, was at the centre of a case that highlights how difficult it can be to ensure justice is served

Source: Boris Roessler/picture-alliance/dpa/AP Images

---

innocent person would want to take every opportunity to defend themselves. Therefore, this model would assume that silence would only be used by the guilty. In order to ensure the conviction of guilty people, crime control theorists would argue that it should always be acceptable to infer guilt from silence.

A due process model believes in checks and balances to protect suspects from the abuse of power by the state and to ensure that the innocent are acquitted. Until recently, the law in England and Wales prevented people assuming guilt from a suspect's refusal to answer questions. Following the Police and Criminal Evidence Act 1984, all interviews have been recorded (now they are often video recorded), protecting suspects from unfair or oppressive questioning. Therefore, the power differential in the interview is now more equal so it should be fair to allow the court to infer guilt in cases where a suspect refused to answer acceptable questions. The balance of power is more equal so the *right* to silence is not needed.

A rights model protects individual rights from state power. Whilst Art. 3 of the ECHR is absolute, most other rights in the European Convention can be altered, but only if necessary for the protection of higher goals. Under a rights system, if an individual should enjoy a particular right then they do not lose that protection just because the balance of power shifts a little, they enjoy it as of right. Therefore, if the right to silence was protected under the Convention it could not be jeopardised even if other things had altered.

Normative models—a conclusion

Table 3.2 summarises the five normative models we have considered, each of which sets out an ideal for the criminal justice system to follow. Each model tends to prioritise the interests of certain groups over others and will be used by people to make specific points. In evaluating

	Crime control	Due process	Medical	Rights	Victims' interests/rights
Aim	To keep law and order—punishing offenders swiftly and harshly to deter criminal conduct, control crime, and to try to protect the public.	To administer justice in each case by using fair legal rules and procedures—the state and courts should be impartial arbiters. The onus is placed on the state to prove the defendant is guilty.	To rehabilitate offenders and thereby reduce crime.	To ensure state power is fair and not arbitrary—to uphold democratic freedoms for everyone.	The punitive aspect: to improve the criminal justice system so as better to serve the interests and needs of victims. This involves punishing offenders. The non-punitive aspect: to prevent crime and repair the harm it causes through community cohesion.
Strategy	Police and courts guard law and order. They should not be over-controlled by rules.	Checks and balances protect suspects from abuse of power.	Therapeutic methods are designed to rehabilitate offenders.	Basic standards of rights for each person are set. The actions of a state can be tested against these rights, and they cannot be violated.	The punitive aspect: real and effective rights and interests for victims are provided. The non-punitive aspect: community policies are constructed to both resolve and prevent crime and conflict.
Assumption	Guilt is implied—police professionalism should be trusted.	Presumption of innocence.	There is something wrong with people who offend.	Presumption of innocence. Individuals should be guaranteed to enjoy their rights and have an absolute right to a fair trial.	The punitive aspect: victims should be central to the criminal justice system. The non-punitive aspect: communities can be trusted to use positive methods to deal with offending.
Legal controls	Minimal. Procedural rules should be kept to a minimum and if breached by the authorities, this should not prevent evidence being admitted.	Control on powers, especially police powers. These are checks and balances which must be followed in each case. If procedure is broken, evidence may be excluded. Procedures may be legally altered.	Very few in this model.	Individuals have rights which cannot be violated or altered. Evidence obtained in breach of rights should be excluded.	The punitive aspect: control of offenders' legal rights to the extent necessary to provide adequate legal rights for victims. The non-punitive aspect: recognition of alternative and hybrid systems which place communities at the centre of harm resolution.
Process	Speedy apprehension, conviction, and punishment of offenders, what Packer (1968) calls a conveyor belt.	Fair trial with complicated criminal processes (but can be compromised).	No legal process except that rehabilitation be a major concern at sentencing stage.	Right to a fair trial—this is absolute.	The punitive aspect: a fair trial must include victims. The non-punitive aspect: the process should include victims and community.

3.3 CRIMINAL JUSTICE MODELS

	Crime control	Due process	Medical	Rights	Victims' interests/rights
View on guilt/innocence	The guilty must be convicted (even if some innocent people are convicted or some people's civil liberties are interfered with). Victim rights supersede those of the accused.	The civil liberties of every person should be respected (even if some guilty people are acquitted).	No stance on this, except that 'guilt' is a less judgemental finding because the offender is not entirely to 'blame' because they were 'ill'.	Individual rights should be protected. (Leading to a problem when victim and suspect rights collide.)	The punitive aspect: we must ensure that only the guilty are convicted so that they can be fully blamed and punished. The non-punitive aspect: more interested in the resolution and prevention of harm than guilt and innocence.
Idea of justice	Denunciation of crime. Community safety and crime control are paramount.	Procedural justice—following the rules even if they deliver an unfair outcome.	Holding offenders to account whilst also supporting them to move on to a prosocial life in the future.	Respecting and seeking to uphold all rights—not quite substantive justice, though closer to it.	The punitive aspect: offenders should take full responsibility for their crimes by being punished to the maximum extent legally possible. The non-punitive aspect: the harm suffered by the victim and their community should be minimised or removed.
Benefits	Pulls law-abiding people together. May be a deterrence for others. Denunciation of crime and aims to make communities safer.	By requiring the state (police, courts, etc.) to abide by laws and rules that curtail state power it protects individuals. Requires legal rights to be respected.	Recognises that offenders may not be fully to blame.	Requires that rights are respected even when not fully enshrined in state law. Curtails the way in which agents of the state (police and prosecutors) pursue offenders.	The punitive aspect: victims are central to the system. The non-punitive aspect: less focus on blaming and punishing the offender and more on supporting victims who have been harmed.
Limitations	Innocent people could be wrongfully convicted.	Some guilty people could avoid conviction.	Focuses on the individual as the problem and does not recognise structural problems in society (or other issues) which may be behind some offending.	Does not always balance the rights of victims and offenders.	The punitive aspect: fails to address how both offenders' rights and victims' rights can be respected and, if they cannot, which rights should prevail. The non-punitive aspect: assumes too much cohesion in communities and does not recognise that modern western states often do not have clear and strongly cohesive communities.

Table 3.2 Outline of the five main normative criminal justice models

how a criminal justice system operates and considering what might be a just approach, you need to consider all the models, both normative and descriptive.

These models are all useful and important to consider, but as we can see from the 'Limitations' row in **Table 3.2**, each falls short of really getting to grips with justice. Some may deliver procedural justice but is that *real* justice? Procedural justice just means that the procedures (often due process procedures) are correctly followed and applied equally in each case. It generally means that there is a system which is designed to resolve conflict or to divide burdens or benefits. If the procedures are unfair, then the outcome will be unjust, so procedure alone does not necessarily deliver justice.

We need to consider **substantive justice**, which is concerned with how an individual evaluates important issues and focuses on the principle, and the idea of a just outcome, which means fair and just treatment leading to a fair and just resolution of a situation, particularly as experienced by those who are involved. Ideally, process and substantive principles deliver just outcomes.

Justice is about public decision-making regarding the distribution of goods and of negative things like punishment (**distributive justice**). It is also about trying to deliver moral outcomes and correcting problems which arise, for example deciding what should happen when A takes something from B (**corrective justice**). We need to look a little more closely at justice to study these more complex ideas, so in the next section we will look in depth at four theoretical ideas of justice.

3.4 Philosophical ideas of justice

Many theorists, from the time of ancient Greece to the present day, have tried to define the concept of justice and identify what perfect justice might look like. Here we will look at just four of these thinkers: Aristotle (384–322 BC), John Rawls (1971), Amartya Sen (2010), and communitarianism (for example, Etzioni 1994). We are focusing on these theorists and theories because they are most commonly used when we discuss justice in relation to the criminal justice system, but also because they are important when we consider ideals of social justice and how these might be achieved. The role of social justice is important in many theories of criminology.

Aristotle on justice

Aristotle's ideas about justice

The famous ancient Greek philosopher Aristotle proposed that justice consisted of treating equals alike, and unequals differently in proportion to their inequality; that is, their difference (384–322 bc, see web pages by Sandel). Some see this as meaning that all people should be treated equally, which is one of the main claims made by the law—the criminal law will be applied to everyone equally. However, there is a second part to this idea of justice: that those who are different deserve different treatment.

This second idea could have been used to say that rich and poor should enjoy different justice when faced with the criminal law, but that is not what Aristotle meant. For him, difference should only be considered when it is important to the decision being made and, in criminal decisions, wealth does not increase or decrease guilt. This part of his rule is more concerned with what is known as distributive justice (or substantive justice), which for Aristotle means that each person should enjoy or be given their desert (what someone deserves). The first part of the rule—to treat everyone equally—he saw as something the courts should ensure; the second part of the rule—to do with distribution of goods—should be done by the lawmakers, the legislature.

Problems with Aristotle's ideas about justice

Aristotle's theory on justice looks logical and reasonably simple until we try to apply the rule, particularly the second part of it. Think of the example in **What do you think? 3.1** about food being stolen. A simple application of criminal law would lead to the perpetrators (Amy and Colin, who take the food) being found guilty. Wealth or poverty are not issues that need to be considered when we decide whether someone is guilty or innocent—but how should they be punished? Aristotle says we should take into account inequality between people when deciding how to treat them.

There are three main ways in which one might answer this question:

1. *If an individual's need explains and excuses the crime, they should not be punished.* Many people, including Judge Bazelon (1976, 1981), would not support punishing someone who steals food because they are hungry, such as Amy in our example. They would

argue that in this kind of scenario, the individual's need is greater than that of the owner and, while they are guilty, they should not face punishment, although we might ask them to apologise. As an interesting example of this kind of philosophy in action, and of the apparent support for it, see the following very widely shared tweet (over 20,000 retweets and 83,000 likes at the time of writing):

> Today in court I defended a homeless man being prosecuted for stealing from bins so congratulations must be in order to Leeds police for solving literally all other crime in the city as that's the only circumstances in which I can imagine this being a proper use of resources
>
> (Thotep, N. R. (2018) 12 October 2018. Available at: https://twitter.com/Psychonaut99/status/1050827574841094144)

2. *If goods have been unfairly distributed, society has failed to ensure justice so it is not entitled to impose punishment.* For thinkers such as Anthony Duff (2001), a British legal philosopher, applying the second part of Aristotle's rule—that the lawmaker in that country has a duty to ensure that goods such as food and money are fairly distributed (not necessarily evenly but fairly)—is essential to a just and moral society. Where the lawmakers have failed to ensure such justice, it means that the whole society has failed in their moral duty and therefore should not be permitted to punish others when they commit crimes to fulfil their needs. By failing to ensure the second part of Aristotle's ideas, they have lost the moral high ground and therefore lost the power to punish either Amy or Colin. The victim—Ben or Debbie—cannot complain as they are complicit in the unfair distribution of goods.

3. *Distribution of goods should not affect criminalisation and punishment.* The third category of response would argue that the way in which food and wealth are distributed is immaterial to either the guilt or innocence or the decision to punish.

In many ways, Aristotle's idea drew out some important issues about justice—that it should take account of equality, or lack of it—but while this is useful, it only deals with one facet of the debate. It is of some help in deciding difficult cases but it does not provide answers. It is unable to guide us in deciding which inequalities should lead to different treatment so we need to examine other ideas which take the analysis further.

Applying Aristotle to sentencing, generally sentences should be equal for crimes of equal harm. However, if there are differences which are important, a different sentence might be accepted. For example, it would not be just to alter the amount of punishment someone should get because the judge likes or dislikes the colour of their eyes, but it might be acceptable to punish someone less if they are less culpable (less to blame).

John Rawls on justice
Rawls' ideas about justice

John Rawls (1921–2002, pictured in **Figure 3.7**) was an American moral and political philosopher. He worked for a time at Oxford University and was influenced by both Isaiah Berlin (1909–97, political theorist and historian) and H. L. A. Hart (1907–92, legal philosopher). Two major occurrences are also thought to have shaped his ideas: the fact that he lost three brothers to illness when he was a child, and his experiences in the Second World War. Each of these instilled in him the idea that a civilised society was one which respected social justice. What this meant and how one might achieve social justice became the core of his professional work. Rawls wrote his most famous work, *A Theory of Justice*, in 1971 and it is still regarded as one of the foremost texts on political philosophy. His ideas have many followers and his position on justice is often referred to as Rawlsianism.

Rawls argues that the first duty of any state or any group who rule others is to ensure that justice is respected, and for him, justice is not only about equality but also about fairness. Without justice, he argues, nothing in a society can be seen to be truly good. Rawls wanted to find an ideal theory of justice with which to judge whether a society (or part of it) was just or not. Even more than that, Rawls

Figure 3.7 The moral and political philosopher John Rawls believed that a civilised society was one which respected social justice

Source: Photo by Steve Pyke/Getty Images

wanted his theory to be of practical use in resolving all issues: to test whether actual policy choices are just or not, or to decide which policy choices would be most just.

To build his idea of justice, Rawls starts with what is called a **social contract**; an agreement or set of principles between all people in a society as to how that society should be run. Before the people in Rawls' imagined state make their social contract, he sets a few ground rules. First, he says that everyone makes the contract from what he calls the 'original position', where each person is ignorant of what they presently enjoy before they contract with others to form the society. In his imaginary world, people do not know which sex, class, religion, or social position they belong to, they do not know whether they are rich or poor, powerful or powerless, etc. He calls this the 'veil of ignorance'.

Rawls says this 'veil of ignorance' is important because when each person makes the contract they do not know whether they stand to gain or lose from the contract. In that situation, he claims, they will use rational self-interest, setting the contract so that it will give them the best chance of attaining 'the good life' (what they consider necessary for their own happiness) whatever their social position turns out to be. They will choose what is fair and this will mean the contract will be just—for Rawls, that means it will be positive for everyone but be most advantageous for the least well off in society. For an example of how this might happen, see **What do you think? 3.3**.

From this original position, Rawls says people will build a society based on two basic principles—liberty and equality:

1. First Principle (liberty):

This refers to the fact that each person should have an equal right to as much basic liberty as is possible when making sure that everyone else enjoys the same amount of liberty.

This is the most important principle and, put simply, this means equality of liberty for everyone. The liberties Rawls included here are sometimes referred to as political rights or basic rights, such as voting rights, freedom of speech and assembly, freedom of conscience, freedom from arbitrary arrest, etc. These he felt were so important no government should ever be able to interfere with them or take them away. Other rights or liberties, such as rights over property, he thought to be less important. Rawls' first principle is therefore about justice, meaning something which can and should deliver fairness.

2. Second Principle (equality of sorts):

This refers to the idea that social and economic inequalities are to be arranged so that:

(a) ideally they are to be to everyone's advantage but where this is not fair, they are to the greatest benefit of the least advantaged;

(b) offices and positions, such as jobs, must be open to everyone, regardless of race, gender, and who you know (there should be equality of opportunity).

Although he discussed it second, Rawls considered 2(b), the right to equality of opportunity (including the opportunity to acquire skills necessary to advancement), to be more important than 2(a), the difference principle (how to fairly distribute difference). He even noted that everyone should have not just an opportunity, but an effective chance of success equal to others with similar talents, no matter what their background. So, in any occupation there should be a percentage of people from rich and poor (etc.) backgrounds that is equal to the percentage of that group

WHAT DO YOU THINK? 3.3

Applying Rawls' ideas about justice

Freda has a cake which she has to cut up and share fairly between nine people. How would we ensure that Freda did this as fairly as possible?

Rawls would argue that we should tell Freda (who likes cake) that she would get the last piece. This places her in a sort of original position in that she might end up with the smallest piece. This way, when it came to their turn, each person would take the largest piece available, so the only way Freda could be sure that she will get her fair share is to cut the cake into nine equal parts.

- Do you agree with Rawls?
- Could this outcome be achieved any other way?
- Is it necessarily just for each person to get an equal-sized piece?
- If one person is starving, or got the smallest portion of cake or none at all last time the group met, would it be just to ensure that this person got a larger portion?

in the population. This wide idea of equality of opportunity may be adversely affected by application of the difference principle and therefore, to protect it, Rawls placed it as more important: it should come first.

2(a) is the difference principle, which decides what should happen when decisions have to be made about inequality. The difference principle means that material differences (such as differences in wealth) can only be justified on the basis that they benefit the least advantaged (for example, means-tested benefits), and that there should be fair equality of opportunity for everyone. The fact that the least well off (in all goods) always stand to gain from the contract is designed to ensure that the worst off are properly provided for. Rawls is striving to compensate for both inequalities which arise naturally (short people unable to reach things in shops) and those that arise through the way society is formed, socially (having systems which tend to protect those who inherit wealth). He aims to ensure that there is some redistribution of all basic goods, with some wealth moving from the rich to the poor, but he does not expect that all goods will or should be equally distributed—the worst off should be given preference though there may still be large inequalities in society. Rawls is not arguing for equality; indeed, he argues that inequality might be fair, as long as it does not prevent the least well off from enjoying their basic liberties. However, where there is any levelling of inequality, it must tend to benefit the least advantaged.

Importantly, Rawls argued that people would see their liberties (the first principle) as more important than their equal right to goods and opportunities in society (the second principle). Everyone involved in drawing up a social contract would agree to a flat policy in terms of ensuring everyone enjoys as many liberties as possible. However, every intelligent and fully reasoning individual will agree to some flexibility regarding the fairness of application for social and economic inequalities (part (a) of the second principle) in case they are in the worst advantaged group. Rawls argues that 2(a) is essential as liberty alone would be a form of total free market and does not distribute wealth nor interfere if you are lucky, for example to be born rich this is not a fair/just way to distribute wealth. Rawls also rejects the idea of relying purely on 2(b), equality of opportunity, as this places the distribution of advantages on natural talent. Whilst he considers this better than absolute liberty, he argues that the luck of being born with talents that are, at that time, rated highly (for example, being brilliant at coding in a time, such as now, when coders are in high demand) is not just or fair.

Rawls envisaged that his two principles would be used to set up just institutions, and establish just rules for the institutions to apply. The constitution, institutions, and rules (laws) would be set in stages where the veil of ignorance is slowly lifted, allowing the society to set up a scheme (constitution) that will deliver justice, and then institutions to give shape to that constitution, followed by rules (laws), and finally by an application of those laws in the society. At each stage, the individuals in the society learn more about their situation before they have to set up the next system. All decisions are to be guided by the basic principles.

Problems with Rawls' ideas about justice

Rawls' ideas have, as we have noted, acquired a large and loyal following, but they are not without flaws. Let's consider the issues associated with them.

- Rawls places great faith in institutions and systems, which he asserts will deliver justice; if the process is fair, the outcome should be fair. He suggests that the process should only be questioned if they fail to apply his two basic principles. As we have noted throughout this chapter, it can be dangerous to assume that procedures in themselves are always or usually fair.

- Rawls' ideas are based on a contract between people currently in a society, so people outside the contract, such as foreigners, future generations, nature, and the environment, do not have a say and are not considered important (although there is a little protection for future generations through the just savings principle). This assumes that each society is cut off from other societies and that they do not affect each other, which is clearly not the case. It might, for example, mean that one society can create lots of pollution for the world and this would not be unjust as long as those within the society were justly treated, and to take a criminal justice example, it would permit a state to decide that in the interests of protecting its law-abiding citizens and to punish all criminals, it could deport offenders to other states outside the contract, regardless of the safety of either the people being deported or the people living in the state to which they are sent (this actually happened in the 17th century, when Britain transported about 160,000 people to penal colonies in Australia).

- There is no guarantee that people in the original position will agree on a fair and just social contract. Many very intelligent and rational people in the original position may choose to take a gamble and choose absolute liberty (even at the expense of other people's liberty), hoping to be at the top of society. If we take the idea that it is unjust for a person to take a large advantage just because they happen to be born with a talent which is prized, then Rawls' solution assumes that it is more just for everyone to gain from that talent, for it to be communally owned; is that fair? If the advantages which arise from talent are to be shared, is it just to force the talented to make full use of their talents so that we all gain? Should an inventor have to share their ideas with everyone or could they be allowed to hide them away so no one or only a small number of people can enjoy them?

- The idea of just organisations giving rise to just solutions has never been proven, nor is it likely to be correct. Everything would depend on the rules being applied: if the rules are not just, they would never deliver justice; if they are just for some situations but do not permit flexibility then they will be unjust in some situations.

If we return to the example given earlier in **What do you think? 3.2** about food being stolen, a simple application of the procedural rules would lead to the perpetrator (Amy, the one who takes the food) being found guilty and punished. Rawls' theory would agree that wealth and poverty are not issues which need to be considered when one decides whether someone is guilty or innocent. However, what about the punishment? Rawls accepts inequalities in wealth as being just, so would not undermine the general right to punish simply because some people are less wealthy, but he would argue that before deciding how to distribute punishment, the decision-maker should take account of all the facts (for instance, the fact that Amy is hungry) and might mitigate the punishment in light of them.

Whilst it may generally be just to fine (or punish) everyone the same amount when their crime is the same, Rawls would accept that fining a poor person less would be acceptable as then their fine hurts them the same amount as the normal fine would hurt the rich person. The difference here advantages the poor person (the least advantaged). Note that it might not, however, be just to increase the fine to the rich person as then they might have to pay more than would be fair for the harm they caused. The starting point should therefore be the amount of harm caused by the crime. It should be reduced if there is good reason for doing so, but should not be increased as any more punishment would be unjust. Rawls assumes that if one has fair processes to decide cases, the outcomes will be just.

Amartya Sen on justice

Sen's ideas about justice

Amartya Sen (1933–) is an economist and a philosopher (pictured in **Figure 3.8**) still working to refine his ideas. He was born in India and is particularly interested in real-world and rational solutions. Like Rawls, he aims to

Figure 3.8 For the economist and philosopher Amartya Sen, fairness is the central concept for justice
Source: LSE Library@Flickr Commons/Public domain

deliver social justice for everyone. He wants to improve well-being for all. He wants to free people from hunger, disease, indignity, and discrimination and to deliver real and greater positive freedoms and well-being by increasing their capacity or capabilities. He published *The Idea of Justice* in 2010.

Sen's central concept for justice is fairness. He questions Rawls' faith in institutions and processes as being capable of delivering justice. Whilst he recognises the importance of trying to set up just institutions and systems, he argues that these alone are not enough. Institutions will not necessarily deliver good social outcomes. Importantly, he questions the idea that there is any ideal theory of justice—meaning that he questions the basis of Rawls' thinking. He argues that things are not always just or unjust; it is not a binary idea. Justice exists on a continuum and whether something is just or not may depend both on circumstances and on who is assessing the situation, on different perspectives. He also argues that people can recognise justice (or injustice) without having clear theoretical guidance—you can recognise injustice without knowing what a perfectly fair society would look like or how it would justify itself.

This almost sounds as if he is giving no concept of justice at all but that is not the case. He believes strongly in the need to ensure individual and collective justice for all, and for justice to serve all communities across the globe, questioning Rawls and other thinkers for only serving western justice—he sees it as a global idea and something which should improve everyone's lives in all parts of the world.

In contrast to Rawls, Sen does not see people as driven by self-interest; he thinks they care for each other and generally observe social **norms** (rules or ethical or moral standards). He does not believe that they are always seeking to improve their own lot, but rather that they are able to put other people or a community before their self-interest. Justice is complex, nuanced, and somewhat subjective—it cannot be defined in a concrete way, nor is it just linked to commodities (things). However, the concept exists because people want to counter evils such as hunger, disease, victimisation, indignity, discrimination, and lack of safety, all of which are measurable. Sen argues that if one counters these negatives (through ensuring 'justice'), one increases people's capacity or capabilities and also increases equality.

Sen draws on elements of Sanskrit literature (the Niti and Nyaya schools of thought, deriving from Burma and India, respectively) which give him his two conceptions of justice:

1. correct procedures and formal rules can give a starting point (Niti);
2. but the decisions arising from these need to be tested by 'impartial spectators' to ensure they emerge with just results (social realisation).

Fairness and justice are therefore assessed by the 'impartial spectators' who view the decision from different vantage points to give a plurality of points of view—a complex assessment of justice. Impartial spectators are people who are separated from their own self-interest and can make a dispassionate assessment of justice, able to recognise justice and injustice. They are able to take a 'social choice' perspective—to combine individual preferences, interests, or welfare needs and reach a collective rational decision which will improve or uphold social justice. Each of these impartial spectators may come to a different decision on justice because motivation, rationality, and well-being are complex and can be analysed in differing ways. Judges and juries may be seen as 'impartial spectators' but, for Sen, they need to be willing to open their minds to all possible outcomes and, often, 'impartial spectators' might be further removed for the decision-making, outside the system.

Sen sets out an example (Sen, 2010: 13). He explains that three children, Ann, Bob, and Carla, are quarrelling over the fate of a flute, making different claims as to why each of them should have it:

- Ann claims the flute on the basis that she is the only one who can play it;
- Bob claims it because he has no other toys to play with whereas the others do; and
- Carla's claim is based on the fact that she made the flute in the first place.

Sen observes that the situation can be assessed as follows:

- If one took a utilitarian approach (greatest good for the greatest number) or looked at the purpose of the flute and decided on that basis, then Ann would get the flute as she can play it (fit its purpose) and will bring joy to people who hear her play (utilitarian).
- If equality is brought to the fore then Bob will get the flute as he does not have anything else to play with.
- If it is all based on legal rights, then Carla will get the flute as it belongs to her.

Sen argues that there is merit in *all three* answers as each outcome would increase the well-being of at least one person. He argues that there are many correct and just answers to any problem and we should embrace the fact that justice has many faces—pluralism. He only rejects outcomes that are clearly unjust in all cases, for example that we destroy the flute so no one has it.

Well-being is strongly associated with justice for Sen, and achieving it for everyone depends on constantly striving to increase people's entitlement and freedom, so increasing their capacity to engage in their communities. Justice and well-being are measured by the social outcome—the measurable increase in positive outcomes for people. There is no ideal formula, no one answer to a problem. In deciding on justice, we should always take account of moral or ethical values and judgements but should recognise that they are value-laden and there is a need to respect alternative values. In deciding on justice, rights are central and should never be ignored, but are not pre-eminent or paramount. However, other things are also important: sociability; moral constraint; respect for others; freedom; safety and security; distribution of goods; social and communal living; and equality. These are not always easy to interpret. So with equality there is always the question of 'equality of what'? Is it that we give each person an equal chance or that we look at the outcome and ensure that one group is not unfairly disadvantaged by decisions? If one group is disadvantaged, then Sen argues that we need to advantage individuals from that group over others until the disadvantage is dealt with, a practice known as positive discrimination. The only aspects which are always important and are essential are social justice, well-being, and capacity.

Therefore, Sen recognises that any theory or idea about justice has something useful to say about the real choices we face and how we might resolve those choices. Almost any problem involving justice and resolution of social justice and freedom can have plural resolutions which may be incompatible but each may have merit, so each should be considered and respected. This means that justice will always be a work in progress, incomplete, and an act of learning to compromise. Recognition that there is no ideal is an important aspect of life and justice. In any socially relevant decision, and certainly those involved in the criminal justice system, different individual and collective needs and priorities will vie for prominence and at each juncture there is a need to take account of social policy. Understanding and testing the decisions and outcomes will help to improve justice. Recognising and rationally debating conflicting just outcomes allows the nuances of problems to be fully considered and understood; it is likely to lead to better, more fully just, outcomes. For Sen, justice lies in well-being and depends on how a person functions. This has two main aspects—a person's 'being' (being linked to their community, educated, happy) and a person's 'doings', their acts (doing things they value, entering relationships they choose, working, playing, having fun). Sen argues that a person's ability to function depends on what they are able to do with the commodities they have and their state of being as a result. Their well-being depends on whether they can do and be something they value; in other words, whether they have sufficient agency and freedom of choice.

If we return to the example about food being stolen (**What do you think? 3.1**), Sen would not assume that criminal law would necessarily be the just way to resolve this dilemma. The issue might be resolved by a more restorative or community-based outcome, such as an apology to the victim and support for Amy to increase her financial capacity so that she would not need to steal, she would have other choices, other ways she could behave or 'be'. If criminal law were to be used, he would admit that justice would be served if Amy, the one who takes the food, is found guilty. Once found guilty, however, the issue of whether or not to punish would open up more conflicting outcomes, each of which might have a claim to be just. He would accept that there might be many just ways of punishing Amy; each would serve justice in some way but in so doing would prevent a different idea of justice being served. In such a situation, Sen calls on decision-makers such as the police and judges to become 'impartial spectators', willing and able to consider all outcomes and take both individual and collective perspectives into account before making a final decision.

As the ultimate drive is to increase each person's capacity to engage, Sen prioritises listening to how people themselves believe things should be resolved or what they consider important (give them agency/choice). Because his argument is basically one of equality, even offenders could be given choice. For example, where punishment is necessary the offender might be given some choice as to what work they need to engage in; this still requires them to do something but allows them to shape what they might have to do so that it is something they value. Sen would argue that this would increase the capacity of the individual to live a pro-social life which will be better for the offender, the victim, and the rest of society (see Williams and Daniel, 2020).

Problems with Sen's ideas about justice

The complexity of Sen's ideas and the need to take account of all aspects of a problem mean that they are not easy to use. Unlike Aristotle and Rawls, Sen does not provide a simple rule to apply that will deliver a just outcome, rather he focuses more on what emerges from these institutions and their decision-making, and assesses whether this leads to a just world. This means that it is difficult to distil justice in any particular situation, indeed his willingness to embrace a number of just outcomes can be difficult to grasp and adds layers of complexity. For example, whilst Sen embraces equality he is likely to consider it too simplistic to fine (or punish) everyone the same amount when their crime is the same. This would be too simplistic and loses sight of the fact that, for Sen, one needs to focus on ensuring that people's well-being is enhanced overall and that their idea of what that should look like (agency freedom) is central to the concept. So, he might well agree that there should be a ceiling on the amount of punishment, based on the extent of the harm caused. However, he would argue that the decision-maker should then take everything into account, including the agency freedom (choices) of the offender.

This is a complex system focused on a just outcome, it may appear to be overly complex but, as illustrated by Williams and Daniel (2020), it is possible to apply Sen's ideas to a criminal justice system. This involves moving away from more traditional means of punitive justice, such as retributive justice, in favour of systems which are more flexible and emphasise the well-being of the offender, whilst still taking account of the needs of the victim and community. We could apply Sen's call for subjective preferences ('choices and agency') to be taken into account. For example, considering the fear one offender may have of another when deciding whether to place them together in a cell or to ask them to work as part of a group on a community intervention. Sen's theory would also require any punitive interventions to be realistic and provide 'real' opportunities. For example, requiring an offender to attend a training course appears positive but if they have no transport and the first bus would arrive late or they could not afford the fare, it would be both setting them up to fail on a requirement of their community order and would be an 'unreal' opportunity; it would be unjust.

This approach could be attacked as allowing an offender to 'choose their punishment'. However, it is still punishment so the offender is not escaping being called to account for their offending and, if we consider prevention of future crime to be a key aim of the criminal justice system, then it might be seen as just and fair, as it is more likely to protect the community in the future. If, however, the purpose of the criminal justice system is seen as purely punishing wrongdoing, then Sen's concept of justice may not be as useful.

Sen's justice places a lot of discretion in the hands of judges and magistrates, some argue that such unfettered discretion would be unjust. Furthermore, his ideas might be seen as too idealistic and to posit a very positive view of the world and of people, one which does not see everyone as driven by self-interest. However, it would be a mistake to forget that he has seen absolute poverty and its effects first hand and that his life's work has been to address the injustices of the world. He seeks to reduce poverty and deliver sustainable development to all parts of the world through embracing a more just global approach; one which does not solely concern the distribution of commodities. For Sen, justice involves both the fair distribution of commodities and respect for an individual's freedom and choice: justice is complex, culturally embedded, and, to a degree, individual. This renders Sen's theory difficult to apply but it is important not to ignore it and, through its application, society might both better tackle the crime problem and break down some of the largest injustices.

Communitarianism

So far most of the theories (for example, Aristotle and Rawls) and models of justice we have discussed focus on individualistic ideas of justice. Communitarianism, which we will now explore, sees these ideas as being too focused on individual rights and freedoms, too inward-looking and absorbed with self-interest. Despite Sen's calls for a multicultural and open approach to justice, even he is seen, by most communitarians, as focusing too closely on the individual in his search for justice.

Communitarians suggest that social order is best upheld by protecting and nurturing informal communal bonds. Communitarians see both left-wing (welfare and rights) and right-wing (the market) solutions to making society fairer as being wrongly focused because they ignore the social needs of human beings. They emphasise the connections between individuals and their communities, focusing on the fact that humans live in close communities and societies because we need each other. They see us as social beings, not separate individual beings, and argue that most ideas of justice, especially the individual and rights-based systems so far considered, ignore this social aspect of human needs. Communitarians focus on solidarity and belonging; they call on us to stop searching for liberty and individual rights and focus instead on cultural controls in small close-knit communities. The idea is that small, local communities should make their own decisions. Whilst ideas of social solidarity have a long pedigree and the word communitarianism has been used for at least 150 years, the ideas of communitarianism we will consider here have a fairly modern basis.

In this section, we will consider the ideas of an influential communitarian, Amitai Etzioni, as well as the ideas of radical communitarianism which, as the name suggests, is the term used to refer to some more radical versions of this theory.

Amitai Etzioni

One of the best known modern conservative communitarians is the Israeli–American sociologist Amitai Etzioni (1929–) (see **Figure 3.9**). Etzioni (1994) does not reject individual rights but sees these as needing to be nested in and understood against a sense of community. He claims that through strengthening the community and its institutions, such as schools and local employers, each individual in that community is strengthened. At points, he is very clear that he wants to recreate what he sees as the more stable, law-abiding, and orderly past experienced in the

Figure 3.9 Amitai Etzioni is one of the best known modern conservative communitarians, seeing strong communities as the key to a just and stable society

Source: Amitai Etzioni, University Professor and professor of international affairs at The George Washington University

US in the 1950s where there was a more culturally agreed moral consensus and widely agreed norms (1994: 22). This form of communitarianism focuses on ensuring that society and everyone in it behaves in a law-abiding and orderly fashion. The expectation is that individuals should respect each other and the whole community:

> communitarians call to restore civic virtues, for people to live up to their responsibilities and not to merely focus on their entitlements, and to shore up the moral foundations of society.
>
> (Etzioni, 1995: ix)

Individual rights (at least democratic and social) should be tempered by a call on community, so the right to free speech, for example, should be permitted as long as it does not damage others in the community (though note here that conservative communitarians do not question property rights, which they generally wish to preserve). Etzioni questions the strong sense of entitlement that rights **ideologies** give rise to, at the expense of community responsibility, and calls for a strengthening of a sense of moral obligation owed, he argues, by each person to others in their society. In terms of criminal justice, this leads to calls for close community policing and a use of strong, draconian ideas of shaming offenders and those who break other **social mores**. He sees that justice will be delivered through security, which can only exist if there is a tight, homogenous community.

This form of communitarianism ignores the racial, homophobic, and gendered nature of these homogenous communities in the past. It also runs counter to many modern ideas of justice as it rejects the multiculturalism and **globalisation** agendas that are common today. Sen, for example, calls on us to take account of the way in which various individuals or groups might define justice before deciding how best to resolve a situation; for him, there is not one just outcome but many and the secret is to choose the most valid in any particular situation. Sen's ideas question Etzioni and communitarianism for their protection of relatively narrow Anglo/American cultural mores and the fact that they ignore other perspectives. His thesis would argue that they miss the possibility of alighting on real just outcomes which take account of the wider perspective, seeing issues from the different perspectives of each person in each situation. Etzioni is also rather vague about how justice within communitarianism will be assured.

Radical communitarianism

There are other forms of communitarianism which arise more from the left of politics and focus on solidarity and mutual respect or reciprocity. These can be grouped together under the term **radical communitarianism**. Radical communitarians suggest justice is better achieved in small-scale communities in which each member participates in democratic decision-making. Radical communitarians recognise that there may be multicultural values (not homogenous values) in a community and that the plurality of values can be resolved into a just solution through discussion and full participation in decision-making.

The ideas of Elliot Currie

The ideas of radical communitarians are not linked to just one theorist but come from the ideals of socialist solidarity. However, the American criminologist Elliott Currie (1942–) is often strongly linked to radical communitarianism so we will briefly consider his ideas, especially in relation to justice and criminal justice. Currie, and other modern proponents of radical communitarianism, recognise that democracy and community decisions do not always respect minority or individual interests and therefore they argue that individual rights and moral autonomy need to be guaranteed to protect each person in the community from the dangers of the powerful majority (Currie 1997).

Radical communitarians embrace the multicultural and pluralistic nature of society and see community solidarity and respect for each other as the best way to guarantee tolerance and just decision-making. They point to modern western liberal states as allowing one section of the community (the rich and powerful) to exploit the others (the poor, largely disenfranchised, powerless, and excluded). Radical communitarians argue that democracy in these **neoliberal** societies is unjust for large numbers of people and that the exploited have lost any real autonomy and quality of life; their individual and group moral authority has been silenced. For these theorists, like Currie, many of the ills in society arise due to the loss of solidarity within it. The absence of any idea of a common good or a common goal and the feelings of exclusion, marginalisation, and inequality (remember the views expressed by the London rioters in **Controversy and debate 3.1**) release people to offend; the lack of solidarity is a root cause of crime and other ills in society.

Here justice involves redistribution of the goods in society and where problems arise there needs to be a focus on reintegration rather than shaming. Through redistribution and reintegration, radical communitarians argue that each individual will be better placed to participate in decision-making and support the community; each will be more likely to choose a path that is supportive of both themselves and others in the community. Their first ideal of redistribution is based on social justice (fairer distribution of all goods) though often needs greater explanation of how to ensure that the new distribution is fair or just. The second assumes that reintegration is sufficient to right all wrongs but again fails to properly engage with justice as it often ignores the harm that might have been caused. There is in this radical communitarianism no concept of how these ideals might be delivered nor any real proof that their achievement would necessarily deliver safer, more just, more cohesive, and less crime-ridden societies. Whilst much of what is argued by this group may sound as if it might lead to greater justice, this is difficult to fully assess as there is not enough detail to analyse whether their ideals would lead to a more just society or more just outcomes.

Restorative justice and communitarianism

One criminal justice resolution which is often strongly linked to or claimed by communitarianism is restorative justice (Braithwaite, 2002), which we consider in more depth in **Chapters 23** and **30**. Certainly in its original Maori usage (as shown in **Figure 3.10**), where a whole community agrees on the outcome of a transgression and the whole community unites to support both the victim and offender to ensure a more positive outcome in the future, we can see aspects of communitarianism. However, most modern societies do not permit this whole community resolution, nor are they as culturally homogenous or unified as the old Maori communities.

Restorative justice in most western societies seeks to heal and put right the wrongs which arise from the offending; the resolution seems voluntary, but the offender is often faced with a full criminal trial if they refuse to cooperate. Often the community or the state ensures that the victim's interests are met but does not necessarily then mend the problem by supporting either the offender or the victim to build more positive lives, or at least if it does this, it is not usually a necessary part of the restorative justice process.

The process of **reintegrative shaming** or restorative justice as used in many western systems allows a community to stigmatise an offender for what they have done. This part

Figure 3.10 Maori-based justice at the Rangatahi Court, Nga Koti Rangatahi o Aotearoa hui on Te Aranga Marae, Flaxmere, Hastings, 2018. Is a whole community solution realistic in western states?
Source: Hawke's Bay Today Photograph by Warren Buckland/NZME

of the process delivers the stigma called for by conservative communitarians. It is then restorative for the victim but often fails to fully restore the offender back into their community. Radical communitarians would argue that this failure prevents the systems being truly restorative; it is not restorative for the community as a whole because the offender may reoffend, and even if they do not they may still feel aggrieved and cause other problems for the community. In this situation, it is questionable whether this is true justice. In radical communitarianism there would be a focus on using restorative justice to redistribute goods and the reintegrative element would be focused on the offender (without any stigma). This approach would sideline or ignore the position of the victim and again might not be truly just. True restorative justice gives equal weight to all three, it recognises the need to restore victims, offenders, and communities and that each has to support the needs of the other two (see Braithwaite, 2002).

3.5 Systems of criminal justice

Most of what we have so far been considering revolves around the content of decision-making rather than the process. Whilst Rawls set out a process for deciding how to achieve justice, even his ideas largely embraced ideals such as equality, rather than being practical. In the case of criminal justice, there is a need for the state to intervene in what might once have been private matters; this requires very practical rules which Rawlsian justice, and the other theories we have so far considered, might fail to provide.

However, once we have a process or system these theorists' ideas can be used to test how just the system is. The criminal justice system needs practical and clear rules because serious wrongs need to be addressed. Serious wrongs, crimes, are ones in which the public shares: Duff stated, 'as members of the community, we should see them not merely as the victim's wrongs but as "our" wrongs' (2001: 63) and argued that we should make it clear that we, as a society or state, are not willing to tolerate certain types of behaviour, that those who perpetrate certain wrongs 'should be called to account and censured by the community' (2001: 61). Here Duff is claiming that there are certain types of behaviour which are so unacceptable that the whole of society should be unwilling to tolerate them, that justice requires us to act, though, for Duff, this does not necessarily involve punishment.

Where this happens, the state has to decide how to dispense such justice; how to decide when and why to censure someone and who to censure. Therefore, each state or community where justice is dispensed needs to have a system or mechanism to decide what would be just, who should be punished; a mechanism to dispense justice. The criminal justice system in each jurisdiction generally constitutes:

- control processes and agents such as the police, who investigate and channel people through to the rest of the system (maybe choosing to divert, reintegrate, or process through the full criminal justice system);
- court processes where decisions are made concerning guilt or innocence;
- agents and systems to punish, rehabilitate, or control.

The whole criminal justice system should exist to empower rather than control a population: ensuring that as many people as possible live full and free lives and enjoy their rights as long as they respect the freedom and rights of others. In other words, the system should only intervene when necessary. To deliver on that ideal there need to be mechanisms to guide the criminal justice system towards the best outcomes. Each section of the system has rules and standards within which it needs to operate.

Clearly, the criminal justice system is vast, in terms of its workings and processes, but here we will limit ourselves to considering the system which is used in court. In most western states, one of two central types of system is normally used: an **adversarial system** or an **inquisitorial system**, summarised later in **Figure 3.12**.

In the UK and in all **common law** countries (laws come from statutes and decisions from higher courts), the system is largely based on an adversarial system. In most of continental Europe and many civil law or codified legal systems, the criminal justice systems are largely based on the inquisitorial system. Whilst there was a time when these two systems were fairly pure in the areas in which they were used, modern criminal justice systems borrow from one another so that, as Tulkens states, 'nowhere is the model any longer pure; it is, for better or worse, contorted, attenuated, modified' (1995: 8). The two systems have some things in common: they are both designed to convict the guilty and each tries to protect against convicting the innocent; they both intend to protect the interests of wider society and so make their society safer and empower innocent people to live their lives free of fear. They disagree about how best to deliver on these ideals.

Adversarial systems

The adversarial system explained

The adversarial system originated in Britain but has been exported to many other jurisdictions. It is based on a contest between the accused (the defendant) and the accuser (in crime, the victim and the state) and its core aspects are:

- the trial, which is crucial;
- oral evidence (from the victim, witnesses, and accused) heard at trial;
- clear rules which determine what each person (judge, lawyers, jury) is permitted to do and to decide what evidence can and cannot be heard in court.

The defence and prosecution (usually the state, though it can be a private prosecution) set out their cases and then an impartial judge, jury, or magistrate(s) determine where they believe the truth lies and pass judgement (convict or acquit) on the defendant.

In this system, the state has to draw together sufficient evidence to prove, *beyond reasonable doubt* (remember our discussion of the due process model), that the accused is guilty. The system is about the contest and is not primarily designed to establish the *truth*, though there is a belief that the truth will come out in the contest and the jury/magistrate(s) decide where it lies. The real search for the truth (if it happens at all) occurs earlier; the police follow the evidence until they are sure that they have unearthed what happened and who is guilty. At that point, the state uses all its powers to prove the guilt of the accused. Whilst the police might sift through all possible outcomes and conduct an inquiry before finding their suspect, they are not required to do that. They merely investigate an occurrence, and the evidence they find is then tested in court. The state has to convince a magistrate(s) or a jury beyond reasonable doubt that the person they are accusing is guilty. It is important to remember that the accused does not have to prove that they are innocent, they simply need to raise sufficient doubt about their guilt; raise sufficient questions to throw doubt on the prosecution evidence.

The decision-makers and the decision

When most people think of our system they picture a judge in wig and gown presiding over a court and 12 jurors (ordinary people—see **Figure 3.11**), deciding whether they believe the accused is guilty; this is the Crown Court system. If the accused does not plead guilty, cases in the Crown Court generally take days if not weeks to conclude. However, the Crown Court is in

Figure 3.11 In an adversarial system the jury has a lot of power: does this affect whether justice is delivered?
Source: Sirtravelalot/Shutterstock

fact only used for the more serious cases (only 3–4 per cent of all criminal trials); it is not the normal arena for criminal cases. Most criminal trials (96–7 per cent) take place in magistrates' courts. In a magistrates' court, the trial is heard by either a professional stipendiary magistrate (who sits alone) or by a bench of lay magistrates (usually three), who are advised by the Clerk to the Court (a local solicitor) on legal matters. In the magistrates' court, the magistrate(s) decide whether the case is proven beyond reasonable doubt. Cases in the magistrates' court tend to be over quite quickly, as many people plead guilty. Even in cases where the accused pleads not guilty, the magistrates' court will usually conclude the case in less than a day.

Regardless of which court hears the case, the trial is adversarial and the contest is led by the lawyers: prosecution lawyers for the state and defence lawyers for the accused. These lawyers present the evidence that they want the court to consider (not necessarily everything they know); they only have to present the jury with the information that is most beneficial for their case, which is not always the same as the truth. The judge is there to make sure that the lawyers only use permitted evidence and to sum up the case to the jury, explaining some of the law (in magistrates' courts this is done by the Clerk to the Court). On the face of it, the jury (or magistrates' bench) decides which set of facts they believe, whether a case has been proven beyond reasonable doubt. However, they actually do more than that: if they think a law is unfair or unjust, they can choose to acquit even if the proof is overwhelming.

An example of this was the case of Clive Ponting in 1985. Ponting was accused of offences under the Official Secrets Act 2011. He was accused of leaking government documents to the press about the sinking of an enemy ship, the Belgrano, during the Falklands War. The judge directed the jury that if they believed he leaked the documents the law required them to convict, they had a duty to convict. There was overwhelming proof that Ponting leaked the documents. Despite that, the jury acquitted Ponting. It has always been assumed that they did this because they felt that it would be unjust to apply the letter of the law in that case. In England and Wales jury members are not permitted to discuss their work so we can never be sure of why they acquitted Ponting, but it seems to be the only logical explanation. We can see that the jury are in a powerful position to make decisions they think are just, even if that does not follow the facts they are presented with at trial, and they are seen as bringing fairness and impartiality to the case. They deliver a decision of one's peers.

Evaluating the adversarial system

Many argue that the adversarial system allows the accused the best chance of justice. They can take control of their defence and present all the aspects they feel are important, and they have a chance to prove their innocence and be acquitted.

However, does the adversarial system seek justice more broadly? What about truth? The main problem is that it is a sort of game so may not be best suited to delivering truth and or justice in all cases. The outcome may depend on how charismatic and persuasive the lawyer is rather than the weight of facts in the case (as we can see in many TV dramas and films from both the UK and US). Witnesses, particularly vulnerable witnesses who may be telling the truth, can be frightened and flustered by the experience of having to appear in court. They may forget things under pressure or appear to be less confident about the truth simply because they are nervous. Whilst some witnesses can use special measures (for example, pre-videoed evidence) this is not available to all.

Whilst allowing a jury to decide on cases is powerful—convictions depend on the decisions of our peers—there are also problems with their position. For example, juries and magistrates do not have to explain their decision to anyone so the defendant does not know why they have been convicted. This means the decision may be based on an irrelevant factor: they could convict because they think the accused looks guilty or acquit if they think the accused looks innocent. It also means that a party who feels the decision is unjust has no means of appeal because they do not know which aspect of the case they need to undermine. Partly for this reason, appeals against convictions are very difficult in common law countries. In some jurisdictions, including England and Wales, the convicted person has to find new evidence before anyone will even consider an appeal or re-trial.

The inquisitorial system

The inquisitorial system explained

The inquisitorial system, mainly used in countries with civil legal systems such as France and Italy, is completely different. This claims to be a search for *truth* and is used in some civil law systems (those who set out written codes to set the boundaries of the law). Whilst each inquisitorial system is slightly different, they generally revolve around building a file. Everything that the police have done to investigate the case should be written up and be contained in the case file or *dossier*, containing all the investigative information. The dossier is then made available to all interested parties (or at least to their lawyers). In this way, everyone knows all the evidence against the accused as well as any evidence which might point in other directions (at least that which the police have followed up and thought important enough to put into the dossier). To ensure that the police include all important information, both that which suggests guilt and that which suggests innocence, the police are tightly regulated about what they can and cannot do, and in many systems (such as France and the Netherlands) they appoint a judge at the start of an investigation who oversees the investigation and may also be able to direct the police to follow up various lines of inquiry.

The decision-makers and the decision

The dossier should contain all the relevant evidence which will convict or acquit the accused. It is the contents of the dossier which is considered; often there is no confrontational trial of evidence in court. In some inquisitorial jurisdictions, there is no jury at all and in others the jury and judge together decide on an outcome. Inquisitorial systems often see juries as unpredictable and capable of returning unjust verdicts so that they are not generally trusted to make the decision as to guilt or innocence alone. Decisions, and the reasons for them, are often given in open court, thereby facilitating any appeal.

The core of the inquisitorial system is the investigation and the dossier to which it gives rise. Witnesses are generally questioned in less stressful situations, often with just the inquisitorial judge present. The defence lawyers may be able to ask questions or to get the judge to ask questions for them, but the accused is often not present. The decision as to guilt or innocence is generally made either by one or more professional judges or by a judge(s) along with some lay people (but not by just lay people).

Evaluating the inquisitorial system

At first glance, the inquisitorial system seems to address some of the issues we identified with the adversarial system. Here, the decision as to guilt or innocence is made by judges, either alone or sitting with lay people (not only by jury members), so it is likely to be made on the basis of the facts, rather than being influenced by a charismatic lawyer or an impressive and appealing witness. The dossier contains the facts as presented by the state as well as those claimed by the accused, and the investigative judge is supposed to use their powers to test the case and to use the police to follow leads which may prove innocence as well as those which may prove guilt. Since the dossier is available before the trial and can be studied at length, the verdict is more likely to be carefully considered and will not be affected by dramatic uncovering of evidence in court. Additionally, when a decision is given in an inquisitorial system it is often explained, meaning that the losing side may be able to appeal the decision.

However, this system also has potential flaws. In theory, the dossier contains everything that is relevant to the case, allowing the truth to be uncovered, but what is irrelevant will depend on the perspective of the decision-maker. Important information may be discounted or even missed (in a world with almost limitless information on virtual media sites and, where police resources are limited, missing or incorrectly discounting information must be possible), and the absence of this information from the dossier might affect the outcome of the case and 'truth' may be lost. For this reason, the police are tightly regulated about what they can and cannot do, and in many systems (such as France and the Netherlands) they appoint a judge at the start of an investigation who oversees the investigation and may also be able to direct the police to follow up various lines of inquiry.

For a comparison of the adversarial and inquisitorial systems, see **Figure 3.12**.

Systems borrowing from each other

The two systems are very different and following major miscarriages of justice in England and Wales, such as those involving the Guildford Four and the Birmingham Six (see **Chapter 25**), there have sometimes been suggestions that we should look carefully at our adversarial system and maybe adopt the inquisitorial system (see, for example, the Royal Commission on Criminal Justice 1993). As we noted at the start of this section, what has actually happened is that we increasingly borrow ideas from the inquisitorial system and alter them slightly to work in

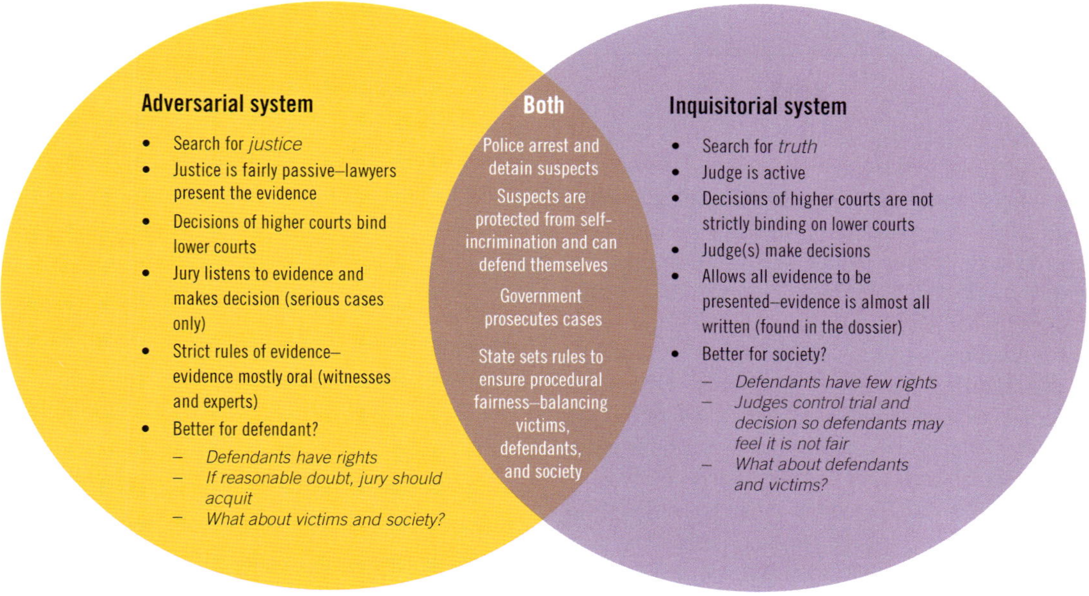

Adversarial system
- Search for *justice*
- Justice is fairly passive—lawyers present the evidence
- Decisions of higher courts bind lower courts
- Jury listens to evidence and makes decision (serious cases only)
- Strict rules of evidence—evidence mostly oral (witnesses and experts)
- Better for defendant?
  - Defendants have rights
  - If reasonable doubt, jury should acquit
  - What about victims and society?

Both
- Police arrest and detain suspects
- Suspects are protected from self-incrimination and can defend themselves
- Government prosecutes cases
- State sets rules to ensure procedural fairness—balancing victims, defendants, and society

Inquisitorial system
- Search for *truth*
- Judge is active
- Decisions of higher courts are not strictly binding on lower courts
- Judge(s) make decisions
- Allows all evidence to be presented—evidence is almost all written (found in the dossier)
- Better for society?
  - Defendants have few rights
  - Judges control trial and decision so defendants may feel it is not fair
  - What about defendants and victims?

Figure 3.12 Comparing adversarial and inquisitorial systems

our adversarial system, such as requiring the defence to disclose their case to the prosecution before trial or permitting vulnerable witnesses to give evidence via video link. These changes generally occur so as to better deliver justice, though there are some, such as Zander (see his dissenting opinion in the Report of the Royal Commission on Criminal Justice, 1993: 221–35, in the discussion of the due process model in **section 3.3**), who see them as undermining that ideal.

Recently, there have been suggestions for changes, particularly regarding the use of juries, which might speed up justice and save money rather than, necessarily, increase the likelihood of justice being served (R. Cooper, 'Trial by Jury Faces Axe in up to 70,000 Cases Per Year to Cut Costs', *Daily Mail* online, 16 January 2012), an idea that we consider further in **New frontiers 3.1**. Our system, like systems in other countries, is constantly evolving, and although they retain their fundamental differences, the adversarial and inquisitorial systems of criminal justice are constantly converging and becoming more similar. Whether they are delivering more just outcomes as a result is not clear.

For a full consideration of each of these systems and of others, such as Islamic justice systems, see Pakes (2004).

3.6 Drawing ideas together

We have covered a lot of material in this chapter and you might be finding it difficult to work out exactly how the criminal justice models and philosophical writings about justice fit together, particularly in terms of how they relate to justice as it applies in criminology; that is, criminal justice.

The models we examined set out some of the important issues which have traditionally been attached to testing whether the criminal justice system is just. However, they leave much out; they do not fully consider the *need* for such a system—what just purpose it serves—and they do not always help in assessing justice in particular cases.

Similarly, the philosophical ideas about justice are interesting but it can be difficult to see how they link to justice within a corrective system such as the criminal justice system and it is particularly difficult to use them to resolve individual cases.

In this final section, we will try to throw light on these issues and help you to apply some of the ideas, mostly using the example of sentencing and punishment to illustrate our points; these are often the end results of criminal actions. (The offender commits a crime, is caught, and found guilty, and then the state has to decide how to deal with the offender.)

NEW FRONTIERS 3.1

Virtual courts

With technology enriching all areas of our lives, it is natural to explore its use in a criminal justice context. As we will study further in **Chapter 25** (see particularly **New frontiers 25.1**), the Ministry of Justice has long been working towards greater use of technology in the court system, and video links and pre-recorded evidence have been used for some time in certain situations (for example, for vulnerable witnesses and children). However, in 2020 the Covid-19 pandemic pushed the system into more serious experimentation with virtual courts.

The state's interest in virtual or digital courts is understandable. The advantages include cost and convenience (though Terry et al., (2010) found virtual bail applications were more costly); solving the issues presented by court closures; time; and legal efficiency. But justice is arguably more important than these considerations. Over time, lack of justice is actually likely to be more costly, in terms of happiness, well-being, economics, social justice, likelihood of future offences, etc. Furthermore, many rights lawyers and justice groups have expressed concern that virtual trials would be unwise and unjust. Gibbs (2017), for example, suggests that suspects who appear via video link are at a disadvantage and are more likely to plead guilty and to get a prison sentence, and less likely to be represented by a lawyer. Possibly the most important objection raised is that there is insufficient evidence about the effects on defendants, victims, and witnesses when they give evidence via video link. There is not yet enough research to answer questions like whether it affects: defendants, victims, and witnesses' stress levels in court; how they present their evidence and what they say; their ability to remember details; the likelihood they will tell '. . . the truth, the whole truth and nothing but the truth'. And does hearing evidence via video link affect how it is received, and whether it is more or less likely to be believed?

It is also worth remembering that one aspect of criminal justice is that justice should be *seen* to be done. This is why criminal trials are open to the public. How will this basic ideal of justice be preserved in a virtual court? At the moment, the justice system is considering the use of public participation rooms in libraries and similar public buildings which might provide a room in which there could be a real-time link to a case as it progresses.

Given the various potential issues, in an ideal world we would have been cautious about 'digitising' courts until we knew more about its effects on justice. If the outcomes are likely to be worse—more innocent people convicted; more guilty people acquitted; harsher sentences etc.—then they are less just. However, we do not live in an ideal world, and Covid-19 pushed the system into enforced experimentation with the use of virtual trials (audio hearings, video hearings, and paper hearings) in both a civil and criminal context. From what we know so far (at the time of writing in autumn 2020), the system has worked well in some areas of law, especially in hearings concerning health, education, or social work. For example, domestic abuse victims have been able to obtain protection orders and children's safeguarding hearings have been able to proceed. Anecdotal evidence from Judge Meleri Tudur (Swansea University, 2020) suggests that court users such as women and children appreciated the ability to appear in court without leaving their homes, or another safe environment. They felt less nervous than they might if they had to go to court or to a lawyer's office or judge's chambers, and more able to participate freely and fully. Also, they did not have to travel, find and pay for public transport or parking, find someone to care for young children, or find somewhere to eat. There might be similar advantages for witnesses in criminal trials, some of whom may feel intimidated or very nervous by having to appear in open court.

At the time of writing, the government has opened 'Nightingale courts' to deal with hearings through the pandemic. These are largely virtual courts which will permit less serious criminal trials (and civil cases) to proceed with witnesses and even the accused appearing from other locations via video link, minimising difficulties with social distancing. However, issues and potential issues with this approach include:

- Virtual court facilities are not available everywhere and in areas where broadband coverage is poor they may never be available.

- Corporate firewalls may not permit some organisations to 'join', or people from those organisations to participate.

- It is essential that participants have access to all important documents and sharing written documents may be problematic in a number of cases, particularly criminal cases, where some participants (offenders, victims, and witnesses) may not be literate.

- The video links between all sites must be real-time and simultaneous. If one link breaks down, is intermittent, or the video or audio quality is poor, then people at that location will not be able to follow proceedings and justice will be put in jeopardy.

Despite these issues and potential issues, the system is currently allowing court cases to proceed and this has freed up the physical courts to deal with more serious criminal cases. In trials involving cases where the accused is already in custody, or where there is a strong likelihood that they will be sentenced to custody, it is necessary to have cells for the accused and secure dock facilities to keep victims, juries, witnesses, and the public safe. At the moment, it is believed that for these more serious cases, a physical court is required to ensure justice, but who knows whether this will change in the future (the pandemic is ongoing at the time of writing), and what advantages and issues will emerge once the data from this enforced 'experimental' use of virtual courts is analysed. In this area, the pandemic has forced us to move faster to solve the justice problems with using virtual courts and so invent the future. The findings from this time could be transformative for justice and our understanding of how best to deliver it.

As you reflect on these issues and competing concerns, think about how you use technology to communicate. For example, the situations or interactions that you consider too important to deal with remotely, and which you prefer to manage in person and the implications that has for whether justice can be served digitally. Also think about the way in which justice was managed during the Covid-19 pandemic and whether justice was one of the victims of the pandemic or whether it proved that virtual trials could be fair and effective.

Justice through treating like cases alike

As we noted in **section 3.1**, many people see justice as being about equality and fairness—they see equal treatment as paramount to fairness. So where a crime is committed, the belief is that the punishment should be proportionate to the action (the crime and the harm caused by it). Remember the scales of justice that we discussed in **section 3.2**: here, the amount of punishment goes on one side and the seriousness of the offence and the harm caused goes on the other; to deliver justice the scales should balance. To illustrate the point, if Gabby steals a pint of milk and Helen murders someone it would generally be seen to be unjust if they both faced life in prison. The scales would not balance in Gabby's case because the harm caused does not match the punishment. In such a situation, Gabby would feel (quite rightly) that she had been unfairly treated and might even regret not having done something more serious—why not, if you are to receive the same punishment? It would also be unjust from the societal perspective; it would fail to help to teach people moral standards—it would indicate that murder and petty theft are equal.

If the punishment should fit the crime, it follows that like cases should be treated alike, and this popular idea has been part of our system since the **Enlightenment** thinkers such as Beccaria (1767) suggested it. Aristotle and Rawls took this view, and in terms of the criminal justice models it fits well with crime control, as long as the punishment is also swift and sufficiently unpleasant. It would also be seen as useful to Durkheim's stigmatisation model, as each person can see clearly what is wrong and how important a transgression it is (how much people should be stigmatised for participating in that behaviour). More recently, it has been part of the drive behind an increasing limit put on the discretion of judges and other decision-makers by setting out sentencing guidelines to inform their decisions, and by increasing the number and type of offence for which there is a minimum sentence.

However, this tendency and call to treat like cases alike may also fail to deliver justice; it may lead to injustice. Let's return to Amy and compare her case with that of Colin (see **What do you think? 3.2**): each has stolen some food so on the equal treatment or **proportionality** argument they should receive the same punishment. However, to give them the same punishment would ignore the underlying context and issues which may be relevant to why the crime was committed. Such a course of action may also ignore injustices or victimisations which may have been caused by the structure of society (for example, a society that does not effectively prevent abject poverty). Amy was poor and very hungry, whereas Colin may well be neither of these things. In England and Wales, the guidelines do not mention poverty and hunger as mitigating circumstances but the system does allow a sentence to use other mitigating circumstances if they appear appropriate so whether this was taken into account would be left to the discretion of the judge or magistrate.

Taking account of social justice

The context for **What do you think? 3.2** touches on issues of social justice, in that Amy appears to have been offending because of poverty and need. Both Rawls and Sen considered these kinds of issues as relevant to an assessment of justice. Treating two cases in the same way, giving out the same punishment, may also ignore injustices and victimisations that society should have dealt with and has not, and for which this offence is a retaliation. For example, if someone who has been the victim of domestic violence for many years and commits an offence in retaliation. Rawls and Sen each argue that justice requires a state to deal with injustices. Dealing with injustices is also relevant to communitarian ideas because if stigmatisation is intended to reinforce social cohesion then it needs to be seen to be just. Punishment needs to take account of and recognise the harm that a person has done in committing the crime, but it must not be too harsh. If punishments are too harsh, either generally or in individual cases, people will view the whole system as unjust and distrust it. The sentencing guidelines are intended to take all of this into account but we can use the theorists to assess how well or poorly they achieve this, as well as to evaluate individual sentencing decisions.

Under radical communitarianism and the power model, if punishment is more severe for certain groups (the poor) by failing to take account of their situation then it is unjust. Therefore, many criminal justice models and philosophers consider that the underlying context in which crime is committed is at least important to some degree in ensuring just punishment. So whilst we work towards delivering social justice, we may need to treat the disadvantaged more leniently. Duff (2001) would suggest that this does not go far enough and would question the state's right to punish at all unless and until it delivers social justice. Although many philosophers and theorists might agree that the severity of punishment should take account of injustices, few would agree that punishment cannot be used until a society delivers social justice. (And it would also be very hard to agree on when social justice has been delivered.) Theorists are also unlikely to agree about which differences or injustices are sufficiently serious to count as social injustices and how much punishment should be reduced to take account of each injustice.

Consider whether the sentences given to Amy and Colin (again, see **What do you think? 3.2**) should differ in the following situations: if one has been sexually victimised as a child; if one is being abused now; if one is racially disadvantaged; if one is addicted to drugs; if one has dependent children. If these differences should lead to different punishments, then how do we decide how much to reduce a punishment? Applying the philosophical ideas to this question:

- Rawls would answer that we take account of those differences which would be chosen in the 'veil of ignorance': that is, the differences that everyone would agree were important if they did not know what their own situation would be.
- Sen would recognise that justice might be served by many answers and that decision-makers or 'impartial spectators' should openly discuss the outcomes and explain why one outcome would deliver more entitlement and well-being than another to ensure that they are seen to take justice seriously—one might then disagree but can respect the outcome.
- Conservative communitarians would argue that only those aspects important to the homogeneous community should be considered, whereas radical communitarians would respect the rights of the individual and take account of those elements which need to be corrected in order to redistribute goods or restore an equal and balanced community.

Each of these arguments is valid. As students of criminology, we need to understand the different arguments, work out what they would mean in practice, and play with the ideas to build our own concepts of justice.

3.7 Conclusion

So why does justice matter? Why should we try to make sure that our sentencing decisions and all other decisions in criminal justice and in wider society are just? Why is justice central to our subject?

The criminal law and the criminal justice service impact most directly on certain groups of society. For some people, the main way in which they relate to or experience the state is through the criminal justice system. If that system is experienced as or seen to be unfair to them or to people like them (other poor people or people from their racial/sex group), they will learn to disrespect it. Still worse, if the state is seen to be violent or brutal towards them or people like them, they may learn that power, violence, and brutality are acceptable and effective ways of teaching people and of getting things done. In that situation, criminal law and its enforcement may actually be the problem rather than the solution. From this it is clear that whilst the criminal law and a criminal justice system are generally intended to support people to live harmoniously together, if they are unjust they may cause more harm than they resolve—some of the models discussed may be more likely to lead to these consequences (see the examples in **Controversy and debate 3.1**).

We constantly need to search for resolutions to criminal conflict that are just to victims and offenders alike and that have a positive outcome overall, increasing well-being for everyone. To do that we must never be blind to contextual aspects of situations—what brings people to act the way they did. Issues of past victimisation, social injustice, and deprivation need to be addressed to increase the well-being of particular individuals, to support them to live more positive lives. However, on a broader idea of justice a state should seek to prevent or address injustices for all people. These ideals would be accepted by many theorists because many envisage at least some fair distribution of goods and burdens (for example, the second rule of Rawls; Sen's broad writings about the importance of increasing the entitlement of each individual, and radical communitarians).

We need to seek to uphold human rights of victims and offenders and, where they conflict, the conflict needs to be resolved in a way which preserves as much of the rights for each group as possible, even if that is at the expense of the state. Here the justice of removing things like legal aid has to be seriously questioned—does it interfere with the ability of suspects to defend themselves and, if so, can a trial be just and fair?

Punishment and the criminal justice system generally need to operate justly; be felt to operate justly. They should empower, not control, people, communities, and society. If they are experienced as being about control they may be causing more of a social problem than is caused by crime (at least in some areas or for some groups) and may actually be adding to the likelihood of criminality. If the system and punishment are too harsh, they cause social division rather than social cohesion.

All groups and sections of our society need to have a strong voice in the discussions about how our society should be shaped—where justice and fairness lie. We need to be open to cultural differences and to different ways of resolving a situation, especially if one of the parties to a situation comes from a different culture.

SUMMARY

After reading this chapter and working your way through its features you should now be able to:

- Explain and appreciate why justice is so important

From a very young age, children tend to almost instinctively understand that justice is important, that they should enjoy the same as others in their community. Why do children believe justice is important? It is generally accepted that any society or group of people—family, school, university, community, state, the world—is improved if it embraces justice as one of its core ideals because in a just society each person is valued equally. Justice ensures that no person or group enjoys more rights than another and that no person or group should be denied rights enjoyed by others. A fully just society calls on each person to respect the rights of everyone else, it is a standard to live up to. From this, most believe that when people break standards of justice they should face consequences. Similarly, when they are good they should be appreciated.

- Critically consider the criminal justice approaches to justice and evaluate how these help our understanding of the concept and its outcomes

In relation to crime, a society expects people to refrain from breaking the law. So part of justice is that we should not—for example—kill each other or that we should drive carefully. If we all live up to the ideal of justice in relation to crime, it should ensure that each individual in a society is safe both from other people and from the tyranny of the state or of the majority. In a just society, the offenders are punished (to prevent them gaining from their wrongdoing) and supported to change their behaviour in the future (to prevent future offending). Whether the punishment or intervention is experienced as fair or just may depend on the circumstances. It is often argued that the amount of punishment in a just society should reflect the seriousness of what someone has done and the amount of harm they have caused. However, justice is not this simple, to decide what the most just outcome would be is a very complex consideration and people often disagree about what is just or unjust.

- Describe the six criminal justice models and be able to critically assess each one

There are three descriptive models: bureaucratic, denunciation and status passage, and power. None of these sets out what a system of justice should look like, rather they *describe or critique the systems they find*.

The bureaucratic model argues that the system manages crime and criminals in the most efficient and cost-effective way possible, setting out processes to be followed by law enforcement officials. The status passage model sees the function of criminal justice as being to draw the good together, to denounce crime and criminals and so re-enforce societal values. The power model accuses the criminal justice system of controlling the poor or other disadvantaged groups in order to benefit the wealthy or advantaged groups.

We covered three normative models: due process, crime control, and rights. Each of these sets out what they consider a system of justice *should* look like and which aspects of the system are most important. The due process model sets out rules which try to ensure that suspects and defendants are fairly treated and considers it important that innocent people *are not* convicted even if some guilty people go free. Crime control models are about reducing controls on the powers of professionals (like the police) in order to ensure that all guilty people *are* convicted—even if some innocent people are also convicted. The medical model treats offenders as being unwell and is concerned with their rehabilitation. Rights theorists want to protect democratic freedoms and, in particular, to protect individuals from the misuse of power by the state. They want to ensure all guilty people are convicted and all innocent people are acquitted. Victims' models either call for equal rights for victims and offenders, with a focus on harsh punishment when someone is convicted, or argue that the criminal justice system should be more focused on repairing the harm caused to the victim and their community and preventing such harms in the future.

It is important to be able to identify and describe the models as this will permit you to use them to evaluate and analyse criminal justice decisions you come across in your studies.

- Outline and evaluate the four philosophical approaches to justice that take a broad view of the concept and allow you to see how justice and injustice can impact on society, crime, security, and well-being

To help us decide what would or would not be just, many philosophers and others have discussed at length how to achieve justice. We saw that, for *Aristotle*, people should generally be treated equally. However, if they are different (in a way that is important to the decision) then they should be treated differently to the extent that they are different. For *Rawls*, justice should be guaranteed under a social contract—an agreement that underpins a society. He asserts that every person should enjoy equality in relation to the core rights, and that where there are inequalities, any decisions should benefit the least advantaged. *Sen* agrees with the general idea that everyone should be equal and enjoy equal rights and social standards but argues that one needs to take account of all the factors in each particular case. He also argues that we need to understand and embrace the idea that there is rarely one just outcome, and that in deciding on the outcome, we should keep social justice, well-being, and capacity in mind. *Communitarianism* emphasises solidarity with small units or informal community networks at the centre of society and of decision-making. Radical communitarianism is about the foregrounding of equality and the redistribution and restitution of justice without any method of deciding what is just, and focuses on restorative justice. These latter approaches are more about systems and types of political stances than about raw justice.

- Explain and critically compare the two main systems of criminal justice

The two main systems used in western cultures are the adversarial system, used mostly in common law jurisdictions, and the inquisitorial system, used mostly in countries with a criminal code. The adversarial system, used in England and Wales, pits the prosecution against the defence. The system is a contest between the state and the accused which is led by the lawyers for each side, with the judge or magistrate making sure that they conduct a fair trial. The jury or magistrate decides which side it believes. The advantage is trial by peers but as the jury do not explain why they make a decision, appeals are difficult. The system is also not necessarily focused on finding the truth so can become more of a legal game, with the outcome arguably depending more on how charismatic the lawyer is than the facts of the case. The *inquisitorial system*, used in most of Europe, claims to be a real search for the truth and centres on a file or dossier that is built up by the police and investigative judge. This dossier is presented to all interested parties and it is generally the dossier which is assessed to decide upon guilt or innocence. The advantage is that everyone knows all the facts; however, the investigative judge (or police) may discount important information and fail to put it in the dossier, and then the decision-makers will never be aware of it so that 'truth' may be lost. Clearly neither system is ideal, and over the last 100 years or so each has borrowed from the other so that no country's system is entirely one or the other type.

 Test your understanding of the chapter's key points by attempting the self-test questions on the **online resources** at www.oup.com/he/case2e

REVIEW QUESTIONS

1. Name and outline the key points of the three descriptive models and the three normative models outlined in this chapter.
2. Compare and contrast crime control and due process models of criminal justice and explain whether one of them is more likely to deliver just outcomes (with reasons).
3. What are the main differences between justice as set out by Rawls and that set out by Sen?
4. Why do well-being and justice matter in considering criminological theory?
5. Choose one of the quotations in **Controversy and debate 3.1** and discuss how and why it is important to criminological discussions.

 Access the **online resources** at www.oup.com/he/case2e to check your answers to the review questions.

FURTHER READING

Bix, B. (2019) *Jurisprudence: Theory and Context* **(8th edn). London: Sweet & Maxwell. Especially Ch. 8.**
Simmonds, N. E. (2018) *Central Issues in Jurisprudence* **(5th edn). London: Sweet & Maxwell.**
There are many textbooks which consider justice, a concept which is generally discussed at length in all jurisprudence books. These two are particularly helpful and approachable. Each of them provides an accessible introduction to some of the important theories of justice. They are both well written, aimed at a legal audience, but as they address students directly they are also both still approachable.

Pakes, F. (2019) *Comparative Criminal Justice.* **Abingdon: Routledge. Especially Chs 1 and 7.**
For a full consideration and evaluation of the adversarial and inquisitorial systems of criminal justice (as well as discussion of other systems, such as Islamic justice systems).

Tyler, T. R. et al. (1997) *Social Justice in a Diverse Society.* **Boulder, CO: Westview Press (reprinted by Routledge, 2019).**
This book looks in detail at issues of justice and fairness from modern perspectives and taking account of diversity, gender, personal satisfaction and well-being, and culture. The book considers how justice should be considered in different fields such as in the resolutions of crimes or other social disputes, economic and labour issues, and politics.

Howard League, 'What is justice? Working papers': https://howardleague.org/research/what-is-justice-re-imagining-penal-policy/what-is-justice-working-papers/
The brief video and audio links on the Howard League's website provide more nuanced and modern consideration of justice.

 Access the **online resources** to view a wealth of extra information relating to your study of criminology, including self-test questions, answers to review questions, and links to other resources that will help you enjoy and fulfil your potential within your studies.

www.oup.com/he/case2e

CHAPTER OUTLINE

4.1	Introduction	96
4.2	Producing criminological knowledge	97
4.3	The evolution of criminological theories	99
4.4	Subjectivity	100
4.5	Supposition	105
4.6	Study	107
4.7	Conclusion	119

4

How criminology produces knowledge

KEY ISSUES

After studying this chapter, you should be able to:

- consider from a critical viewpoint what is knowledge in criminology, and how it is produced;
- understand what is meant by subjectivity, supposition, and study (through research) in relation to knowledge production;
- critically evaluate the benefits and limitations of different research study methods for creating criminological knowledge;
- explore how subjectivity, supposition, and study interact with, and impact on, understanding and knowledge production in criminology.

4.1 Introduction

In this chapter, we will focus on how researchers create knowledge in criminology; knowledge that we then learn about in lectures, seminars, textbooks, journal articles, research reports, policy documents, and other source materials. We will cover two key themes: first, the **empirical** research methods used in our discipline, and how we can develop our understanding and knowledge of crime by applying, analysing, and evaluating criminological information. Secondly, we will discuss how this knowledge and understanding is influenced by the three important and interlinking factors of subjectivity (personal and disciplinary perspectives and opinions), **supposition** (guesswork, assumption), and study (for example, scholarship, and conducting empirical and other types of research).

'Empirical methods' usually means the generation of evidence through (sensory) experience, particularly using experiments and observations (Rennison and Hart, 2020; Chamberlain, 2013). In this chapter, we explore how we can expand the definition to include survey methods, and will then move beyond it to also consider secondary data analysis, which is non-empirical. We will explore both the benefits and limitations of the many ways we can collect information in criminology. In the discussion of study in **section 4.6**, we will look at the different research methods available to criminologists, covering both primary and secondary sources. All this will be useful to you as a criminology student when you begin producing knowledge in your own research work.

As for the second theme, we will explore in some depth how subjectivity, supposition, and study influence criminology, dictating the choices and arguments that researchers make when conducting research and creating knowledge. We will pay particular attention to the relationships between these three factors (shown in **Figure 4.1**, depicting this triad of knowledge creation), which are rarely acknowledged within a subject area that is often seen as research-led and evidence-based. These ideas may at first seem quite complex, but they are well worth exploring because developing a solid understanding of how these factors come into play will greatly enhance your understanding and therefore enjoyment of the subject, and will ultimately make you a more effective criminologist. Reading this chapter will help you to develop the critical perspective that is an essential tool in navigating your way through criminological knowledge, allowing you to recognise and evaluate any influences that may have had an impact on the knowledge you receive and produce.

This chapter is not intended as a series of criticisms of the quality of the knowledge generated in criminology and we are certainly not urging you to reject everything you read or hear—to do so would be counterproductive to the purpose of this book. Besides, influences like subjectivity are not only inevitable, to a degree, but can even be helpful in knowledge production. Knowledge in any discipline can only be advanced by strong-willed, opinionated individuals who are committed to a particular viewpoint and who value the knowledge they generate (see, for example, **Chapter 11** where we discuss how feminist criminologists helped advance knowledge on crime and gender). With this in mind, we simply need to be aware of how subjectivity, supposition, and study create knowledge of certain kinds in criminology and to make sure that we reflexively consider these influences (that is, critically consider their **validity** and impact) in order to produce valid, realistic, and practical knowledge—to keep our perspective in perspective, if you like. Being able to better analyse and evaluate criminological knowledge production in terms of its value and utility motivates us to become thoughtful and reflexive criminologists in our daily lives (Stout, Yates, and Williams, 2008). This practice also gives us a heightened awareness of our own research agenda, which will serve you well when evaluating knowledge and when writing essays and conducting research projects or dissertations.

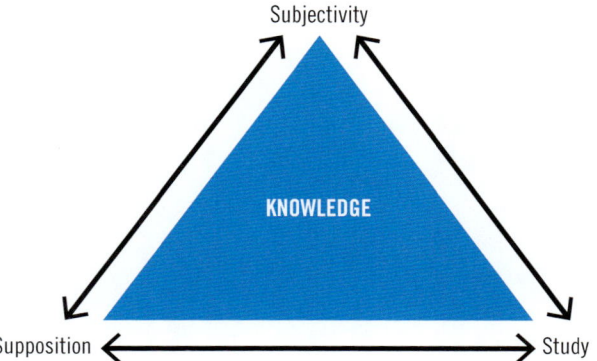

Figure 4.1 Criminological knowledge is influenced by three interlinking factors: subjectivity, supposition, and study

4.2 Producing criminological knowledge

To 'know about crime' means not only absorbing existing knowledge on the topic, but exploring and manipulating it to create more. By actively manipulating and owning information in these ways, you move beyond repetition and description into demonstrating your understandings as being critical, original, and reflective, and knowing about criminology.

Maintaining an ABC mindset

It is important to remember that the material that we read, hear, observe, and produce in criminology has been created or *socially constructed* for a purpose. It is knowledge, but of a specific and possibly limited kind. For this reason, we should keep the ABC (*Always Be Critical*) mantra in mind when considering criminological knowledge and always ask questions like:

- Who has created it?
- How have they created it?
- Why have they created it?
- Who have they created it for?
- Whose knowledge is it?

To expand on the final question, it is essential that we consider the source of all knowledge we engage with in criminology, particularly the perspectives, agendas, and possible biases of the producer of that knowledge, and the ways in which they might be influenced by their employer, academic institution, or other pressures—an idea we consider further in **Controversy and debate 4.1**. We should also go further and consider the source of the source, meaning the methods used to create or obtain knowledge (Walker, 2020; Westmarland, 2011), what form of knowledge it is, the extent to which it is based on evidence, its strengths/benefits, and its limitations/weaknesses. Only by asking such critical questions can we begin to evaluate the quality of the knowledge we are learning and, perhaps more importantly, evaluate how it benefits criminology in general and us specifically.

A key issue here, therefore, is what is known as *validity*, which essentially means the accuracy and trustworthiness of knowledge, of the methods we use to obtain it, and how it can be used to inform the criminological knowledge base. It is absolutely crucial to be able to judge the quality and value of the knowledge that we draw upon to help us understand crime, in order to determine how much faith should be placed in this knowledge, how it can be used, and

CONTROVERSY AND DEBATE 4.1

Who decides what criminologists study?

Many of us would be shocked at the idea that there is modern-day censorship of ideas and opinion, but could it be argued that this is in fact what is going on with criminological research? Today, research is probably even more crucial to a university's financial situation than the teaching of students, and if you speak to academic staff you will learn about the way that research drives the institution and its policy, together with the way that it is complicated by issues of ethics, safety, and the need to employ what are considered to be 'acceptable' research methods. Of course, we can't just barge around, demanding information from anywhere we choose—but we do need to think about the ways in which research is shaped by factors other than the academic learning it aims to promote. If we are only 'allowed' to research in certain ways, does it follow that we are only 'allowed' to research certain things with certain people? Who decides? And what happens to the people we don't listen to because we cannot access them?

These complications can be vividly illustrated when we think about research involving law-breaking, dangerous people (or at least, people who have been labelled as such). Academics may be personally nervous about working with murderers, rapists, and conmen. Universities may not want to be associated with people who have committed offences, and funding organisations may believe that someone who has been in prison is going to be naturally dishonest and therefore will skew the findings. Not least of these anxieties is the fear of being sued, or of being ridiculed or criticised.

Proponents of a school of thought called **convict criminology**, which is often associated with **critical criminology** (see **Chapter 18**), would argue that criminological research is being shaped and even censored by all these factors. They and others would call this a 'market led' research environment and are concerned that it silences (or censors) any kind of movement towards a wider, riskier debate in which the voices of prisoners and their families are heard, taken note of, and given an equal footing. One of the main aims of convict criminology is to challenge and, where possible, reverse this process.

whether we actually agree with it. Such questions are pivotal if you as a criminology student are to move past simply existing as a *consumer* of knowledge towards functioning as a critical *evaluator* and ultimately a *producer* of criminological knowledge (see **Chapter 1** and **Chapter 32**).

What is knowledge in criminology?

We should pause briefly here to reflect on how knowledge differs from fact. Fact is a universal truth, accepted by everyone everywhere. Such facts often emerge from the STEM subjects (science, technology, engineering, mathematics) that study the natural world, physical structures, artificial processes, and numbers. Our discipline does contain facts, of course—the names of organisations and structures (for example, the criminal justice system), the names of crimes (for example, burglary), and illegal substances (for example, heroin) at a given point in time in a given country, though even these facts are often dynamic, changing over time and between cultures. However, criminology is a social science, a study of conscious human beings living in complex societies and the knowledge that we generate is shaped by debate, opinions, and **theories** (Chamberlain, 2015). These tend to be **social constructions** (the artificial creations of concepts and ideas by subjective human beings) rather than objective facts, meaning that much of what we consider to be criminological knowledge is more accurately defined as interpretation rather than cold, hard fact.

The creation and evaluation of knowledge in the social sciences is guided by **epistemology**, which is 'a branch of philosophy which examines the concept of knowledge—what it is, where it comes from and whether absolute, true knowledge can be achieved' (Crow and Semmens, 2008: 23). In other words, it examines what constitutes appropriate knowledge about the social world and how it is created (Robson, 2015). There are many different epistemologies (theories about knowledge creation, usually words ending in 'ism'), but the following are the three that have traditionally been associated with criminology:

- **Empiricism** is the dominant, overarching epistemology in criminology. According to this position, the only acceptable knowledge is that obtained through objective sensory perception and through research methods that measure this form of perception.
- **Positivism** is the dominant epistemology within empiricism. This school of thought says that the empirical research methods of the natural sciences (observation and experiment) can be employed to study and create knowledge about the social world—particularly in the form of universal laws and cause-and-effect relationships between variables. As we will see later in this chapter, positivist epistemology is most commonly associated with the use of **quantitative research** methods—collecting and analysing numbers and statistics.
- **Interpretivism** has challenged the positivist epistemology across the social sciences more generally and specifically within criminology. It focuses on how individuals create and interpret their social worlds, for example through their interactions with others, and argues that reality is a subjective, personal construction (Noaks and Wincup, 2004). Interpretivist epistemology is most closely linked to **qualitative research** methods—collecting and analysing the written word and visual texts such as photographs.

The positivist and interpretivist epistemologies have long been viewed as incompatible and conflicting by social scientists—Oakley (1999) famously labelled this conflict 'the paradigm wars'—and consequently, academics and researchers have tended to prefer a specific epistemology in their work, while excluding the other. However, since the 1990s, another epistemology has gained popularity as both a challenge to and a compromise between this unhelpful dichotomy (division between opposing ideas) (Tashakkori and Teddlie, 1998). The epistemology of **realism**, also known as pragmatism, claims that it is possible to study and create knowledge about an objective, externally measurable reality through any combination of methods, including by combining positivist and interpretivist methods in order to fit the aims of the research (cf. Bryman, 2021; see also later discussion of mixed methods and **Chapter 22**'s discussion of realistic evaluation). The four 'isms' are shown in **Figure 4.2**.

Realist/pragmatist epistemology is presented as a practical, fit-for-purpose approach to creating knowledge. It consolidates the other two epistemologies to an extent, by showing positivist/quantitative and interpretivist

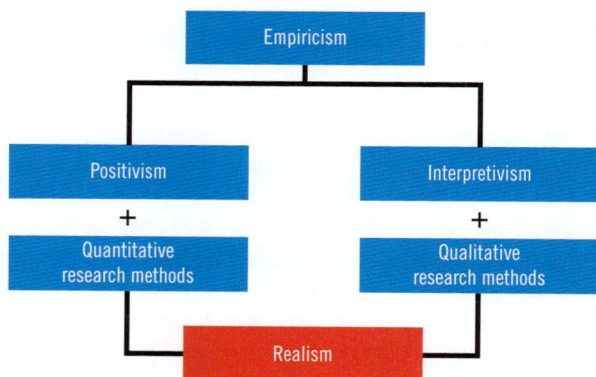

Figure 4.2 The creation and evaluation of criminological knowledge is guided by four main epistemologies

/qualitative approaches as compatible methods for conducting research, which is now widely agreed upon by criminologists. For example, quantitative and qualitative researchers can agree that reality is complex and (to some extent) constructed, and that single theories and methods offer only limited explanations of different social behaviours in the real world (see Reichardt and Rallis, 1994).

By extension, single epistemologies may not provide the most comprehensive and valid means of knowledge creation. Although our focus here is on epistemological debates within criminology, there are similar discussions across the social sciences, see, for example, Creswell's book, *Research Design: Qualitative, Quantitative, and Mixed Methods Approaches* and Robson's *Real-World Research*.

4.3 The evolution of criminological theories

In the introduction to this chapter, we briefly explored the idea that subjectivity, supposition, and study affect each other and influence the generation of criminological knowledge. We can also see this in their reciprocal (give-and-take) relationships with theoretical explanations of criminal behaviour. Study, which is influenced by subjectivity and supposition, directly influences theory, leading to and affecting the development of theories, but study methods are in turn influenced by theory. For example, theoretical developments can enhance the validity and **practicality** of different research methods (for instance, informing suitable survey content) and different research designs (for instance, identifying appropriate sample groups), while theory itself can be used to fine-tune study methods, and to guard against the distorting (biasing) influences of subjectivity and supposition by providing a framework for how to conduct applied studies (Chamberlain, 2015; Stout et al., 2008). In this way, theory and study (including study influenced by subjectivity and supposition) function in a virtuous circle with one another, each benefiting from, validating, and mediating each other, as is shown in **Figure 4.3**.

We can see this reciprocal relationship in the way that the academic study of criminology itself has developed over time. The discipline emerged, at least in part, because of concerns about the levels of crime reflected in the 19th century by the newly created official crime statistics (themselves subjective social constructions—see **Chapter** 5) and the need to explain and respond to criminal behaviour with methods supported by scientific evidence. Over time, criminologists have attempted to develop theories that strike a balance between the elements so that neither subjectivity, supposition, nor study are too strong, and we will consider each one briefly in turn, in chronological order.

Classicism: subjectivity and supposition

Classical criminology, which we explore in more detail in **Chapter 15**, is the original school of criminology that emerged in the 18th century and explained criminal behaviour as based on an individual's **free will** and **rational choices**. These explanations have been criticised on methodological, evidential grounds as being based on 'armchair theorising' (Chamberlain, 2015) rather than being underpinned by applied, empirical study (see Case, in Vaidya, 2015). The argument behind 'armchair theorising' refers to the idea of theorists sitting in their comfy armchairs and trying to explain real life from a distance, implying the use of personal opinion (subjectivity), common sense, guesswork, and speculation (supposition) instead of the collection and analysis of empirical evidence of real-life behaviour through applied research (study).

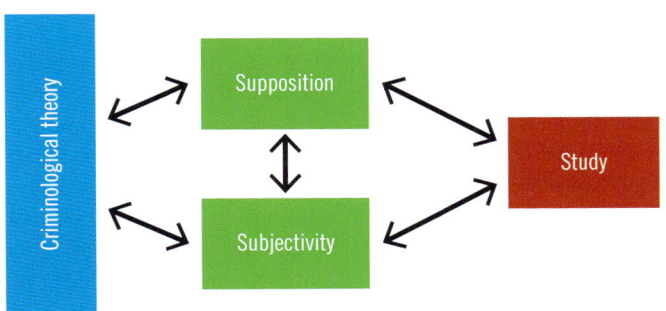

Figure 4.3 The reciprocal relationship between study and theory

Positivism: study through research

Positivism emerged in criminology around the 19th century in response to classicism, using data gained from empirical study to find the evidence that was absent from classical approaches. As we saw in the discussion of knowledge in relation to criminology in **section 4.2**, it generates this evidence by using methods adopted from the natural sciences (experiment, observation) along with other applied methods from psychology and sociology, such as interviews, **questionnaires**, and the secondary analysis of data and documents. This theory helped criminology become a 'social science' by giving it a methodological legitimacy and credibility (Hagan, 2013), but positivists haven't always agreed on the best research methods to use or the most convincing theoretical explanations for criminal behaviour, for example biological, psychological, sociological, and variations of each of these, which we discuss in **Chapters 16** and **17**).

These major disagreements indicate that subjectivity has run throughout criminology, shaping the choice of methods used, the identification of suitable populations and behaviours to examine, the results achieved, and the theories supported and rejected. However, there has been only limited **reflexivity** within positivism regarding these subjectivities and their influence on validity and knowledge creation. What positivists *do* agree is that the concept of crime can be understood as an unproblematic, taken for granted, fact.

Critical criminology: the rebirth of subjectivity

Critical/radical criminology came along in the 1950s/1960s to argue that positivism had it all wrong and that crime and criminals were labels or social constructions applied by powerful groups (for example, whites, middle classes, adults) to less powerful groups such as ethnic minorities, the working classes, and young people (see **Chapter 18**). This theory took an *interpretivist* perspective, which is an approach to the study of the social world (typically qualitative) seeking to understand human behaviour by exploring individual experiences, perceptions, and meanings. It was therefore argued that criminology should be focusing on who has the power to label—to define who is and is not criminal—not what causes crime (Williams, 2012). However, critical criminologists tended to focus on critiquing other studies, rather than producing their own evidence through research. The inherent problem with this viewpoint is that it is similar to the 'armchair theorising' that criminology once rejected.

Today's theories

None of these theories ever go away. They regenerate and redefine themselves based on a variety of academic influences, such as the creation of new evidence and studies, new interpretations of old evidence, and new research methods, along with non-academic influences such as political favour, media representations, and public opinion. Take, for example, the critical criminologist view that people who commit crime are somehow victims of being labelled 'criminal' by powerful groups: in recent years, this has been criticised by realist criminology, which we discuss in **Chapter 20**, working from the evidence-based perspective that crime is a real phenomenon which is experienced negatively by victims, families, communities, and societies, so should be dealt with on this basis (Williams, 2012).

Theory development in criminology is influenced by and in turn influences subjectivity, supposition, and study—combining in reciprocal and reflexive relationships to create and refine knowledge. We will now explore each of these three 's' elements in more detail.

4.4 Subjectivity

As you may have noticed from your reading so far, every source of knowledge in criminology has been created by someone who has a degree of subjectivity—personal opinions, preferences, and experiences. As well as being an inevitable part of a varied social science subject driven by human beings, subjectivity in criminology is also partly the product of the discipline's history as a hybrid, synthetic subject (see **Chapter 1**), where academics tended to train in a related area like sociology, psychology, or law, and would then move on to specialise in a criminological area, bringing to it their existing disciplinary preferences for particular theories and methods. It is important to be aware that this subjectivity means that knowledge produced in criminology *may* have an **agenda bias**, but this is not necessarily a bad thing. Subjectivity plays a large part in making criminology such a dynamic and fascinating discipline, and can have a valuable influence on knowledge production as long as criminologists reflexively explore its role in their decision-making, assessments, explanations, and conclusions (Westmarland, 2011), a practice that we explore later in this chapter.

As students of criminology, we consciously and subconsciously decide what we think about the information that we read about in the criminological studies, hear about in lectures, and choose to find out about through our own research. Our subjectivities lead us to make certain decisions and choices, and these can be further manipulated and influenced by a number of factors in our past and current lives. These subjective factors can be grouped into three categories: external, external-internal, and internal.

External subjectivities

External subjectivities are the perspectives that originate from outside ourselves that can have an influence on how we think and the knowledge we have, without us necessarily realising that they are having this effect. They can come from many sources, including professional subjectivity, dominant viewpoints and the media, which we will discuss in turn.

Professional subjectivity

Your lecturers and the scholars and researchers whose work you read may have preferences and even biases (unconscious or deliberate, hidden or acknowledged) towards particular theories, explanations, topics research methods, policies, and practices. These subjective preferences—professional subjectivity—can direct and restrict the

---

CONVERSATIONS 4.1

My subjective academic journey
with author **Steve Case**

Let me offer you the best example of academic bias that I can—myself. I began my academic journey as an undergraduate student of psychology. Due to what I was taught and the ways I was taught it, I became committed to understanding human behaviour in specific ways that focused on the individual (for example, thoughts, feelings, emotions). Studying psychology offered me micro-level understandings and explanations of human behaviour focused on and within the individual person. I was drawn in by the definite and technical nature of the conclusions psychologists made about human behaviour, often through using experiments and statistical tests. My developing disciplinary preference/bias for psychological methods and understandings fuelled a preference/bias for the study of memory, itself driven by a preference/bias for working with a particularly charismatic, expert professor. Consequently, I decided to study for a master's degree, generating micro-level, individual, experimental understandings of the eyewitness testimony memory of primary schoolchildren.

Sometime later, a research assistant post with a PhD attached to it was advertised in my university's criminology department. The PhD focused on the evaluation of a local youth crime prevention programme. Once again, I was lucky enough to be paired up with a charismatic, knowledgeable professor, only this time he was a criminologist, not a psychologist. He chose to examine the impact of this crime prevention programme in meso-level social ways, considering the influence of external factors such as neighbourhood characteristics, school processes, and family relationships alongside the individual's thoughts, feelings, and psychological features. He also preferred a broader range of research methods than was typical from my experience in psychology, arguing that using experiments and generating quantitative, numerical data with human beings does not provide a valid representation of real-life behaviour and circumstances. What results instead is a restricted understanding of human behaviour that focuses far too much on the individual and not enough on external, macro-level influences such as social factors or relationships and interactions with other people. Simultaneously, these individual, psychologised explanations tend to ignore the views, experiences, understanding, perceptions, and perspectives of the people they are researching.

It took me a while, but once I opened up my world view, I committed to a criminological journey, just like you are doing now. I began to conduct multi-method research studies; always focused on soliciting the views of children and young people (a new bias that I had been given and readily signed up to) and I became increasingly critical of the reductionist (limited, superficial, oversimplified) research and understandings of human behaviour that in my view typified the discipline I had come from. Where had I picked up this critical, sociological form of criminological preference/bias? I had adopted it from my PhD supervisor, developed it in conversation with him (and other like-minded individuals), and consolidated it through my choice of research focus, methods, conclusions, and target audiences (see Case, 2007; Case and Haines, 2009). These biases shaped me into a critical youth criminologist and anti-positivist researcher. It has been a voyage of discovery that continues to this day.

information you receive (and do not receive) through your studies, the theories employed, the debates you engage with, the methods you use, and the knowledge you generate (see Case, in Vaidya, 2015). Consider how professional subjectivities might be shaping your knowledge as a criminology student as you read **Conversations 4.1**.

Dominant viewpoints

Every generation of criminology and topic within the subject has its own dominant theories and arguments, as we discussed in **section 4.3**, which act as an external influence on the knowledge being produced. These theories are inextricably bound up with dominant research methods and the hot-topic questions that the subject, politicians, and broader society want answered (Chamberlain, 2015; Hagan, 2013). Prime examples of these hot-topic issues are the crime and justice issues revealed and/or exacerbated by the Covid-19 pandemic, the recent emergence of substance use, and the emergence of cyberterrorism in criminology, requiring urgent investigation and explanations to inform laws, policies, and practices/responses. Consider, for example, the group Anonymous, famed for protesting in masks similar to that depicted in **Figure 4.4**, who hacked into (and subsequently brought down) more than 5,500 Twitter accounts under the banner of #OpISIS, allegedly belonging to the terrorist organisation, so-called Islamic State.

Of course, the dominant viewpoints that influence knowledge within our subject are themselves influenced by external dominant viewpoints in politics, different cultures, different societies, historical periods, and economic climates. Criminology is influenced from the outside in, far more than it can ever influence the outside. In addition, criminological knowledge and understanding has been influenced historically by the **androcentricism** (privileging the male viewpoint in knowledge creation) and **ethnocentrism** (privileging the white, westernised viewpoint in knowledge creation) of the individuals who study crime (see **Chapter 1**), such as academics, politicians, and criminal justice practitioners. In turn, these biases have influenced who has been studied (for example, working class, white boys) and what has been studied (the violent and property crimes associated with this group as a category of offender) in order to populate and evidence classical, positivist, and critical theories of crime (Chamberlain, 2015). The preferences of those who have the power to decide the criminological knowledge agenda (that is, middle-class professionals in the western world—see **Chapter 13**) have, at least historically, tended to limit diversity in criminology's explanations of and responses to crime, relatively neglecting areas such as the potentially differential experiences of the criminal justice system on the basis of a person's ethnicity, gender, or disability (Pollock, 2016).

Media (mis)representation

Some critics argue that mass media and social media consistently misrepresent the extent and nature of crime (King and Wincup, 2008), partly due to the partial information that it receives from criminologists and politicians, which can lead to misunderstanding, exaggeration, and extrapolation (using existing evidence to make conclusions about things that might happen) (Williams, 2012; see also **Chapter 7**).

Examples are ever-present in modern-day media scaremongering around the terrorist threat posed by young Muslim men (see **Figure 4.5**), which is itself a reincarnation of 1970s media (mis)representation of the epidemic of violent street robbery (labelled 'mugging' by the news media) supposedly caused by young black males (see Hall, 1978). These representations are also prominent in the US, with stark differences between how white and black victims and suspects are portrayed (see **Controversy and debate 4.2**). The media's biased representations could be partly a product of ignorance (wilful or otherwise), or partly a product of the particular political leanings of the media organisation discussing crime. We can be sure that media representations of crime are highly motivated by the desire to entice their audience or readership. Whatever the motivation for media misrepresentations and preferences, the subjectivity and supposition of the mass media can seep into our psyche, create or confirm our own suppositions and stereotypes (for example, relating to the perceived criminal behaviours certain ethnic groups), and can shape our subjectivity going forwards.

Figure 4.4 Dominant viewpoints within criminology, such as the recent focus on cyberterrorism, act as external influences on the knowledge produced

Source: oneinchpunch/Shutterstock

Figure 4.5 Young Muslim men have become targets of modern-day scaremongering in the media as a result of the rise in terrorist activity
Source: Naiyyer/Shutterstock

External-internal subjectivity

Whilst the influences we have just discussed are external, our viewpoints and knowledge are also shaped by elements that are external-internal, meaning that they are outside factors that are specific to the individual, unlike the more wide-reaching influence of the media, for example. These can include our demographic status, our peer groups, and social interactions.

Individual demographics

Our broader personal and social characteristics, known as individual demographics, can influence our views, experiences, and how we interpret and make meaning of them (that is, an interpretivist epistemology). How we behave, what we believe, how others behave towards us, and what others believe about us are all shaped by each person's demographic characteristics such as age, gender, ethnic group, social class, cultural background, religious orientation, sexuality, disability, and locality (Gray, 2013; Hagan, 2013). Each of these demographic characteristics is a socially determined and constructed, external label that can influence the experiences (see the discussion later in this section on internal subjectivity) and perspectives (internal) that shape us as human beings.

To take an example, the demographic make-up of prominent academic criminologists and other criminal justice professionals in the history of criminology has been

 CONTROVERSY AND DEBATE 4.2

Approaching newspaper headlines critically

Take a look at the following newspaper headings taken from news sources from around the US. They serve as examples showing how the media can spin a situation to evoke certain emotions. The role of the media is explored in full in **Chapter 6**, but these headlines demonstrate how important it is to always look beneath the surface and question who has produced the knowledge and why. Take a look at the sources of each heading and have a think about the different agenda biases that may be at play. Pay particular attention to how the suspects are described, and the elements of their past that were chosen to be highlighted.

Headlines covering white suspects

> Brock Turner, guilty of three counts of sexual assault: 'Three-time All-American Stanford swimmer found guilty of rape'
>
> (Associated Press, 31 March 2016)

> US President's response to violence at a white supremacist rally: 'Trump blamed violence in Charlottesville at white supremacist protests on "many sides"'
>
> (CNN, 13 August 2017)

Headlines covering black victims

> Keith Lamont-Scott shot and killed by police: 'Violent past arrest record includes assault with a deadly weapon'
>
> (Associated Press, 22 September 2016)

> Aaron Tucker saved car crash victim from burning car: 'Ex-con skips job interview, takes shirt off his back to save car crash victim'
>
> (CBS News, 15 July 2017)

(The Twitter discussion that ensued when CBS News posted this story is also worth reading, once you have looked at the headline itself: see https://twitter.com/cbsnews/status/886001120254070784?lang=en)

We delve deeper into the issues surrounding race and ethnicity in the criminal justice system in **Chapter 10**.

predominantly white, westernised, middle class, and male (although this gender disparity is diminishing professionally, and most notably amongst the undergraduate student body). It is these very individuals who hold the power to decide who to study and how to understand and respond to the behaviours of those they have decided to study. However, it's possible that the demographic characteristics of these powerful knowledge producers can bias the criminological agenda, creating understandings that are androcentric, ethnocentric, and otherwise neglectful of the diversity of perspectives and behaviours of any populations outside their immediate focus of study (Mitchell Miller, 2014).

Peer groups and social interactions

The development of our own subjectivity can also be influenced by our *peer groups and social interactions*—the subjectivities of friends, family members, peers (such as fellow students), work colleagues, and team mates with whom we interact socially. Social interactions can provide us with validations of our own subjective viewpoints, often because we gravitate towards friends and peers with similar views to us. They may also provide new and improved perspectives by offering us new information or by challenging our own viewpoints. Social interactions can also provide us with information about how a peer group or work team are expected to think (groupthink) and behave (group norms)—in other words, the preferences and biases that members of a group are expected to adopt (cf. Janis, 1972). This is an essential element of group initiation and membership. The implication here is that we do not always fully commit to or believe in the biases we adopt—we may simply be following others, fitting in, or trying to get ahead by choosing the most convenient or acceptable bias for our own purposes and goals. However, we do not always recognise external influences on the way we develop biases. As we have been arguing in this chapter, it is crucial to be aware of your own subjectivity—where it comes from and the influence it can have on your study and application of the knowledge you produce from it—linking back to our previous discussion of reflexivity.

Internal subjectivity

Unlike the other subjective factors we have explored so far, internal subjectivity refers to our individual thoughts and experiences. We all have different backgrounds and journeys in life that shape how we approach the world, as shown in **Figure 4.6**, and this is something we need to keep in mind when we think about producing criminological knowledge. The ABC mantra isn't just for the facts and opinions we come across, it applies to ourselves, too.

Personal experiences

Our past and current *personal experience* can colour and shape the ways in which we perceive and understand the world (an interpretivist epistemology once again). It is important that we do not confuse personal experience and anecdotes (personal stories about our experiences) with evidence to support our academic arguments (Lamputtang, 2019; Stout et al., 2008). Personal experiences can offer useful illustrations of the arguments we are making, but they do not count as supporting evidence in any academic or empirical research sense, mainly because they are so personalised and subjective. That said, it is really useful to reflect critically on your experiences and how they may have influenced the stereotypes, preconceptions, values, prejudices, attitudes, and perceptions that you possess and how you understand different issues in criminology.

A classic example of this is that victims of crime are likely to have a greater fear of crime than non-victims (Ferraro, 1995), despite both groups (arguably) having an equivalent likelihood of experiencing crime in the future. However, this may not be a valid claim for certain types of crime, such as burglary and hate crime, where the repeat victimisation effect has more evidence (Farrell and Pease, 2014). Another example is that students who have had a specific negative or unsatisfactory experience of, and interaction with, the police may be more likely to express negative views of the police in general, even when they are required to offer a balanced, open-minded academic debate or perspective. This example seems to be the university student equivalent of research evidence suggesting that certain ethnic groups

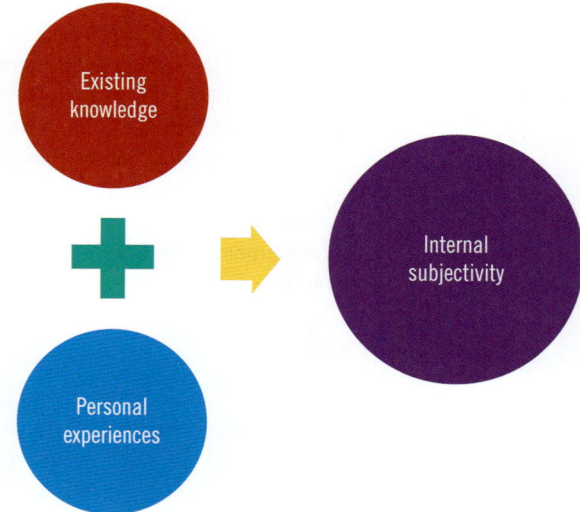

Figure 4.6 Do you recognise how your existing knowledge and personal experiences interact to shape your internal subjectivity as a student of criminology?

WHAT DO YOU THINK? 4.1

How should we respond to crime?

What do you think is the best way to respond to crime and why? To reach your answer, try to list the main potential causes of and influences on crime that you can think of and prioritise those that you see as most important or most likely, then consider how you can tackle these influences in the most effective ways. Finally, ask yourself:

- Is this an easy question to answer?
- Why do you think what you do about how to respond to crime?
- Where have your views come from and what has influenced them?
- To what degree are your views based on evidence or opinion?
- Do we need research evidence to support our views? Why? Why not?
- Are your views based on your personal opinion/perspective of particular evidence or just based on personal opinion?

(for example, young black males) hold more negative views of the police than others who have been in similar situations if they perceive that they have experienced unjust treatment by the criminal justice system (Pollock, 2016). A lesson here is to ensure that you acknowledge and evidence your internal, personal subjectivities as a student, but keep them in perspective so that they do not become bias and supposition. In your studies, you are expected to present all sides of an argument.

Existing knowledge

Part of your personal experience, of course, is the understanding and *existing knowledge* that you have developed, for example through dominant subject viewpoints. Your subjective preferences develop in part due to what and how you learn at home, in formal education, and at work. You pick up a knowledge base of information from external influences (for example, books, teachers, peers) that you then reflect on, consolidate, and extend through your study choices (Aronson, Wilson, and Akert, 2010), from the knowledge you choose to collect, to how you choose to interpret, and (selectively, subjectively) present it. It is essential to maintain a reflexive approach to study and learning so that your knowledge base does not become a knowledge *bias*. An ABC method of maintaining reflexivity as a criminology student is to examine the (research) methods used to obtain knowledge for any instances of bias (for instance, relative to gender, ethnicity, class, age) and other failures to acknowledge and explore potential diversity (for instance, based on sexuality, disability, locality, religion) that could affect the validity of the knowledge production process.

Your choices and decisions as a student of criminology can be affected by any and all of these entirely subjective influences, just as the choices and decisions of each of the influencers (for example, lecturers, scholars, researchers, politicians, criminal justice practitioners, journalists) has been shaped by these factors. The result can be a vicious circle of subjectivity if left unacknowledged and unchallenged, but engaging with and utilising this subjectivity and bias can create a virtuous circle of **reflection** and learning.

After reading this section it is worth considering the questions raised in **What do you think? 4.1**.

4.5 Supposition

> A good story is often less probable than a less satisfactory one.
> (Kahneman, Slovic, and Tversky 1982: 98)

Human beings have an innate need to understand and control their environment. When we lack sufficient information and knowledge to allow us to do this properly, it causes us anxiety. The solution is often to fill the gap in our knowledge using supposition (guesswork and assumption), often drawing on examples from history and personal experience and subjective opinions. Criminologists are not exempt from this. When knowledge is lacking, we may fill the gaps with plausible explanations and extrapolations, with the 'codification of commonsense' and with appeals to stereotypes and preconceptions (Hoefnagels, 1973), rather than necessarily with detailed research and the generation of convincing evidence.

Supposition can help to bridge the knowledge gap between subjectivity and study (see Taleb, 2001) and it helps us to manage and deal with the uncertain and complex aspects of our social worlds. When we study criminology, we may over-value supposition because it is presented so convincingly by 'experts' and authority figures. We may be tempted to accept information uncritically because of the apparent legitimacy and credibility of the source. This is not to say that we should reject expert knowledge that is based on supposition, because this may be only part of what influenced its construction; plus, the supposition of experts may be well informed. Nor is expert knowledge in criminology ever entirely based on supposition; indeed, much knowledge is fully or predominantly based on study. But the existence of supposition does suggest that you should remember the ABC mantra. Always evaluate the origins and validity of the knowledge being imparted. In this way, even if the author has not been (sufficiently) critical and reflexive, you can introduce reflexivity into the creation and application of criminological knowledge.

The lesson from this section and **Controversy and debate 4.3** is, as ever, to *Always Be Critical* in our study. Subjectivity and supposition, especially taken together, produce certain forms of knowledge (Taleb, 2001; Hoefnagels, 1973). This knowledge typically conforms to an interpretivist epistemology, but it is knowledge that is not necessarily grounded in research evidence so it may have a limited validity and even certain biases that must be acknowledged and accounted for by reflexive criminologists. Subjectivity and supposition can reinforce one another, but on their own they can only produce a partial knowledge base for criminology, which brings us on to look in depth at study, our final element of the triad.

CONTROVERSY AND DEBATE 4.3

The supposition of risk prediction

The dominant theoretical explanation used to understand and respond to offending by young people—a topic we consider in **Chapter 9**—is known as the Risk Factor Prevention Paradigm or RFPP (Hawkins and Catalano, 1992; see Case and Haines, 2009 for a detailed critique). The RFPP considers 'risk factors' to be negative experiences, situations, and interactions. In particular, it states that exposure to risk factors from an individual's childhood, school, neighbourhood, and personal life predicts criminal behaviour in later life. Therefore, these risk factors are the logical targets for intervention and prevention work (Farrington, in Maguire et al., 2007; Baker, 2005). Supporters of the RFPP argue that identifying and targeting risk factors is a proven effective, evidence-based, and practical method of reducing current offending and preventing future crime (see Utting, 1999; Youth Justice Board, 2005). However, there is disagreement on methodological and analytical grounds (see Case, 2006, 2007; Case and Haines, 2009).

It is submitted that the claim that risk factors predict or increase the risk of youth offending is based on supposition, which itself is born of subjectivity. The RFPP is supported by hundreds of studies, all measuring the presence of risk factors in early life and then statistically linking them to a measure of offending taken at a later point (see **Chapter 21**—**integrated theories**). This is what's known as identifying a statistical correlation/relationship. It simply shows that a person who has certain characteristics/risk factors (for example, has experienced their parents arguing in childhood) is more likely to possess another characteristic (for example, offending behaviour in adolescence) than other people without those initial characteristics/risk factors (for example, parents arguing). Supposition occurs when we extrapolate these findings by assuming that certain characteristics predict offending behaviour in the real world. Whilst a risk factor may be correlated with offending behaviour, there is no convincing evidence that this alleged relationship has a definitive direction—such as the risk factor causing or influencing offending.

The overwhelming majority of research studies have adopted an **artefactual risk factor theories** approach to converting risk into a factor/number and then examining its (correlational) relationship with offending (see Case and Haines, 2009; Kemshall, 2008). Artefactual risk factor research often measures risk factors and offending simultaneously in cross-sectional studies, making it much more difficult to conclude which comes first. So in our example, a young person may be experiencing parents arguing in their current life, alongside committing offences—they are both happening at the same time, along with exposure to a potentially huge range of additional risk factors/influences, so the direction of any relationship is extremely difficult to untangle in the absence of further longitudinal, qualitative research and more sophisticated statistical analyses.

Some studies (such as those with longitudinal designs) have measured exposure to risk factors *before* they measure offending behaviour, then assume that young people experience risk factors before they offend (that is, that risk factors have **temporal precedence** over offending behaviour), concluding that risk factors must be causing or in some way influencing the offending behaviour. However, the reality here is that the risk factor was simply *measured* first, not necessarily experienced first. To conclude that it predicts offending on this basis (other studies even extrapolate this conclusion into presenting risk factors as *causes* of offending) is supposition—a plausible explanation based on common sense rather than evidence. Until we can convincingly measure which actually occurred first in the young person's life, we cannot accurately assess the nature of the risk factor-offending relationship. Indeed, offending could actually predict or cause increased exposure to risk factors (for example, if you commit crime, being caught and punished may cause your parents to argue), or even that other unmeasured influences (for example, poverty, unemployment, sibling offending) predict or cause both exposure to risk factors and offending behaviour (Case and Haines, 2009). If either of these alternative explanations are valid (accurate) then the label of 'risk factors' is surely misleading because the label would relate to factors that do not actually predict or increase the risk of a future behaviour. Here, supposition fills the gap in our knowledge of how (and even if) risk factors and offending are related.

Regardless of the methodological issues that pervade (artefactual) risk factor studies, the supposition that risk factors predict offending has attained uncritical acceptance amongst researchers, policymakers, and practitioners across the world (for further discussion, see **Chapter 9**).

4.6 Study

Subjectivity and supposition do not only influence one another; as we saw in **section 4.3**, they each have an influence on (and are influenced by) the central means for the generation, application, and critique of knowledge in criminology: study.

We study criminology by reading about it, observing it, hearing about it, talking about it, examining it, and by actually conducting empirical research. Study can involve the collection and examination of secondary information and evidence or the creation of original, primary information and evidence (Chamberlain, 2013). Creating primary knowledge can involve research, but may also be based on the original critique and application of the arguments of others. Study requires you to function as a criminologist and to fulfil the main goal of this book—to move from being a consumer of knowledge to being a producer of knowledge.

When academics, scholars, and researchers talk about studying criminology, they are more often than not implying that this is systematic, controlled study, gathering data through some form of observation or experiment—otherwise known as empirical research (Crowther-Dowey and Fussey, 2013). By study, criminologists are often talking about scientifically capturing information, analysing it so it becomes evidence, and the process of turning it into knowledge that progresses our understandings and informs our theories and explanations. The process of study underpins the arguments throughout this book due to our commitment to understanding criminology through discussion of the methods and findings of applied research conducted in the real world.

Research as study

Applied research is a key vehicle of study in criminology. As we have discussed, (empirical) researchers are influenced by a degree of subjectivity at every step in terms of their decisions and choices regarding what research question to investigate, who to study, what research method to use, how to analyse and interpret the data, what to conclude, whom to tell about this, and how to share the information. These decisions do not invalidate or weaken the research, nor do they make the researcher/research wrong—because criminology does not really do right and wrong as much as it seeks reasoned opinion—but their influence on the research process and on the knowledge produced should be recognised and accounted for.

Criminology has traditionally presented itself as a legitimate, credible social science to rival its older sibling subjects of sociology and psychology (Rennison and Hart, 2018). The traditional empiricist, positivist dominance of epistemology and choice of research methods has enabled academics to assert that criminology is a valid and scientific subject, as these approaches give control over the subject matter, generate generalisable, non-biased results, produce universal laws, and base study on independence and objectivity (Rennison and Hart, 2018; Caulfield and Hill, 2014). However, as we will go on to explore in more depth, applied (especially empirical) research can never be a perfect means of generating criminological knowledge—such a method does not exist. All criminologists have a preference for certain epistemologies and methods; these serve to inform and shape their arguments, whilst also providing a basis for researchers to reflexively evaluate their work (Savin-Baden and Howell-Major, 2013). All research methods have allegiances to a particular epistemology and specific strengths/benefits and weaknesses/limitations, all of which determine the types of knowledge they can and cannot create.

Earlier in the chapter, we introduced the concept of empirical research methods—research that obtains knowledge through sensory experience and experimental and observational methods (Bryman, 2021). Empirical research methods can be quantitative or qualitative, or a mixture of both. The most common aim of empirical research in criminology is to evaluate concepts, phenomena, issues, behaviours, and groups (see Gray, 2013; Robson, 2015). Empirical research can have a mixture of these aims. It can be used to generate brand new knowledge and understandings (**inductive research**), to test existing knowledge and understandings (**deductive research**), or to do both in the same study.

In an ideal world, the most valid forms of research would use the most appropriate research method for the question(s) that needs to be answered, to meet the objectives and agendas of the study, and to pursue the forms of knowledge (epistemology) that the research(er) wants to create. However, research does not take place in an ideal world untouched by external, non-academic influences. For example, a major influence on choice of research method beyond academic concerns is practicality. Research projects, such as funded evaluations conducted for government sponsors, are often short on time, money, and physical resources (people, rooms, equipment). Consequently, researchers must choose the most suitable research method under those circumstances (Chamberlain, 2013; Hagan, 2013), possibly regardless of their own research-based subjectivities and suppositions. In a way, practical requirements can encourage researchers to adopt a realist/pragmatist epistemological approach to the study of criminological topics. However, in the spirit of ABC and reflexivity, we should acknowledge that choices of research method are also guided by many subjective factors, such as:

- professional (disciplinary) training;
- professional experience of a particular method;
- personal preference;
- the preferences of the academic discipline or sub-topic within a discipline;
- theoretical standpoint;
- what the researcher feels has been effective in the past (however 'effective' is defined);
- perceived suitability of a method for a certain group of participants, in addition to the demands or (subjective) requirements of the research funders (see **New frontiers 4.1**).

For example, governments may have a preference for funding experimental evaluations of programmes and interventions, prioritising the measurement of differences between control and experimental groups, or before and after differences within individuals (the 'what works' model of evaluation). This preference may override researching how practitioners understand how intervention inputs (may) produce different outputs or asking recipients of an intervention how it has influenced or changed them. Seeking to understand how interventions work in these ways relates to the theory of change model discussed in more detail in **Chapter 22**.

In **New frontiers 4.1** we explore further the role of reflexivity in knowledge creation.

NEW FRONTIERS 4.1

The role of reflexivity in knowledge creation

The process of evaluating research decisions, known as **reflection**, acknowledges that social research is a set of compromises that are made within complex, imperfect situations—compromises such as maximising the strengths and mitigating the limitations of different research methods in the context of practical constraints on the research (Davies et al., 2011). The extension of reflection is reflexivity, which is 'a process that helps researchers to consider their position and influence during the study . . . to know how they have constructed and even sometimes imposed meanings on the research process' (Savin-Baden and Howell-Major, 2013: 76).

Reflexivity is an essential process to enable academics and researchers to critically assess the influence of their own subjectivities (constructed meanings) and suppositions (imposed meanings) on study (the research process); essential because all research findings, conclusions, and recommendations are the consequences of these decisions (Davies and Francis in Davies et al., 2011). It is equally crucial that the results of this process are acted upon to improve future theory, research, policy, and practice, and in this way, reflexivity can be seen as a new frontier in criminology—an increasingly important and recognised influence on the quality and validity of knowledge creation.

Epistemological reflexivity is a particular form of reflexivity that encourages researchers to critically examine how they produce knowledge (for example, their 'epistemology' or theory of knowledge creation) and how that belief system has shaped their research design and interpretation of findings (Willig, 2001). Researchers may wish to travel even further back, reflexively, to consider how their own demographic characteristics (such as age, gender, ethnicity) and their experiences related to these may have influenced their belief system. As you might remember from your reading earlier in this chapter, our demographic position is one of the external-internal subjective factors that can influence our knowledge. Reflexivity is closely aligned to the concept of **positionality**, the stance/position that the researcher has chosen to adopt within a specific study. Addressing their positionality involves researchers reflexively examining the influence of their own subjective position in relation to the subject matter being studied, the research context, and the research participants, including the influence of their chosen epistemology, disciplinary perspective, and preconceptions (Nightingale and Cromby, 1999).

Reflexivity (including consideration of the influence of positionality) should be employed by criminologists to assess the *validity* of the conclusions they draw as a result of research study (their own and that of others). 'Validity' in this case means the extent to which conclusions are plausible, credible, and generalisable to other contexts and populations (Savin-Baden and Howell-Major, 2013). Criminologists should also use reflexivity to reflect critically on what counts as knowledge within their specific study, how this knowledge was produced, and why.

The most common research methods used to generate empirical knowledge in criminology are experiment, survey, observation, and secondary data analysis, so let us critically examine these methods and the nature of the knowledge that they produce. **Figure 4.7** summarises these methods and their sub-branches—you may like to refer back to this diagram as you read the sections on each research method, to remind you how they fit together.

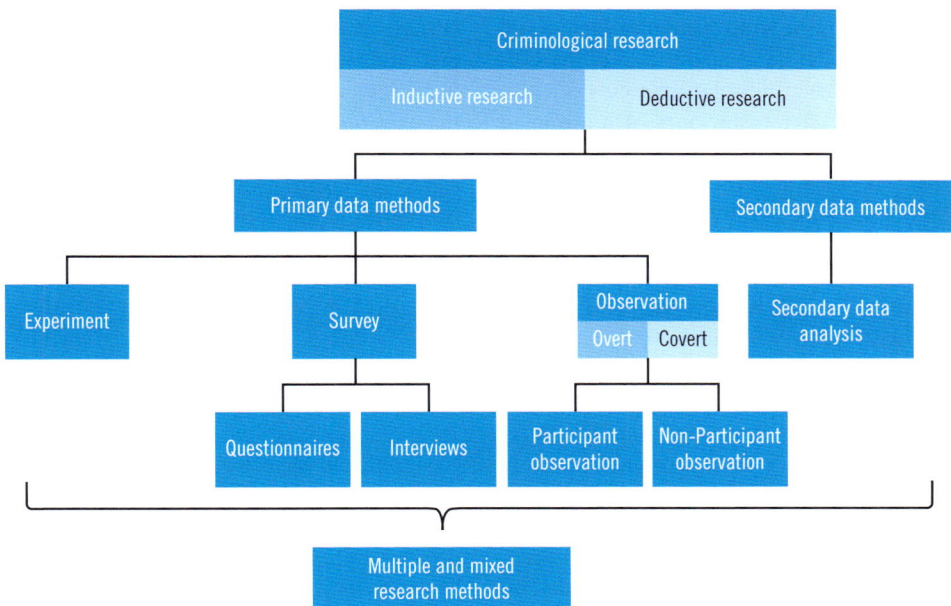

Figure 4.7 Criminological research methods

Experiment: researching by doing and manipulating

The experimental method in criminology involves manipulating an aspect of a person's surroundings/environment, what they experience, or what they are subjected to, in order to see if it has an effect on their behaviour (Caulfield and Hill, 2014). What is manipulated is called the **independent variable** (IV) and the behaviour that is measured as a result of this manipulation is called the **dependent variable** (DV). For example, a particular form of sentence, treatment, or intervention programme (the IV) could be given to offenders or substance users to see if it leads to reductions in their offending behaviour or substance use (the DVs). A simple way to remember the difference between these two types of variable is that 'I' manipulate the IV and we get our 'd'ata from the DV. Variables are almost always measured in numerical/statistical form, which means that experiments are a quantitative research method.

Experiments typically take place in highly controlled situations (the laboratory) or in a—controlled—version of a real-world environment (also known as being 'in the field'). The objective of an experiment is to control all other possible influences on behaviour (extraneous variables) so that the researcher can conclude that manipulating the IV caused a change in a person's behaviour, or DV—the classic 'cause and effect' relationship that underpins the knowledge pursued by positivist epistemology. Experiments in criminology are often designed to provide a service, treatment, or intervention (IV) to a particular group (the **experimental group**) and to withhold this service or treatment or intervention from an equivalent group (the **control group**), in order to measure any differences that result between the two groups. Experiments can also measure the before and after behaviours of a group or individual to see if there was a change after the service, treatment, or intervention was given, which can then be attributed to the IV (Robson, 2015).

In this way, experiments are the embodiment of positivist, scientific methodology in criminology. Experimenters in criminology claim to be able to exert such control over the research situation that they can identify the causes of human behaviours (for example, crime, substance use, antisocial behaviour, and **desistance**). This claim is explored in **Chapter 22**. It is argued that the large amount of control over behaviour made possible by an experiment allows experimental processes to be standardised (conducted in the same way each time), which improves the **reliability** of the experiment. 'Reliability' in this instance refers to the replicability and consistency of experimental methods and results; a crucial benefit if researchers are seeking generalisable, universally applicable explanations for behaviour and recommendations for potentially effective responses.

A criminological example: an effective experiment in preventing shoplifting

Let's look briefly at an example of an effective criminological experiment. In their 'Experiment on the prevention of shoplifting', Farrington et al. (in Clarke, 1993) compared the effectiveness of different **situational crime prevention** methods on levels of shoplifting in nine shops from the same UK electrical goods chain. These shops were 'reasonably comparable' in size, sales, and shoplifting rates. Having taken a baseline level of shoplifting (number of missing items compared to number of items sold) in each shop in the pre-test week before the experiment, the researchers allocated a crime prevention condition to each shop for the experimental week: electronic tagging of all items (two shops), shop redesign (two shops), uniformed guard (two shops), and no intervention/control condition (three shops). The researchers then compared levels of shoplifting in the pre-test week, with levels measured immediately following the experimental week, and a follow-up measure three to six weeks later. This is known as a **before and after experimental design**.

The results of the crime prevention experiment were that electronic tagging 'caused a lasting decrease in shoplifting' (Farrington et al. in Clarke, 1993: 94), still evident six weeks post-experiment. Shop redesign demonstrated an immediate effect post-test that diminished after six weeks, whilst the uniformed guard and control conditions made no difference to shoplifting levels. The researchers did reflect on a series of experimental limitations regarding the generalisability and reliability of their results, including resource constraints, unforeseen reductions in pre- and post-test periods (so these were not actually a full week), and weather disruptions—all acting as potential extraneous variables. Having accounted for these, the researchers concluded that the experiment indicated that electronic tagging was an effective method of preventing shoplifting in the long term, while shop redesign had the potential to be effective in the long term if this method was enhanced, as this was a less expensive option for the company.

Control in experiments

A significant issue for experiments in a criminological context is the need to have control over variables in order to fulfil the measurement objectives. Controlling for all possible influences on behaviour in the real world could be seen as virtually impossible (see **Chapter 22**), and even when significant control is achieved, it may introduce problems by causing the measured behaviour to be artificial. The overarching criticism is that experiments in criminology can lack **ecological validity**—they do not produce results that are a complete and accurate reflection of real-life behaviour. In fact, experiments could actually create forms of behaviour that are not realistic, which is problematic for a research method employed to study crime—a real-life, real-world behaviour committed and experienced by real people (Robson, 2015).

Experimenters can also rely on a degree of supposition when assuming how far external influences can be controlled, how an IV affects a DV, and that any differences between control and experimental groups are necessarily the result of (caused by) their own manipulations (see **Chapter 22**). Changes in people's behaviour in an experimental context could be the result of a series of other influences, including but not limited to:

- existing differences between the control and experimental groups;
- chance;
- the influence of other unmeasured, uncontrolled, and unforeseen variables (bad weather at a specific shop's location in the shoplifting experiment);
- researcher measurement error;
- participants changing their behaviour due to the pressure and demands of the experimental situation (cf. Hope, 2009).

Consequently, experiments can encourage 'black box' understandings of crime (see Pawson and Tilley, 2004). In other words, we have an input (the manipulation of the IV; a particular sentence, treatment, or intervention) and a measurable output (the DV; any changes in behaviour, such as crime reduction). However, we have very little knowledge and explanation of what goes on in the black box between these inputs and outputs (for further discussion, see **Chapter 22**).

In order to illustrate these arguments, let us return to the shoplifting prevention experiment. The IV was the type of crime prevention condition put into each of the shops. The DV was the difference between shoplifting levels in the pre-test and post-test periods. Any changes in shoplifting levels were attributed to the impact of the intervention. However, the reasons/explanations for any changes were impossible to identify from the intervention alone and no qualitative study was conducted to explore them further. Consequently, there is an explanatory black box sitting between the IV (interventions) and the DV (changes in shoplifting levels), along with no consideration or understanding of the influence of **extraneous variables** (EVs) like context, location, or customer demographics. By leaving the black box empty, the researchers were not in a position to explain to the company exactly *why* particular interventions may have worked, or to advise the company *how* these interventions should be applied and improved in the future.

Reductionism

Consider the previous issues when experimental criminologists proclaim, often unreflexively, that a programme or sentence or intervention 'works' or is 'effective' following an experimental study or evaluation. Also consider that the experimental preference/bias for converting behaviour to numbers/quantities artificially can reduce the ecological validity of what is measured and wash away its complexity and detail (Pawson and Tilley, 2004). In criminological, methodological terms this is called **reductionism** (see also **Chapter 9**). Experimental criminologists deliberately reduce and simplify/quantify variables to make them easier to analyse and understand using statistics. Arguably, such reductionism makes perfect sense as it makes our complex world more manageable and the research more practical. However, this process necessarily can disregard *qualitative* outcomes such as what participants understand, experience, and perceive about their lives (Westmarland, 2011). In other words, quantification on its own leaves out subjectivity and so does not represent the (subjective) reality of a real-life situation from a participant's perspective, rendering participants more like 'subjects' of a research experiment that is *done to* them rather than *done with* them (Case, 2007). It can also be considered unethical to manipulate people's behaviour or, if they are in the control group, to deny them access to something helpful or vital such as a specialised treatment or support service, just to measure if their behaviour is harmed by not having it.

Surveys: researching by asking

Surveys in criminology involve researchers asking people questions about their experiences, opinions, feelings, memories, and perceptions relating to a specific issue (Walker, 2020; Rennison and Hart, 2018). In this way, surveys facilitate an **ethnographic** approach—understanding the world from the perspective of the research participant, usually studied in their natural environment (see also **Chapter 32**). Questions can be asked and answered in written form (questionnaires) or spoken form (interviews, focus groups), and can be asked to individuals (questionnaires, interviews) or groups (focus groups). The main objectives of surveys are to measure participants' perspectives on a subject at a set point in time (**cross-sectional research**) or changes in these perspectives over time (**longitudinal research**), and to identify associations/correlations between specific elements of these perspectives and their behaviours (Crowther-Dower and Fussey, 2013). For example, a survey questionnaire could explore whether young people who offend report higher levels of impulsive behaviour than young people who do not offend, or whether older people express a higher fear of crime than younger people. Here we look in more detail at each of these different types of survey and the knowledge they create.

Questionnaires

A questionnaire is a form of survey where participants provide written/typed responses to written questions (on paper or electronically/online/computer-assisted), typically by reading the questions themselves (self-completion/reported/administered) or having them read by the researcher (face-to-face completion.). Perhaps the most well-known example of a criminological survey completed face-to-face (but including self-administered online elements) is the Crime Survey for England and Wales (www.crimesurvey.co.uk). The design of the questionnaire will determine the type and quantity of information the researcher receives back.

A survey can feature:

- **closed questions**—with a set way of responding (for instance, a yes–no scale or a ratings scale);
- **open-ended questions**—with participants able to elaborate on their responses at length.

Interviews

An interview is a one-to-one survey where participants respond verbally to spoken questions from a researcher. Interviews may be conducted face-to-face and in person, via telephone or online (for example, via Zoom).

Interviews may also contain closed and open questions and can take the following formats:

- **structured interviews**—following a set list of questions in a rigid format;
- **semi-structured interviews**—following a set list of questions, but supplementing and expanding upon these with extra questions that the interviewer feels might be useful at the time;
- **unstructured interviews**—flexible, improvised, open-ended, not following a set of questions;
- **focus group**—a form of interview conducted with a group of participants (see **Figure 4.8**).

The epistemologies underpinning surveys depend on how that survey is designed and executed (such as how the data are collected and analysed). For example, questionnaires or interviews consisting entirely or predominantly of closed questions that require quantifiable responses (such as ratings scales, yes/no answers) can be categorised as quantitative methods with a positivist epistemology, as they produce quantified, numerical data that can be statistically tested to identify cause–and–effect relationships between variables. Conversely, surveys that contain open questions can be more qualitative in approach and interpretivist in epistemology because they explore how participants construct and make meaning of their experiences in the social world (Lamputtang, 2019; King and

Figure 4.8 Focus groups are a form of interview conducted with a group of participants. Here, the group is being observed by researchers

Source: Linda Nylind for The Guardian

Wincup, 2008). Where surveys contain both closed and open questions and response formats (for example, a **semi-structured interview**, a questionnaire with ratings and narrative sections), they offer perhaps the best example of a mixed methodology. Mixed surveys represent a realist/pragmatist epistemology that applies the respective strengths of both quantitative and qualitative methods to practical research objectives in the real world.

Surveys provide specific benefits to knowledge in criminology. For example, structured surveys offer similar advantages to experiments in terms of the standardisation of methods and the consequent reliability and generalisability of methods and results. This is a particular advantage of quantitative questionnaires and more structured forms of interview. Certain forms of survey are cheap to administer (for example, questionnaires, especially online versions) and can collect a large amount of information quickly (for example, questionnaires, large focus groups). More flexible, qualitative versions of surveys can benefit knowledge further by identifying the personalised understandings that people have in relation to different elements of their lives (Hennink et al., 2020; Case, 2006). Collecting such data can extend knowledge creation beyond the more reductionist understandings produced by narrow, quantitative, closed questions.

As with all applied research in criminology, it is vital that we reflect on the validity of the knowledge that would be generated and, in this regard, surveys can have similar limitations to experiments. Both research participants and researchers can—whether deliberately or inadvertently—damage the validity of survey results.

Research participants (typically called 'subjects' in experiments) may change their behaviour and perspectives to fit in with what they perceive that the researcher, the research context, or other participants (in the case of focus groups) desire(s), displaying what are called **demand characteristics** (Gilbert, 2001). Where demand characteristics are caused by the perceived needs of the researcher, this can reflect the power dynamics in the survey situation—the questioner/interviewer holds the majority of the power to determine the survey context, process, content, and outcomes. A typical demand characteristic in a job interview, for example, is to artificially present the best version of yourself possible—this is known as **social desirability bias** (Gray, 2013).

In addition to actively changing their behaviour to *fit* the perceived desires or needs of the researcher or study, survey participants may also damage the validity of a study by withholding or distorting information—a kind of inverted demand characteristic. This can be a result of belligerence (deliberate hostility or argumentativeness) or mistrust of authority figures, for example in a police interview (another power dynamic in an interview context), but can also be due to apprehension or embarrassment caused by power dynamics in a sensitive survey situation and/or interviewer characteristics that may discourage full disclosure of information. For example, there may be significant power differentials and issues of researcher suitability in interview contexts where an older male interviewer questions teenage girls about their experiences of sexual abuse by older men (gender and age issues), where adult professionals ask children about their illegal activities (age issues), or where a white interviewer explores negative experiences of the criminal justice system with black and ethnic minority participants (ethnicity issues).

As we have noted, researchers themselves hold a lot of power in a survey or experiment context. They choose what questions to ask, who to ask (which group of the population), how to ask, how they allow participants to respond (such as response categories in questionnaires, time allowed for answers in interviews), and how to select and interpret the answers. As well as influencing responses through their role, context, or characteristics, researchers can also artificially manipulate participants' behaviour either deliberately (for instance, through leading or biased questions) or unintentionally (for instance, through non-verbal behaviour in interviews or confusing questions) (Westmarland, 2011; King and Wincup, 2008). **What do you think? 4.2** provides a good example of how leading questions can be used—read the transcript and consider whether this technique actually helped or hindered the interviewer's pursuit of complete and valid information.

The very choice of a particular form of survey as a research method illustrates a researcher's subjectivity, showing their preference/bias for creating particular forms of knowledge and for a certain form of data. For example, questionnaires tend to collect large amounts of quantitative data from closed questions, whereas interviews and focus groups produce more qualitative data, which may then be quantified (Creswell, 2013). An example of how the methodological preferences of a survey researcher have influenced knowledge production is provided by the *Cambridge Study in Delinquent Development* (West and Farrington, 1973; see also **Chapter 9**). The researchers drew heavily on interviews and questionnaires to identify the best predictors of youth crime, and national preventative interventions have centred around these predictors ever since. However, the study population was predominantly white and male, so although subsequent understandings of and responses to youth crime based on this study might be suitably interpretivist and qualitative (Hennink et al., 2020; Walker, 2020), they may also be androcentric and ethnocentric. The study's explanations and recommendations would need to be examined further before they could be used to inform interventions to girls or black and ethnic minority young people.

WHAT DO YOU THINK? 4.2

Using leading questions to interrogate evasive politicians

The 13 May 1997 edition of the BBC current affairs programme *Newsnight* remains one of the best examples of the effective use of leading questions. The political interviewer Jeremy Paxman used this technique to interrogate former UK Home Secretary, Michael Howard (the man who claimed 'prison works'), and the interview became famous for Paxman's repeated attempts to lead Howard into admitting that he had threatened to overrule the head of Her Majesty's Prison Service (Derek Lewis) regarding the dismissal of the governor of Parkhurst Prison (John Marriott). Howard ultimately sacked both Lewis and Marriott. The implication throughout was that Howard had exceeded his powers as Home Secretary. The interview is equally famous for Howard's repeated attempts to evade Paxman's central question, yet all the while continuing to assert that he had not overstepped his authority. The crux of the interview was:

Paxman (P): Did you threaten to overrule him [Lewis]?

Howard (H): Mr Marriott was not suspended.

P: Did you threaten to overrule him?

H: I have accounted for my decision to dismiss Derek Lewis.

P: (overlapping) Did you threaten to overrule him?

H: (overlapping) . . . in great detail before the House of Commons.

P: I note that you're not answering the question whether you threatened to overrule him

H: You can put the question and I will give you an answer.

P: It's a straight yes or no question and a straight yes or no answer. Did you threaten to overrule him?

H: I discussed the matter with Derek Lewis . . . but I did not instruct him because I was not entitled to instruct him.

P: With respect, that is not answering the question of whether you threatened to overrule him.

H: It's dealing with the relevant point of what I was entitled to do . . .

What do you think about the validity and dynamics of this interaction? Specifically:

- Was Paxman using leading questions to get to the truth?
- Did Paxman's repeated use of the same question amount to one huge leading question or leading interview?
- What do you think of Howard's attempts to evade the question? Was he giving answers to 'lead' the interview in a different direction?
- Do you think that such aggressive questioning or evasive responding is justifiable in a political context? What about in the context of criminological research?

We can see that each of the methodological choices a survey researcher makes can influence the scope and usefulness of survey methods and the knowledge produced, be it positivist, interpretivist, or realist/pragmatist. These are not necessarily criticisms/limitations of the survey method, unless researchers choose not to reflect critically on them. Researchers should consider all the issues we have discussed and aim to address them through piloting—pre-testing the practicality and validity of their research methods and processes in order to refine them before fully implementing them.

Observations: researching by watching

Conducting observations in criminology involves researching by watching—observing individuals or groups in real-world settings (in the field) to examine different aspects of their behaviour (Creswell, 2013). Observers may look for certain predicted behaviours to occur (a form of deductive research), recording these on an 'observation schedule' (a list of important behaviours to record), and be prepared to record new and unexpected behaviours, thus generating new knowledge (inductive research). An observation can be **overt** (open), with research participants fully aware that they are being observed, or the observation may be **covert** (closed), with participants being unaware that they are being observed, so not really being participants in any willing/consenting sense.

Researchers can become part of the individual or group environment that they are observing, for example by joining a group or gang and recording them by filming, making an audio recording, or making written notes, which is known as **participant observation**. They can observe without taking a direct part in proceedings, for example watching a group from the outside and filming a documentary, which is known as **non-participant observation** (Noaks and

Wincup, 2004), as shown in **Figure 4.8**. As with surveys, the manner in which the data are collected and recorded determines the form of research conducted. If data are collected in numerical form (for example, using a tick box or tally chart to record items on the observation schedule) then the research is quantitative/positivist, whereas if the data are recorded in written or spoken form (for example, the observer looks for illustrative examples of observation schedule themes) then the research is qualitative/interpretivist (Davies et al., 2011). Similar to surveys, observations can incorporate both forms of research, adopting a realist/pragmatist epistemology that draws upon the benefits of both positivism and interpretivism to meet the specific requirements of the research project.

Observations offer researchers the potential for studies that are more ecologically valid than what is possible with more controlling and artificial research methods such as experiments and surveys, because these observations tend to study real-world behaviour in real-world contexts (Noaks and Wincup, 2004). This can be a particular benefit of low-profile observations that deliberately or unintentionally minimise the observer's interference with the research context (for example, covert, non-participant observations) and therefore also minimise the extent to which participants may react artificially and change their behaviour in some way because they are being observed. The degree to which the researcher is embedded in the research context and their closeness to the research participants can also enhance the researcher's ability to access and understand the perceptions and experiences of those participants in their everyday lives (Crowther-Dowey and Fussey, 2013). The richness of this data can allow researchers to produce knowledge from an interpretivist perspective, enabling a degree of first-hand experience and explanation of (rather than supposition about) behaviours that quantitative methodologies may not be able to achieve.

As with other types of researcher and research method, observers and observations are inherently subjective in terms of what and whom they choose to observe, what they choose to record and not record, and how they choose to understand what they see. However, observational research can go beyond subjectivity and into (unintentional) bias if researchers influence and change the behaviour of who and what they observe by their evident presence, whether the researcher is participating or not. For example, a researcher changes the situations in the daily lives of a person or group by their very presence—known as the **Hawthorne effect** (Chamberlain, 2013)—along with changing the group dynamics and interactions that different people have. This may limit the ecological validity of the method and its findings, particularly if the observer does not reflect on and account for their influence.

The completeness and accuracy of the data collected can also be limited by the observer becoming physically and practically unable to record all aspects of the observation situation, for example because there is too much behaviour to record at any one time, there are too many people in the observation group or situation (who may not all be in the same place at the same time, or are having overlapping conversations which can't be heard properly), or because it is too dangerous to record behaviour in certain situations at certain times. In what is perhaps the most famous and compelling example of an observation study in criminology, Howard Parker's inevitably androcentric 'A View from the Boys', Parker used to write his observation records from memory after the event, but he acknowledged that this process was imperfect, often incomplete, and vulnerable to his own distortions and biases (see Parker, 1974).

CONTROVERSY AND DEBATE 4.4

Observing football hooligans: the film *I.D.*

In the 1995 British film *I.D.*, a group of police officers go undercover to infiltrate a dangerous gang of football hooligans called 'The Dogs', who follow the fictitious London football club Shadwell FC. The officers pose as painter-decorators and begin visiting 'The Rock', a backstreet pub where the gang is based, in order to observe its members, analyse the gang's behaviours, and establish the group's hierarchy and leadership structure. The main character, John, is eventually accepted into the gang following several individual displays of violence against rival gangs and is then invited to accompany the group to matches and pre-arranged fights. This acceptance gives John a closer and more detailed insight into the group members' histories, motivations, personalities, and behaviours.

At set points (first daily, then weekly, then further apart), John joins his colleagues at the police station and other locations to record their observations. However, the validity of John's observations is increasingly weakened by a range of extraneous variables: extended lengths of time between recording episodes, an emerging alcoholism affecting recall during and after observations, and a growing affinity and identification with the characters and behaviours under observation. These extraneous variables lead to more subjectivity and ultimately to John 'going native' by becoming a real-life member of the gang, behaving how the gang members are expected to behave (that is, demonstrating demand characteristics), and influencing the individuals and situations he is meant to be observing (that is, exerting **observer effects**).

Life imitates art: This small screen scenario may not be as far-fetched as you'd think. Have a look at this online article (www.theguardian.com/uk/2011/jan/19/undercover-policeman-married-activist-spy): it covers a real-life example of an undercover police officer who married a woman he was observing as part of an investigation! Do you think that this compromised the validity of his observations and the ethics of the investigation?

Observing people without their knowledge, as in the 'I.D.' example in **Controversy and debate 4.4**, raises ethical issues about invasion of privacy, lack of informed consent (agreement to participate in the study based on full understanding of the research processes, although not necessarily its aims), protection of participants from harm, and researcher safety. It is pretty much impossible to gain informed consent from participants if you do not tell them that you are conducting research (cf. Parker, 1974). In the case of covert observations, participants do not even know that they are participants and they are actually more like the classic experimental 'subjects'. As a researcher, you need a really good reason *not* to obtain informed consent from the individuals you are researching. The best reason is often based on a '**cost–benefit analysis**'—that the benefits to criminological knowledge that will come from the research, which cannot be obtained if participants are fully aware of the research processes or research aims, are greater than the potential costs to the research participants or subjects in terms of them being deceived, manipulated, or not fully informed in the short term (Davies et al., 2011). These costs can then be addressed after the research has been conducted by a process called **research debriefing**, where the researcher explains the research aims and rationale for not obtaining informed consent initially and checks that participants have not suffered long-term harm. Participants could then give their consent retrospectively or withdraw it, as the right to withdraw is a key ethical consideration in our criminological research (Lamputtang, 2019; King and Wincup, 2008).

Secondary analysis: researching by analysing someone else's data

The three criminological research methods we have considered so far (experiment, survey, and observation) involve primary data—in other words, data that you yourself, or your team, has collected. The most common alternative research method in criminology to these three is **secondary data analysis**, which involves the collection, review, and analysis of secondary data; that is, data collected by someone other than the person conducting the analysis. As its name suggests, this is not strictly a research method—instead it is the analysis of the arguments of others or data collected through someone else's research method (Caulfield and Hill, 2014). Secondary data analysis cannot be considered empirical or applied research either, although the original, primary research may have been.

Types of secondary data analysis

Secondary data analysis can be conducted on data obtained from either quantitative or qualitative research. Numerical, statistical data can be collected from, for example, a statistical database, **official statistics** reports, and questionnaires completed by other researchers, and then analysed statistically—representing a positivist approach. Researchers would be looking for causal relationships (that is, whether something or a certain factor, for example low income, appears to cause or influence something else), differences between groups, and correlations between variables. To take an example from our own author team, from 2011 Steve Case was granted access to the youth offending data for England and Wales and analysed it for statistical differences between the reoffending rates of young people in each country, in order to evaluate any differences in the effectiveness of national youth justice policies (Haines and Case, 2015; see also **Chapter 9**). This was an original analytical focus, but as the researcher did not collect the data that was analysed, the research method was secondary analysis of quantitative data.

The data or information used in secondary analysis can also be in qualitative, written form (for example, in books, journal articles, policy documents, newspapers, diaries, blogs, **literature reviews**) and can be analysed for key themes, arguments, and issues (for example, common ideas, dominant perspectives, particular use of language) that allow the researcher to explore and explain a subject area. There are three main types of qualitative secondary data analysis:

- **Thematic analysis** involves identifying patterns or 'themes' within data—you do this when you conduct research for an essay or dissertation and you identify and analyse relevant criminological literature, drawing out themes and arguments that address a set question.

- **Content analysis** involves systematically describing written, spoken, or visual communication, typically depicting the data in quantitative terms. An example might be research exploring and quantifying the use of exaggerated and sensationalist language in newspaper reporting of crime committed by certain groups such as young people and ethnic minorities.
- **Discourse analysis** involves collecting and analysing conversations such as focus group transcripts, social network discussions, and email/telephone/postal correspondence, or from observations of interactions. An example would be criminologists examining the use of inflammatory language on a discussion forum in order to investigate cyber-bullying.

These methods of secondary analysis are often given the overarching term of **documentary analysis**.

Considering the validity of secondary data analysis

Secondary data analysis offers a flexible, and potentially innovative, range of alternative research methodologies to substitute for or supplement the traditional, primary, empirical methods used in criminology. A key advantage of secondary data analysis over methods that collect primary data is that it is an unobtrusive methodological and analytical tool (Robson, 2015), which may therefore minimise the influence of subjectivity on the part of the researched parties, although it is always possible that they displayed subjectivity during the original, primary research process—the secondary data analysis will only be as valid as the original research. Secondary data analysis is relatively cheap and quick compared to other methods, as the main financial and resource costs concern accessing statistics and documents, many of which are freely available electronically or can be made available through local data sharing arrangements and the Freedom of Information Act (HM Government, 2000).

Secondary data analysis also allows researchers to cross-validate data collected through other methods—a process known as **triangulation** (Robson, 2015). In other words, research findings and conclusions can be further tested or developed through secondary data analysis (in the same study), enabling the researcher to reflect on their validity. Of course, it is also possible to generate new questions and understandings/acknowledge existing issues by exploring existing data from new angles. However, we must always bear in mind that the original data has been produced for a different purpose by a different researcher,

to answer a different question, which is a major challenge to the validity of any analysis and our interpretation of data. Indeed, the data may not always be based on empirical research evidence at all, but instead generated through subjectivity and supposition, such as the data contained in certain government policy documents and position statements, pressure group websites, and personal blogs. All of this means that cross-validation/triangulation is essential when using documentary analysis.

A major issue with secondary data analysis could be labelled 'double subjectivity' (**Figure 4.9**). The validity of the data collected (which data sets or documents were chosen, and how), the analysis (the chosen method of analysis), and the interpretation of data (which findings we choose to present or reject) can be influenced by the subjectivity of the researcher who is conducting the secondary data analysis. However, because researchers rely on secondary data to produce secondary data analysis, this validity could be further influenced by the subjectivity of the original researcher—hence double subjectivity. It is difficult and painful enough for researchers to reflect honestly on the impact of their own subjectivity on their research. It is more difficult, even impossible at times, to fully know the subjectivity of others. The subjectivity, influences (external and internal), and even the research methods of other researchers are not always documented, clarified, fully discussed, or acknowledged. For example, how did the researcher collect, analyse, and interpret the quantitative statistics or qualitative literature and why did they make these decisions and not others. It can be difficult to discern the agenda of an author or contributor to discourse (Westmarland, 2011) unless it has been made explicit on the page, in the conversation, or identified at some other point via a survey—unless the researcher has fully disclosed their methods and been reflexive regarding their subjectivity, epistemology,

Figure 4.9 A major issue with secondary data analysis is 'double subjectivity', where research findings are influenced by the subjectivity of both the current and the original researcher

Source: PixabayPexels

and positionality. Certain documents, conversations, and statistical datasets are authored anonymously, anonymised, or are the product of multiple authors, so it is impossible to pin down who wrote what and why.

Unless we are aware of the extent and nature of the subjectivity of other researchers when we analyse their work (sometimes they might have provided a 'positionality statement' reflecting on the different elements of their positionality—Savin-Baden and Howell-Major, 2013), our capacity to judge the validity of the research is limited, as is what we can know about criminology from their data and our subsequent analysis of it (see Case in Vaidya, 2015).

Multiple and mixed research methods: researching by combining methods

Quantitative and qualitative research methods can be used alongside one another at different stages of a research project to answer different questions, described as **multi-method models**, or combined with other methods to produce more comprehensive and triangulated knowledge in answer to the same question, known as **mixed methods** (Heap and Walters, 2019). This can be a very useful research technique because, as you know by now, research methods used in isolation have certain limitations regarding what and how they can study, what they are able to conclude, and the forms of knowledge they are able to produce. Combining them can allow methods to build on the strengths and compensate for the limitations of one another (see Robson, 2015), although of course you must also guard against the combined limitations of different methods overwhelming their benefits when applied.

Multiple and mixed method designs have increased in popularity across the social sciences in recent years, including in criminology (Heap and Walters, 2019; Creswell, 2013). A particular appeal of multiple and mixed methods beyond the benefits of triangulation is the ability to explore several questions or the same question from different angles within the same study, therefore producing a broader range and depth of cross-validated data and (hopefully) knowledge as a result (Robson, 2015). Multiple and mixed method designs, therefore, can potentially benefit research designed to be conducted over long periods with multiple data collection points (that is, longitudinal research), as these designs have the objective of measuring trends and developments in behaviours and perspectives over time (Heap and Walters, 2019; Bryman, 2021). For example, if you were interested in researching why people commit crime, you could start with a documentary analysis of relevant empirical research or theoretical publications in order to identify the most popular explanations for crime. You could then formulate these explanations into a questionnaire full of closed questions that measure the most common explanations across a certain population in a certain place. You could follow this with an interview asking a select group of people (such as those identified by the questionnaire as the most typical offenders) if any of the most common explanations apply to them and, if so, how and why they influence offending behaviour. See **What do you think? 4.3**, which raises similar issues as well as questions specific to the example of a local crime prevention programme.

As we noted earlier in the discussion of knowledge in criminology in **section 4.2**, in the second half of the 20th century there was a debate between social science researchers regarding the relative merits of quantitative and qualitative methods and the (un)suitability of combining the two approaches—Oakley's (1999) 'paradigm wars'. Some researchers have opposed the idea of combining research methods that aim to create knowledge in different ways (cf. Lincoln and Guba, 1985). In other words, it was once considered wrong to merge quantitative positivist methods, focused on identifying cause-and-effect relationships, with qualitative interpretivist methods, focused on identifying meanings and understandings.

In the 21st century, we are more concerned with realist pragmatism in criminology—what works practically to generate knowledge of our real, complex world (cf. Gray, 2013). That said, as we now know, a big problem associated with using research methods to study and learn about criminology can be a lack of critical reflection/reflexivity—that researchers may ignore or neglect the limitations of their chosen methods and exaggerate the usefulness of their research projects, whilst also ignoring the influence of their own subjectivity, suppositions, and methodological principles on their research choices, analyses, and conclusions (Savin-Baden and Howell-Major, 2013). Clearly, this could be even more problematic when attempting to use several methods in multiple or mixed method models, with each model full of the same influencing factors. The rationale for choosing multiple and mixed methods and for conducting them in specific ways is not always discussed in detail (it is not unusual in criminology to find multiple and mixed methods employed for no obvious or stated reason other than that they seem fashionable or exciting); this could indicate that subjectivity and supposition are driving research study choices in preference to pragmatism.

Innovations in research

So far, we have covered the most common research methods, but criminology is a constantly evolving

WHAT DO YOU THINK? 4.3

Using multiple and mixed methods to design a local crime prevention programme

Let us say that you become part of the team in your local authority Community Safety Department and you are asked to prevent crime in a socially deprived neighbourhood that has been identified as having a growing crime problem. How would you go about researching the issue? Specifically:

- How would you identify the most important targets (for example, behaviours, areas, organisations, people, ages, ethnic groups, genders) for any interventions?
- How would you explore potential explanations for offending behaviour amongst these target groups?
- How would you establish how a particular intervention was meant to 'work' to prevent offending?
- Would you use a multi-method or mixed method design? Neither?
- Would this design give you advantages over using a specific research method in isolation?

---

discipline, and the ways of doing research evolve with it. In recent years, criminologists have been employing new methods for studying crime and working with research participants, for example visual and digital methodologies (see Jacobson and Walklate, 2020). However, even though these new methods offer exciting ways of producing new knowledge and conducting research, as we have learnt, the criminologists who use them will need to remember that no method is free from supposition and subjectivity. We discuss more recent methodological innovations and their related ethical considerations in **Chapter 32**. If you are interested in learning more about these developments, you may also want to read Jacobson and Walklate (2020).

4.7 Conclusion

Research is an imperfect, complex process with many external and internal influences on the methods chosen and the validity of the findings and conclusions produced—that is, the knowledge created. Reflecting critically on the subjectivity, supposition, and study methods that guide the generation of knowledge in criminology can help us to become active and productive criminologists. It is important to remember that subjectivity is not only inevitable, but also constructive—it guides and shapes the arguments that researchers make to further knowledge in criminology. Subjectivity is itself guided and shaped by various external and internal influences that change over time and that we are either aware or unaware of—an issue that we must reflect on through a constant process of reflexivity. Subjectivity is also influenced by supposition—the way that humans consciously and subconsciously fill the gaps in the knowledge we have, so that we can retain the illusion of control over and understanding of our world.

Reflecting critically upon and challenging the accepted knowledge base and the accepted means of knowledge creation is central to being a student of criminology and to becoming a criminologist. The need to challenge is a challenge in itself. Criminology is a multi-headed, multi-directional, unstable, fascinating subject. Just as you should challenge and question established methods and knowledge (including your own), so criminology and criminologists constantly challenge accepted wisdom to push the boundaries of knowledge creation. As a student and as a criminologist, you can contribute in a meaningful way to this dynamic enterprise. Criminology is a subject that is broad-minded, transparent, and open (even vulnerable) to criticism and enhancement, and, what's more, the knowledge to which you may contribute can make a real difference to real people. Criminology exists and develops in the real world—the world that you study and study within. Be brave and ambitious—value your potential to contribute to knowledge in criminology by analysing what exists and by producing new understandings. If we can 'know' anything from this chapter, it is that reflexivity is crucial in our study of criminology, so with this in mind, remember your ABC!

SUMMARY

After reading this chapter and working your way through its features you should now be able to:

- **Consider from a critical viewpoint what is knowledge in criminology, and how it is produced**

This chapter invited you to consider critically how we produce knowledge in criminology. We argued that criminological knowledge is the product of theory and research guided by subjectivity (external and internal), supposition (educated guesswork, prediction), and study (research and scholarship), each of which can be enhanced by the producer's ability to be reflexive. We presented 'knowing about crime' not as a collection of facts, but as understanding how debates, issues, and theories are socially constructed products of subjectivity and the particular epistemology adopted by the researcher.

- **Understand what is meant by subjectivity, supposition, and study (through research) in relation to knowledge production**

In criminological terms, subjectivity refers to the personal opinion, preferences, experiences, perspectives, and agendas of knowledge producers, whilst supposition refers to guesswork, assumption, estimates, speculation, and prediction. For our purposes, study mainly relates to the generation of evidence through research.

- **Critically evaluate the benefits and limitations of different research study methods for creating criminological knowledge**

The chapter outlined and reviewed the key methods used for quantitative and qualitative research study in criminology: experiment, survey, observation, secondary analysis, and mixed methods. The strengths and limitations of each approach were evaluated, with a particular focus on the importance of researcher reflexivity for minimising validity issues caused by subjectivity and supposition.

- **Explore how subjectivity, supposition, and study interact with, and impact on, understanding and knowledge production in criminology**

We argued that subjectivity and supposition interact with and influence (research) study, mainly the validity and applicability of the evidence and knowledge produced through different methods. We presented subjectivity and supposition as largely inevitable—but not necessarily negative—elements of a practical and realistic research process that can lead to comprehensive and fit-for-purpose knowledge in criminology if the researcher is suitably reflexive.

 Test your understanding of the chapter's key points by attempting the self-test questions on the **online resources** at www.oup.com/he/case2e

REVIEW QUESTIONS

1. What do you understand by the term 'subjectivity' and can you provide examples of such?
2. What effect can supposition have on research?
3. What is meant by the term 'black box' supposition?
4. Outline the advantages and disadvantages of the different types of surveys: questionnaires, interviews, and focus groups.

5. How would you assess if an observational method of data collection is viable for your research requirements?
6. Why is it important to acknowledge your own subjectivity when conducting research?
7. What are the potential benefits of employing a mixed methods approach?

 Access the **online resources** at www.oup.com/he/case2e to check your answers to the review questions.

FURTHER READING

Chamberlain, J. M. (2013) *Understanding Criminological Research: A Guide to Data Analysis.* **London: Sage.**
A clear and accessible step-by-step guide to conducting criminological research and analysing data, illustrated by useful case studies.

Chamberlain, J. M. (2015) *Criminological Theory in Context: An Introduction.* **London: Sage.**
A lively, concise, and definitive guide to the historical development of criminology as an academic discipline. The book presents an overview of a range of different theories of crime and analyses the strengths and weaknesses of each theory discussed.

Caulfield, L. and Hill, J. (2018) *Criminological Research for Beginners: A Student's Guide* **(2nd edn). Abingdon: Routledge.**
This is a comprehensive guide to understanding and undertaking research in criminology and will be a helpful aid for a third-year project or dissertation.

Davies, P. and Francis, P. (2018) *Doing Criminological Research.* **London: Sage.**
A collection of high-quality and accessible accounts of doing criminological research in the real world.

Finch, E. and Fafinski, S. (2019) *Criminology Skills* **(3rd edn). Oxford: Oxford University Press.**
This text covers practical, academic, and research skills for the study of criminology, including comprehensive coverage of research methods, ethics, and data analysis.

 Access the **online resources** to view a wealth of extra information relating to your study of criminology, including self-test questions, answers to review questions, and links to other resources that will help you enjoy and fulfil your potential within your studies.
www.oup.com/he/case2e

CHAPTER OUTLINE

5.1	Introduction	124
5.2	How to approach crime statistics	124
5.3	The development of national crime statistics	127
5.4	Police recorded crime statistics	130
5.5	The Crime Survey for England and Wales	136
5.6	Conclusion	142

5

Crime statistics

KEY ISSUES

After studying this chapter, you should be able to:

- understand how statistics relate to the study of criminology, and how to use them effectively;
- appreciate why governments may want to collect data on crime, how they collect it, and how their methods have changed over time;
- identify the main problems with police recorded crime statistics and understand what is meant by the 'justice gap';
- critically assess the Crime Survey for England and Wales (CSEW) as a way of measuring crime and its trends in those countries.

5.1 Introduction

In **Chapter 4**, we discussed the different ways of producing criminological knowledge. In this chapter we are going to look at a specific form of such knowledge: statistics. Statistics are an important part of criminological studies, as they enable us to move from exploring, to explaining, to responding to crime (see **Figure 1.1**). They can give us an indication of how much 'crime' is happening, for example how many robberies or car thefts have been counted in a particular year and area. They also help us identify and assess trends and patterns, such as shifts in types of crimes and perpetrators (like whether there are increasingly more burglaries than assaults, or more women committing violence), rises or falls in the total number of offences, and increases or decreases in what we may consider to be more serious acts of deviance, like assault or murder. Essentially, statistics help us learn more about the scale and nature of a perceived social 'problem' and the trends associated with it. This knowledge then enables us to decide on the appropriate response(s), and for 'society' and its state agencies to implement them—whether this be in terms of attempting to eradicate the issue, control it, or simply to give the impression of addressing and managing it in some way.

Although statistics can be extremely useful, in this chapter we will be continually emphasising the need to approach them with caution and an ABC (*Always Be Critical*) mindset. As we saw in **Chapter 4**, this is the approach we should take with all criminological information—whether this is what we hear in lectures, what we read in academic studies, or our own thoughts and beliefs—but it is particularly true of statistics. Statistical representations can be very persuasive as they look very much like 'facts' and are often accompanied with powerful claims about what they tell us about the 'real world'. From a very young age, we are taught to place great value on such 'hard facts'—information that we believe has been objectively collated—so it can be tempting to take them at face value, but as a criminology student you need to take a closer and more critical look. All statistics have a background and a story to tell about how they were produced; they can be misleading; and they do not always reflect the whole picture.

In addition to making you aware of the potential issues with crime statistics and helping you cultivate a critical approach towards them, over the course of this chapter we look at the development of UK crime statistics and see how these have culminated in the wealth of statistical data that we have at our disposal today. We then look at the two main sources of UK crime statistics: police recorded crimes and the Crime Survey for England and Wales.

5.2 How to approach crime statistics

We have established that statistics play an important role in the criminological quest of exploring, explaining, and responding to crime (as reflected by **Parts 2**, **3**, and **4** of this book). Criminologists are social scientists and as such will use (and often generate) statistics as evidence to develop and support their arguments (see **Chapter 4**). However, this 'evidence' does not speak for itself; it has to be analysed and tested before it can be used. If we think about this in forensic terms, we can compare it to the fact that a splash of blood is just a splash of blood until we examine it—see **Figure 5.1**. Only when we know if it comes from a stubbed toe or a dead body can we use it to help decide if a murder has taken place. With crime statistics, the numbers become interesting and revealing when we interrogate and unpick them, using them to test our ideas and to help us ask challenging questions—and then to evaluate the response.

Think about the number of TV advertisements that claim to 'prove' that a particular shampoo/toothpaste/fruit drink is more popular or effective than its rivals. If you read the small print carefully, you will usually see that where a face cream claims that '75 per cent of women said their wrinkles had got smaller', the figures are in fact based

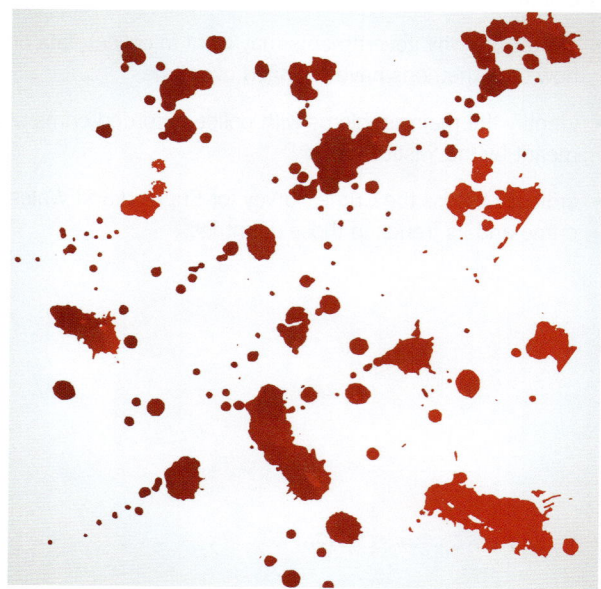

Figure 5.1 We must always analyse the source of our statistical evidence, just like we would with forensic evidence in a crime scene

Source: Starline/Free Ink

on a very small sample of eight or nine people testing the product. This obviously makes them less compelling!

Let's explore the potential issues associated with crime statistics through an example. Suppose we simply wanted to find out how much crime had been recorded in England and Wales over the last century. We could look up the data (using one of the sources we will be discussing later in this chapter) and easily plot a graph (a frequency distribution) which would look something like the one in **Figure 5.2**. However, what do such graphs actually tell us? Simply look at this one for a moment. Make a note of the sorts of stories it may tell.

First, hopefully we can all agree that the graph's sinister-looking upward line shows that crime has increased over this period. You *could* therefore argue that it proves our era is more criminal (and by implication dangerous) than that experienced by previous generations, who lived in more peaceful times. What else can we say? Look carefully for the points of greatest increase. Where are these, according to this source? It would appear from the graph that crime in England and Wales is predominantly a post-war (1945 onwards) phenomenon with significant increases each decade from 1955 to 1995 but with an odd dip around 1997. If we wanted to, we could infer many other tales from such a graph as shown in this figure. The big question is whether or not we would be fully *justified* in doing so.

So, let us think about what the graph does *not* tell us—the chart's limitations. For instance, it does not tell us what types of crime are being committed. Would we look at it differently if it were a chart showing murder rates, or a chart showing incidents of failure to pay parking tickets? What sorts of crimes are being included, and which are being left out? It is crucial to remember that crime is a social construct that changes with time (see **Chapter 2**); so things such as health and safety offences or domestic violence will not have been recorded as crimes for the majority of years in this graph.

By now you are probably wondering if you can trust anything you see and take it at face value. Good! That's exactly the kind of cautious, critical response you need to have when dealing with this kind of simple timescale frequency distribution (in other words, a line plotting incidence over time), especially one which shows crime on an ever-upward march. Another example of a graph to which you would need to apply this critical approach is provided in **Figure 5.3**. Here, the line—perhaps surprisingly—is travelling downwards more smoothly after 1990 than **Figure 5.2**. It is based on survey data from the British Crime Survey (BCS) which has been superseded by the Crime Survey for England and Wales (CSEW), surveys that were taken in the years across the bottom axis of the graph, and its vertical axis measures the total number of crimes that year, in millions. So, you can use it to explain

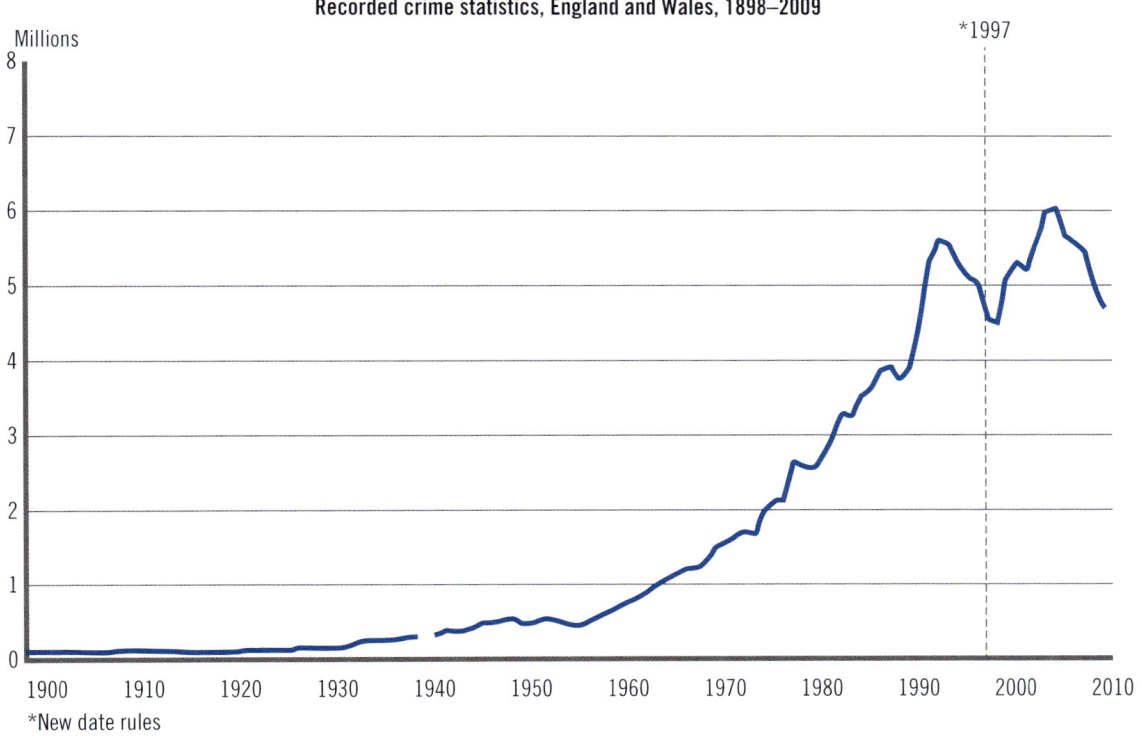

Figure 5.2 This graph purports to show us how much crime has been committed in England and Wales during the last century. But what does it really tell us?

Source: The Home Office, content available under the Open Government Licence v3.0

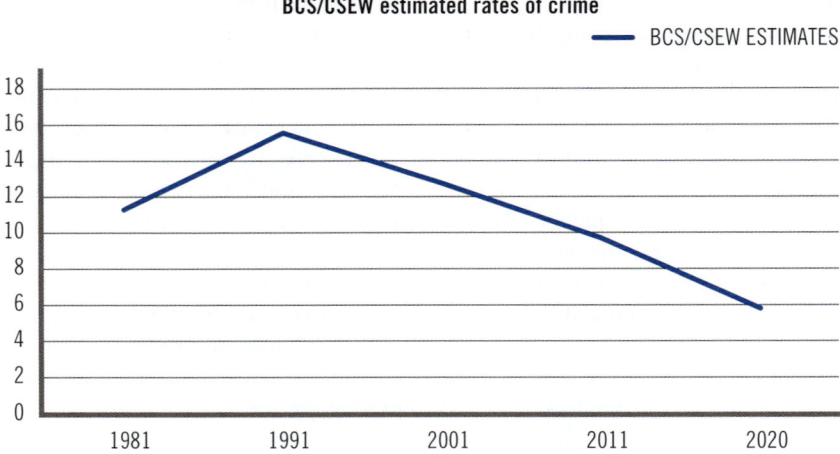

Figure 5.3 Figures from the British Crime Survey and the Crime Survey for England and Wales (1981–2020) suggest that there was far less crime in 2020 than in 1981. Can we take this data at face value?

Source: Office for National Statistics (www.ons.gov.uk), content available under the Open Government Licence v3.0

that in 1981 there was an estimate of around 11 million counts of crime, with the latest figure showing it as under 6 million. Hopefully, you are immediately questioning the accuracy of these figures.

What these examples show us is that there are no easy answers when assessing trends in crime, as the data depends on so many factors like how we define crime and which crimes we include. To further illustrate this example, **Figure 5.4** highlights some of the known differences in the official measurements of crime—the CSEW and police recorded crime. We use this particular graph because of the way it conveys information—the different colours and shades clearly illustrate the changes that have been made over the years to both the CSEW (the line)

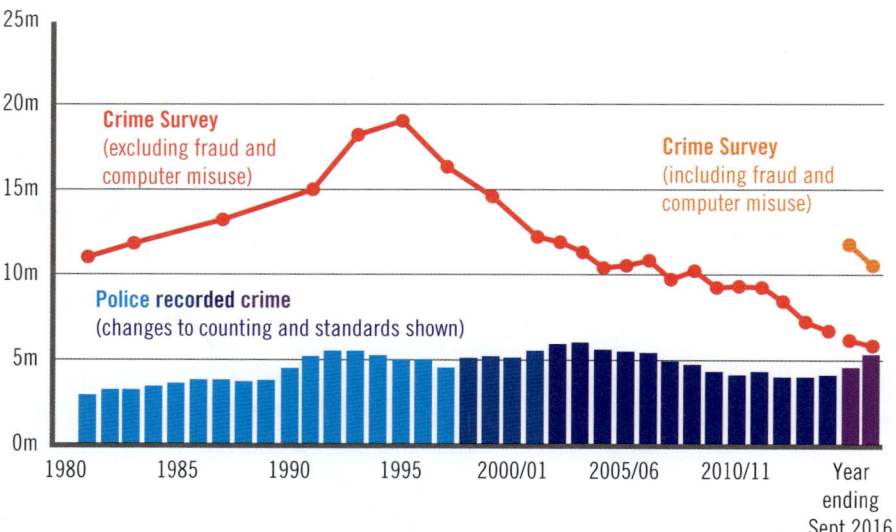

*Police recorded crime: old counting rules pre-1998, National Crime Recording Standard post–2002. Police figures are not reliable indicators of crime trends.

Figure 5.4 The offences estimated by the Crime Survey and recorded by the police (calendar years 1981–97, financial 1998/99–2014/15, ending September thereafter) illustrate the differences between 'official' measurements of crime

Source: Full Fact.org

and to police recorded crime (the bars), for example that the CSEW was expanded to include fraud and computer misuse in 2015. Additionally, **Figure 5.3** demonstrates that police recorded crime has fluctuated annually upwards and downwards since the mid-1990s, yet the more 'complete' CSEW measures of crime indicate a consistent downward trajectory over this period. This discrepancy points to the key dilemma faced by researchers in this area; that statistics need to have '*comparability* of what is being measured year to year ... [but] if one sticks rigidly to the same approach every year, the statistical series will lose both *comprehensiveness* and *relevance to current crime problems*' (Maguire and McVie, 2017: 171, emphasis in original). These three points of comparability, comprehensiveness, and relevance are all essential if we want to assess claims about rates of crime over periods of time.

It should be clear by now that there is more to crime, criminals, and criminal statistics than initially meets the eye. The best way to approach crime statistics is therefore to deconstruct and critically question them, and to be aware that crime data perhaps tells us much more about government priorities, public fears, and criminal justice practices than it does about the 'true' picture of crime itself.

With these issues in mind, let's look at the development of statistics on crime, and what statistics are available to criminologists today.

5.3 The development of national crime statistics

There are two main sets of data relating to crime in England and Wales:

1. Police recorded statistics, which are collated by police forces from the crimes committed that they record.
2. Mass victimisation surveys—principally the CSEW, which asks people to relate their experiences of crime as victims.

Before we look at these sources in more detail in **sections 5.4** and **5.5**, respectively, it is important to have an understanding of how they developed—in other words, how the gathering, analysis, and use of crime data has progressed from the simple recording of crimes and punishments to detailed, mass recording of both crime and social issues at a national level. We will also look at the relationship between these two sets of statistics, and the influence they have had on policy over the years.

Although our focus here is on England and Wales, it is worth bearing in mind that most industrialised countries today also produce such statistical measures, but making meaningful international comparisons is very difficult given that different forms of crime are defined and measured differently across jurisdictions. A branch of criminology that looks at crime on a more comparative, international scale is global criminology, which we cover in more detail in **Chapters 13** and **14**.

The historical development of crime statistics

The prison at Newgate in London was in use for over 700 years, and even today its site is still concerned with the delivery of justice as it is now the location of the Old Bailey (properly known as the Central Criminal Court of England and Wales). What is interesting from a statistical point of view is that from 1773, a monthly list of all the executions that had taken place at the prison was published. This gruesome 'Newgate Calendar' was hugely popular and went on to become a book giving biographical details of famous criminals like Dick Turpin and Moll Cutpurse, but in its original form it was probably one of the first examples of a public statistical record relating to crime and criminals (see **Figure 5.5**).

The first census

More formal (and less sensationalised) figures began to be kept throughout the course of the 19th century. This was partly due to improved communications, making it possible for the central collection and storage of national or regional data, but it also reflects the Victorians' fondness for record-keeping and measurement. The first national census was held in 1801, and in 1836 it became a legal requirement to register births, marriages, and deaths, creating significant amounts of data that needed analysis. Statistical techniques were developed in order to make sense of the information; in 1841, for instance, the census questions were worded in such a way that it helped to identify risks to public health, while the requirement to record causes of death on a death certificate meant that the dangers of particular occupations could be measured. One of the men responsible for this approach to data collection, William Farr (1807–83), redefined statistics as 'a *method of analysis* rather than a social discipline in itself' (Magnello, 2011: 270) and that is a useful summary when we think about the use of figures in a criminological sense.

Figure 5.5 The 'Newgate Calendar', in circulation from 1773, is probably one of the first examples of a public statistical record relating to crime and criminals in England and Wales

Source: Public domain

using the new tools of statistics and their analysis to help them do so.

The first large-scale crime survey

At the same time that Snow and Whitehead were using data to improve public health, the social researcher and reformer Henry Mayhew (1812–87, see **Figure 5.6**) was publishing his vast survey on *London Labour and the London Poor* (1851). Ten years later, this work had a fourth volume that recorded Mayhew's interviews with an enormous range of characters from the poor of the city, giving details of their dress, habits, and even their accents and dialects. His overall aim was to 'give the rich a more intimate knowledge of the sufferings, and the frequent heroism under those sufferings, of the poor' (1861: li); in other words, to try prove the need for change.

The fourth volume of Mayhew's work included a detailed focus on crime and criminals, where he sought to classify his subjects, identifying a 'criminal class' that included such people as beggars, thieves, and fraudsters—whose refusal to work was, he believed, due to a moral defect. However,

Much of this new analytical work was put to use in the public health arena. For instance, over two weeks in 1854, an outbreak of cholera killed over 700 people in one London parish alone. Doctor John Snow and the Reverend Henry Whitehead used statistics to prove that the source was one particular parish water pump; the pair mapped the outbreak, showing how it clustered around the infected pump, helping to save lives and to found the emerging science of epidemiology (the study of patterns in diseases and deaths in a given population). In this case, the Board of Guardians, the Medical Committee of the General Board of Health, and the Parish Paving Committee were also involved in investigating what had happened, a situation that reflected the growing trend for a bureaucratic and official response to public matters. It is perhaps no surprise, then, that an increasingly well organised state system, one that protected its people from polluted water, would also seek to protect them from the 'moral pollution' of crime (and thus to control criminals),

Figure 5.6 *London Labour and the London Poor*, published by social researcher Henry Mayhew, was effectively the first large-scale crime survey in England and Wales

Source: Public domain

he also recognised a second group, people who committed 'crime' as a result of poverty or circumstances—for example, classifying as prostitutes the widows of servicemen who lived with their new partners without marrying them because remarriage would mean the loss of their pensions. As part of this work, Mayhew and his collaborators mapped incidents of crime and correlated this data with other social concerns, such as illegitimacy (people whose parents were not married at the time of their birth) or illiteracy (people unable to read and write), again using the results to highlight links between crime, poverty, and social deprivation.

Throughout your study and use of statistics, it is essential to remember that when a correlation is found between things, there is an association between them. It means they are connected somehow, but it is not the same thing as causation. This is a fundamental point that can often be forgotten. Mayhew found there were correlations between incidents of crime and levels of illegitimacy and levels of illiteracy; but his data did not show that either of these two social concerns caused the incidents of crime.

Soon it became clear there was also the potential for such data to be used to influence positive social reform through public policy. The term 'policy' means the strategies in place for improving public life and Mayhew's research showed how such plans could be more informed by using these statistics. Despite his good intentions—using data to prove the need for change—it could be argued that Mayhew's work strengthened existing prejudices amongst the powerful by appearing to confirm existing ideas about the powerless and the poor. However, it was perhaps the work of social reformers such as Mayhew and other pioneering figures such as Charles Booth (1849–1916) and Seebohm Rowntree (1871–1954) that highlighted the need for governments to collect more accurate data on a range of social issues and problems. As a result, the first British national criminal statistics, based on data derived from the police and court records, were published in 1876. The Home Office was responsible for these figures, with their central authority making it possible to find out how much crime was being recorded nationally. This resulted in methods of statistical analysis, such as a frequency distribution, as we saw earlier in **Figure 5.2**.

Crime statistics today

The developments in statistical analysis over the following years mean that today we inherit a situation in which we are faced with huge amounts of knowledge about crime. Ways of manipulating and evaluating statistical data have become vastly more sophisticated; for example, we can easily now obtain data on how much crime there is, what types of offence are being committed, who is being sentenced by the courts, how many injunctions are issued, and the frequency with which various court disposals (community sentences, imprisonment) are being used. The Ministry of Justice, the Home Office, the Office for National Statistics, and other agencies are now producing statistical bulletins on a monthly basis, which are presented in a range of formats (**Figure 5.7**). Other sources of information are available from the Home Office and the Office for National Statistics, both of which provide websites with links to many reports relating to the police and security. Indeed, you could spend hours perusing the thousands of interactive and often very compelling graphs, tables, and data visualisations on crime and its control which are now at your fingertips.

Although there are arguably some downsides to living in today's so-called Information Age (see **What do you think? 5.1**), as a criminology student it means you can soon find reports not just on criminal justice statistics, but also others that relate to civil justice, courts, race and the criminal justice system, gender and the criminal justice system, the prison population, the probation service, reoffending, sexual offences, youth justice, and much more. In other words, there is a wealth of data available for all the modules you will study on your undergraduate degree, and we recommend that you make the most of it.

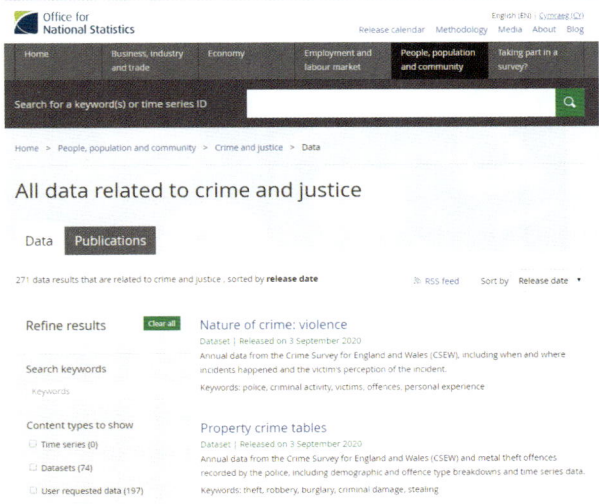

Figure 5.7 The ONS website has a range of reports on crime statistics that are freely available for public use

Source: Office for National Statistics (www.ons.gov.uk), content available under the Open Government Licence v3.0

WHAT DO YOU THINK? 5.1

Crime statistics in the 'Information Age'

Living in the 'Information Age' means we are awash with data. It has become so important that it has been described as 'the new oil' (Kaiser, 2019: 12)—in the sense that it is a valuable commodity—and skills in data manipulation, extraction, and presentation are prized by employers.

Yet there are some potential downsides to the abundance of information. It can tell us a great deal if we know how to approach it critically and cautiously, but the consequences of information overload might be an uncritical acceptance of the data with which we are provided. There is, perhaps, too much information for the average person to sift through and verify, and given the speed at which striking statistics can now be circulated online—often in a condensed form and lacking context (think about the brevity of tweets, for example)—'truth' could be said to be established by the information which receives the most publicity. For example, a 2020 study into how people consumed their news in the 2019 UK General Election campaign found that people relied on familiar sources for their news, with 66 per cent of this time being spent on the websites of BBC News, the MailOnline, *The Guardian*, *The Sun*, and *The Mirror*. Those who used social media (**Figure 5.8**) for news (41 per cent) accessed more online sources than those who did not, and therefore had a more varied consumption of news (Fletcher et al., 2020).

Findings like these suggest that, despite (or even because of) the fact that we have so much data at our fingertips, we still tend to rely on a small number of familiar sources. This behaviour might leave us open to accepting statistics that deliberately distort or manipulate the reality of the facts they supposedly represent, as with the face cream example we discussed in **section 5.2**. And as data becomes ever more sophisticated, the knowledge gap could be said to be widening between the general public and those who understand how to manipulate large data sets, leading to a power imbalance between these two groups that could potentially be exploited, for example for political purposes.

Reflect on these ideas and consider the following questions:

- Where do you most often see crime statistics, and from which sources? Do you tend to rely on particular sources or do you use a variety?
- How much do you trust the statistics you read, especially those in relation to crime? Do you examine them closely or check them against other sources, or do you base your trust on the credibility of the source?
- Are you more or less likely to accept certain crime statistics depending on whether they support your own experiences or viewpoints?
- What might be the potential consequences of the public absorbing misleading information about crime through statistics? (See whether you can predict the kinds of issues we discuss in **Chapter 6**, about crime and the media.)
- Do you think that the events of the Covid-19 pandemic made us better at interpreting and assessing statistics, and more aware of the difficulties involved in developing reliable data, or more likely to accept statistics at face value?

Figure 5.8 Social media sites have been found to encourage users to read a larger variety of online news sources (Fletcher, 2020).
Source: Pixabay.com

5.4 Police recorded crime statistics

Now that you understand how statistics developed to where they are today, it's time to take a more detailed look at the two most widely used sources of statistics, starting with police recorded statistics, which are the statistics that many people expect to see when seeking to understand the rates of crime. There are several important factors you need

WHAT DO YOU THINK? 5.2

How much crime (by category) do you think there is?

There are ten categories of offences that are used by the police to officially record crime; so, if a pie chart was being used to explain this, potentially they could all have equal sized slices. But how likely is that? Have a go at estimating the frequencies in which they get reported by completing the shaded column in **Table 5.1**. The category you think is most frequently reported should be marked as 1, with the second most frequent marked 2, and so on, until you reach the least frequently reported and input a 10.

Once you have done that, have a look at the end of this chapter, where we provide the **official statistics** for the reporting in these categories. You will then be able to complete the whole table by entering these figures into the blank column. This means you will have a clear comparison. Did these statistics differ from what you had imagined? After completing the table, spend a few minutes reflecting on whether any of these categories surprised you and make a few notes on how they differed to what you expected to find.

Offence category	General description	Estimate its frequency (from 1 (most frequent) to 10 (least frequent))	The 2019 recorded crime figures
1. Violence against the person	A very broad category ranging from murder to minor assaults.		
2. Sexual offences	Another very broad term covering rape and indecent assault, but also having sex with a corpse or being a voyeur.		
3. Robbery offences	These are distinct from theft or burglary as they also involve the use of force or fear.		
4. Theft	Includes burglary, vehicle offences, theft from the person, bicycle theft, shoplifting, and other thefts.		
5. Criminal damage and arson	Includes damage to a dwelling, to buildings other than a dwelling, and damage to a vehicle. If inflicted by fire, the offence is recorded as arson.		
6. Drug offences	Includes offences for the possession, distribution, and production of illegal drugs.		
7. Possession of weapons offences	Includes possession of a firearm (both real and imitation) and possession of a knife or bladed article.		
8. Public order offences	Ranging from causing a riot (when 12 or more people threaten violence), violent disorder (3 or more people), to threatening, abusive, or insulting behaviour.		
9. Miscellaneous crimes against society	For all other police recorded crimes where there is no direct victim that do not fit into any other category. Includes dangerous driving, breaching bail, and perjury.		
10. Fraud and computer misuse	Includes fraud by a company director, cheque and credit card fraud, and computer misuse such as: spreading viruses or other malicious software, and hacking or gaining unauthorised access to information.		

Table 5.1 Estimated and recorded figures for the ten categories of offence used by the police

Source: Data from Crime in England and Wales: Appendix tables, Year ending December 2019, Summary Table 3: Police recorded crimes https://www.ons.gov.uk/peoplepopulationandcommunity/crimeandjustice/bulletins/crimeinenglandandwales/yearendingdecember2019

to appreciate before you can analyse any possible accuracy of these statistics, including: the intentions of those recording them, the methods that are used to generate them, and the natural limitations of this type of data. In this section, we will explore each of these factors, but before we consider them, work through **What do you think? 5.2** to start thinking about some of the aspects of recording crime.

The purpose of police recorded crime statistics

Police crime statistics provide data for intelligence-led policing, and so are used for deciding when and where resources will be deployed. This is particularly important in today's times of reduced budgets and decreasing police numbers. One form of statistical analysis is crime mapping, which relies on accurate crime reporting, especially **street crime** and burglary, to pinpoint problematic areas and specific times at which such crimes occur, see **Figures 5.9** and **5.10**. Crime maps were first used in France in the 1830s, thanks to the work of statisticians such as André-Michel Guerry (1802–66) and Adolphe Quetelet (1796–1874). These recorded experiences of crimes against people and property in the different regions of the country; whereas today, street level maps covering all of the UK are readily available through resources such as the national policing website at www.police.uk. Postcodes can be searched on the website's home page to reveal the latest monthly police recorded figures for around a dozen types of crimes that have been reported in that area. Previous time periods can also be searched, with brief details given for each crime and a summary of its outcome. This is undoubtedly an interesting development, as from a police perspective it is

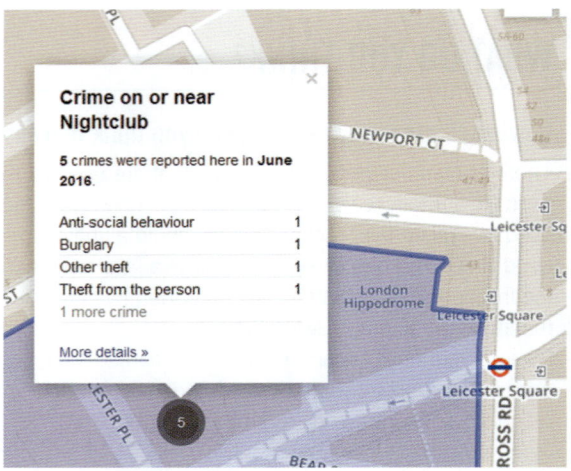

Figure 5.10 Police can use crime mapping to focus on a particular area and pinpoint the types of crime that occur, and when

Source: Crime Mapping—Met police

a positive intervention, leading to more proactive, intelligence-led (that is, based on statistical evidence) forms of policing that aim to prevent crime. In terms of police budgets, it helps the police to deploy their resources in more efficient and cost-effective ways.

On the flip side, however, there is the potential here for the police to target particular areas at particular times which, in turn, might lead to more recorded incidences of a particular form of crime, thus creating the perception of a particular 'crime wave'. It has also been argued by many criminologists, such as Mike Maguire (2002), that the resulting figures are often taken by both journalists and politicians as being an accurate reflection of what is happening, and that this can lead to responses of greater control, increased sentences for particular offences, and a greater fear of crime amongst the public. However, arguably, the 'what is happening' demonstrated by police recorded crime statistics is not necessarily related to the extent and nature of crime in a given year as much as it is reflective of the extent and nature of police activity. This argument is well rehearsed, especially by critical criminologists, who maintain that official crime statistics are social constructions that tell us more about the activity of the criminal justice system than they do about the 'reality' of crime (see **Chapter 18**). Therefore, when evaluating the effectiveness and appropriateness of police targeting of specific neighbourhoods, for example, we should ask ourselves at least two questions.

Figure 5.9 Area around Leicester Square, London. Methods of statistical analysis such as crime mapping can help the police decide when and where resources will be deployed

Source: Crime Mapping—Met police

1. Is targeting justified, for example because a neighbourhood is high risk/high crime, so the approach allows the police to use resources more efficiently?
2. Is targeting a discriminatory and prejudicial practice that 'creates' high-crime neighbourhoods (that is, a '**self-fulfilling prophecy**')?

How police recorded crime statistics are generated

The police recorded crime figures in England and Wales are reliant upon data collected by the police forces that report to the Home Office (not all do, such as the British Transport Police). They also only include what are called 'notifiable offences', so a whole range of what are known as 'summary offences', which are usually thought of as being of a less serious nature, and so are heard at a magistrates' court, are not included. In addition, the police do not record every type or incident of crime that is reported to them, so there will be some incidents that are reported by the public, but not included in the statistics. You might already have realised that these elements of how the statistics are recorded mean that the data are incomplete, and we are only getting part of the story. What's more, we have seen already that the criminal law is a flexible concept that changes over time, and so does the 'notifiable offence' list, as well as Home Office rules on the counting and classification of crimes. These changes make it difficult to compare today with previous eras, but would it surprise you to learn that now, in England and Wales, there are over 100 different categories of recorded crime? Let's examine some of the key things that affect how police recorded crime statistics are generated.

terms) is where a crime takes place, but the record of it somehow gets filtered out during the various phases of the criminal justice process(es). These are cases that may be reported but which do not result in any formal court action like a sentence or fine; this is also sometimes referred to as the 'justice gap'. This can seem shocking—how can a crime simply be ignored? To understand that, we need to think about how and why we consider a crime to have happened in the first place.

It is perhaps useful to think of the criminal justice system as a set of processes (as opposed to being a coherent, seamless system). The first process starts with the reporting of crime by the public and then moves on to the recording and investigation of it by the police. From there, we can move to the decision taken by the Crown Prosecution Service on whether or not to prosecute a crime, before we end up with sentencing processes in the courts (see **Chapters 23–25**).

These stages of the 'system' can be seen as a set of *social processes* in which all the agencies can exercise a degree of discretion. Decisions are also affected by other considerations such as costs, the level of public interest in a case, and the likelihood of securing a conviction. To appreciate the limitations of the figures, it is important to remember the reasons why the police may decide not to record a crime. Read **Conversations 5.1** to find out more about this.

The justice gap (attrition)

The generation of the police figures is also affected by the problem of attrition. Put simply, attrition (in criminological

Under-reporting

We should also keep in mind that something has happened before a crime can be recorded. Crime writers

---

CONVERSATIONS 5.1

A view from the police

with **DC John Harbison**

In my first days of being a police officer I discovered people could call the police, adamant they were a victim of crime, when actually no crime had been committed. Usually, it would be a civil dispute at most, such as a customer refusing to pay for a meal due to poor service or a neighbour playing their music too loud. Be that as it may, when an allegation of crime is made, an officer is duty-bound to record it. Before recording it, however, the officer needs to understand what offence has been committed. Even though officers receive detailed training, they must assess very quickly what offence—if any— has been committed. We can sometimes get it wrong, and fail to understand what crime is being alleged. At the end of the day, police officers are human beings and like everyone can make mistakes.

However, this tends to be rare. Even if officers didn't get the right crime, they will often record something and leave it for more experienced officers to tidy up the report. During my time as a supervisor in a busy Criminal Investigation Department (CID), I spent most of my day going through these reports and justifying why there was either no crime in the first place, or that an incorrect offence had been recorded. It is extremely hard to have a report changed to a 'no crime' and many just get 'screened out', meaning no further investigation would take place but it will still be counted and included in the statistics.

> The process of recording crime has changed many times and, over the years, new crimes have been added to the list of recordable offences. Furthermore, recording systems are much more automated than they were in the past. Today, you can report a crime online without even having to speak to an officer. If you do decide to phone, a Computer Aided Despatch (CAD) gets created. CAD includes a comprehensive geographic information system which allows an operator to log a call, record the information, and use the latest mapping systems to see the location of the reported offence. It is impossible to close a CAD without an outcome, such as someone being charged with the offence, and most CADs will also require a crime reference number before they can be closed. Despite this, from an administrative point of view it is easier to create a crime report in order to close it than it is to justify why there is no report. This means that officers will always be more inclined to create a report in order to cover themselves and show that they have taken some action, however minimal, with the added benefit that this makes it easier to close the CAD too. It is therefore very unlikely that an officer will fail to record a crime out of laziness, as this involves much more work and carries a higher risk.
>
> Even though senior officers will scrutinise recorded crime to make sure it is being reduced, at the end of the day, police officers who are out and about 'on the beat' will care more about helping the public and arresting offenders than about how crimes are being recorded. But police officers are, however, under a lot of pressure to reduce crime and accurate recording is an essential tool in achieving this. So, if we put value on data, we need to make sure we protect it and help those who are compiling it to do so with integrity.
>
> *Detective Constable John Harbison, a police officer with over 15 years' experience in the Metropolitan Police Service*

and historians are often asked what they consider to be the 'perfect crime'. The answer is, of course, that we don't know, because to be perfect, the crime must have gone undiscovered and certainly unsolved! We need to bear this in mind when thinking about crime statistics. If we don't know that there's been a crime, we can't report it.

It might surprise you to learn that out of every 100 crimes committed, fewer than half are reported to the police. This figure roughly halves again (25 of 100 offences) when you look at how many of these are actually recorded as crimes by the police (ONS, 2020), due to some of the issues we explored in the previous section. What's more, of all of these offences, fewer than five of every 100 end up with a caution or conviction (ONS, 2020). This gap between reporting and punishment sees significant variation for different types of offence. For instance, you may have read about concerns being raised about the high attrition rates for sexual offences such as rape (Hohl and Stanko, 2015).

So, what these statistics tell us is that, even when we do detect a crime, we might not choose to report it. The reasons for this can vary widely from fear, to thinking the matter too trivial, to simply not having the time (Flately et al., 2010). One interesting factor that affects people's willingness to report a crime, however, is complicity. If you make a claim on your insurance because you've lost your wedding ring, and you find it after receiving your pay out, you have a choice. You can keep quiet, wear your ring, and keep the money; or you can send the cash back. If you choose the first course, you have committed a crime that nobody will ever know about. Whether or not you even consider yourself to have done something deviant will depend on all sorts of factors, such as your upbringing, your religious faith (or lack of one), your financial situation, and how much you trust your partner not to report you.

All of which goes to illustrate something else we need to think about: how we choose to categorise an act as a crime or otherwise (as discussed in **Chapter 2**), and also whether we think it important to report that crime can be a complicated and variable process that is not always straightforward. It is a series of social processes, which are rooted in our backgrounds, class, education, and personal beliefs, and can affect how we view the police (see **Figure 5.11**). To explore these processes yourself, take a look at **What do you think? 5.3**.

Figure 5.11 Our attitudes towards the police can affect whether or not we choose to report a crime

Source: James R Gibson / Alamy Stock Photo

WHAT DO YOU THINK? 5.3

To report or not to report . . . that is the question

Have you ever been the victim of a crime, or witnessed a crime taking place? What did you do? Did you report it? Why—or why not?

Make a list of some of the reasons why you made the reporting choice you did.

Compare your response to the list below. It is taken from various BCS/CSEW reports on the main reasons why people choose not to report crimes. Would your response have been different if it had been a different category of crime you experienced or saw?

Reasons for not reporting (derived from Flately et al., 2010):

- it seemed trivial;
- the police will be ineffective;
- the police would not be interested;
- nobody would believe me;
- I was too busy;
- I was embarrassed;
- I was too scared or fearful;
- I chose to deal with it in another way.

Now, consider the following list of crime categories:

- bicycle theft;
- vandalism;
- burglary with loss;
- wounding;
- theft from the person;
- theft of vehicle;
- assault with minor injury or no injury.

Which types of crime do you think are most likely to be reported to the police, and why do you think that this might be the case? Jot down your answers and then look at the answers to the exercises at the end of this chapter and compare your responses.

Counting rules

It is important to remember that, in some cases, one incident can lead to more than one crime; for example, the Home Office counting rules for incidents of violence against the person state that if a drunk driver kills his two passengers in one accident, it is recorded as two crimes, one for each victim. This means that there is no definite correlation between numbers of incidents and the resultant number of crimes that show up in the statistics. Changes in the counting rules can therefore result in an increase in the overall levels of recorded crime as well as for specific offences, and this can make attempts to draw comparisons over time meaningless.

How reliable are police recorded crime statistics?

So far, we have considered the factors that might impact the *reliability* of police recorded crime statistics. But how much of an issue are these in practice?

In April 2012, concerns over the police's recording of crime led to the responsibility for the production of the statistics being transferred from the Home Office to the Office for National Statistics (ONS). The problems the police were having were highlighted by scathing assessments in the 2014 report by Her Majesty's Inspectorate of Constabulary (HMIC), which found that the police failed to record one in five crimes that were reported to them. Perhaps the most controversial finding was that it is victims of violent crime (33 per cent) and sexual offences (26 per cent) who are more likely not to have the offences committed against them investigated by the police. In some cases, this could be due to the victim being unwilling to talk to the police, but the HMIC report (2014) found there were other reasons for not recording offences: police practitioners with insufficient knowledge or experience (21 per cent) and inadequate supervision (51 per cent) were cited as the main reasons.

The UK Statistics Authority is the government department responsible for running and overseeing the ONS; it also maintains a national code of practice for official statistics, and accredits the statistics that comply with it as National Statistics. Due to these problems with reliability, it withdrew this status for police recorded crime statistics in 2014. In 2016, the accreditation was restored for the statistics on unlawful deaths, but all other categories remain undesignated (ONS, 2020: para. 3.1), meaning the only official statistics for these offences are those in the CSEW.

So what does this mean for criminologists looking to use police reported statistics to support their work? Inevitably, they—and you—will need to assess the strengths and weaknesses to decide whether they are the best source of data to use—and then proceed with caution!

Strengths of police recorded crime statistics

You may remember that, in **section 5.2**, we discussed the importance of comparability, comprehensiveness, and relevance for a crime statistical series. Over time, the ways that police record crimes have changed, which prevents us from comparing their figures with those from different times. This might be seen as a disadvantage, but arguably these developments have actually made them more accurate and comprehensive. For example, as Maguire and McVie note, the decision 'to promote the summary offences of common assault, harassment, and assault on a constable to the status of notifiable offences . . . added at a stroke over 250,000 extra offences' (Maguire and McVie, 2017: 171).

The recorded crime figures also provide a good indicator of police workload. In addition to use in local crime map analysis, they are seen as a good measure of trends in well-reported crimes (ONS, 2020). This data helps with lower-volume but higher-harm violent offences; where the frequency of offences is low, but inflicts significant harm (for example, murder). This makes police reported statistics a great complement to those in the CSEW because, as we will see in the next section of this chapter, either the survey does not cover these kinds of offences or does not capture them well.

Limitations of police recorded crime statistics

It is also important to remember these statistics have several limitations. They only include 'notifiable' offences (and exclude 'summary' offences), which means they can be affected by legislative change and alterations to the notifiable offence list. This is an important loss in their ability to accurately measure the rate of crime and means they only record crimes deemed to be over a certain level of seriousness. Their credibility is also limited by the research that showed the police do not always record incidences of crime that are reported to them (although simplistic assumptions about the extent of this problem can be challenged by **Conversations 5.2**).

The statistics face the considerable problem that not all crimes that occur are reported to the police. They can also be heavily influenced by current police activities and priorities; these can affect some categories of crime, such as drug possession offences (for example, in contexts where cracking down on drugs offences is a high priority for the police), to the extent that 'in such cases, recorded crime figures may not provide an accurate picture of the true extent of criminality' (ONS, 2020: para. 3.1).

So, overall, we can say that any picture of crime provided by official police recorded crime statistics is far from being a clear one; it is blurred, slanted, and incomplete. Much like when we look at a body of water, we can see beneath the surface, but the depth of detail, the subtleties, and the nuances are absent (**Figure 5.12**).

Figure 5.12 Police recorded statistics can give us a glimpse below the surface of crime, but the limitations of recording practices mean that the insights are not very deep or detailed
Source: luiisrtz/Pexels

5.5 The Crime Survey for England and Wales

By the 1980s, the real limitations of police recorded statistics in England and Wales were widely recognised in government circles, and a new attempt was made to develop a clearer and more accurate research and statistical tool. It was argued that this would help to uncover the so-called 'dark' figure of crime (also known as the 'hidden' figure of crime), as well as provide a more accurate guide for both policymakers and the general public. In 1981, the British government introduced a national crime survey in an attempt to address these issues. This was called the British Crime Survey (BCS), but since 2002 it has been retitled as the Crime Survey for England and Wales (CSEW).

The purpose of the CSEW

As we noted earlier in this chapter, historically speaking, one of the reasons for generating statistical evidence is to help create policies that actually address a particular social problem. The main aims of the CSEW are to uncover the so-called 'dark' figure of crime (those that go unreported or unrecorded) and provide a more accurate picture in terms of the trends of the various types of crime that are being committed. Respondents, who are selected from the general public, are asked about their own **victimisation** (see also **Chapter 7**) as well as their attitudes to issues related to crime, like their general perceptions of crime levels and their thoughts on criminal justice agencies. For instance, respondents are asked to rate their overall confidence in the police and local councils and whether they think these agencies are doing a good, effective, and fair job in addressing local and national crime problems. This information can then feed into public policy to help to control, regulate, and prevent crime. It can help the state to provide appropriate support for victims of crime, as well as to respond to public perceptions of unfairness in the justice system as a whole.

As a research tool, it is now a large (in terms of its sample size) and methodologically sophisticated attempt to estimate a more accurate and realistic reflection of the extent of crime experienced by the population of households in England and Wales. In short, it tries to overcome the very real problems and issues with the reporting and recording of crime that we explored in **section 5.3**.

How CSEW statistics are generated

The CSEW is typically administered by face-to-face interviews, which are now carried out with the assistance of computer-assisted interviewing, which is thought to give the survey results more consistency, compared to a paper-based **questionnaire**. From 1981, the survey ran at (mostly) two-year intervals, but since 2001 it has been a continuous annual survey. In 2020, the survey was carried out via telephone calls as a precaution during the Covid-19 pandemic.

Using a representative sample

The full, complex methodological issues need not concern us too much here, but it is perhaps worth briefly mentioning the basic logic of social survey methodology. As we previously noted, arriving at a complete list of crimes committed in a given area through police reported statistics is an impossible task, especially given the problems of attrition and the number of crimes that are not even reported to the police in the first place. What a social survey does is to take a representative sample of a given population, in this case selected households in England and Wales. It will ask household members to answer its questions and then, through various statistical techniques, it claims to make valid and reliable generalisations from the sample to the population as a whole.

Many students are often sceptical about the claim that from a well-designed survey we can make valid and reliable generalisations that are applicable to the target population (investigate this yourself by trying the activity in **What do you think? 5.4**). The mathematics behind it is very complicated, but remember that the CSEW involves a large team of well-qualified and experienced research designers, researchers, and interviewers to ensure its thoroughness

WHAT DO YOU THINK? 5.4

How easy is it to generate accurate crime statistics?

Imagine that the Chancellor of your university has asked you and your fellow criminology students to design a survey that will produce accurate information about crime rates at your institution. The Vice Chancellor has hinted that this data will be made available to future students and their families, as well as to the press, and will become part of a national survey on campus crime. As we have seen, there are many considerations to bear in mind when trying to produce accurate data on crime. Let us suppose that you make the following decisions:

- you will be surveying all full-time students;
- you will ask about their experiences of theft, car theft, drug use, sexual assault, and violence (and use offence categories which mirror official police recorded crime statistics) whilst on campus;

- you will ask about incidents that took place within the last academic year;
- you will ask respondents to fill in an online survey, which they can access in the main library on campus through their main student account;
- the survey will use a simple yes/no format to certain question items and standard attitudinal scales (ranging from respondents being asked to strongly agree to strongly disagree with particular statements) for others;
- the results will be published on the university website.

Before reading any further, take a moment to write down what you consider to be the strengths and weaknesses of this approach. Try to think as well about how you would use this format in future years—for example, to measure trends.

Now imagine that having drafted the framework of your survey, you have issued it to your peers as a pilot test to gauge the overall clarity of your questions and the general survey design. They challenge your decisions with more questions. Have a look at this list and see how it compares to the strengths and weaknesses you've already noted down.

- If the survey is only for full-time students, how will you justify excluding staff and visitors?
- How are you going to make sure you get a truly representative sample of the student body in terms of gender, ethnicity, and socio-economic status?
- What would you use as your sampling frame?
- Many students say that they would simply not take the time to complete an online survey—how could you increase your response rate? Would carrying out more time-consuming face-to-face interviews be more effective?
- Most mature students are part time. How will you seek their views?
- What about damage to the university itself—such as vandalism, arson, fraud?
- Very few students drive as there is limited parking on campus. Most use bicycles. Why are you not asking about crimes involving bikes?
- What is your definition of violence?
- To what extent are you confident that your questions (including the use of particular crime categories) are worded in a way that actually measures what you want them to measure?
- How will you make sure respondents are clear about the meaning of terms used in your survey—for instance, explaining the difference between an offence and an attempted offence?
- Why are you not examining incidents of **hate crime**?
- There are ethical concerns around surveys and how they are carried out. How will you protect anyone who is affected by discussing crimes they have experienced?
- Are you going to warn students that they are going to be asked about sensitive topics such as sexual assault?
- If students are going to use their personal logins to complete the survey, how can you reassure them about confidentiality? Will this also affect how people respond?
- The university has a significant number of disabled students who use assistive technology like screen readers. How will you adapt the survey to ensure that they are able to use it?
- Similarly, how will you ensure that students with learning needs such as dyslexia are able to understand and complete the survey?
- We have a large number of foreign students here as part of an exchange programme with universities in Europe. How will you check that they have been able to understand the survey?
- What about student attitudes to crime? How will these be measured?

The Vice Chancellor also has a few concerns that you will need to consider. Before reading on, try to anticipate what these may be. Write a short list, then think about how you will answer this memo from the VC:

Dear Students

Thank you for your proposed survey design. I would be obliged if you would consult with your tutors and provide me with the following reassurances:

We need to maintain public confidence in our university. Without a strong reputation for campus safety, we are less likely to attract new students. Without them, and the income they attract, we would see a reduction in our ability to offer financially viable courses. Similarly, our capacity to carry out research would be impaired, which would affect our standing as a centre of international excellence in criminology.

I would ask you therefore to consider how you will carry out your research in such a way as to allow us to reassure students and their families that we do not have a crime issue on our campus. I would also ask that you identify a suitable way of publishing the findings without causing unwelcome and hostile publicity.

Now refer back to the initial plan. What do you think should be changed in light of these questions and challenges? Do you think that it is practicable to accommodate everyone's concerns? If not, how will you justify your decisions?

and credibility. As you have probably realised, all research instruments (and research studies) are far from being perfect, but that is, after all, why criminologists and other social scientists read and critically evaluate each other's work in order to critique, develop, and improve on it.

Who is included in the survey sample?

The first BCS survey questioned a representative sample of households (and the people living within them) numbering 10,000; by 2005–6 this sample size had increased significantly to over 47,000, and now it aims to achieve a sample size of around 35,000 households. This is still a significant number of people to question and, as we have noted, it is a technically sophisticated and large piece of social research.

The survey carefully tries to be representative of all household types in England and Wales, and for its sampling frame it draws on the Postcode Address File (PAF). This approach is very practical and pragmatic but, as a result, the survey will not include those people who live in other types of setting, such as care homes or university halls of residence. It could be argued that this does not hamper the survey or skew its results in any way, although given the rise in concerns about hate crime and elder abuse it could be argued that valuable sources of victim information (for example, from older people, students) are being overlooked, and the experiences of vulnerable individuals might be left out (**Figure 5.13**).

The survey has made attempts to respond to identified weaknesses in its methodology. For instance, in 2009 it was extended to examine the views of children aged 10–15. Although this allowed a greater level of awareness of children as victims of crime, the extension does have some limits, notably in that parental or guardian permission is sought before a child is allowed to take part. Whilst this may help to support children who are being interviewed, there is a correlated risk that a child victim may be prevented from participating. This issue is particularly worrying given that children are most likely to be harmed by people in their own family. Nor are the voices of younger children heard.

Which crimes are included in the survey?

By focusing on individual households, the survey can ask questions about household crimes (such as burglary or criminal damage to a car) as well as personal crimes (such as any member of that household who has been the victim of assault). However, it is openly acknowledged that it cannot cover every criminal offence and that, by necessity, there are some exclusions. Currently these include so-called 'victimless' crimes (such as the possession of and consumption of drugs) as well as types of business crime. There have been some changes to the survey over time, as it has added offences into its inquiries, such as sexual crime, stalking, fraud, and computer misuse crimes. The statistics in these additions are excluded from the main survey count to maintain its status as a consistent statistical series.

The survey attempts to use the main categories of crime as recorded by the police—the main survey covers crimes of:

- violence;
- robbery;
- theft from person;

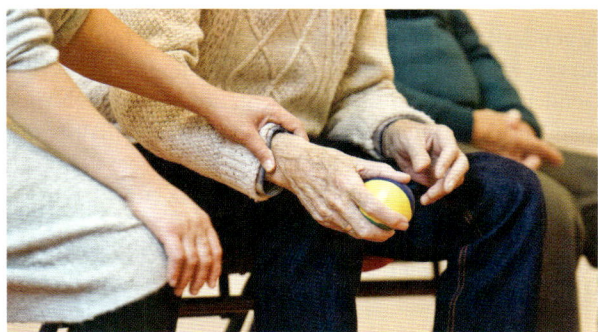

Figure 5.13 Although the CSEW aims to provide a representative sample of households in England and Wales, the exclusion of care homes and other settings might mean that crimes targeting certain members of society aren't being recorded

Source: Matthias Zomer/Pexels

- domestic burglary in a dwelling;
- vehicle-related theft;
- bicycle theft;
- criminal damage to a dwelling; and
- criminal damage to a vehicle.

In doing so, it is argued that we can directly compare the incidence of specific crimes and various crimes trends (both at a general and more offence-specific level) between the police recorded statistics and the CSEW. Many official reports and newspaper articles now draw on both sources when reporting on crime. The ONS also produces the helpful and detailed, *User guide to crime statistics in England and Wales* (ONS, 2020), which usefully covers police recorded crime statistics as well as the CSEW.

How reliable are CSEW statistics?

The CSEW is a very sophisticated research instrument and, as such, it is perhaps the best source of information (to date) we have when studying crime rates and trends in England and Wales. Unlike police recorded statistics, CSEW statistics are accredited as National Statistics by the UK Statistics Authority. The survey is also constantly evolving to reflect changing times and concerns; for example, in April 2019, the existing 10–15s survey was extended to include online behaviour. Sensitive questions focused on five main sections:

- Online bullying.
- Meeting with online strangers.
- Speaking with online strangers.
- Sending sexual images and messages.
- Receiving sexual images and messages.

A gender-identity question was also added to the main survey in October 2019, which was developed by the Gender Identity and Sexual Orientation team at ONS for the Census. But despite these changes, the CSEW is not without its limitations, both in terms of the types of households surveyed, and the offence categories considered.

Strengths of the CSEW

The CSEW has followed a consistent methodology throughout its existence, which means that over three-quarters of CSEW offences can be placed in comparable categories to those recorded by the police (ONS, 2020: Table 2). The stability of the CSEW is shown by its traditional victimisation module, which measures the personal and household offences included in the survey, and has remained the same since it was first launched—any additions are excluded from the main survey. This consistency means that, for these offences, it could be possible to measure trends and compare findings from different periods. These are known as the comparable subset of crime, and the results have shown that victims experience three to four times more offences of these kinds than the numbers recorded by the police (Maguire and McVie, 2017: 169).

The face-to-face interview method of the CSEW is also one of its strengths as it means people may feel more comfortable telling the interviewer about problems they would not want to report to the police—although this may be less likely for highly sensitive crimes such as domestic violence or sexual abuse, especially where a female victim is being interviewed by a male. The survey's face-to-face approach in collecting data has demonstrated reliability when measuring the frequency of crimes; particularly when compared with police counting practices and the distortions they can bring to the figures. The CSEW is therefore able to more accurately describe the quantity of crimes that have been experienced.

The CSEW is the only nationally approved measure of crime and this credibility has proved a useful political device. Its results can support different arguments; such as how well the government have been doing in reducing crime or for justifying decreases in public spending on the police. There have also been political benefits from its measure of subjective things such as fear of crime and confidence in the police. This has provided the Home Office with its own public opinion polls on the apparent 'satisfaction' of the public on its work to improve the criminal justice system.

Limitations of the CSEW

There are some critics who believe the CSEW has serious limitations. One of the issues with the survey is that it is not available online, which means that some people may find it harder to participate, for example those who work long hours or shifts that make it difficult to plan an interview. In **Conversations 5.2** we hear from Professor Tim Hope, who argues that the CSEW is simply not a very good or effective way to measure crime and calls for a new type of crime survey. He argues that we still don't know enough about the true extent of crime, especially about interpersonal violent crime amongst family members and people known to each other. In this conversation, he proposes several ideas for improving the research—suggestions that could be used for valuable undergraduate research projects.

Regardless of the methodological issues that Professor Hope discusses, we can see why some commentators

CONVERSATIONS 5.2

Why we need a different crime survey

with **Professor Tim Hope**

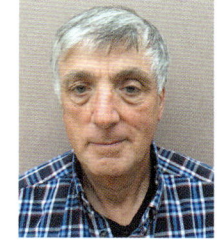

The Crime Survey for England and Wales (CSEW) doesn't cover all types of crime, it doesn't include all victims, and it doesn't count all crime incidents. Neither is it large enough to offer full insight on all local crime experiences, and it records very few serious sexual offences.

Over the years, the CSEW has got progressively better at measuring the reporting of crime, and much worse at measuring crime victimisation. This is because it has got better at representing the experiences of the general population and worse at representing the experiences of victims. The overall distribution of crime victimisation amongst the population is highly unequal: about 20 per cent of the population are chronically victimised, suffering around 80 per cent of all crime (Hope and Norris, 2013). Yet despite knowing about this glaring inequality, we don't know a great deal about the experiences of these victims. This is partly because the politics of large numbers prevail. Politicians can relax because crime seems to be going down for the majority of their constituents, and is therefore viewed as less of a concern by the public. But this is only because they are experiencing less of what was always a rare misfortune; crime is still a huge matter of concern for the less fortunate 20 per cent. For them, crime victimisation is as it always has been: a constant and depressing concern of their everyday lives.

So, we need to reform the crime survey. We should:

- **find more victims:** when the CSEW took over from the BCS, it ceased to be a *crime* survey and became a police performance survey instead. The CSEW stopped looking so much at inner city, high crime areas and instead over-sampled suburban and rural areas. The CSEW became more interested in how the government's law and order policies were going down amongst ordinary citizens and less about the needs of people who experience crime on a daily basis. So we don't know how this has affected the typical profile of victims (e.g. those who live in the inner city in neighbourhoods with high crime rates); particularly, we don't know how many more chronic victims are now being over-looked.
- **include crime that is hard to reach:** we need to find ways of assuring victims that they can talk to the survey frankly, safely, and openly, especially about sensitive offences. This could be achieved through alternative ways of finding and interviewing victims.
- **contact the people that are hard to reach:** since the start, the BCS/CSEW has always failed to contact, or had refusals from, around a quarter to a third of its sample, and that just includes the residential population. It does not reach the homeless, the institutionalised, and the transient. But non-response cannot be ignored in a crime victims' measurement survey: not only does every response count but the kinds of people who refuse or cannot be contacted are probably the kinds of people who are most likely to be vulnerable to crime victimisation.
- **count crime accurately and truthfully:** the counting procedures themselves need to change. Usually, an arbitrary 'cap' is put on the number of victimisations that victims report in order to ensure that the national averages are not affected by a very small number of respondents who report extremely high numbers of incidents. But it is precisely these chronic victims to whom we need to listen; when the capping is removed there are 60 per cent more violent crimes overall; violence against women, along with family and domestic violence, all increase by 70 per cent. In sum, violent crime becomes much less of a problem of 'stranger-danger' and much more a problem of intimate human relationships (Walby et al., 2015).

Obviously, much more needs to be done technically to implement a truly victim-oriented national survey but the issue goes beyond this. Politicians always talk like accountants and never talk about the moral purpose of their policies. We need very much to restore personal experience to our contemporary measurement of crime if we are to bring the moral dimension back to our criminal justice policies.

Professor Tim Hope is Visiting Fellow at the Open University, and a former Professor of Criminology at the University of Salford and Keele University

Source: Hope, T. (2015), 'We need a different crime survey', Centre for Crime and Justice Studies; London (www.crimeandjustice.org.uk/resources/we-need-different-crime-survey)

Figure 5.14 The CSEW provides valuable insight into the general public's experiences of crime, but does the methodology behind it mean we're just looking at the 'tip of the iceberg'?
Source: Spitfire Photography/Unsplash

regard the CSEW to be a stronger and more robust indicator of national estimated levels of crime and trends in specific offences over time than most other measures. It simply cannot, however, cover everything in terms of the types of crime experienced across all groups in society.

Difficult choices have to be made and clear parameters set for it to be meaningful. We have to be aware that there are a potentially huge number of crimes hidden beneath the tip of the CSEW iceberg (**Figure 5.14**).

5.6 Conclusion

You may feel like learning about crime statistics is little more than a (dull) rite of passage that you must go through before you can move on to study seemingly more interesting and dynamic areas of criminology, but in this chapter we have tried to offer a different perspective. We argue that by carefully working through the processes of deconstructing and reconstructing official statistical representations of crime, we can raise many important and interesting questions, which should be at the forefront of your mind throughout the rest of your studies. These processes are central to the development of your own critical criminological imagination. We have aimed to provide you with a critical lens through which you should view all claims to knowledge about crime, criminality, and crime control—not just those statistical claims generated by governments, but also those made by other interested groups, even criminologists themselves (see **Chapter 4**). You should also be able to think about how statistics can be used for the purposes of governance and control; issues considered further in **Chapter 24**.

As part of this critical approach, we need to remember that sets of official crime data are neither perfect, flawless authorities, nor the useless or meaningless constructions that some commentators and journalists would have us believe. Although they are far from perfect, if we carefully deconstruct them they can—and do—tell us a great deal. Data can be highly suggestive in terms of certain crime trends and patterns, and how these may affect people who are the victims of crime. The quality, reliability, and use of data can only be improved if we all exercise our critical imaginations.

SUMMARY

After reading this chapter and working your way through its features you should now be able to:

- Understand how statistics relate to the study of criminology, and how to use them effectively

Statistics are powerful tools for criminological study because they help us learn more about the scale and nature of a perceived social problem and its associated trends. Through statistics, we can assess extent and frequency of the problem and look at the patterns in its occurrence, for example its rises and falls over time. This knowledge then helps us decide what would be an appropriate response. Statistics can therefore be extremely useful for criminologists but to use them effectively, it is important to approach them with an ABC mindset: statistics can be very persuasive but often they do not tell the whole story.

- Appreciate why governments may want to collect data on crime, how they collect it, and how their methods have changed over time

Statistical data are useful for governments as they give an insight into the scale of a social problem. They can be transformed into tools like crime maps, which can pinpoint problematic areas and specific times at which such crimes occur. These figures can then be used to inform or justify policy decisions, as well as allowing for more intelligence-led policing. Governments use a range of techniques for gathering data, including surveys and the analysis of crimes as recorded by the police but, again, the critical response can be that these are of limited accuracy and can be skewed by the methods used to gather them.

- Identify the main problems with police recorded crime statistics and understand what is meant by the 'justice gap'

Police recorded crime figures are of themselves incomplete and inaccurate, for many and complex reasons including the formal categorisation of incidents and the discretion afforded to criminal justice agencies, which means that not all crimes that are notifiable are always considered to need further action. The definition of crimes, and the actions of the criminal justice system, may be affected by political or social pressures which mean that outcomes vary over time. Problems of under-reporting also impact the statistics, due to public perception towards acts of deviance, attitudes towards the criminal justice system, and the perceived power or powerlessness of victims. These factors influence the distinction between what is reported and what is actually recorded, forming the 'justice gap' and highlighting the associated issue of attrition.

- Critically assess the Crime Survey for England and Wales (CSEW) as a way of measuring crime and its trends in those countries

Whilst generally regarded as the best statistical picture of crime we currently have (especially when taken together with police recorded statistics), the CSEW has important flaws. The CSEW sample population does not reach those individuals who have a higher probability of being victimised; nor does it currently fully examine crimes such as bullying or sexual offences—perhaps because of reluctance on the part of respondents to reveal and discuss what are emotionally difficult topics.

 Test your understanding of the chapter's key points by attempting the self-test questions on the **online resources** at www.oup.com/he/case2e

REVIEW QUESTIONS

1. List three reasons why governments collect and collate crime data.
2. What is meant by the term 'justice gap'?
3. Give three reasons why members of the public may decide not to report a crime to the police and consider how (and why) this varies between offence type.
4. Give three reasons why the police may decide not to record an incident that has been reported to them.
5. What is meant by 'attrition' in the context of the criminal justice system?
6. What are the potential benefits and drawbacks of the police developing crime mapping techniques?
7. In what ways is the CSEW thought to provide us with a more accurate picture of crime levels than police recorded statistics, and does it manage to achieve this?

 Access the **online resources** at **www.oup.com/he/case2e** to check your answers to the review questions.

FURTHER READING

Maguire, M. (2012) 'Criminal statistics and the construction of crime' in M. Maguire, R. Morgan, and R. Reiner (eds) *The Oxford Handbook of Criminology* **(5th edn).** Oxford: Oxford University Press.
A clearly written and accessible chapter exploring questions about 'crime levels', 'crime patterns', and 'crime trends' and how they are measured. It also links changes in the way that crime data are collected and presented to changing perceptions about the nature of the 'crime problem' and the politics of crime control.

Maguire, M. and McVie, S. (2017) 'Crime data and criminal statistics: a critical reflection' in A. Liebling, S. Maruna, and L. McAra (eds) *The Oxford Handbook of Criminology* **(6th edn).** Oxford: Oxford University Press.
Expanding on Maguire's (2012) chapter, Maguire and McVie address empirical and methodological questions about how much crime there is and how this changes over time. They also consider the relationship between what crime data are collected and published and changes in perceptions of and responses to the crime problem as a result of developments in the politics of crime control.

Ministry of Justice website: www.justice.gov.uk/
Office for National Statistics: www.ons.gov.uk/
Home Office web pages: www.gov.uk/government/organisations/home-office
Government ministries produce various monthly statistical bulletins on a range of issues of criminological concern, and there is really no substitute for you dipping into these from time to time. You will find many such bulletins on these websites.

ANSWERS TO EXERCISES

WHAT DO YOU THINK? 5.2

Offence category	General description	Frequency (from 1 (most frequent) to 10 (least frequent))	The 2019 recorded crime figures (% and totals) (Total was 5,775,550)
1. Violence against the person	A very broad category ranging from murder to minor assaults.	2	28.7% 1,658,478
2. Sexual offences	Another very broad term covering rape and indecent assault, but also having sex with a corpse or being a voyeur.	7	2.7% 153,794
3. Robbery offences	These are distinct from theft or burglary as they also involve the use of force or fear.	9	1.5% 83,930
4. Theft	Includes burglary, vehicle offences, theft from the person, bicycle theft, shoplifting, and other thefts.	1	32% 1,850,775
5. Criminal damage and arson	Includes damage to a dwelling, to buildings other than a dwelling, and damage to a vehicle. If inflicted by fire, the offence is recorded as arson.	4	9.2% 530,618
6. Drug offences	Includes offences for the possession, distribution, and production of illegal drugs.	6	2.9% 170,197
7. Possession of weapons offences	Includes possession of a firearm (both real and imitation) and possession of a knife or bladed article.	10	0.8% 44,445
8. Public order offences	Ranging from causing a riot (when 12 or more people threaten violence), violent disorder (3 or more people), to threatening, abusive, or insulting behaviour.	5	7.3% 422,252
9. Miscellaneous crimes against society	For all other police recorded crimes where there is no direct victim that do not fit into any other category. Includes dangerous driving, breaching bail, and perjury.	8	1.7% 98,795
10. Fraud and computer misuse	Includes fraud by a company director, cheque and credit card fraud, and computer misuse such as: spreading viruses or other malicious software, and hacking or gaining unauthorised access to information.	3	13.2% 762,266

Table 5.1 Recorded figures for the ten categories of offence used by the police

 Access the **online resources** to view a wealth of extra information relating to your study of criminology, including self-test questions, answers to review questions, and links to other resources that will help you enjoy and fulfil your potential within your studies.
www.oup.com/he/case2e

CHAPTER OUTLINE

6.1	Introduction	148
6.2	Criminological studies of the media	149
6.3	Media representation of crime	153
6.4	Media effects on crime	173
6.5	Conclusion	180

6

Crime and the media

KEY ISSUES

After studying this chapter, you should be able to:

- develop a critical and reflective view of media representations of crime and criminals;
- explain how criminologists have researched this through content analysis and discourse analysis, and by developing an awareness of the capacity of media to distort and shape public perceptions of crime, criminality, and the criminal justice system;
- relate a range of concepts to your own consumption of media;
- assess the importance of media in forming new narratives, such as through citizen journalism;
- compare and analyse differences between traditional and emerging branches of criminological research on the representation of crime across a variety of media.

6.1 Introduction

For most of us today, crime, criminality, and its control are 'mediated' experiences. We have relatively little direct exposure to crime, whether as witnesses, victims, or perpetrators, and unless we choose to take a professional role in the justice system it will not form a major part of our daily lives. Despite this, a quick look at most online news sites, local newspapers, or TV schedules will show you that it forms a significant part of our media consumption. There are hundreds of thousands of books (fact and fiction) on 'crime', thousands of films with crime as a focus, and hundreds of video and online games in which crime and violence are central themes. Museum exhibitions on the subject, such as the Wellcome Collection's 'Forensics: The Anatomy of Crime' (2015) (an exhibit from which is shown in **Figure 6.1**), attract people of all ages and there was so much interest in the collection of nooses, death masks, and murder weapons housed in the Metropolitan Police's London Black Museum and shown to a select number of people that the items were put on public display through the Museum of London. All of this is part of our long-lived fascination with crime and its effects, and these activities and forms of entertainment could be regarded as forms of popular criminology. People love to look at crime, think about it, and read about it, as long as it's safely in a book, in a museum, or on a screen.

Humans have historically used all the media at their disposal to meet this urge to document crime. From the 13th century, when the printing press was invented, through the 1820s (the typewriter), 1840s (photography), 1930s (television), 1970s (first computer shop in the US), and the 1990s (the launch of Google), we in the developed world have used all kinds of media to record, discuss, and fantasise about crime and its effects. Since we have little direct experience of crime, we rely on media to tell us what is happening and what we should think about it, and these sources inform discussions in school playgrounds, workplace canteens, pubs, buses, and on social media. In today's increasingly multi-media world, the types of media available to us have become diverse, interconnected, and fragmented, but at the same time accessible to practically everyone. Whilst fewer people now read a daily newspaper or regularly go to the cinema, most households have at least one TV and can access hundreds of channels, including many which are devoted to crime and its detection, and the vast majority of houses in the UK and at least half of the world's population (World Bank, 2018) have access to the internet. Most of us cannot only access crime-related information and stories through a wide variety of media, but can publish and distribute our own views and accounts, if we choose.

Figure 6.1 The public's fascination with all things crime-related extends to museum exhibitions, such as the forensics exhibition at the Wellcome Collection at which this piece of knife-wounded kidney and the offending knife were displayed

Source: Steve Parsons/PA Archive/Press Association Images

In this chapter we will consider the research into various forms of media and their long, complex relationships with crime. First, we will outline some of the ways in which criminologists examine the media and analyse the ways in which it has been used to represent—either directly or indirectly—'facts' and opinions about crime. We will then look at how this can reflect wider and less obvious considerations, such as social concerns and attitudes to different groups, like young people and migrants, before exploring how crime is depicted in fiction and popular entertainment—in literature, on screen, in music, and in gaming. We then discuss the effects of media representation of crime, considering the ways in which the media could be seen as **criminogenic** (causing crime)—for example, that it can facilitate and provide a platform for crimes, such as cybercrime—and the ways it could be seen as having a positive influence on crime. We conclude by discussing the implications of the evolution in technology which now means that everyone can be a media producer: what does this mean for the future of media criminology?

Ultimately, in this chapter we will encourage you to critically consider media representations of crime.

6.2 Criminological studies of the media

Studies of the relationship between crime and the media began to appear in the 1950s (Davis, 1952) and 1960s (Greer, 2009), and over time this area of interest has become closely associated with a strand of our discipline known as 'cultural criminology' (Ferrell, 1999). Interest in this area has been driven by a number of factors including a wider interest, beyond criminology, in how media representations play a part in shaping how we understand the world. In the field of crime and criminology, of course, this is related to questions about which crimes are viewed as most significant or harmful, who the 'typical' offenders and victims might be, how we view actors and agencies which deliver criminal justice, and how criminals should be punished.

As criminology itself became a more established and diverse discipline, these questions became a logical focus of inquiry. A question of particular interest is why the media tend to highlight particular types of crime or offenders, and this is closely associated with the wider question of how the media themselves shape or reflect public opinion.

Key questions for media criminology

The relationship between crime and media is far from straightforward and it is continually changing, as new forms of both crime and media emerge. Criminologists have studied this relationship over the last 50 years or so, and much of their research has centred around the following questions:

- Do the media exaggerate and distort particular forms of criminality?
- Do the media create and reinforce false and harmful stereotypes?
- Do the media cause a fear of crime?
- Do media representations encourage violence?
- Are the media themselves criminogenic (a cause of crime)?
- What is the relationship between fictional and factual accounts of crime and their effects on public perception?

By the end of this chapter you should have some ideas about the answers to these questions, or at least what kind of research you would need to do or information you would need to gather to attempt to answer them, but for now, read **What do you think? 6.1** to reflect on your initial responses.

Certainly, some criminologists see the relationship between crime and the media as highly problematic. The interactive nature of the relationship, and the role of different interests, has raised significant questions. Reiner's (1997: 376–7) views on the relationship between crime and the media are reflected in much criminological research in this area. He has suggested that there are two broad anxieties around the way that media represent crime and crime control:

1. 'the media as subversive'; and
2. 'the media as (a not so subtle form of) social control'.

The first position sees media representations as being a threat to wider issues of morality, law, and order. For example, it could be argued that by portraying 'deviant' behaviour as glamorous or exciting, describing the ways in which this behaviour can be conducted (and concealed), and giving deviant people fame or notoriety through their coverage, the media make crime appear more attractive, which encourages and amplifies deviance and disorder.

The second position argues that the media exaggerates existing fears and anxieties, which leads to forms of social control being legislated into existence and intensified. One example of this 'knee jerk' legislation, the name given to laws that are quickly implemented and not carefully

> ### WHAT DO YOU THINK? 6.1
>
> **What media criminologists study**
>
> If you relied solely on particular media outlets for your ideas about crime, how do you think your views might be affected?
>
> - Consider first what views of crime you would develop if your only information about it came from popular TV dramas such as *The Bridge*, *Line of Duty*, or *Poirot*.
> - Now, search for the key terms 'crime', 'public', and 'harm' within the 'News' category of any leading search engine.
> - Finally, look at the crime-related stories (or perhaps the absence of them) on your local newspaper's website and social media channels.
>
> Consider how your impressions of crime and its prevalence vary from reading or watching different forms of media—think about news media, entertainment media, and social media. What about media with different objectives or viewpoints, such as a popular newspaper which traditionally has a right-wing readership (like *The Sun*) compared to a more liberal paper (such as *The Guardian*)? And what about the impression of your local area that is suggested by your local newspaper: does this reflect your own views on and experience of the area?

thought through, often as a reaction to media concerns, was the Dangerous Dogs Act 1991. By 2018, it was being reported that this law had both failed to reduce the level of attacks by dogs on humans, and at the same time was imposing unfair restrictions on responsible dog owners (*The Guardian*, 11 May 2018). We consider further the role of public opinion, and the extent to which it is formed by and accurately reflected in the media, in **section 25.2**.

Although the Reiner positions, which can be seen to demonise the media, are reflected in a lot of criminological research, it has also been argued that the media can have a positive and benign role as a vehicle for communication between criminal justice agencies and the public. Police use of social media, for example, might be an effective way of getting across urgent and important messages about public safety and crime detection (Bullock, 2018).

Key concepts in media criminology

There are two particularly important concepts that have long been present within media criminology: those of '**moral panic**' and '**folk devils**'. In this section, we outline these concepts and look briefly at the most famous study exploring their use.

'Moral panic' and 'folk devils'

The concepts of moral panic and folk devils are closely related, and both are used to refer to perceived threats and 'dangerous people'. The terms come from *Folk Devils and Moral Panics*, a highly influential book by Stanley Cohen which is seen as having been pivotal in highlighting the role of the media (the press, at the time he was writing) in dramatising and potentially amplifying the behaviour of young people, or certain groups of them, as deviant and a threat to respectable society.

A moral panic is an aggressive over-reaction to an event, person, or group of people who appear to threaten the 'moral fabric' of society—that is, society's ideas of right and wrong. The people who present that 'threat' are termed the folk devils. This public reaction is a 'moral' one; that is to say, grounded in a set of assumptions about what is conventionally acceptable behaviour so that, when the line is crossed, social order is seen to be threatened. Leslie Wilkins (1964) used the term '**deviancy amplification** *spiral*' to describe the processes through which media reporting, together with police, public, and political reactions, can actually increase rather than control crime. For instance, when an event or form of behaviours is reported in an exaggerated and sensationalised way by the media, they are creating, maintaining, and perpetuating both the panic and the associated stereotypes. The public then demand that something is done about the 'problem' so governments react accordingly, sometimes giving the police new powers to deal with this perceived 'dangerous' situation. This in turn leads to more sensationalist reporting and the whole spiral continues to whirl.

The focuses of recent moral panics have included the threats supposedly posed by online hackers, knife crime, and terrorism. In each case, an identifiable and real source of harm is magnified and dramatised in ways which are likely to be both misleading and misrepresent those who are portrayed as potential threats. The supposed threat from young, radicalised Muslims has led to stereotyped images associated with terrorism being applied to an entire faith group in a discriminatory way (Sian et al., 2012). For example, in 2015 *The Sun* published a story claiming that one in five British Muslims had sympathy for the terrorist organisation ISIS—pictured in **Figure 6.2**. The Independent Press Standards Organisation investigated after receiving 3,000 complaints about the article and found that the headline was 'significantly misleading' (Ipso, 2016).

Studies of moral panics and folk devils: Stan Cohen and the Mods and Rockers

Over the years there have been many studies which draw on these concepts, but the most famous (and certainly the first detailed one) was Stan Cohen's (1972) study of the social reactions to the youth subcultures of the Mods and Rockers in 1960s England. We will explore media representation of young people and crime in **section 6.3**, but Cohen's study had wider implications, providing a clear example of how media can give a very distorted picture of crime, fuelling moral panic and animosity towards folk devils that has no actual basis. His book is regarded as a criminological 'classic' which all criminologists should read at some point—see the publication details in **Further Reading**.

In his study, Cohen charts and analyses the exaggerated press coverage of what were portrayed as violent mobs marauding through tranquil south coast seaside resorts over bank holiday weekends (see **Figure 6.3** later in the chapter). His book describes the press and public reaction to all of this. Cohen recounts that his research involved staying out all night partying on the beach with the young people, then reading the tabloid headlines in the morning. Then he would put on a suit, sit in a magistrates' court, and listen to how the cases of 'wanton destruction and vandalism' were presented there. This reconciliation between

Figure 6.2 The media can play a significant role in creating and sustaining moral panics, in this case by highlighting suggestions that Muslims sympathise with terrorist organisations

Source: The Sun/News UK and Ireland Ltd

competing versions of reality is at the core of sociological criminology. As Cohen warned, this was not about competing versions of reality in the material sense but more a case of reconciling how the world looked to, and was experienced by, the young people involved, the newspaper readers, and middle-class magistrates.

Research methods in media criminology

In **Chapter 4** we considered the various methods that criminologists use to conduct their research. We discussed a method called **secondary data analysis**, in which a researcher reviews and analyses existing data rather than collecting it themselves. Like Cohen, media criminologists are interested in the existing data of media coverage, so they predominantly rely on two forms of secondary data analysis to analyse it: **content analysis** and **discourse analysis**. We will briefly look at both of these methods here—for further discussion of research methods, see **Chapter 32**.

Content analysis

Media criminologists often use a method known as content analysis to examine and critically analyse the extent and patterns of crimes in the news, how often they are reported, and which crimes are focused on (see also **section 32.9** for more on content analysis). Although it involves analysing qualitative data, the strategy is mainly quantitative: it focuses simply on counting the frequency of particular things, such as how many times a particular word (like 'crime') or theme (such as violence) is used in written, spoken, or visual communication, for example a news report, TV programme, Twitter feed, or magazine article. This method therefore allows us to draw conclusions about the extent of coverage of particular forms of criminality by counting the number of headlines or articles which focus on it. We can also count the average number of words used in these articles and study precisely on which page and where on the page of a newspaper or magazine they are placed (these placements show both how important the item is judged to be, and whether it should be treated as 'news' or 'opinion'). We might decide to focus our analysis on a particular time period, or to study crime reporting across more than one media outlet.

Proponents of content analysis (for example, Bengtsson, 2016) argue that it is both systematic and objective (see **sections 4.1** and **4.6**). The claim for it being systematic is important. When researching crime coverage, we must do more than simply look at or read a document, otherwise the claims which we make would be subjective and therefore not reliable or valid (**reliability** and **validity**

are important indicators of a study's quality—again, see **Chapter 4**). We must be very clear as to what we are counting and make sure that our categories are clearly stated or coded. The reason for this is that if other researchers should wish to replicate, or build on, a piece of research, it is important that they are able to do so with ease and accuracy. Being clear and specific can only strengthen and verify the findings of a piece of research.

Content analysis has allowed researchers of media criminology to make claims such as:

- Media 'framing . . . reinforces current prejudices against Muslims' (Nickerson, 2019);
- Female offenders are often portrayed in the media 'as evil, cunning, and methodical, or as sexualized objects' (Collins, 2014); and (from an earlier period where the written press exerted greater influence)
- Whilst violent or sexual crimes constitute 2.4 per cent of recorded crime, the proportion of newspaper coverage of crime devoted to these has been calculated as 45.8 per cent (Ditton and Duffy, 1983).

It is important to understand the process and methods used to produce such statistics so that you can appreciate the work behind them and critically evaluate those you come across in your own studies. With this in mind, try the exercise in **What do you think? 6.2**.

Discourse analysis

Whilst claims from the content analysis method are interesting and can highlight patterns in media coverage of crime, its critics point out that because it focuses on counting, it does not really consider deeper meanings and interpretations of events. This is where discourse analysis, as a more **qualitative research** tool, is helpful (see also **section 32.9** for more on discourse analysis).

Discourse analysis concentrates on the language and meanings of texts, speech, and documents, allowing it to offer a deeper, more nuanced picture than content analysis. Discourse analysis can highlight not only what is included in crime coverage but also what is *excluded*, by examining events in their broader contexts. It considers who says what about a particular subject, why they feel they have the authority to make their claims, and who their intended audience is.

Discourse analysis is a very different research methodology to content analysis and is perhaps rather less straightforward. Mayr and Machin (2012) have explored its use in detail, providing fascinating examples of how language is used in media and popular culture and using these findings to discuss the ways in which crime, criminality, and its control are portrayed. Amongst other things, they look at the use of language in the media discussions on young

WHAT DO YOU THINK? 6.2

Content analysis and counting crime

Look up the TV schedules for the main terrestrial channels (BBC, ITV, Channel 4, Channel 5) and either count the number of times that crime (fictional or factual programmes) is mentioned or look at the amount of time taken up by crime stories as a proportion of the programme time or number of programmes. How might you break down your findings further? For example, could you analyse them according to whether the programmes are police- or court-based, according to the type of crime featured, or whether they are fiction or non-fiction? Once you have your data, consider the following questions:

1. What issues did you encounter in trying to gather this data? (For example, how easy was it to categorise crime and decide which items to include in your counting?)

2. What immediate conclusions do you think you could draw from this—or similar—data? For what kinds of research might this method be useful?

3. What other questions do your findings suggest? What do you think would be worth investigating further?

4. What potential issues or limitations can you foresee with conducting this kind of content analysis, and with the data it produces?

Reflecting on these questions should give you an idea of both the strengths and potential limitations of content analysis in the context of researching the relationship between crime and the media. There are clearly complications associated with this kind of research and it is important to understand these so that you can bear them in mind when you read statistics and studies that have been generated in this way. Content analysis can be a very useful research tool in your own project or dissertation, but it is important to bear these considerations in mind.

---

people and the criminal justice system (on which, see the discussion in **section 6.3**). Jewkes (2015) pays attention to what she calls 'media misogyny' in her analysis of the portrayal of female offenders, thinking about the way their physical attractiveness, motherhood, or mental health are foregrounded in ways which do not happen when men are under scrutiny (see **Further Reading** for details). Tornberg and Tornberg (2016) have also carried out an extensive discourse analysis of social media representations of Islam and its association with violence and terrorism.

Now that we know a little more about media criminology as an area within criminology and have an understanding of its key issues, concepts, and research methods, we can begin our own exploration of the relationship between crime and the media. Our discussions in the next section will help you form more developed opinions on two of the key issues for media criminology: whether the media exaggerates or distorts particular forms of criminality, and whether it creates and reinforces false and harmful stereotypes.

6.3 Media representation of crime

In order to understand and begin to analyse media representation of crime, and ultimately to look at its potential effects, we need to consider not only *how* crime is represented—for example, how certain types of crime, people, and groups are portrayed—but also *why* it might be shown in this way. In this section, we explore:

- what existing criminological research suggests about how media represent crime;
- the factors that influence media representation of crime;
- how media representation of crime varies across different social groups;
- how crime is represented in fiction and entertainment media—since this is just as important as news media in shaping our view of crime in society.

What the research shows

In their thorough review of research carried out over the last 30 years within media criminology, Greer and Reiner (2015: 255–6) come to six conclusions about the extent and patterns of crime representation in media. Given the number of forms of media now available and the

> ## WHAT DO YOU THINK? 6.3
>
> ### How crime is represented on social media
>
> We have briefly noted some of the similarities and differences between more traditional media forms and social media in terms of how crime is represented, but since the latter media form is newer, and is changing and expanding rapidly, there are many questions still to be answered. For example, there are growing concerns about the immediacy of social media and its relationship to online bullying, sexual exploitation, **hate crime**, and other forms of harassment such as stalking. Linked to this, there have been a number of calls for better ways to police social media, and for major online platforms and internet providers to provide more effective protection for their users.
>
> Based on what you have read so far, and on your own experience of social media and knowledge of the controversies surrounding it, what questions do you think we should be considering as we try to learn more about the relationship between social media and crime?

significant changes in communication and content consumption even since 2015, including via an increasingly wide range of social media platforms, we cannot treat this as a definitive summary of media representation of crime today, but it is a very useful starting point for our discussion.

Greer and Reiner (2015: 255–6) claim existing studies have shown that:

1. news and fiction stories about crime appear very widely across all forms of media;
2. within news and fictional representations of crime there is an over-concentration on crimes of violence and this (as we have seen in **Chapter 5**) is very different from the picture we get from **official statistics**;
3. media tend to focus on older and richer victims and offenders, but are also more likely today to give greater attention to children who are victims (or perpetrators);
4. media make it seem as though the risk of becoming a victim or being affected by crime is far higher than official sources suggest but, conversely, they underplay our chances of suffering property crime (burglary or theft, for example);
5. there has been an increasing focus on individual victims and their suffering;
6. the news generally paints the police and the criminal justice system in a positive light, although there is some movement towards criticism, for example in the way that miscarriages of justice or police racism are reported.

Studies of social media content in recent years suggest that although crimes are not often mentioned by individual users, posts from news agencies and journalists about crime and its effects exhibit the same kind of trends as those that Greer and Reiner identified, for example focusing on violent crime (Prieto Curiel et al., 2020).

However, it has also been observed that in the crime-related content that individuals do post, the accounts may be more accurate depictions of the crime suffered, and could provide a picture of crime in a particular area that is closer to reality, with victims and indirect victims more inclined to share their experiences (Curiel et al., 2020). Consider these ideas further in **What do you think? 6.3**. From this brief overview, we can see that crime is widely represented across all media; that media tend to focus more on crimes of violence than property crimes; and that media overplays our risk of becoming a victim of crime. As a result, certain types of crime and offender are more likely to result in 'front page outrage' and controversial tweets, and we are left with the impression that we live in riskier and more dangerous times—an idea we will consider in the effect of media representation on crime in **section 6.4**.

So why do media represent crime in these ways? In the next section we investigate the factors that influence decisions about what to cover in the media and how to cover it, focusing on the concept of 'newsworthiness'.

What shapes media coverage of crime?

If you really liked the style and tone of *The Times* (a 'broadsheet' newspaper), do you think you would continue buying or subscribing to this publication if they began reporting violent crime with the kinds of headline and images shown in **Figure 6.3**? What about if you saw that a new 'Scandi noir' drama from the producers of *The Killing* was available on Netflix and it centred around a burglary in which electronic equipment was taken but no one was threatened or injured—would you be surprised and disappointed?

We place a certain amount of trust in our chosen media outlets and expect them to represent news and

Figure 6.3 Media sources vary widely in how they report on crime, with tabloids like the *Daily Mail* generally using more controversial, sensationalist headlines (and images)
Source: Daily Mail, 14 February 1997

information accurately and honestly. This may not be unconditional, but it is likely that our particular choices reflect some level of agreement with what we see as their underlying values. Our expectations influence our choices, and are in turn influenced by the outlets' coverage of crime. We might like to think that some forms of media (for example, news media) present bare, neutral facts about crimes and crime-related issues from which we can form our own opinions, and that while entertainment media does not present facts, it does not influence our views because we know it is fictional, but in reality no media presents (or, arguably, could ever present) the 'truth' about crime. All forms of media, both factual and fictional, shape our views of crime and society. Those producing media know their audience's expectations and bear them in mind when deciding what information to present and how to present it. This means that the media we consume is heavily influenced by a variety of different factors; some **ideological** (based on putting forward particular ideas, perhaps on political issues) and some commercial (based on sales and profit—generating purchase of, subscriptions to, or clicks onto the media because it is appealing and fits with the consumer's views).

Criminologists give considerable thought to these choices, since they can have significant affects on the consumers of that media (see the discussion of the effects of the media on crime in **section 6.4**), on crime itself, and on criminal justice policy. They often use the terms '**newsworthiness**' and 'news values' to explore how such choices are made. Before we break down these terms and look at the traditional and more modern views of what they entail, take a look at **What do you think? 6.4** and put yourself in the shoes of a news editor to see whether you can come up with some of the key ideas of 'newsworthiness' yourself.

20th-century newsworthiness: Chibnall's 'imperatives'

The first detailed criminological study of how media cover crime was Chibnall's *Law and Order News* (1977). In this study, Chibnall lists eight 'professional imperatives' (which you can think of as being news values) and argues that these guide journalists' decisions on what they think ought to be in the news. His study focused on print newspapers, and therefore what is 'newsworthy' in those publications, but the values he highlighted also have relevance for newer forms of news media as well as other, non-news forms of media, for example films, TV, books, music, and games.

WHAT DO YOU THINK? 6.4

Newsworthiness and news values

The perceived attraction of particular stories to readers or viewers is often a guiding factor in whether or not they are reported. Even on a quiet news day, editors have an almost unlimited supply of events that they could cover.

Imagine that you are the editor of a national news outlet. You have owners to please, reader or viewer targets to maintain, perhaps advertising revenue to earn, and you need to make the decision within the next half an hour. All of these things mean you have to choose your stories carefully, especially the leading headline for your front page (in print) and website homepage. Today, out of all the thousands of events and occasions happening all over the world, you need to select from these four:

1. A report has found that officially recorded knife crime is more prevalent in certain poorer neighbourhoods with a significant ethnic minority population.
2. A pretty blonde child has gone missing from a park which is also being used as a traveller site.
3. A stockbroker is found guilty of evading a huge tax payment. This would have been enough money to fund 12 National Health Service (NHS) nurses.
4. A firm employed to monitor safety at a nuclear power plant is accused of using unqualified staff.

Which story do you choose and why? Have you been guided by what you see as the lead story's potential news value, the 'public interest', or your own views and political preferences? Now consider whether your choice would be different if, for example, you were working for a tabloid or a broadsheet newspaper. What about if you worked for a TV news programme or an online-only publication: would you go for a different story because of the images and video footage that could be used?

With these questions in mind, make a list of the sorts of factors which would influence your decisions as to the potential newsworthiness of a particular event.

This exercise should have given you an insight into the difficulty of making editorial decisions, especially under time pressure, and a sense of the many factors that can influence them.

Read the list in **Table 6.1** and think about whether—and if so, how—these considerations link with the list you made when considering the four news stories in **What do you think? 6.4**.

So how do these values apply to modern newspapers, as well as to the many other forms of media available today?

The imperatives of immediacy, dramatisation, and simplification have arguably become even more significant since the rise of online news. Chibnall was writing at a time when newspapers published once a day and TV news was scheduled for particular times. Now, we have 24-hour news channels, a huge number of online news sources (including the websites of national newspapers), and can access continuous updates via social media. We expect to be able to access reports online within minutes of an event happening, so the need for speed is an even more important imperative, and even more likely to result in the sacrifice of some depth, detail, and accuracy.

We can see that these three imperatives play a big role in crime coverage in non-news media, too: in books, on TV and film, in music and games, and on social media. Studies have shown that the ways we consume content have changed since we began to read so much material on screens, and convey our opinions in character-limited tweets. These trends also reveal generational variations.

In Sweden, for instance, whilst 51 per cent of the general population is reported to rely on social media for access to 'news', this figure rises to 91 per cent for 16–25-year-olds (Bergstrom and Belfrage, Belfrage 2018). We seem to have increasingly short concentration spans (Touitou et al., 2016) and therefore lower tolerance for large amounts of text and detail, so we tend to dip into and skim-read the bits of content that grab and interest us—which are often those that are simple and dramatic. This has clear implications for media content on crime. We want and expect media to be fast-paced and action-packed (much of the fictional media of the 1970s and before would now be considered very slow-paced), and our consumer habits could be to blame for the fact that oversimplified, sensationalised crime stories that omit key facts often gain popularity and go 'viral' online. In **Controversy and debate 6.1** we consider the potential implications of this trend for the boundaries between the media reporting crime and helping to generate crime stories.

Another development since Chibnall's study which has implications for many of his imperatives, but particularly for immediacy, dramatisation, and simplification, is the increasing importance of images and videos over the written word, especially amongst younger generations. The pace of change is so rapid that even some older forms

Imperative	Description	Implications for media coverage of crime
1. Immediacy (speed/the present)	Papers need to publish information about a story as quickly as possible to get their story out before other papers and gain maximum impact in terms of sales and engagement.	The focus on speed can lead to a lack of detail and accuracy. Crime stories often take a while to unravel, but newspapers publish them as quickly as they can so the reader is only given some of the facts.
2. Dramatisation (drama and action)	Dramatic, action-packed news stories draw readers in, keep them returning to the publication, and get the public talking about the issue.	Dramatic crimes get most attention, so media coverage makes it seem like car chases and violent crimes happen more often than they do—and more frequently than, say, burglaries and financial crime. Political protests only get media attention when it seems there is a chance of violence, giving the misleading impression that nearly all political protests are violent.
3. Personalisation (cult of celebrity)	People like to read, watch, and hear about the rich and famous; media can personalise crime victims to the extent that people feel they know them; media can give celebrity status to notorious criminals.	Human interest stories, especially those involving prominent people, appear more frequently than 'drier' material reporting crime frequencies or trends.
4. Simplification (elimination of shades of grey)	Crimes and their impact are reported in shortened form, avoiding complicating or contradictory details.	There is a risk of stereotyping, and of polarising judgements of guilt, blame, and victimhood.
5. Titillation (revealing the forbidden/voyeurism)	'Titillation' is not a word you often hear, but it means to deliberately excite and intrigue someone, and it is often associated with sexual images and descriptions. This value relies on piquing the reader's curiosity to draw them in and encourage them to engage with the content.	Reports tend to highlight the exotic, unusual, or morally dubious aspects of behaviour, inviting reactions of horror, censure, or even amusement.
6. Conventionalism (hegemonic ideology)	Assumptions are made about supposed common knowledge understandings of right and wrong, of behaviour that is unacceptable, or of what responsible people might think and do in certain situations.	Conventional norms are reinforced, and the viewer/reader is expected to take an uncritical view of the material being presented.
7. Structured access (experts, power base, authority)	Particular contributors are given privileged positions: key agencies such as the police; scientific experts such as forensic psychologists; victims and their families; and, perhaps, celebrities with similar experiences to those being reported.	The authority we are expected to give the key participants of the stories comes from their expert or insider knowledge and experience. Their judgements, both factual and moral, are expected to be decisive.
8. Novelty (new angle/extreme feature/speculation/twist)	A new angle is viewed as a major selling point in media terms, so unusual features or apparently dramatic developments are given prominence.	An emphasis on the spectacular or unusual may detract attention from the mundane aspects of crime which are both more common and more significant (such as the relative overemphasis on 'stranger danger').

Table 6.1 The 'professional imperatives' Chibnall identified as driving and shaping media coverage

of visual media such as TV are now declining in popularity. In the US, 'adolescents in the 2010s spent significantly less time on print media, TV, or movies compared with adolescents in previous decades. The percentage of 12th graders who read a book or a magazine every day declined from 60% in the late 1970s to 16% by 2016, and 8th graders spent almost an hour less time watching TV in 2016 compared with the early 1990s' (Twenge et al., 2019: 329). It is quick and easy to share dramatic images and video footage online, quicker than writing about an event, and countless market research studies and polls show that online content with images or a video gets more attention (clicks, likes, and shares), which means more visitors to a channel or site and therefore greater exposure and opportunities to increase advertising income.

Visual content can now be secured either by professional film crews, freelance journalists—including some who specialise in getting footage of crime scenes; look up the film *Nightcrawler* (Dir. Gilroy, 2014)—or ordinary citizens. Since nearly everyone now has a phone with a good quality camera, the public are usually the first photographers on the scene and you will often see their images

CONTROVERSY AND DEBATE 6.1

Reporting crime vs generating crime news

The line between simply reporting crime and its consequences, and contriving or colluding with the orchestration of events which generate 'crime news', is becoming increasingly blurred. When the BBC responded to a police tip-off by filming and broadcasting a police raid on Cliff Richard's home in 2014, claiming 'public interest', it raised considerable public concern. This concern was only heightened when the raid itself did not result in subsequent criminal proceedings. Was this really in the public interest?

The media has also been involved in entrapment, where journalists themselves have solicited offences in ways which cast serious doubt on their role in the process. One example is the efforts of undercover journalist Mazher Mahmood, who styled himself as 'King of the Sting' and posed as different characters in order to expose, embarrass, and even help to convict public figures. This included meeting singer Tulisa Contostavlos at a London hotel, posing as an influential film producer, and allegedly inducing her to arrange for him to be sold cocaine worth £800. He handed evidence to police and Tulisa was arrested and charged with being concerned in the supply of a Class A drug. The drugs trial collapsed in July 2014 and in 2016 Mahmood was jailed after being found guilty of interfering with evidence. It was announced that 18 other civil claims were being launched against Mahmood and News UK, his employer. Tulisa's defence lawyer commented:

> The real scandal in this case is that Mahmood was allowed to operate as a wholly unregulated police force, 'investigating' crimes without the safeguards which apply to the police . . . Investigative journalists do important work, but Mahmood clearly went too far.

(BBC, 5 October 2016)

---

and footage on news channels. Instant communication means that this content is disseminated around the world within moments of an incident taking place and we have become accustomed to seeing dramatic pictures and videos of people, streets, and property who/which have been affected by a crime just moments before—or are even experiencing it before our eyes. In some cases, a particularly dramatic image has become so closely associated with the event that it becomes iconic—for example, the film shot by Abraham Zapruder which captured the assassination of President Kennedy. But how do the people featured feel about being used to illustrate a news story? Does the need to document and record what is happening override any personal considerations for them? We consider this issue in **Controversy and debate 6.2**.

The personalisation imperative is also very interesting to consider in light of today's media. Social media means that celebrities can communicate directly with their fans, using shared media, and effectively manage their own public relations. Those involved in crimes can have their own voice and make their 'story' public, whilst encouraging viewers to feel more directly and personally involved as virtual witnesses, and we can all feed our curiosity about crime to suit our individual preferences, using the power of Google. We and media producers can find photos and videos of and online content shared by those involved in crime stories, all of which supplement the basic facts of the events, make us feel more invested, and perhaps also encourage us to form strong opinions about them. The power of the media also means that the notoriety and celebrity status that some criminals gain can be even more of a problem, especially if this gives publicity to a harmful ideology. This was the reason why, in 2019, New Zealand Prime Minister Jacinda Ardern refused to speak the name of the man who shot 51 people in attacks on mosques in Christchurch (*The Guardian*, 19 March 2019).

The famous and potentially privileged status of an alleged perpetrator can also affect how sympathetically or harshly they are treated in both newer and more traditional media forms. Celebrity status can mean that people are not subjected to the same level or type of press exposure, helping to ensure that convictions have little impact on their careers or reputations, or that they are not investigated or convicted. We can see the former scenario in the case of Ant McPartlin who received a conviction for drink-driving following a collision with two other cars but was treated sympathetically by the media and remains a popular TV presenter. A prime example of the latter is the case of the BBC radio and TV presenter Jimmy Savile, about whom there were suspicions and allegations for many years before he was finally exposed as a predatory sex criminal, as his celebrity status protected him from real scrutiny or criticism. (Though, as we saw in **Controversy and Debate 6.1**, in the years following Savile's exposure the media arguably overcompensated for this mistake and became too uncritical in some of their reporting of potential child abusers.) On the other hand, some celebrities come in for harsher media treatment because of their status. This was the case for the disgraced cycling superstar,

CONTROVERSY AND DEBATE 6.2

The ethics of immediacy

Georgian journalist Ketevan Kardava's images, taken immediately after the bombing of Brussels airport on 22 March 2016 in which 32 civilians were killed, were widely distributed across all forms of media. Try to imagine, first, her perspective on her actions, and, secondly, that of the women shown in **Figure 6.4**. Read the following statements and note down which views you would share, from each perspective. If you have other views (perhaps from your own perspective, rather than either of these parties), note them down too.

- The pictures could provide vital evidence for the police.
- The pictures are voyeuristic and show no respect for victims.
- It is important to show the impact of such events to a wider audience.
- People have the right to earn money from their photos if they get a chance.
- People only take photos like this so they can sell them to the media.
- Both photographer and victim should be credited whenever the picture is shown and share any royalties.
- Victims should have the right to ban the use of their images.
- TV channels should only show the images after the watershed (a time in the evening, 9 pm in the UK, before which content that is considered unsuitable for children cannot be shown).
- Media should not show the images as they involve real people.

Did your answers differ according to the perspective you had in mind, or could you see both sides? Do you, personally, feel that the use of this image and others by

Figure 6.4 Are shocking images like this one—showing the aftermath of the Brussels airport bombing—ethical or offensive?
Source: Ketevan Kardava/Stringer

Kardava was ethical or offensive? Should they have been used in newspapers, TV reports, and websites? Should they even be in this book?

You may have thought about whether Kardava should have stopped to help the injured, rather than photographing them. In some countries, this would be a criminal offence—a breach of so-called 'Good Samaritan' laws, such as section 323c of the German Penal Code, which makes it illegal to fail to assist someone in danger where this can be done safely. Despite the obligations on some professionals, such as social workers, there is no such general law in the UK, despite politicians over the years saying that something similar would be introduced. You may want to think about why this has not become UK legislation.

When you have formed your own views on this issue, you might find it interesting to read the accounts of Kardava and one of the women pictured. Their meeting in 2017, a year after the bombing, was reported in *Time Magazine*, 'A Year After Brussels, "Her Face Tells Us Much About That Day"', 22 March 2017.

Lance Armstrong, who had taken performance-enhancing drugs for years and was perhaps less willing than some others to follow the accepted redemption script, and the TV presenter Caroline Flack who faced intense criticism for an act of domestic violence she allegedly committed against her partner. The media coverage was reported to have been a major factor in her decision to take her own life in 2020.

Regarding titillation, this value has been and continues to be present in many forms of media, but an interesting modern manifestation, in terms of its effect on crime coverage, is the way that online media use deliberately outrageous/provocative headlines or post social media descriptions of stories which are designed to act as 'click bait', encouraging people to click on the associated link. And in today's world, if traditional news publications

> **WHAT DO YOU THINK? 6.5**
>
> **Media reporting of criminal justice issues**
>
> Media coverage is rarely sympathetic towards offenders and the conditions in which they live. Why? Consider whether an NGO press release would meet any of the eight imperatives discussed in this section. Would a report highlighting poor and overcrowded prison conditions, rates of self-harm—especially amongst female prisoners—and diagnosed mental health conditions amongst young offenders, for instance, be deemed newsworthy by a journalist working in the mainstream media?
>
> We will return to the issue of media representations of prisons and prisoners in the discussion of crime in fiction and entertainment media later in this section, but it appears to be very difficult for such reforming organisations to get sustained mainstream media coverage and to use it in order to influence wider debate and policy. Reflect on why this might be the case, bearing in mind the ideas we have discussed in this chapter but also the ideas about crime and justice that we covered in **Chapters 2** and **3**. Consider, for example, the role that the media might play in relation to regulating behaviour in a society, or achieving 'justice' for all.

decide against publishing the most graphic/outrageous images in print or on their website, on legal or ethical grounds, other media may not—content and rumours can very easily 'leak' and spread online, and our curiosity is now fuelled by the fact that we know it is possible to find it there.

Although there are now many more forms of media than when Chibnall conducted his study and almost anyone could be considered a media producer (for example, a vlogger), or at least to inform media content (for example, having your tweet included in a newspaper article), our mainstream crime coverage is arguably even more constrained by the facts given to us by authorities—relating to the 'Structured' value. Today's news media outlets have far fewer specialist crime correspondents than they used to and, like the rest of us, their staff have little direct experience of, and access to, crime. This means that crime coverage does not come from 'on the ground' reporting by the media—most information and statistics relating to crime (and we saw in **Chapter 5** that statistics can be misleading) initially comes from press releases and various press agencies, including from police forces and the Ministry of Justice. If you carefully read different mainstream media accounts of the same story on a particular day, you may find that they are very similar in both style and content, perhaps due to an increasing over-reliance on such sources. Non-governmental organisations (NGOs) in the sphere of penal reform and policy (such as the Howard League for Penal Reform and the Prison Reform Trust) are also more media-savvy than they have been in the past, so they attempt to get their perspective heard and reflected within crime coverage, but the extent to which they can set or influence media agendas on issues like prison conditions is highly debatable (see Colbran, 2015 for a fuller discussion of these issues)—we consider this further in **What do you think? 6.5**.

Newsworthiness today: Jewkes's 'news structures'

We saw in our discussion of Chibnall's (1977) 'imperatives' that these values are still relevant today, and that some have in fact gained further significance owing to recent developments, but Jewkes (2015) has revisited the study to bring it into a 21st-century context (although inevitably there is some clear overlap in focus). Jewkes points out that today's social, political, and economic environment is very different to the one in which Chibnall was writing in the 1970s. There are many more media outlets reporting on the same crime stories, in very different ways, 24 hours a day. This change in landscape, according to Jewkes, means we need to reconsider the elements which were previously thought to decide whether a story was newsworthy—although it is worth noting that different communities and countries will have different values, which in turn mean that a story can receive wide coverage in one place but generate little attention in another. Issues surrounding drug use, for example, may generate little media interest in Portugal compared to other countries because drug use has been decriminalised in that country. Jewkes does not see criminality, negativity, and novelty as separate factors, but rather as ideas that run through and shape all aspects of newsworthiness; as she points out, any crime is broadly negative in and of itself.

Illustrating how criminological concepts can be updated, developed, and expanded to reflect the rapidly changing world in which we live, Jewkes suggests that there are now 12 'news structures' which are behind the shaping and reporting of today's crime news. These are set out in **Table 6.2**.

For both Chibnall and Jewkes, then, media interest in and representation of crime are shaped by a number of factors. These mainly derive from both an interest in what 'sells', or establishes a distinctive identity for a particular media outlet; and from the ideological position it has adopted. So, although every news provider may have an underlying commitment to reporting 'the facts', criminological understanding of the relationship between media and crime must always take these additional factors into account.

Imperative	Description	Implications for media coverage of crime
1. Threshold	A story must be considered important or dramatic enough to warrant being published. (There are additional considerations, such as the grotesque, the unusual, or the involvement of a celebrity.)	Stories that do not meet the threshold are rarely covered, leading the public to gain an incomplete and misleading picture of crime and related issues.
2. Predictability	Some aspects of crime reporting can be planned in advance. For example, it is certain that during a general election every political party will make policy statements on dealing with crime.	Certain crime issues receive more coverage at particular times, and media outlets tend to seek out and emphasise stories which support their initial narrative or approach (for example, that young people are wreaking havoc in seaside towns—see the discussion of moral panic and folk devils in **section 6.2**). As Jewkes describes it: 'once the media expect something to happen, it will' (2015: 51).
3. Simplification	This structure is a development of Chibnall's (1977) categorisation. For an event to become newsworthy, it must be possible to break its story down into separate themes or conventions. It must be brief, have relatively few possible interpretations, and it must be unambiguous.	This kind of simplification means that the audience is making a judgement without having all the facts or nuance. It also means people are more likely to respond uncritically, and to join with the journalist and their editors in following a particular point of view.
4. Individualism	In parallel with Chibnall's idea of personalisation, this structure encourages us to see and interpret crimes in terms of the personal (sometimes called 'human interest') context instead of within a wider political or social context.	The media tend to devote more coverage to crime stories involving individuals, and particular types of individual (both victims and criminals), who will ensure maximum engagement from the audience. For example, crime stories in the media disproportionately feature young, female victims (who are likely to look good in a photo or on screen). (See the discussion in **Chapter 7** on the hierarchy of victimhood.)
5. Risk	Stories are more newsworthy if they imply that the crime could happen to anyone (for example, unpredictable attacks by a stranger, random crimes with no apparent motive, and crimes where the perpetrator has not been caught), because this generates drama, fear, and excitement.	People develop an unrealistic sense of their risk of becoming a crime victim, and of the types of crimes that they are most likely to experience. Prevalent and important crimes that are believed to be more likely to happen to someone else (such as domestic violence, or crimes that take place in very different settings or circumstances, like those in a different social group to that inhabited by most of the viewers/readers, or in developing world countries) receive less coverage.
6. Sex	This structure relates to Chibnall's (1977) titillation imperative and refers to the fact that the media reflects prevailing societal attitudes in considering stories to be more newsworthy if they feature sexual images and descriptions.	The media are likely to over-report sex offences and to focus more heavily on crimes committed against women and girls, giving the impression that these crimes are more prevalent than is actually the case.
7. Celebrity	As Chibnall (1977) noted, this structure seems to be an ever-growing feature of all media; the connection of a famous person to an incident practically guarantees that it will receive coverage.	Crimes connected to high status, well known people are given disproportionate attention compared to crimes involving or affecting 'ordinary' people.

Table 6.2 The 12 'news structures' that Jewkes (2015) suggests are behind the shaping and reporting of today's crime news (*cont.*)

Imperative	Description	Implications for media coverage of crime
8. Proximity	The location of a crime can affect its newsworthiness. This can be on a local or national basis; a story has to feel relevant to the audience.	A lot of national media focuses on crime stories in particular densely populated areas—UK news is often London-centric, which is perhaps not surprising given the size of the city's population and the fact that many media producers are based there. The media also tends to focus on national crime issues (except where crimes abroad affect a country's own citizens), giving little airtime to crimes occurring elsewhere or to transnational crime, despite the latter being much more prevalent in today's globalised world (see **Chapter 14**).
9. Violence or conflict	Stories involving violence or conflict are much more likely to gain media attention.	The media gives the impression that violent crimes occur frequently, and gives little coverage to crimes that may be more prevalent and may be equally harmful in a non-physical sense, such as theft, burglary, fraud, cybercrime, and psychological abuse.
10. Visual spectacle and graphic imagery	As the media become more visual, and as new technology enhances the capacity to generate graphic imagery, news reporting tends to prioritise stories that can be illustrated. What is acceptable in terms of images, photos, and videos is constantly changing, and there are fewer restrictions on what is considered too graphic to publish, so media can rely on these elements even more to intrigue their audience.	Graphic videos and images stoke the public's imagination, increasing fear of crime, and crimes which do not provide 'visual spectacle' receive limited attention. These include fraud, cybercrime, and psychological abuse. We are much more regularly exposed to violent imagery than in previous years, perhaps legitimised by the use of disclaimers: terrestrial TV channels and some newspaper websites (for example, *Daily Mail*) now precede certain stories with a warning that they contain potentially shocking content.
11. Conservative ideology and political diversion	Stories which either champion the so-called 'traditional way of life' or which highlight perceived threats to it are likely to gain news coverage. These stories may focus on deviant activities of 'others', for example immigrants, the unemployed, or the young.	The public are given the impression that their lifestyle is under near-constant attack, which makes people fearful and leads to more negativity towards and stereotyping of the groups and individuals perceived as posing this threat.
12. Children	This is perhaps Jewkes's most significant revision to Chibnall's list: stories involving young people have become increasingly newsworthy.	Children are regularly featured in media reporting, whether as innocent victims or as evil, monstrous, and feral (or simply neglected?) offenders. We consider this later in the section when we discuss young people in the media.

Table 6.2 The 12 'news structures' that Jewkes (2015) suggests are behind the shaping and reporting of today's crime news

Media representation of social groups

In our assessment so far of the relationship between the media and crime, we have seen that the factors influencing what is newsworthy have implications for the ways in which particular groups are represented. Of course, the ways in which groups and individuals are represented in the context of crime are closely related to wider social attitudes and beliefs. These may be to do with assumptions about the typical qualities of certain members of the population; and for some groups there might be a broader tendency towards 'othering' them, in which their supposed criminality is associated with additional negative and undesirable characteristics. There are many groups which receive certain treatment in the media, especially in the context of crime, including women (remember the 'titillation' and 'sex' news values) and particular ethnic groups. We touch on their representation in **Chapters 11** and **10**, respectively. In this section, we will focus on the media representation of just two groups as examples: young people and migrants.

Young people in media

As we will see in **Chapter 9**, youth crime and youth justice is often seen as a distinctive subject area within criminology, and this is largely because wider ideas about childhood and adolescence see young people as a very specific group within the wider population. Given the prevalence of these kinds of assumptions, it is perhaps unsurprising that we often see them reflected in media reporting of youth crime and antisocial behaviour.

A study on youth crime, youth justice, and public opinion (Hough and Roberts, 2004) found that people were generally not very well informed about trends in youth offending or the workings of the youth justice system, and that the media was the main source of their generally poor perceptions. The study suggested that there are many misperceptions about levels of youth offending (that it is continually rising) and the types of crime committed by young people (that they are increasingly becoming more violent), and that overall people have a very negative and pessimistic view of young people. Elsewhere, a 2007 study in the USA found that 91 per cent of US voters believed that youth crime was a major problem (Krisberg and Marchionna, 2007), whilst 64 per cent supported harsher sentences for young offenders. The authors suggest that the context for this was shaped by alarmist media accounts throughout the 1990s.

More recent studies paint a somewhat more complex picture. Roche et al. (2016) have found that whilst 'traditional' media exposure (TV news and crime programmes) is associated with heightened levels of anxiety about crime, this is much less the case with internet use. Jennings et al. (2018), on the other hand, suggest that public attitudes are influenced more directly by crime rates themselves, implying that the media are more likely to reflect rather than lead popular opinion. Recent reductions in recorded levels of youth crime may therefore mean that conventional media have become less preoccupied with the crimes of the young. So, how do the media portray young people? The criminological evidence on this is quite consistent. In analysing the media output of 2,130 news items across all major TV channels in 2006, Wayne et al. (2008) argue that young people have increasingly been demonised in the media; that they are portrayed as not quite being full citizens and as something to be feared. (See **What do you think? 6.6.**) In support of this argument, they say that of the 286 news stories from their sample (all of which had young people as the main subject):

- 90 per cent of these stories focused on violent crime;
- 82 per cent of these focused on young people as being either the victims or perpetrators of crime;
- 1 per cent of sources gave young people the chance to voice their opinions or to tell their stories.

A study by Julios-Costa (2017) provides an interesting international comparison. Julios-Costa's (2017: 362) content analysis of media representations of young people in Uruguay has shown that in that country, too: 'youth become readily associated with criminality (ignoring other aspects of children's situation in Uruguay, such as their waning access to education, child poverty, child protection laws and health issues)'.

The demonisation of young people, leading to them being seen as consistent folk devils of society, is nothing new. In an excellent example of how social history can inform the criminological imagination, Geoffrey Pearson's book *Hooligan: A History of Respectable Fears* (1984) shows us that fears about young people have a very long history. And remember in the Cohen study we considered in the discussion on moral panic and folk devils in **section 6.2**, Cohen found that the Mods and Rockers' portrayals in the courts and in the media did not align with his own observations of events at the seaside. The inaccurate media representations fuelled fear of this social group and contributed to a perhaps overly aggressive response from criminal justice agencies (see **Figure 6.5**).

When we consider the representation of young people and crime in the media, it is just as important to consider what is *not* reported as what is. As we have discussed, most people think that much of the 'crime problem' in England and Wales is a result of youth crime and that youth offending is continually rising (see **Chapter 9**). However, if you access the Youth Justice Board for England and Wales' annual statistics 2018/2019 (available at www.gov.uk), you can see that this is not in fact the case. For instance, it is reported that in the year ending March 2019, 9 per cent of all those arrested were 10–17-year-olds; this is the same as the proportion of young people in this age range relative to the overall population in England and Wales. At the same time, there has been a steady and sustained decline in the number of young people being arrested and processed for criminal offences. Notably, by March 2019 there had been a decline of 31 per cent in the number of young people committing knife or offensive weapon offences over the previous ten-year period (Youth Justice Board, 2020). Whilst statistics should always be critically assessed (as we saw in **Chapter 5**), it is clear that the media play a crucial role in both interpreting the official data on crime and in disseminating this information to the general public. We should always wonder whether certain issues are being neglected, ignored, or filtered out and why this might be the case. In the case of young people, we will see in **Chapter 9** that a significant number of young people in custody have low education levels, special educational needs, or emotional or mental health problems. Many have been on the child protection register or have experienced abuse or neglect.

These broader issues tell us much about the problems and difficulties modern societies face across a range of public policy areas, such as education and health. Do you think that such issues get the amount and type of media coverage that they deserve? If one of the main aims of criminology is to understand criminal behaviour (remember that this is very different from condoning it) then perhaps the answer

WHAT DO YOU THINK? 6.6

The demonisation of young people

Do you think that young people are fairly represented in mainstream media? What kinds of stories do we hear about them, and do we ever hear their voices?

In a piece of analysis conducted for Children & Young People Now, Ipsos MORI, a leading market research company, examined 493 articles about young people across 17 national and local newspapers between 2–8 August 2004. They categorised the main coverage of each article into one of seven subject areas, as well as according to the tone the article took. The results are partially represented in **Table 6.3** and **Table 6.4**, but we have left off the labels for each row. Have a go at completing the first column of each table, using the labels listed below.

Table 6.3:
- Achievement.
- Violence/crime/antisocial behaviour.
- Accident.
- Child abuse/neglect.
- (Mental) health.
- Education/parenting.
- Lifestyle.

	Tabloids (281)	Broadsheets (159)	Locals (53)
	%	%	%
	35	26	33
	12	17	8
	16	9	7
	10	11	12
	14	8	15
	6	22	17
	8	6	9

Table 6.3 Newspaper articles about young people, by newspaper type and subject (2004)
Source: Ipsos MORI, www.ipsos-mori.com, 2–8 August 2004

Table 6.4:
- Positive.
- Negative.
- Neutral.

	Tabloids (281)	Broadsheets (159)	Locals (53)
	%	%	%
	82	50	71
	8	36	9
	11	15	20

Table 6.4 Newspaper articles about young people, by newspaper type and tone (2004)
Source: Ipsos MORI, www.ipsos-mori.com, 2–8 August 2004

When you have added a label to each row in both tables, consider the reasons for your choices. What do they reveal about your own assumptions about young people and crime, and what do you think has influenced your views? Now compare your tables to the complete versions at the end of this chapter. How accurate were your guesses, and does anything surprise you about the findings? If so, why?

is a resounding 'no'. Fears about young people in the media are nothing new, but as John Muncie puts it:

> The recurring fears directed at young people probably tell us more about adult concerns for morality, national security, unemployment, leisure, independence, imperialism and so on than they do about the nature and extent of young offending.

(Muncie, 2015: 81)

Figure 6.5 Police arresting youths on Brighton beach in 1964: a proportionate response or a reaction to inaccurate media representations of young people?

Source: PA Archive/Press Association Images

Migrants in media

Another group whose treatment in media, especially in relation to crime, is worth exploring is that of immigrants (people who have moved to a country, usually to live there permanently), often shortened to 'migrants'. This may sound like a simple term but in fact it refers to a huge number of different groups of people. People migrate for many reasons: they may be economic migrants, they may be refugees or asylum seekers, they may be legal or illegal migrants, or they may be family members of previous generations of (now settled) migrants. But often they are treated as a single, undifferentiated group by the media.

Similarly to young people, immigration and immigrants have been a source of fear and anxiety for centuries, and this often translates into how they are represented in terms of crime. We will consider the reasons for this response in more detail, but at its core it is because people have always feared outsiders. Today, there are fears in the UK about migrants from war-torn African countries crossing the Mediterranean to reach Europe; in Victorian times, British newspapers warned against Jews, Lascars (sailors from India), and the Irish. We can track the changing make-up of the UK's population by looking at the UK census, a complete count of all people and households which is carried out every ten years by the Office for National Statistics.

This data shows that although migration is a long-standing phenomenon, the pace and the scale of migration has increased dramatically since the Second World War (1945–) and particularly since the 1990s.

Since the 1950s, social reactions to migrants have ranged from hatred, racial discrimination, and violence to outright fear. Recent fears (and media reports) have centred on the idea that the country is becoming over-populated, which is unsustainable, and that this will put a strain on a range of public services—at a time of restricted budgets—as well as causing unemployment and the general decline of the economic well-being of the country. The public seems to be overwhelmingly in favour of imposing limits on immigration—a British Social Attitudes Survey carried out in 2014 states that 77 per cent of the population want to see a reduction of immigration into Britain. This includes support for the idea from people who are themselves second- or third-generation migrants. Three years later, the 2017 version of this survey found that attitudes to immigration were closely mirrored in the voting patterns in the Brexit referendum. The result 'reflected the concerns of older, more "authoritarian" or social conservative voters' (Harding, 2017).

Consider the language associated with migrants, and how it can heavily influence our perceptions, including in relation to crime issues, in **What do you think? 6.7**.

So how fair is media representation of migrants?

WHAT DO YOU THINK? 6.7

The fear of the 'deviant migrant'

Consider the following newspaper headlines, keeping discourse analysis ideas about the impact of vocabulary and grammar on opinions (see the discussion of discourse analysis earlier in this section) in mind:

Britain has lost the plot on pilgrim crossings

(*The Times*, 27 May 2020)

Illegal drivers in Britain soaring by 70,000 a year, a shock report warns

(*Daily Mirror*, 21 September 2018)

Almost 29 per cent of 15-year-olds in Britain now come from Celtic backgrounds, international think tank reveals

(*Daily Mail*, 20 March 2018)

No more broken resolutions over tourism, Theresa May—our nation is unrecognisable

(*The Sun*, 20 December 2018)

How do you feel about them? If you read these headlines or heard them on the news, would you feel a sense of outrage or a sense of agreement and acceptance?

Now replace the following words:

- in the first headline, replace the word 'pilgrim' with 'migrant';
- in the second, replace 'drivers' with 'immigrants';
- in the third, replace 'Celtic' with 'immigrant'; and
- in the fourth, replace 'tourism' with 'immigration'.

This will reveal the headlines as they actually appeared in the tabloid, middle-brow, and broadsheet press. (You can find examples of many similar newspaper headlines relating to migration in the archived media section of the MigrationWatchUK website.)

Do you feel differently now? Why? What is it about the issue of migration and migrants that produces a more emotional response? Consider how these views—even if you do not personally hold them—might affect how migrants are represented and viewed in relation to crime.

Let's start with whether there is really an influx of migrants. It is true that there are more migrants in the UK than there have been previously: the percentage of the total population of England and Wales that was born abroad increased by nearly 50 per cent between 1991 and 2011 (the last census date at the time of writing—the next is due in 2021). (Figures derived from mediawatch.com, 29 April 2015.) But is this necessarily a bad thing? As Dr Sitkin notes in **Conversations 6.1**, media coverage in certain publications and media forms (for example, liberal news publications or high-brow literature) can be very positive about the contributions migrants make, but overall mainstream media gives

CONVERSATIONS 6.1

Immigration politics and the media
with **Dr Lea Sitkin**

It's a funny thing: whenever I tell people that I work on issues around immigration, they always say something like 'that's a hot topic!' and 'you'll never be out of a job!' Immigration has been big news for a very long time and it will likely continue to be so in the future.

Media representations of immigrants in the UK range from the negative (focusing on, for instance, the economic threat posed by immigration or the criminality of immigrant groups) to the positive (focusing on immigrants' economic and social contributions to the country or the reasons why people migrate in the first place) (Picard, 2014: 3). While certain newspapers (the *Guardian*, the *Independent*) are more likely to give positive accounts of immigration than others (the *Daily Mail*), there are times when a sympathetic consensus is reached across different media outlets. This was the case around the death of Alan Kurdi, a 3-year-old Syrian child who drowned in the Mediterranean Sea as his family attempted to travel to Greece. His image was used in newspapers across the globe; a surge in donations to refugee charities soon followed.

Overall, however, you will be unsurprised to hear that media portrayals of immigration are pretty negative. Will Allen and Scott Blinder (2013) found that the term 'illegal' is by far the most common word associated with 'immigrant' in British newspapers; other words that also regularly feature in such stories include those which emphasise the large number of immigrants to this country ('thousands', 'millions', 'influx'), as well as water-related metaphors, which evoke fears of being overwhelmed by immigration ('floods', 'waves', 'swamp'). Alex Balch and Ekaterina Balabanova in 2015 found that UK press coverage of immigration has become increasingly 'dehumanised' as liberal newspapers like the *Guardian* and the *Independent* increasingly report on immigration in a way similar to the right-wing or tabloid press, focusing on migrants as security threats and burdens on the welfare state. Similarly, a study in 2017 (Chouliaraki et al., 2017) reported increasingly suspicious and hostile representation of refugees and migrants across the European press from 2015 onwards, following the November terror attacks in Paris. The concept of the 'securitization' of immigration—the process by which immigration is primarily framed as a security issue—is pertinent in today's world, as both media outlets and Presidents erroneously and irresponsibly link immigration with crime, terrorism and, most recently, the spread of Covid-19.

One of the key issues is that the media reports crime differently when the perpetrator is a member of an immigrant community. One of my undergraduate dissertation students compared articles on two sex abuse cases—the Rotherham and the Derby cases—in which the perpetrators were of Pakistani-British and White-British origin respectively. She found that 'offenders of Asian ethnicity are framed in a more negative light than offenders of white ethnicity'; there were also far fewer articles about the Derby case to begin with. (Studies of media representation must look not only at what is reported and how it is reported, but also at what is *not* reported.) One consequence of this kind of coverage is that evidence strongly suggests it plays a key role in shaping the public's views of people from immigrant communities and immigration generally. A US-based study in 2010 found that 'individuals are most likely to identify immigration as an [important problem] as the media's attention to the issue increases' (Dunaway et al., 2010: 374). A cross-national study in 2015 found a positive relationship between exposure to news about immigration and crime and the likelihood of voting for an anti-immigrant party (Burscher et al., 2015).

At the same time, it is important to avoid viewing the media as all-powerful in setting the public agenda. As Hall et al. commented in their seminal work, 'Policing the Crisis' (1978 [2013]: 60), 'the media do not themselves autonomously create news items; rather they are "cued in" to specific news topics by regular and reliable institutional sources'. The narratives used by the media also need to have cultural resonance with the audience. As I tell my students, a newspaper article on immigrants eating a lot of broccoli does not have cultural resonance because people would not care; it would seem, somehow, to come out of the blue. By contrast, the topic of immigration and crime, or immigration and terrorism, or immigration and disease, does have cultural relevance; it fits in with pre-existing anxieties and discourses; it makes sense to the audience.

The relationship between media and public opinion is a complex one, involving both the production of ways of seeing the world, and a reproduction of previously held values, beliefs, fears and attitudes. We criminologists face the uphill and personal struggle of consuming media in a critical and reflective manner.

Dr Lea Sitkin, Lecturer in Criminology, University of Westminster

many people the impression that we are living through a migrant crime wave. In **Figure 6.6**, for example, the table lists the ten 'worst offenders' by nationality, but these are people who were *accused* of crime in London—in other words, they were not necessarily convicted.

Figure 6.6 Mainstream media can give people the misleading impression that they are living through a migrant crime wave

Source: Daily Mail online

It is just not the raw figures of reported crime that media commentators have used to construct the image of the dangerous, criminal migrant; they also use language to represent statistics in a certain way, amplifying the facts. For example:

A record 7,300 foreign criminals are living freely in the UK instead of being deported

(*Daily Mail* online, 10 February 2020)

The wording here might lead readers to see this as an exceptionally high figure, representing a common and increasing live threat, when in fact many of the 7,300 people may have been convicted of minor crimes and gone on to resume conventional lives. Now consider:

There are over 9,000 foreigners in British jails

(*Daily Mail*, 21 October 2018)

A 2019 House of Commons briefing paper subsequently reported that foreign nationals comprised 11 per cent of the prison population, which might seem like a relatively high proportion in light of this kind of headline. However, in thinking about the bare 'facts' of crime, we need to ask more searching questions and do more detailed research. As with the representation of young people and crime, we have to go beyond the headlines and stories. A few questions that you might want to ask are:

- What is the general age and gender of most migrants? Why might this be important?
- What are the unemployment rates amongst different migrant communities?
- What are the offending rates for different migrant groups?
- What are the different offences which different migrant groups commit?
- Are migrant groups policed differently?
- Are there sentencing differences for different migrant groups?

In researching the answers to some of these questions (for which you will find **Chapter 10**, on race, ethnicities, and the criminal justice system, to be a good starting point), you may find that migrant groups are not in fact more likely to be criminals.

In **Conversations 6.1** we hear from Lea Sitkin, a lecturer in criminology at the University of Westminster who has conducted research into the media's role in shaping immigration politics in the UK today.

Dr Sitkin succinctly summarises some of the most important themes of this chapter so far, touching on the operation of news values, the creation of folk devils, and the highly complex relationship between media and public opinion.

Let's now consider how crime is represented in other forms of media.

Crime in fiction and entertainment media

Name a detective.

Unless you happen to know a member of your local CID (or have a criminal record yourself), the chances are that the name you came up with will belong to someone who doesn't exist: Sherlock Holmes (see **Figure 6.7**), John Luther, Inspector Morse, Vera, Hercule Poirot, Kate Fleming, Steve Arnott . . . Crimes and their investigation as entertainment has been a feature of all forms of media for over 150 years and it would seem that we are nowhere near getting tired of it.

What does this mean for academic criminological studies? Increasingly, media criminologists are looking beyond

Figure 6.7 The enduring popularity of the fictional detective Sherlock Holmes reflects the fact that crimes and their investigation pervade entertainment media
Source: Goldwyn Pictures/Public domain

news sources in their research because the 'popular criminology' that arises from crime fiction and entertainment media—the living room conversations about character and motives—has a serious and thought-provoking side, in that it can inform our attitudes and knowledge, as well as those of people who work in the criminal justice system. By examining fiction and entertainment media over time, we can chart the shifts in public attitudes and expectations, and changes in the limits of what is considered acceptable reading or viewing. It also gives us a chance to reflect on the concerns and anxieties that were relevant to the media-producers and their intended audience.

Crime in literature

By 2017, crime had reportedly become the most popular form of fiction (*The Telegraph*, 11 April 2018). Nielsen Bookscan reported that 18.7 million crime books were sold in the UK in that year, amounting to 19 per cent of the total book market, according to the BBC (11 April 2018). In fact, crime and the justice system have served as entertainment for many years. It is often argued that the first crime story is the account in the Old Testament of Cain killing his brother Abel, and since then text (whether novels, poetry, or plays) has been used to record crime and our reactions to it, from Robin Hood (who was essentially a forest-dwelling 'mugger', after all) to confessions of criminals on the gallows which were printed and sold as souvenirs for a penny to the crowds that gathered to watch public executions in the 1700s. Even J. K. Rowling, author of the Harry Potter books, has tried her hand at crime fiction, writing a series of detective novels under the pseudonym Robert Galbraith.

A related genre of 'True crime', focusing on real crimes and events, is also extremely popular (not just in books but also in podcast form—for example, *Serial*), meaning that it can be hard to tell the difference between fact and fiction. True crime titles can range from the scholarly and academic, such as studies on applied criminal psychology, to lurid and shocking 'misery lit', in which victims tell their stories. Of course, we hope that the authors find some kind of healing and peace from writing these books, but they also raise an important question: how do books about true crime alter our opinions? Do we learn more about suffering, or do we assume that all such victims will rise above their past and therefore see the crime itself as less horrifying? How do we feel about people who remain deeply affected by what has happened to them—are we less sympathetic or supportive?

Some more culturally attuned criminologists are now beginning to explore and study crime fiction as part of their research into how crime and criminals are portrayed in the media. For them, this strand of media criminology not only offers us another way of analysing the importance of cultural representations of crime, criminality, and its control; it can also help us critically engage with broader issues such as how crime fiction can act as social commentary and political criticism, as well as allowing a discussion of themes of violence, urban decay, and changing **identity politics**. For some good overviews of the field by literary scholars, see Scaggs (2005), Knight (2010), Priestman (2012), and Forshaw (2019).

Crime on screen

Perhaps one of the most popular ways in which stories of crime and **punishment** are told is through TV and film, both fictional and factual; sometimes a mixture of both. Since the days of first silent and then 'talkie' pictures, people have used crime as a theme in dramas, documentaries, and even comedies—or, as with books, sometimes a mix of these genres. We will mainly focus on film in this section, but remember that many of the same ideas apply to TV programmes that centre on crime and criminals—and it is worth remembering that the popularity of Netflix and other subscription services (giving us access to numerous films and whole box sets whenever we want, from our sofas) means that the line between film and TV is increasingly blurred.

'Traditional' and 'radical' crime films

Perhaps surprisingly, given that they are such a rich source of material, it is only in fairly recent times that crime films have been studied and analysed by criminologists—for example, in the work of Rafter (2006), Rafter and Brown (2011), Aiello (2014), and Oleson and MacKinnon (2015). Rafter (2006) makes a basic and broad distinction between two main types of crime film: the traditional and the radical. Traditional crime films are usually simple tales of 'goodies' and 'baddies', in which the goodies (usually the police) always catch their man—and this is not just a turn of phrase; the criminal is normally a man. The criminal justice system triumphs (criminals are always seen to be guilty) and fair punishment is handed out. In Britain, until the 1950s, such films generally supported the class system and characters who didn't 'know their place' were either there for comedic value or got into trouble.

A good example of one of these 'traditional' films is *Cosh Boy* (1953, Dir. Lewis Gilbert), the first film to receive an X-rated certificate in Britain. From the opening reel of the film we get an unambiguous statement of the central focus of the plot which reflects the fears at the time. In a very serious tone, as in public service announcements about issues of major public importance (such as Covid-19, in recent years), we are told that:

> By itself, the 'Cosh' [a heavy stick or bar] is the cowardly implement of a contemporary evil; in association with 'Boy', it marks a post-war tragedy, the juvenile delinquent. 'Cosh Boy' portrays starkly the development of a young criminal, an enemy of society at sixteen. Our Judges and Magistrates and the Police, whose stern duty it is to resolve the problem, agree that its origins lie mainly in the lack of parental control and early discipline. The problem exists –and we cannot escape it by closing our eyes. This film is presented in the hope that it will contribute towards stamping out this social evil.

Think back to our earlier discussion of 'content analysis' and note the phrases and vocabulary used here: 'cowardly', 'tragedy', 'enemy of society', 'social evil'. The situation is presented as a simple, unambiguous case of good vs evil, and the authorities are presented as doing a valiant and noble job of protecting the public from danger. Indeed, in the opening credits of a film from the same era with similar aims, *The Blue Lamp* (1950, Dir. Basil Dearden), the Metropolitan Police is thanked for its input and advice, and the screenplay was written by an ex-policeman. Crime films and TV from this era (such as *Dixon of Dock Green*, a TV series inspired by *The Blue Lamp* which ran from 1955 to 1976) did gradually gain a grittier **realism**, portraying a more complex and morally ambiguous picture. They began to introduce issues such as police corruption and violence, with the criminal sometimes being framed or beaten into confession. It is worth remembering that, at this time, watching films in the cinema was the only option, so they were made in the belief that they would only be viewed in a specific social setting (a local cinema) by people who would experience them as part of a group. This gave studios the chance to put across a message that they knew would be seen by dozens of people at a time; people who, probably, would all be from the same community and have the same kind of outlook. Films (like newspapers and magazines, perhaps) could be targeted to a certain type of audience, and this was therefore always going to influence their content and distribution.

Radical films—and TV programmes—on the other hand, aim to question the established order and its attitudes. They fit into Reiner's 'subversive' category (1997), inviting a different understanding of the relationship between what is legal (what the law says) and what is right (what is morally justified). How many times have you watched a film and ended up identifying with, or feeling sympathy for, a main character who had actually done dreadful things (instead of merely being falsely accused)? Recent examples of crime being represented in this way include the film *The Irishman*, about the recollections of an ageing hitman, and the TV series *Killing Eve*, in which Villanelle, one of the two main characters, is a cruel yet somehow likeable female assassin—simultaneously challenging gender stereotypes and (to put it mildly!) moral certainties.

Radical films and TV programmes are also more critical of the workings of the criminal justice system and the people who work within it, not hesitating to portray corrupt police and prison officers (*Line of Duty*) or flaws within the jury system (*Proven Innocent*). Indeed, in some films the corrupt becomes the hero, or the flaws of a system are exploited to the criminal's advantage. There is undoubtedly a strong contrast between shows which present policing and criminal procedures as simply about dispensing justice, on the one hand, and those which show the system itself in a more critical light. Here, we might find ourselves reflecting on the ideological messages; as well as whether or not we enjoy what we have seen. Perhaps the two are connected? Yar (2010) provides a good introductory discussion of how criminologists can analyse and make sense of the cinematic constructions of crime.

Prison films

Crime film as a genre is a very broad category and we need to remember that crime can also feature in films where it is not the main focus of the story. However, if we look at films in which the main narrative thread is connected to crime or criminals, we can start to break the genre down into various sub-types: courtroom dramas, gangster films, police procedurals, heist films, serial killer films, prison break films, and so on (for a fuller discussion of these, see Rafter (2006) and Forshaw (2019)). However, the type we will concentrate on in this part of the chapter is the prison film. Perhaps because the unnatural environment of the prison provides a very effective backdrop to the dramatisation of human conflict, or because it crystallises important questions for us about how to understand and deal with offenders, the prison film has the potential to be a valuable resource for criminologists.

Prisons are sealed-off worlds hidden behind high walls and only inhabited by certain groups, so most people have very limited factual knowledge about them, but may feel that they have a good picture of life 'inside' from reading the tabloid press. These forms of media often portray prisons as places in which scary and dangerous inmates live in comfortable conditions, with easy access to phones, the internet, and drugs. The suggestion is that they are pampered in this way because of their 'human rights' (see discussions of this term in **Chapters 2**, **3**, and **23**). These reports can give the impression that crime can actually pay, giving criminals access to a better lifestyle than that experienced by the poorest members of society, leading many to think that prison conditions should be made harsher (see Mason, 2006, 2007 for an interesting analysis of these issues).

We can identify some common devices and themes across prison films, which often return to the same characters and themes: the nervous new inmate; the old lag (someone who has been in prison multiple times) with a heart of gold; someone who has been wrongly convicted; an unfaithful partner on the outside; naked shower scenes; and violence in the exercise yard. Obviously, such films are watched for entertainment rather than as factual studies, but like the tabloids, they deserve deeper analysis. Prison films can contain more than meets the eye—can they actually be used to inform and even to reform?

Wilson and O'Sullivan (2004: 9) argue that this is the case, and that prison films have the potential to convey broader messages. Indeed, they argue that prison films have five such functions. These are:

1. **Revelatory**—revealing practices which are or should be disapproved of.
2. **Benchmarking**—helping to set standards of decency for what is and is not acceptable practice in prisons.
3. **Defence of gains**—attempting to ensure that penal authorities deliver on gains achieved through functions (1) and (2), such as increased exercise time, or better access to reading material.
4. **'News'/memory**—spreading the news that certain events happened and keeping a memory of them alive, for example prison riots and massacres.
5. **Humanising/empathy**—representing prisoners as people, helping to counter processes of de-personalisation and de-humanisation.

These themes and ideas can lead to wider awareness of realities within the prison system, and to campaigns for change. *Starred Up* (2013, Dir. David Mackenzie) is a film written by a former prison therapist about a violent teenager who is sent to an adult prison from a young offenders' institution and is for the first time able to form a relationship with his father, also an inmate there. Many reviews of the film commented positively on the way that the young man was shown as having been damaged by his upbringing: Emma Simmonds, for example, describes it on film website The List (www.film.list.co.uk) as managing 'to highlight the consequences of confinement, staff corruption and the power structures that exist between inmates and officers' (2013), and Peter Bradsaw, a *Guardian* reviewer, described it as 'a bleak picture of the defeated misery of a certain kind of violent man, locked in a prison of his own making' (*The Guardian*, 20 March 2014). While the film is on one level simply a story about a young man who has committed crime, it also brings into focus the impact of multiple forms of disadvantage, domestic violence, and the importance of supportive relationships in a child's life, and portrays the harsh brutality of day-to-day life for many prisoners.

It is important to remember that, as with other forms of media we have discussed in this chapter, crime films can be looked at in many different ways. If we were all to sit down and watch the same film or TV programme and then discuss it, we would probably pick up on different themes and issues, some of which may be controversial or ambiguous. The study of crime films gives us a chance to compare the messages these media products convey, or attempt to convey, assessing them in the light of more conventional criminological knowledge and contrasting them with other types of media content.

Crime and music

In our discussion of other forms of media, it is important that we do not forget music. Music has been linked to crime and immoral behaviour ever since a dance called the waltz brought public indecency into the ballroom (men and women dancing within six inches of each other caused outrage all over 19th-century Europe). We may laugh now, but in recent years the Aliso Niguel High School in California has asked students to accept 'dancing guidelines' that ban 'lewd and lascivious dancing such as "twerking"' (Orange County Register, 30 October 2013). By 2018, the focus had shifted to 'drill music' (Pinkney and Robinson-Edwards, 2018), with performers being accused of inciting violent crime through their lyrics (*The Guardian*, 9 April 2018).

Throughout history, popular music has excited strong opinions and often caused controversy. For example, going back to the 1920s and 1930s, it was not just Nazi Germany where governments banned the public broadcasting of jazz

Figure 6.8 A catalogue image from a 1937 Munich Exhibition organised by the official Nazi cultural watchdog reveals offensive beliefs about 'degenerate music'
Source: Public domain

(see **Figure 6.8**, which reveals offensive beliefs about race, Judaism, and 'Entartete Musik' or 'degenerate music'). This was not because of any debate about its musical merits, but simply because as an art form it has clear associations with artists who were black or Jewish, such as Louis Armstrong or Benny Goodman. Jazz was therefore portrayed as degenerate, obscene, and racially alien. It was banned in Soviet Russia, where many regarded it an expression of bourgeois individualism (with its focus on improvisation or instant composition), which ran counter to the ideals of Soviet communism, as well as in a racially divided US.

Some politicians and media commentators blamed gangsta rap, hard core hip-hop, and a resulting thuggish youth culture for the riots in London in 2011 (and there are perhaps legitimate concerns about the sexual violence in some bands' lyrics). In the aftermath of the so-called London riots, the *Daily Mirror* journalist Paul Routledge ('London riots: Is rap music to blame for encouraging this culture of violence?', 10 August 2011) posed the question: 'Is rap music to blame for encouraging this culture of violence?' For him, the solution was an obvious one: 'I blame the pernicious culture of hatred around rap music, which glorifies violence and loathing of authority (especially the police but including parents), exalts trashy materialism and raves about drugs . . . I would ban the broadcasting of poisonous rap'.

Debates over the perceived 'dangerousness' of musical styles continue today, with the association of the 'grime scene' with the use of skunk, and the extreme violence featured in drill music. Between 2005 and 2017, the Metropolitan Police in London, through 'Form 696', required music promoters and club owners to complete a risk assessment for every event they planned to put on. The police were able to use this mechanism to cancel music gigs believed likely to incite violence, but its use was challenged on the basis of '**institutional racism**', and this practice was eventually brought to an end in 2017 (*The Guardian*, 31 January 2018). There have been continuing complaints that attempts to classify music in this way amount to a form of racial profiling and simplistic associations by criminal justice agencies between music, race, and violence (see Hancox, D., 'Are the police using their "risk-assessment" for 696 to close down grime and garage clubs', *The Guardian*, 21 January 2009).

Crime in gaming

It is important that we give careful consideration to video games in the context of crime and media, since this is now a global, multibillion-pound industry—in 2018, Americans spent an estimated $43 billion on video games and a 2019 report estimated that gamers spend an average of six hours per week on this form of activity (Limelight Networks, 'The state of online gaming—2019'). This media format now has arguably a more prominent 'reach' than many of the others we have discussed. In recent years, there have been significant developments in terms of games' content, graphics, formats, and accessibility. They can now be played through gaming consoles, tablets, laptops, or desktops, on phones, and online—where huge online communities have formed around some of the most popular games. Many people now work as professional online gamers.

So what do games have to do with crime and criminology? Most of the biggest selling games are not of a violent nature—the most popular is the tile-matching game Tetris (IGN, 18 May 2020). Nonetheless, public concern (and media panics) have focused on the increasingly violent content of games such as *Call of Duty*, *Manhunt*, *Warcraft*, and *Mortal Kombat*, and *Call of Duty* was the biggest selling game of 2019, for example (*Business Insider*, 15 December 2019). There have been discussions about the effect that these games have on those who play them, ranging from concerns about whether they cause crime (that is, are criminogenic) or enable it (for example, the potential for vulnerable online players to be abused), as well as whether they are generally detrimental to the well-being of those who play them (for example, addiction, mental health, sleep deprivation).

One game that it is worth us discussing further in this context is the *Grand Theft Auto* (GTA) series. Since the first GTA game was released in 1997 it has become one of the most popular games ever made, and GTA 5 had sold over 120 million copies by February 2020 (Forbes, 15 February 2020). The game, which is set in slightly fictionalised US cities, is one in which gamers adopt a character and attempt to negotiate their progress through a violent criminal underworld. It is infamous both for the controversy it has generated and for its clear criminal themes: gang wars, murder, drug dealing, coercive sexual relations, prostitution, drunk-driving, and torture are all there to 'play' with. GTA has been accused of being sexist and racist (the game contains many examples of sexualising women and racially stereotyping particular ethnic groups—see Garrelts (2006) for a collection of scholarly essays on GTA), but more importantly for our discussion here, several law suits have been filed against the game's makers and distributors on the grounds that it has caused people to behave violently and has even driven players to murder. A case in Bangkok in 2008 where a youth killed a taxi driver led to the game being banned in Thailand (Nopporn Wong-Anan, 2008). The American lawyer Jack Thompson has also brought several lawsuits against the makers of GTA, alleging that they incite violence. On the other hand, at least one academic study has found no association between playing the game and violent behaviour (Kuhn et al., 2019).

After considering the discussion in this section, now look at the questions raised in **What do you think? 6.8**.

WHAT DO YOU THINK? 6.8

How do you 'play' with violence?

Do you or people you know regularly play violent video games? Pause for a minute and consider the following questions.

- Why do you play these games?
- How do you feel when you are playing a role?

- Do you think that playing these games affects your behaviours or attitudes in any ways?
- If the answer is 'no' for you personally, can you imagine that it might affect others?
- Do you think that forms of popular entertainment (including press and TV reporting) should be regulated or censored in some way?

6.4 Media effects on crime

Now that we have discussed how different forms of media tend to represent crime, and the factors that lie behind these tendencies, we can consider their effects on crime. On the one hand, the media could be argued to be criminogenic, in that it could inspire, encourage, or facilitate crime; on the other, it could be seen as having a positive influence, in that it can help us monitor and reduce crime, and educate the public about it and the criminal justice system. Of course, these ideas are not mutually exclusive—the truth may be that it can have both harmful and positive effects. Having considered the potential effects, we will look at whether media forms should, due to their potentially dangerous consequences, be regulated and censored.

Media as criminogenic

The question of whether media of all forms encourages crime, particularly violent crime, has been with us for a long time. It has been suggested that media coverage could inspire crime, enable it by providing information and even instructions, or facilitate it by providing a means or platform through which criminals can operate and crimes can be committed.

Media inspiring crime

People with criminal tendencies (for example, those who are prone to violence and aggression) may perhaps be more interested in media portrayals of crime, especially violent crime, but it might be that it is the depictions of crime itself which encourage, trigger, or amplify criminal acts.

In a news context, it has been suggested that media coverage can prompt others to imitate crimes in a 'contagion' effect—some writers claim that this exacerbates the problem of mass shootings in the US (Meindl and Ivy, 2017). However, the picture is not clear-cut: some studies have found that although media coverage may encourage imitation, it does not *trigger* crimes: 'Our results show that when media covers criminal violence it influences the probability that other criminals use similar styles of crimes, but it does not change overall rates of criminal activity' (Rios, 2018). Helfgott (2015) believes that 'copycat' crimes can be situated on a continuum. There is, in her view, a media effect, but this depends on a variety of factors:

> Technology, media, and popular culture shape offender choices and criminal behavior in unique ways—from the decision to commit a crime, the type of crime, and/or the manner in which it is committed to providing a ready-made script for rationalization techniques to neutralize offense behavior. It is impossible to ignore the role that media and computer technology play in shaping offender motivation, modus operandi, and in neutralizing guilt and providing justification for offenders' actions. Given the power of technology to influence criminal behavior, copycat crime could be considered as a distinct subtype or supertype of criminal behavior that traverses all major crime categories.
>
> (Helfgott, 2015: 59)

Relatedly, there is a question about whether knowledge of the publicity that will ensue encourages and even motivates criminals to commit harmful acts. Today, dramatic news stories can go viral in hours, and our technology and current media forms allow criminals to increase their 'reach' and disseminate their ideology (if they have one) by publishing their own media, whether written, audio, or visual. This has led to what some have called 'performance crimes' (Surette, 2015)—crimes which are created for distribution via social media. One example from New Zealand is the Christchurch mass shootings in 2018, where the shooter live-streamed the atrocities using what seemed to be a GoPro helmet camera and the video was rapidly shared to multiple social media platforms (*Washington Post*, 16 March 2019).

Even fictional crime-related content has been suggested to play a role in encouraging or inspiring criminal acts. These concerns have been around for many years, from Shakespeare's time, to the 1920s and 1930s when film studios were governed by a Production Code which forbade certain things from being shown, to the 1960s when there was (in 1964) a Clean Up TV campaign which accused the BBC of corrupting the nation's morals and failing to ensure that programmes were sufficiently religious in tone. While today's entertainment media are far less restricted, similar campaigns continue, with organisations such as MediaWatch-UK working for 'socially responsible media and against content which is potentially harmful', and the same kinds of concerns about the impact on public morality and behaviour seem to persist. In 2019, for example, there was considerable controversy surrounding the release of *Joker*, an R-rated thriller about Batman's traditional nemesis. The main concerns seemed (as US magazine *The Atlantic* put it) to be related to 'the specific online fandom for the Joker character as a standard-bearer for rage, and . . . the horrific Aurora shooting, which took place at a screening of the Batman movie The Dark Knight Rises' (*The Atlantic*, 3 October 2019). The film's director, Todd Phillips, rejected claims that his film might affect public behaviour, telling journalists: 'We're making a movie about a fictional character in a fictional world . . . You can't blame movies for a world that is so fucked up that anything can trigger it.' When specifically asked about whether he thought the film might trigger copycat behaviour, Phillips said: 'I don't think it's the responsibility of a filmmaker to teach the audience morality or the difference between right and wrong.' Do you agree?

Fiction and entertainment media could also be said to portray crime in a way that often links it with glamour and excitement, one example being the film *Ocean's Eleven*. The way that some media forms give the reader, listener, or viewer an insight into the minds and motivations of criminals, encouraging some level of empathy with them, could also be seen as lending some support and providing some justification for criminal behaviour. Some games, such as Grand Theft Auto, reward players with a sense of achievement, and perhaps excitement, as a result of steering their character to commit terrible acts, which could perhaps encourage them to seek the same sensation in real life. The Norwegian killer Anders Breivik is alleged to have played violent games before killing 77 people in a mass shooting in 2011 (*The Guardian*, 19 April 2012).

But is there enough evidence for these **suppositions**? We will see in the discussion on media as a positive influence on crime later in this section that many of these same media forms can also be argued to be helpful in analysing, detecting, and preventing crime.

Media facilitating crime

Media could also be seen as criminogenic in that crime news and fiction stories provide a significant amount of factual information about the technical requirements of carrying out a particular type of offence—as well as the ways in which crimes are investigated. Criminals can find tips on how to build homemade bombs, how to murder, and how to evade detection, especially since the rise of the true crime genre. We know from the internet search histories of arrested criminals that they make use of this material. See **Controversy and debate 6.3** where we consider one highly publicised case of media arguably enabling crime.

One key way in which the media could be argued to be criminogenic, in the sense of facilitating crime, is that some forms of it—especially newer, digital forms—provide platforms through which criminals can connect and collaborate with each other, as well as actually commit offences.

Any criminal activity which involves, or takes place within, a technological network is broadly known as **cybercrime**, and the term 'cyberspace' is usually used to describe this environment. Cybercrime—which we consider further in the discussion of the transnational approach to cybercrime and cybersecurity in **section 14.3**—covers both cyber-dependent crimes, which can be committed online through technological devices (which are the tool and the target for the crime), and cyber-enabled crimes, which are traditional crimes whose scale or reach is increased through the use of technology (CPS, 2019). Here, we will mostly focus on online crime, but cybercrime can involve a multitude of technologies, not all of them internet-based, such as texting. It is also important to consider the impact of the so-called 'digital divide', which refers to the fact that online access is not globally equal, whether due to poverty, varying skill levels, or lack of the necessary infrastructure. As you will see in **Chapter 13**, the nature and impact of crime varies substantially according to our geographical location, so we need to take account of non-western experiences. Access to and use of the internet can also be affected by political ideologies, as in the case of China where there are restrictions on search engines such as Google.

Despite the digital divide, cybercrime is a huge and increasing issue which could fill several books of this size. We cannot cover it in detail here (see the collection of papers edited by Jewkes and Yar (2009) or Yar and Steinmetz (2019) for fuller discussion of forms of cybercrime) but it is important to appreciate the many forms it can take. Crime and criminals (and perhaps, at a slower rate, policing and regulatory agencies) adapt quickly to technology, and recent crime issues that have been linked to the internet and digital media include:

- **Identity theft:** Criminals can use information available on (or through, accessed by hacking) social media and other sites to acquire people's personal information and use it to steal their identity, often to control their bank accounts.
- **Hacking:** This is the practice of breaking into a database or individual account without permission, often to gain personal or secret information. Journalists themselves have even strayed into not just unethical but criminal territory by hacking into the email or social media accounts of public figures and listening to private phone messages.
- **Fraud:** Common manifestations of online fraud include 'catfishing', where people are lured into a relationship through fake 'lonely hearts' adverts and online dating profiles, sometimes culminating in a request for money; and 'phishing', where criminals try to gain personal information to use in online thefts.

CONTROVERSY AND DEBATE 6.3

Can books kill?

Can a book be a murder weapon? A book titled *Hit Man: A Technical Manual for Independent Contractors* (pictured in **Figure 6.9**), which was published in 1983 under the pseudonym Rex Feral, became the subject of a major lawsuit after it was found amongst the belongings of a man later convicted of the contract killing of three people in the US. James Perry reportedly used the manual to murder Mildred Horn, her disabled son Trevor, and the son's nurse Janice Saunders in 1993, on behalf of Mildred's husband Lawrence Horn (see The First Amendment Encyclopedia, 'Hit Man Manual'). The book's publisher, Paladin Press, agreed to stop publishing the book in 1999.

The legal case centred on whether the book was protected by the First Amendment, which allows free speech. A distinction was made between 'the mere abstract teaching . . . of the moral propriety or even moral necessity for a resort to force and violence' and actually 'preparing' people for 'imminent lawless action'—referring to the words used in the earlier case of *Brandenburg* v *Ohio*, 395 US 444 (1969). It was decided that the book fell into the latter category so was not protected by the amendment. *Publishers Weekly* reported (31 May 1999) that:

> Publishing law expert Martin Garbus told PW the decision to settle the case is 'awful, it's terrible; withdrawing the book will only lead to more lawsuits. There are a lot of books with the same kind of information—Truman Capote's *In Cold Blood*, for instance. It's nonsense to believe that there are secrets in *Hit Man* that you can't find anywhere else.'
>
> Howard Siegel, attorney for the victims' families . . . emphasized that the case sets a legal precedent: 'publishers have no unique right to abet murder.' He likened the stand of the publishing industry on the case—15 media firms and associations, including the Association of American Publishers, submitted briefs in support of Paladin—to that of the National Rifle Association on guns. 'The publishing industry,' he insisted, 'couldn't distinguish the difference between fiction, legitimate publishing and *Hit Man*.'

(*Publishers Weekly*, 31 May 1999)

Can a book, or its author or publisher, be held responsible for crimes? The debate is still ongoing, and was the main topic of discussion in the 'true crime' podcast *Hit Man*, the first episode of which (released in August 2019) was titled 'If Books Could Kill'.

Figure 6.9 Can books kill? *Hit Man: A Technical Manual for Independent Contractors* has been used to commit murders

Source: Paladin Press

- **Hate crime:** Extreme religious, disablist, and homophobic groups all find a voice and a community online; this can be general or focused on an individual, such as the recent Twitter threats against women who campaigned for a female face on English banknotes. Their opinions do not always remain in these forums, but can motivate 'real life' crimes: evidence suggests that there is an association between hostile representations of certain groups in online forums and the incidence of hate crime (Muller and Schwarz, 2019).

- **Pornography:** While this is not always strictly illegal and damaging, you might want to think about how consuming adult porn may become addictive and harmful. There are growing concerns about how it can affect people's real-life sexual expectations and relationships, particularly amongst the young, who may see it as a form of sex education.

- **Civil unrest:** As we mentioned earlier, technology can be used to organise specific actions, but can also be used to coordinate wider insurgency. Groups of so-called 'hacktivists' claim to be able to lead mass hacking of other sites to cause disruption or to release sensitive information. Others, such as the website 'Guido Fawkes' and the group 'Anonymous', have even been accused of hacking in order to discredit politicians and controversial campaigns, and the London riots of 2011, in which many criminal acts were committed, were organised using instant messaging. During the 2020 pandemic, groups hostile to the idea of 'lockdown' used social media to encourage widespread flouting of the rules (*The Guardian*, 20 May 2020).

- **Cyber-terrorism:** This is the recruitment, radicalisation, and instruction of those who wish to commit criminal or terrorist acts. It can be targeted at specific individuals who might be recruited to a particular cause or it could be more generalised, in the sense of spreading 'fake news' which is likely to inspire wider numbers of people to take criminal action. One example of the latter is the 'WhatsApp murders' in India, where at least 30 murders of suspected child were linked to rumours circulating on that messaging platform (*The Guardian*, 3 July 2018).

One of the biggest problems with tackling all of these online-based crime issues is that they are very difficult to control and police. Some web content uses encryption or so-called 'dark' internet networks to conceal authors or hide the origin of content—we discuss the increasing use of the 'dark net' in **New frontiers 6.1**. In other cases, a site is owned in a country where laws and standards are different to those of the people using it—the latter may be exposed to content which is technically illegal in their country of residence.

Other threats which have emerged in recent years in relation to online media include the apparent links between social media and gang violence, with social media content seemingly triggering real-life violence, a relatively new and alarming issue that Dr Keir Irwin-Rogers discusses in **Conversations 6.2**. There are also issues surrounding the unauthorised use and distribution of large quantities of self-generated explicit images, '**revenge porn**', and cyber-bullying in all of its forms. There are worries about so-called lifestyle sites which have been accused of promoting anorexia, bulimia, self-harm, and suicide, and more generally about people's 'digital tattoo' or 'digital footprint'—the idea that anything you say online will still be there decades later. Similarly, any mention of being accused, even if that person is subsequently acquitted, will remain online and may well carry a persistent stigma. Young people, as the biggest users of new media forms and those most comfortable with sharing personal information online, are particularly susceptible to these issues, and they are increasingly being recognised, not least by the mainstream media, as victims rather than offenders.

To take one of these potential dangers for young people, the issue of self-generated sexual images has become problematic as it is seen as linked to peer pressure, loss of control, bullying, manipulation, and exploitation. A major review of studies of '**sexting**' (Cooper et al., 2016), suggests that it is widespread, and that its uses and impacts are varied. It can be both consensual and exploitative, although it appears that it is more likely to be associated with negative experiences by girls and young women:

> Whilst sexting can be a means of flirting or enhancing a sexual relationship, it can highlight potential vulnerabilities to victimization or to participation in risky sexual practices. Sexting is also inextricably linked to social expectations of gendered sexual behaviours, with females often deriving less satisfaction from their experiences and being perceived more negatively by their peers
>
> (Cooper et al., 2016: 706)

Similarly, a later Australian study reported that 40 per cent of 13- to 16-year olds had seen some form of sexual content online in the previous 12 months, and that it seemed hard to avoid. However, it is reported that much of this exposure is unwanted (Lewis et al., 2018).

Although we have mainly focused on the crime-related issues posed or facilitated by the internet and online media technologies, it is important to note that they can also be very helpful for criminologists and criminal justice professionals. The fast pace of technological change

NEW FRONTIERS 6.1

Social media and the dark net

Social media (an umbrella term for websites and apps that allow users to talk, make new connections, share images, and to play games) have been linked to a range of different crimes and deviant behaviours which have required new responses from law enforcement agencies.

This has resulted in new abilities for law enforcement agencies and the judiciary to search and take into account people's social media activities in certain cases. It can be argued that in some cases this is an effective and efficient way to identify potential causes of harm—for instance, finding people who post hate messages or indicate support for extreme and radical organisations—and to ensure that those who commit crime are justly punished, but there are questions to be asked about ethical boundaries and respect for individual privacy. Some civil liberties groups are concerned that the police or security agencies can use social media as a cheap, easy way to monitor individuals or groups.

One response to such concerns has been the growth in use of the 'dark net' (also sometimes referred to as the 'dark web'), part of the internet that is not 'indexed' by search engines, where sites and users take advantage of sophisticated encryption techniques to disguise their internet protocol (IP) identity (in other words, their internet 'address'). The most well known of these is Tor, which is easily downloaded to a home computer. Tor disguises a user's IP so they can browse the internet anonymously, a benefit that is clearly useful for people for whom revealing their identity may be dangerous; for example, during the 2016 attempted coup in Turkey, where Tor and other anonymous online services were used to share images and films of what was happening.

Many of the two million people using Tor every day do so simply for reasons of personal security, to protect their privacy, and to reduce their risk of falling victim to online criminals. However, some have realised that the secrecy of the service can allow people to pursue illegal activity covertly, including the promotion of terrorism and the sale or distribution of guns, stolen credit card details, Class A drugs, or images of child abuse. In response, we have also seen the emergence of 'citizen-led policing initiatives' (Hadjimatheou, 2019), where private individuals have used their own resources and internet skills to track down criminals, notably paedophiles.

As a society, we need to debate where the boundary lies between personal privacy and the detection or prevention of crime: how far we should allow freedom of speech to extend into cyberspace; what the relationship is between statutory agencies and 'civilian policing' (Hadjimatheou, 2019); and how we can best respond to the changing behaviours that the internet brings.

CONVERSATIONS 6.2

Social media and gang violence

with **Dr Keir Irwin-Rogers**

During the summer of 2015, I spent some time in a number of schools for young people who had been excluded from mainstream education. During one conversation with a pupil, he lifted his t-shirt to reveal a stab wound on his abdomen. The pupil had recently featured in a music video uploaded to a popular social media platform, which mocked a local rival gang. In retaliation, a young person associated with the rival gang had found the pupil and stabbed him.

The conversation prompted me to conduct a study that involved, among other things, a six-month period of online social media platform analysis exploring some of the content being uploaded to these platforms, as well as its real-world consequences (see Irwin-Rogers and Pinkney, 2017; Irwin Rogers et al., 2018). The findings, I argued, were clear: social media was acting as a catalyst and trigger for serious incidents of violence in real life. In short, by collapsing space and time, social media was facilitating the proliferation of opportunities to taunt, provoke and disrespect others. At the touch of a button, young people were able to upload content onto social media that was consumed instantaneously by others using the platform, wherever they might be in the world.

Specifically in relation to violence between young people associated with rival gangs, the study identified various forms of content that young people were uploading to taunt and disrespect others. One common means of provocation involved young people making their way into areas associated with rival gangs and posting images or videos evidencing their presence in these areas. The uploaded content was intended to bolster the status of the young people doing the uploading, while denigrating those who claimed to have control over the area in question. This often led to tit-for-tat escalations in tensions, which in some cases resulted in face-to-face incidents of serious violence. A similar process underpinned the relationship between serious violence and other forms of online content, such as images and videos displaying young people being attacked and having their possessions stolen, and music 'diss' tracks set to videos in which one group taunted or threatened another.

Being a relatively new and unfamiliar phenomenon, young people's use of social media platforms seemingly leaves many adults feeling unsettled and fascinated in equal measure. Indeed, in recent years, there has been a raft of criminal justice policy statements and media stories that have sought to shine a spotlight on young people's use of social media and its links to serious gang violence (see Home Office, 2018; Gordon, A. (2018) 'Britain's feral gangs "are now a bigger danger than terrorism": Criminals' online boasts of shootings and stabbings inspire the next generation of gangsters say crime expert', Daily Mail, 4 April 2018). During the summer of 2016, I was asked to speak at a number of conferences and events including the Home Office's 'Ending Gang Violence and Exploitation' Quarterly Forum and an evidence session organised by the House of Commons Science and Technology Committee. In each case, I stressed the vital importance of situating the links between social media and gang violence in their appropriate context.

As I have argued elsewhere (Irwin-Rogers, 2019), activity on social media is a symptom of deeper and more pressing social problems that shape the lives of many young people. For example, a brutalising climate of individualism, competition and status anxiety, generated by rampant consumer capitalism, acts as one of the primary and fundamental drivers of much serious youth violence, which particularly affects those born into relative poverty in grossly unequal societies. People in positions of power, however, often balk at the arduous and complicated task of facing up to and addressing such deep-seated drivers of violence. Minor technical fixes—such as enhancing the degree of monitoring and censorship of young people's activity on social media platforms—appear more attractive, precisely because they are relatively simple, straightforward and have the potential to produce short-term (albeit limited) results.

I have nothing against considered and proportionate tweaks to policy and practice that might save young people's lives. In fact, there are a number of steps that I have recommended social media companies and a range of professionals take in an attempt to sever the links between activity online and violence offline. It is crucially important, however, to avoid a myopic focus on social media when trying to understand and address something as complicated and deep-rooted as serious violence. Indeed, the potential value of future research on social media and gang violence may lie not in pointing the spotlight on the role of social media per se, but in using social media as a lens through which some of the more fundamental and pressing drivers of serious violence might be better evidenced and understood.

Dr Keir Irwin-Rogers, Lecturer in Criminology, The Open University

and the volume of digital data now available (for example, through social media accounts, internet search histories, gaming consoles) offer many new opportunities for understanding and controlling crime, some of which we will discuss in the next section. However, harnessing this wealth of data and grasping the ever-evolving opportunities it presents can be challenging, and often legislation and criminal justice agencies are playing a game of 'catch up' in terms of resourcing and expertise.

Media as a positive influence on crime

Whilst much criminology is concerned with unpicking media representations of crime in order both to question them and to test the idea that some aspects of the media are actually crime-producing in some way, it is worth reflecting briefly on the prosocial aspects of crime 'news'.

In **Chapter 2** we considered the role of social rules and **norms** in forming ideas of crime and deviance, and encouraging people to abide by them. The media, and especially social media, can be argued to act as a social control mechanism in that praise is bestowed on those who behave appropriately and in line with social norms and criticises and cajoles those who do not. The media could certainly be observed to be active in this way during the coronavirus pandemic, with much emphasis being placed on prosocial behaviour and self-policing (social distancing, for example), and sharp rebukes aimed at those who appeared to be breaking the rules:

> Anger has been mounting both in Whitehall and among the public over Cummings' behavior under lockdown rules two months ago. Following a media exposé revealing that he drove his family across England while potentially infectious with coronavirus, and defensive Downing Street press conferences given by both Cummings and Johnson, 39 MPs on Wednesday night called for the top aide's resignation.
>
> (CGTN News, 28 May 2020)

While the publicity that media forms give to crime and criminals can, as we have seen, have harmful effects, it can also give the law-abiding public a sense of unity in condemning the actions of a small number of deviant people—see, as another example, coverage of Mancunians' 'defiant' response to the Manchester Arena bombing in 2017 (*The Independent*, 24 May 2017).

Media publicity can assist criminal justice agencies by encouraging and enabling the public to assist in crime detection, for example coming forward as witnesses or with information, perhaps regarding a missing person, and the media are also used as a public information service, to

Figure 6.10 Media coverage of crime can have a positive effect, such as when it is used to disseminate anti-crime content, for example the Home Office's 2018 campaign amidst warnings of a knife crime 'epidemic' in London

Source: The Home Office/PA

discourage people from committing crime, or to educate them about it and assist them to keep themselves safe. Amongst the most prominent crime-related examples of these, perhaps, are the regular seasonal 'Don't Drink and Drive' campaigns, but the Home Office also uses the media, especially digital media, to publicise campaign material relating to all sorts of crimes that are prominent at the time. Examples include their #knifefree campaign in 2018 (see **Figure 6.10**) and their educational campaign about online fraud in 2020, in response to increased instances of this type of cybercrime as criminals attempted to exploit the Covid-19 pandemic (www.youtube.com/watch?v=NLMx8p2oZQk).

It has been noted, too, that police are increasingly interested in the opportunities to use social media for the purposes of crime prevention and detection. This includes using it to rapidly communicate possible risks to the public, or encouraging people to share phone images of crimes taking place (Hadjimatheou et al., 2019). Prieto Curiel et al. (2020) suggest that four main types of information have been extracted from social media in the context of crime analysis and control.

1. Locating risky areas and crime hotspots using the location of and density of Tweets (that is, using location information not the content of the media posts).
2. Analysing the content of media posts to, for example, predict the locations of certain types of crimes.
3. Revealing the relationships between criminals and **organised crime** networks (looking at who follows and retweets who).
4. Analysing the public's reaction to specific incidents.

The researchers note that other uses of big data and social media in crime analysis and prevention have included detecting the marketing and distribution of illegal drugs and crowdsourcing information on specific incidents. Fiction and entertainment media may also have positive effects on crime. We have seen that literature, films, and TV, for example, can be used to educate and encourage empathy—we discussed that prison films could help highlight issues in the criminal justice system. And while some forms of music have been said to be linked to criminal behaviour, music can also help raise awareness of and condemn crime and violence. In some cases, the message may be quite ambiguous. 'The Pusher', for example, a song featured in the film *Easy Rider*, acts as a stark condemnation of exploitative drug dealers, even though the film itself celebrates drug use.

There are many examples of musicians using this form of media to respond to and condemn violence towards black people in the US and to support the 'Black Lives Matter' movement, especially following the murder of George Floyd in 2020. Many bands produced musical responses to the events (see *Vulture* magazine's list titled 'All the New Protest and Benefit Music Released in Response to Police Brutality', 11 June 2020), using the form to express grief, rage, and support for protests, as well as to amplify black voices (for example, British electronic band Clean Bandit added classical accompaniment to a simple protest song performed by 12-year-old gospel singer Keedron Bryant, helping to publicise it) and encourage donations to relevant organisations. Other examples in recent years have included Childish Gambino's anti-racism song 'This Is America', which went viral in 2018, and a song called 'How Many' by R&B singer Miguel which includes the lyrics: 'I'm tired of human lives turned into hashtags and prayer hands/I'm tired of watching murderers get off'. Even violent games like Call of Duty and Grand Theft Auto, which have been argued to be criminogenic, have also been said to have brought about a reduction in crime levels. Opinions vary on the reasons why this might be the case, but it has been suggested that the games allow people to 'rechannel violent urges' or that they simply take up a lot of time, keeping people indoors and away from places where crimes take place (*The Spectator*, 7 December 2013).

Should media be censored?

If media coverage has a damaging effect on crime, should it be regulated or censored? This is very difficult to answer since the question of whether media coverage of crime leads to more crimes being committed (and whether this is balanced out somewhat by its more positive effects) has not been satisfactorily resolved, and is a matter of continuing debate. Early experimental research by behavioural psychologists in the 1950s and 1960s argued that people somehow learned behaviour, including violent and aggressive behaviour, through watching TV and interacting with other media forms, and in the 1990s Sonia Livingstone commented that:

it seems fair to say that the majority of researchers in the area are now convinced that excessive violence in the media increases the likelihood that at least some viewers will behave more violently.

(Livingstone, in Curran and Gurevitch, 1996)

But is it as straightforward as this? Can we really separate media effects from other possible influences such as the parental, cultural, or psychological factors in our lives? How long do such effects last for? And are we just as able to learn positive behaviour from media and to learn to reject criminal acts?

Imagine that we all sat down together to watch a particular news item, read a lead story in a paper, listen to the same piece of music, read a social media post, or watch the same crime film. Do you think that we would all interpret it in the exactly the same way? The answer is probably not. The fascinating thing about media items is that they spark debate and conversations. In short, we all decode media messages in different ways; just look at the variety of opinions online about crime stories and entertainment media. Today, the consensus in academic circles appears to be that 'Decades of research have amassed on the topic, yet there is no clear agreement about the impact of media or about which methodologies are most appropriate. Instead, there continues to be disagreement about whether media portrayals of violence are a serious problem and, if so, how society should respond' (Phillips, 2017). Since the debate (and the media forms available to us) continues to evolve, we suggest that you look at the latest scholarship available at the time you are reading. If you search using the keywords 'violence', 'crime', and 'media', you will find a great deal of material on either side of the argument, and that the research in this area has increased in detail and sophistication—for example, as we have seen, researchers now distinguish between 'trigger' and 'copycat' effects.

6.5 Conclusion

Let's end this chapter by briefly considering a key development in the fascinating and broad field of media criminology that gives us an idea of the future direction of media coverage of crime: the rise of the 'citizen journalist'.

There is no doubt that the rapidly changing and fragmenting digital mediascape has opened up new (often virtual) spaces for crime stories to be reported and told, whether these be factual or fictional. One implication is that now almost anyone and everyone can get involved with mainstream and alternative media platforms, without having had journalistic or literary training. Anyone with online access can post comments on online articles or produce a blog, vlog, or podcast which can be read, viewed, or listened to by people all over the globe. The opportunities opened up can be quite dramatic, and may well also be highly problematic, as in the example of the use of social media to track down alleged paedophiles: 'There's a global movement of Facebook vigilantes who hunt pedophiles' (*Quartz*, 24 July 2019).

Mainstream printed and TV news media now also rely, to some extent, on input from the public. Often, news channels that are otherwise conventional will ask people to send in their photos, films, and opinions, and will embed tweets from members of the public in online articles. Many respected journalists (and, indeed, some criminologists) interact directly with their followers on social media, and you will notice that opinions from politicians and others are often presented on news bulletins via tweets rather

NEW FRONTIERS 6.2

Social media as a tool for criminologists

We noted in **section 6.4** in the discussion of media as a positive influence on crime, that social media is increasingly being used by criminal justice agencies to monitor and control crime, but it also represents a vast resource, widely available and easily accessible, for criminological researchers. Prieto Curiel et al. (2020) suggest that social media and big data can be useful tools for measuring and assessing fear of crime, especially since this method generates insights much more quickly and cheaply than through expensive **victimisation** surveys.

However, Prieto Curiel et al. (2020) caution that social media presents some challenges and is subject to some of the same tendencies as traditional media, in terms of a heavy focus on violent crime, and the sheer scale and variety of material on the internet creates challenges as well as opportunities for researchers. You may well see the web as a very useful resource for your own research projects, so it may be helpful to know about some of the techniques developed by academic researchers to make the task manageable, and importantly to produce valid results.

Of course, simply carrying out a keyword search on the internet is a perfectly reasonable strategy, and introduces a systematic element into a research study, so long as the keywords are relevant and additional criteria, such as a time frame, are included to make the results manageable. Researchers have built on this kind of principle to develop 'data mining' tools for extracting key data from websites. Techniques include 'scraping' sites for relevant information, in order to answer specific questions—such as the extent of human trafficking in Romania in a study carried out by Ruth McAlister of Ulster University (McAlister, 2015).

Often asscciated with scraping is the technique described by the term 'crawling', which is effectively what large internet providers do to make connections between key terms, or characteristics, so as to identify predictable patterns and, of course, better target us with information and promotional material. As a research technique, though, this is a useful means of establishing associations—as in the case of a study by Decary-Hetu and Aldridge (2015) which was designed to monitor online drug offenders.

The field of online research methods is developing rapidly. There is already a considerable amount of web scraping and crawling software available to researchers, and this is inevitably an expanding field.

---

than filmed interviews. If you think back to some of the controversial areas covered in this chapter (such as media representations of prisons and prisoners or immigration) and search the digitised version of an established newspaper for stories relating to them, you will usually find hundreds of comments from the public underneath—especially on the newspaper's social media channels, where they will generally share links to each story as it publishes.

These kinds of developments could be argued to democratise media production, since they mean that a wider range of voices can be heard. Everyone's views are now visible, unlike in the past when all you could do was to post a written 'letter to the editor' and hope that it would be published. Online comments sections in particular can be a rich source of data and a way to monitor 'public opinion' about an issue: it is important to be aware that they do not represent all members of society (certain people are more likely to comment), and that the comments may be more extreme than they would be if made in person, or do not reflect people's views at all (as in the case of 'trolls'), but they can give an interesting insight into the public's views. They may be supportive of news stories, or may challenge conventional understandings. They can reveal the levels of public knowledge about an issue and highlight the effects of media distortion and exaggeration, sometimes even adding to the distortion by perpetuating stereotypes and spreading hate. With messages going 'viral' almost instantaneously, and limited capacity to 'fact check', we are all now faced with an increasingly challenging task of sorting what might be called 'fake news' (and which may incorporate abusive content) from information which is supported by credible evidence or authoritative expertise.

It has been suggested that so-called 'citizen journalism' may lead to increased political engagement and activism which could, in turn, bring about real social change and reform. Citizen journalists can, after all, often be 'on the scene' well before professional news crews turn up, and there are even cases where they can broadcast information in politically sensitive situations where professional journalists have been banned. Their input can challenge the dominance of the shrinking number of news sources (we noted in **section 6.3** in the discussion of 20th-century newsworthiness and Chibnall's imperatives that many mainstream news stories are built around official press releases) and can critically question official stories and narratives, challenging power relations and state corruption or cover-ups. One crime-related issue in which citizen journalism has played a key part is the racist and violent nature of policing in parts of the US. Shocking and disturbing video footage taken by members of the public of police officers assaulting, shooting, wounding, and even killing people has been uploaded for all to see,

Figure 6.11 Citizen journalism has been important in recording the events of political demonstrations, for example in the Taksim Gezi Park protests in Turkey in 2013
Source: Fleshstorm/CC-BY-SA-3.0

resulting in some prosecutions, as in the case of George Floyd. Forms of citizen journalism have been important over the past decade in capturing moments of civil unrest and political demonstration in response to perceived human rights abuses and state corruption across the globe; for example, across the Middle East and North Africa (Arab Spring), in Turkey (Gezi Park Protests, see **Figure 6.11**), in the Ukraine (Euromaidan protests), and the civil war in Syria.

So is this a positive development? As with all media reporting, the main issues here are the trustworthiness and reliability of the sources. It is vital that we maintain an ABC (*Always Be Critical*) mindset whichever form of media we are assessing, and carefully consider not just what the media we are analysing contains, and the influences and agendas that might have shaped this, but what they ignore. Are they presenting the whole story?

As you will have gathered, media criminology is a huge and continually shifting area of study, with many areas of today's media landscape still barely explored by academics. This is an area where you, as a student criminologist and likely more of a 'digital native' than some of your lecturers, can have a real impact and produce valuable additional knowledge for our discipline.

SUMMARY

After reading this chapter and working your way through its features you should now be able to:

- **Develop a critical and reflective view of media representations of crime and criminals**

We have seen how media have, throughout history, been used to inform and govern social attitudes, for example by promoting the 'hegemonic ideology' of a particular time and place. However, the chapter also examines the ways in which the media themselves can be influenced by external social factors such as 'newsworthiness' and the overriding need to remain relevant, adapt to changing market conditions, and appeal to a reading or viewing public which has an ever-expanding range of sources to choose from. This is changing in the light of citizen journalism, the rise of independent news sources such as social media, and a much greater capacity for everyone to contribute to and participate in media exchanges.

- Explain how criminologists have researched this through content analysis and **discourse analysis**, and by developing an awareness of the capacity of media to distort and shape public perceptions of crime, criminality, and the criminal justice system

Media tend to focus on particular elements of a news story, and in doing so can perpetuate stereotypes and prejudice. This is particularly true in the reporting of certain types of crime and criminality; for instance, we assessed the discrepancy between the reported trends and pattern of youth crime and the selective and often differing impression given of young people by news stories. Media representations also reflect, and in some cases amplify, social anxieties of the time. Criminologists use a variety of methods to research this phenomenon and in this chapter we have briefly examined two of these: content analysis and discourse analysis.

- Relate a range of concepts to your own consumption of media

Key theoretical concepts covered in this chapter include the power of disccurse, the social and ideological construction of crime reporting, moral panics and folk devils, and the caution with which we need to treat statistics. The chapter also examines the blurring of fact and fiction in the shaping of public views about crime and how fictitious representations themselves can reflect or reinforce social norms. You should be able to think about the functions of crime media in promoting key messages and to consider the question of whether, and in what circumstances, media are either criminogenic or a potentially beneficial to the prevention and detection of crime.

- Assess the importance of media in forming new narratives, such as through citizen journalism

Just as the media have always been used to discuss and describe crime, so they are always evolving into new forms, sometimes very rapidly. Whereas in the past the use of media was generally confined to the rich and powerful (those who could afford to buy books or who were actually literate), since the development of mass media like cinemas more and more people have been able to witness and comment upon news and ideas. Examples of this are the use of media to either encourage action against perceived offenders (such as newspapers naming alleged paedophiles) or individuals becoming more personally involved in reporting or reproducing news stories, often offering an alternative and sometimes controversial viewpoint to that given in mainstream accounts. Some of these new narratives can inform and even change public policy, such as prison films that highlight the true nature of life behind bars.

- Compare and analyse differences between traditional and emerging branches of criminological research on the representation of crime across a variety of media

You may wish to think about this question in the light of other chapters in this book, such as **Chapter 18** on critical criminology. However, this chapter does highlight the different environments in which criminologists find themselves working when considering crime and the media; the vastly more varied news sources, the greater access to global media, the need to develop new ways of working with the increasing variety of media outlets and changing practices, and the use of crime reporting of all types in shaping public opinion.

 Test your understanding of the chapter's key points by attempting the self-test questions on the **online resources** at **www.oup.com/he/case2e**

REVIEW QUESTIONS

1. Give three examples of how the media exaggerate or distort crime.

2. What are the two research methods criminologists predominantly use to record the reporting of crime? What are the main differences between these?

3. Name four of the eight 'professional imperatives' that Chibnall identified.

4. What are today's moral panics and who are the folk devils? What is moral about a moral panic?

5. Give two arguments for and against the proposition that it is acceptable for 'true crime' to be portrayed as popular entertainment.

6. Identify three crime films which can be said to challenge dominant discourses about crime, criminality, and its control, and list the ways in which they do so.

7. List some of the most significant ways in which young people are thought to be at risk from being exploited online.

8. How has citizen journalism affected the future of crime reporting? Give a current example of how this can happen.

 Access the **online resources** at www.oup.com/he/case2e to check your answers to the review questions.

FURTHER READING

Cohen, S. (2011 [1973]) *Folk Devils and Moral Panics: The Creation of the Mods and the Rockers*. **London: Routledge.**
The 'classic' study of folk devils and moral panics. This 2011 reprint in the 'Routledge Classics' series includes the revised introduction written by the late Stan Cohen in 2003.

Critcher, C., Hughes, J., Petley, J., and Rohloff, A. (eds) (2016) *Moral Panics in the Contemporary World*. **London: Bloomsbury Academic.**
This collection revisits and updates ideas about moral panics as they have evolved since Cohen introduced the concept.

Forshaw, B. (2019) *Crime Fiction: A Reader's Guide*. **Harpenden: Oldcastle Books.**
This is an authoritative overview of the origins and development of crime fiction as an important element of popular culture.

Greer, C. (ed.) (2010) *Crime and the Media*. **London: Routledge.**
A comprehensive collection of edited articles, both classic and new, which covers a broad range of issues. Some are higher level than others but well worth dipping into.

Jewkes, Y. (2015) *Media and Crime*. **London: Sage.**
This book offers a thorough review and critical examination of much that is covered in this chapter (and more). It is a very good place for you to start if you want to develop your knowledge and understanding of this subject.

Moore, S. E. H. (2014) *Crime and the Media*. **London: Palgrave Macmillan.**
A good, broad coverage of the field which has particularly useful introductory chapters on analysing the media in terms of content analysis, **narrative analysis**, and discourse analysis.

Rafter, N. and Brown, M. (2011) *Criminology Goes to the Movies: Crime Theory and Popular Culture*. **New York: NYU Press.**
This is an interesting collection of essays which attempt to teach criminological theory through (mainly US) crime films. If you want a greater understanding of the criminological theories explored in **Part 3** of this book then this text would be the best place to start.

Yar, M. and Steinmetz, K. (2019) *Cybercrime and Society* **(3rd edn). London: Sage.**
This offers a very clear introduction to the issues of hacking, cracking, virtual piracy, hate speech online, and all things cyber (including the problems of policing and regulating cyberspace).

ANSWERS TO EXERCISES

		Tabloids (281)	Broadsheets (159)	Locals (53)
		%	%	%
Subject	Violence/crime/antisocial behaviour	35	26	33
	Child abuse/neglect	12	17	8
	Lifestyle	16	9	7
	(Mental) health	10	11	12
	Accident	14	8	15
	Education/parenting	6	22	17
	Achievement	8	6	9

Source: Ipsos MORI, www.ipsos-mori.com, 2–8 August 2004

Table 6.3 Newspaper articles about young people, by newspaper type and subject (2004)

		Tabloids (281)	Broadsheets (159)	Locals (53)
		%	%	%
Tone	Negative	82	50	71
	Neutral	8	36	9
	Positive	11	15	20

Source: Ipsos MORI, www.ipsos-mori.com, 2–8 August 2004

Table 6.4 Newspaper articles about young people, by newspaper type and tone (2004)

 Access the **online resources** to view a wealth of extra information relating to your study of criminology, including self-test questions, answers to review questions, and links to other resources that will help you enjoy and fulfil your potential within your studies.

www.oup.com/he/case2e

CHAPTER OUTLINE

7.1	Introduction	188
7.2	Defining victims	188
7.3	Theories, concepts, and debates in victimology	192
7.4	Measuring victimisation	198
7.5	Victims and the criminal justice process	205
7.6	Conclusion	206

7

Victimology

Angus Nurse

KEY ISSUES

After studying this chapter, you should be able to:

- identify who counts as a victim;
- understand the scope of victimology and its importance within criminology;
- evaluate theories of victimisation and explain how different theoretical approaches and practices have contributed to understanding secondary victimisation;
- appreciate the range of victimological approaches and how each contributes to our understanding of victimisation;
- identify how and why the role of victims has changed within criminal justice processes and also assess the extent to which the victim has been marginalised in criminal justice;
- understand the contribution of victimisation surveys in measuring the extent of victimisation;
- critically assess the beliefs about the 'ideal' victim and understand why some victims of crime might be seen as more 'deserving' than others.

7.1 Introduction

When you think about victims of crime, what examples and types of people spring to mind? The burglary victim? Victims of violent crime? Victims of sexual assault? Your ideas may well be based upon the idea of somebody who has directly experienced the effects of crime. Each of these examples shows an idea of the victim as somebody who has had crime done 'to' them, and suggests the victim is an innocent party who suffers from crime through no fault of their own. This may be the idea of crime victims you had as a starting point in your study of criminology, but in this chapter we will expand our understanding to consider a range of ideas on victims and **victimisation** by introducing you to victimology, which has become an important sub-discipline within criminology. We will examine the scope of different debates in victimology and a range of theories on victimisation.

Victimology includes the study of victimisation, as well as the challenges of legal and institutional definitions of the 'victim'. The perspective also engages with debates concerning victims' rights and activism (Tapley and Davies, 2020) and how victimhood has come to be understood and responded to. Over the last 30 years, following the publication of the Victims' Charter in 1992 and the introduction of the British Crime Survey (now the Crime Survey for England and Wales), there has been a move away from seeing victims of crime as simply part of the criminal justice process towards considering a wider range of victim issues, including the psychological effect of crime on victims, the relationship between victims and criminal justice processes, and different types of victimisation (Morgan and Zedner, 1992; Maguire and Kynch, 2000). Criminologists (and victimologists) have explored the long-term effects that victims suffer from their experiences. Victimology also accepts that victimisation extends beyond the immediate victim (the person who has directly experienced the crime) to family members and friends who also suffer when a crime has been committed.

This last point may seem obvious. For example, when a loved one is killed as a result of **homicide**, the family clearly suffers a loss and will need to go through a period of grieving. But in this example, criminal justice processes mainly focus on catching the killer and not on the needs of family and friends affected by the crime. Victimology aims to address the neglect of victims within criminology and criminal justice, and tries to place the victim in a more central role in criminal justice processes and in the study of crime. We will see, for example, that victimology examines how the needs of victims can be better considered. This includes active thought about how to include victims in the criminal trial and investigative process, as well as how best to provide victims with information and support in respect of how crimes that have affected them are being dealt with. We will also see how victimology looks at different types of victim and their experiences of criminal justice (see also **Chapter 8**).

In this chapter, we consider both narrow and wider ideas of victimisation, and examine whether and how criminal justice processes and public policy have developed in response to victims' needs. We will see that while victims are really the people that the criminal investigation and trial are meant to serve, they are often not part of the process. At the same time, we will examine developments in making the victim's voice heard and in reforming criminal justice processes with victims in mind. Alongside this discussion, we will also look beyond a focus solely on the criminal justice system to consider some wider issues in victimology, exploring the main theories surrounding victims and victimisation, as well as the work of various pressure groups in highlighting victim needs. We will also investigate a key part of victimology, which is the use of statistical evidence on the levels of victimisation; particularly **victim surveys** that have sometimes revealed evidence of a 'dark figure' of unreported crime, as well as useful information on the fear of victimisation. We have already looked at crime statistics (**Chapter 5**), which are collected by police services and government agencies for various reasons, and while we learnt that we may need to be cautious in how we use them, crime statistics are important in providing information on who is suffering the effects of crime, including those who experience repeat victimisation.

Before looking at these areas in detail, we should consider what we mean by the term 'victim' and how criminology deals with victims as an area of study, including the theoretical approaches that criminologists use in their research. We also look at the **concept** of '**victimity**' and ideas about how victims experience the state of being a victim and the exercise of power (Turvey, 2014). Finally, we will end the chapter with a brief look at victims in the criminal trial process.

7.2 Defining victims

As you may have noticed from your reading so far, a lot of the words that we might think we understand become trickier to define when we look at them from a criminological perspective. The term 'victim' is no different, and the person you think of when you imagine a victim might depend on your academic and political leanings or social background. The *Cambridge English Dictionary* online, defines victim as:

> someone or something that has been hurt, damaged, or killed or has suffered, either because of the actions of someone or something else, or because of illness or chance.

But critical observers like criminologists, political activists, and NGOs are constantly putting this term under scrutiny, which means that our understanding of the word 'victim' and whom it refers to is always changing, and can be a bit more complicated than the dictionary definition. For instance, you will probably have already spotted that we suggest the term victim is commonly applied to a 'person' but this idea is contested, for example by **green criminologists** who explore ideas of environmental victimisation. This approach considers non-human nature, including animals and the environment itself, as a victim of human-centred harms (see **Chapter 12**). You may also encounter the idea of victimity, which refers to the state, quality, or fact of being a victim, and you may see this term used at times. What's more, much like we learned in **Chapter 2** when discussing definitions of crime, victimhood is partly a **social construction**, which adds some complexity when we discuss victims. All of these different terms can seem a bit confusing, but as you work your way through this chapter, the use of these words and the ideas behind them should start becoming clearer. Let's look at some of these definitions now, beginning with indirect victims (and the idea of secondary victimisation), then moving on to look at the use of the word 'survivor' instead of victim, and the concept of the 'ideal' victim.

Direct and indirect victims

When we think about victims, we probably think of someone who has a personal experience of crime, like a homeowner who has been burgled, or somebody who has been assaulted in the street or outside a pub. These would be people who are looking for and probably deserve justice and practical protection from the state. Such individuals are 'direct' victims, and this idea of directness is the main one in identifying crime; for crime to occur there has to be a perpetrator who commits it, and a victim who experiences it (Xie and McDowall, 2008). But this basic idea of the victim is not the only one; the perpetrator can be an organisation rather than an individual, and the victim may also themselves be an offender. We should also note that there can be crimeless victims (for example, credit card theft where losses are written off and there is no formal crime report) and victimless crimes (for example, possibly recreational drug use), and so the idea of who is a victim extends beyond the direct idea of victim and offender.

Criminology also looks further outside the scope of direct victims, and takes quite a wide understanding by considering how criminal justice systems and social policy also think of *indirect* victims of crime (called secondary victims or co-victims in some cases)—others who are affected by the crime or event. For example, the *Lubanga* case (ICC-01/04-01/06) before the International Criminal Court (ICC) considered the use of and victimisation of child soldiers as a specific crime because it is prohibited under international law. But the ICC also considered whether those who had suffered harm from the actions of the direct victims (that is, the child soldiers) should also be considered 'indirect' victims (Spiga, 2010). It may be obvious that if somebody has been murdered then their immediate family are also indirect victims who will feel the loss of their loved one, and may also need support to deal with their absence. There will also be a range of other issues that the family will have to deal with that go beyond experiencing the loss. But what about the murdered person's friends? Their work colleagues? Their former romantic partners? We could argue that all of these people are indirect victims of the crime. But in considering this broader definition we also need to think about how far it should extend.

Take, for example, an elderly woman who hears about a burglary in her street or sees a news report about the high incidence of crime in her neighbourhood and so becomes afraid to go out. We could argue that this woman is a victim more generally as the incident has impacted her fear of crime, even though she has not directly suffered from it. If we take this approach, we could argue that we are all victims as we become more aware of the levels of crime in our areas, or think about new threats from crime and our fear increases—like the ripple effect depicted in **Figure 7.1**. Something like the government publicly raising the terrorism threat level and warning us all to be vigilant after incidents like the 2005 London bombings or the 2017 Manchester Arena bombing could have the effect of making us all fearful about the likelihood of a terrorist

Figure 7.1 We might think of crime as having a ripple effect, with its impact spreading out from the initial offence to indirect victims

Source: YJ.K/Shutterstock

attack. This idea of indirect victims therefore expands the picture we may have when we initially think about a victim of a crime, and introduces an additional category when exploring victimisation.

Victim or survivor?

The term 'victim' is itself slightly problematic because it has a suggestion of helplessness attached to it. Further dictionary definitions of the word include the following phrases:

> one that is injured, destroyed, or sacrificed under any of various conditions
> one that is subjected to oppression, hardship, or mistreatment
> one that is tricked or duped
>
> (*Merriam-Webster Dictionary*, 2020)

We can see that all these descriptions suggest that the victim was vulnerable and powerless, and so the term 'victim' is seen as a loaded one. Feminist criminology and feminist groups who work with women who have experienced sexual assault have rejected the term 'victim' as unhelpful to the individuals concerned. The term 'survivor' is sometimes preferred as being more appropriate and constructive. However, the term survivor can also be problematic where those who have experienced victimisation may be made to feel somehow inadequate if they do not feel like a survivor or where their suffering is seen as somehow being in the past. Jordan (2013) suggests that being recognised as a rape survivor has sometimes been presented as a straight line from the negative state of victimisation experienced in the presence of the offender, through to the more positive state of survivor. Potentially this creates an impression of the victimisation and its impacts as a past event.

However, in examining the experiences of women who survived a serial rapist in New Zealand, Jordan identified a diversity of responses. These included the fact that the women involved also experienced **secondary victimisation**, further victimisation in their dealings with individuals and agencies afterwards, which complicates the dynamic of being a victim of an offence, and a survivor seeking criminal justice (2013). We should also note at this stage that sexual victimisation is a complex area and that researchers have also explored the relative lack of research or public attention on the rape and assault of adult males. In this area as well, some researchers have identified that negative attitudes can cause the secondary victimisation of men who have experienced sexual victimisation (Lowe and Rogers, 2017).

Jordan's study and the literature analysis of Lowe and Rogers (2017) raise some important points we should consider as we explore victimisation and ideas about victimhood. First, it is important not to assume that all of those who experience crime have the same reactions and needs. One individual who experiences a burglary may become angry about the loss of goods and short-term financial inconvenience the burglary may cause, but could be otherwise unaffected. But another person may be less concerned about the loss of goods, and could instead experience long-term emotional effects that make it difficult for them to remain in their home. Secondly, victims' experiences can sometimes be made worse by their treatment at the hands of the criminal justice system. For some, this could be a result of poor information about the crime and its investigation, or insensitive attitudes or behaviour from criminal justice agencies when taking statements or providing information, an issue we identified above as secondary victimisation. Lowe and Rogers (2017) also identified how negative stereotypes can be factors that contribute significantly to secondary victimisation. The experience at trial can also be a problem where the victim is made to relive events in a way that adds to any trauma. Victimology examines all of these issues and tries to develop our understanding of what it means to be a victim and how policy and practice may need to change to address such problems.

The 'ideal' victim

Not only is our understanding of what makes a 'victim' part of academic and political debate, it is also influenced by public perceptions—in other words, victimhood is a social construction. This means that the public might see some victims as more deserving of public sympathy, political support, and policy protection than others. Recognising this issue, sociologist and **critical criminologist** Nils Christie developed the concept of the 'ideal victim', identifying that 'being a victim is not a thing, an objective phenomenon. It will not be the same to all people in situations externally described as being the "same"' (Christie, 1986: 18). Christie examined the factors that could make a victim appear to be legitimate and valued, and also considered that victimhood can be investigated in terms of both the personality of the victim and in a societal context. Christie's definition of the 'ideal victim' is one who:

- is weaker than the offender—so they are likely to be elderly, female, or a child;
- is going about their normal day-to-day business (even though this may not be entirely legitimate);
- is considered to be blameless for what happened to them;
- is not known to the offender—in other words, the offender is a stranger (and an individual person, rather than a company or organisation);

- has suffered from the behaviour of someone who is clearly deviant;
- is not a threat to the dominant social **norms** and values.

Christie's idea implies that some victims are valued less than others, and indeed raises questions about who can be regarded as a victim even when it is clear that they have suffered harm due to a criminal offence. Christie's **theory** of the 'ideal victim' has been taken forward by other criminologists, and while it would be outside the scope of this chapter to engage with their work in much detail, we suggest that you take a look at other resources such as Marian Duggan's edited collection 'Revisiting the "Ideal Victim": Developments in Critical Victimology', which includes essays from various researchers that respond to and update this concept from different perspectives.

Building on Christie's work, Van Wijk (2013) argues that it is only when potential 'status givers' are aware of the victims' existence that victim status can be granted. By this, he identifies the importance of power relationships and of the social construction of the victim. For example, the label of victim is in one sense 'officially' applied. On reporting an incident to the police, an individual is initially a complainant and where a case goes to trial they are likely a witness. Although the individual may be referred to as the victim during investigation and the prosecution process, it is not until the offender pleads guilty or is found guilty at trial that the individual is given 'official' victim status. In this sense, even if someone feels like they are a victim, they might not be acknowledged as one by others if they do not have some way of confirming their status, or the confirmation can only come from others. This situation places power onto those who are in a position to give this status, with victims becoming dependent on them to, in a way, recognise their experiences and feelings.

We might also consider that in crimes involving children (some of whom are generally perceived as being innocent and fragile) there is a greater sense of shock and outrage than if the same offence had taken place against an adult who may be seen as less vulnerable (and in some cases less innocent). Crimes of sexual violence where men prey on women will also attract shock, given the general perception of men being in positions of power, and because in particular employment situations they are able to exploit a woman's vulnerability. But some groups are still seen as a threat to society or as having characteristics that may mean others question whether they truly are victims. These individuals could include women who are sexually liberated, people from particular religious or ethnic minorities, and young people who appear to be out of control or who act in ways that challenge accepted ideas of how they should behave. In a crude sense, people may see them as deserving of the crime they have suffered, or to have somehow provoked this. We discuss this later in this chapter, but we will also see how the sense of threat that they pose is linked to the group's powerlessness and oppression, and the extent to which their claims are recognised and their voices heard. But first let's consider the idea of a victim hierarchy in **What do you think? 7.1**.

WHAT DO YOU THINK? 7.1

The hierarchy of victims?

Think about Christie's idea of the ideal victim and also how victims of crime are presented in news media, sometimes in a way that is designed to gain our sympathy for the victim. Christie identifies the importance of the victim being weaker than the offender, and suggests that the victim should be blameless while the offender should clearly be deviant. On a scale of 1 to 5 where 5 is 'very sympathetic', rate how sympathetic you think the following victims of crime are and how much support you would give them. In addition to giving your score, make a few notes on your reasons for your score.

- A two-year-old child run over by a drunk driver.
- A crime witness who is attacked by the suspect whilst waiting to give evidence.
- A bank teller who is assaulted during a robbery.
- A woman who is attacked on a first date by a man she met online.
- A teenager who is assaulted in the street by an aggressive beggar after she refuses to give him money.

Now look at a second set of victims and repeat the exercise, scoring each victim and giving your reasons for doing so.

- A drug dealer who is beaten up by a rival.
- A woman who is attacked by a man she has invited into her home for coffee after a night of drinking.
- A man who is attacked by his partner after she finds out he has been cheating on her with another woman from her workplace.
- A woman who is the victim of fraud after she loaned her credit card to a friend.

- A man who has his car stolen after he leaves the keys in the ignition having parked on double yellow lines to run into an off-licence and buy alcohol.

Did you find some of these easier to score than others? Those in the first group probably seem more 'innocent' than those in the second group. They also probably seem less blameworthy. But some of those in the second group may have challenged you a little more (see **Figure 7.2**). A few of these examples may indicate some stereotypes or negative ways of thinking about victims as contributing to their own victimhood. For example, the idea that people who have been drinking are somehow to blame or should take some responsibility for what happens to them. We may also think that the man who has had an affair is now receiving karma for his bad behaviour. This example might also be influenced by preconceptions or stereotypes about the legitimacy of men as victims of abuse at the hands of women.

Before you read on in this chapter, think about how our views on victims can be affected by what we learn about the victim and their relationship to the offender. Think also about how our sympathy for victims can be manipulated by how much we relate to the victim, or think that they fall outside the ideals of behaviour that we have been encouraged to think of as acceptable.

Figure 7.2 Does everyone fit societal outlines of a victim equally?
Source: pashabo/Shutterstock

7.3 Theories, concepts, and debates in victimology

The term 'victimology' is believed to have first been used by an American psychiatrist, Frederick Wertham, in 1949 (Fattah, 1989), although Hans Von Hentig, one of Wertham's contemporaries, was most influential in shaping what we might think of as victimology today. At this point, criminology had mainly focused on the offender, but Von Hentig argued that criminologists should also focus on the characteristics of the victim to try and identify things that may have led to their victimisation, as well as looking at the relationship between the victim and offender in order to identify factors that might contribute to the likelihood of being a victim (Von Hentig, 1948). Von Hentig suggested that victims could be classified into certain typologies; groups that shared the same characteristics, mainly based on psychological and social variables. His theory was that some individuals might be 'victim prone' and that studying various factors would help to identify these individuals and the features that cause their victimisation. Today's victimological research has evolved since Von Hentig's work, but we can see some of its roots in early victimology studies.

Victim precipitation

Early victimology studies were broadly based around three main approaches:

1. The search for individual factors that might increase a person's likelihood of being a victim of crime.
2. A focus on crimes against the person.
3. Interest in the idea of **victim precipitation**, or of the behaviour of victims as being a central cause of their victimisation.

Criminologists are still interested in the third point, particularly in the area of violent and sexual offences. In 1957, Wolfgang noted that 'the term victim-precipitated is applied to those criminal homicides in which the victim is a direct, positive precipitator in the crime' (1957: 1). Wolfgang's work influenced subsequent studies that considered the role of the victim as a factor in the commission of an offence. For example, Gobert (1977), in a *Columbia Law Review* article, suggested that victim precipitated crime was significant and had not been properly recognised. Building on the concept, Brotto et al. (2017: 86) identify two core ideas around victim precipitation (referencing Siegel's 2010 work): active precipitation and passive precipitation. Active precipitation 'is observed in a situation where it is the victim who initiates threatening behaviours and/or the actual use of physical force' (Brotto et al., 2017: 86). This might be, for example, if a person shouts at or threatens another, who then assaults them. Passive precipitation occurs when victims possessing a particular characteristic or behaviour unknowingly threaten their attacker. We might think of this, for example, in a situation where immigrants move into an area and compete for jobs and are then subject to attacks from other workers who feel threatened.

As you can perhaps imagine, these ideas are controversial and have been criticised because they contain an element of victim blaming. Potentially this reinforces differences in power between victim and offender, and risks having a negative impact on how crimes are investigated and prosecuted. For example, there have been problems with police attitudes towards victims of sexual assault, including suggestions that the victim put themselves in a position where they 'should have known' that sex was likely or expected. So, the suggestion becomes that the victim is in part to blame for what has happened.

More recently, Suarez and Gadalla (2010) identified that rape myths—false beliefs used mainly to shift the blame of rape from perpetrators to victims—are also prevalent in today's society and in many ways contribute toward the prevalence of rape. They looked at 37 studies into **rape myth acceptance** (RMA) and found that men displayed a significantly higher endorsement of RMA than women. They also concluded that RMA was strongly associated with hostile attitudes and behaviours toward women. Phillips (2017) has also explored the phenomenon of **rape culture**; the cultural normalisation of violence against women. The **MeToo** hashtag began trending on Twitter on 24 October 2017 in response to allegations of sexual assault by Hollywood producer Harvey Weinstein (Mendes et al., 2018). The MeToo movement and protests against rape culture represent a backlash against such cultural normalisation, as illustrated by **Figure 7.3**. We look at this issue in a little more depth in **Controversy and debate 7.1**.

Theoretical approaches to victimology

Victimology studies have established victimisation as an important area of criminology, and they expand our ideas about victims and how victimisation is experienced by considering evidence of victimisation at local and global levels. Victimology also incorporates various theoretical approaches, and we discuss some of these within this section. There are numerous academic books and several

Figure 7.3 Activists protest against rape culture and the continued blaming of victims of sexual assault
Source: Stephanie Kenner/Shutterstock

journals dedicated to victimology, including: *International Review of Victimology* and the *Journal of Victimology and Victim Justice*. Looking at some recent issues of these two journals identifies the wide range of topics currently being discussed in academic victimology studies. If you examine these publications, you will find cutting-edge research on topics including: sexual exploitation of children; terrorism; victim selection (based on a case study of prisoners); survivors of homicide; effects of childhood sexual victimisation on adulthood; and so-called honour-based abuse. You will also see research on victimisation of particular groups, such as Roma people, black people in South Africa, British Muslim women, and rape survivors. Victimology research within these journals also looks at some issues surrounding new laws and policies, like policing online fraud, engaging victims with restorative justice, and compensating victims of crime.

Each of the researchers who wrote these articles will have taken a different approach to their study, including the theories on which they base their arguments. You might remember from your reading of **Chapter 4** that criminology produces knowledge in different ways, and there is no one overarching method or theory that researchers use in their studies. Victimology is much the same, and there are several theoretical approaches to be aware of in this subject area, most prominently positivist approaches and radical or critical approaches. But we also highlight the importance of feminist victimisation theories and emerging areas like cultural victimology and narrative victimology.

Positivist victimology

Positivism in victimology mainly focuses on the scientific study of victimisation (see also **Chapters 16** and **17**). The main aim of the positivist approach is **aetiology**, which is

CONTROVERSY AND DEBATE 7.1

The victims' movement and MeToo

Part of what we examine in this chapter is the concept of a victim's movement that aims to improve the way we listen to and treat victims of crime. The victims' movement has been said to have four main ideas supporting it, which are:

1. **The care ideology**—this idea suggests that the community should protect and help citizens who are facing hardship. The emphasis is on providing for victims of crime rather than focusing on the nature of the offence.
2. **The rehabilitation ideology**—this view puts victims' interests alongside the use of the penal law, and sees crime as a conflict where both parties, victim and offender, should be 'treated' and rehabilitated.
3. **The retributive or criminal justice ideology**—the idea of this is to punish the offender in line with a 'just deserts' approach. In this approach, the victim would be involved in sentencing and punishment and may also be given the opportunity to pursue civil claims against an offender.
4. **The abolitionist ideology**—the abolitionist or anti-criminal justice approach suggests that criminal justice agencies should not intervene in situations involving criminal behaviour, and should instead leave mediation, reparation, aid to victims, and crime prevention in the hands of neighbourhood groups and other social networks.

(Adapted from van Dijk, 1988: 117–18)

These ideas have become relevant today in light of the MeToo movement, which has identified how frequently powerful men who victimise women have been able to escape the attention of criminal justice agencies. The movement has also exposed how workplace policies are ineffective when dealing with sexual harassment, especially in what we might think of as informal settings (Tippett, 2018). Victims are often silenced through fear, particularly within industries where powerful individuals can make or break careers, like media and creative industries. In some cases, the behaviour of powerful predators like the film producer Harvey Weinstein have been known about for several years, but their positions of power and access to legal systems have protected them from prosecution (Peters and Besley, 2018; Cobb and Horeck, 2018). While this perhaps simplifies things a little, the victims' movement has begun to fight back against powerful men by bringing allegations out into the open, without waiting for justice systems to intervene (the abolitionist approach). Publicly supporting victims in this way also embodies the care ideology and, at least in the UK and US, has led to a situation where there is now a presumption that women will be believed and their victimisation taken seriously. Previously, the system was accused of protecting powerful men and silencing women.

This is not without its controversy. The counter-argument that might be raised is that allegations alone should not be taken as proof of victimisation, and careers should not be derailed without the benefit of due process and a trial. Where you stand on this debate may be affected by your perceptions of some of the victims and offenders that you have read about, as well as how their crimes have been reported. Your own social status and identity may be a factor. For example, for many black Americans, the idea that Bill Cosby, a famous family entertainer and civil rights activist, was also a serial sex offender was at best a challenging idea to accept. However, Cosby's status, wealth, and wholesome image were arguably strong tools to discourage survivors from coming forward. Think about how this may have increased levels of victimisation for Cosby's victims.

the attempt to find out the cause of things (Von Hentig, 1948). This approach is behind some of the victimisation and crime surveys that attempt to measure the extent of victimisation, as well as those studies that may look at the relationship between offender and victim. The positivist approach uses data and evidence to try and understand patterns of victimisation that can tell us when and where crime and victimisation occur and the identification of factors that may be relevant to a non-random risk of victimisation (Miers, 1989). We look at these surveys in more detail later in the chapter.

Critical victimology

Critical victimology brings us back to the issues of vulnerability, power relations, structural inequalities, and the rights and needs of victims (see also **Chapter 8**). Critical victimology considers how individuals act within the structural conditions that they live in and their ability to resist or navigate these conditions. This includes an examination of the 'processes that go on behind our backs, which contribute to the crime and victims that we see as opposed to that which we do not see' (Mawby and Walklate, 1994: 19). Taking issues of 'agency' and 'structure' into account, critical victimology considers connections between political economic and social processes and victimisation. For example, wealthier citizens are arguably structurally more at risk of crime because they represent an attractive target. But when looking at data from the Crime Survey for England and Wales, it could be argued that structural problems in society account for the high proportion of unemployed people and people in deprived areas being the victims of crime. While these may appear to be contradictory ideas, they illustrate critical victimology's approach that identifies that multiple factors interact to complicate victim status and victim responses to the conditions they live in. This includes consideration of the wider social context in which victimisation occurs, which acknowledges such issues as the different experience of and vulnerability to different types of victimisation of social groups. Feminist perspectives also consider this issue in detail.

Radical victimology

Radical approaches to victimisation consider structural conditions that victimise large amounts of people. Quinney (1980) criticised victimology's focus on victims of traditional, conventional crimes and how this had the effect of presenting the capitalist system's view of reality. Research from a radical perspective questions the social construction of victimhood, raising questions about how the label of victim is applied as well as who has the power to apply the label (Mawby and Walklate, 1994). Radical victimologies are based on critical approaches (see also **Chapters 4** and **18**) that challenge ideas that the law is just, and identify how legal processes can be used to preserve hierarchies and traditional power relationships. The radical approach rejects some of the theoretical basis of positivist victimology (and in this sense is critical), and looks at expanding our understanding of victimisation by thinking about how relatively powerless groups in society should be considered, and examining the different types of oppression they suffer. Radical approaches argue that there are a broad range of victims and victimisation, and suggest that the state constructs the status of the victim and decides who is 'deserving' and 'undeserving'. For example, McShane and Williams (1992) considered the potential of radical victimology to explore the role of the victim in furthering the interests of the police and prosecution agencies, as well as the interests of the media and capitalist business enterprises. Within Marxist radical perspectives, some attention has been paid to the role of the state and capitalist systems. For example, workers in a capitalist system are victims due to their exploitation by those who own the means of production. As a result, deaths and injuries that occur at work could be viewed as criminal victimisation (Friedrichs, 1983).

Feminist victimology

Feminist victimisation theories are integral to understanding the importance of gender as influencing victimisation risk, types of victimisation experienced, and other key factors (see also **Chapter 11**). In your studies, you will look at literature and research that examines the differences between men and women in society, and that also illustrate how privilege and marginalisation in society can have an impact on victimisation. For example, Belknap (2014) examined women's experiences with the criminal justice system and considered how victimisation impacts on the female experience with justice and offending. Chesney-Lind (1997) discussed the importance of trauma and abuse in the lives of female offenders and examined how the criminal justice system can further marginalise women (and produce secondary victimisation). Research in this area is important in highlighting how victimisation is not confined to the initial incident but can be added to by policies and practices that further subjugate or marginalise.

Feminist victimology has also highlighted the challenges and limitations of simplistic social constructions of victims and classifications that fail to consider gender differences in the experience of victimisation and trauma (see, for example, Lamb, 1999; Lauritsen and Carbonne-Lopez, 2011; see also **Conversations 8.1**). Research has also challenged some previously accepted knowledge such as the victim precipitation theory mentioned earlier in this chapter. As both Lasky (2019) and Brotto et al. (2017) note, research by Wolfgang's student, Amir (1971), which examined police reports and included a **typology** of forcible rape, drawing conclusions around victim precipitation, was greatly criticised. This is because it focused on the offender's interpretation of the victim's behaviour rather than considering the victim's perspective or 'any form of objective evaluation of the behavioural evidence' (Brotto et al., 2017: 86). Lasky (2019) suggests that the backlash against Amir's work led to broad developments in victimological theory.

Narrative victimology

The focus on considering victims' stories and experiences leads us on to narrative victimology; an emergent area concerned with the role of narratives and their relationship to policy. Walklate et al. (2018: 200) argue that victimology has been slow to recognise the value of narratives 'both as sources of data for making sense of victims' experiences and policy responses to those experiences, and as forces which act upon such experiences and responses.' This is despite some recognition within criminology (and law) that 'narrative is particularly relevant to the study of how people understand their own experience and actions in relation to their identity and the wider collectives to which they belong' (Pemberton et al., 2018: 392). Narrative victimology 'focuses on how people experience wrongdoing' (Pemberton et al., 2018: 393) and stories have value both in terms of allowing individuals to construct understanding of what has happened to them and for examination of the experience of victims. But it has been argued that 'some narratives count more than others and the socio-political context in which such "counting" takes place is important to appreciate' (Walklate et al. (2018: 211).

We explore the acceptance of stories and experiences within policy in the following section.

Policy approaches to victimology

Criminologists are not the only parties who concern themselves with victims, as international organisations and state governments are also responsible for policies around victimisation. While each country will have its own laws in these areas and will implement their own approach to victims and victimisation, there are some key international and regional policies that are important in victimology.

The United Nations on victims

There has been significant concern for victims at an international level, although victims' rights are not necessarily protected in binding international policies. However, the United Nations, the main international organisation concerned with peace and security, developed some definitions of victims in its 1985 Declaration on victims:

1. 'Victims' means persons who, individually or collectively, have suffered harm, including physical or mental injury, emotional suffering, economic loss or substantial impairment of their fundamental rights, through acts or omissions that are in violation of criminal laws operative within Member States, including those laws proscribing criminal abuse of power.

2. A person may be considered a victim, under this Declaration, regardless of whether the perpetrator is identified, apprehended, prosecuted or convicted and regardless of the familial relationship between the perpetrator and the victim. The term 'victim' also includes, where appropriate, the immediate family or dependants of the direct victim and persons who have suffered harm in intervening to assist victims in stress or to prevent victimisation.

(United Nations, *Declaration of Basic Principles of Justice for Victims of Crime and Abuse of Power*, 1985)

The UN Declaration identifies some interesting points about the nature of victimisation. The definition uses the word 'harm' rather than 'crime' and so makes a point about victims being those people who have suffered some form of disadvantage or negative impact. It also talks about 'acts or omissions' and so extends beyond just deliberate criminal acts. For example, failure to take an action that would safeguard a child could have the consequence of that child suffering harm, and would therefore count as an 'omission' that might violate laws. You may also have noticed that the second paragraph talks about 'secondary' victims; the idea that crime can have an impact on the immediate family members of the direct or 'primary' victim. We look at this in more detail as we continue our victimology discussion in this chapter.

The UN Declaration helps us to consider ideas around victimisation in more detail. The Declaration identifies the victim as *any* person who suffers from the violation of criminal laws, and so the distinction between victims and offenders may not always be as straightforward as we might initially think. For example, there is an idea that many offenders/perpetrators also suffer victimisation and we mentioned this earlier in our discussion of child soldiers in the *Lubanga* case. There is evidence that some people who inflict domestic abuse on their partners have themselves suffered abuse while growing up in violent or antisocial households (Simons et al., 1995). Some critics also suggest that young offenders who end up in young offender institutions also suffer from different forms of deprivation and are affected by different importation and deprivation factors (Gover et al., 2000). One might even argue that criminal justice professionals like the police are victims of crime through being the targets of violence and seeing their fellow officers injured and even killed.

The United Nations also has a Victims Rights Advocate (VRA), whose role is to put the rights of victims, their experiences, and their needs at the heart of the UN's efforts to address sexual exploitation and abuse, promoting a policy of **zero tolerance** towards these issues. Jane Connors, the UN Victims' Rights Advocate at the time of writing (pictured in **Figure 7.4**), has stated: 'My priority is to give visibility to those who have suffered, included through connecting with them personally. I wish to amplify their voices in a way that cannot be ignored, and to support them as they rebuild their lives' (United Nations Victims' Rights Advocate Annual Report, 2019).

While the UN works at a global level, there are also regional policies like those of the EU that help to shape victims' rights.

7.3 THEORIES, CONCEPTS, AND DEBATES IN VICTIMOLOGY

Figure 7.4 The United Nations Victims' Rights Advocate (VRA) works to ensure that victims are properly recognised through UN policies and processes
Source: Foreign, Commonwealth & Development Office/Flickr

The European Directive on victims

The EU Directive on Victims' Rights sets out minimum rights for victims, wherever they are in the EU, and was adopted on 4 October 2012 by the EU's Council of Ministers. One idea behind the Directive was a concern that criminal law had become too focused on the criminal and did not consider enough the rights or needs of victims. The Directive intends to ensure that in all 27 EU countries:

- victims are treated with respect and that police, prosecutors, and judges are trained to properly deal with them;
- victims get information on their rights and their case in a way they understand;
- victim support exists in every EU Member State;
- victims can participate in proceedings if they want to and are helped to attend the trial;
- vulnerable victims are identified—such as children, victims of rape, or those with disabilities—and are properly protected;
- victims are protected while police investigate the crime and during court proceedings.

The importance of the EU Directive is that all EU Member States had until 2015 to demonstrate that they had updated their national (domestic) laws so that they put in place all of the measures included in the Directive. For the first time, **restorative justice** was also regulated at an EU level as the Directive aims to provide a framework for restorative justice to be used across the EU as a way of involving victims in the justice process (Gavrielides, 2017). Some of these principles are implemented in the UK in the Victims' Code which was brought in under the Domestic Violence, Crime and Victims Act 2004. The Code spells out what criminal justice agencies must do for victims and the time frame in which they must do it. The Code has specific provisions such as giving victims the right to information about taking part in restorative justice schemes (see **Chapter 30**) and the right to seek a review of the decision not to prosecute. The Code was revised in October 2015 to bring in new measures needed to comply with the EU Directive.

The historical failure to consider victims in the trial process has been a focus of criminologists and victimologists, but before we examine this area in more detail, have a think about the United Nations Declaration and the EU Directive in **What do you think? 7.2**.

WHAT DO YOU THINK? 7.2

The needs of victims

Having read the ideas from the United Nations Declaration of Basic Principles of Justice for Victims of Crime and Abuse of Power, write down your ideas of what it means to be a victim of crime. Think about:

- How would you define a victim of crime?
- Do you think the United Nations Declaration is too broad, too narrow, or about right? Give reasons for your answer.
- The United Nations Declaration identifies somebody as a victim even if the perpetrator is a member of their own family. What do you think about this idea?

Next, think about the EU Directive on Victims' Rights and make a few notes on the following points:

- What is the purpose of the Directive?
- Why might it be important for victims to be protected during the criminal investigation?
- The Directive says some important things about the support given to victims and the need to provide information for victims. Why might this be important?

As you think about these questions, you may begin to see how the United Nations Declaration creates a kind of 'umbrella' approach to victims that says that everybody who suffers from harmful behaviour is a victim. This is important because in the past there have been ideas that suggested husbands had rights over their wives and children, and so any 'harm' they caused to them should not be considered a crime. The United Nations definitions also mention individuals and groups, and take into account abuse of power, and so the definitions of crimes that cause harm and victimisation can include abuses by the police, prison service, and other state agencies. What the EU Directive does is to provide for a practical application of some of the ideas outlined in the United Nations Declaration. It requires EU Member States to give victims of crime information about how the crimes that have affected them are being investigated and prosecuted. Importantly, it also says that if victims wish to attend a trial they can, and they should be given support to do so (see also **Conversations 7.1** for more on the needs of victims' families).

Before you read on in this chapter, think about what types of actions might be needed to support victims and why these principles had to be written into law.

7.4 Measuring victimisation

Criminology has greatly developed our understanding of the extent of victimisation. By looking at statistics, criminologists can reveal trends in specific forms of crime over time and within given locations. These trends can then inform both policing and government policies on crime prevention initiatives aimed at protecting the public from becoming victims of crime. But statistics are not a foolproof way of measuring victimisation, as in victim surveys they rely on participants being willing to provide information on their victimisation. They also rely on robust questions and reliable samples (see **reliability**) and can raise questions about the difference between different surveys and official figures, a topic we discussed in **Chapter 5**. In this section, we will explore both their uses and their flaws.

Statistics on victimisation

The British Crime Survey (now called the Crime Survey for England and Wales or CSEW) collects information about fear of crime and victimisation from crime (see also **Chapter 5**). The survey measures crime by asking people about their experiences of it, and it is one of the largest victimisation surveys (the current sample size is 40,000 households). The CSEW collects more information than the limited statistical picture that we can get from police recorded crime, and offers us more information about the nature and scale of potential victimisation. For example, CSEW figures for the year ending March 2020 estimated that over 10.2 million offences were experienced by adults aged 16 years and over in the previous 12 months, based on interviews from that period (Office for National Statistics, 2020). This number was a significant decrease of 9 per cent from the previous year. The CSEW also measures the prevalence of crime, with the latest estimates showing that eight in ten adults did not experience any of the crimes asked about in the survey in the previous 12 months, although it is important to note that victimisation rates vary across the population and by geographic area.

The survey further breaks down victimisation by ethnic background. Some key findings on this are:

- people of a white ethnic background were the least likely to have experienced crime (excluding fraud) in the year ending March 2020, at 13 per cent;
- people of mixed or multiple ethnic backgrounds were the most likely to have experienced crime, with 20 per cent having experienced crime in the same period;
- people of an Asian ethnic background were also significantly more likely to have experienced crime in the year ending March 2020 than those of a white ethnic background, with 15 per cent having experienced crime in the last year;
- there were no other significant differences in the likelihood of being a victim of crime between ethnic groups.

The CSEW also takes into account a range of other demographic features, including age, sexual orientation, disability status, and religion. These characteristics also showed some key differences in the likelihood of having experienced crime (excluding fraud) in the year ending March 2020:

- younger people were more likely to be victims, with 18 per cent of 16–24-year-olds having been a victim of crime, compared to only 5 per cent of those aged 75 years or older;
- people who identified as heterosexual or straight were less likely to have experienced crime (14 per cent) than those who identified as gay or lesbian (21 per cent), or those who identified as bisexual (21 per cent);
- people with a disability were slightly more likely to have experienced crime (14 per cent) than people who did not have a disability (13 per cent);

- Christians were less likely to have experienced crime (11 per cent) than those with no religion (15 per cent) and Muslims (17 per cent).

We can see from these figures that becoming a victim of crime has some patterns attached to it. For instance, while older people may have a greater fear of crime, the figures show that the risk of being a crime victim actually decreases with age. We can probably guess some of the reasons why this might be the case; older people are less likely to be in certain situations where violence erupts suddenly, like pubs and nightclubs. They are also more likely to drive safer cars and we could speculate that they may have more to lose from drink-driving. They are also likely to live in more secure houses. By contrast, younger age, disability, being gay, lesbian, or bisexual, or being Muslim also appear to be factors that increase the risk of victimisation. We should, though, note here that fitting into one of these categories does not automatically mean that you are more likely to become a victim. But with some of these categories, we can see why people may be more likely to become victims of crime as, for example, religion, race, and sexual orientation are all areas that are the focus of hate crimes (see **Figure 7.5**; see also **Chapter 8**).

Let's look at one of these factors more closely. The likelihood of victimisation decreases with age, which means that children are particularly vulnerable, and especially online, a topic that we look at more closely later on in **Conversations 7.2**. A recent area of debate in victimology has focused on whether the state should weigh the rights of one group against another in order to try and reduce victimisation. **Controversy and debate 7.2** explores this issue by considering a policy attempt to reduce victimisation of young children.

You can find out more about the CSEW and the official victimisation statistics by visiting the websites of the Office for National Statistics (www.ons/gov.uk) and the CSEW (www.crimesurvey.co.uk/index.html). (We also discuss hate crime statistics in **Chapter 8**). As well as providing us with some user-friendly guidance and infographics on what is measured by the survey, we can also look at the figures in detail and download detailed spreadsheets and images that provide some of the information we have already discussed, and on other areas of the CSEW.

The problems with statistics on victimisation

While these statistics are interesting in themselves and you will probably come across these and other crime statistics many times in your criminology studies, it is important to consider their value. Crime statistics like these can inform policy and policing practices and, perhaps more importantly, can tell us something about the impact that being a victim of crime can have on a person. To develop policies on addressing victims' rights and needs, we need a range of qualitative information about the lived experiences and emotional and behavioural reactions that victims have towards crime. Victimisation surveys are useful in providing information about fear of crime and the experience of it, but they can only tell us so much. As we identified earlier,

Figure 7.5 Statistics can tell us about the prevalence of crime in a population, but to develop effective policies on addressing victims' rights and needs, we need to look more closely at their lived experiences

Source: James Cridland/Flickr

CONTROVERSY AND DEBATE 7.2

Megan and Sarah's Laws

Megan's Law is the name generally given to federal law and some US state laws that require law enforcement authorities to make information available about registered sex offenders. These laws were created following the murder of seven-year-old Megan Kanka, who was raped and killed in 1994 by Jesse Timmendequas, a known child molester with two previous convictions who had moved across the street from Megan's family without their knowledge.

The principle behind Megan's Law is that families should be informed when paedophile sex offenders move into their area, although this is just one aspect of the laws. We should note that Megan's Law has been implemented differently in each of the US states, but several US states now list offenders' details online. The idea is that victimisation may be reduced if families are aware that offenders are living in their area. But there have also been arguments that Megan's Law encourages acts of vigilantism (members of the public enacting what they see as 'justice' without legal authority), and reduces the opportunities for those who have served their prison sentences the chance to rejoin society and to put their past behind them. The UK's version of Megan's Law is the child sex offender registration scheme known as 'Sarah's Law', named after the abduction and murder of Sarah Payne. It was initially piloted in four police force areas in 2008 before being rolled out more widely in 2010. When Sarah's Law was implemented, the then Home Secretary Theresa May said:

> The roll-out of this scheme is an important step forward for child protection in this country. Being able to make these checks reassures parents and the community and more importantly keeps children safer.
>
> (Lipscombe, 2012: 8)

Does Megan's Law reduce victimisation, and are there other effects of applying the law? One effect might be that notifying the community will deter potential offenders and increase monitoring of them. Levenson and Cotter (2005) examined a sample of 183 convicted male sex offenders from Florida to identify the impact of Megan's Law on them. About one-third of participants in their survey identified negative impacts such as the loss of a job or home, threats or harassment, or property damage. While physical assault didn't happen often, the majority of participants in the survey declared that they had suffered stress, isolation, loss of relationships, fear, shame, embarrassment, and hopelessness. Several offenders in the study also commented that the information posted about them contained inaccuracies. On the other hand, some offenders did identify positive effects, including motivation to prevent reoffending and increased honesty with friends and family. Yet few of the sex offenders believed that communities were safer as a result of Megan's Law.

The arguments on each side of this debate are complex but raise some interesting points about victimisation. On one side of this debate is the argument that communities cannot protect themselves if they are not fully informed of the threats that they face. Sexual predators who target children are viewed as a particular risk because children are especially vulnerable. So, we could argue that knowing when a convicted sex offender lives in the area can help parents to examine any increased risk. We could also argue that parents and guardians may fail to consider the risks posed by those close to them, as they focus on the 'known' risk of the identified sex offenders. As the UK's former Home Secretary Theresa May argued, access to this knowledge allows child protection agencies and parents to protect children and makes them safer. On the other side of this debate, there is a possible argument that making this information available exposes offenders to vigilante justice and increases their victimisation. The evidence here suggests that offenders suffer stress and anxiety, and could be prevented from reintegrating back into society. Elsewhere in this book, we explore ideas from **labelling theory** (see **Chapter 9**), which argues that describing people in terms of their behaviour can be damaging. Applied in this context, labelling theory suggests that the rehabilitation of offenders could be affected by continuing to view them in terms of their past behaviour.

---

the effects of being a victim of crime will vary between the type of crime experienced and the individual or group experiencing it. We also need to think about both short- and long-term needs of victims, and how best to involve them in criminal justice processes while also protecting them. The independent national charity Victim Support provides some services for victims, and there are also a range of other support charities and non-governmental organisations (NGOs) that promote victims' rights and better treatment for victims.

Another element that may be missing from statistics is where individuals are victimised by criminal justice

Figure 7.6 The Black Lives Matter protests in 2020 raised awareness of police victimisation of black citizens on an international scale
Source: Michal Urbanek/shutterstock

organisations. In recent years, police killing of black people in the US, and particularly that of black men, has gained increased public attention, as shown in **Figure 7.6**. Some of the killings have been caught on camera—some by bystanders and other witnesses, some by body cameras worn by police officers. The victimisation of black people is definitely not a new or emerging issue, but it is one that has recently gained more engagement. The greater visibility of these killings has led to widespread public concern and has reignited a debate about the perception and claim that criminal justice agencies, particularly the police, are engaged in victimisation of an entire community.

Criminology has long been engaged in examining whether policing tactics and the use of police powers can result in a form of victimisation (see also **Chapter 10**). For example, Bowling and Philips (2007) examined the use of stop and search powers by police, and concluded that the statistics showed that the use of stop and search powers against black people was disproportionate, indicating unlawful racial discrimination. In the wake of the killing of George Floyd (and other incidents such as the killing of Eric Garner and Breonna Taylor), questions have been raised again about how the police use their powers and whether systematic racism has created a culture of victimisation (Ray et al., 2017; Ince et al., 2017; Rickford, 2015). The UN Declaration on Basic Principles of Justice for Victims of Crime and Abuse of Power clearly sets out ideas on victims as including those who experience harm from criminal abuse of power. The Declaration's definition of victims therefore applies to black citizens unlawfully killed by policing agencies, even if no perpetrator is identified or if no disciplinary or other action is taken.

Criminology has examined these issues before, and victimology studies in the US and elsewhere have already examined the prevalence of black citizens in officer-involved shootings, as well as the level of use of force. Studies have also examined how far cultural issues within police forces risk increasing the victimisation of black citizens by law enforcement, with its members potentially considering black citizens to be more dangerous and more likely to be criminal (Blum, 2020). From a theoretical perspective, we can see society's preference for truly innocent victims and the limited ability of the justice system to avenge them (McShane and Williams, 1992). But, as we have already discussed in this chapter, those who may be seen as a threat to society's norms can be considered to be less deserving victims. As a result, some victims of alleged racist action by policing agencies receive criticism suggesting that they are somehow deviant, and somehow to blame for the incidents that led to their deaths (see also **Controversy and debate 4.1**).

This is a controversial area and is one that criminology and victimology has again begun to study in detail, examining statistics on the use of force by the police, possible issues of racial bias in the way that black citizens are dealt with, and the extent to which victimisation rates for black citizens are higher than other groups when dealing with law enforcement and criminal justice. As you continue your studies, think about why we revisit these issues again and again, and consider what may need to be done to address these types of victimisation. You might be able to draw some inspiration from David Baker, a senior lecturer at the University of Liverpool, whose research focuses on death after police contact. You can read about his journey into studying such issues in **Conversations 7.1**.

Repeat victimisation

Statistics from the CSEW and other victim surveys also tell us something about how often somebody might be a victim of crime or the statistical likelihood of becoming a victim. Some people unfortunately experience crime multiple times, and we consider this as a problem called **repeat victimisation**. Wiesel (2005: 3) provides the following definition of this term:

> By most definitions, repeat victimization, or revictimization, occurs when the same type of crime incident is experienced by the same or virtually the same victim or target within a specific period of time such as a year. Repeat victimization refers to the total number of offenses experienced by a victim or target including the initial and subsequent offenses. A person's house may be burglarized twice in a year or 10 times, and both examples are considered repeats.

These terms can sometimes be confusing. Repeat victimisation refers to the same perpetrator targeting the victim repeatedly (for example, in domestic violence or hate crime). Revictimisation is where somebody experiences a particular crime at the hands of one perpetrator, and then

CONVERSATIONS 7.1

Death after police contact

with **Dr David Baker**

I began researching this subject after the death of Ian Tomlinson during the 2009 G20 protests in London. He had committed no crime; he was simply walking home. Ian was moving away from police with his hands in his pockets when he was hit from behind by a police baton and shoved to the ground. He died shortly afterwards. Immediately following this incident, it was obvious that the story the police constructed about his death was very different to that of eye-witnesses and Ian's family. Ian was portrayed as a homeless alcoholic, as though that would sufficiently explain being struck and knocked down by a police officer. A pattern of smearing the deceased in these cases became apparent to me the more I looked at this issue. It was a way of distracting attention from the police and focusing it on the 'undeserving' victim: portraying the incidents as tragic, yes, but ultimately just one of those things that happens to 'other' people. I wanted to understand how the families of such victims got justice in these cases, which led me to do a PhD on this issue.

In the period 2008–19 a total of 1,989 citizens died during or after contact with the police in England and Wales, according to figures from the Independent Office for Police Conduct (IOPC). Very few police officers are successfully prosecuted in these cases. In 2015, it became apparent that US authorities did not even count how many citizens die after police contact, a situation the Director of the FBI called 'embarrassing'. This issue was also highlighted by Black Lives Matter activists and civil liberties campaigners following the 2014 deaths of Michael Brown and Eric Garner, and subsequent deaths of several unarmed black men in the following years. The complaint is that officers are rarely prosecuted or dismissed when this happens, so what was called 'embarrassing' is not only shocking but may be business as usual.

In the UK, Australia, and the US we know that if you are from a black, minority, or ethnic (BME) group, or have mental health issues or substance dependency problems, you are disproportionately more likely to die after police contact than other citizens. Victims' relatives and pressure groups such as Inquest have repeatedly asked why lessons cannot be learned that prevent future deaths, and why police use of force cannot be held more to account. The 2017 Angiolini review into deaths and serious injury in police custody in England and Wales identified that police use of force or restraint against people in mental health crisis was problematic and posed a life threatening risk. The report also noted that all police officers prosecuted in connection with a death in custody in the fifteen years prior to its publication had been acquitted. In fact, the review identified that there had never been a successful manslaughter prosecution relating to a death in police custody, despite unlawful killing verdicts in Coroner's Inquests.

The people who die leave behind a family who often experience a sort of double victimisation. Not only has their loved one died, but they are often painted as someone who is either 'unfortunate' (e.g. homeless) or dangerous (e.g. having mental health issues). But the dead cannot defend themselves. Whilst families want to grieve for their loved one, they also want to know the truth: how exactly did they die? Investigations into these cases can last years, as is the case with Sean Rigg, who died in a police station in Brixton, South London in 2008. The case was subject to two investigations by the IOPC's predecessor organisation, the Independent Police Complaints Commission (IPCC). The initial CPS decision was that no criminal charges were brought, although two officers faced trial and were acquitted. In March 2019, five police officers involved in Sean Rigg's arrest were cleared of gross misconduct by a Metropolitan Police panel. This leaves the family without clear answers. In a way, the families themselves become victims of a justice system that seems to deliberately obstruct attempts to get at the truth. This seems some distance from the state pursuit of justice, as in, for example the 2011 riots, when special night courts were set up to deal with 'rioters and looters' as quickly as possible. It seems that justice works one way for some, another way for others.

In 2011, the coroner's court found Ian Tomlinson to have been 'unlawfully killed'. This means that criminal liability could not be ascribed for his death. So, we have a situation where somebody has been killed, but in law there is effectively no killer. This seems to sum up the state justice response to citizens who die after police contact: these cases are investigated in the coroner's court rather than being treated as potential crimes from the outset. This suggests that the state protects its own, using distraction techniques to imply that the victims of such incidents are 'undeserving', and consequently so are their families. We need to think about how the state dispenses justice and why, and how this affects victims and their ability to get justice when their loved one dies after police contact.

Dr David Baker, Senior Lecturer in Criminology, University of Liverpool

experiences the same type of crime again but is targeted by another offender. Victimology studies consistently find that while most people and places do not get victimised by crime, those who are victimised face the highest risk of being victimised again. To think about why this might be the case, consider burglary. A burglar who has successfully entered a house and has been able to make off with possessions may consider entering the house again. The burglar understands that the householder is probably insured and can assume they will replace the stolen goods. So, unless the householder tries to use some kind of situational crime prevention (see **Chapter 15**) by, for example, installing an alarm, improving the locks, or blocking access, then it perhaps makes sense for the burglar to return to the property. Statistics regularly show repeat victimisations happening quite soon after the first incident.

Now let's look at a more complex example. Incidents of domestic violence take place within the context of a relationship, where two people are regularly in contact with each other, sometimes living together. Repeated assaults are more likely in cases where the male partner (usually the perpetrator in domestic violence cases, see **Chapter 11**) may be prone to being aggressive as a form of control or expression, may have a drink or substance abuse problem, or is subject to other stresses or triggers that cause him to be violent. Farrell et al. (2005) found that 40 per cent of crimes reported to the International Crime Victims Survey (ICVS) in 2000 were repeats against the same target within a year, with variation by crime type and country. Knowledge of repeat victimisation allows us to examine the extent to which individuals may make changes such as installing a new security system and reassess the potential risk of crime following victimisation, and whether the failure to make such changes predicts repeat victimisation (Turanovic et al., 2018; Turanovic and Pratt, 2014; see also the discussion of the concentric zone model in **Chapter 17**). We examine some of the ideas about risk and vulnerability in **Conversations 7.2**.

This discussion of victimisation identifies a particular area of vulnerability in the online environment, where

CONVERSATIONS 7.2

Online victimisation and the sharing of intimate images

with **Dr Tine Munk**

Angus Nurse (AN): First of all, do you think that there is a problem concerning online victimisation?

Dr Tine Munk (TM): Yes. There is a problem of victimisation where people are vulnerable but may not have information or skills to protect themselves. Cybercriminals are exposing online users' trust, computing skills and lack of knowledge about cybercrime [for more on cybercrime, see **section 6.4**]. Every day millions of online communications and images are distributed online, through email accounts, social media, photo sharing sites and other platforms. Social engineering (tricking online users into providing personal information or taking actions) has been recognised as a top tier threat by Europol in their Internet Organised Crime Threat Assessment (IOCTA) 2020 report.

Online victimisation can arise particularly when users are taking part in activities that could later be used against them. One example is sexting, which involves the exchange of sexual pictures, messages, or videos using apps, emails, computer devices or webcams. When consensual, this may be perceived as harmless. But if the communication is unwanted, there might be other offences to consider, such as harassment. Although sexting is not a criminal activity, creating or sharing explicit sexual images of children is illegal. This also applies if the person sharing is under the age of 18 years, even though the age of sexual consent in the UK is 16 years. Other areas related to sexual images have also been criminalised. For example, 'upskirting', where sexually intrusive photographs are taken up someone's skirt and circulated without consent, is now included in the Voyeurism Act 2019.

Sexting among consenting adults is based on trust between the people involved. Yet the sender loses control when an image or text is sent, and it could be redistributed to anyone. For example, the image or the text can be sent to friends, family members or employers—or shared on online porn sites, the Dark Web or in particular forums beyond the victims' knowledge. Sharing intimate sexual images or videos of someone else online without their consent is known as revenge porn (or sextortion), and this act was criminalised in the UK by the Criminal Justice and Courts Act 2015. Frequently the victims are unaware that pictures are being circulated, and it is often difficult to stop the distribution.

The impact on the victims can be worsened by the intimate and private nature of the images or texts, and they may be reluctant to come forward and seek help from law enforcement. Victims may also be embarrassed about the sexual material in the offender's possession and fear what the offender might do with it, which can cause negative consequences like self-blaming and victim blaming.

AN: You mentioned that creating or sharing explicit images of children is illegal. Is online victimisation a particular problem for children?

TM: Yes, children are particularly vulnerable to online victimisation. They can be caught by a form of social engineering where the groomer builds up a secret relationship and then exposes the child or takes nude photos or videos. Minors might also take and send intimate photos and videos themselves, either voluntarily or because they have been pressured into doing so, and this material can then be used to blackmail them.

Offenders might also put these images online, and the victim cannot get away from this; once the image has been shared in this way it is online forever, and maybe friends and family will see it. While internet companies may take it down, somebody will have saved a copy of the image, and it will be uploaded and circulated again. This increases victimisation, and makes it very difficult to escape.

AN: So how might these forms of online victimisation of both children and adults be addressed?

TM: Law enforcement, victim support, and several charities and organisations are working to help online victims. Europol has launched several campaigns together with European police forces to enhance the knowledge about various types of cyber crimes and online protection, including sexting and the sharing of intimate images. For example, the 'Say no!' and 'Your life is online' campaigns related to online sexual coercion and extortion.

Improvements in computer literacy and further education about vulnerabilities and online risks on personal and technical levels may help. Online users need to consider their online presence and activities, control their data, avoid oversharing information, limit online activities, and be critical about befriending people online. Cyber criminals are often hiding behind fake identities, and they get information about their target victims on social media and other online forums, where users are sharing personal information that later can be misused. We need to become more aware of online vulnerabilities and cyber criminals' techniques to minimise online dangers.

Dr Angus Nurse, Head of Criminology and Criminal Justice, Nottingham Trent University, and author of this chapter

Dr Tine Munk, Lecturer in Criminology (Cybercrime), Middlesex University

Figure 7.7 Children and young people are particularly vulnerable online, but is enough being done to protect them from cybercrime?
Source: Burdun Iliya/Shutterstock

individuals can conceal their intentions or even their identities. Children are especially at risk of being victimised (see **Figure 7.7**), and we might want to think about whether parents can be more involved in protecting minors. However, this is not always possible where parents are unaware that a threat exists, which might add another level of complexity to the debate on policies like Megan's Law, which we discussed earlier in **Controversy and debate 7.2**.

7.5 Victims and the criminal justice process

Throughout our discussion of criminology, we have referred several times to the idea that victims are sometimes marginalised in the criminal justice process. This happens even though the victim starts the process, and the criminal trial is about getting justice for the victim by seeing the offender punished. The legal system that we have in the UK can be described as the 'law way' of resolving disputes. It is based on a set of rules, including ones that the prosecution and defence in a trial must follow, strict regulations on the power of police constables, and a clear role for the trial judge or jury who hear the case. We may think of the 'law way' as being the natural or correct way of seeking justice and of resolving disputes, although this raises a question: who is at dispute and what is the role of the victim in a trial that is meant to resolve the dispute—see **Figure 7.8**?

Norwegian critical criminologist Nils Christie who gave us our 'ideal victim' theory (discussed in **section 7.2**) also wrote a paper in 1977 entitled 'Conflicts as Property'. In it, Christie argued that the state and legal profession had 'stolen' the conflict (or dispute) away from the main protagonists in any criminal trial. He was particularly critical of the way the system treated the victim, and wrote:

> The party that is represented by the state, namely the victim, is so thoroughly represented that she or he for most of the proceedings is pushed completely out of the arena, reduced to the triggerer-off of the whole thing. She or he is a sort of double loser: first vis-à-vis the offender, but secondly and often in a more crippling manner by being denied rights to full participation in what might have been one of the more important ritual encounters in life. The victim has lost the case to the state.
>
> (Christie, 1977: 3)

Christie raises some important points that we should consider as we think about the role of victims. First, he suggests that victims should have 'rights', an idea that we explored when looking at the EU Directive on Victims' Rights and the Victims' Code and Witness Charter. Secondly, he suggests that the victim's voice is perhaps not an important one in criminal processes, and that once the state has decided to proceed with a case, the victim is largely silenced.

Christie claims that the role of the victim in criminal trials is mainly to give evidence, although since the year 2000 the criminal justice system has started to pay more attention to the rights of victims and their treatment within it. The Victims' Code and Witness Charter provide guidance on support for victims of crime and criminal conduct in England and Wales. Since October 2001, the Victim Personal Statement (VPS) scheme helps victims to provide evidence on how they have been affected by a crime. The purpose of a VPS is to:

1. give victims the opportunity to state how the crime has affected them—physically, emotionally, psychologically, financially, or in any other way;
2. allow victims to express their concerns in relation to bail or the fear of intimidation by or on behalf of the defendant;
3. provide victims with a means by which they can state whether they require information about, for example, the progress of the case;
4. provide victims with the opportunity of stating whether or not they wish to claim compensation or request assistance from Victim Support or any other help agency;
5. provide the criminal justice agencies with a ready source of information on how the particular crime has affected the victim involved.

(www.gov.uk/government/publications/victim-personal-statement)

A VPS gives the court discretion to take into account the consequences of the crime on the victim when passing sentence on an offender, subject to the police having taken a VPS and the CPS drawing it to the attention of the court, although this does not always happen.

Importantly, the fourth stated purpose of the VPS is to provide victims with the opportunity to ask for help from agencies like Victim Support. The charity was set up in 1972 to offer help, advice, and support to victims, and now helps over a million victims of crime every year (see www.victimsupport.org.uk/homepage for more details of their work). A lot of their activity focuses on the immediate effects of becoming a victim, and so they offer practical help and advice like assisting people to fill out forms (such as claims for compensation), helping to get broken windows and doors fixed, arranging medical treatment, and offering advice on how to deal with the often complicated and confusing criminal justice process if a case comes to trial. Alex Mayes, a spokesperson for Victim Support, explains more about what they do in **Conversations 7.3**.

Figure 7.8 Where might we see the victim of a crime in this courtroom? Are they really at the 'centre' of the trial?

Source: kenny1/Shutterstock

CONVERSATIONS 7.3

Support for victims in the criminal justice system

with **Alex Mayes**

Successive governments have promised to put victims at the heart of the criminal justice system, but has this actually addressed the many challenges victims face?

There can be no doubt that the treatment of victims has improved somewhat in recent years. The introduction of the Victims' Code, which sets out the level of service that victims should receive from statutory agencies, has been a vital step forward. 'Special Measures', such as screens and video links in court, have also made the process of giving evidence easier for many vulnerable victims.

However, there is much more to be done to improve the experience of victims in the criminal justice process, and the support and service provided to them.

Too often support for victims is viewed as a 'nice to have' rather than being recognised for what it is; not only a moral duty but also essential to the operation of the criminal justice system. The justice process cannot function without the consent and co-operation of victims; victims are relied upon to report crimes, to provide evidence to the police for their investigation and to be a witness in court.

For this to happen, victims must be supported in their journey through the criminal justice system. If this does not happen they may choose not to engage in this or future cases. The warning signs are there: crime continues to be under-reported, satisfaction with the police is low, every year hundreds of thousands of cases are being closed due to victims not supporting police action, and the CPS's own research found that only half of victims who were a witness in a criminal trial would definitely do so again.

Currently, there are various documents setting out how victims should be treated and agencies' commitments to them. However, what is written in these documents often does not happen in practice. Year after year, Victim Support's research with victims shows that as many as six in ten victims do not receive their entitlements under the Victims' Code. This is potentially leaving victims without access to independent support services, information about the progress of their case, or the opportunity to make a Victim Personal Statement.

Those who give evidence in court also encounter significant challenges. Many victims are anxious and stressed about being cross-examined and fear contact with the defendant or their supporters in the court building.

To help alleviate this, victims should be given more choice over where and how they give evidence, including options to pre-record their cross-examination or give evidence remotely from a building entirely separate from the court. It is also vital that they always have access to specialist, independent support through the process. Long waits for trial, which at the time of writing have been exacerbated by the coronavirus pandemic but have been a long-standing problem, are also of significant concern, leaving many victims in limbo and unable to move on from the incident.

Given these challenges, victim care should not be viewed as an optional extra, but as a central component of the criminal justice system.

We need to work quickly to improve the court experience for victims, to make giving evidence a less daunting and intimidating experience. And, crucially, victims' rights must be strengthened by being moved from Codes and Charters into primary legislation; enshrining in law the level of service and support that victims should receive throughout the process. By doing this, we can build on recent progress and move towards a criminal justice system that works for its participants, and gives victims the support and treatment that they deserve.

Alex Mayes, External Affairs Manager at Victim Support

7.6 Conclusion

Throughout this chapter we have examined victimology as an area of study, focusing on how we understand and measure different ideas on victimisation and the fear of crime. We have explored different ideas of the victim and have identified that these are not always straightforward. From the outset, we have encouraged you to think about terminology; the words that we use when we discuss who is a victim and who defines what a victim is. In your studies, you may need to go beyond the ordinary, everyday (dictionary) definition of the word victim and instead think about wider ideas of victimisation and who could or should be referred to as victims and in what way.

Much of this chapter discusses victims in the context of the criminal justice system and via involvement in crime. But we have also identified some wider ideas of victimisation and how victimology theories have shed light on ideas such as secondary victimisation and the social construction of victimisation.

Theory is important to your study of criminology, and here we have explored how early victimisation theories were centred on the offender perspective and considered victims mainly through the lens of how the offender behaved and what action was needed to address this. But our understanding of victimisation has expanded and so too victimology theory has also developed. In particular, we have highlighted feminist theories of victimisation, and your study in this area should take into account the importance of gender in considering the 'risk' of victimisation and victimisation rates. You should also consider the importance of secondary victimisation and the negative impacts of justice processes and procedures, alongside the state's decisions on which aspects of victimhood it accepts. The exercise of power and ideas on agency and structure are important aspects of victimology, and you may delve into some of these ideas in more detail later in your studies.

Victimology is a dynamic area of criminology, and as your studies continue you may well identify new ideas or emerging problems in the study of victims and victimisation.

SUMMARY

After reading this chapter and working your way through its features you should now be able to:

- Identify who counts as a victim

In this chapter we explored the idea that 'victim' is potentially a contested term and goes beyond a simple dictionary definition. We have explored the reality that the idea of a victim is socially constructed and is influenced by a range of factors. Within the chapter we also explored the role of structure and agency and particularly how the state and structural factors influence who is seen as a victim as well as who is 'counted' as a victim. A core idea that you should take away from this chapter is that the concept of or our understanding of victims and victimisation goes beyond a simple idea of the crime victim.

- Understand the scope of victimology and its importance within criminology

In this chapter we explored the idea that criminal justice is really 'for' victims because it is their experience of crime that sets the criminal justice process in motion, from their initial crime reporting through to conviction of an offender. But by studying victimology, we begin to understand that there are different types of victim, and that victimisation includes an indirect effect: families and friends of victims who also feel crime's impact. We also looked at how criminal justice processes could be accused of ignoring the victim and sometimes even of making things worse for them. Victimology helps to develop our understanding of this issue and how justice processes may need to change to be fairer to victims.

- Evaluate theories of victimisation and explain how different theoretical approaches and practices have contributed to understanding of secondary victimisation

We have examined some theories of victimisation in this chapter and have identified that there are different theoretical approaches to victimology. The positivist approach uses data and evidence to try and understand patterns of victimisation, and also looks at the relationship between offender and victim. Critical approaches take us beyond historical ideas of there being one type of victim; they consider a broader range of victims and victimisation. The radical approach looks at expanding our understanding of victimisation, and considering how relatively powerless groups in society should be thought of as victims by examining the different types of oppression they suffer. Feminist theories expand our knowledge of the gendered nature of victimisation and highlight the importance of secondary victimisation and the further marginalisation and subjugation of victims by criminal justice and policy practices. Important in our theoretical consideration is an understanding of how victims experience justice systems and various forms of victim support in different ways and how their perceptions may be marginalised within processes. Narrative criminology underpins these ideas with its examination of the importance of narratives, noting that victims' stories can be important factors in the recognition or acceptance of different types of victimisation.

- **Appreciate the range of victimological approaches and how each contributes to our understanding of victimisation**

This chapter has explored a range of theoretical approaches as well as policy approaches that contribute to our understanding of victimisation. From this discussion, you should understand that victimology extends beyond the study of crime and criminal justice and also considers other approaches to victimisation. For example, we have briefly mentioned victimisation caused by capitalist systems and the exercise of power. The state, operating from a position of power, can cause victimisation and continue to uphold social structures that have the effect of marginalising social groups. Victimological approaches that consider race, gender, class, or economic inequality as factors in victimisation go beyond the somewhat binary approaches of offender and victim and extend our understanding of how victimisation might be experienced differently.

- **Identify how and why the role of victims has changed within criminal justice processes and also assess the extent to which the victim has been marginalised in criminal justice**

We have explored how the visibility of the victim has changed over time, and how victimology has helped to make the victim the focus of criminological attention. Victims' rights have become an important part of criminal justice policy, through international measures such as the UN Declaration and the EU Directive on Victims' Rights. These efforts have also been helped by organisations like Victim Support and the work of victimologists to try and bring victims back towards the centre of criminal justice. This is a slightly controversial approach because too much of a focus on the victim could lead to punitive policies that might seem to promote seeking revenge for the victim rather than achieving proportionate justice. But there have been some improvements that allow for victims to express their views, for example by providing victim impact statements so that the effect of the crime on the victim can be considered in sentencing.

- **Understand the contribution of victimisation surveys in measuring the extent of victimisation**

In our discussion of crime statistics we have explored the use of victimisation surveys as a tool to measure victimisation. One benefit of such surveys is that they can reveal information about who is a victim of crime and also about the nature of victimisation and how victims have experienced it. Victimisation surveys may also reveal the 'dark figure' of crime by exposing victimisation that is sometimes missing from police recorded crime. Victimisation surveys are also a valuable source of the fear of crime, which is missing from quantitative police data.

- **Critically assess beliefs about the 'ideal' victim and understand why some victims of crime might be seen as being more 'deserving' than others**

In this chapter we have examined the idea that some victims are seen as being more 'deserving' than others. We have also explored Christie's concept of the 'ideal' victim, which helps us to consider social, political, and media constructions of victimhood. The 'ideal' victim concept relates to the theory that there are particular social ideas of somebody who deserves our pity and support, and who is deserving of justice; that is, the 'innocent' victim who is blameless. By contrast, there are victims who are seen as a threat to dominant societal norms and values and who may embody risky lifestyles that are thought to contribute to their victimisation. This includes sex workers, the homeless, travelling communities, and drug users. The concept of the 'ideal' victim prompts us to consider ideas of power and how power relationships can be a factor in constructing our ideas of who is an 'ideal' victim versus a non-ideal victim.

 Test your understanding of the chapter's key points by attempting the self-test questions on the **online resources** at www.oup.com/he/case2e

REVIEW QUESTIONS

1. What are some different ways of defining victims?
2. List three different impacts that crime can have on a victim.
3. What is repeat victimisation and why is it an important idea in criminology?
4. Think about the concept of the 'ideal' victim. Why are some victims of crime thought to be more deserving than others?
5. In what ways does the criminal justice system sometimes appear to 'fail' victims of crime?

 Access the **online resources** at www.oup.com/he/case2e to check your answers to the review questions.

FURTHER READING

Davies, P., Francis, P., and Greer, C. (2017) *Victims, Crime and Society: An Introduction.* **London: Sage.**
This book provides a good introduction to victimology and the study of different types of victimisation. It includes helpful chapters on defining and constructing victims, fear and vulnerability, sexuality, white-collar crime, and the implications of crime policy on victims.

Hilinski-Rosick, C., and Lee, D. (2020) *Contemporary Issues in Victimology: Identifying Patterns and Trends.* **Lanham, MD: Lexington Books.**
This book provides a useful overview of current topics in victimology, including (amongst others): intimate partner violence and dating violence, rape and sexual assault on the college campus, internet victimisation, elder abuse, victimisation of prison, fear of crime and perceived risk of crime, human trafficking, mass shootings, and child-to-parent violence.

Spalek, B. (2017) *Crime Victims: Theory, Policy and Practice* **(2nd edn). Basingstoke: Palgrave.**
This book provides an overview of the historical, social, political, and cultural issues and trends in approaches to victims and victimisation. It examines the impacts of crime on victims as well as the challenges of providing victims' services.

Tapley, J. and Davies, P. (eds) (2020) *Victimology: Research, Policy and Activism.* **Basingstoke: Palgrave Macmillan.**
This book explores the achievements of victimology as an academic discipline and activist movement. It focuses on nine dynamic and contemporary case studies covering topics like violence against women and girls, bereaved family activism, and environmental victims and climate change activists. O'Leary and Green's chapter 'From Invisible to Conspicuous: The rise of victim activism in the politics of justice' covers two of the case studies discussed in this chapter (MeToo and Sarah's Law) and also Stephen Lawrence's murder investigation (see **Chapter 10**).

Walklate, S. (ed.) (2017) *Handbook of Victims and Victimology.* **Abingdon: Routledge.**
This is a comprehensive collection of original essays from leading academics on a range of victimology topics. It is broken down into helpful sections covering a range of perspectives on victims and victimisation, policy, and service delivery, including some case studies that compare victimisation in different countries.

 Access the **online resources** to view a wealth of extra information relating to your study of criminology, including self-test questions, answers to review questions, and links to other resources that will help you enjoy and fulfil your potential within your studies.

www.oup.com/he/case2e

CHAPTER OUTLINE

8.1	Introduction	212
8.2	Understanding hate crime	212
8.3	Disablist hate crime	219
8.4	LGBT+ hate crime	223
8.5	Racially motivated hate crime	226
8.6	Religiously motivated hate crime	229
8.7	Conclusion	231

8

Hate crime

Angus Nurse and Mark Walters

KEY ISSUES

After studying this chapter, you should be able to:

- appreciate the importance of hate crime as an area of study within criminology and criminal justice;
- critically discuss the main features of hate crime and evaluate the need for hate crime legislation;
- identify different forms of hate crime and analyse the underlying social and political issues which affect both public and policy responses to the affected groups;
- explain some of the tensions in society and structural inequalities that may be factors in causing hate crimes;
- critically discuss the evidence of hate crime's occurrence and identify some of the reasons why hate crime may be on the rise.

8.1 Introduction

Many countries have a long and very troubling history of violence against certain groups of people in society who are targeted because of their identities (Bowling 1998). Offences that are either motivated by hostility towards an identity or where perpetrators demonstrate such hostility when committing an offence are now commonly referred to as 'hate crimes'. Hate crimes are complex, as these offences can be linked to both personal gain or even profit, as well as concepts such as 'difference' and othering (see Chapter 10 for a more detailed discussion on race and crime). By examining this type of criminality, we can more fully understand why some people are victimised because of their identity and ideas that they are different (see also Chapter 7). You might be surprised to learn that it was not until the latter part of the 20th century that criminal conduct driven by prejudice (unfairly biased opinions) or hatred was even recognised as a specific type of offending. This newish area of criminology came about primarily because the civil rights movements in the US and the UK (that made their most important gains in the 1950s, 1960s, and 1970s) raised the profile of racist and (later) homophobic violence so that they became important political and social issues. More recent social justice movements like #MeToo and the 2020 'Black Lives Matter' protests have heightened our awareness of persisting societal inequalities and injustices that are rooted in people's identities, and hate crime should continue to be a part of this discussion. The extent of hate crime remains a worrying concern for the stability and inclusiveness of society, and in this chapter we aim to introduce you to the importance of this issue in criminology.

Studying hate crime can expand our understanding of crime and deviance more generally, and in this chapter we look in detail at a broad range of the types of criminal act that are committed, and the motivations behind those crimes. While some of the crimes we examine in this chapter may seem less serious than the interpersonal violence examined elsewhere in this book, they can have serious impacts on the victims who have been targeted mainly because of their identity. We will look at a range of different types of hate crime, including offences based on prejudices towards victims because of their disability, race or ethnicity, religion and beliefs, sexual orientation, and gender identity. Such crimes can include, for example: racist abuse causing victims harassment, alarm, and distress; property damage involving homophobic graffiti; fraud and theft targeted against disabled people; and physical violence targeted towards transgender people, to highlight just some. This is by no means a complete list of all hate crimes, but in this chapter we will highlight key issues that are relevant to most, if not all, types of prejudice-based offending.

Along the way, we will be complicating our investigation of hate crime by looking at some of the factors that can affect these offences in ways that are not immediately obvious. These elements include the influence that politicians can have, especially when using language that excludes minority groups and portrays them as threats to the public or as somehow being 'other' (different and arguably not to be trusted). We will illustrate these examples by studying the effects that recent events, like the EU referendum and Covid-19 pandemic, had on hate crime, delving into the broader, political debates around these topics to identify their links with such offences. The issues we discuss here go hand in hand with what you learned about victimology in Chapter 7, and we encourage you to keep this in mind when working your way through this chapter. Before we delve into these problems in more detail, let us first take a look at some different ways we can gain an understanding of hate crime.

8.2 Understanding hate crime

Much like the concept of 'crime', which we discussed in Chapter 2, defining 'hate crime' can be tricky because its meaning is partly a social construction. The term 'hate crime' does not have a single, universal definition, and what is recognised or classed as a hate crime varies from country to country. So, the idea and definition of 'hate' can be influenced by history, culture, and politics. For example, while the law in England and Wales lists five areas for protection (race, religion, sexual orientation, disability, and transgender identity), various other countries across the world include crimes motivated by gender, social class, health status, and political ideology, amongst others (see www.hatecrime.osce.org/#participating-states).

Hate crime's evolution has also been heavily influenced by identity politics, which is where people identify with particular identities, such as race or religion, and form political movements around such categories. These movements then form various interest groups that play an important role in lobbying (petitioning, urging) governments to include specific identities in legislation

(Jenness and Grattet, 2001). For example, civil rights movements have highlighted the damaging impacts that prejudice and bias can have on the lives of those from marginalised communities. Both the MeToo and Black Lives Matter movements show how important social campaigns (both off and online) can highlight issues of prejudice and discrimination, and in turn advocate for (structural) reform. The MeToo movement in particular has brought focus on the discriminatory treatment of women in society, which has partly led to the UK government requesting the Law Commission (the body in charge of law reform proposals) to review all hate crime legislation in England and Wales. One of the key questions for reform is to look at whether 'gender' or 'sex' should be added to the list of protected characteristics under the law (Law Commission, 2020; see also **Conversations 8.1**).

Laws on hate crime

In many areas of the world, the law includes specific legislative provisions to address hate crimes. For example, Art. 4 of the EU Framework Decision on Racist and Xenophobic Crime (2008) says that Member States 'shall take the necessary measures to ensure that racist and xenophobic motivation is considered an aggravating circumstance, or, alternatively that such motivation may be taken into consideration by the courts in the determination of the penalties'. All EU Members States must have legislation that allows a court to increase the sentence of an offender who has committed an offence due to a racist or xenophobic (showing a prejudice against people from other countries; see **xenophobia**) motivation. Most countries have gone beyond race or ethnicity in protecting groups against hate crimes.

In England and Wales, victims are protected from crimes that are motivated by hostilities towards the following characteristics:

- race;
- religious beliefs;
- sexual orientation;
- disability;
- transgender identity.

The Crime and Disorder Act 1998 (ss. 28–32) sets out 11 racially or religiously aggravated offences (including assaults, criminal damage, harassment and stalking, and public order offences relating to the causing of harassment, alarm, and distress). Section 28 of the Act defines a 'racially or religiously aggravated' offence as one that is either (partly) motivated by hostility towards the victim's (presumed) racial or religious group, or one that demonstrated racial hostility towards the victim's (presumed) racial or religious group when the offence was committed, or immediately before or after. In addition to the Crime and Disorder Act, the Criminal Justice Act 2003 (ss. 145 and 146) gives powers to the courts to increase the penalty for *any* type of offence that has been aggravated by hostility linked to any of the five characteristics.

The main aim of such laws is to recognise the extra harm that may be caused by these offences and to prevent aggravated incidents from occurring (Lawrence, 1999). In the leading case of *Rogers*, Baroness Hale outlines the importance of hate crime legislation:

> The mischiefs attacked by the aggravated versions of these offences are racism and xenophobia. Their essence is the denial of equal respect and dignity to people who are seen as 'other'. This is more deeply hurtful, damaging and disrespectful to the victims than the simple versions of these offences. It is also more damaging to the community as a whole, by denying acceptance to members of certain groups not for their own sake but for the sake of something they can do nothing about. This is just as true if the group is defined exclusively as it is if it is defined inclusively.
>
> (*Rogers* [2007] UKHL 8, [12])

An important part of the English and Welsh legislation is the word 'hostility'. The Crown Prosecution Service, which is the public prosecutor for England and Wales, acknowledges that there is no legal definition of 'hostility', and so in prosecuting hate crime cases it uses the everyday understanding of the word, which includes 'ill-will, spite, contempt, prejudice, unfriendliness, antagonism, resentment and dislike' (CPS, 2020). Despite this literal interpretation, the courts have at times been confused by what types of hate-based conduct counts as 'hostility'. In many cases, especially those involving disability bias, the courts have been seemingly reluctant to accept evidence of targeted violence or abuse aimed at disabled people as proof of 'hostility' towards disability (Walters et al., 2017; see **section 8.3**).

To confuse matters further, the criminal justice system in England and Wales uses a slightly different definition of hate crime than the one that is outlined by legislation. The agreed definition is:

> Any criminal offence which is perceived by the victim or any other person, to be motivated by hostility or prejudice, based on a person's disability or perceived disability; race or perceived race; or religion or perceived religion; or sexual orientation or perceived sexual orientation or transgender identity or perceived transgender identity.
>
> (CPS, 2020)

This victim-centred definition means that the police must record a crime as a 'hate crime' where the victim or anyone else believes it is motivated by prejudice based on one of the recognised characteristics that we listed earlier, which

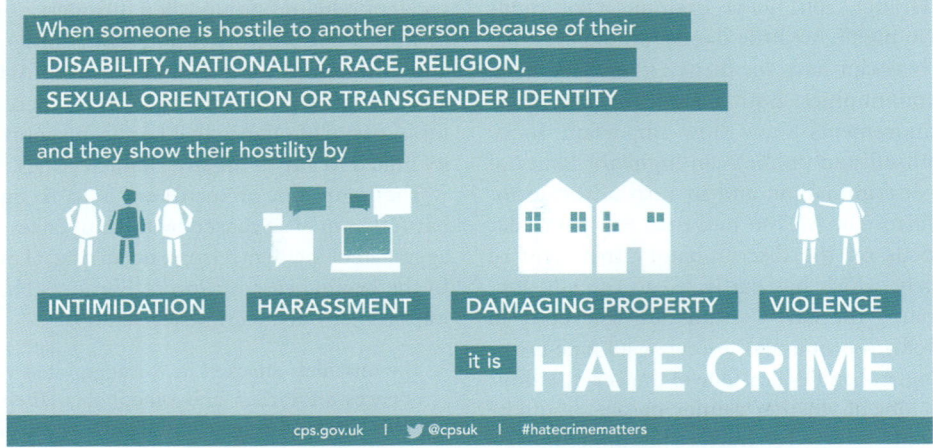

Figure 8.1 The CPS monitors hate crime in the UK, and publishes leaflets to raise public awareness of this offence
Source: https://www.cps.gov.uk/hate-crime-matters, content available under the Open Government Licence v3.0

are illustrated in **Figure 8.1**. Interestingly, some police forces also record characteristics beyond the five official ones, such as gender/misogyny (Nottingham) and subculture (Manchester). The broader, victim-centred definition is aimed at reducing the discretion (freedom to decide) of the police and other justice agencies in determining whether a crime is based on prejudice or not. The use of this definition was one of the key recommendations from the Macpherson Report in 1999, which found that the police were 'institutionally racist'. The purpose is to improve victim confidence in reporting such offences to the authorities (Giannasi and Hall, 2016).

Criminological perspectives on hate crime

While we look in detail at victims and victimology elsewhere in this book (**Chapter 7**), we should note that hate crime is an important topic for criminology's study of power relationships. The legal definition of hate crime outlines only that these are crimes based on hostility or prejudice directed at certain individuals because of their identity characteristic, but this tells us very little about the nature and dynamics of hate crime. Perry (2001) argues that hate crimes must be understood in relation to people's positions of power in society. She argues that over many years a hierarchy (or social order) has developed in society based on individuals' identity. Certain identity characteristics put individuals at the top of the hierarchy (most prominently characteristics like being white, male, heterosexual). Those who do not have these dominant characteristics are deemed as 'different', or as the 'other' (see the glossary definition of **othering**), and will be placed lower in the order. Perry explains that hate crimes are committed against people who are seen as 'different' by perpetrators who want to ensure that 'others' stay at the bottom of the hierarchy.

Walters (2011) argues that the key to understanding hate crime is the emotion of fear (or what social psychologists refer to as 'perceptions of threat'). He maintains that hate crimes are typically the result of 'fear or [a] belief that the victim (and others like him or her) will encroach upon the offender's group identity, cultural **norms** and/or socio-economic security' (Walters, 2011: 315; see also Walters and Brown, 2016). Walters adds that those with low levels of self-control may be more likely to accept or agree with ideas that generalise certain groups as posing a threat to the ideas or values of the dominant group to which they belong (see Gottfredson and Hirschi, 1990; Gottfredson, 2017). These individuals may be most likely to try to resist such threats through acts of physical violence. Other people less inclined to physical violence may try to achieve a similar outcome by encouraging or causing those prone to violence to act out, and by supporting social structures and institutions that continue to oppress certain identity groups (Walters, 2011). We might see an example of such encouragement of violence in the response of the Polish President, Jarosław Kaczyński, to protests that erupted in Poland in 2020. The protests, known as the 'Women's Strike' (Strajk Kobiet), were prompted by the Polish Constitutional Tribunal's ruling in favour of tightening abortion controls. Kaczyński called for citizens to 'defend Polish churches', which prompted far-right and nationalist groups to attack and injure protestors ('Poland delays abortion ban as nationwide protests continue', *The Guardian*, 1 November 2020).

Perry and Walters argue that the link between hate crime and group identity is central to understanding its unique character. Such an approach is supported by research—for example, the Sussex Hate Crime Project showed that victims of both anti-LGBT and anti-Muslim hate crimes were impacted to a greater extent *because* of their connection with a particular identity group (Paterson et al., 2020). Multiple studies found that following a hate crime incident those who shared an identity characteristic that had been targeted felt less safe and more vulnerable in society, because of a perceived sense of threat directed at their identity. This heightened sense of threat was linked to strong emotional responses including anger and anxiety (Paterson et al., 2018). These emotional impacts are often felt across entire groups of people who are more likely to empathise with those who are attacked because of their shared identity, leading to a sense of what Walters et al. (2020b) have called 'shared suffering'.

Other researchers have argued that instead of understanding hate crime in terms of group identity, we should think of it in terms of 'vulnerability' and 'difference'. Chakraborti and Garland (2012) assert that hate crimes often occur for multiple reasons and can be linked to intersecting identities, which is where a person has several characteristics that can go beyond a single group identity (for example, being targeted because of one's race *and* sexual orientation; see **intersectionality**). They argue that, to better understand the nature and dynamics of hate crime, we need take into account the social contexts in which individuals become 'vulnerable' to targeted abuse. In other words, according to Chakraborti and Garland, hate crimes are not only to do with a victim belonging to a certain group or having a particular identity (that is, race, sexuality), but can have multiple factors that can highlight how they are seen as *not* belonging to the offender's group. The victim's intersectional characteristics, whatever they may be, simply make them 'different' and therefore vulnerable to being targeted—the specifics of their identity are not as relevant as their 'difference'. In the offender's eyes, this

Figure 8.2 UK legislation makes it clear that individuals cannot be targeted for their identity, but does it oversimplify these categories?
Source: Northumbria Police

sets them apart and raises questions about their place in society.

We might understand hate crime as being the result of **social hierarchies** and feelings or perceptions of threat relating to group identity, or because offenders see victims as vulnerable because they are somehow 'different'. But, however we see this, we should keep in mind that the victims who are most commonly targeted are those who generally have less political or economic power than the majority (see **Figure 8.2**). These individuals are likely to come from the most marginalised groups who, on average, have less political power and have fewer social connections to draw upon during difficult times.

The idea of power is therefore an important one in considering and studying hate crime. Perry (2001) uses the term 'sprees of violence against the Other' when explaining how hate crimes reinforce and perpetuate difference and segregation. In **Conversations 8.1** we discuss this idea of the Other and some possible problems with legal definitions used to classify hate crime into discrete characteristics.

CONVERSATIONS 8.1

Defining hate crime
with **Dr Erin Sanders-McDonagh**

The following discussion revolves around legal definitions of hate crime and how we deal with this offence.

Angus Nurse (AN): Let's begin by looking at the Government's classifications of hate crime. How effective do you think these are?

Dr Erin Sanders-McDonagh (ESM): I think the ideas that underpinned the original legislation are admirable. For me, the issue is when you use a discrete identity strand to assess how we understand 'hate' as a criminal offence. It's reductive, and critically ignores intersectional issues.

AN: What does that mean in terms of defining the nature of a hate crime?

ESM: One of the problems is that the definitions include sexual orientation and transgender, but we don't have gender as an intersecting factor. For example, if a Muslim woman is the target of a hate crime and the attackers pull down her hijab that is one issue. But if they then use offensive language towards her as a woman, and they target her not just because she's Islamic, but because she's an Islamic *woman*, then the law separates the victim into discrete categories of racism or religion, as if these things are discrete. There are structural issues, and certain groups continue to face stigma, discrimination, and abuse—to suggest that language is the best way of understanding hate misses these structural factors, and tries to create a simple **typology** for something that is much more complex.

AN: So is part of the problem that this defines hate crime in terms of a specific victim type rather than the nature or motivation of the hate?

ESM: Yes. And it's a difficult problem to legislate because it largely focuses on language and the explicit use of certain kinds of language in certain situations, but that doesn't actually tell us much about hate . . . If you assault somebody because they're black but don't explicitly use terminology that suggests that the motivation for the attack is based on race, then how do we know it's hate crime? To have to rely on language or an explicit expression from the attacker to prove 'hate' really limits our ability to look at this issue more holistically.

AN: Is there a question there about how hate crime legislation is framed and whether it's needed?

ESM: Well it's a blunt tool for trying to assess complex behaviour and we perhaps need better tools that allow for more nuance. A key question that's been asked for years is why gender is not included within the definition. We know women experience victimization from men—whether it be sexual assault, rape, domestic violence—women are primarily the victims of male offenders. We also know that offensive language is used to denigrate and harm women. Why do we exclude that from our definitions of hate crime when we know that women are often the victim of attacks that we could consider as hate crimes? There's just no rationale for why we haven't included gender as a specific category—so we have to recognise there is also a politics that underpins who we see as 'legitimate' victims, and who is left outside.

AN: Is there an argument for considering the impact on the victim and how they feel about crime as a classifying factor?

ESM: If you look at the British Crime Survey [now known as the Crime Survey for England and Wales or CSEW; see **Chapter 5**] and consider the impact for people who have been victims of hate crime, this provides us with some additional insight. The psychological impacts of hate crime can be considerable and may stay with people for several years. So, language does matter and so does the impact on the victim. It would be interesting to speak to a black woman who has been the victim of crime and ask her about how she perceives the 'hate' of the crime, whether it's in terms of her race or in terms of gender—or if it's both. Intersectionality would help us to work out what's happening, while the problem with legislation is that it allows us to identify a word or phrase, but this doesn't necessarily allow us to clearly identify the motivation.

AN: So we need to consider broader ideas of hate crime and how to deal with it?

ESM: Yes. For example, one police force has recognised sex workers as a specific category of hate crime target. This expands our understanding of hate crime beyond factors that people cannot control, like their race. It's interesting for our hate crime definition to include something that is not an inherent identity . . . This recognises the reality that some specific groups are stigmatised as the target of hate and also identifies that some people are 'others' who are marginalised and pushed to the side. If we want effective hate crime legislation, then it must look at other groups and we can't be fixed on narrow ideas of what identity strands are credible . . . we need to take a good initial piece of legislation and develop it until it covers different aspects of hate and moves forward in understanding how it relates to issues like class, geography, poverty . . . We are still at the infancy of hate crime, but we need to ensure that we do more to publicise the issues, adapt legislation as we learn more about it, and recognize that what we have right now is a good start, but there's so much more that needs to be done. Legislation needs to be adaptable so that we can start seeing real change—both in terms of the incidents that are recorded, but also in terms of public opinion. Both are key to really getting to grips with this complicated issue.

Dr Angus Nurse, Head of Criminology and Criminal Justice, Nottingham Trent University, and author of this chapter

Dr Erin Sanders-McDonagh, Senior Lecturer in Criminology at the University of Kent

This discussion has identified some of the challenges in studying hate crime. If we start from the idea that different groups experience and perceive hate crime from their own viewpoints, then legal classifications of hate crime become difficult. We can see how legal definitions may not always fully reflect how victims experience hate and prejudice. How the victim feels is important, as they are the ones who suffer the effects of hate crime. But what the offender thinks and feels is also important, and as **Conversation 8.1** identifies, this may not always be recorded or identified in a way that allows us to understand the exact motivation or nature of the crime. Now that you

WHAT DO YOU THINK? 8.1

The scope of hate crime laws

As we have seen, crimes that are said to be motivated by hate are now covered by legislation that classifies hate crimes according to clear categories. We have begun to consider the idea that hate crimes are linked to wider issues of structural inequality and fears about the Other—those we might see as different. Consider the following questions.

- Is there really a need for specific hate crime laws or should these crimes be dealt with by existing laws on assault, theft, abusive language, and so on?
- Are there problems with using the 'strand' approach that identifies specific types of hate crime?
- What about other groups such as the homeless, women, or specific subgroups like sex workers?
- Should courts be given the powers to impose additional sentencing for crimes against these groups and does this amount to special treatment?
- How should we respond to an aggravated crime if a victim who is targeted for being black is also gay or disabled?

Think about some of the problems that we perhaps have with the current law and whether it needs to be reformed or developed in any way. How do we decide which groups are 'worthy' of having the 'extra' legal protection for the purposes of hate crime? Who else might you wish to include when looking at this problem?

---

have read Dr Erin Sanders-McDonagh's perspective, use the exercise in **What do you think 8.1** to develop your own opinions on the topic.

Rates of hate crime

Hate crime rates are analysed by researchers working for the Home Office and the Office for National Statistics. Full reports are available on the government's website at www.gov.uk, but let's discuss some key points on the most recently available figures (at the time of writing).

In 2018/19, there were 103,379 hate crimes recorded by the police in England and Wales, an increase of 10 per cent compared with 2017/18 (94,121 offences). The figures detailed in **Table 8.1** show how rates have continued to rise in recent years, with the number of hate crimes recorded by the police having more than doubled since 2012/13 (from 42,255 to 103,379 offences). In **Chapter 5**, we found that there are difficulties in drawing conclusions from changes in recorded crime, and so we should use the same caution in how we interpret the statistics we see here. An increase in the number of crimes can be the result of an improvement in how the police record offences, meaning that they have become better at identifying hate crimes that may, for example, have previously been recorded as 'ordinary' assaults. Changes in legislation or recording practices may also take time to filter through into both how victims report the abuse they suffer and how it is understood in recording practices (Home Office, 2017, 2019). There are additional social issues that impact on the prevalence of and recording of hate crimes; for example, in producing the figures in **Table 8.1**, the researchers comment that 'there has [sic] been spikes in hate crime following certain events such as the EU Referendum and the terrorist attacks in 2017' (Home Office, 2019: 1). The majority of hate crimes were racially aggravated, accounting for around three-quarters of offences (76 per cent; 78,991 offences) and the table shows the recording across all of the strands we have already mentioned.

Table 8.1 shows us that the total number of motivating factors is greater than the total number of offences. This difference reflects the fact that many hate crimes involve multiple prejudices. Each police force has a crime-reporting information system where officers officially record offences. Typically, these include tick boxes where the officer can select the type(s) of characteristics thought to be involved in the crime (for example, race, religion, sexual orientation). Analysis of recorded hate crime data in London by Walters and Krasodomski-Jones (2018) revealed that over half of all religious hate crimes were also recorded by the police as racially aggravated crimes, while 20 per cent of sexual orientation hate crimes were additionally recorded as racially aggravated.

Recorded levels of hate crime provide only part of the picture. In order to get a full picture of the numbers of hate crimes that occur each year, we must turn to **victimisation** survey data (see also **Chapter 7**). Data from the CSEW are published every other year, which includes the 'dark figure' of hate crime (see **section 5.5**). The survey of 40,000 households is combined over several years to provide an estimated number of hate crimes that occur each year.

Hate crime strand	2011/12	2012/13	2013/14	2014/15	2015/16	2016/17	2017/18	2018/19	% change 2017/18 to 2018/19
Race	35,944	35,845	37,575	42,862	49,419	62,685	71,264	78,991	11
Religion	1,618	1,572	2,264	3,293	4,400	5,949	8,339	8,566	3
Sexual orientation	4,345	4,241	4,588	5,591	7,194	9,157	11,592	14,491	25
Disability	1,748	1,911	2,020	2,515	3,629	5,558	7,221	8,256	14
Transgender	313	364	559	607	858	1,248	1,703	2,333	37
Total number of motivating factors	43,968	43,933	47,006	54,868	65,500	84,597	100,119	112,637	13
Total number of offences	N/A	42,255	44,577	52,465	62,518	80,393	94,121	103,379	10

Table 8.1 Hate crimes recorded by the police in England and Wales, 2011/12 to 2018/19
Source: Home Office statistics, All content is available under the Open Government Licence v3.0, except where otherwise stated

Data estimates show that there were around 184,000 incidents of hate crime a year between 2015–18, representing 3 per cent of all CSEW crime (Home Office, 2018). This included 101,000 race hate crimes, 52,000 disability hate crimes, 39,000 religious hate crimes, and 30,000 sexual orientation hate crimes (note that numbers were too few to provide reliable estimates of transgender hate crimes). The risk of being a victim of personal hate crime (that is, violence, robbery, and theft) was highest among men aged 16–24, those with the religious group Muslim (0.6 per cent compared with 0.1 per cent of Christian respondents); and people with Asian backgrounds (0.4 per cent compared with 0.1 per cent white adults) (Home Office, 2018: 23).

Have a think about these figures and what we have already discussed earlier about how crime is recorded by the police and through victimisation surveys (see also **Chapter 7**). Do you think that these figures accurately reflect the number of hate crimes that occur each year in society? What about online hate? Can statistics adequately reflect the intersectional experiences of hate crime? Now consider some of these issues in **What do you think? 8.2**.

We will now look at some of the individual types of hate crime in a little more detail. We will begin with disability hate crime, and will then move on to cover LGBT+ hate crime, and racially motivated crime, ending with religiously motivated crime.

WHAT DO YOU THINK? 8.2

Hate crime statistics

We have already discussed the 'dark figure' of crime and discussed some of the issues with hate crime figures. Now jot down your ideas on these questions.

- How accurate do you think the figures on hate crime might be?
- Why might the figures on race be the highest?
- Why might the figures for disability hate crime be so high in the CSEW, but relatively low in the police recorded data?
- What barriers could there be towards people reporting hate crime to the police?
- Why might there be a steady increase in the number of recorded hate crimes?
- How might we improve the recording of crimes that are motivated by more than one part of the victim's identity?

8.3 Disablist hate crime

Hate crimes directed at disabled people are also sometimes referred to as **disablist** crimes. The College of Policing, in its guidance for police on dealing with disablist hate crime, defines it as crimes directed towards a person because of their physical disability, learning disability, or mental ill health. As we explore this topic, we need to think about what we mean by the term 'disability' and how it includes a range of factors that are not just physical—see **Figure 8.3**.

It may be obvious to us that if somebody has a missing limb, is in a wheelchair, or has suffered a form of sensory loss (for example, visual impairment), that they will likely be facing challenges that people without these conditions do not face. These are perhaps obvious physical disabilities, and what is called the **medical model** of disability identifies a person as being disabled by physical or mental limitations (Manchester Disabled Persons Access Group, 2019a). However, some consider the **social model** of disability to be a better way of understanding how disabled people are treated in society (Manchester Disabled Persons Access Group, 2019b). The social model suggests that it is society's response to disabled people and their needs that creates challenges, rather than the specific nature of the physical or **cognitive** issues.

According to the social model, when the social response to disability is changed, then disabled people can achieve independence and dignity. For example, the medical model might suggest that a wheelchair user cannot climb the steps of a court, and a blind or visually impaired person cannot effectively pick a suspect out of a line-up, and so potentially they cannot be an effective witness at court. However, the social model of disability would suggest that there is no reason why they should not be able to take part in court proceedings if they were a witness to a crime, and so may seek to improve access to court buildings through the provision of ramps, or provide other support services that might allow a blind or visually impaired person to participate in identification processes, for example through voice recognition. These approaches to understanding disability are important to keep in mind when thinking about disablist hate crime; how society views disabled people can be part of the motivations behind such crimes, and as criminologists we should always

Figure 8.3 There are many disabilities that may not be immediately visible, and we should be careful to include them when we think about disablist crimes

Source: Arithmedes/Shutterstock

remember to consider all factors that can be key to uncovering new knowledge about such offences.

The extent of disablist hate crime

Data from the CSEW suggest that disablist hate crime is the second most common form of hate crime after racist offences (Home Office, 2018). When analysing crime figures for the CSEW in 2016, the charity Victim Support found that although violent crime had fallen by almost half (48 per cent) for the non-disabled population over the previous decade, the proportion of people with a limiting disability or illness who were victims of violence over the same period had increased by 3.7 per cent (Rossetti et al., 2016). The charity also learned that, in stark contrast to the rest of the population, people with a limiting disability or illness were at greater risk of suffering violent crime than they had been ten years before the 2016 crime survey. They identified that having a limiting disability puts you at statistically greater risk of violence than visiting a nightclub once a week or more.

Clement et al. (2011) also identified that crime and harassment are increasingly becoming recognised as significant parts of the discrimination faced by people with mental health problems. They found that a survey of 27 countries showed that 26 per cent of the 732 people with schizophrenia interviewed reported experiencing unfair treatment, which included verbal or physical abuse attributed to having a mental health diagnosis.

Hall (2018) identified that many disabled people experience fear, harassment, and occasionally violence in a variety of public and private spaces. Recent research has also indicated that disablist hate crime can be particularly problematic on public transport (Wilkin, 2020), while many incidents remain hidden, taking place in care homes, residential facilities, or in an individual's own home (EHRC, 2011). Sir Thomas Shakespeare, Chair of the Central Research Committee for Drill (Disability Research on Independent Living and Learning) and senior lecturer in medical sociology at Norwich Medical School wrote about intellectual disability in *The Guardian* in 2010. He commented on harassment being a commonplace feature of people's lives and wrote about discovering stories of such treatment, which you can read in **Conversations 8.2**.

As we can see, Shakespeare identifies the debate of whether actions against disabled people constitute 'hate

CONVERSATIONS 8.2

The cruel toll of disability hate crime

with **Sir Thomas Shakespeare**

The death of David Askew, who had an intellectual disability, in Manchester, after suffering years of harassment, is a sickeningly familiar story. For years, I have been sceptical about the notion of disability hate crime. While acknowledging occasional grotesque crimes such as the death of David Askew, I refused to believe that this was a common problem. As a person with restricted growth, all my life I have faced stares and mockery from people. Every day, children stare and laugh at me. If I'm in a city at night, some drunken stranger is sure to hurl abuse. But I have always shrugged my shoulders and followed my father's advice—'just ignore them'.

Two things changed my attitude. One night, coming home from Newcastle on the Tyne and Wear metro, a group of young women came and sat around me at the front of the train. As they started to harass me, asking facetious questions and making lewd comments, the encounter became increasingly humiliating. For the first time, I felt scared as well as hurt. These girls were

probably 14 or 15, they had almost certainly been drinking or taking drugs, and they had no compunction at all about making me the butt of their games. Nobody on the train intervened. I felt very shaken by the time I got off the metro, and very relieved indeed that my abusers decided not follow me into the deserted car park.

Deeply unpleasant though this episode was, I classed it as bullying, rather than hate crime. From my research with disabled children in schools, I was well aware that bullying was a constant feature of their lives, in both mainstream and segregated settings. Later research with people with restricted growth confirmed that nasty words and harassment were a common experience. My response was to argue for better disability equality education in schools, so as to challenge negative attitudes. I still felt that the term 'hate crime' was overstated and that violence was rare. The research evidence was scanty, and I thought the problem was exaggerated.

It was only when I was interviewed by a group of media students who were making a documentary film about hate crime, that I realised how wrong I was to downplay the seriousness of this very British problem. They challenged my complacency and forced me to question my attitude. I heard from them about the everyday stories of hate crime that they had investigated. I realised that these forms of violence were mostly directed towards people with intellectual disabilities.

Later, I asked several colleagues who work as advocates and supporters of people with intellectual disability about what they knew. They confirmed immediately that harassment was a constant feature of the lives of every person they worked with. They told me about conferences and gatherings where people had shared horrific experiences, which to them were commonplace. People being sellotaped to trees while people laughed, people being urinated on, people who had dog faeces put through their letter boxes, people who were beaten up. Faced with this constant exposure to the risk of abuse and violence, people with intellectual disability remained stoical and uncomplaining. Sometimes they were unable to make a complaint. Often, they were disbelieved, or were not taken seriously as witnesses. In most cases, the police were unwilling or unable to take effective action.

David Askew's tragedy follows the deaths of Raymond Atherton, Rikki Judkins, Steven Hoskin, Barrie-John Horrell, Kevin Davies, Fiona Pilkington, Christine Lakinski, and Christopher Foulkes over the last few years. Each of these individuals was targeted because they were vulnerable and disabled, exploited, humiliated, and finally killed. Looking again at the evidence, and thinking more deeply about the problem, I realise how mistaken I was to trivialise hate crime. It's not just a matter of bullying. It's not something that people can just ignore or laugh off. It is a scourge on our society. We are members of a community where the most vulnerable people live in fear of their lives and where they are being terrified on a daily basis by the bored or the loutish or the dispossessed. I think my mental block arose because I did not want to believe that human beings could be so vile. I was wrong.

Sir Thomas Shakespeare, sociologist and broadcaster

Source: Shakespeare, T. (2010) The Cruel Toll of Disability Crime. Copyright Guardian News & Media Ltd 2020

crime'. He indicates that, before he had understood the level and nature of harassment taking place, he had thought of such incidents as bullying. However, he suggests that he changed his mind when hearing about the nature of everyday violence directed towards people with intellectual disabilities. But what do criminologists think?

The nature and dynamics of disablist hate crime

Like Shakespeare, Sherry (2011) believes that disabled people do experience actions driven by hate. Sherry argues that disability crimes are a global problem and that they are often violent and hyper-aggressive, with life-changing effects on victims—see **Figure 8.4**. For Sherry, such crimes have unique characteristics that distinguish them from other hate crimes. But there are other perspectives: Hall (2013: 96) argues that these actions are instead rooted in prejudice, and offers alternatives to the term 'hate crime', suggesting instead: 'motivated,' 'bias,' or 'targeted' crimes. Hall (2019) suggests that we can map the incidents of disablist hate crime into something like a geography of the offence. He concludes that although the fear, harassment, and violence experienced by disabled people seemingly happens everywhere, from public spaces to individuals' homes, in most cases these acts are not random, placeless acts perpetrated by 'mean spirited bigots' (Perry, 2001: 1). Instead he suggests that hate crimes are a product of how disabled and non-disabled people interact in particular micro-spaces (such as designated parking spaces) and times, therefore identifying local spaces and the specific nature of interactions in close settings as important. He also considers many disablist hate crimes to be 'in the

Figure 8.4 Researchers identify different motives behind disablist crimes, which can be complicated to understand, but the seriousness and extent of these offences shows that they are an important area of criminological research

Source: Klimkin/Pexels

moment' hostile expressions of widely held attitudes towards disabled people.

Hall also identifies that in many cases the victim and the perpetrator are known to each other as neighbours, carers, or friends. In some cases, perpetrators 'befriend' the victim in order to exploit the victim's financial resources. This has been referred to by some as 'mate crime' and reflects the 'pretend' relationship that is developed over a period of time between the perpetrator and victim (Thomas, 2011). Numerous cases have revealed a pattern whereby disabled people's homes are taken over by groups of perpetrators (known commonly as 'cuckooing'), with some victims being tortured and killed in horrific ways once the perpetrators no longer have any use for the victim (EHRC, 2011).

Disablist hate crime is a complex area of criminality. Hate crimes committed against disabled people can often involve property offences (such as theft and fraud), while sexual abuse is also a common experience for victims (Balderston, 2013). The issue of *perceived* vulnerability is important in understanding such offences. This is to say that victims are commonly viewed by their offenders as an easy target because they are seen as weak and less capable of resisting their abusers. The word 'hostility' used in hate crime legislation, which we discussed in **section 8.2**, does not always fit neatly with such situations and research has shown that judges typically see incidents involving 'mate crime' or 'cuckooing' as a result of the victim's 'vulnerability' rather than due to the offenders' prejudice or hatred towards disabled people (Walters et al., 2018). Research on the enforcement of hate crime laws found that just 0.2 per cent of reported disablist hate crimes resulted in a conviction and a more severe (enhanced) penalty, indicating that the courts rarely accept evidence of targeted abuse against disabled people as proof of 'hostility' (Walters et al., 2018). But the violent abuse of disabled people because they are viewed as somehow less continues, and is rooted in an offender's prejudiced beliefs about disabled people. While the complex nature of perception and abuse applies to other types of hate crime, it is particularly relevant to understanding disablist hate crime. Consider these points as you think about how we deal with disablist crime in **What do you think? 8.3**.

WHAT DO YOU THINK? 8.3

Responding to disablist hate crime

Read the following short scenario and write down your immediate reactions to the questions.

A young man leaves a pub late one evening. His speech is slurred, and he appears drunk. He is heard shouting at another group of men and a fight breaks out. The police arrive and the witnesses all state that the man was behaving strangely and making inappropriate comments, and this is what caused the fight. The young man is uncooperative with the police and, even though there are four men in the group he fought with, he is considered to be the aggressor and is arrested.

- Do you feel any sympathy for the man?
- Was the man to blame for what happened to him?
- What do you think of the police response?

Now read the same story with a few more details.

A young man with learning disabilities and a form of ADHD (hyperactive-impulsive ADHD) leaves a pub late one evening. He has been drinking but is not drunk. He cannot find his phone to call a taxi and approaches a group of men for help, raising his voice and speaking in a manner they thought unusual. The men respond by laughing at him and begin name-calling linked to his speech patterns. The young man responds by shouting at the men, one of whom reacts physically to the young man's shouting. The police arrive and witnesses say that they had heard the inappropriate comments from the young man and this is what caused the fight. The young man is uncooperative with the police and shouts at them in response to their questions, which he says he does not understand. He becomes increasingly agitated and the police decide he is the aggressor and is behaving inappropriately and he is arrested.

- Do you feel any sympathy for the man?
- Was the man to blame for what happened to him or do you see any elements of hate crime in this?
- What do you think of the police response?

This is a complex example to consider, but it highlights some of the difficulties in analysing hate crimes against disabled people. In one version of the scenario, you might consider we see a young man who starts a confrontation. In the second version, a young man who has possibly been picked on and assaulted because of his disability.

8.4 LGBT+ hate crime

LGBT+ is an initialism that encompasses many sexual orientations and gender identities, and may refer to anyone who does not identify as heterosexual or cisgender (people whose gender identity matches their sex assigned at birth)—see **Figure 8.5**. The '+' extends the term to include anyone who is questioning their identity or identifies as queer, or who is intersex (people who have a combination of what is culturally thought of as male and female anatomy or physiology). Individuals who are part of the LGBT+ community have often been the victims of hate crime, but in order to understand the reality of these crimes today, we need to look back at the UK's history.

The history of criminalising LGBT+ identities

Hate crime towards members of lesbian, gay, bisexual, and transgender (LGBT+) communities has a long history. The negative treatment of LGBT+ people has been linked to the general belief that non-heterosexual activity was not only sinful but criminal. In fact, same-sex sexual intimacy between men was illegal until 1967 and was punishable by a prison sentence, although we will see as we continue this chapter that the courts could also give other **punishments**. It is important to note that the situation for gay women was slightly different; same-sex intimacy between women has never been a criminal offence in the UK. However, it was stigmatised in the past and gay women continue to be targets of homophobia in the present day.

The law in England and Wales originally classed sexual activity between men as 'gross indecency' according to the Offences Against the Person Act 1861. Anal sex or 'buggery' had previously been made a capital offence by Henry VIII in 1553. Homosexuality was generally viewed as an illness (and something that could possibly be 'cured') and was something that might be pitied or seen as an unnatural character defect (King and Bartlett, 1999). But it was also viewed as dangerous and deviant, and something that the state should control; by the end of 1954 there were 1,069 men in prison in England who had been sentenced for committing gay sex acts (British Medical Journal, 1957; Day, 2013). Even war heroes were the targets of homophobia and had to hide their sexuality. Take, for example, the case of mathematician Alan Turing (depicted in **Figure 8.6**), who was famous for cracking the Enigma code and helping to shorten, if not end, the Second World War. In 1952, Turing was convicted of gross indecency under s. 11 of the Criminal Law Amendment Act 1885. He was given a choice between imprisonment or **probation** with the condition that he 'voluntarily' agree to chemical 'treatment' for his homosexuality. Turing lost his security clearance and was barred from entering the US (BBC News, 'Alan Turing's homosexual court files go on display', 23 September 2016). When he died in 1954, an inquest determined that Turing had committed suicide; he was eventually granted a posthumous pardon in 2013 (BBC News, 'Royal pardon for codebreaker Alan Turing', 24 December 2013). (Alan Turing's life was depicted in *The Imitation Game* where Benedict Cumberbatch plays Turing.) The homophobic treatment of Alan Turing shows how the historical attitude towards gay people has been one of mistrust and hostility, and involved the **criminalisation** of parts of their identity as somehow being unnatural.

It was only with the passing of the Sexual Offences Act 1967 that it finally became legal to engage in same-sex

Figure 8.5 The rainbow flag or colours are often used as symbols of LGBT+ pride

Source: Nadia Snopek/Shutterstock

Figure 8.6 The UK government's treatment of the code-breaking mathematician Alan Turing, pictured here, shows that homophobia was institutionalised

Source: Public domain

sexual intimacy. However, partners still had to be over 21, and they could only have sex in private, with some professions (such as the UK Civil Service) still barring homosexuals from applying for or serving in certain positions until as late as 1991 (see, for example, Southern, 2017). This caveat meant that the law in England and Wales operated with different ages of consent for gay people when compared with their 'straight' peers. In this way, the state made it clear that it considered homosexuality to be different and enforced this difference through the law. It was only in 2000 that the law in England was changed to provide equality and bring the age of consent for gay people down to 16, in line with that of heterosexual people. However, this move was still met with protest from religious and community leaders who wrote to the *Daily Telegraph* opposing the new law and arguing that it failed to protect 'the young of both sexes from the most dangerous of sexual practices' (BBC News, 'Gay Consent at 16 becomes law', 30 November 2000). Among the 17 signatories to the letter were the (then) Archbishop of Canterbury George Carey, Cormac Murphy-O'Connor head of the Roman Catholic Church in England, and Yousof Bhailok, secretary general of the Muslim Council of Great Britain. This reference to 'dangerous sexual practices' is an important indicator of how society still views some forms of sexual expression as dangerous and deviant.

At this point, consider the fact that 72 countries across the world still criminalise private, consensual, same-sex sexual activity (see Human Dignity Trust, 'Map of Countries that Criminalise LGBT People'). Eleven of these jurisdictions can impose the death penalty for such 'crimes'.

The case is similar for transgender people who are directly and indirectly criminalised in many countries. In addition to often being subject to the laws that criminalise consensual same-sex sexual intimacy, transgender people are also criminalised by laws that regulate their gender expression (through so-called 'cross-dressing' or 'impersonation' laws). A recent report found that within the Commonwealth, 'at least 15 jurisdictions impose criminal sanctions against people whose gender expression does not align with their sex as assigned at birth' (HDT, 2019: 15). Transgender people are also subjected to prosecution for public order, vagrancy, and misdemeanour offences. Wide-ranging laws are used, sometimes in combination with other offences and laws, not only to arrest and detain transgender people but to block or restrict their access to justice.

Countries that continue to criminalise LGBT+ people are less likely to protect individuals from hate crimes; Gitari and Walters' (2020) situational analysis of anti-LGBT+ hate crimes across Commonwealth countries found that the police often commit such violence (most commonly in the Global South). The link between the criminalisation of same-sex sexual activity, gender identity, and expression, and anti-LGBT+ hate crimes shows how the law sometimes maintains a hostile environment towards LGBT+ people. It means that these individuals not only live with the constant fear of community-based violence, but in many countries they are at risk of further harassment and brutalisation by law enforcement (Gitari and Walters, 2020).

While significant social changes have occurred in the UK and laws now provide protection against sexual orientation and gender identity discrimination, there are still significant levels of homophobia and transphobia in society. For example, British Attitude Survey data shows that only two-thirds of the population believe that sexual relations between two adults of the same sex are 'not wrong at all', meaning that a significant proportion of the population still believe that such relations are immoral (Curtice et al., 2019; see also **Conversations 8.3**). Fifteen per cent of the population stated that they were very or a little prejudiced against transgender people.

It is perhaps unsurprising then that laws aimed at protecting individuals against sexual orientation or gender identity hate have only relatively recently come into force. Sexual orientation hate crime was not officially recognised in law until 2003, while transgender hate crime was only recognised in 2012. Several high-profile cases also helped to ensure that anti-LGBT+ hate crime became a prominent issue for UK public policy, such as the murder investigations of victims David Morley in 2004 and Jody Dobrowski in 2005 (Duggan, 2010).

The extent of LGBT+ hate crime

In 2017, the UK government launched a survey to gather more information about the experiences of LGBT people in the UK. Over 108,000 people participated, making it the largest national survey of LGBT people in the world to date. (Note that we use the term LGBT+ throughout this chapter, but LGBT was the terminology used by the government in the survey and associated reports.) The government's report on the survey identified that:

- LGBT respondents to the survey were less satisfied with their life than the general UK population (rating satisfaction 6.5 on average out of 10 compared with 7.7). Trans respondents had particularly low scores (around 5.4 out of 10);
- more than two-thirds of LGBT respondents said they had avoided holding hands with a same-sex partner for fear of a negative reaction from others;
- at least two in five respondents had experienced an incident because they were LGBT, such as verbal harassment or physical violence, in the 12 months

preceding the survey. However, more than nine in ten of the most serious incidents went unreported, often because respondents thought 'it happens all the time';

- 2 per cent of respondents had undergone conversion or reparative therapy in an attempt to 'cure' them of being LGBT, and a further 5 per cent had been offered it;
- 24 per cent of respondents had accessed mental health services in the 12 months preceding the survey.

In launching the report, the government recognised that despite the UK making progress in legal protection for LGBT+ people, research and evidence continued to suggest that LGBT+ people not only face hate crime, as well as other forms of discrimination, bullying, and harassment in education and at work, but also higher inequalities in health satisfaction and outcomes.

The Office for National Statistics (ONS) added an extra question to the CSEW on the gender identity of victims that covered the period 1 October 2019 to 18 March 2020, and this question showed that transgender people were 'significantly more likely' to have been a victim of crime in England and Wales in that time period. Moreover, in 2019, the BBC used freedom of information requests to ask all UK police forces for statistics on the number of transgender crimes they had seen reported. The BBC said that 36 out of 44 police forces in England, Scotland, and Wales fully responded to its freedom of information requests. The information that the BBC obtained showed that there were 1,944 crimes across 36 forces in the year to April 2019 compared with 1,073 in 2016/17. The BBC reported this as an increase of 81 per cent (BBC, 'Transgender hate crimes recorded by police go up 81%', 27 June 2019). The LGBT+ charity, Stonewall, commented that these statistics showed the 'consequences of a society where transphobia is everywhere', whereas the Home Office said it was largely due to better reporting and recording. We see this potential conflict wherever we look at crime figures (see **Chapter 5**) and undoubtedly there is a 'dark figure' of unreported crime. In its 2017 report, 'LGBT in Britain—Hate Crime and Discrimination', Stonewall identified that two in five trans people had experienced a hate crime or incident because of their gender identity in the 12 months covered in the report. Based on YouGov polling of over 5,000 LGBT people, the charity also concluded that four in five anti-LGBT hate crimes and incidents go unreported, with younger LGBT people particularly reluctant to go to the police (Stonewall, 2017).

Research by the Sussex Hate Crime Project on anti-LGBT+ hate crime similarly found that 85 per cent of transgender people and 62.5 per cent of non-trans LGB people had been the victim of verbal abuse over a three-year period (Walters et al., 2020a). Of those, 52.5 per cent of transgender people and 27 per cent of non-trans LGB people had also experienced online abuse. Not only were transgender people more likely to experience hate crime, but they were also likely to experience incidents more frequently. For example, 54 per cent of transgender people reported more than three instances of direct verbal abuse in the previous three years and 13.5 per cent reported more than three direct physical assaults. By comparison, 19.5 per cent and 1.5 per cent of non-trans participants experienced more than three instances of direct verbal abuse and direct physical assaults during the same period (Walters et al., 2020a).

It is clear that all LGBT+ people continue to experience disproportionately high levels of hate crime. Transgender hostilities remain worryingly common, with many transgender people experiencing multiple incidents of abuse both off and online. The impacts of such incidents can be far-reaching for all LGBT+ people. Not only do direct victims experience heightened levels of fear, anger, and anxiety, but these impacts ripple out to entire LGBT+ communities who are likely to experience these same emotions when hearing about such incidents (Walters et al., 2020a). A spokesperson for the LGBT+ anti-violence charity Galop discusses these issues in **Conversations 8.3**.

CONVERSATIONS 8.3

Galop's work and the fight against anti-LGBT+ hate crime

with Melanie Stray

The last 50 years have seen remarkable progress in the advancement of LGBT+ rights in the United Kingdom, but the fight is far from over. LGBT+ people in Northern Ireland do not yet have the same rights and protection as in the rest of the UK, and in England & Wales, LGBT+ and disability hate crimes do not have legal parity with race and faith hate crime.

Recent polling showed that the majority of the UK population holds positive beliefs about LGBT+ people, with 4 in 5 believing that LGBT+ people should be free to live as they wish (Stray 2019). However, a sizeable minority still hold anti-LGBT+ beliefs. For example, 1 in 20 people said that LGBT+ people should not be free to live as they wish; 1 in 5 would be uncomfortable with an LGB+ neighbour; and 1 in 4 would be uncomfortable with a trans neighbour. Hate crime remains a common experience in the lives of LGBT+ people in the UK.

Galop's mission is to make life just, safe and fair for LGBT+ people. We provide advice, support and advocacy to people experiencing hate crime, domestic abuse and sexual violence. We have seen a sharp increase in demand for our services since the EU referendum, and this was further exacerbated by the Covid-19 pandemic. The effects of the latter included that LGBT+ communities, along with other minoritised groups, were targeted with Covid-19-related violence and abuse. Those hostile to the LGBT+ community blamed LGBT+ people for the virus, linking it to the AIDS epidemic and saying that Covid-19 was a 'punishment' from God.

We also saw an increase in the severity of hate crime committed by neighbours during lockdown. This was primarily in pre-existing abusive situations that escalated. The impact was amplified by victims being unable to escape their home or access the necessary help and support. Another Covid-19-related development was that couples reported being accused of breaching social distancing rules in the street by strangers who assumed they were not part of the same household. This escalated into homophobic abuse once the accuser realised their mistake, causing LGBT+ people to be fearful of being open in public.

In recent years, but particularly during the pandemic, we have also seen a huge increase in online hate speech and hate crime, including coordinated attacks via 'Zoombombing'—when people join a Zoom video meeting uninvited. Homophobic, transphobic and often racist slurs are used by the perpetrators, who sometimes perform unwanted sexual acts. This is especially distressing to LGBT+ survivors as the attacks take place in their home—somewhere that should be a safe space—and represent a threat to their privacy, for example when screenshots of the call are taken by perpetrators.

These are just some of the examples of the prejudicial treatment faced by LGBT+ people, but hate crime against them is still not taken sufficiently seriously. An analysis of Metropolitan Police Service data found that homophobic or biphobic hate crimes result in more serious injuries than other types of hate crime (Walters and Krasodomski-Jones 2018: 43), but have comparatively poor outcomes in terms of charging. This may in part be due to the differences in legal framework that applies to LGBT+ hate crime, as police often have a shorter window of time in which to investigate. The percentage of offences resulting in charge or summons for LGBT+ hate crime is between a quarter and half of the percentage for other hate crime strands, across violence against the person, public order offences, and criminal damage and arson (Home Office, 2018: 20).

Our key priority is supporting LGBT+ people to live in safety and with dignity. Ensuring that communities can rely on effective anti-hate crime laws is one crucial part of this. We call for legal parity across hate crime strands, so all protected groups have the same protection under the law. For example, aggravated offences should be consistent across all strands. 'Stirring up' offences should be extended to recognise all groups, so that stirring up transphobic violence is an offence, like inciting other types of hate. The same threshold for these offences should apply across all strands. Our hate crime laws must explicitly include asexual people; trans, non-binary, and gender non-conforming people; and intersex people.

Alongside legal reform, ensuring access to justice is equally important if we are to build an effective response to hate crime. Many LGBT+ people mistrust the criminal justice system and don't want to pursue criminal justice routes for many different reasons, so access to both criminal justice and non-criminal justice solutions is essential. Community organisations play a crucial role in providing alternative resources and trusted access points for help, and support to navigate the justice system for those that choose to report. We call for more specialist services to support LGBT+ communities, to create a comprehensive and holistic support system for all LGBT+ people facing violence and abuse.

Melanie Stray, Hate Crime Policy & Campaigns Manager, Galop

8.5 Racially motivated hate crime

In 2020, the killing of George Floyd, a black man, by a white police officer in the US, and the Black Lives Matter protests around the world that followed this incident and other killings of black citizens, highlighted concerns about systemic racism within society and its public institutions (Aymer, 2016). One aspect of these concerns is how criminal justice systems deal with racially motivated crimes. Unfortunately, criticisms of policing activity in this area are nothing new. Race hate is a complex area that extends from what are called everyday **micro-aggressions** that treat people of a different race as 'others' and can have the effect of putting them down (Torres-Harding and Turner, 2014; Campbell and Manning, 2014; Nadal, 2011), through to the actions of far-right groups and politicians that view BAME people as somehow less deserving than other citizens (Pitcher, 2019; Asthana, 2016). The UK has experienced a series of race riots over the years and questions have been raised about how effective policing of black communities has been in the UK (Bowling, 1998; see also **Chapter 10**).

The historical background of racially motivated hate crime

As with anti-LGBT+ hate, the UK has a long history of racism and racial segregation; from the use of slaves and the international slave trade during the 17th and 18th centuries, to the widely used signs outside homes and businesses of 'no Irish, blacks or dogs' in the 1950s and 1960s, and the widespread violent racist attacks in the 20th and 21st centuries (Bowling, 1998). Hundreds of years of racial oppression and racist **ideology** has inevitably become deeply rooted in many of society's institutional systems, and more broadly in the way many people (often unconsciously) think about black, Asian, and minority ethnic (BAME) people. This is referred to as 'structural racism'.

Yet it was not until 1981 that the British government conducted an inquiry into the problem of racism and racial violence. The inquiry found that black people were 50 to 60 times more likely than white people to be the victims of racially motivated attacks (Gordon, 1990), even at the time when many racial attacks were not reported to the police. In his review of the statistics on the nature and extent of racial violence in Britain, Gordon (1990) stated that the police response to racial violence showed a number of problems; delays in responding, denial of racial motives, an unwillingness to prosecute offenders, mistreatment of victims, and unnecessary special measures. Many of these issues are now being raised again by Black Lives Matter activists, who argue that the position has changed relatively little in the last three decades—see, for example, **Figure 8.7** (Chama, 2019; Baldwin, 2018).

The issue of violent racism returned to public attention in the 1990s after the brutal murder of Stephen Lawrence and the following 'botched' police investigation into his death. An inquiry into the investigation later reported that the police were 'institutionally racist' and that the police were failing victims of hate crime (Macpherson, 1999). In response to the social problem of violent racism

Figure 8.7 Racially motivated hate crimes can take any form, like this graffiti that was painted on the front door of a black family's home in 2019
Source: Jackson Yamba

in Britain, the newly elected Labour government introduced a number of new measures including the introduction of racially aggravated offences under the Crime and Disorder Act 1998. This meant that offences that demonstrated racial hostility, or where the offender was motivated by such hostility, could be prosecuted as an 'aggravated offence', which for some offences carried a 400 per cent increase in maximum sentence (for example, racially aggravated assault has a maximum sentence of two years' imprisonment compared with six months for the basic offence).

Racially motivated hate crime today

Since the Crime and Disorder Act came into force, CSEW data suggests that there has been a significant decrease in the number of racist hate attacks in England and Wales (Home Office, 2018). Yet over recent years, a resurgence in racist ideologies has become prominent again, resulting in spikes in reported racist hate crime. For instance, figures show that reported hate crimes surged by 44 per cent in the month following the EU referendum in 2016, during a time when hostilities towards immigrants and non-UK citizens grew, with most of these reported crimes relating to race hate (Home Office, 2017). The number of reported race hate crimes has continued to increase since this date (Home Office, 2019). One of the factors that may have influenced this increase is the language that was used during the EU referendum debates, which were often framed in ideological terms. We consider the relationship between nationalist ideology and racially motivated hate crime in **New frontiers 8.1**.

More recently, issues of racism and violence occurred during the Covid-19 pandemic, causing similar spikes in racially motivated hate crime. This major global crisis created intense fear and panic amongst members of the public, with some individuals seeking to blame Chinese people (or those thought to be Chinese) for the harms caused by the outbreak (alongside the rise in LGBT+ hate crimes, which are discussed in **Conversations 8.3**).

In January 2020, the Chinese government announced that a new coronavirus, Covid-19, had been identified and was quickly spreading through the Chinese city of Wuhan. By March, the World Health Organisation had announced it as a global pandemic. Within weeks, countries across the world went into lockdown and health services were overwhelmed by patients with life-threatening symptoms. The ensuing panic and anxiety felt amongst most populations soon gave rise to hostility, with an instant rise reported in racist incidents directed towards those perceived to be of Chinese descent (Grierson, J., 'Anti-Asian hate crimes up 21% in UK during coronavirus crisis', *The Guardian*, 13 May 2020). One report stated that 'Mandy Huang was shouted at by a man who told her to "Take your f****** coronavirus back home!" Her friend who tried to intervene bore the brunt of the offender's rage when she was punched in the head and knocked unconscious' (Gregory, A., 'Coronavirus: Man racially abuses woman then knocks her friend unconscious after she confronts him', *The Independent*, 24 February 2020).

Incidents like these highlighted the immense anxiety and anger people felt towards those they thought were to blame for risking the health of the nation. As we have already noted, research has shown that when individuals think a group of people pose a physical threat to their safety (often referred to as 'realistic threats' by social psychologists), some individuals will retaliate violently towards members of that group (see **section 8.6**). Tensions can increase where politicians use racially charged language. In fact, research has shown that when leading politicians make disparaging or biased comments against certain groups, the number of hate crimes increase (Müller and Schwarz, 2020). We can see a potential example of this happening in the US, where President Donald

NEW FRONTIERS 8.1

Hate and the hostile environment

One area of hate crime scholarship that has developed in recent years looks at hate crime in a post-9/11 and Brexit world (Laverick and Joyce, 2020; Perry, 2017). When we look at these events, we can see how existing prejudices are confirmed by the state, as well as how new forms or expressions of hate can develop or increase. Research by the Institute of Race Relations into over one hundred incidents of racial violence reported in the mass media in the month after the (2016) EU referendum showed that the 'spike' in such attacks had more than one explanation (Burnett, 2017). The debates over leaving the EU were often nationalistic in tone (prioritising the importance of national interests and identity while othering different countries and their citizens), and some messages from the Leave campaign spoke of putting Britain first and 'taking back control' (Menon and Wager, 2020; Goodwin and Milazzo, 2017). Politicians spoke of waves of immigration and the social problems that they would cause, which helped to encourage a climate in which 'others' from outside the UK were to be resisted. We outlined earlier how the perception that 'others' are a threat to group identity can result in violence; given this, it is unsurprising then that attacks on non-UK Europeans and others viewed as outsiders grew in number (Devine, 2018). For some perpetrators, it is likely that the EU referendum result served to legitimise their public expressions of racism and xenophobia.

Official responses to violence following the EU referendum tended to view the issue as a matter of a few bigoted individuals, rather than seeing it as the result of wider prejudice within society (Burnett, 2017). Incidents were dealt with as a matter of law and order, rather than recognising the role that institutions of the state play in promoting hostile environments within which hate crimes can flourish. This is similar to how the issues of racism in policing have often been dismissed as the problems of 'a few bad apples'—rogue officers who do not follow accepted standards of behaviour, rather than there being a systemic problem (Ray, 2020; Bains, 2018). Anti-racist campaigners and Black Lives Matter activists argue that this response denies any responsibility for the creation of state racism.

Trump framed the threat of the coronavirus as an issue of race by repeatedly referring to it as the 'Chinese virus'. The virus was for many reimagined not as a threat posed by a biological pathogen, but as a threat posed by an entire racial group, thereby potentially promoting the othering and exclusion of Asian Americans. Indeed, San Francisco State University found that the number of news articles related to the coronavirus and anti-Asian discrimination increased by 50 per cent between 9 February 2020 and 7 March 2020, an increase that some argue can be linked to Trump's remarks (Tavernise, S. and Oppel Jr A., 'Spit On, Yelled At, Attacked: Chinese-Americans Fear for Their Safety', *New York Times*, 23 March 2020; Gover, Harper, and Langton 2020).

We can see from these examples that racial tensions and hostilities quickly surface during times of immense social unrest. During the Covid-19 pandemic, racist attacks, online abuse, and conspiracy theories increased, showing just how easily some individuals can translate a crisis into a motive for racially aggravated actions. What's more, despite governments passing laws that protect people against hate crimes, studies suggest that the same individuals who belong to these institutions (like MPs, presidents) can in fact play a part in stirring hostilities towards BAME citizens through the language they use. They can also be responsible for creating or supporting institutions that reinforce and perpetuate racism through policies and practices that fail to recognise their negative impacts. Such insights on recent developments show us just how relevant and important criminological studies of hate crime are today.

8.6 Religiously motivated hate crime

While religion has been a source of tension in society for millennia, criminality motivated by prejudices against religious identity has increased in significance in the 21st century. It is important to remember that religious tensions in different jurisdictions will vary depending on the demographic make-up of that country. In some cases, a religion can be followed by the majority in one country and they can be responsible for persecuting another group for their beliefs, but this situation can be reversed in another country where the demographic proportions are different. You should therefore keep in mind that, just like with the other hate crimes we have discussed so far, there is no universal approach to understanding religiously motivated crime. Each country will have nuances and complicated relationships between faiths that will affect the dynamics of religiously motivated hate crimes there, and you should be careful not to make assumptions based on what you have learned about other countries. For our purposes here, we will focus on the main religious hate crimes affecting individuals in the UK: **Islamophobia** and **antisemitism**.

Islamophobia

In the UK, the main target of this kind of hate crime is the Muslim faith, though antisemitic hate incidents also remain prolific (CST, 2019). A 1997 report describes 'Islamophobia' as a shorthand way of referring to 'the dread or hatred of Islam . . . and, therefore, to fear or dislike all or most Muslims' (Commission on British Muslims and Islamophobia, 1997: 1; see **Figure 8.8**). The report also added that Islamophobia is evident in closed views that presented Muslims and Islam as being an enemy, as violent, aggressive, unchanging, threatening, separate, or 'other' among others (Commission on British Muslims and Islamophobia, 1997).

We have already seen in this chapter how one of the triggers for hate crime is the idea of difference and the fear of threats to security and values. In the case of Islamophobic hate crime, some aspects of hate are linked to discussions of terrorism associated with Islamic extremism in the wake of the 9/11 attacks in the US, and related episodes in the UK including the London bombings in 2005. In fact, it has been frequently observed that Islamophobic hate crimes

Figure 8.8 The burqa, a religious head covering worn by women in some Islamic traditions, is a common symbolic target of Islamophobia

Source: Shutterstock

increase directly after terrorist attacks (Hanes and Machin, 2014). Such attacks become 'trigger events' which provoke some individuals to retaliate against other group members who they perceive as collectively to blame; the identification of Muslims as being responsible for certain terrorist attacks reinforces this idea of Muslims as the enemy. The existence of a particular 'claimed' interpretation of Islam as providing the basis for the actions of terrorist groups such as ISIS is also a factor in the idea of Muslims as terrorists (Venkatraman, 2007; Jackson, 2007).

Part of the problem in addressing this type of hate crime has been the lack of a clear policy to do so. Allen (2017) notes that political recognition of the need to address religious hatred at the national level first emerged following the publication of Salman Rushdie's allegedly anti-Muslim book *The Satanic Verses* in 1989, when some Muslim organisations called for legislation to make religious discrimination unlawful.

However, it was not until 9/11 that the issue of anti-Muslim hatred became a prominent public policy issue. Perry (2014) identified that after the 9/11 attacks on New York, most western nations saw dramatic increases in prejudice-motivated violence against Muslims and those thought to be Muslim. The response to 9/11 identified the 'radical Muslim' as a threat to society and set off what might be seen as a **moral panic** about the threat posed by Islam and radicalised Muslim youth. Perry argued that a long (and continuing) process of vilification of Muslims by the media and the state is a reactionary reminder of Muslims' outsider status (see **Chapter 6**). Hatred towards Muslims can be made worse by 'trigger' events like the UK's Brexit vote, Donald Trump's presidency, and ISIS-inspired terrorist attacks in European countries such as France, Germany, Sweden, and the UK (Awan and Zempi, 2018). The evidence also suggests that Muslim women are disproportionately verbally and physically attacked, threatened, and harassed, which again highlights the often intersectional nature of hate crime (Awan and Zempi, 2018).

Antisemitism

Religiously motivated hate is not confined to Muslims and Islam; Jewish people also suffer from what is called antisemitism. The Community Security Trust (CST) produces a yearly report on antisemitic hate crime. In their 2019 report, they recorded 1,805 antisemitic incidents in the UK, the highest total ever recorded in a single calendar year (CST, 2019). The CST highlights that the biggest increase in incidents has occurred online, particularly on social media. They posit that 'such a high escalation may reflect rising engagement in and intensity of arguments on social media, particularly where antisemitism is expressed in the context of political disagreements' (CST, 2019: 4).

More broadly, the problem of antisemitism has been highlighted within the political system. In 2016, the UK Labour Party launched an inquiry into this issue, after complaints about antisemitism within the party. This inquiry was followed by an investigation by the Equality and Human Rights Commission (EHRC), the UK human rights watchdog, in May 2019. The EHRC's report, published in October 2020, found that the Labour Party had been guilty of unlawful acts of harassment and discrimination, reporting serious failings in the party's leadership in addressing antisemitism, and an inadequate process for handling antisemitism complaints. The Labour Party was served with an unlawful act notice and its leader Sir Keir Starmer accepted the EHRC's findings. The CST (2019) noted that the higher levels of antisemitism reported to the organisation coincided with periods when discussions around Jews and antisemitism were most prominent in the media, due to the continuing controversy over allegations of antisemitism in the Labour Party.

Moreover, like the rise in racially motivated hate crimes against Asian individuals during the Covid-19 pandemic, antisemitism also increased. As the UK entered lockdown, there were fewer opportunities to express religious hostilities in public but, as with most crimes, individuals found new ways to inflict harm. Online incidents soon spiked, including so-called 'Zoom bombing', where individuals hacked into online meetings, including in one case where a virtual Synagogue service was inundated with antisemitic slurs and symbols (Wakefield, J., 'Coronavirus: Racist "zoombombing" at virtual synagogue', BBC New, 31 March 2020). At the state level, some politicians and religious leaders promoted antisemitic conspiracy theories that Israel was responsible for developing and spreading the Covid-19 virus in an attempt to decrease the non-Jewish population and to control the world. The UN Special Rapporteur on freedom of religion or belief, Ahmed Shaheed, stated in response, 'I am extremely concerned to see that certain religious leaders and politicians continue to exploit the challenging times during this pandemic to spread hatred against Jews and other minorities' (United Nations Human Rights, 'Rise in antisemitic hatred during COVID-19 must be countered with tougher measures, says UN expert', 17 April 2020). The CST data highlights the problem of hate speech online as forming a large part of anti-religious hostilities, an issue that we examine in **Controversy and debate 8.1**.

CONTROVERSY AND DEBATE 8.1

Examining hate speech

The European Convention on Human Rights and the Human Rights Act 1998 give us the right of free speech. We are allowed to 'receive and impart ideas' free from state interference, which means that we are generally allowed to say what we like as long as we do not interfere with the rights of others. This means that we can challenge the government and criticise its policies without fear of punishment. We may even say something that others might find offensive, like arguing that organised religion is inherently corrupt. However, the right of free speech is what is called a **qualified right**, one that can be interfered with where the state thinks it is necessary to do so. One area where this happens is in what is called hate speech, which is speech that is considered so offensive and harmful that it can meet the level of being criminalised.

McGuire and Salter (2015) ask the question:

> To what extent should citizens as a matter of law and policy be 'free' to abuse, ridicule, threaten, defame, mock and insult the religious beliefs, icons, prophets, practices and esteemed figures of believers, even where such attacks contribute to ongoing debate of topics of 'public interest' and political controversy?

With this complex question, they draw attention to the competing interests and rights of those who wish to practise religion free from persecution, versus the rights of others to criticise such practices. For example, UK politicians and media commentators may talk about 'radical Islam' in a way that they would not talk about 'radical Christianity'. The possible effect of this and of media commentators talking about the religion itself as being a problem is that it could create and reinforce the idea of the Muslim terrorist and promote hatred towards Muslims within society.

The idea of free speech is to encourage debate and to allow different ideas to be discussed, even those that may offend some. However, free speech can also be used as an excuse or shield to allow attacks on others, and in the response to 9/11 and the London bombings we see explicit criticism of one group of Muslims that extends into criticism of the entire faith (Featherstone et al., 2010; Wood and Finlay, 2008). At the other end of the scale, there have been prosecutions under terrorism law for what are seen by some as expressions of anti-western sentiment. In a French human rights case (*Leroy* v *France* (App. no. 36109/03)), Denis Leroy, a magazine cartoonist, published a cartoon of New York's Twin Towers being hit by a plane with the caption 'We all dreamed it, Hamas Did it'. The cartoon was published within days of the 9/11 attacks, and Leroy was prosecuted for inciting or glorifying terrorism. Leroy argued that he had a right of freedom of expression and was protesting American imperialism. But the court disagreed and said that publishing the cartoon so close to the 9/11 attacks and with a caption that appeared to support terrorism was going too far.

This case is not about hatred towards individuals or a group because of the identities that we have discussed so far in this chapter, but it is interesting because of its anti-American sentiment. It also shows how even cartoonists may need to consider the impact of their work and be forced to limit how they express themselves.

8.7 Conclusion

In this chapter we have explored the complexity of hate crime and highlighted its importance as an area of criminological study. As we have seen, there is a long history of violence against some groups because of their identity (or identities). Offences that are driven by hostility towards particular identities, or that show this type of hostility when the offence is committed, are classed as 'hate crimes'. We have looked at a range of these kinds of crimes, including racist abuse, religious hatred or abuse, the targeting of LGBT+ citizens and violence aimed at transgender people, as well as crimes against disabled persons. This is not a complete list of all types of hate crime, but as you have read through our discussion of these examples you will have gained an understanding of the policy approach to hate crimes in the UK, which is identity-driven and protects certain identities.

As we have shown, the law has perhaps been slow to catch up in the area of hate crime, and has developed over the years as social problems were revealed. The UK's history of race riots and racial persecution gave rise to policy attention when the civil rights movements highlighted issues of racial abuse. Anti-Muslim hatred became the focus of policy after 9/11, but religious hatred and abuse is broader in scope and, as we have discussed, includes antisemitism. Several pieces of law and policy have engaged with hate crimes and we have set out some in this chapter. You may find it useful to reflect on some of these laws and think about how they are enforced.

What you should gain from this chapter is an understanding of the current landscape of hate crime, one in which it is mainly classed as abuse, prejudice, and violence aimed at people because of who they are and the fear and dislike that is felt by some citizens towards them. This fear reveals itself in various activities, not all of which include physical violence. We have also discussed how information about hate crimes is recorded, and have considered information from the recent CSEW, which indicates that hate crime is on the rise. Some of the recent research on hate crimes and prejudice also identifies rising levels of victimisation linked to hate and prejudice. We suggest caution in how we look at these statistics and note the 'dark figure' of crime that means that our data may not be complete. But our discussion and the available evidence suggests that hate crime is widespread, is complex, and affects a range of groups in society, mainly on the idea of their difference.

Our discussion has also considered the limitations of hate crime definitions and policing responses based on singular identity factors. In your study of hate crime, it is important that you also consider intersectionality and the idea that multiple identity characteristics can be present and should be considered. As you continue your criminological study and explore hate crime and ideas of victimisation in more depth (see also **Chapter 7**), think about the full range of issues involved in hate crime scholarship.

As part of your studies, this book encourages you to *Always Be Critical*, but we should also add *Try To Get Involved*. In the area of hate crime, there are many charities and support groups where you may be able to volunteer and could also contribute to campaigns and research that helps to develop policy.

SUMMARY

After reading this chapter and working your way through its features you should now be able to:

- **Appreciate the importance of hate crime as an area of study within criminology and criminal justice**

The study of hate crime expands our understanding of the reasons why people commit crime. Hate crimes are motivated by attitudes towards people identified as being 'other' and we have seen how some extreme views towards certain groups can be a powerful motivator for people to commit crimes. We also identify how certain groups have experienced long histories of prejudice and violence, which unfortunately remains part of our society and public institutions. Some groups, such as the LGBT+ communities, have taken longer to gain official recognition as hate crime victims due to long-lasting prejudices that remain in society. Other groups, such as disabled communities, have similarly struggled to achieve legal protection and continue to remain unrecognised by state agencies as hate crime victims. This is due to a complex relationship that exists between victims' *perceived* vulnerability and the prejudices that motivate offenders. We have also seen some of the challenges of dealing with hate crime and how the law and policy have been slow to recognise and deal with the intersectional aspects of hate crime.

- **Critically discuss the main features of hate crime and evaluate the need for hate crime legislation**

As we discussed in **Chapter 2**, the concept of crime is a social construction and so too is hate crime. One of the main ideas we have explored is that hate crime is motivated by forms of prejudice against people linked to ideas about their identity (for example, whether they are seen as being black, disabled, or Muslim). Legislation recognises this and attempts to provide us with classes of hate crime so that we can see when somebody has been victimised because of their identity. Hate crime laws also allow us to consider this victimisation as something that is of greater seriousness, which is taken into account when punishing offenders. But as we discuss in this chapter, the recording of hate crimes is not straightforward as some groups may be reluctant to report offences to the police and the offender's motivation may not be clearly identified at the time of the offence; this makes it difficult to monitor and record some hate crimes. Whether we need specific hate crime legislation is also a controversial issue of debate.

- Identify different forms of hate crime and analyse the underlying social and political issues which affect both public and policy responses to the affected groups

The main officially accepted and centrally monitored strands of hate crime are: race or ethnicity; religion or beliefs; sexual orientation; disability; and transgender identity. In this chapter, we have discussed whether these strands are enough to reflect the reality of hate crime and the range of potentially vulnerable individuals and groups that suffer from crime that is motivated by hate. We have explored the idea that there are different types of hate, and that policy perhaps does not recognise all forms of hatred as hate crime. Issues of social and political power are important in terms of deciding what is recognised as being hate crime and what is not. For example, we have discussed whether hatred towards women motivated by misogynistic attitudes should be included as a specific category of hate crime. Should we also consider hatred towards specific groups of women, such as sex workers, as a hate crime? These are complex questions that indicate the importance of intersectionality and the need for our policy responses to not oversimplify hate crimes.

- Explain some of the tensions in society and structural inequalities that may be factors in causing hate crimes

This chapter also highlights how hate crime needs to be thought about alongside some of the other tensions in society. Hate can be motivated by feelings of being threatened by 'others' or a belief that certain groups in society are responsible for the problems that some people face. We can see an example of this motivation in the increase in hate crimes towards people of Asian descent during the Covid-19 pandemic. There are clearly tensions between different groups in society, and hate crimes like Islamophobic attacks can be a reaction to this.

- Critically discuss the evidence of hate crime's occurrence and identify some of the reasons why hate crime may be on the rise

We have discussed how evidence of hate crime comes from the **official statistics** as well as material collected by a range of charities and support groups. As with other areas of crime, it is difficult to know if any increases in recording are due to the authorities getting better at collecting information about hate crimes, for example by adding questions to the CSEW. Does an increase mean that more people are willing to report hate crimes and understand that this is what they are experiencing, even though some people may not wish to report these crimes? On the other hand, it is possible that hate crimes are actually increasing as a result of different tensions in society. We have discussed the 9/11 'effect' and the hostility directed at Muslims following terrorism incidents. We have also discussed how events such as the EU referendum and the Covid-19 pandemic could have the effect of making some people more hostile towards what they see as 'others'.

Test your understanding of the chapter's key points by attempting the self-test questions on the **online resources** at www.oup.com/he/case2e

REVIEW QUESTIONS

1. What are the main categories of hate crime according to government policy?
2. How important is the perception of the victim in defining hate crime?
3. List three reasons why victims might decide not to report a hate crime to the police.
4. Is disablist hate crime really a form of hate crime? Why, or why not?
5. Do we really need specific hate crime legislation? List three reasons for hate crime legislation and three reasons against it.

 Access the **online resources** at **www.oup.com/he/case2e** to check your answers to the review questions.

FURTHER READING

Chakraborti, N. and Garland, J. (2015) *Hate Crime: Impact Causes and Responses.* **London: Sage.**
This book offers a clearly written account of the nature, extent, and harms of hate crime and the effectiveness of criminal justice responses to it. It broadens discussion of hate crime beyond the 'standard' discussions of racist, religiously motivated, homophobic, disablist, and transphobic hate crime to also include gendered hostility and elder abuse, as well as attacks upon alternative subcultures and violence against sex workers and the homeless.

Kusminder, C. (2016) *Supporting Victims of Hate Crime.* **Bristol: Policy Press.**
This short book provides an overview of UK hate crime legislation and the EU Directive on Victim Support, as well as a practical guide to tackling hate crime issues.

Laverick, W. and Joyce, P. (eds) (2020) *Racial and Religious Hate Crime: The UK From 1945 to Brexit.* **Basingstoke: Palgrave.**
This is a good place to start for a more advanced, in-depth study of racial and religious hate crimes. It conducts an examination of the factors behind the emergence of these two issues and the challenges of dealing with them in the current environment following the 2016 EU referendum.

Sherry, M. et al. (eds) (2019) *Disability Hate Speech: Social, Cultural and Political Contexts.* **Abingdon: Routledge.**
This book's original essays present legal, cultural, and historical analysis of disability hate speech. It includes the testimony of victims in order to articulate the impact of disability hate speech. It also presents the results of original surveys of disability hate speech from different countries.

Walters, M. and Brown, R. (2016) *Causes and motivations of hate crime.* **London: Equality and Human Rights Commission.**
This report sets out an overview of the current evidence based on hate crime causation and perpetrator motivation. It seeks to help readers understand the causes and motivations

of hate crime perpetration for the different protected characteristics included as 'strands' under current hate crime legislation.

 Access the **online resources** to view a wealth of extra information relating to your study of criminology, including self-test questions, answers to review questions, and links to other resources that will help you enjoy and fulfil your potential within your studies.

www.oup.com/he/case2e

CHAPTER OUTLINE

9.1	Introduction	238
9.2	What do we mean by 'childhood'?	238
9.3	Individualised explanations for youth offending	244
9.4	Contextual explanations for youth offending	250
9.5	Mainstream responses to youth offending	259
9.6	Progressive approaches to youth offending	264
9.7	Conclusion	267

9

Youth offending and youth justice

KEY ISSUES

After studying this chapter, you should be able to:

- outline how 'childhood' and 'youth' have been socially constructed;
- critically explore the key criminological explanations for youth offending;
- appreciate the contextual influences on offending by children and young people, including cultural influences and the role of social structures and processes;
- explain the dominant role of early intervention and risk management approaches in responding to youth offending;
- interpret contemporary progressive models for responding to youth offending, notably diversion and positive youth justice.

9.1 Introduction

In this chapter, we focus on youth offending and youth justice: that is, offending behaviour committed by children and young people and how they are treated in the Youth Justice System (YJS). You may be wondering why these issues get their own chapter. Aren't children and young people just people? Surely, we implicitly discuss their offending behaviour and their treatment in the justice system when we talk about crime and justice generally? Youth offending and youth justice get special consideration in this book, and in criminology generally, because as a society we view children and young people differently to adults. This means that we treat them differently to adults, and this differential treatment extends to crime and justice. You will have seen the child–adult distinction in practice numerous times, perhaps without registering it or considering its significance. Imagine, for example, hearing that someone had committed a knife crime whilst a member of a drugs gang that was led by adults. Would your views of this behaviour and how it should be punished differ depending on whether the offender was 14 or 41? What about if the 'offender' was ten years old?

As we will discuss in this chapter, society's view of children and young people is not straightforward. We hold views that range from protective and sentimental (children and young people are vulnerable beings in need of care, support, and protection), to fearful and threatened (children and young people are out of control and a potential threat, so need to be brought into line). These views can change over time and depending on the specific situation and cultural context. The most consistent feature is a general preoccupation with children and young people, who are sources of adult concern and anxiety, and the presence of a 'them and us' mentality. Society's assumptions about what it means to be a child or a young person and what should be expected of children and young people in terms of their development and behaviour—in other words, how they should come to terms with, and comply with, increasing levels of responsibility and social obligation—shape its views on and responses to youth offending. As criminologists, it is our job to explore these assumptions and their implications and we aim, first, to understand and explain offending behaviour by children and young people and, secondly, to draw conclusions about how we should respond to this behaviour through formal, official processes (that is, youth justice). This chapter will give you the basic understanding and critical skills you need to start grappling with these ideas.

We begin by looking at how the **concepts** of 'childhood' and 'youth' have been seen, theorised, and socially constructed over time (cf. Case, 2018; Hendrick, 2015), before moving on to consider explanations for youth offending and 'delinquency' (a broad, vague term that can encompass crime, but also antisocial behaviour, nuisance, etc.). We will see how youth offending has tended to be explained in **individualised** terms, through **developmental**, and **agentic** explanations, but will then consider the influences of **culture** and of social structures and processes. These discussions will lead us to consider whether the youth offending problem may in fact be constructed by 'us' rather being the sole responsibility or fault of 'them' (children and young people). In the latter parts of the chapter, we will evaluate the main formal responses to youth offending as well as looking at more progressive, contemporary approaches to youth offending and delivering youth justice. Throughout our discussion, the overarching question will be 'who is the problem: "them" or "us"?', and we will conclude by drawing together the evidence to reflect on whether it is individual actions or systemic and structural influences that contribute towards and establish ideas of youth offending and youth justice.

9.2 What do we mean by 'childhood'?

Before we dive into explanations for and responses to youth offending, we need to be clear (or as clear as possible) about what we mean when we talk about 'childhood' and 'youth'—distinct, separate terms that refer to the individual's developmental stage or age. Understanding not only what these concepts mean today, but how they have been shaped over time and influenced by historical events, science, and psychology, is a crucial context for the rest of our discussion and will enable us to consider whether childhood, like 'crime' and 'justice', is in fact a social construct. Whatever we conclude on this point will clearly have implications for our views on explanations for and responses to youth offending.

Begin by considering your own ideas of the 'child' or 'young person' via the questions in **What do you think? 9.1**.

Childhood in history

We noted in **section 9.1** that today children and young people are viewed and treated differently to adults, but this has not always been the case. Before the mid-1700s,

WHAT DO YOU THINK? 9.1

Defining the 'child' or 'young person'

When do you start and stop being a child or young person? The age range has varied over time, and still varies geographically. Consider your views on the following.

- What is the age range during which someone should be considered to be a child?
- Across what ages should someone be considered a young person or youth?
- Should these age ranges be different for specific forms of behaviour, such as offending or attending school or leaving home or voting?
- What do you think could be the main influences on how these categories are socially constructed and decided?

Once you've thought about these questions, you may find it helpful to consider the definitions of 'childhood' and 'youth' provided by the NSPCC (the National Society for the Prevention of Cruelty to Children) and the United Nations:

- www.nspcc.org.uk/preventing-abuse/child-protection-system/legal-definition-child-rights-law/legal-definitions/
- www.un.org/esa/socdev/documents/youth/factsheets/youth-definition.pdf

---

children were essentially thought of as little adults, working and socialising with older adults, dressing like adults, and even being treated the same as adults when they offended—often in terms of **punishment** and imprisonment. However, the Industrial Revolution (from around 1760) followed by the introduction of compulsory schooling in the UK (in 1880) prompted a shift in views. People started to see childhood as a separate life stage with its own very specific characteristics (Hendrick, 2015), and some clear differences from adulthood began to emerge in terms of biological (as indicated by **Figure 9.1**), psychological, and social development and behaviour.

In contrast to expectations of children in the 17th century and earlier, today there is a clear understanding that children and young people are not to be subjected to the same expectations as adults in terms of their legal responsibilities or their obligations to provide for themselves through paid work. Their position in family life is marked out as one of dependency, and they are seen in terms of their relative immaturity and developmental growth towards a fully completed (and responsible) adult state. This view is now widely accepted around the world, to the extent that nearly all nations (the exception being the US) have signed up to the United Nations Convention on the Rights of the Child, which sets out a series of state and public obligations as to the treatment of members of the population defined as children—by which the Convention means everyone under the age of 18. However, despite this apparent agreement, we will see that there are still broad international variations as to exactly when children and young people gain certain rights and become subject to certain expectations.

Commentators have taken contrasting positions as they have tried to make sense of our changing perceptions

Figure 9.1 At what point does a child become an adult?
Source: © Robert Adrian Hillman/Shutterstock

of childhood. Philippe Ariès (a French medievalist and historian of the family, 1914–84), for instance, believed that childhood as a concept was effectively invented in the Middle Ages (generally seen as being the 5th to 15th centuries). Observing that children were rarely visible in artistic works before this time, he suggested that this, along with the absence of any distinctive form of clothing for them, indicated: 'a marked indifference . . . to the special characteristics of childhood' (Ariès, 1962: 73). Children and young people were treated in the same way as adults, meaning that they were given the same social standing but were also subject to the same expectations. This could help explain why children in pre-modern times seemed to be punished in the same, often extreme, ways as their elders. Ariès argues that it is only in more recent times that childhood has come to be seen differently, with families beginning to 'coddle' their young, taking a more sentimental view of them. Children's ignorance, weakness, and innocence began to be emphasised, so that they were viewed as 'fragile creatures . . . who needed to be both safeguarded and reformed' (Ariès, 1962: 133).

The implications of this argument are that childhood and adolescence have only come to be seen as a separate life stage in tandem with, and as a result of, wider social changes—such as industrialisation, the specialisation of labour, and the associated need for longer periods of education and preparation for work (cf. Case, 2018). This theory fits well with the fact that in recent times we have increased the levels of distinction between children/young people and adults within the justice system, characterising separate youth and adult criminal justice systems, but we should not accept Ariès' account unthinkingly as it has come in for substantial criticism:

- Pollock (1983) thinks that Ariès (as an academic from Western Europe) may have been inclined to take a relatively narrow western perspective on childhood. She comments that just because children have been treated differently by other cultures, does not mean that they were not seen as children. Indeed, Athelstan, the first king to rule over the whole of England (in the mid-900s), is believed to have been more lenient towards young offenders on the basis of their age and status.
- Heywood (2001) has also criticised Ariès's position that somehow previous eras and cultures were times of depravity and lack of civilisation (when they were not necessarily), in contrast to contemporary enlightenment and more humane treatment of those who offend.
- Cunningham (2005) has suggested that there has been persistent evidence of a divergence of views about how to bring up children, and evidence of recurrent tensions between advocates of punishment or nurture, so Ariès's position is oversimplified.

It is clear that there have been different perspectives on children and young people throughout history, as well as different perspectives between those attempting to study and summarise these changing views. However, in acknowledging the contrasts between views of children and young people over time, we should also note the characteristics that have remained constant. Even before the mid-1700s, when we could generalise that children and young people were viewed and treated similarly to adults, we can still find evidence of a 'them and us' attitude. Consider, for example, the following lines from Shakespeare's play *The Winter's Tale*, which was first performed in 1611:

> I would that there were no age between ten and three-and-twenty, or that youth would sleep out the rest; for there is nothing in between but getting wenches with child, wronging the ancientry, stealing, fighting.
>
> (Shepherd, *The Winter's Tale*, Act III, Scene 3)

Developmental and psychological explanations of childhood

Another way of considering childhood is through the lenses of development and psychology, seeing it as a developmental life phase during which a series of identifiable biological, psychological, and psychosocial processes and milestones lead towards a mature state of adulthood.

There are certain recognisable stages in our physiological development, such as puberty, where physical growth and biological and hormonal changes occur, and in the 21st century parallels have been found in neurological development, too. In fact, children's brains have been found to be more highly organised than those of adults in some respects, purely because they need to learn things so quickly: 'The number of connections in a baby's brain greatly exceeds adult levels. Many of these excess connections have to be cut back' (Blakemore and Frith, 2005: 18). Blakemore (2019) provides a detailed account of the evidence from neuroscience supporting the idea of a 'teenage brain' (**Figure 9.2**), and notes that this is associated with certain characteristics such as susceptibility to peer influence and risk-taking; which in turn are linked with the potential for antisocial or criminal behaviour. Blakemore has summarised the key arguments in a lecture titled 'The Neuroscience of the Teenage Brain' which you can find on YouTube.

Developmental psychology has also shaped ideas of how 'childhood' can be constructed (understood, explained, and negotiated). Piaget (1959), for instance, set out a number of stages in children's linguistic development which are thought to reflect increasing levels of sophistication and social integration as they move from an

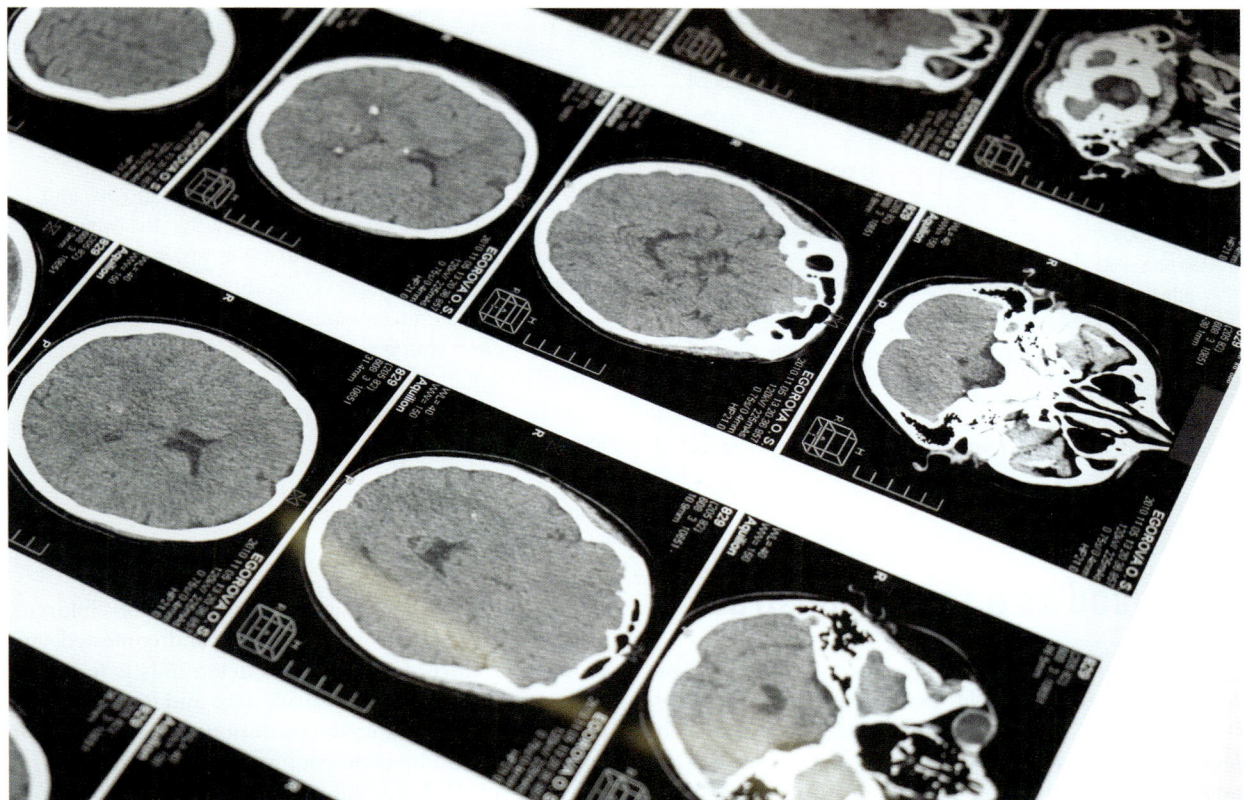

Figure 9.2 Evidence from neuroscience suggests that there is such a thing as a 'teenage brain', which is associated with characteristics like susceptibility to peer influence and risk-taking
Source: Cottonbro/Pexels Stock Photo

'ego-centric' and concrete form of thinking towards more abstract and other-oriented forms of expression. Vygotsky (1986), too, has analysed the processes of young children's learning and development, but he differs from Piaget in that he attributes the changes more to social interaction and acculturation than to internal and innate qualities of the individual.

Others who have strongly shaped this 'ages and stages' model of child development have included Freud (1977), whose analysis of sexuality adopted this kind of framework, and Erikson (1995), whose work is seen as important as it provides an explanatory framework for the tensions and conflicts associated with adolescence. Erikson (1995) presents adolescence as a period characterised by ego-identity versus role confusion; the individual gains a stronger sense of self and of their individual qualities, but at the same time they are also facing the challenge of finding a place and an accepted role in society. Failure to negotiate this divide can result in increasing uncertainty, and a need to experiment with different lifestyles and activities—perhaps including criminal activities. Erikson's ideas about the transitions of youth have echoes in concepts such as 'storm and stress', a phrase used by G. Stanley Hall in 1904 which has had considerable influence on psychology and related fields ever since (Arnett, 1999). Such analyses have helped to cement the idea that conflict and disruption are more or less 'normal' features of making the transition from childhood to fully developed adulthood (Smith, 2011: 12). While this portrayal of youth has been questioned to an extent (for example, by Rutter et al., 1976 and Dasen, 2000), there is no doubt that adolescence is characterised by certain types of 'events' which can have an effect on young people.

For our purposes as criminologists, it is important to think in terms of a range of factors that might have an impact rather than giving too much emphasis to a single source, such as biological drives or psychological phases. Some have suggested that it may be more helpful to think in terms of **critical moments** or turning points when the combination of individual characteristics and social influences shaping young people's experience is exposed to specific forces which may lead to significant changes in their lives (Thomson et al., 2002; Sampson and Laub, 1993, 2005). See **What do you think? 9.2** to reflect on the extent to which you think that biological or social characteristics shape young people's experience.

> **WHAT DO YOU THINK?** 9.2
>
> ### Nature or nurture?
>
> The argument has raged long and fiercely over whether children and young people are predominantly driven by biological, instinctive urges that need to be contained and controlled in order to produce socially adjusted adult citizens (that is, nature; see **Chapter 16**) or whether they are essentially products of their environment (such as social deprivation, poverty) and the influences around them (that is, nurture; see **Chapter 17**). This introduces questions as to whether children and young people who offend are deprived or depraved; whether they are in need or at risk; and whether they require care or control.
>
> Which explanations seem more plausible to you, and what are the implications of your view for the way we respond to youth offending and try to arrive at justice? Think about the contemporary example of 'county lines', a high-profile crime problem involving the exploitation of children and young people as mules to carry and sell drugs. How can and should we explain this behaviour when it's committed by a 13-year-old member of a gang led by adults?

Childhood as a social construct

Although childhood can, to an extent, be mapped out using developmental and psychological markers, we have seen that even these are subject to debate. The lack of agreement throughout history and between academic disciplines about what constitutes childhood has led some to conclude that the concept is essentially a **social construction**, with its specific qualities not fixed but dependent on a society's **norms**, expectations, and requirements (Hendrick, 2015). Stages of development and competence vary according to the assumptions we make about children and young people's place in the world and their relationships with adults, and children and young people's legal status also varies significantly between different countries, reflecting differing assumptions about when they should be seen as becoming responsible for their behaviour (Case, 2017). The age from which children and young people can be arrested and charged with a crime, known as the age of **criminal responsibility**, is relatively low in the countries of the UK, whereas elsewhere in Europe it is much higher—as you can see from **Figure 9.3**. Further complexities arise when we consider the ages at which children and young people assume legal rights and responsibilities across other aspects of their lives. For example, across the UK the age of sexual consent is 16, but the age at which someone can vote is 18 (except in Scotland, where it was lowered to 16 in 2015), suggesting that children and young people are expected to behave lawfully sooner than they are considered capable of participating in democracy.

These significant variations between and even within countries reflect different ways of conceptualising and constructing childhood (Smith, 2010). As James and James (2004: 58) have noted, explanations for children's attributes and actions are conflicting and contested (are they the product of inherent and deterministic forces, or the expression of rational calculations and **free will**?), and all of them lead to different conclusions and strategies for approaching children and young people's upbringing. Is it possible to talk about 'childhood' as a solid concept with common features that stay constant between times and locations?

It might perhaps feel as though our discussion so far has raised many questions yet not brought us much closer to addressing our key issues: understanding and explaining youth offending, and drawing conclusions about how to respond to this behaviour. However, appreciating that childhood is not a fixed concept and that its nature and parameters can change depending on the lens through which it is viewed is useful in itself. Understanding this context means we are better equipped to develop nuanced explanations for offending behaviour by children and young people, and to draw thoughtful conclusions as to how society should respond.

Given the varied, complex, and clearly unresolved accounts of childhood and youth more generally, it may not be too surprising to find that when we narrow our focus to potential causes of children and young people's offending behaviour, explanations are similarly diverse. However, there is some consensus, and views on the origins and causes of youth offending can be broadly categorised as either individualised or contextual. Individualised accounts include those that are developmental and those based on the idea of agency—the idea that we have choices about how to behave. Contextual accounts include those which focus on cultural or socio-structural influences.

9.2 WHAT DO WE MEAN BY 'CHILDHOOD'?

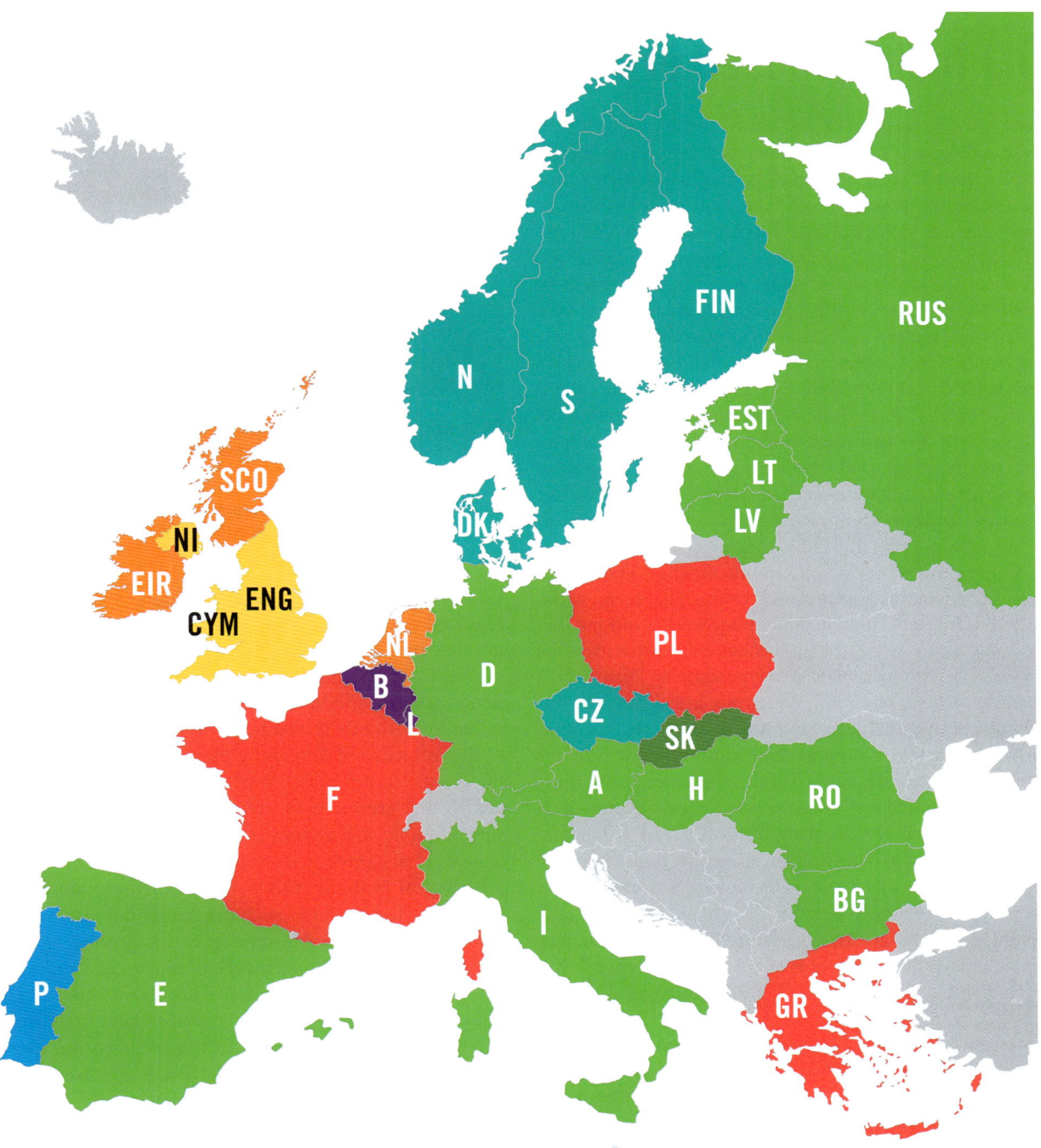

Figure 9.3 Ages of criminal responsibility for children and young people in European countries
Source: Adapted from Goldson 2013: 18

9.3 Individualised explanations for youth offending

As we saw in **section 9.2**, individualised accounts of children and young people's actions and behaviour (that is, explanations associated with the individual child or young person, rather than external influences on them) can be grounded in biological and psychological explanations; in other words, they are **positivist**, applying the methods of natural sciences to the social world (see **Chapters 16 and 17**). For example, there has long been a belief (Jenks, 1996) that children are born with urges that are inherently self-centred, destructive, and antisocial, making them an inevitable threat to discipline and social order. This aligns with the idea that children and young people are naturally unprepared for the demands and responsibilities of later life, and therefore need schooling and shaping in order to meet these expectations. When they do not receive this guidance and education, or it does not achieve its purpose, crime is seen as the inevitable consequence.

Other innate or genetic characteristics that might predispose some children and young people to wilful and deviant behaviour include inherited conditions that are associated with certain behavioural patterns, such as ADHD (Attention Deficit Hyperactivity Disorder), a disorder whose common symptoms are difficulty concentrating, hyperactivity, and impulsivity. Twin studies provide evidence to support these kinds of theories by, for example, comparing monozygotic (shared egg) and dizygotic (non-shared egg) twins to assess the extent to which heredity contributes to their attributes and behaviour. Such studies have consistently claimed to find a heredity effect, meaning that those with more genes in common are also more likely to demonstrate shared criminal traits (Hopkins-Burke, 2013), suggesting that genetics do play a role in how likely a child is to commit an offence. It has been pointed out that it is very difficult to separate out hereditary and environmental influences, particularly in cases where twins share the same environment (Case, 2018), but nonetheless, one twin study has come up with a very precise calculation of the proportionate effect of different factors on delinquent behaviour:

> The best fitting model suggested that 18%, 56% and 26% of the variance in delinquency among both boys and girls is associated with additive genetic, nonshared environment, and shared environmental factors, respectively.
>
> (Taylor et al., 2000: 433)

This quote illustrates the essential nature–nurture debate—assigning varying degrees of influence to genetics (nature) and environment (nurture).

A further strong and apparently indisputable biological factor that appears to have an influence on

Figure 9.4 Biological factors such as gender seem to have an influence on behaviour, but contextual influences also appear to play a part
Source: Cottonbro/Pexels

subsequent criminality is gender (**Figure 9.4**); girls are reported to be about half as likely to commit offences as boys (Arnull and Eagle, 2009). This prompts a challenging series of questions about how far differences in genetic make-up and hormonal balances between genders might influence their likelihood of offending, as opposed to the influence of different patterns of **socialisation** and life events (Rutter et al., 1998). It has been noted, for example, that 'greater male involvement in crime is a universal finding that applies across cultures and over time' (Rutter et al., 1998: 276), suggesting that there may be a biological basis for this pattern. On the other hand, the nature and extent of such disparities has also 'varied markedly over time and among ethnic groups', as well as according to age and the type of antisocial behaviour (Rutter et al., 1998: 276)—males are much more likely to be responsible for certain types of violent behaviour, but only slightly more likely to engage in minor theft, and no more likely at all than females to be involved in shoplifting.

It will be becoming clear that it is impossible to single out one explanation of offending or antisocial behaviour, or even one type of explanation, that fits consistently. Biological differences might contribute, but these seem to be modified by cultural differences, and life experiences also appear to play a part—perhaps in amplifying exposure of boys to conflict and discord in light of innate tendencies towards greater levels of aggressive behaviour (Rutter et al., 1998: 277). For a more detailed discussion of gender issues in the youth justice context, we recommend that you read *Offending Girls. Young Women and Youth Justice* by Gilly Sharpe (2011).

Developmental explanations

In recognising that the factors contributing to a child or young person becoming delinquent are many and varied, a strand of criminological thinking has emerged which suggests that youth offending is the product of interlocking developmental processes. Its proponents see youth offending as the result of the interaction between individual characteristics, personal experiences, and social and cultural influences specific to late childhood and adolescence, noting that most types of antisocial and criminal behaviour are committed in this life stage. This framework provides a theoretical model for explaining youth offending, both in general and in its specific manifestations, and developmental theories are strengthened by the observation that the peak period of offending falls in the teenage years (cf. Case, 2018; Bateman, 2015).

All of this suggests that offending behaviour and criminality can be thought of as following a particular pattern, depending on the factors which comprise the individual's personal life course. Adolescence in particular is a period of transitions, with important potential triggers or turning points, and it is in this period that the preconditions for young people's involvement in criminal activity are thought to be established. However, it is the impact of these factors on particular individuals that determines how likely they are to become offenders. Although the factors will be different for each individual, researchers have attempted to specify what they might be; Coleman and Hendry (1999: 210) group potential influences of children and young people's pathways into or out of crime (see also Chapter 21) as:

- **Normative events**, such as biological and physiological changes or school transfers. These will affect all children and young people.
- **Non-normative events**, such as low income, family change, illness, or being excluded from school, affect particular groups to varying degrees. These will affect children and young people in varying combinations and at different times.
- **'Daily hassles'**, such as isolation, bullying, or other forms of oppression, are persistent experiences which may have an increasingly significant but largely hidden effect on certain children and young people.

Similarly, Sampson and Laub use 'the concept of *emergence*' (2005: 43, emphasis in original) to explain children and young people's involvement in crime. This tries to account for the interplay between different influences and different types of influence, which may be unpredictable and rely on chance combinations of factors, alongside individual characteristics such as group dynamics, 'time-varying events', and 'human agency' (Sampson and Laub, 2005: 43). This means that outcomes that may be difficult to predict with any degree of confidence (whether a certain child or young person will commit an offence) can be reliably explained, albeit after the event has happened. Interestingly, this kind of account leaves room for individual freedom of action; social structures and chance events set the terms but it is the situated choice exercised by the child or young person that determines whether or not they will engage in offending behaviour.

Since the beginning of the 20th century (Case and Haines, 2009), explanations of and responses to youth offending in the industrialised western world have been dominated by empirical research that tends to be both developmental and pseudo-positivist in nature ('pseudo' because these theories focus on predictors rather than causes—see **Chapters 21** and **22**). Positivist developmental theories appeal to politicians, policymakers, and practitioners for their common-sense explanations, vast evidence base (they can call on many studies of young males, which obviously makes them relevant to youth offending, where the majority of offenders are male and—obviously—young), and practical nature (Case and Haines, 2009, 2010). However, they have been criticised in a number of ways. The most common criticism points to the reductionism of positivism's methodology, explanations, and conclusions—it reduces complex systems and behaviours to fixed statistical quantities and overly simplistic and often exclusive (in the sense of excluding other explanations) biological, psychological, or sociological categories and explanations (see **Chapters 16** and **17**). Another criticism is that what positivists present as causal influences on crime could be more accurately described as correlating with, rather than causing, criminal behaviour; this clearly limits their usefulness in explaining crime (see **Chapter 22**).

In the past 20 or so years, positivist explanations have been further challenged by radical and critical theories which offer alternative explanations of youth offending. These theories (see **Chapter 18**) have tended to explain youth offending as a social construction resulting from differential power relations in western society (Case, 2017). The result is that children and young people who offend are often viewed as victims of the differential creation and application of laws in YJSs, based on factors such as socio-economic status, gender, ethnicity, and age. Critical theorists have attacked the theoretical, ethical, and practical weaknesses of modern youth justice, suggesting that children and young people who have offended become stigmatised due to:

- positivist explanations seeing individual factors as more significant causes of youth offending than wider social, economic, and political influences

(Goldson and Muncie, 2015), which can lead to labelling and blaming children and young people, rather than adopting a broader explanatory view of their behaviour;

- the use of custody (prison sentences) for juveniles across Western Europe and North America rather than **rehabilitation** and adherence to basic human rights (Muncie and Goldson, 2006), which is harmful and criminalising;
- the human rights of children and young people in trouble with the law in the UK, Western Europe, and North America often being neglected; this labels them as offenders first rather than as children or young people who have offended (Haines and Case, 2015; Case and Haines, 2010);
- the increasing interventionism of YJSs internationally, which take action in response to an ever-expanding range of behaviours, not always criminal. The effect is that children and young people are labelled as risky, problematic, and in need of adult control (Muncie and Goldson, 2006).

Despite all these criticisms, pseudo-positivist developmental theories continue to dominate in youth offending. They can be seen most clearly in the Risk Factor Prevention Paradigm, or RFPP, a policy approach which has become the go-to model for explaining and responding to offending by children and young people in England and Wales. We return to the RFPP as a response to youth offending in **section 9.5**, but we highlight it here because it is the practical embodiment of developmental explanations known as **artefactual risk factor theories**. These theories assert that there are certain 'risk factors' in the family, school, neighbourhood, lifestyle, and psychological domains of a child or young person's early life (up to early adolescence) which predict their likelihood of offending in later life (late adolescence and adulthood). Artefactual risk factor researchers use positivist, empirical methods (see **Chapter 4**) to identify these risk factors and statistically manipulate them to predict offending.

The UK government's heavily RFPP-influenced approach to youth offending has been shaped by and evidentially grounded in two developmental, artefactual risk factor studies: *The Cambridge Study in Delinquent Development* (West and Farrington, 1973) and *Crime in the Making* (Sampson and Laub, 1993).

The Cambridge Study in Delinquent Development

The much-respected 'Cambridge Study' began in 1961 at Cambridge University under Donald West, who was later joined and then replaced by David Farrington. Its theoretical and methodological origins can be traced to the *Unraveling Juvenile Delinquency* study (Glueck and Glueck, 1930) in the US, which 'pointed to the strong and continuing influence of early upbringing and family circumstances in determining who became delinquent' (West, 1982: 3). In his seminal work *Present Conduct and Future Delinquency*, West (1969: 1) set out his central aim as being 'to trace the influence of community, family and individual factors, as seen at this early age, on personality, performance and social adjustment in later years'. The prospective longitudinal study design (a method involving information being collected over a long period of time from the start of a study into the future/prospectively—highly innovative for the 1960s) was intended to enable the study to trace the development of individual offending over time, to explore the key features of the 'criminal career' (that is, onset, duration, continuity, **desistance**) and to investigate the extent to which offending in adolescence could be predicted by early life experiences. This represented a developmental approach to explaining youth offending in that it located causes in individual characteristics that developed from early childhood—with these influences typically seen as predictors of, and 'risk factors' for, offending.

Methodologically, the Cambridge Study investigated 'a traditional White, urban, working class sample of British origin' (Farrington in Thornberry and Krohn, 2003: 139), all of whom were male and born in 1953–4 in South London, England. The majority of the 411 boys (97 per cent) were from state primary schools, with the other 12 boys sampled from a local school for the 'educationally subnormal'. The boys were interviewed in school at ages 8–9, 10–11, and 14–15, then re-interviewed in the study research office when aged 16, 18, and 21 years and in their homes at age 25, 32, 46, and 50 years. The early interviews explored a variety of psychological and social factors in childhood and adolescence, supplemented in the adult interviews (aged 18 years and over) by gathering data on employment histories, adult relationships, and the children of the sample (Farrington in Rutter, 1988). The researchers used a variety of other methods to complement the interview data, including in-school tests of individual characteristics (for example, intelligence), annual parent interviews, teacher **questionnaires**, peer ratings, and **official statistics** of delinquency of parents and siblings (see Farrington in Thornberry and Krohn, 2003).

In *Who Becomes Delinquent*, West and Farrington (1973) made statistical comparisons between delinquents and non-delinquents in order to identify 'risk factors' (experienced by delinquents) measured when the boys were aged 8–10 years and which allegedly were able to statistically predict future offending (official and self-reported) at age 14–15 years. The 50-year review of the Cambridge Study concluded that at age 8–10 the 'most important

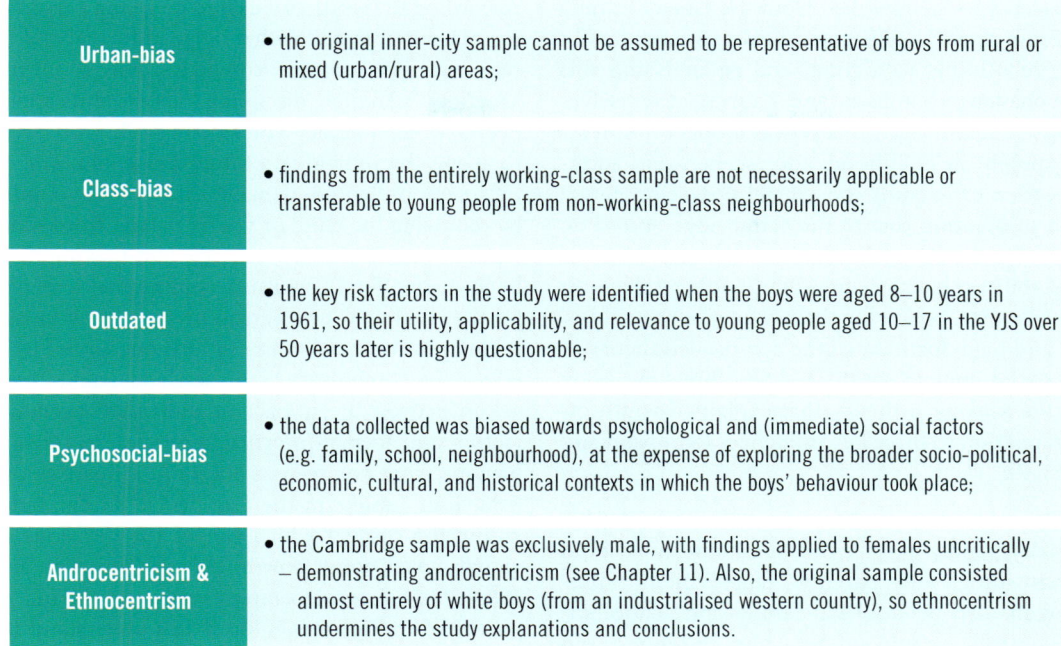

Figure 9.5 Methodological criticisms of the Cambridge Study

predictors' of later offending fell within six categories (Farrington in Thornberry and Krohn, 2003):

- **antisocial behaviour in childhood**—including 'troublesomeness', dishonesty, aggressiveness;
- **hyperactivity-impulsivity-attention deficit**—including poor concentration, restlessness, risk-taking;
- **low intelligence** and low school achievement;
- **family criminality**—including convicted parents, delinquent older siblings, siblings with behaviour problems;
- **family poverty**—including low family income, large family size, poor housing;
- **poor parenting**—including harsh discipline, poor supervision, parental conflict.

The Cambridge Study's use of a prospective longitudinal design and multiple data forms (official and self-reported; quantitative and qualitative) obtained from multiple sources (children, young people, parents, teachers) enabled the study findings to be **triangulated**—validated against one another—which should have resulted in a more holistic and accurate understanding of children and young people's behaviour. However, there have been several methodological criticisms of the study which undermine the **validity** of its findings, specifically urban bias, class bias, the fact that it is now outdated, psychosocial bias, **androcentricism**, and **ethnocentrism**, concerns that are detailed in **Figure 9.5**.

So why is this study still significant? It is still being replicated with the children and young people of the original sample after over 50 years, during which time it has been the theoretical and empirical inspiration for artefactual risk factor theories and the RFPP. The predictive risk factors it identified in childhood have strongly influenced virtually all subsequent risk-focused research with children and young people and have found their way into the policymaking of politicians and senior government policymakers, who have been attracted by the length of the study, the common-sense nature of its findings, and the confidence with which their replicability and apparent validity has been asserted.

Crime in the Making

We come to the second significant developmental, pseudo-positivist study that has shaped UK governmental explanations of and responses to youth offending. Like the Cambridge Study, this research also focused on identifying risk factors for future offending, but in this case it identified a broader range of psychosocial and socio-structural influences. And like the Cambridge Study, this one also emerged from *Unraveling Juvenile Delinquency* (Glueck and Glueck, 1930; see also Case and Haines, 2009), as Robert Sampson and John Laub obtained access to the raw data from the Gluecks' study in 1985. From there, they began an extensive process of restoring, rebuilding, validating, and re-analysing this data. The challenge Sampson and Laub set themselves was to construct and test a theoretical model of individual development in childhood, adolescence, *and* adulthood in order to expand the Gluecks' developmental focus (not to mention that of the Cambridge Study) on childhood experiences and to explore the possibility of not only stability but also *change* in offending behaviour over the life course. Following their extensive re-analysis, Sampson and Laub formulated the 'age-graded theory of informal social control' in their groundbreaking book *Crime in the Making*, a theory that explained youth offending in relation to three key influences (Sampson and Laub, 1993: 7):

- **Structural background factors** such as social class, ethnicity, gender, poverty, broken home, household overcrowding, and parental employment, influenced in turn by informal family and school social controls, explain offending in childhood and adolescence.
- **Strong continuity** in criminal behaviour from childhood to adulthood in a variety of life domains.
- **Informal social bonds** to the family and employment in adulthood explain changes in criminality over the lifespan despite early childhood propensities.

According to this theory, a child or young person's offending behaviour is met with a range of formal and informal responses (for example, conviction may result in official sanction, parental discipline, approval/disapproval of peers), which interact with existing risk/protective factors to shape the individual's future behaviour. For example, incarceration could damage educational opportunities by removing the child or young person from school (potentially creating a vicious circle and making them more likely to reoffend), whilst a community sentence could set the child or young person on a pathway towards pro-social, positive behaviours (a virtuous circle) by making education compulsory. Sampson and Laub's theory also acknowledged the impact of individual agency, so risk factors and formal/informal responses to offending behaviour were not seen as the only influences on future behaviour (unlike in the Cambridge Study), but as providing the context which shapes the decisions an individual makes about how to behave (Sampson and Laub, 1993, 2005). A more complex version of the full model is presented in **Figure 9.6**, but if you understand the three central points above, that is good enough.

Sampson and Laub's 'age-graded theory of informal social control' introduced the idea of measuring risk factors across the life course, rather than focusing predominantly on early childhood risk factors like the Gluecks and Farrington. As such, it is considered a **life course theory** of youth offending. Sampson and Laub identified

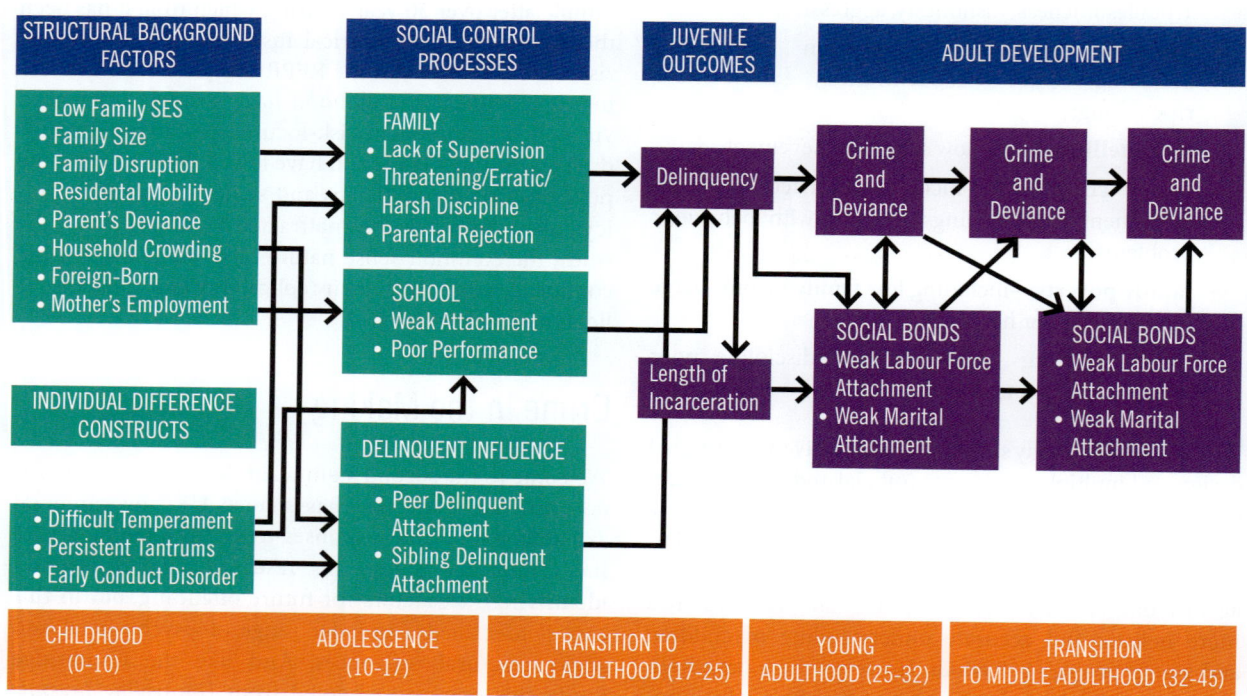

Figure 9.6 Sampson and Laub's (1993) age-graded theory of informal social control

Source: Sampson and Laub (1993), pp. 244–5, Harvard University Press

life events that could interrupt the supposedly predetermined criminal career path, questioning the idea of a stable path of criminal development and an offending **trajectory** that were popular focal points of developmental criminology in the early 1990s following the Cambridge Study (Farrington, 2007). Sampson and Laub argued that turning points and times of transition—important, influential periods or events in an individual's life (such as leaving school, getting a job)—could change an offending trajectory by promoting offending or desistance from offending. Re-analysis of the Gluecks' data identified employment, marriage, and military service as the key turning points which motivated choices to desist from offending. Whereas previously, developmental risk factor explanations of youth offending relied on quantitative (artefactual), developmental, and deterministic understandings of the impact of childhood risk factors (see France and Homel, 2007a), the life course model moved the theory on. It represented a move towards **constructivist** explanations which emphasise the individual's ability to actively construct (create, negotiate, resist) and influence their pathways into and out of crime (see **Chapter 21**)—even if this ability is shaped and constrained by existing risk factors and societal responses to previous behaviour.

Although the Cambridge Study and Sampson and Laub's work remain very influential, developmental explanations have had to adapt in order to recognise variations in patterns of crime. Offending cannot simply be associated with age, for instance, as Smith (2014b) demonstrates by citing widely varying peak ages for different types of offence. This observation has prompted some developmental theorists to suggest that there are alternative pathways, and that it is important to distinguish between what might be seen as 'life-course persistent offending' and 'adolescence-limited offending' (Smith, 2014b: 675), with gender differences much more likely to be evident in the former than the latter. This observation provides potential support for theories which see youth offending as a predictable response to perceptions of unfairness, or restricted opportunities associated with disadvantage.

Explanations using the idea of 'agency'

We have touched on the role played by children and young people's own choices—their agency—throughout our discussion of explanations for youth offending. Many theories, including those of Sampson and Laub (1993) and Wikstrom and Lober (2000), present children and young people as active agents who are capable of making rational choices and decisions (in line with classical and **rational choice** explanations of crime), while also suggesting that external influences such as neighbourhood disadvantage can affect their ability to make and act on these choices and decisions.

To better understand the idea of agency, including its limitations, it is useful to consider **strain theory** and **anomie** (both of which we look at in more detail in **Chapter 17**). Strain theory is the idea that when society puts pressure on people to achieve certain goals, they may turn to criminal behaviour to achieve them if they cannot by legitimate means. Crime can therefore be understood as the product of frustrations generated by the dominant competitive social structure (Merton, 1938). Anomie is when an absence of social norms, rules, or ethical standards create an environment in which people feel free to behave however they like. Agnew (1992) drew on these ideas when he argued, in a well-respected contribution to the debate about causes of offending, that a multilevel model of strain could help to explain deviant choices. He suggested that:

> the general strain theory . . . focuses on three categories of strain or negative relationships with others: (1) the actual or anticipated failure to achieve positively valued goals, (2) the actual or anticipated removal of positively valued stimuli, and (3) the actual or anticipated presentation of negative stimuli.
>
> (Agnew, 1992: 74)

By this, Agnew means that crime becomes more likely in a context where:

1. legitimate social aspirations are not achievable;
2. there are no socially acceptable sources of enjoyment or fulfilment available; and
3. these appear to be offered through undesirable activities (for example, drug use).

He argues that this framework can help us understand the development of delinquency, as these stages illustrate the combined effect of different forms of adversity and the necessity for all three to be in place before a child or young person becomes involved in offending. At the same time, this model also offers a potential explanation for those cases where negative experiences or 'failures' of one kind or another may *not* lead to delinquency, for example where positive personal relationships remain in place.

The idea of choice, situated or otherwise, does not seem to play a part in Agnew's ideas—in fact, its absence is striking. His use of terms like 'stimuli' indicates a deterministic view of criminality, in the sense that children and young people's actions are seen as being shaped and driven by factors outside their control (see also Matza, 1964, 1969). Arguing that the 'general conditions' of social organisation are best represented by a spectrum ranging from freedom to constraint (in relation to an individual's ability to make decisions and exercise choice), Matza suggests that adolescence is an unusual period in which an individual may drift in and out of criminal activity depending on immediate circumstances and events. He says: 'The delinquent *transiently* exists in a limbo between convention and crime, responding to the demands of each, flirting now with one, now the other, but postponing commitment, evading decision' (Matza, 1964: 28, emphasis in original). This portrayal sits more easily with our earlier developmental and life-course observations that certain types of crime are particularly associated with youth, and that becoming an offender does not signal a lifelong commitment or an unbreakable pattern of behaviour.

It might be more appropriate for us to think of delinquency as a product of predisposition, circumstances, and opportunity. The idea of differential opportunity was first put forward by Cloward and Ohlin (1960), who argued that delinquent acts might in fact represent the same kind of decision-making process used in different contexts: 'if goal-oriented behavior occurs under conditions in which there are socially structured obstacles to the satisfaction of these drives by legitimate means, the resulting pressures, we contend, might lead to deviance' (Cloward and Ohlin, 1960: 151). This is strain theory in a nutshell—if there are structural barriers to achieving desired goals legitimately, individuals may turn to illegal means to achieve them. As we will see, this suggests that we need explanations of youth offending which are contextualised and seek to understand the kind of choices and decisions available to children and young people;

recognising that it is the nature of the behaviour or opportunity which is significant from their point of view, rather than its legal status. Some writers have taken this kind of argument further, to suggest that the contextual nature of the choices made by children and young people means that much of what is defined by law as criminal behaviour is actually typical, and is the result of situated decisions which take no account of the legal status of the activity in question. Pitts (2008: 17) points out that youth offending is 'statistically "normal": self-report studies consistently show that between 40 and 98 per cent of adolescents admit to having broken the law in the preceding 12 months'.

To conclude, in this section we have seen that the key criminological explanations of youth offending have been largely individualised and developmental theories, which are grounded in positivism. Whilst some studies have moved beyond the traditional psychosocial and individualising biases of positivism by considering the role of agency, and have begun to acknowledge contextual, socio-structural, and situational influences (cf. Case, 2017), fewer have sought to address the androcentricism and ethnocentrism of explanatory models (although there have been some attempts to challenge these, for example Steffensmeier et al., 2017). This means that there is still a degree of reductionism in explanations of youth offending—a tendency to only explain offending by white males, and only in psychosocial ways.

9.4 Contextual explanations for youth offending

Let's move on to the other broad 'category' of explanation for youth offending: contextual explanations. In **section 9.3**, we saw that some individualised explanations have acknowledged contextual influences to a degree, but generally their emphasis has been on a child or young person's agency. In this section, we consider contextual factors in more depth, looking at the extent to which both cultural and socio-structural factors and processes can help to explain youth offending.

Cultural influences on youth offending

As we saw in **Chapter 6**, cultural influences—that is, the ideas, customs, and environments to which we are exposed—can have a significant impact on our views, allegiances, and patterns of behaviour. Depending on your view of childhood and adolescence, you might feel that children and young people are more likely than adults to be affected by these influences, since their minds and identities are not yet fully formed and they are trying to navigate and establish their place in the world.

Cloward and Ohlin's (1960) subcultural theory (discussed further in **section 17.6**) points to the existence of what they call 'delinquent subcultures' (a subculture is a cultural group within a larger culture which often has different beliefs and customs) in which people do not live by conventional norms and the broadly accepted moral order and do not consider these ideas to be legitimate. Instead, they live according to 'new patterns of conduct which are defined as illegitimate by representatives of official agencies' (Cloward and Ohlin, 1960: 19) but are accepted and even valued by others within the subculture. Examples of such behaviour might be truancy from school, substance use, antisocial behaviour, and offending. Since conventional expectations and routes to achievement do not apply, status and reward become associated with an alternative value system that operates outside (or regardless of) the given legal framework. Cloward and

Ohlin (1960: 20) suggest that deviant subcultures can be subdivided into three categories; those that:

1. hold purely 'criminal values' and involve seeking material rewards by illegitimate means;
2. consist of people whose status is earned by exercising force and gaining domination through violence;
3. represent alienation and a retreat from conventional societal roles. (We can sometimes see this in drug cultures.)

These categories may seem a little simplistic and they are not necessarily mutually exclusive, but all three represent an explicit and conscious rejection of mainstream norms, values, and behavioural expectations. Similarly to the ideas put forward by Agnew and, before him, Merton (1957), Cloward and Ohlin suggest that when regular opportunities or status are denied to young people and alternative routes to some sort of social standing seem attractive, the combination represents a pathway into criminality, and even an alternative rebel identity. Two powerful western-world subcultures that could be described as deviant and are often linked to youth offending are gang culture and radicalisation.

Gang culture and youth offending

Although the term itself is in widespread use, and probably conjures up similar images in your mind and those of your coursemates, the idea of a 'gang' has proved difficult to pin down, at least as an accepted academic term. As long ago as 1927, Thrasher offered the following suggestion, defining a gang as an:

> interstitial group originally formed spontaneously and then integrated through conflict . . . and characterized by . . . meeting face to face, milling, movement through space as a unit, conflict, and planning. The behavior develops a tradition, unreflective internal structure, esprit de corps, solidarity, group awareness and attachment to local territory.
>
> (Thrasher, 1927: 46)

Interestingly, this influential definition does not link gang membership automatically with criminal activity. It does, however, identify self-selection and identification with the idea of being a gang member as important, and this has largely been accepted subsequently. An inbuilt commitment to criminal activity has become more prominent in later definitions, such as Hallsworth and Young's:

> A relatively durable, predominantly street-based group of young people who see themselves (and are seen by others) as a discernible group for whom crime and violence is integral to the group's identity.
>
> (Hallsworth and Young, 2004: 13)

This formulation may appear to be concise and objective, but the way that it presents criminality as an inherent and necessary feature of gang culture reflects a tendency that has been criticised. The government's Gangs Working Group, for example, raised concerns that the idea of 'gangs' had become sensationalised and that this had led to a degree of stereotyping of those believed to be members (Gangs Working Group, 2009).

Pitts's (2008) study of gangs in a UK context therefore attempts to walk a line between sensationalised and over-simplified accounts on the one hand, and the realities of life and life choices in difficult circumstances on the other. He recognises the contextual and structural influences which seem to lead to the formation of a certain type of outsider group with its own sense of identity and embedded meaning, and notes that this is particularly common within black and minority ethnic (BME) communities. For these young people, social conditions may be significantly worse than for their white counterparts and 'the effects of structural youth and adult unemployment and family poverty [can be] exacerbated by negative experiences in school and confrontations with the police in the street' (Pitts, 2008: 64)—we discuss these ideas in **Chapter 10**. Associated with these experiences is what Pitts describes as a negative alternative world view that generates a sense of threat and readiness to resist and respond. The end result may be that these young people 'only feel at ease in the gang' (2008: 65).

As Pitts (2008: 102) goes on to argue, though, the motivations for becoming involved in a gang may be quite complex, rather than a relatively straightforward reaction to societal exclusion. For example, some gang members are 'reluctant gangsters' and have become associated with a gang in order to minimise risks to themselves; whether these risks take the form of threats from other gangs or pressure from their own gang leaders:

> So he tells 'em to 'fuck off'. Anyway, the next thing he knows, someone's shot up his mother's flat. There's lots of families round here can't use their front rooms because of this sort of thing.
>
> (Local resident, quoted in Pitts, 2008: 102)

When we consider this factor together with other less direct and obvious motivations, such as the lack of access to legitimate future prospects (remember our discussion of strain theory in **section 9.3**) and the attraction of 'belonging' to a recognised social group (as suggested by Cloward and Ohlin's subcultural theory), it is clear that there can be a complex, interlocking, and persuasive set of reasons for establishing criminal allegiances. Behaviour which is outlawed at a societal level becomes relatively 'normalised' in the context in which such choices are made. The authors of one major research project noted, for example, that young people 'tended to live in areas of high crime'

(France and Homel, 2007a: 20). Crime was therefore part of everyday life and most of the young people in these areas had regular encounters with criminal activity, as witnesses or even as victims, so it is perhaps not surprising that they engaged with it in 'managing their relationships' with deviance (ibid). The accounts given by two young men in Young et al.'s (2013) qualitative study of the role of family in gang-formation reveal yet more reasons why gang membership can appeal:

> I was thinking to myself, obviously, this is the only way I could get money. I'm not working and what else can I do? Signing on money ain't going far enough; that couldn't even support a sixteen-year-old much less me . . . One of my friends from a long time ago. He used to go to my secondary school, he kind of, not told me to, but he said I should do it . . . [he said] like it's quick, easy money.
>
> When you maybe reach fourteen or thirteen or fifteen, you just feel, 'I'm free!'. You just want to go out now, and you just want to enjoy, you just want to mingle with friends, whatever they're into you're just gonna get into it. It's only when you start growing up you realise what you've done when you're young.
>
> (Young men, quoted in Young et al., 2013)

We can see clearly see the same kinds of motivations in Omar Sharif's account, in **Conversations 9.1**. His story and the quote above give some support to conclusions from Thornberry et al. (2003: 184), who argue that young people join gangs due to a combination of 'push' and 'pull' factors: 'street gangs—populated by friends and families, offering a ready source of fun and action, as well as protection from a hostile world—may be a viable response to the bleakness often confronting these urban, generally poor adolescents'. We can also see these characterisations of situated decision-making in 'pathways' models of youth offending (France and Homel, 2007b). From this perspective, it is unrealistic to try to develop fixed and linear explanations for young people's involvement in crime because human development 'is always contextualised and constructed in dynamic, interactive processes. . . . The person's life is not pre-formed, but rather, its dimensions emerge, are built up, become refined, and either persist or are superseded as the person engages with social others (persons and institutions)' (Lawrence, 2007: 32).

All of this suggests that when we analyse young people's motivations for joining gangs in which criminal behaviours are normal, we should not just think in terms of multiple influences but of factors working in parallel; sometimes mutually supporting, sometimes in conflict, and with different degrees of strength and persuasiveness. We also need to remember that chance events and opportunities may alter the landscape of risk and opportunity from the young person's perspective. If we develop this argument further, we start considering 'contexts' (Goodnow, 2007) and their role in establishing the conditions in which young people make choices. Such ideas could be seen as deriving from concepts like 'habitus' (Bourdieu, 1977), which tries to capture the sense of all the combined factors (social, material, cultural, personal experience) that create the context and preconditions for our decisions and actions.

Radicalisation and youth offending

Radicalisation, the process by which someone comes to adopt extreme political, social, or religious views, is one of the biggest concerns in relation to youth offending today (see Christmann, 2012, for example) because of the number of attacks in recent years on communities in western and European cities which have been linked to 'Islamic extremism' (Christmann, 2012: 6). Although this 'pathway' into crime has only gained prominence in recent years, the search for criminological explanations behind it has followed a similar model to those focusing on more established paths, in other words, looking at 'which contextual features interact with which individual factors through which mechanisms' (Christmann, 2012: 6). Researchers have paid particular attention to the social groupings which are believed to act as catalysts for radicalisation—associating youth criminality with deviant subcultures in a way similar to that suggested by Cohen (1955) and others. They argue that the subcultures of radical groups provide a source of validation and fulfilment for young people who are either alienated or cannot achieve according to conventional expectations. With nothing to gain from living according to mainstream society's rules and norms, they can be expected to turn to alternative means of expression and oppositional belief systems.

We can find echoes of this perspective in the models of the radicalisation process that Christmann (2012: 12) proposes, one of which suggests a four-stage progression:

1. **Pre-radicalisation**—defined in terms of the person's 'vulnerable' life situation.
2. **Self-identification**—the individual begins to associate with new ideas and new social groups, possibly in response to particular alienating trigger events.
3. **Indoctrination**—intensification of beliefs and commitment to the group which represents an alternative value system.
4. **'Jihadisation'**—membership of the group involves complete rejection of conventional society and the individual forgoing their own interests in order to commit to radical social change (in which violence is seen as playing a legitimate part).

CONVERSATIONS 9.1

Gang members? Call us humans
with Omar Sharif

My first gang was my family. This gang provided love, connection, protection, and a sense of belonging. All my key needs were met (all five of Maslow's 'hierarchy of needs'), so this should have been a space where I could feel safe and flourish. However, family support couldn't make up for the fact that I felt failed by the system and excluded by society. I joined a 'real' gang at the age of 14 for my own safety and in order to feel more significant. Yes, it was partly to boost my fragile and immature masculine ego, but this only needed boosting because I felt excluded and purposeless.

One memory that will always stay with me is when I was stopped and searched on Edgware Road, a stone's throw away from my house. I offered no resistance but still the officers felt the need to put my face against the cold, wet slab of concrete, multiple knees pressing into my body. This was simply because I fitted the description of someone they were looking for, and it happened in front of my mum—I'd gone to help her carry her shopping.

This is only one example, and I've experienced many similarly unjust events, but I have never forgotten the humiliation of it and the anger I felt towards those white police officers. The situation deepened my hate for the police force and anything that had to do with the law because yet again, I was the victim of police autocratic behaviour and received no apology. It was just a 'routine check', in the words of the officer.

Many people, including members of the police, have no clue what it feels like to experience constant injustice because of your social class, ethnicity, or religion, and the impact this can have. From interviewing gang members and prisoners, I've found that many of them grew up with unfairness and oppression, feeling like outcasts because of the way society viewed and treated them, and threatened with arrest when they wanted to express their emotions. The common thread in their stories is that there was a real sense of love and purpose missing from their lives at the time when they joined their gang.

Although the purpose of a gang is not to commit nefarious activities or terrorise society—it's normally the result of one individual creating an idea which resolves conflict, solves a struggle that the gang members all have in common, and provides an adrenaline rush—having been involved in gang culture I can easily see why eventually crime becomes a natural part of the territory. There are multiple factors working in parallel which make it an appealing option for young people.

When my involvement in a gang led me to start taking part in criminal activity with financial reward, I justified this to myself because it was to support my parents. I have a vivid memory of my mum huddling me and my four siblings into the corner of a room, telling us to be quiet as there was a monster at the door. That 'monster' was a bailiff man who had come to take our belongings due to unpaid bills.

You may be wondering, why not support your parents another way? The answer is, turning to crime is a natural progression for anyone involved in gang culture, and this felt like the best option as other doors were closed against me. I'd been refused multiple job opportunities based on the colour of my skin or because of my lack of experience, and you cannot gain experience if employers don't want to invest in potential.

Becoming an adult is challenging enough for many reasons, but to gain a sense of fulfilment and independence, we must be able to support ourselves financially. Some of us feel we are denied this right because of wilful ignorance and not being given a chance to earn an honest living. When an opportunity to make decent money presents itself to someone exhausted by trying to be an upstanding member of society and facing constant rejection, it takes a lot of courage to say no.

So how can we stop people turning to gang membership and criminal activity? This is hard to address in brief, and even harder to achieve in practice. It would mean rewiring the psychology of humanity and undoing decades of unjust behaviour and understandings of class and race.

How can we begin this process? This is a more realistic goal, and I think the starting point is focusing on accountability. Every individual must be responsible for their own values and beliefs, and communities need to do a better job of coming together and educating young people in the right way.

Most importantly, we must remember that everyone is a human. Gang members are just people looking for a sense of belonging in a society which constantly excludes them. If we strive for humanity then instead of creating division and amplifying a way of life that is particularly damaging for young people, we will be able to offer support and guidance to those who need it most.

Omar Sharif, Breakthrough Coach and Director of Omar Inspires. Winner of the Pride of Britain Award 2018

In some cases, this sort of process is set out as a pathway model (Gill, 2007), making it seem consistent with the routes into 'normal' crime set out by France and Homel (2007a). Radicalisation, like youth offending in general, is explained in terms of a combination of biological, psychological, and societal theories (Christmann, 2012), with emphasis placed on a number of risk factors (as well as being male; Bakker 2006). These risk factors include: emotional vulnerability; dissatisfaction or disillusionment; identification with the suffering of other Muslims; the conviction that action—including violence—against the state is legitimate; gaining benefits from being part of an identifiable group or cause; reinforcement through valued and meaningful social links (Christmann, 2012: 33). Some of the factors and contexts thought to combine to explain radicalisation are shown diagrammatically in **Figure 9.7**.

Described in this way, the process of radicalisation seems to follow a similar trajectory to processes of becoming delinquent that, as we saw, have been mapped out by earlier scholars. Again, 'push' and 'pull' factors seem to be operating:

The group members begin to exhibit a greater cohesiveness and sense of mutual dependence. They learn to define more closely those who are friendly or hostile to their activities. The experience of arrest, court adjudication of some members of the group casts a new light on the meaning and consequences of their activities.

(Cloward and Ohlin, 1960: 142)

Pitts (2008: 112), however, cautions us against applying what is essentially a 'deficit model' to the behaviours of those whose criminality takes the form of challenging state power—in other words, that we should avoid focusing on perceived weaknesses and flaws of the individual. Not only does this overlook the political dimensions of their actions, but it also denies them agency, with the result that interventions to address their behaviour tend to be misjudged and ineffective. Pitts (2008: 112) suggests that we should instead consider developing 'politicised responses which aim to establish solidarity with these embattled young people, rather than ones which simply aim to cure or suppress them in equal measure'.

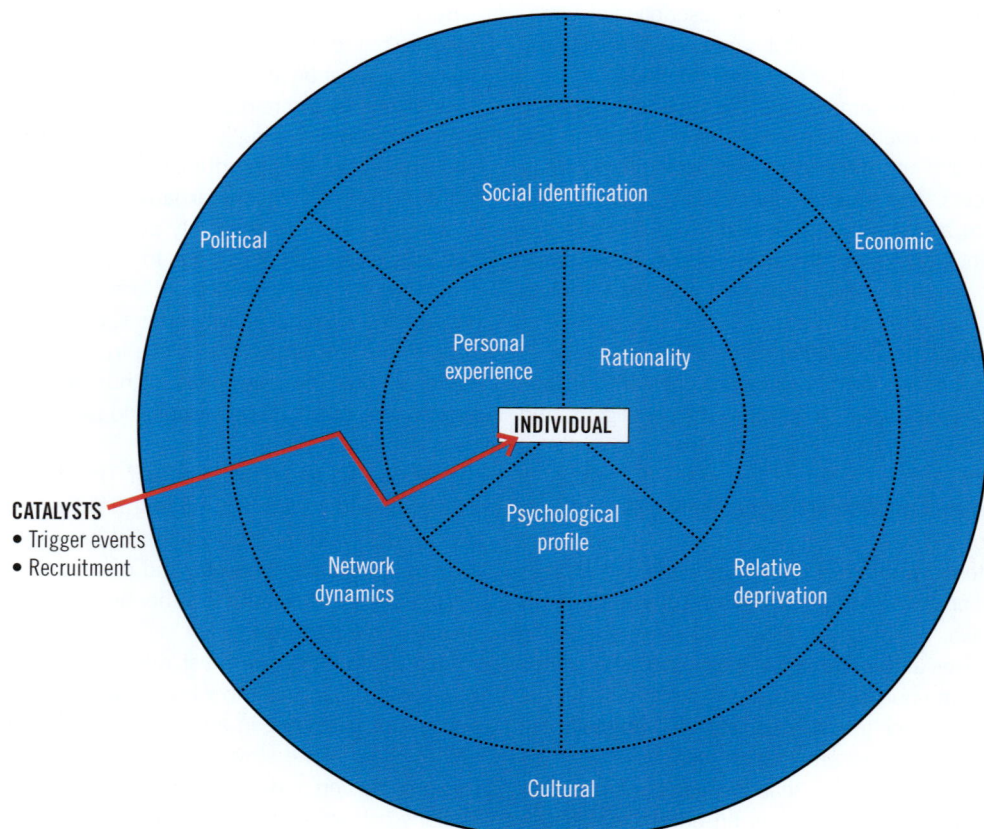

Figure 9.7 Like youth offending more generally, radicalisation is often seen as the result of biological, psychological, and societal factors combining with catalyst events to affect an individual's choices and views
Source: ELSJ

The role of social structures and processes

As we have seen, a lot of criminological work focuses on young people and their behaviour with the aim of discovering what it is about some of them that makes them turn to crime. There is, however, another way of asking the question, and this is to turn the spotlight on the social structures and processes which, it could be argued, criminalise young people. Here, we look at the social construction of the 'youth offender' and the ways in which society could be seen as amplifying deviance.

Constructing 'youth offenders'

The concept of crime itself is a social construction (a theme we first explored in **Chapter 2** but return to throughout this book), so definitions of what is legal, what is not, and who is defined as an offender are all dependent on the way in which that concept is put into practice (Case, 2018). In this sense, ideas of crime and delinquency are problematic since they depend on the perspective and power of those who create and enforce the distinctions between legality and illegality. This comes into play at all levels of the system, from the initial action of determining what is or is not an offence, through the decisions about how to implement and prioritise enforcement action, to encounters between criminal justice workers and young people which contribute (or not) to their criminalisation. Viewing children and young people who offend as (to some degree) *victims* of the criminalising, stigmatising, and marginalising processes of the YJS—which include labelling, excessive intervention, and targeting 'at risk' populations—is an increasingly popular way of exploring youth offending and justice.

A vocal group of youth justice academics and researchers with a critical criminology agenda (such as John Muncie, Barry Goldson, John Pitts, Tim Bateman, Jo Phoenix, and two of this book's authors, Steve Case and Roger Smith) have challenged the negative, individualising, and criminalising nature of dominant positivist explanations of youth offending. They also criticise the resulting individualised responses to youth offending (including youth justice policies and practices) on the grounds that they tend to place too much responsibility on children, young people, and their families for this behaviour and the success of any responses to it—what Muncie (2004) called responsibilisation. They argue instead that responsibilisation ignores a wealth of evidence that children and young people are not sufficiently mature (physically, psychologically, and emotionally) to accept full responsibility for criminal actions, whilst also ignoring external (contextual, cultural, and socio-structural) influences on offending behaviour.

One example that could be seen to support this argument is the experience of children and young people from BME communities in the UK, who (as we explore further in **Chapter 10**) statistics show to have been consistently over-represented amongst those drawn into the justice system and criminalised. One major study commissioned by the Youth Justice Board found a series of inconsistencies in the way certain ethnic groups were treated, including:

- a higher (than the average) rate of prosecution and conviction for mixed-parentage children and young people;
- a higher (than average) proportion of black and Asian males remanded in custody;
- a slightly greater (than average) use of custody for Asian males;
- a much greater proportion (than average) of mixed-parentage females being prosecuted (Feilzer and Hood, 2004: 27).

Other studies have found similar patterns: see, for example, May et al. (2010). The 2017 Lammy Review of the 'treatment and outcomes' of black, Asian and minority ethnic people in the YJS also found evidence of consistent over-representation of minority groups at every stage of the criminal process. The review, 'commissioned by two Prime Ministers' (as it states) and led by David Lammy MP, reported that:

> The BAME proportion of children and young people offending for the first time rose from 11% year ending March 2006 to 19% year ending March 2016 . . .
> The BAME proportion of young people reoffending rose from 11% year ending March 2006 to 19% year ending March 2016 . . .
> The BAME proportion of youth [under 18] prisoners has risen from 25% to 41% in the decade 2006–2016.

We might conclude from these statements that material injustices (for example, poverty, lack of opportunities, and systemic discrimination—see Lammy, 2017) can be exacerbated by additional social processes which ascribe certain criminalised identities to certain groups, almost irrespective of their members' own life histories and characteristics. Indeed, such discriminatory racial disparities and their associated processes of criminalisation have been recently placed under the spotlight in the YJS and the wider societal context by the Black Lives Matter movement and have arguably been exacerbated by the global Covid-19 pandemic (see Bateman 2020). This kind of mechanism was first described in the context of labelling theory, which was associated with a number of leading criminological theorists of the 1960s, including Becker (1963), Lemert (1967), and Kitsuse (1962). We can find what might be seen as a more contemporary version of this mechanism in the concept of '**othering**' which is particularly associated with Garland (2001). Labelling theory has tried to set out a two-stage process in which the initial commission of an offence (primary deviance) is then compounded by the experience of being processed and formally identified as an offender (leading to secondary deviance, as the identity placed on the person becomes self-fulfilling).

Becker's (1963) argument was that a wide range of behaviours could be said to deviate from conventional expectations, but that in themselves these behaviours might not have any particular consequences for the individual—substance use could be seen as one example. Lemert (1967: 17) agrees, suggesting that primary deviation can occur in a range of social settings and in itself, it has only 'marginal implications [for the individual] . . . it does not lead to symbolic reorganization at the level of self-regarding attitudes and social roles'. In other words, someone's choice to act in a way that is outside social norms does not, in itself, make them see themselves as a criminal. On the other hand, Becker (1963) and Lemert (1967) suggest that secondary deviance is a reaction to society's response to perceived primary deviation. This means that the initial causes of the outlawed behaviour become less influential, and society's disapproval and punitive interventions become more important, in relative terms, in shaping the offender's future behaviour. Of course, as McNeill and Barry (2009) point out, it is not just that giving someone a label might enhance the likelihood of them taking part in further deviant activity; labelling also contributes to the **stigmatisation** of children and young people in trouble so that they are more noticeable, and perhaps more likely to come to official attention again and be further criminalised, even if their behaviour is unexceptional.

Research has demonstrated that such suggestions are more than just speculation. McAra and McVie (2007, 2017), drawing on findings from the *Edinburgh Study of Youth Transitions and Crime* (see also **Chapter 21**), have been able to describe the effect of system contact in some detail. Their analysis shows that criminalisation of children and young people depended extensively on selective police responses, such that 'boys and disadvantaged children' were found to be discriminated against by patrolling police officers in terms of the initial decision on whether or not to bring charges (McAra and McVie, 2007: 326). More dramatically, however, they found that children 'who reported that they had been charged in previous years were *over seven times* more likely to be charged at age 15' than those who had not been charged previously (2007: 327, emphasis in original).

This labelling effect appears to operate independently of children and young people's actual level of involvement in criminal behaviour. According to McAra and McVie (2007: 337), their observations suggest that there is in effect a kind of recruitment process in operation: certain young people become identified as the 'usual suspects' and become repeatedly reprocessed by the justice system, irrespective of their actual levels or pattern of offending or need. By contrast, they note that where decisions are taken to divert young people from formal interventions (including custody), their levels of serious offending appear to decline. These findings could be seen to support the arguments made by Lemert (1967) in particular, but they also challenge the idea that it is system contact that brings about further deviancy. The implication here is that once the system has formed a judgement on a child or young person, it will continue to treat them as an offender (or not), regardless of their behaviour.

The 'amplification of deviance'

The findings of the *Edinburgh Study* appear to reflect the 'amplification of deviance' thesis (Wilkins, 1964); this is the suggestion that the YJS not only reacts to children and young people's deviant behaviour, but plays a significant part in escalating it, both directly (for example, by encouraging the child or young person to reoffend) and in the way in which it is dramatised and represented in the public domain and the media.

Alongside the responses from formal representatives of the YJS, which we consider in **section 9.5**, we must also take account of the role of the media in problematising children, young people, and their behaviour. This process was revealed by Cohen's (1972) 'Folk Devils and Moral Panics', a study we considered in **Chapter 6**—see **section 6.2**. Cohen showed the media to have been responsible, first, for portraying a massively overblown and over-problematised picture of a confrontation between two groups of children and young people, the Mods and the Rockers and, secondly, for escalating the situation by acting as a sort of rallying call, inviting children and young people to take part in further re-enactments of the supposed 'battles' that had taken place. The same accusations could perhaps be made of the media, and specifically social media, in the context of the riots around the UK in summer 2011. Consider further examples of **deviancy amplification** in **What do you think? 9.3**.

In Cohen's (1972) view, the media response was effective partly because of its interaction with other agents of control; it repeated what the courts said about the deviant behaviour, effectively telling stories about stories until the reports became true. Cohen (1972) reports that a relatively minor incident in Clacton (a series of scuffles on the seafront between Mods and Rockers) produced a mass of headlines which created an expectation of further disruption and violence and led to the demonisation of

WHAT DO YOU THINK? 9.3

Deviancy amplification in the media

As we saw in **Chapter 6**, the news media have historically represented children and young people as problematic, risky, dangerous, and out of control, as well as helping to fuel the view that the youth offending 'problem' is both new and worse now than it has ever been. What do you think about such (mis)representations? Take a look at the selected headlines, photographs (**Figures 9.8, 9.9, 9.10,** and **9.11**), and printed social commentaries from newspapers in this box and see if you can spot a pattern in the representation of 'youth'; a pattern that arguably challenges the view of 'problem youth' as a contemporary social construction. Consider the media coverage you have seen of children and young people lately, for example in relation to those breaking Covid-19 restrictions—are they still represented in the same kinds of ways?

19th century

> Morals are getting much worse. When I was young my mother would have knocked me down for speaking improperly to her.
>
> (Newspaper editorial, 1843)

Early 20th century

> The passing of parental authority, defiance of pre-war conditions, the absence of restraint, the wildness of extremes . . . are but a few characteristics of after-war conditions.
>
> (Boys' club leader, 1932, referring to the First World War 1914–18)

Figure 9.9 (Mis?)Representations of youth over the years: 20th century
Source: Nationaal Archief @Flickr Commons/Public domain

Figure 9.8 (Mis?)Representations of youth over the years: 19th century
Source: Gavin Wilson (Flickr)

Figure 9.10 (Mis?)Representations of youth over the years: 1950s/1960s
Source: Mary Evans Picture Library

1950s/1960s

The adolescent has learned no definite moral standards from his parents, is contemptuous of the law, easily bored.

(British Medical Association, 1961)

There has been a decline in the disciplinary forces governing a child. Obedience and respect for law have decreased.

(*The Times*, 1952)

21st century

British youths are 'the most unpleasant and violent in the world': Damning verdict of writer as globe reacts to riots.

(*Daily Mail* headline, 10 August 2011)

[P]eople nationally are sick of kids making their life hell . . . it never happened in the 1950s.

(Letter to provincial newspaper, 2005)

Figure 9.11 (Mis?)Representations of youth over the years: 21st century
Source: Andy Sewell

large groups of children and young people. Other studies have reached similar conclusions about the media's role in orchestrating reactions to what might be called signal events, and in the process contributing to the formulation and perpetuation of stereotyped views of threatening or dangerous youth. In the case of 'mugging' (the media-constructed label for violent street robbery), graphically illustrated by Hall et al. (2013), the threat was also racialised, helping to support and amplify another stereotypical assumption, locating criminality amongst black young people (Hall et al., 2013: 324).

The 1990s was a particularly significant period in terms of reconstructing children and young people who offended as 'youth offenders' who were irresponsible, immoral, evil, and dangerous (cf. Case, 2017). This radical reconstruction of youth offenders was in part based on the intense politicisation of the issue during that decade, with one Home Secretary proclaiming 'prison works!', whereas the New Labour mantra was 'Tough on crime, tough on the causes of crime'. However, the urgent need for a new approach to youth justice policy and practice, driven by the reconstruction of youthful offenders as dangerous, was largely sparked by a single horrific event in England—the murder of Jamie Bulger (see **Controversy and debate 9.1**).

As we have discussed, the most widely accepted explanations of youth offending in the western world have mainly been positivist. They have produced a series of explanations focused on the *individual* child or young person, their biology, psychology, exposure to developmental (psychosocial) risk factors, and their experiences of critical life events/turning points. Consequently, the explanations for youth offending offered by academics, politicians, the media, and those working in the YJS have typically 'othered' children and young people who offend (Kelly, 2012) and marked them out as a problematic, dangerous, irresponsible, and risky population which is in need of control and punishment (Haines and Case, 2015). The source of youth offending, according to these explanations, is clearly 'them'— children and young people.

However, we have also seen that alternative explanations have emerged which suggest children and young people's individual choices to offend are mediated and perhaps mitigated by external, structural, and systemic influences that are both **criminogenic** (crime-causing) and constructed by adults—for example, neighbourhood disorganisation, social deprivation, and discrimination (see the Black Lives Matter movement as a response to this issue—Bateman, 2020). This interplay between individual choices and (largely) structural issues suggests that there is a similar interplay between 'them' (children or young people) and 'us' (adults, agents of the state, society) in terms of contributions to explanations of youth offending. This less individualising and more holistic explanatory trend has been advanced by cultural explanations which have again focused on the criminalising role of contextual and structural factors beyond the individual child or young person's control to suggest that these things can perpetuate criminogenic outcomes such as gang membership, radicalisation, and deviancy amplification by the media. In this respect, the emphasis of explanations turns 180 degrees towards 'us'—the adult key 'stakeholders' (people with interests in a particular matter) and decision-makers who create or socially construct these criminogenic contexts and structures.

Given that youth offending may be (at least in part) either the fault or creation of 'them', the product of an interaction between 'us' and 'them', or the social construction of 'us', the big question emerging from this complex issue is: how should we respond to offending behaviour by children and young people?

CONTROVERSY AND DEBATE 9.1

Jamie Bulger and the abolition of *doli incapax*

On 12 February 1993, two-year-old Jamie Bulger was abducted, tortured, and murdered by two ten-year-old boys in Bootle, a town just outside Liverpool in North West England. The **moral panic** that ensued in the news media led to children and young people who offend being represented as 'evil', where previously ten-year-olds were more likely to be considered innocent children requiring welfare and protection (Jenks, 1996). With one horrific act, children or young people who offended became seen as wicked, immoral, but still wilful individuals who were fully responsible and accountable for their actions (known as responsibilisation); and as such they should be punished as if they were adults (**adultification**).

The Bulger murder instigated 'the politicization of juvenile crime' and significantly influenced the way in which child 'offenders' were socially constructed subsequently (Goldson, 2013). A climate of 'institutionalized intolerance' emerged (Muncie, 2004) in which it became impossible to debate decriminalising measures such as raising the age of criminal responsibility. Consistent with this, the Crime and Disorder Act 1998 abolished **doli incapax**—the presumption in law that said children or young people aged from 10 to 14 years old could not tell the difference between right and wrong so could only be convicted of an offence if this presumption was found to be wrong by the court in specific cases. (The Latin literally translates as 'incapable of crime'.) In a sense, *doli incapax* represented the presumption of innocence in childhood and was designed to keep children or young people under 14 out of the YJS. Abolition represented 'an effective lowering of the age' of criminal responsibility (Bateman, 2012: 5) and led to the statutory construction of the ten-year-old child 'offender' as a fully responsibilised and adultified agent, whereas the age of criminal responsibility elsewhere in Europe was higher (Crofts, 2009: 268).

The abolition of *doli incapax* epitomised the contradictory views of children and young people which prevailed in England and Wales. The Crime and Disorder Act contrasted with the welfare-based Children Act 1989, which gave anyone under the age of 18 the status of 'child'. In fact, both of these Acts of Parliament accord with Art. 1 of the United Nations Convention on the Rights of the Child (UNICEF, 1989) by distinguishing a child as 'every human being below the age of 18 years'. On the other hand, there are clear differences in their prescriptions for the treatment of children if their behaviour becomes problematic—in terms of punishment, control, and the prevention of risk (Crime and Disorder Act) versus vulnerability, need, and protection (Children Act).

9.5 Mainstream responses to youth offending

In the previous section, we looked at ways of explaining youth offending, exploring the three main types of criminological explanation as well as the ways in which culture and societal structures and systems can also contribute to and even cause children and young people's deviant behaviour or criminalisation. In this section of the chapter, we will consider both formal and more informal, progressive responses to children and young people's offending behaviour, looking particularly at the dominance of early intervention and risk management approaches in shaping responses to youth offending.

Although, as we saw in **section 9.4**, a 'new youth justice' movement has emerged in both academia and practice to challenge the traditionally negative depictions of 'young offenders' and individualised explanations of offending, it is still the case that positivist and developmental risk-based theories dominate when politicians, policymakers, and other key stakeholders decide how to respond to youth offending in England and Wales (and in many other westernised countries). These theories still hold considerable appeal for their seemingly common-sense, evidence-based, and practical nature (see Case and Haines, 2015, 2009). As we discussed in **section 9.3**, the RFPP, or Risk Factor Prevention Paradigm, has become *the* model for explaining and responding to youth offending, to the extent that 'the risk-factors and prediction paradigms have taken hold of criminology' (Laub and Sampson, 2003: 289). Governments across the UK, Western Europe, North America, and Australasia use risk-assessment tools within YJSs to quantify risk factors and decide on appropriate responses to offending (see Kemshall, 2008). The responses to youth offending that are considered 'appropriate' and 'effective' have therefore been mainly risk-focused; aiming to identify, measure, and reduce children and young people's exposure to risk factors before they offend (that is, early intervention) or once they have offended (that is, risk management). The guiding objective here is *preventing* youth offending by responding to the risks that children and young people supposedly present to themselves and others (Goldson, 2005), as opposed to trying to address the welfare needs of children and young people or to deliver justice based on the offence committed.

The introduction of the Crime and Disorder Act 1998—which, as we saw in **Controversy and debate 9.1**, abolished the presumption of *doli incapax*—played a significant role in establishing this prevention-focused mindset in the YJS. Previously, governments had claimed they would be 'tough on crime, tough on the causes of crime' and would 'nip offending in the bud' (see **Chapter 25**), and the 1998 Act meant that these aims would be delivered through an emphasis on prevention and a deprioritisation of welfare and justice. This emphasis has persisted ever since:

> It shall be the principal aim of the YJS to prevent offending.
>
> (Crime and Disorder Act 1998, s. 37)

> Prevention is the cheapest and most effective way to deal with crime.
>
> (David Cameron, UK Prime Minister, 2012)

> Labour will introduce youth clubs across the country in an effort to combat knife crime
>
> (*The Times*, 8 October 2019)

Prevention and early intervention activity with children and young people within and outside the YJS (in England and Wales) can be associated with one of three main popular approaches, shown in **Figure 9.12** as a triad of risk-based crime reduction and prevention:

1. **Reduction of crime:** Targeted reduction of established negative behaviours/outcomes for (convicted) children and young people within the YJS.

2. **Reduction of risk:** Targeted reduction of the risk factors (that predict negative behaviours/outcomes) experienced by (convicted) children and young people within the YJS (for example, the 'Scaled Approach', which we discuss later).

3. **Early intervention to prevent crime/risk:** Targeted early intervention within the behavioural trajectories of children and young people outside the YJS who are considered 'at risk' of negative behaviours/outcomes—in other words, targeting children and young people who are experiencing exposure to risk factors but have not yet committed an offence.

You might have noticed that all three approaches are in some way negative, risk-based, and aiming to reduce and prevent crime (Case and Haines, 2015). They claim to be focused on prevention but in practice they often prioritise reducing existing problems (largely for short-term political gain or 'quick wins') rather than striving to prevent future ones (Case and Haines, 2015), meaning that the majority of youth justice prevention work takes place with identified offenders (or those considered 'at risk' of offending) and is situated within the formal YJS. There appears to be some confusion over what should be classified as prevention of offending, compared to early intervention and reduction of reoffending.

In the next subsection we will examine the main tools currently used to achieve the objective of prevention: *Asset*, which focuses on children and young people already in the YJS and aims to prevent reoffending or reconviction (approaches 1 and 2 in the previous list), and *Onset*, which focuses on children and young people who are outside or on the brink of the system but who have yet to offend and assesses risk factors for the 'onset' of offending, hence the name (approach 3). (Unlike the complex labels applied to much youth justice policy and practice guidance, *Asset* and *Onset* are not acronyms.)

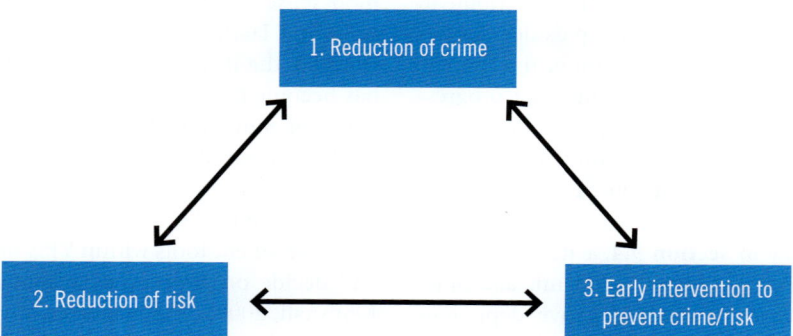

Figure 9.12 Prevention and early intervention activity with children and young people can be associated with three main approaches, shown here as a triad

Risk-focused interventions for children and young people in the YJS: *Asset*

We have noted that in practice, much early intervention in the YJS takes place once a child or young person has been officially identified as 'at risk' of offending and deals with the child or young person (largely) as an offender, using a range of offence- and offender-first interventions (for example, offending behaviour-management programmes, cognitive-behavioural therapy, and restorative justice). Supporters of risk-focused early intervention argue that it offers a logical, effective, and economical preventative approach (Farrington, 2007), especially when used in conjunction with rigorously evaluated, evidence-based 'what works' intervention programmes (Sherman et al., 1998; see also **Chapter 22**).

The Youth Justice Board or YJB, the body that monitors and manages the YJS of England and Wales, has produced a series of Key Elements of Effective Practice (KEEPs) to promote a consistent, evidence-based approach to working with children and young people (YJB, 2003), with the most important KEEP being the practical realisation of the RFPP. Each KEEP focuses on a key area of youth justice practice, which can include: education, training and employment, mental health, substance use, young people who sexually abuse, offending behaviour programmes, parenting, restorative justice, mentoring, targeted neighbourhood intervention, final warning interventions, swift administration of justice, intensive supervision and surveillance, custody, and resettlement (Stephenson et al. 2013; Case and Haines, 2009). The central KEEP is 'Assessment, Planning Interventions and Supervision' (APIS), which is underpinned by the RFPP and outlines 'foundation activities which guide and shape all work with young people who offend' (YJB, 2003: 6) and which are considered crucial to the successful execution of the other KEEPs. These foundation activities are basically to assess levels of risk in young people's lives so that the system can use the most effective services and interventions to reduce the assessed risk through 'dependable methods'.

These dependable methods are essentially the use of *Asset*. The YJB introduced this assessment tool in April 2000 because:

> All children and young people entering the YJS should benefit from a structured assessment . . . to identify the risk factors associated with offending behaviour and to inform effective intervention programmes.
>
> (YJB, 2004: 27)

Asset is a questionnaire that measures risk factors in different psychosocial developmental domains (areas) of a child or young person's life in order to explain offending and inform service development and intervention planning. It is completed by practitioners from multi-agency youth offending teams (YOTs) whenever a child or young person aged 10–17 enters the YJS (Baker, 2005). The practitioner holds an interview with the child or young person which centres around a series of questions relating to their current or recent exposure to 'dynamic' (capable of changing) risk factors in 12 domains:

1. **living arrangements** (living with known offenders);
2. **family and personal relationships** (family/carers involved in criminal activity);
3. **education, training, and employment** (regular truancy);
4. **neighbourhood** (signs of drug dealing);
5. **lifestyle** (associating with delinquent peers);
6. **substance use** (detrimental effect on daily functioning);
7. **physical health** (physical immaturity);
8. **emotional and mental health** (concerns about the future);
9. **perception of self and others** (difficulties with self-identity);
10. **thinking and behaviour** (impulsivity);
11. **attitudes to offending** (reluctance to accept responsibility for behaviour);
12. **motivation to change** (understanding of problematic behaviour).

The 'core profile' of *Asset* is supplemented by four additional sections (see YJB, 2007):

- **positive (protective) factors** (positive attitudes);
- **indicators of vulnerability** (vulnerability to physical or emotional harm);
- **indicators of serious harm to others** (evidence of actual harmful behaviour);
- **what do you think** (the child or young person reports their thoughts and feelings regarding issues about their life and offending).

The complex interrelationships between *Asset* risk domains and (persistent) offending behaviour are depicted in **Figure 9.13**.

When practitioners have responded to the questions in each domain (that is, have given yes/no answers to whether a given risk factor is present), they complete an explanations box in which they provide narrative evidence of what they judge the influence of these risks to be. This narrative is the evidence base for subsequent decisions and judgements regarding how to respond to that child or young person. (This is a potential weakness of *Asset*: the

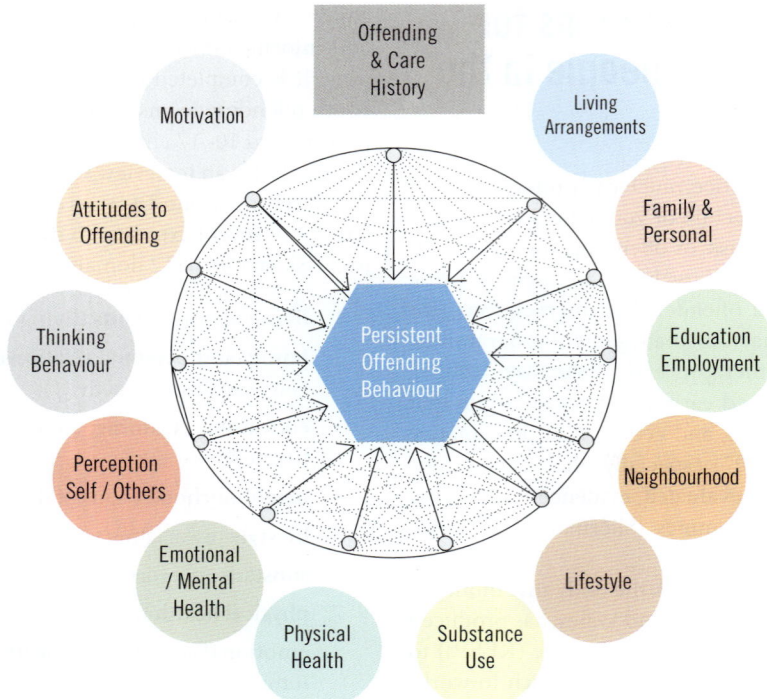

Figure 9.13 The interrelationships between *Asset* risk domains and (persistent) offending behaviour are complex

Source: Centre for Youth and Criminal Justice 2016

level of practitioner subjectivity required in its execution could promote bias and inconsistency within and between the multi-agency YOTs that implement the tool.) Finally, practitioners have to make a generalised quantitative judgement on a five-point scale (though 4 is the maximum rating, since 0 is included) about the extent to which they feel the group of risk factors in each domain, when taken together, are associated with 'the likelihood of further offending'. The significance of each rating is as follows:

- 0 = no association;
- 1 = slight or limited indirect association;
- 2 = moderate direct or indirect association;
- 3 = quite strong association, normally direct;
- 4 = very strong, clear, and direct association.

The ratings for each psychosocial domain are added up to give the child or young person an overall risk score from 0–64 (since there are 16 domains in total, and each is scored 0–4). This overall, or 'aggregate', score determines whether the child or young person is assessed as being a low, medium, or high risk of being reconvicted in the 12 months following the assessment.

In 2009, the UK government brought YJS practice even more closely in line with the RFPP by introducing the 'scaled approach' to assessment and intervention. Under this framework, YOT practitioners tailor (or 'scale') the frequency, duration, and intensity of planned interventions according to the levels of risk suggested by the child or young person's *Asset* score, with interventions categorised as: standard/low likelihood of reconviction (*Asset* score of 0–14), enhanced/medium likelihood (15–32), and intensive/high likelihood (33+). Consequently, an intervention categorised as standard/low likelihood of reconviction would be less intense, not so long, and delivered less frequently than those for intensive/high likelihood.

Risk-focused interventions for children and young people outside the YJS: *Onset*

When it comes to children and young people outside the formal YJS, the focus on prevention has manifested in two large-scale programmes: Youth Inclusion and Support Panels (YISPs) and Youth Inclusion Programmes (YIPs). Young people are referred to these programmes through the use of a pre-offending risk assessment tool called *Onset*.

Onset was introduced in April 2003 for key stakeholder agencies such as the police, social services, education, and health to use with children and young people aged 8–13 years (despite ten years being the minimum age of criminal responsibility) in order to identify whether they are 'at risk' of offending in the future. *Onset* involves risk-focused early intervention, with 'early' taken to mean pre-offending, so preventing the onset of offending, rather than preventing existing offending behaviour from continuing or getting worse (Case and Haines, 2009). The *Onset* assessment is divided into sections that broadly correspond in content and structure to those in *Asset*, with risk rated by practitioners in a similar way, on the same 0 to 4 scale, in order to identify the areas that should become the priority for *Onset*-informed interventions.

The *Onset* process was developed specifically for use by YISPs with children and young people who are considered to be pre-crime and 'at risk' of offending. YISPs began in April 2003 in 13 pilot areas and subsequently expanded across the country. They are panels with representatives from different agencies working with children and young people; in particular the statutory agencies of police, education, health, and social services. They aim to prevent offending and antisocial behaviour by 8–13-year-olds (or 14–18-year-olds in the case of the YISP+ programme) who have been identified by referring agencies (using *Onset*) as 'at risk' of offending in order to ensure that these children and young people and their families can access mainstream services at the earliest possible stage (although participation is voluntary).

YIPs are tailor-made programmes for children and young people living in particularly socially deprived, high crime (and therefore 'high risk') neighbourhoods. They were established by the YJB in 2000 in response to demands for further investment in targeted preventative activity with young people in these areas, and they focus on 8–17-year-olds (Junior YIPs for 8–12-year-olds; Senior YIPs for 13–17-year-olds) living in over 100 neighbourhoods in England and Wales (YJB, 2006). The YJB has outlined a series of key objectives for YIPs:

- to engage with those young people considered to be most at risk of offending and reoffending in a particular neighbourhood;
- to address the risk and protective factors identified by *Onset* assessments;
- to prevent and reduce offending through intervention with individuals, families, and communities (YJB, 2006).

Criticisms of risk-focused responses: *AssetPlus*

The assessment and intervention frameworks used with children and young people in the YJS (*Asset* and the scaled approach) and outside/on the brink of the system (*Onset* and YISPs/YIPs) are underpinned by a risk management approach to prevention and early intervention—the need to identify and manage 'risk factors' that could lead to future and further offending. In our analyses of risk-based explanations of, and responses to, offending elsewhere in this chapter and book, we have noted that these approaches can be criticised for their *reductionism* (see **Chapter 4**; see also Case, 2017; Case and Haines, 2015, 2009): the fact that they gradually move understandings of youth offending further away from the child or young person's own interpretations and experiences of their lives (see France and Homel, 2007a). For example, *Asset* involves adult practitioners simplistically reducing the realities of children and young people's lives to a series of generalised ratings that supposedly indicate their likelihood of further offending. The act of oversimplifying potentially complex and dynamic aspects of children and young people's lives into quantifiable and targetable risk factors has been criticised as an exercise in reductionism which produces results that do not necessarily represent the 'lived realities' of children and young people (see Case, 2018; Kemshall, 2008; France and Homel, 2007a).

We could also criticise the risk management approach on the basis that its assessment tools involve individualising the explanations of, and responsibility for, offending. The fact that these tools measure psychosocial risk factors places the responsibility (blame) for offending with the child or young person and their inability to resist these risk factors, rather than examining the potential influence of broader issues. Such broader issues could include socio-structural factors (for example, social class, poverty, unemployment, social deprivation, ethnicity), the absence of support mechanisms, or the external influence of others (for example, youth justice agencies, schools, youth provision) (France and Homel, 2007a, 2007b). We might argue that it is strange to give so much responsibility (that is, apply *responsibilisation*—Muncie, 2004) to a demographic group (children and young people aged 10–17) who are not given many other social responsibilities or capabilities because of their age. In England and Wales, this age group cannot vote, drive a car, own a house, have sex, or marry, but they are seen as possessing full responsibility for committing a complex, subjective, and socially constructed act that is influenced (at least in part) by factors outside their control (Case and Haines, 2009).

Another criticism levelled at risk management is that scaling intervention proportionately in response to assessed, quantified levels of risk is not only ineffective but also unethical because it can be pre-emptive and disproportionate—see, for example, Case (2018) and Bateman (2011). It is pre-emptive in that risk-based early intervention, such as the scaled approach, intervenes in the lives of children and young people on the basis of what they are predicted to do in the future rather than what they have actually done. This, critics argue, could be seen as subverting the criminal justice principles of due process, proportionality, and evidence-based practice. The approach can be disproportionate in that it can result in excessive intervention for a child or young person who, despite being considered 'high risk', may never have actually offended in the future (a 'false

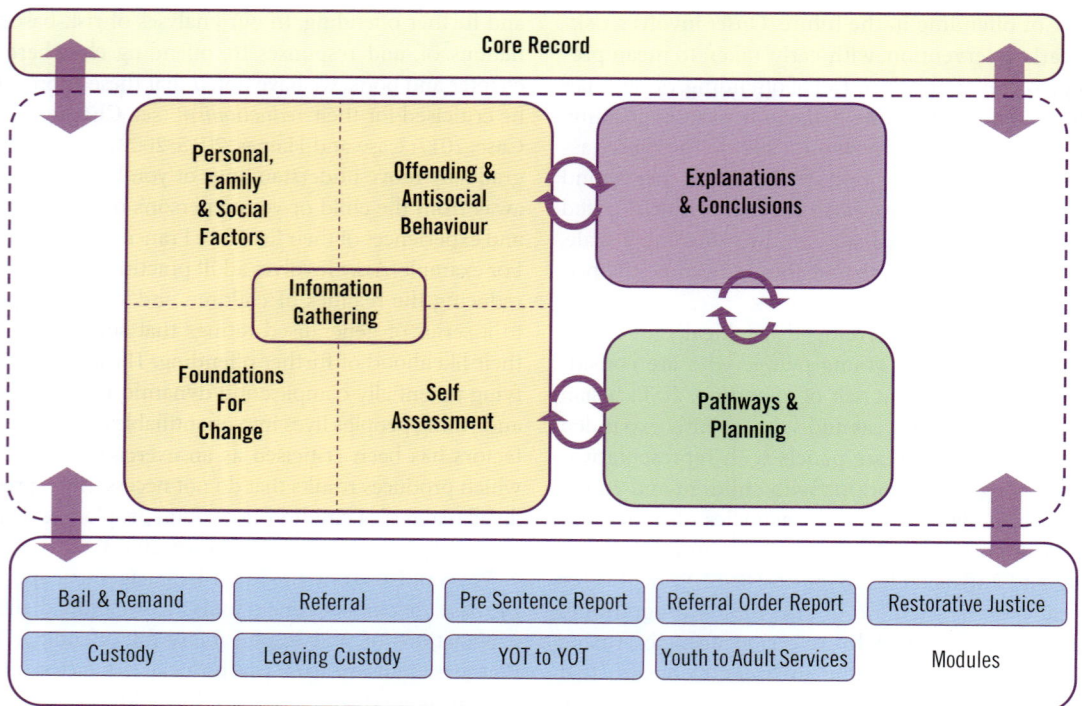

Figure 9.14 The *AssetPlus* framework arguably represents a more positive, less criminalising approach to delivering youth justice than that of *Asset*
Source: Youth Justice Board 2013, Government website

positive'), and insufficient intervention, in the form of support, for a child or young person considered 'low risk', but who may actually go on to offend (a 'false negative').

The YJB has recognised and responded to criticism of its risk-based approach to explaining and responding to youth offending by introducing *AssetPlus* (YJB, 2013). This revised assessment and intervention framework (summarised in **Figure 9.14**) differs from *Asset* in that it:

- focuses on enhancing children and young people's strengths rather than prioritising risks or deficits;
- addresses needs alongside risks;
- promotes desistance from offending;
- tries to access children and people's voices rather than privileging adult prescriptions and understandings of 'risk' and children and young people's lives;
- enables more practitioner discretion in assessment and intervention planning; and
- focuses on achieving positive outcomes for children and young people.

AssetPlus looks and sounds like a contemporary, progressive, and practical evolution of assessment and intervention in the YJS. It provides a framework for explaining and responding to youth offending which goes beyond artefactual risk-factor theories and the RFPP, looking towards more nuanced and constructivist ways of exploring risk and explaining offending—in other words, attempting to understand how children and young people create, experience, negotiate, and respond to their exposure to risk. It has even been argued that *AssetPlus* is, at least partially, a rejection of risk-based explanatory models (Case 2018). But is this true? Read **What do you think? 9.4** to apply your ABC (*Always Be Critical*) mantra in order to reflect on whether *AssetPlus* does indeed represent a progressive approach and has overcome the problems with *Asset*.

9.6 Progressive approaches to youth offending

Having explored the dominance of early intervention and risk management in official, formal responses to youth offending, we ended the previous section by discussing a newer and potentially more progressive approach—*AssetPlus*. As we saw, the introduction of *AssetPlus* represents an arguably more positive, less criminalising

WHAT DO YOU THINK? 9.4

Is *AssetPlus* as progressive as it claims?

Look up and download the *AssetPlus* 'Model Document' (YJB, 2014) by searching for these terms online—you'll find it on the government website. Look through this document, particularly at pages 4 to 10, then use the following questions to help you consider the value of *AssetPlus*:

- In what areas of assessment is *AssetPlus* intended to improve upon *Asset* and the scaled approach?

- Does *AssetPlus* really move youth justice assessment and intervention away from its risk focus?

- To what extent is *AssetPlus* fit for purpose in terms of improving how children and young people who offend are assessed (understood) and responded to?

If you feel there are ways in which *AssetPlus* could be improved, what would a better response look like? Keep your thoughts in mind as you read **section 9.6** and see whether the more progressive responses align with your views.

---

approach to understanding children and young people's lives and to delivering youth justice than previously, and this shift is part of a broader trend in contemporary youth justice—as well as in the justice system more widely, as we will see in **Chapter 30**.

Whether positive approaches are motivated by financial necessity (for example, due to austerity, shaped by the restrictions imposed by the Covid-19 pandemic), political goals, socio-contextual pressures (such as the influence of the Black Lives Matter movement—Bateman, 2020), practical concerns, academic advances, or ethical issues (or a mixture of all of these), these positive approaches generally aim to reduce the number of children and young people entering the YJS for the first time, the number who go on to reoffend after entry, and the numbers receiving custodial sentences, alongside seeking to promote positive behaviours and outcomes for children and young people in their personal and social lives. Broadly speaking, progressive youth justice models have focused on two key areas: diversion from the formal YJS and delivering positive youth justice in promotional, friendly ways for children and young people.

Diversion from the formal YJS

Diversionary models go beyond acknowledging that the system may have criminogenic and iatrogenic (damaging) properties (cf. McAra and McVie, 2007) through practices and processes such as labelling, stigmatising, and marginalising children and young people. Supporters of diversion within youth justice argue that children and young people who demonstrate problems and problematic behaviour (for example, low-level offending, antisocial behaviour, substance use) should be worked with by practitioners offering supportive services. They should be simultaneously diverted *away* from the potentially damaging influence of contact with the formal YJS, and diverted *into* positive and supportive interventions (cf. Smith, 2014b; Richards, 2014).

There has been a significant change in the direction of youth justice since around 2010, when the Conservative–Lib Dem coalition government came to power in the UK, with the current period of youth justice being dubbed 'a new age of diversion' (Creaney and Smith, 2014: 83). The coalition government was heavily critical of the three-strike approach to out-of-court disposals (sentences given to children and young people who offend prior to a formal court conviction) introduced by the previous Labour government which moved from Reprimand, to Final Warning, to Court. In the Legal Aid, Sentencing and Punishment of Offenders Act 2012 (also known as LASPO) they recommended a more flexible, discretionary system of disposal—with categories of No Further Action, Community Resolution, Youth Caution, and Youth Conditional Caution—which children and young people could move into and out of without going to court.

In this way, LASPO set the scene for 'dialogue around costly, net widening, criminalising, counterproductive, and damaging institutional practices' (Yates, 2012: 5). Subsequent guidance given to YOTs regarding the implementation of the new out-of-court system alongside existing diversionary measures (MoJ and YJB, 2013) recommended that their assessments of children and young people focus not just on risk but also on the appropriateness of the intervention and the agency seeking to meet the child and young people's needs, as well as on children and young people's engagement with interventions (for example, looking at their motivation to participate and the likelihood of them receiving family support). These pre-court processes are underpinned by the *AssetPlus* assessment and intervention framework.

The government's diversionary pre-court system is still interventionist in that it promotes diversion from the formal YJS through informal, out-of-court contact with that same system. Such 'interventionist diversion' (Kelly and Armitage, 2015) raises the issue of whether mechanisms intended to be supportive and non-criminalising could actually lead to the child gaining a criminal label through risk-based assessments. It could even be argued that the 'improved' system does little to improve children's access to the range of non-offending-based services that could benefit them (such as education and training, peer mentoring, positive youth activities, and mental health provision), as the focus on intervention and restorative justice could unintentionally cement the child or young person's negative identity (National Association for Youth Justice, 2016) and involve them in the harmful system from which they are being protected (Haines et al., 2013).

Recent diversionary trends in the YJS—such as the strategies detailed in **Conversations 30.3**, with representatives of the County Durham Youth Justice Service—indicate that its advocates are moving away from restricted, criminalising, punitive, and controlling justice-based approaches. However, many have observed that this 'new age of diversion' is not the principled, needs-led, holistic, and universal model that supporters may claim. Instead, the post-2010 prioritisation of diversionary schemes could be seen as a form of 'fast track' justice rather than a considered, consultative, and evidenced diversionary approach (Haines et al., 2013). The shift towards diversion may represent a practical drive for cost-effectiveness (following a re-examination of costly and counterproductive institutional practices—see Yates, 2012) and be viewed as a 'minimum (cheapest) intervention' (Smith, 2014a: 110), rather than demonstrating a principled or progressive commitment to reorientating how children and young people who offend are perceived and responded to. (We will see in **Chapter 25** that efficiency, including cost efficiency, is a key priority for the Ministry of Justice.)

Positive youth justice

The emerging (re)emphasis on diversion from the formal YJS indicates a broader shift towards a less stigmatising and labelling approach to working with children and young people who offend; an approach that aims to avoid the negative outcomes associated with system contact. Diversion is one way of challenging the negative, risk-based, and interventionist forms of youth justice that have been dominant since the Crime and Disorder Act 1998, but a broader model of positive youth justice known as Children First, Offenders Second (CFOS) is another approach that has been gaining traction. CFOS has been developed in the child and young people-focused and rights-facing social policy context in Wales, where national government decision-making is devolved—that is, separate and autonomous—from England in relation to health, education, and social care, but not criminal justice. CFOS emphasises diversion, but also puts forward a broader set of progressive principles for delivering youth justice (Haines and Case, 2015). These are:

- **Child-friendly, child-appropriate practice:** Children and young people who offend should be viewed primarily as children (hence the model's title) rather than offenders. All system responses should therefore be child-friendly, child-appropriate, and should engage in child-sensitive ways, not by treating children and young people as mini-adults (adultification) in a mini-adult criminal justice system.

- **Positive promotion:** CFOS rejects the negative-facing, risk-focused prevention practice of the YJS in favour of promoting positive behaviours (such as educational success and involvement in constructive activities) and positive outcomes (such as employment and the ability to access their rights) for children and young people in the YJS. Children and young people are viewed as capable of making choices and as part of the solution to their problems, not part of the problem itself.

- **Systems management:** The YJS is an interconnected series of decision-making points (including decisions to arrest, bail, remand, sentence, divert, imprison, punish) and these decisions should be directed by CFOS principles in order to achieve positive goals for children and young people.

- **Diversion:** Systems can achieve positive goals through the use of appropriate diversion for children and young people that is holistic, inclusionary, and applied to all children and young people who offend, not only those considered to have committed low-level offences and those at an early stage in the YJS. CFOS normalises offending as an everyday behaviour, so asserts that responsive intervention should be at the minimum necessary level and not excessive.

- **Engagement:** CFOS aims to be engaging and inclusionary, accessing the perspectives of children and young people by encouraging their meaningful participation (not simply consultation) in decision-making, assessment, and intervention (Haines and Case, 2015), in accordance with the United Nations Convention on the Rights of the Child (UNICEF, 1989).

- **Legitimacy:** The state and the agents of the state (including police, YOT staff, and teachers) must treat children and young people in a way that is fair and just. If children and young people consider the authority of these people to be legitimate, they are more likely to engage with crime-prevention interventions and to live crime-free lives (see Tyler, 2007; Hawes, 2013; both in Haines and Case, 2015).

- **Evidence-based partnership:** Genuine partnership between children or young people, families, communities, and key stakeholder staff (including police, YOT staff, teachers, and researchers) that is evidence-based can shape and guide interventions that are more likely to be meaningful, engaging, and legitimate to children and young people (Haines and Case, 2015).

- **Responsibilising adults:** Children and young people cannot fully make their own independent decisions about their behaviour or lead their own independent lives (Freeman, 2007), given that so much about a child or young person's life is decided by adults and is the responsibility of adults. Recognising the responsibilities of adults for decision-making and outcomes for children and young people is a central feature of CFOS.

The progressive principles of the CFOS positive youth justice approach have been applied in different areas of England and Wales (including Surrey, Oldham, Manchester, Cheshire), as well as in Wales (Case and Haines, 2018).

The contemporary focus on diversion and positive youth justice that we have explored in this section has produced examples of progressive and allegedly 'positive' models for responding to youth offending. These approaches are considered progressive and positive by their advocates because they prioritise child-friendly and children first (rather than offender first) understandings of children and young people's lives that normalise typical youthful behaviour, as opposed to labelling and stigmatising children and young people and their behaviours. They inform and recommend less formal and negative responses which try to ensure children and young people have meaningful participation in youth justice processes and decisions and try to better understand how they construct their lives. Although there is some way to go before practice catches up with these ideas (if the current trend continues), these ideas and approaches can be seen as representing a healthy, principled contrast to the negative, positivist, individualised, developmental, and risk-led ways in which children and young people have typically been understood and responded to.

9.7 Conclusion

In this chapter, we have explored the ways in which perceptions of children/childhood and young people/youth have been socially constructed through historical, political, social, media, public, and academic influences. In attempting to understand why children and young people offend, we critically explored the key criminological explanations of youth offending; saw how positivist, developmental theories that individualise causation have been dominant in academic discussions and in policy and practice; and discussed the potential contextual influences on offending by children and young people, including cultural influences and the roles of social structures and processes. We then examined current responses to youth offending, both formal and traditional, and more informal and progressive. In this latter part of the chapter, we also considered some of the ways in which the YJS may discriminate against certain sectors of the wider population of children and young people.

You may have noticed that the development of social constructions of childhood and youth and the main explanations of youth offending and responses to it can be seen as an evolution or trajectory—an ongoing 'them or us?' debate, as we hinted at in **section 9.1**. Youth offending has been theorised and constructed as a problem located within the irresponsible, immature, and out-of-control child or young person ('them'), an idea rationalised and promoted by positivist, developmental explanations, but also as a problem socially constructed by adult-led contextual influences. Debates around the most appropriate and effective responses to youth offending have therefore also been presented as dichotomies (opposing elements): common phrases include 'deprived or depraved?'; 'care or control?'; 'in need or at risk?' The YJS of England and Wales has tried to some extent to address both sides of these dichotomies in its responses (see https://assets.publishing.service.gov.uk/government/uploads/system/uploads/attachment_data/file/966200/YJB_Strategic_Plan_2021_-_2024.pdf), but it has tended to fall into positivist, individualised, and developmental responses that prioritise control through early (risk-based) interventions and expanding levels of risk management which indicate that key stakeholders—whether they are academic, political, or media—prefer to view youth offending as the problem of 'them' that can only be fixed by 'us'. Contemporary 'positive', progressive, and principled explanations and responses provide optimism that traditional dichotomies and more recent risk-based, negative constructions of offending by children and young people are being eroded and made more fit for purpose in our modern society.

However, it must also be stressed that our knowledge and understandings of offending by children and young people are being influenced significantly by 'the global pandemic of the COVID-19 virus . . . [and] the heightened prominence of the Black Lives Matter movement in social and political discourse' (Little in Bateman, 2020: ii), and we have little knowledge of the impact of these developments on youth justice responses at this early stage.

SUMMARY

After reading this chapter and working your way through its features you should now be able to:

- **Outline how 'childhood' and 'youth' have been socially constructed**

Since the mid-1700s and the onset of the Industrial Revolution and compulsory schooling (in the UK), 'childhood' and 'youth' have together become quite clearly distinguished as a separate life stage, with their own very specific characteristics. Previously, children were thought of as essentially little adults, working and socialising with older adults. Distinctions have been drawn based on identified differences in relation to biological, psychological, and social development, and behaviour, leading to a whole range of special provisions and institutional arrangements reserved for children and young people in the criminal justice context. The constructions of childhood and youth have been dynamic and contested over time and place and, as such, formal constructions of children and young people's legal status vary quite significantly between different countries. This in turn reflects differing assumptions about when they should be seen as becoming responsible for their behaviour.

- **Critically explore the key criminological explanations for youth offending**

We explored individualised explanations for youth offending, looking first at developmental theories, which tend to view childhood as a developmental life phase during which a series of identifiable biological, psychological, and psychosocial processes lead towards a mature state of adulthood. Physical growth, and biological and hormonal changes, are therefore correlated with certain recognised stages in children and young people's development, such as puberty. In more recent years, such physiological features of childhood and adolescence have been found to have parallels in neurological developments too. We then explored explanations which emphasise the idea of agency—the way that developmental factors interact with children and young people's capacity (or otherwise) to make rational decisions and choices about whether or not to behave in a particular way. Here, we considered strain theory—the idea that when a person is unable to achieve societal goals through legitimate means, they may turn to criminal behaviour to do so. We noted that youth offending has been dominated by positivist theories which have been criticised in a number of ways, notably for their reductionism in terms of methodology, explanations, and conclusions—reducing complex systems and behaviours to fixed statistical quantities and overly simplistic (and often exclusive) biological, psychological, or sociological categories and explanations.

- **Appreciate the contextual influences on offending by children and young people, including cultural influences and the role of social structures and processes**

Our discussion of contextual influences focused first on cultural influences and then on the role played by social structures and processes. In exploring cultural influences, we considered the role of peers and culture in shaping allegiances and patterns of behaviour amongst children and young people who offend. We suggested that children and young people who join certain groups or 'subcultures', including 'gangs' and terrorist organisations, could be seen as having reassigned their commitment to ideas and groupings that lie outside those associated with conventional norms and the prevailing moral order. In the second part of our discussion, we identified how adult-constructed theories of youth offending in the western world have produced a series of explanations focused on the individual child or young person, their biology, psychology, exposure to developmental (psychosocial) risk factors, and their experiences of critical life events/turning points. We also highlighted the role that the media can play in problematising children and young people and their behaviour—a process of 'deviancy amplification'. Consequently, explanations for youth offending have typically 'othered' children and young people who offend, labelling and stigmatizing them as a problematic, dangerous, irresponsible, and risky population in need of control and punishment—creating a 'them' (children/young people) and 'us' (adults) mentality. We used the experiences of black and ethnic minority children and young people in custody to illustrate these arguments.

- **Explain the dominant role of early intervention and risk management approaches in responding to youth offending**

Negative depictions of young 'offenders' and individualised explanations of offending, and positivist and developmental risk-based theories have become the dominant approach when politicians, policymakers, and other key stakeholders construct youth justice responses to youth offending in England and Wales. In particular, the RFPP has become the go-to model for both explaining and responding to youth offending in the YJS. This has resulted in the widespread use of risk assessment instruments within YJSs to quantify risk factors and to determine appropriate responses to offending. What constitute 'appropriate' and 'effective' responses to youth offending have therefore been predominantly risk-focused, aiming to identify, measure, and tackle children and young people's exposure to risk factors prior to them offending (that is, early intervention) or once they have offended (that is, risk management), with the guiding objective being the prevention of youth offending.

- **Interpret contemporary progressive models for responding to youth offending, notably diversion and positive youth justice**

We concluded the chapter by presenting more positive alternative models for responding to youth offending. We focused in particular on the move towards diverting children and young people away from the formal YFS and diverting them into constructive, less formal interventions. We also explored the concept of positive youth justice in the form of the CFOS model, which is asserted to be child-friendly, promotional, diversion-based, engaging, legitimate, and founded in evidence, and to have a focus on partnership, systems management, and making adults responsible for positive outcomes for children and young people.

 Test your understanding of the chapter's key points by attempting the self-test questions on the **online resources** at www.oup.com/he/case2e

REVIEW QUESTIONS

1. What do you understand by 'the social construction of childhood and youth'?

2. Can you name and outline three key ways in which youth offending tends to be explained?

3. What contextual factors can influence youth offending?

4. What is the relationship between developmental theories of offending and risk management responses to offending by children and young people?

5. In what ways are the diversion and positive youth justice approaches considered progressive models of youth justice?

 Access the **online resources** at www.oup.com/he/case2e to check your answers to the review questions.

FURTHER READING

Bateman, T. (2020) *The State of Youth Justice 2020: An Overview of Trends and Developments*. **London: National Association of Youth Justice.**
Bateman provides a comprehensive, insightful, and accessible review and analysis of trends and developments in the YJS of England and Wales. He examines the extent and nature of offending by children and young people, patterns of and explanations for the use of pre-court, court, and custodial sentencing, ending with a critical **reflection** on the system's aspirations to pursue the principle of 'Child First' as primary in all youth justice activity.

Case, S. P. (2018) *Youth Justice: A Critical Introduction*. **Abingdon: Routledge.**
This book, written by one of our authors, Steve Case, is essentially a more detailed version of this chapter. It is written in the same style and provides a detailed account of the definitions of, explanations for, and justice responses to youth offending.

Case, S. P. and Haines, K. R. (2009) *Understanding Youth Offending: Risk Factor Research, Policy and Practice*. **Cullompton: Willan.**
Another text written by Steve Case, this time with a colleague. This highly critical book will give you a comprehensive overview of the different forms of risk factor theory that have been used to explain youth offending and to inform youth justice responses. It also covers the main theoretical, methodological, and ethical criticisms of these explanations in detail.

Goldson, B. and Muncie, J. (2015) *Youth Crime and Justice*. **London: Sage.**
A highly accessible edited text authored by an impressive group of international youth justice experts. This book covers a wide range of important themes related to youth offending and youth justice and is a must read for students interested in the topic. We suggest you look particularly at Harry Hendrick's chapter on the social construction of youth offending.

Haines, K. R. and Case, S. P. (2015) *Positive Youth Justice: Children First, Offenders Second*. **Bristol: Policy Press.**
This evidence-based text provides a critical context for progressive, child-friendly approaches to youth justice. Reading it will provide you with much more detail to complement the final section of this chapter.

Smith, R. (2014b) *Youth Justice: Ideas, Policy and Practice*. **London: Routledge.**
This book is also written by a member of our author team, Roger Smith. It is a comprehensive textbook that explores the key issues from the current chapter in much greater depth and breadth.

Youth Justice Journal

For students wishing to expand their knowledge of youth offending and youth justice still further, we recommend exploring the website of the *Youth Justice Journal*, an international, multi-disciplinary publication containing articles that are accessible to a wide range of key stakeholders in the area.

 Access the **online resources** to view a wealth of extra information relating to your study of criminology, including self-test questions, answers to review questions, and links to other resources that will help you enjoy and fulfil your potential within your studies.

www.oup.com/he/case2e

CHAPTER OUTLINE

10.1	Introduction	274
10.2	Understanding racial inequality in the UK	275
10.3	How do we 'know' about race, ethnicity, and crime?	279
10.4	Victimisation, offending, and ethnicity	281
10.5	Race, ethnicity, and the criminal justice system	284
10.6	Addressing racial inequality in crime and the criminal justice system	294
10.7	Theorising race, ethnicities, and the CJS: critical race theory	299
10.8	Conclusion	304

10

Race, ethnicities, and the criminal justice system

Neena Samota

KEY ISSUES

After studying this chapter, you should be able to:

- understand the racialised nature of crime and criminal justice today, with reference to its historical and socio-political contexts;
- approach 'knowledge' about race, ethnicities, and crime with caution and appreciate the ways in which it can be problematic;
- recognise the key decision-making points in the criminal justice process that potentially increase or decrease ethnic disproportionality and affects patterns of victimisation;
- appreciate the ways in which people from ethnic minorities are treated less fairly by criminal justice agencies;
- develop a critical view of official and policy responses designed to address institutional racism, ethnic disproportionality, and the patterns of victimisation;
- explain what critical race theory is and apply this framework to analyse the disparate outcomes for ethnic minority groups involved in the criminal justice system.

10.1 Introduction

It is unlikely that you will come to this chapter with no prior knowledge of racial inequality, or how it manifests in relation to crime and criminal justice. The **concepts** of 'race' and 'ethnicity' have long played major roles in both classroom and broader societal discussions about crime, **punishment**, and justice, but they have arguably never been more present and visible than today. At the time of writing, there is heightened awareness of racial injustice and **white privilege**, a development both reflected and amplified by the 'Black Lives Matter' protests which sprang up across the US and Europe in summer 2020. 'BLM' began, in 2013, in response to police violence in the US, and it was this issue that prompted the 2020 protests, but the movement has come to represent resistance against the racism faced by black people and those from minority ethnic groups in all aspects of society. (Consider the BLM movement, your learnings from it, and its implications for addressing racial inequality in **What do you think? 10.1**.) This backdrop makes now a particularly pertinent moment to study race and ethnicities as a criminologist.

So what does studying race and ethnicities mean in a criminological context? The question 'Do some groups simply commit more crime?' might be a good starting point, but there are more significant lines of inquiry that we need to consider. We saw in **Chapters 2** and **3**, when considering the concepts of 'crime' and 'justice', that how we define, explain, and respond to crime are shaped by the powerful group(s) in society, so to study crime we need to consider the nature of the social order in which it takes place. In the UK—and most other western societies—the white majority are the dominant, powerful group. Studying race, ethnicities, and their relationship to crime and criminal justice involves taking this into account as we explore how racial divides and dynamics have evolved over time; how crime problems have often been—and continue to be—problematically constructed and represented in relation to race; how black people and those from ethnic minorities experience the criminal justice system; and how the deep-rooted and damaging racial inequalities in society and the justice system might be addressed. To claim that justice is 'colour-blind' and therefore to focus exclusively on the outcomes, such as statistics on arrests or the lengths of prison sentences for different ethnic groups, is too simplistic and ignores the disparities in the processes that lead to those outcomes.

Thinking about race, ethnicities, and crime also involves critically examining criminology itself and questioning

---

WHAT DO YOU THINK? 10.1

Reflecting on Black Lives Matter

The Black Lives Matter movement gained new levels of visibility and impact in 2020 following the killing in the US of a black man, George Floyd, by a member of the police. Despite this event occurring in the middle of a global pandemic, there were public demonstrations in cities across the US, UK, and Europe, organised under popular social media hashtags #blacklivesmatter and #icantbreathe—the latter being George Floyd's last words, and a symbolic representation of the oppressive effects of racism. The protests unified people from diverse backgrounds in their anger about the persistence of racism, not only in the form of police violence and criminal justice, but in the inequalities and systemic disadvantages faced by black people in all aspects of society, including housing, employment, and education. Stories of black people's experiences of racism in society circulated on social media and books, films, and music centring on these issues gained new audiences.

Think about your knowledge and experience of the BLM protests that took place in summer 2020.

- What was your experience of and knowledge about racial inequality prior to these events?

- What did you learn through and as a result of the movement? Did anything surprise or shock you, and did it prompt fresh **reflection** on some of your personal experiences? (Whether these are experiences of white privilege or experiences of racial inequality.)

- Did you learn anything new about the experiences of people from black, Asian, and other minority groups in terms of crime and criminal justice, both in the US and in the UK?

Now reflect on what has happened since the events of summer 2020. Given the changes, or lack of change, since that moment, do you think that it can be seen as a turning point in our race relations, or were the protests just transient expressions of public anger against racism in the UK? Consider what both alternatives mean for race relations in the UK, and what the implications might be for racial equality in the context of crime and justice.

how criminology has studied race, the ways in which it may have been complicit in entrenching racial inequality (such as through presenting a white-focused version of events), and racial hierarchies within academia. Scholars of race (such as Agozino, Cain, and Carrington et al.) and racial justice activists have been writing about the deeply embedded nature of racism in western societies for some time, and have highlighted that criminology's focus on race and ethnicity has previously been limited to describing the nature and extent of the crime problem. Its foundational thinkers have arguably done more to reinforce racial divides and racial profiling—positivist theorists such as Cesare Lombroso claimed direct links between criminality and race (see **Chapter 16**)—than to question and explore the reasons for any connections between ethnicity and crime and help to redress inequality. Although claims like Lombroso's have now been rejected and discredited, they have helped establish unhelpful constructs which continue to fuel the popular imagination and media interest (as we saw in **Chapter 6**).

In this chapter we will first explore the broader context and history of race-related issues in the UK, considering why racial disparities persist in diverse societies like the US, Australia, Canada, and the UK, before narrowing our focus to race and ethnicity in the sphere of crime and criminal justice. We will then consider the problems with the statistics available on race, ethnicity, and crime, noting the ways in which they may not tell the whole story, before considering the statistics themselves as we discuss the relationships—or supposed relationships—between ethnicity and victimisation and offending. We move on to how ethnic minorities experience the various elements of the criminal justice system, and the disadvantages they often face, then outline the attempts that have been made to address these disparities at a state level. In the final section, we consider critical race theory, a key theory in modern criminological examinations of race and its relationship to crime and justice, which grew out of the US but has much broader value and relevance as a framework of analysis.

Before we go further, it's important to clarify what we mean by 'race' and 'ethnicities' as these terms are often conflated but in fact have distinct meanings. Historically, the concept of race has changed across cultures, space, and time. It is a social construct based on observable features such as skin colour and hair type. According to Omi and Winant (1994: 106), race surrounds us in a way that means it 'becomes "common sense"—a way of comprehending, explaining and acting in the world'. The term 'ethnicity' describes shared culture-encompassing practices, values, and beliefs of a group. It may also include shared language and religion. 'Race' and 'ethnicity' have become common methods for individuals and governments to identify people and organise social life in postcolonial societies. Given that these terms permeate our collective understanding of society, nation, and population, it is important to understand their relationship with criminology, crime, and criminal justice.

10.2 Understanding racial inequality in the UK

To understand and discuss race and ethnicity in relation to crime and criminal justice, we need an understanding of the wider socio-political context and history of the issues, since this sets the tone for contemporary debates and continues to shape the experiences of different ethnic groups today. In this section we will look briefly at the history of race-related issues in the UK, from the 17th century until the late 20th century (we cover more recent history in the course of the chapter), in order to understand how and why issues of racial inequality arose and have been so difficult to eradicate, before discussing how these problems manifest today, particularly in the context of crime and justice.

A brief history of race issues in the UK

The history of race, racism, and race relations in Britain can—and does—fill entire textbooks, so here we cannot do more than try to provide a brief summary. This history is inseparable from the histories of migration and the British Empire, and specifically of colonialism.

In the 17th, 18th, and 19th centuries, Europeans migrated outwards to America, Africa, and Asia. In order to colonise and occupy these lands, the imperial powers (that is, powers associated with an empire) established mechanisms to control and discipline the people already living there—the countries' indigenous populations. These mechanisms included the use of European ideas about punishment, the penal law, and the concepts of justice and the rule of law. They were all used to suppress powerless and marginalised populations. As European empires invaded and conquered land, they crushed uprisings and imposed a new order on the indigenous peoples, disregarding their existing cultures and ways of life.

In the case of Africa, the imperial powers' efforts to achieve domination extended to enslaving indigenous peoples and shipping them to other richer countries where they were traded and inherited as property. This practice, known as the Atlantic or transatlantic slave trade, existed between the 16th and 19th centuries and saw America and European countries, including Britain, transporting nearly 12 million (Segal, 1995) African slaves between Europe, Africa, and the Americas, putting them to work in the British Caribbean and American colonies on plantations. Britain was one of the most successful slave traders: together, Britain and Portugal were responsible for approximately 70 per cent of all Africans transported to the Americas (National Archives, 2020). The slave trade was officially abolished in the British Empire in 1807 and slavery itself was abolished through the Slavery Abolition Act 1833 which came into effect in 1834, but in reality it continued for several more years (ibid). Research on the legacy of slavery (O'Connell, 2012; Reece, 2019) shows that it continues to shape contemporary forms of disadvantage and dehumanisation of black people while simultaneously accumulating advantage and privilege for white people. (Slavery itself also sadly still exists, albeit illegally, in the form of modern slavery, as we discuss in **section 10.4**.)

Another significant time in history in terms of its impact on race relations in the UK today was the period after the Second World War and up to the early 1960s, when Britain—like many other European countries—encouraged migration from its previously colonised territories, known as the **Commonwealth**, in order to fill its postwar labour shortage. It welcomed citizens from Ireland; the so-called 'Old Commonwealth' countries of Australia, Canada, and New Zealand, which were independent nations at this point; and later from the 'New Commonwealth' countries, territories that had not yet been decolonised. The Old Commonwealth countries brought in 'white' immigrants while the New Commonwealth countries brought in non-white immigrants. Why is this significant? First, because this marked the beginning of Britain becoming more diverse—meaning that the multicultural nature of the population today is largely a result of Britain's imperial past (Bleich, 2003). Secondly, because studying racism always involves making a judgement about the extent to which the non-white population integrates. Thirdly, because it was during this time that the black population in Britain came to be constructed as a 'social problem', a view that arguably still persists today.

As people from the Caribbean, Africa, and the Indian sub-continent arrived and settled in Britain, they experienced rejection both politically and socially, finding themselves both victimised and criminalised. They were perceived as a problem and viewed as 'bad stock' that would pollute the 'British race', and a **moral panic** (a phenomenon we discussed in **section 6.2**) developed in the 1970s that Britain was becoming a 'coffee-coloured' nation (Bowling and Phillips, 2002: 7), stoked by similar language in politicians' speeches. The Commonwealth Immigration Act 1962, the Commonwealth Immigrants Act 1968, and the Immigration Act 1971 were passed by Parliament as a response to restrict 'coloured' immigration. Further legislation in the form of the British Nationality Act 1981 consolidated the discriminatory basis of the previous nationality legislation and removed the automatic right of citizenship.

Anti-immigrant views became popular, fuelling hostility and racist violence towards these groups (Phillips and Bowling, 2012: 372), and policing practices singled out minority communities for special attention as they were increasingly perceived as disorderly. Stuart Hall et al.'s seminal work, *Policing the Crisis* (1978), illustrated clearly how police believed black people to be criminal and therefore sought actively to police, control, and punish them. These beliefs were further legitimised and gained currency through the media, politicians, and criminal justice agents. Throughout the 1970s and 1980s, black young men were characterised as the new '**folk devil**' and as inherently criminal. The idea that racism in policing and criminal justice practices adversely affected the safety and liberty of ethnic minorities was simply denied by the British state, and although the Race Relations Act 1976 attempted to address racial discrimination by making it unlawful to discriminate on the basis of race, colour, nationality, and national or ethnic origin, the police as an institution did not fall within its scope (2002: xv). In 1998, the Runnymede Trust, a think tank for promoting racial justice in Britain, set up the Commission on the Future of Multi-Ethnic Britain. The role of the Commission was to assess the state of race relations in multi-ethnic Britain and to offer recommendations to make Britain a confident and vibrant multicultural society that was comfortable with its diversity.

It should by now be clear that in order to understand race relations, and specifically those that arise in the context of crime and criminal justice, we have to acknowledge the racial hierarchy that has been established over previous centuries between 'white' and non-white' people. In early colonial times, scholars drew deliberate distinctions between colonisers and the colonised, developing racial constructs that were linked to ideas of superior and inferior groups, and this hierarchy was reinforced and deepened by the slave trade. These constructs were a central element of imperialism, and imperialism is largely responsible for the diverse make-up of Britain's population today. More than a century ago, writing about the conflict within America following the abolition of slavery, W. E. B. Du Bois wrote that 'the problem of the twentieth century is the problem of the color-line—the relation of the darker to the lighter races of men in Asia and Africa, in America and the islands of the sea' (1903: 10). Use of the term 'color-line' by Du Bois is helpful when we examine racism connected to colonialism and **criminalisation**, and helps us understand how racism against black and Asian minorities became embedded in British social and political power structures. Even as postwar diversity was seen to benefit British culture and its economy and came to be celebrated across media, sport, universities, and the workplace, it continued to incite fear and suspicion of 'others' and to increase tensions across primitive lines of race, ethnicity, language, nationality, and religion. We could, in fact, call all of these lines 'color-lines' since Du Bois later acknowledged that 'the race problem . . . cut across lines of color and physique and belief and status and was a matter of cultural patterns, perverted teaching and human hate and prejudice' (Du Bois and Zuckerman, 2004: 46).

Let's return our focus to crime and criminal justice. We have seen that during colonisation, criminal justice was used to allow imperial powers to gain and maintain dominance, obliterate other cultures, and economically exploit other groups (Moore, 2014; Brown, 2014). Through empire, penal law, and colonial domination, numerous injustices in the former colonies appeared to be legal and justified. Examples of brutal responses to rebellion include the brutal killing and hanging of 312 slaves in Jamaica in 1831, and on tea plantations in British India, the West Indies, and Africa planters enforced the law using public and private floggings, confinement, cuffing, kicking, and other assaults (Moore, 2016). As King (2017) notes, many studies have highlighted a connection between racialised structures of inequality, punishment, and colonisation—we could see the use of criminal justice as a way to control less powerful groups during the racist violence of the 1970s as an illustration of this point. In his seminal work *Slavery and the Penal System*, Sellin (1976) argues that modern criminal justice systems and prisons have been developed from societies which relied on slavery, and have used penal law to integrate domestic slave punishments into state practices:

> The legislator simply made the practices employed by slave-owners within the domestic establishment—flogging, castration, cutting off the hand, blinding, death, and physical force to elicit confessions—into public punishments and judicial procedures.
>
> (Sellin, 1976: 35, cited in Moore, 2016: 45)

This use of the criminal justice system is arguably still an aspect of social control. It helps us to understand the entrenched patterns of disproportionate outcomes in the criminal justice system today.

The clear theme throughout our brief account of the history of British race relations is the domination and neglect of non-white groups. Prejudice based on race and ethnicity has been present for centuries and is rooted in colonial encounters (Chowdhury and Beeman, 2007). It is also impossible to ignore the fact that criminology itself has been complicit in racial inequality, punishment, and colonisation (Agozino, 2004; Cuneen, 2013; King, 2017). In studying patterns of crime in the US, the sociologist John Davis (1976) argues that criminologists have consistently failed to consider the impact of slavery and racist policies on black self-esteem. The cultural domination of black people was more damaging to their self-esteem than economic domination, and white Americans interpreted the law to justify attacks on black people and their culture. The result of this process was the lack of faith that US law would deliver justice to black people. Garner (2015) and Phillips et al. (2020) point to similar marginalisation and neglect in theorising race and racism within British criminology.

It is clear that as students of criminology as well as criminologists, we must reckon with race, racism, and racial hierarchies if we want to gain a systemic understanding of race inequalities.

Race-related issues today

Racial inequality in the UK today may be less immediately visible than it was in the 1970s, but the disproportionate deaths of ethnic minorities caused by the Covid-19 pandemic (Public Health England, 2020), together with the BLM protests in the aftermath of the killing of George Floyd, have highlighted that it still persists, returning it to the centre of our national conversation. Attitudes towards race and racism today can best be described as mixed and divisive. On the one hand, there seems to be increased willingness from individuals, organisations, and government to acknowledge and address racial inequalities. On the other, support is increasing for far-right organisations and ideals (Trilling, 2012)—a trend also visible in Europe and the US. Burnett (2017) suggests that Brexit unleashed racism, and that the 'moral panic' of the 1970s—and, by extension, the colonially constructed roots of this panic—was apparent in some voters' rationales for voting leave. He presents evidence that the EU referendum and its nativist (supporting the interests of native inhabitants) debate generated a racist climate which was a result of the divisive policies and programmes of successive governments—New Labour, coalition, and Conservative. He argues that the 'newness' of the racism that followed the referendum has historical echoes and is sustained by the structural racism of the 'old' (Burnett, 2017: 89).

As the UK has become more ethnically diverse, the government's race disparity audit (Race Disparity Unit, 2017) reports disparities between ethnic groups in all areas of life that are affected by public organisations. We can see significant disparities and unequal outcomes in the education, employment, housing, policing, criminal justice, and health sectors, as well as in overall levels of persistent poverty (Race Disparity Unit, 2017). In 2019, people from all ethnic minority groups except the Indian, Chinese, White Irish, and White Other groups were more likely than White British people to live in the most deprived 10 per cent of neighbourhoods in England (Cabinet Office, 2020). In the public sector workforce, ethnic minority employees are concentrated in the lower grades or ranks and tend to be younger. These disadvantages have an impact from an early stage. Those living in poverty are more likely to have lower levels of educational outcomes (Joseph Rowntree Foundation, 2010), and non-white children, in particular children of mixed and black ethnicity, are slightly over-represented in the number of children in the social care system in England (Ofsted, 2020). In contrast, the workforce in children's social care is predominantly white: 72 per cent, compared to 11 per cent from black ethnic backgrounds (Ofsted, 2020). Feeding into all this inequality is the white-focused curriculum taught at both school and university level, which has led to increasing calls to decolonise the curriculum—see **section 10.7** and **Controversy and debate 10.1**.

This brief outline should have given you an idea of the extent of racial inequality that still exists in different spheres (as demonstrated by **Conversations 10.1**)—an inequality that stems from Britain's colonial past and its racial constructs, and which both relies on and tends to reinforce negative racial stereotypes and perceptions (as we saw in **Chapter 6**). These differences are at their most stark in the context of the criminal justice system, but it is important to be aware that they are shaped by and form part of a much wider picture of racial inequality.

CONVERSATIONS 10.1

Can we talk about racial inequality?

with **Mark Blake**

My son is a talented footballer signed to a Premier League academy and because of his talent I have spent a lot of my spare time driving him around the country to play and train over the past few years. Football dominates the national conversation; it's one of the few topics, apart from the weather, that the British can strike up instant conversation around. It cuts through the barriers of class, region, religion, wealth, or ethnicity.

But, of course, there are issues that as a society we find it much more difficult to talk about, and these are often the most divisive issues in our society. On one occasion I was watching my son play football and noticed something out of the ordinary about the coaching staff of the opposing team. I shared my thought with another parent and she looked at me with a blend of approval and annoyance. My observation was simply that the opposing team had two black coaches. The parent with whom I shared the observation was also black. Would I have made this comment if she had been white? In all likelihood, the answer is probably not.

The conversation on the touchline neatly illustrates the difficulties and social anxieties we face in talking about race, discrimination, inclusion, and racism. These are issues that affect all parts of our society and its institutions, which have on the one hand become more visible, but conversely are now more difficult to raise with statutory bodies than at any time over the past decade or so. Acknowledging and breaching the barriers to such discussions have been the biggest challenge for me in my work over the past five years.

But the football analogy is also interesting because the football industry has, over the past few years, developed into what is arguably the one theatre in British society where there has been a really informed and open debate about race, inclusion, and racism. In an attempt to broaden diversity within the game, the National Football League (NFL) in the US has brought in the 'Rooney rule' which requires the National Basketball Association and the NFL clubs to shortlist black and minority ethnic candidates for coaching positions, a policy which has also recently been agreed for English football academies. These innovations should be seen in the light of some statistics: fewer than 3 per cent of coaching positions in professional football are held from people from BME groups yet in the Premier League more than 25 per cent of the players are of a BME background. I can count on the fingers of one hand the number of black coaches I have seen in more than three years of observing academy football, so it will be interesting to see how English academies take the Rooney rule forward in this country.

All of this means that within the 'beautiful game', race and inclusion have been a constant source of debate. Football undoubtedly has a long way to go, but you could argue that it is miles ahead of some of our institutions, both in its practical reactions and its willingness to engage in a wide-ranging and open debate on the challenges we face if we are to bring about full inclusion and equality.

In contrast, we could be forgiven for thinking that within the criminal justice system, discussions around race and discrimination are uncomfortable and to be avoided. This is certainly the impression that the institutions of law give to anyone who investigates or researches questions of inclusion and diversity in the context of crime and punishment. Such institutions acknowledge that there is a challenge around equality, but it is hard to find evidence of anything being done to overcome it. It is fair to ask: is any action actually being taken to improve the situation?

The road to equality will be a long one but like any journey it begins with one step; in this case, that step is the pressure that has been put on our institutions to openly discuss the issues and challenges, a debate which is the precursor to action and change. The justice system can learn something from what has been happening in the football industry, so that these difficult conversations can be embraced with a clear sense of purpose and a passion for lasting change.

Mark Blake, Councillor, Haringey Council

10.3 How do we 'know' about race, ethnicity, and crime?

To understand the issues of racial inequality associated with crime and the criminal justice system, we need to have comprehensive data which is broken down with details of race and ethnicity. But there are existing or potential (depending on your view) problems with 'knowledge' about race, ethnicity, and crime which are important to appreciate before we consider the available information about these issues.

We can gain information about race, ethnicity, and crime through:

- academic scholarship based on research;
- official data on ethnicity and crime (published by the Office for National Statistics, Home Office, Ministry of Justice, and the Cabinet Office); and
- reports published by other bodies and organisations (for example, regulatory bodies, think tanks, charities, and media) that are based on independent research and evaluation.

These sources can all help us form a picture, but they need to be approached with the ABC (*Always Be Critical*) mantra in mind. Statistics are a good starting point to understand trends and patterns but the data on which they are based are subject to change, updates, and corrections. We also saw in **Chapter 4** on criminological knowledge and **Chapter 5** on crime statistics that criminological knowledge can be biased or subjective and may not present the whole picture or reflect people's lived experiences. For this reason, it has been suggested that it is not helpful to collect data on race and ethnicity, as the simplistic, outcomes-focused picture can reinforce existing constructs and stereotypes—consider this further in **What do you think? 10.2**. We also need to be mindful that criminological knowledge in this area is fairly limited; the origins of criminology ignore race and the processes of racialisation, and scholarship in the discipline has been dominated by white people (mainly men), so the knowledge it has traditionally produced is **androcentric** and **ethnocentric** (Phillips et al., 2020).

Let's consider the official data that is available to us. The first **official statistics** on the racial and ethnic backgrounds of the prison population in England and Wales were produced in 1984, but it was only after the Criminal Justice Act 1991 was passed that statistical data on race and gender was systematically collected and published. This Act required the Secretary of State to publish data and information annually to help ensure that those involved in administering justice did not discriminate against anyone on 'improper grounds', including race or sex. This data set was published for the first time in 1992 and has developed over time. It remains one of the main sources of information available on black and minority ethnic group experiences across the criminal justice system and is available as a report called *Statistics on Race and the Criminal Justice System*, published by the Ministry of Justice. Since 2010, this report has been published every two years.

As we saw in **Chapter 5**, statistics on crime should be treated with caution because of variations in the reporting and recording of crime, and because the criminal justice agencies use discretion. In the context of race and ethnicity, examples include the fact that not all criminal justice agencies record and monitor information based on race and ethnic background (for suspects, victims, witnesses, **defendants**, offenders, and prisoners) in a consistent way. It is also difficult to secure data from courts at different stages of decision-making during the sentencing process which is disaggregated by race and ethnicity.

WHAT DO YOU THINK? 10.2

Is it helpful to collect data on race, ethnicity, and crime?

Collecting data on race and ethnicity relating to crime is a complex task which requires sensitivity but also provokes controversy in public policy and social science discourse. Over the years, there has been disagreement about whether such data helps us to understand the causes and outcomes of racial inequality or actually serves to promote racial divisions and hierarchies.

The writer and journalist Afua Hirsch argues that it is unhelpful and naive to claim not to 'see' race or to suggest that we live in a post-racial society (Brit(ish), 2018). This position, she says, can lead to denial that racial inequality exists. If we take this view, we might be in favour of collecting data on race and ethnicity, to help shine a light on racial inequality.

But could we also argue that the data supports the negative stereotypes and constructs that exist in relation to black, Asian, and minority ethnic groups and criminality? As criminologists interested in the context and reasons for such statistics, we know that they can be explained by a variety of reasons, including systemic inequalities, but this is not clear to the average member of the public, who looks at the numbers alone. Given this, is it helpful to perpetuate unhelpful images of BAME groups by collecting and publishing this data, even if we do so with good intentions?

What do you think?

Bowling and Phillips (2002) summarise the main problems with official statistics on race, ethnicity, and crime as follows:

- they only focus on a small proportion of individuals who get involved in the different stages of the criminal justice process;
- there are definitional and conceptual problems that mean the data does not reflect more nuanced detail on race and gender;
- statistics on race present data and information on ethnic minorities in contrast to their white counterparts and do not present data informed by intersectionality, for example relating to race and gender. *Statistics on Women and the Criminal Justice System*, now also published every two years, reports data on outcomes for women in contrast to men in the criminal justice process without detailing the experiences of black women.

These points, particularly the second and third, emphasise that a key problem is that the data available does not reflect the complexity of the issues. This difficulty is often cited by those in power. In evidence presented to the Home Affairs Committee (2007), for example, the causes of over-representation of young black people in the criminal justice and youth justice systems were described as multiple, complex, and interrelated. In one piece of evidence related to causes of over-representation, the Home Office told the Committee:

> Due to the complexity of the relationship between race, ethnicity and crime and the lack of reliable data, we are unable to say with confidence whether people are being treated differently by the system because of their ethnic group or why disproportionality occurs.
>
> (Home Affairs Committee, 2007: 29, para. 95)

There is no denying that the relationship between crime, race, and ethnicity is nuanced, but explanations and arguments that rely on data complexity and **reliability** ultimately appear to benefit those in power; that is, the officials who make policy and decisions in the criminal justice system. **Empirical** research in relation to police detention and court processes now provides evidence that those of non-white ethnicity are over-penalised and overcriminalised on the basis of their race, but when criminal justice practitioners are challenged by campaigners and scholars to account for decision-making processes, the typical response is a claim that the available data is not reliable, is incomplete, or is not nuanced enough. For several decades now, attempts to methodically, systematically, and comprehensively uncover points of discretion in the criminal justice process that enhance opportunities for racial bias (whether conscious or unconscious) have been frustrated due to limitations of data availability and the inability to acknowledge ethnic disproportionality as a problem in the first place.

10.4 Victimisation, offending, and ethnicity

Now that we have the necessary context and are prepared to exercise caution when looking at statistics, we can begin to look at race and ethnicity in relation to victimisation and offending.

Ethnicity and victimisation

The government's data indicates that black and Asian people and those of mixed race are marginally more likely to be victims of crime than white people (17 per cent average for the former groups vs 15 per cent for white people in 2018/19) (Race Disparity Unit, 2020). The Crime Survey for England and Wales (CSEW) shows the same results for that year. The figures for those with mixed ethnicity are consistently higher than for all other groups, with 28 per cent of this group saying they were victims of crime in 2014/15, whereas the figures reported for other groups do not exceed 19 per cent at any point in the time period. Data on **hate crime**, which we consider further in **Chapter 8**, also shows that ethnic minorities are more likely to be subject to racially and religiously motivated hate crimes. The most recent data published by the Home Office shows that recent spikes in hate crime took place after the EU referendum and the terrorist attacks in 2017. Race hate crimes accounted for 76 per cent of the 78,991 offences recorded by the police in 2018/19, which was an 11 per cent increase over the previous year. Consider this data further in **What do you think? 10.3**.

The hate crime data shows that a proportion of the victimisation experienced by non-white people is directly linked to their ethnicity. But what of other crimes to which they are subjected? While it might be hard to find further direct links, it is important to remember the likely impact of wider, social factors on how likely ethnic minorities are to become victims of crime. We noted in **section 10.2** that ethnic minority groups tend to live in more deprived, often urban, parts of the country. These facts help to explain inequalities between groups in Covid-19 exposure and health outcomes (Platt and Warwick, 2020) because of population density and how these groups are connected in urban areas. Dr Zubaida Haque, former interim director of race equality think tank the Runnymede Trust, has suggested that these are also among the reasons for the higher rates of crime victimisation, as well as offending, among ethnic minorities (*The Independent*, 11 October 2017).

As we noted in **section 10.3**, one problem with data on race, ethnicities, and crime is that it is incomplete, so in some areas we do not yet have the data to enable us to assess the patterns of victimisation—and offending—in relation to ethnicity. The most notable example is the complex and largely hidden crime of **modern slavery**, a form of organised and extreme exploitation of other people that is linked to 'people trafficking'. The UK government passed the Modern Slavery Act in 2015 and set out a compelling case in its Modern Slavery Strategy (2014) to:

- pursue individuals and groups accused of committing modern slavery offences and prosecute them;
- prevent victims/survivors or offenders caught up in modern slavery;
- protect those who are vulnerable from exploitation by strengthening safeguards and increasing awareness of and resilience against this crime;
- prepare in harm reduction caused by this crime through better victim identification and enhanced support.

So-called 'first responder' organisations, such as the police, refer potential victims to the National Referral Mechanism (NRM) for support. Quarterly statistics on this issue are published by the National Crime Agency, but although the data on victims and offenders is disaggregated by nationality, gender, and age, it is not yet filtered by ethnicity. This brings us back to the point we considered in **What do you think? 10.2** about whether we should collect data on race and ethnicity. In this instance, the absence of disaggregated data and monitoring by race and ethnicity in the statistics, policy, and practice (including that of charitable organisations) associated with modern slavery prevents us from gaining a fuller understanding about the experiences of victims/survivors referred to the NRM and the subsequent decisions regarding their status if they happen to be non-European nationals.

The '**social harm**' perspective (Hillyard et al., 2004; Pemberton, 2007), which we consider in **section 10.5** in relation to race and in more depth in **Chapter 19**, provides an alternative way of thinking about ethnicity and victimisation. It focuses on harm rather than crime, which allows us to expand our analysis to a broader range of socially harmful acts and circumstances, rather than being limited to those committed by individuals or to legal definitions of crime. Taking a zemiological approach—**zemiology** is the study of social harm—we can consider the significant

WHAT DO YOU THINK? 10.3

Considering ethnicity and victimisation

Figure 10.1 shows the number of racially or religiously aggravated offences and equivalent non-aggravated offences that were recorded by the police in England and Wales from April 2015 to July 2020. As is noted in the Home Office statistical bulletin in which the data were published (Home Office, 2020a), there are some clear spikes in aggravated offences which are not reflected in the number of non-aggravated offences. They can be seen in:

- July 2016, following the EU referendum;
- July 2017, following the terrorist attacks in that year;
- June and July 2020, following the killing of George Floyd on 25 May of that year and the resulting Black Lives Matter protests.

The data from April to July 2020 was provisional when this bulletin was released, as although police data is sent to the Home Office monthly it is only quality checked each quarter, but if accurate it shows a significant increase in racially or religiously aggravated offences compared to previous years. The report states that most forces reported an increase in these offences on prior year, and 27 forces reported an increase of 25 per cent or more.

Study the graph and consider the questions below.

1. What do these patterns tell us about the nature of hate crime in England and Wales? Study the differences between the aggravated and non-aggravated offences, and the extent to which the figures fluctuate. What do you think are the reasons for these patterns—why might the events listed above have prompted an increase in racially and religiously aggravated offences?

2. What, if anything, surprised you in exploring this data? Consider the reasons for your surprise. What assumptions or experiences informed your preconceptions?

3. What continuities and discontinuities do you observe between 'old' and 'new' types of racism from the chart?

Once you have considered these questions, we suggest looking up the statistical bulletin to assess the data for yourself, and to read the Home Office comments on the potential reasons for the trends.

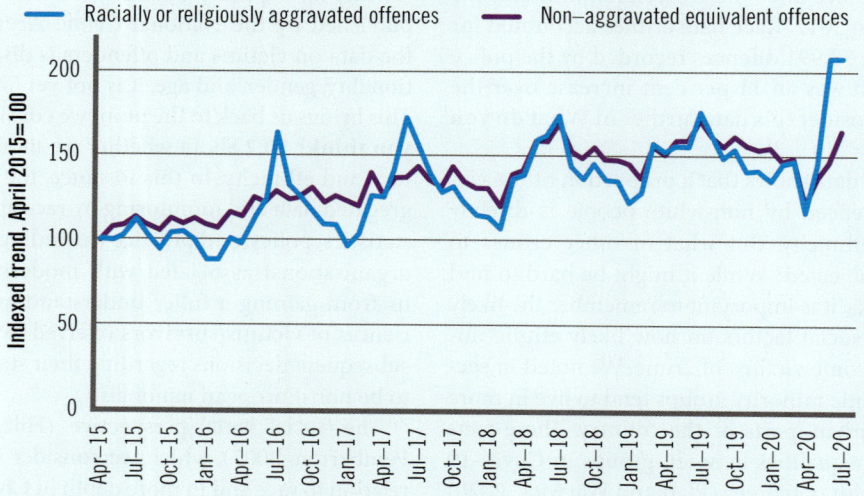

Figure 10.1 Indexed trends in the number of racially or religiously aggravated offences recorded by the police each month (April 2015 to July 2020) show clear spikes at certain points

Source: Adapted from Figure A2, Home Office (2020a), Hate Crime: England and Wales, 2019/20

harms caused to black and ethnic minority people by the systemic disadvantages we outlined in **section 10.2**. In **Chapter 19** we explore the case study of the 2017 Grenfell Tower disaster (see **section 19.4**). Many of whose who lived in the tower and lost their lives in the fire were black or minority ethnic; Leslie Thomas QC, the lawyer representing bereaved families, said that the fire was 'inextricably linked with race' (BBC News, 7 July 2020). He further identified 'parallel themes' between the fire, the killing of George Floyd in the US in 2020, and the high number of coronavirus deaths among people from minority ethnic backgrounds, stating 'Race and state obligation are at the heart of all three cases' (ibid). As Lynne Copson explains in **Conversations 19.2**, zemiology allows us 'to think of structural systems such as **neoliberalism**, **patriarchy** or racism as harmful, whether or not they can be conceived as "criminal" . . . [which encourages] us to imagine how we might respond to these issues in new, joined-up ways that allow us to see the connections between diverse social phenomena—from housing to education, welfare to healthcare—all of which can play a role in understanding a variety of social problems from "cradle to grave"'.

A final point to consider in relation to ethnicity and victimisation is access to justice: given that racial inequality exists, do ethnic minorities have equal access to justice and support? This could include confidence and belief in the criminal justice system to approach the police and report victimisation (which could be affected by negative previous experiences with the justice system—see **section 10.5**—or other public services); the funds to pay for legal representation; and the knowledge to seek support and assert their rights. All of these things could be adversely affected by systemic racial inequality and may mean not only that the actual figures of victimisation of ethnic groups are higher than the data suggests, but that those who have been victimised are less likely to receive adequate support and to achieve justice.

Ethnicity and offending

The information available on ethnicity and offending, which we will consider in more depth in **section 10.5**, demonstrates that minority ethnic groups are over-represented at all stages of the criminal justice process. The data for England and Wales shows that, for example:

- in 2019/20, black people were nine times more likely to be subject to stop and search than white people (54 per thousand vs six per thousand) (StopWatch, 2020);
- in early 2020, black and minority ethnic people comprised 13 per cent of the population of England and Wales but 27 per cent of the prison population (House of Commons, 2020);
- between 2015 and 2018, Asian male offenders received custodial sentences averaging 29.5 months, versus 19.1 months for white males (Ministry of Justice, 2019).

So does this imply a greater proportion and level of offending among black and minority ethnic groups? While the over-representation of ethnic minority groups in the criminal justice system is a reality, the meaning and value of the data are contested. First, as we noted in **What do you think? 10.2**, it could be argued that it is unhelpful to reproduce such 'facts', since they reinforce the tendency to conflate 'black' and 'poverty' with criminality in public policy and political discussion of the 'crime problem'. Secondly, as we saw in **section 10.3**, the meaning of statistics which show disproportionate representation is deeply contested.

To take the first point, labelling and racial profiling—which are arguably reinforced by crime data—are critical issues when we consider race, ethnicity, and offending. They point to the core orientation we have towards certain groups in our society, particularly young black men. The example in **What do you think? 10.4** illustrates that many people, whether consciously or subconsciously, think of young black men as aggressive and potentially criminal. However subtle and internalised they are, these kinds of labels and assumptions inform both our public and private lives, playing a part in the decisions made by criminal justice practitioners about life-changing matters such as arrests, prosecution, and sentencing. (For a full discussion of 'black' criminality and prevalent views about their family structures, values, and culture, see Gilroy, 1987.)

On the second point, if the statistics cannot be read as demonstrating that black and minority ethnic groups commit more and more serious crimes, why are the numbers for these groups higher? A report from the Home Affairs Committee (2007: para. 96) indicated three causes of over-representation:

- social exclusion both past and current;
- factors specific to the black community, such as family patterns and culture fuelled by socio-economic deprivation;
- the operation of the criminal justice system itself, including reality and perception of discrimination.

We have already explored some of the systemic disadvantages faced by black people and those from minority ethnic groups. We will consider the operation of and inequalities within the criminal justice system in more detail in the next section, but for now the important point to note is that crime statistics in relation to ethnicity are widely agreed to be distorted by the unequal treatment faced by black and minority ethnic groups in the criminal justice system.

It is important to note that the statistics have been viewed by some as suggesting that different ethnic groups specialise in different types of offending. For instance, offences related to fraud and forgery, drug offences, and robbery are often associated in arrest figures with black people; Asians are over-represented in arrests for sexual offences and for fraud and forgery; and for burglary and

> ### WHAT DO YOU THINK? 10.4
>
> #### The public's association between 'black' and 'criminal'
>
> Read the following account from one of this book's authors about a recent experience in London:
>
> > A young black male, travelling home with his three friends after college, found my mobile phone on the train. I had noticed it was missing and rang my number, hoping someone would answer it. The young man answered and said he had noticed my phone on the seat as the train doors were closing. So he decided to get off at the next station to return it to me.
> >
> > I was simply impressed by the goodness of the young man and thanked him profusely for waiting for me, but in narrating this experience to my local station officer I was left with much more to think about. Although he was pleased I had got my phone back he asked me if the person was 'black'. Upon confirming that the young man was indeed 'black' he expressed further surprise that despite being 'black' the young man did such a good deed.
>
> How did you react to reading this account and what were your initial thoughts? If you are completely honest with yourself, would you have thought the same as the station officer? If so, why? What experiences or knowledge do you think informed your assumption?
>
> Labelling is common and such race consciousness is deeply problematic because it influences not only how certain people are perceived, but how they are treated—it means that individuals can be rejected and excluded on grounds of race and ethnicity. The example in this box illustrates that leaping to conclusions and thinking about a young black male as a potential opportunist for criminal acts informs our public and private lives.

criminal damage offences, both groups are under-represented, a pattern that has been consistent since 1985. With the exception of robbery and homicide (Phillips and Bowling, 2012: 376), however, there is no empirical evidence that ethnic minority groups specialise in different types of offending.

10.5 Race, ethnicity, and the criminal justice system

We saw in **section 10.3** that the statistics that show higher offending and incarceration rates for black and minority ethnic groups should not be taken at face value. In this section, we look at the inequalities in the criminal justice system that account for the disproportionate over-representation of these groups in the statistics on crime. The criminal justice system in England and Wales investigates, tries, punishes, and **rehabilitates** people who are convicted or suspected of committing a crime. We explore the system in depth in **Chapters 23**, **24**, and **25**, but the key points to note about it for the purposes of our discussion are:

1. The criminal justice system is situated across two different government departments, the Home Office and the Ministry of Justice. It has evolved over time and is constantly being changed and reformed in line with government policy priorities.
2. The criminal justice system is a vast system of organisations and processes. It comprises:
   - the police forces;
   - the Crown Prosecution Service (CPS);
   - courts;
   - prisons;
   - **probation**;
   - the Youth Offending Service.

   There are also other agencies involved in delivering justice: HM Inspectorate of Constabulary and Fire & Rescue Services (HMICFRS), which independently assesses the effectiveness and efficiency of police forces and fire and rescue services; the Youth Justice Board; the Independent Office for Police Conduct; and victim and witnesses services.
3. To ensure justice is delivered fairly to everyone, criminal justice agencies not only need to work independently of each other but also depend on each other to deliver justice in a timely and efficient manner.
4. The system contains many conflicting objectives, such as the tension between punishment and rehabilitation, or between crime control and crime prevention.
5. Although much has been done over the years to improve and revise policy, there is much discretion in decision-making at every stage of the criminal justice process.

This final point, about the prevalence of discretion in the system, is particularly important when we consider that—as Hudson (1993) explored—it is predominantly run by white males. The ethnic diversity among practitioners and staff of the criminal justice organisations is slowly increasing (see the Ministry of Justice's 'Race and the Criminal Justice System' statistical report; at the time of writing the most recent data was from 2018), and its institutions are aware of and working to address the issue (see **Chapter 24**), but a huge proportion are still white—see **Figure 10.2**. This absence of diversity likely influences how the different agencies function—for example, it may mean that practitioners view individuals from ethnic minority groups through stereotypical, imperialist myths and representations (Hudson, 1993), and this will affect how they use their discretion and the decisions that they make.

We have already noted that compared to their proportions in the general population, some ethnic groups are disproportionately represented in the criminal justice statistics. **Figure 10.3** reinforces this point, showing that the greatest disparities, compared with the white ethnic group, appear at the points of stop and search, custodial remands, and the prison population. If we look at more recent data, the picture remains much the same: black people comprise 3.4 per cent of the general population but were 17 per cent of all those stopped and searched in 2019/20 (Home Office, 2020b). Even more startling is the resulting rate of arrests: 52 per cent of white people stopped and searched that year were arrested while the figure for black people was only 19 per cent (Home Office, 2020b). This strongly suggests that stop and search is driven by a perception of criminality that is not matched by actual criminality.

We will now consider the experiences of black and minority ethnic groups in terms of policing, prosecution, sentencing, and prisons and probation. We will pay particular attention to stages of the process where a great deal of discretion is employed, meaning that criminal justice agents have power over individuals and increasing the potential for racial discrimination. To what extent does the perception of criminality, introduced at the policing stage of the system, affect outcomes for black

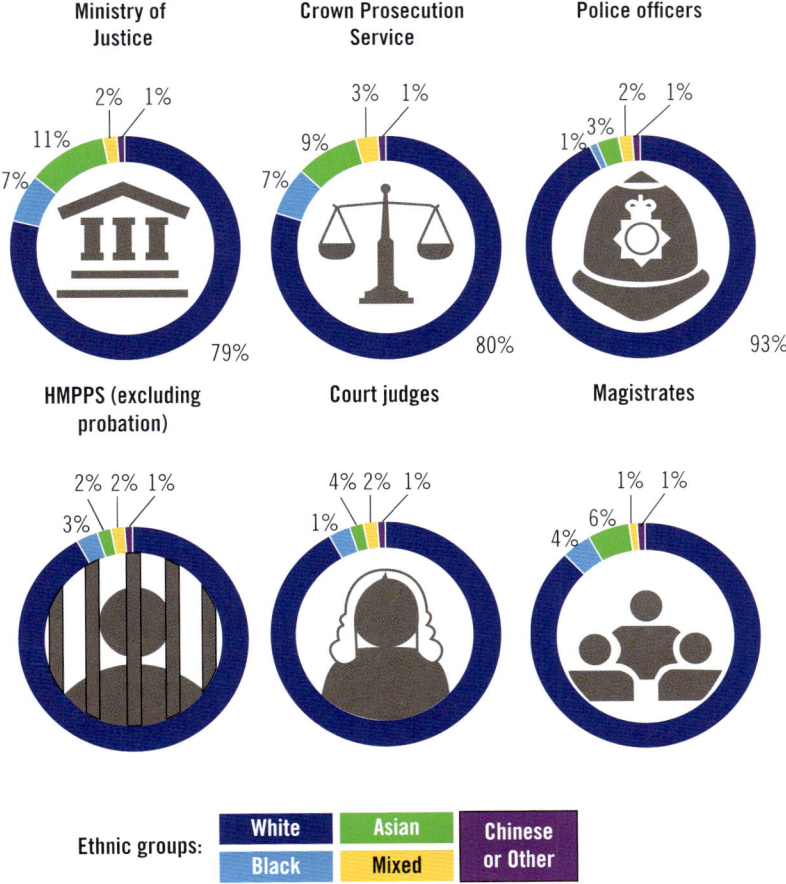

Figure 10.2 Although diversity is slightly increasing each year, statistics continue to show that criminal justice system staff and practitioners are predominantly white

Source: Ministry of Justice: Statistics on Race and the Criminal Justice System, 2018

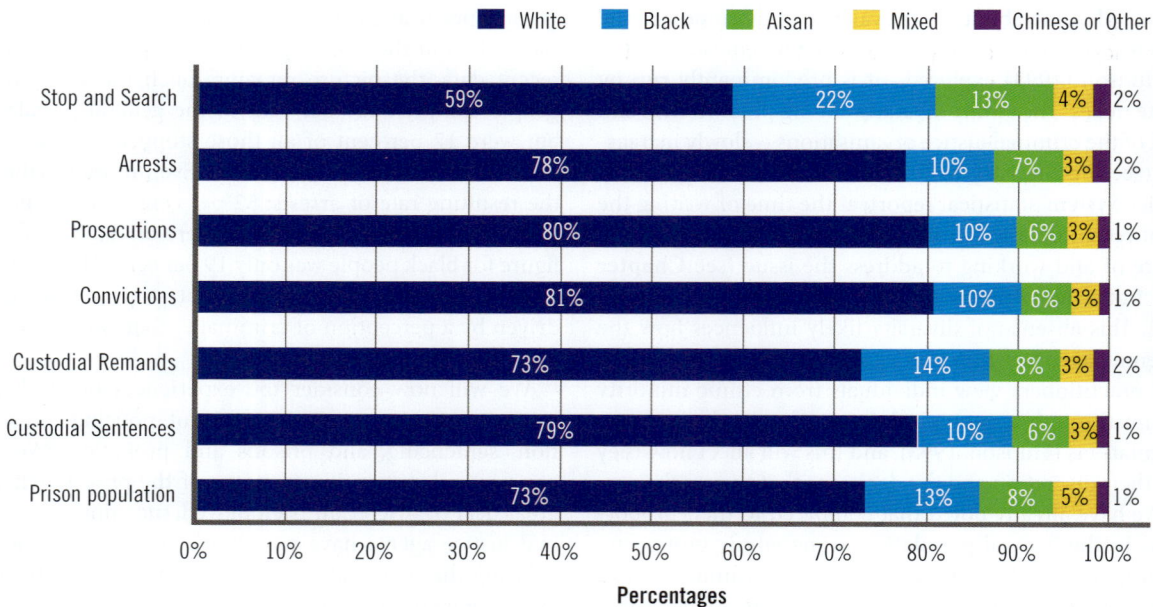

Figure 10.3 Statistics on the criminal justice system from 2018 show that at most stages ethnic groups are disproportionately represented compared to their proportions in the general population

Source: Statistics on Race and the Criminal Justice System 2018, Ministry of Justice (2019)

and minority ethnic groups at later stages of the criminal justice process? Considering the issues of discretion and discrimination is crucial for our understanding of over-representation across these groups.

Policing

In most countries, the police are the most visible organisation within the criminal justice system. In the UK, the police operate on the principle of '**policing by consent**', an idea introduced by Sir Robert Peel when he established the Metropolitan Police in 1829 (see **Chapter 2** for a full discussion), which indicates that the police's power and legitimacy comes from the support and consent of the general public, rather than the state. This consent depends on an expectation that the police operate in a responsible, impartial, and transparent manner. When unfair and discriminatory policing practices are used, they undermine trust and confidence in the police. The ways in which complaints against police investigations are dealt with, the use of force and deaths in police custody, and the treatment of children and young people by the system, including the use of stop and search, are ongoing issues that ethnic minority groups experience with the police. The Black Lives Matter movement and the killing of George Floyd have given fresh impetus to understanding how these issues disproportionately affect ethnic minorities in the UK.

When it comes to making complaints against the police, public opinion remains divided on whether people anticipate being treated fairly. The Independent Office for Police Conduct (IOPC) is the body responsible for overseeing police complaints in England and Wales. It sets the standards on how the police should handle complaints and investigate serious cases, including deaths following police contact. Public perception tracker data for 2018/19 (IOPC, 2019) shows that members of the public would complain if they were unhappy about the conduct of a police officer, but that there is significant variation between different ethnic groups' perceptions of the police and expectations about how they will be treated:

- 47 per cent of black and minority ethnic respondents compared to 36 per cent of white respondents said they were not confident that the police would deal fairly with complaints;
- 32 per cent of black and minority ethnic respondents compared to 23 per cent of white respondents were not confident about the IOPC's impartiality;
- respondents from black and minority ethnic groups were more likely to worry about police harassment and other consequences following a complaint against the police;
- 58 per cent of black respondents were not confident in the police's handling of complaints and 42 per cent did not have confidence in the IOPC's impartiality.

Although the death of George Floyd while in police custody shone a light on the issue of police force in the US, there are also long-standing concerns about the use of force and deaths in police custody in the UK. Independent groups including the Institute of Race Relations (2015) and INQUEST have highlighted that a disproportionate number of people from black and minority ethnic groups have died in police custody in England and Wales. Ongoing casework and monitoring by INQUEST (2020) shows that black and minority ethnic people constituted 14 per cent of deaths in police custody. The deaths were caused by the use of restraint, use of force, and mental health problems. The Angiolini Review of Deaths and Serious incidents in Police Custody (Home Office, 2017) further recognised that the deaths of people from minority ethnic groups, in particular black young men, were linked to experiences of systemic racism and reflected concerns of over-policing, stop and search, and criminalisation. The deaths of black men following police contact, for example Sean Rigg (2008), Olaseni Lewis (2010), Rashan Charles (2017), and Edson Da Costa (2017), invite us to examine the acrimonious relationship between the police and black communities.

There is more evidence of the ways in which discriminatory practices disproportionately stigmatise and criminalise young people from minority groups when they conflict with the law and the criminal justice system. Evidence presented to the UN Committee on the Rights of the Child highlighted several areas of concern for the UK where children's rights were not being protected, especially when they came into contact with the police. The Children's Rights Alliance for England (CRAE) reported specific areas of discriminatory practices in relation to the treatment of children from black and minority ethnic backgrounds. Areas of concern included the over-use of stop and search on children from black and minority ethnic groups, specifically in the age group 15–19 years (CRAE, 2018). The use of the so-called 'gangs matrix', a database of suspected gang members across London, by the Metropolitan Police Service has been shown to breach data protection laws and disproportionately stigmatise children and young people from black and minority ethnic backgrounds; 78 per cent of those on the matrix were identified as black and 75 per cent had been victims of violence (Williams, 2018; Amnesty International, 2018; ICO, 2018). The use of force on children when using a spit-hood remains an area of concern and controversy, and data collected by CRAE between 2017/18 show that children from black and minority ethnic groups accounted for 34 per cent of spit-hood use and that 51 per cent had had a taser used on them (CRAE, 2018).

You will have realised from its mentions in this and other chapters that stop and search (**Figure 10.4**) is a particularly controversial aspect of policing as it is seen as unfair and discriminatory. The term refers to the police activity of stopping and searching members of the public who they suspect may have committed or are about to commit an offence. Police can search an individual or vehicle if they suspect them of carrying illegal drugs, a weapon, stolen property, or something that could be used to commit a crime. This power was established in the use of 'sus' law (since abolished, but with 'sus' referring to the requirement for 'suspicion' from a police officer), which was shown in the Scarman and Lawrence Inquiries (see **section 10.5**) to be a racist and abusive policing tool, triggering much unrest and rioting. Despite this, it is still heavily used—many say overused—against ethnic minorities. Stop and search powers are drawn from different pieces of legislation that is collectively regulated by the Police and Criminal Evidence Act (PACE) Code of Practice A. This includes the PACE 1984 (s. 1), Misuse of Drugs Act 1971 (s. 23), the Firearms Act 1968 (s. 47), the Terrorism Act 2000 (s. 43), and the Criminal Justice and Public Order Act 1994 (s. 60).

Stop and search has been described as a form of **adversarial** contact between the police and public, 'bringing citizens face-to-face with the coercive power of the state' (Delsol and Shiner, 2015: 1), receiving strong criticism over the years from politicians from all parties as well as campaigners. The late Bernie Grant MP argued in 1997:

> Nothing has been more damaging to the relationship between the police and the black community than the ill-judged use of stop and search powers. For young black men in particular, the humiliating experience of being repeatedly stopped and searched is a sad fact of life, in some parts of London at least. It is hardly surprising that those on the receiving end of this treatment should develop hostile attitudes towards the police.
>
> (Bernie Grant MP, quoted in Nacro, 2002: 3)

Grant's words were quoted in the House of Commons in 2010 by Richard Fuller MP, who suggested that 'If the very first part of a person's interaction with the criminal justice system is disproportionate, there may be consequential effects at other stages in that system' (Hansard, vol. 519, 1 December 2010), and in 2018 Afzal Khan MP, a former police officer, stated: 'black people are eight times more likely than white people to be stopped and searched, and Asian people are twice as likely . . . Random stop and search does not work, and the Minister has no evidence that it will. We do know, however, that it can poison community–police relations' (Hansard, vol. 649, 1 November 2018). The findings of the Macpherson Report in 1999 (which we consider in **section 10.6**) that the history, experience, and impact of policing black communities are 'over policed and to a large extent under protected' unfortunately remains true (David Muir, Macpherson Report, 1999: 45.7).

Figure 10.4 Stop and search: a practice that is abused and misapplied?
Source: Rob/Alamy Stock Photo

As a gateway to the criminal justice system, policing activity—and particularly the use of stop and search—fuels the disproportionate number of ethnic minorities visible at all stages of the system. The accounts of those subjected to stop and search powers, such as the story of Leon-Nathan Lynch (see **Conversations 10.2**) and the stories featured on campaign organisation StopWatch's website (www.stop-watch.org/experiences/), show that the experience is intrusive, coercive, and humiliating. It constitutes an invasion of individual liberty and privacy and has been subject to many judicial challenges in courts. And, as Afzal Khan MP's statement suggests, there is also a big question about whether stop and search is even an effective tool in combating crime.

The Home Office publishes statistics on stop and search, arrests for notifiable offences, and other PACE powers in an annual bulletin called 'Police powers and procedures, England and Wales'. These statistics showed that between April 2019 and March 2020 the use of stop and search in England and Wales increased by 52 per cent compared with the previous year. StopWatch tracks racial disparities in the use of stop and search

CONVERSATIONS 10.2

The police *force* or the police *service*?

with **Leon-Nathan Lynch**

I have been stopped and searched by police seven times. On the first occasion I was 14 years old, in my school uniform and walking home with a group of friends. The police stopped and searched me and my black friends for weapons whilst my white friends watched on.

On another occasion I was on my way to work and was singled out on a busy train platform. I was told that I was being searched for drugs. Whilst I was being searched, the officers allowed their sniffer dog to place its paws all over my suit. Imagine having to explain to your work colleagues why you were late and why you were covered in paw prints . . . It appears that that neither the innocence of a school uniform nor the professionalism of a suit is enough to protect you from police racial profiling.

In my most recent encounter with the police, I was detained by armed officers on my local high street. They said that they had reason to believe that I had a firearm in my possession. They searched me at gunpoint. In my bag, instead of finding a firearm, they found law books. The officers refused to release me and focused their attention on a small hammer which was in my bag. I quickly explained that the hammer was going to be used to put up a plaque which was also inside my bag along with some nails. The officers rejected my account and arrested me in connection with a burglary. I was told that the hammer was used in the commission of an offence, despite the initial reason for my detention being in connection for an alleged firearm. It felt like the officers had decided that I was a problem and were trying to create a narrative to fit. I'd done nothing wrong, I'd cooperated, and yet they tried their best to put me in a situation that could have devastated my career. Thankfully, they didn't succeed and I'm a barrister now.

Unfortunately, my encounters with the police are not unique amongst young black men. Many young black men are very familiar with the concept of the police *force*, largely because of experiences like mine, but much less familiar with the concept of the police *service*. Statistics continue to show the presence of racial profiling, which is problematic when the police are the main gateway into the criminal justice system. These kinds of policing practices explain to some degree the reason we see a disproportionate number of ethnic minorities within the Criminal Justice System.

Racial profiling is not a new issue and it is especially clear in the use of stop and search powers. For years, these powers have been used by a disproportionately white police force to harass black and other ethnic minority communities. Let us not forget, only 13 per cent of all stop and searches result in an arrest (Home Office, 2020b). I say that's an unfair intrusion of liberty, particularly when searches disproportionately affect black and other ethnic minority communities.

Discontent is growing about stop and search, and the explosion of support for the Black Lives Matter movement has helped to highlight and focus our attention on the injustices caused by UK policing. In summer 2020, during the outcry that followed the killing of George Floyd in the US, my wife shared an account of my experiences on social media and it went viral. I'm glad that my experiences seem to have increased awareness that racism exists in the UK too. A vast number of young black men, many of whom have no involvement in crime, are coming into contact with the police much more frequently and in increasingly violent situations. Whilst many people recognise the unfairness of stop and search and the way that it criminalises young black men, the narrative painted by the media of knives and violence has undoubtedly created a level of fear that is difficult to shift. This fear has caused many to turn a blind eye to the unfairness of these policing tactics on particular communities.

If stop and search is to remain as a policing tool, I would like to see an intelligence-based, targeted search approach adopted in replacement of racial profiling. We need to get to a place where, when the police stop and search someone, the colour of their skin is of no more significance than the colour of their eyes.

Leon-Nathan Lynch, Barrister, 25 Bedford Row

Reference

Home Office (2020b) 'Police powers and procedures statistical bulletin, England and Wales, year ending 31 March 2020'.

---

and analyses these official statistics on an ongoing basis. In relation to the 2019/2020 statistics, they observed (StopWatch, 2020) that:

- a vast proportion of searches were for drugs (62 per cent), s. 1 PACE searches for offensive weapons (16 per cent) and stolen property (10 per cent);
- the arrest rate as a result of s. 1 PACE searches was 13 per cent compared to 16 per cent in the previous year;
- there is still evidence of disproportionality in the rate of stop and search, with black and minority ethnic groups continuing to be over-policed. Black people are stopped and searched nine times (those of mixed ethnicity 3.3 times and Asians 2.7 times) more than white people.

The Colour of Injustice report (Shiner et al., 2018) which published the previous year had drawn similar conclusions, noting that although the number of stop and searches declined significantly for all groups it had gone down most sharply for white people, and that ethnic disproportionality had increased. The report also found that rates of stop and search for black people did not vary with levels of deprivation. In London, for example, disproportionality was highest in the affluent boroughs, where black people continue to be singled out for stop and search—a pattern that is consistent with ethnic profiling.

So what is being done to address this issue? In a 2019 submission to the Home Affairs Committee Inquiry examining the progress made over the last 20 years on addressing recommendations made by the Macpherson Report, StopWatch (2019) contended that police use of stop and search remained disproportionately targeted against ethnic and religious minorities and that this problem had magnified over the two decades.

The killing of George Floyd in 2020 prompted a renewed focus on addressing racial disparities, and the IOPC intensified its efforts to investigate complaints against police officers in stop and search cases. In 2020, it reviewed and completed five investigations that considered disproportionality, legitimacy, and use of force in stop and search of black men by the Metropolitan Police Service. It found that the legitimacy of police was undermined by ongoing poor communications, lack of understanding about the impact of disproportionality, consistent use of force during encounters, failure to use body-worn video from the point of contact, and continuing with questioning when the initial grounds for stop and search were unfounded (IOPC, 2020). In August 2020, police recorded data for the first quarter of 2020/1 released by the Mayor's Office for Policing and Crime suggested that stop and searches in London increased by 40 per cent between April and June, during the Covid-19 lockdown, but the number of resulting arrests had decreased (MOPAC, 2020). Commentators suggested that the decrease in the number of stops leading to an arrest 'suggests that stops are being carried out based on officers' pre-existing biases rather than on genuine suspicion of criminality' (*The Guardian*, 25 August 2020). In light of the Black Lives Matter movement and the increasing use of digital policing tools (see **New Frontiers 10.1**), the realities of racialised discriminatory policing practices need to be consistently monitored.

NEW FRONTIERS 10.1

Digital policing and discrimination

There are widespread concerns that the use of new technologies and digital policing will further entrench racism. Crime analytics, mobile fingerprinting scanners, social media monitoring, predictive policing algorithms, and mobile extraction are already being used to profile and monitor populations, and their use is increasing.

The problem is that law enforcement agencies are presenting technology as 'race-neutral', independent of bias, and objective in their pursuit to prevent crime and offending behaviour. However, Williams and Kind argue that the use of these technologies could in fact result in the 'hardwiring of historical racist policing into present day police and law enforcement practice' (2019: 6). Since these methods are developed using data that reflects ethnic profiling, they are likely to perpetuate the same issues of over-policing and labelling.

Commenting on the use of digital policing strategies, particularly social media surveillance, in the US, Patton et al. (2017) suggest that 'the use of online surveillance as part of policing strategies raises critical policy, legal, and ethical questions', pointing to their increased use for surveillance on minority ethnic groups on the basis that the majority of prison inmates are 'men of colour'—which is, as they observe, a 'self-validating argument' (2017: 8). The authors suggest that offline patterns of racial profiling translate directly into digital policing, saying:

> the same cognitive and social controls that dominate the everyday lived experiences of people of color in the United States are those which dictate who is watched and what is seen online. Being on the digital street has become no different to people of color to being in the world—the same cognitive and social controls apply. Unlike stop-and-frisk [the US equivalent of stop and search] as a practice, which is physically invasive and threatening to the subject questioned and searched, the effects of social media policing on a watched individual are not immediately apparent. However, the lack of direct physical intrusiveness may hinder any kind of mobilization, grassroots or otherwise, around the use of online, preemptive policing.
>
> (Patton et al., 2017: 8)

If these arguments are true and can be taken as applicable to the UK, we can see that digital policing could inadvertently hardwire racist bias into present and future policing and enforcement practices.

Prosecution

Let's move on to another key stage of criminal justice in which there is real potential—and evidence—for discriminatory practices. When individuals are arrested by the police it is simply a demonstration of an outcome regarding police activity; it does not necessarily mean that the person arrested is guilty as charged by the police. As the agency responsible for establishing the charge and deciding whether an arrest and subsequent prosecution is in the public interest, the CPS plays an important part in delivering justice. As with the police and the use of stop and search, there are areas of great discretion in this decision-making process.

The CPS begins a review process when police bring forward a case. The process includes a decision to reduce or increase the charge, whether to grant or oppose bail, the mode of trial, whether to discontinue a case, and the acceptance of a plea. The extent to which ethnicity plays a role in CPS decision-making was examined in a 1998 study by Bonny Mhlanga of 1,175 young defendants charged with burglary and theft offences (Barclay and Mhlanga, 2000). The study found that if the defendant was from an ethnic minority, there was an increased chance of case termination by the CPS. This was the case despite the study taking into account previous convictions and the type and seriousness of offence. For all offences, black (17 per cent) and Asian (19 per cent) defendants were more likely to have their cases terminated early. For both black and white defendants, 60 per cent of cases were discontinued on evidential grounds but for Asian defendants it was higher at 74 per cent. The research showed that this was because police officers were charging black and Asian suspects without sufficient evidence, meaning they were more likely to be acquitted compared to white defendants.

The Denman Inquiry (2001) concluded that as the CPS had failed to correct the bias in police charging decisions, the agency itself could be accused of discrimination on racial grounds. Racial bias in the CPS decision-making process was also studied in 2003 by Professor Gus John (Race for Justice, 2003). John examined case files, gaining access through the CPS Equality and Diversity Unit. His study found no evidence of racial discrimination in prosecution decision-making but found that there were worrying trends in the prosecution of racist crimes: in the majority of case files examined, the victim was a black or Asian person and the perpetrator white; and, in the process of charging racist crimes, there was a general failure to acknowledge and record racial aggravation, and as a result the racial aspect of the prosecution was dropped and a lesser charge accepted (ibid). This was the case in almost 24 per cent of cases (Race for Justice, 2003: 16–18). The role of the CPS's decision-making in the past is crucial to understanding whether such patterns continue to exist.

Unfortunately, despite the considerable efforts made to tackle these issues (see **Conversations 24.1** for an account from Grace Moronfolu MBE, the Chair of the National Black Crown Prosecution Association, one of the staff networks of the CPS) the issues certainly do continue. A study by Eastwood, Shiner, and Bear (2013), *The Numbers in Black and White*, showed that policing and prosecutions of drug offences in England and Wales are focused on black and minority ethnic communities. They studied data from 2008–10 which showed, for example, that black people are subjected to court proceedings for drug possession offences at 4.5 times the rate of whites and are also subject to immediate custody following prosecution and sentencing at five times the rate of white people. The report suggests significant harms associated with drugs policing and prosecution, particularly drug possession offences. Black groups are at greater risk of criminalisation and harsher sanctions. Shiner et al. (2018) uncovered similar findings in a follow-up to *The Colour of Injustice* report. They established that black people are searched by police for drugs on weaker grounds and that the 'find' rate for drugs is lower for black than white people. While the rate at which further action is taken is similar across ethnic groups, the type of action varies by ethnicity. The study shows that black people are more likely to be arrested, less likely to be given an out-of-court disposal, and therefore more likely to be prosecuted. Black people were prosecuted for drug offences at more than eight times the rate of white people in 2017. More black people were prosecuted for cannabis possession than for the higher threshold offences of supplying Class A or B substances combined.

Between 2010 and 2017, fewer defendants were prosecuted as there has been a downward trend in the number of people being taken to court for indictable offences or either way offences. But despite the downward trend in prosecution of drug offence cases, people are being prosecuted, convicted, and punished for possession and other drug-related offences in high numbers. Shiner et al. (2018) argue that reductions in prosecutions have not been evenly distributed and that this was exaggerating ethnic disparities. Following similar patterns in conviction rates for indictable offences where the overall conviction rate was marginally lower for black and minority ethnic groups than white people, the conviction rate in 2017 for drug offences was 93 per cent for white and 88 per cent for black defendants (Shiner et al., 2018: 44). The lower conviction rate compared to the high number of prosecutions suggests, similarly to Mhlanga's study (Barclay and Mhlanga, 2000), that weaker cases are brought to court for minority ethnic groups as a result of police and CPS decisions.

In 2017, the Labour MP David Lammy undertook an independent review to understand why people from ethnic minorities were disproportionately charged, tried, and punished (Lammy Review, 2017). The review acknowledged that the policing legacy affected how people view the rest of the criminal justice system. When cases were referred to the CPS by the police, it was found that men and women from ethnic minority groups were slightly less likely to be charged than white men and women. While the overall decision-making by the CPS produced equitable results, there were significant differences in the prosecution and conviction rates for rape and domestic abuse, with black and 'Chinese and Other' defendants prosecuted at higher rates compared to other groups. The review recommended that the CPS examine its decision-making in tackling gang crime more effectively and proportionately, given that black people are adversely affected by the policing of gang crime. The CPS should also consider how modern slavery legislation can be used to protect vulnerable young men and women who are exploited rather than dealing with them as perpetrators of crime. The review encouraged the CPS to undertake race-blind decisions in which police remove identifying information from case files that are passed on to the CPS for further decision-making—a practice that is common in many other areas of society, such as recruitment.

Sentencing

There is a similar story in sentencing and, again, some context is useful to understand the situation today—and the frustration it provokes—as the same kinds of issues have been around for some time.

The fact that there is racial inequality in sentencing has been acknowledged since the 1980s and 1990s, when research proved that ethnic minority groups in England and Wales were being disproportionately victimised and criminalised. At this time, debates within criminology focused on the increasing numbers of African-Caribbeans appearing before courts and ending up in prison. This overrepresentation was explained in two ways: either greater numbers of African-Caribbeans were in prison because they were more likely to be guilty of criminal behaviour, or this was the result of racial discrimination at various stages, from policing to sentencing. When Roger Hood's *Race and Sentencing* was published in 1992, both of these explanations were shown to be simplistic. Using a large Crown Court sample of 2,884 cases, Hood's major study revealed a complex and disturbing pattern of racial differences in decision-making on custody, sentence length, and choice of alternative punishments (Hood, 1992). Detailed analysis showed that black males had a 5 per cent greater probability of being sentenced to custody compared to their white and Asian counterparts, with the difference being particularly marked in one of the five Crown Courts in the study. In addition, black males received longer custodial sentences, largely on account of their propensity to plead not guilty thus reducing the likelihood of receiving a discount in the sentence.

Despite the clarity of this data, unfortunately many of the same issues are still present today. In 2018, 38 per cent of white defendants were remanded in custody for indictable offences at Crown Courts, a lower figure than for Asian (40 per cent), black (46 per cent), mixed ethnicity (45 per cent), and Chinese or Other (46 per cent) defendants (Ministry of Justice, 2019). When defendants appeared at court to be sentenced following being remanded in custody, 73 per cent of white defendants were sentenced to immediate custody compared to a slightly smaller proportion for all minority ethnic groups (69–72 per cent) (ibid). Custody rates for indictable offences for ethnic minority groups have increased from 28 per cent in 2014 to 34 per cent in 2018 (ibid).

In the same year, 2018, ethnic minority groups comprised 14 per cent of the general population of England and Wales but made up 27 per cent of the prisoner population (Ministry of Justice, 2019). The average custodial sentence length is highest for Asian offenders (29.1 months) and black offenders (28 months) compared to white offenders (18.3 months) (ibid). This means that from the court stage minority ethnic groups are more likely to be sentenced to immediate custody and also serve longer sentences compared to white defendants. Similar to Hood's findings from 26 years earlier (Hood, 1992), black and Asian defendants are less likely to plead guilty compared to white defendants (Ministry of Justice, 2018). This data is consistent with the Lammy Review finding on the important subject of plea decisions. Lammy maintained that the difference in plea decisions across ethnic groups reflected minority ethnic communities' lack of trust in the criminal justice system. Defendants from these groups were less likely to cooperate with the police or trust the advice of legal aid solicitors, who were perceived as part of the 'system' (Lammy Review, 2017: 25).

In relation to youth justice, Feilzer and Hood's (2004) analysis of over 31,000 Youth Offending Team records found substantial over-representation of young black people and under-representation of young Asians in caseloads. Young people from minority ethnic groups were more often subject to proactive arrests, mostly for drug and traffic offences. Feilzer and Hood showed that black, Asian, and mixed-race youths were disadvantaged at a number of key stages in the criminal justice process; these include pre-court disposals, case termination, remands, acquittals, committals to Crown court, pre-sentence reports, and higher tariff sentencing.

There have been other peculiarities in the statistics on first-time entrants (FTE) in the youth justice estate. Following the Home Affairs Committee report (2007), the Youth Justice Board introduced diversion and out-of-court disposal schemes (see **Chapter 30**) to reduce the number of first-time entrants into the criminal justice system. While this was in some ways an effective way of addressing the overcriminalisation of young people, it is interesting to note the disparities it has generated over a period of time. Diversion worked well for keeping white young people away from the formal justice system but this wasn't the case for young people from black and minority ethnic groups. From 2007–8, the number of white children in custody fell by 37 per cent, whereas the number of children from black and minority ethnic groups fell by only 16 per cent (Allen, 2011: 7).

The pattern has remained steady since then, and these trends can be found in *Youth Justice Statistics* which is an annual report published by the Ministry of Justice. The most recent statistics available at the time of writing show that FTEs from white backgrounds fell by 89 per cent between 2008 and 2018 (Ministry of Justice, 2019). While numbers of FTEs from other ethnic backgrounds also fell, it happened at a much slower rate. The proportion of FTEs from a black background doubled from 8 per cent in 2008 to 16 per cent in 2018, and for Asians it increased from 4 to 7 per cent in the same period (Ministry of Justice, 2019: 13). The types of offences committed by FTEs that are more likely to exclude them from diversion schemes include possession of weapons, drug offences, and violence against the person. Such offences usually attract tougher punishment.

The *Colour of Injustice* report (Shiner et al., 2018) suggests that the policing of drugs and the use of stop and search is a key driver of disproportionality through the prosecution and sentencing stages of the criminal justice process. Conviction rates for cannabis possession for black people were 11.8 times the rate for white people despite their lower rates of self-reported use. The analysis at prosecution and sentencing stages show that ethnic disparities introduced at earlier stages via policing are perpetuated further by sentencing. Between 2010 and 2017, the number of convictions for cannabis possession fell by 59 per cent for white people but only 23 per cent for black people. Taking into account cannabis convictions, it appears that black people comprise a greater proportion of defendants taken to court and punished for cannabis possession offences. Shiner et al.'s analysis shows that by 2017 black people constituted approximately one-quarter of those who were convicted (26 per cent), fined

(27 per cent), and imprisoned (25 per cent) for these offences (2018: 45).

Evidence presented by CRAE (2018) shows the significant impact that a criminal record has on future outcomes for children and young people. A recent Supreme Court judgment relating to the disclosure of criminal records ruled that youth cautions should be filtered from criminal record checks as the impact is disproportionate; the message was that youth cautions should not be used to stigmatise or criminalise children (ibid: 7). Black and minority ethnic children make up 18 per cent of 10–17-year-olds in the general population and currently account for 45 per cent of children in custody. In the youth justice estate, the disproportionate representation of this group in arrest, prosecution, and prison figures is particularly acute.

Whether disparity in outcome is due to the types of offences committed by black and minority ethnic children and young persons, geographical variations in the rates of custody reduction, or other reasons, the differences, and what explains them need further exploration. It is also relevant that, as the Laming Review (2016) noted, young people in care are significantly over-represented in the criminal justice system and particularly in prison, where many have poor experiences. In the care system, 9 per cent of children are from a mixed background and 7 per cent are black. Lord Laming noted that looked-after children and young people who are black or from other minority ethnic backgrounds, and those of Muslim faith, are over-represented in the criminal justice system. These young people also feel discriminated against, particularly by the police (2016: 14).

Prisons

As Phillips and Bowling (2012) point out, at the end of the criminal justice process we can see the cumulative effects of social exclusion and both direct and indirect discrimination through the disproportionate rates of imprisonment by ethnicity. The Young Review (2014: 10) noted greater disproportionality in the number of black people in prisons in the UK than in the US. In 2014, 13.1 per cent of prisoners identified themselves as black, despite comprising just 3 per cent of the general population aged 18 and over. When the Young Review reported in 2014, Muslim prisoners (who are a diverse group in prison and identify as Asians, black, white, and those of mixed heritage) accounted for 15 per cent of the prison population. By 2019, they accounted for 17 per cent of the prison population compared to 5 per cent of the general population. Contrary to their representation in some parts of the media (see **Chapter 6**), only 1 per cent of Muslims in prison are there for terrorism-related offences. Black and minority ethnic prisoners (70 per cent) also serve a greater portion of their sentence in custody compared to white (63 per cent) and Asian (61 per cent) prisoners (Ministry of Justice, 2019). Research by Williams and Clarke (2016) also demonstrates that individuals convicted under the joint enterprise doctrine serve longer sentences and also consider their sentences to be illegitimate. Currently, 37.2 per cent of black British prisoners are serving custodial sentences for joint enterprise. The authors observe that the proportion of black British people in the prison population is 11 times greater than their proportion in the general population (which is 3.3 per cent), challenging notions of 'procedural fairness' and 'moral legitimacy' (Williams and Clarke, 2016: 7). You can find the most recent figures on prison population trends in the *Offender Management Statistics* bulletin which is published by the Ministry of Justice on a quarterly basis. In the remainder of this section we will move away from overall trends in the population and focus on the nature of the problems relating to racial equality in our prison system.

Research evidence shows that people from minority ethnic backgrounds have a more negative perception of race equality while in prison. Prison regimes and the discretionary decisions about incentive and earned privileges, discipline, information, and requests were key to perceptions of fairness (Edgar and Martin, 2004). Similar themes were uncovered by the Race Review undertaken by the National Offender Management Service (2008), which noted that black prisoners were 30 per cent more likely than white prisoners to be on the basic regime without privileges, 50 per cent more likely to be held in segregation, and 60 per cent more likely to have force used against them. The review also found that minority ethnic group prisoners held negative perceptions about prisoner–staff relationships.

Year on year, the conditions inside prisons have consistently worsened as violence in prisons has increased and prisons have become more overcrowded (a theme we consider further in **Chapter 24**). Research published by the Runnymede Trust (Joliffe and Haque, 2017) shows that black and minority ethnic and Muslim prisoners experience racial disparities and racism as part of their daily life in prison. Black prisoners are more likely to experience negative outcomes and are less likely to be in education or employment. Perceptions of racism and discrimination in prison were the main issues for black and minority ethnic prisoners, and black prisoners were frequently misunderstood by white staff who held stereotypical views about black prisoners as 'threatening, aggressive, duplicitous and culturally different' (2017: 14). This made prisoners from black and minority ethnic groups feel alienated and marginalised. Prisoners also shared their views about cultural gaps in knowledge and the need for more diverse prison staff.

The following quotes illustrate some of the reported experiences of BME prisoners:

> Some staff are racist but I haven't experienced it personally. People are mistreated in the block. Everyone else says they have a problem so it must be an issue. Generally guards are racist, openly racist. They don't care. People are not acting professionally, they should be professional.
>
> You feel subversive and cautious if you question anything; you feel alienated. You're seen as a problem or a potential problem . . . during family visits there's more scrutiny. The way people speak from Black cultures—they're seen as more aggressive. Prison officers says things like, 'You're not what I thought you would be like'—which means they have perceptions of you.
>
> (Joliffe and Haque, 2017: 14)

Another problem identified by this report related to the Incentives and Earned Privileges (IEP) scheme: the way in which it was used by prison officers was deemed discriminatory. Prisoners were downgraded to 'basic' status very easily and felt that it was almost impossible to achieve enhanced status. There was argued to be a lack of transparency and accountability in decision-making about a person's IEP status. The quotes below illustrate how this is experienced by prisoners:

> It's very difficult now. You have to go above and beyond. It takes over a year to become Enhanced, but yet you get moved to Basic within minutes.
>
> You do something wrong; you get written up right away. But if you do something good, it doesn't get written up, unless you make them write it up.
>
> (Joliffe and Haque, 2017: 16)

As with making complaints against the police, the complaints system in prison is also viewed with suspicion and deemed unfair by black and minority ethnic prisoners.

The Prison Reform Trust and the Zahid Mubarek Trust published a report in 2017 on tackling discrimination in prisons (Edgar and Tsintsadze, 2017). It uncovered that trends that had been observed in the 2008 Race Review still continued. Black prisoners were over-represented in segregation units while in prison, had force used against them, and were more likely to be on the basic regime under the IEP scheme. Muslim prisoners were more likely to say they were victimised by staff. Both Muslim and black prisoners were also more likely to believe that officers would not treat them fairly.

Many of these issues are explained or exacerbated by the string of 'systemic shortcomings' in prisons which the Mubarek Inquiry (see **section 10.6**) highlighted back in 2006. These included an over-burdened prison service, lack of resources, and a poorly administered race relations strategy as well as poor procedures to tackle racist incidents and complaints. It observed a 'culture of indifference and insensitivity to black people and people from ethnic minorities which institutional racism breeds' (Mubarek Inquiry Report, 2006: 413). Despite the inquiry's damning verdict, the same shortcomings appear to persist. Legislative and policy changes brought in with the intention of improving race equality have not been entirely successful and, despite the passage of the Equality Act 2010, there is evidence that racism still fuels violence and abuse in prisons.

As we will explore in **Chapter 24**, many sentences or parts of sentences are now served outside prison, and offenders are managed and supervised by the probation service. The particular experiences of minority ethnic groups in this part of the system have been recognised from the 1980s but policy development has been inconsistent. Probation inspectorate reports on racial equality have noted poor-quality supervision and shorter contact periods at later stages of probation orders for black offenders. As noted by Phillips and Bowling, a key issue, yet again, has been the experience of racism. Calverley et al. (cited in Phillips and Bowling, 2012: 388) found that while minority ethnic offenders had similar socio-economic disadvantage to their white counterparts, one-fifth had experienced racism in school and that racial discrimination limited opportunities to engage legitimately in the labour market.

10.6 Addressing racial inequality in crime and the criminal justice system

We saw in **section 10.2** that by the 1980s, race relations in the UK were in a bad way. Political promises of 'more law and order' and 'an end to immigration' (Bowling and Phillips, 2002: 8) resulted in inner-city disturbances, riots, and public disorder, and set the tone for policing of ethnic minorities in British society. In the decades since, there have been a number of attempts to understand and address racial inequality in society and the criminal justice system, most visibly in the form of public inquiries commissioned by the government. Each inquiry has been prompted by particularly significant and highly publicised incidents of unrest or injustice. In this section, we consider the findings and policy impact of the three notable inquiries into race and criminal justice—the Scarman Inquiry (1981), the Lawrence Inquiry (1999), and the Mubarek Inquiry (2006)—before looking at more recent attempts to expose and address race relations issues in the UK.

The Scarman Inquiry (1981)

The Scarman Inquiry, led by Lord Scarman, was commissioned by the UK government as a direct response to the collapse of social order following the 1981 riots in Brixton, London (see **Figure 10.5**). Similar riots, between 1980 and 1981, in the English cities of Birmingham, Manchester, Bristol, and Liverpool, had brought young African-Caribbean and Asian men into direct confrontation with police. Tensions were heightened by 'Operation Swamp 81', a police operation to reduce crime in the Brixton area which saw 943 people stopped and searched in four days (Bowling and Philips, 2002) through the use of 'sus' law, the precursor of today's stop and search laws (see the discussion on policing in **section 10.5**). More than half of those stopped were black (ibid).

Scarman's report focused on the flawed policing methods used in Operation Swamp and concluded with a call to address racial disadvantage. It recommended that this be achieved through positive action and by enforcing existing laws on racial discrimination but made no recommendations for new legislation. The Scarman Report received enthusiastic support from politicians and the police but mixed reactions from the black community. For scholars like Paul Gilroy (1987), Lee Bridges (1982, 1983), and Stuart Hall (1999), the report was flawed and reinforced racist pathologies of black people. Despite noting that not all people involved in the riots were black, Scarman placed race at the centre of his analysis and depicted events in racialised terms

Figure 10.5 Police with riot shields line up during the Brixton riots in 1981. The Scarman Inquiry was commissioned in response to the collapse of social order that ensued

Source: Kim Aldis/CC BY-SA 3.0

(Bowling and Phillips, 2002). Actions of the young African-Caribbean and Asian men involved in the riots were depicted as 'something new and sinister'. Scarman also failed to address some of the most problematic areas of policing, such as use of stop and search powers, the investigation of complaints against the police, and police accountability. Policing still remained outside the scope of the 1976 Race Relations Act and the state seemed unable or unwilling to bring the police under democratic control.

In the House of Lords in 1982, Lord Anthony Gifford, who had chaired inquiries into other riots of the 1980s in London and Liverpool, argued that the Scarman Report amounted to 'no more than tinkering' with the fact that the police in inner-city areas 'abused the rights and freedoms of black citizens' (Hansard HL, vol. 682, cols 1435–7, 20 October 1982). By citing social deprivation as the cause of the riots, Scarman was felt to downplay the reality of racial discrimination in inner cities. When the report was presented to Parliament, the suggestion that the Metropolitan Police Service was a racist force was flatly denied.

The Scarman Inquiry was arguably the first missed opportunity to address racial inequality in the criminal justice system. The inquiry recognised that black communities were experiencing racism at the hands of the police, yet nothing substantive was done by the state to address it. This failure led to a further deterioration in race relations, continued inequality, and the disproportionate criminalisation of black communities. Between 1985 and 1999 the number of white males in prison increased by 31 per cent whereas it increased by 80 per cent for Asians and by 101 per cent for black groups (Bowling and Phillips, 2002). Attempts were made by the Commission for Racial Equality to make racist violence a defined criminal offence and to strengthen the Race Relations Act 1976, but John Major's Conservative government rejected both recommendations.

The Lawrence Inquiry (1999)

The Lawrence Inquiry, discussed briefly in **Chapter 3** (see **section 3.2**), followed the murder of black teenager Stephen Lawrence in April 1993 in an unprovoked knife attack by a group of five white youths. An inquiry led by Sir William Macpherson on the circumstances that led to Stephen's death produced its report, titled the Stephen Lawrence Inquiry, in 1999. Eighteen years after the Scarman Report, the Lawrence Inquiry revealed that attitudes of fear, suspicion, and hostility towards the police remained as strong as ever. It represented a turning point in the examination of race relations in Britain.

While the Scarman Inquiry constructed the social problem around race, the Lawrence Inquiry viewed racism as the social problem to be addressed. The inquiry identified racism in:

- the police investigation and treatment of witnesses in relation to the murder of Stephen Lawrence;
- the disproportionate application of the police powers to stop and search on the African-Caribbean community;
- under-reporting of racist incidents due to a lack of trust in the police; and
- the lack of police training in racism awareness.

Scholars like McLaughlin and Murji (cited in McGhee, 2005: 17) have noted that the Lawrence Inquiry was a matter of great public importance for three reasons. First, the Metropolitan Police were subjected to unprecedented public scrutiny; secondly, the established view of the police that young African-Caribbean men were street criminals and drug dealers was challenged; thirdly, previous campaigns for justice were reconnected to the public debate. In contrast to the Scarman Inquiry, the Lawrence Inquiry identified the existence of **institutional racism** not only in the police force but also in a wide range of institutions, including housing and education. It defined institutional racism as:

> The collective failure of an organisation to provide an appropriate and professional service to people because of their colour, culture, or ethnic origin. It can be seen or detected in processes, attitudes and behaviour which amount to discrimination through unwitting prejudice, ignorance, thoughtlessness and racist stereotyping which disadvantage minority ethnic people.
>
> (Macpherson, 1999: para. 6.34)

This definition has been cited countless times since, including in the Grenfell Tower Inquiry (ongoing at the time of writing in late 2020) into the fire in June 2017, in the context of the Black Lives Matter protests of 2020, and in discussions of the disproportionate impact of Covid-19 on ethnic minorities (BBC News, 7 July 2020). It is sometimes now termed 'structural racism'.

The Lawrence Inquiry's valuable contribution to the efforts to identify and address racial inequality included a victim-oriented definition of racist incidents and specific recommendations for the criminalisation of such incidents. The inquiry concluded with 70 recommendations for accountability and restoring confidence in the police. The first recommendation was to make it a ministerial priority for all police services 'to increase trust and confidence in policing amongst minority ethnic communities' (Macpherson, 1999). The inquiry also brought about a significant change in race equality legislation. With the amended Race Relations Amendment Act 2000, Parliament made it unlawful to treat anyone less favourably than another on the grounds of race, colour, nationality, and national or ethnic origin. Direct and indirect discrimination and victimisation were outlawed in public authority functions. The Act placed a general obligation on the police and other public authorities to promote race equality and good race relations as well as a specific obligation for public sector organisations to produce race equality schemes.

Zahid Mubarek Inquiry (2006)

Within a year of the Lawrence Inquiry Report, an Asian teenager, Zahid Mubarek, was murdered in Feltham Young Offender Institution in March 2000. He was attacked by a cellmate who had a history of violence and racist behaviour.

Similarly to the Lawrence Inquiry, the public inquiry into Zahid's murder was the result of his family's persistent campaign for justice in the face of resistance by the state and criminal justice system. There were three investigations before the public inquiry: the Butt investigation, led by a senior Prison Service Investigating Officer; an investigation by the Commission for Racial Equality; and an investigation by the Metropolitan Police. Zahid's family was excluded from these investigations. Their campaign for a public inquiry was successful; it was led by the Honourable Mr Justice Keith, who presented his report to Parliament in 2006.

Racism was made the central focus of the inquiry. The report explained:

> This was not simply because Zahid's killer was himself a racist, and because his racism may have played an important part in his selection of Zahid as his victim. It was also because of the need to explore whether *explicit* racism on the part of individual prison officers had been the reason either for Zahid sharing a cell with Stewart in the first place. . . . There have been lurid allegations about prisoners of different ethnic origins being put in the same cell to see if violence would ensue.
>
> (Zahid Mubarek Inquiry, 2006: para. 3.2, emphasis in original)

The Mubarek Inquiry aimed to determine whether Feltham and the Prison Service as a whole were institutionally racist, and it was as important for the Prison Service in England and Wales as the Lawrence Inquiry was for policing. It specified 13 failings in race relations at Feltham and made 88 recommendations for change to the Prison Service, ten of which related specifically to race and diversity. The then Director General of the Prison Service, Martin Narey, did not deny that the Prison Service had failed in its duty of care towards Zahid and that his death was preventable. Following Mubarek, the Prison Service implemented orders from the Ministry of Justice for specific policies for, among other things, the treatment, safety, and well-being of prisoners. These changes are monitored regularly by the Prisons Inspectorate.

These two tragic racist murders of a black teenager and an Asian teenager reveal the nature of official responses to allegations of racism as well as the collective and institutional failures to prevent it.

Continuing the discourse: reports and responses after Lawrence and Mubarek

The cumulative effect of these inquiries, particularly the Stephen Lawrence Inquiry, and the duties imposed on public sector institutions under the Race Relations Amendment Act 2000, was to open up opportunities for criminal justice agencies to examine their make-up and operational practices with specific regard to race. This specific focus was superseded when the Equality Act 2010 extended public sector duties relating to equality to nine protected characteristics, including race, but race has still remained prominent in the national discourse on inequality and discrimination. This was particularly the case following the murder of George Floyd in the US in 2020 and the ensuing Black Lives Matter protests. In **Conversations 10.3**, Beverley Thompson OBE, a former member of the Home Secretary's Stephen Lawrence Steering Group, reflects on the progress that has been made since the inquiries and the substantial work still to be done in order to identify and eradicate racial inequality in the criminal justice system and society more widely.

Even if they did not result in the significant and long-lasting changes they appeared to promise, the Lawrence and Mubarek Inquiries undoubtedly had an

---

CONVERSATIONS 10.3

Continuing efforts to eradicate racism and inequality

with **Beverley Thompson OBE**

The tragic events surrounding the murder of George Floyd in the US have seen a resurgence in concerns about the existence and impact of race and systemic inequality across organisations, both public and private. Through the efforts of the Black Lives Matter movement, organisations across the sectors have clamoured to pledge their commitment to addressing race inequality by identifying and eradicating instances of systemic racism and inequality. While the issues and concerns so powerfully articulated by BLM are timely, the issues and narrative are not new to the UK, particularly within criminal justice organisations—despite some narrative to the contrary.

BLM should serve as a timely reminder for criminal justice organisations to reflect on how the complacency of their past efforts has all but erased from organisational memory the lessons learned from past tragedies and inquiries. It beggars belief that any section of the criminal justice system should have no knowledge of the pervasive nature of systemic racism or inequality, or what they should do to address racial disproportionality in the justice system. What *is* plausible is that many criminal justice organisations have either lost leadership direction and commitment, organisational expertise and energy (seeking comfort in the dangerous mantra of 'race has been done'), or that previous terminology is 'no longer helpful' in addressing racism and broader discrimination.

I was a member of the Stephen Lawrence Steering Group, and the publication of Macpherson's report in 1999 was the last significant period of activity in the history of race relations in the UK. At that time all public sector bodies, particularly criminal justice organisations, committed to identifying, acknowledging and addressing institutional racism. The limited progress made since the Inquiry shows that challenging and addressing racism and race inequality is not achieved through 'moments in time'; nor is it achieved through circular debate about terminology which favours the powerful and largely privileged majority. The public requires all criminal justice system organisations to articulate an unequivocal position on addressing racism and discrimination, and for them to be held to account through transparent, robust and ongoing scrutiny mechanisms.

Beverley Thompson, former member of Home Secretary's Stephen Lawrence Steering Group and Race Equality Advisor to HM Prison Service. Current member of the Sentencing Council for England & Wales

impact and retain resonance today; they gave expression to the views and experiences of racism from black and minority ethnic communities that were not frequently heard. Although there have not been any public inquiries dedicated to racial inequality in the criminal justice system since the Mubarek Inquiry in 2006, numerous high-profile reports and reviews have tackled race issues in the operation of the criminal justice system. These include:

- **Denman Report (2001):** A review of race discrimination in the CPS, led by Sylvia Denman. It focused on the impact of race discrimination on CPS staff and whether racism filtered into prosecutors' work in courts. The report questioned why the CPS failed to correct the bias in police charging decisions and allowed weaker cases against ethnic minority defendants to go to trial.
- **Young Black People and the Criminal Justice System (2007):** A Home Affairs Committee report, chaired by John Denham MP, to understand the reasons for the over-representation of young black people in the system.
- **The Race Review (2008):** Implementing race equality in prisons, five years on from the formal investigation of the Commission for Racial Equality which was led by the Prison Service Race and Equality Action Group.
- **The Young Review (2014):** A review into improving outcomes for young black and Muslim men in the criminal justice system supported by an independent advisory group.
- **The Laming Review (2016):** An independent review chaired by Lord Laming to challenge and change the over-representation of looked-after children in the youth justice system in England and Wales.
- **The Lammy Review (2017):** A review led by the Labour MP David Lammy to identify racial disparities in the criminal justice system from the point of arrest through to rehabilitation within prison and community.

We have mentioned the Lammy Review at several points in this chapter as it was and has been particularly impactful. The review's 35 recommendations ranged from staffing prisons with personnel more representative of society, a 'problem-solving' approach to dealing with prisoner complaints, the quality of data on race, the manner in which the CPS approaches gang prosecutions, and using modern slavery legislation to protect the public and prevent the exploitation of vulnerable young people. Notably, it recommended that:

> If CJS agencies cannot provide an evidence-based explanation for apparent disparities between ethnic groups then reforms should be introduced to address those disparities. This principle of 'explain or reform' should apply to every CJS institution.
>
> (Lammy Review, 2017: recommendation 4, p. 7)

The government's response to Lammy indicated that it would 'take forward every recommendation in some way', including finding 'alternative approaches' to achieve the same aims. It accepted the principle of 'explain or reform' as a structured approach to identify and address racial disparities (Ministry of Justice, 2018: 4).

This appeared to be a positive response, although successful implementation ultimately depends on a commitment to adequately address social problems beyond the criminal justice system itself. The Grenfell Tower Inquiry (still ongoing at the time of writing in late 2020) appears to provide evidence of this broader **social justice** remit that includes disparities in housing and issues of class—social exclusion, in short. But the government's announcement, in June 2020, of a Commission on Race and Ethnic Disparities was met with criticism. David Lammy characterised it as a knee-jerk plan to satisfy the BLM movement, saying 'We do not need another report, or review or commission to tell us what to do' (*The Guardian*, 2020). He and others pointed out that conducting another review of racism in the UK when the necessary evidence and data on inequalities have already been exhaustively collected amounted to an avoidance of action.

It is perhaps surprising that more intervention is not forthcoming, given the level of consensus among experts on the need to address structural racial inequality. This consensus was apparent in the evidence given by practitioners, community activists, and academics to the reports after Mubarek (the ones listed earlier). These reports and the Grenfell Tower Inquiry show that people who have personal experiences of racial prejudice and discrimination are now driving change in the discourse and policy outcomes on race and racism. The BLM phenomenon of 2020 pushed in exactly the same direction.

Having gained a good understanding of the extent and nature of racial disparities, in the next section we consider the issues through the lens of critical race theory. First, though, complete **What do you think? 10.5** to reflect on the impact of the recent attempts to address racial inequality in the criminal justice system.

WHAT DO YOU THINK? 10.5

The impact of reports and inquiries into racial inequality

Look up the latest reviews and inquiry reports into policy and practice on race inequality in the criminal justice system and critically evaluate their findings. Consider the following questions:

1. What long-lasting impact has the Lawrence Inquiry had on the policing of racial minorities?
2. What does the Lammy Review mean by the principle of 'explain or reform'?
3. How have the various inquiries and reviews changed policing?
4. How have the inquiries and reviews informed the broader debates around justice and injustice?

10.7 Theorising race, ethnicities, and the CJS: critical race theory

Criminologists have developed a number of theories in their efforts to better understand and respond to the complex issues of race, ethnicity, and crime. These include **classical criminology**, **biological positivism**, **psychological positivism**, **cultural criminology**, and **structuralism**. In this section, we focus on **critical race theory** (CRT), generally preferred by criminologists and sociologists studying race, for its rigour and substance. We will attempt to locate CRT within the critical criminological theoretical tradition and consider how this perspective can help challenge established legal and social **norms** that perpetuate conditions of oppression and disadvantage. We will consider the criticisms made of it, before applying the theory to some of the issues discussed in this chapter.

What is CRT?

Critical race theory is an interdisciplinary movement which emerged in the US in the 1970s to study and theorise the relationship between race, racism, and power. Unlike classical and positivist criminological theories, CRT is set within a broader socio-economic and historical perspective, seeks to challenge racial hierarchy and subordination in all its forms, and aims to transform unequal societal structures. Critical criminological perspectives (see **Chapter 18**) help us understand how the unequal distribution of power in society tends to criminalise and victimise those who are less powerful.

CRT helps to examine the nature of institutionalised racial oppression within social structures that are defined by race. These are structures (how decisions are made in policing and prosecution, for example) in which intentional and unintentional racism is prevalent but subtle, meaning that some forms of it cannot be tackled through legal remedies such as race equality legislation. CRT provides a way of examining the dominant **ideology**, assumptions, and discourse that shape racial oppression; through this, it helps us understand the dynamics of structures and institutions such as the criminal justice system, as well as the concepts of race, crime, and justice that characterise it.

CRT can be a useful tool for understanding critical issues such as racial profiling, the over-representation of ethnic minorities in the criminal justice process, and official responses to racial violence. Specifically, it helps us ask questions like:

- Why are racial minority groups over-represented in the criminal justice system?
- Why do institutions such as the police profile and target specific groups disproportionately when using tactics like stop and search?
- Why, despite numerous official responses to racial violence in England and Wales, does victimisation of racial minority groups persist?

CRT is generally viewed as sitting within the tradition of **critical criminology**. As we discuss in **Chapter 18**, the foundations of critical criminology emerged in the 1960s and 1970s with works on **labelling** by Howard Becker, and on conflict, including Marxist criminology, explored by William Chambliss, Richard Quinney, and Jock Young.

Criminologists on the left offered perspectives on how inequality based on class affected crime and deviance, whereas right-leaning criminologists overlooked structural factors and focused on the individual (see **Chapter 20**). In the late 1980s, critical criminology focused on how power shapes the construction of crime and the operation of criminal justice. Zemiology, the study of social harm (see **section 10.3** and **Chapter 19**), then expanded the remit of criminal justice to include acts that cause social harm and undermine social justice. Cultural criminologists added to our understanding of factors that sustain criminal activity—not only background factors such as socio-economic disadvantage, but also how foreground factors such as emotion and thrill-seeking can lead to criminal activity (Ugwudike, 2015).

In the 1970s, CRT brought together insights from critical legal studies (which sees inherent social biases in the law) and radical feminism (Delgado and Stefancic, 2012). Insights from the latter include the relationship between power and the construction of social roles, and patterns and habits that support forms of domination. But CRT differs from both these approaches in the way it makes the treatment of race its central theme, not only to law and policy but also to the expression of racism and power in wider society. Early proponents of CRT—Derrick Bell, Alan Freeman, Mari Matsuda, Kimberle Crenshaw, Patricia Williams, and Richard Delgado—aimed to pursue new strategies to address more subtle forms of racism that were becoming more evident.

The aims of CRT

According to Ugwudike (2015), CRT theorists study how society constructs race and attributes certain traits to groups, and how it establishes ideas about racial difference. The concepts of **intersectionality** and **anti-essentialism** are important to CRT theorists. These propose that individuals do not have fixed identities; they are an accumulation of identities. The ways in which different features of individual identity (for example, one's race, social class, sexuality, and gender identity) intersect to produce different experiences for minority ethnic groups is key to CRT. For these theorists, racism is a normal feature of social relations; it is prevalent but insidious. They also believe that race equality laws are effective only on blatant forms of racism.

In their rejection of legal liberalism (a belief that governments should be constrained by legal boundaries), CRT scholars argue that US law, including anti-discrimination law and the way it is implemented, is structured to maintain white privilege. In bringing together a review of the key writings that informed the CRT movement, Bennett Capers (2014: 26) identifies the following five recurring themes and tenets:

1. Formal equality laws often marginalise and obscure social, political, and economic inequality.
2. Legal reforms that seemingly benefit ethnic minorities happen only when such reforms benefit the interests of the white majority. This is called the principle of 'interest convergence'.
3. Race is biologically insignificant and, to a large extent, socially and legally constructed.
4. CRT scholars reject **essentialism**, or the belief that race itself defines how racial discrimination is experienced; they argue that it is experienced according to a multitude of personal and social circumstances. CRT is a critique of power relationships that considers the many levels on which oppression and subordination exist.
5. Reference to race is often omitted in the law, so CRT scholars try to make race visible by incorporating personal narratives or 'legal storytelling' into their methods.

CRT also recognises that racism is not simply embedded in individual prejudices and biases; it is also embedded and reproduced within social structures and within political and legal institutions. It exposes how race and racism represent social thought and power relations and maintain racial inequality in ways that 'appear normal and unremarkable' (Rollock and Gillborn, 2011: 1). We can try to eliminate these racialised hierarchies through a robust scrutiny of procedures and laws. Since CRT initially emerged as a challenge to US law, critical race theorists use the concept of 'legal indeterminacy' to suggest that courts have the power to determine different outcomes for a given case. According to Ugwudike (2015), the selection of different legal arguments for different outcomes leaves scope for potentially discriminatory decision-making on racial or other grounds. Critical theorists also explore how 'deficit thinking' can put minority ethnic groups at a further disadvantage. This involves constructing negative narratives which suggest certain groups possess inherent deficits that are linked to their pathology or biological constitution (Ugwudike, 2015: 227).

In the UK, CRT is used mainly in the field of education, but it has the capacity to be a useful framework for helping us understand ethnic disproportionality and unequal outcomes in the criminal justice system.

Criticisms of CRT

CRT is not without its weaknesses. The theory is criticised for being separatist in that it encourages **identity politics** based on the shared experiences of one group to pursue self-determination. Nor does it prescribe solutions to structural problems (Capers, 2014). It has even been described, by Richard Posner, as a 'lunatic fringe' (ibid: 26). Other criticisms levelled at CRT include:

- 'playing the race card' (exploiting the idea of racism for gain);
- encouraging a narrative of victimisation;
- propounding irrational ideas;
- sacrificing objective theoretical analysis for subjective storytelling; and
- implying that black people all think alike (Ugwudike, 2015).

CRT is subject to criticism from within, in that activists who support its ideals sometimes question its practical value. They ask how CRT can help activists to challenge a social order that treats some groups unfairly, and how it can help us deal with problems such as racial profiling or police brutality. Activists maintain that the distrust of existing civil rights laws in CRT is not helpful because these laws are in fact effective in enforcing formal equality in the treatment of all citizens (Delgado and Stafanic, 2017).

CRT scholars have also been accused of abandoning their focus on the materialist issues that impact disenfranchised groups and turning to matters that interest middle-class people, such as '**microaggression**'. In response to these criticisms, critical race theorists are combining theory and practice and developing solutions for the social injustices that black groups face (Ugwudike, 2015: 229–31).

Despite the criticisms it faces, the influence of CRT is growing in law to challenge substantive criminal law and procedure. As a discipline, it is now widely taught at law schools and CRT scholarship exists beyond the US. CRT has also led to other critical approaches to the law, such as LatCrit theory, Asian-American jurisprudence, Queer Critical Theory, Critical Race Feminism, and Critical White Studies (Capers, 2014: 26).

Now that we have explored what CRT is, what it aims to do, and the criticisms levelled at the theory, we will apply it to the issues discussed throughout the chapter.

Applying CRT to ethnicity and crime in the UK

CRT offers a toolkit to help us understand, question, and challenge racially discriminatory practices within the UK criminal justice system. From all the information and statistics we have considered so far, it will be clear that unequal outcomes are a core feature of the criminal justice system in England and Wales. Despite inquiries and reviews, legislation (such as the Race Relations Amendment Act 2000 and the Equality Act 2010), and improved policies, ethnic disproportionality remains. Like its US counterpart, the criminal justice system in England and Wales has become a system of racialised social control in which black people and ethnic minorities are treated inequitably (even if implicitly) and, once they are in the system, they are kept in it for longer. It is no longer legal or socially acceptable to discriminate, exclude, and condemn explicitly on the grounds of race, but the use of labels and language to make associations between race and criminality persists through the criminal justice system. In this context, Michelle Alexander's observation that the idea and system of racial caste in the US has not ended but has merely been redesigned, is powerful and astute (Alexander, 2010).

CRT opens new areas of scrutiny and allows us to examine the construction and operation of criminal law, policy, and practice. It allows us to see how crime categories are constructed and helps us uncover new locations of discretion—stages or processes at which racial bias can creep in and influence decisions. We have seen discretion even at the gateway to the criminal justice system: disparities of race and ethnicity in policing activity, notably in the use of stop and search. Criminalisation of young black men continues through the discourse shaped around gangs (an issue we also touch on in **Chapter 9** and **Conversations 9.1**), and the outcome is an over-representation of ethnic minority groups in prison. Williams and Clarke reveal 'dangerous associations of a series of negative constructs, signifying racialised stereotypes that endure and underpin contemporary policing and prosecution strategies' (2016: 3); although their research was in relation to serious youth violence, similar strategies and negative constructs disproportionately punish and criminalise black groups of all ages and at all stages in the criminal justice system.

The extent to which discretion is informed by implicit bias is becoming a popular tool to scrutinise how decisions are made and by whom. Much of the research on implicit bias has been shaped in the US context and its implications are a matter of debate. But it reveals how implicit racial bias can operate in judgements made on bail, pre-trial motions, evidentiary issues, and witness credibility in a way that has a cumulative effect on statistics on imprisonment rates and sentence length. Davis (cited in Capers, 2014) suggests that a prosecutor may choose to prosecute a defendant more aggressively in cases where white victims are involved and may be less aggressive when prosecuting a similar case when the victim is from a racial minority. The decision-making may not be transparent or available to review but Davis suggests that such differences are rarely the product of direct discrimination; they have more to do with implicit biases we all share about race, individual worth, and crime (Capers, 2014: 30). You can examine your own implicit bias now by following the instructions and answering the questions in **What do you think? 10.6**. One way of identifying racial biases is through 'race-switching' exercises, in which an individual (ideally a criminal justice system decision-maker) assesses whether they would take the same view if the racial roles were reversed. This

WHAT DO YOU THINK? 10.6

Examining your own implicit bias

Are you aware of your own implicit bias? Take one of the online 'implicit association tests' available at https://implicit.harvard.edu/implicit/takeatest.html. Note down the results of your test and consider the following questions:

- Were you surprised by the results of your test?
- Can you apply the principles of CRT to understand your test results?
- Can you see how the implicit biases identified in your test have affected or might affect your views on matters of crime and justice?

Figure 10.6 'Race-switching' exercises, such as the technique used in the novel *Noughts and Crosses*, which was dramatised for the BBC in 2020, are one way of identifying and neutralising racial bias

Source: WENN Rights Ltd/Alamy Stock Photo

technique aims to neutralise racial biases by foregrounding them. We can see the efficacy of this approach in the responses to the TV adaptation of Malorie Blackman's race-reversal novel *Noughts and Crosses* (see **Figure 10.6**), which aired in 2020 in the wake of the BLM protests.

CRT also prompts us to examine new forms of discretion, such as the use of stop and search to gather intelligence on gangs and **joint enterprise**. The **social constructions** of threat and of 'black' criminality (constructions that are often media-led—see **Chapter 6**) allow the system to focus its energies and resources on policing and control strategies, meaning that it spends less time and money on criminalising other white-collar crimes. Capers suggests that the definition and ranking of crimes in the US is dependent on race and that this has resulted in crack cocaine offences being ranked higher than possession of cocaine powder (Capers, 2014: 29). Such ethnic disparities are mirrored in the UK. The *Colour of Injustice* report shows that black and Asian people in England and Wales use cannabis at a lower rate than white people but are convicted for possession at 11.8 and 2.4 times the rate, respectively (Shiner et al., 2018).

By applying CRT, we can better see how policies are designed. Policies should operate for the benefit of all groups in society, but we could argue that criminal justice policy in England and Wales is implemented in a way that perpetuates the stigmatisation of groups such as young black men. The same groups also disproportionately suffer as victims of crime and perceive that criminal justice agencies will treat them unfairly compared to white groups. As social constructions of crime, race, gender, and other minorities gain legitimacy, narratives of difference become amplified. The treatment by state agencies of children leaving care—and the black and mixed-race groups among them—who end up in the criminal justice or mental health systems is a good example of how marginalisation can be made worse by institutionalisation.

In England and Wales, the high rates of stop and search, arrest, and imprisonment of young black males are attributed in popular culture to problems associated with family structure or black culture. But the statistics cannot be satisfactorily explained by racial profiling, joblessness, or the operation of laws and policing activities that target black young people in groups, particularly those in gangs. Inquiries, reports, and reviews have exposed a contradiction between the *ideal* of equality and fairness and the reality that some groups are disadvantaged and seen as undeserving. The CRT framework has been the subject of much discussion and debate, particularly in 2020 (see **Controversy and debate 10.1**), but there are compelling arguments that it is a useful tool for policy analysts, first, as a way to identify the underlying causes of socio-economic disadvantage and, secondly, to address the unequal outcomes of criminal justice.

CONTROVERSY AND DEBATE 10.1

'Decolonising the curriculum': critical race theory under the spotlight in 2020

The controversial nature of CRT became more visible in the UK in the wake of the Black Lives Matter protests of 2020. In October 2020, a parliamentary debate was held in response to online petitions entitled 'Teach Britain's colonial past as part of the UK's compulsory curriculum', 'Add education on diversity and racism to all school curriculums', and 'Making the UK education curriculum more inclusive of BAME history' (Hansard, vol. 682, 20 October 2020). The fractious debate resulted in a fundamental split on whether 'decolonising the curriculum' in schools (the efforts to reassess and reconstruct what is taught to mitigate the dominance of white people and white-focused perspectives), was necessary or even relevant. Labour and Scottish National Party MPs argued in favour and Conservative MPs against; for some of the latter it amounted to a tedious slogan.

Government Minister for Equalities, Kemi Badenoch, who is black, argued that the school curriculum does not need to be decolonised 'for the simple reason that it is not colonised' (Hansard, col. 1011, 20 October 2020). She went on to say:

> The recent fad to decolonise maths, decolonise engineering and decolonise the sciences that we have seen across our universities—to make race the defining principle of what is studied—is not just misguided but actively opposed to the fundamental purpose of education.

The minister explicitly blamed CRT for this. She claimed that CRT was a 'dangerous trend in race relations', criticising the way in which it (she argued) has been absorbed across society, in business, as well as in education, and suggesting that it is 'an ideology that sees my blackness as victimhood and their whiteness as oppression'. She declared the government's 'unequivocal' opposition to critical race theory (Hansard, col. 1011, 20 October 2020):

> We do not want teachers to teach their white pupils about white privilege and inherited racial guilt. Let me be clear that any school that teaches those elements of critical race theory as fact . . . without offering a balanced treatment of opposing views, is breaking the law.

Badenoch also warned schools that to 'openly support the anti-capitalist Black Lives Matter group' was to ignore their statutory duty to be politically impartial (Hansard, col. 1011, 20 October 2020).

The UK government had issued guidance, in September 2020, that 'Schools should not under any circumstances work with external agencies that take or promote extreme positions' or 'use resources produced by organisations that take extreme political stances'. Examples included 'promoting divisive or victim narratives that are harmful to British society' (Department for Education, 2020).

The right-leaning media were generally supportive of this guidance. Douglas Murray, a right-wing commentator, argued that the UK should follow the lead of US President Donald Trump when he ordered federal agencies to stop funding training programmes that draw on race-based ideologies: 'The government of this country should follow suit. It is clear where CRT ends. It is not in harmony and fairness. It is a system that attaches electrodes to the brains of a tolerant liberal and diverse society and then fries them' ('It is about time we fought back against the unthinking adoption of critical race theory', *The Telegraph*, 3 October 2020).

A letter to *The Guardian* from academics at the UCL Institute of Education expressed deep misgivings about how the national debate on racism had developed, and the way in which CRT was being represented:

> We are particularly concerned by the misrepresentation of critical race theory, a well-established, diverse body of work . . . To target this body of theory at this moment in time amounts to an attack on black scholars and activists who are already struggling against racial injustice.
>
> ('Diversity of thought is vital in education', *The Guardian*, 13 November 2020)

So while the BLM protests in the summer of that year had re-ignited a national conversation about the nature and extent of racism in the UK, there was a clear backlash to its implications. It is important to note that the opposition to decolonising the curriculum and to CRT that was evident in the government side in the House of Commons was not founded on a denial that black lives do indeed matter. It was a product of almost irreconcilable ideas of what British colonial history means for race relations in the present, and a perception—or misrepresentation—of CRT as an alien intellectual import that is dedicated to worsening those relations. The subject could hardly be more contentious.

10.8 Conclusion

We have seen in this chapter that racial inequality in the UK has a long and multifaceted history. It has taken many decades for the state and society to recognise and understand the extent and shape of inequality in the UK, which is at its worst in relation to criminal justice. The criminal justice system has been complicit in entrenching these inequalities, while the discipline of criminology has marginalised race and crime as one of its own sub-disciplines. However, criminology can now play a central role in exposing and illuminating racial injustice by explaining the dynamics of race, patterns of racism, and racialisation in the UK, including through the themes and tenets of CRT. Solutions can follow only from such understanding.

So what progress can we hope to see in the coming years? The Black Lives Matter protests of 2020 re-ignited a national conversation about race in the UK and undoubtedly prompted a national reckoning with racial inequality in all its forms. Its ripple effect was visible not only in the mainstream media but also across politics, culture, social media, sports, and business. Individuals and organisations have issued statements of support for efforts to tackle racism; the term 'white privilege' has perhaps never been so widely used; and people have begun to describe themselves—and push others to do the same—as not just non-racist, but as 'anti-racist', implying a need for action. But will these developments bring about meaningful and long-lasting change?

It has been suggested that although there is much work to be done, the events of 2020 have at least helped to reinforce the fact throughout wider society that significant racial inequality still exists in the UK, and not just in the US. As writer and broadcaster Afua Hirsch has powerfully argued, it is naive to think that we live in 'post-racial' society, or to strive to be 'colourblind' (see **What do you think? 10.2**). We can also see this shift in the starting point in the more recent high-level strategic reviews in the criminal justice system: the Young Review (2014) and the Lammy Review (2017) were led by black individuals who acknowledge the centrality of racism in the criminal justice system. This is an important departure from previous inquiries and reviews that failed to acknowledge this status quo. In working closely with organisations and agencies dominated by white groups, the Young and Lammy Reviews have the potential to challenge conscious or unconscious white privilege. In soliciting and airing the views of racial and ethnic minorities, the reviews offer an insightful counter-narrative that empowers the voice and experience of those who have experienced racism and understand how they have been marginalised in and by the criminal justice system.

SUMMARY

After reading this chapter and working your way through its features you should now be able to:

- Understand the racialised nature of crime and criminal justice today, with reference to its historical and socio-political contexts

The chapter opens a discussion about why racial disparities persist in diverse societies. This connects to the histories of migration and the British Empire, slavery, and its eventual abolition. 'Race' and 'ethnicity' today are common ways of identifying people and organising social life in multicultural, postcolonial societies. Criminologists and students of criminology are invited to reckon with race, racism, and racial hierarchies to gain a systematic understanding of race inequalities. These terms permeate our collective understanding of society and nation; it is therefore important to understand their relationship with criminology, crime, and criminal justice.

- Approach 'knowledge' about race, ethnicities, and crime with caution and appreciate the ways in which it can be problematic

When engaging with information on race and crime, it is important to question how knowledge on these issues is obtained and constructed. ABC (*Always Be Critical*) is a good strategy. Statistics on race and ethnicity can serve as useful starting points but they do not reflect the whole picture. We have seen that there are many reasons why ethnic minorities are over-represented at nearly every stage of the criminal justice system, and that it is misleading and inaccurate to take these figures at face value, as indications that certain groups simply commit more crime. We also need to be aware that criminological knowledge on race is historically limited partly because, in common with other disciplines, its origins are dominated by white scholars, mainly men. Fresh perspectives are now emerging.

- Recognise the key decision-making points in the criminal justice process that potentially increase or decrease ethnic disproportionality and affect patterns of victimisation

The chapter establishes that ethnic minorities are more likely to be subject to racially and religiously motivated hate crimes. Higher rates of victimisation are linked to adverse outcomes in health, housing, and economic status. Ethnic minorities can be both victims and perpetrators of crime—a good example is the largely hidden crime of modern slavery. In regard to offending, ethnic minority groups are disproportionately represented at every stage of the criminal justice process and we have seen that there are numerous explanations for this. Policing of drugs and the use of stop and search remain key drivers of disproportionality in prosecution and sentencing. In considering race, ethnicity, and offending, it is important to understand that labelling and racial profiling serve to reinforce and reproduce the associations between 'black' and criminality.

- Appreciate the ways in which people from ethnic minorities are treated less fairly by criminal justice agencies

Experiences of ethnic minorities in policing, prosecution, sentencing, and in prison remain negative. Black people remain over-policed and under-protected and once in the criminal justice system are treated harshly at courts and given longer sentences than white people. Ethnic minorities, particularly young black men, face greater risk of criminalisation and harsher sanctions. Bias and discrimination in the criminal justice process, including in complaints procedures and an unrepresentative workforce, go some way to explaining why ethnic minorities lack trust and confidence in the promises of equality and fairness made by the criminal justice system.

- Develop a critical view of official and policy responses designed to address institutional racism, ethnic disproportionality, and the patterns of victimisation

We explored the official responses of the Scarman, Lawrence and Mubarek Inquiries to the problem of race and racism and analysed their short- and longer term impact. The Lawrence Inquiry placed the concept of institutional racism into the public domain. Several other reports and reviews, most recently the Lammy Review, have made recommendations on redressing the entrenched patterns of racial disparities in criminal justice. But the Black Lives Matter protests of 2020 forced British society to return to the question: 'What exactly has changed?'

- Explain what critical race theory is and apply this framework to analyse the disparate outcomes for ethnic minority groups involved in the criminal justice system

Classical, positivist, cultural, and structural theories are not wholly adequate in explaining the complex intersections of race, ethnicity, and crime. We identified the five key tenets of CRT and saw that racism is not simply embedded in individual prejudices and biases; it is also embedded and reproduced within social structures and within political and legal institutions. CRT helps us to challenge established legal and social norms that perpetuate conditions of oppression and disadvantage. In applying CRT to the issues discussed throughout the chapter, we demonstrated that it can provide a sophisticated understanding of how and why patterns of ethnic disproportionality and unequal outcomes remain entrenched in criminal justice. CRT has limitations like any other theoretical framework, and we saw that its increased prevalence and acceptance in UK society has been the source of much debate, but it is robust in illuminating patterns of racial injustice.

 Test your understanding of the chapter's key points by attempting the self-test questions on the **online resources** at www.oup.com/he/case2e

REVIEW QUESTIONS

1. Outline the key historical events which shaped—and continue to shape—the nature of race relations in the UK today, affecting all aspects of society but especially crime and the criminal justice system.

2. What are the main problems with 'knowledge', and particularly statistical knowledge, about race, ethnicities, and crime?

3. What are the apparent links between ethnicity and victimisation and offending?

4. In the context of England and Wales, what are the main reasons for the over-representation of black, Asian, and minority ethnic groups at each stage of the criminal justice process?

5. In which decade and where did CRT first gain prominence?

6. In his review of the key writings that informed the CRT movement, what five recurring themes or tenets did Bennett Capers identify?

7. What are the main criticisms of CRT?

8. Two more recent reviews focusing on race issues in criminal justice have been led by Baroness Lola Young and the MP David Lammy. Using CRT, discuss why these reviews stand out and what makes them significant.

 Access the **online resources** at www.oup.com/he/case2e to check your answers to the review questions.

FURTHER READING

Bowling, B. and Phillips, C. (2002) *Racism, Crime and Justice.* **Harlow: Pearson Education.**
A key textbook that offers rich analysis of racism in the criminal justice process and accounts for experiences of criminalisation of ethnic minority groups.

Decolonization of Criminology and Justice.
The first volume of this journal was published in 2019 and is supported by the School of Social Sciences and Public Policy, Auckland University of Technology, Aotearoa, New Zealand. The journal is an important source of information on the decolonisation of criminology and justice, which encompasses theoretical, qualitative, and quantitative inquiries into traditional and emerging justice topics and studies on epistemologies, methodologies, and methods related to criminological research and tertiary teaching.

Delsol, R. and Shiner, M. (eds) (2015) *Stop and Search: The Anatomy of a Police Power*. London: Palgrave Macmillan.

An important read to understand the key controversies around police power to stop and search. It provides important insights into the history of policing black communities and the up-to-date developments, including regulation and reform, in assessing the effectiveness of these powers.

Equality and Human Rights Commission (2019) *Is Britain Fairer? The state of equality and human rights 2018*. London: HMSO.

This is the most comprehensive review available (at the time of writing) of how Britain is performing on equality and human rights. It presents data and information across all areas of life, including education, work, living standards, health, justice and security, and participation in society. These issues are contextualised against the long-term impact of austerity measures, spikes in hate crime, and the impact of leaving the EU.

Parmar, A., Earle, R., and Phillips, C. (2020) 'Race matters in criminology: Introduction to the Special Issue', *Theoretical Criminology* 24(3).

A special issue of Theoretical Criminology which brings together articles by leading scholars who attended and contributed to the 'Race matters: A new dialogue between criminology and sociology' international symposium held at the LSE in 2018.

Shiner, M. et al. (2018) *The Colour of Injustice: 'Race', drugs and law enforcement in England and Wales*. London: StopWatch and Release (www.stop-watch.org/uploads/documents/The_Colour_of_Injustice.pdf).

Uses statistical analysis of police data and documents the disproportionate impact that drug law enforcement continues to have on black and minority ethnic communities in England and Wales. This causes acute racial injustice.

Williams, P. and Kind, E. (2019) *Data-driven Policing: The hardwiring of discriminatory policing practices across Europe*. Brussels: European Network Against Racism (www.enar-eu.org/IMG/pdf/data-driven-profiling-web-final.pdf).

This interesting text suggests that the use of technology to assist policing and wider law enforcement practices across Europe is not new. The problem is that law enforcement agencies are presenting technology as 'race-neutral', independent of bias, and objective in their pursuit to prevent crime and offending behaviour.

Access the **online resources** to view a wealth of extra information relating to your study of criminology, including self-test questions, answers to review questions, and links to other resources that will help you enjoy and fulfil your potential within your studies.

www.oup.com/he/case2e

CHAPTER OUTLINE

11.1	Introduction	310
11.2	Gender and criminology: an overview	310
11.3	Feminist criminology	324
11.4	Theoretical traditions of feminist criminology	327
11.5	Feminist epistemologies	334
11.6	Newer perspectives in feminist criminology	337
11.7	Conclusion	340

Gender and feminist criminology

Pamela Ugwudike

KEY ISSUES

After studying this chapter, you should be able to:

- understand key criminological explanations of how gender intersects with crime and criminal justice;
- identify the definition, origins, and key principles of feminist criminology;
- outline the main theoretical traditions influencing feminist criminology, namely liberalism, radicalism, Marxism, and socialism;
- recognise feminist epistemologies such as feminist empiricism, standpoint feminism, and postmodern feminism;
- critically evaluate criticisms of feminist criminology and the ways in which newer perspectives have tried to address them.

11.1 Introduction

As we have seen in the context of other topics, such as crime statistics (**Chapter 5**) and crime and the media (**Chapter 6**), criminologists have long been interested in studying how social categories such as gender, race, and sexuality influence and relate to crime and criminal justice. The categories to which you belong can have a significant effect on how you are portrayed and perceived in society, and on your experiences in relation to crime and the criminal justice system. In this chapter, we will focus on criminological studies of gender, particularly women's experiences of crime as offenders and victims, and the extent to which women's offending and **victimisation** are interlinked.

Why the focus on the female gender? You might have noticed from your studies so far, and your reading of other parts of this book, that mainstream criminology is male-dominated—it is dominated by theories and studies of men as victims or offenders. It therefore takes a primarily male perspective and is mostly silent on female-related issues. For much of this chapter we will try to redress this imbalance by focusing on women and feminist viewpoints, but it is important to be aware that the study of how gender intersects with crime and criminal justice goes beyond these themes. Some scholars writing about gender and its relationship to crime have focused on the male gender, demonstrating how **masculinities** (dimensions of the male gender) intersect with crime (Messerschmidt, 1993). Further dimensions of this area of study have been introduced through societal changes such as the growing acceptance of transgenderism (a broad term encompassing individuals who identify as a gender that is different from their birth-assigned gender category) and the emergence of trans-rights activism. These shifts have challenged the idea that birth-sex identity or non-transgender identity (also known as cisgender) is the norm, and there is an increasing awareness that some identities do not conform to conventional ideas of gender and sexuality (Koyama, 2003). Many scholars have noted that criminological analysis of gender and crime should therefore be expanded to consider the experiences of those who fall outside the male/female binary (see, for example, Jauk, 2013; Knight and Wilson, 2016).

Our discussion of gender and crime begins with an overview of how gender features in criminological studies. In this respect, we will consider the experiences of women as victims of crime, women as offenders, and men as offenders. Next, we consider the various elements of feminist criminology. We will explore its origins and principles, since they have heavily influenced criminological studies of gender and crime, followed by its main theoretical traditions and the epistemological orientations that influence feminist research. This exploration will include considering the criticisms levelled against the theories and approaches, and in the final section we explore how more recent strands of feminist thought have tried to respond. Although our main focus throughout the chapter will be on issues relating to women, we will refer to other dimensions of gender where relevant, to give you a sense of how much more there is to explore within this topic. This chapter is intended only as an introduction to some of the key ideas surrounding gender and criminology, and a window into why now is a particularly interesting time to be studying crime through the lens of gender—whatever its form, and regardless of your own gender.

11.2 Gender and criminology: an overview

As we noted in **section 11.1**, some criminologists believe that social categories (for example, ethnicity, gender, and class) can have a significant influence on how and whether people experience or enact criminal behaviour. In this section, we will consider the broad associations between gender and crime, but before reading further, consider the ways in which gender impacts our lives through **What do you think? 11.1**, then bear these ideas in mind as you progress through the chapter.

Women as victims

The data tell us that there are notable differences between the likelihood of men and women becoming a victim of certain kinds of crime. Men are more likely to be victims of personal crime, including violence and robbery: in the year ending March 2018, 4.4 per cent of men were victims of personal crime compared to 3.5 per cent of women (Ministry of Justice, 2018). However, as **Figure 11.1** shows, women are far more likely to be the victims of violence perpetrated by intimate male partners. Despite growing awareness of its harms by policymakers, within criminological research, and through numerous high-profile campaigns about the issue (see **Figure 11.2**), domestic violence in general continues to disproportionately affect women (Gadd, 2017; Ministry of Justice, 2018; ONS, 2019). In the year ending March 2019, approximately 2.4 million adults experienced domestic abuse and more than half (1.6 million) were women, whereas 786,000 were men (ONS, 2019). The victim was female in 75 per cent of the domestic abuse-related crimes recorded

WHAT DO YOU THINK? 11.1

What impact does gender have on your life—and why?

Do you think your gender has had and continues to have a significant impact on your life? Consider:

- The similarities and differences between your upbringing and those of friends and relatives of the opposite gender, for example in terms of:
  - the ways in which you were taught to think of yourself;
  - the restrictions and freedoms you had;
  - the nature and number of the anxieties you suffered.

- The extent to which reactions to your behaviours from those in 'authority'—such as your parents, carers, school teachers—appeared to have been shaped by your gender.

- How you respond to adverts and media pressure about your gender today. What controls—formal and informal—do you experience on your life and actions?

Now apply these opinions and observations to the context of crime. How do you think the **socialisation** processes you have experienced and witnessed in terms of gender might translate into and account for statistical patterns in victimisation and offending behaviours?

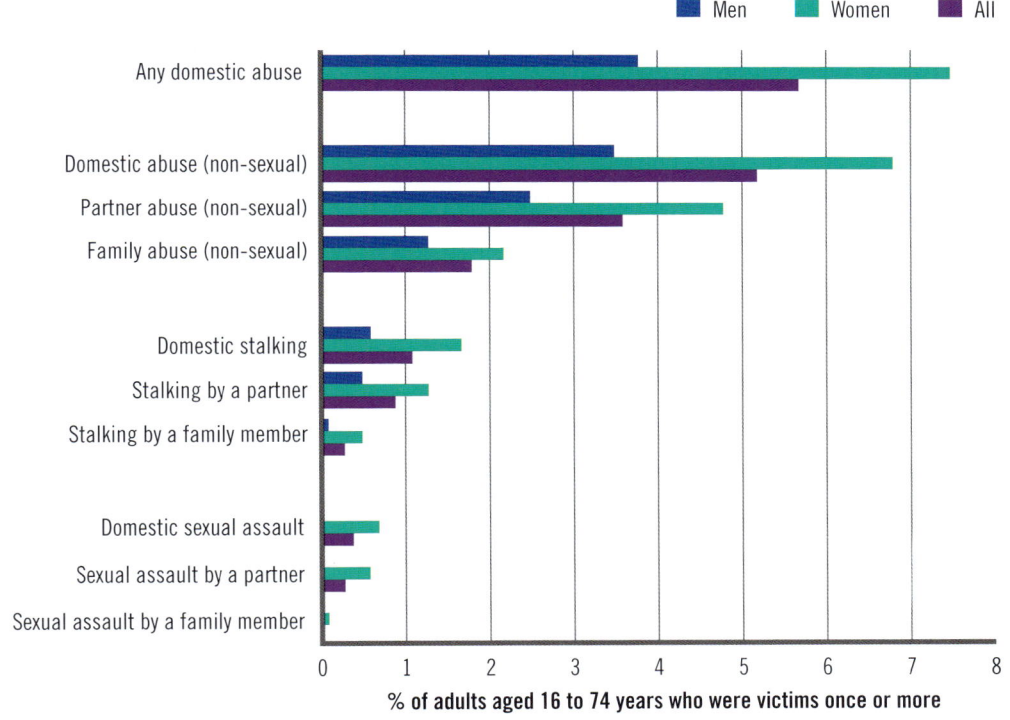

Figure 11.1 This graph depicts the prevalence of domestic abuse in the year ending March 2019 for adults aged 16–74 years by sex and type of abuse. As we can see, women are disproportionately represented in all categories
Source: Office for National Statistics

by the police (ONS, 2019). One study claims that the real figures are even more alarming than these **official statistics** suggest, finding that 61 per cent of women killed by men in the UK in 2018 were killed by a current or ex-partner (Femicide Census, 2020). These gender differences may be even more stark in the next statistical releases, in light of the reported increase in domestic abuse caused by the lockdowns imposed during the Covid-19 pandemic—we consider this issue in **New frontiers 11.1**.

Although national victimisation studies such as the Crime Survey for England and Wales (CSEW) have tried to capture more detailed information about the nature

Figure 11.2 The actor Sir Patrick Stewart is among the public figures who have lent their voices to campaigns aimed at ending violence against women

Source: PA Images

and extent of domestic violence, producing dedicated statistical bulletins on the issue, it remains a largely 'invisible crime' in the sense that it continues to be under-reported, under-recorded by the police, and under-prosecuted, internationally (Chesney-Lind and Hadi, 2017). There have been some signs of slight improvement in reporting rates, with CSEW data from the year ending March 2019 showing that reports of domestic abuse-related crimes increased by 24 per cent compared to the previous year, a rise which according to ONS (2019) may 'reflect improved recording by the police and increased reporting by victims'. However, it is also notable that in the same year, 11 per cent fewer suspects of domestic abuse-related cases were referred by the police to the Crown Prosecution Service (CPS) (ibid).

This CPS statistic points to one of the main reasons why this crime is said to be under-reported: the limited response from the criminal justice system. Studies (for example, Hester, 2013) and official inspections of policing activity in the UK continue to reveal that forces do not treat incidents of domestic violence with as much seriousness as we might expect. For example, an inspection of how the police deal with domestic abuse cases across England and Wales found that only eight out of the 43 police forces in England and Wales acted effectively to bring perpetrators to justice (Her Majesty's Inspectorate of Constabulary, 2014; see also Her Majesty's Inspectorate of Constabulary, and Fire & Rescue Services (HMICFRS), 2017). The situation seems to be similar in the US, where perpetrators of domestic violence against women are often treated more leniently than other violent offenders. This leniency can be seen not only in police activity but at other stages in countries' criminal justice systems. For instance, a study of the discretion (meaning freedom to make choices, for example about whether to arrest and

NEW FRONTIERS 11.1

Domestic violence and Covid-19: 'Dual pandemics'?

The restrictions and lockdowns imposed around the world from December 2019 onwards to contain and control the Covid-19 pandemic are widely accepted to have led to increased levels of domestic violence which, as we have seen, disproportionately affects women to the extent that some have implied that domestic violence against women and girls could constitute one of the legacies of the pandemic (for example, Mahase, 2020). Compounding this problem, many routes for help and support—such as schools, GPs, and workplaces—were closed and domestic abuse support services struggled to respond to the unprecedented challenges because they were already experiencing a funding crisis and 'had little or no financial resilience' (Women's Aid, 2020). The pandemic also led to major court delays, meaning that victims were waiting longer for perpetrators to be brought to justice. Campaigners argued that Covid-19 'exacerbated what was already an unacceptable backlog pre-lockdown' (End Violence Against Women, 2020).

In a survey conducted around this time, 67.4 per cent of those experiencing abuse said it had worsened since Covid-19, and 76.1 per cent said they were having to spend more time with their abuser (Women's Aid, 2020). Campaigners suggested that perpetrators were using the pandemic as a tool for abuse through asserting increased control; blaming their victim for the economic impact of the pandemic on the household; and using the virus itself to abuse, for example by refusing to take precautions or forcing the household to live under unnecessarily strict measures (ibid). In April 2020, the United Nations recognised the scale and severity of the issue in a statement from its Secretary-General António Guterres. He said:

> For many women and girls, the threat looms largest where they should be safest. In their own homes . . . We know lockdowns and quarantines are essential to suppressing COVID-19. But they can trap women with abusive partners. Over the past weeks as economic and social pressures and fear have grown, we have seen a

horrifying global surge in domestic violence. In some countries, the number of women calling support services has doubled. Meanwhile, healthcare providers and police are overwhelmed and understaffed. Local support groups are paralyzed or short of funds. Some domestic violence shelters are closed; others are full. I urge all governments to make the prevention and redress of violence against women a key part of their national response plans for COVID-19.

(United Nations, Secretary-General's video message on gender-based violence and COVID-19, www.un.org/sg/en/content/sg/statement/2020-04-05/secretary-generals-video-message-gender-based-violence-and-covid-19-scroll-down-for-french, 5 April 2020)

The UK government and Local Government Association issued guidance on getting help with domestic abuse during the coronavirus outbreak and clarified that household isolation instructions as a result of the virus 'do not apply if you need to leave your home to escape domestic abuse' (Home Office, 2018). However, even when lockdown measures began to ease in the latter half of 2020, the pandemic continued to affect women experiencing domestic abuse. One survivor was reported as saying that when her partner had been abusive, 'no-one would come and help due to the Covid-19. Even when the police said it's ok for someone to come to sit with me no-one would come' (Women's Aid, 2020). The pandemic is ongoing at the time of writing but it seems likely that its impact will outlast the virus itself, especially given the financial effect on the already-struggling domestic abuse support sector. Writing for the *New York Times*, Amanda Taub summed up the problem as follows:

Eventually, the lockdowns will end. But as the confinement drags on, the danger seems likely to intensify. Studies show that abusers are more likely to murder their partners and others in the wake of personal crises, including lost jobs or major financial setbacks. With Covid-19 ravaging the economy, such crises are set to become much more frequent.

(A. Taub, 'New Covid-19 Crisis: Domestic Abuse Rises Worldwide', *New York Times*, 6 April 2020)

charge suspects) used by police and prosecutors in US domestic violence cases found that 'there is substantial room for investigative improvement by police' and significant work has to be done to increase prosecution rates in relation to this type of crime (Nelson, 2014: 1). In that study, approximately 97 per cent of cases that were taken to court were resolved through plea bargaining, which involves an agreement between the prosecutor and **defendant** that the defendant will receive a more lenient sentence if they plead guilty to a less serious offence.

One of the reasons why perpetrators of domestic violence have historically been treated more leniently is that, before the late 1970s, many laws on domestic violence were not as strict as they are today. In the US, most cases of domestic abuse were classed as 'misdemeanours' (less serious offences), and the police were required to have witnessed the incident before they could arrest the suspect without a warrant—which is clearly difficult when an incident happens in someone's home. But in supposedly more serious felony cases, they had the discretion to choose to make an arrest without a warrant. In their analysis of these laws and the responses of criminal justice services to domestic violence cases, some suggested that many male police officers and prosecutors had sexist views and often used their discretion in favour of men, which meant fewer male offenders were arrested and prosecuted, leaving female victims more vulnerable to these crimes (see, for example, Houston, 2014). Another explanation for the limited criminal justice intervention in these cases is the issue of female victims not wanting to testify, resulting in 'case **attrition**', where felony arrests end up with no conviction or a conviction on reduced charges (Houston, 2014; Smith and Skinner, 2012). Some other key causes of case attrition—which is a problem for sexual assault cases in the UK as well as the US—include:

- the fear of revenge;
- court delays;
- lack of information about the progress of the case; and
- victim blaming (see Houston, 2014; Smith and Skinner, 2012).

We consider the phenomenon of victim blaming, where the victim is held completely or partly responsible for what happened to them, in **Controversy and debate 11.1**.

This situation began to change in subsequent years, thanks to the work of scholars like the Dobashes (1979), and others who were encouraging official intervention to protect the female victims of male violence. By the late 1980s, and in the 1990s and 2000s, almost all of the states in the US had enacted 'pro-arrest and mandatory arrest' laws. These laws allowed the police to arrest those suspected of domestic violence without a warrant, even if the police had not witnessed the incident (Houston, 2014: 262).

As well as prompting the introduction of new laws, victimisation statistics highlighting the extent of domestic violence, and the work of radical feminists in the US (including their research studies), have helped to challenge

! CONTROVERSY AND DEBATE 11.1

Is it a woman's responsibility to stay safe?

In **Chapter 7**, we explore in more detail the **concept** of 'victim blaming', where a victim is held fully or partly responsible for what has happened to them, as it is a concern for victims and victimology in general, but this phenomenon is particularly prevalent in sexual assault cases against women. As we have seen, it can arise in relation to domestic abuse, and Suarez and Gadalla (2010) have identified that the false beliefs and myths involved in victim blaming are in part responsible for the prevalence of crimes such as rape.

BBC News explored this issue in a 2018 article titled 'Victim blaming: Is it a woman's responsibility to stay safe?' which considered whether the suggestion that women should take precautions when alone in public is 'a form of victim blaming or necessary advice in an imperfect world' (BBC News, 10 October 2018). The Metropolitan Police had been strongly criticised for issuing such advice following a series of ten seemingly-linked attacks on lone women in London in which the man had usually approached a lone woman, tried to chat to her, asked for a kiss or a hug, then sexually abused her. The Metropolitan Police arrested a man, later releasing him under investigation, but Detective Constable Laura Avery is quoted as saying:

> I would appeal to women in the local area to take care when they are walking, especially if they are alone. Always stick to well-lit streets. If possible, let someone know when you are coming home and the route you are taking and always be alert in your surroundings, so don't use earphones or handheld devices.
>
> (BBC News, 9 October 2018)

While this might be sensible advice, it can be seen as placing 'an unfair onus on women to change their day-to-day, law-abiding, behaviour' (BBC News, 10 October 2018). This was certainly the view of many Twitter users, as shown in the following tweets:

> Women! Don't drink, don't flirt, don't walk home alone, don't wear a short skirt, don't use headphones, don't talk on the phone . . . How about, just once, tell men not to attack us! I'm so sick of this victim-blaming BSs. Male violence is not our fault.

> Women told to stop doing something they enjoy because men won't stop doing something illegal and violent. Can we see how this might be at odds with civilised society?

> While I'm sure the advice is well intended, it's very problematic. The narrative puts the victim at fault, rather than the criminal. We so frequently hear reports of attacks which detail the behaviour of the victim: what they were wearing, where they were, what time of day, if they were alone, if they had consumed alcohol. All of these things suggest that those choices were naive, foolish, dangerous, or incorrect in some way.
>
> (BBC News, 10 October 2018)

A quick Google search will show you that the issue of victim blaming, particularly in relation to assaults on women, remains live and controversial, despite the policy changes attempting to address it. As **Figure 11.3** illustrates, women still tend to be seen and presented as being in some way responsible for their victimisation, and tend to be advised to live in ways that minimise their risk of being subject to—usually male—violence.

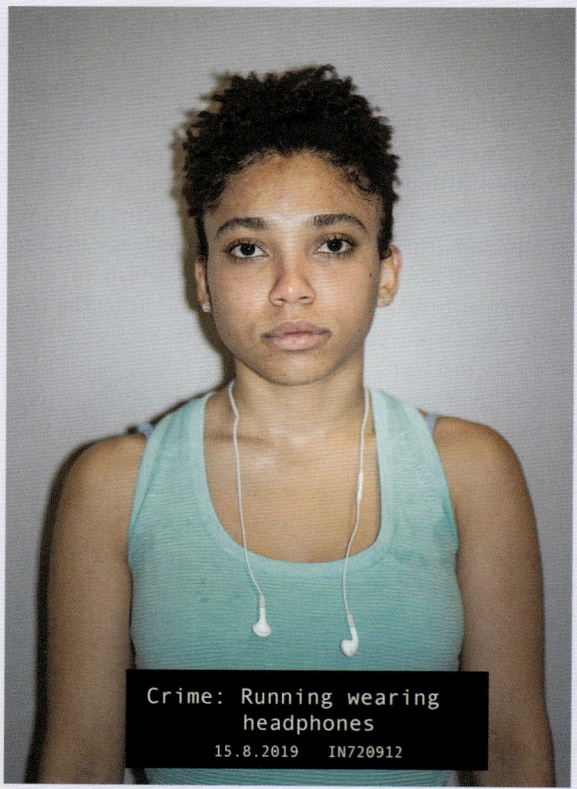

Figure 11.3 A photography exhibition entitled 'Asking for it' highlights the way that female victims of sexual assault often seem to be at least partially blamed for what has happened to them

Source: Jayne Jackson photography

the myths of the 'safe home' or 'stranger danger'. These myths emerged from interpretations of older crime statistics which ignored the hidden victimisation of women in the home by their intimate partners. The statistics implied that violent victimisation mainly involved random acts perpetrated outside the home by strangers who primarily victimised men, suggesting that men were more vulnerable to violent crimes, particularly violent **street crimes** (Myhill and Allen, 2002). Similar to the work of the feminist academics in the US, the scholarly work of UK feminists and those inspired by feminism, for example Stanko (1990) and Walklate (1991), has helped to move domestic violence from being a crime that occurs in the private space of the home to a public issue. Their efforts, alongside the work of campaigners, for example the charitable organisation known as Women's Aid, triggered a series of policy and legislative changes in the UK. Key examples are outlined below:

- 1970s: Laws such as the Domestic Violence and Matrimonial Proceedings Act 1976 were introduced, which empowered the police to arrest those suspected of not obeying orders in cases involving domestic violence.
- 1991: Marital rape became a crime and the previous presumption that marriage implied consent was abolished.
- 1996: Changes were made to the Family Law Act, Part IV to give police automatic powers to arrest suspects in domestic incidents where violence, or threats of violence, had occurred.
- 2004: The Domestic Violence, Crime and Victims Act empowered the police to arrest a person suspected of common assault without a warrant.
- 2005: The document 'Domestic Violence: A National Report' was published by the Home Office, showing the government's commitment to creating policies that deal with domestic violence.
- 2010: The government made plans to give funding to support 'rape crisis' centres for female victims.
- 2013: The UK government expanded the definition of domestic violence to include not only physical domestic abuse, but also non-violent domestic abuse, like behaviour that amounts to controlling the victim or coercing them in some way (Home Office, 2014).
- 2015: New laws were enacted to criminalise non-violent domestic abuse, such as emotional abuse and 'Clare's Law' (named after Clare Wood, who was killed by her ex-partner in 2009) was introduced in 2015 across England and Wales, allowing people to request information from the police about their partner's history of domestic abuse.
- 2016: The UK government published its new strategies in the policy paper titled, 'Strategy to end violence against women and girls: 2016 to 2020' (HM Government, 2016), available at: www.gov.uk/government/publications/strategy-to-end-violence-against-women-and-girls-2016-to-2020.
- 2019: A draft Domestic Abuse Bill was published, in which the government set out 123 legislative and non-legislative commitments aimed at raising awareness and understanding about the impact of domestic abuse; making the justice system more effective in protecting victims of domestic abuse and bringing perpetrators to justice; and improving support for victims of abuse.
- 2020: The government reintroduced the Domestic Abuse Bill, and at the time of writing it is making its way through the House of Lords, having completed its House of Commons stages. The Bill's factsheet is available at: www.gov.uk/government/publications/domestic-abuse-bill-2020-factsheets/domestic-abuse-bill-2020-overarching-factsheet.

Alongside developments in the law, policies have been introduced to try to prevent victim blaming (Coyle, 2007; Mawby and Walklate, 1994). Yet despite this progress, if we look back to **Figure 11.1** and consider the likely picture for 2020 (bearing in mind the issues described in **New frontiers 11.1**), it is clear that there is still more that should be done to further protect women and prevent this crime. For example, some argued that the 2020 Domestic Violence Bill does not acknowledge the reality that women are more likely than men to experience violent victimisation perpetrated by intimate male partners and other men (for example, Oppenheim, 2020). Criminological studies on women and crime are therefore integral to making sure criminal justice measures on domestic violence are continuously improved.

Before leaving this discussion about female victimisation to explore the issues associated with female offending, read **Conversations 11.1**, with writer, campaigner, and artist Eve McDougall, for an insight into the devastating impact of domestic abuse on women and their families. We return to Eve's story, and the events that preceded her abusive relationship, in **Chapter 18**.

Women as offenders

So far, we have explored gender and crime by looking at women's experiences as victims, focusing particularly on domestic violence as a form of victimisation which disproportionately affects women compared to men, and is hidden but widespread. As well as being victimised, women do commit crime but they are more likely than men to be

CONVERSATIONS 11.1

A personal journey through intimate abuse

with **Eve McDougall**

When I got married I thought it would be a special day, I thought I knew him, thought he was the man for me, but how wrong was I. I was punched, kicked, and battered all over the place that very evening. It was unbelievable; this man told me he loved me, he had taken special vows to take care of me, and this is how he showed his love. The days ahead were the most traumatic nightmare anyone could endure, with daily beatings, rape, and hours of psychological and mental abuse. I was in shock and traumatised.

I couldn't understand how someone you think you know could do all of these things to you and didn't even blink an eye, or that he was also injuring our unborn baby. It was extremely painful and shocking that my own husband was raping, beating, and traumatising me—hard to take in, and even harder to accept that this man who says he loves us and will do anything for us can switch rapidly into a person I don't know anymore, behaving like a psychopath. He would always say it was my fault, that I 'made him do it' and that I deserved to be taught a lesson. When I asked him what I had done, he would attack me and abuse me, kicking, punching, strangling, and raping me all over again, then he would get on his hands and knees, begging forgiveness and saying he didn't know what came over him and he would never do it again. He would even cry real tears, tears that I would believe and give him another chance.

It was degrading, humiliating, and all trust had flown off into the wilderness. How could I trust or believe this man who was injuring me, physically and emotionally scrambling my brains to the point of wanting to take my own life? I would run to my Mum and siblings but he always found me in the end. I felt I had nowhere to run. He battered me in front of my Mum and even strangers in public. It had a terrible effect on all of my family, especially my Mum having to watch helplessly as her daughter was hurt by a husband who claimed to love and protect her. She would break down crying, saying he was so nice to us all, he promised to take care of you. She would tell me, 'You have to get away to a place of safety, he will end up killing you. I don't know this man anymore; he's not the same guy who made all those promises. It just shows how you think you know someone but you really don't.'

I felt injured, betrayed, and so depressed by the fact that someone I thought I loved and knew so intimately, a supposed loving husband, could intimidate and inflict such brutality on the woman and child he says he loves. Any little thing that he didn't like, for instance, if the dinner wasn't to his liking, it would be like the trigger of a gun. He would blast all his anger and frustration at me and his unborn child, the child he said he longed for and would do anything to protect and keep safe from the dangers that he acted out and represented.

The years ahead didn't have any meaning in the world that I was existing in; I feared every second, minute, hour. I really didn't know this man I had married, he was a time bomb full of destruction and not the loving caring man I first met who spoke of a future of happy marriage and children. This guy was the total opposite of every promise he had ever made. I didn't understand any of it and I actually believed every 'sorry' and that he would never do it again.

It was a long journey back to reality when I finally did get away from him. It took about 20 years to finally get on a healing path to a place of safety, where I could finally thaw out and work on the trauma and disorder that the experience had caused. Now I look at what I want to do and what can I do, and I ignore that he always told me I would amount to nothing, that I was worthless, illiterate, thick, and stupid. I had believed that. But now I am not a victim, I am a survivor.

Eve McDougall, writer, campaigner, and artist

---

prosecuted for less serious crimes. For example, in 2017, TV licence evasion accounted for 30 per cent of all female prosecutions, compared to 4 per cent of male prosecutions, and shoplifting for 38 per cent of all female indictable prosecutions, compared to 17 per cent for men (Ministry of Justice, 2018). Women's victimisation has also been shown to be closely linked to their offending behaviour (Corston, 2007; Prison Reform Trust, 2017). Many female offenders have experienced domestic abuse, both physical and emotional, as well as coercive control and sexual abuse, and most women in prison have been victims of much more serious offences than those they are accused of committing (ibid).

Over the years, female offending has been explained in a variety of ways, many of which focus on stereotypical ideas about the female sex and its supposed attributes. Although most of these explanations have been disproved, the beliefs which underpin them continue to have some impact on the treatment of women in the criminal justice system. In this section, we therefore consider historical explanations of female offending as well as some more recent criminological accounts, before looking at women's experiences in the criminal justice system. First, read **What do you think? 11.2** to reflect on what the data tells us and what your assumptions are about female offending.

Historical explanations of female crime

Before feminist criminology emerged, there were very few explanations of female offending, and those that did exist were based on **positivist** ideas. Positivist criminology draws on biological, psychological, social, economic, or other similar factors outside the control of the individual to explain criminal behaviour (see also **Chapters 16** and **17**). This means that the positivist explanations of female offending were deterministic; they implied that there were certain attributes or characteristics that could make some women more likely to commit crime. When writing about the concept of **determinism**, Smart (1976) noted that women were portrayed as a homogenous group (having the same or very similar characteristics) whose behaviour was driven by biological and psychological forces beyond their control. Broader issues such as power relations and other inequalities, which had different effects on women's behaviours and experiences in each individual case, were ignored, and so were women's abilities to think and behave rationally (Klein and Kress, 1976; Carlen, 1983). Instead, as Klein and Kress (1976) point out, female offending was seen as part of women's sexuality or unique biological make-up.

WHAT DO YOU THINK? 11.2

The nature and extent of female offending

How does male and female offending differ? Assess **Figure 11.4**, which shows the representation of men and women in the overall population and at different stages of the criminal justice system, then consider the following questions.

1. Do these statistics surprise you? Why or why not?

2. Bearing in mind everything we have discussed so far, what gender differences do you think there might be in terms of types of crimes committed? Why?

3. Consider the comments we have made about women being more likely than men to be prosecuted for less serious crimes, such as TV licence evasion and shoplifting. What factors do you think might explain these patterns?

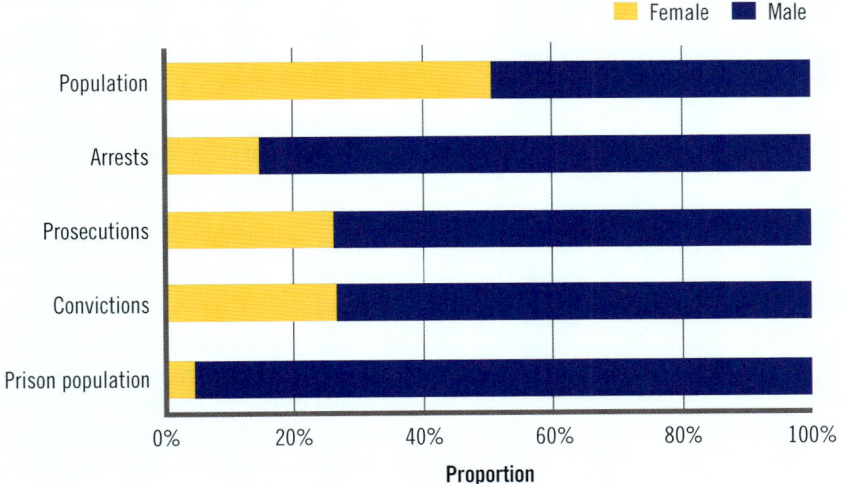

Figure 11.4 Ministry of Justice statistics from 2017 show that men outnumber women at every stage in the criminal justice system

Source: Ministry of Justice

Therefore, one way in which some of the earliest criminologists used stereotypes to explain female offending was by viewing it through a biological lens, arguing that women's biological sex controlled their psychological state. This included women's inherent qualities such as their supposed passivity and their maternal instincts, which were thought to be opposed to criminal behaviour (Lombroso and Ferrero, 1895). Women's offending was therefore seen as abnormal, and the women who did commit crimes were thought to have biological and physical deficiencies which meant they did not have the characteristics assigned to their biological sex (ibid). Instead, it was suggested that they had the traits and anatomical features associated with the male sex (see **Figure 11.5**). These early theorists clearly believed that established views about womanhood and femininity (the female gender), such as the idea that women were passive and maternal, were attributes of their biological sex rather than **social constructs**.

Subsequent explanations of women's offending also applied stereotypical assumptions about the female gender to their biological sex, and implied that biological faults or deficiencies made women more likely to be criminals. Pollak (1950), for instance, portrayed women as fundamentally criminal by nature, and Dalton (1961) argued that hormonal changes due to menstruation or menopausal development contributed to women's offending. As we will see in **section 11.3**, a key principle of feminist criminology is the rejection of the idea that there are links between women's offending and their supposedly deficient biological sex. By implying that women commit crime because of a biological abnormality, these studies pathologise women's offending—in other words, they treat it as a symptom of an illness or defect. This depiction justifies imposing court sentences that have the stated purpose of treating female offenders in criminal justice institutions to 'cure' their condition. Women's rationality and the wider structural contexts of their offending are therefore ignored.

Although more recent explanations of women's offending have challenged biological perspectives, they continue to have an impact on women's experiences in the justice system. The cases covered in **Controversy and debate 11.2** provide a useful example of points we have raised so far.

Modern explanations of female crime

Modern perspectives on female offending have moved away from ideas of biological and psychological abnormality. For example, some emphasise that the social and economic contexts in which we live, such as the inequalities of capitalist and **patriarchal** societies, disadvantage women: they tend to have a lower socio-economic status and may commit crime to survive (Chesney-Lind and Pasko, 2004; Sharpe, 2019). In these circumstances, a woman's marginal socio-economic position can make offending a **rational choice** (Carlen, 1988; Gelsthorpe, 2019). This contradicts earlier criminological theories that ignored women's rationality.

Some scholars also argue that the representation of women in criminal justice statistics could be further influenced by institutional biases around race and class, like racial profiling, which can cause ethnic minority and socio-economically marginal women to experience more criminal justice intervention than white women of higher social status. Official statistics do reveal that ethnic minority women in particular are prosecuted at a higher rate than other women (see, for example, Ministry of Justice, 2018). Noting that race and socio-economic marginalisation can intersect to make offending a rational choice for individuals affected by these problems, Sharpe (2019) argues that: 'as active agents, women (and men) negotiate

Figure 11.5 Early explanations of female offending attributed criminal behaviour to biological deficiencies which made women more masculine, such as the 'projecting cheek-bones', 'enormous lower jaw', and 'over-jutting brows' shown here

Source: Image taken from Lombroso and Ferrero's The Female Offender (1895)

CONTROVERSY AND DEBATE 11.2

The depiction of women in the criminal justice system

Below you can read excerpts from the news reports about two nurses who were convicted of killing their patients in 2006 and 2007. Look at the judges' sentencing remarks in the two cases and consider possible explanations for the differences between them. Did the judges accord similar levels of rationality to both offenders during sentencing? What do the judges' remarks tell us about the portrayal of female offenders compared with the depiction of male offenders?

The case of Beverley Allitt

> The serial killer nurse Beverly Allitt must serve a minimum of 30 years in jail for the murder and abuse of children in her care, the high court ruled today. A high court judge ruled that Allitt, dubbed the 'Angel of Death', should serve a minimum sentence of 28 years and 175 days, taking into account the one year and 190 days she spent in custody before being sentenced.
>
> Allitt was given 13 life sentences in 1993 for murdering four children, attempting to murder another three, and causing grievous bodily harm with intent to a further six at Grantham and Kesteven hospital in Lincolnshire.
>
> Allitt will be 54 before she will be considered for parole.
>
> The former nurse was diagnosed as suffering from Munchausen syndrome by proxy (MSbP) when she carried out the attacks between 1991 and 1993.
>
> The 39-year-old is now being held at the Rampton high-security hospital in Nottingham. Allitt murdered the four children by injecting them with high doses of insulin.
>
> The judge made the following statement:
>
> I have found that there is an element of sadism in Ms Allitt's conduct and her offending. But that sadism is itself, if not the result, certainly a manifestation of her mental disorder, and it would be unduly simplistic to treat it in the same way as one would if the offender were mentally well.

(*The Guardian*, 6 December 2007, www.theguardian.com/uk/2007/dec/06/ukcrime.health)

The case of Benjamin Geen

> A nurse who killed two of his patients 'to satisfy his lust for excitement' was jailed for life today. Judge Mr Justice Crane told Benjamin Geen, 25, that he would serve a minimum of 30 years for a 'terrible betrayal of the trust of others in the medical profession and his patients'.
>
> Geen received life sentences for two counts of murder and 15 counts of grievous bodily harm. The staff nurse injected 17 victims with drugs including muscle relaxants, insulin, and sedatives to stop them breathing.
>
> Although doctors revived 15 of his victims, two did not survive. Mr Justice Crane told Geen at Oxford Crown Court:
>
> Your purpose was to cause a collapse of the patient in order that you could take part in the revival of the patient. It seems that you relished the excitement of that feeling of taking control but you must have known quite well that you were playing with their lives.
>
> This was a terrible betrayal. You betrayed your nursing and medical colleagues and the vital profession of which you had been a member. Most of all, you betrayed the trust of the patients. They were in your care and you intentionally caused them huge damage.
>
> During the trial, the jury heard how Green 'came alive' and looked 'elated' as his patients went into respiratory arrest. During his closing speech, prosecutor Michael Austin Smith QC said that Geen must have known the fatal consequences of what he was doing but that toying with patients' lives was a 'price he was willing to pay in order to satisfy his perverse needs'.

(*The Guardian*, 10 May 2006, www.theguardian.com/society/2006/may/10/health.crime)

---

structural barriers and opportunities in ways which render lawbreaking a more or less attractive or necessary course of action. In some circumstances, women's options may be so constrained that offending becomes almost impossible to avoid'. There is also the (somewhat contested) view that female offending can sometimes be traced to male coercion; in other words, a male partner coercing a woman into committing crime (for example, Corston, 2007).

We can learn more about the **aetiology** (the causes) of female offending by looking at the profile of the women involved in the justice system. In the UK, for example, a high proportion of female prisoners experience or have experienced several (sometimes interconnected) problems, such as:

- a period in care;
- abuse (domestic, emotional, and childhood sexual abuse by men);
- exploitation and violence in intimate relationships;
- poverty and debt;

- homelessness;
- unemployment;
- educational deficits.

(Cabinet Office Social Exclusion Unit and Ministry of Justice, 2009; Corston, 2007; Gelsthorpe, 2019; Ministry of Justice, 2018)

The situation appears similar in the US (see, for example, Messina et al., 2019). Recent statistics in the UK suggest that women deal with these problems in negative ways, including substance misuse and offending behaviour. For example, female prisoners are more likely to say they have an alcohol problem when they enter prison (24 per cent) compared with males (18 per cent). The same applies to drug problems (39 per cent compared to 28 per cent for males) (Ministry of Justice, 2018).

Women in the criminal justice system

Researchers have clearly shown that gender affects people's experiences of the criminal justice system, with numerous studies documenting the unsuitability of the system for women (Corston, 2007; Gelsthorpe, 2019) and the futility of the short sentences they often receive, such as those imposed for TV licence offences (Pantazis and Gordon, 2002). Women in prison have access to fewer services and opportunities compared with men (Moore and Scraton, 2014). They lack access to suitable sanitary protection or support for issues to do with their reproductive health, and other health needs that are specific to their gender. There are also few female prisons, and none at all in Wales, meaning that most women are held in establishments that are a long way from home, which in turn means they receive fewer visits from family and friends and can find resettlement more difficult. These problems are made worse by the fact that a high number of female prisoners are the primary carers of their children, and most of the children do not remain in their home or in the care of their father.

Many children are unable to visit and there are only six Mother and Baby Units, which are not automatically accessible (see generally, Corston, 2007; Gelsthorpe, 2019). Worryingly, there is evidence that separating children from their mothers can affect childhood development and many affected children have an increased likelihood of becoming NEET (Not in Education, Employment or Training) (Prison Reform Trust, 2015).

Because of these and many other issues, there have been increasing calls for a 'gender-responsive' approach to criminal justice (such as Corston, 2007). Campaigners argue that this is necessary since the drivers and patterns of women's offending are usually different from men's and imprisonment seems to have a particularly damaging impact on them and their families, leading to worse outcomes than for men:

> Most of the solutions to women's offending lie in improved access to community-based support services, including women's centres. These enable women to address underlying problems which may lead to offending but which the criminal justice system cannot solve.
>
> (Prison Reform Trust, 2017)

Proposals which would have moved things in this direction were made over a decade ago in the Corston Report (2007), which included recommendations for exactly what the Prison Reform Trust suggests is needed: the creation of community-based centres designed for women, where they can serve their sentence close to their home. Some of these proposals were adopted (see Gelsthorpe, 2019) but the others have since been abandoned, and some suggest that much more still needs to be done to develop a gender-responsive criminal justice system. We consider this issue further in **Controversy and debate 11.3**.

Two interrelated theses (perspectives or explanations) have emerged from theoretical and empirical analyses of women's experiences in the criminal justice system: the chivalry thesis and the double deviance thesis, sometimes

CONTROVERSY AND DEBATE 11.3

Gender-responsive justice: a 'gap between aspiration and reality'

As we have discussed, many studies and inquiries have concluded that 'prison is rarely a necessary, appropriate or proportionate response to women who come into contact with the justice system' (Prison Reform Trust, 2017). The short prison sentences imposed on most female offenders not only have a significant negative impact on the offenders and their families but are also of limited efficacy in terms of addressing the issues and preventing reoffending. The latest official statistics show that more than half of the women released from prison in 2016 reoffended, a figure which increases to 72 per cent when we look at those who served sentences of less than 12 months (Ministry of Justice, 2017). Community sentences, including unpaid work and addiction or **rehabilitation** programmes, are widely agreed to be preferable to short prison sentences for women. They are dramatically cheaper for the state (the cost of keeping a woman in prison ranges from £38,00 to £46,000 per year, whereas the estimated project cost of giving a woman community-based services through a women's centre is around £1,500 per year (Prison Reform Trust, 2017)). They are also better able to address the causes of offending and provide meaningful help and support for women—see, for example, **Figure 11.6**. However, despite the Corston Report (2007) and many studies since recommending this kind of gender-responsive approach to female offending, little appears to have changed. In 2018, the government abandoned plans to create new 'community prisons' for women, which it had said would allow women to be closer to home and maintain better links, and would reflect the emphasis 'from custody to the community' (Dearden, L., 'Government scraps proposed women's "community prisons" in new strategy to reduce female offending', *The Independent*, 26 June 2018). Instead, they stated that custodial sentences should be used as a last resort, with community sentences preferable. Nevertheless, charities and campaigners suggested that the funding available even for this more limited vision was 'wholly inadequate'. Kate Paradine, CEO of the Women in Prison charity, stated:

> Women's centres are key to delivering the strategy, and the funding crisis they currently face is serious—that is the key issue that I don't see being addressed here. The messaging is very positive, but for us it's about what is going to be delivered on the ground. It's all about action matching vision, and that requires funding and a plan.
>
> (*The Independent*, ibid)

The criticisms appeared to be largely well founded as nearly two years later many of the same issues were being raised, with Jenny Earle, director of the Prison Reform Trust's programme to reduce women's imprisonment, saying:

> It is widely acknowledged that most of the solutions to women's offending lie in the community. Addressing the economic marginalisation that can drive women into crime, and the lasting impact of a criminal conviction, is therefore critical [and] makes sense for families, the economy and society as well as women themselves. The government knows the solutions, and has already committed to many of them, but . . . a significant gap remains between aspiration and reality.
>
> (Oppenheim, M., 'Women leaving prison almost three times less likely to be employed on release than men', *The Independent*, 17 February 2020)

Figure 11.6 Blackpool Women's Centre wins lottery funding in 2018: do governments need to provide more support to make a truly 'gender-responsive' justice system a reality?

Source: Blackpool Gazette

known as the 'evil woman' thesis. Both are based on the idea that stereotypical beliefs about femininity influence women's treatment in the system.

The chivalry thesis

According to the chivalry thesis, women receive more lenient treatment in the criminal justice system than men because of the chivalrous (courteous and respectful) attitudes and behaviour of the predominantly male criminal justice workforce (Crew, 1991), who are influenced by dominant but misleading depictions of women as passive and in need of men's protection. The chivalry thesis is associated with Otto Pollak's (1950) account of female offending. In his book titled *The Criminality of Women*, he explained the gender gap in offending (still referenced today—see Heidensohn and Silvestri, 2012) by arguing that women are naturally more prone to criminality than men. However, they are more skilled in avoiding discovery and manipulating men into committing crimes on their behalf, resulting in fewer female prisoners. In his view, women's supposed ability to, unlike men, fake orgasms and to conceal their menstruation despite the discomfort associated with it, showed that they were predisposed to deceitful behaviour and therefore found it easier to conceal their crimes.

Pollak's assertions have been criticised as uncritical, unsubstantiated (Smart, 1977), and **ideological**, in the sense that they simply reflect his own beliefs (Heidensohn, 1985). Nevertheless, his work informed the chivalry thesis because he put forward the idea that in a male-dominated criminal justice system women were treated more leniently than men. He argued that this could also explain the gender gap in offending, as the gender gap could partly be due to officials treating women chivalrously, allowing them to avoid criminal justice intervention.

Although chivalrous treatment might be beneficial to some women, it can generate several problems. First, men are more likely to be chivalrous when the behaviour, appearance, and circumstances of female offenders, and their offences, do not appear to contradict the stereotypical view of women as naturally passive and nurturing. Therefore, women who do not display these qualities may not be treated chivalrously. Secondly, some maintain that the very idea of chivalry reinforces negative stereotypes of women as passive, inferior, and reliant on men for their protection (Steffensmeier, 1980; Gilbert, 2002; Rodriguez et al., 2006). In contrast, men are portrayed as independent and inherently more powerful. Thirdly, some argue that with the chivalry thesis what we might see as chivalrous leniency towards women is mostly **paternalism** (for example, Chesney-Lind and Shelden, 2004). Paternalism in this context can involve limiting women's freedom supposedly for their own good although in reality it benefits those limiting their freedom, in this case, men. As we have already noted, men are more likely to treat women leniently if they see them as occupying acceptable feminine roles or statuses. Examples of these roles include being submissive and sexually conservative, as would supposedly be the case if a woman were heterosexual and married with children, rather than a single mother (Chesney-Lind, 1988, 1999; Daly, 1987).

The double deviance thesis

The double deviance thesis, also known as the evil woman **hypothesis**, is another framework researchers use to communicate the experiences of female offenders in the criminal justice system. Like the chivalry thesis, the evil woman hypothesis suggests that gender plays a key role in how women are treated in the criminal justice system (Belknap, 2001; Rodriguez et al., 2006). But the double deviance or evil woman hypothesis also claims that women whose lifestyles or circumstances do not complement the **normative** standards of femininity set by men are considered doubly deviant. Consequently, sentencers and the rest of society may subconsciously (without explicitly realising) use this as a reason for doubly condemning and punishing them (see **Figure 11.7**). First, for violating socially defined gender **norms** and, secondly, for violating the law (Carlen, 1983; Heidensohn, 1985; Worrall, 1981). The women who are more likely to receive a harsher **punishment** than they normally should for their crimes include:

- homosexual women;
- those convicted of sexual misconduct;
- single mothers;
- those labelled as 'bad mothers';
- others whose circumstances and lifestyles do not fit in with the ideal gender role that is socially prescribed for women.

(Eaton, 1986; Heidensohn and Silvestri, 2012: 351)

Figure 11.7 We have discussed several theories and explanations of female crime, but do you think that they are valid?

Source: Sakhorn/Shutterstock

As we will see later (see **section 11.6**), black feminism, queer feminism, transfeminism, and disability feminism are developments in gender studies that emphasise that women whose identities appear to violate normative identities, including normative gender identities, are vulnerable to harsher treatment in the criminal justice system compared with women who conform to established gender norms.

Criticisms of the theses

Studies have explored the **validity** of the chivalry and the double deviance theses with mixed findings. While some commentators suggest that women do in fact receive more lenient treatment (see, for example, Curry et al., 2004), others argue that women are given harsher punishments if they violate gender norms (for example, Lightowlers, 2019), and some have found that women receive similar sentences to men, particularly when they are convicted of serious crimes (for example, Mellor and Deering, 2010). These differences suggest that more research needs to be conducted to explore the accuracy of the theses.

Men as offenders

In the 1990s, perspectives on **masculinities** and crime emerged on the links between the male gender and crime. The study of masculinities and crime is influenced by several theoretical approaches, particularly feminist perspectives in criminology (see **section 11.3**). It is also influenced by the work some men have done on feminist issues, and by studies of gay and lesbian issues (Flavin, 2001; Heidensohn and Silvestri, 2012).

Masculinities theorists believe that there is no definition of 'masculinity'. This means that there are no values and characteristics associated with maleness that can be ascribed to all men. Instead, multiple 'masculinities' exist and these are structured around a socially constructed hierarchy. Masculinities theorists also examine the gender gap in offending (Messerschmidt, 1993; Messerschmidt and Tomsen, 2012). Messerschmidt and Tomsen (2012), for example, assert: 'Male offenders commit the great majority of crimes . . . and men have a virtual monopoly on the commission of syndicated, corporate and political crime' (2012: 190). As Naffine (1997) notes, masculinities theorists argue that the gender gap exists because there is a close link between masculinities and crime, but similar to feminist criminologists, they believe that this link is often taken for granted and overlooked by mainstream criminologists (see also Messerschmidt, 1993).

In their analysis of this gender gap, masculinities theorists argue that men commit more violent crimes than women and that such crimes are sometimes attributable to the fact that some men feel pressured by society to attain the 'masculine status and power' associated with **hegemonic masculinity** (Messerschmidt and Tomsen, 2012: 151). This aspect of masculinity is said to sit at the top of a hierarchy of masculinities (Connell, 1995, 2000) and is associated with 'heterosexuality, toughness, power and authority, competitiveness and the subordination of gay men' (Connell, 1995; Frosh et al., 2002: 75–6; Heidensohn and Silvestri, 2012). Hegemonic masculinity symbolises socially approved maleness—the characteristics society thinks men should have—and justifies male dominance in patriarchal societies (see also Messerschmidt and Tomsen, 2017). It is argued that men are socially conditioned to want this masculinity, but only a few men in positions of power can attain it (Connell, 1995).

According to Connell and Messerschmidt (2005), the idea that a hierarchy of masculinities exists is partly influenced by the violent attacks and prejudices that were targeted at homosexual men by heterosexual men in the 1970s. Some argue that in this period, homophobia emerged as a socially accepted attitude, and some men, for example homosexual men, were seen as having '**subordinated masculinities**' because they did not have the characteristics associated with hegemonic masculinity, or the resources to attain the privilege and high social status also associated with it (see Heidensohn and Silvestri, 2012: 348). Key examples of these kinds of resources include academic achievement and the opportunity to engage in legitimate leisure activities (Messerschmidt, 1993; Messerschmidt and Tomsen, 2012). Some masculinities theorists have since argued that men with subordinated masculinities may resort to crime to obtain these resources and attain hegemonic masculinity (Messerschmidt, 1993).

The basic idea is that some male crime may be the result of some men attempting to 'accomplish' gender (Renzetti, 2012: 135). In other words, their crimes are committed as a result of them trying to achieve masculinity in its hegemonic form and become a 'real man'. For instance, it could be argued that young men who have been excluded from formal and legitimate pathways of achieving 'success' (through lack of employment opportunities, for example) may attempt to assert and reassert their masculinity and masculine status in criminal ways. A young man, angry and humiliated at being kicked out of school, may make himself feel better by getting into a fight; a man who is belittled at work and overlooked for promotion (or unable to find legitimate employment) may take out his frustrations by beating his wife when he gets home. Crude examples as these may be, they illustrate the social and psychological processes going on; the release of rage and fear through an action which usually involves adrenaline, danger, or risk.

We return our focus mainly to women for the remainder of this chapter, but this brief discussion should have given you a sense of how studies of men and crime, and specifically of masculinities, interlink with the issues we have been considering in relation to women. Reflect further on these ideas in **What do you think? 11.3**.

WHAT DO YOU THINK? 11.3

What does it mean to be a 'real man'?

Whatever the gender with which you most identify, consider what it means in contemporary society to be a 'real man'. Note down your ideas then consider where these thoughts have come from. How are accepted 'masculine' (and 'feminine') traits defined by societies and **cultures**?

This is a question we often ask our students and whilst their responses do of course vary, every year some clear themes emerge and have so far remained constant. Often young men will talk about the pressures they feel to look a certain way, not to show any signs of perceived 'weakness', to be supremely confident, and to compete to achieve their goals in life. On the other hand, many young women will often say that their idea of a 'real' man is someone who is confident and who 'knows what they want', but they also say that their 'ideal' man (in relationship terms) is someone who will 'protect' them as well as having a 'sensitive' side.

The point to consider here is that all of these traits are not biologically specific but are, in many ways, culturally constructed and maintained. In other words, they are perhaps learnt culturally (through the media and those around us), but we internalise them and accept them as 'common sense'.

Other interesting questions to ask and consider on this theme include:

- What, in your opinion, is the worst thing you could call a young boy in a playground?
- How could you offend most teenage girls?
- Why is there still a need for Stonewall (the LGBT+ organisation) to run campaigns against homophobic bullying?

Finally, consider whether ideas of 'real' men and women are changing, as social norms shift. Do you think we're becoming better at questioning set gender roles, both male and female, and more accepting of fluidity between genders—and those who identify as non-binary? If so, what implications might this development have for the kinds of gender and crime issues we have considered so far?

11.3 Feminist criminology

So far in this chapter, we have examined key criminological analyses of the relationship between gender and crime, but it is important to point out that many of those studies are influenced by feminist criminology. We therefore need to analyse feminist criminology and its key debates to understand how the female gender intersects with crime and criminal justice. In this section, we will explore the origins, definition, and principles of feminist criminology.

Feminist criminology comprises several theoretical and **epistemological** strands, so you might not be surprised to hear that it does not have a precise definition. However, some scholars have suggested definitions that capture its unifying themes. Gelsthorpe and Morris (1988: 224) state that: 'the essence of feminist perspectives is that they reflect the view that women experience subordination on the basis of their sex'. Daly and Chesney-Lind (1988: 502) go on to define feminist criminology as: 'a set of theories about women's oppression and a set of strategies for change'. As we can see from these definitions, feminist criminologists emphasise that gender inequality exists in society and it disadvantages women. This gender inequality is said to inform women's experiences in society, including their experiences as victims and offenders. We will, however, see later in this chapter that feminist criminologists do not all agree on what the precise sources of gender inequality are and how we can effectively achieve gender equality (Flavin, 2001).

Origins of feminist criminology

The origins of feminist criminology have been traced to the second wave of feminism, which emerged in the US in the 1970s (Daly, 2006) and spread internationally (Heidensohn, 2012; Heidensohn and Silvestri, 2012). It is generally agreed that there have been four waves (movements) of feminism. The first wave is said to have emerged in the 19th to early 20th centuries in the US, and its focus was on securing women's suffrage—their rights to vote. Notable campaigners in that period were Elizabeth Cady Stanton, Lucretia Mott, Lucy Stone, and others (see Freedman, 2003). Part of the movement at the time also involved the fight against slavery. A key figure in the anti-slavery movement and the campaign for women's suffrage at the time was Sojourner Truth, whose speech 'Ain't I a Woman?' (1851) helped to raise awareness of the predicament of black women as victims of both racial and gender inequality.

The second wave also emerged in the US, but this time it emerged during the civil rights campaign for equality regardless of race and gender. As we will see in **section 11.6**, the third wave emerged amidst debates about **intersectionality**, which is defined as the 'interaction of multiple identities and experiences of exclusion and subordination' (Davis, 2008: 68; Burgess-Proctor, 2006; Crenshaw, 1989). Some now see the social media **#MeToo** movement, which was prompted by exposures of sexual victimisation of women by famous celebrities, as a movement that was enabled by a new, 'fourth' wave of feminism that is based mainly on online activism against male-perpetrated sexual violence and intersectional analysis (for example, Andersen, 2018).

Gelsthorpe and Morris (1988) note that the British researcher Carol Smart's (1976) seminal text *Women, Crime and Criminology* marked the beginning of feminist criminology in Britain. The book highlighted the limited explanations of female offending within criminology and the discriminatory treatment of women in the justice system, particularly in England and Wales. Daly (2006) has since described Carol Smart as a 'pioneering feminist critic of criminological **theory**', but it is important to be aware that Frances Heidensohn (1968), who is now one of the key writers in the field, had earlier drawn attention to the lack of interest in the study of female deviance and the sentencing of female offenders.

Smart's 1976 text highlighted the male-centredness of criminological theories and the lack of adequate scholarship on female offending and victimisation. Her critique of how mainstream criminology tends to overlook the role of women as 'producers and subjects' of criminological knowledge is now a recurring theme within feminist criminology (Gelsthorpe and Morris, 1988: 225; Heidensohn and Silvestri, 2012). As Chesney-Lind and Morash (2013: 287) put it: 'the founders of criminology almost completely overlooked women's crime, and they ignored, minimized, and trivialized female victimization'. Some also argued that the existing theories were male-centred and the few theories that did address female offending and victimisation (though not in any depth) contained many stereotypical portrayals of women and their behaviour (see, for example, Smart, 1976). We explored these theories in **section 11.2** and considered their claims that female crime was caused by predisposing traits that were supposedly unique to women. The theories also implied that women were unable to behave rationally, meaning that the offending behaviour of women could only be the outcome of predisposing factors, including their supposedly unique physical and mental deficiencies.

Principles of feminist criminology

There are a number of different feminist perspectives in criminology, but we can identify some key unifying themes or principles across the approaches. They can be summarised as:

- theorising (developing theories) around the concept of gender and its relationship to crime in order to reverse criminology's 'gender blindness';
- addressing criminology's tendency to portray gender as a binary concept (a concept that comprises only two different social categories: the male and female gender);
- challenging and trying to rectify criminology's male-centredness, or androcentrism; and
- theorising the gender gap in crime statistics.

We will now consider each of these principles in turn.

Theorising gender and crime

Mainstream criminology has historically overlooked gender and has consequently been accused of 'gender blindness'. But some researchers inspired by feminism have tried to address this by developing theories on the concept of gender and its impact on crime and criminal justice (Chesney-Lind and Pasko, 2013; Gelsthorpe and Morris, 1988: 98). For example, early feminist criminologists tried to reverse the existing stereotypical accounts which assumed that gender was the same as biological sex and explained the purported links between the female gender and crime in terms of supposed abnormalities inherent in the biological constitution of female offenders. Feminist criminologists rejected this approach and highlighted the difference between the concepts of gender and biological sex (see, for example, Oakley, 1972); mirroring the broader field of feminist theory in the 1970s. Smart (1995) notes that by the 1970s feminist criminologists began to argue that 'sex' refers to the biological make-up of an individual, while 'gender' represents socially constructed ideas that do not necessarily relate to the biologically determined sex of an individual (Oakley, 1972; Daly, 2010).

By outlining the differences between gender and biological sex, feminist criminologists could challenge the tendency to assume that these two categories were the same. They were also able to refute the accompanying belief that women who violated gender norms by, for example, committing crime, must have a biological (sex) abnormality, as had been implied by the earlier accepted theories of women's offending (such as those put forward by Lombroso and Ferrero, 1895).

Analysing the gender binary

Researchers inspired by feminism, such as Smart (1990), have further theorised the concept of gender by challenging the tendency to dichotomise it. This means that they reject the historical and cultural construction of gender as a binary concept made up of two different social categories: the male gender and the female gender. Some feminist scholars argue that depicting gender as a binary concept can lead to misleading beliefs about gender difference that benefit men, like the belief that women should be passive, nurturing, and subordinate to men. Daly (2010) also argues that seeing gender as a binary is **essentialist** since it implies that each gender (male or female) consists of a homogenous group of people who share the same identity, subjectivity, and other attributes. When looking at public figures, for example, we might see that there is a variety in their characteristics and pursuits that suggests gender is not homogenous—see **Figure 11.8**.

However, some scholars who study the ways in which pathways to crime are gender-specific highlight the benefits of seeing gender in this way. For instance, they have argued that there are certain societal factors that affect women specifically, and these conditions are at the root of women's offending behaviour (Belknap, 2015; Chesney-Lind and Pasko, 2013; Daly, 1992). A key example is their violent victimisation by men in patriarchal societies. The scholars further claim that ignoring the universal experiences that women share exposes them to poor treatment within societal institutions that are designed mainly for men, like the criminal justice system (Daly and Chesney-Lind, 1988). From this perspective, it is important to view men and women as distinct groups and to emphasise that women share unique experiences that require gender-responsive policies and services,

such as women-only community rehabilitation centres (see **Controversy and debate 11.3**, and also Flavin and Artz, 2013).

Challenging androcentrism

Another principle of feminist criminology is the rejection of mainstream criminology's **androcentricism** (or male-centredness) (Daly and Chesney-Lind, 1988; Heidensohn and Silvestri, 2012). Early feminist criminologists, for example Carol Smart (1976, 1990) and Maureen Cain (1986), described criminology as 'malestream' or male-centred and accused the discipline of promoting a male-centred view of the world or an 'amnesia of women' by deliberately overlooking their existence (Gelsthorpe and Morris, 1988: 96–8). In an effort to reverse this situation, feminist criminologists theorised and researched the concept of gender and studied its impact on criminal behaviour. Some researchers who were influenced by feminist theories, such as Messerschmidt (1993), also explored possible connections between the male gender and criminality. But feminist criminologists tended to focus mainly on women, contributing to our understanding of the nature and extent of female victimisation, offending, and punishment. Examples of these studies include Brownmiller (1975), Dobash and Dobash (1979, 1998), Gelsthorpe (2006, 2019), Eaton (1986), Russell (1975), Sharpe (2019), and Stanko (1990). The concept of **femicide** is also an example of a term that is used to challenge androcentricism. Some researchers use this term rather than homicide as it refers specifically to the killing of women and girls, usually by men and because they are female. Feminist thinkers (such as Radford and Russell, 1992) argue that using it highlights and allows deeper investigation of the particular sexual politics involved in the murder of women—for example, the fact that they are sometimes killed for specific reasons (their sex), often by particular perpetrators (for example, their partners), and in different settings (for example, the home), as we saw in **section 11.2**.

Theorising the gender gap in crime statistics

Some of the early feminist criminologists also criticised mainstream criminology for failing to theorise the gender gap in crime statistics (Heidensohn and Silvestri, 2012). As Heidensohn and Silvestri (2012: 348) point out, 'That men and boys are responsible for the majority of offending behaviour remains an uncontested feature within criminology and debates about gender and crime.' According to some scholars (see, for example, Heidensohn and Silvestri,

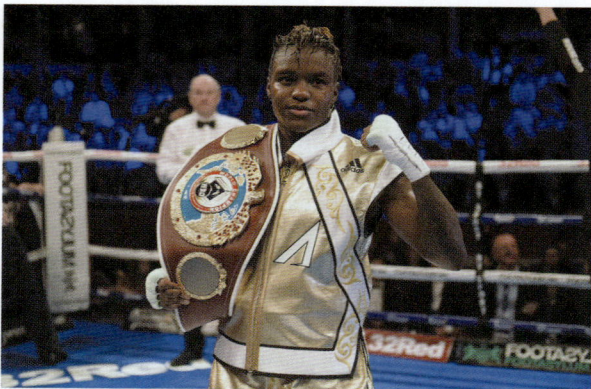

Figure 11.8 The Olympic boxing champion Nicola Adams, who competes in a stereotypically 'male' and aggressive sport, could be seen as proof that women are not a homogeneous group who share the same identity and characteristics
Source: Philip Sharkey/TGS Photo/Shutterstock

2012), rates of female crime have increased steadily since the 1970s, and this had led to a narrowing of the gender gap, a fact that we will discuss when we consider 'liberal feminist theory'. Yet as we have seen, the latest statistics on women and criminal justice in England and Wales reveal that men continue to dominate official crime statistics, indicating that the gender gap remains and should be further studied by criminologists.

11.4 Theoretical traditions of feminist criminology

We will not be able to outline all of the theoretical traditions that have inspired feminist perspectives in criminology in this chapter, so we will focus on the key traditions:

- liberal feminist theory;
- radical feminist theory;
- Marxist feminism; and
- socialist feminism.

These traditions have been described as 'the best known of the early theoretical influences on criminology' (Chesney-Lind and Karlene, 2001; Chesney-Lind and Morash, 2013: 290) and their impact on the key principles of feminist criminology that we covered earlier is evident, particularly the view that gender inequality, which disadvantages women, exists in many societies and should be addressed. However, they disagree on the sources of gender inequality and how best to eliminate it or reduce its harmful impact on women. We will consider both the contributions of these perspectives and the criticisms they have received.

Liberal feminist theory

A key principle of liberal feminist theory, or liberal feminism, is that although men and women are naturally equal, gender inequality that disadvantages women exists in many societies. We can see this inequality in the way that culturally determined ideas of gender give men roles that empower them. Being 'competitive and aggressive' are examples of characteristics that are thought of as socially acceptable male personality traits (Burgess-Proctor, 2006). In contrast, women are expected to be adopt roles that are considered to be submissive and as such disempowering, such as being 'nurturing and passive' (Burgess-Proctor, 2006: 29).

This belief holds that sociological factors, particularly the socialisation of women into these roles ascribed to the female gender explain the limited extent of female offending (the gender gap in offending) (Adler, 1975, 1977; Simon, 1975). According to liberal feminists, during socialisation we internalise the idea that criminal activity is more consistent with the aggressiveness and other attributes of the male gender (masculinity) than with the conventionally passive characteristics assigned to the female gender (femininity). They also argue that women are subjected to stricter social controls than men as they develop and undergo socialisation. Such social controls can involve censuring (criticising or condemning) women if they display characteristics that are usually culturally recognised as masculine. This social censure may be different across cultures and societies, but usually focuses on the social control of women, for example social disapproval of any expressions of female aggression or sexuality (for example, Honkatukia and Keskinen, 2018). As we have seen, the double deviance thesis also emphasises that social censure affects female offenders and highlights that they are vulnerable to severe court sentences that are made harsher due to the belief, perhaps held subconsciously by the judge, that the women have violated gender-role expectations. For liberal feminists, the social control of women is an element of their oppression and part of the effort to uphold male domination in public and private aspects of social life (Heidensohn, 1996).

So far, we have seen that liberal feminists believe gender inequality stems primarily from the socialisation process, which breeds gender-role expectations that disadvantage women. However, they consider the limited opportunities available to women compared to men to be the main factor in maintaining this unequal status quo. They argue that women lack access to opportunities in all aspects of social life, and in all social institutions, from educational and legal institutions to the institution of marriage, and this disadvantages them in society. In the 1960s and 1970s, liberal feminists made significant progress in striving to address this issue and achieve gender equality (see **Figure 11.9**), opening doors to social and economic opportunities that were not previously available to women. In fact, some of the initial studies of women and crime went on to suggest that in taking advantage of these opportunities, women took on qualities that were traditionally associated with masculinity (the male gender), notably aggressiveness and even criminality, which led to a narrowing of the gender gap in official crime statistics (Adler, 1975; Simon, 1975).

A range of theses and hypotheses were put forward to explain the narrowing of the gender gap in crime statistics, including the liberation hypothesis. This hypothesis suggested that the gender gap was narrowing because of the progress towards greater gender equality, which meant that women were now engaging in activities previously dominated by men, and showing supposedly masculine characteristics

Figure 11.9 A women's liberation march in Washington, DC in 1970. Liberal feminists made significant progress in addressing gender inequality during the 1960s and 1970s.
Source: Warren K Leffler/Public domain

(Adler, 1975; Simon, 1975). Criminal activity in the workplace (or elsewhere) was identified as one example of those behaviours (Adler, 1975), as was 'boisterousness' after excessive alcohol consumption, which was in the 1990s, depicted by the media as representative of a 'ladette culture' (Heidensohn, 1996; Silvestri and Crowther-Dowey, 2008; Worrall, 2004). The news media sensationalised the so-called 'ladette culture' by portraying it as a social disorder that was rising at an alarming rate, which supported the liberal feminist view that women could become more likely to commit crime if they engaged in behaviours traditionally associated with masculinity. Thus, it was argued that the gender gap only existed because women lacked the opportunities to occupy certain more powerful roles or engage in certain activities; they were socialised into roles that disempowered them (Adler, 1975). However, in more recent years other explanations have been suggested for the narrowing gap: consider this in **What do you think? 11.4**.

Despite the claims about a narrowing gender gap, liberal feminist theory is still associated with the view that women are socialised into roles that restrict the opportunities available to them to commit crime. Therefore, to achieve gender equality, the existing socialisation process has to be challenged and rebalanced. This is because the process establishes and maintains culturally determined gender roles that fuel gender inequality and disadvantage women.

Let's consider the criticisms of this standpoint. Liberal feminists are mainly criticised for not challenging the patriarchal status quo; they are accused of accepting without question the idea that men's views and experiences represent the norm or the benchmark for measuring appropriate standards of gender equality. Smart (1995: 42) comments that:

> Basically the equality paradigm always affirms the centrality of men. Men continue to constitute the norm, the unproblematic, the natural social actor. Women are thus always seen as interlopers into a world already organized by others.

For critics of liberal feminism, male dominance must be challenged and we should push for gender-responsive provision for women, both in the criminal justice system and wider society. From this perspective, it is not enough to campaign for gender equality in the existing, androcentric system. As we have seen, some of the studies that have explored the experiences of women in the criminal justice system, and the provision available to them, reinforce the importance of gender-specific policies that acknowledge and make room for the unique needs of female offenders (Corston Report, 2007; Gelsthorpe, 2019; Martin et al., 2009).

Critics of the liberation hypothesis also reject the claim made by some of its supporters that the women's liberation movement and the consequent emancipation

WHAT DO YOU THINK? 11.4

The links between gender equality and criminality

An article for the government learning platform Apolitical highlights that although the gender gap in crime statistics, particularly violent crime, remains significant, some have pointed out that it has narrowed slightly and that in some parts of the world the conviction rate for women has actually increased (Apolitical, 2018).

It is generally agreed that the development is a result of increased gender equality, but beyond this, theories vary. As we have seen, it has been claimed (for example by Adler, 1975) that any narrowing in the gap is because gender equality has led to an increase in aggressive and even criminal behaviour from women. However, others point to the fact that male convictions for violent offending are decreasing, so it may instead be that gender equality is not leading more women into crime, but 'enticing men away from offending' (ibid). It has been suggested this might be down to changes in the way we all, but particularly young men, regard masculinity and traditional social roles (Estrada et al., 2016), such as the efforts made in recent years to reduce the stigma surrounding men's roles as stay-at-home parents (see **Figure 11.10**), challenging the idea that children's primary caretakers should be women.

What do you think? Could 'feminism be making the world safer' (Apolitical, 2018)?

Figure 11.10 Domestic work is traditionally thought of as a woman's role, but if we start changing how we approach gendered tasks, could this have a broader impact on criminality?

Source: Mint Images Limited/Alamy Stock Photo

(freeing, liberation) of women, which allowed them access to opportunities previously barred to them, have contributed to the narrowing gender gap in offending. These critics cite research evidence which suggests that the change in crime figures came about too soon after the introduction of liberal feminism for it to be a factor in female crime (for example, Chesney-Lind and Pasko, 2004). Others point out that the rise in female offending could be associated with factors other than their emancipation, such as the adverse economic and other circumstances that affect their lives (Burman and Batchelor, 2009). They support this view by pointing to the increasing involvement of women in property crimes like shoplifting; that is, crimes associated with economic hardship rather than serious violent crimes (for a UK example, see Ministry of Justice, 2018). These crimes are portrayed as rational reactions to unfair socio-economic circumstances (Carlen, 1988).

Other studies of female violence further challenge the liberation and emancipation theses, and suggest that female offending is the result of intersections of socio-economic disadvantage and male dominance. For example, in a study that explored why women in prison committed violent crimes, Batchelor (2005) found that some women would resort to violence so that they could protect and empower themselves, suggesting that rather than being liberated, they actually felt disempowered and vulnerable to violent victimisation, especially those who were socio-economically marginalised (see also Burman and Batchelor, 2009). Importantly, the studies also revealed that unlike the stereotypical portrayal of women by the early positivists, women can and do make rational choices and may actively *choose* violence to protect themselves.

The discussion between Roger Smith, one of this book's authors, and Professor Jo Phoenix in **Conversations 11.2** draws attention to how some vulnerable women's experiences of victimisation could prompt them to 'act out' by committing crime, but they also refer to the fact that there is a continuing tendency to overlook women's agency and

CONVERSATIONS 11.2

Female victimisation, offending, and agency
with **Professor Jo Phoenix**

This discussion between Roger Smith (one of the authors of this book) and Professor Jo Phoenix revolves around the victimisation of women when they enter the criminal justice system, or the experiences of victimised women who enter the criminal justice system, focusing on the sexual exploitation of young girls and their involvement in gangs.

Jo Phoenix (JP): You can see how, sociologically, a girl of 15, 16 years old will allow herself to be 'passed around' a gang to be brutalised, or at least misused sexually, for 'the gains' of being an object to be consumed within a consumer society. That identity, that subject position begins to make sense. When you translate this into the world of policy, law and practice, the only thing that the people [in the criminal justice system] have at their disposal to deal with is the offender. Sexual agency or not. And the discourses around girls and victimisation and sexuality are so big that they, in a sense, override all the other potential possibilities.

Roger Smith (RS): And the problem, it always seems to me, is that you don't then have an easy route towards solutions and ways out for young people who necessarily have ambiguous perceptions of themselves and need to resolve that. So in terms of being able to offer them an insightful response, that classification doesn't work at all.

JP: No, because it is tough to go up to a 16 year old and say, yes, you may have been enjoying yourself, or maybe you weren't. Maybe actually you were really hurt. But the law knows you as a victim. And that's a very difficult label to carry. Particularly if you're a victim of child sexual exploitation.

RS: And you thought you were exercising agency and now you're told you weren't, and you don't know what to do. You lose that one thing that you felt you had control over, in a way.

JP: Yes, so whether the interventions happen through the courts or whether they happen through social work, it's a very difficult subject position for the girl to operate. And then when you actually combine, and pull the lens a little bit back from just the girl and her subject positions and what are possibilities and what aren't, and you start looking again at some of the complex realities of the girls, who really are being harmed—and that's not to say that that other category [who believed they were exercising control over their situation] aren't—then there's a whole other category, isn't there, really?

RS: Yes, who are coerced, directly coerced and feel powerless, and feel and are completely vulnerable, and the term 'victim' works for them.

JP: Yes, absolutely. And for them they may be in situations where they're being offered the same solutions that they were offered before they got into that situation. More social work.

RS: Yes, and something that apparently didn't work previously?

JP: Yes. And they then may choose, because you and I both know that people in extreme situations are resilient. They make choices. Not in conditions of their own choosing, and often those choices are so constrained that the only choices they have are between very toxic or extremely toxic choices. So in some circumstances, as we know, these girls may act out. They may commit crime. Because what they're actually experiencing is more equivalent to rape than it is for the other category of girls. And what do we know about rape? We know that very few people will disclose rape. So they get caught up in the justice systems for the other crimes that they're committing, rather than the crimes that are being committed against them, and they don't disclose what's actually happening to them.

RS: No. And similarly, I wonder if some of the drugs offences, the large scale arrests for carrying large amounts of drugs through customs in countries which have very severe penalties, may be partly a product of getting into a situation where you're trying to exercise and buy, if you like, a little bit of space to be able to exercise some freedom. That bigger picture never really gets detailed. You just think about somebody who is a serious drug offender but what they're probably doing is trying to buy themselves a little bit of space.

JP: Yes, and I mean what do we know from feminists, criminology, and feminist studies generally? We know that those who report rape are only the tip of the iceberg. And so why should we assume that somebody who's caught up in the criminal justice system is going to be more likely to report rape? In fact, there's a whole series of arguments to say they would be less likely. So that link between their victimisation and their criminalisation, methodologically, it's a minefield of a study. But those are the things that I don't think we as critical scholars have really fleshed out very much empirically.

Roger Smith, one of the authors of this book, and Professor Jo Phoenix, Chair in Criminology at the Open University, gender and crime expert, and contributor to The Oxford Handbook of Criminology *(Liebling, Maruna, and McAra, 2017)*

rationality, particularly in criminal justice contexts. This factor is important for understanding the self-identity of the women, or the way they see themselves, and the effectiveness of interventions that aim to tackle their victimisation and offending behaviour.

Radical feminist theory

Similar to liberal feminism, radical feminism contends that gender inequality exists and negatively affects the experiences of women in the criminal justice system and wider society. However, a key difference between liberal feminism and radical feminism is that radical feminists identify patriarchy as the fundamental root of gender inequality and women's oppression, regardless of their ethnicity, social class, or other attributes (MacKinnon, 1989). Radical feminism emphasises that gender relations in patriarchal societies are characterised by men's efforts to control women's sexuality and capacity to reproduce, with men resorting to violence and abuse to achieve their objectives (Brownmiller, 1975). Consequently, as we might deduce from the name, radical feminism proposes more radical action than that encouraged by liberal feminism. Its supporters believe that simply rebalancing the existing social order to achieve gender equality, as the liberal feminists propose, is insufficient. They feel that an overhaul of the existing patriarchal order will achieve better outcomes for women. An example of this could be by removing the 'glass ceiling' for women—see **Figure 11.11**.

Perhaps because radical feminism centres its analysis of gender inequality on unfair patriarchal structures, some of its advocates seem reluctant to recognise the rights of trans women to identify as women, and do not agree that they have a place within women's spaces and feminism in general. They contend that biological sex and gender identity are fixed at birth and the male birth identity awards male privilege. From a feminist perspective, the term 'male privilege' describes the significant but largely invisible benefits of being male, as culturally determined beliefs about gender give men roles that empower them. It is a form of privilege that disadvantages women even if men are unaware of its nature and implications (McIntosh, 2003). It is inaccessible to women in patriarchal societies, but available to men regardless of whether or not they subsequently adopt a female identity and, therefore, in the radical feminist view, trans women have benefited from male privilege (Jeffreys, 2014). This perspective has been heavily criticised, as we will discuss later in this section.

The influence of radical feminism is evident in the findings of studies we have discussed which highlight the violent victimisation men perpetrate against women, and the limited protection the criminal justice system offers to the victims (see also Brownmiller, 1975; Dobash and Dobash, 1979, 2004; Maidment, 2006). Through their seminal studies of female victimisation by intimate male partners, US-based researchers, Rebecca Dobash and Russell Dobash (1978, 1979, 1983), for instance, have highlighted the role of men as the main perpetrators of domestic violence and drawn attention to how domestic violence is used to control women to reinforce male dominance in a patriarchal society, in line with the principles of radical feminist theory (see also Brownmiller, 1975; Hanmer, 1978; Rafter, 1990). Reinforcing this in a text that explored the dynamics of rape as an instrument of male domination over women in a variety of jurisdictions, Brownmiller (1975: 15, emphasis in original) described the violent sexual assaults perpetrated by men against women as: 'nothing more or less than a conscious process of intimidation by which *all* men keep *all* women in a state of fear'.

Advocates of radical feminism have also drawn attention to the social conditions that make women vulnerable to male control and abuse in patriarchal societies. Illustrating this idea in their studies, the Dobashes (1979) argue that male dominance over women is a feature of family life. They depict the family as a setting where men who have been socialised to be oppressive husbands control their wives, who have in turn been socialised into submissiveness. Alongside this aspect of family life, existing socio-economic arrangements allow men to secure high-status and better paid employment, while restricting women to low-status, low-paid positions. This means that women are more likely to become financially reliant on men, making them more subordinated in the home, and therefore more vulnerable to male domination and abuse (Dobash and Dobash, 1979).

Figure 11.11 The 'glass ceiling' is the idea of an invisible barrier that prevents women (and individuals belonging to minority groups) from rising beyond a certain level in a hierarchy due to existing social structures. Radical feminists emphasise the need for rebalancing the social order to avoid such issues

Source: Hyejin Kang/Shutterstock

Radical feminism has been criticised on several grounds. Some criticise the approach for presenting a simplistic account of gender that portrays all men as predatory oppressors whilst overlooking female criminality. From this perspective, feminist studies highlighting the violent victimisation of women by men are accused of implying that women are passive and incapable of exercising their agency, although it is worth noting that some of the same feminists also study female offending (for example, Gelsthorpe, 2004).

As we have hinted, other scholars and activists challenge what they see as radical feminism's reluctance to recognise the rights of transgender women, and the term trans-exclusionary radical feminism (TERF) has been used to describe this position (Williams, 2014). To counter this stance, some have worked to highlight that trans women are vulnerable to multiple types of discrimination (Serano, 2007, 2013). In the specific context of criminal justice, for example, they point to studies that have found connections between transgenderism and the experience of social marginality, which they argue can contribute to offending behaviour (Knight and Wilson, 2016). Some contend that trans people experience discriminatory treatment whilst interacting with criminal justice services like the police and courts, and they are more likely to be held in prisons that correspond with the biological sex that they were assigned at birth, rather than the gender with which they identify (Knight and Wilson, 2016). It has also been suggested that inadequate facilities in prisons for this group expose them to abuse from other prisoners, who target them because of their gender identity (Bromdal et al., 2019). Recognising these and other oppressions experienced by trans people, some have called for an inclusionary feminism which acknowledges that resisting gender-related oppressions of any kind is a worthwhile **social justice** project of the contemporary age (Hines, 2019) (see **Figure 11.12**).

Figure 11.12 A protest against **transphobic** media coverage in London 2018. Trans rights campaigners often emphasise that trans women should be considered women

Source: Penelope Barritt/Shutterstock

Added to the controversy over trans women's rights, radical feminism has also been accused of overlooking the progress that has been made to protect women from oppressive patriarchal social arrangements (Renzetti, 2012). We saw in **section 11.2** that a range of laws and policies have been introduced since the 1970s to address domestic violence perpetrated by men against women in intimate relationships.

In sum, radical feminism believes in the existence of a patriarchy that sustains male dominance while oppressing and subordinating women, and asserts that it should be not just rebalanced but dismantled. It is a theoretical tradition that has influenced the work of many scholars who have highlighted the overwhelming extent and harms of male violence against women. As we have seen (in **section 11.2**), insights from the work of radical feminists and others who campaign for women's rights have led to changes in the law that seek to protect women from domestic violence and sexual assaults perpetrated by intimate male partners. However, radical feminism is not without its opponents, and has been criticised for ignoring female criminality and the agency of women whilst depicting them as passive victims of male oppression, and for excluding trans women.

Marxist feminist theory

Unlike radical feminism, **Marxist feminist** theory does not depict gender inequality and the patriarchy as the only causes of female oppression. Instead, the theory identifies **capitalism** and the social class inequality it creates as the key factors that cause unequal gender relations and provoke the oppression of women by men in capitalist societies (Schwendinger and Schwendinger, 1983). From a Marxist perspective, in capitalist societies an individual's social status and ability to exert power is based on their position in relation to the production of the goods and services that humans need to survive. The wealthy ruling-class capitalists are said to control the means of production in these societies, and so they have more power than, for example, those who work to deliver goods and services, particularly those employed in low-status positions or occupations. Marxist feminist theory believes that men are often the ruling-class capitalists and usually occupy high-level positions in the production process, therefore enjoying a high social status and possessing substantial power.

Unlike men, women tend to have menial jobs, and contribute to the production process at the lower end of the occupational (work-related) ladder. Marxist feminists agree with radical feminists that the jobs available to women tend to be limited to low-paid domestic and caring positions, which reflect the dominant view that women are naturally programmed to perform nurturing roles. Women's typically low occupational statuses are therefore seen as corresponding with their relatively low social status and powerlessness in wider society compared with men, and these unequal gender arrangements influence gender relations. Marxist feminists therefore argue that the powerful positions that men in capitalist societies hold in relation to production, like factory bosses or CEOs, allow them to dominate and oppress women, making them vulnerable to male violence (Chesney-Lind and Morash, 2013). They also contend that the unfair class structure of capitalist societies triggers female offending because it leaves many women in economically marginal positions, with a low social status, meaning they have lower incomes and are in worse financial positions than men (Carlen, 1988). Therefore, the crimes women usually commit, like shoplifting and other property crimes, are seen to reflect their economic marginality (Burgess-Proctor, 2006). We explore the economic marginality of women in **Controversy and debate 11.4** on the gender pay gap. The arguments about the link between economic

CONTROVERSY AND DEBATE 11.4

Economic marginalisation, gender, and crime: the gender pay gap

Radical, Marxist, and socialist feminist criminologists all highlight the fact that women are economically marginalised and see this as significant in studies of gender and crime (see **Figure 11.13**). They argue that women's economic marginalisation stems from the fact that they have a lower social status and are less powerful than men, affecting their experiences of life in general and particularly within the criminal justice system. It makes them financially dependent on abusive partners and is also said to be among the drivers for female offending, for example prompting mothers to steal to feed their children (Prison Reform Trust, 2017).

In the UK, the most visible evidence of this economic marginalisation is the gender pay gap. This is the difference between the average hourly earnings of men and women, and since 2017 all organisations with more than 250 employees have had to publish their gender pay gap figures annually. Although the gap has decreased over recent decades, it remains significant, with men still paid considerably more (see House of Commons Library, 2020). As of the April 2019 data release, the key facts about the UK gender pay gap were as follows:

- Median hourly pay for full-time employees was 8.9 per cent less for women than for men.

- Median pay for all employees, both full time and part time, was 17.3 per cent less for women than men. (More women than men are employed part time and part-time workers tend to earn less per hour.)

- There was no significant improvement between 2017 and 2018: the gap shrunk from 9.7 to 9.6 per cent.

- Almost eight in ten companies pay their male employees more.

- More than one-quarter of companies pay women over 20 per cent less than men based on median hourly pay.

(Duncan et al., 2019 and House of Commons Library, 2020)

When these statistics were released in August 2019, they were met with fierce criticism and calls for more to be done to tackle the gender pay gap. The chief executive of the Fawcett Society, a charity campaigning for gender equality and women's rights, was quoted as saying:

> The regulations are not tough enough. It's time for action plans, not excuses . . . Employers need to set out a five-year strategy for how they will close their gender pay gaps, monitoring progress and results. But we also need to tackle all the causes of the pay gap—introduce more generous leave for fathers that they can afford to take, make every job flexible by default, unless there is a strong business case not to do so, and deal with any outstanding pay discrimination that employers may find.

(Duncan, P., McIntyre, N., and Davies, C., 'Gender pay gap figures show eight in 10 UK firms pay men more than women', *The Guardian*, 4 April 2019)

Figure 11.13 Although the gender pay gap is slowly narrowing, it reflects the fact that women have historically been economically marginalised, working in lower paid and lower status roles, affecting their positions in society
Source: Photofusion/Shutterstock

marginality and many women's offending also feature in the principles of socialist feminist theory, which we discuss in the next section.

We can summarise Marxist feminism as a theory that understands capitalism as a mode of production which produces unequal gender relations that disadvantage women and can contribute to their involvement in offending. To redress this unfair status quo, Marxist feminists, like radical feminists, propose a total transformation of the economic system, rather than an adjustment. Unlike radical feminists, however, they argue that capitalism should be replaced with socialism, which is a mode of production that should produce fairer production processes and a more even distribution of societal resources, so should result in more equal gender relations (Schwendinger and Schwendinger, 1983).

As for the criticisms levelled against Marxist feminism, we will consider these further in the context of the similar criticisms made of socialist feminist theory, but the main objection raised is that this approach emphasises the importance of economic class inequality (in which men enjoy greater economic power), and the gender oppression it generates, over other forms of oppression that occur when gender inequality intersects with other inequalities (Maidment, 2006). We explore this issue in more depth in **section 11.6**.

Socialist feminist theory

Socialist feminist theory combines aspects of radical and Marxist feminist theories. Like Marxist feminist theory, it identifies class difference as a fundamental feature of capitalist societies that can underpin women's offending and victimisation. Socialist feminists also argue that patriarchy or male domination has a negative impact on women, which is in line with radical feminism. But socialist feminism is not simply a combination of these two approaches: it also contends that oppressive gender relations resulting from the patriarchy *intersect* with the class inequality resulting from capitalism to disadvantage women and shape their lived experiences (Acker, 1990, 1992; Hartmann, 1981; Messerschmidt, 1986). For this reason, socialist feminists support both gender equality to reverse the patriarchy, as well as economic reform so that gender and social class equality can be achieved. Researchers who view female offending as a rational choice when facing economic hardship, subscribe to socialist feminist thinking.

Similar to Marxist feminist theory, socialist feminist criminology has been accused of presuming that both genders are homogenous groups, and both strands of feminist criminology have been criticised for suggesting that social class is the only factor that separates the male and female genders, ignoring the impact of other attributes such as race (Sudbury, 2005).

A theme spanning all the criticisms made of the key feminist traditions is that the early versions were generally criticised for portraying all women as the same. Contemporary studies now increasingly highlight the factors that intersect to make women's experiences different depending on the individual, a topic we will explore in **section 11.6**.

11.5 Feminist epistemologies

Alongside the theoretical positions we have discussed, feminist researchers examining issues of gender and crime are also influenced by several epistemological positions. We discuss epistemologies in **Chapter 4**, but it is worth noting here that they are philosophical positions that reflect a researcher's views about what constitutes valid knowledge of the social world (with 'valid' in this context meaning the accuracy, suitability, and relevance of the information) and the best way of generating such knowledge. It is therefore important to understand that, in practical terms, epistemological positions are approaches to generating knowledge. They are not theories in their own right but, as we will see later, certain theoretical approaches tend to go hand in hand with certain epistemologies.

The main epistemological positions that are associated with feminist criminological research are:

- feminist empiricism;
- standpoint feminism; and
- postmodern feminism (Comack, 1999; Harding, 1986).

Let's explore the key features of each of these positions.

Feminist empiricism

Feminist empiricism is an epistemological position which presumes that if we study crime through scientific methods, we can produce unbiased, gender-neutral knowledge of the nature of crime (Harding, 1991; Naffine, 1997). According to Smart (1995), this is the main **epistemology** associated with liberal feminism and its analysis of female crime. The **ontological** basis of this position—that is, its view of what exists in the social world—is that objective knowledge of social reality does exist and is discoverable. This means that it views concepts such as gender and crime as realities that exist objectively and have unique qualities, rather than being social constructs. If we translate this position into the real world of social research, we can see that there is an assumption that a researcher can remain neutral and objective when collecting and analysing research data (Harding, 1991). The belief that the scientific approach is characterised by vital researcher objectivity and represents the ideal way of studying the social world dominated mainstream criminology and influenced feminist empiricism and liberal feminist theory, although it was later challenged by the feminist traditions we discuss in the following sections. As Smart (1995) notes, feminist empiricists, who were prominent in the 1970s and have been described as the earliest feminist criminologists, endorsed the approach. They believed that more 'scientific' studies of women's experiences were needed to balance the focus of scientific inquiry on men. Comack (1999: 288) points out that:

> Feminist empiricists, by and large, left the scientific enterprise intact and called for more studies 'on' women in order to fill the historical gap which had been created by the exclusion of women as research subjects.

Some scholars, such as Carrington (2008), suggest that feminist empiricists did not question how useful the so-called 'objective' scientific methods were, unlike the standpoint feminists whose position we will explore next, because they (the feminist empiricists) were focused on their broader aim: generating empirical insights that would aid the emancipation of women.

Standpoint feminism

Standpoint feminism is an epistemological stance that prioritises the experiences of women, as expressed by women (Cain, 1990a, 1990b; Hartsock, 1987; Harding, 1987, 1991). This emphasis on women's subjective accounts sets standpoint feminism apart from feminist empiricism, which focuses on the 'scientific' notions of researcher objectivity and unbiased knowledge.

Standpoint feminism is based on the belief that women experience various forms of marginalisation, and those who are marginalised are more likely to offer accurate accounts of their experiences (Flavin, 2001). Given their shared experience of gendered oppression, women are said to have a unique perspective that allows them to provide accurate accounts of social reality within a patriarchal society (Harding, 1987). Unlike the dominant group (men) who may wish to maintain unfair conditions so that they can sustain their privileged positions, marginalised groups have nothing to gain from concealing the difficulties they face (Harding, 1991). Researchers who take a standpoint feminist approach therefore view women's descriptions of their experiences as 'epistemologically privileged', or more reliable and authoritative (Cain, 1990b: 126). Women's views, or 'stories' (Comack, 1999: 296), which probably reflect their struggle for emancipation, are seen as more accurate representations of reality that should inform criminal justice policy reform and wider policy change.

Scholars inspired by standpoint feminism therefore put forward empirical methods that they believe can produce knowledge from the standpoint of women, with the overall aim of promoting women's viewpoints and interests (Cain, 1990b; Harding, 1987, 1991, 2004; Hartsock, 1987). Smart (1995) notes that they reject the research methods promoted by feminist empiricists since the methods were influenced by the underlying assumption that objective, gender-neutral 'facts' are discoverable. Standpoint feminists also believe that the methods are male-centred and argue that women are best placed to conduct research on women's experiences (Smith and Skinner, 2012). Smart (1995: 43) observes that 'the epistemological basis of this form of feminist knowledge is experience', which is essentially the belief that female researchers possess unique insight and a clearer understanding of the experiences of female research participants because both parties share similar personal experiences.

It is important to be aware that several scholars who contributed to the early development of standpoint feminism, for example Maureen Cain (1990a, 1990b), have changed their earlier position that women share similar experiences of oppression. They still argue that women's views or perspectives offer more authoritative knowledge of social reality than men's accounts, but they have come to acknowledge that women experience 'multiple realities', or have diverse experiences of oppression, depending on their lives and circumstances (Cain, 1990a, 1990b; Comack, 1999).

Some of the studies conducted by radical feminist researchers who exposed the extent of male violence against women were influenced by standpoint feminism (see, for example, Dobash and Dobash, 1992). These studies produced knowledge of domestic violence that was based on the accounts of the female victims themselves and revealed the power dynamics that underpin domestic violence.

Standpoint feminism has been criticised for prioritising women's perspectives over those of others and of wrongly depicting women's views as definitive knowledge of social reality, implying that the knowledge produced by academic researchers who adopt this stance is superior (Comack, 1999). Some also argue that, again, standpoint feminists depict women as a homogenous group and try to 'impose: a different unitary reality' on women (Smart, 1995: 95). This claim essentially means that standpoint feminists portray women as a group that can, with one voice, speak about their shared experiences in an unfair androcentric social world. Therefore, the standpoint feminist perspective on women and their experiences ignores the racial, cultural, and other structures of disadvantage that impact on women differently (Carrington, 2008), factors that intersectional researchers believe should be taken into account when studying women's experiences.

Postmodern feminism

Postmodern feminists aim to **deconstruct** the dominant language or discourses (forms of communication) that give meaning to social categories such as gender (Butler, 1990; Comack, 1999; Howe, 1994; Young, 1996). They believe this can help uncover the structures of power that fuel gender inequality which disadvantages women. Like feminist empiricists and standpoint feminists, postmodern feminists explore the epistemological question of how best to produce knowledge of social reality, but they are also interested in uncovering the power dynamics underpinning knowledge production (Carrington, 2008).

Unlike some standpoint feminists who believe that women's narratives of their experiences offer definitive knowledge of the social world, postmodern feminists view *all* accounts, whatever the source or sources, as constructed and biased (Howe, 1994; Smart, 1995; Young, 1996). This stance means that they also differ from empirical feminists who believe that scientific methods of inquiry can produce an objective, universal 'truth' about social reality. Instead, they argue that truth depends on context and interpretation, so knowledge or 'what we know' about the things that exist or occur in the social world, including our knowledge of gender issues, cannot be separated from the circumstances from which it emerges. Whereas other feminist perspectives emphasise the androcentric bases of power (the idea that power is mainly held by men), postmodern feminists believe that power is 'ubiquitous' (everywhere or universal) and exists in diverse groups and contexts in society (Smart, 1995: 46). These ideas point to the fact that they are influenced by post-**social structural theory**, particularly the French philosopher Derrida's (1976) idea of 'deconstruction', which is a technique for studying the social world. This concept is based on the belief that the *language* or discourse we use to describe and explain accepted knowledge of the social world is not objective, and instead reflects the values and biases of those who have the power to produce such knowledge.

Influenced by these themes, postmodern feminists challenge the idea that a discoverable universal 'truth' about social reality exists. From their point of view, any knowledge that claims to be the 'truth' about gender is not in any way objective. Instead, they view beliefs about key social categories, such as gender and crime, as subjective beliefs that have been transformed by those in power into 'truth' (see also Young, 1996). This essentially means that the powerful have ways of manipulating our understandings of the words we use, even when it seems like the definitions are neutral or objective. In the same way, the language that is used to define gender difference reflects the values and preferences of the knowledge creators. The more powerful members of society have control over knowledge production and it is their subjective definitions and understandings of social categories that represent dominant knowledge. In fact, postmodern feminists argue that the idea that gender is binary comes from the language and discourses of the powerful. They argue that gender (both male and female) has no natural qualities or traits, but that normalising characteristics are assigned to it, like the ideas that men are aggressive and women are passive, which benefit men and disadvantage women, fuelling gender inequality.

In order to address these dominant discourses that put women at a disadvantage, postmodern feminists try to develop new ways of describing and understanding women's 'realities' (Maidment, 2006). Unlike the feminist empiricists with their search for scientifically generated 'truth' and the standpoint feminists who depict women's viewpoints as the definitive 'truth', postmodern feminists contend that no universal 'truth' exists and that there are multiple realities, including those of groups who do not have the power to spread their views as 'truth'. These groups usually contain individuals who are affected by racial, social class, and gender inequality. For these groups, their realities reflect the truths of their particular social, economic, and political circumstances, and postmodern feminists believe that they are valid sources of knowledge (Comack, 1999). To apply this idea in more concrete terms, take a look at **Figure 11.14**—do you think everyone would interpret this painting in the same way or would it depend on their experiences and point of view? This view is very much in line with arguments of feminists who draw attention to how intersections of gender, and socio-structural factors such as ethnicity and social class, affect women in different ways, an approach we explore in **section 11.6**.

Summarising the tenets of postmodern feminism, Smart (1995: 44–5) notes that its core idea is:

> the rejection of the one reality which arises from 'the falsely universalizing perspective of the master' (Harding 1987: 188). So the aim of feminism ceases to be the establishment of the feminist truth and becomes the aim of deconstructing Truth and analysing the power effects that claims to truth entail.

Figure 11.14 Postmodern feminists argue that there is no universal truth, just multiple realities created by our own individual experiences
Source: Mahlia Amatina https://www.facebook.com/mahliaamatina/photos/a.4762590125 30342/1143576799131890/?type=3

Here, Smart highlights that postmodern feminism's aim is to deconstruct universally accepted claims that are made about social categories, particularly gender and female criminality. Deconstructionism is used to interpret the language we use and to unmask power structures of knowledge production. This process involves analysing texts and discourses in criminology (and other social sciences) that are used to define and categorise human beings and social occurrences, with the goal of uncovering and challenging underlying myths about female characteristics, behaviours, and experiences in society that disadvantage women—myths that are constructed by the powerful and held out as 'truth' (Smart, 1995).

Like the other feminist epistemologies, postmodern feminism also has its critics. This viewpoint has been accused of *relativism*—the belief that there is no absolute knowledge or truth, implying that these exist only in relation to their context—because it views knowledge as socially constructed. Critics suggest that this perspective on knowledge could prevent postmodern feminists from studying and challenging dominant discourses, whereas its intention should be to challenge these discourses and replace them with accounts that highlight women's experiences (for example, Cain 1990a, 1990b). From this perspective, not challenging dominant accounts is an *apolitical* (not interested in politics) approach that is inconsistent with the feminist goal of placing gender and the unfair experiences of women at the core of analyses.

Some also point out that it would be impractical (difficult and unrealistic) to apply the theoretical beliefs of postmodern feminism to real-world social research (see, for example, Flavin, 2001). Since postmodern feminists describe all social categories as social constructions, they would see efforts to study how gender intersects with categories like race and social class to oppress women as effectively accepting social categories that are nothing more than social constructions (Comack, 1999). The counter-argument is that dismissing social categories as social constructions does not mean that the categories disappear; they still affect women's lives and need to be studied to uncover how women give meaning to the social categories that oppress them and generally affect their lives, even if the effect is different in individual cases (Comack, 1999). For some critics, by implying that there are multiple realities, postmodern feminism also suggests that striving for gender equality and improving women's experiences in androcentric societies is futile. This is because, in the view of postmodern feminists, neither outcome (gender equality and improvements in women's experiences) would have a universal impact on women since they all experience different realities (Comack, 1999). We explore the idea of different realities for different women further in the next section.

11.6 Newer perspectives in feminist criminology

We saw in **sections 11.4** and **11.5** that a recurring theme underlies most of the criticisms of feminist theories and epistemologies. This is the argument that feminist theorising, particularly in its early forms, mainly focused on the impact of socially and culturally constructed ideas of gender on women's experiences in society and tended to portray women as a homogenous group, believing that despite their different attributes (such as ethnicity, class, and political or sexual orientation), their gender exposes them to the same type of oppression. Smart (1995: 45) argues that a presumed 'sisterhood' was a key feature of early feminist discourse, and we can see that there was an assumption that feminist scholarship and activism could be a joint project for all women. More recent feminist thinkers have challenged this view and have sought to make feminism a more inclusive 'umbrella' project which acknowledges and highlights the existence of the different types of experiences women encounter. In this section, we consider these developments, looking first at intersectional approaches then at feminist perspectives which focus on the experiences of those who do not conform to normative gender identities.

Intersectional perspectives

As we noted in **section 11.3**, intersectionality is the 'interaction of multiple identities and experiences of exclusion and subordination' (Davis, 2008: 68). Debates centring around this concept began to emerge in the 1980s and 1990s, sparking what is now described as the third wave of feminism (Burgess-Proctor, 2006), as some writers felt that feminist criminology was ignoring the existence of multiple realities for women. They pointed out that feminism was dominated by white, middle-class women and argued that it overlooked how race, social class, and other social categories made other women's experiences different (see, for example, hooks, 1981; Baca Zinn and Thornton, 1996).

The main works responsible for this development were those of African American feminists such as bell hooks (1981, see **Figure 11.15**; note that hooks' name is intentionally lower case), and Hull and Colleagues (1982), who wrote *Ain't I a Woman?* and *All the Women are White, All the Blacks are men, But some of Us are Brave*, respectively. Both scholars and others highlighted the gap created by white, middle-class feminism that dominated feminist analyses at the time. They described it as a brand of feminism that spread universalising perspectives and did not—and could not—effectively portray or represent the interests of other women whose ethnicity, social class, and other aspects of their identities, interacted to worsen their disadvantage, for example black women. These feminists argued that the conceptualisation of 'womanhood' within early feminism only represented the 'white, middle class, Anglo-Saxon' woman (Smart, 1995: 45). This definition of womanhood was not broad enough to encompass the lived realities of those who did not belong to that category

Figure 11.15 Scholar and activist bell hooks' seminal text, *Ain't I a Woman?* (1984), rejected the dominant feminist view that all women share similar experiences of disadvantage

Source: Alex Lozupone (Tduk)/CC-BY-SA 4.0

(Crenshaw, 1994). Reinforcing this argument, Comack (1999: 288) remarked that:

> For feminists in both criminology and elsewhere, the task of producing feminist knowledge initially appeared to be a straightforward one. There was a broad consensus, which emanated from the point that we knew what it was we were rejecting: the androcentricism of the traditional research enterprise. However, as feminists began to respond to this common problematic, cracks in the consensus began to appear.

In order to challenge this definition of womanhood, Kimberlé Crenshaw (1989) devised the term intersectionality to describe the impact of factors like race and class, which can, alongside gender, worsen some women's exposure to discrimination in social institutions, including the criminal justice system. For example, there is evidence that compared with white women, black and other minority ethnic women in the UK and the US receive harsher court sanctions, such as longer prison sentences (Chigwada-Bailey, 1997; Seitz, 2005). They are also said to face additional disadvantages as victims, since they are disadvantaged by the racial, class-based, and sexuality-related factors that influence stereotypes about how men and women should behave in domestic violence incidents. Women involved in these incidents are expected to be passive, like the socially constructed ideal white, middle-class heterosexual female (Dasgupta, 2002, cited in Romain et al., 2016). Ethnic minority women who do not show this quality could be labelled as masculine and excessively violent, and consequently denied adequate protection (Romain et al., 2016). This means that unlike other women who may be vulnerable to perceptions of double deviance when they violate prescribed gender roles, minorities would encounter what could be described as 'triple deviance' given the added influence of their ethnicity.

In her seminal text, bell hooks (1981) highlighted these issues and rejected the dominant feminist view that all women share similar experiences of disadvantage. hooks persuasively argued that the extreme marginalisation and deprivation of African American women is distinctly and qualitatively different from the social experiences of other women (see also Davis, 1983). In her view, black women were disproportionately disadvantaged by inequalities that stemmed from their gender *and* their ethnicity. It was therefore misleading to present women as a group sharing a social reality, who could campaign for change with one voice. Chesney-Lind and Morash (2013: 293) have since stated that: 'African American scholar and activist bell hooks' book, *Ain't I a Woman?* (1984), highlighted and forever invalidated the sole focus on gender'.

In the 1980s, additional African American feminists and others echoed this critique and inspired more comprehensive accounts of gender relations and women's experiences in patriarchal societies. As Daly (2010: 229) put it, their critique challenged any simple idea of a 'woman's perspective' and any 'unified feminist politics for change'. In a paper which aimed to develop 'a black feminist criminology', Potter (2006: 107) argues that 'traditional feminist criminology is built on mainstream feminism, which historically placed issues of race as secondary to gender'. She notes that:

> For Black women, and arguably for all women, other inequities must be considered principal, not peripheral, to the analysis of women. This includes incorporating key factors such as race and/or ethnicity, sexuality, and economic status into any examination.

According to Potter (2006: 110), a black feminist criminology that explores the nature of crime and victimisation among African Americans (and 'other groups of colour'), and responses to it, would also take into account the societal, familial, and other circumstances of black women since, in her view, these circumstances shape their victimisation. Added to race and social class, age and disability are examples of factors that can interact with gender to expose some individuals to different forms of oppression (Crenshaw, 1994; Daly, 2006; Maidment, 2006; Potter, 2006).

Although intersectionality is now often used to explore how identity interacts with oppression, some critics argue that whilst women may possess multiple identities and experience diverse realities they still share certain universalising qualities. In their study of women's experiences of violence in South Africa, which is made up of multiple cultural groups and in which women occupy positions at all levels of the **social hierarchy**, Flavin and Artz (2013) were able to identify shared experiences of violence that affected the women's lives. They found that the legacy of apartheid (a political system that implemented racial segregation) is visible in the 'indiscriminate violence, including sexual violence' that many women experience, and the mostly ineffective criminal justice system that exists in the country (2013: 23). They argued that their findings highlighted the importance of remaining alert to the fact that there are some universalising gender inequalities in many societies across the world, and these disproportionately disadvantage women.

We have continued our focus on women when discussing intersectionality, but it is worth noting that scholars have also shown that men are not immune from the negative effects of intersecting social categories. As we saw when discussing men as offenders in **section 11.2**, essentialising the male gender by attaching certain characteristics to it (for example, privilege and power) overlooks the reality that some men do not possess those qualities. The concept of 'subordinated masculinities' suggests that there are men who do not have access to the privileges associated with ideal masculinity in patriarchal societies (Connell, 1995, 2000), and some men who do not possess those qualities may resort to crime to obtain them (Connell and Messerschmidt, 2005).

Additional feminist perspectives

Since feminist criminology expanded through the 1980s and 1990s to include the theoretical frameworks and epistemological positions we have described, additional feminist perspectives have emerged. Added to the study of masculinities, further developments in the field include queer feminism (typically associated with LGBT feminism), transfeminism, and disability feminism. These theoretical frameworks integrate intersectionality into their analyses of gender issues, exploring how constructions and intersections of identities, such as sexual orientation, disability, race, social class, and other social categories, affect the experiences of groups whose identities do not conform to gender norms.

Scholars taking these perspectives into account have studied these groups' experiences as offenders in the criminal justice system, where they are likely to be exposed to harsh treatment (for example, inadequate police protection from **hate crimes** and punitive court sentences) because they do not conform to gender norms (see Knight and Wilson, 2016; Wolff and Cokely, 2007). Scholars also explore the groups' experiences as victims who are particularly vulnerable to hate crimes, again because their identities contravene normative identities including socially and culturally constructed gender identities (see generally Ball, 2016; Balderston, 2013; Butler, 1990, 1999; Jauk, 2013; Koyama, 2003; Knight and Wilson, 2016)—we consider these in **Chapter 8**. The emergence of these perspectives demonstrates that feminist criminology is a growing field of study that has taken on board the intersectionality debates of the 1980s onwards. It has expanded to accommodate the diverse identities that could expose people to victimisation and to unfair treatment in both the criminal justice system and wider society (see **Figure 11.16**).

Figure 11.16 Feminist criminology now accommodates the diverse identities that could expose people to unfair treatment in the criminal justice system and society, including transgender identities
Source: © istock.com/tomeng

> ### WHAT DO YOU THINK? 11.5
>
> **Your perspective on feminist criminology**
>
> Reflect on what you have read about feminist criminological theories and epistemological positions. Which do you find most convincing? Make some notes about the characteristics and criticisms of each theory and epistemological position and consider which aligns best with your perspectives on studying matters of gender and crime, and your beliefs about the 'reality' (or realities) and the best ways of generating knowledge of the social world.
>
> You might not fully identify with any of the approaches we have discussed, but if this is the case, consider the aspects of each with which you agree and disagree. How would you define your own theoretical position on feminist criminology (see **Figure 11.17**)?
>
>
>
> **Figure 11.17** There is no default approach to generating knowledge about feminism; each researcher develops their own position. Do any of these feminist epistemologies align with your own viewpoint?
> Source: Yuliya Chsherbakova/Shutterstock

Now that we have explored differing feminist theories and perspectives, read **What do you think? 11.5** to reflect on your own standpoint: which of the perspectives, or what combination of them, best aligns with your own views on how best to study gender and crime?

11.7 Conclusion

Think back to your responses to **What do you think? 11.1** about the impact gender has on your life. Would you answer in a different way now? Having read this chapter, it should now be clear that gender and the ways in which it intersects with other social categories has a significant impact on people's lives, both in society more generally and in relation to crime and justice. Although, as we have seen, men are not immune from this impact, gender inequality disproportionately affects women and shapes their experiences as victims and offenders. Feminist criminological perspectives disagree on the main causes of this inequality, the best ways to generate knowledge about it, and what constitutes valid knowledge on the subject, but they agree that it exists and must be addressed. Generally, feminist criminologists have helped to reduce the androcentrism that was a large part of mainstream criminology (Daly and Chesney-Lind, 1988), and have attempted to rebalance criminology's skewed focus on male offending (Gelsthorpe and Morris, 1988: 98). As a result of their work, we know much more about women and crime: several feminist perspectives on female crime and victimisation now exist with researchers adopting diverse epistemological positions and drawing attention to the disadvantages women encounter because of the gender norms that disempower them in a male-dominated society. Despite their disagreements, these perspectives and studies share the motivation of producing knowledge that improves the welfare of women and helps to dispel the myths about gender and its relation to crime and criminal justice by drawing attention to women's experiences (Cain, 1990b; Smart, 1995).

Feminist perspectives have also led to very real changes in some of the ways in which the criminal justice system responds to female offenders and victims, and have contributed immensely to widespread calls for a gender-responsive justice system. For instance, police forces now have dedicated domestic violence units, victims of rape are now allocated to a Sexual Offences Investigative Techniques (SOIT) Officer, there are now 'havens' (Sexual Assault Referral Centres) which ensure that victims of rape and sexual assault get the help they need in a safe and supportive environment, and so on. These are all very real and important changes—it is sobering to think that there was little recognition of the need for such developments in the 1970s when Carol Smart was writing her critique of 'malestream' criminology. As we have also seen, however, there is still a very long way to go with regard to dispelling myths about gender and crime and improving the ways in which female offenders and victims are treated in the justice system and wider society. There are a huge number of areas for further exploration within this area of criminology, and much more reading to do—see the **Further Reading** at the end of the chapter. Feminist, and feminist-inspired, criminological theories—whether produced by academics or students—will undoubtedly continue to be a crucial strand of critical thinking and it is likely that their ideas and findings will help to inform policy, paving the way for greater gender equality.

SUMMARY

After reading this chapter and working your way through its features you should now be able to:

- Understand key criminological explanations of how gender intersects with crime and criminal justice

There are now several gendered accounts of crime (the link between gender and crime), focusing primarily on women's experiences with some also studying the links between masculinity (the male gender) and crime. This development means that there are now studies of women's experiences as perpetrators or victims of crime and their experiences in the criminal justice system. Key examples are the perspectives influenced by radical criminology which emphasise that women are disproportionately more vulnerable to violence from their intimate partners than men, noting that this kind of violence is used to control women in patriarchal societies. Others who support the beliefs of liberal feminist theory argue that the emancipation of women, which was brought about by the feminist activism in the 1960s and 1970s, have created opportunities for women to engage in activities that were previously dominated by men, including crime. They contend that this change can explain the growing representation of women in crime statistics, which has triggered a narrowing of the gender gap. But some whose studies are more aligned with Marxist feminism and socialist feminism, point to the links between the economic marginality of women and their involvement in offending.

- Identify the definition, origins, and key principles of feminist criminology

Feminist criminology emerged in the 1970s during the second wave of feminism that originated in the US and spread to other countries such as the UK. It is made up of several theoretical and epistemological strands and it therefore lacks a precise definition. These different strands do, however, share some key principles such as the rejection of mainstream criminology's gender blindness and androcentricism, and the effort to address these by theorising gender and its links to crime and criminal justice.

- Outline the theoretical traditions underpinning feminist criminology, namely liberalism, radicalism, Marxism, and socialism

Although feminist traditions differ in some important ways, they share in common the belief that gender inequality that disadvantages women exists in society and should be dismantled. Liberal feminist theory's main argument is that if we are to achieve gender equality, we need to challenge and rebalance the socialisation of women into gender roles that are associated with passivity and conformity. In comparison, radical feminism identifies patriarchy or male domination as the fundamental factor driving gender inequality, oppressing women regardless of their ethnicity, social class, or other attributes. Unlike radical feminism, Marxist feminist theory argues that women are disadvantaged by capitalism which provokes an unequal class structure. Social feminist theory combines aspects of radical and Marxist feminist theories, founding its analysis of women's experiences on the view that a combination of the patriarchy and capitalist-class inequality are the factors that fuel the gender inequality that disadvantages women.

- Recognise feminist epistemologies such as feminist empiricism, standpoint feminism, and postmodern feminism

Feminist criminologists take on diverse epistemological positions which reflect their views about the most appropriate ways of generating knowledge of women's experiences in the social world. Feminist empiricists prioritise forms of knowledge that emerge from supposed neutral and objective scientific methods of inquiry. Standpoint feminists privilege women's views as the authoritative source of knowledge. Unlike the other two, postmodern feminists call into question all sources and forms of knowledge, arguing that deconstructing what we consider authoritative knowledge is necessary to uncover how power structures influence the production of forms of knowledge about gender which disadvantage women.

- Critically evaluate criticisms of feminist criminology and the ways in which newer perspectives have tried to address them

We have also explored the criticisms levelled against the key traditions within feminist criminology and feminist epistemologies. In doing so, we have seen that although feminist traditions and epistemologies have received several criticisms, a unifying one is that apart from postmodern feminism, they depict women as homogeneous group. They do not pay enough attention to the wider social categories that intersect with gender to negatively affect certain women, like race and social class. The main ways in which this and other criticisms have been addressed in recent years are through an emphasis on intersectionality and the emergence of additional perspectives. Intersectionality is the idea that someone's lived experience and the disadvantages they face are shaped by the ways in which their numerous attributes intersect, and the additional feminist perspectives draw attention to the experiences of those whose identities do not align with gender norms, such as LGBT people.

 Test your understanding of the chapter's key points by attempting the self-test questions on the **online resources** at www.oup.com/he/case2e

REVIEW QUESTIONS

1. What is meant by the term 'gender blindness'?
2. What are the main similarities and differences between liberal feminist theory and radical feminist theory?
3. How did positivism seek to explain female criminality?
4. What is the 'chivalry thesis'?
5. Outline the main criticisms of standpoint and postmodern feminism.

 Access the **online resources** at www.oup.com/he/case2e to check your answers to the review questions.

FURTHER READING

Brownmiller, S. (1975) *Against our Will: Men, Women and Rape.* New York: Simon & Schuster.
This text provides an informative account that depicts the rape of women as a long-standing instrument of male domination worldwide, and documents the tendency of medical and legal institutions to ignore this reality.

Burgess-Proctor, A. (2006) 'Intersection of race, class, gender, and crime: Future directions for feminist criminology'. *Feminist Criminology* 1: 27–47.

This article offers an insightful account of the intersectionality debates that instituted the so-called third wave of feminism.

Burman, M. and Gelsthorpe, L., (2017) 'Feminist criminology: inequalities, powerlessness, and justice' in A. Liebling, S. Maruna, and L. McAra, (eds) *The Oxford Handbook of Criminology* **(6th edn). Oxford: Oxford University Press.**

This chapter has hopefully provided you with enough grounding knowledge to build on. An ideal next step would be to consult this chapter in *The Oxford Handbook of Criminology* to broaden your understanding.

Dobash, R. E. and Dobash, R. P. (1979) *Violence Against Wives.* **New York: Free Press.**

This text is a notable example of the scholarly work of the 1970s which reflected the tenets of radical feminism and improved awareness of the violent victimisation of women by their male partners.

Smart, C. (1976) *Women, Crime and Criminology.* **Abingdon: Routledge.**

This is a seminal text that provided the impetus for the emergence of feminist criminology. Once again, we encourage you to read the original. It is a clearly written text that sets out the context from which the need for studies of gender and crime emerged.

Ugwudike, P. et al. (eds) (2019) *Routledge Companion to Rehabilitative Work in Criminal Justice.* **Abingdon: Routledge.**

We recommend reading the chapters below from this edited collection for deeper insights into women's experiences of the justice system, effective practice for women in the system, and the merits of gender-responsive approaches:

Gelsthorpe, L., 'What works with women offenders? An English and Welsh perspective'
Messina, N. P., Bloom, B. E., and Covington, S. S., 'Gender-responsive approaches for women in the United States'.
Welsh, M., 'Women's experiences of the Criminal Justice System'.

Access the **online resources** to view a wealth of extra information relating to your study of criminology, including self-test questions, answers to review questions, and links to other resources that will help you enjoy and fulfil your potential within your studies.
www.oup.com/he/case2e

CHAPTER OUTLINE

12.1	Introduction	346
12.2	What is green criminology?	346
12.3	Green criminology and the 'market society'	352
12.4	Key concepts in green criminology	357
12.5	Green crimes or green harms?	362
12.6	Policing green crimes	366
12.7	Conclusion	370

12

Green criminology

Angus Nurse

KEY ISSUES

After studying this chapter, you should be able to:

- appreciate the importance of green criminology as a distinct field within criminology;
- identify how and why green criminology often focuses on harm rather than crime;
- critically assess the extent to which ideas around crime and wrongdoing extend beyond interpersonal violence and property crimes to include crimes against environments, humanity, and other animals;
- evaluate key green criminological concepts and theoretical approaches such as ecological justice (including species justice) and environmental justice and understand the concept of ecocide;
- identify the causes of green crimes, their links with other crimes, and how green criminology can inform mainstream criminology.

12.1 Introduction

When you think about crime or law and order, what kinds of examples come to mind? Violence? **Hate crimes**? Theft? Sexual assault? Your ideas about crime might be broader and more expansive than the average person's, depending on the stage you have reached in your studies, but they are still likely to focus on illegal acts or behaviours that directly harm humans. Environmental issues have gained prominence in recent years and we are all much more aware of our impact on the natural world, but most societies and their criminal justice systems, as well as mainstream criminology, remain preoccupied with illegal acts that affect human life.

Green criminology aims to address this oversight. At a basic level, this strand of criminology looks at crimes against the environment, animals, and non-human nature that are largely ignored by mainstream criminology. Green criminology 'takes as its focus issues relating to the environment (in the widest sense possible) and social harm (as defined in ecological as well as strictly legal terms)' (White, 2007: 33), and in doing so, it highlights that our understanding of crime and deviance is often limited to crimes that affect humans and human interests. We will see, for example, that even though some crimes committed against animals (such as animal cruelty and illegal wildlife trafficking) cause significant harms and threaten species survival, the animals that suffer from these crimes cannot be classed as crime victims (see also **Chapter 7**). Instead, we view these crimes in terms of their impact on humans, primarily those who have property rights. We will also see that much activity that causes harm to animals and to the environment is actually legal and falls outside the criminal law. For example, whereas issues like murder and manslaughter are covered by homicide laws and are clearly classed as crimes that will be dealt with by mainstream policing agencies, environmental harms such as pollution offences and the taking of protected wildlife are often dealt with by civil or administrative justice systems. This means they are dealt with as a breach of regulations, rather than as a crime in a strict sense.

Green criminology takes a critical approach, inviting us to look beyond narrow, human-centred definitions of crime and to consider a wider conception which for some sees green crimes as a form of **social harm** (a **concept** we introduce in this chapter but consider in depth in **Chapter 19**). Its critical approach, which considers wrongdoing and deviance outside mainstream justice and 'ordinary' crimes, means that it is often seen as part of the collection of theoretical approaches known as **critical criminology** (see **Chapter 18**). Green criminologists examine a wide range of environmental issues from wildlife crime, wildlife trafficking, animal rights, and species justice to corporate environmental crime and illegal pollution, ecological justice and ecocide, food crime, and the links between **organised crime** and the waste industry (including disposal of toxic waste and nuclear waste). In this chapter, we will examine some of these issues and see why they are important for green criminology. We will consider how environmental issues are sometimes neglected by markets, the criminological concepts and theoretical approaches associated with green criminology, and the debate about whether we should focus on green crimes or harms. We also consider how environmental harms are regulated and the different ways of responding to and policing green crimes. Having a good understanding of these aspects will not only give you a solid grounding in the increasingly important sub-discipline of green criminology, but will enhance your understanding of other more mainstream criminological issues—this is an ideal area in which to cultivate and develop your ABC (*Always Be Critical*) mindset.

12.2 What is green criminology?

Before we can begin considering these issues, we need a clear sense of green criminology as a distinct sub-discipline. Where does it come from, how does it fit with and reflect wider societal views, and what are its main aims? In this section, we consider the context and origins of green criminology and outline its scope.

The context and origins of green criminology

Have you noticed a separation between the natural/physical world and the human/social world in your university studies? Many universities have distinct academic departments that teach and research the natural sciences (chemistry, physics, biology, and so on) and the social sciences (criminology, sociology, and so on), with the study of law often linked with business or criminology or considered to be a subject in its own right. This separation reflects established ideas within western society that humans are above and have rights over nature and the animal kingdom, as well as ideas from within the Christian tradition that although we have a responsibility to care for the natural world, only humans have souls and are sentient (in other words, able to think, feel, and reason).

While university structures generally remain the same, in recent years there has been a move away from the assumption of human superiority and towards a view that all life forms interact with and affect their environment—a position expressed by the Gaia hypothesis, a theory proposed by the scientist and environmentalist James Lovelock in 1972. This view is present in both old and new religious traditions, such as Buddhism and Neo-Paganism, which stress the importance of showing reverence for and respect for the natural world, and has become increasingly widely held. A holistic approach to and empathy with the environment and natural world can also be found in the traditions of indigenous people in diverse areas including North America, Australia, and elsewhere. We can now see this in popular culture (for example, the environmental themes of the 2009 film *Avatar* and its sequels—at the time of writing *Avatar 2* is scheduled for release in 2022), science, politics, and even in legislation. There is significant scientific interest in the causes of environmental threats such as climate change and the increased variety in weather patterns, and the general public—especially young people—show a high level of engagement in environmental matters (see **Figure 12.1**). There is a huge amount of support for campaigning groups such as Extinction Rebellion, which seek to hold states and corporations to account for the harm they inflict on the environment and their failure to protect it through public policy, and to encourage greater honesty about environmental harm issues. A Gaia-esque view is also present in specific campaigns such as the one underway at the time of writing (spring 2020) to recognise animal sentience in UK law, public policy, and criminal justice systems. The idea that the natural and social worlds interact with each other in complex ways, which can have disastrous consequences, has become an integral part of public discourse and argument, and environmentally conscious views are now so mainstream that in 2020 ethical veganism gained legal recognition in the UK as a protected form of belief.

Green criminology incorporates some of these ideas by placing the environment at the centre of its thinking and has established itself as a distinct form of critical criminology which has a clear presence in the contemporary criminological imagination.

The term 'green criminology' was first coined by American criminologist Michael Lynch in 1990 as a way of describing criminological work that deals with environmental harm (Lynch, 1990). In 1998, a special issue of the academic journal *Theoretical Criminology* expanded on Lynch's 1990 work by bringing together a range of criminological scholars to explore issues such as the causes of animal abuse, ecofeminism, masculinities and crimes against the environment, animal rights, and the ecological impact of illicit drug cultivation. This collection of articles sought to introduce 'the notion of a new "green field" of study for criminology' (South and Beirne, 1998: 147). Their discussions helped to map out the theoretical terrain for green criminology by highlighting the variety and complexity of green crimes and harms and the importance of 'placing crimes against the environment

Figure 12.1 The general public, especially young people, show a level of engagement in environmental matters, with widespread support for activists like Greta Thunberg, Ridhima Pandey, and Aditya Mukarji, and their demands for political action on climate change

Source: Liv Oeian/Shutterstock

and crimes against animals on the criminological agenda' (South and Beirne, 1998: 147).

It is worth noting that although the term 'green criminology' is generally attributed to Lynch (1990), the idea that criminology should cover harms against the environment had been raised before this, and outside the US. Slovenian criminologist Janez Pečar (1981), for example, argued that environmental crime or deviance against the environment was only partially studied within criminology, but his essay was not published in English and so perhaps did not receive the attention it deserved. As you progress through your studies, you may find that the majority of the texts on your reading lists are from American, British, and Australian scholars, but you should be aware that these are not necessarily the first original contributions on some issues and are almost certainly not the only valuable perspectives to consider. You should explore other works whenever you can—particularly those of **Global South** scholars such as Riera (1979), Olmo (1999), and Liu (2009).

Another important thing to note is that 'green criminology' is really an umbrella term in that it covers several different ideas and represents an interdisciplinary approach to environmental problems—it reflects the interests of people who work within environmental science, biology, law, and politics as well as criminology. Its broad nature means that other terms, denoting specific aspects of crime or criminal behaviour, are sometimes used, for example 'environmental criminology' and 'eco-crime', and it has a number of specialist subfields including conservation criminology (Gore, 2017) and wildlife criminology (Nurse and Wyatt, 2020). Leading green criminologist Rob White (featured in **Conversations 12.1**) states that green criminology 'basically refers to the study of environmental harm, environmental laws and environmental regulation by criminologists' (2008: 8). But beyond this simple definition, green criminology explores how environmental laws are made and enforced and it examines the types of environmental crisis that are potentially ignored by environmental enforcement and mainstream criminal justice regimes.

The scope of green criminology

As we have seen, the concerns of green criminology are wide-ranging, but its main focuses are:

- the harm caused to the environment and animals;
- the rights of the environment and animals;
- the people, groups, or entities who commit environmental crimes;
- illegal exploitation of natural resources (fauna and flora);
- the role the state plays in facilitating environmental crimes;
- newer, less obvious forms of environmental crimes;
- failures in environmental laws and regulations;
- wider problems facing the planet, most notably climate change; and
- what constitutes 'crime' and 'harm'.

The first point will come as no surprise from what you have read so far. Although environmental harm is often ignored by mainstream criminology, you will see as you read on that environmental harms and crimes are very important. This is not just because living animals are killed and hurt by harmful human actions such as illegal wildlife trafficking, and many of these activities are in fact crimes, but because the people involved in green crimes and harms are often involved in other types of harmful and often illegal behaviour. If we view actions taken against animals only as an environmental or welfare issue, our justice systems risk ignoring part of an offender's criminal profile and activity. If we ignore the harms caused to the environment itself, we do not consider the true impact of crime and deviant behaviour. In addition, some environmental harms, such as air pollution and human-caused climate change, have a direct impact on us as humans. Thousands of people die as a result of air pollution each year and climate change has been said to cause floods, extreme weather patterns that can kill people, and changes in climate that lead to food shortages (White, 2018). For all these reasons, green criminologists argue that it makes no sense for an environmental problem like climate change to be considered outside criminology's remit and to be omitted from mainstream crime and justice considerations. However, the reality is that environmental problems do remain fringe issues within criminology, so one key concern of green criminology is the problems of not taking environmental problems seriously within our discipline's examination of crime and justice issues.

Green criminology also looks in detail at *who* is committing environmental crimes. In much of your criminology study you will be looking at individual offenders and offending, although you will also consider aspects of gangs and group offending. But in green criminology we also consider how corporations are the cause of much crime and how organised crime units are moving away from their traditional activities like drugs and weapons trafficking (see **Chapter 14**) and into areas like illegal wildlife trafficking. They do so because of the ease in adapting their traditional means of committing crime (transit routes, supply chains, etc.) to wildlife and environmental crimes. But moving into wildlife and environmental crime is also considered to be relatively low risk since these areas are not enforced in the same way as other mainstream crimes. In this way, wildlife and environmental crimes can appear to be relatively low risk and high reward. This is particularly the case in areas where the enforcement of environmental and wildlife crimes attracts relatively low penalties compared to crimes such as drugs or weapons smuggling. Indeed, some environmental crimes do not carry the option for prison sentences to be imposed. This final point raises the idea that punitive and carceral (prison-focused) approaches are not the only mechanism for dealing with crime, deviance, and harm. At a number of points throughout this book, most notably in **Chapter 30**, we discuss alternative ways of responding to deviant or criminal behaviour, including approaches based on **diversion** and **restorative justice**. We touch on these ideas in this chapter and invite you to consider that there are different concepts of justice, not all of which rely on **punishment**.

Green criminology looks at the role of the state and highlights that environmental harms are often the result of problems at a political level. As with organised crime units and wildlife trafficking, this issue also reflects problems in law enforcement mechanisms. For example, there are international laws that cover such things as people trafficking and the transnational drug trade. But the international agreement on wildlife trade is the Convention on International Trade in Endangered Species of Wild Flora and Fauna (**CITES**), which regulates the trade in wildlife rather than prohibits it. CITES does this by listing species of wildlife in one of its three appendices, the parts of the treaty that specify the level of regulation:

- Appendix 1 lists species that are considered highly endangered and threatened by trade and that are only traded within limited circumstances, for example for breeding purposes;
- Appendix II are species that are less threatened but where quotas are imposed on how many individuals can be traded;
- Appendix III are species that may be approaching the Appendix II threshold of being threatened.

Each country that has adopted the Convention is required to create a Management Authority that oversees a permit process and a Scientific Authority to advise on the status of the species that are traded (Wyatt, 2013: 7–8). As a result, the law operates from the presumption that trade in wildlife is acceptable as long as it is properly regulated and differs from some other international laws that are designed to prohibit activities and create a framework for offences. The focus of CITES on allowing trade to continue creates a number of problems for enforcement, not least telling the difference between a legal species and a prohibited one.

Green criminology adopts a critical criminology approach that looks beyond traditional crimes and mainstream justice responses. This includes considering alternatives to traditional punitive approaches and consideration of attempts to repair harm and change behaviour, such as restorative justice or the use of mediation. In addition to important areas of eco-crime like wildlife trafficking and animal cruelty, as well as the disposal of toxic waste, green criminology also considers less obvious, more contemporary areas of eco-crime. One example is biopiracy, where traditional knowledge of indigenous people is taken without their knowledge or without payment and is exploited to produce medicines or is used in food and drink production. This activity is often carried out by corporations from the **Global North** (that is, the developed and generally wealthier societies of Europe and North America), who prefer the term bio-prospecting and who have the power to use patent systems to legally protect the new products that they have arguably only been able to create because they have stolen from native peoples (Shiva, 2007). These activities are often not dealt with as criminal actions but instead fall into the area of intellectual property law, which is concerned with the ownership of an idea or concept. But activities like biopiracy are of interest to green criminologists because they concern the exploitation of natural resources in a way that raises questions about the legality of corporate action and concerns about how justice systems deal with such exploitation. They also reflect the concerns of activists like Nina Gualinga who draw attention to threats facing indigenous peoples. We explore this idea in **New frontiers 12.1** and look at the problems of biopiracy.

NEW FRONTIERS 12.1

Biopiracy

Biopiracy is about the actions of biotechnology corporations who exploit natural products with medicinal and healing properties. Major Global North corporations are the main players in exploiting natural resources, often at the expense of the rights of indigenous peoples, and often in the Global South. Green criminology has begun to look at biopiracy as a form of **corporate crime** in which corporations are exploiting naturally occurring biochemical or genetic material for commercial gain, especially by obtaining patents that restrict its future use, while failing to pay fair compensation to the indigenous communities of the Global South (see **Figure 12.2**).

Figure 12.2 In 2016, a French institute was accused of biopiracy for patenting a drug developed from *Quassia amara*, a tree native to Central and South America, without acknowledging the help of indigenous communities in developing the drug (www.sciencemag.org/news/2016/02/french-institute-agrees-share-patent-benefits-after-biopiracy-accusations)
Source: Pescov/CC BY-SA 3.0

Biopiracy raises complex questions about who 'owns' natural products like plants or fungi and the ideas and development of those natural resources to a point where they become valuable. The key issue is whether indigenous people should be paid for the efforts that they make to find and grow plants and other natural compounds—sometimes changing them in the process—which then become valuable. Companies prefer the word 'bioprospecting' to describe the discovery of an unknown plant or organism which is then subject to scientific processes to identify unknown benefits, such as acting as a stimulant or sleep aid. These previously unknown properties (or at least unknown to the Global North) can then be turned into a new legally protected (patentable and trademarked) product. For example, the discovery of caffeine-like properties in a previously unknown plant could lead to the development of a new energy drink. The company producing the drink has developed a new product from a naturally occurring plant and will quite reasonably wish to protect its investment and recover the costs of turning the chemical in the plant into an ingredient in a drink that it then mass-manufactures. However, we might say that the plant only exists because the local people have cared for it over many years. These local people are then denied access to a share of any profits from the drink that really only exists because of them helping the original plant to thrive.

There is a question over whether biopiracy is a crime, but green criminology considers both the crime and harm aspects (discussed later in this chapter). Biopiracy can involve criminal activity such as land theft, human rights abuses, bribery, and fraud. So, it is a crime of the powerful where illegal or at least unethical means are used to pursue a legitimate goal of creating new products. Green criminology looks at biopiracy as an ecological justice issue and thinks about how biopiracy's corporate environmental crime issues should be dealt with by justice systems.

It is difficult to know how much biopiracy takes place because most of the activity occurs outside the sight of monitoring agencies and official bodies. Indigenous people also do not always have access to lawyers and other ways of challenging the behaviour of the corporations, so it is also likely that many biopiracy problems will only come to light in the rare cases where there is a challenge to the exploitation of a natural resource. This means that, as in other areas of crime, under-reporting may be masking the true extent of this activity and there is likely to be a 'dark figure' of biopiracy. But even so, we can see that biopiracy is a significant global problem, with studies suggesting that Africa alone could be losing more than $15 billion from its biodiversity as medicines, cosmetics, agricultural products, and indigenous knowledge surrounding these are being patented (possibly illegally) by multinational companies. India is also thought to be losing more than $250 million annually from biopiracy, and estimates in 2011 suggested that the illegal exploitation of the Amazon's resources through biopiracy in Amazonia was costing Brazil $16 million per day (Danley, 2015). This is mostly due to a lack of policy surrounding biopiracy and poor enforcement of the few protections that are in place.

In the course of its exploration of harms which affect the environment, green criminology often looks beyond the national concerns that are the focus of much criminology, turning its attention to the global problems, including transnational crimes (see **Chapter 14**) and wider questions about what constitutes 'crime' and 'harm'. It is also concerned with climate change, which has been identified as one of the major threats facing humanity in the modern world. While much activity that causes climate change may be legal, achieving climate justice for those who most feel the effects of climate change—many of whom live in poorer, marginalised communities and in the Global South—and examining mechanisms for bringing so-called carbon criminals to justice is a core concern of green criminology (White, 2019). In terms of wider questions, green criminology gives a great deal of consideration to the idea of harm. Many green criminologists argue that what matters most is the *impact* of environmentally harmful activities and how we can address these harms and prevent their reoccurrence rather than simply punishing offenders when we catch them doing something illegal (see, for example, Hall, 2015; Lynch and Stretesky, 2014). This is one way in which green criminology considers alternatives to the dominant responses to harmful behaviour, which tend to focus on punitive and carceral approaches.

It will be becoming increasingly clear that green criminology is a very broad discipline. It considers not only what we might call distinctly 'green crimes' but also wider crimes that have an impact on the environment and non-human nature, and it spans a number of different areas, reflecting on and critiquing some of the approaches and assumptions of mainstream criminology. As you progress through your study of green criminology, you should consider how the acts and omissions of economically powerful groups can cause harm to human beings, other animals, and the environment itself, as well as how societies respond to these issues (for example, through legislation, regulation, and the enforcement of laws through inspection, prosecution, and sentencing practices). How effective are the measures they take? By the end of this chapter, you should also be thinking about alternatives to the traditional approaches and considering how green criminological ideas can help us to find alternative approaches that have the potential to be effective. In **Conversations 12.1** we hear from Rob White. As we have noted, Professor White is a leading figure in green criminology, and here he explains why he engages in green criminology, what he sees as its fundamental ideas, and what he considers to be the most important issue for the discipline today.

CONVERSATIONS 12.1

The development of green criminology

with **Professor Rob White**

Environmental harm is ubiquitous—it is everywhere—and it affects everyone and everything on Planet Earth. This is, of course, not simply academic; it is intensely personal. I am affected by environmental harms such as pollution and threats to biodiversity, and so is my partner, my children, my grandchildren, my dog Matilda, my community, and our land, air and water. Crimes against nature affect the living and the non-living (for example, rivers) and, ultimately, we are destroying and degrading that which makes life possible and which makes life worth living. Home and habitat are worth defending. This is what motivates me to engage in green criminology and to participate in social activism.

'Ecocentrism' refers to valuing nature for its own sake and is the philosophy that makes most sense to me. It requires that all social practices incorporate ecological sensitivities and heightened awareness of the intrinsic value of flora, fauna, ecosystems and non-living entities such as rivers and mountains. Yet, there are important qualitative differences in regards to the nature, dynamics and seriousness of the harm as these pertain to non-human animals, ecosystems, plant species and human populations. I feel that my most significant contribution to green criminology has been to translate this sentiment into an eco-justice framework, one that is comprised of three key elements: environment justice (humans); ecological justice (specific environments); and species justice (non-human animals and plants).

In analysing environmental issues, I draw upon concepts such as 'ecocide', 'state-corporate crime' and 'carbon criminality'. A fundamental premise of green criminology is that environmental crime needs to be defined and studied in relation to *harm*, and not solely on the basis of legal definitions. For example, this means that attention needs to be directed at how, where and why natural resources are used in any circumstance and the impacts of this on the wider environment.

For me, climate change is definitely the most pressing and important issue of the contemporary era and I believe that criminologists can make significant contributions to the pursuit of climate justice. Time is rapidly running out and the extinction curve is a reality that can only be curtailed by bringing about fundamental social, economic and ecological changes. We all have a part to play in this.

The significance of environmental issues for all that we love and cherish cannot be understated. In the context of rapid climate change, for instance, freshwater resources stand out as one of the vital pinch-points arising from global warming. These resources are under threat worldwide due to the shrinking of glaciers and polar ice sheets, extended periods of drought, human diversion and pollution of waterways, flooding, saltwater contamination due to sea level rise, and expanding industry and consumer demands. The environment and its resources are what sustains us all. We have a moral obligation to protect the planet. The four elements—air, water, land, energy—are essential to life. It is our duty to protect and preserve places, to prevent and repair harm, and to address issues of social and ecological justice.

Doing green criminology requires a sense of scale, and of the essential interconnectedness of issues, events, people and places. It is important therefore to continually learn from others and to interact regularly, especially since things are changing so rapidly. Environmental crime is also about power and social interests. This means that whatever we do as green criminologists is bound to come into conflict with the vested interests of transnational corporations and conservative governments. The quest for a better ecological future necessarily involves concerted struggle insofar as we speak truth to power and fight to transform the status quo.

Professor Rob White, Distinguished Professor, Criminology, University of Tasmania

12.3 Green criminology and the 'market society'

When we think about 'crime' we are concerned with illegal acts and harm that people suffer, for example as a result of being a direct victim of violence or property crime. But 'harm', and particularly environmental harm, can sometimes be the result of activities that are legal and have some wider benefit attached to them. For example, cars cause harmful pollution but making, selling, and driving cars is legal and the car market is a lucrative one. Most of us, especially those of us in the Global North, live in what are known as 'market societies' in which many activities are driven by what consumers need and want. This creates a cycle of demand, production, and supply which causes continuous harm to the environment, making the market society the subject of much discussion for green criminologists. Activities like this are sometimes described as being 'lawful but awful'.

In this section we explore how the market society operates and what green criminologists see as its impact; what the social science of economics, including the idea of the 'treadmill of production', can add to this discussion. We then look at a case study of the oil industry which will allow us to examine some of these ideas in more detail and see how difficult it can be to address the environmental harm caused by industry.

How the market society operates

We can see how the market society works by considering the simple example of a desk—you probably have one in your room or home, and you may be sitting at it right now.

You might have made your desk yourself, but more likely you bought it from a furniture or homeware shop. If your desk is made of solid wood, it may have been made from trees grown in the UK and then produced to order for the retailer, who needs a steady supply of these products. However, the wood may have come from abroad and been shipped to the EU or direct to the UK from a country like Indonesia, which has around 91 million hectares of forests, constituting 53 per cent of the country's total land area and is a valuable yet heavily exploited natural resource. The country harvests and exports a huge amount of wood every year: the International Trade Centre (ITC) estimates that in 2015 export of primary timber products from Indonesia accounted for a total value of $2,483 million. Plywood was the most important product and also sawnwood (but to a lesser extent), both of which are often used to make desks and furniture. In 2017, 3.4 per cent of Indonesia's wood and wood product exports ended up in the UK.

Your desk (and indeed possibly some of the paper you use) neatly illustrates how markets and the market economy work. As consumers in the west we contribute to the demand for products such as wooden furniture and paper because we are willing to keep buying these products. But UK suppliers do not have the facilities or the resources to produce all of these items themselves, so some are either entirely produced by suppliers from other countries, as finished products, or the raw materials required to make them (in this case, Indonesian timber) are supplied by other countries. Basically, this is the market in operation. We, the consumer, want to buy a product and suppliers and retailers have an interest in providing us with that product because when they do we hand over money for their goods. So, the consumer gets what they want; the retailer gets their commission for selling the product; and the supplier gets paid for supplying the raw materials or making the product that we buy. In theory, everybody is happy. But, as we have suggested, there are implications for the natural world. The paper you use, and potentially your desk too, come from trees which have been chopped down, transported, hammered, and glued to make the desk or pulped to produce the paper. It is then coated or varnished, advertised, packaged, and transported to a shop or warehouse for us to come and buy in person or have delivered. **Figure 12.3** illustrates this.

Figure 12.3 Wood products, like our desk, come from trees that are chopped down, the logs are then transported to a manufacturer who shapes them into the products that are then sold to us as consumers

Source: A7880S/Shutterstock

What economics tells us about the market society

We have already identified that green criminology draws on different disciplines and so is an interdisciplinary approach to criminology. The social science of economics helps to explain how increasingly scarce resources are distributed and how the market society, with its process of buying, selling, and supplying goods, works. It also helps us consider whether it should and could be regulated or better controlled to reduce harm to the environment. The three key economic concepts that are relevant to our discussion are Adam Smith's idea of the 'invisible hand' of the market; what is known as the price mechanism, and the idea of the 'treadmill of production'.

Those of us who live in the west or Global North live in a society in which goods and services are traded by what are often called 'economic agents'—this can be companies, governments, organisations, or individual people who operate inside the market. These individuals or groups are 'free' economic agents who are free to act and enter into agreements, although with some small restrictions. For example, the sale of alcohol is generally restricted to those over a certain age (although this age varies between different countries, and between different states in the US), and while you can buy a gun in a supermarket in the US and there is a general right to carry firearms (the right to bear arms is guaranteed in the US Constitution), you cannot do this in the UK where gun ownership is subject to strict control. For most products there is competition for customers, and one principle of the market is that, in theory, the price is determined by competitive market forces so that in a sense the market regulates itself. The idea is that if goods are too expensive consumers will not pay for them and so the market will collapse.

For most economics writers, one of the key thinkers is the economist Adam Smith (1723–90) who spoke of what he called the 'invisible hand'. Smith said:

> Every individual necessarily labours to render the annual revenue of the society as great as he can. He generally neither intends to promote the public interest, nor knows how much he is promoting it . . . he intends only his own gain, and he is in this, as in many other cases, led by an invisible hand to promote an end which was no part of his intention. By pursuing his own interest he frequently promotes that of the society more effectually than when he really intends to promote it. I have never known much good done by those who affected to trade for the public good.
>
> (*An Inquiry into the Nature and Causes of the Wealth of Nations*, 1776)

Smith is suggesting that both producers and consumers act in the marketplace to get their best competitive

All of these stages have the potential to harm the environment. The production, marketing, and distribution chains for these products may well involve waste or pollution. The removal of trees from their natural environment can also have an impact on the ecosystem and indeed some species of tropical hardwoods such as Cuban, Honduran, and Mexican mahogany and Siamese and Honduran rosewood are considered endangered or threatened by trade. As a result, these species are protected under international law (CITES—see the discussion of the scope of green criminology in **section 12.2**), but they can still be traded as long as the rules are followed and they come from sustainable sources—in other words, from forests where care is taken to ensure that the amount of wood taken from the forest does not impact on its overall survival. However, the demand for wood for legal products (our desk and our paper) can cause people either to cut down more trees than they should in order to increase their profits or lead to organised crime groups resorting to illegal actions to produce wood and make a profit. In this case, green criminologists might argue that the market itself is at fault for creating the demand for wood products and for failing to prevent the illegal actions or excessive consumption that takes place. As green criminologists, we are perhaps more concerned with the harm that is caused by deforestation and the excessive consumption of wood products and not necessarily with whether or not this issue is dealt with as a crime.

advantage and ideally the price mechanism facilitates this. So, logically, producers will aim to get the most profit for their products, while buyers will want to buy at the cheapest possible price (and consumers will favour a bargain). However, as we noted earlier, Smith's idea was that the market would regulate itself so there was no need for regulatory intervention should things go wrong, because the 'invisible hand' of the market would sort out any problems. As you can probably imagine, historians and economists have been arguing about this idea pretty much ever since Smith committed it to paper. We need to consider the extent to which it applies and is helpful in green criminology in the context of power relations and how the market deals with environmental costs.

Some scholars argue that Smith is wrong, and that without regulation of the relationship between producers and buyers there may be problems (see, for example, Benedict, 2010 on the market in higher education). From a green criminology perspective, it is important to be aware that Smith's idea of the market is mainly concerned with the goods that enter and are traded in the market; it does not take into account the wider environmental harms that green criminologists consider. For example, private and social costs are higher when trading in goods made from natural resources and this often leads to environmental damage. Economists would call this a '**negative externality**'; this means that neither producers nor consumers take on the full social costs of their decision-making and market prices may not take into account the long-term consequences of continued consumption. If they did, some goods would cost much more than they currently do in order to consider the harm caused in their production. If, for example, we factored in the full impact of removing trees to make our desk by considering the loss of a valuable tree species and the environmental impact of transporting our tree and our desk to the place where we buy it, then our desk would cost a whole lot more. But in a competitive market the focus is on keeping costs manageable, so the environmental costs of production might not be incorporated into the price the consumer pays.

By applying Smith's arguments, we can perhaps draw the conclusion that environmental harm is an inevitable consequence of continued commercial production and the exploitation of natural resources. Arguably, **capitalism** is an ecologically destructive means of producing goods and services because it is concerned primarily with the profits to be made from continued use of natural resources and with the human benefits derived from continued production. In other words, whether the environment is harmed might not be considered as long as consumers get their products and a profit is made. The market does not really consider placing any limits on production in the interests of maintaining a healthy environment as this is not its main purpose. The purpose of production and the operation of markets that allow for continued growth in production is to produce goods, with environmental resources seen as primarily existing to serve such production, the needs of the market, and continued consumption.

This is where the 'treadmill of production' theory (Schnaiberg, 1981) comes in. This theory suggests that changes in production accelerate environmental degradation, or the erosion of the natural environment and the destruction of ecosystems. In other words, environmental degradation is a consequence of production when the methods used for production negatively impact on the environment. For example, one consequence of our desk and paper example from earlier is that trees are chopped down and forests may be destroyed if trees are being removed faster than new trees are planted. The treadmill of production theory uses the terms **ecological withdrawals**, **ecological disorganisation**, and **ecological additions** to describe the effects of production. These effects take place where increasing levels of pollution and natural resource extraction are related to western capital that has been invested in chemical- and energy-intensive technology.

- *Ecological withdrawals* are defined as the resource harms capitalism produces in the process of extracting raw materials (Lynch, 2014). Chemical and technological developments have arguably increased the extent to which environmental harms are caused in the process of extracting materials from the natural environment. At the same time, increasingly mechanised and technical processes have become more efficient in withdrawing resources.
- This intensification of the ecological withdrawal process accelerates *ecological disorganisation* by increasing the destruction of nature (Lynch, 2014).
- *Ecological additions* are the pollutants that are emitted into the ecosystem from the legal operation of production processes. White and Heckenberg (2014: 157) identify that 'the problem of pollution is directly related to how humans use and dispose of natural resources in systemic processes of production and consumption'.

Over time, as the treadmill of production accelerates, it generates larger quantities of ecological additions, and emits increased (and more concentrated) quantities of pollution. It has been claimed that 'just 122 corporations account for 80 per cent of all carbon dioxide emissions. And just five private oil corporations—Exxon Mobil, BP Amoco, Shell, Chevron and Texaco—produce oil that contributes some ten per cent of the world's carbon emissions' (Bruno, Karliner, and Brotsky, 1999: 1). Ecological additions also produce ecological disorganisation by changing nature and accelerating other ecologically destructive tendencies; for example, climate change which is caused by additions (see **Figure 12.4**).

Figure 12.4 The smoke and smog produced by a polluting factory is an ecological addition and can contribute to air pollution
Source: Paul White/Alamy Stock Photo

A market society case study: the oil industry and environmental harm

Let's explore these ideas in more detail using the example of the oil industry and extraction of oil.

Fossil fuels including coal, oil, and natural gas come from decomposed plants and other organisms that have been buried beneath layers of sediment. According to the International Energy Agency (IEA, 2018) they account for around 80 per cent of the world's energy and provide electricity, heat, and fuel for transportation (for example, petrol). But generating power from these 'dirty' fossil fuels has environmental impacts. Burning fossil fuels to create energy releases carbon dioxide and other greenhouse gases which trap heat in our atmosphere and contribute to an increase in global warming and climate change. Crude oil, which is a liquid primarily composed of carbon and hydrogen, needs to be extracted from offshore and onshore wells before it can be refined into petroleum products such as gasoline, diesel, and heating oil. This process involves drilling wells to extract the oil from where it has been buried underground (and sometimes from ocean floor beds). The oil then needs to be refined using chemical processes, which often involves transporting it to special facilities, before it can then be converted into its final products and sold to us, the consumer. Even the selling part of the process has an environment impact as it often requires more transportation, for example transporting the refined petroleum from the oil refinery to petrol stations.

From this description, you will have gathered that producing products in the extracting industries requires major infrastructure and that the companies operating in these industries can cause disruption in the communities where they work. For example, the partnership between the Nigerian government and major oil companies to produce oil in the Niger Delta involves creating drilling sites that are close to villages and oil pipelines that transport oil across the countryside to the refineries. Over 50 years of oil exploration in the Niger Delta has had some quite severe environmental impacts in the form of pollution to the water supply, fish ponds, and vegetation as a result of oil spills. It is estimated that there were as many as 9,343 spills in the delta over the ten-year period 2006–15 (Steiner, 2010; National Oil Spill Detection and Response Agency, NOSDRA, in Kalejaye, 2015), and that over a 50-year period the spills amounted to 9–13 million barrels of oil. Other environmental impacts from oil extraction include gas flaring, which is conducted to burn off flammable gas and can contribute to air pollution; carbon emissions from petroleum use; and disasters linked to the transportation of oil. For example, the *Exxon Valdez* oil spill in 1989 caused devastation to marine wildlife when the *Exxon Valdez* oil tanker spilled 10.8 million US gallons (or 37,000 metric tonnes) of crude oil in an area near Prince Williams Sound in Alaska. The Deepwater Horizon disaster (see **Figure 12.5**) is another example: on 20 April 2010 an oil rig blowout killed 11 rig workers, injured several more, and resulted in an oil spill that took until 15 July that year to halt when the well was closed by a cap. The oil spill had a polluting effect on approximately 28,958 square miles, an area the size of the US state of South Carolina. It killed wildlife and caused considerable damage to the marine environment. It has been suggested that the Gulf of Mexico's oil spill's 'magnitude, duration of release, source of emission (the deep-sea floor), and

Figure 12.5 The Deepwater Horizon oil spill (pictured from space on 24 May 2010) shows the severe impact that commercial activities can have on the environment
Source: NASA/GSFC, MODIS Rapid Response/Public domain

management techniques used (dispersants and controlled burns)' put this disaster in a different category to other similar oil spills (Goldstein et al., 2011: 1334).

Oil extraction is legal, although the industry is often linked to claims of corruption, human rights abuses, and serious environmental impacts. Several court cases have been pursued against the oil companies for actions that have harmed the villagers in Nigeria and caused damage to the local environment. However, as indicated earlier, there are challenges in doing so which include:

- the major oil companies have subsidiary companies that can sometimes be blamed for the harm that is caused;
- bringing prosecutions can be difficult in cases where the government is a partner in the oil-extracting activity and gets considerable money from the oil industry in the form of taxes or investment in the country's infrastructure;
- there are well-documented problems of corruption in the Nigerian legal system, making it difficult to pursue cases;
- many villagers that are affected by oil pollution do not have the resources to bring legal cases.

As a result, some cases are brought against the parent company in the country where it is headquartered—cases have been heard in London and the Netherlands. Interestingly, some of these cases are brought using civil rather than criminal law in an attempt to pursue claims for damages and compensation rather than achieve a criminal punishment. The civil law approach also means that cases can be brought on behalf of a group of affected villagers by an NGO or by lawyers operating on a 'no win, no fee' deal, so that the villagers do not have to meet the costs of legal action themselves. For example, in the Dutch case of *Milieudefensie et al.* v *SPDC, RDS and other Shell companies* (2012), Milieudefensie (Friends of the Earth Netherlands) and four Nigerian residents filed five lawsuits with the District Court of The Hague against the Shell Petroleum Development Co. of Nigeria Ltd (SPDC) and Royal Dutch Shell plc (RDS), the parent company of the Royal Dutch Shell group. The lawsuits argued that RDS was responsible for the actions of its Nigerian subsidiary so was liable for oil spills caused in Nigeria, and that the SPDC had failed to prevent the spills from taking place. Despite RDS's objections, the Dutch court heard the claim and in January 2013 the court issued a decision ordering Shell to pay compensation to one of the farmers, although it dismissed the majority of the other claims. In December 2015, a Dutch appeal court reversed this dismissal and allowed the rest of the claims to go forward.

This case illustrates several important points about power, the market, and how green criminology considers these issues. As we have noted, oil spills are a common occurrence in the Niger Delta and one reason for this is the old infrastructure that continues to be in use. In the *Milieudefensie* case, one argument put forward by the oil company was that it was not responsible for part of the oil spills because the spill was the result of sabotage. Interestingly, the court accepted this argument but found that the oil company had failed to take action to prevent sabotage. Some commentators have identified that it is likely cheaper for the oil industry to accept minor losses of product from oil spills than it would be to fully repair all of the infrastructure (replace leaking pipes, etc.) and put in place effective measures to prevent or address sabotage. The economic power of the oil companies as major transnational corporations means that they can afford these losses while the villagers whose lives are affected by the oil spills bear the social and economic costs. In this example, the market is mainly concerned with the continued supply of oil, as this ensures that the corporation continues to get value from its product and the consumers get their oil. The harm caused to the villagers is a *negative externality* even though there are severe environmental impacts with significant implications for human life—in some parts of the Niger Delta life expectancy is as low as 59 (up from 50 as of year 2000 estimates). Where oil spills occur, it is difficult to bring criminal action against the companies in Nigeria but civil claims brought by NGOs, sometimes in other countries, have been successful in some cases. From a green criminology perspective, the goal is to achieve redress for the environmental harm caused and prevent continued incidents rather than simply adopt the punitive approach of sending somebody to prison; the use of civil action which makes the polluter pay for the environmental harm they have caused fits with this focus.

The Deepwater Horizon case is arguably easier to consider from a 'traditional' criminological viewpoint because the death of the oil-rig workers fits within traditional thinking about crime: it involves murder or manslaughter so should be dealt with by mainstream policing agencies. The injuries to the other workers also fit within the area of safety crimes (see **Chapter 19**). However, again, in this case there are challenges in addressing the wider environmental costs. Should the oil company have to pay the costs of cleaning up the polluted ocean? Should it have to compensate the state and the various local authorities for the loss of marine life and the pollution of their beaches? Should it have to compensate those whose livelihoods have been destroyed, such as the shrimp fishermen who will have lost earnings or the deep-sea fishermen and beach-front traders who can no longer continue to operate? In the end, Deepwater Horizon and the Gulf oil spill was resolved through a complex mixture of criminal and civil legal action (in other words, responses that were

WHAT DO YOU THINK? 12.1

Energy extraction and environmental harm

Think about the two oil industry cases we have examined: the oil spillages and oil-related harms in the Niger Delta and the Deepwater Horizon disaster. What these cases reveal is that industries which operate legally can be involved in illegal or harmful acts. They also show us that traditional criminal justice activity seems to be inadequate to bring cases to court. How do you feel about these cases? Reflect further on them using the following questions:

- Do you think that a small amount of pollution or environmental damage is a reasonable price to pay to continue to have oil products that we still need?
- Would you refuse to use oil from a company that you know has been involved in human rights abuses or pollution incidents in a Global South country?
- Do you think that corporations should be made to pay for the environmental harms they have caused in the countries where they operate?

Before you read on in this chapter, think about what types of actions might be needed to deal with the problems that we have identified in the energy markets and the practices of their extraction industries. Remember that we are mostly dealing with legal organisations, some of whom have state support to continue operating. And remember that these problems are not unique to the energy market and their associated production industries. How might we deal with the wider problem of legal and powerful organisations doing either illegal or environmentally harmful things when it is difficult for state policing agencies to bring them to court?

---

punitive and resolution-based), settlement agreements between the US Department of Justice and the oil companies, and a compensation scheme which allowed those who had lost earnings and been affected by the disaster to pursue claims of loss. Consider this and the Niger Delta example further in **What do you think? 12.1**.

12.4 Key concepts in green criminology

Within green criminology a range of theoretical concepts and frameworks have been developed to explain why green crimes occur and to examine the causes of the environmental problems that green criminology aims to address. Before we delve into these concepts, it is worth pointing out that some of the theories that we discuss elsewhere in this book will still apply. So, for example, rational choice theory can still be used to explain why people may choose to cause harm to the environment (see **Chapter 15**) and the concept of relative deprivation may also help explain why some people in poorer communities turn to wildlife trafficking as a route out of poverty (see **Chapter 20**). But green criminology has its own concepts that will help to develop your understanding of green crimes and harms.

There are three key concepts to consider: environmental justice which is primarily concerned with human concerns, ecological justice and its associated idea of *species justice* which focus on the responsibilities to non-human nature, and ecocide. These three core concepts are part of an eco-justice perspective; a stance which considers how social and environmental justice can be achieved and any environmental harm can be addressed. Let's discuss the three key concepts in turn.

Environmental justice

The idea of *environmental justice* began outside green criminology but has been embraced by green criminologists as a concept which helps to explain the importance of the environment and environmental protection. The concept has its origins in the US, where environmental justice is linked with other ideas of social justice. Environmental justice in the US is mainly concerned with 'two overlapping parts of the grassroots environmental movement: the antitoxics movement and the movement against environmental racism' (Schlosberg, 2007: 46). Like the term 'green criminology' itself, environmental justice is really an umbrella term which covers securing fairness and ending discrimination in access to environmental resources. The term also links to securing justice in terms of environmental harms.

The environmental justice theory is anthropocentric in nature. This means that it is mainly concerned with human interests. Environmental justice puts humans at the centre of environmental concerns, for example as victims of a poor environment who require justice. It also identifies humans as the main cause of environmental damage, for example as the creators of the pollution that causes air-quality problems and as the creators and dumpers of toxic waste. A central idea in environmental justice is that access to environmental resources is unequal, as is access to environmental rights, including the right to live in a healthy environment. Environmental justice also identifies inequality in resolving environmental harms and securing 'justice'. It questions whether all citizens who suffer harms linked to a poor environment can access the means of pursuing a remedy. For example, not everyone can access the courts in order to sue a corporation that is negatively affecting the local environment. Poorer people and those from lower educational backgrounds may find it harder to access lawyers or understand court processes. As a result, environmental justice is easier to pursue for more educated people from wealthier backgrounds.

We noted in the introduction to this section that environmental justice, together with the other two key concepts for green criminology, is part of a wider eco-justice perspective that links environmental concerns with social ones. This is particularly important for environmental justice concerns. Green criminologist Rob White suggests that environmental justice is primarily concerned with:

- environmental rights as an extension of human rights or social rights;
- intergenerational responsibility;
- environmental justice: equity for present and future generations;
- environmental harm, an idea constructed in relation to human centred notions of value and use.

(2008: 15)

Environmental justice can also be said to have a procedural element that refers to fairness in decision-making (Heydon, 2018) and access to legal mechanisms and remedies (Nurse, 2016). So, when we think about environmental justice we can think of it as having different elements that include distributive, recognitional, and procedural elements. This reflects the idea that environmental justice is about the extent to which people are able to access justice and their marginalisation is recognised or their rights addressed. It also considers whether they are able to get access to justice systems and receive a remedy, and the fairness of any processes.

There is a considerable amount of evidence that pollution sources like toxic factories and sewage and municipal waste facilities are often situated near to the working poor, marginalised groups (including ethnic minorities and indigenous people), and other politically disempowered groups. These are also the groups who tend to suffer the most from pollution. As we have seen in other chapters of this book (especially **Chapter 10**), racial disparity and discrimination has become the focus of public attention, with fresh attention since 2020's worldwide protests about racial inequality. Black, minority ethnic, and indigenous communities tend to be in the more socially disadvantaged sectors of society. Generally, these communities and the citizens who live within them are likely to be poorer and have less disposable income. They are also likely to be situated within the more disorganised zones of a city (an idea explored by the Chicago School of criminology—see **Chapter 17**) rather than within the more affluent suburban or rural areas. As a result, these communities are less well served by the tools of social mobility and the mechanisms of civil society and social justice than other communities. They are less likely to have access to lawyers, to be able to navigate local government processes, and to have their voices and concerns heard, represented, and taken into account in decision-making processes.

Environmental justice theory also incorporates the concept of **environmental racism**, which explains how ethnic minority and indigenous people are often deliberately discriminated against in terms of their lack of access to environmental resources (Bullard, 1993a, 1993b). Environmental racism has been defined as follows:

> Racial discrimination in environmental policy making and the enforcement of regulations and laws, the deliberate targeting of people of colour communities for toxic and hazardous waste facilities; the official sanctioning of life-threatening presence of poisons and pollutants in our communities; and the history of excluding people of colour from the leadership of the environmental movement.

(Chavis, 1991)

As this definition identifies, environmental racism is concerned with deliberate and concerted action that is racial in nature. At the 55th Session of the United Nations Commission on Human Rights, the Earth Justice Legal Defense Fund defined environmental racism as being 'any government, institutional, or industry action, or failure to act, that has a negative environmental impact which disproportionately harms—*whether intentionally or unintentionally*—individuals, groups, or communities based on race or colour' (United Nations, 1999, emphasis in original). We explore this issue in **Controversy and debate 12.1**, where environmental racism was claimed in the response to a Native American protest about an oil pipeline.

CONTROVERSY AND DEBATE 12.1

The Dakota Access Pipeline

Opposition to the $3.7 billion North Dakota oil pipeline illustrates aspects of environmental racism, as well as the problem of indigenous people sometimes lacking access to environmental justice. It also highlights issues concerning colonisation, land use rights, and marginalisation of the rights of indigenous communities.

The 1,886 km Dakota Access Pipeline (DAPL) aims to transport half a million barrels of fracked crude oil from the Bakken oil fields in North Dakota (in the US) to Illinois, crossing multiple waterways including the Missouri River, which is an important drinking water source for millions of people. The pipeline route also runs within less than 1 km of a Native American reservation and protestors argued that the pipeline would endanger sacred cultural sites and the water supply of the Standing Rock Sioux tribe.

In April 2016, the Standing Rock Sioux protested against the pipeline. This began with a small prayer camp but the camp eventually swelled to thousands and drew support from some 300 tribes, representing the largest Native American gathering in a generation. When activists began to occupy property and to protest at the construction site, policing agencies cracked down and there were more than 400 arrests. Several commentators suggest the policing response was excessive and involved law enforcement brutality directed at the protesters. In November 2016, Maina Kiai, the UN Special Rapporteur on the rights to freedom of peaceful assembly and association, voiced the same view, saying that law enforcement and private security firms used unjustified force in their response to the protests. In a 2016 press release, the United Nations Office of the High Commissioner on Human Rights expressed concern about excessive use of state security apparatus to suppress protest against corporate activities that are alleged to violate human rights. Stories emerged of the beating of protestors, use of water cannon and rubber bullets, and of a heavy police presence that intimidated protesters (see **Figure 12.6**).

Despite the protests, early in 2017 newly elected President Trump signed an Executive Order to speed up the approvals process to begin work at the site and protestors were then forcibly removed. In June 2017, oil began to flow through the pipeline. Since then, there have been various legal actions concerning the alleged environmental damage caused by pipeline construction

Figure 12.6 The Dakota Access Pipeline—and the ways in which the authorities responded to protests against it—can be seen as an example of environmental racism and the marginalisation of indigenous rights

Source: Vlad Tchompalov/Unsplash

and to challenge attempts to increase the amount of oil produced by the pipeline. In March 2020, a federal judge ordered the Army Corps of Engineers to conduct a full environmental study on the pipeline and, in July 2020, a federal judge ordered the Dakota Access Pipeline to shut down and remove all oil within 30 days. (At the time of writing, this decision is the subject of an appeal.)

This major controversy developed because of the sharply differing perspectives of the oil company and the US government compared to the protestors. The government wants to reduce dependency on foreign oil and to develop US capacity to produce its own. As a result, it views the protestors as standing in the way of necessary oil production and transportation. The protestors, on the other hand, are concerned about a potentially environmentally damaging construction. They are particularly concerned that this is taking place on traditional Native American lands and will affect their cultural heritage as well as their water supply. Similar clashes of perspective are at the heart of many environmental controversies.

Ecological justice

In contrast to the environmental justice concept, *ecological justice* is ecocentric in nature, meaning that it considers the environment itself and non-human nature to be most important. Ecological justice asserts that the environment and non-human nature should not only be protected where there are human benefits to doing so—for example, we should not protect forests just because humans need the wood or benefit from the oxygen that trees produce. Ecological justice argues that the environment should be protected because nature has *intrinsic value*: the protection of the environment is a worthwhile goal in itself. Ecological justice also includes the idea of *species justice*, which considers the well-being of plants and animals and advocates for their protection within legal systems.

There are three main types of ecological justice approach:

- an ecological justice approach that seeks to address ecological harms that affect humans;
- an ecological justice approach that examines ecological harms against the environment; and
- a species justice approach that is concerned with exploring ecological harms against non-human animals.

(Lynch et al., 2019: 1–2)

We can see from these three approaches that ecological justice is more than just a surface-level consideration of the natural world within environmental law; it actively seeks to include it within an expanded idea of what justice should be. Ecological justice includes considering new types of crime and bringing environmental harms into the remit of justice, and involves what is referred to as **ecological jurisprudence** or earth jurisprudence—the idea that nature should be at the centre of legal thinking and that laws can (and should) be interpreted to give better environmental protection. This concept is sometimes known as 'wild law' or 'earth law' (Rogers and Maloney, 2017) and was inspired by feminist judgement projects that analysed and rewrote legal cases, applying a particular perspective.

Ecocide

The ecocide concept relates to mass environmental destruction. This idea actually originated outside academia, emerging from the work of lawyer and environmental campaigner Polly Higgins (1968–2019), but it has become a core concept in green criminology as well as a framework concept for creation of a new crime in international law. A draft Ecocide Convention was produced in 1973 and submitted to the United Nations but was never formally adopted. Article 2 of the draft Convention contained the following definition of ecocide:

1. For the purpose of this Convention, ecocide means the intentional acts committed in the context of a widespread and systematic action that have an adverse impact on the safety of the planet, such acts being defined as follows:

   a. The discharge, emission or introduction of a quantity of substances or ionizing radiation into air or atmosphere, soil, water or the aquatic environments;

   b. The collection, transport, recovery or disposal of waste, including the supervision of such operations and the after-care of disposal sites, and including action taken as a dealer or a broker in the framework of any activity related to the waste management;

   c. The operation of a plant in which a dangerous activity is carried out or in which dangerous substances or preparations are stored or used;

   d. The production, processing, handling, use, holding, storage, transport, import, export or disposal of nuclear materials or other hazardous radioactive substances;

   e. The killing, destruction, possession or taking of specimens of wild fauna or flora species whether protected or not; other acts of a similar character committed intentionally that adversely affect the safety of the planet.

As you can see, the definition contains quite a comprehensive explanation of ecocide which includes intentional action that harms the environment or wildlife. The draft Convention aimed to include acts which affect the safety of the planet by involving widespread and constant harm to air, soil, or water quality, and also sought to cover acts causing death, permanent disability, or illness which could be linked to environmental harm. Higgins (2015) provides a simplified version of this definition:

> Ecocide is the extensive loss or damage or destruction of ecosystem(s) of a given territory, whether by human agency or by other causes, to such an extent that peaceful enjoyment by the inhabitants of that territory has been or will be severely diminished.
>
> (Higgins, 2015: 63)

The idea of ecocide follows naturally from our discussion of ecological justice and its aim of having environmental harms better recognised by legal systems. Green criminology considers mass environmental destruction to be one of the most significant contemporary threats and something that should be dealt with by mainstream justice mechanisms. In **Conversations 12.2** we hear from Professor Nigel South, a leading green criminologist, who explains why he sees ecocide as an important

CONVERSATIONS 12.2

Arguments for a law of ecocide

with **Professor Nigel South**

At a time when I was writing about a range of harms and crimes having environmental and human rights impacts in different parts of the world, I realized I wanted to use a word that paralleled 'genocide'. So really, I used the 'idea' of ecocide as a *concept* before I became aware of the history of proposals to create an international criminal *law* to address problems of environmental crime or harm. This legal history is fascinating. Gauger et al. (2012) trace it back to Richard Falk's (1973) draft of an early model law of ecocide to respond to the enormous environmental damage caused by US military use of the chemical compound Agent Orange in Vietnam. Initially—as a sociologist and 'green criminologist' rather than a lawyer—I was simply interested in a legal concept or proposition that could be applied in a wide-ranging but authoritative way to a call for the prohibition or criminalization of what Gray (1996) called the 'causing or permitting' of 'harm to the natural environment on a massive scale'. But it was meeting Polly Higgins that enthused me about the possibilities of a *law* of ecocide (Higgins et al, 2013).

Polly had looked at the idea of adding an amendment to the 1998 Rome Statute as a route to creating a crime of ecocide (it was nearly included alongside 'genocide' when the statute was first drafted but was then left out). This made sense to me because (a) the statute already covered what could be seen as similar or parallel crimes against the planet and our future; and (b) as a criminologist, a key consideration is that laws need an enforcement mechanism—and the International Criminal Court (ICC) was an obvious candidate. Of course, there have been criticisms of the ecocide proposal and some argue that existing international law could be adequate if used rigorously and appropriately. Alternatives to relying on the ICC have also been proposed—not least because several nations, including some of the worst environmental offenders, do not recognise it—but I would foresee these suffering similar drawbacks unless real global cooperation and leadership is exercised to address ecocidal acts. Polly was very clear that the idea of 'leadership' is vital because so much environmental damage and destruction is the result of a failure of international political leadership and responsibility.

There have been some political and constitutional acknowledgments of the idea of ecocide with varying degrees of credibility, with President Macron of France declaring in August 2020 that he supports the campaign 'to ensure that [ecocide] is enshrined in international law so that leaders . . . are accountable before the International Criminal Court.' (https://www.stopecocide.earth/press-releases-summary/president-macron-shares-ambition-to-establish-international-crime-of-ecocide). This is encouraging but before becoming too optimistic, I would just add two more words for us to consider alongside 'ecocide'. First, 'anthropocentrism'—how would a law of ecocide apply to non-human species? Second, 'ethnocide'. This term usually refers to the destruction of the culture of a group, but in the case of Indigenous peoples their culture is entwined with their environment and, historically, national and international laws have been inadequate in protecting both. A law of ecocide must do better.

*Professor Nigel South, Professor of Sociology,
University of Essex*

References

Falk, R. A. (1973) 'Environmental Warfare and Ecocide—Facts, Appraisal, and Proposals'. *Security Dialogue* 4: 80–96.

Gauger, A. et al. (2012) 'Ecocide is the missing fifth Crime Against Peace', The Ecocide Project, Human Rights Consortium, School of Advanced Study, University of London. Available at: https://sas-space.sas.ac.uk/4830/1/Ecocide_research_report_19_July_13.pdf

Gray, M. A. (1996) 'The international crime of ecocide'. *California Western International Law Journal* 26: 215–71.

Higgins, P., Short, D., and South, N. (2013) 'Protecting the planet: a proposal for a law of Ecocide'. *Crime, Law and Social Change* 59(3): 251–66.

> ### WHAT DO YOU THINK? 12.2
>
> #### Ecocide as an international crime
>
> Having systematic or mass environmental damage classed as the international crime of ecocide would have serious implications, perhaps the most significant of which would be that systematic, widespread, or serious environmental crimes could be prosecuted at an international level without having to rely on an individual state to prosecute these crimes. What other implications—both positive and negative—might there be? Consider the following questions.
>
> 1. What are the advantages of having ecocide as a crime that could be prosecuted at the ICC?
> 2. What difficulties might there be in taking ecocide cases to an international court like the ICC?
> 3. Are there any disadvantages to having ecocide as a separate international crime rather than seeing environmental damage as part of other international crimes?
> 4. Can you think of any other better ways of dealing with the problem of ecocide?

concept in green criminological examination of environmental harm.

A strong ecocide movement now exists which continues to push for ecocide to be recognised within international criminal law as a crime against peace. The most serious crimes that threaten international peace and security are dealt with by the International Criminal Court (ICC). This permanent court sits in The Hague, a city in the Netherlands, and has responsibility for hearing international criminal cases. At the time of writing in spring 2020, 123 countries had agreed to accept the jurisdiction of this court by signing up to its founding treaty, the Rome Statute of 1998. Like any criminal court, the ICC has the power to conduct trials, hear evidence, render judgment, and to impose sanctions and punishments.

The types of cases that the ICC can consider are written into international law in the Rome Statute. This treaty identifies the following as the most serious international crimes that the ICC has legal power to consider:

1. the crime of genocide;
2. crimes against humanity;
3. war crimes;
4. the crime of aggression.

The precise nature of each of these crimes is set out in more detail in the Rome Statute and has been explored further in cases considered by the ICC. To date, all efforts to have ecocide included in the Rome Statute have failed. However, there has been some consideration of environmental damage in cases where the ICC has been invited to examine the environmental harm caused during military campaigns. A 2016 policy paper also indicated that the ICC would give some priority to cases that resulted in 'illegal exploitation of natural resources' and 'land grabbing and the destruction of the environment' (Office of the Prosecutor, 2016: 4).

The ICC has been criticised for the length of time it takes to conduct its investigations as well as the nature of the cases it considers (it has, for example, been accused of being a 'colonial court' because the majority of its cases involve African states). However, it is recognised as part of international justice so the inclusion of environmental harm within the court's remit would have the benefit of bringing environmental crime under the umbrella of serious crimes recognised by the international community. Consider the implications and potential difficulties of enshrining ecocide within international law in **What do you think? 12.2**.

12.5 Green crimes or green harms?

The nature of environmental victimisation poses important questions which are relevant for your criminological studies more widely. First, 'the harms suffered can involve an extended group or even a community of victims, sometimes representing rival interests'; secondly, 'the perpetrators are often corporations or states' (Natali, 2015: 64–5).

It can also be difficult to identify a causal link between policy, action, and victim, meaning that lawful activity can often cause considerable **victimisation**.

The reality of criminological study is that—as we saw in **Chapter 2**—it is often concerned with crime as defined by legal systems. In other words, an act is only a crime if the law says that it is, usually through the criminal lawmaking something an offence. So, it may be obvious that breaking into somebody's home and removing their iPad without their consent is wrong. But it becomes a 'crime' specifically because the Theft Act 1968, the law that governs the illegal taking of possessions, spells out the conditions for the offence of burglary to have taken place: unlawful entry into a property and taking possessions with the intent to permanently deprive somebody of their property. The same principle applies to green crimes, meaning that acts like pollution, illegal taking of wildlife, and climate change-causing activities are only crimes if the written law states somewhere that this is the case. (And, as we have noted, also means that responses to such harms also tend to be crime-based and punitive.) However, some criminologists argue that by discussing and responding to harmful acts as defined by legal frameworks, we are being anthropocentric—focusing only on the concerns of human beings—whereas we should be *biocentric* and thinking about the natural and physical world and non-human nature.

There are disputes about the use of the word 'crime' rather than 'harm' and some criminologists prefer the approach of **zemiology**, the study of social harm. We discuss this school of thought in depth in **Chapter 19**, but the key idea to understand here is that zemiologists argue for a move beyond narrow and limiting discussions of 'crime', towards broader consideration of things that can cause considerable *social harm*. With this approach, our focus shifts from whether what has happened is a deliberate criminal act to the impact of the activity and the harm that has been caused. This means that in addition to considering intentional acts, we can think about acts or omissions, including 'accidents' and 'upset incidents' such as equipment breakdowns. This allows us to consider, for example, the faulty repairs which have led to oil spills in the Niger Delta (see our earlier discussion in the market society case study of the oil industry and environmental harm in **section 12.3**).

This *social harm* approach is integral to some forms of green criminology. Green criminologists observe that criminal law and regulatory systems with a criminal law basis are often based around punishing an offender after an incident has occurred, meaning that they do not take action to address the harm that has been caused. For example, someone who is the victim of a burglary has the potential to have their goods replaced following a successful insurance claim. The process of reporting the crime, receiving a police crime number, then providing those details to the insurer potentially makes the replacement of goods a relatively straightforward process (see **Chapter 19**). This is not the case when the environment is harmed, or when a person or group is affected by environmental harm. Dead wildlife cannot easily be replaced, and the impacts of pollution or climate change can be irreversible. Critical green criminologists have gone a step further, arguing that not only is there too much focus on punishment and not enough on addressing the harm, but some laws and regulations do not work as the levels of fines or sentences imposed on the offending corporations or their employees are inadequate as tools to change behaviour (see, for example, Lynch and Stretesky, 2014; White, 2018).

In these cases, critical green criminologists might argue that alternative punishments and ways of repairing the harm should be considered and there are examples of where they have been tried. Some green criminologists argue for greater **criminalisation** of the corporations themselves, involving a higher level of punishment in terms of heavier fines (fines that are consistent with a corporation's economic power and profit margins) or even for imprisonment for the senior executives involved. Other green criminologists argue for forms of punishment that also include measures based on the 'polluter pays' principle— the idea that those who cause the pollution or environmental harm should meet the costs of remedying that harm. In these cases, polluters may, for example, be made to pay to clean up rivers that they have polluted and restock any fish that they have killed. Where it is not possible to directly remedy any harm they have caused, they may instead be asked to pay compensation or pay for action that helps the nearby environment. Does a focus on harm over crime make sense to you in this context? Work out your own view on this issue with the help of **What do you think? 12.3**.

It should by now be clear that green criminology sometimes challenges the nature of 'crime' versus 'harm' as an issue of definition rather than as one of behaviour. The criminal law identifies a range of behaviours that meet its definition of 'crime', such as *intentional* killing of wildlife or *knowingly* and/or *recklessly* disposing of toxic waste in contravention of legislation. But, as we saw in **Chapter 2**, in a sense the concept of 'crime' is a social construct. It is developed through a range of social processes so that behaviours can be criminalised or decriminalised at various times and according to political processes and changing societal **norms** and beliefs. For example, fox-hunting and other forms of hunting wild animals with dogs were practised in the UK for hundreds of years and only became illegal with the passing of the Hunting Act 2004. This law effectively made hunting wild mammals with dogs illegal. But since this Act was passed there have been attempts to bring back the activity, mostly by Conservative politicians who see fox-hunting as a legitimate countryside pursuit. Political opposition and opposition from the public have so far prevented the changes in the law that would make this form of hunting legal again, but it could still change in the future.

> **WHAT DO YOU THINK?** 12.3
>
> ### Should we focus on harm or crime?
>
> A standard definition of environmental crime would classify it as:
>
> > An environmental crime is an unauthorized act or omission that violates the law and is therefore subject to criminal prosecution and criminal sanctions. This offense harms or endangers people's physical safety or health as well as the environment itself. It serves the interests of either organizations—typically corporations—or individuals.
> >
> > (Situ and Emmons, 2000: 3)
>
> Is this an adequate definition? Critically analyse it by answering the following questions:
>
> - Does the definition adequately cover all types of environmental harm? If not, why not and what types of harm are missing? (Hint: to what extent does it consider 'lawful but awful' activities?)
> - Does the definition cover all types of environmental victims? Who or what might be missing?
> - How would you improve this definition? What additional aspects might you include?
>
> As you consider your answers, think about the distinction between 'crime' and 'harm' and the wider definition of wrongdoing that green criminology aims to explore.

In this sense, crime is not a fixed concept. Criminology generally accepts crime as being how the state defines it at that time, but what constitutes crime is determined by a range of social and political considerations which combine to influence the laws that get passed and the importance attached by policing agencies to enforcing those laws. Some green criminologists argue that, in contrast, environmental 'harm' is a constant so our definitions of crime or response to harmful behaviour need to change. Critical green criminology essentially argues that the impacts of some environmentally harmful activities are so serious that they should be treated as if they were crimes, irrespective of how they are defined in law.

The issue of clean air and pollution highlights the issue of 'crime' and 'harm' and shows how a green criminological perspective can help make sense of these issues.

Air quality is poor in most major cities around the world (see, for example, the Delhi smog pictured in **Figure 12.7**), and this has a major impact on people's health—especially for those with lung conditions such as asthma. Most of the

Figure 12.7 Air pollution in major cities, such as Delhi, has harmful consequences for humans and the environment yet this issue mainly falls outside mainstream criminology

Source: Amit kg/Shutterstock

pollution which lowers the air quality is the result of legal activity, such as the pollution caused by cars (Leybourn-Langton et al., 2018). So, because car use is legal, and the vehicle MOT test in the UK (and its equivalent in other countries) is designed to regulate emissions from exhausts, the use of cars (with a valid MOT certificate or new enough not to need one) is not a crime and would not generally come to the attention of policing or crime control agencies. But the harm caused by air pollution, including the pain suffered by many asthma sufferers (there are over 5.4 million in the UK), is considerable and the evidence suggests that air pollution causes many thousands of early deaths each year in the UK. In the long term, air pollution can also contribute to climate change and cause wider harm to the environment.

Green criminology would argue that because air pollution causes deaths it is something that criminology should consider, in the same way as we would consider other areas where people die as a result of human activity. But rather than penalising individual car owners, green criminologists might see addressing the issue as being the responsibility of corporations and the government through a preventative regulatory approach. The government could try to address the harm of air pollution by:

- helping to speed up the move to electric cars, to reduce the pollution caused by petrol and diesel engines, but market considerations (discussed in section 12.3) mean that we are some way off electric cars being the norm;
- supporting (and funding) scrappage schemes for older cars and forcing industry to move away from producing petrol and diesel vehicles towards electric ones;
- imposing additional regulation to address pollution. So far, the government has been slow to do so. In fact, the UK government has been taken to court several times by ClientEarth, a UK-based NGO for failing to meet EU air quality standards.

In **Conversations 12.3** we hear from Katie Nield, a clean air lawyer at ClientEarth, who comments on the efficacy of current regulations, the difficulty of holding the government to account on air pollution, and the changes that ClientEarth would like to see.

While the global Covid-19 pandemic which began in December 2019 inflicted major harm on people, it had some environmental benefits, including temporary improvements to the air quality in London and several other major cities as construction activities paused and there were fewer vehicles on the roads. From a green criminology perspective, we need to think about how this type of harm can be addressed without relying on action from an NGO—or the intervention of a pandemic, resulting in severe lockdowns and equally severe implications for the global economy. We also need to ask why some laws can be

CONVERSATIONS 12.3

The legal fight against air pollution

with **Katie Nield**

Air pollution is recognised by the World Health Organization (WHO) as the biggest environmental health risk in the world. It also tops the list of environment health hazards in the UK and is estimated to cause the equivalent of up to 40,000 early deaths a year (Royal College of Physicians, 2016).

Breathing dirty air is linked to higher rates of cancer, heart disease, heart attacks, asthma attacks and strokes. Air pollution can also lead to low birth weights (NHS, 2013) and stunted lung development (British Lung Foundation, 2019) in children and it has a disproportionate impact on already vulnerable communities, including ethnic minorities and those on low incomes.

As well as harm to human health, air pollution can cause damage to plants and animals. The UK Government estimates that around 80 per cent of Special Areas of Conservation in England receive damaging amounts of nitrogen from the air (DEFRA, 2019).

But, in spite of all of this, most areas of the UK are still breaching legal limits for harmful nitrogen dioxide (NO_2) pollution. EU-derived domestic law requires the UK Government to take urgent action to achieve prescribed clean air standards—but the UK has failed to meet the limits for NO_2 for over 10 years, ever since this law came into force (ClientEarth, 2019). In many parts of the UK the levels of particulate matter—another toxic air pollutant—are also well over the levels recommended by the WHO, though they are within current legal limits.

Since 2011, ClientEarth has launched three successful legal challenges against the UK Government over its failure to tackle illegal levels of NO_2 pollution.

In response, the courts have ordered ministers to come up with new, improved plans to reduce this harmful pollutant to within legal limits in the shortest possible time. These were ground-breaking victories and have led some cities to finally take this public health threat seriously, with leaders committing to Clean Air Zones—where the most polluting vehicles are deterred from entering the most polluted areas—in places like Birmingham, Bath and Sheffield.

However, the court-ordered plans drawn up by ministers have left local authorities to do much of the heavy lifting when it comes to identifying and implementing solutions. In many cases, this approach has led to delays to decision-making and weak proposals as many authorities lack the resources, capacity and leadership to get to grips with the problem.

Other government bodies have also failed to pull their weight. For example, the government has tasked Highways England with coming up with a plan to address illegal pollution levels along the 4,436 miles of roads it manages—but it is still to publish any concrete proposals.

Yet the solutions needed to tackle the problem are evident. We know that road transport emissions account for 80 per cent of illegal levels of NO_2, with diesel cars being the biggest culprit. The government's own evidence shows that Clean Air Zones are the quickest and most effective way to tackle the problem. This is backed up by recent data showing rapid drops in NO_2 levels since the introduction of the Ultra Low Emission Zone (ULEZ) in London (Greater London Authority, 2020). Ministers need to push forward a national network of Clean Air Zones, coupled with help and support for those who need it.

When it comes to particulate matter pollution, the government needs to adopt stronger legal limits that drive action to better protect people's health and make sure that no part of the country exceeds the levels recommended by the WHO. ClientEarth, alongside the WHO itself and other health organisations, believes that this must be achieved by 2030 at the very latest.

Finally, it is important that as we leave the European Union, public bodies' performance against environmental obligations is overseen by a watchdog with sufficient clout to hold them to account where they fail to comply with their air quality duties. Our health is at stake; the law is our best defence.

Katie Nield, UK clean air lawyer at environmental law charity ClientEarth

References

British Lung Foundation, 'How does air pollution affect children's lungs?'. Available at: www.blf.org.uk/support-for-you/risks-to-childrens-lungs/air-pollution. [Accessed 29 September 2020].

ClientEarth (2019) *UK Air Pollution: How clean is the air you breathe?*

DEFRA (2019) *Clean Air Strategy 2019.*

Greater London Authority (2020) *Central London Ultra Low Emission Zone (ULEZ) Ten Month Report.*

NHS (2013) 'Air pollution associated with low birthweight'. Available at: www.nhs.uk/news/pregnancy-and-child/air-pollution-associated-with-low-birthweight/. [Accessed 29 September 2020].

Royal College of Physicians (2016) *Every breath we take: the lifelong impact of air pollution.*

---

easily enforced and others cannot, and why it is difficult to force governmental action in an area that affects so many people. Underpinning all of this is, again, the question of whether we need to challenge our understanding of 'crime' and how it occurs, giving more consideration to the importance of 'harm' in examining environmental wrongdoing.

12.6 Policing green crimes

Given that green criminology includes many diverse ideas, it won't surprise you to learn that there are many arguments and debates about how best to respond to green crimes and develop this area of study. As we have noted at various points throughout this chapter, there are disputes about whether green criminology should be concerned with 'crime' or 'harm', and scholars have stressed that when we deal only with 'crime', we must ensure that we do not narrow our view on the extent to which environmental damage is considered within justice systems.

As we saw in **Chapter 3**, the concept of 'justice' is a contested one and while we have already touched on some suggested approaches to achieving it in our discussions of environmental justice, ecological justice, and species justice (see the discussion of key concepts in green criminology in **section 12.4**), you should also be familiar with some debates on the best practical approaches to policing and remedying green crimes and harms. In traditional criminal law and criminal justice, there is a straightforward focus on the law enforcement model of detection, apprehension, and punishment. Simply put, the police and other justice agencies identify that a crime has occurred, they apprehend (catch) the offender, and then they progress them through the justice system. This typically results in punishment by a fine or, for serious crimes, a prison sentence. This punitive approach to crimes is based on ideas of protecting the public and seeking retribution (or revenge, if you prefer) on their behalf (**Chapter 27**). However, while many green criminologists would argue that green crimes are often closely linked to and can even worsen criminal and social (in) justices, there are still uncertainties and debates about the best way to respond to the consequences of environmental harms and damage. Some environmental harms are dealt with by regulators rather than mainstream policing agencies. The regulatory approach can include negotiation and offering help to businesses rather than responding in a purely punitive way. There are also debates about how best to deal with the types of criminality and lack of consideration for the environment and non-human nature that are found in green crimes. In this section, we will consider first the main ways of responding to and policing environmental offending, and then the ways that, in practice, we currently punish or seek to address the harm that offending causes—and the problems associated with these responses.

Types of response to environmental offending

The arguments for and against the different types of response to environmental offending and environmental harm are influenced by the degree to which each one is *biocentric* or *anthropocentric*. For some green criminologists, the focus is on the use of existing enforcement agencies (for example, police, customs) and standard criminal justice mechanisms (the criminal law, use of prison) a potentially anthropocentric approach. For others, there are advantages to using specialist environmental enforcement agencies and alternative justice systems such as a restorative justice approach (see **Chapter 30**) or specialist environmental courts that can adopt a more biocentric approach and consider the environment as a victim. White (2008: 182) also identifies three broader approaches that we can consider. These are:

1. **Socio-legal approach**—This approach emphasises using the current criminal law, but improving its ability to investigate, enforce, prosecute, and convict in relation to illegal environmental activity.
2. **Regulatory approach**—This approach argues that environmental harm can be prevented and halted by relying mainly on social regulation. This means trying to reform existing production processes and our levels and ways of consuming natural resources through enforced self-regulation and other measures such as certification schemes and involving NGOs in the regulatory process.
3. **Social action approach**—This is a long-term approach which advocates dealing with environmental crime and harm through social change, to be achieved mostly through democratic institutions and citizen participation.

(Adapted from White, 2008: 182)

Think back to our illegal wood products and timber trafficking example in **section 12.3** about how the market society operates. Each of these perspectives could be applied to dealing with this problem.

The *socio-legal approach* would deal with timber trafficking by detecting, apprehending, and prosecuting those who are involved in deforestation and illegal logging and also prosecuting those involved in the transport and eventual sale of illegally sourced wood. In this model, timber trafficking-related offences are dealt with as crimes; the criminal law would contain offences relating to all stages of the supply chain. Even the possession of illegally taken wood could potentially become an offence so that the actions of consumers are also caught by legal systems, promoting responsible consumption of wood and reducing demand.

The *regulatory approach* would introduce a form of social regulation of the type that already exists as a certification scheme, such as the Forest Stewardship Council (FSC) scheme which is designed to indicate that hardwood products have come from a forest that is managed sustainably. In theory, FSC certification operates as a monitoring system and sets standards that producers need to meet in order to satisfy consumers that responsible forest management has taken place. This helps to prevent illegal logging. Monitoring systems such as FSC certification and the Sustainable Forestry Initiative (SFI) certification are a form of self-regulation where industry participants voluntarily sign up to the scheme and modify their work practices in order to raise standards across the industry. A potential weakness of these schemes is that they may not be well equipped to deal with 'rogue' entrants to the industry. In reality, those who are engaged in deliberate illegal action are unlikely to comply with these kinds of certification schemes and they are potentially easy for determined offenders to circumvent.

The final mechanism, the *social action approach*, seeks long-term change and social transformation. In this context, it might try to educate consumers about the damaging impact of our continued consumption of tropical hardwoods in order to introduce responsible consumerism. Eventually this could result in a move away from solid wood products or result in synthetic alternatives being developed. It could also put the responsibility on retailers to check their supply chains more carefully and ensure that they only stock wood products that they know have been sourced legally and from a sustainable outlet.

Practical responses to environmental offending

While in theory these three different mechanisms are already all in play, in practice environmental crimes are often dealt with via the criminal law or through a regulatory system that is enforced by an environmental regulator. For example, in the US the Environmental Protection Agency (EPA) has responsibility for enforcing pollution crimes and harmful emissions that contravene the US Clean Air Act and the US Fish and Wildlife Service (USFWS) deals with wildlife and fisheries crime. In the UK, the Environment Agency has enforcement duties on environmental crimes and wildlife crime. Some police forces also have Wildlife Crime Officers and there is a police National Wildlife Crime Unit (NWCU). Serious wildlife crime (that is, involving organised crime) is also dealt with by the National Crime Agency (NCA) and some wildlife trafficking offences will be dealt with by HM Customs and Excise where they involve import and export offences.

One problem for environmental crimes is deciding, first, on the appropriate action to take in each case and, secondly, on who should be the target of enforcement action, whether it be punitive or regulatory in nature. As we have seen, environmental and wildlife crimes are covered by a range of laws and a range of agencies. Environmental cases sometimes involve a mixture of criminal, civil, and administrative law and prosecutors may be able to choose from a range of options in deciding how to proceed with a case. It can be difficult to use the criminal law because it requires identifying an offender who can be prosecuted, which is not always straightforward in the context of environmental offences. In the case of our wood products example, a number of people are involved, from the person in Indonesia who first cuts down the tree through to the shop assistant who sells us our desk or paper. In the case of major environmental crime (say, large-scale pollution or wildlife trafficking), identifying the person or entity to prosecute is even more complicated. A corporation may be involved and there may have been potential infringement of other laws, such as health and safety laws or business laws, raising the question of whether company directors or the company itself should be the target of prosecution. This is a key criticism of using legal processes to deal with green crimes and harms, particularly where corporations are concerned.

The people who are responsible for major environmental harms or crimes are often too powerful to be punished. Powerful groups often have the ability to not only define what 'crime problems' are (as we discuss in **Chapter 2** when we consider crime as a social construct) but also to use their power to evade the criminalisation of their own criminal and harmful behaviours, whereas the powerless often cannot escape their victimisation. For example, if an oil company is involved in an oil spill which destroys the marine environment and the spill can be traced back to a faulty repair by a rig worker, should this worker be prosecuted? In one sense they are the offender, but in another sense they might be a victim if they were not given the right tools or were under extreme pressure from within the company to cut corners and get the work done quickly or risk losing their job.

The reality is that modern transnational corporations like the major oil companies have complex bureaucratic structures which can involve layers of managers, directors, senior operating executives, and other staff, right down to the low-level employees who carry out the work on the ground. Is it possible to draw clear lines of culpability between them so that we can legally identify the manager or executive responsible for the decisions that cause our rig worker to break environmental and health and safety laws? Can we actually hold the corporation to account for acting with a malign intent or as having a 'guilty mind' (one of the criminal law's requirements and important to determine if the corporation is responsible), or has the decision (if we can find one) been taken at a level which is so distant from those at the top that the corporation can argue that it is not responsible for the actions of its employee and can effectively shift the responsibility onto them? These questions should give you an idea of why corporate environmental cases are often complex, lengthy, and very expensive, involving court cases, appeals, and counter-appeals.

Another problem with using the regulatory regime in this context is that environmental harms are not always dealt with as simple criminal problems to which the detection, apprehension, and punishment model can be applied. The power dynamics involved in discussions of corporate environmental crime mean that governments are often unwilling to treat corporations as criminal and pursue environmental problems as criminal ones. The reality is that businesses are significant sources of income for political parties (through the taxes they pay) and they can sometimes have an impact on a party's policies regarding legislation. The oil industry in the US, for example, brings with it a powerful political lobby that has been able to restrict industry regulation and in recent years is alleged to have had a hand in restricting or reducing the power of the EPA. Major corporations are also significant employers and corporations that are threatened with extensive regulation have been known to wield the threat of locating their businesses elsewhere. Few politicians would be willing to take responsibility for a significant loss of jobs in the name of environmental regulation. As a result, the criminal law approach is often focused on the individual who commits the criminal act—often a low-level employee—rather than the executive who may have created the conditions that caused the offence to occur. Of course, the punitive approach is not always suitable and an alternative enforcement approach is to encourage compliance and prevent future wrongdoing through negotiation and support.

Where regulators such as the EPA and Environment Agency are used, the regulations that they enforce are often designed to allow the corporation to continue its operations while changing its behaviour. In this respect, environmental regulation can differ from criminal law as it is intended to be corrective rather than punitive, encouraging compliance with the regulations as opposed to punishing non-compliance with legislation in the criminal world. As a result, regulators often have considerable discretion as to whether they use the criminal law tools at their disposal and instead may choose to use civil or administrative law mechanisms which focus on repairing the harm. This means that when a breach of regulations is identified, corporations may be served a warning notice which informs them of their offence and gives them an opportunity to come into compliance by fixing the problem. For example, a corporation that is found to be emitting pollution beyond the limits allowed for by its permits may be informed of this fact and given a set period to put in place additional pollution controls. If the corporation fails to fix the problem within the specified time period, it may be served with another notice which identifies the formal enforcement action that will be taken or fine that it will face if it does not comply. Repeated failure to fix the problem could result in criminal prosecution. In **Controversy and debate 12.2** we consider an example where a water company was found to have bypassed regulations and carried out pollution activities for several years.

As you might expect, there are debates about the effectiveness of the risk-based and regulatory approach, given that it can result in corporations repeatedly committing offences over a long period of time before any action is taken, while continuing to operate and make profit while flouting the law. But fines and what is called 'responsive regulation' (choosing from multiple options in a flexible regulatory approach) are generally seen by governments as being the right approach to take with corporate offending; generally their approach to regulation is risk-based and criminal prosecution is seen as the last resort for the reasons we have already discussed and the generally positive approach that governments have to corporations (Hampton, 2005).

Even when cases do get to court, it does not always result in victory for those opposed to environmental harm. As long ago as 1992, Lord Woolf, at the time one of the UK's most senior judges, argued that the UK judiciary was 'environmentally myopic' (Woolf, 1992). 'Myopic' means short-sighted, so he was saying that prosecutors and judges often did not know how to deal with environmental cases and overlooked or misunderstood their importance. Both prosecutors and judges were sometimes confused by

CONTROVERSY AND DEBATE 12.2

Responding to the polluting activities of Southern Water

In the UK, water companies are monitored through a regulatory regime that means they have to provide information on how they follow the regulations and operate their facilities. If they fail to do so, they can be made to pay financial penalties. In 2017, the UK water regulator Ofwat launched an investigation into the actions of water supplier Southern Water after it identified that the company had failed to operate a number of its wastewater treatment works properly. The company was found not to have properly invested in its plants, and its failures led to equipment breakdowns and unpermitted spills of wastewater into the environment. Ofwat also found that Southern Water had altered its wastewater sampling processes so that it gave inaccurate information to the regulator about the performance of several of its sewage treatment sites. This meant that the company avoided penalties that the regulator could have imposed.

The problems took place over a number of years (2010–15) and were found after the regulator's exten-sive investigation. Ofwat's agreed settlement with Southern Water means that the company will pay £126 million in penalties and rebates to existing and former wastewater customers for serious failures in the operation of several wastewater treatment works and for deliberate misreporting of performance information. The penalties comprised:

- £91.2 million in what are called 'underperformance penalties'. This is money that Southern Water should have paid as part of Ofwat's price review incentive regime.

- £31.7 million as additional compensation to customers (instead of a greater fine) for failing in its legal obligations.

- £3 million as an additional fine in recognition of the company's serious and significant breaches of its licence conditions and statutory duties. However, the fine has been reduced from £37.7 million in recognition of the steps taken by Southern Water to put things right, including its proposal to make significant rebates to customers.

> ### WHAT DO YOU THINK? 12.4
>
> **Specialist environmental courts**
>
> How effective do you think that specialist environmental courts might be in applying a green criminological approach to crime and justice? Consider:
>
> - the type of cases that environmental courts deal with;
> - the advantages and disadvantages of having specialist courts;
> - how environmental courts deal with cases. In particular, whether their approach is based on notions of 'crime' or 'harm' or a mixture;
> - what kind of penalties or sanctions might be imposed in a case.
>
> Think about the way in which cases might be resolved and note down some ideas on possible solutions to cases that involve going beyond the simple use of fines and prison. Think about the types of remedies that consider the environment as a victim and also attempt to repair the harm. What do you think would be important things to include in remedies?
>
> For more ideas and information, you may find it useful to explore the website of the NSW Land and Environment Court: www.lec.justice.nsw.gov.au/.

the complexity of these cases and the lack of experience amongst lawyers in these types of prosecution could mean that prosecutors were simply beaten by a well-prepared defence. One way in which governments and the judiciary have attempted to address this issue has been to use specialist environmental courts which have emerged since at least the early 2000s. Many green criminologists see these so-called 'green courts' as a way of bringing specialist knowledge and experience of environmental issues to bear on the justice process. Green courts such as those of the New South Wales (NSW) Land and Environment Court in Australia have the advantage of having a specific responsibility to consider environmental cases. This includes cases on land use, mining disputes, planning cases, and threats to biodiversity. As a result, the judges and prosecutors involved in the court develop specialist knowledge and practice in environmental justice and can develop a body of case law that determines how cases should be dealt with. Potential benefits of this approach are:

- improved justice processes;
- better consideration of evidence;
- clear consideration of environmental harm and the environmental impacts of both crime and regulatory breaches;
- the ability to move away from a purely punitive approach and to integrate mechanisms to repair harm such as restorative justice procedures (see **Chapter 30**).

Remedies can involve straightforward adjudication; determination of the legal issues in the case and the imposition of a sanction. But they can also involve other remedies such as the use of arbitration or mediation, in other words employing a dispute resolution approach rather than a punitive one. The harm-repairing mechanisms can involve bringing together offenders and affected communities so that they jointly find solutions to problems. They can also have the effect of changing businesses' behaviour by making the leaders of corporations understand the consequences of their wrongdoing whilst also being required to take action to repair or address any environmental harms they have caused.

12.7 Conclusion

In this chapter we have explored how green criminology has emerged as a distinct field of critical criminology in response to the increase in environmental harms in the 20th century and the early decades of the 21st century. Green criminology has also grown rapidly as a consequence of the failure of traditional criminology to deal with environmental harms. As we have seen, green criminology addresses new, emerging forms of harm which fall outside of our traditional understanding of crime as something that is contained within the criminal law. It also considers a wider class of offender and victim (including the environment itself) than is considered by mainstream criminology. In part, what green criminology does is to challenge the dominant discourses about crime, criminality, and control. It highlights social injustice and works towards social change for a fairer world, identifying ways in which our justice systems need to change in order to create a wider concept of justice and consider not just anthropocentric concerns but also biocentric and eco-centric ones.

We have covered a large part of the green criminological landscape in this chapter, but this is far from being the final word on green criminology. The discipline continues to adapt to contemporary circumstances (as we have suggested through the New frontier boxes) and new environmental threats. The Covid-19 outbreak, for example, prompted and will doubtless continue to prompt new debates about keeping animals and animal trafficking, as well as the associated risks of disease transfer from animals to humans. Brexit has also prompted further discussions about animal rights and how best to include animal sentience in UK law. These discussions take place within the context of increased consumer awareness of environmental considerations and a corresponding demand for them to be taken into account when products are produced and sold.

As you progress through your studies and develop your criminological imagination, you should see more areas where environmental concerns and mainstream criminological concerns are in sync. For example, a polluting corporation may also be involved in human rights abuses, representing a colonial power abusing its economic might in a Global South country. Armed militia poaching wildlife may also be involved in killing game wardens who oppose them, and organised crime groups that have historically traded in drugs or weapons may now be using their trade routes to smuggle wildlife as an easier, lower risk option than its traditional serious crime pursuits. We would encourage you to try to view green harms and crimes as issues of crime and deviance and not 'just' as environmental problems. As critical green criminologists, you can contribute to this young and exciting field, helping to find solutions to the problems of green crime, while also bringing a green lens to traditional crime and justice problems.

SUMMARY

After reading this chapter and working your way through its features you should now be able to:

- Appreciate the importance of green criminology as a distinct field within criminology

In recent years, we have witnessed a renewed wave of environmental activism typified by groups such as Extinction Rebellion and activists like Nina Gualinga who draw attention to threats facing indigenous peoples. In addition, scientific evidence of climate change and increased knowledge of environmental impacts and environmental threats have joined the mainstream of social and political debate. Green criminology has emerged as a reaction to mainstream criminology's failure to deal with environmental problems. This is part of critical criminology's re-imagining of some core concepts on power, ideologies, social and political change, and the inadequacies of traditional approaches to crime and justice.

- Identify how and why green criminology often focuses on harm rather than crime

Green criminology challenges traditional criminology's focus on 'crime' as defined by criminal law systems and shifts focus to the causes and impacts of environmental harm. In this respect, green criminology has similarities with *zemiology*—in that it looks at the idea of crime as being not just illegal acts but also harm that has serious impacts—but green criminology extends this idea to harms inflicted on the environment and non-human nature that are committed by business, organised crime, and even the state. Green criminology's focus on 'harm' and 'crime' identifies that much criminology is narrow in focus and suggests that our criminological gaze needs to consider a wide range of actions where powerful groups continue to harm and victimise powerless groups in society. By considering harm, we can also examine the effectiveness of justice systems and mechanisms to repair or address harm rather than relying on a purely punitive approach.

- Critically assess the extent to which ideas around crime and wrongdoing extend beyond interpersonal violence and property crimes to include crimes against environments, humanity, and other animals

Green criminology adopts an expansive definition of crime and wrongdoing that considers crimes and harms against the environment and non-human nature. It argues that our justice systems and our way of looking at crime need to consider the impacts of crime and wrongdoing and a wide range of victims of human harms including the environment itself as a crime (and harm) victim.

- Evaluate key green criminological concepts and theoretical approaches such as ecological justice (including species justice) and environmental justice and understand the concept of ecocide

Green criminology has several core concepts relating to how justice systems can better deal with crime, deviance, and environmental harm. Environmental justice is concerned with how access to environmental justice is often denied to those from marginalised groups (including ethnic minorities and indigenous peoples). Ecological justice and species justice provide explanation for how justice systems need to consider the needs of the environment and non-human nature. Ecocide looks at how serious environmental damage can be incorporated into international criminal law and considered as one of the crimes against peace and security that are included in accepted definitions of international crime.

- Identify the causes of green crimes, their links with other crimes, and how green criminology can inform mainstream criminology

Green criminology identifies some green crimes as a factor of capitalist processes of production and consumption where pollution and environmental harm is a common consequence of our continued use of and illegal exploitation of natural resources. Green criminology also identifies how corporations are dealt with differently from other types of offender because of their position as legal actors who contribute to society. However, green criminology identifies the link between the legal and the illegal and argues that we should consider the effect of corporate activity. Rather than the focus on punishment that is the approach of traditional criminology, green criminology is concerned with repairing environmental harm and changing harmful behaviour. As a result, green criminology incorporates restorative principles as well as the 'polluter pays' principle that seeks to make those who cause environmental damage meet the cost of repairing the harm that they cause.

Test your understanding of the chapter's key points by attempting the self-test questions on the **online resources** at www.oup.com/he/case2e

REVIEW QUESTIONS

1. To what extent can green criminology be seen as a distinct subfield of criminology?
2. What are the key differences between environmental justice and ecological justice?
3. How does green criminology extend our understanding of crime and deviance?
4. List three reasons why green criminologists argue that harm is more important than crime when justice systems and criminologists are considering green crimes and offending.
5. What challenges exist in policing green crimes?

Access the **online resources** at www.oup.com/he/case2e to check your answers to the review questions.

FURTHER READING

Hall, M. et al. (eds) (2017) *Greening Criminology in the 21st Century.* Abingdon: Routledge.
This book's original essays examine the nature of green criminology and it also contains case studies on environmental victimisation, extreme environmental activism, eco-crime, and fresh water and agricultural crime.

South, N. and Brisman, A. (eds) (2020) *Routledge International Handbook of Green Criminology* (2nd edn). London: Routledge.
This is a good place to start for a more advanced, in-depth study of green criminology. It includes a wide-ranging collection of original essays and case studies on issues such as corporate criminality, environmental justice, and wildlife trafficking.

White, R. (2019) *Climate Change Criminology.* Bristol: Bristol University Press.
This book offers a clearly written account of the nature, harms, and perpetrators of climate change and makes the case for criminology to deal with climate change as a pressing social and criminological issue.

Wyatt, T. (2013) *Wildlife Trafficking.* Basingstoke: Palgrave Macmillan.
This book provides a thorough analysis of the causes of wildlife crime, its victims, and the offenders engaged in wildlife crime.

 Access the **online resources** to view a wealth of extra information relating to your study of criminology, including self-test questions, answers to review questions, and links to other resources that will help you enjoy and fulfil your potential within your studies.
www.oup.com/he/case2e

CHAPTER OUTLINE

13.1	Introduction	376
13.2	Globalisation, crime, and justice	376
13.3	Comparative criminology	381
13.4	Global convergences: the positivist approach	384
13.5	Global divergences: the interpretivist approach	393
13.6	Conclusion	403

13

Global criminology 1
Comparative criminology

Sacha Darke

KEY ISSUES

After studying this chapter, you should be able to:

- outline the importance of a global approach to the study of crime and justice and appreciate where this sits within the broader debates on calls for the decolonisation of criminology;
- explain and illustrate the distinction between comparative and transnational approaches to global criminological theories;
- identify the differences between positivist and interpretivist comparative approaches to the study of crime and justice at a global level and how these relate to each other;
- apply and critically evaluate positivist and interpretivist approaches to relevant case studies in terms of convergences and divergences.

13.1 Introduction

For much of its history, criminology has had a narrow, localised focus. British criminology, for example, has until quite recently focused mainly on 'crime problems' and the maintenance of 'order' and security within its own borders. It has given very little consideration to how crime and responses to crime in the UK compare to those elsewhere, or to the extent to which events and trends that arise in one country affect or are linked to others (in other words, the connections between the local and the global). But such a narrow focus limits our understanding of crime and our ideas about how it—as well as harmful but not necessarily criminal acts and behaviour, such as green harms (see **Chapter 12**)—might be prevented or addressed. The following statements will give you a sense of the kinds of issues that arise when we begin to consider criminology from a global perspective.

- Homicide rates are five times lower in Japan than in the UK.
- A person is 1,000 times more likely to be shot dead by the police in Rio de Janeiro than in London.
- British prisoners typically receive one-third of the level of health service they would otherwise receive from the National Health Service, whereas Norwegian prisoners have a legal right to the same quality health services as any other citizen—but are twice as likely to take their own life.
- The number of prisoners in Latin America has more than doubled since the year 2000, while the world prison population has increased by only one-quarter, in line with the rise in the world population.
- The availability of heroin on the streets of Blackpool, England, is arguably influenced not only by the actions of the Lancashire Constabulary and the demand of local consumers, but by political stability in Afghanistan and the commercial activities of the Taliban.
- Hundreds of children in Lagos, Nigeria are injured or poisoned breaking apart the tens of thousands of discarded computer screens that arrive from Europe and North America every day.

Until just a generation or two ago, very few criminology postgraduate students would have considered criminological issues from this kind of global perspective, and even fewer undergraduate students, but this is all changing. In the introduction to one of the first books dedicated to exploring matters of global crime and justice (Sheptycki and Wardak, 2005), Hardie-Bick et al. (2005: 1) were able to provocatively but justifiably describe the majority of criminology textbooks as 'rather ethnocentric and quite parochial'. But most criminology degree courses now include a **global criminology** module as part of their offering. It is now widely recognised that considering the 'bigger picture', across and beyond borders, gives us a fuller and arguably more accurate picture of crime and justice in the 21st century, as well as a more nuanced, critical perspective on criminology as a discipline, and the 'knowledge' it produces. Global criminology is different to the other topics we cover in this book in that it is not one that can (or should) be studied in isolation—it is really a perspective on our subject area as a whole, and a way to encourage a reflective and critical view of all criminological issues.

The defining texts in this emerging area of criminology are specialist and suitable either as additional undergraduate reading or for students studying at postgraduate level (in addition to Sheptycki and Wardak (2005), see for example, Aas (2020), Albanese and Reichel (2013), Allum and Gilmour (2015), Barak (2000), Carrington et al. (2018, 2019), Crawford (2011), Edwards and Gill (2004), Nelken (2010), Newburn and Sparks (2004), Pakes (2019), and Reichel (2005)). In the next two chapters we embark on a whistle-stop tour of the many issues associated with global crime and justice that were introduced into the discipline of criminology by these pioneering authors. In this chapter, we introduce the overarching theme and **concept** of globalisation, drawing comparisons between crime and justice in different countries, before moving on to examine some specific issues of crime on a global scale (and how these issues cross borders) in **Chapter 14**. In both chapters, we will reflect on the ways in which our discipline is being challenged and is changing as a result of its increased focus on the global—indeed, these two chapters could in themselves be considered as huge 'New frontier' boxes.

13.2 Globalisation, crime, and justice

Let's begin by discussing a concept that has become important across the social sciences and is the starting point for our discussion of global criminology. You may well have heard the term '**globalisation**' used in all sorts of contexts, but could you give a clear definition of it? In this section we spend some time reflecting on what the concept means in a broader sense, before considering its implications for crime, justice, and criminology.

What is globalisation?

In *Globalization and crime* (2020), Norwegian criminologist Katya Franko Aas cites the political scientist David Held's definition of globalisation as relating to 'the growing interconnectedness of states and societies' (Aas, 2020: 4). She goes on to describe ways in which the peoples of the world increasingly cross paths economically, socially, culturally, and politically. Take, for example, the fact that US and UK corporations like McDonald's, BP, and Apple sell their products, none of which are manufactured or refined in the US or the UK, in practically every country in the world (see **Figure 13.1**), and the fact that international trade is regulated by multinational bodies like the EU, World Bank, and the International Monetary Fund.

On a more personal level, we are all more likely than ever to have friends, family, and acquaintances in other countries, whether they be migrants, work colleagues, or just people we met whilst travelling or connected with through social media. You yourself might be an international student studying in the UK but keeping in close contact with friends and family elsewhere. We spend much of our days absorbed in the **culture**, current fashions, and social events, including criminal events, of other countries. News of an act of terror by an army or rebel group in one part of the world may feed global fear of state or clandestine organised violence within minutes. Politics likewise travels around the globe faster and faster, with politicians in more militarily and economically powerful countries increasingly lending their expertise to or imposing their view of the world on others. Meanwhile, international bodies such as the United Nations, Amnesty International, and Greenpeace play an increasingly important role in naming and shaming governments for breaching internationally accepted **norms** on human rights in the struggle for global justice.

Underlying these trends, Aas (2020) explains, are two major international developments. First, the rapid advance in information technology—the so-called 'information revolution'—and, secondly, the more gradual shift towards an international economy in which industrial and agricultural production are concentrated in the poorer countries of the **Global South**, where land, labour, and raw materials are cheaper, while knowledge and services are produced in the **Global North**, in the service- and consumer-centred free market, **neoliberal** economies of North America and Western Europe. Aas (2020: 14) describes the modern world as a 'global village' in which time and space have become compressed and do not have the same significance as they did previously—take a minute to consider the examples of changes brought about by globalisation that are highlighted in **Table 13.1**.

It is worth briefly noting here that in this chapter and **Chapter 14** we use the terms 'Global South' and 'Global North' to refer to the economically poorer and richer regions in the world, despite the fact that some of the most economically and politically powerful countries (for example, Australia and New Zealand) are situated below the

Figure 13.1 American fast-food corporation McDonald's sells its products in practically every country in the world, such as Moscow in Russia, as a result of globalisation

Source: Sorbis/Shutterstock

Pre-globalisation (c. 50 years ago)	Post-globalisation
A call from the UK to South America cost the equivalent of £2 a minute.	UK and South American residents can communicate instantly online for free (video calls, instant messaging, etc.).
Few news stories were broadcast live locally, let alone in other countries.	News stories are broadcast live and accessible by anyone in the world (on TV, radio, and online).
The UK produced most of its own fuel and most of the agricultural and industrial products consumed by its population.	The UK now gets the majority of its fuel and many of its agricultural and industrial products from other countries, often the Global South.

Table 13.1 Examples of changes brought about by globalisation

equator and many of the poorest (including much of Asia, Africa, Latin America, the Caribbean, and Eastern Europe) are above it. Although these terms are far from perfect, we feel that they are better than 'developed' and 'developing' countries, and certainly preferable to referring to 'first', 'second', and 'third world' countries. The former terms come from the discipline of economics and risk shifting attention away from wider political and cultural analysis, and the latter have rightly fallen out of favour because its method of ranking countries has pejorative connotations.

What does globalisation mean for criminology?

As we noted in **section 13.1**, until recent years very few UK postgraduate criminology students, and even fewer undergraduates, would have been encouraged to consider the kinds of issues we have highlighted so far. They may have been encouraged to study different parts of the UK, or different English-speaking nations, but they were rarely directed to look at other, non-anglophone parts of the world, or at British crime and justice in the light of what happens in Africa, Asia, Latin America, or the Caribbean, or even in other parts of Europe. Criminology classes previously consisted of mainly British lecturers and British students. Most of the texts read were only published in English. The particular experiences of British students from immigrant communities were foregrounded in some of the more radical and **critical criminology** degrees, as were the experiences of colonisation in the (usually British Commonwealth) countries from which their parents or grandparents had emigrated (see **section 10.2** for more detail about colonisation and its impact), but even so, what happens 'there' or 'out there' and what happens 'here' were treated as different and separate areas of inquiry. The main and most obvious development in criminology as a result of globalisation has therefore been the emergence of global criminology as an important and distinct area of criminological study with its own theoretical and methodological frameworks. A more recent development has been the calls for—and increasing attention given to—a different and more inclusive approach that has been termed 'southern criminology'.

The emergence of a global criminology

Aas argues that living in a 'global village' requires a new level of criminological analysis which looks beyond nation states and takes 'the global and transnational as the primary point of reference . . . [for] a sociology beyond societies' (2020: 3, 8). We will see in this chapter and in **Chapter 14** that a growing number of academics share this view and argue that if criminology is to retain its status as a relevant social science in the contemporary age of global politics and social and economic interconnections, it needs to undergo a major shift in both its **empirical** and theoretical focus. A criminology whose starting point is national definitions of crime and justice arguably remains a criminology of the 20th century. Likewise, a criminology that restricts its analysis of the causes of crime and aims of justice to national contexts, as if what happens in one country has limited bearing on another, is inevitably limited and partial.

Research on globalisation, crime, and justice can be divided into two broad areas, and it is these which form the basis for our discussions in this chapter and **Chapter 14**.

1. **Comparative criminology**, which compares *similarities and differences* in crime and justice *between* countries and regions.
2. **Transnational criminology**, which studies **organised, state,** and **corporate** crimes and criminal justice responses to organised, state, and corporate crimes that *cross* national and regional borders.

Comparative and transnational criminology do not necessarily question or interrogate the perceived benefits of globalisation. They arise from the simple idea that as states and societies become more closely connected economically, socially, and politically, they also become more closely connected criminally. These researchers also argue that it is increasingly futile to study developments in commerce, culture, and politics without reference to both the national and international context in which they emerge and operate, and the same applies to incidences and patterns of crime and justice. This has real implications for each of the three established subject areas of the discipline of criminology: rule making, rule breaking, and rule enforcement as originally defined in the now classic pioneering work of Sutherland (1939) or exploring, explaining, and responding to crime, as we put it in this book.

We noted in the introduction that global criminology is not so much a **theory** or topic in its own right as a way of looking at and reframing our discipline, so it follows that the terms comparative and transnational criminology do not refer to any specific theories of crime and justice. Pakes (2010) explains that comparative criminology is simply concerned with *method*. Transnational criminology, on the other hand, is more concerned with *new objects* of study, focusing on incidences of cross-border crime and justice. Pakes (2010: 19) concludes that the 'key point' is that transnational criminology refers to 'the *what* of inquiry, not to the *how*'.

Time for a southern criminology?

Global criminology has been recognised as an important and distinct area of study for two decades now, but it still receives less attention than you might expect in the modern, multinational university environment, and many would argue that we have not yet attained the new global level of criminological analysis advocated by Aas (2020). Most criminology undergraduate courses (and the textbooks which have been developed to support them) still do not explain why it is important for students to think globally, and though they often refer to other places in their discussions of certain topics, this tends to be with the aim of bringing a topic to life by highlighting unusual, 'exotic' cases (from which some argue there is little useful to learn), like the example of the extraordinary violence of the police in Rio de Janeiro (noted in **section 13.1**). In recent years there has been growing awareness of the continued dominance of northern views and approaches within criminology (and academia more widely). Consider the following facts.

- Nine out of every ten published social science articles are written by academics working in North American and West European universities (Aas, 2012), most of which are from just two countries (Carrington et al., 2019)—have a guess which!
- The bibliographies of most criminology textbooks anywhere in the world, North or South, contain mostly Anglo-Saxon surnames.
- Most of the established criminological (and other social science) theories were originally developed in North America and Western Europe, predominantly in the US and the UK, which between them account for less than 10 per cent of the global population (Aas, 2012). Read **What do you think? 13.1** to explore this idea further.

All of this shows us that while criminology may have adopted a more global field of vision, in that it now considers crime and justice issues in other parts of the world and on a global scale, its approach to these issues often remains too narrow. Across the globe, social scientists continue to privilege the knowledge of northern experts. This includes many criminologists in Latin America, a region we focus on in **section 13.5**. Pressure to adopt northern perspectives starts early in a criminologist's career: for example, Latin

WHAT DO YOU THINK? 13.1

Is it time to decolonise criminology?

Think about what you know of criminological theory so far. Looking at **Part 3** which covers explaining crime, and **Part 4** which covers responding to crime, and using the index, research two of the theoretical perspectives listed below, noting down the central principles of the theory and the key authors with which it is associated.

- **classicism**;
- strain theory;
- **situational crime prevention**;
- **abolitionism**;
- labelling;
- feminisms;
- critical race theory.

How many of these explanations are based on crime and justice in English-speaking countries, or on crime and justice in continental Europe? How do you think these theories might differ if they were based on crime and justice in Asia, Africa, Latin America, or the Caribbean? And if they were developed by researchers from these southern regions rather than by researchers based in the Global North?

American public universities usually require PhD students to know at least one other European language besides Portuguese or Spanish, and to publish in 'international'—that is, American or British—peer-reviewed journals. (For broader critique of Latin American reliance on northern criminology, see, for example, Bortoluci and Jansen (2013), Mascareño and Chernilo (2009), Olmo (1999), Rosa (2014), Santos (2012), and Supervielle (2012).) Recently, and particularly since the worldwide 'Black Lives Matter' protests in 2020, there have been renewed calls to challenge such western centrism by 'diversifying' and 'decolonising' the university curriculum and indeed decolonising criminology (Blagg and Anthony, 2019).

In the introduction to this chapter, we noted that there has been growing awareness of the dominance of northern perspectives in the last few decades: that global criminology has come to be recognised as an important and distinct emerging area of criminological study, requiring new theoretical and methodological frameworks. Among the publications we listed in that section, we should introduce the work of Carrington et al. (2016, 2018, 2019) in a little more detail. In these texts, Kerry Carrington and her colleagues have urged social scientists working on matters of southern crime and justice to stop privileging northern perspectives. They note that 'the dominant tendency has been for theory generated in the global North to be imported into [the South]' (Connell, 2015: 51, quoted in Carrington et al., 2016) and have called for a southern criminology that is based on 'ideas and theory rooted in the history and experience of societies of the South' (Carrington et al., 2016: 2). In making this call, Carrington et al. (2016) drew inspiration from the groundbreaking work of Raewyn Connell (2006, 2007, 2014, 2015), who just a decade earlier had turned social science on its head with a wide-ranging critique of the historical dominance of northern thought. Carrington and her colleagues build on Connell's ideas and draw specific attention to the idea that the discipline of criminology is a 'peacetime endeavour' (Carrington et al., 2018: 8). We consider this further in **Controversy and debate 13.1** and explore the issues in depth in **Chapter 14**, where we focus on case studies of transnational corporate crime and state violence.

Carrington et al.'s (2016: 2) assertion that the established frameworks of (northern) criminological methodology are not appropriate for studying the South also raises numerous questions relating to the assumptions made in existing (northern) theories. We will examine a number of these assumptions throughout this chapter (for example, in **section 13.4** where we question the extent to which urban violence is a larger problem in the inner city than in the suburbs, and **section 13.6** where we question the assumption that poor prison conditions result in conflict and violence).

CONTROVERSY AND DEBATE 13.1

Does criminology focus on the right kinds of crime?

The Norwegian academic Katya Franko Aas raised two issues with traditional criminology which she argues can be addressed by taking a global perspective. We explored the first—the idea that there is a 'primacy of western, particularly Anglo-American, criminological perspectives' in the field—in **What do you think? 13.1**. Her second concern is that certain 'types of crime, harm and security threats . . . tend to be overlooked' within traditional criminology (2020: 223).

We have seen that this concern is shared by Carrington et al., who have pointed to criminology as being a 'peacetime endeavour' (2018: 8), arguing that it has been developed during two centuries of mostly uninterrupted (northern) political stability and liberal democracy. This, they emphasise, has resulted in the obscuring 'of the historical role of state violence in nation-building, the expansion of colonialism across the Global South and the neglect of contemporary violent phenomena, like armed conflict, drug wars and ethnic cleansing' (Carrington, 2016: 3). It has also helped to hide **white-collar crime** and corporate crime, including environmental crime (Carrington et al., 2019), all of which are more prevalent in the South.

Criminology is argued to have taken political consensus for granted and focused on social problems that lawmakers and law enforcers considered the most serious (Young, 1988). These have tended to be crimes most often committed by the poor and powerless in society, for example shoplifting, burglary, robbery, and selling illicit drugs in public. In other words, the kinds of problems that are generally called **'street crime'**.

Even if we feel that criminologists are justified in focusing on these kinds of conventional crimes in the European or North American contexts (a conclusion which has been increasingly contested by more radical, critical criminologists such as Young since the 1960s—see **Chapter 18**), can we justify this emphasis in the context of the more politically unstable South? If you were preparing a module on global criminology, which crimes would you focus on?

The irony is that criminology has *always* 'sought to develop general theories of crime causation and control that can be applied far beyond the cultural context and empirical data from which they were first conceived' (Bowling, 2011: 362). This was a key feature of 19th-century European colonisation and northern criminology needs to be at least partly understood as 'an imperialist science for the control of others' (Agozino, 2004: 343). Continued northern bias in the postcolonial production of academic knowledge has two major consequences for the future of global criminology. On the one hand, it prevents us from developing truly general theories of crime and justice. On the other hand, it perpetuates the unquestioned use of theories that were originally developed to explain crime and justice in one context (the Global North) to explain crime and justice in another (the South). As they are tested and revised over time, theories of crime and justice become academic common sense. Few social science theories have been adequately tested beyond the North, yet many are presented as if they can be universally applied.

We return to these epistemological issues of methodological research bias in **section 13.5**, when we introduce the term occidentalism (which can be broadly defined as the denial of, or blindness to, difference). For now, though, let's look more closely at comparative criminology.

13.3 Comparative criminology

Comparative criminology is an area of social science that provides a helpful way of thinking about crime and justice on a global scale but has not yet been widely discussed at an introductory, undergraduate level. It consists of the study of similarities (usually referred to as **sociological positivism**: see **Chapter 17**) and the study of differences (usually referred to as cultural relativism or, our preferred term, **interpretivism**). Before we outline and compare these two approaches, it is important to clarify a few points about comparative criminology more generally, namely:

- its level of analysis;
- its terminology; and
- the types of comparisons it makes.

It is important to remember that comparative criminology's *level of analysis* is global rather than local. It is not interested in identifying and exploring similarities and differences between institutions or social groups *within* a particular country or region; it focuses on *national* similarities and differences; that is, those between countries and regions rather than between areas within a certain country. For example, we will see in **section 13.4** that sentencing is harsher in some countries than in others, and that these differences can be linked, to an extent, to differing levels of crime as well as broader law and order politics, economics, and social culture which lead to distinct penal regimes. Of course, in any country a person's chance of being sent to prison will also depend on the specific court in which they are sentenced, as well as the views of individual judges and the mood they happen to be in on the day, but these are questions for criminologists studying local similarities and differences in sentencing practices across a particular country. They do not concern comparative criminology.

Undergraduate students are often (understandably) confused by the *range of different words* used in comparative criminology to describe the same thing. We have already highlighted that both interpretivism and relativism are often used in this context and have noted that to avoid confusion, we stick to the former in this chapter. It is worth being aware that in place of the terms 'similarity' and 'norm', some comparative criminologists instead refer to commonalities, averages, or convergences; and in place of the term 'difference', they can use peculiarities, variations, divergences, and (for the most extreme cases) exceptions. Our preferred terms in this chapter are *convergences* and *divergences*.

The final important thing to note about comparative criminology is that it *does not necessarily involve comparing two countries or regions to one another*. These kinds of focused comparisons are just one type of comparative research (Pakes, 2019), and they are actually quite rare, even among PhD students or post-doctoral researchers. This is partly because they are the most difficult to conduct, as a good quality study will require the researcher to have knowledge of the political, social, and economic structures and social cultures of both countries. Classic studies of this kind include Downes's (1988) *Contrasts in Tolerance* and Hinton's (2006) *The State on the Streets*.

Downes's (1988) study explored differences in the approach to imprisonment taken by policymakers in England and Wales, where the prison population was rising and prison conditions deteriorating, and the Netherlands, where the opposite was occurring. Downes focused on the concept of 'Dutch tolerance', which he differentiated from the increasingly punitive political climate in England and Wales. Hinton (2006) explored similarities in the reasons for resistance to police reforms since the 1980s in post-dictatorship Argentina and Brazil, both of whose police forces remained notoriously violent and authoritarian.

Hinton provided a number of explanations for the failure of police training programmes to reduce levels of police violence—such as the impact of rising levels of violence during the transition to democracy in the late 20th century—which could be applied to both countries and, she concluded, probably also to other countries in Latin America. Note that both of these authors compared their own native countries (England and Argentina), about which they naturally had a depth of cultural understanding, with a second country in which they had stayed for significant amounts of time both before and during their research. Downes is English and had been working at British universities for two decades by the time *Contrasts in Tolerance* was published. Hinton had only recently left Argentina to work in the UK when she published *The State on the Streets*. Both authors conducted dozens of interviews in both of the two countries they compared and contrasted.

Few undergraduate students will have the time or resources to complete a satisfactory comparative study of crime or justice in two countries or regions, even when one is their own. Nelken (2007: 144) distinguishes between three comparative research strategies: '[being] virtually there, researching there, or living there'. Even a hardworking final year student taking a dissertation module is unlikely to dedicate more than a week or two to data collection, which is not enough to conduct empirical research in the necessary depth—whichever strategy you use, and even if you have lived in both of the countries or regions concerned and speak all of the native languages. The more common types of research in comparative criminology are **meta-analysis**, involving a large number of countries, or case study analysis in which one county or region is focused on in greater depth (Pakes, 2019). In both these types of comparative research, the measure against which a locality is measured is not another country or region but global or regional averages and categories.

Positivist vs interpretivist comparative research

We have already noted that there are two strands of comparative criminology, relating to the epistemologies of **positivism** and interpretivism. (We discuss these schools of thought in their wider senses in **Chapter 4** (see **section 4.2**).) **Positivist comparative criminology** seeks to describe and understand global norms—in the case of criminology, to generalise and develop theories about global and regional patterns of crime and justice—while **interpretivist comparative criminology** seeks to describe and understand *why* certain countries or regions deviate from other places in the world. A hallmark of positivist comparative criminology is its tendency to identify areas of criminal justice policy or practice in different countries or regions that are 'out of line' and should change. Interpretivist comparative criminology, on the other hand, warns researchers and policymakers to be sure they fully understand a country or region's social and political cultures before they promote criminal justice reforms, otherwise they may end up exporting or importing policies that will not work in practice, or may do more harm than good. In the following sections, we talk about the two strands under the headings 'global convergences' and 'global divergences' to help us keep in mind that one refers to a coming together and an effort to align approaches, and one to recognising and understanding differences. **Figure 13.2** shows

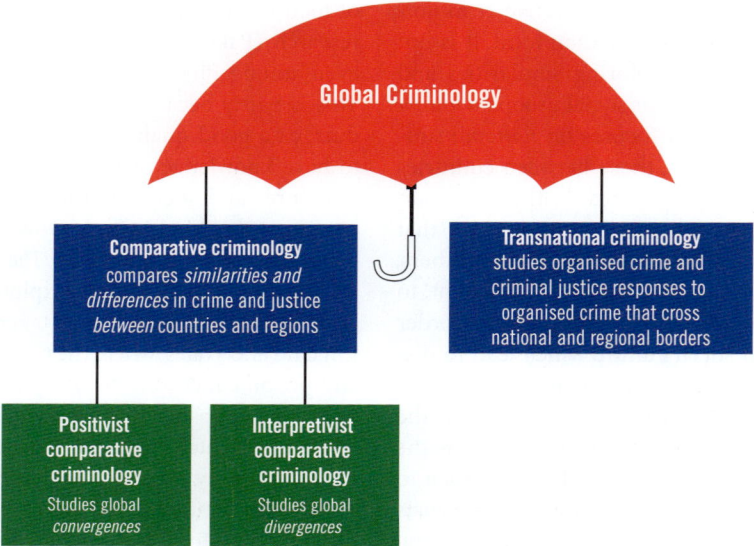

Figure 13.2 The umbrella topic of global criminology contains two main types of research: comparative and transnational criminology'

how these two strands of research fit under the umbrella of global criminology.

Before we go further, it is worth noting that students can sometimes—quite understandably—confuse 'positivism' and 'interpretivism' with the ways these terms are used when criminologists turn to the natural sciences of biology and psychology to study similarities and differences in the behaviour of individuals. The terms are used very differently in this context. A useful way to avoid making this mistake is to always keep in mind that, as we emphasised in **section 13.2** when discussing what globalisation means for criminology, comparative criminology refers specifically to approaches, that is *methods*, of conducting research and on developing 'the ability to see the global in the local and vice versa' (Pakes, 2010: 20). It does *not* refer to specific theories of crime and justice.

Nelken (2010) and Pakes (2019) draw some helpful distinctions between the positivist and interpretivist strands of comparative criminology in their important texts on the discipline, both of which are worth exploring when you have got your bearings (see this chapter's **Further Reading**). Nelken comments:

> Cross-national . . . research is a fundamental way to show whether criminology's claims are more than local truths . . . Trying to understand one place in the light of another allows us to move closer to a holistic picture of how crime and its control are connected . . . The search for universalistic knowledge.
>
> (Nelken, 2010: 14, 19)

> But this kind of 'globalising criminology' can also be less culture-free than it purports to be. . . . By contrast, there are authors who contest this search for universals and suggest the point of comparative research is rather to undermine the pretensions of positivistic criminology . . . [to demonstrate that] the certainties buried in universalising approaches to explanation . . . [often] turn out to be cultural rather than scientific truisms.
>
> (Ibid: 19, 20)

Pakes (2019) further clarifies these points, describing the ideas in a similar way (note both authors' use of 'universal' to describe the positivist approach, and the emphasis on context (or culture)] when explaining the interpretivist standpoint):

> The philosophy underlying [the positivist approach] is that criminal justice can be best understood by focusing on commonalities . . . that, at a certain level, we can find 'universals' in how justice is administered . . . the core set of principles underlying criminal justice . . .
>
> (Pakes: 2019: 16–17)

> The relativist position, in contrast, would be that arrangements should be given meaning in their own context and that we should not assume that what is effective in one context can be lifted into another.
>
> (Ibid: 17)

Positivist and interpretivist comparative researchers tend to lean towards different research methods as a result of their distinct philosophical positions. Positivist comparative analysis often uses meta-analysis since its purpose is to generalise, and generalisation, we have already seen, is the defining feature of positivist comparative analysis. As we will explore further in **section 13.4**, positivist comparative criminology often, but certainly not always, involves quantitative research. It typically seeks to categorise countries and regions, for example as nations whose use of imprisonment may be largely explained by their types of economy (for instance, social democratic as in the case of the Netherlands in the 1980s, or free market neoliberal, as in the case of England today—see **section 19.5** for a further discussion of these terms), as well as to identify rogue or—our preferred term, borrowed from Pakes (2019)—'deviant' cases that fall outside global norms or categories (for instance, the US, whose levels of imprisonment far exceed that of other neoliberal economies).

When a researcher directs their attention towards explaining *why* a certain country or region differs, that is, leaning towards an interpretivist deviant case study analysis, they will usually rely on qualitative research methodologies. Pakes (2019) includes deviant cases as the last of four types of case study analysis, the first three of which involve mostly positivist comparative analysis. (For the sake of simplicity of presentation, we focus on national rather than regional case studies.) The types he lists are:

1. **Representative cases**, in which a country is explored as a typical example of a wider global or regional norm or category (for instance, of a nation whose relatively high levels of domestic violence against women are largely explained by sexism and misogyny—see **Chapter 11**).

2. **Prototypical cases**, in which a country is explored as a leading example (a front-runner) of an emerging global or regional norm or category (for instance, of the trend towards mass incarceration in Latin America—an example we return to later in this chapter in the context of sentencing and imprisonment in Brazil); that is, it is likely to become a representative case in the future.

3. **Archetypical cases**, in which a country is explored as having generated a particular category (for instance, a nation at the forefront of the development of physical security—an example we return to in this chapter in the context of the global trend towards public protection).

WHAT DO YOU THINK? 13.2

Why do we need both positivist and interpretivist comparative research?

Based on what you've read so far, why do you think it's important to conduct both positivist and interpretivist research—in other words, to study both convergences and divergences?

Consider what the potential dangers might be, both in terms of the conclusions that are reached and the resulting effect on policies and practices, if a researcher fails to recognise (a) similarities or (b) differences between countries or regions.

---

4. **Deviant cases**, in which a country is explored as an example of a nation that is unusual in the context of global or regional norms (for instance, of a nation which continues to consider **rehabilitation** the principle aim of imprisonment—an example we return to later in this chapter in the context of Norwegian prisons).

One final point to note about both positivist and interpretivist comparative research is that both must be conducted with reference to another country, global or regional average, or category. Students sometimes think that this does not apply to interpretivist comparative research, but this is a methodological fallacy. It is always necessary to have a reference point against which an observation can be measured, even if only to demonstrate its uniqueness. For example, a criminologist interested in studying why (by global standards) homicide rates are disproportionately low in Japan (an issue raised in **section 13.1**) will need to have a broad understanding of general theories on violence as well as a more in-depth understanding of the regional and locally specific causes of violence in Japan.

It is useful to start any comparative research with (positivist) analysis of convergences, before moving on to

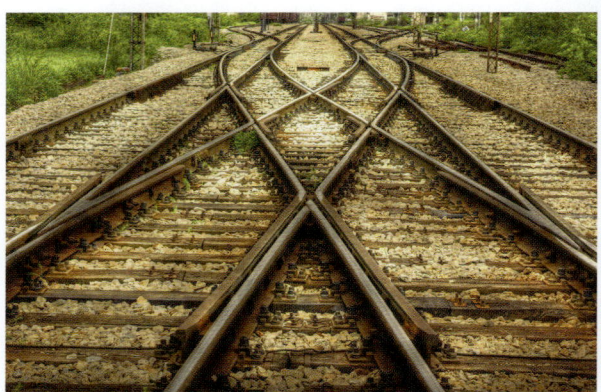

Figure 13.3 It is useful to conduct both positivist and interpretivist comparative criminological research, in other words to explore both 'convergences' and 'divergences'
Source: DrMadra/Shutterstock

(interpretivist) analysis of divergence (**Figure 13.3**). Why is it necessary to do both types of research? We reflect on some of the main reasons at the beginning of **section 13.5** but before you read on, consider this question yourself using the prompts in **What do you think? 13.2**.

13.4 Global convergences: the positivist approach

We have noted that the positivist approach to comparative criminology involves focusing on similarities in crime and justice globally and regionally—on global convergences. More specifically, it explores the means and extent to which crime and justice is converging as a result of globalisation, so as to 'test and validate explanatory theories of crime or social control' (Nelken, 2007: 148). The aim is to understand how much we can generalise from established social scientific theories such as **strain theory** (see **Chapter 17**) and **critical race theory** (see **Chapter 10**), most of which were developed in northern universities and do not necessarily apply equally from one country to another, especially those in the Global South. Only then can a criminologist say with any real degree of confidence that the matters of local crime or justice they are studying are ordinary (representative, prototypical, or archetypical—see Pakes's list in **section 13.3** in the discussion of positivist vs interpretivist comparative research), or whether they are deviant (out of line; unusual and diverging to an unacceptable extent from international standards) and should change.

To critically explore and illustrate global convergences in crime and justice in more detail, we will consider two examples. The first relates to rapid demographic changes, looking at increasing levels of urban violence associated with late 20th-century technological advances and the emergence of the so-called 'global city' (Sassen, 1991). The second explores the move away from more welfare-focused responses to crime and towards more punitive approaches as a result of the increasing influence of political and public demands for retribution and public protection upon legislators, prosecutors, judges, and prison and probation authorities (a theme further explored in a mainly UK context in **Chapter 25** in the discussion of penal populism).

Convergence 1: urban violence

The way in which theories on and responses to urban crime around the world continue to be heavily influenced by theories developed by sociologists at the University of Chicago (the Chicago School, as their department came to be known) in response to the specific circumstances of their city in the 1920s, is an interesting example of a global convergence.

As we will explore further in **Chapter 17** (which focuses on social structural and macro-sociological theories of crime), sociological change became significant for criminology during the early 20th century in the latter stages of the industrial and communication revolutions, by which time the majority of people in North America and Europe, at least Western Europe, lived in urban areas but 90 per cent of the overall world population remained rural. The changes that sociologists at the University of Chicago saw in their city, which had seen its population rise from approximately 300,000 to 2,000,000 in just half a century, led them to develop theories on urban crime that proved popular with sociologists and criminologists in other cities and countries. Their ideas influenced new theories which drew on and developed some of the insights of Chicago School scholars.

The 'Chicago School'—and in particular the work of Clifford Shaw (1922–91) and Henry McKay (1899–1980)—based its urban crime theories on the 'social disorganisation' which it witnessed in inner-city areas. The various migrant and immigrant groups that had moved to the city looking for work tended to settle in these areas initially due to their relatively cheap housing costs, then would move on to greener, richer suburbs once they had established roots and moved up the employment ladder. This meant, first, that inner-city areas were disproportionately populated by young people who had recently been released from the informal social controls exerted by the church, extended family, and so on of smaller, long-established rural communities. It also meant that the cultural make-up of the city was in constant flux as each new migrant group was replaced by others. Inner-city neighbourhoods became melting pots of competing values in which inhabitants were left with conflicting moral choices.

The School's main theory, social disorganisation theory (see **section 17.5**), proved to be the catalyst for numerous criminological theories on urban street crime and the perceived weaknesses in informal community controls. These include aspects of differential association theory and subcultural theory (see **Chapter 17**), as well as more recent control theories associated with the right realist school of criminology, such as broken windows and the existence of an underclass (see **Chapter 20**). Social disorganisation theory also played an indirect role in the development of strain theory at Harvard University in the mid-20th century. As we will see in **Chapter 17**, strain theory focuses on the idea that societal pressure to succeed and the lack of opportunities for people brought up in poor urban areas to do so is what pushes people into crime, whereas social disorganisation and other control theories focus on what holds people *back* from crime. This contradiction was symbolised by the so-called 'American dream', which suggested to people that they were not only expected but *able* to succeed so long as they tried hard enough, and that success was more important than the means by which you achieved it; that is, the ends justified the means (Merton, 1938). Social disorganisation and strain theory broadly agreed that street crime had become a significant social problem within urban communities, in which both offenders and victims were predominantly young, poor men.

The theories that emerged from the Chicago School have been heavily criticised in recent years (see **section 17.5**) but from a comparative criminological perspective we are not interested in the theories themselves so much as the extent to which they need to be modified when applied to countries other than the one in which the original empirical observations were developed. From a comparative criminological perspective, it is notable that the legacy of the Chicago School continues to be felt in social science departments not only in the US but across much of the northern world (Aas, 2020).

As you might have guessed, there are good reasons to question the relevance of northern urban criminological theories like social disorganisation theory and strain theory to the Global South. The socio-economic similarities between North American and European nations (in terms of industrialisation, urbanisation, and immigration) simply do not apply to other regions of the world. Cohen (1988: 195) explains that most established criminological theories and internationally acclaimed crime and justice policies do not take account of socio-economic conditions in Africa, Asia, Latin America, or the Caribbean, yet 'western crime-control models' continue to be exported regardless. Conditions in these regions differed enormously

1950	The world population was 2.5 billion (UN World Population Prospects 2019)—around one-third of today's figure.
	Just 30 per cent of people worldwide lived in urban areas and there were just 76 cities in the world with over one million inhabitants. Of the world's ten largest cities, four were in North America or Europe.
2000	The percentage of Asian (outside Japan), African, Latin American, and Caribbean people living in urban areas had more than doubled by this point.
	Globally, there were approximately 2.9 billion people living in urban areas and 371 cities of over one million.
2007	The urban population of the world overtook the rural population for the first time in human history.
2018	The world population was 7.6 billion, and 4.2 million of this number lived in urban areas (55 per cent).
	The vast majority of cities experienced substantial population growth between 1950 and 2018, but those in Asia, Africa, and Latin America experienced particularly high rates of growth, ranging into the many thousands (in percentage terms).
	Of the world's ten largest cities, none were now in North America or Europe, and only five of the top 50 largest cities were in those regions.
2030	60 per cent of the world population is likely to be urban.
2050	68 per cent of the world population is likely to be urban.

Table 13.2 Changing statistics: how relevant are 20th-century northern, urban criminological theories globally today?
Source: All data from UN World Population Prospects 2019 and UN World Urbanization Prospects 2018

from Europe and North America in the 20th century and continue to differ enormously today—just look at the facts listed in **Table 13.2**.

The key point to absorb about urban crime is that major cities like Lagos, Mumbai, Mexico City, and São Paulo are today not just larger but qualitatively different to major cities in the Global North. These southern cities have not only grown far quicker than northern cities like Chicago did at the turn of the 20th century, they also suffer from far higher levels of absolute as well as relative poverty. In contrast to Europe and North America, African, Asian, Latin American, and Caribbean urbanisation from the mid-20th century has resulted more from a decline in agricultural work in the countryside than the lure of industrial work in the city. While 80 per cent of the world's manual workforce is now located outside Western Europe or North America, most industries are concentrated in South East Asia, especially China, Korea, and Taiwan (Davis, 2006)—how many times have you seen 'made in China' or 'made in Taiwan' on the back or bottom of gadgets compared to 'made in the UK'?

Likewise, there are few points of similarity between, on the one hand, the modern global era of 'urbanization without industrialisation' (ibid: 12) in parts of the Global South and, on the other, the earlier wave of urbanisation in Europe and North America that accompanied the creation of millions of jobs in manufacturing and communications from the late 1700s to the early 1900s. As Darke (2018) notes in a Brazilian context, there is no real equivalent to the American dream in much of the Global South. In other words, there is little social mobility in many southern cities, and few people living in poor, urban areas imagine that they might one day make it into the middle classes. The majority of the so-called 'megacities' of the Global South are not experiencing a second stage in the urbanisation of the global economy that began with the industrial revolution, but rather an 'urbanization of poverty' (Aas, 2020: 54). Four in five of those migrating into the cities find themselves living in makeshift, illegally constructed shanty towns or 'favelas' (see **Figure 13.4**) and often in low-paid work in the informal economy, which by the end of the 20th century provided two-thirds of employment worldwide (Davis, 2006). Urbanisation and 'favelisation' are becoming synonymous (ibid).

Statistics from India powerfully illustrate the same point. During India's economic boom of the 1990s, when the country's GDP rose on average 6 per cent a year, one million new people became dollar millionaires but 56 million people fell into absolute poverty (Davis, 2006). In global business circles, Mumbai is now considered one of the top ten financial centres of the world, but its wealth is concentrated in the upper and middle classes. Nearly one-third of people in Greater Mumbai are defined by the Indian government as living in absolute poverty (defined as living on under $13 a month) (D'Monte, 2011) and six in ten Mumbai residents live in shanty-town slums (Parasuraman, 2007). Two-thirds of employment in the city is in the informal sector; as many as 300,000 residents work as unlicensed street vendors (Sudjic, 2007). Again, this example shows that while the globally connected,

Figure 13.4 Major Global South cities like Rio de Janeiro are not just larger but qualitatively different to cities in the Global North, with little social mobility and most migrants living in shanty towns

Source: Conor Fuller/Unsplash

urban middle classes are becoming richer, urban poverty remains widespread. The global village, Aas (2020) concludes, is a deeply divided one.

We could argue, using these statistics and employing a positivist approach, that the contemporary southern city is experiencing even higher rates of demographic change and economic insecurity than northern cities ever did, and so should—according to social disorganisation and strain theory—be characterised by even more extreme levels of street crime. This conclusion appears to be borne out in official statistics and some of the academic scholarship on urban violence.

- In recent decades, rates of criminal violence have risen across much of the Global South at the same time as they have fallen significantly—by 39 per cent since 2000—in the Global North (Carrington et al., 2019).
- Forty-six of the 50 most violent cities are in the Global South (ibid).
- According to the United Nations (2014), the world intentional homicide rate was 6.2 per 100,000 general population in 2012. Regionally, this figure varied from one to two intentional homicides per 100,000 general population in Western, Southern, and Northern Europe, to between 20 and 30 per 100,000 in the most violent, Southern Africa and South and Central America. Most of the estimated total of 437,000 intentional homicides occurred in urban areas.
- Koonings and Kruijt (2009: 3) describe the levels of criminal violence experienced in many southern cities as akin to 'low-intensity warfare'.

But the picture could be more complex: the authors we have cited in this section, including Koonings and Kruijt, all question whether urbanisation and poverty are related to street crime in the Global South in the same way, or to the same extent, as urban criminologists have demonstrated them to be in the Global North. Three major points stand out in the literature.

1. The average southern country relies far more on the informal controls of local communities than cities in the North (Koonings and Kruijt, 2009).
2. Urban street crime is not so clearly intra-class or intra-age in the South as in the North (Cain, 2000).
3. Southern inner cities have always been equated with gentrification and wealth (Carrington et al., 2019).

Turning to the first point, that southern countries tend to rely more on informal community controls, this is partly because police forces in southern countries are not only less well resourced and less efficient on average; in some countries they are distrusted by the majority of people living in poor urban areas. Residents in poorer communities are also more used to having to turn to their friends and neighbours to make up for shortfalls in some of the most basic of social services that most people in Europe and North America can take for granted, including housing and other welfare benefits. Koonings and Kruijt (2009: 2) emphasise:

> [Our] point of departure . . . is that poverty, exclusion and violence in so-called megacities . . . but more generally in any urban environment, are increasingly intertwined in such a way that conventional distinctions between a formal, legal institutional, peaceful (in short, 'ordered') city and its counterpoint (informal, illegal, non-institutional or 'disordered') more and more fail to have analytical and practical meaning.

The second way in which the Chicago School-type conceptions of links between urbanisation, poverty, and street crime could be argued to be less relevant for the Global South is demonstrated by Cain (2000) in the context of Trinidad and Tobago in the Caribbean. Reflecting on the years she spent working at the University of West Indies in the 1990s, Cain (2000) explores the difficulties she encountered as a British academic making sense of, among other things, relatively similar levels (in comparison to the UK) of offending between youths and adults, as well as **victimisation** between the working and middle classes (again, in contrast to the situation in the UK). Cain came to the conclusion that neither age nor class have the same meaning in the Caribbean as in the UK, and that it was not at all clear to what extent the established social and criminological theories on street crime she had studied as a northern academic were relevant. Cain emphasises that she cannot offer any further explanations as this would require extensive case study research, but warns against the tendency—as we have also done indirectly in this section—to assume that northern theories are universally applicable. It was telling that there were no locally developed theories for her to cite. We return to Cain (2000) in **section 13.5**.

Regarding the final argument against applying Chicago School-type ideas to the Global South, that southern inner cities have always been equated with gentrification and wealth, Carrington et al. (2019: 32) emphasise in their critique of the dominance of northern social science: '[c]riminology has tended to maintain a highly selective focus on violence in the large population centres of the Global North to the exclusion of the . . . global countryside, peripheries and antipodes'. In contrast to the last global wave of urbanisation of the Industrial Revolution which saw migrants initially settle in inner-city areas, today's global poor migrate directly into the suburbs. Seventy-three per cent of Mexico City's and 80 per cent of Mumbai's shanty-town residents live in the outskirts (Davis, 2006). Many families have lived in the same slum areas for generations.

Convergence 2: punitivism and public protection

Our second illustration of global convergence in crime and justice relates to the recent decline of welfare-orientated responses to crime in the northern world, especially in the US and UK.

As we will see when we consider it further in **Chapter 25** (see in particular **Table 25.1**), this 21st-century trend is in stark contrast to the previous era of American and British 'penal modernism' (Garland, 1990: 7) or 'penal welfarism' (Garland, 2001: 3). The welfare-orientated approach was characterised in positivist criminology by the popularity of strain theory which—as we saw earlier in this section and in **Chapter 17**—was concerned with correlations between street crime and socio-economic exclusion; and characterised in criminal justice by the emphasis policymakers and practitioners previously put on '**social crime prevention**' (see **Chapter 20**) and rehabilitating those that had been arrested and prosecuted (see **Chapter 29**). Strain theory, social crime prevention, and rehabilitation were united in the belief that the problem of street crime, seen to have accompanied 19th-century urbanisation, could be resolved through targeted government interventions.

However, official crime rates rose rapidly in both the UK and US in the mid-20th century despite huge reductions in poverty and increased government investment in both social welfare and criminal justice. As a result, '[t]he twin pillars of the modernist project of reason and progress, the use of law in the control and adjudication of human affairs and the intervention of government to engineer a just social order [began to] totter under the weight of their own inconsistencies' (Young, 1998: 262). By the 1970s, high crime rates had come to be seen by criminal justice officials and practitioners as 'a normal social fact' (Garland, 1996: 446) that was out of the control of government. Strain theory fell into political disuse, replaced by theories that questioned the link between poverty and crime, treating them as two symptoms of a wider problem of laziness and welfare dependency which affected many in the poorest sections of society. This culturally disordered, socially dysfunctional 'underclass' was 'viewed as permanently excluded from social mobility and economic integration . . . a self-perpetuating and **pathological** segment of society that is not integratable into the larger whole, even as a reserve labor pool' (Feeley and Simon, 1992: 467).

In recent decades, penal welfare interventions have slowly but surely made way for less ambitious crime control strategies that are intended to satisfy public demands for **punishment** and to keep crime within tolerable limits through managing it, rather than addressing the more difficult, longer term task of changing offenders and potential

Figure 13.5 Over recent decades, northern countries have replaced welfare-focused responses to crime with harsher, more short-term approaches which aim to satisfy the public's demands and keep crime levels manageable rather than to change offenders

Source: Design Pics/Alamy Stock Photo

offenders (see **Figure 13.5**). (For an early, comprehensive outline of such trends, see Cohen, 1985.) According to Garland (2001), these two competing ideas—the welfarist approach aligns with expert analysis of the most efficient method of crime control; the more punitive approach aligns with popular ideas of justice, including the 'common sense' view that the experience of punishment deters offenders from committing further crime—have been the cause of much contradiction in criminal justice in the US and UK today, observing:

> The emergent outcome is a series of policies that appear deeply conflicted, even schizoid, in their relation to one another. On the one hand, there has been an attempt to face up to the predicament and develop pragmatic new strategies that are adapted to it: through institutional reforms aimed at overcoming the limits of the criminal justice state, or else through accommodations that recognise these limitations and work within them. But alongside these *adaptations* to the reality principle, there is a recurring attempt to evade its terms altogether . . . This politicized reaction takes two recurring forms. Either it wilfully *denies* the predicament and reasserts the old myth of the sovereign state and its plenary power to punish. Or else it abandons reasoned, instrumental action and retreats into an *expressive* mode that we might, continuing the psychoanalytical metaphor, describe as *acting out*—a mode that is concerned not so much with controlling crime as with expressing the anger and outrage that crime provokes.

(Garland, 2001: 110)

The contrast Garland draws between the demands of criminal justice workers for measurable solutions and the emotive demands of the public for 'expressive justice' reflects the perspectives of other British and American criminologists working within the **Weberian** sociological tradition (see **Chapter 3**). Feeley and Simon (1992: 463) came to a similar conclusion in one of the most cited criminology papers in recent decades, suggesting that an elite-driven, risk-based, short-term efficiency-orientated 'new penology' had emerged, with an underlying purpose to, 'manag[e] a permanently dangerous population while maintaining the system at a minimum cost'. Weber insisted that everyday institutional decision-making, in this case criminal justice decision-making, was ultimately shaped by a negative tendency towards bureaucratic, depersonalised, and inflexible rules serving the interests of the institution rather than the society it is meant to serve. According to this line of analysis, both British and American criminal justice policymakers and practitioners are slowly but surely coming to terms—rightly or wrongly—with the fact that the 'old penology' of rehabilitation never achieved its stated goals.

Criminologists working within the **Marxist sociological** tradition, on the other hand, question the extent to which everyday institutional decision-making is shielded from political **ideology** (again, see **Chapter 18**). Pratt et al. (2005), for example, treat the trends towards crime management and expressive justice as complementing each other, as two aspects of a 'new punitivism' that has accompanied the move beyond industrial production in northern economies. According to this more critical line of analysis, rehabilitation is less important when there are no suitable areas of work for which to prepare offenders. Young explains: 'the universally orderly population of the modernist period was necessary only with Fordist production and full employment . . . The underclass of today are not needed, their labour unnecessary, the inculcation of punctuality and discipline irrelevant' (Young, 1998: 283–4).

The same line of analysis is also used to explain the increasing resort to **penal populism** (see **Chapter 25**). The division between rich and poor has increased steadily over the past half century, worldwide but especially in neoliberal, free market countries like the UK and US. Economic insecurity is a recipe for anger and frustration. Again, this point is well explained by Young:

> [I]nsecurities in economic position . . . engender feelings of resentment . . . an insistence on clear uncompromised lines of demarcation between correct and incorrect behaviour, an increased intolerance of deviance, a disproportionate response to rule-breaking, an easy resort to punitiveness (verging on the vindictive).

(Young, 2007: 21)

Whether we see them as opposing or complementary, the important point for the purposes of our discussion is that these two contemporary control strategies coexist not only in the US and UK but, as we have already suggested,

Figure 13.6 Crime control strategies throughout the Global North are characterised by a movement away from social crime prevention measures towards situational ones, such as physical and electronic security
Source: Steve Skjold/Alamy Stock Photo

across much of the northern, especially English-speaking northern world—their widespread use is a clear global convergence. One example is the way that crime prevention policies in these countries are characterised by a move away from social measures towards situational ones such as physical and electronic security (see **Figure 13.6**), and the use of algorithms to monitor online activities. At the same time, however, criminal justice measures are also used, for example 'zero tolerance' policing crackdowns on low-level crimes like harassment and begging.

Situational crime prevention essentially tries to 'design out crime' (Hough et al., 1980) through protecting potential victims and blocking or keeping potential offenders under surveillance (see **Chapter 26**). This approach to crime, in particular electronic surveillance, is now the norm in much of Western Europe although some countries, including the Netherlands, France, Italy, and Sweden, continue to place equal emphasis on social crime prevention measures such as family and health interventions (Crawford, 2011). In contrast, electronic security has not taken off to the same degree in the Global South (ibid)—though with some major exceptions, including China and Singapore—but Brazil and South Africa are world leaders in physical security technologies.

In terms of punishment, the move beyond penal welfarism in the northern world is characterised by convergences that are particularly evident in neoliberal countries like the US and England and Wales (Cavadino and Dignan, 2006) but also increasingly common across much of Western and post-Soviet Europe (Ruggiero and Ryan, 2013).

- **Harsh penal policies**, including longer prison sentences and being quicker to resort to incarceration. During the 1990s, the prison population in England and Wales rose more than 50 per cent, despite no corresponding increase in violent crime, and the US prison population doubled, despite a halving of violent crime. This pattern has continued in England and Wales, with the prison population continuing to rise despite a substantial reduction in recorded crime, including violent crime—33 per cent of people convicted for indictable offences received prison sentences in 2018 (Ministry of Justice, 2019) compared with only 13 per cent in 1975 (Cavadino et al., 2013). There were actually similarly high levels of imprisonment during the height of rehabilitation in the 1950s (Davies, 2015), but now prison sentences are not only more frequently used but longer: only 18 per cent of all prison sentences imposed in 1958 were for 12 months or more (ibid); in 2018, the majority of prison sentences were for 12 months or more (Ministry of Justice, 2019).

- **Increasing use of pre-trial detention.** England and Wales has a relatively better record on pre-trial and pre-sentence detention than other parts of the Global North—the Institute of Criminal Policy Research's World Prison Brief online database shows that 14 per cent of prisoners in England and Wales were held on remand in June 2020 (World Prison Brief, 'World Prison Brief data')—but it is still much quicker to resort to remanding people to await trial in custody than it was half a century ago. According to the most recent available figures, 23 per cent of prisoners in the US are held on remand, 34 per cent of prisoners in France, 33 per cent of prisoners in Italy, 21 per cent of prisoners in the Russian Federation, 34 per cent of prisoners in Northern Ireland, and 27 per cent of prisoners in Scotland (ibid).

- **Prisons becoming increasingly full**. England and Wales has one of the poorer records in the Global North on prison overcrowding, although—at 105 per cent occupancy level in September 2020—its prisons are currently less crowded than usual. Twelve European prison systems—in addition to England and Wales—are currently operating over official capacity: Turkey, Belgium, Greece, Hungary, Romania, Cyprus, Italy, Serbia, Bosnia and Herzegovina, Sweden, and Finland (ibid).

For a critical analysis which questions whether UK and other European prisons were in fact ever intended as institutions of rehabilitation, see Mathiesen (1990) and **Figure 13.7**.

To what extent do these convergences exist worldwide? If we consider the use of harsh penal policies (more and longer prison sentences), in the first decade of the 21st century two-thirds of countries saw an increase in their prison populations (Walmsley, 2011), despite relatively minor increases in absolute numbers of homicides (Malby, 2010) and other more serious crimes (Heiskanen, 2010). The worldwide prison population rose from eight million at the end of the 20th century (Walmsley, 1999) to almost 11 million in 2017 (Walmsley, 2018). The overall increase in the worldwide prison population can be

Figure 13.7 The move beyond penal welfarism and towards more punitive responses to crime in many northern countries is an example of a global convergence

Source: Simon Price/Alamy Stock Photo

explained by the rise in the general world population (see **Table 13.2**). The worldwide incarceration rate has remained stable (for the past two decades it has stayed at approximately 145 per 100,000 members of the general population (Walmsley, 2018)). As prison populations have not increased in every country, it is clear that 21st-century penal punitivism is not a global phenomenon, but this does not necessarily mean that it is restricted to the neoliberal nations of the Global North. It is possible that penal punitivism was already a common feature in much of the world, and that parts of the Global North are now catching up. After all, few countries in the Global South ever reached the levels of industrial production (even less so welfare state provision) that came to define northern economies during the 20th century. Since the beginning of the Industrial Revolution, the majority of the world has always been free market. To return to Young's (1998) critical analysis of American and British justice, rehabilitation—and accompanying efforts to minimise the use of imprisonment—was only a major feature of northern penal systems during a specific period of full employment that accompanied Fordist mass-production.

The other two indicators of penal punitivism—pre-trial detention and prison overcrowding—also appear to be common features of prison systems worldwide. According to Prison Reform International (2018), over half of the world's prison systems are operating above official capacity, much of which was calculated allocating an amount of space per prisoner that falls short of the international human rights minimum standard of four square metres (see Coyle et al., 2016).

Before you read on to learn more about the interpretivist approach to comparative research, complete **What do you think? 13.3** to explore some convergences and divergences for yourself, and read **Conversations 13.1** to learn more about two people's experiences of being imprisoned

WHAT DO YOU THINK? 13.3

Convergences and divergences in prisons and punishment

While the worldwide incarceration rate has stabilised in the 21st century, there continue to be major divergences both between and within different regions, as we have already noted in the European context. We outline some of these in **section 13.5**, but before you read on, take a moment to explore them for yourself using the World Prison Brief: http://prisonstudies.org/world-prison-brief-data.

Choose a country from each geographical region listed in the World Prison Brief (Africa, Asia, Caribbean, Central America, Europe, Middle East, North America, Oceania, and South America), then follow these steps:

1. Compare each country's prison populations rates in 2000 with the most recent recorded figures. Take notes on levels of prison overcrowding, and of the percentage of the prison population that has not yet been tried or sentenced.

2. Compare these figures with World Bank data on the countries' GINI index (https://data.worldbank.org/indicator/SI.POV.GINI). (The GINI index is used as a measure of relative poverty, which most economists and social scientists agree is higher in free market, neoliberal economies.) Note down any correlations you find between higher levels of inequality, as measured by the GINI index, and higher levels of imprisonment, pre-trial detention, and prison overcrowding.

3. Consider the results of your comparisons. Does anything surprise you about them? Are there any convergences or divergences you expected to see and didn't, and vice versa? You might wish to compare your results with those of Downes and Hansen (2006), who completed a similar exercise—see https://www.crimeandjustice.org.uk/publications/welfare-and-punishment-relationship-between-welfare-spending-and-imprisonment.

Did anything surprise you about these results? Were there any convergences or divergences you expected to see and didn't, and vice versa?

CONVERSATIONS 13.1

Serving a prison sentence in Italy
with **Marisa Merico** and **Dr Elton Kalica**

Sacha Darke (SD): Can I start off by asking you to summarise your journeys through the Italian prison system?

Dr Elton Kalica (EK): I moved from Albania to Milan in 1995. I was arrested in 1997 and accused of being involved in organised crime. I spent the next 14 years in high security prisons. I was released in 2011. I was the only Albanian prisoner. At the time, high security prisons were overcrowded; we slept three per individual cell, and others slept in the corridors.* They kept moving foreign prisoners like me to make space for locals. I eventually moved away from the Milan region to Padua prison, which had much better conditions. After much struggle, I managed to register for a degree at the University of Padua. They hadn't allowed foreign prisoners to study there before.**

Marisa Merico (MM): I was arrested in 1994 in the UK for offences committed in Italy. My father was a mafia boss. I spent three years in high security at Durham prison, and when I finished my sentence, I was re-arrested and extradited to Italy to face more charges. I ended up in a high security women's unit in Milan.

In some ways, the regime in Milan was harder than it had been in the UK. There was no work, no education, no gym, no washing machines, and only weekly phone calls, which the officials listened to. But we got four hours a day in the exercise yard, unlike in the UK where you only get one hour, weather permitting. And in the evening we could cook, eat, and drink wine in each others' cells. In Italy they turned a blind eye to drinking, whereas in the UK they turn a blind eye to drugs.

SD: How do you think your experiences as foreign prisoners differed to those of Italian prisoners?

MM: I probably had a different experience due to my family status, but the other foreigners I met had to work twice as hard as the Italians to build up good relations with officers. It was worse for the girls from poor countries like Nigeria and Colombia than those from richer countries like the UK and America.

EK: I've mentioned the problems I had with registering for university because previously, only Italian prisoners had been given this privilege. Another difference between the experiences of foreign and Italian prisoners is the food. Like in women's prison, men also cook together in the evenings, but they rely on their family to bring in food. Foreigners have to eat prison food. I agree with Marisa that foreigners from richer countries get treated better. In my experience, Albanians are treated particularly badly.

MM: Elton's right about Italians getting food from their families: families take in weekly parcels of food and clothes. Prisoners cook and heat up this homemade food on camping stoves.

EK: Another problem for me, and for some of the other foreign prisoners, was language. My parents don't speak Italian so I needed to speak to them in Albanian on the phone as there were no Albanian translators, but the prison staff cut me off if I spoke my own language.

SD: So, what are the best and worst things about Italian prisons?

MM: The best things were the family parcels and the four hours of fresh air a day. The worst were the lack of formal activities, which made you feel brain-dead, and the healthcare—it was terrible.

EE: For me, the best things were being able to study and cooking good food together. The visits were the worst thing. We only had an hour a week, behind a glass screen. These were removed in 2012, but have come back during the pandemic.

SD: You've both emphasised the awful conditions you experienced on the one hand, but the enjoyable collective activity of cooking in the evening on the other. How do these characteristics of Italian prisons relate to Italian culture?

MM: Italians are family orientated.

EE: Italians stereotype, and they spend as little on prisoners as possible. Cooking pasta is a fundamental right! But everything else is seen as a privilege.

Marisa Merico (pictured left), 2020 BA Criminology graduate, former prisoner in the UK and Italy and author of Mafia Princess *(2010)*

Dr Elton Kalica (pictured right), Lecturer/researcher in critical criminology, University of Padua, Italy, former prisoner in Italy and author of La Pena di Morte Viva *(2019)*

* The Italian prison system was notoriously overcrowded in the 1990s and 2000s (see Gonnella, 2013). In 2013, the European Court of Human Rights ruled that the levels of overcrowding amounted to inhuman and degrading treatment and violated Art. 3 of the European Convention on Human Rights. Conditions have somewhat improved since: in 2018, Sacha visited one of the prisons in Milan in which Elton Kalica served time and found that prisoners on the high-security unit are now held one per cell.

** Elton went on to complete a PhD at the University of Padua in 2018.

in both Italy and the UK. Based on what Dr Kalica and Marisa Merico say, and the knowledge you have gained in your studies so far about prisons in different countries, what potential convergences and divergences can you identify between countries and regions? To what extent do you think Merico's different experiences of imprisonment in England and Italy were due to divergences between English and Italian social culture?

13.5 Global divergences: the interpretivist approach

As we have seen, interpretivist comparative criminology focuses on recognising and trying to understand differences between countries or regions. The flip-side to positivist comparative criminology, it is concerned with developing local rather than universal theories on crime and justice, and local understanding of the political context in which criminal justice systems operate. Regarding the latter, the interpretivist approach requires the researcher to study how a particular nation's institutions tend to operate (how things get done), as well as how criminal justice policies imported from abroad are reinterpreted and reshaped to suit local practices by officials and practitioners on the ground. Jefferson (2012: 114) explains that 'only by getting to grips with the peculiarities and particularities of different prison institutions can we get to grips with how best to engage in transforming them'.

We emphasised in the conclusion to **section 13.3** that it is useful to start any comparative research with (positivist) analysis of convergences, before moving on to (interpretivist) analysis of divergence. In **What do you think? 13.2** we encouraged you to consider why it is necessary to use both approaches, and in the first part of this section we reflect on the reasons. We will then consider two examples of divergence, the first focusing on punishment in the Nordic region of Northern Europe, in particular Norway, and the second looking at policing and punishment in Latin America, more specifically Brazil.

Why conduct both positivist and interpretivist comparative research?

By this point in the chapter you have probably begun to appreciate that convergences and divergences often appear in the same context and can be hard to untangle and categorise. Most likely you found as many anomalies (divergences) as correlations during the research on prison populations and prison conditions you completed for **What do you think? 13.3**. If you focused on Norway, for example, you will have noted that it has an extraordinarily low number of juvenile prisoners, both in comparison to jurisdictions in free market, neoliberal countries like England and Wales and the US, but also in comparison to other more socially equal, social democratic countries in continental Europe like France and Germany. If we dig a little deeper and compare Norway to its immediate Nordic neighbours, we can see that Sweden, Finland, and Denmark all have few juvenile prisoners too. We can draw two conclusions: first, that there are convergences in youth justice policies and practices within the Nordic region and, secondly, that youth justice in the Nordic region diverges from youth justice in the remainder of Europe, which is, on the whole, more punitive. Continuing the Norway example, a researcher might initially be shocked to find that foreigners make up almost one-third of the Norwegian prison population, but on further investigation they would realise that although northern social democratic countries tend to be more inclusionary than neoliberal countries when it comes to their native populations, they are arguably more exclusionary when it comes to those seen as outsiders (Lacey, 2008; Ugelvik and Damsa, 2018).

The main reason, then, for conducting positivist and interpretivist research is because using both approaches helps us to untangle, categorise, and explain apparent convergences and divergences in crime and justice, assessing them in relation to and separating them from global and regional norms and averages. Using both approaches also helps to counteract the potential issues associated with both approaches (in their more extreme forms); in other words, of either overestimating or denying differences or similarities. Let's briefly consider these potential issues.

Problems with overemphasising similarities

Researchers need to conduct interpretivist as well as positivist research because, as Newburn and Sparks (2004: 11, in Aas, 2020: 216) put it, '[w]e cannot and should not take for granted that surface similarities necessarily imply deeper convergences'. Unless they are conducting a meta-analysis of numerous countries, at some point a good comparative researcher will switch their lens of inquiry from universal, social scientific concepts and theories such as neoliberalism and social democracy to the specificities of the local, whether undertaking a focused comparison or a representative, prototypical, archetypical, or deviant case study. The various countries and regions of the world may have come closer together in the modern era of globalisation (see **section 13.2**), but major cultural divergencies obviously remain. Aas explains:

> The point here is that what may at first glance appear as globalization of penal policies needs to be contextualized... The ethnographic [see **Chapter 5**] study of culture and cultural variation therefore gains a particular importance as an antidote to the abstract nature of many theoretical claims about globalization and its impacts... The lived experience of globalization.
>
> (2020: 217)

In other words, to coin a well-known phrase, a square (empirical) peg does not fit into a round (theoretical) hole.

As we have seen, in its quest for universal theories rather than an understanding of the lived experiences of globalisation, positivist comparative research sometimes stands accused of veering towards **ethnocentrism** or—our preferred term, following Cain (2000)—occidentalism— that is, assuming other countries or regions are like our own. Such assumptions are not only often misplaced but can also be potentially dangerous. They can make us blind to indigenous, cultural differences and may result in us exporting crime and justice policies to another country or region where they will simply not 'work' and may even do more harm than good. This is where interpretivist research, focusing on differences, comes in and becomes really important. 'In order to prepare the ground for effective strategic interventions,' Ruggiero and Ryan (2013: 5) warn, 'penal systems need to be first and foremost interrogated in their own terms.'

The occidentalist threat is even more striking when we consider the cultural reference points against which crime and justice are measured. Whose reference points are these? In **section 13.2** we noted that the discipline of criminology is—or at least was until quite recently— dominated by North American and West European thought. To return to the 'square peg, round hole' expression, the square peg of the local realities of crime and justice in the Global South does always not fit into the round hole of northern criminological theory, most of which— as we saw in the discussion of urban crime in **section 13.4**—was developed from observations of northern, and in particular American and British crime and justice. In the same section, we looked at Cain's (2000) examples of youth and working class crime in Trinidad and Tobago. Cain went on to question social scientific understanding of gender, race, and police–community relations in the country and the Caribbean more widely. Regarding gender and race relations, Cain found feminist activists to be more explicitly concerned with racism alongside **patriarchy** than she was accustomed to in the UK, and more likely to value the contribution of men to the feminist movement (see **Figure 13.8**). Regarding police–community relations, she similarly encountered little resistance

Figure 13.8 The fact that women in Trinidad and Tobago are, it has been claimed, more likely to value the contribution of men to the feminist movement than women in the UK is an important difference between the countries' social realities
Source: © Maria Nunes 2018

to police involvement in neighbourhood watch groups. Her findings suggest that we should not assume too much similarity between this country and the UK.

Problems with overemphasising differences

The fact that the established theories which currently make up the discipline of criminology are sometimes guilty of ethnocentricity and culturally insensitivity does not mean that a comparative researcher should instead start with the assumption that they have no universal application and should never be exported to the Global South. Nor does it mean that criminologists and criminal justice policymakers working in the Global South who turn to northern theories as their starting point should necessarily be criticised if the theories they put into practice turn out not to be a good fit for the local circumstances. As we have suggested, there are also problems associated with giving too much emphasis to difference and failing to acknowledge similarities.

Despite his critique of the transfer of 'western crime-control models' (introduced in the discussion of urban crime in **section 13.4**), Cohen (1988: 195) also warns against moving too quickly towards such a radical relativist (remember that 'relativist' is sometimes used in place of 'interpretivist') position: '[a]t their worst, [relativist] assumptions can lead to ... native intellectuals being urged to take up a caricatured version of local tradition, and what is more, local traditions should not be supported'. Cohen gives by way of example, 'trial by gossip, the stoning of adulterers, and the mutilation of thieves' (ibid). These examples go against two of the oldest and most established international human rights principles relating to the rule of law, namely the

presumption of innocence in criminal proceedings, and the idea that we should impose no more punishment than is necessary to make amends for the harm caused, or to prevent similar crimes from reoccurring. As far as we are aware, there is not a country in the world where (outside the most fundamentally conservative or religious circles) the rights to a fair trial and proportional punishment are not considered universal. Precise definitions of what is fair and what is proportional vary, but the underlying human rights principle that criminal punishment is only justifiable as a 'necessary evil' remains a widely accepted value.

At their most relativist, then, interpretivist approaches are criticised for the tendency of leaning towards orientalism, a term originally defined according to Cain (2000: 238), borrowing from the seminal work of Said (1978), as 'the discursive constitution of an often romanticized but also wayward and unknowing "other" which, because of these besetting albeit (to liberals) endearing characteristics, requires the guidance and advice of the "us" to find and/or accept its proper place in the world'. Put simply, while criminologists should always be sensitive to different cultures, they need to be just as careful not to deny similarities when taking an interpretivist stance as those taking a positivist stance must take care that they do not become insensitive to differences. Otherwise, they may find themselves supporting non-intervention by the global community in matters of crime and justice deemed exceptional to a particular locality, however predatory, punitive, or exclusionary they happen to be.

An important related point about the interpretivist quest for cultural sensitivity is that it can result in difference instead being idealised. This can lead to oppressive or context-specific practices being imported from particular areas to other parts of the world, without proper consideration of the complex local factors that have shaped them. Cain (2000: 239) states: 'Today . . . it is the West that suffers most from its own orientalising tendencies.' She gives the example of informal or **restorative justice**, a practice that sees an offender tried and sentenced by their community and victim rather than professional judges (which we consider in depth in **Chapter 30**). This practice has been taken up with enthusiasm across much of the northern world as an alternative to criminal prosecution since it was first promoted in criminology by Christie (1977) in a comparative analysis of community justice in Tanzania, East Africa, where two-thirds of the population live in rural areas, with criminal justice in predominantly urban Scandinavia. Christie (1977) gave the example of a dispute in a small Tanzanian village in which a man demanded the return of money and jewellery he had given to a woman during their failed engagement. He claimed that the involvement of the former lovers' relatives and village community justice made the judgement fairer, and recommended that Scandinavian courts also included 'more personalised meeting between offender and victim' (Christie, 1977: 9). However, Christie's (1977) argument relied on the view that offenders and victims have equal opportunity to present their cases and decide on the outcome, for which he gave no evidence. Cain dismisses this assumption as 'romantic nonsense (let alone bad sociology)' (2000: 241), especially in the case of domestic disputes, where 'weaker parties (women in divorce proceedings and domestic violence cases, children and women in victim–offender mediation sessions) tend to lose out' (ibid: 240). Indeed, a common complaint made by victims of domestic violence in the UK is that authorities should resort *more* rather than less quickly to legal action. Non-intervention can leave them exposed to the very inequalities of power within their family and wider community that led to their victimisation in the first place.

The fact that penal policies and crime and crime phenomena within a particular region or country are always shaped by a specific mix of local, global, and regional social and institutional cultures is evident from the key roles played by certain individuals and groups. Consider, for example:

- the role played from the 1970s by collaborative academic–prisoner organisations in countering punitive political discourses in Sweden (Hofer and Tham, 2013) and Norway (Mathiesen, 2015);
- the murder of the controversial film-maker Theo van Gogh by a Dutch–Moroccan Muslim in 2004, which triggered an already emerging **moral panic** about Islam and immigration (Boone and Swaaningen, 2013);
- the progressive political climates in Russia (Piacentini, 2013) and Poland (Platek, 2013) that temporarily followed the collapse of the Soviet Union.

Just as Newburn and Sparks (2004) suggest that surface similarities do not necessarily imply deeper convergences, in the absence of focused comparative research on two or more countries (like that completed by Downes (1988)—see **section 13.3**), it is difficult to conclude with any real certainty that surface differences necessarily imply deeper divergences.

Divergence 1: Nordic and Norwegian justice

Most research on Nordic and Norwegian justice takes as its starting point the observation that Nordic justice is, on the whole, less punitive and more humane than other regions, including the remainder of Europe, and that this requires local investigation (see, for example, Lauritsen (2012) on Greenland, Pakes (2020) and Pakes and Gunnlaugsson (2018) on Iceland, and Ugelvik and Dullum (2012) on Norway, Sweden, Finland, and Denmark). In 2008, New Zealand criminologist John Pratt (2008a, 2008b) took the same starting point, publishing award-winning articles on what he described as 'Scandinavian' or 'Nordic exceptionalism', suggesting that the countries' relatively low levels of imprisonment and humane prison conditions (see **Figure 13.9**) are largely explained by the region's peculiar economy (its continued prosperity over most of the past century, unlike most of the rest of the Global North), geography (being sparsely populated and made up of relatively small towns and communities, where people are more likely to know those who have offended against them), and history (being northern countries that, unusually, were not major colonial powers, and until quite recently had little immigration). Most other criminologists who have studied the Nordic region from a distance, such as Cavadino and Dignan (2006) and Lacey (2008), also describe its justice systems as notably progressive, at least in comparison to other parts of Europe and especially England, but opinion among Nordic criminologists is more divided (see **Conversations 13.2**).

A collection of responses to Pratt's Nordic exceptionalism thesis was published in Ugelvik and Dullum (2012). In their introduction to the volume, Ugelvik and Dullum pose the question of whether both Nordic and foreign prison researchers are guilty of an orientalist, 'xenocentric' tendency to assume that the grass is always greener elsewhere. We hear directly from Dr Ugelvik in **Conversations 13.2** (and you might want to compare Dr Ugelvik's comments regarding the treatment of foreign nationals to Dr Kalica and Marisa Merico's comments on this topic in relation to Italian prisons). Perhaps the strongest critique of the Nordic exceptionalism thesis comes from Norwegian sociologist Thomas Mathiesen, who questions whether a non-native-speaking criminologist visiting from abroad is ever likely to gain more than a partial picture of the country's practices, culture, and crime or justice responses (Mathiesen, 2012). Mathiesen accuses Pratt of failing to mention or being unaware of the more negative aspects of Norwegian imprisonment, for instance:

- one in four prisoners is held on remand and one in three prisoners is a foreign national (as we have already noted);
- Norwegian judges take a particularly punitive line to sentencing for drug-related crimes;
- Norwegian prisons make disproportionally high use of solitary confinement; and
- Norwegian prisoners suffer disproportionally high levels of self-inflicted death.

Roddy Nilsson questions Pratt's knowledge of the Swedish prison system on similar grounds, going so far as to describe his findings as 'partly built upon speculative reasoning and anecdotal evidence' (Nilsson, 2012: 94). In his response to this criticism, written with Swedish criminologist Anna Eriksson, Pratt (Pratt and Eriksson, 2012) acknowledges that his research was limited to the extent that it was based wholly on existing literature published in English and on half-day visits to 16 prisons, during which he was always accompanied by a senior prison official. Such a research schedule, Pratt and Eriksson suggest, is better described as 'penal tourism' (ibid: 236) than as participatory or ethnographic, the latter two types being hallmarks of interpretivist research. Still, they insist Pratt's original findings are supported by other research so still indicate that while Nordic prison conditions are by no means perfect, on the whole they remain exceptionally humane (see also Pratt and Eriksson, 2013).

Divergence 2: Latin American and Brazilian justice

In **section 13.4** in the discussion of urban crime, we noted that alongside Southern Africa, the Latin American region is the most violent on the planet. We consider the region's diverging *levels* of crime in more depth in **Chapter 14**, as we analyse the international drugs trade, exploring the cocaine trail from the Andes mountains in South America northwards towards the US and Canada via Mexico,

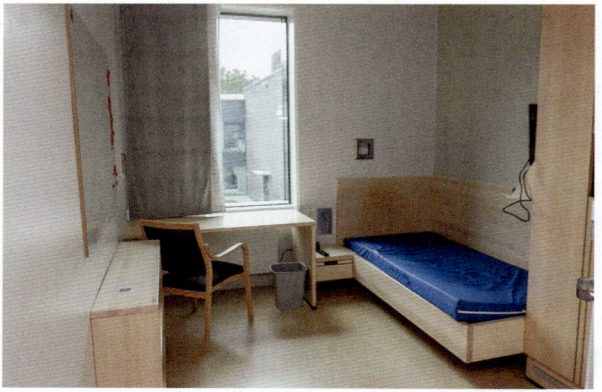

Figure 13.9 A prisoner's student-esque bedroom at Halden prison supports the idea that the Norwegian justice system is notably progressive. But is this interpretation overly simplistic?

Source: Halden Prison. Reproduced with permission

CONVERSATIONS 13.2

Interrogating Nordic exceptionalism
with **Dr Thomas Ugelvik**

Sacha Darke (SD): What, in your view, are the main characteristics of sentencing and prisons in Norway and the wider Nordic region?

Dr Thomas Ugelvik (TU): First of all I would like to say that the Nordic region is an interesting concept, but too often the differences between the Nordic countries are glossed over. Finland is historically closer to Russia in some ways. The three Scandinavian countries (Norway, Sweden and Denmark) are more closely aligned, but over the past 10 to 15 years they have moved in different directions. International tough-on-crime and tough-on-immigration rhetoric has had a big impact on Denmark, while Norway has remained relatively liberal. Sweden lies somewhere between.

It is no longer possible, if it ever were, to talk about Scandinavia having exceptional rehabilitation-orientated policies or exceptionally moderate sentencing. Norway exhibits these ideals to some degree, but less than in the recent past. Sentence lengths have increased and there have been budget cuts across government services, including prisons. Rehabilitation measures have reduced and prisoners are being locked up earlier in their cells.

Still, Norway remains more liberal than many other countries. At least 80 per cent of prisoners are released within a year. The average prison sentence has risen to over 100 days, but this is still low from a comparative perspective. Our prisons are becoming larger, but we still consider 200 spaces a large prison.

The main exception is drug-related crime. Norway is quite puritan. We do not like people who drink too much. We certainly don't like people who take drugs. We have always given people comparatively lengthy sentences for relatively minor drug crimes. Although arguably, we do so more for paternalistic than punitive reasons. We have a highly interventionalist welfare system, and the public see prisons as part of the welfare state. We do not shy away from intervening in drug users' lives.

SD: You have suggested Sweden and Denmark have become tougher on crime partly in response to immigration. Is it not the case that Norway also discriminates against foreign offenders?

TU: Well, yes and no. Anti-immigration rhetoric reached the prison system after the right-wing Norwegian Progress Party took over justice policy 7 years ago. They promoted scaled down services for foreign nationals. They even converted a prison into a foreign nationals prison. What they didn't account for, however, is that Norwegian prisons do not employ their own healthcare workers, social workers, teachers and so on. In contrast to England and Wales, for instance, all welfare services are 'imported' from outside. These external agencies refused to deliver a second class service. They were also held back by our prison staff social service ethos. Here, prison guards do three years' training and need a bachelors' degree. People become prison officers because they want to make a difference. Politicians wanted to deliver a worse service but with a few modifications, but the standard Norwegian package was delivered in the new foreign nationals prison.

SD: The more I speak with Norwegian prisoners, the more I have come to doubt the exceptionalism thesis. Many prisoners are proud of the system, but others complain, for example about the drug laws and the common use of solitary confinement.

TU: I do not like the concept of Nordic or Scandinavian exceptionalism. It's too abstract. It assumes there is a global norm out there to measure against. We need to focus on specifics, which vary from place to place. Every country is different.* Norway 'deviates' from the 'punitive norm' in some ways but not in others.** Take, for example, our tradition of short sentences. We are often criticised for sending people to prison for a week or two for crimes that would not have incurred a prison sentence at all in other countries.

Dr Thomas Ugelvik, Professor in Criminology, University of Oslo, and author of several books on Nordic prisons, including Power and Resistance in Prison *(2014)*

* For a broader critique of the concept of penal exceptionalism that takes global differences rather than similarities as its starting point, see Brangan (2020).

** For an ongoing focused comparative study of penal policymaking and experiences of imprisonment in Norway and England and Wales that explores 'widespread assumptions about the relative mildness and severity of punishment practices in inclusionary versus exclusionary nations', see Crewe (2020); www.compen.crim.cam.ac.uk/Ourresearch.

and eastwards towards Europe via West Africa. Here, we continue our focus on responses to crime, looking at the region's extraordinary levels of police violence and its approach to sentencing and imprisonment.

Levels of police violence

We began this chapter with a startling statistic: that there are proportionally 1,000 times more deaths by police shooting in Rio de Janeiro than there are in London. We based this on the one registered armed police killing in London in 2018 (INQUEST, 'Fatal police shootings England & Wales 2011–2020'), compared to 1,344 armed police killings in the metropolitan area of Rio de Janeiro (ISP Dados Visualizaçã, 'Letalidade Violenta'). What does this tell us? To unpack this statistic and understand the extent to which it indicates a divergence, we need to consider the context. Important factors are:

- Rio de Janeiro has a population that is approximately 50 per cent larger than London.
- In Brazil as a whole, 6,220 police killings (defined as deaths resulting from police intervention) were recorded in 2018 (FBSB, 2019). In England and Wales, 18 people died as a result of police interventions in 2018: there were no armed police killings besides the one recorded in London, but a further 17 people died as a result of crashing their vehicles while under police pursuit (INQUEST, 'Deaths in police custody').
- One in three victims of Brazilian police killings die at the hands of off-duty officers (HRW, 2016), sometimes acting in self-defence, but also working as hit men or as private militia.
- In Brazil, police killings gain broad support from politicians as well as the public. In opinion surveys, half of respondents agree with the commonly heard phrase that 'a good outlaw is a dead one' (FBSP, 2016)—a phrase used repeatedly by the president, Jair Bolsonaro (see **Figure 13.10**), during his election campaign in 2018 (*Huffington Post*, 2019).
- The majority of victims of police killings in Brazil are young, poor, and black. Of the 6,220 victims of police killings in 2018, 82 per cent had left school at or before the statutory minimal age of 14 (FBSP, 2019). The peak age for being killed by the police was 20 (ibid). Black Brazilians are more than twice as likely to be killed by the police than white Brazilians. Of the general Brazilian population, 42 per cent is white and 55 per cent black. Of the 6,220 victims of police killings in 2018, 75 per cent were black and 24 per cent white (ibid). Black Brazilians are also nearly three times more likely to be the victims of homicide than white Brazilians (IPEA, 2020).

Figure 13.10 An important contextual factor for Brazilian levels of police killing is that the phrase 'a good outlaw is a dead one' is commonly used, including by Jair Bolsonaro during his successful presidential campaign
Source: Li Ming/Xinhua/Alamy Live News

- Police killings are also disproportionately high in other parts of Latin America (see Hinton (2006), Hinton and Newburn (2009), Koonings and Kruijt (2015), and Ungar (2009)), though fortunately, no other countries in South or Central America have as poor a record as Brazil.

There are also some peculiarities about Brazil and the wider Latin American region which might help explain this major divergence in police violence. First, there are several foreground issues which could be seen as contributing factors:

- Latin American police forces are typically poorly resourced, poorly paid, and trained as paramilitary units (Ungar, 2009);
- Brazilian police do little crime investigation, instead focusing resources on catching people 'in the act', and regularly hold down second jobs as private security;
- in Brazil, the majority of violent deaths involve firearms. In an average year, 38,000 people die from gunshot wounds (Cavalcanti, 2016). Seventy-one per cent of homicides involved firearms in 2018 (Cerqueira and Bueno, 2020);
- Latin American police are killed themselves in large numbers. There were 367 Brazilian police officers killed on or off duty in 2017 (FBSP, 2019). Willis (2015: 84) writes, 'as many police understand it, [killing] serves an important function: to make them all more secure'.

And there are even more background issues for us to consider, including:

- The legacies of colonisation and slavery, which were notably repressive and violent in Brazil and other parts of the Latin American region (Batista,

2000). An estimated 50 per cent of Brazil's four million inhabitants were held in slavery at the end of Portuguese colonial rule in 1824 (Beattie, 2015). Of the estimated ten million Africans transported into slavery in the Americas from the 16th to 19th centuries, 40 per cent were taken to Brazil. Brazil was the last country in the western world to abolish slavery. Today, it has the largest black population of any country outside Africa (Pereira, 2020). Rio de Janeiro has the largest black population of any city in the Americas (Batista, 2003).

- Despite its cultural diversity, Brazil suffers from high levels of racial inequality (Costa, 2014). White Brazilians earn on average 74 per cent more than black Brazilians (IBGE, 2019).
- Brazil also suffers from extreme levels of economic inequality. The poorest 30 per cent of the population earn just 6 or 7 per cent of national income, while the richest 10 per cent earn close to 50 per cent of national income, making it the third or fourth most unequal country in the world (World Bank, 2020).
- The more recent transition since the 1980s from military dictatorship to democracy (currently headed up by Bolsonaro), which in Brazil was immediately accompanied by a rapid increase in inequality, and urban as well as police violence (Caldeira, 2000).
- The Brazilian public is known to have little faith in democracy and the rule of law, which they consider both ineffective and a legacy of repressive 20th-century dictatorships (O'Donnell, 1998).
- The existence of certain social and cultural attitudes: popular Brazilian expressions include 'for my friends everything; for my enemies the law' and 'human rights are for criminals'.
- Brazilians are (understandably) fearful of violence, which they unashamedly equate with young, mostly poor black men from the poor suburbs of towns and cities (Alves, 2018). They use the terms 'thief' and 'outsider' almost interchangeably to describe these people.
- Poor Latin American suburban areas are themselves barely served by the police. Residents are used to being governed through alternative, quasi-legal systems of justice organised by community organisations, **drug trafficking** gangs, or paramilitary groups formed by serving and retired police officers (see Arias, 2017; Lessing, 2018; Manso, 2020). Over one-quarter of Rio de Janeiro's residents live in areas dominated by paramilitary groups (*Folha de São Paulo*, 18 October 2020).
- In the past few decades, the middle classes have increasingly withdrawn from public spaces into privatised residential and shopping areas.
- More often than not, the public is ready to stand by and turn a blind eye to state violence (Huggins and Mesquita, 1995).

Armed with this contextual information, we can see that rising levels of police violence do not indicate that levels of crime in the region are also on the rise. Given the many issues at play, the fact that police violence is so widespread in the region may now seem less surprising and even inevitable.

Sentencing and imprisonment

The other strongly divergent aspect of crime and justice in Brazil and the wider Latin American region is its approach to sentencing and imprisonment. In **section 13.3**, we noted that Brazil might be regarded a front-runner (a prototypical case) of a wider trend towards mass incarceration in Latin America. Since the start of the 21st century, Brazil has gone from being one of the lowest incarcerators in the Americas to the highest, and this is in addition to the fact that prison populations have risen in South and Central America more than any other global region, from approximately 650,000 in 2000 to 1.5 million in 2014 (Walmsley, 2018). All 20 Latin American countries imprison more people than they did in 2000 (ibid) and have a prison population rate above the world average. In **section 13.4** in discussing urban crime, we saw that the world average was 145 per 100,000 national population in 2018, no higher than it was in 2000. **Table 13.3** illustrates the sharp increase in prison population rates across Latin America since the year 2000 using five countries as examples. In comparison, the European prison population has fallen over 20 per cent since 2000.

In terms of absolute numbers of prisoners, Brazil now lies in third position globally, and is quickly catching up with China and the US, both of which imprison fewer people today than a decade ago. At 726,712 adult prisoners in June 2016, Brazil's official prison population had increased by 1,960 per cent from December 1984, when 37,071 adults were in prison (Pavarini and Giamberardino, 2011). Brazil might today be regarded as the principle player in the emergence of a new, Latin American, mass carceral zone (Darke and Garces, 2017: 2).

This 'great incarceration' (Batista, 2016) has been criticised by human rights and prison reform groups as it does not reflect changing rates or patterns of crime—even less so than the increase in police violence. Homicide rates, for instance, rose by approximately 30 per cent in the 1990s, but have dropped by 10 per cent since 2000. Explanations for the

CONVERSATIONS 13.3

Why are the Brazilian police so authoritarian?
with **Dr Orlando Zaccone**

Sacha Darke (SD): Can I start by asking you to give an overview of your career in the police?

Dr Orlando Zaccone (OZ): I joined the police in 1999. I used to be a journalist. In my 30s, I returned to university to study Law and eventually found work as a civil police delegate in charge of directing crime investigations. The position of police delegate is unique to Brazil. Our police service is divided into two main forces: the military police, responsible for public order, and the civil police, which investigates crime. Each civil police force area and specialised unit is directed by a legally-trained 'delegate'. There are approximately 150 police delegates in Metropolitan Rio de Janeiro.

The existence of police delegate helps to explain our high levels of police violence. Delegates have been instrumental in re-constructing police killings as legitimate defence; more generally, in legitimising a 'state of exception'. In theory, there should be a clear separation between the police and the judiciary. In Brazil, there is little distinction between the rule of law and the rule of the police.

SD: The Brazilian police is criticised internationally for being violent, as you mention, and also for its over-use and discriminatory use of drug laws. We can return to the first issue in a moment. What is your view on the latter one?

OZ: The police do not deal with the people who have a stake in the drug trade—only the street-level seller. They do not have the resources to properly investigate the drug trade. Nearly everyone who is in prison for selling drugs was 'caught in the act' and arrested in possession of small quantities. Possessing drugs for personal use is a non-imprisonable offence here, but the law allows the police to arrest everyone they catch with drugs in poor areas for 'trafficking', while charging those they catch in middle class areas as 'users'.

SD: The prison population has increased by 15 times since the end of the military dictatorship in the mid-1980s. Why do you think this has happened?

OZ: There has been a militarisation of justice. Our military has always been more concerned with 'internal' than 'external' enemies—with protecting Brazil from itself—and the police have always been closely tied to the military. During the 20th Century dictatorships, the people who campaigned for democracy were treated as the enemies of the Brazilian state. Today, it is the poor, black man who is constructed as the internal enemy—and moreover, as the enemy of the people. Re-democratisation did not lead to the police and military being separated either. The military are even involved in training the police.

SD: I suppose this militarisation of justice also helps explain the increase in police killings as well?

OZ: Sure. And the police wouldn't get away with this if it were not for the public support they receive. And the left are not prepared to challenge the public discourse that 'a good criminal is a dead one'. Even human rights defenders say they do not defend criminals. The fact that police officers also die is not an excuse. They die in different circumstances: 75 per cent of the time, this is not during confrontations but when they take out their guns to protect themselves from attempted street robbery. I never carry my gun on the street for this reason.

Dr Orlando Zaccone, civil police delegate in Rio de Janeiro and author of Indignos de Vida *(2015)*

---

expanding power of punishment in the region centre partly on the perceived threat to state sovereignty associated with local drug markets and the international drug trade (Garces, 2014), and partly on punitive populism (remember the issues that contribute to violent policing), but mostly on drug prohibition policies (Darke and Karam, 2016). Depending on the country, up to one-third of Latin American prisoners are remanded in custody or serving sentences related to drug trafficking, rising to 50 per cent or more in the case of female offenders (Karam, 2009). In much of Latin America, pre-trial detention is mandatory for drug-related offences.

In Brazil, the supply of illicit drugs attracts a minimum five-year prison sentence for repeat adult offenders or for first-time offenders deemed to have committed the crime as part of a gang, whatever the quantity and whatever the drug. The country's Drugs Law 2006 also requires judges to take a culprit's social background and place of arrest into account when deciding on guilt or innocence but there is no need to have evidence that a drug deal actually took place—most offenders are convicted wholly on police testimony. Many judges then apply the minimum five-year sentence to everyone they deal with from poor, urban areas (Semer, 2019).

	Prison population rate in 2000	Prison population rate in 2018	Occupancy level in 2020 (% based on official capacity of country's prisons)
Honduras	184	229	204.0 (in 2019)
Argentina	151 (in 2002)	207 (in 2017)	122.1
Colombia	128	239	130.1
Ecuador	64	222	133.2
Brazil	132	354	170.7

Table 13.3 Figures from 2000 and 2018 show a sharp rise in prison population rates (the number of prisoners per 100,000 members of the national population) across Latin America and Brazil

Source: The World Prison Brief (www.prisonstudies.org/world-prison-brief-data)

Recognising convergences: Latin America prison conditions

We noted earlier in this section (and in **What do you think? 13.3**) that convergences and divergences often appear in the same context. Not only can it be difficult to untangle and categorise them, it is also useful to examine case studies from both angles, as this helps counteract the potential issues associated with both types of analysis and gives us a fuller picture of the crime issues in a country or region. Given this, we now delve a little deeper into our Latin America example to illustrate that although in many ways policing, sentencing, and imprisonment in the region represent divergences from global norms, which we can analyse through interpretivist research, we can gain a more complete and nuanced picture of their criminal justice practices through a positivist approach. This reveals that there are in fact some clear convergences in prison conditions within Latin America and with the rest of the world. (Do remember that when conducting your own research, it is generally best to begin by analysing convergences before moving on to divergences.)

The Latin American region is consistently criticised by human rights organisations for breaching international standards on minimum conditions for the treatment of prisoners, including those set by the United Nations Office on Drugs and Crime (the Nelson Mandela Rules: UN, 2016). Of particular concern are the levels of overcrowding and shortages in staffing, health, and rehabilitation services—see the third column in **Table 13.3**. In contrast to the Global North, where the 'old penology' of rehabilitation lasted for much of the 20th century (see the discussion of punitivism and public protection in **section 13.4**), Latin American prisons have always been overcrowded and under-resourced (Aguirre and Salvatore, 2001; Salvatore and Aguirre, 1996). At least one-third of inmates have previously served a prison sentence (IPEA, 2015), suggesting that this region's prisons are not only inhumane but also ineffective—they are better described as institutions of internment (confinement) than of criminal punishment (Birkbeck, 2011). Despite being officially no more than 71 per cent over capacity, Brazilian prisons (see **Figure 13.11**) typically hold inmates in conditions of under one square metre of cell space per person, do not provide them with bedding, sanitary products, or medication, and are visited by a doctor only once a week (Darke, 2018). Most employ too few guards to maintain a permanent presence, manage daily routines, or deal with disputes on the wings (ibid). As a result, prisoners are left to fend for themselves.

We saw in the previous section that Latin American prison populations have on average doubled in the 21st century, while in most of the rest of the world they have remained more stable—taking into account rising general national populations—or, in the case of many European countries, reduced. But although most other countries

Figure 13.11 Brazil appears to be 'ahead of the curve' and provides a particularly extreme example of a global drift towards overcrowded, underfunded, and precarious prison environments

Source: Joa Souza/Shutterstock

have not experienced Latin America's specific phenomenon of hyper-incarceration, they share the defining feature of inhumane prison conditions. This is especially true in the Global South, including much of Africa and Asia. In 2014, five of the ten countries in the world with the most overcrowded prison systems were African (Jefferson and Martin, 2016). In recent times, prisons in Southern African countries have not suffered from overcrowding, however the East African region has a poor record by global standards, with average prison occupancy rates in the mid-2010s reaching 179 per cent (ibid). Levels of prison occupancy also vary in different regions of Asia. Some of the most overcrowded prisons in the continent are to be found in South Asia; the worst example being the remand prison system in Sri Lanka, which has held seven times more people than its official capacity and inmates have to take turns to sleep (Bandyopadhyay, 2016). In reality, few countries in the Global South have the resources or political will to comply with internationally agreed standards on cell occupancy, for instance the minimum of 5.4 square metres in single cell accommodation and 3.4 square metres per prisoner held in a multi-occupancy cell recommended by the International Red Cross and endorsed by the United Nations (UN, 2013).

In other words, inhumane prisons are the global norm. Prison conditions have deteriorated in recent decades as prison populations have risen (Jacobson et al., 2017). To return to Pakes's (2019) **typology** of comparative analysis (see **section 13.3**), Brazil is ahead of the curve (a prototypical case) but it is still part of a 21st-century global drift towards increasingly crowded and underfunded prison environments, which includes but is not exclusive to the Latin American region. Moreover, inhumane prisons have *always* been the global norm. The recent decline in prison conditions in the Global South can be seen as a legacy of European colonisation as well as the result of increasing levels of punitivism and decline in rehabilitation associated with modern-day globalisation. When Latin America's first prison, the Casa de Correção da Corte (Court Correction House), was inaugurated in Rio de Janeiro in 1850, more than half of the city's population were still held in slavery (Menegat, 2012) and the prison proved to be a 'house of disease and death' rather than correction (Salvatore and Aguirre, 1996: 9).

Another striking thing that Latin American prisons and others across the Global South have in common is the way that their inmates form complex social orders: ethnographic and autobiographical accounts show that prisoners create and maintain professional and interpersonal relationships to provide for their everyday needs, including material goods (such as food, medicines, and clothing), services (such as education and legal advice), and personal safety (as discussed in **Conversations 13.4**).

This is reflected in the existence of detailed norms of prison conduct relating to mutual aid and protection among inmates and reciprocal relations between inmates and staff. Brazilian prisoners refer to these informal codes as 'rules of conviviality', and to themselves in the singular: as one 'collective' (Darke, 2018). Though unwritten, these codes are implicitly supported and often instigated by prison managers. They are monitored by inmate councils and enforced through quasi-legal systems of informal dispute resolution. Prisoners who rise through the ranks of inmate hierarchies are usually those with the most experience of prison and the best communication skills.

Like inhumane prison conditions, such inmate self-governance is also common in other regions of the Global South, again including much of Africa (see, for example, Akoensi (2014) on Ghana, Lindegaard and Greer (2014) on South Africa, and Tertsakian (2014) on Rwanda) and Asia (see, for example, Bandyopadhay (2007) on India and Narag and Jones (2016) on the Philippines).

The detailed ethnographic research conducted in the Latin American region in the past decade (for collections of papers that focus specifically on this matter, see Darke and Garces (2017), Darke et al. (2021)) suggests the following possible explanations.

- Prison overcrowding. This may seem counter-intuitive, especially from a northern perspective, as established northern prison theories suggest that overcrowding is a major cause of interpersonal conflict, but research indicates that the collective inmate identity that underpins Latin American prison order is closely linked to the fact prisoners live in such close proximity to one another.

- Collective inmate identity. Prisoners see themselves as a repressed and racialised group of poor people in conflict with the law. In our discussion of urban violence in **section 13.4**, we emphasised that there is less social mobility in the Global South than in the Global North, and that crime is less intra-class as a consequence, and this applies in prison as much as it does in the community.

- The emergence of major criminal gangs. This explanation is linked to the previous one, in that prison gangs, especially those in Brazil, explicitly aim to increase inmate solidarity and collective action by 'raising their consciousness' (of injustice and oppression) and 'unifying' the country's existing system of 'postcode' gangs (created by allocating people from different areas to different wings or corridors) under the banner of one prison-wide, state-wide, or even nation-wide collective.

You can see from this discussion that there is much to be gained from conducting both positivist and

> **CONVERSATIONS** 13.4
>
> ### Understanding Brazilian prison order
> with **Dr Karina Biondi**
>
>
>
> **Sacha Darke (SD):** Can I start by asking you to give an overview of your research in prison?
>
> **Dr Karina Biondi (KB):** My husband was remanded in custody when I was studying at the University of São Paulo in the mid-2000s. This transformed my research as well as my personal life, as I used my weekly visits to see him to study the prison. As an anthropologist, I was particularly interested in studying how prisoners made sense of their lives. I ended up studying the operations and functions of the First Command of the Capital (the PCC), a prisoner collective that had formed in the early 1990s and is now considered one of the largest transnational criminal organisations worldwide. The PCC had already achieved hegemony in prisons across the state. A phenomenon that came to define my research was that very few prisoners were PCC members. Some prisons have no PCC members yet are still considered by their inmates to be PCC prisons. Most prisoners instead referred to themselves as 'running' with the PCC. I quickly realised that the PCC should be understood as an 'idea' more than an 'organisation'.
>
> **SD:** We know that prison conditions are appalling in São Paulo. How are these experienced by prisoners day to day?
>
> **KB:** The PPC came about as a result of precarious prison conditions, and emerged as a way for prisoners to unite to deal with 'state oppression'. The oppression was not just the violent police raids that often made the headlines, but prisoners' everyday experiences of systematic torture: of living 40 to 60 per 20m2 cell, with little access to water or healthy food, and with too few guards to manage the daily regime. Today, it is prisoners who clean the cellblock and distribute meals, and it is often prisoners who unlock the cell doors. Representatives of the inmates negotiate with the prison administration, for example to improve access to essential services such as healthcare. The concept of union is fundamental: prisoners are expected to treat one another as companions.
>
> **SD:** Why do you refer to the PCC as a collective and not a gang?
>
> **KB:** The term 'gang' is American. It doesn't make much sense in Brazil. Brazilian prisoners don't form groups to commit crime, like the gangs described in the American literature. They already consider themselves to be 'criminals'. They do not need the PCC to commit crime.
>
> **SD:** What kinds of rules do prisoners follow?
>
> **KB:** When people are forced to live together, they create rules of conduct just as they would in their own homes. PCC rules seek to distribute resources equally. To return to my example of water shortages, in most cells there is one tap and it is only turned on for an hour or two a day. Prisoners need rules in order to decide who can use it and when.
>
> **SD:** And how are these rules enforced?
>
> **KB:** It's important to emphasise that these rules are not 'imposed'. It's not a case of one group of prisoners trying to dominate another, and they rarely resort to violence. Most are persuaded to follow the rules, and those who refuse to stand accused of thinking they are better than others. They face public humiliation and risk being expelled from the collective and the prison.
>
> *Dr Karina Biondi, Associate Professor, State University of Maranhão, Brazil and author of* Sharing this Walk: An ethnography of Prison Life and the PCC in Brazil *(2016)*

interpretivist analysis, since almost every case study will have some differences from and some common features with other regions or countries. As Dr Ugelvik suggests in **Conversations 13.2**, we need to 'focus on specifics, which vary from place to place' as well as remaining alert to commonalities and global trends.

13.6 Conclusion

In this chapter you will undoubtedly have faced many challenges. The first has been for you to broaden your horizons and to think about issues of crime and justice (and the subject area of criminology) at a more globally informed level, and to consider the possible connections when thinking about definitions of crime, the causes and explanations of it, and how societies respond to it. In short, as we said at the beginning of the chapter, there is now a pressing need for us all to think about these issues beyond the sovereign nation-state level and to reframe criminology so that it reflects a world which is becoming increasingly interconnected.

As we also noted, the development of global criminological theories is still in its relative infancy, and this relates to the second challenge you have faced: it can be difficult to find a sufficiently straightforward conceptual language through which we can meaningfully discuss, debate, and research these important issues. In this chapter, we have explored the distinction between comparative and transnational criminology and, within the comparative approach, between studies which focus on global convergences and those which focus on global divergences. We have also looked at the reasons to conduct both types of analysis and the possible relationships between them. It is important for you to reflect on and fully understand these distinctions as you move forward with your studies. In the next chapter we will build on the framework set out here in order to discuss transnational criminology: studies of organised, state, and corporate crimes, and criminal justice responses to organised, state, and corporate crimes, that *cross* national and regional borders. We will be focusing on case studies of state terror and the 'war on terror', drug trafficking and the war on drugs, **people smuggling** and the war on migration, issues surrounding the disposal of toxic waste, and finally **cybercrime** and cybersecurity.

SUMMARY

After reading this chapter and working your way through its features you should now be able to:

- Outline the importance of a global approach to the study of crime and justice and appreciate where this sits within the broader debates on calls for the decolonisation of criminology

The theories that make up the established discipline of criminology were mostly developed by researchers in northern universities, especially US and UK universities, studying matters of national concern—for example, youth offending in the inner cities of 20th-century New York or London, or the emergence of prison as a main form of punishment in the 19th century. Yet the very same theories have been used to study crime and justice across the world, with little account taken of differences between countries and regions, on the assumption that criminology has already identified the most important matters of crime and justice and the best theories for understanding and evaluating them. Today, criminologists who research other parts of the world are increasingly turning to international definitions of crime, and international understanding of the causes of crime and the effectiveness and legitimacy of the various forms of crime control. In doing so, criminologists are also increasingly aware that they need to diversify the discipline further to include the knowledge and viewpoints of researchers from the Global South.

- Explain and illustrate the distinction between comparative and transnational approaches to global criminological theories

The emerging area of global criminology is divided into two broad areas of research interest. The first, comparative criminology, focuses on identifying and understanding convergences and divergences (that is, similarities and differences) in crime and justice between nations and regions, for example youth offending in the UK compared to youth offending in other parts of Northern Europe, or youth offending in Northern Europe compared to youth offending in South Asia. The second area, transnational criminology, explores the nature of organised, state, and corporate crimes and responses to organised crimes that cross borders, for example torture perpetrated during the post-9/11 international 'war on terror', and the international trades in cocaine and in toxic waste.

- Identify the differences between positivist and interpretivist comparative approaches to the study of crime and justice at a global level and how these relate to each other

Comparative criminology is best understood as a *method* of conducting criminological research. It seeks to explore the true extent that criminological theories can be considered 'universal' at an international or regional level, and the extent to which they otherwise need to be adapted in different national and regional contexts. Examples might include how far established theories such as anomie and rehabilitation apply in South rather than North America, or the extent to which the causes of police violence in Brazil are similar to the causes of police violence in the US. Comparative criminology can therefore be further divided into two broad strands of research: the study of convergences (positivist comparative criminology) and the study of divergences (interpretivist comparative criminology). Positivist comparative criminology typically develops universal theories in order to identify areas of criminal justice practice that are unusual and should be brought 'into line' with regional or international norms. Interpretivist comparative criminology, on the other hand, attempts to understand these diverging practices *in their own terms*. It does so for three reasons: either to identify the limits of *what should be changed* (that is, identifying areas of what at first sight might appear to be bad practice, but in actual fact should be left alone); to identify *what can be changed* (that is, how things get done in the country or region under question); or—in complete contrast to positivist comparative research—to identify areas of unusual but otherwise good national or regional practice that the international community should consider adopting elsewhere.

- Apply and critically evaluate positivist and interpretivist approaches to relevant case studies in terms of convergences and divergences

Pakes (2019) identifies three types of comparative criminological research: focused comparisons, meta-analysis, and case study analysis. Focused comparisons involve comparing a small number of countries or regions to one another. In this chapter, we gave two illustrations: Hinton's (2006) study of the convergences between Argentina and Brazil in police violence, and Downes's (1988) study of divergences between England and Wales and the Netherlands in the use of imprisonment. Meta-analysis involves statistical comparisons of a large number of countries, for example the Institute of Criminal Policy Research's World Prison Brief online database that we referenced in our analysis of convergences in harsh penal policies in neoliberal and post-Soviet northern countries like the Russian Federation, the US, and England and Wales, and in our analysis of Latin American hyper-incarceration. The most common type of comparative criminological research—case study analysis—focuses on individual countries or regions, which it investigates with reference to global averages. Pakes (2019) identifies four types of comparative case study: representative, prototypical, archetypical, and deviant cases. Among the numerous illustrations we have presented in this chapter, we have highlighted India as a representative case of the urbanisation of poverty in the Global South, Brazil as a prototypical case of the trend towards mass incarceration in Latin America, and Norway as a deviant case that bucks the European trend in terms of rehabilitating prisoners.

 Test your understanding of the chapter's key points by attempting the self-test questions on the **online resources** at **www.oup.com/he/case2e**

REVIEW QUESTIONS

1. What are the consequences of globalisation for the discipline of criminology?
2. What are the differences between the comparative and transnational strands of global criminology?

3. What are the differences between the positivist and interpretivist approaches to comparative criminology?
4. To what extent do established criminological theories explain urban violence in the Global South?
5. To what extent is penal punitivism a worldwide criminal justice norm?
6. When studying a particular country, why do criminologists usually conduct positivist as well as interpretivist comparative research?
7. What do you understand by the terms 'orientalism' and 'occidentalism'?
8. Why are Norwegian prisons on the whole more humane than prisons in other parts of Europe?
9. Why are the Brazilian police so violent?

 Access the **online resources** at www.oup.com/he/case2e to check your answers to the review questions.

FURTHER READING

Aas, K. (2020) *Globalization and Crime.* **London: Sage.**
Now in its third edition, this book remains the most comprehensive account of the challenges 21st-century globalisation poses to the established discipline of criminology, and the need for a global criminology.

Carrington, K. et al. (2019) *Southern Criminology.* **London: Routledge.**
This book represents the first major effort to provide a comprehensive overview of crime and justice in the Global South, and to highlight the work of southern criminologists.

Darke, S. (2018) *Conviviality and Survival: Co-Producing Brazilian Prison Order.* **London: Palgrave Macmillan.**
Written by the author of this chapter, this case study of imprisonment in Brazil will help you gain a deeper understanding of the distinction between the positivist and interpretivist strands of comparative criminology.

Jewkes, Y., Crewe, B., and Bennett, J. (eds) (2016) *Handbook on Prisons.* **Abingdon: Routledge. Part 3.**
This remains the only book to include a full set of regional case studies on punishment and prison life in the Global South as well as the Global North.

Nelken, D. (2010) *Comparative Criminal Justice: Making Sense of Difference.* **London: Sage. Especially Ch. 1.**
This book was one of the first efforts to develop and apply a framework of comparative criminology methodology to different areas of crime and justice, and to distinguish its positivist and interpretivist—or, Nelken's preferred term, 'relativist'—strands.

Pakes, F. (2019) *Comparative Criminal Justice.* **London: Routledge. Especially Chs 1 and 2.**
Now in its third edition, this book provides the most detailed overview of the different types of comparative criminological research. Like Nelken (2010), it also remains one of only a few books to explore comparative criminology methodology in the context of different areas of crime and justice, including state–corporate as well as 'street crime', and policing as well as punishment.

Sheptycki, J. and Wardak, A. (eds) (2005) *Transnational and Comparative Criminology.* **London: Glasshouse. Introduction and Parts 1 and 2.**

Published more than 15 years ago, this book is now considered a classic introduction to global criminology and the distinction between its comparative and transnational strands.

 Access the **online resources** to view a wealth of extra information relating to your study of criminology, including self-test questions, answers to review questions, and links to other resources that will help you enjoy and fulfil your potential within your studies.
www.oup.com/he/case2e

CHAPTER OUTLINE

14.1	Introduction	410
14.2	What is transnational criminology?	411
14.3	Key areas of concern for transnational criminology	419
14.4	Critical issues in transnational criminology	435
14.5	Conclusion	437

14

Global criminology 2
Transnational criminology

Sacha Darke

KEY ISSUES

After studying this chapter, you should be able to:

- outline the scope of transnational criminology and explain where it sits within the broader discipline of criminology;
- apply the theoretical concepts employed in transnational criminology to case studies of crime and justice;
- discuss the most prominent academic debates within and associated with transnational criminology.

14.1 Introduction

In this second chapter on **global criminology**, we focus on instances of crime and justice that *cross national borders*. We began our introduction to global criminology in **Chapter 13** with Aas's (2020: 3, 8) call for a new level of criminological analysis that looks beyond nation states and takes 'the global and transnational as the primary point of reference . . . [for] a sociology beyond societies'. We made the point that the increasingly global nature of crime and justice points to a need to move beyond the nation state as the starting point for criminology, both in terms of **empirical** focus (moving from national to international definitions of crime and appropriate responses to crime) and how we analyse crime and its control (focusing on vulnerabilities produced by **globalisation**, and international criminal justice policy transfer and coordination).

Aas (2020) made this call in the context of 21st-century globalisation, which she described, citing Held (2000: 42), as 'the growing interconnectedness of states and societies' (Aas, 2020: 4) (see **Figure 14.1**). This idea is central to both branches of global criminology, **comparative criminology** and **transnational criminology**, but manifests in different ways. As we saw in **Chapter 13**, comparative criminology is concerned with *method*: on the 'how' rather than the 'what' of global criminological inquiry (Pakes, 2019).

It focuses on interconnection in the sense of the globalisation of economic, social, and political **norms**. It argues that crime and justice in individual countries and regions are increasingly *influenced* by developments in crime and justice in other countries and regions, and in the world as a whole, and it assesses the extent to which explanations for crime and justice in one place can be used in another. We saw, for example, that most countries are imprisoning their citizens more often and for longer periods, and explored this global trend in the context of increasing levels of relative poverty and distance between the middle and working classes. We found that both patterns are less apparent in the Nordic region than in other parts of Europe and the world more generally. In this chapter, we will see that transnational criminology is concerned with the *movement of things* rather than norms—of criminal plots, victims, offenders, police officers, and so on—*across national or regional borders*.

Transnational criminology is therefore concerned with how global economic, social, and political connections facilitate the organisation of crime and the coordination of justice. Bowling (2011) uses the term 'linkages' rather than connections. He explains that, '[w]hile comparative criminology seeks to compare one place with another,

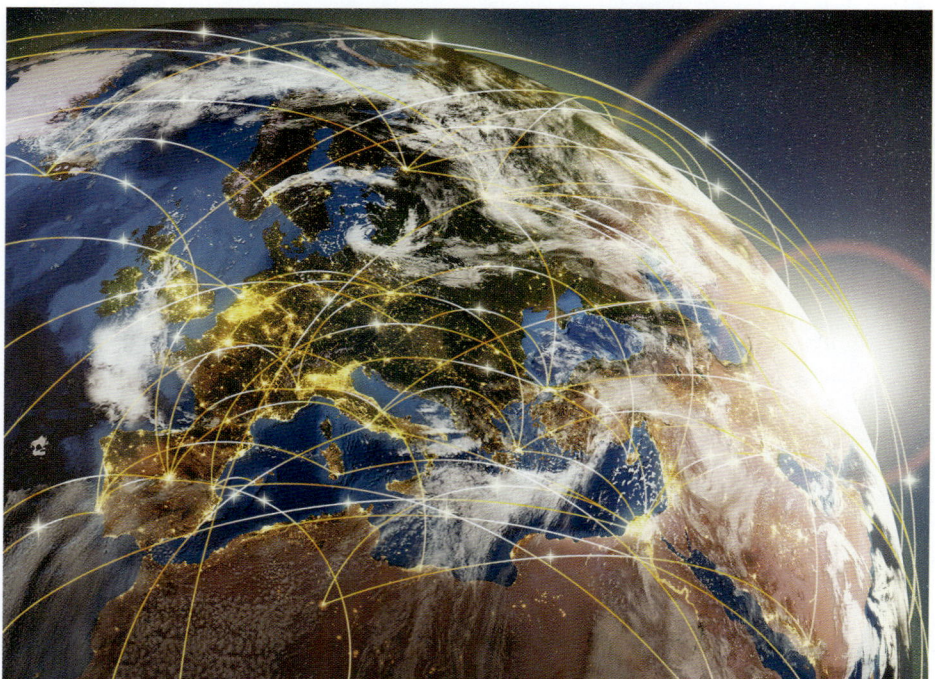

Figure 14.1 International connections are central to both comparative criminology and transnational criminology
Source: MaxxStudio/Shutterstock

transnational criminology . . . explore[s] problems that do not belong exclusively in one place or another and can therefore only be understood by analysing *linkages* between places' (ibid: 362). Bowling applies this distinction to research on illicit drugs. He writes: 'Comparative criminology might seek to describe and explain differences in the prevalence of cocaine use in various countries . . . Transnational criminology, by contrast, might seek to explain the ways illegal drug production, distribution and consumption are linked across time and place' (ibid: 364).

The increasing global connections that have accompanied 21st-century advances in information technology and the globalisation of commerce (see **section 13.2**) therefore have consequences for all areas of economic, political, and social life, including crime and justice, and at both a transnational and national level. In this chapter, we begin by outlining the scope of transnational criminology, looking at the theoretical concepts it employs and its defining characteristics. We then explore some of its major areas of research interest: state terror, drug trafficking, people smuggling, the trade in and dumping of toxic waste, and cybercrime. In the penultimate section, we discuss two of the most prominent academic debates within and associated with transnational criminology: the extent to which transnational crime is hierarchical and organised, and the means by which the international community might best police it.

14.2 What is transnational criminology?

In this section we examine 'transnational criminology' as an area of study and then outline some of its main themes—that is, the traditional social science concepts and distinctions that it calls into question.

The scope of transnational criminology

We noted in **Chapter 13** that comparative criminology is a developing area of study, and the same can be said of transnational criminology. Again, the defining texts that have emerged on the subject so far are mostly suitable for students studying at postgraduate level or as textbooks on specialist undergraduate modules on matters of transnational crime and justice (see, for example, Albanese and Reichel (2013), Allum and Gilmour (2015), Edwards and Gill (2003), Reichel (2005), Sheptycki (2014), Sheptycki and Wardak (2005), and Van Duyne et al. (2002)). They were also largely written by academics working in social science disciplines other than criminology (such as law, human geography, and international relations), so they use a range of theoretical concepts that will be unfamiliar to most undergraduate criminology students.

These texts are groundbreaking, but they do not give equal attention to the full breadth of crimes covered in the discipline of criminology. They focus more on the harms perpetrated by criminal groups than those perpetrated by states and corporations—which Pearce (1976) termed 'the crimes of the powerful'—many of which are not prohibited under criminal laws or are criminalised under laws that are under-enforced. Rothe and Friedrichs (2015: 29) explain that 'the literature on transnational crime and justice has principally focused on such crimes as trafficking in persons, migrant smuggling, drugs and counterfeit goods, cybercrime, money laundering, and the transnational organised crime networks that are at the centre of many of these forms of transnational criminal activity'. These organised crime networks do not include state and corporate institutions, which are responsible for many of the most serious cross-border crimes, for instance colonial and imperial crimes like wars of aggression (see, for example, Kramer and Michalowski, 2005), genocide (Karstedt, 2013), and the transatlantic slave trade. (For broader critique of the failure of criminology to consider colonial and imperial crimes, see our discussion in **section 10.2** as well as Agozino (2018) and Cohen (1988).) Such mass atrocities are usually described in the transnational crime literature as 'international' crimes that, as Reichel (2005: xiv) puts it, 'threaten world order and security . . . whereas transnational crime [only] affects the interests of more than one state'.

We can make the same observation about the general criminology and criminal justice textbooks commonly used on courses in the UK: few dedicate more than a few pages to transnational criminology and, again, this is usually in the specific context of conventionally defined organised crime. In other words, they focus on social harms associated with outlawed organisations and their illicit activities (for example, the transporting of heroin produced in Afghanistan to Europe) more than the social harms associated with states or corporations, most of whose illegitimate activities are only illegal in the sense that they breach international law (for example, the intensive bombing of foreign towns and cities, or the exporting of dirty recycling from the Global North). The same applies to criminology textbooks on globalisation and crimes of the powerful. Most of them make regular use of the term 'transnational' in the context of international *responses* to crime (including transnational policing and surveillance

(Aas, 2020), transnational private security (Pakes, 2019), transnational environmental activists (White, 2013), and transnational civil society (Ward and Green, 2000)) but they usually reserve the term transnational *crime* for the criminalised activities of outlaws.

This observation is not meant as a criticism. The point we are making is simply that it is not theoretically necessary for the developing field of transnational criminology to restrict itself to studying organised crime and criminalised harms. This is acknowledged in most of the classic books on transnational crime we have listed, and is implied by the wide range of terms and categories used by those writing on matters of cross-border crime. The term 'transnational crime' was first used at the United Nations Congress on Crime Prevention (Felsen and Kalaitzidis, 2005), which is mostly attended by government officials and criminal justice practitioners. More often than not, academics working in the field add the word 'organised' between the words 'transnational' and 'crime' to distinguish their research from that produced by people studying global matters of crime and justice from the perspectives of state or corporate crime. Edwards and Gill (2003) and Sheptycki (2014), for instance, named their books *Transnational Organised Crime*. In this chapter, we follow the precedent set by scholars in this area who refer to three categories of transnational crime: transnational organised crime, transnational **state crime**, and transnational **corporate crime** (although it will become clear that in practice there is often little difference between them).

So, we have established that as a subject area, transnational criminology focuses on matters of crime and justice that begin in one country and end in another. We have seen that this definition can be applied to all forms of crime, whether organised crime, state crime, or corporate crime, and irrespective of whether the crime is officially criminalised under international law or the national laws of the countries affected. Whereas comparative criminology studies the influence of global norms on *domestic* crime and justice, comparing trends between one country or region and another, transnational criminology is interested in incidences of crime that *cross* national and regional borders. Naturally, such crimes are relatively large-scale and involve groups of offenders, so transnational criminology essentially explores the nature of organised, state, and corporate crime and responses to these forms of crime that cross national and regional borders. Examples of transnational crime (all of which we return to later in this chapter) include:

- the use of chemical weapons by the United States Army during its 2003–11 occupation of Iraq;
- the transport of hundreds of tonnes of cocaine a year by narco-traffickers across Central America into the US;
- the smuggling of thousands of refugees and migrants every year across North Africa, the Middle East, and Eastern Europe into the EU;
- the dumping of millions of tonnes of toxic, hazardous waste produced in Western Europe and North America each year by transnational corporations (TNCs) in Africa and Asia;
- the sexual exploitation of thousands, if not hundreds of thousands, of children across the world every year for the production of pornography shared online.

Similar to the way comparative criminology uses case study as well as **meta-analysis** to explore similarities and differences between places, transnational criminology often uses case studies to explore the *impact* of global trends in cross-border crime and justice, in their countries or regions of origin, the places they travel through (that is, their 'footprints', their 'trails'), and the places they arrive (their 'end-point'). To understand the impact of transnational crime and justice in one place compared to another, we need to explore the local as well as the global circumstances in which they occur. This might involve considering, for example, why the cocaine trail from South America to the US is the cause of more violence in Mexico than in the other countries on its route. Or why migrants travelling from Africa to Western Europe are more likely to end up in the hands of exploitative people-smuggling networks or to die in transit than migrants travelling in the opposite direction. In this sense, transnational criminology could be seen as a specialist area of comparative criminology rather than a second strand of an overarching global criminology, as we defined it in **section 13.2**.

Key themes for transnational criminology

In its quest to analyse crime and justice in the context of global connections, transnational criminology questions the **validity** and usefulness of distinctions that have traditionally been drawn between key social science concepts at the centre of the established discipline of criminology. These most notably include:

- the national and the international;
- crime and war;
- the crimes of the powerful and the crimes of the powerless;
- the public and the private.

Let's examine each of these distinctions more closely.

National and international

It will probably be clear to you by now that the challenge to the national/international distinction is central to social scientific analysis of the contemporary wave of globalisation. In the past, what happened in one country usually had little effect on what happened in another country, but today countries are increasingly intertwined. We covered this point in detail in **Chapter 13**, both in the broader context of globalisation and in the specific context of comparing and contrasting matters of crime and justice across national borders. We saw, for instance, that the globalisation of the world economy is arguably resulting in reductions in absolute poverty in most countries, but also in increases in relative poverty (which is accepted in both mainstream and critical criminology worldwide to be a significant underlying cause of street crimes like shoplifting, burglary, and predatory youth violence) as well as the use of punitive justice policies and practices like zero-tolerance policing. In the context of transnational crimes, we are also concerned with the negative impacts of globalisation but—to emphasise this important point again—here our focus is on the movement of crimes starting in one country or region and crossing its borders into others.

In our rapidly globalising world, then, it is becoming increasingly futile for social scientists to draw clear distinctions between national and international affairs, including when discussing political or social problems like transnational crime. As we saw in **Chapter 13**, the speed of 21st-century globalisation is leading many social scientists to question the utility of mainstream criminological theories—which, remember, were mostly produced and developed in North America and Western Europe—to study crime and justice in other parts of the world. Even the most established criminological theories have been questioned in the emerging area of global criminology and recently there have been calls (see Carrington et al., 2016, 2018, 2019) for Global South perspectives on crime and justice—a southern criminology—to be developed.

Our discussions in **Chapter 13** demonstrated that the problems with the national/international distinction have implications for comparative criminology relating to definitions of crime, causes of crime, and responses to crime.

- In terms of definitions of crime, we saw that if a criminologist conducting comparative research were to limit their study to acts that are defined as crime by the law in the relevant nation—that is, to follow the standard criminal law approach of our discipline—they would not be able to include in their analysis, for example, 'the stoning of adulterers [or] the mutilation of thieves' (Cohen, 1982: 195) in countries where such acts have not been criminalised.

- Regarding causes of crime, we saw that neither social disorganisation nor strain theories—both of which were originally developed to explain street crime in major cities in the US—provide adequate explanation for street crime in a major Asian city like Mumbai.

- Regarding responses to crime, we saw that a criminologist who insisted that one of the main aims of punishment is to rehabilitate would struggle to explain why few prisons in Latin America employ enough guards to even maintain discipline in the cellblocks and wing corridors.

The same issues affect transnational criminology, where the starting point is that *crime and justice is increasingly internationalised*. Let's consider this using the example of the global clothing industry.

Regarding definitions of crime, an investigation by the *Observer* newspaper found that it is perfectly legal in Cambodia for TNCs like Nike and Puma to pay factory workers less than half of the country's living wage of £300 a month to work in temperatures that regularly exceed 35° centigrade, despite the fact that on average, 100 workers a month are reported to require medical attention for fainting (*The Guardian*, 'Cambodian female workers in Nike, Asics and Puma factories suffer mass faintings', 25 June 2017). US employment and health and safety laws do not cover Cambodia. A concerned criminologist who took a social harm (see **Chapter 19**) approach and considered such working conditions criminal would be severely restricted if they had to wait for the Cambodian government to criminalise them. Or they might decide to take the blatantly absurd position of switching attention to the clothing industry in neighbouring Vietnam, where legislation has been passed that limits maximum working temperatures to 32° centigrade and there are fewer health and safety concerns (see **Figure 14.2**). (Not that we are arguing that these kinds of working conditions should be considered legitimate.)

As for causes of crime, the *Observer* reported that the clothing-manufacturing industry was worth $5.7 billion to the Cambodian economy in 2015, employing 600,000 people. It also makes economic sense for Nike or Puma to produce goods in countries where manufacturing costs are lowest—paying a living wage and providing safe working conditions is not good for business; profit margins are potentially much higher for Global North companies that transnationalise and shift production abroad. The pursuit of profit is recognised as a major cause of crime in studies of working conditions in North America and Western Europe. We return to the causes of transnational crime when we present our first major example, state terror and the 'war on terror', in **section 14.3**.

Figure 14.2 Women make up about 90 per cent of the workforce in Cambodia's garment industry, often working in factories like this one in Phnom Penh, Cambodia's capital

Source: © 2014 Samer Muscati/Human Rights Watch/CC BY-NC-ND 3.0 US

In terms of responses to crime, if state, corporate, and organised crime are becoming increasingly borderless, so too are responses. A criminologist studying the international clothing industry would again not get very far in identifying who is responsible or who should hold the industry to account for criminal activities if they restricted their analysis to the role played by national health and safety inspectorates or national civil society NGOs (non-governmental organisations). Likewise, a criminologist studying the international trade in cocaine between South and North America would produce a limited analysis if they decided only to look at the role played by national police forces in Colombia, Mexico, and the US.

It should be clear that we need to move beyond the national/international distinction in order to carry out meaningful transnational criminological analysis.

Crime and war

The second distinction we need to consider is the one typically made in northern social science between 'crime' and 'war'.

We know that the discipline of criminology is traditionally defined as involving the study of definitions, causes, and responses of/to *crime*. As we saw in **Chapter 2**, in liberal or social democratic countries like the UK, US, France, and Norway, the concept of crime is associated with political philosophical theories surrounding democracy and the rule of law. A nation state is said to gain its legitimacy to govern through establishing and enforcing rules which are designed to protect its citizens from one another and enable them to get on with their daily lives without fear of violence or theft. In performing this role, state officials are entrusted with the right to investigate and detain individuals who are suspected or proven to be planning to break, or to have broken, the law.

Importantly, especially for the purpose of our discussion, these state powers are meant to be strictly limited in terms of when and how people are brought to justice. So, in most North American and West European countries the police are legally and politically expected to exercise discretion in deciding when it is necessary to arrest, detain, and begin prosecution, and only to do so where they have reasonable suspicion or probable cause that the person in question has committed an act or is about to commit an act that is prohibited under criminal law. Similarly, judges and prosecutors are expected to drop cases which it is not thought to be in the public interest to continue, and to only find a **defendant** guilty where the evidence is deemed to be beyond reasonable doubt. The offender should usually be punished in proportion to the harm caused by their criminal actions, although most countries grant judges the power to decrease or increase a sentence to prevent future crimes (for example, to rehabilitate the offender or to deter others from committing similar crimes). Radical criminology questions whether the concept of crime should be restricted to acts that are defined as such by nation state parliaments, but it shares with mainstream, conventional criminology the concern that justice should be proportional and procedurally fair.

The concept of *war*, on the other hand, is traditionally associated with political conflicts that threaten a nation state as well as its citizens. War is a defining feature of the discipline of politics, not of criminology. Threats to states are seen as more serious than threats to citizens, and to call for pre-emptive as well as reactionary responses. These threats are also usually perpetrated by groups (rather than individuals) who are more powerful than the individuals within them so do not require the same level of protection against the power of the state with which they are competing.

The traditional distinction between crime and war is reflected in international human rights treaties such as the European Convention on Human Rights (ECHR) 1950, which we discuss further in **Chapter 23** (see **section 23.5**). The ECHR allows states to restrict citizens' freedoms in the interests of 'the prevention of disorder or crime' or 'national security'. The European Court of Human Rights is more likely to side with the state when citizens' rights are restricted in the interests of national security than for crime prevention. For example, it has approved the use of secret surveillance systems by security forces investigating suspected terrorists (Greer, 2000). In fact, some freedoms associated with the rule of law can be postponed altogether 'in time of war or other public emergency threatening the life of the nation' (Art. 15 ECHR), for example during the aftermath of a major terrorist incident or—as was the case in Northern Ireland in the mid-1970s—during an extended period of terrorist activity (Council of Europe, 2020). This includes the right to liberty (which is broadly defined as the right to be arrested and detained only for as long as is needed to investigate a crime), but not the right to a fair trial (Art. 5 ECHR) or the prohibition of torture and other forms of ill-treatment (Art. 3 ECHR). The latter types have the status of an 'absolute right', meaning that a state cannot contravene them under any circumstances (ibid). The acts and behaviours that are acceptable in war are also regulated by the 1948 Geneva Conventions which say, for example, that states can only kill on the battlefield and can only detain soldiers, unless a crime has been committed, and even then only for the duration of the war.

The relevance of the crime/war distinction has been questioned in comparative as well as transnational criminology. We saw in **Chapter 13** that since the last decades of the 20th century, northern criminologists have noted a more general shift towards 'criminal justice militarization' (Brown, 2005: 985, in Aas, 2020: 109) and that rehabilitation has largely fallen out of favour, with punitive retribution and incapacitation now the main aims of punishment. We can see this shift in the use of exclusionary crime prevention measures such as facial recognition CCTV cameras, the phenomenon of gated communities, the availability to the police of legal powers to stop and search without suspicion, and police use of so-called 'zero tolerance' crackdowns on the antisocial (as opposed to criminal) activities of youths hanging around public areas or homeless people begging in public. In each of these examples, northern states could be accused of policing people rather than policing crime: of treating certain social, religious, or ethnic groups as 'enemies within', and of turning prisons into warehouses for marginalised populations. In **Chapter 13** we also cited Carrington et al.'s (2016: 3) suggestion that established criminology, 'takes for granted a high level of internal peace within what is assumed to be a stable state system [and that] [t]his has led to the obfuscation of the historical role of state violence in nation-building, the expansion of colonialism across the Global South and the neglect of contemporary violent phenomena, like armed conflict, drug wars and ethnic cleansing'. In much of the world, the rule of law is associated with authoritarianism rather than liberalism, as we saw in the case of the policing of poor urban communities in Brazil (see **section 13.5**). This calls into question the relevance of the crime/war distinction in comparative criminology.

Authoritarian trends in transnational justice are even more significant—in the Global North as well as the Global South. Authoritarian national criminal justice practices could in fact be largely seen as intended or unintended consequences of developments in transnational justice, which have often occurred with little legal or political oversight. For example, in **section 13.5** we saw that the Brazilian police are today far more violent and the judiciary far more punitive than during the country's military dictatorship from 1964 to 1985, and we suggested that 21st-century Brazilian authoritarianism can be partly explained by shifting attitudes towards the apparent threat posed to the country by the international trade in cocaine.

In the major examples of transnational crime and justice we consider in **section 14.3**, we draw specific attention to the political use of the phrase 'war on'—for example, the 'war on terror'. We will see how the concept of war has been invoked—rightly or wrongly—especially in the post-9/11 political climate (that is, following the events of the terrorist attacks against the US on 11 September 2001) to legitimise acts of preventative detention and state violence, neither of which are acceptable under international law in times of peace. During the Covid-19 pandemic, the concept was also used in a public health context to legitimise the placing of extreme restrictions of individual freedoms, as we explore in **Controversy and debate 14.1**. Supporters of such measures argue that terrorism, illicit drugs, and migration (and the coronavirus) are exceptional problems that require exceptional measures. Critics argue that even if international terrorism, for example, were a major threat to world order at the height of al-Qaida, we are now two decades on from 9/11 and the exception is becoming the norm (Cercel et al., 2020). It is also worth noting that war has not been declared on state or corporate crimes, including the destruction of the environment, that really do pose a threat to worldwide political stability, not to mention the future of the planet (see **Chapter 12**). Continuing with the example of the 'war on terror', we will see also how the concept of crime is used—again, rightly or wrongly—to depoliticise conflict and avoid granting rights under the 1948 Geneva Conventions to prisoners. Fighters picked up on the battlefields of Afghanistan and Iraq and subjected to extreme forms of interrogation in Guantánamo Bay in Cuba in the aftermath of 9/11, for example, were referred to by US authorities and their allies as criminals and 'enemy combatants' rather than soldiers.

Crimes of the powerful and crimes of the powerless

The third distinction to consider is the boundary that is usually drawn between state and corporate crimes—including some, if not all, of the extreme forms of interrogation practised in Guantánamo Bay—and conventionally defined organised crime such as drug dealing. Crimes committed by states and corporations are often referred to in criminology, especially critical criminology (see **Chapter 18**), as 'crimes of the powerful' (see, for example,

CONTROVERSY AND DEBATE 14.1

The 'war on' coronavirus

We have noted that state powers to restrict the freedoms of individuals are meant to be strictly limited in times of peace, but that there has been a post-9/11 trend for states to invoke the concept of 'war' to legitimise what could be seen as inappropriate or excessive state actions or controls.

Although it was in the context of a transnational public health crisis rather than a crime, it is interesting to note the use of this same technique by world leaders during the Covid-19 pandemic. Again, it was used to legitimise restricting individuals' rights, especially their freedoms, by presenting the situation as an exceptional period which called for exceptional, non-peacetime measures—including the creation and enforcement of new forms of crime, such as attending a large gathering.

British Prime Minister Boris Johnson spoke of the 'front line' of healthcare professionals (*New Statesman*, 11 April 2020), invoked the 'Blitz spirit', and made heavy use of the language and imagery associated with Winston Churchill, the British prime minister famed for bringing the country successfully through the Second World War. He stated, 'I don't think there's really been anything like [this lockdown] in peacetime' and government ministers sought to present the virus as a criminal, referring to it as an 'invisible killer' (*The Times*, 17 March 2020). The same tendency was visible around the world:

- In the US, then-President Donald Trump described himself as a 'wartime president' (*The Conversation*, 8 April 2020);
- Italian Prime Minister Giuseppe Conte also invoked Churchill's words by referring to Italy's 'darkest hour' (ibid);
- French President Emmanuel Macron announced national lockdown measures in front of a military hospital and used the phrase 'we are at war' six times in 20 minutes (*Varsity*, 17 April 2020).
- Xi Jinping, General Secretary of the Chinese Communist Party, used the words of the communist revolutionary Mao Zedong and declared a 'people's war' (*New Statesman*, 11 April 2020).

Commentators have expressed concerns that wartime rhetoric makes it more difficult to question state actions, inhibiting political scrutiny and accountability (*Varsity*, 17 April 2020), and that as with the 'war on terrorism', exceptional levels of state control could gradually become part of the 'new normal'. In an article titled 'War metaphors used for COVID-19 are compelling but also dangerous' on the academic-authored news website *The Conversation*, Dr Costanza Musu suggests:

> It is under the guise of these categorizations that we have already seen, across the world, shifts towards dangerous authoritarian power-grabs, as in Hungary, where Prime Minister Viktor Orbán seized wide-ranging emergency powers and the ability to rule by decree.
>
> Similarly, in the Philippines President Rodrigo Duterte, in the context of a national emergency bill, gained the right to punish people spreading 'false information' about the outbreak, a right that could easily be used to silence political dissent.
>
> (*The Conversation*, 8 April 2020)

Many of the comments on the extent to which war rhetoric was helpful in shaping the global response to the virus have interesting parallels with—and perhaps lessons for—transnational crime. Consider the following suggestion from the war studies academic Professor Sir Lawrence Freedman and keep it in mind as you continue reading this chapter:

> Covid-19 is a universal threat. This is why, as we develop the responses we need to, we should veer away from the language of conflict and think in terms of cooperation in a global effort.
>
> (*New Statesman*, 11 April 2020)

Barak, 2015; Bittle et al., 2018; Pearce, 1976). Critical criminologists sometimes contrast the 'crimes of the powerful' with the 'crimes of the powerless' (for example, Barak, 2015, 2018; Wilson and Braithwaite, 1978), but this distinction is less compelling in the context of transnational crime. The label 'crimes of the powerless' seems far less appropriate for the crimes of organised crime groups such as the huge and wealthy 'Cosa Nostra' from Sicily, Italy, or the 'Red Command' in Rio de Janeiro, Brazil than it does for conventionally defined crimes typically committed by individuals or street-level gangs, such as burglary, shoplifting, or robbery.

As Green and Ward (2004) emphasise, in some parts of the world organised crime is powerful enough to compete with states and corporations, and we will see when considering drug trafficking and people smuggling that it can even corrupt otherwise lawful businesses and government officials. Colombian and Mexican drug-trafficking cartels are among the largest businesses in the Latin American region and their bosses are among the richest people in the world. The profits from the international drug trade have enabled the largest cartels to allegedly pay off politicians, even presidents, and to launder multiple millions of dollars at a time in some of the world's most prestigious banks, including HSBC (*The Guardian*, 11 December 2012). In contrast to the Cosa Nostra and the Red Command, which are known for extorting small businesses and corrupting street-level officials, including local police units, we will see that international drug-trafficking networks like Mexico's Sinaloa are also known to negotiate with senior state officials and the bosses of major corporations. Meanwhile, cartel bosses increasingly act and sound like politicians and corporate executives. Green and Ward (2004) describe the leaders of such Latin American drug-trafficking organisations as 'narco elites'.

The term 'elite' is widely used in critical criminology to describe the leaders of powerful mafia organisations as well as states and corporations. However, it is less commonly used in reference to other forms of organised crime, such as terrorism and people smuggling, and rarely used to describe the organisations themselves. In the absence of established criminological terms for all three areas of organisational criminal activity, we will continue to use state crime, corporate crime, and organised crime, even where we have no need to distinguish between them. When it comes to describing the *perpetrators* of crime, however, we will borrow a more general term from Hallsworth and Lea (2011) and refer to the leaders of all forms of transnational crime, whether state, corporate, or organised, as *powerful offenders*. An advantage of this term's emphasis on the power of transnational offenders is that it draws attention to the similarities between the causes of these types of transnational crime, again challenging the traditional definition of 'crimes of the powerful'. The similarities are also evident when we consider how so-called 'state-corporate crime' has been defined and analysed. Kramer (1992) and Matthews and Kauzlarich (2000) use this term to refer to 'serious social harms that result from the interaction of political and economic organizations' (Michalowski and Kramer, 2007) and have developed a framework for its analysis which, as Green and Ward (2004) explain, involves considering:

1. organisational motivations or goals;
2. opportunity; and
3. social control.

Matthews and Kauzlarich (2000: 293) argue that state–corporate crime arises from 'a coincidence of pressure for goal attainment, availability and perceived attractiveness of illegitimate means, and an absence or weakness of social control measures' (in Green and Ward, 2004: 29), but the same could be said of many types of transnational crime. We will see through our analysis of the causes of drug trafficking, toxic waste, and cybercrime that on a transnational level, there are potentially billions of dollars to be made from criminal activity. We will see through our analysis of state terror, drug trafficking, and people smuggling that political goals can extend as far as the capture, protection, or development of nation states and their economies: what social scientists describe as 'state building'. We will see when considering all of our major examples of transnational crime that it is common for people working for powerful organisations, whether outlawed, state, or corporate, to take advantage of the possibilities money and power bring in order to fulfil the expectations of their employers, through illegitimate as well as legitimate means (**Figure 14.3**). Think how tempting it must be for people working in the finance department of a TNC's London office to invest company profits in banks or investment companies operating in Luxembourg, Jersey, or the Cayman Islands rather than London where they will pay much higher taxes. Our examples will also demonstrate how little power the international political and legal communities have to hold all these types of 'powerful offenders' to account.

The public and the private

As for the final problematic distinction, the line between the public (that is, under state control) and the private (not under state control), our examples will show you the extent to which states contract, negotiate, or compete with corporations, civil society NGOs, and even organised criminal groups to police transnational as well

Figure 14.3 For all kinds of transnational organisations, whether outlawed, state, or corporate, there is a temptation to use wealth and power to advance the group's goals through illegitimate as well as legitimate means
Source: Ichigo121212/Pixabay

as local crime. We will also see that when they carry out public functions like policing, private bodies are on average more likely to resort to violence, criminal neglect, and other human rights abuses.

During the US military occupation and presence in Iraq 2003–11, for example, US and Iraqi authorities jointly turned to local Shi'ite militia groups such as the notoriously violent Madhi Army to fight al-Qaida (the extremist organisation responsible for the 9/11 attacks) and other Sunni rebels, and to transnational security companies such as the US-based Blackwater (since renamed as Academi) to provide tens of thousands of soldiers to guard government buildings and officials (Fitzgibbon and Lea, 2020). Blackwater was involved in hundreds of shooting incidents and three of its employees were prosecuted in the US courts for murder and manslaughter following an incident in which civilians had been shot and 17 killed, although one employee was subsequently acquitted (ibid). In the 2010s, the Russian private military company Wagner was contracted to train soldiers in the Central African Republic (ibid), and also to provide between 800–1,000 soldiers, reportedly backed by Russian army jets, to fight alongside rebel groups in Libya (*The Economist*, 30 May 2020). In the domestic context, companies like G4S and Serco (both London-based multinational security companies) compete to provide criminal justice services like the management of prisons and community sentences. G4S and Serco have also been accused of unlawful killings and other human rights violations, including sexual assaults and the degrading treatment of people held in immigration removal centres (Fitzgibbon and Lea, 2020).

Similarly, state authorities increasingly rely on and sometimes join forces with organised crime groups to regulate local drug markets and other licit and illicit markets, especially in areas where the police choose not to operate or are not welcomed by the local community. This fact not only blurs the line between the public and the private but also—again—the one between the powerful and the powerless. It provides further evidence for the suggestion that it is not only states and corporations that should be considered powerful. Gangs like the Sicilian Cosa Nostra and the Red Command are so authoritative that they can be seen as 'shadow powers' (see Misse (2006) on the role played by the Red Command and other criminal gangs in policing Rio de Janeiro's favelas) or 'shadow states' (for example, Gambetta (1993) on the Cosa Nova, in Green and Ward (2004)) in that they informally govern the communities in which they operate on behalf of or in place of the Italian and Brazilian states.

As a final example of the blurred public/private distinction in transnational crime and justice, NGOs are now playing an increasingly significant role in policing transnational crime, especially crimes perpetrated by states and corporations. Our examples in the next section contain many instances of NGO involvement, but is this the best way of addressing the issues? Consider this question in **What do you think? 14.1** before you read on. We then explore one example of an NGO campaign to address transnational crime in the next section, in **Controversy and debate 14.2**.

It is the sheer scale of such non-state involvement in transnational justice that we are concerned with in this chapter. To distinguish transnational security companies or organised criminal networks from transnational police forces as providing private or community security rather than public security distracts from the fact that they are ultimately performing public functions. (For a detailed discussion of the shift towards such *privatised authority* in the transnational context, see Fitzgibbon and Lea (2020: esp. Ch. 3).)

It is clear that the boundaries between all these social science concepts have become increasingly blurred, especially when they are used to explore matters of crime and justice in a global context. We have seen that in the global context, social scientists are now turning to concepts that straddle these kinds of distinctions or implicitly recognise that they are inadequate for describing the

WHAT DO YOU THINK? 14.1

Ways of tackling transnational issues

In each of the examples of transnational crime we deal with later in this chapter, we will consider both global state responses and those of global civil society NGOs. Consider the following question and note down your initial thoughts, and what implications this has for how you think we should tackle transnational crimes:

- Is global warming more likely to be halted by the chief executives of polluting companies and the representatives of nation states reaching agreements at international climate change conferences, or through public pressure—instigated by environmental pressure groups—naming and shaming governments into action?

Keep this question in mind as you read on and see whether your thoughts change throughout the chapter.

modern world, especially the Global South. These include *internationalised* and *militarised* crime and justice, *powerful offenders*, and *privatised authority*. The relevance of these alternative terms in the global context will become clearer in the next section, where we explore examples of transnational crime in more depth.

14.3 Key areas of concern for transnational criminology

In this section we will explore the theoretical concepts we introduced in **section 14.2** in more detail through investigating five key areas of transnational criminological interest. We will look at:

- state terror and the 'war on terror';
- drug trafficking and the 'war on drugs';
- people smuggling and the 'war on migration';
- toxic waste;
- cybercrime and cybersecurity.

We chose these examples because they represent some of the most serious and prolific transnational crimes. We also wanted to ensure that we looked at major examples of state and corporate as well as organised crime, and that we included within them illustrations of the impact of crime and justice in both the Global North and South, alongside our more general illustrations of the international organisations and networks responsible for them. Our intention is not to explore similarities or variations in the impact of these crimes, or to explore the local contexts in which the specific incidences we describe took place. (In other words, to conduct the kind of analysis we described in discussing the scope of transnational criminology in **section 14.2**.) That would require far more detailed case studies than those we present here. Our main objective in this section is to describe the *global characteristics* of these general areas of transnational crime and justice.

For each area of transnational crime, we will cover both the nature of the crime and the nature of the international responses to it. The former includes the harm caused by that type of crime, the kind of people who are most often offenders or victims, whether it might be defined as a crime according to international law or to international civil society, and its underlying and more immediate global causes. The latter includes the extent to which the responses to that type of crime are coordinated between police and other criminal justice authorities in different countries, the extent to which they involve non-state as well as state actors, their effectiveness, and the extent to which the responses might be regarded as disproportional or excessive and themselves defined as criminal according to international law or to international civil society.

A transnational approach to state terror and the 'war on terror'

Terrorism is practised by states as much as by conventionally defined international terrorist networks like the jihadist group known as Islamic State or Daesh, which operated across much of the Middle East and North Africa in the 2010s, or the Irish Republican Army (IRA), whose violence peaked in the 1970s and operated mostly in Northern Ireland, but also targeted civilian populations in the Republic of Ireland and in other parts of the UK. Terrorism is an age-old crime which is closely linked to war and political conflict.

Green and Ward (2004) distinguish between:

> *'Classic' terrorism*, that is, the clandestine use of violence against civilian targets for purposes of intimidation, or to create a climate of fear, in pursuit of political goals . . . *State terror*, in which civilian targets . . . are attacked for the purposes of intimidation, but the perpetrators are not considered 'terrorists' because they are uniformed servants of the state . . . [and] assassinations or extra-judicial executions . . . by a clandestine death squad linked with the state.
>
> (Green and Ward, 2004: 105, emphasis added)

Besides the numerous international atrocities committed in the name of Daesh or the IRA, examples of transnational terrorism include:

- The bombing, on 7 August 1998, of the US embassy in Nairobi, Kenya, by the Jihadist network, al-Qaida, which resulted in over 200 civilian deaths. Al-Qaida simultaneously bombed the US embassy in Dar es Salaam, Tanzania, killing a further 12 people. The leader of al-Qaida, Osama bin Laden, had made a declaration of war on the US two years earlier.

- The radical Central African rebel group, the Lord's Resistance Army (LRA), which operates in northern Uganda, South Sudan, the Central African Republic, and the Democratic Republic of the Congo. It aims to establish a Christian state, and at its peak in the mid-1990s had as many as 3,000 soldiers. The LRA has become infamous for using machetes to deform people's faces, in addition to committing mass rape and murder. In 2005, the International Criminal Court (ICC) served arrest warrants on the LRA's two most senior commanders, Joseph Kony and his deputy Vincent Otti. Two years later, Otti was reportedly killed by the LRA over internal disagreements concerning peace negotiations. Kony remains at large to this day. We consider the international response to these atrocities in **Controversy and debate 14.2**.

! CONTROVERSY AND DEBATE 14.2

Can awareness turn into action?

In March 2012, a lesser known US NGO called Invisible Children released a short video documentary called *Kony 2012*, which went viral on social media. As its name suggests, the video (which can still be viewed online—search 'KONY 2012' on YouTube) centred on Joseph Kony, one of the leaders of the radical African rebel group known as the Lord's Resistance Army. Its stated aim was 'to stop the rebel group the LRA and their leader', and it focused particularly on the plight of Ugandan children at the hands of Kony and the LRA: in addition to committing mass rape, murder, and mutilation, the LRA is also accused of abducting 60,000 children (*The Guardian*, 8 March 2012) in order to brainwash the boys into fighting for the army and to enslave and rape the girls (*The Guardian*, 7 March 2012). In October 2011, the US had sent 100 troops to Uganda to help its army combat the LRA, mainly by capturing or killing Kony and its other senior leaders, and the video aimed to support this goal by making Kony 'famous', which Invisible Children argued would put pressure on US policymakers to remain committed to the mission.

The video begins with the on-screen statement 'Nothing is more powerful than an idea' and viewers are urged to share it with as many people as possible 'in such a way that we can't be ignored [and] awareness [can be] turned into action'. It highlights the global nature of social media and suggests that platforms like Facebook can bring about the kind of international cooperation needed to address the issue:

> We are living in a new world, Facebook World, in which 750 million people share ideas, not thinking in borders. It's a global community, bigger than the US. Arresting Joseph Kony will prove that the world we live in has new rules, that the technology that has brought our planet together is allowing us to respond to the problems of our friends.
>
> (*Kony 2012* video, Invisible Children, 2012)

The video was certainly successful in raising awareness: it was a near-instant success, gaining the backing of many celebrities and resulting in the Twitter hashtag '#stopkony' trending around the world. But, as for its lasting impact, Kony is still at large and both the US and Uganda ended their hunt for him in 2017, in the belief that he no longer posed a significant threat to Ugandan security (*New York Times*, 17 May 2017). The video was also highly controversial. It was argued to be misleading and Invisible Children faced criticism for its 'Hollywood style campaigning' which focused on dramatic aspects rather than the need for less 'sexy' but more fundamental changes like addressing widespread poverty (*The Guardian*, 8 March 2012).

We have seen that transnational crimes are often complex and that responding involves extensive international cooperation. The video demonstrates the huge global 'reach' that NGOs and social media campaigns can have, but the suggestion was that it simplified the issues involved and the nature of the international response required. It may have been viewed and shared by millions but we could argue that it failed to encourage meaningful engagement or bring about tangible positive action from those in influential positions. Invisible Children's webpage on *Kony 2012* appears to acknowledge the controversy surrounding the video but to claim that the campaign brought about real change:

> The most important thing you need to know about Kony 2012 is what it is enabling us to do today to help save lives and end violence in central Africa. Thanks to the generosity and action of millions around the world in response to the Kony 2012 campaign, we moved world leaders to take unprecedented action to end the LRA crisis and we were able to dramatically expand our life-saving protection and recovery programs across central Africa.
>
> (https://invisiblechildren.com/kony-2012/ Accessed 22 November 2020)

You might like to do some more research yourself into this controversial video and its impact. You should consider the extent to which this type of awareness-raising is effective in tackling transnational crime (does it matter if people are under-informed or don't engage for the 'right' motives so long as they do?), and how far it can help those affected and bring about tangible change.

- The fire-bombing, on 28 April 2020, of a city-centre open-air market in the northern Syrian town of Afrin, which resulted in over 50 civilian deaths, including 11 children. Afrin was under Turkish occupation. Twelve Turkish-backed militia soldiers also died. No one has yet claimed responsibility for the attack. The Turkish government has blamed Kurdish militia groups operating in the region.

Examples of transnational state terror—or 'terrorism from above' (Ruggiero, 2003)—include:

- The Mỹ Lai massacre in 1968 in which US troops killed over 300 unarmed South Vietnamese civilians (see **What do you think? 14.2**).
- The use of 'strategic' or 'terror bombing' during the Second World War, for instance by the UK and US against Germany, killing an estimated 600,000 civilians. In the worst single atrocity, committed after the war had already been effectively won, 1,250 American and British warplanes dropped 3,900 tonnes of bombs, including chemical weapons, on the German city of Dresden between 13–15 February 1945, killing as many as 25,000 civilians. Close to 30,000 British civilians also died from German strategic bombing during the London Blitz in 1940–1.
- The use of an atomic bomb by the United States Army in Hiroshima, Japan, on 6 August 1945, resulting in the immediate deaths of an estimated 80,000 civilians. A further 60,000 died over the next few months from radiation poisoning. Three months earlier, on the night of 9 August 1945, 1,665 tonnes of US incendiary bombs killed over 100,000 civilians at the peak of a terror-bombing campaign against the city of Tokyo.

At the time, the deliberate targeting of civilian populations was still considered extraordinary. Since the Second World War, such terror has since become an ordinary tactic of war. There have been no declared wars since 1942 and today violent political conflicts almost always involve armies fighting insurgents—rebels willing to engage in violence against the government—rather than the armies of other nation states. The conflicts are based more on ethnic or political than national identity (Institute for Public Policy Research, 2008), yet remain transnational rather than civil in the sense that they typically cross into neighbouring countries—by definition, ethnic and political identities do not respect national borders—or usually draw support from other states or rebel groups from other countries, who may send their own soldiers or militia to fight alongside local forces. Less than one-third of countries are politically stable (ibid).

Another development that is relevant to our discussion is that wars now tend to be more asymmetric than they were in the past. Rebel insurgent groups rarely have the military power to meet national armies on the battlefield, so they are more likely to resort to terrorism to achieve their political goals. Meanwhile, the uniformed soldiers that make up national armies also find themselves under strain to turn to terror tactics, as it is often difficult to distinguish the insurgents they are fighting from

WHAT DO YOU THINK? 14.2

State terror as a transnational crime

Below is a harrowing first-hand account provided by an American soldier of his involvement in the infamous 16 March 1968 Mỹ Lai massacre in Vietnam in which US troops killed over 300 (though estimates range to over 500) unarmed South Vietnamese civilians. Consider in what ways the atrocity might be described as a transnational crime and why, from a transnational perspective, it might have occurred.

> I went to turn her over and there was a little baby with her that I also killed. The baby's face was half gone. My mind just went. The training came to me and I just started killing. Old men, women, children, water buffaloes, everything. We were told to leave nothing standing. We did what we were told, regardless of whether they were civilians. They was the enemy. Period. Kill. If you don't follow a direct order you can be shot yourself . . . A lot of people were just doing it and I followed. I lost all sense of direction. I just started killing any kinda way I can kill. . . . I was personally responsible for killing about 25 people. Personally, I don't think beforehand that anyone thought we would kill so many people. I mean, we're talking about four to five hundred people. We wiped out the whole village, a whole community. . . . We just rounded 'em up, me and a couple of guys, just put the M-16 on automatic and just mowed 'em down.
>
> (Quoted in Bilton and Sim, 1993: 130–1, in McLaughlin, 1996: 306)

What the soldier doesn't mention in his testimony was that some of the victims were first gang-raped, and that some of their corpses were mutilated with the name of the army unit carved into their chests (BBC, 20 July 1998). The unit commander served only 40 months under house arrest as a result of the massacre.

others in the communities from which they are recruited. American bombs killed at least 500,000 civilians during the Vietnam war of the mid-1960s to the mid-1970s. In 2003, the Sudanese state responded to an uprising in the Darfur region of the country by arming and recruiting a militia group, the Janjaweed, to murder tens of thousands of civilians. At least 250,000 civilians have been killed by a combination of state and rebel forces since war broke out in Syria in 2011.

It is important to emphasise that few leaders of governments or rebel groups are held to account by the international community for their use of terror tactics. We have already mentioned Joseph Kony, one of only a handful of terrorists to be served with an international arrest warrant by the ICC. Since it came into force in 2002, the ICC has conducted just 11 major investigations and all but one focused on African nations. It has served arrest warrants against just 44 people—all African—and completed criminal convictions against just three, fewer than the four defendants who have died awaiting arrest or prosecution, including Vincent Otti. On 8 July 2019, the ICC found Congolese warlord Bosco Ntaganda guilty of leading a campaign of mass murder, rape, and sex and child slavery, backed by the government of Rwanda. Ntaganda was subsequently sentenced to 30 years' imprisonment. Arguably far more effective than the ICC has been the political pressure states and rebel groups have been put under by international human rights organisations like Amnesty International and Human Rights Watch, whose own investigations and active engagement with the world media have kept terrorist atrocities in the public limelight for years after they occurred—knowing this, you might feel differently regarding the question we posed in **What do you think? 14.1**.

We can identify three major areas of state crime in the global 'war' on (conventional) terror:

- the fighting of terror with terror (already mentioned);
- the 'disappearing' of terrorist suspects;
- the subsequent psychological and physical torture of these suspects.

By 'disappearing', we mean the militarised state practice of detaining people indefinitely, in secret locations, and without resort to law. Remember that in discussing crime and war in **section 14.2** we noted that human rights conventions dictate that we have the right to liberty except in times of war. This practice therefore contravenes human rights conventions, but it is a common tactic of both organised crime and authoritarian dictatorships. It was used, for example, by South American military governments with the support of the US Central Intelligence Agency (CIA) in the later decades of the 20th century, in response to the threat posed to them by insurgency movements. Of those who disappeared during the 1976–83 Argentine dictatorship, 30,000 were never seen again (McLaughlin, 1996), including over 100 left-wing activists (*The Guardian*, 26 May 2016). The US helped to turn disappearing into a transnational, 21st-century practice through its rendition programme—rendition means moving people from one country to another in order to avoid the first country's laws, including those on interrogation and detention.

Open Society Foundations (2013) documented 136 cases in which terrorist suspects were illegally detained by US authorities following President George Bush's declaration of a global 'war on terror' a week after the atrocities of 9/11. Bush counted on the support of 54 countries. Some provided intelligence on the people rendered or allowed them to be taken from their national territory. Others allowed them to be transported through their national airspace. Most significantly, a few (Afghanistan, Lithuania, Poland, and Thailand, as well as US authorities in Guantánamo Bay, Cuba) operated secret 'black sites' to which detainees were taken for 'enhanced interrogation' by American CIA agents. A number of private aviation companies were also contracted to provide logistical support and aircraft (Global Policy Forum, 2008). The CIA is known to have hired aircraft to operate 60 rendition circuits to and from its black sites between 2001 and 2009, involving 120 individuals (Raphael et al., 2019).

Many more thousands of people were also detained extra-legally in US prison camps. These included Camp Bucca, Iraq, where 20,000 people were held at its peak in 2008, and the Parwan Detention Facility in Bagram Airport, Afghanistan, where 3,000 people were held as recently as November 2011, a few months before it was handed over to Afghan authorities. They also included four detention camps in Guantánamo Bay. Most of the 779 detainees that have been held in these camps were originally arrested legally in Afghanistan or Iraq. When Donald Trump was elected President in 2016, close to 50 people were still detained in Guantánamo Bay, some still awaiting trial. Like the previous US President, Barack Obama, Trump did not directly refer to being 'at war' with terrorism, but in 2018 he reversed a previous executive order signed by Obama in 2009 that the Guantánamo Bay detention facilities be closed (**Figure 14.4**).

We have already noted that under the 1948 Geneva Conventions, states are required to release enemy soldiers after the hostilities been two sovereign states have ended. By defining the terrorist suspects as 'enemy combatants' rather than soldiers or common criminals, the Bush administration was able to detain them in a state of legal limbo (*The Economist*, 29 June 2014). Of the eight detainees who were eventually tried and found guilty by a military tribunal at the camp, three remain after Congress refused to allow their transfer to US prisons (the others

14.3 KEY AREAS OF CONCERN FOR TRANSNATIONAL CRIMINOLOGY

Figure 14.4 A protest by Amnesty International against Guantánamo Bay detentions in 2008, a year before President Barack Obama signed an executive order that the facilities be closed

Source: Daniel Tobias/Flickr

have been transferred to other countries). All 41 detainees who remained in Guantánamo Bay in March 2018 had been held for over ten years. Of those, twenty-four had originally arrived following extradition and interrogation in the US network of secret CIA detention; 31 were still being held indefinitely without charge (Amnesty International, 2018).

In his 2018 State of the Union address to Congress, delivered on the same day as the new executive order, President Trump explained:

> Terrorists who do things like place bombs in civilian hospitals are evil. When possible, we have no choice but to annihilate them. When necessary, we must be able to detain and question them. But we must be clear: Terrorists are not merely criminals. They are unlawful enemy combatants. And when captured overseas, they should be treated like the terrorists they are. . . . I am asking Congress to ensure that in the fight against ISIS [Daesh] and al-Qaida, we continue to have all necessary power to detain terrorists wherever we chase them down, wherever we find them.
>
> (Cited in Amnesty International, 2018: 1)

Continuing to justify exceptional extra-legal detention with reference to the continuing threat of international terrorism, nearly two decades after 9/11, adds weight to the argument made by radical criminologists and human rights activists (see the discussion of crime and war in **section 14.2**) that the exception is in danger of becoming the norm.

Arguably, the US-led 'war on terror' has also normalised the practice of transnational torture. The fact that the US government was unlawfully detaining people was only part of the problem. It also used 24-hour solitary confinement and 'enhanced interrogation' techniques in Guantánamo Bay, justifying these practices by defining the detainees as 'enemy combatants' (and so not due the special legal rights to humane treatment also granted under the Geneva Conventions to prisoners of war). The conditions of detention in Guantánamo Bay fell far short of international human rights standards in the Bush era, but United Nations inspectors were prevented from speaking with detainees. An official US parliamentary investigation (Senate Select Committee on Intelligence, 2014) confirmed that the enhanced interrogation techniques included hoodings, beatings, binding in stress positions, and simulated drowning, following prolonged periods of sleep deprivation and subjection to repetitive noise. These came in addition to the sensory deprivation that accompanied the regime of 24/7 isolation. A British parliamentary investigation (Intelligence and Security Committee of Parliament, 2018) uncovered 198 cases in which UK security personnel received intelligence from the US that had clearly been obtained through such forms of psychological torture.

In summary, state terror and the 'war on terror' provide a clear example of the transnationalising of crime and justice in the 21st century, including 'globalizing torture' (Open Society Foundations, 2013). Today's civil conflicts cross borders in much the same way as the inter-national wars of the past, but at the same time violence by both nation states and the rebels they are fighting is increasingly targeted at civilians (Institute for Public Policy Research, 2008). States increasingly enlist powerful non-state actors such as militia groups and private security companies to support their side of the conflict, and they tend to define their enemies as criminals, terrorists, or enemies rather than soldiers. This allows them to suspend the right to lawful detention and to refuse detainees prisoner of war status. Guantánamo Bay symbolises the potential threat to human rights that is posed by such a militarised vision of transnational justice. Before moving on to our next example of transnational crime, drug trafficking, consider the likely causes of state terror and the nature of the 'war on terror' in **What do you think? 14.3**.

A transnational approach to international drug trafficking and the 'war on drugs'

International drug trafficking is a prime example of transnational organised crime. It was also the first transnational crime on which the international community declared war (see **Conversations 14.1**). It involves billions of dollars and numerous individuals and organisations across the globe, and infiltrates into all levels of societies bringing with it significant issues of corruption and

WHAT DO YOU THINK? 14.3

Reflecting on state terror

Why do states commit acts of terror and how can they be held to account internationally? Reflect on the comments made by Green and Ward (2009) and think about your own views.

As to why states commit acts of terror, Green and Ward (2009) suggest that:

> States are in a continual, though not linear, process of development and war-making remains central both to defining states and to fostering their capacity for violence.
>
> (Green and Ward, 2009: 117)

> Revenge and retribution retain a powerful emotional appeal in virtually all societies . . . Bureaucratic organisation and state violence are an inherently unstable combination . . . If the agency seeks to confine its workers to legitimate means . . . it is likely to generate strain between their official objectives and the means for achieving them . . . If, on the other hand, it sanctions the use of clearly illegitimate means, the resulting secrecy and impunity creates motives and opportunities for crime that can easily run out of control.
>
> (Green and Ward, 2009: 122–3)

As for how states might be held to account, the authors offer the following analysis:

> Internal opposition movements and human rights organizations link with transnational networks, which in turn place pressure on . . . powerful states in order to influence repressive regimes.
>
> (Green and Ward, 2009: 126)

CONVERSATIONS 14.1

Why the international 'war on drugs' has to end
with **Maria Lucia Karam**

While working as a judge in Brazil from 1982 to 2000, I became increasingly aware of the vast amount of pain and harm caused by drug prohibition and I frequently wrote and spoke about drug legalisation. In 2007, I joined an international non-profit drug reform NGO called Law Enforcement Against Prohibition (LEAP). LEAP is a network of current and former members of the law enforcement and criminal justice communities (including police, judges, and prosecutors) which campaigns for the end of drug prohibition and the introduction of a system of legalised regulation of the production, sales, and consumption of all drugs. From 2009 to 2016 I served on LEAP's Board of Directors, and I chaired a new LEAP branch in Brazil from its creation in 2010 until it was dissolved in 2018.

Former US president Richard Nixon declared a 'war on drugs' in 1971. Before long, this war-like approach spread throughout the world. However, the 'war on drugs' is not truly a war against drugs. It is not a war against things. As with any other war, it is targeted at *people*. The 'enemies' in this war are the producers, sellers, and consumers of the selected substances that were made illegal. Yet, the real targets of this war, and the ones who suffer the most pain because of it, are the most vulnerable members of these groups; that is, the poor, marginalised, non-white people who act in local illegal markets, such as the small dealers of the Brazilian *favelas*.

In my view, the 'war on drugs' has created quite serious social harm, while failing to solve any of the harms caused by the drugs themselves. In effect, it has actually created much more social harm, while having not solved any of the harms caused by the drugs themselves. In the century since drug prohibition became a global policy (this began in the early 20th century), of which 50+ years have been characterised by a war-like approach, illegal drugs keep getting cheaper, more potent, more diversified, and far easier for everyone to access than they were before prohibition.

However, the 'war on drugs' is not only a failed policy. It is much worse, as drug prohibition causes violence and deaths.

We can see a clear link between prohibition of desire and violence if we look at the examples of alcohol and tobacco. The fact that alcohol is legal and readily available does not lead to people carrying guns; there are no shootings resulting from the existence of pubs or any kind of liquor stores. Similarly, there is no violence around the production or sales of tobacco. So why does it surround the production or sales of marijuana, cocaine, or heroin? The obvious difference is prohibition. The production and supply of any drug are coupled with guns and violence only when they happen in an illegal market, and this was exactly what happened when alcohol was prohibited in the US between 1920 and 1933.

Illegal drugs have been used by millions of people. According to the United Nations Office on Drugs and Crime (UNODC), in 2017 an estimated 271 million people worldwide aged 15 to 64 had used illegal drugs in the previous year (UNODC, 2019b). The intervention of the criminal system in a market that supplies such a large demand brings another inevitable dangerous consequence. The production and supply of illegal drugs have become the main ways of profiting from illicit activities; this means they are the greatest incentive for state officials to become corrupt, and they also bring in money to fund other illicit activities. Prohibition creates and places gangs, cartels, mafias, and other criminal businesses in what was previously a legal market.

Prohibition has been imposed on drugs under the pretext of protecting people's health. However, it paradoxically causes *more* serious risks to health, as it implies the lack of any control and regulation of the market. The gangs and cartels are those who decide what they will produce and sell; what will be the toxic potential of the drugs; what cutting agents (chemicals used to dilute a drug) they will use; what price they will charge; where and to whom they will sell the drugs. Prohibition also hinders drug users receiving or seeking assistance. When treatment is compulsory, as ruled in many countries' laws, it violates human rights and has been proven ineffective in dealing with addiction. On the other hand, users may not search for the most effective voluntary treatment because they would have to disclose their illegal conduct. The fear of being arrested may have tragic consequences as it can prevent people from searching for help and, in the worst cases, can result in fatal overdoses. Last but not least, prohibition causes environmental harm. This includes the manual eradication or, even worse, aerial spraying of chemical herbicides (as has happened in the Andean region) to destroy illegal drug crops. It also drives crop growers to deforest new areas in order to use them for illegal cultivation, often in fragile ecosystems.

It is time to put an end to a policy that, besides not attaining its unreasonable pretension of saving people from themselves, causes too much harm. It is time to legalise—and therefore regulate and control—the production, supply, and consumption of all drugs.

Maria Lucia Karam, retired judge in Rio de Janeiro, Brazil, and former board member of LEAP (Law Enforcement Action Partnership, formerly Law Enforcement Against Prohibition)

---

violence—amongst other social problems. The case of Mexican drug lord Joaquín Guzmán (often known as 'El Chapo', meaning the Shorty or Stocky—see **Figure 14.5**), the now-jailed leader of the country's Sinaloa drug cartel, provides a sense of the vast scale and impact of this issue.

On 11 July 2015, at which point he was the world's 14th richest person, El Chapo climbed down a ladder from the floor of his high-security prison cell and drove a custom-built motorbike to his escape along a rail track through a ventilated and illuminated mile-long tunnel. Over previous months, some of Germany's finest engineers had overseen the excavation of the tunnel from an abandoned building that, with the aid of a GPS watch worn by El Chapo, surfaced directly under his toilet, the only part of the cell that was not monitored by a CCTV camera.

Six months later, El Chapo was re-arrested and later extradited to stand trial in New York. Prosecutors claimed he had amassed a personal fortune of $14 billion through narco-trafficking. He was held in solitary confinement in Manhattan's federal jail.

On 17 July 2019, El Chapo was sentenced to life imprisonment and a forfeiture order of $12.6 billion on the basis of testimony provided from former associates, and from police and prison officials he had corrupted. These included:

- the governor of a second high-security prison El Chapo had previously escaped from in 2001, hidden in a laundry trolley;

Figure 14.5 The case of the Mexican drug lord Joaquín 'El Chapo' Guzmán illustrates the vast scale and impact of international drug trafficking

Source: Octavio Hoyos/Shutterstock

- Colombian drug trafficker Alex Cifuentes Villa, who testified that El Chapo had paid off Enrique Peña Nieto, Mexican president from 2012–18, with a bribe of $100 million, having first turned down Nieto's original demand for $250 million; and
- Jesus Zambada García, one of the most senior figures in El Chapo's Sinaloa cartel, and also its chief accountant, who described how a single shipment of cocaine to the US was worth up to $390 million in net profit, and on whose memory the forfeiture order was calculated. However, García was not required to provide testimony as to how and where the cartel laundered its profits, for instance the $881 million that HSBC bank had been accused of receiving but avoided prosecution for in 2012 after voluntarily paying US authorities a fine of $1.9 billion (*The Guardian*, 11 December 2012).

Figure 14.6 Transnational drug traffickers' use of corruption and violence means they have an unfair advantage over legitimate businesses when they diversify: Mexican drug cartels control much of the country's multi-billion-dollar avocado export industry
Source: Cesar Gonzalez/Pixabay

We can see that the money involved is colossal. The trade in cocaine is estimated to be a $100-billion-per-year industry (UNODC, 2019b). According to the United Nations Office on Drugs and Crime's (UNODC) annual 400-page report on the trade, close to 2,000 tonnes of cocaine were produced in 2017, double the amount produced in 2013 and an increase of 25 per cent in just one year (UNODC, 2019b). In the 1990s, drug trafficking was estimated to account for 7 per cent of Gross Domestic Product (GDP) in the cocaine-producing region of South America (Green and Ward, 2004). Latin America's 'narco elites' became 'indistinguishable from traditional, legitimate economic elites' (ibid: 97). While nearly all cocaine is still produced in the South American countries of Bolivia, Peru, and mostly Colombia, 80 per cent is now consumed in Europe or North America (UNDOC, 2019b).

Of the global cocaine market, 40 per cent is dominated by just one transnational criminal organisation, Italy's 'Ndrangheta (Saviano, 2015). However, the 'Ndrangheta have less control over the northern cocaine trail to the US and Canada than the eastern cocaine trail to Europe. At its height, Mexico's Sinaloa cartel alone made $3 billion profit a year transporting cocaine through Central America (Keefe, P. R., 'Cocaine incorporated', *The New York Times Magazine*, 15 June 2012) and it continues to sell at least $11 billion of cocaine to US consumers every year (*The Guardian*, 7 June 2019). Their greater willingness to resort to corruption and violence also gives drug traffickers an unfair advantage over legitimate businesses when they diversify their commercial activities to compete in other sectors of the economy (Lessing, 2018). Mexican cartels, for instance, control much of the country's iron ore and avocado industries (Watt and Zepeda, 2012), the latter of which is worth $2.4 billion to the export economy of the state of Michoacán alone (Wagner, 2019) (see **Figure 14.6**).

The overall drug trade is worth at least 1 per cent of global GDP (UNODC, 2019b), and this figure is higher in certain countries. In Mexico, for example, the drug trade is worth approximately 3 per cent of GDP, and a 2011 US Senate report estimated that Colombian and Mexican drug traffickers laundered $18 billion and $39 billion respectively per year (Rolles et al., 2016). In Italy, the 'Ndrangheta single-handedly accounts for 3–4 four per cent of the country's GDP (BBC, 9 September 2017).

And the damage is not solely economic. The criminal violence surrounding the control of local drug markets and the significant social problems associated with drug abuse mean that the illicit drug trade literally leaves a trail of destruction on its path into Europe and North America. The UNODC estimates that there were 585,000 deaths worldwide related to drug use in 2017, three times more than from alcohol (UNODC, 2019b). When the cocaine trail from South to North America switched from the Caribbean to Central America in the early 2000s, the murder rate soon doubled in almost every country (*The Economist*, 26 November 2011). As many as half of all intentional homicides in Mexico are drug-related (Open Society Foundation, 2016), and a record 35,964 murders were registered by Mexican authorities in 2018 (*The Guardian*, 21 August 2019).

So what are the underlying causes of transnational drug trafficking and the many associated social harms? We have already noted the importance of financial gain. A kilo of cocaine is worth £325 to a Colombian farmer and £51,695 to a street dealer in London (Rolles et al., 2016). Worldwide, one square kilometre of land dedicated to cocaine production yields on average $37.7 million revenue, compared to $47.66 million for cannabis and $6 million for opium, but a mere $107,000 for coffee, $140,000 for rice, and $56,000 for wheat (McKay, 2014). It is simply impossible for a criminologist to adequately explain the causes of drug-related corruption, violence, and so on in any place without investigating the links between global demand and supply, just as an economist would in studying a legal market in, say, coffee or rice.

Besides commerce, it is also important to note that in politically unstable countries like Afghanistan (the world's leading producer of opium), Colombia, and Mexico, drug revenues have supported conflicts between social, religious, and revolutionary groups competing for a stake in local or national politics. In the case of Mexico, the violence surrounding the drug trade is highly localised. In an average year, there are no recorded homicides in one-third of the country's 2,466 municipalities (Cálderon et al., 2018). In the remaining municipalities, mayors or former mayors are 12 times more likely to be killed than the average citizen (ibid). In some parts of the country, militia groups compete with cartels and state authorities for control over local politics and the local economy, including the drug trade (Gledhill, 2015). The Mexican tradition of political localism had been around long before the transnational drug trade (Pansters, 2018). For most of the 20th century, the country's regions were largely autonomous, but local corruption and drug production was already widespread (Boullosa and Wallace, 2015).

Moving on to the responses, we have already seen how international drug trafficking has led to the emergence of criminal actors who are rich and powerful enough to corrupt both local and national government officials, even presidents, not only in order to facilitate their crimes but also to evade capture, escape prison, and avoid prosecution when they are caught. According to Mexican authorities, drug traffickers pay $100 million a month to local municipal police forces (Rolles et al., 2016) and, in 2012, four army generals were arrested for allegedly facilitating drug trafficking (Lessing, 2018). The US tried and failed to have El Chapo extradited on several occasions before the Mexican state finally did so at the end of 2015. El Chapo even had connections with Interpol (the International Criminal Police Organisation) police officers working in the US embassy in Mexico City (Saviano, 2015).

In assessing the responses to transnational drug trafficking, we also return once again to the concept of war. Here, we are concerned with the negative impacts of the international 'war on drugs'. Not only are the production, sale, and consumption of drugs like cocaine, opium, and cannabis criminalised in most countries in the world—a position that is supported by the United Nations—but they generally attract exceptional police powers and exemplary sentences. Consider that:

- in the US, the world's largest drug-consumption market, the proportion of the prison population sentenced for drug-related offences rose from 8 per cent in the late 1970s, when President Nixon declared the international drug trade to be the greatest threat faced by the nation, to almost 25 per cent by 1990 (*The Economist*, 2 May 2015);

- before the Fair Sentencing Act 2010, the US federal government sentencing guidelines required judges to impose a minimum prison sentence of five years for the possession of just 5 grams of crack cocaine;

- drug dealing is among the three leading offences for which people are prosecuted and sentenced in all Central and South American countries (Darke and Karam, 2016);

- in Brazil, three in ten male prisoners and six in ten female prisoners were sentenced for 'drug trafficking' (Darke, 2018).

The international 'war on drugs' is also largely to blame for the extraordinary increase in police violence in post-dictatorship Brazil that we considered in **section 13.5** and returned to in **Conversations 14.1**. In the early to mid-2010s, the Mexican National Human Rights Commission received 1,000 complaints of police torture a year (Open Society Foundation, 2016). Mexican police and security forces are also accused of direct or indirect involvement in thousands of extrajudicial killings and disappearings (Lessing, 2018), and two in three Mexican prisoners report being beaten by the police at the time of their arrest (Human Rights Watch, 2019). Like the US 'war on terror', aspects of the Mexican 'war on drugs' are arguably as criminal as the problems they are responding to.

A transnational approach to people smuggling and the 'war on migration'

We briefly discussed migration in **section 6.3** in the context of how the media represents different groups of people. The ideas we covered there are relevant to this discussion, especially in terms of the ways in which countries respond to the phenomenon by tightening border controls, but here our focus is on the criminal activities that have sprung up around it, particularly the people-smuggling industry.

According to KNOMAD (2019), international migration has tripled over the past half century, from approximately 80 million to 266 million people living in foreign countries. Around 30 million foreign nationals worldwide were forcibly displaced from their home countries by political conflicts, economic development (such as dam building and natural resource extraction), and environmental disasters (such as earthquakes and flooding) (UNHCR, 2020). This includes 13 million Syrians, half a million of whom made their way to the EU in 2015 before

Figure 14.7 The phenomenon of migration, illustrated here by a packed boat of people arriving at Lampedusa in 2011, has led to the emergence of transnational crimes such as people smuggling

Source: photofilippo66/Shutterstock

the Turkish government agreed to secure its western borders in exchange for €6 billion (Steinhilper and Grujiters, 2018). It also includes 200,000 mostly sub-Saharan Africans who were forced to leave Libya during the 2011 Arab Spring, and of this number 60,000 paid for passage to the Italian island of Lampedusa (Ferraris, 2014)—see **Figure 14.7**.

That year, an estimated 1,500 African migrants lost their lives trying to cross the Mediterranean on small, unseaworthy boats provided by people linked to international people-smuggling networks, having often already paid £1,000 or more for transport across the Sahara Desert. Amongst those attempting this most dangerous of illicit routes into the EU (Steinhilper and Grujiters, 2018) were a group of 47 Ethiopians, seven Eritreans, five Sudanese, seven Nigerians, and six Ghanaian migrants who set off for Lampedusa from Tripoli, the capital of Libya, on 25 March 2011 in an inflatable seven-metre long rubber dinghy supplied by smugglers. Among them were two small children. Some of the women were pregnant.

Within a day, the group found themselves lost at sea, having failed to reach their destination. The smugglers they had paid for the dinghy had not provided them with life jackets or other safety equipment. One of the migrants managed to alert the Italian coastguard, which sent instructions on how to activate the GPS system on the dinghy's satellite phone, only for the phone to run out of battery. The dinghy soon ran run out of fuel and floated aimlessly in the Mediterranean until 10 April, when it drifted back onto a beach in Libya, 160 kilometres from where the journey started.

Only nine adults survived to speak of their ordeal—the others either fell overboard or died from thirst and starvation. The survivors claimed that they had been spotted but ignored by a merchant ship as well as an Italian naval helicopter, whose pilots had just thrown them bottles of water and packets of biscuits. On landing, the migrants were sent to a Libyan detention centre, and a few days later fled to Tunisia, after bribing the centre's guards. There, they took another boat and on 11 June finally made it to Lampedusa.

Aside from those who migrated as a consequence of the Arab Spring, most sub-Saharan Africans who have headed to the EU in the 21st century have been economic migrants. Since the late 2000s, the most popular illicit migrant route into the EU has been from West Africa to Italy, via Saharan Mali and Algeria, across the Mediterranean from Libya and Tunisia. Most migrants remain in the country of arrival, including Italy (Fabini, 2019), but the two most popular final destinations for those who move on are the UK and Germany. In 2019, a record 2,358 migrants were detained by British or French coastal authorities in the English Channel, four times higher than in 2018 (*The Guardian*, 1 January 2020); 3,700 migrants made it across the Channel in the first seven months of 2020 (BBC, 11 August 2020). At least 296 migrants have died trying to reach the UK from mainland Europe since 1999, including 39 Vietnamese people who suffocated in the back of a refrigerated truck on 23 October 2019 while being smuggled from Belgium (Galisson and Institute of Race Relations, 2020).

Both stages of the journey—across the Sahara and across the Mediterranean—have become increasingly dangerous in recent years, as African and EU authorities have stepped up border security. The facts are sobering:

- in the worst period on record, the 18-month period January 2015–June 2016, 6,600 migrants died in the Mediterranean (City University London et al., 2016);

- 34,361 deaths were recorded among economic migrants and political refugees attempting to avoid immigration controls to reach the shores or cross land borders into the EU between 1993 and May 2018 (*The Guardian*, 20 June 2018);

- in a television documentary broadcast in the UK (BBC, 'Europe or Die Trying', 2 October 2009), journalists came across several decomposing and unaccounted for corpses while accompanying a group of Ghanaian migrants who had been abandoned by their smugglers in the desert after they were detected by a Libyan border patrol;

- according to United Nations estimates, for every migrant who drowns in the Mediterranean, two die from starvation in the Sahara (Gunter, J., 'Secret Spectacles: The Story of a Migrant Spy', BBC Africa Eye, 23 May 2019).

Sadly, these issues are far from resolved. Gunter (2019) recounts the story of a Ghanaian man, Azeteng (a pseudonym), who in 2017 began the same journey as the migrants followed by the BBC *Panorama* programme, using a hidden camera to document the perils faced by his compatriots. Having paid $400 to board a truck with 75 other migrants in the northern Chad town of Goa for the first leg of the trip to the border with Algeria, he was required to pay additional fees at a number of rebel group-controlled checkpoints or risk being abandoned in the desert. Those who could not pay were beaten and robbed of their possessions. The few women on the truck were gang-raped. The migrants were required to pay a further $100 by smugglers working at the border to cross into Algeria. Migrants who tried to make their own way on foot were hunted down and often killed. With no means to pay, Azeteng eventually risked the 15-kilometre walk across the desert to the nearest Algerian border town. Later, he buried a fellow traveller, who had been caught and beaten by smugglers, in a makeshift graveyard containing the corpses of many hundreds of migrants who had died in the desert. Once he had made enough money, Azeteng made his way to the capital, Algiers, where he befriended a university student who lent him the money he needed to take the same route home.

Like transnational drug trafficking, the foreground factors behind the 21st-century phenomenon of transnational people smuggling are relatively straightforward. At the same time as international migration has increased, most countries have introduced visa requirements and tightened up border controls (see **Figure 14.8**). The majority of people smugglers are local entrepreneurs, attracted by the opportunity to make money from people who are trying to avoid border controls. Very few are members or work full-time for transnational criminal organisations. A smuggler working on the journey into Algeria or Libya, or across the Mediterranean into Italy, may have contacts in sub-Saharan Africa or Southern Europe, but there is little evidence that any mafia-type group is in charge of the whole route (Campana, 2018).

The underlying causes of people smuggling are more complex. Most important are:

- the increasingly global economic and social ties that cause people to migrate;
- the increasing public demands in the Global North for less immigration (as we saw in **section 6.3**, when we covered media consideration of migration), irrespective of the fact that many migrants are political refugees; and
- that a large proportion of economic migrants work for minimal wages.

To expand on this final point, a significant proportion of migrants work in conditions akin to servitude and slavery—more so than in any period of human history. Today, 24.9 million people are in forced labour—most commonly the victims of withheld wages, threats of violence, or debt bondage—one-quarter of which takes place in foreign countries (International Labour Organization and Walk Free Foundation, 2017). This figure includes 4.8 million people working in the sex industry (ibid). Like transnational people smuggling, much transnational forced labour is facilitated by border controls. Under the United Nations Convention on Organised Crime 2000, only victims of forced labour are granted the right to temporarily remain in the country in which they were exploited—in the UK, they are legally allowed to stay in the country for just 45 days. Sadly, in much of the world migrants have become a major target of the global rise in punitive populism discussed in **Chapter 13** (and also **Chapter 25**). 'The law and order discourse', Aas (2020: 83) explains, 'is . . . intertwined with demands for the reinstatement of a strong nation state with clear assumptions about national identity, otherness and boundaries.'

Similar to transnational terrorism and drug trafficking, international responses to people smuggling are criticised both for their ineffectiveness and for their war-like focus on matching violence with violence. Few people are convicted for people smuggling, let alone for manslaughter, murder, or rape and the UK government does not publish statistics on convictions for people smuggling. In response to a parliamentary question, government officials revealed that prosecutions were commenced against just 88 people between April 2015 and March 2016 (*The Guardian*, 3 July 2016) and we

Figure 14.8 Border patrols are one of the ways that states try to combat transnational crimes like people smuggling, but are they perpetuating it and contributing to its harms?

Source: Michael Dechev/Shutterstock

know that in 2016, a further 97 people were prosecuted for slavery-related offences in the UK, but only 57 were convicted (HM Government, 2018). Approximately one-third of those convictions are likely to have either involved British nationals or foreign nationals who were exploited abroad.

In contrast, governments are dedicating more and more resources to securing their borders.

- In just 15 years, European nations have spent €11 billion on deportations (Andersson, 2016).
- The EU dedicates an annual budget of €4 billion to migration control (ibid).
- In addition to the agreement with Turkey mentioned earlier, in 2015 the EU gave African nations €2 billion to spend on border security. A further undisclosed deal was reached in 2018.

Italy in particular has dedicated considerable resources to securing both its own borders and those of countries from which migrants are likely to come—we consider its actions and their consequences in **Controversy and debate 14.3**. But these trends have not been unique to Italy. Across the Mediterranean, the death rate rose from 0.4 per cent of attempted illicit crossings into the EU in 2014 to 2.4 per cent in 2018 (Kipp and Muller, 2018) and in May 2019 a lawsuit was filed at the ICC accusing the EU of an unofficial 'leave to die' policy aimed at deterring others from attempting the same journey.

A transnational approach to the disposal and regulation of toxic waste

We touched on the huge impact of and difficulty in policing crimes committed by corporations in **Chapter 12**, and the issue is relevant here as 21st-century globalisation has produced new conditions for corporate as well as state and organised transnational crime. The widespread social harms caused by criminal organisations involved in international drug trafficking, people smuggling, and slavery seem almost insignificant when measured against the colossal harms caused by otherwise legitimate global companies (Friedrichs and Rothe, 2013). The 'crimes of globalization' (ibid) committed by TNCs damage the environment as well as people. As we heard in **Conversations 12.1**, green criminologist Rob White (2010) lists waste and pollution alongside global warming and loss of biodiversity as the three largest threats facing humankind today.

One such 'crime of globalisation' was the dumping of 600 tonnes of toxic waste in Abidjan, the capital city of the Ivory Coast. During the night of 19 August 2006, residents across the city and its surrounding neighbourhoods woke up feeling nauseous. Over the coming days, 100,000 people visited a doctor for symptoms of chemical poisoning and there were 16 recorded fatalities. The poisoning was caused by 600 tonnes of a highly toxic sludge containing

CONTROVERSY AND DEBATE 14.3

Italy's response to migration

We have seen that Italy, and particularly the Italian island of Lampedusa, has been a destination for migrants—some have called the island the 'gateway to Europe' (Euronews, 2019).

In 2008, Italy agreed a €5 billion deal with Libya for the latter to bolster its own border controls and to build detention centres to hold illicit migrants. Italy's current government has banned migrant boats from landing, and even people running search-and-rescue missions—such as the global NGOs Sea Watch, Mediterranean, and Doctors without Borders—have been threatened with prosecution, with their planes and vessels grounded and impounded. This includes Sea Watch ship captain Carola Rackete, who was arrested on 28 June 2019 and temporarily held under house arrest after rescuing 42 migrants from another dinghy found drifting off the coast of Libya and dropping them off in Lampedusa (*The Guardian*, 5 July 2019).

Unsurprisingly, the risk of drowning off the Italian coast has risen as a result. Between mid-2013 and mid-2014, during which the Italian navy mounted search-and-rescue operations, the death rate stood at a relatively small 0.2 per cent of attempted illicit crossings (Heller and Pezzani, nd), but in 2015, 800 people drowned in, to date, the most tragic incident off the Italian coast (*The Independent*, 23 April 2015). The number of migrants arriving in Italy by boat dropped to 3,552 in the period 1 January to 24 July 2019, from 18,107 in the same period in 2018 (International Organization for Migration, 26 July 2019), but the number of registered deaths fell much less sharply—from 1,109 to 426 (ibid)—meaning the death rate had doubled, rising from 5.8 to 10.7 per cent of attempted illicit crossings.

hydrogen sulfide that had been dumped around the city. This waste had been transported to the country from the US on a boat (the *Probo Koala*) commissioned by Trafigura, the world's third largest international oil trader. Trafigura had then paid a small Ivorian company ('Tommy') $30,000 to take the sludge off its hands. Had the sludge been dumped in the centre of London, it would have been smelt by people living on the other side of the M25 motorway.

Trafigura was eventually fined €100 million by the Dutch authorities in a criminal law case—not for what had happened in the Ivory Coast, but for previously offloading the waste into chemical containers in Amsterdam without informing port authorities of its toxicity. Trafigura had then chosen to reload the waste and ship it further abroad rather than pay the €650,000 required to safely dispose of it. In 2009, legal action was also taken in British courts in the largest ever global civil class action, on behalf of 30,000 of the victims. At first, Trafigura insisted the sludge had caused no more than 'flu-like symptoms', but the TNC eventually agreed an out-of-court settlement of £30 million. None of Trafigura's employees have been prosecuted individually. Two of its directors were arrested in the Ivory Coast when they visited the country in 2007, but they were released from custody six months later when the TNC agreed to pay $100 million in exchange for an agreement that there would be no criminal prosecutions. The deal did not cover the captain of the *Probo Koala*, however, who later received a five-year custodial sentence, nor the owner of Tommy, who was sentenced to 20 years' imprisonment.

The Abidjan tragedy is not a lone example. At the start of this century, an estimated 440 million tonnes of hazardous, toxic waste was being produced globally every year, of which 2 per cent (five million tonnes) was 'exported' from the Global North to less economically developed nations like the Ivory Coast and then dumped in official or unregulated landfills (Clapp, 2001). According to the United Nations (UNEP, 2019), the two largest producers of toxic waste, the US and China, generate up to 65 million tonnes a year between them. Of the toxic waste produced by the US, 19 per cent are by-products of its coal or petrol industries; 5–10 per cent of all US toxic waste is dumped (ibid). Besides fossil fuels, the two main sources of global toxic waste are the chemical and electronic goods industries. Worldwide, only 20 per cent of the estimated 44.7 million tonnes of e-waste produced in 2016 was safely recycled; most of the rest was informally recycled in Asia or Africa (ibid). Lagos, the capital of Nigeria, receives 500,000 discarded computers from abroad every month (Bakare, 2020).

The Abidjan example tells us a lot about the causes of transnational toxic waste dumping, and why it is countries in the Global South that disproportionately fall victim. The main and most obvious factor (which, as we have seen, is common to many examples of transnational crime) is money. Trafigura has a higher annual turnover than the GDP of the Ivory Coast and its wealth opened opportunities for crime, allowing the company to buy its way out of its legal liabilities. More generally, the world's largest 250 TNCs produce half of all global trade between them (Clapp, 2001). As we demonstrated earlier in the chapter in our discussion of the clothing industry, not only are there literally billions of dollars to be made from the licit global economy, but individual nations find themselves in competition to provide low levels of taxation, wages, and safety standards—or simply to not enforce the law—to make their economies more attractive to TNCs. The employees of TNCs are often also under enormous strain to make money by illegitimate means. Trafigura company directors expected $7 million profit from each cargo, and instructed those in charge of the sludge being transported on the *Probo Koala* to dispose of it imaginatively (MacManus, 2012). There was much at stake for the directors too. Trafigura's most senior employees receive on average one million dollars each in Christmas bonuses (*The Guardian*, 9 December 2016).

Generally, contributing factors for toxic waste being dumped in the Global South include:

- thousands of people working in the informal economy in the Global South rely on salvaging recyclable materials from rubbish dumps to make a living;
- toxic waste disposal costs around $2,000 per tonne in the North and as little as $2.50 per tonne in the South (Lipman, 2015);
- safety standards are not only lower, but '[c]orrupt and/or inept government officials take [a cut in] the money to turn a blind eye' (White, 2009: 116);

Figure 14.9 The Akouedo dump in Abidjan, one of the sites where the global corporation Trafigura disposed of toxic waste

Source: REUTERS/Alamy Stock Photo

- there are often fewer, less rigorous inspections of vessels/vehicles and their cargos, and licences are more easily granted. When the *Probo Koala* arrived in Abidjan in 2006, Ivory Coast customs authorities had a policy of not inspecting oil tankers; Tommy was granted a licence to operate at the port just five weeks earlier, after the *Probo Koala* had left Amsterdam (MacManus, 2014).

And all this is despite the fact that most countries in the Global South, including the Ivory Coast, are signatories to the 1989 Basel Convention on the Control of Transboundary Movements of Hazardous Waste. This Convention makes it legal for parties to import or export hazardous waste *only* if the exporting country does not have the capacity to dispose of it in an environmentally sound manner (which the US clearly had—but it is one of the few countries in the world not to have ratified the Convention), or if the importing country provides written consent that it needs it as raw material (which the Ivory Coast did not) and can dispose of it in an environmentally sound manner (which the Ivory Coast could not).

Like all the other transnational state and corporate crimes we have covered in this chapter, the responses of the international political and legal communities have been strongly criticised. Whereas drug trafficking is, as we have seen, a major focus of the UNODC and its annual budget of approximately $333 million (UNODC, 2019a, citing a figure from 2018), there is no international governmental body dedicated to dealing with the problem of toxic waste dumping. The Basel Convention is the only international treaty that supposedly deals with the problem, but it has not been ratified by the US or China, the world's two greatest polluters, and it relies on global NGOs like Greenpeace and the much smaller Basel Action Network (BAN), which in 2017 operated on a total budget of $958,670, to put pressure on governments to fulfil their obligations (BAN, nd). The final irony, as Clapp (2002) emphasises, is that even if international regulatory measures like the Basel Convention were to be properly enforced, even more northern dirty manufacturing industries, like oil refinery as well as clothing, would simply be sent abroad.

A transnational approach to cybercrime and cybersecurity

Although the 'world wide web' has only existed for the past few decades, it has resulted in a whole new terrain of human activity. A huge amount of human life now takes place on or is facilitated by the internet, even more so since the Covid-19 pandemic pushed numerous workplaces, events, and businesses into operating solely or predominantly online. The internet has created many positive opportunities but it also enables harm and crime, as its inventor, Sir Tim Berners-Lee, acknowledged on the internet's 30th anniversary in 2019:

> And while the web has created opportunity, given marginalised groups a voice, and made our daily lives easier, it has also created opportunity for scammers, given a voice to those who spread hatred, and made all kinds of crime easier to commit . . . Against the backdrop of news stories about how the web is misused, it's understandable that many people feel afraid and unsure if the web is really a force for good.
>
> (Berners-Lee, 2019)

We touched on the relationship between the internet and crime in **Chapter 6** (see **section 6.4**), but here we consider it through a different lens. We know that transnational criminology is interested in material connections between different parts of the world, and by its nature the internet enables exactly these kinds of connections, allowing trade, personal communication, media images and videos, money, music, news, and information to cross boundaries almost instantly, and in most countries, without obstacles. It follows that most 'cybercrimes'—which we can broadly define as any criminal activity that involves, or takes place within, a technological network—have a transnational element. Some definitions even foreground this aspect: the United Nations Office on Drugs and Crime describes cybercrime as 'an evolving form of transnational crime [which] takes place in the border-less realm of cyberspace' (UNODC website. Accessed 22 November 2020).

Some cybercrimes, such as malware attacks and hacking, have been made possible by the very existence of the internet. Others pre-existed the internet but with its help now manifest in different and arguably more harmful forms. (Cyber)fraud, for example, has a far wider reach in the virtual domain as perpetrators are no longer limited by physical constraints such as the need to make a speedy getaway and negotiate border controls. The technology effectively magnifies the effects of any 'negative' action in that it provides increased immediacy of action and effect; and it offers the benefits of distance, disguise, and anonymity to perpetrators (Yar and Steinmetz, 2019: 14). These characteristics are clearly attractive to anyone tempted by criminal activity, but especially to those operating on a large scale, who have a sufficient level of online access and technological know-how. As such, many forms of crime, including drug trafficking, are increasingly carried out (at least partially) online, and the internet gives those involved in (often transnational) illegal and illicit trades access to much greater international mobility and more rapid and secure communications (Global Initiative, 2019; Lavorgna, 2020). Mexico's Sinoloa drug cartel, for example, reportedly uses the online messaging platform

WhatsApp as its main means of communication (*Milenio*, 27 January 2020). Not only does this allow drug traffickers to communicate instantly with members of their network around the world in order to coordinate their activities and evade capture, but the platform's high level of encryption also means that, unlike with conventional calls or SMS messages, it is very difficult for authorities to monitor their communications (ibid).

Cybercrime's global nature means that its perpetrators and victims, and the technological equipment used to facilitate the crimes, can be scattered around the world. The material disseminated online which is based on the sexual exploitation of children illustrates the huge reach and scale of such issues. At least 72 countries have been found to be involved in producing this material (Interpol, 2018a: 10), and Interpol has acknowledged:

> Among these has been a dramatic increase in the number of opportunities for those who would harm children. The Internet makes it easier for offenders to produce, access and share child sexual abuse material, find like-minded offenders, and reduce their risk of detection. It has never been easier for perpetrators to make contact with children, share images of abuse and inspire each other to commit further crimes. And the anecdotal evidence suggests that this has resulted in perhaps millions of children being sexually exploited in recent years.
>
> (Interpol, 2018b: vi)

Hacking provides another illustration of the wide-reaching impact of transnational cybercrime. Hacking is a highly skilled activity which has lawful applications, most notably as a way of testing and enhancing system security, but can be hugely damaging if deployed deliberately to achieve harmful ends on a wide scale, whether for profit (ransom) or political gain (destabilising institutions). Recent controversies have focused on the purported use of hacking to interfere in and influence the outcome of elections in various countries. In the run-up to the 2020 presidential election in the US, for instance, press reports suggested that hackers from Russia, China, and Iran were trying to influence voters in various ways through infiltrating social media and disrupting candidates' campaign organisations, according to Microsoft (*The Guardian*, 20 September 2020). However, the very politicised nature of the context, and the challenges involved in securing concrete evidence of wrongdoing, have ensured that this remains a highly contested subject. Nonetheless, Kragh and Åsberg (2017), among others, claim to have identified signs of Russian attempts to influence political debate in Sweden, including 'troll armies', seeking to target journalists and academics.

These examples give us a sense of the complex nature and huge, far-reaching extent of cybercrime, as well as its likely causes. For these reasons and because of the rapid pace of change and development in this sphere (remember that the UNODC definition (2020) states that cybercrime is always evolving), tackling cybercrime and enhancing cybersecurity is extremely difficult. One key challenge in responding is certainly that of international cooperation. The very nature of the internet as a global phenomenon with victims, perpetrators, and criminal equipment spread across countries, suggests that any concerted attempt to address cybercrime will require close cooperation across borders and jurisdictions. However, as you might anticipate, this is very difficult to achieve in practice.

Figure 14.10 The complex nature and far-reaching extent of cybercrime, as well as the fast pace of change in this area, makes it very difficult to tackle

Source: Dotshock/Shutterstock

One major obstacle to achieving close international cooperation on these issues is the cross-jurisdictional nature of crimes in cyberspace; in other words, the fact that cybercrimes often fall under the jurisdictions of multiple countries (Calderoni, 2010). There are many international variations in definitions of cybercrime, and these slight differences are very relevant in practice as they might mean that the same behaviour is considered criminal in one country but not in another (Grabosky and Smith, 1998). For example, while forms of cyber-trespassing (such as hacking) are covered by substantive law in many countries, other forms of cybercrime (such as cyber-harassment) are not consistently criminalised around the world (Lavorgna, 2020). In an attempt to address this issue, several legislative responses have been adopted at international and regional levels, to work alongside national legislation, the most notable of which is probably the 2001 Budapest Convention on Cybercrime. The Convention advocates adopting appropriate legislation at a national level; improving mutual assistance and investigative techniques; and fostering international cooperation. It urges Member States to criminalise four main types of criminal activities:

- offences against the confidentiality, integrity, and availability of computer data and systems (illegal access, illegal interception, data interference, system interference, and misuse of services);
- computer-related offences (computer-related forgery and computer-related fraud);
- content-related offences (offences related to child pornography);
- offences related to infringements of copyright and related rights.

The Additional Protocol to the Convention also urges states to criminalise acts of a racist and **xenophobic** nature committed through computer systems. Although it is no longer fully up to date and is quite incomplete in its definition of cybercrime, the Convention still represents the best legal international response to cybercrimes that is currently available.

In addition to legislation, international and transnational law enforcement also play a central role in preventing and countering cybercrimes. At the global level, a good example of this is Interpol (the intergovernmental organisation that facilitates cooperation between the criminal police forces of 192 countries), which has expanded its scope to deal with cybercrime by building a new centre in Singapore with the aim of becoming a global coordination body on detection and prevention. At the regional level, the creation in 2013 of the European Cybercrime Centre (EC3) at Europol (the EU agency for law enforcement cooperation) shows the increased attention being directed towards the international policing of cybercrime. The centre was created in order to strengthen the law enforcement response to serious forms of transnational cybercrimes in the EU, and specifically to contribute to faster reactions to online crimes.

In considering the need for harmonised international responses in terms of preventing, identifying, and policing cybercrimes, we also need to remember the importance of the local context where a cybercrime occurs, given that this element still plays a fundamental role in many forms of cybercrime (Lavorgna, 2020)—and we saw in **section 14.2** that is an important aspect of all transnational criminological studies. We need to remember, for example, that the 'digital divide' still exists; in other words, online access is not equal globally. Some countries do not have a high 'internet penetration rate', meaning that many of their citizens do not have online access at home, via a computer, or via a mobile device. Other countries restrict public access to popular websites and in some parts of the world government interference means it may actually be a crime to make use of some of the facilities offered online, including news and social media. (See the interactive map produced by Freedom House of relative levels of internet freedom across the world—https://freedomhouse.org/.) This means that cybercrime often involves exploiting both the global connections provided online but also the national variations in terms of freedom of access and levels of cybersecurity.

We also need to remember that in some regions of the world, international cooperation is not always possible, or fully effective, because of issues of distrust between states, which hinder the exchange of information (Hufnagel and McCartney, 2017; Lavorgna, 2020), or because of political or legal differences. International cooperation is also difficult to implement without acknowledging and addressing the power disparities between the Global North (especially English-speaking nations) and the rest of the world not only in terms of digital divides, but also in setting standards for (online) policing, regulation, and surveillance (Mann and Warren, 2018). These disparities can severely complicate the practicalities of law enforcement and judicial assistance. Also, in a context where international cooperation is still limited in scope and reach, possibilities for sharing data and resources should be improved at least at the regional level, for example throughout Europe. However, the political climate in many countries does not make this easy. Consider, for instance, the need to renegotiate many data- and intelligence-sharing procedures after Brexit (Lavorgna, 2020). As a consequence, while acknowledging the global nature of cybercrime and the fact that it often has a transnational dimension, we cannot ignore the local specificities of where offenders and victims are located.

It should now be clear that cybercrime is a vast and pervasive issue which is ever-shifting, as technology continues to develop, and truly transnational—with all the associated problems that this brings. Before we conclude this section, though, it is worth keeping in mind that although many forms of crime increasingly have a cyber and transnational nature, this does not mean that all crimes are moving online, or that *all* cybercrimes have a transnational element: some still require offline interactions between the actors involved, or might need or prefer geographical proximity (Lusthaus and Varese, 2017). Recent research, for instance, showed that in some cases of cyber-fraud the victims and the perpetrators are in the same country (Levi et al., 2017). In fact, many cybercrimes maintain an offline and local dimension, and the impact of cybercrimes is often suffered at a local level (Lavorgna, 2020).

14.4 Critical issues in transnational criminology

By this point in the chapter, you should have a sense of what transnational criminology involves: the kinds of crime and justice issues it looks at, the ways in which it explores and analyses them, and the kinds of questions it raises—such as about the most effective ways to respond to such issues. This knowledge is a good starting point for your studies, but in order to engage with the issues in depth, you also need to be able to address a number of prominent debates we have alluded to in this chapter. Two of these are particularly important: the critique of the so-called 'mafia' or 'cartel paradigm', and the need for global civil society responses to transnational crime.

Critique of the 'mafia' or 'cartel paradigm'

The mainstream approach is to view the leaders of criminal organisations as hedonistic and violent (**Figure 14.11**), and the groups they lead as hierarchically structured, with clear lines of authority and accountability, organised from the top down (Dúran-Martínez, 2018; Woodiwiss and Hobbs, 2009). From this position, the most effective way of dealing with organised crime is to remove its leaders, so that the remaining layers of the pyramid structure collapse. However, this approach has been strongly criticised in the academic literature on 21st-century organised crime. Criminologists adopting a more radical position question the traditional assumptions, claiming instead that:

- much organised crime is rational and emerges from groups of otherwise law-abiding people taking advantage of criminal opportunities—or just as often, being recruited by government officials and businesspeople to handle their own criminal activities (Zavala, 2018)—rather than power-hungry and dangerous sociopathic individuals who are trying to expand their criminal empire;
- the violence associated with organised crime is usually incidental to the groups' primary objectives, which are to essentially make money or to achieve political gain;
- criminal organisations typically work through networks of individual actors or small groups of friends and acquaintances. These actors are not necessarily directly employed by or loyal to the organisation and do not necessarily know how other parts of the network operate, or even by whom they are run.

(For an overview of research on organised crime in the UK that questions the mafia paradigm, see Silverstone, 2013).

Each of these areas of radical critique become more pertinent when applied to transnational criminal organisations, as not only are they on average larger and more profitable, but their networks are more likely to include people living thousands of miles from each other—as we saw in our examples of drug trafficking and people smuggling. Some criminologists go so far as to describe today's

Figure 14.11 The term 'mafia' might remind you of movies like *The Godfather* (1972), which tend to depict organised crime in much the same way, but some criminologists are moving away from this model

Source: Stokkete/Shutterstock

conventionally defined criminal gangs—transnational or otherwise—as more organis*ing* than organis*ed* (again, see Silverstone, 2013), and as organisations of criminals—or criminal *networks*, as we have referred to them throughout most of this chapter—rather than as 'criminal organisations'. We could argue that this is even the case with the Mexican Sinaloa, as El Chapo's arrest has had little impact on the international trade in cocaine. It also led to a further increase in violence in Mexico, as members of the Sinaloa took the opportunity to split from the cartel and set up their own competing factions (Cálderon et al., 2018).

The need for global civil society responses

The second area of debate relates to the fact that many powerful offenders, especially state and corporate offenders, are largely 'untouchable'. Again, this is even more the case in the 21st-century era of cross-border connections. Our examples have demonstrated how little power or resources the global political and legal communities have to hold transnational criminals to account. The only major success we have highlighted—the extradition and criminal prosecution of El Chapo—came about through bilateral cooperation between two countries. If the main destination of El Chapo's cocaine-trafficking network had not been as rich and powerful as the US, he would probably still be in charge of the Sinaloa today. We have seen that the UNODC's annual budget allocated to tackling drug trafficking is smaller than the net profit the Sinaloa can make from a single shipment.

It is interesting that in discussing responses to transnational crime we have needed to highlight the work of civil society NGOs such as Human Rights Watch, Sea Watch, Greenpeace, and the Basel Action Network as much as the work of official global governmental and judicial bodies like the United Nations and the International Criminal Court. These 'transnational mobilizations for justice' (Aas, 2020: 241) do not have the power to arrest and prosecute (and as we saw in **Controversy and Debate 14.2**, their contributions are not always long-lasting or meaningful) but they increasingly step in to fill gaps in official transnational crime control. This is particularly important for the policing of state and corporate crimes (Green and Ward, 2019). The civil society successes we have highlighted in this chapter include the naming and shaming of the US rendition and transnational torture programmes, and the rescuing of migrants who are abandoned to their fate by European border control forces when the vessels on which they have paid people-smuggling networks to travel, break down in the Mediterranean Sea.

From a criminal law perspective, even the most serious violence is not a matter for criminological inquiry, or for policing, before laws have been passed to criminalise it. But criminologists who work within a social harm (see **Chapter 19**) perspective question whether governments can really be trusted to criminalise their own institutions or the major corporations upon whom they rely to provide jobs and tax revenues, or to allocate the necessary resources to police them. They suggest that this is even more unlikely in the case of transnational crimes, where the states and transnational corporations in question may simply be too powerful to criminalise or police without leading to serious political or economic repercussions. Examples include the US being granted legal immunity by Iraqi authorities for accusations of torture committed during its occupation of Baghdad, and (an example we gave in **section 14.3**) the transnational oil-producing corporation Trafigura being granted legal immunity by Ivorian (Ivory Coast) authorities for accusations of dumping tonnes of sludge containing the world's most odorous chemical, hydrogen sulfide, previously used as a chemical weapon by the British army during the First World War. Consider these issues, and the question of whether certain types of crime are not taken sufficiently seriously, in **What do you think? 14.4**.

WHAT DO YOU THINK? 14.4

Developing a transnational level of criminological analysis

Aas (2020: 235) writes that 'a globally aware analytical perspective may open our eyes to a variety of actors, activities and human rights violations that tend to be neglected due to a nationalist methodological framework . . . a global perspective presents itself not only as a valuable scientific approach but also as an ethical imperative'.

Do you agree that transnational state crime and transnational corporate crime are as serious as transnational organised crime? And do you agree that they are not taken as seriously as they should be by the international community?

14.5 Conclusion

We have discussed that in an increasingly globalised world, a new level of criminological analysis needs to be developed that goes beyond the nation state and takes the global and transnational as its primary points of reference (Aas, 2020). Over two chapters, we have explored the implications of this statement in the context of the two strands of the emerging area of global criminology. In **Chapter 13** we focused on the implications of globalisation for criminological research that aims to compare crime and justice in one place to another. In this chapter, we have focused on the implications of globalisation for understanding specific types of crime: crimes committed by criminal, state, or corporate organisations that cross national and regional borders. In both chapters, we have emphasised a wider lack of diversity within the established discipline of criminology and highlighted the call made by critical criminologists to include the knowledge and standpoints of southern as much as northern experts. Each of the major areas of crime we have covered in these two chapters has greater impact in the Global South than in the Global North. It is essential that southern voices are included and given prominence if global criminology is to develop into a genuine and truly authentic new area of the discipline; one which has the capacity to understand which types of crime require most attention and to identify the most effective and legitimate means of responding to them.

SUMMARY

After reading this chapter and working your way through its features you should now be able to:

- Outline the scope of transnational criminology and explain where it sits within the broader discipline of criminology

Transnational criminology is the second branch of the emerging area of global criminology. It focuses on crimes that cross national or regional borders and their impact in their places of origin, end-point, and the countries they traverse in between. Such crimes are typically large-scale and committed by organisations rather than individuals or 'street-level' gangs. Criminologists who take a criminal law perspective restrict their analysis to the illegitimate activities of criminalised organisations like terrorist and contraband-smuggling networks. Criminologists who take a social harm perspective include the illegitimate cross-border activities of state and corporate as well as criminal organisations. Many of these latter critical criminologists choose to describe such socially harmful state–corporate activities as global rather than transnational crimes. However, it is not theoretically necessary to make this distinction. In this chapter, we have followed the initiative of a significant minority of critical criminologists and described all cross-border crimes as transnational. Where it has been useful to do so, we have utilised the terms transnational organised crime, transnational state crime, and transnational corporate crime.

- Apply the theoretical concepts employed in transnational criminology to case studies of crime and justice

New areas of social scientific analysis require new theoretical concepts. Key concepts being developed by researchers in the field of transnational criminology include *internationalised* and *militarised* justice, *powerful offenders*, and *privatised authority*. None of these concepts are exclusive to transnational criminology—the term militarised, for example, is also used in critical criminology in the context of the domestic war on drugs in the US—but all of them are particularly useful. In this chapter, we explored the relevance and usefulness of these concepts to five major areas of transnational criminological research covering state and corporate as well as organised crime: state terror, drug trafficking, people smuggling, toxic waste, and cybercrime. In each case, we covered both the nature of the crimes in question and the nature of the responses to them.

- Discuss the most prominent academic debates within and associated with transnational criminology

The question whether transnational crime includes the illegitimate activities of state and corporate institutions reflects debates over the wider scope of criminology. Two other prominent academic debates that are more specifically relevant to transnational criminology are the extent to which organised crime is actually that organised, and the extent to which the international political community has the power, resources, or will to hold transnational criminals, especially state and corporate criminals, to account. For each of the major incidences of transnational state and corporate crimes we covered in this chapter, we questioned whether global civil society responses had been more effective.

Test your understanding of the chapter's key points by attempting the self-test questions on the **online resources** at www.oup.com/he/case2e

REVIEW QUESTIONS

1. What does Bowling (2011: 362) mean when he describes transnational criminology as involving analysis of the 'linkages between places'?
2. What do you understand by the terms powerful offenders, militarised justice, and privatised authority?
3. Why are these three theoretical concepts particularly useful to transnational criminology?
4. Why is it argued that the 'mafia paradigm' is even less relevant to transnational than 'domestic' criminology?
5. Why is it argued that global civil society plays a more important role in policing transnational crime than global governmental institutions like the United Nations?

Access the **online resources** at www.oup.com/he/case2e to check your answers to the review questions.

FURTHER READING

Aas, K. (2020) *Globalization and Crime.* **London: Sage.**
Now in its third edition, this book remains the most comprehensive account of the challenges 21st-century globalisation poses to the established discipline of criminology, and the need for a global criminology. We also recommended this text as further reading for **Chapter 13**.

Bowling, B. and Sheptycki, J. (2012) *Global Policing.* **London: Sage.**
This book provides a detailed overview of the global policing responses to the problem of transnational organised crime.

Carrington, K. et al. (2019) *Southern Criminology.* **London: Routledge. Especially Chs 1 and 6.**
This book represents the first major effort to provide a comprehensive overview of crime and justice in the Global South. We recommended the full text as further reading for **Chapter 13**. The introductory and concluding chapters we have also highlighted here focus specifically on the authors' call for a 'southerning' of global criminology.

Fitzgibbon, W. and Lea, J. (2020) *Privatising Justice: The Security Industry, War and Crime Control.* **London: Pluto. Especially Chs 1, 3, and 6.**

This book covers a wide range of issues relating to the phenomenon of privatised authority. The chapters we have highlighted focus largely on issues of transnational crime and justice.

Green, P. and Ward, T. (2004) *State Crime: Governments, Violence and Corruption.* **London, Sage.**
This is considered a classic text on state crime. We used it extensively in this chapter when exploring matters of state violence. It also includes important chapters that explore the intersections between state, corporate, and organised crime.

Stanley, E. and McCulloch, J. (eds) (2013) *State Crime and Resistance.* **Abingdon: Routledge. Especially Ch. 3.**
Although we have only referenced two of the individual chapters in this edited book, we recommend it as a unique collection of papers on the roles played by civil society in the policing of state and corporate crimes, both domestically and globally. The chapter we have highlighted here was authored by Penny Green and Tony Ward.

Access the **online resources** to view a wealth of extra information relating to your study of criminology, including self-test questions, answers to review questions, and links to other resources that will help you enjoy and fulfil your potential within your studies.
www.oup.com/he/case2e

PART OUTLINE

15. Free will, classicism, and rational choice
16. Biological and psychological positivism
17. Sociological positivism
18. Critical criminology
19. Social harm
20. Right and left realism
21. Integrated theories of crime
22. Searching for the causes of crime

Welcome to **Part 3**, in which we focus on the aetiology of crime—that is, its origins and causes. We will consider why some people take part in criminal behaviour and both what leads to some behaviours being controlled by the state (largely through criminal laws) and what the effects of this state control are on the behaviour of individuals.

We begin, in **Chapter 15**, by exploring the purpose of theory and how we can interpret, test, and critically consider ideas, before moving on to discuss classical theories which assert that people freely and rationally choose to offend and therefore can, and should, be punished or have their choices prevented (by, for example, reducing offending opportunities).

In **Chapters 16** and **17**, we take what is known as a positivist stance, using scientific methods to study crime and its causes. From this perspective, crime is seen as determined (made more likely) due to biological, psychological, or sociological causes, meaning that we should rehabilitate offenders or alter our society to reduce the likelihood of criminal behaviour.

Chapter 18 sees us consider critical criminology, which questions everything that has gone before: the idea of crime and the positivist and classical explanations of its causes. Indeed, it questions aspects of our society, such as state definitions of crime, which are assumed to be 'true'. In **Chapter 19** we explore the idea of social harm and consider what it means for definitions of crime, and whether we should think of it as being separate from, or related to, what we have previously thought of as 'criminology'. In **Chapter 20** we then pull together two very different responses to this critical tradition, 'right realism' and 'left realism', which consider real problems faced by society and then suggest solutions.

In **Chapters 21** and **22** we end our consideration of ways to explain crime by trying to identify some explanatory themes and question others. In **Chapter 21** we discuss grand theories, which draw on central principles from other ideas and combine them to build new, integrated theories, and in **Chapter 22** we question criminology's obsession with the causes of crime, especially in light of the problems in defining crime (which we explored in **Chapter 2**).

Overall, this part will give you insight into the many aspects of human beings and societies which either move us to control each other or explain why some people participate in 'unacceptable' behaviours.

PART 3
EXPLAINING CRIME

CHAPTER OUTLINE

15.1	Introduction	444
15.2	Understanding theory	444
15.3	Criminological theory	451
15.4	Classical criminology	453
15.5	Conclusion	469

15

Free will, classicism, and rational choice

KEY ISSUES

After studying this chapter, you should be able to:

- define the concept of theory and understand the purpose of it in the context of criminological study;
- evaluate different theories by understanding how to test their different elements;
- consider the main theoretical schools of thought in criminology including classicism, positivism, interpretivism, and critical criminology;
- critically consider classical criminology; both the key thinkers that shaped it, and the policies to which it gave rise;
- appreciate the importance of free will and rational choice and demonstrate how these ideas in the 17th and 18th centuries underlined the building of the modern new criminal justice system;
- assess the arguments put forward since the 1960s by modern classical thinkers (neo-classical criminology) about the idea that criminals choose to offend and how, when, and where that might occur.

15.1 Introduction

If you are going to be an effective criminologist (in other words, able to identify, interpret, and assess criminal activities and why we control them), it is essential that you understand criminological theories. Theories, very loosely defined, are systems of ideas intended to explain something. They underpin our entire discipline so will play a vital role in your studies; you will be expected to know and make reference to different theories throughout your degree, and this will not only boost your academic grades but your employability, as engaging with theories involves developing analytical and critical skills which will serve you well long after your degree (see **Chapter 31**). For some students, even the word 'theory' sounds intimidating and this aspect of the degree can be a source of worry, but this really should not be the case—learning about theories is not difficult. Once you realise that theories are simply different lenses through which we can look at the world, you will come to see them as valuable tools which help us draw together a logical narrative (a story or set of ideas) from separate pieces of information.

Theory serves as a bridge between the real world and your learning. Theories are constructed using research (collecting information, data, together and making sense of it). Seen in this way, it is clear that all of us work with theory, in that our choices and actions are based on assumptions that allow us to make sense of the world. We sometimes call this common sense—many of us, for example, would choose not to walk alone at night down a dark alley because we have learnt that this might be dangerous (see **Figure 15.1**). In forming this view, we have taken data (information from around us, maybe in news reports or experiences from people we know) and built an understanding of our world—a theory about danger and dark alleys. This is really all that criminological theorists do. They take you on a journey, explaining what they are thinking, how they have formed this view (the evidence on which it is based), and how (in their opinion—remember the ABC mindset (*Always Be Critical*)!) this might help us better understand parts of the world. Please always remember that this is their opinion or their interpretation of the information and it can and should be challenged—remember that you should have an ABC mindset!

Using theories in this way opens up a wealth of stimulating insights into the whole area of criminology. It gives us a much fuller understanding of our world, our society, and people's behaviours. Theories help us to understand how and why things happen so they can help to show us where we need more research or how we might tackle problem behaviour in a way that might prove to be effective. For example, part of rational choice theory is that people are less likely to offend if their behaviour can be witnessed; this has led to changes such as increased street lighting or removal of bushes. You may be aware of this because university campuses have improved lighting or removed bushes in an effort to protect students. So although theories are sometimes seen as abstract and academic, in criminology they are generally very practical.

In this chapter, we will consider what a theory is, how you can assess a theory, and explore some of the overarching ideas in criminology. Since we aim for this book to introduce you to core ideas within criminology and to act as a springboard for further study, we will stick to considering the core elements of each theory, examining its defining features, its strengths, and its weaknesses. This will give you a solid grounding from which to explore them—and other theories introduced elsewhere in this book—in more detail. It is important to be aware that this chapter is *not* a substitute for reading the primary texts—it simply aims to help you understand those texts when you do go to read them (see Newburn (2009) for excerpts from many of the original criminology texts covered in **Part 3** or you can, of course, read the originals in full by accessing the original texts referenced in the chapters).

15.2 Understanding theory

What is a theory?

A theory enables us to make sense of parts of the world that we have not got first-hand knowledge about and explain things outside our experiences. A useful theory therefore helps us to understand part of what is going on around us and can also help to predict when certain events may happen. Theory allows people to unravel and understand things which are otherwise very complicated, such as the nature of unacceptable offensive and criminal behaviour, society's desire to control it, and the means they use to alter, punish, and prevent such damaging behaviour. A theory gathers together a substantial amount of information collected from observing the real world and tries to discern patterns, making sense of what might otherwise be just lots of independent pieces of information.

Criminological and social science theories therefore look for general truths. A useful theory might explain the

Figure 15.1 A 'common sense' decision not to walk alone at night down a dark alleyway is an example of acting on a theory
Source: Atmosphere1/Shutterstock

circumstances or conditions under which a particular behaviour or outcome is likely (laying out the evidence on which their ideas are based and how they have interpreted that evidence) and why those conditions are important to the outcome. The theory should also explain how the ideas fit into other ideas or theories that already exist. With all of this information, the theory should help us to prevent the problem from happening (see **Figure 15.2**). Ultimately, a theory enables us to identify and name a problem, understand and predict it, and plan a way to deal with it.

So what is a theory made from? To help you understand the building blocks of a theory, we will now consider some of the things which often constitute one.

1. **Concepts in theory**—To begin with, there are items called **concepts** which are often part of a **theory**. They draw together a class of data by referring to a characteristic or set of characteristics which marks out the individual items. A concept is a representation (a word) for a thing, for example offender (encapsulates all different types of people who break the law), building (encapsulates all different types of construction) etc., which is used as a shorthand to group together all other things which share its characteristics or as many of its characteristics as possible. Naming a concept or a group of similar things or occurrences allows us to talk about them.

2. **Abstract concept or construct**—These terms refer to concepts with no physical characteristics which may be thought of as ideas, for example freedom, social class, democracy, undeserving. Often an abstract concept or construct forms from concepts or parts of concepts based on physical characteristics that are linked in some way. It is important that the theory specifies or explains what is meant by each term (concept or construct) so that the reader is sure that they are understanding the theory correctly, interpreting it in the way in which the theorist meant it to be understood.

3. **Theoretical principles**—The third part of a theory is the principles or propositions which explain the relationship between two or more concepts or constructs. They explain how the concepts and constructs interrelate, allowing us to understand how specific outcomes arise.

When fitted together, these components make up a theory. Each aspect should be clear so that the theory can be used to predict future occurrences, given the circumstances necessary to the theory, and also to be tested. This

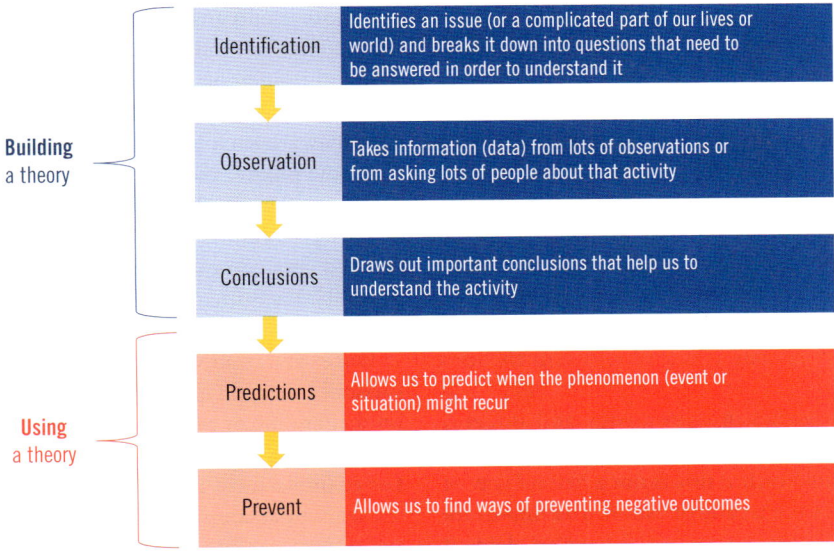

Figure 15.2 The theoretical process, from building to using a theory, comprises five stages

WHAT DO YOU THINK? 15.1

Example of an 'everyday' theory

Imagine that you live in a house share with four other students. The rent is high so money is always tight and you are very careful not to overspend, but you allow yourself a packet of digestive biscuits as part of your weekly food shop. There are 21 biscuits in each packet and you allow yourself three biscuits a day.

You start to notice that biscuits are going missing but none of your housemates will own up to taking them—and they say they're only biscuits anyway, so why does it matter. You become obsessive and watch the kitchen all the time, noting when people go in and then checking your biscuits, and over a few weeks you note that every time one of the biscuits is missing Karin, one of your flatmates, has been in the kitchen by herself. This is a theory—you believe that Karin has been taking the biscuits. Is this definite? Is it proof? Is it enough to confront her?

If you are sure you then *believe* that you know—but it is still a theory. There is no hard proof. However, the knowledge, the theory you have developed, allows you to make choices about how to deal with the problem. In order to try to resolve things, you may not need actual proof; your theory may be enough to give you some options about how to resolve the issue.

- You could confront Karin, however, she may deny it. Also, she is a friend and, as your housemates say, it is only biscuits. She may be hurt that you bring it up or it may lead to an argument. Are digestives worth losing a friend over, even if she has been dishonest? Also, she may have taken the biscuits because she has no money for food and is hungry.

- You could prevent further problems by keeping the biscuits in a locked drawer in your own room (or, if Karin is short, you could just put the biscuits on top of a high cupboard) and the problem would then be sorted out without needing to have an argument, and without losing a friend.

- You could do nothing and put up with the thefts in the name of friendship. This might mean you would either need to reduce the number of biscuits you eat every day or buy more.

The theory gives you an idea of how you may solve the problem. If you think things through, there is usually more than one way to deal with any problem and a theory may help. Consider a scenario in your own life or in the community you live in that is causing problems, collect some data about it, and from that try to work out why it is happening and how it might be tackled.

---

appears complex but **Figure 15.2** illustrates what is necessary to form a theory and then the example in **What do you think? 15.1** shows you that there is no reason why you should find studying theory difficult, it just involves different ways of looking at ideas and information.

What do you think? 15.1 shows you that the main point of a theory is to answer one or more questions. Therefore, instead of thinking about theory, it's best to think about answers to questions. This is a useful starting point partly because it simplifies things, but mostly because criminology is all about questions. For example, why do people kill, or why are some people frightened of going out alone at night? From this, it is clear that because the subject is about questions, criminology needs theories to provide answers.

There are many theories in criminology and students often ask which is correct—they want to know which theory gives the 'right' answer, but this is not a helpful way of looking at things. It is the wrong question. The important thing to remember is that most theories have an element of truth in them and most have areas which do not seem to hold true at all. That does not mean that one theory is right and another wrong, rather it means that one theory is a more useful answer to a particular question than another. Once we understand that each theory is answering a slightly different question or wants to give an answer which will be useful to a different audience, we can see that they are each discussing slightly different aspects of the same puzzle, and therefore that each may have something to offer. So, far from being competing claims they may each be adding a useful perspective to an understanding of a very complex issue (see **Chapter 21** on **integrated theories**). Each theory is therefore useful but needs to be considered alongside the question it was trying to answer.

Once you understand that the subject is best approached through questions, it is easy to see that often our understanding or reading of criminology is not shaped by theory or answers but by the questions we choose to ask. For example, most people beginning criminological studies begin by asking: 'Why do people offend?' But is that the right question? In order for there to be a breach of rules or an offence, there has to be a rule that one is expected to obey. So an important early question might be 'Why are certain behaviours unacceptable?'—we discussed this in **Chapter 2** when considering what 'crime' is. When being asked to consider theory, students might sensibly ask:

- In what sense, if at all, is a general theory of criminology possible or desirable?
- What is the point of theories or conceptual claims (claims based on ideas) and how can we evaluate them?
- If all theories or most theories have some merit, how can we best discover the pros and cons of different criminological theories or ideas?

In this chapter we will begin to answer some of these questions and the more you read about criminology in this book and other texts, the better you will be able to understand how to evaluate and use a theory to resolve an issue.

In brief, a theory should:

- provide a simple explanation of the relations that have been observed which are relevant to the phenomenon;
- be consistent with the observed relations (that is, the interpretation of information found in the research should be true to the data);
- clarify how it relates to an already established body of knowledge. A theory should provide the means for verification and revision. It should stimulate and highlight areas where further research and investigation is needed.

The important thing to remember throughout your studies is that—as we emphasised in **Chapter 1**—you must be an active learner. This means not just accepting and learning what you are told and what you read; it's crucial that you think, and think critically, about all this information (the ABC mindset). This does not mean that you have to criticise everything but that you should consider it all and learn to identify what is good or useful and what may be of little use, or even damaging. As well as coming to these conclusions, you must be able to explain *why* something is useful or something else may be damaging—in other words, you must be able to support your claims with reasoned argument.

Testing a theory

In criminology, as in all social science, a theory needs to be relevant to the real world. A useful theory illuminates or helps us to understand situations, feelings, human behaviour, or human interactions. As we noted earlier, a theory should provide a clear and reasonably simple explanation of the aspect of life being observed and should explain how it fits in (or does not fit in) with other theories. In doing this, it must remain true to the behaviour being observed, it should be true to the data and to the people participating in the activity (they should recognise themselves and their motives). Clearly a theory should, therefore, be simple (or as simple and clear as possible), testable, novel, supportive of other theories, internally consistent, and predictive. There are many different ways to test a theory's value and usefulness; your lecturer may well provide you with a framework to follow. In the absence of that, or to supplement it, here are two frameworks that will be useful in considering a theory. The first is a set of five questions which are designed to help you to better understand a theory and look for strengths and weaknesses. The second sets out a list of nine aspects of a theory to consider in order to test it more thoroughly; this more complex list is simplified in **Table 15.1**.

How to understand a theory

In order to help you understand a theory and look for strengths and weaknesses, you can use the following list of questions.

1. Why is this theorist making this claim? (What questions are they trying to answer?)
2. What is the significance of the claim? (What does it say that might be important, useful, or worthwhile?)
3. What is the problem with the theory? (What does it assume, and are those assumptions acceptable?)
4. What is controversial in the theory and is that controversy useful? (Does it challenge policy or practice and make you think again?)
5. Who or which theories seem to disagree with this theory? (What are the points of disagreement and which is better argued? Do the disagreements arise because each is answering a slightly different question or because each is intended for a different audience?)

How to assess a theory

Answering the questions in the framework above will provide you with a lot of information you can use to critically consider and analyse a theory, but you may wish to go further. The list below is the next step and it will help you to test a theory's value and usefulness. You need to look carefully at the theory and decide *which questions it is trying to answer* and then apply the following tests:

1. Consider whether the theory is *clear and makes sense*, whether the theory as a whole has any contradictions within it.

Logical consistency	• Is the theory clear and *does it make sense*? This might be called *logical consistency*. Do all the parts of the theory hold together, or are there contradictions?
Coverage	• Is everything included in the theory necessary to the questions the theory is looking at? This is often referred to as *parsimony*. • Does the theory *ignore aspects which are essential* and should have been included or at least explained?
Breadth of claims	• Does the theory *try to explain all criminal behaviour or only certain types of crime*? Theories should clarify the limits within which they are relevant. *Whilst failure to state the limits of a theory should be pointed out as being problematic, the theory may still have some worth.*
Verification	• *Is the theory capable of being tested: can it be verified or falsified?* If a later study seems to 'verify' the theory, it does not mean it is 'true' merely that one can rely on it more (it may be falsified in later studies). If it is 'falsified', this does not mean the theory is 'wrong' it may merely draw out a limitation—for example, that it only applies to young men not young women.
Empirical validity	• Is the theory *supported by research evidence*—**empirical** validity? Theories built from robust collection and analysis of data are generally thought to be stronger than those based on claims or on ideas about what will happen in a particular situation but that have not yet been tested (hypotheses).
Relation to other theories	• Is the theory *supported by, or does it relate to, an already existing body of knowledge*? Better theories indicate exactly how they add to or alter our present understanding of the world.
Accuracy	• How *accurate* is the theory? How effective is it at predicting new phenomena (new or future happenings)? This is linked to another question—*how useful is the theory?* Can we use it to predict behaviour and, if so, can it be used to shape policy or practice?
Political and ideological issues	• Where does the *power* lie to define and control behaviour? • *Does the theory ignore* underlying *political, economic, or ideological* issues or issues of justice that may affect the way in which we should interpret the data?
Counter claims	• What are the counter-claims? Many theories are or can be juxtaposed to other ideas/theories and these should be recognised, even if they were put forward after the theory was formed.

Table 15.1 Useful questions to ask when testing a theory

2. It is sensible to look at whether it *covers the right material*. There are two aspects to this: does the theory miss important issues; and does it include irrelevancies. As an example of the former, much criminological theory fails to consider whether age or gender might make a difference to its utility as an idea. On the other hand, if the theory includes aspects which are not necessary to the question(s), then there is unnecessary complexity.

3. Before criticising a theory, you need to look at exactly how much is being claimed. The theorist may have *set limits* to the claims made though these may be implicit rather than explicit. Does it apply:
   - in all places (urban and rural or UK and other countries);
   - at all times (only day-time crime or only night-time crime);
   - to all different types of people (as opposed to only applying to youths, women, or certain racial groups, for example);
   - only to those with particular individual characteristics or who are members of certain groups (such as those with scars or brown eyes, members of a particular club, or those who live in a particular area).

   Better theories will state the limitations or they will be clear from the study. However, weaker theories do not state that they are limited in these ways; they are often written as if they are generally applicable. However, if all the data supporting a theory is from particular groups (male, the young, a particular ethnic group, or a particular type of environment) then there is good reason to question its more general applicability. If the theory is based on data collected in one country, its findings may not apply in other countries as parts of it may depend on local cultural or ethical values. Theories should clarify all of these aspects; if they fail to do so then that is one aspect that you can question about the theory. But please remember that failing to confine a theory does not mean that the ideas have no worth, merely that their worth is confined to a particular time, place, type of behaviour, or type of person.

4. Ideally one should be able to *test (verify or falsify) a theory*. In science, a theory is usually an idea that

can be tested in a controlled experiment—once you control everything except what you are testing, the results will hold true (verify) or not (falsify) the theory. In social science, the ability to replicate findings exactly is unrealistic as people are less predictable than objects. One cannot 'control' for important aspects but the overall theory should be capable of being tested. Note that even if the theory is 'verified', it does not mean that it is 'true'; no idea or generalisation can ever be proven to be entirely 'true' (Popper, 1959). Despite this, it is important that a theory is able to be tested so that it can be disproved or gain weight by having its findings replicated—the theory is then thought of as more reliable. However, even if a theory is 'falsified', it may still be useful. The 'falsification' may merely point to a limitation such as the theory only being relevant in a particular type of community or for men and not women. The theory may still be replicated in a different community or for a different group.

5. Consider whether the theory is *based on data collected and analysed*. If there is supporting data, were the collection methods strong (for example, was all the data from one site—weak—or was it from multiple sites—strong) and were they analysed objectively or was the data forced to 'fit' into a preconceived agenda? Effective methodology and analysis adds to the weight of the theory. Some theories have no supporting evidence. For example, some theories just make grand claims based on ideas alone (see some of the ideas from early classical theorists later in the chapter); others make a suggestion to be tested by others (they set out a **hypothesis**). Even untested theories or those with limited testing have worth but it is important to know the extent to which a theory is supported by evidence.

6. No theory exists in a vacuum, they are all added to our knowledge to date so it is important for theorists to indicate how their ideas *fit together with (or undermine) what we already think we know*. It may be that it will question some ideas we think are 'true' and will support others. It is important for the theory to indicate how and why it questions or supports other theories.

7. You should assess whether the theory is *accurate and useful*. Utility might be tested by, for example, asking whether the theory allows us to predict new or future occurrences of the behaviour being explained. Strong theories do this and so permit new policies and practices to be designed to encourage or discourage the activity (depending on whether it is thought to be pro-social or antisocial). However, some theories may be accurate and important but not be able to be used to build policy. There may be counter-theories, **ideological** problems, cultural issues, or political or economic reasons why it cannot or will not be put into operation. For example, no one can dispute that once a person is dead they do not pose any further crime threat but there would be ideological reasons against executing all convicted offenders.

8. It is important to consider a theory from the outside—looking at *power and critical analysis*. Whilst the theory may clearly and usefully describe or explain a certain behaviour, does it consider the power dynamics in the society or the community being studied? Does it look at the political, economic, or ideological factors underlying the behaviour? These are useful ways of questioning a theory—is it describing behaviour or control?

9. Consider whether the theorist took other theories into account when they were building this theory and, if not, whether there might be any reason for this failure. Theorists sometimes ignore theories that disagree with their claims so you need to consider whether this is the case and, if so, think about what impact the other theory has. You can also consider whether there have been any theories since the one you are analysing that might question or support the theory you are looking at.

Different types of theory

Criminology is a very wide subject; its only real connecting feature is that it is the study of crime (as defined by law) or deviance (the breach of a moral code; a social norm or rule), a basic human right, or something which a powerful group does not like and can prevent a powerless group from doing, which may also be criminal. Under this linking element, we find multidisciplinary approaches—we saw in **Chapter 1** that criminology relies on a wide range of disciplines, from political science to psychology—each trying to explain and predict criminality or its control. Each of these approaches will offer a different, and possibly conflicting, answer as to how and why crime occurs and what should be done to prevent it. Some appear to be common sense but this does not make them right, nor does it mean they are too simple and therefore wrong. Others appear to be far-fetched or to challenge the way in which you have so far understood something; their strangeness does not make them wrong nor does the fact that you find them clever make them correct. You should not judge theories on face value or be alarmed by their conflicts: each one may have something to contribute so should be tested carefully against the list in **Table 15.1**, but most importantly against the evidence of human behaviour.

Criminology's multidisciplinary nature leads to diverse theoretical ideas but each adds something useful to the puzzle of explaining crime, criminality, and control. This makes criminology a contested and fought-over area, an interesting and disputed discourse. This means that it is always possible to use one idea to question or validate another and therefore to build a convincing and intelligent critical discussion. It also means that there are opportunities for new cross-disciplinary research and theoretical ideas. Here we will briefly introduce some of the schools of criminology to give you an understanding of some of the types of theory that you will be reading.

Normative and descriptive theories

Some theories are **normative**, meaning that they set out ideal standards about the way in which things *should*, in that theorist's opinion, happen. These theories may set out beliefs or values and might attack theories which claim to explain 'real' occurrences as being based on unacceptable or unfair systems.

A lot of criminological theory is based on empirical (observed) data and might be thought of as **descriptive theory**. The researcher chooses an area of study, gathers data (what they hope is typical data), and describes what is happening—as opposed to what *should* happen. This type of theory uses the data to build categories and predict and explain behaviour (as we saw in **Chapter 3**, when we considered descriptive and normative types of criminal justice models).

Many researchers use their data to update and build upon old theories or to question and expand what we think we know and understand. So a researcher may take an old theory or a general theory and apply it in a particular situation, discover that parts of the theory do not hold true, and so suggest alterations to the theory for that situation. For example, a theory may have been built on data from an urban environment a few years ago and it may need to be altered to take account of a rural environment or to explain what is happening now. For example, gangs have traditionally been defined by things like gang colours, clothing, territory or 'turf' (Pyrooz, 2014: 355), or by illegal activities (Klein and Maxson, 2006: 4). This was represented as a general definition of gangs on which other aspects of theory could be built. However, these definitions have been constructed from studying urban gangs and may not fit into more rural setting. Furthermore, they do not help us to understand the extent of modern gang membership or to unpick gang members from the use or exploitation of people outside the gang area to boost the gang activities (often referred to as county lines, see the explanation by the National Crime Agency, 'County Lines').

Grand theories or integrated theories

Grand theory is a different type of explanation. Only a few criminological and sociological theories fall into this category. A grand theory, sometimes referred to as an integrated theory (see **Chapter 21**), offers an explanation to a problem which is applicable in most situations—so it is 'grand' in the sense of being large-scale, rather than impressive or fancy. It is generally fairly abstract, based on formal theorising by one person or a group of people rather than growing out of measured phenomena. It often draws together other ideas or theories which are based on observed and measured facts and tends to draw together different disciplines. Most grand theories are so broad that they are not really capable of being tested, though theoretical concepts based on them may well be open to testing.

You will come across many grand theories in your study of criminology because it includes very broad ideas. For example, structural functionalism sees society as a complex system, each part of which works together to build a solid and effective society. It assumes that the ideas, values, and understandings of symbols and customs are shared by most in a society and are necessary—the glue that helps to bind the individuals together to form a healthy society. They are almost more important than each individual (for an example and a full consideration, see the discussion of Durkheim (1858–1917) and functionalism in **section 17.5**).

Although these types of theories often draw on many disciplines, there are also grand theories which are wholly criminological, such as Tittle's control balance theory (which we will consider briefly in **Chapter 21**). Useful grand theories organise materials in ways that people can use to illuminate their area of study. They offer an understanding that is usually based on generalised assumptions about what they consider to be the important problems facing the discipline.

Particular theories

The final type of theory we need to consider is the smaller, particular theories which either try to explain one thing or respond to a few contained questions. These tend to be simpler and more focused, and they are more likely to be capable of being tested or verified. They may form part of, or sit beneath, a grand theory. For example, instead of trying to explain why people commit crime (generally), we might theorise about young people's use of illegal substances. Here, some have argued that, to a certain extent, trying illegal substances has been 'normalised' for certain ages and in certain **cultures** (Parker et al., 2002; Aldridge et al., 2011). This example also shows how ideas and theories alter over time as the 'normalisation' thesis in 2002 is different from that in 2011, despite the fact that a number of the authors remain the same in each.

15.3 Criminological theory

We have seen that theory allows us to name what we observe to describe and explain what is going on in the world. *Criminological* theory improves our understanding of why laws are made, how and why we enforce rules and punish those who break them, what the effects of crime control are, how and why people choose to break or obey rules, and what the effects of rule breaking may be. It allows us to identify and understand problems, providing a platform from which we can try to suggest policies and practices which might change the situation and resolve the problem.

The questions that criminologists use to help them answer include:

- Why do we control (declare illegal) one type of behaviour and not another, and who chooses?
- When, why, and how do we enforce those rules and is that enforcement legitimate?
- Why do some people in certain situations break societal rules and why do others conform?

There are so many different questions posed by theorists and different approaches taken to answer those questions that it can help to draw similar ideas together. Before we delve into one theory (classicism) in more depth, let's briefly reflect on four major types of theory: classical, positivism, interpretivist, and critical. In these sections and in the chapters which follow, we may refer to 'classical criminologists' or 'positivist criminologists', but this is not a fixed group of people. It just refers to researchers whose main body of work aligns most closely to that particular standpoint. It is also important to remember that these schools of thought are not unique to criminology. Most areas of social science refer to schools of thought as being 'classical', 'positivist', 'interpretivist', or 'critical' and use those terms in broadly the same way as they are used in criminology. However, here we will be discussing them within a criminological context.

Classicism

As we will explore further in the next section, classical criminology originally emerged in the 18th century, based on arguments about the causes of crime and how it should be dealt with. Classicism portrays offenders as rational and choosing to offend in order to gain something; given this, classicists argue that the state should (almost has a duty to) punish that individual proportionate to the wrongdoing. Classicism was not grounded in research or evidence, but instead focused on ideas about how to control and punish. Classical criminologists focus on the offence and how to deal with it. They generally portray offenders as rational and calculating; they see the offence as having been committed because the offender has calculated that it will enable them to gain something. Classical thinkers believe that because offenders freely choose how they behave, they can be held responsible for any offences they commit and they can therefore be punished. Once the state has proven their guilt, they should be punished in a way that is proportionate to their wrongdoing.

Originally, the theorists behind the classical school of thought argued that their work was designed to fight against arbitrary (random) use of power which gave rise to unfair outcomes and inequality. However, many critics of classical theory argue that the system it produced is about the continuation of existing power and authority and leads to inequality. They argue that it is about the preservation and protection of social elites. We will consider these ideas in more depth in our discussion of classical criminology later in this section.

Positivism

Positivist criminology, which we consider in depth in **Chapters 16** and **17**, collects large amounts of information to study past crime and criminals so as to predict and possibly prevent future behaviour. It generally studies offenders and posits that their behaviour is determined by social/psychological/biological issues which need to be resolved to prevent future problems. It suggests rehabilitation or change rather than punishment. It began to emerge through the 19th century and was heavily influenced by the power of science that was appearing in other fields. Positivists tried—and try—to gain knowledge about the social world in the same way that scientists gain information about the natural world—through collecting facts. In contrast to classical criminologists, they tend to study the offender or society, rather than the crime. The original group of positivist theorists believed that the social world could be measured and that by collecting information we would uncover an objective (factual) external reality which would explain behaviour. They believed that it was possible to be 'value neutral' when conducting research; that is, to ensure that the research is not influenced by a person's own values or opinions, which could affect the findings. To remain 'value free' they often collect a lot of data and often build their ideas and theories on the quantitative (numbers) analysis of that data.

Positivists collected information about the social world and when they found links they often drew causative conclusions—conclusions that argue that one phenomenon produced, affected, or caused another. Therefore, many positivists took (and still take) the results of their analysis and, finding that two things were related, wrongly assumed that there was a causal link (see also **Chapter 22**). Causal links need greater proof than just a finding that two things change at the same time. For example, they may find that there is more crime in unlit streets, a useful finding which could lead to more lighting being provided in order to prevent offending. However, the positivist standpoint can lead researchers to take findings like this too far and suggest that the lack of lighting *causes* criminality instead of realising that the cause is something else and the lack of lighting merely provides an opportunity to offend without being caught and punished.

At its heart, positivism finds that two things are related. It often claims to explain that relationship but rarely collects the data that would be needed to give a full explanation—it is usually just descriptive. Despite the descriptive nature of their findings, positivists often link behaviour to biological, psychological, or social influences and can see this behaviour as not only influenced but *determined* by one of those factors. If this is the case, the behaviour is **pathological** (for example, caused by a mental or physical condition) and we should not blame the offender as their behaviour was determined by something outside their control. They are not really responsible for their actions so should be treated or rehabilitated rather than being punished. Treatment or rehabilitation may be very invasive and the necessary intervention will not be limited by the seriousness of the crime but rather by the underlying problem as discovered in the research. Most positivist ideas are largely based on **quantitative research** and it is often used to test a hypothesis.

Interpretivism

Interpretivist criminology rejects the idea that complex social and human interactions can ever be fully measured. Those who take this standpoint argue that science can never measure the subjective thoughts and feelings that influence human behaviour and human interactions. We cannot treat people as objects and their behaviour cannot be explained by taking simple measurements. Interpretivist criminologists reject the idea that there is any measurable objective reality because they argue that social reality is constructed and negotiated—each person who experiences something constructs their own 'truth' about it and sometimes the 'truth' is agreed when people discuss their experiences. They argue that it is only through a study of all aspects of each person (who they are and who they portray themselves as being) and the world they inhabit that we can begin to interpret someone's actions. Key to this school of thought is a desire to interpret or understand behaviour or a situation through the eyes of those participating, so that the individuals would recognise themselves in the way that they are portrayed by the researcher. It seeks to give meaning to situations and is subjective, opinion-based, and founded on **qualitative research**.

Critical criminology

Critical criminology is a group of ideas and theories which emerged in the 1960s. Their unifying elements are that they study the effects of power in a society and they challenge the classical, positivist, and interpretivist theories and the way in which their theorists gather knowledge. Critical criminologists accept that social reality is constructed, so there is no measurable, objective reality, and recognise that situations may be seen differently in alternative times or places, by different people or if they are interpreted through different approaches. They argue that we need to question and examine the accepted understandings or constructions of society, testing them from different perspectives—Marxist, feminist, racist, etc. Critical criminology often involves studying how power and authority are constructed; how inequality and discrimination is experienced and frequently accepted; and, more broadly, how and whether society should be controlled. It is critical of the way in which society is structured and the effect this has on the way in which people behave and how their behaviours are judged (for a full consideration, see **Chapter 18**).

In considering each theory and theorist we need to remember that no theory emerges from a vacuum. Each theorist will have been influenced by certain types of theory, certain ways of interpreting the world, and will have used particular methods or ways of interpreting data. When reading a theory, it is useful to be aware of broader influences—such as those discussed here—as this may help you both to understand and to critique the ideas. In the remainder of this chapter, we will consider classical criminology and the modern ideas with which it is associated. We will explore the other theories in more depth later in Part 2: positivism (biological and psychological theories in **Chapter 16** and sociological theories in **Chapter 17**), critical theories (**Chapter 18**), social harm (**Chapter 19**), left and right realism (**Chapter 20**), and grand or integrated theories (**Chapter 21**). We will end these discussions by taking a closer look at the causes of crime in **Chapter 22**.

15.4 Classical criminology

We noted briefly in our earlier discussion of classicism that classical criminology is believed to have emerged in the 18th century. This period, in particular 1715–89, is known as the **Age of Enlightenment** as it saw a major philosophical shift in ideas about God, nature, and humanity in Europe and parts of North America. Its key idea was that reason could help us to understand and interpret our world so allowing us to resolve the problems faced by people. It is a time when many 'thinkers' or 'theorists' emerged to shape new systems of social living. The early theorists such as Locke (1690) and Newton (1686) in England began to consider the place of science and ideas and then the core theorists such as Voltaire (1694–1778), from France (see a modern translation of his main works by Williams, 1994). Rousseau (1712–78), from what was then the Republic of Geneva (see a modern translation of his main works by Gourevitch, 2019) in the mid-18th century, though disagreeing on a lot, argued that 'modern' societies should be based on reason rather than on faith or blind obedience.

Whilst there are many theorists involved in this movement and the ideas of the Enlightenment in England, Scotland, France, Germany, Switzerland, Italy, and the US are different, there are certain themes which bring them all together as a movement. The most important is the idea that there can only be progress through dialogue and rational questioning of all things (they therefore embraced the differences between themselves and viewed conflict of ideas as the best way to ensure progress) as well as rational solutions to all problems. Many challenged the power of the church and argued for a separation of church and state. The Enlightenment's focus on reason rather than faith also opened the door to freedom of speech and thought and to a recognition of science as the best way to understand our world. They also supported constitutional government and the introduction of legally enforceable limits on the power of monarchs; however, many (such as Voltaire) still largely supported monarchies (at least if they were informed by reason) rather than democracy (Williams, 1994).

Linked to this was a recognition that each person in a state is important to that state, which led some Enlightenment theorists to argue for liberty, toleration, fraternity, and progress, especially scientific progress. Each individual exercised free will and used rational thought to choose what was best for themselves. They believed that if an intelligent rational person used all their senses to experience and learn from the world, they would be able to write rational theories about how the world works, why things happen, and how things might be altered for the better. These ideas arose at a time when other events, such as the start of the Industrial Revolution, meant that the old systems of governance were already being challenged. Community and family ties were being stretched, as were feudal systems of control (as people moved to towns to earn a living working in mines or factories), and these ideas which placed the individual at the centre of systems were seized on as new ways of governing and controlling the new industrialised communities. These ideas and the rational consideration of problems seeped into all walks of life, even consideration of crime. This was the first time that crime and criminal justice were seriously considered by theorists, so many modern systems of crime investigation, procedure, and punishment can be traced back to the Enlightenment period and the ideals and ideas they suggested.

Before the Enlightenment, in the 17th and early 18th centuries, the problem behaviour (if dealt with at all) was solved by the use of power, often an arbitrary use of power. The state and those in authority often used fear to control the people, including the use of torture to elicit a confession (see **Chapter 28** for early forms of punishment). The punishment was openly used to back up the power of the state (the monarch) and the wealthiest landowners or the church. The old systems were **feudal**—power came with land ownership (and wealth), and land was held by just a few people, nobles. Ordinary people enjoyed very few rights and were expected to obey their feudal lords. When someone broke the rules, the way that they were dealt with often depended on who they were and whether they could protect themselves. Justice was unpredictable. Punishment was, by today's standards, cruel and often physical—public flogging, burning hands, death, and banishment were all common punishments. Punishment in continental Europe was particularly severe. These methods sound barbaric to us but, at the time, many people believed that they were justified and necessary to retain order. In some instances, they were in fact less severe than what had been used in earlier times; death would normally be faster and there might be fewer lashes of the whip. Many thought they were already living in a more forgiving world than their parents and grandparents.

Enlightenment thinkers, now usually known as classical thinkers, challenged the arbitrary use of barbaric punishment, questioning whether this represented justice and whether it was right that monarchs and noblemen held such absolute power. Their argument that societies should be run on fairer grounds was such a shift from the accepted **norms** of the time that some of these classical criminologists hid their identity and their writing for fear of being punished by those in power. We begin our consideration of classical criminology by examining the ideas of some of the key thinkers from this period—John Locke, Cesare Beccaria, and Jeremy Bentham—before looking at the influence of classical criminology, its limitations, and then some newer manifestations of its ideas.

Key thinkers in classical criminology

John Locke

One of the early Enlightenment thinkers was the English philosopher John Locke (1632–1704, see **Figure 15.3**). In very simple terms, his argument was that all nations and all societies should be run so that each person only gives up a portion of their liberty; only the amount necessary for their society to be fair and to function. Each person should then be able to rely on the state to protect their interests from people (or organisations) who were greedy or unfair, like a form of social contract (Locke, 1690). He was also one of the first thinkers to argue that each and every person in a society was capable of conscious thought, and therefore able to make choices based on previous experience or knowledge—the concepts of free will and rational choice.

Locke's ideas, which were revolutionary at the time, helped to form the basis of classical criminological thought: the idea that every person should exercise free will and use rational thought to think for themselves, make their own choices, and not be controlled by either the fear of arbitrary state punishment or religion. He argued that we should all retain the right to choose how to live and behave; the state should only rarely intrude on and limit that choice. Locke and other Enlightenment thinkers saw each individual as reasonable and assumed that before a person chose how to act they would weigh up the possible benefits and costs of that action for themselves. They would decide which action would be most beneficial for them, which one made most sense, and only then would they act—rational choice.

Cesare Beccaria

The two theorists most commonly linked with classical criminological thought are Cesare Beccaria (1738–94) and Jeremy Bentham (English philosopher, 1748–1832)—we consider the latter in the next section. Both believed passionately that each person could and should make rational, sensible decisions and that the state should get rid of barbaric and unpredictable punishments. They recognised the potential for criminality in each person—everyone is capable of greed and bad behaviour—but called on people to refrain from criminal behaviour, and to respect each other. Despite their agreement on these points, however, the two thinkers disagreed on many other details.

For Beccaria, an Italian criminologist and philosopher, the state should exert power to protect people from any unacceptable behaviour produced when others fail to make respectful, rational choices; it is only with such protection that everyone can live freely and without fear. In his short treatise (another word for a theory) entitled *Dei Delitti e Delle Pene* (1764), or in English *On Crimes and Punishments* (see its front cover in **Figure 15.4**), Beccaria argued that unacceptable behaviours (crimes) should be clearly set out and the punishment for breaking the law should be clear and proportionate to the harm. He said that only then could people rationally choose to respect the law. He went on to argue that when a crime is committed, no punishment should be allowed until the incident is investigated (this part of the process is only touched on by Beccaria) and the perpetrator is found guilty in a court of law following evidence to prove that guilt (legal evidence that they broke the law and factual evidence that when looked at rationally proves guilt).

Beccaria argued that throughout this process, the accused had rights which should be respected, but that if they were ultimately found to be guilty, punishment should follow. In that situation punishment was not only acceptable, because the person had chosen to infringe the rights of

Figure 15.3 The English philosopher John Locke argued that societies should be run so that each person only has to give up a portion of their liberty
Source: Sir Gottfried Kniller/Public domain

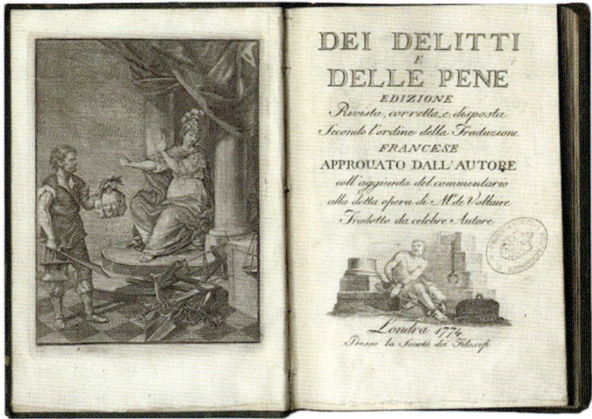

Figure 15.4 In *Dei Delittie e Delle Pene*, Beccaria argued that unacceptable behaviours should be clearly set out and punishment for law-breaking should be proportionate to the harm caused

Source: Public domain

others, but was *expected* in order to protect others and redress the harm inflicted by the crime. However, he stressed that although punishment is deserved, it should not be excessive. It should only be as severe as is necessary to mark the harm caused; any more or less would be unjust.

Beccaria believed the process of investigation, proof, and punishment should be swift in order to keep the link between the act and the punishment and to help to prevent criminality. He argued that with clear, legal, and just systems, rational men would see the likely cost of 'bad' behaviour and choose not to transgress. A just system which caught and punished real offenders would be likely to deter others, and Beccaria suggested that it was more important to prevent crimes in the first place than to punish once they happen. He argued that this kind of system had the following attributes:

1. **A just and fair process**—if the wrong people are punished or the system is believed to be arbitrary or corrupt it would not deter people from offending.
2. **Exactly the right punishment**—too little punishment and the system might fail to reflect the seriousness of the harm and also fail to deter would-be offenders; too much punishment would be an unjust act of violence and reduce respect for the law so would also fail to deter offenders. Beccaria argued that to have maximum deterrent effect, punishment should be just a little worse than the harm inflicted. He also stated that the death penalty should be removed and never used.
3. **Speedy justice**—Beccaria saw this as essential in order to retain the link between the crime and the punishment in the mind of both the offender and of others.
4. **Certainty**—in that people should believe that offenders will be both caught and punished. Beccaria argued that **deterrence** only works if people are certain that they are going to be punished. If they believe they will get away with something, then they will offend.

Underlying all of Beccaria's ideas is, of course, the assumption that people are rational and that they always consider what the outcome will be before they participate in any activity. Read **Controversy and debate 15.1** and consider the issues it raises.

Beccaria's arguments should all sound very familiar; the modern criminal justice systems in many countries are built upon them, and you will see them reflected in **Chapters 24** and **25** on the criminal justice system of England and Wales. His theory is very legalistic (Beccaria was legally trained) and draws out many modern ideas such as justice for all, rights for those accused in court, and fair and just punishment. His call for the punishment to reflect the harm done in each case was the start of what is called retribution or retributive justice (see **Chapter 28**). Beccaria suggested a particularly pure form of retributive justice in which the punishment could not be increased for repeat offending; instead, it should meet the harm done on that individual occasion. This is one of a number of problems that have been raised with Beccaria's ideas, another being his assumption that all people have the ability to reason and therefore should be called to account for their actions. Children and people with mental illnesses were assumed to be rational and able to choose not to offend so could be fully punished if they transgressed. Now, we consider that these groups are less able to make fully reasoned decisions about whether to offend and therefore should not be punished in the same way as adults (see **Chapter 9**).

Jeremy Bentham

As we have noted, many of Beccaria's ideas were shared by the English philosopher Jeremy Bentham, but Bentham also added other aspects to the classical school (Bentham, 1789, reprinted 1907). He suggested a slightly different form of classical theory; one based on the idea of **utilitarianism**, meaning the greatest good for the greatest number of people. Bentham believed that everyone wants to maximise pleasure and minimise pain or unpleasantness. Law breaking occurred, he argued, when someone thought they would be happier if they offended than if they did not. The state therefore has to ensure that the pleasure or happiness initially brought by the crime is outweighed by the punishment or unpleasantness it will ultimately produce.

Whereas Beccaria strongly bound the level of punishment to the level of harm committed, believing that to deter offending and for justice to be served the punishment should fit the crime, Bentham would allow more

CONTROVERSY AND DEBATE 15.1

Are we always rational?

Some psychologists question the extent to which people are rational. They suggest that **cognitive** bias interferes and prevents people making a truly rational choice. This idea was forcefully suggested by Tversky and Kahneman (1974). Basically, the suggestion is that each individual creates their own view of reality: each person has a different background and their thinking is affected by their previous understanding and experience. This means that in every decision they make there will be systematic errors (or biases), based on their background beliefs and ideas, which prevent their decisions being objectively rational. Their decision-making will also be affected by that 'bias' which may cause them to repeatedly or continuously act in (what to others appears to be) an 'irrational' way, usually repeatedly making the same error of judgement. The argument is that it is the individual's construction of reality, the way in which they view the world, that leads them to decide how to behave; the decision is not based on an objective and unbiased idea of reality. For example, people's ideas and thinking are often affected by what other people think; this is particularly true in the information age where media, and particularly the internet and possibly 'fake news', affects people's idea of reality and may alter how they behave. Other examples are that people often fixate on one or two pieces of information (often things they found out early on) and these may lead their decision-making even if from a purely rational viewpoint other factors are more important or later information suggests the earlier ideas/beliefs are wrong. Part of this is that people often fail to take account of issues where it is unclear what the outcome might be, for example they do not know what will happen if they get caught or do not know the likelihood of being caught. There are many cognitive biases but the idea suggests that people are likely to act: in ways that they learn are acceptable from an early age (if their families have a tendency to offend or to use violence to resolve conflict, they may see that behaviour as normal and acceptable); in ways that people whose opinions they value act (if their friends do it then it is acceptable); or if they know people have not been caught then they may have a biased idea of the chances of being caught.

All of this suggests that people do not make fully rational choices, rather they make biased decisions based on their perception of reality. Where does this leave classical theories or ideas based on classical theories? Are people's choices still rational though within slightly restricted parameters? Is the rationality reduced because of cognitive bias and, if so, what does that mean for rational choice and therefore for punishing people for making the 'wrong' choices?

---

severe punishments if they would prevent offending. He believed that for the greatest good to be achieved for the greatest number of people, conformity to the law was essential, so if punishment was a little more unpleasant than any happiness that would be gained by offending, that would ensure compliance. If compliance required more punishment than was necessary to redress the harm done, Bentham would argue that this greater punishment should be inflicted in order to prevent future offending. He would also embrace increasing the punishment for repeat offenders in an attempt to convince them not to reoffend, though suggested that if conformity could be guaranteed without punishment, through education or rehabilitation, then this should be used rather than punishment, as it represents a lesser intervention in the offender's freedom. His idea of punishment was therefore based on what one aims to *achieve*—deterrence or the prevention of offending—rather than based on what someone has *done*—retributivism, as suggested by Beccaria.

While Beccaria was of the firm opinion that the death penalty should never be used, Bentham felt it was generally too severe but was acceptable in cases of murder where there are aggravating circumstances (this was a concession in his 1775 essay but he removed it from his 1831 essay—see Bedau, 1983; Calvert, 2006). Each used evidence and rational thought to support his argument, for example Bentham, in his 1831 essay, noted that when Tuscany abolished the death penalty between 1765 and 1795 the crime rate was largely the same as when it had the death penalty and therefore it served no purpose (this was one of a number of arguments, see Bedau, 1983; Calvert, 2006). Bentham firmly believed in prison as a form of punishment and even designed a prison, referred to as **Bentham's Panopticon** (see **Figure 15.5**), in which each prisoner could be constantly watched from a central point. He had a more sophisticated concept of reason than Beccaria and recognised that those lacking full mental capacity (the legal term for someone unable to make some decisions for themselves) should not be punished. He also rejected punishment if the victim consented, which is interesting when one considers that sadomasochism (a practice in which one person inflicts physical or mental suffering on another, with their consent—see **Chapter 3**) is still illegal in England and Wales.

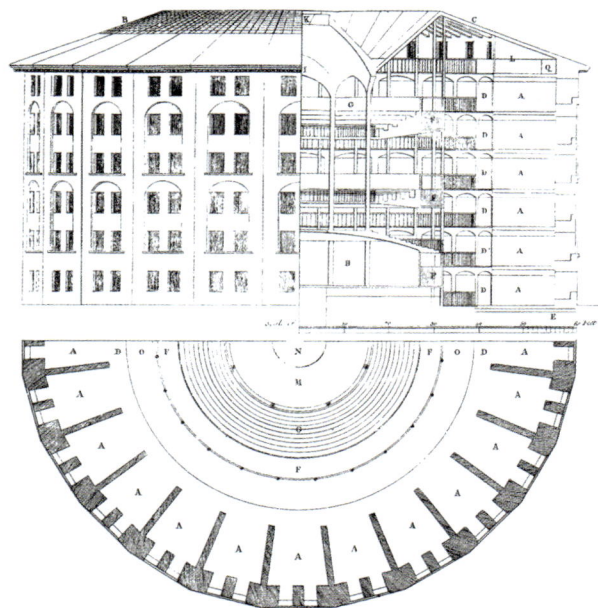

Figure 15.5 Bentham's Panopticon prison design, which ensured that each inmate could be constantly watched from a central point, still influences modern prisons, including the Presido Modelo Prison in Cuba

Source: Jeremy Bentham and Friman/CC BY-SA 3.0

The influence of classical criminology

How much credit should we give classical criminology?

The ideas of classical criminology and the Enlightenment thinkers shaped European law and jurisprudence (the philosophy of law), including the criminal justice system, impacting all parts of the process from suspicion through to arrest, and trial to punishment. We can easily identify the key ideas from this period in what we would now consider to be a modern system of criminal justice, but keeping our ABC mantra in mind, it is important to be aware that classical criminology's popularity could be attributed, at least in part, to the context in which its ideas emerged.

The Enlightenment thinkers and classical criminologists were producing their theories in societies that were facing problems and looking for new ways of dealing with offending. The Industrial revolution (a period of major industrialisation which saw changes in transport and manufacturing, and the decline of handmade products in favour of those produced by large, machine-filled factories) was underway and beginning to build in West European states. Traditional ways of operating were therefore already under threat. The ruling classes were being challenged, first in the American Revolution of 1776 and later, closer to home for the Europe-based Enlightenment thinkers, in the French Revolution of 1789. These revolutions challenged the authority of the state and the supremacy of monarchs. Other European states also experienced upheavals through changes to land use.

The existing method of controlling ordinary people through the feudal system was breaking down as the working poor chose to migrate to cities to seek factory labour. This was the start of a fully waged (capitalist) economy (one based on payment for work rather than on land use) needing new forms of control. Industrial systems, property ownership, and the newly emerging population bases all needed to be legally regulated. The ruling classes were unsettled by these changes and wanted to retain their power even if that meant giving up previous systems of control and supporting (or at least appearing to) the instigation of more humane and just systems.

It is undeniable that around this time states, especially new states like the US and France, were willing to alter their systems of governance and generally chose those suggested by the classical school and Enlightenment, but the widespread adoption of classical systems could be seen as resulting from the social upheaval rather than directly from classical criminology or the Enlightenment theorists. Classical criminology was shaped by its social context, which also made it more likely that states would accept the ideas. Its ideas were a product of their time; they were successful, preserved, and widely disseminated because they served a purpose—the continuation of the power systems, even if in an altered form and more rigidly answerable to law.

Classical criminology's impact on modern justice

So what tangible impact did classical criminology have on justice in the years following the Enlightenment, and on our modern justice systems? Whether we attribute the change to social upheaval or to the influence of specific thinkers, new ideas about crime and justice meant that by the late 18th century the legal authorities in many countries could no longer punish arbitrarily: they had to prove guilt through a trial based on due process (which is still the case—see **Chapters 2** and **25**) which respected the rights and interests of suspects. Torturing people into confessions was replaced by investigation and fair trial. Once guilt was proven, states treated offenders as rational actors and ensured that their punishment reflected the crime. This was generally done through retributive justice; punishment shaped by the harm done. More severe bodily punishments, such as corporal punishment and the death penalty, declined.

These practices are still evident in many justice systems today. They have diverged from the original ideas in some notable aspects, sometimes extending the same ideas (for example, the fact that the death penalty is no longer used in England and Wales) and sometimes changing course (for example, the fact that many modern criminal justice systems, including that of England and Wales, embrace a complex idea of deterrence which leads to more severe punishment of repeat offenders than might be expected as a result of the harm done), but the long-lasting influence of classical criminology is evident. Two central aspects of modern criminal justice are particularly clearly linked to classical thinking: the idea of free will and choice, and the idea of deterrence as a core aim of the law.

The centrality of free will and choice is reflected in one of the core legal aspects at a criminal trial: the idea of *mens rea*. In almost every criminal trial two things need to be proven: **actus reus** and **mens rea**. *Actus reus*, Latin for 'guilty act', are the factual actions that need to be proven, the actions that the law says must have been taken for the relevant offence to have been committed (for example, to commit theft one needs to take property from someone). It is *mens rea*, Latin for 'guilty mind', that is affected by classical thought. Almost all criminal offences require the prosecution to prove a guilty mind (for example, to commit theft one needs to choose to take the object and intend permanently to deprive the other person). Some crimes (for example, driving without brake lights) do not need *mens rea*. *Mens rea* is the intention to act in a way which is proscribed (forbidden) by law; it is the fact that a person chooses to do something which is illegal.

This means that in order to convict a person of most crimes, the prosecution needs to prove beyond reasonable doubt both that they *performed* the proscribed acts (did what they are not permitted to do, *actus reus*) and that they *intended* to do those acts (that they chose to act illegally, *mens rea*). The guilty mind is about choice, not motive. There may be some criminal acts that are done for love and compassion but are still crimes. A person might intentionally steal food in order to feed their starving children. That is still theft because of their intention; their motive is not taken into consideration in decisions as to whether to convict, although, in some cases, it may be a reason for a less severe punishment. Therefore, the choice to act illegally is central to being able to call an individual guilty and being able to punish them for their choice. This is very much in line with classical theorists' ideas.

The other key idea from classical criminology which is visible in many modern justice systems is that deterrence is the core aim of the criminal law: it should deter future unacceptable behaviours. For this to occur, the punishment needs to be sufficiently severe to ensure that the criminal does not gain from their crime and yet not so severe that it could be seen as unjust. This is known as **proportionality** in sentencing and in many states (including England and Wales) it is central to the sentencing of each and every offender. It is also central to Parliament's consideration of the maximum sentence it should set when prohibiting an act; it considers how harmful the act can be and sets the maximum punishment in line with the possible harm. Without this proportionality, murder might be given the same sentence as theft and criminals might then choose to kill witnesses (to a theft) in order to prevent the authorities from discovering that they committed the crime. Proportionality deters this kind of behaviour as, if the offender kills witnesses, their punishment will be far more severe than it would be just for the theft.

The idea is that proportionality of sentencing prevents criminals from gaining from their crimes and so should deter them from choosing to offend in the future. For deterrence to work in this way, punishment needs to be both fairly swift (happen soon after the offence so that the offender links the punishment and the choice to act) and certain (the authorities need to solve most crimes and punish offenders otherwise people will continue to offend and take the chance that they will get away with it). In sentencing each individual, the level of harm done indicates the upper limit of punishment, but the actual punishment may be reduced to take account of mitigating circumstances, good behaviour, or reduced guilt.

These two examples demonstrate the real, lasting, and important impact that classical theories have had on modern justice. However, many criminologists have observed that classical criminology has its limitations, especially when its ideas are adhered to very rigidly, and modern systems embrace ideas such as rehabilitation and **restorative justice** which do not fit with classical theories. In the next section, we reflect on the limitations of classical criminology.

Limitations of classical criminology

The ideas associated with classical criminology may have been enthusiastically embraced following the Enlightenment and have had a long-lasting influence, but they are not without limitations or beyond question.

As with any theory, it is important that we consider this school's assumptions and claims critically, assessing the extent to which it applies and is useful in other contexts.

Over-reliance on classical criminology's assertion that every person is capable of rational thought led (in the late 18th and 19th centuries) to children and those with mental illnesses or impairments being punished as if they were able to make fully reasoned choices about whether to offend. However, these Enlightenment-based laws have changed over time, and in England and Wales the age of **criminal responsibility** is ten; this means that from the age of ten, children are treated as if they have full adult responsibility. Mental illnesses may also be taken into consideration when deciding whether someone should be held responsible for their actions. Rigidly punishing each person for the harm done prevented judges from being able to take account of different factors and almost certainly led to injustice. For example, in **Chapter 3** we suggested that justice would be better served if circumstances could be taken into account, for example when a starving person steals food, we should treat them less severely than someone stealing something they don't need for survival simply because they felt like it. Strict adherence to classical ideals would have prevented many of the advances in our systems:

> There would have been no … adjustment of fines to the means of offenders, no suspended sentences, no **probation**, no parole, no special measures for young offenders and the mentally ill.

(Radzinowicz, 1966: 123)

Of course, classical thinking has not stood still. Theorists such as the British philosopher H. L. A. Hart (1907–92) (see **Figure 15.6**) have re-evaluated classical thinking and taken it into what is known as neo-classical (literally, 'new classical') thought. We will see when we discuss neo-classical criminology in the next section, that neo-classical thinkers recognise complexities in behaviour and so argue for more complex sentencing decisions, ones which can take into account differences in responsibility. Neo-classical approaches tend to try to moderate the core classical ideals by seeking either just outcomes or outcomes that may be more likely to achieve a particular aim, such as prevention. However, the changes have never interfered with the basic classical principle that people should be called to account when their choices (their free will and rational decisions) are unacceptable to others, but even with these modernisations of the theory there remain issues.

Culpability

Whilst neo-classical thinking has addressed some issues, such as capacity and more complex sentencing decisions, it still leaves the basic problem of the school's rigidity around the idea of culpability—whether someone is deserving of blame. Classical criminology and court and punishment systems based on it have problems dealing with differences between **defendants**, because treating people differently conflicts with the core idea that conviction and punishment should be based on free will. Classical criminology assumes that if you are capable of rational decision-making then you always make rational decisions. However, in reality many of us act on impulse, without thinking things through; it could be considered unjust to punish an individual as if they had considered all eventualities before committing an offence. We consider this issue further in **Controversy and debate 15.2**.

Intentions

Classical criminology also has problems with taking into account differences in crimes. It sees one case of assault or murder as being the same as another, and yet for both the victim and offender they may be very different. For example, intentionally killing someone in order to rob a bank is murder, but so too is intentionally killing someone you love who has repeatedly asked to die in order to be put out of extreme pain and misery. To classical thinking, and therefore to our legal system, both are murder and both require life imprisonment (more recently 'mercy' killing is taken into consideration in deciding whether to prosecute, though on strict legal grounds it should not be). Whilst overall the system may be just, it cannot deal with nuance and subtlety and this leads to injustice in some cases.

Timing

Classical theory believes that it is important that punishment happens very soon after the crime is committed so that people can see and understand the connection between the two. In practice, there is always a conflict

Figure 15.6 Neo-classicist thinkers like the British philosopher H. L. A. Hart recognise complexities in behaviour and argue for more nuanced sentencing decisions

Source: Robespierre 7/CC BY-SA 4.0

CONTROVERSY AND DEBATE 15.2

The limits of culpability

So far, the idea has been clear: classical thinkers, neo-classical thinkers, and the law in most western states assume that we punish because we see the offender as 'guilty' of choosing to act in a criminal way. Is this always the case? We have already looked at the impact of age, illness, and development on choice and therefore on criminal responsibility. However, are there other, more difficult, circumstances in which we could question the ideas of 'guilt' and culpability/responsibility?

Let's consider issues of impulsive behaviour, in particular impulsive aggression. The word 'impulsive' implies that the individual does not really 'choose' to act aggressively and this prompts the question of whether they are accountable and therefore should be punished. If an individual has difficulty in controlling their aggressive impulses, particularly when frustrated or provoked, then this is likely to result in interpersonal conflict, disruptive relationships, and domestic abuse. It may also be related to aggression towards themselves.

Imagine that there has been a particularly violent knife attack resulting in grievous bodily harm. Normally, most people would agree that the perpetrator deserves to be severely punished. However, if the violence is the result of a neurobiological issue (structural or functional abnormalities in the brain), the individual may not be fully culpable. It may be possible to prove that the individual suffers from abnormalities that might sometimes lead to aggression (violence), but it may not be possible to prove that the brain abnormality caused the behaviour at the moment that crime was committed. Can/should we still punish them?

When considering the answer to this, remember that someone who has a tendency to be aggressively impulsive is more likely to repeat acts of violence—they can't help it. So, those who act violently without thinking things through may be less *culpable* but they could be considered far more *dangerous* for the rest of us, simply because they cannot control the aggression. What does that tell us about what we should do and why? For a full discussion of similar ideas, see Shuman and Gold (2008).

---

between the speed in obtaining a conviction and the fairness/justice of the process (also important to the classical ideals). Ensuring that the correct procedures are followed and are just is often time-consuming, resulting in a delay in conviction. Classical theory cannot resolve this conflict.

Power structures

An issue that is often overlooked is classical criminology's relationship with power. Classical approaches tend to ensure that the present power structures remain largely unchallenged. Those in power tend to make criminal laws that protect their interests, and reliance on the ideas of free will and rational decision-making as the underlying basis of crime fails to explain why the poor tend to be accused and convicted of crimes more frequently than the rich. Classical thinking seems to suggest that rational decision-making is more likely if you are rich. Can this really be the case? An alternative explanation might be that those in power (generally the rich) make laws they are less likely to break. We discuss the complex and often unjust-seeming relationship between classical criminology and power at various other points in this book: see **Chapters 18** and **19** (and **Chapter 10**, where race is considered, and **Chapter 11**, which discusses gender).

Neo-classical criminology

We have already touched on the school of thought known as neo-classical criminology, and the fact that this is a more modern incarnation of the original ideas of classical thinking, with some of its ideals developed and adapted. Out of this broader school, other theories (we discussed particular theories in **section 15.2**) have sprung up, including rational choice theory, routine activity theory, and situational crime prevention. These theories are briefly defined, and the relationship between them summarised, in **Figure 15.7**. Before discussing the theories themselves, though, let's briefly consider the context from which they emerged.

For many years, classical ideas took a back seat in criminological work and became more of a tool used by lawyers and jurisprudence. They were mainly used to discuss processes and punishments, since these elements were at the core of the criminal justice system, whereas for most of the 20th century, criminological thought focused on *why* crime occurred and what we should do about it. As Garland (2000) notes, from about 1890 through to the 1970s there was confidence that through a combination of improved social conditions and rehabilitation it would be possible to reduce crime by altering the offender's

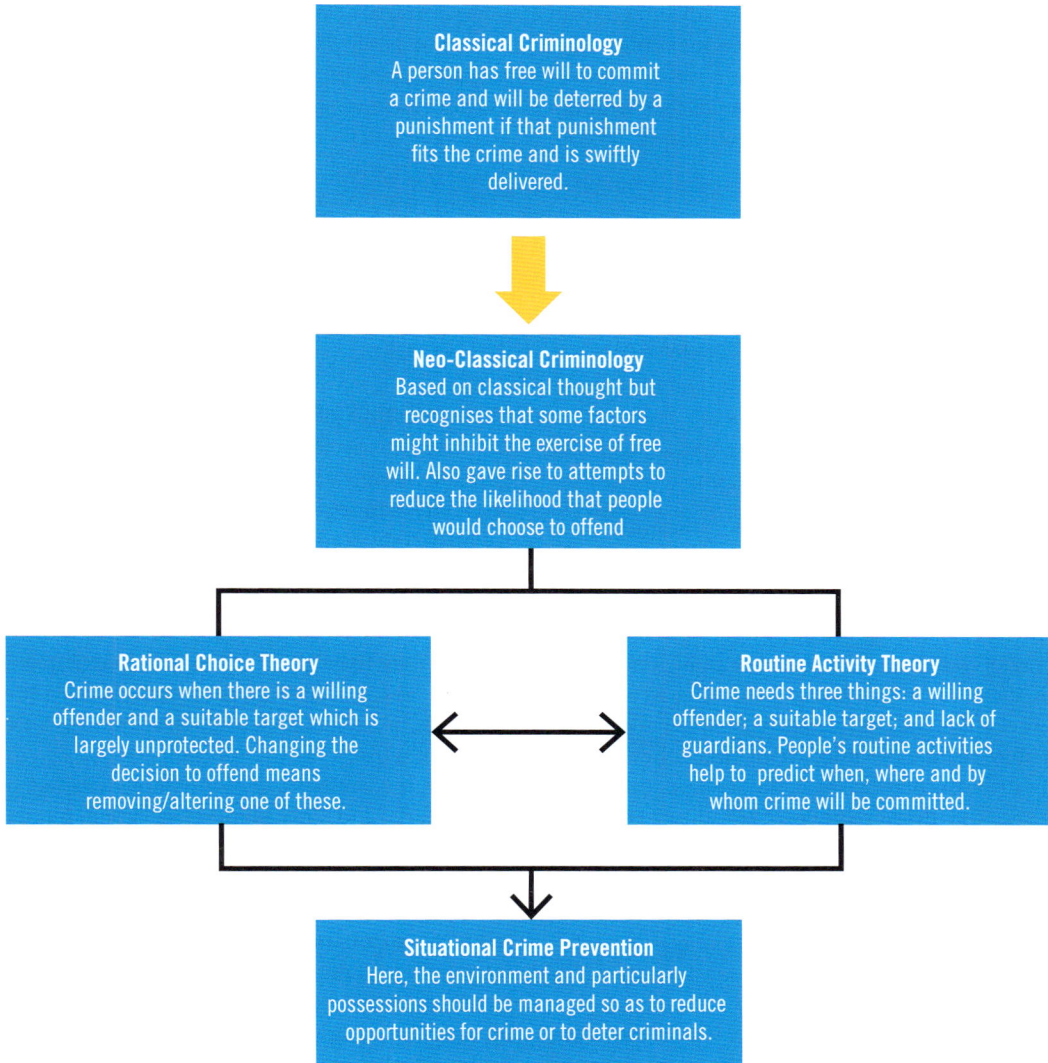

Figure 15.7 The schools of thought relating to, and developed from, classical criminology

likelihood of reoffending, or by softening the worst effects of structural problems like poverty and unemployment. However, the end of the 1960s saw this confidence fade and an era began in criminology where the idea that 'nothing works', sometimes called 'penal pessimism', began to take over and by the late 1980s these ideas led policymaking—we discuss these shifts in **Chapter 25**, and they are summarised in **Table 25.1**.

For offenders, this meant a move away from a focus on welfare and rehabilitation towards the idea that punishment was the underlying factor in the way in which they would be treated—a move back to a purer form of classical decision-making in court. If during the punishment someone was also rehabilitated, this was seen as a bonus, but punishment itself was key. Neo-classical thinkers also advocated using classical ideals to reduce crime in ways that did not rely on working directly with offenders; they focused on reducing the opportunities for crime and increasing the likelihood of offenders being caught. Most of these theorists do not see crime as the result of individuals having a certain disposition (mind and character) to offend (see, for example, Lombroso discussed in **Chapter 16**) but as the result of an individual's choices, so they argue that policies should be adopted that make the criminal choice less likely, which should reduce offending. Neo-classical criminologists are in favour of altering the environment (for example, increasing street lighting tends to reduce street crime as it makes people more visible) to reduce criminality, taking the view that this influences people's choices and makes them less likely to choose to offend.

Classical criminology remains at the core of modern neo-classical criminological theories as they all start from the idea that offenders want to gain an advantage from their offending behaviour. They want to maximise pleasure with minimum pain. It ignores any other motivations and focuses on this **cost–benefit** analysis (weighing up benefits against harms) to explain everything. Its core assumptions are that:

- each human being is rational;
- rational consideration involves weighing up gains against possible dangers;
- rational assessment decides how each person will behave (both their legal and illegal behaviours);
- before acting, each person weighs up the likely pleasure against the possible pain;
- their choice will depend on which action will give the person most individual pleasure;
- possible future punishment (if it is sufficiently swift, severe, and certain) may reduce the likelihood that illegal behaviour is chosen.

Here the offender is considered to be a rational actor with power to make decisions. The fact that punishments are available if they are caught doing something wrong may act as a prevention for some people in some situations, or at least may reduce the number of times they choose to offend. However, neo-classical theorists in the 1980s wanted to take this further and look at rational choice in the shaping of crime prevention policy. This brings us to rational choice theory.

Rational choice theory

At the heart of rational choice theory are the British criminologists Cornish and Clarke (1986, 2014), who argued that for most people even quick decisions, based on minimum data, would follow a pattern of self-interested rational choice. Rational choice, they claim, is at the core of whether to offend and when, where, and with whom to offend. Offending would occur if there was a suitable target which was not protected. Their suggestion was therefore that if you make something harder to offend against (in other words, you protect it), then the potential offender will move on to something else (for example, improving locking systems on cars helps to reduce car theft).

Rational choice theorists study why some people in some circumstances decide to behave in criminal ways and how we can change those choices. Cornish and Clarke began working together as early as 1985 and developed their rational choice theory over the next 20 years, until 2006. Their basic argument was that an individual will only choose to participate in any particular act if they will benefit from it. A crime indicates that the individual thinks that they will benefit from that offending activity; it does not indicate that they think they will benefit from other criminal acts. When deciding whether to participate in a crime, each individual has to weigh up many issues. Not all aspects of a situation are clear and each potential offender has to weigh up risks and uncertainties and try to arrive at the decision which is most likely to benefit them. The way in which decisions are made and the outcomes that are reached differs depending on the situation and the type of crime they are considering participating in—there are no set patterns. There are generally two layers of decision-making, involvement decisions and event decisions, and each is a complex set of choices that occur at different times.

Involvement decisions

Involvement decisions are those about whether to engage in crime rather than other types of activity. They generally concern the values, attitudes, and personality traits that lead a person to be more likely to accept criminal, or particular types of criminal, behaviour. So someone may believe that substance use should not be regulated and so be open to involvement in that activity, and they may have friends who participate, but that does not mean that they necessarily offend themselves. However, it means that they are open to offending if they so choose.

These involvement decisions are depicted in **Figure 15.8** (Clarke and Cornish first used the depiction in 1985 but it also appeared in later works, for example 2006). This flow chart notes factors which may lead someone towards or away from crime. For example, a young man who lives in an area where crime is common and whose father offends: (1) may have learnt some criminal techniques from his father; (2) so when he needs money; (3) he sees the easiest way to get it to be burglary (4 and 5); he sees his chance (6 and 7); and so offends (8). By inserting different facts, **Figure 15.8** can also explain why or how a person may choose not to offend (either choosing not commit this burglary or to never commit a burglary). It is also important to be aware that the factors noted in **Figure 15.8** may alter over time. Factors that opened someone up to become involved (such as their temperament or upbringing, or the fact that they need money) are different from those which may make such involvement a normal part of their life—they realise they are good at offending; it brings them money or happiness or escapism; it may result in a change of peer group which supports the offending. Other factors may lead them to stop their involvement: they may become more settled, for example with a partner, and may not want to risk being caught; security may be increased so that opportunities to offend are no longer so easily available; they may get caught or almost get caught; they may secure a job; and some or all of these factors may lead them to stop offending, to desist. It is important to note that involvement decisions are specific to each separate

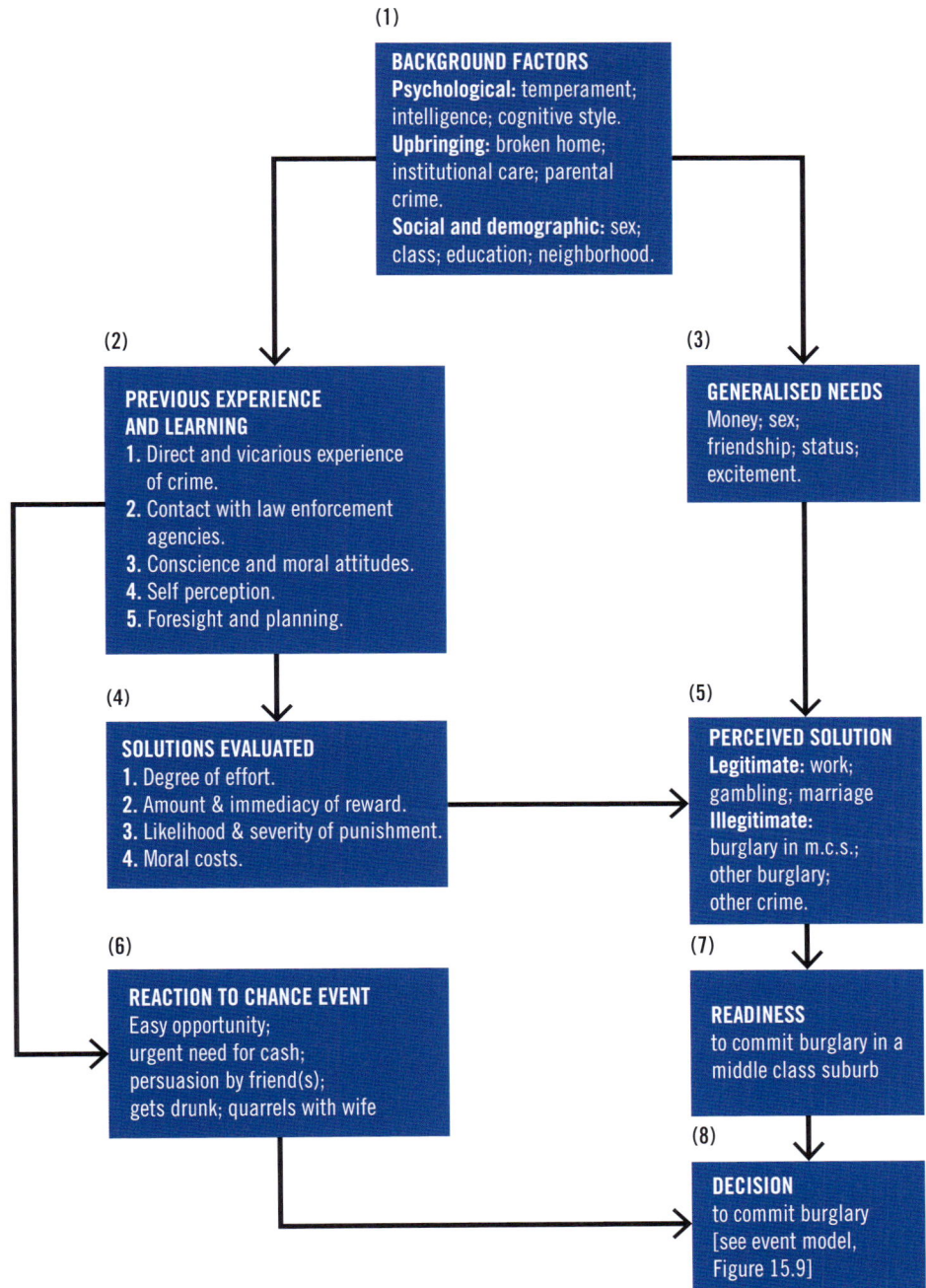

Figure 15.8 Clarke and Cornish's flow chart of factors at play in involvement decisions can explain why or how a person may choose to participate in criminal activity
Source: University of Chicago Press

crime so that just because someone may be willing to or open to committing burglary, this does not mean that they are open to committing murder or rape.

Event decisions

Involvement decisions were general, being willing to participate in criminal activity. Event decisions are more specific, they are the factors which influence the decision about whether to commit a specific crime, for example to commit a burglary from this particular house now. Having made the decision to commit a burglary (see the involvement decision in **Figure 15.8**), the potential offender then has to select the area in which it will be committed—this is the event decision which is depicted in **Figure 15.9**. As you can see from this flow chart, the first part of the decision will take account of how easy (or difficult) it is to commit the crime

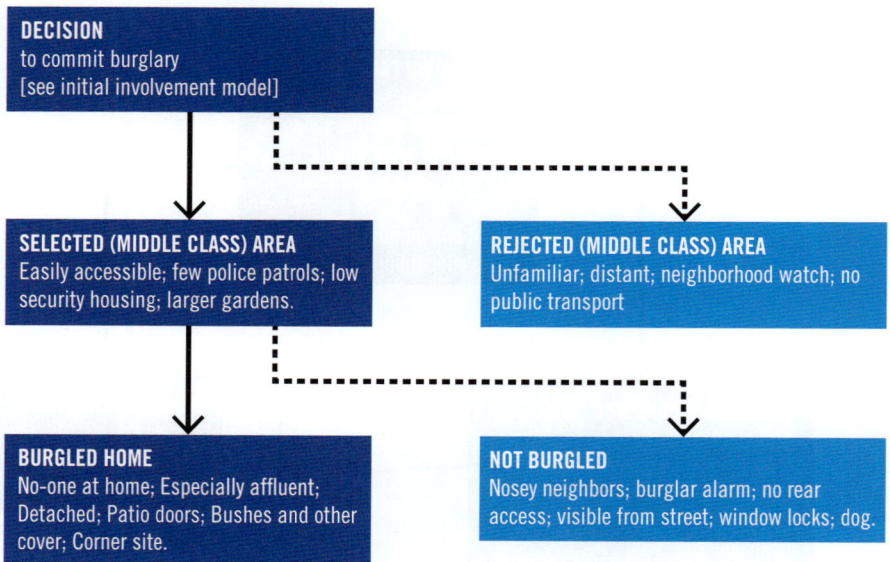

Figure 15.9 Clarke and Cornish's flow chart of factors at play in event decisions can explain why or how a person may choose to commit a specific crime

Source: University of Chicago Press

in a particular area or environment. The next level of decision-making is to select an exact target. This could be chosen by asking the following questions: Is it/he/she protected? Is it possible to approach and commit the crime without being seen or recorded? And so on. Following target selection, the potential offender has to decide how and when to commit the crime, how to escape, and how to prevent themselves being tracked down by the authorities afterwards. If the individual offends in a similar way multiple times, they may become more skilled and professional, choosing more difficult but more rewarding or lucrative areas and targets.

In rational choice theory, crime always serves a purpose; it is not pointless. Originally, many classical thinkers had a limited idea of purpose—it was to gain an economic advantage. However, purpose for Cornish and Clarke (2006, 2014) is a broad concept and includes greater happiness, respect and admiration amongst your peer group, excitement, and sexual or other gratification. This takes account of benefits and punishments that might accompany offending, but also recognises that the way in which these benefits and punishments are viewed and rationally weighed up may alter over time or as peer group, learning, and professionalism alter.

Our discussion about decisions taking place and the organised-looking flow charts might suggest that people sit down and consider all the options at length before deciding to offend, perhaps even making lists or spreadsheets of the pros and cons. That is not what Cornish and Clarke (2006) are suggesting. They recognise that in many cases the decision is made quickly or with reduced capacity to be rational (the offender may be drunk or on drugs, very young, or mentally impaired). However, even in these instances the thinkers still argue that there is a rational choice, even if that choice may be bounded or conditional. 'Bounded rationality' refers to the idea that a person's rationality may be 'bounded' or limited by the information a person has available to them, the limitations of their mental abilities (which may be affected, for example, by alcohol, other substances, or lack of sleep), or by the time available to make the decision (many decisions to offend are spur of the moment). These limitations to the rational decision mean that many decisions are only the best possible under the circumstances rather than being the absolute best decision. Clarke and Cornish argue that criminals, like everyone else, are making the most rational or sensible decision for them at the time, with the information and with the capacity they have at that moment. In many instances, the decision to commit a particular crime is made fairly quickly, but even a quick decision is a decision. Even if the crime is planned (and many are not), the offender is likely to encounter unexpected problems and needs to decide how to deal with those; for this, many rely on experience and instinct, each decision made will be rational but may not be the optimum decision because the thought process is bounded (the decision-maker may not have all the information, their mental abilities may be impaired, or they may have to make the decision very quickly).

Whilst the original classical criminologists claimed that offenders would weigh up benefits (often long term) and punishments, Cornish and Clarke (2006) suggest that offenders tend to focus on the immediate risks and benefits; what the crime will give them now compared to the immediate likelihood of being caught. Other factors that are often considered are frequently referred to as **situational variables**, and might include their skills, the tools available to them (they cannot commit **cybercrimes** without access to a digital device), their personality and background, whether they need or are motivated to offend, whether they have the opportunity, and whether something triggers the actual event. The possible punishment, Clarke and Cornish argue, is less relevant to the immediate decision made by the offender.

Cornish and Clarke used all these elements to build **crime scripts** (first used by Cornish, 1994), which are accounts of how the decisions leading up to a crime and following the crime (for example, decisions about the getaway and what to do with a body or stolen goods) might be taken. Most human activity can be broken down into a script, a logical sequence of events which when put together describe and possibly explain an activity. For example, the crime script for eating in a restaurant might be: enter the restaurant; get shown to a table; study the menu; order; be served; eat; get the bill; pay; and leave the restaurant. Crime scripts are similar; they walk us through what might happen and consider and explain the rational choices included in the activity. They often explain and answer the questions as to who, what, when, where, why, and how, so theorists often create them to try to predict and prevent crimes from occurring. The crime script for a pickpocket might be:

Figure 15.10 Developing crime scripts—accounts of the decisions leading up to and following a crime—can help us predict crimes and take measures to prevent them from occurring, for example issuing public warning notices
Source: Steve Vidler/Alamy Stock Photo

Preparation	Select a general area in which to pickpocket;
	Dress and behave appropriately for that setting.
Pre-activity	Arrive at the location;
	Loiter and watch the crowd but ensure that you blend in;
	Identify a suitable target;
	Move in close and create an opportunity, for example bump into them.
Activity	Take hold of the target goods—wallet, purse, mobile phone, etc.
Post-activity	Move away from target;
	Do not draw attention;
	Find a more private location;
	Secure important items such as cash and cards;
	Dispose of unwanted items such as the wallet or purse;
	Hold onto the most immediately useful items, for example cash;
	Sell other items such as cards and phones;
	Spend the money.

This script might be used to suggest that people should be more careful to keep valuable portable goods, cash, and credit cards in zipped pockets within bags or zipped pockets inside clothes to ensure that they are not available to pickpockets. This prevention can only be achieved by asking the public to be careful, for example in advertisements or warning notices (see **Figure 15.10**).

Theorists have constructed these scripts for many types of crime in an effort to try to prevent or predict such offences (take a look at **What do you think? 15.2** to have a go yourself). We can see that rational choice theory does not explain why certain people or types of people offend; rather it aims to explain why crime happens. It is interested in the situations and circumstances in which crime is likely to be chosen and suggests policies which might deal with those possibilities. Some policymakers have used rational choice theory to justify increasing the severity of punishments. The argument goes:

(a) if offenders make rational choices about whether to offend or not; and

(b) they choose to offend because they will gain more by offending than they will lose by being punished; then

(c) the punishment is too lenient.

There is logic to this argument, but it could be said to display a lack of understanding of the theory's finer points. A serious limitation of the theory lies in its almost complete disregard for what it terms 'background factors' (see **Figure 15.9**). These individual and structural aspects linked to crime are mentioned but then largely ignored by rational choice theorists. The theorists are not trying to find ways in which policy might alter these underlying elements and potential causes of crime; they even claim that policies such as rehabilitation programmes have failed to prevent criminality.

Despite these shortcomings, rational choice theory is important as it reminds criminologists and policymakers

> ### WHAT DO YOU THINK? 15.2
>
> **Crime scripts**
>
> Create a crime script for one of these offences:
>
> - bank robbery;
> - house burglary;
> - shoplifting.
>
> Consider what aspects need to be present for this crime to be committed. Classify each aspect of the crime into: preparation; pre-activity; activity; and post-activity.
>
> Remember that neo-classical thinkers are keen to prevent crime happening in the first place, so using your script consider what might be done to prevent the activity.
>
> Neo-classical thinkers also argue that people who choose to offend should be punished. Go back over your script and consider whether there are any aspects of the script that might require a lot of thought and planning. And are there any aspects that might be able to be performed by someone without making a rational choice? Then consider whether these aspects should be used to increase or decrease punishment.

that if we simply focus on individual and structural underlying causes of crime, we miss the fact that people do make choices. People's behaviour is not determined purely by other forces; they are active decision-makers and we should search for ways to alter their decision-making processes.

Routine activity theory

The American criminologists Cohen and Felson (1979) built on rational choice theory and suggested **routine activity theory**. They argued that for crime to occur, three things were necessary: a motivated offender; a suitable target (it might be a human victim or an object such as a car or a house); and the absence of guardians (as well as the police this includes other people who might see what happens and also surveillance systems such as CCTV). All three had to be present at the same time and in the same place before a crime would occur (see **Figure 15.11**). This wonderfully simple way of trying to understand and so prevent crime is now most closely associated with Marcus Felson, based at Texas State University. He argues that a motivated offender, a suitable target, and the absence of guardians will tend to converge in the routine patterns of people's lives. As with rational choice theory, crime is placed at the centre, supplemented by the motivated offender but, here, people's routine activities help us to predict where, when, and against whom crime might be committed. (It is worth noting that criminologists tend to use a similar theory, known as **lifestyle theory**, when looking at victims and trying to predict **victimisation**.) Although both rational choice theory and routine activity theory are focused on similar aspects of the problem, the latter is wider. It is termed 'routine' because it studies the everyday activities or patterns of activities that people follow, but 'routine' also means the normal rather than the unusual. For routine activity theory, crime is therefore linked to (and opportunities to offend arise from) normal things that occur in society, not to abnormal or pathological aspects of life.

Felson was interested in explaining changes in crime rates over time. He observed that following the Second World War, when welfare provision was increasing and poverty was being tackled, crime was increasing (Felson was particularly interested in the increase in acquisitive crime such as theft). From this, he argued that crime could not be explained by weighty and pathological problems such as poverty, inequality, unemployment, or social exclusion, which had all been at least partially tackled by the welfare system. He suggested that crime resulted from

Figure 15.11 Cohen and Felson's (1979) routine activity theory suggested that for crime to occur, three things were necessary: a motivated offender, a suitable target, and the absence of guardians

human weaknesses such as temptation, which led people to be motivated to do things they should not and noted that, following the Second World War, the key ingredients of motivation, suitable targets (more portable and high-value goods in people's homes), and the absence of guardians (more houses were left 'unguarded' because both adults in a house often worked all day, and more adults lived alone so went out for work and companionship) all came together, so crime increased. The rise in car ownership was another factor in the crime wave at this time, providing both a way to carry goods away from the crime scene and being themselves targets of crime, both in terms of car theft and stealing the goods left in cars. Here, social prosperity actually opens up more opportunities for crime rather than helping to reduce offending.

Felson's writings could give the impression that routine activity theory only explains acquisitive crime—crime which involves acquiring other things—and it is true that the early versions of the theory did just that. However, more recently Felson has suggested that similar analysis can be made for every crime type. He claims that each crime has its own chemistry, meaning that to understand and begin to address each crime we just need to work out what encourages or discourages a motivated offender, a target (often a place where one can offend), and an absence of capable guardians to come together in time and space.

As with rational choice theory, there are important truths here in that a crime does need a willing or motivated offender, a target, and the absence of guardians. These clear ideas have allowed the theory to be used by others, for example Maxfield (1987), Smith et al. (2000), and Pratt et al. (2012). Despite these positives, there are weaknesses in the theory, for example despite the theory's focus on a motivated offender as one of the three necessary ingredients of crime, there is not much discussion of what this might mean or how a person might become motivated except to note that offenders often desire immediate pleasure and avoid imminent unpleasantness. It does not discuss how this motivation might arise so it does not link with work that focuses on motivation which might take into account what might move someone to be motivated.

It is possible to use routine activity theory which focuses on the activities of everyone, all those who might be potential victims, to study offenders. Its proponents have tried to understand 'normal' decisions made by offenders and to map these into their routine activities so that they can better understand their behaviour, and therefore predict the crimes that they might commit. They argue that offenders usually have mental maps of where they are comfortable, so will offend in spaces that are familiar to them. Familiar areas may include areas they live in (or have lived in), areas where they work, areas near where they go to a sports centre or a pub, areas near a school they used to attend, or a place they used to go on holiday.

The routine activities of offenders then need to be layered onto the routine activities of other people (their potential victims), and the areas where there are overlaps are those that are most in need of attention to reduce the attractiveness of offending. The logical outcome of routine activity theory is to work to reduce criminal opportunities by making targets more difficult to offend against. This leads us into situational crime prevention and ideas of 'defensible space'.

Situational crime prevention

Out of rational choice theory and routine activity theory, **situational crime prevention** arose. It is questionable whether situational crime prevention is really a theory, it is more of an idea which pulls on other theories to provide a logical way to prevent or avoid criminal activity. Under situational crime prevention, the environment and particularly possessions should be managed so as to reduce opportunities for crime or to deter criminals. The idea is that by removing the opportunity for criminal behaviour, we can make the costs of crime outweigh the benefits so that individuals will not choose to offend. This might be done by:

- designing goods which are harder to, for example, steal (such as better car locks);
- persuading people to be more responsible about their possessions and themselves;
- using locks on property, cars, and so on;
- installing CCTV to make it harder to steal something or more likely that the offender will be seen and caught.

This perspective sees crime as a sensible choice in certain situations; it is therefore a normal part of social living and the only way of dealing with crime is to reduce the number of situations in which crime might occur. Situational crime prevention expects everyone—the state, local authorities, health service, education, voluntary services, and individuals—to work together and take responsibility for reducing criminal opportunities.

This might sound unquestionably sensible, but—as you may conclude from engaging with the examples in **What do you think? 15.3**—situational crime prevention or 'hardening' targets (making something more difficult to offend against and get away with it, for example improving security or surveillance) can result in some unexpected and unwelcome outcomes, so should be employed carefully. These kinds of efforts might have partial success but could just shift offending to another place, another time, or to another crime type. Situational crime prevention may only be a partial answer because it says nothing about

WHAT DO YOU THINK? 15.3

Situational crime prevention strategies

Consider the following crime issues:

- A problem with thefts from shops in one area of town.
- Buses being vandalised late at night on some routes.

If supporters of situational crime prevention decided to address these issues by installing CCTV in the area around the shops and introducing conductors on the buses, what do you think would happen? Consider the extent to which these measures might reduce the crimes, but also what unintended impacts it could potentially produce. Do you think these measures would help to stop the crimes, or would they simply alter or divert them?

Now think about any examples of other situational crime prevention strategies that you have come across, whether in your local town or in the media. What unintentional outcomes might result from them?

Increasing the effort	Increasing the risks	Reducing the reward	Removing excuses
Target hardening	*Entry/exit screening*	*Target removal*	*Rule setting*
Steering locks	Baggage screening	Keep car in garage	Customs declaration
Anti-robber screens	Merchandise tags	Removable car radio fascia	Hotel registration
Access control	*Formal surveillance*	*Identify property*	*Stimulating*
Entry phones	CCTV	Product serial numbers	Roadside speed displays
Computer passwords	Automatic number plate recognition	Vehicle licence plates	Drink-drive campaigns
Deflecting offenders	*Employee surveillance*	*Removing inducements*	*Controlling*
Cul-de-sacs	Park wardens	Rapid repair of damaged property	Drinking age laws
Routing away fans at soccer matches	Club doormen	Removing graffiti	Parental controls on internet
Controlling means	*Natural surveillance*	*Rule setting*	*Facilitating compliance*
Weapons availability	Street lighting	Tenancy agreements	Fine deduction from salary
Photographs on credit cards	Windows	Software copyright agreement before installation	Ample litter bins

Table 15.2 Target hardening techniques

Source: Pease (2002: 953) who summarised Clarke (1997)

the offender (it does not look to motivation or to explaining why people offend, merely to how to prevent certain items or certain people being targeted by an offender if one comes along), but this lack of focus on the offender means that rational choice theory and, by extension, situational crime prevention, views offending and offenders as normal people, not monsters or people with a problem, which could be seen as positive. They argue that we should tackle the target (make it less attractive or less available) or increase the risk of being caught (increase guardianship), rather than stigmatising the offender. **Table 15.2** suggests a number of techniques that are often suggested as means of target 'hardening'.

The situational crime prevention approach can be used to alter whole areas. For example, Alison Coleman (1990), building on the work of Newman (1972) and his **defensible space theory** (see also Newman, 1996; Cozens, 2008; Glasson and Cozens, 2011), argues that through careful design of spaces to live, shopping centres, and towns we can decrease the likelihood of crime. She suggested three aspects which needed to be addressed.

1. Reducing the number of anonymous spaces—this means allocating space to specific homes or businesses, as the residents (or owners and workers) would then be more likely to care for it.

Figure 15.12 Coleman (1990) sees high-rise blocks of flats (Trellick Tower, London pictured here) and pedestrian subways (St Dunstan's Subway, Cranford, London) as increasing the likelihood of crime
Sources: Steve Cadman (Flickr)/CC BY-SA 2.0 and Shirokazan (Flickr)/CC BY 2.0

2. Increasing surveillance—this involves designing buildings so that they overlook each other and so that shared spaces can all be seen and so guarded. This might mean removing hedges and other barriers to guardianship.
3. Removing the possibility of easy escape without being seen.

Coleman suggested that public housing organisations should return to building houses or low-rise flats rather than high-rise blocks of flats. She also suggested that things like walkways and subways should be avoided as they could not be overlooked (see **Figure 15.12**). She produced a table of design suggestions which she argued should be taken into account in all public space development, and even in deciding on planning applications for large private developments.

Others support situation crime prevention. For example, Linden (2007) argued that it should be a central part of Canada's crime prevention strategy and Davey and Wooton (2016) argued that it should be integrated into town planning in the UK. However, if you take into account the limited money available for housing projects, the large number of people needing homes, and the limited space available in the UK, how realistic are the ideas of defensible space theorists in the near future?

15.5 Conclusion

Classical criminology, and subsequently the neo-classical theories it inspired, have had a profound effect on modern life. They have an appeal that makes them attractive to policymakers in that they sound like common-sense solutions and suggest policy changes that are relatively simple and do not undermine modern social structures. They treat crime as normal and produced by the normal routines of modern life. An offender is not then different or problematic, just someone who is motivated to commit crime and assumes that they will avoid the consequences of their offence. As we have seen, these theories mainly ignore the offender and concentrate on making the targets less appealing and decreasing the risk of offending.

Both the early classical criminology and modern, neo-classical theories are products of their time. We discussed in both the neo-classical and the routine activities theories that in many western states there was a loss of confidence in the 1980s and 1990s that providing welfare could resolve social problems, including crime. This was the Thatcherite era in Britain (the period when the Conservatives were in government and Margaret Thatcher was prime minister), when there was a general move towards empowering the individual, withdrawing the state, and allowing people more room to make choices for themselves (for example, national companies were sold off at prices and in ways that allowed ordinary people to become shareholders, and councils were forced to sell off their houses at prices affordable to people who were living in them if they chose to buy them). Along with this came the idea that if people made the wrong choices, they should face the consequences. If people behaved appropriately, society would respect their freedom and allow them to live lives largely uncontrolled by the state. However, if they behaved unwisely, if they offended, then the state would step in to blame and punish them harshly, excluding them from society. The neo-classical theories we have discussed saw crime as a result of misdirected use of free will, which makes sense when we consider the Conservative political environment from which they emerged. (These ideas are very closely related to right realism, which we discuss in **Chapter 20**.)

Whilst the focus on the offender as the author of the behaviour and the crime is important and the neo-classical theorists have drawn out some very interesting and practical suggestions for tackling crime, we need to stay critical and recognise both the clear strengths of these theories as well as their limitations and weaknesses. Although traditional classical theory is over 200 years old, when analysing the ideas in this chapter it is important to keep up to date because neo-classical theorists are constantly building on the useful elements of the theory and working to address its limitations and weaknesses. It is particularly important to take stock at this point because the chapters which follow all question the very roots of classical theory and suggest that other very different ideas explain or underlie criminal behaviour.

SUMMARY

After reading this chapter and working your way through its features you should now be able to:

- **Define the concept of theory and understand the purpose of it in the context of criminological study**

Theory is a way of explaining parts of our world. In criminology, most theories try to answer a particular question or set of questions. That means that although theories may appear to be in conflict, they may just be answering a different set of questions. Most criminological theories have elements in them that are useful to our understanding of crime. However, no theory answers all the questions.

- **Evaluate different theories by understanding how to test their different elements**

To assess a theory, you first need to make sure you understand which questions it is trying to answer. Then you might consider: Why is this theorist making this claim—what questions are they trying to answer? What is the significance of the claim? What does it say that might be important/useful or worthwhile? What is the problem with the theory? What does it assume and are those assumptions acceptable? What is controversial in the theory and is that controversy useful? Does it challenge policy or practice and make you think again? Which theorists or theories seem to disagree with this theory? What are the points of disagreement and which viewpoint is better argued? Do the disagreements arise because each is answering a slightly different question or intended for a different audience?

And then, to test the theory, you should ask questions which asses each aspect of the theory.

- **Consider the main theoretical schools in criminology including classicism, positivism, interpretivism, and critical criminology**

There are many types of theory; some focus on the individual, others on society or the control system.

Classical criminology arose in the late 17th and early 18th centuries out of a desire to introduce a fairer system for all people living in a state. Classical, Enlightenment theorists saw the system then operating as arbitrary and unfair. They therefore suggested a system of clear legal rules to be applied in every criminal case.

Positivists use science to study what leads people to offend. They collect a lot of information about their societies and where they find something (biological, psychological, or social) is related to criminality, they suggest a link, often a causal link. All of these theories reduce (though generally do not rule out) the extent of free will—if the link arises, offending is more likely. Many positivists suggest rehabilitation because the person cannot be fully 'blamed' so punishment may be unjust.

Interpretivism suggests that to blame and punish the individual for wrong choices is too simplistic, but that the positivist alternative is also too simplistic. They argue that each person's social reality is constructed and negotiated through the many interactions of their daily lives and look for explanation there.

Critical criminology challenges all other ideas. Whilst these thinkers accept social realities are constructed, they challenge all accepted understanding or descriptions of our society and put forward different interpretations and means of constructing societies and communities. They often argue that current social realities are structured to favour the more powerful at the expense of the less powerful (whether the power be financial, political, gender, racial, etc.). This leads to them questioning the basis on which our society stands, including the controls and criminal justice systems designed to enforce controls.

Each of these types of theory contain many competing individual theories and the criminologist needs to learn to assess and consider each with care and objectivity.

- Critically consider classical criminology; both the key thinkers that shaped it, and the policies to which it gave rise

Enlightenment thinkers encouraged every person to think for themselves, make their own choices, and not be controlled by the fear of arbitrary state punishment or religion. Classical criminologists argued that each person should retain the right to choose how to live and behave; each individual exercises free will and uses rational thought to decide how to make their choices and how to act. Before acting, each individual decides which action would be most beneficial for them. If they choose something which harms others, it should be criminal and they should be punished for their choice but only after a fair trial.

Many critics of classical theory argue that the system it produced is about the continuation of power and authority and that it led to inequality (something Enlightenment thinkers claimed to be fighting against). They argue that, in reality, it is about the preservation and protection of social elites.

- Appreciate the importance of free will and rational choice and demonstrate how these ideas in the 17th and 18th centuries underlined the building of the modern new criminal justice system

The reliance on free will and rational choice was crucial for Enlightenment thinkers. These two concepts were at the centre of reforms to the criminal justice system and other legal reforms in the 17th and 18th centuries. Classical theories are very legalistic and draw out many modern ideas such as justice for all, rights for those accused in court, fair and just punishment to reflect the harm done (Beccaria), or to ensure compliance and so protect non-offenders (Bentham). These can all be seen in modern criminal justice systems throughout the world.

- Assess the arguments put forward since the 1960s by modern classical thinkers (neo-classical criminology) about the idea that criminals choose to offend and how, when, and where that might occur

Modern classical thinkers (neo-classical criminology) focus on how, when, and where criminals choose to offend. Rational choice theory looks at intervening in the decision-making process in order to make a criminal choice less attractive. Routine activity theory looks at motivated offenders, suitable targets, and capable guardians.

Both rational choice theory and routine activity theory have a common-sense appeal to policymakers because they suggest practical and more manageable changes to, for example, harden targets, increase surveillance, increase punishments, or increase the likelihood of being caught. However, neither theory explains why the changes might succeed. Their popularity is partly due to the rise of conservative ideals (Thatcherite policies) across the full political spectrum. Right-wing policymakers would be likely to embrace conservative or neo-classical explanations of criminality.

 Test your understanding of the chapter's key points by attempting the self-test questions on the **online resources** at www.oup.com/he/case2e

REVIEW QUESTIONS

1. Describe what theories do and how they can be tested.
2. Explain the main aspects of classical criminology and consider to what extent they are valid in the modern world.
3. Explain the term 'bounded rationality' and give examples of how it might operate.
4. What is a 'crime script'? Choose a crime type and construct a crime script for it.
5. Explain the three things necessary to for a crime to be committed, according to routine activity theory.
6. How could you use both routine activity theory and situational crime prevention to reduce crime on a university campus?
7. How is situational crime prevention related to rational choice theory and routine activity theory and what is its function?
8. How do the neo-classical ideas or modern classical theories link to the traditional classical school of thought?

 Access the **online resources** at www.oup.com/he/case2e to check your answers to the review questions.

FURTHER READING

Cornish, D. B. and Clarke, R. V. (2014) *The Reasoning Criminal: Rational Choice Perspectives on Offending.* **London: Transaction Publishers.**
This is a reprint of their 1986 book but with a new introduction by Clarke. The whole book offers detailed consideration of each aspect of neo-classical thought. It is a very good primary text as it is a collection of contributions by leading proponents of these theories and it provides a critical and analytic introduction to what was, in 1986, a groundbreaking new direction of criminological thought.

Dorling, D. et al. (2008) *Criminal Obsessions: Why Harm Matters More Than Crime* **(2nd edn). London: Centre for Crime and Justice Studies. Especially Ch. 5, pp. 70–90.**
A useful questioning of societies' focus on resolving crime rather than seeing other social problems which cause harm as being equally important. This relates to our discussions in **Chapter 19** on social harm and challenges the commonly accepted ideas about why and when a society should control behaviour, pushing the reader to think differently and to develop answers to the solutions and ways of thinking which the text suggests.

Newburn, T. (2009) *Key Readings in Criminology.* **Abingdon: Willan Publishing.**
For excerpts from original criminology texts, the key readings for the theories covered in this chapter are Ch. 4, 4.1 (Beccaria) and all the readings in Ch. 17.

Williams, K. S. (2012) *Textbook on Criminology* **(8th edn). Oxford: Oxford University Press. Ch. 2 especially pp. 20–39.**
Most general criminological textbooks have useful chapters which consider both classical and neo-classical ideas. This text considers the subject from a broad perspective—both legal and criminological perspectives.

 Access the **online resources** to view a wealth of extra information relating to your study of criminology, including self-test questions, answers to review questions, and links to other resources that will help you enjoy and fulfil your potential within your studies.
www.oup.com/he/case2e

CHAPTER OUTLINE

16.1	Introduction	476
16.2	Positivism and positivist criminology	476
16.3	Causation and correlation	477
16.4	Positivism, punishment, and rehabilitation	478
16.5	Early positivism	480
16.6	Biological theories	485
16.7	Psychological theories	494
16.8	Learning theories	500
16.9	Conclusion	509

16

Biological and psychological positivism

KEY ISSUES

After studying this chapter, you should be able to:

- recognise the contribution of both biology and psychology to our understanding of crime;
- understand the contribution early positivists such as Lombroso made to criminology;
- explain how brain structure is linked to behaviour;
- understand the extent of the evidence linking chemicals in the body to offending behaviour;
- identify the nature and extent of the link between genetics and offending behaviour;
- understand whether psychoanalysis helps to explain crime;
- explain whether, and if so how, personality impacts on criminal behaviour;
- compare and contrast the various learning theories and consider which is most useful to reduce criminal behaviour.

16.1 Introduction

In the previous chapter we discussed a number of classical theories (including **free will**, **classicism**, and **rational choice**) which argue that crime arises because individuals choose criminal behaviour. If criminality results from a choice this means that society can:

- blame the individual for the bad choices they make;
- punish the individual for their actions;
- support the individual in learning how to make better choices in the future;
- help potential victims to consider how to keep themselves safe (for example, by better securing their property).

Through these mechanisms, classical theorists believe crime can be reduced and possibly even eliminated.

In this and the next chapter we move away from classical thinking and away from looking to *blame* the individual for incorrect choices. We consider what is known as **positivist** criminology: using scientific methods to study crime and its causes. Positivism sees crime as determined (made more likely) by biological, psychological, or sociological causes.

In this chapter we will be studying individual positivism: that is, those aspects of positivist criminological explanations that look for differences between criminal and non-criminal populations.

One of the (many!) exciting things about studying criminology is that the discipline draws from many other disciplines. In this chapter we'll look in particular at how interesting theories from biology and psychology can help us understand crime.

Biological and **psychological positivists** believe that by measuring biological and psychological differences between offenders and non-offenders they will discover a clear explanation of criminal behaviour, a truth that explains criminal actions. Early positivists such as Cesare Lombroso (1835–1909), a famous Italian criminologist, collected large amounts of information. When a researcher discovered physical or biological differences between offenders and non-offenders, they tended to assume that those characteristics were causative and explained the behaviour. However, as we will see, there is a large step between finding differences and taking things further by assuming that the difference explains behaviour. Correlation does not equal causation—you may have heard this useful phrase (and if not, it is definitely worth remembering). In other words, a correlation (a relationship) between two factors does not necessarily mean that one factor *causes* the other. For example, you might note that a very high proportion of those in hospital on any given day are injured or sick, but you would be wrong to suggest that visiting a hospital is what makes people sick or causes their injuries. Many early positivists made this mistake, they found two things correlated and assumed causation—they found differences between offenders and others, assumed that the difference caused the criminal behaviour (predetermined the individuals to act in a criminal way), and so tried to design ways to counter the problem and thereby to reduce crime. As we will see, this is a common mistake in positivism but also in other areas of criminological research.

In this chapter we will study the journey of biological and psychological positivist thinking from its roots in the 19th century through to more modern approaches in the 21st century where these biological and psychological traits are merely seen as one factor which may increase the likelihood of criminality rather than causing it. In this chapter we will only consider positivism in relation to individuals. We will look at whether crime can be explained by biological and psychological factors in individuals. The next chapter (**Chapter 17**) will look at whether crime can be explained from the perspective of society, or the social world.

As with the previous chapter, since this book aims to introduce you to core ideas within criminology and to act as a springboard for further study, we will stick to considering the core elements of each **theory**, examining its defining features, its strengths, and its weaknesses. This will give you a solid grounding from which to explore them in more detail in later chapters of the book and when reading the primary texts.

16.2 Positivism and positivist criminology

Like classical theories, positivism grew out of the **Enlightenment**. As people moved away from spiritualism, they started to rely more on rational scientific findings. Positivism really became prominent during the 19th century when scientific study was coming to the fore and when scientists, such as Charles Darwin, were collecting information and facts about the natural world in order to better understand it. At the same time, information about the social world was also being collected by governments (the decennial UK census started in 1801) and by social researchers wanting to better understand all aspects of the societies they lived in. Positivists believed that they would be able to discover patterns in society or certain characteristics in some people which would help them to understand all sorts of behaviour, from suicide to communal living, to crime (for a critical examination of positivist methods, see also **Chapters 4** and **22**). Basically, positivism collects large amounts of data and uses it to explain our lives to help us to better understand the world around us.

Positivist criminology is the use of the scientific methodology (in collecting data about people or societies) to throw light on why people offend or why crime arises. It assumes that all human behaviour, including crime, can be studied scientifically: by recording what has happened we can understand the past, and from understanding the past we can predict what is likely to happen in the future—maybe even alter crucial factors to prevent future criminal behaviour. Positivist criminology draws on biological, psychological, social, economic, or other similar factors outside the control of the individual to explain criminal behaviour. Positivist criminologists tend to suggest that criminal behaviour is not an act of free will (or not free will alone) but is predetermined due to certain (personal or social) characteristics. This means that they tend to suggest rehabilitation rather than punishment.

In this chapter we will focus on biological and psychological positivism. Biological positivism suggests that some physical characteristic or genetic or chemical abnormalities or imbalances might cause some people to offend. Early theorists suggested that their data proved that criminals are born with the characteristics that would cause them to offend, more recently (from the 1970s onwards) they have been less certain about the idea that offenders are necessarily born with the causal characteristics—they may still consider it as a contributing factor, though probably not the most important element (Rock, 2007). Psychological positivists suggest people commit crime because of internal psychological factors, some of which may be genetic but others arise because of upbringing.

16.3 Causation and correlation

As noted in the introduction to this chapter, it is essential to recognise that correlation does not equal causation. The scientific method, positivism, relies on the collection and comparison of all sorts of data. It is very common to find that two things vary at the same or at a similar rate, that they are correlated. However, this does *not* mean that one causes the other; that is, they are not causally related. This means that two factors may change at the same time but these may be totally unrelated. So, for example, crime may rise when unemployment rises but it does not mean that crime causes unemployment nor does it necessarily mean that unemployment causes crime. To illustrate how problematic it might be to claim a causal relationship, one famous example will be considered: a graph was produced which plotted two things in Maine in the US between 2000 and 2009: the divorce rate and the consumption of margarine per person. On the graph, these two lines fluctuate in tandem and then it was suggested that margarine consumption caused divorce, but that is ridiculous, eating more margarine does not increase the likelihood of getting divorced. Clearly, something different is behind each of the fluctuations recorded on the graph and it is unclear why anyone thought plotting them together would be of value. Whilst everyone can see that this is not an example of causation and the error is very obvious, many people do not question other such findings in the same way.

To claim a causal relationship between two elements, the following three conditions are necessary: one element must start to change before the other (even if only a short time before); they must vary together (covary); and there is no explanation which better explains the covariance. Even these three are not sufficient to prove a causal relationship (they are necessary but not sufficient). Earlier, we referred to a correlation between the divorce rate and the rate of margarine consumption which suggested that not only were the two correlated but also that greater margarine consumption caused more divorces. Then we stated that it should have been clear that there was no causation between the two. However, one can go further and argue that they are not even meaningfully correlated, each is caused by very different factors and there is not really any relationship at all between the two, it is just chance that one rises at the same time as the other. They should never have been plotted together because doing this did not aid understanding; rather, it might have been misleading, suggesting some relationship. In reading about positivist theories, we will come across many instances where two factors change at the same time but where there is no causative relationship, there may not even be any meaningful correlation. One of the things it is often useful to consider is both whether there is any strong argument for suggesting a causative relationship but also whether anything meaningful can be learnt by correlating two or more variables.

16.4 Positivism, punishment, and rehabilitation

Classical theories of crime (see **Chapter 15**) focus on free will and therefore suggest punishing people for incorrect choices. If a person chooses to offend, then they should face punishment which is proportionate to the harm they do. Positivism is very different; it suggests that people offend when aspects of their lives which they cannot control make offending more likely. If this is the case, should society punish the offender? Is punishment appropriate if the offence was, at least partly, out of the control of the offender? Positivists consider how a society or state should respond to crimes that are not within the full control of the offender: punishment or rehabilitation.

We can take a historical example which careful research has refuted but which still resonates with many people. For many years, there was a claim that black people were more likely to commit crime than white people, in other words something in their racial make-up caused their bad behaviour. If it were true, if black people were more likely to offend because of something in their biological or psychological make-up, then surely they should not be punished, or at least not punished as severely as suggested by the harm caused. Therefore, if true, positivism suggests that something in the biological (or psychological) make-up of black people makes them more likely to offend—this is something over which they have no control—the offending is not the result of free will and so punishment to fit the harm caused would be unjust. However, it is important to note that it is not true that black people are more likely to offend because of their racial origin. The original claim of a link between race and offending arose partly because there was a greater ratio of black people arrested and punished than you might expect compared with the ratio of black people in the general population. This argument assumed that the criminal justice system (being stopped by police, charged, convicted, and punished) was objective, and therefore black people must be offending at a higher rate than other groups. This has since been proven to be incorrect and it is in fact a result of how the criminal justice system operates rather than the behaviour of one race. The anger towards this over-policing and more violent and controlling policing (and sentencing) of racial minorities has underpinned a number of protests, such as those in the UK in 1981 and 2011 (often referred to as riots; see Scarman, 1982; LSE and the Guardian, 2011) and across the world in 2020, following the killing of George Floyd by a police officer in the US (see **Figure 16.1**). The racial prejudice of our criminal justice system is also central to some judicial reviews and academic work (see Taylor, 1999; Bowling and Phillips, 2002; Phillips and Webster, 2014; Scarman, 1982; Macpherson, 1999; and, for a full consideration, see **Chapter 10**).

Figure 16.1 Images captured on video in 2020 of police officers using excessive force, resulting in the death of George Floyd, sparked protests round the world under the 'Black Lives Matter' banner

Source: Justin Berken/Shutterstock

In cases where a person is more likely than others to offend, perhaps because of specific biological or psychological (or, as we'll see in the next chapter, sociological) factors, criminologists refer to that behaviour as 'pathological'. By this, they mean that a particular type of behaviour is caused by a physical or mental condition. So positivists question the use of punishment and instead suggest using treatment or rehabilitation to support them to resist the biological or psychological (or sociological, see **Chapter 17**) pull to offend. If one does that, the treatment or rehabilitation needs to continue until the pathology is overcome; therefore, the length of treatment and the seriousness of the treatment may bear no relation to the seriousness of the offence. It is now clearly understood that the colour of a person's skin does not affect the rate of offending. What is now suggested is that people living in similar social situations and who are treated in similar ways (discriminated against) are likely to have similar rates of offending. Where problems such as discrimination and poverty or similar issues may be the 'intervening causative factor' (the factor which causes the behaviour), full (or any) punishment may be unjust; the individual was acting at least partly due to things outside their control. Here again, rehabilitation may be necessary but arguably society should change to reduce discrimination and so reduce offending related to it (for a discussion concerning **sociological positivism**, see **Chapter 17**).

Whilst rejecting the idea that whole racial groups are **pathologically** more or less inclined to offend, biologists and psychologists still point to specific differences that may mean some individuals are more likely to offend than are others. If these theories are correct, such individuals should not be punished, rather they should be treated or rehabilitated.

Before moving on, consider the examples in **What do you think? 16.1**. These examples indicate that rehabilitation, removing the problem, or requiring assessment is not necessarily less severe, sometimes it is more invasive and more

WHAT DO YOU THINK? 16.1

How far should treatment go?

Take a look at these hypothetical scenarios and think about how you react to them.

- Anya steals a pencil from a shop. She is found to have a problem with her brain that is believed to cause such behaviour. In that situation, her behaviour is out of her control so justice suggests that she should not be punished. She is forced to undergo invasive brain surgery to prevent her offending in the future.

- Chaman kills his wife. He has always been a very gentle person but has recently been prescribed medication which has had an extreme effect on his behaviour and 'caused' him to become violent. Again, the behaviour is not his fault so maybe he should not be punished. His problem can be rectified through altering his medication, so he is given a new prescription and sent on his way.

- Cameron is 30 and has been offending since he was ten. In his teens, he (and his friends) tended to participate in a mixture of petty offences, antisocial behaviour, and substance misuse. In his 20s, he moved on to more serious crimes such as burglary. Recent studies claim to have discovered that specific gene structures are clearly associated with persistent offending. Cameron is now in a permanent relationship. Justice Devon, the judge sentencing Cameron following his most recent burglary, has decided that Cameron should be sterilised so that he does not pass on this genetic problem to any offspring. Justice Devon is determined to protect future generations from this type of persistent offender.

Do you think the responses to these scenarios are acceptable? Why, or why not?

Building on the third scenario, Cameron's case, assume now that the findings linking specific gene structures with persistent offending have led the government to consider mandatory testing of all people to locate these genetic structures. Would mandatory testing be acceptable in these circumstances?

The government introduces the mandatory testing with a view to adopting one or more of the following laws:

- sterilising all people with these gene structures to prevent them being passed on;

- genetic engineering of all people with these gene structures to eradicate the unwanted genes;

- laws specifying legal and illegal breeding groups; or

- execution of all people with these gene structures.

Assuming mandatory testing is acceptable, would these policies be acceptable? Would they be fair and just? Consider your reaction to each of these cases very carefully and reflect on why you answer them in a particular way. Reading the rest of the chapter will help in collecting your thoughts.

unpleasant for the offender. As part of a piece of research, one of this book's authors spoke to a group of sex workers who said they would far rather pay a fine or serve a short prison sentence than face a sentence of 'rehabilitation'. They had chosen to sell sex for money, had done this after weighing up the alternatives open to them such as working in a factory, and decided that sex work was their best option. They did not feel they harmed anyone although they recognised that many sex workers had not made a similar free choice and might need protecting. The point here is that punishment, rehabilitation, treatment, and other responses to offending (other sentences) or other interventions all involve interfering with someone's free will and all need to be justified. If the claim is that crime results from a biological or psychological trait, this needs to be proven and care taken to ensure that the subsequent intervention is both proportionate and legitimate. For a full discussion of moral reasoning in relation to crime and criminal justice interventions, especially the use of rehabilitation, see Palmer (2003).

16.5 Early positivism

Biological positivism emerged out of the growing interest in science in the 19th century and as a backlash against the harsh effects of classical criminology. As classical ideals became more widely applied, they were being used to control many types of social problems. People were being ever-more closely monitored, not only for their actions but also for their attitudes (to protect the moral fibre of society). Many different types of people and activities were being controlled—alcoholics, drug addicts, the mentally ill, the poor, immigrants, people moving from one parish to another, prostitutes, people suffering from sexually transmitted diseases, petty offenders, and hardened criminals. Control in the 19th century usually meant being incarcerated (sent to prison). Despite growing levels of imprisonment, the problems were still increasing—control was failing so researchers looked for other answers. Positivism offered different solutions. If people could not be controlled, then the problem might lie inside them—there might be something biologically or psychologically wrong with them. The idea of biological or psychological problems causing criminality began to emerge at the beginning of the 19th century but really took hold towards the end of that century.

Cesare Lombroso

Cesare Lombroso (1835–1909) was an Italian criminologist and is often referred to as the father of criminology. His work was the turning point for the discipline to move away from a legalistic focus on the crime towards a scientific study of the criminals. Classical theorists concentrated on the crime and responsibility; biological and psychological positivists focused on the criminal. Lombroso though that normal people would not participate in crime so he searched for a pathological explanation, something different about criminals which made them break the law. In 1876, he published *L'Uomo Delinquente* (*The Criminal Man*) and in 1899 he published *Le Crime, causes et Remèdes* (*Crime, Its Causes and Remedies*). He replaced the legal and moralistic approach to crime with one based on a scientific stance which used careful analysis of **empirical** evidence (remember from **Chapter 4** that this refers to knowledge generated through sensory experience, particularly using experiment and observation).

Lombroso is best remembered for claiming that criminals were atavistic throwbacks, meaning people whose genetic make-up was from a more primitive stage of human development. In sum, they were more 'savage' than non-criminals. Lombroso also claimed that this primitive aspect of their genetic make-up was evident not only in their criminal behaviour but also in their physical appearance, particularly in anomalies or 'defects' which Lombroso often referred to as **stigmata** (for illustrations, see **Figures 16.2** and **16.3**). On a basic level, Lombroso's early claims were that you could pick out a criminal from their appearance.

According to Lombroso, thieves (see number 5 in **Figure 16.3**, bottom left-hand corner) and murderers (see number 3 in **Figure 16.3**, middle left) are characterised by:

> their expressive faces and manual dexterity, small wandering eyes that are often oblique in form, thick and close eyebrows, distorted or squashed noses, thin beards and hair and sloping foreheads.... [H]abitual murders have a cold, glassy stare and eyes that are sometimes bloodshot and filmy, the nose is often hawk-like and always large; the jaw is strong, the cheekbones broad; and their hair is dark, abundant, and crisply textured. Their beards are scanty, their canine teeth very developed, and their lips thin ... [N]early all criminals have jug ears, thick hair, thin beards, pronounced sinuses, protruding chins and broad cheek bones.
>
> (Lombroso, 1876: 51)

Figure 16.2 Illustration of some 'physical defects' which Lombroso believed indicated a criminal tendency
Source: Public domain

Figure 16.3 Physiognomy (facial features) of criminals, according to Lombroso
Source: Public domain

Lombroso was not the first to propose a biological underpinning of criminal behaviour. These explanations really began with the phrenologists in the 18th and early 19th centuries (for full history, see Fink (1938)) who claimed that there was a relationship between the size and shape of the skull (and therefore of the brain) and social behaviour. Lombroso built on these ideas. He conducted post-mortem examinations on criminals and also took measurements from living offenders in prison. He compared these findings to similar studies of law-abiding people, mostly those in his own affluent circle of associates. He found abnormalities in criminals' skull shapes (compared to non-criminals) and also noted that criminals had asymmetrical facial features and different facial bone structures (for example, broader cheekbones, deeper set eyes, large jawbones, etc.). He proposed that these physical differences 'proved' the existence of a distinct anthropological type (type of human being) who was likely, or even bound, to commit crime, the '**born criminal**'. Lombroso claimed that we could look for these characteristics in people in order to detect those likely to offend.

The idea that we can tell whether someone is likely to be a criminal based on the shape of their skull or how symmetrical their facial features are has since been rejected. In fact, his whole theory claiming that there is a 'born criminal' type has largely been discredited (see Rock, 2007). However, it is not his findings for which he is remembered, rather it is for the methodology he used. Lombroso did not just put forward a theory, he collected data to test it. Although others before him had used this methodology, his was the first major work to be entirely based on the scientific collection of information.

His legacy, and the reason he is recognised as the father of criminology, is his insistence on taking a scientific approach to explaining crime through the collection and measurement of data. Although his methodology was flawed, because his comparator group was too different and he assumed that the differences were causative, the idea that large data sets are useful to our understanding of criminology is important, and since Lombroso's time this scientific approach has been at the centre of criminology, especially positivist criminology.

Lombroso was also willing to be flexible and amend his theories when new evidence arose, which is an important aspect of scientific research and contributes to his role as the father of modern criminology. In his later work (1906 *Crime: Causes et Remèdes*), whilst he continued to focus on physical factors as causing criminality, he added social and psychological factors such as climate, grain prices, sex and marriage customs, education, and moral and mental strength, recognising that they also had a part to play. By including these factors, he embraces and measures aspects of the three disciplines which underpin positivist criminology: biology, psychology, and sociology (Morrison, 2004).

Before we move on, let's think about what might follow from Lombroso's theory. If we accept both: (a) that some people are born with a predisposition to offend; and (b) that this can be seen in their features from a young age, then it might influence the way in which a state chooses to control crime. In this type of scenario, the state might move away from punishing people for the crime they committed (making the punishment fit the crime) towards controlling some people (the 'born criminals') to protect the rest of society. In this circumstance, following a crime, a state might:

- permit a sentencing judge to choose to incarcerate people for longer to protect society from them (most recently Imprisonment for Public Protection was introduced into the UK in s. 225 of the Criminal Justice Act 2003, it was abolished in 2012 under the Legal Aid, Sentencing and Punishment of Offenders Act 2012);
- permit a judge to require them to undergo treatment to teach them to control their natural urges (for example, programmes attached to **probation** orders such as Cognitive Behavioural Programmes to counter things such as violent behaviour);
- require them to take drugs or undergo operations in order to 'cure' them (for example, chemical 'castration' of sex offenders, see Grubin and Beech, 2010);
- permit sterilisation to prevent them passing on their substandard genes (in the US the Supreme Court permitted sterilisation for a number of reasons, including violent behaviour, see *Buck* v *Bell*, 274 US 200 at 205 (1927));
- even put them to death.

If it were possible to identify a 'born criminal', a state might also argue that it could legitimately intervene even before a crime was committed.

This might seem shocking, particularly knowing that the idea of a 'born criminal' has been discredited. However, most of these punishments or treatments have been tried somewhere in the world, with genetic or biological explanations of offending used as the supposed justification. It was partly what the eugenics movement (this began in the late 19th century but really took hold in Europe and North America from about 1925 to 1950) was based on and it was at least partly behind the rationale for the Nazi concentration camps (Burleigh, 1995; and see the *Holocaust Encyclopedia Online*, 'Euthanasia Program and Aktion T4'). Therefore, despite being largely discredited (see Rock, 2007), these types of theories have underpinned some appalling state policies designed to protect society. They stand as a warning of the awful consequences that arise when theories are misused.

William Sheldon

The idea of a 'born criminal' who can be identified by their physical features was attractive to other famous criminologists. For example, William Sheldon (1898–1977), an American psychologist, argued that we can classify people by their body shapes and use this to predict future behaviour, including criminal behaviour. This area of study is referred to as **somatotyping**. Sheldon (1949) identified three main body types and argued that they were linked to certain temperaments. His three body types (somotypes) are as follows: (a) endomorphs are physically soft and round, often fat, they are described as having friendly and sociable temperaments; (b) mesomorphs are physically muscular and athletic, they are described as having assertive and active temperaments; (c) ectomorphs are physically thin and rather weak, they are described as being temperamentally focused on privacy and restraint and are very self-aware (see **Figure 16.4**). Sheldon suggested that mesomorphs were most likely to be criminals whereas others have suggested that somatotypes are linked to particular types of or patterns of offending (Madden, Walker, and Miller, 2008).

This type of theory, like that of Lombroso, was largely discredited (Sampson and Laub (1991) accredit that to Sutherland; see **Chapter 17** for a discussion of his work). In particular, there is little evidence to link body type to offending (Cortes and Gatti, 1972). However, the idea that offending might be linked to types of personality has been revived and used in developmental criminology and life-course criminology (Sampson and Laub, 1991, 2005; McAra and McVie, 2017; see also **Chapters 9** and **21**).

Francis Galton

It is important not to dismiss outright these early theories. You might think of them as ludicrous, but there may be a link: this link between crime and physical appearance is still important, though far more complex than so far discussed. To understand it better, we need to look at the work of Francis Galton (1822–1911), a 19th-century English researcher with a particular interest in sociology and anthropology. Galton's idea was that it is possible to predict and read behaviour from facial features; he even suggested that these might determine a person's fitness for a particular profession.

Galton searched for facial features which were common to people who were successful in certain types of profession, or ranks within a profession; for example, he recorded different features for soldiers and commanding

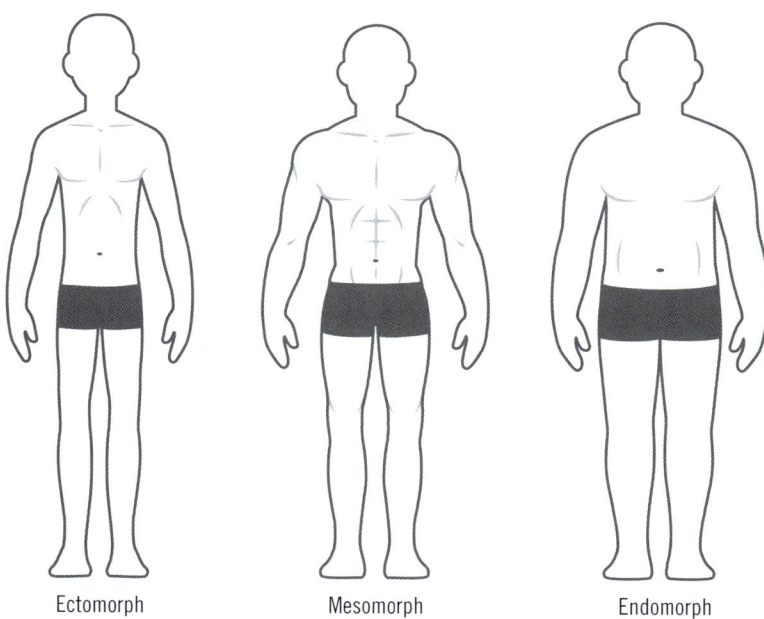

Figure 16.4 Sheldon argued that these three main body types ('somatotypes') are linked to certain temperaments, with mesomorphs most likely to be criminals

officers. He also argued that it is possible to pick out a criminal from facial features alone (Galton, 1883). Whilst his ideas have been largely discredited—and indeed many of his main views would be considered completely unacceptable in today's society—there is some very interesting research about how we react to different facial features. Consider the exercise in **What do you think? 16.2** before we move on to explore this idea in more depth.

As you will have seen from the above, on a personal level we all make judgements about people, in everyday situations, based on how they look. However, more worryingly, some evidence suggests that physical appearance (including facial features) may affect outcomes in court. Berry (1988) found people were more likely to believe that suspects with baby faces, rounded faces with large eyes and small chins, can be involved in crimes of negligence because they are seen as naive. However, people were less likely to believe that suspects with baby faces could be involved in crimes involving mental intent or those of violence because they are perceived as more honest and gentle (Berry, 1988).

If true, this evidence would suggest that decision-makers in court may be partially influenced by looks. The key point to absorb here is that the research shows that people *assume* a link between behaviour and looks, rather than that there is any such link. These assumptions are worrying for law, criminal justice, and society. Baumeister (1982) suggested that these assumptions can be proved wrong by the use of strong proof one way or the other. That is, the assumption concerning facial features was only important in cases where the proven facts were unclear. In cases where either the prosecution or defence had hard proof, factual evidence, the assumption (prejudice) would not stand and the decision-maker would follow the evidence (Baumeister, 1982). What is interesting is that the assumptions (prejudices) may *need* to be proven wrong. When people are introduced to the theories of Lombroso and Galton, most consider them to be ridiculous, but what more recent research suggests is that many people are affected by the way someone looks (Berry, 1988; Baumeister, 1982; Eberhardt et al., 2006). Our prejudices about looks and behaviour are likely to be learned and their existence shows how people may believe there is a link between physical features and crime. However, these assumptions (prejudices) do not mean that the links are real, they only show that people believe in them or use them. If there is any link between physical features and crime, it is very complex. Acceptance of its existence or an unwillingness to question your prejudices can lead to very serious outcomes. For example, in the US, assumptions about appearance linked to crime have been found to affect whether someone faces the death penalty. Eberhardt et al. (2006) found that having black features made murderers more likely to face death row: African American

WHAT DO YOU THINK? 16.2

Do you judge people on their looks?

Most of you have recently started at university and have had to start to build up new friendship groups. When you have walked into a room full of people you do not know, how did you decide who to talk to? How have you chosen your friends?

Some of you may have tried to narrow down the field by joining clubs and so trying to find people who enjoy the same things you do. Even if you did that, you still needed to decide who to talk to when you got to the club or participated in activities. Think about how you decided (probably very quickly) who to approach. With limited information available, most of us do this based on appearance—facial appearance and the way others are dressed. Try to think carefully about what you do in these situations.

Now look at the images in **Figure 16.5** and consider the following:

- Which, if any, of these people would you choose to befriend if you knew nothing about them but were merely placed in a room with them?

- Do you ever judge people or think of them differently depending on their facial features? Be honest, even if it is only when you are watching television programmes. If this does ever happen, which facial features might lead you to feel differently about an individual? Which might be enough to make you treat them differently?

- In your experience, are people treated differently by you or others dependent on their facial features (think about school and all the other environments where you encounter or have encountered people)? If people *are* treated differently depending on their facial features, does this influence their behaviour and their personality? Do you think it might have an effect on how they feel about themselves and, therefore, maybe on how they behave? If so, what is affecting their behaviour—their looks or the way people treat them because of their looks—is it biology or environment?

Figure 16.5 Which, if any, of these people would you choose to befriend if you knew nothing about them?
Source: Nathan Cowley/Pexels.com, Italo Melo/Pexels.com, and Anderson Guerra/Pexels.com

men convicted of murdering a white person were more than twice as likely to get the death sentence if they had stereotypically black features than if they had less stereotypically black features.

Therefore, despite our rejection of the theories of Lombroso, Galton, and others, their theories reflect aspects of thoughts and prejudices we all use in our daily lives, in our interactions with other people. Generally, our prejudices are relatively harmless but when they affect justice in police or jury decision-making, they cause serious problems. We therefore need to be more aware of our prejudices and try to resist them, at least in situations where their use may cause injustice. Finally, it is important to recognise that the lasting legacy of Lombroso is the understanding that the collection and analysis of data are essential to criminological work.

16.6 Biological theories

We'll now move on to discussing how biological factors might influence whether we commit crime. We saw in the previous section that early positivists argued that aspects of someone's appearance (whether our skull shape, body shape, or facial features) predict the likelihood of them committing crime. We've seen that this has been discredited. Biological theories of crime instead look inside the body to consider the impact of things like our brain structure and chemical influences like hormones on criminality. We'll also come back to the early positivists' idea of a 'born criminal' but this time consider whether, and if so how, our genetic make-up might play a part in criminality.

Brain structure and function

Every one of us has a certain degree of choice over the way in which we react to things or behave. This choice emanates from the decisions a person makes, which are ultimately the result of brain activity. It follows, then, that the way in which the brain functions may have a strong influence on our behaviour. Most alterations to the structure of the brain, or its function, will affect behaviour and decision-making. A basic understanding of the structure and function of the brain (and the rest of the nervous system) is therefore very important and useful if we are to understand some aspects of behaviour.

There are two parts of the nervous system and of decision-making: the **central nervous system** and the **peripheral nervous system** (see **Figure 16.6**):

1. The central nervous system (CNS) is made up of the brain and spinal cord.
2. The peripheral nervous system (PNS) is made up of all the nerves running through the body, which communicate signals from our senses back to the CNS, and relay signals from the CNS out to the rest of the body. These signals from the brain to other parts of the body—including muscles and glands—allow a person to react to the environment they are currently experiencing. In turn, the PNS has two components—the somatic and automatic.

Let's now focus on the CNS, and its two components: the spinal cord and the brain. The spinal cord is basically the conduit for the flow of information between the brain and the rest of the body. If this is damaged, the flow of information will be interrupted, or even blocked completely. As a result, the senses won't be able to tell the brain what they see or feel or the brain won't be able to tell the muscles and glands how to react.

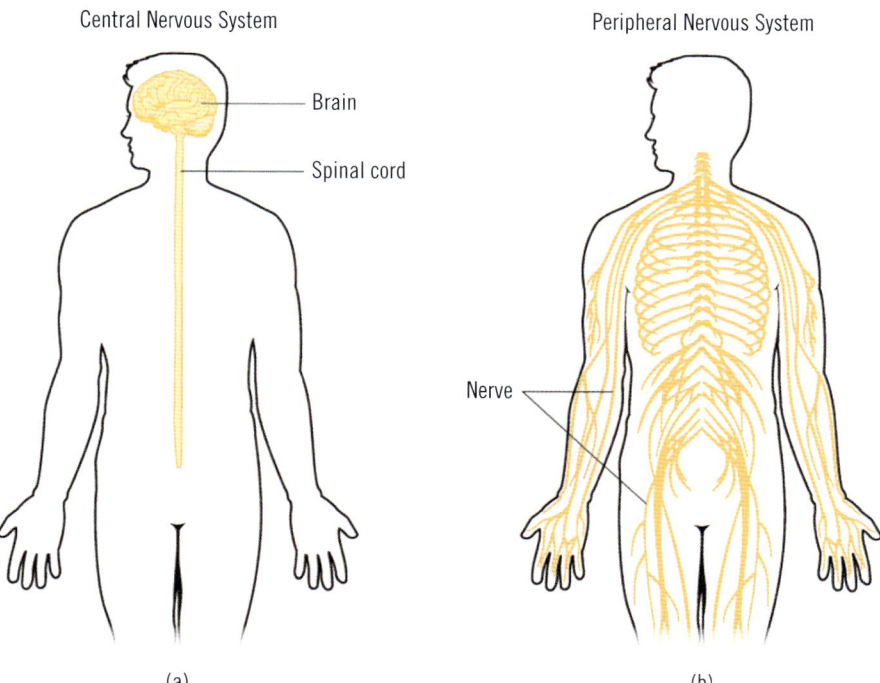

Figure 16.6 The decisions we make are the result of brain activity, which involves the central and peripheral nervous systems

Source: © Aug 31 2020, OpenStax

The brain logs and sorts the information it receives, decides what to do, and sends messages to the rest of the body telling it how to respond. It is a command-and-control centre—it interprets the information the senses pick up from the external environment and from the internal environment (the rest of the body); it then analyses all the data, decides how to respond, and sends instructions to the rest of the body. It is also the centre for storing memories and it allows people to reason and think.

Each part of the brain performs a different function (see **Figure 16.7**). Whilst each part is important, the frontal lobe (thinking and behaviour), parietal lobe (language), and temporal lobe (feelings) are most important to behaviour and to communicating with the outside world. The frontal lobe is particularly important as it is the site of thinking, reasoning, social behaviour, planning, and cognitive decision-making.

How do we know that the frontal lobe is so important for these particular behaviours? The answer lies in what we learn when the frontal lobe is damaged, as illustrated by the famous case of Phineas Gage (**Figure 16.8**). Gage was a railway worker who in 1848 was involved in an accident during which an iron bar was driven through his skull. It entered his head behind his left ear, travelled through his frontal lobe, and exited the top of his head. He survived and functioned normally—except that his personality was completely altered. Before the accident, he was a normal, pleasant, and well-adjusted family man. Following the accident, however, he became rude, impatient, reckless, and unpleasant. This case, and other incidents, led scientists to recognise that different parts of the brain were responsible for different functions. While our understanding has advanced a long way since Gage's unfortunate accident, there are still many things we are discovering about brain function and structure.

Problems with the structure or functioning of the frontal lobe are very frequently linked to negative behaviours (Tukstra et al., 2003). For example, damage to the frontal

Figure 16.8 Phineas Gage. The sudden change in Phineas Gage's personality following a brain injury led scientists to recognise that certain parts of the brain had specific functions
Source: Public domain

and pre-frontal lobes is likely to: impair a person's ability to understand the consequences of their actions or

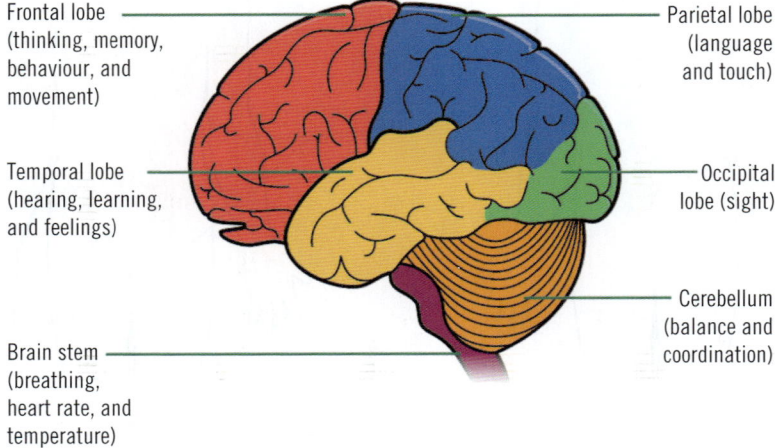

Figure 16.7 Illustration of the different sections of the brain and their functions
Source: Public domain

their ability to learn from previous experience; reduce their concentration, self-control, and feelings of empathy; and make them less able to feel shame or guilt. Damage to other parts of the brain, particularly the cortex or the amygdala, may also cause behavioural difficulties (Raine and Scerbo, 1991; Scarpa and Raine, 2000). But it isn't just physical impairment that causes the brain to function less effectively. It has been discovered more recently that such problems can occur through maltreatment, neglect, or even lack of love shown to children when they are young, when their brain functions are still forming (Baglivio et al., 2014, 2015; Fox et al., 2015).

It is now well recognised that maltreatment alters the way in which the brain develops (Anda et al., 2005). This has a knock-on effect on the way in which the child experiences the world, their ability to feel emotions (Scarpa and Raine, 2000) and the behavioural choices they make, and their ability to think rationally and to learn from their mistakes (Dube et al., 2003; Kolb et al., 2009; Kolla et al., 2013). These inabilities which may be caused by brain development (or lack of development) may be one of the factors that make criminal behaviour more likely, especially in adolescence. **Figure 16.9** illustrates the impact of severe neglect in childhood on the structure of the brain. Maltreatment might also be one of the factors that prevents individuals from maturing out of or learning not to offend, suggesting that it—and other traumatic childhood experiences which are likely to have an adverse effect on brain development—may be a factor leading to a life-course of persistent offending (Reavis et al., 2013; Baglivio et al., 2014, 2015; Fox et al., 2015).

However, it is important to be aware that, as we noted in **Chapter 9** (see **section 9.2**), even normal development affects adolescents. The adolescent brain (up to the age of about 25) exhibits various 'cognitive deficits': teenagers lack impulse control; have impaired ability to control emotions and to problem solve; and their thinking is more rigid and inflexible, meaning they are less able to recognise the consequences of their behaviour (Arian et al., 2013; Reavis et al., 2013; Baglivio et al., 2014, 2015; Fox et al., 2015). The adolescent brain is often able to reason like an adult, but with a heightened need for reward (meso-limbic reward sensitivity) and a lower ability to see past immediate influences. This means it is poor at considering consequences and prone to risky decision-making (rather like a car without a skilled driver). Arian et al. (2013) conclude that 'the adolescent brain is structurally and functionally vulnerable to environmental stress, risky behavior, drug addiction, impaired driving, and unprotected sex'. All of this heightens the likelihood of adolescent offending and may help to explain why the crime rate in most countries spikes during teenage years and declines from age 20 onwards. The downward move is most marked after the age of 25.

Even after the structure of the brain is largely formed (by adulthood, especially over the age of 25), it can be affected (or at least the *way* in which it functions can be affected) by behavioural choices made later in life. **Figure 16.10** illustrates that the use of certain substances affects the way in which the brain functions. Certain molecules called dopamine D2 receptors are found in the brain; these receptors receive signals, primarily in the form of the chemical dopamine. Dopamine is a chemical messenger (or, more formally, a 'neurotransmitter') that is used by the nervous system to regulate many behaviours and bodily functions: it's involved in the sensations of pleasure and pain, in movement, in learning, attention, and motivation, and myriad other things besides. When it is 'detected' by dopamine D2 receptors in particular, it has an effect on movement, learning and memory, attention, sleep, and reproductive behaviour (Mishra et al., 2018).

The images in **Figure 16.10** show the effect of substance use on the availability of dopamine D2 receptors in the brain. Look at this figure and notice how those who are addicted to the substances listed in the figure

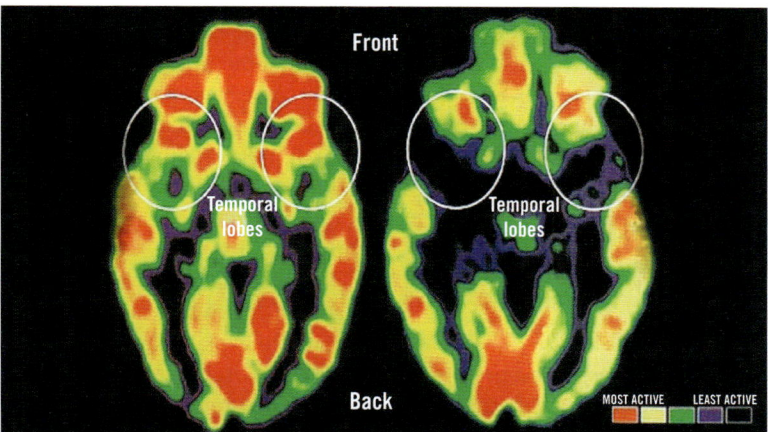

Figure 16.9 The structure of a normal brain (left) compared to that of a child who has been abused (right) shows that maltreatment alters the way in which the brain develops

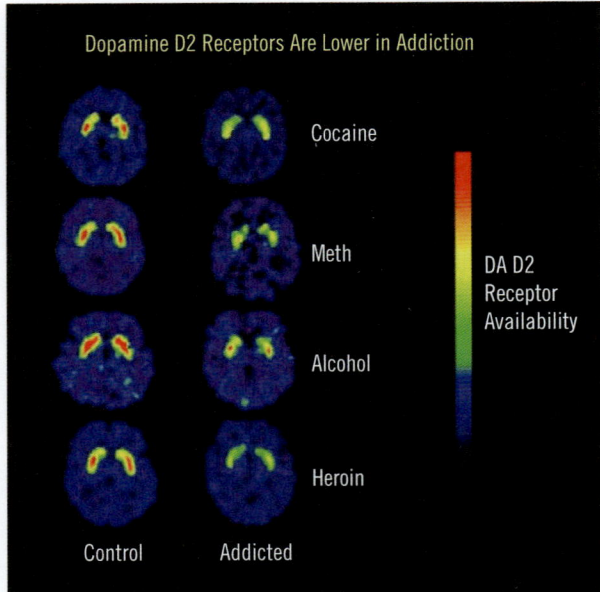

Figure 16.10 Scans show the effect of addiction to different substances on the availability of dopamine D2 receptors in the brain—a change that can affect someone's behaviour and body function

Source: Science Source/Science Photo Library

have a lower number of dopamine receptors compared with those with a healthy brain: there are more regions of yellow/green than in a control (someone not addicted to the substances listed), where we see more regions of red, indicating a higher number of dopamine receptors. If someone's brain has fewer active dopamine D2 receptors, their brains won't be able to respond to dopamine as they might otherwise do—and this leads to changes in behaviour and body function.

This example illustrates how environmental and behavioural choices can affect the way in which the brain functions and its ability to produce and respond to neurotransmitters like dopamine or serotonin normally. Neurotransmitters support the healthy functioning of the brain, but too much or too little may well affect emotion and behaviour.

We can begin to see a clear link between behaviour (which, as in the case of increased violence, may be linked to crime) and the structure and functioning of the brain. What is less clear is:

- whether this link is caused by genetics, biology, or environment;
- the extent to which the individual's ability to control their behaviour might be impaired; and
- the extent to which any damage to the brain and its functioning can be reversed or repaired and whether this would prevent or help to prevent further offending.

Having considered the main effects of the structure and development of the brain on behaviour and how that might affect criminality, let's now move on to look at how chemical and biochemical influences might affect behaviour and whether they have any impact on criminality.

Chemical and biochemical influences

Before we consider whether chemical and biochemical factors can influence criminality, let's think about what we mean by these terms. In scientific terms, a chemical is any kind of substance (a liquid, solid, or gas, from sodium chloride to alcohol). A biochemical, in simple terms, is a chemical which is active in living beings (for example, hormones, DNA, or insulin) or a process which occurs in the body. Every chemical taken into the body affects an individual either physically or mentally. Many foods and other substances merely affect the body physically, providing strength and nutrients. However, others will also affect the biochemical balance of the mind and therefore may have an effect on behaviour. This might be as mild as the calming influence of a good cup of tea or as potentially dangerous as the way in which some substances alter one's ability to perform everyday tasks, such as driving under the influence of alcohol or certain illegal drugs or substances (for example, alcohol) which may alter behaviour patterns and increase, for example, the likelihood that someone will be violent.

Take a look at **What do you think? 16.3**. It is clear that many substances that we drink or eat, such as chocolate and coffee, affect our minds and therefore may also affect our behaviours. Behavioural changes may also be associated with low blood sugars (hypoglycaemia), food allergies, and excesses or deficiencies in vitamins (Marsh, 1981; Mednick et al., 1987; Gesch et al., 2002; Herbison et al., 2012). Therefore, many substances that are introduced into the body (or their deficiency) can affect the way in which the brain functions and therefore influence behaviour, sometimes behavioural problems (Herbison et.al., 2012); some have discovered that behavioural changes can increase the likelihood of antisocial behaviour or crime (Marsh, 1981; Mednick et al., 1987; Gesch et al., 2002).

We will next focus on the effects of testosterone, which is one the internal chemicals or hormones produced by the body.

In almost all parts of the world, **official statistics** suggest that men commit far more crime than women. Researchers seeking to explain the difference began to suspect that it might be caused by testosterone, the hormone which some have related to characteristics often associated with men and their aggressiveness (Olweus, 1987; Schalling, 1987; Raine, 1993). Many of the early scientific studies involved

WHAT DO YOU THINK? 16.3

Which substances give rise to the following symptoms?

Here you will see a list of symptoms for three drugs. From the descriptions, try to work out what substance is being referred to, before checking the answers below.

Symptoms

- **Drug A:** Whilst often unpleasant to start with, once people become accustomed to this drug they usually get addicted and find it hard to stop. Most users find it difficult to get though the day without this substance; they often need it as soon as they wake, and multiple times through the day. If they don't get the drug, they can become irritable, inattentive, and moody. This drug probably kills more people than any other drug. This drug is unpleasant and risks causing serious harm to non-users—every year a number of innocent people are killed.

- **Drug B:** This depressant drug can affect mood and behaviour negatively. It is physically addictive and withdrawal is particularly unpleasant—in some of the worst cases, drug users suffer epileptic seizures and hallucinations when withdrawing. This drug is strongly linked to aggression and violence.

- **Drug C:** This stimulant drug is psychologically addictive. These drug users feel that they can't face life unless they have their fix. Most of these drug users have to take the drug at least once a day. If they can't get hold of their drug, these users become edgy, irritable, depressed, and restless. Heavy users suffer palpitations, dizziness, headaches, migraine, and insomnia.

Think carefully before looking at the answers at the end of the chapter.

*Source: Inspired by Professor Julian Buchanan's inaugural lecture. Available at: http://www.academia.edu/181097/Inaugural_Professorial_Lecture_Questionnaire_Powerpoint_Lecture_Notes_preview_and_download_below_*

---

primates, but we will consider those that studied the relationship between testosterone and human behaviour, particularly aggression (Olweus, 1987; Schalling, 1987).

Dan Olweus (1987) found a link between testosterone and both verbal and physical aggression especially when a male was provoked. While he suggested that provoked violence (verbal and physical) was directly correlated with levels of testosterone, he noted that unprovoked aggression had a more complex connection with testosterone. Olweus concluded that, while there was a clear relationship between testosterone and aggression, this link was complex and many other factors also affected aggression. Daisy Schalling (1987) suggested that testosterone was only associated with verbal aggression, not physical aggression. In her research, testosterone increased when young men felt that their status was threatened. Boys with low testosterone avoided conflict and those with high testosterone were more assertive, extrovert, and social but tended to become angry when they were questioned or threatened. As with Olweus's work, Schalling suggests that the link between testosterone and aggression is complex and many other factors also play a part. Neither of the researchers tested whether higher levels of testosterone *caused* aggression.

More direct links between testosterone and crime have been found by Ellis and Coontz (1990) who linked testosterone to high crime rates across many societies and across time, and Dabbs and Dabbs (2000) who linked high testosterone to criminal aggression, violence, delinquency, substance abuse, and other unacceptable or challenging behaviours. Ellis and Coontz (1990) claimed a causal link between testosterone and behaviour and suggest that the explanation for that link lay in the fact that testosterone affects the developing brain of the foetus; however, this link is not yet substantiated and, even if the substance does affect the developing brain, it is unclear what the effects of this would be on later behaviours. Therefore, it is unclear whether testosterone causes unacceptable behaviours. Hollin (1992) suggests that the claimed links arise partly because young males show many challenging behaviours (including heightened aggression, antisocial behaviour, and criminality) and also experienced high levels of testosterone. But that the way in which testosterone causes behaviour change is far from understood; the two may have a different cause or link.

Overall, whilst the empirical evidence suggesting a link between testosterone (and many other substances) and unacceptable behaviours is strong, the evidence does not always prove a causal link. Explanations as to how or why the substances cause the change in behaviour are still often far from clear. In the introduction, we noted that just because two things change at the same time does not mean that one change caused the other. Remember the graph that plotted two things—the divorce rate in Maine and the consumption of margarine from 2000 to 2009—and the fact that, although the two lines fluctuated in tandem, it did not mean that eating more margarine increased the likelihood of getting divorced. It may merely be a correlation: the two things may just happen to change at the same time, each being caused to change by a different stimuli or each may be caused by the same third factor. The important thing to remember is that a correlation (a relationship) between two factors does not necessarily mean that one factor *causes* the other. While everyone can see that some things are clearly not causally related, there is a tendency to accept causative relationships when the data only prove a correlation.

Genetics

As we saw earlier in this chapter, early positivists believed in the idea of a 'born criminal'. Researchers such as Lombroso, Sheldon, and Galton considered how we might identify 'born criminals' from their physical features. Other researchers took this idea further and questioned *how* specific individuals could come to be 'born criminal' (for example, Dugdale, 1877; Goddard, 1912; Goring, 1913). In the mid-19th century, Charles Darwin's *On the Origin of Species* attracted widespread interest and may have influenced criminologists to consider whether criminality in individuals is inherited. We're all quite used to the idea that we share physical characters (eye colour, height, etc.) with our parents and siblings. But what about our behaviours? Are there similarities in the way you and your parents or siblings behave or your likes and dislikes? Have you considered why? In this section we'll look at whether our genetics might play a role in how we behave and, in particular, whether we commit crime or whether it is upbringing (social factors) that shapes an individual's behaviour.

Family studies

How could criminologists establish whether criminal behaviour is inherited? Early criminologists such as Dugdale (1877) and Goddard (1912) decided to study what they called 'criminal families'. The most famous such study was of the Juke family and was conducted by an American sociologist, Richard Dugdale (1841–83). Dugdale (1877) found that a high proportion of the family were either criminals (males) or prostitutes (females). From this, he suggested that there were links between criminality and prostitution, and that these behaviours might somehow be inherited and be passed onto the next generations. Can you see any problems with this study? Finding that many members of the same family are criminals does not necessarily mean that there is a genetic link. Family members don't just share their genes, they share the same 'environment' (upbringing, taught values, quality of housing, level of income, etc.) and might learn social behaviours from each other. However, other theorists used similar correlations to those found by Dugdale (finding crime within families) to strengthen the claim that there is a genetic link and claimed it as the most important (even if not the only) causative factor.

Charles Goring (1870–1919), a British criminologist, discovered that there were many fathers and sons in prison as outlined in his work *The English Convict: A Statistical Study* (1913). Like Dugdale, he claimed a clear correlation between the behaviour within families (at least among the male members). He claimed the correlation was too close to be explained by environmental factors: they occurred even if the father was removed from the family when the child was very young. He therefore concluded that there must be a genetic link. He argued that criminality was passed on in the same way as eye colour so there must be a criminal gene and therefore someone could be born a criminal.

More recent studies also support the idea that the family has a role to play in criminal behaviour. In a longitudinal study—a study conducted with the same individuals over a number of years—a group of 397 children from 344 families were studied at regular intervals between the 1960s and the 1990s. The researchers found that criminal behaviour was concentrated in a small number of families, with half of the convictions found in just 23 families. They also found that three-quarters of convicted mothers and fathers in the study had a convicted child (Rowe and Farrington, 1997). The modern study recognises the possibility that the links may be environmental or learnt rather than genetic.

Adoption and twin studies

How can we investigate whether family patterns of criminality are caused by inheriting 'criminal genes' or by sharing the same environment? Usually, members of the same family share both their genes and their environment so it is difficult to determine which is responsible. Psychologists have developed some clever research techniques to try to separate these influences—adoption studies and twin studies.

As you are probably aware, there are two types of twins—identical and non-identical. Monozygotic (MZ) twins (literally 'one egg') are genetically identical because they come from a single egg and a single sperm (and are known as identical twins). Dizygotic (DZ) twins (literally 'two eggs') are formed when two eggs are simultaneously fertilised by two sperm so share only about 50 per cent of their genes, like any brother or sister. (DZ twins are known as non-identical twins.)

Adoption studies are important because the environment for the twins or siblings (brothers and sisters) is different, so similarities are more likely to be explained by genetics. Studying identical twins is an attractive prospect because they are genetically identical, so any differences in behaviour will most likely be due to environment whereas similarities should be explained by genetics.

In a twin study, researchers compare the behaviours of the two types of twins living with their birth parents. Both sets of twins share the same environment, so if there are more similarities in behaviour between MZ twins than between DZ twins, we can conclude that the similarities are likely to be explained by genetics.

There is a lot of disagreement amongst criminologists about the strength of findings from these studies. Few today suggest that there is a criminal gene; rather, they suggest that certain types of behaviour that are often related to criminal tendencies (such as extraversion) may be genetically passed on (Loehlin, 1992). Many believe there is a strong suggestion that genetics play a part in forming these broader behavioural traits. For example, Loehlin (1992) suggests that MZ (identical) twins are at least twice as likely to share behavioural traits as are DZ (non-identical) twins. The conclusion from this and other work is that both genetics and environment play a part in the formation of any behavioural traits: both nature and nurture are important to eventual behaviour (Fishbein, 2001; Joseph, 2000).

So, there is likely to be some family connection in terms of criminality, but it is difficult to assess exactly what this is or how it operates. If it is genetic, how does it manifest itself in our genomes? The human genome—the 'genetic code' for all of the genes in our bodies—has now been mapped and no individual genes have been found for any behaviour, certainly no criminal gene. Is this even possible if we consider crime to be a **social construction** (see **Chapter 2**)?

Most geneticists predict that genes found at certain places in the genome may be linked to personality types—and we can carry out broad sweeps of the genome (using what are called genome-wide association studies (GWAS)) to identify those genes (or variants of genes) that show a particularly strong association with individuals who exhibit certain behavioural traits or personality types. Some of these personality types may be more common among criminals than others—but this is still a long way from there being a criminal gene. If anything, GWAS approaches are revealing just how *many* genes can be involved in determining various physical and behavioural traits: the picture is often much more complicated than geneticists originally anticipated.

In any case, it is difficult to define a trait as being exclusively 'criminal' in nature. For example, a heightened drive or aggression might be useful in sport, for physical labour, for competitive financial or business practices, or for violent crime, etc. Therefore, such drives do not inevitably lead to criminality but may make it more likely.

If a genetic link *is* found to such personality traits, then it may lead to certain policy changes.

- It may be decided that we should not fully punish these individuals—they could not help their criminal behaviour as it resulted at least in part from their genetic make-up. They should therefore be helped to find more positive outlets for their personality traits or be given drugs to control the trait.

- If people cannot be controlled or redirected, then they should be removed to protect everyone else. If people are to be removed for the benefit of everyone else, they should presumably enjoy very comfortable surroundings. To an extent, this is used today as we extend punishments to protect the public, although the policy is not related to genetic or to environmental factors, merely to an acceptance that this person is somehow more dangerous than another and needs to be removed for as long as the law permits. These people are generally contained in prisons and do not enjoy better conditions.

- There might even be renewed calls for selective breeding or genetic manipulation, although as there are always legal outlets for these behavioural traits this would be more difficult to argue (and this is setting aside any consideration of the significant ethical issues surrounding such manipulation).

Therefore, if we were to find or accept that the personal choice of an individual is interfered with because their mind/body is predisposed to certain types of behaviour, then one of the above outcomes (which accept **determinism**) would be logical. However, scientists tend to agree that it is not possible to be certain whether (and to what extent) behaviour is affected by genetics (nature) and whether (and to what extent) it is affected by environment and upbringing (nurture). As such, it is almost impossible to quantify how much of any individual's behaviour results from free choice. In this circumstance, it is difficult to agree to what extent a state can justly punish. Most believe that behaviour is a combination of:

> gene and environment acting together. It is impossible to sort them into convenient compartments. An attribute such as intelligence is often seen as a cake which can be sliced into so much 'gene' and so much 'environment'. In fact, the two are so closely blended that trying to separate them is more like trying to unbake the cake.

(Jones, 1993: 171)

The most that can be claimed for biology or genetics is that someone's genetic make-up *might* make them more physically or psychologically *prone* to certain types of emotions, which *may* be linked to criminal behaviour (but also to perfectly legal behaviours). But it is also clear that there is no strong or direct link between genetics and criminal behaviour. We'll soon see how the possible link is made even more complicated when we add the study of evolutionary psychology to our discussion.

Evolutionary psychology

Evolutionary psychology is a fairly new field: it emerged in the 1970s but really began to take hold in the late 1990s. It applies Darwinian ideas of natural selection—the broad idea of 'survival of the fittest'—to the development of the human psyche. Elements of these ideas apply to the evolution of humanity as a whole (for example, the general evolution of humans has suggested that some things are important to survival) and some apply to small groups of people, often families (for example, some aspects of this general evolutionary background may be more important to survival in one family or one neighbourhood than in another). The overarching idea behind evolutionary psychology is that in order to understand modern humans and their behaviours, we need to consider the environment in which our ancestors lived, and how this shaped their evolution.

Evolutionary psychologists argue that some aspects of our behaviour and our preferences have evolved because they made us more likely to survive. Let's look at two examples used by Toates (2007).

- First, humans generally have a love of sweet food. In hunter-gatherer communities that existed in the past, sweet foods were a positive thing: they signalled that a food was unlikely to be poisonous, and could therefore be consumed without risk to health (which, in itself, promoted survival). Sweet foods were also sufficiently uncommon that they couldn't be consumed in quantities that might make people unhealthily overweight. Compare that to today's societies, where the consumption of abundant sweet foods is leading to rising diabetes, obesity, and dental decay.
- Secondly, the attractiveness of symmetrical faces is explained because people with this appearance tend to be younger and it reflects a strong developmental history: they are an indicator of someone with 'good' or 'strong' genes, who are therefore good people to mate with—returning to the **concept** of the natural selection of the fittest.

Evolutionary psychology recognises that the mind has evolved various methods or mechanisms to process information in a way that permits us to resolve problems that we, as humans, often meet. Therefore, those behaviours or characteristics that have over time benefited a group of people will tend to be selected: people with those traits will be chosen as possible mates and will pass their genes on to the next generation so that they, too, can benefit from the same behaviours and characteristics. In this way, the process of evolution has enhanced those thoughts and feelings that help humans survive. For example:

- caring for and protecting our children helps their survival and the survival of our genes;
- social living enhances the safety of the group. Respecting and protecting others in our group enhances our own likelihood of survival;
- aspects of social living such as religion which might tie people more closely to each other might also be evolutionary positives; and
- distrust of those not in our group also enhances survival in a world where resources are limited—the 'them and us' attitude may therefore increase our chances of survival.

Much of our behaviour is learned in the here and now: in the context of our **culture** as it exists today. However, evolutionary psychologists suggest that our behaviour when under extreme stress can be at least partially explained by our underlying, natural, evolved psychology. The lines between cultural/learned and evolved psychology are not really understood and are constantly moving. Most people would view what we've learned in the 'here and now' to be the strongest contributors to the behaviours we exhibit (except in extreme situations). As such, the argument seems to be that evolutionary psychology sets the *background* for likely behaviours but learning and culture shape how these evolutionary traits normally manifest themselves—that is, the aspects of our evolved behaviours that are brought to the fore.

Ultimately, then, we are all affected by our underlying evolutionary psychology but how that manifests itself may depend on an individual's background or their upbringing. So, for example, while social living may be important to all humans and means that we respect and protect others in our group, how we do this and how we learn it may depend on our circumstances. For example, two people may be born into different close-knit communities, one in a neighbourhood where violence is used to protect the community from outsiders and the other in a neighbourhood where outsiders are welcomed and taught to become part of the community and so strengthening it. The behaviours of each of these people will be shaped by their underlying evolutionary psychology but the way in which it comes out will be very different.

Some evolutionary psychologists (Ridley, 2004) even suggest that our inherited, evolved characteristics—those carried from generation to generation in our genes—alter through a person's life. Until the end of the 20th century, it was believed that an individual's genes, and the information they convey, were completely set from the moment the sperm and egg joined. However, evolutionary psychologists question this idea; they believe that either genes alter or the way in which they affect the person alters through a person's life, with these changes arising in response to external stimuli. These theorists recognise that while the structure of the body and the brain are *largely* shaped and predetermined by genes, they are also affected by external factors.

For example, the basic structure of the brain is moulded by genes but will develop differently depending on the way in which it is stimulated. Formative experiences, especially those taking place as the brain passes through important developmental stages, will affect the physical structure of the brain (see the discussion of brain function and structure earlier in this section). So, although a brain's physical potential—the way a particular brain can develop—may be constrained by the genes the person is born with, the way in which it *actually* develops (that is, whether or not it reaches its potential) depends on experience, opportunities, and life choices: free will, cultural opportunities, and family upbringing (especially the amount of affection) may well shape the brain. Therefore, nature gives us the building blocks but environment and nurture decide how these are finally shaped (Ridley, 2004).

This area of science is called *epigenetics*—it studies the influence our environment or upbringing may have on the way our genes direct our development, function, and behaviour. These influences do not alter our basic genetic material, they do not 'rewrite' our DNA; rather, they change how our genes can be interpreted or expressed. Epigenetic elements are essentially tags (instructions) that are attached to the genes. These tags help the body to decide how the information stored in those genes should be interpreted—which bits should be enhanced or suppressed. Epigenetic tags are somewhat like directions in a theatrical script as to how a line should be delivered, or a musician adding comments or instructions to a sheet of music which guide how the music is played (**Figure 16.11**). The annotations don't change the original musical notes, but they do change how the musician interprets them.

Recently it was recognised that these epigenetic tags can be altered (or even added to) by our environment; as such, environment or upbringing can change the way in which genes are interpreted by the body and therefore how they affect a person. While many of these epigenetic tags are stripped off when our genes, in the form of DNA, are passed on to the next generation, scientists are now finding that some get passed on to children and grandchildren. As a result, behaviours that have a strong environmental contribution—a propensity for

Figure 16.11 Epigenetic 'tags' are like annotations added to a piece of music, in that they guide how the music is played rather than changing the actual notes
Source: Dragon Images/Shutterstock

smoking, for example—might get passed down through the generations: the epigenetic tags that are added as a consequence of environmental factors in one generation can persist to the next. Therefore aspects of behaviour and traits that were thought to be entirely nurture- or environment-based in the 'here and now'—in the context of a particular generation—are increasingly being found to be influenced by epigenetics: they are inherited.

This is beginning to further blur the lines between natural ('born') and environmental ('made') criminals and may well have scientific and policy implications as more is understood about this area. The important thing to remember for the moment is that it demonstrates how difficult it is to reliably determine whether the environment in which a person is brought up or their genes has the greatest impact on their propensity towards criminal behaviour. However, what the theorists clearly agree on is that some people are more likely to choose criminal behaviour than are others. They also agree that this predisposition has implications for how much punishment would be just and how frequently and to what extent we should intervene in other ways (especially to rehabilitate).

Biological positivism: conclusion

This section of the chapter has considered the effects of physical attributes on behaviour: the genetic make-up or *tags* on genes which affect behavioural choices; the physical development of the brain and its effect on emotion and behaviour; and the production of substances such as testosterone or serotonin which affect the functioning of the brain and so alter behaviour. Whilst it is clear that biological factors have some role to play in determining behaviour, including criminal behaviour, the extent of their effects may be fairly minor and exactly how their effects might intervene to cause particular behaviours is far from understood. What almost all theorists who claim a biological underpinning for behaviour or crime now agree on is that the effects of these substances and physical attributes are altered or enhanced by broader social and environmental factors. Therefore, modern claims made by biological positivists are much less powerful than those made by Lombroso and other early positivists and even these limited claims need to be more carefully assessed before being finally accepted. We will now move on to explore psychological theories.

16.7 Psychological theories

Psychology suggests an alternative scientific basis for criminal behaviour. In contrast to biological theories, psychological explanations focus more directly on the workings of the mind and how that affects behaviour. Here we move away from the physical make-up to deal directly with individual characteristics such as personality, reasoning, thought, intelligence, learning, perception, imagination, memory, creativity, and how they may give us some insight into human behaviour.

There are many aspects of psychology, many theories which have been associated with criminal behaviour. Some of these are **cognitive** and place the issues clearly in the mind of the individual. These theories see behaviour as the result of thought processes, compelling mental forces or drives (the result of anger, frustration, desire, despair, etc.). Others, often referred to as behavioural psychologists, consider behaviour to arise out of both internal factors and external social or environmental factors, which may reinforce or discourage the behaviour. Each of these approaches has many different ideas about how psychology and criminal behaviour may be linked. Some theorists are closely linked to biological explanations and related ideas such as genetics and neurological factors. Others work more closely with some of the sociological theories such as social bonding. In this section, we will present a brief introduction to two areas of psychology which often form part of other theories: psychoanalytic perspectives and learning theories.

As with biological theories of crime, psychological theories are grounded in positivism—they claim that crime is the result of some mental or behavioural construct and is not entirely the result of free will or human choice (although psychological factors can influence and interact with free will).

Sigmund Freud and psychoanalysis

We will start our discussion about psychology with perhaps the most well-known ideas in psychology, psychoanalysis (although as we will see later, modern psychology has moved very far away from these ideas).

In psychoanalysis, researchers argue that it is the forces within an individual that explain their behaviour. These inner forces are usually a mix of drives to fulfil their desires. The desires arise in an unconscious part of the brain and are merely experienced as strong needs or wants. The desires or base instincts grapple with reason and feelings of right and wrong to decide whether the desire will be met. The mental conflict is therefore often between reason and standards of behaviour on one side and fulfilling the desires of base instincts on the other. According to psychoanalysts, this mental conflict is experienced by everyone. Some people control their desires quite well; others fail to control themselves and their behaviour then often causes concern. According to this theory, crime and other unacceptable behaviours often arise when someone fails to control their desires.

The mental conflict, how it arises and is resolved, is the core of psychoanalysis. These ideas are strongly associated with Sigmund Freud (1856–1939), an Austrian neurologist and psychologist whose theories have had a profound effect on psychology, literature, philosophy, and on the way in which we understand our world. In fact, his influence is so complete that psychoanalysis is often referred to as Freudian (Freud, 1935; and for information about application of his ideas to crime, Kline, 1984).

We will start by considering the theory of psychoanalysis, before looking at how it can help us to understand crime.

Levels of awareness

Psychoanalysis breaks the workings of the mind into three levels of awareness: conscious thought, preconscious thought, and unconscious thought.

- **Conscious thought:** Freud claimed that current thoughts and experiences are held in this part of the mind and the individual is always aware of these. This is where the three aspects of the personality (see next list) are resolved and where reason and conscience either control or fail to control the desires. If desires are not controlled in line with social expectations, then crimes occur.

- **Preconscious thought:** For Freud, ideas, thoughts, and functions are held just outside your conscious mind but close enough to allow your conscious mind to decide to pull them to the fore when they are needed. Some of these are memories that are partially triggered by something in the conscious mind.
- **Unconscious thought:** Thoughts, memories, feelings, and wishes that are safely stored in your mind but which, at the moment, you are wholly unaware of Freud labelled as unconscious. This is also where natural instincts and drives are held and where there will be repressed memories. For the most part, things held in your unconscious mind are not available to the conscious mind, or not without considerable help. These may be used by the mind unconsciously, for example when a smell invokes a memory.

Components of personality

Alongside the levels of awareness (though not perfectly mapped onto them), Freud singled out three components of personality: Id, Ego, and Superego. See **Figure 16.12**.

The Id

Freud claimed the Id is the pleasure-seeking part of the personality. The Id is basically in the unconscious part of the mind and is the most primitive portion of our personality. We are born with our Id. It is driven by desire and operates on a pleasure principle—it knows what the person likes and seeks to deliver the most pleasure possible. The Id houses the drives to eat, drink, excrete, be comfortable, enjoy sexual pleasure, etc. The Id has no control or restraint (no reason or ethical or moral standards) and seeks to deliver as much pleasure as possible, as soon as possible. Freud argued that in order to live with other people the Id needs to be repressed or controlled so that people do not harm each other.

The Ego

According to Freud, the Ego acts as a break on the Id. We are not born with an Ego; it has to be learnt. The Ego recognises what happens in the real world and reasons with the Id. If April likes chocolate, the Id will require her to take it from the shelf in a shop and eat it immediately. The Ego recognises that taking chocolate from a shop (without paying) leads to punishment. The Ego tries to prevent the Id from taking the chocolate but the Id is strong so the Ego also wants to ensure that April gets her chocolate. So the Ego will take the chocolate to the counter and pay before eating it. This delays the pleasure and ensures that what happens relates to the real world—the necessity to pay. The Ego uses the 'reality principle' and tries to ensure that the desires are met in the most appropriate way possible. This may mean delaying fulfilment of the desire or only fulfilling it after another action has happened (paying). The Ego learns both how to control and how best to serve the Id in the real world. For example, the Ego learns that we are more likely to get what we want if we say please or that we will not be punished if we pay. The Ego tries to provide as much pleasure as possible whilst staying within the expected boundaries—the reality.

The Superego

The Superego controls the Ego. For Freud, the Superego is the conscience and it begins to develop at about two years old. The Superego exists in both unconscious (guilt) and conscious (moral or ethical codes) parts of the brain. Whilst there is a conscious element, it is largely unconscious in the way in which it operates—feelings of guilt or pride rather than consciously working out what is right. However, it is where societal values reside, where the rules of a society (family, community, country) get stored. The Superego tries to ensure that the individual is a perfect social being. It has an ideal image of the perfect person and constantly measures actions against that image. Of course, perfection looks different to each person, each of us learns from different people and learns slightly different rules. The Superego is where we internalise rules so that if we live up to what is expected we feel pride—we have come close to the perfect social being—if we break the rules we feel guilt or shame—we are a long way from perfection. In this

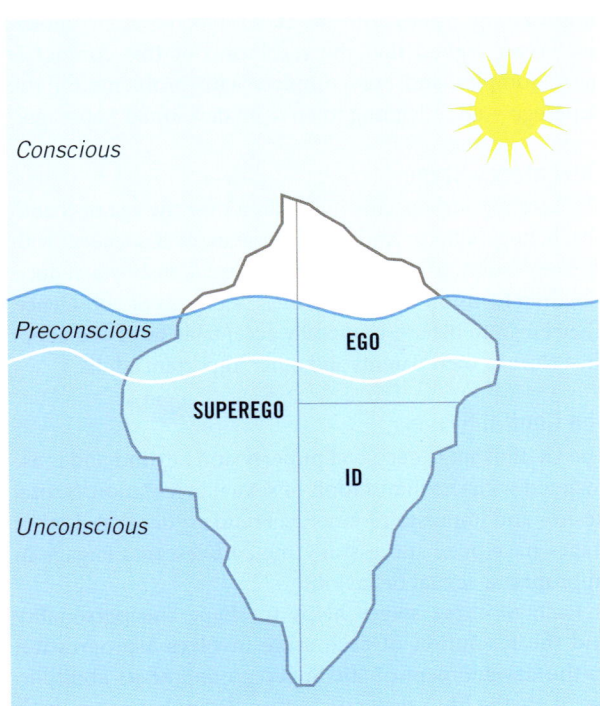

Figure 16.12 Freud highlighted three main components of personality: the Id, the Ego, and the Superego
Source: Simply Psychology.org

way, it is the Superego which allows us to feel pride, guilt, or shame and it is through these feelings rather than conscious thought that the Superego often operates. The guilt and shame are remembered as unpleasant so the next time the person considers the action they experience anxiety that the bad feelings will return, the person represses the action and controls their desires. Often the Superego goes further, by actually repressing the thought or desire before it comes to being a conscious thought. In this way, thoughts and desires may also be repressed.

Those who use Freudian analysis to explain negative or criminal behaviours often claim the individuals have underdeveloped Superegos (Aichhorn, 1936). That means that the person is likely to be a persistent offender as their internal moral code is not developed. Similar to how biological theorists claimed that neglect or other problems with upbringing caused the brain to fail to develop connections, psychoanalysts claim that problems with upbringing mean the brain fails to develop the Superego. An individual might fail to develop what society would class as an adequate Superego if the parents are overindulgent and do not set boundaries. However, an individual might also fail to develop an adequate Superego for society if the parents or others close to the individual have a different moral code from the wider society. They may have more permissive (easy going) views or, alternatively, their views might reflect a totally different moral code from that of society in general. Taking an extreme example, a person who has been groomed by terrorists might possess a normal, fully developed Superego with respect to the rules of the terrorist organisation. They therefore obey the rules of the terrorist organisation: however, they may have inadequate or underdeveloped Superegos with respect to the rules of society. Or they might repress the Superego they developed as part of the wider society and supplement it with this new Superego. In whichever way this happens, the individual will feel free to break some of the most fundamental rules of the wider society because their Superego will not prevent them from doing so.

The five stages of development

Freud also set out five stages of development for the personality. Each is associated with a particular age and any problems experienced at that age cause problems for that stage of development.

The Oral Stage
The Oral Stage occurs at ages 0–17 months and affects the mouth (sucking, biting, and chewing). Freud believed that because at birth babies have a sucking reflex and with a desire to suckle on their mother's breast, so the mouth becomes the pleasure centre. Freud claims that if a child's oral needs are not met during infancy, they may develop negative habits such as nail biting or thumb sucking to meet this basic need.

The Anal Stage
The Anal Stage occurs at ages 18–35 months and affects the anus. At this stage, Freud argues that children begin to play with urine and faeces and are fixated on bowel and bladder control. The control they learn to exert over their bodily functions is important. Freud claims that problems at this stage, such as parents toilet training their children too early, can result in a child who is uptight and overly obsessed with order.

The Phallic Stage
The Phallic Stage occurs at ages 3–6 years and affects the genitals During this stage, Freud argues that children begin to enjoy their genitals and to struggle with sexual desires towards the opposite-sex parent. Boys get attracted to their mothers (Oedipus complex) and want to replace their fathers who are seen as rivals for the mother's attention. However, they also feel guilty and worry the father will punish them by removing their penis. The fear of castration forces the child to control his desire for his mother. Freud believed that it is through resolving this conflict that the Superego (the restraint and conscience) is developed. Failure to resolve the conflict leads to problems in the Superego and serious behavioural problems may arise. Girls get attracted to their fathers (Electra complex—proposed by Jung) and want to replace their mothers. Freud argued that the resolution of this conflict is more complex and less complete with problems for the Superego—often leading to an over-developed Superego.

The Latency Stage
The Latency Stage occurs in children over the age of 6 until just before puberty and, Freud argues, is associated with the repression of sexual feelings. Sexual instincts reduce. Children focus on developing their Superego or conscience. They begin to behave in morally acceptable ways and adopt the values of their parents and other important adults.

The Genital Stage
The Genital Stage occurs at puberty and beyond and is associated with the maturation of sexual orientation. Sexual desires and impulses re-emerge. Freud argues that if other stages have been successfully met, adolescents engage in 'appropriate' sexual behaviour.

Each of these stages helps to shape the personality and the resolution of each stage involves a progression in the development of the Superego and of its ability to persuade the Id to seek satisfaction through means which are acceptable to the Superego. Basically, the Ego sits between the powerful forces of natural, biological urges on one side (the Id) and reality and social requirements (the Superego) on the other.

Defence mechanisms

Freud proposed that there are a number of defence mechanisms that are used to build an acceptable balance between desire and repression. When there is a conflict between the Id and the Superego, the Ego feels overwhelmed and gets anxious; in order to resolve the anxiety, a range of defence mechanisms are used. The defence mechanisms generally operate at the unconscious level but have an effect on the conscious decision about how to resolve the conflict. The balance, once it is reached, is mostly kept by the Ego. The perfect personality balance is reached when the desires of the Id are satisfied but that satisfaction is achieved by means which are acceptable to the Superego, so allowing the person to enjoy what they want but also feel good about themselves. As part of the building of a Superego, the mind uses a number of defence mechanisms, examples of which are provided in **Table 16.1**.

Defence mechanism	Description	Example
Repression	This was the first mechanism Freud proposed. It is a mechanism which arises in the unconscious part of the mind and prevents threatening or disturbing thoughts getting to the conscious mind. This is done unconsciously so people have no control over it and are unaware that it has been done.	Repression is used to stop an individual becoming conscious of thoughts that would result in guilt. For example, in the Oedipal stage it prevents thoughts about harming the same-sex parent reaching the conscious mind. Repressed memories have been blocked for the conscious mind and often contain things which are damaging to the person or that they cannot face.
Projection	Where an unacceptable thought, motive, or feeling reaches the conscious mind, it is attributed to somebody else. This arises when someone is not able to acknowledge their own feelings or is unaware or not conscious of them.	Often aggressive or inappropriate sexual thoughts and desires are dealt with in this way. Strong feelings of dislike or hatred are unacceptable so when they arise you tell yourself the other person hates you and you are merely returning the feelings. Or you may be angry at your partner for not listening when it is you who is not listening.
Denial	Refusing to accept reality. Here someone acts as if a nasty fact, feeling, thought, motive, etc. is not real. This is one of the most dangerous and primitive defence mechanisms and is often used by young children.	People use this to deal with truths in their lives that they cannot deal with. For example, an alcoholic may deny the problem and state that they can hold down a job or keep a relationship going so they can't be an alcoholic.
Regression	When a person is faced with unacceptable thoughts, impulses, or realities, they merely move backwards to an earlier stage of development. Stress moves them backwards.	A teenager who becomes overwhelmed by the changes in their feelings (anger) and desires (especially sexual) may move back to problem childhood behaviours such as thumb sucking or bedwetting. People may also refuse to get out of bed and face the world.
Acting out	Performing an extreme behaviour in order to express or release thoughts or feelings they cannot otherwise deal with. Taking the action releases tension and stress.	Children often have temper tantrums when they feel they cannot control something or cannot express themselves to let people know how they feel. As an adult, instead of telling someone they are angry, they break something, punch an object, or self-harm.
Displacement	This mechanism causes thought feelings and impulses about a person or object to be directed at another person or object. This mechanism can be helpful if redirected to a useful purpose but generally causes more problems when it is directed towards an innocent person.	The classic example is someone who is angry with a boss or someone else who has power over them and who then comes home and takes things out on the family or on pets. The anger is redirected from the person who caused the problem to others who are not to blame. This causes guilt whilst not resolving the anger.
Sublimation	Channelling unacceptable impulses, thoughts, and emotions into acceptable ones.	In the example under 'displacement' above, if the anger is redirected into driving the person to do better in a sport then whilst still not resolving the anger it does not increase the problem by adding guilt. Sexual frustrations and other problems may be usefully dealt with in this way. Another example is the use of humour to defuse tension.

Table 16.1 Examples of the mind's defence mechanisms, according to Freud

Very often the desires of the Id are channelled into more acceptable behaviours. For example, a person may be persuaded that they should satisfy their sexual desires only in a relationship, or destruction and violence might be satisfied by taking apart toys and learning to rebuild them or through competitive sports. However, as is evident from **Table 16.1**, psychoanalysts argue that sometimes the mechanisms cause unacceptable or criminal behaviours or store problems up for the future.

Freud used these ideas to treat people who were experiencing problems. While he never specifically used them as a tool to analyse the criminal mind, he did recognise that they might underlie odd or unacceptable behaviours. Therefore psychoanalysis may be useful to explain criminality. For example, if a criminal has no personality problem (no conflict between the Superego on the one side and the Id and Ego on the other) then Freud might explain the behaviour as arising out of a complete criminal personality. Here the Superego is fully formed but is very permissive of behaviour others find unacceptable or criminal. Here the offender's cultural and social upbringing taught them to regard certain types of offending as acceptable and so they do not see it as wrong. For example, they may consider theft from a company as acceptable whilst still condemning theft from individuals. Along with the rest of society, they may condemn many other acts; they merely feel free to commit particular offences. Furthermore, some of the defence mechanisms can also be connected to particular types of criminal act; see displacement in **Table 16.1** where anger at a boss and frustration about not being able to resolve the problem is displaced to a family member. Other defence mechanisms may provide an offender with a way of coping once they do offend, for example someone who has been violent or attacked someone sexually may project the problem onto the victim so claiming that they caused the violence or sexual attack (see Gracia, 2014).

Freud set out most of this analytical psychology though others have added to it (many defensive mechanisms have been added by others). His theories have influenced many aspects of modern life such as philosophy and literature and his ideas are often referred to in conversation. However, this does not make them true. Furthermore, Freud did not write a great deal about crime but others have often connected psychoanalysis with crime and therefore it has been discussed here. Psychoanalysis is a science but the central concepts described earlier cannot be directly observed so that it is not possible to prove or disprove their existence. Freud claims that the Id, Ego, and Superego exist because of particular external manifestations which also exhibit the extent to which each part of the personality has developed or is discovered when a psychoanalyst uses dream analysis, verbal association, hypnosis, etc. It is important to note that each psychoanalyst will interpret behaviours, dreams, verbal association, etc. differently so that even if the techniques were useful in explaining behaviour (crime), the precise connections would be almost impossible to prove. More importantly, the proof of the ideas sets up a circular argument:

- we are looking to explain criminal behaviour;
- psychoanalysts explain it using things like the Id, Ego, and Superego and the way in which they interact;
- when we ask psychoanalysts to prove that their explanations are correct or true, they point to the very behaviour (crime for us) which we wanted them to explain.

For psychoanalysis, the criminality is the outward manifestation of a disease or problem of the mind and personality, which exists in the subconscious or the unconscious. Furthermore, even if there is truth in Freud's explanations it does not help us to understand crime generally or help us to prevent crime, it is mainly of use at an individual level, to help 'treat' or alter the behaviour patterns of a single person (for discussion of Freud's work, see Kline, 1984). Despite this, the theory is interesting and Freud's ideas have been used by many other people. It was Freud who first set out a well-organised and reasonably complete theory to untangle the human personality. Inspired by Freud, other theorists such as Carl Jung (1875–1961), a Swiss psychologist who worked with Freud, extended or altered his ideas.

Extroversion, neuroticism, and psychoticism

Carl Jung diverted from Freud on several points but most importantly for the study of crime was the addition of the introvert and extrovert personality types. Whether or not you have heard of Jung, the idea that some people are extroverts and some are introverts is likely to be very familiar to you. Where would you place yourself on this scale? And what about your friends or members of your family?

According to Jung, extroverts love people and love being surrounded by people. They are most energised when others are with them because they love an audience. They are often the life and soul of the party and other people find them very engaging, charming, good company, and likeable. However, they can be a lot of work because they always like to be centre stage, they get easily bored, and do not like repetitive tasks. They tend to have a short concentration span and do not like solitary tasks. They will happily invest in people. Extroverts talk and act without properly considering things. They are sociable people who can be impulsive.

Introverts, on the other hand, like some people, often have a few close friends and prefer to know when people will come around. Introverts do not like attention unless they know everyone. They may not be shy but are more reserved and are happy to listen, to be part of the group but not at the centre. Introverts focus on their world at that time so can read a book in a busy room, they can shut the world out and focus on a task, they are happy doing just that. Introverts are often more lonely in a crowded room than when they are alone. They often choose not to engage with people but when something or someone interests them they have a lot of concentration. They make friends for life. Introverts think things through before they speak or act. They are private people, defend their territory, and think before they act. Jung said that there was a continuance from introversion to extroversion, and that everybody could be placed somewhere along the spectrum.

Jung did a little work which applied the extrovert/introvert spectrum to explain criminal behaviour and the main work in this area is that of Eysenck (1959, 1977, 1987) and Eysenck and Gudjonsson (1989). Eysenck argued that the personality you develop is partly explained by genetics and partly by social factors. He said that people learn societal rules (in Freud's terms, develop a Superego) through conditioning, in particular punishment for bad acts and reward for good ones (we will discuss conditioning in more detail in the next section). However, their capacity or ability to learn is set by their genetic make-up; how well they are able to learn through conditioning is part of who they are. He used Jung's extroversion–introversion spectrum (the E scale) as one part of this. According to Eysenck, each person is born somewhere on that spectrum. He also added in another spectrum for neuroticism which runs from neurotic or unstable to stable (the N scale) (see **Figure 16.13**). Neurotics tend to be anxious and moody and are often overly emotional whereas stable people are emotionally calm and tend not to react. He argued that everyone lies somewhere on each of these scales; most fall somewhere in the middle but some people are placed at the extremes of each scale. The positioning of people on the scales set their ability to learn social norms. According to Eysenck's hierarchy of conditionability:

(a) stable introverts (low N, low E) are the easiest to condition;
(b) stable extroverts (low N, high E) and neurotic introverts (high N, low E) are less malleable (less easy to change) but do not encounter great difficulty in social learning;
(c) neurotic extroverts (high N, high E) experience most difficulty in social learning.

In his later theories, he added a third dimension—psychoticism (the P scale, see **Figure 16.14**) which runs from low impulse control (psychoticism) to high impulse control. A person with low impulse control (psychoticism)

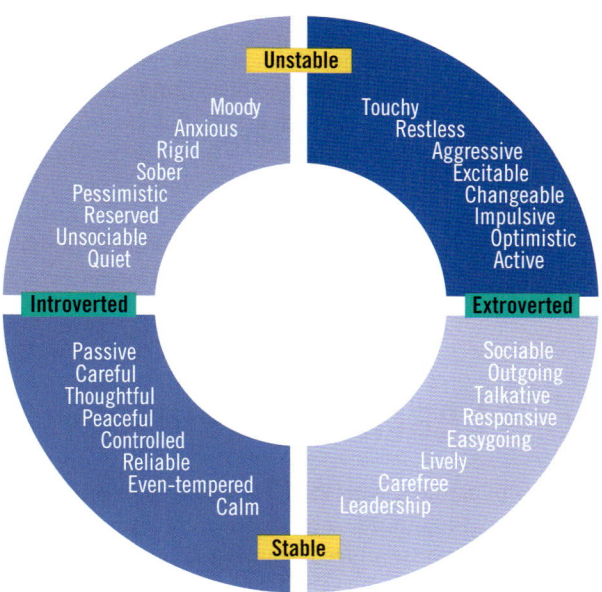

Figure 16.13 Eysenck argued that every person is born somewhere on the extroversion–introversion spectrum

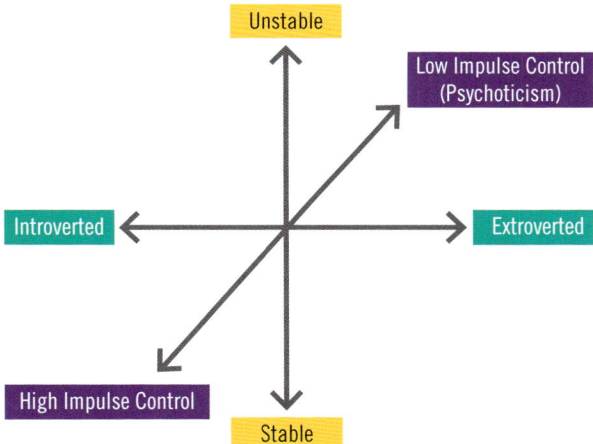

Figure 16.14 In his later works, Eysenck argued that people are born somewhere on three different spectrums, and that their position can predict how likely they are to offend

lacks empathy and can be cruel, aggressive, and sensation-seeking, whereas a person with good impulse control is empathetic, gentle, and caring. Neurotic, psychotic extroverts (high N, high E, high P) are the least likely to learn societal norms and so most likely to offend. Later, he also suggested that in order to enhance predictability it was necessary to split the extrovert scale (E scale) into sociability and impulsiveness and it is only impulsiveness (lack of thought before acting) that is linked to criminal behaviour.

There is some support for Eysenck's ideas. For example, McGurk and McDougall (1981) found that neurotic extroverts and psychotic neurotic extroverts were only found to be delinquent (people who had offended or broken important societal rules) whilst stable introverts were non-delinquent (they did not participate in offending behaviour and they tended to obey important societal rules). They therefore suggested that the classifications could be used to identify those who had or were likely to offend. The link between offending and impulsiveness has also been supported (Farrington, 1994). However, there is still quite a bit of controversy both about the extent to which these underlying and broad personality traits may be linked to delinquency and whether the personality traits are genetic or learnt as part of an individual's **socialisation**. In addition, it is important to understand that Eysenck proposes that an individual's underlying personality makes them more or less likely to offend. However, whether they actually do offend is not governed by their personality trait; they have other choices, but offending behaviour is made more likely as a result of it.

16.8 Learning theories

You will be familiar with the idea of learning something, whether learning to ride a bike as a child, learning a musical instrument, or, indeed, learning about criminology while reading this book. These are all positive things to learn and are usually encouraged by parents and society. But what about negative things like committing crime? Might criminals have *learnt* to commit crime? And, if so, how have they learnt this—it certainly isn't included on the school curriculum! Learning theories argue that most behaviours (whether positive or negative) are in some way learnt and suggest a number of ways in which this happens. It is important to remember that learning about an activity includes many things:

What needs to be learnt	Example of riding a bike
The physical element—what to do.	To balance and turn the pedals.
The results to which those actions will give rise—what will happen.	You will move forwards without directly touching the ground.
Why and how those results may be beneficial or harmful.	That you may get somewhere more quickly or enjoy the sensation of riding.
Whether the activity is encouraged and valued by others, permitted, tolerated, or banned.	That cycling is generally considered beneficial both in that it helps people to get around but also that it is a healthy pursuit.

People learn in various ways. However, the environment in which a person is raised and lives is thought to have the strongest impact on what they learn and therefore on how they learn to behave. Young children are most affected, first by their family, particularly parents, and then by teachers (Shaw and McKay, 1969). As a child grows, the influence of their peer group increases until in adolescence the peer group (Young, 1999) is probably the strongest influence on social learning (the changes over times are best recorded in life-course criminology, see Farrington, 2010). Whoever is the strongest influence or whatever the learning environment, theorists have suggested four different theories that explain how behaviour, attitudes, and skills may be learnt: classical conditioning; operant conditioning; social learning; and **cognitive learning**. We will consider each of these in this section.

Classical conditioning

Classical conditioning was discovered, accidentally, by Ivan Pavlov (1849–1936), a Russian physiologist (1927). Pavlov was studying the digestive systems of dogs and wanted to gather their saliva for his experiment. Dogs salivate when they eat, as an innate response to the food. But he noticed something strange: after repeating the procedure a number of times the dogs started salivating before eating. They would salivate at the sight of the food or even just seeing the researcher. Somehow the dogs had learned that the researcher would give them food.

Pavlov set out to investigate this response further. He rang a bell when feeding the dog. After this was repeated many times, the dog would salivate when the bell rang, even if there was no food in sight. He explained this as a learned or conditioned response.

Figure 16.15 demonstrates the processes involved in classical conditioning. Some behaviours are innate, such as a dog salivating when they are fed. This is an example of an unconditioned response (dog salivating) to an unconditioned stimulus (food). Unconditioned here merely means that it happens naturally and is not learned. When Pavlov presented the dog with a neutral stimulus (a bell), there would be no conditioned response (no salivating). The unconditioned stimulus (the food) is then repeatedly paired with the neutral stimulus (the bell) when feeding the dog. Eventually the dog salivated (conditioned response) when the bell rang (conditioned stimulus). This is a learned or conditioned response. Pavlov had taught

Figure 16.15 Classical conditioning, a process discovered by Pavlov through experimentation with dogs, is the idea that certain stimuli produce a learned or conditioned response

the dog that the sound of a bell meant food; the dog associated bell ringing with being fed. If these behaviours are firmly embedded, it is difficult to unlearn them. These are learned responses to our environment, so they often arise without feeling as if they are being learnt; the learned responses are often strongly attached to emotions and are therefore very powerful (Raine and Venables, 1981; Kim et al., 1998).

Most people associate some sounds or smells with happy or sad occurrences and the mere sound (for example, of a voice) or smell may bring on powerful feelings of fear or joy. It is thought to be how most phobias arise; a strong emotional response to a stimulus and the emotional response is generally far more powerful than logic would suggest is sensible. The response arises due to something experienced or learnt from someone else. However, the emotional response is sometimes rather inexact, arising outside the exact and expected learned reaction, for example abused children often associate an angry face with violence and can experience extreme fear when others would merely feel uncomfortable (Pollak et al., 1998; Pollak and Tolley-Schell, 2003).

Ideas from classical conditioning are sometimes used in teaching animals and small children, for example by pairing rewards (such as treats) with good behaviour. Punishment can also be used to teach people (or animals) not to behave in certain ways. When an individual is punished, they relate the punishment to the unacceptable behaviour and learn not to repeat that behaviour. Here, behaviour is shaped not just by the inner forces but by the environment, therefore increasing the extent to which the environment 'punishes' unacceptable behaviour (either by repeated small, negative 'punishments' such as disappointment or by one large action such as preventing a child from enjoying activities they normally participate in or not letting them go out with friends) should reduce that behaviour. It is often referred to as **avoidance learning**. Treatments based on classical learning are limited because the person who is learning is passive (in other words, they do not play an active part in their learning). However, useful treatments include exposure therapy (flooding is where a person is exposed to their painful memories and learns to deal with them using knowledge they now have) and systematic desensitisation (exposing someone to their phobia and teaching them to relax rather than react). These are mostly used to treat phobias or post-traumatic stress disorders (PTSD) so are little used in criminal justice.

Operant conditioning

Classical conditioning remains an important aspect of learning (Martin and Carlson, 2019: ch. 7). However, it is limited by only explaining passive learning. American psychologist B. F. Skinner (1904–90) studied an active type of learning, known as operant conditioning. He placed rats in an 'operant chamber' (1938) (sometimes called a 'Skinner box', see **Figure 16.16**) and they were given food if they pressed a lever. They learnt that pressing the lever provided food so they pressed the lever frequently. This is an example of positive reinforcement—a reward stimulates more of the activity. In other trials, the floor of the Skinner box had a low-level electric current running through it, which was unpleasant for the rats. The rats soon learnt that pushing the lever turned off the electric current through the floor. This is an example of negative reinforcement—an action removes an unpleasant stimulus.

The individual interacts with the environment to either increase or decrease a particular behaviour. It operates through rewards and punishments. If a person is rewarded that behaviour is reinforced, they learn it is good and that nice things happen when they participate so they perform more of this type of behaviour (positive reinforcement). Through use of negative reinforcement, people learn that to prevent something nasty they need to participate in a particular activity.

Bad behaviours are dealt with through punishment. Positive punishment is the use of something nasty to persuade people that they should not participate in that behaviour any more. For example, having to pay a fine might persuade someone that it is not worth parking on a double yellow line. Negative punishment is the removal of a desired activity in order to persuade that person and others not to act that way again. For example, the removal of a driving licence for speeding or the removal of the right to be a company director for breach of regulations. Here the person learns not just what happens when certain types of behaviour occur but also how to increase positive outcomes, for example to continue with the bad behaviour when no one is watching so a child who is punished if they just take a biscuit might learn that they can take a biscuit as long as no adult sees them, they have learnt that taking biscuits is frowned upon but have not learnt any inner values.

Each individual tries to maximise rewards whilst minimising unpleasantness. The techniques of positive and negative reinforcement and of positive and negative punishment are used to try to shape behaviour. However, there is little detail as to how the conditioning works. Here the changes in behaviour are a reaction to the environment and the learning does not include any element explaining why the behaviour is unacceptable or why it should be avoided.

To alter behaviour, you need to manipulate the environment to either encourage or discourage a particular activity. Systems such as Antecedent-Behaviour-Consequence (A:B:C) are used (often referred to as functional analysis, see LaVigna and Willis, 2012; Wardale et al., 2014). An antecedent is something that happens before behaviour and may trigger the behaviour. Behaviour is something someone does; consequence is something that follows the behaviour. So, if a peer group persuades a young person to misbehave and then the peer group applauds the behaviour and society and possibly their family punishes that misbehaviour: if the fun or the approval of the peer group is stronger than the punishment, the behaviour will be repeated, but if that is not the case it will not. For each individual, you can find out why that behaviour is encouraged or worth participating in and then try to counter it to find ways in which the behaviour might be discouraged in the future (Hanley et al., 2013).

Many of the studies concerning both classical conditioning and operant conditioning have been conducted on animals and whilst they have been used to explain some behaviours in humans we now move to discuss learning which has been applied more centrally to the human sphere and to offending behaviour.

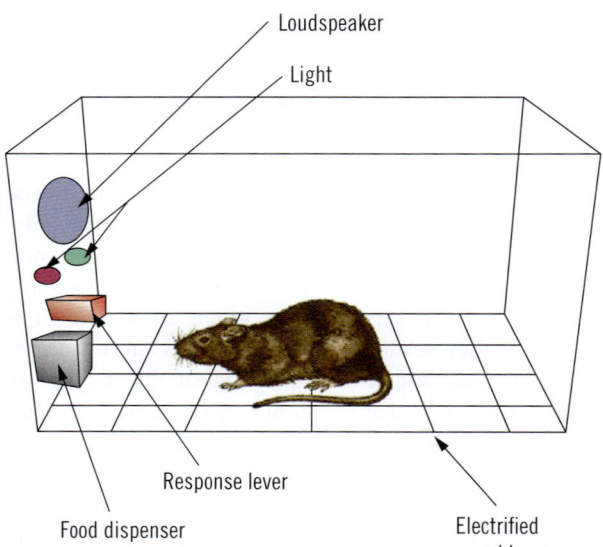

Figure 16.16 Operant conditioning, studied by Skinner through experimentation with rats, involves an individual interacting with the environment to produce particular results

Source: andreas1/CC BY-SA 2.0

Social learning theory

The learning theories so far considered have focused on directed learning, but we will now move to a **social learning theory** which draws on the individual's environment and on those around the person. Social learning theory suggests that humans learn through social interactions and tend to mimic behaviours of others. The psychologist Albert Bandura (1925–) argued that we can learn any human behaviour and that all behaviour is learned rather than inherited (1961). He claimed that the learning happens through imitating and copying others. His famous Bobo doll experiment was designed to test these ideas. There are different variations of the experiment but here we will consider just one (1961). Bandura put some children into a room with an adult who verbally and physically attacked a large doll. They hit the doll with a mallet put in the room for that purpose. He put others in a room with an adult who was neither verbally nor physically aggressive towards the doll and just played quietly with other toys in the room. A third group were in a room with no adult present. All the children were then exposed to a mild stimulus which might increase their feelings of aggression—as soon as the children started to play with toys they were told that they could not. Each child was then taken to another room with a variety of toys (including the Bobo doll and the mallet). Children who witnessed the aggressive behaviour tended to either be verbally or physically aggressive (or both). Boys were three times more likely to be physically violent towards the doll than were girls. Both boys and girls had the same rates of verbal aggression. Those who witnessed no aggression or where there was no adult in the room (the control) were less likely to show any aggression (see **Figure 16.17** and Bandura et al., 1961).

The experiment supports the ideas set out in social learning theory—that people learn social behaviour, even aggression, through observation and learning. Some believe that this has important implications for child rearing and for showing things such as aggression in the media. That, at least, is one interpretation of the findings. Another way of understanding the findings is to say that people have the urges to be aggressive and far from learning aggression they learn to control aggression. When they see aggression by others (particularly if it is not punished), they feel free to be aggressive so they imitate the levels of aggression they have witnessed. This would mean that showing aggression does not cause the problem. There is therefore disagreement about the effects of showing aggression and some argue that it is therefore unacceptable to curtail the freedom of the media, others that such freedom should be curtailed in the hope that it might prevent violence by others, whether that is social learning or merely imitation. This is a complex issue and one with conflicting evidence on each side.

Figure 16.17 In Bandura's Bobo doll experiments, children who had witnessed an adult being verbally or physically abusive to the Bobo doll (as in the top row of photos) were more likely to be abusive themselves than children who had not witnessed the abusive behaviour
Source: okhanm/CC BY-SA 4.0

What is important here is that it suggests that through this and the other behavioural learning theories (such as classical and **operant learning**), it may be possible to retrain offenders to avoid certain unacceptable behaviours.

Each of these theories is, however, limited. They fail to take account of the individual and how their brain works, how they think. We will now move on to look at theories which take more account of the thought processes of human activities and which claim to better explain human behaviour.

Cognition

Cognition is very important as it adds understanding to the activities of humans. Cognition takes account of thought processes, experience, and all information coming to the person through their senses. It takes account of how the person identifies knowledge or learning, how they understand it and perceive it and then process it before deciding how to act. Cognition accepts that behaviour usually arises from the mind taking account of the complexity of everything a person has learnt and understands, it is the result of a thought process and a decision is made about how to act. The early learning theories are known as behavioural psychology and treat every learner the same, assuming that if you use the same techniques to prevent or encourage certain behaviour then every person will react the same way. So, behavioural psychology tends to assume that if someone is exposed to positive reinforcement it will encourage the behaviour they are participating in at the time. Whilst many people will be encouraged to repeat that behaviour, some will not and behavioural psychology does not explain this difference in learning and therefore difference in behaviour. Behavioural psychology does not take account of how an individual learns, the thought processes that go on inside the brain of the person who experiences the stimulus. Cognition assumes that learning is more complex, that in deciding whether or not to act a person generally takes account of many things.

Taking cognition into account is different from behavioural learning. Here we move to looking at how cognitive psychology teaches us that all aspects of, and processes of, the conscious mind are engaged in choices about how to behave. It is therefore necessary to interact with many aspects of learning (including, but not limited to, behavioural learning) to fully alter behaviour. The idea is that an informed learner is more likely to retain the positive activity because it becomes part of what is important to them. Here learning involves not only behaviours and skills but also attitudes and moral standing. Cognition requires a focus not just on external experiences as affecting behaviour but also the way in which each of us processes those experiences. It focuses on how we can alter the internal processes which affect behaviour

and thought. The idea of cognitive theorists is that morals and attitudes are learnt from others in the environment. They argue that one of the strongest protections against criminal behaviour is a moral standing that rejects such behaviour as unacceptable so that the person chooses not to offend. This is not just response learning. This requires an individual to understand, to give meaning to what they experience in the world. Here individuals learn about the physical world and the skills necessary to interact as well as learning meaning, attitude, and beliefs. It includes learning to: control impulsive desires and behaviours; develop powers of moral reasoning; solve interpersonal problems; respect others; take responsibility; and make rational choices about behaviour.

There are various aspects to cognitive decision-making. A person must learn to process information logically, what behaviour is expected of them in particular situations, how to resolve problems in a way that brings them the most benefit without disadvantaging others, as well as learning motor skills so that they can perform practical tasks. All of these are used when a person is deciding what to do in a particular situation. Added to these is moral reasoning; deciding what action is right in a particular situation. Moral reasoning is important because we all live in a community with other people and to do that it is essential that we live at peace with those around us. Living in harmony and, indeed, the importance of doing so, is something that is learnt, it is part of our moral psychology. Put simply and for our purposes, morality and higher cognitive thought underlies our decisions about how to act and what to do, it means that we think about what we ought, morally, as a citizen of a community, to do. One early researcher of cognitive science or moral psychology was Kohlberg (1958, 1963, 1981). Kohlberg set a basic question for children to answer:

> In Europe, a woman was near death from a special kind of cancer. There was one drug that the doctors thought might save her. It was a form of radium that a druggist in the same town had recently discovered. The drug was expensive to make, but the druggist was charging ten times what the drug cost him to make. He paid $200 for the radium and charged $2,000 for a small dose of the drug. The sick woman's husband, Heinz, went to everyone he knew to borrow the money, but he could only get together about $ 1,000 which is half of what it cost. He told the druggist that his wife was dying and asked him to sell it cheaper or let him pay later. But the druggist said: 'No, I discovered the drug and I'm going to make money from it.' So Heinz got desperate and broke into the man's store to steal the drug-for his wife. Should the husband have done that?
>
> (Kohlberg, 1963: 19)

Kohlberg was not interested in whether the children answered that Heinz should or should not have stolen the drug but rather in how they explained their answer. Through a series of questions, he found out the level of reasoning each child had met. He argued that there were six stages of moral development:

Level/stage	Type of answer given	Description
Level 1—Obedience linked to punishment.	Heinz was wrong to steal the drug because 'it's against the law' or 'it's bad to steal and he'll get punished'. Or He could steal the drug because 'he asked first and it's only small'.	Obedience brought about by punishment (how can I avoid punishment?). Assumes rules are set by the powerful and cannot be questioned.
Level 2—Self-interest, individualism and exchange.	Heinz, might think it's right to take the drug, the druggist would not. One boy said that Heinz might steal the drug if he wanted his wife to live, but that he doesn't have to if he wants to marry someone younger and better looking (Kohlberg, 1963: 24). Heinz was right to steal the drug because the druggist was unwilling to make a fair deal; he was 'trying to rip Heinz off'.	Interests shifts to rewards and the person seeks to ensure the best outcome for themselves. They weigh up consequences and assesses pros and cons from a selfish perspective (what is in it for me if I modify my behaviour?). They may also look at what is fair, a sort of fair deal.
Level 3—Conformity and good interpersonal relationships—interpersonal harmony.	Good motives and interpersonal feelings such as love, empathy, trust, and concern for others should lead the decision. 'Heinz was a good man for wanting to save her,' 'His intentions were good, that of saving the life of someone he loves.' The 'druggist' was selfish, greedy, and 'only interested in himself, not another life'.	The person tries to fulfil societal roles (good or bad). A person makes the effort to secure the approval of others and to maintain friendly relations with others (usually those they know or live in their local community). The individual ensures their behaviour accords with society—conformity (but to what standards—which social norms—which society?).
Level 4—Maintaining the social order—authority.	Heinz's motives were good, but they cannot condone the theft. What would happen if we all started breaking the laws whenever we felt we had a good reason?	Level 3 above works best in small groups (for example, family or friends). Here the concern is with broader society and the laws it expects one to obey and duties one should perform. Here there is a moral obligation to obey societal rules because they are just. There is an acceptance that law breaking is morally wrong because of an acceptance that harmony is necessary for the entire society. Here they obey rules because they accept them, they are necessary to ensure everyone's safety, people accept the moral authority of social order, they understand how it enables society to function more effectively.
Level 5—Social contract—mutual benefit.	People at this level would say that they would not generally condone law breaking because laws ought to be obeyed. However, they also recognise that the wife has a moral right to life. It is Heinz's duty to save his wife. The fact that her life is in danger is more important than other standards you might use to judge his action. Life is more important than property.	The person recognises and accepts the mutual benefit of certain rules. Laws become viewed as a social contract—democracy, compromise, etc. However, there is the beginnings of the understanding that the law is not always morally correct. So individuals question rules, tested against an inner idea of right. Some basic rights (such as the right to life) and democracy may be more important than the law.
Level 6—Universal ethical principles.	If each of the parties changed places or did not know who they were, it is likely that they would all agree that Heinz should take the drugs to save his wife.	This moves into the ability for abstract reasoning, recognition of universal ethical standards/principles. The idea is that morality and the right thing is sometimes more important than what might be beneficial to the individual or to others. This entertains the possibility of civil disobedience (principled conscience). It also recognises that some rights might be important even if in the individual case they lead to injustice, such as not being allowed to use evidence which is illegally obtained (for example, evidence of who committed a murder if the evidence came from an illegal search).

The higher the stage of development, the more moral the reasoning, and, in theory, the more likely others are to support the decisions made and how they drive one's actions. Moral reasoning is therefore one essential element of positive behaviour achieved through cognition. Very few people reach Kohlberg's level 6 but that is not necessary for living a prosocial life. One can be good and recognise and internalise justice, have a functioning internalised moral personality at lower levels. Also, Kohlberg's levels are not accepted by everyone though they do allow us to understand the basic building blocks of moral reasoning and thereby aid an understanding of one of the elements necessary for full cognition. The learning and moral development depends on how effectively a person is socialised through explaining why behaviours are acceptable or unacceptable, and through the cultural norms of their community, and learning the desire to please or appease rather than disappoint or anger other people.

The tenets of cognitive science are often used to try to alter the behaviour of offenders. Here it is necessary to use multimodal learning which teaches a person about various aspects of their behaviour. For example, it might teach them how and why to process information or to problem solve as well as teaching practical skills, social skills, and moral reasoning. If only one of these is taught, the learning might not be complete. Many aspects of probation or youth justice work use cognitive behavioural therapy (CBT) to address particular behaviours.

Cognition used to alter behaviour is based on a broader school of cognitive psychology. This makes it clear that learning, like any other part of brain processing, is complex and may affect each person differently. Cognitive psychology studies (or gets to know) an individual's mental processes such as their attention, language use, memory, emotion, perception, creativity, and problem-solving. It studies these processes and their effects on how people think, feel, and behave. It seeks to understand how things such as memory, attention, problem-solving, and language work. How do people process information? How do we remember things? Why does one person focus on one aspect of a story or an occurrence whereas another focuses on other aspects? Cognitive psychologists are therefore interested in the processes that occur from the time someone experiences something (a stimulus) until there is a response.

Cognitive psychology asks questions such as:

- How do different people perceive the world around them? How do they perceive colour or shapes? In criminology and criminal justice, we might want to understand how they perceive what they witness at a crime scene and why one eyewitness account may differ from another.

- Why do people remember some facts and not others? Why does one person remember faces better than another? Why do eyewitnesses remember different things even if they experience the same crime scene?

- Why do some people learn from a particular input and others do not? This is very important if a state wishes to alter or regulate behaviour.

Take a look at **What do you think? 16.4**. Once you have taken the tests, it should be clear that what is in the world

WHAT DO YOU THINK? 16.4

Do you believe that what you see is always accurate?

What we see and how we see it is complex. Take some of the tests below.

- Look at **Figure 16.18**, what do you see? Did you see faces or a vase?

- What do you see in **Figure 16.19**? Most people answer that they see a triangle and a square, but that is not correct. In fact, there is neither a square nor a triangle; your eyes see the potential for these shapes and your brain fills in the gaps.

- Which of the circles turns most quickly in **Figure 16.20**? None of them are turning—it's a still photograph. Your eyes see the shapes and your brain perceives movement where there is none.

Figure 16.18 Do you see faces or a vase?

Source: Gordon Johnson/Pixabay

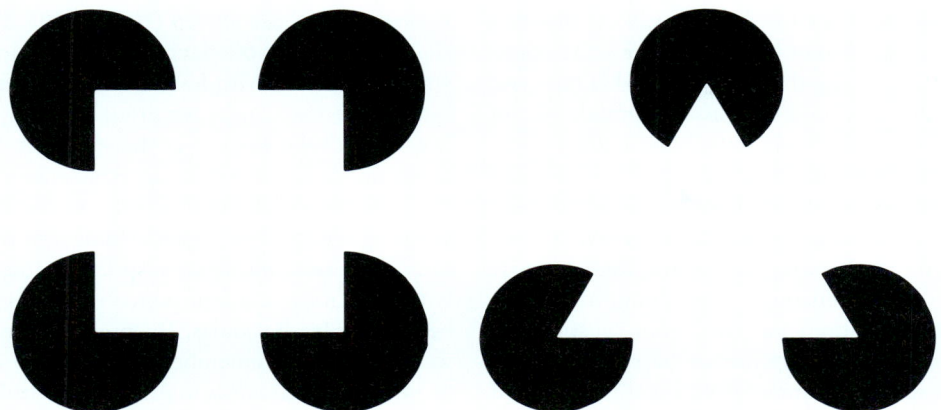

Figure 16.19 Do you see shapes, or gaps with potential for shapes?
Source: Public domain

Figure 16.20 Do you see these circles turning?
Source: Public domain

and what we *see* as being in the world may be different. Each of us selects, organises, interprets, and responds to information in the outside world. We do this very quickly and constantly and we organise the information we take in in such a way that it makes sense. For example, it seems to make more sense that there is a square and a triangle in **Figure 16.19** rather than various circles with segments cut out. We may also not see things which we do not know or understand. This happens particularly if we are watching a play, reading a story, or watching a film. We will tend to try to make the story fit what we know, so we will enhance things that make sense and might ignore or see as less important things which are difficult to understand or which we have been taught are less important (Bartlett,

1932; Ghosh and Gilboa, 2014). We also do that when we witness things in real life such as a crime. So, if two eyewitnesses give very different accounts of the same crime, they might both be telling 'the truth' about what they saw, however what they saw differs because our minds are not like a camera (Mack and Rock, 1998; Moore, 2001; Lleras et al., 2013). This has important implications for court cases which rely so heavily on witnesses telling 'the truth, the whole truth and nothing but the truth' and whilst they may be telling the truth it may not be everything because they may not 'see' and remember everything. Whilst this has important implications for the criminal justice system, we will not open this up further here (if you want to learn more, see, for example, Hollin, 2013; Pakes and Pakes, 2014; Webber, 2019). Here, we are not studying the giving of evidence but rather the way in which we learn and interpret the world, so we need to understand how our memory and our background affect that understanding. One person may learn from a particular input whilst another does not, one may understand and empathise with a victim whilst another may not, and sometimes it may be due to differences in what they have already learnt or understood (Bartlett, 1932; Ghosh and Gilboa, 2014). True cognition takes all of this into account and tailors the learning to fit the individual, to make sure that this person's previous background, culture, and other important aspects are taken into account so that they are fully able to understand and learn about a particular type of behaviour. The need for this learning of understanding and moral stance as well actions in trying to control behaviour explains why punishment alone often fails to alter behaviour.

Cognitive learning could influence some or all of the following behaviours relating to criminality or the absence of it: law-abiding attitudes and emotions; greater interactive or social skills; acceptable types of behaviour; acceptable reactions to certain stimuli which they may encounter; and life skills so they are more able to cope with everyday problems such as finding and keeping a job. The effectiveness of such learning depends on a number of factors, including the skill of the teacher and the willingness of the criminal to learn, also how far the learning takes account of the psychological processes and ways of thinking of the person who needs to learn new controls. Cognitive learning uses skills-based approaches to address problem-solving and social interaction while also challenging belief structures and attitudes. For real success, it is necessary for the individual's understanding and attitude to change not just the behaviour in relation to a particular response (see Vennard and Hedderman, 1998; Hollin, 1995). One of the problems with cognitive learning is that if it is not properly and fully effective, it may teach people how to avoid detection, make them more effective offenders, so great care needs to be taken with the use of CBT to ensure that attitude, values, and moral reasoning have also altered (Hollin, 1995, 2002). With serious offences, this often requires a lot of one-to-one work with a specialist. With less serious offences, group work can be effective. Cognitive group work is often used to teach those who drive over the speed limit or to reduce aggression in cases of lower level violence.

Cognitive psychology is very important to understanding how best to obtain reliable testimony from victims, witnesses, and from suspects or the accused. This is used in most modern police work but still needs to be adopted by the courts. The problems involved in how we perceive and remember things is also not explained to jurors and this may interfere with justice. Cognitive psychology and what it tells us about learning and behaviour is central to much rehabilitative work being done by probation and youth justice. CBT is routinely used to alter behaviour in the hope of teaching people to be more law abiding.

Learning theories: conclusion

Table 16.2 sets out a precis of learning theories, their core ideas, their application to human learning, and their relationship to criminology. From all of this, the impact of learning theories on criminology are clear: they can throw light both on why some people learn to offend and what we could do to counter that problem.

Behavioural learning, especially classical and operant learning, do not take account of how each person processes the information but they do lay out ways in which people learn which behaviours are acceptable and which are not. They also display human capacity to understand when and where particular behaviours may be appropriate as they are firmly linked to the environment in which the learning takes place. Clearly, cognitive learning goes further as it involves interacting with the attitudes, values, and moral reasoning of an individual in order to alter their behaviour not just in that environment but in all environments.

Learning, especially cognitive learning, involves learning not only the behaviours and skills but also attitudes and moral standing. Morals and attitudes are learnt from others in the environment. One of the strongest protections against criminal behaviour is a moral standing that rejects such behaviour as unacceptable so that the person chooses not to offend. From this, it is clear that learning theories have a powerful input to rehabilitation and make a positive contribution to the problem of criminality—to our understanding of how crime might be learnt and how society can alter that learning. It is important to recognise that this is not about treatment for offenders but rather about increasing their learning so that they can live in

	Closely associated with	Core of the idea	Application to human learning	Relationship to criminology
Classical conditioning.	Pavlov (1927)	Behaviours can be learned by association. In humans, this type of learning is often linked with strong emotions.	Here behaviour is shaped not just by the inner forces but by the environment.	Punishment is often used to teach people not to behave in certain ways.
Operant conditioning or operant learning	Skinner (1938)	Behaviours can be encouraged through positive reinforcement or discouraged through negative reinforcement.	It operates through rewards and punishments. There is often little detail as to how the conditioning works.	The techniques of positive and negative reinforcement and of positive and negative punishment are used to try to shape behaviour.
Social learning theory	Bandura (1961)	All human behaviour is learned rather than inherited.	He claimed that the learning happens through imitating and copying others.	Humans learn from each other so it is important to receive positive social inputs.
Cognitive science and cognition in decision-making (also the use of cognitive behavioural theory (CBT))	Most modern learning theorists	Cognition is very important as it adds understanding to the activities of humans. Cognitive learning is not just a response, it requires an individual to understand, to give meaning to what they experience in the world.	Learning the interactive skills as well as meaning, attitude, and beliefs all of which is necessary to social living. It includes learning to: control impulsive desires and behaviours; develop powers of moral reasoning; solve interpersonal problems; respect others; take responsibility; and make rational choices about behaviour.	An informed learner is more likely to retain the positive activity because it becomes part of what is important to them. Many aspects of probation or youth justice work use CBT to address particular behaviours.

Table 16.2 A precis of learning theories and their contribution to understanding criminal behaviour

Source: Pavlov, I. (1927) *Conditioned Reflexes*. Oxford: Oxford University Press; Skinner, B. (1938) *The Behaviour of Organisms*. New York: Appleton-Century-Crofts; and Bandura, A. et al. (1961) 'Transmission of Aggression through Imitation of Aggressive Models'. *Journal of Abnormal and Social Psychology* 63(3): 575–82

society without harming others. However, learning will not always be able to prevent future offending, to equip people to make more socially constructive (or less destructive) choices in the future.

If criminal behaviour and social behaviour are both learnt, then the earlier biological theories in this chapter suggesting that crime is innate or genetically passed from one generation to the next are questionable.

16.9 Conclusion

The aim of the chapter was to move away from theories that blame the offender for wrong choices and to look instead at those which consider at individual traits that might make a person more likely to offend; here we studied biological and psychological theories. Theorists who suggest biological and psychological theories today tend to accept that no single theory can ever explain all criminality (see **Chapter 21** for discussions of **integrated theories** of crime). No one theory is able to explain murder, speeding, insider dealing, and **cybercrime** or online fraud.

Therefore, modern biological and psychological positivists usually claim that the science is only a partial explanation; environment and societal situations also influence choices and behaviour. Biological or psychological explanations may influence behaviour, but they do not determine what is going to happen. For example, people who have an increased psychopathic (or sociopathic) element to their personalities are often associated with criminal or antisocial behaviour. They tend to be antisocial, lack empathy and remorse, lack respect for the social expectations and social controls (they do not feel so bound by the rules), and are impulsive. Whilst it is true that many offenders display these characteristics, so too do many of our top sports personalities or athletes and many of those who excel in business or in the financial markets. From this, it is clear that an individual with an enhanced psychopathic (sociopathic) aspect to their personality has a choice. The personality trait does not determine whether they become a chief executive or an offender. At best, the personality trait is a partial explanation, a background factor.

Our discussion in this section suggests that although the theories in this chapter are useful to our understanding of behaviour, they should be studied as part of a much broader explanation which will include social and other factors as well. Recognition of the fact that any theory is at best only a partial truth is good reason to be careful of any intervention in the life of an individual. It is reason not to use extreme treatments or extreme punishments as specific responses to any specific explanation of crime (see also in **Chapter 1** the discussion of the 'triad of criminology').

SUMMARY

After reading this chapter and working your way through its features you should now be able to:

- Recognise the contribution of both biology and psychology to our understanding of crime

Both biological and psychological theories of crime are grounded in positivism—crime results from physical, mental, or behavioural constructs and is not entirely the result of free will or human choice (although psychological factors can influence and interact with free will) so question the use of punishment.

Whilst both biological and psychological factors play some role in determining behaviour, including criminal behaviour, the extent of their effects is difficult to prove and exactly how their effects intervene to cause particular behaviours is far from understood. Because of this, neither biological nor psychological links to crime should be considered without also taking account of broader social and environmental factors.

- Understand the contribution early positivists such as Lombroso made to criminology

Lombroso collected data from many offenders and from this he suggested that certain facial and body characteristics were an indication of throwbacks to an earlier evolutionary stage, and were indicators that people were dangerous, less civilised, and likely to offend. From these and similar ideas, the eugenics movement arose which wanted to rid society of these dangerous people by either controlling their breeding or killing them to prevent their genes being passed on to future generations. The idea was to create a more positive, crime-free society. We now understand that Lombroso's theory (and others which claimed to discover a 'born criminal') were too simplistic and their ideas have been largely discredited (Rock, 2007). However, Lombroso remains important because of his use of scientific methods. Whilst the methodology he used was seriously flawed, his recognition of the importance of detailed data is still used today.

- Explain how brain structure is linked to behaviour

The central nervous system is made up of the brain and the spinal cord. The brain is a complex structure which sorts and retains information and makes decisions about how to act, etc. Different areas of the brain perform different functions. The areas which are most important in the study of criminology are the frontal lobe (thinking and behaviour and central to deciding how to behave), the parietal lobe (language), and the temporal lobe (feelings).

The way in which and the rate at which the brain develops affects our ability to process information. An underdeveloped or damaged brain impairs a person's ability to concentrate, control themselves, make rational decisions, understand the consequences of their actions, solve problems, feel empathy, sort and access information, and learn from previous experiences. Each of these might be one aspect which makes criminal behaviour more likely.

- Understand the extent of the evidence linking chemicals in the body to offending behaviour

Whilst there is evidence to suggest a link between testosterone (and many other substances) and unacceptable behaviour, this evidence does not generally prove a causal link. Explanations as to how or why the substances cause the change in behaviour are still often far from clear.

- Identify the nature and extent of the link between genetics and offending behaviour

The link between genetics and offending behaviour is not necessarily causative and the most that can be claimed is that in some people their genetic make-up may render them more likely to experience certain types of emotions which may be linked to criminal behaviour (but also to perfectly legal behaviours). From this, it is clear that there is no strong or direct link between genetics and criminal behaviour.

- Understand whether psychoanalysis helps to explain crime

Freud is the theorist most strongly linked to analytical psychology though others have added to it (for example, Carl Jung). Whilst Freud's theories are well known and have influenced many aspects of modern life, this does not make them true. The central concepts of psychoanalysis, such as the Id, Ego, and Superego, cannot be directly observed so their existence cannot be proved or disproved. Freud claims concepts exist because of particular external manifestations and then uses the constructs to explain behaviour. Even if psychoanalysis is correct, it does not help us to understand crime generally or help us to prevent crime, it is mainly of use at an individual level, to help 'treat' or alter the behaviour patterns of a single person (for discussion of Freud's work, see Kline, 1984).

- Explain whether, and if so how, personality impacts on criminal behaviour

For Eysenck, development of the personality depends on both a person's genetic make-up and the environment or social context in which they live, social factors. He claimed that three scales impact on learning capacity: the extroversion–introversion spectrum (E scale); the neurotic (unstable)–stable scale (N-scale); and the impulse control (P scale or psychotic scale). High scores impede social learning—a neurotic, psychotic extrovert (high N, high E, high P) is the least likely to learn societal norms and most likely to offend. He later split the extrovert scale into sociability and impulsiveness. Only impulsiveness is linked to criminal behaviour.

There is some support for his ideas (see McGurk and McDougall, 1981; Farrington, 1994). However, there is still controversy both about the extent to which these underlying personality traits are linked to delinquency and whether personality traits are genetic or learned as part of socialisation.

- Compare and contrast the various learning theories and consider which is most useful to reduce criminal behaviour

There are four main theories about learning: classical conditioning; operant conditioning; social learning; and cognition. Classical and operant conditioning are both associated with strong emotions and learning but use limited means to teach social norms so their success is limited. They ignore how people process information, why rules are chosen, and why they should be followed. Bandura explained social learning and emphasised the need for positive social inputs for a child to copy. Finally, cognition (used in CBT) embeds meanings, attitudes, morals, and beliefs as part of learning, which helps the learner to apply the rules to new situations. Learning theories help us understand why people offend and how we can counter or prevent that behaviour. It is important to note that learning theories put in doubt the idea that crime is innate, whether that is genetically passed on or the result of brain development, etc.

 Test your understanding of the chapter's key points by attempting the self-test questions on the **online resources** at www.oup.com/he/case2e

REVIEW QUESTIONS

1. Consider whether the evidence supports the idea that criminals and non-criminals are physically different.

2. If science proved that there was a physical, genetic, biochemical, or similar cause to crime, what policy implications would this give rise to? Take time to consider the ethical implications to any policy which might be implemented.

3. Does the history of biological and genetic links with crime teach us more about the dangers inherent in policy applications in this field than it does about the causes of criminal behaviour?

4. How, if at all, do extroversion, neuroticism, and psychoticism link to criminal behaviour? If there is any link, what use might be made of that information either to prevent offending or to deal with offenders?

5. If you want to reduce crime in a community, is it useful to teach the members of that community how to process information? Assuming it is useful, how might this be achieved?

 Access the **online resources** at www.oup.com/he/case2e to check your answers to the review questions.

FURTHER READING

Bernard, T. J., Snipes, J. B., and Gerould, A. L. (2015) *Vold's Theoretical Criminology* (7th edn). Oxford: Oxford University Press.
Chapter 4 considers how biological factors may alter behaviour and Chapter 6 discusses the link between offending behaviour and psychology.

Hollin, C. (1992) *Criminal Behaviour: A Psychological Approach to Explanation and Prevention.* London: Falmer Press.
Chapter 3 of this text discusses criminal behaviour in relation to biological aspects and the rest of the volume is of interest in its discussion of psychological aspects.

Hollin, C. R. (2013) *Psychology and crime: An introduction to criminological psychology* (2nd edn). London: Routledge.
Chapters 2, 3, 4, and 7 are all of interest when discussing psychology or learning and criminal behaviour.

Hopkins-Burke, R. (2018) *An Introduction to Criminological Theory.* Abingdon: Routledge.
Chapters 5 and 6 of this text provide a clear and accessible introduction to biological (Ch. 5) and psychological (Ch. 6) theories.

Newburn, T. (2009) *Key Readings in Criminology.* Abingdon: Willan Publishing.
For excerpts from original criminology texts and the key readings for the theories covered in this chapter relating to biological positivism and psychological positivism.

ANSWERS TO EXERCISES

WHAT DO YOU THINK? 16.3

- **Drug A = Tobacco:** This drug acts as a stimulant and is quite addictive but it is very harmful to the user. When you smoke tobacco, you inhale tar, nicotine, carbon monoxide, and other gases. Many smokers find it releases anxiety and helps them to concentrate.

However, it is harmful and each year in the UK about 120,000 people die prematurely through smoking related diseases (see Drugwise at www.drugwise.org.uk). Smoking is also harmful to other people. Passive smoking is believed to cause about 1 per cent of deaths worldwide (Laurance, J., 'Passive Smoking 'Causes 1 Per Cent of all World's Deaths', *The Independent*, 26 November 2010), with over 11,300 per year in the UK (Jamrozik, 2005). Cigarettes have caused many deaths through fires in people's homes. Dropped cigarette ends are thought to be responsible for fires that have led to mass deaths, including the Bradford City Football Club stadium fire in 1985, which killed 56 people and a fire in the King's Cross underground station in London in 1987, in which 31 people died.

- **Drug B = Alcohol:** Alcohol is a depressant drug (depressant means that it slows down the activity of the CNS). It can damages the heart, liver, brain, and other major organs. In 2017, in the UK there were 7,697 alcohol-specific deaths (death as a direct result of alcohol misuse), that is just over 12 for every 100,000 people (Office for National Statistics, 2018a). Alcohol Concern records that it is linked to crime in a number of ways (see www.alcoholconcern.org.uk):

  – Alcohol-related crime in the UK is estimated to cost between £8–13 billion per year.

  – In England and Wales in 2017/18, in 39 per cent of violent crimes the victims believed the offender to be under the influence (31), in 2016/17, 12.4 per cent of theft offences, 20.6 per cent of criminal damage, and 21.5 per cent of **hate crimes** were alcohol-related and in 35.8 per cent of sexual assault cases the offender was under the influence of alcohol (Office for National Statistics, 2018b).

  – There were 8,800 injuries due to drink-driving in the England and Wales in 2016 and 230 fatalities (Drink Driving Organisation, 2019). Alcohol has been related to harm more widely than this. Alcohol Concern estimates that alcohol-related harm costs England around £21 billion per year, with £3.5 billion to the NHS, £11 billion tackling alcohol-related crime, and £7.3 billion from lost work days and productivity costs. Alcohol-related deaths have increased every year since 1979; direct deaths are now 5,543 per year in the UK and those where alcohol is a factor are as many as 22,000 (Drugwise). Despite these figures, alcohol is part of the dominant culture, for example it is offered at many celebrations and parties. We demonise other substances (many of which are less harmful) and yet alcohol is promoted and advertised. Why is that?

- **Drug C = Caffeine:** Caffeine is found in chocolate, some soft drinks such as cola, tea, coffee, caffeine pills, and energy drinks. Caffeine is a stimulant drug (meaning it speeds up the CNS). It increases the heart rate and blood pressure, it can counter tiredness, and it increases brain activity. People who drink more than about six cups of coffee a day start to become dependent (they will have withdrawal symptoms if they stop drinking coffee), it can happen with as little as one cup a day (Studeville, G., 'Caffeine Addiction Is a Mental Disorder, Doctors Say', *National Geographic*, 19 January 2005). In large quantities, caffeine may make people irritable and it can cause headaches. Caffeine is a relatively harmless stimulant.

 Access the **online resources** to view a wealth of extra information relating to your study of criminology, including self-test questions, answers to review questions, and links to other resources that will help you enjoy and fulfil your potential within your studies.

www.oup.com/he/case2e

CHAPTER OUTLINE

17.1	Introduction	516
17.2	Sociological theories	517
17.3	Key concepts in sociology	518
17.4	Social process/interaction theories	523
17.5	Social structural theories: social strain and social disorganisation theories	527
17.6	Social structural theories: culture and subcultural theories	539
17.7	Conclusion	555

17

Sociological positivism

KEY ISSUES

After studying this chapter, you should be able to:

- recognise the contribution of sociology to the development of criminology as a subject in its own right;
- identify the main strands of sociological thinking and distinguish their differing contributions to criminology;
- appreciate the contribution of the Chicago School to the study of criminology;
- understand and critique the concepts of anomie and strain;
- understand differential association and understand how it might help to prevent offending;
- critically consider how subculture advances our understanding of offending behaviour;
- appreciate the complex relationship between social exclusion and criminal activity.

17.1 Introduction

In this book we have been looking at various theories of criminology to help us understand criminal behaviour. The theories studied so far have focused on individuals, their choices, and how their differences might impact on their likelihood to offend. In many of these chapters, the individual was seen as problematic, either because they made poor choices for which they needed to be punished or because there was something inherently wrong with them.

First, in **Chapter 15** we studied theories based on classical thinking; these theories assert that criminality is explained by the choices people make. From these theories come the ideas that if we can alter those choices, making people less likely to opt for criminal behaviour, we can reduce or eliminate crime. Classical theorists put this into action by devising fair criminal justice systems leading to **punishments** aimed at preventing people from gaining from criminal behaviour. For **neo-positivists**, a branch within classic **theory**, the outcome of this action often involved and continues to involve manipulating the environment to render it harder to successfully gain anything from criminal behaviour, therefore making it less likely that people will opt to offend (see the discussion of **situational crime prevention** in **section 15.4**).

Secondly, in **Chapter 16** we considered the ideas of early **positivists** and theories based on biological or psychological ideas. These theories study the individual and suggest that criminals are biologically or psychologically different from everyone else. They assume that if we could identify a difference between offenders and the rest of the population we could design a way to counter it. In most of these (biological and psychological) theories, the 'difference' identified is deemed **pathological**, a term denoting disease, either physical or mental. In this way, positivists assume that there is something wrong with offenders, claiming that there is something about the person which predetermines them to act in a criminal way. In early theories this was taken almost literally—so that there was a drive to rid societies of people with criminal characteristics; criminals were seen as less civilised or less evolved than other people (atavistic (ancestral) throwbacks); and it was thought that they should not be allowed to breed. Note that if this were true, then—as a consequence—punishment would be wrong as these offenders would not be in control of their actions. More recently, theorists have accepted that whilst these biological or psychological traits may make a person more likely to offend, they do not predetermine behaviour and lots of other factors are also involved.

In this chapter we will move away from explaining criminality in terms of the individual and instead will study how society or social processes might affect behaviour. We will be asking why there might be more known offenders in some geographical areas than in others and why more people from a certain background might become offenders than those from other backgrounds.

Whether a person turns to crime or chooses a law-abiding life may depend on decisions taken by government about economic issues or by companies about where to locate or how to operate. The choices made by governments and companies may open up law-abiding choices (removing the need for criminality) or close down law-abiding opportunities (making offending more likely). Decisions by governments and companies and sociological issues (such as poverty) affect individuals but may also affect whole communities; they may influence the likelihood of many people to choose to offend or be law abiding. Therefore, the health of the economy or the rate of unemployment, for example, may influence the behaviour of an entire population, not just one individual, and so may lead to a rise or fall in criminal behaviour.

Sociologists often study the underlying social conditions in which people may be more likely to choose to offend, such as if they lose their job. Sociologists are therefore suggesting that individual behaviour may be affected by broader social conditions or political decisions and lead to changes in crime rates. As with the biological and psychological theories we discussed in **Chapter 16**, many sociological theories are also positivist and suggest that the behaviour of each individual is, to an extent, predetermined. This means that offenders are at least partially (often almost wholly) directed by forces outside the control of the individual. For example, offenders have no control over the economy though it may cause them to become unemployed and that may propel them towards criminality.

Like the biological and psychological theories, sociological theories are not absolute—sociologists do not argue that everyone who loses their job will offend. Rather, they look for patterns and study factors (like losing a job) that may increase the likelihood of offending. What sociological theories most often suggest is that particular social or societal changes or factors may *influence* criminal behaviour. Here tangible and measurable aspects of society can be scientifically recorded and the information obtained can be used to understand criminal activity. If you go on to work in any field relating to criminology, it will be essential to understand how aspects of society can influence crime. Along with the other important theories we explore in this part, the sociological theories will help you to develop a strong understanding of crime and criminal behaviour. It may even help you to reduce crime. If we can identify which factors in society influence crime, and how they do so, it may be possible to alter those social factors and so decrease criminal behaviour.

Before we begin to consider some of these theories, we should remember that because crime encompasses many activities (graffiti, murder, burglary, blackmail, substance misuse, etc.) no single theory will ever be able to explain all crime. There are therefore many theories and it is important not to disregard the biological and psychological ideas (from **Chapter 16**) or to try to choose any single sociological theory to explain criminality.

We will first take a quick look at three types of sociological theory and give a very brief overview of what they are trying to do and trying to explain. This should help you to see links between the theories we discuss later. We will then take a step back from the theories to explore some key concepts in sociology; these are concepts that will pop up in many of the theories and it will really help your understanding of the theories if you grasp these first. We will then move on to the main part of the chapter in which we will explore the key sociological theories of crime.

17.2 Sociological theories

Think about what and who influences you to act in a particular way, for example which clothes you wear, what you do in your free time, or why you chose to study at university. You might think about how individuals close to you (your friends or family) impact on your decisions. Or maybe about what wider society expects and requires of you (to get a particular type of job, you might need a degree). For any choice you think about, there are likely to be a number of different sorts of influences from other people or society more broadly. Sociologists also look at these different sorts of influences and sociological theories are often split into three distinct types: social interaction or social process theories; social structural theories; and social conflict theories. We will briefly describe each of them here (see also **Figure 17.1**). Keep these distinctions in mind as you read through the theories later on in the chapter and consider how the theories fit into each of these categories (often they do not fit neatly or exactly within one or other of these), as well as how we might want to draw from theories in different categories to help us understand crime.

Social interaction theories

We will first look at social interaction theories (also known as social process theories). These are micro-sociological theories—they look at elements close to the individual and explain crime in terms of the immediate social situation an individual finds themselves in and how that impacts on choices and behaviours. Interaction theories focus on small groups and individuals and consider the way in which people behave and how they interact with each other, which then creates the groups and communities they live in. Any interaction between two or more people will be affected by the 'rules' or expectations that surround that interaction, for example each family will have slightly different boundaries and expectations, etc.

These may be affected by changes to the dynamics of the group, such as divorce, which might affect interactions of all members of that group in the future. They are called interaction theories because they accept that the choices made by an individual impact on their immediate social situation and on that of others around them, so affecting the micro-sociological environment in the immediate future. The effect is reciprocal in that the social situation around a person affects the way in which they behave and their behaviour, in turn, affects their social environment. Social interaction theories include differential association theories, social control theories, and labelling perspectives. We will discuss the first of these in this chapter and the other two theories in later chapters.

Social structural theories

Next, let us consider social structural theories, which are often referred to as structuralism. These are macro-sociological theories—they stress the impact of broad social conditions

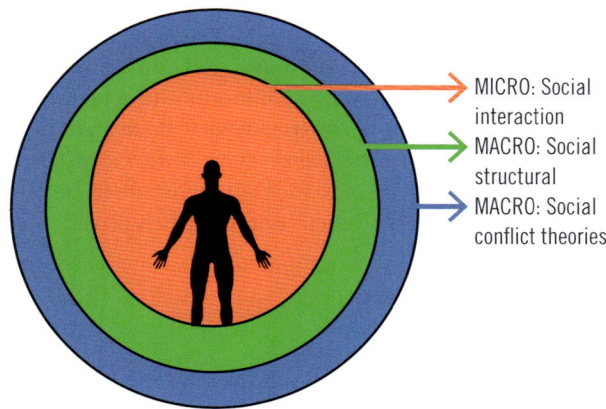

Figure 17.1 The relation between the individual and the three main sociological theories

(such as unemployment rates) on the behaviour of individuals. Structuralism looks at how society makes us what we are—they look at the way in which the structure of a society has an influence on our daily lives. These theories assert that the way in which the big social picture affects the individual's behaviour may have more of an effect than their immediate social situation (their home, upbringing, school, etc.). Social structural theories include social strain theories, **social disorganisation theories**, and **subcultural theories**. We will explore these theories in this chapter.

Social conflict theories

Lastly, let's consider **social conflict theories**. These are generally macro-sociological theories stressing the impact of the way in which societies are structured. Conflict theorists consider that those in power pass laws (including criminal laws) and use the legal system and other organs of the state (any parts of the executive, legislature, or judiciary of a state) to ensure both that they—the leaders—remain in power and at the top of society and that they also keep the powerless controlled and at the bottom of society. They argue that the poor, the disadvantaged (sometimes including women), and minorities, such as non-dominant racial groups, are more likely to be closely controlled, arrested, convicted, or imprisoned, simply because of their poverty, gender, or race. These theorists therefore study the distribution of power and of other goods in society and see these factors as associated with what behaviours we choose to control (and how we control them). The powerful (in a state or in any community) tend to define actions as criminal or deviant (and use the police and courts to control it) if they might interfere with their power. In a democracy, they also may control behaviours that others call on them to control (as long as doing so does not interfere with their basic interests), they capitulate in order to persuade people that they 'care'. Therefore they control (often through laws and use of police and the courts but sometimes also through ideas of deviance) the behaviours they see others participating in and which they feel they are less likely to participate in and any behaviour that may interfere with their power. For example, everyone recognises that loss of revenue through either tax evasion or benefit fraud is similar. Those who commit tax evasion often defraud the country of large amounts of money (tax revenue) and yet they are often permitted to repay the amount and no further action is taken, no criminal record arises. However, most of those who commit benefit fraud are prosecuted, punished, and even incarcerated despite the fact that their frauds are often for far smaller amounts.

The core of their argument is that societies revolve around relationships of conflict and domination where those in power use their authority to ensure that they retain control and that others, the powerless subjects, are carefully controlled. Their power may arise due to their class, gender, ethnicity, etc. or because they have money or knowledge but they use that power to shape society and control others in ways which are beneficial to them. These theorists therefore study the distribution of power and of other goods in society and see these factors as associated with what behaviours we choose to control (and how we control them), and with why some people choose to transgress. Social conflict theories are briefly referred to but not fully discussed in this chapter, they are linked to **Chapters 9, 10, and 20** and form the basis for **Chapters 18 and 19**.

17.3 Key concepts in sociology

Before we delve into the sociological theories and how they help us understand criminology, let's take a look at a few concepts which are always important to sociological study. Whilst different theorists may view them and weigh them up differently, these concepts are always significant in sociological discussions so it is important to understand them and to keep them in mind when considering sociological theories.

Status and role

How would you describe yourself to someone you don't know? You might mention things like your age and gender, that you are a student, or, depending on the context, that you are a particular person's child or a supporter of a particular football team. Sociologists would refer to each of these descriptions as your 'status'. Every person in a society inhabits various positions associated with a status. Status may be largely given or ascribed, for example gender, race, and age. Ascribed status is generally thought of as fixed though today gender has become a more fluid idea and individuals may question their ascribed gender. Also age, of course, alters each year but one cannot alter the year of one's birth. Status may also be earned (in that it arises due to something you do or affiliate with or are believed to do or affiliate with) and be more transient (temporary), such as class, professional status, or marriage status, which may change throughout a person's life. Being a student is an earned status, and so too is being a criminal in that it is a status others give you due to something which you do, or which you are believed to do by being convicted of an offence. It's helpful to recognise that some of the terms are being used in a slightly different way from their everyday use. For example, status is not necessarily high or low status.

In each society there are expectations which will be linked to each status and, even before we meet someone, their status will affect the way in which we view them. Each status will have a different meaning or connotation in different societies. For example, in some societies (especially Asian **cultures**) the elderly are respected and valued; in others (many western cultures) they are considered more of a burden or at least viewed in a more negative light (Giles et al., 2003). Similarly, status may be linked to roles; that is, actions which one is linked to such as being a civil servant, a learner driver, a person struggling with substance abuse, etc. Many of these roles are earned in that they arise due to something you do or affiliate with or are believed to do or affiliate with (for example, that you are a criminal, have been convicted of a crime) rather than ascribed (though people may be born into a particular role, such as a king), and bring with them certain expectations. Note that an individual who has 'earned' the status of criminal is often expected to continue offending and is treated accordingly (not trusted and often not able to get a job, etc.). This can happen even if they were innocent in the first place and so never 'earned' the status of criminal but, rather, were wrongly identified as such.

From knowing a person's role or status we expect certain things to follow and certain behaviours. So, we expect something different from a mother, a doctor, a teacher, a builder, etc., and if an individual acts outside their expected role/status then it can make us uncomfortable. To give an extreme example, you expect a lecturer to teach you but not to take your blood pressure whereas a doctor might be expected to take your blood pressure but not to lecture you. So if a shop assistant is helping customers find the goods they want and selling goods to customers then they are living up to the expectations placed on that role and, if they perform those functions well, they will be respected and thanked for their help. If that same shop assistant suddenly starts to shout at customers and berate them, they have moved outside their expected role and the customers and the company will react against them. Many sociological theories revolve around roles and statuses, how they are 'earned' or changed, and the meanings given to each.

Rules/norms

Social rules or **norms** are the standards by which people in a society are expected to live. Many are just types of behaviour which are expected or frowned upon. Some have existed for a long time, such as the expectation that it is not polite to pick your nose in public or that people are expected to wear clothes and cover their genitals in public. Others may be newer, such as the expectation that people should walk on the left (in the UK) in busy buildings. Some change frequently and come into and fall out of fashion. Some, often referred to as **social mores**, are taken more seriously; people may get angry if they are broken or some people in society might act negatively towards you if you breach them (a social sanction). For example, think about the attitudes that some societies have towards women who have many sexual partners; women who do this may be looked down upon or even excluded from parts of that society. Some social mores may even become criminal laws and will be enforced by the state through the use of sanctions if they are broken (see **Chapter 2**).

When setting criminal laws, a state should, ideally, consider the social mores of society in general, which may become difficult when there is disagreement about a particular issue. When criminal laws reflect most citizens' social mores (that is, their ideas about what is right and wrong), it follows that most people will obey the law and accept that those who break the law should be punished. But what about if the state makes a law that most people disagree with? In that case, people may protest or they may feel free to break that law, while still respecting other laws. An interesting example of this comes from the US. Between 1920 and 1933 the federal government in the US made it illegal to make, transport, import, or sell alcohol; this was known as prohibition (see **Figures 17.2** and **17.3**). It was not illegal to own or to consume alcohol and doctors could also prescribe it. Many people disagreed with this law and many broke it. Some people illegally made alcohol (known as 'moonshine'), others opened underground bars (known as 'speakeasies') or smuggled alcohol into the country. The manufacture, transportation, and selling of alcohol was taken over by crime rings and **organised crime** fed the desire for alcohol and made

Figure 17.2 If a state makes a law which goes against social mores—as was the case with prohibition in the US in the 1920s and 1930s—people may protest or feel free to break it

Source: Public domain

Figure 17.3 Although many Americans had to dispose of liquor during prohibition, a large number disagreed with the law and broke it
Source: Wikimedia commons

a lot of money from it. To avoid being detected, the gangsters often paid-off public servants (especially, though not only, the police) to turn a blind eye. Police were willing to be bribed to ignore breaches of this law because, like many other Americans, they thought the law was incorrect and should not be enforced. So this little-supported law helped to build organised crime and made the corruption of public servants a frequent occurrence. It helped to forge strong connections between organised crime and public officials, something which was very difficult to break and led officers to 'turn a blind eye' to practices they disagreed with (harmful crimes) because they were concerned their earlier corruption would be discovered. The prohibition of alcohol clearly caused many problems and, in 1933, the federal government transferred the power to decide issues concerning the sale of alcohol to individual states; it made laws about the sale of alcohol a local rather than a federal matter. Some states still control or prohibit alcohol, as demonstrated by **Figure 17.4**.

> The majority of Kentucky's 120 counties are still dry or partially dry, despite the state being home to some of the world's best-known liquor brands, such as Jim Beam and Maker's Mark bourbon.
>
> (Wheeler, B., 'The Slow Death of Prohibition', BBC News Washington, 21 March 2012)

However, some (especially large corporations) are now pushing for the laws concerning the making, distribution, and use of alcohol to move back into federal hands. In 2015, Wal-Mart (a multinational retail organisation) challenged the laws in Texas because they were not permitted to sell alcohol in their shops. In January 2020, Wal-Mart's claim failed but they are still hoping to get a full hearing of their case in Texas. Furthermore, Wal-Mart is using online sales to sell alcohol and is still lobbying for the laws on the sale of alcohol to be altered and for it to become a federal issue, this time to force states to adopt 'acceptable' alcohol retail legislation.

This is an example of an almost a 100-year battle over the content of the criminal law in respect of alcohol in the US. Similar discussions and disagreements over the content of the criminal law take place from time to time in all countries. The history of prohibition laws in the US demonstrates the importance of understanding the accepted standards or *mores* in a society before making criminal laws and being careful not to curtail people's freedom by passing criminal laws merely because a strong and vociferous group pushes for the change. Therefore whilst mores are important as guidance for people within a society, they should not always be used as the basis for a criminal law, it may be that alterations in the law which legalise or criminalise certain behaviours might be important for other reasons and may not follow the standards set by the people. For example, when homosexuality was legalised and again when same-sex marriages were made legal in the UK, many people were angry about the change to the law. However, there were not widespread protests and the legal change helped to break down the prejudice against the LGBT+ community. Therefore, whilst it is usually good for a government to ensure it follows general social mores in making its criminal laws, there may be important exceptions to this, times when one might move away from the expectations and use the law to lead social change.

Socialisation

Socialisation is another key concept in sociology—it refers to the way in which we all learn the norms and rules of our society, learn what is expected of us, and learn how to behave in order to live up to those expectations. Psychologists look at the mechanics of the process of socialisation (for example, reward and punishment). Sociologists look at *where* the learning happens. They study the sorts of things that are likely to be learnt in different environments. For sociologists, socialisation can take place anywhere but they tend to split the environments into types or levels—many argue that there are two levels at which socialisation occurs—informal and formal.

Informal socialisation takes place within less formal social units such as families, groups of friends, peer groups, or groups brought together by a single idea or value, for example religious groups or single-issue protest groups. In a family, children learn how to distinguish between right and wrong and how to behave. Family members help children to fit into the family and to the wider social groups that the family interacts with; ideally it teaches members how to live prosocially (positively, not breaking the norms of behaviour) within a society. However, some families or

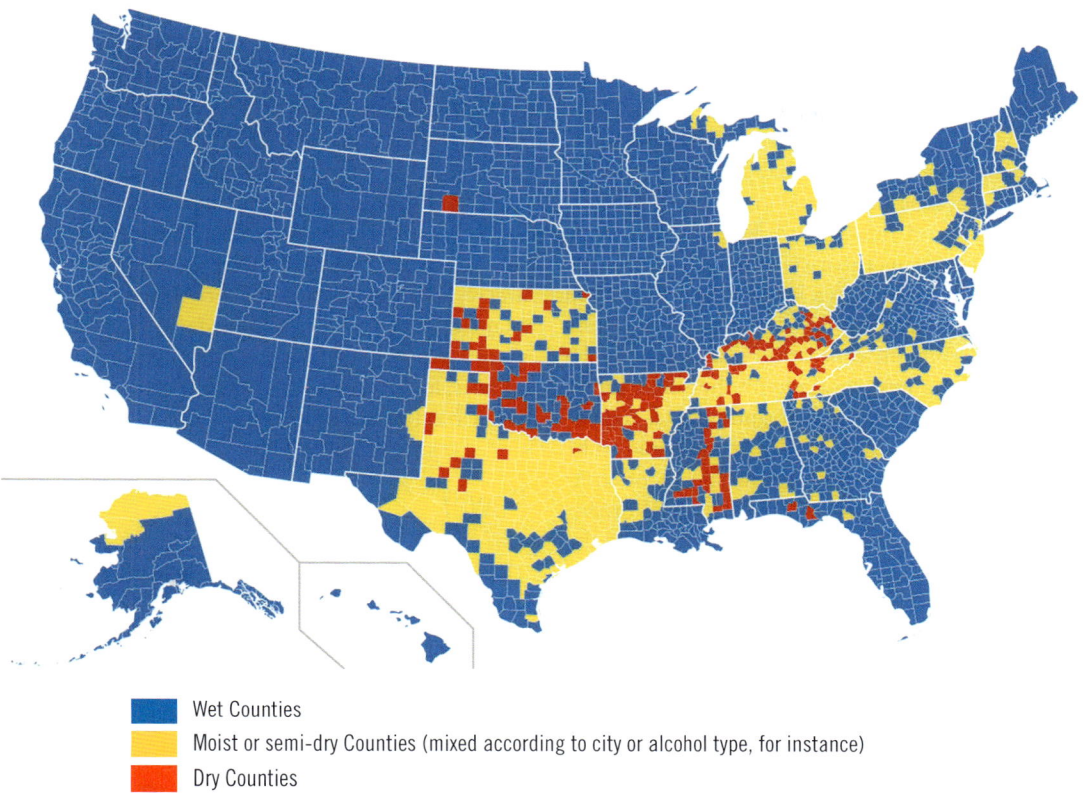

Figure 17.4 A snapshot of wet and dry America. In 'wet counties', alcohol can be sold legally. In 'dry counties', it is illegal to make or sell alcohol
Source: Wikimedia commons

groups may have different values from those of the wider society. The different values may arise in people from different cultural or religious backgrounds from those of the wider society or simply arise because they hold different moral standards which, while they do not breach the norms of the broader society, may be misunderstood by that wider society merely because they are different. These differences do not necessarily cause society major problems but the group may be discriminated against because of their different views, such as New Age travellers, or because they may challenge the views of the many, such as animal rights protesters. However, sometimes what starts as a minority or 'outsider' group may become accepted by wider society and become more mainstream, for example environmentalists. Other families or groups who participate in crime may have values that allow or encourage some types of criminal behaviour, they may teach values which permit certain forms of crime, which does cause problems for others in society.

Families and peer groups may transmit different expectations; the peer group may expect certain clothing to be worn and may expect some rule breaking, whereas the family may expect people to obey the criminal laws. Each of these will also influence the way in which their members think about certain laws. The family often helps the individual work out who they are, what their role or status is, and what is expected of them. These expectations may differ from those of the peer group which may encourage an individual to break out of their 'expected' status to build a different view of themselves, one which embraces different behaviours and may lead to different statuses being adopted.

Formal socialisation takes place within organisations such as schools and businesses. Every organisation tries to socialise people into their ways of working or operating but many also help socialise individuals into society. Again, there may be conflicts. For example, a corporation may socialise some of its employees into bending or breaking laws to advantage the company; these employees may be otherwise very conforming members of society but are socialised by the firm and its corporate expectations into different behaviours. Some of these behaviours may be illegal, others merely unacceptable. See, for example, the way that some multinational organisations are reported to have manipulated their company structures to avoid paying taxes (Barford, V. and Holt, G., 'Google, Amazon, Starbucks: The Rise of "Tax Shaming"', *BBC News Magazine*, 21 May 2013). The criminal justice agencies, on the other hand, will use sanctions and coercion to try to force or persuade people to abide by societal rules.

Conflict and consensus

Another key concept in sociology is the idea that we can see society in terms of either 'consensus' or 'conflict' and there are theorists which consider each of these ideas. Consensus theorists often believe that society is held together or 'works' because the people in that society share a set of key values and beliefs, and agree on the same norms or rules. Consensus theorists emphasise harmony, integration, and stability within a society. They also often view a core group of values as largely set and something that will be passed from one generation to another as each generation teaches the next to abide by the same values and rules. Here social order, stability, and social regulation are emphasised and social order is considered to be in the best interests of all members of the society or community. They are generally supportive of societal organisations and institutions, seeing them as working for the society, for the consensus. Whilst they recognise that no healthy society should be preserved for all time without change, they argue that any change should be incremental and follow an agreed direction for development. Any change should be based on and reflect the shared norms and values which are seen as fundamental. The main **consensus theory** we will be considering later in this chapter is Durkheim's functionalism (see also the discussion in **section 17.5**).

Conflict theorists, on the other hand, see society as being organised to benefit some groups over others. They were briefly discussed earlier in this chapter as one of the main sociological theories and will be further considered in **Chapter 18**. They argue that members of the favoured groups (for example, the rich and powerful) almost always thrive in the society or community and that they often thrive at the expense of other groups who may not enjoy such a comfortable existence. Members of favoured groups tend to help to set the values or make the rules and laws so they can ensure that their ideals and ways of life are protected at the expense of other people. In the eyes of conflict theorists, dominant groups and individuals have the control and power to decide how everyone lives their lives. These theorists believe that all societies are basically built on disagreement, conflict, and struggle but that the secret to hiding that fact is to convince or socialise everyone to believe that the society is to benefit everyone.

Traditionally, conflict theorists see the UK as a society in which certain social classes do better than others, but in which those in power spend considerable time convincing others (often referred to as the middle and lower classes) that the society is fair and designed to work best for everyone, including them. For example, some conflict theorists argue that education is designed to socialise the young into accepting the society as it is presently constructed, teaching them the morals and ethics necessary for their control so that they adopt the views of fairness and justice set up by the powerful in their society for their own benefit but which children are taught is to benefit everyone, including them. Conflict theorists argue that the basic institutions in a society (religion, education, government, law, media) help to maintain this unequal situation, keeping some groups in a privileged situation whilst others suffer or are less fortunate. The conflict theorists study the way in which conflicts of interest between certain groups are resolved to protect the privileged. Theories such as Marxism and those based on Marx's original ideas clearly depict this type of thought (see **Chapter 18**) as do racial (that is, focusing on race) or feminist critiques of society (see **Chapters 10** and **11**).

Power

The way in which power is distributed and what it means for a society is vital to many sociological theories. Power is key part of consensus and conflict theories, as we just saw, but is so integral to sociological explanations of crime that it deserves to be considered separately. In sociological terms, power is the ability to influence people's behaviour or to have the authority to set standards and rules to be followed by others. If you have power, it often means that you or your group manages to enjoy freedom to participate in activities of your choice, regardless of whether or not other groups approve, and even when others may suffer as a result. Power exists in many relationships or social interactions. Power in sociology often refers to major institutions or those who work in them such as legislators, police, judiciary, teachers, religious leaders, those who work in or on the media (today that is more diffuse due to the power of the internet), and social influencers (on the internet and in real life), etc. However, some also include other, smaller and less formal institutions such as the family.

Most effective uses of power are authorised, made legitimate, or at least appear to be authorised in democratic societies; however, sometimes power is forced or coercive, in authoritarian societies for example. Power can accrue (be built up) through many means. It may arise, for example, due to authority vested (power which is officially given to someone) through some accepted institution or organisation, through social class (often material wealth), through knowledge, through social status, or through charisma. However power is achieved, it permits one individual or group to control their own destiny but also often to shape the way in which others think and act in order to ensure the well-being of those in power (maybe also of others). Some, particularly conflict theorists, argue that the powerful shape society, or parts of it, to suit themselves or their group. As we discussed when looking at conflict theories, those in power may also try to manipulate others into believing the society is being run to serve the needs of the powerless, through education, the media, and employment.

Clearly, where one person or group has power, others are powerless and this means there are likely to be inequalities. Many conflicts in society are struggles over power because the authority a group or individual enjoys determines how effectively they can impose their wishes and values on others. Sociology has many theorists who study power (for example, Nash, 2010; Lynch and Michalowski, 2006; Galbraith, 1983; Foucault, 1975). It will become central in the study of radical theories in **Chapters 9 and 18** though you should search for it and be aware of it in discussion of all sociological theories. Many sociological theories fail to consider issues of power and fail to question decisions made by those in power, for example lawmakers or those applying the rules, such as the police, and assume that the decisions of these people are objective and justified. They fail to consider how these decisions might result in inequalities which can cause problems for those who lose out; they focus on explaining the actions of alleged perpetrators and do not take account of issues which may arise due to use or abuse of power. Therefore, a possible weakness of many sociological theories is that they do not question or consider the way in which power is used or why it is done and this may well be a weakness of these theories; it is often something worth exploring or considering when you are analysing a theory. Now we've considered some of the key parameters and concepts in terms of society's effect on criminal behaviour, we will spend the rest of this chapter considering some of the most important and influential sociological theories of crime. We will begin with those focused on the close social environment (micro-social theories) and then move on to those associated with broader sociological issues (macro-social theories, see **Figure 17.1** for a reminder).

17.4 Social process/interaction theories

Social process theories are micro-social theories. Remember from our discussion earlier in the chapter, micro-social theories focus on social interaction between individuals in a society. Rather than looking at broad social categories, they consider social factors in an individual's immediate social situation and how these impact on their behaviour generally, though we are interested in their research about criminal activity in particular. They study how individuals and groups interact; they might consider social interaction within a family or school to understand its impact on behaviour and how that behaviour impacts on the group or social setting. There are a number of these theories in this chapter and we will consider just one: **differential association**. In later chapters we will look at other examples of social interaction/process theories: **labelling perspectives** in **Chapter 18** and social control theory in **Chapter 21**.

Differential association

Edwin H. Sutherland (1883–1950) was an American sociologist and part of the **Chicago School of sociology and criminology** in the 1930s (see **section 17.5** for a discussion of this school of thought). Many of the Chicago School were concerned with explaining the physical distribution of crime, for example whether there is more crime in cities or villages. In comparison, Sutherland (1939a) was more interested in the social distribution of crime, particularly whether there is more crime in a particular social class. He argued that crime existed and was committed by people at all levels of society (1939a, 1939b).

He studied **white-collar crime**, that is offences which are committed by those in a position of responsibility and respectability (Sutherland, 1949); for example, if a rich company director, for his own benefit, used inside information he had learnt through his job to make personal dealings on the stock market thus ensuring he made a profit (the crime of insider dealing) this would be white-collar crime, but if the same person stole from his local supermarket it would not, it would merely be a wealthy person committing a crime. In his studies, Sutherland sometimes included activities which he felt 'ought' to be criminalised because they are as socially or individually damaging as other offences. He was interested in studying how people in upper or middle classes might turn to crime. He set out to demonstrate that they are affected by the same processes as are individuals from the working or lower classes. He considered the processes and interactions in the individual's immediate social situation and in particular looked at differential association. Before we go on to consider what this means, take a look at **What do you think? 17.1** for an example which introduces these ideas.

Sutherland's theory

Differential association is a learning theory (1939b: 4–8). Whereas some behaviours are natural—breathing or swallowing—and depend on biology, not all behaviours fall

WHAT DO YOU THINK? 17.1

Conforming to company expectations

Javed is a 45-year-old man who was brought up in a traditional middle-class home. He went to school where he fitted in well, achieved academic success, and never really got into any trouble. He studied law and business at university, achieving a high grade in his degree. Following graduation, he trained as a solicitor and also completed his accountancy examinations. He got a job working as a company lawyer for a multinational company called Moonpounds and did very well for himself. His clear understanding of both law and business allowed him to rise through the company ranks quite quickly. He also learnt very quickly the company mantra of 'keeping the customers happy whilst also ensuring large profits for shareholders'. He became director of law and finance at the age of 35 and has spent the last ten years shaping the company structure to ensure that the organisation globally makes the highest profits possible.

Do you think his background is likely to lead to criminality or deviant activity in any aspect of his life?

What if the company expects all its employees to be willing to stretch the rules so as to maximise profits? In this environment, he might lead a decision to structure the multinational company so as to avoid high taxes in certain countries. Whilst this may not be illegal, the company's customers in countries where it is avoiding taxation may see the activity as immoral, as breaching social expectations. Javed might be very surprised by the reaction to him. He clearly sees himself as law abiding and conforming. However, conforming too strictly to the company expectations may have led him to breach the expected standards of the broader society even if no laws have actually been broken.

What has led Javed into this position? Do you think he will continue to see himself as good and law abiding? If he does, do you think that he will accept that the avoidance of tax was immoral or is he likely to continue to look at the legality and see nothing wrong?

---

into this category. Sutherland argued that most behaviours are learned and therefore depend on the knowledge, skills, habits, and recognition of opportunities that result from experience. For example, whilst swallowing may be a natural process, what to swallow is something parents and others we are close to teach us; similarly, purchasing a ticket before travelling on a train is not a natural process, it is something society expects us to do and we are taught through social interactions. Sutherland argued that crime was no exception: it needed to be learnt. For Sutherland, criminal behaviour is normal learned behaviour and arises when someone is in an environment where it can be absorbed; it is learnt, like all other behaviours. Sutherland argued that crime is discovered through association with other people. Note that this is a sociological theory which discusses the social circumstances in which the behaviour might be learned but does not consider *how* the learning occurs (that would be a psychological learning theory).

There are two parts to Sutherland's theory. He argues that people, first, learn to imitate or replicate behaviours by learning the techniques to perform that behaviour and, secondly, learn the motives, rationalisations, values, and reasons for committing it (the reasons behind the crime). For Sutherland, this learning occurs through direct interaction between individuals; he thought that the media had less impact. Some individuals might come into direct contact with criminal activity but not learn or adopt that behaviour. Whether a person adopts the behaviour is dependent on the amount of contact they have with such behaviour compared with law-abiding behaviour and whether the individual's main contacts (or those they most admire) support that activity or not. Essentially, differential association suggests that a person will be more likely to take part in criminal activity if they spend a lot of time with people who support criminal activities and can teach them the skills and techniques necessary for criminal behaviour and that their learning will be stronger if they admire the person. That person will learn from a lot of sources (family, friends, school, etc.); some may support and teach criminal activity and others may support and teach prosocial activity, but the strongest (in terms of time, close association with, and admiration of) are the ones likely to be acted on. Basically Sutherland saw crime as the outcome of a learning process in which the person learns values, attitudes, motivation and motives, and techniques which support criminal activity of one sort or another. The idea is that an individual will choose crime if there are more learning experiences which are supportive of breaking the law than those which support law-abiding behaviour and that those law-breaking learning experiences come out of interactions with people who are admired or liked.

Sutherland's basic theory is often set out in nine propositions.

1. Criminal behaviour is learned.
2. The learning happens in interaction with other people.

3. Most learning of criminal behaviour occurs within close groupings.
4. The learning includes:
   (a) the techniques necessary to commit the crime (may be fairly simple);
   (b) the motives, drives, and attitudes necessary to the offending.
5. The direction of motives and drives (learned standards of behaviour) is learned from understanding the legal codes (rules of their community or society) as being favourable or unfavourable.
6. A person becomes delinquent because of an excess of definitions (more associations or stronger associations) favourable to violation of law over definitions unfavourable to violation of law.
7. Differential associations may vary in priority, frequency, duration, and intensity. People are more likely to offend if they are exposed first (*priority*), more *frequently*, for a longer time period (*duration*), and with greater *intensity* (the importance of the person or of the behaviour, attitude, or values) to law-violating than to law-abiding associations.
8. Learning criminal behaviour involves all the same mechanisms that are used to learn any other behaviour.
9. The needs and values expressed or satisfied through criminal behaviour often also explain or underlie law-abiding behaviour: therefore, those needs and values do not explain the behaviour.

Sutherland recognises that each direct contact a person has with someone else may be partially criminal and partially law abiding. He took account of the effects of both the behaviour and the attitudes and values others display and the effects these have on other people. Whilst people generally believe, for example, that those who kill should be punished, they may not want to punish those who take the life of someone who is dying in pain and who asks to be euthanised (mercy killing). Each of these is technically murder but many would take a different attitude to each behaviour and might pass on that way of thinking to others.

Every individual will be exposed to some criminal behaviours and attitudes and some law-abiding behaviours and attitudes, as well as many that are not clearly one or the other. These experiences will only lead to criminality if an individual admires, and has more personal contact with, people who support and participate in criminal behaviour than those who are law abiding. The learning is affected by the frequency, duration, and intensity of the definitions (associations) either for law-abiding or law-breaking behaviour. They are also affected by how early in a person's life (or their experience in a particular environment) the interaction occurs; the respect for the other person and how close their relationship is; as well as whether the behaviour resulted in positive or negative outcomes.

Sutherland: a critique

Differential association is based on the *assumption* that all behaviour, including criminal behaviour, is learned. To an extent, therefore, it is claiming that criminality is both a 'normal' and learned behaviour. This idea challenges two claims made in earlier chapters: that it is fully chosen (**Chapter 15**) or that something in the individual's pathology causes the criminality (**Chapter 16**).

First, the normality challenges the idea that the behaviour itself is necessarily unacceptable (even killing is sometimes condoned—mercy killing or killing in war). If the behaviour is intrinsically normal and merely made unacceptable in certain social situations, it then becomes necessary to consider why some behaviours are controlled and others are not (even though both behaviours may be equally harmful). Sutherland was interested in this as he noted that many practices carried out by the upper and middle classes, often whilst at work, were damaging but not criminalised (these might include insider dealing, fraud, embezzling, etc.). He suggested that the power structures were benefiting these privileged groups.

Secondly, claiming that behaviour is learnt undermines the idea that criminality is somehow biologically or psychologically predetermined. Remember, in sociological learning theories the way in which the learning occurs is not central, it is the context in which this happens that is of interest. The theory is therefore of great interest and importance as a counter to other ideas: it questions the often-claimed objectivity of the criminal law; and the idea that some people are predisposed to criminality. It allows one to move the focus from **street crime** to white-collar crime and to look at how and where the necessary elements for white-collar crime might be learnt, and therefore how they might be controlled or the behaviours curtailed.

Differential association cannot explain all crime but it is a very wide-ranging idea and it is true that a learning process is a factor in many behaviours. It has certainly been supported by some researchers; see, for example, McCarthy (1996). Clearly, being a theory based on learned behaviour it cannot explain how crimes first arose or how new forms of crime arise. Nor can it explain the crimes of those who offend despite never being subjected to direct interpersonal experiences of offending. It does not explain why some youths will learn offending or deviant behaviour from a peer group despite very strong and close interpersonal family relationships which are law abiding (or vice versa). Nor can it explain impulsive, opportunist, or angry behaviour committed on the spur of the moment, without any real thought or planning; these require different explanations (Nagtegaal and Rassin, 2004).

Despite these shortcomings, the idea of differential association certainly has some merit, at least to explain what types of offending a person may be involved in. However, it is not possible to test the theory because it is not possible to measure whether someone has more inputs favourable to criminality than to law-abiding behaviour. This is particularly difficult to evaluate given that it is not merely a matter of counting inputs but also of gauging how strongly they might affect an individual and why. It is also very difficult to test whether motives and values existed before a particular set of interactions or only arose as a result of those interactions. We might, for example, question whether someone becomes a member of a delinquent peer group because they want an outlet for their already existing delinquent tendencies or (as Sutherland argued) they become a member due to the need for friendship and, once a member, they *then* learn the deviant behaviours. Of course, for some individuals it may be the former and for others it may be the latter. Even if the individual joins a delinquent group because of their pre-existing delinquent tendencies, they may have learned those deviant tendencies in previous interactions. It is often very difficult to tease out the effect of any particular interaction on the behaviour of an individual. However, in more closed areas of interaction this may sometimes be possible.

Much of Sutherland's work focused on upper- and middle-class crime at work. His theories have been supported by other sociologists, for example Steven Box (1983), who agree that law-abiding people may learn criminality at work. Box and others argue that such behaviour, conflicting with societal expectations, seems nonsensical unless the offending behaviour, along with the reasons why it should be committed, are learnt at work. The behaviour may well not be fully considered criminal but just one of the 'realities of business', necessary in order to ensure the firm survives and prospers (Box, 1983; Bauman, 1994). The firm may even reward those who participate in such activities by promoting them so that the behaviour becomes considered respectable or necessary to an extent that it is not really condemned by either those working in the field or wider society (Slapper and Tombs, 1999; Croall, 2001). Complying with these workplace expectations is then understandable though still in breach of societal expectations (see the reaction to tax avoidance by large multinational corporations such as Google, Amazon, and Starbucks discussed in Campbell, P., 'Anger as Starbucks Boss Says: We may not pay UK tax for up to three years', *Daily Mail*, 1 December 2014). Therefore in areas of life which might be seen as somewhat separated from broader society—areas which set their own expectations for individuals—such different behaviour may be both understandable and explainable based on interactions within that environment.

What is more difficult to explain is that even where someone has the knowledge, values, and morals which would support criminality, they nonetheless spend most of their time in law-abiding behaviour. Even if within their working environment these people may be willing to and learn to breach a few rules, they are basically law abiding; Sutherland does not really address this underlying conforming existence. Sutherland's theory also fails to explain why two people from very similar backgrounds, with very similar interpersonal and learnt experiences may behave very differently. In addition, his theory ignores most individual aspects and assumes that all people learn in similar ways—as long they personally experience a behaviour and the values that support it, they will adopt it. Apart from a lack of respect for the person conducting the behaviour, little will interfere with the learning; if there are more facets supporting criminality than law-abiding behaviour, this will give rise to criminality. In reality, it is unlikely to be quite this simple but Sutherland allows no real room within his theory for **free will** or different personalities.

Despite these problems, some theorists have adopted part of Sutherland's theory in presenting their own (as we will see in **section 17.6** in the discussion on Cloward and Ohlin). Others have conducted **empirical** research which partially supports Sutherland's theory; for example, McCarthy (1996) found that differential association only partly explained criminal behaviour, and found that other important factors included lax supervision within the family, coming from a 'broken' home, and insecurity. What Sutherland's theory can help to explain is why some people who suffer these or other structural problems offend whilst others do not; only some will have been exposed to the learning necessary for them to offend. Others (such as Box, 1983 and Bauman, 1994) have used these or similar ideas to help to explain why someone who is law abiding in most aspects of their life may be willing to offend in one area; a very honourable and upstanding member of society may, for example, be willing to offend at work. It is not surprising that these are the conclusions we draw, given that this is the aspect of criminality which Sutherland started out trying to explain; white-collar offending especially by those who are basically law abiding (see **What do you think? 17.1** and the discussion associated with it).

We can see that Sutherland's theories have provided a foundation for some interesting methods to prevent re-offending. For example, **reintegrative shaming** is the idea of shaming the criminal act while supporting the offender as a person (Braithwaite, 1988; Fisse and Braithwaite, 1993). Law-abiding individuals who are important to the offender (perhaps particular friends or family members) can awaken the offender's guilt about their offending behaviour, whilst also supporting them to change to more law-abiding behaviour. Another example that we might see as being inspired by Sutherland's theories is mentoring services. By giving an offender a mentor it is hoped that the mentor's prosocial behaviour will have a positive impact and encourage the offender to conform in future. The mentor can guide the offender's values to help them adopt a conforming outlook and can be an example of how to behave and the benefits which might flow from conformity.

Others have tried to use social learning to support controlling practices such as media censorship (Magoon, 2010: Ch. 7; Cantor and Sheehan, 1996). They argue that the media can teach 'unacceptable' values and practices. The evidence often suggests an association between media and crime (Paik and Comstock, 1994) or even an influence (Murray, 1994) but it does not generally prove any causation (Brown, 1996; Freedman, 1994). However, Sutherland rejected the media as a tool through which people learnt, insisting that direct interpersonal connections were more important. This would call into question any media censorship on the basis that it might lead some to copy the values or actions seen on the screen. Of course, if someone is intending to offend, and has already learnt the values which would support offending, they may learn how to offend from watching the media, using it to pick up the mechanics of the activity. Furthermore, others who use Sutherland's basic ideas might well recognise the importance of the media, especially the internet, so the consideration of censorship might be important (Kiesbye, 2010; Calvert, 2001). However, before censorship is used people should be clear exactly why it is intended to be imposed and be realistic about whether these considerations are really likely to affect behaviour.

Overall, therefore, differential association and other **social learning theories** may be useful in altering future behaviour. It is important to remember that this theory, like other theories we will discuss in this chapter, does not mean individuals are not responsible for their offending—they are. What it does mean is that it may be more fruitful to spend time and money on altering future behaviour through mentoring, for example, rather than blaming wrong choices, seeking punishment, or claiming the behaviour is caused by something inherently 'wrong' with the individual and therefore trying to 'cure' them. Differential association calls for taught-behaviour patterns that will encourage positive behaviour and values and so lead to more conforming and socially beneficial decisions in the future.

17.5 Social structural theories: social strain and social disorganisation theories

We will now move on from our discussion of social interaction theories; in the rest of the chapter we will consider social structural theories. Social structural theories are much broader than the interaction or process theories. They are macro-sociological theories which, as we discussed earlier in the chapter, means that they focus on whether (and how) broad, societal issues such as poverty or unemployment might have an effect on our daily lives and on individual behaviour. These sorts of theories consider how the wider social picture affects both individual behaviour and shapes the more immediate, micro-social environment in which interpersonal interactions occur. Social structural theories include strain and disorganisation theories such as anomie, social strain theories, and social disorganisation theories, which we will discuss in this section, as well as cultural-based theories such as subcultural theories and social exclusion theories, which we will discuss in the final section of the chapter. Here we will start with Durkheim's work on functionalism and anomie.

Durkheim and functionalism

Emile Durkheim (1858–1917) (see **Figure 17.5**) was a French academic who trained as a biologist but is most famous as a sociologist, criminologist, and philosopher. He is thought of as one of the founders of modern social science and sociology. Durkheim's aim was to understand what made societies operate and keep their members integrated and cohesive. To achieve this, he observed societies and took particular care to gain an insight into social institutions such as the judicial system or the criminal justice system, to understand them and to understand how they helped preserve a society. Sociologists generally use the term social institutions to mean complex social groupings that can reproduce (and sometimes alter) themselves, for example governments, the family, legal systems, schools, hospitals, corporations, and similar systems. In contrast to Sutherland, Durkheim wasn't interested in explaining why an individual behaves in a particular way, but rather how society as

Figure 17.5 Emile Durkheim (1858–1917)
Source: Wikimedia commons

a whole can impact on and therefore possibly explain our behaviour. To do this, he studied rates of crime, suicide, and deviance in a society, compared rates in different societies, and sought to explain differences in terms of institutions, aspects of society, or social rules and regulations.

Durkheim was a structuralist, meaning that he argued that human behaviour and culture can best be understood by looking at the broader system or structure in which it is found, often unobservable elements which have observable consequences. He was also a consensus theorist (someone who is interested in maintaining the social order in society as they see it serves a positive purpose) who adopted a **functionalist** sociology approach. This is a sociological approach which sees society as a system of interconnected parts working together to ensure that the balance and equilibrium of a social group is not interfered with (it supports and promotes solidarity and stability). He used his scientific, biological background to help his understanding of societies, seeing them as organic structures; that is, a complex society in which each person relies on others within their society for the things they need. He studied various social institutions such as family, schools, universities, and the legal system, trying to find out what function each of these served. He wanted to understand how societies functioned and how they succeeded in curbing the most powerful needs and drives of the individuals who lived within them in order to allow people to live together in relative harmony. He viewed society as a delicate system whose separate parts (or institutions) worked together for the good of all its members. Here, according to his perspective, society was more than all the individuals who were a part of it. A society was important of and for itself and needed to be preserved, even if some of its members may be damaged, to achieve that goal. Its healthy survival would ultimately benefit the common good. Durkheim recognised that the healthy survival of society benefited everyone and argued that the function of institutions, practices, values, and norms (rules) should be to help to ensure society as a whole functions properly, for the good of all.

Durkheim argued that to understand a society, and especially to understand any phenomenon which happened within a society, it was necessary to understand both the cause which produced it and the function it fulfilled. Here, we can understand 'cause' in its normal meaning, but we need to take a closer look at what Durkheim meant by 'function'. Function, for Durkheim, includes all the objective consequences (of an aspect of society) which are capable of being observed (whether intended or not). If we take punishment as our example, the cause of punishment is generally something negative happening, a crime; but the function of punishment is more complex. At an individual level, punishment ensures the criminal does not gain from their crime and so it hopes that it will tend to deter that individual. However, more broadly, if someone is publicly punished it serves to maintain social order by deterring other people (so its effect will be broader and it may deter more than just the person being punished) and also showing the community that the original action is wrong so reinforcing shared values and beliefs basically helping to maintain 'social solidarity'. It is this broader function which particularly interested Durkheim. Crime is the element which triggers punishment and the positive effects of punishment—social solidarity and maintaining social order—are important to society, so crime is also functional and important to a healthy society.

Simple, ancient, and pre-industrial societies tend to be very close-knit. Their members share the same culture, religion, attitudes, and values so that each individual and the whole tend to think and act in similar ways and, as a result, Durkheim calls this social solidarity 'mechanical solidarity': in a mechanical society, because everyone accepts common values and beliefs, they internalise the same rules and so social solidarity can almost be taken for granted. Each member is similarly linked to all others by close obligations and responsibilities. In modern, more complex, societies each person serves a different function, there are many cultures, many religions, many attitudes. These cultures are held together by 'organic solidarity', by the realisation that people depend on each other and need to live harmoniously. In these complex societies, links between individuals and between one person and the social institutions are not obvious nor are they always strong; they have to be worked on. However, even in complex societies there are basic collective values and ideas (like democracy, human rights, the **rule of law**, etc.) which are agreed on and represent the collective consciousness. For Durkheim, this collective consciousness ties people together and is the basis of the social order. Institutions such as punishment serve to unite people and strengthen this social consciousness.

Durkheim makes two very important contributions to criminology: seeing crime as necessary to a healthy society; and his consideration of **anomie**, a dysfunctional society in which the rules have broken down. We will discuss these in two ideas in this section, starting with the idea of crime as being normal and healthy.

Crime as normal and healthy

Durkheim noted that crime and deviance exists in all societies. From this, he decided that they must be 'normal' aspects of a society. He argued that it would be impossible to have a society with no crime or deviance. All societies have some rules (criminal laws) and provide sanctions (punishments) if they are broken. These sanctions and rules would not be necessary if people did not naturally want to participate in those criminal activities. Furthermore, given that they are part of every society at all times, crime and deviance must, he argued, serve a positive function or a useful purpose. Therefore, he argues that a certain, fairly low, level of crime is normal and functional; necessary to the good order, health, and function of a society.

Durkheim cites two main reasons for believing that crime is a social good:

- first, crime attracts punishment and serves as the catalyst for an expression of collective indignation against the crime (or deviance) that has been committed and against the criminal/deviant who committed it. This collective moral outrage serves to build and strengthen the bonds between law-abiding members of society and so strengthens that society's solidarity;
- secondly, crime sometimes acts as a catalyst for social change, helping to display problems with the present rules and preparing people for the change, thus helping any change in rules to be accepted as part of the collective values and rules.

In recent years there has been an ongoing discussion around whether assisted suicide should be illegal (for a personal account, see Purdy with Paul (2010) and for a round-up of European laws, see 'Euthanasia: A Continent Divided', BBC News, 11 February 2009). A strict application of the criminal law would consider helping someone to die to be murder, but public opinion is slowly altering and many now believe this should not be illegal (see **Figure 17.6**), at least where the 'victim' is already either terminally or seriously ill and is explicitly asking to end their lives. The most recent poll conducted in 2019 by Populus for Dignity in Dying found that 84 per cent of the population support a change in the law. Today, in these circumstances, perpetrators are less likely to face murder charges than was the case in the past (Director of Public Prosecution, 2010, updated 2014). In the future it seems likely that assisted suicide (within particular carefully defined circumstances) may move from being murder to being legal, partly because many people are outraged that relatives and doctors face prosecutions when they help someone who is already very ill to achieve their desire to die (in the UK, there is already an understanding that such cases will not always be prosecuted (Director of Public Prosecution, 2010, updated 2014)). In these cases, bonds have been strengthened in sympathy for the perpetrators rather than in moral outrage at what they have done and

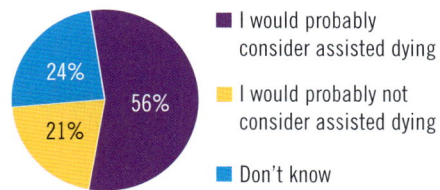

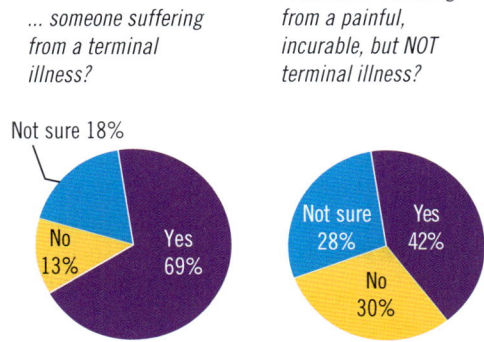

Figure 17.6 Public opinion is becoming more supportive of 'the right to die' (legalising assisted suicide), as shown in these YouGov figures (July 2014)

Source: YouGov, July 2014

the law is slowly following suit. In the case of *R (Purdy) v DPP* [2009] UKHL 45, the courts suggested that the rules on bringing a prosecution should be clarified. Following that case, the DPP set out a policy which suggests that if the 'victim' had voluntarily and clearly chosen to die and the 'suspect' acted compassionately, reluctantly, and did not do anything major, then the decision to prosecute would probably not be in the best interests of the public and a prosecution might not take place. However, no one can rely on this and anyone who assists a suicide takes a chance that they may be prosecuted. The courts cannot decriminalise assisted dying and, so far, have refused to alter the law any further (*Newby v Secretary of State for Justice* [2019] EWHC 3118 (Admin)). Only parliament can change the law and it is currently considering a private member's bill entitled the Assisted Dying Bill [HL] 2019–21 and a debate pack has been prepared (Rough and Sutherland, 2020). So whilst outrage at crime generally strengthens bonds and draws people together in moral outrage, where this ceases to be the case there is an impetus to change the law, to preserve the powerful social solidarity that moral outrage against crime provides. We can see in this example how Durkheim's analysis of the positive effects of crime are relevant today.

Durkheim notes that the need for this communal outrage is so strong that if a society existed in which there was no crime, they would instead describe some behaviour as unacceptable in order to produce the same moral outrage:

> Imagine a society of saints, a perfect cloister of exemplary individuals. Crimes, properly so called, will there be unknown, but faults which appear venial to the layman will create there the same scandal that the ordinary offense does in ordinary consciousness. If, then, this society has the power to judge and punish, it will define these acts as criminal and will treat them as such.
>
> (Durkheim 1895, from the edition edited —by Lukes, 2014: 100)

So in a religious society, such as a convent, there may be no real crimes but the members would find small transgressions which they can treat as unacceptable. They may be things such as being late for prayers which would be seen as deviance and those who are late may be shunned. The deviance would bring the others together to enjoy 'moral anger' and 'righteous indignation' which in turn allows them to develop a tighter bond of social solidarity. When something unacceptable happens in society people get together to talk about it, they gossip about how unacceptable it is and so the deviance or crime draws together those who are indignant and makes them feel good about themselves and each other, it encourages their feeling of being 'one of the good in society'.

Durkheim argues that societies need to have conformity and values and those values need to be backed by general agreement. It helps to build social solidarity if individuals in a society are reminded of the values and of their agreement to them. Crime gives rise to media reports and to prosecutions which are reported and which permit society to show all its members what will happen if they break the rules and serve to remind individuals of their agreement that certain behaviour is unacceptable and that they are rightly angry with the offender. Therefore, for Durkheim, the functional aspect of crime happens through the ritual or moral indignation provided by trials and punishment; these are essential to crime being seen as functional. In the past, this was done by public punishments (stocks and public hanging) while we now use local gossip, the media, and social media to publicise unacceptable behaviour and what is being done about it. Durkheim therefore found that a limited amount of crime is useful or functional for society in reinforcing its collective values and that a society would suffer if the crime rate was either too high (that would be destructive) or too low (some crime is needed to fuel the moral outrage). Here crime serves a function because it helps people feel that they have something in common and that they really belong to a particular group or a particular community; it supports social integration.

Others academics such as Albert Cohen (1966) and Kai Erikson (1966) have added to the positive functions of crime as identified by Durkheim and claim that deviance and crime:

- unite the broader society against the deviants (criminals) and promote solidarity around shared values;
- help societies locate their 'boundaries' through apprehending and punishing deviant and criminal individuals;
- help to define and point out the virtue in conformity and normality;
- can help to point out problems in society, things which may need to be changed (Cohen, 1966);
- provide jobs for many people as police officers, prison guards, **probation** officers, social workers, youth justice workers, workers in many charities, criminology lecturers, and researchers;
- clarify the rules and serve as a reason to remind people about the rules and why they are there (Cohen, 1966);
- act as a safety valve for societal pressures, when people are stressed or under strain they might find an outlet in criminality (Cohen, 1966); and
- act as an educating process (Erikson, 1971).

There are a number of very interesting examples of the application of Durkheim's functionalist theory. One by Kai Erikson (1966) applies these ideas to a historical setting. Erikson studied the Salem witch trials in colonial

Massachusetts (1692–3), distilling Durkheim's ideas down to three elements which he wanted to test: (1) all communities set their boundaries for acceptable behaviour through the process of punishing deviants; (2) rates of deviance remain fairly steady over time; and (3) each community has its own way of defining and dealing with deviants. He therefore studied the new settlers who were cut off from their old societies in Europe and were in the process of building new communities. These new communities needed new values which required building new bonds of social solidarity. He discovered that they were a fairly closed community with a powerful shared culture and strict religious and moral codes. He found some low-level crime and breaches of the strict moral code but little real crime. In this atmosphere, minor transgressions were focused on. When the behaviour of a few young girls fell into question and they faced exclusion from the group, they accused others in the community of bewitching them. The women they accused were tried, convicted of witchcraft, and punished. The trials were one way of expressing and displaying how important religion and strong moral codes were to the group. However, when the young women started to accuse others, including trusted elders in the community, their stories were no longer believed. At that point, the prosecution and punishment would serve no purpose, rather than uniting the community against transgressors it would destroy the community by undermining those intent on its protection.

The second example is more contemporary. Kingsley Davis (1971) analysed prostitution which he notes has existed in society through time; he wanted to discover whether this criminal activity could be seen as beneficial for the community. He notes that prostitution exists and has always existed despite it being almost universally criticised. He argues that it exists because it provides a positive function in society—the prostitutes (a small number of women) take care of the sexual needs of a lot of men, including those who are not physically attractive. Furthermore, he argues that by providing a safety valve for married men to enjoy what he referred to as their more perverted sexual appetites, it actually serves to support married life allowing it to be more harmonious, successful, and functional. He also suggests that the prostitutes benefit by earning more money than other employment might provide. From this, he suggested that the provision of sexual activities for money was functional and would always exist, though this (and indeed much of his argument), of course, is not universally accepted by others.

Consider these ideas further by looking at the questions raised in **What do you think? 17.2**.

Anomie

As we mentioned earlier, Durkheim's other key contribution to criminology is that he was one of the earliest theorists to write about anomie (see the 1933 and 1970 editions of his works). As a reminder of things discussed earlier in this chapter, anomie refers to the breakdown of social standards or controls. Remember (from when we discussed functionalism), simple societies are largely homogeneous and 'mechanical'; they are held together because each individual is similar to the others, therefore each has similar values, aims, and roles. In simple societies, law is used to ensure any areas of diversity fit together harmoniously and is generally not heavily used. With modern industrial, technological, and economic complexity, the interrelationships in any given society have become more complex and diverse resulting in largely 'organic societies' coming into being. Whilst there is still some overlap (some mechanical aspects), most individuals fulfil different roles. This means that each individual depends on the others to

WHAT DO YOU THINK? 17.2

What is functional?

Take a look at the following behaviours. Do you think any of them are functional? If so, explain how.

- Drug taking.
- Rioting.
- Being drunk and disorderly in a public place.

You need to consider the level of public support for the crimes you are being asked to consider. Do all sections of society support those actions being criminalised, if not do they divide rather than unite the society (are they functional or dysfunctional in Durkheimian terms)? In the case of rioting, does it depend on the 'cause' of the rioting; again, might it be supported in some parts of society and not in others? What about a peaceful protest that merely boils over? Should it be considered on a case-by-case basis, does it matter who offends or the reason for the action? Look at the previous discussion and then decide what factors should be considered in deciding whether the above actions are 'functional'?

support an aspect of their lives. Think about the number of different people you need to rely on in an average day:

- food producers so that you can eat;
- electricity suppliers so that you can use your devices;
- phone companies and internet service providers who help you stay connected;
- bus drivers to get you to university;
- lecturers to support your learning;
- parents, banks, and others to help pay for all of this;
- the police who make sure you can study in relative safety;
- the health service if you are sick;
- your friends and colleagues who help keep you happy.

Thinking about this should bring into focus the complexity of our society. It should be clear from this that many people perform many different functions to support each of us to live our lives. It is also true that each of those people may come from or have been influenced by slightly different aspects of the community and have learnt slightly different cultural norms; we are all different. Although we are more different from each other than was true in the past, we are also more interdependent so that we need greater social cohesion to ensure that we can rely on each other.

Durkheim viewed the change from largely 'mechanical' to largely 'organic' societies as inevitable and as positive, bringing greater freedom because individuals can enjoy goods produced by others. When this transformation is gradual, it is likely to lead to a healthy society. When it is too fast, the society might well become unhealthy. In an unhealthy society, the laws would be inadequate to regulate the diversity of the society and that society would collapse into anomie. One of the results of anomie is an excess of criminality. For Durkheim, if a society changed too quickly anomie was likely to arise. The change might arise out of a financial crisis that results in industrial conflict; an overly rigid class or other societal division which might lead the oppressed to rebel; and an abnormal division of labour which might well mean many would be unemployed and thereby alienated as feeling dysfunctional and not part of 'normal' society. For Durkheim, any major upheaval of this sort might give rise to anomie. For other writers, anomie is possible without these large economic and political upheavals.

Durkheim viewed anomie as a collapse of social solidarity, a state in which the fundamental bonds that generally unite individuals into a collective social order break down. He argued that this occurred when there was a major upheaval and people no longer felt regulated by the rules of a society; their desires and aspirations were no longer controlled by the social order. For Durkheim, a functioning society, in which individuals could be happy, had to control or set moral standards and reasonable expectations, that is, set out what people could reasonably be allowed to enjoy (set some things as being illegal) but also set out what people could reasonably expect to enjoy (a bricklayer could not reasonably expect to become king). Where these moral limits and expectations were absent, he argued that the situation was always miserable for a society and for all those within a society and brought with it unhealthy levels of ills such as suicide and crime. Like crime, he viewed suicide as a natural phenomenon and as generally functional—all societies have some suicide and this was to be expected. He particularly focused on suicide and explained it from four perspectives, set out in **Table 17.1**.

Whilst suicide is no longer looked on as deviant, his ideas are nonetheless useful. One can study Durkheim's **typology** of suicide and apply similar categorisations to those who offend. For example, an egoistic offender feels released to commit crimes for their own benefit even if they harm others; an altruistic offender may be one who offends for a cause such as an environmentalist; an anomic offender would be one who is convinced by something like the 'American dream'—anyone can achieve anything and one should aim high—if a person believes this but legal ways of succeeding are unavailable, then offending may result (see the discussion of Merton later in this section); and fatalistic offending may occur when a person feels that society has nothing to offer and may result in dropping out completely, for example becoming homeless or reliant on substances (legal or illegal). One might also look at his broader ideas to apply them to offending.

Anomie has a profound effect on criminality and deviance. Durkheim never clarified what level of crime and deviance would be functional for a society. However, too little crime and deviance was indicative of an over-regulated society which was too intolerant. On the other hand, too much crime was indicative of a society in which there was insufficient trust and people could not depend on each other so that social solidarity would collapse, the ties that bind people to conformity would be broken, and many would feel free to offend.

Durkheim therefore viewed anomie as existing when a society lacked norms (laws and rules) and common shared values. He argued that this occurred when there had been a profound and abrupt change, such as that resulting from the technical revolution, the breakdown of the modern state as a socialising force, or **globalisation**. Some, such as Bauman (2001), suggest that in the modern era there have been many changes and people are less unified and so feel released to offend. However, it might be argued that globalisation has given rise to stronger feelings of national identity and national unity, if this were the case then it might, in fact, deliver shared values and

Durkheim's types of suicide	Description	Examples	Type of social issue
Egoistic	The individual is insufficiently integrated into the social group. They feel alienated, separate.	Those with mental or physical illnesses or the bereaved who feel they are not supported by society and cannot continue.	Egoistic and altruistic suicides are connected to the level to which individuals are integrated into a society. Egoistic suicides are under-integrated.
Altruistic	Individuals who are overly integrated and who put the group or society before themselves, before their own well-being.	Here an individual may commit suicide out of a sense of duty to the group. Their action serves a greater good—social cohesion and the success of a community. Here the action is not selfish, it is altruistic. This might include actions we do not immediately consider to be suicides, such as heroism in war or someone who undertakes a seemingly impossible task for the benefit of the group. It would also include the actions of a suicide bomber who sacrifices themselves for the greater good of the group—to promote the political group.	Altruistic suicides are over-integrated.
Anomic	Suicides that occur due to an upheaval in society. Durkheim argued that: 'No living being can be happy or even exist unless his needs are sufficiently proportioned to his means' (*Suicide*, original 1897, reprinted, 1970: 246). Where the society is in a state of flux or upheaval, people lose their way, the society fails to regulate either what they could legitimately desire or how they could legitimately achieve it. In such a situation, some turn to crime, others to suicide. Here the increased suicides result from the sudden change in society which undermines the collective order and leads to high levels of uncertainty and unhappiness about what is going to happen.	For example, suicide rates often increase when there is an economic crisis such as the Wall Street crash in the 1920s and even the less catastrophic crash in 2008–9.	Anomic and fatalistic suicides are connected to levels of regulation and effective setting of social values and standards in a society. Anomic suicides result when the norms and values are lax or non-existent.
Fatalistic	Individuals who are heavily over-controlled feel they have no life. Durkheim did not discuss this type in depth.	This might include slaves.	Fatalistic suicides occur when individuals feel they have no individuality, no self.

Table 17.1 Although suicide is no longer considered deviant, Durkheim's typology for it contains some useful ideas that we can apply to those who offend

norms so helping to control crime. However, the new national identity is often fractured and may actually cause disunity—see the experience of Brexit in the UK and in Europe, it has not really served to unify the society, rather it has resulted in disunity. The effects of Brexit on offending have been unclear except that it has given rise to protests (some boil over into criminality) and to an increase in racial hatred. Over the modern era, there have been a number of instances of crime increases during periods of recession and unemployment and these might be seen as upheavals sufficient to lead to anomie and therefore increased criminality and increased suicides. If Durkheim is right, then to prevent these we need to strengthen social controls and strengthen people's commitment to shared values. But the example of Brexit shows that the shared values need to embrace all aspects, cultures, and religions in our complex, modern multicultural societies.

Durkheim: critique

Durkheim powerfully questions the blaming of individuals for criminality. He shows clearly how individual behaviour is affected by social forces and might, in turn, affect those forces. However, there are weaknesses in his approach.

Durkheim is not explicit about what is necessary, he suggests many functions but none of these is essential. Therefore, whilst his ideas may help us understand some fundamental aspect of our society and certainly provide information and ammunition to question other theories, they also leave too many questions unanswered. Running through Durkheim's work is a recurring ambiguity as to exactly what needs to be done to build a harmonious society. How much crime is healthy and how do we know? Does society deliberately create deviance and crime to ensure its members bond to the culture? Is deviance necessary before we can say that a society exists and functions? Are some crimes and acts of deviance so destructive as to be unhealthy and, if so, which are they?

Authors such as Erikson (1966) and Davis (1971) have applied some of Durkheim's ideas to real-life situations, however the ideas are generally too vague and ambiguous to be carefully validated and tested. It is unclear how much crime is functional or when a society is in anomie or enjoys healthy social bonds. There are too many unanswered questions for this to be the only explanation of criminality.

Merton and strain

The American sociologist and criminologist Robert K. Merton (1910–2003) borrows and develops some of Durkheim's ideas to build a **strain theory** built on his own concept of anomie. Like Durkheim's, his theory is macro-sociological, explaining crime in terms of social structural issues.

Merton's theory

Merton sought to explain the crime problem in the US in the 1930s and 1940s when crime rates were increasing very quickly. As with Durkheim's theory, Merton puts anomie at the centre of his explanation. However, anomie as described by Merton is rather different. For Durkheim, in a healthy society the moral norms regulate the individual's *desires*—each person knows what they can legitimately expect and accepts their place in society. However, for Merton, the norms regulate *the means* of achieving an individual's desires (or as Merton called them, an individual's goals). For Merton, it doesn't matter if the goals of a society are limitless as long as most of its members only or largely use legitimate means to achieve those goals (the idea that 'it's not winning that matters, but how you play the game'). For Merton, the society only becomes anomic if its members use illegitimate means to achieve their goals (if people think 'it is winning that matters, not how you play the game'): it is the relationship between desires and the means of achieving those desires which is fundamental (Merton, 1938, 1949). Therefore, for Merton there is no need for social upheaval to occur for a society to be anomic. Rather, anomie arises when people's desires, which they honestly feel they should be able to attain, go beyond what they could possibly achieve through legitimate means. For Merton, there are two parts to take into account to decide whether a society is anomic.

1. The culturally defined goals of a society—the things which the whole or most people in a society value. These are elements that the society considers it is important for all its members to achieve or enjoy. For some in the UK, it might include a good education, to get a good job and a certain standard of living, perhaps by owning a house. For others, it might include the enjoyment of rights such as the right to religion, freedom of thought, free expression, privacy, liberty, or security.

2. The institutional means by which the goals can be achieved. For example, it might be ensuring good educational opportunities for everyone or a legal and political system which guarantees rights are enjoyed.

His theory is therefore about means and ends. For Merton, anomie occurs, or a state is anomic, where there is a mismatch between these two concepts, where the generally accepted goals (or ends) cannot be achieved through the legitimate means available to individuals. Where the society encourages individuals to achieve goals which are not attainable by legitimate means, the society is anomic and individuals will be under strain to achieve or deal with the conflict in other ways. This may occur if people are led to believe that they deserve a lot, for example that they deserve the 'American dream' (that everyone is capable of succeeding and becoming wealthy) but there is no way for most people to achieve that. If, for example, the educational and employment systems are biased and discriminate against certain groups or it is unlikely that many will actually achieve the 'American dream', there may be discontent. Some people start further up the ladder, already enjoying better lives and having enhanced opportunities; others will start lower down, with few opportunities and may even be discriminated against (so climbing the ladder with one hand tied behind their back, so to speak). These latter groups and individuals will feel unfairly deprived relative to others in the society. In that situation, these deprived groups may be dissatisfied and feel disaffected, which might lead them to feeling no longer bound by the rules and therefore feeling and so being free to break them. If this happens, these individuals and groups are in a state of normlessness or anomie. Merton used this to explain the higher rates of criminality of the lower classes in the criminal statistics: for these groups criminality was a 'normal' and rational response to their situation. However, he suggested that people in these anomic groups might respond in various ways. There are five ways they might respond, as illustrated in **Table 17.2**.

For Merton, fundamental flaws in a society arise if the goals and means are not realistic; if they are not in accord with each other. His theory depends, therefore, on there being a 'strain' between what people want and what they can achieve; it is thought of as a social strain theory even though Merton himself did not accept that analysis of his theory (Cullen and Messner, 2007). Merton argued that a healthy society emphasises and rewards conformity, whereas an anomic society emphasises reaching the goals by any means. If *how* the goal is achieved is unimportant, problems arise. So if being wealthy brings with it power, social status, and prestige, even if the wealth is achieved through drug dealing or bank robbery (or no one asks how it is achieved), then there are problems.

Merton, like Sutherland (see the discussion of differential association in **section 17.4**), argues that all people are basically trying to achieve similar goals but may choose different ways of achieving them, not because they learn different ways of achieving success (as suggested by Sutherland) but rather because of strain due to blocked opportunity.

Merton: critique

Merton's ideas may be useful in explaining lower class crime and, if the **official statistics** were a true reflection of crime, the ideas might be useful. However, Merton only really explains acquisitive crime committed by those who feel relatively deprived through social structural problems. He fails to explain crimes committed by middle- and upper-class groups or crimes which have no basis in the means/end dichotomy. In a more recent interview, however, Merton stated that he intended for the theory to apply more widely (Cullen and Messner, 2007); and elsewhere he did apply it to aspects of white-collar crime (Merton, 1957). However, the criticism still holds true: generally the theory is not useful on a wider scale, even if he did intend for it to apply more broadly. Furthermore, even for acquisitive crime in the lower classes, Merton relies too heavily on statistics which do not take account of how crime control agencies operate. The statistics on

Type of response	Culturally prescribed goals	Institutionally available means
Conformity	Accept the goals.	Acceptance of the legitimate means of achieving them.
Innovation	Accept the goals.	Rejection of societal means and substitution of new means. Instead of getting a job, an individual might turn to crime to make money.
Ritualism	Rejects the goals because of an awareness that they can't be achieved. These individuals just accept that limitation.	Acceptance of the legitimate means of achieving the ends. Work hard but with no real aspiration.
Retreatism	Rejects the goals, drops out of the usual intentions and aspirations.	Rejection of the accepted societal means of achieving the accepted goals. In fact, these individuals generally reject almost everything about the society but are not destructive of the society, they tend to drop out of society and give everything up (many homeless people fall into this category, they may feel hopeless and become dependent on alcohol or drugs and then become vagrant).
Rebellion	Rejection of societal goals and substitution of new goals.	Rejection of societal means and substitution of new means. These individuals physically live in the society but do not accept anything to do with the society and suggest an alternative way of living, for example New Age travellers or those who embrace 'van life'. In some cases, they may turn against the society and try to substitute their own ideas—they might even use violence to force their interests.

Table 17.2 Responses to anomie

Source: Merton, R. (1938) 'Social Structure and Anomie'. American Sociological Review 3(5): 672–82) and Merton, R. (1949) Social Theory and Social Structure. New York: Free Press

which Merton relied are therefore disputed and this places his theory into question.

Moreover, Merton does not fully explain what causes the strain and his theory of structural strain fails to locate a causative link between the strain and the type of action (meaning that it does not prove that the strain causes the type of action). Is the strain different for the rebel than for the innovator and, if so, is that what explains the different reactions? Furthermore, it is not clear what is cause and what effect (think back to our discussion of cause and effect in the previous chapter). Does rebellion cause the social strain or does the social strain cause the rebellion and how does the causation work in practice?

Like Durkheim, Merton accepts society as it is and merely tries to explain the crime levels. He does not question why society is constructed the way it is. He does not even really criticise the inequalities and why social disparities exist. There is no critique of the political or social systems that lead to this situation or that allow it to continue.

The Chicago School: social disorganisation

The Chicago School is an example of another social structural theory. The Chicago School was a group of sociologists who studied various aspects of life in Chicago at a time when the city was undergoing considerable economic, industrial, and demographic changes. Their work is often referred to as social ecology because they studied how the city changed and developed over time and how each area had its own characteristics. They conducted a systematic analysis of the geographic distribution of the rates of various factors such as infant mortality, illness, adult crime, and juvenile delinquency (youth crime and youthful actions which are unacceptable but may fall short of criminal). They mapped the rates for each factor in each area and searched for statistical correlations between these and specific characteristics of the areas. Alongside this, they conducted **ethnographic** work, learning about people's everyday lives. They studied these elements because:

> it is assumed that people living in natural areas of the same type and subject to the same social conditions will display, on the whole, the same characteristics.
>
> (Park, 1929: 36)

Social disorganisation theories

Robert Ezra Park (1864–1944), an American sociologist, and Ernest Burgess (1886–1966), a Canadian–American urban sociologist who was part of the Chicago School, studied what they referred to as 'natural areas' which they described as geographical areas which were physically very similar and whose inhabitants shared certain social and cultural features. They argued that these 'natural' areas had distinct physical boundaries such that you would be aware when moving out of one area into another. Building on this, they developed one of the Chicago School's most famous ideas, the zonal theory. In this, they split the city into concentric circles and argued that each of the zones represented a distinct type of 'natural' area (see **Figure 17.7**).

In the centre was the business district made up of high-value properties mainly used for commercial and economic transactions. This zone had very few residents. The next zone was the transitional zone, so called because its inhabitants were moving through and constantly changing. This zone had a large population living in crowded and inadequate accommodation; properties were run-down and in need of repair. The residents were poor, often immigrants. Outside this were zones 3, 4, and 5. These were all largely residential areas whose inhabitants became more affluent as you moved out from the centre: poor working families lived in zone 3; the better off working classes and middle classes in zone 4; and the affluent in zone 5. The population in zone 2 tried to move on as quickly as possible and, in the early 20th century, altered from being largely new immigrants from Northern Europe to being new immigrants from Southern Europe and then predominantly African Americans. These populations were transient and, as soon as they were able to, they moved into zone 3 to more stable accommodation paid for from a more stable income. You might recognise the idea of distinctive areas from cities you know although, as we will come to see, it is likely to be a lot more complex than the concentric circles idea.

One of the most famous pieces of criminological work conducted by the School was carried out by Clifford Shaw (1922–91) and Henry McKay (1899–1980) who studied the way in which juvenile delinquency rates were distributed (Shaw and McKay, 1942). Juvenile delinquency includes young people who commit crimes but also those whose actions are unacceptable but may fall short of being criminal (occasionally it may also embrace those who support but do not participate in wrongful activities). They conducted their study in three different time periods: 1900–6, 1917–23, and 1927–33. They were particularly interested in whether there was a causal correlation between the way in which different neighbourhoods were socially organised and their rates of delinquency, wanting to know whether the delinquency was caused by a breakdown in social integration. They thus developed the social disorganisation theory, building on the zonal theory to explain delinquency (they split the city into different zones, each zone denoted a type of neighbourhood, see **Figure 17.7**). It is important here to recognise that the Chicago School never claimed that the physical elements

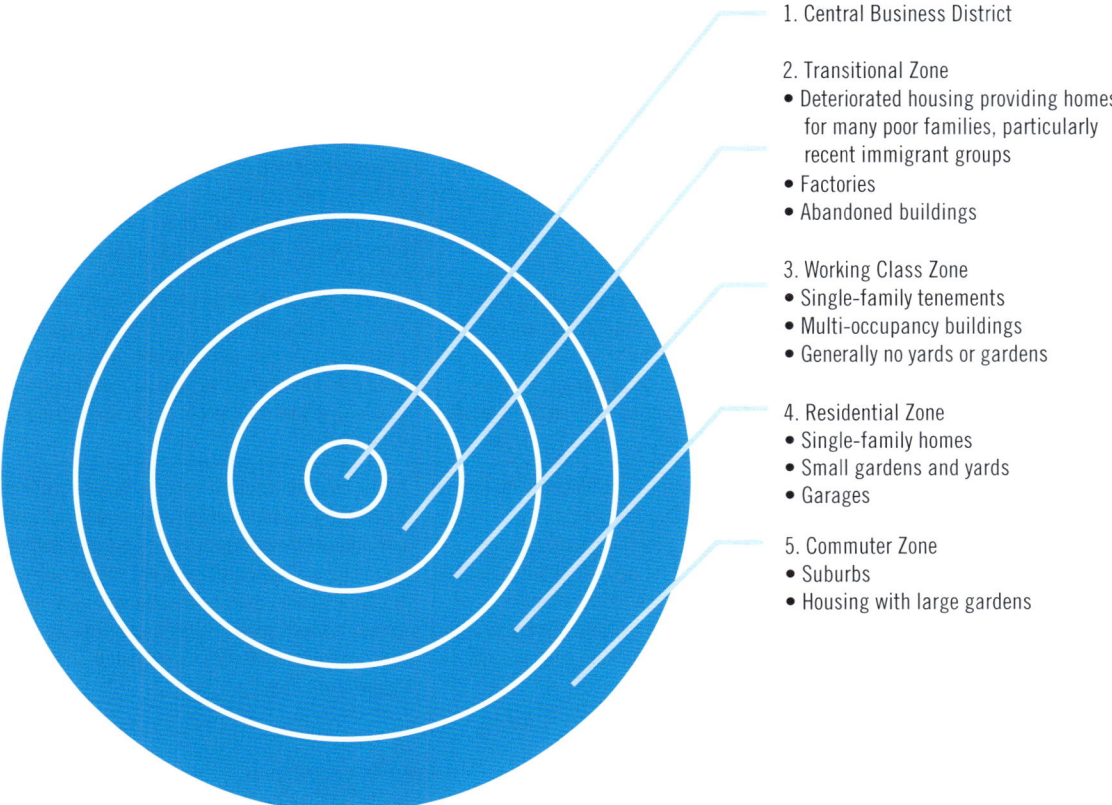

Figure 17.7 The concentric zone model splits a city into different zones, each denoting a type of neighbourhood, and attempts to use this theory to explain delinquency

of an area caused the behaviour of the inhabitants. Rather, the claim is that these physical manifestations are an outward illustration of the type of community living within the area and it is therefore the social communities, their levels of organisation, cultural features, and how rules and values are accepted within the communities which cause these manifestations. Healthy natural areas or communities were socially cohesive, with their own values and social order. However, others were not socially cohesive, divided on ethical, racial, cultural, religious, intergenerational, or political grounds. These communities were fragmented and dysfunctional. Shaw and McKay were interested in levels of social organisation and their link to negative outcomes such as crime and deviance, as illustrated by **Table 17.3**.

Shaw and McKay discovered that the highest rates of delinquency could be found in zone 2 and that these rates decreased as you moved out through zones 3 and 4 to zone 5. The highest rates of delinquency were found closest to industrial or commercial areas. This pattern of delinquency rates mapped onto the rates for social disorganisation so zone 2 had very high social disorganisation (low social organisation) whereas zone 5 had high levels of social organisation. They also discovered that the same areas that had high rates of delinquency also suffered from other negative social factors, such as high levels of mental and physical illness, high infant mortality, high rates of suicide, and high rates of adult involvement in crime, as well as being associated with negative economic conditions such as high unemployment and poverty.

Interestingly, because they conducted their study at three separate times they could consider delinquency rates over time and discovered that low delinquency rate areas remained low over time and high delinquency rate areas remained high over time. What does this tell us? High rates of delinquency in zone 2 survived changes in the population and could not, therefore, be associated with the individuals living there. In their first time period, zone 2 was largely populated by immigrants from Northern Europe and had high rates of delinquency and was very socially disorganised. In their second time period, zone 2 was largely populated by immigrants from Southern Europe; it still had high rates of delinquency and was very socially disorganised. In their third time period, zone 2 was largely populated by African Americans; once again, it had high rates of delinquency and was very

Type of measure	Socially organised natural areas with high levels of cohesion	Socially disorganised natural areas lacking cohesion
Formal social controls—provided by organisations such as schools, churches, and the police	The formal mechanisms work effectively to teach individuals acceptable forms of behaviour and positive values. There is mutual respect between the community and the formal social control mechanisms such as school and police.	A breakdown in the operation of these formal control mechanisms. For example, schools being unable to engage the young people and failing to teach social mores (standards of behaviour) or the police acting to contain problems within an area rather than enforcing and protecting from within.
Informal social controls—provided by the family and peer groups, etc.	Families, peer groups, and other informal social mechanisms work effectively to socialise members of the community into the cultural expectations, rules, and values of their communities so producing cohesive and socially sound communities. High levels of respect and support for formal groups such as the police.	A breakdown in informal control mechanisms. For example, these informal groups fail to teach the generally accepted social values. They may even socialise into alternative, unacceptable rule-breaking mores. Low levels of social cohesion around conformity.
Levels of social capital and internal supports	High levels of social capital—people participating in activities and groups within the community. Showing pride in their area, caring for their homes and for their streets. Also, caring for and about others in their community. People come together to volunteer or to happily participate in activities with others and with groups that help conformity such as religion, sports activities, etc. Citizens are willing to participate in informal and semi-formal groups.	A lack of social capital—people being unwilling to participate in groups in the community. Not showing any pride in their area so letting the physical surroundings deteriorate and not connecting with or caring about others in the community. Children are likely to encounter conflicting moral standards and negative adult role models (adult crime and involvement in drugs).
Values	Accepts and embraces the conventional values of the wider society.	No real commitment to the values of the broader society. Wide diversity of norms and values.

Table 17.3 Types of control and their effects by type of area

Source: Shaw, C. R. and McKay, H. D. (1942) *Juvenile Delinquency and Urban Areas*. Chicago: University of Chicago Press

socially disorganised. This was a very important finding as it proved that the ethnic mix of the community did not affect the rate of delinquency or affect the levels of disorganisation. Delinquency was, however, the result of social conditions such as the social disorganisation of a community; it was a feature of the community not the culture and values of a particular type of person or group.

Shaw and McKay found that the links between delinquency and the communities was strong but they did not claim that it was causative. These findings have been replicated in work by, for example, Sampson and Groves (1969) whose work probably provides the strongest support for social disorganisation theory. Like Shaw and McKay, they included structural factors (such as ethnic heterogeneity (measured by both the number of first- and second-generation immigrants and the diversity of ethnic backgrounds), family disruption (including divorce, legal separation, and parental or infant death), and residential mobility, families moving to better neighbourhoods within the same city) as well as measures of social disorganisation (such as the strength of friendship groups and participation in community organisations). For Sampson and Groves, structural elements might themselves be linked to criminality and delinquency or might lead to social disorganisation which in turn would be linked to crime and delinquency, as shown in **Figure 17.8**.

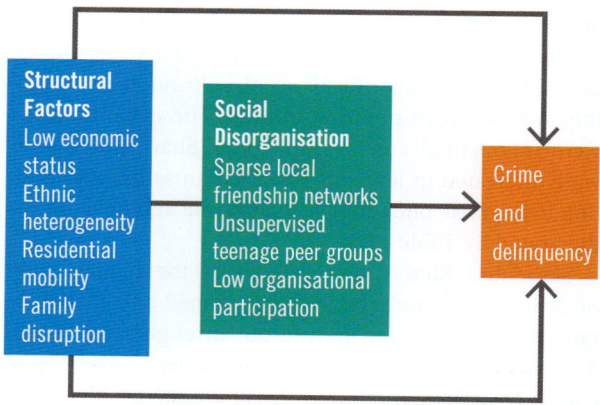

Figure 17.8 Sampson and Groves (1989) suggested that structural factors might be linked to crime and delinquency

Source: Adapted from Sampson and Groves 1989: 783

Social disorganisation: critique

At the centre of Shaw and McKay's work is the belief that we can only understand juvenile delinquency if we first understand the social context in which it arises. They accepted that the social context was linked to structural factors such as transient populations, poverty, and unemployment but believed that the more important connector was with social disorganisation. Offenders lived in areas where the official and informal institutions were weak or dysfunctional, which left them uncontrolled and free to offend or to be delinquent.

From this, Shaw and McKay suggested that efforts should be made to strengthen community ties in these areas and to support the inhabitants to build a more organised social setting. They set up the Chicago Area Project (CAP) which used community leaders to try to tackle problems, provide activities for young people, and encourage residents to take pride in their area. Whilst these efforts have never been carefully evaluated, it is believed that they had limited success (Schlossman et al., 1984).

Despite being supported by later research and being a respected theory, some serious critiques of Shaw and McKay's work might be made.

- First, the researchers accepted and relied heavily on official statistics to assess rates of delinquency and crime. However, these were unlikely to be correct; they probably better reflected the way in which areas are policed than the crime rates of those areas. Some self-report studies on rates of juvenile delinquency show that rates of self-reported delinquency are not very different when you compare the different areas (Fitzgerald, 2009; Moffitt and Silva, 1988). These studies suggested that most young people transgress (offend or commit acts of delinquency) and rates of self-reported delinquency and crime remain fairly constant between socially organised and disorganised areas (though the type of deviance might differ). However, more recently there has been partial support for the original idea that socially disorganised areas displayed higher levels of delinquency and crime (Valdimarsdóttir and Bernburg, 2015) and differences in rates may reflect the official means of controlling crime and of helping or failing to help children to become prosocial (McAra and McVie, 2010; Johns et al., 2017).

- Secondly, the zonal theory does not work particularly well for other cities. All cities have neighbourhoods with high and low levels of social organisation and in many cities the most socially disorganised areas have the highest levels of officially recorded juvenile delinquency. However, most cities' deprived areas cannot neatly be placed in zones or concentric circles.

- Thirdly, it over-predicts delinquency (that is, it predicts more delinquency than is seen in the statistics) and fails to explain why some young people in socially disorganised areas do not transgress.

- Finally, whilst it provides evidence that race does not explain the differences in rates of juvenile delinquency, it does not consider whether within these communities there might be different levels of ethnicity, religion, or other factors.

Therefore, although the theory is important in linking crime and other ills in a neighbourhood to lack of community cohesion, the details of the theory, such as the zonal nature of city layouts, are questionable.

17.6 Social structural theories: culture and subcultural theories

What do you think of when you see the word 'culture'? You might think of all the things we share in a particular society, such as knowledge, beliefs, morals, law, habits, expected standards of behaviour, forms of art (such as literature, film, music), and customs (common ways of doing things). Sociologists explain culture in a similar way and might define it as the shared ideas, customs, history, and behaviours of a society or a group. All the theories we've discussed so far in this chapter have, to some extent or another, considered how effectively a community has passed on its culture. The theories have then linked high levels of crime or delinquency to communities where there is no real shared culture (anomie), or where one aspect fails to ensure legitimate behaviour is effective (strain and anomie), or where the community is ineffectively built or passed on (social disorganisation). Each of these theories indicated that delinquency and crime might be rational solutions to particular social situations and that therefore you could, in these situations, expect high rates of criminality. However, these theories seem to over-predict criminality and fail to explain why not everyone living in a situation of anomie, strain, and social disorganisation offends or commits act of deviance. As we will discuss in this section, subcultural theory offers some answer to this. We will first discuss what subcultures are and how they relate to crime and then move on to discuss four different theories of subculture. All of these theories are, like the theories in the last section, examples of social structural theories.

Subcultures

Before we consider some sociological theories of subculture, let's take a look at what sociologists mean by subculture and think about how it might relate to crime. A subculture is a division of the broader culture with some of its own values, customs, and expectations to which individuals feel committed and which influence the way in which they think and behave. Many subcultures expect certain types of behaviour, styles of dressing, music, and other preferences, values, opinions, or ways of expressing themselves. Displaying some or all of these allows an individual membership of the group. Subcultures may be built on class, ethnic origin, religion, music, or other unifying elements. Every complex society supports many subcultures. Some, such as many religious groups and professional groups (such as judges, parliament, the police, and professional bodies like the General Medical Council in the UK), are welcomed and embraced. However, some aspects of these sorts of groups may occasionally be questioned or be damaging. For example, the parliamentary expenses scandal in 2009 led people to question politicians. More worrying is the example from the US where, in many states there appears to be a widespread 'culture' of negative policing of minority races evidenced by police brutality towards racial minorities. For example, the killing of George Floyd by a police officer (witnessed by three other officers who did not intervene) in Minneapolis in May 2020 was met with outrage and sparked protests worldwide (the killing is captured on video and the suspect was not resisting arrest, he was dying). Despite examples of damaging behaviour, these organisations are generally considered as positive for society, as largely serving the greater good and accepted as being necessary for the good functioning of the society. However, some cultures are viewed and treated negatively by the dominant elements of society; much youth culture falls in this category and even when it is not criminal it may be seen as deviant. The most studied subcultures are these juvenile subcultures or youth subcultures each of which generally has a very distinctive image, style, behaviour, appearance, demeanour, values, and their own figures of speech or jargon. Many are also associated with particular types of music and often embrace excitement, power, and freedom.

There are many examples of youth cultures over time in the UK. A famous example from the 1960s and 70s were the Mods and Rockers—these were two British youth subcultures who were in conflict. The Mods often rode scooters and were interested in fashion (often setting fashion), they wore suits and looked 'clean cut' with short hair. They often listened to soul, rhythm and blues, and beat music. The Rockers generally rode motorbikes so needed protective clothing; their group got linked to wearing black leather jackets (often with slogans), they listened to rock and roll and often had their hair swept back from the face into 'big' hairdos. The two groups were in disagreement and there was frequently tension between them. This tension sometimes resulted in violent clashes. Reports of their conflicts in the media led to '**moral panic**' about these two groups which led to them being labelled '**folk devils**'. Many adults considered the members of these groups to be dangerous and called for them to be controlled.

Punks came in the 1970s and 80s. The punks were a subculture that grew out of punk music (see **Figure 17.9**). This subculture was fractured and had a number of **ideologies** and fashions. For most punks, it was important

Figure 17.9 A subculture, such as punk (which emerged in the '70s), is a division of broader culture with its own values, customs, and expectations which influence how individuals think and behave

Source: Roger Tillberg/Alamy Stock Photo

to allow individuals to express themselves through their bodies, clothing, music, and dance. The main unifying idea was probably negative—that they were against the controlling nature of the establishment. However, they also promoted individual freedom. Punk music is loud and in both its nature and the lyrics it is often confrontational or even aggressive. Because their appearance was often challenging, sometimes even aggressive, and the music they listened to was loud and aggressive, many adults wanted punks to be controlled.

'Road' Life and 'Bad Boys' appeared from 2000 onwards. These young, black Caribbean men largely in East London are deviant, commit crime, and build a style, lifestyle, and set values which revolve around badness and arise due to their need to support each other and be able to recognise each other in order to survive (see Gunter, 2008; Young, 1999).

However, many of the gangs and peer groups who may cause trouble today do not necessarily belong to a particular, recognisable national group or subculture, for example the 'Bad Boys' discussed above are only noted in East London though may be copied in a few other urban locations. These more local groupings which may display a specific local subculture are sometimes strongly linked and may be referred to as groups or gangs. According to the government, antisocial behaviour and group violence have been a central issue from the 1990s onwards, meaning it has been a problem in society which the government have sought to solve (Hollingan, 2015; Westminster Government, 2015; Squires, 2006; Klein et al., 2006). Groups of youths may well be involved in antisocial behaviour, and though they may not be a national phenomenon or a visually recognisable group, the behaviour is still often believed to be from groups of youths, maybe because they are visible on the street. This belief and the visibility of these groups led politicians to try to control young people. The Crime and Disorder Act 1998 first tried to curb and control these groups by allowing the authorities to control antisocial behaviour. The controls were strengthened in the Anti-Social Behaviour Act 2003 (which relates to adults and children but has been used most frequently to control children) and in later legislation. Antisocial behaviour is not clearly defined in any of the legislation; it is a subjective feeling experienced by victims who complain to the authorities that they have been harassed, alarmed, or distressed. Part 4 of the Policing and Crime Act 2009 (see also the Magistrates' Courts (Injunctions: Gang-related Violence) Rules 2015) provides for injunctions (stopping them doing something or requiring them to do something) to control those who participate in group- or gang-related activities (the Act defined a gang as a group of three or more who have characteristics (a 'style') by which they can be identified) and for punishment if the injunction is breached. See also the controls, including injunctions, in the Anti-social Behaviour, Crime and Policing Act 2014 (as amended by the Serious Crime Act 2015). These controls have had mixed success but have led to the criminalising of many young people who first have injunctions against certain behaviours and are then criminalised when they breach those injunctions (Burney, 2009).

Riots often indicate major discontent in young people. Lord Scarman (1981) argued that the 1981 riots, which started in Brixton but soon spread to cities around the country, arose out of distrust of the police and were related to racial tension and inner-city deprivation. It was also a strong feeling coming out of the riots of August 2011 which broke out in a number of cities in the UK and lasted a number of days. The joint *Guardian* and LSE (2012) research which followed, pinpointed the discontent of young people in British society:

> These young people are coming out to prove they have an existence, to prove that if you don't listen to them and you don't take into account our views, potentially this is a destructive force.
>
> (Man, mid-20s, north London, *The Guardian* and LSE, 2012: 13)

> There's a massive police station there, and they couldn't do anything. It was ours for a day. Salford was more like a party atmosphere. Everyone was stood around, drinking ... smoking weed, having a laugh. People weren't threatening the public.
> There was people there to get on a rob [loot], there for the spectacle, there to have a go at police. And then people there for all of the above. We hate the police, hate the government, got no opportunities ...
> These aren't gangs. The kids just did what they wanted to do 'cos they wanted to do it, not because some gang boss orchestrated it to get back at the police.'
>
> (Unemployed man, 22, ibid: 20)

> The government needed someone to blame and [put] everything together under 'gangs'. I don't believe there was much planned gangland activity. I believe there was a lot of angry, very working-class, disillusioned young men that realised 'hang on a minute, it's going off'.
>
> (Man, 21, ibid: 22)

> When I left my house ... it wasn't anything to do with the police ... I literally went there to say, 'All right then, well, everyone's getting free stuff, I'm joining in', like, 'cos, it's fucking my area. These fucking shops, like, I've given them a hundred CVs ... not one job. That's why I left my house.
> It's not like I haven't got GCSEs ... Why haven't I even got [an] interview? ... I feel like I haven't [been] given the same opportunities and chances as other people ... If I had a job ... I honestly wouldn't have stolen nothing ...
> And that's what I feel like: people are not worth anything in this area.
>
> (Man, 22 from London, ibid: 26)

In all of the examples we have discussed so far (Mods and Rockers, punks, Road Life and Bad Boys, the riots, and a lot of antisocial behaviour), young people group together most often to help them solve the problems they face. Even in riots, there is a sense of belonging to a group which is united to reveal or solve a problem. In the case of gangs, to get them through their lives they adopt values and behaviours different from those of the general population. Whilst adults often accuse these youths of intentionally challenging the broader culture or trying to undermine it, this is not generally what underlies youth subculture—most often they are just trying to deal with the social environment they inhabit (Hazelhurst and Hazelhurst, 2017; Gunter, 2008; Young, 1999).

Whilst all subcultures are 'deviant' by the standards of the broader culture, many only 'breach' conventions concerning relatively minor issues such as style, music, and speech patterns, remaining otherwise quite conforming. Some, however, do encourage or condone crime and damaging forms of delinquency. It is these subcultures which generally interest criminologists, partly because these young people often become the adult offenders of tomorrow and partly because the rate of offending is still relatively high in young people (10–17 years old) than in other age groups although their offending tends to be relatively less harmful and today many of them are diverted rather than facing a caution or a trial. We can see the effects of youth crime in the numbers of young adults (18–25 years old) most of whom began their offending as children and who make up almost one-third of those sentenced to prison each year, one-third of the probation caseload, and one-third of the economic cost of crime (see Prison Reform Trust, 2012).

Policymakers are constantly seeking new ways to tackle this youth criminality which often seems to serve no purpose and yet is very destructive for others, especially if it involves violence. Juvenile subcultures largely revolve around peer group or even gang delinquency. This means breaking with the mores of the larger society (though not necessarily offending, so it includes low-level improper behaviour as depicted in their choice of style, music, and language (Bennett, 1999) all the way up to criminality) which is generally considered to be a lower class and male pursuit. The link to lower class is important because since the 1960s academics have increasingly accepted that poverty is not the result of individual failure but rather it is the fault of the system, the society, and the way society is structured. It is important to note that it is not arguing that the poverty causes the criminality but that it is associated with the lack of opportunities open to those in their localities and the children/young people's need to survive in difficult circumstances (Yates, 2014; Ilan, 2015). This has also been accepted by many politicians and some aspects of the media. This acceptance of poverty as a social structural problem brought to the fore ideas based on Merton's idea of anomie—one in which everyone was told they could achieve 'the American dream' and were encouraged to strive for this goal, but many of the poor could never legitimately attain that goal. The gang subculture theories that we will discuss in the rest of the chapter draw heavily on this idea. Before considering them, take a look at **What do you think? 17.3** for a real-life example which may provide some context.

Cohen and delinquent subcultures

We will start our discussion of subculture theories by looking at the work of Albert K. Cohen (1918–2014). Cohen was a prominent American criminologist who drew heavily on Merton's concept of anomie to suggest that young people used delinquency to resolve social problems. He also drew on Sutherland's differential association (see earlier in this chapter) believing that associating with a criminal or delinquent subculture would lead a young person to offend.

Cohen's theory

In his major work, *Delinquent Boys: The Culture of the Gang* (1955), Cohen argued that juvenile delinquency could be largely explained by the adoption of the values of their peer group. The core of his thesis was that to resolve the problems caused by the strains a society placed on certain young people, they turned to each other to form a 'subculture' in which they could succeed and feel comfortable. However, he needed to explain where the delinquent subculture came from, how it arose, and why it persisted over time.

Cohen suggested that gangs provided a vehicle allowing young people to belong and grow, and to solve the problems caused by the broader culture. The gangs that had values which were likely to lead their members into delinquent behaviour were concentrated in urban, lower class areas and were largely the preserve of young men angry at the constraints of middle-class culture which prevented them from succeeding. When Cohen refers to middle-class culture and values, he means the values of the dominant culture in the US:

> Though we refer to them as 'middle class' norms, they are really manifestations of the dominant American value systems and even working class children must come to terms with them.
>
> (Cohen, 1955: 87)

He argued that the problems started to arise very early because working-class boys faced a conflict once they went

WHAT DO YOU THINK? 17.3

Tackling crime

The following letter was a real letter sent out to many people in a particular area. Read the letter and then consider the questions that follow.

Consider your thoughts about the following questions.

- Do you think that this is a positive way of tackling serious crimes of violence?
- How would you feel if you received this letter?
- What does it tell us about the way in which the police view these 'gangs'?

Remember this letter as you read what follows.

Working together for a safer London
TERRITORIAL POLICING

Brent Borough
603 Harrow Road
Wembley
Middlesex
HA0 2HH

19th August 2015

Dear

You may be aware of an incident on the Kilburn High Road on Sunday 16th August during which a 24 year old man received serious stab injuries. This is being treated as an attempted murder.

Our intelligence suggests you are linked to gang related criminal activity in the South Kilburn area. We are determined to bring the cycle of violence affecting this area to an end. We are not suggesting you were directly involved in the latest incident but we believe that you are involved in criminal behaviour that puts you at greater risk of becoming a victim or a perpetrator of violent crime yourself.

We would like to invite you to take the opportunity to meet with Brent Police, Brent Council and other agencies to discuss the events of 16th August, possible risks to yourself, and ways we can help you move away from criminal behaviour.

This meeting will take place on **Thursday 27th August at 3pm at the Marian Centre 1 Stafford Road NW6 5RS.**

If you choose not to attend we will see this as a clear message that you intend to continue with a criminal lifestyle. As such, we will work hard to disrupt your activities utilising every legitimate means available to us.

Yours Sincerely

Borough Commander

to school—the socialisation at school was different from and often clashed with that in their homes. This confused the boys. At school they were faced with values such as ambition, responsibility, rational behaviour, control of aggression (physical and verbal), and respect for others. At home there was recognition that the ambition was unlikely to be rewarded with success. In this confusing atmosphere, they sought a way of resolving the conflict or of coping with their situation. Cohen suggested that they would adopt one of three solutions:

College Boys—these young men wholly accept the values of the wider culture and compete for success on those terms—they conform and compete. Cohen argued that only a minority of boys chose this solution.

Street Corner Boys—accept their limitations and live within them—they conform, lose any real ambition, and just make the most of what legitimately they can attain. This solution is considered deviant but not problematic for the broader society.

Delinquent Corner Boys—are angry at their situation and hit out against what they see as the problem. These working-class young males see middle-class values and ways of achieving success work unfairly against them. The way they choose to resolve this problem is to join with others and engage in negative and malicious behaviours, things destructive to the middle-class values they see as causing the strain and the problem. These boys want what the society says is valuable, they want success, but feel that it is being unfairly blocked which leads to strain. The means of coping with the situation is an anger focused on the dominant middle-class culture which is vented through the youth subculture which sees delinquency as attractive partly because it is 'non-utilitarian, malicious and negativistic' (Merton, 1938: 25).

To break this down, we can explore each of these terms:

- non-utilitarian—this delinquency is done for themselves, for fun or to vent anger, not for gain. If property or money is stolen, this is done for 'kicks', for the excitement, and the 'profit' would be given away or 'wasted';
- malicious—to harm or undermine other people, authority, or middle-class values. Here destructiveness is intentional not a by-product. They might well scrawl graffiti all over a property they broke into for no other reason than they could and it would upset others;
- negativistic—the behaviour is good because it is unacceptable to the dominant culture, the values are not accidentally at odds but intentionally in opposition to the dominant culture.

We might add that he viewed this gang delinquency as short term and hedonistic (the main reason for the delinquency is pleasure, excitement, and immediate gratification) and included acquisitive, destructive, and aggressive behaviours as well as causing problems or 'hell-raising'. Importantly, for these young people loyalty was to the group or gang rather than to society or family.

Therefore, for Cohen the style, music, culture, slang, and behaviour chosen are attractive to the subculture partly because it is in conflict with or undermining of the standards and norms of the wider culture. Many of the juvenile subcultures value aspects such as excitement, toughness, and immediate gratification whereas those of the wider culture, particularly the middle classes, prioritise drive and ambition, individual responsibility, achievement and success, postponement of gratification, respect for others and for their property, and control of both physical and verbal aggression. They therefore engage in delinquency which others find irrational and disrespectful of conventional, middle-class culture, activities such as truanting from school, fighting, being disrespectful or rude to others, or vandalising or destroying property.

Here the strain caused by a class-based system, which excludes some from the success it claims and teaches (in schools and other institutions) is available to everyone, is the catalyst for delinquent subcultures; these will exist over time as long as this class-based strain persists. This theory of class-based strain claims to explain why delinquent subcultures arise, why they are in conflict with mainstream culture, and why they persist over many generations. Cohen also claims that the feeling of inclusion, friendship, and excitement that is offered by these delinquent subcultures (gangs) may attract some boys who do not feel the strain but merely wish to be a part of something which is 'fun'.

Cohen: critique

Cohen's theory is attractive because it neatly matches with youth justice statistics in most western cultures. For example, it leads us to expect higher levels of criminality among lower class (poorer) children than among middle and higher class (richer) children because the better off children are more likely to succeed through conventional, legal routes. Whilst his ideas still neatly follow the crime statistics in this way that does not mean that he was correct. Cohen assumes, though he never really proves it, that working-class boys, and particularly those involved in gangs, first try to succeed by middle-class values and when they fail they become hostile to those values. Cohen suggests that it is frustration at failure which leads to the gangs and the delinquency (crime). However, Box (1981: 150) suggests that it may be that these young men never really try to succeed but feel resentment and anger at being called a failure and that it is this labelling which leads to the delinquency and crime. However, they may be both frustrated and resentful; a mixture of both of these theories.

Cohen does not write a lot about women though his theory suggests there would be a far lower rate for young females which again reflects the criminal statistics in most western countries. His explanation in the 1950s was that they were more concerned with marrying well than with an occupation so needed to keep a good reputation. Of course, this reasoning no longer really holds for young females and, whilst there has been an increase in girls who offend, their rates are still well below those of males and Cohen's ideas probably no longer explain that gap.

Empirical testing of the theory has not been particularly successful in either proving or disproving his ideas. The most useful piece of empirical work was conducted by Short and Strodtbeck (1967) and supported Cohen's general theory of links to the subculture though did not back the idea that the members were against societal values. It found that they both supported the group culture and the wider societal culture which is not strong support for his ideas and suggested a far more complex explanation than that provided by Cohen.

Cloward and Ohlin and 'differential opportunity'

Richard A. Cloward (1926–2001) and Lloyd E. Ohlin (1918–2008) were famous American sociologists and criminologists who worked together in the 1950s and 1960s. Like Cohen, they also drew on Merton's anomie.

Cloward and Ohlin's theory

Cloward and Ohlin (1960) recognised that crime and delinquency existed throughout society. They argued, however, that for middle-class youths it arose as part of an individual struggle, whereas for working-class youths it was part of a lack of opportunity leading them to form peer groups or gangs to react against the problems this caused. Like Cohen, they concentrated on the delinquency of these lower-class youths partly because they were interested in studying the subculture of the peer group or gang but also because this group appeared most commonly in crime statistics. They also argued that these strong groupings were possible in lower-class neighbourhoods because they met with less disapproval from adults within their neighbourhood than would be the case for middle-class delinquency.

Cloward and Ohlin drew on both Merton and Sutherland. From Merton they recognised the pressure and strain that these young people were placed under because of:

> the disparity between what lower-class youths are led to want and what is actually available to them.
>
> (Cloward and Ohlin, 1960)

This disparity caused the young men problems that needed to be resolved. Their strain theory is much closer to that of Merton than that of Cohen, in that it depends on failures in society, particularly economic failures, rather than the conflict caused by school. Cloward and Ohlin argued that this anomie and its resulting strain was *necessary* to understanding the behaviours, but that it was not *sufficient* to explain the delinquency of young people because:

> it does not sufficiently explain why these pressures result in one deviant solution rather than another.
>
> (ibid: 34)

Cloward and Ohlin add to the discussion of juvenile gang and peer delinquency by taking strain theory further, using it to explain why one delinquent solution is chosen over another.

From Sutherland they learned that whatever role a person chooses (legitimate or illegitimate) they need access to the means of succeeding in that role. If you want to become a teacher you will need education, training, and opportunity. To succeed as a burglar you might need some training and also access to people willing and able to sell the stolen goods. Cloward and Ohlin therefore suggest that the type of gang or peer group depends on access to these opportunities.

Therefore, in brief, the background social situation necessary to this criminality is a blocking of legitimate opportunities. The blocking of opportunities is experienced as unfair because it is based not on merit or need but on subjective criteria such as speaking with the 'right' accent, coming from the 'right' background, or 'who you know'. The legitimate institutions such as schools and employers therefore fail the working-class youths who are then 'free' to choose other ways of achieving some sort of success and to do so without feeling any guilt about how they achieve 'success'. However, to explain the type of criminal activity an individual engages in, we need to consider the type of alternative opportunities available in their area. Cloward and Ohlin suggest three types of solution to the strain, depending on opportunities available to youths: criminal subcultures, conflict subcultures, and retreatist subcultures, as set out in **Table 17.4**.

Cloward and Ohlin therefore embraced Merton's idea of strain theory and argued that the perceived unjust denial of access to legitimate opportunities to 'succeed' in society was a powerful pressure which explained why someone might be willing to commit acts of deviance

	Type of adaptation: criminal subculture	Type of adaptation: conflict subculture	Type of adaptation: retreatist subculture
What is involved	Generally this gang or peer group is involved in the illegal taking of property or other means of making money.	Young men who lack purpose in life, who then become angry because society has let them down. They use power and violence to vent this negativity. They come together to use power and violence in a conflict gang.	This is a drug-oriented gang.
Where	In organised slum areas where there are opportunities for offences like burglary and for selling on any goods which are stolen.	In disorganised slum areas. These areas are transient or unstable due to shifts in population or because of lack of pride in the community. These areas lack both criminal and legitimate role models so the youths turn to using conflict.	In any areas or neighbourhoods where drugs can be obtained.
What is necessary	Adult offenders to serve both as role models and as people who can facilitate such behaviour or an established gang who can support in these ways. It also often requires a wider community which is at least tolerant of this way of making money so that there is some respectability associated with succeeding in criminal endeavours.	Absence of both legitimate and illegitimate (criminal) opportunities. With no supportive criminal opportunities, the youths form gangs which use violence to build a reputation for themselves. Fear gives them an identity and social standing.	For those who fail in legitimate, illegitimate (criminal), and illegitimate (conflict or status) spheres, retreatism is the only deviant coping strategy open to them. For Cloward and Ohlin, this retreatism involves a retreat into drug use to blot out the reality of their lives. Note this drug use is different from the occasional use that may be part of all these subcultures, it is more all-consuming. Some of these young people may conform but give up any hope of achieving any goals—see Cohen's 'Delinquent Corner Boys' (1955). Whether they become part of a retreatist gang or peer group or conform depends partly on their own personality but also on the availability of drugs and a drug culture.
Types of individuals involved	Those on whom the group can rely; unpredictable individuals will not be accepted as they will place the whole criminal endeavour in jeopardy.	Mostly disorganised people who are seeking status and willing to participate in violence to achieve it. They are often angry because they lack both legitimate and illegitimate opportunities. This gives rise to a desire to prove their worth and status.	Could be drawn from any area. This can involve almost anyone (no particular personal traits are involved). However, membership is a personal choice and clearly requires an opportunity, a drug culture, which can arise in any type of area.
Legitimate goals and means	Accepts the traditional goals of the broader society. Rejects legitimate means of achieving them.	Rejects the traditional goals of the broader society. Rejects legitimate means of achieving their ends. Rejects the 'conventional' illegitimate means of succeeding which might lead to financial success.	Some may accept the goals of society but generally this group rejects all legitimate and illegitimate goals. Generally—though not in every case—members of this group reject both legitimate and illegitimate means of achieving goals.
Illegitimate goals and means	Adopts illegitimate means of succeeding.	Adopts destructive goals, linked to achieving personal and gang (peer group) status, often through fear. Adopts violence and activities which lead to fear to achieve status.	Generally this group rejects both legitimate and illegitimate goals. Generally—though not in every case—members of this group reject both legitimate and illegitimate means of achieving goals.

Table 17.4 Cloward and Ohlin's solutions to strain

Source: Cloward, R. and Ohlin, L. (1960) *Delinquency and Opportunity: A Theory of Delinquent Gangs*. New York: Free Press

or crime. However, they recognised that this theory was limited and could not explain why some people chose one way to resolve this strain and others another. They therefore added in a focus on the availability of illegitimate opportunities, a form of differential association theory, to explain why certain solutions were chosen to resolve the strain of restricted opportunities to succeed. Whilst they applied their theory to juvenile subcultures (peer groups and gangs), they also believed that differential opportunity theory could help us explain how and why adults resolved similar conflicts.

Cloward and Ohlin: critique

Cloward and Ohlin's focus on economic success, in terms of achieving a good living, is possibly more realistic than Cohen's focus on the lack of achievement at school. However, as Box (1981) notes, their theory is still a little implausible as the lower class youths are not likely to ever believe that they would have the opportunity to earn large amounts of money so they are unlikely to experience strong disappointment when they do not succeed. The disappointment is more likely to appear in the middle-class children who were told that they might expect success but who fail anyway.

Furthermore, Cloward and Ohlin's theory cannot explain why many youths stop offending as they reach adulthood or in their early 20s. Their situation is unlikely to have suddenly improved, the legitimate opportunities open to them will not suddenly have opened up, and they will continue to be at the economically poorer end of society. It is possible that, when young, they are more likely to be angry that their lives seem blighted but, that as they mature, they come to accept their situation. However, this is something outside that theory itself, certainly not something that the theory explains.

Neutralisation and drift

Gresham Sykes (1922–2010) and David Matza (1930–), American sociologists and criminologists, worked on the concept of 'neutralisation'. The original idea of 'neutralisation' arose out of work by Matza and Sykes in 1957 and 1961 but was refined, extended, and more fully considered by Matza (1961, 1964, 1969) when he added the concept of 'drift'. Their joint work is now often referred to as Matza's, presumably because he built on and refined the ideas, and we will follow that convention in this section. However, it is important that you recognise that the original concept of 'neutralisation' was conceived by Matza and Sykes together.

Neutralisation and drift theory

Matza argued that strain theory and Merton's concept of anomie over-predicted the amount of crime and delinquency found in most societies. Strain theorists and other subcultural theorists could not explain why most people were law abiding and adhered to conventional values most of the time and why most offenders stop offending in their early 20s. Matza started from the premise that most people of all ages (including youths) are basically conventional and likely to conform to most of the rules most of the time. He also questioned the idea that subcultural values of gangs and youth peer groups were set up in opposition to the values of the broader society and in doing so rejected these elements of the subcultural theories of Cohen and Cloward and Ohlin. He did not accept the idea that young people in certain surroundings would face so much 'strain' that they would be forced into an otherwise unattractive coping strategy (a delinquent/criminal strategy).

However, he does not totally reject strain as part of the reason for offending but he does include factors such as desperation as application to some parts of his theory. He set out to explain:

1. why people who face this overwhelming strain are nonetheless law abiding most of the time;
2. why, despite remaining in the areas where strain is strongest, they tend to grow out of deviant and criminal behaviour and become more conventional and law abiding.

He noted that most people's behaviour was not always or even usually delinquent or criminal. He argued that even fairly prolific offenders do not behave unacceptably all the time. So, instead of totally relying on strain as an explanation for criminality, Matza suggested that all people retain free will and that delinquency and crime, like all other behaviour, is largely chosen; it is the outcome of free will. To explain the criminal behaviour of otherwise law-abiding people, Matza suggested that they were in a state of drift—they were able to drift between commitment to conventional behaviour and unacceptable behaviour, never wholly committing to either.

Matza suggested that young, working-class males did not reject conventional culture in order to form delinquent and criminal subcultures—this predicted more crime than actually occurred. Instead, they were in a state of 'drift'. This state of drift arises because the dominant values are fluid and have no real hard requirements. So, for example, dominant culture allows people to have fun (through enjoying hobbies) and to be aggressively competitive (to get a promotion or to win at sport) or to enjoy excitement and adventures (in extreme sports, by travelling, or at funfairs). In the dominant culture, these norms are 'subordinate' to the more important aspects of hard work and earning the right to enjoy oneself. People in a state of drift take these 'subordinate values' and extend or distort them so that excitement, aggression, violence, and so on become more dominant and become used in inappropriate ways. Violence and aggression are supported by society if channelled into winning in sport or doing well at work, when the violence is not done for and of itself. Those in a state of drift extend the acceptable use of violence to include, for example, fighting to protect your reputation or credibility with a subgroup or to get a wallet in order to get the money you need. Each person in a state of drift may extend the rules in slightly different ways but they all generally retain aspects of a rule they do not feel it is legitimate to breach (it may be that violence towards other gangs is acceptable but towards elderly people is not); they do not become rule-less.

Furthermore, in every rule-based culture there are exceptions and defences to every activity; every rule is qualified. Intentional killing is generally illegal—murder—but might be excused if committed in self-defence or mercy killing, or might even be glorified if committed in war. Again, those in a state of drift extend these grey areas at the edges of rules; the area of permissible behaviour is widened. From the dominant culture they learn that no rule is absolute and therefore use the permissiveness which is part of the dominant culture, extending it to include permissions which are favourable to delinquency or crime. They, therefore, are simultaneously bound to the dominant culture and free to violate it if they choose.

Matza sees this as a subculture of delinquency—a subculture that permits delinquency and will excuse it if an individual chooses to break rules. He therefore rejects Cohen's and Cloward and Ohlin's ideas of delinquent subcultures which depend on and positively encourage rule breaking.

The other part of drift involves 'neutralisation'. Here people (including juveniles) generally accept and live within conventional values but learn ways of explaining their lapses into delinquency and crime. They use 'techniques of neutralisation' which would release them from the conventional rules and allow them to break the rules without feeling guilt. For example, they might extend the sorts of justifications that officials and conforming individuals use. Matza found that the authorities often blamed parents for the actions of their children or accepted some transgressions as accidents and, as previously discussed, these are extended to allow transgression without guilt—young people, when they offended or broke societal rules, would blame their parents rather than accept responsibility for their own actions. Similarly this placing of guilt on others is extended to various situations. So, for example, young people might see that society treats homeless people very badly and take that negative feeling further by becoming actively violent towards them. They might see big businesses being attacked in the press for avoiding taxes and then decide that it is acceptable to steal from these big shops whose shareholders can afford the loss and would anyway be insured. Matza suggested five techniques of 'neutralisation' which individuals might use as justifications before the act or excuses after they had transgressed, set out in **Table 17.5**.

Type of neutralisation	What it entails	Examples
Denial of responsibility	'It is not my fault'. Here offenders may claim that: • they had no choice and could therefore not be blamed; • it was the fault of someone or something else—a result of parental neglect or of poverty or being led astray by friends; or • the transgression was unintended and was an accident—'I didn't mean to do it'.	Following the Second World War, those who committed war crimes tried to claim that it was not their fault because they were 'only following orders'. Claims such as: • 'I only wanted to steal her purse but she wouldn't give it to me so I had to hit her, I didn't want to'; • 'He was disrespecting me so I had to hit him'; and • 'If only you did what you were told I wouldn't have to hit you' (this could also be denial of victim), would fall into this category. Claims which deny responsibility are very common.
Denial of injury	The offender may claim that no one was harmed—for example, the victim was insured. They might also claim that the victim knew what they were letting themselves in for and therefore has no right or justification to complain about their injuries; it is a private affair.	If an individual starts a fight, disrespects someone, or participates in a gang fight then any injuries are accepted and therefore there is no real victim. Claims such as: • 'I stole a car but the victim will be insured so they have not lost out—what is the problem?';

17.6 SOCIAL STRUCTURAL THEORIES: CULTURE AND SUBCULTURAL THEORIES

	Here very often the perpetrators are law abiding and genuinely believe that their extended view of what is acceptable should be the law.	• 'They have so much they will never miss it'; and • 'We enjoy it and no one else is involved or those involved all consent' (such as sadomasochistic behaviours, drug taking, or a gang fight).
Denial of victim	Offenders might claim that the victim is bad or a lesser person so has no right to complain. They may claim that the victim deserved their victimisation or even that all those involved participate so there is no victim and it is no business of broader society.	Examples of such claims might be that the 'victim' started the fight so only got what was coming to them. In domestic violence, the offender might tell the victim that if they would only do things properly they would not need to be punished, it is for their own good. Other examples would be claims such as: • 'We were all enjoying taking drugs, it didn't harm anyone so what is the problem?'; • 'We had a fight but no one really got hurt, it was just a bit of fun so what is the problem?'; • 'You can't rape a prostitute; it is just a matter of negotiating the price'; and • 'She was dressed provocatively and chose to come back for a coffee so can't complain of rape'.
Condemnation of condemners	Offenders might claim that 'we have all offended so no one can take the high ground and condemn others'. They might take an 'everyone is doing it so why pick on me' stance. Finally, they might claim that police and judges are corrupt or don't punish their friends or those who are rich.	Examples might involve: 'everyone speeds so you should not just punish me; if you don't punish all of them it is not fair. You are unjust'. Pointing out that those who evade taxes can merely pay them back whereas making a bogus benefit claim will be treated as a crime. Claiming police corruption or brutality so seeing police as 'bad' and criminal and so unable to call others to account.
Appeal to higher loyalties or a mood of humanism	The claim here is that someone is acting on a 'higher' calling, something that is more important than obeying the laws or expectations of society. So it may be to redress a balance or for (for example) human rights reasons. This kind of justification can subsume some people that deny responsibility.	The example of 'only following orders' would fit here as well as above. Other claims which might fall under this head: • 'I was hungry'; • 'I was taking it to feed my family'; • 'The system is so unfair and I was trying to redress the balance and make things fairer'; • 'My friends expect me to do it and I can't let them down'; • 'It is a gang (peer group) ritual or necessary to support the gang (peer group) and I can't let them down'; • 'The law is unjust and I am bound to and answerable to a higher and more important standard'; • 'I acted because "god" expects me to'; • 'It is being done to protect the faith'; • 'It is necessary to free my people'.

Table 17.5 Techniques of neutralisation
Source: Matza, D. and Sykes, G. (1961) 'Juvenile Delinquency and Subterranean Values'. American Sociological Review 26(5): 712–19)

All of this 'drift' and 'neutralisation' frees the individual to choose to offend but Matza recognises that not all individuals will choose to offend; some will lack 'the position, capacity or inclination' or even the opportunity to act in ways which break the law (1964: 29). Matza saw these people as permanent drifters. Just being free to offend does not mean it will happen; it does not explain the offending itself. Matza's theory is often thought of as a control theory. However, it differs from other control theories because here merely having controls removed does not mean offending will occur, it has to be both possible and chosen.

For Matza, before offending is chosen there is a combination of 'preparation' and 'desperation'. For Matza, 'preparation' means that the individual:

- is aware that a particular type of offending is possible, that it can be done;
- knows how to commit the crime;
- is able to perform all aspects necessary to the crime and has all the tools and the opportunity to commit that offence;
- feels confident that they can perform the task; and
- can cope with the fear of being discovered.

'Desperation' occurs when there is a very strong feeling of despair or hopelessness and a need to offend in order to prove that you can take control and show that you are a person, an individual.

'Neutralisation' and 'drift': critique

There are difficulties with Matza's theories of 'neutralisation' and 'drift'. Some are internal; the claim to be answering a higher calling rarely fits with the action being taken. Also all the techniques of neutralisation are very 'convenient' as, from the perspective of the offender, they let them off the hook, removing the need to feel guilty. However, clearly they do not excuse their guilt or explain the behaviour such that the offender should be excused. What is interesting is that from the perspective of the offender they *believe* that they are reasonable explanations of the behaviour and should be enough to excuse it. Clearly, looked at objectively, we might even wonder whether they are explanations or excuses, whether they existed at the time of the behaviour or are used as mechanisms after the event so that the offender does not need to feel guilty. In particular, it is often difficult to decide whether something such as the denial of responsibility: 'I had to, I was being pushed around and I had no choice' exists before the offence is committed and 'frees' the offender to act or is used to avoid feeling guilty and to avoid condemnation from accusers once they are found out. Clearly, this is difficult to unpick and cannot be proven. What is, however, clear is that these techniques could both act to free someone from conventional bonds and assist the offender to escape full blame and censure either from themselves (guilt) or others.

Another issue arises from the ability of the theory to explain certain 'facts' recorded by officials. Matza's theory clearly deals with the problems of over-predicting crime. However, his theory probably under-predicts crime and may fail to adequately explain serious offending, because many offenders would find it difficult to 'neutralise' serious crimes. Furthermore, it cannot explain why some people do not grow out of offending or only take to offending later in life. It does not explain the 6–10 per cent of offenders who are prolific and persistent. It therefore seems to solve one problem but ignores other aspects of the crime problem that do not fit with the theory.

It is also important to recognise that Matza is not really a subcultural theorist, but rather is often seen as a control theorist. This is because, for Matza, delinquency is an individual choice which occurs when someone is in a state of drift. However, it is a subculture theory because some of the forces that move someone into drift or that prepare someone for or place them in a position of desperation arise out of youth subculture. The difference for Matza—as opposed to other subcultural theorists—is that the subculture permits and facilitates delinquency and offending but these activities are not a required element of the subculture.

Social exclusion and the underclass

So far in our analysis we have concentrated on the social environment which arises due to different economic conditions and the impact it has on offending. At this point we will move away from environment to concentrate directly on external factors such as poverty, unemployment, and general despair. These factors have existed in all cultures over time but became particularly important to studies of crime once societies became industrialised and people tended to live in large urban areas where communities were less connected and more diverse. Migration, population growth, and rapid urbanisation led to the concentration of population in smaller geographic areas. This made offending easier, as there was 'more' close at hand—more property to steal or destroy and more people to be violent towards—and this made it more of a problem for the law abiding as there was more fear. In these concentrations of population, there emerged—over time—large differences between the rich and poor. The differentials gave rise to large areas of slums in which, 19th-century commentators feared, dangerous sub-groups formed, commonly referred to as the 'Residuum' or the **underclass** (see Phillips, 1977; Tobias, 1972; Jones, 1982).

In western cultures (similar concepts may apply in other parts of the world), the existence of an underclass which causes society problems is not a new idea but rather persists over time. Take a look at the following quotes about the underclass and consider the variety of opinions:

In 1844, Friedrich Engels (1820–95), a German philosopher, stated:

> If the demoralisation of the worker passes beyond a certain point, then it is just as natural that he will turn into a criminal—as inevitably as water turns into steam at boiling point.

(1844, from 1971 translation: 145)

In 1850, Henry Mayhew (1812–87), an English social researcher, stated that the dishonest poor man was:

> distinguished from the civilised man by his repugnance to regular and continuous labour—by his want of providence in laying up a store for the future—by his inability to perceive consequences ever so slightly removed from immediate apprehensions—by his passion for stupefying herbs and roots and, when possible, for intoxicating fermenting liquors.
>
> (*Morning Chronicle*, 1850)

In 1982, Ken Auletta (1942–), American writer and media critic, stated:

> among students of poverty there is little disagreement that a fairly distinct black and white underclass does exist; that this underclass generally feels excluded from society, rejects commonly accepted values, suffers from *behavioural*, as well as *income* deficiencies. They don't just tend to be poor; to most Americans their behaviour seems aberrant.
>
> (1982: xiii)

In 1990, Charles Murray (1943–), an American political scientist, said this of the 'underclass':

> They were defined by their behaviour. Their homes were littered and unkempt. The men in the family were unable to hold a job for more than a few weeks at a time. Drunkenness was common. The children grew up ill-schooled and ill-behaved and contributed a disproportionate share of the local juvenile delinquents.
>
> (1990: 1)

In 1990, Runciman (1934–), a British historical sociologist, stated that the term underclass:

> stand[s] not for a group or category of workers systematically disadvantaged within the labour market but for those members of British society whose roles place them more or less permanently at the economic level where benefits are paid by the state to those unable to participate in the labour market at all ... They are typically the long-term unemployed.
>
> (1990: 388)

In 2002, Jock Young (1942–2013), a British sociologist and criminologist, set out what the way in which others had described the underclass as:

> an underclass left stranded by the needs of capital on housing estates ... those who because of illegitimacy, family pathology, or general disorganization were excluded from citizenship, whose spatial vistas were those of constant disorder and threat, and who were the recipients of stigma from the wider world of respectable citizens. The welfare 'scroungers', the immigrants, the junkies and crack heads: the demons of modern society. ... an underclass of despair.
>
> (2002: 465)

In 2011, Kenneth Clarke (1940–), a British Conservative politician and the then Justice Secretary, following the riots (see **Figure 17.10**) of that year stated:

> I've dealt with plenty of civil disobedience in my time, but the riots in August shocked me to the core. What I found most disturbing was the sense that the hardcore of rioters came from a *feral underclass* cut off from the mainstream in everything but its materialism.
>
> (*The Guardian*, 5 September 2011)

Looking briefly at the 19th-century writers (Engels and Mayhew) we have just considered, two very different narratives emerge. Engels (1844) wrote about the gross injustices of the unfair social system and saw crime as the start of a rising-up against that system. This is a conflict concept of crime and social systems. Mayhew (1861–2) also recognised that many people were being driven into poverty and from there to crime and agreed that crime can be caused by social factors. However in contrast to Engels, Mayhew did not argue for dramatic social change or revolution. Despite not blaming individuals, he recognised certain lifestyles as dangerous to the fabric of the rest of society—these lifestyles formed an underclass. This concept of an underclass, separate from the 'honest' poor, still exists today. It can be seen in the writings of Murray (1990) and Young (2002) and of some politicians (Clarke, K., 'Punish the feral rioters, but address our social deficit too', *The Guardian*, 5 September 2011).

As with the writers of the 19th century, Murray and Young take very different views of the underclass. Murray views the underclass as a danger, something which needs to be dealt with by removing welfare payments and applying strong punishments and controls (for a fuller discussion, see the consideration of **right realism** in **Chapter 20**). Young, on the other hand, studies it in order to discover how best to move to a more inclusive and just social order.

Murray's theory

Charles Murray (1943–) is an American political scientist who stigmatises various aspects of modern society as the

Figure 17.10 The individuals involved in the 2011 London riots were depicted by the then Justice Secretary as belonging to a dangerous 'underclass'

Source: Henry Langston

'new underclass' (see Murray 1984, 1990, 2001). As was the case for many 19th-century authors, he considers dependency on welfare payments as the seat of this 'evil'. Welfare payments that are used to support people for a brief period while they get themselves back on their feet is, to Murray, acceptable as supporting the deserving poor. However, he is less tolerant of what he sees as the underclass or the undeserving poor. He argues that welfare payments support some people's lives outside the legitimate job market for far too long so that they become dependent and stop taking responsibility for themselves. He even accuses young women of becoming pregnant in order to claim benefits and housing. In the parts of society where this happens, he argues that children are not being properly socialised and lack prosocial role models, which leads them to expect to be looked after by the state and not need to provide for themselves. He argues that they learn to depend on the state and become unwilling to work, preferring state support supplemented by the proceeds of crime. These are the undeserving poor and—according to him—they are a danger to society and a danger to their communities. As these problems proliferate, he argues that crime begins to take over and, through the victimisation of some by others in the neighbourhood, these communities tend to fragment and are destroyed or altered. The victimisation and offending build up and as more people participate in crime so the norms of that community alter, leading them to tolerate more crime (the community is permanently altered).

Murray draws together a number of the common problems which he refers to as 'demons' within criminology such as dysfunctional families (Murray sees single mothers as particularly dysfunctional), dependency on welfare payments, inconsistent discipline, and the negative effects of gangs and peer groups and ties them to a *moral deficiency*. For Murray, crime and other social ills are not the result of poverty, rather they arise out of the moral depravity of some people. The morally deprived are, for him, those undeserving in society who take advantage of others and who need to be properly controlled and appropriately punished. Murray therefore sees the 'underclass' as the problem; the people and the choices they make cause the difficulties. Murray states that it is not a structural problem caused by the economic choices of the society, it is not lack of work or low pay which is the problem but rather that it is the people who are the problem, the immoral choices they make; the lack of a willingness to work is the problem. He considers societal structure to be a side issue except that welfare payments may help to sustain rather than control this group.

Young's theory

Jock Young (1942–2013) was a British sociologist and criminologist who approached discussions of an 'underclass' from a very different perspective. He would see the actions of the group that Murray defines as the 'underclass' as an understandable reaction to the appalling inequalities some face in our society. In particular, Young (1999, 2002, 2007) and others like him, such as Taylor (1999), see massive structural unemployment (especially that which is long term) and inequalities which some face due to our social structures as destroying the lives of some in society who are made poor, homeless, and desperate. Here the 'underclass' are not criminal but people who lack hope and choices, and in this situation they turn to criminality (Young, 1999; Taylor, 1999). These commentators see lack of work, not lack of a willingness to work, as the issue. Here the problem is structural not individual.

The problems faced by some in society were recognised by 'New Labour' (a rebranding of the UK's Labour Party in the mid-1990s) when they came to power in 1997. They set up the Social Exclusion Unit to work towards reintegrating socially deprived individuals and communities and to deal with the issues of long-term unemployment, welfare-dependent single mums, truanting young people, and unpleasant housing estates. The idea was to set out policies to counter the problems faced by those whom society had failed: one of its most important strategies was entitled *A New Commitment to Neighbourhood Renewal: National Strategy Action Plan 2001*. The action plan aimed to increase employment in areas hit by unemployment, increase work-based skill levels, reduce burglary in the areas most blighted by that problem, reduce health inequalities, and raise the standard of housing in deprived neighbourhoods. The idea of the action plan was to tackle some of the structural problems in society that led to the social exclusion of some groups. However, alongside this, 'New Labour' asserted that there was also a section of the socially excluded who breached the norms of the wider society. These they viewed as individual and moral breaches and so they set policies to deal with what they saw as unacceptable choices made by these people and groups—they brought in controls to deal with problems such as antisocial behaviour (Crime and Disorder Act 1998, Anti-social Behaviour Act 2003, and Part 4 of the Policing and Crime Act 2009 (as amended by the Crime and Security Act 2010)). These individual controls were used most commonly for the working/lower classes and particularly the young and the underclass (Squires and Stephen, 2005). Young (2002) viewed this solution as setting up the illusion of a binary problem; this is the idea that society divides people into two opposite categories, often with the implication that one is 'good' and the other is 'bad'. It classifies people as either 'society at large' or 'the underclass', as 'stable families' or 'single mothers', as 'victims' or 'criminals' (see more examples in **Table 17.6**) and doesn't acknowledge that people may be in both groups at the same time. Young argued that this binary illusion actually exacerbates the issue.

Society at large	The underclass
The unproblematic	The problem
Community	Disorganisation
Employment	The workless
Independence	Welfare dependency
Stable family	Single mothers
The natives	The immigrants
Drug free	Illicit drug use
Victims	Criminals

Table 17.6 Young's binaries of social exclusion

Source: Young, J. (2002) 'Crime and Social Exclusion' in M. Maguire, R. Morgan, and R. Reiner (eds) The Oxford Handbook of Criminology (3rd edn). Oxford: Oxford University Press

The underclass, although in reality a group heterogeneous in composition and ill-defined in their nature, is a ready target for resentment.... Re-constituted, rendered clear cut and homogenous by the mass media, they became a prime focus of public attention in the sense of stereotypes: 'the undeserving poor', 'the single mother', 'the welfare scrounger' etc., and an easy focus of hostility.... the very opposite of the 'virtues' of the included, thus casting the social world into the binary mould.

(Young, 2007: 36–7)

He argues that seeing the problem as two separate groups, one conforming and the other delinquent, is too simplistic. Whilst he recognises that some areas and some people belong more to one group than another, he argues that there is a lot more intermingling of problems than is often acknowledged and 'society at large' has many of the issues that are generally associated with the underclass and vice versa. His point is that the borders of behaviour are permeable so that people in the wider society participate in negative and damaging behaviours. Furthermore, the physical borders are also permeable, people move across them and there are no clear and 'real' splits in the population. Moreover, he suggests that by asserting that there are differences and trying to target the problems a clear differentiation is created where there may never have been one, or at least not one that was so clearly defined. Therefore the provision of social exclusion units placed some inside the wider 'good' society and others outside. Naming or labelling (see **Chapter 18**) that divide made it more real and actually caused greater exclusion, increasing the problems rather than dealing with them. He also talks of 'social bulimia', a society in which the most deprived groups and individuals are the most desperate to acquire the appearance of success, for young people it may be the most fashionable trainers. For Young, a 'bulimic' society is one where the most excluded and marginalised people strongly desire the possessions that will make them feel included and that their only way to succeed may be through crime. Young argues that *cultural* inclusion sits beside systematic and *structural* exclusion. In this situation, society and those living in it are constantly unclear about what is happening and there can be claims that inclusion is working when in fact people are still experiencing clear social exclusion. So people may understand and fully accept the values of their community and of wider society (cultural inclusion) whilst simultaneously being rejected by it through prejudice, racism, exclusion from real opportunities, or other exclusionary practices (structural exclusion). Here people feel part of the society but that society alienates them, rejects them, or part of them (Young, 2007: 164). Those who are so excluded fight back by trying to turn things more in their favour in an attempt to regain respect, dignity, and to be included. They may do this by fighting a personal battle, using crime to gain the trappings of the society that structurally excludes them or by replacing some values with their own and offending to prove that their values are worthwhile (Ferrell et al., 2015). Or, they may do this by trying to alter the society through, for example, terrorism (see also Brotherton and Naegler, 2014). This concept of 'social bulimia' has a powerful explanatory quality, it is probably most useful in allowing us to understand the complexities or inclusion and exclusion. It explains that they are not binary issues, rather they are complex interwoven ideas that need to be examined in more depth for them to be useful either as explanatory concepts or a means to resolve problems in society.

Bearing in mind what you have just read, take a look at **What do you think? 17.4** and consider the questions raised.

WHAT DO YOU THINK? 17.4

Thinking again about tackling crime

This is a real letter sent to certain people in 2015. Previously you were asked how you would feel about receiving a letter like this and what it told you about the way the police were operating. Now you need to consider whether the letter should be seen as a positive move by the police. Different people in society might view it very differently. Also think about whether it is singling certain people out for different treatment and, if so, whether you think it is likely to cause greater problems as Young claimed would be the case with the social exclusion units.

TERRITORIAL POLICING

Brent Borough
603 Harrow Road
Wembley
Middlesex
HA0 2HH

19th August 2015

Dear

You may be aware of an incident on the Kilburn High Road on Sunday 16th August during which a 24 year old man received serious stab injuries. This is being treated as an attempted murder.

Our intelligence suggests you are linked to gang related criminal activity in the South Kilburn area. We are determined to bring the cycle of violence affecting this area to an end. We are not suggesting you were directly involved in the latest incident but we believe that you are involved in criminal behaviour that puts you at greater risk of becoming a victim or a perpetrator of violent crime yourself.

We would like to invite you to take the opportunity to meet with Brent Police, Brent Council and other agencies to discuss the events of 16th August, possible risks to yourself, and ways we can help you move away from criminal behaviour.

This meeting will take place on **Thursday 27th August at 3pm at the Marian Centre 1 Stafford Road NW6 5RS.**

If you choose not to attend we will see this as a clear message that you intend to continue with a criminal lifestyle. As such, we will work hard to disrupt your activities utilising every legitimate means available to us.

Yours Sincerely

Borough Commander

Social exclusion and the underclass: critique

Subcultural theories focus on the effect of groups on individuals; for most of the theories we have discussed in this section, these are groupings *chosen* by the individual. Their choices of subculture may be constrained by those available in their neighbourhood but there is a choice. However, theories about social exclusion and the underclass focus on groups into which people *are fitted* rather than those which they choose. Although Murray suggests some fault on their part (they might have moved into the honest poor rather than the underclass), these are still groupings that the individual might not even recognise let alone choose to inhabit. For Young, the underclass is a structural creation of the powerful; for **critical criminologists**, this group is important to society as it is a grouping into which others in society do not want to sink so it helps to control the honest poor. What they have in common is that both the underclass and subcultural criminology largely apply to the lower classes. In the case of much subcultural theory and of Murray's underclass, they seek to explain criminal statistics which are seriously flawed and may explain more about the agencies of control than about those who offend.

Most of these theories assume that social exclusion largely arises out of poverty or lack of money relative to others. If true, then simple redistribution of wealth may alleviate the problem. However, it may arise out of exclusion from other things, for example work, and governments could thereby try to resolve issues by rendering work and other opportunities more 'real' for those who have suffered most. However, Young suggests a far more complex interlinking of exclusion and inclusion, something he calls 'social bulimia'. This idea recognises the possibility that both exclusion and inclusion may appear and be working on a person or group simultaneously. Here it is important to recognise that their effects are complex and simple policy interventions such as redistribution of wealth or creating more job opportunities are unlikely to work. Partially this means that a more individual approach is necessary (shaped to a particular individual or group) and partially it underlies that we need to take far more notice of the effects of exclusion such as loss of dignity, respect, and rights in order to work out solutions to these issues.

17.7 Conclusion

Each of the theories studied in this chapter has aspects which are useful to understanding crime but they are each also seriously flawed. Collectively, their most important strength is that they draw our attention to the fact that the individual is not a totally separate actor making decisions without any input from others. They clearly illustrate that social, environmental, economic, and cultural aspects impact on each and every one of us and help to shape who we are, how we think, and therefore play a part in whether we are likely to participate in criminal activities. They draw attention to particular aspects of our social architecture (physical, structural, cultural, human) which make it more or less likely that we will offend. Each theory draws attention to a different aspect of society as being important. In doing this, they draw attention away from both our ability to fully blame an individual for the choices they make and our blaming behaviour on flawed individuals (individual physical or psychological flaws which may be associated with criminality). They awaken a realisation that the society which complains of the crime may be part of the problem, may be partially complicit or flawed such that crime is more likely.

Collectively they also have problems. Many of these theories rely too heavily on official statistics as a true indicator of who offends, where they live, and what type of laws are being breached. Many of these theories conveniently forget that many offences are committed by the wealthy and powerful or the middle classes but that they are rarely caught or prosecuted. Anomie, strain, subcultural, and social exclusion theories all have this flaw. Some of these theories are accused of being atheoretical—too descriptive and not based in real theory. So, for example, social disorganisation is not a real theory, it is more a description of the problem. Most theories in this chapter also focus on men, they fail to really consider how these same social and structural issues impact on women and why there is such a large difference in the rate at which women resort to crime compared to men when they live in the same circumstances. Of course, maybe male and female criminality is, in fact, a lot more similar than suggested by the official statistics but if that is true then the statistics are problematic and, again, many of these theories lose much of their credibility. Many of these theories also use simplified ideas of, for example, culture or subculture, they do not always fully engage with the deeper sociological literature, they select the aspects of society, culture, and structure they wish to highlight and collect data which will or might appear to throw light on its effects.

Overall, these theories are important to our wider understanding of the causes and effects of crime, they certainly ensure that we take account of social as well as individual facts. None of these theories alone explain criminality generally or in any individual case, neither do they together offer a full explanation of criminal behaviour. However, each throws light on certain aspects of criminality and therefore may offer a way of countering criminal activity.

Therefore, you need to read all of these theories with care and with a critical eye, looking for both strengths and weaknesses. You need to consider exactly how far it is sensible to use any one theory to explain criminality and to prevent offending or deal with those who transgress.

SUMMARY

After reading this chapter and working your way through its features you should now be able to:

- **Recognise the contribution of sociology to the development of criminology as a subject in its own right**

Sociologists suggest that individual behaviour is affected by broader social, structural, or cultural conditions. Many sociological theories are positivist in that they suggest that behaviour is, to an extent, predetermined. Criminal behaviour is therefore at least partially attributed to forces outside the control of the individual. For example, an individual may be born into a poor community where many people offend and through a peer group, or learning from others or merely to survive and acquire money or food, something (or a combination of things) may propel them towards criminality. Sociologists do not claim that these external factors absolutely cause crime but rather that they are an environment in which that behaviour becomes more likely, they *influence* some people to offend.

Their contribution is therefore to guide policymakers towards aspects of our social environment which, if altered, may reduce the likelihood of offending.

- **Identify the main strands of sociological thinking and distinguish their differing contributions to criminology**

In criminology there are three main strands of sociological thought: social intervention or social process theories (micro-sociological theories), social structural theories or structuralism (macro-sociological theories), and social conflict theories (generally macro-sociological theories).

Social interaction or social process theories search for explanations of criminality in an individual's close social situation or environment. They consider how groups and individuals interact and how this affects behaviour. Social interaction theories include differential association theories, social control theories, and labelling perspectives.

Structuralism considers the way in which broad social conditions such as poverty impact on the way in which people behave. Their argument is that the way in which a society chooses (largely through policy set by governments) to structure itself opens up or closes down the choices people enjoy. For example, policy may shape what sort of home an individual lives in, the type of school they attend, and the types of work available to them. Each of these will open up or close down various opportunities and therefore influence the direction of a person's life. Social structural theories include social strain theories, social disorganisation theories, and subcultural theories.

Conflict theorists consider that society is weighted in favour of certain groups of people—the powerful, those who pass laws. The core of their argument is that societies revolve around relationships of conflict and domination where those in power use their authority to ensure that they retain control and that others, the powerless subjects, are carefully controlled.

- **Appreciate the contribution of the Chicago School to the study of criminology**

The Chicago School is about social disorganisation and is significant for criminologists because it places the cause of offending squarely within the ecology surrounding the offender. For Shaw and McKay, social context, linked in to broader structural factors such as transient populations, recession, poverty, and unemployment, was of central importance. However, the most crucial factor was the social disorganisation within a community or neighbourhood leading to weakened informal social controls leaving young people free to offend and be antisocial. However, the theory fails to explain why many people in those areas remain law abiding. In spite of differing opinion, however, no one can deny its influence has been and remains strong as a factor to explain juvenile crime and was heavily drawn on in some of the subcultural theories.

- **Understand and critique the concept of anomie and strain**

Durkheim argues that far from being a negative occurrence, crime is actually necessary for a healthy society; a certain level of crime is functional and helps to make law-abiding citizens feel more connected. However, he views high levels of crime as dysfunctional, as an indication of a society in which the rules have broken down; an anomic society. Durkheim does not indicate how much crime is healthy and exactly how we know when a society is anomic.

For Merton, anomie is slightly different; it takes account of social structural problems. Here, a society becomes anomic when people's desire cannot be met through legitimate means. Whilst under this strain many people will continue to conform, some will choose one of the other ways of coping: innovation, ritualism, retreatism, and rebellion. Merton does not really explain what causes the strain or why it leads to a particular type of response.

- **Understand differential association and understand how it might help to prevent offending**

Sutherland (1939a, 1939b, 1949) argued that, as with almost all other human activities, crime is a learnt behaviour. If crime occurred in the environment in which someone lived or worked then it would be learnt along with other behaviours, in that way he saw crime as normal behaviour. If at work criminal activity is normal, it will be learnt but may not be transferred into other social environments. However, his theory says little about how or why one person learns criminal behaviour when someone else in the same environment does not. This learning involves both the values (values loose enough to permit, or even expect, criminality) and the skills (the abilities necessary to commit a particular crime) so by undermining the values, teaching an individual why the activity is wrong, one might be able to persuade them not to reoffend; this forms the basis of mentoring and reintegrative shaming.

- **Critically consider how subculture advances our understanding of offending behaviour**

Subcultural theories base their explanations on smaller groupings in society, often the young. Cohen suggested that peer groups adopt looser values freeing young people to offend. For Cloward and Ohlin, the young people were under strain and offending was one coping strategy. Matza and Sykes add the idea of neutralisation and Matza adds drift. Matza argued that all people drift between being law abiding and offending and some feel free to offend in particular situations because it is the only real solution, the offending is therefore 'not their fault'. It is unclear whether this explanation of it being 'not their fault' arises before the offending and explains why they feel free to offend or is a mechanism used to assuage any feelings of guilt.

Subcultural theories, to a greater or lesser extent, free the offenders from guilt, their criminal activity being explained by something outside their control. These theories have shown some ways in which one might intervene to help young people build more law-abiding lives.

- Appreciate the complex relationship between social exclusion and criminal activity

There are a number of sides to social exclusion. Murray sees the 'underclass' or those who are socially excluded as being the problem, as dangerous, people everyone else needs to be protected from. Others see this group as suffering the problems of poverty and unemployment and wish to help them (New Labour's social exclusion units). A third group, including Young, consider that while you might intervene to relieve problems for an individual or a family, any blanket official differentiation will exacerbate the divide and thus cause more problems, more exclusion.

Test your understanding of the chapter's key points by attempting the self-test questions on the **online resources** at www.oup.com/he/case2e

REVIEW QUESTIONS

1. Name and explain three key concepts in the sociology of crime.
2. Explain the extent to which the following offences/acts of deviance might be explained by differential association and consider the limitations of that explanation:
   - stealing the secrets of a rival company for use by your company;
   - burglary.
3. How does Durkheim suggest that crime is functional for a society?
4. Explain the differences between Durkheim's and Merton's concepts of anomie.
5. How useful are the subcultural theories to explaining youth offending in the UK?
6. What are the main differences between Cohen's subcultural theory and that of Matza?
7. What is meant by the term 'underclass' and why does Young see it as divisive to deal with the issue through social exclusion?

Access the **online resources** at www.oup.com/he/case2e to check your answers to the review questions.

FURTHER READING

Bernard, T. J., Snipes, J. B., and Gerould, A. L. (2015) *Vold's Theoretical Criminology* (7th edn). Oxford: Oxford University Press.
Discusses the issues in detail and provides some examples and references though it is written from an American perspective and the examples are generally from the US. See Ch. 6, Durkheim and anomie; Ch. 7, Chicago School; Ch. 8, strain theories including Merton, and parts of Ch. 9, social learning.

Downes, D., Rock, P., and McLaughlin, E. (2016) *Understanding Deviance* (7th edn). Oxford: Oxford University Press.
This book has excellent chapters on each aspect of this sociological positivism (Chs 3, 4, 6, and parts of 9). These chapters provide challenging and often radical consideration of the classical texts. The section about 'Culture and Subculture' (Ch. 6) is particularly useful.

Lilly, J. R., Cullen, F. T., and Ball, R. A. (2011) *Criminological Theory: Context and Consequences.* Thousand Oaks, CA: Sage. Especially Chs 3 and 4.
Provides clear analysis of the classical texts, though it is written from an American perspective.

McLaughlin, E. and Muncie, J. (2013) *Criminological Perspectives: Essential Readings* (3rd edn). London: Sage. Especially readings 6, 9, 10, 14, 15, 16, 21, 23, 24.
It is very important to read the original texts written by these theorists. Whilst you may not have time to read their whole texts, it is essential to read the essential or key extracts.

Newburn, T. (2009) *Key Readings in Criminology* (2nd edn). Cullompton: Willan Press. Especially sections 8 and 9.
As with McLaughlin, it is very important to read the original texts written by these theorists. Whilst you may not have time to read their whole texts it is essential to read the essential or key extracts.

Rock, P. (2012) 'The Sociology of Crime' in M. Maguire, R. Morgan, and R. Reiner (eds) *The Oxford Handbook of Criminology* (5th edn). Oxford: Oxford University Press.
Rock, P. (2017) 'The Foundations of Sociological Theories of Crime' in A. Liebling, S. Maruna, and L. McAra (eds) *The Oxford Handbook of Criminology* (6th edn). Oxford: Oxford University Press.
These chapters discuss the issues in detail and provide more examples and references.

Williams, K. S. (2012) *Textbook on Criminology* (8th edn). Oxford: Oxford University Press. Chs 11 and 12.
As with Rock, this book discusses the issues in detail and provides more examples and references.

 Access the **online resources** to view a wealth of extra information relating to your study of criminology, including self-test questions, answers to review questions, and links to other resources that will help you enjoy and fulfil your potential within your studies.
www.oup.com/he/case2e

CHAPTER OUTLINE

18.1	Introduction	562
18.2	What is critical about critical criminology?	563
18.3	Social construction and power	564
18.4	Labelling perspectives	566
18.5	Marxist-inspired critical theories	572
18.6	Examples of the diversity of critical criminological theories	576
18.7	Conclusion	586

18

Critical criminology

KEY ISSUES

After studying this chapter, you should be able to:

- appreciate the philosophical and political arguments that underpin critical criminological theories;
- understand the different foundational strands within critical criminology, and their development within a cultural and historical context;
- develop an awareness of how important the ideas of power and power relations are to the study of critical criminology;
- discuss the problems of 'deviance' and its interpretation and control;
- relate theoretical ideas to the real world through specific examples, such as state crime, feminist perspectives, subcultures and emotions (cultural criminology), and convict criminology.

18.1 Introduction

Before you read any further, go and look at yourself in a mirror. Ask yourself these questions:

- Where did you get your clothes and why did you choose them?
- What sort of jewellery and make-up are you wearing?
- How many different toiletries have you used today?

Let's consider your clothes: do you know where they were made and under what conditions? Was your jacket a genuine bargain, or might there be a reason why it was cheap, for example because it was made by an exploited worker in an unsafe factory or sweatshop? Perhaps some of your clothes came from a charity shop, which could be argued to be more ethical. However, have you ever questioned why, in the 21st century, people with illnesses and disabilities still have to rely on charities for help, or why there are still starving populations? Now think about why you chose your clothes—maybe for cultural reasons, to make a point, or to identify with a particular group. These choices tell other people something about us—for example, a yarmulke (or kippah, see **Figure 18.1**) tells us that a man or boy is Jewish—but these signifiers can also provoke prejudice and disapproval. Society judges us based on appearance (a skirt is too short, a hoodie hides a face) and so tries to 'control' those choices. Muslim women are or feel pressured to take off their scarves and veils (**Figure 18.2**), little boys are told they want dinosaurs and not fairies on their new trainers, and there is pressure to have a particular toned physique, especially for the summer months.

Consider your jewellery. Are you lucky enough to be wearing any gold or diamonds? If so, how were they mined? You may notice now that some high-street jewellers offer 'ethical gems'—does the average shopper know what makes an 'unethical' one? Do you know if the make-up, hair products, or other toiletries you have used were tested on animals? And if you take selfies, how much do you know about the precious and toxic metals that are used to make your phone? Where did they come from, who mined them, and what happens to the old phone when you upgrade?

You may be wondering how all these issues relate to crime and criminology. Crimes involving the exploitation of workers, and the breaching of human rights or international treaties, are examples of crimes of the powerful and, in many cases, **state crime**. The thoughts and opinions of others, and the effect that these may have on how we see ourselves and may behave, form the basis of a strand of sociological thinking known as **labelling perspectives**. Race and gender are important elements of criminological study (and are discussed further in **Chapters 10 and 11** respectively), as is **green criminology** (**Chapter 12**), which considers the impact of human activity on the environment. That one short look in the mirror touched on the preoccupations of a range of different theoretical approaches which are generally seen as strands of **critical criminology**, and demonstrated that these theories (as with all theories) are relevant and can be applied to all aspects of our daily lives.

Criminologists draw on many of these kinds of theories in their work, but the strands that are widely regarded as most important in the development of critical criminology (all of which arose in the 1960s and 1970s) are labelling perspectives, Marxist-inspired critical theories, power perspectives, and feminist perspectives. We consider all four strands in this chapter (though we only cover the

Figure 18.1 The choices we make about our appearance tell other people something about our culture or beliefs, but these signifiers can also provoke prejudice and disapproval

Source: Gimas/Shutterstock

Figure 18.2 The pressure that can be placed on Muslim women to take off their headscarves or veils is an example of society trying to control our choices about our appearance

Source: Amir Ridhwan/Shutterstock

third briefly; for more depth, see **Chapter 11**). The ideas and insights contained within these theories inspired and prepared the ground for more recent developments in the field, including cultural criminology and convict criminology, which will be considered in this chapter.

We now know which principal theories constitute critical criminology, but what do these theories have in common that places them under this same banner? Critical criminology does not just suggest that we make small alterations to our criminal justice systems. Instead, it requires us to question everything we think we 'know' about these systems and the societies and communities in which we live. It questions how and why we control behaviour, it looks from the perspective of the oppressed or the powerless and suggests alternative narratives that should be part of our accepted knowledge base—different solutions based on 'out of the box' thinking. For example, rather than increasing crime control and punishment, it might suggest that society is altered to tackle the root of the problem, to tackle poverty, inequality, and oppression. This takes attention away from individual misdeeds and focuses instead on the misdeeds of powerful corporations, the state, etc. Looking at the 2020 race protests which arose in the wake of the killing of George Floyd by a police officer in the US, we can see these two factions—the powerless and the powerful—writ large. President Trump defended the actions of the officer and called for 'law and order' to be resumed by quashing the protests, by force if necessary; he did not accept that the killing reflected any prejudice or unfairness in US society. The protesters talked about the cold-blooded killing of Floyd by an agent of the state and what it showed about the way the state (through the action of the police) devalued and dehumanised black people and failed to value black lives; they protested to awaken US society to this injustice. Whilst neither side necessarily holds the whole 'truth', we are indoctrinated with the status quo (the perspective of the powerful) from birth, so critical criminology which gives voice to the less powerful is essential to help us question what we think we 'know' about ourselves and our society. Studying critical criminology will help you to question and think differently about your society and how it operates.

18.2 What is critical about critical criminology?

What is *critical* about critical criminology? Perhaps the best way to answer this is to explain what critical criminology is not, as there is no standard or agreed definition of what it actually is. Nor is there one critical criminology. Instead there is a range of diverse perspectives, all of which have some features and themes in common (so it is probably more accurate to talk about critical criminological theories, plural) and we shall be exploring some of these further in this and other chapters.

As we saw in **Chapters 15**, **16**, and **17**, the mainstream, traditional, and conventional criminological perspectives of classicism and positivism have, over the years, been subject to trenchant criticism. This is the first common theme—and indeed the starting point—of critical criminological theories; that they were developed, in part, from a thorough, critical review of both classicism and positivism. We will set our sights on positivism here if only because it was, in many ways, the dominant and mainstream paradigm of viewing crime in the 20th century. Many would argue that perhaps it still is today. One of the foremost critical criminologists, Jock Young, has argued that positivism has become hubristic (over-confident), with its increasing use of sophisticated mathematical formulae which attempt to accurately measure our subject matter, and has effectively almost 'closed down' the criminological imagination (Young, 2011: 10–21).

As you will remember from **Chapters 15**, **16**, and **17**, the perspective of positivism (in either its biological, psychological, or sociological forms) can be reduced to four main ideas. These are:

- determinism;
- scientism;
- consensus;
- treatment/rehabilitation.

Before we see how critical theorists challenged these ideas, let's briefly recap what they mean.

In general, positivist theories argue that our behaviour is *determined* (or driven) through forces which are, to a great extent, beyond our control. These forces may be biological or psychological, such as through having a specific genetic predisposition (as in the individual variant of positivism) or social, such as where we live or who we associate with (as in the sociological variant). By speaking the powerful language of numbers and statistics, the 'holy grail' of much early criminological research was to *scientifically* find out the causes of crime (or aetiology). There is a logic to all this: if you can scientifically, in an *objective*, *neutral*, and *value-free* way (see **Chapters 4** and **22** for a further discussion of these ideas) prove that A causes B, then it follows that you will be able to prevent B if you do something about A (for instance, treat or improve it). We can still see the logic of such arguments today. For instance, it has been argued that antisocial behaviour in young people (ASB) is a 'syndrome' (note the use of a medical language here) which can be 'treated' pharmacologically—that is, through the use of prescription drugs (see Viding et al., 2005). Similarly, if it is thought that crime is caused by poor living environments, then these can be addressed through a range of social policies which focus on environmental design, such as improving housing standards and the areas in which people live. The last and most important foundational idea of positivism is that there is a general agreement (a *consensus*) not only on what 'crime' is, but also on who the 'criminals' and our 'public enemies' are. So, what, according to critical criminologists, are the main problems with all of this?

First, for the critical criminologist it makes little sense to argue that our behaviour is totally determined through forces over which we have no control. To be sure, our behaviour may, in part, be driven or influenced by internal and external influences and social structures. For instance, the world and lived realities of an 18-year-old, single parent, black woman living in poverty are very different to those of a wealthy, white, middle-class male of the same age—race, class, and gender are, as we shall see later in the chapter, very important. But we all have degrees of choice. Indeed, it could be said that some forms of 'criminal' behaviour can be logical and very meaningful and cannot simply be the result of faulty reasoning or defective genes or where we grow up. The idea that we can 'scientifically' study all of this so that the 'criminal' can be treated in some way can also be questioned. As we saw in **Chapter 5** when we considered self-report studies, most of us, at some point in our lives, will have done something which has transgressed the criminal law and which could have warranted a criminal sanction. To quote the late Sir Terry Pratchett (a novelist), 'everyone's guilty of something'. But even if we do think about ourselves with this much honesty, do we really see ourselves as 'criminals' who need to be 'treated' or do we see ourselves as somehow different, whose actions don't count as being *deviant* (something which is not the norm)? How do we and society draw these boundaries?

As well as helping and curing, we need to remember that treatment in its various guises can also be used as a form of control. Imagine, for a minute, the possibility that scientists discovered *the* criminal gene or that neuroscientists, through sophisticated brain-imaging techniques, could clearly show us a 'criminal mind'. What do you think the logical conclusions and 'treatments' could be? Whilst advances in medical science have been incredible over the last 60 years (since the discovery of penicillin to treat disease) and have the potential for doing good in terms of the identification and treatment, prevention, and management of various diseases, we should not forget that there is also a potential dark side to all of this. For instance, if a 'criminal gene' could be 'discovered' then the logic, when pushed to extremes, could result in the compulsory sterilisation of those carrying the gene or even worse—their complete eradication. This all may seem a little over the top, but history tells us otherwise; there are many historical examples of states implementing policies of eugenics and pseudoscientific forms of racism, with Nazi Germany being the obvious one. More recently, in 2012, a UKIP council candidate's personal manifesto proposed that any foetus with a disability be aborted, in order to prevent it being a 'burden' on the state (*The Independent*, 18 December 2012).

All of these questions are raised by the critical criminologist. For this branch of criminological **theory**, the very idea that there could be a consensus on what is crime, and what causes it, is something that is in itself open to debate (see **What do you think? 18.1**). We often hear the word *law* coupled with the word *order* as if 'law and order' were one and the same thing. But, if you think about it, we can only really have a conception of 'order' if we have a clear picture of what 'disorder' might look like, and such things are rarely as clear-cut as they may, at first, seem.

Having gained a clearer idea of what critical criminology is (or, at least, what it is not), we can move on to consider some of the main ideas and theories with which it is associated. We will begin this by exploring the concept of power and how this can affect crime—for example, whether behaviour is defined as crime, and how or whether it is punished. We then move on to labelling perspectives and consider how the powerful shape our thoughts and conceptions of right and wrong, how we think about other people and, in turn, how this affects the way people think and feel about themselves and, maybe, how they behave. From there, the chapter considers Marxist-inspired theories and ends with examples from state crime, feminism (also studied in more depth in **Chapter 11**), and consideration of two relatively new areas of critical criminology: cultural criminology and convict criminology.

18.3 Social construction and power

The concept of power is crucial to critical criminologists who argue that rather than being based on an agreed consensus, society (and the social order) is perhaps best viewed as being made up of a variety of groups which do not always agree with each other and have different values; this is usually called *pluralism*, although you may wish to think of it in terms of diversity. After all, we live in diverse societies which have diverse **norms** and values.

WHAT DO YOU THINK? 18.1

What is antisocial about antisocial behaviour?

We often read in the press about the idea of antisocial behaviour (ASB) but what does it actually mean?

- Try to jot down a precise definition of it and list forms of behaviour which you regard as being antisocial.
- What images come in to your head as you do so?
- Did you find this an easy thing to do or was it trickier than you initially thought?
- Why might this be the case?
- Do you think if you were to do this as a seminar exercise that you would find a general agreement (a consensus) across your class?

ASB hit the headlines in the late 1990s. It remains a cause for concern to the extent that most local authorities now have multi-agency partnerships which work with the police and other agencies to try to deal with it. The Crime and Disorder Act 1998 defines ASB as:

> Acting in a manner that caused or was likely to cause harassment, alarm or distress to one or more persons not of the same household as (the **defendant**).

As you can see, this is a rather broad and even vague definition. What is antisocial to one person may well be acceptable to another. The main point of all of this is that terms such as ASB (and even the very **concept** of crime) are *socially constructed*; that is, they are constructed through a series of social processes and are essentially contested concepts. This means that whilst the broad idea of ASB may be generally understood by most people, what exactly it encompasses for each person or group of people may be slightly different and will depend on the community, **culture**, subculture, etc. in which they are living. According to the critical criminologist, the same can be said of the concept of crime. This is seen through the fact that what counts as a crime is constantly changing: it is a dynamic concept (see **Chapter 2** for a more developed discussion and analysis of this crucial point). As we shall see in this chapter, laws do indeed change and they are far from being carved in tablets of stone. One of the reasons for this is to do with the final and perhaps most important and central concept which informs critical criminology; that of *power*.

Can we really speak in terms of there being 'moral absolutes' today? In a stronger form, it could be argued that people rarely agree and are in constant *conflict* with each other. This is where the concept of power comes in. Here it is argued that the important thing for us to study is how particular versions of social reality are constructed in the first place; particularly the questions of who has the power to help define what crime actually is (see **Chapters 2** and **19**), and to declare what the crime problem is. In short, critical criminologists argue that power is distributed unequally in societies and that inequality in terms of social class, as well as race and gender, can lead to 'crime problems' and to distinct and often harsh penal policies in terms of policing and sentencing. Critical criminology can therefore be said to be a 'political project', as one of its key aims is to demystify how 'crime' itself is defined and to question the very nature of *justice*. In doing so, it aims to somehow change society at a structural (social and cultural) level to bring about a more socially just society (see the discussion of the concept of justice in **Chapter 3**).

It could therefore be argued that the most important criticisms levelled by critical criminologists are that the orthodox and mainstream criminological theories (such as positivism) didn't pay nearly enough attention to the crucial concept of *power* and the resulting *power relations* which characterise society. The very idea of power is a central one to all social sciences and is vital to critical criminological perspectives. In general, critical criminologists draw on this concept of power and foreground it in two particular ways:

1. **The power of some groups to criminalise (and decriminalise) forms of behaviour** Here it is argued that certain people in society (the powerful) have the authority to at least partially define what counts as 'crime' and what makes up the 'crime problem'. It follows that there are thus certain groups (the powerless) whose behaviour is sometimes defined as criminal. A good way to think about this is to look back through history. You will see how things we now consider to be perfectly okay were once illegal—homosexuality, for instance. To be gay was against the law in the UK until 1967 and it was not until 1982 that it became legal in Northern Ireland. Homeless and starving children in the 18th century could be hanged for stealing food, whereas today we would be prosecuting the family members (parents or carers) who had neglected to feed and house them (child neglect). Critical criminologists would find fault with both of these approaches. Unless the family members

(parents or carers) have money and are cruelly refusing to feed their children, the children's hunger probably arises from the poverty of the whole family, caused, critical criminologists might argue, by the way in which a society is shaped rather than simply because of the behaviour of individuals; it is a structural issue in the hands of the powerful. The idea of who decides who and what are acceptable (and what causes the shifts in these beliefs) is something critical criminologists are very interested in and, as can be seen from the example of the starving child, something they consider and try to shape.

2. **The power of some groups to evade being criminalised** This refers to the idea that the acts and behaviours of powerful groups are sometimes not defined as being criminal, even when these acts cause enormous harm and even deaths. For example, until relatively recently, only direct employees were able to claim compensation from companies who were negligent in their handling of asbestos—a fibre which if you breathe it in can cause illness and death. Nobody else affected was able to seek compensation for the effects of asbestos, regardless of the fact that women washing their husbands' work clothes were also inhaling the harmful fibres and suffering from the associated diseases. We have also read stories of large multinational corporations avoiding the payment of corporation tax. For example, three large multinational companies and household names (Starbucks, Google, and Amazon) have all had the ways in which they sought to reduce their overall tax burdens scrutinised by the British government. In other words, millions of pounds which could (and should) have gone into the public coffers to pay for things such as healthcare, schools, libraries, and housing and so on have been withheld through what are considered to be 'legitimate' tax-avoidance schemes.

The obvious form of power that springs to mind when considering these issues is political power, closely followed by economic power (although these often merge and become blurred), but it can also be seen in terms of race, class, and gender, where certain types of people are able to exercise power over others—for example, in a **patriarchy** where older men have a power over women, girls, and younger boys, which may be reflected in the law. We will be looking at how critical criminology considers all these groups later on in the chapter. For now, though, it's important that we give the question of power more attention (see **What do you think? 18.2**).

18.4 Labelling perspectives

Although there has been a long history of critical thinking around issues of crime, criminality, and its control (dating back to the late 19th and early 20th centuries), this never really had a huge influence on the way in which the majority of people thought about these subjects. Such ideas therefore had very little impact on governmental responses

WHAT DO YOU THINK? 18.2

If power were a shape, what would it look like? Quickly draw your ideas and ask your classmates to do the same. Why have you all chosen to represent it in the way that you have?

Many of you will have chosen to draw a triangle, with the point (apex) representing the 'top of the tree' with power being situated at the top and trickling downwards. Some of you may have drawn a triangle pointing downwards, suggesting that although power is in the smallest part, it supports the greatest area. How many of you drew a constantly moving spiral or changing shape? This is perhaps more accurate and interesting as it captures the idea that power can ebb and flow. For instance, it reflects the way that we as individuals experience differing levels of power throughout our lives—being powerless as children, more powerful as adults, and losing power again as we age. This supports the idea there is no one single powerful group in society but that there are many who have varying degrees of power at different times.

Power is indeed a tricky and slippery concept but, as we have seen, critical criminologists draw on it to highlight how an individual or group of individuals utilise power to achieve acceptance and compliance, or to persuade people to behave in ways in which they would not ordinarily do and which may not even be in their interests. A key issue for you to think about here is how does power become legitimised. In other words, how do powerful groups gain, exercise, and maintain their control over others. These questions are at least partly examined by the first perspective we shall look at, that of 'labelling'.

to crime and never really successfully challenged and changed mainstream, powerful ideas. Indeed, many of the earliest critical thinkers were marginalised voices at the time they were writing. They included Prince Pyotr Kropotkin (1842–1921), a Russian aristocrat who believed society did not need government but thought instead that it should be based upon ideals of mutual cooperation and support between the workers, and Willem Bonger (1876–1940) who was a Dutch criminologist heavily influenced by Karl Marx and who formed the view that crime was a result of the capitalist system. Whilst the legacy of these writers should not be ignored (we will return to Bonger a little later), things started to really change in the 1960s.

1960s radicalism and revolutionalising criminological thought

This decade undoubtedly witnessed a huge amount of social change. As you will be aware from your reading of **Chapters 15**, **16**, and **17**, we often need to consider the broader context of the times in which theoretical perspectives develop—after all, they rarely emerge fully formed from thin air. It is perhaps worth briefly mentioning here that in the US in the 1960s (where and when the labelling tradition emerged), many people started to question the very social order in which they lived and the power relations which structured their lives. The civil rights movement, the gay rights movement, anti-war movements (**Figure 18.3**), and alternative (hippie) subcultures all emerged with a sceptical and questioning attitude towards power and authority. Perhaps more importantly, critical sociologists such as Howard Becker (1928–), David Matza (1930–2018), and Edwin Lemert (1912–96) began to develop concepts which challenged the prevailing positivist orthodoxy. Such ideas began to take hold in the UK, as higher education was expanding, and these radical and critical ideas were being discussed by young people taking sociology degrees. Eventually, they came together to form the basis of what became known as 'labelling' perspectives.

The development of these labelling perspectives in many ways did more than simply challenge the prevailing orthodoxy of positivism. By posing more challenging and different ethical questions it could be said that they turned the problem upside down. For instance, instead of merely seeking to answer the questions of who were the criminals and why did they behave in the ways that they did, and then looking for ways in which they could be punished and controlled more effectively, labelists began to tentatively ask questions about definition and process. For example, who has the power to define crime and deviance in the first place? How might people react to being labelled in a particular way and what

Figure 18.3 It is important to consider the societal context in which theoretical perspectives develop, and in the 1960s many people were beginning to question power and authority
Source: Public domain

are the possible societal and individual consequences of this? By shifting the focus of inquiry towards the very processes of how crime becomes defined in the first place, and subsequently the social and individual reactions to it, this critical perspective literally revolutionised the development of criminology. The main line of argument of these perspectives is that it is the social reaction to certain behaviours which actually creates deviance. Or, as Lemert (1967) sums it up, that whilst the 'older sociology' (that is, positivism):

> tended to rest heavily on the assumption that deviance leads to social control.... [T]he reverse idea—i.e. that social control leads to deviance—is equally tenable and the richer premise for studying deviance in modern society.

As such, criminal behaviour was beginning to be characterised as often being meaningful, and the driven, **pathological** criminal 'other' of positivism was becoming humanised. This perspective is, however, often misunderstood, so before we start to talk about the theoretical niceties in more detail, let's take a step back and start to think about what it may actually mean to label something or someone:

> Labels are devices for saving talkative persons the trouble of thinking.
>
> (1st Viscount Morley of Blackburn, 1838–1923)

In the developed world, we use labels all the time. Adverts for anything from cough mixture to pimple cream tell us sternly to 'always read the label'. We have labels on food to tell us how much sugar is in a pudding and our clothes contain tags to tell us how to wash them. A label, in this sense, gives us a lot of information very quickly. And yet how accurate are these labels? Why do we believe things because of the way they are presented to us and why do they make us behave in certain ways (usually, why do they make us spend money)? In the world of retail, this kind of marketing trick is studied and researched with great care because it makes profit. Manufacturers know that they can charge a premium for something labelled in a certain way. One classic example of this is the packaging of painkillers; the branded (more expensive) painkillers often contain the same or very similar ingredients to the supermarket or pharmacy own brands. Similarly, there is little difference in the tablets marketed as being specific to migraines, period pain, or muscle aches—other than the price, of course.

We are taught from a very early age to decode signs and symbols. As a result, we unconsciously associate certain colours and shapes with particular aspects of life. Human beings are visual creatures, and we are drawn to how things look. We instinctively know what different labels signify. Likewise, and through a similar process, we think we know what is right or wrong about a person or group because of the way we (as individuals and as a society) decode and interpret them.

The nature of deviance

At this point it is worth taking a few moments to think about the nature of deviance and why certain acts are labelled as such. As we saw in **Chapter 2**, in its broadest sense deviance means an act which goes against what society considers to be normal, but this needs to be unpicked a bit. **Chapter 2** noted that it is not the nature of the behaviour which is deviant or criminal, rather it is the society which chooses to view it as deviant; it is a social choice (see **What do you think 2.2**). We therefore need to take into account the social context before deciding if an act is deviant or not—as we saw earlier on, ideas about deviance and acceptability change through time and only a few things (murder, theft, and so on) are more or less constantly disapproved of—although even this is argued about, such as whether killings by soldiers in times of war can be considered murder (see **Controversy and debate 2.1**) or whether stealing food to feed a starving child should be regarded as being a form of 'social crime'. We also need to bear in mind that there are degrees of deviance. Pinching an envelope from the office stationery cupboard is theft. So is embezzling vast sums from a pension fund and leaving millions of people without financial support in their old age.

Very few of us can hand on heart say we have never, ever committed any kind of deviant act. Which brings us to an important question: if we are all (at least to some degree) deviant, then why is it that only a minority of us is labelled? If we have all stolen something at some time or another—even if it is just that we stole a toffee from the corner shop when we were six—why are relatively few people defined as thieves and treated as such? Think about celebrities accused of tax avoidance—are the actions of the labelled really any different from the things the rest of us do? You are probably thinking that to steal a toffee is not as important or meaningful as the theft of millions of pounds, but we need to think about why we make that assumption; if we swap 'toffee from the shop' for 'diamond ring from my granny' does it make any difference? Where do we draw the line between the important and the unimportant deviance? In **Chapter 2** we considered how a society might decide which behaviours to control through social norms or by the criminal law; where the line is between deviance and criminality. In this chapter we will not reopen that debate though we will, in some places, look at who makes those decisions and at why certain acts which are harmful are not criminalised (see also **Chapter 19**). However, this section focuses on a different question: what happens when someone gets labelled as being deviant or an offender? How does being labelled criminal or deviant affect that person and the choices they make?

Primary and secondary deviance

Edwin Lemert, in his book *Social Pathology* (1951) proposed that there are in fact two kinds of deviancy, which he simply called *primary* and *secondary deviance*. The primary kind is that which is temporary, unwitting, and often 'secret'. It causes no long-term harm for the offender because either the act does not cause a social reaction or, if it does, then the reaction is not particularly strong or *stigmatising*. The offender does not get labelled, or—and this is where the personal reaction is important—they do not end up seeing themselves as offenders.

Secondary deviance has deeper long-term consequences. In these cases, the offender's act is caused by the way they (and others) may come to think about themselves. The impact of socially being labelled may well have an individual psychological impact on their self-identity. Having internalised the label, they may then act deviantly because they see themselves as deviant, or as part of a group that is viewed that way. As Howard Becker (1963), who is widely regarded as being the founder of the labelling tradition, would argue, the label has had a transformative effect on how they perceive themselves. Think back to where we discussed how we are taught to view signs and symbols in the supermarket; we are also taught to think in certain ways about ourselves (and other people), either by our family and community or the wider world, media, and education we are exposed to and interact with. These ideas were brought together in the work of George Herbert Mead (1934), who developed the sociological theory of *social interactionism* which influenced writers such as Becker, in which the reactions of others teach us what is 'normal' and what 'isn't'. We learn these ideas and, in our turn, pass them on to others who want to be accepted. Frank Tannenbaum, in his 1938 book *Crime and the Community*, had already proposed the idea that those who break the norms—the ones we have been learning to call the labelled—are placed in groups with names like 'junkies', 'troublemakers', and so on. Once in a group, it is harder for the labelled to be accepted back into the wider community. After all, would you want a convicted drug dealer or sex offender living next door to you?

The impact of stigma

We should remember that it is human nature to seek companionship and support from others who are like us and share similar interests—for example, a genre of books such as fantasy (like *The Lord of the Rings*), or a particular sport like football. You almost certainly will avoid places where you will be mocked or *stigmatised* for your passion, but instead will stick to places and people—and actions—where you feel accepted and understood. You are thus illustrating labelists' views that we live up to our own internal labels and by doing so may reinforce them. You feel better amongst other Tolkien or Crystal Palace fans and so your behaviour as such a fan can become more visible—you buy a scarf in your team's colours, you learn Elvish, and so on. Now imagine that the label you have is 'car thief'. You can't get a job because of it and nobody will lend you any money to get a vehicle, so you can't travel to work and are therefore unemployed. Or your label is 'immigrant' and you are shouted at in the street by a middle-class supporter of a far-right movement. Or, your label is 'teenage mother' and you are not allowed to return to school to take your A levels. How are things like this likely to affect you and your actions?

Stigma is therefore a pivotal factor when we consider the potential impact of labelling and its usage as a criminological perspective. Many of the writers considered in this section on deviance (all writing in the 1960s) gave a lot of thought to the ways in which deviancy is created by social reactions.

By accepting the importance of stigma to the creation of deviance, we can of course move on to look at how the removal of such stigma can prevent crime in the first place. Labelling proposes that instead of asking why someone committed an offence, we should instead be asking ourselves: 'Why do we consider this action to be wrong? Who says it is unacceptable?'

It can thus be argued that labelling is a process whereby we undertake two unconscious actions: we classify what we see, which makes us have expectations, and we react accordingly when those expectations are met (or we think they are met). In criminological terms, the argument is that this process relates to how groups or individuals classify and categorise other people's actions, behaviour, and appearance. The people doing the classifying (who are usually the more powerful) stereotype the people who are classified (the powerless) and expect them to behave in a certain way. When that happens, the powerful have their expectations confirmed, and react accordingly.

Recently in the UK, in the name of austerity measures, the Coalition and Conservative governments attempted to cut welfare spending budgets. The welfare state and its associated policies were intended to alleviate poverty, which people may find themselves in through no fault of their own; however, it can be argued that the impact of the cuts can itself lead to the **criminalisation** of the people that welfare was actually intended to support. The difficulties that people reliant on welfare may face can be summed up in chart form—see **Figure 18.4**.

Once a label is applied, it is very hard to remove: you can have what is often referred to as a *spoilt identity*. If you have ever applied for a job (and even on your university application) you may well have been asked to declare any criminal convictions; think for a moment about why this might be something employers (and even universities) are interested in. Sometimes it's obvious—a bank isn't going to want to employ a convicted forger—but if you were convicted of something irrelevant a long time ago, should that make any difference to your chances of getting the job or the university place? (This is something that is becoming increasingly important in the light of our 'digital tattoo'—see **Chapter 6** for more on this).

Bearing in mind the issues raised so far, see the discussion in **What do you think? 18.3**.

```
┌─────────────────────────────────────────────────┐
│  The Powerful: We need to save money so I am     │
│  going to make it harder for you to claim tax    │
│  credits and benefits. Get a full-time job.      │
└─────────────────────────────────────────────────┘

The Powerless: I don't get the minimum wage until I'm 25…so I need to claim otherwise I can't afford to feed my children.

The Powerless: I've got a part-time job but it's a zero-hours contract and I haven't got enough money to pay my bills. My employer can't afford to pay me more so I claim what I can to make ends meet.

The Powerful: But your employer has to pay you the national living wage. You won't need the credits.
```

Figure 18.4 We can think about the difficulties that people reliant on welfare may face as a 'welfare cycle'

WHAT DO YOU THINK? 18.3

Have you ever been labelled or been a labeller?

If you have ever been labelled, stop for a moment and think about how it made you feel and react.

Have you ever labelled somebody else? Perhaps you called them a punk, emo, nerd, gangsta, stoner, teenage parent, educational failure, autist, wheelchair user . . .

These may not all be obviously connected to criminology—until we think about Muslim women having their veils torn off in the street, or women in short skirts 'asking' to be assaulted, or the murder of a young woman (Sophie Lancaster in 2008—**Figure 18.5**) who was beaten to death for her Goth clothes and lifestyle, or the high rate of **hate crime** against the disabled or gay people (see **Chapter 8**)—the stories go on and on.

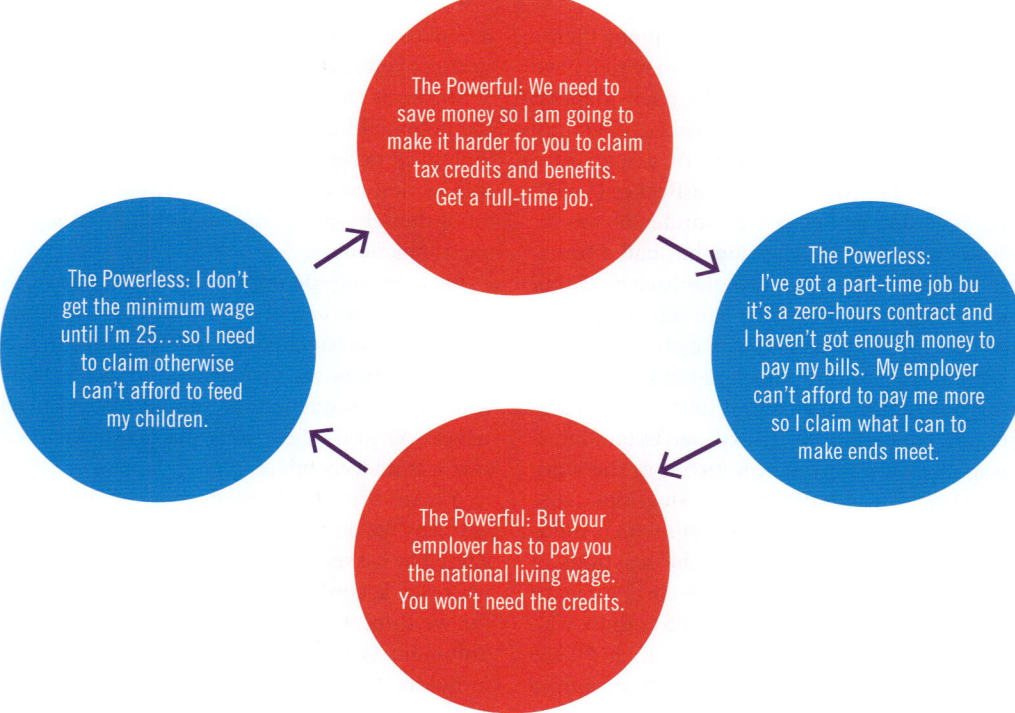

Figure 18.5 Sophie Lancaster was murdered in 2008 for no other reason than her appearance as a 'goth'
Source: PA Images

Labelling according to race and ethnicity

One of the most visible ways in which labelling can be observed is in terms of race and ethnicity (see **Chapter 10** for fuller discussion of these issues and critical race theory). Someone's physical appearance is the first thing we notice, so before we have even said our first hello we will have registered that another person is black, Asian, Chinese, white, or whatever. This can bring its own baggage in terms of our attitudes and prejudices, which in turn will have been shaped by our personal experience and the messages to which we have been exposed. Let's try to apply this to an area of current criminological concern; the controversial policing practice of stop and search.

You might also want to think about how the media represent and label various groups, and the extent to which this influences public perceptions and our general 'social constructs'. So, for instance, something like gender is a social construct, in that societies have broadly agreed ways in which males and females are supposed to look and behave—despite the fact that medical science is now showing that, biologically speaking, things are far less definite. Transgressing expected and emphasised gender expectations can often result in bullying, harassment, and violence.

It is often argued that in today's high-crime and high-risk societies, police stop-and-search tactics are a good and effective method of crime prevention and crime control. Is there, however, any evidence to support this claim? As was seen in **Chapters 4** and **10**, black people are stopped and searched far more frequently than white people, at just under three times the rate of white people across London (www.stop-watch.org). Here, we focus not on the possible bias and discrimination this might evidence, as that was considered in **Chapter 10**; rather, we are interested in the lasting effect the police behaviour has on the individuals who undergo the processes, and on their families and communities. The question here is what does it feel like to be stopped and searched and what impact does this police activity have on the individuals involved, and on their families and communities? **Controversy and debate 18.1** explores one personal account of this.

Kwabena's testimony in **Controversy and debate 18.1** highlights some of the things which we have been talking about in this section on labelling. Questions he echoes include 'where do labels come from' and 'what does it feel like to be labelled' and 'what are the potential consequences of this'. He does not adopt a 'deviant identity', as not all labels stick, but it clearly shows how such practices can make a difference to how the world is viewed; in this case, his attitude (and that of his community) towards the police. His experiences also highlight some of the potential pitfalls and problems with this approach. We will conclude this section with some thoughts on why labelling perspectives, even though they ask more searching questions about the social construction of crime and deviance and the individual or social reactions to it, only take us so far on our journey into critical criminology.

CONTROVERSY AND DEBATE 18.1

Being stopped and searched by the police

Kwabena Oduro-Ayim is an accountancy student who lives in Tottenham, North London. He is a founding member of a youth-led group that works to combat knife and gang violence in London. Below he talks about his experience of being stopped and searched by the police and how this made him feel.

> There is a kind of feeling of us against them. There's been various generations that have had negative experiences with the police. And when you've got so many fragmented stories of negative experiences with the police, it really does give a negative mosaic of the police. I mean, if you're an 8-year-old child and you go to play football, and the police officer stops and searches you. If you experience that from the age of 8, all the way through your secondary school career, then you're not going to have a positive view of the police. You will not invest faith in the police if something happens to you. You start to feel you have to take the law into your own hands. Being stopped three times in the same day, that's bound to mess up your psyche. You're criminalizing people who are already in an environment where it is extremely easy to slip into crime anyway. You don't want to give them a motive to engage in crime. For my entire childhood I would never have turned to the police for any assistance. If someone tried to rob me, my mind frame would be to phone members of my community to help me go and get back my stuff.

(Open Society, Justice Initiative, and Stopwatch (nd) 'Viewed With Suspicion; The Human Cost of Stop and Search in England and Wales'. Available at www.stop-watch.org)

Beyond the label

As we said at the beginning of this section, the impact which labelling perspectives had on the study of crime and deviance should not be overstated. At the time that they were forming their ideas, the key authors certainly started to ask a set of more penetrating questions and to raise many interesting and important issues which were neglected by more traditional criminologists. For instance: how are crime and deviance socially constructed? Who may have the power to pin a label on another? How might societies and individuals react to a particular label? And so on. We also began to see the human being behind the label. The driven, pathological, evil monster of some early positivist criminological theories became a person who made meaningful choices. This is, however, far from being the final word on critical criminological theorising. What are some of the problems with it?

You are probably thinking that some acts are obviously more serious than others, and in doing so you are raising one of the key criticisms of labelling theory. The ideas of labelling have some significant shortfalls, principally that the prime focus is on so-called 'victimless' crime and the 'underdog'. It's easier to think about labelling for offences that have less impact on us—most of us couldn't care less about whether the person who burns down our house or murders our friend has been labelled or not; we will probably see the act as deserving of stigma and punishment. Labelling also does not really give enough explanation of why only some behaviours get stigmatised, or provide answers to questions of whose law and order is being imposed on the labelled. Lastly, we need to bear in mind that, as with all other criminological perspectives, definitions and contexts remain fluid and that this will always affect what is 'normal' and what is 'unacceptable'.

It is also often argued that labelling has little practical application in terms of broader criminal justice responses to crime. This link between theory and policy implications is a very important one when studying theory; often, once such links are made, all of the other bits of the theory fall into place! For instance, as we saw in the last three chapters, the logic of classicism plays out in policy terms in the form of **deterrence** and punishment, whilst that of positivism does so in terms of treatment and rehabilitation.

The logic of labelling would be that crime is caused by processes of labelling and that, in order to do something about the 'crime problem', society should simply not label. This is perhaps not as ridiculous as it might first sound. The idea of not labelling is important and is at the core of the concept of 'radical non-intervention'; that is, simply not responding to certain forms of behaviour via the criminal justice system (proposed by Schur in 1973). Non-intervention informs some current responses to crime such as **restorative justice**, a form of justice which aims not to stigmatise perpetrators and instead brings the parties together and then reintegrates both victim and perpetrator back into their communities (you will get the chance to consider this in more detail in **Chapter 30**). Non-intervention can also be seen in the even more radical *children first, offenders second* approach (considered in **Chapter 9**) which aims, whenever possible, to divert children and young people out of the youth justice system, thereby avoiding the effects of negative labelling. Children first is important because it prioritises the responsibility of adults to ensure that children and young people enjoy their rights and that their needs as children and young people are met; it focuses far less on the risks they pose.

Perhaps the most telling criticism of labelling perspectives is that, by concentrating mainly on the effects of a label on an individual or a group of individuals, they fail to examine the way in which labels come to be used within the broader context of power. In other words, they fail to ask why particular people or groups are prosecuted and labelled, and what shapes the present laws or criminal justice practices (such as police stop and search). Furthermore, they fail to focus on the fact that many people who have harmed others in society (or committed crimes) have never been prosecuted, never labelled. They do not draw attention to the fact that crimes committed by powerful groups are rarely prosecuted—see the discussion about the power to evade criminalisation earlier on in this chapter. In short, it can be argued that their analysis of power and power relations was merely suggestive rather than being fully developed (Taylor, Walton, and Young, 1973). This leads us to **section 18.5** where we will consider some Marxist-inspired critical criminologists who developed the insights derived from labelling perspectives in a very particular and even more critical way.

18.5 Marxist-inspired critical theories

Although Marx never discussed crime in any detail, later theorists apply his ideas to the criminological field of study. There are far too many of these to include them all, so here we will focus on the most important British developments.

Jock Young and the 'naughty schoolboys'

At the University of York, in July 1968, the first ever National Deviancy Conference (NDC) was held; this was the first of 14 such conferences which took place between 1968–73. It was a meeting of like-minded critical criminologists who wanted to challenge the prevailing academic (that is, positivist) and official (that is, Home Office and Ministry of Justice) views about crime and its control which we outlined at the beginning of this chapter. They included some now legendary figures—such as Stan Cohen, Jock Young, and Mary McIntosh. Perhaps we should note that Mary was the only woman involved, and the only one of the founding members of the movement who was not later awarded a post as professor anywhere, which suggests that academic institutions are not exempt from discrimination, although she did go on to do some very important work in the study of gender and feminism. These critical thinkers were part of a new wave of British criminologists and sociologists, benefiting from wider access to higher education; traditionally something only available to the rich and privileged.

Described by one rather disapproving academic of the day as 'naughty schoolboys' (Radzinowicz, 1999: 229)—presumably Ms McIntosh was gallantly exempted—the leaders of the deviancy conference wanted to think about why society considers some acts to be deviant, why it reacts to deviancy in the ways it does, and to highlight the experiences and opinions of the deviant (who are, of course, often the powerless too). The critical movement argued that labelling didn't give enough consideration to issues of power, and instead attempted to develop a *fully social theory of deviance*, which drew on insights derived from both labelling perspectives and neo-Marxist theories of the state. This is all perhaps sounding a little bit complex so let's take a step back for a moment to consider what inspired them and, in particular, the writings of Marx.

The philosopher and political economist Karl Marx (1818–43) actually wrote very little about crime and criminality in his vast body of work; his concerns were far grander. Over the years, however, some of his ideas relating to the inequalities which he regarded as being inherent and inevitable in capitalist societies, have been drawn on in different ways by many criminologists—especially critical criminologists—attempting to explain the constructions of crime and societies' responses to it. According to Marxist ideas, such societies are characterised by the existence of a class of capitalists who own the *means of production* (the components required for the production of goods and services) and a working class who do not, but who feed it by giving their lives to keeping production going. You will often read of these two classes being referred to as the *bourgeoisie*, who are the ruling or capitalist class, and the *proletariat* or working class, although many writers influenced by Marxism today will simply use the terms the 'powerful' and 'less powerful' or even 'powerless'. Critical criminologists draw attention to the injustices of these capitalist societies (see **Figure 18.6**) and claim that the unjust institutions (health, education, legal) they develop sustain these injustices, keeping the powerless in their place. Consider this further by trying the exercise in **What do you think? 18.4**.

In terms of our journey through criminology, the critical, Marxist-based argument is that in capitalist societies there is a distinct *mode of production* (a way of producing things) which is linked to 'crime' and how those with power (the state and its agencies) respond to it. The basic argument is this: the powerful produce the goods and services we all consume and do so for profit. In doing so, they employ workers who sell their labour power for a wage (often low) and are thus exploited because they need the money to buy the goods they have themselves made. This results in there being a conflict in society between capital and labour, which is, in part, resolved through law. The law

Figure 18.6 Critics of capitalism have represented it as a pyramid with the workers supporting the rich and powerful, providing their comfort and wealth. This example is from the *Industrial Worker* (1911)

Source: *Industrial Worker*

> ### WHAT DO YOU THINK? 18.4
>
> **Developing the pyramid of capitalism**
>
> Look at the reproduction of the 1911 poster in **Figure 18.6**, noting the clear power relations between power and wealth at the top, and poverty and labour at the bottom. Obviously, **capitalism** has developed since 1911. If you were to draw this poster today what would it look like? What would you include? For instance, where would you place global conflict and inequalities, an economy changing from manufacturing to services based on short-term contracts and zero-hours contracts, consumerism and crime? Where would you place the police and the army?

in turn reflects and encourages the capitalist system and the power relations it involves because, of course, it is the powerful who make the laws in the first place. The argument goes on to say that it is this very economic system and its fundamental unfairness which produces conflict and crime.

The links between money and crime go back a long way—the poison arsenic, for example, used to be known as 'inheritance powder' due to its popularity as a means of killing people who had left their not-so-grieving relatives a little something in their will! But it's the wider implications of power and money that have concerned critical criminologists, for what may seem a surprisingly long time. So, let's take a moment to think about how economics is intricately related to crime and punishment.

Willem Bonger: capitalism and crimes of the powerful

Perhaps the best way to answer this would be to turn to the Dutch criminologist Willem Bonger (1876–1940) to whom you were introduced earlier on in the chapter. Bonger is widely regarded as being the first person to really apply Marx's ideas in terms of how it is that the social, political, and economic structures of a society (in this case, a capitalist one) can create 'crime' and form social responses to it. In arguing that capitalism is **criminogenic** (that is, that it causes crime), he came up with the following six propositions (or statements of opinion) (Bonger, 1916, from Muncie, 2015: 128). They are:

1. That ideas of immorality and criminality are socially and historically variable (we saw this is **Chapter 2**).
2. That the criminal law exists to protect the interests of the powerful.
3. That capitalism is held together by coercive exploitation rather than cooperative consensus.
4. That capitalism encourages egoism and greed. In the pursuit of such 'pleasures' both the proletariat and bourgeoisie become prone to crime as the mutual sense of responsibility towards each other is diminished.
5. That poverty prompts crime to the extent that it creates a desperate need for food and other necessities.
6. That crime also results when there is a perceived opportunity to gain an advantage through illegal means or when opportunities to achieve pleasure are closed off by a biased legal system (very similar to Merton's anomie or stress).

Here Bonger is raising many important and interesting critical issues. For instance, he suggests that capitalist societies are based primarily on exploitation, greed, and conflict. He also holds the view that, as we have argued earlier in this chapter, 'crime' is something which changes over time, but that under capitalism the criminal law comes to reflect the interests of powerful groups (so we punish the child for stealing the bread instead of punishing the person or institution who allowed them to go hungry in the first place).

Perhaps the most interesting points noted by Bonger are points 4 and 6. Here he argues that in a capitalist society some members of both the powerful and powerless groups commit crime through greed when they have the opportunity to do so. Whilst this may be true, what is most important for critical criminology is that the actions of the powerful are rarely prosecuted even if they are criminal and, more importantly, the 'greedy' and harmful actions of the powerful are often not criminalised because they form the laws. Studying 'crimes of the powerful' gives us a chance to look at the way that such actions (or omissions) can cause great harm, but are often not even classed as crimes at all (see **What do you think? 18.5**).

The 'new criminology'

Since Bonger's work over 100 years ago, many critical criminologists have revisited the work of Karl Marx and developed some of his ideas in novel ways with regard to the analysis of crime and its control—see, for instance, the

WHAT DO YOU THINK? 18.5

Crimes of the powerful

The year 2015 saw the 800th anniversary of Magna Carta. This 'Great Charter' is perhaps the most famous document setting out restrictions on power—in this case, that of the king of England. However, Magna Carta, like any similar document over the years, is a reflection of its time and context.

The examples below are all taken from Magna Carta or other legal frameworks. Which do you think are genuine pieces of lawmaking? Which are modern, which are mediaeval? Which do you think are still in force? And what do they tell us about the power relations of the time and place in which they happen?

- A woman may not accuse a man of murder or manslaughter, unless the case involves her husband.
- Only men who are members of the Church of England can stand for Parliament.
- Companies responsible for the environmental disasters in the developing world can avoid liability for cleaning operations or compensating the victims.
- The British police may cut off food supplies to people in protest camps.
- The UK Foreign Secretary can issue secret warrants allowing phone tapping.
- The US government can legally refuse to allow international law to prosecute US citizens who commit war crimes.

All of the above examples are, or were, genuine. (In case you are wondering, the first is from Magna Carta and has long since been superseded; the second was true until the Roman Catholic Relief Act 1829, followed by the Jews Relief Act 1858. All the others are modern.) We will return to issues concerning crimes of the powerful later in this chapter, as they are such an important part of critical criminology today; they also form part of the consideration of **zemiology** (**Chapter 19**) and green criminology (**Chapter 12**).

---

work of the American critical scholars Quinney (1974) and Chambliss (1975). In Britain, the most ambitious and influential ideas came out of the work of three criminologists who were at the centre of the NDC. They were Ian Taylor, Paul Walton, and Jock Young. In 1973, they published *New Criminology*, a book that was to become almost a manifesto for critical criminology and has influenced and inspired generations of critical criminologists. Whilst their book was a product of its time in that it reflected a social and political backdrop of discrimination and social injustice (which still exists but is less extreme), it was the first text to offer a thorough and rigorous critique of both classicist (seen in **Chapter 15**) and positivist thinking (**Chapters 16** and **17**). However, it goes much further than this. In the last chapter of *New Criminology* the authors, by integrating elements of interactionism, labelling, and neo-Marxism, call for the development of a *fully social theory* of deviance.

They set out seven core and formal requirements for a *fully social theory* of crime and deviance. These formal requirements are (Taylor et al., derived from Mooney, in DeKeseredy and Dragiewicz, 2012: 18):

1. The wider origins of the deviant act—'in other words to place the act in terms of its wider structural origins'.

2. The immediate origins of the deviant act—to 'be able to explain the different events, experiences and structural developments that precipitate the deviant act'.

3. The actual act, to explain the relationship between the behaviour and the causes—'a working class adolescent for example, confronted with blockage of opportunity with problems of status frustration, alienation from the kind of existence offered out to him in contemporary society, may want to engage in hedonistic activities or he may choose to kick back at a rejecting society (e.g. through acts of vandalism)'.

4. The immediate origins of the social reaction—that is, how the act is responded to.

5. The wider origins of deviant reaction—that is, 'the position and attributes of those who instigate the reaction against the deviant'.

6. The outcome of the social reaction on the deviants' further action.

7. The nature of the deviant process as a whole; how 1–6 connect.

Let's apply these ideas to a real example using the story of Eve McDougall. We heard about Eve's experiences of intimate partner abuse in **Conversations 11.1**, but here we consider some earlier childhood events. When Eve was

15 years old she was sent to an adult prison in Scotland for attempting to steal food, although her 'real' crime was criminal damage. Can we connect what happen to Eve with the complicated list of formal requirements for a *fully social theory* of deviance and crime as set out Taylor et al. back in 1973?

1. **The wider origins of the deviant act**—Eve grew up in a part of Scotland characterised by poverty and a sense of hopelessness. She did not meet her father until she was 17 (although he was pointed out to her by a school friend long before she actually met him). Her mother suffered from physical disabilities for which the family received no support and which were not, at that time, recognised by the state in terms of her receiving appropriate social security benefits.
2. **The immediate origins of the deviant act**—Eve wanted to escape her background and to have all of the things which she saw others having. She felt excluded. The absence of her father, and her mother's disabilities, meant that she did not have effective support to help her deal with the family's situation. By the age of nine she was stealing food and clothes and getting drunk on cheap wine. Her birthday and Christmas were ignored by her father and her mother's disabilities meant that the family had little money.
3. **The actual act, to explain the relationship between the behaviour and the causes**—when she was 15 Eve was hungry. She saw what she thought were buns and cakes in a shop window and broke it, in order to steal something to eat; however, the food was fake and she was shocked to be arrested.
4. **The immediate origins of the social reaction**—Eve was seen by the 'authorities' only as a thief and as someone who had committed criminal damage, rather than as a socially vulnerable young woman. She was believed to be behaving in a way not thought of as 'suitable' and 'appropriate', and deserving of punishment to teach her a lesson. Eve was assaulted by police officers after her arrest, who failed to treat her as the child she was.
5. **The wider origins of deviant reaction**—Eve had challenged society's expectations and it was felt that she needed to be made an example of. As a result, she was treated as an adult rather than as a child (although she was only 15) and no attention was paid to her poverty, hunger, or social exclusion which could have been viewed as causing her act. The only question was how she should be punished, rather than how she could be helped to overcome her family's problems.
6. **The outcome of the social reaction on the deviant's further action**—in the first instance, Eve was taken to a police cell where she was hurt by officers who had a duty of care towards her. After her sentence, she was sent to an adult prison where she encountered offenders who treated her with either kindness or harshness; she learnt more criminal behaviour from them but did not receive any help for her feelings of anger or for the poverty and frailty of her family's background.

As for point 7, if we think of Eve as a young person with particular thoughts and feelings who was living in a particular context—socially and economically—we can see how the factors all interlinked to form what the new criminologists would call a *fully social theory* of how she came to be imprisoned. Removing any one of the factors—for example, if Eve had not been hungry or if her father had been a supportive presence in the family—would perhaps have influenced the outcome.

18.6 Examples of the diversity of critical criminological theories

Critical criminology is a broad-ranging subject, covering many different issues. To give a flavour of its diversity, here we will include discussion of four important and very different aspects of this theoretical approach. Two of those we will look at are examples of traditional areas of critical criminology: state crime, which studies governmental misuse of power, and feminist perspectives, which throw light on the effects of misogyny and patriarchy. Two are examples of more contemporary critical criminological theories: cultural criminology, which studies subcultures and emotions, and convict criminology, which looks at control and punishment—especially imprisonment—from the perspective of the offender. The more prominent new area of zemiology (the study of **social harm**) will be considered in **Chapter 19**.

What each of these examples does is to uncover the unjust use of power against certain parts of society, and to do that the researchers focus on the views of the powerless or the oppressed and give them a 'voice'. With this information, they build a knowledge, a 'truth', which counters the ideas and 'truths' of wider society or of the powerful in society. Once these counter-truths are exposed, they can begin to push for changes to our society, ones which take account of the perspective of the less powerful.

State crime

Throughout this chapter we have discussed power and looked at the way critical criminologists perceive it to be used to the detriment of ordinary people; how it shapes laws and the way in which laws are applied and people are controlled; and how it influences who is labelled and how those labels will affect people's lives. However, what we have not yet considered in detail are the harms and transgressions of the powerful: corporate and state harms and violations. As Hillyard et al. (2004) note, **corporate crime** causes a lot more harm and suffering than individual offending, and yet most criminological work is bound up in studying and explaining individual transgressions and how to deal with them. Indeed, as noted by Freudenberg (2014), many of the most harmful activities of corporations (and of states) are not criminal. Critical criminologists argue that this focus—the reliance on the powerful to create law and protect us, and the gaps in the criminal law and crime control that arise—blinds us to the real harms most of us suffer, which are perpetrated by corporations, or even states. In **Chapter 19** you will explore what is called social harm and look particularly at the transgressions of corporations. Here, we will briefly consider state crime and harmful activities by the state.

States do not tend to criminalise their own activities; they rarely protect their people against violence or terror committed or ordered by the government or by their servants. However, most states do control the actions of their servants in an effort to prevent state crimes. Servants of the state (such as the police, fire service, prisons, teachers, health workers) may be controlled through criminal laws where their actions fall within the definitions of these laws (Drumble, 2007). However, powerful state agents—those at the centre of power—rarely face enforcement through the criminal law; they are more likely to be controlled through disciplinary procedures or loss of promotional opportunities. Today, when the state harms its citizens and there is no criminal law which can be used, the only possibility of control of these activities comes from the international community (Drumble, 2007), but it rarely steps in when the actions are internal to a state. Critical criminologists note that due to this complexity, many victims of state actions go unheard, and a lot of the work in this area is giving voice to these victims and calling the state to account for unacceptable policies (Anthony and Cunneen, 2008; Bovenkerk, 2007; Cunneen, 2007; Tombs and Whyte, 2003).

Throughout history, those in power or seeking power—the state or strong religious or other sects—have terrorised their peoples. Many were religiously motivated: about 1,000 years ago the Order of Assassins (in Persia and Syria) subjugated people through terror to defend and propagate a particular version of Islam, killing those who disagreed; the Thuggee cult (connected to the Hindu goddess Kali the destroyer) in India operated and governed parts of the country for about 600 years up until the 19th century; and the Catholic Church used the Inquisition to suppress heresy and discourage challenges to the authority of the church and its hierarchy. Similar tactics arise out of political **ideologies** or tyrannical state powers. For example, the 20th-century experiences of the Stalinist regime in the Soviet Union, the Nazi regime in Germany, Pol Pot's Khmer Rouge in Cambodia, Pinochet in Chile, the Hutus in Rwanda, and, in 2017, the persecution of the Rohingyas in Myanmar, etc. Over the last 100 years, state terror has become all too commonplace (Green and Ward, 2004; Williams, 2013, 2010). The acts of atrocity committed by state actors under these regimes were not 'crimes' in the states in which they were committed; they may even have been rewarded by the state. Those who carry out the atrocities are conforming to the standards and laws of state power at the time. Many of the perpetrators would argue that they were 'merely following orders', one of the defences rejected at international tribunals such as the Nuremberg trials, the International Criminal Tribunal for the Former Yugoslavia (ICTY) in 1993, the International Criminal Tribunal for Rwanda (ICTR) in 1994, and the Special Court for Sierra Leone (SCSL) in 2000, and, since 2002, by the International Criminal Court (ICC).

What these examples prove is that states often damage, devalue, wound, and kill their own peoples and people outside their territories. Whilst these states may act in the international arena (to condemn atrocities by other states), they rarely protect their people against violence or terror committed by themselves or their servants in their name. It is easy to see these big, international, violations of human rights and human dignity as unacceptable, and easy to condemn those involved. However, state breaches also happen at individual or more local levels and are then often ignored. Laws or policies which are harmful are followed by all states at different times. For example, the **victimisation** of street children in Brazil, the Indian government's choice to enter the space race rather than using the money to alleviate poverty, state crime in causing populations to flee (such as the 2017 persecution of the Rohingyas which caused them to leave Myanmar), and the use of inhuman and degrading actions to interrogate people in Northern Ireland who were interned (detained because they were suspected of having connections to terrorist activities without any real proof) which was labelled as a breach of Art. 3 of the European Convention on Human Rights (*Ireland* v *United Kingdom* (App. no. 5310/71) (1978)). For other examples, see Criminal Justice Matters (2010). These all caused some groups to suffer but are rarely talked about in terms of crime or even of intended harm.

There are then examples of a state being discriminatory or allowing discrimination to flourish. These may seem less problematic and less violent, but discrimination can devalue certain people, limit their life chances, increase the likelihood of them being violently attacked by members of the public or by agents of the state, and sometimes even increase the likelihood of their early death. An example of this is the historical legacy of the slave trade, which is seen today in **institutional racism** (for a full discussion concerning race and ethnicity, see **Chapter 10**). In the UK, this has been present for over 200 years but, for most of this time, has been ignored. Over many years, racial minorities fought to be heard. The first important time their plight was accepted at an official level was in Macpherson's review into the police handling of the death of Steven Lawrence (Macpherson Report, 1999). But there have been other reports and instances that have highlighted both the racism and institutional racism that exist in society. For example, racism being blamed for deaths of black people in custody, such as the killing of Zahid Mubarek by his white, racist cellmate after Feltham Young Offenders Institution put them together (Keith, 2006), racism being widely accepted as one of the triggers for the 2011 riots (LSE and *The Guardian*, 2011, Criminal Justice Matters, 2012), racism underlying the international movement entitled 'Black Lives Matter' (for a link to criminology, see Criminal Justice Matters, 2015). Looking further back, in the US racism was the core of Martin Luther King's stand against oppression. It was also the core of the 2020 riots that arose in many countries across the world following the killing of George Floyd.

In the case of George Floyd, there was a call for the police officers to face prosecution (and they did: Derek Chauvin, the officer who knelt on Floyd's neck, was convicted of murder in 2021); this is the traditional calling to account. However, critical criminologists point out that the protests and riots which followed the awful death of George Floyd would not have happened if certain groups had not suffered institutional racism over the past 200 years. The harm caused by the state (by institutional racism) and the demand for change goes very deep. Therefore, critical and radical criminologists would call on us to view the individual actions of the officers both as criminal (individuals to blame and be prosecuted) and as the product of a system which denigrates certain races (institutional racism). In certain parts of the US, institutional racism is very strong and, according to Black Lives Matter, causes some races to be treated as almost inhuman, especially by the police. At the same time, and often in the same areas of the US, police officers are trained to use extreme force to control order; they are not trained to use negotiation and conciliation tactics. This training is likely to inflame any conflict. Taking into account both the level of institutional racism in the US alongside the training of police officers in many areas, the critical criminology perspective (backed up by some human rights organisations; see, for example, Human Rights Watch, 2020) views the state as culpable both in the death of George Floyd and other deaths in police custody and during arrests. Critical criminologists also view the state as culpable in the continued discrimination within public bodies which, at the very best, the state does little to counter, especially following President Trump's dismantling of President Obama's policies to curb discrimination (such as the withholding of funds unless cities addressed segregation). At worst, it can be seen as encouraging discrimination through negative portrayals of black people, such as President Trump's wish to set the army on the 2020 race protesters, which some saw as backed by media images (see **Figure 18.7**). Whilst much of this has been about the US state and its institutional racism, it is important to remember that in the early summer of 2020 many other countries witnessed race riots/demonstrations (under the banner of Black Lives Matter). Critical criminologists point out that all of these countries also have institutional racism which at best prevents many people reaching their full potential and at worst results in their deaths at the hands of the state.

Critical criminologists also point to other social and criminal failings of many western states, including both the UK and US, for allowing children to be incarcerated despite the fact that they have suffered: social inequality; educational failure; drug, alcohol, and mental health problems; and experience of abuse, bereavement, and neglect which the state is aware underlie many high offending

Figure 18.7 A police vehicle in the US city of Seattle is set alight during the Black Lives Matter protests of summer 2020. Images like this were common in media coverage of the protests

Source: james anderson/Alamy Stock Photo

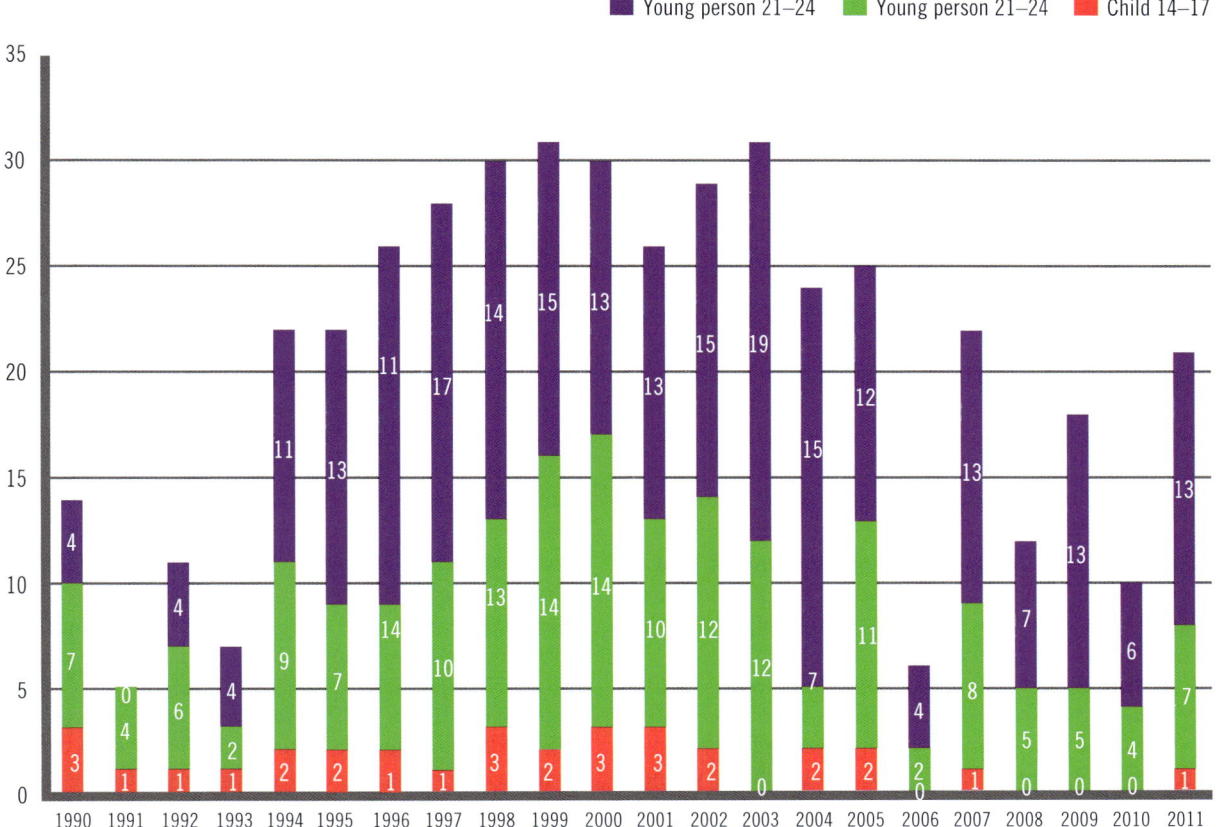

Figure 18.8 Children continue to be incarcerated in the US and UK despite the high numbers of deaths of children and young people in prison
Source: © 2012 Prison Reform Trust and INQUEST

rates of children (Young, 1999). They also continue this incarceration despite there having been many suicides and self-harming of young people when they are incarcerated (Prison Reform Trust and INQUEST, 2012; see **Figure 18.8**).

> These deaths are the most extreme outcome of a system that fails some of society's most troubled and disadvantaged children and young people. This shocking death toll has been obscured for far too long and for the first time, we now have a clear picture of the extent of the problem and the fatal consequences of placing vulnerable young people in unsafe institutions ill equipped to deal with their complex needs.
>
> (Deborah Coles, co-director of INQUEST)

The claim by critical criminologists is that the state causes more harm than all other offending; that it may do it through inaction and its activities are not criminalised but they are a result of the use and abuse of power. Critical criminology brings these abuses to the fore, and fights for the victims of these acts to be heard and protected. This section gives some flavour of the issues raised when critical criminologists think about state crime, but there are many more.

Feminist perspectives

You may have noticed, during your studies, that mainstream criminology has been largely conducted by men, and therefore dominated by male perspectives. You may even have asked yourself, 'Where are the women?' Feminist criminological theories seek to redress the balance by foregrounding the experiences and perspectives of women. For a full discussion of the feminist perspective, see **Chapter 11**; after reading that chapter, you may want to choose one of the other chapters and reread it with the feminist perspective in mind and see if this raises any new ideas or concerns for you. Here, however, we will briefly discuss feminist criminology as an important part of the critical criminology legacy.

For most of its history, criminology has focused almost exclusively on male actors in the criminal justice world, such as male offenders, male victims, male judges, and male police officers (these latter two roles being still predominantly male-dominated). Any study that involved women tended to look on them as weak, feeble creatures who were unable to control themselves or their actions, so the female criminal was seen in terms of her biology and sexuality. Many were considered hysterical (named after the Greek word for 'womb', 'hysteron'), an almost exclusively female illness associated with anxiety, irritability, insomnia, depression, and in women with 'non-feminine' behaviour such as prostitution and criminality. Women said to be hysterical were often placed in mental asylums and the trope of the 'madwoman in the attic' found in 19th-century literature (such as *Jane Eyre*) encapsulates this well.

Daft as such ideas can seem, they took a long time to die. Indeed, Cesare Lombroso and his collaborator Guglielmo Ferrero, in their 1893 book *Criminal Woman, the Prostitute and the Normal Woman*—a telling title if ever there was one—pictured women as being slaves to their biology, as you would perhaps expect from such early positivist approaches. So, much early criminology reflected male criminologists' sexist assumptions that the majority of women were biologically predisposed to be conformist and law abiding, whilst those who transgressed the criminal law were somehow mentally unstable beings who often displayed masculine traits.

This criminological understanding mirrored the wider social ideas that women were incapable and needed to be controlled. Questioning of the position of women in society and demands for greater freedom for women can be traced from Mary Wollstonecraft's 1792 book *A Vindication of the Rights of Women* to the suffrage campaign of the late 19th and early 20th centuries (first wave feminism). In 1928, all women over the age of 21 were eventually allowed to vote in general elections in the UK. At this point the changes were, though very important, limited and involved public rights to vote or to work in certain professions. At that time, there was no real change in criminological literature or in policy or practice in criminal law.

Second wave feminism (1960s–1980s) focused more on the way in which women's personal lives reflected male power and sexist political and social structures, all of which were detrimental to the lives of women and children. This led to a very visible movement within criminology. The resulting perspective, which is considered to belong to the 'critical' school, has come to be known as feminist criminology. Feminist criminology moved away from the positivist methodologies and focused on the 'real' experiences of women who suffered due to male power. It questioned traditional male 'knowledge' about crime and criminal justice, calling on academics, policymakers, and practitioners to recognise that that only represented the experiences of half of the population. It called on them to understand and recognise a different 'truth', a gendered truth which included male aggression and abuse of power. To do this, it drew on the individual experiences of women who suffered gendered domestic violence and rape, and shone a light on the victimisation of children by focusing on their sexual and other abuse (Hanmer, 1978, 1990; Smart and Smart, 1978; Stanko, 1985; Pain, 1991; Dobash and Dobash, 1992; Criminal Justice Matters, 2011; Williams, 2015). Feminist criminology and the feminist movement led to practical support for female victims through rape crisis and women's aid, and refuges for those victimised by domestic abuse (Williams, 2015; Gladstone, 2013; Hague and Malos, 1998; Fattah, 1992; Stanko, 1985: 16). These organisations, and the pioneering academics who worked alongside them, gave a voice to women. They used that voice to speak 'truth to power' (Bowell, 2014; Harding, 2004; Collins, 1986), to get men to listen to the experiences of the many women who suffered gender-based violence at the hands of men. To begin with, that 'truth' was largely ignored, sometimes even ridiculed, but slowly it has become nationally and internationally recognised such that it has now (many years later) supported changes to government policy and improvements in the way in which female and child victims are viewed and provided for. For example, in 2019, Nottinghamshire Police were the first to recognise misogyny (ingrained prejudice against women) as a hate crime (see Citizens UK, 'Better hate crime protection for all'). The 'truth' of female victimisation was even a catalyst for the whole victim movement. However, despite having managed to be heard, feminist criminologists argue that, in many respects, their stories are listened to with a gendered ear which only listens to part of the 'truth', which is then moulded to serve the interests of male power (Welsh, 2008; Hague and Malos, 1998; Foley, 1996). Feminists continue to work to allow the full stories of women and children to be heard.

Third wave feminism (1990s–) criticises second wave feminism for its emphasis on the lives of upper- and middle-class women and calls on us to view women's lives as being intersectional (affected by multiple social factors). It calls on us to see women as complex political beings affected not just by gender and gender differences, but also by race, ethnicity, class, religion, gender orientation, etc., and that all of these factors should be considered when examining women's lives (Potter, 2013, 2015). Intersectionality grew out of women-of-colour feminist theory, but Potter (2013, 2015) suggests it should be applied to all criminological research where social identity and status are discussed. Differences of status and identities are so important that some groups of women (particularly the socially excluded, black, or less highly educated) feel that no feminism really speaks for them or promotes their interests; they may align more naturally with another grouping—racial, religious, ethnic, etc.—or feel they may fall between all stools so that only an intersectional perspective would truly reflect this complexity.

It is clear from this potted history that, as with critical criminology itself, there is not just one feminist criminological perspective but many. These have different ideas and points of view, and include specific areas of interest such as black feminist or lesbian criminological theories. However, even if we acknowledge that feminism means different things to different groups (especially groups of women), we can argue that there are nevertheless strands of common thinking and aspirations that arise. For example, a broad recognition that state organs are heavily ordered through gender, assume that men are superior, and that this needs to be challenged and altered. Taken as a whole, feminist criminological perspectives can be regarded as being critical, whether they are based on liberalism or Marxism or indeed any other 'ism', because they have definite characteristics in common with other critical criminological theories. The principal ideas they share are the importance of social construction (in this case, the social construction of gender) and power relations (the focus being here on patriarchal power).

Among the achievements of feminist criminology are the following (qualified) points:

- Victims, particularly female and child victims, are now central to both scholarly and policy work in crime and crime control. However, there remain too many examples throughout the world of gendered crimes which though now better recognised are still not properly addressed, for example rape, domestic abuse, genital mutilation, and police or policy failure to tackle honour killings and beatings.
- In England and Wales, since the Corston Report of 2007, there is a recognition that women who are caught up in the criminal justice system need to be treated differently. They need different support to move them out of offending. Many of Corston's recommendations were accepted and made government policy and the third sector rallied to ensure that bespoke services for women were available. However, since 2010, ground has been lost in this work: the third sector has suffered following the 2008 financial crisis, reducing one way women speak to power, and government policy has focused elsewhere. Arguably, by focusing on responding to a specific problem for women involved in the criminal justice system, such as domestic violence, the state and community misses the broader underlying and deep-rooted reality of the abuse of male power in women's lives (Welsh, 2008; Stanko, 1985). The argument here is that the state fails to tackle broader gender inequalities and so fails to prevent the problem; instead, it just responds when male domination leads to male violence against women. Feminists argue that this is insufficient, and that a more holistic approach needs to be taken. Furthermore, the laws on sentencing still fail to take account of issues which might impact more on women's lives (for example, taking the caring duties of an offender into account at the sentencing stage) and so still have a male bias (see Feilzer and Williams, 2015).

Clearly feminist criminology has had some positive effects, both for our understanding of the subject and for some policy and practical changes; see, for example, the 2011 Home Office series of posters and adverts which try to combat domestic abuse, see Norfolk County Council, Health Information Leaflet Service and see **Figure 18.9**).

There are also grassroots movements such as 'Reclaim the Night' (see **Figure 26.12**), which are women-only marches to protest against street violence, and so-called 'Slut Walks' in which women wear 'provocative' clothes in order to make the point that what we wear should not mean we are open to attack or assault. However, feminist criminologists argue that there is still a lot of gender bias within crime and crime control (Welsh, 2008), and that many researchers and criminological writers still fail to truly acknowledge gender as an issue. They also point to

Figure 18.9 Poster from a UK government campaign highlighting the psychological and emotional form that domestic abuse can take

Source: The Home Office, content available under the Open Government Licence v3.0

many gaps, both in research and in policy, particularly in recognition of intersectional issues but also in equality (Potter, 2013, 2015). There is also a danger, seen mostly in the US at the moment, of a backlash against feminist agendas, which Chesney-Lind (2006) termed 'vengeful equity'; an attempt to prevent policy and research taking on board a gendered approach.

Cultural criminology

Culture has a number of different meanings. In sociology it is generally linked to a collection of concepts relating to tradition, norms, values, ideas, beliefs, style, images, and so on, that are revered or accepted by a group of people. In this section, we will use it in a more precise but limited sense to simply refer to how *webs of meaning* (the way in which what we do and say is understood, interpreted, and reacted to) in society are created and maintained, and how they can change. This last point is important, as it is clear that *culture*, in terms of our understandings of the world (including our understandings of, and the meanings we give to, crime and its control; see also the reference in **Chapter 4**) is not something which is static and on which everyone agrees (see **Chapters 2** and **3**). In other words, it is something which is dynamic and, perhaps more importantly, it is something which is contested vigorously and is in a constant state of flux.

One of the important emerging strands of critical criminology since the 1990s is something that has been called *cultural criminology*. As with the very concept of culture, cultural criminology is hard to define in any straightforward or precise manner, as the idea of culture is at its very core. Cultural criminology is a complex theoretical approach which seeks to simultaneously embrace and juggle many different aspects of how, where, when, and why we do things, and how they are understood by others. It draws on and reworks many of the insights from the original variants of critical criminology, such as interactionism, and critical methodologies such as **phenomenology** and **ethnomethodology**. It incorporates modern sociological analysis from culture, style media, identity, and space (meaning areas where people engage; they are particularly interested in urban spaces), and it engages with concepts of power and social injustice. It studies the way in which things are understood or expressed from alternative standpoints, and uses meanings from these to question accepted ideas about crime and criminal justice. Furthermore, it sees **ethnographic** methods as essential but needing to be extended to capture the emotion and the lives and experiences of the studied group/individual. At its core is a study of meaning, representation, and power, so it embraces the meanings, feelings, and emotions of those involved in transgression. For example, cultural criminology would question the usefulness of positivist criminology and its focus on data collection. It argues that positivist criminology fails to capture the meaning of the activity to the individual or subculture, which means that the people being written about would not recognise themselves, their lives, and their motivations in that research. Cultural criminologists, on the other hand, seek to explain and understand the actions of any subculture from the perspective of that group. They aim to present the world as it is experienced by the group being studied (generally those breaking the rules of society), and represent what is important or meaningful to that group. They consider that to question or analyse that meaning would be to detract from the reality for the group.

A core aspect of the reality studied by cultural criminologists is the emotions that members of subcultures (particularly youth subcultures) feel when they participate in behaviours that are associated with their group. In the behaviour of young people, this draws out the fun, power, and freedom experienced in law breaking; it sees it as 'seductive' (Katz, 1990), as something that has special meaning for participants, and as an addictive behaviour because of the adrenaline and the emotions it releases (Jackson-Jacobs, 2004). This type of risk-taking behaviour is sometimes referred to as 'edgework'. Cultural criminologists also note that members of certain subcultures may break rules for a number of reasons: to prove that it is possible, to face the risk and so take control, to enjoy the feelings they experience in the process, to feel alive, and to show and entertain others ('crime as carnival', Presdee, 2000). From the outside, their behaviour may appear reckless and be referred to as such but critical criminologists report that many of the participants see their activity as careful; they hone their senses and their skills to ensure they are neither injured nor arrested, so they can participate again. They then often talk about or boast about their exploits to the group, replaying the excitement.

Amongst other concepts, cultural criminologists study style (in clothes, speech, music, media, and common rituals) and its symbolism for particular subcultures. For example, youth subcultures are characterised and differentiated by complex systems of symbols and the shared meaning the symbols have for the group. For example, certain trainers and jackets may be a sign of membership of a group or subculture when accompanied by aspects of behaviour or use of particular language. They study how culture, style, the meaning of that style, and its questioning of traditional culture, travels through the streets, but they also study how it travels through the internet/media with no need for face-to-face links. The style unites the group (often the young) and protects them from those wishing to control them (usually adults) (Jewkes, 2003). Much of the style and the behaviour is not illegal, merely different from more powerful mainstream society. That wider society (often adult society but always the more powerful group) may use their style to control the subcultural groups, such as by banning people wearing hoodies from shopping centres. Wider society may also misappropriate and market the style in mass-produced goods, in the process profiting from the youth (or other) culture and undoing its exclusivity (Alvelos, 2004).

Whilst studying the nuance and complexity of youth culture, cultural criminology has been criticised for taking a simplistic view of wider society and criminal justice actors, not affording these groups the same complex meanings (O'Brien, 2005). More importantly, the approach largely ignores victims who may not enjoy or revel in the activity (Downes, 2005) or, if they are included, they are not given the same deep ethnographic focus, and the discussion is not as nuanced or textured as that of the subculture. Critics have also noted that whilst this type of work allows us real insight into the activities and the subcultures from within, it does nothing to explain how or why people move out of the broader culture into these alternative cultures and what the journey into the subculture looks like; nor does it explore how they interact with people outside the group, their families, or communities (O'Brien, 2005).

This gives you a small taste of cultural criminology. As Muncie (2015: 215) notes, the aims and scope of cultural criminology are indeed many and varied but they can, he argues, be summarised by the following eight key features (some of which were illustrated earlier):

1. Explorations of the convergence of cultural and criminal processes and dynamics in everyday life.
2. A fusion of aspects of cultural studies, *postmodernism*, critical criminology, interactionism, *anarchism*, and media/textual **discourse analysis**.
3. The use of *ethnographic methodologies* to reveal issues of meaning and representation.
4. Investigations into *deviant subcultures as sites of criminalisation*.
5. Explorations of the role of the emotions of excitement, fun, and pleasure in *processes of transgression*.
6. Journeys into the spectacle and carnival of crime.
7. The linkages (and disconnections) between *marginality*, illegality, media representations, and the criminalisation of popular culture. For example, popular culture being 'blamed' for unacceptable behaviour and so criticised (see **Chapter 6**).
8. Crime control as a cultural enterprise (consider this when you read **Chapters 27** and **28**).

Cultural criminology is a powerful critical tool, something you can use to test other theories, to see whether they really hold meaning for those being written about.

Convict criminology

There are many different ways that people who have been imprisoned are represented and portrayed through art, film, and television programmes. And yet, despite the growing prison population (see **Chapter 28** for a further discussion of this), it's probable that most of us don't actually have any first-hand connection with prisons or prisoners. So, it's far more likely that we develop our views about prisoners based on what we read and watch in the media. There may be an occasional news story about an inspection report criticising a particular prison, but there is little public debate about overcrowding, lack of rights, lack of dignity, poor healthcare, and the impact of an ageing prison population needing ramps, hand rails, and disabled toilets (things that are not often found within our secure estate). We are far more likely to read that prisoners live well and at no cost, can access drugs, and use the internet. We do not hear positive messages, such as that art, education, and therapy can often change and heal prisoners' lives or that, on release, some ex-prisoners visit schools to give a first-hand account of the reality of incarceration in an attempt to deter young people from committing crime. Most of the messages are negative: we are told that prisons both inflict deserved punishment and keep the rest of us safe from 'dangerous' people, and that prison may not be a sufficiently harsh punishment.

We hear these messages from the media and those in power, yet how much do we hear about the way prisoners see themselves and their lives? The emerging critical perspective of convict criminology tries to alter this situation. As a movement, it was started in the US in 1997 by two former prisoners who became academics (Steven C. Richards and Jeffery Ian Ross). Richards and Ross pointed out how much wisdom was absent from conventional literature and research that dealt with prisons, including much criminological research. The perspective has only recently spread across the Atlantic.

The idea is that criminology needs to be informed by multiple sources and that there is no such thing as a single 'truth'. There is a 'truth' in all accounts: in those of the criminal justice system (the police, courts, prisons, and so on), the victims of crime, and also the voice of the prisoner, something traditionally ignored.

Historically, prisoners have been passive, sometimes unwitting, subjects of studies and tests. To convict criminologists, this meant that criminology, despite seeing itself as a dynamic and challenging discipline, helped to maintain the accepted view of prisoners, which in turn went on to feed and shape public opinion. Critical convict criminology set out to bring about 'radical' change by highlighting the need (as they see it) to take account of the knowledge, opinions, and experiences of prisoners themselves; to focus on their views and ideas, and to ensure that the knowledge of the outcast and deviant is given as much status as that of professors, doctors, and lecturers.

The notion here of 'knowledge' is important and takes us back to thoughts about power, so we need to pause for a moment and think about what we mean by knowledge. We all have knowledge, some of which is common to us all—don't put your hand into the fire, for instance—and some of which is hidden and almost unconscious: for example, that there is a certain dark road that people 'know' not to walk down or that black people 'know' they will be turned away from a particular club, despite its inclusion policy. Yet, like the voice of the prisoner, this knowledge (real or imaginary) is not shared or spoken, unless in ways that reinforce it—when someone is attacked or sues for discrimination. Power relations, such as the power of a white bouncer to turn away a black clubber, reinforce the knowledge. Yet by not being voiced, this hidden knowledge is not shared with those who can make a difference. Street lighting will not be improved if the council doesn't know that people avoid a particular lane because it is dark and scary. Prison policy will not change if the Home Secretary is only told safe, voter-pleasing things by criminologists.

Convict criminologists argue:

1. that without data based on ideas, opinions, and lived experiences of prisoners we are not going to be able to make fully informed judgements; and
2. if we fail to use all the information we can get, some knowledge will be given more status than the rest of it, and this is where we risk silencing those ideas and people which we value less.

Convict criminologists actively involve prisoners in the research programmes, not by treating them as research subjects, but by respecting their knowledge and allowing them to design or co-design research, and even carry it out themselves. This recognises that prisoners have knowledge which is as important as that of the expert. As well as increasing its relevance and broadening our knowledge, this approach means that information is less likely to be tainted or skewed by the beliefs or prejudices of the researcher (see Aresti et al., 2015 for a fuller discussion of these and other issues which convict criminologists are interested in).

The acceptance that prisoners have something valid to say leads to another aim of convict criminology: to ensure that prisoners' voices are heard in the public arena as well as just by academics. In other words, it seeks to make sure that they are reported accurately and respectfully in the *Daily Mail* as well as in the *British Journal of Criminology*. This means that the media needs to allow an honest portrayal of prisons and prison life. It follows that this open, well-informed, and frank debate would be a platform for prison reform, yet for this to happen, it would mean challenging what the public and therefore the electorate 'knows' about prisons.

Ironically, the one thing this section has yet to do is to think about the impact of all of this on prisoners. So let us be convict criminologists for a moment and bring them to the foreground.

Convict criminology seeks to challenge and shape public perceptions (and misconceptions) about prisons and prisoners. It aims to humanise and make real the otherwise faceless and frightening idea of the hidden deviant, who is behind bars for our protection, and to 'bridge gaps', especially between the public and the prison population. What it does not do is argue that only prisoners should be involved in research or policy direction. Instead, it looks to promote the balanced generation of knowledge through the equal participation of prisoners, academics, and policymakers, to arrive at a broader and more accurate understanding of (and from) people who have experience of being convicted and locked up. It seeks to use this knowledge to challenge complacency and to improve the ways in which we use prison as a form of crime control. Convict criminology is a relatively new perspective, and one which is still finding its feet amongst the better known, more established criminological theories; but as a movement it is one which perhaps presents the greatest degree of challenge and debate to the current political and social views on prisoners and their lives.

In **Conversations 18.1** we hear from Dr Andreas Aresti. Andy is one of the founders of British Convict Criminology (BCC) and is a senior lecturer in criminology at the University of Westminster. He is also a former prisoner. As you read the account of his journey, see if you can make any connections with what we said about labelling perspectives and the concept of stigma earlier in this chapter. Also, make some notes of your responses to what he has to say about the need for a 'convict criminology'. Do you agree with him? Why, or why not?

CONVERSATIONS 18.1

A journey into criminology . . . via prison
*with **Dr Andreas Aresti***

I wouldn't say crime was my profession as such. I was a tradesman, and had been working as a roofer since leaving school at the age of 15. Even then, however, my mates and I were always involved in some form of 'illegal activity'. Typically, these activities were usually motivated by the desire for financial gain, but of course, they were also inextricably linked to other complex factors, such as status, identity, and masculinity.

In August 1998, I walked out of the prison gates, having served three years in mainly category B prisons, and straight into university. At that moment in time, I had little awareness of what lay ahead and how my life would turn out. I remember my first day at university vividly. I was consumed with anxiety and fear, questioning myself as I looked around the grounds and at the other students waiting to enrol. I thought to myself *'what the hell am I doing here?'*—or words to that effect! These were not my kind of people and this was not an environment that I was familiar with. At this point, my old life appeared quite attractive despite my strong urge to change and find fulfilment in other ways.

Needless to say I stuck with my course, and gained my momentum. I walked out of university with a very good first degree in psychology, and full of confidence and self-belief. I had worked my backside off. It wasn't easy, it was definitely a struggle, and there were times I wanted to give it up. But I did it. I had proved something to myself, and that something was that 'I can do this. I can change my life'. Education was pivotal in this process. For me, desistance from crime could only be achieved through my education and by developing a career on the back of that. You may be surprised, but this is the case for a number of people like me who are former prisoners (or as they may also be known, ex-convicts).

When I left prison I thought I was the only ex-con(vict) who had gone on to go to university. Other ex-cons have said the same. Look around you . . . one of your peers may be one of us! One of us, an ex-con: someone who is morally contaminated in the eyes of the wider society. This 'spoiled identity' that I have inherited from my days in prison never really impinged on my life in the early days of my transition to conventional life, and it was never really a source of great tension either. I didn't really give my ex-con identity much thought until it slapped me in the face, at the moment when I was considering my career options after doing my Masters' degree. Up until this point, life was looking good. I had goals and I was achieving them. I was determined to achieve them. The past was becoming a distant memory, I was moving forward.

I had a first class, first degree (BA, Hons) in Psychology and an MSc in Cognitive Neuropsychology, and my goal was to be a clinical psychologist. I started looking into the clinical psychologist training programme and quickly discovered that my past criminal convictions were an issue. I realised that because of my criminal record, I would never be able to work as a clinical psychologist. This is also the case for a number of other positions that are exempt from the Rehabilitation of Offenders Act (ROA) 1974. Entry in to certain jobs and professions are literally barred to those who have been behind bars.

As you might imagine I was devastated. I simply couldn't believe it. I had invested so much effort into changing my life, experienced struggles and difficulties, and yet had overcome these only to be confronted by these structural constraints. It made me question the system.

Once again, as on my first day at university, my old life on 'the wrong side of the law' seemed a lot more attractive. My ex-offender status would never be an issue there—in fact in many instances it would be respected. What an injustice! All this talk about 'rehabilitation' and helping people to desist from crime was bullshit. And this is still the case now. In my view nothing has changed. If anything, things have got a lot worse! It is almost as if my past follows me around like a shadow. Frequently, I have to negotiate this 'spoiled identity' in social situations; do I disclose my past? If I do, what are the implications? In other instances, I am forced to disclose my status on forms that require you to advise if you have a criminal record—for instance on job applications, insurance forms, visas applications if I want to go abroad, and so on. So like many others, despite the dramatic changes I have made in my life, I still have to live with the damaging effects of the label, 'ex-offender'.

Anyway, feeling quite deflated I ended up contacting UNLOCK (this is an independent award-winning charity which provides information, advice, training, and advocacy, dealing with the ongoing effects of criminal convictions) and had a lengthy conversation with someone who empathised with my situation. They helped me to put things into perspective; I needed to take 'the bull by the horns'.

In the end I decided to study for a PhD, the focus of which was on former prisoners' experiences of self-change and identity negotiation. Specifically, my work considered what it is like to live with the stigmatised status of ex-prisoner, exploring how these 'forced' identities are negotiated in everyday life; this undoubtedly being a means of making sense of my own situation as well as a career choice.

It was whilst doing my PhD that I came across convict criminology (CC). In short, CC is a theoretical perspective and an academic network that takes a critical approach to criminal justice issues and challenges the traditional understandings of crime, criminal justice issues, prisoners, and ex-convicts. Many of the convict criminologists have had direct experience of prison and use this as a basis for their work. They use their personal experience to generate knowledge on the lived realities of prisons, prisoners and life after prison.

To date, little of the knowledge or policy work on prisons, prisoners, and the criminal justice system comes directly from people that have had first-hand experience of prison. In many respects, the voice of prisoners (including former prisoners) is muted and often silenced altogether. We need to question why this happens, and consider whether work that fails to hear that voice can truly capture the lived realities of prisoners and ex-convicts.

On developing a relationship with the convict criminologists in the USA, I, along with two colleagues, decided to push CC forward in the UK. Like convict criminologists in America, we believed that much of the knowledge on prisons and prisoners did not resonate with our personal experiences. In terms of our lived realities, the dominant discourses on such matters were, and still are, predominantly negative, and the existing policies that directed our lives were constraining and typically ineffective. Having had such experiences, and subsequently having made that transition into 'conventional life', I believe that like many others before me, I can utilise this personal experience to provide an alternative lens through which to view an authentic understanding of the lived realities of prisons, prisoners, and the criminal justice system, from an 'insider perspective'.

And whilst my aim is not to discredit some of the very good and valuable good work being generated by other academics, especially those of a critical orientation, I also believe there is no substitute for personal experience. So, having had such experiences, and achieving the academic credentials, I believe that I can utilise this personal experience to, as many a convict criminologist has commented, really '*tell it like it is*'.

Dr Andreas Aresti, Senior Lecturer in Criminology, University of Westminster

18.7 Conclusion

In this chapter we have explored some of the foundations of critical criminology in the form of labelling perspectives, the 'new' criminology, state crime, feminist perspectives, and cultural and convict criminological theories. It could be said that these were a powerful agenda for a criminology which was politically engaged and which sought to change the world and to challenge forms of injustice. Although critical criminology is not perhaps the dominant paradigm within criminology today, it retains a vital presence in the criminological landscape. Despite the drift towards a narrow and **empirically** based 'crime science' and the recent revivals of classicist ideas (see **Chapter 15** on this), many would argue that critical criminological perspectives are crucial to understanding today's rapidly changing, globalising, and fragmented world. To be sure, we have witnessed enormous and far-reaching social, economic, and political changes since the times in which the likes of Becker, Taylor, Walton, Young, and Smart were writing. Throughout the chapter, we have discussed some of the changes brought about by critical criminological theories, but we have also shown that there are still many issues which need to be addressed—there remain many areas where power is used in ways that are harmful to a large part of the population, for example the problem of institutional racism as highlighted by the Black Lives Matter protests of 2020. The critical agenda is therefore still very relevant to studying criminology today. Some of the critical criminological studies that are most relevant today are considered in more depth in other chapters of this book: social harm is discussed in **Chapter 19**, race and ethnicity in **Chapter 10**, feminist criminology in **Chapter 11**, and green criminology in **Chapter 12**. Each of these areas shows that critical criminological theories remain an important part of the criminological imagination; they explore areas important to our lives today, broaden our horizons to include acts and behaviours which are not normally regarded as being crime, and—to echo Becker's rallying cry in the 1960s—encourage us to stand up and to advocate on behalf of the 'underdog'.

SUMMARY

After reading this chapter and working your way through its features you should now be able to:

- Appreciate the philosophical and political arguments that underpin critical criminological theories

The chapter examined the way that critical criminological theories challenge the more traditional, positivist and classicist approaches to the study of crime. It considered the critical view that differences in lifestyle, background, and social inequalities affect reactions to crime and its control, as well as placing the origin of the critical movement within the context of the social and political upheavals of the 1960s.

- Understand the different foundational strands within critical criminology, and their development within a cultural and historical context

We have seen how critical criminology is a multifaceted approach which embraces a wide range of issues and arguments (more of which will be covered and developed in **Chapter 19**). This chapter described some of the major ideas that concern the critical criminologist, particularly how different groups have different experiences, needs, and reactions when it comes to the issue of crime and social control, and how there needs to be an appreciation of those differences to ensure equality and fairness within the criminal justice system and society. Key areas examined were feminism, state crime, cultural criminology, and convict criminology.

- Develop an awareness of how important the ideas of power and power relations are to the study of critical criminology

Power and power relations are key to understanding the critical approach. Critical criminology argues that the underpinning issue for any study of crime is that of power: how it is used, by whom, and how the powerful maintain their position of authority over the powerless. For example, critical criminologists study the impact of patriarchal power on women and children within the criminal justice system, and how the use of power by the police can be interpreted and experienced differently by different groups.

- Discuss the problems of 'deviance' and its interpretation and control

In this chapter we have asked you to consider various aspects of critical theory. For example, we looked at the ways in which deviancy is ascribed to certain people and certain acts more than others. We introduced the concept of 'labelling' and discussed how this basic human behaviour can influence social reactions and expectations, often through the use of media and the positive or negative coverage received by various groups. We also discussed the reaction of individuals to such labelling, with a focus on how ideas of deviance are formed and amplified by reaction to any breach of the social norms accepted within a particular group of people.

- Relate theoretical ideas to the real world through specific examples, such as state crime, feminist perspectives, subcultures and emotions (cultural criminology), and convict criminology

We have looked at the ways in which state power causes problems in the lives of many individuals and how concepts such as feminist criminology have affected public discourse, particularly in the arena of domestic abuse, and the fresh arguments which such new approaches have raised. We've discussed how cultural criminology draws attention to the importance of understanding crime from the perspective of subcultures, and why those perspectives are important and should be considered. Another area of study we've looked at that calls for different perspectives to be respected is convict criminology, which questions how knowledge is produced in prison studies. It calls for participatory forms of research, which involve prisoners and former prisoners on an equal footing with academic researchers. Each of these aspects of critical criminology considers the experiences of groups whose views and ideas are either challenging to the accepted order or are not generally heard or valued due to the powerlessness of their members.

Test your understanding of the chapter's key points by attempting the self-test questions on the **online resources** at www.oup.com/he/case2e

REVIEW QUESTIONS

1. What are the four defining ideas of positivist perspectives and how are critical criminological theories critical of them?

2. To what extent can it be argued that the 'rich get richer and the poor get prison'? Why might this be the case?

3. In what ways can labelling someone be said to have a transformational effect on their self-identities?

4. Critically apply Taylor et al.'s (1973) notion of a 'fully social theory' of crime and deviance to a real-world example of criminality.

5. Give two examples of state crime. Why should criminologists study this?

6. Feminist perspectives in criminology have altered over time. Explain two different feminist approaches and how they impact on crime and criminology.

7. By focusing on emotions such as anger, excitement, and boredom some cultural criminologists have nothing practical to say or offer to criminal justice policymakers. Critically consider this statement.

8. Explain why convict criminologists argue that prisoners and former prisoners should be involved in prison research as more than participants.

Access the **online resources** at www.oup.com/he/case2e to check your answers to the review questions.

FURTHER READING

DeKeseredy, W. S. (2010) *Contemporary Critical Criminology.* **London: Routledge.**
A clearly written account of both the foundations and contemporary theoretical positions of critical criminology.

DeKeseredy, W. S. and Dragiewicz, M. (eds) (2018) *The Routledge Handbook of Critical Criminology.* **London: Routledge.**
A good, although more advanced, collection of original essays which cover a range of critical perspectives and contemporary issues at both national and international levels.

Hillyard, P. et. al. (eds) (2004) *Beyond Criminology; Taking Harm Seriously.* **London: Pluto Press.**
This is good starting point for those of you wishing to take forward your study of the notion of social harm. It contains many interesting essays on a wide range of areas (from state and workplace harms to poverty and disease) to which the harm perspective can be applied.

Scraton, P. (2016) *Hillsborough; The Truth.* **Edinburgh: Mainstream Publishing.**
This is a very powerful and moving account of the Hillsborough tragedy and its aftermath, written by an eminent British critical criminologist. It is an excellent example of what critical criminology is all about and what it can achieve.

Ugwudike, P. (2015) *An Introduction to Critical Criminology.* **Bristol: Policy Press.**
This book offers a clearly written introductory account of both the foundations and contemporary theoretical positions of critical criminology.

 Access the **online resources** to view a wealth of extra information relating to your study of criminology, including self-test questions, answers to review questions, and links to other resources that will help you enjoy and fulfil your potential within your studies.
www.oup.com/he/case2e

CHAPTER OUTLINE

19.1	Introduction	592
19.2	What is social harm?	592
19.3	How social harm theorists critique criminology	595
19.4	How the social harm approach works	602
19.5	The production and reduction of social harm	609
19.6	Critique of the social harm approach	612
19.7	Conclusion	614

19

Social harm

KEY ISSUES

After studying this chapter, you should be able to:

- outline the key elements of the social harm approach, identifying its various levels and dimensions;
- explain and illustrate the nine fundamental criticisms made of criminology by social harm theorists;
- analyse case studies using the principles of the social harm approach;
- explain how different forms and levels of social harm can originate from, and are related to, different forms of social, economic, and political organisation;
- critically evaluate the extent to which social harm approaches sit within criminology.

19.1 Introduction

In this chapter we will be exploring the idea of 'social harm'—a concept we have touched on in other chapters, such as **Chapters 2** and **12**—and considering whether we should think of it as being separate from, or related to, what we have previously thought of as 'criminology'. This process will involve a critique of existing criminological approaches—indeed, most of the theoretical approaches you have been studying in **Part 3** of this book can be critically interrogated through the lens of social harm. The social harm approach, a perspective that has become increasingly prominent over the past two decades, argues that state-generated, legal definitions of 'crime' are much too narrow, as they do not reflect significant (though not always illegal) social, physical, emotional, psychological, cultural, and financial and economic harms that can be inflicted by social structures, multinational bodies, and the state.

So far, much of the work in this area has focused on broader theoretical and conceptual issues, but social harm perspectives have also informed important studies of a wide range of social occurrences and events. These have ranged from studies of the harms produced by corporations (Freudenberg, 2016), learning care settings (Feeley, 2014), human trafficking (Boukli, 2019), and even genocide, meat eating, intimate partner violence, and penal harm (Presser, 2013). It is clear that as the social harm perspective develops further, we will see the emergence of a greater range of case studies which are informed by its approach.

In this chapter we will consider the ways in which the social harm perspective can inform our criminological imaginations. We will begin by examining what social harm is, and the many criticisms that its proponents make of traditional interpretations of 'crime' and 'criminology'. We will then move on to consider the various dimensions and levels of social harm, the possible causes of social harm, how such causes can be prevented, and the ways in which they can potentially be mitigated through interventions focused on reducing harm. We will conclude by considering whether these harm perspectives belong within the theoretical perspective of critical criminology, or whether it is time to develop a distinct discipline (or 'replacement discourse'), which considers the cause, prevention, and reduction of harm as a separate area of multidisciplinary study. In considering all of these issues, we will give particular attention to the example of the Grenfell Tower fire disaster in 2017, since this provides a powerful example through which we can focus on the concept of 'harm' as distinct from 'crime'.

19.2 What is social harm?

The concept of social harm was developed by a group of critical criminology scholars at the start of this century (see Hillyard et al., 2004; Hillyard and Tombs, 2017) and centres around the idea that criminology needs to move beyond narrow, partial conceptions and constructions of 'crime' and towards a consideration of acts and behaviours which can cause great *social harm*. It is a difficult concept to define and delineate, but one of the clearest explanations is provided by Pemberton (2016). Pemberton does not precisely define social harm itself, but describes what a society free of social harm—one that he would see as healthy—would look like. He suggests that a harm-free society is one in which people's physical and mental integrity is preserved, their autonomy is protected and respected, and they enjoy a sense of connectedness with others (Pantazis, paraphrasing Pemberton in Pemberton, 2016: xiii). Overall, it is a space in which humans can flourish and their well-being is preserved; they are free to realise their full potential.

A harm-free society is an ideal which a state might need to take positive action to achieve; its ethos and the way in which its institutions behave would need to be shaped around this ideal. Proponents of social harm are therefore interested in the ways in which states, organisations, and individuals fail to live up to this ideal, behaving—whether through action or inaction—in ways that can kill and damage people, limit their life chances, and impede their ability to flourish. These scholars point out that actions and inactions which cause harm are often not thought of as 'crime'; in fact, they are rarely covered by the criminal law or processed through criminal justice systems. Instead, we tend to see them as 'accidents', 'disasters', or the 'failings' (rather than criminal acts) of individuals or groups of people. Such events or occurrences—which we might call 'phenomena' as a shorthand—can include things like air pollution, poverty, infant mortality, excessive winter deaths of the elderly, disease, and the hundreds of deaths and injuries every year which are a direct (though often cumulative) result of the violation of health and safety legislation in the workplace.

This is far from an exhaustive list, and it will be becoming obvious that the social harm approach can cover an extremely broad range of issues. Consider examples of what we could think of as social harm in **What do you think? 19.1**.

In the next section we will gain a clearer picture of this perspective's theoretical principles through

WHAT DO YOU THINK? 19.1

What constitutes 'social harm'?

Think about recent events in the news and consider which might be good examples of social harm. For example, at the time of writing there are news reports about the following events:

- a drugs company putting up the price of a medication to a level where it is unaffordable by healthcare providers and insurers, leaving patients unable to access the drugs that were keeping them alive;

- local councils having to provide free lunches for children in deprived areas during the summer holidays, as their parents rely on free school meals and are otherwise unable to afford to feed them;

- a national company collapsing, leaving hundreds of people out of work overnight. However, its senior managers say that it was not their fault that the company failed, and they will be keeping thousands of pounds paid to them in bonuses.

What aspects, if any, of these scenarios (and of your own examples) could be viewed as causing social harm?

Now imagine that these incidents are taking place in 2030. The law has been changed and the social harms you identified are now considered in the same way as other crimes such as burglary, with individuals and groups of individuals being held to account and being punished by the state.

Consider the following questions:

1. What might the implications be if we started treating social harms in the same way as we do other crimes? Would this be possible? Why, or why not?

2. Should individual people be held accountable for a social harm caused by an organisation? If so, who? Or should the organisation be held accountable for causing harm? How would they be identified and how could they defend their actions or inactions?

3. If we decide that a group of people should take responsibility for a social harm, how should they be punished?

examining the issues raised by the study of social harms, sometimes referred to as **zemiology** (*zemia* means harm in Greek). First, though, we will set this concept into a real-life context by considering some examples of phenomena that could be seen as a form of social harm. As you read, try to identify some common features across the examples.

Example 1: deaths due to austerity measures

Researchers such as Watkins et al, (2017) have observed that although mortality rates in the UK steadily declined by 0.77 per cent each year from 2001 to 2010, this trend dramatically reversed in 2010. As **Figure 19.1** shows, from 2010 to 2014 the number of deaths *increased* by 0.87 per cent each year, a rise that equated to 45,368 extra deaths during this four-year period.

The researchers have directly attributed the rise in mortality rates to the introduction of austerity measures (strategies to reduce government spending, such as reductions in social spending and increased taxes) in 2010 and the cuts to public service funding that followed—actions that the government called 'efficiencies'. It has been estimated that for death rates to return to 2010 levels there would

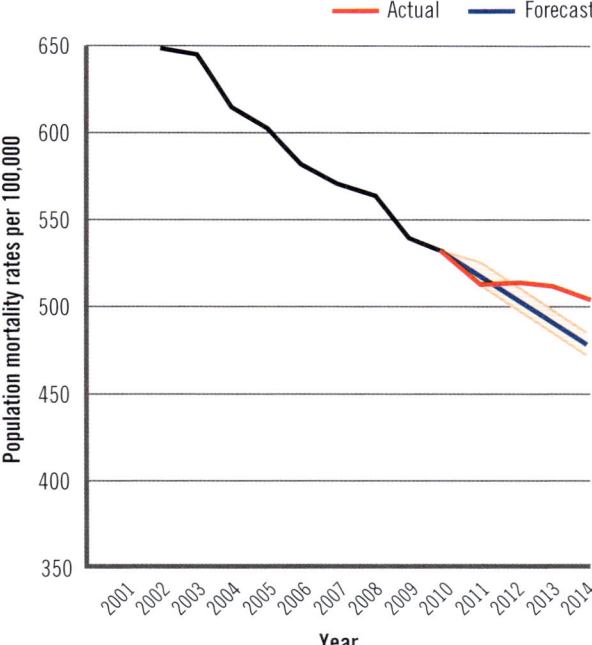

Figure 19.1 The increasing gap between actual and forecast mortality rates from 2010

Source: Watkins J., Wulaningsih W., Da Zhou C., et al. (2017) 'Effects of health and social care spending constraints on mortality in England: a time trend analysis', BMJ Open 2017;7:e017722. doi: 10.1136/bmjopen-2017-017722

need to be an increase in public spending of £25.3 billion, and although these findings have been greeted with caution, one study has gone so far as to call the results of the cuts 'economic murder' (Watkins et al., 2017).

Example 2: failure to meet educational needs

In recent years, funding cuts have also had an impact on children's access to high-quality education. In England, children who have special educational needs can apply for an Education and Health Care Plan (EHCP), a legally binding document which sets out the support that the child is entitled to receive in order to allow them to access the best possible education. Such support can range from the provision of specialist equipment, to being given a place at a special school. EHCP applications are assessed by local councils and parents whose child's application is turned down can appeal to a tribunal.

Cuts to public service funding have put local authorities under pressure to award fewer EHCPs, which has resulted in many more cases being taken to a tribunal appeal, even though the appeals process is lengthy and expensive, particularly for local authorities which have to take money from their budgets in order to fund legal representation, and for parents, who face both financial and emotional burdens. Between 2011 and 2016, around 800 cases were heard, but in 2016–17 this number doubled. Ninety per cent of appeals made in court are successful, but until the case is heard the child will remain without support and in some cases will not be able to attend school, and in December 2018 a report by Ofsted stated that over 2,000 children who had been awarded an EHCP were receiving no additional help at all. These children are being denied access to a full, high-quality education, a 'failure' (in the words of the local news headline shown in **Figure 19.2**) on the part of the state which will have a severe negative impact on their futures.

Example 3: the industrial legacy of asbestos

For most of the 20th century, a mineral substance called asbestos that we now know to be extremely harmful was widely used in industry for its remarkable insulating and heat-proofing qualities. When inhaled into the lungs, asbestos particles can eventually cause scarring, breathing failure, and cancers such as mesothelioma, but workers in settings such as Royal Navy dockyards and factories came into regular contact with it. In some forms, asbestos looks rather like cotton wool, and workers were unaware of its harmful nature. Fibres and dust regularly settled on their clothes, meaning that it would travel to their homes and their families were also exposed to the particles.

By the 1930s, it was legally accepted that employers should know that asbestos can cause lung disease, and in 1945 dockyards and the shipbuilding industry were warned that anyone working with asbestos should wear respirators (Herbert, nd)—a device worn over the nose and mouth, or even the whole face, to prevent inhalation of harmful substances (see **Figure 19.3**). Despite this, few workers were issued with warnings or protective equipment, and as a result it is now estimated that more than 5,000 people die in the UK every year as a direct consequence of asbestos exposure. Such is the extent of the problem that it is now rare for the Ministry of Defence to deny liability for an asbestos-related disease in anyone who worked in a dockyard or other military installation. However, people affected as a result of working in factories or other settings may have to fight harder to prove their case, despite the fact that the use of, and exposure to, asbestos has been strictly controlled since the 1990s (*The Independent*, 22 November 2009).

Defining social harm

What can we learn from these examples about the concept of social harm? It is clear that in each of these situations, harm arose from preventable factors (for example,

Figure 19.2 A campaign by parents of children with special educational needs makes headlines: could state failure to provide adequate educational support be seen as a social harm?

Source: Sutton Guardian

Figure 19.3 The dangers posed by asbestos are now treated very seriously, but workers were knowingly exposed to it in the past. Such action by employers is now seen as a form of social harm
Source: Mike Dotta/Shutterstock

the failure to properly fund special needs education) and that the impact of such harm could have been significantly reduced (for example, by providing protective equipment). In other words, all of the examples discussed earlier are 'foreseeable' harms which could have been prevented. Some such foreseeable harms involve the failure to abide by legal rulings or advice, although this may not itself be illegal; or there may be acts and omissions with significant, harmful consequences. So far, in most cases there has been little responsibility taken, or accountability enforced, for these acts and omissions. It is difficult to identify specific actions or individuals which/who were directly responsible for the harm inflicted and could be labelled the 'criminal'; rather, they feature a chain of events and actions that are not necessarily 'criminal', as we would usually conceive of it within criminology, but which led to the suffering of harm by individuals, families, and communities.

19.3 How social harm theorists critique criminology

The group of critical criminologists who developed the concept of social harm came together in order to assess where critical criminology had got to and where it was going (see Hillyard et al., 2004; Hillyard and Tombs, 2017). The rise of right- and left-realist criminologists in the 1980s had (as we will see in **Chapter 20**) pushed much critical thought to the side and, in a sense, these scholars saw the critical criminology project as unfinished business. In revisiting some of the themes we explored in **Chapter 18**—such as the social and **ideological** construction of crime, and the ability of the powerful to avoid **criminalisation** whilst criminalising the behaviour of the relatively powerless—and by focusing attention towards social harms, they arrived at what could be called a radical critique of critical criminology. Some argued that the study of social harm could become a progressive development within critical criminology, in that it critically questions the very concepts of 'crime', 'criminality', and 'criminal justice'. For others, though, a sustained focus on social harm could only be fully achieved within a separate, alternative academic discipline—that is, zemiology.

The concept of an alternative discipline arises from the very different ideas at the core of 'crime' and criminology on the one hand, and social harm—especially as set out in zemiology—on the other. This separation is highlighted by Copson (2016, 2018), whose views we hear directly in **Conversations 19.3**. For Copson, this separation comes about because crime and criminology look to protect citizens from harm through protecting people's liberties and ensuring that their rights are not interfered with. This is a negative protection; protection from harm. The interference being protected against is close in time and space, so we can trace a clear link between the perpetrator and victim. We can clearly see that the action of the perpetrator caused the **victimisation** and, in most cases, that the decision-making of the perpetrator makes them responsible. On the other hand, social harm and zemiology protect people's human needs; their right to enjoy undiminished autonomy and well-being. These are positive rights; protections to allow them to flourish. In this context, the interference being protected against is distant in time and space, and we cannot trace a clear link between the perpetrator and victim. It is difficult to work out exactly what caused the 'victimisation' or to link the harm (for example, environmental pollution, child poverty, worker deaths, or obesity) to the decision-making of a social structure or an individual; it is difficult to define or prove clear responsibility, and therefore to hold 'perpetrators' to account. There are clear differences between this perspective and criminological ideas of crime or 'responsibility', so writers like Copson have argued that social harm is better studied within a completely separate discipline—that of zemiology.

We consider this debate further in **section 19.6**, but here we focus on how the concept of 'social harm' can be used as an important tool to question crime and criminology. In their important contribution to this topic, Hillyard and Tombs (2004: 10–18) list nine fundamental criticisms of the academic discipline of criminology which, they argue, need to be readdressed by critical scholars. They are worth summarising here before we discuss them further.

1. 'Crime' has no ontological reality (it does not exist in itself).
2. Criminology perpetuates the myth of 'crime'.
3. 'Crime' consists of many petty (unimportant and trivial) events.
4. 'Crime' excludes many serious harms.
5. Constructing 'crime' through the criminal law is myopic (short-sighted).
6. Criminalisation and **punishment** inflict pain.
7. 'Crime' control is ineffective.
8. 'Crime'—and therefore criminology—gives legitimacy to the expansion of crime control.
9. 'Crime' helps to maintain power relations.

The first thing to note here is that the authors place the word 'crime' in inverted commas; this suggests that they regard the very concept of 'crime' as a problematic one which should be replaced, because—as they argue in the first point—it has no objective 'reality'.

Let's unpack the nine fundamental criticisms.

'Crime' has no ontological reality

As we have already discussed (see **Chapter 11** and our discussion of gender and feminist criminology), the term **ontology** simply refers to the study of what exists in the social world. It is concerned with whether or not concepts—such as 'crime'—are existing objective realities, or whether they are socially and ideologically constructed. Similarly, we have used the **theory** of **social constructionism** in many chapters of this book to refer to the idea that crime and its associated concepts (such as criminal justice) are the changeable and subjective creations of institutions and individuals in societies at specific points in history.

Hillyard and Tombs's (2004) claim that 'crime' has no ontological reality therefore means that they see it as a myth of everyday life. They are not denying that people commit forms of behaviour which can 'harm' other people ('offending' behaviour or 'criminal harms', for lack of a better phrase), the suggestion is simply that giving such behaviours the label of 'crime' is misleading. This is because constructions of 'crime' (and 'justice') do not exist in themselves—what is and is not 'crime' is continuously defined and redefined by a particular set of social relations which involve, in varying degrees, the exercise of power together with forms of social inequality and social exclusion (Scraton and Chadwick, 1991).

To illustrate this, let's consider some examples.

- The age of criminal responsibility for young people varies hugely across western European countries (see **Chapter 9**).
- If you have gay or lesbian sex today, you are unlikely—in most, but not all, parts of the world—to be prosecuted as having committed a criminal offence, whereas if you had committed the same act before 1967 in England you could have been found guilty and possibly imprisoned (see **Chapter 2**).
- Blasphemy has been legal in England since 2008, but it remains an offence in many other countries around the world (see **Figure 19.4**).
- Someone taking their own life in Oman would be breaking the law, but they would not be considered a criminal in the Netherlands.

For social harm theorists, such basic **reflections** are of great importance as they have significant implications for the study of criminology, and its future as a distinct subject area. They argue that constructions of 'crime' and 'crime problems' are limited, partial, and selective and offer a distorted lens through which to view the social world and its problems, meaning that the central elements which characterise the study of criminology make little sense. This also applies to the search for the causes of 'crime'—the 'holy grail' of much early criminology—as well as to other central aspects of the subject area, such as why crime rates increase or decrease, theories of **desistance**, and so on.

Criminology perpetuates the myth of 'crime'

The second criticism is linked to the first: given that crime has no ontological reality, it could be argued that some versions of criminology in themselves help to perpetuate the myth of 'crime'. For instance, some criminologists research and write as though if what they are studying—that is, 'crime'—is a fixed concept which can be measured in unproblematic ways. Indeed, in **Chapter 2** we focused on the obvious question on which all new criminologists have to reflect: 'what is crime?'

Although almost all students new to the subject area will consider this question, it is sometimes seen—and presented—as just being a compulsory rite of passage that they must go through before they are allowed to study what are perceived to be more interesting and fruitful areas, such as what causes 'crime' (**Part 3** of this book covers *explaining crime*) and how it can be prevented and controlled (**Part 4** of this book discusses *responding to crime*). Having started off their criminological journey by critically interrogating the concept of 'crime', students

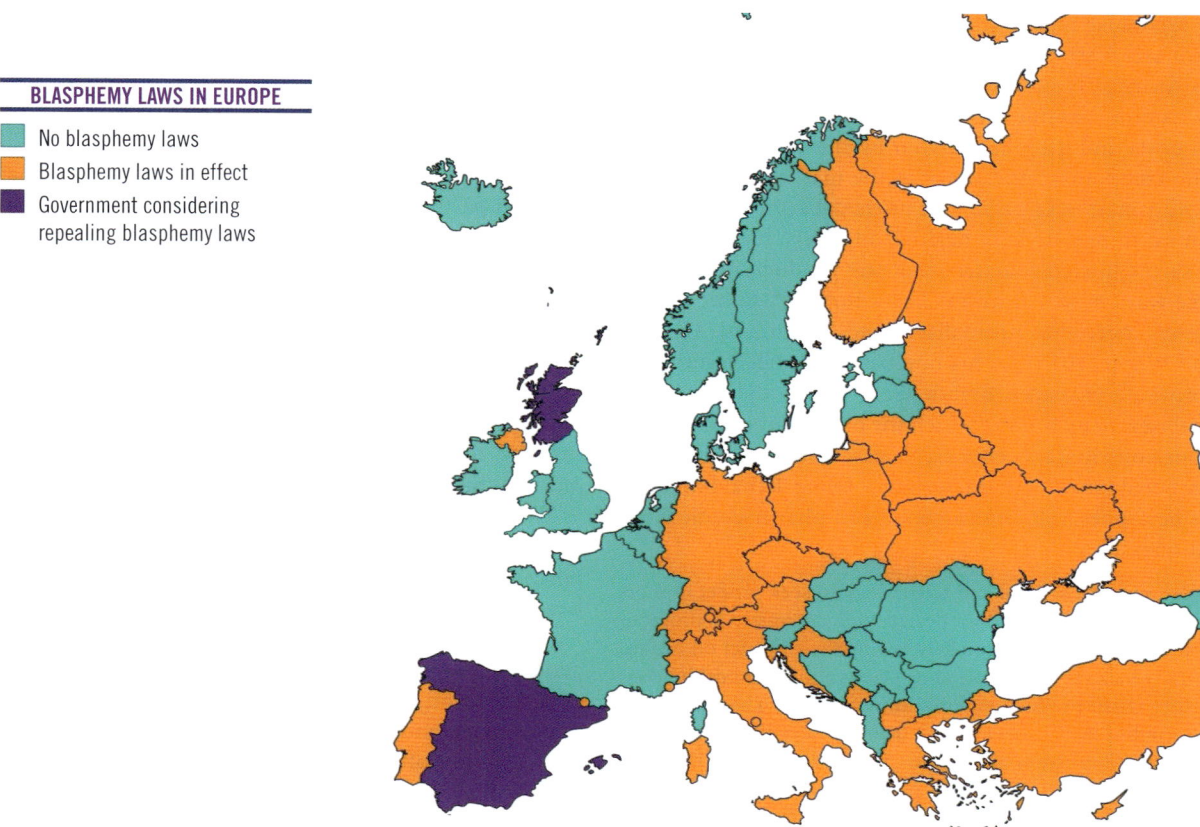

Figure 19.4 If 'crime' is a construct and has no ontological reality (as shown here, laws on acts such as blasphemy vary widely between countries), is it a helpful label to use?
Source: Humanists UK

are almost expected to forget these valuable first lessons as they engage with ideas of **free will** and **determinism** (**Chapter 15**), and issues such as serial killers, terrorism, stalking, and debates about the police and prisons, as if such institutions are a natural, inevitable, and correct response to criminality and offending behaviour. In this book, however, we aim to continually return to the ABC (*Always Be Critical*) mantra, which means you should remain critical of the concept of 'crime' itself throughout your criminological studies—especially in this particular chapter.

'Crime' consists of many petty events

Hillyard and Tombs (2004) argue that much 'crime', as officially recorded, is of a relatively petty, unimportant nature. As we saw in **Chapter 5**, where we focused on criminal statistics and how 'crime' is officially recorded and measured, there are many different categories of offences and all of them include sub-categories. For instance, offences within the category of 'violence against the person' range from very severe and harmful acts, such as murder, to relatively harmless assaults without injury. The media plays a pivotal role in interpreting and disseminating crime statistics (which it presents as facts), and the news values that influence their coverage (see **Chapter 6**) result in the general public getting the mistaken impression that 'crime' mainly consists of serious and harmful events. In fact, as Tombs and Whyte (2015) have argued, the risk of someone contracting a terminal illness or being struck by lightning is far higher than the likelihood that they will become the victim of an intentional homicide.

'Crime' excludes many serious harms

Elaborating on their third criticism, Hillyard and Tombs (2004) say that placing so much importance on petty events, because they are defined as 'crime', means we fail to recognise many other forms of behaviour which are seriously harmful. The most obvious examples of this are forms of corporate criminality. Corporations tend to focus on economic rather than social and environmental costs and are often driven by the profit motive. To gain competitive advantage in the market, manufacturing businesses in particular often 'cut corners' and may ignore things such as health and safety regulations. It is through such practices that the production of harm (the ways in which harms like injury or fatalities come about) becomes normalised and routinised (Tombs and Whyte, 2015). In his book about public health and corporate practices, Freudenberg (2016) discusses and analyses many ways in which the behaviours of corporations contribute to chronic disease and global epidemics; behaviours he characterises as being 'lethal but legal'. As he argues, the food, alcohol, and pharmaceutical industries all:

> use modern science and technology to seek profits in ways that harm health. They design and aggressively promote products without adequately testing their impact on health. They make false or misleading claims about the health benefits of their products and minimise the known harms or seek to obfuscate the science that demonstrates this harm. They price unhealthy products cheaply to maximise their market penetration but charge high prices that put healthy products out of reach of many who need them.
>
> (Freudenberg, 2016: 63)

In **Conversations 19.1,** Professor Steve Tombs talks about his research on workplace injury and death from a social harm perspective. He highlights why this particular issue is a powerful example of the fact that 'crime' excludes serious harms and reflects on some of the other fundamental criticisms of criminology that we discuss in this section.

Constructing 'crime' through the criminal law is myopic

In **Chapter 2** we began by posing the question 'what is crime?' but ended by critically considering whether we need the criminal law at all, which is effectively what Hillyard and Tombs (2004) are suggesting with this criticism.

According to Hartjen (1978, in Muncie and McLaughlin, 1996: 8–9), certain conditions have to be met in order for an act to be defined legally as a crime:

- the act must be legally prohibited at the time it is committed;
- the perpetrator must have criminal intent (often referred to as *mens rea*);
- the perpetrator must have acted voluntarily (often referred to as *actus reus*) and;
- there must be some legally prescribed punishment for committal of the act.

Social harm theorists argue that this definition is too narrow and partial, because—as Professor Tombs discusses in **Conversations 19.1**—the criminal law concentrates on certain forms of harm, to the exclusion of other equally harmful behaviours. Social harm proponents see the concept of *mens rea*, crucial in criminal law, as particularly problematic because its focus on the individual and issues of individual guilt effectively prevents any kind of criminal liability being attributed to groups of individuals—such as corporations—whose collective decisions and practices harm millions of people.

The complexity, diversity, and relative invisibility of **corporate crime**, alongside the diffusion of responsibility and victimisation, make it very difficult to regulate through criminal law. As a result, many corporate harms go undetected or, if they are recognised, either generate no response or lead to action which falls short of prosecution. This means that there are generally low rates of prosecution, and even when this is successful, sanctions are often relatively lenient (see Hughes and Langham, 2001).

Criminalisation and punishment inflict pain

We saw in **Chapter 18** that power and power relations are a central theme of critical criminology, and Hillyard and Tombs's (2004) next criticism of the discipline is that a narrow conception of 'crime' allows relatively powerful groups to criminalise and inflict pain (punishment) on relatively powerless groups while avoiding criminalisation for their own harming behaviours. Processes of criminalisation—detection, arrest, prosecution, conviction, and punishment—are all social processes which involve the exercise of power and discretion by state institutions, so they can behave in ways that serve their own interests. 'Crimes' committed by powerful groups—such as forms of corporate crime, as we have seen, and also green crimes and harms, as we discussed in **Chapter 12**—are less easy to detect and prosecute, but often they are not seen as being 'criminal' at all and, even when prosecutions are brought, the 'criminal justice' system responds in a different, more lenient way. As Tombs (2016) notes, it is not unusual to see a corporation punished financially, such as through a fine, and such financial penalties are often miniscule compared to executives' annual salaries and a corporation's overall profit margin. In practice, the financial burden of the fine is often

CONVERSATIONS 19.1

The serious harms of workplace injury and death

with **Professor Steve Tombs**

There's an old trade union saying: if you want to kill somebody and get away with it, set up a company and then employ them. Flippant and gruesome, maybe—but with more than a ring of truth to it. And this was the key reason why I ended up toying with the concepts of social harm and the discipline of zemiology as alternatives to the concept of crime and the discipline of criminology.

In Great Britain, one of the most developed economies in the world, tens of thousands of people are killed as a result of work every year. The Health and Safety Executive (HSE) records a limited sub-set of fatal injuries—in 2018–19, there were 147—but this is in addition to 13,000 deaths per year from occupational diseases [a disease caused by work or certain working conditions]. Both figures are significant under-estimates; other calculations reach a figure almost four times the HSE's data, that is, about 50,000 such deaths a year (SHP Online, 10 December 2008).

This annual total is higher than almost all other recorded causes of premature death in the UK. It is certainly far greater than the numbers of deaths caused by 'real' crimes—which is not to deny the awful reality of any specific early death. This comparison is not simply a numbers game, but it *is* a recognition that numbers do matter. Such numbers also highlight the dangerous distortions of the category of crime, as Paddy Hillyard and I originally identified in *Beyond Criminology* (2004).

Even the bare statistics underscore two of the criticisms we made in that work—that 'crime' excludes many serious harms while it includes many petty events. For example, data from the Crime Survey for England and Wales released in 2019 reveals that the most prevalent forms of crime are computer misuse, fraud, theft, and criminal damage. Each of these 'umbrella' categories covers a wide range of offences of varying severity, and indeed they may generate significant, detrimental consequences for some victims. But for the most part, none of the offences under any of these categories are likely to have life-changing impacts on their victims—as we put it, following Louk Hulsman, none score particularly highly on a scale of personal hardship (Hulsman, 1986).

Furthermore, a failure to place crime in perspective, seeing it alongside other prevalent social harms (including workplace deaths) is, most significantly of all, illustrative of two further key criticisms of the category of crime to which Paddy and I pointed.

First, the criminal justice system gives a great deal of attention to 'real' crimes, including the inter-personal violence that may result in death. Failing to consider workplace deaths alongside these, is to maintain existing power relations. It effectively removes a class of offenders (corporations), and offences (corporate killing), from the attention of the criminal justice system. True, there are a handful of prosecutions for workplace deaths under health and safety law every year in the UK, and in the first 10 years following the passing of the Corporate Manslaughter and Corporate Homicide Act there were 26 convictions. However, when we compare these to the numbers of recorded work-related fatalities, we can see that the corporate killing of workers is effectively decriminalised. These deaths do not feature in the criminal justice landscape. They are rarely even investigated, let alone properly recorded. These facts are what the trade union saying I cited above recognises. And they are an effect of power—an effect which is effectively reproduced by criminology's focus on crime and criminal justice.

This latter observation also raises a further question. What is the difference between the person killed by a fall in a street fight, the death of a patient from legionnaires' disease (a disease which is often caught in places like hotels, hospitals or offices where the bacteria have got into the water supply), the cyclist killed by a motorist distracted by lighting a cigarette, or the worker killed when an employer fails to check that scaffolding has been properly erected? All involve a sequence of avoidable events. None involve the intention to kill. All result in a dead body, a life lost, relatives and friends distraught, lives changed forever, communities bereft. But each is treated vastly differently by the law and in relation to the category of crime—evidencing the crucial observation that crime has no ontological reality. Rather, crime is a legal construct; one that is created, maintained, and reproduced through a great deal of political, police, judicial and wider criminal justice activity. Yet criminology remains in crime's thrall. It is defined by a focus on crime. It can never entirely deconstruct crime. And for that reason, we argue that criminology was and remains an essentially problematic enterprise.

Professor Steve Tombs, Professor of Criminology, The Open University

passed on to workers and consumers through raised prices, redundancies, etc., so the impact on the groups of individuals whose actions or inactions caused the harm is minimal.

In contrast, the pain inflicted by criminalising individuals who have committed 'crime' is considerable. As we will discuss in **Chapters 24–8**, the UK has an **adversarial** criminal justice system, meaning that its focus is on establishing the guilt of the 'offender' (possibly to the relative neglect of the victim; see Christie, 1977), and imposing punishment. It could be argued that this focus means the state exacerbates and reinforces the pain of relatively powerless people who are likely to be already suffering as a result of state actions, such as austerity measures. These processes of criminalisation also effectively shut off alternative responses to 'crime problems'. An approach that takes the wider socio-economic factors which are often linked to 'offending' behaviours into account may be more effective and just.

We can examine this idea briefly by thinking back to the systemic issues faced by young people which we explored in **Chapter 9**, and by looking at Jacobson et al.'s (2010) analysis of children in custodial provision (see **Figure 19.5**) in England and Wales. This study points out that prior to imprisonment:

- 51 per cent of children lived in a deprived household or unsuitable accommodation;
- 47 per cent had, at some point in their lives, run away from home;
- 27 per cent had, at some point in their lives, been in local authority care;
- 12 per cent had experienced the death of a sibling or parent;
- 48 per cent had been excluded from schools.

Figure 19.5 Criminalisation inflicts considerable pain on individuals, including children, who are often already suffering as a result of systemic issues

Source: Rui Vieira/PA Images

A later report published by the Ministry of Justice (2013) cited further research which established that:

- 50 per cent of 15–17-year-olds entering public sector Young Offender Institutions were assessed as having the literacy levels expected of 7–11-year-olds;
- 18 per cent of sentenced young people in custody had a statement of special educational needs, compared to 3 per cent of the general population;
- 27 per cent of young men aged 15–17 in custody felt they had emotional or mental health problems; and
- 39 per cent had been on the child protection register or had experienced abuse and neglect.

These issues say a great deal about the problems modern societies face across a range of public policy areas, such as education and health. They also foreground the multiple forms of disadvantage (and forms of social injustice, and a lack of recognition of children's rights) faced by young people who are perceived as 'troublesome'—issues we considered in depth in **Chapter 9**. Indeed, Goldson has made a powerful case for the abolition of child imprisonment, arguing that:

> locking up children is spectacularly ineffective . . . children invariably leave prison not only more damaged but also more angry, more alienated, more expert in the ways of crime and more likely to commit more serious offences . . . in fact, more of everything that the children themselves and the community need much less of.
>
> (2002: 159–60)

'Crime' control is ineffective

Hillyard and Tombs (2004) argue that not only does the idea of 'crime' lead to considerable pain being inflicted on individuals through criminalisation, but these methods are not even effective in terms of eradicating or reducing the undesirable behaviour and harm.

Are they right? To assess this, we need to examine the statistics. The kinds of figures that show a criminal justice system and systems of crime control working effectively will depend on your point of view. Many people would look for decreases in recorded crime rates; increases in police clear-up and detection rates; evidence of 'successful' diversionary strategies (see **Chapters 9** and **30**); or a falling prison population. But perhaps you think that the opposite would provide stronger evidence of efficacy and 'success': increases in police recorded crime rates, an increasing prison population and so on. The complex and problematic nature of accurate measurement is a key issue here. For instance, as we saw in **Chapter 5**, even these statistical indicators are socially constructed; they are affected by issues relating to police power and discretion, which is inherent at all stages of a criminal 'justice' process.

Criminologists will often look at rates of reoffending for evidence of the effectiveness of 'crime control'. Social harm theorists would argue that statistics such as those shown in **What do you think? 19.2** indicate that the way in which societies deal with both powerful and 'conventional' offenders needs to be radically rethought, a shift that will require wide-ranging and transformative social, political, and economic changes.

WHAT DO YOU THINK? 19.2

Is 'crime' control effective?

Consider **Figure 19.6**, which is derived from Ministry of Justice data (2018). What strikes you most about the statistics, and to what extent do you think they provide evidence of an effective system of 'crime control'? Bear in mind the criticisms we have considered so far, and remember to maintain an ABC mindset: what occurrences of 'crime' (or harmful behaviour) might these categories exclude?

The first thing to note is that 'proven reoffending' is likely to be a lot lower than actual reoffending rates indicate, as this term relates to police detection, cautions, and sentencing practices and outcomes: the figures therefore do not include those who reoffend and who are not caught. Perhaps the most striking statistics in the figure are the high 'proven reoffending' rates following custodial sentences. If the overriding objective of imprisonment is crime control and reduction, then surely this means that it simply does not work?

The second consideration is that, as we discussed earlier in point 6 about criminalisation and punishment inflicting pain, corporate 'crimes' are rarely dealt with through the criminal justice system. Since this means that harm inflicted by corporations is often not punished at all, we could argue that this approach to crime control is ineffective too.

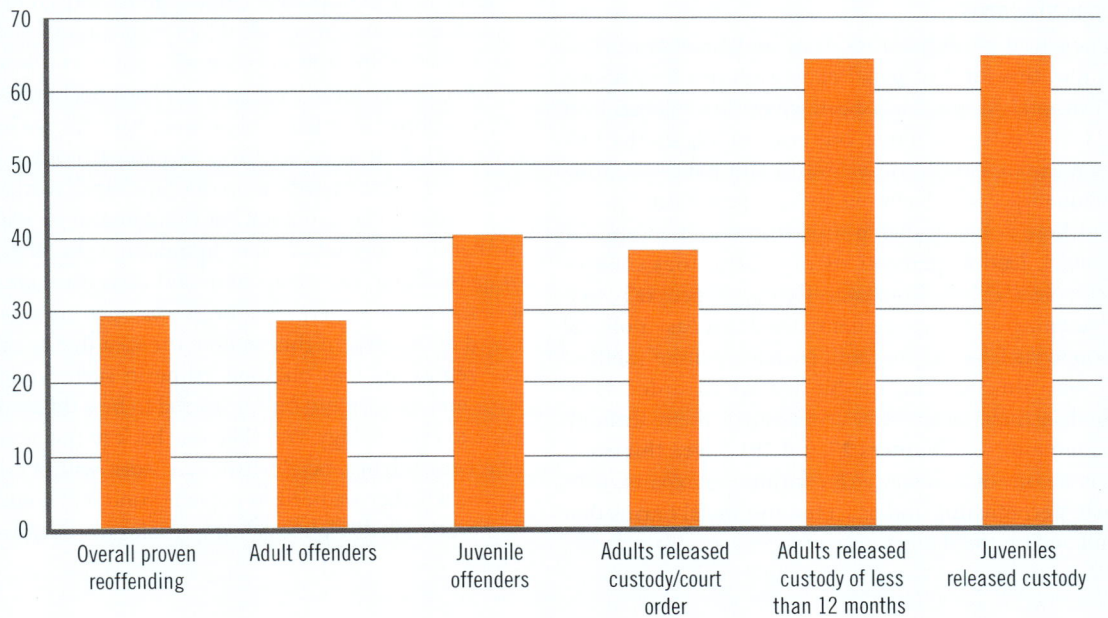

Figure 19.6 Proven reoffending for adult and juvenile offenders who were released from custody, received a non-custodial conviction at court, or received a caution between October and December 2016

Source: Ministry of Justice

'Crime' legitimises the expansion of crime control

Hillyard and Tombs (2004) claim that 'crime', and by extension much criminology, enables systems of crime control to keep expanding. This argument was first put forward by the Norwegian criminologist Nils Christie, who in 1993 published a book entitled *Crime Control as Industry* (since republished many times—see Christie, 2000). By this title phrase, Christie meant that systems designed to 'control crime' were becoming important industries in their own right; not only do they employ thousands of people but they also cost a lot of money to run and maintain. Focusing on growing global prison systems and populations, Christie (2000) argues that instead of existing to **rehabilitate** 'offenders' or even to reduce levels of offending, the overriding aim of the crime control industry has become to make a profit. It is unlikely to be a coincidence that the expansion of 'crime control' has taken place against the background of the increasing privatisation of the system—its components (prisons, etc.) are increasing owned and run by private companies, rather than the state, so there is more of a motive to make profit. Angela Y. Davis (2003) has made similar arguments in relation to the US, which in 2016 imprisoned 698 people per 100,000 of the national population, the highest ratio in the world. In contrast, England and Wales imprisoned 140 per 100,000 of their national populations and Finland 51 (Walmsley, 2018).

Some social harm theorists draw on Christie's work to argue that this kind of penal expansion not only shows how 'criminal harms' have been given precedence over other forms of social harm, but also highlights the link between expansion of crime control and issues of growing inequalities and declining welfare provision. The argument here is that growing inequalities creating public fears which lead to perceptions of a 'dangerous class' of poor people. The behaviour of this group of people is seen as threatening and they are demonised. An easy political reaction to such 'social junk' and 'social dynamite' (Spitzer, 1975) who threaten the 'established social order' is to criminalise their behaviours and control them through imprisonment (see **Chapters 27 and 28**). Given this cycle, the crime control industry will continue to expand, with the state perpetuating and exacerbating social harms that are inflicted on the 'dangerous poor'.

'Crime' maintains power relations

As we have seen through unpacking the preceding eight criticisms, the concept of 'crime' can be seen to both create and maintain power relations. But can the same be said about criminology? Whilst some critical criminological theories have challenged the basis of such relations and the exercise of forms of power—including economic, political, and patriarchal power—it is hard to argue against the fact that criminology, in the main, involves studying and analysing a concept which is defined and mobilised by the state and its institutions. By remaining fixated on legal definitions of crime and the workings of a 'criminal justice system', criminology itself could be seen as a narrow, partial, and selective subject area which lacks the conceptual frameworks to adequately study the full range of harms committed in today's complex world.

This idea is probably best illustrated by Box's seminal work *Power, Crime and Mystification* first published in 1983. Through the use of examples including corporate crime, rape and sexual assault, and crimes of the powerless, Box argues that the powerful in society—such as the state, the media, corporations, the police, and the rest of the criminal justice system—all disseminate messages which focus on the 'crime problem'. Their actions and discourse increase fear of certain types of behaviours, the ones they define as crimes, and of certain types of people, those who have been labelled as criminal. All of this deflects attention away from the harms caused by the powerful so that their transgressions or failures to protect citizens go unnoticed or are accepted as 'normal', an accident, or (in relation to something like poverty) the fault of those who fall victim to it. Box's (1983) claim is not that crime is not harmful, but that many other actions are as harmful or more harmful; we have just been socialised to accept them as part of modern society. He calls this the 'mystification of crime'. Box's work calls on us to question criminology but it might also be seen to go further and question its very foundations; in other words, to question the way that 'crime' and its control are central focuses in our society. This begins to open up a point we raised at the start of this section: the idea that social harm and zemiology may question 'crime' in such fundamental ways that they should be considered to be a different discipline to criminology. We will come back to the question of whether studying social harms can 'work' within criminology, or whether we need to move beyond it and embrace a new academic discipline called zemiology in **section 19.6**.

19.4 How the social harm approach works

The next important aspect of social harm that we need to consider is how the approach works; how we can apply it to issues and study them. To help us identify the complex and overlapping levels and dimensions of studying social harms and to ground these ideas in reality, we will first familiarise ourselves with a case study of social harm, that of the Grenfell Tower fire, an example that has been analysed in depth by Tombs (2019). With this example in mind, we will consider the different categories of social harm—physical harm, psychological and emotional harms, cultural harms, harms of recognition, and financial and economic harms—before reflecting on how social harm is produced and whether it can be reduced or prevented.

As you read the case study, try to make connections between this example and the three other scenarios we considered in **section 19.2**, as well as any other examples you may be aware of. For instance, think about issues such as political will, power, and why some harmful behaviours may not immediately be acknowledged as crimes.

A social harm case study: The Grenfell Fire

On 14 June 2017, a major fire engulfed Grenfell Tower, a high-rise block of flats in North Kensington, London, and killed 72 people. The tragedy shocked the UK and the world, particularly when it emerged that actions and inactions of the state and state agencies contributed to—or perhaps even caused—the deaths. As with the other examples of social harm that we have considered, significant harm was inflicted on a large group of people, people we could call victims, but this event would not fall within existing definitions of 'crime'. As writer and Grenfell Foundation activist Dan Renwick's passionate account in **Conversations 19.2** suggests, the fire was not the result of a direct, single action by an individual or small group of identifiable issues, but of a chain of actions and inactions, and of systemic social issues. Let's consider this example in more detail.

Grenfell Tower was built in the early 1970s and contained 129 flats across 21 floors. These flats were home to a diverse community of mainly working-class residents, most of whom were council tenants of the Royal Borough of Kensington and Chelsea (RBKC), although some families owned their homes or rented them privately. In 2012, the building underwent significant renovations, being fitted with new windows and heating systems, as well as with new external cladding (a covering or coating) that was designed to increase energy efficiency and improve the overall appearance of the tower—**Figure 19.7** shows it before this refurbishment. According to the RBKC Joint Strategic Needs Assessment (JSNA): Housing Support and Care report, published jointly with Westminster City Council in 2016 (a year before the fire), this was intended to support residents' well-being by helping to address the problem of fuel poverty. The JSNA also made frequent mention of financial pressures affecting the councils, but without discussing the fact that at the time of the fire, RBKC had £274 million in reserves.

The renovations were overseen by the Kensington and Chelsea Tenant Management Organisation (KCTMO), which was commissioned by the council to manage and run over 9,000 buildings in the borough. Relations between tenants, the KCTMO, and the council were often poor, with tenants making complaints about the way that they were treated by both organisations. There was a sense that as poorer, working-class (and, for some, non-white) people living in an otherwise extremely affluent area, they were seen as undesirable residents and received less favourable treatment than their wealthier neighbours. RBKC is one of the richest local authorities in the UK, but the ward (an area within an authority) in which the tower was located was one of the poorest, resulting in significant disparities between the life chances and life choices of people living only a few miles apart.

We can learn more about these inequalities by looking at national statistics compiled for all areas in England, and in particular the Index of Multiple Deprivation. This is one of seven official measures of deprivation used by statisticians, with other indices focusing on specific aspects

Figure 19.7 Grenfell Tower shown before the council-commissioned refurbishment that is argued to have contributed to the tragedy

Source: PA Images/Alamy Stock Photo

of deprivation, such as child poverty or poverty amongst older people. Most recently published in 2015, the Index of Multiple Deprivation works by examining small areas called Lower Layer Super Output Areas (LSOAs) across the country, ranking them from 1 (the most deprived) to 32,844 (the least deprived). The index reveals that Grenfell Tower was in the Notting Dale ward, which is ranked at 3,171 (out of 32,844), placing it firmly in the 10 per cent most deprived wards in England. If we look at the other LSOAs in RBKC, we can see that only ten scored lower on the Index than Notting Dale. The least deprived LSOA in RBKC scores 26,751 on the index—a sharp contrast in deprivation levels.

Another important piece of context for the Grenfell fire is that residents had been raising safety concerns about the building for at least five years. The writers of a local blog pointed out fire hazards such as blocked exits and the lack of easy access for emergency vehicles (Grenfell Action Group, 28 January 2013); by November 2015 they were so concerned that they wrote an article that predicted, with chilling accuracy, that the only way the KCTMO would be put under scrutiny would be for lives to be lost in a major fire. Earlier in 2017 notices were put up in the entrance and by the lifts, advising that in the event of a fire residents should stay in their homes; this was based on the belief that the design of the building would contain any outbreak and prevent flames and smoke from spreading around the tower.

So, on the evening of 13 June 2017, the residents of Grenfell Tower went to bed in a building that was nearly 40 years old, sited in a profoundly deprived area, and about which they had been raising safety concerns. Just before 1 am, a resident on the fourth floor dialled 999 to report that his fridge-freezer had caught fire. The fire brigade arrived within minutes, but it is likely that the fire had spread outside the building even before they reached the kitchen. Less than half-an-hour after the first fire engine arrived, flames had reached the top floor, travelling up and along the cladding that had been fitted to the exterior of the flats, then moving to engulf the south and east sides of the building. Some residents ignored the advice to stay in their flats and left the building, but those who did not were trapped as the flames, smoke, and fumes spread. The 'stay put' guidance was formally abandoned just before 3 am, but although 144 people had escaped before that point, only a further 36 were able to leave once the decision to evacuate was made. By 4.30 am, the entire building was on fire.

A public inquiry began in 2017 into the cause, spread, and aftermath of the disaster. As we can see clearly from **Figure 19.8** and **Conversations 19.2**—an account from activist and Grenfell Foundation representative Dan Renwick—there has been widespread public anger about how the fire was allowed to happen. Note the title of Dan's documentary ('Failed by the state') and his emphasis on and description of justice for the community. Much of the anger has been directed at RBKC and the KCTMO,

Figure 19.8 The Grenfell Tower tragedy produced widespread outrage, especially as it emerged that the cladding on the building which is thought to have contributed to the scale of the disaster was chosen to reduce costs
Source: The Associated Press

CONVERSATIONS 19.2

Failed By the State: seeking justice for Grenfell

with **Dan Renwick**

I have worked, played and lived in North Kensington. It is an area very close to my heart. Prior to the Grenfell disaster I was working on a number of youth-focused projects in Notting Dale, the area of the borough in which Grenfell tower is located (now more commonly referred to as 'Latimer' by locals), and in the years since the fire I have campaigned with the Grenfell Foundation to support and seek justice for those affected.

My friends and I made *Failed By the State*, a documentary created with the local community and presented by Ishmael Francis-Murray, who was born in Grenfell Tower, in a bid to right some wrongs and seek justice. The documentary's title refers to the fact that we feel the scale and severity of the fire was a direct result of actions and inaction by the state—and also by corporations.

In 2009 the local authority commissioned a master plan for the area which recommended demolishing Grenfell Tower, but following local resistance they resorted to redeveloping it. The concrete building, which the plan stated 'blighted' the local skyline and stood (to their clear annoyance) above the spire of the Notting Hill Methodist Church, was insulated and covered with cladding to make the aesthetic more amenable to the new classes who were taking to the area. The cladding also reduced energy costs so aligned with climate change agreements like Kyoto.

From the onset of the renovations, Grenfell residents raised their voice and sought external scrutiny over the quality of the work being done on the tower. They were muted by authorities. When their pressure finally led to external assessments, the local council praised the construction company for its work on the tower and only asked that the developers 'mitigate' the inconveniences.

Freedom of information requests from residents regarding the materials used for the refurbishment were denied. Had these requests been met, they would have revealed the catastrophic decisions that went on to kill. The corporations responsible were safeguarded, and what was effectively kindling and fuel were clad and stuck to the concrete structure. In one night, 71 lives were lost, including the loved ones of my friends.

When the disaster struck, the whole community united in their understanding that criminal decisions were made that led to this entirely preventable loss of life. Yet a callous indifference from the institutions of state instead presided. After the fire, when people needed humanity, they got interlopers who agitated for immediate change, using the event to gain media attention and score political points. The disaster struck less than a week after the election in which the British public had made clear that they wanted real, substantive change by voting in a way that led to the Conservatives losing their parliamentary majority, and this feeling gathered strength in the local community following the fire.

The bereaved and survivors called for the local authority to be put under special measures, but again their calls were muted. Instead, the community had to interface with the very same people who were so neglectful in their duty of care that it resulted in lives being lost. This led the community to organise itself. Grenfell United and the Grenfell Foundation were born out of a failure of state. People like myself serve them, because they are our vessel to justice.

Justice to the community is a number of things. It is cradle to grave support for those affected. It is criminalisation of those who knowingly risked life. Anyone who knew the risks of the cladding or insulation must face the same justice we see meted out to working class people who kill through negligence. Those who were unaware of the consequences of their actions should tell the truth in a process of meaningful reconciliation, but that should be done so that the real culprits can be laid bare.

Daniel Renwick, writer, community youth worker, and representative of the Grenfell Foundation

---

particularly over the installation of the cladding which almost certainly caused the fire to spread so quickly across the exterior of the tower. The fact that this type of cladding was chosen as a cost-saving measure has been a source of great pain and outrage, as has the reaction of senior politicians, who were perceived as showing a lack of care or empathy for those who lost their homes. The greatest grief of all, however, is the loss of the 72 people who were killed. Survivors and well-wishers take part in a silent walk on the 14th day of every month to show them the respect, honour, and dignity that many feel they were denied in their lives and in the way of their death.

Levels and dimensions of social harm

Now that we have this context in which to ground our discussion, we can begin to explore the various 'levels' and dimensions through which social harm can be measured; in other words, how the concept can be operationalised and made to 'work' when studying and analysing social harms. Whilst every social harm scholar may identify different types or levels of social harm, the most commonly included levels are physical harm, psychological and emotional harms, harms to autonomy, and relational harms. However, other levels of harm that are frequently considered include cultural harms, social harms, financial and economic harms, environmental harms, harms to dignity, and harms caused by the refusal to recognise a person's voice.

Mapping the various levels of social harms is very much a work in progress and is currently the source of much debate. For instance, Hillyard and Tombs initially (2004, 2017) suggested a relatively straightforward fourfold **typology** (classification) of harm, which would include physical, financial, psychological, and cultural and environmental harms. Taking this forward, in what was the first book-length theoretical consideration of the social harm perspective, Pemberton (2016: 28–30) expressed these categories and levels of harm slightly differently. Examine his categories in **Table 19.1** with the scenarios we have been considering, in particular the Grenfell tragedy. How many of Pemberton's levels can be seen within these situations? We look at this in detail in **What do you think? 19.3**.

As you can see, categorising levels and dimensions of harm is not as straightforward as it may first appear. Some of the categories in the typologies clearly overlap and, as

Category of harm	Dimension of harm/needs that can arise from the harm
Physical and mental health harms Recognising that life-limiting illness and injury can severely compromise our ability to exercise life choices or maintain relationships.	**Lack of:** • a healthy diet; • time to participate in physical exercise; • appropriate healthcare systems; • shelter; • a non-hazardous physical environment to ensure a sufficient level of health is maintained. **Illness**: • psychotic disorders leading to a complete loss of the self and a total inability to participate in social relations; • clinical forms of depression, anxiety leading to feelings of helplessness and worthlessness. • Loss of control or autonomy over life
Autonomy harms Harms that result from situations where 'people experience "fundamental disablement" in relation to their attempts to achieve *self-actualisation* . . . and a sufficient level of *autonomy*'.	**Access to effective education** • The ability to formulate and act on choices. • Illiteracy and innumeracy. • Communication and critical evaluation. • Practical skills. **Opportunities for meaningful and productive social activity** • Family life. • Paid work. • Recognition and reward. • Ability to participate in the decisions that affect their life. • Control of economic and social resources.
Relational harms	• Enforced exclusion from social relationships. • Access to social support and help. • Opportunities to learn and develop. • Fulfilment of emotional needs. • Being able to present one's identity in a way one chooses. • Shame, stigma, being the 'other'.

Table 19.1 Pemberton's categories of harm

Source: Pemberton, S. A. (2016) Harmful Societies. Bristol: Bristol University Press. Pp. 28–30

WHAT DO YOU THINK? 19.3

Identifying the types of harms caused by the Grenfell fire tragedy

Having now read about the context of the Grenfell fire and its aftermath, including **Conversations 19.2**, think about the various social harms which have resulted from it and fill in the grid below, as far as you can. As you do this, think beyond the immediate victims—the 72 people who died in the fire—and consider the residents who survived, the immediate community, the rescue and medical services, and the wider costs to central and local governments.

In completing this exercise, you have probably started to realise that a single incident, such as the Grenfell fire, has wide-ranging consequences that ripple out to cause harm to people and organisations who may initially appear to be unconnected to the event. If you repeat this exercise with the other scenarios we have looked at as well, can you identify any patterns?

Category of harm	Dimension of harm/needs that can arise from the harm
Physical harms	
Psychological and emotional harms	
Cultural harms	
Harms of recognition	
Financial and economic harms	

you will see when we apply this to the Grenfell fire case study, there is often a clear 'rippling out' effect of various harms. For instance, physical and psychological harms suffered by individuals and groups of people can extend to have a further impact on their financial harms, such as when a person is too ill to work. Constructing typologies is, however, a very useful analytical device through which social scientists attempt to understand the social world and, in this case, harmful events. It is clear that typologies of harm will continue to be developed and refined as work in this field progresses. For now, though, it is perhaps best for us to be creative and to reconfigure social harms categories as we apply them to examples of harmful behaviours and events. We do this in **What do you think? 19.3**, drawing on the typology adopted in Tombs's (2019) analysis of the Grenfell fire.

Let's walk through the various levels and dimensions of harm, and how these manifest in the Grenfell disaster, in more detail.

Physical harm

This is probably the most obvious form of harm that can arise from a catastrophic incident such as a fire or road accident. In the case of the Grenfell disaster, there were, of course, the fatalities and injuries from burns or smoke inhalation, but other injuries and illnesses may still be diagnosed or identified at a later date. These may include those associated with harmful substances that may have been released as a result of the fire.

As well as the physical impact of smoke and flames, Tombs (2019) identifies further harms in the form of psychological damage inflicted by the events at Grenfell Tower—these are in addition to mental or emotional harms, which we discuss below. Trauma is likely to have exacerbated dependency on alcohol or drugs; similarly, illnesses linked to poverty and poor housing will have been worsened for sufferers who found themselves living in temporary accommodation with limited space and poor access to cooking facilities.

Psychological and emotional harms

Anyone who was in the tower that night or who witnessed the fire, whether as a bystander or as a member of the rescue services, will have been affected by the experience. For some, the impact has been unbearable; according to one charity (Silence for Suicide), over 20 survivors have attempted suicide (BBC News, 5 September 2017). Survivors' guilt, grief, and the trauma of what was seen and heard have increased the needs of what was, in many cases, an already vulnerable population. Relief workers have described drug dealers coming to the area to prey on the community, which included large numbers of people who had existing mental health problems or who had previously experienced trauma as refugees or victims of persecution.

As well as those directly affected, there are a large number of people who saw the fire take hold or who had to try to explain what had happened to their children when watching news reports. Residents of tower blocks across the country have since lived with the fear that they are also at risk, and in some places have even been evacuated from their homes or had fire patrols imposed on their building, heightening their sense of anxiety. The burned, plastic-sheeted tower remains a very visible reminder of the fire and the suffering it caused; its covering states, 'Grenfell: forever in our hearts'.

Cultural harms

These are harms caused by having one's way of life, social networks, and daily routines disrupted or destroyed. This type of harm was certainly experienced by the hundreds of Grenfell Tower residents who lost their homes and who were forced into temporary accommodation, sometimes many miles away from their community, jobs, schools, and friends.

In the immediate aftermath of the fire, a group of local women, some of whom had survived the fire, came together at a nearby Muslim Cultural Heritage Centre to cook for the survivors and the relief workers

Figure 19.9 The Duchess of Sussex's assistance at a community kitchen supporting those affected by the Grenfell Tower fire could be seen as an attempt to redress cultural harms

Source: Jenny Zarins

(*The I Newspaper*, 21 September 2018). The women and their community found this therapeutic, not least because in some cases it was the only place they had to prepare food for their families. However, the kitchen could only afford to open for two days a week until the Duchess of Sussex, who had carried out secret visits to the centre, suggested creating a recipe book to be sold in aid of the project (see **Figure 19.9**). One newspaper found her involvement significant as it showed a member of the royal family to be championing causes that prioritised women of colour, which is particularly important in the context of Grenfell where, it was alleged, safety complaints from black or minority ethnic residents were ignored (*The I Newspaper*, 21 September 2018).

Being able to physically protect oneself and one's family is a fundamental human need, and the loss of such basic facilities as a kitchen from which to feed relatives and friends is one of the 'cultural harms' affecting people displaced by the fire. These routine aspects of our daily lives make us feel secure and safe, so their loss at a time of trauma and distress can make the experience doubly difficult. The fact that such a loss coincided with other emotional or psychological needs placed additional burdens both on those who were suffering and those whose role was to try to alleviate the distress caused by the disaster.

Harms of recognition

As we have already seen and heard, some residents of Grenfell Tower felt that when they raised safety complaints, they were ignored because of their ethnicity—a claim which would perhaps have received more attention today, in the wake of 2020's global 'Black Lives Matter' movement and the resulting increased awareness of the systemic disadvantages faced by members of non-white ethnic groups (discussed in more detail in **Chapter 10**). Since the fire, others have suggested that council tenants were discriminated against and even encouraged to leave the area to make way for richer, whiter people. Indeed, it has been suggested that the new cladding was installed in order to make the tower look nicer in the opinions of its wealthy neighbours— what the local MP called 'prettification' (*The Times*, 16 June 2017). Others have noted how social workers from the borough failed to include poverty and environmental risks in assessment reports, instead focusing on alleged parental harm to children (Social Work Action Network, 11 October 2017), while social assets such as the library had been 'stripped' by the local authority (*The Independent*, 19 July 2017).

Tombs (2019: 14) has described 'a systematic contempt' for the poor, disadvantaged tenants of the area, and the tension between rich and poor remains a key point of argument for those investigating the fire and attempting to analyse its causes. When Sir Martin Moore-Bick was appointed as the judge in the public inquiry, people were quick to note that in 2014 he had upheld Westminster Council's decision to move a single mother 50 miles out of the area because her benefits had been capped and she could no longer pay rent on her flat. The ruling was later overturned, but not before the woman's solicitor had claimed that the decision amounted to 'social cleansing of the poor' and 'could have dire consequences for poor families across the country' (*Evening Standard*, 29 June 2017).

We have already noted the stark inequalities within the borough, and the political and economic factors which fed them. It is particularly shocking to note that a council with £247 million in its reserves made the decision to install lower quality rather than fire-resistant cladding as a cost-saving exercise. This apparent disregard for the needs of the poor has continued even after the fire, with displaced, homeless, and traumatised people forced to stay in temporary accommodation for far longer than had been initially promised and being subjected to hostile press reporting and attitudes from the general public. Notable incidents have included:

- Over 1,300 people complained to the Independent Press Standards Organisation about an intrusive *Daily Mail* article which criticised the owner of the flat where the fire is believed to have broken out (*Daily Mail*, 15 June 2017).
- Online comments in response to an article about the fire in *The Sun* newspaper expressed views such as, 'I'm baffled as to why so many immigrants were living in social housing to start with. Again, what about those British people on the waiting lists or worse those living on the streets?' (*The Sun*, 23 June 2017). A video emerged of an effigy of the tower being burned at a London party, in which voices can be heard mocking the screams of victims and saying 'That's what happens when they don't pay their rent' (BBC, 6 November 2018).
- Whirlpool Corporation, the company which made the fridge-freezer which is believed to have started the fire, tried to evade any responsibility by claiming that it is possible the fire could have been started by a carelessly thrown cigarette—a claim dismissed by a lawyer for the fridge's owner as 'pure speculation' (*The Independent*, 12 December 2018).

Financial and economic harms

It is likely that we will never know the full cost of the fire since the elements are so wide-ranging, covering diverse expenses incurred by all those affected by the disaster. These costs can involve the public purse, such as paying for fire and rescue services, housing for victims, and medical costs, or the finances of the victims themselves (replacing lost items, increased costs of travel to appointments, school, and work, and loss of earnings, particularly for those on zero-hours contracts or who were not entitled to sickness payments). On a wider scale, there has been significant cost to local and national economies, with the short-term closure of nearby schools, services, and businesses, while the cost of the public inquiry alone is likely to run into millions of pounds.

Perhaps the single biggest cost could be the unlimited fine which could be imposed if any agency, such as the council, is found guilty of corporate manslaughter, which would be in addition to further costs in terms of loss of reputation and rising costs of insurance premiums. Other local authorities have spent large sums of money improving safety, with the London Borough of Croydon, for example, spending £10 million on sprinkler systems in council flats, whereas in another Croydon building the £2 million costs of such improvements threatened to fall on residents until the construction company Barratt agreed to fund the work (*Construction News*, 20 April 2018). Like many other councils, Croydon has lobbied central government for financial support with this work, and although such help has been promised, it appears that this will simply be through funds diverted from other social programmes. This approach reinforces the impact on those who rely on state help—not least those whose vulnerabilities match those of the victims who died in the tower that night.

19.5 The production and reduction of social harm

In this section we will look carefully at the links between different types of societies and the harms they produce. By the 'production of harm' we simply mean how harms are produced; what leads to injuries, fatalities, poverty, etc. and how these factors might be linked to the social order in a state. When we refer to the 'reduction of harm', we mean the things that can be done to reduce or mitigate the effects of a particular social harm; for example, how a social order based on equality might lead to a reduction in poverty, or how a system which regulates dangerous activities might reduce injuries. Here, we are particularly interested in the links between high-level aspects of social order (whether a society can be described as liberal, capitalist, social democratic, etc.) and the production or reduction of social harm that arises in these different types of societies. Because it is the social system that produces or reduces the social harms, the society becomes used to them, seeing and accepting the harms as normal (Tombs and Whyte, 2015).

As we have seen throughout this chapter, the very concept of 'crime'—in terms of how it is defined and responded to, through an adversarial criminal justice system—leads us to focus primarily on interpersonal relationships. In other words, to look at a clearly identifiable individual offender and a clearly identifiable individual victim. By contrast, social harm and zemiological approaches can help turn our attention to different ways of conceptualising and understanding 'problems' and our responses to them, which take us beyond thinking about issues at a purely individual level. Instead, this approach suggests that the production of social harms is related to how societies are organised socially, politically, and economically. Pemberton, in his thought-provoking analysis *Harmful Societies* (2016), takes this idea further by arguing that such harms are not inevitable. He sees them as being influenced and patterned by the various forms which societies can take; in short, he suggests that different varieties of capitalist societies (societies whose economies and political systems are based on private companies making profit and where industry and trade are not controlled by the state) produce different forms of harm, and other varieties of capitalist societies lead to the reduced occurrence of some forms of harm.

Pemberton identifies seven broad models of capitalist regimes: **neoliberal**, liberal, post-corporatist, Southern corporatist, meso-corporatist, Northern corporatist, and social democratic. All of these 'regimes', he argues, differ in terms of their:

- mode of production (how economic systems, and the relationships between capital and labour are organised);
- welfare systems (a system where the state—in varying degrees—takes responsibility for the economic and social welfare and well-being of its citizens, through policies relating to health, education, social security, pension provision, etc.);
- criminal justice systems (a system which sets out how those people who transgress the criminal law are dealt with);
- forms of regulation (the degree to which economic and social systems and relations are regulated by the state);
- degrees of social solidarity (the extent to which societies are characterised by high/low relationships of trust and levels of social cohesion, tolerance, and inclusion/exclusion).

We will now consider Pemberton's typology further, reflecting on how the harm inflicted by certain regimes might be amplified or reduced. Let's simplify Pemberton's analysis for the moment and focus on two of the harm production/reduction regimes in his typology: liberal and social democratic. Mapping specific regimes to specific countries is both complex and inexact: for instance, it could be argued that whilst the UK is liberal in terms of its mode of production, welfare state, and harm reduction regime, its criminal justice system is more neoliberal in that it relies on high rates of imprisonment as a form of incapacitation rather than pursuing criminal justice policies informed by notions of rehabilitation. It is also important to be aware that countries can change the direction of their regimes over times. These regimes/models are *ideal types*, so it is impossible to precisely match specific nation states to any one of them, or to label them in a permanent way. They do, however, offer us ways in which we can think, at a much deeper and more penetrating level, about the broader issues of social harms, their occurrence in societies, and the potential to reduce them.

To help your understanding of this sophisticated set of arguments, we can more or less think of the UK, the US, Canada, Australia, and New Zealand as being examples of liberal regimes (with the caveat stated above, that all of their criminal justice systems appear to be more neoliberal than liberal.) Similarly, it may be useful for you to think of countries such as Sweden, Finland, Denmark, and Norway as being more social democratic in their orientations (see **Figure 19.10**). By doing this we can, importantly, also reflect on how regimes can be considered and compared, ranging from the more harmful regime to the least harmful. You will have gathered that Pemberton's arguments are in-depth and quite complex: here, we are simply setting out his basic arguments—summarised in **Table 19.2**—for you to use as a platform for your further study and reading. The main question you should consider as you look through the table is how the harm inflicted by certain regimes could be amplified or reduced.

19.5 THE PRODUCTION AND REDUCTION OF SOCIAL HARM

Figure 19.10 Countries such as Norway, where inmates at Bastoy Prison have access to hiking trails, nature, and sports facilities, can be seen as having what Pemberton (2016) terms a social democratic harm reduction/production regime
Source: Bastoy Prison

If nothing else, the table illustrates that both 'crime' and 'harm' are related to broader social, political, and economic factors and how societies are organised. It also alerts us to the fact that, as criminologists (or zemiologists), we need to think critically about more than just criminal justice policies; we should make links and connections across a wide range of policy domains. As we pointed out in **Chapter 1** (see **section 1.2**), the study of how social orders are constructed, maintained, and change—whether we give it the label of 'criminology' or 'zemiology'—is truly an interdisciplinary endeavour.

Table 19.2 may have encouraged you to think more carefully about these kinds of links. For instance, you may have made a deeper connection between countries such as the UK and US, which have a more liberal welfare system, characterised by high degrees of economic inequality,

Regime type	Liberal (Examples include the UK, US, Canada, Australia, and New Zealand)	Social democratic (Examples include Sweden, Finland, Denmark, and Norway)
Mode of production	• Highly competitive economies; • economic decisions dominated by the pursuit of short-term profit; • low levels of worker representation in the workplace and unionisation; • economies integrated into global financial markets, which dominate economic decision-making.	• A focus on the social and social partnerships in economic relations and production; • high levels of worker representation in the workplace and macro-economic planning; • appeals to building social partnerships; • state commitment to pursuing policies of full employment; that is, to achieve low levels of unemployment.
Welfare	• Residual systems of welfare which target the perceived needs of low-income households; • entitlement to benefits are means tested—that is, people applying for benefits have to prove that their income is below a certain level—and the recipients of benefits are stigmatised; • level of benefits modest and designed to encourage participation in the labour market; • voluntary organisations and the family play key roles in the delivery of welfare.	• Commitment to the principle of universality; that is, benefits are not means tested, and there is a rights-based welfare system; • the level of benefits provided by the state are relatively generous; • the state pursues full-employment economic policies: that is, macroeconomic policy seeks to maintain low levels of unemployment; • the state plays a key role in the delivery and funding of welfare.
Criminal justice	• Penal policy influenced by law and order rhetoric; • over-reliance on imprisonment and exclusionary methods of punishment; • harsh punishment and higher levels of imprisonment; • crime viewed as perpetrated by individual, autonomous, rational actors.	• Penal policy based on welfarism and the needs (as opposed to the deeds) of offenders; • lower levels of imprisonment and forms of punishment which, being informed by the ideal of rehabilitation, are more inclusive; • a collective (societal) responsibility for crimes which partially rejects viewing 'criminals' as acting out of free will and choice; • crime control through social policy measures; that is, policies which aim to address poverty, environments, addiction, social, economic and political, etc.

Table 19.2 Harm production/reduction regimes *(continued)*

Regime type	Liberal (Examples include the UK, US, Canada, Australia, and New Zealand)	Social democratic (Examples include Sweden, Finland, Denmark, and Norway)
Regulation	• Forms of regulation characterised by voluntarism; that is, not imposed by the state—and self-regulation; • regulatory agencies; that is, agencies which regulate things such as education, finance, health, housing, transport, utilities, and other areas of social life. In the UK, these include the Food Standards Agency and the Health and Safety Executive. They are funded and resourced at a minimal level; • minimal levels of legal enforcement.	• Regulation characterised by negotiation between various interest groups; • high levels of funding/resources for regulatory agencies; • high levels of legal enforcement.
Social solidarity	• Highly **individualised** societies; • low levels of trust and social cohesion; • high levels of socio-economic inequality and forms of social exclusion; • weak collective responsibility for others.	• Societies which are characterised by a high degree of social citizenship; • low levels of economic inequality, strong commitment to social inclusion; • high degree of collective responsibility and concern for the 'other'.

Table 19.2 Harm production/reduction regimes
Source: Pemberton, S. A. (2016) Harmful Societies. Bristol: Bristol University Press. Pp.60–63

resulting in harms associated with poverty and **relative deprivation**, such as child poverty and suicide. However, countries such as Sweden and Norway, which have a more social democratic welfare state, would see a reduced incidence of such harms. Similarly, you may have thought about how some of the social harms we have considered in this chapter, such as workplace injury, and forms of corporate criminality in general, could be reduced in regimes which follow social democratic forms of regulation more closely.

The point to make here is, as Pemberton (2016) argues, that we can **empirically** test the indicators of social harm 'so that at the very least, the levels of harm that vary between societies may be evaluated, and in doing so, we may understand the ways, to varying degrees, that particular harms are "designed into" and "designed out" of, specific societies' (2016: 78). As he concludes, 'a social harm perspective has much to contribute to speaking this important truth to power: austerity and the resulting injuries are political choice, rather than economic reality' (2016: 158).

In the final section of this chapter, we will consider where (if at all) social harm perspectives 'fit' in to criminology, and why this debate is important.

19.6 Critique of the social harm approach

As with all ideas, the concept of social harm and the discipline of zemiology have strengths and weaknesses. Without doubt, a social harm discourse offers a progressive and alternative perspective to that found in traditional criminology or in 'crime' as defined by law. This makes it a powerful and useful tool with which to consider and reflect on these older and more accepted ideas. For example, it gives us ammunition to question the concept of 'crime' and whether it is truly focused on resolving conflicts and addressing social injustice. It also allows us to draw out and understand the ways in which the criminal justice system itself is at best ineffective, but often actively harmful in that it can add to rather than help to address social injustice and harm.

However, the idea of social harm and zemiology suffers from some of the same failings as the concept of 'crime'. Critical criminologists question 'crime' because it cannot be defined, yet 'harm' and 'social harm' also defy definition. This is a problem despite Pemberton's description (2016; set out in **section 19.2**) of a society free of social harm as one which aspires to help humans flourish by protecting their physical and mental integrity, autonomy, and desire to live in community with others. This definition links 'social harm' to human integrity and well-being, and therefore also to respect (and protection from disrespect) and to human rights, but it still lacks precision. Despite this, Pemberton (2016) applies his definition by studying how well—or badly—a number of states perform against some social harms, in particular those which he relates to capitalism. Essentially, he admits that the idea of 'social harm' has some way to go before it can be of real practical value.

Despite these issues of definition, the link between social harm and rights, even international human rights, is a strong one and has been made by many writers (Soliman, 2019). In some respects, this link strengthens the utility of social harm as a concept as it means we can use 'social harm' discourse to pinpoint weaknesses in criminal law where it fails to protect people from harm or fails to ensure that their human rights are upheld. For example, it has been used to call on the authorities to pay more attention to certain types of harm, such as domestic abuse, and to better protect its victims. It can also help to open up brand new areas of criminal law such as genocide, corporate crime, or state crime, so that it covers protections that were not previously recognised. With this view, social harm or zemiology can be seen as an adjunct to criminology, a part of critical criminology, but this may not always be useful.

This brings us to back to the key debate we touched on in **section 19.3** surrounding the use of 'social harm' as a concept: how and where it fits within or alongside criminology. For many, the claims that zemiology offers a *new* perspective seem problematic: they argue that criminologists have been doing this for years. But Dr Lynne Copson (see **Conversations 19.3**) has analysed the key differences between how harm is conceptualised within criminology, critical criminology, and zemiology (2016, 2018) and suggests that since crime and social harm have very different focuses and involve different relationships or links between the harm and perpetrator, criminology and zemiology may be best thought of as separate disciplines. With this view, criminology has its own core power and knowledge bases focused on crime, one in which considerations of 'social harm' may be a useful critical aspect (for example, when considering harmful behaviour that

CONVERSATIONS 19.3

Zemiology *or* criminology?

with **Dr Lynne Copson**

I first encountered zemiology in 2004, the same year that *Beyond Criminology* (Hillyard et al., 2004) was first published and zemiology was beginning to emerge as a perspective.

I was drawn to zemiology as a result of my frustrations with the limitations of 'crime' as a concept for addressing the harms caused by the powerful, in particular state harms. This was not long after 9/11 and I remember reading Phil Scraton's (2002) *Beyond September 11* and being struck by the moral inequality of the outpouring of grief and mobilisation of resources for tackling the 'war on terror' and the little attention paid to the thousands of lives lost on a daily basis from avoidable diseases such as diarrhoea and measles (Stanley, 2002: 208), or the patenting of lifesaving drugs by wealthy Western liberal democracies that prevent those in poorer countries accessing lifesaving medication (Whyte, 2002: 154). It seemed obvious to me that the concept of 'crime' could never begin to recognise, let alone tackle, the harmful outcomes of global systems of inequality. Consequently, I found zemiology's criticisms of the concept of crime—as a way of shaping our understanding of harmful events and deciding which lives matter and which do not—very compelling.

There was much about the approach of zemiology and its search for the structural causes of harm that resonated with the things I'd learned in my undergraduate studies of sociology: that people, their life chances and experiences are shaped by social structures far more than by individual traits. This seemed particularly apparent in the study of crime and justice. But zemiology did not appear to offer much that was different to critical criminology, which left me wondering to what extent this could really be said to be a 'new' perspective or whether it was just a rebranding of a critical approach that had a long-standing presence within criminology.

Criminology has spent a lot of time exploring the relationship between crime and criminal justice and systems of power and inequality—see, for example, Taylor, Walton and Young's (1973) 'new criminology', to Stuart Hall's (1978) groundbreaking work on *Policing the Crisis*, and the feminist criminological theories, theories of crime and ethnicity, and other critical perspectives that have continued to develop and multiply to the present day. But there is also a long-standing commitment to expanding the focus of criminology beyond acts and behaviours defined as crimes by the state through criminal law. From Edwin Sutherland's ([1949] 1983) work on white-collar crime, to subsequent debates about an alternative definition of crime outside formal definitions, critical criminologists have often challenged the formal, legal concept of crime to suggest better ways of recognising the harmful practices of the powerful.

For many criminologists, therefore, the claims that zemiology offers a *new* perspective seem problematic: they argue that criminologists have been doing this for years. On the other hand, proponents of zemiology emphasise that the language of harm, as a 'replacement discourse' for that of crime, provides an important distinction to criminology. They argue that even using the language of 'crime' reproduces particular, problematic ways of thinking about and responding to social problems that criminology cannot escape (see, for example, Copson, 2016).

The relationship between zemiology and criminology is still not clear. For some, zemiology presents an extension or continuation of existing critical criminology—continuing the latter's project of drawing attention to the harmful acts of powerful social actors, such as states and corporations (see, for example, Yar, 2012a, 2012b).

For others, zemiology provides an *alternative* to criminology in the way it frames, understands and responds to social problems (see, for example, Pemberton, 2016; Hillyard and Tombs, 2017).

Perhaps because it was so new when I was first encountered it, it felt to me that zemiology offered a way forward when arguably criminology had reached an impasse. In particular, I found the emphasis zemiology places on *what* harm was caused rather than *how* harm was caused a more productive way of thinking about social problems and what to do about them. As Hillyard et al. (2004: 1–2) highlight in the introduction to *Beyond Criminology*: for the person who dies it makes no difference how that death is caused; the consequences for them and those left behind often remain the same. Even now, I consider this to be one of zemiology's distinctive features, and a way in which it differs from criminology. It also opens up a wider range of responses that move beyond concerns about responsibility or accountability or identifying harms as discrete events. For example, by allowing us to think of structural systems such as neoliberalism, **patriarchy** or racism as harmful, whether or not they can be conceived as 'criminal', zemiology encourages us to imagine how we might respond to these issues in new, joined-up ways that allow us to see the connections between diverse social phenomena—from housing to education, welfare to healthcare—all of which can play a role in understanding a variety of social problems from 'cradle to grave', without worrying whether or not they fit within the field of 'criminology'.

Dr Lynne Copson, Lecturer in Criminology, The Open University

is not covered by the criminal law, such as some environmental harms—see **Chapter 12**) but should not be used to overhaul the discipline. Zemiology should be seen as a discipline in its own right, not an offshoot of criminology, with different foundations. Whilst these two disciplines may 'speak' to each other and may have important areas of connection, neither should be seen as more important than the other.

19.7 Conclusion

We have seen the relevance of social harm to other criminological topics at several points throughout this book, for example in **Chapter 12** in relation to **green criminology**, but in this chapter we have considered the perspective in more detail. We have explored the various aspects of social harm—what it is, the criticisms it makes of 'crime' and mainstream criminology, how the approach works, and how social harm could be produced or reduced. In **section 19.6** we returned to the debate we first touched on in **section 19.3**: whether these perspectives sit within or beyond criminology. Do they belong within the theoretical perspective of critical criminology, or is it time to develop a distinct discipline (or 'replacement discourse') which considers the cause, prevention, and reduction of harm as a separate area of multidisciplinary study?

In **Conversations 19.3**, Dr Copson outlined these complex debates and the main disagreements and tensions which exist between scholars over whether social harm perspectives can logically fit within the academic discipline of 'criminology' or whether 'social harm' opens up separate and more productive and useful ways for us to conceptualise social problems. Dr Copson also considers possible ways in which societies can effectively address such questions. Having read this chapter and Dr Copson's account you should give some thought to your own conclusion about social harm: think about which arguments you find most compelling, and whether such debates matter. If so, why? Keep reflecting on these questions as you progress through your criminological studies and do not be surprised if your thoughts and ideas change over time.

SUMMARY

After reading this chapter and working your way through its features you should now be able to:

- Outline the key elements of the social harm approach, identifying its various levels and dimensions

In this chapter we have critically explored social harm perspectives, which have become increasingly prominent over the past two decades. Such approaches argue that state-generated, legal definitions of 'crime' are too narrow as they do not reflect significant (though not always illegal) harms that can be inflicted by social structures, multinational bodies and the state. By drawing on the typologies of Hillyard and Tombs (2004) and Pemberton (2016), we set out the various levels and dimensions of social harm, which can include physical, emotional, psychological, cultural, and financial and economic harms.

- Explain and illustrate the nine fundamental criticisms made of criminology by social harm theorists

As we have seen, some harm theorists are highly critical of the subject area of criminology, and they consider the concept of 'crime' itself to be highly problematic. In this chapter, we have outlined the controversial issues raised by harm theorists in terms of what have been described as 'the nine fundamental criticisms' of criminology, including whether the concept of 'crime' exists at all and whether criminalisation and crime control are effective ways of dealing with and preventing harmful behaviours. In **Conversations 19.1**, Professor Steve Tombs further developed these arguments by applying them to his research on workplace death and injury. In the chapter's text and its What do you think? features, you have been encouraged to continually reflect on the nature of criminology by adopting the ABC approach to 'crime problems' and responses to them.

- Analyse case studies using the principles of the social harm approach

In this chapter we have applied the various levels and dimensions of harm to a specific harmful event—the Grenfell Tower fire in London in 2017—and saw the ways in which these harms can manifest. By identifying various categories of harm—for instance, physical, psychological and emotional, cultural, harms of recognition, financial and economic—we have seen the rippling-out effects that these types of harm can have, and how they overlap and are often connected to each other. You have been encouraged to apply the same ideas to other harmful events you encounter in your studies or read about in the news.

- Explain how different forms and levels of social harm can originate from, and are related to, different forms of social, economic, and political organisation

In **section 19.5** we took our knowledge and understanding of social harm further, considering the idea that different forms of economic, political, and social organisation produce different kinds and levels of harm. In developing this important point, we explored the basic ideas from Pemberton's (2016) theoretically complex and sophisticated analysis to help you to conceptualise harm production and its potential reduction at a deeper level. You have considered the ideal types of liberal and social democratic capitalist regimes and how they differ in terms of their mode of production, welfare systems, the ways in which their criminal justice systems are regulated, and their degrees of social solidarity. The important point for you to take from this is the argument that we can empirically test and evaluate levels of social harm which arise between different types of societal organising, and that particular harms seem to be 'designed into' and 'designed out of' specific forms of capitalist societies.

- **Critically evaluate the extent to which social harm approaches sit within criminology**

We concluded this chapter by considering the wider and theoretically complex debates on how social harm approaches relate to critical criminology. In **Conversations 19.3** we heard Dr Lynne Copson's reflections on whether harm approaches sit comfortably within the growth and diversification of critical criminological theories, or whether they are best suited to sit outside it, as a 'replacement discourse' of zemiology. It is important to continually reflect on this debate—and why it matters—as you progress with your studies.

 Test your understanding of the chapter's key points by attempting the self-test questions on the **online resources** at www.oup.com/he/case2e

REVIEW QUESTIONS

1. What is social harm and how does it differ from 'crime'?
2. Outline and provide examples in support of the claim that 'crime' consists of many unimportant and trivial events and that it excludes many serious harms.
3. Give two examples for and two against the critique made by proponents of social harm that crime control is ineffective.
4. What are the opportunities offered by a social harm approach? How could it be achieved and what are the potential barriers?
5. List the main categories of harm and, drawing on a case of your own choosing, illustrate the needs that can arise from them.
6. To what extent does zemiology provide an *alternative* to criminology in the way it frames, understands, and responds to social problems?

 Access the **online resources** at www.oup.com/he/case2e to check your answers to the review questions.

FURTHER READING

Copson, L. (2018) 'Beyond "Criminology vs. Zemiology": Reconciling crime with social harm' in A. Boukli and J. Kotze (eds) *Zemiology: Reconnecting Crime and Social Harm* London: Palgrave Macmillan. Pp. 33–56. An interesting discussion about the relationship between crime, criminology, social harm, and zemiology which considers some differences but also, importantly, identifies some shared goals and ideals.

Hillyard, P. and Tombs, S. (2016) 'Social Harm and Zemiology' in A. Liebling, S. Maruna, and L. McAra (eds) *The Oxford Handbook of Criminology* (6th edn). Oxford: Oxford University Press.
An excellent analysis to read once you have a good basic grasp of this subject.

Hillyard, P. et al. (eds) (2004) *Beyond Criminology: Taking Harm Seriously.* London: Pluto Press.
An edited collection examining the 'narrow focus of conventional criminology'. It looks at the early stages of social harm and zemiology and uses case studies to bring the ideas to light.

Tombs, S. (2016) 'Social harm' in K. Corteen et al. (eds) *A Companion to Crime, Harm & Victimisation.* Bristol: Policy Press. Pp. 218–20.
An excellent short reading on social harm written by Steve Tombs, a major figure within social harm and the author of **Conversations 19.1**.

 Access the **online resources** to view a wealth of extra information relating to your study of criminology, including self-test questions, answers to review questions, and links to other resources that will help you enjoy and fulfil your potential within your studies.
www.oup.com/he/case2e

CHAPTER OUTLINE

20.1	Introduction	620
20.2	The rise of realism in context	620
20.3	Right realism: key ideas	623
20.4	Right realism: policy implications	624
20.5	Evaluating right realism	630
20.6	Left realism: key ideas	631
20.7	Left realism: policy implications	634
20.8	Evaluating left realism	637
20.9	Beyond 'left' and 'right' realism?	639
20.10	Conclusion	642

20

Right and left realism

KEY ISSUES

After studying this chapter, you should be able to:

- identify the key ideas of both right and left realism;
- appreciate the links between criminological theorising, and broader law and order politics;
- understand the political context surrounding the emergence of realist criminological theories;
- critically evaluate the influence of realist ideas on aspects of criminal justice policy.

20.1 Introduction

Realist criminological theories emerged in the late 1970s and early 1980s; the two main strands were **right realism** and **left realism**, so called because of the political leanings that influenced them. Realist criminological theories were, in basic terms, theoretical developments grounded in and informed by sociological **positivism** (right realism) and critical criminological theories (left realism).

Realism itself is an important social scientific **concept**, developed to try to provide a basis for understanding social realities which are not directly observable or precisely measurable, but undoubtedly have material substance, and affect human behaviour, such as the law. So, for example, laws are indeed made with the intention of regulating what people do, and setting boundaries to permissible activities; but in order to be workable, they rely on a set of social relations that influence whether they are seen to be legitimate and how they are enforced. Realists are interested in seeking to identify and analyse these social relations in order to account for the behaviour they bring about.

However, at least partly because these social realities are not directly observable, realists take different positions and offer alternative and sometimes conflicting explanations for specific social phenomena, such as 'crime'. Right realists might, for example, attribute increasing crime and social disorder to the deteriorating quality of family life or declining religious affiliations. Left realists are more likely to attribute the same outcomes to the harm to communities arising from economic upheavals and increasing levels of poverty. Both, however, agree that crime is a problem that must be addressed directly, and cannot be explained away simply as a **'social construction'** or unavoidable feature of changing societies.

More recently, we have seen a further variation emerge in the form of 'ultra-realist' criminology (Winlow and Hall, 2019), which seeks to challenge and extend the definition of 'crime' to encompass the idea of **'social harm'** (see **Chapter 19**), thereby making a connection with concerns about the environment, or damaging state and corporate activity.

In this chapter we will set out the key ideas of both right and left realism and encourage you to critically engage with the very real impacts that they have had on criminal justice policy formation in both the UK and the US. We will begin our discussion by considering the theoretical and political context to the rise of realism, so that you can understand how and why the theories emerged. We'll then discuss right realism and left realism in turn, looking at the **theory** and policy implications for both, before concluding with a brief discussion of what lies beyond in the shape of emerging ideas, including ultra-realism.

20.2 The rise of realism in context

Before delving into the key ideas and concepts associated with left and right realism, it is important to better understand the theoretical and political context in which they emerged. This should help you to understand the motivations of criminologists to develop new ideas and to appreciate how theories often emerge as a response to other theories, policies, or political events. By understanding the context, we can better make sense of the social and political origins of these strands within criminology, and perhaps begin to relate our own assumptions and beliefs to key debates at the heart of the study of criminology. It is probably fair to say that realist positions in criminology are driven more clearly by a sense of political purpose, on all sides. Realist criminologists may be viewed as actively engaged in formulating ideas and explanations which both account for crime in all its forms and provide the rationale for specific policy and operational initiatives. These may be geared towards improving the destructive conditions that put communities at risk of crime (left realists), on the one hand; or on taking decisive action to halt the pervasive spread of immoral attitudes and debilitating social **norms** (right realism). Both positions, though, are clearly action-focused and politically committed. We will start by looking at the theoretical context and then move on to the political context.

The theoretical context to the rise of realism

In **Chapter 18** we described and analysed the foundational ideas and subsequent development of critical criminological theories. Although there are clear differences in focus between them (especially in the later variants of **zemiology**, **green**, **cultural**, and convict criminological theories) these perspectives have many things in common. For example, all critical criminologists have an interest in researching and highlighting crimes and social harms committed by powerful groups in society, and use a focus on structural inequalities to analyse such crime and the official responses to it. They are also committed to challenging social research and critical analysis that 'speaks truth to power' through working with marginalised and silenced social groups (the powerless); and they advocate for radical reforms in social, economic, and penal policies to achieve greater **social justice** and a fairer, more equal society.

Critical criminological theories retain a real and important presence in our current thinking about crime and its control. However, they have never represented the dominant paradigm in criminology, which is perhaps a necessary consequence of adopting a questioning and challenging stance to what might be seen as conventional wisdom. As a result, direct policy gains resulting from such critical research have been limited. It might be more realistic to claim that such perspectives have been significant in raising difficult or unacknowledged issues, and drawing attention to important public concerns, such as racism or violence against women.

By the late 1970s, the foundational ideas of **critical criminology** (especially the more Marxist-inspired variants) were being challenged by groups of so-called 'realist' criminologists, who came from both the political right and left wings. The main gist of these critiques was quite simply that critical criminology was utopian and idealistic in both its analysis of crime and the methods recommended for controlling it. For instance, left realists forcibly argued that the early critical criminologists' idea of the **rule of law** was little more than a simplistic reflection of capitalist class relations, and failed to recognise that the law can also protect relatively powerless groups against the misuse of power by other people.

Left-realist authors like Lea and Young (1984) criticised what they regarded as the romantic portrayal of working-class offenders who were characterised as victims of structural inequalities and oppression. It was also argued by left realists that a reluctance to critically engage with the 'real world' of law-and-order politics of the late 1970s and early 1980s was failing working-class (and especially female) victims of crime and not recognising their very real suffering. To simply say that much crime was an expression of class conflict and media-inspired **moral panic** was unsympathetic to those who experienced it and who had to live with the practical and emotional consequences.

It has also been suggested that the lack of acknowledgement of the effects of crime by those on the left allowed for right-realist criminological perspectives to gain dominance and influence policy, in terms of increasing police powers, reducing police accountability, and promoting custody as a solution. Consistent with this, those on the right also argued that criminal justice policies that were informed by positivist theorising and **determinism**, highlighting individual needs and **rehabilitation**, were regarded as simply wrong, and were often caricatured as creating an explanatory framework that effectively excused criminal behaviour.

In short, there was a growing sense amongst a range of commentators that critical criminological theories had nothing practical to offer policy debates apart from a rather detached call for revolution. Critics argued that if a theoretical perspective claims to take crime seriously, it must engage with policy initiatives on a practical level, so that it can address all forms of crime—not just those committed by the relatively rich and powerful. This willingness to initiate action is at the core of theoretical claims to being 'realist'; that is, getting real about the crime problem(s) which exist, being realistic about what can be done about them, and generating solutions which are both workable and have a demonstrable beneficial impact.

One of the central themes of this current part of the book on explaining crime is that whilst criminological theorising can, at first, appear to be abstract and complicated, theories always contain certain underpinning assumptions. These assumptions can, for instance, be about the human actor—such as whether our behaviour is seen as rational or predetermined—or about the nature of society, which can be viewed as sitting at some point on a continuum from 'consensual' to 'conflictual'. Take a look at **Controversy and debate 20.1**, and you may well notice other assumptions as you broaden your reading and

CONTROVERSY AND DEBATE 20.1

'The causes of crime'

An important part of criminological debate, and especially to realist arguments, is the question of whether the causes of crime are essentially associated with individual characteristics and tendencies or are mainly to do with social conditions and contextual influences. The media dramatisation of violence, for instance, might be seen as a conditioning factor, encouraging violent behaviour; or simply as a reflection of people's increasing appetites for violence (see **Chapter 6**).

Reflecting on this question for a moment, where do you think you would look to identify the most important causal factors for crime? At the personal or the social level? Is this likely to be the same for all types of crime? For different types of society?

continue your studies. You may also find it useful to pause here and consider the assumptions you might bring to your own criminological theorising (see also **Chapter 4**).

The political context to the rise of realism

In this section of the book we have already seen how classicism links with policies based around the idea of deterrence (**Chapter 15**) and how the logic of forms of positivism(s) lead us to consider crime control and prevention based on the idea and concept of rehabilitation (**Chapters 16** and **17**). In short, broader social and political contexts are important when studying and understanding criminological theories, and perhaps of even greater importance when considering the rise of so-called 'realist' criminological theories. In this section we will outline such broader contexts (in both the US and UK) in the late 1970s and early 1980s when these perspectives were being developed.

A useful concept to consider is that of a 'critical election' in politics. This idea has a long history in US political science but Evans and Norris (1999) have developed it to broaden our understanding of British politics. For them, one of the main conditions that mark a critical election is a radical realignment of, and ruptures in, the ideological basis of competition between the various political parties. As they note, such ideological changes often have important and long-lasting consequences for public policy agendas, which of course include criminal justice policy. The elections that saw Margaret Thatcher becoming the Conservative Prime Minister in the UK in 1979 and Ronald Reagan being elected as the Republican US President in 1981 (see **Figure 20.1**) are good examples

of critical elections, as they heralded significant shifts in the ways in which both these main parties presented themselves and decided on their priorities for action and legislation.

It was against a backdrop of increasing official crime rates and public fear of crime during this period that new populist and public criminological theories emerged. In these critical elections, law and order, perhaps for the first time, became a fundamental issue; crime and its control were becoming politicised. There was a shift in political ideology away from the *social democracy*, which characterised much of the postwar period in the UK (with its stress on equality of opportunity, fairness, social citizenship, and social justice) to *economic liberalism* (with its prime social values being individual responsibility, freedom, and social order). This shift was to have profound consequences across a range of social policy domains (see, for instance, Hughes and Lewis (1988) for an analysis of how the welfare state was being restructured at this time in the UK).

Related to this shift, new discourses on criminal justice were also emerging; these in some ways developed existing theories but were given various new labels, such as neo-conservative authoritarianism, neoliberal responsibilisation, and neo-conservative re-moralisation. This led to significant shifts in the ways in which those who broke the law were thought about; they went from being seen as vulnerable people whose individual needs and multiple forms of deprivation needed to be recognised and addressed, to being regarded as being irresponsible, amoral, or wicked individuals who needed to be held to account and accept responsibility for their behaviours, usually through forms of punishment—ranging from having their welfare benefits curtailed through to more conventional criminal justice sanctions. Taken together, it could be argued that such approaches combined to form what became known as right realism.

What these ideas share is a shift away from the social democratic consensus on crime control. This consensus, in the main, accepted multiple forms of disadvantage as being a cause of crime, and did not blame offenders exclusively for their actions, prioritising welfare and rehabilitation (see the discussion in **section 20.7** on Young's (1999, 2007) account of the rise and consolidation of the *exclusive society* and the implications of this for criminal justice policy and the criminalisation of welfare. See also **Chapter 29** for a detailed discussion of the decline of the rehabilitative ideal). In time, of course, right realism developed its own critics who began to oppose these discourses, and this often took the form of what became known as 'left realism'. As we will see later in this chapter, the key ideas of left realism developed as a response to the influence right-realist ideas had on policy, especially in the UK under the Thatcher government. We will also see

Figure 20.1 The elections that saw the coming into power of Margaret Thatcher in the UK and Ronald Reagan in the US are good examples of 'critical elections'
Source (Thatcher): Nationaal Archief/CC BY-SA
Source (Reagan): Public domain

that as left-realist ideas developed, they too had a real impact on the policies of the first New Labour government (1997–2001), especially in terms of its policy focus on issues of social exclusion. This focus was encapsulated by the mantra of being 'tough on crime, tough on the *causes of crime*', adopted in an attempt to capture the moral and political high ground on matters of law and order, traditionally seen as a strongpoint for the Conservative Party.

20.3 Right realism: key ideas

In the most influential right-realist work we discuss in this chapter, we can see a re-imagining of certain theoretical ideas and concepts that you will have encountered previously (see in particular **Chapters 15** and **16**). These include:

- a re-imagining of classical criminology themes with a focus on the offender as a rational actor and a call for crime control policies based on deterrence, greater social controls (both formal and informal), and on an increased use of punishment and imprisonment (Wilson, 1975);
- a re-imagining of certain ideas associated with individual positivism, which focus on offending having a genetic basis (as opposed to a social one). In particular, the controversial argument that there is somehow a link between social behaviour and intelligence (as measured by the intelligence quotient—IQ) and that offenders suffer from a form of '**cognitive** disadvantage' (Wilson and Herrnstein, 1985; Herrnstein and Murray, 1994); and
- a refocusing on the idea that crime is linked to (im)morality and that most crime is committed by a growing '**underclass**' who lack a moral conscience—in short, the idea that it is 'moral poverty' rather than economic poverty which is linked with criminal behaviour (Murray, 1990).

Right realism is often regarded as being an inconsistent and rather contradictory criminological perspective; for example, it appears confused over whether criminality is a genetic trait or the product of wilful malicious intent. This may be because of its broader relationship with political philosophies of the 'new right'—which also seem to emphasise conformity, social order, and criminal justice on one hand, and individual responsibility and freedom on the other. The main contradiction lies between a belief in so-called *free market (neoliberal) economics*, which champion individual freedom of choice, and *neo-conservative politics*, which emphasise the need for a strong government to create a disciplined society around a very particular version of 'social order'. Entrepreneurial self-reliance is seen and promoted as a positive virtue in a market economy, on the one hand; but this depends on the guarantees offered by a 'strong state' (Gamble, 1988) that sets the rules by which the markets must operate, and promises swift and certain consequences for anyone who breaks them.

Despite tensions, contradictions, and the varying levels of analytical sophistication within right-realist theorising, Platt and Takagi (1977) originally identified three common themes that unite it and give it a form of coherence. These are:

1. **A focus on 'street crime'**—In the work of James Q. Wilson, 'crime' is simply defined as being 'predatory crime for gain, the most common forms of which are robbery, burglary, larceny [theft of personal property], and auto theft . . . [as] . . . it is a far more serious matter than consumer fraud, antitrust violations, prostitution, or gambling, because predatory crime . . . makes difficult or impossible the maintenance of meaningful human communities' (1975: xix). In short, right realists are united in focusing entirely on legal definitions of crime and in particular on '**street crime**'. It could be argued that these forms of crime are largely concentrated amongst the working classes and their neighbourhoods. You will find very little—if any—focus on crimes committed by powerful groups (such as corporate or state criminality) in right-realist texts.

2. **Anti-intellectualism**—This common thread relates to the right realists' outright rejection of any deep analysis of the 'causes of crime', especially the idea that crime might have social and economic causes (sociological variants of positivism). Such a line of thought, especially the idea of there being any causal links between crime rates and rates of poverty, is dismissed as simply being misplaced. The basis of this dismissal is the rather simplistic and crude argument that crime in the postwar period has risen, despite there being very real increases in the distribution of wealth and income (we will revisit this argument later in the chapter when we consider left-realist arguments about the concept of **relative deprivation**). Poverty, like crime, is seen simply as evidence of moral weakness and reluctance to do a fair day's work.

3. **A focus on punishing criminals**—As we saw in point 1, right realists regard what they call 'predatory street crime' as being the most urgent and damaging threat to a particular 'way of life'. As a result, they call for tough responses to it (see **Figure 20.2**). These

Figure 20.2 The use of batons and anti-riot gear is an example of 'tough' (coercive) policing

Source: somsak suwanput/Shutterstock

proposals focus on policies based on deterrence which, at the soft end, would include different and more aggressive styles of policing and forms of crime prevention suited to the specific context—such as vandal-proof paint, perhaps—(see **Chapter 26**) and, at the hard end, indeterminate prison sentences (sentences which do not have a fixed length of time) and even, in some cases, capital punishment.

In short, investing in and maintaining social order and controlling public spaces are seen as priorities. They are believed to serve the public interest more immediately and certainly than devoting resources to promoting social welfare, equality, or social justice. It is seen as necessary to take a hard line against threats to the rewards of an industrious life.

20.4 Right realism: policy implications

Having looked at the key ideas of right realism, we will now move on to discuss some key theories within right realism and analyse their policy implications. We will begin by considering the work of James Q. Wilson (who was a policy adviser to President Reagan in the 1980s) and, in particular, his very influential (and controversial) work *Thinking About Crime* (1975). We will then move on to discuss and analyse Charles Murray's (1984, 1990, 1994) arguments that much criminality is located within a violent and feckless underclass. The influential and highly controversial right-realist biosocial theory of Herrnstein and Wilson (1985), which argues the controversial idea that low intelligence is related to criminality, will be covered in **Chapter 21**.

James Q. Wilson: *Thinking About Crime*

As we just discussed, the origins of right realism in criminology could be linked to the sense of disillusionment and economic retrenchment associated with the 1970s and the decline of the welfare ideal. Crime became increasingly seen as a fact of life, and as something which could not be treated or reduced. The seeds of this change of mood were sown in the US, but its influence rapidly spread across the developed world. James Q. Wilson, in particular, is associated with articulating the underpinning arguments on which much subsequent realist criminological thinking and policymaking has been based. The arguments he set out provided a rationale for making '*crime control*' the central feature of criminal justice practices (we will explore this in more detail in **Chapter 27**). Wilson deliberately bridged the domains of academia, policymaking, and public debate in order to popularise his position. He wanted to counter what he saw as an unhelpful consensus of opinion which tended both to minimise the effects of crime on victims and communities, and to misrepresent the true nature of criminality.

In his most influential book, *Thinking About Crime*, Wilson set out a five-point critique of the prevailing liberal consensus within criminology of that period—the 1970s (Delisi, 2010: 194). His critique can be summarised as follows:

1. The individual is the source of crime, and social causes are of no significance.
2. Previous criminological thinking was dominated by ideology and conjecture rather than **empirical** evidence; the facts of crime were being ignored.
3. Crime which occurs on the streets and in geographical neighbourhoods is more significant and more harmful than **white-collar crime**, and thus needs to be taken more seriously.
4. Crime should be treated as a moral issue. Blame and responsibility are important elements of any system which accounts for and responds to offending.
5. Some people are criminal by nature—their disposition to do bad things is innate.

Although these ideas were articulated forcefully and systematically by Wilson, it is likely that they gained credence and became influential at least partly because they were not new, but actually picked up on and amplified long-held beliefs about the origins and reality of crime. Indeed, for him, the 'problem of crime' and his perceived solution

CONTROVERSY AND DEBATE 20.2

Indeterminate sentencing

In Wilson's quote, 'Wicked people exist. Nothing avails except to set them apart from innocent people', he seems to be arguing for 'preventive detention', the idea of imprisonment to prevent further criminal acts. This idea establishes the logic of indeterminate sentencing. According to the Ministry of Justice, 'Sentences of Imprisonment for Public Protection (IPPs) were created by the Criminal Justice Act 2003 and were first used in April 2005. They were designed to protect the public from serious offenders whose crimes did not merit a life sentence'.

By 2010, there were 10,000 prisoners serving extended sentences for the purpose of public protection under this legislation. In 2012, it was abolished following a ruling by the European Court that it was in breach of human rights. By 2019, however, there were still 2,600 prisoners detained under this provision who had been sentenced prior to its abolition.

Should **indeterminate sentences** be allowed, in order to protect the public? Or do they breach the human rights of the prisoner? Consider your response to the case discussed in the following newspaper article: 'Sister of IPP prisoner who took his own life calls for urgent action' (*The Guardian*, 10 January 2019).

Tommy Nicol committed suicide several years into the indeterminate sentence imposed on him for an offence of robbery. He was a persistent offender, and may have been viewed as likely to represent a continuing threat to society. Most of his offences, though, were not serious.

See also the following contributions as indeterminate sentencing came under the spotlight once again, following the London Bridge attack of December 2019. In this instance, a successful appeal against his original sentence meant that the attacker, Usman Khan, was released earlier than he might have been if the indeterminate sentence initially imposed for terrorism offences had been allowed to continue. Does this case impact on your judgement about indeterminate sentences?: 'London Bridge terrorist freed automatically after appeal court quashed sentence' (*The Mirror*, 30 November); 'Usman Khan, sentencing and the rehabilitation of serious offenders' (*The Guardian*, 2 December 2019).

---

to it, was simply (and rather simplistically): 'Wicked people exist. Nothing avails except to set them apart from innocent people' (Wilson, 1975: 235). Before we continue our discussion, consider **Controversy and debate 20.2**.

These ideas could be traced back to the 17th-century British political philosopher Thomas Hobbes, who argued that there is a need for state structures and systems of law in order to regulate and control the behaviour of those who are naturally inclined towards unlawful behaviour. The idea is that the vagaries of self-interest and human nature mean that we cannot predict which individuals in particular will be inclined towards unlawful behaviour, but we do know that this is an inherent possibility within all of us. Hobbes felt that a strong and comprehensive system of controls needs to be put in place in view of the inevitability of law breaking, and the need to maintain social order:

> annexed to the sovereignty [is] the right of judicature; that is to say, of hearing and deciding all controversies which may arise concerning law, either civil or natural, or concerning fact. For without the decision of controversies [judicial power to adjudicate conflicts], there is no protection of one subject against the injuries of another; the laws concerning meum and tuum [what is mine and what is yours] are in vain, and to every man remaineth, from the natural and necessary appetite of his own conservation, the right of protecting himself by his private strength, which is the condition of war, and contrary to the end for which every Commonwealth is instituted.
>
> (Hobbes, *Leviathan*: Ch. 18)

Such assumptions, of course, underpin much of the subsequent development of judicial structures and modern forms of policing, with the implicit assumption that coercive powers will be a necessary and central part of their remit.

In a sense, the work of Wilson, and others such as Kelling, served to reawaken and reinforce persistent concerns about public order and the threat to security represented by certain identifiable elements of the population. Indeed, their argument was for a return to an idealised past where police–community relations relied on a sense of common purpose and cooperation, and unquestioning compliance with the rule of law.

For centuries, the role of the police as watchmen was judged primarily not in terms of its procedural legitimacy, but rather in terms of its attaining a desired objective. The objective was order, an inherently ambiguous term but a condition that people in a given community recognised when they saw it (Kelling and Wilson, 1982: 13).

As we might also acknowledge, perceived threats to social order are often associated with difference and the perceived threat from outside, of people who are 'not like us', and who do not naturally share the same cultural assumptions or behavioural norms. '**Othering**' of this kind—that is, associating undesirable characteristics with identifiable differences between groups of the population—is also a powerful driver of right-realist sentiments (we will develop this further later in the chapter when we will consider and evaluate Murray's (1990) use of the term 'underclass').

The emerging tide of concern about lawlessness and loss of control was crystallised on both sides of the Atlantic by the periods of office of Ronald Reagan (US President, 1981–9) and Margaret Thatcher (UK Prime Minister 1979–90), both of whom arguably came to power at least partly because of their appeal to populist fears about endemic threats to the social order. Here, too, political rhetoric became infused with a renewed concern for the interests of victims; and the need to shift the balance away from a misplaced (and supposedly costly) interest in offender welfare.

Taken in combination, these ideological shifts led to a number of changes in the organisation and focus of criminal justice. We can see some coherence in these changes. Politicians stressed the interests of victims and the importance of promoting community safety, following Kelling and Wilson's '**broken windows**' thesis (1982); that is, their suggestion that neglect of even minor infringements in the community multiplies the likelihood of further crime and neighbourhood decline, and therefore should be addressed immediately.

Associated with this argument was a clear commitment to a proactive approach to policing which would target those areas and situations where the likelihood of a crime being committed was greatest. Thus, policing strategies associated with the principle of '**zero tolerance**' (meaning strict and rapid application of the law, even for minor crimes, as we will discuss further in **Chapter 27**) became more prominent, and some key individuals, like the New York police commissioner, Bill Bratton, became closely associated with this idea. Its implementation was claimed to be a significant factor in reducing levels of violent crime, particularly in that city during the 1990s.

Exploring the notion of pre-emptive control of this kind further, we can identify a number of other key features of this model. First, it seems that the idea of unspecified 'danger' is significant, in that there is a pressing need to develop better means of identifying the risk of crime and responding accordingly. Concepts of targeting and *risk management* become important, both in shaping intelligence gathering and designing intervention strategies. There is an apparent need for much better information in order to anticipate and choke off crime, wherever it is most likely to occur. And, where it does occur, a swift and certain response is required, with the objective of preventing a recurrence of the problem.

From this, a number of further features of the right-realist strategy derive. These include the use of physical security measures to enhance security for businesses and communities; a robust and focused police presence in those areas most vulnerable to crime; speed and certainty of enforcement action where infringements occur; definitive action to control offenders and restrict their future opportunities to commit crime; and prison sentences which aim to reduce the likelihood of further criminality.

Many substantial claims have been made for the effectiveness of crime control strategies deriving from 'right realist' arguments. There was a substantial drop in crime in New York, for example, following Commissioner Bratton's adoption of a proactive approach to policing; and similar claims have been made elsewhere for their effectiveness, although these have been challenged (for example, Justice Inspectorates, 'Evidence on zero-tolerance policing').

Another form of 'othering'—focusing blame for crime on a specific group of people—in right realism can be seen in Charles Murray's ideas about the existence of a criminal 'underclass'. We shall turn to this now.

Charles Murray on the (criminal) 'underclass'

Imagine that you are an unskilled worker who decides to move in order to find a job. You leave home, make your lengthy journey, arrive at your destination . . . only to be locked up until you can get someone to lend you the cash to go home again. Your crime? Not carrying a reference from the local justice of the peace, confirming that you had an acceptable reason for leaving, and that you are not actually a beggar.

This might sound like a story from modern times, with its hints of economic migration and fears of benefits scroungers; in fact, it describes the 'Cambridge Statute' from 1388, a piece of legislation that illustrates the lengthy history of attempts to control those who do not fit into wider social ideas of how people should behave. These controls are not always formal and legislative; they may be informal, unspoken, almost secretive ways of regulating behaviour, keeping people 'in their place', and reinforcing the boundaries between the social classes. For instance, what do you think the following passage tells us about these invisible divisions?

> I had one of those moments at a friend's dinner in a gentrified part of East London one winter evening. The blackcurrant cheesecake was being carefully sliced and the conversation had drifted to the topic of the moment, the credit crunch. Suddenly, one of the hosts tried to raise the mood by throwing in a light-hearted joke.

'It's sad that Woolworths is closing. Where will all the chavs buy their Christmas presents?'

(Jones, 2012: 1)

(The 'credit crunch' refers to the UK recession in 2007, a major financial crisis that saw many retail companies collapse, including Woolworths, which was a well-established high-street chain at the time.) The implicit 'rules' and conventions which mark out class differences are not formally set out anywhere. They have accumulated over time, and become a way we can place other people in the hierarchy of the class system, so we know whether they are someone to whom we should look up or whether instead they can be looked down upon and even perhaps feared.

If we acknowledge that there is a class structure in the UK—however flexible and shifting it may be—it follows that there has to be a lowest class, a group which is at the bottom of the social heap. It is this lowest group which was targeted by laws such as the Cambridge Statute, and which has been characterised in art and drama for centuries as reckless, immoral, and lazy. In 1747, the artist William Hogarth published a set of engravings called 'Industry and Idleness' which compare the consequences of hard work to those of drinking and idleness, in which the idle apprentice ends up being hanged whilst his industrious friend becomes Lord Mayor of London (see **Figure 20.3**).

This disdain and hostility towards those who were not 'doing their bit' continued. By the time Henry Mayhew was writing in the 1840s, he categorised non-workers as those who need not, could not, or would not get jobs (Mayhew, 1861: 601). Later, it has been suggested that unemployment during the 1920s and 1930s was the result of the perverse incentives of generous benefit levels rather than the lack of work (see Eichengreen, 1988, for example). And in 2008, when Karen Matthews was convicted of staging the kidnap of her daughter to claim a reward, her role as a member of the 'underclass' was given prominent media attention (see the following extract from *The Telegraph*). These examples serve to show that hostility towards those who rely on state benefits and support is neither new, nor has it subsided in recent years.

> The case of Karen Matthews, convicted of kidnapping her own daughter in order to claim a reward, has again pulled back the curtain to allow us a glimpse of this netherworld of taxpayer-funded fecklessness.

(*The Telegraph*, 6 December 2008)

The term 'underclass' was, by the time *The Telegraph* article was published, in common use to describe a particular group of people—those who were unemployed, who lived on state welfare benefits, were generally poorly educated, and who were unwilling to live up to societal expectations of hard work and industry. In criminological terms, the word was given prominence by Charles Murray in his 1990 work 'The Emerging Underclass'. Murray argued that being in the underclass was not simply about being financially poor, but rather living in a specific type of social and *moral poverty* (see **Chapter 17**). He rejected the suggestion that 'there was no such thing as the ne'er do well poor person [and that] he was the figment of the prejudices of a parochial middle class' (Murray, in McLaughlin and Muncie, 2013: 128). Instead, he argued that there are three distinguishing features of the underclass. These are 'illegitimacy' rates, violent crime, and non-participation in the labour force. Murray's principal concern was that of illegitimacy—children born to parents who are not married to each other. As well as any possible religious implications, Murray saw the decline in traditional two-parent families as meaning many children grow up without suitable male role models, due to the absence of fathers from family life and the prevalence of single mothers. Whilst this may not be a problem in individual households, he argues, it becomes significant in communities where the majority of families lack a father.

Moving on from the notion of illegitimacy, Murray then identified engagement with violent crime as the second feature of the underclass. For him, crime—especially violent crime—amongst the underclass is normal behaviour and is often based on the way young boys and men choose role models from older male members of the community. Murray predicted that England would become a 'more dangerous place in which to live: that this unhappy process is not occurring everywhere, but disproportionately in particular types of neighbourhoods; and that those neighbourhoods turn out to be the ones in which the underclass is taking over. Reality will once again force theory to its knees' (ibid: 136). We can see this association of violence and threat with one particular sector of society if

Figure 20.3 William Hogarth's 1747 engravings, 'Industry and Idleness', show that the lowest class in UK society has long been characterised as reckless, immoral, and lazy

Source: William Hogarth/Public domain

we look at the reaction to the London riots of 2011. Some prominent politicians were quick to identify social dissatisfaction and exclusion as a cause. For others, rioters were described as feral, or alternatively as organised looters planning their activities through social media. Noticeably less attention was given by them to the shooting of a young black man by the police, which at least one local community saw as the trigger for the 'riots' (Newburn, 2015).

One person who was arrested after the riots told the *New York Times*:

> 'No one has ever given me a chance; I am just angry at how the whole system works,' Mr James said. He would like to get a job at a retail store, but admits that he spends most days watching television and just trying to get by. 'That is the way they want it,' he said, without specifying exactly who 'they' were. 'They give me just enough money so that I can eat and watch TV all day. I don't even pay my bills anymore.'
>
> (*New York Times*, 9 August 2011)

Murray would have seen Mr James as one of the 'economically inactive'—someone who likes the idea of being a productive citizen, but who has lost the will to look for work; in Murray's words, they have 'given up'. (Murray, in McLaughlin and Muncie, 2013: 136) He sees this as something associated with young men, living in economically deprived areas and who lack the sense of shame that older men feel when unemployed and claiming benefits. These young people have not been 'socialised into the world of work' (ibid: 139). For Murray, the problem is not so much that these young men are supported by the tax payer; rather that they are not persuaded to develop a sense of pride or to make any contribution to benefit the community in general.

Murray reached a bleak conclusion: that there was a growing underclass and it would only be improved if it were forced into a position to help itself; in other words, to take some form of individual responsibility for the plight of its members. He argued that neighbourhoods did not want to experience high rates of crime, youth unemployment, or illegitimacy, and that they would in fact self-regulate to reduce these problems. In later work, he advocated reducing benefits for single mothers in order to discourage them from having 'illegitimate' babies; instead, he argued that there should be social and financial incentives that encourage behaviour demonstrating what he saw as indicative of moral and social responsibility. Although this approach received strong criticism (for example, see MacDonald's (1997) collection of critical papers on the idea of a youth underclass in the UK), we can see its legacy in more recent policy discussions, such as the adoption of 'workfare' schemes which require claimants to carry out unpaid work in order to be eligible for benefits. Take a moment to look at **What do you think? 20.1** and consider Murray's theories further.

WHAT DO YOU THINK? 20.1

Murray's research and writing was carried out in the 1990s. Since then, there have been many social shifts that may affect our interpretation of, and reaction to, his work. Take a moment to jot down some of these as they occur to you.

Your list will probably be a personal one, influenced by your own background and attitudes. However, some important things to bear in mind when thinking about the concept of an underclass and Murray's key elements are as follows:

- He was writing before the idea of single-sex families became acceptable; we might like to consider how his views would accommodate this important social shift. Would 'illegitimacy' in a single-sex partnership, where a male role model remained, cause him such anxiety?
- Is it surprising that Murray used the term 'illegitimacy', which today would be seen as a highly problematic term?
- Murray quoted statistics that illustrated a rising illegitimacy rate—from 14.1 per cent in 1982 to 25.6 per cent in 1988. In 2012, the Office for National Statistics reported that 47.5 per cent of children were born 'out of wedlock', but by 2017 the rate of increase had clearly slowed, and just over half (51.9 per cent) of live births were still to parents who were married or in a civil partnership. Nonetheless, this meant that nearly half of all births were outside marriage/civil partnership by that point in time. How does this compare to current crime rate statistics, and what are the implications for Murray's argument?
- Murray has associated crime and the underclass with male identities and role models. How would his work be viewed in light of studies of female offenders (see Campbell, 1981; Youth Justice Board, 2009, for example)? Do you think he might consider bearing 'illegitimate' children to be a form of female deviance, and how should we analyse his work in the light of feminist criminological theories (see Bullen and Kenway, 2004)?

As we can see, simple characterisations of an impoverished underclass are controversial. One of the main critical responses to the underclass thesis is that such a description individualises (and pathologises) people who suffer from what are arguably deeply entrenched forms of socio-economic disadvantage, which can limit the real choices they have (Lambert and Crossley, 2016). In doing so, it also brackets off and dismisses the possibility that forms of disadvantage can or should be addressed through various policy initiatives. We will pause here to consider how the concept of an underclass has been developed to have a particular resonance in popular culture in recent times.

Beyond the underclass: the making of the 'chav'

Although, as we have seen, we can still encounter the word 'underclass', other ideas and descriptions have risen to take its place. Some have become replacement language for what can be seen as an outdated and almost offensive term; one of the most pervasive of these in recent times has been the (equally offensive) word 'chav'. Although like most such colloquial terms, the term is perhaps not so prevalent now as in the early 2000s, Hayward and Yar (2006) suggested that 'chav' became what they called 'a popular reconfiguration of the underclass idea'; as such, it is worth considering further here.

The origin of the word chav is disputed, but it is generally thought to have originated as a word meaning child or youth. However, by the early 21st century it had become a slang term for someone wearing particular styles of clothing; baseball caps on backwards, heavy 'gold' jewellery, and counterfeit designer shoes (see **Figure 20.4**). Chavs were generally young and, more importantly for this discussion, likely to exhibit antisocial or offending behaviour.

Hayward and Yar (2006) suggest that most writers consider the underclass in relation to its failure to be part of a productive industry, which in turn causes various undesirable 'side effects' such as crime. In contrast, the discourse around chavs is connected to consumption. This is not in itself a new phenomenon; indeed, in another course of paintings titled 'Marriage a la Mode', Hogarth illustrates the risks of marrying for wealth and prestige by depicting the story of the young woman who is effectively sold to a rich husband: the series ends with a hanging, a suicide, and a child suffering from syphilis (see **Figure 20.5**). Hayward and Yar argue that this desire for money and status can be traced into the modern era, with the development of youth subcultures which value differing styles of clothes, shoes, cars, and so on.

As opportunities for work become increasingly insecure—a recent example would be the rise in 'zero

Figure 20.4 Young adults, such as this young male, have been branded 'chavs'—a word that has become associated with the underclass—because of the way they choose to dress
Source: The Arches (Flickr)/CC BY 2.0

Figure 20.5 Modern discourse around 'chavs' is connected to consumption, but we can see from 'Marriage A-la-Mode', a series of paintings produced by Hogarth in the 1740s, that this is not a new phenomenon
Source: The National Gallery/Public domain

hours' contracts—so its intrinsic value is lessened; the authors argue that self-expression and self-respect are now rooted in the ownership and display of goods, rather than in participation in productive labour. And it is the inability to consume, rather than the inability to create, that is now commonly identified as a cause of social exclusion. Many young people now talk about 'FOMO'—Fear of Missing Out—as a cause of anxiety and strain, and a driver for social behaviour, to the extent that a popular BBC television series, *I've Never Seen Star Wars*, could be based on the notion that not having taken part in a common social activity was so unusual as to be worthy of exploration and discussion.

Yet Hayward and Yar (2006) take a slightly different stance. For them, the chav is marked out by levels of consumerism that are viewed as excessive and vulgar rather than refined and tasteful. As an example, they highlight the chav's association with lager as opposed to good wine, or their fondness for obvious, rather than subtle, make-up and hairstyles. As Owen Jones's dinner party host might see it, the chav is marked out by their failure to appreciate the desirable social qualities of taste, decorum, and sophistication; it is their perceived tastelessness which marks them out as a group which can be looked down upon and stigmatised:

> Current popular discussion of the 'chav' focuses not on the inability to consume, but on the excessive participation in forms of market-oriented consumption which are deemed aesthetically impoverished. The perceived 'problem' with this 'new underclass' is that they consume in ways deemed 'vulgar' and hence lacking in 'distinction' by superordinate classes. . . . 'chavs' and 'chavishness' are identified on the grounds of the taste and style that inform their consumer choices.
>
> (Hayward and Yar, 2006: 7)

Not only is the chav despised for their choices, Hayward and Yar go on to argue that these choices and the associated culture are irresponsible and pathologised. If the consumption of goods is a means of self-expression, then what does it say about someone who chooses to consume things that are seen as unrefined and unattractive? The authors argue that the 'new British underclass' is increasingly understood as 'flawed consumers', unable or unwilling to make the 'right' type of consumer choice (Hayward and Yar, 2006: 11). Such criticism is not confined to those who are financially poor; for instance, in 2012 the singer Cheryl (formerly Cheryl Cole) was 'branded' a chav by the fashion designer Julien MacDonald. And if wider society mocks and despises a group for its aesthetic choices, it is hardly surprising when that group becomes marginalised, excluded, and labelled as dangerous, different, and to be feared. Hayward and Yar conclude by pointing out that there is a fundamental clash at the heart of society's disdain for the 'chav'. On the one hand, there are economic factors—recession, the decline in manufacturing industries—which limit the employment opportunities available to the less well educated or entrepreneurial. Whether they want to be productive or not, there are fewer chances for them to participate in the creative life of the economy. And yet, they also suffer from 'the relentless dissemination of messages that link social worth and well-being to one's ability to consume at all costs' (Hayward and Yar, 2006: 25). Small wonder perhaps that they struggle for an acceptable identity that does not consign them to the role of threat, danger, and mistrust that they seem fated to fill. In face of this, Owen Jones (2012) provides a trenchant critique of what he sees as the lazy and ideological 'demonization' of chavs, largely because of their working-class roots, and their attempts to make sense of their own lives in the face of de-industrialisation and the insecurities of the neoliberal economy.

We will return to the idea of the growing culture of consumption in late modern societies and its potential links with criminality later in the chapter when we consider left realism.

20.5 Evaluating right realism

Right realism has been criticised on a number of grounds. First, questions have been raised about claims made, by Wilson (1975), for example, for the effectiveness of zero tolerance or other aggressive crime reduction measures. For instance, area-wide initiatives to tackle specific types of crime, such as burglary or drug dealing, may just displace these to other areas which are less intensively policed (Bottoms, 2012). Hall and Winlow (2015: 23) similarly argue that increased punitiveness was unsuccessful in its 'principal aim of deterring crime', as crime rates continued to rise, at least until the mid-1990s. More generally, some of the grand claims made for crime control strategies may simply overstate the case. They may also fail to take account of other factors that contribute to changing patterns of crime, such as demographic trends, or the increasing influence of social media. Matthews (2014), too, makes the point that right realism's powerful rhetoric was not always reflected in the delivery of criminal justice. The 'three strikes' law introduced during the 1990s in the US, for example, was intended to ensure that draconian sentences would be imposed on those who offended repeatedly; but Matthews observes that many US states modified this provision carefully, so as to ensure that it would very rarely apply in practice.

In addition, approaches which are based on targeting certain communities or particular offences are questioned because of their likelihood of incorporating discriminatory practices at the heart of law enforcement. This has for a long time been a criticism of the use of 'stop and search' powers by police in London and other metropolitan areas, where black, young people have been disproportionately targeted (see **Chapter 10**). More broadly, an emphasis on anticipatory or pre-emptive policing may provide implicit acceptance of misuse of the authority conferred on enforcement agencies, in pursuit of the wider public interest.

Similarly, too, the emphasis of right realists on certain types of visible and interpersonal offences is believed to distract attention from equally and potentially more harmful white-collar, state, and corporate crimes which are not prioritised (Hall and Winlow, 2015: 38).

This emphasis on certain types of interpersonal crime and certain individuals and groups also, as right realism at least partly intended, shifts attention away from more distant and perhaps less easily proved factors underlying criminal activity, such as structural inequality, systemic disadvantage, and discrimination. For left realists, as we will soon see, it is these neglected structural issues that are a central part of their critique of right realism. We will now set out the key ideas of what became known as left realism, before identifying, analysing, and critically engaging with their policy proposals.

20.6 Left realism: key ideas

We can think of left realism as a response to two very different perspectives. First, it was a response to the kinds of critical criminology that we discussed in the last chapter. Secondly, it sought to act as a counterbalance to some of the ideas associated with right realism that we have discussed in this chapter. Its origins, though, are to be found in its rejection of some aspects of critical criminology in favour of more practical and grounded understandings of crime and its effects.

As we noted at the beginning of this chapter, 'realist' perspectives in criminology were developed in the late 1970s and early 1980s (mainly in the US and UK) against a backdrop of profound social, economic, and political change. With crime rates on a seemingly never-ending upward trajectory and similar increases in forms of urban disorder, attention was increasingly paid to public fear of crime, and certainly 'law and order' became a key political issue in the run-up to 'critical elections' in 1979 (UK) and 1980 (US).

The results of these elections saw a distinct shift to the right in politics and in economic and social policies; and, as we have seen, criminal justice policies became focused on strict crime control and orientated towards punishment. You can read more about this in Downes and Morgan's (2012) detailed discussions of the changing politics of law and order in British politics since 1945. At this time, many criminologists felt that critical criminological theories, especially more Marxist-informed ones, were flawed and not very suitable for these 'new times'. We have already discussed the response of criminologists on the right of the political spectrum (right realism). Whilst criminologists on the left of the political spectrum might be expected to be more sympathetic to left-wing views associated with Marxism, they were equally critical of the more fundamental Marxist-inspired arguments in critical criminology—for instance, that those who broke the law should be regarded as being the victims of an oppressive and exploitative capitalist system (see Quinney, 1977 for an articulation of this perspective). Here the implied argument was that much offending behaviour, amongst working-class and marginalised groups, should be seen as being a form of primitive rebellion or an act of resistance, whereas for left realists this both idealises and romanticises the offender.

Left realists argued that critical criminologists were both utopian and unrealistic in their calls for a wholesale reduction or even abolition of the judicial apparatus (see **Chapter 30**) and the kind of wholesale revolution which would somehow herald a crime-free society. They also argued that critical criminologists were wrong to solely concentrate on how the state criminalises some forms of behaviour, and the harms that directly resulted from the actions of powerful groups. Doing this, left realists argued, neglects the equally harmful behaviour of the relatively powerless, or amongst members of the same community. Radical analyses that targeted the justice system did not appear to take account of the public's most tangible and immediate fears, which realists on all sides identified as being street crime and being a victim of a violent attack; these fears were largely ignored.

As a result, existing Marxist-influenced critical criminological theories were characterised by the left realists with the rather pejorative label of 'left idealism' and a fierce theoretical debate between these two radical positions ensued (see Gilroy and Sim, 1987 for the 'left idealist' response). Jock Young, one of the key thinkers behind left realism, had in fact been one of the co-authors of the seminal neo-Marxist text, *The New Criminology* (1973), before later modifying his personal position.

As we mentioned at the beginning of this section, as well as being a reaction to critical criminology, left realism can also be seen as being a reaction to the right-realist perspectives which we considered in the previous sections of this chapter. These perspectives were at that time gaining public support and were starting to have real impacts on criminal justice and crime control policies. Authors such as Jock Young, John Lea, and Roger Matthews, at Middlesex University, argued that in order to counter the growing influence of right-wing criminological theories, there needed to be a response from those criminologists on the social democratic left of the political spectrum. Such a response had to be seen as taking crime 'seriously' and to see it as a real problem; to be credible, it also needed to be pragmatic in its approach to both crime causation and realistic prevention policies and strategies:

> The central tenet of left realism is to reflect *the reality of crime, that is in its origins, its nature and its impact*. This involves a rejection of tendencies to romanticise crime or to pathologise it, to analyse solely from the point of view of the administration of crime or the criminal actor, to underestimate crime or exaggerate it . . . [M]ost importantly it is realism which informs our notion of practice; in answering what can be done about the problems of crime and social control.
>
> (Young, 1986: 21, emphasis added)

There were, however, clear points of convergence and divergence between right- and left-realist approaches. Both argued that 'crime' (as defined by the state, with its focus on forms of street crime) was a genuine and growing problem. Both accepted that the public's fear of becoming a crime victim was also a very real issue, which needed to be addressed in a measured and practical way. Where they differ markedly is in what they had to say about the causes of crime and what should be done about it. Whilst right realists generally didn't address the issue of what causes crime, we can see in their work an implicit re-imagining of explanations focused on the individual—and their potential to exhibit **pathological** and immoral behaviours. By contrast, left realism drew on and developed work grounded in more sociological forms of inquiry. These included developing insights derived from **subcultural theories** and concepts such as **anomie**, as well as broader issues like social exclusion and marginalisation—see **Chapter 15** and Young's (2003) article, which reworks Merton's notion of anomie in a more culturally attuned way. As such, it could be said that left realism is an **integrated theory** (see **Chapter 21**) which seeks to capture the real complexities of crime and approaches to dealing with the problems associated with it.

So, left realism firmly locates its analysis of crime causation within broader social structural factors, together with questions of class, gender, and racial inequality. Although left realists still claimed to recognise that crimes committed by powerful groups did impact on the relatively powerless, their main focus was on what might be called everyday crimes. Like the right realists, their focus was on the (usually) low-level offences which cumulatively contributed to a sense of fear and abandonment amongst ordinary people. They argued that criminal acts of this kind had an immediate and substantial impact on the working classes and marginalised communities; and, consequently, their fears were rational and should be taken seriously. Crime should therefore not be seen principally or exclusively as taking place between (inter) social classes but proper attention should be paid, by criminologists as well as the justice system, to that which occurs within (intra) communities. The types of crime that people feared most, and which had the greatest impact on their lives, were those committed by people within their own communities.

In seeking to develop left realism as a theoretically grounded empirical project, its claims were based mainly on local crime and **victimisation** surveys (see **Chapter 5**) which asked people about both their problems with crime as well as their perceptions of the effectiveness of the police. For instance, there were local crime surveys carried out by Jones et al. (1986) and Crawford et al. (1990)—both in Islington, North London—which gave some empirical support for the idea that the experiences of being, and fear of becoming, a victim of burglary and street crime were very real ones for residents of this particular community. The surveys also identified that there were high levels of dissatisfaction with how this was dealt with at a local level by the police and the courts; although, of course, these studies did leave open the question of whether similar experiences and concerns were replicated elsewhere.

Whereas for right realists the 'solution' to street crime is the use of crime control strategies which maintain a particular vision of social order through deterrence, left realism, by contrast, sees economic and social policies as having a central part to play in tackling marginalisation and forms of social exclusion. Perhaps the most important concept they draw on and develop in relation to exploring the possible social causes of criminality is that of *relative deprivation*. Relative deprivation is a phrase used to refer to the perception or experience of being deprived of something which an individual believes they are entitled to. It encapsulates the idea that people look both downward (on those who have fewer possessions and opportunities) as well as upwards (to those who have more of these) as well as considering their emotional reactions to this. W. G. Runciman is usually acknowledged as the originator of the concept of relative deprivation:

> If A, who does not have something but wants it, compares himself to B, who does have it, then A is 'relatively deprived' with reference to B. Similarly, if A's expectations are higher than B's, or if he was better off than B in the past, he may when similarly placed to B feel relatively deprived by comparison with him.
>
> (Runciman, 1966: 10)

Our personal, subjective perceptions of, and reactions to, perceived injustices are important when thinking about the idea of relative deprivation. These are explored further in **What do you think? 20.2**.

WHAT DO YOU THINK? 20.2

What does it mean to be relatively deprived?

You will have heard the term 'first-world problem'—something which is viewed as being important and difficult (although sometimes amusing) but which is really reflective of privilege and abundance: 'I cut myself halving an avocado' and 'I can only use two devices on this Wi-Fi router' are examples. But does seeing this sort of thing as a 'problem' distract us from real issues of deprivation, such as the 2.4 billion people in the world who do not have access to a toilet? Do we develop a false sense of priority, seeing things as important when in fact they are perhaps not? Let us think about this idea of need and deprivation by considering a basic part of our existence—our need for nutrition—in the light of some seemingly unconnected facts.

- The British supermarket Waitrose offers an 'essential' range of groceries that includes Essential Raw Prawns, Essential Coconut Milk, and Essential Gnocchi; the budget supermarket Aldi also runs an 'essential' range which features cheddar cheese, lemonade, and frozen Yorkshire puddings.

- Essential foods were rationed during the Second World War; by 1945, an adult's weekly entitlement included 57 grams of cheese, 113 grams of bacon or ham, and one egg. Many people turned their gardens or public spaces into smallholdings where they grew vegetables and kept chickens, and communities would club together to buy and raise a pig for meat.

- The charity Love Food, Hate Waste estimates that 15 million tonnes of food are thrown away in the UK each year, and yet in the UK the Trussell Trust operates over 400 food banks which in 2015 gave out over one million packs of emergency supplies to people who otherwise were unable to buy essential food items (see **Figure 20.6**).

Think about the people associated with these statements; the supermarket shoppers, the wartime housewife, the cook throwing away unwanted food, and the food-bank user.

Then consider how you think the person in each of these groups feels about their access to food—do you imagine the 1940s shopper was resentful about rationing, or welcomed it as doing their bit for the war effort? Do food bank users feel anger about food waste? You might want to reflect on how your personal circumstances or experiences have affected your decisions.

Next, take a look around the space where you are reading this book. Jot down a list of the things around you, such as the furniture, your possessions, the equipment you are using, and again, give them a ranking;

Figure 20.6 The widespread use of food banks in the UK might be seen as evidence of the kind of deprivation which leads to crime
Source: HASPhotos/Shutterstock

1 being essential, 3 being nice but not completely necessary, and 5 a luxury.

As a last activity, think about the people around you. Note their clothes, accessories, what they are carrying. Write down the things they have that you envy—perhaps they have a better laptop than you, or more fashionable shoes. Then the things that you prefer from amongst your own possessions—is your jacket newer, your coffee from a trendier shop, or your mobile phone the latest upgrade? How has this made you feel—angry, resentful, smug, and grateful, or any other emotional reaction you may have experienced?

The point is, of course, that such things are *relative* to circumstance. If we have plenty of money, and are accustomed to eating well, then perhaps items such as truffles and coconut milk are something we learn to take for granted. If, on the other hand, we struggle to buy basic ingredients, the sight of someone spending several pounds on a large cup of coffee may cause us to feel aggrieved about the difference between their circumstances and our own.

What does it mean to feel deprived for people living in the developed world today? In what ways do you feel deprived or excluded and marginalised? As standards of living increase, our expectations and sense of entitlement develops. Compare your expectations with those of your parents and grandparents. What do you have (in terms of both material goods and opportunities) which they did not at your age? Overall, economic growth in developed countries over the last 60 years has been exponential. Many of us now own and have 'things' (and have opportunities) which would have been simply unthinkable and unobtainable for our forebears.

Finally, think about this question: how would a right or left realist view us if we stole something we desire, believe we deserve, or think we need?

Left realists (Lea and Young, 1984; Young, 2007) pick up and develop the idea of relative deprivation and relate it to crime by arguing that late modern societies are increasingly characterised by an *ethos of individualism* and a *culture of consumerism*, and that it is this which perhaps sets our age apart from previous epochs. Webber (2007: 114) agrees with this suggestion, arguing that relative deprivation might encourage: 'a tendency towards crime. It is relevant to the complex process that renders deviancy understandable and intelligible, as opposed to pathological, as is often the case in new-right realist discourse and positivistic explanations.'

You might want to visit the discussion of Young's development of the ideas of *cultural inclusion* and *structural exclusion* in **section 20.7**, as it is relevant here in two ways. First, in terms of the anger and frustration which may be felt by those who are culturally included yet structurally excluded (see Merton, 1957, on the consequences of 'anomie', too). And, secondly, in terms of the feelings of anxiety, fear, and lack of empathy towards these marginalised groups felt by those who are relatively better placed, and who have greater legitimately obtained resources and opportunities.

The desire to consume and possess things can provide individuals with a sense of identity, and possessions can also provide them with a sense of recognition, status, and fulfilment. The ethos of individualism and culture of consumption can, according to Lea and Young (1984), lead to crime mainly, although not exclusively, within excluded groups (the 'have nots'). Such a cultural atmosphere can also lead to calls for greater controls from within included groups (the 'haves'); who, in their efforts to maintain their relatively privileged positions and their fear of falling out of this group, may also transgress the law. For Young (2007), the relationship between relative deprivation and crime is not a simplistic, unilinear one. He does, however, argue that relative deprivation can:

> in *certain conditions* . . . [be seen] . . . as being a major cause of crime. That is, when people experience levels of unfairness in their allocation of resources and utilise individualistic means to attempt to right this condition. It is a reaction to the experience of injustice. Experienced injustice, coupled with individualistic 'solutions', can occur at different parts of society; like crime itself, it is certainly not a monopoly of the poor.
>
> (Young, 2007: 488)

In other words, feeling relatively deprived can contribute to crime. As he and Lea put it:

> The equation is simple; relative deprivation equals discontent; discontent plus lack of political solution equals crime.
>
> (Lea and Young, 1984: 88)

We will now turn our attention to what these political solutions might be and consider to what extent these ideas can be translated into realistic policies and political 'solutions' to the 'problem of crime'.

20.7 Left realism: policy implications

Given its prime focus on the issues of relative deprivation and marginalisation, it is perhaps not surprising that left realism translates into policy proposals and objectives which focus primarily on the socio-economic causes of crime. Therefore, in terms of policy, it emphasises forms of **social crime prevention** through engagement with communities and victims, although it argues that **situational crime prevention** and deterrence also have a minor role to play (see **Chapters 26** and **27**). Left-realist approaches in practice have involved close communication with local communities, for example by using crime and **victim surveys** (Lea, 2016); alongside strategies to promote and strengthen trust between police and communities, and to ensure policing was aligned with the priorities set by the community. This approach to improving the 'democratic accountability' of the police (Lea, 2016: 55) might be supplemented by programmes of activity and support for young people, and better victim services, especially for those victims amongst otherwise oppressed groups in society (DeKeseredy, 2016). In other words, left realism favours policies that seek to demarginalise the marginalised and include the excluded; and seeks to find policy interventions which would bring about more cohesion and less crime within otherwise fractured communities. As we have seen, left realists are also concerned with addressing the public's fear of crime and acknowledging the needs of the victim, and so they argue also for a fairer, more victim-focused, and more accountable criminal justice system.

Whilst Young (1997: 42) argues that issues of social causation should be given the 'highest priority', he also insists that crime control policy should involve interventions 'on all levels'. In developing this idea, he identified what he saw as the four fundamental elements of a 'crime'. These are brought together in what is referred to as the 'square of crime': a framework for the analysis of crime and crime control in terms of the interaction between four 'participants' in the process: offenders, victims,

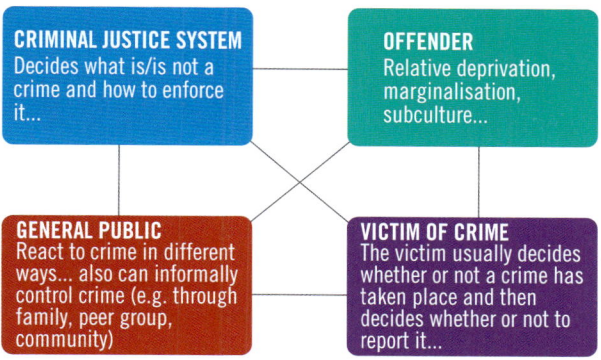

Figure 20.7 Young (1997) identified four fundamental elements of a 'crime' and this 'square of crime' enables anlaysis of crime and crime control

criminal justice agencies, and communities (Lea, 2016: 58). Thus, for example, a lack of investment in adequate street lighting (community) might result in perceived opportunities for potential offenders with nothing else to do, and consequentially a greater risk to properties or people (victims), for whom protection is unavailable because of pragmatic decisions about deployment of limited police resources (criminal justice agencies).

The argument developed here (as can be seen in **Figure 20.7**) is that it is essential for criminologists to explore the various interactions and interrelationships which exist between each of these elements. This conceptual framework attempts to capture the complexities involved, both in terms of action and reaction but also in terms of the constantly changing relationships between both informal and formal systems of control. It is often noted that this conceptualisation of crime and justice heavily influenced the first New Labour government (1997–2001) in directing their policies on crime; for instance, in legislation such as the Crime and Disorder Act 1998 which set up various multi-agency crime prevention partnerships at the local level (see **Chapter 15**).

As we have seen, left realists base much of their analysis of crime on the concept of relative deprivation (Webber, 2007). In his later work, Jock Young (1999, 2007) developed this further in terms of the concepts of *inclusion* and *exclusion*. His main argument was that late modern societies had shifted away from being inclusive and had instead become more exclusive (see **section 20.7**).

When elected in 1997, the New Labour government's Prime Minister, Tony Blair, set up the Social Exclusion Unit (SEU); this was abolished in 2006 and replaced with a Social Exclusion Task Force, which, in turn, was abolished in 2010 when the Coalition government was elected. This may indicate a questionable political commitment to addressing issues of social exclusion.

But what do the terms *social inclusion* and *social exclusion* actually mean—and how, as social scientists, can we meaningfully operationalise them in our research and policy evaluations? The 1997 New Labour government offered the following definition of social exclusion:

> Social exclusion is what can happen when people or areas suffer from a combination of linked problems, such as unemployment, poor skills, low incomes, poor housing, high crime, poor health and family breakdown.
>
> (Social Exclusion Unit, 1997)

For some commentators, issues of exclusion are tightly linked to broader issues of poverty and welfare, seeing the spheres of education, employment, health, and housing as key areas:

> The fundamental dynamic of exclusion is a result of market forces which exclude vast sections of the population from the primary labour market and of market values which help generate a climate of individualism. Such a situation has an effect on both the causes of crime (through relative deprivation and individualism) and on the reactions against crime . . . attempts to control it by barriers, incarceration and stigmatization
>
> (Young, 1999: 26)

Here, Young means physical barriers, such as gated-housing developments; extensive use of custody (as in both the UK and US, for example); and the use of identifiers (such as criminal records, or even addresses) to exclude people from employment or access to services.

Levitas (2005) argues that attempts to explain and respond to social exclusion are framed by a number of competing analytical and ideologically driven discourses, referred to by the acronyms RED, MUD, and SID:

- **RED**—this is a Redistributive Discourse (rooted in a critical social policy tradition) which emphasises poverty as being a key cause of social exclusion. In other words, it suggests that economic and social policies should aim to redistribute wealth and income; for example, through taxation and welfare policies.
- **SID**—this is a Social Integrationist Discourse, which focuses on paid work as being the key to greater social integration (but it does not address the issues of poorly paid employment or unpaid work).
- **MUD**—this relates to the Moral Underclass Discourse, which we considered earlier in the chapter when we looked at the work of the right realist Charles Murray.

Clearly these analytical devices take different positions as to what kind of inclusionary measures might best be offered. It is also likely that shifts may take place between these three discourses in terms of policy initiatives and implementation. The issues of addressing exclusion and the interrelated and problematic issues it involves through policy is considered further in **What do you think? 20.3**.

WHAT DO YOU THINK? 20.3

Implementing inclusivity through policy

A new housing estate is being built on the outskirts of the town where you live. The developers and local council have asked for volunteers to sit on a multi-agency committee responsible for improving the area and addressing some fears which have been raised about crime and antisocial behaviour. You put your name forward and have been selected to take part.

The committee's task is to spend a grant of £500,000 which has to be divided up between its 'stakeholder' members. These are:

- the police, who have an annual target of reducing youth crime by 30 per cent and who want to fund two beat officers for the area;
- the local Children's Centre, which aims to offer education and healthcare to 70 per cent of the children under the age of five on the estate;
- a housing association, which will be offering half of the new homes as affordable housing;
- the local branch of Age Concern, which already has a small social centre for the elderly in the area;
- the new school being built on the estate, which will cater for children who have been excluded from other schools;
- you, representing the young people on the estate who will not have access to any recreational or social facilities such as a youth centre.

You can also nominate up to three new stakeholders—think about who you think could also be involved, for example social workers, local transport providers, etc.

Use a grid like the one below to write down the arguments you think each member will put forward to get the biggest share of the money, and why they might disagree with their fellow stakeholders. How do you think Levitas's models of social exclusion might fit the aims and perceptions of different committee members? Do you think that the various stakeholders' interests differ in terms of the potential for fostering inclusivity or exclusivity?

When you have done this, take some time to consider the things that influence members' attitudes to these issues in terms of the aims of their organisations.

Police	
Health	
Housing	
Education	
Youth	

Lastly, imagine that you are given the casting vote to decide who gets the biggest grant. Who do you choose, and why? What do your reasons tell you about your response to inclusion and exclusion? Do your personal experiences and political position have any influence on your choice?

It is clear that the issues of social inclusion and exclusion are inherently contentious and contested—not only in terms of definition, but also in terms of how they should be dealt with through practical and workable policy measures.

The New Labour government believed that the best way to address these problems—unemployment, housing, and so on—was not by looking at them in isolation but through multi-agency partnerships:

> Our remit is to help improve government action to reduce social exclusion by producing 'joined-up solutions to joined-up problems'. We work mainly on specific projects, chosen following consultation with other government departments and suggestions from interested groups.
>
> (Social Exclusion Unit, 2004)

Levitas (2005) concluded that under New Labour there was a discernible move away from the more socially democratic RED model (which argues for macro solutions to what are seen as being essentially macro problems) to more economically liberal SID and MUD ones (which argue for individual solutions to what are seen as being essentially individual problems).

Similarly, Rodger (2008) argued that during its time in office, New Labour's policies shifted away from issues of social inclusion to embrace a discourse around a so-called moral underclass. As he argues, elements of social policies aimed at *including* vulnerable and marginalised groups also contained within them aspects of criminalisation and hence exclusion. In other words, to paraphrase their well-used sound bite, New Labour came to be rather tougher on *crime* rather than on *the causes of crime*.

Relatively few policy initiatives effectively bring together all four of the dimensions outlined in the 'square of crime' (**Figure 20.7**), and it might be the case that this is very hard to achieve in the 'real world' of policy implementation. As criminologists, we need to be aware of the very real difficulties and complexities which are involved in translating theoretical perspectives and their policy prescriptions into practice. Part of the problem here, in relation to left realism, is related to the constantly shifting power relations between the components of the 'square of crime'. This can result in there being a real gap between what, at first sight, appears to be progressive and socially beneficial policy, and the ways in which it is subsequently implemented. For instance, the same policy can be applied differently (and result in very different outcomes (intended or unintended) at different local levels).

Despite this, even if gains resulting from a particular policy that benefit some people in some conditions are small, they are gains (and important) nevertheless. For argument's sake, imagine that you are evaluating a programme which brings victims, offenders, and the wider community together to resolve their disputes (the notion of **restorative justice** as an alternative to punishment is considered in more detail in **Chapter 30**). Having been clear and meticulous in terms of what a positive outcome looks like, your findings are that in 48 per cent of the cases evaluated, the process was 'successful'. In other words, in these cases the process was fully restorative and, as the result of genuine dialogue and participation, plans were made which led to higher levels of victim satisfaction or community reparation being made. There were also real, supportive opportunities for offenders to address broader issues of their exclusion, and so on. Yet 'only' 48 per cent of the cases met these standards. Is this therefore a 'bad', ineffective, and failed policy which should be abandoned? You may wish to further investigate why the programme had less 'positive outcomes' and was 'less successful' in the other 52 per cent of cases. It is worth considering how your findings might influence the development of the programme. In short, policy gains are often incremental, growing over time, which may make initial results seem less impressive than the final outcome of a project may eventually turn out to be.

If a policy can reach even a relatively small percentage of the people it was intended to reach through good, constructive means (and help to change their lives in positive, inclusive, and demarginalising ways) then is it a good thing? After all, no policy will have a 100 per cent success rate, despite what some governments claim. Evaluating policy is an incredibly difficult thing to do with precision; we live in a highly complex world and, as social scientists, in conducting our applied research, we need to recognise that all such research has limitations (see **Chapter 4**). For left realists, purely theoretical work, whilst both interesting and intellectually rewarding, needs to be related to developing realistic policy interventions which can make a real difference. If nothing else, left realism offers a challenge to responses to crime which are based solely on (punitive) crime control policies and which regard offenders as primarily pathological individuals. As a result, it also raises important questions about the relationship between what we might call 'criminal justice' and wider aspirations to promote human rights in general and 'social justice'.

20.8 Evaluating left realism

In effect, criminological perspectives aimed at explaining crime develop through a critical dialogue with each other, sometimes infused with wider ideological perspectives and political position-taking. For instance, forms of positivism challenged and critically questioned the central tenets of classicism; critical theories challenged and critically questioned the central tenets of positivism; realism challenged and critically questioned critical theories, and so on. Whilst this is oversimplified it is perhaps a useful way for you, as students at the start of your criminological journeys, to think about how such theories interlink.

Over the course of your studies, you will probably be asked to evaluate a particular theoretical position, and an effective way of doing this is through comparison with other theoreticians' work. Such a task may be in relation to considering a particular dimension of a theory. The dimension of realist criminological theories that we have considered most in this chapter is the logic they present in terms of policy development. This is important because some theoretical criminologists might well argue that it is not their place to get directly involved in the world of policy formation and implementation at all—their role is instead simply to concentrate on analysing evidence and constructing and developing theories and arguments, and they leave it up to others to decide if the work has any policy relevance. On the other hand, as we have seen in this chapter, realist perspectives are directly engaged with policy solutions to crime; in other words, as well as being of a pure theoretical nature, they also claim to have a clear applied element.

One of the problems with theoretical debate and critique is that often one thinker might criticise another for not analysing something which their theory was never intended to address in the first place. Sometimes this may be more connected with what the critic feels or believes, rather than the content of the theory itself. After all, as we mention in **Chapter 21**, criminologists are human beings who have their own political opinions, strong personal beliefs, and ideas about what a 'good society' should look like (see also **Chapter 4**).

It is therefore vital to consider every dimension of every argument, as far as possible, and to offer as balanced a viewpoint as possible (based on the available evidence), regardless of the strength of your personal or professional beliefs. We will therefore illustrate this in **Table 20.1** by simply stating the main critical points which have been raised against left realism, and what the left-realist response to these might be. You might also want to think about what the critics' response to the initial reply would be.

Criticism of left realism	Response from left realists
It totally abandons the gains of critical criminology by uncritically accepting state-defined notions of crime. It is therefore regressive.	Left realists would argue that this is not so; they may adopt a 'softer' social constructionist conception of crime, but their first aim was to develop a policy-relevant, radical criminology which challenged the punitive thrust and exclusionary nature of right-wing government policies. Unlike the right-realist perspectives, it does not accept crime figures as measured by police recorded crime statistics as being an accurate measure. Its use of local crime surveys seeks to uncover rates of victimisation from within marginalised groups, as well as obtaining their perceptions about crime and policing in the areas where they live. To challenge right-wing discourses on crime, left realism needed to be seen to be challenging those ideas on a similar terrain; an acceptance of a 'harder' sociological/ideological reconstruction of the concept of crime would simply not make this possible. Its overall aim was to be 'realistic' about crime and its causes, and to advocate for reforms in the shape of 'realistic' policies which address these. In this sense, left realists were moving debate and analysis forwards in practical and applied ways and not backwards.
It totally abandons the gains of critical criminology by neglecting to focus on crimes committed by powerful groups (which are more harmful).	Left realists would refute this by saying that they note the very real social harms which are caused by the actions and inactions of powerful groups. Left realists initially felt, however, that the need to challenge right-wing arguments was the most pressing, as these were impacting on the lived realities of excluded groups of people. For instance, left realists focused their analysis on increasing police powers, a decline of police accountability, and increasingly harsh prison sentences. This, along with the political abandonment of the social causes of crime, had to be vigorously contested. As left realism has developed, it has also started to analyse crimes committed by powerful groups (see John Lea's (2016) argument along these lines, for example).
It has a weak empirical base and it over-relies on local crime surveys and victimisation within poor, marginalised communities.	Left realists would describe themselves as being realistic about crime, and argue that what can be done about it requires an empirical base. Left realists note the limitations of local victim surveys, but feel that they are a 'democratic' research tool. Such surveys clearly reveal (unlike official police recorded crime statistics) 'real' hidden crime problems in communities which require both attention and 'realistic' solutions.
It over-predicts crime, especially crime committed by BME (black and minority ethnic) groups. It is therefore racist.	Left realists assert that their arguments do not in any way perpetuate the myth of black criminality or subscribe to the meaningless and potentially dangerous idea of 'black-on-black' crime. They argue that local surveys have shown that some crime is intra-ethnic (that is, carried out between people of the same race or minority ethnic group). This should not be a surprise if that survey has been carried out in an area with a higher than average population of BME residents. In taking this approach, left realists can also argue that they are drawing attention to higher rates of victimisation amongst **BAME communities**, too. Left realism has thus highlighted an issue which requires further investigation within a broader framework in terms of institutional discrimination and relative deprivation, especially if the intersections of 'race' and 'class' are recognised. Left realists' empirical work has also highlighted perceptions of disproportionate policing against certain ethnic communities. It cannot therefore be said to be racist.
It neglects feminist issues in terms of the social inequalities which affect women.	Left realists would argue that this is not the case; left realism is informed by **socialist feminism**, and so focuses on gender inequalities. However, like all theoretical perspectives, it is a developing one. Early work did not perhaps have a firm enough focus on issues relating to the patriarchal nature of society, and critics were right to point this out. Later work (for instance, Mooney, 2000) addressed these issues more thoroughly, and the developing work within their perspective is clearly in dialogue with contemporary feminist theory. More work on this, and other areas, clearly still needs to be done.

Criticism of left realism	Response from left realists
It integrates diverse theories (that is, labelling, strain, radical, control) which are theoretically contradictory.	Whilst left realists are clearly seeking to develop an integrated theory, they would argue that they are not in the business of trying to reconcile what can be regarded as theoretical niceties and elegant theoretical debates. They might even argue that an eclectic approach to criminological thinking is a strength rather than a weakness.
	By drawing on and developing insights and concepts from a variety of theoretical positions, left realists are aiming to develop a theory which helps to further our understandings of crime, the processes of criminalisation, and crime control in our rapidly changing times. They aim to be able to offer radical, social democratic policy alternatives which will achieve greater social justice. To this end, the left-realist project is not at an end and, as such, it will always be in the process of 'becoming'.
Not all of those who are relatively deprived commit crime.	Left realists would agree with this point, and respond that they have never claimed this to be the case. As they argue, relative deprivation can in certain conditions be seen as being a major cause of crime. Also, they clearly say that crime (and experiences of relative deprivation) are certainly not a monopoly of poor, marginalised groups. Left realists feel that they have made a start on this work in ways that challenge both older critical theories and right-wing criminological theories. There is still much to be done in challenging the dominance of particular capitalist forms of social organisation which prevail in many late modern societies (see again, Lea, 2016).

Table 20.1 Critiques of left realism

20.9 Beyond 'left' and 'right' realism?

In the face of the various criticisms levelled at realist perspectives (as we discussed in this chapter), some criminologists have attempted to develop and improve on these ideas. Matthews, for example, has argued that changing economic conditions and the new social landscapes associated with technological developments, require an increasingly sophisticated approach to the problems experienced by 'the weak, the vulnerable and the victimised', that is to say, those who experience social exclusion (2014: 155). For some theorists, the major political and social shifts of recent years prompt us to rethink our ideas about crime, social harm, and violence—see **New frontiers 20.1**. According to this diagnosis, criminal justice systems need to be flexible, creative, and sensitive to local circumstances, and the needs of distinctive sections of the population. Similarly, interventions which respond to identified 'hurts and harms' need to take close account of the lived realities of those affected.

Lea (2016), another early proponent of 'left realism', has, on the other hand, sought to reconnect its core aspirations to a wider understanding of what we mean by the idea of crime. He believes that it is important to acknowledge and respond to those forms of transgression which may not be the most immediate or obvious at the personal or local level, but which nonetheless have a substantial impact. For example, the failure of landlords to comply with health and safety regulations might not be thought of straightforwardly as a criminal act, but may be a source of significant risk of harm. Lea argues that communities and social organisations should still be seen as lying at the heart of the process both of defining how 'crime' is perceived and prioritised; and of securing just outcomes, rather than simply relying on 'the criminal justice agencies' (2016: 61). Here, he cites the example of 'mass refusal to pay protection money' in Italy as an effective way of 'combatting Mafia power'.

Further criticisms, though (Winlow and Hall, 2016), have suggested that realist approaches need to be refocused more comprehensively. Winlow and Hall, and other ultra-realists, argue for a wider understanding of social harm, but also for a clearer recognition of the effects of crime in this broader sense on the attitudes, beliefs, and expectations of community members. Ultra-realist criminology was developed by Steve Hall and Simon Winlow from their experiences of studying crime and violence in post-industrial areas of England. It takes as its starting point not just the direct experiences and harms affecting those who are victims of injurious actions (or inaction); it looks behind these for the 'forces and processes' that are characteristic of 'advanced capitalism' and can be seen as causing such harms (Winlow and Hall, 2016: 92). Ultra-realists were studying crime in the same places as the left realists and concerned about the same sort of things as the right

NEW FRONTIERS 20.1

Redefining the reality of crime?

According to Redhead, the era of 'post-truth'—originating in the mid-2010s, with 'lying, denying and inventing stories . . . [becoming] a daily occurrence in government'—has meant that established assumptions and belief systems have become open to question, making it 'OK to talk about capitalism again' (2018: 3, 15). The challenges to conventional thinking associated with these trends also appear to have prompted a degree of moral re-evaluation. What counts as 'crime', and who has the right and the authority to make this kind of judgement, when we become more and more doubtful about the sources of legitimacy and power within society? For some theorists, the emergence of a form of politics which appears to represent a major test to accepted moral conventions in the public sphere challenges (or frees) us to rethink what we understand by 'crime', and how its impacts are felt on individuals, communities, and entire sectors of the population. As Redhead notes, 'This perspective has spread across disciplinary boundaries in and around sociology and criminology' (2018: 15).

Might this mean, for example, that we are now able to reconsider the strategic framework for policing and crime control? Policing strategies might need to be adapted so that racism is not simply addressed on a case-by-case basis, but as a form of conspiracy, requiring different, proactive approaches to investigation and detection. How could policing and the justice system be adapted to achieve this? Would it be an appropriate role for the police?

---

realists. Their brand of realism holds that crime is real, harmful, and that it is experienced as real by the people who have to live in communities that are affected by all of these problems. The theory has its roots in some of the early feminist criminology, victimology, left realism, zemiology, and from other philosophical sources beyond criminology such as critical realism, and recent developments in continental philosophy, such as transcendental materialism.

Let's have a closer look at what exactly ultra-realism is in **Conversations 20.1**, in the discussion about the ideas behind it.

CONVERSATIONS 20.1

Ultra-realist criminology

with **Dr Tom Raymen**

Roger Smith (RS): What do you think that ultra-realism did, or tries to do, that left and right realism didn't?

Dr Tom Raymen (TR): I wouldn't say it was a reaction to left and right realism in the way that people might look at left realism as a reaction to right idealism. It was very much a theoretical perspective that was trying to get back to looking at the real consequences of neoliberal capitalism, its structures, its processes and the subjectivities that were emerging within it.

RS: So, making a much stronger connection between the structural factors and day to day experience, which had kind of disappeared a bit with left realism.

TR: Yeah, I think where ultra-realists quarrel with left realism is that, while left realism was focused on structure and political economy—which was a very welcome thing—it then drifted away from that into a kind of 'left administrative' kind of criminology. And . . . where I think ultra-realism also wanted to take a step forward was in its model of subjectivity and its understanding of subjectivity. It challenged some of the philosophical tropes around subjectivity that underpin a lot of criminological theory. A lot of criminological theory is underpinned by the imagination of the subject as either inherently good, benign, and progressive, but oppressed by structures; or inherently evil, hedonistic and greedy, and therefore in need of stringent control and needs to be corralled by informal and formal social control systems.

RS: And most people are a bit more complicated than that.

TR: Exactly. So, they challenged that and drew upon psychoanalytic theory to understand that, basically, there is no natural moral or evil essence at the core of who we are. We're capable of being loving and creative and progressive, and we're also capable of being regressive and quite nasty and mean. We are fundamentally, ultra-realists argue, geared towards plasticity, very adaptable to different kind of social, cultural, political circumstances.

RS: Yes, and that's at the individual, subjective level, but they're also trying to make connections between that and objective circumstances that shape that.

TR: Absolutely. So, without going into it in too much detail, they argue that the core of subjectivity is a void—what Jacques Lacan calls the 'Real'. The Real is just this profound absence, a pre-symbolic experience of raw conflicting drives, which are always in tension with each other, and we're just bombarded by internal and external stimuli of which we cannot make coherent sense. Imagine a baby who is just alive in the world and they don't know what anything means, they have no reference point to make sense of their experiences. Ultra-realists argue that this original experience, this original state of nature as it were, is fundamentally traumatic and something which we are driven to escape. Subjectivity is formed in the transition from this state of nature to a state of culture.

RS: So, they reject Hobbes on the one hand, and Rousseau on the other. We're neither fundamentally evil or fundamentally good?

TR: Yes, and our state of nature is not a site of original freedom as it is portrayed in standard liberal philosophical discourses. In actuality, it is actually profoundly traumatic. So, to escape that original condition, we actively solicit what Lacan calls the 'symbolic order'. This is the kind of social, cultural, and symbolic structure of society, and we actively seek out the symbolic order to bring some coherent structure and meaning to our lives and our identities. The symbolic order 'fills up' the void of subjectivity as it were. What's more, we'll actively seek out whatever symbolic order is available, hence the emphasis upon human plasticity. So, that's how it looks at the relationship between the individual subject and the structures of neoliberal capitalism.

RS: So, to some extent they're helping us to explain why people might look for simple solutions to complex problems. How does this theory relate to how we look for solutions to crime?

TR: Well, for instance, Steve Hall, James Treadwell, and Simon Winlow recently wrote a book called The Rise of the Right. It was an ethnography interested in the rise of far-right nationalism across the UK, but also the wider trend in Europe and the USA. They particularly focused on some of the most deprived, left-behind communities that, 30 years ago, would've been flying the red flag of socialism. So, looking at what's happened there, they argue that it wasn't just the presence of poverty or inequality or anything else that drove them into these far-right ideologies, it was the absence of an appealing political narrative or story that could explain their circumstances. They look around and see their communities in decline, they see the world passing them by. They've experienced massive job loss through deindustrialisation—but also the loss of an entire culture and a way of life. While all this has been happening, the political left has, for a number of decades, shifted its attention away from class and political economy and more to a cultural politics of everyday life, a politics of identity and 'privilege'—a privilege that many white working-class people feel they do not possess. People in these communities are angry. They feel like they've been tossed on the scrap-heap of history. At the precise moment that has occurred there has been the relative disappearance of a coherent political narrative to make sense of their plight—and far-right ideologies have been able to move into that void and people have dipped into that common language of xenophobia and racism, which has been ever-present throughout history.

RS: So these ideologies give them solutions that they could see being practical and achievable.

TR: Beneficial to them, yes. So, that's where ultra-realism challenged the evacuation of political economy from leftist political discourse as well.

RS: I suppose that kind of summarises what ultra-realism offers that other perspectives don't, that it's connecting the subjective, personal, to the social, and giving an explanation for the interface between them. It's also redefining what we understand as crime or harm, by expanding it to include harmful experiences that people have that are not necessarily captured easily or neatly by routine, conventional criminological account.

TR: Yeah. This is one of the other criticisms of left realism; it focused upon political economy and structure, but by virtue of that, left realism could have taken it much further, but they stayed very much focussed upon legally defined definitions of crime.

RS: By legal definitions you mean things like recorded crimes and police figures?

TR: Yeah, absolutely. So, ultra-realism massively advocates not just looking at harmful crime, but also legal but harmful political, economic, social cultural practices. My own work into leisure and consumerism and harm is an example, looking at things like gambling, social media, tourism and environmental harm.

RS: Corporate crime, and that sort of thing?

TR: Corporate crime, certainly, people like Kate Tudor who have looked at fraud, and the blurring of the legal and illegal within that. But also people like Mark Horsley who has done fascinating research on issues like indebtedness; and Anthony Lloyd who has explored the harms of work in the contemporary context of wage repression and the precarious labour market which makes liberal use of tenuous zero-hour contracts and soul-sapping forms of affective labour in places like call centres and retail. These things such as debt and this kind of employment and wage repression are not illegal. In fact, they're absolutely integral to the 'normal' functioning of contemporary capitalism. But they're nevertheless extremely harmful. So ultra-realists believe it is imperative to look at such things, again taking their lead from those who have previously made these arguments, and analysing these harms within their own conceptual framework.

Dr Tom Raymen, Senior Lecturer in Criminology, Northumbria University

20.10 Conclusion

Our aim in this chapter has been to set out and evaluate the key ideas of both right and left realism. Both make claims of 'taking crime seriously' and being 'real' about 'crime problems'. They also both put forward their own views on practical solutions, and we have deliberately focused on the policy proposals associated with them as theoretical approaches. Drawing on the work of Jock Young (1990), John Muncie (2015: 147) has succinctly summarised the key points of similarity and difference between right- and left-realist approaches. These are set out in **Table 20.2**. If we work through these carefully, we can focus on how the two perspectives differ; this is particularly noticeable in terms of which criminological theories they rework, what they have to say about crime causation, and what they both prioritise in terms of policy proposals.

Let's end this chapter by thinking further about their relationship to policymaking through critically applying both 'realisms' in terms of what they might each have to say about a real and very visible issue: that of urban disorder.

In August 2011, thousands of people 'rioted' in several London boroughs and a number of towns and cities across England. News programmes showed acts of arson and looting, as well as the mass deployment of police officers (see **Figure 20.8**). It is clear that there were many complex causes of these disturbances. In the articles that were published in the aftermath, we can see how commentators' views on the causes and remedies of the unrest reflected either right- or left-realist arguments. For instance, some commentators argued that the disorder was a clear example of the moral decay of British society and the resultant increasing levels of criminality and thuggery; these authors felt that the lengthy prison sentences given to some of the 'rioters' were justified. Furthermore, it was argued that 'order' could only be restored to the streets of Britain by increasing police powers and the sentencing powers of the courts (right realism).

Other writers saw the key contributory factors as being forms of social exclusion, high levels of unemployment, and poverty. For these more liberal commentators, such issues can and should be addressed through social policies, such as urban regeneration programmes. They also argued that it was necessary to reverse government 'austerity' measures such as the spending cuts which, they argued, had created and exacerbated social divisions, leading to feelings of anger, frustration, and discontent that many young people now experienced—a strongly left-realist response.

Clearly, the disorder aroused strong feelings amongst theorists and commentators on both sides of the

Right realism	Left realism
Rejection of utopianism in favour of neo-conservatism.	Rejection of utopianism in favour of democratic socialism.
Acceptance of legal definitions of 'crime'.	Acceptance of legal definitions of 'crime'.
Primary focus on 'crime' as represented by **official statistics**.	Primary focus on 'crime' as perceived by victims and local surveys.
Fear of crime as a rational response.	Fear of crime as a rational response.
Reworking of genetic and individualistic theories.	Reworking of subcultural, anomie (lacking usual moral or social standards), and structural conflict theories.
Crime caused by a lack of self-control or wilful disobedience.	Crime caused by relative deprivation, social injustice, and marginalisation.
Prioritising order (rather than justice) via deterrent and retributive means of crime control.	Prioritising social justice via programmes of crime prevention and social inclusion.

Table 20.2 Summary of the differences between left and right realism

Figure 20.8 Media commentary on the August 2011 London riots reflected either right- or left-realist arguments
Source: 1000 Words/Shutterstock

political divide. The then government instituted a Riots, Communities and Victims Panel, which concluded that improving parenting and employment opportunities would prevent further riots—echoing the work of Murray and promoting a right-realist approach. Indeed, the final report's cover features a photograph showing one of the volunteer groups that cleaned up broken glass and debris as an alternative image of local people (see **Figure 20.9**).

A further report was produced by a group of academics from the London School of Economics and Political Science in partnership with *The Guardian* newspaper (*Reading the Riots*, 2011). This involved not only interviews but an analysis of tweets made about the events; whilst another perspective was offered by Fully Focused, a youth organisation which produced the award-winning documentary *Riot from Wrong* (2012). The film-makers attempted to ascertain the 'truth' behind the disorder and its causes; whilst they acknowledge the impact of the violence, they also discuss how cuts such as the removal of the Education Maintenance Allowance were equally significant. Both the report and the film emphasise that poor relationships between communities and the police were seen by those involved as a primary cause—something which the Riots, Communities and Victims Report places much lower in its list of factors.

Figure 20.9 The cover of the government report on the 2011 riots featured a volunteer group cleaning up debris, presenting an alternative image of local people
Source: Content available under the Open Government Licence v3.0

From this example, we can see how both right- and left-realist perspectives can be used to analyse and rationalise such incidents, as well as informing the proposals for measures that aim to prevent them. Given the emotive nature of the 2011 riots—and the heavy impact they had on local communities—it is crucial that we maintain our critical approach when we consider both left- and right-realist perspectives and their use in formulating both national and personal responses.

SUMMARY

After reading this chapter and working your way through its features you should now be able to:

- Identify the key ideas of both right and left realism

In working through the main tenets of both right and left realism, we noted the main concepts which they draw on to develop their arguments. We brought these ideas (such as the existence of an underclass, the concept of relative deprivation) together with our discussion on urban unrest, suggesting ways in which you can critically engage with these by way of comparison. In this chapter we have set up a series of debates with which you can critically engage. For instance: crime is individualistic in its origin *versus* social in its origin; crime is caused by a lack of self-control *versus* social deficits; political priorities are to restore order *versus* to implement policies which address social disadvantage; and the main policies to deal with the 'crime problem' are deterrence and retribution *versus* social crime prevention.

- Appreciate the links between criminological theorising, and broader law and order politics

Throughout this part of the book on explaining crime, we have been suggesting various ways in which you, the student, can critically engage with what can at first appear to be abstract theoretical arguments. As we have also seen, an important point for us to recognise and develop is that criminological theory does not exist in a vacuum. In this chapter we have deliberately focused on relating theoretical perspectives to the broader economic, political, social, and cultural times in which they were being developed; in other words, the broader law and order politics of an era. So, for example, the government's 'zero tolerance' response to the English 'riots' of 2011 could be identified as an attempt to put a 'right realist' political analysis of the problem into practice.

- Understand the political context surrounding the emergence of realist criminological theories

The point that broader political contexts are important when studying and understanding criminological theories is perhaps of greater importance and significance when considering the rise of so-called 'realist' criminological theories. In this chapter we noted that the late 1970s and early 1980s, in both the UK and US, were witnessing a turn to the right in their national politics. Successful right-wing governments were espousing neoliberal economic arguments and socially conservative views and policies. By drawing on material which otherwise might be best thought of as belonging to the study of political science, economics, social policy, history, and so on, we hope to have underscored the truly interdisciplinary nature of criminology and illustrated why it is such a dynamic, interesting, and challenging subject area. In terms of crime and its control in this period, we noted that it was (amongst other things) a perception of increasing crime rates, instances of urban unrest, and a developing fear of crime which informed the development of right-realist perspectives (and all that this entails in terms of calls for tougher crime control strategies and a strengthening of 'social order' and so on). Similarly, we documented how, in part, the left-wing variants of realism emerged as a challenge to right-wing governments' policies, with their calls for crime prevention policies which prioritised social justice. With both perspectives claiming to 'take crime seriously' and to be 'realistic' about its causes and what can be done about these at a practical level, we have also highlighted how criminological theorising can engage with 'real world' issues and impact on policy formation and implementation; for instance, the influence which left-realist ideas initially had on the New Labour government's policy initiatives on social inclusion.

- Critically evaluate the influence of realist ideas on aspects of criminal justice policy

Following on from the above list, this chapter has also focused on the links between theory and the development and implementation of policy, highlighting some of the very real difficulties and tensions which exist when we attempt to bring the theoretical and the practical together. Having worked through the What do you think? boxes (especially **What do you think? 20.3** on implementing inclusivity through policy) you will have had the opportunity to further develop your critical evaluation skills. Policy responses to crime and the development of your critical responses to these are further developed in **Part 4** which discusses responding to crime.

 Test your understanding of the chapter's key points by attempting the self-test questions on the **online resources** at **www.oup.com/he/case2e**

REVIEW QUESTIONS

1. What is meant by the term 'critical election' and why is that important in this instance to the rise of realist criminological theories?

2. What, according to Platt and Takagi (1977) are three common themes which unite right realism and give it a form of coherence?

3. What are the problems of identifying a (criminal) underclass who suffer from 'moral' poverty?

4. Why, and in what ways, did Lea and Young (1984) portray previous critical theories as being 'left idealist'?

5. How can the ideas of individualism, consumerism, and relative deprivation be linked to criminal behaviour?

6. What are the four points of Young's 'square of crime'? Apply and analyse this conceptual device with regard to one particular form of criminal behaviour.

 Access the **online resources** at www.oup.com/he/case2e to check your answers to the review questions.

FURTHER READING

Currie, E. (1985) *Confronting Crime.* **New York: Pantheon.**
This is one of the 'classic' books on left realism. This book directly challenges conservative arguments that crime is a consequence of individual characteristics or shortcomings; and instead provides a lengthy analysis of the social, political, and economic influences which are identified as more plausible explanations for the nature and level of crime.

Hall, S. and Winlow, S., (2015) *Revitalizing Criminological Theory.* **Abingdon: Routledge.**
This book sets out the case for the development of an 'ultra-realist' perspective on crime and criminality.

Herrnstein, R. J. and Murray, C. (1994) *The Bell Curve.* **New York: Basic Books.**
This is one of the classic texts of right realism, so reading it will deepen your understandings of the foundations of this theory, but it should be read with a strong and consistent ABC (*Always Be Critical*) mindset given the heavy criticism it has faced. It has been criticised for containing implicit racism and being poorly grounded in the available evidence.

Lea, J. (2016) 'Left Realism: A Radical Criminology for the Current Crisis', *International Journal for Crime, Justice and Social Democracy,* **5(3): 53–65.**
This article covers further developments in realist thinking.

Lea, J. and Young, J. (1984) *What Is To Be Done About Law And Order?* **Harmondsworth: Penguin.**
This is another of the classic texts for left realism, which recognised that previous critical criminological theories of the left had overlooked the effects of crime on communities.

Matthews, R. (2014) *Realist Criminology.* **Basingstoke: Palgrave Macmillan.**
As with Lea above, this authoritative book covers further developments in realist thinking.

McLaughlin, J. and Muncie, J. (2013) *Criminological Perspectives; Essential Readings* **(3rd edn). London: Sage.**
Shorter, edited extracts of the work of Wilson, Murray, Lea and Young, Young, and Currie can be found in this reader.

Murray, C. (1990) *The Emerging Underclass.* **London: Institute of Economic Affairs.**
This is another of the classic right-realism texts, setting out the argument that the principal focus of both social policy and criminal justice should be a particular segment of the population whose attitudes and wasteful and chaotic behaviour are the source of persistent disruption for respectable society.

Wilson, J. Q. (1975) *Thinking About Crime.* **New York: Vintage.**
This is another of the classic texts for right realism, which sets out the principles of policing practice based on this perspective.

 Access the **online resources** to view a wealth of extra information relating to your study of criminology, including self-test questions, answers to review questions, and links to other resources that will help you enjoy and fulfil your potential within your studies.
www.oup.com/he/case2e

CHAPTER OUTLINE

21.1	Introduction	648
21.2	Integrated theories in context	648
21.3	Integrated positivist theories	650
21.4	Integrated risk factor theories	655
21.5	Conclusion	664

21

Integrated theories of crime

KEY ISSUES

After studying this chapter, you should be able to:

- place integrated theories of crime in the context of the historical development of criminological theories;
- analyse and evaluate integrated positivist theories of crime in explanatory and practical terms;
- analyse and evaluate integrated risk factor theories of crime in explanatory and practical terms.

21.1 Introduction

In this chapter we will look at how we can explain crime in ways that integrate the ideas from more than one **theory**. The integrated explanatory theories (hereafter, just 'theories') that we will explore have evolved from the criminological theories we discussed in previous chapters. These theories have integrated the main **concepts** and arguments from existing theories and challenged their position as the hegemonic (dominant) theoretical explanations of crime.

There are four main groups, or schools, of theories in criminology, each of which we have explored throughout **Part 3** of the book: **classicism**, **positivism**, **critical criminology**, and **realism**. If you need a brief recap of these theories, skim back over the details in previous chapters to remind yourself of the context for our following discussion and evaluation of the integrated theories of crime. **Integrated theories** have merged ideas, explanations, and arguments from more than one theory within a school of theories and even across different schools, thus they may also be called *multi-factor* or *hybrid* theories.

Criminologists (for example, Ferrell and Hayward, 2015) have suggested that there is currently a **bifurcation** of criminology. By this they mean that the field of criminology is developing in two different directions at the same time: towards positivism and positivist methodologies on the one hand and, conversely, towards anti-positivist, alternative paradigms on the other. We will explore these two directions in this chapter.

We will begin the discussion of integrated theories with an exploration of *integrated positivist theories*, which we will divide into two main groups:

- **Sociobiological theories**—an integration of biological factors and sociological and environmental influences (positivist in focus).
- **Social control theories**—an integration of psychological, sociological, and structural factors (a blend of positivist theories).

We will then move onto explore *integrated risk factor theories*, which we will also divide into two main groups:

- **Artefactual risk factor theories**—explanatory frameworks that identify quantifiable psychological and sociological risk factors and present these as predictors of crime.
- **Enhanced pathways risk factor theories**—an evolution of artefactual theories through the integration of socio-structural factors and personal constructions and meanings in order to understand individual **pathways** into and out of crime.

For both sets of integrated theories we will evaluate (that is, assess the strengths, weaknesses, limitations, and utility of) the theories, with a detailed consideration of the role of subjectivity, **supposition**, and study (see **Chapter 4**). We will end the chapter by revisiting the role, context, and influence of integrated theories in the evolution of theories in criminology. We will reiterate the role of subjectivity, supposition, and study in the construction, development, and evolution of these theories and conclude that integrated forms of theory remain inconclusive regarding the *causes* of crime—the focus of the following chapter.

21.2 Integrated theories in context

Before we look at the context in which integrated theories have developed, take a look at **What do you think? 21.1** in order to focus your thoughts as you continue with this chapter.

We will start by placing integrated theories in their historical context in terms of theory development in criminology. The foundation for theoretical development in criminology has been the single theory (or school of explanation) that explains crime in a specific way—often replacing a previous theory that has either been rejected or has fallen out of favour. For example, **biological positivism** replaced the classical theories that it had originally challenged as the hegemonic theory in criminology, then fell out of favour itself and was replaced by psychological and later sociological forms of positivism (Williams, 2012). As we have explored in this part, each criminological theory and school of theory has specific (and shared) strengths and weaknesses. Often, however, weaknesses or criticisms are terms used in criminology to describe what should be called limitations—what the theory will not, does not, or cannot, do due to its focus, objectives, methods, and biases.

Identifying a theory's limitations does not mean that the theory's basic explanation of crime is wrong—it may be valid for a particular person committing a particular crime at a particular point in time, or you could say, for some crimes at some times. But it is not valid to claim that any theory is universally applicable, that it can explain all crimes at all times by all people (see **Chapter 4**). Therefore, when we evaluate a theoretical explanation, we can point out criticisms, parts that are arguably inaccurate or misleading (for example, ignoring an explanation because it

WHAT DO YOU THINK? 21.1

How should we explain crime?

From what you have read so far in this book, what do you think is the most convincing explanation of why people commit crime? Is it easy to answer such a general question? Should the answer be contingent on what form of crime we are trying to explain? For example, how would you explain:

- violent crimes such as murder and assault?
- property crimes such as vandalism and burglary?
- sexual crimes such as rape and child abuse?
- **corporate crimes** such as fraud and environmental pollution?

Is it possible for explanations to be different for different people at different times and even for the same people at different times? What do you think and why do you think this?

---

doesn't fit the theory or policy), but we can also point out limitations, parts that are missing, and areas that cannot be explained using that theory alone. This is where an understanding of integrated theories becomes essential.

A common limitation of theories of crime has been their exclusivity—their single-minded focus on a specific way of explaining crime, whilst ignoring other theories as either potential contributions to their own explanation or potential alternative explanations of crime in their own right (Akers and Sellers, 2013; Agnew, 2011). Of course, it can be a strength to be single-minded in developing a line of argument (it demonstrates commitment and clarity of thought). However, this can run the risk of narrow-mindedness and artificially restricting *explanatory utility* (the usefulness of the theory for explaining crime) if criminologists are too exclusive to develop or reject their own ideas in the face of compelling evidence (see also **Chapter 4**). Exclusivity in theories can be demonstrated between schools; for example, classicists rejecting positivist explanations or positivists ignoring critical arguments. It is also demonstrated within schools; biological positivists excluding psychological or sociological explanations, critical Marxists rejecting the ideas of critical feminists, right realists ignoring left realists, and so on. As **What do you think? 21.1** should have indicated, this exclusivity can result in certain types of crime being easier to explain for certain people using one theory but not another. What is far less common in criminology is a theory that can explain all crimes at all times by all kinds of people. However, such a *universal* theory may not be feasible, or even desirable in our complex and nuanced area of study.

It is important to note that our summary here is a necessary oversimplification. Most theories have developed with a degree of acknowledgement and even integration of concepts and arguments from other competitor theories. Two notable examples are Lombroso's eventual acceptance that social factors are far more influential on crime than biological factors and the linking of **labelling theory** to structural influences on crime by critical criminologists (Hopkins Burke, 2013). The neo-classical compromise and right realism are also good examples of early theoretical integration through their acknowledgement that a person's capacity to make fully rational choices is influenced by biological, psychological, and sociological factors (cf. Agnew, 2011). However, even these theories are still limited in focus. As we will see, the integrated theories we will discuss in this chapter aim to offer a much broader integration of historical and current theories.

The evolution of theories in criminology has been evidenced by integrated theories—explanations of crime that mix together concepts, arguments, research methods, evidence, and explanations from more than one criminological theory. Integrated theories can operate in one of three ways (see **Figure 21.1**):

1. **Within theory**—A theory may integrate arguments from a similar theory/theories within its own strand of explanation. For example, an integrated biological positivist theory may consider explanations of crime that incorporate substance use, hormonal imbalance, and biochemical dysfunction in the brain.

2. **Within school**—A theory may integrate arguments from other strands of explanation within its own school, yet outside its own specific

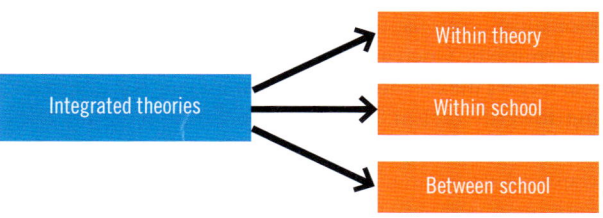

Figure 21.1 Integrated theories can operate in one of three ways: within theory, within school, or between school

theoretical framework. For example, an integrated biological positivist theory may consider the influence of social/sociological factors on offending behaviour and on the very biological factors that were originally thought to be the only influences on offending (such as the refinement of Lombroso's original theory to include social, cultural, and economic factors—Akers and Sellers, 2013). Such theories would be known as sociobiological theories—our first illustration of integrated theories in this chapter.

3. **Between schools**—A theory may integrate arguments from different schools of explanation. For example, the neo-classical compromise position is a tentative attempt to fuse traditional **rational choice** explanations with select positivist influences.

Several theories thought of as critical criminology are actually integrated theories that bring in arguments from outside of traditional critical criminology (for example, from **sociological positivism**). *The New Criminology* is a good example here (Taylor, Walton, and Young, 1973; Walton and Young, 1998), as are the new forms of social control theories that we will discuss in this chapter as the second illustration of integrated theories.

As we stated earlier in this chapter, it is possible and helpful to divide integrated theories into two distinct bifurcated groups or pathways: integrated positivist theories and integrated risk factor theories. Let us start where much research-based criminological explanation starts: positivist theory.

21.3 Integrated positivist theories

Integrated positivist theories have addressed the explanatory and practical weaknesses and limitations of traditional single factor theories by combining their individual strengths (thus compensating for their individual weaknesses and limitations) in order to offer more holistic, universal, and valid explanations of crime. By integrating different positivist explanations (for example, biological, psychological, sociological), epistemologies, and research methods, integrated positivist theories have the potential to offer a more open-minded and less subjective way of knowing about how to explain crime. But we must *Always Be Critical* (ABC) as you know, so let us analyse and evaluate examples of integrated positivist theories in more detail, specifically *sociobiological theories* and *social control theories*.

Sociobiological theories

Where once the ideas and methods of biological positivism were considered groundbreaking and even revolutionary in criminology, they soon became viewed by some as controversial and unethical as psychological and sociological explanations gained in popularity. Certain arguments of biological positivism began to be considered to be overly deterministic (such as suggesting that exposure to biological factors makes offending almost inevitable), even veering towards racism, sexism, ageism, and classism. Their recommended responses to offending behaviour such as chemical castration, electro-convulsive therapy, and genetic engineering, were excessive, even barbaric (Vold, Bernard, and Snipes, 2002). The dominance of biological factors when explaining crime was superseded by a more palatable body of psychological factors, albeit a focus that still tended to view the causes of crime as illnesses or flaws or problems in the person, otherwise known as **pathological** explanations (Bernard et al., 2015). The popularity of these explanations was challenged by a more socially acceptable (less blaming and pathological) focus on sociological factors (Winters, Globoklar, and Roberson, 2014). However, in recent years, exploring biological factors as potential explanations for crime has undergone a resurgence in popularity in criminology, particularly in the US, which has always favoured a more bio-psychological form of criminology over the more sociological and critical forms popular in the UK. This rebirth has been driven by the emergence of sociobiological theories (also known as 'biosocial' theories) offering explanations of crime that combine biological influences with sociological and environmental (socio-environmental) influences as part of multifactor integrated approaches (see Vold et al., 2002; Bernard et al., 2015). The development of sociobiological explanations is best illustrated by its two most prolific strands of theory: the *biosocial theory* of the late 1970s and 1980s and 21st-century *biosocial risk factor theories*.

Biosocial theory

The possibility of explaining crime as the result of interactions between biological and socio-environmental factors was introduced by a criminologist called Sarnoff Mednick (1977), who argued that: 'the value of biological factors is more limited in predicted antisocial behaviour in individuals who have experienced **criminogenic** social conditions in their rearing' (Mednick et al., 1987: 68).

Mednick's main argument was that we all have natural, biological instincts and urges to commit crime, but that most people can control these urges. Those who do commit crime are more likely to experience a combination of socio-environmental problems, for example inadequate learning of appropriate behaviour in the family, interactions with criminal and antisocial peer groups, and biological problems, for example an autonomic nervous system that responds slowly to external stimuli such as **punishment** (for example, Rafter, 2008). Mednick's biosocial theory suggests, therefore, an interaction between nature (biological factors) and nurture (socio-environmental factors). Another criminologist, C. Ray Jeffery (1977), added psychological factors into the mix to produce what could be more accurately described as a *biopsychosocial theory* of crime. Jeffery offered a two-pronged theory suggesting that the biological and psychological characteristics that people are born with (that is, nature) could cause offending behaviour in their own right or could interact with socio-environmental processes such as **socialisation** (upbringing, being taught social **norms**) in the family and school (that is, nurture) to cause offending. For example, according to this theory biochemical imbalances in the brain, acting alone, could cause offending behaviour, but they could also interact with and be exacerbated by socio-environmental factors such as poverty and its associated problems (such as poor diet, increased exposure to pollution), which could then lead to behavioural problems and offending (see Rafter, 2008).

Right-realist biosocial theory

The biosocial interactions proposed by Mednick and Jeffery in the late 1970s were built upon in explanatory terms in the mid-1980s by the forefather of right realism, James Q. Wilson and his colleague Richard Herrnstein. Wilson and Herrnstein (1985) made two conclusions: that most crime is committed by young men and this group should therefore be the focus of theories of crime. Arguably, there are **validity** issues associated with making the claim that young men should be the focus of explanations of crime. There is also much available evidence from **official statistics** and criminological research data to suggest that the former claim is **androcentric** (a male-centred view of the world), not least because it prevents study of female offending. Take a look at **Controversy and debate 21.1** before we consider this theory in more detail.

For the purposes of their right-realist biosocial theory, Wilson and Herrnstein (1985: 69) viewed crime by young men as the product of an interaction between biological and sociological factors, asserting that:

> It is likely that the effect of maleness and youthfulness on the tendency to commit crime has both constitutional and social origins: that is, it has something to do with the biological status of being a young male and with how the young man has been treated by family, friends and society.

In other words, being male (as in your biological sex and your sociological and cultural gender) means that you

CONTROVERSY AND DEBATE 21.1

Androcentric bias or justified focus?

A lot of criminological research focuses on crime committed by males. But is this an 'androcentric bias' (taking a male-centred view of the world)? Or is it simply a justified **reflection** of crimes committed?

- Do we prioritise explanations of crime that apply to males because they commit the majority of crimes? This would be a realist view in both theoretical (explanatory) and epistemological (knowledge creation) terms.

- Is our androcentric focus the product of a **self-fulfilling prophecy**—we assume that males commit the most crime so we target our **empirical** research, our academic explanations, and our criminal justice practices (such as police activities) on this group to the exclusion of other populations?

- Is it possible that the androcentric nature of biosocial explanations of crime is (in part) a product of academic theorising by an exclusive group of middle-class, white, male researchers (for example, **Figures 21.2, 21.3, 21.4**).

- To what extent have we **socially constructed** the extent and nature of crime committed by males and the need to respond to this crime?

Figure 21.2 Sarnoff Mednick (biosocial theory)

Figure 21.3 C. Ray Jeffery (biopsychosocial theory)

Figure 21.4 James Q. Wilson (right-realism theory)

may receive different treatment and experience different interactions in society compared to if you are female. The theory argues that we carry certain biological characteristics into the social world (for example, gender, age, intelligence, personality) that positively or negatively affect our ability to learn the norms of behaviour and to learn from any reinforcement or punishment of behaviour. It can also be that some people are less likely to receive reinforcement for positive behaviour, but may be more likely to be rewarded for negative behaviour, so they are more likely to choose to become criminal (in a given situation) and to persist with criminal behaviours. Consequently, right-realist biosocial theory can be viewed as an integration of rational choice and biopsychosocial factors. Its arguments recommend the prevention, treatment, and punishment of crime that focus on influencing people's (young males') rational choices to commit crime and to comply with social norms (that is, their self-control).

Biosocial risk factor theories

Since the late 1990s, an updated form of biosocial theory has become popular (especially in the US), with three notable tweaks in its focus compared to traditional biosocial theory:

1. an emphasis on risk factors as predictors (statistically correlated with future offending) rather than as causes (direct, linear influences on offending) as the way to explain crime;
2. a desire to explain and predict future behaviour rather than past behaviour;
3. a focus on antisocial behaviour rather than crime per se.

This strand of theories links neatly into the integrated risk factor group of theories (that we will discuss later in this chapter), but it is relevant and appropriate to introduce and discuss it here to give you a better idea of the types of explanation offered. The premise of risk factor theories of crime is that it is possible to identify certain biopsychosocial factors in early life (pre-birth, childhood, adolescence, young adulthood) that place a person at an increased risk of committing crime or antisocial behaviour in the future. The risk factors can be seen as predictors of these behaviours and so are argued to be ideal targets for intervention aimed at preventing crime (see Farrington, Kazemian, and Piquero, 2019).

Biosocial risk factor theories might, for example, explain crime as the result of complications to the foetus during pregnancy, which has a knock-on effect on other areas of life. For example, biological problems with central nervous system functioning and subsequent well-being in early and later childhood and adolescence (Moffitt, 1993) could interact with the mother's rejection to encourage violent behaviour (Raine, Brennan, and Mednick, 1997). These biological issues could also mix with social factors such as poverty (such as living in a deprived environment) to encourage physical aggression (Arsenault et al., 2002). Other social factors that mix with biological ones can include poor parenting, such as unresponsiveness and rejection (for example, Shaw et al., 2003) or harsh, controlling behaviour and lack of acceptance of the child (for example, Younge, Oetting, and Deffenbacher, 1996), which can lead to antisocial behaviour.

Evaluating sociobiological theories of crime

Advocates argue that by bringing together different perspectives, sociobiological theories have benefited criminological theory, providing broader and more versatile explanations of crime (for example, Vold et al., 2002). The explanatory utility of biological (positivist) theories in isolation has been characterised as narrow and *reductionist*—reducing the causes and explanations of crime to their most (over)simplified and basic forms at the expense of a broader focus on other potential influences (Mitchell Miller, 2009). Consequently, integrating psychological and sociological explanations (to a lesser extent, rational choice theories) into broader integrated theories can moderate the **determinism** of biological theories (the extent to which they claim that biological factors inevitably cause, predict, or affect crime) and offers more holistic, comprehensive explanations that fit more crimes at more times for more people (Akers and Sellers, 2013). Contrary to the broad focus of sociobiological theories, however, it is possible that subjectivity may encourage theorists to privilege particular factors and to reject or neglect other potential sources of explanation from other schools of thought. For example, integrated biosocial theories appear to privilege positivist explanations at the expense of giving more detailed consideration to **free will** or rational choice (with the exception of right-realist biosocial theory) or giving full consideration to the role of **criminalisation** in identifying, targeting, and dealing with individuals in the criminal justice system. Therefore, biosocial theories remain reductionist to a degree, in the sense that they are limited in scope and oversimplified in explanation.

The androcentric focus on males within integrated biosocial theories is also worthy of discussion, especially as androcentricism is a critical issue for criminology. As discussed, this androcentricism is in part justified by the dominance of males in crime statistics and research evidence. However, it is also in part a product (social construction) of the excessive prioritisation of young males in lawmaking, law enforcement, and in criminological research—somewhat of a chicken and egg situation. A by-product of androcentrism is that it can weaken theoretical explanations by making them less representative of, and valid for, all people who commit crime or who are criminalised. Integrated positivist (sociobiological) theories, therefore, can exacerbate the androcentric positivist/criminological tendency to develop explanations of crime with male populations and then uncritically apply these explanations to females who offend (relying on *supposition* that they are applicable—see also **Chapter 4**), rather than studying the particular lives, contexts, experiences, and behaviours of those females in developing a theory from there (Hagen, 2013). As we know, similar criticisms can be made of the extent to which theories in criminology are *ethnocentric*—dominated by explanations of crime generated in the industrialised western world and then uncritically applied to non-western populations. Theories can also be accused of being class-centric—dominated by explanations of working-class crime and criminals, whilst ignoring the middle classes.

Notwithstanding any identified limitations, the central argument here is that sociobiological forms of integrated positivist theory have built on and evolved traditional single factor positivist explanations of crime, whilst retaining a degree of their narrow focus and explanatory preferences. So, what other theories are there? Let's turn our attention to social control theories.

Social control theories

A second strand of integrated positivist theories, *social control theories*, is concerned with why people *do not* commit crime. It offers a more promising set of integrated explanations of crime compared to sociobiological theories for at least three reasons:

1. **Longevity**—It has been around since the 1950s, so it has had more time to develop and to be refined (Hagen, 2013).
2. **Empirical research**—There is more evidence to support their explanations, perhaps more than any other theory in criminology (Winters et al., 2014).
3. **Between schools**—It has made more of an attempt to integrate explanations between schools, such as integrating rational choice and positivist explanations and more recently by incorporating elements inspired by critical criminological theories and the Victimised Actor Model (Hopkins Burke, 2013).

Social control theories are unique as criminological explanations of crime because they subvert the question of 'why do some people commit crime?' into 'why don't some people commit crime?' and 'why do people obey the law?' Building on mid-20th-century control theories that focused on the psychological influences (for example, personality) that control people's behaviour and stop them from offending (such as Reiss, 1951; Nye, 1958), social control theories introduced a greater focus on the social factors that bond people to the norms of a given society—factors such as socialisation processes in the family, school, and peer group.

There are a number of social control theories. We'll structure our discussion around two groups of social control theory: traditional and 21st century. Traditional social control theories include the original social control theory (Hirschi, 1969), integrated social control theory (Elliott, Ageton, and Canter, 1979), and the general theory of crime (Gottfredson and Hirschi, 1990). The 21st-century social control theories include power control theory (Bates, Bader, and Mencken, 2003), control balance theory (Tittle, 2000), and differential coercion theory (Colvin, 2000).

Traditional control theories

The forefather of all other social control theories is Travis Hirschi's (1969) *social control theory*, which explains why some people obey the law and, by extension, why others don't. Hirschi argued that obeying the law is the result of a strong social bond to the rules and norms of your society. Social control theory divides this bond into four social elements:

1. attachment to significant and important people, organisations and institutions (for example, relationships);
2. commitment to conventional behaviours and actions (for example, a rational choice to conform);
3. involvement in conventional behaviours and activities (that is, being too busy to commit crime); and
4. beliefs in the importance of conventional behaviour and in each of the other elements of the social bond.

Hirschi (1969: 16) explained that 'delinquent acts result when an individual's bond to society is weaker or broken'.

Social control theory is supported by large amounts of data from a wealth of empirical studies (for instance, Brookmeyer, Fanti, and Henrich, 2006; Unnever, Cullen, and Agnew, 2006; Elliott et al., 1979). It is integrated because it takes arguments from rational choice theory and positivism (mainly sociological forms such as **strain theory**, with some consideration of psychological controls). There are also close links to later risk factor theories (see the next section) in claims that strong social bonds protect against offending (Laub and Sampson, 2003; Hawkins and Catalno, 1992), whilst weak social bonds are essentially risk factors for offending, especially for young people. As with other theories, critics tend to focus on what the theory does not consider, such as the extent of the influence of delinquent friends or the influence of historical and structural contexts on social bonds and on offending behaviour. Critics also focus on what the theory cannot explain, such as the extent and nature of offending behaviour that may result from weak social bonds (see Agnew, 2011).

Just as Hirschi had done ten years previously, Elliott et al. (1979) argued that prosocial behaviour (for example, not committing crime) is the product of strong social bonds, whereas crime is the result of weak social bonds that are themselves the product of poor, negative socialisation in early life. Therefore, strong social bonds are the result of effective socialisation. These social bonds are further weakened or strengthened by later socialisation experiences in the home, school, and community and especially exposure to delinquent peer groups. In structural terms, Elliott et al. (1979) believed that social bonds can be further weakened by a person experiencing blocked opportunities, social disorganisation, unemployment, and economic recession. Therefore, the *integrated social control theory* explains crime by integrating arguments and concepts from social control, anomie, and **social learning theories**.

Twenty-one years after his social control theory, Travis Hirschi collaborated with Michael Gottfredson to produce the *general theory of crime* (Gottfredson and Hirschi, 1990), also known as 'self-control theory'—an attempt to offer a universal explanation of 'all crimes, at all times' (Gottfredson and Hirschi, 1990: 117) in all places by all people. As the title suggests, Goffredson and Hirschi argued that the common explanation of all crimes is low self-control. People with low self-control, it is argued, are much more likely to make rational choices to commit crime, as well as to perform other potentially harmful or deviant behaviours, such as smoking, drinking, or having under-age sex. This situation is made worse by ineffective parenting during childhood, which means that self-control is likely to stay at lower levels throughout the person's life. The general theory of crime attempted to address a key criticism of social control theory in that it is able to explain and account for specific types of crime using the same explanation—low self-control. However, it is not strictly a social form of control theory because it rejects the influence of social factors on crime, preferring to talk about the more psychological motivation to commit crime, as opposed to the causes of crime, and explaining all crime as a personalised, immediate rational choice linked to low self-control. This being the case, the general theory of crime has much more difficulty explaining **white-collar** and corporate crimes, which are typically the product of long-term, detailed, and considered planning and all of which seem incompatible with the immediate rational choices implied by the low self-control **hypothesis**.

21st-century social control theories

A series of modified social control theories have been developed since the end of the 20th century. *Power control theory* (Bates et al., 2003) integrates control and social class theories to argue that patriarchal attitudes in the home can explain gender differences in offending. Put simply, they argue that girls are controlled far more than boys in the family setting (usually by their mothers who were themselves controlled as girls) and so are less likely to take risks and commit crime. However, if the balance of power in controlling the child is shared more equally between parents then girls will not be subjected to excessive control and will be as likely to offend or not offend as boys (Bates et al., 2003).

Control balance theory is the brainchild of Charles Tittle (2000), who asserts that crime results from an imbalance in the amount a person's behaviour is controlled compared to others in society. If a person is subjected to excessive amounts of control (that is, they have a control deficit) then this leads to resentment, anger, weak social bonds, and ultimately to offending. Where a person has an excess of control over others and over their environment (that is, they have a control surplus) then they get greedy, corrupt, and obsessed with dominance, which leads into offending. This is a need versus greed situation—the need to alleviate a control deficit versus the greed to extend a control surplus.

The final 21st-century social control theory that we will discuss, known as *differential coercion theory* (Colvin, 2000), focuses on the criminogenic (crime-causing) influence of exposure to coercion—the pressure to behave in a certain way; in this case, criminally. Colvin asserts that high levels of consistent coercion (actual or threatened) in the family, school peer group, or neighbourhood can be criminogenic. Such coercion can be from individuals and from society. For example, coercion from individuals situated in the family or school could manifest in the form of the removal of social supports or the use of physical force. Similarly, coercion from individuals in the peer group could be evidenced by gang violence. Socially, neighbourhood coercion can occur through exposure to poverty or unemployment. According to the theory, coercion can produce a series of social-psychological deficits (flaws, failings, missing parts) that encourage criminal behaviour. These deficits include anger, low self-control (see also Gottfredson and Hirschi, 1990), weak social bonds (see also Hirschi, 1969), and an increased commitment to using coercion to achieve personal goals, which is known as 'coercive ideation'.

Social control theory has been dubbed 'the most tested theory of crime causation' (Hopkins Burke, 2013: 218), although this claim could now be challenged by the rise to prominence of artefactual risk factor theories (see **section 21.4** for a discussion of integrated risk factor theories). Such a high level of empirical support is a major strength of social control theories—it is indicative of a reliable and replicable set of explanations that are appropriate and applicable (valid) to a range of populations. This may in part be due to the broader range of influences on crime considered by social control theories when compared to single-factor and single-school theories, including their focus on the socio-structural factors that have been traditionally under-researched by positivist theories. However, despite the 'grand theory' claims of certain theorists (most notably, Gottfredson and Hirschi, 1990), social control theories remain unable to explain all crimes at all times (for example, those based on rational choice decisions, white-collar crimes by middle-class individuals with strong social bonds). An associated limitation when compared to other theories appears to be an inability to identify what types of crime would result from the specific explanations of social control theories. The complex concept of crime is, therefore, ill-defined and oversimplified by social control theorists (see also Downes and Rock, 1998). Hopkins Burke (2013) goes as far as to claim that crime (or deviance in most social control theories) is reduced to the gratification of basic appetites—acquisitive (to obtain goals, property), aggressive (for instance, violent), or sexual. This oversimplification and **reductionism** in social control explanations is compounded further by overlooking a key avenue of explanation—the influence of *criminalisation* processes on the social construction of crime.

Evaluating integrated positivist theories

Taking sociobiological theories and social control theories together, let us evaluate what they can tell us about how crime can be explained. The intention has been to provide criminology with hybrid theories of how a range of different factors may interact and interrelate to cause and influence crime. In this respect, they are an improvement over the more limited, subjective, and reductionist single factor theories. However, integrated positivist theories remain subjective and reductionist in their own right to some extent. They may privilege certain explanations over others, for example fusing two single factor theories such as biological and sociological positivism or merging rational choice with a form of social control theory (see Agnew, 2011). Indeed, integrated positivist theories could be accused of ignoring certain explanations altogether, such as the critical criminological concept of criminalisation and the left-realist interactions within the 'square of crime' (see **Chapter 20**; see also Ugwudike, 2015). They still privilege explaining the behaviour of certain groups (such as males, populations in the western world) and ignore or relatively neglect other groups (such as females, non-western populations).

Integrated positivist theories can also be reductionist in their uncritical view that crime is an accepted concept that simply needs explaining, rather than a dynamic and contingent phenomenon specific to historical, socio-structural, cultural, and temporal context (MacDonald and Marsh, 2005).

In conclusion, a major limitation of integrated positivist theories, as with all theories in criminology, is their inability to be universal—to explain all crimes at all times by all people. In fact, certain integrated theories (social control theories in particular) may attempt to over-generalise to such an extent that they cannot identify the specific forms of offending that result from their explanations. In trying to explain too much, they can end up explaining too little. There is a sense, therefore, that integrated theories may occasionally overreach and overclaim when trying to outperform single factor theories. In doing so, they risk magnifying the weaknesses and limitations of the single factor theories they are integrating, without compensating for them by merging their strengths and dramatically improving their explanatory power.

We will now move on to discuss the second main set of integrated theories: integrated risk factor theories.

21.4 Integrated risk factor theories

In the 1990s, a socio-political risk perspective began to gain popularity within criminology in the industrialised western world. Two central tenets of this perspective were:

1. that we live in a 'risk society' characterised by rapid social and economic changes brought on by **globalisation** (Beck, 1992), which results in populations feeling unsafe and uncertain and thus needing to control their environments;

2. that in this risk society, crime is rapidly increasing, especially crime committed by young males, which indicates that official criminal justice system responses to crime (for example, deterrence, imprisonment, treatment, prevention) are not working.

The notion in the 1990s that crime was increasing strongly implied (rightly or wrongly) that the explanations of and responses to crime offered by criminological theories—consolidated by official statistics, political rhetoric, media representations, and public opinion—had not been fit for purpose. Throughout the 1990s, governments in the western world, especially the post-1997 New Labour UK government under Tony Blair, challenged key stakeholders to produce a theory of crime that was straightforward, politically acceptable (for example, that did not necessarily focus on the contribution of governments to creating and exacerbating crime), and most of all, practical. In other words, governments needed an **apolitical** explanation that focused on micro-level (for instance, individuals) and meso-level (for instance, mid-range, community-based) dynamic factors (Andrews and Bonta, 2010) that could be easily targeted and changed, whilst macro-level factors such as unemployment, poverty, social disorganisation, and economic recession were largely overlooked. This was the impetus for integrated risk factor theories.

In this section we will analyse and evaluate integrated risk factor theories. These are a range of explanations, each with a slightly different take on the same basic explanatory framework, that it is possible to identify and measure certain factors in the lives of children and young people that increase the risk of them committing crime in the future. (See **Figure 21.5**.) These so-called 'risk factors', typically psychological and sociological (psychosocial) in focus, therefore, are seen by risk theory advocates to predict crime (or an increased likelihood of crime) and it is argued that they should be targeted by preventative interventions before they occur or by early intervention once they occur, but before they get worse (Farrington, 2000). This practical model of identification and targeting (that is, assessment and intervention) is known as the Risk Factor Prevention Paradigm (RFPP) (Hawkins and Catalano, 1992). Risk-based explanations of crime actually emerged in the 1930s in the US (Glueck and Glueck, 1930). By the 1990s, their time had truly come and since then the political and academic popularity of risk-based theories has grown to such an extent that integrated risk factor theories are now arguably the hegemonic set of theories in criminology (Case, 2018).

For clarity and simplicity, risk-based explanations of crime can be divided into two groups: **artefactual risk factor theories** and *enhanced pathways risk factor theories*. Artefactual theories focus on the conversion of risk to a quantity or number (a risk factor), whereas enhanced pathways theories complement this positivist quantification of risk with **interpretivist** qualitative measures of how risk is personally constructed and experienced. Consequently, artefactual theories tend to be within-school integrations of positivist theories, whilst enhanced pathways theories are more concerned with integration between schools, such as fusing positivist, rational choice, and critical theories. We will begin our discussion with artefactual risk factor theories because these make up the vast majority of integrated risk factor theories and are the form of theory that is dominant within criminology. Conversely, enhanced pathways risk factor theories have been marginalised as minority and militant theories within the risk factor research movement (Case, 2018).

Artefactual risk factor theories

The vast majority of integrated risk factor theories have conceived of risk as an objective fact that can be measured and turned into a numerical factor, or artefact. This 'factorisation' (Kemshall, 2008) is typically for the purposes of statistical analysis—to identify statistical relationships between quantified risk factors and quantified measures of offending. Statistical relationships or correlations are interpreted as demonstrating how risk factors predict an increased risk of offending behaviour in the future. The conflation of correlation with prediction is a key supposition (assumption) of artefactual risk factor theories (see Kemshall, 2008; France, 2008) and one that we will challenge later.

The other basic supposition of artefactual risk factor theories is both developmental and deterministic—that risk factors tend to occur in childhood and adolescence and then develop to the point that they determine offending behaviour in later life (see also McAra and McVie's developmental criminology chapter in *The Oxford*

Figure 21.5 *Minority Report* (2002, Dir. Spielberg). This futuristic action-thriller depicted a mid-21st-century 'pre-crime' police department that is able to predict crime and so intervene and sentence offenders before any crime actually takes place

Handbook of Criminology—Liebling, Maruna, and McAra, 2017). These risk factors can be biological (for example, related to physique or hormones), but they tend to be psychosocial, that is micro-level psychological (for example, related to cognition, impulsivity, hyperactivity, attitude, emotion, mental health) and meso-level sociological (for example, in immediate social domains—family, education, lifestyle, neighbourhood).

But first we need to develop a clear understanding of the types of artefactual risk factor theory that have evolved over the years. They share very similar arguments, strengths, and weaknesses/limitations, so it is unnecessary to discuss each one in great detail (if you are interested in a more detailed discussion, read Case and Haines, 2009), but a broad overview will help us to understand the nature of these theories. Better understanding of a theory should make it easier to evaluate its value and utility. As you will see from **Table 21.1**, despite a clearly evolving focus over time, each artefactual risk factor theory is essentially a within-school integration of various positivist theories.

The table demonstrates the clear evolution of artefactual risk factor explanations of crime—starting with integrated biopsychosocial explanations of officially recorded crime in adolescence (in the first half of the 20th century), moving into psychosocial explanations of both official and self-reported crime in adolescence and adulthood (1970s and 1980s theories), and finally more holistic theories integrating psychosocial factors with socio-structural influences (1990s).

When we evaluate theories it is important to assess their *validity* (for example, accuracy, comprehensiveness; see **Chapter 4**)—to separate their actual strengths from any potentially invalid claims made by their supporters about their supposed strengths. To this end, let us examine the common claims made by advocates as they relate to the validity, **reliability**, and practicality of artefactual risk factor theories.

Artefactual risk factor theorists assert that their explanations have validity—that they are common-sense, simplistic, acceptable, practical explanations of crime

When?	What, who and how?
1930s	**Multi-factor developmental theory (Glueck and Glueck, 1930, 1934)**
	Biological, psychological, and sociological (biopsychosocial) characteristics measured in childhood correlate with officially recorded offending in adolescence.
1940s–1950s	**Developmental crime prevention theory (Cabot, 1940; McCord and McCord, 1959)**
	Biopsychosocial factors measured in childhood correlate with officially recorded offending in adolescence and can be prevented and reduced through official interventions.
1970s	**The criminal careers model (West and Farrington, 1973)**
	Psychosocial risk factors experienced in childhood exert a developmental influence on (that is, correlate positively with) the extent and nature of official and self-reported offending in adolescence and adulthood.
1980s	**Social development model (Hawkins and Weis, 1985)**
	Psychosocial risk factors (for example, opportunity for and involvement in conventional activities, positive interactions, skills to participate, and reinforcement for behaviour) interact with **cognitive** ability, socio-structural status (such as gender, age, race) and external constraints (such as in/formal reactions to behaviour) to cause offending at different developmental stages of a child's life. This is the first self-proclaimed 'integrated' risk factor theory.
Early 1990s	**Age-graded theory of informal social control (Sampson and Laub, 1993)**
	Informal social controls in the family and school interact with structural factors (for example, poverty, unemployment) to cause offending in childhood and adolescence. Social bonds, significant **transitions**, and critical life events in adulthood can encourage **desistance** from offending.
Late 1990s	**Ecological theory (Wikstrom and Loeber, 1998; Sampson et al., 1997)**
	Psychosocial risk factors interact with socio-structural context (for example, community characteristics, immediate situational factors) in childhood and adolescence to influence offending at different times in different places.

Table 21.1 The evolution of artefactual risk factor theories (adapted from Case and Haines, 2009: 102–3)
Source: Haines, K. and Case, S. (2009) Understanding Youth Offending: Risk Factor Research, Policy and Practice. *Cullompton: Willan.*

(see, for example, Farrington, 2007). This validity is increased by the integration of a range of explanatory influences, from the biological to the psychological to the sociological to rational choice and situational influences (see **Table 21.1**). An excellent example of the faith put in the validity of artefactual risk factor explanations is their application in the *Asset* risk assessment process conducted with all young people who enter the youth justice system (YJS) of England and Wales (see **What do you think? 21.2**). In other words, the ways that youth justice practitioners are expected to understand and explain offending of young people who enter the YJS is significantly shaped by artefactual risk factor theory (see Stephenson, Giller, and Brown, 2011).

In contrast to claims that artefactual risk factor theories provide valid, holistic understandings of offending, a number of methodological criticisms have been aimed at these theories; criticisms that could diminish the validity of their explanations and conclusions. For example, there have been psychosocial, deterministic, and reductionist biases to artefactual explanations of crime (see Haines and Case, 2015). Theories have privileged psychological and sociological factors (that is, psychosocial bias—see **Table 21.1**) over socio-structural issues such as poverty, unemployment, social/neighbourhood disorganisation, and economic instability (see Muncie, 2009). There has also been an overriding supposition that risk factors inevitably determine crime in the future (that is, deterministic bias—see **Table 21.1**) at the expense of examining the processes of criminalisation such as the potentially criminogenic influence of contact with the formal YJS due to the labelling of young people as 'offenders' (McAra and McVie, 2007). There is the further issue regarding the common-sense, simplified understandings of crime that typify artefactual risk factor theories and whether they have been *reductionist* by *over*simplifying risk into a quantified factor, thus dumbing down explanations of crime and washing away the complexity of how risk may be experienced and negotiated by young people (that is, reductionist bias). Of course, similar criticisms of psychosocial, deterministic, and reductionist biases could be levelled at the biological, psychological, and sociological theories promoted by positivism, but that does not make these criticisms of artefactual theories any less valid.

WHAT DO YOU THINK? 21.2

Risk-based assessment and intervention in the youth justice system

The artefactual Risk Factor Prevention Paradigm (RFPP) is the driver for understanding and responding to the behaviour of all young people who offend and enter the YJS of England and Wales. Since 2000, all young offenders (aged 10–17) who have contact with the formal YJS (that is, they are not diverted from it or given pre-court interventions) have been subject to a risk assessment called *Asset* which is completed by adult youth justice practitioners during interviews with the young person (see also **Chapter 9**).

Asset measures the likelihood (risk) that factors in different psychosocial areas of a young person's recent and current life (attitudes, emotions, thoughts, motivations to change, family, education, neighbourhood, lifestyle) will encourage reoffending in the future. *Asset* is a clear animation (making real, bringing to life) and application of artefactual risk factor theories, in particular, the criminal careers model (West and Farrington, 1973; see **Table 21.1**) because it measures a set of psychosocial risk factors and uses these measures to predict and prevent future offending. Youth justice practitioners use *Asset* to assign to a young person a risk score, which leads to them being rated as at high, medium, or low risk of future reoffending. This rating can influence their sentence and definitely determines the amount, frequency, and duration of intervention that they then receive from youth justice agencies. This process is known as the 'scaled approach' to assessment and intervention (see Stephenson et al., 2011) because the intervention that results from the assessment is scaled to the assessed level of risk. This artefactual risk focus dominates how we explain and respond to the behaviour of young people who commit crime in England and Wales; it is also popular in other western countries such as the US, Canada, Australia, and parts of Western Europe. So what do you think of it? Specifically:

- Is a risk-based approach the best, most valid, and most practical way to explain the criminal behaviour of young people in our society?
- What are the advantages and disadvantages of this approach theoretically and practically?
- Could artefactual risk factor understandings of youth crime be enhanced by the inclusion of any elements of other theories? If not, should they be replaced entirely by other theories? If so, what and why?

A major strength of artefactual risk factor theories, one very attractive to politicians and practitioners, has been their *reliability*—the ability of thousands of different studies to replicate findings and conclusions and thus support the central explanatory assumptions that risk factors predict later offending. Study after study over different times and places and populations has identified that exposure to psychosocial risk factors during childhood and adolescence increases the likelihood/probability/risk of offending behaviour at some point in later life (see Farrington, 2007). These reliable and replicable psychosocial risk factors are located within the risk domains of individual/psychological (for example, hyperactivity, impulsivity, lack of empathy), family (for example, lack of parental supervision, parents arguing, criminal siblings), school (for example, academic underachievement, disliking school, truancy), neighbourhood (for example, criminal friends, lack of community resources, easy availability of drugs), and lifestyle (for example, drug use, lack of positive activities). For sheer weight of replications, artefactual risk factor theories would seem to be the most reliable explanatory of crime, replacing social control theories as having produced the largest body of supportive research evidence (Kemshall, 2008).

However, remember your ABC. Closer examination could lead us to question exactly how reliable this body of studies has been in terms of content, design, and methods. Varying measures of risk factors have been employed (within or between studies), such as ratings scales of different sizes and dichotomous yes/no measures; all taken over varying measurement periods, such as in the past month, past year, over the lifetime, etc. Furthermore, these varying definitions and measures of risk factors have been linked to varying measures of offending (for example, non-offenders, self-reported offenders, young people identified as antisocial, convicted offenders, reoffenders). They have also been linked to different types of offending (for example, property crime, violent crime, lifetime offending, recent offending) and different definitions of offending, some of which are not actually offending at all, but broader categories such as deviance, delinquency, and antisocial behaviour. Artefactual research studies have used differing understandings of the risk factor–offending relationship—variously understanding risk factors as correlates, predictors, indicators, causes, and even symptoms of offending (see later in this chapter). **Table 21.1** illustrates how theories have evolved by prioritising different sets of risk factors over others—indicated by the evolution from biopsychosocial factors, to psychosocial factors, to psychosocial plus socio-structural factors. Therefore, artefactual risk factor theories have presented themselves as a unified, reliable explanatory movement (cf. Agnew, 2011), in broad agreement on the nature of what a risk factor is and how it relates to offending, but the research has been less reliable than claimed in terms of its working definitions and measures of its central concepts, the methods used to collect evidence, and the explanations of the risk factor–offending relationship that results.

The findings and conclusions from artefactual risk factor theories offer a degree of *practicality* beyond the other theories that have gone before them, particularly when they are targeted in practice through the RFPP, thus linking explanation with responses. Professor David Farrington has robustly championed the practicality of the RFPP since it was imported to the UK from the US in the 1990s, asserting that:

> The basic idea . . . is very simple: Identify the key risk factors for offending and implement prevention methods designed to counteract them. There is often a related attempt to identify key protective factors against offending and to implement prevention methods designed to enhance them.
>
> (Farrington, 2007: 606)

A key argument for the practicality of artefactual risk factor theories is that they identify the predictors of future reoffending, so they can be used to guide youth justice staff in how best to target their time, resources, and money (for example, on high-risk individuals, neighbourhoods, and crimes—see Baker et al., 2005). Consequently, the RFPP has gained popularity as a practical model for official (YJS) responses to youth offending across the western world, for example the use of the *Asset* risk assessment tool in England and Wales (see **What do you think? 21.2**; see also **Chapter 9**). Put simply, the explanations of crime clearly guide the responses to crime. However, there are certain problems with this claim to practicality. First, risk assessment tools are not necessarily very good predictors of crime. The *Asset* instrument, for example, accurately predicts whether or not a young person will reoffend in 67–9 per cent of cases (Baker et al., 2005), which is a higher predictive accuracy than similar tools in the adult criminal justice system. But what about the one-third of young people whose offending future is incorrectly predicted by *Asset*? They may be subject to excessive intervention that they do not necessarily need because they have been incorrectly judged as likely to reoffend, but they do not (that is, false positives). Conversely, they may not receive sufficient levels of intervention because there have been incorrectly judged as *un*likely to reoffend, but they do (that is, false negatives). Such disproportionate levels of intervention could be viewed as ineffective, inefficient, unethical, and inappropriate responses to crime due to a flawed explanatory model (Bateman, 2011; Paylor, 2011).

In explanatory terms, artefactual risk factor theorists may have been overconfident in their claims and conclusions. That these theories have become the dominant explanations of why crime is committed by young people and have guided policies and practices to tackle youth crime globally, indicates that this confidence is shared by a growing number of politicians and policymakers (Farrington, Kazemian, and Piquero, 2019; Stephenson et al., 2011). Is this explanatory confidence misplaced based on the methods employed to reach these deterministic conclusions? The explanatory basis of artefactual risk factor theories is that risk factors identified in childhood and adolescence predict crime in later life. A typical research design for artefactual risk factor studies is to measure a person's exposure to risk factors and the occurrence of offending behaviour over the same time period (for example, the past year), with little (if any) consideration of which occurred first in the person's life (this is known as temporal precedence). If we do not measure which comes first, then how can we support conclusions about the direction or nature of the relationship between risk factors and offending? Let us tease out the difficulties in establishing the risk factor–offending relationship with an example from a hypothetical **cross-sectional research** study that measures risk factors and offending over the past year:

- **Predictive relationship:** The central claim of artefactual theories is that risk factors predict crime. To illustrate this relationship, assume that during the measurement period, a young person experienced a series of risk factors at a particular time (for example, from January to March), after which they offended (for example, in July). In this case, it looks as if the risk factors predicted the offending, because they have temporal precedence. However, even if they predated offending, we cannot be definite (from statistical analysis alone) that the identified risk factors influenced the offending in any real way or that they were the only influences on offending. Something else may have happened before July that influenced the offending. At best, we can conclude that risk factors came first in a young person's life. At worst, that they were identified and measured first (for example, the young person may have also offended the previous year, but was undetected).

- **Interactive relationship:** A young person could experience certain risk factors (for example, experience family breakdown, temporary school exclusion) at a particular time (for example, January–March), then they offend (for example, in July). They may then experience exacerbated versions of the original risk factors or different risk factors (for example, going into care, permanent school exclusion) at a later point (for example, December), then offend again. In this case, risk factors and offending seem to interact in a kind of vicious circle. But again, how this relationship works in reality, beyond being identified via a statistical test, is less clear.

- **Symptomatic relationship:** Offending could predate and/or worsen the effects of exposure to risk. In our example, a young person could have offended in the period immediately before the measurement period, which could have created the risk factors (for example, led to family breakdown or school exclusion)—so the risk factors may actually be symptoms of offending, not predictors of it. But . . . if offending comes first, the resultant symptoms/experiences (for example, family breakdown) are not really risk factors in any predictive sense, as what they predict has already happened. They may, however, be risk factors for further offending at a later date.

- **No relationship:** It could be that risk factors and offending are totally unrelated. This is unlikely, but certainly possible. In our example, exposure to risk factors and offending behaviour may have occurred almost simultaneously or at least so close together that they did not affect one another. Maybe family breakdown, school exclusion, and offending were all the products of other, unmeasured risk factors or problems. We shouldn't assume a real-life, directional relationship (for example, predictive, causal) between risk factors and offending based on their co-occurrence in the life of a young person or even when temporal precedence can be established, especially when our evidence is based entirely on statistical relationships between quantitative factors. Longer term, qualitative measures are required for these theories to move beyond what risk factors and levels of offending are present and into explaining the how and why of the risk factor–offending relationship.

Figure 21.6 illustrates the potential for these different relationships between risk factors and offending outcomes. When risk factors are understood to 'predict' a crime, we mean that they increase the statistical likelihood of future offending, whereas 'influence' is a more vague term suggestive of risk factors contributing to offending behaviour to some extent.

It is arguably most valid to conclude that the risk factors identified by artefactual risk factor theories are correlates with offending—factors that have a statistical relationship with offending and have been present in the life of a person who has also offended at some point. However, correlates are not causes, neither are they necessarily 'predictors' of a later behaviour (offending) as they may occur at the same time as it, rather than before.

Bear in mind the points we raised in this section when looking at **What do you think? 21.3**.

Enhanced pathways risk factor theories

Although artefactual risk factor theories dominate contemporary explanations of (youth) crime, we would be oversimplifying the discussion of risk factor

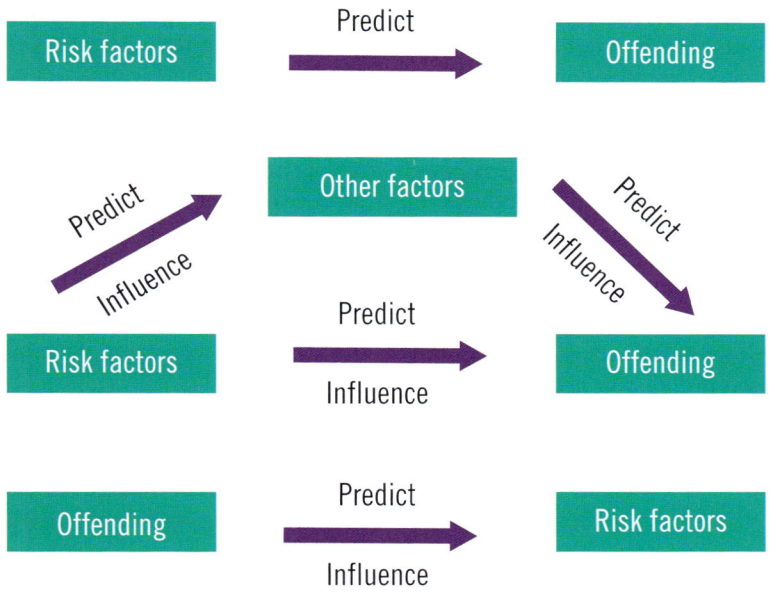

Figure 21.6 Different relationships between risk factors and offending outcomes

WHAT DO YOU THINK? 21.3

Explaining crime using quantified risk factors

Based on the previous discussions of the contested validity, reliability, and practicality of artefactual explanations, how would you assess the utility of this group of theories? Specifically:

- What do you think are the theoretical and practical advantages of understanding crime in terms of identifying risk factors?

- Does converting the potentially complex concept of risk into a numerical factor inevitably oversimplify it and/or is this a helpful process that enables us to target the key indicators of future crime?

- Does the emphasis on risk factors as predictors (statistical indicators of increased likelihood of later offending) rather than causes (factors with a direct, measurable influence on offending) give criminologists more flexibility in their explanations as they do not need to be as precise and definite about how these factors influence crime?

In other words, does the common-sense, practical nature of artefactual risk factor explanations allow us to forgive an element of overstatement about their rigorous methods and overconfidence about their conclusions?

theories if we were to end here. Theories of crime continually evolve through challenge, fresh research, new ideas, and refinements, processes reflected in the risk factor research movement. A new movement of what can be seen as enhanced pathways risk factor theories has gained momentum since the late 1990s and into the 21st century. This group of explanations has attempted to address the alleged explanatory and methodological weaknesses/limitations of artefactual risk factor theories, particularly their oversimplification of risk by converting it to a number ('factorisation'—Kemshall, 2008) and neglecting to elicit the qualitative understandings of those who experience risk (Case, 2006). The enhanced element, therefore, refers to viewing the traditional weaknesses of risk factor theories more as limitations of an otherwise valid explanatory framework (that is, understanding offending as the product of exposure to risk factors) that should be enhanced and improved rather than rejected. The pathways element derives from the explanatory emphasis on exploring and explaining (typically young people's) pathways into and out of crime. These pathways explanations tend to focus on between-school interactions between exposure to risk factors (measured in a positivist way) and personal constructions and understandings of these experiences (measured in an interpretivist way). Remember from **Chapter 15** that interpretivists reject the idea that complex social and human interactions can be measured and instead seek to understand behaviour by exploring individual experiences, perceptions, and meanings. Two progressive sets of enhanced pathways theories have emerged: the *Edinburgh integrated pathways theory* and *constructivist pathways risk factor theories*.

Edinburgh integrated pathways theory

The research team behind the 'Edinburgh study of youth transitions and crime' (D. J. Smith, Lesley McAra, and Susan McVie) have conducted several sweeps of data collection as part of their longitudinal study of over 4,000 young people—starting with a cohort of 12–17-year-olds and most recently when that cohort was aged 24–25 years old. The commonly abbreviated 'Edinburgh study' set out to produce a contemporary, integrated theory of youth crime that was 'not concerned with early childhood influences, but with transitions and personal transformations during adolescence and adulthood' (Smith and McVie, 2003: 169–70). By utilising a range of data collection methods (for example, **questionnaire**, interview, official statistics) from a range of participants (for example, young people, parents/carers, teachers), the study produced a holistic explanation of youth crime—the *Edinburgh integrated pathways theory*. Note that we are using this label for clarity of discussion, however the researchers have not so far named their theory. This theory explains young people's pathways into and out of crime as the result of interactions between psychosocial risk factors and socio-structural factors such as social controls in the community and physical environment, interactions with agencies of informal and formal social control such as the family, school, police, and the YJS. These interactions influence young people's pathways into/out of crime and their self-rated ability to navigate and negotiate these pathways. Therefore, the theory integrates positivist understandings of risk (factors) with interpretations of risk (experiences) and contextualises these by examining macro-level socio-structural influences. The relationship between risk and offending is framed as a complex, qualitative process rather than an oversimplified, quantitative/statistical artefact (France, 2008).

The synthesised, integrated pathways explanation enabled the Edinburgh researchers to 'understand the causes of youth crime and how offending emerges in the process of development from childhood to adulthood' (Smith and McAra, 2004: 14). The most important 'explanatory variables' (essentially risk factors, but the Edinburgh team appear to reject the term) for offending were:

- family-based—poor parental supervision, parent–child conflict;
- school-based—negative attitudes to school, poor relationships with teachers, misbehaviour;
- neighbourhood-based—social deprivation, unemployment, social disorganisation;
- peer- and lifestyle-based—gang membership, contact with the YJS in Scotland;
- individual-based—impulsivity;
- '**critical moments**' in teenage years—especially school exclusion.

A particularly notable finding was that 'repeated and more intensive forms of contact with agencies of youth justice may be damaging to young people in the long-term' (McAra and McVie, 2007: 333) due to their labelling effects and exacerbation of existing explanatory variables. The identification of system contact as a key explanatory variable contradicts the central premise of the RFPP—that risk factors should be identified and then targeted by official intervention. The Edinburgh study discovered that such risk-focused targeting is, in itself, criminogenic. In other words, official intervention can make offending worse.

The Edinburgh integrated pathways theory enhances the explanatory utility of risk factor theories by adopting a broader theoretical perspective and by measuring more areas of risk through the use of multiple research methods (Tashakkori and Teddlie, 1998). The psychosocial bias of artefactual theories is addressed through a focus on socio-structural factors and system effects. In addition, the longitudinal design and complex statistical analysis employed help to identify the temporal precedence of certain risk factors over offending, complemented by interpretivist, **qualitative research** to fill the explanatory gap (the 'black box'—see **Chapter 22**) between exposure to risk factors and offending behaviour (Pawson and Tilley, 2004). As such, traditional risk factor theories are enhanced in terms of their ability to explain the nature of risk factor–offending relationships at different stages of life.

Constructivist pathways risk factor theories

Two groups of integrated studies have enhanced risk-based explanations of (largely youth) crime by considering in detail how young people 'construct' (build, understand, create) their experiences of risk. These constructions influence how they experience, navigate, and negotiate risk and their pathways into and out of crime (see also Sampson and Laub, 1993 in **Table 21.1**). These two main **constructivist** risk factor studies are: *Pathways into and out of crime* (see France and Homel, 2007; Hine, 2005) and the *Teesside studies* (see MacDonald and Marsh, 2005; Webster et al., 2004).

'Pathways into and out of crime: Risk, resilience and diversity' (Hine, 2005) is a partnership of five longitudinal studies in the UK. The studies explored how young people construct, negotiate, and understand their experiences of risk factors and their pathways into/out of crime, with a particular focus on the social processes that mediate (influence, intervene, interfere with) these pathways. The five studies focused on: young people in youth offending teams and pupil referral units (Hine et al., 2007); black and Asian young people (Haw, 2007); young people with a parent in prison (Walker and McCarthy, 2005); young people's social capital or social and material resources (Boeck et al., 2006); and the role of risk in substance misuse by young offenders (Hammersley et al., 2003). The Pathways studies identified 'substantial differences between the reality of their [young people's] everyday experiences and the theory presented within the dominant current policy framework for interventions' (Hine, 2006, in Case and Haines, 2009: 144). The dominant current policy framework in this case was heavily influenced by artefactual risk factor theories and the RFPP and prioritised risk-focused interventions in the YJS of England and Wales.

The theory that emerged from the Pathways studies is risk-based, but views risk as a complex and dynamic *process* that is actively experienced, constructed, resisted, and negotiated by young people. This contrasts with artefactual explanations of risk (factors) as experienced deterministically and helplessly by young people, who essentially hurtle uncontrollably towards offending outcomes once exposed to risk factors as a deterministic explanation that overlooks young people's ability to interpret and shape their own lives.

The constructivist pathways theory enhances risk factor explanations by examining the standard psychosocial risk factors in artefactual theories, but giving equal significance to social factors and influences (for example, interactions, socio-structural, cultural, and historical factors) and to the qualitative voices of the young people whose behaviour is being explained. Like the Edinburgh study, the range of research methods used (such as interviews, questionnaires, official statistics), the range of participants involved (such as young people, parents, teachers, youth justice staff), and the range of factors examined has produced a more holistic version of a risk factor theory (France and Homel, 2007). The resultant theory seems to offer a more holistic, valid, and up-to-date explanation of crime due to its broader focus on qualitative measures of risk processes over longer periods (not single measurement periods) and the detailed integration of young people's views, perspectives, and experiences of these risks as a vehicle to explaining the risk factor–offending relationship.

The Teesside studies conducted in north-east England focused on how young people construct risk and their experience of risk factors in particular socio-cultural contexts such as living in a socially deprived neighbourhood, being from an ethnic minority, and being a member of a lower social class. Three biographical, interview-based studies make up the Teesside trilogy: *Snakes and ladders: Young people, transitions and social exclusion* (Johnston et al., 2000); *Disconnected Youth: Growing up in Britain's poorest neighbourhoods* (MacDonald and Marsh, 2005); and *Poor transitions: Young adults and social exclusion* (Webster et al., 2004—published second but conducted last). *Snakes and Ladders* examined the lives of 98 young people aged 15–25 and focused on their social class and ethnic background; *Disconnected Youth* studied 88 young people aged 15–25 and focused on neighbourhood; *Poor Transitions* followed 34 original members of the other study samples into adulthood (aged 23–9). The theory that resulted from the Teesside studies explained crime as a result of interactions between 'rough approximations' of psychosocial risk factors (for example, dislike of school, truancy, single-parent family, no educational qualifications, traumatic life, domestic violence, parent in prison, difficult parental divorce, living in care) and socio-structural barriers to success (for example, socio-economic dependence, lack of employment opportunities, low wages, poverty).

The most influential socio-structural barrier in the Teesside context was the influx of cheap heroin into the neighbourhood. The researchers also identified 'unpredictable critical moments' in young people's lives (for example, experiencing rape, suffering a road accident) that could influence their future vulnerability or resistance to risk factors. The authors of the Teesside studies concluded that the extent and nature of the socio-structural risks identified:

> could not have been predicted by artefact-based approaches that neglect historical, socio-economic and geographical context . . . [and] that the relationship between risk factors and offending is complex and multifaceted rather than unproblematically causal and predictive, as depicted in traditional risk factor research.
>
> (Webster et al., 2004, in Case and Haines, 2009: 149)

The explanatory utility of the Teesside studies is inevitably limited by their narrow focus on explaining crime amongst one specific sample in one specific neighbourhood in the UK at a specific time. However, the theory that emerges moves beyond the psychosocial, deterministic, and reductionist biases of artefactual risk factor theories by incorporating socio-structural focuses, examination of critical life moments, qualitative interpretations of risk, and, perhaps most importantly, the importance of context in shaping how young people experience and construct (understand, negotiate, respond to) risk. Perhaps this enhanced form of risk factor theory emerged precisely because of the self-imposed limitations of the Teesside studies, in the sense that the researchers limited their ambitions to an intensive focus on explaining in detail the behaviour of a small group of people in a specific context. The Teesside studies have conducted research and produced a theory that was never intended to be replicable, generalisable, universal, or deterministic in quantitative terms—it was deliberately limited in focus. The result is a multifaceted and sensitive explanation of crime in a specific neighbourhood over time based on how risk is constructed by context and by young people's active experiences and responses to it.

Evaluating enhanced pathways risk factor theories

The pathways-focused theories from Edinburgh and Teesside have offered broad, wide-ranging explanations of (youth) crime, enhancing the risk-based explanations of their artefactual counterparts. Enhanced pathways theories have integrated measures of psychosocial risk factors with socio-structural factors and consideration of young people's personal understandings and constructions of how risk factors interact with one another, how they are shaped by context, and how they are experienced by young people. It could be argued, therefore, that these enhanced forms of integrated risk theories are more valid than artefactual alternatives because they incorporate more factors or influences into their explanations and are the products of more personalised, meaningful research with the very people whose behaviour they are trying to explain (France and Homel, 2007). This approach could be viewed as a more appropriate, open-minded, and ethical way of researching and developing theories—asking young people for their own interpretations (whilst always maintaining **reflexivity**—see **Chapter 4**) and considering multiple influences on their lives at the micro-, meso-, and macro-levels.

These enhanced risk factor theories do, however, retain the notion of risk as their central explanatory concept. Whilst this risk focus moves explanations away from potentially more invalid discussions of *causes* (see **Chapter 22**) and onto understandings based on predictors, the concept of risk is also problematic on theoretical, methodological, and ethical grounds (Case and Haines, 2015; see also Muncie, 2009). Explaining young people's lives as collections of risks, however these may be resisted and negotiated, dictates that we as criminologists understand young people's lives as risky and dangerous; as bundles of deficits, flaws, and weaknesses. Whether adults intervene through applying the RFPP or whether young people are capable of intervening themselves (as indicated by enhanced pathways risk factor theories), we are still compelled to understand and explain crime largely as the result of a personal failure to resist risk. This, of course, illustrates the reductionist self-fulfilling prophecy of many theories—we only look in certain ways at certain factors and inevitably generate only particular explanations, but not others.

21.5 Conclusion

Taking a broad overview of the integrated theories that we have covered in this chapter, it is possible to (over)simplify them into two dichotomous groups of positivist theories and enhanced pathways risk factor theories (see **Figure 21.7**).

Group one (positivist theories) has tended to quantify the causes and predictors of crime in order to identify statistical relationships between psychosocial factors and offending at one point in time. Group two (pathways theories) has used more qualitative research methods to identify personal understanding, dynamic processes, and interactions between psychosocial factors and a broad range of socio-structural factors, along with cultural, historical, and economic factors. Group one has produced purportedly generalisable, universal explanations of crime through research with large groups; group two has preferred detailed, nuanced (non-generalisable) explanations

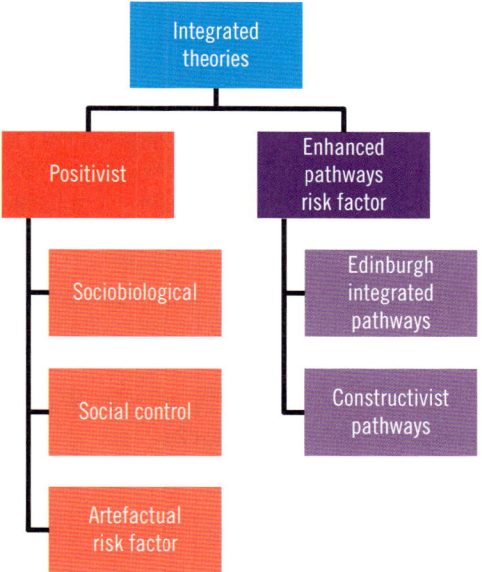

Figure 21.7 Illustrating the relationship between integrated theories of crime

of crime committed by smaller, specific groups in specific places. Both groups have attempted to explain crime by integrating a range of theories from within schools (for example, different positivist theories) and between schools (for example, blending positivism with constructivism).

In this chapter, we have analysed and evaluated the explanatory and practical utility of integrated theories of crime. We have demonstrated that explaining crime by exploring a broader range of possible factors, influences, and interactions has increased the potential of integrated theories to be valid (in the sense of appropriate, relevant, comprehensive, and up to date) compared to outdated and narrower single factor theories. However, integrated theories suffer similar problems of *androcentrism*, *ethnocentrism*, *reductionism*, and *supposition*. These issues all raise questions as to exactly what and how much we can realistically expect theories to be able to explain. Just how feasible is it to pinpoint the factors, influences, and processes that explain all crimes at all times by all kinds of people? Exactly what can we expect from criminologists and criminology in terms of explaining crime? Let's see in **Chapter 22**.

SUMMARY

After reading this chapter and working your way through its features you should now be able to:

- Place integrated theories of crime in the context of the historical development of criminological theories

We argued that the foundation for theoretical development in criminology has been the single theory explaining crime in a specific way. A common limitation of these single theories of crime has been their exclusivity—a single-minded focus on a specific way of explaining crime, to the exclusion of others as potential contributors to their explanations, or as potential alternative explanations of crime. However, many theories have developed by acknowledging and integrating concepts and arguments from other theories. These integrated explanations have been within theory, within school, and between schools.

- Analyse and evaluate integrated positivist theories of crime in explanatory and practical terms

We divided integrated positivist theories into two main groups: sociobiological and social control. Sociobiological theories integrate biological factors with sociological and environmental influences, whilst social control theories integrate psychological, sociological, and structural factors. We argued that these hybrid theories of how different factors interact and interrelate to create crime are more holistic and less subjective and reductionist than single factor theories, thus they may have more explanatory utility and validity. However, integrated positivist theories retain elements of subjectivity and reductionism, privileging certain explanations over others, tending to focus on male and westernised groups (so demonstrating androcentrism and ethnocentrism), and being unable to provide a universal explanation of crime.

- Analyse and evaluate integrated risk factor theories of crime in explanatory and practical terms

We divided integrated risk factor theories into two main groups: artefactual and enhanced pathways. Artefactual theories identify quantifiable psychological and sociological risk factors that purportedly predict crime in the future, whilst enhanced pathways theories integrate socio-structural factors and personal constructions with these risk factors in order to understand individual pathways into and out of crime. We explored the advantages of risk factor theories, notably their superior practicality, validity, reliability, evidence base, and explanatory utility when compared to traditional single theory explanations. However, we also identified several explanatory and methodological limitations, particularly in terms of a degree of psychosocial bias, reductionism, and determinism (mainly within artefactual theories).

Test your understanding of the chapter's key points by attempting the self-test questions on the **online resources** at www.oup.com/he/case2e

REVIEW QUESTIONS

1. Which single-factor explanations of crime have dominated the evolution of criminological theory?
2. Identify two main groups of integrated positivist theories of crime.
3. Identify two main groups of integrated risk factor theories of crime.
4. What explanatory advantages do integrated theories have relative to single-factor theories?
5. Could integrated theories be limited in explanatory utility in similar ways to single-factor theories?

Access the **online resources** at www.oup.com/he/case2e to check your answers to the review questions.

FURTHER READING

Case, S. P. (2018) *Youth Justice: A Critical Introduction.* **London: Routledge.**
This text written by Steve Case, one of this book's authors, provides a detailed explanation and critique of all forms of integrated theories and their links to policy and practice.

Farrington, D. P., Kazemian, L., and Piquero, A. (2019) *The Oxford Handbook of Developmental and Life-Course Criminology.* **Oxford: OUP.**
A handbook offering comprehensive explanations, from the risk perspective, of the development of offending by young people, developmental correlates and risk factors linked to offending, transitions and turning points in young people's lives, and the use of developmental interventions.

Hirschi, T. (1969) *Causes of Delinquency.* **Berkeley, CA: University of California Press.**
Quite simply one of the seminal, must-read criminological texts. Hirschi provides a detailed and accessible, yet challenging, overview of his groundbreaking social control theory.

Hopkins Burke, R. (2018) *An Introduction to Criminological Theory* (5th edn). Abingdon: Routledge.
This is a very well-known and popular criminological theory text that offers an ideal supplement to the theory chapters in this book. It is comprehensive, clearly written, informed, and research-based.

 Access the **online resources** to view a wealth of extra information relating to your study of criminology, including self-test questions, answers to review questions, and links to other resources that will help you enjoy and fulfil your potential within your studies.
www.oup.com/he/case2e

CHAPTER OUTLINE

22.1	Introduction	670
22.2	Thinking about and defining causes of crime	671
22.3	Exploring the causes of crime in research	674
22.4	Explaining crime by identifying causes	679
22.5	Responding to crime	680
22.6	Chaos theory	686
22.7	Conclusion	687

22

Searching for the causes of crime

KEY ISSUES

After studying this chapter, you should be able to:

- explore the reasons why we search for the causes of crime in criminology, with particular focus on positivism;
- discuss the definitional issues relating to the concepts of crime and causes that influence the valid and reliable identification of the causes of crime;
- assess the implications of these definitional and explanatory issues for producing valid and reliable responses to crime;
- evaluate the feasibility and necessity of identifying the causes of crime.

22.1 Introduction

Exploring the causes of crime has been a high priority within criminology as the main way of explaining crime, and of informing responses to crime. In this chapter we will consider why the causes of crime have been so central to work in criminology.

The explanatory theories that we discussed throughout this exploring crime part of this book have focused mainly on the aetiology of crime—the origins of crime explained in terms of its causes. Classical theories (see **Chapter 15**) and right-realist theories (see **Chapter 20**) assert free will and rational choice as the causes of crime. Positivists identify biological, psychological, and sociological causes of crime, as do integrated positivist theories and risk factor integrated theories (see **Chapters 16** and **17**). More recently, critical criminology (see **Chapter 18**) and left realism (see **Chapter 20**), along with some integrated theories like enhanced pathways risk factor theories, have explored qualitative processes and interactions (for example, criminalisation, the 'square of crime'), rather than the influence of single factors (see **Chapter 21**). However, these processes and interactions are still viewed as somehow causing crime (see **Chapter 4**). Whether different criminological theories and theorists choose to understand the role of these factors as predictive (that is, increasing the likelihood of future offending), indicative (that is, identifying that offending may be present or may follow), influential (that is, having some undetermined influence upon offending behaviour), or interactive (that is, in a reciprocal relationship with offending), the main goal of these theories is to identify the causes of crime or the causal mechanisms leading to crime. Consequently, many explanatory theories in criminology have been developed and utilised as if they have unquestionably been able to identify the causes of crime.

From the very start of this book, we have looked at criminology as a three-part process consisting of definitions, explanations, and responses to crime. Once the earliest criminologists had defined crime and different types of crime (see **Chapter 2**), there followed a pressing need to explain such crime. The pressure to explain crime has come largely from politicians, policymakers, practitioners, the media, the general public, and academics themselves. It has never gone away; if anything, it has increased as the concept of crime has become more diverse and problematic in the political sphere and public eye.

Take a look at **What do you think? 22.1** for some questions which encourage you to think about the context of this chapter.

Arguably the most important reason for wanting to explain crime(s) (beyond simple academic and human curiosity) is so that we as criminologists can understand it better and respond to it appropriately through prevention activity, punishment, rehabilitation, policy and practice, and further academic research. If we are able to better understand crime, we are able to respond to it in more effective ways. But in the spirit of ABC (*Always Be Critical*—see **Chapter 1**), it is important to first ask some key questions.

- Why do criminologists prioritise the identification and exploration of causes, and to a lesser extent, causal mechanisms, as their explanatory gold standard?
- Why are causes rated more highly and assigned a greater explanatory power than other potential modes and mechanisms of explanation (for example, predictors, indicators, influences)?

In this chapter, we will explore how we might find the answer to both questions in the dominance of positivism in criminology. In the spirit of our ABC mindset, we will take an analytical, critical look at the issues of prioritising causes and the dominance of positivism. We take a rather different approach to other chapters in this part, in that the whole chapter is like an evaluation section on what we have learnt so far. We aim to show that the strong confidence in the methods used by positivists, and in the importance placed on searching for causes, has taken the attention of criminologists away from their possible flaws and limitations as an explanatory tool. At times, we will offer quite a strong rejection of certain aspects of positivism, but we are not suggesting that you reject positivism (and the conclusions drawn from it). Instead, we hope to help you develop a critical mindset and encourage you to analyse and evaluate the criminological knowledge that you read throughout this book and in other books and articles. You may well disagree with the arguments we make in this chapter (or anything you read as part of your studies), and we welcome this debate, providing that you are able to evidence, support, and justify your opposition. We aim to provide you with the skills to critically analyse both the dominant theories in criminology (as we do in this chapter) and, indeed, critically analyse the critiques.

Our discussion and critique of some of these theories draws on many of the topics that we discussed in **Chapter 4**, particularly those relating to how criminological knowledge is produced. If you feel a bit unsure about some of the key words we use when we discuss theory, or would more generally like to refresh your understanding of how criminology produces knowledge, feel free to go back to **Chapter 4** and reread our discussion there before you dive into this chapter.

WHAT DO YOU THINK? 22.1

Why search for the causes of crime?

- Why do you think that so many criminologists over so many years have prioritised the identification of the causes of crime over other potential ways of explaining crime?

- Do you think that the concept of causes has any explanatory or practical advantages over other forms of explanation, such as talking in terms of the predictors, indicators, drivers, and influences related to crime?

22.2 Thinking about and defining causes of crime

We will start the chapter by considering how criminologists understand crime and the causes of crime. We'll first compare interpretivism with positivism as ways of exploring and thinking about crime. We will then consider the tricky issues of how to define crime, how to define causes of crime, and how these problems make the task of searching for the causes of crime a very difficult one.

Explaining crime using interpretivism and positivism

The evolution of explanatory theories in criminology been dominated by positivism, which pursues an **epistemology** (theory of knowledge generation) based on gathering data in the social world to form the basis of universal laws of behaviour (see also **Chapter 4**). Positivism also pursues an **objectivist ontology** (theory of how to understand reality) that the real world consists of undeniable facts that can be objectively measured. Positivism has dominated criminological research and knowledge generation since the heyday of Lombroso (see **Chapter 16**). In this sense, the hybrid discipline of criminology is perhaps closer to the discipline of psychology than sociology.

Traditionally, sociologists have given equal consideration in their research methods and theory generation to **interpretivism**, the opponent of positivism. Interpretivist epistemology asserts that knowledge is generated internally within the person (in the mind and consciousness), so relies on how people experience their worlds and make them meaningful. Therefore, there are no universal facts or truths, but rather subjective, dynamic, and personalised constructions of phenomena in the social world. The accompanying ontology is *constructionism*—arguing that reality is created by the individual through their social interactions, personal experiences, and **cognitive** understandings of these interactions and experiences. For interpretivists, perception is reality. Accordingly, interpretivists argue that social research should be qualitative in order to explore behaviour from these epistemological and ontological bases. **Figure 22.1** sets out the central characteristics of interpretivism when compared to positivism.

Methodologically, positivists apply the **empirical** research methods of the natural sciences, particularly experiment and controlled observation, to the study of human behaviour in the social world. Consequently, positivism prioritises **quantitative** forms of criminological research that generate numerical data (for example, statistics, ratings), that quantify social phenomena (for example, crime, personal experiences) and that search for statistical relationships between these phenomena (see Bryman, 2021).

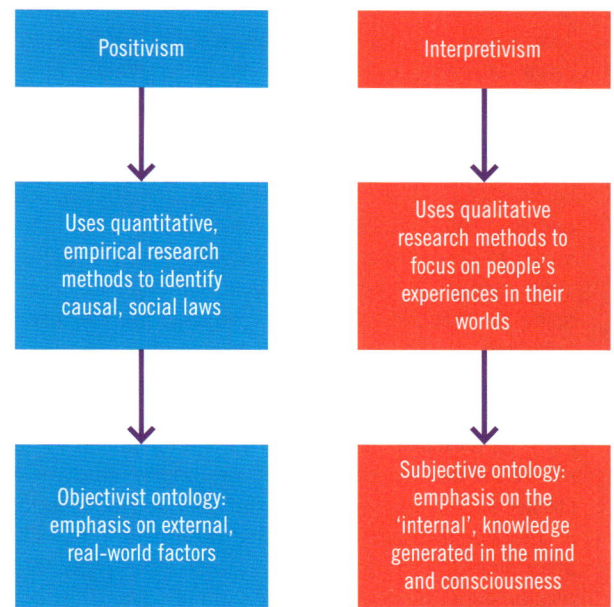

Figure 22.1 An illustration of the different characteristics of positivism and interpretivism

Prioritising causes as vehicles for explanation in criminology can be viewed as the product of a **self-fulfilling prophecy**, itself caused by: subjectivity that social scientific methods should be the priority for criminology, **supposition** that causes are the preferable and most valid tool to explain crime, and study, notably the dominance of positivist methods and conclusions—possibly at the expense of detailed **reflection** and critique (see **Chapter 4**).

In the spirit of this book's objective to make criminology more accessible and less complex, in **Conversations 22.1** we see a short section of a piece of criminological writing, adapted from a chapter in an edited text entitled *Applying Complexity Theory*. In this piece, the author discusses some of the drawbacks of positivism and the arguments that other criminologists have made against this way of approaching research. As you read, have a think about what you have learnt about these theories so far and whether you had considered these arguments against positivism yourself. For a detailed discussion of the sociological challenge to the dominance of positivist thought in British criminology, see also Paul Rock's chapter 'The foundations of sociological theories of crime' in the latest *Oxford Handbook of Criminology* (Liebling et al., 2017).

CONVERSATIONS 22.1

The hegemony of positivist criminology

with author **Steve Case**

> positivism has long ceased to be a viable option, but the message has still not got through to some researchers.
>
> (Robson, 2015: 163)

Positivism's domination of explanation in criminology is at its peak due in large part to the popularity of the experimental method, consistent support from high profile criminologists (for example, Lawrence Sherman, David Farrington) and continued endorsement by large official funding bodies in the UK (for example, Home Office, Ministry of Justice, Economic and Social Research Council) and the USA (for example, Office of Juvenile Justice and Delinquency Prevention). Consequently, positivist theory and research has a far greater influence on crime prevention and reduction policy than any other criminological theory and form of research. Positivist research privileges **empiricism**—validating knowledge by using scientific method, particularly experiment, but also survey (Williams, 2006) as the main routes to acquiring criminological knowledge. The positivist method is seen as the gold standard for developing the evidence-base in criminology and has been animated by experimental criminology, the randomised controlled trial, survey research and statistical testing of relationships between variables and measures of offending. The **reductionism** (reducing a complex process to a simple concept in order to measure it more easily; see **Chapter 5** for a reminder) and simplicity of experimental and survey methods has enabled positivism to identify deterministic (causal), stable, predictable, replicable relationships between variables and offending (Robson, 2015). However, these conclusions have been highly dependent upon the researcher's ability to control complex behaviours, systems and situations (Hope, 2009). The explanations of crime that have emerged from positivist research have been underpinned by two central principles or suppositions:

1. **Linearity**—that there is a direct, straight line, deterministic, causal relationship between variables and offending behaviour—basic cause and effect.

2. **Proportionality**—that increases of a given size in these (causal) variables produce increasing in offending behaviour of the same size/proportion.

Critics have attacked positivist theory and research for being reductionist, using narrow methodology, and debatable representations of reality (for example, Mears and Cochran, 2019; Pycroft and Batollas, 2014; Case and Haines, 2014; Young, 2011; Goldson and Hughes, 2010). Positivist researchers have also been accused of overstating the **validity** and utility of the research findings that inform their explanations (see Robson, 2015; Case, 2015; Pycroft and Bartollas, 2014; France and Homel, 2007) and for assuming an invalid level of control over the real world variables that they study (see Young, 2011; Bateman, 2011; Case, 2007). Some critics who promote *chaos theory* have also challenged the validity of positivism's claims to be able to identify linear and proportional relationships between causes and offending behaviour (see the chaos theory section later in this chapter; see also Robson, 2015; Case, 2015; Young, 2011).

Adapted from Case, S. P. and Haines, K. R. (2014) 'Youth justice: From linear risk paradigm to complexity' in A. Pycroft and C. Bartollas (eds) Applying Complexity Theory: Whole Systems Approaches to Criminal Justice and Social Work

Explaining crime as a dynamic social construction

A major problem with identifying the causes of crime is that criminologists cannot seem to agree on what they understand or mean by either 'causes' or 'crime'—the two concepts central to this entire exercise. Both of these criminological concepts are typically understood from a positivist perspective as objective facts, yet both are arguably interpretivist **social constructions**. This argument implies that positivism may be an invalid or less valid tool (at least when used on its own) for exploring and explaining crime and its causes, especially if searching for universal causes that apply to all crimes at all times by all kinds of people.

We have already discussed the difficulty of defining what counts as crime and the extent to which this idea is socially constructed (see **Chapter 2** for a detailed discussion of this issue). The concept of crime, which is the foundation and centrepiece of the study of criminology, should be permanently written in inverted commas—indicating that it is dynamic, contested, and contingent on the historical period, **culture**, or demographic characteristics of those people socially constructing the concept of crime. The implication here is that searching for and pinning down the causes of this free-floating, shape-shifting, and highly subjective behaviour(s) that sits within these inverted commas is somewhere from extremely difficult to practically impossible—causes that at any given point in any given place may change in definition, may be the subject of disagreement, or may not even exist! (See **What do you think? 22.2**.)

Following the **What do you think? 22.2** exercise, you may think that there is still plenty of explanatory mileage in searching for the causes of crime—albeit a dynamic and more restricted definition of crime that may not be applicable to everyone, everywhere, every time. The alternative is to become so staunchly interpretivist and constructionist that we abandon the idea of any form of measurable reality existing external to the human mind and we give up entirely on trying to explain, respond to, or change any aspect of the social world. Surely there is hope—enough potential similarity and overlap between individual experiences, perceptions, and meanings to make the search for explanations (though not necessarily causes) worthwhile?

Criminologists could, perhaps, limit themselves to a more valid search for the causes of crime(s) committed at specific times in specific places—a temporally specific, time-limited notion of causality that is also sensitive to the type of crime being explained and to the cultural and country context. That is not to say that the identified causes of crime(s) at a specific time in a specific place could not and should not be applied to crimes at other times (for example, new crimes that emerge later in time, such as **cybercrime** (see **Chapters 6** and **14**)) in other places (for example, in different cultures and contexts). The overriding argument is that we should guard against the unhelpful supposition that certain causal explanations need to be generalisable and universal, or in fact that they *are* generalisable and universal.

Instead, we as criminologists should conduct open-minded and reflective research to test and develop more valid explanations of crime. By acknowledging

WHAT DO YOU THINK? 22.2

Identifying the causes of a chameleon concept

As we've just discussed, some criminologists argue that it is virtually impossible to work out what the causes of crime are, given that the definition of crime is so changeable. Given the many difficulties involved in trying to identify the causes of crime, it might seem tempting to give up now and move to the next chapter, but that is not in the spirit of the ABC mindset. Criticality is really important, but it should be as much a tool for progressing arguments, theories, debates, and the practical utility of criminology as it is a tool used for undermining and rejecting them. We should always try to be progressive and forward thinking in our critique, not simply reactionary against the past. With that in mind, why do you think the issue that the effect (crime) in the cause-and-effect relationship we are trying to identify here is so changeable and volatile and difficult to define? Specifically:

- Should we abandon our search for the causes of crime on the basis that we can never agree or be certain about what crime actually is? If so, what is our alternative? (Maybe have a quick peek at **Chapter 23** for some ideas.)

- If we accept that crime is difficult, but not impossible, to define, what are the benefits of searching for its causes?

- What type of constraints and restrictions should be placed on the interpretation of any results that claim to have identified the causes of crime? For example, think about the validity, reliability, and generalisability of practical utility. Also, consider the role of subjectivity, supposition, and study.

the constraints placed on our explanatory conclusions by the difficulties in defining and measuring crime, the result should be a series of (more) sensitive, flexible, valid, and practical explanations of crime. If the nature of crime can be dynamic and contingent, then perhaps we should produce explanatory theories that are similarly dynamic and contingent. In this way, we can use our ABC mindset in the pursuit of both theoretical advancements in criminology and the practical application of criminological knowledge. But regardless of what we understand by crime, should the foundation stone of these theories and practical applications be the search for and identification of the causes of crime?

Operationalising the causes of crime

In the previous section, we focused on the dynamic and socially constructed nature of crime when exploring the search for the causes of crime. Here, we move on to addressing the causes element of this crucial question. We should start by defining what we mean when we talk about and *operationalise* a cause of crime. Remember that to '**operationalise**' refers to defining something in terms of the measures used to examine it. Does causality assume a static, objective, quantifiable factor or mechanism that causes crime to occur at a fixed point in time or does causality relate to a dynamic, subjective, **qualitative** process that causes crime at multiple points in time in multiple different ways? Do we understand cause in the sense of a factor, variable, or mechanism making crime happen for the first time in a person's life? Conversely, does this cause bring about *re*offending and somehow change existing criminal behaviour, such as increasing its frequency (known as escalation), changing its nature (diversification, specialisation), encouraging its continuance (maintenance), or even promoting its ending (**desistance**)?

Does a cause make something new happen or does it change/affect an existing behaviour? Criminologists have neither decided nor agreed. Much like the uncertainty around how we understand and define the concept of crime, if we cannot agree on what we understand by the concept of cause or causation then it is difficult, if not impossible, to produce universal, valid, and reliable causal explanations of crime.

The culture of causality in explanatory theory

It is possible to argue that the majority of explanatory theories in criminology have laid claim to identifying the causes of crime. They may make these claims directly and explicitly, particularly if they are positivist. They may imply that their central explanatory factors, variables, predictors, influences, or mechanisms are somehow causal (for example, as do classical theorists and some integrated theorists)—implying causality through the degree of influence assigned to their explanations and by the definitiveness of the conclusions that targeting these explanatory areas can reduce and prevent crime (see Mears and Cochran, 2019). Indeed, one of the motivations to identify causes can be to inform appropriate criminological, criminal justice and legal responses to crime such as sentencing, crime reduction/prevention activity, and policy. Theorists may even slip into claiming that certain factors have a causal influence as a way of solidifying their own explanations, even where this causality has not been established—**artefactual risk factor theories** are especially prone to falling into this possibly inescapable confusion and omission (see Case and Haines, 2009). But remembering our ABC mindset—are the claims of experimental, positivist, and other fields of criminology that focus on causes valid? Classical theories have never been empirical, research-based explanations and have never claimed to be. The conclusions about the usefulness of free will and rational choice as explanations for crime (see **Chapter 15**) are based on subjectivity and supposition, not study. Free will and rational choice are therefore not causes in any experimental or empirical sense; they are the (possibly expert) guesses and conjecture of armchair theorists (remember from **Chapter 4** that 'armchair theorising' is a critique of theorists sitting in their comfy armchairs and trying to explain real life from a distance, using subjectivity and supposition instead of study). These arguments may be convincing, but they are not causal.

22.3 Exploring the causes of crime in research

Issues of control in scientific experiments

As we discussed in **Chapter 4**, experiments are at the heart of empirical research and positivist theories. The objective of any scientific experiment in the natural and social sciences is to identify universally applicable cause–and-effect relationships between variables—aspects of behaviour that change and that can be changed through manipulation. Scientists conduct experiments by attempting to manipulate some part(s) of the natural environment or behaviour of a living organism in order to measure the impact of this manipulation, such as any changes in the environment or behaviour. What is manipulated is known as the **independent variable** (IV) and what is measured is known as the **dependent variable** (DV).

The typical experimental **hypothesis** or research prediction is that manipulating the IV will either cause a new DV or cause a change in an existing DV—classic cause and effect. But how can scientists be so confident that their manipulating the IV was the only cause of any change (effect) in the DV and not other potentially unmeasured variables having an influence? Well, scientists aim to control for and protect against any additional unmeasured influences (known as **extraneous variables** or EVs) and in this way to isolate the influence of the IV. There are a number of ways to control EVs, for example using comparison groups, rigorous procedures, controlled conditions, standardised instructions, and statistical manipulation. Therefore, control is the bedrock of any experiment. **Figure 22.2** illustrates the classic experimental design, where the researcher manipulates the IV and controls the EV(s) in order to cause a measurable change/effect in the DV.

High levels of control may very well be possible and achievable in the natural sciences in the laboratory or other artificial environments. For example, if we want to observe and measure the effect when two chemicals are combined, we can mix them together in a test tube and stand well back. Provided that we can control for other extraneous influences on the resultant chemical reaction, such as any chemicals already in the test tube, contamination from the experimenter, or from pollutants in the air, we can be confident that mixing these two chemicals (IVs) causes the measured chemical reaction (effect on the DV). That is a valid conclusion—as far as we can tell it is true, accurate, and comprehensive. If we repeat the experiment in an identical manner with identical equipment several times, we should get the same results. That is a reliable conclusion—as far as we can tell it is consistent, replicable, and repeatable.

Now let us move our ABC discussion forwards with a hypothetical example of a criminological experiment. Say we wanted to test the **criminogenic** effects of excessive alcohol intake on young people. We could start with the idea that giving our sample group eight pints of lager each (the IV) is likely to encourage certain criminal acts (for example, violence, criminal damage, public disorder) compared to the behaviour of an equivalent group of young people who are not given alcohol. Let's put to one side the fact that it is highly unlikely that we could get ethical approval for this study, even if we sampled young people above the legal drinking age—we certainly would not get permission to break the law by using young people under the permitted age for alcohol consumption. However, if by some miracle we were granted permission, we could identify two groups of young people of equivalent gender, age, and physical size (we would say that they were matched samples in experimental terms). We could then administer the eight pints of lager to the **experimental group** and give the **control group** no lager. We then measure the behaviour of all of the young people and compare the behaviour of the experimental group with the behaviour of the control group. This comparison should allow us to conclude, provided that we have controlled for any extraneous variables, that any differences in the experimental group's behaviour (effects) were caused by our manipulation (that is, giving them lager—the IV).

But remember our ABC mindset—not just because of the unethical nature of this experiment and its potential to cause harm and suffering to the participants and to innocent outsiders (that is, we are essentially attempting to cause crime). As criminologists, we should *Always Be Critical* about the possibility of fully controlling for all potential extraneous variables that could affect the outcome of this experiment, even assuming that we have taken steps to thoroughly match the groups on key criteria (which does not always happen or is not always possible).

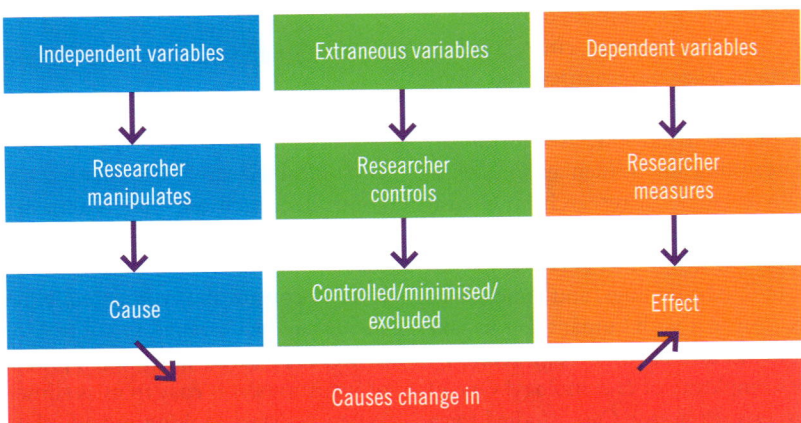

Figure 22.2 In an experimental research design, a researcher manipulates the independent variables and controls extraneous variables to cause a measurable effect in the dependent variables

For example, what if certain individuals within the comparison groups had not eaten for days (for example, were more vulnerable to the effects of alcohol) or were ill or injured or pregnant, thus introducing extraneous physiological variables? What if young people in the experimental group were highly traumatised or overexcited by the experimental conditions, thus introducing extraneous physiological and psychological variables? What if any of the subjects in either group had done the experiment before, thus introducing practical variables? They may have more capacity for lager as a result (practice effects) or less capacity if they did the experiment recently (fatigue effects). Therefore, can we ever control for the influence of extraneous variables?

Compared to experiments in the natural world, we can see that there are a number of issues with controlling for extraneous variables in the human world, such as:

1. Is it even less possible or impossible to control for extraneous variables when studying human behaviour, which we could assume to be more complex and psychologically driven than that of chemicals, plants, and animals in the natural world?
2. Conversely, is it possible to control human behaviour to such an extent that it becomes artificial and no longer represents the real-life, natural behaviour that we are trying to measure? This latter issue, the extent to which measured human behaviour in an experimental environment reflects real-world, everyday behaviour, is known as **ecological validity**.

Figure 22.3 Humans are complex organisms, interacting with other complex human organisms in numerous complex systems, so it is difficult to control all extraneous variables
Source: Grasko/Shutterstock

Ecological validity is a serious issue for the social sciences in general and for criminology in particular (see **Chapter 4**)—a problem to which we will return later in this chapter. But let us start with the first control problem. Is it feasible to fully control for all of the influences on human behaviour, even in an experimental situation? Human beings are complex organisms with complex systems of physiology. We interact with other complex human organisms in complex human systems such as societies, cities, communities, families, media, workplace, universities, and clubs, as represented in **Figure 22.3**. In other words, controlling all the influences on human behaviour is enormously more difficult than controlling for influences in natural science experiments, for example in research on chemicals, plants or animals (Mears and Cochran, 2019).

The problem of control has a potential effect on the validity of the measures, methods, findings, and conclusions relating to experimental research with humans. Let us take an example from the complex area of psychology, before we even get into the hyper-complexity of criminology! One of the authors of this textbook, Professor Case, studied for a MPhil (research-based postgraduate Masters degree) in applied cognitive psychology, which essentially means doing real-world (applied) research into how people's thought processes influence their behaviour. His research looked at the effectiveness of the 'Cognitive Interview' with primary schoolchildren—a popular police interview technique with eyewitnesses of crimes that was invented by Ronald Fisher and Ronald Geiselman in the US (for example, Fisher and Geiselman, 1992). The technique involves stimulating the eyewitness's memory using four mnemonic strategies:

1. Context reinstatement—encouraging the eyewitness to recall the environmental and personal contexts around the event they witnessed, such as where they were and how they felt.
2. Report everything—report every detail that they can, no matter how trivial they may think it is.
3. Different perspectives—recall events from the perspectives of other people, such as other eyewitnesses, the victim, and the offender.
4. Different orders—recall events from different starting points, such as forwards (start to finish), backwards (finish to start), and from the middle to the start and the middle to the end.

The findings are discussed in **Conversations 22.2**.

Steve's personal experience conducting applied psychological research demonstrates that even in a fairly controlled situation, there is a massive difference between the level of control over your ability to manipulate people's behaviour that you think you have, compared to the level of control that you actually have. In theory, experiments can be designed to control for many of the factors in Steve's research; however, in practice, even with the best of intentions, it is easy to miss some extraneous variables. When we start looking outside the artificial bubble that is the laboratory and into the real world where crime is

CONVERSATIONS 22.2

The experimental effectiveness of the Cognitive Interview

with author **Steve Case**

I conducted an experiment with two groups of primary schoolchildren aged 7 years and 11 years drawn from a number of schools across England and Wales. I showed each child a three minute clip from the film *Bugsy Malone*—a gangster film where the entire cast are children pretending to be adults. I then interviewed each child individually to assess how much detail about the clip they could recall. There were four study groups: 7- and 11-year-olds who received a basic interview (the two control groups) and 7- and 11-year-olds who received the Cognitive Interview (the two experimental groups). My hypothesis was that the Cognitive Interview (the IV) would significantly increase the number of items recalled from the clip (the DV) by the experimental groups compared to control groups. In other words, I predicted that the Cognitive Interview technique would cause an increase in eyewitness recall—which is exactly what I found. My conclusion as a devout (highly uncritical and unreflective) experimental psychologist was that the Cognitive Interview causes an improvement in eyewitness recall; a conclusion that was pleasingly in line with much similar research coming from the US and the UK. This approach, I believed, proved to me that my experiment had worked, which was good because the last thing that inexperienced researchers want is to have to explore and explain results that contradict the hypothesis, their colleagues, their preferred theory, or their expectations and preconceptions. But what about ABC? Was I able to control for all potential extraneous variables that could have influenced eyewitness recall beyond the IV? For example:

- Did I check whether any child had already seen the film clip? No.
- Had any of the children done this or a similar experiment before? I do not know, I did not ask.
- Had any child used any of these recall strategies before? Who knows?
- Had any subject been in an interview situation before? No idea.
- Were there any other pre-existing differences between the control and experimental groups, such as intelligence or academic ability, language issues, gender, emotional and physical state on experiment day, fatigue, vision or hearing problems? I do not know.
- Did I introduce any experimenter bias into the study, such as giving some subjects longer to recall than others, prompting or helping in any verbal or non-verbal ways, accepting answers at different levels of detail and accuracy? Probably, but I certainly did not control for this.
- Did I account for any recall strategies and other influences within the basic interviews I employed with the control groups? No I didn't.
- Did I conduct every interview in a similar way, so the study method had reliability? Probably not.
- Could I explain exactly how the Cognitive Interview enhanced memory in the experimental groups? No.

What a minefield! I was not a terrible researcher, nor was I necessarily even a terrible experimenter. What I was in this particular study was uncritical, unreflective, and overconfident in my conclusions about my ability to control for extraneous variables, the causal influence and effects of cognitive interview (IV), and the explanatory utility of the experiment as a research method. All of this affected the reliability of my methods and the validity of my findings and conclusions. But I have only realised this later in my career.

---

committed, defined, explained, and responded to, this control problem is magnified and amplified.

Issues of correlation and causation in survey research

There is a large contradiction at the heart of explanatory theory in criminology. For a subject dominated and shaped by positivist method and the search for causes, the explanatory theories that have emerged from empirical research (not from the armchair or based purely on subjectivity, supposition, experience, and anecdote), have been largely the product of survey methodology (**questionnaire**, interview, **focus group**), and to a lesser extent observation, rather than experimental method.

Positivist and *artefactual risk factor* theories, for example, have relied heavily on data obtained using the survey method, typically the identification of statistical relationships between quantified factors reported in questionnaires and interviews and quantified measures of offending behaviour (see **Chapter 4**). The statistical relationships identified between different factors and crime are correlational, not causal. Let us take an example from artefactual risk factor research (see **Chapter 21**), the dominant explanatory theory in the field of youth criminology. John Pitts (2003) asserts that this body of research has been unable to establish the 'causal primacy' of risk factors—whether they precede offending behaviour or whether they are symptoms or effects of offending behaviour. Even the most influential artefactual risk factor theorist, David Farrington, has confessed that 'it is difficult to decide if any given risk factor is an indicator (symptom) or a possible cause of offending' (Farrington, 2007: 605).

The statistical tests used (for example, ANOVA, t-test, Person's regression) are able to indicate that two factors/variables (supposed criminogenic influences and offending behaviour) either vary in statistically significant ways (in terms of their average/mean) or are correlated in statistical terms. However, statistical correlation does not necessarily indicate a relationship in real life—two factors may just coexist in the life of a person, with no tangible or measurable relationship, so statistical tests should not be used to presume real-world relationships. Furthermore, these tests are not designed to conclude that one variable (criminogenic influence) specifically causes, or causes a change, in the other (offending behaviour) and their results should not be taken to indicate causality (Robson, 2015; Case and Haines, 2014). Where this does occur, it leaves positivist researchers open to accusations of invalid extrapolation (extending their conclusions beyond the scope and capacity of the statistical test used), which has led Freedman et al. in the book *Statistical Models and Causal Inference*, to argue that 'an enormous amount of fiction has been produced, masquerading as rigorous science' (Freeman et al., 2010: 16).

Of course, survey questionnaires, interviews, and focus groups are also able to measure variables and collect data in qualitative, meaningful, personalised formats through the use of open-ended questions. Even then, however, there has been a preference for the quantification or 'factorisation' (Kemshall, 2008) of qualitative data through criminological survey research (see Farrington, 2003)—turning it into handy, usable numerical form (for example, counting the number of incidences of a particular phrase, opinion, or behaviour) for easier manipulation and analysis through statistical tests. Some researchers (Case and Haines, 2009; Young, 2011; Robson, 2015) argue that this oversimplifies the results and loses the complexity and ecological validity of the original measured data.

The criminological research underpinning many explanatory theories has strongly prioritised quantitative forms of data collection and analysis, in part based on an underpinning rationale that collecting and analysing significant amounts of quantitative data from very large samples offers advantages over qualitative methods in relation to scientific credibility. But statistical analyses of quantitative surveys are restricted to identifying correlations. As asserted repeatedly during the critique of artefactual risk factor theories in **Chapter 21**, correlation is not cause! See also **Controversy and debate 22.1**.

CONTROVERSY AND DEBATE 22.1

Correlation is not causality

Having reviewed the use of experiments and surveys to identify the causes of crime, it is useful at this stage to revisit some of the most influential (and controversial) explanatory theories in the history of criminology. In doing so, we are able to take a closer look at the nature of the relationships between criminogenic variables and offending that underpin their explanations.

Biological positivism

Lombroso's theory that physical defects (**stigmata**) indicated criminal tendencies; Goring's idea that criminality could be genetically inherited; and Sheldon's proposal that criminals have mesomorph physiques, were all correlated with crime identified through observation (see **Chapter 16**; see also Hopkins Burke, 2018). Later experiments have correlated (not manipulated and caused) physical measures such as sexual hormones, adrenal sensitivity, and brain injury with offending behaviour (see Jones, 2013). But correlation is not causality.

Psychological positivism

Freud's psychodynamic theory (based on interviews), Eysenck's extraversion–introversion scale (based on questionnaires), and Bandura's **social learning theory** (based on observations or quasi-experiments), for example, each correlated personality, extraversion, and imitation (respectively) with criminal behaviour or criminogenic attitudes (see **Chapter 16**). But correlation is not causality.

Sociological positivism

Merton's **strain theory** (based on observation and focus group), the Chicago School thesis (see **Chapter 17**, based on **secondary analysis** of **official statistics**, geographical mapping and analysis, and case studies), Cloward and Ohlin's **subcultural theory** (based on observations and case studies), and Hirschi's **social control theory** (based on questionnaires) identified correlations between deviant, non-conforming attitudes, social disorganisation, and crime (see **Chapter 17**; see also **Chapter 21**). But correlation is not causality.

Artefactual risk factor theories

Every theory discussed in **Chapter 21** has employed questionnaires, observation, and secondary data analysis of official statistics to identify the psychosocial risk factors in childhood and adolescence that are correlated with (in the sense of predictive of) some form of offending behaviour in later life (see also Case and Haines, 2009). But correlation is not causality.

The most influential, seminal studies in terms of the development of positivist and quasi-positivist (artefactual risk factor) theories have been largely survey-based and to a lesser extent based on observations (but less often experimental) and have tended to identify the correlates of crime. Arguably, any subsequent claims that these studies have identified the causes of crime, often the claims of other criminologists, politicians, policymakers, and journalists (not necessarily the original authors) have been invalid—based on misunderstanding, overstatement, or misrepresentation of the original research.

Many studies in criminology have measured the occurrence of criminogenic (crime-causing) factors and offending behaviour over the same time period, but few studies have been willing or able to tease out the temporal precedence of criminogenic factors over offending behaviour—in other words, establishing that they come first in a person's life and that the direction of any relationship with offending is therefore one-way (uni-directional).

Even studies that have attempted to tease out the temporal precedence of criminogenic factors have not conclusively proved, demonstrated, or even discussed the nature of the influence that these preceding (also known as antecedent) factors may have on the offending behaviour they are alleged to have caused or changed. So these factors may be experienced first in someone's life, but precisely how do they influence offending? We cannot conclude causation just because certain factors occur first. In fact, we should not conclude that someone has actually experienced a factor in any personal, meaningful, qualitative way simply because it has been measured as present in their life through official records, statistics, or the reports of others. Nor have survey studies attempted to or ever been able to control for the influence of extraneous variables (for example, the unmeasured sociostructural risk factors missing from so many psychosocial artefactual risk factor theories), because these studies were not experimental.

These survey studies arguably have more ecological validity than experiments due to their relative lack of control or attempted control over people's behaviour and responses (although survey questions can be highly leading and biased, as we know from **Chapter 4**). However, this same lack of control has introduced more subjectivity and supposition into the interpretation of survey results and has deprived studies of the ability to draw valid conclusions about the nature of the relationships between what they call explanatory factors and offending behaviour. The most valid conclusion possible from the majority of the studies that underpin explanatory theories in criminology should be that they have been able to identify correlates with crime, not the causes of it, but this does not stop criminologists (mainly positivists) and supporters of positivist research (such as policymakers and the media) from laying claim to causal explanations. But being able to conclude that certain factors are more likely than others to be measured in the lives of people who offend is a long way from identifying them as causes, and being able to explain exactly how they are causal. Do you see the invalidity here? The majority of explanatory studies claiming to have identified the causes of crime have relied on a research method that is unable to identify causality.

22.4 Explaining crime by identifying causes

It is useful to summarise where we are so far and what we (think we) know from this chapter. Defining crime is problematic because, as we have already discussed, it is a contested, ambiguous, and socially constructed concept. Defining cause is equally problematic for exactly the same reasons. Explaining crime through the identification of its causes, therefore, is highly problematic because of uncertainty over these two central concepts.

Further complicating the search for the causes of crime is the lack of reliability of the empirical research that claims to have identified these causes. Criminological research within and between schools has been inconsistent in terms of:

- the empirical research methods and designs used—for example, the degree of control researchers have exerted or have tried to exert over the potential influences on crime;
- the types of relationships (for example, causal, predictive, indicative, symptomatic) identified between potential influences and offending—for example, surveys can only identify correlations, not causes;
- the areas of potential influence investigated—for example, the common psychosocial bias in measured experimental and survey variables;
- the types of offending measured—for example, self-reported, official, general and specific forms of offending;
- the demographic characteristics of the populations sampled—for example, the typical, but not universal, bias towards investigating and explaining the behaviour of young males (**androcentricism**) (see also **Chapter 11**);
- the country/legal system in which the research was conducted—for example, the typical, but not universal, focus on exploring offending in the industrialised western world (see also **Chapter 13**);
- the historical period during which the research was conducted—for example, the application of outdated research findings to explanations of crime in modern contexts.

We are ultimately left with a body of explanatory research that is arguably less valid and less reliable than it may claim to be, due to its epistemological and ontological bias, inconsistent operationalisation of its central research concepts (crime and causes) and its variable research methods (Mears and Cochran, 2019). This causes major problems when we get to stage three of the triad of criminology (see **Chapter 1**): responding to crime. In other words, how can we promote desistance from crime by people who have offended (that is, crime reduction) and prevent the occurrence of crime if we cannot identify the alleged causes of crime? We will turn to this question in the next section.

22.5 Responding to crime

How can we respond appropriately and effectively to a behaviour or social construction if we cannot be sure what it is or how to explain it (causally) for a particular person or group in a particular place at a particular point in time? Before reading the rest of this section try focusing your own thoughts by looking at the questions in **What do you think? 22.3**.

WHAT DO YOU THINK? 22.3

How should we respond to crime?

Consider the arguments in this chapter that causal explanations of crime include a certain amount of supposition, which has a knock-on effect on their validity, reliability, and generalisability.

- How can we measure whether our responses work?
- How do you think we should respond to crime?
- Can we ever really identify the cause of crime that we can then target?

What works to prevent crime

The previous dominance of positivist methods within criminology and the associated search for causes has been re-animated in the 21st century by the growing popularity of experimental criminology, particularly in the US (see Weisburd et al., 2017; Sherman, 2009; Farrington, 2003). This popularity has been influenced and animated by the 'what works' experimental method of evaluating crime prevention programmes and responding effectively to crime based on empirical evidence (Gates et al., 2018; O'Shea, 2017). In 1996, the US Congress requested a comprehensive evaluation of the effectiveness of crime prevention programmes across the US that used 'rigorous and scientifically recognized standards and methodologies' and that emphasised 'factors that relate to juvenile crime . . . including "risk factors" in the community, schools, and family'. The resulting report, *Preventing Crime: What Works, What Doesn't, What's Promising* (Sherman et al., 1998) has become extremely influential globally in the field of criminology and policy and programme evaluation; its supporters praise it for applying high standards of robust evaluation as a measure of what works in crime prevention.

Sherman et al. (1998) used the 'Scientific Methods Scale' (invented by Cook and Campbell, 1979) to assess the methodological quality of individual crime prevention evaluations according to three methodological criteria: measurement error (the accuracy of measurement of variables), statistical power (the validity of the results of statistical tests), and, most importantly, control over extraneous variables that might influence the relationship between intervention and outcome (see Hope, 2005). The Scientific Methods Scale (SMS) consists of five levels of analysis, escalating in detail and rigour:

1. Correlation between the programme and level of crime measured at one point in time.
2. Comparing levels of crime measured before and after the programme, but with no control condition.
3. Comparing levels of crime measured before and after the programme in experimental and control conditions.
4. Comparing levels of crime measured before and after the programme in multiple experimental and control groups, controlling for extraneous variables.
5. As level 4, but with random assignment to experimental and control groups—the randomised controlled trial gold standard of evaluation methodology.

For a programme to be considered 'what works' as crime prevention by the SMS, we must be 'reasonably certain' that it prevents crime or reduces risk factors (that is, illustrating the dominance of the 'what works' approach and the Risk Factor Prevention Paradigm in the fields of youth crime prevention and youth justice particularly —see **Chapter 21**; see also YJB, 2017) in the social context in which it is evaluated. The intervention must have findings that are generalisable to similar settings in other places and times, in addition to at least two successful evaluations at level three on the SMS or above. The strong implication here, of course, is that these 'what works' programmes cause reductions in crime levels and risk factors by tackling the causes of crime. Programmes were categorised by Sherman et al. as 'what's promising' if the level of certainty regarding reduction of crime or risk factors was considered too low to support generalisable conclusions, but there was some empirical basis for predicting that they could attain this, plus they had at least one successful evaluation at level three of the SMS. Sherman et al. classified 'what doesn't work' as programmes they were reasonably certain failed or couldn't be demonstrated to prevent crime or reduce risk factors.

The SMS has been commended for promoting the utility of experimental research for evaluating the effectiveness of prevention and intervention programmes and for creating evidence to underpin responses to crime. Supporters also argue that the method can enable the identification of cause-and-effect relationships between programme measures and outcomes (see Gates et al., 2018; Weisburg et al., 2017; Sherman and Strang, 2004; Farrington, 2000), thus linking explanations with responses. The SMS and the concept of 'what works' has become extremely popular amongst policymakers, researchers, and evaluators keen to underpin crime reduction and prevention programmes with a scientific, empirical evidence base and to ensure that programmes demonstrate cost-effectiveness (see Applied Research in Community Safety, 2008). Without getting into yet more definitional ambiguities, regarding what we understand by prevention and reduction, or critiquing the conflation of these subtly different objectives (for example, preventing a behaviour from starting versus reducing an existing behaviour), let's put the explanatory utility of what works under the microscope in **Controversy and debate 22.2**.

CONTROVERSY AND DEBATE 22.2

The problem of the 'what works' explanation: what is in the 'black box'?

Despite the huge popularity of the 'what works' model of evaluating crime prevention programmes, it has been subject to several methodological and ethical criticisms (see Hope, 2009). As discussed, the 'what works' approach employs a positivist experimental methodology in order to physically and statistically manipulate (control) aspects of the environment in order to identify constant and predictable causal relationships between interventions (causes) and outcomes (effects). The most common criticism of the positivist 'what works' approach has been that the focus on interventions (inputs/causes) and reductions in offending (outputs/effects) has been unable or unwilling to examine mechanisms and processes of change that intervene between the two, and has neglected the potential influence of context (for example, socio-structural factors, situations, interactions/relationships) on programme implementation and outcomes (see Tilley, 2009; Hughes and Edwards, 2005; Pawson and Tilley, 1998; Braithwaite, 1993). Pawson and Tilley (1998) use the metaphor of a 'black box' (a complex device whose internal workings are hidden) in their critique of the approach. They argue that 'what works' makes assumptions as to what is going on in the black box between inputs and outputs. For example, in the black box between interventions and reduction in offending, there might be a person's *individualised* interpretations, perception, and decisions. The idea of 'what works' also bleaches out the complexities of context by treating them as variables to be controlled (Reddon et al., 2020; Applied Research in Community Safety, 2008). As a result, it can be difficult to understand *how* (for example, by what *mechanisms*) a particular intervention generates positive impacts.

The evidence-based, experimental, 'what works' evaluation model, therefore, is unable to evidence conclusively the relationship between programme implementation (causes) and programme outcomes (effects) because any explanation of this relationship is located within the black box of unmeasured and unexplored influence. Consequently, the 'what works' approach tends to fill this 'dark figure' of unexplored, imprecise, and indefinite explanation with supposition about how programmes cause changes in crime levels, or simply ignores the need for explanation altogether.

The dark figure of explanation in criminology

Supposition and lack of criticality are evident in explanatory theories in criminology, especially those populated by causes and the proxy indicators of causes. Proxy indicators (or proxy causes) are terms like indicators, influences, predictors, drivers, motivators, risk factors, and criminogenic factors. They are used by some researchers instead of 'causes' in order to suggest that the claims are more tentative, whilst still strongly implying some form of causal influence. To allow us to move forward with an exploration of causes, let's assume that there is a relationship, beyond chance or luck, between these alleged causes/proxy causes and offending behaviour and that we are somehow able to discern the direction of this relationship by identifying the temporal precedence of causes/proxy causes. Of course, these assumptions/suppositions go against the critical spirit of this book and the previous criticisms in this chapter, but it is always useful to contextualise, understand, and explore counter-arguments to yours in order to provide a fully informed perspective. However, despite the focus on causes, what the experimental method can struggle to tell us is anything about the nature of this influential relationship—*how* and *why* different factors influence crime. In other words, experiments can identify and measure potential causes and influences in a quantified way, but they cannot explain (they can only suppose and conjecture) how a cause works qualitatively and, thus, whether it is actually a cause at all. Extending the 'what works' critique of Pawson and Tilley (1998), experiments leave us with an empty, unexplored black box between input (manipulating the IV) and output (the effect on the DV)—as illustrated in **Figure 22.4**.

As students of criminology, we should resist the impulse to overstate our explanations in definitive, causal terms if our current criminological methods and results cannot support such conclusions. As criminologists, it is

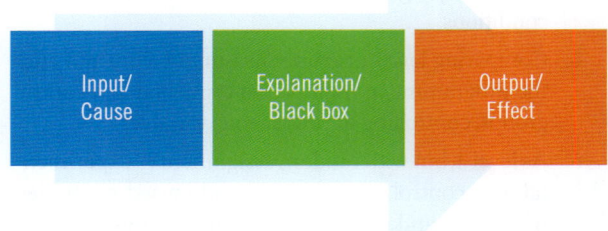

Figure 22.4 A 'black box' explanation of an effect fails to adequately take into account unexplored influences on the final outcome it seeks to describe

important that we acknowledge and address the complexities involved in defining crime, establishing causes, and controlling and measuring human behaviour in the real world. One argument would be to push for more tentative and flexible explanations than we have now, prioritising context, *realism*, and pragmatism, rather than the determined pursuit of definitive and undeniable causes. Only then can we produce explanations of crime that are valid in the sense of being meaningful, applicable, appropriate, and practical to the populations whose behaviour we are trying to explain and then respond to.

Searching inside the black box

How does the dark figure of explanation affect our ability to respond to crime in terms of reduction and prevention interventions that are meant to target its causes? Traditionally, explanations of and responses to crime have been stuck on supposition—enthusiastically assuming and conjecturing (or just ignoring) what is happening in the black box between inputs (factors, variables, sentencing responses, programmes, interventions) and outputs (outcomes, the nature of influence on offending behaviour). Such supposition, jumping from A to C without understanding B (black box) has encouraged overconfident and possibly invalid conclusions regarding the universal causes of crime and what works when intervening to reduce and prevent crime.

In this chapter we argue that we need a much better understanding of the mechanisms, processes, and interactions that could be occurring within the black box, and that ultimately influence offending behaviour, in order to turn these suppositions into actual meaningful explanations that can inform targeted responses. Whether these explanations will be necessarily focused on causes and causality is debatable, but the bigger issues involve searching for explanations that are more sensitive, valid, and therefore more useful in practical terms.

Desistance from crime

An alternative perspective for exploring the influence of causes is to focus on desistance—the 'cessation' (ceasing, ending) of crime. Similar to how social control theory asked why people *do not* commit crime (see **Chapter 21**), it is useful to explore what might cause people to stop offending once they have started. In **Conversations 22.3** we hear from Shadd Maruna, co-editor of *The Oxford Handbook of Criminology* (Liebling, Maruna, and McAra, 2017) and leading criminological expert on desistance, about his views on the relationship between causality and desistance.

In this discussion, Shadd Maruna suggests that explaining desistance from crime is as complex and uncertain as explaining crime itself. Like crime, the explanatory difficulties begin with pinning down a clear definition for such a contested and dynamic concept, not least because desistance presents as a process of change, rather than a static, easily measurable DV. Desistance theories have evolved from identifying correlates into focusing on what Shadd calls 'the primary causes of desistance from crime'. However, more contemporary multifactor, integrated theories of crime (see **Chapter 21**) acknowledge the complex interplay between biopsychosocial factors, sociostructural influences, agency, motivation, and identity, thus spanning positivism and interpretivism. Therefore, bearing in mind previous arguments regarding the limitations of certain explanatory theories and their associated research methods, is it valid to conclude that desistance theories have been able to identify the causes of desistance from crime, rather than simply the correlates of this behaviour? What do you think?

Innovative evaluation methods

In addition to the theoretical and explanatory alternative models gaining prominence in criminology (see **section 22.6**; see also enhanced pathways risk factor theories in **Chapter 21** and in MacDonald and Marsh, 2005; Smith and McVie, 2003), alternative models of implementing, explaining, and evaluating crime prevention programmes are emerging. These models are far less focused on or constrained by causation and the ambitious search for universal, generalisable, definitive recipes for curing crime encouraged by positivist method and the 'what works' approach. In other words, these models acknowledge the necessary complexity and practical realities of explaining and responding to crime; complexities and realities that

---

CONVERSATIONS 22.3

The causality-desistance relationship

with **Professor Shadd Maruna**

Steve Case (SC): What are the main ways in which the criminological literature has defined desistance?

Shadd Maruna (SM): Good question. Desistance is a tricky variable for criminologists because it is an absence of something rather than a tangible event or occurrence in itself. Specifically, desistance refers to the absence of repeat offending for individuals who have previously engaged in a pattern of offending and would be predicted to re-offend. Colloquially, desistance used to be described with now anachronistic phrases like 'going straight' or 'going legit'. The key here is the 'going'. Desistance is not a moment or an event, although some individuals may experience a sort of epiphany where they decide to stop offending, what is important is the process of actually staying stopped once that decision is made. Other words associated with desistance include things like 'rehabilitation' or 'reform', but the difference is that those words typically connote structured interventions or so-called 'correctional treatment'. Desistance refers to the overall process of change whether people 'rehabilitate themselves' or make this change with the support of a structured program. At one point, in fact, the term 'desistance' was seen as something of the opposite of rehabilitation. Either one was rehabilitated by others or else one 'desisted on one's own'. Today, few believe that state

programs can rehabilitate someone who does not want to change or make efforts to change; likewise, it is hard to imagine individuals desisting 'on their own' without the help of others, inside or outside of structured programmes. Both rehabilitation and desistance, then, are socially constructed and negotiated. One of the real difficulties, in fact, for those seeking to desist from crime is to convince others that their change is genuine and not an act put on to avoid criminal detection. After all, desistance is not something that can be easily proven. We tend to 'know it when we see it', but this is a subjective judgement that is notoriously difficult to research or measure.

SC: Based on these definitions, what are the main theories employed to understand desistance?

SM: Traditionally, only a limited number of theories existed to explain desistance, but today the theoretical explanations are growing rapidly in both number and in their sophistication. Some of the earliest theories, based on the strong correlation between age and crime (street crimes, in particular, appear to be a 'young person's game') posited that desistance was a largely biological process akin to puberty. Individuals were said to 'grow out of crime' as they matured out of the exuberance of youth. Later theories challenged this biosocial explanation by pointing out that although the age-crime relationship is strong, it is anything but perfect. Many individuals desist from crime around the age of 17, but others persist well into their 20s or 30s, and some persist even longer. A new body of theories posited that normative changes in the social sphere, such as employment and marriage, and not biological ageing itself, were the primary causes of desistance from crime. This was the idea that desistance required 'a steady job and the love of a good woman' (or man, presumably, although the evidence is less strong regarding the latter). The difficulty here was that things like marriage and employment are not random occurrences; typically, they are the outcome of agentic efforts on the part of individuals. Therefore, newer theories argue that desistance is the product of an interplay between changes in motivation, cognition and identity, as well as biology and social structure. It is a complicated enough business and should keep criminologists busy for numerous decades in the same way that the field has struggled to explain and understand crime itself.

You can read more on desistance in *The Oxford Handbook of Criminology* (Shapland and Bottoms, in Liebling et al., 2017).

Professor Shadd Maruna, Dean of the School of Criminal Justice, Rutgers University, Newark

---

may make it impossible to identify the causes to target. Two particularly useful models are worth considering here: realistic evaluation (Pawson and Tilley, 2009, 1998) and the theory of change model (Blamey and MacKenzie, 2007; Weiss, 1995).

The realistic evaluation approach

Ray Pawson and Nick Tilley (1998, 2009) have created a realist method of exploring and evaluating crime prevention programmes that addresses the black box issues ignored by the 'what works' methodology. In their book, *Realistic Evaluation*, Pawson and Tilley argue that positivist 'what works' evaluation is insensitive to what is going on inside the black box between programme inputs (causes) and changes in crime/behaviour (effects). They advocate for a more sensitive, realistic, and pragmatic evaluation approach that focuses on 'what works for whom in what circumstances'.

Pawson and Tilley's realistic evaluation model is made up of the following three parts (see Table 22.1):

1. **Context:** Where and when is the programme/intervention taking place and with whom? This is the 'with whom and in what circumstances?' part of their evaluation question.

2. **Mechanisms:** What does the programme/intervention do and what does it intend to do? What processes and mechanisms does it activate? How can any changes be explained in theoretical and practical terms?

3. **Outcomes:** What are the consequences and effects of the mechanisms activated by the programme/intervention?

The Context-Mechanism-Outcome (CMO) model of realist evaluation, therefore, actually does more than examine its original (1998) descriptive question of 'what works for whom in what circumstances?' and moves into examining the more explanatory questions of 'in what respects, and how?' (Pawson and Tilley, 2004: 2). Realistic evaluation offers a more sensitive, pragmatic, and (obviously) realistic approach of explaining and responding to crime—one that is neither married to nor constrained by the search for quantifiable causes or the pursuit of single factor theories and explanations (see **Chapter 21**). Instead, realistic evaluation incorporates qualitative considerations of individualised and contextualised mechanisms and influences into its more holistic explanations of crime and how crime prevention/reduction programmes may work.

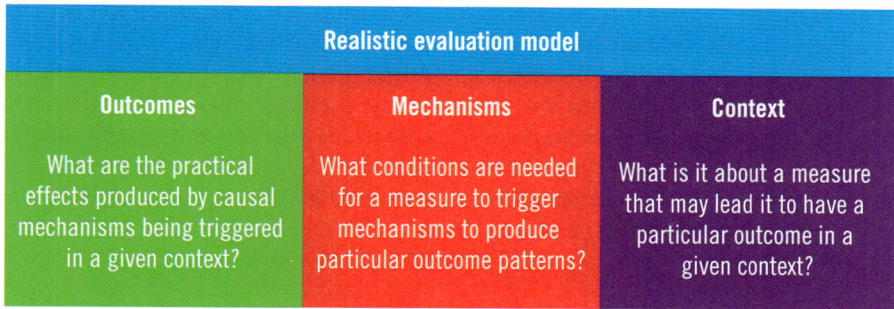

Table 22.1 Pawson and Tilley advocate for a sensitive, realistic, and pragmatic approach to evaluating crime prevention programmes comprising three parts: context, menchanisms, and outcomes

The theory of change model

Theory-based evaluation is a method for addressing the limitations of the experiment-based 'what works' model and for enabling more context-sensitive evaluation of crime prevention programmes (such as interventions in the community) that look inside the neglected black box of explanation. The theory of change model is particularly well-suited to evaluating community-based interventions, an area in which 'what works' struggles, given the longer term outcomes, complex and multifaceted, open-ended nature of such problem-solving interventions and their related theories of change. The theory of change model (Connell et al., 1995; Kubisch, Fulbright-Anderson, and Connell, 1998) starts from the premise that methods-driven evaluation is insufficient to discover and explore the explanatory causal pathways, processes, and contexts through which (community) interventions have an effect. The conclusion is that crime prevention programmes should make explicit their theory of *how* interventions are intended to achieve certain outcomes, that this theory should inform their methods, and that we should evaluate their effectiveness based on this theory.

The theory of change model focuses on programme implementation (Weiss, 1995)—hypothesising links between the 'nuts and bolts' of programme activities and the linkages between these programme activities and their outcomes. The theory or rationale for a crime prevention intervention is evaluated in terms of how it has informed the programme's design (Blamey and MacKenzie, 2007). The linkages between the 'nuts and bolts' of specific interventions and their outcomes are explained as potentially 'causal triggers that fire appropriate mechanisms in certain circumstances' (Blamey and MacKenzie, 2007: 446), leading to particular outcomes. However, this causal aspect is secondary to the main focus on searching for qualitative explanations of how programmes operate and are intended to operate as the basis for evaluating whether or not they work. Whereas the realistic evaluation approach of Pawson and Tilley has been predominantly focused upon individualised interventions and policies (for example, prison education programmes), the theory of change model has been applied far more frequently to the evaluation of community-wide, multiple intervention programmes, which realistic evaluation has proven far less suited to (Blamey and MacKenzie, 2007).

A realistic theory of change?

Both approaches to evaluation make a clear break from positivist epistemology and methodology by offering a post-positivist, enhanced version of positivist explanation (for example, Blamey and MacKenzie's 'causal triggers') that is more sensitive to context and underpinning theory. However, neither realistic evaluation nor the theory of change model offers any qualitative investigation of the individualised interpretations, experiences, perceptions, and thought processes that may explain how a crime prevention programme operates or may work.

Despite their more sensitive exploration of context and theories of change, there remains little exploration within the black box, only the confident identification of the pre-formed theories that should populate this box. That said, both approaches consciously distance themselves from positivist 'what works' methodology and its associated limitations, most notably the quantified over-simplification of complex issues and relationships (*reductionism*). Both approaches remain under-developed, under-researched, under-exposed, and under-supported in criminology (Case, 2015; Young, 2011). However, both approaches offer viable, feasible, and open-minded alternatives to established positivist 'what works' methods, understandings, and explanations of supposed cause and effect relationships and what works in the social world of crime prevention programmes.

So far in our discussion, the overriding argument has been that positivist methodology is focused on identifying the causes of crime and then responding to these through 'what works' interventions that are evaluated using an experimental model. Alternative models have emerged for implementing and evaluating crime prevention programmes; models based on post-positivist, realistic, and 'theory of change'-based methodologies and understandings. However, even these models remain committed, to some degree, to explaining causality.

So is criminological explanation wedded to the pursuit of causality? Not necessarily; we address numerous alternative (for example, non-positivist) explanatory approaches elsewhere in this book, for example those founded in critical criminology (**Chapter 18**) and realist approaches (**Chapter 20**). However, as we have seen, positivist explanations have come under fire for their perceived limitations, such as reductionist methods and invalid presumptions that linear (straight-line) causal relationships exist between variables and outcomes. We will now consider one theory in particular that critiques the presumed linearity within positivism: *chaos theory*.

22.6 Chaos theory

A possible alternative to the dominance of positivism within criminology can be found in 'complex systems science', also known as 'chaos theory' (see Lorenz, 1963; Gleick, 1997; Young, 1991), which argues that:

> The inherent nonlinearity of many social phenomena . . . must explain, in part, the challenges social scientists face when attempting to understand the complexity of social dynamics . . . a simple deterministic equation can generate seemingly random or chaotic behaviour over time.
>
> (Elliott and Kiel, 2000: 4)

Although a full explanation of the development and principles of complex systems science/chaos theory is beyond the scope of this chapter (but see Gleick, 1997; Young, 1991), it is useful to explore two of its central components to gain a better understanding of the theory itself and how it can be used to critique positivist explanations of crime. These central components are fractal measurement and sensitive dependence on initial conditions (the **butterfly effect**).

Fractal measurement

Chaos theory challenges the validity and reductionism of positivist method in criminology through the concept of fractal measurement, which is based on the assertions of mathematician Benoit Mandelbrot (Mandelbrot, 1967, 1982):

1. That objects in the real world could be conceived of as fractals—reduced-size copies of a larger whole.
2. That an object's dimensions are relative to the observer and can be fractional—sensitive to the scale of measurement employed.

The concept of fractals, therefore, provides a non-deterministic model for understanding the measurement of rough (that is, complex) and non-linear phenomena. The significance of fractal measurement for criminological research lies, perhaps, in what it tells us about the importance of method and scale of measurement for the reliability and validity of the measures employed to identify causes and influences on crime (for example, the quantitative ratings scales used in questionnaires) and the confidence we can have in these understandings. Ratings scales and risk assessments, for example, can be a little basic and unsophisticated in their measurement and analysis of causes, risk factors, and correlates as 'smooth shapes' rather than rough phenomena that might be better understood as fractals (see Case and Haines, 2014). Mandelbrot argued that 'smooth shapes' do not exist in the real world:

> Smooth shapes are very rare in the wild but extremely important in the ivory tower and the factory . . .
>
> (Mandelbrot, 2004 (in interview with www.edge.org))

The butterfly effect

Whilst conducting meteorological research in the 1950s, American mathematician Edward Lorenz contradicted one of the fundamental assumptions of modern statistical analysis, that small measurement errors are irrelevant. Instead, Lorenz found that minute differences in the measurement of initial conditions (IVs) caused points of instability throughout complex systems that could result in unpredictable and fundamentally non-linear, unpredicted outcomes (DVs)—implying complexity and chaos. Lorenz also discovered that the introduction of intervening variables (EVs) could intensify the unpredictable (non-linear), complex, and chaotic nature of a system's outcomes. He concluded that the accurate analysis of any behaviours required 'sensitive dependence on initial conditions'; a phenomenon he dubbed the butterfly effect, from the idea that a flap of a butterfly's wings could influence the onset of a tornado thousands of miles away. **Figure 22.5** illustrates the butterfly effect that can occur when two equivalent variables have minutely different starting points (initial conditions) on a journey, thus leading to markedly different trajectories and outcomes.

The possibility of chaos or instability in complex systems indicates that small changes in (the measurement of)

Figure 22.5 The butterfly effect: slightly different starting points producing different trajectories
Source: Hellisp/CC BY 2.5

of linear, stable, and proportionate relationships between variables sits at the core of positivist analysis; an assumption directly refuted by chaos theorists in criminology (Ziliak and McCloskey, 2007; McGrayne, 2011).

The chaos and complexity critique

Taken together, the concepts of fractal measurement (method) and sensitive dependence on initial conditions/the butterfly effect (analysis) offer potential alternatives to positivist criminology and the explanatory, causal-based theories that have emerged from it. Arguably, positivism has paid very limited attention to initial conditions—both in terms of when these initial conditions are measured (in time) and how they are measured (in terms of sensitivity). Nor have positivists acknowledged sufficiently that repeated interactions between measured (and unmeasured) variables produce the unpredictable. Consequently, if potential causal variables and 'risk factors' are imprecisely measured before being fed into statistical analyses mechanisms, this process could lead to invalid conclusions about their linear, proportionate, and causal influences on offending behaviour.

initial variables can lead to large differences in outcomes or conclusions. Consequently, analysing the relationships between criminogenic variables and offending in a manner that is sensitive to chaos theory could enable an exploration of criminal behaviour 'in ways not possible in . . . [positivist methods] . . . and the linear causality they presume' (Young, 1991: 447). Nevertheless, the assumption

22.7 Conclusion

Can we search for the causes of crime and ever hope to identify them? Searching for conclusive evidence of the causes of crime may be an impossible goal in the strict experimental, positivist sense, because there are simply too many unknowns and unmeasured dark figures of crime and explanation to enable us to draw valid and reliable conclusions from research. But the search for the unequivocal, universal, reliable causes of crime is also arguably unnecessary. What is needed in order to enhance our understanding of crime is more sensitive, specific, and reflective explanations of different crimes at different times by different kinds of people; the types of explanations that are facilitated by innovative, contemporary explanatory models such as chaos theory and evaluation models like realistic evaluation and theory of change. This more nuanced and sensitive, less deterministic and definitive approach to understanding requires:

- more sensitivity to and critical reflection on the constraints set by our research methods and what they can and cannot tell us about crime, including more consideration of mixed methods designs;
- more sensitivity to and critical reflection on the roles of subjectivity, supposition, and study on the production of explanatory knowledge of the causes and explanations of crime;
- more sensitivity to and critical reflection on the nature of the explanations we produce—with particular focus on exactly what they explain and how they explain it.

The result of this constructive application of our critical mindsets should be a set of necessarily limited, yet more valid, explanations of crime that move away from the concern with causes and begin to explore and explain crime inside the black box in more mixed (epistemologically and methodologically) and meaningful ways. This would lead us into identifying and exploring influences and processes of change (not causes) that relate to specific crimes at specific times by specific kinds of people. Subjectivity and supposition are inevitable and integral components of criminological study (research and scholarship), so we should be transparent, acknowledge them, and explore their influences on our explanations of crime. Ultimately, our goal should be to offer understandings of crime that are practical and realistic—underpinned by logical, reflective, meaningful, and valid relationships between criminological definitions, explanations, and responses.

SUMMARY

After reading this chapter and working your way through its features you should now be able to:

- **Explore the reasons why we search for the causes of crime in criminology, with particular focus on positivism**

In this chapter, we argued that if we are able to better understand crime, we are able to respond to it in more valid, appropriate, and effective ways. We explored the extent to which the evolution of explanatory theories in criminology has been dominated by positivism, which pursues an *epistemology* (theory of knowledge generation) of gathering data in the social world to identify the causes and to create universal laws of behaviour, and an objectivist *ontology* (theory of how to understand reality) that the real world consists of undeniable facts that can be objectively measured.

- **Discuss the definitional issues relating to the concepts of crime and causes that influence the valid and reliable identification of the causes of crime**

This chapter has examined a key issue with identifying the causes of crime, that criminologists cannot seem to agree on what they understand or mean by either causes or crime. Both of these criminological concepts are typically understood from a positivist perspective as objective facts, yet both are arguably social constructions born from *interpretivism*. Throughout the chapter, it was suggested that criminologists could limit themselves to a more valid search for the causes of crime(s) committed at specific times in specific places—a contextualised, temporally specific, time-limited, transient notion of causality that is also sensitive to the type of crime being explained and to the cultural and country context. In other words, we should guard against the unhelpful supposition that certain causal explanations need to be generalisable and universal and instead prioritise more sensitive, flexible, fit-the-purpose, valid, and practical explanations of crime.

- **Assess the implications of these definitional and explanatory issues for producing valid and reliable responses to crime**

We discussed that a central motivation for identifying causes is to validate the factors targeted through criminological responses such as sentencing, crime reduction and prevention activity, and policy. This causal definitiveness was contested by arguments that the key positivist and quasi-positivist (artefactual risk factor) theories have been largely survey-based and to a lesser extent based on observations (but less often experimental) and have tended to identify the correlates of crime, not the causes. However, the dominance of positivist experimentation within criminology and the associated search for causes has been re-animated in the 21st century by the growing popularity of experimental criminology in the US, most notably the 'what works' experimental method of evaluating crime prevention programmes. Further discussion was provided of contemporary challenges to the experimental, 'what works' approach, namely realistic evaluation, the theory of change model and the chaos theory.

We concluded that experiments are limited as an explanatory tool in criminology; that they tend to identify and measure rather than explain the mechanisms and processes of influence upon crime, which leaves us with a 'dark figure' of explanation—a black box.

- **Evaluate the feasibility and necessity of identifying the causes of crime**

The chapter concluded that searching for the cause of crime is an impossible goal in the strictest sense, because there are simply too many unknowns and unmeasured dark figures of crime and explanation to enable us to draw valid and reliable conclusions from research. We asserted that criminologists could pursue more sensitive, specific, contingent, dynamic, and reflective explanations of different crimes at different times by different kinds of people. In particular, criminologists should have more sensitivity to and critical reflection on the roles of subjectivity, supposition, and study on the production of explanatory knowledge of the causes and explanations of crime.

Test your understanding of the chapter's key points by attempting the self-test questions on the **online resources** at www.oup.com/he/case2e

REVIEW QUESTIONS

1. What are the main differences between positivism and interpretivism in terms of how they seek to explain crime?
2. What are some of the main issues we must address in order to identify the causes of crime? Illustrate your answer with reference to a specific criminological theory.
3. What is the main difference in focus between the realistic evaluation approach of Pawson and Tilley, and the theory of change approach by Connell and others?
4. How do the concepts of 'chaos theory' pose a challenge to the deterministic arguments made by positivists?

Access the **online resources** at www.oup.com/he/case2e to check your answers to the review questions.

FURTHER READING

Bryman, A. (2021) *Social Research Methods* **(6th edn). Oxford: Oxford University Press.**
A comprehensive guide to social research methods, including detailed and accessible discussions of quantitative and qualitative research methods and their related causal assumptions.

Case, S. P. and Haines, K. R. (2014) 'Youth justice: From linear risk paradigm to complexity' in A. Pycroft and C. Bartollas (eds) *Applying Complexity Theory: Whole Systems Approaches to Criminal Justice and Social Work.* **Bristol: Policy Press.**
Using youth justice as its illustration, this critical chapter, co-written by one of the authors of this textbook, explores the central causal claims of positivism in criminology, followed by a detailed exposition of an alternative theoretical and methodological perspective—chaos theory.

Sherman, L. (2009) 'Evidence and liberty: The promise of experimental criminology' *Criminology and Criminal Justice* **9(1): 5–28.**
A critical discussion of the role of experimental criminology in the creation of evidence to inform our explanations of crime and appropriate responses to it. Why not read Hope's (2009) response to Sherman's arguments too? It is in the subsequent edition of the same journal and is entitled 'The illusion of control: A response to Professor Sherman'.

Access the **online resources** to view a wealth of extra information relating to your study of criminology, including self-test questions, answers to review questions, and links to other resources that will help you enjoy and fulfil your potential within your studies.

www.oup.com/he/case2e

PART OUTLINE

23. Criminal justice principles
24. Criminal justice institutions
25. Criminal justice policies and practices
26. Crime prevention
27. Crime control
28. Punishment
29. Rehabilitation of offenders
30. Alternatives to punishment
31. Critical perspectives on punishment

This part of the book, responding to crime, shifts our focus to the practical and theoretical challenges associated with the question of what to do about crime and its impact on individuals and societies.

We begin with a discussion of the underlying principles which inform the decisions and actions in the criminal justice system (**Chapter 23**), then move to the roles and challenges of its key institutions, namely the police, the Crown Prosecution Service, the courts, prisons, and probation services/community sentences (**Chapter 24**). We conclude our overview of the criminal justice system by exploring the policies and practices which inform how justice is delivered (**Chapter 25**).

In the subsequent chapters, we focus on different perspectives on responding to crime. We consider a range of crime prevention strategies and look at the ideas that inform them (**Chapter 26**), before evaluating approaches to intervention which share the goals of minimising opportunities to offend and taking swift action when the limits of acceptable behaviour are breached—the 'crime control' perspective (**Chapter 27**). The chapters that follow critically consider the ways in which criminals are dealt with by the justice system, including the justifications and implications of punishment as a general response to crime (**Chapter 28**), and the issues associated with delivering socially acceptable and effective rehabilitative programmes (**Chapter 29**).

In **Chapter 30** we discuss alternatives to traditional forms of punishment: recent developments in criminal justice thinking and practice which concentrate on problem-solving and resolving the harms caused by crime (diversion and restorative justice), based on the argument that if we respond to offending in a forward-looking way, this can produce long-lasting social benefits. Finally, in **Chapter 31** we review critical perspectives on crime and punishment and invite you to reflect on whether conventional assumptions and approaches actually obscure important questions about how crime is defined and whose interests are served. In light of this, we conclude this part of the book by considering possible alternative models for constructing and delivering socially just forms of criminal justice.

PART 4
RESPONDING TO CRIME

CHAPTER OUTLINE

23.1	Introduction	694
23.2	The rule of law: an overview	695
23.3	The rule of law: an independent judiciary	697
23.4	The rule of law: due process	701
23.5	The rule of law: human rights	707
23.6	Adversarial justice	710
23.7	Restorative justice	713
23.8	Conclusion	715

23

Criminal justice principles

KEY ISSUES

After studying this chapter, you should be able to:

- recognise the source and changing nature of essential criminal justice principles;
- outline the importance of the rule of law doctrine;
- discuss the essential features of an adversarial justice system;
- assess the force of the restorative justice principle.

23.1 Introduction

'Criminal justice', which can be broadly defined as the system of law enforcement for potential crimes, is a complex and dynamic field that (as we saw in **Chapter 3**) is inextricably linked to the discipline of criminology. In this chapter we get to grips with the core principles of criminal justice, looking at how they manifest in our current system but also at how they have evolved over time, because a sound understanding of these *concepts* is essential if we are to fully engage with criminal justice today, critically assessing our policies and practices and considering how they might be improved. It may feel as though the current system has always been here and is the only logical way to operate, but actually our views and methods have changed significantly over time and continue to do so. Today's methods of law enforcement would seem bizarre to the people of 150 years ago, and vice versa, and it seems likely that students in the next century will likewise consider our justice system and responses strange, perhaps even primitive.

In this chapter, **Chapter 24**, and **Chapter 25** we begin to think about criminal justice through examining the work of and relationships between its four main components: principles, policies, practices, and people. We consider the key principles of the criminal justice system in this chapter, we look at its central institutions (and the people within them) in **Chapter 24**, then in **Chapter 25** we explore criminal justice 'in action' by considering policies and practices and also return to the influence of people in this context. A key focus for this part of the book is the idea of making practical modifications to improve our justice system, and looking at it through the lens of these four components will help you see the variety of influences that are involved whenever we try to make such changes. Essentially, they provide a useful framework for deploying your ABC (*Always Be Critical*) approach in the context of criminal justice.

We devote this chapter to principles because these concepts underpin the entire criminal justice system and shape the way in which it operates. Despite their integral importance, however, these principles are fluid and can be subject to change, especially in the UK since there is no written constitution or penal code. Many countries do have these written documents, which provide definitive statements of the essential principles that guide the people, policies, and practices in their criminal justice systems. The Code of Ur-Nammu (**Figure 23.1**), for example, was written over 4,000 years ago and performed this function for a place known as Mesopotamia (recognised today as covering parts of Iraq, Kuwait, Syria, Turkey, and Iran). It is the earliest known legal code and—perhaps surprisingly, as we often assume that law in the past involved brutal responses—financial compensation to a victim or family member was its most common response to unacceptable behaviour. It contained few examples of the principle of *lex talionis* (laws based on retaliation), subsequently made famous in the 'eye for an eye' conceptions of justice. A modern example of a written penal code would be France's Code pénal, which was last updated in 1994 and details all the crimes and procedures in the country's justice system.

Although the UK has neither a written constitution nor a penal code, the country's processes of justice are still guided by authoritative principles. They cannot be located in one document but exist in a variety of sources such as Acts of Parliament, decisions of the higher courts (known as judicial precedents, because they set the precedent, or position,

Figure 23.1 The Code of Ur-Nammu, pictured in its current location at the Istanbul Archaeology Museum, is the earliest known legal code or constitution and provides guidance on criminal justice responses

Source: Istanbul Archaeology Museum/ CC 0

that lower courts must then follow), and international treaties and obligations. Whilst these overarching principles guide UK criminal justice, their power is challenged by the different perspectives and opinions which are so easily provoked by the subject of justice. (See **What do you think? 3.1**, where we considered the wide variety of just responses possible from the apparently simple case of stolen food.) The principles we explore in this chapter represent broad values for the justice system which, when studied, show themselves not as fixed, sacred things but as 'rules' that are frequently modified, replaced, or improved. The key principles behind the abstract aims of criminal justice are:

- the **rule of law**;
- **adversarial** justice; and
- **restorative justice**.

We will now consider each principle in turn, spending the most time on the rule of law due to the broader themes it includes, as well as its global acceptance as a key criminal justice principle. In the final part of this chapter, we consider the roles of the police, the courts, and the CPS in the administration of justice, in order to get a full picture of the ideas behind and workings of the criminal justice system before we then move on to assess it.

23.2 The rule of law: an overview

The rule of law replaced the will of the monarch as the supreme power in the UK in the so-called 'Glorious Revolution' which followed the English Civil War (1642–51). The Parliamentarians (supporters of the English Parliament) triumphed over the Royalists (supporters of the royals, at that time King Charles I), so the law and not the monarchy became the highest form of authority.

So, the rule of law means everybody and everything is subject to the law in open court proceedings—although it is worth noting that the law must be prospective (it applies in the future) and not retrospective (that is, people cannot be punished for previous behaviour which was not recognised as a crime at the time when it was committed). The rule of law is considered such a vital concept that the World Justice Project Rule of Law Index (considered further in **What do you think 23.1**) now monitors how closely countries adhere to its key principles. The Index identifies the following as universal principles:

1. **Accountability**: governments as well as individuals must be answerable to the law.
2. **Laws are 'just'**: laws are applied evenly and protect key human rights.
3. **Open government**: laws are transparently created and enforced.
4. **Accessible and impartial dispute resolution**: cases are resolved by competent and independent adjudicators.

Another key feature of the rule of law is **parliamentary sovereignty**, which means that Parliament, based in the Palace of Westminster in London (**Figure 23.2**), is the supreme authority when it comes to the making of law. Nothing can be done to restrict this power and no court can question the **validity** of Parliament's statutes (legislation or Acts of Parliament). Parliament can also delegate its legislative powers to other individuals and organisations. Its ability to pass any laws it chooses has been restricted in recent years by the UK's membership of the European Union and the requirement that its laws are compatible with these legal obligations, but even this qualification did not affect its ultimate authority: each Parliament can repeal (revoke, or cancel out) any statute previously passed, including the European Communities Act 1972 that initially brought the UK into the EU.

The constitutional doctrine (a set of beliefs or key principles) of the **separation of powers** is also vital to the rule of law. According to this doctrine, the power of a state should be divided into three separate and distinct branches (De Montesquieu, 1748):

- the executive (the government and associated agencies);
- the legislature (Parliament, that is, the House of Commons, the House of Lords, and the monarch); and
- the judiciary (the courts).

Figure 23.2 The UK Parliament, which is based in the Palace of Westminster, London, has supreme authority when it comes to making law

Source: jeffwarder/CC BY-SA 3.0

WHAT DO YOU THINK? 23.1

Judging the rule of law

The World Justice Project's Rule of Law Index (**Figure 23.3**) monitors the extent to which countries adhere to the rule of law in practice. The Index has limitations and cannot provide us with absolute answers, but the research is rigorous so it is well worth spending time exploring its data and documentation. This will help you appreciate the depth and breadth of the principle.

The Index first published overall rankings in 2016–17 and, so far, there has been no change in the top four places in the 'league'; these positions are held by countries which are geographically close to each other. The UK's performance has also been consistent.

Before you look at the data, consider the following questions.

- Which countries do you predict make up the top four in the rankings?
- Why have these countries come to mind?
- What position do you think is generally achieved by the UK?

Now spend some time exploring the Index's latest Insights report and its interactive map (both available via the WJP Rule of Law Index pages at https://worldjustice-project.org), before answering the following,

- Are the countries within the top ten, and particularly in the top four, the ones you would have expected?
- Why do you think these countries are 'winning'?
- Is the UK placed where you would expect for a country from which many of the rules for this principle originated?

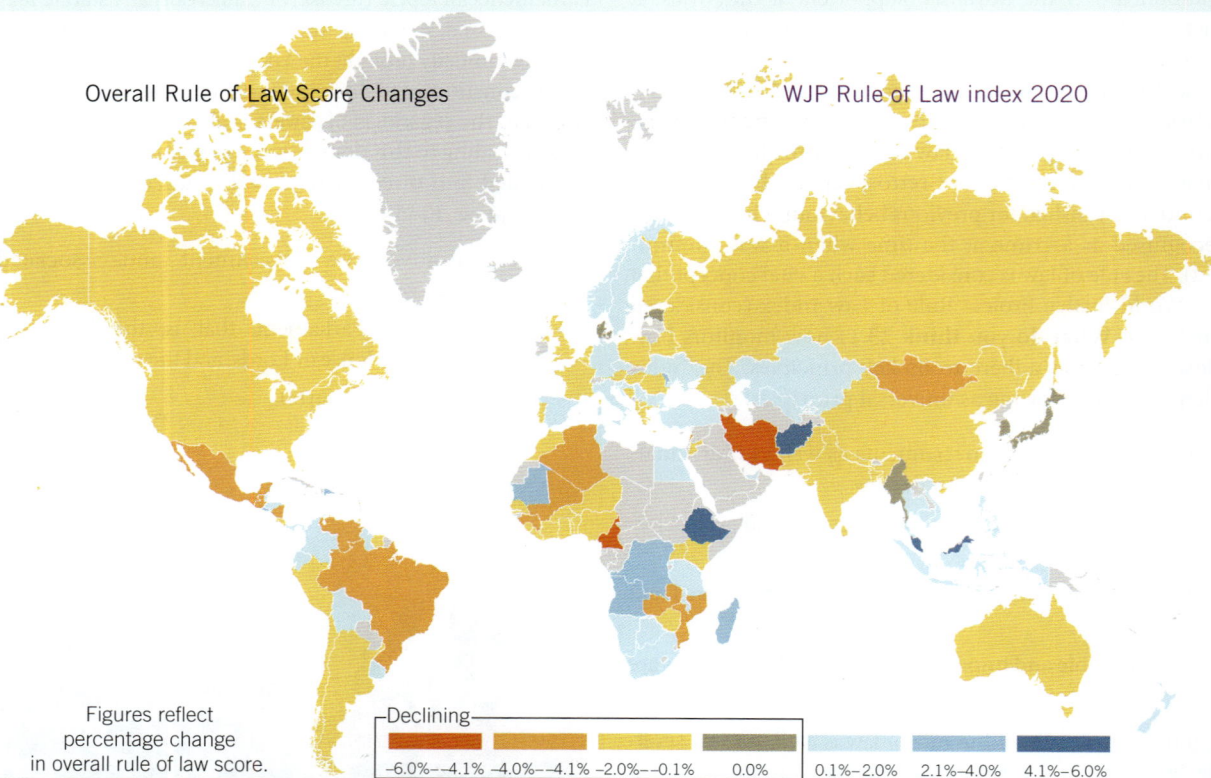

Figure 23.3 The World Justice Project's Rule of Law Index monitors the extent to which countries adhere to the concept in practice
Source: World Justice Project https://worldjusticeproject.org/our-work/research-and-data/wjp-rule-law-index-2020

Sharing the power between these branches means that each one acts as a 'check' and a 'balance' on the others and no single branch has excessive control. For example, the executive can propose law but the legislature then needs to approve it, or not, and an impartial judiciary adjudicates on its disputes. In theory, the doctrine ensures that power is effectively shared and reduces undue bias in the development of the law.

However, in the UK the lines between these branches of the state can be blurred (see **Figure 23.4**), preventing complete separation of powers. Examples include that members of the government, including the Prime Minister and other members of the Cabinet, can also be Members of Parliament, and that until 2005 the Lord Chancellor held power in all three branches. The Lord Chancellor was a Cabinet Minister, a member of the House of Lords, and also the head of the judiciary, so this position sat firmly in the middle segment of the diagram at **Figure 23.4** and clearly contradicted the doctrine. The Constitutional Reform Act 2005 rectified the issue by reforming the judicial appointment process, establishing the Supreme Court as the UK's highest court in place of the judicial arm of the House of Lords, and making the position of Lord Chief Justice the head of the judiciary.

The lack of separation of powers in the UK system means concerns about appropriate uses and balances of power are often expressed. These concerns frequently relate to the dominance of the executive over the legislature, but also to disagreements between the executive (politicians) and the judiciary—see **What do you think 23.2** for a recent and very notable example of the latter. Struggles of this kind have a long history that stretches back to battles between the monarchy and the church in the Middle Ages, and the monarchy and Parliament in the Glorious Revolution. The modern-day tension between the executive and the judiciary is usually traced back to the precedent set by a case titled *Entick* v *Carrington* (1765) EWHC KB J98, in which it was accepted that the

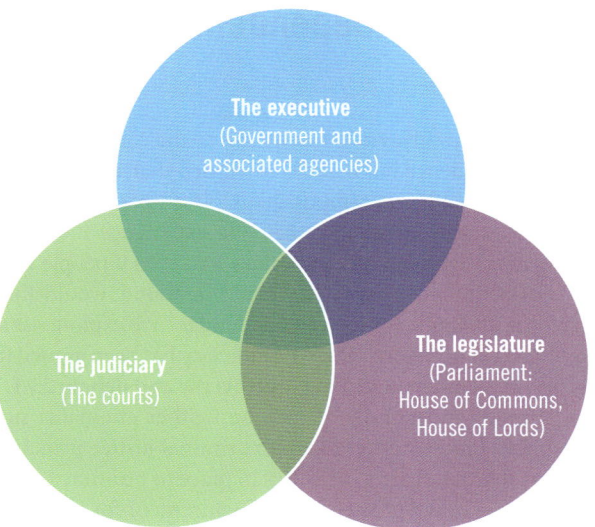

Figure 23.4 The idea of 'separation of powers' is crucial to the rule of law but in practice the different branches of criminal justice are closely linked

executive could be held accountable by the judiciary because the rule of law says that everyone is subject to the law. A high-profile example of this tension occurred in 2002 when Princess Anne was the **defendant** at Slough Magistrates' Court as one of her dogs had bitten two children in Windsor Great Park; despite her position, she was convicted and fined £500.

We can see the significance of the rule of law principle to criminal justice in the UK through its association with three important supplementary concepts:

- an independent judiciary;
- the due process model;
- human rights.

Let's consider each concept in turn.

23.3 The rule of law: an independent judiciary

The requirement to have an independent judiciary is visible in the fourth universal principle of the Rule of Law Index: that of accessible and impartial dispute resolution. To adhere to this requirement of the rule of law, hearings must be run by a judiciary (including magistrates) that is separate and independent from the other branches of a state. In this section, we consider the extent to which this is actually possible, the impact of judicial independence in terms of accountability (how are judges held to account if they are independent?), and what judicial responsibilities are in practice. Having a good grasp of the requirement for an independent judiciary will develop your understanding of the separation of powers concept; it will also help you reflect on whether court hearings in the justice system are delivered in a fair and valid way.

Is judicial independence possible?

The rule of law gives heavy emphasis to the concept of judicial independence but it could be argued that, in reality, absolute independence is impossible. Unless a person has lived hidden away from society, their life experience inevitably influences their opinions and values, and even if people with this detachment from society could be found, would they have the attributes for being a good judge? We explore some examples of occasions when the judiciary has been argued to be less than independent in **Controversy and debate 23.1**.

Absolute independence may be neither attainable nor desirable, but its importance as a criminal justice principle means there are many measures in place to promote it. The most well known of these is the requirement for judges to be apolitical—they have to be seen as completely removed from politics and not to support a particular party or set of beliefs—but again, we could question whether this is always achieved in reality. Until the Constitutional Reform Act 2005 the monarch, acting on recommendations from the Prime Minister or the Lord Chancellor, was responsible for appointing the members of the judiciary. This situation led many observers to claim there was clear political influence on a supposedly separate branch of the state. Both Margaret Thatcher and Tony Blair, when holding the position of Prime Minister, were criticised for 'recommending' the appointment of judges who were suspected of lacking this impartiality. The radical reforms of 2005 therefore upgraded the role of the Judicial Appointments Commission to allow it to nominate candidates or make appointments itself. Since 2009, all new judicial members of the Supreme Court have been appointed through this system, reducing the likelihood of political influence, but judicial appointments remain controversial because members are not very diverse: only 7 per cent of the 3,000 currently serving judges come from a BAME background (Lammy, 2017: 37).

CONTROVERSY AND DEBATE 23.1

Choosing the judges

The importance we attach to the idea of an independent judiciary is clear from how emotionally we respond when the principle appears to have been compromised.

One UK example in recent years was when Judge Robert Altham adjudicated in the trial of anti-fracking protestors in 2018. The judge imposed custodial sentences for each of the three defendants and this was widely criticised as an excessive response given the protest's peaceful nature (and the sentences were overturned on appeal a few weeks later). However, there was considerable further concern when it was revealed that the Althams had a well-established family business in the oil and gas industry (*The Times*, 12 October 2018).

Around the same time, another controversy relating to judicial independence played out in the US at the proposed appointment of Brett Kavanaugh as judge to the US Supreme Court. The then President Donald Trump used his powers to make the nomination, which then needed approval of the US Senate (an institution which, along with the House of Representatives, forms the legislative branch of the US constitution). Kavanaugh's judicial independence was questioned by religious and legal institutions and law academics (*The Guardian*, 9 February 2019) because:

- he had previously made statements that he would not support the investigation into allegations of misconduct in Trump's 2016 election victory;
- he had undertaken some secret work for the US government during the 'war on terror' in the early 2000s;
- his highly conservative views on abortion rights and LGBT issues were well known;
- there was an allegation against him of sexual assault.

The Senate marginally approved Kavanaugh's appointment despite unprecedented scenes at his nomination hearing that saw hundreds of people arrested for public order offences. Kavanaugh's own supporting statement was also unusual as instead of expressing legal views, it focused on his own life story and attacked the conspiracies against him (BBC News, 5 October 2018).

These examples demonstrate the contemporary importance of judicial independence. The word 'independence' is often used in criminal justice decision-making, but it is always important to analyse it and ask: 'Independence from what?' Judicial independence can be affected not only by economic and political influences, as in these examples, but also social influences. Lammy's (2017) findings show that judges' backgrounds are limited in terms of their ethnicity, social class, and age, which could have serious implications for the independence of decisions made by the criminal justice system.

The need for independence means judges are not allowed to be directors of private companies and they are encouraged to maintain a low profile in society. This is something they seem to do extremely well: if you were asked to name three current UK judges, could you even name one? More senior members of the judiciary may do occasional interviews with a serious part of the media, and the Lord Chief Justice holds a press conference annually, but judges are highly unlikely to appear on chat shows or give interviews in newspapers or magazines, etc. while they are in post. (Watching the video footage of the most recent of the Lord Chief Justice's press conferences, available on YouTube, will give you an idea of how the senior judiciary want to come across to the public—note the apolitical language to demonstrate their independence and detachment from politics.) This desire for anonymity is partly why the judiciary wear formal wigs and gowns when hearing a trial.

Judicial accountability

The impact of judicial independence means that once appointed, a judge has **security of tenure**; in other words, their position is secure until they retire as they can only be removed from office following a resolution from both Houses of Parliament. Only one High Court judge (a term that includes the 150 or so senior judges who sit in appellate courts) has ever gone through this procedure. Sir Jonah Barrington, who was particularly vocal in his allegations against the English government for misrule in Ireland, was dismissed in 1830 based on fraud allegations but no prosecution was ever brought against him (O'Brien, 2013).

Security of tenure means that judges are immune to political pressure through the executive and democratic pressure through the legislature; that is, their decisions should not be influenced by a desire to please politicians or the public in order to keep their jobs. The downside is that there is a lack of accountability—with the powers separated in this way, it is very difficult for judges' 'performance' to be evaluated—so the principle of the rule of law tries to counterbalance this freedom by holding the judiciary accountable to the law itself rather than a particular body. This judicial freedom may seem unquestionably positive, but particularly since the 2016 Brexit referendum, people have questioned whether an unelected judiciary should be able to stop the wishes of a democratically elected government. Consider this argument further in **What do you think? 23.2**.

WHAT DO YOU THINK? 23.2

The ultimate legal power

The *Daily Mail* published this controversial headline in response to a High Court ruling which held that the UK's exit from the EU had to be kick-started by Parliament and not by the Prime Minister's executive powers. The *Daily Mail*'s headline alone provoked many complaints, as did the associated report, which referred to one of the judges as 'the epitome of a modern judge' and described him as an 'openly-gay' ex-Olympic fencer. None of the other judges received such descriptions. The full story can be read online here: https://www.dailymail.co.uk/news/article-3903436/Enemies-people-Fury-touch-judges-defied-17-4m-Brexit-voters-trigger-constitutional-crisis.html.

As you can see from the article, the *Daily Mail* was reporting on *R (Miller)* v *Secretary of State for Exiting the European Union* [2017] UKSC 5, a case that was considered so constitutionally important that it progressed all the way up to the Supreme Court and was heard by 11 judges rather than the usual five. We recommend that you read the full judgment of this case, as it provides a fascinating real-life demonstration of the debates surrounding the separation of powers principle and the constitutional roles of the executive, legislature and judiciary (https://www.supremecourt.uk/cases/docs/uksc-2016-0196-judgment.pdf).

Once you have familiarised yourself with the case and the article, consider the following questions:

Source: Daily Mail, 4 November 2016

- Where should the boundaries lie in terms of the government's and the courts' lawmaking powers, given the fundamental importance of the separation of powers?
- Why might an unaccountable judiciary be better than an elected Parliament for protecting the rights and freedoms of citizens?

Judicial responsibilities

In order to understand judges' roles, and appreciate the complexities involved, you need to be able to identify the differences in the courts in which they sit. In the English court system (shown in **Figure 23.5**), the highest ranked court is the Supreme Court. (The European Court of Human Rights (ECtHR) sits alongside this structure of national courts—we discuss human rights and the role of the ECtHR shortly, in **section 23.5**, but for now you should just be aware that it exists—and that it will continue to, as Brexit only affects our relationship with the *European Union*, which is a separate entity.) There are two main categories of court in the English system; the **appellate courts** and the **courts of first instance**. For criminological purposes, the key things to remember are the differences between these types of courts.

There are three appellate courts: the Supreme Court, the Court of Appeal, and the Divisional Court (a branch of the High Court known as the Queen's Bench Division). These courts are more powerful than the courts of first instance. They look again at cases that have already been 'heard' in the lower, 'first instance' courts and deal with appeals that have been filed against the decisions. The courts of first instance have to follow the decisions made by the appellate courts. Expressed in legal language, appellate courts set 'precedents' that are 'binding' for future cases.

The two types of first instance court are the Crown Court and the Magistrates' Court. In courts of first instance, the judiciary, including magistrates, are required to act as either a trial court (if the defendant has pleaded not guilty and a verdict must be reached) or a sentencing court (if the defendant has pleaded guilty). The Crown Court setting is generally what people have in mind when they use the term 'court', although due to the way criminal offences are classified, they are very much the exception; usually over 90 per cent of cases are completed in the Magistrates' Court. Our system classifies offences as:

- **indictable offences** which are considered so serious they can only be tried in the Crown Court in front of a judge and jury (examples include murder, manslaughter, and rape);
- **summary offences** which are of lesser seriousness so can only be tried in the Magistrates' Court (examples

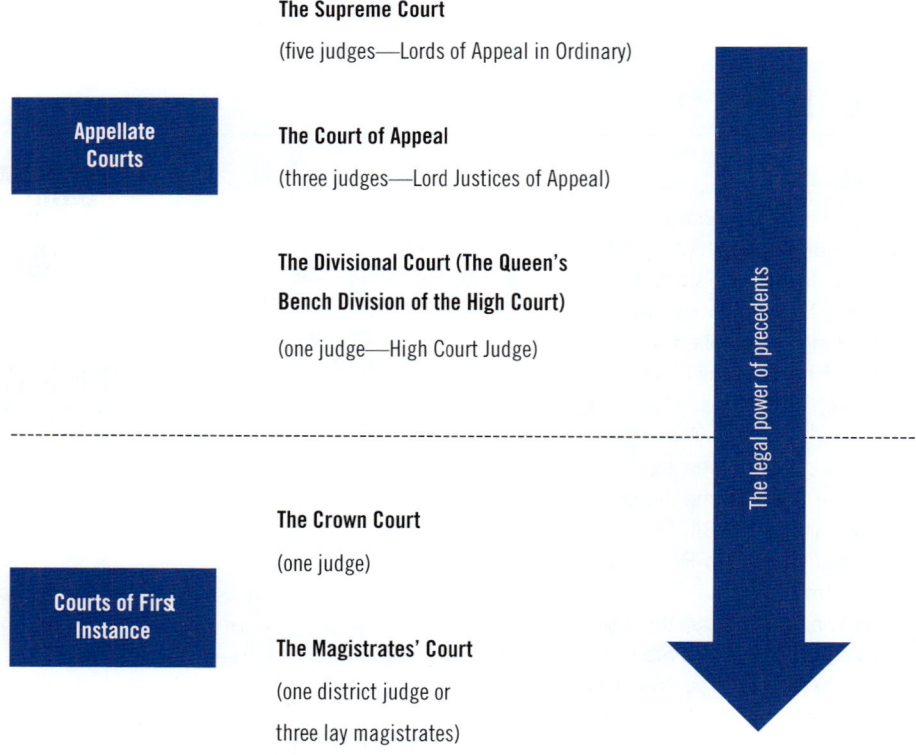

Figure 23.5 The hierarchy of criminal courts in England and Wales helps us to understand the different judicial responsibilities, and to appreciate the complexities involved

include most driving offences, common assault, and minor public order offences); or

- **either way offences** are those of mid-ranking seriousness so can be tried in either court of first instance (examples include burglary, theft, and assault occasioning actual bodily harm).

Although only a relatively small number of cases proceed to a Crown Court trial, it is in these trials that we can most clearly see the responsibilities of the different parts of the judiciary. Here, the judge acts as the **tribunal of law**, with responsibility for deciding all matters of law, such as whether evidence is admissible and what sentence to impose. The jury is the **tribunal of fact** and has to decide all factual questions, such as the defendant's possible guilt. Such clear separation of roles does not exist in other criminal trials, as magistrates simultaneously act as both the tribunal of law and the tribunal of fact (that is, as 'judge and jury'). These are therefore known as summary trials (hence the term 'summary offences'), and whilst the lack of separate decision-makers on issues of law and fact might seem unfair, they are considered acceptable for less serious offences. The fairness of a trial can also be threatened when decisions are made by one person rather than a jury, but as we will discover in **Chapter 24**, this practice has become increasingly common in recent years and recent governments have tried to restrict the 'right' to a trial by jury in more serious cases such as either way offences. This illustrates the separation of powers principle at work, as plans from the executive (the government) have been checked and restricted by the legislature (Parliament), which has so far refused to pass the proposals into law.

The role of a judge in the appellate courts is quite different to that of judges and magistrates in courts lower in the hierarchy. When a court is hearing an appeal, which is traditionally against a conviction (although following the 'double jeopardy reform' we consider later, it can now also be against an acquittal), there are additional issues for it to address. In addition to retrying the facts of an individual case, the court also needs to consider questions of law. The answers to these legal questions can involve setting precedents that become binding in the future. This is particularly true of precedents from the Supreme Court. Alongside this court sits the ECtHR, which has arguably produced the most authoritative precedents since the Human Rights Act was introduced in 1998—though the Supreme Court does not have to always follow ECtHR decisions and there have been times, such as in *Boyd* v *The Army Prosecuting Authority* [2002] UKHL 31, when it did not feel bound by such rulings. We consider the complexity of the relationships between these two courts in **Chapter 24**.

23.4 The rule of law: due process

The rule of law's focus on the fairness of the justice process, reflected in its insistence on the need for separation of powers and an independent judiciary, aligns it most closely with the **due process model** of justice system. In this section we unpack this justice model, considering its focus on **fair procedure**, the ways in which some of its principles have been reshaped over the years, and the closely related idea of **open justice**.

A focus on 'fair procedure'

As we saw in **Chapter 3**, where we considered due process as one of the three **normative** models for criminal justice (see **Table 3.2**), this model holds that the burden is on the state to prove that a defendant is guilty through a process that respects legal rights and protects individuals. Fair procedure—also known as **procedural justice**—is the most important principle of the due process model, and this is seen as essential if a system is to succeed in reducing crime. The term refers to the criminal justice practices that authorities can take to 'build their legitimacy; increase voluntary deference to their authority; motivate more compliance with laws or rules; and heighten cooperation in achieving community-level goals, such as the maintenance of social order' (Tyler, 2017: 2.2). Unlike the **crime control model**, which prizes *efficient* procedure most highly, for the due process model fair procedure is paramount. This is more important than any other consideration, including questions of fact, with guilty verdicts only acceptable if their cases have been dealt with in a 'procedurally regular fashion . . . [by] rules designed to safeguard the integrity of the process' (Packer, 1964: 16).

It is important to note that a justice process that is based on 'fair procedure' will develop over time, as the meanings of both 'fair' and 'procedure' can change. For example, it was not until the Criminal Evidence Act 1898 that it was considered 'fair' to allow a defendant to testify at their own trial, then less than a century later (the Criminal Justice and Public Order Act 1994) it became fair to interpret a defendant failing to testify at their trial as evidence of guilt. Just five years later, further change occurred with the Youth Justice and Criminal Evidence Act 1999 preventing defendants from personally cross-examining their alleged victims in court. However, the restriction only applied to criminal courts and not to family courts in the civil side of the law, and recent research found that one-quarter of domestic abuse survivors had been cross-examined by their ex-partner (*Law Society Gazette*, 30 May 2018). This received critical media coverage to which the government responded in January 2019 with its parliamentary bill, 'Transforming the Response to Domestic Abuse'. In addition to these changing attitudes towards fairness, changes to 'procedure' also occur—we examine these consequences in **section 23.6**.

Elements of the due process model are at play when the law is written and structured so that it 'checks and balances' the powers in the criminal process. These 'brakes' can be applied at different stages of the process to filter out cases that should go no further. Due process systems take the possibility of errors and mistakes extremely seriously so, to reduce this possibility, they are 'designed to present *formidable impediments* to carrying the accused any further along in the process' (Packer, 1964: 13, emphasis added). Depending on a system's perspective on justice, these elements can be like an 'obstacle course' or, much less negatively, 'a factory that has to devote a substantial part of its input to *quality control*' (ibid: 15, emphasis added). This level of 'quality control' does, of course, have an impact on procedural speed and efficiency, so the financial implications can be a major disadvantage.

The priority that due process gives to the rights of innocent people was famously represented in a statement that has become known as the **Blackstone ratio**, which asserts that it is 'better that ten guilty persons escape, than that one innocent suffer' (Blackstone, 1769, Vol. 4: 27). This quotation, from the renowned *Commentaries on the Laws of England* by Sir William Blackstone which published between 1765 and 1769, makes it clear where this writer felt the balance should lie between protecting the innocent and convicting the guilty. The Blackstone ratio reflects due process values as it asserts that a so-called false negative (that is, falsely deciding the defendant *did not* do it) is a far less serious mistake than a false positive (that is, falsely deciding the defendant *did* do it).

It is important to remember, when discussing fair procedure, that although the very idea seems bizarre to modern ideas of fairness, our justice system has not always accepted that mistakes can be made. The Court of Appeal was only established in 1907, and high levels of respect for the rule of law principle meant that the idea that there could be miscarriages of justice was not seriously considered until the end of the 19th century.

At this time, a campaign was led by newspapers, periodicals, and people such as the creator of Sherlock Holmes, Sir Arthur Conan Doyle, to introduce an appeal court to try to reduce the chances of mistakes being made (Thomas, 1998).

Other authors and journalists involved in the early campaigns to prevent or correct mistakes from the justice system included Ludovic Kennedy, whose book *10 Rillington Place* recorded the wrongful execution of Timothy Evans in 1953 for the murder of his wife and baby daughter. Journalist Bob Woffinden, author of *Miscarriages of Justice* (1987) and *The Nicholas Cases: Casualties of Justice* (2016), also played an instrumental role. We would strongly advise that you watch the films *10 Rillington Place* (1971) and *Let Him Have It* (1991) to learn more about cases that were instrumental in increasing awareness of miscarriages of justice in our system. These days, there is widespread awareness that errors are possible in the justice system, with appeal courts considered an essential feature of a fair system, and it is also much easier to build public interest and support in a case through digital media, as we explore in **Controversy and debate 23.2**.

Reshaping fundamental principles

Some principles associated with the rule of law and the due process model are so fundamental that they seem fixed, but in fact even the firmest principles have shifted over the years. Due process principles demand that:

- the court has the jurisdiction to deal with the accused (that is, that it possesses the legal power to do so);
- the accused must be presumed innocent until/unless the prosecution can prove them guilty 'beyond reasonable doubt'—the concept of **presumption of innocence**;
- the accused must be legally competent to stand trial (that is, they must possess **criminal responsibility**);
- the accused must not have committed the offence too long ago or have been previously acquitted or convicted of it—the concept of **double jeopardy**.

Although these principles still stand, attitudes towards them and the ways in which they manifest in the UK system have shifted considerably over recent decades. The results have included a slight revaluing of the presumption of innocence, more criminal responsibility being placed on children, and a revised double jeopardy rule.

CONTROVERSY AND DEBATE 23.2

Miscarriages of justice

In recent years, some miscarriages of justice have gained global interest through semi-dramatised coverage on TV and in podcasts. The most prominent examples are the Netflix series *Making a Murderer* (seasons 1 and 2 were released in 2015 and 2018) and the podcast *Serial* (seasons 1, 2 and 3 were released in 2014, 2015–16, and 2018). The Netflix series provoked public protest rallies around the world, a petition with over 500,000 signatures being sent to then US President Barack Obama within 72 hours of its release and, less than a year later, a US district court overturning Dassey's conviction (Costello, 2018). However, despite this publicity the cases featured in *Making a Murderer* and *Serial* have not been resolved at the time of writing and are likely to produce further court hearings.

This brings us to an interesting controversy: digital media has certainly helped increase awareness of the prevalence of miscarriages of justice, but the difficulties in deciding whether a verdict is mistaken remain. There are also concerns that if the prevalence of errors is exaggerated, this could erode trust in—and therefore respect for the decisions of—a justice system. For example, research has suggested that there are error rates of 4 per cent in the US justice system, where capital **punishment** is used, but this statistic cannot be generalised as a measure of innocent people convicted by justice systems across the world. It is unique to these 'death penalty' cases and their resources for reinvestigations—people do not reopen cases and receive exonerations for shoplifting or assault. The academic research into these numbers of mistakes suggests:

> they may be lower or they may be higher. But with a 4% error rate for death sentences, it's hard to believe that false convictions occur in a mere fraction of a percent of lesser cases
>
> (Gross, 2017: 769)

The presumption of innocence

The concept of presumption of innocence is considered so crucial that it is often referred to as the 'golden thread' of criminal law:

> Throughout the web of the English criminal law one golden thread is always to be seen that it is the duty of the prosecution to prove the prisoner's guilt.
>
> (Viscount Sankey LC in *Woolmington* v *DPP* [1935] AC 462 at 481)

In practical terms, this principle means that the state has the burden of proof whenever it brings a case against an individual and to acquire a conviction must reach the required standard of proof ('beyond reasonable doubt'—a phrase with which you are probably familiar from films and TV, as well as the news). The prosecution is responsible for proving that every element of the relevant crime (the requirements listed in the legal definition of the crime) was present. They must prove that the accused had a particular mindset or intention, known as the **mens rea**, and that they performed certain actions or behaved in a certain way, known as the *actus reus*. The need to prove *mens rea* does not apply in some crimes, known as strict liability offences, but for the rest, it is needed to prove that the accused can reasonably be considered responsible for their actions—known as the **fault principle**.

However, despite society's reverence for the presumption of innocence, there are many instances when it does not apply and when the burden of proof is instead on the defence. This can come about in three ways.

1. Through the unwritten body of law based on precedents, known as the **common law** or case law, when the defence of insanity is pleaded (the M'Naghten Rules (1843) 10 C & F 200).

2. By written laws, known as statutes, in the form of:

    (a) An *express* statutory provision (an explicit clause or statement within a statute). One example is s. 139 of the Criminal Justice Act 1988, which states that unless the defence can show 'good reason or lawful authority' for possessing a knife in a public place, an accused will be convicted. Another is the partial defence of diminished responsibility, only available to charges of murder by s. 2 of the Homicide Act 1957, which states that the accused has the legal burden.

    (b) An *implied* statutory provision. According to s. 101 of the Magistrates' Court Act 1980, the burden has been transferred to the defence whenever a defence relies on 'any exception, exemption, proviso, excuse or qualification'. This kind of policy in English criminal law led to estimates in the influential journal *Criminal Law Review* that around 40 per cent of all indictable statutory offences contain this reverse burden (Ashworth and Blake, 1996).

We can see that in practice the rule of law has revalued its 'golden thread' to a much lower level than its 1935 standard.

Criminal responsibility

Whether someone is legally competent to stand trial—that is, has criminal responsibility—is another seemingly fundamental standard that has shifted and been undermined in recent years. The changing '*doli incapax*' standard has been particularly controversial.

As we noted in **Chapter 9** (see **Controversy and debate 9.1**), *doli incapax* referred to the presumption in law that said children and young people aged from ten to 14 years old are unable to tell the difference between right and wrong so cannot be held legally responsible for their crimes. You will remember that from a legal perspective, *doli incapax* was a rebuttable presumption, meaning that it could be defeated by appropriate evidence, but it strongly suggested that a child or young person of this age would not have the level of understanding needed to allow them to be prosecuted. However, this defence was abolished for those aged ten or over in s. 34 of the Crime and Disorder Act 1998, and the abolition of the whole defence was later confirmed in the case of *R v JTB* [2009] UKHL 20, where a 12-year-old boy was convicted of a dozen counts of causing or inciting a child under 13 to engage in sexual activity. Although the wording in s. 34 is vague and clarification can be needed from judges and the common law, this change to the principle of criminal responsibility now means that in England and Wales, children aged ten rather than 14 can be held legally responsible for their crimes.

The double jeopardy rule

The double jeopardy rule is another established principle that has been undermined in recent decades. This rule prevented individuals being tried again if they had already been acquitted or convicted for the same offence. For example, in *R v Beedie* [1998] QB 356 the landlord of a woman who died from carbon monoxide poisoning was first prosecuted under the Health and Safety at Work Act 1974 and then for manslaughter. The manslaughter conviction was overturned on appeal as it was not considered fair to prosecute the defendant again for the same offence. The double jeopardy rule can be traced to the common law doctrine from the Middle Ages known as the *autrefois* rule (*autrefois* means 'another time'). It evolved to protect people at that time from liability in both courts of its dual system; those under the jurisdiction of the monarch and those under the church. As well as representing 'fairness', it was also thought to encourage diligence and efficiency in criminal investigations and prosecutions (Law Commission, 2001).

The rule was first adapted by the tainted acquittal procedure from ss. 54–7 of the Criminal Procedure and Investigations Act 1996. This means a retrial can be held if a court decides that an acquittal has occurred as a result of interference with, or intimidation of, a juror or a witness. Provisions in ss. 75–91 of the Criminal Justice Act (CJA) 2003 were more controversial as they removed the guarantee that people could not be prosecuted twice and introduced exceptions which mean that, in principle, it is now possible to have more than one 'go' at a defendant. The rule has been modified rather than abolished, as it is only possible to re-prosecute following a not guilty verdict for certain 'qualifying offences' where there is 'new and compelling evidence' and the Court of Appeal believes it is 'in the interests of justice' to prosecute again. It was first used in 2006 against the murderer of a young woman named Julie Hogg and the reform's qualifying offences are listed in Sch 5 to the Act (they currently total 30 different offences) and go far beyond the recommendation from the Law Commission that cases of murder should be the only exception to the *autrefois* rule.

Research into the first decade of the use of these new powers found there had been 13 applications to the Court of Appeal; out of the nine cases that passed the test for a retrial, the defendant was convicted in eight (Dennis, 2014). The fact that this reform can be used retrospectively has meant that even though the *autrefois* rule may have been in force at the time of the offence or acquittal, a defendant can still be retried. Whether a retrial is 'in the interests of justice' is decided by the Court of Appeal's answers to the three questions contained within s. 79:

- Is a subsequent retrial likely to be fair?
- How long ago was the qualifying offence allegedly committed?
- Was due diligence conducted by the police and prosecution in the original trial?

Apart from the exceptions introduced by the CJA 2003, the *autrefois* rule is still enforced by the common law and its **abuse of process** principle. This gives the judiciary the power to stop a prosecution (which is called granting a 'stay') if the court considers it unfair, and the House of Lords' decision in *Bennett v Horseferry Road Magistrates' Court and Another* [1993] 3 All ER 138 is the leading authority. A 'stay' should be granted either because it would be impossible to give the accused a fair trial, or because the circumstances of the prosecution amount to a misuse of process that disregards justice and propriety. Unfortunately, the vague nature of this principle means it is not possible to produce specific or even

WHAT DO YOU THINK? 23.3

Do 'technicalities' prevent the wheels of justice from turning?

> Man who filmed 100 women's feet escapes charges on a technicality.
>
> (*The Times*, 30 June 2007)

So far in this chapter, we have considered how changing attitudes to fairness in the criminal process have resulted in subtle, but significant, changes to the law. In this case, reported in *The Times*, a man had taken photographs of the legs and feet of more than 100 unsuspecting women after claiming that his car had broken down in supermarket car parks across Devon between 2003 and 2006. He had asked the women to sit in the driver's seat and rev the engine whilst he pretended to repair it under the bonnet. The women were unaware that a camera was concealed in the car's footwell.

The man could not be charged with the criminal offence of voyeurism because according to s. 67 of the Sexual Offences Act 2003 this can only be committed if the victim is 'is in a place which, in the circumstances, would reasonably be expected to provide privacy'. The local police decided that a car in a car park was not one of those places. In his interview with the police, the accused was reported as saying, 'I'm doing something totally innocent'.

A criminal prosecution was not brought because what the accused had said was 'technically' correct—but *do you think* this was 'actually' the right decision? What would have been gained (and lost) if the rule of law had been applied 'less technically' in this case?

In the case itself, the police used their civil powers to successfully apply for an ASBO that prohibited the man from approaching or taking photographs of women without their consent for the next ten years. Does this change your view?

---

consistent guidelines on its use. For example, an unreasonable amount of time between an offence and subsequent prosecution can count as an abuse of process if it is considered unfair to the defendant. This is supported by the 'justice delayed is justice denied' maxim that protects individuals against long-drawn-out (and now, repeated) prosecutions.

There is a widely held view that the 'double jeopardy reform involves renegotiating, or reneging on the criminal justice deal' (Roberts, 2002: 405), that is, going back on an agreement between consenting individuals and the state. However, a frequently quoted comment from the Law Commission (cited by both senior judiciary and academics) suggested a different consensus:

> There is . . . the spectre of public disquiet, even revulsion, when someone is acquitted of the most serious of crimes and new material (such as that person's own admission) points strongly or conclusively to guilt. Such cases may undermine public confidence in the criminal justice system as much as manifestly wrong convictions. The erosion of that confidence, caused by the demonstrable failure of the system *to deliver accurate outcomes* in very serious cases, is at least as important as the failure itself.
>
> (2001: para. 4.5, emphasis added)

This comment suggests that mistaken acquittals inflict as much damage on the credibility of the criminal justice system as convictions that are clearly wrong. It therefore suggests a weakening of the Blackstone ratio, which prioritises the protection of innocent people from suffering, and a shift towards prioritising the accuracy of outcomes. In the *autrefois* debates, it was claimed that it is in the interests of justice to use scientific advances in acquiring 'new material'; yet the example given by the Law Commission in the quotation above is actually a person's confession.

Have a look at **What do you think? 23.3** and try to apply some of the issues we have discussed so far in this chapter.

Open justice

We now turn to the final element of due process: open justice. 'Open government' is the third principle of the rule of law listed by the World Justice Project (see **section 23.2**), and they clarify that it means laws must be transparently created and enforced. The Court of Appeal highlighted this important principle in 2014 when ruling on the legality of a criminal trial being mostly heard in secret, with Lord Justice Gross remarking:

> The rule of law is a priceless asset of our country and a foundation of our Constitution. One aspect of the rule of law—a hallmark and a safeguard—is open justice, which includes criminal trials being held in public and the publication of the names of defendants.
>
> (Gross LJ in *Guardian News and Media Ltd* v *AB CD* [2014] EWCA Crim 1861, [2])

Gross LJ gives open justice this prominence and refers to it as a 'safeguard' because it is intended to protect the integrity of the rule of law and ensure public confidence in the legal system. There can be exceptions to this rule, but according to Gross LJ's judgment, these are rare and must be justified on the facts of a case. Any deviations must be necessary and proportionate. The case that led to the appeal in which Gross LJ was commenting concerned two defendants arrested in a high-profile terrorism investigation in October 2013. Eight months later, representatives from the media went to the Court of Appeal to challenge the order from a Crown Court judge that anonymised the defendants' names and required their whole trial to be conducted in secret. The prosecution, supported by government ministers, had requested this order in the interests of national security. The Court of Appeal ruled that a significant part of the trial could be conducted in private, or 'in camera' in legal terms ('camera' means 'chamber' in Latin). Both defendants were convicted of collecting information useful for terrorism, under s. 58 of the Terrorism Act 2006, but one had also been prosecuted for the far more serious charge of preparing a terrorist act, contrary to s. 5. He was subsequently acquitted of this charge but since the public and media were excluded from significant parts of the trial, there is no public knowledge as to why the prosecution was brought, or of the evidence that acquitted him.

In some ways, though, justice is more 'open' than ever before: it is possible to see some cases on camera thanks to the live TV broadcasts from both the Court of Appeal and the Supreme Court (**Figure 23.6**). These courts provide live broadcasts of their hearings (with a delay of around one minute) and recordings for future viewing, which are viewable on their websites and on YouTube. (If you would like to see an example, we suggest looking up the case entitled *In the matter of D (A Child)* UKSC 2018/0064: www.supremecourt.uk/cases/uksc-2018-0064.html. This was an important hearing as it was the first time that a female majority of judges had heard a case in England's highest court. The fact this did not occur until 2018 demonstrates how slow some changes to the legal system can be!)

Increasing public confidence by allowing people to see what happens in court has been a recent policy aim. The open justice principle means that, usually, anyone can visit and observe proceedings in court; local Crown or Magistrates' Courts can therefore be valuable resources for you, as a criminology undergraduate needing to learn about this part of the justice system. At the time of writing, the principle is being extended by the Crown Court (Recording and Broadcasting) Order 2020, which will allow some of the court's work to be shown live on television. The broadcasts will be limited to the sentencing remarks from senior judges in certain criminal cases; the judge is to be the only person in the court who can be seen; and, to avoid breaches of reporting restrictions, there will be a short delay in the live broadcasts. Cameras are not going to be installed in the courts and the TV companies have to bring their own equipment. This extension of open justice is being introduced to improve public understanding of the system, although the fact that it is reserved for the sentencing in serious cases shows us the kind of tough-looking image that the system wants to project. The interest in improving public confidence by increasing the transparency of the court process reflects the well-known quotation:

> It is not merely of some importance but is of fundamental importance that justice should not only be done, but should manifestly and undoubtedly be seen to be done.
>
> (Lord Chief Justice Hewart in *R* v *Sussex Justices, ex parte McCarthy* (1924) 1 KB 256, KBD at 259)

This emphasis on justice being 'manifestly and undoubtedly' seen to be done is often used to promote due process values, but such forceful claims do not actually appear in the current legal test for whether there is bias in a court hearing. This test is restricted to whether the fair-minded and informed observer, having considered the facts, would conclude that there was a real possibility of bias (*Porter* v *Magill* [2001] UKHL 67). Assessing whether the standards of a fair-minded observer (or, more frequently, a 'reasonable person') have been met can be an important part of a judge's role. These supposedly objective decisions are in reality the subjective views of a judge, but the judge's independence, training, and experience are designed to reduce possibilities of bias. The open justice principle can be considered the most important of all criminal justice safeguards:

> Publicity is the very soul of Justice. It is the keenest spur to exertion, and the surest of all guards against improbity. It keeps the judge himself, while trying, under trial. . . . It is through publicity alone that justice becomes the mother of security.
>
> (Bentham, 1843: 115)

Figure 23.6 The decision to provide live TV broadcasts of some hearings at the Court of Appeal and the Supreme Court—the largest courtroom of which is pictured here—is an extension of the principle of 'open justice'

Source: David Iliff/CC BY-SA 3.0

23.5 The rule of law: human rights

Human rights—the basic rights and freedoms to which all humans are entitled—have been a major criminal justice principle, influencing the rule of law since the creation of the European Convention on Human Rights (ECHR). This treaty was drafted in 1950 by an organisation called the Council of Europe, a body that was established by the UK and nine other European countries to protect human rights, democracy, and the rule of law in Europe in the hope of avoiding repetition of the horrors from the 20th century's two World Wars. The Council of Europe is a separate organisation to the European Union so the ECHR, which was not directly incorporated into UK law until the passing of the Human Rights Act 1998 (HRA), will remain within UK law post-Brexit (unless, of course, legislation for its removal is passed). We saw in **section 23.3** and **Figure 23.5** that the Supreme Court is the highest ranked court in the system but that the ECtHR can also be influential. So, what are the implications of this?

Schedule 1 to the HRA lists the human rights (known as Articles) that are protected, so as long as the Convention remains in force, and UK citizens can take their cases about alleged infringement of their rights to a UK court rather than the ECtHR in Strasbourg, France. The legislation has implications for all public authorities in the UK, as they must respect the rights listed in the Convention. A 'public authority' includes courts and tribunals, plus people with public functions; the latter group includes police officers, prison staff, **probation** staff, local authorities, and government departments. The ECHR has also had a significant impact on the judiciary, as the influence of human rights on the rule of law means that judges must, as far as possible, interpret legislation in a way that is compatible with the Convention rights. They have the power to declare legislation incompatible, and whilst this does not affect the validity of the law (unlike the pre-Brexit obligations from the EU), Parliament then has to decide whether to amend its law under a process known as the Remedial Order. The judiciary and legislature can work together through a 'dialogue model', where the courts can be asked by Parliament to specify when legislation is incompatible, but the ultimate power to decide whether and how to respond remains with Parliament.

If an individual's human rights are found to have been breached by a public authority the court has the power to grant a 'judicial review'. This is a court hearing that reviews the lawfulness of a decision by a public authority; if the court judges the decision unlawful, then, among other things, it can make this declaration, cancel the decision, or prevent the authority from acting in a particular way. Generally, when a decision is found to be unlawful at judicial review, the public authority will make the decision again. The alternative (according to s. 8 of the HRA) is that a court can award compensation to the **claimant** if it is necessary, just, and appropriate.

There are three main types of human rights: absolute rights, strong rights, and **qualified rights**. Let's consider each one before reflecting on the challenges involved in the use of rights.

Absolute rights

Absolute rights are, as the name suggests, the strongest and most indisputable form of human rights. The clearest example of an absolute right is arguably Art. 3, which forbids the use of torture on and inhuman or degrading treatment or punishment of a person. Public authorities have to uphold an absolute right like this one, even in times of war or other national emergencies. An absolute right also cannot be 'balanced' against the needs of other individuals or the public interest, except in rare circumstances where two absolute rights are pitched against each other. This category of rights includes those guaranteed by Arts 2, 3, 4(1), and 7.

Another absolute right is Art. 7, which forbids criminalising someone for acts or omissions committed at a time when they were not illegal. However, your reading in this chapter so far should have made you sceptical about the strength of this claim—think about the 'double jeopardy' reforms and the way that the common law creates precedents in cases that have already happened (**section 23.4**).

Strong rights ('special' or 'limited' rights)

Strong rights are similar to absolute rights in that they cannot be 'balanced' against the rights of other individuals or the public interest. But unlike absolute rights, governments do not have to apply strong rights in times of war or national emergency (Art. 15)—in legal language, they are allowed to partially suppress these rights, known as *derogation*. Under ss. 14 and 16 of the HRA, derogation can only be made by the Secretary of State for Justice and this lasts for five years, unless renewed. The right to liberty (Art. 5) and the right to a fair trial (Art. 6) are examples of limited rights for these purposes.

The right to liberty is limited in that states can arrest or imprison someone in order to fulfil the law; the right does not apply to 'lawful detention' following 'conviction by a

	Can be 'balanced' against other rights or the public interest?	Can be 'derogated' from in times of war or national emergency?	Examples of this right
Absolute rights	✗ (except when two absolute rights conflict)	✗	Art. 3—the use of torture on or of inhuman or degrading treatment, or punishment of a person. Art. 7—the retrospective criminalisation of acts and omissions.
Strong rights	✗	✓	Art. 5—the right to liberty. Art. 6—the right to a fair trial.
Qualified rights	✓	✓	Art. 8—the right to respect for private and family life. Art. 9—the right to freedom of thought, conscience, and religion. Art. 10—the right to freedom of expression. Art. 11—the right to freedom of assembly and association with others.

Table 23.1 The three main types of human rights
Source: Human Rights Act 1998, Sch 1

competent court'. We could suggest that the right to a fair trial is similarly limited in that it includes the right to be presumed innocent until proved guilty according to law, and we have already seen that there can be exceptions to this right (see **section 23.4**).

Qualified rights

Qualified rights can be restricted not only in times of war or emergency but also in order to protect the rights of another or the wider public interest. In general, qualified rights are structured so that the first part of the Article sets out the right, while the second part establishes the circumstances in which a public authority can legitimately interfere with that right in order to protect the wider public interest. This category of rights includes those guaranteed by Arts 8, 9, 10, and 11.

The characteristics of these three main categories of rights are summarised in **Table 23.1**.

The challenges of using 'rights'

The influence of the ECHR, and its court the ECtHR, has seen the concept of human rights grow to become one of the rule of law's fundamental ideals, comparable in terms of significance with the protection of democracy (Bingham, 2010). However, some politicians and parts of the media loudly criticise the principle (see **Figure 23.7**)—for example, former Prime Minister David Cameron referred to the European ruling that prisoners should get the vote as something that 'makes him physically sick' (*The Telegraph*, 2 October 2015). It is not always clear whether these objections are directed towards the EU or the ECHR, but they have led to calls for Parliament to strengthen its safeguarding (protective) role for human rights (Hunt et al., 2015) and they show no sign of fading away. We consider the potential future direction for human rights further in **New frontiers 23.1**.

There seems to be less of this kind of outrage in other countries, such as Germany. Like most European nations, it has also had its share of extremely 'hard' human rights cases, including *Gäfgen* v *Germany* (App. no. 22978/05) (2011) 52 EHRR 1, considered in depth in **Controversy and debate 3.1**. In this case, a successful claim for €3,000 was granted in compensation to Gäfgen for breach of his human rights during his arrest and detention in a police station. He was arrested after collecting a ransom of €1 million he had demanded from the parents of a missing 12-year-old boy. Initially, Gäfgen refused to say anything to the police (he had already suffocated the boy and disposed of the body near a lake), and believing the boy to be in serious danger, the police responded with extremely sinister threats of torture to try to make him say where the boy was. On receiving the threats, Gäfgen

Figure 23.7 Although human rights has become one of the rule of law's central principles, some politicians and media sources are strongly critical of their influence

Source: Daily Express, 3 October 2014

Source: https://theday.co.uk/stories/uk-s-pm-targets-europe-s-human-rights-court

NEW FRONTIERS 23.1

A new direction for human rights?

Taking a case to the ECtHR has been an option for UK citizens since the country became a signatory to the court in 1966. Today, over 800 million people in 47 countries across Europe can do the same, yet it is something in the UK that has been repeatedly criticised. This opposition has been led by some politicians and parts of the media in their respective searches for quick popularity and sales. It has included wildly exaggerating the number of cases the UK supposedly loses in the ECtHR, and continued attacks on rights protections being given to the 'wrong' kind of humans (Anon., *The Secret Barrister*, 2020). A famous example of this bias was provided in a speech at the Conservative Party conference by the then Home Secretary (and later Prime Minister) Theresa May:

> We all know the stories about the human rights act. The violent drug dealer who cannot be sent home because his daughter—for whom he pays no maintenance—lives here. The robber who cannot be removed because he has a girlfriend. The illegal immigrant who cannot be deported because—and I am not making this up—he had a pet cat.
>
> (*The Guardian*, 4 October 2011)

However, subsequent fact-checking by various people, including senior judges, media organisations, and politicians, found that this 'cat story' was indeed made up. It came from a 2008 decision of the Asylum and Immigration Tribunal (IA/14578/2008) where the government lost its case not because of the HRA, but because the Home Office had failed to follow its own policy. This has been described as 'the most famous example of the misrepresentation of human rights . . . perhaps ever' (Wagner, 2012: para. 32(a)).

The government's continued hostility was evident in an interview with May 16 months later, published under the headline, 'It's MY job to deport foreigners who commit serious crime and I'll fight any judge who stands in my way' (*Sunday Mail*, 17 February 2013). Its aggressive language showed disregard for the separation of powers, as well as the principle of human rights. The criticism has continued and in 2020 the government's then chief adviser Dominic Cummings stated that holding a referendum on the ECHR was 'high on the agenda' (*The Independent*, 13 September 2020). However, apart from extremely vague claims for a 'British Bill of Rights', it is uncertain which of the human rights in the HRA/ECHR will be up for a public vote.

immediately broke down, confessed to the crime, and disclosed the location of the body. It was unanimously held by the ECtHR judges that this was a breach of Art. 3 as Gäfgen had received degrading treatment for which no derogation was possible. This right's absolute nature re-categorised Gäfgen as a victim and his entitlement to compensation is a striking example of the force of absolute human rights.

23.6 Adversarial justice

We now move on to discuss the second key criminal justice principle for this chapter: adversarial justice. As with the rule of law; it is a standard with many different values.

As we discussed in some depth in **Chapter 3** (see **section 3.5**), criminal justice in the UK, particularly England and Wales, is renowned for operating under a system of **adversarial justice**. In this chapter, we will briefly reflect on the way in which adversarial justice has become a key principle in our system, with its implications reaching beyond court trials themselves. It is a system that frames the criminal process as a battle between an individual and the state (remember that cases where one individual or company battles against another sit within the civil rather than the criminal system), which ultimately results in a showpiece trial where the parties can win and lose their cases. The trial is an important part of the process but (as Jaime Hamilton QC notes in **Conversations 23.1**) it does not set out to establish the 'truth' about a crime in a neutral sense—hence the 'winning' and 'losing' of cases. Instead, it emphasises the importance of the burden of proof (see **section 23.4**) and the need to have sufficient evidence for a conviction. It means the police and prosecution cannot proceed with a case, regardless of their views of guilt, until they have sufficient proof—beyond reasonable doubt—that the crime was committed by the suspect. There is no burden on a suspect to establish or prove their innocence because, as with the rule of law, the presumption of innocence is rated highly (apart from the numerous exceptions we discussed in **section 23.4**).

An adversarial criminal trial can be seen in simple form as 'a game of two halves'. Each half is always the same, in that each side produce their witnesses for **examination-in-chief**, in which they are questioned by their own side, and then **cross-examination**, when they are questioned by the opposition. It is then possible for witnesses to experience **re-examination**, where questions can be asked from the witnesses' own side as a result of what came out of cross-examination. The prosecution always starts first and, if by 'half-time' (the end of the prosecution case), a case to answer has not been established (that is, it seems clear that there are no grounds to prosecute), the tribunal of law must stop the proceedings. It may not surprise you to learn that the adversarial system of trial in England has evolved from procedures that were established by the Ancient Romans. It can be described as a gladiatorial contest, and this can lead to the belief that the person with the most effective gladiator (lawyer) and the 'best', most credible witnesses will win. Aspects of the adversarial system, including the importance it places on witnesses and cross-examination (see **Controversy and debate 23.3**), have been criticised on the grounds of fairness, and in response the tradition in England has been adjusted in a variety of ways over recent years. Changes include:

- New presumptions that a complainant's previous sexual history is inadmissible.
- A range of special measures (such as live video links, video-recorded evidence, and protective screens in court) are now available for any witness considered vulnerable or intimidated (although this protection does not apply to defendants when they testify). This change came about through the Youth Justice and Criminal Evidence Act 1999.
- The defence are now required to take part in a full **disclosure of evidence** process, providing the prosecution with a statement that sets out the nature of the proposed defence, the defences which will be relied on, the facts that are disputed with the prosecution (including reasons), plus indications of any points of law likely to be raised. (This means that only in film and TV courtroom dramas will the crucial bit of evidence arrive just in time!)
- The law's presumption of innocence has been reshaped (see **section 23.4**) so that it no longer includes the suspect's right of silence at arrest, in the police station, and at court—this protection was removed by ss. 34–5 of the Criminal Justice and Public Order Act 1994. Such silences can now be treated as a sign of guilt, as can non-compliance with the rules for disclosure of a defence statement.

The Criminal Procedure Rules and decisions such as *R v Gleeson* [2004] EWCA Crim 579 have adapted this new version of adversarialism still further. It is no longer acceptable for the defence to seek an advantage from a 'technical' or 'legal' mistake in the prosecution; arguably, this further reshapes the presumption of innocence and means a defence lawyer can effectively be expected to help with their client's downfall! These changes have altered the rules considerably for those working in the system (see **Conversations 23.1** for a discussion); and have evolved to the extent where some scholars regard criminal justice in the UK as 'adversarialism lite' (Cape, 2010). Jurisdictions such as the US, Australia, and other common law countries also employ adversarial justice—you

CONVERSATIONS 23.1

Our changing adversarial system: a view from inside the courtroom

with **Jaime Hamilton QC**

Barristers like to think of ourselves as bewigged gladiators, fighting to the death as adversaries vying for the jury to give our side the thumbs up or down.

The words 'adversarial system' are incorporated into every social conversation when a barrister is asked how we defend the guilty. We reply with pride about how we must suspend our beliefs and about how each side has the sword and the shield of the evidence; we are simply there to deploy the material to the best of our abilities. Two advocates presenting our case and attacking the other side, so the tribunal of fact can make the decision.

The truth is that the adversarial system has been modified over the years and this pace of change has quickened since the introduction of the Criminal Procedure Rules in 2005. A statement accompanying the first edition of the rules described the presumption of innocence and a robust adversarial process as the 'essential features of English legal tradition and of the defendant's right to a fair trial'. This was difficult to reconcile with the stated overriding objective of the rules, which included all parties preparing and conducting the case as to 'acquit the innocent and convict the guilty'.

When answering the acquaintance who asks how we do what we do, we would also always quote the phrase 'it is better that ten guilty men go free than one innocent man go to prison'. Until relatively recently, this seemed to be at the heart of the adversarial system, which did not involve a search for the truth and was not a system for sorting between the innocent and the guilty with any degree of certainty. It was about safety before results.

Very much a part of that was the idea that the defence simply had to react to what the prosecution did. The defence did not have to tell the prosecution what the defence was. The defence could exploit any and every deficit in the prosecution's case and preparation.

Not anymore. Now the defence have to be proactive. If the prosecution have failed to do something then it is the duty of the defence to bring it to their attention and, if need be, to the attention of the court. No longer can we ambush the prosecution at trial with their failures.

That has diminished the adversarial nature of the system. Getting the case before the jury has become far more of a collaborative effort in recent years. And that has probably saved many a prosecution in times of austerity.

It is not only in the interaction of the sides that the system has become less adversarial but in the **culture** and demeanour of the courtroom. Each generation of advocates tell those coming after that judges in their day were more fearsome, however it is undoubtedly the case that the modern judge is more courteous and understanding than the tyrants of previous years.

The way the advocates deal with those who are important but occasional players in the criminal justice system has changed beyond recognition. Where we used to never speak to witnesses before they gave evidence, we now are obliged to speak to every witness. As we try to create an environment where witnesses can give their best evidence, the manner and tone of being adversaries has diminished.

The whole emphasis in recent years has been about ensuring advocates speak in an appropriate way, ask questions which are appropriate for the age or other characteristics of the witness, and generally work in a way to allow evidence to be given, rather than attacked. We are no longer provided with a sword and a shield, but online 'toolkits' which instruct us on how to deal with a broad array of vulnerable witnesses.

The adversarial system has always had rules. Now it has a tone which is softer. We are on different sides, we fight without fear or favour, but the courtroom is becoming less of a battleground than it used to be. Politics may not have become any more gentle, but the adversarial system has.

Jaime Hamilton QC, criminal law barrister and Deputy Head of Chambers at 9 St John Street, Manchester

CONTROVERSY AND DEBATE 23.3

Cross-examination is 'the greatest legal engine ever invented for telling the truth'

The highly distinguished American legal scholar John Henry Wigmore (**Figure 23.8**) claimed that cross-examination is the 'greatest legal engine ever invented' for finding the truth. But is this accurate?

Despite the courtroom being one of the most important stages in a criminal process, there are restrictions on jury research and therefore little information exists about whether '12 randomly selected UK citizens' see truth as the outcome from cross-examination. Supporters of cross-examination argue that the 'best' witnesses react well to their versions of events being forcibly tested. Such witnesses provide the tribunal of fact with highly influential evidence, and cross-examination supposedly 'beats and bolts out the Truth much better' than when a witness is not cross-examined (according to Sir Matthew Hale's (1736) influential *History and Analysis of the Common Law of England*).

On the other hand, it is generally agreed by both jurists (legal scholars) and practitioners that a 'good' witness is a person who is articulate, confident, and seems emotionally balanced. If true, these **suppositions** demonstrate clear potential for unfairness as such characteristics are highly subjective and disregard individual differences. Researchers have also noted the toxic effects on witnesses from cross-examination, such as those in sexual offence trials who compared the experience to 'a second rape' (McGlynn, 2017). These observations have prompted the kinds of changes to the adversarial system that we have detailed, and that Jaime Hamilton QC describes in **Conversations 23.1**—for example, the requirement that lawyers speak to every witness before they give evidence and try to create an environment where witnesses can give their best evidence.

Figure 23.8 American legal scholar Major John Henry Wigmore believed that cross-examination was a powerful method of uncovering the truth

Source: Public domain

might like to investigate whether they, too, have diluted their systems.

Whilst the adversarial contest is usually weighted in favour of the prosecution (consider the resources available to the state compared to those available to a local solicitor), this is not always the case. It was clearly reversed in the News International (owned by the billionaire Rupert Murdoch) phone-hacking trial of 2014 when Rebekah Brooks and Andy Coulson, former editors of the *News of the World*, were prosecuted. This led to reports of:

> the power of the private purse knocking six bells out of the underfunded public sector . . . Brooks and Coulson had squads of senior partners, junior solicitors and paralegals, as well as a highly efficient team monitoring all news and social media. The cost to Murdoch ran into millions. Against that, the Crown Prosecution Service had only one full-time solicitor attached to the trial and one admin assistant.

(*The Guardian*, 25 June 2014)

This quotation implies that substantial financial resources can also result in a case being better organised, but it is hard to know the extent to which this might influence its credibility due to the restrictions on criminological research in this area (see **Chapter 32** for further discussion).

An imbalance in resources is less of a problem for the other main system of criminal justice, the **inquisitorial system**, which is used in European countries such as France and the Netherlands. As the name conveys, this system is more of an *inquiry* into an alleged offence rather than a contest between two parties. The inquiry is led by an official investigator who independently discovers as many facts as possible; rather than being an adversarial battle where each party produces the evidence, which naturally has the strong possibility of being biased. Instead of centring on a showpiece trial where the parties confront each other with their witnesses, an inquisitorial process emphasises the importance of preliminary stages, where meetings and written communications between the appointed judge and the parties' representatives produce the evidence for the case. A judge is responsible for questioning the witnesses and this more active role diminishes the power and functions of lawyers. The expense and inefficiency of adversarial trials has led to calls from campaigners, politicians, and some members of the judiciary for a move to an inquisitorial approach (*The Guardian*, 2 August 2018). An 'English style cross-examination' for testing the reliability of a witness's evidence is not possible in inquisitorial trials.

23.7 Restorative justice

Let's turn to the final key principle we will be discussing in this chapter. Here we get to grips with the basic characteristics of restorative justice, its evolution over time, and how it underpins modern approaches to criminal justice. We discuss restorative justice, along with the idea of **diversion**, in more depth in **Chapter 30**.

Restorative justice is a vast term encompassing many different features and practices, but it has a widely accepted general definition as:

> a process whereby parties with a stake in a specific offence collectively resolve how to deal with the aftermath of the offence and its implications for the future.
>
> (Marshall, 1999: 5)

In other words, it is an approach to justice that, in contrast to the standard method where the state takes full responsibility in the response to a crime, emphasises the need for *collective* action for dealing with an offence, seeking to repair the harm it has caused. The harm is generally repaired by providing reparation (in other words, compensation—not necessarily financial; completing a programme of work can be enough) to the injured parties, who are *restored* (hence the name of this approach), as much as possible, to their pre-offence positions.

Restorative justice has become much more extensively used and discussed in recent decades but it is not a principle unique to contemporary times, as we saw in **section 23.1**, when we discussed the compensatory function of the Code of Ur-Nammu (see **Figure 23.1**). However, interest in this potentially game-changing criminal justice principle has grown considerably since around the time the Advisory Council on the Penal System (1970) published their 'reparation and community service ideas [that] were the apotheosis of the post-war attitude to offenders' (Hood, 1974: 380). The optimism of this 'apotheosis' (meaning ideal example) contrasted starkly with the increasingly held belief that 'nothing works' in the **rehabilitation** of offenders (Martinson, 1974). In this discussion of restorative justice, we will focus mainly on the 'community service' ideal, where the harm is repaired to the community as a whole, because in addition to being the most visible and frequently implemented restorative justice response, it has also been called 'the paradigm of community restoration' (Ashworth, 2003: 170—'paradigm' means an ideal, typical model).

We have noted that restorative justice is a very wide term. In addition to the 'community service ideal', it commonly offers responses of:

- victim–offender mediation schemes (where the two parties are brought together in the presence of a mediator);
- other types of meetings, often called conferences, where families or other representatives of an offender and victim are present;
- written communications between these parties.

Restorative justice is a principle that has been adapted over time, becoming increasingly difficult to sum up because of the lack of an agreed standard definition that deals with its different features, and because there is no consensus on the criteria for deciding how much 'restorativeness' is needed for the response (Sharpe, 2004). Restorative justice has become such a disparate set of practices that it is difficult to talk confidently about its theoretical background. Practitioners and supporters usually agree on what practices constitute restorative justice, but 'they tend to disagree about how to characterize those practices' (Garvey, 2011: 510).

Despite these uncertainties, however, restorative responses do have some common features, such as the involvement of the victim of an offence in the criminal process—not just the offender and the state. This principle contributed towards 'the return of the victim' being identified as one of the clearest measures of change in late 20th-century criminal justice (Garland, 2001: 11). Reparation for victims can be provided either indirectly, through community service, or more directly through victim–offender mediation schemes (as illustrated in **Figure 23.9**). In these direct forms of restorative justice, the aim is to create dialogue between an offender and a victim under the direction of an official mediator. This method can provide levels of communication that traditional methods cannot, but there are concerns about its potential unfairness:

> It is plausible to think that people with greater verbal ability will be able to give more expressive—and thus effective—answers to such questions. This is problematic if socio-economic background affects an individual's linguistic development.
>
> (Willis, 2020: 188)

Initially, there was enthusiasm in North America for restorative justice practices being used as an alternative to imprisonment (Umbreit and Zehr, 1982). However, these hopes do not appear to have been realised as the countries that have widely implemented it (the US, New Zealand, Australia, and the UK) are also those which have experienced some of the largest recent increases in rates of imprisonment (Wood, 2015). Nonetheless, interest in the UK for offenders making *reparation* to people affected by their crimes has meant that it has become one of the five statutory purposes of sentencing; the others are *punishment*, *reduction of crime* (including by discouraging and preventing it from happening in the first place), *reform and rehabilitation* of offenders, and the *protection of the public* (s. 142 of the CJA 2003).

We have noted that the restorative justice focus on restoring the whole community has prompted some to refer to the 'community service paradigm' (Ashworth, 2003: 170)—the idea that this is the ideal response for repairing harm through criminal justice. In **Chapter 25** we will consider the influences of policy and practice on this response, but for now it is important to note the changing ways in which the state has tried to 'brand' and present restorative justice approaches, which is most obvious in the variety of labels it has been given. Although sentences of 'community service' (sometimes called CS) are widely understood, this term was officially scrapped by the Criminal Justice and Court Services Act 2000 (CJCSA), which referred to 'community punishment orders', and later described as the unpaid work requirement of a **community order** by the CJA 2003. The CJCSA also rebranded probation orders as 'community rehabilitation orders', which became generic 'community orders' in the CJA 2003. This shift saw clear intentions to distinguish these two responses: probation was considered 'rehabilitation' whereas community service was 'punishment'. This punitive shift was supported by policy from the Home Office (2005) that brought about yet another term, 'Community Payback', as the brand name for this form of sentencing.

Now that you have an overview of this principle, it will be clear that restorative justice already underpins many approaches that are increasingly used in the criminal justice system. We might see its influence as offering hope for 'changing the game' of criminal justice. However, it is important to remember that 'in the context of widespread social exclusion, even restorative, deliberately reintegrative penalties have little hope of making a serious impact on rates of offending' (Lacey, 2003: 101). Social marginalisation results in disadvantages in terms of social welfare, mental health, employment, and education; these factors seriously limit the abilities of criminal justice responses alone to have a clear effect on reoffending. There are restorative justice practices that, in principle, can limit the negative effects of traditional punishment methods and that have social reintegration as an aim, but we know that even a solid, agreed principle is not enough on its own to bring about real change. We return to restorative justice in **Chapter 25** to see what influence it can have in the context of criminal justice policy and practice.

Figure 23.9 The principle of restorative justice underpins many criminal justice approaches, including the Forgiveness Project, a scheme shown here in action at High Down Prison in Sutton, Surrey

Source: Guardian News & Media

23.8 Conclusion

In this chapter we explored the ways in which three key principles, with many supplementary concepts, guide and direct the delivery of criminal justice. We discovered that despite their fundamental importance, the rule of law, adversarial justice, and restorative justice are flexible and evolving concepts. We considered the rule of law in detail to illustrate the extent of this principle, which goes beyond an aim for equality under the law into the controversial areas of judicial independence, due process, and human rights. Now that you are aware of the concept of separation of powers in the justice system, you can appreciate the respective roles and powers of central government, Parliament, and the courts. Reflecting on changes to previously accepted justice standards and practices—such as the presumption of innocence, the double jeopardy rule, and cross-examination in adversarial trials—showed how dynamic this area is. The knowledge and understanding you now have of these core principles, and just as importantly their ability to continually change, mean that you are now equipped with the background information which will allow you to critically analyse the system 'in action' in the next two chapters.

SUMMARY

After reading this chapter and working your way through its different features, you should now be able to:

- Recognise the source and changing nature of essential criminal justice principles

In the initial sections we saw how, despite their fundamental importance, the criminal justice principles of the rule of law, adversarial justice, and restorative justice are dynamic rather than static concepts. Their evolving nature demonstrates that values which have previously been deeply accepted can in fact be changed. Being aware of some of the conflicts arising from these modifications will mean that you can explain how priorities in the justice system can change.

- Outline the importance of the rule of law doctrine

We focused particularly on the rule of law doctrine to illustrate its status as the ultimate authority for democratic systems of justice around the world, but we also reflected on three of its supplementary concepts (an independent judiciary, due process, and human rights) so you should now feel able to question this source of power. Your assessment of the difficulties in creating a judiciary with full independence, or for providing a system of justice that is based on either the Blackstone ratio or on guaranteed human rights, will support analysis of the impact of the doctrine.

- Discuss the essential features of an adversarial justice system

We discussed the key features of adversarialism to encourage you to consider whether its gladiatorial courtroom processes do indeed represent the most effective way for discovering truth. The traditional adversarial contest between two opposing sides means such hearings can lack impartiality as the role of the judge is limited to ensuring the rules are followed. We saw that this differs in inquisitorial systems, where the judiciary have a more active role and undertake 'lawyer-like' functions such as examining witnesses and discovering new evidence.

- Assess the force of the restorative justice principle

We recognised how, in recent decades, this principle has become a much-discussed alternative to the traditional criminal justice processes of state-inflicted punishment on convicted wrongdoers. We saw that the restorative justice principle offers a different dimension, one that prioritises the repairing of the harms suffered by injured parties, and the limits to the principle's status as a key function of justice were revealed in the recent popularity of a much tougher approach to community sentencing.

 Test your understanding of the chapter's key points by attempting the self-test questions on the **online resources** at **www.oup.com/he/case2e**

REVIEW QUESTIONS

1. How does the rule of law principle seek to ensure an independent judiciary?
2. What would be emphasised by a due process model of justice?
3. What is the Blackstone ratio of justice?
4. In recent decades, what examples have there been of the weakening of the principle of adversarial justice?
5. How has the restorative justice principle been used in the work of the criminal justice system?

 Access the **online resources** at **www.oup.com/he/case2e** to check your answers to the review questions.

FURTHER READING

Visit this book's online resources to access additional chapters on the criminal justice systems in Scotland, Wales, and Northern Ireland, respectively.

It is worth bearing in mind that many primary sources, including Blackstone's *Commentaries on the Laws of England 1765–9*, are available free online at Project Gutenberg: www.gutenberg.org.

Cavadino, M., Dignan, J., Mair, G., and Bennett, J. (2019) *The Penal System: An Introduction* **(6th edn). London: Sage.**
The title of this book shows its emphasis on prisons and punishment. It is a comprehensive and authoritative text that will help you research these specific areas, and for critically evaluating the broader criminal justice system.

Joyce, P. (2017) *Criminal Justice* **(3rd edn). Abingdon: Routledge.**
This text investigates issues concerning the measurement, prevention, and detection of crime, before focusing in detail on topics such as policing, prosecutions, the judiciary, and sentencing. It then considers the position of victims in the process; going on to explain the global dimension of criminal justice policy and its potential future direction.

Partington, M. (2019) *Introduction to the English Legal System 2019–2020* **(14th edn). Oxford: Oxford University Press.**
This book clearly explains the key ingredients of the English legal system. It offers detailed information on both the purposes of law and legal processes. Its three chapters on civil law will develop your legal understanding, as will those on the funding for legal services and current challenges for the legal system.

Robins, J. (2018) *Guilty Until Proven Innocent: The Crisis in Our Justice System.* **London: Biteback Publishing.**
This book is written by a renowned legal journalist who also runs the Justice Gap online magazine available at www.thejusticegap.com. Both of these sources are invaluable to undergraduates as they provide many real-life examples of the gaps between legal principles and the practical provision of justice.

 Access the **online resources** to view a wealth of extra information relating to your study of criminology, including self-test questions, answers to review questions, and links to other resources that will help you enjoy and fulfil your potential within your studies.
www.oup.com/he/case2e

CHAPTER OUTLINE

24.1	Introduction	720
24.2	The police	720
24.3	The Crown Prosecution Service	724
24.4	The courts	729
24.5	Probation services and community sanctions	732
24.6	Prisons	735
24.7	Conclusion	739

24

Criminal justice institutions

KEY ISSUES

After studying this chapter, you should be able to:

- assess the ways policing providers engage with the public;
- discuss the purpose of the CPS and consider its effectiveness;
- identify the different courts that can respond to crime and its related problems;
- recognise the different forms of probation and community sanctions;
- appreciate the challenges facing prisons as a key criminal justice organisation.

24.1 Introduction

In the introduction to **Chapter 23**, we suggested that a variety of factors come into play when we try to make changes to the criminal justice system and that these can be boiled down to four main components: principles, people, policies, and practices. These are interlocking cogs in the 'engine' of the system, so changes made to one of these elements will often affect the others. We explored the fundamental 'principles' that underpin the workings of the UK criminal justice system in **Chapter 23**, and in this chapter we move on to 'people' in that we will look at the institutions that give effect to these values. As well as being valuable knowledge for your current studies, a good understanding of the criminal justice system and the challenges it faces may give you ideas for your final year research project or dissertation, as well as a sense of the careers available within the system—see **Chapter 33** for further information relating to careers and employability.

The term 'criminal justice system' (often abbreviated to 'the CJS', but check your institution's position on whether these kinds of informal terms are acceptable in your work) implies that there is a single system so could give the misleading impression that there is one agreed system of justice where organisations work towards common priorities and purposes. Such a system is often called for, but as you know from reflecting on what 'justice' means in **Chapter 3**, it is highly unlikely that we will ever reach a total consensus.

In practice, the criminal justice system contains five distinct institutions that are responsible for delivering justice: the police, the Crown Prosecution Service (known as the CPS), the courts, probation providers, and prisons. Although they are all part of one overall system, each has different aims, roles, and challenges. Theoretically, the fact that these bodies are all accountable to the separation of powers concept (see **section 23.2**) should bring some unity in that it gives Parliament, the independent judiciary, and central government opportunities to shape the system to align with their version of justice. The government (the 'executive') can exert considerable influence through the work of the Ministry of Justice or MoJ (which contains smaller departments such as HM Prison and Probation Service and HM Courts & Tribunals Service). The MoJ is currently the most important governmental agency in the criminal justice system, but the larger and more powerful Home Office is also involved to an extent, mainly with the police (as we will see). Local government organisations can also be involved, such as the different members of Local Criminal Justice Partnerships. The number of different agencies operating in this area adds weight to the idea that it may not be realistic to expect these institutions to operate as one system, particularly as many of them—particularly those at the local level—have their own measurements of success for their work.

24.2 The police

If asked to name organisations within the criminal justice system, most people would list the police first. This is partly because they are the most visible, but also because they are the group with which people are most likely to have some experience. This puts the police in a unique position amongst the big five criminal justice institutions we cover in this chapter and means that it attracts high levels of praise as well as criticism (Hough and Roberts, 2017).

An overview of the police

The first formal system of policing is usually considered to be the one implemented for London by the Metropolitan Police Act 1829, but actually this was an extension of practices that were already in place. Eighty years earlier the Bow Street Runners, established by the Westminster magistrate Henry Fielding, were being paid by central government to detect and prosecute crimes such as robberies on the streets and highways, pickpocketing, shoplifting, as well as visibly patrolling the streets and investigating serious offences (Beattie, 2012). Today's professional approach evolved from growing dissatisfaction with the corruption of 'thief-takers', the people who solved crimes for a fee and claimed rewards for bringing suspects to court. The efforts of Sir Robert Peel, the Home Secretary at the time, were instrumental in the creation of the Metropolitan Police Act, which was rolled out to the rest of the country over the next couple of decades. The police's nickname 'Bobby' (you may have heard the phrase 'local bobby', or 'bobby on the beat') is testimony to the influence of Robert ('Bob') Peel in establishing organised policing with local and central accountability.

These different interests are reflected in the three-part governance structure for the police which was set out in the Police Act 1964 and which, apart from one major modification, is still in force today. It requires power and responsibility to be divided between:

- chief constables or the commissioner;
- the Home Office; and
- Police and Crime Commissioners (PCC).

Each of the 43 regional police forces in England and Wales has a chief constable and the Metropolitan Police in London has a commissioner. The chief constables and the commissioner have the power to establish the policing priorities and policies in their area. Their role is independent when it comes to operational matters and the directing and controlling of their police forces, to guard against political or other forms of influence. They used to work collectively through the Association of Chief Police Officers (ACPO) but since 2015 they have done so through the National Police Chiefs' Council (NPCC).

The Home Office is the government department with responsibility for the police and provides much of the funding to its individual forces (with the Department for Communities and Local Government or the Welsh Assembly Government, plus local council tax revenue known as the police precept, being the other sources). The provision of funding is dependent on targets and other performance indicators set by the Home Office being met; this gives it substantial influence in the delivery of local policing services (Rowe, 2013).

The final part of the system used to be the police authorities. These were local bodies made up of councillors and magistrates with responsibility for maintaining an adequate and efficient police force in their area. However, they were replaced in the Police Reform and Social Responsibility Act 2011 by the role of Police and Crime Commissioner (PCC) and now every police area in England and Wales, with the exception of London and Greater Manchester, must hold a local election every four years where the public can vote for their preferred PCC. London has a unique system due to its population size, the governance powers held by the Mayor of London, and its separate districts of the Metropolitan Police Service and the City of London Police. Greater Manchester is also an exception as, since 2017, the office of the Mayor of Greater Manchester has taken the role of its PCC. The main powers of a PCC are the hiring and firing of chief constables, setting the force's budget, and creating the Police and Crime Plan that sets out the strategies and priorities for their term in office. This plan is established through consultations with an area's chief constable who is then accountable for its implementation.

The PCCs are advised and scrutinised by a Police and Crime Panel (made up mainly of councillors from the relevant local council), who can block proposals to increase the budget or for a new person to be appointed as chief constable. It is not yet clear whether this amendment will ensure the necessary level of power separation, particularly when a PCC and a Police and Crime Panel will both be dominated by the same political party. The PCC elections so far have been renowned for very low levels of voter turnouts and consistent successes for the candidates from the Conservative and Labour Parties, and concerns have been raised about whether PCCs pose a threat to police independence. We consider this issue further in **Controversy and debate 24.1**.

CONTROVERSY AND DEBATE 24.1

Police Crime Commissioners: the voice of the people in policing?

In 2011, the position of Police Crime Commissioner was introduced in every area of England and Wales.

The PCCs aimed to increase public involvement in policing and improve the police's responsiveness to public concerns. The authorities that preceded them were criticised for a lack of accountability, and the hope was that PCCs would give the public a voice in (and window into) policing strategies and priorities. But has the public genuinely been empowered by PCCs, or has their introduction simply increased the powers of local political parties? The public response to the role appears underwhelming to say the least, with very low turnouts to PCC elections. In 2016, the average turnout was around 25 per cent and in 2012, it was half of this amount (*The Guardian*, 9 May 2016). The public voice has also been limited by the dominance of political parties: in the 40 elections in 2016, only four of the winners were independent candidates. The next election should have taken place in 2020 but was postponed for 12 months because of the coronavirus pandemic.

The political associations of PCCs mean there is a risk that they prioritise the interests of their parties and gaining votes over the efficiency and effectiveness of an area's policing. Chief constables report being pressured to increase the numbers of officers in areas likely to vote for the PCC and say that PCCs' views on the system can be 'bonkers' and 'bizarre, unhelpful and dysfunctional' (*The Independent*, 14 September 2018). These reports reveal the tension produced by the hierarchy of these roles: chief constables can feel threatened by the ultimate authority of a PCC to appoint and dismiss them.

Given all this, do you think that PCCs are an effective way of bringing the public voice into contemporary policing, or does the role hold too much power for one elected official?

The role of the police

The introduction of a formal system of policing in 1829 provoked widespread concerns about 'police soldiers' appearing on the streets of England. In response, there was a shift to a more consensual style of policing, a philosophy known as **'policing by consent'**. This effectively turned Peel's original 'boys-in-blue' (a colour intentionally chosen to differ from the army's traditional red), and also the 'girls-in-blue' after the creation of the Women's Police Service in 1914, into 'citizens-in-uniform'.

This approach is said to be enabled by the power that the police have to perform their role—their mandate. Unfortunately, the mandate mirrors other parts of the English constitution in that it is unwritten, poorly defined, and vague. It is said to represent the authority of the people but, because it is hard to pin down, there have always been significant disagreements over the comparative importance of catching offenders, preventing crime, and helping people in emergencies, to name just three of the possible aspects of the policing role. In theory, the police are able to decide for themselves the weight they place on each aspect of their role: their independence is equivalent to the independent judiciary principle (see **section 23.3**) in that they are ultimately accountable to the rule of law and not a particular organisation or body of people. But, as with any information you encounter in your criminology studies, you should use your ABC (*Always Be Critical*) mindset when considering this **concept**. The Covid-19 pandemic provided many examples of the difficulties faced by the police in performing their role, such as the speed at which new rules were being introduced and the confusion regarding their legal status. They sometimes took the form of policy, meaning they were advisory rules rather than ones that could be enforced by criminal justice institutions. This uncertainty, along with the desire to police through consent, meant that in the first six months of the pandemic the police issued around 19,000 fines for breaching coronavirus regulations, whereas in France the figure was more than one million (*The Observer*, 18 October 2020).

Scholarship and research into the role of the police has become a major topic of interest for criminology in recent years, following **ethnographic** research (research that studies social groups and interactions from the perspective of the research subjects) from the 1960s and 1970s. We discuss the benefits of this kind of research many times in this book (see **Chapter 25** for a specific example) and, with regard to the police, the methods revealed the vital importance to the policing role of police **culture**, discretion, and attitudes to the criminal law (Ellison, 2013). The role of the police is a huge topic so it would be a good idea to coordinate your studies of this area with carefully reading the 'Policing' chapter by Trevor Jones, Tim Newburn, and Robert Reiner in the sixth edition of *The Oxford Handbook of Criminology* (2017). This, and the fifth edition of *The Politics of the Police* by Benjamin Bowling, Robert Reiner, and James W. E. Sheptycki (2019), will provide you with comprehensive analysis of current issues and problems. The size of this area of study is also illustrated by the growing levels of knowledge and expertise in sub-areas known as community policing, problem-oriented policing, intelligence-led policing, and evidence-based policing (Keay and Kirby, 2018). It also includes 'pracademic research', which is the name given to research from police professionals into policing practices (Sherman, 2018: 2).

Challenges for the police

It may have been difficult to gain public confidence initially, but for around 100 years between the mid-19th and 20th centuries, the police experienced a 'Golden Age' of high levels of public support. These levels of support may have declined, but even in recent years there is still a far higher level of backing for and confidence in the police than for other criminal justice organisations (Hough and Roberts, 2017).

The major challenge that the police face today is maintaining their current levels of support as public service funding continues to be eroded. Funding cuts mean that they have to employ fewer people and make careful use of their resources, such as reducing the number of police officers patrolling the streets, or 'bobbies on the beat'. This makes them less visible to the public, an impact we consider in **What do you think? 24.1**. These problems are made worse by the changing nature of crime and the fact that certain offences, such as online fraud and child sexual abuse, now require specialist policing (House of Commons Home Affairs Committee, 2018). There are expectations that technology will help the police to direct their resources more efficiently. This includes relying on computerised algorithms for some decision-making; software that determines important issues in the process such as a defendant's risk assessment (Oswald et al., 2018).

Another challenge the police face is the fact that their traditional position as the sole provider of policing services is under threat. The increasing use of private security and other forms of privatisation (when businesses or services are transferred from public to private ownership) risks fragmenting the policing system. Some local people and authorities are privately paying for additional policing, which includes contracting private security firms to patrol the streets in the early hours of the morning. Norfolk Constabulary made headlines in 2018

WHAT DO YOU THINK? 24.1

The end of 'bobbies on the beat'?

The sight of police officers 'on the beat', where they walk the streets in communities they know well, is a classic image for the criminal justice system and one that still seems to be important to the public. In the 'Public Perceptions of Policing in England and Wales 2018' report, over three-quarters of the 17,000 respondents felt it was important to see such a presence in their area (HM Inspectorate of Constabulary and Fire & Rescue Services, 2019: para. 1.5). However, more than one-third of respondents said that they had not seen any police officers on foot in their areas in the past year, and 48 per cent were dissatisfied with the frequency with which they see officers on their streets.

You should read this research in full but, first, it's worth considering your own answers to some of the questions it raises. You will see that the report is really asking how valuable you think that visible policing is in practice.

On the one hand, the sight of 'bobbies on the beat' may be reassuring and make people feel safer, but perhaps these kinds of traditional methods should be replaced with a more targeted approach where officers are allocated to areas where they are more likely to be effective. The potential downside of this strategy is that it could damage the relationship between the public and the police. In addition to feeling less safe, disconnection from the police could also mean that people are less willing to comply with certain regulations, especially those without significant legal consequences, such as the restrictions on individual freedoms imposed during the Covid-19 pandemic. There is also a danger that the public may be less willing to report crimes if they feel disconnected from the police. We know from our discussion of **procedural justice** in **Chapter 23** (see **section 23.4**) that trust and confidence in the police is crucial.

Keep these considerations in mind as you answer the following questions.

1. How important, if at all, do you think it is to have regular police or PCSO presence on foot in your local area?

2. In the past 12 months how frequently, on average, have you seen police officers or PCSOs on foot in your local area? Does this frequency seem about right?

---

when, following their decision to abolish the role of Police Community Support Officers due to the financial pressures they were facing, they contracted the global security company Securitas to supply 'Crime Scene Guards' (*The Guardian*, 10 September 2018). Securitas can employ these guards on zero-hours contracts and also provides non-crime scene services, such as conducting searches, carrying out door-to-door inquiries, and helping with flooding and other environmental incidents. The extent of these developments has led some scholars to describe it as a revolution in policing (Button, 2020). Private policing is now a common practice all over the world and contradicts the traditional view of crime control being something that is exclusively reserved to the state (Nalla and Gurinskaya, 2020).

Despite the difficulties they face, the police are still the central organisation in the criminal justice system. The 'frontline' position of the police enables them to turn the first cog in the engine of justice and their influence spreads through much of the system. This influence can be beneficial, inspiring trust and confidence in the system and encouraging people to want to work with it, or even within it (as you may be thinking of doing). However, it can also be negative, with damaging, criminalising, and even **criminogenic** consequences for individuals and society. In 2020, the killing of an African American man named George Floyd and the global surge of support for the 'Black Lives Matter' movement shone a spotlight on the issue of police brutality against ethnic minorities and the continued existence of **institutional racism**. We have discussed police treatment of BAME people at numerous points in this book and especially in **Chapter 10**, with a focus on the controversial practice of 'stop and search'. We saw examples of the damaging effect of negative experiences of the police in **Conversations 9.1**, where Omar cites this as one factor which led to his involvement in gang crime, and **Conversations 10.2**, where Leon explains the humiliation he experienced as a result of the misplaced use of stop and search. Other groups, including women (see **Chapter 11**) and LGBTQ+ people (see **Chapter 8** and **Conversations 8.1**), also tend to report negative experiences of the police, including that crimes committed against them are not taken sufficiently seriously.

These issues point us towards a final key challenge for the police; one that is shared by other elements of the system but is perhaps particularly pressing for the police as its most public-facing element. This is the challenge of ensuring diversity in the workforce. To take two indicators of diversity, as of March 2019 only 7 per cent of all police officers in England and Wales identified as black and minority ethnic, whereas BME people make up 14 per cent of the overall population, and 30 per cent of officers were women (Home Office, 2019). If the public are not adequately represented by the police workforce, does this prevent them viewing police as 'citizens in uniform' and undermine the principle of policing by consent?

We consider the influence of the police on the justice system further in **Chapter 27**.

24.3 The Crown Prosecution Service

Suspected criminal offences are treated as a matter of **public law** so they are dealt with by a state-implemented system known as the Crown Prosecution Service, often abbreviated to CPS. This legal classification distinguishes crimes from the civil law, which requires individual people or organisations to bring their cases to court. The CPS is an independent prosecuting authority and is not 'the victim's lawyer', as some people assume. (As we touch upon later, in **What do you think 24.2**, although this makes sense from an objective legal position it can contribute to victims feeling excluded from the process.)

An overview of the CPS

The CPS was established as an independent, national prosecuting body in 1986, having been created through the Prosecution of Offences Act 1985 in response to growing criticism of the previous practice of prosecutions. Before 1986, it was the responsibility of individuals and then the police to decide whether cases should be prosecuted, and it was this police involvement which caused most concern, sparking criticism from voices as varied as the law reform pressure group JUSTICE in 1970 and the Royal Commission on Criminal Procedure in 1981. They were concerned about the lack of separation in the police's role for both investigating and prosecuting suspected offences. They argued that this blurring of boundaries brought bias into the police's investigations as, in order to prove an arrest was right, they might try to prove the suspect was responsible rather than conducting an open inquiry into the offence, pointing to the growing numbers of miscarriages of justice and the regional differences in the practice of prosecutions.

The CPS is the main prosecuting body in England and Wales but not the only one, as such powers are also held by agencies such as the Health and Safety Executive, the Civil Aviation Authority, the Maritime and Coastguard Agency, the Financial Conduct Authority, the Office of Fair Trading, and the Department for Environment, Food and Rural Affairs. This is not the case in Scotland, where the only prosecuting authority is the Crown Office and Procurator Fiscal Service. The Prosecution of Offences Act 1985 gives members of the public in England and Wales the right to bring private prosecutions. This right is rarely exercised due to the considerable expense of bringing a prosecution as an individual, but in theory it means that people can seek justice even when the system has decided not to proceed with their case.

The head of the CPS has the title of Director of Public Prosecutions (DPP) and reports to the Attorney General, who is accountable to Parliament for this service. The Attorney General is a member of the government who provides legal advice to its different departments. The fact that this high-level appointment is political again shows how contested the principle of separation of powers can be. Supporters of the Attorney General position argue that the holder of this role has a relatively limited role in the justice process, but Attorneys General have been involved in important matters such as the legality of military responses, potential corruption charges in government departments, and allegations that donors to political parties have received a peerage (been given a title, for example Lord or Duchess) and a parliamentary place in the House of Lords.

The role of the CPS

The CPS is organised into geographical areas for England and Wales and each one is led by a Chief Crown Prosecutor. Each area has the following general responsibilities:

- advising the police on cases for possible prosecution;
- taking cases from the police once a defendant has been charged or 'summonsed' (ordered to attend court);
- presenting cases at court.

Since the Criminal Justice Act 2003, the CPS has not only advised the police on cases that should be prosecuted but has also decided on the appropriate charge in serious or complex cases. Until 2003, the policy was that the CPS waited until the police had decided on the charge. Charging decisions for all police forces across England and Wales are made by a service called CPS Direct, a national network of telephone and online advice which is available 24 hours a day. Before this service was introduced, there was a CPS office in every police station and the efficacy of CPS Direct has been strongly criticised. People question its ability to respond to the police's calls, and some hold it responsible for delaying the system (Justice Committee, 2009).

Once a defendant has been charged or summonsed, the CPS takes a case from the police. It has the responsibility for reviewing all of the evidence it receives and assigns cases to teams in the local area. This team is then responsible for preparing the case for court and managing its progress throughout the prosecution process. This leads us to the final main responsibility of the CPS: presenting cases at court through lawyers known as Crown Prosecutors. This is an essential role for **adversarial** criminal trials which can, as we have noted (see **section 23.6**), represent a gladiatorial contest in that there is fierce competition and the lawyers (gladiators) have a major influence on the outcome. This responsibility is known as **advocacy** and it is this work, along with the quality and timeliness of its decisions, that represents 'the core of the CPS's business' (HM Crown Prosecution Service Inspectorate, 2018: 10).

There are three main types of role within the CPS:

- **Crown Prosecutors**—the barristers and Higher Court Advocates who are responsible for presenting the cases in court on behalf of the Crown (the state). They are not always exclusively employed by the CPS and may also work in private practice as defence lawyers.
- **Paralegals**—these people (who used to be known as caseworkers) have some legal knowledge and training but are not fully qualified lawyers. They can take on a variety of tasks and help to prepare a case for court.
- **Administrators**—the broad category of workers who assist the CPS with financial, managerial, and information technology issues.

The Code for Crown Prosecutors is issued by the Director of Public Prosecutions and contains the key guidelines that prosecutors should follow when deciding whether to prosecute someone. It also provides guidance on charging decisions, out-of-court **disposals**, accepting guilty pleas, and **mode of trial hearings** (where a Magistrates' Court decides where an 'either way offence' will be tried).

The decision to prosecute a case in court is based, first, on whether the case has a realistic prospect of conviction. To decide this, a prosecutor considers whether a court is more likely than not to convict the defendant of the alleged charge. This standard is the level of proof needed in the civil courts of justice, and it is often referred to using the phrase 'on the balance of probabilities'. This part of the decision process borrows the standard of proof from civil cases, as opposed to the 'beyond all reasonable doubt' standard that is eventually required by a criminal court. In very crude numerical terms, this means the court must be 51 per cent sure in a civil court and 95 per cent sure in a criminal court.

If the case passes the first stage then it will be subject to the public interest test; the prosecutor must believe it is in the public interest to prosecute the case. This is obviously a difficult decision and may sound like a grand power but there are certain factors that make prosecution more likely, such as how serious the offence is considered to be and the suspect's level of involvement. Other factors that make it more likely that a case will be prosecuted are:

- if an offence was premeditated;
- if not prosecuting might put the public at risk;
- if there is hostility against the victim's ethnic or national origin, gender, disability, age, religion or belief, sexual orientation, or gender identity;
- if there was a position of trust or authority between the suspect and victim, or the victim was serving the public at the time (for example, as a police officer or nurse).

The prosecutor will also take into account the age of the suspect, national security considerations, the impact of the offence on the community, and whether a prosecution is a proportionate response.

Challenges for the CPS

The criticism that follows 'not guilty' verdicts (that is, acquittals), particularly in high-profile cases, can suggest that the CPS is seriously underperforming. You might form similarly negative views of the service based on the numbers of cases that, for different reasons, do not actually proceed to trial. These numbers can be found in the annual reports for the CPS (at www.cps.gov.uk), as well as headline figures in the mainstream media that question the organisation's effectiveness. But are these measures a fair reflection of the CPS's performance? Can we assume that in all the cases where there wasn't a conviction, the defendant should have never been prosecuted? Alternatively, does the work of the CPS in bringing over half a million cases to court in 12 months, with a conviction rate of 84.8 per cent in the Magistrates' Court and 79.9 per cent in the Crown Court (Crown Prosecution Service, 2018: 7), actually make it a high-performing organisation?

The outcome of a case can be incredibly difficult to predict, particularly if the prosecution have little knowledge of the defence case. The requirement for both sides to disclose the evidence they are going to use—plus, if relevant, the evidence they are *not* going to use—which we discussed in **section 23.6** is intended to improve this. In traditional adversarial trials, there was a risk that evidence

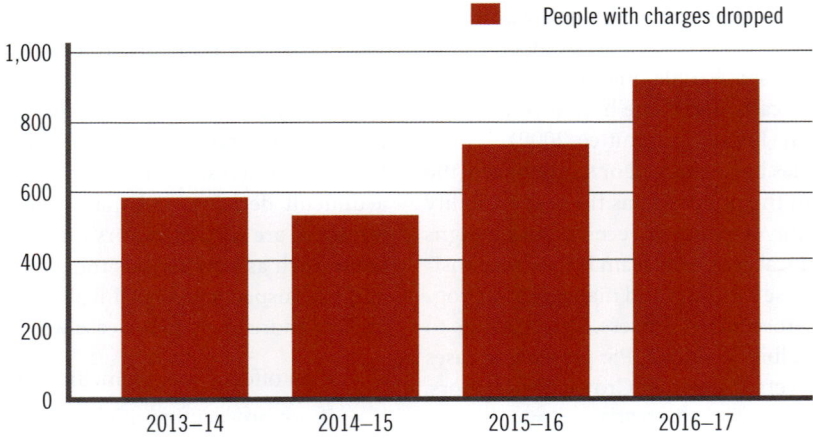

Figure 24.1 The requirement for both sides to disclose evidence has resulted in an increasing number of prosecutions collapsing because the CPS and police are failing to meet the obligation

Source: From BBC News at bbc.co.uk/news

was being suppressed because each side only wanted to present evidence that was favourable to their case. The first formal system for the **disclosure of evidence** began in the Criminal Procedure and Criminal Investigations Act 1996 and imposed these obligations on both sides. This requirement may seem like an indisputably positive change, but as we can see in **Figure 24.1** it is now a major issue in the work of the CPS, with an increasing number of prosecutions collapsing because of their failure to disclose evidence. Some of these errors are made by the police, who are supposed to help them with meeting these obligations (Criminal Justice Joint Inspection, 2017).

The disclosure system requires the defence to provide a statement of their defence before their trial; this speeds up the court hearings and replicates the approach used in the civil courts. However, this responsibility and the effects of the Criminal Procedure Rules contradict the traditional adversarial justice principle that there should be two competing sides, as it means that defence lawyers frequently help the CPS in the course of a prosecution; a situation strongly criticised in *The Secret Barrister*, a first-hand, anonymous account of the criminal justice system that was published in 2018.

As a publicly funded service, the CPS is required to provide value for money and many measures are taken to monitor its efficiency, such as the average number of court hearings required by cases. This initially seems fair, but the CPS's efforts to resolve cases in as few hearings as possible are held back by the fact that the most common reason for delays is defendants not turning up at court (HM Crown Prosecution Service Inspectorate, 2017: para. 4.17). It may be a principle of the Code for Crown Prosecutors that the CPS should not make decisions on matters of justice purely on a financial basis, but this does not prevent it being heavily criticised when large amounts of money are spent and the right kinds of results are not achieved.

Bearing the contents of this section in mind, consider the issued raised in **What do you think? 24.2**.

WHAT DO YOU THINK? 24.2

How would you judge the success of the CPS?

If the rates of discontinuances or the current acquittal/conviction rates do not provide the evidence you feel you need for evaluating the work of the CPS, then you might want to consider alternative sources such as research into victim and witness satisfaction levels. Sometimes the CPS carry out thematic reviews into this topic which can produce revealing findings; examples include the troubling evidence that one in five victims and one in ten witnesses reported that they were dissatisfied with the service they received (Crown Prosecution Service, 2016: 5–6). (As we noted in the introduction to this section, this could be partially linked to the impersonal nature of the criminal process, as the CPS does not act as the 'victim's lawyer'.)

Other sources you can consider include the annual reports for the CPS and other key criminal justice organisations, which often include helpful summaries and graphs—see **Figure 24.2**. However, these reports and statistics need to be read in their context: each one is

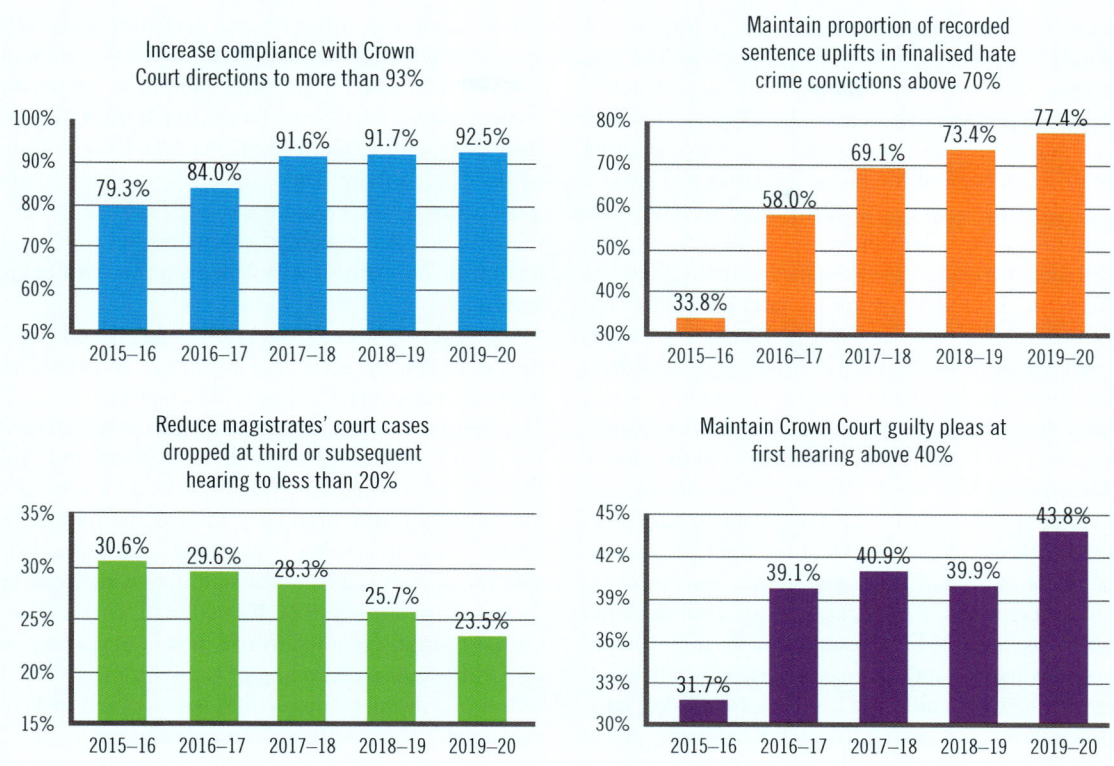
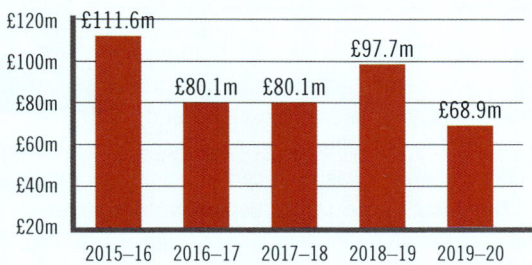

Figure 24.2 The information shared in the annual reports of criminal justice institutions can help us judge their efficacy. These charts are provided in the CPS's Annual Report and Accounts 2019–20 to evidence its performance in relation to the strategic aim of 'Everyone contributing to high quality casework'
Source: © Crown copyright 2020

a review of that service's performance that year, so in isolation their value can be limited.

The information in these annual reports offers an ideal opportunity to deploy your ABC mindset. They are likely to provide bold statements of things we can all question—for example, does the finding that increasing numbers of defendants are now pleading guilty really mean that the right cases are being prosecuted? Is there a danger that this ignores other reasons people may have for pleading guilty? People may not have the financial resources to contest the charge or may want to take advantage of the reduced sentences available to people who plead guilty at the first reasonable opportunity. If they feel that such a sentencing 'discount' could make the difference between going to prison and receiving a non-custodial sentence, then regardless of their actual guilt a defendant may decide to admit legal guilt. In the US, the problem of people pleading guilty to crimes they did not commit reached a point in 2017 where the Innocence Project, a well-known non-profit-making organisation based in the US to help people who have been wrongfully convicted, launched an ongoing public education campaign: see #GuiltyPleaProblem.

The CPS shares some challenges with the police. Like the police, it also has to contend with the private sector increasingly challenging its work. The company TM Eye, for example, claims to be one of the UK's most active and successful, private investigation companies; they run 'My Local Bobby Ltd' and offer policing and prosecuting services to residents and businesses in areas of London. These services can be purchased through monthly subscriptions of a couple of hundred pounds a month for their Enhanced Service and smaller amounts for its Standard Service (*The Telegraph*, 2 January 2020). The focus of companies such as these is usually on the offences that the police are seen as unwilling or unable to prosecute, such as shoplifting and pickpocketing. These businesses show that anyone can arrest and prosecute, subject to the laws that the police and CPS follow, such as the public interest test. The CPS also shares with the police the challenge of ensuring diversity in its workforce. In 2020, the Workforce Diversity Data for the CPS showed that out of its total staff numbers, 66 per cent were female, 18 per cent were BAME, and 11 per cent declared themselves as disabled (www.cps.gov.uk/publication/workforce-diversity-data). Increasing diversity will mean it better reflects the population it serves, increasing public confidence and improving the quality of its output as greater diversity will reduce the chance that bias, for example racial bias, will influence decisions at stages in the system when they have discretion. These points of discretion most notably include whether to prosecute. We considered some of these issues in **Chapter 10** (see **section 10.5**), and in **Conversations 24.1** Grace Moronfolu MBE, Chair of the National Black Crown Prosecution Association (NBCPA), discusses the efforts the CPS has made to tackle inequality both within its workforce and its output, in terms of its role within the criminal justice system.

The scale of the challenges now facing the CPS is shown by the criticism it received in 2019 from Sir Brian Leveson, who had recently retired as Lord Chief Justice (LCJ). The LCJ is also known as the Head of Criminal Justice and is the most senior criminal judge in England and Wales; at the time of writing, the position is held by Lord Burnett. Sir Brian Leveson strongly criticised the fact that some crimes were not being prosecuted and expressed fears that the system risked collapse unless it received greater financial investment (BBC News, 2019). This level of criticism was unprecedented from a person in such a position, providing another example of the relevance of the separation of powers principle that we analysed in **What do you think? 23.2**.

CONVERSATIONS 24.1

The CPS' efforts to tackle institutional racism

with **Grace Moronfolu MBE**

The CPS has one of the most diverse staff groups of all civil service departments—we've won a number of awards for our inclusion programmes and in 2020 we featured on the Business in the Community Top Employer for Race list for the second successive year. If you know a little of our history as an organisation this might surprise you, but these achievements are no coincidence.

I joined the CPS as an administrative officer in 1988 soon after it came into existence in 1985. The 1990s was a challenging time for race relations in the UK. It felt like there was little social or criminal justice for Black African Caribbean or Asian communities.

My personal experiences working for the CPS at that time were not particularly positive. During that period, I experienced a lot of negative behaviours from managers and colleagues, which I was unable to articulate as 'racism' at the time; it was just 'the way things were'. I have been at the sharp end of disadvantage for most of my career due to my circumstances; I was divorced, had a child and little family support. In those days you demonstrated your credentials by staying late at the office and going to the pub after work. As a Black woman and primary caregiver I was excluded in more ways than one.

But things were slowly beginning to change. In the late 1990s, the CPS lost several high-profile race discrimination tribunal cases which also threw a spotlight on community concerns about the quality of our prosecution decision making.

The Equality Act came into law in 2000, and in light of the new statutory obligations and the issues raised previously, the CPS invited Sylvia Denman QC OBE to investigate race equality in the service. Her report found that the CPS was institutionally racist and that this had wide ranging impacts on both the treatment of staff and the approach to criminal casework.

To the CPS's credit, senior leaders responded swiftly and in less than three years went beyond the recommendations of the report—undertaking a complete review of policies and practices which revolutionised our organisational culture. For example, the Denman review brought to light the mistreatment of Black, Asian and minority ethnic staff across the service. The senior team at the time said they weren't aware this was happening so the report recommended that the CPS establish a network for these staff to give them direct access to key decision makers. In 2001, the National Black Crown Prosecution Association (NBCPA), the first CPS staff network, was born.

In 2020, the NBCPA is now one of eight CPS staff networks—covering a broad span of interests including race, religion, disability and most recently social mobility. The CPS senior management team fully supports our networks and our committee members have time during working hours to undertake their duties as well as a small budget to deliver activities.

At the NBCPA we're relatively unusual compared to other civil service networks as we not only look to promote equality and diversity within the CPS but also more broadly in the criminal justice system. We act as a critical friend to the CPS. We work closely with the HR team to develop programmes and training events to support the progression and development of Black, Asian and minority ethnic staff and to educate all CPS staff about the realities of structural racism and intersectionality in the UK today. We also provide feedback and advice on projects relating to the delivery of CPS casework. We support with equality impact assessments, advise on the community impact of decisions, and help the CPS to gain a better understanding of some of the challenges Black, Asian and minority ethnic communities have in accessing justice.

It's fair to say that we've come a long way but we know there is still more that we can do. The NBCPA recently held a conference called 'The journey' to reflect on that fact, celebrating what we've achieved and setting out where we need to go next, for example increasing Black, Asian and minority ethnic representation in senior roles.

I've always felt the need to support colleagues and my experience working with the NBCPA has been transformative in that regard. In 2020, with over 30 years' service in the CPS under my belt, I can truly say I'm proud to work in a diverse, inclusive, transparent and innovative organisation.

Grace Moronfolu MBE, Chair of the National Black Crown Prosecution Association (NBCPA)

24.4 The courts

We can now turn to the courts. We have already outlined the main types of criminal court in England and Wales and the relationships between them in **section 23.3** (see **Figure 23.5** in particular). Here we continue our focus on the criminal court system, since this is our main interest as criminologists, but we also consider the courts' roles in more detail to see how they fit into and contrast with other aspects of the court system.

An overview of the courts

It is impossible to be precise about when the first court was established because places where communities meet to resolve disputes can be found throughout human history. But for students of criminal justice, a common reference point is the career of the famous advocate Sir William Garrow (1760–1840); it was around this time that criminal trials moved away from responses such as branding offenders with hot irons, to meeting the adversarial justice principle we analysed in **Chapter 23**. Whilst historically the courts have mostly worked independently according to local demand, these days they operate under the HM Courts and Tribunals Service (HMCTS), an executive agency of the MoJ which is responsible for the administration of criminal, civil, and family courts and tribunals in England and Wales.

The wide remit of HMCTS points to a distinction that you need to grasp in order to understand the court system: the difference between matters of **public law** and **private law** (also known as civil law). This determines which of the **courts of first instance** will hear a case and which party has responsibility for bringing legal action. Criminal cases are considered to be public law as they are deemed to affect the whole community and are classed as an offence against the state; the trials for these possible crimes take place in either the Magistrates' Court or the Crown Court. If a case is categorised as private law, then the individuals affected have the responsibility for bringing the case to court and the likely venues are the County Court or the High Court. Family law matters can be classed as either public or private law because in addition to individual members of the public, they can involve many different authorities and agencies and, as a result, they have their own specialist courts and procedures. The difference in these types of law is illustrated in the way that criminal and civil law cases are cited.

- Criminal law citations take the form of *R v The Defendant's Surname*. R stands for either rex or regina (depending on whether a king or queen is in existence at the time), representing the state.
- Civil law citations take the form of *Name v Name*, with 'name' being either the surnames of the individuals or the names of the organisations involved. The party bringing the action is known as the **claimant** and the party with potential liability ('guilt' is not a term used in civil law) is the **defendant**. Usually the claimant's name comes first, although this can be reversed if the citation is for an appeal.

We will return to the criminal/civil distinction in the next section, when we consider the roles of the courts, but for now let's look at criminal cases, since we are primarily interested in the criminal justice system. A criminal case is scheduled for trial if it has been investigated by the police and the CPS and the latter has decided (via the process we discussed in **section 24.3**) that the potential offence should be prosecuted. They all start in a Magistrates' Court but can be transferred to the Crown Court if the case is sufficiently serious. (Or, if the defendant is aged between ten and 17, the offence will be heard in a youth court, a type of Magistrates' Court which adopts special rules such as excluding the public from trials and placing restrictions on reporting.) How a case is dealt with, and in which court, depends on how the crime has been classified. The three categories (which we introduced in **section 23.3**) are as follows:

- **Indictable offences** are considered so serious that they can only be heard in a Crown Court. Examples include sexual offences and murder. This means they will generally be presented by barristers in front of a judge, and a jury will decide on a defendant's guilt if they do not enter a guilty plea.
- **Summary offences** are the least serious category of offence and these crimes have to be heard in a Magistrates' Court. Examples include motoring offences. This means they will generally be presented by solicitors in front of either three lay magistrates (volunteers from the community) or one district judge.
- **Either way offences** can be tried in either court. Remembering about this classification of offences will help you evaluate claims that 'crime is rising' as the accuracy of such claims can be affected by whether the statistic includes all of the three categories.

So, the Crown Court is the higher of the two first instance criminal courts and deals with more serious crimes. This dynamic is reflected in the courts' sentencing powers. A Magistrates' Court is only able to impose a maximum of six months' imprisonment (or 12 months for more than one offence), whereas a Crown Court has the maximum power of life imprisonment. Both courts have the power to impose unlimited fines, although before 2015 the less serious nature of proceedings in the Magistrates' Court meant their power was limited to a maximum of £5,000. The two courts can also be distinguished by the separation—or lack of it—between the **tribunal of law** (the judge) and the **tribunal of fact** (the jury); in summary trials magistrates are responsible for both aspects.

The standard image of a criminal trial may involve barristers cross-examining witnesses in front of a judge and jury (as is the case in a Crown Court), but the vast number of summary offences and the much lower frequency of indictable offences means that a scene from a Magistrates' Court is actually a far more accurate representation of the work done by the criminal courts. As we suggested in the previous list, Magistrates' Court hearings can take two forms: traditionally, offences have been heard by three lay magistrates, but they can also be heard by a single district judge. Lay magistrates do not have legal qualifications and do not get paid for their time, whereas district judges do have legal qualifications and get paid—they are effectively professional magistrates. There are around 160 district judges and many more lay magistrates, although their numbers have decreased, standing at 25,170 in 2012 and 13,177 in 2020 (Ministry of Justice, 2020a).

In the last decade, there have been increasing tensions between the two 'camps' and debates about the merits of professional magistrates sitting alone ('sitting' in legal terminology means to hold a court or judicial session, including a parliamentary session). Lay magistrates can be representatives of the local community and this characteristic, along with their additional numbers, can enhance perceptions of a trial's fairness. However, district judges are able to process cases more quickly and their legal training can be an advantage when hearing more serious cases. These arguments have intensified following the implementation of the Single Justice Procedure that we discuss in **Chapter 25** (see **section 25.5**).

The role of the courts

In considering the role of the courts it is helpful to return to the criminal/civil law distinction. The key difference between the two is that civil law does not exist to punish; it is there to compensate injured parties who have suffered a loss. This includes financial **punishment** so compensation is awarded in line with the principle of *restitutio in integrum*, which aims to restore the injured party—as much as it is possible to do so through an award of money—to the situation they would have been in if they had not sustained the relevant harm or injury. A claimant should not be in a 'windfall position' as any award is supposed to make up for what has been lost. There can be some rare situations when compensation is awarded that exceeds a claimant's loss (known as punitive damages) but these are rarely imposed as restitution is the purpose behind the civil courts' judgments. In some cases, money may not be the key issue at all—sometimes, civil litigation may be a way of keeping a case alive in the hope of pressurising the criminal justice system into bringing a prosecution.

In contrast, the main responsibility of the criminal law and its courts is to deliver justice to the satisfaction (or not) of the parties involved. Its public law classification means the criminal law seeks to benefit society as a whole by maintaining order and prohibiting conduct that is detrimental to the public interest. It gives protection to individuals and property by providing a way of resolving disputes in an orderly and agreed manner. In a criminal case, the courts have the power to impose punishment on an individual who has been found guilty of breaching the law. Judges and magistrates decide on the appropriate sentence following sophisticated sentencing guidelines issued by the Sentencing Council. These cover both general and offence-specific matters, setting out factors the court should take into account when sentencing and indicating the required level of sentence depending on the harm caused and the extent to which the offender is to blame. Although judges and magistrates still have some discretion in sentencing, since the implementation of the Coroners and Justice Act 2009 they have been compelled to apply any guidelines that have been set, and judges are expected to explain how they have decided on a particular sentence. Where there are no specific guidelines, a judge can refer to Court of Appeal decisions on similar cases.

As well as understanding the lines of division between the criminal and civil law and courts, you should also be aware of how they can be blurred. A prominent example is the Anti-Social Behaviour Order (ASBO), now known as a Criminal Behaviour Order (CBO). This order was introduced to resolve harassment and behaviour that is considered a nuisance, such as begging. Such behaviour used to be a matter for the civil law and it could only be dealt with in the civil courts; this was partially maintained by ASBOs as legally they were classed as a civil order. But, despite this status, the breach of an ASBO was classed as a crime, meaning offenders could be punished for not following the terms of their civil order. ASBOs became a power of considerable force for local authorities and expanded the reach of the criminal law; not by creating new criminal offences for begging, nuisance, etc., but by empowering courts to punish people for breaching their civil order. ASBOs were replaced by the CBO (a 'Crimbo') in 2014, and can now only be imposed if someone is convicted of a criminal offence and they have been involved in persistent antisocial behaviour.

Now that you have read this section of the chapter, you might find it be useful to revisit **Conversations 23.1** for Jaime's discussion of how working in the criminal courts has changed in recent decades.

Challenges for the courts

One of the main challenges for the criminal courts is dealing with the reduced government spending on the HMCTS. It is estimated that between 2011 and 2019 there were funding reductions of between 18 and 32 per cent in real terms (Institute for Government, 2019). It is difficult to identify an exact figure as during this time the courts increased their fees for civil cases and other non-criminal work. This initially helped to offset the impact of the funding cuts but was only a short-term solution—it could not make up for the significant reduction in financial support from the government.

The courts are also having to deal with more cases of increased complexity, meaning that they take longer to consider. The total number of cases received by the courts may be declining, but the ones they do hear are increasingly more difficult and require high levels of expertise. This feature of the courts' work in the 21st century was highlighted in research from the MoJ; it showed how the average custodial sentence length for indictable offences in 1993 was 16 months and by 2015 had increased to 18.8 months. In the same period, the total prison population almost doubled from 44,000 to 85,000 (Ministry of Justice, 2016).

Partly as a result of the increased complexity of cases, the courts have to deal with considerable backlogs of cases. This issue was worsened by the Covid-19 pandemic as lockdowns meant that only a handful of cases could be processed by the courts and all jury trials were completely suspended. In 2020, a report predicted that the system would produce its highest ever waiting times unless the government spends at least an extra £100 million to enable these trials to take place (Institute for Government, 2020).

The courts' ability to do this additional work is threatened by shortages of court staff, particularly the number of 'duty solicitors'. The duty solicitor scheme provides free legal advice to people suspected of committing a crime, either at court or in a police station. It is a statutory right in s. 58 of the Police and Criminal Evidence Act 1984 for people in a police station to have legal advice, and this is given in person or over the telephone through Criminal Defence Direct (CDD) Services. The scheme is run by the Legal Aid Agency, which awards contracts to solicitors' firms to allow them to provide the service. Reduced funding has made it difficult to gain these contracts, and between 2013 and 2018 two-thirds of existing solicitors' firms were deemed ineligible. This has resulted in '"deserts" in rural areas, with a lack of local firms forcing defendants to travel several hours just to see a solicitor' (*The Secret Barrister*, 2018: 182). In addition, research from the Law Society (2019) found duty solicitors to be 'an ageing profession' as the average age was 47 and suggested that this could become an increasingly significant issue for this important stage of the justice process:

> Many young people pursuing a legal career are drawn to criminal law, yet once qualified, many turn instead to corporate or regulatory law . . . low salaries coupled with high debt levels were a 'significant barrier' to pursuing a career in legal aided areas of law. This is being felt deeply by young criminal lawyers and deterring them from criminal duty work . . . in five to 10 years' time, there will be insufficient criminal duty solicitors in many regions, leaving people in need of urgent legal advice unable to access their rights.
>
> (The Law Society, 2019: 18)

If this issue is not corrected, when the current duty solicitors retire, the courts will lack the sufficiently experienced replacements needed to keep the system moving efficiently. This weakness in the system could also result in a breach of the rule of law principle, in that individuals will be denied their statutory rights, and it illustrates a weakness in the due process safeguards we considered in **section 23.4**. Problems in the court system threaten other core criminal justice principles, too. For example, the faults in the system for disclosure of evidence mean that important evidence is sometimes not being made available until a very late stage, contravening the adversarial justice principle (see **section 23.6**) that requires rigorous testing of the other side's evidence.

A final notable challenge for the court system is the system-wide challenge of ensuring that workforces are sufficiently diverse and eliminating potential opportunities for bias. The gender and ethnicity of court staff are monitored, and although the statistics indicate that diversity in both respects can vary when previous experience is required for a role, overall they show that women comprise 38 per cent of barristers and 52 per cent of solicitors (Ministry of Justice, 2020a: 11) and people declaring themselves to be BAME account for 15 per cent of barristers and 18 per cent of solicitors (ibid: 19). The courts are also working to address issues of potential inequalities in sentencing—as we discussed in **section 10.5** of **Chapter 10**.

There are two professional bodies that can help the criminal courts meet these challenges; the Bar Council which is the professional association for barristers (who generally act in the Crown Court), and the Law Society which does the same for solicitors in the Magistrates' Court. Both bodies have active social media profiles so following these will help you to keep up with the main contemporary issues.

24.5 Probation services and community sanctions

'Probation' refers to serving a community sentence or to being released from prison on licence or on parole, subject to supervision and adhering to certain rules and conditions. Probation services help to implement these sentences and monitor the offenders serving them. We include 'community sanctions' in the section title to recognise the wide range of criminal justice system responses of this kind: responses that keep an offender in the community but restrict their freedom by imposing obligations (such as paying a fine) or conditions (such as participation in probation supervision and programmes). They can also be called 'non-custodial sentences' but this name is problematic as it suggests they are imposed as alternatives to imprisonment rather than a result of correct application of the sentencing guidelines. It also wrongly implies that custody is the main form of sentencing, which is not correct considering that in 2019 90 per cent of people sentenced in England and Wales received non-custodial sentences (Parliamentary Office of Science and Technology, 2020). In fact, community sanctions and measures (with 'measures' referring to the array of non-traditional or court-imposed responses to crime, such as **diversion**—see **Chapter 30**) have become so frequently used around the world that commentators have suggested that criminal justice has entered a new era of mass supervision (McNeill, 2019).

An overview of probation services

Probation first became part of criminal justice in the 1880s but developed into an important function within the system during the 20th century (as we explore further in **Chapter 29**). The National Probation Service (NPS) is the authority for people serving community sentences and those released from prison on licence or parole. It was established in its current form in 2001 and is managed by the MoJ through Her Majesty's Prison and Probation Service (HMPPS). The NPS works with a variety of agencies to deliver probation services. The government's Transforming Rehabilitation policy (TR) meant that between 2015 and 2019 it was only responsible for high-risk offenders, with

21 private Community Rehabilitation Companies (CRCs) responsible for all medium- and low-risk offenders. However, this policy was abandoned following strong criticism (which we consider in the discussion of challenges for the probation services later in this section) and from 2021 the NPS regains responsibility for the supervision of all offenders. The new model involves 12 new NPS regions in England and Wales that each have a 'Probation Delivery Partner'. These are organisations from the private or voluntary sector with responsibility for providing unpaid work and accredited programmes.

Since the Criminal Justice Act 2003, there have been two main forms of probation supervision for offenders; the community order and the suspended sentence order. Until this statute, there were separate powers for things like probation, electronic tagging, community service, etc.; the legislation combined them into what is known as the generic community order. These generic orders have 12 separate requirements that can be attached as conditions to an offender's sentence in the community. The suspended sentence order is legally classified as a custodial sentence but it is served in the community and not in prison, as long as the offender keeps to their conditions. The orders are categorised in low, medium, or high levels with the higher classifications having tougher requirements, such as longer periods of curfew or additional hours of unpaid work, etc.

The conditions that both orders can impose on offenders include obligations such as residence requirements (living at a private address or an Approved Premises), unpaid work, curfews, electronic monitoring, and alcohol or drug rehabilitation requirements. They were combined to give sentencers more options in choosing the terms of their orders; the different conditions effectively became their 'pick n mix' system. In theory, this makes it possible to devise a sentence which suits the needs of the offender, but there is a risk of the offender being overloaded with conditions. This can be a serious problem for an offender as a custodial sentence can be imposed if the order is breached.

The role of probation services

The main role of probation services is to ensure that offenders comply with the conditions of their order. But, in addition, probation work involves attempting to rehabilitate offenders, including through providing accredited programmes. At the time of writing, these include:

- Building Better Relationships (for offenders convicted of violence against an intimate partner);
- Building Skills for Recovery (for offenders whose substance abuse increases their chances of future offending);
- Promoting Human Dignity (for offenders who have committed a hate crime);
- Resolve Programme (to control emotions to counter aggressive behaviour); and
- Thinking Skills Programme (to develop thinking skills that help stop reoffending).

We noted in our overview of probation services earlier that in recent years government policy changes have meant that these programmes and the unpaid work condition have been outsourced to other agencies. The privatisation of these services reflects a shift in probation's role from care to correction (as we describe it in **Chapter 29**—see **section 29.4**). Probation has traditionally held social work values, reflected in its mission to 'advise, assist and befriend' offenders; now it seems to prioritise offender management and managing offenders' risk to society. There are two main types of risk: the risk of future reoffending and reconviction (the probability someone will reoffend and be reconvicted within two years) and the risk of serious harm (the probability that the reoffending will involve serious harm). This shift means that probation work now requires the use of various risk assessment tools, such as the Offender Assessment System (OASys). This is a software package that assesses the probability of reoffending and reconviction within two years of the offence, and the probability that the reconviction will be for an offence of serious harm. OASys is supposed to bring objective reasoning (rather than subjective predictions) into probation work, but like many other risk assessment tools in the criminal justice system it can be criticised for failing in this regard (see **section 21.4**).

This change in emphasis—prioritising risk management—has increased the caseloads of probation workers. Their roles now involve a lot of case management in addition to doing everything possible to support offenders—including listening, being empathetic, and providing them with practical advice. Probation workers also have to produce reports on their cases, which often involves liaising with the courts.

Challenges for probation services

We have hinted at some of the challenges for the probation services throughout this section, for example in our mention above of the increased workloads as a result of the shift towards offender risk management. The caseload of most probation workers now exceeds the recommended limits (HM Inspectorate of Probation, 2020). The probation and prison services also share the system-wide challenge of increasing diversity and tackling inequality in their workforce—the latest figures showed that only 9.6 per cent of the HMPPS staff declared themselves black, Asian, or minority ethnic (Ministry of Justice, 2019).

Another significant challenge is the public perception of probation services and the demand for harsher responses. Although many studies have shown that probation can have a significant impact, including lowering reconviction rates (Raynor, 2019: 9), the service is constantly challenged by politicians, the media, and the public and can be seen as a 'soft' option. (We consider this issue further in **What do you think? 24.3**.) We can identify the same desire for punitive responses in the way community sanctions have been used: despite hopes that they might reduce prisoner numbers, the effect has been almost the opposite as they are widely used for offences where previously the sentence would have been a fine or **conditional discharge** (Carr, 2020: 6). The effect has therefore been a widening of the net of criminal justice, bringing more people into the system and increasing the number of people who are likely to be imprisoned if the community sanctions are breached.

Overall, the major challenge that the probation service faces in the next few years is to recover from the harm inflicted on it by TR—the 'Transforming Rehabilitation' government policy we mentioned in our overview of the probation services. This started in 2015 and extended the reach of probation services by making supervision in the community mandatory for everybody released from short-term prison sentences (under 12 months), as well as dividing up probation work between the NPS and CRCs in the way we described. TR had an extremely short consultation period and faced many objections, so its introduction exemplifies the force of governmental power in the work of the criminal justice system. We noted earlier that TR was abandoned because of strong criticism. This came from various official HMPPS inspections, as well as the media. The many issues with TR included:

- TR failed to divide up the work in the way that was promised—it was supposed to result in two-thirds of probation work going to CRCs, with the NPS getting the remainder, but in fact the CRCs only got around half the work (Carr and Robinson, 2020).
- The CRCs were accused of being dominated by private sector interests, and focusing on the needs of their contracts rather than on procuring genuine engagement with offenders.
- The involvement of the private sector was not as profitable as had been envisioned and two companies, Interserve and Working Links, the owners of eight CRCs between them, went into financial administration despite holding around £3 billion in government contracts (*The Guardian*, 18 March 2019).

The official policy review found that 'probation services have been left in a worse position than they were in before . . . [TR] will cost the taxpayer an additional £467 million' (House of Commons Committee of Public Accounts, 2019: 3). It also criticised the environments that are currently used for probation services, such as Approved Premises (see **Chapter 33**). The quality of buildings used for rehabilitative work had 'faulty

WHAT DO YOU THINK? 24.3

'Getting away with it' thanks to probation?

How often have you heard the claims that someone 'got away with it', even though they have been convicted and sentenced by a court? Such views can include 'they only got probation', and this might even be explicitly described as a 'soft' option. These negative perceptions have been persistent problems for probation work, as is the criticism of its apparent public invisibility (Worrall et al., 2017).

Jimmy McGovern is a renowned screenwriter and producer of many TV programmes that are likely to be of interest to criminology undergraduates; these include *Cracker* (1993–6), *Hillsborough* (1996), *Accused* (2010-12), and *Common* (2014). In 2020, his *Moving On* BBC series featured an episode called 'Time Out' (series 11, episode 1) in which the main character is released from prison on an electronic tag to serve the remainder of his sentence in the community. The episode stands out because it is so rare for this topic to have this kind of attention. Probation receives similarly little coverage in films. The concept of a 'prison film' is a well-established genre led by examples such as *The Shawshank Redemption* (1994); but what about 'probation films'? This is a curious absence considering the increasing severity of these powers, the extended periods of time people can spend on supervision, and the use of a greater number of conditions (Bottoms, 2017).

- Have you come across any representations of probation that you have seen in popular culture? If so, how was it represented and what impression did it give you?
- Why do you think probation is often neglected by films and TV programmes?
- What might be the impact of this limited coverage?

plumbing, broken lifts, vermin infestations and some older premises that are unfit for purpose in a modern probation service' (ibid: 7).

It is not yet clear whether the lessons of TR have been learnt and probation partnerships can recover their focus on factors known to help reduce offending that are beyond the traditional criminal justice system; such as health, education, skills, employment, and housing. In this challenging environment, new staff 'need more support to gain the confidence and skills to supervise the complex and high risk of harm offenders who form the NPS cohort' (HM Inspectorate of Probation, 2020: 10).

24.6 Prisons

Prisons are one of the main forms of punishment in the UK (Johnston, 2016). but despite their widespread use, they are very controversial. For some people, they provide criminal justice's only acceptable outcome whereas others stand for their complete abolition (Brown and Schept, 2017).

An overview of prisons

The first national prison in Britain opened at Millbank in London in 1816 but by this time the institution had been around for centuries in different forms. Like the probation service, prisons are regulated by the MoJ executive agency HMPPS, but their high profile makes the needs of this part of the agency more likely to be heard at the MoJ. Prisons are organised into different categories in the UK, as shown in **Table 24.1**, with those in categories A to C being closed prisons which, as the name suggests, prisoners cannot leave.

Prisons use the rule of law principle to inflict the system's most significant power on offenders: the deprivation of liberty. The rule of law also works to hold prisons to account and to ensure their compliance with relevant laws. A famous example is the case of *Raymond* v *Honey* [1981] UKHL 8, where the country's highest court found a prison governor to be in breach of the law when he intercepted a prisoner's legal correspondence. The case illustrated that prisoners still retain their rights unless they have been expressly taken away by legislation such as the Prison Act 1952, or it can be implied that they have been. The 1952 Act gives power to the Prison Rules 1999, providing the regulations for matters like discipline, physical welfare, and communications. It also gives legal authority to Prison Service Orders, which are long-term rules for specific issues such as mandatory drug testing and prisoners' pay, and to Prison Service Instructions, which are for short-term issues such as the privileges that prisoners can expect from good behaviour.

The collection of rules set out in this legislation apply across the prison estate but what goes on inside individual prisons can vary considerably as a prison governor can introduce local rules. A famous example is the 'Special Unit' which was set up at HMP Barlinnie (Scotland) in the 1970s to try to rehabilitate a group of violent prisoners through

Category A	High-security prisons for male prisoners who, if they escaped, are believed to pose the most threat to the public, the police, or national security.
Category B (local or training prisons)	Local prisons for prisoners taken from the courts in their local area.
	Training prisons to hold long-term and high-security prisoners.
Category C	Training and resettlement prisons to provide skills development opportunities to help prisoners find work and resettle back into the community on release.
	Most of the prison population is housed in this category.
Category D (open prisons)	Prisons with minimal security where prisoners can spend time away from the prison on licence for work, education, or other resettlement purposes.
	To house risk-assessed prisoners deemed suitable for open conditions.
Women and young adults	Women and young adults are housed in either closed conditions or open conditions and categorised according to their risks and needs.
	Those considered high risk, are categorised as 'restricted status' and must be held in a closed prison.
	In exceptional cases, women and young adults can be held in a high-security prison (category A).

Table 24.1 The categories of UK prisons

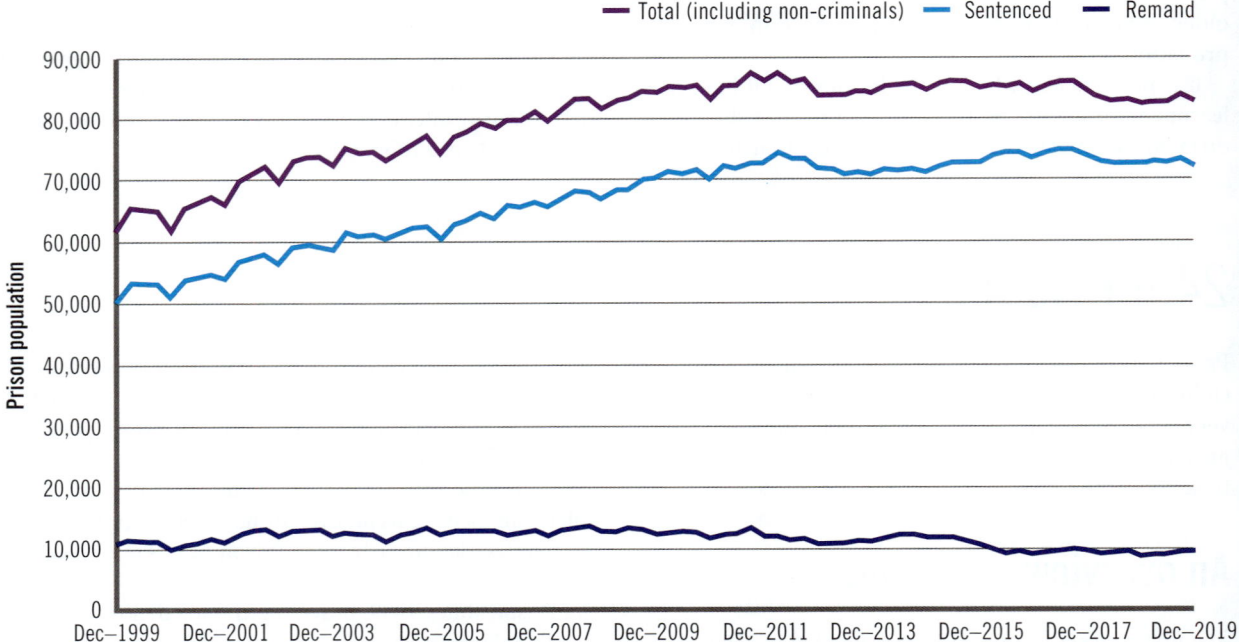

Figure 24.3 The prison population of England and Wales has increased significantly during the 21st century

Source: Ministry of Justice (2020) Offender management statistics quarterly: July to September 2019

therapy, including art therapy, and gave prisoners a voice in making decisions and setting programmes (*The Guardian*, 11 October 2007). Similar innovation currently takes place in the practice of therapeutic communities at HMP Grendon and HMP Dovegate. Like HMP Barlinnie's Special Unit, these communities seek to involve the prisoners much more in the running of their regimes. These examples suggest that prisons do not exist simply to punish and contain offenders and can also help to reform and rehabilitate—we return to this idea and the example of HMP Barlinnie's Special Unit in the discussion of the role of prisons later in this section.

As we have noted at other points in the book, including when highlighting worldwide trends and divergences (see **Chapter 13**), the prison populations in many countries have increased considerably in recent decades. In the last 20 years, this growth has seen the population noticeably increase to a 'new normal' of over 80,000 (see **Figure 24.3**). (This number includes 'non-criminal' prisoners, meaning people who are in prison for a non-criminal matter such as contempt of court or non-payment of council tax, and immigration detainees who have served their sentence and are being kept in prison by immigration authorities.) The growth in the US prison population has been even more dramatic, rising from 329,000 in 1980 to around 1.5 million in 2016 (Brennan Center for Justice, 2016). The increased prison populations around the world (see, for example, the figures available at www.prisonpolicy.org) has prompted researchers to identify a 'prison–industrial complex' (Davis and Barsamian, 1999), a term which derives from the 'military–industrial complex' of the US in the 1950s, where the growth of the military was such that it became a cornerstone of economic life.

We noted that the numbers shown in **Figure 24.3** also include immigration detainees, and when thinking about the numbers of people in prisons, we also have to recognise those being held in Immigration Removal Centres (IRCs). Until 2001, these places were called 'immigration detention centres' but their name was changed to convey a tougher image (as were other parts of the criminal justice system—see **Chapter 25** for more examples of this kind of rebranding). IRCs are problematic for the rule of law as they can infringe a person's liberty even though they have not committed a crime; instead their detention is justified by administrative reasons such as passport status. Technically they are not prisons, but IRCs can have many prison-like features, such as their bunk-bed cells and people being locked up for over 12 hours a day. There are nine IRCs across the UK that house around 25,000 people a year.

The poor conditions in IRCs have been recognised by some parts of the mainstream media, such as the undercover investigation from the BBC *Panorama* television programme in 2017. This received acclaim for its reporting of the whistle-blower evidence from an officer at Brook House IRC, that was then operated by the private security firm G4S. In 2020, this contract was taken over by the firm Serco, which was also awarded Tinsley House IRC; the same company also run Yarl's Wood IRC (see **Figure 24.4**) which has been regularly criticised for its poor conditions (Bosworth, 2014).

Figure 24.4 When thinking about prison populations we also have to recognise those being held in Immigration Removal Centres, such as Yarl's Wood IRC
Source: Varsity Newspaper—(Darren Johnson) www.varsity.co.uk

Immigration is part of criminal justice, yet this is an area in which the principles of due process and equal human rights that we investigated in **Chapter 23** can be absent. It can be criticised for extending the criminal law for some people but not others, and for disregarding the distinction between administrative penalties and criminal ones. This has been very controversial and, for some criminologists, its presence in the system has transformed the nature of justice itself (Bosworth, 2019).

The role of prisons

On the face of it, prisons exist to uphold the rule of law and bring offenders to justice by depriving them of their liberty as a punishment for their crimes. But this is a deceptively simple statement. Prisons are not necessarily solely punitive—we touched on this in our overview of prisons, where we noted the variation in regimes across prisons and the existence within some of therapeutic communities. You might also remember that in **Chapter 13** (see **section 13.5**) we considered the example of Norway, where prisons tend to be more focused on rehabilitation, with the key goal being to make offenders into 'good neighbours' (BBC News, 6 July 2019). Such ideas are very controversial in the UK, with many taking the view that rehabilitative approaches, including art-based therapies like those used in the Special Unit at HMP Barlinnie, make the prison experience too 'easy'. We explore this further in **Controversy and debate 24.2**.

The complexity and diversity of views about the role of prisons in the UK is evident in a major governmental speech on prison reform given in 2018 by the then Justice Secretary David Gauke. Gauke stated that the purpose of UK prisons has three components:

> First, protection of the public—prison protects the public from the most dangerous and violent individuals.

> Second, punishment—prison deprives offenders of their liberty and certain freedoms enjoyed by the rest of society and acts as a deterrent. It is not the only sanction available, but it is an important one.

> And third, rehabilitation—prison provides offenders with the opportunity to reflect on, and take responsibility for, their crimes and prepare them for a law-abiding life when they are released.

> It is only by prioritising rehabilitation that we can reduce re-offending and, in turn, the numbers of future victims of crime.
>
> (Ministry of Justice, 2018)

This range of expectations demonstrates that despite what the rising prison population the figures might suggest, increasing the levels of punishment is not always the sole political intention. Indeed, were it not for recent parliamentary time being dominated by Brexit (and, even more recently, Covid-19), the government would have introduced legislation for the largest reform of the prison system in 150 years (Chamberlen and Carvalho, 2019). This included turning six prisons into 'reform prisons' where governors had greater financial and regime autonomy; collecting 'better data' on prison successes and failures to measure their 'performance'; taking a more interventional approach towards repeat offenders and adopting behavioural 'insights' and 'new technology' to help rehabilitation, resettlement, and **desistance** from crime (ibid: 111). Such ambitions will require strong political support, enthusiasm that may be harder to acquire given the financial costs of the Covid-19 pandemic.

But even if a government is able to clearly identify a preferred role for prisons, implementing it is difficult because 'there is usually a gap between the official intended model and what happens in practice' (Crewe and Liebling, 2017: 891). We can see this in the examples of varied practices at different prisons, such as the use of therapeutic practices (see the overview of prisons earlier): these variations suggest differing views about the role of prisons. Through research like that conducted by Crewe and Liebling, we know that prisons are places where power continually fluctuates between a long list of stakeholders: prisoners, staff, unions, managers, governors, central authority, and politicians. As a consequence, the role of prisons not only varies between prisons, depending on the views of staff, but is also strongly influenced by policy changes such as the trends we will explore in **Chapter 25**.

Challenges for prisons

The many challenges currently facing English and Welsh prisons has led researchers to describe the situation as a crisis (Chamberlen and Carvalho, 2019). The House of Commons Health and Social Care Committee (2018)

CONTROVERSY AND DEBATE 24.2

What should life behind bars be like?

Opposition to the so-called 'easy' prison life, where conditions are said to be like holiday camps, is regularly expressed by politicians and parts of the media. In the mid-1900s, Alexander Paterson, the Commissioner of Prisons in England and Wales from 1922 to 1946, became known for the view, 'Men come to prison as a punishment, not for punishment' (cited in Ruck, 1951: 23). In other words, the very fact of being in prison—and therefore deprived of your liberty—is punishment, without the need for further sanctions. This distinction can be missed when people clamour for tougher regimes inside prisons.

The acclaimed film *A Sense of Freedom* (1979) recounts the prison experiences of Jimmy Boyle, one of the group of violent offenders involved in the Special Unit at HMP Barlinnie. Boyle had much to tell, as he had spent a decade going in and out of prison and was once said to be Scotland's most violent man. He was known for his non-compliant attitude and hostility to prison staff, and the film shows the violence and brutality this involved. However, the Special Unit's regime of arts and therapy brought about a remarkable change in his behaviour. This led to Boyle's release in 1981, and he subsequently created a charity for ex-offenders and established himself as an acclaimed writer and artist.

Despite this apparent success story, the Special Unit was deeply controversial. The regime's opponents felt it was too liberal and gave the prisoners too much autonomy and authority, and it was disbanded in 1994. Even the making of *A Sense of Freedom* was controversial, as due to opposition from the Scottish Prison Service, its prison scenes had to be filmed in a prison in the Republic of Ireland. Although the film is now a few decades old, it is well worth watching as it highlights many of the controversial issues involved in establishing a regime, outlining many of the same debates that run today about the role of prisons and the use of therapeutic communities within them.

---

cited short-staffing and overcrowding in prisons that 'severely limit access to healthcare and the ability of prisoners to lead healthy lives' as a key concern (2018: 7). This means prisons are working primarily on their incapacitation purpose, as prisoners are spending more time than is recommended locked up in their cells. The dilapidated state of the prisons themselves is also a challenge and the number of poor facilities in the prison estate has not been helped by the government's decision to stop its programme of prison closures. This has meant that outdated establishments, which they had previously strongly criticised, have had to remain open (House of Commons Library, 2019: 17). These problems are unlikely to be fixed at least in the short term, as the government's priority was clear in June 2020 when it confirmed its promise to build four new prisons in England to create 10,000 more prison places (see **New Frontiers 24.1**).

An official review of the prison estate between 2015 and 2020 undertaken by the National Audit Office (2020) judged 40 per cent of inspected prisons to be 'poor' or 'not sufficiently good' for safety. These were the worst findings on record, as were the similar views on decency (hygiene and cleanliness). During the same period, there was a 110 per cent increase in prisoner assaults on staff, a 63 per cent increase in prisoner-on-prisoner assaults, a 73 per cent increase in self-harm incidents, and 378 self-inflicted deaths (National Audit Office, 2020: 14). As we saw in **Chapter 10 (section 10.5)**, racial inequality is also a pervasive issue in this part of the justice system. The Mubarek Inquiry highlighted a poorly administered race relations strategy in prisons, describing a 'culture of indifference and insensitivity to black people and people from ethnic minorities which institutional racism breeds' (Mubarek Inquiry report, 2006: 413) and evidence suggests that there has not been sufficient improvement in the years since. More recent research, such as that conducted by the Runnymede Trust (2017), shows that people from minority ethnic backgrounds have a more negative perception of race equality while in prison, and that prison regimes and the discretionary decisions about incentive and earned privileges, discipline, information, and requests were key to these perceptions of unfairness. These alarming failings highlight its inability to deliver safe, fair, and constructive prison regimes that work for all offenders and are focused on rehabilitation.

A solution often put forward for addressing many of these problems is greater involvement from the private sector. However, as shown in **Figure 24.5**, this approach has already been taken in England and Wales. (Remember to apply an ABC mindset when reading this information; the much larger size of the US prison population means that around 196,000 of its prisoners are under the authority of a private organisation, compared to the 15,000 in England and Wales.) The positive image of the private sector with its successful, business-like mindset contrasts sharply with that of the constantly failing public sector. In the last 30 years, beliefs in the superiority of the private sector have been shared by governments around the world. This is despite the lack of evidence for any

NEW FRONTIERS 24.1

Using prisons to build a way out of the pandemic?

The Covid-19 pandemic had serious effects on prisons across the world, as the close proximity between prisoners, who in Britain often share cells, make them obvious candidates for outbreaks of an infectious disease. These concerns are exacerbated by hygiene issues and the health problems that can come having from a poor diet. In the first six months of the pandemic, MoJ statistics recorded the deaths of five officers, 23 prisoners, and 21 people on probation (HMPPS, 2020). They also recorded over 500 positive tests for Covid-19 across 86 establishments (ibid). This was despite reducing the prison population by 3,000, as low-risk offenders within two months of their release date were given early release.

In June 2020, the government confirmed its plans for building four new prisons in both the north and south of England to fulfil its pledge to create 10,000 extra prison places. The new prisons are part of the government's strategy to rebuild the economy from the huge damage inflicted on it by the pandemic; the plan also includes building new roads, hospitals, and schools. It is a clear example of how prisons can now be perceived and the importance of their economic benefits.

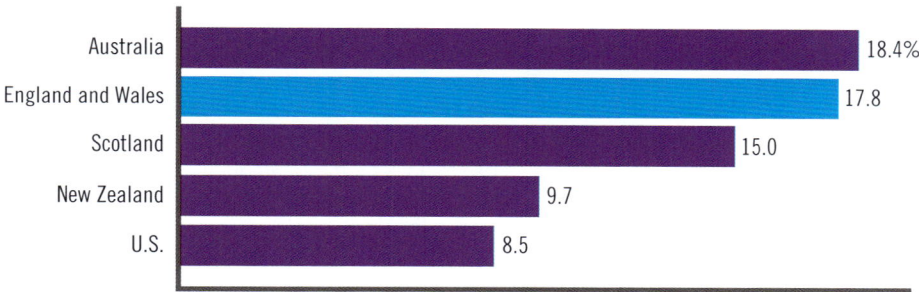

Figure 24.5 Greater privatisation of prisons is often presented as a solution to their many challenges, but in fact this approach is already in use

Source: https://www.bloombergquint.com/businessweek/u-k-private-prisons-are-one-industry-not-worried-about-brexit

'improvement outcomes that marketization processes can deliver' to prisons (Ludlow, 2017: 926). These processes refer to the business-side of a prison and the steps that are required when a private company is providing the service. This focus could be harmful for prison life; the consequence could include a reduction in prisoner and staff interaction, as staff spend increasing amounts of time on administrative tasks for the company.

These challenges come on top of what the core responsibility of a prison should arguably be; the fulfilment of its duty of care to its prisoners. This will vary as the law develops, but the obligation is more important than ever, considering people are now serving longer sentences than ever before. The difficulties this creates for young prisoners, those aged under 25 when sentenced to 15 years or more, have been recently highlighted (Crewe et al., 2020).

24.7 Conclusion

In this chapter we have analysed the actions of the 'big five' criminal justice institutions to see how they work, including how they put into practice the principles we explained in **Chapter 23**. We discovered that such implementation is not always possible, meaning that these core values of justice go unfulfilled. This was particularly clear when we assessed the institution's expected roles, as we learnt that these continually evolve, leading to problems when they are not clearly defined and supported.

We also examined the challenges faced by each organisation to help us think more critically about the impact and effectiveness of their services. We saw that these challenges often impede their ability to deliver the principles of justice. Recurring themes in terms of the challenges faced include funding cuts, resulting in understaffing and difficulties managing workloads and responsibilities—all troubles that have been and will be likely to continue to be exacerbated by the restrictions, delays, and financial impact of Covid-19. We noted that many of the institutions need to tackle issues of diversity in their workforce, which may (as we discussed in more detail in **Chapter 10**) have an effect on whether justice is served and on the treatment of offenders or potential offenders. Finally, we noted that all of the institutions, bar the courts, now have competition from the private sector, which invites critical analysis of their work through these comparisons and contrasts. This knowledge and understanding will prepare you for the next chapter, where we conclude our analysis of criminal justice by assessing the competing influences of the system's policies and practices.

SUMMARY

After reading this chapter and working your way through its features you should now be able to:

- **Assess the ways policing providers engage with the public**

We explained that the support of the public is essential for consensual policing. It underpins the police mandate that empowers the police to perform their work. Recent moves for increasing public engagement with policing include the introduction of Police and Crime Commissioners. This has changed the traditional structure of policing but, so far, there is limited evidence that they enhance public engagement. We concluded the policing section by considering the various challenges to policing, including the work and increasing use of private policing providers.

- **Discuss the purpose of the CPS and consider its effectiveness**

We discussed the CPS as the independent body responsible for prosecuting the vast majority of criminal cases, exploring its role in advising the police then taking cases to court. All of its prosecutions have to pass the public interest test, which affirms the importance of public views. We outlined the challenges facing the CPS and the criticisms made of its work. In doing so, we considered the problems of using conviction rates to measure its work, and whether this is fair; the CPS's ability to comply with adversarial justice responsibilities; and the system of disclosure of evidence.

- **Identify the different courts that can respond to crime and its related problems**

Being able to correctly identify the categories of criminal offences is essential for understanding how the court system operates. Their classification as indictable, summary, and either way offences determines which of the two criminal courts will hear the case. We noted that most people picture a Crown Court hearing when they think of a courtroom, but highlighted the set up and role of the Magistrates' Court because of its more frequent use in practice. We also noted the increasing preference for these courts to be held by district judges, or professional magistrates, rather than lay magistrates. In this section, we also outlined the differences between private law and public law, so that you can appreciate their different conceptions of justice.

- **Recognise the different forms of probation and community sanctions**

In this part of the chapter we explained how the recent expansion in probation and community sanctions has resulted in what has been called an era of mass supervision. We investigated how the community order and the suspended sentence order have facilitated this growth through the variety of conditions they can impose on offenders. We discussed the shift in recent years from 'care to correction' in terms of the priorities of this part of the system, and saw the importance of partnership work for this criminal justice organisation. This included assessments of the involvement of the private sector and the harms that this has caused to the system.

- **Appreciate the challenges facing prisons as a key criminal justice organisation**

In this section we navigated some of the extensive range of academic literature and research findings on prisons to help you find themes and make connections in your further reading. We saw that prisons are heavily used in many countries, including in England and Wales, and that prison populations are increasing. We observed that it is very difficult to identify and implement the precise role that prisons should fulfil. Not only are there a wide range of views about the extent to which they should be punitive or rehabilitative, but each one operates slightly differently and there is a gap between the intended model of the system and what happens in practice. We saw that prisons are facing a whole host of different challenges, ranging from overcrowding to violence between inmates and towards officers, and explored the ability of the private sector in resolving the current crisis.

 Test your understanding of the chapter's key points by attempting the self-test questions on the **online resources** at www.oup.com/he/case2e

REVIEW QUESTIONS

1. How has the traditional organisation of policing been challenged by political and private interests?
2. Why does adversarial justice require the CPS to take part in the disclosure of evidence process?
3. In what ways do civil and criminal courts differ in their approaches to the provision of justice?
4. Explain the term 'mass supervision' and outline its implications for an offender on probation or a community sanction.
5. Explain the term 'mass incarceration' and outline its implications for both public and private sector prisons.

 Access the **online resources** at www.oup.com/he/case2e to check your answers to the review questions.

FURTHER READING

Visit this book's online resources to access additional chapters on the criminal justice systems in Scotland, Wales, and Northern Ireland, respectively.

Bowling, B., Reiner, R., and Sheptycki, J. W. E. (2019) *The Politics of the Police* **(5th edn). Oxford: Oxford University Press.**
This is a popular and highly acclaimed book written by leading figures in this field. Its chapters are divided into four parts that detail policing theory and research, contemporary policing practice, and law and politics. It can advance your critical reflections through its theoretical and empirical arguments.

Hamerton, C. and Hobbs, S. (2019) *Privatisation in Criminal Justice: key issues and debates.* **Abingdon: Routledge.**
This text analyses the social, cultural, and political context of privatisation in the criminal justice sector. It contains separate chapters on how it has affected the police, prisons, probation, and defence lawyers. Both theoretical and practical issues are included in its analysis that provides essential information for evaluating contemporary justice responses.

Jewkes, Y., Crewe, B., and Bennett, J. (eds) (2016) *Handbook on Prisons* **(2nd edn). Abingdon: Routledge.**
This is a comprehensive collection of chapters on prison life. As well as academics, they are written by ex-prisoners, prison governors and ex-governors, and prison inspectors. Its topics include prison design, technology in prisons, the high-security estate, and therapeutic communities.

McNeill, F. (2019) *Pervasive Punishment: Making Sense of Mass Supervision.* **Bingley: Emerald.**
This text explains the harms being uncovered by research into community sanctions and their related measures. It highlights how the focus of criminological research on mass incarceration has neglected the issues raised by the new era of mass supervision. It explains how this has harmed the prospects of reintegrating the people serving these orders.

 Access the **online resources** to view a wealth of extra information relating to your study of criminology, including self-test questions, answers to review questions, and links to other resources that will help you enjoy and fulfil your potential within your studies.
www.oup.com/he/case2e

CHAPTER OUTLINE

25.1	Introduction	744
25.2	Criminal justice policies	744
25.3	Criminal justice practices	754
25.4	People in criminal justice	761
25.5	Conclusion	763

25

Criminal justice policies and practices

KEY ISSUES

After studying this chapter, you should be able to:

- examine key influences on contemporary criminal justice policy, including modernisation and penal populism;
- analyse the effects of policy on criminal justice practices in policing, courtroom, and community settings;
- assess the influence of criminal justice professionals in the delivery of criminal justice;
- engage with the idea that there are four core components of the criminal justice system (principles, policies, practices, and people) and that all four are involved in any process of change within it.

25.1 Introduction

In the introduction to **Chapter 23** we discussed the idea that the criminal justice system in England and Wales can be seen as having four interrelating components. Having spent time in the previous two chapters on getting to grips with the principles that underpin the system and looking at how these manifest in its key institutions, we can now move on to explore the system 'in action': in this chapter, we examine criminal justice policies, practices, and the people who work within the system. It is important that you think of these components as the interconnected parts of a single entity (the criminal justice system). **Figure 25.1** shows them as four interlocking cogs, each of which has a knock-on effect on the workings and overall direction of the 'engine' of criminal justice. For example, principles tend to be presented as fixed and stable, but we have seen in **Chapter 23** and **24** that in reality they are often reshaped or even ignored—for example, the system's abandonment of the principle of the rule of law in the use of Immigration Removal Centres (see **section 24.6**).

The oil can in **Figure 25.1** is a reminder that to keep running smoothly, any system of gears needs appropriate adjustment and maintenance. In this chapter we will critically assess the extent to which this happens in criminal justice, investigating whether its policies, practices, and people respond effectively and appropriately to the principles we have identified. In discussing policy, we will be considering **penal populism**, as well as returning to the **concept** of 'adversarial-lite' (which we introduced as a principle in **Chapter 23**) to look at its influence on the UK system. We will then critically assess their use in practice in the courtroom and the community to see how key principles can play out in reality. Finally, we will reflect on the effects of all the components upon the people who work in the criminal justice system.

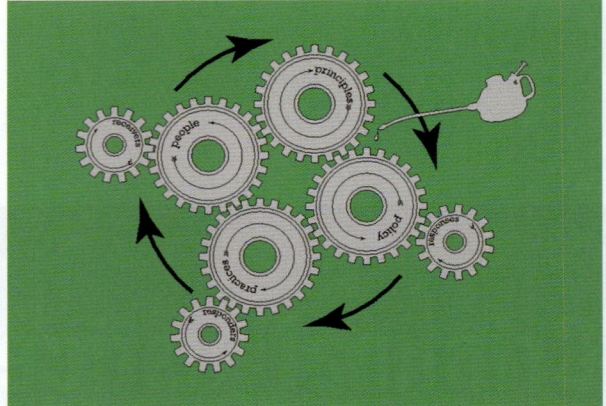

Figure 25.1 The criminal justice system can be seen as a complex engine of interlocking components (principles, policy, practices, and people) which needs regular attention and adjustment to operate smoothly

25.2 Criminal justice policies

'Policy' is the catch-all term used to describe strategies and proposed courses of action. A policy isn't necessarily large scale and governmental (you could, for example, suggest that the best 'policy' for dealing with your messiest flatmate is to let their dirty dishes pile up in a corner until they eventually run out of crockery), but here we use the term to refer to regional or national strategies for responding to crime. We consider the origins and influences of criminal justice policies; the significant impact that 'penal populism' can exert on policy; and how government policy is shaping the ways in which the 'adversarial-lite' principle is implemented.

Policy origins and influences

Criminal justice policies predominantly come from the government, but other organisations and individuals such as academics, the media, corporations, and lobbyists can influence them. The motivations behind these policy influencers may vary, but they all share the ultimate aim of ensuring that their preferred strategy is implemented (carried out) in practice. Academics shaping policy through independent research might sound desirable, but the politicised nature of criminal justice means that other forms of influence can be more important (Wincup, 2017). Finding the source of criminal justice policies is not always straightforward as they can originate from a mixture of political, social, and cultural contexts.

When a policy has been developed, it has to go through an implementation stage which sees it passed down to the relevant parts of the civil service, such as the Ministry of Justice, Home Office, and Youth Justice Board. These bodies are responsible for administering the system and contribute at the policy-creation stage as well as implementation. Policies can then be filtered down to the smaller parts of these organisations, like HM Prison and Probation Service and HM Courts and Tribunals Service. They continue to regional areas and, depending on how the service is structured, onto borough or town level, before reaching individual offices and officers. This might suggest that individuals are merely passive recipients in the policy process, but as we discuss in **section 25.4**, they are the ones with power to interpret it and apply it to specific cases.

So, policy development is usually a top-down process with the government applying pressure and setting the direction, but to effectively make this transition from idea to practical strategy, policies need to appeal to shared values in society. It would be an extremely complicated and difficult task to secure agreement on what these shared values might be, particularly in today's diverse, multicultural society, but happily for the government there is no need to even attempt this mission. We will see in **section 25.2** that its policies are quite strongly influenced by penal populism, but ultimately the constitutional power of the executive (the government) means that it can put forward its proposals for validation from the legislature (the three parts to Parliament: the House of Commons, House of Lords, and the monarchy), and as a result of the lack of **separation of powers** in the UK (see **section 23.2**) this validation is generally given. The government is therefore the main policymaker for criminal justice, and responsibility for contributing to this is shared across many of its different parts. The policy area for law and the justice system is shaped by about 20 different government departments including the Ministry of Justice (MoJ) and the Home Office; it is also influenced by other public bodies such as the Crown Prosecution Service, HM Prison Service, National Probation Service, and the Parole Board.

The key drivers for these policymakers have been summarised as: 'We must be *tough*; we must be *modern*; we must get *value for money*; we must get *re-elected*' (Cavadino and Dignan, 2006: 75, emphasis added). It could be argued that these demands have directly led to flaws in justice policy in recent decades, and throughout this chapter we will explore the extent to which they are still relevant. The MoJ's current policy preferences are summarised in its single departmental plan for 2019–22, and focus on the courts, prisons, and reoffending levels (Ministry of Justice, 2019a), but modernisation and efficiency continue to be key influences (see **New frontiers 25.1** for a more in-depth discussion of these priorities). Crime responders such as the police and the CPS are increasingly judged on the extent to which they support these priorities by reducing delays, reducing the number of hearings, and making trials more effective. This is a very difficult task considering that the biggest reason why first court hearings can be ineffective is the **defendant**'s failure to attend (HM Crown Prosecution Service Inspectorate, 2017).

NEW FRONTIERS 25.1

The direction of criminal justice policy

The Ministry of Justice regularly issues new plans for its policy direction; plans that can be amended when there is a change of government, as was the case in 2019 (see Ministry of Justice, 2019a). In recent years, the desire to change and improve the criminal justice system has been shown by the frequency with which the word 'transforming' appears in important policy developments, for example:

- 'Transforming Our Justice System' (2016a), which focused on ensuring the court system operates in a just, proportionate and accessible manner;
- 'Transforming Rehabilitation' (2015), which focused on reforms for managing medium- and low-risk offenders and which, in 2015–21, transferred this power to private Community Rehabilitation Companies;
- 'Transforming Summary Justice' (2015), which aimed to speed up the processing of criminal cases by the Magistrates' Court in England and Wales.

These plans have formed part of the MoJ's general drive for greater digitisation of the court system, an ambition that was made clear in the joint vision statement issued in 2016 by the Lord Chancellor, the Lord Chief Justice, and the Senior President of Tribunals:

> As the courts and tribunals are modernised we will need fewer buildings, used more efficiently with courtrooms which are more adaptable. In many cases, attending hearings in person will only be needed where there is no other alternative; parties will be able to engage virtually or online rather than have to take time to attend hearings in person.

(Ministry of Justice, 2016a: 6–7)

The plan was to get all civil courts online in the next few years, a shift that would start with all claims for under £10,000 (Ministry of Justice, 2018a: para. 2.1), and it was expected that parts of the criminal process would follow suit. However, we saw in **New frontiers 3.1** that the Covid-19 pandemic hastened the digitisation process: in 2020, the restrictions and lockdowns forced the system to experiment with virtual courts in both a civil and criminal context. The hope is that digitisation, which has seen many UK courts close (see **Figure 25.2**), will solve numerous problems of delays and inefficiency—such as participants travelling long distances to court only to discover that the case has been put on hold. It means new ways of working for everyone employed in courts and tribunals; changes that are long overdue considering that the police often handwrite their own and other witnesses' statements. These confidential documents are scanned into the official digital case management system and prompt security concerns about hacking, as well as causing additional work as time must be spent making them legible to the prosecution and defence (Criminal Justice Joint Inspection, 2016).

In their 2016 statement, the Lord Chancellor, the Lord Chief Justice, and the Senior President of Tribunals recognised that the checks and balances imposed by the separation of powers (see **section 23.2**) may delay new initiatives. Although we saw increased digitisation as a result of the Covid-19 pandemic, the judiciary remain cautious about widespread use of virtual courts, particularly in the criminal context. According to a leaked report of the Judicial Ways of Working policy consultation exercise, in 2018 the judiciary expressed concerns that online criminal trials

Figure 25.2 Moves towards digitisation have seen many courts close in recent years

Source: UK Justice Policy Review: Volume 7—Centre for Crime and Justice Studies

were unfair to defendants since they limit engagement with the seriousness of the proceedings and mean they cannot communicate properly with their lawyers (*The Guardian*, 20 December 2018). There has not yet been sufficient research to fully address these and other concerns.

Penal populism

Until the last decades of the 20th century, little effort was made to assess or factor in the public's views on criminal justice. Instead, policymakers such as politicians, senior administrators, penal reformers, and academic criminologists saw themselves as 'Platonic guardians'—with 'Platonic' in this context not meaning 'non-romantic', as we often use it today, but referring to the ideas of the philosopher Plato. Plato claimed that a 'just' society has three classes, top of which are the 'guardians' (also known as philosopher-kings). Their perceived wisdom and intellect, and their detachment from normal public life, meant they were considered the people best able to direct society. In keeping with these ideas, early policymakers believed the role of the government was 'to respond to crime (and public anger and anxiety about crime) in ways that, above all, seek to preserve "civilized values"' (Loader, 2006: 563).

This detached position changed in the 1990s with the emergence of what was initially known as populist punitiveness. This resulted in the creation of policies that suited politicians' own purposes by aligning with the assumed punitive stance of the public (Bottoms, 1995: 40)—an assumption which reflects some of the perspectives on justice that we considered in **Chapter 3**.

What is penal populism?

Bottoms's view did not expressly use the term 'penal populism' but nonetheless is recognised as the original source of this concept. Penal populism can be concisely explained as 'penal policies to win votes rather than to reduce crime rates or to promote justice' (Roberts et al., 2003: 5). The word 'populism' makes for interesting debate, as instantly it seems like a 'good' word—after all, what's wrong with being popular? But in criminal justice, and other areas of life such as politics, the label has such negative associations that it 'typically carries a strong whiff of disapproval' (Loader and Sparks, 2017: 98). Nonetheless, examples of populist movements around the world are not hard to find (you will probably be able to name a few immediately), and in addition to the UK and US, many European, Asian, and South American countries have taken this approach to criminal justice (see **Chapter 13**). Populism is not recognised as a philosophy or a distinct school of thought with organising principles and a clear history, but Loader and Sparks (2017: 100–1) have identified its three distinct features:

1. **Populists speak on behalf of the people**—This claim illustrates populism's potential for broad appeal. From a left-wing political perspective, being on the people's side means defending the working class against exploitation by a richer elite; whereas right-wing populists focus on ethnicity and race and consider speaking for the people to mean being against minorities and migrants.

2. **Populists contest the powers of self-interested elites**—Populists present themselves as holders of genuine public views rather than those of a group that is part of the establishment (for example, a political party). Establishment groups are presented as privileged, self-serving, and out of touch with real public views; they are accused of protecting the interests of minorities rather than dealing with the fears of ordinary people.

3. **Populists are committed to the ideal of popular sovereignty**—They believe politics can, and should, express clearly and then fulfil the general will of the people. This is expected to be achieved through firm political leadership, where strong personalities overcome perceived problems such as the restrictions imposed by human rights, and other checks and balances on political power.

Considering populism's vagueness, it is unsurprising that it is hard to identify a clear starting point for its offshoot, penal populism, but the 'prison works' speech in 1993 at the Conservative Party conference by the then Home Secretary Michael Howard is often seen this way. There is a huge amount of academic literature about this policy approach, and though it is not the most recent of these works, we strongly recommend that you read 'Penal Populism' by Pratt (2007) (see the **Further Reading** at the end of this chapter) for the numerous examples it provides of this policy approach in action. These include the rapidly increasing prison populations in many countries (discussed at many points in this book, including **section 13.4** and **section 24.6**) and the practices in some US courts to force offenders to wear T-shirts to indicate the crime they committed and to make some sex offenders 'display a "scarlet M" sign in their window' (Pratt, 2007: 31). The 'M' stands for molester and this policy shift reflects the influence of right-realist criminology (see **Chapter 15**), and its view that being tougher with offenders is something favoured by the public.

We have attempted to summarise the key characteristics of policy preferences over time in **Table 25.1**, to give you a sense of these changes and repetitions. Please note that this is intended as a rough guide only, and the information, including the dates cited, should not be accepted as established fact. The dates simply indicate two major events—the French Revolution (1789) and the collapse of communism in Eastern Europe (1989)—which cover, approximately, the recognised modern period for justice policymaking. The '89 pattern' is a simple but effective way of remembering these shifts, and if you know the 'old' era as well as the new one, you will have plenty to write about in your assessments.

Reading public opinion

Favouring certain policies because they are believed to have popular appeal might seem like a victory for democracy, particularly as policymaking has previously been

	Pre-modern (pre-1789)	Modern (1789–1989)	Post-modern* (1989+)
Level of **punishment**	Severe	Restrained	Excessive
Basis for policies	Emotional	Rational	Rational and emotional
Style of punishment	Physical punishments: in public view	Private punishments: behind prison walls	Mass incarceration Mass supervision
Key influences	The monarch	Experts: psychiatrists, **probation** officers, psychologists	Politicians
Extent of public involvement	Public involved as witnesses	Public excluded	Public involved as stakeholders
Main sentencing priority	Retribution	**Rehabilitation**	Punishment (plus the other aims of s. 142 of the Criminal Justice Act 2003)

*Some people prefer 'late modern' rather than the total separation implied by 'post-'.

Table 25.1 Policy preferences in different time periods

a closed and elitist process (Ryan, 2005), but this is not necessarily the case. Whether the resulting policies are democratic depends heavily on the accuracy of readings of public opinion. Criminal justice policy that does not align with public opinion risks losing its authority under the rule of law, as it is public support that legitimises the criminal justice system's use of its power. Gaps between the public's expectations and the policies produced have been evident in the Crime Survey for England and Wales (see **Chapter 5**), which has often found that around three-quarters of respondents believe court sentences to be too lenient (Roberts and Hough, 2013: 240).

Efforts to assess public opinion on responses to crime can be limited by a number of factors, one of which is the extent and accuracy of the average person's knowledge of current practice. Most people, for example, underestimate the severity of sentences that are usually imposed (Hough et al., 2012). (You can test your own knowledge and expectations in **What do you think? 25.1**.) In addition, a survey's question order, wording, and accompanying information can all have an influence on people's opinions on crime and justice. These issues suggest that public opinion is much more varied and complex than is generally assumed, particularly by penal populists who claim to speak for the public. Hough and Roberts (2017) suggest that contrary to widespread assumptions:

> One of the most significant recent trends in public opinion is a swing *away* from support for imprisonment. Even in the US, where the public has traditionally been more punitive in its attitudes to offenders, members of the public appear to be growing more skeptical of the use of custody
>
> (Hough and Roberts, 2017: 247–8, emphasis added)

If you can recognise the characteristics of the three phases of policy preferences outlined in **Table 25.1** you will have a way of analysing current strategies for their modern or backward-looking features. For example, the growing recognition that criminal sanctions can produce disproportionate amounts of harm has led to many calls for limits on their use (McNeill, 2019). But we can see the lack of political support (even though it would be considerably cheaper) for the modern principle of *restraint* in the numerous new offences created by Parliaments, the rising prison population, and the introduction of additional community sentencing powers

WHAT DO YOU THINK? 25.1

You be the judge

Do you have a good enough sense of current responses to crime to be able to say whether UK sentencing is too lenient, just right, or too harsh? The MoJ has created a 'You be the Judge' simulation online (**Figure 25.3**) which allows you to test your assumptions: visit http://ybtj.justice.gov.uk.

At the time of writing, eight cases are available. Each has video footage from a mock courtroom plus written information for the defendant's plea and the offence's aggravating and mitigating factors. You are asked a quick question after the video, then you will be invited to pass sentence by choosing from four options, before receiving a judicial explanation as to how the sentencing guidelines would be applied.

When you have worked through one of the cases and selected a sentence, consider the following:

- Were you surprised at the sentence that was actually imposed in the case?
- What influenced your views on the appropriate sentence?

After reflecting on your opinions, consider these broader questions:

- Why has the MoJ set up this simulation?
- What effects might it have?
- What are the implications of this resource's finding that members of the public completing the simulation tend to select sentences that are more lenient than those chosen in court?

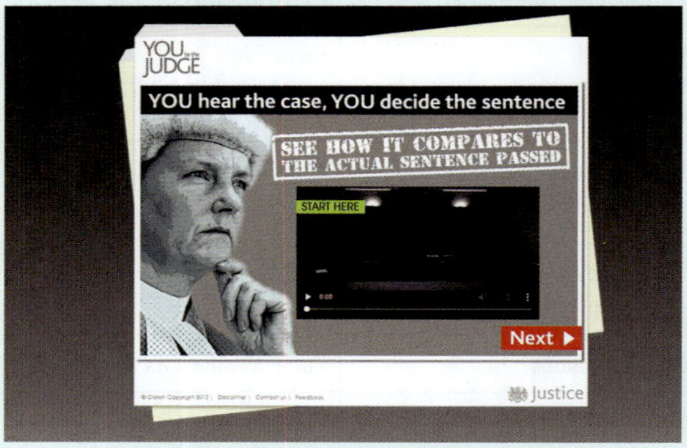

Figure 25.3 The Ministry of Justice's 'You be the Judge' online simulation allows you to test your assumptions about UK sentencing
Source: You Be The Judge © Crown Copyright 2012

(see **section 24.5**) and harsher disposals for first time offenders. A *rational* justice system would take such possibilities of disproportionate harm seriously and its official policy agendas would be grounded in research. It would also avoid implementing contradictory policies where decisions from the executive could not be justified (such as the so-called 'book ban' considered later in this section).

At this point, it is worth remembering the reforms to the judiciary that we considered in **Chapter 23**, specifically the merging of the positions of Lord Chancellor and Minister for Justice in 2005 (see **section 23.2**). Although this reform secured more separation of powers than previously, the role of the Lord Chancellor (also called the Minister of Justice) is still political as it is a Cabinet position, with the powers and responsibilities for running the court system. The fact that this political power exists in the justice system means that policy may be created with very different motives to those underpinning the key justice principles we explored in **Chapter 23** and its direction can vary dramatically from Chancellor to Chancellor. Under Ken Clarke (2010–12), for example, the aim was 'to halt the populist tone and "prison works" mantra that had prevailed from the early 1990s' (Annison, 2018: 1070). In sharp contrast, Chris Grayling (2012–15) made numerous 'tough on crime' speeches and during his tenure legislation was created for: increasing the minimum length of extended sentences for dangerous offenders; restricting the use of cautions; introducing a minimum sentence for a second offence involving an offensive weapon; increasing the range of offences where a mandatory life sentence had to be imposed; and increasing the amount of force householders could use when responding to a burglary (Annison, 2018: 1071).

Grayling's tenure also featured what became known as the 'book ban' in 2014, where policy changes resulted in prisoners no longer being able to receive books sent to them by family and friends. This was an attempt to show the public that prisons were austere places where prisoners did not easily acquire luxury items. The MoJ countered the criticism that the ban attracted by claiming prisoners could still buy books from the money they earned from working in prison (which at the time was £8 a week) and could request books from the prison library. The separation of powers principle was able to exert a 'check' on this policy as it was declared unlawful by the High Court in *R (on the application of Gordon-Jones) v Secretary of State for Justice* [2014] EWHC 3997 (Admin). This case effectively demonstrates how the separation of powers principle can empower the judiciary to block irrational policy from the executive. The court held that there was no good reason to change the policy for prisoners' conditions and endorsed the view of the Prison Reform Trust that some books, for some prisoners, can help the rehabilitation process (at [21]).

Current policy hints at different priorities and there can be exceptions to the increasingly tough forms of punishment that populists assume the public want to see. Serving prisoners can now access opportunities such as studying at the Open University, thanks to the use of the same software that can fulfil the digitisation agenda we assessed in **New frontiers 25.1**. Previously, prisoners would have to rely on receiving printed materials through the post or accessing their prison library, both of which could clearly have limitations. But now that policy is gradually accepting some advancements in secure in-cell technology, full access to online Open University courses is now available in some prisons. And Open University degrees are not the only new learning opportunities for people serving a custodial sentence. Since 2017, the organisation Prisoners' Education Trust (**Figure 25.4**) has supported various educational partnerships through its prison–university partnerships network. The 'Learning Together' programme also supports the development of modules with university students learning alongside prison students, which are generally established by university staff. The accounts from an academic, student, and prisoner in **Conversations 25.1**, and the evidence that is gradually emerging about the impact of these schemes, indicate that there are potential advantages for all who participate.

Another example of a policy with non-populist priorities is the Safer Living Foundation, a partnership between the school of social sciences at Nottingham Trent University and HMP Whatton (*The Guardian*, 9 February 2019). This initiative aims to increase community reintegration for recently released prisoners, with a specialism for those with sexual convictions. For most of the 20th century, this kind of rehabilitation of offenders was the 'organizing principle' for government criminal justice policy (Garland, 2001: 35), but this ideal was displaced by the tougher attitudes in its latter decades—exemplified by the 'tough on crime, tough on the causes of crime' sound bite in the Labour Party's landslide election success in 1997. One of the most frequent criticisms of this claim was that, in practice, the exclusive focus was that its first half—'tough on the causes of crime'—was almost completely neglected.

Figure 25.4 The Prisoners' Education Trust supports learning opportunities for those serving custodial sentences, representing an exception from the otherwise increasingly tough modern forms of punishment

Source: The Prison University Partnerships network

CONVERSATIONS 25.1

Learning Together

with **Dr Charlotte Barlow, Emma Pease**, and an **anonymous prisoner**

Learning Together is one of the models of the prison–university partnership facilitated by the Prisoners' Education Trust. Here, a criminology academic and student from Lancaster University and a prison student from HMP Lancaster Farms discuss their experiences of participating in the programme.

An academic's view

Learning Together is an initiative whereby students in universities and prisons learn alongside one another in the prison environment. It was originally developed at Cambridge University, but has since been extended to various UK-based higher education institutions. Learning Together is based on the notion that although education can be a practice of freedom, it can sometimes become a means of oppression in itself, particularly if knowledge is delivered in ways that are exclusive and didactic. For prisoners in particular, education is often isolating, therefore this initiative suggests that by learning together, all students can engage with knowledge in ways that are individually and socially transformative (Armstrong and Ludlow, 2016).

To develop the Learning Together course at Lancaster University, I worked collaboratively with education staff at HMP Lancaster Farms to facilitate learning opportunities that were inclusive for everyone. As some examples of how I attempted to achieve this inclusivity, I worked with the university to ensure the module was accredited for all learners (both university and prison-based students receive 15 Lancaster University credits for completing the course) and that all students had equal access to resources and readings (all students are provided with reading packs and these are the only sources that can be used for lesson and assessment preparation). I regularly encourage reflexivity, exploring issues such as knowledge production and underlying presumptions and stereotypes of particular groups or communities in order to help all students appreciate the importance of different types of knowledge and life experiences.

The student feedback on the course has been fantastic and for me personally, it has been the most enriching teaching experience I have ever been part of.

Dr Charlotte Barlow (pictured left), Lecturer in Criminology, Lancaster University

A university student's view

I began studying criminology in 2015 but it was my final year that affirmed my passion for the subject because not only was I studying fascinating topics and writing a dissertation, but I also took part in a new module called 'Learning Together'. This involved weekly visits to the local prison, where university and prisoner students were taught together in lecture/seminar-based sessions.

Learning Together had a profound impact on me both personally and academically because it allowed me to experience education in prison first-hand and learn from the perspective of a prisoner. Whilst it was useful to hear from various lecturers, it was the prisoners who were at the heart of the module as they were able to contribute personal experience to debates. I soon found that I was making connections between discussions and academic content, and this became clear during the assessment which involved putting together a presentation in mixed groups of prisoners and students.

According to the Prisoner Learning Alliance (2016), education has four key functions; social capital, human capital, employability and knowledge and well-being. Whilst Learning Together promoted knowledge and well-being through academic discussion, skill development such as public speaking, it particularly promoted social and human capital through the relationships built between prisoners and students.

Social capital, meaning a sense of belonging in society, was strengthened through its ability to bring people together, particularly through the graduation ceremony which closed the module, and to which all involved invited family and friends. It is clear how this could act as a 'ritual of reintegration' (Maruna, 2011) that encourages the sense of belonging to society which is vital for rehabilitation and desistance.

Human capital, defined by a prisoner's motivation to change, was also enhanced through Learning Together, evident in the prisoners' opinions on the module. They said it 'opened my eyes to what I could achieve' and '[made] me think differently about my own life and offending'.

> Learning Together was an incredible experience which I believe will have a life-long impact on me. I would recommend it to anyone who gets the chance to take part.
>
> *Emma Pease (pictured right), former Criminology BSc student, Lancaster University*

A prisoner's view

I initially signed up for Learning Together because I wanted to try something new whilst in prison that would help me pass the time. I also wanted to further my education whilst serving my prison sentence and to take any positives that I could out of a negative situation. I didn't expect to enjoy or get as much out of the course as I did.

The module involved 12 students from Lancaster University and 12 prison-based students learning a criminology module together. It was run over an eight week period at the end of which we had to deliver a group presentation and portfolio on one of the lectures/seminars we had been taught during the module. My group involved two university students and two prison-based students.

The module opened my eyes to other things possible to me both whilst in prison and more importantly when I am released. The course has made me realise that other opportunities are available to me. I thoroughly enjoyed the experience and it has made me feel more positive about the future.

A student from HMP Lancaster Farms, a men's Category C prison in Lancaster

References

Armstrong, R. and Ludlow, A. (2016) 'Educational partnerships between universities and prisons: How learning together can be individually, socially and institutionally transformative'. *Prison Service Journal* 225: 9–17.
Maruna, S. (2011) 'Reentry as a rite of passage'. *Punishment & Society* 13(1): 3–28.
Prisoner Learning Alliance (2016) 'What is prison education for? A theory of change exploring the value of learning in prison': www.prisonerseducation.org.uk/data/Theory%20of%20Change%20Report%20FINAL.pdf

---

Politicians' desire to be 'tough on crime' has meant that over the past few decades, some principles that would previously have been considered fundamental to sentencing policy have been overridden. Principles such as the need for sentences to be imposed by an independent judge (see **section 23.3**), and the requirement that punishments have a specified end point, have been eroded by increases in the practices of **mandatory sentencing** and **indeterminate sentencing**. A mandatory sentence is one that is set by law and therefore not decided by a judge, whereas an indeterminate sentence does not have a fixed length of time and runs until the Parole Board believes a prisoner can be safely released.

Murder used to be the only offence that had a mandatory sentence (in this case, a life sentence) but judicial discretion has been restricted through a range of new statutes over the last 20 years, with other offences now carrying an automatic minimum prison term. In ss. 109–11 of the Powers of Criminal Courts (Sentencing) Act 2000 you will find a list of offences that have automatic life sentences, along with offences that carry a minimum prison term, for example a minimum seven-year term for a defendant's third Class A **drug trafficking** offence. Sometimes courts try to avoid imposing an automatic sentence in light of exceptional circumstances. This was the case in the trial of *R v Usherwood* [2018] EWCA Crim 1156. In this case, the 20-year-old defendant had been found guilty of possessing and producing several drugs and breaching a Crown Court sentence, but was originally sentenced to four years because he was seen as having mitigation in the form of his age (quite young) and the fact that he was under pressure to pay drug debts. The prosecution appealed against this sentence for being unduly lenient and were successful in the Court of Appeal, which ruled that such factors should be disregarded and the statutory minimum had to be imposed.

The disregard of principles that were devised to ensure that responses to crime were proportionate and flexible would have been seen by the 'Platonic guardians' as a sign of weakness in the justice system. This is not an opinion shared by populists, who see policies such as mandatory sentencing as signs of strength that become 'emblems of political virility' (Pratt, 2000: 131). Assumed popularity with the public is a key policy driver and repeated claims about being on 'the public's side' always indicate tough responses. Although it may sound sensible and democratic to listen to the public, taking 'sides' in policymaking can have divisive effects. This approach also seems self-defeating because if the populist message consistently conveys to the public that crime is increasing (despite the evidence potentially suggesting otherwise), then harsher strategies will be seen as yet another failure from the government.

'Adversarial-lite' justice

In **Chapter 23** we assessed the UK's traditionally strong leanings towards the principle of **adversarial** justice, an approach involving public criminal trials in which both the prosecution and defence rigorously present their cases (see **section 23.6**). Having this background knowledge means that we can now critically reflect on how governmental policy is currently shaping how this principle manifests in the system. We will investigate these changes so that we can form a view on whether 21st-century criminal justice is developing a new and distinct method for implementing the principle, one that is perhaps better described as 'adversarial-lite'.

A notable shift to consider is that the powers of the police and Crown Prosecution Service (CPS) have become increasingly diverse, in that they can now issue the various out-of-court **disposals** listed in **Table 25.2**. There are concerns that these powers actually amount to sentencing—which the adversarial system says should be done in court—and therefore contravene the principles of **open justice** and **due process** (see **section 23.4**) as they are made out of public view, by relatively low-level representatives of the police and the CPS, and with no independent judicial scrutiny. There are also fears that decisions could be made in the interests of economy, not justice. Despite not being issued as the result of a full legal process, a **conditional caution** can result in formal powers that, according to s. 17(2) of the Police and Justice Act 2006, seek to rehabilitate, punish, or require reparation from an offender. This means that people who might previously have been dealt with informally (via 'a telling off') may now receive a formal disposal and be moved into the criminal justice system; this is another example of the 'net widening' effect that we considered in **section 24.5**. Cautions count as criminal convictions and can be cited in future court proceedings; like criminal convictions they may also have to be disclosed in other situations, such as when applying for jobs, so critics (such as the advisers at https://hub.unlock.org.uk) argue that they have the potential to do a lot of harm if awarded inappropriately. Even a **community resolution** is formally recorded and will show up on enhanced DBS checks (DBS stands for the Disclosure and Barring Service, which runs background checks on people for employers and organisations).

There are plans to simplify the current options for out-of-court powers (listed in **Table 25.2**) by reducing them to either a community resolution or a conditional caution (National Police Chiefs' Council, 2017). This is a four-year strategy that requires all of the police forces in England and Wales to radically change their current practices. Community resolutions would be grounded in legislation and these disposals could be used by the police for minor offences if the victim and offender agree. This would align with the principle of restorative justice, in that victims would be given a say in how the offender should be dealt with and the result could involve an apology to the victim, the provision of reparation (such as working to repair the harm), or financial compensation. The proposed second tier of response for more serious offences would involve the use of suspended prosecutions. These would allow the police to attach one or more conditions to the disposal for the purposes of reparation, rehabilitation, or punishment, and to prosecute only if the condition(s) are not complied with.

The frequency with which out-of-court powers are used, as well as the high proportion of these disposals that are community resolutions, is illustrated by **Figure 25.5**. This shows they were used over 150,000 times in the year ending March 2020, which is around 10 per cent of the 1.49 million people that were formally dealt with by the criminal justice system (Ministry of Justice, 2020). That year's statistics excluded cautions as the Covid-19 pandemic meant full data collection was not possible; in the previous year, the total number of cautions was 67,300 (Ministry of Justice, 2019b).

The reshaping of the adversarial justice principle and the growth of penal populism have been accompanied by significant increases in the use of imprisonment, which has become the most dominant general criminal justice practice. This trend is evident from the fact that the prison population doubled between 1993 and 2012 and in recent years the total has consistently been in the low to mid-80,000s despite the decreases within these periods for both recorded crime and the numbers of people being formally proceeded against. The 1.49 million people who were formally dealt with by the criminal justice system in the year ending March 2020 is the lowest figure ever recorded; it matches similar record decreases in levels of reported crime, as found by both police figures and the Crime Survey for England and Wales (CSEW).

Although it may seem illogical at first, it is important to appreciate that rates of crime and numbers of people in prison measure different things and are not inseparably linked—changes in one do not automatically produce changes in the other. There have been several points when relatively low crime rates and high prison populations have coexisted (and vice versa), and despite the current all-time high of the latter and the decreasing number of people being formally proceeded against, the government predicts further increases in the prison population until 2023 (Ministry of Justice, 2018b). The high levels of imprisonment are being maintained by increases in more serious offences coming before the courts, plus the increasing number of offenders with more serious criminal records. A serious criminal record is defined as having 15 or more convictions and cautions, and in 2019 it accounted for 39 per cent of adult offenders being convicted for an indictable offence, its highest ever level (Ministry of Justice, 2019b), compared to 25 per cent a decade earlier (Ministry of Justice, 2016b). A key factor influencing the high rate of imprisonment, though, is that punitive policies appear to have been accepted and implemented by the

Type of power	Description	Is it a criminal conviction?
1. Community resolutions	An informal agreement between an offender and victim (where there is one) to use restorative justice techniques to resolve an offence for which the offender accepts responsibility. These are intended for cases of less serious crime and antisocial behaviour.	✗ (But it's formally recorded on the Police National Computer and will show up on enhanced level DBS checks.)
2. Simple cautions	A formal warning given to an offender once MoJ guidelines have been followed and the police have decided that this is a suitable response. The police can consult with the CPS and, if it is an indictable offence, only the CPS can decide if a simple caution is appropriate. It is possible to appeal to a court against the awarding of a caution and if successful, the offence should be reinvestigated. The pre-conditions for the issue of a caution are:<ul><li>there must be sufficient evidence to prosecute;</li><li>the offender must admit their guilt; and</li><li>the offender must consent to the caution being given.</li></ul>	✗ (But it's recorded on the Police National Computer and will show up on enhanced level DBS checks.)
3. Conditional cautions	A type of caution with the same three preconditions for use as simple cautions, but which stipulates conditions that must be fulfilled if the offender is to avoid prosecution. They can be issued when the prosecutor believes reparation to the victim or rehabilitation of the offender will be best achieved by action from the offender (such as paying compensation to a victim, participating in treatment for substance misuse, performing up to 20 hours of unpaid work, etc.). Since 2006, the police have had the power to issue conditional cautions, but not for indictable offences and those involving hate crime and domestic violence.	✗ (But it's recorded on the Police National Computer and will show up on enhanced level DBS checks.)
4. Penalty Notices for Disorder (PNDs)	A notice to an individual to pay an immediate fine (within 21 days). PNDs were introduced in 2001, and although they were originally intended for cases of disorderly behaviour, they can be used in minor cases of theft and criminal damage, wasting police time, or selling alcohol to a minor. If the PND is paid then no further action is taken—if not, the fine can be increased or referred to the courts.	✗ (When paid as required, all liability is satisfied, and the offence is not part of a criminal record.)
5. Fixed Penalty Notices (FPNs)	A notice to pay a fine for both traffic and other offences. A recipient usually has 28 days to challenge it. A failure to pay can result in the fine being increased or a prosecution for the original offence. They can be issued by police officers, PCSOs, local authority-authorised officers, parish councils, waste collection authorities, and the Environment Agency.	✗ (When paid as required, all liability is satisfied, and the offence is not part of a criminal record.)
6. Cannabis and khat warnings	Warnings that can be issued to adults for possession of small quantities of these substances for personal use. These have been available since 2004 and 2014 respectively.	✗ (The only records that are kept are those on local police systems.)

Table 25.2 A summary of the current (as of autumn 2020) out-of-court powers for adult offenders

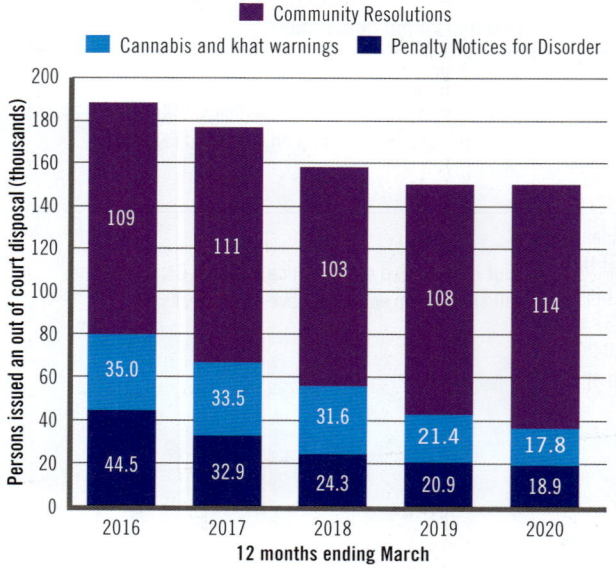

Figure 25.5 Government figures reveal that a significant number of individuals are being dealt with outside the courts system, often through community resolutions, suggesting that policy has reshaped the adversarial justice principle into an 'adversarial-lite' version

Source: Contains public sector information licensed under the Open Government Licence v3.0.

courts, which are increasingly prepared to impose imprisonment and to do so for longer average times. We made this point in **section 24.4** where we saw that the average length of a custodial sentence for an indictable offence was 16 months in 1993, and by 2020 it was 22.2 months (Ministry of Justice, 2020).

By now, it should be clear that policy can exert a strong influence on the work of the criminal justice system. These strategies can have significant effects on how key principles play out as they are attempting to address other requirements and values, such as securing the perceived political and economic advantages from responding to crime. The assumption that highly punitive values are popular with the general public does not have a convincing evidence base, but this has not prevented approaches of penal populism taking root and heavily influencing policy by seeking to involve the public in matters which previously were the responsibility of experts in the field. The resulting tough, 'common sense' approaches have a further contradiction in that their financial costs make them unsustainable. These conflicting policy imperatives show that there are many sticking points when we try to make changes in criminal justice. It is not only that each component of the system offers resistance against the others; as we have seen, the obstacles can come from within the 'cogs' themselves.

25.3 Criminal justice practices

We now turn to the criminal justice practices that result from the ever-evolving and interconnected principles and policies we have discussed. We will examine high-profile policing, courtroom, and community practices because they symbolise key values and expectations for contemporary justice systems.

Policing practices

Let's begin by exploring a prominent real-life example of how the due process principle (see **section 23.4**) can conflict with the principle of adversarial justice when both are applied in practice. The due process principle is supposed to be at its strongest when a police investigation produces confession evidence because an admission of guilt has long been seen as the 'best' evidence, in that it has major probative value against a defendant—in other words, it has the potential to prove a case on its own. However, in practice the weight of importance that is placed on a confession can be problematic, especially if it is the only piece of evidence in the prosecution case. What if the confession is not true? There are numerous reasons why a confession could be inaccurate, such as people feeling compelled to admit to crimes they did not commit in the hope of getting a more lenient sentence.

The risk of relying on false confessions was recognised in several cases from the 1970s; particularly that of the Birmingham Six (see **Figure 25.6** and **Figure 25.7**). They were sentenced to life imprisonment for bombings in Birmingham pubs in 1974 which killed 21 people, and it was not until many years later, in 1991, that their convictions were overturned by the Court of Appeal. This was because the confessions from four of the accused had been withdrawn, as had unreliable forensic evidence against the two others. Evidence of the violent tactics used to acquire the confessions is displayed in the infamous image in **Figure 25.6**. The case of the Birmingham Six and other similar cases had a significant influence on criminal justice practices, not just in relation to confessions, but to treatment in a police station more generally. They revealed flaws in the idea of the adversarial process as a contest between two equal parties and highlighted the need for safeguards to ensure genuine equality. This helped bring about the Police and Criminal Evidence Act 1984 (PACE), a piece of legislation that strengthened the defendant's right

Figure 25.6 The case of the 'Birmingham Six'—pictured here with battered faces, three days after going into prison—had a significant influence on criminal justice practices
Source: PA Images

to consult a solicitor (see our discussion in **section 24.4** on the role of duty solicitors); required interviews to be recorded (to stop the practice of 'verballing', where police officers could attribute false statements to a suspect); and introduced special protections for vulnerable people held in police custody.

The safeguards introduced by PACE mean that, generally, everyone in police custody has the right to have someone informed (s. 56) and the right to access legal advice (s. 58), but in practice there are some exceptions. Both rights can be lawfully refused if there are reasonable grounds to believe they could lead to interference with, or harm to, witnesses or other people; the alerting of other suspects; or might hinder the recovery of the proceeds of crime. This granting, but then denying, of the due process rights in PACE (and its official codes of practice) might seem understandable in some cases (see, for example, the case described in **Controversy and debate 25.1**) but it calls into question the influence of this principle in the policing legislative framework.

In addition to the successful appeals for the Birmingham Six, the adversarial justice principle took more criticism in the late 20th century's other infamous miscarriages of justice cases such as the Cardiff Three (see the 2012 BBC *Panorama* episode 'Justice Denied: The Greatest Scandal?') and the Guildford Four (see the 1993 Hollywood film *In the Name of the Father* and the 2018 BBC documentary *A Great British Injustice*). The references in the nicknames for these cases to the number of people involved indicates the extent of this problem and the fact that the adversarial system struggles to counterbalance the readiness of both the police and the CPS to secure a conviction.

Courtroom practices

The controversies surrounding the practice of using disputed confession evidence at a criminal trial (whether they were actually made at all; their legitimacy; and their reliability—plus the fact that these practices conflict with the need for accurate outcomes; see discussion of the **double jeopardy** rule in **section 23.4**) have resulted in reforms to its due process. Disputed confessions can now only be admitted when they 'pass' a set of tests. This practice, which can be illustrated by the mnemonic 'OUTSEX' (although we have cheated slightly as **cross-examination** is represented by 'X'), and its six tests are set out in **Table 25.3**. These tests certainly help to regulate the use

Figure 25.7 The 'Birmingham Six' were released in 1991 after the withdrawal of confessions from four of the accused and unreliable forensic evidence against the two others
Source: PA Images

of disputed confession evidence, but you may notice from the table that there are many gaps in its protection—such as the partial definition of oppression (it includes torture, inhuman or degrading treatment, and the use or threat of violence) and the very wide discretion in s. 78 in deciding whether the evidence would adversely affect the fairness of proceedings.

We can find other examples across the system of safeguards and similar multi-requirement approaches where the due process principle is applied to limit police and prosecuting powers. It is apparent in ss. 1–7 of PACE, which detail the limits to the police's stop and search powers under this statute. It is also evident when admitting disputed identification evidence into court; another well-known factor in miscarriages of justice. The influence of due process is clear in the guidelines laid down by R v *Turnbull* [1977] QB 224; they ensure that the judge carefully directs the jury on the dangers of relying on eyewitness testimony. This is supported by the College of Policing's advice, shown in **Figure 25.8**, that the police should follow the mnemonic ADVOKATE when investigating this kind of evidence.

Community practices

We briefly discussed community practices in **section 24.5** when exploring the role and significance of probation services and community sanctions within the criminal justice system. We saw that giving offenders sentences that they have to serve in their communities rather than in prison has become an extremely common criminal justice practice. We also highlighted their negative effects, which include that offenders can be overloaded with conditions due to the many options sentencers have when imposing a suspended sentence order or a community order. This makes completing a sentence much harder and could be seen as an obstacle to an offender being rehabilitated—one of the aims of these orders. The specific condition which contributes to this problem is the requirement for an offender to do unpaid work; this is imposed the most often and varieties of the practice are in common use around the world (Canton and Dominey, 2017). It took until the Criminal Justice Act 1972 for the practice to be introduced in England and Wales as an official sentencing response, but it had appeared in other forms long

CONTROVERSY AND DEBATE 25.1

Catching a serial killer but losing a career

The due process principle played a major role in the investigation and subsequent trial for the murder of a woman named Sian O'Callaghan in 2011. Like the *Gäfgen* case we considered in **Chapter 3** (see **Controversy and debate 3.2**), the correct procedures were not followed as the police felt they hindered their chances of finding the victim alive. Five days had passed since Sian was reported missing, during which evidence was accumulating against Christopher Halliwell, a taxi driver who had picked Sian up in the early hours of the day she disappeared. The police officer leading the investigation, DS Fulcher, formally arrested the suspect in a supermarket car park but instead of taking him immediately to a police station as required by PACE, Fulcher tried to build a relationship with Halliwell and took him to a local beauty spot, hoping he could get him to talk about Sian's whereabouts. He believed this was justified by Sian's right to life under Art. 2 of the ECHR.

These unusual methods worked up to a point, as the suspect took the police to where he had disposed of Sian's body. Then, and again in contravention of his rights under PACE, the suspect confessed to another murder and took the police to where he had buried the body of Becky Godden in 2003. However, at the trial for the murders in 2012, both confessions were ruled inadmissible because of the manner in which they were obtained and their breaches of PACE. There remained sufficient evidence for the suspect to be convicted of Sian's murder, but not for Becky's. Two years later, an internal police investigation found Fulcher guilty of gross misconduct, resulting in his resignation despite his exemplary policing record.

At the retrial for Becky's murder in 2016, Fulcher was vindicated as the confession was admitted and helped to secure a murder conviction, for which a whole-life order was imposed. The judge's sentencing remarks can be read online (see https://www.judiciary.uk/wp-content/uploads/2016/09/r-v-halliwell-sentencing-remarks.pdf), and demonstrate what we can expect when these parts of the justice process are televised in the future. It may appear that justice was done eventually, but in his 2017 book *Catching a Serial Killer*, Fulcher stated that the case left such a mark on his reputation that he become unemployable in the UK. Arguments persist about whether this case was inspired policing or an abuse of power comparable with those committed in the 1970s. These were heightened in 2019, when it was the subject of a four-part ITV series titled *A Confession*.

---

before this, for example in the British Royal Navy's use of 'impressment' in the 17th and 18th centuries (Cabana, 2018). (This was a way of forcing convicted offenders to serve in and therefore help the navy, and was also known as the 'press gang'—the origin of the phrase 'press-ganged' into things.)

This form of restorative justice has had three official name changes in the last 20 years. The media still tends to call it 'community service'—see **What Do You Think 25.2**—and we use this term here, for convenience, but when you are writing about it formally, you should use its current official term: the unpaid work condition of a **community order**. Community service in its current form originates in a proposal from part of the traditional policymaking elite in the UK, the Advisory Council on the Penal System (1970). As we saw in **section 24.5**, it has become very widely used and is the most commonly imposed requirement in community sentencing (HM Inspectorate of Probation, 2016). It is a practice with which the public are familiar, and it has become the form of community sentencing they understand the most (McIvor, 2016). This support is mainly due to the flexibility of community service as a justice response; and the fact that it can be adapted to suit different demands and expectations like 'a chameleon, which is able to merge into any penal philosophic background' (Pease et al., 1976: 1). This description has some merit, but community service's adaptability goes deeper than just changing colour, to the extent that the sanction transforms into a different 'animal' in each new context. A more accurate term for such extreme adaptability would be *protean*, a word which originated in Ancient Greek philosophy, where it was considered a highly desirable quality.

Conceived in different forms, and viewed in different ways, community service can be supported by all three main sentencing philosophies (discussed in **section 23.7**) in ways that other sentences, such as imprisonment and fines, cannot.

O	**Oppression**—s. 76(2)(a) of PACE	Partially defined in s. 76 and is said to occur if (1) there has been a breach of authority or disregard of rules which *causes* the suspect to feel more oppressed than is inevitable from time spent in police detention, *and* (2) the investigators know they are acting improperly.
U	**Unreliability**—s. 76(2)(b) of PACE	Answered if anything said and done by the investigators could have the consequence of making the confession unreliable. The criminal justice system adopts the correct question as not whether the confession is *true*, but whether it was obtained in a way that is likely to make it unreliable.
T	**Trial-in-a-trial**	The Crown Court setting is the clearest example of this process (often called a *voir dire*, literally meaning 'to see to speak' in French). It is a mini-trial but on a matter of law (such as admissibility), so the jury leave the court whilst it takes place. In a *voir dire* for a disputed confession, the burden of proof is on the prosecution to establish that it was not obtained in breach of s. 76 (that is, that it did not involve oppression and is not likely to be unreliable). They can also take place in summary trials, but as magistrates have the functions of both 'judge and jury' the process is not as clear—bizarrely, they can be required to disregard evidence they have only just heard when deciding on its admissibility!
S	**s. 78 of PACE**	This is a general power of the judiciary to exclude any evidence which they think would have an 'adverse effect on the fairness of proceedings' (a key tenet of the due process principle). It is a discretionary power so there is little specific guidance as to when it can be used, but the power has to be used 'reasonably' to comply with the rule of law (the **common law** principle of '*Wednesbury* unreasonableness' and the '**proportionality**' principle which comes from the European Court of Human Rights). The circumstances that could have an 'adverse effect' on the fairness of proceedings can vary infinitely, so s. 78 applications tend to be dealt with on a case-by-case basis—for example, cases where trickery produced a confession will generally be inadmissible.
E	**Examination–in-chief**	A key stage of adversarial court trials in which a witness is questioned about the evidence by their own side and their credibility is assessed. The adversarial skills of a lawyer are important when dealing with confessions because even if they are ruled to be admissible by the trial-in-a-trial, their credibility can still be challenged before the jury.
X	**Cross-examination**	A key stage of adversarial court trials in which a witness is questioned about the evidence by the opposing side and their credibility is assessed. If the confession is presented in a credible way, will this part of the criminal process be the 'greatest legal engine ever invented' (see **Controversy and debate 25.1**) for discovering whether it was true?

Table 25.3 The 'OUTSEX' tests for whether disputed confession evidence can be admitted in court show the due process principle in practice

- **Rehabilitation:** Unpaid work can provide an offender with benefits such as improved job prospects.
- **Reparation:** Unpaid work for the community can be seen as restoring the harm caused by the offence.
- **Retribution:** Unpaid work that is deliberately unpleasant, such as hard physical labour, can act as retribution for the harm caused.

The protean nature of this response to crime is further illustrated by the changing views on what is meant by offenders 'paying back' the harm they have caused. This idea was a central part of the original proposal and whether the reparation was made directly to a victim or more broadly to general society, the restorative opportunities were seen as giving a new dimension to sentencing. The optimistic attitudes about what payback would involve was a key reason why the proposal was so quickly enacted then used so frequently by the courts. It was hoped that offender-only work groups would be the exception and that, wherever possible, individual offenders would work alongside non-offenders, but in practice this did not happen.

A	Amount or length of time the witness had the suspect under observation
D	Distance between the witness and the suspect during the observation
V	Visibility conditions during the observation
O	Obstructions to the observations – whether they temporarily or partially inhibited the observation
K	Whether the suspect is known to the witness in any way
A	Any particular reason the witness has for remembering the suspect or event
T	Time the witness had the suspect under observation and the amount of time elapsed since the event
E	Errors in the description provided by the witness compared with the actual appearance

Figure 25.8 The police's ADVOKATE strategy for testing the reliability of an eyewitness to an offence shows the influence of the due process principle in practice

Source: https://www.app.college.police.uk/app-content/investigations/working-with-suspects/#identification-of-suspects

WHAT DO YOU THINK? 25.2

Sentences that 'pay back' or serve the community?

The prominence of community service has seen it described as 'the shop window of the probation service' (Varah, 1987: 70). The media attention it gains (see the publicity surrounding the experiences of the Manchester United footballer Wayne Rooney, who was given this sentence after being convicted of drink-driving—BBC News, 18 December 2017; 'Wayne Rooney "really enjoying" community service') and the fact that it takes place in public, not behind prison walls, means that it offers an insight into sentencing that other responses cannot (as David Scott notes in **Conversations 25.2**).

This 'shop window' status offers clear possibilities for engaging the public in constructive responses to crime but, as we have seen, the positive impact of the display varies considerably depending on who is in charge of the 'shop'.

Imagine that you are the manager of the 'Community Payback' shop on your local high street (**Figure 25.9**) and consider the following questions:

1. What kinds of 'products' (that is, projects) would you display in your window and why?

Figure 25.9 How would you use the 'shop window' of community service to package and promote the justice system?
Source: Kaique Rocha/Pexels

2. Which people or organisations have the power to influence the success or otherwise of your shop?
3. How would you convince them of the value of your shop?

In 1993, a collection of good practice (that is, examples and case studies of where the practice had proved effective) from both academics and criminal justice professionals was published under the title, 'Paying Back: Twenty Years of Community Service'. It reported numerous projects involving offenders' close relationships with the beneficiaries of their work, which included decorating or gardening for those in need; driving for, or attending to, people in need of care; general assistance in geriatric and psychiatric hospitals; supervising adventure playground activities; and running football teams (Whitfield, 1993). These projects provided reparative opportunities to the offenders, who also gained new skills, developed empathy with vulnerable members of society, or acquired a sense of responsibility; issues that were also noted as beneficial for reducing recidivism (McIvor, 1992). This good practice was so persuasive that it resulted in official policy adopting a method of delivery for the sanction that was known as 'enhanced community punishment' (ECP). It meant that projects had to benefit offenders by developing their skills and helping them develop supportive relationships with their supervisors and beneficiaries.

A powerful example of the value offenders can have whilst working in the community is Donna's Dream House, a Blackpool holiday home for terminally ill children that was established in honour of Donna Curtis, who died from cancer at the age of 20. The home, shown behind its founders in **Figure 25.10**, was built entirely by volunteers working alongside offenders on community service and day release from the nearby HMP Kirkham. In addition to helping the offenders gain practical skills, these community orders had a real purpose and clear beneficiaries.

The dominant form of this criminal justice practice now operates under the name of 'Community Payback'. It has two priorities, both of which aim to ensure public confidence in this method of sentencing.

1. Offenders' work must be visible.
2. Members of the public should be given the opportunity to directly nominate projects for the offenders to take on.

Community Payback extended the practice's visibility in quite literal terms by requiring offenders to wear high-visibility orange vests and encouraging the work to take place in the areas and at times when the greatest number of people will be able to see it (HM Government, 2008). It seeks to gain public confidence by showing them the hard work required from offenders. So, today, offenders are often sent to 'grot spots'; places so untidy that the required work is inevitably unpleasant and physically demanding. It is a practice that has emerged from populist policy which is based on largely assumed public confidence ratings, rather than research findings, and its second element also prioritises public confidence by allowing the public to choose the work that offenders must do. The process can vary slightly

Figure 25.10 'Donna's Dream House', a home for terminally ill children in Blackpool (pictured here behind its founders), was built by volunteers working alongside offenders on community service and day release from a nearby prison
Source: *Donna's Dream House*

in different areas, often it involves online voting where members of the public can choose from a selection of projects or can submit nomination forms. Suggested projects are usually judged on their ability to:

- benefit the local community;
- avoid replacing paid work opportunities;
- be challenging and worthwhile;
- avoid making a profit for anyone;
- show offenders giving back to the community.

This is a prominent example of the 'activation strategy' that was first observed in the early 2000s (Garland, 2001). This refers to the growing willingness from governments to involve the community in duties previously performed solely by the state. It has resulted in policies and practices that 'challenge the central assumption of penal modernism, which took it for granted that crime control was a specialist task' (Garland, 2001: 126). The public are encouraged to make the 'right' choices in their votes, as illustrated by the promotion of grot spot projects through the community service social media channels and the fact that the majority of the shortlisted projects in national voting initiatives involve physically tiring and unpleasant work; such as clearance of dense overgrowth of trees and shrubs, 'deep cleans' of the project area, and removal of graffiti and litter (Carr and Robinson, 2020). If you search Twitter for #CommunityPayback, you will find examples of current projects, as well as information on how to nominate future ones.

In this section we have critically assessed how criminal justice practices can be shaped by the policy agendas held by our political and legal establishments. Change can occur quickly in this part of criminal justice, so recognised practices once supported by principles and policies can morph into very different entities. We examined different practices in both the courtroom and the community, to illustrate the controversies associated with them and the demands on them from the other components of the system. We also saw that criminal justice practices can be a force of their own, acting as another competing influence in the system.

25.4 People in criminal justice

Let's now turn to the final component of the criminal justice system: its people. The combined power of the impersonal-seeming criminal justice principles, policies, and practices (represented in **Figure 25.1**) might give the impression that there is little opportunity for people to have an impact, but this is not always the case.

It is true that often individuals working in the system are propelled forward by the power of its other components and are unable to resist the changes imposed on them. One example is the Transforming Rehabilitation (TR) programme which, as we noted in **section 24.5**, was introduced by the Ministry of Justice despite widespread misgivings about the policy. These fears proved justified as it caused considerable harm to the overall organisation of probation services, as well as to the people working within them. The many problems it caused probation professionals (including significantly increased workloads) were highlighted in the **ethnographic** research prompted by the implementation of the scheme (Millings et al., 2018).

However, we saw in our discussion of community service and the early days of the restorative justice principle being implemented in practice (see **section 25.3**) that individuals can play a major role in bringing about new criminal justice responses. Barbara Wootton from the Advisory Council on the Penal System and the participants in the first pilot schemes for community service played a major role in establishing this practice (Pease et al., 1976).

The current populist approach of Community Payback still relies on the involvement of individuals in that it empowers the public to choose and witness projects, thereby completing the justice process for many offenders.

Criminal justice professionals can also effect change. Their position as the last cog in the 'engine' of criminal justice (**Figure 25.1**) makes their support essential as both individually and collectively, consciously and unconsciously, they can resist pressure to work in the desired new direction. We saw this in DS Fulcher's decision to ignore the requirements of PACE in the case of Sian O'Callaghan (see **Controversy and debate 25.1**). The following quotation from a police detective in research investigating new methods for overseeing policing provides another powerful example of this kind of resistance:

> We have a saying, which I probably shouldn't say ... but it's FIDO, and I don't know if you know what *FIDO* means? Well, '*Fuck It, Drive Off*'. Yeah, and that's exactly what happens.
>
> (Campeau, 2015: 681, emphasis added)

These kinds of decisions to actively avoid or turn a blind eye to situations in which the other components of the system (criminal justice principles, policy, and practices) dictate that professionals must respond in a certain way demonstrate the potential influence of people working in the justice system. They highlight that crime statistics can never provide a full picture as they cannot capture these kinds of situations. This unreliability is, of course, increased if other parts of the system have their own version of 'FIDO'.

Another example of the influence that criminal justice professionals can exert is the probation service's previous (before the TR programme) emphasis on 'reaching not breaching' offenders (Bale, 2000). This meant that a lenient approach could be taken in order to build supportive relationships with offenders and help them complete their orders, rather than taking formal action (a breach) against them for non-compliance. These kinds of decisions could obstruct official policies for stricter enforcement. This lenient ethos has, however, largely been discredited thanks to the punitive shift in criminal justice policy and practices such as those in the Criminal Justice Act 2003, which create a presumption of custody for an offender following a second unacceptable breach. It has been calculated that 16 per cent of the increased prison population between 1995 and 2009 can be attributed to these enforcement changes from probation officers (Fox et al., 2013: 18).

The power of principles, policies, and practices may alter what criminal justice professionals do, sometimes with positive results, but the fast pace of change within the system has similarities with the popular 'Whack-a-mole' game, where as soon as one problem is solved, others instantly appear. For example, the current system may be good at reducing its financial costs and working more quickly, but this could be affecting the quality of information used in its processes. This seems present in current probation work as officers frequently deliver their reports verbally to a court; consequently, decisions are being made without the assistance of detailed, written documents (Robinson, 2017).

Conducting research into the roles played by the people (the professionals) within criminal justice can give us significant insight into the workings of the system as a whole. Ethnographic research can produce particularly useful findings, as we can see from Dr David Scott's description of a research project of this type in **Conversation 25.2**. David's account is a great example of how we can learn through the people of the criminal justice system, but it is also a useful reminder that we are all research novices at first, and by having a go we develop the attributes to be able to use our new skills and knowledge in other situations. It also shows how **mixed methods research** can have different components such as ethnography, surveys, and **structured interviews**. As criminologists we can choose which approach to take. Further guidance for conducting your own research is provided in **Chapter 32**.

CONVERSATIONS 25.2

Learning about the criminal justice system through studying its people
with Dr David Scott

The criminal process is a largely hidden world and the working practices and cultures of magistrates, police officers, prison officers, probation officers, and other occupational groupings are largely closed to those on the outside; the same is true for the lived experiences and culture of prisoners and some groups of lawbreakers. Doing a piece of ethnographic research can give you a real insight into a given role in the criminal process and how people adapt (or fail to adapt) to its specific demands and requirements.

The first piece of ethnographic fieldwork I undertook was on community policing in Lancashire whilst I was an undergraduate student on a BA (Hons) Applied Social Sciences and History degree. I wanted to uncover whether community policing was about consensus policing, or if it was the 'velvet glove' covering the state's 'iron fist'.

Three themes formed the basis of my research questions:

1. Studies of policing had historically found that people who had the most contact with police officers—largely people from socially excluded backgrounds—held the lowest opinions of the police.
2. There were many concerns at the time that 'community police officers' were being used as means of gleaning surveillance.
3. The academic literature indicated that many police officers were hostile to the 'social work' emphasis on community policing and that many were reluctant to undertake such duties.

To investigate these ideas, I undertook surveys with 300 people in three different areas of South Lancashire—Ormskirk, Burscough, and Skelmersdale. I chose these areas because of their different socio-economic contexts.

Alongside the surveys I undertook observations, including joining the police officers on their community beats in the three districts, and held structured interviews with numerous community police officers.

The findings were fascinating:

- In line with previous research, perceptions of the police in the district with the highest social exclusion produced the lowest pro-police scores.
- The community police officers interviewed were open about their real role: the policing practices in Skelmersdale were 'worlds apart' from the rest of the region and this area was the 'thorn in the bum of the county'.
- In the most deprived area community, police officers 'were laughed off the estate' and some members of the community 'would sooner stab a community officer in the back than talk to him [sic]'.
- Suspicions of community surveillance were confirmed: I was told how school liaison trips by community officers were used to find out about the movements of the children's parents.
- Community police officers recognised that they were 'bottom of the pile' and that most police officers 'don't want to walk around' on the beat. The police service in Lancashire moved designated officers off their beats to fill in mobile patrols as and when required.
- It was clear that certain groups of people—those from Liverpool—were considered by the police as a problem. Officers talked about 'the scouse problem'; that 'all scousers are thieves'; and that 'Liverpudlians come here to commit crime'.

Conducting this ethnographic study has had long-lasting value for me. It allowed me to experience what I had previously only read about and to connect the critical literature to actual practice, which considerably deepened my understanding of existing scholarship. I credit this experience with giving me the skills and confidence to pursue the critical analysis of other state institutions and those who work for them.

*Dr David Scott, Senior Lecturer in Criminology,
The Open University*

25.5 Conclusion

In **Chapters 23**, **24**, and **25** we have seen that each component of the criminal justice system can present obstacles to developing more effective ways of achieving justice as they take conflicting positions on how best to address recurring problems. Even when principles and policy occasionally align in jointly advocating changes that make our system more focused on delivering justice that is proportionate, restorative, has a defined end-point, ensures defendants maintain certain rights, and is carefully and fairly judged through transparent processes (open justice) and an independent judiciary with well-separated powers, the system continues to prioritise punitive practices and to favour speed and efficiency—sometimes at the expense of fairness and due process rights.

Let's reflect on some examples. We know that restorative justice is one of the key principles underpinning the UK system, and for over 50 years policymakers have advocated community sentencing as an improvement on some custodial sentences, particularly short ones. However, these ideas are yet to be reflected in practice and in the way that criminal justice professionals work. Prison sentences of less than 12 months are still regularly imposed, despite almost two-thirds of such offenders being reconvicted a year after release and at a rate 6 per cent higher than for community orders (Prison Reform Trust, 2018: 48). We can see this preference for punitive justice in many of the system's modes of practice, such as the controversial use of the **suspended sentence order**. As we know from **section 24.5**, these sentences were introduced in the Criminal Justice Act 2003 and were meant to have been used sparingly, but their use has been described as 'a classic case of penal net-widening' (Ashworth and Roberts, 2017: 859) as more people have been made subject to this new power than was originally intended.

The current prioritisation of speed and efficiency in the justice system has led some researchers to suggest that it delivers 'McJustice' (Robinson, 2019). This term owes its roots to the American sociologist George Ritzer and his thesis 'The McDonaldization of Society' (1993). He created the term 'McDonaldization' to explain how the principles of the fast-food restaurant have been adopted by societies all over the world. These include making efficiency the overriding priority of an organisation, high levels of management control, and practices that reduce levels of employment by asking more from their customers (such as ordering and carrying their own food, plus cleaning their tables after). Think about the way that Community Payback employs an 'activation strategy' to get the public to provide ideas and support for offender work projects.

A particularly clear illustration of the focus on speed and efficiency is the 'Transforming Summary Justice' (TSJ) initiative which launched in England and Wales in 2015. We mentioned this initiative in **New frontiers 25.1** and noted that it reflected the clear policy desire in recent years to bring about change within the criminal justice system. When implemented in practice, this policy—which is still in place at the time of writing—involves all the main agencies involved in Magistrates' Court trials (the CPS, the police, solicitors, HM Courts and Tribunals Service, the judiciary, magistrates, and the National Probation Service) and it has had a rapid and visible effect. TSJ has been accompanied by the 'Better Case Management' (BCM) initiative (also launched in 2015), which seeks to focus on improving the way cases are processed through the system. It builds on the changes to the adversarial justice principle that were explained by Jaime Hamilton QC in **Conversations 23.1** which had already begun to erode or reshape the concept that a criminal trial is a contest between two completely opposing sides. The process of reshaping or eroding has been advanced by BCM, which states that a key responsibility of defence lawyers is to have 'early and continuous engagement with the prosecution' (Judiciary of England and Wales, 2020: para. 4.1).

Official research into the impact of TSJ, entitled 'Business as Usual?', found that following the policy had reduced the amount of time taken from first court hearing to completion of a case by an average of nine days, meaning the court system was saved from holding 39,000 hearings that would have otherwise been needed (HM Crown Prosecution Service Inspectorate, 2017: para. 3.28). At one level, this has been a very positive change, but it is worth noting that some of the supposed failings in the system which TSJ aims to address are not the result of organisational inefficiencies: for example, we saw in **section 24.3** that the failure of the defendant to attend court can be the main reason why over one-third of first hearings are ineffective (para. 4.17). The focus on reducing time periods and increasing efficiency is unlikely to resolve problems like these, which require attention and input from both criminal justice policy and people. The efficiency drive can also actively cause problems for criminal justice professionals, for example prosecutors. The emphasis on making quicker decisions does not always reflect the complexities involved in finding the right charge on which to proceed against a defendant, and the reliance on services like CPS Direct (see **section 24.3**) adds another layer of communication that can slow the process down.

The overall emphasis on quicker justice is clear in the Criminal Justice and Courts Act 2015, which introduced the Single Justice Procedure. This empowers a single magistrate to deal with **summary offences** that are non-imprisonable (such as driving without insurance, speeding, and television licence evasion) without the need for a court hearing. Instead of going to court, these cases are dealt with 'on the papers', which is legal speak for written communications between the court and defendant. It provides considerable financial savings through avoiding the costs and formalities of court hearings but raises serious questions for the **open justice** principle we considered in **section 23.4**. The offences may be non-imprisonable but they can still have serious implications for defendants, so they may wish to exercise their right to choose a standard court hearing instead.

In our three chapters on the criminal justice system we have seen how the fundamental principles (**Chapter 23**) play out in reality. We have seen how these theoretical values can be changed through the actions of criminal justice policies, practices, and people. The fast pace of change has been a recurring theme, and this is easily illustrated by counting the number of times that you have read the word 'transform' in these chapters! Our analysis has included the pressures these modifications are placing on the system; burdens that are likely to remain unless the current prioritisation of punitive punishment, speed, and efficiency change. Now that you understand the complexities and problems with the criminal justice system in action, you are in a strong position to appreciate the issues and debates we discuss in other chapters, especially **Chapter 30** on alternative methods of punishment.

SUMMARY

After reading this chapter and working your way through its different features you should now be able to:

- Examine key influences on contemporary criminal justice policy, including modernisation and penal populism

We started the chapter with the idea of the 'engine' of criminal justice to illustrate how change in criminal justice involves and affects multiple components. **Figure 25.1** shows the four central cogs (principles, policies, practices, and people) as travelling in the same direction, but the idea that they work in such harmony has been thrown into question through our examination of various aspects of the criminal justice system in action, including the differences in opinion about the value of modernisation and penal populism. We also discussed the ability of policy to reshape established principles, and saw that it has led to the principle of adversarial justice being implemented in a 'lite' version.

- Analyse the effects of policy on criminal justice practices in policing, courtroom, and community settings

We analysed practices in these three settings to illustrate the evolving nature of criminal justice and its impact on individuals in the system. Policing dilemmas where due process rules can hinder investigations show the difficulty in establishing the right kind of practice. The procedures in the courts, such as in cases which rely on confession and identification evidence, show a strict quality control system and the many stages of due process. We saw that the unpaid work condition of the community order is the most common form of community sentencing and that its current practice involves forcibly adapting the restorative justice principle to meet increasingly tough policy requirements.

- Assess the influence of criminal justice professionals in the delivery of criminal justice

We reflected that since criminal justice people (professionals) are the final cog in the engine, they do in fact have more power than you might expect. We assessed this influence by reflecting on the value of research into professionals' experiences and practice (particularly ethnographic research) for understanding the criminal justice system. This can reveal how people involved in criminal justice practices perceive their work and the ways in which they sometimes resist the changes imposed upon them. The demands for the justice system to prioritise efficiency and to have a businesslike approach were shown to compete with its accepted principles, policies, and practices. It requires adaptability from criminal justice professionals, who must meet new expectations in a system of justice that is regularly manipulated and transformed.

- Engage with the idea that there are four core components of the criminal justice system (principles, policies, practices, and people) and that all four are involved in any process of change within it

The chapter concluded with a discussion of the interplay of the four main components in the system and its overall direction of change. Although the relationship between the components is far more complex than that suggested by the engine image (**Figure 25.1**), keeping this in mind when considering the justice system will help you think about it critically by making you aware of the extensive force required to bring about change. In any system of interconnected factors, things cannot move forward when one 'cog' works against another. This means that despite the considerable support for addressing recurring criminal justice problems (such as short-term prison sentences and inappropriate use of community sentencing), it is incredibly difficult to generate enough momentum to overcome the forces exerted by the other components in the process. The lack of importance given to research evidence is a reminder that the system can be led by many things other than knowledge; to get the engine of criminal justice operating smoothly, we have to recognise political pressures and legal implications.

 Test your understanding of the chapter's key points by attempting the self-test questions on the **online resources** at www.oup.com/he/case2e

REVIEW QUESTIONS

1. How has penal populism changed the role of the public in making criminal justice policy?
2. How have recent policies affected the principle of adversarial justice?
3. What does due process require for admitting disputed confession evidence in a criminal trial?
4. Why can the sanction of unpaid work (formerly known as community service) be said to have 'protean' qualities? Do you know of any other punishments with this characteristic?
5. What are the two key elements of Community Payback?
6. Why might the label 'McJustice' be appropriate for today's criminal justice system?

 Access the **online resources** at www.oup.com/he/case2e to check your answers to the review questions.

FURTHER READING

Visit this book's online resources to access additional chapters on the criminal justice systems in Scotland, Wales, and Northern Ireland, respectively.

Anon. (2018) *The Secret Barrister: Stories of the Law and How It's Broken*. **London: Macmillan.**
This anonymous book is from an experienced barrister and provides a scathing assessment of criminal cases' current progression through the system and the effects of its prioritisation of efficiency and speed. Anonymity could affect its credibility, but this is countered by acclaim from members of the legal profession and its significant social media presence: see @BarristerSecret on Twitter.

Campbell, L., Ashworth, A., and Redmayne, M. (2019) *The Criminal Process* **(5th edn). Oxford: Oxford University Press.**
This is a detailed explanation of key issues in the criminal justice process. It covers the procedures followed in the various stages of criminal justice; such as police investigations, prosecutions, trials, and appeals. It is valuable for students of criminal justice as it uses the law, research, principle, and policy in its analysis.

Canton, R. and Dominey, J. (2017) *Probation*. **London: Routledge.**
This is a critical exploration of the policy and theoretical influences that inform probation practice. The role of probation in the provision of sentencing is comprehensively addressed with international examples also provided. It contains specific chapters on specialised aspects of this part of the justice system.

Pratt, J. (2007) *Penal Populism.* **Abingdon: Routledge.**
Although this book is over a decade old, it provides an accessible and useful account of how governments around the world have allowed penal populism to influence criminal justice policy. It offers much help for understanding the phenomenon's roots and contains many national and international examples; particularly useful are the chapters on the countries which have not experienced it.

Access the **online resources** to view a wealth of extra information relating to your study of criminology, including self-test questions, answers to review questions, and links to other resources that will help you enjoy and fulfil your potential within your studies.

www.oup.com/he/case2e

CHAPTER OUTLINE

26.1	Introduction	770
26.2	What is crime prevention?	770
26.3	Perspectives on crime prevention	776
26.4	Frameworks for policy and practice	779
26.5	Implementing crime prevention measures	790
26.6	What does prevention achieve?	792
26.7	Consequences of crime prevention	794
26.8	Reviewing the limitations of crime prevention	797
26.9	Conclusion	799

26

Crime prevention

KEY ISSUES

After studying this chapter, you should be able to:

- discuss the arguments in favour of a preventive approach to criminal justice;
- appreciate the implications of crime prevention for different stakeholders, including potential victims, potential offenders, communities, politicians, interest groups, and others;
- recognise the implications and effects of different approaches to preventing crime;
- consider and assess the evidence base in support of preventive measures;
- evaluate the theoretical dimensions of perspectives on prevention;
- examine the critical arguments questioning the aims and effectiveness of crime prevention strategies, including a consideration of escalation, adaptation, and displacement.

26.1 Introduction

Although this chapter sits inside the responding to crime part of the book, crime prevention occupies a very different position to other perspectives, which focus principally on the consequences of offending. A preventive approach is proactive, rather than reactive, and is based on the assumption that crime is to a great extent predictable, and can therefore be avoided by taking precautionary steps in advance. Preventive strategies thus represent an approach that is less concerned with dispensing justice, but rather with minimising the risk of crime being committed in the first place. Preventing a crime being committed in the first instance could save emotional or physical distress for victims, sanctions for offenders, and time and resources for the criminal justice system.

Crime prevention strategies are based on a combination of assumptions about human motivations and research evidence about observed patterns of offending behaviour. However, it is unlikely that we'd ever have enough resources to prevent all crimes, so decisions (whether implicit or explicit) have to made about which types of crime, and indeed, which victims, to prioritise. Critics suggest that these choices may lead to subsequent problems. Because of this, the almost self-evident desirability of crime prevention may come to be seen as less straightforward than at first sight, and more complex and uncertain in both its aims and effects. We therefore need to take the criticisms seriously, as we conclude in this chapter.

In the first section of this chapter we will explore definitions of crime prevention and what it is intended to achieve. We will look at the political and strategic factors that may influence decisions about which crimes to try to prevent. We will consider the complexity of decision-making in this area, including by putting yourself in the position of a local politician making tough choices.

We will then introduce some of the key conceptual frameworks underpinning approaches to crime prevention, and we will also consider these further in relation to three key elements: potential victims, potential offenders, and 'risky' places. We will also consider perspectives on crime prevention focusing on potential offenders (in terms of **deterrence** and diversionary approaches), potential victims, and the idea of community safety and well-being.

We will incorporate some of the most influential models of practice in crime prevention, including the example of the influential Kirkholt project.

In the final sections of the chapter we will consider some of the continuing and unresolved questions about the purported achievements and effectiveness of crime prevention strategies, and will conclude with a discussion of their possible limitations and wider impacts.

26.2 What is crime prevention?

One of the key elements of the UK Crime and Disorder Act 1998 (s. 37(1)) is the requirement that:

> It shall be the principal aim of the youth justice system to prevent offending by children and young persons.

Although this requirement related specifically to youth crime, it captured the sense of how important prevention had become as a feature of the criminal justice agenda in the late 1990s. There had been a growing conviction that, with the right technology effectively used, with relevant expertise, and with sufficient resources, crime could largely be anticipated and so prevented. For Tilley (2002: 15), this was essentially the height of a movement to place crime prevention 'centre stage', as it became increasingly clear that other strategies to tackle persistently high levels of crime were failing to address public concerns: '**Punishment** did not appear to deter; confidence in treatment had disappeared. In relation to criminology, "Nothing works"... had become the dominant orthodoxy'.

Although both deterrent sentences and **rehabilitative** treatments aim to 'prevent' future offending, they also have certain fairly clear shortcomings (as we will discuss in later chapters in this part). Neither is actually very effective at stopping offenders from committing further crimes according to known rates of reoffending. Nor do they come into effect until at least one offence has already been committed. Instead, the argument goes, it is better for everyone to invest in finding out what causes crime in the first place, and what measures can be undertaken to reduce the possibilities that offences will be committed. As Hope (2019) argues, from around the 1980s there was an increasing recognition that efforts to prevent crime could be better targeted to the specific circumstances and motivations behind certain crimes. Crime prevention should seek to develop better mechanisms for anticipating and averting future offences, rather than simply reacting to what has already happened.

As Tilley (2002) has pointed out, other developments in the late 20th century also fuelled a belief in the potential value of crime prevention as the core strategy for tackling crime. These included the increasing availability of knowledge and expertise to help understand the drivers of crime, as well as a growing recognition of the threat to social cohesion associated with 'fear of crime' (Lee, 2007). There was also desire on the part of the UK government to cut the costs of a very expensive justice system.

In addition to these influences on beliefs and policy in the public sphere, crime prevention—to many—simply makes sense as an idea. For virtually everyone, the thought of being able to live safely without coming to harm or losing property through criminal actions is a powerful aspiration. As a consequence, we might be inclined to agree on the desirability of measures which offer more certainty of achieving this goal. And even if crime itself cannot be eradicated, a reduction of popular fears about its incidence and impact may appear to be an almost equally desirable objective for many.

Crime prevention strategies

Crime prevention strategies are organised around the belief that crime and its causes can be understood and that, in turn, appropriate measures can be taken to eradicate it (or certainly substantially reduce its frequency) based on this knowledge. Of course, behind this belief are the further assumptions that we can identify those at risk, either of committing or of being a victim of crime; that the causes of crime are capable of being quantified; and that we can then identify effective measures to be put in place based on this knowledge. If it is possible to anticipate crime with any degree of certainty, then it seems to make sense to use what means we can to ensure that it is prevented.

In practical terms, we can liken this to the actions we might take to avoid children running into a busy road. In this instance, we would probably expect to combine education about the potential dangers, risk reduction by keeping young children away from the road, risk management in the sense of controlling their movements (and those of road users—by recruiting a lollipop person, perhaps), and direct action by restraining children at the point of crossing the road (see **Figure 26.1**). Even in this context, there are a number of factors to consider and a number of different strategies that could be used, singly or in combination. But, of course, most situations in which crime might occur are not as easy to identify or 'read' as this example. Likewise, our knowledge of what constitutes a practical or effective preventive measure may also be limited.

Figure 26.1 Crime prevention strategies assume that it is possible to understand crime and its causes, and that this knowledge can be used to eradicate or reduce crime

Despite this, the idea of being able to prevent crime 'at source' is highly attractive, and so considerable emphasis has been placed on this as a desirable objective, and similarly a great deal of time and money has been invested in trying to discover what is effective in reducing the likelihood of crimes being committed. Tilley (2002: 14), for example, has identified 37 separate 'key developments' in crime prevention policy and practice in the UK from 1976 to 2001. Some prominent developments were the initiation of the British Crime Survey in 1983, the Safer Cities programme in 1988, the Morgan Report on 'Safer Communities' in 1991, and the Crime and Disorder Act 1998 with the prevention of crime explicitly becoming the cornerstone of criminal justice policy.

Crime prevention, then, appears to be inherently desirable. But we need to unpack the **concept** itself, since it is certainly not as simple as it might appear. First, there is the question of just what it is that we might wish to prevent. 'Crime' might be the obvious answer, but even this inevitably leads to further questions. Which crimes should be targeted? All of them? Or should we prioritise certain crimes and, if so, how? Crimes of violence? Racist crimes? Only the most serious crimes, however they are defined? Should we direct our energies towards stopping offenders committing crimes? Should we enable potential victims to better protect themselves against known risks of harm? Should we focus instead on reducing fear of crime which may not be proportional to these risks? Should we rely on official definitions of crime or the perceptions and experiences of crime held by communities?

As we know, the extent of crime goes well beyond what is officially recorded, and also merges with other types of problematic behaviour, such as bullying in schools and the workplace, antisocial behaviour, harassment, and even violence in sport. A global prevention strategy would therefore need to be very extensive, and would be very expensive, and it would probably still be unable to cover all the areas which a broad definition of crime would encompass:

> Crime in general is complex, with many features, causes, motivations and conditions ... it will not be possible for any agency on its own successfully to address all aspects of all crime prevention problems.
>
> (Tilley, 2002: 17)

Importantly, this observation suggests that crime prevention is not just a matter for criminal justice agencies, but needs to incorporate a much wider range of organisations and interests if it is to be properly targeted and have any chance of being implemented successfully. Stopping crime is a matter for everyone, it seems.

When making choices about how to approach prevention, though, we are still faced with a number of dilemmas when it comes to determining its practical 'face', and deciding which crimes should be prevented. One option would be to base our decisions on certain thresholds or qualifying criteria, so that only certain types of crime or harms are to be prioritised. First, of course, we would need to establish a basis for making this kind of judgement. Should we concentrate on individual crimes of violence, for example those acts having the most significant effect on the people affected? Or should we base our decisions on the principle of minimising wider disruptions to community life, which may be less harmful in individual cases, but cause more misery overall, such as acts of damage to communal property? Or maybe we should concentrate our efforts on minimising the harm and losses caused to business and commercial interests in order to avoid the risk of damaging the local economy, with the consequences that might involve? The underlying question here is which potential victims' interests should be given preference? It quickly becomes apparent that the outcome of this kind of moral and ethical choice will have a significant impact in terms of the form and content of preventive strategies and practices. Try the exercise in **What do you think? 26.1**

WHAT DO YOU THINK? 26.1

Making difficult choices with limited resources

If you were a local politician and member of a community safety partnership, you might find yourself having to decide which crimes to concentrate on, when allocating limited financial resources.

Imagine, for example, that you had to make a choice between committing police officers and other resources in response to one of the following scenarios:

- Antisocial behaviour in your town or city centre on a Saturday night which has resulted in damage to buildings and other public property, with individuals involved in a brawl.
- A sexual attack on an individual in a park that has taken place in a usually quiet and safe neighbourhood.

Which of these situations would you prioritise? What are the implications of this? How do you think other interested parties might respond to your decision?

The focus of crime prevention

The idea of 'crime prevention' has already become more problematic than it might have appeared at first; and this is further complicated when we think more deeply about how we might put the concept into practice. From the start, there are differences of opinion as to whether crime prevention activities should concentrate their attention on victims, offenders, or the combinations of circumstances which create the conditions for crime to occur. We will now look at each of the three areas in **Figure 26.2** in more detail.

Vulnerable groups

The growing emphasis on the needs and rights of victims of crime (and potential victims) might lead to the conclusion that we should prioritise high-risk groups and introduce measures to protect them in the first instance. Even within this category, we need to consider whether we should prioritise those most 'at risk' of being victimised (typically, young men, for example), or those who are most worried and perhaps more at risk of serious harms (for example, older people and women).

Fear of crime amongst older people is one well-recognised area of concern. Concerns have been quite widely expressed about some sectors of the population limiting themselves because of the possibility of being affected by crime. Older people, for instance, may decide not to go out at night, and this may have an effect in terms of reducing the risk of **victimisation** somewhat, but at the expense of restricting their freedoms and diminishing the quality of life they are able to enjoy (Chakraborti et al., 2011: 34).

As the study on which this evidence is based points out, though, responding to the needs and wishes of victims (or potential victims) is not straightforward. Some people may not recognise or accept that they are at risk, for example:

> When you're talking about someone who is elderly or with a disability, trying to get them to understand that they are being targeted and it is a **hate crime** is difficult. It's getting people to understand that they shouldn't suffer.
>
> (Local authority representative quoted in Chakraborti et al., 2011: 34)

However, there is also the risk that concentrating efforts on those most fearful of crime may exacerbate their fears rather than reducing them.

Potential offenders

Alternatively, it might make sense to target those believed to be most likely to commit crime—although, as with 'victim' groups, there are clearly a considerable

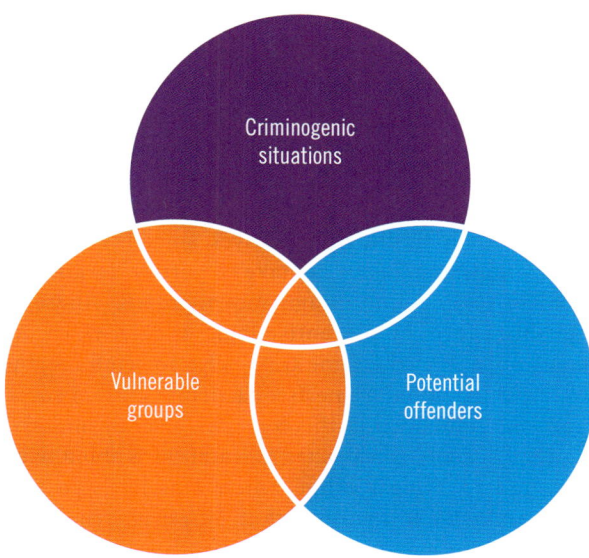

Figure 26.2 There are three main areas where crime prevention strategies could be focused in order to achieve the most effective results

to better understand the sort of decision that a local politician might be faced with.

Linked to these considerations is a further series of questions to do with the targets of prevention; that is to say, where preventive work should be concentrated to achieve the most effective results. There are at least three potential focal points where such efforts might be concentrated (see **Figure 26.2**):

1. criminogenic environments ('risky' situations);
2. potential offenders ('risky people'); and,
3. vulnerable groups or communities ('at risk' people).

We will revisit these three classifications in the course of this chapter. Examples falling within each category come to mind quite readily, such as:

- late-night drinking zones in city centres;
- drug users with expensive addictions;
- children from care at risk of sexual exploitation.

Whilst there may also be significant interplay between contexts and populations at risk from crime, these are just examples of a very wide range of possibilities when it comes to the potential for crime to occur. This breadth of possibilities, in turn, helps to highlight considerable variations in the way we might understand the issue of crime prevention, depending on the stance taken towards the problem. **Figure 26.2** illustrates three main areas where crime prevention strategies could be focused, yet as you can see these are not distinct from one another, they also overlap. Can you list some additional examples for each of these areas not provided in the list earlier?

number of sub-categories of this population as well. As such, 'within group' targeting and prioritisation is likely to be required. So, for example, whilst young people in general may be seen as liable to get involved in crime and antisocial behaviour, it might be best to focus on preventing the onset of criminal and antisocial behaviour amongst children who have never previously acted in that way. On the other hand, we might focus our attention on young people who have already been involved in minor antisocial behaviours and aim to prevent them from graduating to more serious antisocial and criminal activities (Prior and Paris, 2005).

The problem here is how to decide on such categorisations and whether or not this might build discriminatory assumptions and practices into the crime prevention agenda.

Criminogenic situations

Finally, preventive measures could seek to prioritise those situations and circumstances where crime is believed to be more likely, apparently irrespective of the identity of either perpetrators or victims. This approach is normally based on the application of prior knowledge of patterns of crime and the use of a variety of predictive tools to identify 'real world' risks associated with known features of the lived environment. The aim is to reduce the potential for crime to take place in contexts which are known to be criminogenic. So, a strategic perspective which shifts the focus from crime-prone populations or groups to a concern with the predisposing contexts and circumstances of crime—that is, situational crime prevention (see also **Chapter 28**):

> departs radically from most criminology in its orientation.... Proceeding from an analysis of the circumstances giving rise to specific kinds of crime, it introduces discrete managerial and environmental change to reduce the opportunities for those crimes to occur.
>
> (Clarke, 1997: 2)

Challenges in crime prevention

In each case, though—looking at potential crime victim, potential offender, and potential offence location—there are common challenges en route to achieving the goal of effective crime prevention. These are linked to developing the tools and techniques necessary to do the job. 'Risk' has to be specified and quantified; 'what works' has to be developed, evaluated, and implemented systematically; and desired outcomes must be clearly identified and achieved. Considered in this way, crime prevention can be seen as a technical task, concerned with problem identification and resolution. The only challenges to effective interventions are those of limited knowledge, imperfect information-gathering, insufficient resources, and inefficient programme delivery—substantial issues, but all capable of being resolved with the right combination of will and skill.

On the other hand, it might be argued that these are potentially limiting alternatives, since their shared assumptions incline us to take a particular kind of problem-solving and pragmatic approach. There is arguably a form of 'preventive logic' at play which depends on, and at the same time helps to reinforce, the way we think about crime as a particular kind of social problem. Embedded in this logic are a set of underlying (and socially constructed) assumptions about what constitutes a 'typical' crime, where it is likely to take place, and who will perpetrate it. However, 'crime' and its effects are not necessarily quantifiable in this way, nor are instances of harm, conflict, exploitation, and loss and their effects reducible to an exchange between stereotypical offenders and victims. It may be extremely difficult to disentangle and assign criminal intent and blame; and, as a result, it may be restrictive to rely on conventional assumptions about 'normal' crimes and their causes when approaching the question of crime prevention. This is underlined for us when we broaden the idea of prevention to incorporate wider questions of how to tackle social harms and their origins. Much recent work has been undertaken, for example, to place the issue of 'hate crime' on the agenda, and to shift the preventive 'gaze' accordingly.

> The reality faced by many people across Britain is one of being targeted on a daily basis because of who they are.
>
> (Chakraborti et al., 2011: v)

Tilley (2002: 19) suggests that initial views of crime prevention by policymakers were quite narrow and technical:

> [T]here was no political dimension to the conception of crime prevention.... Several matters which could, in other circumstances, have played a large part in crime prevention were not considered. For example, questions of large-scale social structural change affecting the class, 'race' and gender distributions of power, the decriminalization of some behaviour, and much crime committed by the powerful, did not find a place on the crime prevention agenda, in part because this is set by the political and bureaucratic context.

So, in reflecting on just what 'crime prevention' is, we must also pay attention to how it comes to be constituted in specific social and political contexts, and how this might lead to a rather partial view of both its objects and the manner in which it is delivered (see **What do you think? 26.2** for an exercise in prioritising different factors to help in such decision-making).

WHAT DO YOU THINK? 26.2

What factors should be prioritised in crime prevention?

If you had to make a decision about what type of crime to prevent, what would it be, and why?

Would your choice be influenced by any of the following factors:

- the severity of the effect of the crime;
- the vulnerability of those affected;
- the extent to which victims may or may not contribute to their own problems;
- your thoughts about your own or family members' safety and security;
- the common good;
- the economic and social well-being of the community;
- the need to challenge oppression and promote human rights;
- the threat of exploitation or environmental damage represented by corporate interests?

Is there any other consideration you would take into account? There are eight factors listed above; try ranking these in order of importance by assigning each a number from 1 to 8 (where 1 = most important). Was this an easy task?

The emergence and development of crime prevention

Crawford (1998: 30) locates the origins of crime prevention in the establishment of the modern police force under the Metropolitan Police Act 1829. At this time, prevention was identified as a primary objective of policing. Subsequently, though, policing priorities shifted towards responding to crime and the preventive function of the police was given less emphasis (Crawford, 1998: 32). For others, the origins of modern crime prevention practices date back to the period following the Second World War and the emergence of a more active role for the state in creating the conditions for communal well-being (Hughes and Edwards, 2011: 16). As the state gained a more prominent role in social life there was also a growing sense of confidence in the capacity of science and rational planning to understand the conditions giving rise to crime; and so also to devise effective forms of intervention to tackle these: 'There was a widespread belief that the political will and scientific means now existed to remould and improve virtually all aspects of society' (Hughes and Edwards, 2011: 17).

However, the subsequent development of crime prevention has been rather uneven, with a concentrated focus on systematic and scientific approaches to the subject only emerging relatively recently, in the 1960s and 1970s, according to Welsh and Pfeffer (2013), as conventional methods for controlling crime became discredited.

Gilling (1997: 76) suggests that it was the growing recognition of opportunist crime as a persistent problem, and the work of the Cornish Committee on crime prevention and detection (Home Office, 1965), that eventually changed the emphasis of criminal justice policy in favour of preventive strategies. This, in turn, led to the establishment of an infrastructure for implementing this approach, and with the support of the Home Office, 58 crime prevention panels had been established by 1969, rising progressively to over 400 by the 1990s (Gilling, 1997: 78).

Much of the responsibility for achieving these changes was given to the 'new professions of the welfare state', such as those working in children's departments, for instance. It was believed that these workers, with a clear understanding of family dynamics and therapeutic need, would be able to prevent outbreaks of juvenile delinquency originating in 'problem families'. As West (1967: 240) put it, 'the children's departments of each local authority watch over the whole', providing necessary additional support 'for children whose parents are prevented' from giving adequate care. There was a mood of optimism, buoyed by the idea that 'problem families' could be readily identified, and their difficulties resolved through judicious use of expert guidance and firm behaviour management.

In this spirit, the Children and Young Persons Act 1963 incorporated requirements for local agencies 'to seek out and advise parents of children who appear to be at risk of becoming delinquent' (West, 1967: 241). However, West (1967: 254) also noted the absence of any evidence to justify such interventions. At the same time, the US experience of similar programmes was not encouraging, with significant examples of failure becoming apparent, notably the Cambridge–Somerville project (McCord, 1992; we will discuss this in **Chapter 29**) and other substantial prevention schemes in Washington and New York.

These reported failures subsequently contributed to a growing mood of despondency (amongst the probation service and other welfare professionals) and the sense that 'nothing works' in the field of social interventions to discourage crime. However, this did not lead to the conclusion that crime prevention was an unrealistic objective. Rather, there was a 'shift' of focus (Crawford, 2007: 867), incorporating a wider range of agencies and a broader understanding of the risk of crime as a generalised threat, rather than depending purely on the delinquent tendencies of identifiable individuals. The Morgan Report (1991) commissioned by the Home Office, was seen as particularly influential in de-emphasising the role of statutory agencies and formalised interventions, and instead establishing the principle that crime prevention was the responsibility of the whole community.

By 2000, the emphasis in crime prevention work had been transformed, according to Garland (2001: 16):

> Over the past two decades [the 1980s and 1990s], while national crime debates in Britain and America have focused upon punishment, prisons and criminal justice, a whole new infrastructure has been assembled at the local level that addresses crime and disorder in a quite different manner ... this network is designed to foster crime prevention and to enhance community safety, primarily through the cultivation of community involvement and the dissemination of crime prevention ideas and practices.

Underpinning these developments, there had emerged new theoretical constructs of prevention, too. The loss of faith in the idea of welfare-led interventions and rehabilitation (see **Chapter 31**) was associated with a growing interest in alternative conceptual frameworks associated with risk identification and risk management. Originating with the Safer Cities programme of the late 1980s (Tilley, 2002) an array of community-based partnerships and programmes were established to reduce crime; although evidence of their effectiveness appears somewhat limited (Berry et al., 2011).

Some more recent initiatives have focused on specific types of crime, such as 'deradicalisation' (Thomas, 2017), and knife crime prevention (Squires, 2009); whilst the 2011 'riots' in England prompted the government to launch the extensive 'Troubled Families' programme, with crime prevention being one of its key objectives (Crossley, 2015). Although there has been a significant reduction in conventional crimes over recent years, this is an international phenomenon and does not take account of any possible shift in the patterns of offending, perhaps towards a greater prevalence of online crime, for instance. We are urged to be cautious in attributing a falling crime rate specifically to crime prevention initiatives. The Troubled Families programme was found to have no visible effect on offending in its initial implementation phase, for example (Crawford and Evans, 2017).

26.3 Perspectives on crime prevention

Implementing crime prevention is inevitably more complex and nuanced than it might appear at first glance. Not all crimes are the same, victims' interests vary, some crimes are 'victimless', and prevention involves making choices about policy and resource priorities. Inevitably, then, when we start to think beyond the definition of prevention, and move on to its aims and implementation; we find that these also vary considerably, and the implications of different approaches are quite diverse. Preventive measures may be directed at any of a lengthy list of alternative goals. Some of these can be seen to overlap, whilst others involve potentially conflicting choices, such as when criminal activities are 'displaced' from one target to another. The objectives of prevention may include:

- diverting potential offenders from crime;
- avoiding 'bad lives';
- safeguarding potential victims;
- providing reassurance to the general public;
- promoting community safety;
- protecting commercial interests;
- building social capital; and
- defending the moral order.

Crime prevention might be thought of in broad and symbolic terms, as a means of maintaining the moral order and promoting the common good by reaffirming general principles of 'right and wrong'. This requires that we make significant choices about priority areas for action, related to those crimes which are believed to represent the most substantial and persistent threat to our combined sense of integrity and shared morality as a society. We might think of 'extreme' crimes such as child abuse or disability hate crime in such terms, for instance.

As we have seen, the question of 'what is crime prevention for?' is a deceptively simple one. In fact, it generates many further questions about the underlying assumptions and moral judgements we make about what crime is, and which crimes are the most serious, and who we should be protecting from their effects. Prevention strategies and interventions, however, have to be based on just such value judgements, as well as more pragmatic considerations of effectiveness and what constitutes a successful intervention.

Crime prevention, like many other areas of public interest and policymaking, is subject to negotiation and debate depending on the interests of different stakeholders. It is therefore important to try to understand these and how they inform the different sets of assumptions about crime prevention. Hughes (1998: 18) has pointed out that: 'crime prevention strategies may be geared towards addressing quite distinct dimensions to the phenomenon of crime'. Depending on the viewpoint brought to bear on the subject, prevention initiatives may be directed towards modifying 'the context of the crime act, the criminal motive, problems in the environment or the unprotected "at risk" victim'. In Hughes's view, 'all correctional **ideologies**', that is to say, every competing view about the best way to respond to criminal acts by changing behaviour, can also claim to be consistent with the goal of preventing crime, even though these will be associated with widely differing approaches in practice. Our aim in this section is to introduce the agendas lying behind crime prevention initiatives and consider how these may represent differing and potentially conflicting interests.

Making choices and setting priorities

Tilley (2011: 3) reflects on the contradictory nature of prevention, which he describes as 'both disarmingly simple and bewilderingly complex'. On the one hand, as we have already observed, it is straightforwardly attractive to think in terms of developing effective mechanisms for anticipating crime and thereby stopping it; whilst, on the other hand, this glosses over problems of defining crime, prioritising interventions, the ethical challenges of different preventive activities, political contexts, the costs and choices involved, and the trade-off between intended outcomes and what are often described as unintended consequences (Tilley, 2011: 5).

For some, the challenge is more or less technical; depending on developing the best technical knowledge and skills in order to be able to find the most effective means of pre-empting actions which are clearly defined as criminal. However, this is not readily accepted by others who see both defining and preventing crime as reflecting processes of social and moral judgement: 'Crime is socially defined, socially committed and elicits social responses' (Tilley, 2011: 5).

Furthermore, the ability to define something as a crime and therefore as worthy of attention and preventive action is not fairly distributed; it depends on the relationship between different, and sometimes competing, interests within society. Many forms of suspect and possibly unlawful activity rarely or never seem to fall under the scope of crime prevention activity, such as breaches of professional codes of practice, corporate or environmental crime, tax offences, or, indeed, most crimes without an obvious victim. Tilley seems to suggest that the very idea of crime prevention conjures up a particular image for most of us of the type of activity which should be the focus of our anxieties, as well as the type of people we should be worried about as potential offenders (young males or certain ethnic and religious groups, for example). And even the term itself may be seen as potentially problematic, with the distinction being made between *crime prevention* which is seen as police terminology, and *community safety* which 'is preferred in local authorities … to signify a broader set of interests in crime consequences' (Tilley, 2011: 7).

The local politics of crime prevention: a case study

The different origins and implications of varying underlying assumptions certainly raise significant questions about the ways in which preventive initiatives are organised and how they impact not just on 'crime' but on wider communities, as well as those directly involved in the justice system. Coleman and his colleagues (2002), for example, have drawn on the experience of crime prevention in Merseyside, North West England, to analyse the complex politics of that area. In their view, whilst crime prevention has assumed the position of a 'taken for granted' (Coleman et al., 2002: 86) element of community intervention by local agencies, there are particular assumptions and dynamics underlying this development, which must, in turn, be subject to critical evaluation.

Noting the coincidence between the origins of community safety initiatives in Merseyside with its economic regeneration programme from the late 1990s, they suggest that this implied a merging of a particular group of interests. As a result, this helped to shape the local agenda. The authors also observe that the key data used to establish priorities for intervention were those which proved to be most easily countable; namely, police crime statistics and their geographical distribution. Generated in this way, the evidence lent itself to 'situational', rather than 'social', prevention measures, which were geared towards protecting business interests and commercial activities, supposedly in the interests of promoting a vibrant local economy. And so, a partial definition of the problem lends itself to an apparently obvious solution (Coleman et al., 2002: 91):

CCTV was to be the centrepiece of this strategy. SMP [Safer Merseyside Partnership] supported this development politically and also funded schemes to enhance training and codes of practice for CCTV operatives in the city centre.

The eventual aim was to set up an integrated system of 'up to 240 cameras' in the city and in some 'hot spot' residential areas. Coleman and colleagues, however, expressed scepticism about the underlying priorities of the scheme. Although, as they put it, it was 'trumpeted on the back of promoting the safety of women and children' (2002: 92), its core rationale was to demonstrate that Merseyside was a 'safe place to do business' and therefore to encourage investment.

These developments provide an example of how resources are prioritised with, in this case, funding assigned to one form of technological intervention at the expense of other projects less reliant on hardware, and grounded instead on principles of fostering good community relations. The authors note that the finalisation of plans to place CCTV cameras in the Dingle area of Liverpool coincided with the loss of public funding to 'the only local youth centre' in the area (2002: 94). Developing the contextual argument further, the authors also pointed out that Dingle itself at the time was located within sight of an array of chemical plants which had been responsible for a range of environmental breaches; whilst at the time Liverpool also 'had the highest levels of traffic pollution for any city outside of London' (2002: 95). The conclusion drawn by the authors is that a particular definition of 'crime prevention' came to dominate in Merseyside in this period, with the 'priorities of crime prevention partnerships [sweeping] aside the priorities identified by local communities' (2002: 102); suggesting at the same time

that this reordering of priorities also helped to shift attention towards a convenient (and conventional) definition of the crime problem.

On the other hand, as Coleman and colleagues acknowledge, there are powerful reasons for taking crime as it is commonly understood and experienced seriously: 'we are not denying the impact of conventional crimes such as burglary on the socially and economically powerless'; and they also acknowledge government attempts 'to introduce crimes such as racist violence, domestic violence and rape onto the political and social policy agenda' (Coleman et al., 2002: 104). So, it seems, crime prevention cannot simply be explained as a process of misdirection and mystification of the relationships between powerful interests and exploited communities. It also represents a core of legitimate and genuinely felt concern about risk, vulnerability, and harm to particular sectors of the population.

Now consider the issues raised in **Controversy and debate 26.1**.

Community interests and crime prevention

From a 'community safety' perspective, the proper focus of 'crime prevention thinking' might be viewed as the development of practical strategies for assessing vulnerability and introducing concrete measures to prevent harm for those most at risk. Crime is not necessarily taken as a given, or as a homogeneous category, but as an indicator of a wide range of potential 'harms' which themselves must be subject to detailed understanding

CONTROVERSY AND DEBATE 26.1

An article published in 2020 suggests that the focus for community crime prevention has shifted, with local plans and intervention strategies focusing more on the protection of vulnerable members of the community, and less on commonly used measures of criminality, such as burglary and theft figures:

> Whatever the reasons behind it, moving from an emphasis on volume crime and [antisocial behaviour] to high harm and vulnerability entails a radical change in the work being carried out under the umbrella of community safety. This is now less quantifiable and more genuinely preventative in nature, less focused on incivility and behaviours, and more on harm reduction.
>
> (Menichelli, 2020: 51)

These developments can be viewed either as the result of the withdrawal of funds and associated loss of influence on the part of central government, or as the reassertion of local autonomy and the voice of the community. However, the associated risk is that lack of resources will mean that good intentions in terms of public protection become increasingly difficult to realise. At the same time, public concerns about disruptive behaviour in the community may become more acute if it appears this is being given less priority than previously.

and prioritisation, based on the consensual view of the community as a whole.

Edwards (2002), writing in the same volume as Coleman, has suggested that there is scope within community partnerships for a distinctive approach to defining social harm which is not restricted in its focus and helps to create a broader and more grounded approach to dealing with the threat of crime. Moves towards greater local control mean that the capacity for differential approaches becomes greater, with increased potential, too, for specific local and communal interests to influence strategic decision-making. In Edwards's view, it is important to understand actual practices in community crime prevention and their consequences in order to generate a clearer insight into what is possible and achievable, rather than imposing prior assumptions.

Based on detailed investigation of local crime prevention and community safety partnerships, Edwards (2002: 146) set out several key challenges which may be expected to arise, but which are capable of being resolved in very different ways. *Competition* over priorities and resource allocation is to be expected, for example, and can exacerbate 'tensions between different communities'; but it can also stimulate new thinking and creativity in problem-solving. *Innovation*, though, also depends on being open to the ideas and aspirations of a range 'of interest groups' (2002: 147), rather than reflecting narrow and entrenched interests. New thinking, in turn, needs to be guaranteed by a degree of '*flexibility*' to adapt within partnerships, rather than becoming restricted by 'nationally set performance criteria' (2002: 149). This, though, raises yet further dilemmas of the nature of *accountability*, and its limits, where local communities may set aims and objectives which are themselves punitive and exclusionary towards certain, often already marginalised, groups (2002: 150).

Edwards provides an example of conflicts of interest in the form of misalignments between agency and community expectations of crime prevention strategies in Leicester in the East Midlands, UK. Whilst 'a coalition of local residents' wanted to act against sex workers by way of '**zero tolerance**' policing and antisocial behaviour orders, the police and social work agencies were more inclined to see this as connected with a need for enhanced welfare services such as 'employment, housing and drug advice' (Edwards, 2002: 154).

Edwards concludes, though, that on balance partnership arrangements do offer genuine opportunities to develop effective crime prevention strategies. Partnership models offer inherent advantages such as the inbuilt potential for ongoing dialogue. This, in turn, establishes the basis for engaging and educating community members so as to generate more sophisticated understandings of shared social problems than might be gleaned from relatively crude and exploitative media portrayals (Edwards, 2002: 154).

The delivery model for crime prevention, as well as its underlying principles, should therefore be grounded in what Edwards describes as 'critical pluralism'. Instead of making assumptions about what is best for people, this identifies the proper conditions for discussion and the development of common understandings and measures of what would benefit the community. This is not just a practical compromise, but it also 'provides a core set of **normative** principles around which advocates of community empowerment can coalesce' (2002: 161). In practice, then, crime prevention initiatives could be focused at any or all of the following: potential offenders, vulnerable members of the community, or risky situations but, whichever of these is prioritised, it must be based on a fair and inclusive form of 'participative democracy' (2002: 162).

Tilley (2011: 9) agrees that a partnership approach is essential. No organisation 'on its own has the capacity to address the full range of conditions giving rise to local crime problems', so working together is a fundamental requirement. At the same time, however, he observes that the actual conditions under which partnerships are expected to operate, including structural constraints and political differences, still present major challenges in achieving these aspirations.

Although 'community' is a relatively ill-defined term, the gist of these arguments is that strong community relationships and effective collaborative mechanisms will provide a greater sense of security as well as practical safeguards against crime and antisocial behaviour. This, in turn, will depend on practical measures to establish effective dialogue and to guard against the dominance of particular interests, neither of which is straightforwardly achieved, as we have seen.

26.4 Frameworks for policy and practice

You should now have a good understanding of the some of the core challenges and choices facing those who attempt to formulate and deliver crime prevention strategies. We will now move on to explore several of the most influential theoretical frameworks relating to crime prevention.

Brantingham and Faust's model

Brantingham and Faust (1976) proposed a framework for policy and practice drawing on the field of healthcare, and based on ideas of 'primary', 'secondary', and 'tertiary' prevention. Primary prevention would focus on managing and modifying the 'criminogenic conditions in the physical and social environment' (1976: 284); secondary prevention would aim to identify and then intervene to reduce the likelihood of individuals or groups going on to offend; and tertiary prevention would be concerned with reducing the likelihood of reoffending (see **Figure 26.3**). As you will see, their framework reflects two of the three main areas of crime prevention that we discussed earlier: potential offenders and criminogenic situations. It does not include vulnerable groups explicitly.

Having articulated the model, the first question the authors posed for themselves was whether it was helpful to establish such a broad framework that it would cover almost any intervention within (and sometimes beyond) the remit of the criminal justice system. Their considered response was that it enabled a proper analysis to be made of the state of knowledge and practice associated with each level; which would, in turn, facilitate a more nuanced understanding of what kind of approach would be most effective in each case. In their view, the state of knowledge at the time did not indicate that tertiary prevention was very effective, consisting as it did of 'treatment' measures with little knowledge of their likely effectiveness (Brantingham and Faust, 1976: 293). Similarly, they argued that in the case of secondary prevention, we did not have good enough knowledge to provide effective 'diagnosis and intervention', partly because of the 'premature and inappropriate assignment of the "potential offender" label' (Brantingham and Faust, 1976: 293; see also Lösel and Bender, 2012). Their conclusion, then, was that primary prevention offered the most promising prospects, and this therefore heralded a significant shift in emphasis towards wider-ranging environmental and social programmes (see **What do you think? 26.3**).

The coincidence of a loss of confidence in targeted programmes aimed at known or potential offenders, and the parallel growth of concern about personal security, led to a shift towards a more extensive and diverse preventive philosophy. Drivers identified by Hughes and Edwards (2011: 17) included: a persistent increase in recorded crime and criminality (until the early 1990s, at least); identifiable weaknesses in the justice system, such as poor detection rates; increasing emphasis on the 'costs of crime'; and a recognition of the limited impact of formal criminal justice interventions. As the system itself became associated with failure and inadequacy, so the focus shifted and crime prevention objectives began to infuse other aspects of social policy: 'The inflated cultural, social and political salience accorded to crime and insecurity since the 1970s has resulted in policies and strategies previously defined in terms of other outcomes increasingly redefined in terms of their possible crime preventive effects' (Crawford, 2007: 871). In contemporary terms, we might recognise the same tendencies at work in the context of welfare and educational interventions with those believed to be at risk of being 'radicalised' (Shain, 2011). Take a look at **Controversy and debate 26.2** for a discussion of 'Prevent', an anti-radicalisation programme.

A number of authors, including Crawford (1997) and Rodger (2008), have described these trends as a form of 'criminalisation of social policy', whereby a whole range of measures come to be seen not simply in terms of their primary objectives, such as 'the quality of education, nutrition, health' or housing (Crawford, 2007: 871), but also as crime prevention projects.

Another way of thinking about this, as Crawford (1998) has observed, is in terms of a shift away from the offender as the target of intervention, towards the 'offence'. Therefore, because we cannot be even reasonably sure who will offend, where, and when, but we are able roughly to estimate that a certain number of offences will be committed against some people from vulnerable groups in certain areas, then this knowledge should shape intervention. However, because we still cannot be precise about either victims or sites of crime, there need to be broad and generalised strategies of crime-proofing and protection across communities.

This does not mean that efforts to improve the anticipation and prevention of offending at either secondary or tertiary levels have been abandoned (as is evident from

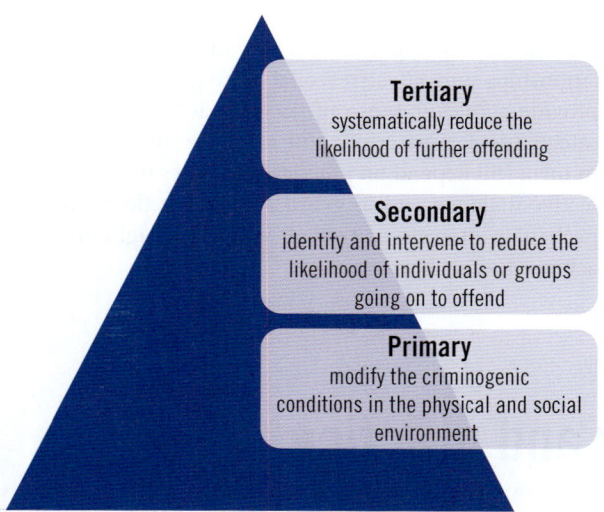

Figure 26.3 Brantingham and Faust proposed a framework for the policy and practice of crime prevention which draws on the field of healthcare and has three levels

WHAT DO YOU THINK? 26.3

Police presence in schools

The Safer Schools Partnerships (SSP) initiative, launched across the UK in 2002, established a police presence in a number of schools across the country (see **Figure 26.4**). The main objectives behind such partnerships were to keep young people safe, reduce crime (and the fear of crime), and improve behaviour in schools and communities. Having police in schools is believed to provide a means of enhancing the relationship between the police and young people, in light of an acknowledged degree of historic hostility and mutual distrust. An additional benefit of police coming into schools may be a greater level of availability and, as a result, readiness on the part of school students to share their concerns and alert police to potential crimes.

In 2006, the Cambridge Constabulary introduced their own partnerships and following that secured a presence in ten secondary schools across the county. The presence of officers was hoped to provide a focus on early intervention and prevention of crime, ultimately resulting in students who respect police officers, and their wider communities. According to the Cambridgeshire Constabulary website, the SSP aims to ensure:

- the safety of pupils, staff, schools and surrounding areas
- there are safe and secure school communities
- young people achieve their full potential
- young people develop respect for themselves and the community
- there is help for young people to deal with situations that may put them at risk of becoming victims of crime, bullying or intimidation
- young people understand there are consequences for their actions

Figure 26.4 The Safer Schools Partnerships established a police presence in schools (such as Smithdon High School in Norfolk, pictured here behind a Police Community Support Officer) with the aim of keeping young people safe, reducing crime, and improving behaviour in communities
Source: Norfolk Constabulary

- students at risk of offending are given appropriate support
- there are better standards of behaviour in schools
- there are positive relations between young people and the police.

(Cambridgeshire Constabulary, 2018; www.cambs
.police.uk/information-and-services/
Community-safety/Student-safety)

Think about these aims of the SSP initiative and then consider the following two questions:

- Do you think it is helpful to have police officers routinely present in schools?
- Should education and schools be used as a vehicle for promoting crime prevention messages?

---

the range of criminogenic assessments that continue to be carried out with detected offenders—OASys, *Asset* (subsequently *AssetPlus*), and the like, and continuing research into the developmental causes of youth crime in particular; Welsh and Farrington, 2012), but it does illustrate the logic behind the substantial growth in 'situational crime prevention'.

The driving force behind this shift in emphasis is often seen as the Home Office in the UK (Crawford, 2007: 872), although Crawford believes that this was also associated with a growing number of local and relatively modest initiatives, grounded in pragmatic attempts to reduce or eradicate discrete problems of crime in specific communities. Hughes and Edwards (2011: 19), too, identify a significant level of government interest in developing crime prevention strategies culminating with the enshrinement of prevention in law in the Crime and Disorder Act 1998, as the principal objective of the youth justice system, as we noted earlier. Interestingly, this section of the Act includes a further subsection (s. 37(2)) requiring all relevant agencies to 'have regard' to this aim, including some such as the health service for whom crime prevention is by no means the principal focus of their activities.

Associated with legislative change has been a heightened expectation placed on local authorities to

CONTROVERSY AND DEBATE 26.2

Who should be responsible for deradicalisation?

In 2003, the UK began its 'Prevent' strategy as one strand of its counter-terrorism strategy. It was designed to prevent people joining extremist groups and committing terrorist acts and made it a statutory duty for schools, colleges, universities, health, local authorities, police, and prisons to prevent people from being drawn into terrorism.

Although it is sometimes associated narrowly with discouraging involvement with terrorist groups claiming affiliation with Islam, Prevent was originally designed to target all forms of terrorist threat, including those linked to extreme right-wing groups. Its three original objectives were to:

- respond to the *ideological challenge* of terrorism and the threat we face from those who promote it;
- *prevent people from being drawn into terrorism* and ensure that they are given appropriate advice and support; and
- work with *sectors and institutions* where there are risks of radicalisation which we need to address.

(Home Office, 2011)

Prevent aims to balance concerns over potential involvement in terrorism, on the one hand, and the fear of stigmatising an entire community or faith group, on the other. Schools, for example, are a focal point for the strategy, because they can combine educational input with a targeted approach to challenging inappropriate and extreme views where they are expressed, as the Scottish government has suggested:

> Within the curriculum, Social Studies, Health and Wellbeing, and Religious and Moral Education have particular roles to play in helping children and young people develop their understanding of the world by learning about other people, **cultures**, beliefs, attitudes and values.
>
> It is important to use learning and teaching methodologies that support collaborative learning and critical thinking, help to create supportive learning environments, and to address controversial issues effectively.
>
> Helping to challenge misinformed views and perceptions amongst learners and challenging commonly held myths, for example regarding particular communities, requires skilled practitioners who use techniques that open up discussion.

(National Improvement Hub, Scotland)

Prevent has been claimed as a success, according to some commentators:

> Prevent has performed a valuable service in turning people away from committing acts of terrorism or from travelling to join terrorist groups abroad.

(Simcox, 2019)

But, others argue that the Prevent strategy is counter-productive:

> 'Prevent' can unintentionally add to structural and cultural **Islamophobia**, which are amplifiers of both Islamist and far right radicalisation.

(Abbas, 2019: 396)

As Abbas reports, Muslim referrals through the Prevent programme are hugely disproportionate (41 times the rate for far-right groups), and the associated risks of **stigmatisation** and alienation may themselves have a 'radicalising' effect.

---

coordinate action to address problems associated with crime, and the establishment of local crime reduction and community safety partnerships (Gilling, 1997), intended to involve all relevant agencies and other community interests in managing the threat of crime and victimisation in the locality.

The extensive scope of this goal of reducing levels of crime has also meant that crime prevention has come to feature multiple stakeholders, and diverse objectives, with a wide range of interventions falling under its umbrella. '**Target hardening**' may be supplemented by strategies to reduce temptation and 'opportunity', for example by:

- increasing the required effort to commit the crime (such as erecting better fencing or creating 'gated' communities);
- increasing the risks of being obstructed or caught in the act of offending (such as better street lighting);
- reducing the potential rewards of the crime (such as security marking of valuable goods or animals);
- reducing 'provocation' (such as hiding presents on the back seat of the car);
- removing excuses (such as sending reminders to pay taxes or renew TV licences).

(Adapted from Crawford, 2007: 873)

The example of gated communities and secure compounds is interesting, since it raises the question as to whether this is actually a measure designed to prevent crime, or rather to act as a form of social control. Instead of situational prevention, Rose (2000: 329) refers to this type of initiative as a form of 'situational crime control', whereby secure communities do not so much act to prevent crime in general but rather just to guarantee their inhabitants' safety and 'eliminate or expel those who have no legitimate ... reason to be there' (Rose, 2000: 330). Paradoxically, though, while this may be an effective strategy for some affluent neighbourhoods, it has been suggested that in poorer areas of public housing, the use of gates and barriers might actually make it more difficult to respond effectively to crime and disorder (Morgan, 2013: 33).

As Crawford goes on to point out, the change of emphasis we have observed does not mean that crime prevention has simply shifted its focus from changing people and their behaviour to changing the physical world, in order to improve the security of potential victims and make transgression more difficult. He cites the example of speed bumps, for instance, where the change in the physical environment complements speed awareness initiatives and encourages adaptive behaviour on the part of the motorist, promoting a greater sensitivity to speed limits in general.

This kind of reasoning process has been described as a manifestation of '*nudge* theory' (Thaler and Sunstein, 2008), which it is argued can exploit unconscious as well as conscious thought patterns to discourage opportunistic criminal behaviour, such as shoplifting (Sharma and Scott, 2015). So, for example, publicly displayed video footage of criminal activities such as shop thefts in progress might increase 'natural surveillance' by the general public whilst also prompting second thoughts amongst those inclined towards shoplifting. This is consistent with a wider trend associated with the cost-reducing effects of austerity which are represented in the devolution of responsibility from government to local communities and individuals, with increased reliance on initiatives such as Neighbourhood Watch, supported by electronic media, whilst more concrete forms of support are withdrawn (Home Office, 2011). Squires (2017) suggests that crime prevention strategies can be seen as becoming more selective over time, with a more limited but specifically targeted role for state intervention, including measures such as the Troubled Families programme and the Prevent counter-terrorism initiative. These are 'aligned around behavioural compliance, moral reform and responsibility and labour market re-entry' (Squires, 2017: 45).

Situational crime prevention

It is perhaps unsurprising that there is in parallel a comparably high level of interest in controlling the 'situations' in which crime is likely to occur. Situational crime prevention is based on a range of theories about the processes leading to crime described as 'opportunity theories' (Clarke, 2011: 41), consisting of 'the rational choice perspective (RCP), the routine activity approach (RAA), and crime pattern theory (CPT)' (Smith and Clarke, 2012: 292). Taken together, these capture a sense of the 'contingent' nature of much behaviour that is defined as criminal, and how it depends on particular combinations of factors working together to act as catalysts for antisocial behaviour or delinquency. We will look at each of these dimensions of situational crime prevention next.

Rational choice perspective

The rational choice perspective assumes that decisions about whether (or not) to offend are based on a more or less deliberate calculation by the potential offender of the 'risks, rewards and efforts of alternative courses of action' (Smith and Clarke, 2012: 294); remember from earlier in this chapter that situational crime prevention also assumes that offending is essentially rational. Whilst the rational choice perspective does not assume that all such choices are fully rational given constraints of 'time, ability, and knowledge about the circumstances', it does suggest that offenders are, in effect, constantly ready to take advantage of crime opportunities (see, for example, **Figure 26.5**) when they are confronted with them, if rational calculation suggests this will be to their advantage.

Routine activity concept

The concept of 'routine activity' locates the potential for crime in the coincidence of three factors: a 'likely (motivated) offender, a suitable target for the offense, and the

Figure 26.5 The rational choice perspective suggests that offenders are ready to take advantage of crime opportunities—such as open windows

Source: Darryl Brooks/Shutterstock.com

Figure 26.6 The routine activity concept suggests crime is more likely to occur when there is no 'capable guardian' on hand to prevent a crime from occurring—as shown in this image of a lone tourist being pick-pocketed
Source: Jacob Lund/Shutterstock

Figure 26.7 Crime pattern theory has led to the idea of crime 'hot spots', such as dimly lit streets late at night
Source: Horia varlan/CC-BY 2.0

absence of a capable guardian to prevent the crime from occurring' (Smith and Clarke, 2012: 296). By 'guardian', the authors mean someone whose presence is likely to discourage potential offenders and whose absence may mean that there is less perceived risk for the offender. Such co-incidences might be more likely to occur if the 'routine activities' of the various parties to the offence converge 'at a particular time and place', thus increasing the probability of a crime taking place—see **Figure 26.6** for an example.

Crime pattern theory

Crime pattern theory is based on the idea that human behaviours in general, and crime in particular, 'show regularities when viewed across time and space' (Smith and Clarke, 2012: 297), and these can be identified in the pattern of rules governing behavioural decisions, movements related to particular locations, and the ways in which crimes are concentrated. From this develops the idea of crime 'hot spots', where predictable combinations of events are known to take place, which might create the right preconditions for crime. Paradoxically, for instance, this could include the relative absence of people ('guardians') from suburban housing estates during school hours. More predictably, perhaps, dimly lit streets late at night are also thought to be sites of particular risk (**Figure 26.7**).

Situational crime prevention uses these conceptual frameworks to develop systems of classification and prediction. These then enable a methodical approach to reducing opportunity, creating inhibitors, and creating greater uncertainty as to the outcomes of crime (greater risk/lower rewards). This, in turn, underpins a variety of practical strategies to influence these different 'enablers' of crime—for instance, in the design of laptop bags to be more secure, in the use of advisory stickers on bike stands, and in creating

uncertainty of gainful outcomes for offenders, for instance through the use of passwords for electronic equipment (Ekblom, 2012). **Figure 26.8** shows the potentially complementary relationship of these alternative theories of crime prevention. See **New frontiers 26.1** for an exploration of how situational crime prevention applies to social media.

Situational crime prevention in action: the Kirkholt Project

The Kirkholt Project, implemented in North West England in the 1980s, achieved 'iconic status in worldwide contemporary thinking on crime prevention' (Hope, 2002: 44). The aim of the project was to activate a policy goal established by the Home Office in 1984 of promoting a collaborative inter-agency approach to reducing burglaries in a specific

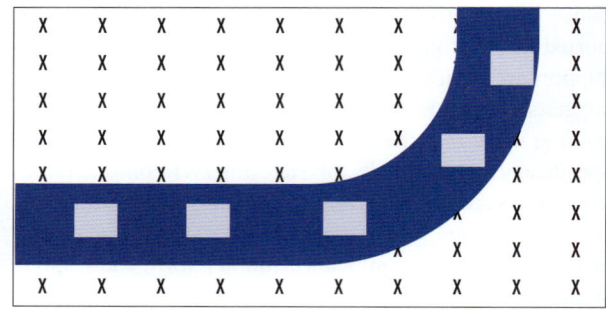

Figure 26.8 The various alternative theories of crime prevention have the potential to be complementary

NEW FRONTIERS 26.1

Social media

The advent of social media has perhaps inevitably created another site of potential crime, where the concepts underlying situational crime prevention—**routine activity theory**, for example—might also apply. This means that we need to think again about the risks involved and strategies of prevention which might be deployed. Reporting on an Australian research study, researchers have identified a number of challenges faced by students in negotiating social media:

> Facebook, Twitter, and other social networking sites have changed the way we interact online. Technological advances have also facilitated the emergence of cyberstalking and online harassment, a growing issue on college campuses. [We used] **focus group** data to examine college students' experiences with online harassment and cyberstalking. Students voiced concerns with online tracking, falsifying identities, and harassment. They also noted that incoming first-year students and those negotiating some of their first romantic relationships are especially vulnerable. In addition, students were asked to propose appropriate prevention, education, and intervention strategies at the college level. Surprisingly, many students recommended offline programs to battle this online problem.
>
> (White and Carmody, 2018: 2291)

The web offers all sorts of positive resources and opportunities, not least to students seeking out relevant knowledge sources, but its scale and the difficulty of imposing controls create new risks, perpetually. Is it helpful to think about what 'developmental', 'social', or 'situational' measure might best insure us against the range of crimes potentially associated with social media?

---

geographical area (Forrester et al., 1988: 1). It took the form of an action research project which involved a wide variety of activities coordinated by the project team, including target hardening measures such as improved household security and property marking; behavioural interventions directed at known offenders in the area; social capital initiatives such as the establishment of a credit union and school-based activity programmes; and improved surveillance for and by local residents. As such, in effect, the project incorporated elements of all three crime prevention approaches outlined and, according to Hope (2002: 45), it was also supplemented by a range of other initiatives to improve living standards (social capital) in the local area.

Over the course of the project, some quite dramatic changes were reported by the research team, including a 75 per cent reduction in the household burglary rate from 1986–7 to 1989–90 (Forrester et al., 1990: 42). The successes achieved were not uniform, though, and for some groups and some types of dwellings (short-term tenants and maisonettes), burglary rates had actually increased over that period. However, the researchers still concluded that the overall achievements of the project demonstrated its success. It was not possible, according to the evaluation, to be able to identify which specific measures had been associated with which beneficial outcomes reported, although the researchers argued that 'the adoption of a series of measures is likely to have much greater impact than simply taking one or two steps' (Forrester et al., 1988: 11). They suggested, though, that community-oriented prevention initiatives of this kind are likely to depend on continuing maintenance of a 'flow of information' and 'established inter-agency links' as well as building new ones (Forrester et al., 1990: 43) in order to retain its capacity to respond to changing patterns of crime and victimisation—providing heightened surveillance of their homes for 'holidaying older people in September', for example.

Although not disputing the effectiveness of the Kirkholt Project, Hope (2002) does sound a note of criminological caution, suggesting that the mechanisms by which crime reductions are achieved are not always as clear-cut as might sometimes be suggested (2002: 51):

> If we asserted that Kirkholt was commendable simply because it brought about huge reductions in burglary—similarly large reductions in incidence, concentration and prevalence can be found to have occurred in other places—sometimes not even as a result of purposive prevention efforts.

Other burglary reduction initiatives have also been shown to be effective, not because they specifically targeted **repeat victimisation**, as in the case of Kirkholt, but because they also represented 'intensive, efficient and sustainable multiple interventions to bring about' the desired objective of a significantly lower burglary rate in the locality (Ekblom et al., 1996). 'Alley-gating', for example, has been subject to intensive review and is reported to be an effective means of reducing burglary by restricting access to vulnerable properties (Sidebottom et al., 2015).

Crawford's levels of intervention

Building on the framework suggested by Brantingham and Faust (1976), Crawford (1998) developed a more elaborate **typology** of crime prevention, distinguishing not just between the different groups involved (the 'audience' for

	Primary	Secondary	Tertiary
Potential offender	Citizenship education. Early intervention social programmes (see **Figure 26.8**). Reducing incentives to offend.	Work with 'at risk' groups, constructive leisure activities, alternative opportunities.	Aftercare, monitoring of ex-offenders, resocialisation.
Potential victim	Target hardening. Campaigns. Secure technology.	Risk assessment and protection of 'at risk' groups.	Repeat victim support, 'hot spot' interventions.
Communities at risk	Neighbourhood Watch (see **Figure 26.9**). Surveillance technology.	Identifying and modifying risk potential in specific community settings. Planning strategies.	Regeneration. 'High crime' area strategies. Building social capital.

Table 26.1 Levels at which intervention might be targeted

Source: Adapted from Crawford, A. (1998) Crime Prevention and Community Safety: Politics, Policies and Practices. *London: Longman*

crime prevention messages), but also the population 'level' at which intervention might be targeted (see **Table 26.1**). Here, 'primary' refers to the community in general, where risks are generalised; 'secondary' refers to those groups and individuals who represent a specific risk; and 'tertiary' refers to those who are identified as being involved in crime, as offenders or victims, and so at even higher levels of continuing risk.

As we have already recognised, the object of intervention might be the potential offender, the potential victim, or the community in general. In this section we will consider each of these objects of intervention, but will first look at the distinction between social and situational crime prevention, which cuts across every category.

Social and situational crime prevention

As well as setting out the objects and levels of intervention, Crawford distinguished between addressing the social factors associated with offending, on the one hand, and controlling the situations which are criminogenic, on the other. Crawford recognises that these are based on different assumptions about the causes of crime. The idea of **social crime prevention** assumes that criminality is the product of a range of interacting influences that impact on individuals and shape their predispositions towards offending behaviour; whilst situational crime prevention relies on the premise that offending is essentially rational and contextual, and can therefore be reduced by making it more difficult to commit crimes (Crawford, 1998: 18).

The kind of early intervention and educational programmes outlined in the 'primary level' column of **Table 26.1**, for example, are designed to address personal and social factors which have been linked with crime (see Farrington et al., 2012, for example). Social crime prevention:

is most commonly directed at trying to influence the underlying social and economic causes of crime, as well as offender motivation. This approach tends to include crime prevention measures that take some time to produce the intended results. This may include action to improve housing, health and educational achievement, as well as improved community cohesion through community development measures.

(Morgan et al., 2015: 15)

Figure 26.9 The use of Neighbourhood Watch schemes is one of the primary-level strategies Crawford suggests for reducing the risk of crime in communities
Source: Amanda Sadler (NHWN) enquiries@ourwatch.org.uk

Figure 26.10 The 'Values Versus Violence' programmes in the West Midlands integrate the police into schools in the Birmingham area
Source: The Dot Com Children's Foundation: www.dotcomcf.org

The focal point for such interventions might be the individual, families, or communities (see **Figure 26.10**), and it is suggested that some 'community-based interventions . . . have adopted a risk-focused approach' that effectively sees the community as an aggregate of 'individual risk profiles' (Crawford and Evans, 2017: 808).

Situational measures, by contrast, are based on the more pessimistic assumption that criminality is endemic and is, indeed, a natural form of self-interested behaviour. The underlying belief here is that we would all be willing to commit crimes if they offered risk-free potential gains. In this context, crime prevention can only be expected to be effective if it restricts opportunities or increases the potential risk—the use of physical security measures to protect homes and businesses being an obvious example of this kind of strategy.

Situational prevention highlights the importance of targeting very specific forms of crime in distinct circumstances. This involves identifying, manipulating, and controlling the situational or environmental factors associated with particular types of crime (Morgan et al., 2015: 13).

We will see how both social and situational crime prevention measures are important in relation to each of Crawford's groups in turn: potential offenders, potential victims, and communities.

Potential offenders

Drawing on Crawford's typology and starting with those who are seen as potential future offenders, preventive approaches aim to ensure that the incentives and attractions of offending are minimised, or that alternative opportunities are provided for this group to undertake 'constructive' activities and to live productive lives, free from crime. Here, though, we are already confronted by the possibility of adopting very different strategies to reduce the likelihood of someone going on to offend. One possibility is a *deterrent* approach: discouraging crime, perhaps through the threat of harsh punishment. Another possibility is a *diversionary* approach: turning potential offenders towards a different activity, such as sport, music, or another creative activity. We will now discuss these two approaches in more detail. Note that they should not be seen as opposing approaches, as prevention programmes targeting those at risk of offending could opt for a combination of the two.

Deterrence

Conventional deterrent measures include various forms of confinement or community punishment (we will discuss these in **Chapter 29**) but, of course, deterrence can only have any prospect of being effective if potential offenders understand the consequences of their actions.

So, for example, the UK government developed an anti-fraud strategy which devoted considerable attention to getting across the message to potential fraudsters that they would be found out and punished (see **Figure 26.11**). The strategy was summarised as follows:

> From September 2001, the campaign [to prevent benefit fraud] focused on dishonest **claimants**. Messages of deterrence and detection aimed to raise the fear of getting caught and portray the likely consequences. Scenarios used in television advertisements showed benefit fraudsters being caught or punished, or both. In addition, the campaign used radio and regional press advertisements, the latter featuring real newspaper headlines from fraud prosecutions.
>
> In June 2003, the next phase used the slogan 'We're on to you'. It featured a spotlight that followed fraudsters in realistic scenarios, such as at work, to show them that they would be found out if they were continuing to claim benefits to which they were no longer entitled, and to warn potential cheats that benefit fraud is a serious crime.
>
> (HM Treasury and National Audit Office, 2008: 22)

Another rather eye-catching and certainly controversial example of the deterrent approach is the 'Scared Straight' programme established in the US in the 1970s and which is still in use in many places. Under this programme, groups of young people 'at risk' of offending are taken to custodial institutions to give them a flavour of just how tough and unpleasant it is to be incarcerated—a type of 'aversion therapy'. The programmes usually involve a tour of the institution and the 'at risk' juvenile is made to live the life of a prisoner for a full day. The visit could include aggressive 'in your face' presentations by inmates as well as one-on-one counselling (*Office of Juvenile Justice and Delinquency Prevention News*, March/April 2011).

Figure 26.11 The anti-fraud strategy employed by the UK government in the early 2000s is an example of a deterrent measure
Source: Department for Work and Pensions (content available under the Open Government Licence v3.0)

The intention is to enhance the deterrent effect of custody for those young people who are believed to be at risk of committing crime at some point, and are open to persuasion of this kind. Interestingly, though, the available evidence suggests that this is a particularly unproductive strategy, which may even have the effect of increasing the likelihood of offending by those undergoing the programme. Petrosino et al. (2004) carried out a 'meta-analysis' of programme evaluations of 'Scared Straight' initiatives and concluded that 'programs like "Scared Straight" are likely to have a harmful effect and increase delinquency relative to doing nothing at all to the same youths'. These findings were based on a 'systematic review' of nine studies carried out over a 25-year period (1967–92) in the US. Although they were unwilling to speculate on the reasons for this outcome, the reviewers concluded that 'we cannot recommend this program as a crime prevention strategy' (Petrosino et al., 2004: 8). Ironically, as the authors noted on completing their review, despite the evidence such programmes remained in demand, regardless of their apparent ineffectiveness.

Diversion from crime

By contrast, a significant body of work has been developed over the years which seeks to promote a 'diversionary' strategy—that is, interventions geared towards encouraging those children or young people identified as potential offenders to find more constructive uses for their time, particularly leisure time, when it is believed they may be at risk of 'drifting' into unlawful activities (see Matza, 1964). Informed by such insights, there has been a long tradition in the UK of developing and delivering just such programmes, originating with Intermediate Treatment in the 1970s and continuing in the same vein subsequently, with variations on the theme; such as Intensive Intermediate Treatment, then Supervised Activity Orders, and subsequently activity requirements for those subject to court orders, and an array of activity-based programmes for those merely 'at risk' of offending. Intermediate Treatment (IT), for example, was introduced under the Children and Young Persons Act 1969 to provide alternative forms of activity and 'compensatory education' (Pitts, 1988) for young people on the fringes of delinquency. By 1976/7, 8,000 children and young people were participating in IT schemes.

What do you think? 26.4 invites you to consider the value of this kind of programme in light of reported public criticisms of them.

Other approaches

Deterrent and diversionary approaches are not the only ways in which this subject can be considered. Other perspectives view crime prevention differently, depending on their assumptions about the nature of the 'processes which a crime prevention measure seeks to affect' (Crawford, 1998: 17), as well as the available evidence on the effectiveness of different types of intervention.

Crawford contrasts 'developmental' and 'community' models of crime prevention. Developmental models aim to address those aspects of the individual's characteristics and behaviour which are believed to predispose them to commit crime. On the other hand, the modification of individuals' criminality is held to be dependent on influencing aspects of the social life of the community to reduce those features which might be criminogenic. Strengthening schools, for instance, is a recent example of one such community approach which has been adopted tentatively in some areas. Improving the 'whole school' ethos is believed to have a generally beneficial effect on student discipline and behaviour, including reductions in criminal activity in and beyond the school itself. Targeting schools in this way may also be seen as sharing assumptions with a

WHAT DO YOU THINK? 26.4

Alternative activities for young people at risk of offending

In the 1980s, in response to a series of outbreaks of unrest, the French government introduced a programme called *Étés Jeunes*, to provide a programme of cultural and sporting activities for young people during the summer months. In 1983, in its second year, the programme involved 100,000 young people and by 1986 it was estimated by the police that there had been a 10 per cent fall in youth crime during the period when the programme was active (Pitts, 1988: 168).

This programme seems to have had much in common with the Summer Splash programme introduced in the UK in 2000 with a similar crime prevention focus.

Some people criticise the idea of spending money on 'treats' for those at risk of offending. Do you agree? If so, what problems can you identify with this strategy?

Or do you think it is a worthwhile programme? If so, how would you go about justifying this and countering such criticisms?

'situational' prevention strategy, especially if they are also connected with or located within what are believed to be high-crime neighbourhoods.

In the case of school-based prevention, though, there has been limited research and thus little evidence as to the impact of such approaches (see Luiselli et al., 2005; Gottfriedson et al., 2014, for example).

Regardless of which of these strategies is favoured, any strategy which targets potential offenders has to take account of the limited capacity we have to predict exactly who will commit what sort of crime, where, and when. These predictions could be based on those imperfect tools such as *Asset* and *Onset* (see **Chapter 9** on youth justice for an explanation of these terms) used by criminal justice practitioners. Or they could be based on academic investigations which have generated a substantial body of work identifying broad but inconclusive associations between individual characteristics and circumstances and the likelihood of offending (for example, Sutherland et al., 2005; see also Case and Haines, 2009: 116). Given that the ability to predict offending at the individual level remains crude, it makes sense to also address the wider needs of the public to feel and to be 'safe'.

Potential victims

While 'social' measures are more likely to be directed at potential offenders, this is not exclusively the case, and they may be directed at enhancing the capacity of victims and communities to protect themselves or exercise 'informal social control'. We can distinguish, therefore, between measures which are purely 'situational' and concentrate on 'target hardening' (Clarke, 1995)—security fencing, for example; and personal safety measures—concealing expensive jewellery, say—which place an emphasis on the potential victims' own responsibility for self-protection. Understandably, this latter approach has possible controversial consequences, in turn, with the risk of 'victim-blaming' and the sense that people are being asked to forego their own natural rights, for example to freedom of movement, which they are entitled to expect the state to guarantee. This point has been powerfully illustrated by women's groups which have deliberately set out to 'reclaim the night' in the face of advice to avoid certain places at certain times in their own interests (see **Figure 26.12**):

> In every sphere of life we negotiate the threat or reality of rape, sexual assault and sexual harassment. We cannot claim equal citizenship while this threat restricts our lives as it does. We demand the right to use public space without fear. We demand this right as a civil liberty, we demand this as a human right.
>
> The Reclaim the Night march gives women a voice and a chance to reclaim the streets at night on a safe and

Figure 26.12 Crime prevention approaches emphasising potential victims' responsibility for self-protection have been controversial—as illustrated by 'Reclaim the Night' marches in which women 'demand the right to use public space without fear'

Source: Barbara Cook/Alamy Stock Photo

empowering event. We aim to put the issue of our safety on the agenda for this night and every day.

(Reclaim the Night, www.reclaimthenight.co.uk/why.html)

Communities at risk

The third strand of prevention identified by Crawford prioritises changing communities rather than targeting individual offenders or victims. The objective here is to generate a greater sense of well-being and communal security in general. This strategy can perhaps be associated with the idea of building or enhancing the supply of 'social capital': the collective resources available to enhance the quality of life enjoyed by community members. One of the original proponents of the concept of social capital describes it in terms of: 'features of social organisation such as networks, **norms** and social trust that facilitate coordination and cooperation for mutual benefit' (Putnam, 1995: 67).

Some support for this perspective is offered by the findings of Sampson and colleagues (1997), whose research seemed to demonstrate the protective value of 'collective efficacy' in the form of strong, established informal networks of support operating within defined communities. The aim of preventive initiatives based on these findings would be to find ways of building and maintaining stronger interpersonal bonds which would both create greater security through building effective connections between people and generate a sense of mutual obligation and regard. Of course, in causal terms, it is debatable as to whether building social capital could be expected to lead to a lower crime rate, or whether effective crime prevention strategies might themselves generate enhanced social capital. The answer to this question could lead to very different priorities for community intervention.

Community interests may not always coincide. It is possible to make a case for prioritising commercial and business interests, for example, because of their key role as neighbourhood assets. As a result, particular objectives might be emphasised, such as a reduction in theft and vandalism, because of the importance of retaining key contributors to the local economy, such as shops and other small businesses. Other risks, to vulnerable members of the community, say, may therefore gain relatively less support; this takes us back to our earlier discussion about whose interests should come first in a context of finite resources and diverse needs.

If instead we were to concentrate our efforts and available funds on protecting those most 'at risk' according to the available evidence (Reza and Magill, 2006), then black and minority ethnic groups and people living in poorer neighbourhoods would be the first to benefit from crime prevention measures. Critical commentators such as Wacquant (2008) would view even this kind of remedial action as inadequate, though. In his view, community decline and marginalisation are the consequence of social and economic changes at the macro-level which combine to produce racialised neighbourhoods ('the American hyperghetto') in which crime and disorder become institutionalised.

> Many [crime prevention] interventions are more accurately understood as humanitarian programming; the type of things that should be done in a just and compassionate society. Hence, it is poignant to see the following programmes reduced to being elements of crime prevention initiatives: adult basic education, vocational training, drug treatment, improving the self-esteem of disadvantaged youths, homework instruction, academic tutoring, family planning, mentoring, after-school programming (including music lessons, sports, dance and scouts), job training for disadvantaged youths, litter and graffiti removal, midnight basketball, group counselling for students with alcoholic parents and so on.
>
> (Haggerty, 2008: 119)

26.5 Implementing crime prevention measures

As understandings of crime prevention have shifted, and arguably become more elaborate and sophisticated, we have also seen the range of strategies put in place expand. It is still the case that preventive initiatives can be categorised according to three domains of 'developmental', 'social', and 'situational' measures (Welsh and Farrington, 2012) but, equally, these may not always be quite as discrete and self-contained as each broad term might suggest. Community crime prevention, for example, is sometimes thought of as a 'combination of developmental and situational prevention' (Welsh and Farrington, 2012: 9), but could also easily be described as 'social' in the ways that they are organised and delivered.

It is perhaps the very complexity and multilevel nature of community crime prevention initiatives that makes it difficult to draw precise conclusions about their effectiveness or the methods by which beneficial outcomes are achieved. Developmental and situational crime prevention approaches might, on the face of it, offer more readily understandable means of intervention (and impacts) than measures designed to promote community cohesion. Developmental crime prevention, for example, is based on the assumption that: 'Traits or propensities conducive to antisocial conduct and crime develop in the womb and early in childhood. The roots of crime thus extend over the life course.' (Cullen et al., 2012: 25). This means that in order to stop someone committing crime, we need to develop interventions which both alleviate these predisposing characteristics and provide alternative 'social opportunities for change' (2012: 26). By applying the right evidence-based interventions it should therefore be possible to provide effective routes out of crime for many individuals, both in the early years and at later stages in their lives.

We have considered situational crime prevention in detail earlier in this chapter. In this section we will take a look at social and developmental crime prevention measures. In the following section, we will consider the intended outcomes of crime prevention strategies in more detail.

Social crime prevention

Many researchers agree that there is now ample evidence available of the risk factors for offending, which have been characterised as 'individual', 'familial', and 'social' (for example, Farrington et al., 2012). As these are now well understood, it becomes possible to specify those which should be seen as priorities for intervention. Individual risk factors include: impulsiveness and school achievement; familial risk factors include child-rearing methods, young mothers, child abuse, parental conflict, and disrupted families; and social risk factors include poverty, delinquent peers, and deprived neighbourhoods (Farrington et al., 2012: 62). At first glance, this appears a daunting and hugely resource-intensive list of areas of social welfare needing to be addressed. Nevertheless, there are a considerable number of initiatives that claim to demonstrate some positive effect of intervening in these areas (Sherman et al., 1998).

So, for example, it has been possible to identify beneficial outcomes of what is described as 'poverty deconcentration' (Ludwig and Burdick-Will, 2012); that is, rehousing people on low incomes in wealthier areas. One example of this is the Moving to Opportunity (MTO) experiment in which 4,000 families in public housing in the US were randomly awarded housing vouchers to enable them to move from 'high-poverty, dangerous neighbourhoods' to more affluent areas with less obvious signs of social stress. Following family moves, the evaluation reported a reduction in violent crime 'for all youth in the sample' (2012: 190), although at the same time, rates of property crime committed by young males appeared to increase. Despite this, the scheme did 'appear to reduce the social cost of offending for youth living in high concentrations of poverty' (Ludwig and Burdick-Will, 2012: 190).

Developmental crime prevention

Alongside such generalised ('primary') interventions, more specific and focused initiatives are also believed to be effective in changing developmental trajectories and reducing the likelihood of young people being drawn into criminality. Social skills training (including parenthood education), pro-social modelling, and coaching for children are reported to be consistently beneficial in terms of reducing the likelihood of young people turning to crime (Lösel and Bender, 2012). Such programmes are argued to be at their most effective when they incorporate a number of elements: 'Structured, multimodal, cognitive-behavioural approaches revealed the most robust and largest effects . . . research supports basic principles of addressing **cognitive**, emotional, and behavioural facets of social competence in an integrated manner' (Lösel and Bender, 2012: 119). The authors of this review of social skills-based interventions do not suggest, however, that programmes should necessarily be selective or concentrated only on those most 'at risk' of becoming offenders, because universal programmes can be shown to benefit 'high-risk participants' and because they avoid the risk of 'stigmatisation' or labelling (2012: 120).

Developmental approaches to crime prevention typically focus on early years interventions (this was one of the goals of the national Sure Start programme in the UK, for example), parent training, and behavioural programmes, and they are in fact relatively rarely focused on changing the material circumstances of potential offenders. So, the emphasis is on aspects of children's upbringing or **socialisation** through changing parenting behaviour, or managing challenging behaviour as a means of anticipating and discouraging antisocial behaviours.

More recently, too, the UK government has established and then expanded the Troubled Families programme, targeting those families most at risk of experiencing a range of problems, including the involvement in crime or antisocial behaviour of one or more family members (Department for Communities and Local Government, 2012). The Troubled Families initiative was explicitly geared towards achieving prosocial behavioural change, although it was associated by some critics simply with a strategy of '**responsibilisation**' without offering additional resources to help families achieve change (Smith, 2015).

Although some programmes targeted at promoting life-course changes are reported to have beneficial effects, these are not easily predictable or consistent: 'Unfortunately mixed success is the current state of the field' (Homel, 2011: 97). This somewhat downbeat assessment is echoed elsewhere in relation to developmental strategies: 'The difficulty of establishing causes, not to mention the co-occurrence of risk factors, is a major impediment to understanding and replicating effective DCP [developmental crime prevention] programs' (Welsh et al., 2017: 147).

26.6 What does prevention achieve?

In the same way that the 'targets' of prevention differ, we can reasonably expect the success criteria to vary according to the model adopted. Early interventions geared towards achieving behavioural change amongst potential offenders will be measured in a very different way to those approaches which are concerned with reducing the likelihood of crime associated with a particular location or social occasion, such as a football match. Other questions spring to mind when we try to determine what criteria to apply to the question of whether a particular prevention initiative 'works'; is the aim to just reduce or to eradicate a certain type of unacceptable behaviour, to make people feel safer irrespective of changing crime patterns, to reduce levels of crime in general or target particular offences, to protect 'the public' in general or particular vulnerable groups, to promote social or economic benefits, or even to try to balance these diverse objectives in some way?

And, indeed, measurement of success becomes more complex still when we factor in the costs (human and financial) associated with achieving specified outcomes—achieving crime reduction goals in absolute terms might begin to feel like less of a bargain if this means that other desirable outcomes have to be foregone, or that there are substantial hidden costs involved. (So, for example, the *Daily Mirror* reported in January 2015 that it could cost as much as £250 to replace a set of car keys designed with improved security in mind.)

In this section we will look in more detail at the impacts and outcomes of prevention initiatives, and we will critically evaluate claims of success.

Early prevention programmes

Despite our concerns about defining success, significant claims have been made over the years for the achievements of crime prevention projects, some of which have achieved almost iconic status. For instance, the Head Start programme, originating in the US in the 1960s, has long been associated with a range of socially desirable outcomes, including a reduction in participants' propensity to commit crime as they grow up. A linked initiative, the High/Scope Perry Preschool study, was established in the early 1960s to track the progress and outcomes of children identified in their early years as being at risk of school failure, and then randomly allocated to an intensive pre-school intervention programme. These children, and the associated **control group**, were followed up regularly to the age of 40, with consistently more positive outcomes for the programme group (Schweinhart et al., 2005). At this point, educationally, they were more likely to have graduated from high school (77 per cent vs 60 per cent), they were more likely to be employed (76 per cent vs 62 per cent) and more likely to own their own homes and cars, they were less likely to have used social services at any point in their lives (71 per cent vs 86 per cent), and they were significantly less likely to have been arrested or imprisoned (7 per cent vs 29 per cent with five or more arrests, for example).

Similarly, a number of larger scale reviews of the evidence relating to early prevention programmes ('meta-analyses') have also suggested that these programmes generate a range of socially desirable benefits, including reductions in both involvement with the criminal justice system and self-reported delinquency (Manning et al., 2010). Weisburd and colleagues (2017) have undertaken a 'review of reviews' which has evaluated some 118 systematic evaluations of the outcomes and effectiveness of crime prevention measures, concluding that: 'It is time to abandon the idea that "nothing works," not only in corrections but also in developmental, community, and situational prevention; sentencing; policing; and drug treatment'; whilst adding the cautionary note that: 'Nevertheless, key gaps remain in our knowledge base' (Weisburd et al., 2017: 435).

Some reservations have been expressed, though, about the quality of the evidence available, the scale of the beneficial outcomes achieved, and the mechanisms by which positive change is brought about: 'there is a need to identify the particular ingredients that make the specific early parent programs successful at inhibiting antisocial and delinquent behaviours ...' (Piquero et al., 2008: 87).

Targeting risky behaviours

As the focus shifts from stopping 'at risk' individuals getting into trouble to concentrating on problematic and potentially criminogenic patterns of behaviour then, naturally, approaches to establishing and evaluating the achievement of success criteria are somewhat different, too. For example, one community action project in Sweden adopted a 'multicomponent strategy' to reduce alcohol-related problems, assessment of which required an evaluation of the extent to which positive changes were 'institutionalised' (Wallin et al., 2004), that is to say, sustained over time. Different dimensions of the programme were therefore considered independently in order to identify if and how each of these had a discernible impact; namely, 'adoption, sustainability, key leader support, structural change, and compliance' (Wallin et al., 2004: 411). Specifically, the programme evaluation tried to determine change at all levels, including organisational practices, the commitment of managers, and the continuity of the programme, as well as the compliance of problem alcohol users.

This project used a range of strategies including awareness training of staff in the night-time economy, a mutually agreed protocol between statutory agencies and alcohol retailers, and stricter enforcement. As a result, the programme evaluators were able to claim that: 'the effects of the project are promising. Alcohol service to underage patrons, alcohol service to markedly drunk patrons, and violence have all decreased significantly' (Wallin et al., 2004: 398). Extrapolating from this experience, we might assume that community-based crime prevention initiatives in general will depend for their success on a consistent and comprehensive 'buy-in' from those concerned with implementation and programme delivery.

Similarly, a systematic large-scale international review of anti-bullying programmes in schools (Farrington and Ttofi, 2009) has indicated that such programmes could be effective in reducing bullying incidents (by 20–3 per cent) and the number of victims of bullying (by 17–20 per cent), and that specific programme elements were particularly closely associated with successful outcomes. However, one programme element, 'work with peers', was in fact associated with an increase in bullying: 'it seems from our results that work with peers should not be used' (Farrington and Ttofi, 2009: 69). The conclusion of this review was that a range of programme elements were associated with a reduction in the levels of bullying, including: 'parent training/meetings, improved playground supervision, disciplinary methods, classroom management, teacher training, classroom rules, whole-school bullying policy, school conferences, information for parents, and cooperative group work' (Farrington and Ttofi, 2009: 66). However, once victimisation was also taken into account, there were fewer programme elements associated with a decline in both respects: 'parent training/meetings, disciplinary methods and the length and duration of the programme'. Nonetheless, this appears to support the idea that crime and antisocial behaviour can be prevented by systematic programmes of intervention which are broadly community-based, target particular types of crime or antisocial behaviour, have widespread commitment from participants, and are implemented rigorously.

Making places safer

In the case of 'situational' prevention, the first thing that becomes clear is that the nature and variety of 'places' where crime may occur demand very different preventive strategies depending on the characteristics of specific locations. Eck (2002: 245), for example, has suggested four 'categories and nine subcategories of places' where crime prevention activities might be carried out at some point:

1. money spending places (shops, banks/money handling premises, bars);
2. residential places;
3. transportation places (airports, car parks, public transport); and
4. other public places (open spaces, coin-operated machines).

This categorisation has since been revised to suggest five rather than four 'place types' (Eck and Guerette, 2012: 360): residential, public places, retail, transport, and recreational, with differing and overlapping interventions applied under each heading. Each of these place categories may require different preventive strategies. For example, the presence of railway staff on trains may discourage aggression towards passengers and good lighting might reduce the risk of attacks in pedestrian subways. On the other hand, some technologies such as CCTV might well be utilised across the range of 'place types'.

For each of these, a range of 'securitisation' strategies or methods to control activities have been attempted, and researchers have reported substantial changes in a number of cases (Eck, 2002). For example, in the 'Clawson Point' housing development a 54 per cent reduction in crime was reported as a result of changes to the accessibility and appearance of the estate. In another example, a substantial majority of residents in public housing complexes in Chicago reported reductions in 'shootings and fighting' following a number of physical security measures and closer scrutiny of the use of buildings (Eck, 2002: 248). However, Eck concludes that the robustness of such findings is not sufficient to be able to suggest that such measures 'work' consistently.

Other 'situational' measures are thought to be more demonstrably effective, however. Both Eck (2002) and Welsh and Farrington (2010) are persuaded that CCTV has been shown to reduce crime, particularly 'in car parks' (Welsh and Farrington, 2010: 27). Here, too, though, it is acknowledged that the 'exact optimal circumstances for effective use of CCTV schemes are not entirely clear at present' (2010: 27). Similarly, improved street lighting has been found to be effective to a robust standard of certainty. According to Welsh and Farrington (2010: 25), 'improved street lighting is effective in city and town centers, residential areas, and public housing communities, and is more effective in reducing property crimes than in reducing violent crimes. In pooling the effects of ... 13 [high-quality evaluations], it was found that improved street lighting lead to a 21 per cent reduction in crime.'

Distinguishing between what is 'known' to work and what is 'promising', Eck (2002: 276) also found a range of evidence that street closures may be effective in preventing a range of different types of criminal activity, including kerb-crawling, 'drive-by shootings', violent crime, burglaries, and car thefts.

Do preventive measures work?

Despite these apparently encouraging examples, a note of caution has been sounded about taking such evidence strictly at face value. As Eck (2002: 281) points out, even though we can find evidence that targeted place-based interventions are associated with reductions in levels of crime, 'we know little about the place- and crime-specific effects of these tactics' and which changes exactly can be seen as causal: 'Even when the effects of a single tactic were identified, other changes were [often] reported that could have confounded the evaluation results. Thus we might learn that crime was prevented, but we do not know what caused the prevention' (2002: 282). There has therefore been a clear and influential move towards developing a consistent 'evidence-based approach to crime policy' (Welsh and Farrington, 2012: 510); whilst at the same time, it is acknowledged that the quality of much of the evidence available is 'very thin' (Eck and Guerette, 2012: 367).

Over the years, though, proponents of an 'evidence-based' approach to situational (and other forms of) crime prevention have made increasingly confident claims, both for the effectiveness of specific interventions and for the overall value of an evidence-informed strategy. As some of the pioneers of this approach argued in the 1990s:

> Many crime prevention programs work. Others don't. Most programs have not yet been evaluated with enough scientific evidence to draw conclusions. Enough evidence is available, however, to create provisional lists of what works, what doesn't and what's promising.
>
> (Sherman et al., 1998: 1).

Some 20 years later, more evidence has been gathered, certainly, and similar sentiments continue to be expressed:

> In the areas of developmental and social prevention, community interventions, situational prevention, policing, sentencing, correctional interventions, and drug treatment interventions, we find consistent evidence of programs and practices that work. Importantly, our conclusion is that not everything works. We think the idea that everything works would be as naïve as the 'nothing works' narrative of the last century. Rather, we find that there is much evidence of practices that are effective. There is also evidence of less effective practices and, importantly, of practices that may even cause harm.
>
> (Weisburd et al., 2017: 437)

26.7 Consequences of crime prevention

Despite the evidence of increasing confidence in the value and success of well-planned, systematic, and evidence-led crime prevention strategies, there have been some concerns raised about the implications of such approaches, and their unintended consequences (Cozens and Love, 2017), alongside the more deep-seated political objections mentioned earlier (Coleman et al., 2002). In this section we will discuss some of these unintended consequences, including escalation, adaptation, displacement, and deflection.

Escalation

Grabosky (1996), for example, has identified a number of possible outcomes of prevention measures which might be counterproductive. These include what he describes as: 'crime escalation, displacement, overdeterrence and perverse incentives' (1996: 25). In the first of these categories, he discusses the Cambridge–Somerville Youth Study (McCord, 1978) which evaluated an intensive programme targeting 'at risk' young people, including educational support, leisure activities, family counselling, and additional health services. Despite the array of services provided, when compared with a control group those targeted for intervention compared unfavourably not only in terms of their likelihood of offending, but also on a number of other criteria, including 'mortality, stress-related disease, and evidence of mental illness and alcoholism' (Grabosky, 1996: 27).

Kelly's (2012) more recent qualitative study has identified similar dynamics and suggests a number of possible factors at play in this process of 'escalation'. In this case, a programme was implemented based on targeting the 50 most 'at risk' young people in the 'most deprived' neighbourhoods and undertaking intensive programmes of intervention with them, in this instance with a sporting theme. Despite a number of individual 'success stories', Kelly also concluded that programmes were associated with a number of adverse effects, including 'accelerating' formal interventions—that is, drawing young people into contact with the justice system and 'labelling' them as potential offenders, for example, 'defining deviance up'—heightening concerns and sensitivities to what might otherwise be seen as normal adolescent behaviour; and contributing to processes of exclusion, where young people undergoing the intervention programme, or in some cases rejecting it, would be persistently marked out as different from the mainstream population ('othered': Garland, 2001). At the same time, the concentration of service provision in this one area would necessarily divert resources from generic and universally accessible services.

As Grabosky (1996: 27) also observes: 'Other forms of escalation are less subtle and more immediately apparent. The construction of physical barriers may invite their defacing or destruction'. He also suggests that suppressed criminal intent may find its expression in more intensified and potentially harmful activities, such as 'expressive violence'. In other words, the preventive measures put in place may actually be perceived as 'provocative' and produce 'defiance not deterrence' (1996: 27); excessive police action can prompt rather than prevent violence in the course of demonstrations, for instance. Similarly, stark warning messages ('don't press the red button') can produce 'perverse effects' (1996: 28), first by bringing what is deemed unacceptable behaviour to people's attention, and then by associating it with a desirable expression of rebellion. In this context, Grabosky refers to the potentially counterproductive effects of stern 'warnings from law enforcement authorities about the perils of various illicit drugs' (1996: 28). Similarly, measures taken by the UK government in 2016 to ban what were previously known as 'legal highs' have been criticised as less likely to prevent harm than to lead to an increase in criminal activity: banning something people enjoy does not mean they will stop doing it. It just means that instead of buying what they want from shops and legal websites, they now need to trade with criminals. Criminals have much less incentive to make sure their products are genuine and unadulterated or to refuse sales to minors (*New Scientist*, 21 January 2016).

Adaptation

Another unintended consequence of preventive measures is when the measure actually facilitates the act of certain types of crime, for example better lighting making certain targets more, rather than less, accessible, or being associated with higher levels of violent crime (Davis and Farrington, 2018). In some cases, well-intended information about the potential vulnerability of certain products or locations might act as an alert to potential offenders; and it may well also be the case that prevention leads to complacency on the part of enforcement agencies, with the effect of reducing rather than enhancing their capacity to anticipate crime.

Preventive measures can be unhelpful in other ways, too. Grabosky (1996: 33) draws attention to the effects of 'over-deterrence' in restricting everyday legitimate activities or creating additional inconvenience for people going about their normal routines (over-enthusiastic internet security software is one such minor irritation, for example). It is also quite likely that social consequences might follow as a result of a general over-sensitisation to the risks of crime; levels of fear might be unnecessarily escalated and community cohesion and mutual trust might be put at risk.

Preventive measures might also be no more than the precursor of what Grabosky (1996: 32) refers to as 'creative adaptation'; that is, a process of refining criminal activity to avoid detection. Offenders may well actually find ways of 'borrowing' from preventive methods to reduce their chances of getting caught (Marx, 2007).

Displacement

A continuing concern in preventive intervention is the problem of **displacement**, where either the criminal activity or its effects are merely shifted from one area, one point in time, or one population to another in the face of specific targeted prevention initiatives. In fact, as Grabosky acknowledges (1996: 31): 'The risk that undesirable activity, rather than prevented absolutely, will be shifted into other areas within or beyond one's jurisdiction or policy domain has become part of conventional criminological wisdom.' So, we might anticipate that strengthening particular targets for crime could just lead to the substitution of other available targets which offer less of a challenge. In the not too distant past, certain older makes and models of car were known to be less well protected by security devices than others, so became more attractive options for car thieves as newer models became increasingly difficult to steal. Interestingly, Grabosky has also cited the example of tax legislation as 'an ongoing drama' (1996: 32), involving the continuing efforts by tax authorities to close loopholes and the equally diligent efforts of 'a small industry' of accountants and financial interests working to create new 'avenues of avoidance and evasion'. Such practices appear to persist, and attempts to control the establishment of 'shell' companies for the purposes of money laundering are reported as consistently ineffective because of displacement: 'if we stop something … then they'll look to something else, so it's the normal supply and demand economics isn't it? They're businessmen like everybody else' (Tax investigator, quoted in Lord et al., 2019: 1231).

See **Controversy and debate 26.3** for further discussion of 'displacement' and its consequences for a specific subgroup of the population.

The problem of displacement is of particular concern to those wishing to develop the science of prevention because, if it is demonstrated to be widespread and perpetually unavoidable, then it seriously undermines any project of improving or perfecting preventive measures. This 'worst case scenario' is mapped out by Johnson et al. (2012), who describe a 'hydraulic' perspective on criminality, such that 'people who would have committed crime in the absence of intervention will continue to do so at the same rate. All that would change is how, when or where they commit those offenses; crime would be displaced' (Johnson et al., 2012: 337). Building on Repetto's (1976) initial formulation, five forms of displacement are identified as potentially problematic:

- how offences are committed;
- when they are committed;
- the types of target selected;
- where crimes are carried out; and
- the type of offence committed.

The possibility of a further form of displacement, in terms of 'who' commits offences, is also acknowledged, as might occur in the case of **organised crime** or gangs, for example.

The idea of a 'steady state' of criminal activity with perfect displacement of one crime for another does depend on

CONTROVERSY AND DEBATE 26.3

Crime prevention, crime displacement, or crime promotion?

Periodically, it appears, 'respectable' communities' fears about the impact of sex work on the locality lead to the introduction of 'zero tolerance' policies. Sex workers are effectively criminalised and excluded from certain areas of towns and cities, and dispersed to other locations. But the effect of this may be to expose the sex workers themselves to greater risk of victimisation through theft and violence. Consider the following extracts from letters to *The Observer*, 26 January 2014:

> The article 'Mariana Popa was killed working as a prostitute. Are the police to blame?' . . . is a turning point in getting senior officers . . . to admit that criminalisation puts women at risk: 'It would be good to allow a small group of women to work together, otherwise . . . they are working away from other human support.' It has taken 40 years of campaigning to get this truth out. From the trial of Peter Sutcliffe, who murdered 13 women, many of them sex workers, to the Ipswich murders in 2006, we have complained that the police hound rather than protect sex workers.
>
> (Niki Adams, English Collective of Prostitutes, London NW5)

> My report, 'Shadow City', found that police received £500m to tackle trafficking prior to the Olympics. They found no more trafficking cases than the year before—four—but did raid a huge number of brothels. This meant sex workers were displaced and became more vulnerable to violence. The laws on prostitution need to change. Until they do, we need to change dramatically how we police sex workers.
>
> (Andrew Boff, Conservative Londonwide Assembly member, leader of GLA Conservatives, London SE1)

- How do you think the different groups' rights to protection from the effects of crime and antisocial behaviour might be assured in this context?
- Who should we see as the potential victims in this example?
- How do you feel about 'respectable communities' and the effects of their actions on both potential victims and other communities?

---

a number of assumptions, though. Where an opportunity is blocked, there must be a more or less direct alternative available, offenders must know about such alternatives, and have the means and ability to exploit them, and they must be indifferent to the further consequences of making such choices, such as the implications of offending nearer to/ further from where they live (Johnson et al., 2012: 338). Not only must offenders be 'sufficiently adaptable and capable of committing a variety of crimes in a variety of places or at different times', but they must also be 'driven by irresistible pressures' to offend, even to the extent that they are prepared to make extra efforts to overcome 'the initial thwarting of intention' achieved by an active crime prevention strategy (Crawford, 1998: 81).

Choice and 'deflection'

Doubt has been cast on the presumption of a steady state by those who support a 'rational choice' theory of crime (see the discussion of the rational choice perspective in **section 26.4**), as articulated originally by Clarke and Cornish (1985). According to this perspective, offenders will not automatically look elsewhere for the opportunity to commit crime if it is blocked at their preferred time and place. They will, instead, be guided, and possibly constrained, by a calculative decision-making process which may or may not lead to them committing an alternative offence: 'The everyday constraints on perfect rationality can include limitations of time, ability and knowledge about the circumstances in which decisions are made' (Smith and Clarke, 2012: 294); but the 'irrational' influences on potential offenders do not completely override the 'rational elements' involved.

We should think perhaps in terms of actors' 'bounded rationality' (see **Chapter 15**), when trying to understand the potential for displacement of particular criminal activities to other settings, or towards the use of alternative methods. It is likely, then, that for certain types of crime that involve a deliberative process, effective preventive measures will not necessarily lead to straightforward displacement. This is supported by Johnson et al. (2012: 349), who observe that for certain types of place-based intervention 'crime appears just as likely (or perhaps slightly more so) to decrease in the areas that surround a treatment area following intervention'. It is argued in this respect that some 'displacement' effects may be viewed as positive in the sense that the 'benefits' of the preventive intervention are also dispersed beyond the specific site of intervention—in other words, a sort of 'halo' effect is achieved as crime rates go down in the surrounding area, as well as in the target location (Johnson et al., 2012: 349).

Johnson and colleagues point out, however, that this conclusion is 'based on a relatively small number of studies', focusing particularly on measures designed to improve 'surveillance', such as CCTV (2012: 350). It seems plausible that preventive measures are less likely to result in spatial displacement for certain types of criminal activity (unplanned property crimes, for example), but that this conclusion cannot be generalised.

Barr and Pease (1992) have additionally raised questions about the adequacy or effectiveness of displacement as a concept. They appear to be concerned about the risks of taking a one-dimensional view of crime, arguing that it is the interaction between the potential offender and the 'situation' which is crucial (Barr and Pease, 1992: 277):

> Crime patterns take the form they do because of a combination of circumstances: offender motivation, the absence of legitimate routes to personal satisfaction, the availability of vulnerable targets, the degree of preparation and investment required to commit different crimes, and the perceived consequences of crime commission.

As such, they suggest, it may be better to think in terms of 'deflection' when a particular criminal opportunity is 'blocked', which may involve legal or illegal alternatives. It may also be better to think in terms of whether these alternatives are 'optimal'. Displacement can thus be viewed as 'benign' or 'malign', depending on the impact of the alternative activity—less serious offending might therefore be viewed as an acceptable consequence of preventive activity even though the overall crime rate has not seen a decline: 'displacement is not necessarily an undesirable consequence of social intervention' (Crawford, 1998: 83). However, displacement may have problematic consequences even when it is regarded as unproblematic from a 'majority' point of view. For example, as we saw in **Controversy and debate 26.3**, the displacement of sex workers from one area to another put the sex workers at greater risk of violence and murder, whatever the apparent benefits to the wider community.

In sum, therefore, crime prevention has consequences which are not always (or often) straightforwardly measurable—to return to our starting point, what seems like a simple and common-sense aspiration may not be without its complications.

26.8 Reviewing the limitations of crime prevention

Despite its inherent attractiveness, the idea of 'crime prevention' has been the subject of criticism, as we have already observed. Such criticisms can effectively be categorised in two ways: first, that crime prevention initiatives are impractical, ineffective, or even counterproductive, some examples of which we have already considered; and, secondly, that their inherent assumptions reflect ideological perspectives and trends in criminological thought that are open to question. Of course, these two problems may be linked, in the sense that initiatives which appear to be politically attractive or to offer a ready-made 'quick fix' may also be precisely those measures which are associated with poor or undesirable outcomes.

The 'quick fix' problem 'dispersal orders' were introduced by the UK government under the Anti-Social Behaviour Act 2003 as an apparently popular and practical solution to the problems of 'gangs' of young people responsible for 'low-level but persistent group-related anti-social activity and intimidatory behaviour' (Crawford and Lister, 2007: 4). As a community-based preventive measure, the police were given powers to 'disperse groups of two or more people from areas where' such behaviour was believed or perceived to be taking place (2007: 5). In order to obtain the authority to administer these powers within a 'designated zone', the police had to gain the approval of the relevant local authority and specify the area covered and the duration for which such permission was sought. If agreed, the police would be authorised to require people in a group to 'disperse', to require anyone not living locally to leave the area, and to require them to stay away from the area for up to 24 hours. Crawford and Lister (2007: 9) have reported rather patchy use of the powers, and a number of practical challenges associated with implementation, such as the limited capacity of police to sustain the level of engagement required to ensure compliance, and an increase rather than a reduction in the number of 'confrontational situations' (2007: 22).

Additionally, evaluation of the use of dispersal powers in certain police areas suggested that there was strong evidence of 'displacement', not only for the specific problem of young people 'hanging around', but also for certain types of crime, including burglary and criminal damage, with indications of 'a considerable displacement effect' (2007: 49). In this instance, not only did the intervention have little effect other than moving crime and antisocial behaviour around, leading to the issuing of dispersal orders to cover neighbouring areas (a 'domino' effect, 2007: 52), but this escalated rather than reduced residents' feelings of insecurity:

> People were concerned that while the area around the shops had become safer during the dispersal order period, the back streets and some of the green spaces had become less safe: 'The groups of young people who were dispersed simply moved to an area just beyond the boundaries of the order and regrouped' (Resident).

Interestingly, there also seems to be some evidence from this study that a superficial concern with dealing with the outward manifestations of community conflict might generate some initial interest and support, but does little to address underlying and arguably more important problems of (lack of) social cohesion:

> It doesn't actually resolve anything.... Six months later we've still got groups of young people that won't engage with adults and vice versa. Very little has happened as a direct result of the dispersal order.
>
> (Housing officer, quoted in Crawford and Lister, 2007: 61)

Indeed, it was concluded that none of the benefits associated with the introduction of dispersal powers, such as 'galvanising community capacity and dialogue about the appropriate use of public space', actually depended on their use, and these positive outcomes could have been achieved in other ways (Crawford and Lister, 2007: 74).

This is, of course, only one case example, and proponents of systematic crime prevention strategies might well argue that the problems identified in this case were to do with faulty implementation rather than any fundamental problem with the principles of targeted, evidence-based approaches. So, it has been argued that a considerable number of preventive measures do work, and a similarly extensive number have been found to be 'promising', in the sense that concrete but less comprehensive evidence points towards their effectiveness (Sherman et al., 1998; Weisburd et al., 2017).

Replication and transferability

Similarly, we need to be careful about making unjustifiable generalisations: what 'works' in one set of circumstances with a specific community may well not be transferable to another very different setting, since these external influences may alter the very basis on which an intervention is established—such as cultural perspectives on the use of drugs. This illustrates a further problem for the 'science of prevention', and this is the matter of replicability. That is to say, if a particular measure can be demonstrated to be effective, then it ought to be capable of being implemented elsewhere, at least in similar settings, with a similar degree of success. However, as Sherman and colleagues (1998: 3) have noted, 'Until replications become far more common in crime prevention evaluations, the field will continue to suffer' from uncertainty about the implications of previous findings, both positive and negative.

Replication, though, does appear to present a very substantial challenge. Cherney (2006: 3), for example, acknowledges the persistent problem of external influences. Failure to think through the impact of contextual factors 'is a key reason that program replication in the crime prevention field has such a dismal record', he observes, citing Tilley's (1993) reflections on this problem. In this instance, Tilley was reporting on attempts to replicate the Kirkholt Burglary Prevention Project (see **section 26.4** on crime prevention in action: the Kirkholt Project), at least one of which deliberately used Kirkholt as a prototype (Tilley, 1993: 6). He concluded that the outcomes of these replications demonstrated variable levels of success, but that the project most closely modelled on Kirkholt was notably the least successful of these. However, this prompted the further reflection that: 'Contextual variation is crucial' (1993: 20), and that even where attempts were made to follow the template offered by its predecessor, it was not possible to do so with a sufficient degree of accuracy (1993: 11); it was a different type of area; the crime profile of the area was different; and the resources put into the scheme were also not comparable. In practical terms, then, faithful replication of previous initiatives is hard, if not impossible, to achieve, as Ekblom (2002: 144) agrees.

For those still committed to the 'science of prevention', the challenge remains one of developing better mechanisms for understanding the contexts and processes involved in implementing preventive schemes. Work should be written up so that 'conjectures concerning measures, mechanisms, context and outcome pattern are made explicit' (Tilley, 1993: 19), for example. Or, perhaps we should '*assemble generic principles of intervention then apply them alone or in combination as appropriate to specific circumstances*—fitting theories and/or abstract distillations of preventive mechanisms to particular problems and contexts' (Ekblom, 2002: 148, emphasis in original).

Even in the context of encouraging claims, researchers express significant caveats about the successes of crime prevention: 'The most important limitation of science is that the knowledge it produces is always becoming more refined, and therefore no conclusion is permanent' (Sherman et al., 1998: 3). That is to say, even in the most convincing examples of the effectiveness of preventive initiatives, we have to accept that our findings remain 'provisional'. This does not, of itself, make the search for better interventions and better evidence pointless. As Popper (2002) made clear, no causal explanation can ever be proved to be true; all 'theories can be disproved or, more likely, revised by new findings' (Sherman et al., 1998: 3).

Responsibility for prevention

The lack of certainty associated with preventive strategies and their outcomes means that initiatives are likely to remain open to external influences and interests which could well determine priorities, and so shape practice:

> We need to place evaluations within a broader political framework. Debates about 'what works?' only reveal that the politics of success and failure are often struggles about the

status of criteria which can rarely be reduced to 'universally accepted scale of efficiency'.

(O'Malley, 1992: 263, quoted in Crawford, 1998: 214)

Indeed, it seems to be fairly widely accepted that crime prevention is peculiarly susceptible to 'political challenges' (Welsh and Farrington, 2012: 511). Advocates of preventive measures may have to deal with the fears of politicians, for example, that they may be perceived as soft on crime by supporting prevention instead of 'law-and-order measures' (Welsh and Farrington, 2012: 512). But it is not just the delivery mechanisms and strategic frameworks that are subject to political or ideological influence, according to some. It is rather the way in which the whole conceptual basis and scientific logic of 'crime prevention' is constructed which is subject to this kind of influence. So, for instance, Garland (1996) has argued that it is important to understand the growth of interest in prevention as part of a 'responsibilisation' project, by which government and the state relinquish their primary role in preventing and controlling crime, and transfer responsibility (and potential blame) to a wide range of community interests (Garland, 1996: 453):

> Property owners, residents, retailers, manufacturers, town planners, school authorities, transport managers, employers, parents and individual citizens—all of these must be made to recognise that they too have a responsibility in this regard, and must be persuaded to change their practices in order to reduce criminal opportunities and increase informal controls.

The idea of individuals and communities filling the gap left by a process of state withdrawal is consistent with the reduction in the proportion of total UK government funding for 'public safety', including policing and crime prevention, from 5.5 to 4 per cent between 1995 and 2015, as reported by the Office for National Statistics.

The political problem

Just which of the many potential targets for intervention are identified as most important, and how does this help to construct a perception of particular groups and particular forms of behaviour as the most problematic? Young people, for instance, are routinely brought under the spotlight when the potential for antisocial behaviour and crime is put on the public policy agenda. As Goddard (2012) has observed, it is 'at-risk' youth who are considered to be particularly prone to committing serious offences or joining gangs, and he notes, at the same time, the spotlight is also most likely to fall on those from minority ethnic groups, with radicalisation, notably, featuring as a particular contemporary concern (Abbas, 2019). Politicians and business leaders can perhaps use the idealised concept of 'crime prevention' itself as a powerful strategic tool, to shape public concern and institutional behaviour in directions that are favourable to their interests whilst diverting concern about criminality, moral disorder, and unacceptable behaviour (such as tax avoidance) away from themselves.

Linked to these possibilities is the potential for popular images of criminality to fuel a somewhat unbalanced 'fear of crime' (Lee, 2007), which does not map accurately or directly onto the wider realities of crime and irresponsible and dangerous behaviour.

26.9 Conclusion

So, in conclusion, crime prevention in the sense of stopping bad behaviour before it happens seems like a 'no-brainer'; a self-evidently desirable aspiration. But, lying behind this apparently obvious and consensual objective are the political interests, influences, and dynamics that construct particular groups, particular neighbourhoods, or particular kinds of activities as the targets of intervention. It is these factors which transfer the mundanely good and desirable into something which needs to be closely examined and evaluated before we can invest our belief, energies, or commitment in it.

In the course of the chapter, we have discussed a number of approaches to identifying the incidence of crime and developing interventions to anticipate it and prevent offences taking place. These are based on increasingly substantial and sophisticated bodies of evidence, and they are targeted typically at people, places, or communities, or sometimes a combination of these. Research has shown that some of the programmes implemented have an identifiable effect on crime levels.

At the same time, there have been concerns about the impact of crime prevention measures on particular sections of the population, on civil liberties, and on the quality of community life. Others have argued that many of the claims made about the effectiveness of crime prevention are overstated. So, what seems like an obvious and desirable common objective has to be approached with some caution. Recognition of potential benefits accruing from crime prevention measures may need to be tempered with a critical awareness of the ancillary effects and possible unintended consequences.

SUMMARY

After reading this chapter and working your way through its features you should now be able to:

- Discuss the arguments in favour of a preventive approach to criminal justice

Supporters of crime prevention believe that it is possible to identify risky situations or risky people and on this basis to predict and reduce the likelihood of crime, notably supported by ideas such as rational choice theory.

- Appreciate the implications of crime prevention for different stakeholders, including potential victims, potential offenders, communities, politicians, interest groups, and others

Deciding which crimes are most problematic to the community in general or particular interests involves making a number of choices about whose needs to prioritise, what level of intrusion into everyday activities is acceptable, and how we can judge what counts as a successful outcome. The implications and success criteria are variable.

- Recognise the implications and effects of different approaches to preventing crime

Crime prevention can be distinguished according to whether it is 'situational', 'community-based', or 'developmental'. Each of these points towards different intervention strategies, and is associated with alternative practices and technologies. Policy and practice decisions can also be differentiated according to the 'level' of intervention, identified as 'primary', 'secondary', and 'tertiary' by Crawford (1998).

- Consider and assess the evidence base in support of preventive measures

A considerable body of work has developed, building up a detailed evidence base which in turn has made claims about 'what works', what's 'promising', and what 'doesn't work'. As well as reflecting on this evidence, we have also reflected on the question of how such approaches have shaped our understanding of the prevention agenda.

- Evaluate the theoretical dimensions of perspectives on prevention

We have shown that the idea of prevention incorporates some contestable assumptions about what types of behaviour are unacceptable and who it is that presents the most risk to the community. These assumptions draw on theoretical traditions in which concepts of criminality, responsibility, and control are grounded.

- Examine the critical arguments questioning the aims and effectiveness of crime prevention strategies, including a consideration of escalation, adaptation, and displacement

For some, the idea of prevention is itself a political concept which invites us to prejudge and problematise certain populations (young people, minority groups) or communities and neighbourhoods in a way which supports a divisive and exclusionary approach to targeted interventions and oppressive forms of control and boundary maintenance. We have examined some unintended consequences of crime prevention through a consideration of three issues: escalation, where crime prevention strategies have in fact worsened crime rates; adaptation, where preventive measures have actually facilitated the act of certain types of crime; and, finally, displacement where criminal activity or its effects are merely shifted from one area, one point in time, or one population to another as a consequence of specific targeted prevention initiatives (Hodgkinson et al., 2020, for example).

 Test your understanding of the chapter's key points by attempting the self-test questions on the **online resources** at www.oup.com/he/case2e

REVIEW QUESTIONS

1. What do you understand by the term 'crime prevention'?
2. Who are the principal targets of crime prevention: offenders, potential victims, or communities?
3. In line with Brantingham and Faust's framework for crime prevention, give an example of 'primary', 'secondary', and 'tertiary' prevention tactics.
4. Outline the main differences between deterrence and diversion measures in relation to potential offenders.
5. What are the main features of 'situational' crime prevention?
6. What is the main assumption underlying the rational choice perspective?
7. What do you think of the idea of 'scaring straight' potential offenders?
8. To what extent do you think that displacement of criminal activity is a problem for crime prevention initiatives?

 Access the **online resources** at www.oup.com/he/case2e to check your answers to the review questions.

FURTHER READING

Forrester, D., Chatterton, M., and Pease, K. (1998) *The Kirkholt Burglary Prevention Project.* **London: Home Office.**
An important and influential case study of an extensive and thoroughly evaluated crime prevention initiative in one particular location.

Lea, J. and Young, J. (1984) *What is to be Done about Law and Order?* **Harmondsworth: Penguin.**
An influential re-evaluation of the effects of crime on working-class communities, and critique of the argument that the criminal justice system is simply a tool of the dominant class.

Schweinhart, L. et al. (2005) *Lifetime Effects: The High/Scope Perry Preschool Study Through Age 40.* **Ypsilanti, MI: High/Scope Press.**
A longitudinal review of one of the earliest and most comprehensive (and extensively evaluated) early prevention schemes and its long-term effects.

Tilley, N. and Sidebottom, A. (2017) *Handbook of Crime Prevention and Community Safety* **(2nd edn). Abingdon: Routledge.**
This is a very useful resource, summarising theories, models, and evidence on the subject of crime prevention and protecting communities.

Welsh, B. and Farrington, D. (eds) (2014) *The Oxford Handbook of Crime Prevention.* **Oxford: Oxford University Press.**
An authoritative and comprehensive sourcebook covering a wide range of theoretical perspectives and research evidence on crime prevention strategies and their impact.

Winterdyk, J. (ed) (2016) *Crime Prevention: International Perspectives and Trends.* **Boca Raton, FL: CRC Press.**
This is an extensive overview of international approaches to crime prevention, covering both practical developments and policy objectives.

 Access the **online resources** to view a wealth of extra information relating to your study of criminology, including self-test questions, answers to review questions, and links to other resources that will help you enjoy and fulfil your potential within your studies.
www.oup.com/he/case2e

CHAPTER OUTLINE

27.1	Introduction	804
27.2	What is crime control?	804
27.3	Objectives of crime control	808
27.4	The role of the police in crime control	811
27.5	The role of other agencies and interests in crime control	816
27.6	The objects and technologies of crime control	820
27.7	What does crime control achieve?	822
27.8	Does crime control 'work'?	828
27.9	The limitations of crime control	831
27.10	Conclusion	833

27

Crime control

KEY ISSUES

After studying this chapter, you should be able to:

- explain what constitutes 'crime control';
- interpret the crime control model and the due process model, understanding the implications of each;
- analyse the different methods of delivering 'crime control', including deterrence, target hardening, offender surveillance, and incapacitation and associated intervention programmes;
- recognise the role played by the police in crime control;
- critique the effectiveness of different crime control methods, including deterrent measures and zero-tolerance initiatives;
- appreciate the practical and moral limitations of crime control.

27.1 Introduction

The previous chapter on crime prevention might be seen as representing an optimistic view of crime and offenders. The assumptions which lie behind crime prevention strategies are that people can be dissuaded from taking up crime, or they can be discouraged from offending because of the risks involved and potential costs to themselves. Crime control perspectives, while also geared towards stopping crime, are much more pessimistic. In this case, a gloomier view of human nature and desires seems to prevail. Some people, for whatever reason, are committed to crime, it seems. The task of the criminal justice system is to stop crime and, where it cannot do so, to take decisive action to apprehend the criminals, and at least stop them from repeating their crimes.

The different approaches to dealing with crime that we are considering in this part of the book are each informed by a particular set of assumptions about the causes of crime, and what to do about it. As we saw in **Chapter 26**, crime prevention strategies are based on the assumption that potential offenders can be educated or persuaded not to break the law, that opportunities to offend can be anticipated, and that the possibility of crimes being committed can therefore be minimised or eradicated. On the other hand, as we will see (**Chapter 28**), more punitive perspectives on crime accept that crime is inevitable, and concentrate on what penalties should be imposed and how much the offender should suffer by way of atonement.

In this chapter we will consider an approach that lies between these perspectives, based on the idea of 'controlling' crime. Criminologists and criminal justice practitioners who adopt this standpoint accept that crime is inevitable; but they are also committed to minimising its effects, either by restricting opportunities to offend or by acting decisively where crimes are committed. Accepting that crime, or at least criminal impulses, is/are inevitable, a crime control perspective seeks to 'manage' the threat of harm and limit the impact on victims and communities.

Crime control and retributive interventions may well coincide, despite their differing motivations, as in the case of imprisonment, for example. But crime control also extends well beyond deterrent sanctions to include other measures geared towards the assessment and management of potential risks, **target hardening**, proactive policing, offender surveillance, and restrictions—measures such as curfews and antisocial behaviour orders. In this respect, crime control perspectives align quite closely with the crime prevention agenda. Where the two differ, though, is in their principal motivations. Whereas crime prevention approaches are concerned with understanding the causes of crime and intervening to address these, crime control strategies are much more narrowly focused on enhancing security and managing risk in order simply to stop crime.

In this chapter we will first explore in more detail what a crime control approach means. We'll then consider what this approach is intended to achieve, for example reassuring the public, minimising harm caused by offences, and incapacitating offenders. We'll look at the role of the police in crime control including **zero-tolerance**, intelligence-led policing, and community policing and the role of other agencies, such as architects, the community, private security providers, and the judiciary. We'll consider how predictive tools might be used to minimise the risk of reoffending. In the final sections of the chapter we will consider some of the impacts and outcomes of crime control strategies, and will conclude with a discussion of their possible practical limitations and moral challenges.

27.2 What is crime control?

In this section, we will explore in a bit more detail just what it means to take a crime control approach to criminal justice. At the heart of this perspective is a belief in the idea that criminality is essentially predictable, and that offenders are to be held fully responsible for their behaviour. Where possible, threats to individuals, their property, or public order should be recognised, and action taken to reduce or remove them. Potential offenders should be identified and pre-emptive action should be taken to stop them from committing crimes. If necessary, this can involve the use of forceful persuasion, or coercion. In effect, they can be led to believe either that a crime 'just isn't worth it' or that it is not possible if, say, the security system on a particular make of car is enhanced to such a level that it becomes too risky or difficult to disarm. And if the force of logic fails, then simple force should achieve a similar outcome—a police blockade, for example. Where pre-emptive action fails and crimes are committed, decisive action is necessary to bring the offenders to justice, with the aim of preventing them from reoffending, either by way of incapacitating them or by means of deterrence.

Underpinning the philosophy of crime control are a number of additional assumptions which we will examine further throughout this chapter and will look at briefly now. First, the crime control perspective relies on a non-problematic view of crime; that is, that there is a clear common understanding of what constitutes illegal behaviour, and that there is similarly a clear, uncontroversial and readily identifiable common interest in taking action to manage, control, or eradicate this behaviour. (Interestingly, at this point a similar question of 'proportionality' arises as is the case in relation to retributive forms of punishment (see **Chapter 25**), but this time complicated by calculations of risk and the likelihood of possible criminal actions being carried out.) Secondly, is the assumption that such measures are themselves relatively unproblematic and will result in the achievement of the desired outcome; that is, the prevention or minimisation of the likelihood of crime being committed and the reduction of harm associated with it.

Advocates of 'crime control' would argue that the principal aim of the criminal justice system is to stop crime, by whatever lawful means are necessary. The 'rule of law' is central to this position, since this is what marks crime control out from either vigilantism or the arbitrary use of force to gain or maintain power. The legal framework of the state confers legitimate authority on agents of control such as the police. Otherwise, there is nothing to distinguish such interventions from the purely arbitrary exercise of coercive power by one group or individual over others.

Crime control strategies therefore claim to represent a simple, impartial, and authoritative approach to stopping criminal activity. Crime control can be distinguished from crime prevention in that it is essentially *reactive*, being geared to responding to crime and dealing with its consequences, although there is certainly some common ground between the two, as in the case of physical security (and there are some obvious areas of overlaps with **Chapter 26** on crime prevention).

'Broken windows'

In this context, the task of the justice system (starting with those whose role is associated with the detection and prosecution of crime) is to maintain order and to regulate the life of the community; so that ordinary 'law-abiding' citizens are able to feel safe and go about their business without being exposed to undue risk of harm. This thesis is famously associated with the position adopted by Wilson and Kelling (1982) in their article entitled 'Broken Windows' (see **Figure 27.1**). So, the principal aim of the police should be seen as being one of controlling or driving away 'someone challenging community standards':

> the most important requirement is to think that to maintain order in precarious situations is a vital job. The police know this is one of their functions . . . the police—and the rest of us—ought to recognize the importance of maintaining, intact, communities without broken windows.
>
> (Wilson and Kelling, 1982: 38)

Figure 27.1 Broken windows—a symptom of a bigger problem?
Source: Tomas Castelazo, CC BY-SA 3.0

And so it is understood, for example, that the actions of the police (and by implication other practitioners within the justice system) should be judged according to their outcomes, rather than the immediate effects of their actions. We should put aside our utilitarian concerns and commitment to treating people 'fairly' in favour of preserving the integrity of the community and serving the interests of the majority in maintaining public order:

> Arresting a single drunk or a single vagrant who has harmed no identifiable person seems unjust, and in a sense it is. But failing to do anything about a score of drunks or a hundred vagrants may destroy an entire community.
>
> (Wilson and Kelling, 1982: 35)

Whilst this line of argument was originally developed to address the perceived problems experienced in neglected or rundown neighbourhoods, its logic may also seem attractive when applied to the wider challenges associated with the problems of managing and controlling crime.

Crime control and due process models

Herbert Packer (1964) analysed two distinct types of models related to the delivery of criminal justice: the due process model and the crime control model. In this chapter, we will discuss the crime control model, but it is important to understand where it differs from ideas of due process and what this might mean for the practices of those involved in the criminal justice system.

Before considering how these two models differ, we will first consider their similarities (Packer, 1964; and see **Chapter 23**). Both models presume that the legislative methods and procedures for defining behaviour as criminal can be kept separate from the process of detection and dealing with those who infringe the law. Equally, criminal justice should be delivered impartially, and simply as prescribed by the requirements of the law. Otherwise, law enforcement processes would rely entirely on ad hoc decisions by those in positions of power who would be able to define what should be treated as criminal (or not), without reference to key principles such as that of fair and equal treatment of all citizens under a common legal framework.

In line with this, though, a crime control approach further assumes that it is possible to articulate a single, overarching aim for the justice system which takes precedence over all other considerations, as Packer notes:

> The value system that underlies the Crime Control Model is based on the proposition that *the repression of criminal conduct is by far the most important function to be performed by the criminal process*. The failure of law enforcement to bring criminal conduct under tight control is viewed as leading to the breakdown of public order and thence to the disappearance of an important condition of human freedom.
>
> (Packer, 1964: 9, emphasis added)

This appears to be a powerful argument. Based on an assumption that there is a consensus in society about what constitutes unacceptable behaviour and how it should be dealt with, it prioritises enforcement activities to protect the community. These are to be judged principally in terms of whether or not they preserve public order. In effect, the ends justify the means, and less concern is paid to other aspects of the wider justice system, such as the protection of **defendants**' rights.

Setting out the crime control model in this idealised form helps us to understand its aspirations and working principles, but we should also acknowledge that, as with other theoretical models, it is unlikely that we will find it operating in its pure form in any particular real-world setting. Nonetheless, it is helpful to use this as a starting point in order for us to be able to tease out the implications and to consider how the different, pure positions could, and do, interact in the administration of criminal justice as it is realised in practice.

Efficiency, or fairness?

Packer suggests that the crime control model, given its underlying aspiration to protect fundamental freedoms (for the law abiding), is in the first instance to be judged according to the 'efficiency' with which it operates to identify suspects, achieve findings of guilt, and ensure appropriate **disposals** are imposed. Speed of response to an alleged crime and certainty of outcome, in terms of detection and court disposals, are viewed as central to effective crime control. As Packer observes, 'efficiency' often significantly determines actual practices, to the extent that it, necessarily, shapes the capacity and operation of enforcement agencies. In this respect, routine procedures and speed and informality of operation might all be beneficial attributes of the justice system, in that they increase efficiency. As Packer famously noted, the 'image that comes to mind is an assembly line or conveyor belt down which moves an endless stream of cases', on which a predictable series of operations is performed to produce 'a finished product, or, to exchange the metaphor for the reality, a closed file' (1964: 11).

In this respect, then, a crime control approach is in clear contrast to what Packer describes as the 'Due Process Model', which places much more emphasis on the fair administration of justice and fair treatment of those believed to be responsible for committing crime. According to this position, if the judicial system is to claim the authority to administer punishment, then it must be able to justify this in the quality, fairness, and legitimacy of the fact-finding and adjudication processes which support this: 'If the Crime Control Model resembles an assembly line, the Due Process Model looks very much like an obstacle course' (Packer, 1964: 13). **Figures 27.2** and **27.3** provide a visual metaphor to help you remember the fundamental principles behind the crime control model (the factory line) and the due process model (the obstacle course).

Stopping crime, or protecting individual rights?

Underlying these two perspectives are quite different understandings of society's best interests and the central purposes of the criminal justice system. Under the crime control model, the principal objective is to maintain security,

Figure 27.2 Packer compared the crime control model to an assembly line— like the one in this factory

Source: Hamick/Shutterstock.com

Figure 27.3 Packer likened the due process model to an obstacle course
Source: CA Eccles/Shutterstock.com

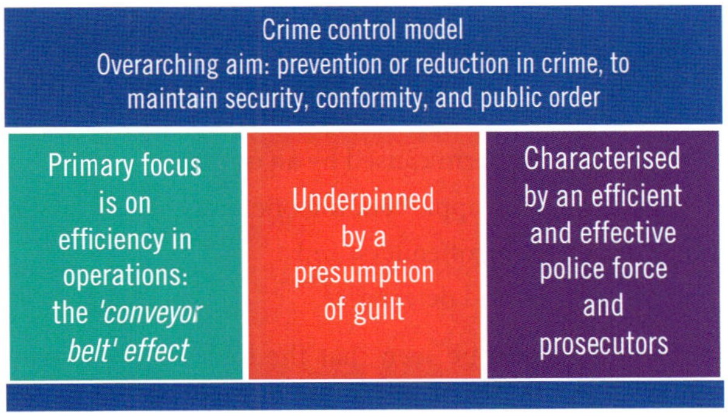

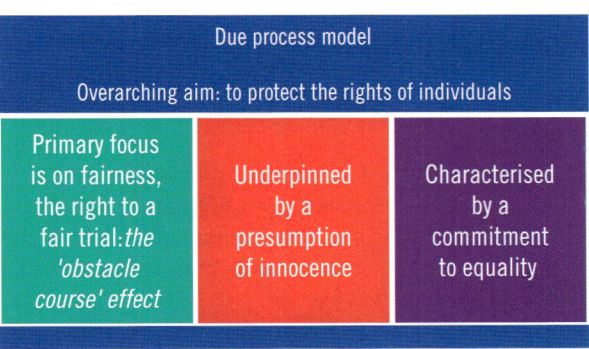

Figure 27.5 The due process model—summarised here—pays more attention than the crime control model to the rights of the individual

Figure 27.4 The main objective of the crime control model—summarised here—is to maintain security, conformity, and public order

conformity, and public order (see **Figure 27.4**), whilst the due process model pays greater attention to the rights of the individual, even as an alleged offender (Roach, 1999) (see **Figure 27.5**). As Roach observes, the operational emphasis of the crime control model is quite distinctive, in that very substantial weight is placed on the establishment and maintenance of an efficient and effective police force able to act quickly and decisively to investigate and respond to instances of law breaking or disorder, and to do so decisively without undue constraints. So, for example, the police should be able to require citizens to produce evidence of their identity or lawful activities to the extent that this will enable them to identify potential wrongdoers—we should expect our civil liberties to be restricted in this manner in the interest of social stability and personal safety:

> The police should have wide powers to conduct searches because only the factually guilty have something to hide. Illegally seized evidence should be admissible at trial. Unlike coerced confessions, guns, drugs and stolen property reveal the truth no matter how the police obtained them.
>
> (Roach, 1999: 678)

Roach does caution us against concluding that this represents a 'thuggish model that is unconcerned with police abuse' (1999: 678)—rather, this is viewed almost as a separate issue from the central question of whether the guilty are properly identified and held to account for their behaviour. Like the police, the prosecutor should be trusted to act consistently and effectively in evaluating evidence and determining guilt, and the roles of the judiciary and the jury system are relatively less important, because we can expect that this preparatory work will be sufficient in the vast majority of cases, without the need to go to trial.

In this idealised version of the criminal process, there is relatively little merit in establishing elaborate mechanisms for allowing criminal charges to be contested or findings of guilt challenged on appeal. Of course, extending the logic of this perspective would point towards the rather more controversial conclusion that the occasional mistake might be acceptable if it means that in the great majority of cases crimes are being prevented, criminals apprehended, and effective measures are put in place to ensure that further offending is minimised.

Take a look at **What do you think? 27.1** to consider the issues in relation to the use of evidence.

The principal focus of an approach driven by a crime control agenda is, therefore, the establishment of a criminal justice system which is best placed to identify criminals and potential criminals, to assess and take action to respond to potential threats to community safety or public order, and to intervene to ensure that the potential for future crime is kept to a minimum. In delivery terms, the emphasis is therefore on well-organised, well-resourced, proactive policing, effective identification of risk, comprehensive measures to ensure public safety, rapid and effective responses to crime and disorder, and efficient mechanisms of containment and control for those identified as perpetrators of crime (or representing a future risk of offending). Swift and robust intervention lies at the heart of this philosophy of criminal justice.

> ### WHAT DO YOU THINK? 27.1
>
> #### UK vs US
>
> Conventionally, in the UK, courts have been willing to accept credible evidence even if it has been obtained illegally (see Jackson, 2013, for example). On the other hand, in the US, if evidence is obtained unlawfully it cannot be submitted in court.
>
> This suggests a clear distinction between the two jurisdictions with the UK favouring a 'crime control' perspective in this instance, and the US reflecting 'due process' principles in this aspect of the administration of justice.
>
> - How do you think the courts should deal with evidence which may be significant but may also have been obtained by unacceptable means?
> - What are the arguments for and against permitting use of such evidence in criminal trials?

27.3 Objectives of crime control

The operating principles of crime control models

Having set out a model of criminal justice practice which is grounded in an underlying logic of 'crime control', our next step will be to consider the operating principles of such a model, that is to say, what it is intended or expected to achieve. In one sense, this may seem self-evident in that its aim is to minimise or eradicate crime in all its forms; that is, it is a manifestation of the principle of 'zero tolerance' of antisocial or unlawful behaviour. The crime control model also supports anticipatory action to prevent or minimise harm; alongside direct intervention to reduce its immediate effect and measures taken to prevent its reoccurrence (we will discuss some examples of this later in the chapter, including target hardening and deterrent sentences). The challenge of implementation does become somewhat more complicated, though, when we start applying abstract principles to concrete situations. In practice, the police have to make 'real world' decisions about how best to allocate their available resources, such as the choices they might have to make between targeting 'known' offenders or trouble spots, or being ready to respond rapidly to instances of crime and disorder in progress wherever they occur.

Crime control is, indeed, expected to achieve its goals in a number of different ways and, in so doing, to serve several distinct objectives, including:

- reassuring the public;
- preventing crime;
- directly controlling disorder in progress;
- minimising harm caused by an offence;
- detecting and apprehending offenders;
- incapacitating offenders; and
- corrections and deterrence.

In this way, it can be seen that the logic of crime control as an operating principle might be expected to run throughout the cycle of intervention from the pre-crime phase to the continuing effects of actions intended to reduce the possibility of the repetition of crime and further harm.

Target hardening and defensible space

Considered in this way, we might also argue that crime control strategies are likely to be varied and ambitious. Its focus includes, but extends beyond, the individual offender, to include the context and consequences of crime. Its starting point, therefore, might be seen as the denial of opportunity, and the work that often goes under the heading of 'target hardening'. Target hardening is a form of situational crime prevention (for a fuller account of situational crime prevention, see **Chapter 26**) which is also linked to the idea of 'defensible space'. Target hardening, as the phrase suggests, aims to make the physical act of committing crime increasingly difficult, if not impossible. Most of us probably employ a form of 'target hardening' a number of times every day—secure passwords for phones or Wi-Fi, padlocks on our bikes, front door locks, car security devices, and so on.

Figure 27.6 This housing development in Barking, London, displays some of the key characteristics of defensible space: clearly demarcated spaces, windows that face public areas, and well-maintained buildings to avoid the appearance of vulnerability
Source: Hufton+Crow-VIEW/Alamy Stock Photo

Managing and regulating the environment

Similarly, the idea of **defensible space** assumes that crime can effectively be designed out of the living environment, particularly in urban areas (see **Figure 27.6**):

> One of the more widely known and enthusiastically received theories in the field of man-environment relations is the idea of defensible space: the notion that crime can be controlled through environmental design.
>
> (Merry, 1981: 397)

According to this line of argument, it is possible to build into the physical design of communal areas, 'spaces which are easily observed, clearly demarcated as public or private' (1981: 397), and which can become identified by and for community members as their own 'territory' which, supplemented by human security personnel, can be defended effectively from the impact of crime:

> Defensible space is a design concept consisting of four features: the definition of a space which demarcates areas of influence of the inhabitants and creates territorial attitudes, the positioning of windows to allow natural surveillance of public areas, the adoption of building forms and idioms which avoid the stigma of peculiarity and the suggestion of vulnerability, and the location of developments away from areas that provide continued threat.
>
> (Merry, 1981: 398)

Moving beyond ideas associated with the establishment of orderly and safe environments, and partly because of the unpredictability of human behaviour, we can also identify 'crime control' as being about the management of people and their actions, not least to ensure that the space for regular and conventional social interaction remains secure. Business relies on the certainty of people being able to access commercial premises or park safely in the vicinity. So, crime control is concerned with regulating the actions and movement of people in space.

We may observe interesting parallels here with a quite different criminological **concept**: that of **Bentham's Panopticon**, the prison design drawn up by Jeremy Bentham in 1787 which was intended to provide an effective vehicle for monitoring and controlling all aspects of the convict's behaviour (see **Figure 12.5**), characterised by high visibility and surveillance of communal areas as a way of maintaining order, albeit *within* the prison rather than outside.

Physical design, then, is one means by which the possibility of criminal or antisocial behaviour can be anticipated and pre-empted, and quickly identified when it does occur, in the interests of maintaining harmony and security in the everyday lives of community members. Of course, as with any such preventive measures, there is another side to this; by defining effective 'ownership' of space which is supposedly communal, and by simultaneously effectively prescribing what (and who) is acceptable, the creation of defensible space also creates a concept of what (and who) is to be defined as unacceptable and defended against. The presence of 'kids hanging round' and infringing on the sense of orderliness, just by being there, may contribute to a sense of fearfulness and threat; simply in the way that it is treated as being out of the ordinary, and because it does not comply with ideas about how public space should be managed and used.

Control through incapacitation

Although the preceding example raises awkward questions about rights of access to public places, it does shift the focus on to a further logical function of a 'crime control' approach; that is, the incapacitation of offenders or potential offenders. This can be achieved straightforwardly by imposing direct limits on identified offenders' freedom—by means of imprisonment or less reliable alternatives such as wearable 'tags' and curfews; or it can be achieved through the use of general prohibitions, such as powers of crowd dispersal or the creation of 'no go' areas. See **Figure 27.7** depicting the practice of 'kettling' demonstrators by police (controlling large crowds by confining them in a small area) which has become a controversial issue in recent years. Is this crime control or a more oppressive form of state coercion?

In this sense, crime control strategies aim to identify and eradicate specific threats, applying risk-based assessments of where threats to public order exist and which members of the population are most likely to present this kind of threat. Measures of control are supported by techniques of risk identification and quantification—linked in turn to judgements about the most efficient and effective use of resources. Their specific application also depends on wider mediating influences associated with considerations of political expediency, public accountability, and policy priorities. O'Malley (2010) has argued that the emergence of 'risk' as a driver of criminal justice practices was first acknowledged as a significant development during the 1980s. This reflected a shift in the priorities of those concerned with the administration of criminal justice away from understanding and attempting to modify offenders' behaviour towards a more restricted interest in dealing with their behaviour simply in its own terms. That is to say, the priority became one of assessing the likelihood and impact of crime and taking action to minimise the harm associated with this (Smith, 2006).

In the same vein, the final objective of crime control as an operating principle of criminal justice is to eradicate, or at least cut down, the level of risk by reducing the possibility of further offending. In this respect, interventions are driven by the threefold aims of: corrections, that is, changing offenders' behaviour so that it becomes socially desirable and conforming; containment, in the sense of incapacitation; or, deterrence, in which case, irrespective of their motivations, current offenders (or potential future offenders) will be dissuaded from reoffending in light of the potential costs to them.

We might summarise the purposes of crime control as revolving around the idea of 'risk' or 'threat' and how this is averted, managed, minimised, or removed. Following on from this, we might also want to consider questions such as who or what might be the object of any such risks or threat, and how judgements are made as to whose interests should take priority in determining how to organise and deliver effective crime control strategies. Is there a trade-off, for example in terms of dedicating police resources to crowd control at top-level football games, or preventing shoplifting, or responding to calls about racist attacks or domestic violence? And on what basis could such judgements be made? These questions, in turn, prompt a wider consideration and this demonstrates the extent to which an apparently neutral term such as crime control represents a range of judgements

Figure 27.7 The police practice of 'kettling' (controlling large crowds by confining them in a small area) has become controversial in recent years

Source: Gavin Rodgers/Alamy Stock Photo

and choices at different points in the social and political structure which themselves are necessarily selective. That is to say, apparently unproblematic calculations about what constitutes the most significant risk to community safety and public order are themselves based on prior assumptions about common community interests and whose safety and security should be prioritised, as well as who represents the most significant threat. Particular understandings of risk, and of the need to control it, become normalised and, in turn, certain types of troubling behaviour become priority targets, whereas other, perhaps equally concerning, forms of unacceptable activity do not come under the spotlight. So, as well as asking 'what' is crime control for, we also need to think about 'whose' interests it serves.

27.4 The role of the police in crime control

When we start to think about tackling crime and the responsibility for doing so, the police are probably the first body to come to mind. Certainly until relatively recently developed societies have tended to see the police as the exclusive authority for maintaining order and controlling crime, although historically many societies have functioned without an equivalent role: 'The concept of policing is closely related to that of social control' (Newburn and Reiner, 2007: 913).

Despite the growing role of private provision and an increasing emphasis on self-help, for most people, most of the time, the routine responsibility for preventing and responding to crime and antisocial behaviour still rests with the police, whose legitimacy derives from their status as a public body acting under the authority of the state.

Their duties in this respect are generalised and involve a number of distinct functions, including anticipatory action, immediate response, monitoring, and surveillance. Approaches to how they control crime will therefore differ, depending on the specific task in hand, and the priorities set for them by way of organisational and policy demands. A recent overview suggests that the approach to dealing with crime adopted by the police is not fixed but varies according to the expectations placed on them ('politicians and the public still expect and demand a police service that focuses on fighting crime': Karn, 2013: 3), the emerging evidence as to what is 'effective' in practice, and the resources available to them. Sometimes this may also mean engaging the community in crime control partnerships, as **New frontiers 27.1** illustrates.

NEW FRONTIERS 27.1

Using volunteers to keep communities safe

Volunteers are helping to keep their communities safe by working in partnership with the police. Indeed, Neighbourhood Watch has been a feature of many localities for some time, originating in New York in the 1960s. In 2007, the Home Office established the Neighbourhood Watch Network to provide an umbrella organisation for local groups in the UK.

Other more informal community groups with similar objectives have also been established in response to specific local problems of criminal activity or antisocial behaviour. According to a newspaper report from Stockton-on-Tees (in North-East England), a group of volunteer street patrollers have issued the warning 'we are out, we are watching and we will report to the police'. The team from the local Residents Association responded in the middle of night after a perimeter alarm system was triggered at one property in the area; they watched the suspects and kept the police control room updated about the suspects' location which, along with CCTV evidence, led to two men being charged.

A spokesman for the Residents Association told the paper:

> The Volunteer Street Patrol operates every evening, patrolling the streets of Low Hartburn in an attempt to reduce crime and to allow residents to be able to sleep safely in their beds. They also provide an emergency response to incidents assisting and supporting Cleveland Police. The street patrols were set up following an increase in crime in the area and since they have started we have seen a crime reduction.
>
> (www.gazettelive.co.uk/news/teesside-news/were-watching-warn-stocktons-volunteer-16029458)

Thinking about this example, we can see that the involvement of local volunteers may be helpful to the police in adding to their capacity and providing a quicker response to criminal incidents. On the other hand, should we be concerned that lack of training might expose the volunteers to risk themselves or that certain individuals or groups within the community may become targeted unfairly as potential suspects?

Conventionally, it is suggested, the police have adopted an approach to crime control which principally derived from theories of deterrence. By being visible and catching criminals, they have been assumed to achieve the dual functions of solving crimes that are committed and discouraging further offending. In order to achieve these aims, the police mainly relied on 'random patrols, emergency response, stop and search, investigation and detection and intensive enforcement.... Evidence from research, however, suggests that these strategies are relatively ineffectual in reducing crime and detecting offenders' (Karn, 2013: 3). See **What do you think? 27.2** for a more detailed consideration of stop and search.

Currently, approaches to policing have become more diverse, according to competing ideas about how best to balance a range of responsibilities and expectations. Karn (2013) suggests, for example, that policing strategies have more recently been influenced by principles of 'risk' identification and management; in effect, by shifting the focus of attention towards 'specific individuals (prolific offenders and repeat victims) and places (high crime areas)'. That is to say, the police concentrate their efforts on those people and contexts which are particularly likely to be the focal point of criminal activity (Kennedy et al., 2018). Two strategies which illustrate this approach are 'hotspot' policing and 'focused deterrence' of potential offenders.

'Hotspot' policing refers to targeting particular areas that are thought to be 'hotspots' for crime. This kind of 'targeted' approach was at least partly inspired by prior evidence of the 'limited impact of random patrol, reactive and intensive enforcement on crime rates' (Karn, 2013: 14), which prompted the emergence of initiatives such as the Minneapolis Hot Spots Experiment. In this case, 'focusing interventions' on the 'micro-locations' responsible for the greatest concentration of police calls delivered 'clear, if modest, general deterrent effects' (Karn 2013: 14). Policing interventions are also increasingly effective where a problem-focused approach responds directly to the worries and fears of the community, Karn observes (2013: 19).

'Focused deterrence' (Karn, 2013: 17) is where police concentrate their efforts on known or repeat offenders, with the aim of increasing the level of 'certainty' in their minds that further offending will inevitably come to the attention of the police and will be dealt with swiftly and severely. Once again, it seems, the value of this approach is borne out by research evidence (of the deterrent effects of heightening offenders' belief in the likelihood of being caught; Karn, 2013: 18).

Zero-tolerance policing and its influence

The term 'zero tolerance' has become firmly established in our understanding of a particular stance taken in relation to evidence of wrongdoing, not necessarily criminality, but rule breaking of one kind or another, such as breaches of school discipline (Curran, 2019). The rationale behind this position is that prompt and certain action achieves the objectives of both containing and limiting any harm caused, and symbolising the broader societal rejection of unacceptable behaviour. As Newburn and Jones (2007) demonstrate, the term itself has come to be applied in a range of contexts, such as the US President, George W. Bush's arguably ill-advised comments warning against law

WHAT DO YOU THINK? 27.2

Stop and search: police powers

A police officer has powers to stop and search you if they have 'reasonable grounds' to suspect you're carrying:

- illegal drugs;
- a weapon;
- stolen property;
- something which could be used to commit a crime, such as a crowbar.

See www.gov.uk/police-powers-to-stop-and-search-your-rights, and discussions of 'stop and search' in **Chapters 3** and **10**.

The allegedly arbitrary use of police powers of 'stop and search' has caused considerable controversy over the years, leading to accusations of oppressive and discriminatory practice.

On the other hand, some claim that these powers are of great value to the police in enabling them to anticipate crime, from the minor to the extremely serious, and this justifies their use of this power.

Do you think that the use of 'stop and search' can be justified, even if it means that innocent people will inevitably be subjected to this experience?

breaking in the aftermath of Hurricane Katrina in 2005; and, subsequently, the then Home Secretary Theresa May was reported to be taking a zero-tolerance approach to illegal immigration (*Daily Telegraph*, 25 May 2012). Others, too, have adopted the term enthusiastically, including Superintendent Ray Mallon in the North-East of England. The term was also applied by the Trump Administration to migrants accused of crossing the Mexico–US border illegally (*The Guardian* online, 2019). Zero tolerance seems to have gained widespread use as a form of shorthand for firm and decisive action by enforcement agencies to prevent criminal or antisocial behaviour (Newburn and Jones, 2007: 222).

According to Newburn and Jones, the origins of the term lie in the 1980s and the Reagan Administration's war on drugs in the US, subsequently being picked up and applied in a number of policy domains by George Bush Snr, on becoming president. The direct application of the term in the law enforcement arena is attributed to the New York Police Department under William Bratton, from 1994 onwards.

The argument behind the term 'zero tolerance' was that communities in New York and other major cities had become too passive and accepting of routine infractions of public order, which then translated into a broader normalisation of crime. It was believed to be something which was just an undesirable fact of life, like bad weather. To redress the balance, advocates of zero tolerance argued that any manifestation of antisocial behaviour should be stopped at source to provide both practical and symbolic reinforcement of the idea that unlawful behaviour at any level was not acceptable. The strategy adopted involved taking immediate action to put a stop to any infringement of the law, however trivial, reinstate any harm or damage caused, and take strong measures to prevent any repetition. At the same time, a robust and reliable body of statistical knowledge would be built up to inform targeted interventions by the police, based on a 'management information and control system for regulating and directing policing at precinct level—Compstat' (Newburn and Jones, 2007: 226). Of course, one of the consequences of this 'aggressive' policing strategy was inevitably a change in the relationship between the police and the community, and this may have been why this approach has proved controversial in the UK and elsewhere (Crichlow, 2016; Fraser et al., 2018).

It seems that this idea gained limited support amongst the wider ranks of the police, with some being openly critical of its likely impact on police–community relations. Alongside this, though, the concept did prove attractive in political circles, offering a ready-made slogan to politicians seeking to maintain or establish their credentials as being 'tough on crime'.

This period of political grandstanding in the UK was 'ushered in' by senior figures in the Labour Party (Newburn and Jones, 2007: 228), who went on to play a leading part in the government that took power in 1997. It is wryly observed that: 'Continued sightings of the term are testimony to its enduring power and resonance' (Newburn and Jones, 2007: 229). And these characteristics in turn can be attributed to certain attractive features of the idea of zero tolerance: 'it is an apparently simple notion; . . . it is flexible—it has no fixed meaning; . . . it has strong symbolic potential; . . . in policy terms it became associated with a clear "meta-narrative; and . . . it resonates with contemporary concerns"' (2007: 234). In practical terms, it is also argued that it is an approach that works, with zero-tolerance policies and practices being widely credited for achieving substantial reductions in crime and greater public confidence, especially in New York itself, during the 1990s; although such claims have also been the subject of detailed criticism (see Bowling, 1999, for example).

Whilst the term 'zero tolerance' itself has been less prominent in policing, more recently it has been argued that the methodologies that it foreshadowed and underpinned have continued to exert a considerable influence on policing practices (Braga et al., 2011; Fraser et al., 2018). The idea of focusing police energies on countering criminality through the use of systematic tools, such as the planning and management system known as Compstat, for measuring trends and changing patterns of crime, has remained influential (Silverman and Eterno, 2019). However, there has also been a substantial degree of criticism of the pervasive impact of this philosophy (Weisburd et al., 2019). Zero-tolerance strategies are also widely deployed in schools to address both classroom misbehaviour and bullying. However, such approaches are criticised for creating an undue focus on criminality in the school environment and, as a result, helping to institutionalise a form of school-based racism (Ofer, 2011).

As the idea of an expanded crime management role for the police has taken hold, police forces have acknowledged a parallel need to move away from a preoccupation with detecting crimes to one which incorporates a much wider crime control function (Braga et al., 2011: 29). Regardless of the development of more sophisticated arguments, simplistic terminology still plays a part, offering a kind of political comfort blanket at times of crisis: 'We haven't talked the language of zero tolerance enough but the message is getting through', said the UK Prime Minister following the 'riots' in English cities in 2011 (*Daily Telegraph*, 3 August 2011), as he recruited William Bratton to advise him on how to deal with the problem. Consider the issues raised in a newspaper report on Bratton's more recent visit to the UK in **What do you think? 27.3**.

WHAT DO YOU THINK? 27.3

Learning from others' experience?

In March, 2019, *The Sun* reported that William Bratton has suggested that his 'zero tolerance' approach could be effective against knife crime in the UK. Take a look at some quotes from the article and consider the issues they raise.

> Bill Bratton is a legend among US law enforcement for overseeing drastic reductions in crime in New York and LA . . .
>
> In New York, Bratton, 71 used high tech data gathering techniques to identify when and where crime was taking place and who was committing it.
>
> It would identify trends and when there were four low-level incidents cops would be deployed to nip things in the bud before they turned violent.

How easy do you think it would be to transfer a policy idea from one country to another? What problems could you envisage, in general?

> Now, after a man was stabbed to death in London last night, and two 17-year-olds, Jodie Chesney and Yousef Makki, were killed in separate horrific incidents over the weekend, Bratton believes the UK is on the edge of a precipice, with parallels to the dark days of 1980s New York.

Do you think comparisons of this kind are valid, given the geographical and historical distance between 1980s New York and 2020s London?

> But he IS convinced there is a way back from the brink . . .:
>
> The knife issues you're dealing with are just reflective of what I would describe as the eyeball of a storm that's been gathering for several years in your country.
>
> It is quite clear that you have police forces that are at a very low morale position.
>
> You also have a changed society with more drug issues. You've got a very large mixed youth population. You're a country going through a lot of demographic change.
>
> To prevent serious crime, you must prevent crime and disorder.
>
> (*The Sun*, 7 March 2019)

Do you think this might mean that particular communities are targeted? What problems might be associated with that kind of approach?

Intelligence-led policing

Intelligence-led policing (Ratcliffe, 2016) is distinguished, as the term might suggest, by the apparent need to develop a more systematic and evidence-based approach to dealing with crime. It developed in response to:

- a perception that historic methods were simply inadequate to deal with rising crime and public expectations;
- wider expectations of a more professional approach to management across the public services;
- the availability of methods and technology which should facilitate greater efficiency; and
- a feeling that criminals were becoming more sophisticated and better organised, necessitating an equivalent response from justice agencies.

So intelligence-led policing has come to be recognised as a distinct approach to law enforcement relying on very specific crime reduction objectives (Ratcliffe, 2016: 271). Police activities within an intelligence-led framework are underpinned by systematic analysis of available information, offender targeting (based on known characteristics), and strategic use of resources to anticipate or respond to identified crime problems. This approach is largely proactive, and by anticipating crime and disorder it might be seen as problematic from a civil liberties perspective (Sellers and Arrigo, 2018); but, of course, it is consistent with an overarching concern to prioritise crime reduction and thereby protect the public (Farmer, 1984). Despite this, public support for policing tactics of this kind cannot be taken for granted (Geller et al., 2018: 28). In one survey of community perceptions in New York, it has been found that people 'are sensitive to police legitimacy' and that this depends on levels of trust afforded to the police. Differences in perception were also related to ethnic differences in this study and 'Respondents reporting that the police stop a lot or almost all of the young people in their neighbourhoods' are also less willing to tolerate police 'misconduct' (Geller et al., 2018: 21).

Community policing

The idea of community policing appears to take a very different starting point to defining the role of the police and their relationship with the citizens they serve. It is associated with an underlying belief in the importance of establishing good relations between the police and the public. The central function of the police may, indeed, be less about crime fighting and the maintenance of order, and more about providing a sense of security and reassurance to ordinary people, reducing their fears about crime rather than prioritising its actual incidence. Nonetheless, a community policing philosophy can also be seen as contributing to various aspects of a 'crime control' approach through actively discouraging wrongdoing by being highly visible in the neighbourhood. Community policing is described as a customer-led approach, directed towards establishing partnerships with community interests to assist the community to both prevent and detect crime as well as decreasing levels of fear and improving the quality of life (Longstaff et al., 2015: 9).

Close knowledge of the locality and its inhabitants provides a potential source of intelligence for the police, in terms of being able to identify potentially risky situations and early signs of problematic behaviour. In this respect, being visible and 'present' in the community seems to afford a greater degree of awareness and preparation to police at the point where they might need to respond to incidents of crime or antisocial behaviour. There is also a potential 'pay-off' to the extent that the community subjectively feels better protected, almost irrespective of the impact of this policing strategy on crime. Some studies support the argument that a visible police presence alone can boost public confidence and satisfaction with the level of police effectiveness (Mackenzie and Henry, 2009: 5).

Problem-oriented policing

Problem-oriented policing also adopts a clear focus on the concerns of the community about crime and disorder. Its principles were initially set out and later expanded upon by Herman Goldstein (1979, 1990). The intention was to move away from perceived inefficiencies in trying to apply a standardised and labour-intensive model of policing across a diverse and increasingly challenging range of demands.

> The public calls upon the police to respond to an astounding range of problems and to perform an extraordinary diversity of tasks, all the while assuming that police have the expertise and resources to do so. Many of these problems and tasks fall to the police through the default of others: from gaps in government services, to the abandonment of responsibility by private citizens, corporations, and other organizations. This has always been a concern. In recent years, through a more methodical approach to policing, police are increasingly pressing for a more rational distribution of responsibilities based upon a detailed examination of the differing facets of police business.
>
> (Scott and Goldstein, 2005)

The idea of using available knowledge about risks and vulnerabilities, communities and their residents, and observable patterns of behaviour to focus efforts on providing efficient and effective responses to persistent problems is clearly highly attractive (Tilley, 2010: 183). In a context of increasing demand and stretched resources, it seems quite reasonable to target effort on the most acute problems and to use trusted methods to tackle them.

Tilley notes the expansion of interest in problem-oriented policing in the UK as well as the US, and also observes that as ideas about responsibility for crime control have shifted, the police have become seen as 'partners' in the task of achieving crime reduction, rather than taking sole responsibility for this.

One systematic review of problem-oriented policing has found that studies consistently identified a positive effect associated with policing strategies based on these principles (Weisburd et al., 2010: 140), although the researchers also noted that these benefits were fairly modest on average (2010: 162).

Neighbourhood policing

Neighbourhood policing is described as a further development of the principles of community policing (Longstaff et al., 2015: 10). The aim of those promoting this model was to enhance the level of police engagement with the community further, but also to incorporate elements of other policing approaches which could contribute to improved performance and better outcomes. The 'foot patrol' is at the heart of neighbourhood policing not least because of its capacity to conjure up an image of a friendly and available public servant always on hand to offer protection and reassurance. Alongside this, though, neighbourhood policing offers a number of other elements which are more directly geared towards dealing with crime, including 'hotspots policing' which, as described earlier in this chapter, focuses on 'micro-locations' where particular problems of offending or antisocial behaviour are concentrated (Longstaff et al., 2015: 22). These sites could be subject to intensified police activity, heightened surveillance (in the form of CCTV), and environmental measures to provide a coherent and integrated strategy.

This approach is also linked to problem-oriented policing, in that it tries to relate to the most acute problems of law and order affecting communities, in order to target interventions more effectively:

> The model requires a thorough analysis of the causes of crime and disorder, identifying strategies for intervention (beyond law enforcement) and involving other agencies and the community in delivering them. It also requires checking whether the intended benefits have accrued.
>
> (Longstaff et al., 2015: 26)

Here, in effect, we can see intelligence-based approaches being tailored to local contexts and very specific problems, where connected patterns of offending can be identified;

sometimes, however, the implementation process has been found to be somewhat flawed, especially in terms of the quality of analysis applied (Tilley, 2010).

One study of neighbourhood policing has identified significant benefits in terms of community perceptions and a sense of empowerment (Turley et al., 2012), although there is some evidence that others have found the police to be somewhat unresponsive to community members when engaging with them (Longstaff et al., 2015).

The police as moral guardians

The police act by their presence as a reminder of social expectations and the consequences of infringement. In addition to their direct impact on behaviour, through their crime control activities, there are other ways in which they exercise a more nuanced and indirect influence. Of course, they are mandated with the task of investigating crimes and bringing offenders to justice but their crime control functions also extend beyond this, in the sense of exerting a more generalised influence over particular populations, communities, or events. This influence can be seen to operate in a number of ways, both by setting the moral agenda and by defining which crimes and misdemeanours are to be taken most seriously. Indeed, it may be that their role in maintaining a sense of order and responsibility is as important to the public as their actual interventions to ensure public safety. As such: 'Across England and Wales, the police may not primarily be seen as providers of a narrow sense of personal security, held responsible for crime and safety. Instead the police may stand as symbolic "moral guardians" of social stability and order, held responsible for community values and informal social controls' (Jackson and Bradford, 2009: 493).

Reiner (2000: xi) has argued that the perceived effectiveness of the police depends not so much on what they do but on their role as acting as the guarantors of social order, acting as a kind of back-up to the everyday informal controls through which social institutions 'regulate most potential deviance'. When the police do become active, though, they cannot be everywhere at once, so they are engaged in an active process of prioritising their work and deciding where to commit time and resources. In this sense, policing becomes directly implicated in determining the nature and purposes of crime control. In other words, the symbolic function of the police associated with their actions helps to determine and then reinforce wider views about what is acceptable behaviour, and which elements of the population represent the most significant threats to social order. And this can, in turn, become controversial, since it may involve practices and outcomes which will be open to question, such as the disproportionate use of police powers in relation to particular ethnic groups (see **Chapter 10**) or decisions about how to maintain public order which might involve restrictions on freedom of movement or freedom of expression, as in the case of climate protests, for example. In one notable case, Stephen Gough, the 'naked rambler', has been arrested 'dozens of times' according to BBC News (October 2014), resulting in a cumulative total of over eight years in prison at substantial cost to the public purse—this is 'crime control' in action and, by taking this action, the police are helping to define, or at least reinforce, the moral boundaries of society.

27.5 The role of other agencies and interests in crime control

As you may have gleaned from the preceding sections, crime control philosophies tend to make assumptions about the rationality of human behaviour and the technical nature of the problems associated with crime. Essentially, the crime control perspective relies on a belief that it is possible to develop a systematic and predictable understanding of how crime comes about and who the offenders are. This, in turn, suggests that it is possible to use that understanding to develop structures, systems, and mechanisms which are capable of maintaining or restoring an ordered universe where the threat of crime is minimised or even eradicated.

In Philip K. Dick's science fiction novel *Minority Report*, this is taken to its extreme, with every crime being anticipated by a group of 'precogs' who can see into the future, with punishments being imposed in anticipation of the offence. As in real life, though, as the story unfolds things turn out to be a bit more complicated . . . (no spoilers!).

Despite the unpredictable nature of real-life events, though, the belief that it is possible to take pre-emptive action to anticipate and avert crime is well established. This, in turn, has resulted in the development of a range of interventions, some geared towards making crime more difficult to commit and others directed at controlling the behaviour of actual (and potential) offenders. Therefore, crime control has often been framed in terms of securitising the physical environment, on the one hand, or constraining the behaviour of likely offenders, on the other. Here we will move on to consider some of the strategies which have been adopted to predict and deal with the threat of crime.

Planning out crime

'Target hardening' is a term to describe the process of making property and places more crime-proof, and we can think of obvious examples of this sort of strategy, such as car alarms or padlocks on the garden shed. Whilst people have probably always taken action of various sorts to safeguard their property, the origins of contemporary thinking about enhancing physical security and creating 'safe' places are attributed to the architect Oscar Newman (1972), and the idea of 'defensible space' (which we introduced earlier in this chapter). Newman believed that the way in which buildings and neighbourhoods were (or were not) designed could have a major effect on the safety and stability of community life:

> Crime control can be achieved by creating a situation in which it is possible for the potential victim to recognize in advance the potential criminal. . . . Design can facilitate the process of recognition. Rather than the device of uniformity of population, such a design enables a varied and mixed population to know and control its own territory, to distinguish who (in an apparently complex and anonymous urban space) is neighbour and who intruder.
>
> (Newman, 1972: 18)

Newman therefore argued that appropriately designed and secure housing provision ought to be available to all sectors of the population and not simply remain the privilege of those few who could afford it. Specific features of such defensible residential areas would include the capacity to 'observe the public areas' of housing developments (1972: 78), and clearly marked out territorial boundaries so that residents would feel a sense of belonging and responsibility for their own areas.

These assumptions made their way across the Atlantic and the concept of 'situational crime prevention' became popular with the UK Home Office (Tilley, 2002: 68), which launched the Safer Cities programme in 1988, involving the implementation of a range of 'target hardening' measures in a number of selected locations believed to be particularly prone to crime. So, for example, residents in certain 'disadvantaged areas' were offered the opportunity to increase the security of their homes through replacing doors or fitting locks and bolts (Tilley and Webb, 1994: 8). The evaluation of the scheme determined that such forms of target hardening, especially when focused on those most at risk (previous victims), did have some effect in reducing burglary levels (Tilley and Webb, 1994: 26; and see **Chapter 22**).

The contribution of 'environmental criminology' to debates on community safety and 'designing out crime' has become increasingly substantial over recent years, linked to arguments about what makes a community 'sustainable' and healthy:

> As a potential tool for delivering such outcomes, crime prevention through environmental design (CPTED) strategies, guidance and policies have become increasingly adopted throughout countries in the developed world and in many developing countries.
>
> (Cozens, 2011: 482)

However, concerns have been expressed about the strength of the evidence available to support the claim that crime can be 'planned out' of communities (2011: 499).

These observations shift our attention away from the built environment, and the physical and technological apparatus available for minimising or eradicating crime. The question here is not just about the efficacy of such measures, but also about the types of crime and human behaviour at which they are targeted. Essentially, security and design measures are concerned with crimes against property, whereas an overarching concern to control crime in general must take account of the many and diverse types of criminal behaviour, the huge range of human activities these represent; and so recognise the need to adopt a much greater variety of intervention strategies than simply manipulation of the physical environment. People are, of course, able to adopt their own forms of personal protection measures, such as weapons (in those jurisdictions such as the US where it is legal to do so), mobile devices which enable them to stay 'connected', or panic alarms (Westmarland et al., 2013). As such, in effect, part of the responsibility for controlling crime is transferred to the individual citizen, whether or not the individual concerned is considered to be at particular risk for any reason (such as age, gender, or disability).

Crime control therefore becomes a personal as well as a community matter, and this is reflected in the ways that the state devolves such responsibility, for instance through Neighbourhood Watch initiatives, public information briefings about cybersecurity, or the promotion of personal safety measures.

The role of the community in crime control

Noting that the responsibility for crime control has historically rested with the community, Bullock (2014) argues that recent trends have simply led to the 'rediscovery of the citizen' and, in particular, the re-emergence of an expectation that people will take responsibility for resolving crimes informally and without calling on the justice system. This,

Bullock (2014: 7) believes, is a historically specific development which increasingly represents 'a challenge to the view that crime control *should* be a state monopoly driven by expert fiat'; that is to say, where all the key assessments and decisions are made by recognised criminal justice professionals. Earlier models of crime control, such as those outlined by Packer (1964), tended to assume that the police would hold exclusive responsibility for identifying and tackling crime. Subsequent developments, though, have taken the wider view that citizens and communities both can and should take responsibility for managing and dealing with their own crime problems. This might be achieved partly through taking individual steps to avoid the risk of **victimisation**, but also partly through taking on a more proactive role as someone who 'discourages' crime (Felson, 1995) or who acts as a kind of 'guardian' of order (Reynald, 2010). Of course, the risks involved in taking on such a role must be acknowledged, both in terms of the potential harm a self-appointed 'guardian' might suffer, but also the possibility that such forms of intervention will lead to vigilantism and harm to 'innocent parties' (Roehl, 1998: 254). Importantly, though, for this perspective the rule of law is not seen as being diluted or compromised by the devolution of responsibility for maintaining order from the state to the community.

The role of private security providers

Even though we might still more readily think of the police as the appropriate resource when it comes to exercising active crime control measures, it is worth noting that this function may be fulfilled by a variety of private operators with a security-providing role (see **What do you think? 27.4** for an example). Zedner (2006: 268), for instance, has argued that the shift of emphasis from the 'solid state' of the established criminal justice system to the more flexible and 'dispersed' activities of the 'private security sector' is a reflection of wider social changes as markets come to pervade everyday life, even in what has historically been seen as the public sphere:

> successive governments have created a black hole that the private security industry is only too happy to plug and the state to see filled.
>
> (Zedner, 2006: 269)

Private security itself is a fragmented form of activity, featuring 'bouncers' whose role is to maintain public order (and protect the owners' property) in places of entertainment, security guards whose task is to protect physical

WHAT DO YOU THINK? 27.4

'Policing' Glastonbury

Read the following quote and then consider the questions below. Security firm AP Security describes the challenges of providing private security for the Glastonbury Festival, a major cultural event in the UK:

> Put nearly 140,000 people and hundreds of attractions—from the mainstream to the truly surreal—into several thousand acres of prime English farmland for a weekend and, without very carefully managed safety and stewarding, there's the potential for many problems. . . .
>
> 'It's a cliche to say that the planning for this year's event started as soon as last year's finished, but it's absolutely true,' says Andy Stevens, AP Security's general Manager. 'What you have to remember is that Glastonbury is effectively several major events encompassed within one perimeter fence. Each on its own would be a major undertaking for any event organiser, but combined they need massive amounts of very careful pre-planning.'
>
> The answer is threefold: firstly to ensure seamless communication and co-operation between the festival's organisers, the police and security firms. Second, to plan a long way ahead and, third, to divide the site into a number of zones, thus making the task more manageable.
>
> (IFSEC Global, 3 August 2009)

- Have you noticed a private security presence at any large events or festivals you have attended?
- If so, did you consider these security guards to be the same as police? Have you seen them act in a similar way to the police when dealing with issues? Do you think that these security guards have or should have the same level of authority as the police?
- Does it matter in terms of crime control if private security do not have the same powers as the police? Can they serve the same function by simply acting as though they have the right to control what people do?
- Depending on your answers to the above questions, is it actually efficient for private security to fulfil these kinds of roles in relation to what are essentially private functions, thus freeing the regular police to channel their resources elsewhere? Or do you agree with the implication of Zedner's comments that the widespread use of private security represents a failure on the part of government?

property, and others whose expertise is utilised to patrol and securitise the hidden worlds of the financial sector and information technology.

Whilst in most of these cases the rights of those acting to enforce the rule of law are no greater than those of ordinary members of the public, they do assert the authority to exercise control and dispense justice in the spaces and places for which they have assumed responsibility, such as gated-housing developments. Zedner's view is that the role of private security is increasingly problematic, as 'previously public functions are contracted out to private providers' and this is 'a cause of grave concern when private providers fail to accord with the standards expected of public servants' (Zedner, 2006: 272). **Controversy and debate 27.1** provides an example of why we might hold such concerns: in 2016, staff employed by the private security provider G4S were accused of abuse in a young offenders' centre in Kent.

Aside from this example, there are other concerns about the blurring of the distinction between privately and publicly provided forms of security and crime control—so 'elites' begin to organise and pay for their own 'forms of protection' in place of public provision (Loader et al., 2014: 480).

The role of the judiciary in crime control

In common with other elements of the criminal justice system, the judiciary is capable of adopting a range of objectives in its practice. Where crime control is the priority, courts will seek to use their powers to minimise the possibility of further crimes being committed, using a range of measures, both before and at the point of sentencing, to constrain, incapacitate, or deter known or likely future offenders. Those defendants who are believed to pose a continuing risk to the community are then liable to be made subject to a range of requirements intended in particular to limit their opportunities to offend. They can expect to be subject to curtailment of their freedom even before sentencing, by way of custodial remands, electronic surveillance, prohibitions of movement, or curfews, for example; and they will also be subject to sentences which aim to achieve the maximum effect, combining **deterrence** with measures intended to provide continuing safeguards, such as conditional release from custody. Consistent with this perspective, little attention is given to offenders' welfare or their rights. Neither of these carry the same weight as the question of whether or not the measures taken will protect the public and reduce the likelihood of further offences. The logic of crime control readily infuses the judicial process—as in the bald prescription of the Crime and Disorder Act 1998 that the 'principal aim' of the justice system is simply the prevention of offending.

Conditional sentences and periods on post-custodial licence can be viewed as good examples of the application of the logic of crime control to the judicial decision-making process. They offer the combined merits of exercising some measure of control over the offender's current behaviour, whilst also acting to discourage further offending, with the promise of future incapacitation in the event of failure to comply with their requirements. So, for

CONTROVERSY AND DEBATE 27.1

G4S and private security: controversial methods of maintaining discipline in youth custody

A BBC *Panorama* documentary, aired in 2016, accused private security provider G4S of abuse at a young offender's centre in Kent in the UK. Staff at the Medway Secure Training Centre are alleged to have:

- slapped a teenager several times on the head;
- pressed heavily on the necks of young people;
- used restraint techniques unnecessarily—and that included squeezing a teenager's windpipe so he had problems breathing;
- used foul language to frighten and intimidate—and boasted of mistreating young people, including using a fork to stab one on the leg and making another cry uncontrollably;

- tried to conceal their behaviour by ensuring they were beneath CCTV cameras or in areas not covered by them.

Four of the men were arrested on suspicion of child neglect. A fifth person was held on suspicion of assault, a police spokeswoman said.

Zedner's concerns around private providers and a drop in expected standards of security and treatment seem particularly pertinent in light of this example.

On the other hand, it has since been revealed (*The Guardian*, 16 December 2019) that 'unacceptable' pain-inducing restraints were still being used on children at the Medway centre even after G4S was stripped of its contract and the establishment was taken back into public control.

Perhaps these problems are less to do with who operates this type of regime, and more to do with the underlying nature of custodial institutions for children?

instance, when a court administers a **conditional discharge**, the offender is offered a bargain: if you don't reoffend during a specified period of time, you won't be punished. In this case, a positive incentive not to offend is offered, but its underlying purpose is still to reduce the possibility of further crimes being committed by the individual. Although they fall short of the complete loss of liberty, conditional sentences are intended to place very real constraints on offenders' freedoms. As Gemmell has pointed out, these could take a variety of forms:

> Conditional sentence orders could provide for such dispositions as home detention, electronic monitoring in the community and banishment to remote areas, at a much lower monetary cost to the community and personal cost to the accused than the ... cost of our current reliance on imprisonment.
>
> (Gemmell, 1996: 340)

Ironically, perhaps, this kind of imposition could actually be viewed as 'letting off' an offender if it takes the place of a prison sentence. As retribution is not a significant consideration for those occupied principally with controlling crime, the prospect of being seen as lenient may not be a major concern and financial considerations may also play a part.

The availability of conditional disposals has been welcomed by some commentators because the consequences of reoffending during the operational period are both 'known and certain' (Armstrong et al., 2013: 16).

We can see from this brief overview that the principles behind a 'crime control' approach to crime prevention and criminal justice permeate the whole continuum of policy and practice: from the starting point of 'crime-proofing' the lived environment, through security provision and surveillance, to the specific targeted interventions of agents of the justice system and judiciary. There is a strong spirit of rationalism and pragmatism about this orientation, in that the principal concern is to identify the most effective forms of intervention and apply them single-mindedly to securing the overarching objectives of containment, control, and harm reduction. If followed through to its conclusion, though, this line of reasoning might lead to significant concerns about the nature, practicality, proportionality, and indeed the legitimacy of the form of 'justice' being administered.

27.6 The objects and technologies of crime control

In this chapter, we have identified a distinctive strand of thought running through the various components of a 'crime control' approach to providing criminal justice, materialised in the 'instrumental [aim] of reducing or containing rates of criminal behaviour' (Garland, 1990: 18). Garland (1990: 126) argues that there is a distinctiveness and coherence to this perspective on criminality, which means that 'penal institutions and crime control policies have their own internal dynamics which cannot be regarded as expressions or reflections of events occurring elsewhere'. By this he means that the structures and operational logic of control systems are self-contained, and do not depend on external influences or political pressure to justify their processes or outcomes.

Implicated in these institutions and practices are a series of key assumptions, which can nevertheless be related to wider strands of social and political thought and underpin specific mechanisms for identifying and responding to criminal activities. Amongst these assumptions are an embedded view of the offender which stresses the 'freedom, equality and responsibility of the legal subject' (1990: 127) and a belief in the achievability of a 'scientific criminology' (1990: 127), which would enable both the probabilities of crime and effective interventions to be identified and calibrated to achieve maximum effectiveness. This, in turn, points towards and draws upon more generalised assumptions informing policy and practice in modern society, encapsulated effectively in Beck's (1992) characterisation of the *Risk Society*. According to Beck, ideas of measurable 'risk', developing scientific expertise, and the capacity for effective management, enable any identifiable threat to social structures and communal life to be dealt with as essentially a technical matter. This would apply equally to criminal activity, industrial failure, or a health epidemic. The potential for any particular adverse event or harm 'could be redefined as the probability of a negative outcome that was experienced equally by everyone in a defined group'; which could be precisely calculated and to which it was therefore possible 'to forge a complete solution' (Beck and Willms, 2004: 110).

Informed by these assumptions, then, those responsible for anticipating, preventing, managing, or eradicating crime are guided by a common belief in the capacity to calculate the probability of antisocial acts of one kind or another. Based on this, they would also assume the capability of devising and applying interventions with predictable effects and desirable outcomes. Crime could be predicted and controlled scientifically. It would be possible, for example, to identify and quantify the contextual triggers for crime, and thereby target these for specific practical responses. That is to say, the factors which lead to a specific offender committing a specific offence in a specific location should all be capable of precise calculation: 'Consideration of situational precipitators expands the range of techniques available for situational prevention and encourages crime prevention practitioners to think in a more focused way about the antecedents of behaviour' (Wortley, 2011: 63).

Predictive tools and techniques

The logic of this line of argument has prompted an increasing interest in developing the tools:

- to make reliable predictions about **criminogenic** environments, social contexts and events, or situations of conflict;
- to assess offenders' level of criminality and the future threat they might pose;
- to design, construct, test, and improve interventions to manage or reduce the risks identified in the preceding phases; and
- to organise and modify effective systems for administering and delivering these interventions.

On this basis, we could start by identifying, accounting for, and addressing specific 'patterns' of criminal activity (as in the crime pattern **theory** in **Chapter 26** (**section 26.4**)): 'Pattern theory sees crime as a complex phenomenon, but even assuming high degrees of complexity, finds discernible patterns both in criminal events and for criminals that are scale interdependent. That is, the rules behind the patterns can be found at both detailed and general levels of analysis' (Brantingham and Brantingham, 2011: 79). Techniques have been developed for 'mapping' crime and thereby identifying 'hotspots', which can be shown to have certain consistently identifiable criminogenic characteristics. It is increasingly easy to find out where we are and where we're going by the use of technology; and, similarly, geographic information systems (GIS) can analyse the incidence of crimes with a considerable degree of precision—although, of course, this does only apply to crimes which can be geographically located in this way, unlike fraud, say. Although there are competing theoretical explanations for the geographical concentration of criminal activity, such knowledge itself is clearly likely to influence policing policy and practice, and wider discussions about creating sustainable and safer communities.

As Anselin et al. (2011: 98) acknowledge, there are two types of theory offering explanations for the variable distribution of crimes by location: those which attribute this outcome to the 'routine' coincidence of 'suitable targets and motivated offenders' in time and space; and those which offer more structural and contextual explanations, based on the social and economic conditions underlying the emergence of patterns of crime and disorder in particular neighbourhoods (Anselin et al., 2011: 99). Nonetheless, the identification of patterns of criminal behaviour does suggest a discernible logic at work; an approach further developed in consideration of **repeat victimisation**; in drawing out the implications for policing and other protective interventions (Farrell and Pease, 2011); and in asserting the importance of 'designing out' crime when developing new products (Ekblom, 2011).

In the same way as 'place' and 'property' can be focuses of strategies grounded in principles of risk analysis and management, so can people. There seems to be a continuous thread of logic here, by which the vulnerabilities associated with location are bound up with the risks of victimisation, for example because people from particular ethnic backgrounds live in or travel through certain areas, or because there are particular places where people with disabilities are exposed to the risk of being victimised (Sin et al., 2009: 87). It is well known that particular sectors of the population are disproportionately likely to be the victims of crime (see, for example, Sin et al., 2009; Ministry of Justice, 2010; **Chapter 7** on victims and victimisation) and this might be seen to justify a 'problem oriented' (Scott et al., 2011) approach to policing the crimes experienced by minority groups.

Minimising the risk of reoffending

From the preceding discussion we can acknowledge the persuasive logic in favour of developing better techniques for assessing and dealing with offenders, once identified. In essence, the question is a simple one: how do we ensure that the risk of reoffending is minimised? The aim may be to prevent crime but the intended means of achieving this are very much about exerting direct control over potential offenders. The pure 'risk averse' answer would then be simply to incapacitate the perpetrator of the crime, but this does run into significant challenges in terms of capacity and resource-allocation, and (albeit of less concern to crime control purists) 'due process' and **natural justice**. Whilst preventive detention and indeterminate sentences have been made available to the courts from time to time, there are clearly still limits to their use (see **Controversy and debate 19.2**).

Additionally, the growing belief in the capacity of various risk assessment tools to predict future behaviour accurately has encouraged a pragmatic approach to offender management and punishment; with a balance struck between incapacitation, deterrence, and correctional interventions to secure the most cost-effective possible guarantee against further offending. As Merrington (2004) has pointed out, the idea of managing risk to the public has become a much more central feature of the justice system in recent years (Kennedy, Caplan, and Piza, 2018), especially in relation to the management of offenders who are perceived to represent a threat to the community. Thus research and development of assessment tools have concentrated on understanding and enhancing the methods for precisely quantifying risk and determining the appropriate interventions. So, for example, probation has experienced three distinct phases in the development of such 'tools':

1. those relying essentially on subjective and 'professional judgement' but with no explicit criteria on which to base such judgements;
2. 'actuarial models' (risk-prediction techniques originating in the world of accountancy) based on what are called 'static' characteristics, such as 'age' and criminal record (Smith, 2006), including the Offender Group Reconviction Scale (OGRS); and
3. the more recent refinement of this approach to include both static and 'dynamic' factors (such as changing living circumstances or patterns of drug use), also described as 'criminogenic needs' (Merrington, 2004: 48).

There has also been particular interest in the *Asset* tool, developed for the purposes of predicting the likelihood of reoffending by young people (Baker et al., 2005; and see **Chapter 9**). A progressively refined version of the tool resulted in a claim that it was capable of achieving 69.4 per cent accuracy in this respect. *Asset* was also claimed to be sensitive to changing circumstances and so could incorporate a dynamic element into the process. Further work and evaluation of the tool led to a slight increase in this figure, and the assertion that 'Asset is still a good predictor of proven re-offending among young people' (Wilson and Hinks, 2011: 29), in the face of a number of criticisms.

The sheer amount of work undertaken and the range of tools and scales developed (*Asset* and others) certainly suggests that there is a deep-seated belief in the value and efficacy of such predictive measures in government and policymaking circles. This preoccupation has contributed to the suggestion that other ways of understanding and quantifying risk have been overlooked in face of 'the unquestioning confidence that has been placed in actuarial-based risk assessments' (Lewis, 2014: 122; see also Smith, 2006). Some have certainly argued that the emphasis on apparently neutral technological processes as a means of developing increasingly fine-tuned mechanisms for measuring risk 'merely [mask] the intended purpose of assessment technologies as a politically fuelled mechanism of governance and regulation' (Lewis, 2014: 132). Therefore, concepts such as 'risk assessment' and 'risk management' are seen as attractive at least partly because they provide both practical tools and a supporting justification for taking a particular (politicised) approach to crime control. This argument gains further credence in light of the recognition that despite efforts to refine and refocus it, the best available tool (*Asset*), applied in the most rigorous fashion, is still expected to be wrong in about one-third of cases. Use of such tools thereby results in a large number of false positives (a false positive in this case means that an offender is predicted to reoffend but does not); that is to say, a considerable number of young people who would not have reoffended will be made subject to potentially restrictive interventions. Predictive tools are relatively inefficient and could lead to injustices in the form of inappropriately applied sanctions, so it is perhaps surprising that they have not been questioned more extensively than they have. As Case and Haines (2009: 322) conclude: 'Despite over half a century of research, we still lack a clear understanding of risk and its relationship to the behaviour of young people. Furthermore, the evidence that certain risks cause offending and that these risks can be targeted to reduce offending has simply not been provided.' Partly in recognition of these criticisms, *Asset* itself was substantially reformulated as *AssetPlus*, and this revised version was implemented in England and Wales in 2015. By 2018, though, even this new assessment tool was coming in for criticism:

> AssetPlus was reported as being 'practitioner-unfriendly', unwieldy, time-consuming and taking practitioners away from direct face-to-face work with children.
>
> (Deering and Evans, 2018: 17)

27.7 What does crime control achieve?

As we have seen so far, the 'crime control' perspective on criminality and the proper function of the justice system seem to be associated with what might be termed a 'scientific' approach towards calculating risk and managing the threat posed by offenders.

This is informed by a number of presuppositions regarding:

- the underlying rationality of offenders;
- the possibility of calculating the costs and benefits to the community of trying to stop crime;

- the potential for developing effective predictive tools to identify known and potential offenders;
- the ability to tailor interventions to identified offender 'types'; and
- the capacity to impose effective and efficient measures to reduce or eradicate the possibility of criminal behaviour in the future.

Behind this list lies a further series of assumptions:

1. the belief that it is (a) feasible, and (b) desirable to develop a technological arsenal of crime control measures; and
2. the belief that there is an underlying consensus amongst the population in general as to (a) what constitutes 'crime', and (b) the priorities to be pursued in dealing with it.

Given that this represents quite a substantial body of **suppositions**, it is worth considering in a bit more detail the impact and outcomes of attempts to control crime that rely on them. What, for example, have been the achievements of 'zero tolerance' policing measures; what have been the benefits and disadvantages of 'target hardening'; how has electronic surveillance been incorporated into criminal and judicial processes, and with what consequences; what have been the consequences of applying risk measurement/management techniques to policing strategies and sentencing decisions?

The use of technology

The influence and capabilities of emerging technologies have also played a part in shaping ideas about crime control, as we have developed the capacity to maintain extensive information systems and widely dispersed surveillance and monitoring operations. Although there is something of a contemporary preoccupation with 'new' technologies and their seemingly inexorable expansion, the idea of applying scientific methods in the service of criminal justice has been around for quite some time (Grabosky, 1998; Moriarty, 2017). Although they are mundane features of the criminal process now, fingerprints, wireless communication, and even the car are all technological developments which were at various points incorporated into policing practice. The argument for innovation has often been informed by the suggestion that continuous improvement in methods is necessary simply in order to be able to match the creativity and advances made by criminals (Clevenger et al., 2018). Grabosky (1998: 1) offers a kind of **typology**, suggesting that technological developments can be viewed as a combination of: 'mechanisms for surveillance and detection, . . . blocking devices, and . . . technologies of restraint and incapacitation'.

In the first of these categories we find technologies such as the array of detection devices now located in airports, drug-detection equipment, and more generalised surveillance systems such as CCTV (Piza et al., 2019), evidence from which is now relied on extensively in police investigations and in court, and may be accepted as persuasive. On the other hand, the normalisation of such technology has consequences which might be viewed as disturbing: estimates suggest that Britons are caught on CCTV '70 times a day on average' (BBC News, 3 March 2011). The introduction of facial recognition technology is also controversial (see **New frontiers 27.2**).

Blocking devices inhibit the accessibility of the intended object of a criminal act, as with audio systems in cars which will not operate once removed; and even quite simple measures can be used to achieve the same sort of end, such as tamper-proof seals on new consumer products, to avoid the risk of counterfeiting and prevent deliberate contamination.

Technologies which incapacitate or inhibit offenders now include weapons of restraint, such as tasers and acoustic devices used for crowd control, various electronic tagging devices to limit the movements of suspects or convicted offenders, and even chemical substances which have been developed to modify the behaviour of convicted criminals (see **Controversy and debate 27.2**).

It is also likely that technology will play a greater part in crime control as information technologies become ever more powerful. Of course, crime itself is increasingly moving online and into the virtual world—and a wider range of opportunities have been opened up for unacceptable or unlawful behaviour, including fraud, harassment, sex offences, and various forms of online coercion, exploitation, and oppression. On the one hand, there is almost an inexorable logic about the parallel development of new technologies and, on the other, the increasingly inventive and sophisticated application of methods to limit their unlawful use.

Bowling, Marks, and Murphy (2008: 55) have outlined a typology of technological applications in crime control:

- **Communicative**—the collection and sharing of information.
- **Defensive**—the creation of design features and barriers to inhibit crime.
- **Surveillant**—observation to provide security and prevent crime.
- **Investigative**—collection and analysis of information to prevent, detect, or solve crimes.
- **Probative**—gathering of evidence to support conviction of guilty parties.

NEW FRONTIERS 27.2

Facial recognition

Although facial recognition technology has been in use for some time, since at least the late 1980s (Joshi and Gupta, 2016), its application in the criminal justice context has come much more recently, as attempts have been made to improve its accuracy and **reliability**.

Big Brother Watch, a civil liberties and privacy campaigning organisation, argues against the use of facial recognition. In a report, they commented that the Metropolitan Police (in London) carried out their:

> second 'trial' in London. This resulted in over 30 false matches and one positive match—which turned out to be based on out of date arrest information. Big Brother Watch joined with other civil society groups in calling on the Met to scrap the use of facial recognition. The Met also used facial recognition technology at Remembrance Sunday targeting 'fixated individuals'—people not wanted for any criminal purpose, but who suffer mental health problems. In addition, South Wales Police used facial recognition technology in the lead up to and during the Champions League final in Cardiff. They even subjected concert-goers at a Liam Gallagher gig to facial recognition to monitor 'suspected phone thieves'. No arrests were made.
>
> (https://bigbrotherwatch.org.uk/2018/01/the-surveillance-state-in-2018/)

On the other hand, the Metropolitan Police Commissioner, Cressida Dick, defended the use of facial recognition technology:

> Speaking as a member of the public, I will be frank. In an age of Twitter and Instagram and Facebook, concern about my image and that of my fellow law-abiding citizens passing through LFR [live facial recognition] and not being stored, feels much, much, much smaller than my and the public's vital expectation to be kept safe from a knife through the chest.
>
> (www.theguardian.com/technology/2020/feb/24/met-police-chief-cressida-dick-facial-recognition-technology-critics-ill-informed)

- Do you think the problems of facial recognition technology are just to do with trying to implement this technology too soon?
- Do you think we need to set limits to the kind of technologies put in place to control crime and ensure public safety?
- How can we judge what is acceptable or unacceptable in the use of technology to support criminal justice agencies?

CONTROVERSY AND DEBATE 27.2

Chemical castration

Chemical castration has been used in the UK, and according to the *Daily Telegraph* (3 March 2012):

> The treatment is being piloted by psychiatrists at HMP Whatton, Nottingham, a specialist category C prison which holds male sex offenders.
>
> The drug, leuprorelin, which is marketed as Prostap, inhibits the production of testosterone, which is linked to the high sex drives in paedophiles.

This form of 'treatment' has been viewed as contentious, though. Psychologist Dr Ludwig Lowenstein told the *Daily Mirror* (13 March 2012):

> Apart from lengthy jail sentences, the only other way to deal with most of these people is through chemical castration.

> The idea of giving sexual offenders a pill to destroy their ability to have intercourse always provokes fierce objections on the grounds of civil liberties. But a child's right to protection is far more morally important than the freedoms of paedophiles.

But Frances Cook, of the Howard League for Penal Reform, said: 'Sex offending is often not about sex at all, but about violence and domination. The drugs used will not affect those attitudes.'

Chemical castration remains highly controversial. Whilst the state of Alabama passed a law making it a condition of parole for some child sex offenders in 2019, Moldova passed a similar law in 2012, only to repeal it the following year because of its implications for human rights (*The Atlantic*, 11 June 2019).

- **Coercive**—use of force to maintain order and restrain suspects.
- **Punitive**—use of facilities to incapacitate or achieve other purposes of punishment.

As technology becomes more pervasive, of course, there are also likely to be related concerns about its improper use, or deliberate misuse. Some have expressed fears of this kind, even whilst acknowledging the apparent advantages it offers:

> But do we really want technology to lead society? Where will it lead? Who will be in control? Will we have time to know that before it is too late? [And so, the] warning about the danger of self-amplifying technical means silently coming to determine the ends or even becoming ends in themselves, separated from a vision of, and the continual search for, the good society needs to be continually repeated.
>
> (Byrne and Marx, 2011: 34)

The fears expressed here reflect widespread anxieties about the capacity of technologies of crime control to become so pervasive and sophisticated that they impinge upon freedoms enjoyed by the general population.

Whose interests does crime control serve?

The note of caution sounded here helps to remind us of the questions we need to ask about the underlying objectives of a strategic approach grounded in principles of crime control, and in particular, whose interests it best serves: the victim, the community, or the 'system'. The predictive merits of tools for assessing the risk of offending are not beyond dispute; and in various other ways the apparent certainty offered by supposedly neutral technological means can only come at a price. This is represented in both the economic costs of, say, failsafe security and, equally significantly, in terms of associated social costs and consequences. We might all have to accept a certain degree of inconvenience, and perhaps worse, as the legitimate quid pro quo for the exercise of vigilance, as in the collective experience of the extensive security checks operated by airports. And, in turn, it might be felt that this is a price worth paying if we can be (fairly) certain that the justice system will work well most of the time to protect community interests. Victims will be served because risks will be identified and reduced, offences prevented, and offenders managed, incapacitated, and deterred; in this sense, the crime control model might claim to reflect victims' priorities through providing reassurance and promoting public safety, albeit at the expense of higher levels of security and surveillance.

Similarly, it might be argued that crime control offers guarantees of greater levels of community safety, so that the public lives of people in their neighbourhoods can be conducted safely and free from fear of crime. Once again, it may be the case that the community in general has to accept minor inconveniences (such as the fencing off of a popular short-cut, perhaps), but that these are outweighed by the increased security that these provide. **What do you think? 27.5** asks some questions which should help you decide where you stand on these issues.

The problem, though, for both victim- or community-led understandings of crime control is that they rely on a number of assumptions which may or may not coincide with direct experience. As Roach (1999) has pointed out, for example, crime control approaches were developed before victimisation studies had revealed some of the critical realities of the victim experience. Notably, many victims are not well served by a system that focuses on, and indeed prioritises, only a relatively small subset of those crimes committed. Victimisation studies, in fact, have demonstrated 'that the crime control activities of police and prosecutors only affected a minority of crimes'

WHAT DO YOU THINK? 27.5

Inconvenience versus safety

It is an increasingly common feature of our lives that we are expected to accept certain demands in the communal interest, in order to carry out normal activities, such as having our bags searched at the airport when going on holiday. What sort of minor inconvenience might you be willing to put up with in the interests of reducing levels of crime:

- in your neighbourhood;
- when you're out at night;
- at the airport;
- at sport or musical events;
- in a shopping centre?

Why do you think your tolerances change depending on the situation?

(Roach, 1999: 695). The police inspectorate has expressed similar sentiments more recently:

> Victims of crime are being let down. The police are failing to record a large proportion of the crimes reported to them. Over 800,000 crimes reported to the police have gone unrecorded each year.
>
> (Her Majesty's Inspectorate of Constabulary, 2014)

As a result, in 'many cases victims were aware that contacting police about crimes was useless' (Roach, 1999: 695); with some fearing that they would be re-victimised by the justice process itself. As Roach goes on to observe, the high level of unreported or undetected crime revealed by research into victims' experiences can be interpreted in several different ways. Adverse experiences may be due to inefficiencies in the administration of criminal justice or a lack of resources which could be resolved by, for example, increased spending or better techniques and procedures. For some, then, emerging evidence of victims' poor experiences of criminal justice provides a strong argument in itself for greater investment in law and order.

It could also be argued that the justice system is overly concerned with standardised procedures, at the expense of the victim's needs (Holmberg et al., 2020), and that its work needs to be refocused:

> Too often victims found themselves a 'sideshow' as police, prisons, lawyers and the courts focused on the offender, Louise Casey [Commissioner for Victims] said. She said too much time was spent trying to help all crime victims, rather than focusing on those in genuine need.
>
> (BBC News, 20 July 2010)

It is certainly possible that the inbuilt logic and capabilities of crime control approaches help to focus attention on crimes which are relatively easy to define and target, and those which involve measurable losses. This may not reflect very accurately the nature and extent of victimisation or the social rather than material consequences of being affected by crime. Many also argue that the criminal justice system has demonstrably failed to meet the interests of certain classes of victims, notably those exposed to what might be termed 'private' crimes of assault, abuse, and domestic violence (Roach, 1999: 696; Brooks and Burman, 2017). It seems to be the case that social inequality is also mirrored in a greater susceptibility of disadvantaged groups to suffering the effects of crime; and there may also be a persistent ethnic bias to this (Roach, 1999: Smith, 2014).

In terms of the wider community, too, there may well be a tendency for crime management efforts and resources to focus on those outcomes which are more easily and visibly achieved. As Tilley (2002: 71) has pointed out, crime control initiatives incorporate a much greater level of complexity and unpredictability than might be anticipated. Even in the relatively straightforward example of CCTV, both technical and policy aspects of implementation have distinct implications:

> Lighting levels, local offending and offence patterns, lines of sight, patterns of usage, nature and levels of publicity, relationships to supplementary policing and security services and so on will ... vary widely. Even within the apparently simple and mechanical there is huge variation.
>
> (Tilley, 2002: 71)

Some have gone as far as to suggest that the technological and risk-driven frame within which such measures are understood actually steers crime prevention strategies in a particular direction. As we saw in **Chapter 23**, CCTV programmes introduced in Liverpool actually reflected a particular way of thinking about crime and victims. A new CCTV network was developed in the city to protect essentially commercial and retail areas, at considerable cost (Coleman et al., 2002: 91). When this approach was extended to other areas of the city, it represented a choice between investing in technological measures or in alternatives such as improved youth provision. The argument here is that the initiation of apparently neutral programmes of 'crime control' organised around specific technologies also reinforces a range of underlying assumptions about which crimes are most harmful, and which 'communities' should be prioritised for protection. These:

> not only construct very precise definitions of what is (and is not) a responsible strategy for crime prevention, but they are also based on a very precise definition of what is harmful to the communities subjected to these strategies.
>
> (Coleman et al., 2002: 96)

Stenson (2002) has argued that public and democratic debates about how to enhance crime control are underpinned by arguments between competing interests about what the term actually means; and whose interests should be prioritised when determining the allocation of limited resources. Often this results in oversimplified caricatures of what is needed to promote a greater sense of safety and security amongst a disparate population, where communities are not homogeneous but overlap and have both common and different interests. Indeed, as Crawford and Evans (2017: 808) put it, emerging trends suggest that:

> The principle of community safety from below has been replaced by more top-down managerial interventions which, while using the language popularized by community safety interventions, are far removed from its incipient ideals.

For Stenson, this equates to the emergence of a 'lowest common denominator': 'As one community safety officer remarked ... for a lot of councillors responsible ... for community safety, it means little more than CCTV and more bobbies on the beat' (Stenson, 2002: 134).

Tackling antisocial behaviour

Similar tendencies are perhaps evident in the recent trend towards developing an array of measures to deal with antisocial behaviour, which have depended very much on an assumed consensus about what constitutes problematic behaviour, what its effects are, and the importance of using tough measures to control it. In a way, these measures have represented an extension of the earlier logic of zero tolerance into the realms of pre-criminal behaviour, and indeed into the remit of non-police public agencies, such as housing providers. As Brown (2004) has observed, this extension of the scope of crime control encompasses wider social control objectives, with marginalised populations being targeted in particular. Drawing on Cohen's (1985) work, she identifies a process, where the term 'antisocial behaviour' whilst being symbolically powerful also appears to offer definitional precision to a wide range of activities which are a potential source of unease and distress in the community, such as 'violence, vandalism, dog fouling, litter and young people "hanging around"' (Brown, 2004: 204). It becomes straightforward then to parcel up such eclectic and undefined concerns and provide apparently neat and precise solutions in the form of sanctions and prohibitions, including civil penalties such as eviction or behavioural requirements linked to the threat of further punishment (and **criminalisation**) if breached (see **New frontiers 27.3** for a recent example). Notably, legislative measures put in place to tackle antisocial behaviour are not concerned with whether or not the criminal law has been broken. Instead, they are constituted in terms of civil law breaches, with correspondingly lower standards of proof (Brown, 2004: 205).

Requirements in terms of the quality of evidence and standards of proof to justify making these orders are lower than those necessary to make a case in criminal proceedings.

In addition, in the case of types of antisocial behaviour, crime control strategies are deployed not merely on behalf of the community but by the community: 'Neighbours are the catalyst for investigation and the primary source of evidence' (Brown, 2004: 206). The community is supported in its endeavours by what both Brown (2004: 207) and Garland have identified as a newly emerging professional grouping 'a series of new specialists who staff this still rather inchoate and ill-defined set of arrangements' (2001: 171). Under this umbrella, where these emerging specialisms also perform the function of affording legitimacy to formal interventions of one kind or another, the machinery of antisocial behaviour orders 'and associated "civil" means of control are now an intrinsic part of . . . crime and disorder policy' (Brown, 2004: 210), performing a function as an intensified vehicle of both '**responsibilisation**' (holding people solely accountable for all the problems they face) and social exclusion. The identification of crime control with social control, according to this analysis, raises substantial questions about whose interests are being served, and what the underlying effects of this kind of strategy might be. Webster (2015: 41) has criticised the very wide terms in which legislation is drawn, as in the case of the Antisocial Behaviour, Crime and Policing Act 2014 which allowed for action to be taken against anyone over the age of ten who 'has engaged or threatens to engage in conduct capable of causing nuisance or annoyance to any person'.

NEW FRONTIERS 27.3

Knife Crime Prevention Orders

Because of growing fears about an increase in knife crimes, the government introduced the Knife Crime Prevention Order in 2019, with the aim of discouraging those identified as likely to carry knives from doing so. This measure was modelled on previous antisocial behaviour legislation, with the aim of effectively predicting those likely to commit knife crime, and then taking a range of actions to limit their opportunities to do so, whilst at the same time diverting them towards more acceptable activities. The order itself was part of a raft of measures to address the problem of possession and use of offensive weapons. The Offensive Weapons Act became law on 16 May 2019 and was heralded by government as being a 'tough' response to violent crime.

The Knife Crime Prevention Order was intended to be a deterrent to those at risk of getting involved in knife crime. Orders would allow courts to place restrictions on certain individuals, so as to help police to maintain control over those who present a risk to the community.

In support of this legislation, the Home Secretary said:

> I'm doing everything in my power to tackle the scourge of serious violence. Our new Offensive Weapons Act is a central part of this.
>
> These new laws will give police extra powers to seize dangerous weapons and ensure knives are less likely to make their way onto the streets in the first place. The Act will also see the introduction of Knife Crime Prevention Orders—a power the police called for.

(www.gov.uk/government/news/offensive-weapons-act-receives-royal-assent)

27.8 Does crime control 'work'?

As we have seen, an approach to criminal justice grounded in the philosophy of 'crime control' has an attractive and coherent logic to it, which is able to inform policies and practices that span the justice system from one end to the other. As we have also observed, there have been a considerable number of attempts to put these principles into practice, to enhance our capacity to predict the likelihood of crime (and antisocial behaviour), to identify the perpetrators of crime, and to take appropriate action to prevent its occurrence, minimise its impact, and discourage its repetition. Much of the impetus for intervention is geared towards establishing and then implementing 'what works' in reducing the crime levels and preventing reoffending (Burnett and Roberts, 2004; Braga et al., 2019, for example). Associated with this has been a growing interest in the development of increasingly sophisticated mechanisms for assessing levels and types of risk, and techniques and technologies to support effective intervention. In this section, we move on to consider the effects of crime control strategies, whether or not they achieve their explicit objectives, and what other impacts they might have.

'Designing out' crime

In this context we can consider, first, approaches seeking to reduce the initial 'opportunity' to commit crimes, or to make offending more difficult in some way. Conceptually, this has involved a shift of perspective from a focus on offenders to the offence and its context. It has been claimed (Clarke, 2012, for example) that criminology in both its academic and applied senses has been preoccupied with offenders' prior histories and motivations, at the expense of considering those contextual factors which facilitate or constrain criminal activity. Some argue that it is wrong to assume 'that the earliest and most remote causes are most significant. Instead, the more immediate causes are often more powerful in generating crime' (Felson and Clarke, 1998: 3). By 'remote causes' the authors are presumably thinking of the kind of factors which might contribute to the likelihood of committing a crime which might be found in the offender's upbringing or in the social and cultural context.

Put simply, irrespective of the offender's background, characteristics, or motivation, if it is made harder to commit an offence then it seems reasonable to assume that crime rates will fall. And as Crawford and Evans (2017: 800) point out, there is a correlation between the growing emphasis on this kind of strategy and what is known as the 'crime drop'; that is, a consistent and sustained fall in crime rates. So, rather than seeking to address the potential criminality of individuals, the aim is instead to limit the opportunities to offend. This has been the clear emphasis in the work of **rational choice** theorists, who believe that a large proportion of crime is opportunist in character (see Clarke, 2012, for example, and **Conversations 27.1**). Support for this is provided by a range of evidence, demonstrating that changes in patterns of crime can be identified as a consequence of policy initiatives or policing practices, even where this is not their principal objective. So, for example, the introduction of motorcycle helmet laws in Germany, on safety grounds, seemed to have an impact on criminal behaviour, as 'opportunistic thieves would be immediately noticed when riding past without a helmet' (Clarke, 2012: 4).

CONVERSATIONS 27.1

The price of crime?
with author **Roger Smith**

I can well understand the logic behind the idea of situational crime prevention. Some years ago, my son worked behind the counter in Woolworth's (a mass-market retailer), and the constant challenge for him and other staff was to intercept children helping themselves, without paying, to the large, attractive, and easily accessible pick 'n' mix sweets selection located a few paces inside the main door to the shop. Perhaps unsurprisingly, the poorly paid shop assistants did not think that security and crime control was part of their job.

In this case, though, I also began to wonder about making the assumption that the store actually wanted to prevent crime. Was this a kind of unstated 'loss leader', and was the shop prepared actually to accept a low level of crime as an acceptable price to pay for attracting customers?

Extending this line of thought, maybe some kinds of offence are also susceptible to the kind of 'dynamics at play within the market and civil society' that Crawford and Evans (2017: 804) mention. As mobile phones become more affordable and widely available, does this make them also less attractive to potential offenders, to whom they are worth less now?

Thefts of motorcycles declined by about two-thirds in that country between 1980 and 1986, with little apparent displacement to car or bicycle thefts. Similarly, Clarke (2012: 5) reports that the practice of 'alleygating' (installing lockable gates at the entrance to the alleys running between rows of houses) has identifiable and sustainable impacts on crime rates, saving '£1.86 in costs of residential burglary for every £1 spent' in the first year after the gates' installation in one such scheme in Liverpool.

Again, it is suggested that correlations between improved car-security measures and reductions in car theft support the proposition that crime can be designed out, at least in some instances. For example, as the 'proportion of cars in England and Wales *without* immobilisers fell from 77 per cent to 22 per cent between 1991 and 2006', so the 'number of stolen cars fell around two-thirds from half a million to 175,000 per year and theft from vehicles from 2.4 million to 1.1 million' (Farrell et al., 2008: 18). The extension of such work into a wider range of studies, focusing on different types of crime, situated opportunities, and intervention strategies has led to the suggestion that 'situational crime prevention is applicable not just to "opportunistic" street crimes, but potentially to every form of crime, however complex, and however determined the offenders' (Clarke, 2012: 5). This is a strong claim, extended even as far as 'complex crimes such as internet child pornography' (Clarke, 2012: 5), which might initially be viewed as less readily susceptible to 'situational' influences.

There are potential criticisms of this approach to analysing and managing incentives to commit crime; not least that it assumes common levels of motivation, rationality, and capacity for calculation that may not be held by all members of a community or wider society (Hayward, 2007). With what you have read in mind, see **What do you think? 27.6**. Crawford and Evans (2017: 804) also raise the potential objection that what might appear in one sense as a 'crime drop' may instead be better understood as 'crime migration' with much offending activity now going online.

Crime control and deterrence

It is frequently asserted that deterrent punishments are also an effective form of 'crime control'. But does punishment have a deterrent effect? The evidence on this question has been presented in a number of different ways, notably distinguishing between individual level (that is, known offenders' further offending rates) and population level (that is, overall crime rates) outcomes.

Population-level deterrence

Population-level estimates of deterrent effects are seen as important in the US, in particular, given its extremely high rates of imprisonment. The analytical methods applied have necessarily been speculative, because this is not the kind of territory in which controlled experiments are possible. Criminal justice professionals and sentencers would be likely to resist attempts to constrain their discretion, for example; and there would also be significant ethical implications (Lipsey and Cullen, 2007). Instead, large numbers of studies have applied a range of modelling techniques to try to assess what *would* have happened if sentencers and penal policymakers had behaved differently.

A further challenge for those trying to establish meaningful estimates of the global effects of imprisonment is to distinguish effectively between the different ways in which it might have an impact on offending rates. As Tarling observes, it could have any of the following effects:

- deterrent (for both actual and potential offenders) effects (discouraging people from offending or reoffending because of the fear of imprisonment);
- incapacitating effects (stopping people offending simply by way of removing them from the community—although, of course, crimes *are* committed *in* prison); or
- rehabilitative effects (providing the means to change their behaviour or improve life chances on release).

All of these effects, individually and in combination, could have an impact on current and future offending rates. In light of the difficulties in unpicking this complex pattern, Tarling (1994: 175) has acknowledged that to achieve any degree of certainty would be 'professionally challenging'.

WHAT DO YOU THINK? 27.6

'Designing out' crime

- Can you think of any initiatives similar to the 'alleygates' in Liverpool in the areas or buildings you are familiar with?
- If you have travelled abroad recently, did you notice anything specific to the local environment there that might be intended to reduce criminal activity?
- Can you think of any other problems these measures might cause (such as making it harder to leave the area in an emergency)?

Despite these methodological issues, a considerable number of attempts to resolve this question have been undertaken. Some claim to have identified substantial effects on offending rates, attributable to the use of custody. Levitt (1996: 348), for example, related crime rates to enforced reductions in prison populations in a number of US states, and noted that locking up 'one additional prisoner reduces the number of crimes by approximately fifteen per year', effectively claiming a fairly straightforward incapacitation effect. In the UK context, Bandyopadhyay (2012: 4) claims to have identified a complex set of effects, by which shorter sentences appear to be 'counterproductive' whilst longer sentences might still act to reduce levels of crime.

However, when reviewed more systematically, such studies deliver inconsistent results:

> One could use available research to argue that a 10 per cent increase in incarceration is associated with no difference in crime rates, a 22 per cent lower index crime rate, or a decrease only in the rate of property crime.
>
> (Stemen, 2007: 3)

Lipsey and Cullen (2007) have carried out an extensive review of the available evidence on the effects of imprisonment, summarising the findings from other reviews, and they have concluded that custody at best demonstrates 'modest reductions in **recidivism**, and, in some instances, have the opposite effect and increase' reoffending rates (2007: 297). They acknowledge that variations in the quality and content of individual research studies could account for the variability of findings, and they argue that by aggregating studies systematically, inconsistencies can be minimised. They conclude that rehabilitative interventions with offenders are generally more likely to lead to lower reoffending rates than those involving custodial measures (2007: 302).

Individual-level deterrence

When viewed in terms of individual outcomes, which at least has the advantage of relying on identifiable events rather than complex modelling exercises, the signs are rather different, at least in the UK. In this case, the evidence indicates that custodial sentences are associated with relatively high reoffending rates—46 per cent of those released in 2000 had reoffended after one year, rising to 78 per cent after nine years (Grimwood and Berman, 2012: 24), and 71 per cent of juvenile offenders released from custody in 2010 in England and Wales had reoffended within a year. Whether or not it is criminogenic (causes crime), custody certainly appears to be highly ineffective in terms of discouraging further criminal activity, especially in the case of short-term sentences. As the Ministry of Justice (2013: 4) has found, for 2010 offenders receiving sentences of less than 12 months in custody had a higher re-offending rate in the year following release than similar offenders receiving:

- a community order, by 6.4 per cent;
- a **suspended sentence order**, by 8.6 per cent.

Detailed analysis of outcomes for those receiving short-term custodial sentences appears to confirm these findings. Over a one-year follow-up period those receiving short custodial sentences were 3 per cent more likely to reoffend than similar offenders given community sentences in a study carried out by Mews et al. (2015).

There is considerable consistency in reported outcomes for young people, too. The reoffending rate in the year after release for young people (under 18) freed from custody in the year ending March 2018 (69.8 per cent) remained higher than the equivalent rates for those receiving non-custodial sentences (Youth Justice Board/Ministry of Justice, 2020: 68).

For proponents of a crime control model of criminal justice, then, the implications are challenging. It seems that for certain sectors of the offending population, at least, a less 'incapacitating' court disposal might actually be less likely to result in further offences. Of course, this does not necessarily invalidate crime control strategies under all conditions. It is still arguable that what is needed is a better understanding of risks, risk management, 'what works' and with whom, and a more sensitive, flexible, and better coordinated approach to management and delivery of effective, tailored interventions.

Some researchers have begun to try to assess the value of more 'targeted' deterrence strategies. Braga and Weisburd (2015) discuss one type of strategy that has been developed to reduce violent gun crime:

> These strategies seek to change offender behavior by understanding the underlying violence-producing dynamics and conditions that sustain recurring violent gun injury problems and by implementing a blended strategy of law enforcement, community mobilization, and social service actions. . . . the focused deterrence approach identifies underlying risk factors and causes of recurring violent gun injury problems, develops tailored responses to these underlying conditions, and measures the impact of implemented interventions.
>
> (Braga and Weisburd, 2015: 55)

Braga and Weisburd report that while more rigorous studies are needed, there is evidence to suggest that these strategies reduce gun violence. Despite the limited evidence for this kind of deterrence strategy, it certainly appears to be a growing area of interest.

27.9 The limitations of crime control

Is crime control simply a matter of developing increasingly sophisticated methods and analytical tools for understanding crime and criminals, and applying these systematically to obtain 'best knowledge' and enhance 'best practice'? Or are there other, more substantial considerations to be taken into account when we weigh up the merits and downsides of an approach solely geared to the management and reduction of crime? In effect, there are two types of question to be considered here; those that relate to the practical challenges of implementing a pure crime control approach; and those that address the moral and political dimension of this perspective. Some of the issues are interlinked, of course—such as judging an 'acceptable' rate of miscarriages of justice or excessive use of police powers.

Practical limitations of crime control

First, it is helpful to consider the practical issues related to crime control—what does work in terms of reducing levels of crime and criminality, and how easy is it to implement effective solutions? For instance, it seems that there is some evidence that:

- in some circumstances, some forms of incarceration achieve a reduction in reoffending rates;
- risk assessment tools can achieve a reasonable level of accuracy in predicting reoffending rates;
- targeted policing appears to have some degree of deterrent effect; and
- target hardening and environmental planning also seem to deliver benefits in terms of reducing opportunities to offend.

Policymakers, strategists, and criminal justice agencies are understandably keen to seek out continual improvements in system efficiency and effectiveness. In this spirit, for example, the Carter Report commissioned by the UK government in 2003 was rife with criticisms of the operation of the justice system, and with concerns about the use of relatively ineffective sentences such as imprisonment increasing at the same time as there was a general reduction in crime levels, which could not be attributed to the supposedly deterrent effects of custody.

Proposed solutions were couched in terms of better management and operation of the correctional machinery available. In line with this, the Carter Report recommended substantially extending the use of electronic monitoring and a reduction in the use of short-term prison sentences (Carter, 2004: 30). The report concluded that (2004: 43):

> a new approach is needed to focus on the management of offenders... Services need to be focused on the management of the offender throughout [the] sentence, driven by information on what works to reduce re-offending.

By 2015, similar language is evident in the articulation of the government's approach to 'integrated offender management':

> Local partners [should] ensure that there is a coherent framework in place so that no offender of concern falls through the gaps between existing programmes and approaches. The intensity of management [should be] related directly to the severity of risk posed by the individual.
>
> (Home Office and Ministry of Justice, 2015: 7)

It may be, however, that this emerging emphasis on the technical ways of achieving effective means of managing offenders and controlling crime has led to a rather narrow understanding of the key purposes and objectives of the justice system. The particular configuration of issues, interests, and ways of thinking which underpin criminal justice practices are historically and culturally specific, as Garland (2001: 72) has observed: 'new institutional arrangements originated as problem-solving devices growing out of the practical experience of government agencies and their constituencies... The crime control field is an institutionalized response to a particular problem of order, growing out [of] a particular collective experience.' Stenson, too, has argued that what might be viewed as an emergent and relatively narrow preoccupation with 'managing' crime has been linked with the wider trends towards a form of social organisation characterised by fear and anxiety and a desire to minimise threats to the natural and social environment. Therefore, for him, in 'the sphere of crime control... there is a widely shared criminological view that the new lexicon of risk has downplayed older... concerns with justice as retribution or just desserts and also the welfarist concern with **rehabilitation** through criminal justice dispositions' (Stenson, 2009: 25).

He suggests that the technocratic language and logic associated with this perspective lends itself to a depoliticised understanding of the task of dealing with manifestations of unacceptable behaviour:

> The principal goal of professional practice, consequently, is to keep the lid on problems through pragmatic risk assessment and management policies and practices geared to individuals and social collectivities and 'problem' areas.
>
> (Stenson, 2009: 25)

This managerial ethos has some problematic consequences, however. For an approach that is grounded in generalisable calculations of risk and harm, the inexorable logic leads to the development of broad, probability-driven intervention strategies and practices. In other words, crime control measures are likely to be driven by a set of calculations that problematise particular subsets of the general population, who may demonstrate what might be described as 'criminal tendencies'. So, for example, the identification of a particular neighbourhood as a high-crime area might be sufficient to justify a 'crackdown' by the police, or the adoption of particular methods for dealing with potential offenders. This, in turn, has led to a series of controversial outcomes, particularly in terms of discrimination against black and minority ethnic groups.

The moral challenges of crime control

Crime control and discrimination

Over a considerable period of time it has been noted that black and other minority groups are disproportionately likely to be the subject of 'stop and search' by the police (see **Controversy and debate 27.3**). This would seem to suggest that there is an inbuilt bias towards stopping black people simply on suspicion of unlawful behaviour.

As proportionally fewer of those black people who are stopped are subsequently arrested, the implication is that much of the initial action in stopping them is simply speculative, driven in part by crime control logic, which itself is circular. The greater concentration of resources on black populations is inherently likely to generate a higher rate of arrests and convictions (as it would with any group), which in turn provides the logical justification for the initial 'targeting' of those who are believed to represent a particular risk of offending. As such, it need not be a prior policy decision, or manifestation of direct racism, which leads to this outcome; it is simply a consequence of the impersonal rationality of the machinery in place to control crime.

Apart from being implicated in **institutional racism**, a crime control perspective also has to deal with the challenge that it legitimises miscarriages of justice. Once again, if practice is led by an overarching goal of reducing crime, then the problem of unintended consequences becomes of lesser importance. In broad terms, this means that the objective of ensuring community safety and reducing the risk of crime overrides concerns for due process and the rights of those suspected of crime, as Stenson (2009) implicitly acknowledges. Whilst it might be argued by some that the occasional overzealous police action or unsound finding of guilt is a 'price worth paying' for the safety and certainty afforded by a consistent and effective system of justice, this is not a position that can be held comfortably, especially in

CONTROVERSY AND DEBATE 27.3

Racial discrimination in stop and search

In 2017/18, there were 3 stop and searches for every 1,000 White people, compared with 29 stop and searches for every 1,000 Black people . . .

Black people were 9 and a half times as likely to be stopped and searched as White people in 2017/18; the previous year they were just over 8 times as likely, and in 2014/15 they were just over 4 times as likely'

(Home Office, 15 February 2019)

These are striking figures, and they suggest an endemic problem with criminal justice strategies grounded in broad, population or area-based assumptions. These concerns persisted even during the period of restrictions associated with the Covid-19 pandemic, when the Metropolitan Police reported that black and minority ethnic community members were more likely to be the subject of police action than the general population. Between 27 March and 14 May 2020, under the emergency legislation then applying:

> when compared with the composition of the resident population, higher proportions of those in black and minority ethnic (BAME) groups were issued with FPNs [Fixed Penalty Notices] or arrested across London as a whole

(Metropolitan Police Press Release, 3 June 2020)

The criminal justice system's relationship with ethnic minorities has been controversial for a very long time. It is likely that there are complex and interacting ('intersectional') explanations for these disparities, grounded in wider social structures and processes. This means that the problem of disproportional treatment should not be seen as one for the criminal justice alone to resolve, but this still leaves the question of what actions should be taken to ensure that it does not compound already existing social inequalities and discrimination.

those jurisdictions where the death penalty or other forms of extreme punishment are meted out.

Identification issues in crime control

Associated with these substantive concerns is the underlying problem of legitimacy for crime management strategies grounded in standardised and mechanistic forms of problem identification and risk reduction. Decisions about which crimes to prioritise, and which potential offenders are to be the subject of targeted intervention, depend on prior moral and political judgements about how harms are to be defined and which of them should be viewed as justifying a response. In other words, despite their claims to impartiality and balance, crime control strategies are underpinned by specific choices about whose interests should take precedence and how they should be safeguarded. Behind a presumed consensus lie social and cultural differences which limit the capacity of any given system of justice to ensure equitable treatment. In a context of wider social inequalities, there is clearly a risk that an apparently 'neutral' approach to dealing with crime will simply serve to reinforce those inequalities. As Garland reminds us, the justice system itself is grounded in shifting social and political terrain:

> The new politics of crime-control are socially and culturally conditioned; and . . . the content, timing, and popular appeal of these policies cannot be understood except by reference to shifts in social practice and cultural sensibility.
>
> (Garland, 2001: 139)

Outcomes from the US appear to give additional weight to such concerns, as the extreme consequences of a crime control approach seem to highlight:

> Racial minorities are more likely than white Americans to be arrested; once arrested, they are more likely to be convicted; and once convicted, they are more likely to face stiff sentences. African-American males are six times more likely to be incarcerated than white males and 2.5 times more likely than Hispanic males. If current trends continue, one of every three black American males born today can expect to go to prison in his lifetime, as can one of every six Latino males—compared to one of every seventeen white males.
>
> (The Sentencing Project, 2013: 1)

These outcomes cannot be attributed simply to the application of a particular policy framework and machinery for administering criminal justice. Instead, practices in the US in relation to black and minority ethnic groups represent a striking example of a criminal justice regime where the logic and practices associated with crime control have been highly influential, despite its constitutional commitment to the ideals of 'due process', and where the consequences have been a markedly unequal distribution of what we might term '**substantive justice**'.

27.10 Conclusion

We have covered a lot of ground in this chapter in order to explore a range of ideas and practices falling under the heading of 'crime control'. These approaches are based on an assumption that crime itself is an ever present threat, and that the principal task of the justice system is to ensure that the public are protected, and the threat posed to law-abiding communities by criminals is minimised. We have considered the implications of this approach for criminal justice agencies, such as the police, and the means for dealing with offenders. The chapter has also reflected on the consequences and impacts of interventions based on the aim of 'controlling crime', introducing some critical observations about the risk of unintended and potentially counterproductive consequences.

SUMMARY

After reading this chapter and working your way through its features you should now be able to:

- Explain what constitutes 'crime control'

We have built up a picture of the crime control perspective based on its assumption of a morally neutral orientation to dealing with crime, based on the principle of finding the most effective legitimate means of maintaining public safety and reducing the impact of crime.

- Interpret the crime control model and the due process model, understanding the implications of each

Whereas a due process approach to the administration of justice demands adherence to principles of good practice and ethical behaviour throughout, crime control strategies are more concerned with 'just' outcomes, and less so with how results are obtained. This might mean, for instance, less of a concern to protect the rights of alleged offenders.

- Analyse the different methods of delivering 'crime control', including deterrence, target hardening, offender surveillance, and incapacitation and associated intervention programmes

Crime control is essentially pragmatic in approach, adopting the most reliable and fruitful strategies for addressing the core problem of maintaining security and providing reassurance. As a result, it draws on a wide range of methods and approaches, targeting offenders, communities, and potential victims in order to reduce risk. We have reviewed a number of these strategies and their likely effects when applied in practice.

- Recognise the role played by the police in crime control

The chapter has discussed a range of policing strategies designed to extend their role beyond simply catching criminals to develop approaches to policing geared towards crime reduction and providing a sense of security and reassurance to communities.

- Critique the effectiveness of different crime control methods, including deterrent measures and zero-tolerance initiatives

The reported benefits of crime control strategies are considered, as are some of the problematic issues associated with them, such as the infringement of civil liberties, discriminatory impacts of some community-based interventions, and counterproductive nature of some core methods, notably the use of custody as a supposed deterrent measure.

- Appreciate the practical and moral limitations of crime control

As noted, crime control involves a difficult trade-off between effectiveness and certainty of outcomes, on one hand, and ethically sound practice, on the other.

Test your understanding of the chapter's key points by attempting the self-test questions on the **online resources** at www.oup.com/he/case2e

REVIEW QUESTIONS

1. Outline the main differences between the crime control model and due process model.
2. Are there any similarities between 'crime control' and 'crime prevention' strategies? How do they differ?
3. What do you understand by the term 'designing out' crime?
4. What are the issues surrounding the use of technology in crime control?
5. What are the challenges and implications of prioritising some interests over others in crime prevention?

Access the **online resources** at **www.oup.com/he/case2e** to check your answers to the review questions.

FURTHER READING

Coleman, R., Sim, J., and Whyte, D. (2002) 'Power, politics and partnerships: the state of crime prevention on Merseyside' in G. Hughes and A. Edwards (eds) *Crime Control and Community*. Cullompton: Willan.
An interesting study of the local politics of crime control and the outcomes of contested arguments about how best to reduce levels of crime in particular locations. Issues of power and vested interests are explored from a critical perspective.

Clarke, R. (2012) 'Opportunity Makes the Thief. Really? And So What?'. *Crime Science* 1(3): 1–9.
Reflections on the idea that crime is really a matter of rational choice and opportunity, and that the principal focus of criminologists should be to understand and resolve the essentially practical problems associated with reducing opportunities for crime and creating disincentives for potential offenders.

Newburn, T. and Jones, T. (2007) 'Symbolizing Crime Control: Reflections on Zero Tolerance'. *Theoretical Criminology* 11(2): 221–43.
A careful analysis of the emergence of zero-tolerance policing, its contribution to the crime control movement, its reported benefits, and some of the challenges that might be associated with a determined attempt to implement a comprehensive strategy of this kind.

Packer, H. (1964) 'Two Models of the Criminal Process'. *University of Pennsylvania Law Review* 113(1): 1–68.
A thorough account of the crime control and due process models of criminal justice, incorporating a consideration of their relative merits and limitations.

Stenson, K. (2009) 'The New Politics of Crime Control' in K. Stenson and R. Sullivan (eds) *Crime, Risk and Justice*. Cullompton: Willan.
A critical review of the emergence of crime control in the context of new forms of governance, and the associated technologies of risk management, setting out some of the limitations associated with this approach.

 Access the **online resources** to view a wealth of extra information relating to your study of criminology, including self-test questions, answers to review questions, and links to other resources that will help you enjoy and fulfil your potential within your studies.
www.oup.com/he/case2e

CHAPTER OUTLINE

28.1	Introduction	838
28.2	What is punishment?	838
28.3	What is punishment intended to achieve?	840
28.4	How punishments are imposed	844
28.5	The objects of punishment	849
28.6	Punishment: policies, practices, and consequences	852
28.7	What are the effects of punishment?	855
28.8	Punishment, justice, and the public	858
28.9	Conclusion	859

28

Punishment

KEY ISSUES

After studying this chapter, you should be able to:

- appreciate the rationale for retributive approaches to dealing with crime;
- discuss the aims and objectives of retributive approaches to punishment;
- recognise the development of different forms of punishment;
- reflect on the use and impact of penal sanctions;
- evaluate the potential limitations of punitive penal practices.

28.1 Introduction

Our purpose in this chapter is to consider the place that **punishment** occupies as a response to crime. Here, we will think particularly of punishment in the sense of the 'price to be paid' for committing a crime. In many ways, the idea of punishment lies at the heart of our thinking about crime and criminal justice. It acts as a kind of balancing factor to the offence, and seems like an obvious and natural consequence of a wrongful act, as in the biblical idea of 'an eye for an eye'. However, as you will probably recognise by now, the criminologist's task is precisely to interrogate our fundamental assumptions, and to question the obvious. So, we need to consider in a bit more detail, and with a critical eye, some very well-established conventions, such as the principle of '**just deserts**' and the idea that we should make 'the punishment fit the crime'.

So, we will consider key arguments which support the principle of punishment and just deserts generally, and specific punitive practices associated with these ideas, in particular. We will explore aspects of the historical development of punishment and its changing role in society. We will discuss particular forms of penal sanction, notably the death penalty, the use of imprisonment, and community-based alternatives to the deprivation of liberty.

We will go on to consider the role of the judiciary in administering punishments, before exploring its impacts and outcomes. We will consider the consequences of imposing punitive measures, including its effects on offenders and reoffending rates. This will lead us on to a discussion of the potential criticisms of the use of punishment, including miscarriages of justice, its apparent failure to affect the likelihood of reoffending or to reform criminals, and its potentially destructive effect on offenders and those around them, such as their families.

28.2 What is punishment?

As we will see in other chapters as well as this one, punishment can take a number of forms, and it can be associated with various objectives, such as: deterrence, incapacitation, reform, correction, or restoration. Punishment also serves a more general purpose in helping to establish a sense of moral order and collective **norms**. It acts as one way of defining unacceptable behaviour in a particular society. In this chapter, however, our focus will be rather narrower. Here, we will concentrate on punishment as 'retribution'; that is, as the penalty the offender must pay for committing a crime.

Retributive approaches to punishment are based on the assumption that harms caused as a result of criminal acts can and should be redressed by the imposition of an equivalent level of hurt on the perpetrator. This is seen not just as an understandable response to crime, but as morally justified. This vengeful view of crime and punishment has often become seen as a default position, reflecting what might be termed a 'natural' or common-sense view of what it means to administer justice. This is clearly reflected in widely recognised and influential belief systems, such as the biblical endorsement of the principle of 'an eye for an eye, a tooth for a tooth. The one who has inflicted the injury must suffer the same injury' (Leviticus, 24: 20). Of course, this position is not shared by other religions, or even in later Christian teachings. These disagreements about what is appropriate when we think about imposing a punishment are significant.

> Punishment requires justification because it is morally problematic. It is morally problematic because it involves doing things to people that (when not described as 'punishment' [and thereby legitimised]) seem morally wrong.
>
> (Duff and Garland, 1994: 2)

The philosopher Thomas Aquinas articulated the case for seeing retributive punishment as 'natural' in great detail, arguing that this is not just a matter of instinct, but that 'anger' and the urge to punish has a rational basis (Koritansky, 2012: 118). More recently, the title of Ignatieff's book, *A Just Measure of Pain* describing punitive practices in the 18th and 19th centuries, draws attention to the abiding presumption that the infliction of pain as a form of punishment could be considered fair and equitable as long as it complied with certain rules of equivalence.

Embedded in such well-established arguments is a set of supporting assumptions, of course. They imply, for example:

- that responsibility for an action can be clearly and accurately defined;
- that the consequences of such actions are equally clearly and accurately identifiable;
- that these consequences are predictable and understood;
- that the choice to initiate any such action (or not to prevent something happening) is made freely and rationally;
- that there is a commonly agreed framework within which the extent and nature of any transgressive action can be identified (that is, what constitutes 'harm' and how it is quantified);

- that an equivalent amount of punishment can be specified for any harm caused; and
- that any such punishment can be administered in such a way as to constitute an equivalent level of suffering from the subjective point of view of the perpetrator.

Of course, translating such statements into the real world of lived experience leaves most of these assumptions open to question, as we shall explore in this chapter. Importantly, though, the underlying principles set out here can clearly be identified in persistent and often prevailing notions of 'fault', 'just deserts' (meaning a fairly determined penalty), '**proportionality**', determinacy (in the sense that once the agreed price is paid for a crime, then the offence is dealt with and the matter is closed), and 'equal treatment'.

As we can see from this outline, a purely retributive approach to dealing with crime does, by implication, exclude from consideration a number of well-established features of the judicial decision-making process; such as the sentencing tariff, mitigation, **individualised** sentencing, and, indeed, any role of the offence victim in determining the outcome (apart from contributing to an assessment of the 'harm' caused). In fact, most of these modifications represent attempts to establish a basis for applying punitive principles in the real world; that is, in the specific and unique circumstances of every individual offence. Punishment therefore has to tread the fine line between apparently objective measures of harm and blame, on the one hand, and the subjective and contextual aspects of human experience and characteristics, on the other. So, in order to represent retributivist principles formally and precisely, a number of procedures and criteria need to be invoked. If they are not, it then becomes impossible to distinguish punitive measures from other extrajudicial modes of response to perceived hurt, such as revenge-taking or what might be termed 'rough justice'.

In this light, the Icelandic sagas, for example, present a picture of a **culture** infused with a strong sense of justice, in which punishments could nonetheless be determined and inflicted by the wronged party, almost without reference to any sense of a shared penal code; thus taking a form which may bear no apparent relationship to the harm caused (Thorsson, 2001).

Punishment and its claims to legitimacy

If we are to distinguish retributive forms of punishment from other ways of holding offenders to account or responding to crime, we must try to define them according to their claims to legitimacy. This will, in turn, appear to depend on a clear set of working rules, consistently and fairly applied. These can be set out as a series of steps, designed to reach a determinate outcome which is procedurally 'just' (Vermunt and Steensma, 2016) in the sense of being fair and justifiable (both to all parties to the specific offence and in comparison to other punishments administered in other cases).

Considered in these terms, then, the steps to be followed are:

1. Establish the nature of the offence (what was the alleged infraction (crime), and what is the evidence for it?).
2. Establish the extent of the harm caused (what was the injury and how were those involved affected?).
3. Establish responsibility (who did it?).
4. Establish intent (was the alleged perpetrator aware of the consequences, did they mean this to happen, and were they influenced in any way?).
5. In the absence of intent, was the perpetrator reckless, or indifferent to the consequences of their actions?
6. Determine an equitable balance between harm caused and harm intended (decide whether more weight should be given to the intent behind the crime or its actual impact—as in the case of 'one-punch deaths', for example).
7. Decide an equivalent penalty based on this calculation, the facts of the offence, and 'normal' (culturally defined) expectations of punishment.

As a consequence of adopting a formalised approach to determining the level and nature of punishment to be administered, we will have inevitably moved away from simply specifying an exact and equivalent penalty to be paid by the offender, in all comparable cases.

This means that there may need to be modifications to the principles of retributive punishment, in its pure form. We will discuss two of them in this section: how to determine an equivalent harm and how to consider issues of intent.

Equivalent harm

The notion of 'simple' retribution in the form of an exactly equivalent harm is open to question, in that it does not lead to consistently fair outcomes in all cases. This might be because of subjective variations in the nature of harm experienced by the victim, the extent of blame to be accorded to the perpetrator, the capacity to apply an exactly equivalent penalty, or the subjective experience of harm from the perpetrator's point of view. In some instances, for example, the effects of *institutionalisation* may well dilute the punitive impact of being incarcerated—prisoners may become habituated to custody and so become less likely to experience the kind of deprivation that is intended by the imposition of a custodial sentence. For some, it's harder to live in the world outside the prison walls:

> It's true what they say—your sentence begins the day you get out.
>
> (Adult ex-prisoner, quoted in Social Exclusion Unit, 2002: 86)

> I walked into the supermarket . . . and found eleven different types of bread. Eleven. In prison there was one, and you ate it or didn't. I spent ten minutes trying to make a choice, then stressed out and left without buying anything.
>
> (Adult prisoner, quoted in Social Exclusion Unit, 2002: 86)

For those adopting a pure 'retributivist position', this represents a significant challenge—what *is* punishment in this sort of case? How can retributivists take account of the subjective element in determining how to administer the appropriate penalty?

Intent and accountability

Similar considerations apply when we move on to think about the question of 'intent', and whether punishment should be expected to take account of perpetrators' motivations and understanding of their own moral or social obligations. This may be the case in situations where neglect or carelessness may be a factor, rather than a proactive decision to infringe the formal rule of law. Thus, for example, in the context of **corporate crime**, judgements of blame are mediated by the difficulty of attributing 'pure' responsibility to specific individuals. Where a legal obligation has not been met, as in the case of the Grenfell Tower fire, it may be difficult to identify precisely who is responsible for this failure, or to apportion blame amongst a number of potential culprits:

> The ambiguous moral character of work-related fatality cases, and of health and safety law, has long been seen as a barrier to the imposition of orthodox criminal liability, and has led to these offences being commonly categorized as 'regulatory'.
>
> (Almond, 2009: 160)

So, if it is difficult to attribute blame in cases of joint responsibility and neglect, what of those cases where there is no doubt about intent to cause harm, but no harm is done—as in the case where player one jumps out of the way of a bad tackle before player two makes contact? Applying the **concepts** and principles of retributive justice in practice can therefore be problematic.

Whilst there may be an absolute and clearly specified basis for imposing a specific and measurable penalty equivalent to the harm caused by an offence, this will inevitably be modified by the human dimension of the crime itself. That is to say, in every case there are specific factors which come into play which will modify this kind of calculation. How do we estimate the precise extent of blame in cases where carelessness, rather than intent, has led to the offence—as in the case of dangerous driving? What account should we take of the personal circumstances which may have contributed towards the offender's actions—such as stealing food to provide for a hungry family? (See **What do you think? 3.1** for more on this example.) Even the simple administration of punishment according to fixed and apparently definitive principles implies necessarily taking positions about fairness and justice, rather than simply implementing a neutral set of unquestionable universal standards.

28.3 What is punishment intended to achieve?

Retributive ideas of punishment are widely established, grounded in what seems to be a fairly attractive and straightforward principle that offenders should pay the appropriate price for their crimes. These ideas, in turn, provide a clear framework for establishing mechanisms of judgement and sentencing; that is, the assumption that each and every offence will have a consistent, fair, and calculable penalty associated with it. Whilst there are problems of equivalence and a common basis for determining guilt, as we have observed, it is nonetheless believed to be possible to develop rational guidelines for resolving these, in line with the overarching principles of fair and equitable treatment. Beyond determining the basis for imposing a particular form of punishment, though, we might also reasonably have concerns about what it is intended to achieve and what it should achieve. Is it simply a matter of trying to find a balance by righting a wrong, and responding to one harm with another, for example? Or, does retributive punishment serve a wider function, in terms of maintaining social norms and a shared sense of what is right and fair? Is punishment designed to maintain a common sense of accountability and responsibility?

This would imply that retributive punishment may have a more extensive function than simply imposing a penalty on the offender which matches the harm done by the crime. Is it also intended to remove any 'unfair advantage' gained by the offender by committing the offence? Does it provide restitution, in the sense that its aim is to achieve some form of direct compensation and, if so, to whom is restitution owed, the direct victim or the wider community? Is it intended to inflict an equivalent level of harm to that experienced by the victim? Is it also symbolic, in that it stands as affirmation of the rule of law and justice in society in general? Is it intended to establish and maintain a sense of moral balance, in order to sustain a common belief in the idea of a fair and equitable rights-based society?

In this context a distinction is being made between the different interests at play; we could ask whose interests and perspective should take precedence: is it the victim's or those of the wider community, or even the perpetrator, whose sense of right and wrong might be restored by way of accepting that a particular punishment is fair and deserved. In the remainder of this section, we will consider these groups in turn.

Strengthening the role of the victim

If retribution is to be administered on behalf of the victim (by a legitimate and properly constituted body), then there is clearly an associated argument for the direct involvement of victims in determining the level and nature of the punishment to be administered. Indeed, this kind of argument is increasingly recognised as legitimate.

Recent legal developments appear to have strengthened the position of victims of crime in two respects. They have become more clearly entitled to direct compensation; and they have also been more centrally involved in the justice process, in the sense of having their voices heard and their views and feelings taken into account. Thus, for example, the Anti-social Behaviour, Crime and Policing Act 2014 made provision in England and Wales for a Community Trigger and a Community Remedy, whereby:

> Victims will be able to use the Community Trigger to demand action, starting with a review of their case. Agencies including councils, the police, local health teams and registered providers of social housing will have a duty to undertake a case review when someone requests one and the case meets a locally defined threshold.
>
> (Home Office, 2014: 3)

And:

> The Community Remedy gives victims a say in the out-of-court punishment of perpetrators for low-level crime and anti-social behaviour. The Act places a duty on the Police and Crime Commissioner to consult with members of the public and community representatives on what punitive, reparative or rehabilitative actions they would consider appropriate to be on the Community Remedy Document.
>
> (Home Office, 2014: 11)

At the other end of the scale of punishments, though, there has also been much debate about the place of victims in determining more severe penalties. Some have strenuously rejected the right of victims to take part in the sentencing process for severe crimes, for example Moore (1999: 89) argued that 'doing justice is the essence of retributive punishment and . . . victims have neither any moral right nor expertise to say how our legal institutions should achieve that justice'. However, others view it as a matter of principle that those most closely and deeply affected should have a role in determining the scale and nature of the punishment to be administered and there is perhaps an emerging consensus about their entitlement to have a say in this regard. Fletcher (1999), for example, argues that victims should be given a role in the sentencing process as a form of empowerment, and as a way of 're-establishing equality between' (1999: 63) them and the perpetrators of crime who have exerted a form of 'dominance' over them. In addition, it is suggested that the administration of a suitable form of punishment is a way of achieving 'closure' for victims and allowing them to move on. Bandes (2000: 1599) quotes a victim advocate in the US who identified the impending execution of a murderer as an opportunity for the victim's family, in that it would 'open the door to being able to go on with the rest of their lives'.

It is also worth noting at this point that different jurisdictions, particularly those differentiated on cultural and religious grounds, may also vary in their prevailing views of the place of victims in determining the punishment to be invoked. Thus, Islamic law provides in some circumstances for victims to have a direct say in the sentencing decision. Esmaili and Gans (1999) discuss the implications of this in some detail, helping to dispel simplistic assumptions about Sharia (traditional Islamic law). Whilst all parties to an offence are entitled to representation in the criminal justice process, the capacity for victims to have a say in the sentencing process varies—depending on whether the offence is subject to a mandatory or discretionary punishment (Esmaili and Gans, 1999: 153). Where it is decided that victims have a part to play in determining the sentence to be imposed, even in extreme cases such as murder, they are entitled to ask for an equivalent retributive sanction (such as the death penalty), an alternative retributive measure (monetary compensation), or 'they can ask for forgiveness' (that is, a non-retributive outcome; 1999: 164).

If, victims are to take a central role in the sentencing process, but not in every case, this does create a sense of ambiguity about whose interests take precedence in deciding on punishments. Similarly, where victims choose not to seek retributive sanctions, it leaves open the question of who should determine what should be considered 'just deserts'.

As Edwards has pointed out, there has been a recent move towards 'victims being encouraged, permitted, required or entitled to have input into criminal justice decision-making processes' (2004: 968), which implies that the state has begun to reassign its claims to authority and legitimacy in this area to those directly affected and harmed by an offence being committed. This, of course, not only reflects a shifting balance of power, but it also means that the consistency and coherence of punishment decisions are likely to be diluted in the process.

Victim personal statements

In the UK, the government has increasingly sought to provide victims with a voice throughout the criminal justice process, and particularly in court. The following outline from Victim Support illustrates how the Victim Personal Statement (the equivalent in Scotland is known as a Victim Statement) works, and how it can play a part in influencing sentencing decisions (see also **Figure 28.1**):

> All victims who report a crime are entitled to make a Victim Personal Statement at the same time as giving a witness statement to the police. The VPS allows you to say how you and your family have been affected by the crime. This is different to a witness statement, which describes what happened at the time of the crime. Giving a VPS is optional and it will include your routine personal details such as name, date of birth and address.
>
> Once you've completed a VPS you cannot change it, but you can give a further VPS at any time before sentencing. This will add to or clarify your initial VPS, and gives you the chance to describe any further impact the crime has had.

If you're a victim of a serious crime (including bereaved close relatives), persistently targeted, or vulnerable or intimidated, you are entitled to make a VPS to the police at any time before sentencing, whether or not you make a witness statement about what happened.

The VPS will form part of the prosecution case but will only be considered by the court once the offender has been found guilty of the offence.

Figure 28.1 neatly encapsulates some of the key tensions involved in the practical application of retributive principles. Victims may be afforded a say in the process, but this remains at the discretion of the court, as does the degree to which this may influence judicial thinking. The extent to which victims' views are actually influential also adds a layer of complication to the idea of equitable treatment of offenders.

Whilst the state can adopt a consistent framework for sentencing decisions, this is less likely to be sustainable where influence over or even control of the process is given to victims. Taken to its extreme, the victims of crime would then be free to apply their own subjective judgements and ethical codes in determining the appropriate outcome in relation to the harm caused.

Although, as Edwards notes (2004: 968), much of the rhetoric concerning a more prominent role for victims has to do with 'balancing' their interests against those of alleged offenders, in practice any shift of emphasis of this kind also modifies the role of the state as an interested party in the justice process. This might be a reflection of our increasing awareness of the limited role played by the state in preventing and controlling crime in general; but it

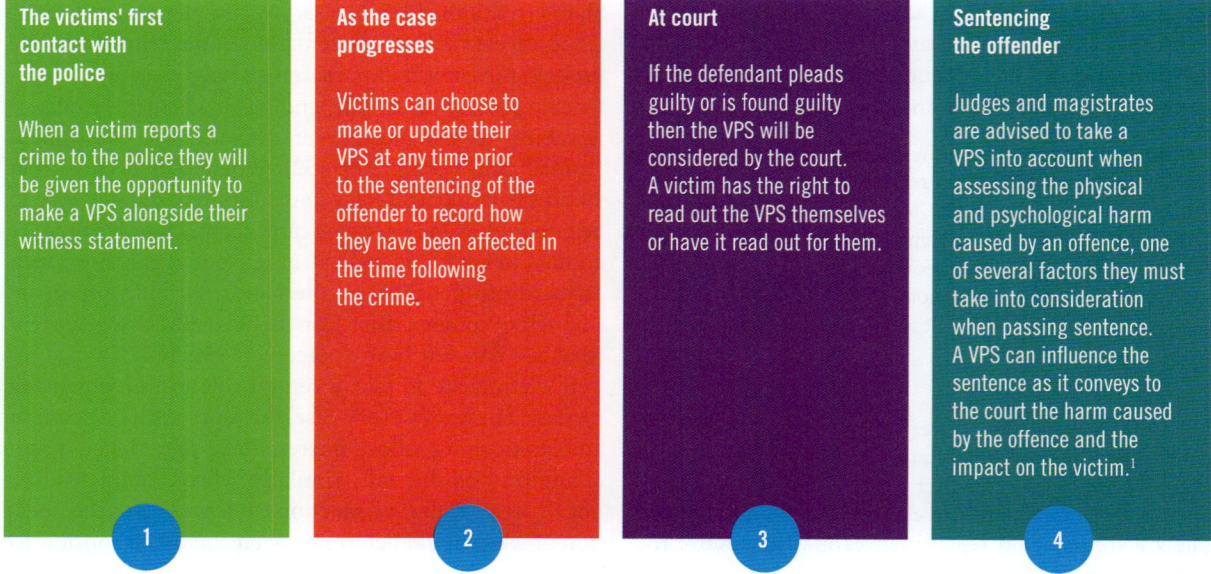

Figure 28.1 The Victim Personal Statement aims to give victims a voice in the criminal justice process and can play a part in influencing sentencing decisions
Source: Adapted from Victim Support

might also be linked to an assumption by some politicians that 'placing the victim centre-stage' (2004: 969) will help to satisfy public aspirations for a more punitive approach to offending:

> In the United States and elsewhere, there has been a considerable overlap between those calling for improvements in the position of victims and those demanding curbs on defendant's rights and protections. Several writers have argued that victim reforms in the 1980s and 1990s have been essentially punitive measures, serving to counter or restrict the protections and rights afforded to defendants.
>
> (Edwards, 2004: 970)

Acknowledging that such moves may partly be driven by political calculations rather than any underlying concern for the interests of victims (including the great majority where offenders are not caught or brought to court, for example), Edwards goes on to suggest that the victim's role and the nature of their 'participation' in the process must be viewed as rather more nuanced; in practice, the victim role is usually restricted to that of an 'expressor', one who is enabled and encouraged to express their feelings about the offence but who does not have control either in procedural or decision-making terms. In essence, the unresolved 'problem lies in defining the relationship between the public interest and the victim's interest' and in the difficult task of achieving 'procedural and **substantive justice** for victims *and* offenders: can victims be given particular participatory roles whilst upholding principles of rationality, consistency and objectivity?' (Edwards, 2004: 980, emphasis in original).

Both in principled and practical terms, then, it is hard to make a case for the argument that punishment in general, or retribution in particular, can remain entirely at the discretion of the victim(s) of an offence. It may be viewed as preferable for the state judiciary as an independent rational authority to take responsibility for the determination and imposition of retributive forms of punishment. In this sense, the state can be seen to be acting on behalf of specific victims, but also the wider community and the common interest, which it represents. Assuming that the state is capable of acting more rationally and consistently than individual victims (who have different interests, experiences, and expectations) and assuming that it is also able to represent a consensual view about the aims and conditions of punishment, this appears to offer a basis for a more equitable approach to the imposition of penal sanctions, based on a set of guaranteed rights held by all parties to the offence; and thus to ensure fair treatment in the decision-making process and proportionality of **disposal** at the point of determining the sentence to be applied. We should perhaps acknowledge here that this does depend on an idealised assumption of the state and its institutions which clearly cannot be taken for granted.

Maintaining moral and social order

Retributive punishment imposed by the state can be said to operate 'on behalf of' society as a whole, because it is intended to maintain a uniform balance between citizens in terms of harms caused and penalties imposed. This is in contrast to specific instances of victim-determined sanctions which might be inconsistent and less consistently fair or 'just'. Retribution is intended to maintain a sense of social order which is based in turn on underlying assumptions about the common good and '**natural justice**':

> Once society has decided upon a set of legal rules, the retributivist sees those rules as representing and reflecting the moral order. Society's acceptance of legal rules means that the retributivist accepts the rules, whatever they may be: accepts that the rule makers are justified in their rule making; and claims that those who make the rules provide the moral climate under which others must live.
>
> (Banks, 2004: 109)

The harm caused by a crime can therefore be viewed not just as an offence against a specific individual, but as a breach of a shared set of rules and obligations. The specific hurt experienced by individual victims falls under a broader heading of damage to the collective moral fabric of society. The state is authorised to inflict punishment on the offender in order to restore the moral order. Punishment thus involves the imposition of substantive penalties, which also act as a symbolic expression of disapproval or condemnation.

Accepting the price of crime

Although coming close to the idea of **deterrence** (see **Chapter 15**), this view of punishment is distinguished by its emphasis on repairing breaches in the integrity of the social fabric, in that 'punishment serves to teach offenders a moral lesson so that in the process of being punished... they will come to see what is good' (Banks, 2004: 111); whilst at the same time, the rest of the community will be reassured that the moral order has been restored. Banks is concerned, however, that this 'approach does not account for the punishment of those who are already repentant' (2004: 111). That is to say, for offenders who show genuine remorse, punishment is not needed in order to convince them that they have done wrong. Retributive punishment might be viewed as justified by those offenders who accept that any harm they have caused merits an equivalent punishment—and in some instances are prepared to accept this risk as a rational calculation of the benefits of committing an offence. William Tenn's 1956 science fiction story, *Time in Advance*,

> ### CONTROVERSY AND DEBATE 28.1
>
> **Seeking the death penalty in Turkey: what reasons might lie behind this?**
>
> On 15 July 2016, a coup d'état was attempted in Turkey against the government. The attempted coup was carried out by the Turkish Armed Forces, but after attempting to gain control of key areas in Turkey, the coup was quashed by supporters of President Erdoğan.
>
> In the wake of this severe threat to his position, government, and safety, President Erdoğan told a rally of more than one million people that he would approve the death penalty if approved by Parliament. Erdoğan said:
>
> As the sovereignty unconditionally belongs to the nation and as you request the death penalty [for the coup leaders], the authority which is going to decide on this issue is Turkey's National Assembly. If our parliament takes such a decision, the necessary step will be taken. I am expressing in advance, I will approve such a decision coming from the parliament.
>
> (*The Independent*, 8 August 2016)
>
> In light of the theories discussed in this chapter, why do you think President Erdoğan and the Turkish National Assembly might want to impose the death penalty in response to the alleged coup?

is a speculative account of an offender who chooses to serve his punishment before committing the crime to which it relates; whilst the slogan 'don't do the crime if you can't do the time' suggests that some offenders may well accept the legitimacy of sanctions imposed upon them.

Reports of offenders' views on punishment seem to support this suggestion:

> [What do you think is the purpose of a sentence like yours?] Well, safe-guarding shopkeepers. I'm nae entitled to walk oot to shops and jist help myself. I realise that I've got to be punished for daein it.... 55 year old woman, 120 days imprisonment
>
> (Quoted in Armstrong and Weaver, 2010: 11)

Paradoxically, the same respondent also felt that this punishment was having no effect on her and that it had made her 'worse'. Importantly, this helps us to distinguish between the legitimacy (or otherwise) of punishment and its effects.

For retributivists, punishment is justified simply because of the impositions it makes on the offender; whereas for those more interested in deterrence (see **Chapter 15**), for example, its effects on their behaviour are more important.

See **Controversy and debate 28.1** for a discussion about the purpose of sentencing in a specific scenario.

So, in considering the question of what punishment is 'for', and whose needs and expectations it is intended to meet, we can state that: punishment can be defined as a legitimate and reasonable penalty imposed at the instigation of any of those with a direct or indirect interest in a crime. Its justification in terms of being 'the price to pay' metaphorically and sometimes literally for breaching the commonly held formal rules of society is widely accepted. However, this still leaves open a series of questions about the 'practice' of punishment, its effects, and consequences; and whether and in what ways it is justifiable—questions we will consider in the remainder of this chapter.

28.4 How punishments are imposed

The nature of the punishment inflicted is dependent on two things. First, on the way in which crimes are defined and, secondly, on the value system which determines the appropriate sentence. In one sense, perhaps, it may be that the very idea of 'crime' implies an equivalent form of penalty but, as we have already acknowledged, there are debates to be had between the different aims and objectives of the justice system. Adopting a retributive model of punishment is therefore a matter of choice and, in taking this position, it seems that certain forms of penal sanction are consistent with this preference; especially those which involve some form of deprivation, suffering, or physical harm. As we have seen, there are clear variations even within the retributive perspective over the meaning of harm and **victimisation** and therefore just what punishment can and should achieve, and for whom. And it is therefore understandable that the kind of penalties to be imposed should vary, from those relying on the infliction of physical harm, or even death, to those involving deprivations—of freedom, residence, dignity (in the form of the 'stocks' or high-visibility unpaid labour, perhaps), or time—and those involving some form of recompense—fines or unpaid labour, for instance. In this section we will consider different ideas about the kind of penalties that should be imposed and how these have changed over time.

A historical perspective

All societies seem to have grappled with the idea of crime and punishment and how to deal with those who offend. However, their approaches have varied over the course of history. In Victorian Britain, the question of whom and how to punish was 'exacerbated' (Tomlinson, 1981: 126) by the problem that three of its preferred punishment options were called into question at the same time—that is, hanging, transportation, and imprisonment on the 'prison hulks' (as shown in **Figure 28.2**—Britain started converting old merchant ships and naval vessels into floating prisons known as hulks. Many of these were on the River Thames. Convicts spent time on the hulks before being transported to Australia, the new destination for Britain's criminals). Similarly, there are acknowledged problems over proportionality and what type and degree of punishment equates to the harm caused and the intentions of the offender. To explore this, it is worth considering the history of punishment.

The history of punishment does provide a striking insight into social norms and the ideas people have held over time about what is acceptable in terms of the way offenders are treated. What we understand—or what has been understood in the past—by the idea of just and fair punishment is shown to be subject to wide variation. Cultural differences are sometimes stark. Certainly, when we consider historical and geographical variations, it becomes clear that there is considerable divergence in prevailing ideas as to what is deemed reasonable and appropriate.

Physical punishment and executions

It is suggested: 'Back in the day, retribution tended to be exacted through cruel and violent forms of punishment' (Materni, 2013: 267). Materni also cites Foucault's (1979) work, *Discipline and Punishment*, itself widely recognised as a major contribution to our understanding both of the historical development of punishment and of its wider role in maintaining social order and the rule of law.

Foucault's graphic description of the punishment administered to 'Damiens the regicide', in 1757, is striking and shocking, as was intended, no doubt (see **Figure 28.3** for a visual representation). Damiens had attempted to assassinate the French king, Louis XV, who had in fact survived the attack with only a minor knife wound. This case represented only the extreme form of an established tradition. Although it was, in today's terms, a horrifying form of execution, it was:

> not the exception; in the eighteenth century, the administration of criminal law in continental Europe was barbaric. Gallows, torture, branding, mutilation, and the wheel were commonplace in the administration of 'justice; the death penalty was implemented even for the most trivial of crimes, such as, for example, stealing a handkerchief.
>
> (Materni, 2013: 268)

In Elizabethan England, similarly, the nature of the punishments described seems extreme from our present-day perspective. Being 'hung, drawn, and quartered', for example, was to experience a brutal and ritualistic process of dismemberment:

> The greatest and most grievous punishment used in England for such as offend against the State is drawing from the prison to the place of execution upon an hurdle or sled, where they

Figure 28.2 In Victorian Britain, old merchant ships and naval vessels were converted into floating prisons known as hulks

Source: Public domain

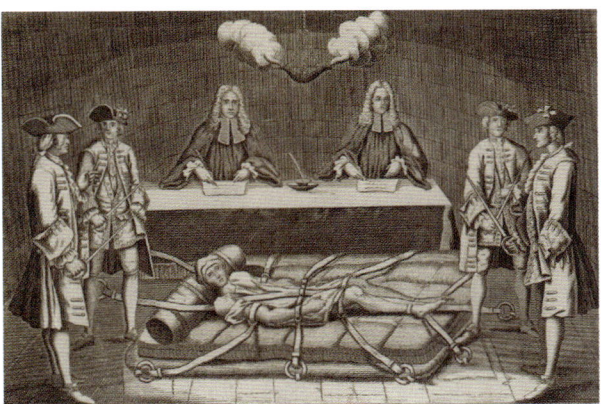

Figure 28.3 In the 18th century, 'barbaric' methods of administering the criminal law were common—as illustrated by the horrifying execution of 'Damiens the regicide' in 1757

Source: Bibliothèque nationale de France/Public domain

are hanged till they be half dead, and then taken down, and quartered alive; after that, their members and bowels are cut from their bodies, and thrown into a fire, provided near hand and within their own sight, even for the same purpose.

(Harrison, 1577)

And for lesser offences, 'rogues and vagabonds' might be 'stocked and whipped' while thieves would be 'hanged', except in Halifax, Yorkshire, where they could expect to be 'beheaded after a strange manner' by way of a form of guillotine (Webb, 2011: 40).

The latter example highlights the issue of proportionality of punishment, which poses a particular challenge to retributivists. That is to say, the punishment that 'fits' the crime can be seen to vary enormously in different historical periods; and this suggests that there is likely always to be a chance element to any fixed tariff of criminal sanctions, however reasonable this may appear at the point where it is established. The era of the 'Bloody Code' in England, for example, saw the number of offences subject to the death penalty increase from around 50 to 220 between 1688 and 1815. The use of such measures was both fairly common and a source of growing concern: 'Executions were enormously popular events, a fact that deeply frightened reformers' (Wiener, 1990: 95; see **Figure 28.4**).

Nonetheless, it may have been the very extensiveness of the Bloody Code that progressively strengthened feelings of unease about the scope and scale of punishments then administered: 'Juries appear to have been increasingly unwilling to convict on an array of minor capital charges' note Godfrey and Lawrence (2005: 70). As King and Ward (2015) also show, there was considerable regional variation in jury behaviour in the 18th century, with those in some areas, including Wales, seeking to convict on lesser charges to avoid the imposition of the death penalty.

Figure 28.4 Balcony at 30, Old Elvet, Durham, from which wealthy spectators would watch hangings on the 'new drop'-style gallows outside the courthouse in the 19th century

Source: Roger Smith

Prisons

As Wiener notes, it was not so much the retributive nature of such dramatic punishments, and others including the 'convict ship' and transportation, that prompted their decline and eventual abolition, but their 'arbitrariness and their tendency to incite dangerous passions' (1990: 100), at least partly because of their visibility. Instead, retribution came to be represented by the prison, with the denial of freedom taking over from the infliction of pain as the medium of punishment. Foucault (1979) has written graphically of this **transition**, suggesting that the prison itself represented almost perfectly the translation of rational thought into penal form. The idea of imprisonment mirrored and was 'bound up . . . with the very functioning of society' such that it was able to '[banish] into oblivion' other forms of punishment, real and imagined (Foucault, 1984: 215). The clearly defined nature of custody, and the ability to quantify it in terms of 'time served', made imprisonment attractive to penal policymakers:

> This 'self-evident' character of the prison, which we find so difficult to abandon, is based first of all on the simple form of 'deprivation of liberty'. How could the prison not be the penalty *par excellence* in a society in which liberty is a good that belongs to all in the same way and to which each individual is attached . . . by a 'universal and constant' feeling? Its loss has therefore the same value for all; unlike the fine, it is an 'egalitarian' punishment . . . By levying on the time of the prisoner, the prison seems to express in concrete terms the idea that the offense has injured, beyond the victim, society as a whole.
>
> (Foucault, 1984: 215)

Of course, for retributivists prison had the added advantage that it is possible also to promote it as meeting deterrent (see **Chapter 26**) or correctional (see **Chapter 27**) aims in addition to their own, and it need not therefore be the focus of **ideological** disputes about its true purpose. In Foucault's terms, the prison has a 'double foundation—juridico-economic on the one hand, technico-disciplinary on the other' which made it appear to be 'the most immediate and civilized form of all penalties' (Foucault, 1984: 216). What he means here is that prison can be justified as an efficient way of delivering clearly specified legal penalties; whilst at the same time, its organisation and structure impose a predictable and consistent form of correctional discipline.

The change in techniques of punishment in western societies from the early 19th century appears to be quite dramatic, although other forms of 'bodily punishment' continued well into the 20th century, with the abolition of capital punishment in the UK occurring only in 1965. Nonetheless, it is from the early 19th century that the prison was developed as the central element of the machinery of punishment. Its specific features of containment, routine and uniform treatment, and loss of time were more consistent with the spirit of the age. As a result, there was a 'swathe of prison building during this period' (Godfrey and Lawrence, 2005: 75), with a number of what could be described as 'state of the art' institutions being developed. Custodial sentencing became the norm very rapidly, so that in the '1860s, over 90 per cent of those convicted of indictable offences went to prison' (Godfrey and Lawrence, 2005: 75).

At this point, debates about the core purpose of punishment did not concentrate on the purposes of sentencing or the proper sanction to be imposed, but were found instead to focus on what went on within the prison establishment. It was not just the imposition of a custodial sentence which constituted the full extent of punishment, but in many cases the parallel operation of a harsh and intensive regime of 'hard labour'. Measures to intensify the prison experience were passed by Parliament and the 'task of enforcing the new-style penal servitude' was given to Sir Edmund Frederick Du Cane in 1863, who hoped that it would become 'the last and most dreaded result of a heinous crime against life and property short of capital punishment' and did his utmost to ensure that it would be (Tomlinson, 1981: 141).

Comparing regimes in the mid-19th century to prison conditions 100 years later, Godfrey and Lawrence certainly suggest that the role and nature of imprisonment 'was by no means unchanging' (2005: 81), citing an example of a petty offender required to 'turn a hand crank weighted at thirty pounds pressure ten thousand times every ten hours'. This was not untypical of this kind of prison regime in the Victorian era; and, in its pointless repressiveness, this intensification of prisoners' suffering can only really be seen as conforming to the logic of retribution as a form of atonement taken to extreme lengths.

Despite the apparent enthusiasm for this kind of meaningless penance in some quarters, others such as Henry Mayhew argued against the simplistic association of 'hard labour' with punishment (Wiener, 1990: 118). Pointless activities involving nothing but suffering would make 'regular labour' less attractive to the criminal rather than more so, he believed. This was not to suggest that demanding work should not form a key element of the overall sanction, but that it should incorporate some sort of meaningful productive purpose. The implications of this logic can be seen in subsequent developments such as the chain gangs of the US or labour camps in Russia, but also in the incorporation of mandatory and unpaid labour into a range of punishments administered in the UK.

Punishment in modern times

Contemporary thinking about punishment continues to be influenced by retributive thinking, whilst adapting to ideas about rehabilitation, reform, and deterrence. At the same time, some of the harsher aspects of punishment have clearly been modified; most obviously in the UK with the effective abolition of the death penalty in 1965 (1973 in Northern Ireland). As we shall see, this has led to some models of punishment which deliberately aim to incorporate differing objectives alongside each other.

Community service

As we discussed in the previous section, the idea of unpaid work as a punitive sanction became very attractive and so gained increasing prominence in penal policymaking over the course of time. Unpaid work in the community by convicted offenders has become a popular option for policymakers. The former Secretary of State for Justice, Chris Grayling (serving between 2012–15—see **Figure 28.5**), stated: 'I share public concern that offenders given community sentences often feel they are getting away with it, slapped on the wrist rather than properly punished.' The government would ensure that: 'Courts will be required to make sure there is punishment in every community order—whether community payback, a curfew that curtails an offender's freedom, or fines' (Grayling, 2012: 3–4). Furthermore, 'community payback' would 'in future involve

Figure 28.5 Chris Grayling, the Secretary of State for Justice from 2012 to 2015, wanted to ensure that all community orders were 'properly punitive'
Source: Policy Exchange (Flickr)/CC BY 2.0

a full five day week of hard work and job seeking'. The aim would be to ensure that, irrespective of any other aims, offenders' unpaid labour would be a demanding and uncomfortable experience, 'properly punitive' in the minister's words; and this in turn would be effectively complemented by the requirement for those engaged in Community Payback activities to wear high-visibility vests so that justice could be 'seen to be done'— ironically reminiscent of the kind of 'spectacle' associated with historic forms of punishment such as the stocks and pillory.

There are other possible motivations for the use of community service as a form of sanction. The scope for ambiguity may well contribute to its apparent popularity as a sentence of the courts—it is capable of being construed simultaneously as retributive, correctional, deterrent, rehabilitative, and restorative. However, the way it is administered is likely to suggest a bias towards one or other of these very diverse sentencing objectives. The type of work undertaken, for example, might be routine and unrewarding, on the one hand (retributive/deterrent), or it might be constructive and clearly of benefit to the community (rehabilitative/restorative).

Consider the questions in **What do you think 28.1** before moving on.

Fines

Having covered capital punishment, imprisonment, and community punishments, the final example of a retributive measure to be considered here is the fine, which has rather less of a sense of ambiguity about it. On the face of it, it seems to represent a fairly straightforward manifestation of the retributive principle of 'paying the price' for an offence committed. In medieval Iceland, for example, fines were central to the administration of justice and in some instances could be seen as a legitimate sanction in the case of serious crimes, including murder (Friedman, 1979).

The significance and universality of money makes it an ideal vehicle for translating the abstract notion of 'just and fair punishment' into a form which appears to represent a precise and easily measurable level of hardship to those on which it is imposed. As a consequence, fines are an extremely commonly used disposal, representing 77 per cent of all sentences administered in England and Wales in 2018 (Ministry of Justice, 2019). Interestingly, fines take the form of a debt to be paid to the state rather than to the victim of a crime, suggesting implicitly that this form of retributive punishment at least is seen as a forfeit owed for breach of one's obligations as a citizen in general, rather than between individuals. It might be argued that compensation orders fulfil that sort of function instead—but they are used very much less often than fines and are not identified as a 'principal disposal' but rather as a supplementary measure (Lee, 2013). Fines, too, offer some of the same attractions to sentencing theorists as imprisonment, in the sense that they can be viewed as simultaneously retributive and deterrent in effect (whilst coincidentally helping to cover some of the costs of administering the criminal justice system); although unlike other sanctions they cannot be seen as rehabilitative and by imposing financial hardship may actually have the opposite effect.

Despite the obvious significance of monetary penalties as a feature of the punishment repertoire, it seems that they have been little considered in research and academic literature. There has been some work undertaken by economists seeking to evaluate the 'utility' of the fine, particularly in terms of its influence on calculative decision-making by offenders (or potential offenders; see,

---

WHAT DO YOU THINK? 28.1

Community Payback

Read the extract from the Ministry of Justice website:

Community Payback is unpaid work like:

- removing graffiti
- clearing wasteland
- decorating public places and buildings—for example, a community centre

You will usually work in your local area, and be managed by a Community Payback supervisor. You must wear a high visibility orange vest while you work.

You can expect to complete anything from 40 to 300 hours of Community Payback, depending on how serious your crime was.

You have to work 3 or 4 days each week if you're unemployed.

The Community Payback work will be arranged outside your working hours if you have a job, for example evenings or weekends.

(Ministry of Justice website, www.gov.uk/community-sentences/community-payback)

In this brief outline, there are certain implicit messages about what sort of punishment Community Payback represents. What do you think these are? Why are offenders required to wear high-visibility vests? Why should they have to work three or four days a week on Community Payback if they are not in paid work? Why is the length of the sentence linked to the seriousness of the crime?

Becker, 1968, for example); but little discussion of the symbolic or material function of the fine as an element of the justice system, at least according to O'Malley (2009). He argues though that there has been a persistent tendency to overlook its significance in penal thinking, identifying Jeremy Bentham, for example, as someone whose interest in financial penalties has been overlooked in light of his more widely acknowledged interest in 'the disciplinary prison' and the Panopticon (see also **Chapter 27**):

> Yet he saw money sanctions as the ideally liberal form of punishment for they delivered no physical coercion. Rather than giving pain, they took away pleasure. They were, in the event of injustice, completely reversible.
>
> (O'Malley, 2009: 67)

Bentham also suggested that the level of fines could be calculated so as to deliver equitable punishments to rich and poor alike by calculating monetary penalties as a proportion of the convicted person's wealth, and not simply as a fixed sum. This was the idea of the 'day-fine', a fine based on the offender's daily personal income, which was briefly brought into law in the UK in the early 1990s. Fines were in theory precisely calculable, providing for fine-grained proportionality between the offence and the penalty imposed, and at the same time they were both cheap to administer and promised at least a modest future income to the public purse. O'Malley has observed, too, that the fine represents 'more than 70 per cent of sentences in all criminal courts' in Australia: and yet, he complains, 'the fine is virtually ignored theoretically' (2009: 68). This may be because the fine's monetary characteristics reflect the wider 'taken-for-grantedness' of money, such that the 'price of crime' is self-explanatory.

This kind of calculative logic is, though, less evident in the US where fines form a much smaller proportion of the overall number of sentences administered, amounting to only 29 per cent of disposals for 'misdemeanours' (minor offences) and being virtually unused in the case of more serious offences ('felonies' in the terminology of the US justice system). O'Malley suggests that this limited use of fines in the US is because fines cannot be viewed as 'reformative'; that is to say, they are not a means of offering positive support to behaviour change (2009: 72). In England and Wales, on the other hand, where their punitive aspects are more clearly acknowledged, the interaction between the use of fines and imprisonment seems to offer confirmation of their retributive character. Accordingly, a relative decline in the use of fines during the 1990s was mirrored by an intensification in the use of other forms of punishment, including custody (Ashworth, 2001), contributing to what has come to be known as 'the punitive turn' in criminal justice (Carrier, 2010).

During the 1990s, there was an international trend towards more repressive treatment of offenders, drawing on a mood of political populism. Although sentencing patterns did vary from country to country, evidence from England and Wales suggests that during this period there was a displacement of monetary penalties by other more severe sanctions, such as imprisonment; notably for offence categories that might be expected to generate strong reactions from the public. Between 1990 and 2000, 'for sexual offences the use of the fine dropped from 29 per cent to only 3 per cent [and] for burglary from 14 per cent to 3 per cent' (O'Malley, 2009: 79), reflecting, in turn, a wider upward trend in sentencing tariffs.

O'Malley also makes the more general point that imprisonment is often the penalty imposed for failing to pay off a fine, calculated as a daily monetary equivalent. As O'Malley points out, this draws our attention to another potential feature of the justice system, and this is its unequal impact because 'many of the high risk offenders are members of the "underclass" who in any case could not afford to pay fines. Prison is their fate once again' (O'Malley, 2009: 79).

As we have observed, then, retributive punishments can take a number of forms, involving both direct physical effects of one sort or another (corporal and capital punishment, for example), restrictions of freedom and incapacitation, material forfeits (money, work, or time), and even loss of dignity and ridicule (the stocks or high-visibility vests). Collectively, retributive punishments can be seen to share the features of the imposition of some sort of loss or harm, equivalent to the hurt caused by the offender's actions. Interestingly, though, we have also noted how different forms of punishment can be specific to certain cultures or historical periods and how these become more or less fashionable over time. We will now move on to consider the relationship between our belief systems and ideological assumptions and the changing practices in the administration of penal sanctions.

28.5 The objects of punishment

For many, the natural starting point for this section would be the work of Michel Foucault, and especially his book *Discipline and Punish*. Foucault offers a striking depiction of the emergence of modern forms of punishment and their underlying rationale and consequences. Starting with an account of the execution of 'Damiens the regicide', mentioned earlier, Foucault develops the argument that the mode and purposes of punishment have shifted, as it has become less about inflicting direct and dramatic public harm on the offender, and more diversified and subtle in its attempts to deliver an appropriate response to the crime committed. A period of:

> a few decades saw the disappearance of the tortured, dismembered, amputated body, symbolically branded on face or shoulder, exposed alive or dead to public view. The body as the major target of penal repression disappeared.

Instead, the characteristics of punishment became:

> Of a less immediately physical kind, [with] a certain discretion in the art of inflicting pain, a combination of more subtle, more subdued sufferings, deprived of their visible display.

(Foucault, 1979: 8)

As Foucault points out, the public shaming, humiliation, and harming of offenders in earlier times was both widespread and appeared to serve a particular kind of symbolic social function, in very demonstrably setting criminals apart; and in a sense asserting the implicit legitimacy of the punishments administered for the sanctions applied. The public nature of the spectacle and the direct involvement of the community as spectators combined two functions. On the one hand, this offered a direct and visible demonstration of the gravity attributed to the offence and, on the other, as spectators the general public were encouraged to show their approval of the pain and humiliation inflicted on the convicted criminal. However, their dramatic brutality tended also to implicate spectators in consenting to acts as vicious and unpleasant as the offences for which these forms of punishment were inflicted. Writing at the time in the mid-18th century, Cesare Beccaria (1738–94) (see **Figure 28.6**)—who is often thought of as the founder of the modern system of law and punishment—set out his essay: 'On Crimes and Punishment' and was an eloquent voice for such sentiments:

> The death penalty is not useful because of the example of savagery it gives to men. If our passions or the necessity of war have taught us how to spill human blood, laws, which exercise a moderating influence on human conduct, ought not to add to that cruel example, which is all the more grievous the more a legal killing is carried out with care and pomp.

(Beccaria, 1995: 70)

As the modern state became established, its role in the criminal justice system also became more extensive as it took on powers which had historically rested with monarchs or emperors. Logically, and perhaps more comfortably for the community in general, the state also began to take closer control at this point over the calculation and administration of penal sanctions, which would now 'tend to become the most hidden part of the penal process ... It is ugly to

Figure 28.6 Cesare Beccaria argued that the death penalty sets a cruel and unhelpful example of 'savagery' to the wider public
Source: Public domain

be punishable, but there is no glory in punishing' (Foucault, 1979: 9). What Foucault saw was a growing unease with extremely brutal forms of punishment, and an increasing reluctance to be associated with these amongst members of the wider society, so the administration of justice became more discreet and less likely to be acted out in public.

In addition, Foucault argues, this transition was associated with the emergence of a more 'civilised' rationale for the administration of punishment. The balance shifted from pure retribution towards correction, reclamation, or even 'cure' of the offender.

Although punishment continued to be administered bodily even after the abolition of the most dramatic forms of harm as public spectacle, it came to take different forms—'imprisonment, confinement, forced labour, penal servitude, prohibition from entering certain areas, [and] deportation' (Foucault, 1979: 11). In this way, the effect of punishment changed significantly so that: 'the pain of the body itself, is no longer the constituent element of the penalty. From being an art of unbearable sensations punishment has become an economy of suspended rights' (Foucault, 1979: 11). So, to the extent that the law still found it to be necessary to impose restrictions on the offender's freedom, this would be done 'at a distance' and properly regulated and monitored. Loss of liberty, then, largely took the place of the infliction of physical harm.

Foucault draws attention to the incorporation of 'caring' professionals into the administration of physical punishments; and the role of the doctor, for example, in alleviating the pain of those subject to the death penalty. Punishment should not be expected to lead to excessive suffering and so should be administered with moderation and care; and these assumptions have been incorporated into contemporary thinking:

> Lethal injection is the predominant form of execution in the United States, in part because it is considered more humane than hanging, electrocution, and chemical asphyxiation.
>
> (Waisel, 2007: 1073)

Wider processes of social and structural change necessitated the development of a different form of punitive logic, underpinned by changing patterns of social belief and political ideology, captured in the following quotation from Foucault:

> Shift the object and change the scale. Define new tactics in order to reach a target that is now more subtle but also more widely spread in the social body. Find new techniques for adjusting punishment to it and for adapting its effects.
>
> (Foucault, 1979: 89)

The emergence of rationality and a belief in scientific calculability associated with 'modernism' came to be applied to the field of criminal justice, as in all other spheres of human activity. As the 19th-century state adapted to industrialisation and the emergence of capitalism, taking on a more central role in organising human behaviour, it progressively assumed authority for the establishment and oversight of social norms. These became aligned with the requirements of the emerging market economy, and Pratt (2002) suggests that the development of modern forms of 'civilisation' associated with these drivers can be seen to coincide with changing ideas about punishment and justice.

As the new rationality became dominant, so too did the logic of proportionality and the belief in the capacity to match the punishment both to the crime and to the offender. Aligned with wider beliefs about the capabilities of science and the importance of applying knowledge with precision, crime and punishment also became infused with ideas about measuring criminality and matching punishment to the identified characteristics of the offender.

As the shape of punishment changed, it also became clear that retributive and correctional objectives could now be brought into alignment. In this way, too, the focus of punishment was transformed with the emphasis now on its impact on the offender's mind rather than simply on the body, an argument developed in some detail by Michael Ignatieff in the book *A Just Measure of Pain*.

In Foucault's view, the emergence of the modern prison was a logical and almost 'natural' reframing of the idea of punishment, so as to act on the attitudes and beliefs of the offender as well as exercising a regime based on the deprivation of liberty for a specified period of time:

> By levying on the time of the prisoner, the prison seems to express in concrete terms the idea that the offence has injured, beyond the victim, society as a whole. There is an economico-moral self-evidence of a penalty that metes out punishments in days, months and years and draws up quantitative equivalences between offences and durations.
>
> (Foucault, 1979: 232)

David Garland also claims that 'modern state punishment no longer addresses itself to the body of the criminal offender' (2011: 767), suggesting that this is partly a result of the 'civilisation' process of modern societies which have become sensitive to barbaric forms of human suffering and less willing to be associated with the administration of punitive measures which inflict direct pain. On the other hand, as he also acknowledges, it is difficult to avoid imposing some form of physical restraint in the course of applying penal sanctions if they are to be meaningful. Redefining imprisonment as 'deprivation of liberty' does not change the physical act of containment. Garland believes that 'bourgeois' sensibilities ensured that forms of punishment 'involving bodily exposure of suffering—the stocks, the pillory, flogging, birching, and branding—were mostly abandoned' (2011: 776). The death penalty, too, became less frequently used and eventually abolished in some countries, including the UK, as we have seen. Garland also refers to the process of 'refinement' of the death penalty in the US, and the 'transformation of execution techniques' both to reduce suffering and to achieve a sense of distance between the community and the state and the act of killing in the name of the law.

In practice, the development of punishment and penality in modern societies has been quite complex. First, as the direct infliction of pain and suffering on the body of the criminal has come to be seen as excessive and uncivilised, new forms of punishment have emerged, in the form of deprivations of time, unpaid labour or money. Secondly, however, these have not resulted in the complete abolition of punishments which involve the body in some way. There has been a tendency to underplay the direct bodily effect of punishment, in Garland's view, whether by deflecting attention from the physical conditions of imprisonment or by developing techniques which give the effect of 'sanitising' the punishment inflicted. Far from leading to a more 'civilised' system of justice, Garland concludes that this ensures that repressive treatment continues to be legitimised:

> The fiction of imprisonment as 'deprivation of liberty' occludes millions of suffering bodies and the regimes of discipline and neglect that produce them. Similarly, the fiction of a disembodied death penalty and an execution that 'ends life without touching the body' help ensure the 'dignity' and acceptability of capital punishment ... in this country [the US] long after it has been abolished elsewhere in the West.
>
> (Garland, 2011: 790)

Drawing on the example of the US, where (at the time of writing) the death penalty is still legal in 28 states, we should acknowledge that even in and between societies

WHAT DO YOU THINK? 28.2

A number of countries still have the death penalty, and this can be imposed for a range of offences, according to Amnesty International:

> Every day, people are executed and sentenced to death by the state as punishment for a variety of crimes—sometimes for acts that should not be criminalized. In some countries, it can be for drug-related offences, in others it is reserved for terrorism-related acts and murder.
>
> Some countries execute people who were under 18 years old when the crime was committed, others use the death penalty against people with mental and intellectual disabilities and several others apply the death penalty after unfair trials—in clear violation of international law and standards. People can spend years on death row, not knowing when their time is up, or whether they will see their families one last time.
>
> (Amnesty International, www.amnesty.org/en/what-we-do/death-penalty/)

Countries still using the death penalty at the time of writing include the US, China, Egypt, Saudi Arabia, Iraq, and Iran.

From what you know of these countries, do you think of them as similar or different regimes? Why do you think some countries continue to use the death penalty, whilst 106 had completely abolished it by 2019?

According to Amnesty International, the following methods of execution are still in use:

- beheading;
- electrocution;
- hanging;
- lethal injection;
- shooting.

Do these seem to you to be designed to minimise pain in the way that Garland suggests (execution 'without touching the body')?

(This article may help: BBC News, 'Death penalty: How many countries still have it?', 11 December 2020.)

---

which are often thought of as similar, there may be significant differences in their methods of punishment. We must be careful not to think of 'western societies', for instance, as sharing uniform criminal justice systems and practices (see **What do you think 28.2**).

In this section we have observed a diverse array of understandings and beliefs about what purposes punishments serves. It is both symbolic, in the sense of acting as a guarantor of fundamental ideas about the value of life, property, and freedom and how these should be respected; and at the same time, highly practical, in the sense simply of paying the penalty for an illegal act.

We have seen, too, that ideas about punishment have changed over time and so have the methods of punishment typically favoured. Punishment can have a number of objects, including the body, mind, and even soul of the offender (Collica-Cox and Sullivan, 2017), whose rightly-earned suffering may therefore be imposed in a number of different ways. Similarly, punishment can incorporate a range of objectives, with retribution sitting alongside other purposes such as reform, deterrence, and reparation. Whilst other aims appear to have become more influential, retribution retains a central position in criminal justice policy and practice.

What all retributive sanctions have in common is the principle that the offender must make amends by way of some sort of forfeit. The price of crime must be paid; retributive goals are still seen as legitimate in their own right without the need for further justification (Collica-Cole et al., 2017).

28.6 Punishment: policies, practices, and consequences

We will move on now from our discussion of the aims and ideological trappings of particular forms of punishment to focus more closely on the ways in which punishment is framed and delivered. How is it used and how is it experienced? In most cases, it is impossible to define punishments in terms of entirely separate objectives (as solely retributive, deterrent, restorative, or rehabilitative, for example); but it is possible to distinguish between them in terms of their principal or significant effects. For the moment, we will concentrate on those forms of punishment which may be viewed principally in retributive terms.

It is clear from policy pronouncements, judicial rulings, and the sentencing practices of the courts that retribution and 'just deserts' are never far from the thinking of those who are responsible for the organisation and delivery of 'justice' in our contemporary society. See **Controversy and debate 28.2** for a great example of this in relation to Chris Grayling, a recent UK Minister of Justice.

As far back as 1988, the UK Home Office issued a Green Paper setting out its objectives for the future of the justice system, entitled 'Punishment in the Community', and subsequent penal policy measures have demonstrated considerable continuity in this respect, illustrating two key points: that retributive punishment remained the benchmark against which court disposals tend to be judged; and that there is an underlying political will for sentences to incorporate elements of 'punishment', even when this is not their principal objective—usually for fear of appearing 'soft on crime'. It has been observed that the New Labour government (1998–2010) continually sought to present itself as 'tough on crime' because of the party's perceived historical weakness in this respect. The sound bite 'tough on crime and tough on the causes of crime' was central to both the ideological rebirth of the Labour Party as 'New Labour' and its landslide victory in the 1997 General Election (McLoughlin et al., 2001: 301). According to McLoughlin, one of New Labour's most notable achievements during its first term of office was to successfully challenge the idea that social democratic political parties are by definition 'soft on crime' (McLoughlin et al., 2001: 301).

Giving further substance to a sense of continuity and rigour in dealing with crime as a political issue, the proposals for community sentences published by the Ministry of Justice in 2012 under the subsequent Conservative/Liberal Democrat coalition government were titled *Punishment and Reform: Effective Community Sentences*:

These retributive sentiments can be observed in the pronouncements and sentencing practices of those in the judiciary, too. The 'default position' in respect of punishment is helpfully illustrated by the debate about the use and character of 'alternatives to custody' which has taken shape over recent years.

As Brownlee (1998: 9) has observed, there is a kind of 'beauty-contest' at play, in which those who wish to promote non-custodial sentencing options seek to present them 'in a light which will make them attractive' to courts who are predisposed towards conventional assumptions

CONTROVERSY AND DEBATE 28.2

The power of punishment rhetoric

The then Secretary of State for Justice, Kenneth Clarke, was widely seen as being quite liberal on social issues, but when introducing his programme of reforms in 2012, he promised:

> we will: ensure that there is a clear punitive element in every community order handed down by the courts. As a matter of principle, it is right that those who commit crime should expect to face a real sanction.
>
> (Clarke, 2012: 1)

A February 2015 radio interview with Chris Grayling, then Secretary of State for Justice, described his continuing commitment to short prison sentences (in a context of significant overcrowding and discomfort in the prison estate), because of the supposed desire of the public to see criminals pay the price for their crimes, irrespective of the very limited evidence of the reformative value of such sentences. Although Grayling was seen as taking a more punitive line than some of his predecessors, and indeed his immediate successor Michael Gove, the hard-line rhetoric was taken up again by Home Secretary Priti Patel in 2019, claiming to be on the side of crime victims in wanting longer sentences:

> The worst offenders should be spending more time behind bars. Victims will lose trust and confidence in our justice system if we don't make sure they do.
>
> (inews, 15 October 2019)

Some authors believe that this is a predictable feature of the relationship between politicians and the public:

> feedback processes in democratic politics—between crime rates, public opinion, and public policy—can account for the growth of **penal populism** in Britain. . . . the public recognize and respond to rising (and falling) levels of crime, and that in turn public support for being tough on crime is translated into patterns of imprisonment.
>
> (Jennings et al., 2016: 463)

Is this the best way to make criminal justice policy, though?

about the use and purposes of punishment. He describes the process of adding extra conditions to probation orders (as in the Criminal Justice Act 1972), as a means of enhancing the 'punitive bite' of the probation order itself (1998: 12) by incorporating restrictions on offenders' liberty within the terms of the order. This was intended to act as an incentive to sentencers who might not be persuaded of the order's merits solely by its rehabilitative objectives. Allen's (2008) account of later attempts by government to shore up support for non-custodial measures confirms that this is a recurring feature of criminal justice policy. Government repeatedly appears to emphasise the punitive qualities of alternatives to custody, encouraging greater use of fines by the courts and increased 'use of *robust* community sentences' (Allen, 2008: 389, emphasis added). Similar messages have been reiterated over the course of time:

> tougher community sentences may give more options to sentencers who currently feel that prison is the only robust choice.
>
> (Chris Grayling, Secretary of State for Justice, 2012)

> I do not want community orders which are in any sense a 'soft option.... Prison will always play a part in serving as punishment for serious crimes and in rehabilitation, and our reforms will deliver that. But we need to think more imaginatively about different and more modern forms of punishment in the community. Punishments that are punitive, for a purpose.
>
> (David Gauke, Minister of Justice, 2019)

To illustrate this point, we can consider the example of the community order, introduced under the Criminal Justice Act 2003, which offered a graded, tariff-based sentence which would enable courts to attach detailed additional requirements to an order in keeping with the seriousness of the offence: 'Twelve requirements are available to be used with the Community Order including unpaid work [and] a curfew backed by a tag' (Allen, 2008: 390). On the other hand, as Allen observes, some believed that even ostensibly tough measures such as this would not convince sentencers that non-custodial sentences could be 'effective', including senior members of the judiciary (Phillips, 2007, quoted in Allen, 2008: 390).

A subsequent analysis of alternatives to custody has also found that 'confidence was a key theme' (Taylor et al., 2014: 45) and that courts need to be persuaded that particular non-custodial options (in this instance, the pilot Intensive Alternative to Custody (IAC) scheme) would represent 'a sufficiently punitive alternative' to custody.

The IAC represented a further variation on the 'Order +' model of previous measures, in that it enabled courts to build upon the requirements of the community order by 'combining' sentencing components in new ways. In the evaluation undertaken by Taylor et al., it was indeed noted that the IAC orders incorporated on average 3.4 requirements, as compared to 1.7 requirements per offender given the 'standard community order' (2014: 46) and, of these, it was the more punitive elements such as 'Community Payback' and 'curfew' which seemed to be more attractive to the courts.

Interestingly, one of the findings of this study was that sentencers were not readily persuaded by the introduction of yet another innovation in what seemed to be an endless stream of new sentencing options, viewing the IAC as 'just another fad', according to one criminal justice professional (Taylor et al., 2014: 48). There 'was a prevalent perception amongst sentencers that the IAC was simply an attempt to "dress up" community orders' (Taylor et al., 2014: 48). In fact, the new sentencing option IAC seemed to fall foul of the same kind of response as many of its predecessors had done, as far back as the Community Service Order and enhanced Probation Order of the early 1970s. This viewpoint was captured in the terse response of a district judge: 'there's no alternative to custody; custody has to be used' (quoted in Taylor et al., 2014: 49). Custody is the benchmark against which sentencers appear to judge the severity of a sentence, and it seems that amongst them there is a consistent view that alternatives are just not the same thing in terms of toughness and impact on the offender.

This conclusion is supported by the recurrent finding that 'alternatives to custody' do not often function very effectively as a genuine alternative to incarceration. Brownlee has observed, for example, that following the introduction of new community sentencing options such as the Community Service Order, the proportion of convicted adult offenders receiving immediate custodial sentences actually increased, from 16 per cent in 1975 to 21 per cent in 1985 (1998: 11); and in the 1990s when the proportion of community sentences given for more serious (indictable) offences was increasing, *so also* was the absolute number of custodial sentences, as a feature of whole system expansion (1998: 135). Similarly, Allen (2008: 390) noted that the community order did not have the desired effect in terms of making significant inroads into the number of shorter prison sentences administered; and Taylor et al. (2014: 55) found that recommendations for the IAC made in court reports were not consistently taken up by sentencers. Indeed, the tendency for policymakers (and practitioners, it should be noted) to continually seek out ever more intensive 'alternatives' both plays into the underlying punitive ideology and, at the same time, underlines the implicit and self-defeating message that existing (and potential) non-custodial measures are simply not tough enough. Thus:

> An ever increasing demand for punishment is clearly set out in the current government consultation on community sentences and the sentiment is one of 'harsher' and 'tougher' community sanctions... In this context alternatives to

custody will need to be effective in articulating how they will punish and inconvenience offenders.

(Taylor et al., 2014: 55)

In a further note of irony, researchers have found a quite widespread belief amongst sentencers that they do only use custody as a genuine 'last resort', with some clearly expressing 'difficulty and distaste' when feeling compelled to impose custodial sentences (Hough et al., 2003: 35). Given that they already seemed to believe that they were only using imprisonment where absolutely necessary and where no other option could apply, the authors of this study observed that 'it is no surprise that many . . . sentencers were resistant to the idea that they should reduce their use of custody in order to reverse the rise in the prison population' (Hough et al., 2003: 39).

Despite significant shifts in sentencing trends and the prison population over time, it seems that there is an almost irresistible force at the heart of the judicial process. Retribution remains a powerful motivating force even if changing social norms and conventions have perhaps reduced the level of severity of the punishments administered. Sentencing policies and practices, and their underlying justifications, all seem to acknowledge the power of this dominant discourse embedded in the criminal justice process.

28.7 What are the effects of punishment?

As we have seen, the spirit of retribution is central to most debates about punishment. Indeed, it seems to act as the backdrop against which alternative objectives and methods of dealing with offenders have come to be judged. In the face of this, it makes sense to ask the question: what does punishment achieve? What are the effects and consequences of retributive disposals? Of course, in one sense, a punitive measure can be said to be 'successful' simply because it has been implemented. This is self-evidently the case in those historical and, indeed, contemporary measures which are simply about causing physical harm or pain. Execution 'works' if it results in the death of the offender on whom the sentence is passed, although there are some notorious historical cases of people surviving their own executions and subsequently being spared—as in the case of Maggie Dickson, for example (see The Scotsman, 'Half-hangit Maggie: The Scots woman who survived hanging', 7 April 2016).

Imprisonment can also be said to 'work' if the specified period in custody is served. A fine 'works' if it is paid in full. However, once we pause for a moment to reflect on the apparently neat symmetry of intention and outcome, we do find room for doubt. To what extent should the punishment 'fit' the crime, for example? Can it be said to be properly retributive if it is either too lenient, on the one hand, or too severe, on the other? Although the principle of balance can be effectively articulated, as Bentham illustrates it may be harder to achieve:

> The perfection of frugality, in a mode of punishment, is where not only no superfluous pain is produced on the part of the person punished, but even that same operation, by which he is subjected to pain, is made to answer the purpose of producing pleasure on the part of some other person.
>
> (Bentham, 2003 [1859]: 93)

Although Bentham here refers to 'pleasure', this might be better viewed in terms of 'satisfaction' with the outcome on the part of crime victims or the community in general.

How do we know what is a sufficient punishment, though, and on what basis can we calculate that the penalties imposed are 'just', equitable, and fair? What is an appropriate period of imprisonment for a specific crime, for example, and how do we weigh mitigating and aggravating factors? What consideration should we give to indications of repentance and remorse? And what of sentences that are irreversible—death, chemical castration, amputation, for example—what if there is a miscarriage of justice in such cases? Can such sentences be justified in general terms notwithstanding the heavy probability that they will be administered to innocent people in some cases? We will go on here to consider two areas which are both central to considerations of the effectiveness and fairness of retributive justice and which may prove to be particularly challenging for this as a core principle of sentencing: the difficulty of establishing proportionality and miscarriages of justice.

Proportionality

As recognised by Bentham in the quote in the introduction to this section, the question of the 'commensurability' of a punishment to the crime committed is of considerable importance when setting the criteria by which sentences should be determined. Of course, it is possible to develop a framework for grading punishments in relation to each other when they are of the same kind—for example, in terms of the duration in days, months, or years of a custodial sentence but, as Bentham acknowledged, this becomes problematic when punishments are of 'different kinds' which 'are in few instances uniformly commensurable' (Bentham, 2003/1859: 92). His recommended solution to this problem was to apply a scale of penalties within which a 'greater punishment' always incorporates the 'lesser punishment' which precedes it in the scale. Whilst this may prove to be an effective basis for determining the relationship between different forms and quantities of penal sanction, it does not address the more fundamental question of the relationship between any kind of punishment and the crime to which it applies.

The umbrella term 'crime', of course, covers a wide range of problematic behaviours (see **Chapter 2**) with and without victims, individual or corporate, against property or person, reckless or intentional, and expressed in these terms, establishing parity in terms of sanctions can be seen as highly problematic. In the UK, definitional distinctions between 'summary' and 'indictable' offences are intended to provide some guidance as to the seriousness of the alleged offence and therefore the scale of penalties to be imposed. Similarly in France, the distinction is made between 'délits' (less serious) and 'crimes' (more serious), and in both countries the level of court proceedings and scale of punishments available reflects this distinction. In addition, the sentencing framework is structured to enable courts to make individualised assessments of the seriousness of the offence in each case proven, in light of specified mitigating or aggravating factors, and to pass sentence accordingly.

There is clearly a mismatch here, on the one hand, between the apparently rational and objective basis for standard sentencing decisions and, on the other, the very wide variation in the pattern of sentencing decisions across jurisdictional boundaries, and in some cases even within the same jurisdiction. In the field of youth justice in England and Wales, for example, the arbitrary outcomes of 'justice by geography' have been recognised for many years (see Morris and Giller, 1987, for example); and this is a phenomenon which has again been acknowledged quite recently. As Bateman (2011: 10) has observed, there is a very wide disparity in the use of custody between different areas in England and Wales, with as many as 20 per cent of the young people (under 18) appearing in court in Merthyr Tydfil being incarcerated, as compared with less than 1 per cent in Dorset. Whilst 'demographic factors and the local prevalence and nature of youth crime account for some of the divergence between areas' (2011: 10), the disparity seems too great to be explained by these variables alone. Such disparities are a persistent feature of the youth justice system and, in 2015/16, Bateman (2017: 51) reports that 'rates of custody ranged from 2.28 per every 1,000 children [aged 10–17] in Islington, to 0.02 in Somerset and 0.00 in Wokingham'.

In practice, the principle of proportionality is compromised by 'real world' factors which distort the judicial process and lead to inconsistent outcomes. It becomes even more concerning when we observe that geography is not the only variable at play; in particular, ethnicity can be a significant factor in relation to inconsistent use of custody. A study commissioned by *The Guardian* newspaper found in 2011 that 'black offenders were 44 per cent more likely than white offenders to be sentenced to prison for driving offences, 38 per cent more likely to be imprisoned for public disorder or possession of a weapon and 27 per cent more likely for drugs possession' and a similar pattern applied in the case of Asian offenders (*The Guardian*, 26 November 2011). Uhrig (2016) found that 'black individuals account for about 3% of the total population of England and Wales yet make up about 9% of defendants prosecuted for indictable offences'. And, the influential Lammy Report has also noted that for 'drug offences, the odds of receiving a prison sentence were around 240% higher for BAME offenders, compared to White offenders' (Lammy, 2017: 36).

Inconsistencies in sentencing of this kind are also to be found in international comparisons, with courts in France, for example, actually being much more likely to impose prison sentences than England and Wales, but for much shorter periods, with the result that it consistently has a much smaller prison population per 100,000 of the overall national population (National Audit Office, 2012; Aebi and Tiago, 2018). Figures produced by the Institute for Criminal Policy Research in 2016 show a very wide variation in the rate of imprisonment globally, and even within a fairly homogeneous region of the world such as Europe. For example, prison population rates per 100,000 of the national population ranged from 21 in Liechtenstein to 445 in Russia; between those extremes there were 55 in Sweden, 76 in Germany, 133 in Spain, and 147 in England and Wales.

Sentencing patterns are thus widely disparate and raise significant questions about the notion of 'proportionality' as a guiding principle in sentencing policy and practice, since the application of such rules seems to be highly situated, specific, and biased.

Miscarriages of justice

The justice system relies for its standing on a broad level of shared belief in its **reliability** and consistent capacity to achieve the proper result. For it to retain its legitimacy, we have to be able to trust it, and largely it seems that we do, with 64 per cent of the public expressing confidence in the criminal justice system in 2013/14, for example (Janssen, 2015).

> 'People think that miscarriages of justice are rare and exceptional,' says Dr Michael Naughton, founder of the UK Innocence Project. 'But every single day, people are overturning convictions for criminal offences. Miscarriages of justice are routine, even mundane features of the criminal justice system. They are systemic.'
>
> (*Daily Telegraph*, 4 September 2014)

The retributive basis for punishment rests, as we have seen, on a series of assumptions, crucial amongst which is that it is possible to be sure of the guilt of the convicted offender on whom the punishment is imposed. Of course, it is impossible to guarantee total certainty so we might have to accept that penalties will be erroneously imposed in a very small number of cases. The risk of unfairly being criminalised incurred by law-abiding people who just happen to be in the wrong place at the wrong time might in fact be seen as a legitimate price to pay (see **What do you think? 28.3** and consider whether you agree with this point). That is to say, if society determines that punitive sanctions should have a place at the heart of the criminal justice system, then we must equally recognise that there will be occasional innocent victims of miscarriages of justice. If this were the case, the next task would be to consider the question of what is a reasonable ceiling on the number or proportion of cases in which punishment is wrongfully administered.

In response to a wider sense of unease about a number of high-profile miscarriages of justice, the Criminal Cases Review Commission was established in 1997 to consider dubious convictions from the Magistrates' Court, the Crown Court in England, Wales, and Northern Ireland, and the Court Martial and Service Civilian Court.

WHAT DO YOU THINK? 28.3

Miscarriages of justice

If some people are arrested and punished for crimes they have not committed, is this a reasonable price to pay in the interests of a safer society? Are we prepared to accept that some people might wrongly experience quite severe penalties as an unfortunate by-product of a robust and authoritative response to crime?

What we do

Our principal role is to investigate cases where people believe they have been wrongly convicted of a criminal offence or wrongly sentenced.

(https://ccrc.gov.uk/about-us/)

In 2020, for example, the commission referred the cases of 39 Post Office workers to the Court of Appeal in relation to previous convictions for theft, fraud, and false accounting, which were subsequently found to be questionable because of problems with the computerised accounting system they were using. This was reported to be the largest number of cases referred for appeal by the Commission at any one time.

Naughton suggests that there are in fact many more miscarriages of justice than is commonly thought to be the case, and that there are 'many thousands of victims of wrongful criminal conviction who are able to overturn their convictions in the appeal courts each year' (2005: 166). He implies that reports of notorious high-profile cases where convictions are reversed tend to deflect attention from acknowledgement of the extent to which initial decisions of courts are routinely reversed. '[A]ll criminal cases in magistrates' courts', 'all those cases . . . that did not incur a custodial sentence', and 'all those criminal convictions that incur a custodial sentence of less than four years' are typically excluded from consideration (Naughton, 2005: 169). He maintains that the conventional notion of a 'miscarriage of justice' does not account for all those instances where the judicial process fails to operate fairly and consistently and an injustice follows, whether in the form of an unsafe conviction or an inappropriate sentence. He concludes that:

> The impossible pursuit of innocence can be discarded and a more appropriate debate about 'justice in error' can proceed. This . . . can feed into attempts to promote confidence in the criminal justice system by provoking a more adequate discussion on miscarriages of justice.
>
> (Naughton, 2005: 179)

Naughton has also pointed out that proving a miscarriage of justice will probably not mean that those affected will be fully compensated: 'almost all (over 99 per cent) successful appellants who overturn criminal convictions in the appeal courts in England and Wales are not even eligible for compensation for the losses and harms that they and their families experience, let alone receive a financial award to put them back into the position that they might have been had they not been wrongly convicted' (2014: 1160).

This might, perhaps, support the proposition that if we cannot be sure of the justice of the outcome in a great number of cases going through the justice system then the use of very harmful or stigmatising forms of punishment should be avoided.

28.8 Punishment, justice, and the public

Even though the previous section drew attention to the possibility of punishment being applied unfairly in some cases, it remains popular and is easily justified in light of public opinion (Hough et al., 2013). It is commonplace in political discourse to hear of the need for justice to be 'seen to be done' in the eyes of the public.

To a considerable extent, this seems to be borne out by the evidence from research. In the context of very low levels of public confidence in the delivery of youth justice, Roberts and Hough (2005: 214) have reported that, 'they [the public]... think that the system is too lenient'; a finding echoed in a subsequent study (Hough et al., 2013) and mirrored in similar investigations in other countries such as Canada and the US. When considering the British public's optimal 'purposes' for sentencing, the authors found that in relation to adult offenders, 'there was more support for proportionality [the idea that the penalty should be equivalent to the harm caused by the offence] ...: 46 per cent of the sample endorsed proportionality for adults' (2005: 216), compared to 31 per cent favouring deterrence, for example. At the same time, there was less support for the principle of 'just deserts' in relation to young offenders and relatively more backing for rehabilitative goals for this group. Other studies, too, suggest that 'the public' are prepared to distinguish between young and adult offenders. Whilst there is evidence of generalised concern about the behaviour of young people, punitive sentiments are tempered by other considerations such as the 'potentially damaging long-term impact of a criminal record on a young person's prospects' (Jacobson and Kirby, 2012: 3). On the other hand, when it comes to sentencing in general, there is a well-established popular belief that 'sentences are much too lenient' (Hough et al., 2013: 23). This sentiment was once again confirmed in the run-up to the 2019 General Election, when one poll found that 70 per cent of Britons believed that punishments should be more severe (YouGov, 'Brits want harsher punishments for criminals', 1 October 2019).

It has also been established that 'public opinion' has direct and indirect effects on courts and sentencing decisions. In one study of the behaviour of the judiciary: 'All the sentencers interviewed... were acutely aware that their sentencing decisions are not made in a vacuum, but in a highly pressured political and social context' (Hough et al., 2003: 53). Sentencers described a feeling of 'there being too much political interference', for example, and of government tendencies towards 'knee-jerk reactions' (2003: 53). But they also experienced a sense of direct pressure from the public: '[s]everal of the sentencers, particularly district judges and magistrates, talked of being criticised by the media or the public for not being tough enough with the offenders who come before them' (2003: 54). Sentencers have been shown to have particular concerns about the credibility of community disposals, fearing that these would be viewed as a 'soft option' or 'cop out' (2003: 54). Thus:

> A senior judge commented that his 'biggest regret' was over a six-month sentence he once imposed for death by dangerous driving. He felt in hindsight that he should have used a non-custodial penalty; however he opted for custody because 'I was scared of what the world would say'.
>
> (Hough et al., 2003: 57)

Although not all the judiciary felt beholden to public opinion in the same way—for one Crown Court judge, media criticism would be 'water off a duck's back', for example (2003: 56), the strong overall message is that if sentencers anticipated a particularly punitive response from the media or the public, they would take this into account when passing sentence.

This poses additional challenges to the principles of fairness and equity in sentencing. First, an assumed consensus around sentencing practices does not necessarily reflect the views or expectations of individual victims in specific cases—should we therefore seek to rely on some kind of objective construct of public expectations of the appropriate level of harm to be inflicted on the offender, or should we rely on the specific views of the 'real life' victim in a 'their' case? However, this then raises concerns about equity from the point of view of the offender. Perhaps a more 'objective' set of sentencing criteria would be fairer in the interests of consistency?

This, though, brings us to our second dilemma—concerning the subjective effect of punishment and whether there should be incorporated an assessment of the specific impact of a particular sanction on a particular offender. This might be another argument for taking account of mitigating factors, such as those to do with lesser blameworthiness, on the one hand, or particular adverse impacts on the offender, on the other:

> Suppose two people commit the same crime and are sentenced to equal terms in the same prison facility. I argue that they have identical punishments in name only. One may experience incarceration as challenging but tolerable while the other is thoroughly tormented by it. Even though people vary substantially in their experiences of punishment, our sentencing laws pay little attention to such differences.
>
> (Kolber, 2009: 182)

Bronsteen et al. (2008) make the important point that the impact of punishment is inevitably modified by the capacity of humans to 'adapt' to their circumstances and to the privations (penalties or deprivations of freedom) to which they are subject. Thus, for example, they argue that a bigger fine will not 'ultimately diminish an offender's happiness much more than will a small one, nor will a long prison sentence impose much more suffering than a short one' (Bronsteen et al., 2008: 43).

In practice, then, it seems that establishing an entirely fair and equitable system of punishments which meets collective expectations as well as the wishes of individual victims and at the same time exacts reasonable and equitable forms of retribution on the offender is, for all practical purposes, unachievable. Punishment in its retributive sense can only be understood in terms of its symbolic function rather than its actual effects; that is, it makes sense because it appears to embody a 'natural' and consensual view that an equivalent level of harm must be imposed to compensate for harms caused.

28.9 Conclusion

We can conclude by reflecting on the argument that if punishment does, indeed, perform an effective symbolic and cohesive function on behalf of the wider society, then this is good enough. We might accept the qualification that certain forms of punishment should be ruled out because of the unnecessary or irreversible harm they cause, but otherwise retribution might be viewed as a perfectly legitimate aim and driver of sentencing. If it satisfies such popular aspirations, isn't that sufficient to justify its position as the cornerstone of sentencing practice?

Perhaps so, but this line of argument must also mean modifying the purist view that public opinion should always determine the sentence to be imposed—as in the case of capital punishment where opinion surveys consistently demonstrate a majority in favour of it amongst the general population, although support may be declining (*The Guardian*, 12 August 2014).

Other questions would still remain concerning if and how the punishment can be made to 'fit the crime'—what length of prison term should apply to what offence, for example; a question which appears to lead to very different answers in France or Norway and the UK, for instance.

More significantly, though, persistent questions also arise over what exactly punitive penal sanctions achieve, especially in the case of imprisonment. The use of custody is recognised as being disruptive not just to those sentenced but to others around them, especially if they have family or caring responsibilities (although some might actually prefer a short prison sentence rather than incur a debilitating fine). The use of custody is similarly acknowledged as being associated with high reoffending rates: 48 per cent of adults and 59 per cent of children are reconvicted within a year of release (Prison Reform Trust, 2018). Use of custody carries very substantial associated costs, directly attributable to the sentence itself—£38,042 annual cost per prisoner in 2016–17 (Prison Reform Trust, 2018)—and to its consequences (see Anderson (2011) on the social care needs of short-sentence prisoners); and it is socially divisive—custodial sentences, for instance, are disproportionately likely to be imposed on offenders from black and minority ethnic groups:

> Out of the British national prison population, 11% are black.... For black Britons this is significantly higher than the 2.8% of the general population they represent.
>
> (Prison Reform Trust, www.prisonreformtrust.org.uk, 12 February 2015)

In terms of the overall ethnic minority population, whilst they comprise 19.5 per cent of the population as a whole:

> Over a quarter (26%) of the prison population, 21,992 people, are from a minority ethnic group.
>
> (Prison Reform Trust, 2018: 7)

This observation, of course, acts as a direct reminder of the social context of punishment, as opposed to its abstract legal basis. The effects of punishment are distributed unevenly amongst the population and, as the Prison Reform Trust has reminded us, this is manifested in the form of institutional (and direct) racism (Edgar, 2010).

We are thus faced with what appears to be a 'natural' desire for crimes to be punished and justice to be done in the form of a penalty imposed in direct proportion to the harm caused by the offence—although this may be mediated by assessments of culpability and mitigating factors, such as mental health needs, on the one hand. On the other hand, we have to take account of the implications of taking a purely punitive approach to dealing with crime. Whatever modifications are made to sentencing frameworks and practices, punishment cannot be made perfectly equitable and fair. And, at the same time, there are a number of social consequences attributable to the administration of different forms of punishment. Punishment practices themselves are socially determined and, as we have seen, different cultures and periods of history have shown a readiness to use forms of retribution which might be viewed as brutal and unacceptable in the extreme. Sentencing regimes vary and seem only to be based on a very tenuous link between the harm caused and the penalty imposed—an equation which itself is subject to cultural, geographical, and historical variation.

This tension, in turn, poses a constant challenge to policymakers, practitioners of criminal justice, philosophers, and even criminologists, both in terms of questioning the moral basis of a retributive approach to punishment and in terms of the organisation, administration, and delivery of punishments that are able to meet certain commonly agreed minimum standards of consistency, fairness, and decency. We might then seek to review retributive philosophies and practice in light of the following questions:

- Is retributive punishment justifiable, even in its own terms?
- What are its principal features and effects? What are its limits?
- Can it be made fair and equitable? How can effective safeguards be put in place?
- What are the social costs of retributive sanctions? Who is affected?
- What are the implications of the use of penal sanctions for other criminal justice goals?

SUMMARY

After reading this chapter and working your way through its features you should now be able to:

- **Appreciate the rationale for retributive approaches to dealing with crime**

We have reviewed the main arguments advanced by proponents of retributive punishment, namely that it offers a fair and equitable means of redress for those harmed by offences; and it represents a commonly agreed form of sanction given legitimacy by the authority of the state.

- **Discuss the aims and objectives of retributive approaches to punishment**

The distinctive features of retributive as opposed to other approaches to punishment, such as deterrence or maintenance of social control, have been highlighted.

- **Recognise the development of different forms of punishment**

We have considered historical changes in the form and uses of punishment, notably the shift from dramatic, public, and brutal measures to the use of restrictive sanctions such as containment and loss of time.

- **Reflect on the use and impact of penal sanctions**

The extent of the use of punishment and its impact on offenders have been considered, including issues of proportionality, subjective vs objective assessments of fairness, and the implications of miscarriages of justice.

- **Evaluate the potential limitations of punitive penal practices**

Evidence of the relatively high reoffending rates associated with imprisonment, and the discriminatory effects of punishment on black and minority ethnic groups, have been introduced, along with a series of challenges to be taken into account by those seeking to develop effective frameworks for the administration of penal sanctions.

 Test your understanding of the chapter's key points by attempting the self-test questions on the **online resources** at www.oup.com/he/case2e

REVIEW QUESTIONS

1. What are the distinguishing features of a retributive theory of punishment?
2. Why do you think the idea of 'making the punishment fit the crime' appears to be popular?
3. What have been the most significant historical changes in the administration of punishments?
4. Why is it difficult to establish a basis for judging the fairness and consistency of specific punitive measures?
5. What are some of the problematic consequences of the use of sanctions such as imprisonment?

 Access the **online resources** at www.oup.com/he/case2e to check your answers to the review questions.

FURTHER READING

Beccaria, C. (1986) *On Crimes and Punishment*. Indianapolis, IA: Hackett.
A highly significant publication as it represents one of the earliest attempts to systematise the administration of law and punishment and to introduce a rational basis for the calculation of the penalty commensurate with the offence.

Foucault, M. (1979) *Discipline and Punish*. New York: Vintage Books.
An influential account of the emergence of modern ideas about punishment, and in particular the replacement of dramatic and highly visible forms of bodily punishment with imprisonment, whilst his analysis of more contemporary forms of crime control illustrates the later modification of pure retributive principles.

Hough, M. et al. (2013) *Attitudes to Sentencing and Trust in Justice*. London: Ministry of Justice.
A research review of public attitudes to sentencing which attempts to understand the prevalence of punitive attitudes amongst the general population and the widespread preference for harsher rather than more lenient sentences.

Kolber, A. (2009) 'The Subjective Experience of Punishment'. *Columbia Law Review* 109: 182–236.
An important reminder of the relevance of the subjective dimension of punishment and the problems this causes for calculations of equivalence in the sentencing process.

Prison Reform Trust (2019) *Prison: The Facts*. London: Prison Reform Trust.
An annual publication from a prominent lobbying organisation, setting out in considerable detail the realities of imprisonment in contemporary Britain.

 Access the **online resources** to view a wealth of extra information relating to your study of criminology, including self-test questions, answers to review questions, and links to other resources that will help you enjoy and fulfil your potential within your studies.
www.oup.com/he/case2e

CHAPTER OUTLINE

29.1	Introduction	864
29.2	What is rehabilitation?	864
29.3	What is rehabilitation for?	867
29.4	How has rehabilitation developed?	870
29.5	The objects of rehabilitation	873
29.6	Models and practices in the delivery of rehabilitative services	876
29.7	How do we judge whether rehabilitation is successful?	880
29.8	What is the impact of rehabilitation?	884
29.9	The limitations of rehabilitation	886
29.10	Conclusion	891

29

Rehabilitation of offenders

KEY ISSUES

After studying this chapter, you should be able to:

- explain the concept of rehabilitation as applied in criminal justice;
- recognise different objectives to which rehabilitation might aspire;
- identify and describe alternative models of rehabilitative practice;
- evaluate the achievements and outcomes of rehabilitative interventions;
- assess the critical perspectives on rehabilitation and its aims.

29.1 Introduction

As we have seen throughout the book, much discussion of crime and criminality focuses on the culpability of the offender, the management and control of crime, and the nature and legitimacy of **punishments**. However, there is another strand of criminological inquiry (and practice) which is more concerned with understanding offenders, appreciating 'what makes them tick', and seeking out tools and methods for reintegrating them into society as conventional law-abiding citizens. In effect, such approaches are concerned with identifying causes and consequences of criminal behaviour and developing interventions which will enable offenders to change their behaviours and thought processes so as to be able to take advantage of legitimate opportunities and to live decent lives. In this chapter, we will explore some of the beliefs and assumptions that underlie this kind of orientation to crime and criminality. We will consider some of the implications in terms of criminal justice practices and we will evaluate the outcomes of rehabilitative approaches. Finally, this chapter will also reflect on some of the limitations of this perspective on crime, both **empirically** and theoretically. Important questions to be considered include whether seeking to **rehabilitate** offenders means being 'soft on crime'. We might also be concerned about whether some forms of intervention to change offenders might actually be more intrusive than other forms of punishment. Are good intentions sometimes a mask for oppressive treatment, perhaps?

29.2 What is rehabilitation?

Rehabilitative ideas and practices are principally concerned with making sense of and addressing the origins and causes of offending at the individual level. That is to say, the focus of attention is not on general patterns of behaviour, or on the nature of crime in the abstract, but on the drivers and influences which lead to particular people committing particular crimes at particular points in time. What, in effect, are the causal factors which lead to criminal behaviour? And what sort of interventions can help offenders to overcome these influences and resume conventional law-abiding lives? We should perhaps also distinguish here between rather different rehabilitative outcomes. We might think of rehabilitation as being to do with being able to reclaim the status of a law-abiding citizen in the eyes of others; we might think about it as being able to resume productive and socially useful activity (such as work or caring); or we might think of it in terms of achieving changes in behaviour (stopping drug use, for example):

> If asked to describe a 'rehabilitated offender', it is likely that the majority of lay people would indicate a person with some history of offending behaviour which has now ceased. We might think of this as a return to 'normal', law-abiding behaviour ... it is about a change in the way a person behaves. So, the action of rehabilitation might involve the provision of interventions to remove the propensity, desire or necessity to offend.
> But the notion of rehabilitation also has a symbolic dimension, such that it implies a return to a former status that of a law-abiding citizen.
>
> (Robinson and Crow, 2009: 2)

The Rehabilitation of Offenders Act 1974 enshrined this principle in law in Britain (the Northern Ireland equivalent is the Rehabilitation of Offenders (Northern Ireland) Order 1978). Subject to certain caveats and exclusions concerning the type and severity of the offence, offenders could therefore 'spend' their convictions and reclaim full citizenship status and rights after a certain period of time following conviction. In practical terms, this means that most ex-offenders would no longer have to disclose former convictions to potential employers, or for any other purposes such as applying for insurance, obtaining housing.

In short, rehabilitation is intended to restore offenders to a more socially desirable way of living. However, the idea of 'restoration' does involve making the assumption that the offender's previous lifestyle or personal circumstances were adequate or socially acceptable. This may not have been the case especially for those whose offending may have been triggered by their adverse circumstances in the first place. With this in mind, it might not be enough simply to 'restore' the offender to their previous living conditions; but it might be necessary to go further and achieve concrete improvements—'this would suggest a definition of offender rehabilitation as "change *for the* better"' (Robinson and Crow, 2009: 3). Underlying ideas about what rehabilitation looks like are a number of other implicit assumptions. We will now move on to explore some of these.

Rehabilitative assumptions

There are five main assumptions underlying the principle of rehabilitation:

1. **A change in an offender's circumstances is likely to have future positive effects:** The achievement of

changes in the offender's circumstances is likely to have a positive effect on future offending; in other words, the removal of harmful features of the individual's life is also likely to remove the triggers to offending—say, in the form of a craving for drugs or alcohol which might be viewed as **criminogenic**.

2. **Offenders do not choose to commit crime:** The rehabilitation perspective views an offender as more or less constrained to act in the way that they do due to biological, psychological, or social influences which have behavioural consequences. Offenders are assumed not to have **free will** or full responsibility for their behaviour; or they are believed to be unable to respond rationally to the identifiable risks of being caught or to deterrent sentences. Rehabilitation is therefore not concerned with addressing the superficial manifestations of offenders' behaviour but engaging with them to understand and resolve underlying causes, of which offenders themselves may be unaware and which they are unable to control.

3. **Offenders are not fully culpable for their crimes:** In part following from the second assumption, is the belief that offenders are neither fully responsible for their behaviour nor therefore fully liable for it, in terms of the blame accorded to them or the punishment to be imposed. Punishment is not justifiable in retributive terms as the price to be paid for wilfully criminal actions simply because offenders are not in full control of what they do; but nor is it likely to be effective as a deterrent because the underlying 'drivers' of the offender's actions are not addressed by a punitive response.

4. **Change will help address the offender's needs and serve a community purpose:** It is assumed that effective rehabilitative measures will both meet an offender's practical and emotional needs and serve wider social purposes, such as improving the quality of life of those around the offender, for instance other family members. Practical help may be complemented by counselling or other measures to support behaviour change.

5. **Ultimately, rehabilitation 'works':** Implicit in the **concept** of rehabilitation is the belief that it is actually possible to return offenders to conventional, socially acceptable ways of life by virtue of the interventions provided with this end in mind. That is, most, if not all, offenders are believed to be capable of responding to positive help, guidance, or correctional treatment. Underlying the idea of rehabilitative practice is the presumption that it can be developed and delivered in a manner that will 'work'. For those convinced of its value, any difficulties in obtaining persuasive evidence of the efficacy of particular intervention strategies are likely to be attributed to design or implementation problems rather than any underlying shortcomings of the rehabilitative ideal itself.

Reform, resettlement, reintegration

As we shall see, the concept of rehabilitation remains keenly contested, and in setting out its apparent scope and intent we must be careful to avoid giving the impression that it can be straightforwardly understood or implemented in practice. Rehabilitation is 'surprisingly difficult to pin down' in the words of Robinson and Crow (2009: 2). They observe that this is partly because the idea of rehabilitation is complicated by its association with several other closely related terms, such as 'reform', 'resettlement', or 'reintegration', which all share the same prefix and all seem to promise some form of normalisation of the deviant individual. The common goal is to enable the (ex-)offender to take up or resume their place as a conforming and productive citizen. At the same time, however, these aims do differ in emphasis, and therefore perhaps also in the kind of processes and practices with which the terms are associated. Where 'reform', for example, can very easily be construed in terms of changing someone's behaviour, and (hopefully) making it more acceptable, 'resettlement' is more suggestive of effective service provision to enable the (ex-)offender to have access to the material requirements of everyday life, and ensure the same entitlements and access to facilities as anyone else. The '**social justice** charity', Nacro, for example, provides a dedicated housing and resettlement service for ex-offenders, particularly those released from prison without stable accommodation.

'Reintegration' might be seen as taking this process a step further, so that the (ex-)offender would now become able to play a full part in community life in exactly the same way as, and indistinguishable from, any other citizen. As we shall see, these differing interpretations of the idea of rehabilitation are reflected in a varying pattern of responses from the criminal justice system and other agencies responsible for meeting welfare needs or promoting change in offenders' lives.

McNeill (2012: 1) suggests that we must approach rehabilitation cautiously and with a readiness to accept that it is riven with what he describes as 'paradigm conflicts'. These conflicts are associated with a number of unresolved issues in the way the concept is implicitly defined; for instance, its 'underlying *crime theories* . . . have to engage somehow with the problem that crime is (at least in part) a social construct' (McNeill, 2012: 6). Therefore, interventions geared towards 'reform' and normalisation of offenders are based partly on a selective understanding of what constitutes criminal behaviour and its causes.

Rehabilitation for drug offenders, for example, could on the one hand be viewed simply in terms of promoting desistance from crime or, on the other, it could be undertaken with a view to ensuring that the identified offender is able to pursue a drug-free life, with the prevention of further offending being a secondary factor.

Models of rehabilitation

In an attempt to map out a route towards resolving this kind of conceptual (and operational) challenge, McNeill argues that we should adopt a multidimensional view of rehabilitation:

- **Psychological rehabilitation** 'is principally concerned with promoting positive individual-level change in the offender' (McNeill, 2012: 14).
- **Legal or judicial rehabilitation** relates to the formal 'decriminalisation' of the offender, by means of setting aside a criminal record or ensuring that one is not incurred in the first place.
- **Moral rehabilitation** effectively requires the offender to demonstrate acceptance of the reciprocal mutual obligations that citizens hold in common; and this could be demonstrated practically by some form of reparation or visible atonement for the offence and harm associated with it.
- **Social rehabilitation** 'entails both the restoration of the citizen's formal social status and the availability of the personal and social means to do so' (McNeill, 2012: 15).

Linked to this apparent uncertainty about how we should conceptualise the term itself, there is a similar degree of uncertainty as to how it should be operationalised. What does rehabilitation look like in practice? Where and how is it delivered by the justice system? For Robinson and Crow (2009: 5), the problem arises of how it relates to the punitive aspects of responses to offending. Is rehabilitation to be associated with a particular form of punishment or is it perhaps incompatible with the idea of punishment? Perhaps rehabilitation should be viewed as an alternative to punishment, maybe as a feature of court-ordered programmes which seek to address welfare needs rather than imposing a penalty of some kind. Or, in the event that the offender is subject to a form of punishment, does rehabilitation follow on from this as a means of reinstating the offender in the community, and perhaps minimising the harm caused by the experience of punishment itself?

As Robinson and Crow acknowledge, different approaches may lead to distinctive forms of intervention. For instance, where offending is seen to be linked to other needs, such as mental health issues, the case may be made for diverting reported offenders away from the justice system so that they can obtain treatment for the underlying problem. Mild and strong versions of this argument can be put forward, too, with one simply emphasising the underlying health need and the other stressing the positively harmful consequences of drawing someone into the justice system who may already be suffering difficulties in their life and so be particularly vulnerable as a result.

Where rehabilitation is viewed as an integral element of a punitive measure, it is also concerned with making changes in the offender (Robinson and Crow, 2009: 7), but these are directed mainly towards reducing the likelihood of reoffending. In this respect, rehabilitation could be seen to share some of the characteristics of a 'crime control' approach (see **Chapter 27**). It may be viewed as principally concerned with reforming the offender, and producing a law-abiding and productive citizen; that is to say, enabling behavioural change which will be beneficial both for them and for the wider community in the sense of reducing the likelihood of further offending.

Where rehabilitation follows punishment, it is likely to be viewed as a necessary form of intervention to enable the offender to return to a 'normal' life; that is, to take their place as respectable members of the community again, with no adverse effects as a consequence of experiencing punishment (such as homelessness). Rehabilitative measures might be required to address the problems which may have led to the individual offending in the first place (including homelessness, potentially). This view of rehabilitation, of course, stands in contrast to the concept of rehabilitative punishment since it reflects a belief that punishment itself is often more likely to be a source of continuing hardship than a vehicle for reintegration. Punitive sanctions, such as the imposition of fines or prison sentences, can themselves compound the difficulties experienced by offenders, and possibly their families as well. As a result, reintegration into the community may become more problematic, necessitating additional rehabilitative provision merely to offset the disruptive effects of the initial punishment. Western et al. (2015: 1540) provide a detailed illustration of the negative consequences of imprisonment in terms of substantial hardship after being released from prison, for example. Their analysis suggests that there is 'a mechanism linking incarceration to its negative social and economic effects: incarceration creates a stress of transition. Prison release is a disruptive event that is often unpredictable and unfolding in a context of severe hardship.'

Despite the obvious differences in approaches to the idea of rehabilitation, it is clearly distinguishable from other philosophies of intervention in the justice system, notably because of its concern for the outcomes for the offender, its assumptions about the 'causes' of crime, its belief in reintegration, and its relative lack of emphasis on stronger forms of punishment.

29.3 What is rehabilitation for?

Given the range of 'models' of rehabilitation we have identified, it will not be surprising that this also means that the ends and means adopted by their proponents also differ in emphasis and content. Rehabilitative objectives encompass a number of potential outcomes:

- the reinstatement of the offender as a competent and socially accepted citizen;
- achieving positive change in the individual's behaviour; or
- the amelioration or removal of the (external or internal) conditions which stand in the way of the offender's reintegration into the community.

Whilst they might share what could be described as 'normalising' goals, achievement of these varying aims (or steps on the way to them) may well involve different approaches to intervention and different success criteria.

Formal rehabilitation

'Formal' rehabilitation works in two ways to reinstate the offender. It may involve the termination of some form of prohibition or ban or it may involve some form of reinstatement of previous entitlements. That is to say, the rights, entitlements, and status of full citizenship are restored. So, someone who receives a ban for driving offences is formally rehabilitated once their driving licence is returned to them or the penalty points have expired. The end of a ban on movement or participation in certain events might also be viewed in this way; whilst the end of a period of supervision on licence following a prison sentence is also significant in signalling that an (ex-)offender is no longer viewed as a social problem or a threat to the community.

The underlying objective of this kind of measure is exemplified by the Rehabilitation of Offenders Act 1974 (as amended in 2012) in the UK, which 'aims to give those with convictions or cautions the chance—in certain circumstances—to wipe the slate clean and start afresh' (Lipscombe and Beard, 2014: 2). Significantly, the opportunity to make a fresh start is not afforded to all offenders in all circumstances, and there are certain types of offence and certain contexts which are expected to set limits to this principle. Under the Act, in general, convictions or cautions would become 'spent' after a specified period of time—the 'rehabilitation period', which itself varies according to the age of the offender and the nature of the caution or conviction. There are exceptions. Following the 2012 amendments, any conviction resulting in a prison sentence of more than four years could never become 'spent'. Rehabilitation periods could be lengthened if the offender commits a further offence before the end of the period, but on completion a conviction would be 'spent', and remain so, irrespective of any further offences. When a person's conviction or caution becomes spent they will become a 'rehabilitated person'. Calculating the exact circumstances and which precise rehabilitation period applies might seem an unnecessarily complex procedure for those obliged to follow the official guidance on the subject (Ministry of Justice, 2014).

The central objective of the legislation is to ensure that ex-offenders need not disclose previous 'spent' convictions when applying for employment, except in relation to 'excepted positions', which might involve working with children or vulnerable adults or in other positions of trust. On the other hand, spent convictions still remain a matter of record and will be likely to be taken into account at any subsequent court appearance.

The original legislation was introduced in the UK in 1974 to remove what had been seen as a significant barrier to rehabilitation, with former offenders being excluded from employment simply on the basis of having committed a crime of any kind at some point in their lives, potentially many years previously. However, this legislation in turn came in for criticism because it was believed to impose undue limits on rehabilitation periods (too long) and qualifying prison sentences (too short). With the arrival of a new government in 2010, with an explicit commitment to rehabilitation (Ministry of Justice, 2010), changes were introduced (effective from 2012) because the 1974 Act was felt to 'fail in its aim to help reformed offenders resettle into society . . . rehabilitation periods are too long and do not reflect the point at which reoffending tails off following a conviction' (Ministry of Justice, 2010: 34).

Further legislation was introduced in the form of the Offender Rehabilitation Act 2014, which seeks to provide a more comprehensive system of support on release for offenders receiving relatively short custodial sentences who are believed to pose relatively low levels of risk to the community but are liable to experience limited support on release.

The legislation in this area does indicate a broader government commitment in the UK to removing barriers to rehabilitation, particularly in relation to employment. Such measures only offer what might be termed a negative form of recognition, however, rather than constituting positive provisions to support resettlement or tackle continuing personal problems. In this sense, rehabilitation is seen as a formal process whose objectives are to create a level playing field and provide the same or similar opportunities to former offenders as any other member of society would enjoy,

Figure 29.1 The potentially stigmatising high-visibility tabard worn by this young offender undertaking Community Payback can be seen as undermining rehabilitative aims

Source: Photo by Jeff Moore/Jeff Moore/PA Images

especially in terms of access to work. The overarching aim of the UK government's rehabilitation proposals in 2010 was to 'put more offenders on the right path' and to enable them to 'become law-abiding citizens and contribute to society' (Ministry of Justice, 2010: 32). In this sense, then, we might think of rehabilitation in terms of removing the stigma that might be attached to offenders and therefore inhibit their ability to resume normal everyday lives. Such objectives can be contrasted to those which might work in a very different way to mark out those convicted as different or as posing a continuing risk to society. So, visible and potentially stigmatising signs of criminality, such as electronic monitoring devices or high-visibility tabards, can be seen as running counter to rehabilitative aims even when supporting objectives such as learning about the discipline and routines of work. Despite this apparent contradiction, such measures may still be associated with practical reintegrative objectives, such as the provision of work opportunities (paid or unpaid, see **Figure 29.1**) and the chance to acquire skills and enhance employability.

Rehabilitation as a social and moral project

The association of reform and reintegration with work has been identified as a particular feature of the 19th century, when concerns arose about the brutal treatment of convicted criminals in prison at the same time as wider developments in the industrial world brought demands for new and disciplined forms of labour to the fore. Michael Ignatieff's (1978) account of the transformation of punishment in the age of the Industrial Revolution links this explicitly to wider currents of social change, citing the example of Elizabeth Fry and her proactive attempts to change the nature and function of the prison. The introduction of 'order' into the penal establishment lay at the heart of her work to change the lives of women who had been imprisoned, inspired by the goal of promoting their subsequent rehabilitation into the community as law-abiding and productive citizens (see **Figure 29.2**).

Figure 29.2 In the 19th century a woman named Elizabeth Fry attempted to rehabilitate women in Newgate Prison, London, through methods which included reading to them, as shown here

Source: Jerry Barrett/CC BY 4.0

In order to achieve this, she initiated a systematic approach to identifying and then working with women who could be helped:

> First, the tried and the untried, the young and the old, the first offender and the 'hardened, drunken prostitute' were divided and placed in separate wards. The women's children were placed in a school within the prison, run by one of the prisoners.
>
> (Ignatieff, 1978: 143)

In an attempt, almost, to cleanse them of their previous criminal tendencies, and remake them as productive and conformist members of the community, steps were taken to impose a more ordered and sober appearance amongst the inmates, and so attention was paid to their outer appearance as well as their inner feelings and attitudes. The women's hair was cut short and they were required to wear white uniforms. Soon, too, they were put to work, sewing (Ignatieff, 1978: 144).

In an instructive twist to the idea of self-discipline, Elizabeth Fry also appointed 'monitors' from within the ranks of the women prisoners to watch over them. She wanted to show that even those most difficult to reform could be 'turned round'.

Many of those who visited were inspired to the same conclusion. They had seen Elizabeth Fry working with those she had identified as 'the very lowest order of the people ... the scum of the city and country' and she appeared to be demonstrating that their lives could be changed and they could show penitence and become respectable members of society (Ignatieff, 1978: 145).

In the early 19th century, then, rehabilitation had very much the flavour of discipline and instruction, whereby old unsavoury habits and problem behaviour could effectively be overridden by clear and consistent practices designed to mould and direct wrongdoers into more acceptable ways of managing their own lives. Rehabilitation therefore had a strong correctional flavour with its punitive aspects being viewed as an essential element of the reform process. Attention in this era was focused very much on controlling the behavioural manifestation of criminal impulses rather than remedying their underlying causes.

Rehabilitation as a psychological project

Subsequently, however, from the late Victorian period onwards the principal focus of rehabilitation could be said to have shifted, with a growing interest in psychoanalysis and those internal influences on thought and emotions which might in turn be associated with wrongdoing and harmful behaviour. Freudian notions of the Id, Ego, and Superego (see **Chapter 16**) suggested a set of complex internal interactions affecting individuals' propensities to behave in a particular way. In those instances where the Id was not subject to sufficiently rigorous controls by the other elements of the psyche, uncontrolled and sometimes criminal behaviour could be anticipated. The unconscious could be viewed as the source of problem behaviour. This assumption implies that interventions designed simply to change behaviour would run the risk of leaving underlying causal mechanisms untouched. 'Treatment' would necessitate an approach designed to understand and resolve those internal syndromes or characteristics which operate as the underlying causes of criminal behaviour. In Mary Gordon's (2010) terms, simply applying force or correctional interventions of the kind associated with Elizabeth Fry would be pointless where offenders were 'insusceptible of being managed by force'. Writing in 1922, Gordon argued that:

> The time is ripe for us to convince ourselves of this. We should turn a fresh leaf in our treatment of the offender, fortified not by precedent, or by age-long prejudice, but by the findings of science which is, at last, in the act of discovering the mechanism of the whole man. We know enough already about how he 'works' to be able to consider when, under stress, he falls, what to be at in the matter of restoring him.
>
> (Gordon, 2010: 57)

Arguing that most recognised forms of 'penal discipline' could only be viewed as unproductive, failing to 'impress, punish or deter the vast majority of petty offenders', she proposed the substitution of one principle of intervention with another, which would be geared to the application of 'scientific' methods of understanding and treating the offender. Advocating the 'deferred sentence', which would act as a reminder to the offender of the importance of compliance, she argued that the offender should then be handed over to 'the doctor' or 'the educator', and reap the benefits of an effective casework relationship. This view of the key purposes and shape of intervention became increasingly influential throughout the first half of the 20th century, and certainly played a significant part in shaping the development of the probation service, with a growing belief in the capacity of skilled professionals to achieve positive behavioural change.

These ideas are clearly represented in contemporary approaches to changing offender attitudes and motivations, as epitomised by the techniques associated with **cognitive** behavioural therapy, for example (see **What do you think? 29.1**; we will also come back to this topic in **section 29.6** in our discussion of models and practices in the delivery of rehabilitative services).

WHAT DO YOU THINK? 29.1

Cognitive behavioural therapy

Methods such as cognitive behavioural therapy can be used in rehabilitation. Read the following description of the therapy and then consider the questions below.

> Cognitive behavioural therapy (CBT) is a talking therapy that can help you manage your problems by changing the way you think and behave . . .
>
> CBT cannot remove your problems, but it can help you deal with them in a more positive way. It is based on the concept that your thoughts, feelings, physical sensations and actions are interconnected, and that negative thoughts and feelings can trap you in a vicious cycle.
>
> CBT aims to help you crack this cycle by breaking down overwhelming problems into smaller parts and showing you how to change these negative patterns to improve the way you feel.
>
> (NHS, 'Overview: Cognitive behavioural therapy', 16 July 2019)

- Do you think the objectives of rehabilitation can be achieved simply by changing the offender's patterns of thought? Yes or no?
- Why do you think so?

Rehabilitation through meeting material needs?

As the focus on the psychological dimensions of behaviour became increasingly well established in the early part of the 20th century under the influence of Freud and others (Ross et al., 2008), methods and mechanisms of intervention proliferated, offering a wide and varied array of individual and sometimes group-based programmes, drawing on diverse practice models. These shared an orientation towards enabling offenders to gain insight into their own actions and to develop the personal resources and capacity to exercise self-control and change that behaviour. However, an alternative view of rehabilitation would see it not simply as a matter of remaking the offender psychologically so as to fit in and feel comfortable with the idea of conforming with social **norms**, but that it should also take account of the needs of the offender. This argument is supported by the claim that interventions of any kind would be unlikely to succeed if the material needs of the offender could not be met. So, for example, returning a former prisoner to a jobless and homeless existence would leave them more exposed to the risks and temptations of reoffending. Rehabilitation, then, should be about meeting offenders' needs and ensuring that they are effectively resettled into the community; and this is not simply in their own interests but is also likely to discourage reoffending. This position was extensively argued by the incoming UK Coalition government in 2010, for example (Grimwood and Berman, 2012), lying at the heart of its 'Breaking the Cycle' reforms (Ministry of Justice, 2010). Interventions which prioritise offenders' needs can be controversial, though (see **Controversy and debate 29.1**).

29.4 How has rehabilitation developed?

It is widely acknowledged that there was a process of significant social change, emerging from the political restructurings and economic transformations of the 19th century, which also contributed to new ways of thinking about crime and criminality (Hendrick, 2006). According to this analysis, the idea of crime as a deliberate act of transgression, based on free will, came to be extensively modified or even rejected to the extent that crime was viewed as **pathological** and predetermined, driven by individual characteristics of the offender (Garland, 1985). The consequence of this line of reasoning was a call to develop an **individualised** approach to sentencing and intervention:

> We thus reach an individualization of punishment, which, once and for all, replaces the entire punitive procedure prescribed by the law according to the outer character of the crime—an individualization adjusted not to the crime but to the organic, latent or manifest criminality of the individual. This point alone persists; the conception of responsibility disappears.
>
> (Saleilles, 2010: 46)

This argument also therefore gave rise to critical observations about the unsuitability of standardised and purely penal regimes for dealing with offenders, with calls from some, for instance, for the criminal to be handed over 'to

CONTROVERSY AND DEBATE 29.1

Rewarding bad behaviour?

Sometimes rehabilitative interventions have come in for criticism either because they do not work or because they seem to be rewarding offenders for their crimes, as in the following example:

> A serial burglar dubbed 'Safari Boy', after being sent on a trip of a lifetime to Africa in a failed bid to stop his offending as a boy, was jailed today for his latest offence—breaking into an elderly widower's home.
>
> Mark Hook, now 38, was taken on an 88-day safari to Egypt and Kenya at public expense when he was just 17—sparking a national outcry which included condemnation in the House of Commons by the then prime minister John Major.
>
> But it proved to be a waste of taxpayers' money as Hook has continued to offend ever since.
>
> Today Gloucester crown court heard that in April this year, he smashed his way into 86-year-old Frederick Talbot's remote home near Dorsey, ransacked it and stole property and cash, including photographs of sentimental value.
>
> (*Daily Mail*, 4 December 2014)

In this case, a fairly unusual example of a rehabilitative programme designed to develop an offender's interests in constructive activities came in for extensive criticism, because it appeared to provide a widely unaffordable experience, compounded by its apparent failure to prevent him from reoffending.

By contrast, other less spectacular positive activity programmes have been reported to contribute to a reduction in crime levels.

> Kickz is a national programme, funded by the Premier League and Metropolitan Police, that uses football to work with young people at risk of offending in deprived areas. In the evaluation data crime rates on the days of the project were compared with general trends in the same area from official statistics. This method allowed the programme providers to argue that on the days that Kickz sessions were running, the overall results for crimes often associated with young people reduced by 23% for robbery, 13% for criminal damage, 8% for anti-social behaviour and 4%. Such a method shows a correlation between youth crime and the Kickz interventions.
>
> (Project Oracle, 'Sports-based Programmes and Reducing Youth Violence and Crime', October 2013: 12)

Certainly, the evidence of apparent success in this case may help to support the argument in favour of activities which might be enjoyable but still divert potential offenders from crime. Is there perhaps an important difference between giving those at risk of offending a chance to take part in regular activities—such as football projects—and offering them what might seem to many people as the 'experience of a lifetime'?

---

the doctor' or 'to the educator' (Gordon, 2010: 58), thereby effectively articulating the need for a new type of professional role in criminal justice. As Garland (1985) has observed, the late 19th century was a period of considerable growth in interest in crime and its causes amongst the expanding psychological professions of the time. Specialist skills and knowledge were reputedly required to gain an in-depth understanding of the offender's individual characteristics and mental processes, as the basis for precisely targeted interventions.

The origins of probation

Associated with the growing interest in criminological analysis and the penal reforms of the late 19th century, the probation service emerged as a new profession which progressively took on a central role in offender rehabilitation. For younger and less serious offenders, imprisonment seemed increasingly inappropriate to Victorian legislators, and in 1887 the Probation of First Offenders Act became law, creating space for rehabilitative interventions, even if it did not actually provide the means to deliver these (May, 1991: 5). To occupy this space, it was first police court missionaries, linked to the Church of England, who took on the role of providing advice and support to those placed 'on probation'. In 1907, the Probation of Offenders Act made provision for the appointment of paid probation officers to 'advise, assist and befriend' those for whom they were made responsible. Although never precisely defined, this phrase set the framework for probation officers to provide a range of services to offenders, including practical and personal guidance, counselling, and, in some cases, material assistance. Using their knowledge, influence, and interpersonal skills to promote reform became the core elements of their role:

> This era in the formation of the service took its impetus from a convergence between the inappropriateness of existing penal sanctions to a particular class of offenders—habitual,

drunken and petty—and a reforming zeal motivated by religious belief.

(May, 1991: 9)

Over the course of time, the role of the probation officer and the probation service became increasingly formalised and institutionalised. In 1912, the National Association of Probation Officers was established, which gave an organised professional focus to the development of this form of work with offenders and, by 1914, the service was sufficiently well developed to form the subject matter of a book setting out its form and functions (Leeson, 1914). The aims and scope of the emergent service were by this point fairly clearly articulated; and it should be noted that they incorporated certain assumptions about the limits of its operation. That is, it was believed to be of particular value as a means of dissuading and reforming offenders who were, as yet, uncommitted to a life of crime, or affected by particular adverse personal circumstances or influences. By implication, 'hardened' or experienced criminals would be considered less eligible for this kind of intervention and could, perhaps, expect straightforward penal sanctions for their behaviour:

> Probation is a system by which reclaimable offenders are given an opportunity to reform. It is applied to those in whom wrong-doing is not habitual, and whose youth, previous good character, or other circumstances, give reasonable hope of reformation.

(Leeson, 1914: 3)

Leeson also provided a flavour of the nature of the intended relationship between probation officer and probationer. This would be essentially paternalistic operating from a position of authority and underpinned by the threat of court-imposed further sanctions in the case of non-compliance. Probation orders could be imposed by the courts in place of a substantive sentence, but failure to comply with the terms of the order would mean a return to court. The approach of the probation officer to the offender on probation would be that of a reliable but authoritative friend, bringing insight and common sense to bear. It would not be expected that the probation officer would either idealise the relationship and be too forgiving of the probationer or that they would be too directive and so undermine the value placed on the relationship by the probationer. The aim would be to use the relationship productively as a vehicle of persuasion and to provide a good example; but the threat of court-imposed sanctions could also be called upon where thought necessary. Although the probation officer 'will not threaten without just cause, he will, when the occasion demands it, not hesitate to remind offenders refusing his suggestions of the court which is behind him' (Leeson, 1914: 114).

The emergence of probation in the early part of the 20th century is associated with a growing recognition that offending could be attributed, in many cases, to factors outside the offender's control; and simultaneously potentially responsive to non-punitive intervention in the form of counselling, guidance, and practical support. At the same time, though, such reforming or rehabilitative interventions would not be carried out on an entirely voluntary basis, free from any threat of further sanctions (Vanstone, 2004). This sense of ambiguity and compromise with the punitive underpinnings of the justice system has persisted in the subsequent growth and development of rehabilitation in criminal justice.

A casework approach

Further changes saw the probation service becoming increasingly clearly established as a statutory service; the Criminal Justice Act 1925 required all criminal courts to have probation officers attached to them (May, 1991: 11), with probation areas created and the work administered by local Probation Committees. As the number of offenders placed on probation increased, so too did the rationale for probation practice become more clearly oriented towards problem diagnosis and 'treatment'. As May (1991: 15) observes, the probation service had by now become clearly wedded to a social casework approach to intervention:

> Officers no longer engaged in special pleading on behalf of individuals in the courts, but provided a scientific assessment of their predicament. With the casework method the offender became the subject of professional diagnostic appraisal, all of which drew upon a phase in criminological thought which provided for the treatment of the offender who was in some way maladjusted.

As the 'casework' ethos of the service became increasingly well established, probation practice became more and more closely aligned with the broader domain of welfare-oriented social work. This influenced subsequent policy reviews and legislation such as the Criminal Justice Act 1948, which extended the role of probation officers to provide aftercare for prisoners, in keeping with broader rehabilitative aspirations and a view of probation as essentially a helping profession.

The Scottish model

Scotland went even further than England at this point, following the publication of the Kilbrandon Report in 1964 on child care and juvenile offending. This report set the scene for the effective removal of children in trouble from the remit of the criminal justice system, paving the way for the establishment of the Children's Hearings system in place of the criminal courts. This philosophy was extended to the adult criminal sphere, too, with the probation service being integrated with generic social work departments and the associated dominance of a welfare approach to the provision of community support of offenders. Ironically, as it happens, in parallel with these 'welfarist' developments, it has been acknowledged that from '1905 to 2004 most informed observers have recognized that the Scottish courts sent disproportionate and unacceptable numbers of the population to jail' (McNeill, 2005: 34).

As McNeill also acknowledges, the period from the 1990s onwards saw a change of emphasis in criminal justice policy in Scotland with significant implications for agencies with primary responsibility for working with offenders in the community. He identifies this change of direction as being inspired by 'a growing emphasis on public protection' (McNeill, 2005: 34). This was reflected in a growing use of measures of compulsion and conditions attached to community-based court disposals such as supervision and probation orders. Reflecting on these trends further, he goes on to speculate about the apparent contemporary threat to both the organisational forms and the underlying aims and objectives of probation and social work in criminal justice: 'Perhaps the most pressing question ... is whether the objectives that probation was established in Scotland to pursue—improving justice and helping offenders to change—can survive' (McNeill, 2005: 35).

From care to correction

These trends towards a more correctional and controlling orientation for probation are mirrored in England and Wales, as both organisational change and the framing and delivery of practice seemed geared towards reducing the role of rehabilitation in service provision. Probation and social work training were separated in 1997 and there were subsequent changes in structural arrangements for service delivery. These changes in training and delivery clearly signalled a downplaying of rehabilitation, since this function was being marginalised in the one organisation best placed to deliver it. Emerging trends towards more restrictive and coercive community sentences in the early 2000s led Robinson and Crow (2009: 162) to conclude that in light of 'penalties with more conditions and restrictions than at any time in the past ... it is difficult to see rehabilitation as a priority for policymakers or sentencers'. In parallel with this concern, the fear was expressed that rehabilitation had come to be viewed in purely utilitarian terms, with offenders no longer being seen as its 'main beneficiaries'. So, the value of a rehabilitative intervention would be judged according to whether it directly contributed to a reduction in reoffending or met victims' needs. It was no longer simply to concentrate on getting offenders back on their feet.

Rehabilitation was restored to a central position in criminal justice policy with the incoming government's publication of *Breaking the Cycle* in 2010. However, this did not translate into a return to its former role for the probation service. Continuing structural changes in relation to delivery of community punishments and supervision of offenders continued to create uncertainty as to the role and place of probation in service delivery. Between 2010 and 2015, community-based offender management services were reorganised and (partially) privatised, including aspects of the probation function, creating considerable uncertainty about how welfare and rehabilitative functions could be retained within the restructured delivery arrangements. Many experienced practitioners were highly concerned about the threat to their ability to provide an effective service, even though much of their workload had been transferred to community rehabilitation companies:

> I've been in this job for 25 years and I've never known morale so bad and so low ... You just don't want to go to work on Monday mornings. We've just had enough.
>
> (Probation officer, quoted in *The Guardian*, 9 April 2015)

By 2019, the government seemed to acknowledge the problems associated with its chosen model of privatisation of probation, and it seemed that the service would once again become a statutory function in the near future.

> Under the proposed future model, the NPS (part of HMPPS—which is an executive agency of the MoJ) will have responsibility for managing all offenders on a community sentence or licence following release from prison.
>
> (HM Prison & Probation Service, 'The proposed future model for probation: A draft operating blueprint', 2019)

Although rehabilitation has clearly retained a place in the delivery of criminal justice, changing policies, patterns of organisation, and intervention suggest a considerable degree of historical volatility, and a distinct susceptibility to change in the way in which it is conceptualised, in its place and standing in the wider justice system, and in its practices.

29.5 The objects of rehabilitation

As the history of rehabilitative provision reveals, the objectives and practices which it encompasses are both quite diverse and subject to change and reorganisation over time. What was originally defined as moral weakness which could be dealt with by way of strong guidance and sound advice, has gone through a process of transformation and development, becoming increasingly associated with more precisely delineated 'scientific' formulations of offenders' 'inadequacies'. In both cases, though, the concentration on offenders' characteristics and perceived shortcomings has maintained a focus on achieving individual change as opposed to addressing wider needs or social circumstances. In fact, even under the broad heading of rehabilitation there are a number of significant differences in the understanding of need and the appropriate targets for change. This can essentially be summed up in the form of the distinction between material needs and their resolution through practical support and reintegration, on the one hand, and moral and psychological needs and interventions focusing on changing thoughts, attitudes, or behaviours, on the other. McNeill's (2012) **typology** of moral, psychological, social, and legal rehabilitation, as mentioned previously, clearly suggests that we can expect to find a range of approaches to the task of delivering 'rehabilitation'.

Faith and *moral* redemption

In its early days, rehabilitation was characterised by a strong spiritual element, even when this was linked with programmes of practical help. Prior to the 20th century, 'nearly all reform efforts were justified as religiously informed, if not inspired, undertakings' (Cullen and Gendreau, 2000: 114). Based on his experience as a 'police court missionary' in the early 20th century, Holmes (2010: 47) argued for fair rents, better schooling, and controls on the strength and sales of alcohol, at the same time as he sought moral redemption for those involved in acts of 'hooliganism':

> From apathetic content may God deliver the poor! From such possibilities may wise laws protect them! 'Righteousness—right doing—"exalteth a nation"', and a nation whose poor are content because they can live in cleanliness, decency and virtue . . . is a nation that will dwell long . . . and among whom the doings of hooligans will no longer be remembered.
>
> (Holmes, 2010: 47)

Similarly, writing originally in 1925, Poulton (2010: 60) argued for close attention to be given to offenders' 'spiritual' as well as material needs 'perhaps above . . . all'. The idea of rehabilitation itself has long been associated with religious ideals of forgiveness and redemption; these would be reciprocated in the form of penitence and reform on the part of offenders. The underlying assumption is that the inherent goodness of all, even those who had strayed into wrongdoing, could be unlocked by enabling offenders to transform themselves spiritually. This was clearly reflected in the strong sense of 'missionary zeal' in many of the forms of practice associated with rehabilitation in the 19th century and beyond (McWilliams, 1983).

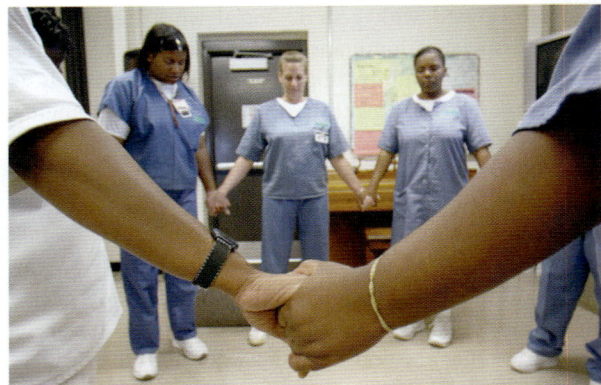

Figure 29.3 'Faith-based correctional' programmes and 'faith-based prisons' are quite common in the US, and UK policy documents also mention the potential rehabilitative value of 'religious groups'
Source: Inside CCA (Flickr)/CC BY-ND 2.0

However, this has been associated by some with a notion of pre-scientific ignorance (Mannheim, 1946). Early proponents of prison reform are attributed with 'only a rudimentary understanding of human behaviour', associating offending purely with a lack of moral fibre, itself attributed to the absence of a proper understanding of religious teachings (Cullen and Gendreau, 2000: 116; see also McWilliams, 1983). It would be a mistake, though, to conclude that these early proponents of rehabilitation had no understanding of the material factors, such as poverty, which were associated with crime or that the association of religion and redemption was entirely superseded by the more scientific approaches to 'treatment' which emerged in the 20th century.

In the US, 'faith-based correctional' programmes (see **Figure 29.3**) are still to be found quite widely (Duwe and Johnson, 2013), as are 'faith-based prisons', and there is some evidence that taking up religion is associated with reductions in criminal activity (Johnson and Jang, 2010: 119). On the other hand, Volokh (2011) has found no evidence that faith-based prisons 'work', in the sense of reducing reoffending. The benefits of religion-based intervention programmes may be viewed in terms of the material as well as emotional support afforded by a sense of spiritual belonging. It is interesting that the potential rehabilitative value of 'religious groups' is still mentioned in contemporary policy documents in the UK (Ministry of Justice, 2013: 8).

The *psychological* basis of rehabilitation

As we have moved from understanding crime and criminality in terms of offenders' morality to more 'scientific' approaches, so the focal point for intervention has also shifted, from the soul to the mind. The emergence of the social and psychological sciences and their growing position of authority in the late 19th century was associated with an increasing belief in the capacity to identify the causes of an individual's criminality, and accordingly to devise means of influencing their attitudes and thinking, thereby changing their behaviour. Reform and rehabilitation were seen as going hand in hand. Thus emerged the 'rehabilitative ideal', which has to a great extent underpinned efforts to understand the causes of crime and design effective interventions ever since, notwithstanding a period of 'ontological' crisis' and doubt during the 1970s when some discouraging findings led to the widely held conclusion that nothing 'works' (Martinson, 1974). The rehabilitative ideal first:

> embraced the belief that crime was caused by an array of psychological and social factors that ... intersected to push a person to the other side of the law. Second, and relatedly, the way to prevent future crime was to change the unique set of factors that drove each individual into crime. Third, the process of corrections should be organized to identify these crime-causing factors and to eliminate them. That is, the goal of the correctional system should be rehabilitation. Fourth, since each offender's path into crime was different, the rehabilitation that was delivered had to be ... *individualized*. Fifth, to provide individualized treatment, the state, through its agents in the correctional process, was to be invested with virtually unfettered *discretion*.
>
> (Cullen and Gendreau, 2000: 117, emphasis in original)

The actual nature of the crime committed, and indeed the harm associated with it, would be almost irrelevant to the process of analysing the root causes of individual behaviour and the development of less punitive and de-criminalising forms of intervention to ensure that offenders were effectively reintegrated into society. This meant, in addition, investing a great deal of trust in those experts whose task it was to assess and understand offenders' criminal characteristics, and put individualised programmes together to promote their reform. The concepts of 'treatment' and 'cure' became central to the process and sat sharply at odds with the idea that we explored in the last chapter, that the punishment should 'fit' the crime, or that the interests of victims should be taken into account in the sentencing process.

The language of welfare and treatment became much more integral to the criminal justice process, and informed the kind of diagnostic practices evident in the production of reports for the courts, assessing the offender and their needs in relation to the offence committed. Similarly, of course, a range of interventions was developed, collectively designed to provide insight into the offender's behaviour and to build within them the capacity to act responsibly and play a full and legitimate part in society as a reintegrated citizen. In this sense, although apparently quite similar to correctional measures, rehabilitative interventions could be seen as more

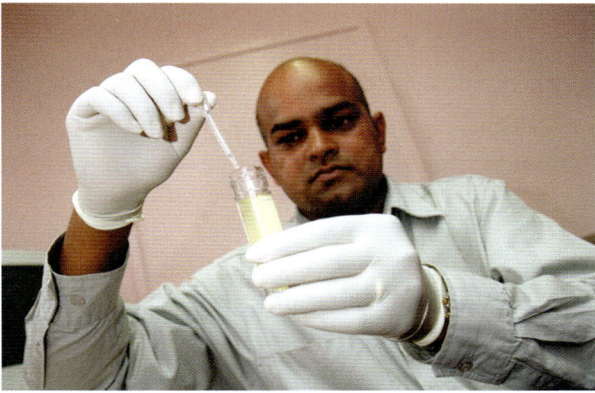

Figure 29.4 Interventions involving alcohol and drug treatment, including drug testing (shown here), are increasingly being incorporated into court disposals
Source: Janine Wiedel Photolibrary/Alamy Stock Photo

ambitious and more inclusive than those aimed mainly at curbing criminal tendencies or controlling behaviour. Although compliance with interventions might be ordered by the court, this would be for the offender's 'own good' rather than simply as a means of exerting authority and control. Significantly, offenders would be invited to recognise this by 'voluntarily' agreeing to comply with the terms of a probation order, until compliance became compulsory in 1997 (in England and Wales), prior to the eventual replacement of the probation order by the community order in 2005. The retention of the probation order in Scotland is another indicator of the distinctive philosophy of criminal justice practice applying there.

The emergence of alcohol and drug treatment as an addition to criminal justice disposals is perhaps a good example of the strand of rehabilitation which was about changing the harmful ways of thinking and associated behaviours of offenders whose criminal activities were believed to be linked to problems of substance abuse. Increasingly, interventions of this kind have been formalised and incorporated into the mandatory requirements of court disposals. For example, drug testing (see **Figure 29.4**) and treatment began to be included as conditions of community orders in the 1990s, and the Drug Testing and Treatment Order itself was introduced in England and Wales by the Crime and Disorder Act 1998. Here, too, an element of compulsion had crept into the process (see **What do you think? 29.2**), perhaps due to the assumed loss of self-control associated with addictions.

Resettlement and *social* rehabilitation

In addition to forms of rehabilitation which focus on the supposed psychological or attitudinal 'problems' of the offender, and their impact on their behaviour, there has also

> ### WHAT DO YOU THINK? 29.2
>
> **Should rehabilitation be compulsory?**
> Some rehabilitative interventions are compulsory and attendance or participation in the prescribed programme is mandatory.
>
> - How far, and in what circumstances, do you believe that it is acceptable to impose mandatory forms of treatment, reputedly for the offender's own good?
> - What safeguards would you apply, if any?

been a consistent strand of rehabilitation practice which has focused on the practical needs and entitlements of those who are to be reintegrated into the community, particularly on release from custodial establishments. This form of intervention, too, has tended to vary in popularity over time. However, it is well established and well supported by principled arguments, based on the recognition that resettlement and a 'fresh start' depend to a great extent on the material conditions of those who are attempting to begin new lives as 'ex-offenders'. From Victorian times, discharged prisoners' aid societies were established, whose aim was to organise charitable support for ex-offenders to promote their resettlement and enable them to meet their immediate material needs. By 1884, every prison except one had established an aid society, and their work was coordinated by a national Central Committee of Discharged Prisoners' Aid Societies (established in 1877). Over the course of time, this body developed and became established as a central feature of the criminal justice system in respect of prisoner rehabilitation. It adopted its contemporary name, the National Association for the Care and Resettlement of Offenders (Nacro), in 1966. Nacro has become one of the biggest providers of rehabilitation services in criminal justice, and has also become an influential body in terms of providing policy advice and information to government and statutory bodies.

> Nacro's activities are designed to reduce crime, the fear of crime and reoffending. Our services give offenders and those at risk of offending skills, support and motivation to change their lives and move away from crime. We support the work of our services by working with policy makers and commissioners to improve reoffending outcomes and develop cost effect criminal justice services.
>
> (From Nacro's Charity Commission entry, 2015)

Importantly, the idea of resettlement offers a rather different view of the aims and objectives of rehabilitation to those approaches which focus on changing the beliefs, morality, thoughts, characteristics, or behaviour of offenders. In essence, the emphasis shifts from changing the individual to make them fit the expectations of society, on the one hand, to promoting change in their material circumstances so that they are better supported to resume life as a ('normal') member of society, on the other.

29.6 Models and practices in the delivery of rehabilitative services

As we have seen, the idea of 'rehabilitation' is open to a variety of interpretations; and, inevitably, this means that there are an equal (or greater) number of approaches to practice which claim to be rehabilitative. It might be helpful to think in terms of a spectrum, with interventions which are solely focused on individual change at one end, to those which are principally concerned with creating the right social conditions for effective reintegration at the other (see **Figure 29.5**). At one end of the spectrum, where the emphasis is very much on achieving individual change, rehabilitative and correctional interventions come closely into alignment with the only clear distinction being that the correctional approach seeks only to put a halt to criminal behaviour; whilst rehabilitative measures are also interested in improving quality of life.

At the other end of the spectrum, rehabilitation shares much in common with radical perspectives whose approach is geared towards limiting harm caused by the criminal justice system itself.

At the correctional end of the spectrum, some approaches to rehabilitation are based on assumptions about the relationship between the offender's 'needs' and the 'risk' of reoffending. Where these two are closely aligned, interventions which target either of these are also presumed likely to have a beneficial effect as far as the other is concerned:

> The assumption is that risk is a rough indicator of clinical need and, therefore, according to this principle, high-risk individuals should receive the most treatment . . . while those designated as low-risk warrant little, if any, intervention.
>
> (Ward and Maruna, 2007: 71)

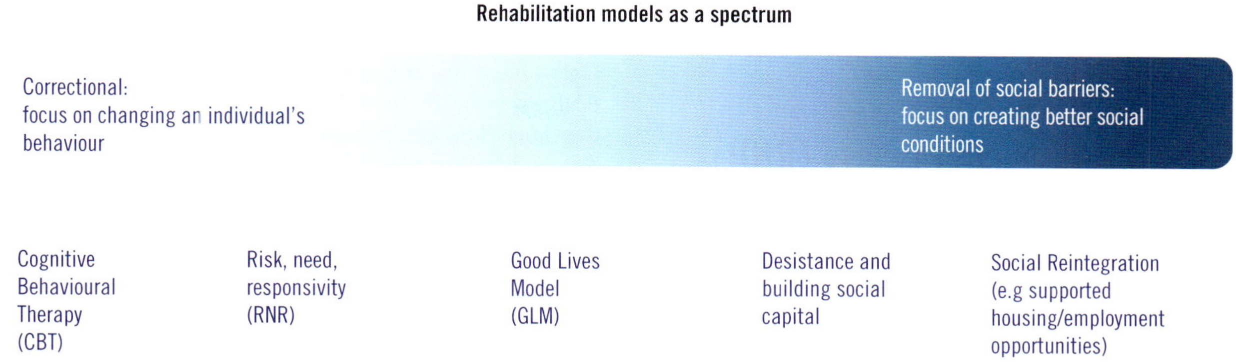

Rehabilitation models as a spectrum

Correctional: focus on changing an individual's behaviour → Removal of social barriers: focus on creating better social conditions

- Cognitive Behavioural Therapy (CBT)
- Risk, need, responsivity (RNR)
- Good Lives Model (GLM)
- Desistance and building social capital
- Social Reintegration (e.g supported housing/employment opportunities)

Figure 29.5 Rehabilitation models can be visualised as a spectrum, from correctional interventions to measures focused on improving social conditions

Cognitive behavioural therapy

Cognitive behavioural therapy (CBT) has gained considerable popularity as an evidence-based intervention which, according to extensive evaluation, is capable of reducing levels of recidivism when implemented rigorously (Lipsey et al., 2007).

CBT programmes have been developed to address the problems associated with faulty reasoning which is believed to predispose criminals to offend. That is to say, offenders are able to persuade themselves by a variety of tricks of the mind that their actions are justifiable, even if illegal. The offender may feel that they were victimised previously, and so the offence is just a way of redressing the balance. The offender may rationalise property theft on the basis that it does no real harm or by assuming that the victim is insured against loss. Or perhaps the offender perceives antisocial behaviour as broadly accepted or even encouraged; for example, if they are a member of a wider group which condones that sort of behaviour.

CBT attempts to unpick the thinking processes which lead to such forms of distorted thinking and so strip away the underlying justifications for the offending behaviour. Typically, the focus will be on trying to develop prosocial forms of reasoning and problem-solving; and developing techniques for dealing with problematic and stressful situations without resorting to unacceptable responses (anger management, for example).

A considerable number of bespoke CBT programmes have been developed to address different aspects of offending and targeting identified offender 'types'.

CBT has been widely endorsed by government and other agencies, such as the Youth Justice Board (Wikstrom and Treiber, 2008) because of its wide scope and the substantial evidence base in support of its effectiveness (see Lipsey et al., 2007):

> Cognitive behavioural interventions can affect many different areas of cognition and behaviour, as they may target, for example, emotional characteristics of behaviour, decision-making processes or the application of cognitive activity to behaviour.
>
> (Wikstrom and Treiber, 2008: 27)

Despite its popularity and reports of its effectiveness, some doubts are raised about CBT, particularly in relation to precisely what its effects are and the mechanisms by which it changes behaviours:

> some supporters of CBT play down the huge variation and complexity in process models that clinical psychologists have developed over the last 30 years and introduced into CBT. For example, dialectical behaviour therapy, schema therapy, acceptance commitment therapy, mindfulness, radical behaviour therapy (just some of many), although quite different, all fall under the general umbrella of CBT.
>
> (Gilbert, 2009)

There is some concern, too, about the 'black box' issue (see Bonta, 2008)—that is, the extent to which programme delivery complies with specifications; and uncertainty about precisely what aspects of the intervention might be having an impact (Haqanee et al., 2015).

At the same time, questions are raised about the almost exclusive focus on offending rates as a measure of success (Wong, 2019) and the limited attention given to making improvements in other aspects of offenders' lives—that is to say, the social dimensions of rehabilitation. How successful is cognitive behaviour therapy, then? Summarising the available evidence, the College of Policing concludes that:

> Overall, the evidence suggests that CBT has reduced crime. Specific and significant reductions were observed in both general and violent reoffending amongst adults, young people, and participants of different ethnicities. CBT aims to alter the way in which offenders view violence by building cognitive skills, increasing victim empathy, and challenging immature attitudes to crime. Results suggest that CBT is effective in both high-risk and mixed-risk offender groups.
>
> (College of Policing Crime Reduction Toolkit, 'Cognitive Behavioural Therapy', 19 March 2018)

There is, though, a lack of clarity about the mechanisms by which these outcomes are achieved, as the College of Policing overview also acknowledges.

Risk, need, responsivity (RNR)

For those who seek to develop a comprehensive approach to risk and need, it is important to distinguish between 'static' and 'dynamic' risk factors; that is, those which are unchangeable (static) and those where appropriate forms of management or treatment might achieve beneficial changes (dynamic). Static risk factors are those which are more or less fixed but are still associated with a greater likelihood of being involved in crime—such as being male or having offended previously. Dynamic risk factors are more likely to change, or be capable of being influenced, and might include such attributes as peer relationships, 'impulsivity or deviant sexual preferences' (Ward and Maruna, 2007: 71). According to what Ward and Maruna describe as the 'Risk-Need-Responsivity Model', the next stage of the intervention process is to target 'treatment' programmes on 'changing criminogenic needs', such as impulsiveness or poor problem-solving capabilities; but not to prioritise other possible needs which are not associated with offending. The individual's well-being is therefore seen as less important than the primary objective of reducing the chances of further offending. The third element of this model, 'responsivity', establishes the principle that interventions should be adapted to the 'relevant characteristics' of the offender, such as their 'cognitive ability' and 'preferred learning styles' (Ward and Maruna, 2007: 71). Responsivity itself can be further subdivided according to its 'internal' aspects, such as individual circumstances and characteristics, and its external features, such as **culture**, peer influences, and opportunities. Although this suggests that programmes need to be carefully tailored to account for variations between offenders, it is also suggested that, to be successful, programmes can be expected to share common elements. They will be (Ward and Maruna, 2007: 73):

(1) cognitive-behavioural in orientation;
(2) highly-structured, specifying the aims and tasks to be covered in each session;
(3) implemented by trained, qualified and appropriately supervised staff;
(4) delivered in the intended manner ... to ensure treatment integrity;
(5) manual based; and
(6) housed within institutions with personnel committed to the ideals of rehabilitation ...

Programmes incorporating these components have been implemented widely, especially in Canada. Typically, they offer a range of options so that interventions can be tailored to meet individual requirements. In British Columbia, for example, interventions based on the RNR framework have been delivered for some time; they include core programmes incorporating cognitive-behavioural techniques, violence prevention, respectful relationships modules, substance abuse management, and specific interventions designed for female offenders (Government of British Columbia, 2012). Some studies suggest that the RNR model offers considerable success in reducing reoffending (for example, Bonta et al., 2011); although the model is often inconsistently implemented (Viglione, 2019).

The Good Lives Model (GLM)

There has been some criticism of an apparent tendency for the RNR model to fail to take full account of offenders' 'needs' (Hannah-Moffat, 2005), with an undue focus on the correctional/individual end of the rehabilitation spectrum introduced earlier. Ward and Maruna (2007: 107) have proposed an alternative formulation, described as the 'Good Lives Model', stating that it was originally developed 'as an alternative approach to correctional treatment that has the conceptual resources to integrate aspects of treatment not well dealt with by the RNR perspective'. Essentially, the GLM looks more towards promoting beneficial outcomes for offenders and less towards managing risk through behaviour change:

> RNR is associated with a risk management approach and as such tends to regard offender welfare as of secondary interest, as a 'means' to the 'end' of increased community safety. By way of contrast, the GLM proposes that advancing offenders' needs will also reduce risk.
>
> (Ward and Maruna, 2007: 172)

The claim here is that while one approach focuses on addressing 'deficits' in offenders' capacity to achieve positive change, the other is concerned with creating the favourable conditions within which that might be achieved. This approach is based on the argument that there are a number of common 'primary goods' which overall contribute to our well-being but which may be sought or met in inappropriate ways by those who become involved in offending behaviour. The ten 'primary goods' are:

> life (including healthy living and functioning), knowledge, excellence in work and play (including mastery experiences), excellence in agency (i.e., autonomy and self-directedness), inner peace (i.e., freedom from emotional turmoil and stress), friendship (including intimate, romantic, and family relationships), community, spirituality (in the broad sense of finding meaning and purpose in life), happiness, and creativity. Instrumental or secondary goods provide

concrete ways (or the means) of securing these goods, for example, certain types of work (i.e., good of mastery), relationships (i.e., good of intimacy), or leisure activities (i.e., good of play).

(Ward and Gannon, 2006)

The goals of the GLM approach are to understand and address the reasons and motivations for adaptive but unacceptable behaviour. As such, the GLM adopts an orientation towards achievement and making improvements in offenders' lives which in turn reduce the incentives to reoffend, but without necessarily addressing offending behaviour directly. Ward and Maruna (2007: 170) cite the 'Make it Work' programme in Victoria, Australia as an example of a GLM initiative to 'support positive lifestyle change ... and to reduce recidivism through a combination of vocational training and a mentoring system'. There have been a number of studies which appear to have demonstrated successful outcomes of interventions based on the GLM (see Purvis et al., 2011), in the sense of generating an improved quality of life for ex-offenders and therefore potentially increasing the likelihood of sustained desistance from offending.

In North West England, the G-map project, established in 1988, applied the GLM to its work as a specialist service for young people who had exhibited sexually harmful behaviour (Wylie and Griffin, 2013). Although distinguishing itself from the initial articulation of the GLM, the G-map approach is designed to enable young people to pursue a number of 'primary goods' or 'needs', supporting the achievement of outcomes which are both beneficial to them and prosocial. The five 'primary needs' identified are (Wylie and Griffin, 2013: 347):

- having people in my life;
- being healthy;
- having fun and achieving;
- being my own person; and
- having a purpose and making a difference.

The particular focus of G-map has been to develop a model of practice with young people who have been responsible for sexually harmful behaviour. Over the course of time, typically 18–24 months (2013: 353), therapeutic work is undertaken with the young person to focus on those specific needs which have been met previously by way of sexual offending. Accordingly, very explicitly and directly, the rehabilitative intervention works to identify a causal connection between the young person's needs and the risk they might pose to others arising from these. The concept of 'criminogenic need' is operationalised and underpins the rationale for this approach to service delivery and reintegration of young people who offend. It is suggested that very often the traumatic nature of young people's backgrounds underlies their adoption of 'maladaptive strategies'. Thus: 'Trauma-informed practice can be directly relevant to addressing the Good Lives need of being healthy, addressing indirectly other needs such as belonging and being my own person ... and potentially mitigating risk' (Wylie and Griffin, 2013: 354). The experience of G-map is also taken to suggest that this intervention model could equally easily apply to 'other populations' of offenders.

Desistance and social capital

Although there is a 'dearth of outcome research' providing evidence of its effectiveness (Wylie and Griffin, 2013: 354), the rationale for desistance-based interventions which link offenders' needs and motivations is well established. The emphasis in this kind of practice model is on addressing and working with the needs, interests, and distinctive characteristics of the offender, so as to achieve and support prosocial change thought likely to discourage future offending. McNeill (2009: 17) explained the idea as follows: 'Put simply, the argument is that criminal justice social work services need to think of themselves less as providers of correctional treatment (that belongs to professional experts) and more as supporters of desistance processes (that belong to desisters).'

In acknowledging the contribution of the RNR and GLM models, McNeill and colleagues have also argued in favour of a broader approach to avoid the risk of an excessive concentration on changing the individual, and recognises that there is a social dimension to desistance as well. Observing that 'social capital' may also be as important as changes at the individual level, McNeill and Weaver (2010) make the case for including work with families and wider networks in the repertoire of rehabilitative interventions. 'Such work may involve helping offenders, ex-offenders and their families, where appropriate, to repair the bonding social capital represented in family ties ...' (2010: 21).

Further than this, the social capital available to ex-offenders can also be developed through the forms of intervention that actually promote positive ties in the wider community, and which thereby provide those concerned with additional resources and support in making changes in their lives. An example of this approach is the Circles of Support Model, developed particularly in Canada. In this model, offenders are directly engaged with community members whose role is to provide mentoring and encouragement and to hold them to account should their thoughts or behaviour appear to show signs of reverting to previous unacceptable patterns. More generally, it is suggested, identifying prosocial roles in the community for offenders, perhaps by way of volunteering, may be another mechanism by which their 'civic reintegration' may be encouraged and they (and others) may become able to see themselves as 'positive contributors to communities rather than risks or threats to them' (McNeill and Weaver, 2010: 21).

Social rehabilitation

A more wide-ranging and welfare-oriented approach to rehabilitation would take as its starting point the well-being and reintegration of the ex-offender rather than focusing only or mainly on reoffending. In this kind of approach, the principal aim is to ensure that those who have been involved in crime, and especially former prisoners, are resettled effectively and enabled to take up opportunities to enhance their lives and claim or reclaim a valued place in society. The emphasis here is on providing practical access to accommodation, work and training, health services, and other welfare provision; and at the same time, supporting or encouraging social reintegration within the community and establishing a positive network of relationships. In some ways, this may be seen as an extension of the desistance model, but by reversing the priorities for intervention it argues more explicitly for a reassertion of the everyday rights of ex-offenders as the basis for resuming full and equal citizenship. This may, in turn, reduce the likelihood of further offending but this would be seen as a beneficial by-product of intervention rather than its principal goal.

The Beyond Youth Custody Partnership has produced a set of good practice principles illustrating how this kind of rehabilitative model can be implemented. Rather than focusing directly on preventing further offending, these are concerned with building positive relationships and continuity of support for young people on release from custody:

- Ensuring a continuous service
- Preparing for release
- Supporting transition
- Ensuring engagement
- Co-ordinating services and brokerage

(Bateman et al., 'Beyond Youth Custody: resettlement of young people leaving custody', 2013)

29.7 How do we judge whether rehabilitation is successful?

We will now turn to the question of how rehabilitation efforts are evaluated. It is immediately apparent that we can judge whether rehabilitation is successful using a wide variety of criteria, depending on whether or not we are simply interested in assessing reoffending rates or extending this to consider other outcomes which can also be seen as positive (Wong, 2019), such as stable housing, successful drug treatment, or employment. Typically, though, the key criterion of success is seen to be whether or not rehabilitative measures act directly or indirectly to reduce levels of reoffending. On this basis, there has been a recurrent controversy as to whether any form of intervention actually 'works', in the sense of positively influencing the future behaviour of offenders undergoing such programmes. The gloomy prognosis that 'nothing works' came to prominence with a number of widely reported studies, particularly in the US. The Cambridge–Somerville Study, for instance, reviewed the outcomes of an intervention programme with a cohort of young offenders based on individual counselling, as against the results for a comparison group offered no such support, matched on a number of criteria, including age, personal characteristics, and family background. The study found that no improvement could be detected for those subject to the intervention programme in terms of a series of 'undesirable outcomes', including reoffending, early death, or diagnosis of alcoholism or mental health problems; and, indeed, rather more of the 'treatment' group experienced these adverse outcomes than those from the **control group** (McCord, 1992: 202). Ironically, the more likely the young offenders and their families were to be cooperative, the less likely the outcome was to be beneficial: 'These findings strongly suggest that the treatment itself had been harmful' (McCord, 1992: 202). Explanations for the failure of the programme tended to imply that there are inherent weaknesses in rehabilitative approaches which cannot easily be resolved, for example:

- the creation of dependency—whereby the offender in receipt of the intervention becomes over-reliant on the provider
- 'value conflict' between service providers and recipients—where conflicting objectives may lead to withdrawal from the service on offer;

- the effects of labelling—where the nature of specialist interventions mean that the recipient continues to be associated with an offender identity;
- the consequences of raised, or unmet, expectations—where the programme is unable to provide the kind of benefits expected, and recipients are disappointed and may become disengaged; or
- 'contagion'—in the case of specialist programmes which group recipients together and may actually reinforce their unacceptable behaviour.

(Zane et al., 2015)

Nothing works?

Of course, the Cambridge–Somerville Study was only one study and it only evaluated one intervention method, so it might be reasonable to argue that either the method used, or the study itself, were deficient in some way. It did not stand alone, however, and in fact contributed to a growing mood of doubt and despair. A consensus emerged by the 1970s that there was very little evidence to support rehabilitative interventions in general, encapsulated most forcefully by Martinson (1974) who concluded that 'nothing' or at least 'not much' works in rehabilitative terms and particularly in reducing recidivism. Martinson evaluated over 200 studies spanning a wide range of intervention programmes and methods, institutional and non-institutional, and found: 'very little reason to hope that we have in fact found a sure way of reducing recidivism through rehabilitation' (Martinson, 1974: 49). Martinson did acknowledge that there could be several reasons for this, including the models of treatment then in use being insufficiently well developed. If that were the case, all that would be required was a redoubling of efforts to eradicate the flaws in existing programmes of supervision, education, or personal development. However:

> It may be, on the other hand, that there is a more radical flaw in our present strategies—that education at its best, or that psychotherapy at its best, cannot overcome, or even appreciably reduce, the powerful tendency for offenders to continue in criminal behavior.

(Martinson, 1974: 49)

The effect of this seminal article was to cast a shadow of gloom over rehabilitative practices for a considerable period of time. Instead, currents of opinion favouring deterrent or retributive measures of punishment and, indeed, approaches grounded in principles of crime control and risk management became increasingly dominant. Only after a considerable period of time had elapsed—in the early 2000s—did rehabilitation make a significant comeback. Even though Martinson's claims came under critical scrutiny (Hollin, 1999), the belief that 'nothing works' became cemented in place as a form of orthodoxy in criminal justice: 'Against this academic and political backdrop, the policy and practice generated by acceptance of the futility of treatment were implemented on an increasing scale' (Hollin, 1999: 362).

Having been confronted with this challenge, practitioners and researchers went on to make extensive efforts to develop effective treatment-based interventions, and to show 'what works, for whom, and under what conditions?' (Hollin, 1999: 362). Lipsey (1995), for example, carried out a further review of 400 studies of delinquency treatment and claimed to have identified a number of factors associated with positive outcomes. These did not necessarily reflect highly sophisticated treatment programmes or techniques, but did demonstrate associations with particular 'treatment types'. Lipsey (1995: 75) found that consistently certain types of intervention were associated with 'positive outcomes', especially but not exclusively defined in terms of reduced levels of recidivism. So, for example, employment-based programmes, those described as 'multimodal' (that is, having a number of different elements), and those geared towards behaviour change and skills development were the most successful, although all except 'vocational counselling' and 'deterrence' were judged to have some kind of positive effect. In addition, Lipsey observed that successful outcomes were associated with more extensive and intensive programmes (longer term with higher levels of weekly contact), which appeared to be more beneficial (1995: 76) and that close attention to effective programme delivery by supervisors was also important. In other words, it was not so much 'rehabilitation' per se that was problematic, but the nature and integrity (consistency with programme specifications) of the programmes being delivered. It seems, then, that over time rehabilitation itself was being rehabilitated.

Rehabilitation revived

McGuire and Priestley (1995) built on this renewed spirit of optimism. They argued that it was possible to design and construct the kind of cognitive-behavioural and 'multimodal' programmes which could achieve success by addressing different aspects of offenders' needs and behaviour and therefore working through the complexities of their lives and the factors associated with offending behaviour. The focus of intervention should be on 'risk' (assessed on the basis of prior offending history) and 'criminogenic need' rather than needs which are 'more distantly related, or unrelated' to offending (McGuire and Priestley, 1995: 15). So, the shift in approach was encapsulated in the movement from 'nothing works' to 'what works?' (with or without a question mark). This process eventually culminated in the UK government endorsing rehabilitation (see earlier; Ministry of Justice, 2010) and supposedly launching a 'Rehabilitation Revolution' in 2012.

Given that there are a very wide range of factors in offenders' lives which may be criminogenic, this does suggest that there could be a very wide range of targets for intervention in rehabilitation work, especially if we believe that we can only reduce reoffending rates by addressing linked 'needs' of those who offend. One evidence review suggests that:

> **Holistic interventions that address multiple criminogenic needs are more likely to be effective in reducing offending.** The evidence suggests that offenders often experience multiple problems, many of which are considered 'criminogenic' in the sense that they contribute directly towards offending.
>
> (Sapouna et al., 2011: 12, emphasis in original)

Success might therefore be judged according to certain interim measures such as the level or extent of offenders' 'habilitation' (access and use of mainstream services, for example) or 'integration' (2011: 14), especially because offenders in custody 'have a greater number of needs' than the general population (2011: 13). This might suggest a need for a comprehensive and sustained approach to post-release help and support.

Harper and Chitty (2005: ix) have calculated that offenders are assessed as experiencing on average four criminogenic needs, and that this rate is higher for those in custody. This again provides support for 'multimodal' approaches to intervention and the establishment of a range of intermediate success criteria, aside from reoffending rates: 'multi-modal interventions offer the prospect that work on several fronts could be tackled simultaneously, with the potential to achieve more than the traditional "linear" approach' (Harper and Chitty, 2005: 59).

Key areas identified for intervention by Harper and Chitty in this review were: employment, education, accommodation, drug misuse, and mental health. Taking employment as an example, there are a number of possible approaches to supporting offenders into employment or training. However, there are challenges—where programmes are targeted at those in custody, for instance, they are unable to provide direct experience of work in a conventional setting so are limited to providing skills training or work preparation. Success might, therefore, be viewed in terms of programme attendance, certificated skills attainment, or jobs arranged for prisoners on release. In practice, one study of the circumstances of prisoners nearing release found that only limited help of this kind was available, and even when it was, it did not lead directly to employment for two-thirds of those receiving vocational preparation (Niven and Olagundoye, 2002). Consider **What do you think? 29.3** for an example of another issue offenders may face when looking for employment.

Similarly, it is suggested that community-based, employment-support initiatives might be beneficial for offenders. Indeed, throughout its history the probation service in the UK has viewed work and training as priority areas for intervention, with a particular focus on 'employability', although the evidence as to what sort of skills to develop, and how to do so, is limited and has been for some time. A report from the early 2000s stated: 'We have as yet no information on employment or offending outcomes from such schemes, on which to make a soundly-based choice between the options' (Johnson and Rex, 2002: 198). And yet, evidence presented to the parliamentary committee on the employment of ex-offenders in 2017 made a familiar point:

> The skills they are teaching, particularly in women's prisons, are not particularly applicable to today's world. They are not teaching them anything that you need in 21st century Britain. They are teaching them hairdressing. We don't need hairdressers. We have too many hairdressers in this country. They are teaching them sewing. Life has moved on ... Women in prison should be taught how to do Excel spreadsheets, coding and business administration.
>
> (Evidence of Jocelyn Hillman, Working Chance, to the House of Commons Work and Pensions Committee, Fifth Report of Session 2016–17)

See **What do you think? 29.4** for more detail on an organisation providing rehabilitative services for prisoners, and then consider the questions raised.

In other areas, too, whilst it may seem fairly straightforward in theory to base intervention programmes on general aims such as improving offender education or providing secure accommodation, this becomes rather more problematic and evidence becomes less conclusive when practice examples are considered in detail (Harper and Chitty, 2005: 62). Grimshaw (2002) found, for example, that accommodation support needs vary over the life course, so we could expect that different interventions will be required at different points in time for ex-offenders; that housing needs were connected with and interacted with other needs; that specific groups, such as sex offenders and mentally disordered offenders would have specific needs; and that continuing support might be necessary, beyond the initial provision of somewhere to stay for offenders.

As one survey of newly sentenced prisoners found, there has been limited recognition of:

> the complex and interlocking problems facing prisoners ... The majority of offenders enter prison with a range of health and social problems, including poor mental health, drug and alcohol misuse and low levels of literacy and numeracy ... These problems are known to be associated with offending behaviour.
>
> (Stewart, 2008: 1)

WHAT DO YOU THINK? 29.3

Ex-offenders and employment

Finding work may not simply be a question of appropriate training or preparation. Obstacles may also arise in the form of external factors, such as employer attitudes:

> When Michaela was 19, she got into a fight in a nightclub with a stranger and was handed a four-year prison sentence for GBH. 'It was a 30-second mistake I'll always regret,' says Michaela, who spent two years behind bars and another two on licence.
>
> Now 26, she was released from prison almost four years ago and has found applying for jobs a stressful ordeal, despite doing everything she could to rehabilitate and make herself employable.
>
> She isn't the only one—only around a quarter (26.5%) of prisoners enter employment after release, according to government figures. The criminal record tick box, often used on mainstream application forms, can automatically filter ex-offenders out of jobs, condemning them to unemployment.
>
> (*The Guardian*, 28 June 2017)

Do you think employers should be prevented from discriminating against ex-offenders? If so, how could this be implemented or enforced?

WHAT DO YOU THINK? 29.4

Who should provide rehabilitation services?

The North East Prison After Care Service (NEPACS, see **Figure 29.6**) has been established as a rehabilitative resource for ex-offenders since the 19th century.

> NEPACS and its forerunners have been working in the north east of England to support a positive future for prisoners and their families for over 130 years. During this time, the structure of the organisation and the activities we undertake have changed, but our commitment to helping people affected by imprisonment remains constant.
>
> - NEPACS works in prisons across the north east of England and we welcome over 140,000 visitors through our centres each year.
> - Nearly 20,000 children use NEPACS' play facilities at prisons in the north east each year.
> - NEPACS provides tea bars and staffs play areas within the prison visits rooms and organise special visits for children so they can spend quality time with their parent, learning through organised play activities.
> - NEPACS helps about 500 offenders and/or their families each year with a small grant to help them through financial difficulties and get their lives straight.
> - NEPACS provides free caravan holiday breaks for up to 40 families with a relative in prison each year.
> - NEPACS promotes good practice in resettlement through our Annual Awards and raises awareness through public lectures and events.
>
> (www.nepacs.co.uk)

Figure 29.6 The North East Prison After Care Service has operated as a rehabilitative resource for ex-offenders since the 19th century
Source: www.nepacs.co.uk

Do you think rehabilitation services such as this should primarily be a state responsibility, or is it more appropriate for them to be provided independently, by voluntary or other organisations? Why?

It seems clear that if we agree that offenders are likely to have complex and interlinked needs, which are in turn likely to contribute to a predisposition to reoffend; and if we agree that these needs should be addressed as part of a wider goal of achieving effective rehabilitation; then establishing and delivering suitable interventions and appropriate measures of success will almost certainly remain highly challenging. The diverse nature of offenders' needs and circumstances make it extremely difficult to identify exactly what outcomes should be prioritised; although initiatives such as the GLM and other desistance-based approaches do seek to provide a route towards this goal.

29.8 What is the impact of rehabilitation?

At this point we should consider what kind of evidence we have available, and what it tells us about the wider objective of promoting the reintegration of offenders.

In the previous section we saw that there is considerable support for the principle of rehabilitation of at least some categories of offenders. However, the evidence to inform policy and practice decisions about the best way to achieve positive outcomes is not always as robust as it could be.

In some cases, the air of pessimism has been quite pervasive:

> The scarcity and generally poor quality of previous research means that it is difficult to come up with firm advice about 'what works' which goes beyond the usual principles of programme integrity, targeting offenders and matching teaching and learning styles.
>
> (Webster et al., 2001: iii)

This comment is unsurprisingly drawn from a study whose findings were not encouraging: 'prison workshop experience emerges as unhelpful in securing future work'; and the 'most common complaint from inmates is that the tasks they do in workshops are boring and repetitive' (2001: 65). However, even this study moderates its tone, recognising that there is some hope in the findings of other studies which identify characteristics of employment-based programmes for offenders that might generate sustained benefits. A combination of individualised planning and advice, practical help, post-release support, and incentives for employers may be associated with greater success in obtaining and keeping work and reduced recidivism (Webster et al., 2001: 73).

Another inquiry into the effectiveness of the 'Pathfinder' resettlement initiative—a programme to support short-term prisoners on release introduced in 1999—suggested that programme integrity and consistency of support were associated with 'meaningful work' and the acknowledgement by over 70 per cent of prisoners that 'they had gained benefits from the project' (Lewis et al., 2003: v); and that 'participants showed significant positive change in crime-prone attitudes and self-reported problems' (Raynor, 2004: 313). The study concluded, like many others, that the resettlement needs of prisoners arise 'typically' from 'a combination of difficulties which have their roots in the prisoner's attitudes, beliefs and habitual responses to problems', suggesting the need for 'holistic' and continuing support (Lewis et al., 2003: vii). However, this study did not report on reconviction rates, even though the authors argued that 'the reduction of offending is [likely] to assume a central role in resettlement work' (2003: 4).

Reflecting on the findings from this and other 'Pathfinder' projects, Raynor (2004) noted a sense of disappointment amongst policymakers that evaluations had been unable to provide more conclusive evidence of their achievements (or, indeed, failings): 'we had not so much an end product as a variety of interesting interim products, with a mixture of positive and negative findings and few clear answers' (Raynor, 2004: 314). This, in his view, demonstrated the importance of reading research carefully and critically rather than being seduced by 'headline results' (2004: 316). On the other hand, Raynor was careful at this point not to throw the whole premise of 'what works' research into question, as some did at the time, such as the probation officers' union, NAPO. The union's concerns included the argument that such research: 'programmes are inherently conservative, pathologizing individual offenders and ignoring social causes of crime … NAPO refers to "a simplistic model of offending that isolates individual behaviour from its social, economic and political context"' (Raynor, 2003: 336).

Programmes might prove difficult to evaluate positively for other reasons, too, such as flawed implementation. Raynor was writing at a time of particularly rapid policy innovation following a change of government, and he also drew attention to the important distinction between 'demonstration' and 'practical' project developments:

> The former are the special pilot projects, which are often the source of the research covered in systematic reviews, and the latter are the routine implementations which follow organizational decisions to adopt new methods, as in the rapid roll-out of the Probation Service's new programmes. Better results are more commonly found in the 'demonstration projects'.
>
> (Raynor, 2004: 318)

Despite such reservations, Lipsey and Cullen (2007) have argued that 'practical projects' are able to demonstrate consistently positive effects if, and when, properly implemented. Similarly, Sherman et al. (1998) have provided a wide-ranging overview of interventions in criminal justice, summarising the kinds of rehabilitative interventions that have been shown to be effective. Included in this list are:

- therapeutic drug treatments in prison;
- rehabilitation programmes tailored to identified 'risk' factors; and
- ex-offender job training for older males.

At the same time, this review identified a number of other 'promising' interventions where the evidence was not yet robust enough to support unqualified claims of effectiveness. These included:

- community-based mentoring;
- prison-based vocational programmes; and
- intensive supervision and aftercare for juvenile offenders (Sherman et al., 1998: 12).

A more recent review of previous studies (Berghuis, 2018: 4671) also seems to suggest that there is some value in taking an integrated approach to offender rehabilitation:

> many of the trials [of different methods] which did see trends towards reductions in recidivism found that continuity of care is integral for a smooth transition from prison to the community. . . . This requires clear communication between institutional personnel and those institutions outside of prison helping with the transition, meaning both probation and community-based services. This reflects the principle of cooperation from the community. . . .

Increasing certainty

Over the course of time, the body of evidence relating to rehabilitative interventions has certainly increased. In 2013, the Ministry of Justice published an updated report on effective rehabilitation strategies. This time, the distinction was made between 'static' and 'dynamic' risk factors, with the suggestion that interventions should be targeted towards those 'factors, such as education, employment and drug use, [that] are amenable to change' (Ministry of Justice, 2013: 3). In addition, the emerging interest in 'desistance' has helped in identifying aspects of change in offenders' lives which are particularly associated with a reduction in reoffending and which rehabilitative interventions might therefore seek to promote or reinforce; such as 'hope and motivation' to change (2013: 8). This line of argument is consistent with the case made by McNeill and others (see the earlier discussion of desistance) that interventions to support dynamic change processes are likely to be more effective than simply focusing on offending behaviour, particularly in the form of punitive sanctions which are consistently shown not to work well in terms of reducing recidivism (Lipsey and Cullen, 2007).

According to the Ministry of Justice (2013: 16), there is now 'good evidence' of the effectiveness of a number of 'interventions' to reduce reoffending through addressing problem drug-taking and that custodial treatments are 'most effective' if they are consolidated with effective aftercare provision. There is 'mixed/promising evidence' of the effectiveness of targeted housing support for offenders with mental health issues, of the effectiveness of employment/education programmes, and of the potential benefits of disposals which 'require offenders to engage with mental health treatment' (Ministry of Justice, 2013: 20). See **New frontiers 29.1** for an example.

Although there is a range of evidence to support particular approaches to rehabilitation, there also remain unresolved questions, not just about 'what works' but about 'how' and 'why' anything works. On the one hand, there is an understandable tendency for programme evaluations to frame their conclusions in terms of the achievement of the programme itself, as a discrete intervention model. This, then, encourages the assumption that all that is needed to replicate successful approaches is a 'top-down' process of rolling them out; that is to say, reproducing exactly the same methods and processes throughout any given service. However, as Lipsey (1999) has shown, there is considerably less evidence of success when interventions are not carried out in experimental conditions—which might be favourable in a number of ways, such as funding, practitioner commitment, institutional support, researcher bias, and so on. Many of the research studies

NEW FRONTIERS 29.1

Supporting ex-prisoners into employment

The Centre for Mental Health has developed a programme to support ex-prisoners with mental health issues into employment (Durcan et al., 2018). This programme offered 'Individual Placement and Support' and assisted 39 per cent of its participants into paid work following release from custody. The programme employed several specialists to provide guidance, assistance with job searches, and post-employment support to enable ex-prisoners with 'severe mental health difficulties' into work. Although the success rate might not appear particularly high, those who were provided with this help were twice as likely to get jobs as those who were unable to make use of the scheme; and they were also less likely to require subsequent hospitalisation.

and project evaluations which you may encounter in the course of your criminological studies will have been carried out on new initiatives, set up specifically to test a new model of practice. This can mean that they are relatively favourably treated in terms of funding, practitioner recruitment, and participant selection. And, in turn, this may create inbuilt advantages when these 'experimental' projects are compared to what might be called 'business as usual' in mainstream practice (Weiss et al., 2008; Losel, 2018).

Indeed, it may be the case that successful interventions do not depend so much on the design and delivery of standardised programmes, but on the ways in which extra financial investment and motivated criminal justice practitioners might achieve more beneficial outcomes, not least because recipients feel that this means that someone cares about them.

Desistance and effective practice

An apparent need for responsive and individually tailored interventions is central to the arguments put forward by those who promote a 'desistance' model of practice. According to this 'paradigm' (Durnescu, 2011), effective practice achieves its objectives by adopting a strategic but focused approach to intervention, geared to the specific features of the offender's life and circumstances, rather than relying on uniform programme-based models which by definition are less able to be responsive to the individual. To maximise the chances of successful outcomes, intervention must therefore adopt a series of principles, such as the following:

1. Agency is as important as ... structure in promoting or inhibiting desistance from crime.
2. Individuals differ in their readiness to contemplate and begin the process of change.
3. Generating and sustaining motivation is vital to the maintenance of processes of change.
4. Desistance is a difficult and often lengthy process, not an 'event', and relapses are common.
5. While overcoming social problems is often insufficient on its own to promote desistance, it may be a necessary condition for further progress.
6. As people change, they need new skills and capacities appropriate to their new lifestyle, and access to opportunities to use them

(Maguire, 2007: 408)

Farrall's (2002) research, for example, suggests that 'successful desistance was the product of individual motivation, social and personal contexts, probation supervision and the meanings which people hold about their lives and their behaviours' (Farrall and McNeill, 2010: 211). This, in turn, suggests that relationships and sustainable engagement with offenders should be prioritised as the basis of effective intervention, rather than highly structured and rigorously enforced change programmes. Criticising attempts to put such programmes into operation systematically in England and Wales, Farrall and McNeill (2010: 212) argue that, instead, 'personal motivation', the 'social context', the 'organisational context', and practitioner relationships and skills are crucial in supporting the 'change process'. Desistance-based arguments do not fall into the trap of relying entirely on the intervention to facilitate change in people's lives:

> The way in which we think about interventions and case management needs to be embedded within an understanding of the change process that it exists to support—and even desistance itself is not the ultimate concern. People do not simply desist, they desist *into* something ... Ultimately, desistance is perhaps best understood as part of the individual's ongoing journey towards successful integration within the community.
>
> (Farrall and McNeill, 2010: 213)

29.9 The limitations of rehabilitation

On the face of it, rehabilitation seems to offer a 'win-win' option in criminal justice. Beneficial and usually less punitive interventions are provided for the offender, which are in turn likely to facilitate reintegration into the community and at the same time reduce the likelihood of recidivism. It is difficult on the face of it to find grounds for objecting to it as a central element of the justice system. But, as we have seen, it has not always been popular or viewed as particularly desirable by those determining policy. As we have also seen, for example, the suggestion, associated with Martinson (1974) in particular, that 'nothing works' did appear to have some influence in justifying a move away from needs and welfare-based interventions towards more mandatory, correctional, and risk-oriented models of rehabilitative practice. It is unlikely that Martinson's contribution on its own generated what has been described as an 'era of "nothing works pessimism" and "lock 'em up" punitiveness' (Ward and Maruna, 2007: 8); but it certainly seemed to capture the spirit of the times and gave added force to the case against well-intentioned but ineffective measures intended to improve the lives of those in trouble with the law. It must be acknowledged, too, that achieving certainty about what interventions are effective (as well as why and how) remains challenging (Harper and Chitty, 2005).

Five years after Martinson published his forceful argument that 'nothing works', he published another paper retracting his original claim. In the new paper (1979) he argued forcefully for the effectiveness of some forms of intervention as against others. However, this paper was far less influential, despite being based on a considered re-evaluation of his previous conclusions. It is plausible to suggest that the claim that rehabilitative programmes made no difference suited the influential claims of those who viewed any kind of measure which offered help or self-improvement to offenders as being insufficiently punitive, and in some cases akin to 'letting them off'. In light of its own sensitivity on this point, the UK Ministry of Justice, in setting out detailed reform plans and under the guise of promoting rehabilitation in 2012, also committed itself to incorporating more demanding elements in community disposals; probably to allay fears that rehabilitative measures might be viewed as not being tough enough.

The question of proportionality

Similarly, it may be argued that paying undue attention to offenders' needs and well-being is to discount the wishes and interests of victims in seeing the offence dealt with by way of an appropriate punitive sanction (see **Chapter 28**). Additionally, as Raynor and Robinson (2009: 11) argue, rehabilitative principles are not necessarily consistent with moral arguments which stress the importance of fairness (treating offenders equally and proportionately) and the unbiased administration of justice. That is to say, a pure rehabilitation position would take account of considerations such as the needs and circumstances of the offender, and perhaps even the wider public interest, rather than the strict demands of a 'just deserts' model of criminal justice.

Ironically, though, there are also those who argue that rehabilitative interventions imposed without taking account of the need for proportionality in sentencing may actually be excessively punitive rather than unduly lenient. Once beneficial effects are claimed for interventions, it becomes easier to advance justifications for a wide range of practices, many of which might otherwise be unacceptable:

> faith in rehabilitation has manifested itself in a wide variety of practices for which 'rehabilitative effects' have been claimed, from the treadmill and the crank through extended periods of solitary confinement, to psychosurgical and medical interventions. . . . The history of rehabilitation includes the use of drugs to 'chemically castrate' sexual offenders; to tranquilise 'dangerous' offenders; and to arouse pain and fear in the context of 'aversion therapy'.
>
> (Robinson and Crow, 2009: 11)

This raises the further question of whether incorporating coercion in the administration of measures of treatment or reintegration can be justified, especially where it involves the imposition of sanctions such as confinement or physical restraint which go beyond what would be legitimate as a purely punitive measure. Rehabilitative interventions could, therefore, breach the principle of 'just deserts'. Irrespective of this, current practice is widely characterised by the use of mandatory additional conditions and requirements to supplement the treatment element of community orders, as in the case of the Drug Treatment and Testing Order introduced under the Crime and Disorder Act 1998, and replaced in 2003 by the Drug Rehabilitation Requirement, for example. One systematic review of compulsory drug treatment has found very mixed results based on a number of studies:

> Of an initial 430 potential studies identified, nine quantitative studies met the inclusion criteria. Studies evaluated compulsory treatment options including drug detention facilities, short (i.e. 21-day) and long-term (i.e., 6 months) inpatient treatment, community-based treatment, group-based outpatient treatment, and prison-based treatment. Three studies (33%) reported no significant impacts of compulsory treatment compared with control interventions. Two studies (22%) found equivocal results but did not compare against a control condition. Two studies (22%) observed negative impacts of compulsory treatment on criminal recidivism. Two studies (22%) observed positive impacts of compulsory inpatient treatment on criminal recidivism and drug use.
>
> Conclusion—There is limited scientific literature evaluating compulsory drug treatment. Evidence does not, on the whole, suggest improved outcomes related to compulsory treatment approaches, with some studies suggesting potential harms. Given the potential for human rights abuses within compulsory treatment settings, non-compulsory treatment modalities should be prioritized by policymakers seeking to reduce drug-related harms.
>
> (Werb et al., 2016: 2)

This account summarises the potential problem of disproportionate treatment of offenders on purportedly rehabilitative grounds, when there is an element of compulsion, which could similarly be applied to other settings and contexts, such as detention in a mental health facility or mandatory attendance for education or counselling.

The problem of compulsion

As Raynor and Robinson (2009: 9) argue, the problem of compulsion in the delivery of treatment programmes is linked with assumptions about the therapeutic value of the intervention in question. We can sum this up in the phrase: 'This is for your own good'; the treatment is justified by a belief in its potential benefits. This, though, is based on a further set of assumptions about both the effectiveness of the programme of intervention and the effectiveness of its delivery, which may be unrealistic based on what the evidence suggests. The idea of 'treatment' that is sometimes incorporated into rehabilitation programmes is suggestive of a 'medical model' of intervention which McNeill (2014: 6) associates with 'dubious expertise'. The offender is the focus of what might be deemed 'coerced correction', according to a predetermined set of expected outcomes; and in pursuit of which it is assumed the appropriate treatment dosage or behavioural technique will be administered precisely and unproblematically. The offender's distinctive characteristics are disregarded, and their sense of 'agency' and capacity for 'self-determination' (Farrall and McNeill, 2010: 212) are ignored.

Robinson's (2008) view is that the recent and continuing remaking of rehabilitation has represented a process of realignment, bringing intervention into line with a number of other influential strands of thought in criminal justice. It may be seen as 'utilitarian rehabilitation', 'managerial rehabilitation', or 'expressive rehabilitation' (we will explore these ideas in the following paragraphs). Each has developed its own rationale but each represents a significant modification of rehabilitative aims. Lines between treatment and control become blurred and offenders become subject to various forms of coercion in the apparent pursuit of their own best interests.

- 'Utilitarian rehabilitation' focuses on reducing levels of offending behaviour and pays little attention to other potential objectives, such as reintegration or resettlement. This strategy uses cognitive-behavioural programmes to promote prosocial attitudes and behaviour, purportedly in the interests of the offender and the community. Rehabilitation becomes principally a means of ensuring the protection of the public and potential future victims, rather than promoting the welfare of offenders themselves.
- 'Managerial rehabilitation' situates rehabilitative practices within discourses of risk assessment and risk management: 'contemporary rehabilitation has evolved by learning to speak the language of risk' (Robinson, 2008: 434). Associated with this trend, we can perhaps see particular types of intervention becoming more prominent, given their particular focus on risk reduction; these might include drug rehabilitation programmes or therapeutic interventions with sexual offenders.
- 'Expressive rehabilitation' associates reintegrative interventions with explicitly punitive objectives: 'rehabilitative sanctions and interventions have entered a new discursive alliance with punitiveness, which has been essential to their continuing legitimacy' (Robinson, 2008: 435). In this way, the inclusion of punitive requirements into ostensibly rehabilitative interventions is only to be expected. Tracing this trend back to the late 1980s, Robinson (2008: 436) suggests that the emerging policy goal of delivering 'punishment in the community' and the alternatives to custody movement of that era helped to usher in rehabilitative programmes, such as intensive supervision, which integrated punishment and treatment within the same disposal. In her view, the separation of the probation service and probation training from their social work roots in 1995 (in England and Wales) was not a coincidence. This effectively highlighted the marginalisation of concerns for offenders' welfare: 'Indeed, it is arguably now the case that the "pure" rehabilitative sanction is extinct' (Robinson, 2008: 437). As Cohen (1985) anticipated some time earlier, rehabilitation may become inextricably linked with 'control'.

Rehabilitation: putting the offender first?

Common to all these tactical realignments of rehabilitation has been the relative absence of concern for the well-being of the offender. This is seen as ancillary to the central objective of reducing levels of crime and promoting public safety. This, as Robinson and others note, completely obscures 'a vision of rehabilitation *as a right of the offender*' (Robinson, 2008: 431, emphasis in original), and as something for which the state has a responsibility because of the disadvantages associated with being an offender—that is to say, both existing disadvantages and those likely to arise from being identified as an offender. So, questions of 'stigma' and 'social exclusion' which might legitimately be seen as consequences (if not causes) of being processed as an offender are, in turn, de-emphasised as reasonable objectives for rehabilitative interventions. As a consequence, those aspects of reintegration which might address the challenges facing ex-offenders also become de-emphasised, and this is reflected, for example, in the relatively poor provision of services, accommodation, and opportunities for those leaving custody—see **Figure 29.7**.

By contrast, the case made increasingly strongly by desistance theorists is that effective reintegration of offenders into society and the associated cessation

Figure 29.7 The lack of accommodation for those leaving custody reflects the low importance attached to aspects of reintegration which might address the challenges facing ex-offenders

Source: Photograph: Fabio De Paola/The Guardian

of offending careers is dependent on life changes to a much greater extent than specific programmes targeted at certain features of their behaviour or mental functioning. The evidence from desistance research suggests that there are 'a range of factors associated with the ending of active involvement in offending' and that these factors are associated with changes such as gaining 'employment, a life partner or a family' (Farrall, 2002: 11). In addition, it is suggested, it is the subjective meaning of such changes which matters, depending on the kind of 'narrative' that offenders build around them; how do they value such changes and what do they imply for their understandings of their own identities (McNeill, 2009: 18).

Relatedly, it seems that the insights expressed in **Conversations 29.1** with Nicole Westmarland are also increasingly acknowledged in policy development, with the Prison Reform Trust (Edgar et al., 2012), for example,

CONVERSATIONS 29.1

Arguments for rehabilitation: the case of community interventions and domestic violence

with Professor Nicole Westmarland

Roger Smith (RS): Fundamentally the question for the purposes of this conversation is 'What do you think we should do about gender-based or gendered violence?' and particularly 'How should we exercise control over it?' or is that the right way to think about it?

Professor Nicole Westmarland (NW): People say that the place for domestic violence perpetrators is in prison, we should stamp it out, we should never accept it, domestic violence is wrong. So we have all of these messages on the one hand at a very kind of high level policy level, which are all obviously correct, but then I think once that starts filtering down into practice we get a much more complicated and nuanced picture about the problems that are linked with this crime, happening within families, which has ripple effects not only to the children living within that family but huge ripple effects in families and friends. And I think that we can often be accused of over simplifying the problem of domestic violence and falling into a trap of stereotyping victims and perpetrators and the impacts on them.

RS: I know that you're interested in perhaps challenging some of the conventional criminal justice responses and I wonder if you could say a bit more about some of the work that you're doing that questions the sort of routinely tough perspective?

NW: I think the problem is that we have a tough perspective in policy but not actually in practice. Recently I've spent a lot of time with individual police officers and also, I've spent a lot of time in court observing judges and magistrates and sentencing around domestic violence related crimes. And what we see in a *lot* of those cases is actually much more of a therapeutic based approach to dealing with men's violence than a punitive approach. So we see things like alcohol, mental health . . . bereavement etc., being used as more the rationale, actually, for men's use of violence than things we see in policy, in academic life, around it being about gender inequality, power and control. So I think on the one hand we think of a court as somewhere where kind of quite tough sentences are given potentially, for domestic violence, and in fact I find that to be a myth in a lot of the cases.

RS: It is almost supported by the media a bit though isn't it? Because the impression I would get from the media, as just a disinterested reader, is the courts just do dispense tough sentences.

NW: It is and I think it's also a myth, even among some parts of researchers and activists as well, there is this idea that there is a 'tough on crime' stance. Once, when talking to some Home Office ministers, the idea was raised of a hostel for perpetrators of domestic abuse to be taken to, rather than removing women and children into refuges and, the statement was given 'Well we already have hostels for domestic violence perpetrators, they're called prison'. But, but in reality men who commit domestic violence offences, in the large, aren't going to prison. They're given fairly low-level community sentences and rarely even domestic violence perpetrator programmes, actually. I suppose that brings me onto kind of one of the topics that I've been looking at a lot recently, which is the issue of domestic violence perpetrator programmes. The ones which we've looked at are those which are outside of the criminal justice system, so they're not ones which men have been mandated to attend by a court but they're not really truly voluntary either. These aren't men who are waking up one day and thinking 'Next thing on my to-do list is to tackle my use and misuse of power and control within the relationship'. It's men who are at risk of losing their children, it's men who want to regain contact with their children, it's men who are told 'This is the end of the line, the relationship is over unless you get professional help to change your behaviour'. And these types of programmes have often been kind of dismissed as, the soft edge of responses. They're sometimes seen as, tackling the middle-class men who are willing to be educated on topics, rather than, the majority of perpetrators. And that's really not what we found in our interviews with men, we found that men had been very open, actually, about their use of violence, some of the men had tried to kill their partners. And these were on community programmes and many of these had never had any contact at all with the criminal justice system, at any point. So, this isn't really a diversionary sentence, this isn't really an alternative to a tough sentence, this is men who, for whatever reason, have never been in touch with the criminal justice system, possibly because their partners are so fearful of the criminal justice response, of what might happen, that they're never going to make a report. So, to me, one of the advantages of domestic violence perpetrator programmes is you are at least doing *something* rather than in many of these cases, which it would be, doing nothing, it's not an alternative to; it's not a diversion to. We can't change the fact that some people do want to remain with that partner and we can't change the fact that even if they separate, the chances are that that man will have more relationships in the future and it's what we do about those future relationships as well.

RS: So do you think those types of programmes demonstrate their value? I wouldn't say that they were successful or not successful but do they change things in some way?

NW: I think they do change things and I think our research has shown that they change things in a number of ways. Sometimes that was that they were giving the women power to change, so sometimes that was that they were emboldening women to be able to make decisions to leave.

RS: Like the Freedom Programme? I know that is victim oriented but is it similar?

NW: No, it's more that when a man goes on a programme the woman gets an independent safety worker to support her and she knows that there is a weekly check-in where somebody is looking at what the behaviour of that man is. So I think, for some women, they feel this kind of safety net of somebody else knows what is happening in this relationship, somebody else is there, there is a weekly contact point. Somebody else is holding him accountable, it's not just them all the time. So that can embolden women, it can empower them to leave, it can enable them to say to themselves, to their families, to the perpetrator's family, 'Look, I've done everything I can, I've even gone to the extent of engaging with this programme and he's got professional support and he still hasn't changed'. So it can give them the confidence to leave or to change their behaviour. It can make men change their behaviour, we found particularly in relation to physical and sexual violence that there [were] dramatic reductions, over time, in their use of physical and sexual violence. In terms of things like respectful communication, their use of coercive and controlling behaviours, they all did reduce but not to the same extent as physical and sexual violence did.

Ultimately, we found there's a bit of a myth around perpetrator programmes that they will make men *worse*, that they'll learn new tactics, that they'll somehow skew the programme to make them better abusers. And we found very little evidence of that and that's why we called our . . . report 'Steps Towards Change' because we're not saying that these programmes are entirely successful, we're not saying that they make all of these men into, perfect, model men. But we are saying that for most of the lives of the women, children and men who were in our study, their lives were better to some extent. And maybe, at this moment in time that's all we can ask for because I don't know of any other interventions that we're doing, which can do anything more than that and I guess that's the next big question, if not these then what?

Professor Nicole Westmarland is the Director of the Durham Centre for Research into Violence and Abuse (CRiVA), and Professor of Criminology, at Durham University

See also

Kelly, L. and Westmarland, N. (2015) *Domestic Violence Perpetrator Programmes: Steps Towards Change. Project Mirabal Final Report.* London and Durham: London Metropolitan University and Durham University

explicitly accepting the importance of desistance theory as a guide to good practice.

Strikingly, though, the available evidence suggests that welfare provision, within and beyond the justice system, is not systematically available to provide continuing support to facilitate desistance. Suitable accommodation is often not provided for ex-offenders on release from custody, for example, especially those with mental health problems (Edgar et al., 2012: 21); and the employment rates for prisoners on release has remained consistently low (2012: 54). In 2018, the UK Ministry of Justice reported that only 17 per cent of ex-prisoners get jobs within a year of their release. Further to this, in September 2014 a thematic review of resettlement provision was published jointly by the inspectorates responsible for oversight of criminal justice services, which found consistent failings in the quality of services available for those released from custody. The study observed, for example, that despite its importance in helping to rehabilitate ex-offenders, there was 'no evidence' of prisoners' families being involved in the resettlement process (HM Inspectorate of Prisons et al., 2014: 5), a finding which seems directly at odds with the conclusions of the desistance literature.

There is a significant mismatch between approaches to rehabilitation which focus on the offender alone, perhaps applying a 'deficit model' to the individual taken out of context, on the one hand, and the sort of intervention strategy suggested by both desistance theory and much of the available evidence, on the other. This would prioritise working with the ex-offender in situ, developing individualised programmes which take account of specific circumstances and address 'social' needs. The key question seems to be 'what works, for whom and under what conditions' (Hollin, 1999: 362)?

29.10 Conclusion

In this chapter we have considered the idea of rehabilitation and how this applies to the treatment of offenders. The principles of rehabilitation are based on the idea that lives and circumstances can be changed for the better, and those who commit crime can be helped to change their ways. Sometimes this might mean working with them to change attitudes, thought processes, and behaviour; sometimes it might mean improving their life chances or relationships; and sometimes it might mean removing the stigma or labels that attach to them by virtue of having offended. All share the view that offenders are not condemned to a life of crime and that 'desistance' is possible.

We have considered some of the practical initiatives that have been introduced to support rehabilitation and some of the evidence base to evaluate these. This has revealed a mixed picture, leading us to reflect on some of the potential criticisms of rehabilitative approaches, and areas for further exploration and inquiry where we don't yet know enough to be certain about their value. If you're interested in a career in criminology, this might be where you come in . . .

SUMMARY

After reading this chapter and working your way through its features you should now be able to:

- **Explain the concept of rehabilitation as applied in criminal justice**

We have introduced the argument that the principal consideration in dealing with offenders is their effective reintegration into society by means of interventions which promote their well-being and address their needs and personal problems.

- **Recognise different objectives to which rehabilitation might aspire**

We have acknowledged various approaches to rehabilitation, from those which focus on changing aspects of the offender's lifestyle or habits to those which are concerned with improving their circumstances and life chances.

- **Identify and describe alternative models of rehabilitative practice**

We have provided an account of a range of interventions, which are designed to deliver the stated outcomes of rehabilitation including resettlement initiatives and treatment programmes.

- Evaluate the achievements and outcomes of rehabilitative interventions

We have reviewed the claimed and actual outcomes of rehabilitation programmes, including those which appear to have negative consequences in terms of reoffending and the explanatory accounts which seek to make sense of these apparently anomalous effects.

- Assess the critical perspectives on rehabilitation and its aims

We concluded the chapter with a discussion of the possible shortcomings of arguments for rehabilitation in terms of its uncertain benefits, possible failures to reflect the interests of all stakeholders, and its potential to act as form of disguised punishment.

Test your understanding of the chapter's key points by attempting the self-test questions on the **online resources** at www.oup.com/he/case2e

REVIEW QUESTIONS

1. What do you understand by the term 'rehabilitation'?
2. What are the five main assumptions underlying the principle of rehabilitation?
3. What are the arguments for and against compulsory treatment of offenders for rehabilitative purposes?
4. What are some of the key methods used in rehabilitation?
5. How can rehabilitative interventions avoid the accusation that they represent an easy option for offenders?
6. How do you think the effectiveness of rehabilitation is best measured?

Access the **online resources** at www.oup.com/he/case2e to check your answers to the review questions.

FURTHER READING

Carter, L. (ed.) (2019) *Female Offenders and Reentry.* **Abingdon: Routledge.**
Female offenders are often overlooked in criminological literature, but this collection reports on the specific issues and challenges associated with their reintegration into society following conviction and imprisonment.

Hannah-Moffat, K. (2005) 'Criminogenic needs and the transformative risk subject'. *Punishment and Society* **7(1): 29–51.**
An interesting analysis of the relationship between 'risk' and 'need' and how tensions are managed between these apparently competing perspectives on understanding offenders and accounting for their crimes.

Kelly, L. and Westmarland, N. (2015) 'New approaches to assessing effectiveness and outcomes of domestic violence perpetrator programmes' in H. Johnson, B. S. Fisher, and V. Jaquier (eds) *Critical Issues on Violence Against Women.* **Abingdon: Routledge. Pp. 183–94.**
This chapter describes some of the challenges and achievements of attempts to adopt a rehabilitative approach with offenders whose crimes generate strong expectations of an exclusively punitive response.

McNeill, F. (2009) *Towards Effective Practice in Offender Supervision.* **Glasgow: Scottish Centre for Crime & Justice Research.**

Provides a detailed overview of the arguments in favour of 'desistance'-based approaches to offender management.

Ministry of Justice (2013) *Transforming Rehabilitation: A summary of evidence on reducing reoffending.* **London: Ministry of Justice.**

A government-commissioned overview of the available evidence on the contribution of rehabilitative practice to the reduction of further offending.

Ward, T. and Maruna, S. (2007) *Rehabilitation.* **Abingdon: Routledge.**

A full and helpful overview of the principles and practices central to rehabilitation in criminal justice.

Access the **online resources** to view a wealth of extra information relating to your study of criminology, including self-test questions, answers to review questions, and links to other resources that will help you enjoy and fulfil your potential within your studies.

www.oup.com/he/case2e

CHAPTER OUTLINE

30.1	Introduction	896
30.2	Alternative responses to crime: an overview	896
30.3	Restorative justice and diversion	901
30.4	Delivering alternatives to punishment	906
30.5	The meaning and impact of alternatives to punishment	917
30.6	Conclusion	925

30

Alternatives to punishment

KEY ISSUES

After reading this chapter, you should be able to:

- describe the approaches to the delivery of criminal justice which challenge conventional assumptions about crime and punishment;
- explain the origins and development of restorative ideas and practices;
- understand the emergence and impact of diversion as an intervention strategy;
- consider examples of the implementation of 'alternatives to punishment' and their impact;
- critique the arguments in favour of alternative forms of intervention, appreciating the potential criticisms of alternative forms of intervention;
- develop your own arguments for and against these more informal methods of dealing with offences.

30.1 Introduction

In recent years a number of interesting arguments in favour 'alternative' means of responding to offenders and their crimes have emerged within criminal justice and have been gaining wider recognition. In this context, we are using the term 'alternatives' as an umbrella to incorporate a range of strategies and practices to deal with crime which are not driven by traditional concerns with attributing guilt and imposing **punishment**. Those who favour innovations of this kind in fact tend to reject conventional assumptions and approaches, proposing new principles for the operation of the justice system. They believe that it is not enough just to concentrate on the crime and the criminal aside from the context of the offence. Instead, the offender and other 'interested parties', including victims, should be seen as active participants in the justice process, able to play a significant part in offence resolution.

In this chapter, we will consider two distinct but in some ways similar challenges to conventional models of justice which have developed from this viewpoint. We briefly considered the first, **restorative justice**, in **Chapter 25** and saw that its supporters argue for a less rigid and more collaborative way of responding to crime than has been the case up to now in western societies.

> Restorative justice is a process to involve, to the extent possible, those who have a stake in a specific offense to collectively identify and address harms, needs and obligations in order to heal and put things as right as possible.
>
> (Zehr, 2003: 40)

This definition neatly sums up several key elements that set restorative justice apart from more established ideas of offence resolution, in the sense of making amends for one's misdeeds. Restorative justice is based on the presumption that dealing with crime is a *process* rather than a single act or decision, that it centres on *collaboration* between those with a stake in the offence, and that it emphasises *healing* (making things better) as well as 'putting things right'.

The second strand of contemporary practice that we will consider in this chapter has developed over a slightly longer period of time. Those who support the idea of **diversion** advocate the use of informal means of dealing with criminal behaviour, outside the formal justice process, drawing their inspiration from **labelling theory** (Lemert, 1967) and the idea of 'radical non-intervention' (Schur, 1973). Zimring (2000) and Smith (2018) among others have claimed that, especially for young offenders, diversion from formal judicial processes has progressively become a central objective of criminal justice practice. Diversionary interventions, which can include community service, restitution, and education, as well as elements of restorative practice, provide an opportunity for the offender to avoid criminal charges or formal judicial processes, albeit sometimes by meeting certain conditional requirements. Here, though, the principal focus is on promoting less intrusive or potentially damaging outcomes for offenders, rather than addressing the concerns of all those affected by the offence, as in the case of restorative justice.

Although they differ in key respects, restorative and diversionary approaches offer similar challenges to conventional models of justice, and are often found closely linked in practice. They are essentially *problem-solving* approaches to dealing with crime and its consequences, where questions of guilt and punishment are substantially modified in favour of forms of negotiated justice, intended to satisfy the needs and expectations of a range of stakeholders (offender, victim, family, community, and state).

In this chapter we will consider the reasoning behind the contemporary development of these models of intervention, illustrating this by reporting on a number of practice initiatives. We will then discuss their impact and review potential criticisms, such as their modification of principles of 'due process', their reliance on administrative rather than judicial procedures for dealing with offences, their suggested failure to hold offenders properly to account, and their apparent lack of concern with conventional criteria of success, such as reoffending rates.

30.2 Alternative responses to crime: an overview

Before taking a closer look at these new models and practices, it may be helpful for us to consider their origins and the ways in which they claim to represent a different form of criminal justice.

'Old' vs 'new' justice

In the case of restorative justice, influential recent contributions to criminal justice debates have aimed to shift the focus from the *offender* to the *offence* in relation to decisions about attributing blame, determining responsibility, and agreeing on appropriate **disposals** (Christie, 1977). Whereas conventional perspectives on crime and punishment emphasise the behaviour and characteristics of the offender, these newer voices argue for a sharper consideration of the offence, its actual impact, its context, and its consequences. So, although factors such as intent, guilt, responsibility, and mitigating circumstances might still be seen as relevant, they are not expected to determine the final outcome. Daly (2002) draws some helpful contrasts between historic forms of criminal justice and these more modern approaches:

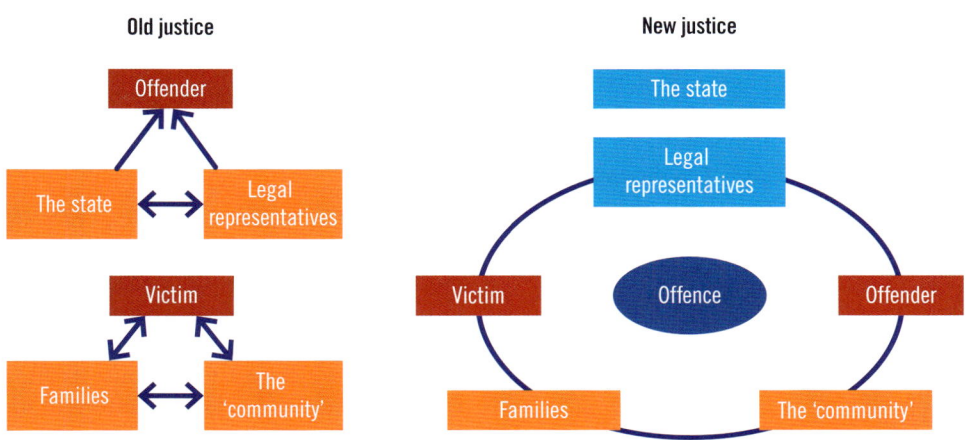

Figure 30.1 The parties involved in 'old' and 'new' justice

By the *old justice*, I refer to modern practices of courthouse justice, which permit no interaction between victim and offender, where legal actors and other experts do the talking and make decisions whose (stated) aim is to punish, or at times, reform an offender. By the *new justice*, I refer to a variety of recent practices, which normally bring victims and offenders (and others) together in a process in which both lay and legal actors make decisions, and whose (stated) aim is to repair the harm for victims, offenders and perhaps other members of 'the community' in ways that matter to them'

(Daly, 2002: 61)

According to this characterisation—what Daly calls the 'new justice'—the purposes of sentencing, and indeed the criminal justice process as a whole, should no longer be considered in terms of clearly prescribed measures for dealing with the offender, but in terms of the need to prioritise and 'resolve' the problems associated with the commission of an offence, and to compensate for any harm that might have arisen from it. Not only does this suggest a realignment of the central purposes of the criminal justice system, but also a reconfiguration of the relationships between key interests ('stakeholders') in determining what should be done in response to an offence, as you can see from the diagrams in **Figure 30.1**. The victim, for example, becomes a much more central and active figure in deliberations and the decision-making process whilst, if anything, the state becomes a less influential player. Other interests, too, such as families and the 'community', gain a more significant place in the problem-solving process, whilst the offender is expected to take on a much more active form of 'responsibility' for putting things right than simply accepting a predetermined penalty (see **What do you think? 30.1**).

The state's role can be seen as shifting from one of initiator and agent of justice, towards acting more as a guarantor and facilitator of decisions arrived at by others (principally, the offender and victim). Importantly, too, these relatively new models of justice can be seen as concrete and targeted, being tailored to the specific offence, the specific context, and the specific dynamics of the interactions between stakeholders. These new models appear in sharp contrast to principles of conventional justice models which rely on generalisable and fixed measures of guilt, **proportionality**, and desert. In fact, ideas of equivalence between offence and punishment are not relevant in this context—two identical acts of criminality could legitimately result in contrasting outcomes, depending on the wishes and decisions of the key players in each case.

In the case of diversion, as with restorative justice, the ideas which informed its recent development were represented in calls for a simplified, offence-focused approach to criminal justice. Claiming that the justice system had become too concerned with offenders' characteristics and circumstances, Morgan (1981: 64) argued that: 'The only respectable way out of the morass [a morass is an area of boggy ground] is for the law to restrict itself to one narrow aspect of the individual, his [sic] criminal acts.'

WHAT DO YOU THINK? 30.1

'Being held responsible' vs 'Taking responsibility'

Approaches which prioritise offence resolution can be seen as distinguishing between 'taking responsibility' for your actions rather than being 'held responsible' for your actions (the conventional perspective)—something like being encouraged to willingly clean up graffiti as opposed to being required to do unpaid labour as a form of punishment.

- Does this is distinction make sense to you?
- If so, do you think it is right to claim that a 'taking responsibility' approach makes us think differently about the ways in which the justice system operates?

This viewpoint was, significantly, shared across political divisions at this point in time, with others arguing that: 'Compulsory intervention in the lives of children must be limited in nature, not subject to indiscriminate intervention . . .' (Morris et al., 1980: 8). Importantly for diversion, these sentiments reflected an emerging consensus which spanned political, academic, and practitioner interests and so gave added impetus for an offence-led focus for intervention, especially in relation to young offenders (Smith, 2018).

Challenging conventional assumptions

The increasingly prominent offence-based models of criminal justice also differ from other perspectives because of what we might call their temporal frame—that is, they are very much about resolving the immediate issues generated by the offence and achieving a solution in the here and now. This sets them apart from strategies of deterrence, treatment, or prevention, which are purely future-oriented; and those which are essentially backward-looking and desert-based being concerned mainly with matters of guilt, 'antecedents' (previous offences, characteristics, and circumstances), and historic factors when determining the nature and scale of any disposal.

Offence-based models mean that formal determinations of guilt, assessment of offender culpability and need, mitigating circumstances, and standardised calculations of penal sanctions (whether deterrent, rehabilitative, or retributive) all become irrelevant. In other words, an offence-resolution perspective not only assumes a distinctive set of objectives for the criminal justice system but it calls into question conventional approaches to evaluating the offence itself, which measure guilt and administer a 'just' response. The proper considerations are, instead, the determination of whose interests are to be taken into account, how these can be determined in light of negotiated understandings of the offence itself, and how any outstanding needs or expectations can be met in light of this.

Taken together, the key features of an 'offence resolution' approach represent something of a challenge to other philosophies of justice and punishment, particularly if implemented in its purest form. It will be becoming clear that this can be understood as a situated contextual 'problem-solving' approach rather than a standardised and calculative model of decision-making. The administration of justice therefore becomes a tailored, individual process, adapted to the precise circumstances of the offence and consideration of the interests of those affected, rather than being based on generalised principles and replicable forms of disposal.

How offence resolution works

The increasing prominence afforded to criminal justice practices which concentrate on dealing with the offence rather than focusing on the offender is associated with the development of new 'models of practice', most notably those falling under the headings of 'restorative justice' and 'diversion'. By 'models of practice', we mean agreed processes for dealing with offences, often but not always instead of a court-imposed order, which result in mutually agreed outcomes between those involved or affected by the offence and which seek to minimise its impact and its adverse consequences. Associated intervention programmes may be agreed, which could involve the offender making amends directly or indirectly, or undertaking other activities to reduce the likelihood of further offending.

Whose interests should be prioritised?

Under the broad term 'offence resolution' there are naturally differences of emphasis, particularly concerning whose interests should be prioritised and what, therefore, represents a successful resolution of the offence. For those for whom 'diversion' is the main aim, the central concerns are to minimise the consequences of the offence for the offender. In particular, the consequences of 'labelling' (Lemert, 1967) and interventions which might themselves encourage further offending, are seen as potentially harmful not only to the offender but more widely when the social costs of crime are considered. Diversion is therefore identified as both economically and socially useful. Minimum intervention is a desirable objective. It is both a relatively cheap option, avoiding the mobilisation of further effort on the part of criminal justice agencies and, at the same time, reduces the likelihood of the offender being further criminalised, according to the available evidence (see McAra and McVie, 2007).

Those who prioritise other interests, such as those of the victim or the community, would consider the primary purpose of offence resolution to be to find ways to make amends or put right the harms and disruption associated with the offence. Restorative justice has come to be viewed by many as the most effective means by which these aims can be achieved (Johnstone, 2011; Gavrielides, 2017).

Practical implications of a 'resolution' approach

The implications of taking a 'resolution' approach to an offence go beyond setting distinctive aims and objectives for interventions; in fact, they point towards a broader reconstitution of the justice process. Clearly, the conventional machinery of state-sponsored prosecution, formal court hearings, attributions of guilt and responsibility, and the imposition of penal sanctions do not sit well with the goals of achieving less prescriptive and more informal, flexible, negotiated outcomes. Because of this, there has been considerable growth in the number of alternative mechanisms which offer discretionary (non-compulsory) means of dealing with an offence.

At their most straightforward, these include the recognition of police discretion and encouragement of its use, particularly in relation to minor offences which can be dealt with on the spot by way of the (now, but not always) metaphorical 'clip round the ear' (Smyth, 2011); a term associated with Victorian and early 20th-century policing practices. Despite this term's original association with physical mistreatment, it is now understood in terms of an informal telling off and an expression of leniency.

The purposes of offence resolution

Approaches to criminal justice decision-making which emphasise problem-solving rather than attributing guilt and blame, imply a particular view of crime, what it represents, and how offenders should be understood. Healing, redemption, normalisation, and reintegration take centre stage and override concerns over imposing sanctions, extracting compensation, or compelling penitence on the part of the offender. Whilst the precise rationale for offence-resolution strategies may vary, they share a commitment to putting things right by way of mutually determined and mutually legitimised solutions.

The key features of the 'new justice' approaches focusing on 'resolving' the issues associated with an offence, rather than questions of responsibility, blame, and punishment, can be summarised as:

- mutuality;
- inclusion;
- legitimacy;
- restoration;
- trust.

These features clearly set offence resolution apart from conventional criminal justice decision-making forums, which could only really claim to share the attribute of legitimacy from this list. Even in this respect, many of the arguments for the institution of new offence-based resolution approaches depend on deriving legitimacy from different sources than the formal institutions of the state; that is, from victims, communities, and even offenders.

Figure 30.2 Nils Christie, Norwegian sociologist and criminologist, advocated allowing those affected by an offence to participate in court proceedings
Source: Don LaVange/CC BY-SA 2.0

Nils Christie (1977) (pictured in **Figure 30.2**) famously advanced the argument that court procedures need to be fundamentally rethought to ensure effective participation of those most affected by the supposed offence. His work has drawn attention to the impersonality of courtroom settings and their processes, and the way in which those most centrally concerned with the case and its outcomes appear only intermittently in proceedings and at 'the periphery': 'The parties are represented, and it is these representatives and the judge or judges who express the little activity that is activated within these rooms' (Christie, 1977: 3). Although acknowledging the interests of the state in resolving conflict and protecting the victim's interests, Christie thinks that other interests intercede. Lawyers, he suggests, 'are particularly good at stealing conflicts' (Christie, 1977: 4). By this, Christie means that the formalities of the legal process often appear to exclude the voices of those most directly affected by the offence.

Christie also argues that those who adopt therapeutic roles in the justice system are skilled at defining problems in ways which justify their position, particularly in the way that they redefine the conflict between offender and victim as the consequence of 'the criminal's . . . defects', and so effectively the actual lived realities of the conflict are 'defined away' (1977: 5). Cohen also notes that sophisticated systems of classification are emerging which are preoccupied solely with defining more and more offenders as belonging to 'special populations meriting specialised treatment' (1985: 195), at the expense of any concern for what actually happened when the offence was committed. The precise nature of the offence and its consequences for both victim and offender are considered to be of lesser importance. The victim is effectively disenfranchised (unable to take part) from the establishment of decision-making authority and the conduct of criminal processes.

Writing as he was in 1977, Christie was one of the early proponents of the reinsertion of the victim into the judicial process so that attention could be shifted to 'the victim's losses' which, in due course, 'leads into a discussion of restitution' (Christie, 1977: 9), and the offender 'gets a possibility to change his [sic] position from being a listener to a discussion . . . of how much pain he ought to receive, into a participant in a discussion of how he could make it good again'. Christie stresses that his principal interest is in producing a more authentic means of responding to crime, as opposed to 'a belief that a more personalised meeting between offender and victim would lead to reduced **recidivism**' (1977: 9). That is very much a secondary consideration.

Christie's central point is that there is a need to restore 'ownership' of the crime and its consequences to those who are closest to it and are most likely to be strongly affected. By implication, he is suggesting that what has happened is of no real concern to most people, and therefore there is no need for them to be involved in resolving the matter, even by proxy in the form of the state. Indeed, the withdrawal of the state (at least to an extent) is an important precondition for the creation of a forum for victims and offenders alike to regain control of the process of sharing experiences and feelings and agree a means of resolving the harm done and restoring social harmony. Perhaps idealistically, the opportunity is created for a negotiated outcome with responsibility acknowledged and accepted (and not necessarily all on one side), and the determination of a sustainable and mutually acceptable outcome.

In this way, offence resolution is about asserting a distinctive rationale for the criminal justice process. Its aims can be summarised as follows:

- the victim comes first;
- questions of guilt and responsibility are negotiated;
- perceptions and subjective feelings are given as much weight as objective 'facts';
- decisions and outcomes are specific to the offence;
- solutions are agreed rather than imposed.

From the point of view of the offender, the most important aspect of the process is the acceptance of responsibility. Rather than simply being 'held responsible', the expectation is that perpetrators will genuinely recognise the harm caused and its direct impact on the victim and this, in turn, is anticipated to lead to a genuine sense of remorse and commitment to putting things right (see **What do you think? 30.2** for a powerful and thought-provoking example). Although not the primary aim, the argument also holds that the insight gained by the offender will have some effect in reducing the likelihood of reoffending.

WHAT DO YOU THINK? 30.2

Using problem-solving traditions from indigenous communities

The 1997 documentary *Circles*, directed by Shanti Thakur, provides a useful insight into alternative approaches to sentencing offenders used in the Yukon, a northern territory in Canada. The National Film Board of Canada provides this description on their website:

> In the Yukon, an innovative program is bringing a traditional form of Aboriginal justice—circle sentencing—to the Canadian justice system. Sentencing circles don't focus on punishment. Instead, they bring together the perpetrator of a crime, his or her victims, and peers and family in an effort to bring healing to the community.

For many Aboriginal men in the North, going to jail was a natural extension of attending missionary-run schools. Brothers Harold and Phil Gatensby, who have both done their share of jail time, now participate in circles as a way to allow offenders to break the cycle of crime, court and prison. The program works so well that Aboriginals from the Yukon have helped set up similar programs elsewhere in Canada and in the US. The circle is a powerful alternative to prison terms imposed by courts—not only for Aboriginal people in the North but, potentially, for all communities. Consider the following questions:

- Would you feel comfortable taking part in a circle of this kind?
- If so, would this depend on how 'serious' the offence was? Or who the victim was?

30.3 Restorative justice and diversion

Restorative justice

The contemporary emergence of restorative justice in the UK has seen the creation of mechanisms to address the consequences of offending, supplementing conventional criminal justice processes. Typically, these are designed to consider the offence and its ramifications and to provide the basis for reaching an agreed conclusion as to how to put things right, whether by way of reparation, apology, or some other compensatory mechanism. Restorative justice may give the victim a chance to meet their offender in person, often within a controlled environment (as shown in **Figure 30.3**). In such an environment, the victim can explain the real impact of the crime committed. This can be an empowering experience for the victim, helping them to better understand the reasons for the offence (Daly, 2002). Restorative principles underpin decision-making forums which carry the authority of the community and therefore gain respect and legitimacy, without necessarily drawing on the forceful and symbolic resources of a more formalised and remote state institutional framework.

In England and Wales, restorative justice has been formally incorporated into government policy and legislation, notably through the introduction of the referral order in 1999 (see **section 30.4**), based on explicitly restorative ideas. Subsequent policy developments have been somewhat uneven. Restorative justice seemed to have taken a significant step forward in association with the 'rehabilitation revolution' announced by Kenneth Clarke as Minister of Justice in 2010.

> While it is a well-established concept in youth justice, restorative justice for adults is sometimes viewed as an afterthought to sentencing. We are looking at how we might change this so that in appropriate cases restorative justice is a fundamental part of the sentencing process.
>
> (Ministry of Justice, 2010: 22)

Figure 30.3 Restorative justice emphasises the need for collaboration and gives the victim a chance to meet the offender(s) in a controlled environment
Source: The Centre for Justice & Reconciliation: (www.restorativejustice.org)

Government then adopted a series of action plans, and held a series of 'Restorative Justice Weeks', until 2015. Following that, though, a series of less enthusiastic ministers appeared to give it lower priority and government funding for the national coordinating body, the Restorative Justice Council (described by its Chair in **Conversations 30.1**), was also substantially reduced. By contrast, Scotland has maintained a more active commitment to restorative justice, aiming to have 'restorative justice services widely available across Scotland by 2023, with the interests of victims at their heart' (Scottish Government, 2019: 4).

Where does restorative justice come from?

The origins of contemporary models of restorative justice have been traced to indigenous populations who have created consultative mechanisms for resolving community disputes and allegations of wrongdoing. Howard Zehr is often credited as being the originator of a 'new paradigm of criminal justice' (Johnstone, 2002: 87), adopting and contrasting ideas from these traditional practices with the retributive model on which western systems of justice are based.

Barnes (2013) also locates the origins of contemporary restorative practice within the problem-solving traditions of indigenous communities, including the New Zealand Maoris, Canadian First Nations peoples, and Australian Aboriginals. Family Group Conferencing, for example, has emerged from Maori problem-solving traditions to become recognised as a highly promising model for practice in both criminal justice and child welfare contexts. These developments, Barnes argues, have not only introduced new forms of justice into conventional western criminal procedures but have also gone some way to redressing discriminatory treatment of minority groups in the alienating setting of the formal courtroom. Citing a number of Canadian initiatives, including 'circle courts', based on First Nations traditions (an example of which is discussed in **What do you think? 30.2**), he argues that these 'were designed to impact positively the justice system's unequal treatment of first nations people' (Barnes, 2013: 105).

Importantly, restorative justice is seen as an international movement, connecting and providing mutual reinforcement for a range of indigenous and culturally varied practices, all of which are believed to share common features, grounded in **concepts** of healing and reconciliation. Another example of the international nature of restorative justice practices is the way that attempts to develop effective responses to serious crimes in the

CONVERSATIONS 30.1

The work of the Restorative Justice Council
with **Dr Kerry Clamp**

A group of practitioners established the Restorative Justice Council (RJC; see **Figure 30.4**) in 1997 to encourage the adoption of restorative justice within the criminal justice system and to provide standards for practice. In 2001, this extended to schools, communities and the workplace.

Restorative justice practices are now used across the UK (in schools, children's services, workplaces, hospitals, communities and the criminal justice system) and the RJC's practice guidance documents are highly respected. Having therefore achieved our initial ambitions, we have positioned ourselves as an independent charity that promotes access to good quality restorative justice provision for everyone. We do so in three principal ways:

1. At a professional level, we promote *quality* through the development of practice, training and service standards and through provision of resources such as e-learning, guidance and CPD events;

2. At the level of the public, we are the *national voice* for restorative justice through our media work (proactive and reactive), partnership working on campaigns and parliamentary lobbying, stakeholder engagement and advocacy, our website, e-comms, publications and events; and

3. At the level of practice, we help restorative practice to *grow* through consultancy and advice, and enabling services and individuals new to restorative practice to develop quality provision.

In England and Wales, the main restorative processes used are victim-offender mediation, conferencing, and (to a lesser extent) circles. Each of these processes aim to enable participants to understand the causes and consequences of offending and to come to an agreement about how to respond to what has happened. The RJC has developed clear, evidence-based standards and guidance to support the delivery of good quality restorative processes, underpinned by six key principles:

1. Restoration—the primary aim of restorative practice is to address and repair harm;

2. Voluntarism—participation in restorative processes is voluntary and based on informed choice;

3. Neutrality—restorative processes are fair and unbiased towards participants;

4. Safety—processes and practice aim to ensure the safety of all participants and create a safe space for the expression of feelings and views about harm that has been caused;

5. Accessibility—restorative processes are non-discriminatory and available to all those affected by conflict and harm; and

6. Respect—restorative processes are respectful to the dignity of all participants and those affected by the harm caused.

Research tells us that when individuals are involved in a process where they feel respected and heard, they are likely to feel empowered to make choices that enable them to move on from the incident. It empowers victims by providing them with a process that allows them to have a say in how their incident is dealt with. It empowers offenders by providing them with an opportunity to make amends for the harm that they have caused. Restorative justice can therefore be used in two different ways: firstly, to prevent harm and conflict by enabling individuals to consider explicitly how their actions might affect others; secondly, as a way to deal with conflict and harm after it has arisen.

Despite the progress we have made, there is still much to do in promoting restorative justice throughout the criminal justice system. There are various barriers to victims being offered restorative justice; the Crime Survey for England and Wales suggests that the number of victims offered the opportunity to meet their offender is still low; only 7.5 per cent in 2018. We want to see this figure much increased. As we evolve, we also want to devote attention to the other areas in which restorative justice is increasingly practised to help people communicate more effectively: those of health, education, the workplace, and welfare.

Dr Kerry Clamp, Associate Professor in Criminology, University of Nottingham, and Chair, Board of Trustees, Restorative Justice Council

Figure 30.4 The Restorative Justice Council encourages the adoption of restorative justice within the justice system

Source: The Centre for Justice & Reconciliation: www.restorativejustice.org

Figure 30.5 Rwandan gacaca courts are based on principles similar to those of restorative justice
Source: STR/AP/Press Association Images

aftermath of the genocide in Rwanda relied on the reassertion of traditional modes of dispensing justice, in the form of the *gacaca* courts (see **Figure 30.5**) (Brehm et al., 2014). Although they acknowledge that the outcome was by no means a perfect solution, nor a pure form of restorative justice, Brehm et al. suggest that the approach helped those involved to find viable responses to many of the harms caused:

> In short, the gacaca courts represented a powerful response to mass crime and an important element in the struggle to address society-wide tragedy and move forward. While these courts represent a 'home-grown' Rwandan solution in many ways, their blending of punitive and restorative aims and traditional and contemporary elements holds important insights for justice pursuits around the world.
>
> (Brehm et al., 2014: 346)

It is also helpful to recognise that alternative structures for dealing with offences and resolving the problems associated with them do not necessarily lead to outcomes which are radically different from those that might achieved under conventional justice processes (Daly, 2002). What makes restorative justice and offence resolution different may therefore be the sense of community engagement and legitimacy afforded to the process, at least as much as the range and flexibility of outcomes that are available. So, for example, in one case involving traditional methods of 'healing' and restorative practices used by the Heiltsuk First Nations people of Bella Bella in British Columbia, Canada, the outcome for an offender responsible for offences of assault was 'banishment' for seven months to a nearby uninhabited island, in accordance with Heiltsuk tradition (Barnes, 2013: 107). So, in this case the eventual resolution of the offence agreed with the offender may have been at least as punitive as would have been imposed by a conventional criminal court, although undoubtedly different in character and cultural meaning. **Read What do you think? 30.3** to consider the extent to which restorative practices and evidence of offender remorse should affect the punishment administered.

WHAT DO YOU THINK? 30.3

Do—or should—restorative practices lead to different punishments?

Consider this quotation from the official guidance on the referral order by 'Youth Offender Panels', which are established to oversee its implementation:

> Youth offender panels operate on restorative justice principles, enabling young people, by taking responsibility and making reparation, to reintegrate and lead a safe, crime free life and make a positive contribution to society. Victims must be given the opportunity to participate actively in the resolution of the offence and its consequences, subject to their wishes and informed consent. The youth offender panel process is an opportunity to:
>
> - address the victim's needs for information;
> - provide answers to questions;
> - reassure of future safety; and
> - ensure reparation for harm done.

> Victims who attend restorative justice processes such as a youth offender panel, can often derive considerable benefit and generally report high levels of satisfaction with the process. The presence of victims also can substantially enhance the beneficial impact of the panel on both children and parent/carer.
>
> (Ministry of Justice, *Referral Order Guidance*, 2018: paras 6.1–6.2)

Some victim interests have expressed the concern that they are being 'used' to address concerns about the offender rather than being provided with a service geared to their own needs.

- Why do you think that might be the case?
- Is it possible that offenders might feel under pressure to comply with the expectation to participate? Is that a problem?

Diversion

Whilst restorative models of offence resolution are often grounded in a vision of bridge-building and reconciliation, with a significant tone of redemption and emotional healing, diversionary approaches are geared more towards minimising the adverse impact of the formal justice system on the offender. Grounded in principles of minimum intervention and evidence of the unhelpful consequences of formal **criminalisation** (McAra and McVie, 2007), diversion seeks to promote normalisation and social inclusion of the offender and to avoid the damaging consequences of 'labelling'. Diversion may, though, incorporate elements of reparation, apologies, or community service as an adjunct to the principal aim of avoiding formal proceedings (Smith, 2018).

Despite their common temporal frame, diversion can be distinguished from purely restorative approaches in the sense that it is more forward- than present-oriented. It is concerned principally with future consequences for the offender rather than resolving the immediate harms caused by the offence. So far, diversion has also been viewed principally as a vehicle for dealing with young offenders, and decriminalising their behaviour, on the basis that they are capable of growing out of crime (Rutherford, 1992). For this reason, diversionary initiatives have been much less in evidence in the adult domain.

Support for diversionary objectives has been provided by McAra and McVie (2007), who have measured the effect of 'system contact' on young people in Scotland. The Scottish approach is quite distinct in its reliance on a children's hearing system which is fundamentally based on welfare principles and seeks to avoid criminalising young people who offend. Where children are reported for offences in Scotland, they may well be asked to attend a children's hearing which is a meeting to consider the offence in light of the child's circumstances and identified needs. The principal aim of the hearing is to reach an outcome with the agreement of all participants which will promote the child's future well-being. The basic assumption of the children's hearings system is that children and young people who commit offences, and children and young people who need care and protection, should be dealt with in the same way—as they are often the same children and young people (see http://www.chscotland.gov.uk/the-childrens-hearings-system/).

In this sense, the hearings system appears closely aligned to diversionary principles. However, despite its predominantly rehabilitative aims, McAra and McVie (2007: 333) have found that those 'who were brought to children's hearings' at a particular point in time 'were significantly more likely to report involvement in serious offending one year later than were their comparable counterparts'. As they put it, '**desistance**' from offending is actually more likely amongst those who have minimal or no contact with the system than those who receive interventions which are precisely directed towards reducing their levels of problem behaviour. They conclude that this evidence goes a long way towards validating the theoretical arguments about the effects of 'labelling' on offenders, and on young people in particular:

> The findings have shown a complex filtering process . . . in terms of gate-keeping practices, which means that certain groups of youngsters . . .— 'the usual suspects'—become the principal focus of agency attention . . . recycled into the hearing system again and again.
>
> (McAra and McVie, 2007: 337)

They argue that early intervention strategies which target those believed to be at risk of offending are themselves likely to draw young people into the system and, if anything, intensify the likelihood of further criminal involvement on their part. By contrast, McAra and McVie point out that diversionary mechanisms which rely on police warnings rather than formal referrals into the hearings system are associated with lower rates of serious subsequent offending. They conclude that the underlying principles of work with young offenders should be grounded in 'maximum diversion and minimum intervention' (2007: 340). The starting point for the justice system, then, especially as it applies to young offenders, is to avoid counterproductive interventions which actually increase the potential for their subsequent behaviour to cause further harm.

'Minimum intervention', then, seems to be a fairly distinctive starting point for thinking about diversion in principle and practice. Here, the central objective is to achieve *diversion from* the harmful impacts and consequences of the criminal justice process; and this principle is quite explicitly underpinned by a series of international agreements on the treatment of children and young people in the criminal justice system. The United Nations, for example, has consistently expressed its commitment to 'diversion' and the avoidance of formal processes of criminalisation wherever possible, as set out in the 'Beijing Rules' (1985), the 'Tokyo Rules' (1985), and the 'Riyadh Guidelines' (1990) on juvenile justice (see Smith, 2010 and Hamilton, 2011, for example):

> The need for and importance of progressive delinquency prevention policies and the systematic study and the elaboration of measures should be recognized. These should avoid criminalizing and penalizing a child for behaviour that does not cause serious damage to the development of the child or harm to others.
>
> (From the United Nations Guidelines for the Prevention of Juvenile Delinquency (the 'Riyadh Guidelines'), UN General Assembly, 1990)

Although diversion is often thought of principally in these terms, that is, the avoidance of involvement with and possibly contamination by the criminal justice system, it can also be understood in other ways (Smith, 2014b). In particular, it is viewed in terms of 'diverting' young people from further criminal behaviour; and also a matter of concern to McAra and McVie (2007) is the question of diversion *towards* beneficial services and opportunities. In these two senses, then, diversion is not simply about doing nothing, since it can also be geared towards proactive forms of intervention and positive outcomes, it is suggested. As an example, the Diversion Project provided by Halton and Warrington Youth Offending Team was developed in 2008. The project was established with two Diversion Workers, one with a social care background and the other a seconded mental health nurse from the child and adolescent mental health service (CAMHS). The CAMHS worker was identified as a major feature of the scheme who could assess young people for mental health or communication needs and link them directly into appropriate health services. The key aim of the project was to divert children and young people with particular needs away from the youth justice system and to make suitable welfare interventions available to them (see Youth Justice Resource Hub, 'Youth Justice Liaison and Diversion Scheme').

Despite the degree of ambiguity generated by these alternative interpretations of diversion, there remains considerable common ground with restorative strategies (Smith, 2011a). Both are concerned to set limits to the role and reach of formal state institutions, both are predisposed towards informal means of resolving problems associated with offending, and both seek to devolve control and decision-making to those most closely concerned with the offence. Procedures are simplified and those directly involved are empowered, it is argued, since the offence can be effectively 'processed' without ceding control to distant, complex, and only partially informed administrative and judicial mechanisms: 'The true story [of restorative justice] offers some hope, not only for a better way to do justice, but also for strengthening mechanisms of informal social control, and consequently, to minimize reliance on formal social control, the machinery and institutions of criminal justice' (Daly, 2002: 72). As an ancillary benefit, of perennial interest to those responsible for public finances, these alternative offence-resolution processes are believed to be much less costly to operate than courts and prosecuting bodies (Centre for Mental Health et al., 2010, for example)—although arguably a secondary consideration, this is no doubt a persuasive element of the argument in favour of informal forms of justice.

Diversion and restorative justice: similarities and differences

In distinguishing between the objectives of restorative and diversionary approaches, it is helpful to acknowledge their different orientations towards intervention. On the one hand, restorative justice is based on a belief in the importance of the process itself as a vehicle for reconciliation, acceptance of responsibility, making good, and the rebuilding of social bonds. On the other hand, diversion seems more strongly grounded in the notion of avoiding harm by minimising the effects of intervention, and only taking such action as is absolutely necessary in the circumstances. This could, of course, lead to a restorative intervention but only where this is justified and desirable. Clearly, here there is less emphasis on meeting the needs of the victim, but this is consistent with the underlying rationale of limiting the impact of any formal intervention and providing the opportunity for a 'normalising' outcome. In this respect, though, the aims of diversion and restorative justice come back into alignment, since both are committed to the principle of reintegration of the offender.

In its purest sense, diversion might simply aim to minimise intervention on the part of formal systems, based on the assumption that avoiding system 'contamination' is both the most effective and the least resource-intensive course of action (or inaction). On the other hand, somewhat paradoxically, arguments are made for a more proactive approach to diversion which seeks actively to promote the reintegration of the (usually) young offender ('*diversion to*' rather than '*diversion from*'). In this case, an intervention programme may well be offered, which may be a condition, in order to address any problems associated with the offending behaviour such as exclusion from school, perhaps. The Halton and Warrington project referred to earlier in the chapter was part of a national pilot programme geared towards delivering welfare-oriented interventions outside the justice system, especially providing specialist input to tackle any mental health issues the offender might have (Haines et al., 2012).

Comprehensive models of diversion, such as those established in Northamptonshire in the 1980s (Smith, 2011a) and Swansea more recently (Haines et al., 2013), would incorporate a range of objectives, including both restorative and welfare outcomes, depending on the issues identified on notification of an offence. In these cases, restorative practice might be viewed more as a means to an end (achieving diversionary outcomes), rather than as an end in itself.

Alternatives to punishment or alternatives to custody?

The place and function of restorative justice and diversion within the wider justice system draws attention to a broader philosophical question about the underlying principles and aims of criminal justice practices which do not follow conventional approaches, and are sometimes explicitly promoted as 'alternatives'. Are they designed to stand as authentic means of resolving problems of criminality in their own right, as a fully-fledged alternative to the conventional criminal justice system? Or are they intended to operate in a more limited fashion as a way of modifying the existing justice system to compensate for some of its acknowledged shortcomings; and to enhance its capacity to respond flexibly and humanely to the problems associated with crimes?

This tension can be identified in the recent history of the 'alternative to custody' movement which has, according to Mills (2011: 34), 'been a mainstay in thinking about criminal justice since at least the 1970s'. Initially, the idea of replacing all forms of custody with more humane and socially beneficial alternatives was associated with the 'decarceration movement' and the abolition of penal sanctions in all their forms (see **Chapter 28**). Mills argues, though, that this more extreme version of the idea is not the only way in which it could be interpreted, and that its practical application is 'ambiguous'. She suggests that the term can be understood in one of three ways:

- As a means of extending prison constraints and conditions into the community by imposing additional requirements on community sentences
- As a means of diverting 'some people' from custody, particularly more minor, short-term offenders
- In its original, strong version, as a principled means of challenging 'the use of custody'

(Mills, 2011: 34)

This confusion of aims can have practical as well as theoretical consequences, and reforms have often failed to produce the desired effect when 'alternatives to custody' have been introduced or adapted in order to replace the use of imprisonment. The Criminal Justice Act 2003, for example, failed to influence the proportional use of custody over the period following its implementation (24 per cent in 2004, 25 per cent in 2009), despite the 'key stated intention of these reforms . . . to provide credible community alternatives to custodial sentences of less than 12 months' (Mills, 2011: 35). Irrespective of the underlying purposes of such measures, their limited impact in practice seems fairly clear:

> Those concerned with identifying credible long-term strategies for addressing the use of prison . . . will not find answers working only within the limited confines of the 'alternatives to custody' debate.

(Mills, 2011: 36)

Historic and deeply-entrenched conceptualisations of law and justice are not easily discarded; and arguments for the expansion of 'alternatives to custody' have consistently faced pressure to modify their aims and make practical compromises; that is, to adapt themselves to look and feel more like the forms of punishment they are intended to replace.

Importantly, then, we must recognise that the landscape of 'alternatives to punishment' and 'offence resolution' is not formed independently of the existing, mainstream criminal justice system. Common ground may be defined in terms of processes of determining guilt and responsibility, for instance; and there may also be similarities in terms of the punitive quality of decision-making processes, even though these may be constructed very differently from the formal procedures associated with contemporary, westernised judicial structures. These constraints can prove problematic for those concerned to see alternatives such as restorative justice and diversion as driven by quite different principles, such as offence resolution and healing.

30.4 Delivering alternatives to punishment

By definition, 'alternatives' aim to set themselves apart from conventional approaches to criminal justice; although portrayed in these terms, they are implicitly defined in relation to the norm from which they seek to distinguish themselves. The relationship between 'alternatives' and established understandings of **individualised** rights and responsibilities, 'due process', **adversarial** justice, notions of guilt and mitigation, and the sentencing tariff is inherently problematic. Neither a diversionary nor a restorative perspective sits easily with these ideas and processes, all of which are central to the operation of the machinery of law and justice as historically organised. In practice, perhaps unsurprisingly, there are different degrees to which diversion and restorative justice make compromises with this established and ideologically powerful model. The Referral Order, introduced as a youth justice disposal in 1999, is a particularly good example of an attempt to insert restorative processes into the existing framework of disposals available to the courts, but without disturbing underlying principles of guilt and the sentencing tariff.

The emergence and the eventual acceptance of these alternatives to conventional approaches to punishment and the administration of justice has been the result of a process of engagement with a well-established body of ideas and judicial mechanisms. These are often organised in ways which do not easily allow for informal, negotiated justice, where ideas of responsibility are not necessarily clear-cut; and where 'tailored' outcomes do not sit well with the principle of a unified framework of mandatory penalties. Although both conventional and 'alternative' approaches might argue that the punishment should fit the crime, they have very different ways of seeking to achieve that goal.

Given their origins and the challenge to accepted practices that they represent, diversionary and restorative initiatives have often had to present themselves as small scale and experimental, so as not to disturb or threaten the prevailing consensus; and at the same time they have been subject to continuing challenges on the basis that they do not comply with accepted standards for the administration of justice. For example, the idea that diversion might allow for repeat cautioning or the reversal of the sentencing tariff has faced consistent questioning and resistance prior to its explicit adoption under the Legal Aid, Sentencing and Punishment of Offenders (LASPO) Act 2012. As **Controversy and debate 30.1** illustrates, the level of unease about repeat cautioning amongst influential interested groups, such as the Magistrates' Association, has remained high.

Delivering restorative justice

Making the case for restorative justice

[J]udges often emphasize that 'it is not merely of some importance but is of fundamental importance that justice should not only be done, but should manifestly and undoubtedly be seen to be done.'

(Gabbay, 2005: 355)

For alternatives to conventional forms of punishment in general, and particularly for restorative justice, the judiciary has tended to express concerns about the apparent threat to consistency in sentencing, on the one hand, and guaranteeing outcomes that meet both public expectations and the specific needs of the victim, on the other.

Gaining a foothold and achieving credibility have been problematic for approaches to the administration of justice which are innovative and offer potential challenges to deep-seated beliefs (and vested interests, such as the judiciary). One tactical solution to this has been to build alliances and to seek to generate support for these forms of practice amongst those who might be reluctant to do so, amongst established criminal justice agencies and the judiciary.

Like diversion, restorative justice has its origins in relatively small-scale and experimental schemes, which actually predate the widespread adoption of the term itself. And, like diversion, restorative justice has faced the challenge of establishing a legitimate and credible place for itself within an established criminal justice system, where its claims have not always been seen as having obvious merit.

A number of 'mediation' and 'reparation' schemes were funded by the Home Office in England in the 1980s with the aim of promoting new ways of resolving the harms associated with crime. The forerunner of these schemes was a victim/offender mediation project established by what was at the time the highly innovative South Yorkshire Probation Service in 1983. This project prompted ministerial interest and the Home Office established a programme of four reparation projects in Cumbria, Leeds, Wolverhampton, and Coventry for two years from 1985 (Graef, 2000: 24). A further adult reparation project was established in Northamptonshire in 1987, building on the initial success of the county's Juvenile Liaison Bureaux. These developments were restricted in scope—they were clearly seen as experimental and their funding was time limited. In such circumstances, demonstrating a track record of achievement was problematic, and none survived in their original form. At this point, the underlying justification for 'restorative' practice had not been established and, as Graef observes, the timing was unfortunate as political attitudes on crime 'hardened' during the early 1990s.

It seems that subsequent renewed interest in restorative interventions was grounded as much as anything in a strengthening recognition of the place of the victim in the justice process; restorative justice offered a vehicle for giving substance to this, whilst at the same time incorporating a more inclusive approach to offence resolution. In arguing for restorative justice, Graef (2000: 30) placed great reliance on the benefits to victims, noting that in 'the Leeds Victim-Offender Unit in 1996–7, 58.3 per cent of victims said they were very satisfied with the service, 33.3 per cent fairly satisfied and 8.3 per cent satisfied—there was no dissatisfaction'. Similar results were reported in North Wales and Aberdeen. So, just as diversionary initiatives appear to have been careful to avoid directly challenging conventional assumptions to do with the sentencing tariff, so early restorative practices were celebrated largely because of the enhanced benefits they appeared to offer to victims rather than offenders (Umbreit, 1989, for example).

Restorative justice in practice

The emerging models of criminal justice described here—which rely on informal and negotiated processes to achieve consensual outcomes—are believed to offer benefits to offenders, victims, and wider agency and community interests. These direct gains, though, are also associated with wider and more fundamental aspirations for a transformation in the way we 'do' justice. There may be an underlying belief that achieving change of this kind in an important symbolic sphere such as the administration of criminal justice can also prefigure and energise wider shifts in the configuration of social relations; that is to say, the way we understand and have expectations of each other (Boyes-Watson, 2000). The justice system is the practical realisation of our collective sense of morality and fairness; and there is undoubtedly an aspiration embedded in models of restorative and integrative practice to replace what may be termed the 'blame culture' with a more conciliatory and mutually respectful approach to human relations:

> The social movement for restorative justice does practical work to weld an amalgam that is relevant to the creation of contemporary urban multicultural republics.
>
> (Braithwaite, 2004a: 46)

Braithwaite's aspirational language here suggests that he believes that the promotion of principles of collaboration and restoration in criminal justice might have a wider impact in influencing the way we relate to each other, encouraging tolerance and respect. Supporters of consultative or mediated offence-resolution mechanisms have argued that these are transferable to any such context where disputes or conflicts of interest arise (neighbour disputes, bullying in schools, consumer complaints, or employee conflicts, for example)—see **New frontiers 30.1**.

On the other hand, such reintegrative aspirations do not necessarily imply a readiness to take crime less seriously, or to diminish commitment to victims' interests, which is sometimes a criticism levelled at extra-legal crime resolution initiatives. Braithwaite's pioneering work, for instance, is strongly grounded in a commitment to promoting concern for the victim, encouraging the offender to accept responsibility and make amends, and reducing the risk of future harm. The offender should be placed very squarely in the spotlight, and the basis for reintegration and reconciliation lies in what he terms 'shaming . . . Societies with low crime rates are those that shame potently and judiciously' (Braithwaite, 1989: 1).

In this formulation, restorative justice, whilst aspiring to reintegration, focuses strongly on ensuring that the offender takes responsibility. Braithwaite first outlined a model of restorative 'conferencing' which draws out the

---

NEW FRONTIERS 30.1

Restorative practice and the community

As we heard from Dr Kerry Clamp in **Conversations 30.1**, the Restorative Justice Council's aim is to articulate guiding principles which will inform practice, and to prioritise the needs of communities' and their members' interests, without reference to the justice system or any other statutory adjudicatory forum. The focus of intervention is very much on promoting and rebuilding strong ties and community relationships, echoing Christie's (1977) plea for conflicts to be reclaimed by those most directly affected and resolved within their community settings.

> Restorative practice . . . enables people to understand the impact of their behaviour on others. It delivers effective outcomes owned by the local community and creates stable, positive community environments . . . Restorative practice can be used to build strong communities and to ensure that disputes and disagreements are dealt with positively and constructively.
>
> (Restorative Justice Council, 'Restorative practice in the community')

The RJC's website highlights the story of woman called Susan who was a victim of theft—but is also a restorative justice practitioner herself—and met her offender in a restorative justice setting. You can read her full account at https://restorativejustice.org.uk/resources/susans-story, but her summary of the experience is (in her own words):

> By meeting the offender they become powerless—insignificant and humanised—and you can move on. You feel empowered by being able to say what you feel. I felt like Joe was wriggling like a worm on a hook and could barely look me in the eye—it wasn't an easy process for him to go through.
>
> Although I'm a bit biased, I'd recommend restorative justice every time. Crime can feel very personal and usually it's not. Restorative justice can help you find a perspective that makes you feel less targeted and safer in your home.

WHAT DO YOU THINK? 30.4

Using restorative processes in existing practices: the referral order

Szmania and Mangis (2005: 352) describe a restorative meeting taking place outside any formal criminal justice setting. It involves the offender and the mother of a victim who died in a car accident caused by the offender:

> The victim then begins to show the offender pictures of her daughter who was killed in the crash, and she reads several personal letters sent to her family after the car wreck. The victim's opening dialogue shows no hostility or anger towards the offender; she even explicitly forgives him. The offender responds to these gestures with his apology: I get so mad sometimes at the choices I made. I know in my heart that I'd never would [sic] have hurt anyone on purpose. God, I'd give anything to change what I did. I'm just sorry. God has brought me through too. But when I look at y'all, I see so much goodness, and so much (offender pauses), she had so much potential. And I know that no matter how much I play 'what-if' I can't change what I did. And I know there's been a lot of good has come out of it. I'm just sorry, [victim's name]. Part of me just wishes that you would just get mad and beat on me and uh. It's just so hard, you know.

This account is very powerful, and clearly demonstrates the offender's remorse, but how would it change your views about the punishment to be administered in this case, if at all?

---

experiences of those who have been harmed and uses these to focus the collective disapproval of the community on the offender. Because the process of engagement at this level involves the direct evidence of victims' experiences and it may also be mediated by those closest to the offender, the product of the restorative meeting is intended to be one of genuine recognition of the human consequences of the offence, and genuine feelings of remorse and commitments to put things right as far as possible on the part of the offender. Achieving this creates the basis for acceptance and reintegration 'of the offender back into the community of law-abiding or respectable citizens through words or gestures of forgiveness', or even 'ceremonies to decertify the offender as deviant' (Braithwaite, 1989: 100).

The idea of '**reintegrative shaming**' as formulated by Braithwaite has clearly made some uncomfortable, and the idea is 'not uncontroversial within the restorative justice community' (Harris and Maruna, 2006: 456). Whilst it is recognised that Braithwaite has advocated an approach to 'shaming' which maintains a sense of respect for the offender, avoids condemnation, and seeks to promote forgiveness, its consequences are less easy to predict and may not be positive. For example, there is a risk of piling guilt and blame onto someone who is already feeling remorse: 'shaming in contexts that are already highly shaming is unnecessary and may even be interpreted as stigmatizing' (Harris and Maruna, 2007: 457). The threat to an offender's possibly fragile sense of self-worth may well be problematic. In such cases, the use of shame may be counterproductive and unlikely to lead to the sort of reconciliation to which restorative justice aspires, especially if the offender feels 'unfairly treated' in the process (2007: 459).

Of course, a parallel question arises as to whether it is possible to predetermine an essentially unscripted encounter such as a restorative meeting between offender and victim, so that feelings of shame can be generated and then used constructively, irrespective of the feelings participants will bring to the table. Indeed, as Harris and Maruna recognise (2007: 460), Braithwaite's thinking appears to have shifted over time, too, from an emphasis on 'shaming' to a concern with 'shame management' (Ahmed and Braithwaite, 2011) within a reintegrative framework; a more conciliatory approach is viewed as likely to generate a more constructive response from the offender. The process may lead to more positive responses if all concerned in the restorative encounter are able to 'tell their stories' (2007: 460) and share (and hopefully resolve) their feelings, rather than experiencing a one-sided moralistic 'holding to account'. See **What do you think? 30.4**.

An open-ended approach is also more likely to be attuned to the ambiguous and confused feelings and understandings that participants may bring to a restorative encounter. Guilt and **victimisation** may not be neatly apportioned to one party or the other, and neither is it easy to quantify the expectations of those coming to a structured interactive process with which none are likely to be familiar (see **What do you think? 30.5** for a description of one such encounter).

In **What do you think? 30.5**, we can see that the offender, whilst acknowledging his wrongdoing, explained it in a context of adaptation to his own prior victimisation and the need to adopt a particular social role from his own interests. On the other hand, as often appears to be the case

> ## WHAT DO YOU THINK? 30.5
>
> ### Putting offending behaviour in context
>
> One study of restorative justice describes how:
>
> > One case sent for a conference involved two teenage boys—one English speaking and the other Spanish speaking. The English speaking boy had been harassing the other boy and eventually started a fight with him . . . The victim's mother was very worried that this conference may result in more bullying, so working closely with each family was very important . . . The day of the conference the tension in the room was very high. . . . As the offender began talking it became clear that there was no personal reason for the bullying and fight that took place. . . . After . . . some prompting, the offender revealed that many of the boys at school bullied the victim because he was from Mexico. He had simply joined in the group and quickly became their ringleader. At first it did not appear that he would show any remorse . . . but he surprisingly revealed that he too had been bullied a few years before. He discovered that becoming a bully himself was an easy way to divert the bullying. . . . onto someone else. The discussion that followed seemed astonishingly honest and heartfelt. While the boys did not become friends after this incident . . . the kindness and forgiving nature of the victim's family stood out to the offender's family.
> >
> > (Mongold and Edwards, 2014: 209)
>
> - What are the advantages of this form of conflict resolution in your opinion?
> - And what might be some of its limitations? Does it help to resolve wider, systemic problems, for example?

with restorative encounters, the opportunity to personalise the offence and to acknowledge the impact on the victim was important to the offender and enabled him to recognise and take responsibility. The participants were both able to gain from the sense of having a common experience.

The referral order

As with diversion, subsequent attempts to formalise restorative justice, such as the referral order, have relied on extensive compromise with existing structural arrangements. Aspects of practice under the referral order have also reflected conventional assumptions with offenders experiencing the intervention as essentially routinised, coercive, and punitive rather than inviting or encouraging the kind of reflective and deliberative approach outlined by many proponents of restorative justice. An extensive evaluation of referral order projects found that, at least in the early stages, implementation was highly problematic:

> The referral order represents both a particular and a rather peculiar hybrid attempt to integrate restorative justice ideas and values into youth justice practice. It does so in a clearly coercive, penal context that offends cherished restorative ideals of voluntariness.
>
> (Crawford and Newburn, 2003: 239)

The 'context' to which the authors refer is one of a strict alignment of the order with the tariff—administered only once, and on the young person's first court appearance (subsequently relaxed to enable repeat use in certain circumstances: Ministry of Justice, 2018)—and a set of requirements incorporated into its delivery which heightened the sense of compulsion and conditionality as far as the young offender was concerned. In this respect, the order represented no real challenge to conventional penological assumptions. For the young people concerned, it resembled just another form of punishment.

On the other hand, as Crawford and Newburn (2003) acknowledge, the mandatory nature of the referral order following a first court appearance meant that 'a steady supply' of young people to youth offender panels (established to oversee the order) would be guaranteed. In principle, this would offer the potential to cement restorative practices into the justice process: 'Coercion provided the capacity to move certain restorative values to the very heart of the youth justice system, and the loss of voluntariness was the price paid' (Crawford and Newburn, 2003: 239). This, in turn, did create the opportunity for the panels to engage young people and parents in a 'very different, and more positive' process of discussing and attempting to resolve the problems and harms associated with the offence, although concerns have been raised about the extent to which young people are genuinely involved in this kind of dialogue or simply feel coerced to take part (HM Inspectorate of Probation, 2016). A major question for the referral order, like other restorative measures, is whether the price paid in terms of compromising the voluntary and collaborative principles of the restorative ideal is worth it, in order to gain some degree of legitimacy (see **Controversy and debate 30.1**).

Despite concerns about its operation and impact (HM Inspectorate of Probation, 2016), the referral order has become an established feature of the youth justice

CONTROVERSY AND DEBATE 30.1

The role of compulsion in restorative justice

There are strong differences of opinion about the role of compulsion in restorative justice, and the extent to which offenders should be made to apologise or make amends for their actions. Some argue that this should be entirely voluntary and only offered on the basis of a genuine desire to make things right on the part of the offender.

A compulsory apology might be a way of underlining the message that the offence is unacceptable, and the offender therefore 'owes' something to the victim and the wider society:

> An apology shows that the offender has received, understood and the moral message directed at him and that he accepts the values implicit in it. It affirms his readiness to change his ways and to re-build relationships. This suggests that the criminal justice system could be made more meaningful if it was organised around a demand for a suitable apology from the offender.
>
> (Bennett, 2006: 129)

Arguing against forcing offenders to apologise, the following quote questions the value of any of the participants of a set exchange which all sides see as meaningless:

> Coerced apologies are particularly problematic in terms of RJCs [Restorative Justice Conferences]. They are less likely to be perceived as sincere by victims because youth offenders appear to lack or convey genuine understanding of the impact of their crimes. . . . Furthermore, coerced apologies may negatively affect . . . the 'ethical identity' of youth offenders, where such coercion functions to discourage offenders from critically and positively absorbing and reflecting on their experiences of RJC.
>
> (Suzuki and Wood, 2018: 458)

Where do you stand on this issue?

---

process, comprising 43 per cent of all court sentences for young offenders (under 18) during 2018–19 (Youth Justice Board, 2020).

Delivering diversion

Making the case for diversion

Interestingly, the pioneering cautioning scheme in Liverpool was established with the support of the police authority and the direct supervision of the chief constable, partly to ensure that the scheme was seen as legitimate (Mays, 1965). The Juvenile Liaison Officer scheme in Liverpool 'began in a small exploratory way', as Mays notes (1965: 186), with a stress on intervening early with young people 'on the verge of delinquency'. Cautioning was presented as one of the options available to the scheme to try and discourage further offending where children had perhaps 'got away with things' (1965: 188) previously. A caution, however, would only be administered in place of prosecution for minor offences (burglary being specifically excluded, notably), and the decision to do so could only be taken at a very senior level in the police force. See **Controversy and debate 30.2**.

Acknowledging potential criticisms that the police could be seen to be usurping the 'authority of the courts' (Mays, 1965: 195), the limited extent of the scheme was stressed repeatedly, and its function as an adjunct to the existing justice process was clearly signalled as 'filling a gap in existing services' (1965: 187). So, in this case at least, the potentially radical message of diversion from the judicial process was significantly modified in order to create a legitimate (and non-threatening) space for the scheme. In the case of diversion and cautioning, the persistence of this form of defensive rationale can be identified in the recurrent stress on the restricted nature of such schemes—being targeted only at minor offences, first or early career offenders, and remaining under the aegis of the police.

The same cautious logic can be seen to have applied much later, too, when limits to diversion were effectively institutionalised under the New Labour government's Crime and Disorder Act 1998. Here, the establishment of a rigid framework for 'Reprimands' and 'Final Warnings' ensured that they could only be administered progressively and only on the occasion of a young person's first and second offences; after this point, further offences could only be dealt with by the court. In addition, the expectation laid out in government guidance was that the final warning would be accompanied by a programme of intervention to discourage further offending, thus effectively instituting a pre-court tariff.

Diversion in practice

Unlike restorative interventions, but consistent with the approach outlined previously, diversion initiatives have focused more on the (young) offender with the aim of promoting an out-of-court disposal of the offence. One

CONTROVERSY AND DEBATE 30.2

Repeat cautioning

One of the criticisms practitioners come up against in youth diversion is that offenders are 'getting away with it', and taking advantage of the leniency afforded to them. This is said to be unfair on victims and to encourage reoffending.

> Thousands of violent criminals, sex offenders, and burglars were let off with a caution amid concerns from magistrates that police were infringing upon sentencing powers which should be left to the courts.
>
> John Fassenfelt, chairman of the Magistrates' Association, has written to Chris Grayling, the Justice Secretary, to call for an inquiry into police use of cautions, which can help stretched forces cut down on paperwork.
>
> 'It seems to have got out of hand, to be honest,' he said. Cautions were 'constantly being used for violent and sexual offences', he added, robbing victims of their chance for compensation and to see the offender in court.
>
> Mr Fassenfelt went on: 'When you see continuous cautions being given out you do begin to think the police are using them for some other reason'.
>
> (*Daily Telegraph*, 27 January 2013)

- Do you think repeat offenders should be 'let off' with a caution? Does it matter if it's the same type of offence? Does it matter if it's a violent offence?

- To what extent should the victim's views be taken into account when deciding on whether or not to administer a caution?

- Are there any offences which should not be eligible for a caution? Why?

---

of the best known models of diversion was established in Northamptonshire during the 1980s, in the form of three Juvenile Liaison Bureaux (JLB), in Wellingborough, Corby, and Northampton. A subsequent, and rather less successful, attempt was made to establish an adult equivalent in the county although with a rather more 'restorative' flavour—the Kettering Adult Reparation Bureau (Dignan, 1990). The JLBs were developed as a response to the previous very low use of out-of-court disposals in the area, and had a strong commitment to avoiding formal intervention, by way of prosecution or childcare measures. They were set up on a multi-agency basis, bringing together police, **probation**, youth and social services, and education (and in one case, health and the voluntary sector as well); and their remit was to consider the cases of young people reported for offences by the police and to make recommendations about the appropriate response. Recommendations would be informed by the principle that the least intrusive intervention possible would limit the risks of escalation into the justice system and the consequences of 'labelling'.

This approach has been compared to the philosophy of 'radical non-intervention' (Schur, 1973) by Davis and colleagues (1989). Although the Northampton JLB was apparently committed to a purist diversionary position, based on 'the Bureau's distrust of intervention of *any kind*' (Davis et al., 1989: 231), this was not the case elsewhere in the county, with Corby, for example, offering a more active approach to offence resolution and problem-solving. Reparation became a prominent element in that particular JLB's repertoire (Blagg, 1985). Despite these internal differences, the Northamptonshire 'model' became highly influential, based on its dramatic success in reducing levels of prosecution in the county (without any evidence of 'net-widening'; see Austin and Krisberg (2002) for a detailed discussion of this phenomenon). Those interventions which were undertaken by the more proactive bureaux were associated with high levels of victim and offender satisfaction (Blagg et al., 1986; Smith, 2014a).

Although diversion appeared to fall into disfavour in the 1990s and early 2000s in England and Wales, it re-emerged as a prominent feature of the youth justice landscape from 2007 onwards, encouraged by a shift in government policy and rhetoric and a desire to rationalise policing practice (Flanagan, 2007); and as 'austerity' struck, to save money.

New initiatives emerging from that point included the Youth Restorative Disposal (see later), the 'Triage' model of initial decision-making (Haines et al., 2013), and the Youth Justice Liaison and Diversion (YJLD) scheme (Haines et al., 2012). Several of these appeared to be infused with a 'welfarist' assumption that in certain cases and under certain conditions young people should be referred out of the justice system into more appropriate forms of service provision, as in the 'second-tier' outcomes provided for by the Triage model and the mental health provisions linked to the YJLD services. Interestingly, similar models of welfare-oriented diversion also seem to have shown a parallel growth elsewhere, as with the Ohio Behavioral Health Juvenile Justice Initiative (Kretschmar et al., 2016).

A further development, associated with 'an emergent difference between . . . policy in Wales and England'

(Haines et al., 2013: 170) was the Swansea Bureau, whose principal aim is to 'divert young people out of the formal processes of the Youth Justice System' (2013: 168). Described as a 'new approach in diversion', although acknowledging a debt to the Northamptonshire model, the Swansea Bureau also adopted a partnership frame for its development and sought explicitly to treat young people referred for offences as 'children first'. The underlying aim would be to work with parents and children to focus on beneficial outcomes and avoid the negative consequences of formal criminal processes (see **Conversations 30.2** with Professor Kevin Haines).

CONVERSATIONS 30.2

The Swansea Bureau diversion initiative (Haines et al., 2013)

with **Professor Kevin Haines**

Roger Smith (RS): Please could you briefly summarise what the Swansea Bureau Initiative is, and what that stands for?

Professor Kevin Haines (KH): The Swansea Bureau is designed as a non-criminal justice based response to offending by young people. It's based partly on the view that any significant involvement with the formal criminal justice system has negative implications for young people, in terms of their immediate behaviour, but also long term consequences for employment and such things. It's also based on the view that it's better to engage with young people with a positive agenda rather than a negative agenda. And placing the family at the core of responding to what is, for most young people, fairly normal adolescent behaviour.

RS: You mentioned 'children first, offenders second' in your discussion of the project, is that a good way of summing it up?

KH: Well, it is about responding to what is, for the vast majority of young people, a fairly normal adolescent behaviour. And it's about not overreacting to that with a punitive criminal justice system, whether it intends to be punitive or not, it's about responding to them as children and the fact that children need guidance and support and help. But it's best to do that in a constructive manner rather than in a negative manner.

RS: What does that mean in practice, in terms of the way something like the Bureau operates?

KH: For most young people, what [the agencies] found when they started to run the Bureau, was that in most cases the arrest of the child was the first time that the parents got to find out that their youngster was doing things that we wouldn't really want youngsters to get involved in. And in most instances, parents put in place boundaries, some cases sanctions, but broadly, a variety of responses that reinforced their role as parents and were broadly constructive. There was no particular need for the youth justice system to do any more than parents were already doing.

RS: It's supported by all the relevant agencies; do you have a sense that there's a collective will to succeed behind this?

KH: The main agencies involved in the Bureau itself and the decision making that goes with it are the police and the Youth Offending Service and they're absolutely committed to it. The police are very keen to support it because it's administratively an effective response, but also it's a practical response, and what the police want is young people to get constructive interventions that help them to lead better lives.

RS: Were the success criteria broader than just preventing reoffending; would 'that they lead better lives' be a better way of summarising the success criteria?

KH: If you're trying to engage a young person, either parents are trying to or professionals are trying to, you're not going to engage a young person on the prevention of offending. You could engage a young person on improving positive outcomes. So that's what makes it 'children first', it's about something that children will engage with.

RS: Can you summarise the achievements of the Bureau?

KH: Yes, the evaluation that we've done so far was on the first twelve months, and what that showed was that the reconviction or re-arrest rates for young people was below ten per cent.

RS: Does that refer to everybody who's eligible go through the Bureau—all young people, first offenders or repeat offenders?

KH: Originally the police went with first time offenders, first time arrestees, with a gravity score of one to three on the police gravity score scale, but the experience of the police in the Bureau was so positive that they opened it up to a broader range of offence gravity scores and to reoffenders.

Professor Kevin Haines, Professor of Criminology and Youth Justice, Swansea University, Director of the Centre for Criminal Justice and Criminology

Interestingly, this model explicitly sought to 'de-couple' the issues associated with young people involved in crime from the needs or wishes of the victim. Thus, restorative interventions would not be pursued as a specific element of bureau work; although they would be facilitated if an opportunity to make amends did arise. Nor would the Swansea model adopt an overtly 'rehabilitative' approach; instead, it would focus on ensuring children would be able to enjoy the normal entitlements and opportunities to which they should have access. The emphasis on informal problem-solving and inclusionary approaches underlying the Bureau's approach can generate a range of substantive benefits, reputedly:

> Early indications are that the Swansea Bureau has been able to employ proactive, yet informal, non-criminalising and prosocial measures, to divert young people from the formal YJS [Youth Justice System] and to reduce levels of reconviction. In this way, practitioners have begun to address some of the negative unintended consequences of contact with the YJS through sensitive and principled intervention, rather than a non-intervention ethos.
>
> (Haines et al., 2013: 185)

In this and similar contexts, then, diversion has been developed as an essentially informal process for delivering negotiated and focused interventions in response to alleged offences, tailored to children's specific circumstances and needs; as an alternative to criminalising judicial procedures measures involving prosecutions and court proceedings (Smith, 2018).

Diversion and youth justice

(For a fuller discussion on youth justice, see **Chapter 9**.)

It has certainly proved easier to develop models of diversionary or restorative practice in the field of youth justice than in the adult sphere. This may well be because of the inherent assumptions that young people are less responsible, less culpable, less 'hardened', and more open to developmental change. They are perhaps assumed not to understand the full implications of their antisocial or criminal behaviour and therefore to be open to the kind of deliberative process represented by restorative justice. At the same time, their commitment to criminal behaviour is thought to be less well established and, so the argument goes, effectively managed diversionary interventions may be sufficient to direct them towards a more law-abiding future. Practice is therefore geared towards facilitating change through a kind of moral educative process which encourages offenders to reflect on the harm caused by their behaviour, what they could do to put it right or make amends in other ways, the effects of offending on their social identity and life chances, what life choices are open to them, and how they can avoid the longer term hazards of further criminalisation.

Sometimes interventions are based on the assumption that young people are not necessarily committed to change and that an element of coercion is needed to reinforce the socialisation and educative work to be undertaken. This element of coercion also helps to reassure potential critics that what is offered by 'alternative' programmes is not a 'soft option'. Indeed, much is also made of the challenging aspects of facing up to your own wrongdoing and acknowledging responsibility for harm caused; as represented by Braithwaite's (1989) concept of 'reintegrative shaming'. In sum, there is a strong moral message of repentance and redemption underlying much practice in diversion and restorative justice, even though this may be problematic if such expectations do not coincide with offenders' perceptions of their own culpability (Suzuki and Wood, 2018). Restorative practice in its idealised form will typically be organised around a 'conference' of some kind, where the offender, family members, victim, supporters, and other key individuals will meet to share understandings of the offence and gain insight into each other's experience.

> Our definition of an RJC [Restorative Justice Conference] is this: a planned and scheduled face-to-face conference in which a trained facilitator 'brings together offenders, their victims, and their respective kin and communities, in order to decide what the offender should do to repair the harm that a crime has caused'.
>
> (Strang et al., 2013: 8)

The opportunity will be created for the offender to express regret or apologise and to commit to doing something to put right any harm caused; and, similarly, the victim will have a chance to acknowledge the offender's contrition and express forgiveness if they wish to do so (see **Conversation 30.3** later).

According to Strang et al. (2013), based on their systematic review of restorative justice conferences, these typically follow a prescribed format, lasting from one to three hours, encompassing (Strang et al., 2013: 8):

- preparatory work with victim and offender to explain the process and identify whether they agree to participate in the conference;
- planning the meeting on the victim's terms;
- establishing a democratic forum for the event (seating on the same level, privacy, neutral setting, for example);

- inviting participants to share their experience of the crime and the harm caused;
- encouraging a restorative discussion of how things could be put right;
- agreeing 'next steps' and registering these with a formal body in order to encourage compliance.

Strang et al. (2013) acknowledge, however, that the generic term 'restorative justice' covers a 'wide range' of practices which might share common aspirations but which operate in very different ways. There is a significant difference between the formalised processes associated with set-piece restorative conferences and more informal ad hoc arrangements.

Specifically mentioned by these authors is the recent development in the UK where police have been trained and then encouraged 'to undertake "restorative disposals" or "community resolutions" that may involve negotiations on the street immediately after a crime has occurred, in which an apology is made, no further action is taken and that is the end of the matter' (Strang et al., 2013: 7).

Instant justice? Combining diversion and restorative justice

The Youth Restorative Disposal (YRD) was introduced as a pilot scheme in eight police forces in 2008, and subsequently extended nationally as one of the options available under the catch-all term 'Community Resolutions' in 2011. The YRD has concentrated on rapid and proportionate resolution of crimes and misdemeanours as near as possible to the point at which they occur. It can be argued that the benefits of immediacy and making a direct connection between the offending behaviour and the response is as beneficial as a lengthy process of preparation and a highly formalised restorative conference. See **Conversations 30.3**.

The YRD was 'intended to be a quick and effective means for dealing with low-level, anti-social and nuisance offending, offering an alternative to arrest and formal . . . processing' (Rix et al., 2011: 2). Typically (in 75 per cent of cases, according to one study), the YRD would be carried out 'instantly', 'on the street' (Rix et al., 2011: 4), consisting of a verbal or written apology made to the offence victim by the offender. Importantly, it is reported, the administration of a YRD depended on the wishes of the victim; in fact: 'many victims did not want the offender to be criminalised . . ., and simply wanted an apology, or an assurance' that the offence would not be repeated (Rix et al., 2011: 4). In its early days, the YRD was reported to meet with considerable approval, both from police officers who appreciated the opportunity to exercise professional discretion and from victims and offenders, and not just in the latter case because it represented a 'second chance'. Young people also acknowledged the value of being made aware of the effects of their actions on others. Parents, too, were reported to be satisfied with the outcome and the positive effects of the experience on young people's behaviour.

CONVERSATIONS 30.3

How restorative and diversionary approaches are used in practice

with **Kate Howarth** and **Rob Hunter**

At County Durham Youth Justice Service (CDYJS), we work with young people and partner agencies (including the local County Council, the police, and the prison service) to prevent offending and reduce re-offending.

We always prefer to work in collaboration with the young people who use our service—in other words, with them rather than against them—as we feel this builds more effective relationships and leads to more meaningful outcomes. We also often work closely with victims. All our staff are trained in restorative approaches, and we've trained children's home staff in restorative

practices to try and prevent the unnecessary criminalisation of children in care.

The restorative and diversionary strategies we use evolve as we look for innovative ways to prevent offending, reduce re-offending, and give victims a voice. At the moment they include trauma-informed practice; Pre-Caution Disposals; Referral Orders; support for young victims of crime; and working with parents and carers.

Many of the young people we work with have suffered adverse childhood experiences (ACEs), and these traumas can mean they have difficulties in cognitive flexibility, impulse control, and have additional speech, language and communication needs. All of this can make it difficult to work with them around empathy and victim awareness. We have therefore been trialling an approach based around the trauma recovery model which involves a team, including a clinical psychologist, producing a report about a young person and planning interventions. With this approach, offence-specific work is often not the priority; one of the challenges is to balance the victim's needs with those of the young person, and we have to carefully consider the timing of restorative approaches.

One of our other trauma-informed practices is a new diversionary scheme called Violent Incident Support & Intervention. We have started this in response to the fact that our most prolific offenders often come to us first for a violent offence and share similar ACEs, including domestic abuse, parental substance misuse, and exclusion from school at a young age. The scheme is targeted and non-criminalising, aiming to engage these young people at an early stage. Interventions are based around a model of offender rehabilitation called the Good Lives Model; on desistance theory; and will build on positives, focussing on engagement and on establishing close working relationships with practitioners.

An important aspect of our work involves young people who are 'pre-court': this amounts to roughly half of our work with young people who have offended and a third of our work with victims. Typically, the intervention in these cases is short-term, and rather than being solely offence-based, it often involves working closely with other (non-criminal) services to meet the young person's needs. The fact that over 80 per cent of young people on Pre-Caution Disposals do not re-offend within the first year shows how effective this approach can be.

Following the suggestion by HMIP in 2016 that the restorative element of Referral Order panels had been lost, we've been working hard to redress this by increasing the emphasis on restorative principles and victim involvement. We've designed a new set of communication-friendly resources to help all participants understand and engage in the process, and we've shifted our emphasis away from 'getting a contract signed at all costs' towards facilitating a meaningful restorative process. We can now extend timescales to allow for additional work to take place with the young person who has offended and the victim, so that they are better prepared and the perpetrator has a better understanding of the impact of their behaviours. Within panels, the focus of the discussion is now around restoration and reparation rather than specific interventions. We've still got work to do, but we're seeing better levels of engagement and more meaningful restorative outcomes.

We support young people who have been victims of crime through an activity-based peer support group called With Youth in Mind (WYIM). This group was set up in 2015 and is led by young people who originally used it for support. WYIM has so far supported over 180 young people, some of whom originally came to us having committed offences, and many accessed the group due to violence within their family. There can be a link between young people being victims of crime and going on to commit offences: we often work with victims and perpetrators from the same families and communities, with similar issues. WYIM tries to help address this by providing a safe and comfortable space where young people receive ongoing support from peers and professionals.

Finally, although it is not perhaps a traditional diversionary scheme our Parent Support Group (PSG) is a restorative intervention in the broadest sense. This group was set up for parents/carers who have been direct or indirect victims of their son/daughter (such as criminal damage within the home, assault, and theft) and helps them to understand their child's behaviour better, equipping them with the skills and knowledge to improve communication and relationships. We see very positive results from this intervention, as this quote from Craig, one of the young people whose parents attended the group, shows:

> Instead of doing what they used to do they started to give me time to calm down and explained some strategies to help me do it. We didn't argue as much. Sometimes they would get the file out and remind themselves of what to do. They noticed the good things I was doing more and praised me for it.
>
> I am trying to make it up to my mam and dad but you smashed it and helped them loads. They still talk about all the stuff they learnt.
>
> (Craig, 16 years)

Kate Howarth (pictured left), Deputy Manager, Interventions Team, County Durham Youth Justice Service

Rob Hunter (pictured right), Youth Justice Consultant, County Durham Youth Justice Service

30.5 The meaning and impact of alternatives to punishment

As we have seen, in the case of desistance (**Chapter 29**) there is some controversy about how best to judge the outcomes of interventions in the criminal justice system. For some, the test of effectiveness is relatively straightforward, being based simply on reoffending rates. But, in the case of 'alternatives' to punishment, it is less clear that this should be the only, or even a principal, consideration. After all, the main aims of restorative intervention, or diversionary non-intervention, are not framed in terms of the criminality of the reported offender but rather in relation to wider potential benefits, such as victim satisfaction and harm reduction in a broader sense. Nonetheless, reoffending rates are often cited in support of claims for the overall effectiveness of these models of practice.

So, for example, analysis of the impact of the Swansea Bureau—whose principal aims are diversionary—pays close attention to the impact of the project's encouragement of 'non-criminal disposals' (NCDs), arguing that 'a general trend can be tentatively discerned that reconviction rates for NCDs are lower than those for all other disposals . . .' (Haines et al., 2013: 178). Thus, it is argued 'the combination of engagement, participation, informal action, appropriate intervention and the adoption of a pro-social approach appear to be critical ingredients in the ability of the Bureau to reduce FTEs [first-time entrants to the justice system] and reconviction' (2013: 185).

On a wider scale, a **meta-analytic** review' undertaken in the US found 'strong support for the efficacy of diversion programs, whether these involved cautioning or direct interventions. . . . In nearly all cases, these programs led to lower levels of reoffending than traditional processing through the juvenile justice system' (Wilson and Hoge, 2013: 514); thus, leading to the conclusion that there is 'little reason to abstain from adopting a strategy that is more effective than traditional processing and considerably cheaper'.

In the same vein, the Restorative Justice Consortium (2006), perhaps not an entirely disinterested contributor to the debate, published an overview of more than 45 studies, offering clear support for the claim that restorative interventions are associated with a reduction in reoffending rates. The important point here is not the **validity** and strength, or otherwise, of these claims, but that one of the leading proponents of restorative justice should consider it so important to produce this kind of affirmative material with its specific emphasis on reoffending. If anything, this suggests something of a lack of confidence in the inherent value (or effectiveness) of other purported benefits of restorative practice.

Indeed, as Robinson and Shapland (2008) have observed, there is a degree of ambiguity in the position adopted by advocates of restorative justice on the relative importance of reoffending as a measure of success. Noting Schiff's (2003) claim that restorative justice is distinctive precisely because it does not focus simply on what happens to offenders, they acknowledge that it is not principally presented as 'an offender-centred approach' (Robinson and Shapland, 2008: 337). At the same time, however, the concern with reoffending rates is recognised as a continuing matter of significant interest for policymakers. It has, therefore, been viewed as something of a 'tactical' adjustment for proponents of restorative justice to promote offender rehabilitation and prevention of reoffending as important goals. On the other hand, critics have suggested that 'reducing recidivism is a somewhat unrealistic goal for restorative justice' (Robinson and Shapland, 2008: 340); and that taking this approach also runs the risk of diminishing the 'importance or salience of other goals, particularly victim-centred ones'. In practice, though, there appears to be a considerable degree of enthusiasm for the idea that restorative practices might be effective in reducing reoffending. Indeed, 'victims, in common with other participants, actively wished to focus on addressing the offender's problems and so minimising the chance of reoffending' (Robinson and Shapland, 2008: 341). Offenders' expressed intentions to 'do something' about their behaviour actually constituted a form of reparation from the point of view of some victims. Restorative justice, then, might be viewed as capable of encompassing rehabilitation at least as a subsidiary aim, without compromising its underlying principles:

> There is a case to be made for a subtle shift in ways of thinking about the recidivism reduction potential of restorative justice. Instead of thinking about restorative justice as a new-style 'intervention'—something which is 'done to' offenders—we might be better advised to re-frame restorative justice as an opportunity to facilitate a desire, or consolidate a decision, to desist.
>
> (Robinson and Shapland, 2008: 352)

Diversion, too, reflects a degree of ambiguity when it comes to its potential contribution to desistance. In the case of the Northamptonshire Juvenile Liaison Bureaux in the 1980s, diversion from crime featured as one of the four principal aims of the initiative, but only as a subsidiary objective to enabling 'agencies' to respond effectively to youth offending. Partly, this relative lack of concern with reoffending derives from the underlying acceptance of the validity of labelling theory. In other words, non-intervention should help to reduce the level of reoffending ('secondary deviance'; Lemert, 1967) more or less automatically. However, it is also clear from accounts of early schemes such as that in Northamptonshire, and of subsequent diversionary initiatives as in Swansea, that the success criteria of these projects extend much more widely than that and encompass a much more substantial form of social reintegration of young people.

In Northamptonshire, diversion also encompassed the promotion of 'informal networks of control, support and care' and encouragement of 'the normal institutions of society to respond constructively to adolescent behaviour' (Bell et al., 1999: 96). So, too, the Swansea Bureau describes its first aim as being to 'divert' young people away from the justice system and to actively promote positive behaviour (Haines et al., 2013: 171). In both cases, the initial achievement of a lower rate of formal processing of young people through the justice system was the primary criterion on which they sought to be judged. And, indeed, in both cases substantial reductions were recorded in this respect. By 1992, over 90 per cent of those referred for offences to the Northampton JLB were not prosecuted (Bell et al., 1999: 98); and in Swansea the introduction of the Bureau was associated with a 70 per cent reduction in the number of 'first time entrants' to the justice system from 2008–9 to 2011–12. The continuing and sustained fall in the number of 'first time entrants to the youth justice system from 2007 onwards has been attributed, in part, to wider adoption of diversionary practices by police and other youth justice agencies' (Sutherland et al., 2017).

Considering the evidence

Ironically perhaps, it is more straightforward for alternatives to punishment to demonstrate (or at least claim) success in conventional criminal justice terms, than it is to show similarly positive outcomes in relation to aspirations to achieve a radically different way of 'doing justice'. Robinson and Shapland (2008), for example, are dubious about the capacity for restorative conferences to build 'social capital' or to provide systematic opportunities for engagement between the offender and the 'community', despite the claims of restorative justice supporters. Despite this concern about the quality of available evidence, a number of sources have identified benefits for victims and offenders arising from restorative processes which do distinguish them from other disposals. Larsen's (2014) review of restorative justice in the Australian context suggests that not only was there evidence of lower reoffending rates in at least some practice settings, but that 'both victims and offenders reported that [restorative] conferences were fairer than court proceedings and that there were greater benefits for victims who attended conferences (including feeling less fearful and having their sense of security restored)' (Larsen, 2014: 25). The effects of 'humanising' the offender are thus believed to offer significant benefits to victims who take part in restorative processes, and gain a sense of the person behind the offence; at the same time, active engagement of victims seems to provide an effective counterbalance to the sense of alienation and uninvolvement they typically experience under conventional criminal justice processes. Shapland et al. (2007) have also reported very high levels of victim (and offender) satisfaction, particularly associated with restorative conferencing: 'Around three-quarters of both victims and offenders thought the process was useful for them and were satisfied with the outcome.' Interestingly: 'Conferencing was perceived as significantly more useful by groups [involved] with more serious offences' (Shapland et al., 2007: 36).

Larsen's review also draws attention to the potential benefits for offenders of a closer sense of engagement through restorative processes, with some evidence of higher levels of 'compliance' with agreed responses to offences than in the case of court-ordered outcomes; and a greater degree of 'satisfaction' with the restorative justice experience itself (Larsen, 2014: 27).

Some work has been undertaken, too, to determine the relative cost-effectiveness of both restorative and diversionary interventions. As Larsen (2014: 28) acknowledges, this is often a significant political consideration, and in some cases research has suggested a substantial cost saving associated with restorative practices. It is also claimed that reductions in reconviction rates associated with restorative justice represent a future saving in relation to the anticipated costs of future crimes (which will not be committed).

Studies have attempted to estimate the actual and potential savings achievable through the implementation of diversion and restorative justice (such as Matrix Evidence, 2009), although these are inevitably hampered by the need to estimate what *would* have happened if a different course of action had been pursued. Nonetheless, it has been claimed that diversion of young adults (18–24) from formal court disposals to restorative pre-court interventions in England could have led to 'lifetime' savings of around £275 million at 2009 prices (Matrix Evidence, 2009: 3). That is to say, the combined effects of lower processing costs and reduced future offending would produce a significant net saving. Similarly, the Centre for Mental Health et al. (2010) has estimated that the costs of diversion to appropriate alternative provision for offenders with mental health problems would be offset by savings in direct provision of criminal justice services and an estimated 30 per cent reduction in reoffending (Centre for Mental Health et al., 2010: 2). This evidence is supported

> **WHAT DO YOU THINK?** 30.6
>
> ### 'Justice reinvestment'
>
> 'Justice reinvestment' became an influential policy framework at one point, based on the claim that effective investment and targeted incentives could persuade statutory agencies to use less intrusive and intensive forms of punishment; that is, adopt diversionary principles, as a means of realising cost savings as well as reducing the level and intensity of punitive sanctions. This approach was piloted for two years from July 2012. A subsequent programme evaluation concluded that: 'The overall cost of both adult and youth demand reduced in the majority of sites in both years of the pilot' (Wong et al., 2016: 41).
>
> Consider the following questions:
>
> - Is cost-effectiveness a good basis for judging whether or not to deal with offences in one way rather than another? (How can we balance victims' interests against a cost-based decision not to proceed against an alleged offender, for example?)
> - Can and should human and economic costs be correlated in order to enable us to decide what is the best way of dealing with crime?

by reports from specific schemes, with the local authority reporting annual savings to the public purse of over £2.8 million following the introduction of 'robust pre-court disposals' in Swansea (Haines et al., 2013: 185).

It is interesting to reflect on the expectation that 'alternatives to punishment' should justify themselves in terms of their cost-effectiveness; whereas this does not seem to be the case for conventional elements of the justice system, whether in the form of the judicial machinery, the community and custodial disposals in use, or the consequential costs of further offences and reconviction. It is only relatively recently, with the emergence of arguments for 'justice reinvestment', that these default assumptions have come into question in public policy debates (House of Commons Justice Committee, 2009)—see **What do you think? 30.6**.

The implications of alternatives to punishment

In one respect, it might seem that the justifications for alternatives to punishment are self-evident. They are—reportedly—cheaper than conventional approaches, they are—apparently—capable of reducing reoffending rates (Allen, 2017), they offer recognised benefits to both victims and offenders, and they represent a rebalancing of the relationship between the state and the community. As a result, alternatives could be seen as offering a powerful challenge to established assumptions about the underlying objectives and operation of the justice system. They seem to call into question widely held beliefs about '**just deserts**', deterrence, the sentencing tariff, legal authority and expertise, and the relationships between victims, offenders, and the formal agencies of criminal justice. As such, they might be viewed as prefiguring a radical shift in the way in which criminal justice is organised as well as its underlying purposes.

To some extent, this hinges on whether or not the arguments in support of alternatives to punishment are articulated in their 'weak' or 'strong' forms (Smith, 2011b: 171); that is, whether they are viewed as representing a direct challenge to conventional justice models or whether they are viewed as a form of 'modification', perhaps acting as a kind of brake on the most harmful or wasteful aspects of established practice.

Restorative justice, for instance, is viewed as a 'critique of traditional forms of justice . . . and many of its proponents depict it as an oppositional paradigm to retributive justice. . . . The benefits of restorative justice are typically set out with reference to the failings of the traditional criminal justice system. Advocates of restorative justice argue that it resolves many of these criticisms by addressing the needs of the victim, offender and wider community' (Campbell et al., 2006: 5). Crawford and Newburn (2003: 19) have equally suggested that restorative justice is 'one of the most significant developments in criminal justice' in recent times, because it offers a different perspective on conflict resolution and the repair of harm to that of the traditional fault-finding **ideology** and machinery of the justice system. Although they express doubts about the delivery of restorative justice in practice, Crawford and Newburn (2003: 20) have suggested that its underlying principles and aims act as a direct challenge to:

- the ineffectiveness of conventional models of justice;
- the limited capacity of the justice system to respond effectively to crime;
- the 'theft' of conflicts from those most affected by the offence (following Christie, 1977);

- the failure to engage effectively with offenders in resolving the issues associated with their crimes;
- the reliance on 'punishment', such that 'one harm is met by another harm', to no beneficial effect;
- the limited capacity of conventional processes to acknowledge or incorporate cultural differences and diversity;
- the distance in space and time of formal processes from the actuality and context of the offence.

Essentially, then, restorative justice appears to be based on a different set of values, to do with resolving problems through negotiation and making good the effects of harm as opposed to pursuing formal and criminalising processes of fault-finding, blame, and punishment.

This points towards a significant reformulation of the core principles of criminal justice. The idea of a 'tariff' of disposals, for example, clearly comes into question since this does not allow for the specific circumstances of the offence or the expressed interests of the victim (and others affected) to take precedence in determining the outcome.

Similarly, diversion represents a challenge to the principle of a graduated sentencing tariff whereby disposals are progressively more punitive, depending on the gravity of the offence, and the persistence of the offending. First, the concept of 'minimum intervention' underpinning diversion suggests that any form of statutory proceedings needs to be justified in every case, rather than simply following from the number of prior offences committed by the individual concerned. Secondly, the arguments associated with the idea of 'labelling' would support the principle that no record should be kept of any 'out of court' disposal (Allen, 2017: 10). And, thirdly, even where an offender has a history of prior formal involvement in criminal proceedings, this should not preclude a diversionary outcome in relation to any subsequent offence. For proponents of both diversion and restorative justice, the point here is that the response to the reported crime can be much better 'tailored' to its specific characteristics if there is no requirement to follow a standardised and formulaic procedure which is, by definition, incapable of taking these into account.

Wider benefits

Not only are alternatives presented as more effective and better tailored responses to crime, but they are also believed to support broader objectives, such as enhanced social cohesion and reintegration of those at risk of being marginalised. The active involvement of the community is seen as an important objective for criminal justice, offering the opportunity to return control to those most directly affected, as Christie (1977) advocated. This aspiration was undoubtedly at the forefront of the ambitious restorative justice initiative in Northern Ireland where 'community justice' was also believed to be an important element of the wider post-conflict reconciliation strategy. The highly positive evaluation of the youth conferencing service introduced in Northern Ireland in 2003 recognised that the service had quickly 'become established as a mainstream approach to young people who come in contact with the criminal justice system'; and that the high rates of satisfaction recorded, for both offenders and victims, suggested that 'the process itself may be seen to have inherent value' (Campbell et al., 2006: 144).

Indeed, it has been argued that restorative justice may have a central role to play in enhancing peace-building initiatives in societies which have experienced long-standing conflict, such as Northern Ireland and South Africa:

> The extent to which the language and concept of restorative justice has permeated transitional justice in recent years has been nothing short of remarkable. Overall, this advance is to be welcomed: restorative justice approaches evidently contain a capacity to bolster peace-building in offering a flexible and pluralistic means of resolving conflict at macro and micro levels.
>
> (Clamp and Doak, 2012: 359)

However, the same authors are sceptical about the extent and substance of change achieved as a result of the introduction of restorative practices, questioning whether the adoption of 'singular components' of restorative justice, such as mediation, apologies, or reparation, are sufficient to achieve a genuinely different kind of outcome than those associated with conventional justice systems.

Although some advocates of alternatives to punishment certainly aspire to radical objectives (O'Mahony and Doak, 2017, for example), others take a more moderate view of their scope and realistic goals. Thus, in effect, the aim is to achieve a better 'balance' in the justice process rather than to see it transformed. Alternatives are seen as a useful way of moderating the justice process to avoid the risk of disproportionate or unfair outcomes, but explicitly within rather than in opposition to the accepted framework of judicial decision-making. Diversion, then, might be adopted reasonably and realistically as a means of extending the sentencing tariff rather than as an alternative model for dealing with crime. It would therefore be available at the lower end of the scale for early and minor offences (Taylor, 2016) and where offenders accept responsibility and demonstrate remorse (O'Mahony and Doak, 2017: 114). Similarly, restorative justice might be understood as a useful adjunct to conventional processes and disposals, offering a stronger voice for victims and an opportunity for offenders to make amends but only within the context of the attribution of culpability and enforced punishments.

Pragmatic compromises

In practical terms, it does seem that diversionary and restorative interventions occupy a specific operational 'space' where they come into play, but only at the invitation and on the terms of established judicial procedures and interests (the police, the courts, and prosecutors). As we have observed, the referral order represents a particularly clear-cut example of just this sort of accommodation between the apparently radical aspirations of restorative justice and the reluctance of the judicial system to cede any ground, either symbolic or substantive, to other perspectives. The initial location of the referral order at a very specific point in the tariff of disposals made this point very clearly. Despite subsequent reforms, the underlying logic of the tariff remains essentially unaltered.

Similarly, diversionary measures are very often presented as only being justified in relation to minor or early offences:

> We are particularly encouraged that many youth offending teams and police forces are using a restorative approach to resolving minor offending.
>
> (House of Commons Justice Committee, 2013: 8)

However, in more serious circumstances, especially in cases where the offence involves violence, the boundaries are clear. There are, indeed:

> circumstances in which even a low level offence would not be appropriate to be dealt with in this way. Examples included where it was part of a pattern of repeat offending or was associated with racial or domestic violence.
>
> (Northern Ireland Office, 2008: 20)

Recent evidence, too, suggests that wider trends in criminal justice have been characterised by a substantial proportionate reduction in the use of lower level diversionary or restorative disposals, whilst spending cuts have had a much less severe impact on prosecution rates:

> the Magistrates' Association have waged a campaign against the so-called 'caution culture' arguing that, while out of court disposals have a role to play, too many cases are diverted rather than prosecuted, thereby potentially eroding public confidence in criminal justice . . . Partly as a result of this criticism, the last ten years [2006–16] have seen a substantial decline in the use of diversion. The numbers receiving police cautions fell from 340,000 in 2006 to 110,000 in 2016. Those receiving penalty notices fell from 188,000 to 38,000 in the same period. While the number of prosecutions has fallen over this period too, reflecting falls in recorded crime, the cautioning rate has declined even more. The proportion of offenders who were cautioned has fallen from 30% to 13% over the last ten years.
>
> (Allen, 2017: 4)

The influence of established thinking about guilt, responsibility, deterrence, and retribution is also evident in the administration of alternatives. Some proponents of restorative justice, for example, believe that it can incorporate mandatory requirements to engage in consultative processes and to make amends without compromising its essential qualities of negotiation, recognition, and reconciliation. There is perhaps understandable support for the idea that reparation should be made conditional, in the interests of victims, and that alternative sanctions should be available in the event of failure to comply (O'Mahony and Doak, 2017: 114). This principle has been extended, too, to purportedly diversionary measures such as the **conditional caution** introduced under the Legal Aid Sentencing and Punishment of Offenders Act 2012.

Walgrave has argued that even though voluntarism is the preferred option for restorative practice, to be pursued wherever possible, there must be provision (and safeguards) at some point for the introduction of 'coercion' where it 'finally appears to be the only possible way of doing justice' (Walgrave, 2003: 62). He goes on to argue that 'restorative justice proponents are increasingly aware that due process and some kind of proportionality are important constraints to safeguard rights and justice in general' (2003: 76). On the other hand, though, he does assert that such limitations should be integrated with the logic of restorative practice rather than dominating or marginalising it.

In various ways, then, conventional assumptions rooted in the ethos of blame, individual responsibility, and holding offenders to account have become incorporated into a range of disposals which simultaneously are promoted on the basis that that they introduce radical and original principles and operational logic into the justice system.

Limitations of alternatives to punishment

Lack of consensus

One of the most important questions for proponents of alternative approaches to punishment in criminal justice is just what they understand their aspirations to mean. The only real area of agreement in relation to restorative justice, for instance, is that it is a complex and disputed concept. There are fundamental disagreements, for example, as to whether compulsion has any part to play in the process of bringing offenders into the process of offence resolution and reparation, albeit in the cause of achieving beneficial outcomes for other stakeholders (including victims). The underlying threat of alternative sanctions for non-compliance is believed by some to fatally undermine the key objectives of securing mutually and freely agreed outcomes which are viewed as fair and beneficial by all concerned. Others, though, would argue that the role of the state and the law as 'guarantor' of satisfactory procedures and appropriate outcomes logically extends to securing compliance, as would be the case with many forms of contractual agreement.

In practice, much of what takes place under the broad umbrella of alternative mechanisms for resolving crime does incorporate conventional assumptions about holding offenders to account, reinforcing a sense of responsibility, and making good; so, questions perhaps need to be asked about the limits beyond which this sort of compromise actually subverts the underlying principles of restorative or diversionary practice. This becomes more significant when we acknowledge the evidence that offenders themselves often experience 'alternative' interventions as no more than another form of punishment and humiliation. Maruna et al. (2007) identify limitations associated with youth conferencing, to do with its apparent similarities to other aspects of young people's experience, such as being continually blamed, berated, and imposed upon:

> It was all: 'How you'd feel if this happened to you?' And I was like, 'Yes I know. I get the point'. For an hour maybe every week. It was just talk crap in me ear. . . . You know. It took an hour of my week. I think I had to go on a Friday. You know I love my Friday!
>
> (Young person quoted in Maruna et al., 2007: 52)

As Maruna et al. go on to explain, the experience of being vilified in this way and being unable to get across their own accounts of what happened could be very negative for some offenders. Their attempts to rationalise and contextualise their offences seemed to be dismissed as mere 'excuses' and this left them feeling angry that they had not been taken seriously in the restorative conference.

Lacey (2012) also expresses concern about the potential variability in the way in which 'restoration' is achieved, identifying ambiguous and contrasting experiences in different settings:

> At YOT [Youth offending Team] B 'restoration' was achieved in that young people did work that they tended to feel made a tangible contribution and that they were therefore 'better off' as a result. In contrast, young people at YOT A viewed their reparation work as a punishment and did not feel that they were 'restoring' the harm that had been caused by their crime.
>
> (Lacey, 2012: 161)

Smith and Gray (2019) have also identified different 'models' of service delivery in youth justice which are likely to translate into variations in restorative practices.

Alternatives *as* punishment

The implication of such findings is that alternatives to punishment may not, in fact, be experienced by those on the receiving end as any less of a punishment, whilst at the same time they may not be assured of the safeguards available to those going through conventional adjudication and sentencing processes. In other words, 'alternatives' may actually be less fair than conventional criminal justice mechanisms. Conventional principles of appropriate and proportionate punishment may be breached because of the absence of proper legal safeguards. Pratt (1989) was one of the early trenchant critics of the idea of 'administrative justice', describing the Northamptonshire diversion scheme as 'corporatist' and concerned principally with achieving the agencies' internal policy goals rather than ensuring that the participants' rights were protected: 'instead of a shift from the inhumanities and injustices of the institution, we find these features of the carceral system now being reproduced in the community—in those projects that are supposed to be alternatives to the institution' (Pratt, 1989: 252).

Whilst these conclusions were disputed by others, based on **empirical** observations of diversion schemes in operation (Hughes et al., 1998), there remains a degree of support for the idea that alternative forms of justice are not necessarily just. Where alternative interventions do not act as genuine alternatives but as an adjunct to conventional processes, it is argued that they expose offenders to more intrusive and less effectively regulated forms of punitive sanction than would otherwise be the case. Thus, pursuing the apparently laudable objective of 'making amends' may achieve what is expected of it in a formal sense whilst actually involving excessive and demeaning impositions on the offender (Menkel-Meadow, 2007).

In a similar vein, concerns are raised about the extent to which supposed 'alternatives' to formal interventions simply run alongside them, contributing to a general 'system' expansion. 'Net-widening' has been identified as a significant potential risk associated with attempts to develop informal and extra-legal disposals, outside the remit of conventional adjudicating forums. Austin and Krisberg (2002) depict the criminal justice system as a series of 'nets' which are able to develop their own criteria for sifting and 'catching' those deemed eligible for one kind of intervention or another. Their suggestion is that each new theoretical model and reform movement in criminal justice either adds another 'net' to the array of options available, or strengthens or expands existing nets. Alongside other reform initiatives (in the domains of decarceration, due process, decriminalisation, deterrence, and just deserts), diversion is viewed as a contested area of practice where a range of agency interests come into play. In similar vein to

Pratt (1989), Austin and Krisberg (2002: 259) view this as territory ripe for exploitation by 'corporate' interests:

> Diversion has been implemented through the addition, by criminal justice agencies, of new programs and new resources to the existing system . . . The pre-trial criminal justice process is . . . an 'open' system, in which agencies compete and conflict with one another and in which various and diverse decision makers exert considerable discretionary powers.

At the time of their original study (1981), Austin and Krisberg identified examples of diversion programmes 'expanding' and 'strengthening' nets as well as creating new ones. Schemes were extending their terms of reference to deal with new forms of apparently problematic behaviour, 'formalizing previously informal organizational practices' (Austin and Krisberg, 2002: 260) and establishing new procedures to ensure engagement. In the process, questions of guilt and responsibility appear to have been subordinated to the procedure and conditional requirements imposed on those 'diverted', at the expense of 'due process'.

In this context, there is a related concern that the lack of effective safeguards surrounding out-of-court decision-making may also lead to inequalities and discriminatory outcomes on ethnic grounds. The risk of minority ethnic groups being drawn arbitrarily and disproportionately into the justice system has clearly been recognised (Bowling and Phillips, 2003; Lammy, 2017); and even a 'diversionary' outcome in such cases can result in a criminal record with longer term consequences.

In fact, there has been evidence of system expansion at various points in time. The use of juvenile cautions increased dramatically in the UK from the 1950s onwards, following the implementation of the pioneering Juvenile Liaison Scheme in Liverpool, but with little impact on prosecution rates. It was this cumulative trend associated with other developments in the use of care orders which prompted Thorpe et al. (1980) to draw attention to the dramatic parallel growth in the criminalisation of children and their institutionalisation on welfare grounds, particularly during the 1970s.

Similarly, following the Crime and Disorder Act 1998, the prescriptive framework of reprimands and final warnings, the development of an array of targeted 'early prevention' programmes, and the introduction of the anti-social behaviour order were also associated with a period of system expansion and increasingly punitive treatment of a growing number of young people across the range of interventions (Bateman, 2015).

At other times, however, it is clear that 'net-widening' is not a necessary consequence of the introduction of diversionary initiatives. Indeed, Thorpe et al. (1980: 130) made an important distinction between 'process' and 'practice' intervention, arguing that diversion could be effective if its goal was to change system behaviour rather than simply to develop yet more ways of working with young people. This kind of 'systemic' approach was a feature of the diversionary initiatives of the 1980s and is arguably once again a feature of the reduction in formal processing of young offenders in England and Wales from 2007 onwards.

However, when diversion does appear to be successful in these terms and offenders are subject to less obviously punitive interventions, it is exposed to another form of criticism, namely that offenders are 'getting away with it'. Not only is justice not being served, it is asserted, but victims are believed to lose out significantly in the context of an approach which is designed primarily to meet the interests of offenders. In a context in which victims feel poorly served by the justice system, sharp concerns about diversion and restorative practices are perhaps to be expected. As Victim Support (the national victims' organisation) has put it:

> Confidence in the criminal justice system among victims remains far too low. The rule of law rightly demands that victims do not dictate justice or sentencing, but the engagement and confidence of victims in it is nevertheless vital. Victims and witnesses have been historically marginalised in the field of sentencing. While this has begun to change and the need to consider victims' perspectives is acknowledged more widely, the views of victims continue to be misrepresented and misunderstood.
>
> (Victim Support, 2012: 5)

A survey of views on community sentences carried out by Victim Support has suggested a considerable degree of wariness about restorative justice, and comments to the effect that it should not be used as a justification for reducing the level of punishment imposed on the offender. Concerns about the marginalisation of victims' interests are persistent; as is the fear that alternative measures will be associated with undue leniency (Jacobson and Kirby, 2012). Such fears are endemic, undoubtedly, and coincide with a broader mood of public (and political) opinion in favour of more punitive responses to most types of crime (Hough et al., 2013).

Alternative models have also been applied in increasingly complex and challenging settings, as in the case of domestic violence, as outlined in **Controversy and debate 30.3**.

However, it may be that such criticisms are based on unrealistic expectations. For example, 'alternative' interventions with known offenders are not well placed to address victims' interests because of their structural location in the justice system. In many cases, it is not possible to match offenders with victims simply because crimes are not solved; and thus models of restorative justice are not well placed to consider the interests of victims in general. In the interests of fairness, it might actually seem

CONTROVERSY AND DEBATE 30.3

Restorative practices and domestic violence

Is there a place for restorative practice in cases of domestic abuse and other violent offences? The BBC's *Panorama* programme reported on innovative approaches to domestic violence which involve restorative practices in an episode titled 'Can violent men change' which aired in October 2018 (see **Figure 30.6**).

The accompanying BBC News article (BBC News, 8 October 2018) outlined the case of a man called Andrew who featured in the programme. Andrew was increasingly abusive to his partner, Emma, and moved out of their home, leaving Emma struggling to cope with their children. Social services later intervened and removed the children from their parents' care.

Emma was offered courses to support her in moving on from the abusive relationship, but Andrew also wanted help to confront and change his abusive behaviour. He enrolled on a weekly programme with Phoenix Domestic Abuse Service. The BBC reported that despite a shaky start:

> after seven months on the course he has formed a bond with the group and says he is beginning to understand the effects of his behaviour. Every week he was challenged on his behaviour and had to confront his actions. The course uses role-play, problem-solving tasks, and challenging discussions to teach the men about the impact of their actions. 'I'm not proud of who I was then, but I am proud of who I am now,' he says.

Emma says she recognises the transformation in Andrew. 'He's different. We talk more, he listens,' she says. They were separated for two years but are now together again and are working to get their children back.

Lidia, who helped Andrew through the course, said it is important to intervene because 'if no one does any work with that person then they are likely to go on and find another victim. Their next relationship is likely to become abusive.'

Phoenix sees both sides of abusive relationships on a weekly basis, believing the abuser and the abused partner both need support—either together or apart—if they hope to break out of the violent cycle.

But as the BBC's article and programme highlight, the courses do not receive universal support: they are costly and some see this type of intervention as unhelpful and even counterproductive. The BBC spoke to a victim who not only saw no change in her partner when he was referred to a programme by her local authority, but felt that 'If anything it made him angrier.' The abuse continued throughout and after the course and she thinks these interventions are not enough to bring about meaningful change: 'Their whole brain needs unpicking. It's got to be long-term mental health intervention, not a six-week course, because they are so manipulative they will pull the wool over people's eyes.'

Those in favour of the courses, such as a practitioner named Denise who features in the *Panorama* programme, do acknowledge that some people 'cannot change and will not change, for a variety of reasons', but still argue that the courses are valuable. Denise told the BBC: 'those that want to, those that are willing to give it a go, they need to be given the opportunity and I think for those people, yes they can change.'

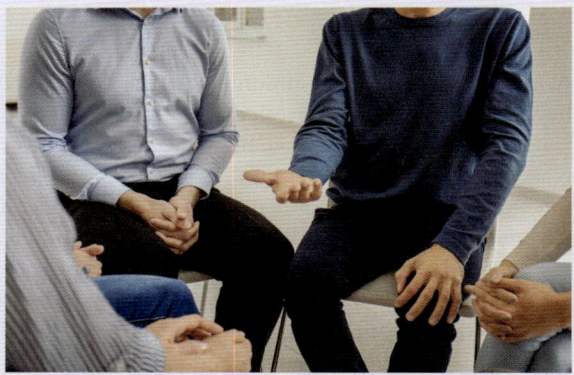

Figure 30.6 Can violent men change? Restorative practices have been used in cases of domestic violence, but this approach does not receive universal support

Source: Africa Studio/Shutterstock

inequitable or unjust to afford victims who are matched with offenders a greater role in deciding what happens to the offender than when this is not the case.

So, perhaps the justice system's principal focus on the offender is unsurprising; although this might also lend weight to the suspicion held by some that victims' involvement in restorative interventions is a secondary consideration. Can we perhaps conclude that alternatives to conventional forms of punishment may struggle to reflect public expectations or address victims' concerns effectively, despite their claims to this effect?

Finally, though, for those arguing from a critical perspective (see **Chapter 18**), the complaint is that 'alternatives' do not go far enough. This derives from the inherent ambiguities of a supposedly radical approach to dealing with crime which operates predominantly within the confines of an established criminal justice framework; but with which its core principles (such as negotiated justice, challenging the sentencing tariff, or decriminalising young offenders) appear to be in conflict. Thus, for example, diversionary and restorative alternatives retain a primary focus on the individual offender and implicitly accept the structures and procedures according to which decisions are made, and through which they obtain their 'clientele'. Established assumptions about who offenders are, what causes crime, and how to address it are not fundamentally challenged by the way in which alternatives operate, albeit they may be subject to some modification and relaxation. As Wood (2015: 11) observes, restorative justice 'cannot readily fix . . . structural problems', going on to cite Braithwaite's acknowledgement of its 'modest' approach to changing the shape of criminal justice. Whatever its positive and progressive qualities, the suggestion is that restorative justice 'cannot resolve the deep structural injustice[s] that cause problems' (Braithwaite, 1998: 329).

A critical view of diversion and its expanding use, on the other hand, might portray it as merely a pretext for the withdrawal of the **neoliberal** state from any role or interest in addressing the effects of offending and **social harm** on individuals and communities (Smith, 2018: 151) whilst at the same time sustaining and legitimising continuing racial inequalities in the delivery of criminal justice (Lammy, 2017).

30.6 Conclusion

What we have described here as 'alternatives to punishment' play an important part in the criminal justice system, precisely because they offer a different perspective on crime and punishment to those which concentrate on guilt, blame, and holding the offender to account. Some, indeed, would argue that not only do they provide a more rounded and inclusive approach to dealing with offences, but they address the needs of all concerned, including crime victims, more effectively. Moving away from a focus on punishment and the responsibility of offenders for their actions towards a problem-solving approach, based on the idea of putting things right, appears to be better suited to the variety of causes and consequences of crime. They are also promoted as more appropriate across a broad range of cultures, where the 'western' ideal of criminal justice is inconsistent with established indigenous practices. As they have become more widely used, alternative models have become applied in increasingly complex and challenging settings, as in the case of domestic violence, as outlined in **Controversy and debate 30.3**.

On the other hand, these developments are open to the well-versed criticisms that they avoid the question of guilt and culpability, and the principle that offenders should pay the price of their crimes. 'Alternatives' such as diversion and restorative justice are criticised as offering the criminal a 'soft option' and as failing to respect the wishes of victims and, indeed, the wider public. They have thus struggled to gain a place at the heart of many contemporary criminal justice systems, being utilised largely in cases involving relatively minor crimes or in youth justice settings where calls for punishment may be moderated. Future developments in this context are relatively hard to predict and may well depend on wider political currents as much as on continued innovation and emerging evidence from within the criminal justice community.

SUMMARY

After reading this chapter and working your way through its features you should now be able to:

- Describe the approaches to the delivery of criminal justice which challenge conventional assumptions about crime and punishment

The chapter has introduced ideas about dealing with crime and its consequences which do not depend on conventional theories of blame, or individual responsibility, but instead take a problem-solving approach to the specific implications and consequences of an offence.

- Explain the origins and development of restorative ideas and practices

We have explored the origins and contemporary development of restorative justice, with particular reference to its origins in diverse cultural practices based around notions of healing, reconciliation, and forgiveness.

- Understand the emergence and impact of diversion as an intervention strategy

The chapter has provided an overview of the emergence of diversion as both an informal and formalised mechanism for dealing with offences, usually of a less serious nature, and involving young offenders. The chapter has also considered recent patterns and trends in the changing use of 'out of court' disposals.

- Consider examples of the implementation of 'alternatives to punishment' and their impact

Restorative and diversionary practices have been considered in detail and we have considered the implications of the problematic relationship between these forms of intervention and conventional ways of organising and delivering criminal justice.

- Critique the arguments in favour of alternative forms of intervention, appreciating the potential criticisms of alternative forms of intervention

Critical arguments questioning the purposes and uses of alternatives to punishment have been introduced, especially in relation to their ability to provide fair and just outcomes for everyone affected by an offence; and regarding their possible role not as alternatives but as an extension to the existing justice system ('net-widening').

- Develop your own arguments for and against these problem-solving rather than fault-finding methods of dealing with offences

This chapter has provided you with the persuasive arguments put forward by others, but you should apply this knowledge to develop your own viewpoints. Use the answers to the questions in the What do you think? boxes as a starting point. Creating your own arguments is good practice for essays and examinations.

Test your understanding of the chapter's key points by attempting the self-test questions on the **online resources** at www.oup.com/he/case2e

REVIEW QUESTIONS

1. What do we mean by the term 'alternatives to punishment'?
2. What are the distinctive features of offence-resolution strategies?
3. Why do you think these approaches have gained more ground when working with young offenders rather than adults?
4. What are the advantages and disadvantages of informal attempts to deal with offences?
5. What do you think of the suggestion that employing 'alternative' means of dealing with offences is just letting criminals off lightly?

Access the **online resources** at www.oup.com/he/case2e to check your answers to the review questions.

FURTHER READING

Braithwaite, J. (2009) *Crime, Shame and Reintegration.* **Cambridge: Cambridge University Press.**
This book has been seen as highly influential in setting out a clear rationale for restorative justice and seeking to bring together diverse interests (victim, offender, and community) in a way which provides an effective justification for this form of offence resolution.

Christie, N. (1977) 'Conflicts as Property'. *British Journal of Criminology* **17(1): 1–15.**
Nils Christie's seminal article made a strong case for communities reclaiming offence resolution from the conventional justice system, which was believed to be impersonal and sometimes unresponsive to the interests of those most directly involved, particularly victims.

Haines, K. et al. (2013) 'The Swansea Bureau: A Model of diversion from the Youth Justice System'. *International Journal of Law, Crime and Justice* **41(2): 1–21.**
This article provides a detailed account of one model of diversionary practice in youth justice which has been thoroughly evaluated and makes credible claims for the effectiveness of dealing with many offences 'out of court'.

O'Mahony, D. and Doak, J. (2017) *Reimagining Restorative Justice.* **London: Bloomsbury.**
This relatively recent book sets out a clearly articulated argument for extending the 'reach' of restorative justice into the heart of the criminal justice system, based on an 'agency-accountability framework'.

Smith, R. (2018) *Diversion in Youth Justice.* **Abingdon: Routledge.**
This book analyses the history and development of diversion in youth justice and offers a critical exploration of different models of practice and their underlying justifications.

Wood, W. (2015) 'Why Restorative Justice Will Not Reduce Incarceration'. *British Journal of Criminology* **55(5): 883–900.**
This article makes the argument that restorative justice will have only a marginal effect on the operation of the wider criminal justice system and, whatever its merits, it cannot compete for centre stage with conventional approaches to dealing with crime.

 Access the **online resources** to view a wealth of extra information relating to your study of criminology, including self-test questions, answers to review questions, and links to other resources that will help you enjoy and fulfil your potential within your studies.
www.oup.com/he/case2e

CHAPTER OUTLINE

31.1	Introduction	930
31.2	What are critical perspectives on punishment?	930
31.3	Unjust punishment	933
31.4	Social control theory, punishment, and legitimacy	936
31.5	Crimes of the privileged and powerful	938
31.6	What is to be done about crime?	942
31.7	Limitations of critical perspectives on punishment	951
31.8	Conclusion	954

31 Critical perspectives on punishment

KEY ISSUES

After studying this chapter, you should be able to:

- explain what is meant by the idea of critical perspectives on punishment;
- consider a range of critical perspectives on the justice system including the abolitionist position, social control theories, and transformative justice;
- identify the disparities in treatment between white, BAME, and other sectors of the population in the criminal justice system;
- explore how 'crimes of the powerful' and state crimes can remain unseen and unpunished;
- evaluate radical responses to the problems associated with crime, such as truth and reconciliation, community justice, and abolitionism;
- analyse the limitations of critical analyses of crime and punishment.

31.1 Introduction

In this final chapter on the justice system and its outcomes, our aim is to explore a range of perspectives which effectively question the underlying assumptions behind the **concept** of '**punishment**'. This represents a shift in emphasis from the system 'as it is' to a critical evaluation of its social and **ideological** foundations, along with some ideas about how it might be different if we follow through the implications of these critical arguments. In light of this, questions also arise (and some answers are offered) as to the precise relationship between criminal and **social justice**; and, indeed, whether or not these are compatible concepts.

The chapter will explore ideas about the use of punishment as a vehicle for maintaining the dominance of particular interests within society, and using it to exert social control. Implicated within this is the suggestion that claims of legitimacy, fairness, and justice must be called into question, especially in light of the evidence of unequal treatment of certain groups, such as members of black and minority ethnic communities.

Critical perspectives also invite us to consider why some forms of behaviour, such as corporate negligence and tax fraud, appear to be much less heavily penalised (if at all) than crimes more typically associated with other groups and communities, such as benefit fraud or drug offences.

31.2 What are critical perspectives on punishment?

Critical perspectives on punishment and the way it is used draw on a number of theories and sources of evidence. Some researchers, for example, are mainly concerned with evidence of systemic injustices. A particular example of systematic injustice is the persistent evidence of discrimination against minority ethnic groups in the administration of justice (see **Controversy and debate 31.1**). Criticisms of this kind may be associated with a 'rights' perspective, which argues in effect for an overhaul of the justice system to eradicate the potential for systemic oppression of particular groups.

As will already be clear from **Chapter 10**, the scale of disproportionate treatment of offenders in terms of their ethnic background is significant, and this is illustrated graphically in the experience of the US. In a country with what is acknowledged to be an extremely high prison population, black men are six times as likely as white men to be locked up: 'Almost 3 per cent of black male U.S. residents of all ages were imprisoned on December 31, 2013, compared to 0.5 per cent of white males' (Carson, 2014: 1).

For some, this kind of pattern of unfair treatment is evidence that the criminal justice system in its current form does not, and cannot, serve the common interest and is always likely to favour those who are in positions of power and privilege, both within and outside the system itself.

Other critiques might well agree with this kind of sentiment, but would also make links with the underlying symbolic role of the justice system in maintaining belief in the legitimacy of a particular social order (see **Chapter 17** on sociological **positivism**). In other words, the organisation and delivery of criminal sanctions according to an established set of rules and assumptions is self-serving, in that it helps to perpetuate an inevitable sense of order and logic about the way it operates. Critics argue that the way that the institutions of law and justice are given status and the trappings of authority (as in courtroom dress, for example) is a direct example of this attempt to establish and maintain a sense of legitimacy, and effectively to institutionalise unfairness—the very opposite of the underlying qualities claimed for the justice system, of course.

> ### WHAT DO YOU THINK? 31.1
>
> **Unequal treatment within the youth justice system**
>
> Figures issued by the Youth Justice Board (Youth Justice Board, 2018) which cover young offender institutions, secure detention centres, and secure training centres in England and Wales, show a shocking number of ethnic minority children and young people being held in the youth justice system. In the year ending March 2017, 45 per cent of prisoners aged under 18 were from black, Asian, and minority ethnic backgrounds (BAME), that is, two-and-a-half-times what would be expected based on general population figures.
>
> - What is your initial reaction to seeing these figures?
> - What do you think they tell us immediately?
> - How would you go about trying to investigate further the reasons for the disparities reported here?

Figure 31.1 Critics say the justice system diverts attention from the crimes of the powerful, such as the Union Carbide gas leak (a protest against which is pictured here)

Source: Photo by Gagan Nayar/Hindustan Times via Getty Images

Again, associated with such criticisms are arguments about what the justice system does not do. Its existing form and practices also serve the function of diverting attention from the 'crimes of the powerful' (Pearce, 1976). Such crimes, of corporate entities and covert but powerful networks, may have extensive and dramatic consequences but somehow do not readily result in findings of guilt or punishment of those responsible, it is suggested.

There have been many disasters over the years which have been attributed to corporate negligence or recklessness. The massive gas leak at Bhopal in India in 1984, for which the US corporation Union Carbide was responsible and which resulted in an estimated 16,000 deaths (see **Figure 31.1**):

> was first a criminal justice issue. Crime No. 1104/84 was registered, *suo moto*, by Hanumanganj Police Station House Officer Surinder Singh Thakur on December 3, 1984, 1 less than 24 hours after the onset of the disaster, while hundreds of corpses still lay scattered across the roads, parks, and gullies of the old city.
>
> On the day that Crime No. 1104/84 was registered, five local junior officers of Union Carbide India Limited (UCIL) were the first company officials to see the inside of a jail. They were also the last: their release on bail after 12 days marked the final day in custody for any Union Carbide representative before or since. Though convictions were secured for seven UCIL officials over 25 years later, each of the convicted were granted immediate bail and remain at liberty at time of writing, with vigorous appeals still pending.
>
> (Edwards, 2015: 53)

Similarly, it might be argued that the criminal justice system does not even hold accountable those responsible for a wide range of activities which may be widely socially unacceptable, morally suspect, or of questionable legality, such as tax avoidance, environmental harm, and exploitation of labour in developing countries. **Green criminology** (see **Chapter 12**) claims to examine 'complex issues in criminological enquiry that extend beyond the narrow confines of individualistic crime which dominate criminological discourse and are the main focus of criminal justice policy. Simply put, green criminology thinks bigger' (Nurse, 2014: 3).

It always seems easier to criticise what is there, in this case the established criminal justice framework, than it is to put forward positive alternatives, in the form of progressive ways of 'doing justice', intended to achieve socially desirable as well as legally valid outcomes. Nonetheless, in this chapter we will also consider a number of arguments and proposals which, in the eyes of their proponents, do point to more acceptable ways of resolving the problems of antisocial and problematic behaviour and harm occurring at both individual and wider societal levels. First, we will consider some of the key positions taken by critics of conventional criminal justice systems.

Abolitionism

There are a range of critical perspectives to consider. First, and perhaps most straightforwardly, there is the abolitionist position (Mathiesen, 1974) which shuns any idea of punishment and blame entirely. **Abolitionism** is based on the view that any justice system that relies on **individualised** concepts of guilt and responsibility, and is supported by institutional forms of punishment and restraint, is inherently unfair and unjustifiable. All aspects of conventional systems of fault-finding and imposition of penal sanctions are therefore to be opposed. Abolitionism is unashamedly concerned with the principle of rejecting conventional punitive practices; and, according to its leading proponent, does not seek to engage in a process of compromise with alternative views: 'When something is said to be "necessary", you should beware. . . . The abolitionist stance goes beyond (some of) the parameters [of the system]. For example, it is possible to say "sorry, but public opinion is not my concern", or perhaps better "public opinion can be changed . . ."' (Mathiesen, 2008: 59).

So, rather than seeking to improve unacceptable prison conditions in the short term, abolitionists simply adopt a position of outright opposition to the use of imprisonment in any form. To accept custody in any form as legitimate, is to accept and effectively condone oppressive institutional treatment and the inequitable social system that it represents. Even radical attempts to change prison regimes for the better are rejected by abolitionists as merely contributing to the justification of supposedly humane forms of institutional confinement (Sim, 2009: 133).

Although abolitionism does provide an effective basis for questioning some of our implicit assumptions about crime and punishment, it appears less obviously capable of providing a practical and achievable basis for resolving problems of 'transgression', where shared understandings of acceptable behaviour are breached. Pure opposition may serve a purpose, but it is unhelpful as a basis for articulating alternative frameworks for dealing with crime and the problems associated with it. Both morally and practically, there are clearly questions to be answered as to whether we wish to dispense with ideas of blame and accountability entirely; and, relatedly, whether this is even possible in the face of wider societal wishes and expectations. How, for example, can we provide protection for vulnerable and less powerful groups if we dispense with concepts of individual responsibility and justice entirely? Nor, indeed, is it likely to be possible to wish away deeply held grievances or feelings of hurt without offering some way of seeking redress. Victims' interests may thus seem poorly served by abolitionist arguments.

Transformative justice

On the other hand, ideas of **transformative justice** do take a more proactive view of the question of how to understand and resolve the 'harms' which are the result of human actions of one kind or another. Lea (2002), for example, has argued for a return of the power to resolve conflicts to 'communities': 'Communities could take the law into their own hands again . . . But these systems will function *only* if substantive equality exists between groups and individuals such that disputants have equal power and some willingness to sort out conflicts. This requires fundamental social and political change' (Lea, 2002: 189, emphasis in original).

What this approach would help us to do, in principle, is to set out common, agreed, and exhaustive frameworks for collectively identifying wrongdoing and acting to remedy this, irrespective of its origins and impacts. We might, here, turn to some of the known examples of indigenous justice mechanisms which depend on communal negotiation and consensus—somewhat similar to some of the aspirations for **restorative justice** we discussed in **Chapter 30**, and often seen as the inspiration for restorative initiatives. Despite this, once again, there are limitations in the 'transformative' argument when it comes to the task of implementing and realising justice, especially in complex industrial societies. Of course, if 'fundamental change' of the kind Lea aspires to is a prerequisite, then this only illustrates the scale of the task—it is not simply a matter of internal reform of the justice system or improving its effectiveness, but of wider change, too, in order to cement principles of social justice at the heart of the social system itself.

Community justice

In order to gain a better sense of what may be practically and more immediately achievable, we will now turn to consideration of attempts to embed critical principles of human rights and social justice in the workings of the criminal justice system. In this context, we will consider attempts to develop models of 'community justice', particularly in post-conflict situations; and we will also consider a number of specific initiatives which have sought to articulate critical challenges 'from within'.

In a sense, this echoes Lea's argument that transformation can be achieved locally and in piecemeal fashion, although clearly this depends on achieving the necessary degree of independence to be able to establish separate self-contained frameworks and processes for resolving conflict. Whether this is ultimately feasible is perhaps open to question, as some recent experiences of 'community justice' appear to have confirmed. The community justice initiatives in the North-West of England established in 2005, for example, were closely tied in to existing court structures and were unable to establish a distinctive identity outside the conventional sentencing framework. The introduction of a 'problem-solving' ethos and the promotion of community engagement through these schemes did not seem to have a notable effect on changing the ways in which justice was delivered, or in its outcomes:

> It is very clear from our interviews that there was some agreement and frustration that only a minority of local residents were being 'engaged'. Respondents spoke about scratching the surface, about community apathy, about people only taking an interest in the [Community Justice] Centre when they had a problem—and, of course, this is exactly how support services are used by the general public.
>
> (Mair and Millings, 2011: 100)

Such initiatives may not have the capacity to achieve whole system change. But in favourable circumstances and free from undue constraints they may be seen as an early indication of what might be possible, or at least of sufficient influence to open the way for radical developments in policy and practice: 'Community justice in general, and the North Liverpool Community Justice Centre in particular, could have a potentially transformative effect on criminal justice' (Mair and Millings, 2011: 101).

In the following sections, we will explore further both the critical analyses of the existing criminal justice system and the alternative models of justice outlined here. Unlike previous chapters, in this section these will be organised according to each argument in detail, before ending with some concluding reflections on the overall strengths and limitations of critical approaches to punishment.

31.3 Unjust punishment

The credibility and sustainability of the criminal justice system depend on it being able to demonstrate that it operates according to its own rules of fairness and **procedural justice**. It is, of course, open to criticism over the extent to which these principles are breached. It would naturally be unreasonable to expect any system, and especially one so dependent on human interaction and judgement, to operate perfectly. But, at the same time, we would probably also expect to see this kind of system at least meet minimum standards of fairness, or to be called seriously into question. The available evidence of inconsistency and discriminatory outcomes is therefore of great interest and relevance.

It is fair to say that there have been persistent concerns in this respect, over a considerable period of time, especially in regard to discrimination on ethnic grounds, although other groups, too (such as young people in the care system) have problematic experiences of criminal justice interventions. In fact, as reported by Bowling and Phillips (2007; see also Phillips and Bowling, 2017) in some detail, the justice system appears to operate in a way in which discrimination gets progressively worse at each stage of the process.

Discriminatory practice and BAME communities

Disparities in how different ethnic groups are treated are apparent throughout the justice system, right from the very point of entry onwards. As Bowling and Phillips (2007: 434) have observed, the practice of 'stop and search' is the most problematic of all aspects of the relationship between police and minority ethnic groups. They noted that black people were over six times more likely, and Asians twice as likely, to be stopped and searched as white people. *The Independent* reported on 6 August 2015 ('Stop and search: Can transparency end this abuse of police powers?'), that this is a persistent problem. Despite considerable regional variations, the article reported that in all parts of the country police were continuing to subject black people to 'stop and search' unnecessarily and disproportionately. By 2020, there appeared to be little change, according to figures for England and Wales released by the government:

> between April 2018 and March 2019, there were 4 stop and searches for every 1,000 White people, compared with 38 for every 1,000 Black people.
>
> (www.ethnicity-facts-figures.service.gov.uk/crime-justice-and-the-law/policing/stop-and-search/latest#main-facts-and-figures)

Such practices are not justified by the number of arrests resulting from the use of police powers in this way—with only 13 per cent of 'stops' involving black people resulting in subsequent arrests, according to Bowling and Phillips (2007: 435). By 2017/18, 21 per cent of stop and searches involving black people resulted in an arrest, compared to 6 per cent of white people (Full Fact, 'Stop and search in England and Wales', 24 June 2019).

Similar disparities, specifically in relation to young black people, were documented by May et al. (2010), who also found evidence of discrimination at other stages in the criminal process, including decisions about custodial remands, for example. Unequal treatment of different ethnic groups has been modified from time to time, as Phillips and Bowling (2017: 199) point out, although for some the differences still remained fairly striking. Racial 'disproportionality' decreased over the period 2011–15 and an overall decline in the number of people being stopped was also observed during this period; but in 2018/19, police were still 25 times more likely to stop and search black people then white people in Dorset.

As Bowling and Phillips also point out, there may be cumulative effects of unequal treatment at the entry point to the justice system. Black suspects may be less likely to 'cooperate' with the police, in the sense of exercising the right to silence or seeking legal assistance, with the result that they are less likely to be spared prosecution in the absence of an admission of guilt. So: 'Whilst these decision points can be regarded as racially neutral, minority ethnic individuals are effectively denied the benefits of cooperation because of long-standing mistrust' of police (Phillips and Bowling, 2017: 203). This, in turn, is a form of 'indirect racial discrimination'.

The progressive effect of discriminatory practices at the point of sentencing has been identified, too. There is no doubt that ethnic minorities are substantially over-represented at the conclusion of the justice process, when sentencing decisions are made; and as the **official statistics** consistently show, this trend seems to be intensified at each stage of the process (Ministry of Justice, 2013). Stolzenberg et al. (2013) provide a detailed analysis of the cumulative effects of discrimination as **defendants** progress through the US justice system; whilst Irwin-Rogers (2019) provides an account of the racism that black people experience at different points in the judicial process.

Thus, the 2011 census reported that 87 per cent of the population of England and Wales aged over ten was white and 13 per cent ethnic minorities; although those proportions will have changed somewhat, a House of Commons Briefing reported that, in 2019, 27 per cent of the prison population were from ethnic minority groups combined

(Sturge, 2019). These findings have been supported by other analyses; for example, in 2014, black 'men and women comprise[d] 11 per cent and 6 per cent of the British male and female prison population, despite the fact that they comprise[d] only 3 per cent of the general population' (Phillips and Bowling, 2017: 202). Further analysis has confirmed that there is a greater risk of being sentenced to custody for minority ethnic defendants (see Hopkins, 2015).

We need to exercise some caution in drawing precise conclusions from population-wide figures but the consistency of such findings does suggest that the justice system progressively compounds the discriminatory effects of disproportionate initial police activity.

As Bowling and Phillips (2007: 450) have argued, there appear to be a number of discriminatory mechanisms at play. From the start of the involvement of black people in the justice system, they suggest that police stereotyping has a part to play. This is compounded by the interaction between policing practices and the 'availability' of certain groups—such as young people from ethnic minorities—in the sense that these groups are more likely to be the subject of police attention, especially when they are in places or doing things that the police, applying prejudiced racial stereotypes, consider unexpected or untypical (Shiner et al., 2018). For example, members of certain groups appear to be more likely to be stopped by the police simply because they are driving an expensive car (see **Controversy and debate 31.1**).

Moreover, what Bowling and Phillips describe as 'supposedly neutral' decision-making criteria actually compound systemic disadvantages. For example, decisions on whether or not to grant bail may be based on housing status and so implicitly work against those defendants from minority groups which are known to experience less secure accommodation. Indeed, from this point of view there is a clear link between socio-economic disadvantage, the 'visibility' of certain types of behaviour and discrimination resulting in the progressive **criminalisation** of minority ethnic, and particularly African and Caribbean groups. Noting that outcomes for different ethnic groups vary, the role of distinctive stereotypes and their differential effects is stressed:

> '[R]ace', class and ethnicity are not *ahistorical* essences, but socially constructed categories upon which iniquitous social structures are based. Racism interacts with class disadvantage to produce patterns of social inequality experienced differently by minority ethnic groups . . . [their] experiences of crime and criminal justice do not result *solely* from their socioeconomic position, as shown by research on criminal justice decision-making.
>
> (Bowling and Phillips, 2007: 451)

The effect of difference has been conceptualised as a form of 'ethnic penalty' which systematically disadvantages members of particular groups as compared to majority (white) people with the same backgrounds and characteristics (Roberts, 2015: 19).

A more recent development has been the increasing attention paid to young Muslims by the justice system. By the mid-2000s, the Muslim Council of Great Britain was expressing the fear that **institutional racism** was becoming evident in the way that young Muslims were treated (Smith, 2009: 42). In its 2014 report, the Young Review on young black or Muslim men in the justice system concluded that Muslim prisoners then comprised 13.4 per cent of the prison

CONTROVERSY AND DEBATE 31.1

Black and minority ethnic celebrities report being apprehended by the police, seemingly just for being in a wealthy area or driving an expensive-looking car.

> Chris Rock took a selfie after being pulled over by police while driving Tuesday, marking the third time in seven weeks he's posted while being stopped by a police officer.
>
> Rock posted the photo to his social media accounts early Tuesday, writing: 'Stopped by the cops again wish me luck.' In the shot, the comedian can be seen behind the wheel of a car with blue police lights shining through his rear window.
>
> (*Huffington Post*, 4 April 2015)

In contrast to this, some influential figures, including the Metropolitan Police Commissioner, have defended police practice on the basis that it is important to respond where necessary to reported criminal activity and not to be selective in meeting responsibilities to the public. According to *The Guardian* (13 April 2018):

> She said that officers knew 'absolutely' that for certain types of crime in certain areas the tactic was effective. 'We scrutinise the levels of stop-and-searches all the time and involve local people in looking at what we're doing, why we're doing it and I can tell you the public are overwhelmingly supportive of it.'

Why do you think she is making this claim of public support? Is it enough to make this kind of claim without providing evidence to back it up? Or does it suggest instead that the speaker has a selective view of who 'the public' are?

population compared to 4.2 per cent of the general population; and commented that Muslim prisoners felt that they were being 'stigmatised as extremists' (Young, 2014: 11). The review reiterated the evidence of a range of 'drivers' for the disproportionate representation of black and minority ethnic young people in the justice system, including stop and search practices, use of powers of arrest, and prejudicial assumptions about gangs (2014: 31). In addition, Young (2014: 31) reports that black and Muslim prisoners feel that they experience 'differential treatment as a result of their race, ethnicity or faith'. One of the authors of this textbook recalls interviewing a Muslim young person who recounted the difficulties being created for him in carrying out his religious observances in one prison establishment (Smith and Fleming, 2011), and this experience is echoed by the evidence gathered for the Young Review. Internal prison practices and disciplinary decision-making processes ('adjudications', in prison terminology) appear to compound the effects of prior discrimination: 'the continued presence of discrimination within our prisons has a significant effect' (Young, 2014: 31).

It is important to note here that the Young Review was just one of a consistent line of high-profile inquiries into racism in the justice system which have come to similar conclusions, including the Scarman Report (1982), the Stephen Lawrence Inquiry (Macpherson 1999), the inquiry into the death of Zahid Mubarek whilst in custody (Keith, 2006), and the report produced by David Lammy MP in 2017 which continued to identify a significant problem of 'disproportionality' in the treatment of some minority ethnic groups in the justice (especially youth justice) system (Lammy, 2017). As these inquiries have often graphically illustrated, too, the sense of injustice associated with unequal and unfair treatment is worsened by the experiences of ethnic minority communities as victims of unlawful acts and the perception that they do not receive a respectful or active enough response when they suffer the effects of crime (Yarrow, 2005).

Discriminatory practice and other groups

In addition to the justifiable concern about unequal treatment on grounds of ethnicity, critics of the justice system would suggest that other groups are also likely to be singled out for particular attention, and this may be for similar reasons, such as the perceived threat they represent or the visibility of certain forms of behaviour which may be seen as problematic. Pettit and Western (2004), for instance, have suggested that, in the US, class and ethnic factors interact to influence the likelihood of experiencing imprisonment over the life course:

> class bias in criminal sentencing is suggested by findings that more educated federal defendants receive relatively short sentences in general . . . Imprisonment may be more common among low-education men because they are the focus of the social control efforts of criminal justice authorities
>
> (Pettit and Western, 2004: 153).

In the UK context, it has been consistently shown that certain sectors of the population are much more likely to be sentenced to custody, and these characteristics are interlinked. The Prison Reform Trust produces a regular overview of the pattern of sentencing (Bromley Briefings), which have shown that (Prison Reform Trust, 2014: 1–6; Prison Reform Trust, 2017: 34–45):

- fewer than 1 per cent of all children in England are in care, but they make up around two-fifths of children in secure training centres (38 per cent) and young offender institutions (42 per cent);
- 25 per cent of children in the youth justice system have identified special educational needs, 46 per cent are rated as underachieving at school, and 29 per cent have difficulties with literacy and numeracy;
- 53 per cent of women and 27 per cent of men in prison reported having experienced emotional, physical, or sexual abuse as a child;
- 65 per cent of women in prison reported that they had mental health issues;
- 20–30 per cent of all offenders have learning disabilities or difficulties that interfere with their ability to cope with the criminal justice system;
- 26 per cent of women and 16 per cent of men in prison said they had received treatment for a mental health problem in the year before custody.

These findings are supported by Williams et al. (2012), who also note that many of those in custody have complex and problematic personal histories which are representative of a cumulative experience of 'social exclusion' which features poverty and other difficult circumstances.

This combination of factors, and the persistently uneven impact of imprisonment on specific elements of the general population, have led theorists to conclude that the underlying function of punishment in general and custody, in particular, has been to exert a form of generalised social control. This is in contrast to its more conventional portrayal as a fair and equitable mechanism for maintaining social order and safeguarding communal interests, especially on behalf of the most vulnerable. Rothman has concluded, for example, that with the historic emergence and institutionalisation:

> [O]f prisons, mental hospitals, [and] reformatories . . . it is now apparent that no simple links connect these places to a spirit of humanitarianism. That all of their wards were filled with the lower classes . . . that within a few decades of their

founding, they were invariably places of last resort (overcrowded, brutal and corrupt)... these considerations remain beyond the explanatory powers of a concept of 'reform'.

(Rothman, 1985: 113)

Criminalisation and control, then, are associated with a process of '**bifurcation**' (Rock, 2007: 23). Bifurcation is a term used quite frequently within criminology to account for a process whereby the justice system identifies offenders with specific characteristics as particularly problematic for some reason, as compared to the offender population in general. This selection process may, in turn, be used to justify differential and often harsher treatment for those who fall into this category.

31.4 Social control theory, punishment, and legitimacy

Critics have built on the argument that punishment is selective and oppressive to suggest that this not only serves a practical function of exercising targeted social control, but it also serves as a form of implicit self-justification. In other words, the simple assertion of authority to act in a certain way grants the justice system a claim to legitimacy (see also **Chapter 4**, where we discuss the topic of legitimacy and consent in more detail). The formalisation and ceremonial aspects of its procedures and decision-making act to establish the basis of belief in the fairness and authority of the judicial process. This viewpoint was associated with an emerging radical strand in criminological thought, including authors such as Quinney (1970), Taylor et al. (1973), and Chambliss (1976): 'Crime control was said to be an oppressive and mystifying process that worked through legislation, law-enforcement, and ideological stereotyping to preserve unequal class relations' (Rock, 2007: 23), which could also be said to extend to other forms of oppression and discrimination against disadvantaged groups.

The machinery of justice, then, might be said to operate according to a form of internal logic, apparently grounded in the rhetoric of fair and equal treatment; and yet at the same time favouring particular powerful interests. By treating unequal populations equally, the system does not compensate for pre-existing effects of disadvantage or discrimination but in fact compounds these inequalities.

Foucault and the shift of punishment from drama to routine

The symbolic value of punishment and its effects is a theme of Michel Foucault's work, as we have also seen in **Chapter 28**, In his view, the form of punishment which dominates at any particular time offers considerable insight into the nature of society and the social order. Foucault suggests that in pre-modern times, punishment was frequently exercised in dramatic and often brutal fashion so as to demonstrate the force of the law in action and the direct authority of the sovereign.

Legitimacy in this case was associated with the divine power of the monarch and continually demonstrated through the visible exercise of authority. Punishment was not simply a matter of applying the appropriate penalty but was also about asserting the *right* to do so, and as such needed to be seen to be delivered. As we discussed in **Chapter 28**, Foucault (1977) offers several graphic accounts of punishment as spectacle, supporting the idea that highly visible and dramatic displays of justice being done was historically significant.

By contrast, Foucault argues, with the major social changes of the late 18th and early 19th centuries, the idea of 'punishment as a spectacle' (1977: 8) died out, or certainly became less prominent (apart from community punishments and prison clothing, perhaps—see **Figure 31.2**).

Figure 31.2 The idea of punishment as a spectacle has become much less prominent, but arguably still exists—for example, in the form of community punishments and prison clothing

Source: Patrick Denker/CC BY 2.0

Associated with this apparent shift of emphasis, Foucault observes: 'The body as the major target of penal repression disappeared' (1977: 8). Instead, punishment became 'the most hidden part of the penal process' (1977: 9) reflected in the close ordering and severe discipline to be applied through the custodial regime. Foucault gives the example of the very tightly specified timetable for a day's activities at the 'House of young prisoners in Paris'. The rationale for imposing punishment shifts at this point as well. The form of discipline to be imposed through the institutional regime closely matches the organisation of work in modern (capitalist) society:

> If the penality in its most severe forms no longer addresses itself to the body, on what does it lay hold? The answer ... seems to be contained in the question itself: since it is no longer the body, it must be the soul. The expiation that once rained down upon the body must be replaced by a punishment that acts in depth on the heart, the thoughts, the will, the inclinations.
>
> (Foucault, 1977: 16)

As the age of modernity became established and new forms of social organisation took shape, so, Foucault argues, the mechanisms of social control and punishment also adapted. In particular, they became infused with assumptions about technologies of power and the capacity to shape and correct human behaviour, in the same way as the material world could be managed and transformed. The emphasis shifted from highly visual demonstrations of the legitimate power to punish towards the use of more technical forms of assessment, discipline, correction, and behavioural adjustment.

This has most recently been a trend identifiable in the technologies of risk and risk management, for example (see Beck (1992) on the 'risk society'). Further than this, Foucault suggests, the relationship between the logic and machinery of control and wider social relations were mutually reinforcing. The same forms of discipline and incentives for good behaviour were extended into other institutional settings ('orphanages', 'establishments for apprentices', 'factory-convents'). As a result:

> the carceral archipelago transported this [penitentiary] technique from the penal institution to the entire social body ... This vast mechanism established a slow, continuous, imperceptible gradation that made it possible to pass naturally from disorder to offence and back from a transgression of the law to a slight departure from a rule, an average, a demand, a norm.
>
> (Foucault, 1977: 298)

Associated with these developments, we observe a modification of the function of the law so that it has a more 'educative' role, and the rapid development of 'disciplinary networks', comprising a range of professional experts who all have the capacity to assess and determine the nature of the delinquent's problem and the proper correctional intervention to be applied.

Cohen and the techniques of social control

Stanley Cohen (1985) developed this line of argument further (in *Visions of Social Control: Crime, Punishment and Classification*) suggesting that the machinery for administering and delivering criminal justice has a particular 'bifurcatory' function; that is, it serves to act as a pivotal point distinguishing between, and justifying, the treatment of the (socially) included and excluded. The assumption of this role by the state has been the outcome of the kind of historical process proposed by Foucault, where the 'centralised, rationalized' bureaucracy (Cohen, 1985: 12) would preside over processes of assessing and classifying deviant individuals into specific intervention categories. Each of these would be the domain of a particular 'body of "scientific" knowledge and its own recognised and accredited experts' (Cohen, 1985: 12). Such precise and apparently well-informed judgements would then inform provision of specific forms of institutional care, treatment, or correction, depending on the classification achieved.

Significantly, such a framework for adjudication and disposals achieves the paradoxical outcome of strengthening its underlying justifications by explicitly allowing room for disagreement, sometimes quite vehement, between competing 'expert' assessments or principles of intervention. Thus, for example, the recurrent conflict between 'welfare' and 'justice' positions in relation to young offenders can readily be accommodated within a wider and cohesive rationale for the organisation and delivery of youth justice. So, as Cohen (1985: 37) was able to point out, critical voices arguing for a reformed justice system emerging in the 1960s and 1970s were not able to dislodge the established system: 'Instead of any destructuring ... the original structures have become stronger'. And, indeed, consistent with Beck's (1992) arguments, Cohen views these trends as symptomatic of a wider shift towards a risk-sensitive and risk-driven social and penal ethos, in the face of 'rapid economic, demographic and technological change' (Blomberg and Hay, 2007: 178).

Gramsci and hegemony

For social control theorists, the question of how a particular form of criminal justice maintains legitimacy is important. Antonio Gramsci (1971), for example, makes an important contribution with his work on the concept of 'hegemony' (the term hegemony refers to ideological domination or control). The hegemony of the justice system is realised through the set of ideas and mechanisms by which the state and allied interests maintain a sense of both the inevitability and the legitimacy of the established social order. 'Hegemony' is of particular value because it provides a vehicle for the maintenance of conformity and domination without the routine alternative to measures of coercion; although, the legitimate use of force is also available where 'consent' breaks down (Gramsci, 1971: 12).

The criminal justice system is an important element in the networks of control, in that it unites both the legitimacy derived from the implicit authority of the judicial machinery; and at the same time is able to call on the directly coercive power of law enforcement agencies and punitive institutions. The effective exercise of coercion, in this sense, depends on broader popular consent to the claims to legitimacy made by the institutions of criminal justice; at the same time, of course, in the absence of effective challenge, coercive action helps to reinforce these claims, too.

The English riots of 2011 (which we discussed in **Chapter 20**) have sometimes been depicted in Gramscian terms, where the outbreak of rioting in the aftermath of the shooting of Mark Duggan represented a 'crisis of authority' (Jefferson, 2015: 21), to which the immediate response was the use of coercive force by the police. On the second day of the riots: 'The policing strategy entailed flooding the streets with riot-clad officers . . . From midnight, Scotland Yard introduced an additional weapon, namely, the power to stop and search without reasonable suspicion . . . in Lambeth, Haringey, Enfield and Waltham Forest' (Jefferson, 2015: 7). By day four, 'London was relatively calm. The police presence increased from 6,000 to 16,000 and [then Prime Minister] David Cameron returned from holiday, offering police the option of using plastic bullets for the first time in the UK, outside Northern Ireland' (Jefferson, 2015: 8).

Direct confrontation of this kind represents both a physical and a symbolic challenge to the legitimacy of the state's role in maintaining order; and, in turn, the immediate response involved the state effectively ascribing new powers to itself to act outside the previously constructed (and legitimated) framework for doing so. Again, in Gramscian language, the task for those in positions of power was not just to take appropriate and effective coercive measures but to account for their actions in a way which reasserted or restored their rightful authority to act in these ways.

In strategic terms, this is argued to have taken the form of a sustained campaign to depoliticise and instead 'criminalise' the actions of those involved in the riots; and, thus, to justify their subsequent treatment straightforwardly as offenders by the criminal justice system. And so, the construction of the rioters as greedy and materialistic thieves rather than politically motivated protesters (who might have a point) was a critical element of the response from the then Prime Minister outwards and downwards. Cameron is reported to have said in his initial response to the outbreak of disorder: 'I have this very clear message to those people who are responsible for this wrongdoing and criminality: you will feel the full force of the law' and subsequently stated that 'anyone convicted should expect to go to jail' (quoted in Lamble, 2013: 578–9).

Following the riots, over 3,000 people were charged on related criminal matters over the next year. These were typically conventional and mundane criminal charges but the response of the judiciary was one 'of quite stunning harshness' (Jefferson, 2015: 15), with 70 per cent of those appearing before magistrates being remanded to custody and a similar figure being imprisoned and for periods of time often considerably longer than 'normal'. The 'spectacular show of criminal justice' power initiated by the police, legitimised by the courts' actions, and facilitated by agencies such as the Crown Prosecution Service represented both a reassertion of coercive power and, in parallel, of the right to be able to do so. Sim (2012) has argued that extremely severe sentencing of the kind seen in this instance might have the effect of calling into question the authority of the justice system. However, it could also be argued that it was actually operating to reinforce the narrative that the riots represented a major outbreak of criminal activity and so needed to be dealt with accordingly:

> these punitive responses were consistently framed as rational and appropriate responses to the 'mindless criminality' that had emerged on the streets. In doing so, the government was able to cloak its own class anxieties . . . These [responses] were the hallmarks of a civilized outrage . . . This was the riotous behaviour of the elite classes, who mete out legally sanctioned modes of violence while naming it otherwise.
>
> (Lamble, 2013: 583)

Therefore, from a critical perspective, the process of criminalising those who represent a specific threat to the social order, serves to support the exercise of a particular form of legitimised authority; in this instance, against a subgroup of the population largely comprising young, black, and poor people (Jefferson, 2015).

31.5 Crimes of the privileged and powerful

In addition to the consequences of the justice system's hegemony that we discussed in the previous section, critical theorists argue that it deflects attention from the crimes of those in positions of power and dominance, whether these be influential individuals, corporations, or even states themselves. The scope of such wrongful behaviours is enormously wide—such as the unlawful kidnapping ('rendition') of foreign nationals or the industrial-scale dumping of toxic waste—but what they have in common is that they are rarely treated as criminal actions, and equally rarely is any attempt made to bring perpetrators to some form of justice. Here, one apparent exception might seem to be war crimes where there is well-developed machinery in place to hold those responsible to account.

The estimates of the level of harm caused during wars suggest that extraordinarily high numbers of people are victimised as a result of 'armed conflict and state-sponsored aggression . . . Approximately 191 million people lost their lives to collective violence in the twentieth century, more than half of whom were civilians' (Hoyle and Zedner, 2007: 469). It is also noted that an estimated 70 per cent of those who have been casualties in recent wars have been non-combatants, mostly women and children (2007: 467).

In some instances, the crimes associated with these shocking figures are acknowledged and action taken, although the international methods for dealing with war crimes have been subject to criticism.

The Lieber Code and war crime tribunals

The Lieber Code ('Lieber Instructions') was introduced during the American Civil War by Francis Lieber of Columbia College in New York (see **Figure 31.3**). The code was established to set limits to the behaviour of troops in the course of combat and to prevent atrocities being committed in the pursuit of military action. The code was subsequently highly influential in setting the standard for further international development of binding rules of conduct for those engaged in formalised conflict. The Lieber Code led to the establishment of an international convention on the legal framework for the conduct of war, presented to an international conference in Brussels in 1874 and eventually leading to the agreement of the Hague Conventions on land warfare of 1899 and subsequently 1907 (see www.icrc.org/ihl/INTRO/110).

As such, the history of the idea of war crimes and the attempt to codify legal frameworks for dealing with them stretches back around 150 years, and is associated with attempts to criminalise excessive behaviour on whichever side amongst those engaged in armed conflict. Since the original Lieber Code was formulated, a substantial machinery for administering justice in relation to war crimes has also been put in place. Most notably, perhaps, the war crimes tribunals established at the end of the Second World War at Nuremberg (see **Figure 31.4**) and Tokyo have been widely recognised as a successful attempt to use formal penal mechanisms to punish those most centrally involved in war-related offences, whilst at

Figure 31.3 Francis Lieber introduced the 'Lieber Code' to set limits on the behaviour of troops in the American Civil War and prevent atrocities being committed in the pursuit of military action

Source: Library of Congress Prints and Photographs Division, Brady-Handy Photograph Collection/Public domain

the same time enabling the countries involved (principally Germany and Japan) to re-establish peaceful democratic societies. Importantly, this was seen as a mechanism for bringing culpable *individuals* to account rather than imposing drastic punishments on entire societies, with the negative consequences that were experienced, for example, following the First World War: 'Nuremberg initiated a process whereby individuals, as opposed to nation-states, were subject to criminal prosecution for the atrocities of war and violations of the laws of war' (Penrose, 1999: 330).

It has been suggested that war crime tribunals have brought a sense of order and legitimate and impartial international authority to the process of holding perpetrators to account for extreme actions committed in the course of conflict, such as systematic mistreatment of the inhabitants of occupied territories and brutalities committed against prisoners of war. For example: 'the experience of the two ad hoc International Criminal Tribunals for the former Yugoslavia and for Rwanda has proved constructive in many respects, despite the difficulties encountered and the weaknesses and flaws inherent in the two structures' (Tavernier, 1997: 661). Although recognised as

Figure 31.4 The tribunals held after the Second World War at Nuremberg (pictured) and Tokyo are considered a successful attempt to hold culpable individuals to account for war-related offences
Source: The Truman Library/Public domain

What we do know is that it is dangerously naïve to ignore the possibility that ICTs might not only lack any significant **deterrence** benefits, but might actually exacerbate conflicts in weak states.

(Ku and Nzelibe, 2006: 833)

And, of course, the additional problem for international tribunals, specifically those to do with conflict, is determining an agreed basis on which to operate; that is, finding a common definition for what constitutes a 'war crime' and determining the framework for taking legal action across state boundaries. This was exemplified in the not too distant past by the calls to hold Tony Blair and George Bush responsible for war crimes allegedly committed in pursuit of their joint commitment to military action (and all that entailed) in Iraq (see **What do you think? 31.2**).

imperfect, war crimes tribunals are seen as a relatively recent development whose flaws can be gradually addressed and eliminated over time as they gain more widespread endorsement and respect.

On the other hand, sceptics argue that these tribunals have proved inadequate to the task of delivering effective and consensual forms of justice in the aftermath of conflict, for a number of reasons. First, it appears that the problem of 'enforcement' has not been effectively resolved; and, as a result, any 'deterrent' potential of the tribunals has been diluted to the point of ineffectuality (Penrose, 1999: 326). Although war crimes tribunals have certainly handed down highly retributive punishments, some argue that it is clear from the level of continuing conflict in the world that they have had no deterrent effect, and perhaps could not be expected to do so given the nature of the hostilities and hatred which tend to fuel armed conflicts. Nor, though, are tribunals believed to do much to tackle the underlying causes of conflict, at least in part because their conventional, individualising approach to the administration of justice does nothing to address the deep-seated sources of antagonisms such as those based on ethnic and religious differences. Tribunals offer no intrinsic basis for healing wider social divisions and achieving reconciliation (as alternative approaches seek to do, as we shall see later in this chapter). And, further, some suggest, placing unjustified faith in a relatively untested institution such as an international tribunal might actually weaken the potential for initiating other forms of conflict resolution. This leads to the question:

> Should the international community completely abandon ICTs [international criminal tribunals] in favour of purely political or local approaches to combating humanitarian atrocities? We do not presume to answer that question.

State crimes

Beyond the specific context of international military action, there are a range of other activities which are increasingly understood as constituting **state crimes**. These are usually seen in terms of unjustified use of surveillance, force, or restraint against its own (or foreign) citizens by agents of the state. A particularly high-profile example is the sustained imprisonment without trial of suspected terrorists by the US in the detention camp at Guantánamo Bay—widely reported to be in breach of the Geneva Convention, the international Convention Against Torture, and other international human rights agreements (Pearlman, 2015).

For those who highlight the excessive and unlawful use of state power, though, this forms part of a recurrent pattern of activity, more or less prevalent across regimes and political systems, where internationally agreed checks and balances against improper use of state power do not exist or fail to operate effectively.

Although this kind of misuse of power may well be more or less constant, concerns about the harms caused and the failure to hold those in authority to account tend to crystallise around key events which seem to typify state-sanctioned illegalities. The brutal suppression of demonstrations against the Vietnam War in Chicago in 1968 by the police is one such example which has remained a point of reference ever since (see **Figure 31.6**).

Similarly, in the UK, the repeated use of excessive force by police brought in from around the country in the course of the 1984–5 miners' strike also has powerful historical connotations.

> During the first few days of the strike, on 14 March 1984, ministers pressed Home Secretary Leon Brittan to get chief constables to adopt a 'more vigorous interpretation of

WHAT DO YOU THINK? 31.2

'I will be with you, whatever'

A bombshell White House memo has revealed for the first time details of the 'deal in blood' forged by Tony Blair and George Bush over the Iraq War [see **Figure 31.5**].

Figure 31.5 Could Tony Blair (left) and George W. Bush (right) reasonably be prosecuted for 'war crimes'?
Source: Photo by Mark Wilson, Getty Images

The sensational leak shows that Blair had given an unqualified pledge to sign up to the conflict a year before the invasion started. Tony Blair wrote to George W Bush eight months before the invasion into Iraq, saying 'I will be with you, whatever'. This flies in the face of the Prime Minister's public claims at the time that he was seeking a diplomatic solution to the crisis. He told voters: 'We're not proposing military action'—in direct contrast to what the secret email now reveals.

(*Daily Mail*, 17 October 2015)

Based on what you know of the circumstances of the Iraq War, triggered by claims that Iraq had developed (and was ready to use) 'weapons of mass destruction', do you think that Blair and Bush could reasonably be prosecuted for 'war crimes'? (The decision to invade or attack another country has to be based in international law on certain criteria being met (Lucas, 2011), and the question here is whether or not that was the case).

Figure 31.6 The brutal suppression by police of demonstrations against the Vietnam War in Chicago, 1968, remains an important example of the excessive and unlawful use of state power
Source: Ed Molinari/NY Daily News Archive via Getty Images

their duties'. A clampdown followed that prevented pickets reaching the working coalfields of Nottinghamshire and Leicestershire in large numbers.

(Channel 4 News, 3 January 2014)

The critical perspective would argue that this simply provides evidence of the alliance between the state and other powerful vested interests to reinforce the dominance of private and business interests over those of working people and their communities. Their position of control is maintained not principally by simple force, but through the process of constructing a logical and authoritative rationale for the preservation of established social order and class domination. This, in turn, is intended to secure the consent and compliance of the general population and their continuing assent to common principles of law and order (see earlier). However, when the basis for consent fractures, the state and its allies resort to more basic means, and in particular the use of coercive measures, to maintain control. Althusser (1971) has described this distinction in terms of the twin elements of Ideological and Repressive State Apparatuses (ISAs and RSAs), which carry out complementary and mutually reinforcing functions—each one acting as justification and reinforcement for the other. The former ISAs might consist of those elements of society which develop, promote, or defend agreed rules and standards of behaviour in society—such as the family, schools, religious bodies, local authorities, or moral leaders (some 'influencers', perhaps). RSAs, on the other hand, would include institutions and agencies capable of exercising control in more directly coercive ways: the police, the army, courts, and other disciplinary and regulatory bodies.

Importantly for the critical perspective, those who are victimised by these means have neither the physical capability nor the basis in legitimate authority to hold perpetrators of state crimes to account. Often this relies on the work of journalists, such as John Pilger and Hadi Al Khatib whose work documents human rights abuses and other crimes committed during the war in Syria, for example (see www.journalismfestival.com for a brief synopsis of Hadi Al Khatib).

The establishment of the International Criminal Court in 1998 has to some extent offered the possibility of taking action against those individuals who have abused state power to cause harm or oppression to their own citizens, and committed unjustified acts of aggression against other countries (Gegout, 2013). Its scope and impact have been relatively limited to this point, but it represents a significant statement of intent.

Crime and power

Viewing crime through a critical lens also leads us to consider the 'crimes of the powerful' (Pearce, 1977) more broadly, both as a feature of the unfettered expansion of commercial ('big business') interests and as a reflection of efforts to distort systems of reward and resource distribution, as in the case of tax evasion (which is illegal) or avoidance (which is legal, but morally dubious).

In a way, critical arguments identify the 'crimes' of the powerful as a consequence of a series of processes of the kind outlined in our discussion of war and state crimes. Powerful interests are able to control the mechanisms of justice, and the media representations of crime so as to shape conventional and accepted ideas of what a criminal offence is and who a 'typical' offender might be. As a result, the attention of criminal justice agencies and systems is directed towards certain types of crime and away from the wrongdoing of those in positions of power. **Critical criminologists** would suggest that this creates space for this type of criminal activity to become 'taken for granted' as routine, unproblematic, and perhaps an inevitable feature of society (such as attempts to avoid paying tax). By diverting attention onto particular groups, such as young people or ethnic minorities, the 'hegemonic' (see Gramsci, 1971) project of the powerful thus contrives to hide from view or at least minimise its own much greater crimes, according to this line of argument.

A notable example often given by critical commentators is that there is much greater interest in the relatively small amount of benefit fraud amongst poorer members of society than there is in the comparatively much larger sums involved in fraudulent business activity or questionable schemes to reduce tax liabilities (tax evasion). In both cases, the public purse has been denied money to which it is entitled, but media attention, the collective anger of the community, and state enforcement activity seem only to be targeted in one direction—at the crimes of the poor (Cullis et al., 2015).

Such evidence as has been assembled by critical commentators suggests that crimes of the powerful do have a drastic impact (Tombs and Whyte, 2015) and yet lead to uncertain and at best only partial attempts at enforcement action. Where such crimes do become more widely known about, attention is directed towards individual culprits rather than systematic or widespread criminality. The idea of the 'rogue trader' cheating stock markets on a major scale has become established in a number of recent cases. The implausibility of single individual culprits being responsible for major stock market frauds seems clear to critical commentators (Bruce, 2007), but this is typically the way in which the activities of Nick Leeson and others have been portrayed (see Greener, 2006, for example).

31.6 What is to be done about crime?

Having explored the wide-ranging critical analyses of what is wrong with the ways in which the justice system conceptualises and responds to crime, we will also now move on to consider the kind of solutions advocated by the critics. In this context, we will look at both radical alternatives to the organisation of responses to crime and at arguments which simply reject the idea of punishment and put forward a different way of thinking about and acting on the social problems which 'crime' represents.

Critical solutions (1): truth and reconciliation

First, we will reflect upon models for resolving conflicts which are conceived as 'collective'; that is, crimes against communities or societies rather than against individual victims. This, in a sense, represents an extension of restorative justice principles into the wider arena; and it is largely represented in a range of models for delivering 'truth and reconciliation' in the aftermath of conflict.

There have been a number of country-wide, state-led attempts to resolve internal conflict and 'crimes' committed by one section of the population against another, for example in South Africa, Northern Ireland, Rwanda, and Bosnia and Herzegovina. These conflicts are often associated with the historic legacy of colonisation or invasion, resulting in the overwhelming dominance of one section of the community by another, possibly on grounds of religion, ethnicity, or nationality (or a combination of these). Such dominance has often also been associated with routinised exploitation, oppression, everyday violence, and brutality. There is therefore a very substantial legacy of blame, guilt, and culpability to be addressed when the period of domination ends. This is why states and communities have sought to find a coherent and negotiated process for resolving the strong feelings and hostilities associated with this history, without resorting to acts of counter-violence or revenge. As such, this offers an alternative mode of conflict resolution to those based on conventional processes of fault-finding, the attribution of guilt, and the imposition of punitive sanctions.

The Truth and Reconciliation Commission (TRC) for South Africa (see **Figure 31.7**), for example, sat for seven years from 1995 to 2002, hearing testimony from victims of conflict during the apartheid regime, and considering requests for amnesty from those responsible for harm in the same period. As well as determining levels of compensation and recommending further political and social reforms: 'The TRC encouraged victims, offenders, and the community to be directly involved in resolving conflict. In its quest to make peace with the past, the TRC looked at the restorative dimension of both traditions in South Africa: the Judeo-Christian tradition and African traditional values of *Ubuntu* . . .' (Vora and Vora, 2004: 306). The commission effectively acted as an umbrella for a painstaking and highly detailed exercise in allowing those affected by the previous regime to express themselves and, where they wished for it, to seek redress (or absolution). Many of the mechanisms for encouraging dialogue and achieving change remained in place following the completion of the commission's work, and it could therefore be argued that this approach to conflict resolution had a lasting impact.

On the other hand, as a number of commentators have observed, the process itself was significantly flawed in a number of respects and its outcomes represented only a partial achievement of its goals (Vora and Vora, 2004; Gibson, 2005). The sheer scale of an initiative such as a commission to achieve reconciliation across an entire nation might be expected to involve constraints and limitations:

> All truth commissions might be considered compromises and deals worked out within the framework of political negotiations surrounding the transitions. South Africa was faced not only with a transition but also with an immense transformation from an oppressive minority-ruled racist regime to a democratic government.
>
> (Vora and Vora, 2004: 304)

So, for instance, choices had to be made about whether or not to guarantee amnesty to those responsible for acts of oppression or barbarity during the apartheid era, which other reconciliation initiatives had done. In South Africa's case, amnesty was not offered automatically but determined on the basis of representations made to the TRC, so perhaps reinserting conventional principles of individual responsibility and blame into the process.

Interestingly, the rationale for making amnesty conditional seemed to be that this offered a greater incentive for those concerned to tell the truth about their own unlawful actions. In the event, what seemed like a pragmatic compromise emerged, where many of those applying for amnesty were denied it but were not subsequently prosecuted either (Wilson, 2001: 562). At the very least, the introduction of a mechanism designed to align the discovery of uncomfortable truths with achieving reconciliation appears to represent a challenge to prior understandings of the place of prosecution and due process in the search for justice: 'On the one hand the revelation of the truth in sufficient details may lead to calls for, and may even be designed with a view to, prosecution. On the other hand, the cathartic, or liberating, effect of revealing the truth and the pursuit of reconciliation may lead to arguments against prosecution' (O'Shea, 2008: para. 24).

Figure 31.7 The Truth and Reconciliation Commission for South Africa was a state-led attempt to resolve internal conflict and 'crimes' committed by one section of the population against another

Source: Eye Ubiquitous/Alamy Stock Photo

The South African TRC is seen as an important example because of its sheer scale and, as a result, considerable effort has gone into assessing both its character and its achievements. Did it in reality represent a genuinely different way of 'doing justice'? And, if it did, to what extent can it be seen as having achieved its fundamental objectives in retrospect? Both are, of course, highly significant questions in relation to any attempt to replicate this model of resolving crime elsewhere. As Gibson (2009: 124) notes, there is certainly a considerable degree of belief in the capacity of truth commissions to 'contribute to the development of a rule-of-law culture that respects human rights' and 'advance political tolerance'; and this perhaps accounts for their increasingly widespread international use: 'The world has clearly registered its opinion about the desirability and effectiveness of truth commissions. From South Korea to Peru, truth commissions (and functionally equivalent institutions) have been established as a means of addressing historical injustices' (Gibson, 2009: 123).

As Gibson (2005: 356) concludes elsewhere, the evidence does suggest that there is potential value in attempts such as this to achieve truth and reconciliation, because it creates a forum for dialogue and mutual understanding which does not involve a struggle for dominance in terms of either ideas or material power. Gibson's extensive survey of public opinion in South Africa led him to the conclusion that: 'Perhaps the most important achievement of the truth and reconciliation process . . . is that all racial groups have come to see the past in equivocal terms, not as a struggle between absolute good and infinite evil' (Gibson, 2005: 355).

Resolving conflict in Northern Ireland

Although the structures and processes which characterise the 'peace process' in Northern Ireland are rather different, it is also widely recognised as a 'model' for post-conflict reconciliation between hostile communities (Hughes, 2015). It is noted that the process of continuing dialogue and essentially piecemeal negotiation gained widespread international approval, including from US Presidents. In criminal justice terms, the process crucially involved initially setting aside any previous acts of wrongdoing, and 'talking to terrorists. . . . It was a case of building peace from the extremes rather than from the moderate centre ground' (Hughes, 2015: 247). Important, too, was the role of external interested parties in establishing the basis for dialogue and acting in a mediating role where necessary. Usually in this sort of case, a respected and mutually agreed go-between seeks to enable conflicting parties to work towards an agreed resolution. The role of George Mitchell as the US mediator in the initial stages of peace-building in the Northern Ireland case, has come to be viewed as pivotal. The promotion of mediated dialogue is also central to the principles and practices of restorative justice.

Hughes notes, too, that as in the case of South Africa, lessons from Northern Ireland were subsequently applied elsewhere, in attempts to resolve ethnic and religious confrontations in Sri Lanka and Iraq, for example (Hughes, 2015: 248). As well as the promotion of dialogue, Northern Ireland saw the initiation of 'a de facto amnesty for perpetrators' and the establishment of a well-funded mechanism for the support of victims' groups and the promotion of their distinctive interests (Hughes, 2015: 266). But for Hughes and others, there are concerns about the extent to which high-level claims about the effectiveness of new models of peace-building and reconciliation accurately reflect a more complex and uncertain reality. McGrattan (2012), for example, argues that in both Northern Ireland and Bosnia and Herzegovina there is less evidence of open dialogue and mutual engagement between opposing interests than of a kind of institutionalised coexistence, with little significant exchange. In consequence, whilst reordered institutional structures may give the appearance of integrated and collaborative models of governance, in reality they may instead merely cement existing divisions:

> the consociational structures of governance in each case reflect and, arguably, reproduce the segregation that characterizes everyday life.
>
> (McGrattan, 2012: 103)

Consociational democracy (which involves parallel social and political structures) can be found in countries that are deeply divided into distinct religious, ethnic, racial, or regional segments—which may give rise to conflicts unfavourable for achieving stability in society. Others, too, have recognised the complex and shifting nature of debates and experiences of 'transitional justice' (Nagy, 2013; Skaar, 2013) and the consequent challenges of making sense of partially achieved aspirations. Skaar (2013: 10) acknowledges that academic understandings of what is involved in pursuing justice in post-conflict situations are continually evolving, and that an initial 'focus on retributive justice has' been extended 'to include other elements such as forgiveness, healing and reconciliation'. This, however, has meant that evaluating practical achievements against these criteria has remained an uncertain task.

At the same time, the sheer diversity of lived experiences and localised variations in implementation have made it very difficult to establish common core elements of reconciliation processes and transitional justice. As Skaar (2013: 47) comments, even the term 'justice' itself has generated a range of interpretations in this context: 'forward-looking justice, backward-looking justice, retributive justice, restorative justice, retroactive justice, reparatory justice, administrative justice, local justice, traditional justice, historical justice, and more'.

Nagy (2013) comments, too, on the complexities of translating uncertain understandings of a novel process into an established institutional framework in the Canadian context. The Canadian Truth and Reconciliation Commission was established in 2006 to address the unresolved issues of oppression and harm associated with the Indian residential school system imposed on the country's indigenous people from the 19th century until 1996. In reflecting on the impacts of this aspect of colonial activity, Nagy acknowledges the potential value of the commission in enabling evidence to be heard and victims' accounts and claims to be validated. But at the same time, she identifies significant limitations to the process, where it is limited in scope to resolving 'legal–political' issues rather than promoting 'social justice': 'The most strenuous objection is that the pacifying' language of reconciliation helps to reduce white guilt while deflecting responsibility for the 'broader harms perpetrated against Indigenous Peoples' (Nagy, 2013: 53).

We might conclude, therefore, that the idea of 'truth and reconciliation' as establishing a distinctive framework for the delivery of justice on a society-wide and collective level is obviously both attractive and has prompted innovative structures and processes for resolving deeply felt historic harms. At the same time, however, both supporters and critics have identified a range of understandably deep-rooted challenges to the effective implementation of programmes designed to achieve 'transitional justice'. Not least, as Nagy (2013: 52) observes, implementation necessarily occurs within a pre-existing institutional context, where embedded interests may wish to set limits to what is known and what is done about past injustices.

Critical solutions (2): community justice

Often grounded in similar historical experiences and traditions, forms of 'community justice' share significant characteristics with transitional justice. Community justice is based on the belief that rather than placing responsibility in a distant and potentially disinterested state body, it is better to allow solutions for harm and disorder to emerge from the collective wisdom and wishes of those most directly affected.

Community justice in Northern Ireland

Northern Ireland is again an interesting starting point for a discussion of community-based offence-resolution processes because of its acknowledgment of these as a component of the wider peace-building project but, also, because its experience is similarly viewed as a potential model for adoption elsewhere.

McEvoy and Mika (2002) have charted the emergence of community-based restorative justice in Northern Ireland, identifying its emergence as an alternative way of practising justice in direct contrast to the similarly 'community-based' legacy of 'beatings, shootings and exclusions by paramilitary organisations as a response to local crime and anti-social behaviour' (Mika, 2006: i). As such, the concept of 'community' was not idealised but seen as a site of active engagement for projects designed to promote a more cohesive and integrative approach to dealing with the problems associated with unacceptable and harmful behaviour in localities.

The work of dedicated projects in Northern Ireland, philanthropically funded and promoting an 'alternative' justice model (Chapman, 2012), is seen as crucial to the reported successes of community justice (Mika, 2006). In this case, the model depended on establishing a credible local forum for engaging all parties to the reported offence, including paramilitary organisations which still held a degree of authority in the area, and negotiating an appropriate response. Importantly, the emphasis on voluntary involvement and agreed solutions was central to the process and, in this sense, it represented a more radical form of restorative practice than is sometimes achieved under the auspices of conventional justice systems:

> In conducting its work, Northern Ireland Alternatives subscribes to published principles of good practice, including an inclusive approach, non-violence, confidentiality, responsiveness to community needs, child protection, voluntary participation, accountability and transparency, a holistic approach, rights of the individual, value of the individual, a person-centred approach, human rights, working within the rule of law, and evaluation.
>
> (Mika, 2006: 9)

The importance of genuine community ownership of the process is emphasised, and although these were project-based initiatives so did not emerge spontaneously from the local context, it became clear that they had provided a catalyst for a broader reshaping of the life of the community. The evaluation of the Northern Ireland projects' work concluded that they quickly became recognised as 'essential community assets' (Mika, 2006: 28). Despite these initial achievements, concerns have subsequently been raised about the incorporation of community justice in Northern Ireland into the mainstream state-run justice system, with the associated risks of losing credibility amongst the community and undermining 'its capacity for maintaining social cohesion and for socialising young people' (Chapman, 2012: 587).

Nonetheless, certainly at their inception, initiatives in Northern Ireland illustrated some of the key attributes associated with community justice which set it apart from more conventional top-down and **adversarial** models. In particular, this form of justice needs to:

- be grounded in the networks, relationships, and shared beliefs of those in the locality concerned;
- have participatory, consensual, and open processes;
- ensure all those with an interest are able to contribute to the process and have their voices heard;
- allow doubts or uncertainties to be aired;
- provide support for anyone who needs help in stating their views;
- ensure outcomes are agreed, fair, and reasonable;
- be certain that the resolution decided upon is seen as the end of the matter.

Indigenous models of community justice

Contemporary models of community justice are often seen as deriving from traditional or indigenous forms of social practice, which commonly assume some element of negotiated and collectively sanctioned resolution of conflict or harm. One example is the 'family group conference' derived from Maori dispute-resolution traditions in New Zealand/Aotearoa, which were then incorporated into law in that country in 1989. Another is the 'sentencing circles' which originate in the 'traditional sanctioning and healing practices of Canadian Aboriginal peoples and indigenous peoples in the Southwestern United States', according to Bazemore (1997: 26; and see **Chapter 30** on restorative justice). Circle sentencing, too, received a modern-day revitalisation in Canada in the 1990s. Sentencing circles are described as a supportive vehicle for the expression of strong feelings about the offence and harms caused; for achieving a degree of 'healing of the offender, victim, and community'; but also as a means of reasserting 'social control through help and support' (Wilson et al., 2002)—a form of 'tough love', it would seem.

Bazemore, though, makes a clear distinction between two types of justice. On the one hand, there is a 'one-dimensional definition of community justice' (1997: 28) which simply consisted of changing the location of justice services, introducing greater informality, or increasing the flexibility of arrangements. On the other hand, there are forms of practice which would substantively 'change the role of neighbourhood residents from service recipients to decision makers with a stake in, or feeling of ownership in' the process of determining outcomes and engaging with criminal justice intervention (Bazemore, 1997: 28). Weaver (2011) has similar views and also stresses the importance of active community engagement in justice processes if they are to have real meaning and offer a proper sense of involvement for people affected by experiences of conflict and harm. For Weaver, the principle of 'co-production' of just outcomes is of central importance. Recognising that communities are not only harmed by crimes but also may be the focal point of the 'ills that provoke it [crime]' (Weaver, 2011: 1052), she argues that community justice should be a vehicle for promoting genuine dialogue about the offence and what led up to it; and at the same time a vehicle for all parties to consider what they might contribute to 'the process of change' (2011: 1052).

Karp and Clear (2000) have set out a 'conceptual framework' for community justice, recognising its emergence as a distinctive strand of ideas and practice in the criminal justice arena. The integrative goals and achievements of resolutions delivered for and by communities are seen as the most important feature of the 'community justice ideal', as they put it. They note the potential for communities to be able to act autonomously to address the problems associated with crime; and they stress the rejection 'of punishment as a sanctioning philosophy' (Karp and Clear, 2000: 325). Community justice is believed to offer a vehicle for unifying different ideological perspectives in linking common concerns to promote public safety and the quality of communal life. Key elements of Karp and Clear's community justice model are:

- its neighbourhood focus;
- its problem-solving ethos;
- the diffusion and decentralisation of authority;
- prioritisation of the quality of community life as an outcome; and
- the direct involvement of citizens themselves in the justice process.

These aspects of the model are in turn underpinned by a series of operating principles which are 'democratic' and 'egalitarian'. Community justice is therefore seen as participatory and equalising in the sense that it factors differences between participants into the frameworks and processes for achieving just and agreed outcomes. Importantly, then, the background characteristics of offenders are recognised and, at the same time, justice interventions seek to promote inclusion:

> A community justice approach favours public safety but rejects the simplistic claim that removal of the 'bad guys' is the core strategy for solving community safety problems. Residents existing on the margins of community life are potential resources for community development. The challenge is not to isolate as many dubious residents as possible but to

find ways to include as many community members as possible in efforts to improve . . . quality of life.

(Karp and Clear, 2000: 335)

The principle of inclusion implies that offenders should also be actively engaged in the process of resolving the problems associated with crimes, including 'having a say' (Weaver, 2011: 152) in how the offence should be dealt with and what forms of response—**rehabilitation**, reparation, or punishment—are most appropriate. By implication, too, this also modifies conventional assumptions about guilt and responsibility, which become understood more in collective terms, with the focus on building community cohesion and creating opportunities for mutual benefit, rather than fault-finding and exacting punitive sanctions.

Indeed, some would take the argument even further to suggest that 'crime' is not the starting point for thinking about community justice. In other words, it is the creation of effective relationships and working models for problem-solving which establishes the basis for dealing with problematic behaviour or harm when it occurs. Community justice, then, is not just a mechanism or a technique, but depends on a form of social organisation that is embedded in a wider network of positive relationships and underlying trust (Blagg, 2009; see also Lea, 2010). Criticising the limitations of 'traditional' justice systems, Gilbert and Settles (2007: 5) also advocate a community justice approach because 'crime is a deeply embedded social problem', involving complex and conflicting needs. They argue that it is very much local knowledge and locally based relationships which will underpin effective responses to any breakdown of the social order.

Chantrill's (1998) depiction of the establishment of a community justice programme in Kowanyama, Queensland nicely captures the idea of the community appropriating space for its own distinctive approach from government, partly because the community already felt detached and of little interest to the centralised state authorities. As a result, aboriginal traditions of mediation, offence resolution, and prevention were incorporated into, and often usurped, conventional adversarial and hostile criminal justice practices. Chantrill (1998: 55) concluded that this was not simply a matter of 'returning' to traditional ways, but setting out a new model for the administration of justice in a changing social context, which was nonetheless crucially informed by those traditions and in which local community members and interests retained leading roles. In other words, community justice was here, as elsewhere, very much about establishing legitimacy and authority for the measures adopted to deal with and resolve the harms associated with unacceptable behaviour; and the benefits associated with more appropriate justice outcomes also extended into 'broader community development processes that are making Kowanyama a safer and better place to live' (Chantrill, 1998: 55). This particular form of community justice initiative has subsequently been recognised as offering substantial benefits and has become more or less institutionalised within the wider governance framework (Ryan et al., 2006).

Critical solutions (3): abolitionism

The final strategy we shall consider here is essentially captured by the term 'abolitionism'. Abolitionists' principal aim is to seek an end to the use of penal sanctions in the administration of criminal justice and the decommissioning of its associated mechanisms and institutions. Prisons, for example, should simply be shut down (Sim, 2009: 153).

As this implies, abolitionists argue that any attempt to respond to crime by way of a punitive or '**responsibilising**' (guilt-based) intervention is unacceptable. Instead, we should be concerned first and foremost with the conditions under which the alleged offence takes place, the means by which it comes to be defined as a crime, and the organisation and delivery of mechanisms of control. Abolitionists argue that the current justice system is not, and cannot be, a neutral system for identifying and dealing with crime, as the principles of individual accountability and guilt underlying the justice system are a political vehicle for regulating and maintaining the social order. It is the system itself which should be problematised, both in general terms and in respect of the practices it puts in place. Any criminal justice intervention initiated under these conditions is therefore considered to be inherently biased in some way, resulting in inappropriate or disproportionate outcomes for those judged to be offenders. This disregards the socially constructed nature of the justice system and the collective responsibility of the members of society for an offence.

Abolitionism therefore fundamentally rejects the rationale on which conventional forms of intervention and adjudication of the offender take place. It takes this position irrespective of the ethos on which intervention is based, whether this be punitive, rehabilitative, deterrent, or restorative. Whichever of these applies, they share a common concern with determining individual responsibility and putting measures in place which are directed at influencing, changing, or controlling offender behaviour. Abolitionists argue that anyone concerned with rights and social justice should oppose any sanctions that are based on this narrow framing of criminality. Both the response of the system and the underlying rationale of the justice system should come into question. There is no scope for negotiating or modifying the impacts of the justice process; instead, the only valid position, they argue, is to oppose those sanctions for which it is responsible, especially those which involve the denial of liberty. As such, there is no scope for compromise positions, such as those adopted by proponents of 'alternatives' to punishment, just because these offer implicit justifications for the underlying penal logic. Mathiesen (1974) has therefore argued that it is important not to enter into negotiations with the existing system of justice over making improvements to penal facilities. To take this sort of position would simply be to collude with the discourse of individualised blame and punishment. Abolitionists are unapologetic about taking this 'extreme' position.

The grounds for abolition

The rationales for taking an abolitionist position may vary. It is possible, for instance, to oppose certain kinds of punishment (or punishment in general) primarily on the basis that it is ineffective, and even counterproductive; that is, it is opposed on practical grounds and on the basis that it does not 'work'. On the other hand, the use of penal sanctions may be opposed on more fundamental and principled grounds, in the sense that the aims and ethos of punishment are essentially inhumane and therefore unacceptable.

Punishment doesn't work

To support the former line of argument (that punishment does not 'work'), abolitionists draw attention to the absence of any real evidence to support the effectiveness of any particular form of punishment, including custody, despite the well-known claim by a former Home Secretary Michael Howard that 'prison works' (this phrase featured prominently in a speech made by Michael Howard to the Conservative Party Conference in 1993). Bianchi (1994: 337), for example, takes an abolitionist position, at least partly on the grounds of the inherent problems associated with the imposition of compulsory measures of punishment. 'Even the docile convict,' he argues, is unable to make any meaningful contribution to their 'own social salvation', because they have no say in the administration of the punishment imposed and must simply accept the harmful 'stigma' associated with it. So, the recipient of punishment is denied any role in putting things right, and instead must accept a permanent stain on their character (see **Controversy and debate 31.2**).

Not only is punishment damaging in this respect, but Bianchi also argues that it has demonstrably failed to achieve any of the other positive outcomes claimed for it, such as therapeutic healing or rehabilitation. In effect, because of their misleading claims to do good: 'Adaptation and therapy programmes have even strengthened the destructive power of the criminal law system' (Bianchi, 1994: 338). Abolitionists argue that penal measures are therefore called into question as they fail to meet many of the positive claims advanced for them: there is little or no evidence to suggest that they have any rehabilitative effect; they do not offer an effective deterrent; and they provide no opportunity to make amends. Indeed, in many ways it could be suggested that punishment is more likely to escalate than reduce offending (McLeod, 2015).

As a consequence, it might seem simply a rational economic argument to suggest that the very substantial investment of money and human resources into prisons and other penal facilities might be better directed elsewhere, into social prevention measures, for example. Although cautious about the risks of becoming absorbed into the

CONTROVERSY AND DEBATE 31.2

The use of criminal records

> Most of all, young people need a different future to aspire to, but our criminal records regime is holding them back. Half of employers would not consider employing someone with a criminal record. But over the past five years 22,000 minority ethnic children have had their names added to the national police computer database.
>
> (David Lammy, *The Guardian*, 8 September 2017)

Lammy argued that young people should be able to apply to have their criminal records 'sealed' so that their childhood offences should not be held against them for the rest of their lives, particularly when seeking employment.

This measure would result in the 'rolling back' of the justice system in one small but significant respect. The argument for its introduction for young offenders is grounded on the longer term effects it has on their employment and career prospects, but the same principle could be applied to other offenders as well.

Counter-arguments might be that employers and others are entitled to know about offenders' criminal records because of the continuing threat they are believed to pose to community safety.

conventional justice system and thereby reinforcing it, Bianchi (1994: 345) does offer some possible indicators of alternatives which might be supportive of the abolitionist principle, such as 'neighbourhood centres' to resolve minor local disputes and harms. It is likely, though, that others such as Mathiesen (1974: 211) would take issue with this on the grounds that most such changes would run the risk of being 'absorbed by . . . the main system', consolidating support for it. So, for example, the alternatives to the custody movement in the UK led to practitioners being 'held responsible' (Mathiesen, 1974: 20) for the administration of the new arrangements and so, by extension, maintaining the justifications underpinning the existing punitive regime.

Punishment is morally wrong

We will now move on to the second of the two rationales for the abolitionist position. This stronger argument against punishment is based on the principle that deliberate imposition of harm, on whatever grounds, is wrong. According to this idea, it is not sufficient to establish a system for arbitration and determination of just deserts, no matter how fair in principle, because it is simply not the role of the state to allow or authorise the infliction of hurt on any of its citizens, even where they have themselves already caused harm. Imposing any form of punishment is viewed as morally unjustifiable and an unacceptable expression of primal instincts of revenge and vindictiveness. In other words, those responsible for seeking and imposing punishments are in effect no different from the perpetrators of an offence, especially if we are to accept that offences are socially contextualised and socially constructed. The principle of 'an eye for an eye' is rejected by the abolitionists, who argue instead for a spirit of tolerance and forgiveness in the administration of criminal justice. So, both the avoidance of negative outcomes such as the infliction of pain and the promotion of more harmonious human relationships through the expression of forgiveness and reconciliation are associated with the aim of ending the use of state-sanctioned punishments. The abolitionist, therefore, rejects the retributivist position on the basis that it is morally unacceptable. There is no place for the imposition of harm as a means of atonement, and certainly not simply for its own sake.

Wider justifications are also sought for the abolitionist position in the acknowledgement of the inherent injustices embedded in the justice system, to the extent that it reflects and reproduces wider social inequalities, through institutional discrimination, for example. The justification for abolitionism is thus not simply humanist, grounded in moral arguments, but also material, in that it actually supports wider political aspirations such as social justice. If fairness is viewed as a fundamental requirement of legal systems and criminal processes, then institutional practices which operate unfairly should be brought to an end, according to this logic.

Making progress

For abolitionists, however, there has been relatively little scope to make progress in practical terms, given its limited popular appeal. However, one example of an attempt to end the use of custody was the 'Massachusetts experiment' in which the recently appointed head of the Department of Youth Services, Jerome Miller, shut down all penal establishments for young people in the state in 1971 and 1972. Instead, a range of genuine alternatives was put in place of custody, under a global policy of 'deinstitutionalisation'. Importantly for the success of this policy, Miller did not enter into a process of negotiation with the existing penal structures but simply used his authority to close them down, despite resistance and without having instituted a process of establishing a range of 'alternatives' first. In this sense, his actions complied with the expectations of abolitionists. Interestingly, too, the deinstitutionalisation policy has remained largely in place in Massachusetts since then. Of course, it could be argued that the success of the scheme itself was limited. Much of the machinery of justice was unaffected by the reform, and an array of alternative forms of penal sanction remained in place; the policy only applied to young offenders and not adults; and the Massachusetts experience has not gained support more widely.

On the other hand, researchers claim that the initiative has not led to an increase in crime levels. It did result in the establishment of new ways of dealing with youth crime, some of which were influential in the UK; and it did generate improved outcomes for those young people no longer subject to punitive regimes (Krisberg and Austin, 1993; Jones, 2012).

Aside from this example, the abolitionist case has typically been advanced more in the pursuit of policy change and targeted campaigns of opposition, focusing on the adverse and harmful effects of penal regimes on many of those who experience them—prison, essentially, has been the principal target. Sim (2009) has argued that abolitionism need not simply be about expressing 'opposition' (Mathiesen, 1974: 14), but has also been associated with a series of positive developments in theory and practice with demonstrable concrete outcomes. The abolitionist campaigning group established in 1970, Radical Alternatives to Prison (RAP), is highlighted as being very active in pursuing targeted short-term reforms, such as the ending of the use of drugs as tools to control behaviour and an end to the use of solitary confinement. In this case, and more widely, Sim appears to endorse a shift from the purist position of simply rejecting the idea of penal sanctions, especially prison, to one which supports a more engaged activist approach intended to make the prison 'more effective, responsive and accountable' (Sim, 2009: 11).

This is somewhat at odds with the position taken by Mathiesen in 1974 on the publication of his highly influential book *The Politics of Abolition*. Here he argued that abolitionism must necessarily pursue a path of pure opposition, setting out its principles in their own right, and not simply as a counter-argument to the established justice system. Abolitionism, therefore, should be thought of in terms of the 'unfinished'; that is, as a continuous questioning of conventional penal assumptions and practices, rather than seeking to find an accommodation with these at any point: 'The alternative is "alternative" in so far as it is not based on the premises of the old system, but on its own premises, which at one or more points *contradict* those of the old system' (Mathiesen, 1974: 13). Being unpopular and being dismissed as idealist is reckoned to be a necessary price to pay in order to sustain the integrity of those arguments; which, nonetheless, are likely to be influential and actually secure important changes in penal policy. In **Conversations 31.1** we hear from Thomas Mathiesen, one of the principal architects of 'abolitionism'.

CONVERSATIONS 31.1

Abolition

with **Thomas Mathiesen**

'Abolition', and 'to abolish', means 'to erase', 'get rid of'. 'Abolitionism' is a word covering the movements dedicated to the abolition of an institution or a sentiment which is considered immoral or politically wrong. It is opposed to but also akin to 'reform', which means to change and make a situation better without really getting rid of it.

Reforms at times develop into abolitions—one moves from attempts to make a situation better to getting rid of it. An example would be slavery, which in several places started out as attempts to improve the conditions of slaves, but later moved to an abolitionist stance to slavery. But the opposite development, where an abolitionist stance moves to a reformist stance, also takes place.

Historically, five examples may be mentioned: the death penalty; slavery; segregation of populations based on race; torture; and imprisonment have been goals of abolitionism.

The death penalty, slavery, and racist segregations

In many parts of the world, *the death penalty* has increasingly been met by an abolitionist stance, whereby it has receded in importance. An example would be the USA. *Slavery* is also an example, again in the USA, where it today is forbidden. *Racist segregation of the population for example in schools* is a third example. In the USA, the abolition of segregation in schools was prompted by a long political and moral debate, and finally took place in the 1960s. US president John F. Kennedy was among the politically active politicians. These abolitions are regularly met and strengthened by new legal standards of human rights and equality before the law. But the movement against racist segregation has also in part been reversed by popular political opinion/resistance groups. The conditions creating such popular political opinions are complex.

Source: Photo by Astrid Renland

Torture

Torture, for example during interrogation, is now forbidden under most conditions in countries where the rule of law has a strong standing. But a long abolitionist struggle took place before we reached this stage. Unfortunately, torture is still widespread in some parts of the world and among some population groups, but at times secretly and in hiding.

Imprisonment

Imprisonment is our final example. Here I will go into some detail. Popular groups exist in western countries such as Norway, England, and the USA, which have abolition of imprisonment as a goal. In connection with abolition of imprisonment, several questions are regularly raised.

A point of departure is that in the Western world, some prisons (in some places many prisons) have very detrimental conditions for the prisoners. Is all imprisonment, then, to be abolished? Some people for various reasons answer 'yes' to this question, but there are also several other answers to it. The answers are often that some of the poor prisons, with bad conditions, should be abolished, but not all of them, and—more radically—while imprisonment has to be used for some very dangerous and repetitive criminals, it may be abolished for large groups of the prison population.

The latter question in turn raises the issue of prediction, which is hotly debated among psychiatrists, psychologists, and criminologists. It also raises the question of alternatives to prison, such as *conflict resolution boards* and *new technological inventions* such as electronic fetters.

Conflict resolution boards is an entirely different type of reaction than prison, where the point is that the lawbreaker and the victim meet with a third party—a moderator—to discuss the issue and find the best reaction. Discussions may be long. But they often lead to fruitful results. To be sure, it perhaps does not fit all offenders, and some offences do not have clear cut victims. But it may be used much more widely than today, and reduce prison populations very sizeably.

Modern electronic fetters may be used while the law breaker stays at home instead of in prison. There are also several other attempts at finding alternatives to prison, which exist or are being tried out.

And in fact, changes are taking place in connection with the use of prison in countries such as Sweden and the Netherlands, and even in the USA, which has the largest prison population in the western world. Sweden in fact now has some empty prisons, and prison populations are at least receding a little in some parts of the USA.

Of course, such developments may be caused by a decreasing crime rate in the countries concerned. But the development is much more likely to be caused by the political situation and climate in the outside society. Norway has recently had a more or less constant crime rate or a crime rate which is increasing only for some crimes. Yet Norway has in recent years had a sizeable increase in the number of prisoners (from 44 per 100,000 population in 1980 to 73 per 100,000 population in 2010 (Scott, 2013)), partly due to longer sentences and the political climate in the community. Norway in fact exports a sizeable proportion of its prisoners to the Netherlands, which has vacant prison facilities! Some of the Norwegian increase could have been solved by a minor reduction of prison sentences.

Further questions along the same line are at times raised, such as: are new technological inventions, such as electronic fetters or surveillance of various kinds, any better than prisons? Some of the movements which started out as abolitionist movements have for reasons of such questions ended as critical reformist movements, emphasising vital reforms—improvements of various kinds in living conditions—for prisoners.

A further question is that of the effectiveness of prisons. In many places and under many conditions, recidivism—a relapse to prison after release—is high, and has been a very important argument for abolitions or critical reform.

Social change

Finally, I briefly wish to mention *social change* (or perhaps better, societal change), which may be caused by a more or less abolitionist stance, or by more or less reformist opinions. This is an important historical question.

The Chinese revolution, which ended in a victory in 1949 and the escape of Chang Kai Chek and his forces to Formosa (now Taiwan), is an example of the former.

Another, different example is Norway, which in the first part of the 1900s had quite a radical labour party, but then quickly entered a long reformist stage before and after World War II, with a social democratic welfare state and welfare law as the main goal.

But the further questions concerning broad social change belong to a different order and are not discussed further here.

Thomas Mathiesen, Norwegian sociologist

Suggested further reading

Mathiesen, T. (2015) *The Politics of Abolition Revisited.* Abingdon: Routledge.
Mathiesen, T. (2005) *Prison on Trial* (3rd edn). Hook: Waterside Press.
Scott, D. (2015) *Why Prison?* Cambridge: Cambridge University Press.

31.7 Limitations of critical perspectives on punishment

Of course, it is in the nature of criminological argument that the positions we take prompt criticism; but the critics themselves must be prepared for yet further counter-arguments. For those adopting critical perspectives on punishment, the challenges they encounter are principally of two kinds: that they go too far, on the one hand, and that they do not go far enough, on the other. They also risk the accusation that they advance a lot of objections to existing practices and conventional theories, but they offer very few answers to the problems they raise.

Romanticising crime

Critical criminology is often portrayed as both unrealistic and idealistic. Lea (1999) has suggested that there is a strand in critical criminological thinking which is influenced by radical historians' acknowledgement of 'social crime' as a form of political resistance to oppression, as in the 'Robin Hood legend' (Lea, 1999: 309). Indeed, radical criminology has been called to account for its political leanings and for allowing these to compromise its objectivity and integrity, with Walker (1974: 47), for example, describing supposedly critical criminologists as being 'glamorous partisans'. As such, it seems the radicals were believed to be unconcerned with the practical applications and implications of academic analyses and they were seen as 'refusing to engage practically with the real public and private circumstances of criminal activity' (O'Brien and Penna, 2007: 248). Some might respond that there is no such thing as a 'neutral' position in criminology, or any other academic discipline, and that the key question, following Becker (1967), is merely 'whose side are we on?', a position subsequently endorsed by Scraton (2002), among others.

Crime is 'real'

Sykes (1974) would also have concurred with the suggestion that critical criminology did not have an obvious basis in the available evidence, but instead reflected an aspirational political choice: 'the viewpoint of critical criminology as it stands today probably cannot be said to be true or false. Rather, it is a bet on what empirical research and theoretical development in the field will reveal in the future' (Sykes, 1974: 212). However, even though he thought this bet might be 'not a bad one', Sykes was also clear about some of his reservations. Critical criminology, he believed, was too ready to look for the worst and oversimplify complex patterns of social interaction in order to convey an impression of a deliberately stratified social system, with the criminal law and its processes acting simply as a vehicle for maintaining control on behalf of vested interests. That, in turn, led to a number of other problematic misreadings of the reality of crime and criminality. Critical perspectives seemed unwilling to recognise that there was a demonstrable relationship between official accounts of crime and their impact on the daily lives of those affected by it: 'Persistent criminals or criminals considered serious may be singled out for the law's attention without reducing a criminal conviction to a mere label that has no connection with an objective reality' (Sykes, 1974: 213). That is to say, official records of crime do represent, however imperfectly, real events where harm is caused to real victims.

This was the point recognised by the 'left realist' school of criminologists, emerging in the 1980s (see **Chapter 20**), some of whom such as Jock Young were effectively revising their own previous assumptions about the meaning and impact of 'crime'. Left realists began to question some of their own earlier ideas (Taylor et al., 1975) which had portrayed crime as the product of an undeveloped and emerging radical consciousness. They cast doubt on sympathetic interpretations of deviant activity, such as those associated with Quinney and others drawing on Marxist theory:

> Crime is . . . an incomplete but not altogether mistaken response to a bad situation . . . coming into active existence only by overcoming the resistance of inherited values and internalized sanctions.
>
> (Quinney, 1977: 99)

Instead, a process of adjustment took place where a 'romanticised' view of 'criminal as revolutionary' was progressively rethought and replaced by a recognition that 'crime' should be understood as a form of 'social harm' that 'negatively affects working class people's lives' (Pavlich, 1999: 33). Whilst still claiming to be 'of the left' and committed to progressive change, those associated with the left-realist position were clearly prepared to accept crime at face value. As such, Young argued, 'the major task of radical criminology is to seek a solution to the problem of crime and that of a socialist policy is to substantially reduce the crime rate' (1986: 28). In this way, the focus of attention for critical criminology shifted towards what were described as the harms done to 'the most vulnerable members of capitalist societies' (Young, 1986: 29).

Taking crime at face value

This, however, leads to another possible criticism of critical and radical approaches: that they are unduly prepared to compromise with established criminological conventions, such as taking conventional definitions of 'crime' at face value. Some 'critical' commentators do not go far enough. The fear was that by conceding ground to mainstream criminological ideas about the risks to communities, progressive arguments would lose their value: 'left realism's engagement with administrative criminology [is] compromising a commitment to critical practice' (Pavlich, 1999: 34). By taking this approach, it is argued, critical criminologists have become virtually indistinguishable from the mainstream in their concern to find technical (administrative) solutions to the (undoubtedly real and damaging) harms experienced by particular individuals and communities as victims. And so, what might well be a perfectly legitimate concern with community safety and protecting those at risk, has the effect of diverting attention from questions to do with the prior definition of what counts as crime and which offenders should be targeted for intervention. Feminists, for example, challenged the readiness of left realists to accept conventional definitions of crime because they risked failing to address the distinctive concerns of women and the gendered nature of crime and 'fear of crime' (Walklate, 2004). So, too, criticisms could be levelled at radical perspectives which simply take crime for granted to the extent that the preoccupation with its effects on communities deflects attention from punishments and their consequences. In fact, conventional assumptions about the need to be 'tough on crime' became implicit elements of a 'left realist' position, at least to the extent that it was incorporated into Labour's criminal justice policy in the early 1990s (Blair, T., 'Why Crime is a Socialist Issue', *New Statesman*, 29 January 1993).

Therefore, for many critical criminologists the problem is with what is not addressed as much as it is with deliberations over the legitimacy or otherwise of conventional understandings of crime. For example, the relative lack of attention paid to antisocial activities and corporate crime which do not routinely generate interest is a critical point for some commentators. In their discussion of corporate crime, Slapper and Tombs observe that there are many obstacles in the way of criminologists who wish to investigate this area of human activity, concluding that 'most of what constitutes criminological theorising has signally failed even to attempt to account for corporate offending' (1999: 110). They suggest that this may partly be related to criminology's concern to identify the 'pathological' and to seek explanations for behavioural abnormalities; whereas, in fact, 'corporate crime is widespread and routine' (Slapper and Tombs, 1999: 129). Corporate crime is a feature of normal organisational behaviour, they argue, and so cannot really be accounted for by theories of deviance, even those which have critical leanings, such as labelling theory. In this sense, then, criminology, no matter how critical or radical, does not have the 'explanatory power' (1999: 130) to account for the routine immoralities of corporate interests. As Tombs and Whyte (2009) have argued, this realisation prompts consideration of the relationships between powerful groups and interests, their capacity to organise things in their own favour, and their ability, at the same time, to define other groups as undesirable and their behaviour as unlawful. It is this kind of analysis, in these authors' view, which must precede any kind of discussion of crime and its effects, even where these are played out at the 'micro' level in particular communities and neighbourhoods; even localised and personal relationships must be understood as being organised and 'lived' according to the interests and wishes of those in positions of power.

Reaching the limits of critical criminology

Tombs and Whyte's (2009) analysis of the interplay of state and corporate interests in the context of regulatory regimes and their enforcements offers a sense of how these relationships operate in constructing and implementing 'criminal justice' in one area of activity. In this study, the authors examined the ways in which business practices are governed by laws and regulations covering issues such as proper treatment of employees and health and safety. In Tombs and Whyte's view, under capitalism there is a necessary reciprocal relationship between state institutions and the corporate sector, whose continuing legitimacy depends at least in part on the authority of the state itself. Theories which are principally critical of the criminal justice apparatus of the state on the grounds of its inadequate functioning, or even its periodic corruption, effectively overlook this close, symbiotic relationship between the two. Critical arguments which are concerned with inadequacies in the ways in which the machinery of the state functions, or its powers are misdirected, are still guilty of failing to understand its underlying rationale, which is to preserve the basis for capitalist accumulation and all the potential injustices which follow from that.

In a complex formulation, Tombs and Whyte describe the process involved as creating the impression of 'externality—the positioning of the state in direct opposition to capital' in order to create an 'imaginary legal order' in which the state acts 'in the public interest' while actually still serving the purposes of capital (2009: 109). It could be argued that the machinery of justice is designed and constructed in ways which enable corporations to avoid being held responsible for their wrongdoing rather than ensuring that they can be held to account for any wrongdoing.

In a way, this brings us full circle back to the case of Bhopal, and the failure of conventional systems of national and international justice to hold those responsible to account over many years. Criticisms and campaigns which have focused principally on the failure of these mechanisms to work properly are held to fall short according to arguments of this kind from radical criminologists. That is to say, they believe that the systems of justice in operation are inherently geared to serving business interests and concealing or misrepresenting the inevitable consequences of capitalism in terms of human distress and harm: 'our analysis has attempted to indicate that in thinking about corporate crime and its regulation, what is really at issue is not "crime"—rather, it is an issue of state, corporate and class power' (Tombs and Whyte, 2009: 115). As we write this, and as discussed in greater detail elsewhere in the book, the issue of whether or not corporate or political interests or individuals will be held to account by the criminal justice system for the Grenfell Tower fire is very much a live question; and the outcomes will clearly have significant implications for those directly affected, of course, but also for our deeper understanding of how the institutions of the state and the criminal justice system operate, supposedly in the public interest.

Barton and colleagues (2007: 199) conclude starkly that it is, in fact, an endemic problem for criminology that its 'structural relationship to the capitalist state . . . can only be described as parasitical'. In this sense, criminology is constrained only to consider problems of order and disorder from within the confines of what they describe as a 'liberal conceptual framework'; no matter how progressive some of its insights and observations may appear, they seem to be bound by conventional concepts of individualised responsibility, guilt, and redemption. As such, criminology must at all times, according to them, incorporate understandings of 'structurally embedded harm' into its 'consciousness' and incorporate these into its evidence-gathering and explanatory frameworks (Barton et al., 2007: 206). And so, they conclude:

> If the development of the critical criminological imagination is to play a part in escaping the straitjacket that criminology has created, then we have once again to think in terms of *social* justice rather than *criminal* justice, to enhance, rather than undermine democratic and legal accountability, and to develop research agendas that provide the potential to challenge, rather than consolidate, the interests of the powerful.
>
> (Barton et al., 2007: 211, emphasis in original)

31.8 Conclusion

In this chapter we have introduced a range of critical criminological perspectives which have illustrated a number of problematic aspects of conventional approaches to the study of criminal justice and offending behaviour. In various ways, these critical arguments have pointed towards the proposed need for radical overhaul, or even in some cases, the abolition of existing systems for delivering and maintaining law and order. However, critical perspectives, too, can be criticised; for being unrealistic, for underestimating the impact of crime on ordinary lives, and for failing to provide credible solutions to the problems they claim to identify.

SUMMARY

After reading this chapter and working your way through its features you should now be able to:

- **Explain what is meant by the idea of critical perspectives on punishment**

We have considered a number of the problems identified with contemporary forms of punishment, such as their role in maintaining social control and their unequal impact on different sectors of the population.

- **Consider a range of critical perspectives on the justice system including the abolitionist position, social control theories, and transformative justice**

The chapter has discussed the contribution of several key theorists of punishment and social control, it has provided a detailed account of the abolitionist position on punishment, and it has introduced several international examples of attempts to develop a form of post-conflict justice based on principles of dialogue and reconciliation.

- **Identify the disparities in treatment between white, BME, and other sectors of the population in the criminal justice system**

We have reviewed evidence on the disproportionate impact of policing and punishment on specific groups, including minority ethnic communities in particular.

- **Explore how 'crimes of the powerful' and state crimes can remain unseen and unpunished**

We have explored some of the arguments suggesting that privileged and powerful interests are able to divert attention from their own crimes, and that this is sometimes also associated with subversion and misuse of the supposedly legitimate authority of the state.

- **Evaluate radical responses to the problems associated with crime, such as truth and reconciliation, community justice, and abolitionism**

A number of alternative perspectives on the definitions of crime and the organisation and delivery of criminal justice have been considered and critically analysed in light of their achievements and possible shortcomings.

- Analyse the limitations of critical analyses of crime and punishment

We concluded the chapter by discussing a number of criticisms of critical perspectives themselves, such as the tendency of some to romanticise criminal behaviour or their failure to offer practical solutions to the problems they identify.

 Test your understanding of the chapter's key points by attempting the self-test questions on the **online resources** at www.oup.com/he/case2e

REVIEW QUESTIONS

1. What are the distinguishing features of a critical perspective in criminology?
2. Identify some of the key theorists of social control and their contributions to criminological thinking.
3. Why might it be important to try to understand the 'crimes of the powerful'?
4. What do you think has been achieved by international efforts to promote truth and reconciliation?
5. Outline the benefits and limitations of the abolitionist perspective.

 Access the **online resources** at www.oup.com/he/case2e to check your answers to the review questions.

FURTHER READING

Chapman, T. (2012) 'The Problem of Community in a Justice System in Transition: The Case of Community Restorative Justice in Northern Ireland'. *International Criminal Law Review* 12(3): 573–87.
A useful discussion of the possibilities and challenges of putting alternative community-based mechanisms in place for resolving crimes.

Nurse, A. (2014) 'Critical Perspectives on Green Criminology: An Introduction' in A. Nurse (ed.) *Critical Perspectives on Green Criminology*. Internet Journal of Criminology. Available at: www.internetjournalofcriminology.com
An introductory collection on environmental crime and the criminological response.

Pearce, F. (1997) *The Crimes of the Powerful*. London: Pluto Press.
A hugely influential book, which was one of the earliest attempts to provide a comprehensive account of the ways in which those in positions of power are engaged in criminal activity, as well as the ways in which they evade accountability.

Phillips, C. and Bowling, B. (2017) 'Ethnicities, Racism, Crime and Criminal Justice' in A. Liebling, S. Maruna, and L. McAra (eds) *The Oxford Handbook of Criminology*. 6th edn. Oxford: Oxford University Press.
This chapter provides a thorough analysis of the problems of racism in criminal justice.

Sim, J. (2009) *Punishment and Prisons: Power and the Carceral State*. London: Sage.
A critical account of the symbolic and material impacts of the machinery of punishment and its role in maintaining the authority and control of the contemporary state.

 Access the **online resources** to view a wealth of extra information relating to your study of criminology, including self-test questions, answers to review questions, and links to other resources that will help you enjoy and fulfil your potential within your studies. www.oup.com/he/case2e

PART OUTLINE

32. Conducting criminological research
33. Employability and careers

This part is all about making the best use of the detailed body of knowledge and high levels of critical understanding that you will acquire from this book. It offers a range of guidance intended to put you in charge of your undergraduate journey, the reward being the stimulating and original experiences promised in **Chapter 1**. The two chapters support your progress into independent work by taking you through the essential features of and considerations for effective undergraduate research, before looking at how you can boost your employability and career prospects.

Chapter 32, on researching and producing knowledge, looks at your current role and identity: it seeks to enhance your undergraduate studies by encouraging you to think and act as an independent researcher. The chapter walks through the main steps of a research project and provides an array of practical and creative tips for developing your role as a knowledge producer and becoming a person who contributes to what is, and helps to establish what is not, known about crime and the criminal justice system.

Chapter 33 helps you think about what comes next, guiding you through some of the career options you are likely to have after completing your degree. It also contains a strategy for achieving the skills and attributes employers expect to see in contemporary undergraduates. This method will help ensure that your employability is continually refined as you progress through the next stages of your life and future career.

PART 5
RESEARCH AND CAREERS IN CRIMINOLOGY

CHAPTER OUTLINE

32.1	Introduction	960
32.2	Why research?	960
32.3	What makes a good student research project?	962
32.4	Choosing your research topic	965
32.5	Reviewing academic literature	969
32.6	Choosing your research strategy	971
32.7	Collecting data	975
32.8	Analysing data	977
32.9	Writing up your research	980
32.10	Planning your research project	987
32.11	Ethics and legality in research	989
32.12	Conclusion	996

32

Conducting criminological research

KEY ISSUES

After studying this chapter, you should be able to:

- appreciate the breadth of opportunities offered by being an undergraduate researcher in criminology;
- identify effective ways of choosing your research topic and methodology;
- plan the core features of a research project or dissertation;
- consider unconventional methods of disseminating your research;
- engage with ethical standards for researchers in criminology.

32.1 Introduction

Now that you have a grounding in criminology, you are equipped to take the next step in your criminological journey and become a knowledge producer. At the moment this may feel like a step into the unknown, but the different sections of this chapter will demonstrate how producing knowledge naturally evolves from being an engaged and effective undergraduate. It will help you study with increased independence, assist your development of the third characteristic of the E3 student (employability) (see **Chapter 1**), and reveal why research can be such a rewarding undertaking. Through this chapter we also hope to address any preconceptions you might have about doing research, such as it being an elite activity only undertaken by postgraduate students or established academics, or something that you only need to think about in your research methods module. A first step in demystifying research is to think about the word itself—'re*search*'; as the second syllable indicates, it as an act of searching. So, as long as you are looking for information, and can write about what you find, then you are researching!

This chapter is directly relevant to your current course as you will probably be required to undertake a dissertation or perhaps a similar, small-scale research project in your final year. Regardless of the size of your research, the same key principles and elements apply and it is these areas that we will focus on because, once they are grasped, they can be adapted to suit the size of your task. We begin by looking at how you should go about choosing a research or dissertation topic, and how to conduct the necessary academic reading in this area and decide on an appropriate research methodology for that topic. We then consider how your project can be effectively planned and organised and provide some advice on writing up your research and demonstrating your critical thinking. Finally, we will look at the fundamental ethical principles for conducting research, encouraging engagement with ethical thinking that goes further than a tick in a box of a dissertation proposal. These different parts will develop your research experience and skills for your 'next step' and the continuation of your higher education or progression into employment.

We should note that this is not an exhaustive chapter on how to conduct research. Social science research strategies, data collection methods, and approaches to data analysis are the subject of entire books, so we cannot hope to equip you with all the skills and knowledge you need within a single chapter. We simply aim to provide an overview of the main areas of consideration for completing successful undergraduate research, to help you make the transition from learning about others' research to becoming an independent researcher. Before you embark on your student research project or dissertation, we strongly suggest that you read **Chapter 4** and refer to the texts recommended in the further reading list. They provide detailed advice on the considerations and practicalities of each aspect of independent research.

32.2 Why research?

You will gain many benefits from taking part in the research process whilst you are an undergraduate. It will develop your intellectual skill set by allowing you to use the knowledge you have acquired, and test your ability to work more independently. This progress can come from experiencing new things in research and from embracing the freedom it gives you to be creative.

These are valuable personal benefits, but there are broader rewards too; such as your work adding to the knowledge base in the discipline of criminology, which in turn is used to inform practical changes in the wider world. One of the many examples of this in action was when many police forces in England employed extra officers during the World Cup in 2018 and joined a 'Give Domestic Abuse the Red Card' campaign (*The Independent*, 19 June 2018) following research conducted by Kirby et al. (2014)—see, for example, **Figure 32.1**. This study had found reports of domestic abuse to a police station in North West England increased by 26 per cent when the England football team won or drew, and by 38 per cent when they lost. (If this type of topic area intrigues you, see **section 32.4** to guide you on making it a manageable project.)

Doing your research, in the ways advised by this book and your institution, will make you think repeatedly about the true value of what is known in criminology. This search for meaning and truth is shared by every university student: in Arts subjects, for example, students might produce designs or paintings to demonstrate what their course has meant to them; in criminology, our undergraduates have the opportunity to produce a portfolio of completed research projects. It can give you a real sense of personal achievement as you bring together the knowledge you have already acquired and build on it through a project that challenges or supplements what is known in your research area. This satisfaction can feel greater than

Figure 32.1 Criminological research on the link between football and domestic abuse had a clear practical impact, leading to additional policing measures at major football matches and many forces working with charities to raise awareness of the issue

Source: David Bagnall/Alamy Stock Photo

in other parts of your course, as research projects require you to work more autonomously; levels of independence that can also require your creativity, imagination, and curiosity. This freedom can be rare so we advise you to embrace it whilst you can! It might sound overly grand, but current criminology students really can shape and add to the knowledge base of our field—and, as **Conversations 32.1** demonstrates, can genuinely inform and shape real-world decisions. The idea of undergraduates being knowledge producers whilst studying for their degrees means students are fully recognised for their ability to contribute to the fundamental rationale for their university's existence—the pursuit of knowledge.

As exciting prospects show, you can become what is known in business as a 'creative disruptor', using the resources available to you during your studies to investigate the areas of criminology that need more attention. A creative disruptor is someone who does their research in imaginative ways that challenge established presumptions in their research area. A disruptor used to be something undesirable but these days, thanks to technology and particularly the internet, this view has changed. It is a belief in the value of undergraduate research and can result from the ABC (*Always Be Critical*) approach as advocated throughout this book. A creative disruptor maximises their resources and shows productivity by engaging with the formal research process in a new or innovative way. There are many reminders in this book's chapters—for example in those on gender (**Chapter 11**), race (**Chapter 10**), hate crime (**Chapter 8**), and global criminology chapters (**Chapters 13 and 14**)—that more work is still needed to ensure greater equality and fairness in the pursuit of knowledge about crime and

CONVERSATIONS 32.1

Research with a purpose: stand up for what you believe

with **Mike Periera**

As someone who had not previously studied at degree level, I faced the daunting task of my dissertation with some dread. My lack of experience meant I genuinely had no idea what made a good research project or how to go about writing one. The gravity of the task began to dawn upon me as I read other dissertations and the wide variety of personal styles and structures they contained.

The journey which I then embarked upon was both an academic and personal process of discovery. I chose to investigate Police Officers' Perceptions of Institutional Racism within their Constabularies, a sensitive and challenging subject area within policing. However, I am pleased that I had the full support of my Chief Constable to conduct the research.

Understanding the history and significant events of institutional racism in policing was immensely personal to me and therefore the many hours spent on my dissertation never felt like a chore. In fact, knowing that my research could increase the knowledge and understanding of such a highly debated topic, and could lead to improvements in how the police service operates felt like a privilege.

Pleasingly, my research is now being used to inform and shape my organisation's diversity, equality and inclusion strategy, which seeks to improve recruitment, retention and progression of BAME staff. I feel now that, beyond the obvious academic requirements of what a dissertation should structurally contain, a good dissertation is one that is written with passion and personality. Completing this research project has opened my eyes to new possibilities, potentially PhD research, and also showing how research can inform policy and practice, having a real impact on peoples' lives.

Mike Periera, MSc Crime & Community Safety: Evidence Based Policing graduate, Suffolk Constabulary

justice; for example, we saw in **section 21.3** that many key theories and important studies were mainly from white, reasonably privileged men in the western world. These issues have the chance to be addressed as today's generation of student researchers brings more diversity to criminological research.

This can result in both new insights and new ways of spreading research findings; possibilities for your discipline to engage with society more widely and to inform and interest the public in issues of crime and justice—not to mention opportunities to impact on criminal justice practices and the criminal justice system itself.

32.3 What makes a good student research project?

There are many things that contribute towards a good student research project. In this section we attempt to pull several of these factors together into some clear tips and guidance. However, it should always be remembered that what makes a good research project will vary from university to university, so you should pay close attention to the guidance you receive from your lecturers and tutors—you will almost always be given written guidance, which will often be saved on your VLE (virtual learning environment), but there may also be a lecture on what is expected of you. Make yourself aware of the essential components that are required for your specific dissertation or research project and refer closely to any template that your institution provides.

Use all available help

If your project is to be effective, the single most important tip is to take advantage of learning from others and utilise all available help from the people and places around you on your course. It is easy to feel alone whilst researching as it involves plenty of solitary work, but this can be overcome with support at your institution. Opportunities to discuss ideas and problems with your tutors, supervisors, and fellow students should always be taken. In **Conversation 32.2**, we hear some of the advice that Stuart Agnew gives his criminology students, and elsewhere in this chapter you will find many accounts from past criminology students explaining what helped them through their research.

CONVERSATIONS 32.2

What makes a good research project?

with **Stuart Agnew**

There are five key things that underpin a successful student research project.

Focus

It is very easy to allow yourself to be diverted from the specific research questions that you have set. As you are working through the research project, keep referring back to these to ensure you have not lost focus. Do your research questions flow from the literature review? Is the method you are taking appropriate to answer these

questions? Will your choice of data collection tool (interview schedule/questionnaire) enable you to ask the correct questions that will help answer the research questions?

Evaluate

A good research project does not only evaluate the data that is collected but is evaluative throughout. For example, in the literature review can you explain what gaps in knowledge exist in the topic? Can you justify the approach you are taking in terms of the methods adopted and the data collection tools together with the analytical framework you will use? For example, a former student of mine wanted to explore Youth Justice practitioners' views on Youth Justice reforms and believed that semi-structured interviews would be most appropriate. He managed to justify this approach by explaining the limitations other approaches would have had on the study.

Depending on the type of research project you are conducting, you may have a separate results and discussion section. If that is the case, ensure that you report your findings and provide an analysis of what it means, keeping this analysis aligned to your overarching research questions.

Integrate

Although it is good to see each section of your research project as a separate task, they need to read as a coherent paper. So, make sure each section leads naturally into the next. It is important that your discussion section not only critically evaluates your data but that this is discussed in relation to the themes you identified earlier in the literature review. Research projects that integrate key elements from the literature review with the findings are amongst the most successful.

Conclude

Ensure you provide a conclusion to your research project. This is where you bring everything together: initial aims, research questions, approach taken, your findings and discussion. Have you been able to answer all research questions? It is ok if you have no conclusive findings—most research does not!—but you should acknowledge this in your conclusion. However, have you engaged with the whole research process? Go back through your final report ensuring everything is covered, if not, this is the time to add it.

Reflect

Many research projects would like you to reflect on your learning journey. This is a good practice to develop and will stand you in good stead for a professional workplace. This is less about the specifics of the research project and more about your perceptions of what worked, what could have been done differently and what have you learned about yourself as a researcher; it is not about identifying flaws or weaknesses, but rather acknowledging what has been achieved within the constraints available. You gain the most from self-reflection when you are honest with yourself.

If you take the above into consideration, regularly engage with your research project supervisor and take on board their guidance, you will be in a strong position to produce a high quality research project.

Stuart Agnew, Associate Professor (Criminology), University of Suffolk

Plan properly

Good planning is essential for producing a good project, and this in itself requires time! So make sure you put aside some hours to consider how you will invest your time. We'll consider the usefulness of having a full plan later in this chapter, in **section 32.10**, as several stages in the process need to be done before you can draw one up.

Break new ground

The first things to think about in the early planning stage of your project are how you are going to show that your topic, and the aim of your research, are breaking new ground. This is really important, as being able to clearly justify why your project is new will help others to understand its value. 'Breaking new ground' might sound daunting, but this requirement can be fulfilled simply by ensuring that your research offers a slightly different perspective on an issue or is conducted in a slightly different place or context to those of existing studies. You will be able to make such claims after doing an appropriate literature review (see **section 32.5**). Be warned, however, that ambition for researching new things must be balanced with realism: whatever you decide to do must be achievable within your project's time frame.

Ensure your findings are valid and reliable

Your project will be a success if its findings are valid and reliable. We discussed both **concepts** in **Chapter 4** but, as a reminder, valid findings are those that are accurate and measure what they say they are measuring; they require honesty, protection against influences such as bias and chance, and the use of a suitable research method. The need for **reliability** refers to the repeatability of a research finding; whether there is enough consistency in your findings to make it likely that other researchers using your methods and approaches in similar settings would attain broadly similar results. This is a crucial benefit if researchers are seeking generalisable, universally applicable explanations for behaviour and recommendations for potentially effective responses. Both concepts are important in order to ensure that your research is taken seriously, and you should keep them in mind from the early planning stages of your project.

It is important to note that a measure can be reliable but might lack **validity**; think about a broken speedometer in a car: if it is consistent in its mistakes its data can be reliable, but it will not be valid if it is an inaccurate measure of your car's speed. This point is usefully expanded by Clark et al. (2019) in their consideration of undergraduate research projects where the researchers interview people already known to them. There are several threats to the accuracy of these views, such as the interviewees telling you what they think you want to hear or them not telling you everything as they assume you already know how they feel. This does not mean such research cannot be done, but you have to acknowledge these limitations.

You can test the validity of your findings through a process called **triangulation**, depicted in **Figure 32.2**. We introduced this process in **Chapter 4** and saw that it involves using data collected through other methods to test or develop research findings. Triangulation is more generally associated with qualitative research but, regardless of your type of research, reading about how it is done by other researchers will benefit the quality of your project. It will show you the varied options for supporting the accuracy of your project and strengthening the quality of your findings. The accepted possibilities are:

- data triangulation (using different types of data on the same topic);
- theoretical triangulation (using different theories to investigate the same topic);
- methodological triangulation (using different methods for collecting data on the same topic); and
- investigator triangulation (using different researchers to collect data on the same topic).

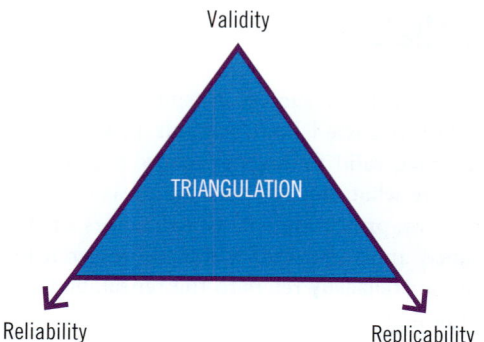

Figure 32.2 You can test the validity of your findings through a process called triangulation

Use creative research methods

The best student projects do not always have to follow the traditional structure of a dissertation—although how far this applies to you will depend on your university. Today, many tutors see overly formal, academic writing as restricting students' individuality and therefore will allow other new ways of carrying out a project. Such opportunities enable you to shine and show your creativity. This is not a case of being creative for the sake of it because, as we will see later in this chapter, visual research and other creative methods can be the best way of answering the research question.

Apply your usual essay-writing skills

When faced with the need to complete a dissertation or other similar research project, you may feel overwhelmed by the seeming size of the task before you. However, these fears can be reduced by recognising the many similarities between a dissertation and the other forms of coursework you have already done to reach this stage. It might help to see the dissertation as an extended essay. It may be three or four times longer than those you normally produce, and you may get to choose the topic, but it is still just another piece of academic work and the academic principles are the same:

- you will still need to collect primary data or analyse **secondary data** (or a combination of the two);
- you will still need to manage the different forms of information you collect and create a logical and coherent argument for the question or **hypothesis** you have chosen to investigate;
- your hypothesis, although written yourself, is still a statement of a possible relationship between two variables (that is, the things you are measuring), and likely written in an 'if . . . then' format ('If a person has been the victim of crime then they are less supportive of alternatives to imprisonment').

In some ways, doing a good research project can actually be *easier* than a conventional essay as some of the sources you will be expected to use will include data you have collected yourself; the greater the effort you make in your data collection, the more issues you will have to critically evaluate, and the better the opportunity to display your criminological skill.

The main difference between a research project and a normal essay is its size and more distinct components. In the rest of this chapter we will provide practical advice for approaching these components and stages, discussing:

- choosing a research topic;
- reviewing the literature around that topic (to inform your research itself, and in order to complete a literature review);
- choosing the research strategies that will be most appropriate for your topic and aims;
- collecting the data;
- analysing the data;
- writing up the research, including disseminating the findings.

In our final sections, we look at how to plan your project (working out how you'll complete it within the time frame and how you'll communicate your findings) and the ethical and legal considerations you need to bear in mind when conducting research.

32.4 Choosing your research topic

Choosing your research topic can be one of the hardest challenges. The freedom you have for choosing your topic means it may be the first time in your education where you are completely in charge; this might sound great, but having this power can be overwhelming if you normally rely on being directed on what you study. However, many parts of this book have been designed to help you to take this control.

For example, **Chapter 1** looks at the 'triad of criminology'. The triad approach is based on defining, explaining, and responding. This means your research project could be based on a topic that seeks to:

- *Define* the extent and nature of crime: are you aware of new things being criminalised or decriminalised?
- *Explain* the influences on crime: are there new research findings out there that interest you?
- *Respond* to crime through the criminal justice system and crime prevention strategies: have new initiatives been implemented that you wish to research?

The 'triad of criminology' structure can be applied to any criminological issue you encounter. For instance, lets apply it to the topic of cybercrime (covered in **Chapter 6** and, through a transnational lens, in **Chapter 14**): If 'exploring' is your preference then it is important to ask fundamental questions about the nature of cybercrime: what it actually is, what it includes and excludes, how it is measured, and the reliability of these measurements—any of these questions could provide your topic. If 'explaining' cybercrime is of more interest, you could look to the key criminological theories for help: can any of the theories we discussed in **Part 3** provide you with a framework? How about looking at it from a feminist perspective (see **Chapter 11**)? Alternatively, if 'responding' to crime is where you feel your passion rests, you could investigate how cybercrime or other offending behaviour is being responded to: your research could assess the work of the police, the courts, the CPS (all covered in **Chapter 24**), or the services provided by organisations like Victim Support—see **Chapter 7** on victimology and **Chapter 8** on hate crime for the kinds of stories and intersectional issues that might be missed in responses to cybercrime.

Whilst in this book we tend to see the three aspects of the triad as part of a 'continuum of crime' rather than separate entities, appreciating these three broad features of criminology can still guide you in your choice of research area.

As we've mentioned, other chapters in this book might also help to inspire your topic, as they have provided you with detailed knowledge of the extent, nature, and distribution of crime. For example, in **Part 3** we considered the usefulness of the best-known criminological theories; if you think back to each of these theories (classicism/neoclassicism in **Chapter 15**, positivism in **Chapters 16** and **17**, critical criminological theories in **Chapter 18**, and realist theories in **Chapter 20**), are you interested in their different methods of research? Contemplating which of these theoretical backgrounds you would prefer to use in your quest to advance the knowledge base in criminology may seem a very simple thing to do, but it engages you with the discipline and could narrow down the range of topics open to you. You may also want to look back at some of the Conversations features we have included throughout the book. For example, think about how David Baker chose to investigate the issue of death after police contact after becoming passionate about the topic (**Conversations 7.1**). Is there a topic you feel strongly about that you can turn into a research project? The activity in **What do you think? 32.1** is designed to help you reflect on and refine these ideas.

As well as browsing the chapters of this book for inspiration, thinking about your project from one of the following 'angles' might be a useful starting point to help

> ## WHAT DO YOU THINK? 32.1
>
> ### Finding the inspiration for your project
>
> If you feel at a loss in deciding what to research, take some time to reflect on what you have thought about your studies so far. A great strategy is to set yourself a time limit of ten minutes and, on a blank piece of paper (or even your phone), list the five things that have interested you the most. These could be large or small topics, specific readings, or small parts of lectures and seminars that really connected with you—things that represent the 'best bits'. Writing a sentence or two about why you found these to be so interesting will help you focus on the specifics. Next, pick the one of these five ideas that inspires you the most, and apply the 'triad of criminology' to really develop the direction that you could take this idea in. Discussing the topics with your course mates might also help you see new angles for approaching the subject. This might lead to a 'bingo' moment, or it might lead you to discard the idea in favour of another on your list—but this is all part of the process.

you focus in on the area of criminology that most interests you:

- a 'new frontier' of crime;
- a locally inspired topic;
- a personally inspired topic;
- an employability inspired topic.

We will discuss each of these themes in this section. If, at the end of this section, you are still unsure what topic to choose, then the best course of action is to take advantage of the staff expertise available to you and talk it through with your supervisor.

A topic inspired by 'new frontiers' of crime

This book's New frontiers features can help with your choice of topic as all of them highlight future challenges for the discipline of criminology. They can justify the relevance of your project and help you to break new ground. So, if you are feeling devoid of ideas, spend some time reviewing these features (you can use the exercise in **What do you think? 32.1** to help). Similar ideas could also be acquired by searching recent issues of the academic journals subscribed to by your institution, as these will highlight current topics of interest to criminological researchers. Help is also available from searching the websites of academic publishers to discover the latest books being published in the field. These different sources of guidance can be reinforced by advice from the lecturers at your institution and your lecture notes and seminar work.

A locally inspired topic

A research topic could be something that produces knowledge that might be in the interests of your community. There are likely to be many organisations capable of providing a topic area, such as social enterprises, charities, hospices, food banks, etc. They might be running community initiatives that, for example, seek to help people who have offended or victims of crime and antisocial behaviour. This sort of project can investigate their impact and would work well with the 'responding to crime' part of criminology's triad. Often these initiatives seek to reduce low-level crime and antisocial behaviour by implementing changes like improved street lighting or other safety measures. More serious examples also exist, such as the so-called plastic knife scheme in Nottinghamshire where the police offered blunt knives to domestic abuse victims for their protection (BBC, 13 June 2019)—see **Figure 32.3**. A similarly controversial example was the purchase of water cannons by Boris Johnson when he was Mayor of London in response to the London riots of 2011. The cannons were declared unlawful, meaning they were never used and were subsequently sold at a loss of £300,000 to public funds (*Daily Mail*, 20 November 2018). These high-profile

Figure 32.3 Local crime-prevention schemes, like the blunt knives offered to domestic abuse victims in Nottinghamshire, could be a source of inspiration for your research project

Source: Nottinghamshire Police

examples could inspire a variety of projects, such as financial expenditure in the criminal justice system or measuring views from criminal justice professionals and samples of the public.

If you feel that you want to do a project investigating these kinds of initiatives, make sure you read **Chapters 25 and 26** of this book, as they take you through the theoretical and the evidence base for the crime prevention agenda. Combining this knowledge with being aware of what is going on in your local community in terms of current policing priorities or community safety plans will really help in creating an effective project. You can do this by following your local police force and other criminal justice organisations on social media, and by reading your local newspapers. This could be extended by approaching your local MP as they will hold open meetings—known as surgeries—with members of the public to discuss local issues and concerns. If this resulted in written communication, an official House of Commons letterhead or email signature would make an impressive item for your project's appendix!

A personally inspired topic

One of the joys of studying as a criminologist is the chance to research things that are personally meaningful. It is very common to find undergraduate study difficult, but with patience and persistence, moments of discovery can occur and powerful moments of understanding can arise where you make clear connections to use your learning (see **Conversations 32.3**).

CONVERSATIONS 32.3

Developing a research interest in criminology

with **Dr Marian Duggan**

Much of my research has centred on feminist theory, and this interest was sparked for me by the specific gender-based modules I took on my undergraduate degree. I recall sitting in class discussing feminist readings that theorised gendered experiences of sexism, victimisation, fear, and harm. Without initially realising it, we gradually migrated from discussing 'them' (the women in the research) to 'us' (the women in the seminar). Suddenly, we were engaging with the research to theorise our *own* experiences in a way we hadn't been able to do so before; our exposure to this literature furnished us with the language, evidence, and critiques we needed to better articulate our perspectives. The importance of research, and the powerful impact it could have, became abundantly clear to me in those discussions and from that point onwards I felt I had found my passion, both personally and professionally.

Soon after, I was lucky enough to be given the opportunity to do an independent, desk-based research project on the harms of 'Battered Women's Syndrome' prior to my final year dissertation project on 'Rape Victims and Legal Discourse'. The autonomy I was given to undertake these in-depth investigations harmonised various components of my degree whilst allowing me the freedom to shape my own developing area of academic interest.

The level of engagement I felt from doing those projects gave me the confidence I needed to progress onto postgraduate study, where I honed my feminist researcher skills under the mentorship of several other inspiring tutors. I broadened my Master's research to address sexuality-based victimisation in light of legislative changes concerning homophobic hate crime, which was a prominent issue at the time. This led on to my PhD research, which was one of the first academic studies to highlight the socio-legal complexities of addressing lived experiences of homophobia in Northern Ireland.

I've been actively engaged in researching victimisation on the basis of gender and/or sexuality for over a decade now and am still hugely passionate about this topic. My engagement with a range of people working in the community voluntary and charitable sectors regularly reminds me of this power differential and demonstrates the importance of pursuing truly purposeful research activity. For me, this has included: writing articles for relevant community publications on the issues I'm researching to disseminate this information to a wider audience; speaking at a range of community events with a view to exploring a combined academic-practitioner approach to effecting positive change; and liaising closely with the police with regards to effective community interaction and sensitive approaches to awareness-raising which acknowledges and avoids 'victim-blaming'.

My career direction to date has been inspired by my undergraduate studies and the research projects I've completed during it. The scholars I studied and the fantastic tutors I had taught me that I can bring about positive change by pursuing research in this area. If you feel a keen interest in a particular area of your studies I would strongly encourage you to explore it further through a research project—it could be the start not only of a great project, but a fulfilling career path.

Dr Marian Duggan, Criminology Lecturer, University of Kent

Such personal interest might come from your desire to know more about issues concerning crime or justice that are experienced by your own ethnic group or demographic; characteristics such as age, gender, and education level. If you have been a member of a social group then finding out whether they have been similarly affected might stimulate your research interests. Researching issues in areas where you have lived or worked might also provide a meaningful topic.

Whilst personal experiences can lead to effective projects, if you follow this option then you need to continually remind yourself to be objective as your inquiries can be clouded by personal bias. This can be protected against by securing your project's validity and reliability, as discussed in **section 32.3**.

An employability inspired topic

Another motivation for a topic could come from choosing something with potential to help your future career. Your research has the potential to strengthen your employability in any field, even those that are not directly criminology-related, as having successfully completed a research project will be evidence of your project management abilities, communication, problem-solving, and enterprise—as well as your skills as a criminologist. Your research could also increase your business and customer awareness for the particular type of employment or role you are interested in—for example, a topic that provides an insider's view of working in the justice sector would be an extra opportunity to learn about the type of work you might like to do in the future from professionals in the field.

So, if your career interests include police or probation work, why not investigate their current priorities or initiatives. This could be focused on your local area, and if you have a term-time address that differs from your home one then you have double the opportunities for this kind of investigation, meaning you could acquire data from both areas and compare your results with the national position. If you are creative with your approach, such as by using the multiple and mixed research methods that were considered in **Chapter 4**, you could get the chance to study in-depth some of the realities of working in the criminal justice system. This approach is also considered later in this chapter. To do research with an employability focus, you do not necessarily need special access agreements or inside contacts in a justice organisation as much of the data and reports on the work of the system are publicly available online. This could apply to any organisation you are interested in working for, but if enhancing your employability for a policing career is your main concern, then local community safety plans contain current priorities that you might want to investigate.

Developing your topic into a research question

These four inspirational pointers for choosing your topic show the extensive choice you have in a discipline as engaging as criminology. But when choosing your topic, it's also important to be realistic about whether you will be able to complete your project within the given time frame.

The best way to achieve this is to ensure the topic isn't too general, and this will be more likely if you treat the process of choosing your area and possible research questions as an evolving process that refines your ideas: First, you identify your broad area of interest—say, youth justice—then narrow this down into something more focused—say, a particular element of youth justice policy.

Taking these steps will lead you comfortably into the creation of your topic's specific research question. This process is critically important to your project as, whilst your topic area is certainly something you are going to investigate, your project is actually about your investigation into the question you have set. Note that more than one research question or hypothesis can be allowed and your supervisor is best placed to advise on whether this would be manageable. It can also be appropriate to have aims and objectives rather than an explicit question and your university course will make it clear whether this is permissible.

The creation of good questions takes time and is another part of your project where feedback and talking with people can be so beneficial. You need to allow a decent period of time for this as good research questions are rarely, if ever, the first ones we think of; so be prepared for another cycle of work where you go back to revisit and edit them. Your research supervisor is the person you need to convince that your question is appropriate and there are various things you can do to get this approval.

A good research question is one that helps you, and other people, to learn new things about your topic area. It enables you to think and act like a criminologist and to investigate issues that, until your project, have been neglected by research. This sounds great but you must recognise that you can only know about such neglect if you are familiar with the academic literature in your area. Therefore, this is one of those points in your project where you can be simultaneously doing more than one stage—combining your research question choice with your literature review. The more you read, the more your question, and any follow-up questions, might change—and it is through this review that you can show the relevance of your project. This combination of your literature review with your question creation can be one of the most difficult parts of a project; it is overcome by being well organised and reviewing the literature as advised in the next section.

To get approval from your supervisor, make sure your question meets the following criteria.

- It is clearly written and grammatically correct.
- It is an answerable question, meaning it can be answered from a theoretical or **empirical** position.
- It is connected to the academic literature.
- It takes account of the data you will have. For example, you may want to do the kind of research mentioned earlier in this chapter with regard to the relationship between England football matches and reports of domestic abuse (Kirby et al., 2014); but how likely is it you will be able to acquire the required data? Instead, a qualitative project with participants who work in the area could provide you with a similar but different research question.
- Your question needs to interest people such as academics and professionals, so if you don't find it interesting, there's little chance others will.

Once you have a provisional question or title in mind, your supervising tutor will be able to let you know whether it is a manageable project in terms of the resources available to you. This will ensure your project avoids excessively broad topics as the narrowing down of a proposed topic area is very common in research supervisors' feedback. It is likely you will want to use sub-questions as these are extra questions that can add focus to the research question.

32.5 Reviewing academic literature

Being able to review the academic literature on a topic is an important skill to develop, as once mastered it will help improve your marks in almost all of your assessments, from essay writing to presentations, though especially in a research project or dissertation. Such literature includes research articles in criminology journals, chapters in edited books, or indeed entire academic monographs. It also goes outside academic literature as it can include research and data from official sources, like reports published by branches of the government.

Most criminology projects and dissertations have to contain a detailed review of the relevant literature on the issue being investigated and the variables in the study (see **Chapter 4** for the discussion of the different types of variables in research). As with other aspects of your project, your institution may have issued guidance on the content and format of your literature review, and your supervisor or subject librarian will be able to provide assistance if you have any questions. You can complete your literature review when you come to write up your research, but you will need to undertake the exploration phase before you begin gathering your data as your reading might inform your research topic and question(s); you will also need to refer back to the information you gather throughout the project as your written-up report should demonstrate how the literature influenced the direction of your research. Reading the other researchers' literature reviews will inform you about developments in your topic area, how they may have been influenced by research and scholarship, and of any disagreements between criminologists on a particular topic. If you read them during your planning phase, you will also see how this information needs to be organised. Most importantly, an effective literature review will give coherence to your project as it will identify gaps in the current knowledge base and highlight issues that need researching—openings your project intends to fill. It can influence your choice of methodology as well as setting the scene for your project's findings, as advised in **Conversations 32.2**.

We will now walk through the steps involved in completing a literature review.

Create a statement of purpose

A useful first step is to create either a review question for the literature or have a statement of purpose for your research. This question or statement should specify the key words for your study as this will break your topic down into essential elements. These terms need to be based on your research title or question, but they do not have to be identical to it; for example, they do not have to argue for a particular position or opinion. Having this direction will ensure your review is not too broad and, if needed, additional focus could come from adding particular places or professions to your searches.

Find relevant literature

Now, using key words, questions, or statement of purpose, you should find examples of existing literature reviews in your area. These can be found by searching for your key words in your library website or a journal database, along with the words 'literature review'.

Your literature review must be balanced so you will need to include both academic books and journals, and to decide whether your review will also include official documents and other sources. The balance also involves ensuring that if you are researching a particular argument or debate, you include literature from both points of view. You will often find that there is a huge amount of literature out there, so to ensure that you find and review only the literature and studies most relevant to your project, you need to be strategic. One way of doing this is to create criteria for searching the literature. These can come from your research interests and mean you are only reviewing publications within a certain time period or geographical location, or studies with only certain types of participants. Reading abstracts will help you with this process as they are a quick way of familiarising yourself with the different stages of completed research.

The question of how many sources are needed for your review is understandably common, but it is not one that can be answered with a precise number that is suitable for all projects. It will depend on the needs of your research. As a bare minimum, you should use all of the important sources suggested in your research modules and any others that your supervisor has advised you to read. The further reading lists at the end of each chapter in this book will also provide starting points for useful additional sources on each topic. Whilst you are doing this reading, it is essential to remember the purpose of your review: rather than a descriptive account, your review should be *assessing* and *analysing* the literature. You should be especially focused on identifying limitations within it as these deficiencies provide the rationale for your project.

Plan your reading schedule

As reading all the literature you've gathered can be a very time-consuming part of your project, you need to carefully plan your available time to allow you to read and incorporate it; you should start as early as possible and try to get through at least a couple of sources per week. This can be intimidating but is overcome through effective organisation where you take notes on everything you read.

Review the literature

To produce an effective literature review you will need to keep careful records of what you have read. As you are reading each document in your literature list, you should aim to record your thoughts on the following:

- What is the author's academic reputation in your topic area (the importance of your topic can be shown if prominent authors have written on it)?
- Does the author seem to have a particular bias?
- Are opposing positions discussed or ignored?
- Do these views contradict your ideas (literature like this can strengthen your work by showing your awareness of alternative arguments)?

In academic reading, satisfaction comes from detailed discussion of key sources and a comprehensive bibliography that makes you proud when you see it at the end of your project. This can only be achieved through accurate referencing, so don't forget to record these details in your records (the referencing section in **section 32.8** provides guidance on this).

Revise your research question

Your literature review should focus your topic and questions, helping you to avoid overly general project topics such as 'reoffending rates' which would result in you gathering too much data and finding it difficult to analyse. The awareness you gain from following your review's statement of purpose will guide you towards more specific issues—for example, in the case of reoffending rates, 'the Female Offender Strategy', 'stigmatisation', and 'Community Payback' might arise during your reading. This, in turn, would lead you to form a more focused research question, such as, 'Discuss the effect of Community Payback on female offenders'. As you can see, an initial interest in recidivism has now evolved into something more answerable. This kind of question will enable you to show genuine specialist knowledge and understanding of the published material in the issue you are investigating. It will show focus and vision in your research, and will provide you with additional questions to guide your investigations—for instance, in this example, additional questions could include sub-questions to do with the types of community sentences, the types of providers of these sentences, or the effects these differences have on their criminal justice functions.

Write up your findings

When writing up your findings on the literature, take time to organise your review with a clear structure as this gives confidence in its credibility; you have the freedom to come up with this structure and common ways of organising it. For example, this could be categorising sources on factors such as their themes or their methodology.

You must avoid writing a general description of the literature and instead provide a critical commentary that clearly explains why your project is needed. Your review must work in partnership with your methodology section so the philosophy underpinning your research and choice of methods, which we will consider in the next section, needs to be reflected here. The literature's influence on your methodology, such as inspiring the desire for a quantitative study, needs to be made clear. This structure will help you justify your project by providing you with informed reasons for doing it—such as providing new data where it is needed or studying an area with a new and more appropriate methodology.

32.6 Choosing your research strategy

It is important to choose the right overall strategy or approach for your project, particularly as you will be required to explain and justify these kinds of decisions in the writing-up stage. In this section we discuss your options in terms of your overall research strategy—that is, whether you want to use **quantitative research**, **qualitative research**, or **mixed methods research**—and how to decide on the appropriate theoretical background for your project.

Will your research be quantitative or qualitative?

At this point it is likely you have already been thinking about the kind of data you want to use in your project but, if not, you need to decide whether quantitative or qualitative research would be more appropriate for your project, or whether a mix of both will be most appropriate. These strategies are often distinguished by their associations with words and numbers, respectively, and although this contrast is somewhat oversimplified, it can be a helpful way to remember their key differences.

There may be requirements on your course to use a particular type of research; if so, this will be made clear by your institution. If you have a free choice, begin thinking by reading **Controversy and debate 32.1**, which examines the arguments made by proponents of quantitative and qualitative criminological research.

Quantitative research methods

Quantitative methods tend to have an **objectivist ontology**, meaning they assume the thing being researched exists and is discoverable, and a **positivist epistemology**, meaning it can be discovered by applying the methods of the natural sciences. This results in the researcher taking a more detached viewpoint, as opposed to the qualitative researcher who seeks immersion in their field of study. This type of research generates and uses data that is numerical or countable. This approach is criticised by many criminologists (as we saw in **Controversy and debate 32.1**), particularly when it is used to promote policy-orientated research. They contest the validity of its findings, supposedly produced 'under the guise of a social-scientific cloak of objectivity and neutrality, not least of all because there is no such thing as an "ideology-free zone"' (Chamberlain, 2013: 50). If you believe your project can overcome such objections, these strong opinions are a reminder to protect your research against your own influence as a researcher.

As **Controversy and debate 32.1** indicated, there are various criticisms of quantitative methods—most notably the lack of 'meaning' they convey. However, some people regard the evidence that quantitative research produces as more persuasive, thanks to the belief that it is objective and therefore detached from the views of the researcher. It enables you to produce statistical evidence, which, as we saw in **Chapters 5** and **6**, often makes good headlines, but hopefully your ABC mindset will mean you think more about the truth of such claims. If you have read **Chapter 5**, you will know that statistics do not tell the whole story; this is where quantitative methods fall down against qualitative methods, which produce deeper and richer data, even though it is more specific to the context and tends to be less generalisable. However, statistics can provide useful starting points, so take advantage of their online accessibility and their frequent use in many parts of the criminal justice system; this combination offers opportunities that, until the growth of the internet, were beyond most researchers. A quantitative strategy can also be a good choice in an undergraduate project because the type of data it produces can be less time-consuming to analyse (see **section 32.8**).

Qualitative research methods

The driving force behind qualitative research is the desire to see the world through the eyes of the people in the research which means it is more open-ended. This can be a useful quality particularly where the range of potential

CONTROVERSY AND DEBATE 32.1

Quantitative vs qualitative research

The views of the eminent criminologist, Roger Hood, expressed at the start of this century, highlight the fundamental debate within the discipline between the merits of quantitative and qualitative data collection:

> [Q]uite a number of criminologists have joined 'the anti-numbers brigade'. They regard crime as an entity that cannot be counted in any of its definitions or forms . . . They insist that valid data can be obtained only through a 'qualitative' appreciation of the sentiments, actions and 'meanings' attached to actions by the participants.
>
> Such work has its place, but it is not always appropriate to the issue being researched. Nor can it provide the kind of evidence that would be regarded as convincing proof by those who require reliable, replicable observations, based on representative samples from which valid inferences can be drawn, before considering changing their policy or practices . . .
>
> Think of the impact that [medical] research has had on demonstrating the connection between smoking and lung cancer. That could not have been achieved through an 'appreciative account' of how smokers felt about their habit or viewed the effect of it on their health!
>
> (Hood, 2002: 165–6)

More recently, in the opening chapter of the sixth edition of *The Oxford Handbook of Criminology*, Paul Rock suggests that criminology has been 'a surprisingly lively and creative discipline', but is heading towards a future that may be negatively shaped by 'the manipulation of large data sets and a mushrooming of repetitive, profitable, quantitative, and readily assessable work in the service of the state' (2017: 50). Despite these diverging views, many researchers have been able to produce highly successful research with quantitative research—as can be seen throughout the various Conversations in this chapter.

Where do you sit within this argument? Can you see the merits of both sides—and what do you think Rock means when he refers to the 'repetitive, profitable' nature of quantitative research? Can you think of some examples of when qualitative research might be a more suitable option, and when a quantitative study would be more appropriate? What might be the drawbacks in each case?

---

material for investigation is extensive. Arguably, the only 'rule' about what constitutes qualitative research is the requirement for quantification, such as percentages and averages, to be completely absent (Clark et al., 2019: 107). (Though it is worth noting that, in practice, qualitative research often contains some elements of 'quasi-qualification', such as references to 'many' and 'most' (Clark et al., 2021).) It is a form of research based on the view that social phenomena and their meanings are constantly being constructed by people (**constructionism**), and guided by the principles of **interpretivism**, a research approach that tries to understand human behaviour by exploring individual experiences, perceptions, and meanings. (As we explained in **Chapter 22**, interpretivism can be contrasted with positivism—see **Figure 22.1** for the summary of the central characteristics of these two approaches.)

This type of research has traditionally used data that is textual, verbal, or sensory, but increasingly qualitative researchers are also examining media and visual content, thanks to the growing interest in the new frontier of **visual criminology** (Brown and Carrabine, 2017). This is a type of research that uses visual sources, like photographs and films, as an alternative to the more conventional methods. It offers prospects of research rich in interpretation of individual meanings and context as opposed to the more scientifically rigorous approach of quantitative research. However, this means its value can be questioned as it does not provide replicable findings that can be applied more widely to other settings.

A summary of the key differences between these two research approaches is provided by **Table 32.1**.

The mixed-methods approach

The mixed methods approach is an increasingly popular strategy within social research more widely (Clark et al., 2021), and also with criminology undergraduates. It has been defined as 'the systematic and rigorous bringing together of qualitative and quantitative research methods and data into a coherent whole, where this whole is greater than the sum of its individual component parts, in order to answer a central research question' (Heap and Waters, 2019: 15). This means your project has to have qualitative and quantitative parts, but they do not have equal attention; one of them can be more dominant if this is most appropriate for answering your research question. In this sense, mixed methods can be a pragmatic approach in

	Quantitative research	**Qualitative research**
Ontology	Objectivism	Constructionism
Epistemology	Positivism	Interpretivism
Data	Countable things, numerical values	Textual, visual material, sensory material
Standard methods of data collection	Surveys, questionnaires	Interviews, participant observation
Standard methods of data analysis	Univariate analysis Bivariate analysis Multivariate analysis	Discourse analysis Narrative analysis Thematic analysis
Approach	Deductive (theory → research)	Inductive (research → theory)
Standard research questions	'To examine the relationship between X and Y' (such as experience of victimisation and fear of crime). 'To test the hypothesis that there is a relationship between X and Y' (such as age and fear of crime).	'To explore perceptions of X' (policing, probation, prisons, etc.). 'To describe opinions of X' (policing, probation, prisons, etc.).

Table 32.1 The essential differences between quantitative and qualitative research

which your methods are determined by the needs of the research question rather than necessarily being led by a particular ontological or epistemological bias.

With a mixed methods approach, you collect both qualitative and quantitative data. You might, for example, use a survey to collect quantitative data about people's levels of trust in the police, then use interviews to acquire qualitative data from participants who showed a particularly low level of confidence in the police to find out more about their reasons. (You might want to look back at **Conversations 25.2** with Dr David Scott who explains how he used mixed methods to good effect in his research to learn more about the people in the criminal justice system.) The two components must complement each other, so you must have a clear reason for doing both types of research and you must give thought and attention to how you will integrate the data. Data integration is essential both during your analysis and when you come to write up your project—note the reference to a 'coherent whole' in Heap and Waters' (2019) definition.

Remember that it is your research question that determines your method and not the other way round, so whilst the mixed methods approach may seem interesting, that is not how you should think about it. We have seen that if your research questions have a focus on 'what' might be existing, then quantitative investigations could be more appropriate; whereas for 'why' questions, qualitative ones will be more suitable. Therefore, if your question(s) combine both 'what' and 'why', a mixed methods approach might work well. But collecting more data, or more types of data, will not necessarily result in a better research project and it is also important to be realistic and consider whether this approach could be achieved in your time frame. It requires high levels of organisation as well as good levels of knowledge and understanding of the stages in the research process. If you think a mixed methods approach is appropriate for your project and will help you answer your research question(s), we suggest discussing your ideas with your supervisor as early as possible.

Which method is best for you?

In **Figure 32.4** we summarise the sequence of steps in your research so far. It shows that you should not be definitive about your choice of methods until you reach this point. It maps the general order of stages and the process of narrowing down the focus of your project. But some stages, particularly between the research question and the literature review, could have arrows that go both up and down as you move between the stages and make adjustments, for example changing your research question in light of literature.

This sequence shows the work required before choosing your research methods; it shows you must have a clear reason for choosing them which cannot just be because they look good or seem easier. Even after you feel you have come to a decision, you need to consider three further things before you can be confident your project will be able to answer your research question or test your hypothesis:

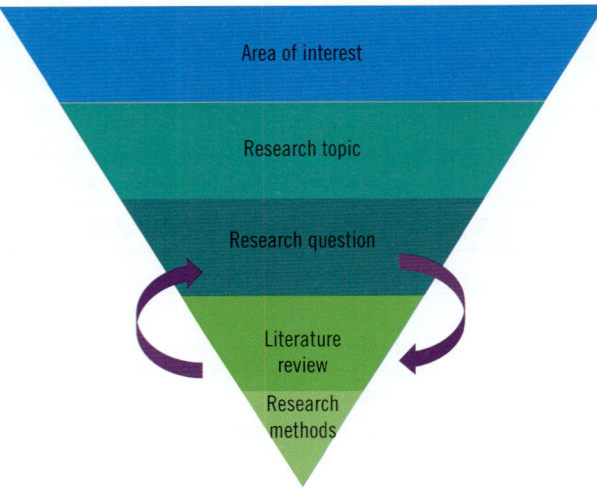

Figure 32.4 A summary of the research stages we have discussed so far shows that you should not be definitive about your choice of methods until you reach this point

the theoretical background to your project; your data collection methods; and your data analysis method.

Which theoretical background will you adopt?

You will already have thought about your theoretical approach in **section 32.4**, but now that you have completed a few stages of the research process, these thoughts need to result in final decisions. It is important to have the right theoretical background as this should ensure you choose the right method for your research. These backgrounds come from the different perspectives on what can and what should be researched in the academic discipline of criminology. **Figure 32.5** shows the four most common theoretical positions: classicism, positivism, criticalism (a broad term used here to refer to the various critical approaches, including feminism and critical race theory), and realism. You should decide which of these 'usual suspects' (or other theories) you will use as a framework for your research.

You will have to write in great detail about your chosen position beyond briefly explaining its relevance to your project but this is still an important decision as it will influence your subsequent data collection and analysis—you will integrate theory into your project by explaining the impact of your data and analysis. These kinds of choices are also made in 'professional' criminological research. For example, the Howard League's Commission on Sex in Prison (Stevens, 2020) recently outlined government preferences in criminal justice research. The researchers could only have access to prisoners if their study used quantitative methods, 'anchored in positivist epistemology and objectivist ontology, [and] overwhelmingly focused on the functional achievement and application of quantitative and technical competence' (2020: 458). This was at odds with the researchers' own positions and illustrates the contested nature of the research concepts of ontology and epistemology.

If you are still not sure which perspective is most applicable to your project, try the simple activity in **What do you think? 32.2** to help you to identify it.

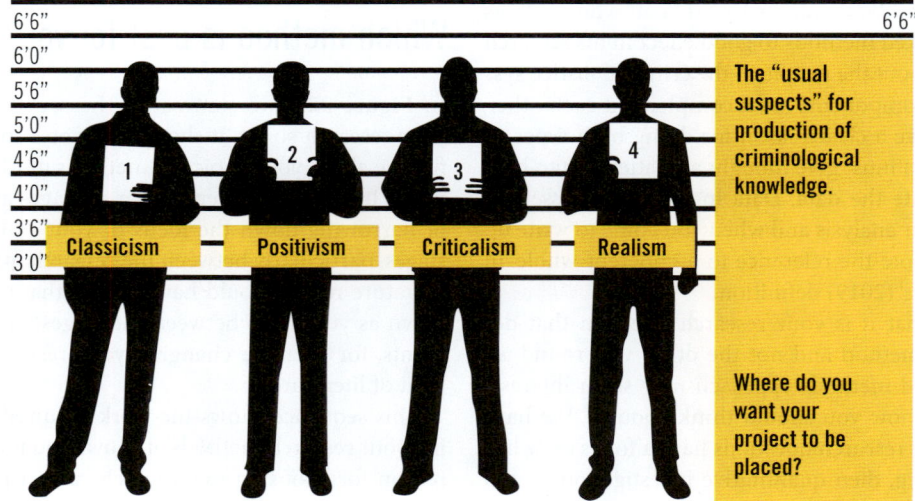

Figure 32.5 Where do you stand? You need to decide which of these 'usual suspects' (or other theories) you will use as a framework for your research

Source: By Skocko/Shutterstock

WHAT DO YOU THINK? 32.2

Choosing a theoretical background

By this stage you will likely have decided on some research questions, so read them through carefully and summarise them. These summaries will enable you to identify their unifying theme which will highlight your research perspective. Popular angles for criminology undergraduates can be questioning or applying a certain theory or researching a topic from a historical or theoretical standpoint, such as when you compare crime and justice in different periods of history.

Now, think about the quantitative/qualitative and the positivist/interpretivist debates we have discussed so far, and apply them to your project: what are the similarities between *your* research and the things you are investigating, and the research undertaken by 'the usual suspects'; that is, the classical, positivist, critical, or realist approaches? Remember that positivists and realists believe that objective research, untainted by the values of a researcher, is possible; therefore, they say criminological research should follow the customs and practices of research in the natural sciences. This view is rejected by the critical approach that does not believe a single shared reality can be discovered from research as it cannot be separated from the influence of the values of a researcher. It can be useful to picture yourself on a scale of these views, as in **Figure 32.5**; where would you choose to stand when placing your project?

To help you with this decision, imagine you want to research the extent of crime and antisocial behaviour in a particular location. A quantitative approach using official data might provide an answer, as could a qualitative one using perceptions of the area's residents. It is not unusual for these measures to differ with areas defined as 'high crime' by official statistics, but 'low crime' by the people who actually live there (Foster, 1995). This impact makes it important for you to have your own views on which is preferable for finding the 'truth'.

32.7 Collecting data

Just like when you write an essay, the data you use in your project can be acquired from either primary or secondary sources. Neither are automatically superior, and the type of data you collect will be determined by your theoretical and methodological approach and the needs of your research question, as well as by practical considerations (such as how much time you have). Your first choice is whether you want to use primary or secondary data (or a mixture of both) and, if you decide to collect your own data, your next choice is which method(s) you will use. To repeat the point we made in **section 32.1**, this chapter only provides an overview of the main considerations and the options available to you; you should refer to specialist research methods texts such as those listed in the **Further Reading** at the end of the chapter for detailed information about the pros and cons of each data collection method, and guidance on implementing it.

Primary and secondary data

Primary data means any material or information you gather from your own surveys, interviews, or observations. Secondary data is evidence or data that someone else has collected, and the use of it is quite common in quantitative research, as findings from other data sets can be tested.

If you are undertaking secondary analysis of quantitative data, the UK Data Archive at https://ukdataservice.ac.uk can be very useful. It is the UK's largest collection of social, economic, and population data resources; it is easy to register an account with them when you are in higher education, which gives you increased access to the collection. The archive goes back to the year *c.*440, so will help if your research has a historical angle; unsurprisingly the available sources for 'crime' increase considerably when contemporary times are included in the search. It includes the Crime Survey for England and Wales, plus the British Social Attitudes (BSA) survey and Understanding Society (formerly the British Household Panel Survey); these measures now have data sets covering several decades. In addition to national surveys, international measures such as the European Social Survey (ESS) can be helpful, plus the more irregular surveys such as the International Crime Victims Survey (ICVS) and the European Survey on Crime and Safety (EU ICS).

These large data sets can be the outcome of well-resourced studies with robust research methods, meaning that their findings can be more representative than those from one isolated researcher. Using such resources can be extremely helpful for assessing potential trends in an issue, and potentially they save you time at the data-collection stage; meaning you have more time for its analysis. However, this has to be balanced against the time it will take for you to find the data you are interested in.

Depending on your research question, the use of secondary data can also be appropriate for qualitative projects. This means your data collection could include books, journal articles, policy documents, and newspapers. Your ABC mindset will be essential for assessing the validity and reliability of this data and using the right theoretical background for your research will help you make these judgements.

Quantitative data collection methods

As we saw in **Table 32.1**, the standard research positions in quantitative studies are an ontology of objectivism and an epistemology of positivism. This means the research is based on the belief that the thing being researched can be measured objectively by a detached researcher. As such, rigour and structure are key to most quantitative methods as researchers want to ensure that they are replicable and repeatable. The main methods used in quantitative research are:

- **Questionnaire**—a form of survey where participants provide written (often typed) responses to written questions without the help of an interviewer. It can be completed online, via email, or (less commonly now) by post. Questionnaires may contain **closed questions** or **open-ended questions**, or a mixture of the two, but closed-ended questions are more common in a quantitative context.
- **Structured interview**—an interview conducted face to face, over the phone, or online (for example, via Zoom) following a set list of questions in a rigid format, known as an interview schedule. The aim is for interviewees to be questioned in as similar and consistent a way as possible, and for the data to be easy to collate for analysis, so questions are often closed (offering the interviewee a range of choices). This is also known as a standardised interview.
- **Structured observation**—often called systematic observation, this technique involves observing individuals or groups in a natural setting for a set amount of time, following rules (an observation schedule) which set out what the observer should be looking for and how they should record what they see. This method is less common than those above, especially in undergraduate research.

Another data collection method associated with this research strategy is quantitative **content analysis**, in which a researcher collects content that meets specific criteria (for example, news articles on a particular subject, from a particular type of publication, within a certain time frame) and counts things within it to produce quantitative data. We consider this in **section 32.8** because, as the name suggests, it is also a form of data analysis.

Qualitative data collection methods

We have seen that qualitative research has a very different take on how research should be conducted. Its ontology of constructivism and epistemology of interpretivism means that it uses data collection methods that allow the researcher to be closely involved and to see things through the eyes of the participants. As we discussed in **Chapter 4**, common qualitative methods include:

- **Semi-structured interview** or **unstructured interview**—interviews conducted face to face, over the phone, or online, which are more like conversations than the unstructured interview. In semi-structured interviews, there is an interview schedule but the interviewer does not have to follow it precisely or ensure consistency between participants: they can change the order of questions, expand on them, and ask extra follow-up questions. In unstructured interviews, the interviewer only has a brief set of prompts as opposed to a schedule of questions and the interviewee is fairly unconstrained. The interviewer might only ask one main question and then prompt or probe as necessary.
- **Focus group**—a form of interview conducted with a group of participants. The participants have quite a lot of control over how the discussion unfolds, but the researcher needs to consider what sorts of topics should be addressed during a session and how any questions should be asked. A moderator or facilitator steers the discussion and keeps it on track, intervening or using prompts where necessary.
- **Participant observation** or **non-participant observation**—again, this involves the researcher watching participants in a natural, real-world setting, but unlike in a structured observation, the researcher does not have to follow a set schedule in terms of what they observe, for how long, and how they record this data. In a participant observation, the researcher becomes part of the group or environment they are observing, and non-participant observations involve them watching the group from the outside. They can be either '**overt**' or '**covert**'; terms which refer to whether the researcher is open about what they are doing.

The latter minimises the researcher's influence on the setting but clearly has ethical implications.

You can also collect documents to use as data, analysing them through qualitative content analysis, but unlike the quantitative variety this approach is focused on the source rather than the method of collecting or analysing the data. Again, we consider it in the next section. Another option that you might want to consider and discuss with your supervisor is whether you want to stick to traditional methods or include creative data produced by your research participants. These could include films, digital stories, photos, paintings, graffiti, theatre performances, and written narratives. These methods provide data that result in different interpretations, such as that which can be found in the Photovoice method, which combines photography and focus group discussion (Fitzgibbon and Healy, 2019).

32.8 Analysing data

Just as your approach to collecting data will change depending on whether you are doing a qualitative or quantitative study, so too will the way you analyse it. There are lots of different methods you can use for analysing your data, and here we discuss those that will likely be the most relevant to your research project. Each of the methods in this section merit a full chapter on their own; in this chapter we simply skate over the main ways of analysing quantitative and qualitative data. Help and guidance on these different approaches will be provided in the 'research methods' modules on your course and by the specialist texts in this chapter's **Further Reading** (see, for example, **Figure 32.6**), and remember that you can always ask your supervisor and other lecturers in your department for help and advice on how best to approach data analysis.

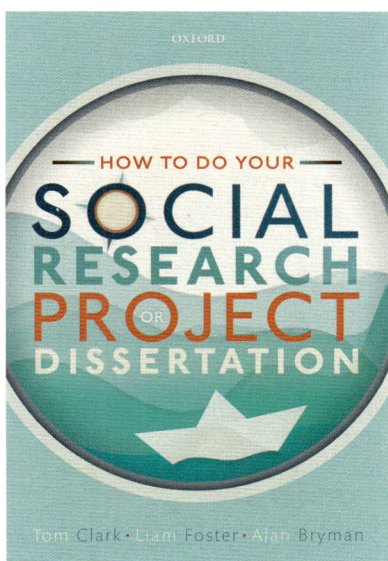

Figure 32.6 *How to do your Social Research Project or Dissertation* is an excellent resource for focused and efficient guidance on completing your dissertation or research project
Source: Oxford University Press

Quantitative data analysis

You have three potential options for approaching the analysis of quantitative data. Depending on your own preference and on the size of your data set, you can do this using Microsoft Excel or a dedicated data software program like SPSS. Using these programs will allow you to summarise and explain your data, for example by providing the averages and the figures for the mean, mode, and median. You will be able to claim specialist knowledge on your CV after gaining experience of this kind of software, but it can seem intimidating at first so we recommend dedicating time to familiarising yourself with the software then you will quickly become comfortable with it—as the experiences of the two students in **Conversations 32.4** show. To help you with this, we suggest accessing the video tutorials and quick reference sheets on SPSS provided within the online resources for *Bryman's Social Research Methods* (Clark et al., 2021).

There are three main options when it comes to performing quantitative data analysis. The first is **univariate data analysis**. This approach should be used when the research has a focus on one variable, so would be suitable for projects that, for example, research the frequency in which a particular offence has been reported to the police. It would allow you to test whether this frequency was evenly distributed across the year, and whether the number of offences you saw in your research was a close fit with what you expected or whether this number deviated significantly from your expectations (Clark et al., 2019: 259).

The second option is **bivariate data analysis**. This should be used when you are researching whether there is an association between two variables; such as fear of crime and gender. This type of analysis would allow you to assess whether the responses may have differed according to the gender of the respondents. **Multivariate data analysis** is the final option, and this explores the relationship between three or more variables in more detail. It is a difficult form of analysis and less commonly used in undergraduate

CONVERSATIONS 32.4

Being creative with SPSS: reflections from staff and students

with **Kate Strudwick**, **Amy Gibbons**, and **Hollie Skipp**

Kate Strudwick (KS): I have been teaching research methods for the last 20 years and one of the first hurdles I seek my students to overcome is to appreciate the value of quantitative research methods and in particular, tools such as SPSS. I have always purported that the aim of good research is about matching the research design to the choice of methods and apply to data.

Amy Gibbons (AG): My experience with SPSS began through using it for a quantitative research-based assessment in one of my research modules. I had never come across it before but had done statistical tests in my A-level psychology which were all done by hand, so it was such a relief to find out SPSS simply does it all for you!

Hollie Skipp (HS): I found it very effective for my research on topics such as fear of crime, bystander behaviour and victim satisfaction research. I used it for inputting data from a range of mediums that included questionnaires on Qualtrics, paper questionnaires and surveys.

KS: As lecturers, we seek to provide you with the skills, knowledge and ability to develop your critical thinking and importantly build upon these skills for you to demonstrate them in your academic studies and research projects.

AG: I was nervous at first as I had heard other students say it was difficult. But I found it very helpful to practice and play around with it for several weeks. I did this using very large data sets, so by the time I had acquired my own data for the assessment, it no longer felt intimidating. This gave me the confidence to use SPSS for a research project that aimed to explore young women's fear of terrorism and attitudes towards extremism and terrorism. I collected quantitative data using Qualtrics, which enabled over 100 responses to be acquired. Using SPSS to analyse this data was straight forward and so helpful to use, especially in terms of using the crosstabulation tables (that everybody calls 'crosstabs').

KS: Quantitative research methods have the potential to go beyond simple measurements. They can evaluate trends and help with explaining and defining. Knowing about different types of statistics and how common statistical tests such as 'Chi square tests' work can enable you as a researcher to expand your knowledge. Take advantage of all the help your course offers, as the quantitative research method and analysis through SPSS, allows you to explore a critical and informed analysis of your data.

AG: I learnt that crosstabs were an effective way of summarising the relationship between variables that have certain types of data. First I just used it to show my demographic data in the form of pie charts. Thanks to the options in SPSS, I could make it more personal and do things such as changing the colours in the charts, so they matched the poster I made for an exhibition at the end of the project.

I also used crosstabs to present data from my questions, such as 'does the UK take a zero-tolerance approach to terrorism'. Interestingly I found 45.9 per cent said yes, 26.6 per cent said no, and 21.1 per cent weren't sure; using crosstabs meant I could present this in a pie chart to clearly illustrate how people feel and think about contemporary issues like the fear of terrorism, which worked perfectly on the poster for the research that I produced at:

https://cpb-eu-w2.wpmucdn.com/blogs.lincoln.ac.uk/dist/a/8035/files/2018/09/Amy-Gibbons.pdf

HS: I agree, using SPSS can save so much time as you don't have to do your calculations from scratch. I also found it a saviour because it does the work for you! From using it regularly I was also able to create graphs, crosstabs and other things such as chi-squared tables. Chi-square is used to categorise data, which helps your analysis as you can use it to investigate the significance level between two variables.

AG: I found SPSS not as difficult as it may seem at first. I think it is a great employability skill to have and it increases your confidence as a student to know you are capable of this type of work.

HS: I'd say not to worry if you don't understand the process first time. But by repeatedly having a go, you can master it. I found talking it through with my fellow students most helpful, because if you can demonstrate to others how to use SPSS, it aids your learning and theirs.

KS: My experience of teaching both how to use SPSS and quantitative research methods has shown me that criminology students should not fear them! Knowing about their role, purpose, benefits, and importantly their limitations, is an asset to your skills, one where you can reap the benefits as a researcher.

Kate Strudwick (pictured right), Associate Professor in Criminology, University of Lincoln; Amy Gibbons (pictured left) and Hollie Skipp (pictured middle), BA Criminology undergraduates, University of Lincoln

research, so before proceeding with it you should consult your supervisor.

As we noted in **section 32.7**, the other main approach to analysing this form of data—which also determines how data is collected—is quantitative content analysis. This is an analytical method that quantifies content through predetermined categories that have been drawn up in a systematic and replicable manner. This means you have a system for sampling documents and also have one for the things you are counting. For example, researchers may precisely count the number of times the research issue is featured in a newspaper or measure the amount of space it is given. This approach was taken by Jones and Wardle (2008) into the publicity given to the infamous trial of Ian Huntley and Maxine Carr in 2003. To ensure the study included different types of newspapers, the researchers sampled qualitative content, such as photos, from *The Sun*, the *Daily Mail*, and *The Times* newspapers. Their quantitative analysis found photographs of Carr to be larger than those of Huntley and also appeared more often—despite the fact she was accused and convicted of a much less serious offence (conspiring to pervert the course of justice) than Huntley who was tried and convicted for the murders of two ten-year-old girls.

Qualitative data analysis

There are various options for undertaking qualitative analysis, and again you can use software to help you—in this context it is known as **CAQDAS** (Computer Assisted Qualitative Data Analysis Software). CAQDAS programs such as NVivo can save qualitative researchers a lot of time in helping them organise and retrieve their data, but it is worth being aware that it may not be worth your while to learn how to use it if you have a relatively small data set, as may be the case for a student project. If you do decide to use it, or experiment with using it, we would again suggest accessing the video tutorials and quick reference sheets on NVivo that are provided within the online resources for *Bryman's Social Research Methods* (Clark et al., 2021).

As we noted in **section 32.7**, options for conducting qualitative data analysis include qualitative content analysis, which unlike the quantitative equivalent refers to the source rather than the method of analysis. This involves analysing existing (as opposed to requested by you)

documents that are relevant to your research questions. These documents can be official (such as government reports or policy documents) or personal (such as diaries), and they can include visual material. Their validity is the key to this kind of research and you need to employ 'sensitizing devices' (Clark et al., 2019: 300) of authenticity, credibility, representativeness, and meaning to help you interpret the documents and think carefully about their validity. Otherwise, the main approaches to analysing qualitative data involve using discourse analysis, narrative analysis, thematic analysis, and grounded theory.

Discourse analysis

Discourse analysis has become increasingly popular in recent years and is more like a broad approach than a 'method' of data analysis since there is no single agreed formula for doing it: it involves collecting and analysing communications, such as focus group transcripts, social network discussions, or email, phone, or postal correspondence, to analyse the 'talk' (the term usually used in this context) on a topic or issue. The example we used in **Chapter 4** is criminologists examining the use of inflammatory language on a discussion forum in order to investigate cyber-bullying. With this approach, you think deeply about the use of language, studying what is being said and written about an issue and looking particularly at how some voices are privileged while others are discounted. It will allow you to understand how a particular problem is talked about and how this discourse shapes and drives the agenda in the first place, so it clearly illustrates your ABC mindset.

Narrative analysis

Your research might call for **narrative analysis** in order to understand the lives of individuals and their social context; this would be done by qualitatively analysing biographical accounts, oral histories, and other personal stories. Stories (narratives) are the primary data source in this type of research and can be found in things like autobiographies, diaries, letters, and even scrapbooks—all of these sources contain a narrative that can be described as their 'plot'. As explained by Clark et al. (2019), the intention behind this method of analysis is less about inquiring into their possible truth and more about 'exploring how narratives are (re)produced, transmitted, and received by particular people at particular points in time' (2019: 283). This means you investigate how a story conveys meaning. To do so, you must consider deeper issues than just what the voices explicitly say; you must investigate their purpose and intended audience as well.

Thematic analysis

Thematic analysis is a useful method for projects with qualitative data on people's views, opinions, and experiences. It can be applied to data such as interview transcripts, survey responses, or social media profiles. Braun and Clarke describe it as 'a method for identifying, analysing and reporting patterns (themes) within data' (2006: 79). A theme is something identifiable in your data that relates to your research question; finding them means you will show your theoretical understanding of your data. Repetitions in the data are one way of identifying a theme, but this alone may not be enough as it must also be relevant for your research question for the issue to be a theme. Other ways of generating themes include theory-related material, where you use things you know from studying your research topic to stimulate a potential theme. Missing data is another stimulator, meaning you investigate if things were missed out by a research participant. The important thing is that the theme 'captures something important in relation to the overall research question' (Braun and Clarke, 2006).

Grounded theory analysis

Grounded theory analysis is one of the most widely used frameworks for analysing qualitative data. The approach was first advocated by Glaser and Strauss (1967) and is an all-encompassing approach to qualitative research in that, like some of the other approaches we have considered, it can be seen as not just a strategy for analysis but also an approach to collecting data, as it has to be built in from the beginning of a research project. It is difficult to define precisely as there are several versions, but it involves selecting cases based on the needs of an emerging theory, coding the data as it's collected by breaking it down into labelled components, and collecting data until no new data is needed (or the data has become repetitious), a point known as theoretical saturation. The researcher uses memos to constantly compare the data that is being coded under a particular category so that the analysis emerges gradually. This approach can be used with a variety of data sources, including interview transcripts, observations, and surveys.

32.9 Writing up your research

Writing up is an important stage in the research process, so you must allow sufficient time to do it. As explained in the previous section, this part will be much easier if you have made effective notes throughout your project. The specific details for how to write up your work will be set by the guidelines of your university and department, but your writing will also be influenced by the approach you have taken to your research, the type of reading you have done, and the type of evidence you have acquired. For example, if your project investigated perceptions for the extent of antisocial behaviour in a community, you may have chosen an objectivist ontology that is supported by a positivist epistemology. This would mean your writing will include official data sources and their quantitative evidence. But this would not be acceptable in a qualitative project, as this kind of research excludes all references to numbers and statistical claims, in preference to written language and themes.

Observing how other studies have presented their evidence in relevant academic journals is the best way to appreciate what can be required, so your earlier efforts in your literature reviews will be rewarded here. Academic studies can vary in format so, first and foremost, you must ensure your project complies with all the relevant guidelines from your course and university.

In this section we will consider practical tips for:

- how to structure your writing;
- the appropriate style for your type of project;
- how to reference properly;
- ways of disseminating your findings.

Structure and content

In the same way that good research involves breaking the task down into stages through manageable steps, effective academic writing requires a similar approach. There is no need to overcomplicate it, as credit will be given for doing the simple things well; remember all good writing has the same basic structure of a beginning, a middle, and an end. It can be easy to neglect introductions or conclusions when word limits are tight, as the middle part of your answer is likely to contain the majority of your critical thinking. This can be a serious mistake as it means you will miss the relatively easier marks for introducing and summarising your work.

The milestones in a formal, academic research project can vary by the requirements of your project and any guidance on structure from your university; such guidance should be followed closely, especially in terms of any required headings and subsections. This chapter's suggested structure is advocated by many departments and the expectations for each feature you will need to include are listed here:

1. **Cover Page**

   Dissertation/project title, researcher's name, degree.

2. **Table of Contents**

   The page numbers for the different chapters, these will change frequently so do this last.

3. **Acknowledgements**

   Recognition to the people who have helped you in your research.

4. **Abstract**

   A summary of your whole project, usually 150–300 words. This should clearly state the aim and scope of your project and be written in a comprehensible way.

5. **Introduction**

   This part needs to capture the reader's attention immediately, and as your supervising tutor is likely to have marked many projects before, make sure yours stands out by explaining:

   - the motivation for your research;
   - a statement of the problem you are investigating;
   - your research question and objectives.

   Naturally this is something for the early stages, but amending it at the end of the project is useful for ensuring it is accurate and that it includes these required features.

6. **Literature Review**

   See **section 32.5** for how you should approach this part of your research.

7. **Methodology**

   This is where you present the general philosophical framework for your chosen research methods (discussed in **section 32.6**). It should include justifications for your choice of quantitative or qualitative methods, or a combination of both.

   It should also explain:

   - the variables in your study;
   - the population and research samples;
   - methods of data collection and data analysis;
   - the limitations of your chosen methods

8. **Ethical Considerations**

   See **section 32.11** for guidance on incorporating ethical principles into your research.

9. **Results and Findings**

   Sometimes the results and findings have to be in separate chapters, so check this with your institution. In either case, when you are writing about the results, simply describe what they were for each of your inquiries. All results have to be described and these descriptions should have clear connections with your methodology chapter.

   In relation to findings, sometimes they can be expected in a separate 'analysis' or 'findings' chapter. It requires your own judgements on what can be learnt from your own data. The personal aspect can make the work for a research project feel different to that for an essay. But they are very similar as both require critical thinking; you just need to find the confidence to ensure you apply the same level of evaluation to your own research as you have to others in your studies of criminology. This is another part where your literature review will have an impact, as reading how other researchers have written up their findings will illustrate what's expected.

10. **Conclusions**

    Some of this part may have been done in the results/findings or analysis chapter, but a final part is needed to summarise:

    - your key findings and how they relate to what you expected to find;
    - the relevancy of your work to researchers and practitioners;
    - your recommendations for future researchers and practitioners;
    - the conclusions you have drawn from this research.

11. **Bibliography**

    As with all academic writing, the 'house style' (in this case your institution's expectations) should be followed for the required manner of referencing the sources used in your research. If you are unsure about this 'house style', then get in touch with your tutor. Not following this could have a detrimental impact on your mark.

12. **Appendices**

    Again, the conventions followed by your institution will determine what needs to go in this part. Often appendices are not marked so if you feel the information is important, include it in one of the earlier sections. The standard things for inclusion in an appendix are:

- blank copies of questionnaires (note: analysis of their results must not be left to this point);
- observation sheets;
- interview transcripts;
- supplementary data that adds value to your work but is not essential to it.

When it comes to structuring and articulating the material *within* these sections, it is useful to have a system for ensuring your content is sufficiently critical. A suggested way for achieving this level of criticality is provided in **Figure 32.7** and its sequence of simple questions. It is included here at the writing-up stage as its prime purpose is to demonstrate how your writing can be organised; but it can be followed throughout your studies of criminology. This means it can be applied to everything you read in your research, so use it on your own work as well as the information in journals, books, media, and other sources.

The first row of questions can be easily remembered as the 'W questions'; straightforward questions with relatively straightforward answers. If answered accurately, they provide clear descriptions that 'account' for what is known in your research area, and what could be known from your study. They are descriptive questions that can be applied to any topic; for example, if the **adversarial** justice principle is your area, then your writing will need to explain what the principle is, when it got explained this way, by who, and where. These same initial questions should be used even if the topic was potentially more complex, such as a particular theoretical position, as answering them provides the foundation to your research.

The second row requires questions that break down and analyse your work, so they add 'balance' to your writing and prevent it from being biased to one perspective. They maintain the questioning approach whilst also introducing more depth to your writing, such as explaining why and how this issue with adversarial justice or particular theoretical point has occurred. This is followed by further consideration of the potential consequences of this issue not being resolved. The ability to imagine 'what if' questions and answers is the highest form of thinking according to leading scholars in artificial intelligence (Pearl and Mackenzie, 2018); the ABC questions in **Figure 32.7** are a simple way of achieving this level of **cognitive** ability.

The final row is where you 'complete' this critical thinking process by evaluating what you have found. It also requires high cognitive skills and hypothetical thinking, where you make informed comments and predictions for what might happen following your project. It means considering questions such as, what if all of your views and recommendations in your project were accepted, what would happen? Your writing will be able to make credible arguments if you have the foundations from the first two rows of **Figure 32.7**. The final question in our ABC system is the 'so what' question, which is the most important question when it comes to evaluating knowledge, as it forces you to think about its true worth. It is a

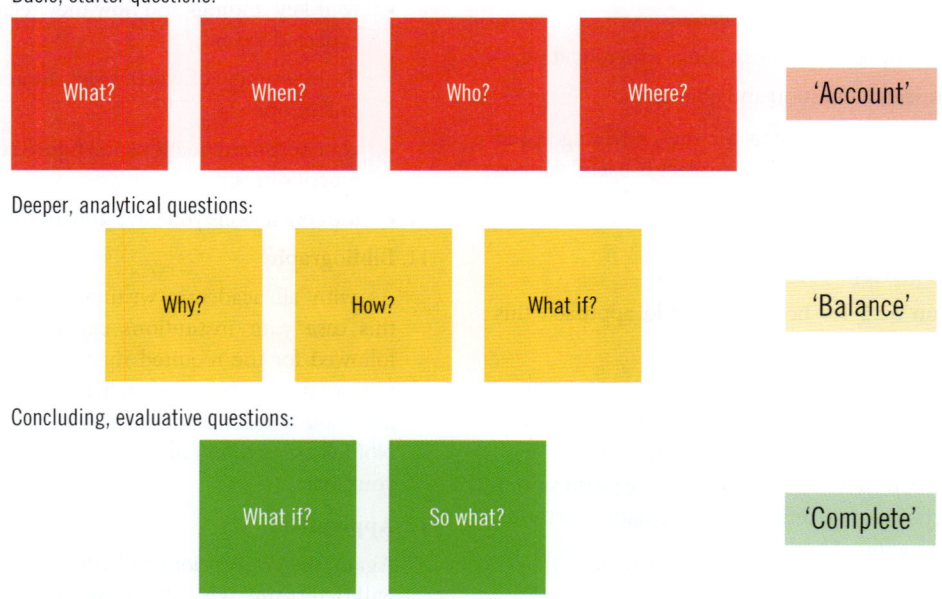

Figure 32.7 Use this sequence of simple 'ABC' questions to organise your writing and to ensure that your content is sufficiently critical

difficult question, but it must be used on your own work, as it will reveal your thoughts on your project's value and whether there was any point to it. Be prepared to spend time thinking about this question, remember your first thoughts will rarely be your best so don't rush it and make sure you think hard about all your project's implications and different levels of importance. The 'so what' question is fundamental to the justifications you give for your research which—as you know—is at the heart of the academic exercise.

Writing style

Writing up your work should hopefully be an enjoyable part of your studies, as it is here where you can showcase your abilities. The quality of your writing is crucial as it will affect how your study appears to the reader—how easy the rationale and findings are to understand and how compelling its arguments are—so you should practise it as much as you can.

Getting the tone right

It is important to note that the writing style and tone you adopt will be different depending on the content of your research, so again you will find it very useful to look at the style used in similar existing studies as you complete your literature review. It is likely to be more formal than that of this book, as we adopt a more conversational style to take you through the different topics.

You should try to write in a way that avoids any perception of researcher bias, particularly as by now you will be accustomed to detecting this in many forms of criminological knowledge; one way to reduce perceptions of bias is to generally avoid the use of the first person in your work. Instead, apply a more formal style by writing in the third person. The first person can sometimes be acceptable in a reflective piece or a research report, for example where it might be appropriate to write 'I interviewed ...' or 'I analysed ...'; but the crucial point is whether such a choice adds value to your work. It could threaten your objectivity and detract from the overall quality of your writing, so both the first person and other personal terms are generally best avoided.

Although we do advise writing in the third person, we would advise against referring to yourself as 'the author' as this is also too personal and can sound pretentious; using alternative statements like 'it can be argued that ...' or 'it was found that ...' will provide the detached, objective impression you need to convey. The use of the formal third person may feel unnatural at first but it will help you avoid the use of informal language and slang. Such terms usually have no place in academic writing where their use can cast doubt on the authority of your writing.

It is also important to be sensitive when writing up your research, as it could lead to harm if your findings were critical of individuals and organisations; the ability to use language sensitively is an essential part of an ethical researcher's toolkit. Keeping a detached tone and neutral language will help your writing remain sensitive if your research deals with such potentially delicate issues, and will ensure that you protect yourself from accusations of bias.

Practise and seek feedback

You should take every opportunity you can to practise your academic writing, such as the work expected for seminars or other parts of your course. If possible, get your writing checked by someone at your institution preferably before your work is formally marked. This might be possible at any academic writing clinics that take place at your institution. When you start receiving your marked work back, the temptation is just to look at your grade and then forget all about it. It can be difficult to take criticism when you have worked so hard, but it is essential that you develop the ability to accept and act on constructive feedback. We discuss this in **What do you think? 32.3**.

Make the most of software tools

The style of your written work can influence subsequent grades so neat presentation is essential. This means getting guidance from your lecturers about issues such as font sizes, line spacing, etc., and applying these properly on good quality, widely used, word processing software. Again, this is something you should ask about at your institution as they might offer discounted packages to their undergraduates. It is advisable to use the best available option as cheaper versions of the software can have formatting issues that damage the quality of how your work is presented.

Additionally, we cannot stress enough the fundamental importance of doing spelling and grammar checks on everything you write. We all know these tools may not be perfect (and therefore should not replace your own complete read-through), but nonetheless they can identify issues in the way you construct your sentences. If further improvements to your building of sentences and paragraphs are needed, then this kind of development will be possible by working your way through sources such as Finch and Fafinski (2019: Ch. 7).

> ## WHAT DO YOU THINK? 32.3
>
> ### Learning from others whilst doing your research
>
> The concept of an academic community is integral to university life; its importance illustrated by the '.ac' characters in the URLs and email addresses for its students and staff. An academic community consists of a supportive group of learners who seek to help each other in their studies and research. Your academic community includes the other students on your course as they can offer useful assistance in your development as an undergraduate researcher.
>
> The writing-up stage of a research project can be a lonely experience, but such feelings can be overcome by acquiring other people's views on your writing. If you can find another student and suggest you exchange some of your writing, you could try the following exercise together to help each other with this stage. It doesn't have to be a huge amount, around 500 words of a project should be enough to obtain comments regarding:
>
> - What's the general perception of the writing's clarity?
> - Are there any repeated mistakes?
> - What is the 'top tip' for improving the writing?
>
> The answers to these questions will provide both of you with critical feedback on developing your writing style; feedback that you would not have otherwise received but for the help of your academic community. The exercise is completed by reflecting on what you've learnt from it, which should help improve the quality of your writing and develop your skills and experience in regard to receiving and giving feedback.
>
> There are also online academic communities that host general discussions and inquiries to help current criminology undergraduates, such as @TheCrimiTalk.

Referencing

To develop an effective style of writing, you have to be able to reference academic literature in the expected ways. These expectations will be set by the requirements of your course and institution, but they are likely to be either 'a form of the "Harvard method" (most likely) or "Chicago style" (less likely)' (Clark et al., 2019: 159). There can be variations of these approaches, so it is important to know which one applies, as the rules for referencing can cause new undergraduates much concern. The Harvard system is not that difficult as long as you first write the detail for the list of citations that is required at the end of a piece of academic writing. The 'house style' will dictate whether this list is a 'Bibliography' or 'References'. Incorporating the reference into the main body of your writing then becomes much easier, although precisely what is needed for an in-text reference will depend on whether you are including a direct quote from that source.

Direct quotes

Direct quotes should follow the pattern used throughout this book. For instance:

> Whilst media reports on wrongful conviction often create popular narratives framed as heroic injustices, occasionally some cases face difficulties in eliciting popular support (Stratton, 2015: 282).

In the above example, a short reference to the source of the quote is inserted directly into the text, in brackets.

The *full* reference will then be included in the list of references in the bibliography. For direct quotes, the in-text reference should include:

- the author's surname;
- the year of publication; and
- the page number.

In the Stratton source, the quote was taken from page 282 of his article that was published in 2015, and hence you see the format '2015: 282'.

Including direct quotes can be an excellent way of proving that you have read widely on the subject, but they should be used sparingly: overuse can damage your claims that your work is original and produced by you, so care is needed to ensure they are not too long. A definitive rule for their acceptable length does not exist, but if one exceeds 30 words you should be cautious as the 'house style' for your project might require special methods of presentation, such as a different font size and an indented, separate paragraph.

In addition to getting the right balance for both the number and length of direct quotes, problems can also arise when they are not naturally incorporated into your writing. When they do not flow with the previous sentence, this can raise questions in a marker's mind as to whether they are only being included for the sake of it. For example, if you are writing about the influence of the due process principle on the criminal courts (as we studied in **Chapter 23**), more needs to be done than merely copying out a few words from a famous source such as Packer (1964). To get full credit for incorporating quotes, such as his view of criminal justice sometimes being 'a factory that has to devote a substantial part of its input to quality control' (Packer, 1964: 15); you would have to explain what the key words in the quote might mean. You would need to explain what Packer meant by 'quality control' and how the due process model has safeguards to prevent the progression of weak cases through the system.

However, quotes can add real value if they support (or contradict) the point you are trying to make in your writing. For example:

> The speed with which cases are dealt with not only brings, at least potentially, economic savings and benefits for the victims of crime, but can be to the advantage of **defendants**, especially those who are remanded in custody (Cape, 2010: 25).

If you are writing about the importance of speed to the criminal justice system, using this quote could be very beneficial as explaining its key words will mean you write about the possible financial savings, benefits to victims, and advantages for defendants. If you expand on these three separate points, you will clearly incorporate Cape (2010) into your writing.

Indirect references

In situations where you are not taking a direct quote but are using your own words to paraphrase or otherwise refer to another source, the conventional way to reference is to just put the author's surname and year of publication at the end of the sentence (no page number). So, adapting the previous example, the text might read something like:

> Sometimes media reports on cases of wrongful conviction show strong beliefs in a mistake by the justice system (Stratton, 2015).

As you can see from this book and in academic sources generally, the indirect use of references is the most common way of incorporating academic literature. If you wish, it is possible to put the surname (or name of an organisation) and year of publication earlier in a sentence but this is rare so, if you are doing it, reread your work carefully to check it does not disjoint your writing. For example:

> Stratton (2015) argued that media reports on cases of wrongful conviction, sometimes showed strong beliefs in a mistake by the justice system.

How to compile a reference list

At the end of your work you will need to provide a list of references which, if done correctly, will prove that your writing complies with the standard referencing conventions. Initially this can be intimidating, but such fears can be overcome by simply following the standard format for each of the different kinds of sources you have used in your writing. There is not the space in this chapter to list them all, for this amount of detail you can use something like https://www.citethemrightonline.com, but the most common forms of patterns for your list of references are as follows.

1. For published books you need to provide the:
   - author (surname—comma—initial(s)—full stop);
   - date of publication (in brackets);
   - full title (in italics);
   - edition number, if it is after the first (in brackets);
   - place the book was published (followed by a colon) and the publisher's name (if you remember 'place' then 'publisher' is in alphabetical order, you will get this convention right).

   An example used in this chapter was:

   Finch, E. and Fafinski, S. (2019) *Criminology Skills* (3rd edn). Oxford: Oxford University Press.

2. For articles published in academic journals you need to provide the:
   - author (surname—comma—initial(s)—full stop);
   - date of publication (in brackets);
   - the title of the article (in inverted commas);
   - the title of the journal (in italics);
   - the volume number, and if there is one the issue number of that volume (this last part in brackets);
   - the start and end page numbers for the article.

   An example used in this chapter was:

   Fitzgibbon, W. and Healy, D. (2019) 'Lives and spaces: Photovoice and offender supervision in Ireland and England'. *Criminology & Criminal Justice* 19(1): 3–25.

3. For a chapter from an edited book, these two patterns are effectively merged and each chapter is treated in a similar way to a journal article.

   An example used in this chapter was:

   Rock, P. (2017) 'The Foundations of Sociological Theories of Crime' in A. Liebling, S. Maruna, and L. McAra (eds) *The Oxford Handbook of Criminology* (6th edn) pp. 21–56.

4. If you are seeking to use a secondary source then you need to provide both the primary and secondary citations in your text, but only include the secondary source in your list of references. For example, suppose you want to refer to work published in 1963 by Goffman, which you read about in the 2019 study by Fitzgibbon and Healy; your writing should include something like:

   Goffman (as cited in Fitzgibbon and Healy, 2019) uses the concept of spoiled identity in his theory of social stigma to explain offenders' feelings of rejection from society.

Or:

The stigmatising effects from criminal sanctions can mean offenders feel their identity is spoiled, leading to their rejection from society (Goffman, as cited in Fitzgibbon and Healy, 2019).

Note that it is far from ideal to use this kind of referencing, as you are completely relying on the source you have read for this second-hand information. You will not be able to check its accuracy and its use is therefore not generally welcomed but, as ever, exceptions can sometimes be allowed so carefully read the referencing guidelines from your institution. If it is permitted, then in your list of references you should only cite the source you have actually read.

It is essential that your list of references is presented in alphabetical order using the surnames or organisations responsible for your sources. These days many automated ways exist for generating references but, just as with a calculator for doing your maths, it's advisable to understand the principles of what you are doing!

Disseminating your findings

It is increasingly important, especially in times of stretched budgets in many sectors, that research provides evidence of impact. This means transparency and openness about study results is now crucial. The process of ensuring that as many people as possible have access to research findings is called dissemination. This phase of research is so important that dissemination activities usually need to be proposed at the outset when trying to acquire funding for postgraduate or professional research studies.

At undergraduate level, meeting funding requirements is not usually an issue and most dissertations are only read by the producing student and their supervising tutor. This can sometimes be extended to include tutors who are involved in the second marking processes, but clearly this is still a very limited audience. Is this a missed opportunity? Considering the amount of effort you have put in, and the fact that you may have conducted your research in the hope of having an impact on the wider discipline or society, should there not be a wider circulation of your work? If you want to ensure your work reaches a wider audience whilst developing your communication skills, you should make dissemination part of your research process. If it is appropriately planned and justified, paying attention to this aspect of research could gain you extra recognition and marks and this is the kind of action through which you become the 'creative disruptor' that we described in **section 32.2**.

Undergraduate research may traditionally be something of a closed affair, but advancements in technology and the popularity of online education and initiatives such as MOOCs (Massive Open Online Course) are changing this traditional position. We'll consider how these developments can benefit your employability in **Chapter 33**, but for now we consider their assistance for developing your role as a researcher. The accessibility of these online courses and the freely available resources that accompany them are seen by some as a revolution in education and learning (Tuomi, 2013). They use various ways of communicating with their students, and by adapting some of these you will have many new options for disseminating your work.

- Create a blog or video diary.

This would be a written or visual record of the progress of your project. It could stimulate interest and acquire useful feedback for your research. If you would prefer an audio record, then making a podcast could be appropriate, with the current popularity of 'true crime' podcasts suggesting that these can be an engaging format. Any of these options for recording your progress would be a way of completing the research diary for achieving the milestones in your project, as suggested in **Table 32.2**.

- Build a wiki.

A wiki is a website developed collaboratively by a group of people that allows its users to add and edit its content. They can be free to create and straightforward to use—many options exist, but ones like https://www.pbworks.com provide user-friendly systems for acquiring helpful comments and feedback. Their collaborative ethos means a wiki works really well in team projects, but they can be used for individual ones as well. Building one will develop your written communication skills and, so as to reach the audience you want, you may have to write in a different style to the more formal one required by your course.

- Produce an **open educational resource** (OER).

The term OER can be applied to any online source with an educational purpose. In recent years, online communities have evolved that encourage the production and use of OERs. This has led to initiatives such as the OER University and numerous other MOOCs. It has also meant presentation-sharing sites, such as SlideShare and Wattpad, have become extremely popular, with these two alone having more than 100 million users. Sharing some of your research by producing an OER for one of these sites could be a useful way of both disseminating what you have learnt and for spreading awareness of your work. These benefits can mean you fully capitalise on work you have to do for your project; for example, creating and publishing a presentation on your methodology or results would show your achievement of these parts of your project.

- Take part in exhibitions and displays.

This option used to be associated only with art students but departments are generally keen to publicise their students' work so they may host such an event for criminology students. If you have photographs from your research, then (if ethical considerations allow—see **section 32.11**) you could create your own online display. You could even use PowerPoint or free movie-making or screen-recording software to upload your work to an video-sharing site like YouTube. Some criminology students' productions have been known to attract thousands of views—see, for example, Tegan Walsh's 'Poor housing and its implications for children's health and well-being' (https://www.youtube.com/watch?v=R4ZZD_CYSB8) and Joanna Barlow's 'Penal Populism' (https://www.youtube.com/watch?v=LQdME-PETsA). You do not even have to wait until the end of your project as you could incorporate aspects of this dissemination into your research but, again, before taking such steps it is important to be aware of the ethical and legal issues, which are discussed in **section 32.11**.

- Involve a community group or organisation.

If there are any community groups that might benefit from your research, you should seek to involve them with its dissemination as their support can mean you reach a wider audience. A project with a community focus, such as a local criminal justice issue, could acquire interest in its results or its up-to-date review of the issue's academic literature. Again, any communication from the group or organisation could be integrated into your project and provide relevant data for your research question. In several European countries, the research findings of a student's PhD automatically achieve this extra level of dissemination as their *viva voce* stage (the oral examination of the research) is conducted in public.

- Write an article.

The conventional academic practice of writing an article on your research is another route for disseminating it. This can be possible by writing for a journal or other scholarly publication at your institution. There are also various open-access journals that publish undergraduate dissertations and articles. These include the *Internet Journal of Criminology*, and *Reinvention*, the online, peer-reviewed journal from all disciplinary areas and all universities that publishes high-quality undergraduate student research.

- Present at a conference.

This dissemination method is also common practice for researchers as it allows their thoughts and ideas to be presented to audiences of people who often have expertise in the field. It can provide feedback that is an important part of the research process in large projects. Conferences held at your institution can provide this experience as could the British Conference of Undergraduate Research. The stature of this conference means some of its work is presented annually in Parliament.

Being creative with your dissemination methods can increase the visibility of your project and help you find your target audience, meaning the chances of acquiring impact are increased. Trying any of these distribution techniques can also be personally beneficial as they will provide opportunities to enhance your employability. They include an element of risk-taking from you, as there is a possibility your methods could be unsuccessful, either from not reaching your intended audience at all or getting one that is completely unreceptive to your research! Coping with this level of uncertainty can show your possession of the advanced skills and attributes that today's employers like to see in their graduate recruits (**Figure 33.3**); particularly the expectations for a positive attitude, enterprise, and communication skills.

They may have many advantages but these steps can take a long time to complete. This can be a major disadvantage, so you need to judge whether attempting creative dissemination will be worth the time you will have to invest. It means balancing these risks of time and possible failure against the rewards of visibility and impact. Several years ago, the importance of dissemination was summed up by a specially commissioned report into undergraduate education in the US:

> Every university graduate should understand that no idea is fully formed until it can be communicated . . . Dissemination of results is an essential and integral part of the research process.
>
> (The Boyer Commission, 1998: 24)

32.10 Planning your research project

You will have gathered that there is a lot to do and think about when conducting research, even a relatively small-scale one, so it is important that you dedicate some time to planning how you will go about completing your project. This section will help you with this.

Right from the start of your project you need to record your plans on a spreadsheet or equivalent document; this should plot when and how the different stages of your project will be completed. **Table 32.2** shows you what such a spreadsheet might look like. But planning is not something only done at the start of the project, it's something you need to keep doing, particularly as time constraints are likely to be an issue. To help you with this planning, and to indicate when your busiest times are likely to be, **Table 32.2** suggests a series of dates for achieving the essential stages in the research process, with the shaded areas indicating when the key parts of your project should be completed. It is a timetable that assumes you have a full academic year to complete the project, but if there is a shorter timescale it should be adapted proportionately. It should be frequently updated, as successful projects require constant planning in order to achieve their targets; this is because the time spent on these different stages in the research process might vary from what was predicted.

Having this clear vision of your project's different parts can help when things don't seem to be running smoothly, such as feeling overwhelmed by the literature or by finding it hard to collect data. It means other parts in your project can be addressed whilst you are working out these difficulties. Some rows are shaded more than once to show them as parts that require your regular attention. You need to be organised in your writings to ensure you can come back to them and further develop them. This need to revisit and adapt is an example of how the research process does not always have a neat chronological pattern. This table is just an outline of the main stages (your institution will be able to give you more detail on each part, or tell you whether their requirements differ), but it should be enough for you to use to get started with the stages in your project.

To begin this process, gather together all the information that you have about the timescale and deadlines for your project, as well as the dates for any meetings or check-ins with a supervisor, and use this information to complete **Table 32.2**. When deciding on deadlines for your project:

- make sure to allow plenty of time for your supervisor to look over your plans and provide feedback;
- be realistic in your estimations of how long tasks will take you. **Table 32.2** highlights the parts that will take the most time but if you are unsure your supervisor will be able to tell you whether it seems sensible or overly ambitious, given the time and resources available to you;
- be realistic about how much time it will take others to do their part, including how long it will take for study participants to complete their tasks, whether those working in an organisation are likely to have a gap in their diary to speak to or see you, whether people will respond to your questionnaire, whether the library will still have the books you need, and so on;
- factor in some buffer time for possible delays or setbacks (some may be out of your control, for example

	Sept–Oct	Nov–Dec	Jan–Feb	Mar–Apr	May–June
1. Cover Page					
2. Table of Contents					
3. Acknowledgements					
4. Abstract					
5. Introduction					
6. Literature Review					
7. Methodology					
8. Ethical Considerations					
9. Results and Findings					
10. Conclusions					
11. Bibliography					
12. Appendices					

Table 32.2 Potential times for the milestones in your project

the people who are providing your data might have to postpone your meeting or call);
- do not plan to complete your project on the day of the deadline!

Remember that the dates you list are likely to change, but clearly planning them all at the start will enable you to foresee any hurdles and react more quickly to any issues that arise. A plan like this will also direct your work and remind you how the key parts to a research project or dissertation are interconnected.

Keeping up a spreadsheet or other such document throughout the whole course of your project will help so much with its later stages, as it will be far superior to using memory. It will provide evidence of what happened (or didn't happen) in your project and when; it means you can monitor the project's progress and react if things are not going to plan. These details will be extremely useful in the writing-up stage, and again later when you're evaluating your role in the research.

This high-level organisation is why employers can rate research projects highly in their preferred experiences of their applicants: its successful completion will prove your abilities in planning deadlines and meeting them successfully.

32.11 Ethics and legality in research

We have seen that ethical thinking has to be a priority for any dissemination practices, but safeguards also need to be taken much earlier in the process to guard against the possibility of harming any of your research participants. This could arise in a number of ways—for example, if assurances for anonymity were essential to informed consent, would these steps mean they become identifiable? It could also lead to harm if your findings were critical of individuals and organisations in your research; this can be a common problem so the ability to use language sensitively is an essential part of an ethical researcher's toolkit. On the other hand, your participants might stand to benefit from your research and might be keen to help you with its dissemination; this is where effective planning for your topic will pay off, as research concerning community groups, campaigns, and professionals can lead you to people with an interest in publicising your findings.

The fact that research in criminology and criminal justice investigates serious issues and often involves human subjects in surveys, participant observation, and other experiments means it is essential that ethical principles and legal requirements are followed. This is more than just a small section in your report; it should influence much of your thinking, both in the planning and carrying out of your research. This section of the chapter will explain the core principles of ethics and legality so they can be applied to your project, as well as to help you see how you can demonstrate a commitment to ethical forms of study in higher education generally.

Conducting ethical research

Criminological research has the potential to cause obvious harm to victims who may feel traumatised by it, and offenders who could implicate themselves through it. This means following ethical standards should be a priority but, as we discover in **Controversy and debate 32.2**, this does not always happen.

CONTROVERSY AND DEBATE 32.2

Ethical breaches in criminology

In a survey conducted in 1988–93 on officers and executives at the American Society of Criminology, '40 percent of the respondents indicated some first-hand knowledge about unethical research practices. Almost 50 percent have heard other colleagues questioning the ethical nature of recent criminological research efforts' (Vohryzek-Bolden, 1997: 132). The respondents claimed to have knowledge of many ethical concerns in criminological research at this time, including the fabrication of data, plagiarism, lack of consent from research subjects, confidentiality issues, and deception. The journal article where this research was published also featured some of the most infamous examples of unethical criminological research.

1. **The Tearoom Trade:** This research, published in 1970, investigated sexual behaviour between men in public toilets in the US. It is renowned for its discovery that, contrary to the thinking at the time, men of all

kinds of backgrounds could take part in this kind of behaviour (Humphrey, 1970). It has become infamous as an example of ethical bad practice because the researcher used deception to disguise his true identity from the people he was observing, and then traced the men's car registration numbers so he could interview them in his study.

2. **The Stanford Prison Experiment:** This was a simulated prison experiment conducted in 1971, where undergraduates at Stanford University in the US were paid to take the role of either guard or prisoner for a period of two weeks (Zimbardo, 1973). It had to be cancelled after six days to avoid the risk of harm as the participants were getting too carried away with their respective roles. This included one-third of the 'guards' displaying sadistic behaviour and many 'prisoners' being traumatised by the experience.

3. **The Milgram Experiment:** This was a series of experiments that began in the early 1960s to research responses to authority figures (Milgram, 1974). The participants were led to believe they were inflicting electric shocks of increasingly high voltage on other people in the research. These other people (played by actors) were hidden behind a wall, and the research found that two-thirds of participants were prepared to use the maximum voltage when told to do so. This was despite hearing screams and banging on the walls from the supposed victims. The participants were deceived into thinking they had inflicted this pain and many were observed shaking and trembling whilst taking part.

Notice how all these cases are from around 50 years ago; similar examples no longer seem to happen. It is generally accepted that universities now have much stronger systems with ethics committees that must be satisfied before any research can be done. A tighter system may have stopped these sorts of extreme cases, and meant the public were more protected, but is this at the cost of beneficial criminological research?

In addition to the controversial studies we described, the other controversy and debate in this feature is whether contemporary ethics committees appropriately protect the public or prevent researchers and the public from getting the answers they need.

Engaging with ethics in research goes far beyond merely proving that you have complied with an institution's regulations. Naturally, you do have to meet the standards required by your course, but considering and developing an ethical approach will influence the duration of your project, from its first planning stage to its potential dissemination. The broad nature of criminology means that this commitment can be demonstrated through your research in many ways.

Who decides what's ethical?

The Statement of Ethics from the British Society of Criminology in 2015 is a document freely available on the society's website. It states that researchers' first specific duty is owed to the discipline of criminology itself:

> Researchers have a duty to promote the advancement and dissemination of knowledge, to protect intellectual and professional freedom, and therefore to promote a working environment and professional relationships conducive to these. More specifically, researchers should promote free and independent inquiry into criminological matters and unrestricted dissemination of criminological knowledge'
>
> (2015: para. 2).

The Statement of Ethics will offer considerable help for assuring your project's ethical standards as it breaks down the research responsibilities of criminologists to fellow researchers, research participants, and funders. It contains 14 separate points about research participants and, if you can meet all of them, you can then be confident in meeting high ethical standards in your project. The Statement of Ethics also provides help through several case studies and a section on frequently asked questions. This resource is additionally extremely helpful for its links to the statutory provisions in the Data Protection Act that can affect researchers, and also for explaining the permissible limits of confidentiality in research—namely, situations where suspected offences of terrorism, money laundering, and the neglect or abuse of children are excluded.

You also have responsibility under the General Data Protection Regulation (GDPR) and the Data Protection Act 2018 to safely store and protect any data containing identifiable information on people. These duties are limited and not comparable with those of businesses as academic research can be exempt from the GDPR. This is something your supervisor can advise you on, and an overview for researchers is provided by the Information Commissioner's Office (https://ico.org.uk).

Principles for ethical research

When you are considering the ethics of your project, it is generally recognised that there are four main areas in which contentious issues could arise within research:

1. informed consent;
2. misrepresentation;
3. accuracy of data;
4. no harm to research subjects, and protection of their privacy.

The first of these requires you to take appropriate steps to ensure there was informed consent on the part of your research subjects. They have the right to be fully informed about the nature and consequences of your research, its methods, potential risks, and its general purpose. This was lacking in the examples in **Controversy and debate 32.2** as many things were withheld from the participants. The principle of informed consent means physical or psychological coercion cannot be used in acquiring the voluntary participation of your research subjects. This can be an issue for research involving prisoners or offenders on community sentences, as they may have only agreed to take part through fear of what might happen if they did not consent. In order to attain this level of informed consent, the use of deception, as practised by the Tearoom Trade study, is not permissible.

This leads us on to the second contentious issue, and means deliberate misrepresentations from researchers are forbidden. This was clearly apparent in the Milgram Experiment with the false statements given to the participants about the pain they were supposedly inflicting. However, it is not always easy to identify deception. For example, is not telling a person something (an omission) as morally unacceptable as actively telling them something that is false (a lie)? Researchers have different views on this distinction, with some believing 'there is a world of difference between not telling subjects things and telling them the wrong things. *The latter is deception, the former is not*' (Hey, 1998: 397, emphasis in original). Others disagree and believe it is unethical and reflects badly on the trustworthiness of researchers, plus it misses out on the benefits of having informed participants in the research. This type of deception is the key issue in contemporary research, not the extreme examples in **Controversy and debate 32.2**; it is argued that participants rarely receive all the information they might want to know about a project. This is because it may not be practical for a researcher to provide full details to every participant, and the researcher may feel it could bias their response (Clark et al., 2021).

Absolute prohibitions on all kinds of deceptions do not exist, as in some areas of life, like with state violence and corporate wrongdoings, valuable information could not be attained without it. This means the use of covert research methods where the researcher does not disclose their identity as a researcher to the people being observed can sometimes be allowed. One of its most famous examples is Holdaway (1982), where the researcher, a serving police officer, conducted undercover research over a two-year period to study the occupational **culture** of the police. It was permitted as there was a limited body of knowledge in the area and alternative research methods were considered likely to be unsuccessful. The approach is controversial for the way it contravenes ethical principles such as informed consent; but has been recently used in studies of people such as football fans, members of extreme political parties, and several others (Calvey, 2017). In Calvey's own research and his case study of bouncers in the Manchester night-time economy, he spent six months working on the doors of different night clubs in the city. The study identified some of the pressures the covert method can place on researchers:

> I laughed along with racist and sexist jokes, physically horsed around on the door, made fun of some drunken customers and 'chatted up' female customers on a regular basis. I needed to fit in like any ordinary doorman doing the doors.
>
> (2017: 127)

So, if the research is seeking knowledge with a clear value to society, then, in exceptional circumstances, minor deviations from the ethical principle (such as deception by omission) can be accepted. The exceptional circumstances have not been completely defined but they include situations where alternative research methods are not possible and the participants do not face any increased risks because of the deception. They also require participants to be adequately debriefed and given the right to withdraw any data obtained from them without their consent. These conditions are extremely difficult to satisfy, so it is highly improbable that deceptive methods of research would be approved by the ethics committee at your institution.

The third contentious issue concerns the accuracy of the data produced in your research, as this must truthfully represent what you found, and any lies or manipulations will invalidate your work. This may seem obvious but occasionally it can be an issue for criminological research. For example, Kahn (cited in McCarthy et al., 2020: 462) reported on the research misdemeanours of Dr Diederik Stapel at Tilburg University in the Netherlands. Over several years, he had published many research papers supporting the **broken windows** theory of crime, and its belief that being in environments with litter and graffiti makes people more likely to commit small crimes and acts of antisocial behaviour (see **Chapter 27**). However, three junior researchers at his university raised concerns about his work and believed certain data were forged. Stapel subsequently admitted to doing this and left his position at the university.

The fourth contentious issue is sometimes divided into two, but we will consider harm to research subjects and protection of their privacy together because in undergraduate projects they are likely to be the same issue. Harm is a broad concept, think of its various types in **Controversy and debate 32.2**, and so the potential for it needs to be appreciated in your choice of methods—for example, the use of interviews would inconvenience your research subjects by simply impinging on their time. In this context, the amount of harm could be negligible but this may not be the case if individuals are identified or identifiable from your research. If the need for anonymity is high, then this could affect your methodology as quantitative research and its more limited nature of permissible responses makes it less likely that individuals could be subsequently identified. This general principle of ethics means the identity of research subjects (people and locations) has to be protected, and assurances of anonymity need to be given to safeguard against the disclosure of personal data. The potential for harm in matters such as a research subject's professional or social reputation includes the duty on a researcher to ensure any records are secured safely, with only access from the researcher allowed.

Potential ethical issues for student researchers

The ethical principles that we have considered also apply to traditional methods of research, such as documentary research and essays. They may seem like they wouldn't, due to secondary research not directly involving research subjects to acquire data, but the values in concepts such as harm and consent still have to be addressed. Ethical issues that might arise in your research project or dissertation will very much depend on your topic and data-collection method(s), but here we will consider a few of the issues associated with particular methods commonly used in student projects.

You must take steps to consider potential harm to the original participants so, if anonymity is an issue, ensure you will maintain and protect it. This means taking reasonable steps to ensure people cannot be identified in your research and is particularly important when the research involves an organisation or any other small sample of people. Again, the focus of your research and research question will influence what precautions are needed; if there are contentious issues to the research, it may be better to use pseudonyms for the names of particular people, organisations, and places. It may be possible to identify people from your general descriptions of their job titles and responsibilities, so you need to make sure your writing does not include these more subtle ways of identification.

Consent can also be an issue in secondary research even though acquiring informed consent from the research participants could be impossible if the research was done years ago. But there is still the obligation to work in an ethically sound manner, meaning you need to find out what consent was given in the original research, justify how your research would not be objected to by the original participants, and explain why the original researchers would not object to your intended use of their data.

Ethical problems can be a concern if your project involves modern methods such as visual data collection and analysis. Since most people now own phones that are capable of taking good-quality photos, videos, and audio recordings, these kinds of data-collection methods, particularly the former, are often used in undergraduate social science research. These methods undoubtedly bring great benefits (being able to be a criminologist wherever you are means that you can quickly capture all sorts of valuable data for analysis, allowing you to use your imagination and creativity and to demonstrate intellectual adaptability) but also give rise to a number of particular ethical concerns. These include:

- criminological data should be inspired by a desire for social change not financial gain, so a good photograph should not be sold off;
- visual methods such as photography could breach the anonymity safeguard;
- consent of the subjects in the photographs;
- harm from people being identified in a particular place and time.

Help for overcoming these ethical concerns for visual research is provided by the Visual Sociology Group. They suggest a range of ways for ensuring the research is consensual and ethical, such as 'the practice of socially responsible research that seeks to provide justice and the fair distribution of the benefits and burdens of research' (International Visual Sociology Association Code of Research Ethics, para. 6(c)). The Code expressly mentions the dissemination of images so, if this is planned in your research, you need to ensure any identifiable participant consents to this kind of action and understands its implications. This additional ethical responsibility and enhanced need to be sensitive with visual images means you should take steps to ensure the anonymity of your participants, like pixelating their faces in photographs.

The legal requirement to take care with the dissemination of visual images is laid down in the decision of the European Court of Human Rights in *Peck* v *United Kingdom* (App. no. 44647/98, 2003). This case was an appeal from a member of the public against a local council's release of CCTV footage to a newspaper and to a regional television programme. The images showed the individual moments after he had attempted suicide in a public street by slashing his wrists with a kitchen knife. Two photographs from the footage were published in a newspaper article about the benefits of CCTV, and the face of the individual was not masked when broadcasted on TV. His appeal was eventually successful, as the court found that there had been a breach of his right to respect for private life. This was because there were no reasons to justify this dissemination without first getting the individual's consent or ensuring his identity was not revealed.

It is important to give careful consideration to these potential issues, not only to ensure that your research does not negatively impact others, but also because your methods and research may be rejected if they are considered unethical. In order to attain ethical approval, visual researchers need to demonstrate their care and compassion for the research subjects and act in ways likely to benefit the individuals or groups being researched. You can be proactive here by adapting the model consent form in **Figure 32.8**, as using this will show your ethical commitment. This form has been designed to cover projects that use creative research methods. If this is not needed, your university is likely to have templates that you can use for conventional methods. An information sheet may also be appropriate as this can explain your research and give participants the information they need for their informed consent. These two forms should be created early in the project, as they secure its ethics and can be required at the proposal stage. They can be flexible documents that are adapted to meet the circumstances of the project.

This section has shown how to incorporate ethical principles into your research; values that are always present but can vary according to the research. Their effect can be summed up as:

> Ethics is a matter of principled sensitivity to the rights of others. Being ethical limits the choices we can make in the pursuit of truth. Ethics say that while truth is good, respect for human dignity is better.

(Cavan, 1977: 810)

Considering copyright

One of the most difficult parts of the undergraduate experience can be learning how to effectively use sources in your work without plagiarising them or infringing copyright agreements. When we refer to copyright, we mean the legal protection people can place on their work that stops others from using it without their permission. In plagiarism we mean putting forward other people's work or ideas as your own, with or without their consent, by incorporating it into your work without giving full acknowledgement.

It is likely that information for overcoming concerns on plagiarism will have been provided by your institution as it is an essential feature of any induction into higher education; if it hasn't been, you might want to ask if the library or your department can provide any guidance. The number of sources you will be expected to use in your project will be guided by the marking criteria and, with regard to academic sources, any plagiarism fears can be dispelled by appropriate referencing.

If your work uses other sources such as photographs, videos, and interview recordings, then copyright issues may also affect the ethical nature of your work. The creators or purchasers of the works are likely to have the 'all rights reserved' protection of copyright, and so have rights in law enforceable against you if you use those works in your text without permission—being in higher education does not exclude your liability. The commonly accepted practice of 'fair use' allows limited use of copyrighted materials, so small amounts of text can usually be used without asking permission, but it is important to check with your supervisor if you are unsure. If you are using the full or a significant part of a piece of work, for example a photograph, table of data, or a large extract of text, permission should almost always be sought from the copyright holder. Advice on the different steps this requires will be in the legal resources provided by the library at your institution.

Requesting permission means you must see if the name of the copyright holder is on the image or can be found through online searching, and then contacting them, explaining how and why you are seeking to use their material. If it proves difficult to find the copyright holder, take extra steps such as using a 'reverse image search' to upload an image in a search engine and finding the other places where it has been used online. Whether your source needs permission or not, it is essential to acknowledge the source wherever it is used in your work. You can see this in action in this book: look at the source lines under the numbered photos we have included and you will see that we always acknowledge the copyright holder from whom we obtained permission to reproduce the images. (The only exception is the thumbnail headshots in our Conversations features, where the contributor is the copyright holder unless otherwise indicated. We have explained this policy and thanked the copyright holders in this book's preliminary pages.) If you have sought permission to use a piece, it is polite to ask how the copyright owner would like to be

CONSENT FORM

VENUE………………………………………………………………………………………..

DATE……………………………………………………………………………..…………...

PHOTOGRAPHER/CREATOR OF RECORDING…………………………………….………

This form is to be signed by the person who has agreed to be photographed and/or filmed and/or recorded for [insert name of project here]. The purpose of this form is to seek consent for the photographs and/or films and/or recordings to be taken and subsequently to be used in a number of media, including print and the web by [insert name of organisation here]. [Insert name of organisation here] in turn offers a commitment to only allow said pictures and recordings to be used appropriately and sensitively.

I, the undersigned, consent to the use of my image and/or recordings of my voice being used within [insert name of project here]. I understand that the image and/or recordings will be used for [insert details] purposes only and that copyright in the image and/or recordings will be retained by [insert name of the organisation].

I acknowledge that the image and/or recording may also be used in, and distributed by, media pertaining to [insert name of project or organisation here] other than a printed publication, such as, but not limited to, CD-ROM or the World Wide Web.

Copyright restrictions placed on [insert name of organisation here] prevent the content being sold or used by way of trade without the express permission of the copyright holder. Images and recordings may not be edited, amended or re-used without prior permission from [insert name of project or organisation here]. Personal details of those taking part are never made available to third parties.

I require/do not require that my name is removed/retained in association with the shots and/or recordings {please delete as appropriate}

FULL NAME AND TITLE _____

NAME OF ORGANISATION_____

CONTACT TELEPHONE_____

EMAIL ADDRESS _____

SIGNED _____DATED_____

Figure 32.8 Conducting ethical research often requires securing informed consent from your participants, usually through a consent form like this one. (Note: this form is for research using creative methods. Your university is likely to have templates that you can use for conventional methods)

acknowledged. Using an online resource such as Thomson Reuters Practical Law will explain how this can be done.

It can be argued that traditional copyright laws are out of step with the digital age, as everything online is a copy of something. The amount of enforcement that should take place for potential breaches of intellectual property is much contested, and there are numerous ethical issues in using and producing online resources in your research. However, it is still your responsibility to be a responsible researcher and be aware of what does sit under copyright and what doesn't.

Is your research legal?

Like ethical considerations, legal considerations should also be given careful thought as they could influence the scope of your proposed study. An example of this can be seen in the laws governing research into how jurors come to their verdicts: despite the importance of this stage of the criminal process, very little is known about it because there are both common law and statutory provisions that enshrine secrecy for all deliberations by a jury. In order to fill this gap in knowledge, the Wichita Jury Study acquired its data by secretly recording jury deliberations in the city of Wichita in the US (Amrine and Sanford, 1956). The study was strongly criticised because it did not have agreement (informed consent) from the jurors about taking part and it also failed to take into account the legal restrictions on this kind of research (see **Figure 32.9**). The hostile reactions demonstrated the concerns people can have when criminological research interferes with this protection; in **What do you think 32.3** we ask you to give *your* opinion on this controversial topic.

Another example of where legal issues can arise is if you are using visual research methods in your project. Photography is illegal in a 'prohibited place' as defined by the Official Secrets Act 1911 (such as a Ministry of Defence establishment), and you might be guilty of an offence under the Terrorism Act 2000 if the photograph includes a member of the armed forces or police. In addition, public photographers have experienced the police using stop and search powers on them.

Figure 32.9 The researchers behind the Wichita Jury Study used secret, illegal recordings of jury deliberations to gather their data. You should always remember to carefully take into account the legal implications of your research to avoid such issues

Source: AP Photo/Joe Burbank, Pool

> ## WHAT DO YOU THINK? 32.3
>
> ### An inaccessible 'black hole' for criminological knowledge?
>
> The UK's statutory prohibition on acquiring any statements, opinions, arguments, or votes cast by jurors in the course of their deliberations is provided by s. 20D of the Juries Act 1974. This provision means that very little is known about this crucial part of the justice system. But should such laws be allowed to interfere with your discipline?
>
> Consideration of its ethical implications should enable you to see the potential for harm in this kind of research. It would include the lack of voluntariness on behalf of jurors, as their service is coerced by a court summons supported by the threat of imprisonment should it not be done. Anonymity is a key principle of jury service and harm from any research would considerably increase if raising the veil of secrecy were found to have influenced any decision-making. This would have serious implications for both the defendants and victims in these trials, plus others in the future. It could also damage wider society through a loss of trust in the jury system; a level of faith often explained by Lord Devlin's famous description of a jury as 'the lamp that shows freedom lives' (1956: 164).
>
> So, do you agree that the law should be able to rule these matters completely off limits to academic researchers? What could the consequences be if this black hole in criminological knowledge began to be filled? And what about other areas—can you think of any other situations where it might be appropriate for the law to interfere with academic research?

Some methods, such as covert research, can result in pressure on the researcher to commit unlawful acts; in a covert study of football hooliganism, Pearson (2009) explains how committing minor offences, such as confronting rival fans and invading the pitch, were necessary to gain acceptance in the group and make his research possible. Supporters of this method maintain that:

> Research governance needs to be realistically relaxed, not removed, for in-depth research into a range of criminological topics. Some topics like the study of crowd behaviour and public disorder, which are standard topics for criminology, are often difficult to achieve in standard overt ways.
>
> (Calvey, 2013: 544)

The debates over research governance provoke many arguments for today's academic researchers. They can inspire creativity and imagination in criminological research. This means developing alternative methods so that deception used in cases like the Wichita Jury Study is no longer required.

32.12 Conclusion

As we have repeatedly said, there is far more to conducting criminological research than we could possibly hope to cover in a single chapter. We strongly recommend that you make the most of the support and guidance your department provides, and that you follow up the recommendations provided in this chapter's **Further Reading** to learn more about approaches and methods that interest you. But as well as giving you a sense of the many considerations involved in conducting independent research, we hope this chapter has conveyed that conducting student research is a hugely exciting and inspiring prospect. As we outlined in **section 32.2**, its benefits include allowing you to explore an area of criminology that particularly interests you, and to add to the existing criminological knowledge base. Many courses require students to evaluate their own role as a researcher in the project; if so, this provides another great opportunity as it allows you to reflect on the debates we have considered throughout this chapter. You can apply your own project to these never-ending arguments about the best types of research methods, and to the views in other parts of this book about researcher influence in the production of knowledge (such as **Chapter 4**). In addition to reflecting on theoretical positions, an evaluation can also have very practical benefits in enabling you to consider how your project could have been improved, and what you might do differently in any future research. Your knowledge of criminological research and its different aspirations will be developed by using the chapter's **Further Reading**.

Finally, the experience of completing such a large task as a research project allows you to develop and appraise your skill set in order to move forward in other areas of life and study. Conducting research can help you refine your ideas about potential career directions, and both the experience itself and, as we have hinted previously, your reflections on it will undoubtedly enhance your graduate employability which we explore in the next chapter.

SUMMARY

After reading this chapter and working your way through its features you should now be able to:

- Appreciate the breadth of opportunities offered by being an undergraduate researcher in criminology

You are now in a position where you can produce things of value to yourself, to the discipline of criminology, and to others. As promised in **Chapter 1**, your studies can now genuinely become fascinating, dynamic, and stimulating. This means researching the subject as a creative disruptor where you apply your research knowledge and skills to multiple situations.

- Identify effective ways of choosing your research topic and methodology

Making the right choices for your topic and methodology will enable you to get the most out of your research and maximise its impact on you. Relevant topics can be things you personally care about, such as community issues, campaigns, and work-related issues. The ability to make an effective choice of methodology for your project will depend on your appreciation of the quantitative/qualitative debate in research. It will mean you can employ either conventional or unconventional methods in your project.

- Plan the core features of a research project or dissertation

You now have a structure for your research project from **Table 32.2**, which can be adapted according to its size and its core features. Effective time management is of absolute importance and it is also essential that your project is written up in an appropriate style and correctly referenced. This sequence of stages may not always run in perfect order, but these parts can be connected; explaining this will show that you have created a coherent research project.

- Consider unconventional methods of disseminating your research

There is a rich potential in openly disseminating your research, and you are recommended to try a wide variety of methods to take advantage of the communicative power in technology. It is now possible for the work you produce as an undergraduate to reach audiences far bigger than the traditional one of the project's supervisor and marker. Being a creative disruptor means incorporating these opportunities for dissemination into your research; this demonstrates your advanced skills and enhances the impact of your project. Plus, if you get involved in these kinds of steps you will be immersed in the ongoing nature of research, which could further stimulate a desire to research the effectiveness of your dissemination. It could be your next topic where, for example, you research when and why the dissemination was successful or not; meaning the cycle of research could start again.

- Engage with ethical standards for researchers in criminology

It is important to engage with the ethical standards for researchers in criminology. These duties, such as informed consent and avoiding harm to research participants, are integral to academic research; following these principles proves you are capable of showing appropriate sensitivity to others. Both ethical thinking and action are things you can routinely apply to your research, for example when using technology such as phone cameras and the internet. Ethical standards are persistent and also flexible as they can adapt to different circumstances so, when a researcher meets them, there is evidence of enhanced sensitivity and creativity.

 Test your understanding of the chapter's key points by attempting the self-test questions on the **online resources** at www.oup.com/he/case2e

REVIEW QUESTIONS

1. What kind of research do you now want to do? Why?
2. What would be the essential stages in this research?
3. How could the approach of a creative disruptor be used in this research?
4. How could you make the research ethically sound?
5. What limitations will the research have?
6. How do you want research to feature in your future career?

 Access the **online resources** at www.oup.com/he/case2e to check your answers to the review questions.

FURTHER READING

Chamberlain, M. (2013) *Understanding Criminological Research: A Guide to Data Analysis*. **London: Sage.**
This text provides a thorough and stimulating guide for appropriate research methods in different stages of your research. The author uses many examples of his own experiences to help you understand the content and apply it to your own research work.

Clark, T., Foster, L. and Bryman, A. (2019) *How to do your Social Research Project or Dissertation*. **Oxford: Oxford University Press.**
This is a practical guide to the full research process with specialist detail for the different stages of a project or dissertation. It is supported throughout with examples from students to show how your research can become more efficient. There is useful advice on how to get the best out of your supervisor meetings.

Clark, T. et al (2021) *Social Research Methods* **(6th edn). Oxford: Oxford University Press.**
This is the most comprehensive book out there for introducing research methods. Its detail means it can serve as a kind of dictionary for research as it takes you through the whole research process, from formulating a research question to writing up.

Heap, V. and Waters, J. (2019) *Mixed Methods in Criminology.* **London: Routledge.**
This is the first criminology textbook to be focused on the mixed methods research strategy. Its chapters on how to combine quantitative and qualitative data are accompanied by case studies that demonstrate how the approach has been used in criminological projects.

 Access the **online resources** to view a wealth of extra information relating to your study of criminology, including self-test questions, answers to review questions, and links to other resources that will help you enjoy and fulfil your potential within your studies.
www.oup.com/he/case2e

CHAPTER OUTLINE

33.1	Introduction	1002
33.2	Reflective learning and employability	1002
33.3	What employers are looking for	1004
33.4	How to boost your employability	1007
33.5	Producing your 'RARE' employability framework	1010
33.6	Can people 'HEAR' your successes?	1011
33.7	Journeying into careers	1011
33.8	Criminology-related careers	1013
33.9	'Joining the DOTS' in your career plans	1019
33.10	Conclusion	1020

33

Employability and careers

KEY ISSUES

After studying this chapter, you should be able to:

- produce evidence of higher-level reflective thinking to support your employability development;
- understand the characteristics that employers most commonly look for in recruits;
- engage with opportunities available outside of your degree course to boost your employability;
- systematically assess and refine your graduate employability through the RARE framework;
- apply the key principles of career development learning.

33.1 Introduction

In this final chapter we aim to help you succeed in the next phase of your life that begins after graduation, by supporting you to develop your employability and career learning. Before we go further, let's consider what we mean by the term 'employability'. There is no universally recognised definition, but broadly speaking we can understand it to mean the skills, attributes, and knowledge individuals need for successful careers.

In discussing employability and careers we are looking to the future, but to give yourself the best chance of achieving your goals it is important to start laying the groundwork as early as possible. Fortunately, there is a lot of support now available within higher education institutions. In fact, many institutions now include employability as an integral part of undergraduate courses, and even if it isn't part of your course you will find that there are plentiful resources available via your university careers service. Start by finding out what support is available to you, and do this as early in your studies as you can. It may feel a little daunting to focus on your employability when you are grappling with the demands of your criminology studies, but we will explain how both challenges can be tackled simultaneously, and how taking part in employability development whilst you are an undergraduate can be a rewarding and efficient use of your time.

The second part of the chapter aims to get you thinking about the type of career you want, and how you can achieve that. If you are reading this chapter at the start of your undergraduate degree, you may feel it is too early to begin thinking about your future career. Believe us when we say that, as with employability, it pays to start learning about potential careers as soon as you can. Developing an understanding of what employers are looking for, particularly in the sectors that interest you, will lead to more effective and targeted employability development, and taking your time to explore your career options will result in better decision-making.

Employability and careers are inherently practical topics and so, throughout this chapter, we will introduce you to various tools and techniques you can use to support your employability development and career planning. We encourage you to have a go at these yourself and see what works for you.

33.2 Reflective learning and employability

In this section we consider the importance of 'reflective learning' in developing your employability. The **concept of reflection** is increasingly important in various contexts within higher education and the world of work. At its most basic, reflection simply means giving something 'serious thought or consideration' (*Oxford English Dictionary*). However, during your degree course, and perhaps in your future job, you may well be asked to take part in more formal reflective practice intended to promote your personal development. For example, you could be asked to complete a 'reflective journal' in which you might note down experiences you have had, how you feel they went, and what you learnt from them. Or you might carry out an assessed reflective assignment designed to help you connect your personal experience with the theoretical or practical topics you are studying. Read **Conversations 33.1** for an example of two students reflecting on their experience of **work-based learning**.

Reflection is a very useful tool in the development of employability, both in helping to hone the skills that employers are looking for and in developing awareness of, and confidence in, the skills that you possess. By reflecting on your current knowledge, skills, and attributes, you can identify your strengths and the areas you need to improve. Critical self-reflection will also hone your evaluation and analytical skills which are vital to success in your degree and beyond.

There are various academic models of reflective practice that can be helpful in developing a more systematic approach to reflection. The well-known Gibbs' Reflective Cycle is set out in **Figure 33.1**.

Building on earlier work done by Kolb (1984), Gibbs developed a six-stage model of reflection. By following the steps in Gibbs' cycle, you will come to a good understanding of your performance in any given situation and develop valuable insight into how you can improve. The cyclical nature of the model indicates that this sort of reflection is best viewed as an ongoing process rather than a one-off event. In this way, you will feed previous learning into your future activities, from which you will continue to learn, further honing your skills and leading to a cycle of continuous improvement. With each full cycle, your confidence in this type of reflective thinking will increase and it will eventually become engrained into how you practice and learn, both in academic studies and subsequently in the workplace.

CONVERSATIONS 33.1

Reflective practice whilst working in criminal justice

with **Hannah Bailey** and **Sarah Greenhalgh**

Phil Johnson (PJ): Please describe your involvement in the work-based learning element of your degree.

Hannah Bailey (HB): I volunteered to work on a community project called Fast 4wd. This was a scheme offering support to vulnerable adults, predominantly ex-offenders. It gave them mentoring opportunities to increase their engagement with local volunteering initiatives.

Sarah Yates (SY): I also worked for Fast 4wd and ran a weekly drop-in session at a local probation-run Approved Premises (AP). I was then offered the position of relief worker at the AP where I helped with the supervision of its residents. This included maintaining discipline, promoting adherence with the AP rules and monitoring the behaviour of high-risk residents.

PJ: When looking back on this experience, what do you think you learnt about the experience of the people you were working with, and did this affect your views about the practices involved?

SY: I learnt from observing the project coordinator that, when mentoring offenders, a less authoritative approach was a better communication technique. This would encourage them to open up and engage more. Many of them had low skills levels and suffered emotional distress when they thought they were being seen negatively.

HB: Almost all the men I worked with had to adhere to licence conditions. Sometimes these were very strict and that made finding opportunities for reintegration very difficult. This made me reconsider my views on government policies, as I now recognised the extent of the problem. This motivated me to find new opportunities for helping the people on the project to succeed.

PJ: What do you feel you learnt about yourself from this experience?

HB: At the start, I was uncertain if I was doing things correctly and would always check with colleagues before making decisions. However, by the end, I found myself no longer having to do this as I built confidence in my own judgement. I also believe I improved at communicating effectively with both service users and professionals in the justice system.

SY: This experience made me want to work directly with offenders as it developed my communication skills. I learnt the importance of communicating effectively when trying to help people to change their lives. I also felt it enhanced my active listening skills as I got used to observing the importance of behaviour and body language whilst communicating.

PJ: How have you been able to put this learning experience into practice?

HB: It meant I became familiar with licence terms and the conditions attached to community sentences. It also helped me build good working relationships with professionals such as police officers and probation officers. This has increased my confidence in successfully acquiring employment in this field after my graduation.

SY: I agree, it has definitely improved my chances of being employed by HM Prison and Probation Service. My experience of directly working with offenders at an AP has shown me many of the challenges they face in turning their lives around. I learnt many new things, such as the difficulties sex offenders face when they are housed in an AP with non-sex offenders. It enabled me to get a first-class grade in my dissertation that inquired into the lived realities of these mixed environments.

Hannah Bailey (pictured left) and Sarah Greenhalgh (pictured right), BA Criminology students, University Centre at Blackburn College

---

In the context of employability, this model is very helpful in structuring your approach to developing the skills and knowledge employers are looking for. But this type of structured reflective practice will also, of itself, be highly valued by potential employers who will be looking for employees who are self-aware and can proactively drive their own learning and development.

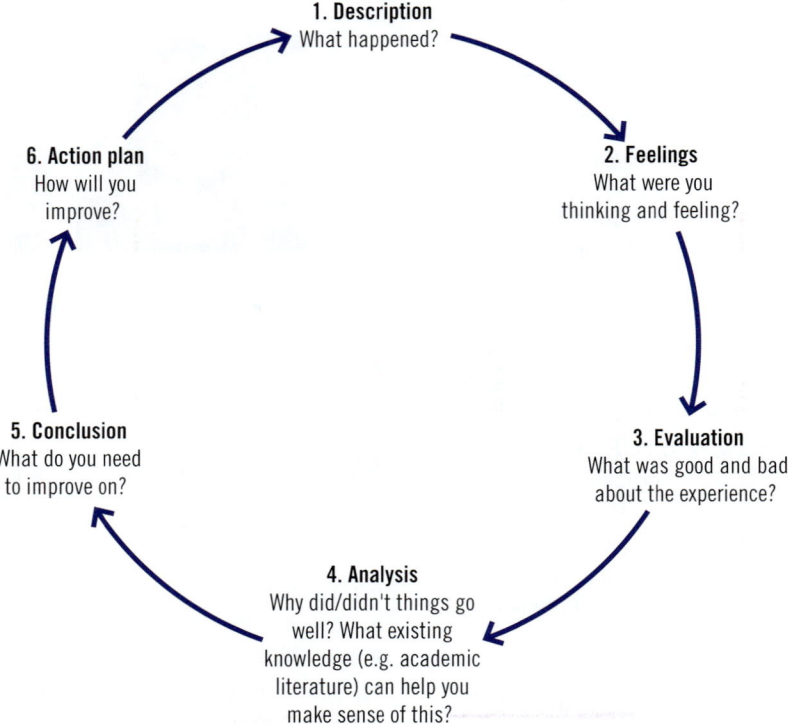

Figure 33.1 Academic models like the well-known Gibbs' Reflective Cycle can be helpful in developing a more systematic approach to reflection

Source: Gibbs, G. (1988) Learning by Doing: A guide to teaching and learning methods. Oxford: Further Education Unit, Oxford Polytechnic

33.3 What employers are looking for

In this section we look at the type of skills that employers tend to value and explain how you can make use of the experiences you have during your degree to develop and demonstrate these skills. In **section 33.4** we will return to these points as we discuss how you can assess your level of employability.

As discussed in **Chapter 1**, you will have to undertake a range of work such as essays, exams, dissertations, presentations, and group work during your degree course. These activities may be essential parts of your course and your primary focus will probably be on getting the best mark possible, but—if considered in the right way—they can also be valuable experiences in terms of developing and demonstrating the skills that employers look for. While we focus in this section on how you can harness and maximise the employability value in your undergraduate course, activities that you participate in outside your studies will also be of value in this context, and we discuss these sorts of activities in **section 33.4**. For an example of a student who made the most of opportunities to develop her employability, both within and outside her degree course, read **Conversations 33.2**.

Since the 1990s, UK universities have been required to consider how their courses can produce graduates who meet employers' expectations. The influential Higher Education Academy Report, Pedagogy for Employability (Pegg et al., 2012) was produced with the aim of supporting institutions in that goal. It cites CBI (Confederation of British Industry) research that highlights seven key skills expected by employers, and these employer expectations are set out in **Figure 33.2**. We will look at each of these points in turn in the context of your criminology degree. The main points are then summarised in **Table 33.1**.

A positive, can-do attitude

This is a difficult term to measure, but a positive can-do attitude can be demonstrated by displaying the attributes of the E3 student (see **Chapter 1**). An effective and engaged undergraduate is one who is employable and by taking on this challenge you will show initiative and proactivity—key elements of a can-do attitude. The same can also be said of a commitment to reflective practice (**section 33.2**).

Figure 33.2 Seven preferences employers look for according to CBI research, as cited by Pegg, A. et al. (2012) *Pedagogy for employability*. York: The Higher Education Academy

Look for opportunities on your course to take your learning further and push yourself out of your comfort zone. Taking on and succeeding at any form of challenge (particularly a challenge you set for yourself), and bouncing back after a failure, are experiences that will show off these attributes.

Business and customer awareness

This point encompasses the importance of commercial acumen, knowledge of the work environment, and respecting and interacting well with other people. You will have many opportunities as part of your course to hone your people skills, some of which are discussed below under communication. Demonstrating this point requires you to explain how you have successfully worked with or for a range of people, and how you related to their differing values and opinions, so make the most of any chances to participate in group work and to interact with people outside your institution (for example, during a research project). Evidence of this kind will be valuable as it demonstrates your flexibility and ability to deal with varied groups (customers, clients, colleagues, officials, etc.). These examples will add substance to bland 'I am a good team player' statements. Commercial awareness may be harder to develop during your studies and best addressed by extracurricular activities. However, you can still go some way to addressing this point on your course by embracing experiences that require you to adapt to new and varied circumstances and environments; this will indicate that you'll be likely to adapt well to commercial and other contexts. If your institution offers any training opportunities to develop commercial awareness then do take advantage of them.

Communication and literacy

High-level abilities in communication and literacy, in both verbal and non-verbal forms, can be acquired from your degree. This is particularly true of non-verbal communication and literacy as production of clear, structured, written work will probably be a requirement of the majority of your assessed work. The variety of complex information you have to read, synthesise, and evaluate as a criminology undergraduate will provide you with extensive experience of advanced literacy. Verbal communication experience may come in different ways—in the course of your studies you may carry out interviews, conduct focus groups, hold formal and informal meetings, as well as regularly communicate with your fellow students and lecturers. Giving PowerPoint or Prezi presentations is another great example of communication that will be of value to employers.

Problem-solving

The development of a questioning mindset is a key part of being a criminology student. Your experience of critically analysing information from diverse perspectives is integral to your studies (as discussed in **Chapter 32** and throughout this book). This critical and analytical mindset, along with an ability to see things from different perspectives, is valuable when it comes to breaking down problems and providing appropriate, possibly alternative, solutions. As you progress through your course, be alert to the problems that you encounter and how you solve them; for example, when carrying out *empirical* research, did you find that you were unable to obtain access to your preferred research subjects? How did you find an alternative course for your project?

Numeracy

Criminology undergraduates have an advantage here over, for example, many arts and humanities students, because all of us at some point will have studied quantitative statistics methods. The ability to understand and manipulate statistics is extremely useful in many employment contexts. Even if you found this a challenging area of study, you may find that the experience you have gained is enough for your chosen role, since required levels of numeracy will vary depending on the kind of work you seek; unless you're aiming at a specialist area, the expected mathematical abilities generally consist of working with things like averages and probabilities, spotting trends and anomalies, as well as more basic calculations.

Information technology

The development of certain information technology (IT) skills will be a natural result of your undergraduate studies. As with numeracy, the level and type of IT skills you need will be influenced by the type of work you are applying for. Some jobs will require specialised skills, such as website development and use of specific packages (such as InDesign), though that's not usually the case for criminology-related roles. Generally speaking, employers want recruits who can use internet search engines effectively and are familiar with standard software packages, such as Microsoft Excel, Word, and Outlook. You will probably have much more experience than this, particularly if your criminology degree has offered assessments via blogs, visual images, and PowerPoint or Prezi presentations, as discussed in **Chapter 1**.

Entrepreneurship and enterprise

It may not be immediately evident how entrepreneurship and enterprise skills result from a criminology degree, but the varied opportunities in your discipline could well mean

Key skill expected by employers	How to apply your degree to these skills
1. A positive, 'can-do' attitude	Being all-embracing and taking the E3 student approach: effective, engaged, and employable.
2. Business and customer awareness	Taking part in team projects that teach the importance of flexibility in working with others.
3. Communication and literacy	Writing clear, structured pieces of work such as essays and literature reviews, as well as critically evaluating academic research. Doing presentations and in-person research.
4. Problem-solving	Using critical and creative thinking to analyse and assess facts and statistics. Providing or exploring multiple solutions to issues in essays.
5. Applying numeracy	Undertaking *quantitative research* using appropriate methods. Working with statistical data and understanding their significance.
6. Applying technology	Using a variety of programs such as Microsoft Office Word, Excel, and PowerPoint, as well as more advanced software such as SPSS.
7. Entrepreneurship or enterprise	Undertaking group work and research projects that add to the knowledge base in criminology.

Table 33.1 Seven key skills expected by employers

you have accrued relevant experience. This element is best considered as two separate points. *Enterprise* is a broad concept that combines the ability to generate ideas with the skills needed to make them happen. It can be demonstrated when creative ideas and innovations are applied to practical situations, and it also includes collaboration and risk-taking. Involvement in group work can be a good way to develop and demonstrate these skills; specifically, it will be helpful to cite evidence of how you took part in the allocation of roles, generated and championed ideas, communicated effectively, and overcame difficulties in the group.

Evidence of *entrepreneurship* prowess may be relatively harder to acquire. Entrepreneurship is recognised as the application of enterprise abilities in the context of setting up a new venture or business. Opportunities for developing this talent whilst studying for a degree may seem limited, but there are aspects of entrepreneurship you can work on during your course, because the same entrepreneurial role is needed to make new projects and ventures happen within existing organisations. This is known as intrapreneurship (being an 'inside entrepreneur').

Table 33.1 provides a summary of how you can apply specific skills and attributes you have learnt during your degree to the seven generic graduate employability skills. Giving these specific examples in interview situations will set you apart from the crowd.

33.4 How to boost your employability

The enhancement of your employability is something you can do both now—during university—and after graduating. To really maximise your employability, you should always be on the look-out for opportunities to develop and display the required characteristics. While you will have opportunities to develop valuable skills and knowledge as part of your course, we suggest that you explore what other activities are available both in and outside your university, because these extra activities can really give you the edge when it comes to applying for graduate jobs. There is a huge, almost endless, range of activities you could particulate in; from classic 'extracurricular' activities such as taking part in university clubs and societies, to paid work, to optional activities that are linked to your course (such as volunteering within the criminal justice sector or campaigning about an issue that matters to you). Some ideas are discussed in **Conversations 33.2**. You may find that there are student engagement roles available at your institution, for example as a group representative. Many universities now offer mentoring work to their students and various types can be available, such as advising new students on your course. Getting involved in academic research projects—that is, working alongside your lecturers as they carry out their own research—is another way of boosting your skills and experience.

If you're looking to expand your skills and knowledge in a particular area, but don't necessarily have the funds or inclination to embark on another formal course, you could sign up to what is known as a MOOC (Massive Open Online Course). These are free courses from prestigious universities, with a lot of flexibility as to when you need to study. Because they are free (in almost all cases), you don't need to worry too much about what happens if you decide the course isn't right for you. But if you do stick at it and complete the course this can be a valuable demonstration of your commitment to continuing professional development (CPD), an attribute welcomed by employers. To find any MOOCs that might be suitable, simply search online for the term or go to specific sites (such as www.classcentral.com).

It can be challenging to navigate the range of options available, and you will find that employing your reflective skills will be useful here. Consider the amount of time you realistically have available, what you hope to get out of your activities (and having fun is also a perfectly reasonable goal, alongside developing your employability!), and weigh your options against these criteria. You might like to consider this alongside the self-assessment work discussed in **section 33.4** in the context of plugging any employability gaps you have identified. The benefits of getting involved in these types of opportunities are discussed in **Conversations 33.3**.

For the remainder of this section, we will discuss work-based learning (WBL) opportunities that may be available to you. The rise in the importance given to employability within higher education has been accompanied by more interest in WBL. Though interest is now growing, WBL is not a new phenomenon and participation in it has long been linked to good final-year grades (Mandilaras, 2004; Balta et al., 2012). The potential reasons for this link were said to be increased focus on studies and enhanced time-management skills. These findings support the view that placements increase the likelihood of attaining full-time paid employment following graduation, and a link between social sciences graduates with work experience and their early employability was found two decades ago (Bowes and Harvey, 2000). If you are still undecided about

CONVERSATIONS 33.2

Engaging with my institution for developing employability skills

with **Zoe Rodgers**

Many of the modules I have undertaken on my undergraduate criminology degree have provided me with essential employability skills. The core 'Graduate Research and Development' modules within my first year set the foundations of my research methods knowledge and sparked a desire to develop my research skills further. Consequently, at the beginning of my second year I pursued and successfully attained a Student Researcher post within the department. This gave me an array of responsibilities such as, contributing to research team meetings, producing recruitment materials, working on the first and second rounds of data collection, inputting data for analysis and aiding the presentation of the findings at a university conference alongside the lead researchers.

This equipped me with fundamental research experience to add to my CV, as I gained valuable insights into the workings of a research project and potential career options within academia. I was also able to undertake a volunteering mentor role, where I supported first year criminology students by delivering one-hour workshop sessions. This diversified my employability further by developing my adaptability, communication and transformational leadership skills. This helped me gain necessary experience of delivering student support, which aided me to make career decisions with regards to my preferred career pathway.

Facilitated by my interest in second year research methods modules, I developed my knowledge of the mixed methods approach and a range of more advanced data collection methods, including establishing my interviewing technique. Subsequently, I was able to apply my research skills to a range of study, employment and volunteering opportunities offered in the department.

Throughout my degree I have taken on board the topics studied within my modules to find my areas of research interest. My academic, personal, and professional skills were especially pertinent during my dissertation module, as I was able to apply the skills from previous modules and work experience to my own mixed methods research thesis. Being aware of the preparation and planning work required to successfully execute a research project, I was able to complete my dissertation to a high standard within a set timeframe. This resulted in me being approached by my Academic Advisor (personal tutor) and Dissertation Supervisor to work with them as an intern on a funded research project, which included the opportunity to write a journal article as a co-author.

This opportunity so far has been extremely beneficial, as I have been required to liaise with a partnership organisation, the research team, participants, and an external transcriber in a professional manner that contributes significantly to the study. I was able to apply the interpersonal skills I developed within my modules; regarding communicating with stakeholders holding a range of value bases and professions in order to work towards a common aim.

Getting involved with the different opportunities occurring around my course has given me new experiences, furthered my skills and abilities, that can be transferred to many types of employment.

Zoe Rodgers, BA Criminology student, Sheffield Hallam University

---

whether it is worth doing then consider the finding from recent research with employers:

> Two-fifths warned that in today's competitive job market, it was either 'not very likely' or 'not at all likely' that a graduate who'd had no previous work experience at all with any employers would be successful during their selection process and be made a job offer, irrespective of their academic achievements or the university they had attended
>
> (High Fliers, 2020: 23)

Placements are a popular way of acquiring WBL experience and the length of these opportunities can range from a matter of days to year-long arrangements. Longer placements often occur in 'sandwich courses' where a year of full-time work, often paid by the employer, is a mandatory requirement. An **internship** can be the name for either summer or year-long placements and traditionally these were obtained by students coming towards the end of their studies, but in recent years it has become more common for first-year students to take them as well. They have acquired some negative publicity for potential exploitation from employers, though payment can be provided in many cases. But if you feel in control and believe it can benefit your career, then an internship is well worth

CONVERSATIONS 33.3

Employability for criminology: boosting your employability

with **Dr Vicky Heap**

When students decide to pursue a criminology degree, their minds are likely to be filled with ambitions of studying high-profile serial homicide cases and exploring the more unconventional (gruesome) explanations as to why people commit crime. Let's face it, employability skills don't quite possess the same wow-factor, which is why criminology undergraduate courses should embed them in different ways such as experiential learning and simulation learning.

I believe a tiered approach throughout the three years of undergraduate study is most appropriate for developing employability. It really should start from day one, through concepts such as reflection, action planning and CV building. Criminological content can be the vehicle to explore these skills in an applied and interesting way. For example, themes such as ethics, equality and diversity can be explored in the context of research methods and a research project following a short placement of relevant work. It can include students researching local policing priorities such as hate crime or cyber-bullying, then presenting their findings to local community groups, schools and colleges to raise awareness. These skills can be developed and refined through research methods and dissertation modules in the second and third years.

Students that get involved in work-related learning and undertake placement opportunities, get the benefits of experiential learning. They develop a reflective approach that can be related to theoretical developments within the discipline of criminology. So, take advantage of any opportunities you get to do a placement, to meet different agencies or to get involved with volunteering opportunities and careers mentors. I would also recommend taking opportunities to work alongside lecturers conducting academic research, for those of you aspiring for a research career, as well as working in the criminal justice system.

All of these elements can ensure criminology students have the necessary graduate attributes to successfully gain employment and transform lives once they have completed their studies.

Dr Vicky Heap, Reader in Criminology,
Sheffield Hallam University

---

doing as it will provide you with a different experience beyond your formal course; it can help you become a well rounded team player who understands how to work with a diverse range of people in different environments and within a given time frame.

Another form of placement is **work shadowing**, where you can directly observe a specific individual or role in an organisation. These arrangements generally last for short periods of time and are unpaid, but as well as providing relevant work awareness they offer excellent networking opportunities.

WBL experience could also be acquired by volunteering work which, despite sharing the same financial barrier as unpaid internships, can be far more accessible due to the sheer number of opportunities. Contemporary criminal justice work now takes place in a mixed economy of voluntary organisations working alongside private and public sector bodies. The organisations work delivering services, campaigning, giving mutual aid, and providing coordination support to other voluntary sector bodies (Maguire et al., 2019). This means there can be numerous WBL opportunities that are an accessible way of producing and refining your graduate employability.

Part-time work in combination with your studies is another way of getting the required work experience. This can enhance your employability as it demonstrates reliability and commitment as well as developing generic transferable skills such as teamwork. It can also be an impressive way of demonstrating your prowess in time management. Concerns about excessive workloads have led to some universities completely banning their students from doing part-time work during academic terms, although most advise a maximum of around 15 hours per week. Part-time jobs may not offer the targeted experience of internships or work shadowing but their successful combination with the demands of a complex programme of undergraduate study could nonetheless enrich your employability. You could seek out part-time work that is related to the skills you identify as requiring improvement (see **section 33.4**). For instance, if you need to brush up on professional IT skills then look for an office job where using a computer is necessary.

In this section we have shown the diversity in the types of work available. Experience in the justice sector (and others) can look extremely impressive on CVs, and time spent in this environment will develop job-relevant skills, help clarify your career choice, and open up networking opportunities. These days, students applying for work placements in their first or second year at university are selected through a similar recruitment process to that used to recruit graduates, so in many ways you can treat it like a mock examination. Going through a process of researching suitable opportunities, completing successful applications, and succeeding at interviews can all be described as career management skills. These experiences should not be left until you're approaching graduation as they can be worked on throughout your time as an undergraduate.

33.5 Producing your 'RARE' employability framework

Now you have started the process of thinking reflectively about your performance and have begun to appreciate what employers are looking for, we recommend that you next use an employability framework to systematically track your overall progress. This process is sometimes referred to as Personal Development Planning (PDP), although PDP may be a broader process that encompasses your academic development as part of your course as well as employability (though, of course, these aspects overlap). Your institution may have developed a framework that you can use. If you don't have a pre-existing, employability-focused framework that works for you, the 'RARE' framework, which is a development system based on the work of Cole and Tibby (2013), is a helpful tool. The system supports you to create a personal action plan by working through four steps.

Stage 1: Reflect

Reflect on both your understanding of employability and the understanding of the stakeholders in your employability (your university, regulatory and professional bodies, potential employers, etc.).

Questions to consider:

- What are the graduate employability expectations where you want to work (see **section 33.8** for help with deciding which career avenues are right for you)?
- Who can help you find out what they are?
- Who are the stakeholders (influential people and organisations) that set the expectations?
- Are their perceptions of employability comparable with yours?

You are advised to revisit this first stage to refine your framework after you have read this full chapter.

Stage 2: Assess

Assess and map your current employability features by assessing your own level against those required for the areas of work you are interested in. Self-assessment means making judgements about your own learning and development, and monitoring your own performance like this will help you grow in confidence and encourage you to take greater responsibility for your learning which is, in itself, a highly marketable skill. It is at this point in the framework that your reflective thinking, as discussed in **section 33.2**, really comes into play.

Questions to consider:

- What aspects of graduate employability do you currently possess and to what level?
- What is needed for the work you seek to acquire?
- Are there any gaps?
- What are the areas you feel most and least confident in?

At this point we suggest that you return to the seven graduate skills and attributes set out in **section 33.3**. Reflection and development in these seven key areas will help you to establish a broad base of transferable skills that you can call on. You can supplement these with any specific skills that you have identified are required for your chosen career path in stage 1. To help you with this self-assessment process, we have developed some tools that you will find on the book's online resources, which provide a structured means of assessing your progress. In these forms, the seven elements are expanded into 21 sub-skills and this detail will add depth to your reflections. These exercises provide a starting point to help you record and assess your performance, but as you gain confidence in your reflective practice and develop your understanding of the skills needed for your future career, you may want to adapt these or develop your own personal tools. Your university may also provide self-assessment tools of this nature to help with employability development. This self-assessment can be a strategy you apply to every piece of assessment you undertake on your course; you merely select three or four skills that are needed for its completion and then assess your performance in those areas.

Stage 3: React

React by filling in the gaps you identified at stages 1 and 2.

Questions to consider:

- Who can help you fill in these gaps?
- Can they be addressed by your undergraduate course?
- Could your life or work experience be used?
- What is your action plan for answering these questions?
- Is it effective?
- Who can help you make this judgement?

Stage 4: Evaluate

Evaluate the development plan you created from stages 1–3. Questions to consider:

- Is your strategy from stages 1–3 defined and organised?
- Is it comprehensive?

The cyclical nature of this strategy means it can be used more than once; in fact, it should be, as the more frequently you work on each stage, the more progress you will make. It has a dynamic nature in which each stage influences the others and so repetition is advised, as neither your employability nor your potential careers remain static. The first time you use it, you should start with the first stage and then work through the others in the advised order; a structured framework for expressing your employability will emerge.

33.6 Can people 'HEAR' your successes?

If you have put the effort into developing your reflective practice, building an action plan, and tracking your progress, you'll want to make sure that you keep a good record of all this work. Whether your institution offers the chance to compile a Higher Education Achievement Report (HEAR), a portfolio of your development and achievements, or any other format, it is important to take advantage of such opportunities. Documenting the things you have done whilst being an undergraduate can mark you out as an engaged learner; it will also save considerable time when applying for future jobs and will mean you can more effectively articulate your experience and skills. A document of this type needs to include the following sections:

- personal information (up-to-date CV; employment history);
- educational history (summary of educational achievements to date; evidence of training or staff development);
- skills audit (self-assessment of your graduate employability skills; see **section 33.5**);
- 'critical incidents' reflection (select at least five memorable incidents that have affected your learning at either university, work, or in general life and apply the reflective learning cycle; see **section 33.2**);
- contributions by third parties (references are normally sent between employers but any testimonials about you and your work are important assets in a portfolio).

An e-portfolio is the most common way of documenting this evidence and we recommend that you start compiling this now.

33.7 Journeying into careers

This section provides you with support and guidance for the final stage of your journey from university to the workplace. This move will be a successful one if you follow the advice for maximising *career learning opportunities* and take the time to investigate and understand the career options that are available. All the work you have done in reflecting on your skills, attributes, and preferences will help you as you consider which avenues to take.

We begin this section by discussing in broad terms the jobs market you will be entering. We then move on to explore the various types of careers you could consider, with a focus on those that are particularly relevant to criminology and criminal justice graduates. Finally, we offer some guidance on how you might go about evaluating your options and deciding which career path(s) you'd like to focus on.

As you plan for your transition into the workplace, it's helpful to have an overview of the jobs market that you'll be entering. We begin by making some general points about the current graduate jobs market, with some pointers as to how this might develop. We then touch on some criminology-specific points to be aware of.

General points about the workplace you will be entering

Here's the good news: recent reports on graduate employment tell a largely positive story. In 2019, the number of graduate positions in the job market saw their highest annual increase since 2010, and public sector employers (where many criminology-based jobs are found) increased their vacancies by 12.5 per cent, compared with 3.6 per cent in the private sector (High Fliers, 2020: 10).

The most recent research into the employment outcomes of new graduates found that six months after graduation, almost three-quarters of graduates were employed, around 20 per cent had progressed on to further study, and 5 per cent were unemployed (Higher Education Careers Services Unit and the Association of Graduate Careers Advisory Services, 2018: 8). Having said this, we cannot ignore the fact that events since then, namely the global Covid-19 pandemic, risk jeopardising this situation. At the time of writing, it is too early to know what the impact of the pandemic will be on graduate employment opportunities over the coming years, but it is clear that the global economy has taken—and will probably continue to take—a severe hit as a result, and this is likely to have some effect on the number of graduate jobs available. How serious and long-lasting these effects will be is difficult to judge at present and depends on multiple factors. While the situation is certainly worrying, there is some cause for hope. In the last recession, in 2008, the graduate recruitment market suffered less than expected. Employers tend to be cautious about taking a short-term view and putting a stop to their intake of new talent because this will hamper their ability to recover and grow once things start to bounce back. Whatever the economy has in store in the wake of the pandemic, the best advice we can give is that economic turbulence makes it even more important that you take the time to focus on developing your employability and careers knowledge.

The current climate aside, concerns about the number of graduate opportunities in the workplace have been around for many years and have been accompanied by fears about the end of the 'job for life' view of employment, in which it was assumed that people would work for the same employer for most of their career. In contrast, these days people are expected to be able to make career changes throughout their working lives, and this is known as a 'protean career' (a concept first coined in the 1970s but increasingly relevant today). A protean career has been described as 'a process which the person, not the organization, is managing' (Hall, 1976: 201). So, the trade-off for less job security may be greater individual control. You may remember that the term protean was used in **Chapter 25** to describe the development of the use of community service as a criminal sanction, a sentence that somehow stayed constantly popular with sentencers and yet was frequently altered to meet the different penal expectations for providing reparation, rehabilitation, and retribution. A similar sense of continual change can be seen in personal career development as individuals are expected to play a range of roles and regularly regenerate their identity:

> Pursuing the protean career requires a high level of self-awareness and personal responsibility. Many people cherish the autonomy of the protean career, but many others find this freedom terrifying, experiencing it as a lack of external support.
>
> (Hall, 1996: 10)

The independence and freedom in these career structures can be unsettling, so the support of your 'travel partners' (see **Chapter 1**) will be invaluable for your journey. The more people you talk to as you progress into and through your career, the more opportunities you will discover. Flexibility is your major asset, as individuals who can adapt to the changing demands of the workplace, and to various working spheres, are those with the highest potential for career success. This serves to underline the importance of developing and demonstrating a broad range of transferable skills that can be employed in a variety of situations.

The quote above from Douglas Hall, written back in 1996, demonstrates that the concept of the ever-changing—or protean—career took hold long before the disruption to employment from technology that has gathered pace in the last 15 years. The development of tech-based industry has heightened the issue thanks to the impact of companies such as Amazon, eBay, and Uber. Many believe that the disruption from online-based businesses such as these will substantially change work practices in the 21st century; for example, an increasing shift towards what has become known as the 'gig economy', described as 'a labour market characterized by the prevalence of short-term contracts or freelance work as opposed to permanent jobs' (*Oxford English Dictionary*). Robin Chase, the co-founder of the extremely successful car-sharing site, Zipcar, said of her 2015 book, *Peers Inc.*:

> My father had one job in his lifetime, I will have six jobs in my lifetime, and my children will have six jobs at the same time.
>
> (*The Guardian*, 29 November 2015)

It may sound unlikely that people in the future could simultaneously have so many different jobs but, arguably, it may not be that remote if they include, for example, trading on eBay; driving for Uber, and renting space in your house as a 'hotel' room for Airbnb. While these sorts of activities may provide helpful additional income streams, they're unlikely to be your preferred, primary career path.

However, self-employment among graduates, whether freelancing or via start-ups, is on the rise, albeit from a low base. Whether you're aiming for a traditional graduate role or prefer something more flexible and individually driven, the unpredictability of the current job market means that to increase your chances of success you need to be prepared to be flexible.

Criminology-specific points about the workplace you will be entering

In addition to these general pressures, the workplace for criminology-related careers can also be subject to political and legal influences. The shifting legal environment was discussed in **Chapter 23** where we considered the narrowing of the traditional gap between the civil and criminal branches of the law. This means that criminology graduates who wish to enter discipline-relevant jobs no longer need to limit their focus to careers in the police, probation service, or prisons; instead, they can aim at a much broader justice sector that includes local government, health, the armed forces, and other emergency services. These different parts of the economy are all under the remit of the organisation Skills for Justice, which is the skills council for the justice sector. A search of their website will soon show the variety of jobs that now exist in this area of work.

The opportunities in criminology-related careers are also affected by changes in the nature of crime itself, such as the developing issue of cybercrime (see **Chapters 6** and **14**).

Changes in the ways we currently respond to crime are also likely, and this will affect the opportunities available in the sector; as the chapters in **Part 4** of this book demonstrate, the debates over methods of punishment and rehabilitation are far from settled. The politics of crime are likely to remain key issues as politicians and governments seek public popularity. This was exemplified by the first speech of Prime Minister Boris Johnson, which included a pledge to recruit 20,000 more police officers over the following three years. However, it's worth noting that political involvement can be unpredictable; that announcement by Boris Johnson conflicted with the pre-existing government policy (of Johnson's own party) of austerity and financial cuts reducing the number of employees across the public sector.

Criminology-related careers are also likely to evolve based on influences within the discipline's research agenda. For example, the attention given to domestic abuse in recent decades means Domestic Abuse Caseworker positions (with either victim or perpetrator perspectives) are now frequently advertised by charities and community organisations. For that reason, when seeking careers in the justice sector, and especially further study opportunities, it pays to understand what the emerging issues are within the field. The New frontiers features throughout this book will help to guide you on this. More pervasively, in **Chapter 1** this book began with the view that criminology is a hybrid academic discipline; that is, something that has evolved out of other disciplines such as anthropology, law, geography, economics, politics, sociology, psychology, etc. This mixture of academic influences has resulted in criminology being inherently interdisciplinary, and this diversity is reflected in the many different careers open to you.

33.8 Criminology-related careers

As a criminology graduate you can access a wide range of different careers, not limited to those linked to your degree subject. There are plenty of general resources that will help you research careers more widely, and your university careers service will be able to help with this. One particularly popular source of careers information for graduates is the Prospects website, and that is a good place to start in researching potential career paths. We have outlined a few criminology-related career destinations to get you started. You can read more about many of these career paths in **Chapter 24**, where we give an overview of the principle institutions of the criminal justice system and describe their key roles and the challenges they face.

Police

If you're keen to put your criminology knowledge into practice in the real world, and feel you have the resilience to cope with what can be an emotionally and physically demanding job, you could consider policing. Police officers perform a wide variety of duties but broadly their remit is to protect the public from crime and ensure successful prosecutions of those who commit crimes. They need to be able to communicate effectively—calmly and confidently—in challenging situations, demonstrate good judgement and problem-solving skills, and possess high levels of dedication and motivation. There are two principal routes into policing designed for graduates: a two-year work-based training programme alongside studying for the Graduate Diploma in Professional Policing Practice which is recruited at police-force level or a two-year national leadership development programme called Police Now (www.policenow.org.uk), which also includes work-based learning but is recruited centrally and has a focus, as the name suggests, on developing future leaders. Read **Conversations 33.4** to learn about Police Now from the officer who founded it, and from a young detective who came through the programme (you can find out more about both routes into policing, and learn about life as a police officer, at www.joiningthepolice.co.uk). If you do your research and think policing could be the route for you, consider first applying to be a special constable to get first-hand experience before making up your mind.

The legal profession

The legal profession of England and Wales includes solicitors, barristers, and—less commonly—chartered legal executives (as well as, at a more senior level, judges). Solicitors are by far the largest group of legal professionals. A solicitor advises their client on the best course of action, depending on their circumstances and the relevant law; they communicate on their client's behalf, in person and in writing, and draw up technical legal documents. A barrister provides specialist advice and representation; they are generally instructed by a solicitor when a case goes to court or when a matter becomes particularly complex. While solicitors are generally employed by law firms and other organisations, most (but not all) barristers are self-employed and work alongside other barristers in 'Chambers'. Lawyers of all types need excellent communication skills, the ability to synthesise and analyse very complex information, and attention to detail, amongst other skills. They need to be able to cope with pressure because the stakes are often high for the client and hours may be long. Barristers spend much of their working life advocating for clients in courts and tribunals, and so confidence in public speaking is essential. Most lawyers start to specialise early in their career and for our purposes the most relevant branch of law is criminal law. Criminal lawyers are responsible for either prosecuting or defending people who have been accused of committing a crime. Defence lawyers work in private practice or for the Public Defender Service, while most prosecutors work within the Crown Prosecution Service (CPS), though the CPS also

---

CONVERSATIONS 33.4

A career in the police

with **David Spencer** and **DC Upile Mtitimila**

As a former detective I know the positive impact the police can have on crime and society, so I co-founded The Police Now National Graduate Leadership Programme to encourage a new generation of diverse, brilliant individuals to enter the service.

The Police Now National Graduate Leadership Programme is a salaried two-year training programme through which participants (usually a cohort of about 300 each year) develop skills in leadership, negotiation, problem solving, decision-making, and emotional intelligence. It begins with a six-week intensive training academy, designed and delivered by outstanding, high performing frontline police officers. Participants are then placed in some of the most challenging communities in England and Wales in the role of a neighbourhood police officer, enabling them to get to know the issues up close and develop innovative ideas and techniques to tackle the most pressing challenges.

This programme has been a driving force for change within the policing sector and 80 per cent of candidates who join the programme continue their journey in policing, either by progressing through their force or going on to other disciplines within the sector. However, experience with Police Now equips participants and alumni with skills for life; skills which are transferable and recognised across the public and private sectors.

DC Upile Mtitimila is a Detective Constable who entered the police through Police Now's National Graduate Leadership Programme, which he joined after studying international relations at the University of St Andrews. Our participants come from a range of academic backgrounds, but a degree in criminology would stand you in very good stead for both the programme and a career in policing. As well as meaning that you are already familiar with the issues we encounter in policing and the role of the police within the criminal justice system, studying criminology will have helped you develop critical thinking skills and an active, independent approach to learning. These skills are crucial on the Police Now programme, as participants need to not only understand different strategies but critically assess them in order to choose the best approach (or come up with their own solution); apply strategies in practice; and regularly reflect on their efficacy, sharing the outcomes with peers.

David Spencer (pictured left), CEO and Co-Founder of Police Now

Since completing Police Now's National Graduate Leadership Programme, I have transitioned into a detective role investigating serious and complex crime. For me, that journey was about doing something where you have an incredible amount of responsibility.

My motivations for joining Police Now, and coming into policing through this particular route, stem from being slightly sceptical of policing. I knew I wanted a position and role where I could make a tangible difference to people's lives, but there was just something that made me reluctant to engage through the regular route.

Police Now's National Graduate Leadership Programme focuses on neighbourhood policing, which appealed to me as I am drawn to problem solving and the more complex issues behind crime. We have weekly or fortnightly meetings with social housing providers, social care, the NHS, and the fire service to bring the right people to the table. The rewards last a long time and affect a whole community. Being a neighbourhood police officer really is about being a leader in the community you are serving and having direct responsibility for changing people's lives for the better.

One of my proudest achievements has been addressing a long-term drug-dealing problem. I spent time mapping addresses that had been linked to the supply of heroin and crack cocaine, working with colleagues to locate the intelligence we'd received. Some of these locations had been open for 15 years, and the difference after we'd closed them down was amazing. I saw people coming outside who had previously been unwilling to speak to the police; they were really grateful. I wrote some guidance on best practice around the closure of these premises which won me the Achieving Cheshire Excellence award.

What sets Police Now apart is that, while learning how to be a police officer, you are encouraged to think critically about how things should be done. You learn about various strategies and then choose the one that will work best, or even come up with your own solution.

I have chosen to stay in policing, but even within the police there are so many specialisms you can go into: examples include covert policing, counterterrorism or child protection, as well as emerging areas such as cyber policing. I'm also now studying towards a part-time master's degree in Policing, Policy and Leadership with the University of Portsmouth—completing the programme has given me the drive to continue developing my knowledge and skills, and keep working to transform society for the better.

DC Upile Mtitimila (pictured right), Police Now Graduate Leadership Programme alumnus and international relations graduate, University of St Andrews

instructs self-employed barristers (you can read more about the Crown Prosecution Service at www.cps.gov.uk).

Probation and Youth Offending Teams

Probation service officers work closely with offenders in various settings to support rehabilitation and reduce re-offending. They assess the risk that offenders pose to the community, collaborate with other personnel within the criminal justice system (within the courts, police, local authorities, and health services, for example), and make recommendations that feed into sentencing and parole decisions. They need to be able to build a rapport with the offenders they manage and help them overcome the practical (for example, housing and employment) and emotional challenges they face. To be a probation officer, you need (amongst other skills): excellent interpersonal and communication skills; a caring and patient attitude; flexibility and the ability to think on your feet; good writing skills to produce effective reports; and the resilience to deal with challenging behaviour. To become a probation officer you need to complete the Professional Qualification in Probation, which takes either 15 or 21 months depending on your existing experience and qualifications. Recent moves to outsource some probation services to private companies mean that opportunities are now available outside the public sector, within Community Rehabilitation Companies) to read more about the role of a probation services officer within the (public sector) National Probation Service, visit www.probationservicesofficer.co.uk).

If you like the sound of the work done by the probation service and are keen to work with young people, you could explore the work of Youth Offending Teams (YOTs). YOTs are housed within local authorities and their purpose is to work with young people who are involved (or at risk of being involved) in crime, to help them avoid (re) offending and find alternative paths. Specific job titles and roles will vary by local authority and it is possible to progress to management and specialist roles.

Prisons

Prison officers have responsibility for maintaining security and order within prisons, and working to rehabilitate prisoners. It is a varied and demanding job that requires recruits to adapt to a range of roles, as prison officer Louisa Laven describes in **Conversations 33.5**. Prison officers will spend much of their day interacting with inmates so they need to have excellent interpersonal skills—to be able to relate well to people in tough circumstances—and be adaptable and calm under pressure. There are no specific qualifications required to become a prison officer and personal qualities are considered more important. Find out more about the work of a prison officer and how the application and assessment process works at www.prisonandprobationjobs.gov.uk, and see **section 24.6** of this book for more detail on prisons.

Academia and research

If you've enjoyed the research aspects of your criminology degree and like the idea of delving deeper into the discipline, you could consider a career as an academic, much like your university teachers. To succeed in academia you need good qualifications, a passion for your chosen discipline, and a talent for carrying out research, critically analysing information and ideas, and developing your own (informed) arguments. Excellent communication (written and oral) and leadership skills are also very helpful. These days, being an academic within a university is a more precarious career path than it once was, with many junior academic positions offered on a temporary basis; it can be challenging to secure coveted permanent positions and takes dedication and persistence. The job is a busy one, with most academics juggling the competing demands of teaching students and conducting research, though some posts will be research-only and others solely focused on teaching. Career paths within academia vary depending on the subject, and there is no single route even within

CONVERSATIONS 33.5

A career in the prison service

with **Natasha Porter** and **Louisa Laven**

Many people work with prisoners—from teachers and trainers to psychologists and charity volunteers. However, the only people who see every single prisoner, including those who are most disengaged, vulnerable and difficult, are prison officers. They have the most access to prisoners and have the ability to spend the most time with them. The Unlocked Graduates programme enables frontline prison officers to make real change in their prisons. We fund our participants to complete a bespoke Master's degree, giving them the knowledge they need to make change, as well as giving them regular, high quality mentoring and support. In exchange, we expect them to be brilliant at this incredibly tough job and to consider how they can make systemic impact.

Since starting the programme, Louisa has not only become an excellent officer but has also begun to have wider impact in her prison. She was awarded funding last year through our Innovation Acceleration Programme to start a prisoner-led TV channel in her prison, and this is now running successfully in her placement prison. We are looking forward to seeing where Louisa's career takes her. Every year we welcome a new cohort of Unlocked

Graduates to our programme and we strongly encourage any criminology students interested in making a difference within the prison system to consider applying.

Natasha Porter (pictured left), CEO and Founder of Unlocked Graduates

I first became interested in prisons when I was at Loughborough University, studying for a Criminology and Social Policy BSc. My first time in a prison was shadowing the chaplain at HMP Erlestoke for a very memorable and alarming day. It wasn't alarming because of the volatile prison environment; it alarmed me to find out about all the failings and inefficiencies within the prison service. Almost 50 per cent of the prison population re-offend within a year; the majority of them suffer from mental health issues with high rates of self-harm and suicide; drug use is extremely prevalent. The list goes on. From that day on, I was hooked—I knew my career would centre around prison reform and the effective rehabilitation of prisoners.

I applied to the Unlocked Graduates programme because it offered the opportunity to be on the frontline, working with prisoners every day, building relationships with them to support them in their rehabilitation. The funded Master's degree was also hugely attractive to me, for the help it might provide in future career paths. The academic side has turned out to be an effective tool for self-awareness and reflection while starting the prison officer role, and I've been able to really engage with existing prison literature because I can constantly apply it and relate it to my daily work.

My criminology degree undoubtedly helped me by equipping me with a level of forensic psychology and HMPPS knowledge, but no amount of academia really prepares you for working on the landings. In my prison a day of work in its simplest form is as follows: unlock the men, get them to and from work and their meals, make the regime run smoothly and safely, then lock them again, while counting them all four times throughout the day. But throughout this day, you will switch roles countless times; from a security guard, to a first aider dressing self-harm wounds, to a support worker helping a prisoner write their CV for release, to a detective receiving and reporting intelligence, to a mediator de-escalating violent situations. Every single day is different and even though it can be seriously tough, I have loved this job since day one. It is such a reward when you feel you've had an impact, better equipping a prisoner with the tools they need to change their lives and not return to prison, that it makes the tough days worth it.

Being on Unlocked has improved me as a person. I've learnt to cope and make decisions under all kinds of pressure, developed confidence and communication skills for every situation, gained a lot of empathy and a superhuman level of patience. These, among many more, are valuable skills and traits that I can bring to any future career choice.

Louisa Laven (pictured right), Unlocked Graduates participant and Criminology and Social Policy graduate, Loughborough University

disciplines, which can make it feel rather confusing at first. We recommend talking to your lecturers about this if you're considering a career in academia. The traditional first step is to complete a PhD which is a significant piece of assessed independent research lasting three years full time or five years part time, and before you can do that you will usually require a Master's degree (though that's not always the case, as **Conversations 33.6** demonstrates). After obtaining a PhD, most would-be academics will look for early career positions within universities, such as a temporary research assistant working on a larger research project alongside other academics or a part-time teaching post you can combine with pursuing your own research and publications. After some years of working in these sorts of roles and making a name for yourself, you can apply for permanent lectureship positions.

If you're keen on research but less sure about pursuing a career in academia, there are alternatives out there. For example, the Civil Service employs Government Social Research Officers and various other public bodies and private companies (often consultancies) also recruit researchers.

Charity work

The charity sector is extremely diverse and among it are many organisations dedicated to, or whose work includes, issues relating to crime and criminal justice. The charity sector has an important role to play in this area and we include the perspectives of those working in relevant charities in various chapters; for example, see **Conversation 7.3** with a representative of Victim Support and **Conversation 8.3** with a representative of anti-hate crime charity Galop. Working for a charity can be very rewarding, especially if it's a cause you're passionate about. However, money is often tight in charitable institutions so pay is rarely high and job security may not be as good as in some of the public sector roles we have outlined. The job roles on offer are as diverse as the organisations, but we'll give a few examples here of jobs that were advertised at the time of writing, to give you a sense of the breadth of roles available. The charity Victim Support offers emotional and practical support to help people recover after becoming victims of crime and traumatic events. They recruit a range of personnel, from Victim Focus Officers who provide direct support to victims in their local area, to office-based administrative assistants. Nacro is a charity dedicated to **social justice**, with a criminal justice arm. It has a variety of mission-specific roles on offer, including Reducing Reoffending Workers who work directly with people coming out of prison, and Bail Accommodation Support Service Referral Officers who manage the allocation of accommodation for people released from custody. The NSPCC is a well-known national charity that aims to protect children from harm. It offers roles including, for example, that of an E Learning and Publications Assistant providing technical support for their e-learning platform, and an Executive Assistant supporting the work of an NSPCC director. From this sample of available roles, you'll get the sense that charities offer both specialised, mission-specific jobs as well as those that aren't specific to the charity's cause (administration, technical support, etc.). All large charities will employ staff in central roles, in areas such as fundraising, communications, research, and policy (monitoring and aiming to influence government policy). So, within the charity sector it's possible to work in your chosen job type and develop transferable skills that will be valuable across sectors, while at the same time contributing to your charity's mission.

We also advise using social media to search for criminology-related career opportunities, and if you have taken the advice in **Chapter 32** about adding criminal justice agencies to your networks, you may only need to extend your search a little. This could be done by adding terms such as 'Recruitment' or 'Jobs' after the name of the organisation and you will soon have these contacts in your networks. This might not work with all organisations so using the popular job finding sites will be helpful. You can also use graduate recruitment websites (such as TARGETJobs, Milkround, and Prospects), plus graduate careers directories (such as The Times Top 100 Graduate Employers and The Guardian UK 300). Some employers are known to use recruitment apps (such as Debut or Placer), but this is currently limited.

You may also consider continuing in higher education by taking a postgraduate course, like the contributor to **Conversation 33.6**. This is an essential step if you are aiming for a career within academia, but also something that many graduates choose to do in order to develop higher level skills, gain knowledge in a different area of study, or hone their discipline-specific knowledge and specialise. All of this can give your employability a boost, though if you are undertaking further study for employability reasons rather than simply because of personal interest, you should carefully consider exactly what you will gain from your specific course and how this will be considered by potential employers versus gaining work experience.

According to the Framework for Higher Education, an undergraduate degree is a level 6 qualification, after this are a Master's qualification at level 7, with a PhD at level 8. Universities can vary on their postgraduate entry criteria but generally all will expect a good undergraduate degree. The access route to level 8 may be conditional on level 7 qualification but, as discussed in **Conversations 33.6**, alternative routes exist.

CONVERSATIONS 33.6

Working with criminal justice organisations for further studies within criminology

with **Vickie Barritt**

After graduating with my BA (Hons) Criminology, I spent several years working in the justice sector; for a community safety partnership, the police, and a Women's Centre funded by the Ministry of Justice. This experience made me aware of the gap in official responses to offending, problems exemplified by the many stories of going into peoples' homes and seeing unopened letters on the fireplace because no-one there can read them. My work was therefore very influential in getting my local Community Rehabilitation Company to be my research partner, which in turn was integral to being accepted on my current programme of study.

Competition is fierce for funded scholarships so, to increase my chances, I applied to two different doctoral training partnerships. I was successful with one because of the strength of my research proposal. To get it right took eighteen months as I talked to as many potential supervisors as I could, about the best ways for developing my idea. It had to follow a similar structure to those on my BA and had to justify my plans for acquiring quantitative data from the probation service, qualitative data from probation staff and service users, and for using case studies that track peoples'

journeys through the criminal justice system. It was also strengthened by the fact that literacy was an identified priority in my CRC's equality and inclusion strategy.

In 2019, I was successful in my application to do a full-time, four-year PhD when I was awarded what is known as a White Rose Doctoral Training Partnership. This pays all of my tuition fees plus an annual tax-free maintenance grant, currently £15,009, for up to four years. It has given me the opportunity to push the boundaries of what is currently known and in four years' time, I will hopefully be one of the leading authorities on my subject area. I will also have a diverse and varied qualification with many different components that will stand me in good stead for the future.

Vickie Barritt, PhD Student, Sheffield University

33.9 'Joining the DOTS' in your career plans

As with developing your employability, it is very helpful to take a systematic approach to career planning. One of the most respected approaches is the DOTS model, which advises four stages of: *Decision learning, Opportunity awareness, Transition learning,* and *Self-awareness* (Law and Watts, 1977). It is a memorable prompt for the different parts of career planning, which requires you to think logically and strategically to be effective—that is, to 'join the dots'. However, while the stages in this model are useful, the ordering of them is less so, and many careers advisers recommend that you approach these stages in the order SODT. The four stages, with slightly tweaked wording to emphasise practical application, are set out in the SODT order in **Figure 33.3**.

The sequence starts with *self-awareness*. You are encouraged to consider your own abilities, personality, interests, and values as a basis for considering what type of career will suit you best. This brings us back full circle to the concept of reflection discussed in **section 33.2**, and the mindset and exercises we discussed in that section will be extremely helpful when it comes to building your self-awareness for career planning. Try the exercise in **What do you think? 33.1** to begin reflecting on what matters to you in a job.

In the second stage of the model, *opportunity awareness*, you will begin to explore the career options that are available. This stage is all about research, so read up about criminology-related careers (see **section 33.8**), visit relevant websites, talk to your university careers adviser, and any other actions you can think of to find out as much as you can about the various opportunities available (for example, could you speak with somebody working in a similar role?). As part of this process you should apply the self-awareness that was the output of stage 1 to begin narrowing down the options to those that interest you most. You should research these careers in as much detail as possible because the more knowledge you have, the more reliable your decision-making will be at the next stage.

In the next part of the model you exercise *decision-making*. At this stage, you will carefully evaluate each of the options you generated at the opportunity awareness stage. This is where you apply everything that you know about yourself (self-awareness) to your possible careers, to decide on which are most likely to be the right fit for you. It will increase the effectiveness of this stage if you take the time to consider your decision-making process. For example, how important are things such as intuition, external advice, 'trial and error', analysing the risks, or weighing up the 'pros and cons'? Try the exercise in **What do you think? 33.2** to consider some possible decision-making scenarios. These reflections will help you appreciate how you think about decisions and whether your approach changes in different circumstances. There is not necessarily a right or wrong way to make decisions, as long as you feel confident that your process yields good results, which you can judge by past performance. However, the decisions about your career are some of the most important you will make so it pays to take some time to carefully weigh the pros and cons. If you feel that you would benefit from some more support in making decisions, there are a number of useful tools you can use (read about these at www.mindtools.com). Your career decision-making will need to start early in your undergraduate days—for example, thinking about how you will acquire work experience—so these skills will soon be put to the test.

Once you have identified your preferred career routes, the final stage in 'joining the DOTS', is *transition planning*. This stage is about building your understanding of how the careers system works in your chosen areas, and what

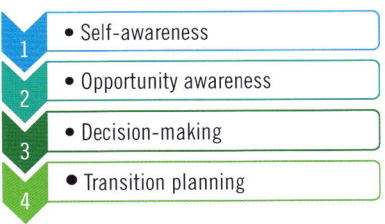

Figure 33.3 'DOTS' is a memorable prompt for the four main stages of career planning, but many careers advisers recommend approaching them in the order 'SODT'

WHAT DO YOU THINK? 33.1

Your vision of meaningful work

Most people are looking for 'meaningful employment'—but what does this phrase mean to you? Consider the following prompts before attempting the reflective task below.

- In your view, are all forms of employment meaningful? If not, why not?
- Do you define meaningful employment by financial reward? Or by things such as autonomy, professionalism, and the purpose of the employment?

Reflective task: if money was not an issue (but you still had to work), what kind of employment would you choose to do, and why?

> **WHAT DO YOU THINK?** 33.2
>
> **Your decision-making**
>
> The following are all realistic and common scenarios you are likely to face in your career.
>
> - Imagine that you are coming to the end of a period of work experience when you are offered two different positions in the organisation. You have to decide which one to take—how do you choose the right one for you?
> - You are involved in a team project for your organisation and, when it reaches a successful conclusion, the whole team is praised by the senior managers. However, you know that one of the team did not take their share of the responsibility. How do you decide what to do?
> - A rival organisation has offered you a position—should you stay with your present employer or move to the new one? How do you make the right decision?

steps you need to take to give yourself the best chance of securing the job you want. You'll want to have a good grasp of how to locate positions in your chosen field as this will vary significantly between different sectors and types of role. For certain jobs there will be very predictable forms of advertising, particularly graduate schemes in large organisations. However, sometimes you'll need to dig a little deeper, and there are sizeable numbers of positions of various types that are filled without any advertising at all.

This demonstrates the importance of networking and, fortunately, the current pervasiveness of social networking services makes this easier than ever to do. Your networking abilities can be worked on throughout your time as an undergraduate, so do take advantage of all opportunities for establishing relevant career networks. If you haven't already done so, now is an excellent time to speak directly with people working within your chosen field or organisation, so don't be nervous to ask; most people are only too happy to help and the worst that will happen is that the person you've asked says they're too busy to speak.

During the transition planning stage, you should also start to prepare for the process of producing applications and being interviewed and assessed for roles. It is vitally important that you understand the key principles behind writing an effective application and doing well at interview, and your university careers team will be able to support you in this, so do make the most of their expertise. The knowledge behind crafting the perfect application or giving a compelling interview is not something that comes naturally; it requires experience, so don't try to go this alone. Hiring graduates can be a ruthless process with some employers using so-called 'weapons of mass rejection' (WMR) to sift applications. This is a powerfully succinct description of what can happen in the shortlisting stage when understaffed HR departments or, in smaller organisations, the employers themselves, are swamped with applications that they do not have the resources to deal with, and use crude sifting techniques such as degree classification and any spelling or grammatical mistakes to eliminate large swathes of applicants. Awareness of this practice illustrates how important it is that you understand exactly what your selected employer is looking for and take the time to craft the most effective—and accurate—application possible.

33.10 Conclusion

In this chapter we have learnt about the twin concepts of employability and careers. Employability encompasses all the skills, traits, knowledge, and experiences that make a person an effective and desirable employee. We have encouraged you to take a considered and strategic approach to developing your employability and to begin this process as early in your degree as possible. Employability development is an inherently personal process (though best achieved when supported by the input of others), and to succeed at it you need to know yourself; to understand your strengths and weaknesses. That is why we began this part by discussing the concept of reflection, something at the core of most of the activities we have recommended throughout the chapter. As much as self-awareness is key, so is an outward-facing mindset, because you need to know what characteristics and experiences will make you employable, both generally—we have seen that there are some things almost all employers value—and specific to the type of job you want. When reflection and self-awareness are combined with an understanding of the needs and priorities of employers, you give yourself the very best chance of success. The value in thinking reflectively and strategically can be maximised if done in a systematic way and so we have recommended that you use a system—we suggest the RARE framework—to help you build an employability action plan and track your progress; and that you record your achievements in a portfolio that you can draw from as you move into the career-planning phase.

Ideally, you will think about potential careers alongside your employability development, though you may not have a clear idea of what you want to do from early in your degree course. These two processes feed each other: the self-awareness built from your employability reflections will inform your thinking about career options, and your career thinking will, in turn, influence which points you choose to focus on in your employability development. The key to finding the right job for you on graduation is to do as much research as you can, because in this context knowledge really is power. This detailed knowledge will help you first make the right decision on which is the path for you, and then increase your chances of securing your chosen role. Finally, you need to understand how to marshal all the knowledge you have gleaned about your chosen job and sector, and the employability you have developed, to succeed in applications and interviews. Here, we have strongly encouraged you to seek expert help and take full advantage of the resources available to you within your university.

The journey towards your ideal career is rarely an easy one but if you follow the advice in this chapter it can be immensely rewarding. If you take just one thing from this chapter, let it be to start the processes of developing your employability and learning about careers as early as possible—it really is a marathon and not a sprint. Finally, we wish you every success, and hope you find a path that leads to happiness and fulfilment!

SUMMARY

After reading this chapter and working your way through its features you should now be able to:

- Produce evidence of higher-level reflective thinking for your employability development

The chapter began with the essential advice that employability is something that should be worked on throughout your time as an undergraduate. We discussed the importance of reflection to your personal development, a practice that underpins many of the activities we recommended throughout the chapter, and suggested Gibbs' reflective cycle as a means to develop your higher-level reflective thinking. This reflective thinking enables you to critically assess your abilities and understand what and how you need to develop.

- Understand the characteristics that employers most commonly look for in recruits

We set out seven core characteristics that research suggests most employers value in their recruits, and then considered the opportunities provided by your criminology degree to develop and demonstrate each of these characteristics.

- Engage with the opportunities available outside of your degree course to boost your employability

This part of the chapter highlighted the many and varied extracurricular activities you could take part in to develop your employability. Participating in work-based learning was recommended as a particularly effective way to gain compelling skills and experiences, and is something that research suggests may also benefit performance on your course. We detailed the various types of work-based learning opportunities available.

- Systematically assess and refine your graduate employability skills through the RARE framework

We recommended that the most effective way to develop your employability is to take a systematic approach, by following a framework such as RARE (reflection, assessment, reaction, and evaluation). This allows you to develop a personalised employability action plan and track your progress. We also recommended that you record your achievements in a Higher Education Achievement Report (HEAR), or similar.

- Apply the key principles of career development learning

The final part of the chapter looked at careers. We offered some insights into the graduate jobs market and looked at the types of job often sought by criminology graduates. We then discussed the DOTS approach to career planning, a system that takes you through four steps to understand your personal characteristics, explore the various paths, decide on the right opportunities for you, and learn how to maximise your chances of getting the job you want.

Test your understanding of the chapter's key points by attempting the self-test questions on the **online resources** at **www.oup.com/he/case2e**

REVIEW QUESTIONS

1. Find out what employability and careers support is available to you within your institution. What is on offer as part of your criminology course, and what services are provided centrally? Make a note of your findings and consider how and when you might take advantage of the various services and opportunities.

2. Practice using Gibbs' reflective cycle. Select a recent or forthcoming activity from your course—ideally something that is assessed—and work your way through each of the steps in the cycle. How did you find the process? How might you use it in future to support your personal development?

3. Apply the RARE framework (reflect, assess, react, evaluate) to assess your current employability, and build an action plan for your personal development. If you have yet to engage with career development learning to any meaningful extent, we suggest that you focus on the seven key characteristics discussed in **section 33.3**. You can add to your RARE document once you have a better idea of the specific points you'll need for your preferred career paths.

Access the **online resources** at **www.oup.com/he/case2e** to check your answers to the review questions.

FURTHER READING

Cottrell, S. (2021) *Skills for Success: Personal Development and Employability* **(4th edn). London: Macmillan.**
Now in its fourth edition, this popular book helps undergraduates create their own personal development programme to nurture the attributes and skills today's employers want. It is divided into four parts, with the first helping students define what success means to them. The second and third parts have ideas for developing people- and task-management skills, and creative and reflective thinking. Part four is particularly valuable as it is focused on what employers want from job applicants.

Diver, A. (ed.) (2019) *Employability via Higher Education: Sustainability as Scholarship.* **Cham: Springer.**
Whilst this edited collection is predominantly aimed at lecturers, thinking like one and appreciating how employability is currently being taught will help you develop ideas for your own employability. It includes an extensive collection of chapters that allows you to select areas of interest; four chapters are based on recent experiences of criminology, criminal justice, and law undergraduate students.

Access the **online resources** to view a wealth of extra information relating to your study of criminology, including self-test questions, answers to review questions, and links to other resources that will help you enjoy and fulfil your potential within your studies.
www.oup.com/he/case2e

GLOSSARY

Abolitionism The position taken by some criminologists that all forms of penal sanction are unacceptable and should be eradicated because they rely on misleading concepts of individualised guilt and responsibility.

Abuse of process A legal principle that gives the judiciary the power to stop a prosecution (to grant a 'stay') if the court considers the procedure to be unfair. It is a vague principle that is rarely enforced.

Actus reus A legal term which means 'guilty act' and refers to the actions or conduct required for establishing that a criminal offence has been committed.

Adultification The practice of thinking of and treating children and young people as if they were adults, for example by explaining and responding to their offending as if they had equivalent maturity and responsibility.

Adversarial system A system of law—and general approach to justice—which perceives criminal procedure as a contest between two opposing sides who have responsibility for producing evidence. Two advocates represent their arguments in a formal court hearing before an impartial judge, magistrate, or jury, who determine(s) the truth and pass(es) justice. It is the system used in **common law** countries such as England and Wales, and in the US.

Advocacy The ability to skilfully present a case in court through either oral or written methods.

Aetiology The study and identification of causes, for example the causes of abnormal behaviours or disorders such as crime or illness.

Age of Enlightenment (also known as the Enlightenment) The basis of enlightenment thinking is that human reasoning can be used to discover all knowledge about the world. It emphasises reason, individualism, and scepticism (especially of religion). The Enlightenment started in the late 17th century but remained important throughout the 18th century.

Agenda bias The degree to which a pre-existing subjectivity or preference on the part of a researcher, scholar, or other key stakeholder can influence how they pursue knowledge creation within criminology.

Agentic Having or displaying agency, that is, rational choice and autonomous decision-making ability.

Androcentricism The practice (conscious or not) of adopting a male-centred view of the world. It involves prioritising the interests of men over the welfare of women and privileging masculine traits.

Anomie The breakdown of social standards or controls (a lack of ethical guidance) which leads to a dysfunctional society in which the rules have broken down and people feel free to act in criminal ways.

Anti-essentialism An explanatory theory within race theory that sees group identities as fluid, and categories such as race, gender, and sexual identity as socially constructed and imposed by those with power. Universal claims on deviance and those who commit crime are seen as leading to marginalisation and exclusion.

Antisemitism Hostility towards, or prejudice against, Jewish people and their faith.

Apolitical The position required from judges which means they are not allowed to show any allegiance or involvement with politics. The requirement is in place to protect the principle of judicial independence.

Appellate courts The higher of the two main categories of court in the English legal system. The three appellate courts (the Supreme Court, the Court of Appeal, and the Divisional Court) hear appeals against decisions made by the **courts of first instance** and their decisions set precedents that must be followed.

Artefactual risk factor theories A set of explanatory, **developmental** theories of youth offending that identify quantifiable, psychosocial risks in the lives of children and young people and assert that these 'risk factors' are predictive of offending in later life.

Attrition Though it has a more general meaning, in criminal justice this term refers to the gap between levels of known crime and the response of the criminal justice system in terms of prosecutions, convictions, and sentencing.

Avoidance learning When a person learns to behave in a positive way through adopting an automatic response to a stimulus. Treatments based on classical learning are limited because the person who is learning is passive.

BAME community Black, Asian, and minority ethnic groups. Thanks to the power of criminological research, we know that these groups can be discriminated against in the criminal justice system and society more widely.

Before and after experimental design Taking measures of the **independent variable** before and after implementation of an intervention in order to compare any differences and explain them as the effect of a cause.

Bentham's Panopticon A prison design drawn up by Jeremy Bentham in 1787 which utilised surveillance to maximise the capability for monitoring and controlling all aspects of inmates' lives and behaviour.

Bifurcation The division of something into two branches. For example, where criminal justice policy may advocate severe punishments for serious offenders but more lenient punishment (even diversion) for less serious offenders.

Biological positivism A group of explanatory theories which identify the biological characteristics internal to an individual as the causes of crime.

Bivariate data analysis The form of analysis used when the relationship between variables is being investigated.

Blackstone ratio A criminal justice concept which holds the protection of innocent people to be a greater priority for the system than conviction of the guilty. Its statement that it is better to release ten guilty people than convict one innocent person signifies the harm caused when the system mistakenly convicts somebody.

Born criminal The idea that crime arises because of something biological or psychological which is 'wrong' with an individual, usually believed to be inherited.

Broken windows theory The theory that neglect of any kind of infringement in the community, such as visible damage to property ('broken windows') for example, increases the likelihood of further crime and neighbourhood decline, and therefore should be addressed immediately.

Butterfly effect The idea that a small change in one part of a system, process, or chain of events can produce large differences further along in that same system, process, or chain of events.

Capitalism A capitalist system of production is a system in which the means of producing goods and services, and the accruing profits, are privately owned by individuals or companies rather than the state.

CAQDAS The acronym for Computer Assisted Qualitative Data Analysis Software. It refers to the programmes that can assist researchers with analysing qualitative data.

Central nervous system (CNS) The part of the nervous system which, in humans, is made up of the brain and spinal cord and it controls the activities of the body.

Chicago School of sociology and criminology A group of theorists and school of thought which emerged in the late 19th century from the department of this name at the University of Chicago. Beginning in the early 20th century much of the Chicago School were concerned with explaining the physical distribution of crime and they established links between environmental factors and criminal behaviour. *See also* **social disorganisation theory**.

Chivalry thesis The theory that women receive more lenient treatment in the criminal justice system because of the chivalrous attitudes and behaviour of the predominantly male criminal justice system workforce.

CITES The Convention on International Trade in Endangered Species of Fauna and Flora. This is the main international law protecting wildlife.

Claimant The individual or organisation that is bringing legal action in a civil law case.

Classical criminology, classicism A theoretical perspective which is based on the idea of rational choice and **free will**. It portrays offenders as rational, calculating, and as choosing to offend because they calculate that they will gain something. As offenders choose to offend they can and should be punished but that punishment should be proportionate to their wrongdoing.

Closed question A question used in an interview or questionnaire that asks participants to choose from a set of fixed responses, which might include a ratings scale. It contrasts with the **open-ended question**.

Cognitive The process of acquiring knowledge and in criminology this places the problem behaviour clearly in the mind of the individual. Crime arises out of processes in the conscious mind which are engaged in choosing how to behave.

Cognitive learning The idea that all aspects of and processes of the conscious mind are engaged in choices about how to behave—learning involves behaviours, skills, attitudes, and morals. It is therefore necessary to interact with many aspects of learning to fully alter behaviour. The idea is that an informed learner is more likely to retain the positive activity because it becomes part of what is important to them.

Common law An unwritten body of law based on precedents. These laws are created when statutes do not cover a case so the court decides how to apply law to it. That interpretation sets a 'precedent' which is used for all cases that follow.

Commonwealth The international association of countries that consists of the UK together with states that were previously part of the British Empire, and its dependencies.

Communitarianism A philosophy that turns away from a focus on self-interest and individual's personal rights and interests and argues that social order is best upheld by individuals respecting each other and their community as humans are social and need controls to live together.

Community order A sentence that is served in the community and requires an offender to comply with one or more conditions set by the court.

Community resolution An informal agreement between an offender and victim (where there is one) to use **restorative justice** techniques to resolve an offence for which the offender accepts responsibility.

Comparative criminology One of the two main types of global criminological approaches (the other type is **transnational criminology**). It compares similarities and differences in crime and justice between countries and regions and explores incidences of local crime and justice in their international context.

Concept An abstract idea that arises when we draw together shared characteristics into groups, allowing them to be considered together. This grouping of information permits us to simplify a mass of data and so helps our understanding.

Conditional caution An out-of-court **disposal** which stipulates conditions that must be fulfilled if the offender is to avoid prosecution.

Conditional discharge An order which releases an offender and says that if they do not commit another offence within a set period (a maximum of three years), no further action will be taken. It is similar to a suspended sentence except that is not possible to attach **community order** conditions.

Consensus theory A theoretical perspective which asserts that society is held together or 'works' because the people in that society share a set of key values and beliefs, and agree on the same norms or rules. Consensus theorists emphasise harmony, integration, and stability within a society.

Consociational An arrangement whereby countries with deep divisions—along religious, ethnic, racial, or cultural lines—share parallel social and political structures in order to create stability and avoid domination of one group by another, as is observable to some extent in Belgium, for instance.

Constructivism, constructivist (Also referred to as **constructionism** and **constructionist**) An ontological position (a theory about how reality should be understood) which takes the view that social phenomena and their meanings are constantly being constructed by people. It contrasts with objectivism.

Contempt of court The criminal offence that is committed when disrespect for the court system has been shown. It is designed to protect the integrity of court proceedings and any conduct interfering with the course of justice can be deemed as a contempt of court. It is a strict liability offence so it can be committed regardless of any fault from an individual or organisation.

Content analysis A technique for systematically describing written, spoken, or visual communication. It typically provides a quantitative (numerical) description of qualitative data. Many content analyses involve media—print (newspapers, magazines), television, video, films, and the internet.

Control group The subgroup within an experimental sample which does not experience any manipulation of the **independent variable**—this variable is 'controlled' or kept constant. This group exists so that its results can be compared to those of an **experimental group**, which does experience a change in the independent variable.

Convict criminology A branch of critical criminological study and social movement which aims to bring to the foreground the voices of those who have been convicted of criminal offences. Convict criminology places the experiences and opinions of prisoners and ex-prisoners at the centre of criminological research and encourages (ex-)prisoners to take an active role in designing and carrying out such studies and to become academic criminologists.

Corporate crime Crimes committed by an otherwise legitimate organisation, such as a business or financial institution, or one of its representatives, acting on its behalf. These crimes are intended to benefit the organisation. It is a type of **white-collar crime**.

Corrective justice When wrongs committed by one individual against another are repaired or made good as far as that is possible. In this case, justice is rectifying an injustice that has been inflicted, for example compensation.

Cost–benefit evaluation A type of evaluation that aims to measure whether the costs of an initiative are justified by its possible benefits by looking at both impact and process. Assessing the costs and benefits in response to crime is highly important considering the limited resources available to the criminal justice system, but it can be extremely difficult to quantify the financial benefits of things such as reductions in crime or improvements in perceptions of safety.

Courts of first instance The lower of the two main categories of court in the English legal system. These courts, which include Magistrates' Courts and Crown Courts, hear cases first and have to follow the precedents set by the more powerful **appellate courts**.

Covert In a research methods context, this refers to a form of study that is conducted secretly (undercover), without the knowledge of study participants or subjects. It differs from an **overt** study, where participants are aware of the research.

Creative disruptor A term used in business and marketing to refer to innovative ideas that bring about positive and creative change in an established model. In this book, we refer to creative disruptors as those who bring new ideas and approaches to criminology, for example by conducting their research in imaginative ways that challenge established knowledge or ways of thinking.

Crime control model A model of criminal justice that advocates efficiency when dealing with criminal cases. It is often characterised as an assembly line and aims to deal with the maximum number of cases with the minimum amount of resources.

Crime script A full, step-by-step account of all the actions and decisions which are involved in a crime.

Criminal responsibility The legal principle that requires a **defendant** to be capable of standing trial. It can be lacking when a defendant is a child or if they did not have the mental capacity to distinguish between right and wrong at the time of the alleged offence.

Criminalisation The process of transforming behaviours and individuals into crimes and criminals.

Criminogenic Causing or likely to cause criminal behaviour.

Critical and radical theories A group of explanatory theories which challenge the assumptions of **positivism** by asserting that crime is the product of the perceptions of lawmaking and law enforcement activities of powerful groups (for example, the ruling classes, whites, adults) to the detriment of less powerful groups (such as the working classes, black and ethnic minorities, children).

Critical criminology A theoretical perspective which emerged in the 1960s and challenges traditional understandings such as the **classical**, **positivist**, and **interpretivist epistemologies**. It claims to uncover false beliefs about crime and criminal justice and often studies the effects of power and context on behaviour.

Critical moment In a criminological context, this is a point in a young person's life when their individual characteristics and the social factors shaping their experiences are exposed to specific influences or forces which may lead to significant changes in their lives, such as the onset of offending or desistance from offending. Also known as a turning point.

Critical race theory A theoretical framework that **deconstructs** and challenges racial inequality in society by illustrating how such inequality is reproduced through accepted structures and assumptions.

Cross-cultural comparisons Theoretical and statistical comparisons made between cultures (typically between countries) in relation to dominant definitions, explanations, and responses to crime.

Cross-examination A key stage of adversarial court trials in which a witness is questioned about their evidence by the opposing side and their credibility is assessed.

Cross-sectional research A research design in which data is collected and analysed at one specific point in time (also known as a 'snapshot' design).

Cultural criminology A criminological perspective that is concerned with the interaction between commonly experienced cultural influences such as media, advertising, and politics, and the acts committed by both criminals and the state. Cultural criminology is particularly concerned with issues of social injustice, the significance of subcultures, and the heightened emotions associated with acts of deviancy.

Culture The values, beliefs, norms, shared history, languages, communication, religions and religious beliefs, rituals, art, and shared stories of a group. Culture encapsulates the way a group sees and understands itself, and the 'ways of life' which guide what members of the group do and the way they do it, and it is continually evolving.

Cybercrime An ever-developing and wide-ranging form of crime that involves the use of technology, particularly the internet and computer networks, in the planning and commissioning of criminal activity and deviance.

Dark web The term given to websites that are publicly visible but hide the identities of the people and organisations that run them. The anonymity of the dark web creates much concern but offers valuable services for people living in oppressive, totalitarian societies.

Deconstruction In social science research, deconstruction involves analysing textual, verbal, visual, and other information to uncover the underlying message the information seeks to convey. Often, the objective of deconstruction is to expose the limitations of dominant beliefs and the agenda that motivates their perpetuation.

Deductive research Research that tests and refines existing **hypotheses** and understandings.

Defendant The legal name for the person or organisation accused of having committed a crime. This is also the name for the party with potential liability in a civil law action.

Defensible space theory A theory based on the idea that the living environment can be designed and constructed to minimise or prevent the possibility of crime occurring. It often builds in design elements which increase surveillance of an area and so allow inhabitants to become actively involved in their own and their neighbours' security.

Demand characteristics An artefact of the research process where participants form an interpretation of the study's purpose and (sub)consciously change their behaviour to fit that interpretation.

Dependent variable The variable within an experiment that is measured with the intention of identifying it as an effect of manipulating the **independent variable**.

Descriptive theory A theory that arises when a researcher gathers data (what the researcher hopes is typical data) and describes what is happening. It uses the data to build categories and predict and explain behaviour.

Desistance The process and the outcome of a former offender achieving a long-term and sustainable cessation of offending.

Determinism The assumption that the causes of crime are predetermined and preceded by identifiable causes, rather than the result of the individual's **free will**.

Deterrence theory The idea that if someone knows they will be caught and liable to be punished, this will discourage them from committing a crime; so we should structure our scale of punishments with this as the principal objective of the justice system.

Developmental A form of criminological theory that identifies the causes and predictors of crime in early life (childhood and adolescence) and seeks to explain their influence on offending in later life.

Deviancy amplification A media-induced phenomenon where an isolated act of perceived deviance is over-reported or exaggerated, leading to further episodes of deviance and a **moral panic** regarding the reported behaviour.

Differential association A theory which assumes that crime is learned behaviour and that people need knowledge, skills, and recognition of opportunities in order to offend. It claims that crime will only be learned if it is part of an individual's environment and discusses the social circumstances in which crime or other behaviour might be learned.

Disablist hate crime A crime directed towards a person because of their disability or a perception of their physical disability, learning disability, or mental health condition.

Disclosure of evidence A legal requirement that arises before a criminal trial and imposes obligations on both sides to inform the other of the evidence in their case.

Discourse analysis A qualitative approach to analysing written, vocal, or sign language use, or any significant event that is 'semiotic' (the study of signs and symbols and their use or interpretation). It operates on the assumption that reality is shaped by language and some strands, such as critical discourse analysis, seek to uncover power relations that underpin talk.

Displacement A concept that, in a criminological context, suggests that intensive crime prevention activity in one geographical area is likely to lead to a relocation of offending behaviour elsewhere rather than eliminating it altogether.

Disposal The final settlement in a criminal case, such as a sentence passed by a court. There are various types of disposals, including out-of-court disposals which impose a punishment (such as a fine or a caution) on an offender without them having to go to a court.

Distributive justice The idea that in modern societies there is an acceptance that goods and evils will be fairly distributed through society, so there are often expectations or rules such as 'equal pay (or other benefits) for equal work'. This idea is more complex than it may at first seem as we have to take account of equality (of opportunity and outcome), proportionality, and fairness.

Diversion In the context of crime, diversion is when offences are dealt with informally, outside the official processes of prosecution and court hearings.

Documentary analysis *See* **Content analysis** and **Secondary data analysis**.

Doli incapax A 'rebuttable presumption' in UK law that children aged from ten to 14 are unable to tell the difference between right and wrong so are incapable of committing a crime. Before its abolition in 1998 (it is now only relevant to historic crimes committed before this year), children within this age range could be convicted if the prosecution could prove that the child knew that what they were doing was seriously wrong.

Double deviance thesis The theory that women whose lifestyles or circumstances do not fit in with the normative standards set by men are (whether consciously or subconsciously) considered doubly deviant, and therefore receive particularly punitive treatment in the criminal justice system. It is sometimes known as the evil woman thesis.

Double jeopardy The long-established rule that a person who has been found not guilty cannot subsequently be tried again for that offence. The rule experienced major reform in the Criminal Justice Act 2003 which, subject to certain safeguards, allows retrials of selected serious offences even after an original verdict of not guilty.

Drug trafficking The illegal cultivation, manufacture, importation, distribution, and sale of controlled or prohibited substances (drugs).

Due process model The idea of a justice system that exercises just and appropriate adjudication of offences whilst ensuring that alleged offenders are treated fairly and equitably, and with suitable safeguards, by the judicial system.

Ecocide The destruction of the natural environment by deliberate or negligent human action. This term is often used to describe large-scale environmental damage.

Ecological additions The pollutants that are emitted into the ecosystem from the legal operation of production processes.

Ecological disorganisation The destruction of nature caused by the intensification of the **ecological withdrawals** process.

Ecological jurisprudence The idea that nature should be at the centre of legal thinking and that laws can (and should) be interpreted to give better environmental protection. This is sometimes referred to as 'earth jurisprudence', or as 'wild law' or 'earth law'.

Ecological justice The idea of social and environmental justice and the idea that society and the environment are interconnected. Ecological justice argues that man owes a responsibility to the environment.

Ecological validity The degree to which a research method, finding, or conclusion provides an accurate representation of real-world behaviour.

Ecological withdrawals The environmental harms caused by extracting raw materials from the natural environment.

Either way offences A category of criminal offence that can vary in their deemed seriousness and so can be tried at either the Crown Court or the Magistrates' Court. A person charged with one of these offences has traditionally had the right to elect for a trial by jury, but the extent of this right has been questioned on several occasions.

Empirical Knowledge that is generated using sensory experience, particularly through experiment and observation.

Empiricist, empiricism The theory and practice of generating knowledge 'scientifically' through sensory experience, typically using experiment or observation.

Enlightenment *See* **Age of Enlightenment**

Environmental racism Racial discrimination in environmental policy and the enforcement of regulations and laws. Environmental racism refers to the deliberate targeting of people and communities of colour for environmentally harmful operations.

Epistemological reflexivity The critical examination by a researcher of how their belief system has shaped their research design and interpretation of findings.

Epistemology In social science research, a researcher's epistemological stance reflects their philosophical position on what constitutes valid knowledge of the social world, and how such knowledge should be generated.

Essentialist, essentialism The belief that social categories such as gender or crime have distinct or intrinsic characteristics with which they can be identified and defined.

Ethnocentric The dominance of a particular cultural perspective (typically that of the white, westernised world) in the creation of knowledge in criminology.

Ethnographic The systematic study of people and cultures from the point of view of the subject of the study.

Ethnomethodology A method of analysis which studies the way in which people make sense of their everyday worlds, taking account of different perspectives.

Evolutionary psychology A theoretical approach which applies Darwinian ideas to the development of the human psyche and claims that the human mind has developed various methods and mechanisms to process information in ways which permit us to resolve commonly encountered problems. Evolutionary psychology claims that in order to understand behaviour today we need to consider the environment in which our ancestors lived.

Examination-in-chief A key stage of adversarial court trials in which a witness is questioned about their evidence by their own side and their credibility is assessed.

Experimental group The subgroup within an experimental sample that experiences the manipulation of the **independent variable**; in other words, it receives the experimental procedure or treatment. This group's results are compared to those of the **control group**, where the independent variable is 'controlled' or kept constant.

Extraneous variable Any variable that is not the **independent variable** but could affect the results of an experiment. The researcher wants to make sure that it is the manipulation of the independent variable that has an effect on the **dependent variable**.

Fair procedure The **common law** doctrine that every individual has the right to fair procedure in the system. Currently, fair procedure for a criminal case is taken to include the protection within the Human Rights Act 1998. The elements of what is considered to be a 'fair' criminal procedure can change considerably with time. For example, until 1898 a **defendant** was not allowed to testify in their defence at trial; conversely, in 1994 the law was changed in order to hold it against a person who did not testify in their defence at trial.

Fault principle The principle that only people who can be considered at fault can be held legally responsible for a crime.

Femicide The killing of women and girls, usually by men and because they are female.

Feudal system A system in which the lowest people in a society serve or work for their 'master' in return for land; the 'master' serves his 'lord' in return for larger pieces of land and so on, up to the monarch.

Focus group A form of interview conducted with a group of participants. The participants have quite a lot of control over how the discussion unfolds but a moderator or facilitator steers it, asking questions and intervening or using prompts where necessary.

Folk devil A group which is negatively stereotyped and portrayed in the media and culture as the embodiment and main cause of social and crime problems.

Free will The ability to choose between various things or courses of action without being restricted.

Functionalism, functionalist A theory which sees society as a complex system of interconnected parts working together to ensure the balance and equilibrium of a social group. Also referred to as structural functionalism.

Gaia hypothesis The argument that all living matter is connected and that living matter on the earth collectively defines and regulates the material conditions necessary for the continuance of life. Gaia theory likens the planet, or rather the biosphere, to a vast self-regulating organism.

Global criminology A criminological perspective arising from the idea that as states become more closely connected through **globalisation**, they also become more closely connected in terms of crime and justice. It encourages analysis within an international context and recognises that many traditional criminological definitions and theories were developed within and mainly apply to the **Global North**.

Global North A term used to refer to the richer countries of the world, mainly located north of the equator, with service- and consumer-centred free market **neoliberal** economies in which knowledge and services are produced. Alternative terms (which we do not use in this book) are 'developed' or 'first world' countries.

Global South A term used to refer to the poorer countries of the world, mainly located south of the equator, where industrial and agricultural production are concentrated as land, labour, and raw materials are cheaper. Alternative terms (which we do not use in this book) are 'developing' or 'second world' or 'third world' countries.

Globalisation The process by which the world is becoming increasingly interconnected—in economical, social, and political terms—as a result of massively increased trade, cultural exchange, easier international travel, the expansion of the media and social media, and other technological advancements.

Grand theory A broad and often quite abstract type of theory that relates to concepts and the relationships between them and is based on formal theorising by a person or a group of people rather than growing out of measured phenomena. In criminology, grand theories are often **integrated theories** that purport to offer an explanation to a problem which is applicable in most situations.

Green criminology The study of criminal offences that affect the natural world, the reasons why these are committed, and the impact on those who are harmed as a result. Green criminology also examines the national and international responses to such crimes and those who commit them.

Grounded theory A systematic, iterative approach to data collection and analysis which generates theory from qualitative data—the theory is 'grounded' in the data.

Harm principle The idea that conduct should not be limited or criminalised unless it is harmful to others. This principle is often used to test whether an activity should be criminalised.

Hate crime Crimes committed against an individual or group of people because of an actual or perceived difference, such as race, disability, sexual orientation, or religious affiliation.

Hawthorne effect A change in behaviour by the subjects of a study due to their awareness of being observed.

Hegemonic masculinity The values and characteristics which a particular society or culture deems to be the most desirable aspects of maleness and which therefore become the dominant features associated with masculinity.

Hegemony The set of structures, relationships, and meanings by which a particular form of social order and domination is achieved, maintained, and legitimised.

Homicide The killing of one person by another.

Hypothesis A statement which is proposed to explain a phenomenon or an outcome. It is generally based on limited evidence and, ideally, it should be capable of being tested or at least should only be intended as a starting point for further investigation.

Identity politics A situation where people of a particular religion, race, social background, or other characteristic may join together or form exclusive political alliances. In doing so, they move away from traditional broad-based party politics to a movement that shares their identity.

Ideology, ideological A set of beliefs or system of ideals, particularly those that provide the basis of political or economic policy.

Independent variable The variable within an experiment that is manipulated by the researcher with the intention of identifying it as a cause of behaviour.

Indeterminate sentencing The name for sentences imposed by a court which do not have a fixed length of time; that is, do not set a date for the offender's release. They will be imposed if the court believes the offender to be a danger to the public. The offender must serve a minimum period of time in prison, known as a tariff, before they can be considered for release by the Parole Board.

Indictable offences The category of criminal offences which, due to their deemed seriousness, can only be tried at the Crown Court in front of a judge and jury. They carry maximum penalties of life imprisonment and unlimited fines.

Individualised In a criminological text, this term means tailored to explaining the behaviour of an individual. Individualised explanations for crime, for example, are concerned with explaining offending behaviour as resulting from individual (biological, psychological, sociological) factors rather than broader socio-structural influences.

Inductive research Research that generates new **hypotheses** and understandings.

Inquisitorial system A system of law in which part of the court, usually a judge, is actively involved in investigating the facts of the case, compiling a comprehensive dossier of information on it, and helping to determine the truth. This system is often used in countries with civil law systems, such as France, whereas the UK uses an **adversarial system**.

Institutional racism A term introduced into public discourse in the UK by the Stephen Lawrence Inquiry in 1999 but used on numerous occasions since, for example in relation to the Grenfell Tower fire. Refers to unwitting, as well as overt, practices and stereotypes within organisations that disadvantage groups of people because of their colour or ethnic origin. The term implies that organisations can collectively be held responsible for unwitting racial discrimination.

Integrated theories Criminological theories that integrate explanations from multiple theories to produce a more holistic, multifactor, hybrid theory of crime. They include integrated **positivist** theories which merge explanations from different positivist theories and integrated risk factor theories which fuse explanations from multiple risk factor theories.

Internship A formal employment position offered for a fixed period of time by an organisation to provide a structured introduction to the work it undertakes. An internship can be paid or unpaid, and these opportunities are often available in the summer months. In addition to providing valuable work experience, internships can provide research opportunities and potential topics for your dissertation.

Interpretivism, interpretivist An approach to the study of the social world which seeks to understand human behaviour by exploring individual experiences, perceptions, and meanings. It is usually associated with qualitative research. Interpretivism rejects the idea that complex social and human interactions can ever be fully measured and tries to see behaviour and situations through the eyes of those participating.

Interpretivist comparative criminology An approach to **comparative criminology** which focuses on global divergences and seeks to understand why certain countries or regions deviate from other places in the world.

Intersectionality The interaction between various factors that impact on a person's experience and identity and the way that the state and society react to that person. Examples of such factors are race, social class, sexuality, and gender.

Invisible hand, the This is the idea, put toward by economist Adam Smith, that the market regulates itself as if there was some unseen force (an 'invisible hand') guiding its operations.

Islamophobia Dislike of or prejudice against Muslims and the Islamic religion.

Joint enterprise Crimes in which one person takes part. Legally, this is a doctrine of criminal law which permits the conviction of two or more **defendants** involved in one incident of the same criminal offence, even though the level of involvement in the incident may be different.

Just deserts A principle of sentencing theory which asserts that the form and amount of punishment administered can be made exactly equivalent to the harm and distress caused by a crime.

Justice gap The discrepancy between the numbers of crimes that are committed and recorded and the numbers which are actually prosecuted through the criminal justice system.

Labelling perspectives These include at least two ideas. First, how and why certain behaviours become controlled whilst others do not and the fact that this may depend on how some (the more influential) in society react to that behaviour. Secondly, how the behaviour of groups or individuals may be shaped by how others react to them. So, for example, when a person is convicted society assigns them the label of 'criminal', if they are then treated differently it may lead to them behaving in ways which are in line with the 'criminal' label in a self-fulfilling way, by committing further 'crimes' (sometimes referred to as labelling theory).

Left realism Theoretical developments grounded in traditions of critical criminology, and put forward partly in response to the ideas associated with **right realism**. It still focuses on everyday 'street' crimes but unlike right realism it is interested in the underlying social and structural 'causes of crime', together with questions of class, gender, and racial inequality.

Legal moralism Prohibiting acts merely because they are offensive to the majority in that society, or because it is believed that if they are not prohibited they might destroy the very fabric of a society.

Lex talionis The term for the ancient system of laws (*lex*) that were based on retaliation (*talion*). It could result in an offender experiencing physical punishment that is deemed to fit the crime. The system is most famously associated with the 'eye for an eye' conception of justice.

Liberal feminist theory The theory that the gender inequality which disadvantages women in many social institutions, including the criminal justice system, stems from the sexist socialisation of women into gender roles that are associated with passivity and conformity.

Life course theory A **developmental** perspective which studies the influence of factors, experiences, and events in early life upon pathways into and out of crime later in life, particularly into adulthood.

Lifestyle theory The idea that each individual's likelihood of being victimised depends on their lifestyle.

Literature review A form of academic writing that analyses the existing research on a particular topic. It is an essential part of the research process as it justifies the chosen research questions.

Longitudinal research A research design in which data is collected and analysed on multiple occasions over a prolonged period of time.

Macro-level analysis The broadest level or unit of analysis in social science, focusing on nation states, countries, and international and global-level issues—for example, the economic forces and interactions that affect societies.

Mandatory sentencing A form of sentencing where the punishment to be imposed for an offence is set by Parliament rather than the judge of the particular case. This applies to all murder convictions which by law, regardless of the circumstances, have to receive a life sentence of imprisonment. Other examples that prevent judicial discretion in sentencing include firearms and knife offences.

Marxist feminism A theory that sees the capitalist system of production, and the higher socio-economic status men occupy within that system compared to women, as the primary reason for the oppression of women in society.

Marxist sociology The form of sociology that is developed from and informed by the ideas of Karl Marx, often described as one of the main founders of the discipline. It focuses on power and class structures under **capitalism**, where one class exploits the other; it studies the relationship between society, politics, and economics.

Masculinities (the study of) Masculinities theorists believe that there is no singular 'masculinity' that can be ascribed to all men. Instead, multiple 'masculinities' exist and these are structured around a socially constructed hierarchy which comprises the highly valued **hegemonic masculinity** and other masculinities including **subordinated masculinity**.

Medical model (of disability) The medical model of disability is a way of explaining how a person's impairment is the cause of them being unable to access goods or services. It puts the emphasis on the disability rather than any social or structural issues.

Mens rea This legal term means 'guilty mind' and refers to the mental element, such as intention, that can be required in order to establish that a criminal offence has been committed.

Meso-level analysis The mid-range level or unit of social scientific analysis which focuses on neighbourhoods, communities, localities, and organisations in particular social contexts.

Meta-analysis A type of quantitative analysis which assesses data from a number of studies or sources on the same subject in order to identify broad trends. It is a systematic analysis of current research in order discover whether there are any agreed threads within present knowledge. In **comparative criminology**, this might involve analysis of a certain crime issue in a number of different countries to understand, for example, which approaches may be fairer or more effective.

MeToo movement (or #MeToo) A social movement against sexual abuse and harassment where people publicly share their experiences of such crimes committed by powerful or prominent men, with the aim of empowering victims and bringing attention to the extent of this issue.

Micro-aggression A statement, action, or incident that is regarded as an instance of indirect, subtle, or unintentional discrimination against members of a marginalised group, such as a racial or ethnic minority.

Micro-level analysis The most detailed and granular level or unit of social scientific analysis. This type of analysis focuses on the individual or on small group interactions in particular social contexts.

Mixed methods research Research which uses a combination of quantitative and qualitative data collection methods within a single project to answer a research question (or questions).

Mode of trial hearings Hearings that decide whether an **either way offence** is to be tried in the Magistrates' Court or in the Crown Court.

Modern slavery Forced unpaid labour, usually taking advantage of vulnerable individuals for commercial gain. This may be linked to human trafficking, which is the movement of people based on deception, fraud, or coercion. For the purposes of exploiting them.

Moral panics A disproportionate social reaction to a perceived problem or issue. A moral panic serves as a distraction, diverting public attention away from what are perhaps more urgent and pressing problems and issues. Moral panics can be used by the state to manipulate public opinion and thus steer policy decisions.

Multi-method research Research in which more than one method of data collection is used within a project.

Multivariate data analysis The form of analysis used when the relationship between three or more variables is being investigated.

Narrative analysis A method of analysing data (and, sometimes, to collecting it) that focuses on the stories or narratives that people construct about their experiences. It can include analysing accounts of specific episodes, events, or whole life spans.

Natural justice The right of anyone involved in a legal case to be heard, to hear and contest the arguments of others involved, and to have their views taken into consideration in the decision-making process, without bias.

Negative externality A cost suffered by a third party because of an economic transaction, for example the harm caused by plastic waste. Transactions usually involve producers and consumers as the first and second parties, but third parties can also be affected in a negative way—for example, when people and marine life are affected by the plastic waste thrown away by others.

Neoliberalism A political and social position which promotes the reduction of state intervention in both public and private affairs, together with the removal of controls on markets and commercial competition.

Neo-positivism A later phase of **positivism** which asserts that social events and human behaviour, including crime, can only truly be studied through measurement. Neo-positivists see similarities, sometimes equivalence, between the natural and social worlds, so they use the former's laws to explain events and behaviour in the latter. They place considerable emphasis on statistical analysis and do not make reference to feelings, motives, values, and will.

Newsworthiness The quality of an event or an individual which is believed to make it of contemporary interest to media consumers.

Non-participant observation A form of observational study where the researcher or observer does not participate in the activities of the individual or group under observation.

Normative theory Any theory that sets out what (in that theorist's thinking) is right and wrong, desirable or undesirable, or just and unjust in a society. It sets out ideal standards about the way in which things should, in that theorist's opinion, happen.

Norms or rules The standards by which people in a society are expected to live. Many are just types of behaviour which are expected or frowned upon. When widely observed in a society or culture, these are referred to as **social mores**.

Objectivism, objectivist An **ontological** position (theory of how to understand reality) which holds that the real world is external to the person measuring it and consists of indisputable facts that can be objectively measured. It is the opposite of **constructivism**.

Observer effects The changes that the act of observation bring about for a phenomenon and individuals being observed. This is often the result of instruments that, by necessity, alter the state of what they measure in some way.

Official statistics Statistics compiled by public agencies. In the context of criminology, these are the figures collected by the police and courts which are regularly published by governments to indicate the extent of crime.

Ontology, ontological In social science research, the term ontology refers to the nature of what exists in the social world. A social researcher's ontological position relates to whether they believe that concepts such as gender and crime are realities that exist objectively without prior description, and have unique qualities (an **objectivist** ontology), or whether they are social constructs (a **constructivist** ontology).

Open educational resource (OER) The collective name for freely available, online educational resources.

Open-ended question A question used in an interview or questionnaire that gives participants flexibility in how they respond, rather than presenting them with a set of fixed options (as in **closed questions**), and allows them to elaborate.

Open justice The legal principle that requires the delivery of justice to be open to the public view.

Operant learning Occurs when behaviour is controlled by an individual learning its consequences. Whether they are rewarded or punished for a particular behaviour (or expect rewards or punishments) will decide whether they are likely to participate in it.

Operationalise To express or define something in terms of the operations and measures used to examine it.

Organised crime Serious crimes that are carried out by a group of people who have worked together over a period of time to plan and coordinate their criminal activities which are often continuing and serious. In many cases, organised crime is planned and controlled by powerful individuals or groups and carried out by those working for them or carrying out their orders. Organised crime is often conducted for financial gain and, although it can be domestic, increasingly it is carried out on a transnational level.

Othering The act of treating people from another group—often identified as the 'Other'—as different, often by assigning them with what are considered to be negative characteristics, to make them seem lesser than your own group.

Overt In a research methods context, this refers to a form of study that is conducted openly and with the knowledge of study participants or subjects. It differs from a **covert** study where participants are not aware of the research.

Parliamentary sovereignty The idea that the UK Parliament—which consists of the House of Commons, the House of Lords, and the monarch—is the most powerful source of law in the UK. The laws it produces must be followed by all of the courts of justice. (This idea is also known as parliamentary supremacy.)

Participant observation A form of observational study where the researcher or observer participates in the activities of the individual or group under observation.

Paternalism A policy or criminal law designed to restrict the freedom of an individual in order to protect people from themselves (in terms of their life, health, or safety) when they may not choose to be protected. The interference is supposed to be for an individual's benefit but reduces their liberty or autonomy.

Pathological Showing signs of illness or abnormality.

Pathways The routes or trajectories a young person may take into and away from offending behaviour.

Patriarchy A system or state of affairs in society that is characterised by unequal gender relations and manifests as the oppression of women by men.

Pedagogy The method and practice of teaching as an academic subject.

Penal populism An approach to the making of penal policy that has been recognised since the 1990s. It means that policy is shaped by its perceived popularity with the general public rather than its actual effectiveness. Sometimes referred to as *populist punitiveness*.

People smuggling The illegal transportation or facilitation (for example, by providing fake documents) of people across international borders, for material, financial, or other gain. It differs from human trafficking in that it involves providing a service to groups or individuals who want to illegally enter or illegally leave one country and travel to another.

Peripheral nervous system (PNS) The part of the nervous system which is made up of all the nerves running through the body. The nerves communicate signals from our senses back to the **central nervous system** (CNS) and relay signals from the CNS out to the rest of the body. The signals from the brain to other parts of the body allow a person to react to the environment they are currently experiencing.

Personal transferable skills Skills developed in one situation (for example, during university study) that can be transported and applied to another situation (for example, the workplace).

Phenomenology The study of structures of experience and consciousness. It looks at how events or phenomena are consciously experienced or understood without needing to explain them free of preconceptions.

Placements These are positions within organisations, usually offered on a short-term basis, that provide practical work experience for undergraduates. In addition to offering valuable work experience, they can also provide research opportunities and potential topics for dissertations.

Policing by consent The idea that the police's power and legitimacy comes from the support and consent of the general public, rather than from the state.

Positionality The stance or position that a researcher has chosen to adopt within a specific study and the researcher's evaluation of how that position influences the subject matter being studied, the research context, and the research participants. The stance or position can include the researcher's chosen **epistemology**, disciplinary perspective, and preconceptions.

Positivism, positivist An approach to the study of the social world which uses the methods of the natural sciences to generate universal laws and cause-and-effect understandings of human behaviour (that is, tries to predict future behaviour by studying past events). It is usually associated with quantitative research. In criminology, this perspective is characterised by a focus on the criminal rather than the crime, and by explanations which draw on biological, psychological, social, or economic factors outside the control of the individual, suggesting that behaviour is determined rather than chosen.

Positivist comparative criminology An approach to **comparative criminology** which focuses on global convergences and seeks to describe and understand global norms—in the case of criminology, to generalise and develop theories about global and regional patterns of crime and justice.

Practicality The extent to which a method, practice, or policy is useful, usable, and applicable in the real world.

Presumption of innocence The principle that requires a **defendant** to be presumed innocent until the prosecution can prove their guilt 'beyond reasonable doubt'. It is a key principle of due process justice.

Price mechanism The way in which price affects the behaviour of buyers and sellers in a market and how the profits of goods or services affects the supply and demand of goods and services.

Private law One of the two categories of legal matters (the other is **public law**). Private law deals with disputes between individuals or organisations rather than between them and the state. If a case is categorised as private law, the individuals affected have responsibility for bringing the case to court, usually the County Court or the High Court.

Probation A period of supervision over an offender when they are either serving a community sentence or have been released from prison on licence or on parole (a release that is subject to supervision and adhering to certain rules).

Procedural justice The idea that people should feel fairly treated in their interactions with the police and other state authorities. It is recognised in many research findings as an important influence on a person's potential for reoffending.

Proportionality The idea that the punishment should equal the crime, and should be sufficiently severe to ensure that the criminal does not gain by their crime (commensurate with the harm caused or sought to be prevented), but not so severe that it could be seen as unjust. This is a central idea in sentencing in many states, including England and Wales.

Psychological positivism A group of explanatory theories which identify the psychological characteristics internal to the individual as the causes of crime.

Public law One of the two categories of legal matters (the other is **private law**). Public law cases are deemed to affect the whole community and to be an offence against the state. The trials for these crimes, which include criminal cases, take place in the Magistrates' Court or the Crown Court. (Public law is also known as civil law.)

Punishment A term that can have many meanings. In this book it generally means that a state has imposed an unpleasant outcome (or one intended to be unpleasant) on a person or group because they have broken the law—or the state believes this to be the case.

Qualified right Rights that have to be balanced against the public interest and so can be interfered with, subject to a number of conditions specified in the relevant provisions. These often include considering whether any interference is legitimate and necessary.

Qualitative research A branch of research concerned with understanding human behaviour and phenomena in terms of words that depict personalised meanings, experiences, and perceptions.

Quantitative research A branch of research concerned with understanding human behaviour and phenomena in quantifiable, numerical, and statistical forms.

Questionnaire A form of survey where participants provide written (often typed) responses to written questions without the help of an interviewer. It can be completed online, via email, or (less commonly now) by post. Questionnaires may contain **closed questions** or **open-ended questions**, or a mixture of the two.

Radical communitarianism The philosophical view that justice is better achieved in small communities which choose just outcomes through each member participating in a full discussion of the plurality of values (often multicultural).

Radical feminist theory A theoretical tradition that identifies patriarchy as the fundamental factor which drives the gender inequality that pervades society and oppresses women regardless of their ethnicity, social class, or other attributes.

Rape culture The cultural normalisation of violence against women.

Rape myth acceptance (RMA) The acceptance of prejudicial, stereotyped, and false beliefs about sexual assaults, rapists, and rape victims. Myths can be used to excuse sexual aggression, create hostility toward victims, and bias criminal prosecution.

Rational choice An idea underlying the theory that individuals normally use rational thought to calculate how best to achieve outcomes that are most beneficial to them, in their self-interest. It assumes that offenders want to gain by their criminal behaviour.

Realism A set of explanatory theories which view crime as a real, measurable phenomenon with tangible effects on victims and society, challenging critical criminology's 'idealist' view of crime as a **social construction**. See also **Right realism** and **Left realism**.

Recidivism An individual's relapse into undesirable behaviour. In a criminal justice context, this means a repeat of offending behaviour. The most common measure of rates of recidivism is the number of offenders who are reconvicted in the two-year period following their punishment by the criminal justice system.

Reductionism The practice of measuring or analysing a concept or behaviour in simplistic terms, for example by reducing it to a category or quantity.

Re-examination In a criminal justice context, this is the stage in adversarial court trials in which a witness can be questioned by their own side on matters that may have been raised during cross-examination.

Reflection A critical process through which the researcher evaluates the quality and validity of their research processes, findings, and conclusions.

Reflexivity A process through which researchers consider their position, preconceptions, choices, and influence during the study and how these have affected the research process.

Rehabilitation Preventing crime by addressing causative factors, whether they be economic, social, or individual. However, in a criminal justice context it has the more specific meaning of working with an individual to alter their behaviour and so reduce their offending.

Reintegrative shaming The idea that positive shaming is important in crime prevention. The shaming should focus on the criminal act not the offender as a person—the behaviour is bad, not the person—and, ideally, the offender apologises and their apology is accepted. The process should include support to help the offender not to offend in the future.

Relative deprivation This term refers to the sense in which people feel disadvantaged in relation to other groups in the wider population, particularly those closest to them in terms of income, location, or lifestyle. **Left realists** draw on this concept to highlight the changing perceptions of injustice and deprivation.

Reliability The repeatability, replicability, or consistency of a research design, method, or finding.

Repeat victimisation A situation where a person, household, business, or vehicle is repeatedly a victim of crime.

Research debriefing A post-research meeting with subjects or participants to discuss the study, to assess its impact, and to offer support if required.

Responsibilisation The phenomenon of placing responsibility and blame on individuals, families, or communities for offending behaviour and the inability of these individuals, families, or communities to resist the criminogenic influences that contribute to it.

Restorative justice An approach to justice in which those most closely involved in and affected by an offence are encouraged and enabled to resolve and make good the harms caused by crime through a process of dialogue and reconciliation.

Revenge porn (also called sextortion) The sharing of intimate sexual photos or videos of another person online without their consent. This act was criminalised in the UK in 2015.

Right realism Right-realist perspectives focus on popular definitions, representations, and experiences of crime, especially 'street crime'; right realists reject deep analysis of the social or economic causes of crime, arguing that what matters are tough and decisive responses to the harm and victimisation experienced by people in their daily lives.

Routine activity theory A theoretical perspective which assumes that the offender has made a choice to offend but focuses on the action, the crime, and particularly the situation in which the crime occurs. It assumes that crime arises out of everyday opportunities and holds that for crime to occur three things are necessary: a motivated offender, a suitable target, and the absence of guardians.

Rule of law The legal principle that means the law itself, rather than governments or individual people, is the ultimate authority. This principle should apply equally, meaning that no one is above or exempt from the law.

Secondary data analysis The analysis of data collected from other sources for the purposes of the current research.

Secondary victimisation The idea that in addition to the impact of a crime itself, individuals may suffer further victimisation at the hands of the criminal justice system.

Security of tenure The employment position of individuals, particularly judges, that protects them against being dismissed from their position. It is informally known as 'a job for life', although 'until retirement' is more accurate. This security is designed to protect judges from external pressures (that is, pressures to take certain actions in order to preserve their jobs) in order to preserve their independence when adjudicating cases.

Self-fulfilling prophecy A prediction that directly or indirectly causes itself to become true due to positive feedback between a belief and behaviour. For example, if an individual offends and is then labelled a 'criminal', they may come to accept that label and reoffend as a result of their new 'criminal' identity.

Semi-structured interview An interview which loosely follows a list of questions, known as an interview schedule, but unlike a **structured interview**, the interviewer does not have to ask them in exactly this way or order, or in the same way for every participant. They can also use prompts and probes if needed.

Separation of powers The constitutional principle for the way power is shared between the government (the executive), Parliament (the legislative), and the courts (the judicial). The doctrine holds that each of these three parts of the state should be kept separate to act as a check and a balance on each other to ensure none has excessive power.

Sexting A combination of texting and sending images. This often involves the exchange of sexually explicit pictures, messages, or videos.

Situational crime prevention Crime prevention strategies or policies which focus on reducing opportunities for criminal behaviour. These often involve redesigning products (for example, improving car locks) or altering environments (for example, removing conductors on buses, or introducing street lighting or CCTV) to either reduce the possibility of criminal activity or to increase the likelihood of offenders being caught.

Situational variables Environmental factors that can affect the result of a study or an activity. They are external things such as the weather, lighting, etc.

Social conflict theory The theoretical perspective which claims that individuals and groups interact on the basis of conflict. The idea is often that those in power use the legal system to ensure that they remain in power and that the powerless remain controlled. In essence, social conflict theory is the study of the distribution and use of power in order to control others.

Social construction The idea that crime and associated concepts (such as justice) are the subjective and ever-changing creations of institutions and individuals in societies at specific points in time.

Social contract An implicit agreement between people within a society to give up part of their freedom to ensure their security. The assumption is that without controls people would do whatever they wanted and some would become very powerful and abusive whilst others would suffer. People agree to social restraints to allow them to live safely in communities.

Social control theory A very broad theory which holds that people's desire to conform means that their behaviour generally aligns with that which is expected in society. The theory starts with the assumption that conformity is learned and considers all the ways this might occur—social, psychological, through families or other groups, and through societal expectations.

Social crime prevention The idea that the origins of crime lie in potential offenders' social circumstances, and that if these can be improved then their likelihood of offending is correspondingly reduced.

Social desirability bias The tendency of research participants to behave or respond in a manner that will be viewed favourably by others, for example by answering survey questions to exaggerate good behaviour and under-report bad behaviour.

Social disorganisation theory A **social structural theory** developed by the **Chicago School of sociology and criminology** which links crime to environmental or ecological aspects of the neighbourhood and to a breakdown in social integration in an area. High crime rates occur in areas which are not socially cohesive and are dysfunctional; they may be divided on ethical, racial, cultural, religious, intergenerational, or political grounds.

Social engineering In the context of information security, this term refers to the use of deception to manipulate individuals into sharing confidential or personal information that may be used for fraudulent purposes.

Social harm An evolution of the traditional criminological focus on the individual harms caused by crime to consider the social harms and injuries that result from the activities of nation states, corporations, and businesses—some of which activities may not be considered criminal.

Social hierarchy The result of the way that societies implicitly or explicitly group and rank individuals based on factors like wealth, race, education level, jobs, and overall social standing.

Social interaction or social process theories Theories which claim that crime and deviance are socially constructed. They also accept that the choices made by each individual have an impact on those around them and that this constructed environment then has an impact on the ways in which people behave.

Social justice A concept relating to the way in which all benefits (wealth, opportunities, and privileges) and burdens in society are distributed. It is often associated with the view that everyone deserves equal economic, political, and social rights. It includes access and opportunities as well as equal opportunities to participate and to be heard.

Social learning theory A theory which suggests that humans learn through social interactions and tend to mimic other people's behaviour. With this perspective, all behaviour is learned, including criminal behaviour.

Social model (of disability) The social model identifies the problems faced by disabled people as a consequence of external factors. It looks at the barriers erected by society in terms of disabled people being able to participate fully in day-to-day life and seeks to remove unnecessary barriers.

Social mores The *social norms*—in terms of customs, rules, and expectations of proper or acceptable behaviour—that are widely observed across a society. Each society sets its own standards and within a society different groups may set different social mores.

Social structural theories (Often referred to as *structuralism*.) Theories which argue that the way in which a society is shaped affects the way in which people behave. These theories—which include **social disorganisation theory** and **strain theory**—look at the ways in which the structure of a society (overarching system) has an influence on our daily lives. Here social structure is often thought to be more important than function.

Socialisation The way in which we all learn about the norms and rules of our society, what is expected of us, and how to behave in order to live up to those expectations.

Socialist feminism A theory which combines aspects of radical and Marxist feminism and argues that oppressive gender relations resulting from the patriarchy *intersect* with the class inequality resulting from **capitalism** to disadvantage women.

Sociological positivism A group of explanatory theories which identify the sociological characteristics that are external to the individual as the causes of crime.

Somatotyping A classification of people according to their body shape which is used to predict future behaviour, including criminal behaviour.

State crime Illegal or deviant acts (or omissions) committed by states or their representatives (or which they are complicit in) which break either their own criminal law or public international law. 'States' are usually defined as the elected or other officials and the bureaucrats, institutions, and bodies that make up a government. However, many see this legalistic definition as too narrow and would include acts such as depriving a population of adequate food, acts committed by warring factions, fighting to become 'the government', or acts which condone or facilitate crime. They include things like genocide, torture, war crimes, censorship, corruption, institutional racism, funding terrorism, funding, supporting or condoning corporate crime, etc.

Stigmata In a criminological context this is something which visibly marks someone out as being deviant or criminal or as having deviant or criminal tendencies. It may indicate marks or physical types that are deemed to make someone more likely to participate in particular types of behaviour.

Stigmatisation Labelling, marginalisation, exclusion, and other negative treatment that portrays certain individuals or groups as harmful, risky, deficient, and pathological.

Strain theory A **social structural** theory which argues that when society (or part of a society) puts pressure on individuals to succeed, they will turn to illegitimate means such as crime to achieve their goals if they cannot meet them by legitimate means.

Street crime Usually refers to 'everyday' crimes committed in public places such as shoplifting, burglary, robbery, and selling illicit drugs in public.

Structuralism *See* **Social structural theories**.

Structured interview An interview which follows a set list of questions in a rigid format, known as an interview schedule. The aim is for interviewees to be questioned in as similar and consistent a way as possible, and for the data to be easy to collate for analysis, so **closed questions** are often used.

Structured observation This technique involves observing individuals or groups in a natural setting for a set amount of time, following set rules (an observation schedule) which dictate what the observer should be looking for and how they should record what they see or hear. Also called systematic observation.

Subcultural theory A theory which points to the existence of delinquent subcultures in which people do not live by conventional norms and the accepted moral order. Instead, they adhere to patterns of behaviour that are illegitimate or illegal, but are accepted and valued within the subculture.

Subordinated masculinity The values and characteristics which a particular society or culture considers to be less desirable aspects of maleness, located at the lower end of the 'hierarchy of masculinities' and considered inferior to **hegemonic masculinity**.

Substantive justice A treatment that is fair, just, and reasonable. What is accepted as substantive justice will vary from person to person but it usually claims to reflect the prevailing moral leaning of a society or community—it is therefore culturally bound and socially constructed. In many modern western cultures it is seen as similar to **distributive justice**.

Summary offences The category of criminal offences that, due to their deemed minor nature, can only be tried at the Magistrates' Court in front of either a district judge (a professional magistrate) or three lay magistrates (volunteers from the community and traditionally known as Justices of the Peace).

Supposition Guesswork, assumption, conjecture.

Suspended sentence order A type of sentence that means an offender does not go to prison immediately and can avoid going at all if they comply with certain conditions set by the court. The order can suspend a prison sentence for up to two years.

Target hardening A term used in the police and those working in security to refer to physical security measures which are designed to increase the difficulty of committing crime against a potential object or victim.

Temporal precedence When one variable or event can be shown to have occurred before another.

Thematic analysis One of the most common forms of analysis in qualitative research. It emphasises pinpointing, examining, and recording patterns (or 'themes') within data. Themes are patterns across data sets that are important to the description of a phenomenon and are associated with a specific research question.

Theoretical principles The principles or propositions which explain the relationship between two or more basic parts of a theory (concepts or constructs), allowing us to understand how specific outcomes arise.

Theory A group of linked ideas which tries to explain something in the world. In criminology, it might explain why someone offends or why society criminalises certain behaviours.

Trajectory The path of development into and out of crime.

Transformative justice An emerging concept which is based on the principle that the mechanisms and processes for resolving crime should also be grounded in and driven by wider objectives of achieving norms by means of social and structural change.

Transition A word with many meanings in everyday life, but often used in discussions of youth offending to refer to a significant change or move in a young person's life, such as entering secondary school, leaving school, leaving home, or getting a job. Transitions can be stressful and uncertain and may contribute to criminal behaviour.

Transnational criminology One of the two main types of global criminological approaches (the other type is **comparative criminology**). It studies incidences of crime and justice that cross international borders, including transnational organised crime, transnational state crime, and transnational corporate crime.

Transphobia Mistrust, fear, hatred, or dislike of or prejudice against transgender people, or those who do not conform to gender identities. It often leads to harassment and discrimination against those who are gender different.

Treadmill of production The idea that the constant search for economic growth means capitalist societies are stuck on a treadmill. Well-being might not be improved by economic growth and the constant drive for production causes environmental problems through unsustainable use of natural resources and increased pollution.

Triangulation The technique of collecting and analysing data from multiple sources in order to test the validity of the results and conclusions (also known as 'cross-validation').

Tribunal of fact The legal term for the jury or magistrate(s) who decides on all questions of fact in a case.

Tribunal of law The legal term for the judge or magistrate(s) who decides on all questions of law in a case.

Typology A system of classification according to general types or categories. Typologies are widely used across the social sciences—for example, to refer to different types of **mixed methods research**.

Underclass A term popularised by certain sections of the press and crime writers who associate criminality with the behaviour of this group, attributed with the characteristics of irresponsibility in their personal lives, laziness, and dependence on state handouts or charity.

Univariate data analysis The form of analysis used when only one variable is being investigated.

Unstructured interview An interview which does not follow a particular list of questions or an interview schedule and is fairly unconstrained. The interviewer just has a brief set of prompts and may only ask one main question.

Utilitarianism An ethical theory which assumes that actions are right or just if they produce the greatest good for the greatest number of people. If the pleasure which arises from an action (for the actor and others) outweighs the suffering caused by it, the action is beneficial (of use) and should be permitted.

Validity The accuracy, honesty, suitability, and relevance of a research method, result, or conclusion. Whether something measures what it says it measures.

Victim precipitation The extent to which a victim is seen to be responsible for their own victimisation. This concept seeks to understand the interaction between victim and offender.

Victim surveys Surveys which aim to address the problem of crimes which the police do not record or the public do not report. They involve asking members of the public to recount their experiences of crime in an attempt to get both a more accurate measure of the crime rate and to assess the impact of crime on victims.

Victimisation Either the process by which a person comes to see themselves as a victim (for instance, through the way certain groups are represented in the media, which also affects the social reaction to those who have experienced crime) or the factors which lead to groups becoming perceived as victims (such as the targeting of young people by police operations).

Victimity The state, quality, or fact of being a victim. This can include the characteristics that affect someone's risk of becoming a crime victim. Victimity can also be seen as a broad concept that considers the results of a crime.

Visual criminology A growing part of the discipline of criminology which looks at visual representations of crime and its associated concepts and uses visual data in its methods of research.

Weberian sociology The form of sociology that is developed from and informed by the ideas of Max Weber, often described as one of the main founders of the discipline. A key facet of this approach is the idea that in order to understand the world we need to study social actions by interpreting the purpose and meanings which individuals attach to their actions.

White privilege A societal condition in which people benefit from access to resources, rewards, and power because they belong to a white ethnic group.

White-collar crime Offences which are committed by those in a position of responsibility and respectability; those of high social status. These offences are made possible because of the position of the individual in society.

Work shadowing The practice of observing and following a person around whilst they are working in order to acquire an understanding of what the job involves. In addition to providing valuable work experience, work shadowing can provide research opportunities and potential topics for a dissertation.

Work-based learning The use of practical experiences in the workplace to complement academic studies. It enables students to apply their learning to real-world situations and illustrates the value of what they have learned on a formal course. In addition to providing valuable work experience, work-based learning opportunities can provide research sources or settings and potential topics for a dissertation.

Xenophobia A dislike of or prejudice against people from other countries.

Zemiology From the Greek word *Zemia*, meaning harm, zemiology examines the nature and causes of harm. Such harm can be social, financial, or physical; zemiology seeks to examine harm caused by and to individuals as well as that which results from the acts and omissions of the state and its agencies.

Zero tolerance In a criminal justice context, this is a policing strategy involving strict and rapid application of the law, even for minor crimes.

BIBLIOGRAPHY

Chapter 1

Clark, T. et al. (2021) Bryman's *Social Research Methods* (6th edn). Oxford: Oxford University Press.
Finch, E. and Fafinski, S. (2019) *Criminology Skills* (3rd edn). Oxford: Oxford University Press.
Hale, C. et al. (2013) *Criminology* (3rd edn). Oxford: Oxford University Press.
Jones, S. (2013) *Criminology*. Oxford: Oxford University Press.
Millie, A. (2016) *Philosophical Criminology*. Bristol: Policy Press.
Redman, P. and Maples, W. (2011) *Good Essay Writing*. London: Sage.
Whiting, A. (2018) 'Introduction to first year criminology', *Birmingham City University blog*. No longer available online.
Williams, K. (2012) *Textbook on Criminology*. Oxford: Oxford University Press.
Young, J. (2003) 'In praise of dangerous thoughts'. *Punishment and Society* 5(1): 97–107.

Chapter 2

Alvesalo, A. and Tombs, S. (2002) 'Working for Criminalisation of Economic Offending: Contradictions for Critical Criminology?'. *Critical Criminology: An International Journal* 11(1): 21–40.
Ashworth, A. and Zedner, L. (2008) 'Defending the Criminal Law: Reflections on the Changing Character of Crime'. *Criminal Law and Philosophy* 2: 21.
Baker, D. (2007) 'Moral Limits of Criminalizing Remote Harms'. *New Criminal Law Review* 10: 370.
Becker, H. S. (1963) *Outsiders: Studies in the Sociology of Deviance*. London: Macmillan.
Berlin, I. (1958) 'Two Concepts of Liberty' reprinted in I. Berlin (1969) *Four Essays on Liberty*. Oxford: Oxford University Press.
Boreham, R. et al. (2007) 'The Arrestee Survey 2003–2006'. Home Office Statistical Bulletin 12(07).
Boukli, A. and Kotzé, J. (eds) (2018) *Zemiology: Reconnecting Crime and Social Harm*. London: Palgrave Macmillan.
Box, S. (1983) *Power, Crime and Mystification*. London: Tavistock.
Brunstrom, R. (2007) 'Drugs Policy: A Radical Look Ahead?'. North Wales Police Authority: www.drugequality.org/files/Drugs_Policy_Paper_2007.pdf.
Cane, P. (2006) 'Taking Law Seriously: Starting Points of the Hart-Devlin Debate'. *The Journal of Ethics* 10: 21–51.
Coleman, R. et al. (2009) *State, Power Crime*. London: Sage.
Dempsey, M. (2005) 'Rethinking Wolfenden: Prostitute Use, Criminal Law and Remote Harm'. *Criminal Law Review* 255.
Devlin, P. (1965) *The Enforcement of Morals*. Oxford: Oxford University Press.
Ditton, J. (1977) *Part-time crime: An ethnography of fiddling and pilferage*. London: Macmillan Press.
Dorling, D. et al. (2008) *Criminal Obsessions: Why Harm Matters More Than Crime* (2nd edn). London: Centre for Crime and Justice Studies.
Downes, D., Rock, P., and MacLaughlin, E. (2016) *Understanding Deviance* (7th edn). Oxford: Oxford University Press.
Duff, R. (2007) *Answering for Crime: Responsibility and Liability in the Criminal Law*. Oxford: Hart.
Durkheim, É. (1895) *The Rules of Sociological Method*. Translated by Steven Lukes (1982). London: Macmillan.
Erikson, K. T. (1966) *Wayward Puritans: A study in the Sociology of Deviance*. New York: John Wiley.
Feinberg, J. (1984–8) *The Moral Limits of The Criminal Law*. Oxford: Oxford University Press. Vol. I: Harm to Others (1984); Vol. II: Offense to Others (1985); Vol. III: Harm to Self (1986); Vol. IV: Harmless Wrongdoing (1988).
Gardner, J. (1994) 'Rationality and the Rule of Law in Offences against the Person'. *Cambridge Law Journal* 53: 502–23.
Goode, E. (2016) *Deviant Behaviour* (10th edn). Abingdon: Routledge.
Green, P. and Ward, T. (2004) *State Crime: Governments, Violence and Corruption*. London: Pluto Press.
Hart, H. L. A. (1963) *Law, Liberty and Morality*. Oxford: Oxford University Press.
Henry, S. (1978). *The Hidden Economy: The Context and Control of Borderline Crime*. London: Martin Robertson.
Henry, S. and Milovanovic, D. (1996) *Postmodernism and Constitutive Theory: Beyond Modernism*. London: Sage.
Herring, J. (2015) *Great Debates in Criminal Law* (3rd edn). London: Red Globe Press and Macmillan.
Hillyard, P. and Tombs, S. (2004), 'Beyond Criminology' in P. Hillyard et al. (eds) *Beyond Criminology: Taking Harm Seriously*. London: Pluto Press.
Hulsman, L. (1986) 'Critical Criminology and the Concept of Crime'. *Contemporary Crisis* 10: 63–80.
Husak, D. (2007) *Overcriminalization: The Limits of Criminal Law*. New York: Oxford University Press.
Jackson, R., Murphy, E., and Poynting, S. (2009) *Contemporary State Terrorism: Theory and Practice*. Abingdon: Routledge.
Jones, H. (2004) 'Opportunities and Obstacles: The Rape Crisis Federation in the UK'. *Journal of International Gender Studies* 8: 55–71.
Karstedt, S. and Farrall, S. (2006) 'The Moral Economy of Everyday Crime: Markets, Consumers and Citizens'. *British Journal of Criminology* 46(6): 1011–36.
Law Commission (2010) *Criminal Liability in Regulatory Contexts: A Consultation Paper*, LCCP 195. London: Law Commission.
Maher, J., Pierpoint, H., and Beirne, P. (2017) *The Palgrave International Handbook of Animal Abuse Studies*. London: Palgrave Macmillan.
Marshall, S. and Duff, R. (1998) 'Criminalization and Sharing Wrongs'. *Canadian Journal of Law and Jurisprudence* 11: 7–22.
Mehta, S. and Merz, P. (2015) 'Ecocide—A New Crime Against Peace?'. *Environmental Law Review* 17(1): 3–7.
Mill, J. (1859) *On Liberty*. London: Longmans, Green and Co.
Millie, A. (2016) *Philosophical Criminology*. Bristol: Policy Press.
Nutt, D. et al. (2007) 'Development of a Rational Scale to Assess the Harm of Drugs of Potential Misuse'. *The Lancet* 369(9566): 1047–53.
Pemberton, S. (2004) 'A Theory of Moral Indifference: Understanding the Production of Harm by Capitalist Society' in P. Hillyard et al. (eds) *Beyond Criminology: Taking Harm Seriously*. London: Pluto Press.

Quinney, R. (1977) *Class, State and Crime*. New York: David McKay Co.
Reiman, J. (2006) 'Book Review: Beyond Criminology: *Taking Harm Seriously*'. *British Journal of Criminology* 46(2): 362–4.
Schwendinger, H. and Schwendinger, J. (1970) 'Defenders of Order or Guardians of Human Rights?'. *Issues in Criminology* 5(2): 123–57.
Tombs, S. and Whyte, D. (2003) 'Unmasking the Crimes of the Powerful'. *Critical Criminology* 11(3): 217–36.
Tombs, S. and Whyte, D. (2003) *Unmasking the Crimes of the Powerful: Scrutinizing States and Corporations*. New York: Peter Lang Publishing.
Vold, G. B., Bernard, T. J., and Snipes, J. B. (2002) *Theoretical Criminology* (4th edn). New York: Oxford University Press.
von Hirsch, A. (1996) 'Extending the Harm Principle: "Remote" Harms and Fair Imputation' in A. Simester and A. Smith (eds) *Harm and Culpability*. Oxford: Oxford University Press.
von Hirsch, A. and Jareborg, N. (1991) 'Gauging Criminal Harm: A Living-Standard Analysis'. *Oxford Journal of Legal Studies* 11(1): 1–38.
Waldron, J. (2012) *The Harm in Hate Speech*. Cambridge, MA: Harvard University Press.
Williams, K. S. (2012) *Textbook on Criminology*. Oxford: Oxford University Press.

Chapter 3

Aristotle (384–322 BC) 'The Politics'. Harvard University's Justice with Michael Sandel: www.justiceharvard.org/resources/aristotle-the-politics/.
Bazelon, D. L. (1976) 'The Morality of Criminal Law'. *Southern California Law Review* 49: 385–405 (esp. 389).
Bazelon, D. L. (1981) 'Forward: The Morality of Criminal Law: The Rights of the Accused'. *Journal of Criminal Law and Criminology* 72: 1143–70.
Beccaria, C. (1767) 'On Crimes and Punishments' reprinted in R. Bellamy (ed.) (1995) *Of Crimes and Punishments and Other Writings*. Translated by R. Davies. Cambridge: Cambridge University Press.
Braithwaite, J. (2002) 'Setting Standards for Restorative Justice'. *British Journal of Criminology* 42(3): 563–77.
Currie, E. (1997) 'Market, Crime and Community'. *Theoretical Criminology* 1(2): 147–72.
Duff, R. (2001) *Punishment, Communication and Community*. Oxford: Oxford University Press.
Durkheim, É. (1982) *Rules of Sociological Method*. New York: Free Press.
Etzioni, A. (1994) *The Spirit of Community: The Reinvention of American Society*. New York: Touchstone.
Gibbs, P. (2017) 'Defendants on Video—Conveyor Belt Justice or a Revolution in Access?', Transform Justice: www.transformjustice.org.uk/wp-content/uploads/2017/10/Disconnected-Thumbnail-2.pdf.
Home Office (2009) 'The Macpherson Report—Ten Years On', Home Affairs Committee Twelfth Report of Session 2008–09, HC 427.
King, M. (1981) *The Framework of Criminal Justice*. London: Croom Helm.
Leveson, The Rt Hon. Sir B. (2015) 'Review of Efficiency in Criminal Proceedings'. Judiciary of England and Wales: www.judiciary.gov.uk/publications/review-of-efficiency-in-criminal-proceedings-final-report/.
Macpherson, W. (1999) *The Stephen Lawrence Inquiry*, Cm 4262-1. London: The Stationery Office.
Packer, H. (1968) *The Limits of the Criminal Sanction*. Stanford, CA: Stanford University Press.
Pakes, F. (2004) *Comparative Criminal Justice*. Cullompton: Willan.
Quinney, R. (1970) *The Social Reality of Crime*. Boston, MA: Little, Brown.
Rawls, J. (1971) *A Theory of Justice*. Cambridge, MA: Harvard University Press.
Sen, A. (2010) *The Idea of Justice*. London: Penguin.
Skogan, W. (2006) 'Asymmetry in the Impact of Encounters with Police'. *Policing and Society* 16(2): 99–126.
Swansea University (2020), Hillary Rodham Clinton School of Law, Justice in Wales Seminar Series: www.youtube.com/watch?v=c8R7JvEGOSk&feature=youtu.be.
Terry, M., Johnson, S., and Thompson, P. (2010) 'Virtual Court Pilot Outcome Evaluation'. London: Ministry of Justice. Available at www.gov.uk/government/publications/virtual-courts-pilot-outcome-evaluation-report.
Tulkens, F. (1995) 'Main Comparable Features of the Different European Criminal Justice Systems' in M. Delmas-Marty (ed.) *The Criminal Process and Human Rights: Towards a European Consciousness*. Dordrecht: Martinus Nijhoff.
Weber, M. (1922) 'The Nature, Conditions and Development of Bureaucratic Herrschaft' in G. Roth and W. Wittich (eds) (1968) *Max Weber Economy and Society*. New York: Bedminster Press.
Williams, K. S. and Daniel, H. (2020) 'Youth Justice as Justice for Children: Towards a Capabilities Approach' in J. Blaustein et al. (eds) *Emerald Handbook of Crime, Justice and Sustainable Development*. Bingley: Emerald Publishing.
Zander, M. (1993) 'Royal Commission on Criminal Justice', Runciman Report, Cm 2263. London: The Stationery Office.

Chapter 4

Aronson, E., Wilson, T. D., and Akert, R. (2010) *Social Psychology* (7th edn). Upper Saddle River, NJ: Prentice Hall.
Baker, K. (2005) 'Assessment in Youth Justice: Professional Discretion and the Use of Asset'. *Youth Justice* 5: 106–22.
Bryman, A. (2015) *Social Research Methods* (5th edn). Oxford: Oxford University Press.
Case, S. (2006) 'Young People "At Risk" of What? Challenging Risk-Focused Early Intervention as Crime Prevention'. *Youth Justice* 6(3): 171–9.
Case, S. (2007) 'Questioning the "Evidence" of Risk that Underpins Evidence-Led Youth Justice Interventions'. *Youth Justice* 7(2): 91–106.
Case, S. (2015) 'Criminology as a Social Science: How Does Criminology "Know" About Crime?' in K. Vaidya (ed.) *Criminology and Criminal Justice for the Curious: Why Study Criminology and Criminal Justice?* New York: Curious Academic Publishing.
Case, S. and Haines, K. (2009) *Understanding Youth Offending: Risk Factor Research Policy and Practice*. Cullompton: Willan.
Caulfield, L. and Hill, J. (2014) *Criminological Research for Beginners*. Abingdon: Routledge.
Chamberlain, J. M. (2013) *Understanding Criminological Research: A Guide to Data Analysis*. London: Sage.
Chamberlain, J. M. (2015) *Criminological Theory in Context: An Introduction*. London: Sage.
Creswell, J. (2013) *Research Design: Qualitative, Quantitative, and Mixed Methods Approaches*. London: Sage.
Crow, I. and Semmens, N. (2008) *Researching Criminology*. Maidenhead: Open University Press.
Crowther-Dowey, C. and Fussey, P. (2013) *Researching Crime: Approaches, Methods and Application*. Basingstoke: Palgrave.
Davies, P., Francis, P., and Jupp, V. (eds) (2011) *Doing Criminological Research* (2nd edn). London: Sage.
Farrell, G. and Pease, K. (2014). 'Repeat Victimization' in D. Weisburd and G. Bruinsma (eds) *Enclopedia of Criminology and Criminal Justice*. New York: Springer.

Farrington, D. (2007) 'Childhood Risk Factors and Risk-Focused Prevention' in M. Maguire, R. Morgan, and R. Reiner (eds) *The Oxford Handbook of Criminology* (4th edn). Oxford: Oxford University Press.

Farrington, D. et al. (1993) 'An Experiment on the Prevention of Shoplifting' in R. V. Clarke (ed.) *Crime Prevention Studies*, Vol. 1. Monsey, NY: Willow Tree Press.

Ferraro, K. (1995) *Fear of Crime: Interpreting Victimization Risk*. Albany, NY: State University of New York Press.

Gilbert, N. (2001) *Researching Social Life*. London: Sage.

Gray, D. (2013) *Doing Research in the Real-World*. London: Sage.

Hagan, F. (2013) *Research Methods in Criminal Justice and Criminology*. New York: Prentice-Hill.

Haines, K. and Case, S. (2015) *Positive Youth Justice: Children First, Offenders Second*. Bristol: Policy Press.

Hall, S. (1978) *Policing the Crisis: Mugging, the State, and Law and Order*. London: Macmillan.

Hawkins, J. and Catalano, R. (1992) *Communities That Care*. San Francisco: Jossey-Bass.

Heap, V. and Walters, J. (2019) *Mixed methods in criminology*. London: Routledge.

Hennink, M., Hutter, I., and Bailey, A. (2020) *Qualitative Research Methods*. London: Sage.

Hoefnagels, P. (1973) *The Other Side of Criminology*. New York: Springer.

Hope, T. (2009) 'The Illusion of Control: A Response to Professor Sherman'. *Criminology and Criminal Justice* 9(2): 125–34.

Jacobson, M. and Walklate, S. (2020) *Liquid criminology: Doing imaginative criminological research*. London: Routledge.

Janis, I. (1972) *Victims of Groupthink: A Psychological Study of Foreign-Policy Decisions and Fiascoes*. Boston, MA: Houghton Mifflin.

Kahneman, D., Slovic, P., and Tversky, A. (1982) *Judgment under Uncertainty: Heuristics and Biases*. Cambridge: Cambridge University Press.

Kemshall, H. (2008) 'Risk, Rights and Justice: Understanding and Responding to Youth Risk'. *Youth Justice* 8(1): 21–38.

King, R. and Wincup, E. (2008) *Doing Research on Crime and Justice*. Oxford: Oxford University Press.

Lamputtang, P. (2019) *Qualitative Research Methods*. Oxford: Oxford University Press.

Lincoln, Y. and Guba, E. (1985) *Naturalistic Inquiry*. London: Sage.

McAra, L. and McVie, S. (2010) 'Youth Crime and Justice: Key Messages from the Edinburgh Study of Youth Transitions and Crime'. *Criminology and Criminal Justice* 10(2): 179–209.

Mitchell Miller, J. (2014) *The Encyclopaedia of Theoretical Criminology*, Vol 1. Oxford: Wiley.

Nightingale, D. and Cromby, J. (1999) *Social Constructionist Psychology*. Buckingham: Open University Press.

Noaks, L. and Wincup, E. (2004) *Criminological Research: Understanding Qualitative Methods*. London: Sage.

Oakley, A. (1999) 'Paradigm Wars: Some Thoughts on a Personal and Public Trajectory'. *International Journal of Social Research Methodology* 2(3): 247–54.

Parker, H. (1974) *A View from the Boys. A Sociology of Downtown Adolescents*. Newton Abbot: David and Charles.

Pawson, R. and Tilley, N. (2004) *Realistic Evaluation*. London: Sage.

Pollock, J. (2016) *Ethical Dilemmas and Decisions in Criminal Justice*. Boston, MA: CENGAGE Learning.

Reichardt, C. and Rallis, S. (1994) *The Qualitative-Quantitative Debate: New Perspectives*. San Francisco: Jossey Bass.

Rennison, C. M. and Hart, T. C. (2020) *Research methods in criminal justice and criminology*. London: Sage.

Robson, C. (2015) *Real-World Research* (4th edn). London: Wiley.

Savin, M. and Howell-Major, C. (2013) *Qualitative Research: The essential guide to theory and practice*. London: Routledge.

Stout, B., Yates, J., and Williams, B. (2008) *Applied Criminology*. London: Sage.

Taleb, N. (2001) *Fooled by Randomness: The Hidden Role of Chance in Life and in the Markets*. New York: Random House and Penguin.

Tashakkori, A. and Teddlie, T. (1998) *Mixed Methodology: Combining Qualitative and Quantitative Approaches*. Thousand Oaks, CA: Sage.

Utting, D. (1999) *Guide to Promising Approaches*. London: Communities that Care.

Walker, M. (2020) *Social research methods*. London: Sage.

West, D. and Farrington, D. (1973) *Who Becomes Delinquent?* London: Heinemann.

Westmarland, L. (2011) *Researching Crime and Justice: Tales from the Field*. Abingdon: Routledge.

Williams, K. (2012) *Textbook on Criminology*. Oxford: Oxford University Press.

Willig, C. (2001) *Qualitative Research in Psychology: A Practical Guide to Theory and Method*. Buckingham: Oxford University Press.

Youth Justice Board (2005) *Role of Risk and Protective Factors*. London: YJB.

Chapter 5

Flately, J. et al. (2010) *Crime in England and Wales 2009–2010*. London: Home Office.

Fletcher, R., Newman, N., and Schulz, A. (2020) 'A Mile Wide, an Inch Deep: Online News and Media Use in the 2019 UK General Election'. Available at: https://ora.ox.ac.uk/objects/uuid:4ed09df1-5fbd-485d-b425-b1aae21ae3d4 [Accessed 21 December 2020].

Her Majesty's Inspectorate of Constabulary. (2014) 'Crime-Recording: Making the Victim Count. The final report of an inspection of crime data integrity in police forces in England and Wales'. Available at: www.justiceinspectorates.gov.uk/hmic/wp-content/uploads/crime-recording-making-the-victim-count.pdf [Accessed 1 December 2020].

Hohl, K. and Stanko, E. (2015) 'Complaints of rape and the criminal justice system: Fresh evidence on the attrition problem in England and Wales'. *European Journal of Criminology* 12(3): 324–41.

Hope, T. and Norris, P. (2013) 'Heterogeneity in the Frequency Distribution of Crime Victimization'. *Journal of Quantitative Criminology* 29(4): 543–78.

Kaiser, B. (2019) *Targeted*. London: Harper Collins.

Magnello, M. (2011) 'Vital Statistics; The Measurement of Public Health' in R. Flood, A. Rice, and R. Wilson (eds) *Mathematics in Victorian Britain*. Oxford: Oxford University Press.

Maguire, M. (2012) 'Criminal statistics and the construction of crime' in M. Maguire, R. Morgan, and R. Reiner (eds) *The Oxford Handbook of Criminology* (5th edn). Oxford: Oxford University Press.

Maguire, M. and McVie, S. (2017) 'Crime data and criminal statistics: a critical reflection' in A. Liebling, S. Maruna, and L. McAra (eds) *The Oxford Handbook of Criminology* (6th edn). Oxford: Oxford University Press.

Mayhew, H. (1812–87 [2012]) *London Labour and the London Poor*. Oxford: Oxford University Press.

Office for National Statistics (2019) *'CSEW: New developments and programme of work'*. Available at: https://ukdataservice.ac.uk/media/622572/child.pdf [Accessed 1 December 2020].

Office for National Statistics. (2020) *Crime Survey for England and Wales*. London: ONS.

Walby, S., Towers, J., and Francis, B. (2015) 'Is Violent Crime Increasing or Decreasing? A new methodology to measure repeat attacks making visible the significance of gender and domestic relations'. *The British Journal of Criminology* 56(6): 1203–34.

Chapter 6

Aiello, M. (2014) 'Policing the masculine frontier: Cultural criminological analysis of the gendered performance of policing'. *Crime, Media, Culture* 10(1): 59–79.

Allen, W. and Blinder, S. (2013) *Migration in the News: Portrayals of Immigrants, Migrants, Asylum Seekers and Refugees in National British Newspapers, 2010 to 2012*. Oxford: Migration Observatory, COMPAS, University of Oxford.

Balch, A. and Balabanova, E. (2016) 'Ethics, Politics and Migration: Public Debates on the Free Movement of Romanians and Bulgarians in the UK, 2006–2013'. *Politics* 36(1): 19–35.

Bengtsson, M. (2016) 'How to plan and perform a qualitative study using content analysis'. *NursingPlus Open* 2: 8–14.

Bergstrom, A. and Belfrage, M. (2018) 'News in Social Media: Incidental consumption and the role of opinion leaders'. *Digital Journalism* 6(5): 583–98.

Bullock, K. (2018) 'The Police Use of Social Media: Transformation or Normalisation?'. *Social Policy and Society* 17(2): 245–58.

Burscher, B., van Spanje, J., and Vreese, C. (2015) 'Owning the Issues of Crime and Immigration; The Relation between Immigration and Crime News and Anti-Immigration Voting in 11 Countries'. *Electoral Studies* 38: 59–69.

Chibnall, S. (1977) *Law-and-Order News*. London: Tavistock.

Chouliaraki, L. et al. (2017) 'The European "migration crisis" and the media: a cross-European press content analysis'. LSE Research Online available at: http://eprints.lse.ac.uk/84670/ [Accessed 4 January 2021].

Cohen, S. (1972 [2011]) *Folk Devils and Moral Panics: The Creation of the Mods and the Rockers*. London: Routledge.

Colbran, M. (2015) *Penal Reform Groups, New Media and Mainstream News: Strategies for Managing the New Media Landscape*. London: The Howard League for Penal Reform.

Collins, R. (2014) 'The construction of race and crime in Canadian print media: A 30-year analysis'. *Criminology & Criminal Justice* 14: 77–99.

Cooper, K. et al. (2016) 'Adolescents and self-taken sexual images: A review of the literature'. *Computers in Human Behavior* 55: 706–16.

Crown Prosecution Service (2019) '*Cybercrime—prosecution guidance*'. London: CPS. Available at: www.cps.gov.uk/legal-guidance/cybercrime-prosecution-guidance [Accessed 1 December 2020].

Davis, F. (1952) 'Crime News in Colorado Newspapers'. *American Journal of Sociology* 57: 325–30.

Decary-Hetu, D. and Aldridge, J. (2015) 'Sifting through the Net: Monitoring of Online Offenders by Researchers'. *European Review of Organised Crime* 2(2): 122–41.

Ditton, J. and Duffy, J. (1983) 'Bias in the Newspaper Reporting of Crime News'. *British Journal of Criminology* 23(2): 159–65.

Dunaway J., Branton R. P., and Abrajano, M. A. (2010) 'Agenda Setting, Public Opinion, and the Issue of Immigration Reform'. *Social Science Quarterly* 91(2): 359–78.

Ferrell, J. (1999) 'Cultural Criminology'. *Annual Review of Sociology* 25: 395–418.

Forshaw, B. (2019) *Crime Fiction: A Reader's Guide*. Harpenden: Oldcastle Books.

Garrelts, N. (2006) *Meaning and Culture of Grand Theft Auto: Critical Essays*. Jefferson, NC: McFarland & Co.

Greer, C. (ed.) (2009) *Crime and the Media: A Reader*. London: Routledge.

Greer, C. and Reiner. R. (2015) 'Mediated Mayhem: Media, Crime, Criminal Justice' in M. Maguire, R. Morgan, and R. Reiner (eds) *The Oxford Handbook of Criminology* (5th edn). Oxford: Oxford University Press.

Hadjimatheou, K. (2019) 'Citizen-led digital policing and democratic norms: The case of self-styled paedophile hunters'. *Criminology & Criminal Justice*. DOI: 10.1177/1748895819880956.

Hadjimatheou, K., Coaffee, J., and De Vries, A. (2019) 'Enhancing Public Security Through the Use of Social Media'. *European Law Enforcement Research Bulletin* 18: 1–14.

Hall, S. et al. (1978 [2013]) *Policing the Crisis*. London: Macmillan.

Harding, R. (2017) 'Immigration' in E. Clery, J. Curtice, and R. Harding (eds) *British Social Attitudes 34*. London: NatCen Social Research.

Helfgott, J. (2015) 'Criminal behavior and the copycat effect: Literature review and theoretical framework for empirical investigation'. *Aggression and Violent Behavior* 22: 46–64.

Home Office (2018) 'Serious Violence Strategy April 2018'. Available at: https://assets.publishing.service.gov.uk/government/uploads/system/uploads/attachment_data/file/698009/serious-violence-strategy.pdf [Accessed: 24 November 2020].

Hough, M. and Roberts, J. V. (2004) *Youth Crime and Youth Justice: Public Opinion in England and Wales*. London: Policy Press.

IPSO (2016) 09324-15 Muslim Engagement and Development (MEND) v The Sun. Available at: www.ipso.co.uk/rulings-and-resolution-statements/ruling/?id=09324-15 [Accessed 24 November 2020].

Irwin-Rogers, K. (2019) 'Illicit Drug Markets, Consumer Capitalism and the Rise of Social Media: A Toxic Trap for Young People'. *Critical Criminology* 27: 591–610.

Irwin-Rogers, K. and Pinkney, C. (2017) *Social media as a catalyst and trigger for youth violence*. London: Catch22.

Irwin-Rogers, K., Densley, J., and Pinkney, C. (2018) 'Gang violence and social media' in J. L. Ireland, C. A. Ireland, and P. Birch (eds) *The International Handbook on Human Aggression*. London: Routledge.

Jennings, W. et al. (2017) 'Penal Populism and the Public Thermostat, Public Punitiveness, and Public Policy'. *Governance* 30(3): 463–81.

Jewkes, Y. (2015) *Media and Crime* (3rd edn). London: Sage.

Jewkes, Y. and Yar, M. (eds) (2009) *The Handbook of Internet Crime*. Cullompton: Willan.

Julios-Costa, M. (2017) 'The age of crime: A cognitive-linguistic critical discourse study of media representations and semantic framings of youth offenders in the Uruguayan media'. *Discourse & Communication* 11(4): 362–85.

Knight, S. (2010) *Crime Fiction Since 1800: Detection, Death, Diversity* (2nd edn). Basingstoke: Palgrave Macmillan.

Kraft, Emilie S. (2009) *Hit Man Manual*. Murfreesboro, TN: The Free Speech Center. Available at: https://mtsu.edu/first-amendment/article/814/hit-man-manual [Accessed 1 December 2020].

Krisberg, B. and Marchionna, S. (2007) 'Attitudes of US Voters toward Youth Crime and the Justice System', Focus: Views from the National Council on Crime and Delinquency. Available at: www.issuelab.org/resources/1068/1068.pdf. [Accessed 1 December 2020].

Kuhn, S. et al. (2019) 'Does playing violent video games cause aggression? A longitudinal intervention study'. *Molecular Psychiatry* 24: 1220–34.

Lewis, L. et al. (2018) '"I see it everywhere": young Australians unintended exposure to sexual content online'. *Sexual Health* 15(4): 335–41.

Livingstone, S. (1996) 'On the Continuing Problem of Media Effects' in J. Curran and M. Gurevitch (eds) *Mass Media and Society* (3rd edn). London: Arnold.

Mason, P. (2006) 'Lies, Distortion and What Doesn't Work: Monitoring Prison Stories in the British Media'. *Crime, Media, Culture* 2(3): 251–67.

Mason, P. (2007) 'Prison Decayed: Cinematic Penal Discourse and Populism 1995–2005'. *Social Semiotics* 16(4): 607–26.

Mayr, A. and Machin, D. (2012) *The Language of Crime and Deviance: An Introduction to Critical Linguistic Analysis in Media and Popular Culture*. New York: Continuum.

McAlister, R. (2015) 'Webscraping as an Investigation Tool to Identify Potential Human Trafficking Operations in Romania'. Proceedings of the ACM Web Science, Article 47: 1–2. DOI: 10.1145/2786451.2786510.

Meindl, J. N. and Ivy, J. W. (2017) 'Mass Shootings: The Role of the Media in Promoting Generalized Imitation'. *American Journal of Public Health* 107(3): 368–70.

Muller, K. and Schwarz, C. (2019) 'Fanning the Flames of Hate: Social Media and Hate Crime'. *Journal of the European Economic Association*. DOI: 10.2139/ssrn.3082972.

Muncie, J. (2015) *Youth and Crime* (4th edn). London: Sage.

Nickerson, C. (2019) 'Media portrayal of terrorism and Muslims: a content analysis of Turkey and France'. *Crime, Law and Social Change* 72: 547–67.

Oleson, J. and MacKinnon, T. (2015) 'Seeing Saw through the Criminological Lens: Popular Representations of Crime and Punishment'. *Criminology, Criminal Justice Law & Society* 16(1): 35–50.

Pearson, G. (1983) *Hooligan: A History of Respectable Fears*. London: Macmillan.

Phillips, N. (2017) 'Violence, Media Effects and Criminology'. Oxford Research Encyclopedia Online, available at: https://oxfordre.com/criminology/view/10.1093/acrefore/9780190264079.001.0001/acrefore-9780190264079-e-189 [Accessed 4 January 2021]

Picard, R. G. (2014) *Public Opinion, Party Politics, Policy, and Immigration News in the United Kingdom*. Oxford: Reuters Institute for the Study of Journalism.

Pinkney, C. and Robinson-Edwards, S. (2018) 'Gangs, music and the mediatisation of crime expressions, violations and validations'. *Safer Communities* 17(2): 103–18.

Priestman, M. (ed.) (2012) *The Cambridge Companion to Crime Fiction*. Cambridge: Cambridge University Press.

Prieto Curiel, R., Cresci, S., Muntean, C.I., and Bishop, S. R. (2020) 'Crime and its fear in social media'. Palgrave Communications 6, Article 57. Available at: www.nature.com/articles/s41599-020-0430-7 [Accessed 24 November 2020].

Rafter, N. (2006) *Shots in the Mirror: Crime Films and Society*. Oxford: Oxford University Press.

Rafter, N. and Brown, M. (2011) *Criminology Goes to the Movies: Crime Theory and Popular Culture*. New York: NYU Press.

Reiner, R. (1997) 'Media Made Criminality' in M. Maguire, R. Morgan, and R. Reiner (eds) *The Oxford Handbook of Criminology* (2nd edn). Oxford: Oxford University Press.

Rios, V. (2018) 'Media Effects on Crime and Crime Style'. Available at: https://scholar.harvard.edu/files/vrios/files/rios_mediaeffectscrimestyle.pdf [Accessed 4 January 2021].

Rios, V. and Ferguson, C. (2019) 'News Media Coverage of Crime and Violent Drug Crime: A Case for Cause or Catalyst?'. *Justice Quarterly*. DOI: 10.1080/07418825.2018.1561925.

Roche, S., Pickett, J., and Gertz, M. (2016) 'The scary world of online news? Internet news exposure and public attitudes toward crime and justice'. *Journal of Quantitative Criminology* 32(2): 215–36.

Scaggs, J. (2005) *Crime Fiction*. London, Routledge.

Sian, K., Law, I., and Sayyid, S. (2012) *The Media and Muslims in the UK*. Leeds: Centre for Ethnicity and Racism Studies, University of Leeds.

Surette, R. (2015) 'Performance Crime and Justice'. *Current Issues in Criminal Justice* 27(2): 195–216.

Tornberg, A. and Tornberg, P. (2016) 'Muslims in social media discourse: Combining topic modeling and critical discourse analysis'. *Discourse, Context & Media* 13B: 132–42.

Touitou, Y., Touitou, D., and Reinberg, A. (2016) 'Disruption of adolescents' circadian clock: The vicious circle of media use, exposure to light at night, sleep loss and risk behaviors'. *Journal of Physiology* 110(4B): 467–79.

Twenge, J., Martin, G., and Spitzberg, B. (2019) 'Trends in U.S. Adolescents' Media Use, 1976–2016: The rise of digital media, the decline of TV, and the (near) demise of print'. *Psychology of Popular Media Culture* 8(4): 329–45.

Wayne, M. et al. (2008) 'Television News and the Symbolic Criminalisation of Young People'. *Journalism Studies* 9(1): 75–90.

Wilkins, L. (1964) *Social Deviance*. London: Tavistock.

Wilson, D. and O'Sullivan, S. (2004) *Images of Incarceration: Representations of Prison in Film and Television Drama*. Winchester: Waterside.

Wong-Anan, N. (2008) 'Thailand halts Grand Theft Auto sales after murder'. Reuters: http://uk.reuters.com/article/us-crime-thailand-grandtheftauto-idUKBKK22888820080804 [Accessed 11 December 2020].

The World Bank. (2018) *Individuals using the Internet (% of population)*. Washington, DC: The World Bank. Available at: https://data.worldbank.org/indicator/IT.NET.USER.ZS [Accessed: 24 November 2020].

Yar, M. (2010) 'Screening Crime: Cultural Criminology Goes to the Movies' in K. Hayward and M. Presdee (eds) *Framing Crime: Cultural Criminology and the Image*. London: Routledge.

Yar, M. and Steinmetz, K. (2019) *Cybercrime and Society* (3rd edn). London: Sage.

Youth Justice Board (2020) *Youth justice statistics: 2018 to 2019*. London: YJB.

Chapter 7

Belknap, J. (2014) *The invisible woman: Gender, crime, and justice*. Stanford, CT: Cengage Learning.

Bowling, B. and Phillips, C. (2007), Disproportionate and Discriminatory: Reviewing the Evidence on Police Stop and Search'. *Modern Law Review*, 70: 936–61.

Brotto, G., Sinnamon, G. and Petherick, W. (2017) 'Victimology and Predicting Victims of Personal Violence' in W. Petherick and G. Sinnamon (eds) The *Psychology of Criminal and Antisocial Behaviour: Victim and Offender Perspectives*. Amsterdam: Academic Press/Elsevier.

Chesney-Lind, M. (1997) *The female offender: Girls, women, and crime*. Thousand Oaks, CA: Sage.

Christie N. (1986) 'The Ideal Victim' in E. A. Fattah (ed.) *From Crime Policy to Victim Policy*. London: Palgrave Macmillan.

Cobb, S. and Horeck, T. (2018) 'Post Weinstein: gendered power and harassment in the media industries'. *Feminist Media Studies* 18(3): 489–91.

Duggan, M. (ed.) (2018) *Revisiting the 'Ideal Victim': Developments in Critical Victimology*. Bristol: Policy Press.

Farrell, G., Tseloni, A., and Pease, K. (2005) 'Repeat Victimization in the ICVS and the NCVS'. *Crime Prevention and Community Safety* 7: 7–18.

Fattah, E. (1989) 'Victims and victimology: the facts and the rhetoric' in E. Fattah (ed.) *Towards a Critical Victimology*. New York: Macmillan.

Friedrichs, D. (1983) 'Victimology: a consideration of the radical critique'. *Crime & Delinquency* 29: 283–93.

Gavrielides, T. (2017) 'The Victims' Directive and What Victims Want From Restorative Justice'. *Victims & Offenders* 12(1): 21–42.

Gobert, J. J. (1977) 'Victim Precipitation'. *Columbia Law Review* 77(4): 511–53.

Gover, A. R., Mackenzie, D. L., and Armstrong, G. S. (2000) 'Importation and Deprivation Explanations of Juveniles'

Adjustment to Correctional Facilities'. *International Journal of Offender Therapy and Comparative Criminology* 44(4): 450–67.

Ince, J., Rojas, F., and Davis, C. (2017) 'The social media response to Black Lives Matter: how Twitter users interact with Black Lives Matter through hashtag use'. *Ethnic and Racial Studies* 40(11): 1814–30.

Jordan, J. (2013) 'From victim to survivor—and from survivor to victim: Reconceptualising the survivor journey'. *Sexual Abuse in Australia and New Zealand* 5(2): 48–56.

Lamb, S. (ed.) (1999) *New versions of victims: Feminists struggle with the concept*. New York: New York University. Press.

Lasky, N. V. (2020) 'Victim Precipitation Theory' in F. P. Bernat and K. Frailing (eds) *The Encyclopedia of Women and Crime*. Hoboken, NJ: Wiley.

Lauritsen, J. L. and Carbone-Lopez, K. (2011) 'Gender differences in risk factors for violent victimization: An examination of individual-, family-, and community-level predictors'. *Journal of Research in Crime and Delinquency* 48(4): 538–65.

Levenson, J. S. and Cotter, L. P. (2005) 'The Effect of Megan's Law on Sex Offender Reintegration'. *Journal of Contemporary Criminal Justice* 21(1): 49–66.

Lipscombe, S. (2012) 'Sarah's law: the child sex offender disclosure scheme', House of Commons Briefing Note SN/HA/1692.

Lowe, M., and Rogers, P. (2017) 'The scope of male rape: A selective review of research, policy and practice'. *Aggression and Violent Behaviour* 35: 38–43.

Maguire, M. and Kynch, J. (2000) *Public Perceptions and Victims' Experiences of Victim Support: Findings from the 1998 British Crime Survey*, London: Home Office.

Mawby, R. and Walklate, S. (1994) *Critical Victimology*. London: Sage.

McShane, M. D. and Williams, F. P. (1992). 'Radical Victimology: A Critique of the Concept of Victim in Traditional Victimology'. *Crime & Delinquency* 38(2): 258–71.

Mendes, K., Ringrose, J.. and Keller, J. (2018) '#MeToo and the promise and pitfalls of challenging rape culture through digital feminist activism'. *European Journal of Women's Studies* 25(2): 236–46.

Miers, D. (1989) 'Positivist Victimology: A Critique'. *International Review of Victimology* 1(1): 3–22.

Morgan, J. and Zedner, L. (1992), 'The Victim's Charter: A New Deal for Child Victims?'. *Howard Journal of Criminal Justice* 31: 294–307.

Office for National Statistics (2020) *Crime in England and Wales: Year Ending March 2020*. Available at: www.ons.gov.uk/peoplepopulationandcommunity/crimeandjustice/bulletins/crimeinenglandandwales/yearendingmarch2020 [Accessed 29 September 2020].

Pemberton, A., Mulder, E., and Aarten, P. G. M. (2019) 'Stories of injustice: Towards a narrative victimology'. *European Journal of Criminology* 16(4): 391–412.

Peters, M. A. and Besley, T. (2019) 'Weinstein, sexual predation, and "Rape Culture": Public pedagogies and Hashtag Internet activism'. *Educational Philosophy and Theory* 51(5): 458–64.

Phillips, N. (2017) *Beyond Blurred Lines: Rape Culture in Popular Media*. Lanham, MD: Rowman & Littlefield.

Quinney, R. (1980) *Class, State and Crime* (2nd edn). New York: Longman.

Ray, R. et al. (2017) 'Ferguson and the death of Michael Brown on Twitter: #BlackLivesMatter, #TCOT, and the evolution of collective identities'. *Ethnic and Racial Studies* 40(11): 1797–813.

Rickford, R. (2016) 'Black Lives Matter: Toward a Modern Practice of Mass Struggle'. *New Labor Forum* 25(1): 34–42.

Spiga, V. (2010). 'Indirect Victims' Participation in the Lubanga Trial'. *Journal of International Criminal Justice* 8(1): 183–98.

Suarez, E. and Gadalla, T. M. (2010) 'Stop Blaming the Victim: A Meta-Analysis on Rape Myths'. *Journal of Interpersonal Violence* 25(11): 2010–35.

Tippett, E. C. (2018) 'The Legal Implications of the MeToo Movement'. *Minnesota Law Review* 103: 229.

Turanovic, J. J. and Pratt, T. C. (2014) 'Can't Stop, Won't Stop: Self-Control, Risky Lifestyles, and Repeat Victimization'. *Journal of Quantitative Criminology* 30: 29–56.

Turanovic, J. J., Pratt, T. C., and Piquero, A. R. (2018) 'Structural Constraints, Risky Lifestyles, and Repeat Victimization'. *Journal of Quantitative Criminology* 34: 251–74.

Turvey, B. (2014) *Victimity: Entering the Criminal Justice System, in Brent Turvey, Forensic Victimology* (2nd edn). Oxford: Academic Press/Elsevier.

van Dijk, J. J. M. (1988) 'Ideological trends within the victims movements: An international perspective' in M. Maguire and J. Pointing (eds) *Victims of crime: A new deal?* Buckingham: Open University Press.

van Wijk, J. (2013) 'Who is the "little old lady" of international crimes? Nils Christie's concept of the ideal victim reinterpreted'. *International Review of Victimology* 19(2): 159–79.

Walklate, S. et al. (2019) 'Victim stories and victim policy: Is there a case for a narrative victimology?'. *Crime, Media, Culture* 15(2): 199–215.

Wolfgang, M. (1957) 'Victim Precipitated Criminal Homicide'. *Journal of Criminal Law, Criminology & Police Science* 48(1): 1–11.

Xie, M. and McDowall, D. (2008) 'Escaping Crime: The Effects of Direct and Indirect Victimization on Moving'. *Criminology* 46: 809–40.

Chapter 8

Allen, C. (2017) 'Political Approaches to Tackling Islamophobia: An Analytical Review of the British Coalition Government 2010–2015'. Preprints online: www.preprints.org/manuscript/201706.0082/v1/download [Accessed 10 August 2020].

Awan, I. and Zempi, I. (2018) '"You all look the same": Non-Muslim men who suffer Islamophobic hate crime in the post-Brexit era'. *European Journal of Criminology*. DOI: 10.1177/1477370818812735.

Aymer, S. (2016) '"I can't breathe2: A case study—Helping Black men cope with race-related trauma stemming from police killing and brutality'. *Journal of Human Behavior in the Social Environment* 26(3–4): 367–76.

Bains, C. (2018) '"A Few Bad Apples": How the Narrative of Isolated Misconduct Distorts Civil Rights Doctrine'. *Indiana Law Journal* 93(1): 29–55.

Balderston, S. (2013) 'Victimised again? Intersectionality and Injustice in disabled women's lives after hate crime and rape' in M. Texler Segal and V. Demos (eds) *Advances in Gender Research*, Vol. 18a. Cambridge, MA: Emerald.

Baldwin, B. (2018) 'Black, White, and Blue: Bias, Profiling, and Policing in the Age of Black Lives Matter'. *Western New England Law Review* 40(3): 431–46.

Bowling, B. (1998) *Violent racism: Victimization, policing, and social context*. Oxford: Oxford University Press.

British Medical Journal (1957) 'Report of the Departmental Committee on Homosexual Offences and Prostitution'. *British Medical Journal* 2(5045): 639–40.

Burnett, J. (2017) 'Racial violence and the Brexit state'. *Race & Class* 58(4): 85–97.

Campbell, B. and Manning, J. (2014) 'Microaggression and Moral Cultures'. *Comparative Sociology* 13(6): 692–726.

Chakraborti, N. and Garland, J. (2012) 'Reconceptualising Hate Crime Victimization through the Lens of Vulnerability and "Difference"'. *Theoretical Criminology* 16(4): 499–514.

Chama, B. (2019) 'The Black Lives Matter movement, crime and police brutality: Comparative study of New York Post and New York Daily News'. *European Journal of American Culture* 38(3): 201–16.

Clement, S. et al. (2011) 'Disability hate crime and targeted violence and hostility: A mental health and discrimination perspective'. *Journal of Mental Health* 20(3): 219–25.

Community Security Trust (2019) 'Antisemitic Incidents Report 2019'. Available at: https://cst.org.uk/data/file/9/0/IncidentsReport2019.1580815723.pdf.

CPS (2020) *Hate Crime*. Available at: www.cps.gov.uk/hate-crime [Accessed 30 May 2020]

Curtice, J. et al. (eds) (2019) *British Social Attitudes: The 36th Report*. London: The National Centre for Social Research.

Day, A. (2013) 'The PinkNews Guide to the history of England and Wales equal marriage'. Available at: www.pinknews.co.uk/2013/07/15/the-pinknews-guide-to-the-history-of-england-and-wales-equal-marriage/2/.

Devine, D. (2018) 'Hate crime did spike after the referendum—even allowing for other factors', *LSE Brexit blog*, available at: https://blogs.lse.ac.uk/brexit/2018/03/19/hate-crime-did-spike-after-the-referendum-even-allowing-for-other-factors/.

Duggan, M. (2010) 'Homophobic Hate Crime in Northern Ireland' in N. Chakraborti (ed.) *Hate Crime: Concepts, Policy*. Abingdon: Routledge.

Equality and Human Rights Commission (2011) *Hidden in plain sight. Inquiry into disability-related harassment*. Available at: www.equalityhumanrights.com/publication/hidden-plainsight-inquiry-disability-related-harassment [Accessed: 30 May 2020].

Equality and Human Rights Commission (2020) 'Investigation into antisemitism in the Labour Party'. Available at www.equalityhumanrights.com/en/publication-download/investigation-antisemitism-labour-party [Accessed 9 November 2020].

Featherstone, M., Holohan, S., and Poole, E. (2010) 'Discourses of the War on Terror: Constructions of the Islamic other after 7/7'. *International Journal of Media and Politics* 6(2): 169–86.

Giannasi, P. and Hall, N. (2016) 'Policing Hate Crime' in J. Schweppe and M. A. Walters (eds) *The Globalisation of hate: Internationalising hate crime?* Oxford: Oxford University Press.

Gitari, E., and Walters, M.A. (2020) *Hate crimes against the LGBT community in the Commonwealth: a situational analysis*. London: Human Dignity Trust.

Goodwin, M. and Milazzo, C. (2017) 'Taking back control? Investigating the role of immigration in the 2016 vote for Brexit'. *British Journal of Politics and International Relations* 19(3): 450–64.

Gordon, P. (1990) *Racial Violence and Harassment*. London: Runnymede Trust

Gottfredson, M. (2017) 'Self-Control Theory and Crime'. Available at: https://oxfordre.com/criminology/view/10.1093/acrefore/9780190264079.001.0001/acrefore-9780190264079-e-252#:~:text=Gottfredson%20and%20Hirschi%20advanced%20self-control%20theory%20in%201990,ability%20to%20act%20in%20 favor%20of%20longer-term%20interests.

Gottfredson, M. and Hirschi, T. (1990) *A general theory of crime*. Stanford, CA: Stanford University Press.

Gover, A. R., Harper, S. B., and Langton, L. (2020) 'Anti-Asian Hate Crime During the COVID-19 Pandemic: Exploring the Reproduction of Inequality'. *American Journal of Criminal Justice* 45: 647–67.

Government Equalities Office (2018) 'National LGBT Survey: Research report'. Available at: https://assets.publishing.service.gov.uk/government/uploads/system/uploads/attachment_data/file/721704/LGBT-survey-research-report.pdf.

Hall, E. (2019) 'A critical geography of disability hate crime'. *Area* 51: 249–56.

Hall, N. (2013) *Hate crime*. Abingdon: Routledge.

Hanes, E. and Machin, S. (2014) 'Hate crime in the wake of terror attacks: Evidence from 7/7 and 9/11'. *Journal of Contemporary Criminal Justice* 30(3): 247–67.

Home Office (2017) 'Hate Crime, England and Wales, 2016/17'. Available at: https://assets.publishing.service.gov.uk/government/uploads/system/uploads/attachment_data/file/652136/hate-crime-1617-hosb1717.pdf.

Home Office (2018) 'Hate Crime, England and Wales, 2017/18'. Available at: https://assets.publishing.service.gov.uk/government/uploads/system/uploads/attachment_data/file/748598/hate-crime-1718-hosb2018.pdf.

Home Office (2019) 'Hate Crime, England and Wales, 2018/19'. Available at: https://assets.publishing.service.gov.uk/government/uploads/system/uploads/attachment_data/file/839172/hate-crime-1819-hosb2419.pdf.

Human Dignity Trust (2019) 'Injustice Exposed. The Criminalisation of Transgender People and its Impacts'. Available at: www.humandignitytrust.org/wpcontent/uploads/resources/Injustice-Exposed-the-criminsalisation-of-trans-people.pdf.

Jackson, R. (2007) 'Constructing Enemies: "Islamic Terrorism" in Political and Academic Discourse. *Government and Opposition* 42: 394–426.

Jenness, V. and Grattet, R. (2001) *Making Hate a Crime: From Social Movement to Law Enforcement*. New York: Russell Sage.

King, M. and Bartlett, A. (1999) 'British Psychiatry and Homosexuality'. *British Journal of Psychiatry* 175: 101–13.

Law Commission (2020) *'Hate Crime: Background to our Review'*. London: Law Commission. Available at: https://s3-eu-west-2.amazonaws.com/lawcom-prod-storage-11jsxou24uy7q/uploads/2019/07/6.5286-LC_Hate-Crime_Information-Paper_A4_FINAL_030719_WEB.pdf.

Lawrence, F. (1999) *Punishing hate: bias crimes under American law*. London: Harvard University Press.

Macpherson, W. (1999), *The Stephen Lawrence Inquiry*, Cm 4262-I. London: The Stationery Office.

Manchester Disabled Persons Access Group (2019a) The Medical Model of Disability. Manchester: MDPAG. Available at: www.mdpag.org.uk/resources/the-medical-model-of-disability/.

Manchester Disabled Persons Access Group (2019b) The Social Model of Disability. Manchester: MDPAG. Available at: www.mdpag.org.uk/resources/the-social-model-of-disability/.

McGuire, K. and Salter, M. (2014) 'Legal Responses to Religious Hate Crime: Identifying Critical Issues'. *King's Law Journal* 25(2): 159–84.

Menon, A. and Wager, A. (2020) 'Taking back control: sovereignty as strategy in Brexit politics'. *Territory, Politics, Governance* 8(2): 279–84.

Müller, K. and Schwarz, C. (2020) 'From Hashtag to Hate Crime: Twitter and Anti-Minority Sentiment'. Available at SSRN: https://ssrn.com/abstract=3149103 orhttp://dx.doi.org/10.2139/ssrn.3149103.

Nadal, K. L. (2011) 'The Racial and Ethnic Microaggressions Scale (REMS): Construction, reliability, and validity'. *Journal of Counseling Psychology* 58(4): 470–80.

Perry, B. (2001) *In the Name of Hate: Understanding Hate Crime*. New York: Routledge.

Perry, B. (2014) 'Gendered Islamophobia: hate crime against Muslim women'. *Social Identities* 20(1): 74–89.

Perry, B. (2017) 'The more things change… post-9/11 trends in hate crime scholarship: Concepts, policy, future directions' in N. Chakraborti (ed.) *Hate Crime: Concepts, Policy*. Abingdon: Routledge.

Pitcher, B. (2019) 'Racism and Brexit: notes towards an antiracist populism'. *Ethnic and Racial Studies* 42(14): 2490–509.

Ray, R. (2020) *Bad apples come from rotten trees in policing*. Washington, DC: Brookings. Available at: www.brookings.edu/

blog/how-we-rise/2020/05/30/bad-apples-come-from-rotten-trees-in-policing/

Rossetti, P., Dinisman, T., and Moroz, A. (2016) *An Easy Target? Risk Factors affecting victimisation rates for violent crime and theft*. London: Victim Support.

Sherry, M. (2011) Disability hate crimes: Does anyone really hate disabled people? Farnham: Ashgate.

Southern, J. (2017) 'Homosexuality at the Foreign Office 1967–1992'. Foreign Office History Notes, Issue 19.

Stonewall (2017) 'LGBT in Britain: Hate Crime and Discrimination'. London: Stonewall. Available at: www.stonewall.org.uk/system/files/lgbt_in_britain_hate_crime.pdf [Accessed 10 August 2020].

Stray, Melanie (2019) 'The Hate Crime Report'. Galop. Available at: www.galop.org.uk/wp-content/uploads/Hate-Crime-Report-2019.pdf.

Thomas, P. (2011) 'Mate crime': ridicule, hostility and targeted attacks against disabled people'. *Disability & Society*, 26(1): 107–11.

Torres-Harding, S. and Turner, T. (2015) 'Assessing Racial Microaggression Distress in a Diverse Sample'. *Evaluation & the Health Professions* 38(4): 464–90.

Venkatraman, A. (2007) 'Religious Basis for Islamic Terrorism: The Quran and Its Interpretations'. *Studies in Conflict & Terrorism* 30(3): 229–48.

Wadham, J. and Mountfield, H. (1999) *Blackstone's Guide to the Human Rights Act 1998*. London: Blackstone Press.

Walters, M. A. (2011) 'A general theories of hate crime? Strain, doing difference and self control'. *Critical Criminology* 19(4): 313–30.

Walters, M. A. and Brown, R. (2016) *Causes and motivations of hate crime*. London: Equality and Human Rights Commission.

Walters, M. A. and Krasodomski-Jones, A. (2018) *Patterns of hate crime: who, what, when and where?* London: DEMOS.

Walters, M. A, Owusu-Bempah, A., and Wiedlitzka, S. (2018) 'Hate crime and the "justice gap": the case for law reform'. *Criminal Law Review* 12: 961–86.

Walters. M. A., Wiedlitzka. S., and Owusu-Bempah, A. (2017) *Hate crime and the legal process: options for law reform*. Brighton: University of Sussex.

Walters, M. A. et al. (2020a) 'Hate crimes against trans people: assessing emotions, behaviors and attitudes towards criminal justice agencies'. *Journal of Interpersonal Violence* 35(21–22): 4583–613.

Walters, M. A. et al. (2020b) 'Group identity, empathy and shared suffering: understanding the "community" impacts of anti-LGBT and Islamophobic hate crimes'. *International Review of Victimology*, 26(2): 143–62.

Wilkin, D (2020) *Disability Hate Crime Experiences of Everyday Hostility on Public Transport*. London: Palgrave.

Wilson, I., Antin, T., and Hunt, G. (2020) 'Some Are Good, Some Are Bad: Perceptions of the Police from Black and Latina Women Living in the San Francisco Bay Area'. *Women & Criminal Justice*. DOI: 10.1080/08974454.2020.1741489.

Wolff, K. B. and Cokely, C. L. (2007) 'To Protect and to Serve?: An Exploration of Police Conduct in Relation to the Gay, Lesbian, Bisexual, and Transgender Community'. *Sexuality and Culture* 11: 1–23.

Wood, C. and Finlay, W. M. L. (2008) 'British National Party representations of Muslims in the month after the London bombings: Homogeneity, threat, and the conspiracy tradition'. *British Journal of Social Psychology* 47: 707–26.

Chapter 9

Agnew, R. (1992) 'Foundation for a General Strain Theory of Crime and Delinquency'. *Criminology* 30(1): 47–87.

Ariès, P. (1962) *Centuries of Childhood*. New York: Vintage Books.

Arnett, J. (1999) 'Adolescent Storm and Stress, Reconsidered'. *American Psychologist* 54: 317–26.

Arnull, E. and Eagle, S. (2009) *Girls and Offending—Patterns, Perceptions and Interventions*. London: Youth Justice Board.

Baker, K. (2005) 'Assessment in Youth Justice: Professional Discretion and the Use of Asset'. *Youth Justice* 5(2): 106–22.

Bakker, E. (2006) *Jihadi Terrorists in Europe, their Characteristics and the Circumstances in which they Joined the Jihad*. The Hague: Institute of International Relations.

Bateman, T. (2011) 'Punishing Poverty. The Scaled Approach and Youth Justice Practice'. *Howard Journal* 50(2): 171–83.

Bateman, T. (2012) 'Who Pulled the Plug? Towards an Explanation of the Fall in Child Imprisonment in England and Wales'. *Youth Justice* 12(1): 36–52.

Bateman, T. (2015) *The State of Youth Justice 2015: An Overview of Trends and Developments*. London: National Association for Youth Justice.

Bateman, T. (2020) *The State of Youth Justice 2015: An Overview of Trends and Developments*. London: National Association for Youth Justice.

Becker, H. (1963) *The Outsiders*. New York: Free Press.

Blakemore, S.-J. (2019) *Inventing Ourselves*. London: Penguin.

Blakemore, S.-J. and Frith, U. (2005) *The Learning Brain*. Oxford: Blackwell.

Bourdieu, P. (1977) *Outline of a Theory of Practice*. Cambridge: Cambridge University Press.

Byrne, B. and Brooks, K. (2015) *Post-YOT Youth Justice*. London: Howard League for Penal Reform. Available at: https://howardleague.org/wp-content/uploads/2016/04/HLWP_19_2015.pdf. [Accessed 2 December 2020].

Case, S. (2017) *Contemporary Youth Justice*. Abingdon: Routledge.

Case, S. (2018) *Youth Justice: A Critical Introduction*. Abingdon: Routledge.

Case, S. and Haines, K. (2009) *Understanding Youth Offending: Risk Factor Research Policy and Practice*. Cullompton: Willan.

Case, S. and Haines, K. (2010) 'Juvenile Delinquency: Manifestations and Causes' in M. Herzog-Evans (ed.) *Transnational Criminology Manual*. Nijmegen: Wolf Legal Publishers.

Case, S. and Haines, K. (2015) 'Children First, Offenders Second Positive Promotion: Reframing the Prevention Debate'. *Youth Justice Journal* 15(3): 226–39.

Case, S. and Haines, K. (2018) 'Transatlantic "Positive Youth Justice": a distinctive new model for responding to offending by children?'. *Crime Prevention and Community Safety* 20: 208–22.

Christmann, K. (2012) *Preventing Religious Radicalisation and Violent Extremism*. London: Youth Justice Board.

Cloward, R. and Ohlin, L. (1960) *Delinquency and Opportunity*. New York: The Free Press.

Cohen, A. (1955) *Delinquent Boys*. Chicago, IL: The Free Press.

Cohen, S. (1972) *Folk Devils and Moral Panics*. London: Paladin.

Coleman, J. and Hendry, L. (1999) *The Nature of Adolescence* (3rd edn). London: Routledge.

Creaney, S. and Smith, R. (2014) 'Youth Justice Back at the Crossroads'. *Safer Communities* 13(2): 83–7.

Crofts, T. (2009) 'Catching up with Europe: Taking the Age of Criminal Responsibility Seriously in England'. *European Journal of Crime, Criminal Law and Criminal Justice* 17(4): 267–91.

Cunningham, H. (2005) *Children and Childhood in Western Society Since 1500* (2nd edn). Harlow: Pearson Longman.

Dasen, P. (2000) 'Rapid Social Change and the Turmoil of Adolescence: A Cross-Cultural Perspective'. *International Journal of Group Tensions* 29: 17–49.

Erikson, E. (1995) *Childhood and Society*. New York: Vintage.

Farrington, D. (1988) 'Studying Changes Within Individuals: The Causes of Offending' in M. Rutter (ed.) *Studies of Psychosocial Risk: The Power of Longitudinal Data*. Cambridge: Cambridge University Press.

Farrington, D. (2003) 'Key Results from the First Forty Years of the Cambridge Study in Delinquent Development' in T. Thornberry and M. Krohn (eds) (2003) *Taking Stock of Delinquency: An Overview of Findings from Contemporary Longitudinal Studies.* New York: Kluwer.

Farrington, D. (2007) 'Childhood Risk Factors and Risk-Focused Prevention' in M. Maguire, R. Morgan, and R. Reiner (eds) *The Oxford Handbook of Criminology* (4th edn). Oxford: Oxford University Press.

Feilzer, M. and Hood, R. (2004) *Differences or Discrimination?* London: Youth Justice Board.

France, A. and Homel, R. (2007a) 'Societal Access Routes and Developmental Pathways: Putting Social Structure and Young People's Voice into the Analysis of Pathways into and out of Crime' in A. France and R. Homel (eds) *Pathways and Crime Prevention.* Cullompton: Willan.

France, A. and Homel, R. (eds) (2007b) *Pathways and Crime Prevention.* Cullompton: Willan.

Freeman, M. (2007) *The Best Interests of the Child.* Leiden: Martinus Nijhoff.

Freud, S. (1977) *On Sexuality.* Harmondsworth: Penguin.

Gangs Working Group (2009) *Dying to Belong.* London: Centre for Social Justice.

Garland, D. (2001) *The Culture of Control.* Oxford: Oxford University Press.

Gill, P. (2007) 'A Multi-Dimensional Approach to Suicide Bombing'. *International Journal of Conflict and Violence* 1(2): 142–59.

Glueck, S. and Glueck, E. (1930) *500 Criminal Careers.* New York: Alfred Knopf.

Goldson, B. (2005) 'Child Imprisonment: A Case for Abolition'. *Youth Justice* 5(2): 77–90.

Goldson, B. (2013) '"Unsafe, Unjust and Harmful to Wider Society": Grounds for Raising the Minimum Age of Criminal Responsibility in England and Wales'. *Youth Justice* 13(2): 111–30.

Goldson, B. and Muncie, J. (2015) *Youth Crime and Justice* (2nd edn). London: Sage.

Goodnow, J. (2007) 'Adding Social Contexts to Developmental Analyses of Crime Prevention' in A. France and R. Homel (eds) *Pathways and Crime Prevention.* Cullompton: Willan.

Haines, K. and Case, S. (2015) *Positive Youth Justice: Children First, Offenders Second.* Bristol: Policy Press.

Haines, K. et al. (2013) 'The Swansea Bureau: A Model of Diversion from the YJS'. *International Journal of Law, Crime and Justice* 41(2): 167–87.

Hall, S. et al. (2013) *Policing the Crisis* (35th anniversary edn). Basingstoke: Palgrave Macmillan.

Hallsworth, S. and Young, T. (2004) 'Getting Real About Gangs'. *Criminal Justice Matters* 55(1): 12–13.

Hanson, E. and Holmes, D. (2014) *That Difficult Age: Developing a More Effective Response to Risks in Adolescence.* Totnes: The Dartington Hall Trust.

Hawes, M. (2013) 'Legitimacy and social order: A young people's perspective'. Unpublished PhD thesis, Swansea University.

Hendrick, H. (2015) 'Histories of Youth Crime and Youth Justice' in B. Goldson and J. Muncie (eds) *Youth Crime and Justice.* London: Sage.

Heywood, C. (2001) *A History of Childhood.* Cambridge: Polity Press.

Hopkins-Burke, R. (2013) *An Introduction to Criminological Theory.* Abingdon: Routledge.

James, A. and James, A. (2004) *Constructing Childhood.* Basingstoke: Palgrave Macmillan.

Jenks, C. (1996) *Childhood.* London: Routledge.

Kelly, L. (2012) 'Representing and Preventing Youth Crime and Disorder: Intended and Unintended Consequences of Targeted Youth Programmes in England'. *Youth Justice* 12(2): 101–17.

Kelly, L. and Armitage V. (2015) 'Diverse Diversions: Youth Justice Reform, Localized Practices, and a "New Interventionist Diversion"?'. *Youth Justice* 15: 117–33.

Kemshall, H. (2008) 'Risk, Rights and Justice: Understanding and Responding to Youth Risk'. *Youth Justice* 8(1): 21–38.

Kitsuse, J. (1962) 'Societal Reaction to Deviant Behaviour: Problems of Theory and Method'. *Social Problems* 9: 247–56.

Lammy, D. (2017) *The Lammy Review: An independent review into the treatment of, and outcomes for Black, Asian and Minority Ethnic individuals in the criminal justice system.* London: Ministry of Justice.

Laub, J. and Sampson, R. (2003) *Shared Beginnings, Delinquent Lives. Delinquent Boys to Age 70.* London: Harvard University Press.

Lawrence, J. (2007) 'Taking the Developmental Pathways Approach to Understanding and Preventing Antisocial Behaviour' in A. France and R. Homel (eds) *Pathways and Crime Prevention.* Cullompton: Willan.

Lemert, E. (1967) *Human Deviance, Social Problems and Social Control.* Englewood Cliffs, NJ: Prentice-Hall.

Matza, D. (1964) *Delinquency and Drift.* New York: John Wiley & Sons.

Matza, D. (1969) *Becoming Deviant.* Englewood Cliffs, NJ: Prentice-Hall.

May, T., Gyateng, T., and Hough, M. (2010) *Differential Treatment in the YJS.* London: Equality and Human Rights Commission.

McAra, L. and McVie, S. (2007) 'Youth Justice? The Impact of System Contact on Patterns of Desistance from Offending'. *European Journal of Criminology* 4(3): 315–45.

McAra, L. and McVie, S. (2017) 'Developmental and life-course criminology: Innovations, impacts and applications' in A. Liebling, S. Maruna, and L. McAra (eds) *The Oxford Handbook of Criminology* (6th edn). Oxford: Oxford University Press.

McNeill, F. and Barry, M. (2009) 'Conclusions' in M. Barry and F. McNeill (eds) *Youth Offending and Youth Justice.* London: Jessica Kingsley Publishers.

Merton, R. (1938) 'Social Structure and Anomie'. *American Sociological Review* 3(5): 672–82.

Merton, R. (1957) 'Priorities in Scientific Discovery: A Chapter in the Sociology of Science'. *American Sociological Review* 22(6): 635–59.

Ministry of Justice and Youth Justice Board (2013) *Youth Out-of-Court Disposals Guide for Police and Youth Offending Services.* London: Ministry of Justice.

Muncie, J. (2004) *Youth and Crime.* London: Sage.

Muncie, J. and Goldson, B. (2006) *Comparative Youth Justice.* London: Sage.

National Association for Youth Justice (2016) *Response to Review of the YJS: An Interim Report of Emerging Findings.* London: NAYJ.

Piaget, J. (1959) *The Language and Thought of the Child.* London: Routledge.

Pitts, J. (2008) *Reluctant Gangsters.* Cullompton: Willan.

Pollock, A. (1983) *Forgotten Children.* Cambridge: Cambridge University Press.

Richards, K. (2014) 'Blurred Lines: Reconsidering the Concept of "Diversion" in YJSs in Australia'. *Youth Justice* 14(2): 122–39.

Rutter, M., Giller, H., and Hagell, A. (1998) *Antisocial Behaviour by Young People.* Cambridge: Cambridge University Press.

Rutter, M. et al. (1976) 'Adolescent Turmoil: Fact or Fiction?'. *Journal of Child Psychology and Psychiatry* 17: 35–56.

Sampson, R. and Laub, J. (1993) *Crime in the Making: Pathways and Turning Points Through Life.* Harvard, MA: Harvard University Press.

Sampson, R. and Laub, J. (2005) 'A General Age-Graded Theory of Crime: Lessons Learned and the Future of Life-Course Criminology' in D. Farrington (ed.) *Integrated Developmental and Life-Course Theories of Offending.* New Brunswick, NJ: Transaction.

Sharpe, G. (2011) *Offending Girls: Young Women and Youth Justice*. Abingdon: Routledge.

Sherman, L. et al. (1998) *Preventing Crime: What Works, What Doesn't, What's Promising*. Baltimore, MD: Department of Criminology and Criminal Justice, University of Maryland.

Smith, R. (2010) *A Universal Child?* Basingstoke: Palgrave Macmillan.

Smith, R. (2011) *Doing Justice to Young People*. Cullompton: Willan.

Smith, R. (2014a) 'Reinventing Diversion'. *Youth Justice* 14(2): 109–21.

Smith, R. (2014b) *Youth Justice: Ideas, Policy and Practice*. London: Routledge.

Steffensmeier, D., Hua, Z., and Yunmei, L. (2017) 'Age and its relation to crime in Taiwan and the United States: Invariant, or does cultural context matter?'. *Criminology* 55(2): 377–404.

Stephenson, M., Giller, H., and Brown, S. (2013) *Effective Practice in Youth Justice*. Abingdon: Routledge.

Taylor, J., McGue, M., and Iacono, W. (2000) 'Sex Differences, Assortative Mating and Cultural Transmission Effects on Adolescent Delinquency: A Twin Family Study'. *Journal of Child Psychology and Psychiatry* 41: 433–40.

Thomson, R. et al. (2002) 'Critical Moments: Choice, Chance and Opportunity in Young People's Narratives of Transition'. *Sociology* 36(2): 335–54.

Thornberry, T. et al. (2003) *Gangs and Delinquency in Developmental Perspective*. Cambridge: Cambridge University Press.

Thrasher, F. (1927) *The Gang: A Study of 1,313 Gangs in Chicago*. Chicago, IL: University of Chicago Press.

Tyler, T. (2007) *Legitimacy and Criminal Justice: International Perspectives*. New York: Russell Sage Foundation.

UNICEF (1989) *United Nations Convention on the Rights of the Child 1989*. Geneva: United Nations.

Vygotsky, L. (1986) *Thought and Language*. Cambridge: MA, MIT Press.

West, D. (1969) *Present Conduct and Future Delinquency*. London: Heinemann.

West, D. (1982) *Delinquency: Its Roots, Careers and Prospects*. London: Heinemann.

West, D. and Farrington, D. (1973) *Who Becomes Delinquent?* London: Heinemann.

Wikstrom, P-O. and Loeber, R. (2000) 'Do Disadvantaged Neighborhoods Cause Well-Adjusted Children to Become Adolescent Delinquents? A Study of Male Juvenile Serious Offending, Individual Risk and Protective Factors and Neighborhood Context'. *Criminology* 38(4): 1109–42.

Wilkins, L. (1964) *Social Deviance*. London: Tavistock Publications.

Yates J. (2012) 'What Prospects Youth Justice? Children in Trouble in the Age of Austerity'. *Social Policy and Administration* 46: 432–47.

Young, T., Fitzgibbon, W., and Silverstone, D. (2013) *The Role of the Family in Facilitating Gang Membership, Criminality and Exit*. London: Catch22.

Youth Justice Board (2003) *Assessment, Planning Interventions and Supervision*. London: Youth Justice Board.

Youth Justice Board (2004) *National Standards for Youth Justice Services*. London: Youth Justice Board.

Youth Justice Board (2006) *YIP Management Guidance*. London: Youth Justice Board.

Youth Justice Board (2007) *ASSET Young Offender Assessment Profile*. London: Youth Justice Board.

Youth Justice Board (2013) *Assessment and Planning Interventions Framework—AssetPlus Model Document*. London: Youth Justice Board.

Youth Justice Board (2014) *AssetPlus Model Document*. London: Youth Justice Board.

Chapter 10

Agozino, B. (2004) 'Imperialism, crime and criminology: Towards the decolonisation of criminology'. *Crime, Law and Social Change* 41: 343–58.

Alexander, M. (2010) *The New Jim Crow: Mass Incarceration in an Age of Colorblindness*. New York: New Press.

Allen, R. (2011) *Last Resort? Exploring the reduction in child imprisonment 2008–11*. London: Prison Reform Trust.

Amnesty International (2018) 'Trapped in the Gangs Matrix'. Available at: www.amnesty.org.uk/files/reports/Trapped%20in%20the%20Matrix%20Amnesty%20report.pdf [Accessed 24 November 2020].

Athwal, H. and Bourne, J. (eds) (2015) *Dying for Justice*. London: Institute of Race Relations.

Barclay, G. and Mhlanga, B. (2000) 'Ethnic differences in decisions on young defendants dealt with by the Crown Prosecution Service'. Home Office, Section 95 Findings No. 1.

Bleich, E. (2003) *Race Politics in Britain and France: Ideas and Policymaking Since the 1960s*. Cambridge: Cambridge University Press.

Bowling, B. and Phillips, C. (2002) *Racism, Crime and Justice*. Harlow: Pearson Education.

Bridges, L. and Bunyan, T. (1983) 'Britain's New Urban Policing Strategy: The Police and Criminal Evidence Bill in Context'. *Journal of Law and Society* 10(1): 85–107.

Bridges, L. and Gilroy, P. (1982) 'Striking Back: The police use of race in crime statistics is a political act'. *Marxism Today* (June): 34–5.

Brown (2014) *Penal Power and Colonial Rule*. Abingdon: Routledge.

Burnett (2017) 'Racial violence and the Brexit state'. *Race & Class* 58(4): 85–97.

Cabinet Office (2020) 'People Living in Deprived Neighbourhoods', *Ethnicity Facts and Figures*. Available at www.ethnicity-facts-figures.service.gov.uk/uk-population-by-ethnicity/demographics/people-living-in-deprived-neighbourhoods/latest#title [Accessed 23 November 2020].

Capers, B. (2014) 'What is Critical Race Theory?' in M. Dubber and T. Hörnle (eds) *The Oxford Handbook of Criminal Law*. Oxford: Oxford University Press.

Children's Rights Alliance for England (2018) 'State of Children's Rights in England 2018: Policing and Criminal Justice'. Available at www.crae.org.uk/publications-resources/state-of-childrens-rights-2018/ [Accessed 20 June 2020].

Chowdhury, G and Beeman, M. (2007) 'Situating Colonialism, Race, and Punishment' in Bosworth and J. Flavin (eds) *Race, gender, and punishment: from colonialism to the war on terror*. New Brunswick, NJ: Rutgers University Press.

Cuneen, C. (2013) 'Colonial Processes, Indigenous Peoples, and Criminal Justice Systems' in S. M. Bucerius and M. Tonry (eds) *The Oxford Handbook of Ethnicity, Crime, and Immigration*. Oxford: Oxford University Press.

Davis, J. A. (1976) 'Blacks, Crime and American Culture'. *The Annals of the American Academy of Political and Social Science* 423: 89–98.

Delgado, R. and Stefanic, J. (2017) *Critical Race Theory: An Introduction*. New York: New York University Press.

Delsol, R. and Shiner, M. (eds) (2015) *Stop and Search: The Anatomy of a Police Power*. London: Palgrave Macmillan.

Department of Education (2020) 'Plan your relationships, sex and health curriculum'. Available at www.gov.uk/guidance/plan-your-relationships-sex-and-health-curriculum [Accessed 26 November 2020].

Du Bois, W. E. B. (1903) *The Souls of Black Folk*. Chicago, IL: A. C. McClurg & Co.

Du Bois, W. E. B. and Zuckerman, P. (2004) *The Social Theory of W.E.B. Du Bois*. Thousand Oaks, CA: Sage.

Eastwood, N., Shiner, M., and Bear, D. (2013) *The Numbers in Black and White*. London: Release Publications.

Edgar, K. and Martin, C. (2004) 'Perceptions of race and conflict: perspectives of minority ethnic prisoners and of prison officers'. Home Office Online Report 11/04.

Edgar, K. and Tsintsadze, K. (2017) *Tackling Discrimination in Prison: still not a fair response*. London: Prison Reform Trust.

Feilzer, M. and Hood, R. (2004) *Differences or Discrimination— Minority Ethnic Young People in the Youth Justice System*. London: Youth Justice Board.

Garner, S. (2015) 'Crimmigration: When Criminology (Nearly) Met the Sociology of Race and Ethnicity'. *Sociology of Race and Ethnicity* 1(1): 198–203.

Gilroy, P. (1987) *There Ain't No Black in the Union Jack*. London: Hutchinson.

Hall, S. (1999) 'From Scarman to Stephen Lawrence'. *History Workshop Journal* 48: 187–97.

Hall, S. et al. (1978) *Policing the Crisis: Mugging, the State and Law and Order*. London: Macmillan.

Hansard, Brixton Disorders: *The Scarman Report*. House of Lords, 4 February 1982, Vol. 426: 1396–474.

Hillyard, P. et al. (2004) *Beyond Criminology: Taking Harm Seriously*. London: Pluto Press.

Home Affairs Committee (2007) *Young Black People and the Criminal Justice System, Second Report of Session 2006–07*, Vols 1 and 2. London: The Stationery Office.

Home Office (2017) *Review of Deaths and Serious incidents in Police Custody*. London: Home Office.

Home Office (2020a) 'Hate Crime England and Wales, 2019/20', Statistical Bulletin. Available at: https://assets.publishing.service.gov.uk/government/uploads/system/uploads/attachment_data/file/925968/hate-crime-1920-hosb2920.pdf.

Home Office (2020b) 'Police powers and procedures', Statistical Bulletin, England and Wales, year ending 31 March 2020. Available at: https://assets.publishing.service.gov.uk/government/uploads/system/uploads/attachment_data/file/935355/police-powers-procedures-mar20-hosb3120.pdf.

Hood, R. (1992) *Race and Sentencing*. Oxford: Clarendon Press.

House of Commons (2020) 'UK Prison Population Statistics', Briefing Paper No. CBP-04334. Available at https://commonslibrary.parliament.uk/research-briefings/sn04334/ [Accessed 23 November 2020].

Hudson, B. (1993) *Penal Policy and Social Justice*. London: Macmillan

ICO (2018) 'Information Commissioner's investigation into the Metropolitan Police Service's Gangs Matrix concludes with enforcement action'. Available at: https://ico.org.uk/about-the-ico/news-and-events/news-and-blogs/2018/11/information-commissioner-s-investigation-into-the-metropolitan-police-service/ [Accessed 23 November 2020].

Independent Office for Police Conduct (2019) 'The Independent Office for Police Conduct: Public Perceptions Tracker, Summary of Research for the 2018/19 Financial Year'. Available at: www.policeconduct.gov.uk/research-and-learning/statistics/public-confidence-and-engagement [Accessed 23 November 2020].

Independent Office for Police Conduct (2020) 'Review identifies eleven opportunities for the Met to improve on stop and search'. Available at: https://policeconduct.gov.uk/news/review-identifies-eleven-opportunities-met-improve-stop-and-search [Accessed 23 November 2020].

INQUEST (2020) 'INQUEST casework and monitoring statistics'. Available at: www.inquest.org.uk/bame-deaths-in-police-custody [Accessed 23 November 2020].

John, G. (2003) *Race for Justice: A Review of Crown Prosecution Service Decision Making for Possible Racial Bias at each Stage of the Prosecution Process*. London: CPS/GJP.

Joliffe, D. and Haque, Z. (2017) *Have prisons become a dangerous place? Disproportionality, safety and mental health in British Prisons*. London: Runnymede Trust.

Joseph Rowntree Foundation (2010) *Poorer children's educational attainment: how important are attitudes and behaviour?* York: Joseph Rowntree Foundation.

Keith, The Hon. Mr Justice (2006) *The Zahid Mubarek Inquiry*. London: The Stationery Office.

King, S. (2017) 'Colonial criminology: A survey of what it means and why it is important'. *Sociology Compass* 11(3). Available at: https://doi.org/10.1111/soc4.12447.

Laming Review (2016) *In Care, Out of Trouble?* London: Prison Reform Trust.

Lammy, D. (2017) The Lammy Review: An independent review into the treatment of, and outcomes for Black, Asian and Minority Ethnic individuals in the criminal justice system. London: Ministry of Justice. Available at: www.gov.uk/government/publications/lammy-review-final-report [Accessed 23 November 2020].

Macpherson, W. (1999) The Stephen Lawrence Inquiry, Cm 4262-1. London: The Stationery Office.

Mayor's Office for Policing and Crime (2020) 'Quarterly Performance Update Report: Quarter 1 2020/21'. Available at: www.london.gov.uk/sites/default/files/q1_pack_performance_and_finance_18_aug_2020.pdf [Accessed 23 November 2020].

McGhee, D. (2005) *Intolerant Britain? Hate, Citizenship and Difference*. Buckingham: Open University Press.

Ministry of Justice (2019). *Race and the criminal justice system statistics 2018*. London: Ministry of Justice.

Moore, J. M. (2014) 'Is the Empire coming home? Liberalism, exclusion and the punitiveness of the British state'. Papers from the British Criminology Conference, 14, 31–48.

Nacro (2002) *Policing Local Communities: The Tottenham Experiment*. London: Nacro.

O'Connell, H. A. (2012) 'The Impact of Slavery on Racial Inequality in Poverty in the Contemporary U. S. South'. *Social Forces* 90(3): 713–34.

Ofsted (2020) 'Children's Social Care Data in England 2020'. Available at: www.gov.uk/government/statistics/childrens-social-care-data-in-england-2020 [Accessed 20 November 2020].

Omi, M. and Winant, H. (1994) *Racial Formation in The United States: From the 1960s to the 1990s*. New York: Routledge.

Patton, D. U. et al. (2017) 'Stop and Frisk Online: Theorizing Everyday Racism in Digital Policing in the Use of Social Media for Identification of Criminal Conduct and Associations'. *Social Media+ Society* (July–September): 1–10.

Pemberton, S. (2007) 'Social harm future(s): exploring the potential of the social harm approach'. *Crime, Law and Social Change* 48: 27–41.

Phillips, C. and Bowling, B. (2012) 'Ethnicities, Racism, Crime, and Criminal Justice' in M. Maguire, R. Morgan, and R. Reiner (eds) *The Oxford Handbook of Criminology* (5th edn). Oxford: Oxford University Press.

Phillips, C. et al. (2020) 'Dear British criminology: Where has all the race and racism gone?'. *Theoretical Criminology* 24(3): 427–46.

Platt, L. and Warwick, R. (2020) 'Are some ethnic groups more vulnerable to COVID-19 than others?' London: Institute of Fiscal Studies.

Public Health England (2020) *Beyond the data: Understanding the impact of COVID-19 on BAME groups*. London: PHE Publications.

Race Disparity Unit (2017) 'Race Disparity Audit Summary Findings from the Ethnicity Facts and Figures website'. London: Cabinet Office. Available at: https://assets.publishing.service.gov.uk/government/uploads/system/uploads/attachment_data/file/686071/Revised_RDA_report_March_2018.pdf [Accessed 20 November 2020].

Race Disparity Unit (2020) 'Tackling Racial Disparity in the Criminal Justice System: 2020 Update'. London: OGL.

Reece, R. L. (2019) 'Whitewashing Slavery: Legacy of Slavery and White Social Outcomes'. *Social Problems* 76(2): 304–23.

Rollock, N. and Gillborn, D. (2011) *Critical Race Theory (CRT)*. London: British Educational Research Association. Available at: www.bera.ac.uk/wp-content/uploads/2014/03/Critical-Race-Theory-CRT-.pdf [Accessed 2 December 2020].

Segal, R. (1995) *The Black Diaspora: Five Centuries of the Black Experience Outside Africa*. New York: Farrar, Straus and Giroux.

Sellin, J. (1976) *Slavery and the Penal System*. New York: Elsevier.

Shiner, M. et al. (2018) *The colour of injustice: 'race', drugs and law enforcement in England and Wales*. London: StopWatch.

StopWatch (2019) *Home Affairs Select Committee: The Macpherson Report: Twenty Years On inquiry—February 2019*. STOPWATCH response. Available at: www.stop-watch.org/uploads/documents/StopWatch_Response_to_Macpherson_20_years_on.pdf [Accessed 20 November 2020].

StopWatch (2020) 'Stop and searches increase 50%—racial disparity remains the same'. Available at: www.stop-watch.org/news-comment/story/stop-and-searches-increase-50-racial-disparity-remains-the-same [Accessed 20 November 2020].

Trilling, D. (2012) *Bloody Nasty People: The Rise of Britain's Far Right*. London: Verso.

Ugwudike, P. (2015) *An Introduction to Critical Criminology*. Bristol: Policy Press.

Williams, P. (2018) *Being Matrixed: The (Over)Policing of Gang Suspects in London*. London: StopWatch.

Williams, P. and Clarke, B. (2016) *Dangerous Associations: Joint Enterprise, Gangs and Racism*. London: Centre for Crime and Justice Studies.

Williams, P. and Kind, E. (2019) *Data-driven Policing: The hardwiring of discriminatory policing practices across Europe*. Brussels: European Network Against Racism (ENAR).

Young Review (2014) *Improving Outcomes for Young Black and/or Muslim Men in the Criminal Justice System*. London: BTEG, Clinks and Barrow Cadbury Trust.

Chapter 11

Acker, J. (1990) 'Hierarchies, Jobs, Bodies: A Theory of Gendered Organizations'. *Gender & Society* 4: 139–58.

Acker, J. (1992) 'Gendering Organizational Theory' in A. Mills and P. Tancred (eds) *Gendering Organizational Analysis*. Thousand Oaks, CA: Sage.

Adler, F. (1975) *Sisters in Crime: The Rise of the New Female Criminal*. New York: McGraw-Hill.

Adler, F. (1977) 'The Interaction Between Women's Emancipation and Female Criminality: A Cross-Cultural Perspective'. *International Journal of Criminologyand Penology* 5: 101–12.

Andersen, M. (2018) 'Getting to the Root of #metoo-Through the Fourth Wave of Feminism'. Master's thesis, University of Copenhagen.

Apolitical (2018) 'Has gender equality made women commit more crimes? In some countries, the gender crime gap is narrowing'. Available at: https://apolitical.co/solution_article/has-gender-equality-made-women-commit-more-crimes/ [Accessed August 2019].

Baca Zinn, M. and Thornton Dill, B. (1996) 'Theorizing Difference from Multiracial Feminism'. *Feminist Studies* 22: 321–31.

Balderston, S. (2013) 'Victimized Again? Intersectionality and Injustice in Disabled Women's Lives After Hate Crime and Rape'. *Advances in Gender Research* 18: 17–51.

Ball, M. (2016) *Criminology and Queer Theory: Dangerous Bedfellows?* Basingstoke: Palgrave Macmillan.

Batchelor, S. (2005) '"Prove Me the Bam!" Victimisation and Agency in the Lives of Young Women Who Commit Violent Offences'. *Probation Journal* 52(4): 358–75.

Belknap, J. (2001) *The Invisible Woman: Gender, Crime, and Justice*. Belmont, CA: Wadsworth.

Bromdal, A. et al. (2019) 'Experiences of transgender prisoners and their knowledge, attitudes, and practices regarding sexual behaviors and HIV/STIs: A systematic review'. *International Journal of Transgenderism* 20(1): 1–17.

Brownmiller, S. (1975) *Against Our Will: Men, Women and Rape*. New York: Simon and Schuster.

Burgess-Proctor, A. (2006) 'Intersection of Race, Class, Gender, and Crime: Future Directions for Feminist Criminology'. *Feminist Criminology* 1: 27–47.

Burman, M. and Batchelor, S. (2009) 'Between Two Stools? Responding to Young Women Who Offend'. *Youth Justice* 9(3): 270–85.

Butler, J. (1990) *Gender Trouble: Feminism and the Subversion of Identity*. New York: Routledge.

Cabinet Office Social Exclusion Unit and Ministry of Justice (2009) 'Short Study on Women Offenders, May 2009'. London: Cabinet Office and Ministry of Justice.

Cain, M. (1986) 'Realism, Feminism, Methodology, and Law'. *International Journal of the Sociology of Law* 14: 255–67.

Cain, M. (1990a) 'Towards Transgression: New Directions in Feminist Criminology'. *International Journal of the Sociology of Law* 18: 1–18.

Cain, M. (1990b) 'Realist Philosophy and Standpoint Epistemologies or Feminist Criminology as a Successor Science' in L. Gelsthorpe and A. Morris (eds) *Feminist Perspectives in Criminology*. Milton Keynes: Open University Press.

Carlen, P. (1983) *Women's Imprisonment*. London: Routledge & Kegan Paul.

Carlen, P. (1988) *Women, Crime and Poverty*. Milton Keynes: Open University Press.

Carrington, K. (2008) 'Critical Reflections in Feminist Criminologies' in T. Anthony and C. Cunneen (eds) *The Critical Criminology Companion*. Sydney: Hawkins Press.

Chesney-Lind, M. (1988) 'Girls in Jail'. *Crime and Delinquency* 34: 150–68.

Chesney-Lind, M. (1999) 'Media Misogyny: Demonizing "Violent" Girls and Women' in J. Ferrel and N. Websdale (eds) *Making Trouble: Cultural Representations of Crime, Deviance and Control*. Chicago, IL: Aldine Transaction.

Chesney-Lind, M. and Hadi S. T. (2017) 'Patriarchy, Abortion, and the Criminal System: Policing Female Bodies'. *Women & Criminal Justice* 27(1): 73–88.

Chesney-Lind, M. and Karlene F. (2001) 'What About Feminism? Engendering Theory-Making in Criminology' in R. Paternoster and R. Bachman (eds) *Explaining Criminals and Crime*. Los Angeles: Roxbury.

Chesney-Lind, M. and Morash, M. (2013) 'Transformative Feminist Criminology: A Critical Re-thinking of a Discipline'. *Critical Criminology* 21: 287–304.

Chesney-Lind, M. and Pasko, L. (2004) *Girls, Women, and Crime*. Thousand Oaks, CA: Sage.

Chesney-Lind, M. and Pasko, L. (2013) *The Female Offender: Girls, Women, and Crime*. Thousand Oaks, CA: Sage.

Chesney-Lind, M. and Shelden, R. G. (2004). *Girls, Delinquency, and Juvenile Justice*. Belmont, CA: West/Wadsworth.

Chigwada-Bailey, R. (1997) *Black Women's Experiences of Criminal Justice*. Winchester: Waterside Press.

Comack, E. (1999) 'Producing Feminist Knowledge: Lessons from Women in Trouble'. *Theoretical Criminology* 3: 287–306.

Connell, R. (1995) *Masculinities*. Cambridge: Polity.

Connell, R. (2000) *The Men and the Boys*. Cambridge: Polity.

Connell, R. and Messerschmidt, J. (2005) 'Hegemonic Masculinity: Rethinking the Concept'. *Gender and Society* 19(2): 829–59.

Corston Report (2007) *Review of Women with Particular Vulnerabilities in the Criminal Justice System*. London: Home Office.

Coyle, C. (2007) 'Feminism, Victimology and Domestic Violence' in S. Walklate (ed.) *Handbook on Victims and Victimology*. London: Sage.

Crenshaw, K. (1989) 'Demarginalizing the Intersection of Race and Sex: A Black Feminist Critique of Antidiscrimination Doctrine, Feminist Theory and Antiracist Politics'. *University of Chicago Legal Forum* 1(8): 139–67.

Crew, B. K. (1991) 'Sex Differences in Patriarchy: Chivalry or Patriarchy?'. *Justice Quarterly* 8: 59–83.

Curry, T., Lee, G., and Rodriguez, S. (2004) 'Does Victim Gender Increase Sentence Severity? Further Explorations of Gender Dynamics and Sentencing Outcomes'. *Crime & Delinquency* 50(3): 319–43.

Dalton, K. (1961) 'Menstruation and Crime'. *British Medical Journal* 2: 1743–52.

Daly, K. (1987) 'Discrimination in the Criminal Courts: Family, Gender, and the Problem of Equal Treatment'. *Social Forces* 66(1): 152–75.

Daly, K. (1992) 'Women's Pathways to Felony Court: Feminist Theories of Lawbreaking and Problems of Representation'. *Southern California Review of Law and Women's Studies*, 2: 11–52.

Daly, K. (2006) 'Feminist Thinking About Crime and Justice' in S. Henry and M. Lanier (eds) *The Essential Criminology Reader*. Boulder, CO: Westview Press.

Daly, K. (2010) 'Feminist Perspectives in Criminology: A Review with Gen Y in Mind' in E. McLaughlin and T. Newburn (eds) *The Sage Handbook of Criminological Theory*. London: Sage.

Daly, K. and Chesney-Lind, M. (1988) 'Feminism and Criminology'. *Justice Quarterly* 5: 497–538.

Davis, A. (1983) *Women, Race, and Class*. New York: Vintage.

Davis, K. (2008) 'Intersectionality as Buzzword: A Sociology of Science Perspective on What Makes a Feminist Theory Successful'. *Feminist Theory* 9: 67–85.

Derrida, J. (1976) *Of Grammatology*. Baltimore, MD: Johns Hopkins University Press.

Dobash, R. E. and Dobash, R. P. (1978) 'Wives: The "appropriate" victims of marital violence'. *Victimology*, 2: 426–42.

Dobash, R. E. and Dobash, R. P. (1979) *Violence Against Wives*. New York: Free Press.

Dobash, R. E. and Dobash, R. P. (1983) 'The Context Specific Approach' in D. Finkelhor et al. (eds) *The Dark Side of Families*. Beverly Hills, CA: Sage.

Dobash, R. E. and Dobash, R. P. (1992) *Women, Violence and Social Change*. London: Routledge.

Dobash, R. E. and Dobash, R. P. (1998) *Rethinking Violence against Women*. Thousand Oaks, CA: Sage.

Dobash, R. E. and Dobash, R. P. (2004) 'Women's violence to men in intimate relationships: Working on a puzzle'. *British Journal of Criminology*, 44(3): 324–49.

Eaton, M. (1986) *Justice for Women? Family, Court and Social Control*. Milton Keynes: Open University Press.

End Violence Against Women (August 2020) 'Access to Justice for Women & Girls during Covid-19 Pandemic'. Available at: www.endviolenceagainstwomen.org.uk/wp-content/uploads/Access-to-Justice-for-Women-Girls-during-Covid-19-Pandemic.pdf [Accessed 12 November 2020].

Estrada, F., Bäckman, O., and Nilsson, A. (2016) 'The Darker Side of Equality? The Declining Gender Gap in Crime: Historical Trends and an Enhanced Analysis of Staggered Birth Cohorts'. *British Journal of Criminology* 56(6): 1272–90.

Femicide Census (February 2020) 'Annual Report on UK Femicides 2018'. Available at: https://femicidescensus.org/reports/ [Accessed 12 November 2020].

Flavin, J. (2001) 'Feminism for the Mainstream Criminologist'. *Journal of Criminal Justice* 29(4): 271–85.

Flavin, J. and Artz, L. (2013) 'Understanding Women, Gender and Crime: Some Historical and International Developments' in C. Renzetti, S. Miller, and R. Gover (eds) *Routledge International Handbook of Crime and Gender Studies*. London: Routledge.

Freedman, E. (2002) *No Turning Back: The History of Feminism and the Future* (reprint edn). New York: Ballantine Books.

Frosh, S., Phoenix, A., and Pattman, R. (2002) *Young Masculinities: Understanding Boys in Contemporary Society*. New York: Springer.

Gadd, D. (2017) 'Domestic Violence' in A. Liebling, S. Maruna, and L. McAra (eds) *The Oxford Handbook of Criminology* (6th edn). Oxford: Oxford University Press.

Gelsthorpe, L. (2004) 'Female Offending: A Theoretical Overview' in G. McIvor (ed.) *Women Who Offend*. London: Jessica Kingsley.

Gelsthorpe, L. (2006) 'Women and Criminal Justice: Saying it Again, Again and Again'. *Howard Journal of Criminal Justice* 45(4): 421–4.

Gelsthorpe, L. (2019) 'What Works with Female Offenders? A UK Perspective' in P. Ugwudike et al. (eds) (2019) *The Routledge Companion to Rehabilitative Work in Criminal Justice*. Abingdon: Routledge.

Gelsthorpe, L. and Morris, A. (1988) 'Feminism and Criminology in Britain'. *British Journal of Criminology* 28(2): 93–110.

Gilbert, P. R. (2002) 'Discourses of Female Violence and Societal Gender Stereotypes'. *Violence Against Women* 8: 1271–300.

Gordon, D. and Pantazis, C. (2002) 'Television Licence Evasion and the Criminalisation of Female Poverty'. *Howard Journal of Crime and Justice* 36(2): 170–86.

Hanmer, J. (1978) 'Violence and the Social Control of Women' in G. Littlejohn et al. (eds) *Power and the State*. London: Croom Helm.

Harding, S. (1986) *The Science Question in Feminism*. Milton Keynes: Open University Press.

Harding, S. (1991) '"Strong Objectivity" and Socially Situated Knowledge' in S. Harding (ed.), *Whose Science? Whose Knowledge? Thinking from Women's Lives*. New York: Cornell University Press.

Hartmann, H. (1981) 'The Unhappy Marriage of Marxism and Feminism: Towards a More Progressive Union' in V. Lippit (ed.) *Radical Political Economy: Explorations in Alternative Economic Analysis*. New York: M. E. Sharpe.

Hartsock, N. (1987) 'The Feminist Standpoint: Developing the Ground for a Specifically Feminist Historical Materialism' in S. Harding (ed.) *Feminism and Methodology: Social Science Issues*. Bloomington, IN: Indiana University Press.

Heidensohn, F. (1968) 'The Deviance of Women: A Critique and an Enquiry'. *British Journal of Sociology* 19: 160–73.

Heidensohn, F. (1985) *Women and Crime*. London: Macmillan and New York University Press.

Heidensohn, F. (1996) *Women and Crime* (2nd edn). Basingstoke: Macmillan.

Heidensohn, F. (2012) 'The Future of Feminist Criminology'. *Crime, Media and Culture* 8: 123–34.

Heidensohn, F. and Silvestri, M. (2012) 'Gender and Crime' in M. Maguire, R. Morgan, and R. Reiner (eds) *The Oxford Handbook of Criminology* (5th edn). Oxford: Oxford University Press.

Her Majesty's Inspectorate of Constabulary (2014) 'Everyone's Business: Improving the Police Response to Domestic Abuse'. Available at: www.justiceinspectorates.gov.uk/hmic/wp-content/uploads/2014/04/improving-the-police-response-to-domestic-abuse.pdf [Accessed July 2014].

Her Majesty's Inspectorate of Constabulary (2017) 'Inspection programme and framework 2017/18'. Available at: www.justiceinspectorates.gov.uk/hmicfrs/wp-content/uploads/hmicfrs-inspection-programme-2017-18.pdf [Accessed 12 November 2020].

Hester, M. (2013) 'From Report to Court: Rape Cases and the Criminal Justice System in the North East'. Centre for Gender and

Violence Research, School for Policy Studies, University of Bristol and Northern Rock Foundation.

Hines, S. (2019) 'The feminist frontier: on trans and feminism'. *Journal of Gender Studies* 28(2): 145–57.

Home Office (2018) 'Domestic abuse: get help during the coronavirus (COVID-19) outbreak'. Available at: www.gov.uk/guidance/domestic-abuse-how-to-get-help [Accessed 12 November 2020].

Honkatukia, P. and Keskinen, S. (2018). 'The social control of young women's clothing and bodies: A perspective of differences on racialization and sexualization'. *Ethnicities* 18(1): 142–61.

hooks, b. (1981) *Ain't I a Woman: Black Women and Feminism*. Cambridge, MA: South End Press.

hooks, b. (1984) *Feminist theory: From margin to center*. Boston, MD: South End.

House of Commons Library (2020) 'The Gender Pay Gap'. Available at: https://commonslibrary.parliament.uk/research-briefings/sn07068/ [Accessed 12 November 2020].

Houston, C. (2014) 'How Feminist Theory became (Criminal Law): Tracing the Path to Mandatory Criminal Intervention in Domestic Violence Cases'. *Michigan Journal of Gender and Law* 21(2): 221–72.

Howe, A. (1994) *Punish and Critique: Towards a Feminist Analysis of Penality*. London: Taylor &Francis.

Hull, G. T., Scott, P. B., and Smith, B. (eds) (1982) *All the Women Are White, All the Blacks Are Men, But Some of Us Are Brave: Black Women's Studies*. Old Westbury: Feminist Press.

Jauk, D. (2013) 'Gender Violence Revisited: Lessons from Violent Victimization of Transgender Identified Individual'. *Sexualities* 16(7): 807–25.

Jeffreys, S. (2014) *Gender Hurts: A Feminist Analysis of the Politics of Transgenderism*. London: Routledge.

Klein, D. and Kress, J. (1976) 'Any Woman's Blues: A Critical Overview of Women, Crime and the Criminal Justice System'. *Crime and Social Justice* 5: 34.

Knight, C. and Wilson, K. (2016) *Lesbian, Gay, Bisexual and Trans People (LGBT) and the Criminal Justice System*. Basingstoke: Palgrave Macmillan.

Koyama, E. (2003) 'The Transfeminist Manifesto' in R. Dicker and A. Piepmeier (eds) *Catching a Wave: Reclaiming Feminism for a 21st Century*. Boston, MA: Northwestern University Press.

Lightowlers, C. (2019) 'Drunk and Doubly Deviant? the Role of Gender and Intoxication in Sentencing Assault Offences'. *The British Journal of Criminology* 59(3): 693–717.

Lombroso, C. and Ferrero, W. (1895) *The Female Offender*. London: T. Fisher Unwin.

MacKinnon, C. (1989) *Toward a Feminist Theory of the State*. Cambridge, MA: Harvard University Press.

Mahase, E. (2020) 'Covid-19: EU states report 60% rise in emergency calls about domestic violence'. *British Medical Journal Online*, available at: www.bmj.com/content/369/bmj.m1712.

Maidment, M. (2006) 'Feminist Perspectives in Criminology' in W. DeKeseredey and B. Perry (eds) *Advancing Critical Criminology: Theory and Application*. Lanham, MD: Lexington Books.

Martin, J., Kautt, P., and Gelsthorpe, L. (2009) 'What Works for Women? A Comparison of Community-Based General Offending Programme Completion'. *British Journal of Criminology* 49: 879–99.

Mawby, R. and Walklate, S. (1994) *Critical Victimology*. London: Sage.

McIntosh, P. (2003) 'White privilege: Unpacking the invisible knapsack' in S. Plous (ed.) *Understanding prejudice and discrimination*. New York: McGraw-Hill.

Mellor, D. and Deering, R. (2010) 'Professional Response and Attitudes Toward Female-Perpetrated Child Sexual Abuse: A Study of Psychologists, Psychiatrists, Probationary Psychologists and Child Protection Workers'. *Psychology, Crime and Law* 16(5): 415–38.

Messerschmidt, J. (1986) *Capitalism, Patriarchy, and Crime*. Totowa, NJ: Rowman & Littlefield.

Messerschmidt, J. (1993) *Masculinities and Crime*. Lanham, MD: Rowman & Littlefield.

Messerschmidt, J. and Tomsen, S. (2012) 'Masculinities' in W. DeKeseredy and M. Dragiewicz (eds) *Handbook of Critical Criminology*. Abingdon: Routledge.

Messerschmidt, J. and Tomsen, S. (2017) 'Masculinities, crime, and criminal justice' in M. Tonry (ed.) *Oxford Handbooks Online* (pp. 1–23), available at: https://doi.org/10.1093/oxfordhb/9780199935383.013.129 [Accessed October 2018].

Ministry of Justice (2018) 'Female Offender Strategy'. Available at: https://assets.publishing.service.gov.uk/government/uploads/system/uploads/attachment_data/file/719819/female-offender-strategy.pdf [Accessed 10 November 2019].

Ministry of Justice (2018) 'Statistics on Women and the Criminal Justice System 2017: A Ministry of Justice publication under Section 95 of the Criminal Justice Act 1991'. Available at: https://assets.publishing.service.gov.uk/government/uploads/system/uploads/attachment_data/file/759770/women-criminal-justice-system-2017..pdf [Accessed 10 November 2019].

Moore, L. and Scraton, P. (2014) *The Incarceration of Women: Punishing Bodies and Breaking Sprits*. Basingstoke: Palgrave Macmillan.

Myhill, A. and Allen, J. (2002) 'Rape and Sexual Assault of Women: Findings from the British Crime Survey', Home Office Research Study, Findings No. 159.

Naffine, N. (1997) *Feminism and Criminology*. Cambridge: Polity Press.

Nelson, E. (2014) 'If You Want to Convict a Domestic Violence Batterer, List Multiple Charges in the Police Report', Sage Open. Available at: http://sgo.sagepub.com/content/spsgo/4/1/2158244013517246.full.pdf.

Oakley, A. (1972) *Sex, Gender and Society*. London: Maurice Temple Smith.

Office for National Statistics (2019) 'Domestic abuse in England and Wales overview: November 2019'. Available at: www.ons.gov.uk/peoplepopulationandcommunity/crimeandjustice/bulletins/domesticabuseinenglandandwalesoverview/november2019 [Accessed 10 November 2020].

Office for National Statistics (2019) 'Domestic abuse victim characteristics, England and Wales: year ending March 2019'. Available at: www.ons.gov.uk/peoplepopulationandcommunity/crimeandjustice/articles/domesticabusevictimcharacteristicsenglandandwales/yearendingmarch2019 [Accessed 10 November 2020].

Pantazis, C. and Gordon, D. (2002) 'Television Licence Evasion and the Criminalisation of Female Poverty'. *Howard Journal of Criminal Justice* 36(2): 170–86.

Pollak, O. (1950) *The Criminality of Women*. Philadelphia, PA: University of Pennsylvania Press.

Potter, H. (2006) 'An Argument for Black Feminist Criminology: Understanding African American Women's Experiences with Intimate Partner Abuse Using an Integrated Approach'. *Feminist Criminology* 1: 106–24.

Prison Reform Trust (2015) 'Why focus on reducing women's imprisonment? A Prison Reform Trust briefing'. Available at: www.prisonreformtrust.org.uk/Portals/0/Documents/why%20focus%20on%20reducing%20women%27s%20imprisonment%20BL.pdf [Accessed December 2019].

Prison Reform Trust. (2017) *'There's a reason we're in trouble': Domestic abuse as a driver to women's offending*. London: PRT.

Radford, J. and Russell, D. (1992) *Femicide: The Politics of Woman Killing*. New York: Twayne.

Rafter, N. (1990) *Partial Justice: Women, Prisons, and Social Control*. New Brunswick, NJ: Transaction.

Renzetti, C. (2012) 'Feminist Perspectives in Criminology' in W. DeKeseredy and M. Dragiewicz (eds) *The Routledge Handbook of Critical Criminology*. New York: Routledge.

Rodriguez, S., Curry, T., and Lee, G. (2006) 'Gender Differences in Criminal Sentencing: Do Effects Vary Across Violent, Property, and Drug Offenses?'. *Social Science Quarterly* 87(2): 318–39.

Romain, D. and Freiburger, T. (2016) 'Chivalry Revisited: Gender, Race/Ethnicity, and Offense Type on Domestic Violence Charge Reduction'. *Feminist Criminology* 11(2): 191–222.

Russell, D. (1975) *The Politics of Rape*. New York: Stein & Day.

Schwendinger, J. and Schwendinger, H. (1983) *Rape and Inequality*. Newbury Park, CA: Sage.

Seitz, T. (2005) 'The Wounds of Savagery: Negro Primitivism, Gender Parity, and the Execution of Rosanna Lightner Phillips'. *Women and Criminal Justice* 16: 29–64.

Serano, J. (2007). *Whipping girl: A transsexual woman on sexism and the scapegoating of femininity*. Boston, MA: De Cappo Press.

Serona, J. (2013) *Excluded: Making feminist and queer movements more inclusive*. New York: Avalon.

Sharpe, G. (2019) 'More sinned against than sinning: women's pathways into crime and criminalization' in P. Ugwudike et al. (eds) (2019) *The Routledge Companion to Rehabilitative Work in Criminal Justice*. Abingdon: Routledge.

Silvestri, M. and Crowther-Dowey, C. (2008) *Gender and Crime*. London: Sage.

Simon, R. (1975) *Women and Crime, and Criminology?* Lexington, KT: Lexington Books.

Smart, C. (1976) *Women, Crime and Criminology*. Abingdon: Routledge.

Smart, C. (1990a) 'Law's Power, the Sexed Body and Feminist Discourse'. *Journal of Law and Society* 17: 194–210.

Smart, C. (1990b) 'Feminist Approaches to Criminology, or Postmodern Woman Meets Atavistic Man' in L Gelsthorpe and A. Morris (eds) *Feminist Perspectives in Criminology*. Philadelphia, PA: Open University Press.

Smart, C. (1995) *Law, Crime and Sexuality*. London: Sage.

Smart, C. (1977) 'Criminological Theory: Its Ideology and Implications Concerning Women'. *British Journal of Sociology* 28(1): 89–100.

Smart, C. (1997) *Women, Crime and Criminology: A Feminist Critique*. London: Routledge.

Smith, O. and Skinner, T. (2012) 'Observing Court Responses to Victims of Rape and Sexual Assault'. *Feminist Criminology* 7(4): 298–326.

Stanko, E. (1990) *Everyday Violence*. London: Pandora.

Steffensmeier, D. (1980) 'Trends in Female Delinquency'. *Criminology* 18: 62–85.

Sudbury, J. (2005) 'Feminist Critiques, Transnational Landscapes, Abolitionist Visions' in J. Sudbury (ed.) *Global Lockdown: Race, Gender, and the Prison-Industrial Complex*. New York: Routledge.

Truth, S. (1851) 'Ain't I A Woman?', Women's Rights Convention, Old Stone Church. Available at: www.nps.gov/articles/sojourner-truth.htm [Accessed 12 November 2020].

Walklate, S. (1991) 'Victims, Crime Prevention and Social Control' in R. Reiner and M. Cross (eds) *Beyond Law and Order: Criminal Justice Policy and Politics into the 1990s*. Basingstoke: Macmillan.

Williams, C. (2014). 'TERF hate and Sandy Stone. The Trans Advocate'. Available at: www.transadvocate.com/terf-violence-and-sandy-stone_n_14360.htm [Accessed October 2019].

Wolff, K. and Cokely, C. (2007) '"To Protect and to Serve?": An Exploration of Police Conduct in Relation to the Gay, Lesbian, Bisexual, and Transgender Community'. *Sexuality and Culture* 11(2): 1–23.

Women's Aid (2020) 'A Perfect Storm: The Impact of the Covid-19 Pandemic on Domestic Abuse Survivors and the Services Supporting Them'. Available at: www.womensaid.org.uk/wp-content/uploads/2020/08/A-Perfect-Storm-August-2020-1.pdf [Accessed 12 November 2020].

Worrall, A. (1981) 'Out of Place: Female Offenders in Court'. *Probation Journal* 28: 90–3.

Young, A. (1996) *Imagining Crime*. London: Sage.

Chapter 12

Benedict, S. (2010) *Regulation by Markets and the Bradley Review of Australian Higher Education*. Melbourne: RMIT University.

Bullard, R. D. (1993a) 'Race and Environmental Justice in the United States'. *Yale Journal of International Law* 18: 319–35.

Bullard, R. D. (1993b) 'The Threat of Environmental Racism'. *Natural Resources & Environment* 7(3): 23–6, 55–6.

Chavis, B. (1991) 'The historical significance and challenges of the first national people of colour environmental leadership summit' in *Proceedings of the First National People of Colour Environmental Leadership Summit*. Washington, DC: United Church of Christ Commission for Racial Justice.

Danley, V. (2015) 'Biopiracy in the Brazilian Amazon: Learning from International and Comparative Law Successes and Shortcomings to Help Promote Biodiversity Conservation in Brazil'. *Florida A&M University Law Review* 7(2): 291–327.

Goldstein, B., Osofsky, H., and Litchveld, M. (2011) 'The Gulf Oil Spill'. *New England Journal of Medicine* 364: 1334–48.

Gore, M. (ed.) (2017) *Conservation Criminology*. Chichester: Wiley-Blackwell.

Hall, M. (2015) *Exploring Green Crime*. Basingstoke: Palgrave.

Hampton, P. (2005) *Reducing Administrative Burdens: Effective Inspection and Enforcement*. London: HM Treasury.

Heydon, J. (2018) 'Sensitising Green Criminology to Procedural Environmental Justice: A Case Study of First Nation Consultation in the Canadian Oil Sands'. *International Journal for Crime Justice and Social Democracy* 7(4): 67–82.

Kalejaye, K. (2015) 'Nigeria records 9,343 oil spill incidents in 10 years'. Lagos: Sweetcrude. Available at: https://sweetcrudereports.com/nigeria-records-9343-oil-spill-incidents-in-10-years/.

Leybourn-Langton, L., Quilter-Pinner, H., and Ho, H. (2018) *Lethal and Illegal: Solving London's Air Pollution Crisis*. London: Institute for Public Policy Research. Available at: www.ippr.org/files/publications/pdf/lethal-and-illegal-solving-londons-air-pollution-crisis_summary_Nov2016.pdf [Accessed 25 May 2020].

Liu, J. (2009) 'Asian Criminology—Challenges, Opportunities, and Directions'. *Asian Journal of Criminology* 4: 1–9.

Lynch, M. (1990) 'The greening of criminology: a perspective on the 1990s'. *The Critical Criminologist* 2(3): 1–4 and 11–12.

Lynch, M. and Stretesky, P. (2014) *Exploring Green Criminology: Toward a Green Criminological Revolution*. Farnham: Ashgate.

Lynch, M., Long, M., and Stretesky, P. (2019) *Green Criminology and Green Theories of Justice*. Basingstoke: Palgrave Macmillan.

Natali, Lorenzo (2015) 'A Critical Gaze on Environmental Victimization' in R. Sollund (ed.) *Green Harms and Crimes: Critical Criminology in a Changing World*. Basingstoke: Palgrave Macmillan.

Nurse, A. (2016) *An Introduction to Green Criminology and Environmental Justice*. London: Sage.

Nurse, A. and Wyatt, T. (2020) *Wildlife Criminology*. Bristol: Bristol University Press.

Office of the Prosecutor (2016) 'Policy paper on case selection and prioritisation'. The Hague: International Criminal Court.

Olmo, R. del (1999) 'The Development of Criminology in Latin America'. *Social Justice* 26(2): 19–45.

Pečar, J. (1981) 'Ekološka kriminaliteta in kriminologija'. *Revija za kriminalistiko in kriminologijo* 34: 33–45.
Riera, A. (1979) 'Latin American Radical Criminology'. *Crime and Social Justice* 11: 71–6.
Rogers, N. and Maloney, M. (eds) (2017) *Law as if Earth Really Mattered*. Abingdon: Routledge.
Schlosberg, D. (2007) *Defining Environmental Justice: Theories, Movements and Nature*. Oxford: Oxford University Press.
Shiva, V. (2007) 'Bioprospecting as Sophisticated Biopiracy'. *Signs: Journal of Women in Culture and Society* 32(2): 307–13.
Situ, Y., and Emmons, D. (2000) *Environmental Crime*. Thousand Oaks, CA: Sage.
South, N. and Beirne, P. (1998) 'Editors Introduction'. *Theoretical Criminology* 2(2): 147–8.
Steiner, R. (2010) *Double standard: Shell Practices in Nigeria Compared with International Standards to Prevent and Control Pipeline Oil Spills and the Deepwater Horizon Oil Spill*. Amsterdam: Milieudefensie. Available at: www.foei.org/wp-content/uploads/2014/01/20101109-rapport-Double-Standard.pdf [Accessed 1 August 2020].
United Nations (1999) '55th Session of the Commission on Human Rights', 22 March–30 April 1999, Documentation. Available at: www.ohchr.org/EN/HRBodies/CHR/55/Pages/Documentation.aspx [Accessed 29 May 2020].
White, R. (2007) 'Green Criminology and the pursuit of social and ecological justice' in P. Beirne and N. South (eds) *Issues in Green Criminology: Confronting harms against environments, humanity and other animals*. Cullompton: Willan.
White, R. (2008) *Crimes Against Nature: Environmental criminology and ecological justice*. Cullompton: Willan.
White, R. (2018) *Climate Change Criminology*. Bristol: Bristol University Press.
Woolf, H. (1992) 'Are the judiciary environmentally myopic?'. *Journal of Environmental Law* 4(1): 1–14.

Chapter 13

Aas, K. (2020) *Globalization and Crime*. London: Sage.
Aas, K. F. (2012) 'The earth is one but the world is not: Criminological theory and its geopolitical divisions'. *Theoretical Criminology* 16(1): 5–20.
Agozino, B. (2004) 'Imperialism, crime and criminology: Towards a decolonisation of criminology'. *Crime, Law & Social Change* 41: 343–58.
Aguirre, C. and Salvatore, R. D. (2001) 'Writing the history of law, crime, and punishment in Latin America' in R. D. Salvatore et al. (eds) *Crime and punishment in Latin America*. Durham, NC: Duke University.
Akoensi, T. D. (2014) 'Governance through power sharing in Ghanaian prisons: A symbiotic relationship between officers and inmates'. *Prison Service Journal* 212: 33–8.
Albanese, J. and Reichel, P. (eds) (2013) *Transnational Organized Crime: An Overview from Six Continents*. London: Sage.
Allam, F. and Gilmour, S. (2011) (eds) *The Routledge Handbook of Transnational Organised Crime*. London: Routledge.
Alves, J. A. (2018) *The Anti-Black City: Police Terror and Black Urban Life in Brazil*. Minneapolis, MN: University of Minnesota.
Arias, E. D. (2017) *Criminal Enterprises and Governance in Latin America and the Caribbean*. New York: Cambridge University.
Bandyopadhyay, M. (2007) 'Reform and everyday practice: Some issues of prison governance'. *Contributions to Indian Sociology* 41(3): 387–416.
Bandyopadhyay, M. (2014) 'Asian prisons: Colonial pasts, neo-liberal futures and subversive sites' in Y. Jewkes et al. (eds) *Handbook on Prisons*. Abingdon: Routledge.

Barak, G. (ed.) (2000) *Crime and Crime Control: A Global View*. Oxford: Greenwood.
Batista, V. M. (2003). *O medo na cidade do Rio de Janeiro*. Rio de Janeiro: Revan.
Batista, V. M. (2016). *A questão criminal no brasil contemporâneo*. São Paulo: Fundação Bienal de São Paulo.
Biondi, K. (2016). *Sharing this walk: An ethnography of prison life and the PCC in Brazil*. Translated by J. F. Collins. Chapel Hill, NC: University of North Carolina.
Birkbeck, C. (2011) 'Imprisonment and internment: Comparing penal institutions North and South'. *Punishment and Society* 13(3): 307–32.
Blagg, H. and Anthony, T. (2019). *Decolonising criminology: Imagining justice in a postcolonial world*. London: Palgrave Macmillan.
Boone, M. and Swaaningen. R. (2013) 'Punishment in the Netherlands' in V. Ruggiero and M. Ryan (eds) *Punishment in Europe: A Critical Anatomy of Penal Systems*. Basingstoke: Palgrave Macmillan.
Bortoluci, J. H. and Jansen, R. S. (2013) 'Toward a postcolonial sociology: The view from Latin America'. *Postcolonial Sociology, Political Power and Social Theory* 24: 199–229.
Bowling, B. (2011) 'Transnational criminology and the globalization of harm production' in M. Bosworth and C. Hoyle (eds) *What is Criminology?* Oxford: Oxford University Press.
Bretas, M. L. (1996) 'What the eyes can't see: Stories from Rio de Janeiro's prisons' in R. D. Salvatore and C. Aguirre, C. (eds) *The birth of the penitentiary in Latin America*. Austin, TX: University of Texas.
Burdett, R. and Sudjik, D. (eds) (2011) *Living in the Endless City*. New York: Phaidon.
Cain, M. (2000) 'Orientalism, occidentalism and the sociology of crime'. *British Journal of Criminology* 40: 239–60.
Caldeira, T. (2000) *City of Walls: Crime, Segregation and Citizenship in São Paulo*. Berkeley, CA: University of California Press.
Carrington, K. et al. (2016) 'Southern criminology'. *British Journal of Criminology* 56(1): 1–20.
Carrington, K. et al. (eds) (2018) *The Palgrave Handbook of Criminology and the Global South*. London: Palgrave Macmillan.
Carrington, K. et al. (2019) *Southern Criminology*. London: Routledge.
Cavadino, M. and Dignan, J. (2006) *Penal Systems*. London: Sage.
Cavadino, M., Dignan, J., and Mair, G. (2013) *The Penal System*. London: Sage.
Cavalcanti, R. P. (2016) 'Armed violence and the politics of gun control in Brazil: An analysis of the 2005 referendum'. *Bulletin of Latin American Research* 36(1): 31–51.
Cerqueira, D. and Bueno, S. (eds) (2020) *Atlas da Violência*. Brasilia: Instituto de Pesquisa Econômica Aplicada.
Christie, N. (1977) 'Conflicts as Property'. *British Journal of Criminology* 17(1): 1–14.
Cohen, S. (1985) *Visions of Social Control*. Cambridge: Polity Press.
Cohen, S. (1988) *Against Criminology*. New Brunswick: Transaction.
Connell, R. (2006) 'Northern theory: The political geography of general social theory'. *Theory and Society* 35(2): 237–64.
Connell, R. (2007) *Southern theory: The global dynamics of knowledge in social sciences*. Cambridge: Polity.
Connell, R. (2014) 'Using southern theory: Decolonizing social thought in theory, practice and application'. *Planning Theory* 13(2): 2010–233.
Costa, A. E. (2014) *Reimagining Black Difference and Politics in Brazil: From Racial Democracy to Multiculturalism*. New York: Palgrave Macmillan.
Coyle, A. et al. (2016) *Imprisonment Worldwide: The Current Situation and an Alternative Future*. Bristol: Policy Press.
Crawford, A. (ed.) (2011) *International and Comparative Criminal Justice and Urban Governance: Convergence and Divergence in*

Global, National and Local Settings. Cambridge: Cambridge University.

D'Monte, D. (2011) 'A matter of people' in R. Burdett and D. Sudjic (eds) (2011) *Living in the Endless City.* London: Phaidon.

Darke, S. (2018) *Conviviality and Survival: Co-Producing Brazilian Prison Order.* London: Palgrave Macmillan.

Darke, S. and Garces, C. (2017) 'Surviving in the new mass carceral zone'. *Prison Service Journal* 229: 2–9.

Darke, S. and Karam, M. L. (2016) 'Latin American prisons' in Y. Jewkes (eds) *Handbook on Prisons.* Abingdon: Routledge.

Darke, S. et al. (eds) (2021) *Carceral Communities in Latin America: Troubling Prison Worlds in the 21st Century.* London: Palgrave Macmillan.

Davies, M. (2015) *Davies, Croall & Tyrer's Criminal Justice.* Harlow: Pearson Education.

Davis, M. (2006) *Planet of Slums.* London: Verso.

Dikötter, F. (2007) 'The prison in the world' in F. Dikötter and I. Brown (eds) *Cultures of confinement: A history of the prison in Africa, Asia, and Latin America.* Ithaca, NY: Cornell University.

Downes, D. (1988) *Contrasts in Tolerance.* Oxford: Oxford University Press.

Downes, D. and Hansen, K. (2006) *Welfare and Punishment: The Relationship between Welfare Spending and Imprisonment.* London: Crime and Society Foundation.

Edwards, A. and Gill, P. (eds) (2003) *Transnational Organised Crime: Perspectives on Global Security.* London: Routledge.

Feeley, M. and Simon, J. (1992) 'The new penology: Notes on the emerging strategy of corrections and its implications'. *Criminology* 30: 449–74.

Fórum Brasileiro de Segurança Pública (2016) *Anuário brasileiro de segurança pública.* São Paulo: Fórum Brasileiro de Segurança Pública.

Fórum Brasileiro de Segurança Pública (2019) *Anuário brasileiro de segurança pública.* São Paulo: Fórum Brasileiro de Segurança Pública.

Garces, C. (2010) 'The cross politics of Ecuador's penal state'. *Cultural Anthropology* 25(3): 459–96.

Garland, D. (1990). *Punishment and modern society: A study in social theory.* Oxford: Clarendon Press.

Garland, D. (1996) 'The Limits of the Sovereign State: Strategies of Crime Control in Contemporary Society'. *British Journal of Criminology* 36(4): 445–71.

Garland, D. (2001). *The culture of control: Crime and social order in contemporary society.* Oxford: Oxford University Press.

Gonnella, P. (2013) 'Between amnesties and emergencies' in V. Ruggiero and M. Ryan (eds) *Punishment in Europe: A Critical Anatomy of Penal Systems.* Basingstoke: Palgrave Macmillan.

Hardie-Bick, J., Sheptycki, J., and Wardak, A. (2005) 'Transnational and comparative criminology in global perspective' in J. Sheptycki and A. Wardak (eds) *Transnational and Comparative Criminology.* London: Glasshouse.

Hinton, M. (2006) *The State on the Streets: Police and Politics in Argentina and Brazil.* London: Lynne Reinner.

Hinton, M. and Newburn, T. (eds) (2008) *Policing Developing Democracies.* London: Routledge.

Hofer, H. and Tham. H. (2013) 'Punishment in Sweden: A changing penal landscape' in V. Ruggiero and M. Ryan (eds) *Punishment in Europe: A Critical Anatomy of Penal Systems.* Basingstoke: Palgrave Macmillan.

Huggins, M. and Mesquita, M. (1995) 'Scapegoating outsiders: The murders of street youth in modern Brazil'. *Policing and Society* 5: 265–80.

Human Rights Watch (1998) *Behind bars in Brazil.* New York: Human Rights Watch.

Human Rights Watch (2016) *Good Cops are Afraid: The Toll of Unchecked Police Violence in Rio de Janeiro.* New York: Human Rights Watch.

Instituto Brasileiro de Geografia e Estatística (2019) *Desigualdades Sociais por Cor ou Raça no Brasil.* Rio de Janeiro: IBGE.

Jacobson, J. et al. (2017) *Prison: Evidence of its Use and Overuse from around the World.* London: Birkbeck.

Jefferson, A. M. (2007) 'The political economy of rights: Exporting penal norms to Africa'. *Criminal Justice Matters* 70(1): 33–4.

Jefferson, A. M. and Jensen, S. (eds) (2009) *State Violence and Human Rights: State Officials in the South.* Abingdon: Routledge-Cavendish.

Jefferson, A. M., and Martin, T. M. (2014) 'Everyday prison governance in Africa'. *Prison Service Journal* 202.

Jefferson, A. M. and Martin, T. M. (2014) 'Prisons in Africa' in Y. Jewkes et al. (eds) *Handbook on Prisons.* Abingdon: Routledge.

Karam, M. L. (2009) 'Estado penal, novo inimigo interno e totalitarismo' in R. T. Oliveira and V. Mattos (eds) *Estudos de execução criminal: Direito e psicologia.* Belo Horizonte: Tribunal de Justiça de Minas Gerais.

Koonings, K. and Kruijt, D. (eds) (2007) *Fractured Cities: Social Exclusion, Urban Violence and Contested Spaces in Latin America.* London: Zed Books.

Koonings, K. and Kruijt, D. (eds) (2009) *MegaCities: The Politics of Urban Exclusion and Violence in the Global South.* London: Zed Books.

Koonings, K. and Kruijt, D. (eds) (2015) *Violence and Resilience in Latin American Cities.* London: Zed Books.

Lacey, N. (2008) *The Prisoners' Dilemma: Political Economy and Punishment in Contemporary Democracies.* Cambridge: Cambridge University Press.

Lessing, B. (2018) *Making Peace in Drug Wars: Crackdowns and Cartels in Latin America.* New York: Cambridge University Press.

Lindegaard, M. R. and Greer, S. (2014) 'Surviving South African prisons'. *Focaal* 68: 35–54.

Manso, B. P. (2020) *A República das Milícias: Dos esquadrões da morte à era Bolsonaro.* São Paulo: Todavia.

Mascareño, A. and Chernilo, D. (2009) 'Obstacles and perspectives of Latin American sociology: Normative universalism and functional differentiation'. *Soziale Systeme* 15(1): 72–96.

Mathiesen, T. (1990) *Prison On Trial: A Critical Assessment.* Winchester: Waterside Press.

Mathiesen, T. (2012) 'Scandinavian exceptionalism in penal matters: Reality or wishful thinking?' in T. Ugelvik and J. Dullum (eds) *Penal Exceptionalism? Nordic Prison Policy and Practice.* London: Routledge.

Mathiesen, T. (2015) *The Politics of Abolition Revisited.* Abingdon: Routledge.

Menegat, M. (2012) *Estudos sobre ruínas.* Rio de Janeiro: Instituto Carioca de Criminologia.

Ministry of Justice (2019) 'Criminal Justice Statistics Quarterly: December 2018'.

Narag, R. E. and Jones, C. R. (2016) 'Understanding prison management in the Philippines: A case for shared governance'. *Prison Journal* 97(1): 3–26.

Nelken, D. (2007) 'Comparing criminal justice' in M. Maguire et al. (eds) *The Oxford Handbook of Criminology* (4th edn). Oxford: Oxford University Press.

Nelken, D. (2010) *Comparative Criminal Justice: Making Sense of Difference.* London: Sage.

Newburn, T. and Sparks, R. (eds) (2014) *Criminal Justice and Political Cultures: National and International Dimensions of Crime Control.* Cullompton: Willan.

O'Donnell, G. (1998) 'Polyarchies and the (un)rule of law in Latin America'. Kellogg Institute. Available at: http://kellogg.nd.edu/publications/workingpapers/WPS/254.pdf [Accessed 28 October 2020].

Olmo, R. (1999) 'The development of criminology in Latin America'. *Social Justice* 26(2): 19–45.

Pakes, F. (2010) 'The comparative method in globalised criminology'. *Australian and New Zealand Journal of Criminology* 43(1): 17–30.

Pakes, F. (2019) *Comparative Criminal Justice*. London: Routledge.

Pakes, F. (2020) 'Old fashioned Nordic penal exceptionalism: The case of Iceland's prisons'. *Nordic Journal of Criminology*. DOI: 10.1080/2578983X.2020.1809199.

Pakes, F. and Gunnlaugsson, H. (2018) 'A more Nordic Norway? Examining prisons in 21st Century Iceland'. *Howard Journal of Crime and Justice* 57(2): 137–51.

Parusuraman, S. (2007) 'Uncovering the myth of urban development in Mumbai' in LSE and Alfred Herrhausen Society (eds) *Urban India: Understanding the Maximum City*, Urban Age Project. Available at: https://urbanage.lsecities.net/newspapers/urban-india-understanding-the-maximum-city-1.

Peirce, J. and Fondevila, G. (2020) 'Concentrated violence: The influence of criminal activity and governance on prison violence in Latin America'. *International Criminal Justice Review* 30(1): 99–130.

Pereira, A. W. (2020) *Modern Brazil*. Oxford: Oxford University Press.

Piacentini, L. (2013) 'The Russian prison system' in V. Ruggiero and M. Ryan (eds) *Punishment in Europe: A Critical Anatomy of Penal Systems*. Basingstoke: Palgrave Macmillan.

Platek, M. (2013) 'Poland: The political legacy and penal practice' in V. Ruggiero and M. Ryan (eds) *Punishment in Europe: A Critical Anatomy of Penal Systems*. Basingstoke: Palgrave Macmillan.

Pratt, J. (2008a) 'Scandinavian exceptionalism in an era of penal excess: Part I—The nature and roots of Scandinavian exceptionalism'. *British Journal of Criminology* 48(2): 119–37.

Pratt, J. (2008b) 'Scandinavian exceptionalism in an era of penal excess: Part II—Does Scandinavian exceptionalism have a future?'. *British Journal of Criminology*. 48(3): 275–92.

Pratt, J. and Eriksson, A. (2012) 'In defence of Scandinavian exceptionalism' in T. Ugelvik and J. Dullum (eds) *Penal Exceptionalism? Nordic Prison Policy and Practice*. London: Routledge.

Pratt, J. and Eriksson, A. (2013) *Contrasts in Punishment: An explanation of Anglophone Excess and Nordic Exceptionalism*. Abingdon: Routledge.

Pratt, J. et al. (eds) (2005) *The New Punitiveness: Trends, Theories, Perspectives*. Cullompton: Willan.

Reichel, P. (ed.) (2005) *Handbook of Transnational Crime and Justice*. London: Sage.

Rosa, M. C. (2014) 'Theories of the South: Limits and perspectives of an emergent movement in social sciences'. *Current Sociology* 62(6): 851–67.

Ruggiero, V. and Ryan, M. (eds) (2013) *Punishment in Europe: A Critical Anatomy of Penal Systems*. Basingstoke: Palgrave Macmillan.

Said, E. (1978) *Orientalism*. New York: Pantheon.

Salvatore, R. D. and C. Aguirre, C. (eds) (1996) *The birth of the penitentiary in Latin America*. Austin, TX: University of Texas.

Santos, J. V. T. (2012) 'Contemporary Latin American sociology and the challenges for an international dialogue' in A. L. Bialakowsky et al. (eds) *Latin American critical thought: Theory and practice*. Buenos Aires: CLASCO.

Sassen, S. (1992) *The Global City: New York*. Princeton, NJ: Princeton University.

Sassen, S. (1997) 'Cities and Regions in Today's Global Age' in LSE and Alfred Herrhausen Society (eds) *Urban India: Understanding the Maximum City*, Urban Age Project. Available at: https://urbanage.lsecities.net/newspapers/urban-india-understanding-the-maximum-city-1.

Semer, M. (2019) *Sentenciando tráfico: O papel dos juízes no grande encarceramento*. São Paulo: Tirrant.

Sheptycki, J. and Wardak, A. (eds) (2005) *Transnational and Comparative Criminology*. London: Glasshouse.

Skarbek, D. (2014) *The Puzzle of Prison Order: Why Life behind Bars Varies around the World*. New York: Oxford University Press.

Smith, S. and Ugelvik, T. (eds) (2017) *Scandinavian Penal History, Culture and Prison Practice: Embraced by the Welfare State?* London: Palgrave Macmillan.

Sudjic, D. (2007) 'India's Urban Shift' in LSE and Alfred Herrhausen Society (eds) *Urban India: Understanding the Maximum City*. Urban Age Project. Available at: https://urbanage.lsecities.net/newspapers/urban-india-understanding-the-maximum-city-1.

Supervielle, M. (2012) 'Revitalizing the sociological view in Latin America' in M. Burawoy et al. (eds) *Facing an unequal world: Challenges for a global sociology*. Taiwan: Institute of Sociology, Academia Sinica.

Sutherland, D. (1939) *Principles of Criminology*. Chicago: Lipincott.

Tertsaklan, C. (2014) 'Some prisons are prisons, and others are like hell'. *Prison Service Journal* 212: 4–10.

Ugelvik, T. (2016) 'Prisons as welfare institutions? Punishment and the Nordic model' in Y. Jewkes et al. (eds) *Handbook on Prisons* (2nd edn). Abingdon: Routledge.

Ugelvik, T. and Dullum, J. (eds) (2012) *Penal Exceptionalism? Nordic Prison Policy and Practice*. London: Routledge.

Ungar, M. (2003) 'Prisons and politics in contemporary Latin America'. *Human Rights Quarterly* 25(4): 909–34.

United Nations (2013) *Handbook on strategies to reduce overcrowding in prisons*. New York: UN.

United Nations (2016) 'United Nations standard minimum rules for the treatment of prisoners' ('Nelson Mandela rules') UN Doc. A/RES/70/175. Available at: https://cdn.penalreform.org/wp-content/uploads/1957/06/ENG.pdf [Accessed 28 October 2020].

Walmsley, R. (1999) *World prison population list*. London: Home Office.

Walmsley, R. (2018). *World prison population list* (12th edn). London: Institute for Criminal Policy Research.

Willis, G. D. (2015) *The Killing Consensus: Police, Organized Crime, and the Regulation of Life and Death in Urban Brazil*. Oakland, CA: University of California.

World Bank (2020) *Shared Prosperity 2020: Reversals of Fortune*. Washington, DC: World Bank.

Young, J. (1997) 'Vertigo and vindictiveness: Some notes on the political economy of punishment'. *Criminal Justice Matters* 70(1): 21–2.

Young, J. (1998) 'Writing on the Cusp of Change: A New Criminology for an Age of Late Modernity' in P. Walton and J. Young (eds) *The New Criminology Revisited*. Basingstoke: Macmillan.

Chapter 14

Aas, K. (2020) *Globalization and Crime*. London: Sage.

Agozino, B. (2018) 'Imperialism: the general theory of crimes of the powerful' in S. Bittle et al. (eds) *Revisiting Crimes of the Powerful: Marxism, Crime and Deviance*. London: Routledge.

Albanese, J. and Reichel, P. (eds) (2013) *Transnational Organized Crime: An Overview from Six Continents*. London: Sage.

Allam, F. and Gilmour, S. (2011) (eds) *The Routledge Handbook of Transnational Organised Crime*. London: Routledge.

Amnesty International. (2018) *'USA: President Trump Signs Order on Guantánamo and Sets Stage for First New Detainee Arrivals since 2008'*, Doc. AMR 51/7822/2018.

Andersson, R. (2016) 'Europe's failed "fight" against irregular migration: Ethnographic notes on a counterproductive industry'. *Journal of Ethnic and Migration Studies* 42(7): 1055–75.

Bakare, A. (2020) 'Why Nigeria needs to manage electronic waste better', The Conversation. Available at: https://theconversation.com/why-nigeria-needs-to-manage-electronic-waste-better-135844 [Accessed 01 December 2020].

Basel Action Network (2018) 'A True Circular Economy: 2017–2019 Biennial Report'. Available at: https://static1.squarespace.com/static/558f1c27e4b0927589e0edad/t/5ceeee7f10cbed00018fa766/1559162522513/Biennial+Report.pdf.

Bilton, M. and Sim, K. (1992) *Four Hours in My Lai*. London: Penguin.

Boullosa, C. and Wallace, M. (2015) *Narco History: How the United States and Mexico Jointly Created the Mexican Drug War*. New York: Or Books.

Bowling, B. (2011) 'Transnational criminology and the globalization of harm production' in M. Bosworth and C. Hoyle (eds) *What is Criminology?* Oxford: Oxford University Press.

Bowling, B. and Sheptycki, J. (2012) *Global Policing*. London: Sage.

Brown, M. (2005) '"Setting the conditions" for Abu Ghraib: the prison nation abroad'. *American Quarterly* 57(3): 973–97.

Calderón, L. et al. (2019) *Organized Crime and Violence in Mexico*. San Diego, CA: University of San Diego.

Campana, P. (2018) 'Out of Africa: The organization of migrant smuggling across the Mediterranean'. *European Journal of Criminology* 15(4): 481–502.

Carrington, K. et al. (2016) 'Southern criminology'. *British Journal of Criminology* 56(1): 1–20.

Carrington, K. et al. (eds) (2018) *The Palgrave Handbook of Criminology and the Global South*. London: Palgrave Macmillan.

Carrington, K. et al. (2019) *Southern Criminology*, London: Routledge.

Cercel, C., Fusco, G. G., and Lavis, S. (2020) *States of Exception: Law, History, Theory*. London: Routledge.

City University London, University of York, and the International Organization for Migration (2016) 'Missing Migrants in the Mediterranean: Addressing the Humanitarian Crisis'. Available at: www.mediterraneanmissing.eu/wp-content/uploads/2015/10/Mediterranean-Missing-Summary-report-290816.pdf.

Clapp, J. (2001) 'Seeping through the regulatory cracks: The international transfer of toxic waste'. *SAIS Review* XXII(1): 141–55.

Clapp, J. (2001) *Toxic Exports: The Transfer of Hazardous Wastes from Rich to Poor Countries*. Ithaca, NY: Cornell University.

Cohen, S. (1988) *Against Criminology*. New Brunswick, NJ: Transaction.

Council of Europe (2020) 'Guide on Article 15 of the European Convention on Human Rights'. Strasbourg: Council of Europe.

Darke, S. (2018) *Conviviality and Survival: Co-Producing Brazilian Prison Order*. London: Palgrave Macmillan.

Darke, S. and Karam, M. L. (2016) 'Latin American prisons' in Y. Jewkes et al. (eds) *Handbook on Prisons*. Abingdon: Routledge.

Durán-Martínez, A. (2018) *The Politics of Drug Violence Criminals, Cops, and Politicians in Colombia and Mexico*. Oxford: Oxford University Press.

Edwards, A. and Gill, P. (eds) (2003) *Transnational Organised Crime: Perspectives on Global Security*. London: Routledge.

Fabini, G. (2019) 'Internal bordering in the context of undeportability: Border performances in Italy'. *Theoretical Criminology* 23(2): 175–93.

Felsen, D. and Kalaitzidis, A. (2005) 'A historical overview of transnational crime' in P. Reichel (ed.) *Handbook of Transnational Crime and Justice*. London: Sage.

Ferraris, V. (2014) 'Lampedusa 2011: A failed stress-test from migration control policies' in D. Sorvatzioti et al. (2014) *Critical Views on Crime, Policy and Social Control*. Nicosia: University of Nicosia.

Fitzgibbon, W. and Lea, J. (2020) *Privatising Justice: The Security Industry, War and Crime Control*. London: Pluto.

Friedrichs, D. O. and Rothe, D. L. (2013) 'Crimes of globalization as a criminological project' in F. Pakes (ed.) *Globalisation and the Challenge to Criminology*. London: Routledge.

Galisson, M. and Institute of Race Relations (2020) *Deadly crossings and the militarisation of Britain's borders*. London: Institute of Race Relations.

Gambetta, D. (1993) *The Sicilian Mafia: The Business of Private Protection*. Cambridge, MA: Harvard University Press.

Gledhill, J. (2015) *The New War on the Poor*. London: Zed Books.

Green, P. and Ward, T. (2004) *State Crime: Governments, Violence and Corruption*. London, Sage.

Green, P. and Ward, T. (2019) *State Crime and Civil Activism*. London, Routledge.

Greer, S. G. (2000) *The Margin of Appreciation: Interpretation and Discretion under the European Convention on Human Rights*. Strasbourg: Council of Europe.

Hallsworth, S. and Lea, J. (2011) 'Reconstructing Leviathan: Emerging contours of the security state'. *Theoretical Criminology* 15: 141–57.

Held, D. (2000) 'The changing contours of political community' in R. Ericson and N. Stehr (eds) *Governing Modern Societies*. Toronto: University of Toronto Press.

Heller, C. and Pezzani, L. (2016) *Death by Rescue: The Lethal Effects of the EU's Policies of Non-assistance at Sea*. London: University of London, Goldsmiths College.

HM Government (2018) '2018 Annual Report on Modern Slavery'. Available at: https://assets.publishing.service.gov.uk/government/uploads/system/uploads/attachment_data/file/907527/2018_UK_Annual_Report_on_Modern_Slavery.pdf.

Human Rights Watch (2019) *World Report 2019*. New York: HRW.

Institute for Public Policy Research (2008) *Shared Destinies: Security in a Globalised World*. London: Institute for Public Policy Research.

Intelligence Security Committee of Parliament (2018) 'Detainee mistreatment and rendition 2001–2010', HC 1113.

International Labour Organization and Walk Free Foundation (2017) *Global Estimates of Modern Slavery: Forced Labour and Forced Marriage*. Geneva: ILO.

Karstedt, S. (2013) 'Contextualizing Mass Atrocity Crimes: Moving Toward a Relational Approach'. *Annual Review of Law and Social Science* 9: 383–404.

Kipp, D. and Muller, M. (2018) 'EU Migration Policy Bears No Relation to Reality'. *Fair Observer*: www.fairobserver.com/region/europe/eu-migration-policy-european-union-europe-news-headlines-today-23009/.

KNOMAD (2019) *Leveraging Economic Migration for Development*. Washington, DC: World Bank.

Kramer, R. C. (1992) 'The Space Shuttle Challenger Explosion' in K. Schlegel and D. Weisburd (eds) *White-Collar Crime Reconsidered*. Boston, MA: Northeastern University Press.

Kramer, R. C. and Michalowski, J. (2005) 'War, Aggression and State Crime: A Criminological Analysis of the Invasion and Occupation of Iraq'. *British Journal of Criminology* 45(4): 446–69.

Lessing, B. (2018) *Making Peace in Drug Wars: Crackdowns and Cartels in Latin America*. Cambridge: Cambridge University Press.

Lipman, Z. (2015) 'Trade in toxic waste' in S. Alam et al. (eds) *International Environmental Law and the Global South*. New York: Cambridge University Press.

MacManus, T. (2014) 'Civil society and state-corporate crime: A case study of Ivory Coast'. *State Crime* 3(2): 200–19.

Matthews, R. A. and Kauzlarich, D. (2000) 'The Crash of Valujet Flight 592: A Case Study in State-Corporate Crime'. *Sociological Focus* 3: 281–98.

McKay, T. (2014) '11 Months After Marijuana Legalization, Here's What's Happening to Mexican Cartels'. Available at: www.mic.com/articles/105510/11-months-after-marijuana-legalization-here-s-what-s-happening-to-mexican-cartels.

McLaughlin, E. (1996) 'Political violence, terrorism and states of fear' in J. Muncie and E. McLaughlin (eds) *The Problem of Crime*. London: Sage.

Michalowski. J. and Kramer, R. C. (2007) 'State-corporate crime and criminological inquiry' in H. N. Pontell and G. Geis (eds) *International Handbook of White-Collar and Corporate Crime*. Bew Your, NY: Springer.

Misse, M. (2007) 'Illegal markets, protection rackets and organized crime in Rio de Janeiro'. *Estudos Avançados* 61: 139–57.

Open Society Foundations (2013) *Globalizing Torture: CIA Detention and Extraordinary Rendition*. New York: Open Society Foundation.
Open Society Foundations (2016) *Undeniable Atrocities: Confronting Crimes against Humanity in Mexico*. New York: Open Societies Foundations.
Pakes, F. (2019) *Comparative Criminal Justice*, London: Routledge.
Pansters, W. G. (2018) 'Drug trafficking, the informal order, and caciques: Reflections on the crime-governance nexus in Mexico'. *Global Crime* 19(3–4): 315–38.
Pearce, F. (1976) *Crimes of the Powerful: Marxism, Crime and Deviance*. London: Pluto.
Raphael, S., Black, C., and Blakeley, R. (2019) *CIA Torture Unredated*. London: Rendition Project and Bureau of Investigative Journalism.
Reichel, P. (ed.) (2005) *Handbook of Transnational Crime and Justice*. London: Sage.
Rolles, S. et al. (2016) *The Alternative World Drug Report* (2nd edn). London: Transform Drug Policy Foundation.
Rothe, D. L. and Friedrichs, D. O. (2015) *Crimes of Globalization*. London: Routledge.
Ruggiero, V. (2003) 'Terrorism: cloning the enemy'. *International Journal of the Sociology of Law* 31: 23–34.
Saviano, R. (2015) *Zero, Zero, Zero*. London: Allen Lane.
Senate Select Committee on Intelligence (2014) 'Report of the Senate Select Committee on Intelligence Committee Study of the Central Intelligence Agency's Detention and Interrogation Program', Senate Report 113–288.
Sheptycki, J. (ed.) (2015) *Transnational Organized Crime*. London: Sage.
Sheptycki, J. and Wardak, A. (eds) (2005) *Transnational and Comparative Criminology*. London: Glasshouse.
Silverstone, D. (2013) 'Globalisation and criminology: The case of organised crime in Britain' in F. Pakes (ed.) *Globalisation and the Challenge to Criminology*. London: Routledge.
Stanley, E. and McCulloch, J. (eds) (2013) *State Crime and Resistance*. Abingdon: Routledge.
Steinhilper, E. and Gruijters, R. J. (2018) 'A Contested Crisis: Policy Narratives and Empirical Evidence on Border Deaths in the Mediterranean'. *Sociology* 52(3): 515–33.
United Nations Environmental Programme (2019) *Global Chemicals Outlook II—From Legacies to Innovative Solutions: Implementing the 2030 Agenda for Sustainable Development*. Nairobi: UNEP.
United Nations High Commissioner for Refugees (2020) *Global Trends: Forced Displacement in 2019*. Copenhagen: UNHCR.
United Nations Office on Drugs and Crime (2019) *Annual Report*. Vienna: UNODC.
United Nations Office on Drugs and Crime (2019b) *World Drug Report*. Vienna: UNODC.
Van Duyne, P. et al. (eds) (2002) *Upperworld and Underworld in Cross-border Crime*. Nijmegen: Wolf Legal Publishers.
Wagner, C. (2019) 'Are Mexican Avocados the Next "Conflict Commodity"', *Maplecroft*: www.maplecroft.com/insights/analysis/are-mexican-avocados-the-next-conflict-commodity/.
Ward, T. and Green, P. (2000) 'Legitimacy, civil society, and state crime'. *Social Justice* 27(4): 76–93.
Watt, P. and Zepeda, R. (2012) *Drug War Mexico: Politics, Neoliberalism and Violence in the New Narcoeconomy*. London: Zed Books.
White, R. (2008) 'Toxic cities: Globalizing the problem of waste'. *Social Justice* 35: 107–19.
White, R. (2010) 'Globalisation and environmental harm' in R. White (ed.) *Global Environmental Harm: Criminological Perspectives*. Cullompton: Willan.
White, R. (2013) 'Environmental activism and resistance to state-corporate crime' in E. Stanley and J. McCulloch (eds) *State Crime and Resistance*. Abingdon: Routledge.
Wilson, P. R. and Braithwaite, J. (1978) *Two Faces of Deviance: Crimes of the Powerless and Powerful*. Brisbane: University of Queensland Press.
Woodiwiss, M. and Hobbs, D. (2009) 'Organized evil and the Atlantic alliance: Moral panics and the rhetoric of organized crime policing in America and Britain'. *British Journal of Criminology* 49(1): 106–12.
Zavala, O. (2018) *Los cárteles no existen: Narcotráfico y cultura en México*. Barcelona: Malpaso.

Chapter 15

Aldridge, J., Measham, F., and Williams, L. (2011) *Illegal Leisure Revisited: Changing Patterns of Alcohol and Drug use in Adolescents and Young Adults*. London: Routledge.
Bedau, H. A. (1983) 'Bentham's Utilitarian Critique of the Death Penalty'. *Journal of Criminal Law and Criminology* 74(3): 1033–65.
Bentham, J. (1789 [1907]) *An Introduction to the Principles of Morals and Legislation*. Oxford: Clarendon Press.
Calvert, B. (2006) 'Bentham and the Death Penalty'. *Canadian Philosophical Review* 45(2): 211–31.
Clarke, R. V. (1997) *Situational crime prevention: successful case studies* (2nd edn). New York: Harrow and Heston.
Clarke, R. and Cornish, D. (1985) 'Modelling Offenders' Decisions: A Framework for Research and Policy' in M. Tonry and N. Morris (eds) *Crime and Justice: A Review of Research*. Chicago: University of Chicago Press.
Cohen, L. and Felson, M. (1979) 'Social Change and Crime Rate Trends: A Routine Activity Approach'. *American Sociological Review* 44(4): 588–608.
Coleman, A. (1990) *Utopia on Trial* (2nd edn). London: Hilary Shipman.
Cornish, D. (1994) 'The Procedural Analysis of Offending and its Relevance for Situational Prevention'. *Crime Prevention Studies* 3: 151–96.
Cornish, D. and Clarke, R. (2006) 'The Rational Choice Perspective' in S. Henry and M. Lanier (eds) *The Essential Criminology Reader*. Boulder, CO: Westview Press.
Cornish, D. and Clarke, R. (2014) *The Reasoning Criminal: Rational Choice Perspectives on Offending*. London: Transaction Publishers.
Cozens, P. M. (2008) 'Crime Prevention Through Environmental Design (CPTED): Origins, Concepts, Current Status and Future Directions' in R. Wortley, L. Mazerolle, and S. Rombouts (eds) *Environmental Criminology and Crime Analysis*. Cullompton: Willan.
Davey, C. L. and Wooton, A. B. (2016) *Integrating Crime Prevention into Urban Design and Planning*. Salford: University of Salford, USIR. Available at: http://usir.salford.ac.uk/id/eprint/38589/3/JPM%20paper%20-%20revised%2023MAR16[1].pdf [Accessed 2 December 2020].
Garland, D. (2000) 'Ideas, Institutions and Situational Crime Prevention' in A. von Hirsch, D. Garland, and A. Wakefield (eds) *Ethical and Social Perspectives on Situational Crime Prevention*. Oxford: Hart.
Glasson J. and Cozens, P. (2011) 'Making Communities Safer from Crime: An Undervalued Element in Impact Assessment'. *Environmental Impact Assessment Review* 31: 25–35.
Gourevitch, V. (ed. and trans.) (2019) *Rousseau: The Social Contract and other political Writings* (2nd edn). Cambridge: Cambridge University Press.
Klein, M. W. and Maxson, C. L. (2006) *Street gang patterns and policies*. Oxford: Oxford University Press.
Linden, R. (2007) 'Situational Crime Prevention: Its Role in Comprehensive Prevention Initiatives'. *Institute for the Prevention of Crime (IPC) Review* 1: 139–59.

Locke, J. (1690) *Second Treatise of Civil Government.* Available at: www.marxists.org/reference/subject/politics/locke/ch08.htm [Accessed 2 December 2020].

Maxfield, M. G. (1987) 'Lifestyle and Routine Activity Theories of Crime: Empirical Studies of Victimization, Delinquency, and Offender Decision-Making'. *Journal of Quantitative Criminology* 3(4): 275–82.

Newburn, T. (2009) *Key Readings in Criminology.* Abingdon: Willan.

Newman, O. (1972) *Defensible Space: People and Design in the Violent City.* London: Architectural Press.

Newman, O. (ed.) (1996) *Creating Defensible Space.* New Brunswick, NJ: Rutgers University, Institute for Community Design Analysis.

Parker, H., Williams, L. and Aldridge, J. (2002) 'The Normalisation of "Sensible" Recreational Drug Use: Further Evidence from the North West England Longitudinal Study'. *Sociology* 36: 941–64.

Pease, K. (2002) 'Crime Reduction' in M. Maguire, R. Morgan, and R. Reiner (eds) *The Oxford Handbook of Criminology* (3rd edn). Oxford: Oxford University Press.

Popper, K. (1959) *The Logic of Scientific Discovery.* Translation of *Logik der Forschung 1935).* London: Hutchinson.

Pratt, T., Holtfreter, K., and Reisig, M. (2012) 'Routine Online Activity and Internet Fraud Targeting: Extending the Generality of Routine Activity Theory'. *Journal of Research in Crime and Delinquency* 47(3): 267–96.

Pyrooz, D. C. (2014) 'From your first cigarette to your last dyin' day: The patterning of gang membership in the life-course'. *Journal of Quantitative Criminology* 30(2): 349–72.

Radzinowicz, L. (1966) *Ideology and Crime: A Study of Crime in its Social and Historical Context.* London: Heinemann Educational.

Shuman, D. W. and Gold, L. H. (2008) 'Without Thinking: Impulsive Aggression and Criminal Responsibility'. *Behavioral Sciences & the Law* 26: 723–34.

Smith, W. R., Frazee, S. G., and Davison, E. L. (2000) 'Furthering the Integration of Routine Activity and Social Disorganization Theories: Small Units of Analysis and the Study of Street Robbery as a Diffusion Process'. *Criminology* 38(2): 489–524.

Tversky, A. and Kahneman, D. (1974) 'Judgment under Uncertainty: Heuristics and Biases'. *Science, New Series* 185(4157): 1124–31.

Williams, D. (ed. and trans.) (1994) *Voltaire: Political Writings.* Cambridge: Cambridge University Press.

Chapter 16

Aichhorn, A. (1936) *Wayward Youth.* New York: Viking Press.

Anda, R. F. et al. (2005) 'The enduring effects of abuse and related adverse experiences in childhood: A convergence of evidence from neurobiology and epidemiology'. *European Archives of Psychiatry and Clinical Neuroscience* 256: 174–86.

Arian, M. et al. (2013) 'Maturation of the Adolescent Brain'. *Neurpsychiatr Dis Treat* 9: 449–61.

Baglivio, M. T. et al. (2014) 'The prevalence of adverse childhood experiences (ACE) in the lives of Juvenile offenders'. *Journal of Juvenile Justice* 3(2): 1–17.

Baglivio, M. T. et al. (2015) 'The relationship between adverse childhood experiences (ACE) and juvenile offending trajectories in a juvenile offender sample'. *Journal of Criminal Justice* 43(3): 229–41.

Bandura, A., Ross, D., and Ross, S. (1961) 'Transmission of Aggression through Imitation of Aggressive Models'. *Journal of Abnormal and Social Psychology* 63(3): 575–82.

Bartlett, F. (1932) *Remembering.* Cambridge: Cambridge University Press.

Baumeister, R. (1982) 'Reducing the Biasing Effect of Perpetrator Attractiveness in Jury Simulation'. *Personal and Social Psychology Bulletin* 8(2): 286–92.

Berry, D. (1988) 'Facial Maturity and the Attribution of Legal Responsibility'. *Personality and Social Psychology Bulletin* 14(1): 23–33.

Bowling, B. and Phillips, C. (2002) *Racism, Crime and Justice.* London: Longman.

Burleigh, M. (1995) *Death and Deliverance: 'Euthanasia' in Germany 1900–1945.* Cambridge: Cambridge University Press.

Cortes, J. B. and Gatti, F. M. (1972) *Delinquency and Crime: A Biopsychosocial Approach: Empirical, Theoretical and Practical Aspects of Criminal Behaviour.* New York: Seminar Press.

Dabbs, J. and Dabbs, M. (2000) *Heroes, Rogues and Lovers: Testosterone and Behaviour.* New York: McGraw-Hill.

Dube, S. et al. (2003) 'Childhood Abuse, Neglect, and Household Dysfunction and the Risk of Illicit Drug Use: The Adverse Childhood Experiences Study'. *Pediatrics* 111(3): 564–72.

Dugdale, R. (1877) 'The Jukes: A Study in Crime, Pauperism, Disease and Heredity', Buck v. Bell Documents Paper 1. Available at http://readingroom.law.gsu.edu/buckvbell/1 [Accessed 3 December 2020].

Eberhardt, J. et al. (2006) 'Looking Deathworthy: Perceived Stereotypicality of Black Defendants Predicts Capital-Sentencing Outcomes'. *Psychological Science* 17: 383–6.

Ellis, L. and Coontz, P. (1990) 'Androgens, Brain Functioning and Criminality: The Neurohormonal Foundations of Antisociality' in L. Ellis and H. Hoffman (eds) *Crime in Biological, Social and Moral Contexts.* New York: Praeger.

Eysenck, H. (1959) *Manual of the Maudsley Personality Inventory.* London: UCL Press.

Eysenck, H. (1977) *Crime and Personality* (3rd edn). London: Routledge & Kegan Paul.

Eysenck, H. (1987) 'The Place of Anxiety and Impulsivity in a Dimensional Framework'. *Journal of Research in Personality* 21: 489–92.

Eysenck, H. and Gudjonsson, G. (1989) *The Causes and Cures of Criminality.* New York: Plenum Press.

Farrington, D. (1994) 'Introduction' in D. Farrington (ed.) *Psychological Explanations of Crime.* Aldershot: Dartmouth.

Farrington, D. P. (2010) *Life-course and Developmental Theories in Criminology.* London: Sage.

Fink, A. E. (1938 [1985]) *Causes of Crime: Biological Theories in the United States, 1800–1915.* Westport, CT: Greenwood Press.

Fishbein, D. (2001) *Biobehavioural Perspectives in Criminology.* Belmont, CA: Wadsworth Publishing.

Freud, S. (1935) *A General Introduction to Psycho-Analysis.* Translated by J. Riviere. New York: Liveright.

Galton, F. (1883) *Inquiries into Human Faculty and Its Development.* AMS Press: New York (republished 1907 and 1973).

Gesch, C. B. et al. (2002) 'Influence of supplementary vitamins, minerals and essential fatty acids on the antisocial behaviour of young adult prisoners: Randomised, placebo-controlled trial'. *British Journal of Psychiatry* 181(1): 22–8.

Ghosh, V. E. and Gilboa, A. (2014) 'What is a Memory Schema? A Historical Perspective on Current Neuroscience Literature'. *Neuropsychologia* 53: 104–14.

Goddard, H. (1912) *The Kallikak Family: A Study in the Heredity of Feeble-mindedness.* New York: Macmillan.

Goring, C. (1913) *The English Convict: A Statistical Study.* London: HMSO.

Gracia, E. (2014) 'Intermate Partner Violence Against women and Victim-Blaming Attitudes among Europeans'. *World Health Organisation Bulletin* 92(5): 380–1.

Grubin, D. and Beech, A. (2010) 'Chemical Castration for Sex Offenders'. *British Medical Journal* 340: c74.

Hanley, G. P., Iwata, B. A., and McCord, B. E. (2013) 'Functional Analysis of Problem Behaviour: A Review'. *Journal of Applied Behaviour Analysis* 36(2): 147–85.

Herbison, C. E. et al. (2012) 'Low intake of B-vitamins is associated with poor adolescent mental health and behaviour'. *Preventive Medicine* 55(6): 634–8.

Hollin, C. (1992) *Criminal Behaviour: A Psychological Approach to Explanation and Prevention*. London: Falmer Press.

Hollin, C. (1995) *Psychology and Crime: An Introduction to Criminological Psychology*. London: Routledge.

Hollin, C. (2007) 'Criminological Psychology' in M. Maguire, R. Morgan, and R. Reiner (eds) *The Oxford Handbook of Criminology* (4th edn). Oxford: Clarendon Press.

Hollin, C. R. (2013). *Psychology and Crime: An introduction to criminological psychology* (2nd edn). London: Routledge.

Jamrozik, K. (2005) 'Estimate of Deaths Attributable to Passive Smoking Among UK Adults: Database Analysis'. *British Medical Journal* 330(7495): 812.

Jones, S. (1993) *The Language of Genes*. London: Harper Collins.

Joseph, J. (2000) 'Not in their Genes: A Critical View of the Genetics of Attention-Deficit Hyperactivity Disorder'. *Developmental Review* 20: 539–67.

Kim, J., Lim, J.-S. and Bhargava, M. (1998) 'The Role of Affect in Attitude Formation: A Classical Conditioning Approach'. *Journal of the Academy of Marketing Science* 26: 143–52.

Kline, P. (1984) *Psychology and Freudian Theory*. London: Methuen.

Kohlberg, L. (1958) 'The Development of Modes of Thinking and Choice in the Years 10–16'. Unpublished doctoral thesis, University of Chicago.

Kohlberg, L. (1963) 'The Development of Children's Orientations Towards a Moral Order: I. Sequence in the Development of Moral Thought'. *Human Development*. 6: 11–33.

Kohlberg, L. (1981) *The Philosophy of Moral Development*. San Francisco, CA: Harper and Row.

Kolb, B. (2009) 'Brain and Behavioural Plasticity in the Developing Brain: Neuroscience and Public Policy'. *Paediatric Child Health* 14(10): 651–2.

Kolla, N. J. et al. (2013) 'Childhood Maltreatment and Aggressive Behaviour in Violent Offenders with Psychopathy'. *Canadian Journal of Psychiatry* 58(8): 487–94.

LaVigna, G. W. and Willis, T. J. (2012) 'The Efficacy of Positive Behavioural Support with the Most Challenging Behaviour: The Evidence and its Implications'. *Journal of Intellectual and Developmental Disability* 37(3): 185–95.

Lleras, A., Buetti, S., and Mordkoff, J. T. (2013) 'When do the Effects of Distractors Provide a Measure of Distractability?' in B. H. Ross (ed.) *Psychology of Learning and Motivation*, Vol.59. San Diego, CA: Elsevier Academic Press.

Loehlin, J. (1992) *Genes and Environment in Personality Development*. Thousand Oaks, CA: Sage.

Lombroso, C. (1876) *L'Uomo Delinquente* (5th and final edn 1897). Turin: Bocca.

Lombroso, C. (1899) *Crime: Causes et Remèdes* (2nd edn printed in 1906). Paris: Alcan.

LSE and the Guardian (2011) *Reading the Riots: Investigating England's Summer of Disorder*. London: The Guardian.

Mack, A. and Rock, I. (1998). *Inattentional blindness*. Cambridge, MA: MIT Press.

Macpherson, W. (1999) The Stephen Lawrence Inquiry, Cm 4262-1. London: The Stationery Office.

Madden, S., Walker, J. T., and Miller, J. M. (2008) 'Does Size Really Matter? A Reexamination of Sheldon's Somatotypes and Criminal Behaviour'. *Science Journal* 45(2): 330–4.

Marsh, T. O. (1981) *Roots of Crime—A Bio-physical Approach to Crime Prevention and Rehabilitation*. New York: Neller Publishing.

Martin, G. N. and Carlson, N. R. (2019) *Psychology* (6th edn). Harlow: Pearson Education.

McAra, L. and McVie, S. (2017) 'Developmental Criminology' in M. Maguire, R. Morgan, and R. Reiner (eds) *The Oxford Handbook of Criminology* (6th edn). Oxford: Oxford University Press.

McGurk, B. and McDougall, C. (1981) 'A New Approach to Eysenck's Theory of Criminality'. *Personality and Individual Differences* 2: 338–40.

Mednick, S. A., Moffitt, T. E., and Stack, S. A. (1987) *The Causes of Crime: New Biological Approaches* (Part V). Cambridge: Cambridge University Press.

Mishra, A., Singh, S., and Shukla, S. (2018) 'Physiological and Functional Basis of Dopamine Receptors and Their Role in Neurogenesis: Possible Implication for Parkinson's Disease'. *Journal of Experimental Neuroscience* 12: 1–8.

Moore, C. M. (2001) 'Inattentional Blindness: Perception or Memory and What does it Matter?'. *Journal Psyche* 7(02): 1–7.

Morrison, W. (2004) 'Lombroso and the Birth of Criminological Positivism: Scientific Mastery or Cultural Artifice?' in J. Ferrell et al. (eds) *Cultural Criminology Unleashed*. London: Glasshouse Press.

Office for National Statistics (2018a) 'Alcohol-specific deaths in the UK: Registered in 2017'. Available at: www.ons.gov.uk/peoplepopulationandcommunity/healthandsocialcare/causesofdeath/bulletins/alcoholrelateddeathsintheunitedkingdom/registeredin2017#main-points.

Office for National Statistics (2018b) 'Data on alcohol related incidents, years ending March 2011 to March 2017, Crime Survey for England and Wales'. Available at: www.ons.gov.uk/peoplepopulationandcommunity/crimeandjustice/adhocs/009372dataonalcoholrelatedincidentsyearsendingmarch2011tomarch2017crimesurveyforenglandandwales.

Olweus, D. (1987) 'Testosterone and Adrenaline: Aggressive and Antisocial Behaviour in Normal Adolescent Males' in S. Mednick, T. Moffitt, and S. Stack (eds) *The Causes of Crime: New Biological Approaches*. Cambridge: Cambridge University Press.

Pakes, F. and Pakes, S. (2014) *Criminal Psychology*. London: Routledge.

Palmer E. (2003) *Offending Behaviour: Moral Reasoning, Criminal Conduct and the Rehabilitation of Offenders*. Cullompton: Willan.

Pavlov, I. (1927) *Conditioned Reflexes*. Oxford: Oxford University Press.

Phillips, C. and Webster, C. (eds) (2014) *New Directions in Race, Ethnicity and Crime*. Abingdon: Routledge.

Pollak, S., Cicchetti, D., and Klorman, R. (1998) 'Stress, Memory, and Emotion: Developmental Considerations from the Study of Child Maltreatment'. *Development and Psychopathology* 10: 811–28.

Pollak, S. and Tolley-Schell, S. (2003) 'Selective Attention to Facial Emotion in Physically Abused Children'. *Journal of Abnormal Psychology* 112(3): 323–38.

Raine, A. (1993) *The Psychopathology of Crime*. San Diego, CA: Academic Press.

Raine, A. and Scerbo, A. (1991) 'Biological Theories of Violence' in J. S. Milner (ed.) *Neuropsychology of Aggression*. New York: Springer Scientific.

Raine, A. and Venables, P. H. (1981) 'Classical conditioning and socialization—A biosocial interaction'. *Personality and Individual Difference* 2(4): 273–83.

Reavis, J. et al. (2013) 'Adverse Childhood Experiences and Adult Criminality: How Long Must We Live before We Possess Our Own Lives?'. *The Permanente Journal* 17(2): 44–8.

Ridley, M. (2004) *Evolution* (3rd edn). Cambridge, MA: Blackwell.

Rock, P. (2007) 'Cesare Lombroso as a Signal Criminologist'. *Criminology and Criminal Justice* 7(2): 117–34.

Rowe, D. and Farrington, D. (1997) 'The Familial Transmission of Criminal Convictions'. *Criminology* 35: 177–202.

Sampson, R. and Laub, J. (1991) 'The Sutherland–Glueck Debate: On the Sociology of Criminological Knowledge'. *American Journal of Sociology* 96: 1402–40.

Sampson, R. and Laub, J. (2005) 'A Life Course View of the Development of Crime'. *The Annals* 602: 12–45.

Scarman, L. (1982) *The Scarman Report*. Harmondsworth: Penguin.

Scarpa, A. and Raine, A. (2000) 'Violence Associated with Anger and Impulsivity' in J. C. Broad (ed.) *The Neuropsychology of Emotion*. Oxford: Oxford University Press.

Schalling, D. (1987) 'Personality Correlates of Plasma Testosterone Levels in Young Delinquents: An Example of Person-Situation Interaction' in A. Mednick, T. Moffitt, and S. Stack (eds) *The Causes of Crime: New Biological Approaches*. Cambridge: Cambridge University Press.

Shaw, C. R. and McKay, H. D. (1942), *Juvenile Delinquency and Urban Areas* (revised edn). Chicago, IL: University of Chicago Press.

Sheldon, W. (1949) *Varieties of Delinquent Youth*. New York and London: Harper.

Skinner, B. (1938) *The Behaviour of Organisms*. New York: Appleton-Century-Crofts.

Taylor, I. (1999) *Crime in Context: A Critical Criminology of Market Societies*. Cambridge: Polity Press.

Toates, F. (2007) *Biological Psychology* (2nd edn). Harlow: Pearson Education.

Tukstra, L., Jones, D., and Toler, H. L. (2003) 'Brain Injury and Violent Crime'. *Brain Injury* 17(1): 39–47.

Vennard, J. and Hedderman, C. (1998) 'Effective Treatment with Offenders' in P. Goldblatt and C. Lewis (eds) *Reducing Offending: An Assessment of Research Evidence on Ways of Dealing with Offending Behaviour*, Home Office Research Study 187. London: Home Office Research and Statistics Directorate.

Wardale, S., Davis, F., and Dalton, C. (2014) 'Positive Behavioural Support Training in a Secure Forensic Setting: The Impact on Staff Knowledge and Positive Behavioural Support Plan Quality'. *International Journal of Positive Behavioural Support* 4(2): 9–13.

Webber, C. (2019) *Psychology and Crime* (2nd edn). London: Sage.

Young, J. (1999) *The Exclusive Society: Social Exclusion, Crime and Difference in Late Modernity*. London: Sage.

Chapter 17

Auletta, K. (1982) *The Underclass*. New York: Random House.

Bauman, Z. (1994) *Alone Again: Ethics After Certainty*. London: Demos.

Bauman, Z. (2001) *The Individualised Society*. Cambridge: Polity Press.

Bennett, A. (1999) 'Sub-cultures or Neo-tribes? Rethinking the Relationship between Youth, Style and Musical Taste'. *Sociology* 33(3): 599–617.

Box, S. (1981) *Deviance Reality and Society* (2nd edn). London: Holt, Rinehart and Winston.

Box, S. (1983) *Power, Crime and Mystification*. London: Tavistock.

Braithwaite, J. (1988) *Crime, Shame and Reintegration*. Cambridge: Cambridge University Press.

Brotherton, D. C. and Naegler, L. (2014) 'Jock Young and Social Bulimia: Crime and the Contradictions of Capitalism'. *Theoretical Criminology* 18(4): 441–9.

Brown, M. (1996) 'The Portrayal of Violence in the Media: Impacts and Implications for Policy' in *Trends and Issues in Crime and Criminal Justice*, No. 55. Canberra: Australian Institute of Criminology.

Burney, E. (2009) *Making People Behave: Anti-Social Behaviour, politics and policy*. Cullompton: Willan.

Calvert, C. (2001) 'Off-campus Speech, On-campus Punishment: Censorship of the Emerging Internet Underground'. *Boston University Journal of Science and Technology Law* 41(2): 243–87.

Cantor, C. and Sheehan, P. (1996), 'Violence and media reports: A connection with Hungerford?'. *Archives of Suicide Research* 2: 255–66.

Cloward, R. and Ohlin, L. (1960) *Delinquency and Opportunity: A Theory of Delinquent Gangs*. New York: Free Press.

Cohen, A. (1955) *Delinquent Boys: The Culture of the Gang*. New York: Free Press.

Cohen, A. (1966) *Deviance and Control*. Englewood Cliffs, NJ: Prentice-Hall.

Croall, H. (2001) *Understanding White Collar Crime*. Buckingham: Open University Press.

Cullen, S. and Messner, F. (2007) 'The Making of *Criminology Revisited*: An Oral History of Merton's Anomie Paradigm'. *Theoretical Criminology* 11(1): 5–37.

Davis, K. (1971) 'Prostitution' in R. Merton and R. Nisbet (eds) *Contemporary Social Problems* (3rd edn). New York: Harcourt Brace Jovanovich.

Durkheim, É. (1933) *The Division of Labor in Society*. Translated by G. Simpson (1960). New York: The Free Press. Available at: http://fs2.american.edu/dfagel/www/Class%20Readings/Durkheim/Division%20Of%20Labor%20Final%20Version.pdf

Durkheim, É. (1895 [1938]) *The Rules of Sociological Method*. Chicago: University of Chicago Press.

Durkheim, É. (1895) *The Rules of Sociological Method*. Reprinted and edited in 2014 by S. Lukes and translated by W. D. Halls, *Émile Durkheim: The Rules of Sociological Method and Selected Texts on Sociology and its Method*. New York: Free Press.

Durkheim, É (1897, reprinted 1970) *Suicide*. London: Routledge &Kegan Paul.

Engels, F. (1844) *Outlines of a Critique of Political Economy*. English translation in D. J. Struik (ed.) (1970) *Birth of the Communist Manifesto*. New York: International Publishers, pp. 197–226.

Erikson, K. L. (1966) *Wayward Puritans: A Study in the Sociology of Deviance*. New York: John Wiley and Sons.

Ferrell, J., Hayward, K., and Young, J. (2015) *Cultural Criminology: An Invitation*. London: Sage.

Fisse, B. and Braithwaite, J. (1993) *Corporations, Crime and Accountability*. Cambridge: Cambridge University Press.

Fitzgerald, R. (2009) 'Self-reported Violent Delinquency and the Influence of School, Neighbourhood and Student Characteristics'. Canadian Crime and Justice Research Paper Series 17. Available at: www.publicsafety.gc.ca/lbrr/archives/cnmcs-plcng/statcan-cjrps-no17-eng.pdf.

Foucault, M. (1975) *Discipline and Punish: The Birth of the Prison*. London: Penguin.

Freedman, J. (1994) 'Viewing television violence does not make people more aggressive'. *Hofstra Law Review* 22: 833–54.

Galbraith, J. (1983) *The Anatomy of Power*. London: Houghton Mifflin.

Giles, H. et al. (2003) 'Intergenerational Communication across Cultures: Young People's Perceptions of Conversations with Family Elders, Non-family Elders and Same-age Peers'. *Journal of Cross-Cultural Gerontology* 18: 1–32.

Guardian and LSE (2012) *Reading the Riot: Investigating England's Summer of Disorder*. London: The Guardian and LSE. Available at: http://eprints.lse.ac.uk/46297/1/Reading%20the%20 riots(published).pdf [Accessed 3 December 2020].

Gunter, A. (2008) 'Growing up Bad: Black Youth, "Road" Culture and Badness in an East London Neighbourhood'. *Crime, Media and Culture* 4(3): 349–66.

Hazelhurst, K. and Hazelhurst, C. (2017) *Gangs and Youth Subcultures: International Explorations*. Oxford: Routledge (first published 1998).

Holligan, C. (2015) 'Disenfranchised Violent Young Offenders in Scotland: Using Actor-Network Theory to Explore an Aetiology of Knife Crime'. *Sociology* 49(1): 123–38.

Ilan, J. (2015) *Understanding Street Culture: Poverty, Crime, Youth and Cool*. London: Palgrave.

Johns, D., Williams, K. S., and Haines, K. (2017) 'Ecological Youth Justice: The social ecology of young people's prolific offending'. *Youth Justice* 17(1): 3–21.

Jones, D. (1982) *Crime, Protest, Community and Police in Nineteenth Century Britain*. London: Routledge & Kegan Paul.

Kiesbye, S. (2010) *Does the Internet Increase Crime?* San Diego, CA: Greenhaven Press.

Klein, M. W., Weerman, F. M., and Thornberry, T. P. (2006) 'Street Gang Violence in Europe'. *European Journal of Criminology* 3(4): 413–37.

Lynch, M. J. and Michalowski, R. J. (2006) *Primer in Radical Criminology: Critical Perspectives on Crime, Power and Identity*. Monsey, NY: Criminal Justice Press.

Magoon, K. (2010) *Media Censorship*. Minneapolis, MN: ABDO.

Matza, D. (1961) 'Subterranean Traditions of Youth'. *Annals of the American Academy of Political and Social Science* 338: 102–18.

Matza, D. (1964) *Delinquency and Drift*. London: Wiley.

Matza, D. (1969) *Becoming Deviant*. Upper Saddle River, NJ: Prentice Hall.

Matza, D. and Sykes, G. (1961) 'Juvenile Delinquency and Subterranean Values'. *American Sociological Review* 26(5): 712–19.

Mayhew, H. (1850) *London Labour and the London Poor*. London: William Kimber.

McAra, L. and McVie, S. (2010) 'Youth Crime and Justice: Key Messages from the Edinburgh Study of Youth Transitions and Crime'. *Criminology and Criminal Justice* 10(2): 179–209.

McCarthy, B. (1996) 'The Attitudes and Actions of Others: Tutelage and Sutherland's Theory of Differential Association'. *British Journal of Criminology* 36(1): 135–47.

Merton, R. (1938) 'Social Structure and Anomie'. *American Sociological Review* 3(5): 672–82.

Merton, R. (1949) *Social Theory and Social Structure*. New York: Free Press.

Merton, R. (1957) 'Priorities in Scientific Discovery: A Chapter in the Sociology of Science'. *American Sociological Review* 22(6): 635–59.

Moffitt, T. E. and Silva, P. A. (1988) 'Self-reported Delinquency: Results from an Instrument for New Zealand'. *Australian and New Zealand Journal of Criminology* 21: 227–40.

Murray, C. (1984) *Losing Ground: American Social Policy 1950–1980*. New York: Basic Books.

Murray, C. (1990) *The Emerging British Underclass*. London: IEA Health and Welfare Unit.

Murray, C. (2001) 'Underclass + 10' in CIVITAS, *Underclass + 10: Charles Murray and the British Underclass 1990–2000*. London: Institute for the Study of Civil Society. Available at: www.civitas.org.uk/pdf/cs10.pdf [Accessed 3 December 2020].

Murray, J. (1994), 'The impact of televised violence'. *Hofstra Law Review* 22: 809–25.

Nagtegaal, M. H. and Rassin, E. (2004) 'The Usefulness of the Thought Suppression Paradigm in Explaining Impulsivity and Aggression'. *Personality and Individual Differences* 37(6): 1233–44.

Nash, K. (2010) *Contemporary Political Sociology: Globalization, Politics and Power* (2nd edn). Chichester: Wiley-Blackwell.

Paik, H. and Comstock, G. (1994) 'The effects of television violence on antisocial behavior: A meta-analysis'. *Communication Research* 21(4): 516–46.

Park, R. (1929) 'The City as a Social Laboratory' in T. Smith and L. White (eds) *Chicago: An Experiment in Social Science Research*. Chicago: Chicago University Press.

Phillips, D. (1977) *Crime and Authority in Victorian England*. London: Croom Helm.

Prison Reform Trust (2012) *Old Enough to Know Better?* London: Prison Reform Trust.

Purdy, D. with Paul, G. (2010) *It's Not Because I Want to Die*. London: Harper True.

Rough, E. and Sutherland, N. (2020) 'The Law on Assisted Dying', House of Commons Library CDP 2020/0009.

Runciman, W. (1990) 'How Many Classes are there in Contemporary British Society?'. *Sociology* 23(3): 377–96.

Sampson, R. and Groves, W. (1989) 'Community Structure and Crime: Testing Social-Disorganization Theory'. *American Journal of Sociology* 94: 774–802.

Scarman, Lord (1981, produced in paperback in 1982) *The Scarman Report*. Harmondsworth: Penguin.

Schlossman, S. et al. (1984) *Delinquency Prevention in South Chicago: A Fifty Year Assessment of the Chicago Area Project*. Santa Monica, CA: RAND.

Shaw, C. R. and McKay, H. D. (1942) *Juvenile Delinquency and Urban Areas*. Chicago, IL: University of Chicago Press.

Short, J. F. and Strodtbeck, F. L. (1967) *Group Process and Gang Delinquency*. Chicago, IL: University of Chicago Press.

Slapper, G. and Tombs, S. (1999) *Corporate Crime*. Harlow: Longman.

Squires, P. (2006) 'New Labour and the Politics of Anti-social Behaviour'. *Critical Social Policy* 26(1): 144–68.

Squires, P. and Stephen, D. (2005) *Rougher Justice: Young People and Anti-Social Behaviour*. Cullompton: Willan.

Sutherland, E. (1939a) 'The White Collar Criminal', Speech to the American Sociological Association in *American Sociology Review* 5(1): 1–12.

Sutherland, E. (1939b) *Principles of Criminology* (3rd edn). Philadelphia, PA: Lippincott.

Sutherland, E. (1949) *White Collar Crime*. New York: Holt, Rinehart and Wilson.

Taylor, I. (1999) *Crime in Context: A Critical Criminology of Market Societies*. Cambridge: Polity Press.

Tobias, J. (1972) *Crime and Industrial Society in the Nineteenth Century*. Harmondsworth: Penguin.

Valdimarsdóttir, M. and Bernburg, J. G. (2015) 'Community Disadvantage, Parental Network, and Commitment to Social Norms: Multilevel Study of Self-reported Delinquency in Iceland'. *Journal of Research in Crime and Delinquency* 52(2): 213–44.

Westminster Government (2015) *2010 to 2015 Government Policy: Knife, Gun and Gang Crime*. London: UK Government.

Yates, J. (2014) 'Structural Disadvantage: Youth, Class, Crime and Poverty' in W. Taylor, R. Earle, and R. Hester (eds) *Youth Justice Handbook: Theory, Policy and Practice*. Abingdon: Routledge.

Young, J. (1999) *The Exclusive Society: Social Exclusion, Crime and Difference in Late Modernity*. London: Sage.

Young, J. (2002) 'Crime and Social Exclusion' in M. Maguire, R. Morgan, and R. Reiner (eds) *The Oxford Handbook of Criminology* (3rd edn). Oxford: Oxford University Press.

Young, J. (2007) *The Vertigo of Late Modernity*. London: Sage.

Chapter 18

Alvelos, H. (2004) 'The Desert of Imagination in the City of Signs: Cultural Implications of Signposted Transgression and Branded Graffiti' in J. Ferrell et al (eds) *Cultural Criminology Unleashed*. London: Glasshouse Press.

Anthony, T. and Cunneen, C. (2008) *The Critical Criminology Companion*. Annandale, NSW: Hawkins Press.

Aresti, A., Darke. S., and Manlow, D. (2015) '"Bridging the Gap": Giving Public Voice to Prisoners and Former Prisoners through Research Activism'. *Prisons Service Journal* 224: 3–14.

Becker, H. (1997 [1963]) *Outsiders: Studies in the Sociology of Deviance*. New York: Simon & Schuster.

Bovenkerk, F. and Levi, M. (2007) *The Organized Crime Community: Essays in Honour of Alan Block*. New York: Springer.

Bowell, T. (2014) 'Feminist Standpoint Theory', *Internet Encyclopedia of Philosophy*, available at: www.iep.utm.edu/fem-stan/ [Accessed 19 June 2020].

Chambliss, W. (1975) 'Towards a Political Economy of Crime'. *Theory and Society* (2): 149–70.

Chesney-Lind, M. (2006) 'Patriarchy, Crime, and Justice: Feminist Criminology in an Era of Backlash'. *Feminist Criminology* Vl 1(1): 6–26.

Clarke, A. and Wydall, S. (2013) '"Making Safe": A Co-ordinated Community Response to Empowering Victims and Tackling Perpetrators of Domestic Violence'. *Social Policy and Society* 12(3): 393–406.

Collins, P. H. (1986) 'Learning from the outsider within: the sociological significance of Black Feminist thought'. *Social Problems* 33(6): 14–32.

Corston, J. (2007) *The Corston Report: A Review of Women with Particular Vulnerabilities in the Criminal Justice System*. London: Home Office.

Criminal Justice Matters (2010) 'The Violence of the British State'. Special issue. *Criminal Justice Matters* 82.

Criminal Justice Matters (2011) 'Women, Violence and Harm'. Special issue. *Criminal Justice Matters* 85.

Criminal Justice Matters (2012) 'The August 2011 Riots'. Special issue. *Criminal Justice Matters* 87.

Criminal Justice Matters (2015) 'Black Lives Matter'. Special issue. *Criminal Justice Matters* 101.

Cunneen, C. (2007) 'The Effects of Colonial Policy: Genocide, Racism and Aboriginal People in Australia' in M. Prum, B. Deschamps, and M.-C. Barbier (eds) *Racial, Ethnic and Homophobic Violence: Killing in the name of Otherness*. New York: Routledge Cavendish.

DeKeseredy, W. and Dragiewicz, M. (eds) (2011) *The Routledge Handbook of Critical Criminology*. London: Routledge.

Dobash, R. E. and Dobash, R. P. (1992) *Women, Violence and Social Change*. London: Routledge.

Downes, D. (2005) 'Review of K. Hayward, City Limits: Crime, Consumer Culture and the Urban Experience'. *Criminal Justice* 5: 3.

Drumbl, M. A. (2007). *Atrocity, Punishment, and International Law*. Cambridge: Cambridge University Press.

Fattah, E. A. (1992) 'The need for a critical victimology' in E. A. Fattah (ed.) *Towards A Critical Victimology*. New York: Martin's Press.

Feilzer, M. and Williams, K. S. (2015) 'Breaking the Cycle for Women through Equality not Difference' in J. Annison, J. Brayford, and J. Deering (eds) *Women and Criminal Justice: From the Corston Report to Transforming Rehabilitation*. Bristol: Policy Press.

Foley, M. (1996) 'Who is in Control? Changing Responses to Women in the Home' in M. Hester, L. Kelly, and J. Radford (eds) *Women, Violence and Male Power*. Buckingham: Open University Press.

Foley, M. (1996) 'Who is in Control? Changing Responses to Women in the Home' in M. Hester, L. Kelly, and J. Radford (eds) *Women, Violence and Male Power*. Buckingham: Open University Press.

Freudenberg, N. (2014, reprinted 2016) *Lethal But Legal: Corporations, Consumption, and Protecting Public Health*. New York: Oxford University Press.

Gladstone, L. (2013) 'Learning from Rape Crisis Volunteers: Remembering the Past, Envisioning the Future'. PhD thesis, University of Toronto.

Green, P. and Ward, T. (2004) *State Crime: Governments, Violence and Corruption*. London: Pluto Press.

Hague, G. and Malos, E. (1998) *Domestic Violence: Action for Change*. Cheltenham: New Clarion Press.

Hanmer, J. (1978). 'Violence and the Social Control of Women' in G. Littlejohn et al. (eds) *Power and the State*. London: Croom Helm.

Harding, S. (2004) *The Feminist Standpoint Theory Reader*. London: Routledge.

Hillyard, P. et al. (eds) (2004) *Beyond Criminology; Taking Harm Seriously*. London: Pluto Press.

Jackson-Jacobs, C. (2004) 'Taking a Beating: The Narrative Gratification of Fighting as an Underdog' in K. J. Hayward et al. (eds) *Cultural Criminology Unleashed*. London: GlassHouse Press.

Jewkes, Y. (ed.) (2003) *Dot Cons: Crime, Deviance and and Identity on the Internet*. Cullompton: Willan.

Katz, J. (1990) *The Seduction of Crime: The Moral and Sensual Attractions of Doing Evil*. New York: Basic Books.

Keith, B. (2006) *Report of the Zahid Mubarek Inquiry*, Vol.1. London: The Stationery Office.

Lemert, E. (1951) *Social Pathology*. New York: McGraw-Hill.

Lemert, E. (1967) *Human Deviance, Social Problems and Social Control*. Englewood Cliffs, NJ: Prentice Hall.

LSE and the Guardian (2011*) Reading the Riots: Investigating England's Summer of Disorder*. London: The Guardian.

Macpherson, W. (1999) The Stephen Lawrence Inquiry, Cm 4262-1. London: The Stationery Office.

Mawby, R. I. and Gill, M. L. (1987) *Crime Victims: Needs, Services and the Voluntary Sector*. London: Tavistock.

Mead, G. (1934) *Mind, Self and Society*. Chicago, IL: University of Chicago Press.

Muncie, J. (2015) *Youth and Crime* (4th edn). London: Sage.

O'Brien, M. (2005) 'What is Cultural about Cultural Criminology?'. *British Journal of Criminology* 45: 599–612.

Pain, R. (1991) 'Space, Sexual Violence and Social Control: Integrating Geographical and Feminist Analyses of Women's Fear of Crime'. *Progress in Human Geography* 15(4): 415–31.

Potter, H. (2013) 'Intersectional Criminology: Interrogating Identity and Power in Criminological Research and Theory'. *Critical Criminology* 21: 305–18.

Potter, H. (2015) *Intersectionality and Criminology: Disrupting and Revolutionizing Studies of Crime*. London: Routledge.

Presdee, M. (2000) *Cultural Criminology and the Carnival of Crime*. London: Routledge.

Prison Reform Trust and INQUEST (2012) *Fatally Flawed: Has the State Learned Lessons from the Deaths of Children and Young People in Prison?* London: Prison Reform Trust.

Quinney, R. (1974) *Critique of Legal Order*. Boston, MA: Little, Brown.

Radzinowicz, L. (1999) *Adventures in Criminology*. London: Routledge.

Ross, I. and Richards, S. (2003) *Convict Criminology*. Belmont, CA: Wadsworth.

Schur, E. (1973) *Radical Non-Intervention: Re-thinking the Delinquency Problem*. Englewood Cliffs, NJ: Prentice Hall.

Smart, C. and Smart, B. (1978) *Women, Sexuality and Social Control*. London: Routledge & Kegan Paul.

Stanko, E. A. (1985) *Intimate Intrusions: Women's Experience of Male Violence*. London: Routledge & Kegan Paul.

Taylor, I., Walton, P., and Young, J. (2013 [1973]) *The New Criminology; For a Social Theory of Deviance* (40th anniversary edn). London: Routledge.

Tombs, S. and Whyte, D. (2003) *Unmasking The Crimes of The Powerful: Scrutinizing States and Corporations*. New York: Peter Lang.

Tombs, S. and Whyte, D. (2007) *Safety Crimes*. Cullompton: Willan.

Viding, E. et al. (2005) 'Evidence for Substantial Genetic Risk for Psychopathy in 7-year olds'. *Journal of Child Psychology and Psychiatry* 46: 592–7.

Welsh, K. (2008) 'Current Policy on Domestic Violence: A Move in the Right Direction or a Step Too Far?'. *Crime Prevention and Community Safety* 10: 226–48.

Williams, K. S. (2010) 'State Crime' in F. Brookman et al. (eds) *Handbook on Crime*. Cullompton: Willan.

Williams, K. S. (2013) 'Punishment of Serious Human Rights Violations by Changing Internal Moral Codes'. *Statecrime* 2(2): 173–95.

Williams, K. S. (2015) 'Victims and the Voluntary Sector: A Torrid Affair' in A. Hucklesby and M. Corcoran (eds) *The Voluntary Sector and Criminal Justice*. London: Palgrave Macmillan.
Young, J. (1999) *The Exclusive Society: Social Exclusion, Crime and Difference in Late Modernity*. Thousand Oaks, CA: Sage.
Young, J. (2011) *The Criminological Imagination*. Cambridge: Polity Press.
Zahid Mubarek Report (2006) *Report of the Zahid Mubarek Inquiry Chaired by The Honourable Mr Justice Keith*. London: The Stationery Office.

Chapter 19

Boukli, A. (2019) *Zemiology and Human Trafficking*. London: Routledge.
Box, S. (1983) *Power, Crime and Mystification*. London: Tavistock. Republished in 2003 by Taylor Francis.
Christie, N. (1977) 'Conflicts as Property'. *British Journal of Criminology* 17(1): 1–15.
Christie, N. (2000) *Crime Control as Industry: Towards Gulags, Western Style* (3rd edn). New York: Routledge.
Copson, L. (2016) 'Realistic Utopianism and Alternatives to Imprisonment: The Ideology of Crime and the Utopia of Harm'. *Justice, Power and Resistance*, Foundation Issue: 73–96.
Copson, L. (2018) 'Beyond "Criminology vs. Zemiology": Reconciling crime with social harm' in A. Boukli and J. Kotze (eds) *Zemiology: Reconnecting Crime and Social Harm*. London: Palgrave Macmillan.
Feeley, M. (2014) *Learning Care Lessons: Literacy, Love, Care and Solidarity*. London: Tufnell Press.
Freudenberg, N. (2016) *Lethal But Legal: Corporations, Consumption, and Protecting Public Health*. New York: Oxford University Press.
Goldson, B. and Jamieson, J. (2002) 'Community Bail or Penal Remand? A Critical Analysis of Recent Policy Developments in Relation to Unconvicted and/or Unsentenced Juveniles'. *British Journal of Community Justice* 1(2): 63–76.
Hall, S. et al. (1978) *Policing the Crisis: Mugging, the State, and Law and Order*. Basingstoke: Macmillan.
Hartjen, C. A. (1978) *Crime and Criminalization* (2nd edn). Westport, CT: Praeger.
Hillyard, P. and Tombs, S. (2017) 'Social Harm and Zemiology' in A. Liebling, S. Maruna, and L. McAra (eds) *The Oxford Handbook of Criminology* (6th edn). Oxford: Oxford University Press.
Hillyard, P. et al. (eds) (2004) *Beyond Criminology: Taking Harm Seriously*. London: Pluto Press.
Hughes, G. (2006) 'Book Review: Paddy Hillyard, Christina Pantazis, Steve Tombs and David Gordon (eds), *Beyond Criminology: Taking Harm Seriously*'. *Social & Legal Studies* 15(1): 157–9.
Hughes, G. and Langham, M. (2001) 'Good or bad business: Exploring Corporate and Organized Crime' in J. Muncie and E. Mclaughlin (eds) *The Problem of Crime*. London: Sage.
Hulsman, L. (1986) 'Critical criminology and the concept of crime' in H. Bianchi and R. van Swaaningen (eds) *Abolitionism. Towards a Non-Repressive Approach to Crime*. Amsterdam: Free University Press.
Jacobson, J. et al. (2010) *Punishing disadvantage: a profile of children in custody*. London: Prison Reform Trust.
Ministry of Justice (2013) *Transforming Youth Custody: Putting education at the heart of detention*. London: Ministry of Justice.
Ministry of Justice (2018) 'Proven Reoffending Statistics Quarterly Bulletin', October 2016 to December 2016.
Muncie, J. (1996) 'The Construction and Deconstruction of Crime' in J. Muncie and E. McLaughlin (eds) *The Problem of Crime*. London: Sage.
Jacobson, J. et al. (2010) *Punishing disadvantage: a profile of children in custody*. London: Prison Reform Trust.
Pantazis, C. (2016) 'Foreword' in S. Pemberton, *Harmful Societies*. Bristol: Policy Press.
Pemberton, S. A. (2016) *Harmful Societies*. Bristol: Bristol University Press.
Presser, L. (2013) *Why We Harm*. New Brunswick, NJ: Rutgers University Press.
Scraton, P. (ed.) (2002) *Beyond September 11: An Anthology of Dissent*. London: Pluto Press.
Scraton, P. and Chadwick, K. (1991) 'The theoretical and political priorities of critical criminology' in K. Stenson and D. Cowell (eds) *The Politics of Crime Control*. London: Sage.
Soliman, F. (2019) 'States of Exception, Human Rights, and Social Harm: Towards a Border Zemiology'. *Theoretical Criminology* online, available at: https://doi.org/10.1177/1362480619890069.
Spitzer, S. (1975) 'Toward a Marxian Theory of Deviance'. *Social Problems* 22: 638–51.
Stanley, E. (2002) 'An Attack on Truth?' in P. Scraton (ed.) *Beyond September 11: An Anthology of Dissent*. London: Pluto Press.
Sutherland, E. ([1949] 1983) *White Collar Crime: The Uncut Version*. New Haven, CT: Yale University Press.
Taylor, P., Walton, I., and Young, J. (1973) *The New Criminology: For a Social Theory of Deviance*. London: Routledge & Kegan Paul.
Tombs, S. (2016) 'Social harm' in K. Corteen et al. (eds) *A Companion to Crime, Harm & Victimisation*. Bristol: Policy Press.
Tombs, S. (2019) 'Grenfell: the unfolding dimensions of social harm'. *Justice, Power and Resistance* 3(1). Open Research Online.
Tombs, S. and Whyte, D. (2015) *The Corporate Criminal: Why Corporations Must Be Abolished*. Abingdon: Routledge.
Walmsley, R. (2018) *World Prison Population List* (12th edn). World Prison Brief, Institute for Criminal Policy Research (ICPR) at Birkbeck, University of London.
Watkins, J. et al. (2017) 'Effects of health and social care spending constraints on mortality in England: a time trend analysis', *BMJ Open*. DOI: 10.1136/bmjopen-2017-017722.
Whyte, D. (2002) 'Business as Usual? Corporate Moralism and the "War Against Terrorism"' in P. Scraton (ed.) *Beyond September 11: An Anthology of Dissent*. London: Pluto Press.
Yar, M. (2012a) 'Critical Criminology, Critical Theory and Social Harm' in S. Hall and S. Winlow (eds) *New Directions in Criminological Theory*. London: Routledge.
Yar, M. (2012b) 'Recognition as the Grounds for a General Theory of Crime a Social Harm?' in S. O'Neill and N. Smith (eds) *Recognition Theory as Social Research: Investigating the Dynamics of Social Conflict*. Basingstoke: Palgrave Macmillan.

Chapter 20

Bottoms, A. (2012) 'Developing Socio-Spatial Criminology' in M. Maguire, R. Morgan, and R. Reiner (eds) *The Oxford Handbook of Criminology* (5th edn). Oxford: Oxford University Press.
Bullen, E. and Kenway, J. (2004) 'Subcultural Capital and the Female "Underclass"? A Feminist Response to an Underclass Discourse'. *Journal of Youth Studies* 7(2): 141–53.
Campbell, A. (1981) *Girl Delinquents*. London: Wiley-Blackwell.
Crawford, A. et al. (1990) *Second Islington Crime Survey*. Hendon: Middlesex Polytechnic.
DeKeseredy, W. (2016) 'Contemporary Issues in Left Realism'. *International Journal for Crime, Justice and Social Democracy* 5(3): 12–26.
Delisi, M. (2010) 'James Q. Wilson' in K. Hayward, S. Maruna, and J. Mooney (eds) *Fifty Key Thinkers in Criminology*. London: Routledge.
Downes, D. and Morgan, R. (2012) 'No Turning Back: The Politics of Law and Order into the Millennium' in M. Maguire, R. Morgan, and R. Reiner (eds) *The Oxford Handbook of Criminology* (5th edn). Oxford: Oxford University Press.

Eichengreen, B. (1988) 'Unemployment In Inter-War Britain', Institute for Research on Labor and Employment Working Paper No. 13-88.

Evans, G. and Norris, P. (eds) (1999) *Critical Elections: British Parties and Voters in Long-term Perspective*. London: Sage.

Gamble, A. (1988) *The Free Economy and the Strong State*. Basingstoke: Palgrave Macmillan.

Gilroy, P. and Sim, J. (1987) 'Law, Order and the State of the Left' in P. Scraton (ed.) *Law, Order and the Authoritarian State*. Buckingham: Open University.

Hall, S. and Winlow, S. (2015) *Revitalizing Criminological Theory*. Abingdon: Routledge.

Hayward, K. and Yar, M. (2006) 'The "Chav" Phenomenon: Consumption, Media and the Construction of a New Underclass'. *Crime, Media, Culture* 2(1): 9–28.

Herrnstein, R. and Murray, C. (1994) *The Bell Curve*. New York: Basic Books.

Hobbes, T. (1651 [1969]) *Leviathan*. Menston: Scolar P.

Hughes, G. and Lewis, G. (1988) *Unsettling Welfare: The Reconstruction of Social Policy*. London: Routledge.

Jones, O. (2012) *Chavs: The Demonization of the Working Class*. London: Verso.

Jones, T., Maclean, B., and Young, J. (1986) *The Islington Crime Survey*. Aldershot: Gower.

Kelling, G. and Wilson, J. G. (1982) 'Broken Windows'. *Atlantic Monthly* 249(3): 29–38.

Lambert, M. and Crossley, S. (2017) 'Getting with the (troubled families) programme'. *Social Policy and Society* 16(1): 87–97.

Lea, J. (2016) 'Left Realism: A Radical Criminology for the Current Crisis'. *International Journal for Crime, Justice and Social Democracy* 5(3): 53–65.

Lea, J. and Young, J. (1984) *What is to Be Done About Law and Order?* Harmondsworth: Penguin.

Levitas, R. (2005) *The Inclusive Society? Social Inclusion and New Labour* (2nd edn). London: Macmillan.

MacDonald, R. (ed.) (1997) *Youth, The 'Underclass' and Social Exclusion*. London: Routledge.

Matthews, R. (2014) *Realist Criminology*. Basingstoke: Palgrave Macmillan.

Mayhew, H. (1861) *London Labour and London Poor*, Vol.1. London: Griffin, Bohn.

McLaughlin, J. and Muncie, J. (2013) *Criminological Perspectives: Essential Readings* (3rd edn). London: Sage.

Merton, R. (1957) *Social Theory and Social Structure*. Glencoe: Free Press.

Mooney, J. (2000) *Gender, Violence and the Social Order*. New York: Palgrave.

Muncie, J. (2015) *Youth and Crime* (4th edn). London: Sage.

Murray, C. (1984) *Losing Ground*. New York: Basic Books.

Murray, C. (1990) *The Emerging Underclass*. London: Institute of Economic Affairs.

Murray, C. (1994) *Underclass: The Crisis Deepens*. London: Institute of Economic Affairs.

Newburn, T. (2015) 'The 2011 England Riots in Recent Historical Perspective'. *British Journal of Criminology* 55(1): 39–64.

Platt, T. and Takagi, P. (1977) 'Intellectuals for Law and Order: A Critique of New Realists'. *Crime and Social Justice* 8: 1–16.

Quinney, R. (1977) *Class, State and Crime*. New York: David McKay.

Redhead, S. (2018) *Theoretical Times*. Bingley: Emerald Publishing.

Rodger, J. (2008) 'The Criminalisation of Social Policy'. *Criminal Justice Matters* 74(1): 18–19.

Runciman, W. G. (1966) *Relative Deprivation and Social Justice*. London: Routledge & Kegan Paul.

Social Exclusion Unit (1997) 'Social Exclusion Unit: Purpose, work priorities and working methods: Briefing document'. London: Cabinet Office.

Social Exclusion Unit (2004) *The Social Exclusion Unit*. London: Office of the Deputy Prime Minister.

Taylor, I., Walton, I., and Young, J. (1973) *The New Criminology: For a Social Theory of Deviance*. London: Routledge & Kegan Paul.

Webber, C. (2007) 'Revaluating relative deprivation theory'. *Theoretical Criminology* 11(1): 97–120.

Wilson, J. (1975) *Thinking About Crime*. New York: Vintage.

Wilson, J. and Herrnstein, R. (1985) *Crime and Human Nature*. New York: Simon & Schuster.

Winlow, S. and Hall, S. (2019) 'Shock and Awe: On Progressive Minimalism and Retreatism, and the New Ultra-Realism'. *Critical Criminology* 27(1): 21–36.

Young, J. (1986) 'The Failure of Criminology: The Need for a Radical Realism' in J. Young and R. Matthews (eds) *Confronting Crime*. London: Sage.

Young, J. (1990) 'Asking Questions of Left Realism'. *Critical Criminologist* 2(2): 1–2, 10.

Young, J. (1997) 'Left Realist Criminology; Radical in its analysis, realist in its policy' in M. Maguire, R. Morgan, and R. Reiner (eds) *The Oxford Handbook of Criminology* (2nd edn). Oxford: Oxford University Press.

Young, J. (1999) *The Exclusive Society: Social Exclusion, Crime and Difference in Late Modernity*. London: Sage.

Young, J. (2003) 'Merton with Energy, Katz with Structure: The Sociology of Vindictiveness and the Criminology of Transgression'. *Theoretical Criminology* 7(3): 389–414.

Young, J. (2007) *The Vertigo of Late Modernity*. London: Sage.

Youth Justice Board (2009) *Girls and offending—patterns, perceptions and interventions*. London: Youth Justice Board.

Chapter 21

Agnew, R. (2011) *Towards a Unified Criminology: Integrating Assumptions About Crime*. New York: NYU.

Akers, R. and Sellers, C. (2013) *Criminological Theories: Introduction, Evaluation, Application*. Oxford: Oxford University Press.

Andrews, J. and Bonta, D. (2010) *The Psychology of Criminal Conduct*. Newark, NJ: Matthew Bender.

Arsenault, L. et al. (2002) 'Obstetrical Complications and Violent Delinquency: Testing Two Developmental Pathways'. *Child Development* 73(2): 496–508.

Baker, K. et al. (2005) *Further Development of Asset*. London: Youth Justice Board.

Bateman, T. (2011) 'Punishing Poverty: The Scaled Approach and Youth Justice Practice'. *Howard Journal of Criminal Justice* 50(2): 171–83.

Bates, K., Bader, C., and Mencken, F. (2003) 'Family Structure, Power-Control Theory, and Deviance: Extending Power-Control Theory to Include Ultimate Family Forms'. *Western Criminology Review* 4(3): 170–90.

Beck, U. (1992) *Risk Society: Towards a New Modernity*. London: Sage.

Bernard, T. et al. (2015) *Theoretical Criminology*. Oxford: Oxford University Press.

Boeck, T., Fleming, J., and Kemshall, H. (2006) 'The Context of Risk Decisions: Does Social Capital Make a Difference?'. *Forum: Qualitative Social Research* 7(1): Article 17. Available at: www.qualitative-research.net/fqs-texte/1-06/06-1-17-e.htm [Accessed 4 December 2020].

Brookmeyer, K. A., Fanti, K. A. and Henrich, C. C. (2006) 'Schools, parents and youth violence: A multilevel ecological analysis'. *Journal of Clinical, Child and Adolescent Psychology* 35(4): 504–14.

Cabot, R. (1940) 'A Long-Term Study of Children: The Cambridge-Somerville Youth Study'. *Child Development* 11(2): 143–51.

Case (2018) *Youth Justice: A Critical Introduction*. London: Routledge.

Case, S. (2006) 'Young People "At Risk" of What? Challenging Risk-focused Early Intervention as Crime Prevention'. *Youth Justice* 6(3): 171–9.

Case, S. and Haines, K. (2015) 'Risk Management and Early Intervention' in B. Goldson and J. Muncie (eds) *Youth, Crime and Justice*. London: Sage.

Case, S. P. and Haines, K. R. (2009) *Understanding youth offending: Risk factor research policy and practice*. Cullompton: Willan.

Colvin, M. (2000) *Crime and Coercion: An Integrated Theory of Chronic Criminality*. New York: St Martin's Press.

Downes, D. and Rock, P. (1998) *Understanding Deviance: A Guide to the Sociology of Crime and Rule-Breaking*. Oxford: Oxford University Press.

Elliott, D., Ageton, S., and Canter, J. (1979) 'An Integrated Theoretical Perspective on Delinquent Behavior'. *Journal of Research in Crime and Delinquency* 16: 126–49.

Farrington, D. (2007) 'Childhood Risk Factors and Risk-focused Prevention' in M. Maguire, R. Morgan, and R. Reiner (eds) *The Oxford Handbook of Criminology* (4th edn). Oxford: Oxford University Press.

Farrington, D. P. (2000) 'Explaining and preventing crime: The globalization of knowledge'. *Criminology* 38(1): 1–24.

Farrington, D. P., Kazemian, L., and Piquero, A. (2019) *The Oxford Handbook of Developmental and Life-Course Criminology*. Oxford: Oxford University Press.

Ferrell, J., Hayward, K., and Young, J. (2015) *Cultural Criminology: An Invitation* (2nd edn). London: Sage.

France, A. (2008) 'Risk Factor Analysis and the Youth Question'. *Journal of Youth Studies* 11(1): 1–15.

France, A. and Homel, R. (2007) *Pathways and Crime Prevention: Theory, Policy and Practice*. Cullompton: Willan.

Glueck, S. and Glueck, E. (1930) *500 Criminal Careers*. New York: Alfred Knopf.

Glueck, S. and Glueck, E. (1934) *One Thousand Juvenile Delinquents*. Cambridge: Cambridge University Press.

Gottfredson, M. and Hirschi, T. (1990) *A General Theory of Crime*. Stanford, CT: Stanford University Press.

Hagan, F. (2013) *Introduction to Criminology Theories, Methods and Criminal Behaviour*. Thousand Oaks, CA: Sage.

Haines, K. R. and Case, S. P. (2015) *Positive Youth Justice: Children First, Offenders Second*. Bristol: Policy Press.

Hammersley, R., Marsland, L., and Reid, M. (2003) *Substance Use by Young Offenders: The Impact of the Normalisation of Drug Use in the Early Years of the 21st Century*. Home Office Research Study No. 261. London: Home Office.

Haw, K. (2007) 'Risk Factors and Pathways Into and Out of Crime: Misleading, Misinterpreted or Mythic? From Generative Metaphor to Professional Myth' in J. Hawkins and R. Catalano (eds) *Communities that Care*. San Francisco, CA: Jossey Bass.

Hawkins, J. and Weis, J. (1985) 'The Social Development Model: An Integrated Approach to Delinquency Prevention'. *Journal of Primary Prevention* 6: 73–97.

Hine, J. (2005) 'Early Intervention: The View from On Track'. *Children and Society* 19(2): 117–30.

Hine, J. (2006) 'Young people, pathways and crime: context and complexity', *Pathways into and out of Crime: Taking Stock and Moving Forward: International Symposium*. Leicester, April.

Hine, J. et al. (2007) 'Risk and Resilience in Children who are Offending, Excluded from School or Who Have Behaviour Problems'. Sheffield: PCRRD Group. No longer available online.

Hirschi, T. (1969) *Causes of Delinquency*. Berkeley, CA: University of California Press.

Hopkins Burke, R. (2013) *An Introduction to Criminological Theory* (4th edn). Abingdon: Routledge.

Jeffery, C. (1977) *Crime Prevention through Environmental Design*. Beverly Hills, CA: Sage.

Johnston, J. et al. (2000) *Snakes & Ladders: Young People, Transitions and Social Exclusion*. Bristol: Policy Press.

Kemshall, H. (2008) 'Risk, Rights and Justice: Understanding and Responding to Youth Risk'. *Youth Justice* 8(1): 21–38.

Laub, J. H. and Sampson, R. J. (2003) *Shared beginnings, divergent lives*. Cambridge, MA: Harvard University Press.

Liebling, A., Maruna, S., and McAra, L. (eds) (2017) *The Oxford Handbook of Criminology* (6th edn). Oxford: Oxford University Press.

MacDonald, R. and Marsh, J. (2005) *Disconnected Youth? Growing Up in Britain's Poor Neighbourhoods*. Basingstoke: Palgrave.

McAra, L. and McVie, S. (2007) 'Youth Justice? The Impact of System Contact on Patterns of Desistance from Offending'. *European Journal of Criminology* 4(3): 315–45.

McCord, J. and McCord, W. (1959) 'A Follow-up Report on the Cambridge-Somerville Youth Study'. *Annals of the American Academy of Political and Social Science* 322(1): 89–96.

Mednick, S. (1977) 'A Biosocial Theory of the Learning of Law-abiding Behavior' in S. Mednick and K. Christiansen (eds) *Biosocial Bases of Criminal Behavior*. New York: Gardner.

Mednick, S., Moffitt, T., and Stack, S. (1987) (eds) *The Causes of Crime: New Biological Approaches*. Cambridge: Cambridge University Press.

Mitchell Miller, J. (2009) *Twenty First Century Criminology: A Reference Handbook*. London: Sage.

Moffitt, T. (1993) 'Adolescence-Limited and Life-Course-Persistent Antisocial Behavior: A Developmental Taxonomy'. *Psychological Review* 100: 674–701.

Muncie, J. (2009) *Youth and Crime*. London: Sage.

Nye, F. (1958) *Family Relationships and Delinquent Behavior*. New York: Wiley.

Pawson, R. and Tilley, N. (2004) *Realistic Evaluation*. London: Sage.

Paylor, I. (2011) 'Youth Justice in England and Wales: A Risky Business'. *Journal of Offender Rehabilitation* 50(4): 221–33.

Rafter, N. (2008) *The Criminal Brain. Understanding Biological Theories of Crime*. New York: NYU Press.

Raine, A., Brennan, P., and Mednick, S. (1997) 'Interaction between Birth Complications and Early Maternal Rejection in Predisposing Individuals to Adult Violence: Specificity to Serious, Early-Onset Violence'. *American Journal of Psychiatry* 154(9): 1265–71.

Reiss, A. (1951) 'Delinquency as the Failure of Personal and Social Control'. *American Sociological Review* 16: 213–59.

Sampson, R. and Laub, J. (1993) *Crime in the Making: Pathways and Turning Points through Life*. Cambridge, MA: Harvard University Press.

Sampson, R., Raudenbush, S., and Earls, F. (1997) 'Neighborhoods and Violent Crime: A Multilevel Study of Collective Efficacy'. *Science* 15: 918–24.

Shaw, D. et al. (2003) 'Trajectories Leading to School-Age Conduct Problems'. *Developmental Psychology* 58: 480–91.

Smith, D. and McAra, L. (2004) 'Gender and Youth Offending', *Edinburgh Study of Youth Transitions and Crime Research Digest No. 2*. Edinburgh: Edinburgh University.

Smith, D. and McVie, S. (2003) 'Theory and Method in the Edinburgh Study of Youth Transitions and Crime'. *British Journal of Criminology* 43(1): 169–95.

Stephenson, M., Giller, H., and Brown, S. (2011) *Effective Practice in Youth Justice*. London: Routledge.

Tashakkori, A. and Teddlie, T. (1998) *Mixed Methodology: Combining Qualitative and Quantitative Approaches*. Thousand Oaks, CA: Sage.

Taylor, I., Walton, I., and Young, J. (1973) *The New Criminology: For a Social Theory of Deviance*. London: Routledge & Kegan Paul.

Tittle, C. (2000) 'Control Balance' in R. Paternoster and R. Bachman (eds) *Explaining Criminals and Crime: Essays in Contemporary Theory*. Los Angeles: Roxbury.

Ugwudike, P. (2015) *An Introduction to Critical Criminology*. Bristol: Policy Press.

Unnever, J. D., Cullen, F. T., and Agnew, R. (2006) 'Why is "bad" parenting criminogenic?'. *Youth Violence and Juvenile Justice* 4(1): 3–33.

Vold, G., Bernard, T., and Snipes, J. (2002) *Theoretical Criminology*. Oxford: Oxford University Press.

Walker, J. and McCarthy, P. (2005) 'Parents in Prison: The Impact on Children' in G. Preston (ed.) *At Greatest Risk: The Children Most Likely to be Poor*. London: Child Poverty Action Group.

Walton, I. and Young, J. (1998) *The New Criminology Revisited*. London: Macmillan.

Webster, C. et al. (2004) *Poor Transitions: Social Exclusion and Young Adults*. Bristol: Policy Press.

West, D. and Farrington, D. (1973) *Who Becomes Delinquent?* London: Heinemann.

Wikstrom, T. and Loeber, R. (1998) 'Individual Risk Factors, Neighbourhood SES and Juvenile Offending' in M. Tonry (ed.) *The Handbook of Crime and Punishment*. New York: Oxford University Press.

Williams, K. (2012) *Textbook on Criminology*. Oxford: Oxford University Press.

Wilson, J. and Herrnstein, R. (1985) *Crime and Human Nature*. New York: Simon & Schuster.

Winters, R., Globokar, J., and Roberson, C. (2014) *An Introduction to Crime Causation*. Boca Raton, FL: CRC Press.

Younge, S., Oetting, E., and Deffenbacher, J. (1996) 'Correlations Among Maternal Rejection, Dropping Out of School, and Drug Use in Adolescents'. *Journal of Clinical Psychology* 52(1): 96–102.

Chapter 22

Applied Research in Community Safety (2008) *Reviewing the Effectiveness of Community Safety Policy and Practice—An Overview of Current Debates and their Background*. Montreal: International Centre for the Prevention of Crime.

Bateman, T. (2011) 'Punishing Poverty: The Scaled Approach and Youth Justice Practice'. *Howard Journal of Criminal Justice* 50(2): 171–83.

Blamey, A. and MacKenzie, M. (2007) 'Theories of Change and Realistic Evaluation. Peas in a Pod or Apples and Oranges?'. *Evaluation* 13(4): 439–55.

Braithwaite, J. (1993) 'Beyond positivism'. *Journal of Research in Crime and Delinquency* 30(4): 383–99.

Bryman, A. (2021) *Social Research Methods* (6th edn). Oxford: Oxford University Press.

Case, S. (2007) 'Questioning the "Evidence" of Risk that Underpins Evidence-Led Youth Justice Interventions'. *Youth Justice* 7(2): 91–106.

Case, S. (2015) 'Criminology as a Social Science: How Does Criminology "Know" About Crime?' in K. Vaidya (ed.) *Criminology and Criminal Justice for the Curious: Why Study Criminology and Criminal Justice?* New York: Curious Academic Publishing.

Case, S. and Haines, K. (2009) *Understanding Youth Offending: Risk Factor Research, Policy and Practice*. Abingdon: Routledge.

Case, S. and Haines, K. (2014) 'Reflective Friend Research: The Relational Aspects of Social Scientific Research' in K. Lumsden (ed.) *Reflexivity in Criminological Research*. Basingstoke: Palgrave.

Connell, J. et al. (1995) *Approaches to Evaluating Community Initiatives: Concepts, Methods and Contexts*. Washington, DC: Aspen Institute.

Cook, T. and Campbell, D. (1979) *Quasi-Experimentation. Design & Analysis Issue for Field Settings*. New York: Houghton Mifflin.

Elliott, E. and Kiel, D. (2000) *Nonlinear Dynamics, Complexity and Public Policy*. Commack, NY: Nova Science Publishers.

Farrington, D. (2000) 'Explaining and Preventing Crime: The Globalization of Knowledge'. *Criminology* 38(1): 1–24.

Farrington, D. (2003) 'A Short History of Randomized Experiments in Criminology: A Meagre Feast'. *Evaluation Review* 27: 218–27.

Farrington, D. (2007) 'Childhood Risk Factors and Risk-Focused Prevention' in M. Maguire, R. Morgan, and R. Reiner (eds) *The Oxford Handbook of Criminology* (4th edn). Oxford: Oxford University Press.

Fisher, R. and Geiselman, R. (1992) *Memory Enhancing Techniques for Investigative Interviewing: The Cognitive Interview*. Springfield, IL: Charles C. Thomas.

France, A. and Homel, R. (2007) *Pathways and Crime Prevention. Theory, Policy and Practice*. Cullompton: Willan.

Freedman, D. et al. (eds) (2010) *Statistical Models and Causal Inference: A Dialogue with the Social Sciences*. Cambridge: Cambridge University Press.

Gates, A. et al. (2018) 'Evaluation of the reliability, usability and applicability of AMSTAR, A2 and ROBIS'. *Systematic Reviews* 7: 85.

Gleick, J. (1997) *Chaos: Making a New Science*. London: Vintage.

Goldson, B. and Hughes, G. (2010) 'Sociological Criminology and Youth Justice: Comparative Policy Analysis and Academic Intervention'. *Criminology and Criminal Justice* 10(2): 211–30.

Hope, T. (2005) 'Pretend it Doesn't Work: The "Anti-Social" Bias in the Maryland Scientific Methods Scale'. *European Journal on Criminal Policy and Research* 11(3–4): 275–96.

Hope, T. (2009) 'The Illusion of Control: A Response to Professor Sherman'. *Criminology and Criminal Justice* 9(2): 125–34.

Hopkins Burke, R. (2018) *An Introduction to Criminological Theory*. Abingdon: Routledge.

Hughes, G. and Edwards, A. (2005) 'Comparing the Governance of Safety in Europe: A Geo-Historical Approach'. *Theoretical Criminology* 9(3): 345–63.

Jones, S. (2013) *Criminology*. Oxford: Oxford University Press.

Kemshall, H. (2008) 'Rights, Risk and Justice: Understanding and Responding to Youth Risk'. *Youth Justice* 8(1): 21–38.

Kubisch, A., Fulbright-Anderson, K., and Connell, J. (1998) *New Approaches to Evaluating Community Initiatives: Theory, Measurement and Analysis*. Washington, DC: Aspen Institute.

Liebling, A., Maruna, S., and McAra, L. (eds) (2017) *The Oxford Handbook of Criminology* (6th edn). Oxford: Oxford University Press.

Lorenz, E. (1963) 'Deterministic Nonperiodic Flow'. *Journal of the Atmospheric Sciences* 20: 130–41.

MacDonald, R. and Marsh, J. (2005) *Disconnected Youth? Growing Up in Britain's Poor Neighbourhoods*. Basingstoke: Palgrave.

Mandelbrot, B. (1967) 'How Long Is the Coast of Britain? Statistical Self-Similarity and Fractional Dimension'. *Science* 156(3775): 636–8.

Mandelbrot, B. (1982) *The Fractal Geometry of Nature*. San Francisco, CA: W. H. Freeman and Co.

Mandelbrot, B. (2004) 'A Theory of Roughness', *Edge*. Available at: www.edge.org/conversation/benoit_mandelbrot-a-theory-of-roughness [Accessed 4 December 2020].

McGrayne, S. (2011) *The Theory that Would Not Die*. New Haven, CT: Yale University Press.

Mears, D. and Cochran, J. (2019) *Fundamentals of Criminological and Criminal Justice Inquiry*. Cambridge: Cambridge University Press.

O'Shea, B. (2017) 'AMSTAR-2: A critical appraisal tool'. *BMJ Nutrition, Prevention and Health 2017*: 358.

Pawson, R. and Tilley, N. (1998) *Realistic Evaluation*. London: Sage.

Pawson, R. and Tilley, N. (2004) 'Realistic Evaluation' in S. Matthieson (ed.) *Encyclopaedia of Evaluation*. Newbury Park, CA: Sage.

Pawson, R. and Tilley, N. (2009) 'Realist Evaluation' in H. U. Otto, A. Polutta, and H. Ziegler (eds) *Evidence-based Practice—Modernising the Knowledge Base of Social Work?* Leverkusen: Barbara Budrich.

Pitts, J. (2003) *The New Politics of Youth Crime: Discipline or Solidarity?* Lyme Regis: Russell House.

Pycroft, A. and Bartollas, C. (2014) *Applying Complexity Theory. Whole Systems Approaches to Criminal Justice and Social Work.* Bristol: Policy Press.

Reddon, H., Kerr, T., and Milloy, M. (2020) 'Ranking evidence in substance use and addiction'. *International Journal Of Drug Policy* 83: 1–7.

Robson, C. (2015) *Real World Research: A Resource for Social Scientists and Practitioner-Researchers*. Oxford: Blackwell.

Sherman, L. (2009) 'Evidence and Liberty: The promise of experimental criminology'. *Criminology and Criminal Justice* 9(1): 5–28.

Sherman, L. and Strang, H. (2004) 'Verdicts or Inventions? Interpreting Results from Randomized Controlled Experiments in Criminology'. *American Behavioral Scientist* 47(5): 575–607.

Sherman, L. et al. (1998) *Preventing Crime: What Works, What Doesn't, What's Promising*. Baltimore, MD: Department of Criminology and Criminal Justice, University of Maryland.

Smith, D. and McVie, S. (2003) 'Theory and Method in the Edinburgh Study of Youth Transitions and Crime'. *British Journal of Criminology* 43(1): 169–95.

Tilley, N. (2009) 'Sherman versus Sherman—Realism and Rhetoric'. *Criminology and Criminal Justice* 9(2): 135–44.

Weisburd, D., Farrington, D., and Gill, C (2017) 'What works in crime prevention and rehabilitation'. *Criminology and Public Policy* 16(2): 415–49.

Weiss, C. (1995) 'Nothing as Practical as Good Theory: Exploring Theory-Based Evaluation for Comprehensive Community Initiatives for Children and Families' in J. Connell et al. (eds) *Approaches to Evaluating Community Initiatives: Concepts, Methods and Contexts*. Washington, DC: Aspen Institute.

Williams, M. (2006) 'Empiricism' in V. Jupp (ed.) *The Sage Dictionary of Social Research Methods*. London: Sage.

Young, J. (2011) *The Criminological Imagination*. London: Polity.

Young, T. (1991) 'Chaos and Social Change: Metaphysics of the Postmodern'. *The Social Science Journal* 28(3): 289–305.

Youth Justice Board (2017) *Prevention in youth justice*. London: YJB.

Ziliak, S. and McCloskey, D. (2007) *The Cult of Statistical Significance: How the Standard Error Cost Us Jobs, Justice, and Lives*. Ann Arbor, MI: The University of Michigan Press.

Chapter 23

Advisory Council on the Penal System (1970) *Non-Custodial and Semi-Custodial Penalties*. London: HMSO.

Anon. (2020) *The Secret Barrister, Fake Law: The Truth About Justice in an Age of Lies*. London: Picador.

Ashworth, A. (2003) 'Is Restorative Justice the Way Forward for Criminal Justice?' in E. McLaughlin, R. Ferguson, and L. Westmarland (eds) *Restorative Justice: Critical Issues*. London: Sage.

Ashworth, A. and Blake, M. (1996) 'The Presumption of Innocence in English Criminal Law'. *Criminal Law Review* 306.

Bentham, J. (1843) *Benthamiana, or Select Extracts from the Works of Jeremy Bentham*. Edinburgh: William Tait.

Bingham, T. (2010) *The Rule of Law*. London: Allen Lane.

Blackstone, W. (1769) *Commentaries on the Laws of England 1765–9*, Project Gutenberg, available at: www.gutenberg.org/ebooks/30802.

Cape, E. (2010) 'Adversarialism "Lite": Developments in Criminal Procedure and Evidence under New Labour'. *Criminal Justice Matters* 79(1): 25–7.

Costello, D. (2018) 'Un-Making a Murderer: New True Crime Sensationalism and the Criminal Justice System'. *American Criminal Law Review Online* 55: 77–101.

De Montesquieu, C. (1989 [1748]) *The Spirit of the Laws*, English translation. Cambridge: Cambridge University Press.

Dennis, I. (2014) 'Quashing Acquittals: Applying the "New and Compelling Evidence" Exception to Double Jeopardy'. *Criminal Law Review* 4: 247–60.

Garland, D. (2001) *The Culture of Control*. Oxford: Oxford University Press.

Garvey, S. (2011) 'Alternatives to Punishment' in J. Deigh and D. Dolinko (eds) *The Oxford Handbook of Philosophy of Criminal Law*. Oxford: Oxford University Press.

Gross, S. R., (2017). 'What We Think, What We Know and What We Think We Know about False Convictions'. *Ohio State Journal of Criminal Law* 14(2): 753–86.

Home Office (2005a) 'Visible Unpaid Work', Ref. 66/2005. London: Home Office.

Hood, R. (1974) 'Criminology and Penal Change: A Case Study of the Nature and Impact of Some Recent Advice to Governments' in R. Hood (ed.) *Crime, Criminology and Public Policy: Essays in Honour of Sir Leon Radzinowicz*. London: Heinemann.

Hunt, M., Hooper, H., and Yowell, H. (eds) (2015) *Parliaments and Human Rights: Redressing the Democratic Deficit*. Oxford: Bloomsbury.

Lacey, N. (2003) 'Principles, Politics and Criminal Justice' in L. Zedner and A. Ashworth (eds) *The Criminological Foundations of Penal Policy: Essays in Honour of Roger Hood*. Oxford: Oxford University Press.

Lammy, D. (2017) *The Lammy Review: An independent review into the treatment of, and the outcomes for, Black, Asian and Minority Ethnic individuals in the criminal justice system*. London: Ministry of Justice.

Law Commission (2001) *Double Jeopardy and Prosecution Appeals*, LC267. London: Law Commission.

Marshall, T. (1999) *Restorative Justice: An Overview*. London: Home Office.

Martinson, R. (1974) 'What Works? Questions and Answers about Prison Reform'. *Public Interest* 35: 22–54.

McGlynn, C. (2017) 'Rape Trials and Sexual History Evidence: Reforming the Law on Third-Party Evidence'. *Journal of Criminal Law* 81(5): 367–92.

O'Brien, P. (2013) 'When Judges Misbehave: The Strange Case of Jonah Barrington', *UK Constitutional Law Blog*, available at: http://ukconstitutionallaw.org.

Packer, H. (1964) 'Two Models of the Criminal Process'. *University of Pennsylvania Law Review* 113(1): 1–68.

Roberts, P. (2002) 'Double Jeopardy Law Reform: A Criminal Justice Commentary'. *Modern Law Review* 65(3): 393–424.

Sharpe, S. (2004) 'How Large Should the Restorative Justice "Tent" Be?' in H. Zehr and B. Toews (eds) *Critical Issues in Restorative Justice*. New York: Criminal Justice Press.

Thomas, D. (1998) *Victorian Underworld*. London: John Murray.

Tyler, T. (2017) 'Procedural Justice and Policing: A Rush to Judgment?'. *Annual Review of Law and Social Science* 13(1): 29–53.

Umbreit, M. and Zehr, H. (1982) 'Victim Offender Reconciliation: An Incarceration Substitute'. *Federal Probation* 46: 63–8.

Wagner, A. (2012) 'Witness Statement to the Leveson Inquiry into the Culture, Practice and Ethics of the Press'. Available at: https://webarchive.nationalarchives.gov.uk/20140122163400/http://www.levesoninquiry.org.uk/evidence/?witness=adam-wagner.

Willis, R. (2020) '"Let's talk about it": Why social class matters to restorative justice'. *Criminology & Criminal Justice* 20(2): 187–206.

Wood, W. R. (2015) 'Why Restorative Justice Will Not Reduce Incarceration'. *British Journal of Criminology* 55(5): 883–900.

Chapter 24

Anon. (2018) *The Secret Barrister: Stories of the Law and How It's Broken*. London: Macmillan.

Beattie, J. M. (2012) *The First English Detectives: The Bow Street Runners and the Policing of London, 1750–1840*. Oxford: Oxford University Press.

Bosworth, M. (2014) *Inside Immigration Detention*. Oxford: Oxford University Press.

Bosworth, M. (2019) 'Immigration Detention, Punishment and the Transformation of Justice'. *Social & Legal Studies* 28(1): 81–99.

Bottoms, A. (2017) 'Punishment' in Non-Custodial Sentences: A Critical Analysis'. *Criminal Law Forum* 28(3): 563–87.

Brennan Center for Justice (2016) 'The History of Mass Incarceration'. Available at: www.brennancenter.org/our-work/analysis-opinion/history-mass-incarceration.

Brown, M. and Schept, J. (2017) 'New abolition, criminology and a critical carceral studies'. *Punishment & Society* 19(4): 440–62.

Button, M. (2020) 'The "New" Private Security Industry, the Private Policing of Cyberspace and the Regulatory Questions'. *Journal of Contemporary Criminal Justice* 36(1): 39–55.

Carr, N. (2020) 'Recruitment, training and professional development of probation staff, HM Inspectorate of Probation, Academic Insights 2020/02. Available at: www.justiceinspectorates.gov.uk/hmiprobation/wp-content/uploads/sites/5/2020/02/Academic-Insights-Carr-Final.pdf.

Carr, N. and Robinson, G. (2020) 'A legitimate business? Representations of privatised probation in England and Wales'. *Crime, Media, Culture* 1–20.

Chamberlen, A., and Carvalho, H. (2019) 'The Thrill of the Chase: Punishment, Hostility and the Prison Crisis'. *Social & Legal Studies* 28(1): 100–17.

Crewe, B., Hulley, S., and Wright, S. (2020) *Life Imprisonment from Young Adulthood: Adaptation, Identity and Time*. London: Palgrave Macmillan.

Crewe, B. and Liebling, A. (2017) 'Reconfiguring Penal Power' in A. Liebling, S. Maruna and L. McAra (eds) *The Oxford Handbook of Criminology* (6th edn). Oxford: Oxford University Press.

Criminal Justice Joint Inspection (2017) 'Making it Fair: The Disclosure of Unused Material in Volume Crown Court Cases'. Available at: www.justiceinspectorates.gov.uk/hmicfrs/publications/making-it-fair-disclosure-of-unused-material-in-crown-court-cases.

Crown Prosecution Service (2016) 'Annual Report and Accounts 2015–16'. Available at: https://www.cps.gov.uk/publications/docs/annual_report_2015_16.pdf.

Crown Prosecution Service (2018) 'Annual Report and Accounts'. Available at: www.cps.gov.uk/sites/default/files/documents/publications/CPS-Annual-Report-2017-18.pdf.

Crown Prosecution Service (2020) 'Annual Report and Accounts 2019–20'. Available at: www.cps.gov.uk/sites/default/files/documents/publications/CPS-Annual-Report-and-Accounts-2019-20.pdf.

Davis, A. and Barsamian, D. (1999) *The Prison Industrial Complex*. Oakland, CA: Ak Press.

Ellison, G. (2013) 'Policing: Context and Practice' in A. Hucklesby and A. Wahidin (eds) *Criminal Justice*. Oxford: Oxford University Press.

HM Crown Prosecution Service Inspectorate (2017) 'Business as Usual? Transforming Summary Justice Follow-up Report'. Available at: www.justiceinspectorates.gov.uk/hmcpsi/inspections/business-as-usual-transforming-summary-justice-follow-up-report.

HM Crown Prosecution Service Inspectorate (2018) 'Annual Report 2017–2018'. Available at: www.justiceinspectorates.gov.uk/hmcpsi/inspections/hmcpsi-chief-inspectors-annual-report-2017-18.

HM Inspectorate of Constabulary and Fire & Rescue Services (2019) 'Public Perceptions of Policing in England and Wales 2018'. Available at: www.bmgresearch.co.uk/wp-content/uploads/2019/01/1578-HMICFRS-Public-Perceptions-of-Policing-2018_FINAL.pdf.

HM Inspectorate of Probation (2020) 'An inspection of central functions supporting the National Probation Service'. Available at: www.justiceinspectorates.gov.uk/hmiprobation/wp-content/uploads/sites/5/2020/01/NPS-central-functions-inspection-report-1.pdf.

HM Prison and Probation Service (2020) 'COVID-19 Official Statistics, Data to 7 August 2020'. Available at: https://assets.publishing.service.gov.uk/government/uploads/system/uploads/attachment_data/file/909207/HMPPS_COVID19_WE_07082020_Pub_Doc.pdf.

Home Office (2019) 'Police Workforce, England and Wales, 31 March 2019'. Available at: https://assets.publishing.service.gov.uk/government/uploads/system/uploads/attachment_data/file/831726/police-workforce-mar19-hosb1119.pdf.

Hough, M. and Roberts, J. (2017) 'Public Opinion, Crime and Criminal Justice' in A. Liebling, S. Maruna, and L. McAra (eds) *The Oxford Handbook of Criminology* (6th edn). Oxford: Oxford University Press.

House of Commons Committee of Public Accounts (2019) 'Transforming rehabilitation: progress review, Ninety-Fourth Report of Session 2017–19'. Available at: https://publications.parliament.uk/pa/cm201719/cmselect/cmpubacc/1747/1747.pdf.

House of Commons Health and Social Care Committee (2018) 'Prison health, Twelfth Report of Session 2017–19'. Available at: https://publications.parliament.uk/pa/cm201719/cmselect/cmhealth/963/963.pdf.

House of Commons Home Affairs Committee (2018). Policing for the future, Tenth Report of Session 2017–19'. Available at: https://publications.parliament.uk/pa/cm201719/cmselect/cmhaff/515/515.pdf.

House of Commons Library (2019) 'The Prison Estate', Briefing Paper No. 05646. Available at: https://commonslibrary.parliament.uk/research-briefings/sn05646

Institute for Government (2019) 'Performance Tracker 2019'. Available at: www.instituteforgovernment.org.uk/publications/performance-tracker-2019.

Institute for Government (2020) 'The criminal justice system: How government reforms and coronavirus will affect policing, courts and prisons'. Available at: www.instituteforgovernment.org.uk/sites/default/files/publications/criminal-justice-system_0.pdf.

Johnston, H. (2016) 'Prison Histories, 1770s–1950s: Continuities and contradictions' in Y. Jewkes, B. Crewe, and J. Bennett (eds) *Handbook on Prisons* (2nd edn). Abingdon: Routledge.

Jones, T., Newburn, T., and Reiner, R. (2017) 'Policing and the Police' in A. Liebling, S. Maruna, and L. McAra (eds) *The Oxford Handbook of Criminology* (6th edn). Oxford: Oxford University Press.

Justice Committee (2009) 'The Crown Prosecution Service: Gatekeeper of the Criminal Justice System, Ninth Report of Session 2008–09'. Available at: https://publications.parliament.uk/pa/cm200809/cmselect/cmjust/186/186.pdf.

Keay, S. and Kirby, S. (2018) 'The Evolution of the Police Analyst and the Influence of Evidence-Based Policing'. *Policing: A Journal of Policy and Practice* 12(3): 265–76.

Ludlow, A. (2017) 'Marketizing Criminal Justice' in A. Liebling, S. Maruna, and L. McAra (eds) *The Oxford Handbook of Criminology* (6th edn). Oxford: Oxford University Press.

McNeill, F. (2019) *Pervasive Punishment: Making Sense of Mass Supervision*. Bingley: Emerald.

Ministry of Justice (2016) 'The Story of the Prison Population 1993–2016'. Available at: www.gov.uk/government/statistics/story-of-the-prison-population-1993-to-2016.

Ministry of Justice (2018) 'Prisons reform speech'. Available at: www.gov.uk/government/speeches/prisons-reform-speech.

Ministry of Justice (2019) 'Her Majesty's Prison and Probation Service. Offender Equalities Annual Report 2018/2019'. Available at: www.gov.uk/government/statistics/hm-prison-and-probation-serviceoffender-equalities-annual-report-2018-to-2019.

Ministry of Justice (2020a) 'Diversity of the judiciary: Legal professions, new appointments and current post-holders'. Available at: https://assets.publishing.service.gov.uk/government/uploads/system/uploads/attachment_data/file/918529/diversity-of-the-judiciary-2020-statistics-web.pdf.

Ministry of Justice (2020b) 'Offender management statistics quarterly: July to September 2019'. Available at: www.gov.uk/government/publications/offender-management-statistics-quarterly-july-to-september-2019/offender-management-statistics-quarterly-july-to-september-2019.

Mubarek Inquiry Report (2006) 'Report of the Zahid Mubarek inquiry', Vols 1 and 2. Available at:www.gov.uk/government/publications/report-of-the-zahid-mubarek-inquiry.

Nalla, M. K. and Gurinskaya, A. (2020) 'Private Police and Security Governance: Mapping Emerging Trends and Future Directions'. *Journal of Contemporary Criminal Justice* 36(1): 101–9.

National Audit Office (2020) 'Ministry of Justice, HM Prison & Probation Service, Improving the prison estate'. Available at: www.nao.org.uk/wp-content/uploads/2020/02/Improving-the-prison-estate.pdf.

Oswald, M. et al. (2018) 'Algorithmic risk assessment policing models: lessons from the Durham HART model and "Experimental" proportionality'. *Information & Communications Technology Law* 27(2): 223–50.

Parliamentary Office of Science and Technology (2020) 'Non-custodial sentences'. Available at: https://researchbriefings.parliament.uk/ResearchBriefing/Summary/POST-PN-0613#fullreport.

Raynor, P. (2019) 'Supervision Skills for Probation Practitioners', HMI Probation Academic Insights 2019/05. London: HMI Probation. Available at: www.justiceinspectorates.gov.uk/hmiprobation/research/academic-insights.

Rowe, M. (2013) 'The Police' in A. Hucklesby and A. Wahidin (eds) *Criminal Justice*. Oxford: Oxford University Press.

Ruck, S. K. (1951) *Paterson on Prisons*. London: Frederick Muller.

Runnymede Trust (2017) 'Have prisons become a dangerous place? Disproportionality, safety and mental health in British Prisons'. Available at: www.runnymedetrust.org/uploads/PressReleases/Prisons%20report%20v3%20final%20typesetter.pdf.

Sherman, L. W. (2018) 'Nudge Failures and Crime Indexes: Inside March–July 2018'. *Cambridge Journal of Evidence Based Policing* 2: 1–3.

The Law Society (2019) 'Justice on Trial 2019: Fixing our Criminal Justice system'. Available at: www.lawsociety.org.uk/topics/research/justice-on-trial-2019.

Worrall, A., Carr, N., and Robinson, G. (2017) 'Opening a window on probation cultures: a photographic imagination' in M. Brown and E. Carrabine (eds) *Routledge International Handbook of Visual Criminology*. London: Routledge.

Chapter 25

Annison, H. (2018) 'The Policymakers' Dilemma: Change, Continuity and Enduring Rationalities of English Penal Policy'. *British Journal of Criminology* 58(5): 1066–86.

Ashworth, A. and Roberts, J. V. (2017) 'Sentencing' in A. Liebling, S. Maruna, and L. McAra (eds) *The Oxford Handbook of Criminology* (6th edn). Oxford: Oxford University Press.

Bale, D. (2000) 'Reflections: Pure Fiction: An Infallible Guide to National Standards'. *Probation Journal* 47(2): 129–31.

Bottoms, A. (1995) 'The Philosophy and Politics of Punishment and Sentencing' in C. Clarkson and R. Morgan (eds) *The Politics of Sentencing Reform*. Oxford: Clarendon Press.

Cabana, P. F. (2018) 'Paying off a fine by working outside prison: On the origins and diffusion of community service'. *European Journal of Criminology* 17(5): 628–46.

Campeau, H. (2015) '"Police Culture" at Work: Making Sense of Police Oversight'. *British Journal of Criminology* 55(4): 669–87.

Canton, R. and Dominey, J. (2017) *Probation*. London: Routledge.

Carr, N. and Robinson, G. (2020) 'A legitimate business? Representations of privatised probation in England and Wales'. *Crime Media Culture* 1–20.

Cavadino, M. and Dignan, J. (2006) *Penal Systems: A Comparative Approach*. London: Sage.

Criminal Justice Joint Inspection (2016) 'Delivering Justice in a Digital Age: A Joint Inspection of Digital Case Preparation and Presentation in the Criminal Justice System'. Available at: www.justiceinspectorates.gov.uk/cjji/wp-content/uploads/sites/2/2016/04/CJJI_DIG_Apr16_rpt.pdf.

Fox, C., Albertson, K., and Wong, K. (2013) *Justice Reinvestment: Can the Criminal Justice System Deliver More for Less?* Abingdon, Routledge.

Garland, D. (2001) *The Culture of Control*. Oxford: Oxford University Press.

HM Crown Prosecution Service Inspectorate (2017) 'Business as Usual? Transforming Summary Justice Follow-up Report'. Available at: www.justiceinspectorates.gov.uk/hmcpsi/inspections/business-as-usual-transforming-summary-justice-follow-up-report.

HM Government (2008) *Fair Rules for Strong Communities*. London: HMG.

HM Inspectorate of Probation (2016) A' thematic inspection of the delivery of unpaid work'. Available at: www.justiceinspectorates.gov.uk/hmiprobation/wp-content/uploads/sites/5/2016/01/Unpaid-Work-Thematic-report.pdf.

Hough, M. and Roberts, J. (2017) 'Public Opinion and Crime' in A. Liebling, S. Maruna, and L. McAra (eds) *The Oxford Handbook of Criminology* (6th edn). Oxford: Oxford University Press.

Hough, M. et al. (2012) 'Attitudes to Sentencing and Trust in Justice: Exploring Trends from the Crime Survey in England and Wales'. Available at: www.icpr.org.uk/media/34605/Attitudes%20to%20Sentencing%20and%20Trust%20in%20Justice%20(web).pdf.

Judiciary of England and Wales (2020) 'Better Case Management: Defence Toolkit'. Available at: www.judiciary.uk/wp-content/uploads/2019/12/Defence-toolkit-FINAL-05122019-f.pdf.

Loader, I. (2006) 'Fall of the "Platonic Guardians": Liberalism, Criminology and Political Responses to Crime in England and Wales" *British Journal of Criminology* 46(4): 561–86.

Loader, I. and Sparks, R. (2017) 'Penal populism and epistemic crime control' in A. Liebling, S. Maruna, and L. McAra (eds) *The Oxford Handbook of Criminology* (6th edn). Oxford: Oxford University Press.

McIvor, G. (1992) *Sentenced to Serve: The Operation and Impact of Community Service by Offenders*. Aldershot: Avebury.

McIvor, G. (2016) 'What is the impact of community service?' in F. McNeill, I. Durnescu, and R. Butter (eds) *Probation: 12 essential questions*. London: Palgrave Macmillan.

McNeill, F. (2019) *Pervasive Punishment: Making Sense of Mass Supervision*. Bingley: Emerald.

Millings, M., Burke, L., and Robinson, G. (2018) 'Lost in transition? The personal and professional challenges for probation leaders engaged in delivering public sector reform'. *Probation Journal* 66(1): 60–76.

Ministry of Justice (2016a) 'The Story of the Prison Population 1993–2016'. Available at: www.gov.uk/government/statistics/story-of-the-prison-population-1993-to-2016.

Ministry of Justice (2016b) 'Transforming Our Justice System: By the Lord Chancellor, the Lord Chief Justice and the Senior President of Tribunals'. Available at: https://assets.publishing.service.gov.uk/

government/uploads/system/uploads/attachment_data/file/553261/joint-vision-statement.pdf.

Ministry of Justice (2018a) 'Ministry of Justice single departmental plan'. Available at: www.gov.uk/government/publications/ministry-of-justice-single-departmental-plan/ministry-of-justice-single-departmental-plan--2#transform-the-department.

Ministry of Justice (2018b) 'Prison Population Projections 2018 to 2023, England and Wales'. Available at: https://assets.publishing.service.gov.uk/government/uploads/system/uploads/attachment_data/file/735428/prison-population-projections-2018-2023.PDF.

Ministry of Justice (2019a) 'Ministry of Justice single departmental plan 2019–2022. Available at:www.gov.uk/government/publications/ministry-of-justice-single-departmental-plan/ministry-of-justice-single-departmental-plan--3.

Ministry of Justice (2019b). Criminal Justice Statistics quarterly, England and Wales, April 2018 to March 2019. Available at: https://assets.publishing.service.gov.uk/government/uploads/system/uploads/attachment_data/file/825364/criminal-justice-statistics-quarterly-march-2019.pdf.

Ministry of Justice (2020). Criminal Justice Statistics quarterly, England and Wales, April 2019 to March 2020. Available at: https://assets.publishing.service.gov.uk/government/uploads/system/uploads/attachment_data/file/910530/criminal-justice-statistics-quarterly-march-2020.pdf.

National Police Chiefs' Council (2017). Charging and out of Court Disposals: A National Strategy 2017–2021. Available at: www.npcc.police.uk/Publication/Charging%20and%20Out%20of%20Court%20Disposals%20A%20National%20Strategy.pdf.

Pease, K. et al. (1976) *Community Service Orders*, Home Office Research Studies No. 29. London: HMSO.

Pratt, J. (2000) 'The Return of the Wheelbarrow Men; Or, The Arrival of Postmodern Penality?'. *British Journal of Criminology* 40: 127–45.

Pratt. J. (2007) *Penal Populism*. Abingdon: Routledge.

Prison Reform Trust (2018) 'Bromley Briefings Prison Factfile', Summer. Available at: www.prisonreformtrust.org.uk/Portals/0/Documents/Bromley%20Briefings/Summer%202018%20factfile.pdf.

Ritzer, G. (1993) *The McDonaldization of Society: An Investigation Into the Changing Character of Contemporary Social Life*. Newbury Park, CA: Pine Forge Press.

Roberts, J. V. and Hough, M. (2013) 'Sentencing Riot-Related Offending: Where Do the Public Stand?'. *British Journal of Criminology* 53(2): 234–56.

Roberts, J. et al. (2003) *Penal Populism and Public Opinion: Lessons from Five Countries*. Oxford: Oxford University Press.

Robinson, G. (2017) 'Stand-down and deliver: Pre-Sentence Reports, quality and the new culture of speed'. *Probation Journal* 64(4): 337–53.

Robinson, G. (2019) 'Delivering McJustice? The probation factory at the Magistrates' court'. *Criminology & Criminal Justice* 19(5): 605–21.

Ryan, M. (2005) 'Engaging with Punitive Attitudes Towards Crime and Punishment' in J. Pratt et al. (eds) *The New Punitiveness: Trends, Theories, Perspectives*. Cullompton: Willan.

Varah, M. (1987) 'Probation and Community Service' in J. Harding (ed.) *Probation & the Community*. London: Tavistock.

Whitfield, D. (1993) 'Extending the Boundaries' in D. Whitfield and D. Scott (eds) *Paying Back: Twenty Years of Community Service*, Winchester: Waterside Press.

Wincup, E. (2017) *Criminological Research: Understanding Qualitative Methods*. London: Sage.

Chapter 26

Abbas, T. (2019) 'Implementing "Prevent" in countering violent extremism in the UK: A left-realist critique'. *Critical Social Policy* 39(3): 396–412.

Barr, R. and Pease, K. (1992) 'A Place for Every Crime and Every Crime in its Place. An Alternative Perspective on Crime Displacement' in D. Evans, N. Fyfe, and D. Herbert (eds) *Crime, Policing and Place: Essays in Environmental Criminology*. London: Routledge.

Berry, G. et al. (2011) 'The Effectiveness of Partnership Working in a Crime and Disorder Context: A Rapid Evidence Assessment', Research Report 52. London: Home Office.

Brantingham, P. and Faust, F. (1976) 'A Conceptual Model of Crime Prevention'. *Crime & Delinquency* (July): 284–96.

Case, S. and Haines, K. (2009) *Understanding Youth Offending*. Cullompton: Willan.

Chakraborti, N. et al. (2011) 'Public Authority Commitment and Action to Eliminate Targeted Harassment and Violence, London, Equality and Human Rights Commission', Research Report 74. London: Equality Human Rights Commission.

Cherney, A. (2006) 'Problem Solving for Crime Prevention'. *Trends & Issues in Crime and Criminal Justice* 314.

Clarke, R. (1995) Situational Crime Prevention, *Crime and Justice* 19: 91–150.

Clarke, R. (1997) *Situational Crime Prevention: Successful Case Studies* (2nd edn). Guilderland: Harrow and Heston.

Clarke, R. (2011) 'Seven Misconceptions of Situational Crime Prevention' in N. Tilley (ed.) *Handbook of Crime Prevention and Community Safety*. Abingdon: Routledge.

Clarke, R. and Cornish, D. (1985) 'Modelling Offenders' Decisions: A Framework for Research and Policy' in M. Tonry (ed.) *Crime and Justice: An Annual review of Research*, Vol. 6. Chicago, IL: University of Chicago Press.

Coleman, R., Sim, J., and Whyte, D. (2002) 'Power, Politics and Partnerships: The State of Crime Prevention on Merseyside' in G. Hughes and A. Edwards (eds) *Crime Control and Community*. Cullompton: Willan.

Cozens, P. and Love, T. (2017) 'The Dark Side of Crime Prevention Through Environmental Design (CPTED)'. *Oxford Research Encyclopedia of Criminology*. DOI: 10.1093/acrefore/9780190264079.013.2.

Crawford, A. (1997) *The Local Governance of Crime*. Oxford: Clarendon Press.

Crawford, A. (1998) *Crime Prevention and Community Safety*. London: Longman.

Crawford, A. (2007) 'Crime Prevention and Community Safety' in M. Maguire, R. Morgan, and R. Reiner (eds) *The Oxford Handbook of Criminology* (4th edn). Oxford: Oxford University Press.

Crawford, A. and Evans, K. (2017) 'Crime Prevention and Community Safety' in A. Leibling, S. Maruna, and L. McAra (eds) *The Oxford Handbook of Criminology* (6th edn). Oxford: Oxford University Press.

Crawford, A. and Lister, S. (2007) *The Use and Impact of Dispersal Orders: Sticking Plasters and Wake Up Calls*. Bristol, Policy Press.

Crossley, S. (2015) *The Troubled Families Programme: The Perfect Social Policy?* London: Centre for Crime and Justice Studies.

Cullen, F., Benson, M., and Makarios, M. (2012) 'Developmental and Life-Course Theories of Offending' in B. Welsh and D. Farrington (eds) *The Oxford Handbook of Crime Prevention*. Oxford: Oxford University Press.

Department for Communities and Local Government (2012) *The Troubled Families Programme*. London: DCLG.

Eck, J. (2002) 'Preventing Crime at Places' in L. Sherman et al. (eds) *Evidence-Based Crime Prevention*. Abingdon: Routledge.

Eck, J. and Guerette, R. (2012) 'Place-Based Crime Prevention: Theory, Evidence and Policy' in B. Welsh and D. Farrington (eds) *The Oxford Handbook of Crime Prevention*. Oxford: Oxford University Press.

Edwards, A. (2002) 'Learning from Diversity' in G. Hughes and A. Edwards (eds) *Crime Control and Community*. Cullompton: Willan.

Ekblom, P. (2002) 'From the Source to the Mainstream is Uphill' in N. Tilley (ed.) *Analysis for Crime Prevention, Crime Prevention Studies 13*. Monsey, NY: Criminal Justice Press.

Ekblom, P. (2012) 'The Private Sector and Designing Products against Crime' in B. Welsh and D. Farrington (eds) *The Oxford Handbook of Crime Prevention*. Oxford: Oxford University Press.

Ekblom, P., Law, H., and Sutton, M. (1996) *Safer Cities and Domestic Burglary*. London: Home Office.

Farrington, D. and Ttofi, M. (2009) 'School-Based Programs to Reduce Bullying and Victimization'. *Campbell Systematic Review* 5(1): i–148.

Forrester, D., Chatterton, M., and Pease, K. (1988) 'The Kirkholt Burglary Prevention Project, Rochdale', Crime Prevention Unit Paper 13. London: Home Office.

Farrington, D., Loeber, R., and Ttofi, M. (2012) 'Risk and Protective Factors for Offending' in B. Welsh and D. Farrington (eds) *The Oxford Handbook of Crime Prevention*. Oxford: Oxford University Press.

Forrester, D. et al. (1990) 'The Kirkholt Burglary Prevention Project: Phase II'. Crime Prevention Unit Paper 23. London: Home Office.

Garland, D. (1996) 'The Limits of the Sovereign State'. *British Journal of Criminology* 36(4): 445–71.

Garland, D. (2001) *The Culture of Control*. Oxford: Oxford University Press.

Gilling, D. (1997) *Crime Prevention: Theory, Policy and Politics*. London: UCL Press.

Goddard, T. (2012) 'Post-Welfarist Risk Managers? Risk, Crime Prevention and the Responsibilisation of Community-Based Organisations'. *Theoretical Criminology* 16(3): 347–63.

Gottfriedson, D., Cook, P., and Na, C. (2014) 'Schools and Prevention' in B. Welsh and D. Farrington (eds) *The Oxford Handbook of Crime Prevention*. Oxford: Oxford University Press.

Grabosky, P. (1996) 'Unintended Consequences of Crime Prevention' in R. Homel (ed.) *The Politics and Practice of Situational Crime Prevention*. Monsey, NY: Criminal Justice Press.

Haggerty, K. (2008) 'Book review'. *Theoretical Criminology* 12(1): 116–21.

HM Treasury and National Audit Office (2008) *Tackling External Fraud: Good Practice Guide*. London: National Audit Office.

Hodgkinson, T., Saville, G., and Andresen, M. (2020) 'The Diffusion of Detriment: Tracking Displacement Using a City-Wide Mixed Methods Approach'. *British Journal of Criminology* 60: 198–218.

Home Office (1965) *Report of the Committee on the Prevention and Detection of Crime* (Cornish Committee). London: Home Office.

Home Office (2011) *A New Approach to Fighting Crime*. London: Home Office.

Home Office (2011) *Prevent Strategy*. London: Home Office.

Homel, R. (2011) 'Developmental Crime Prevention' in N. Tilley (ed.) *Handbook of Crime Prevention and Community Safety*. Abingdon: Routledge.

Hope, T. (2002) 'The Road Taken: Evaluation, Replication and Crime Reduction' in G. Hughes, E. McLaughlin, and J. Muncie (eds) *Crime Prevention and Community Safety: New Directions*. London: Sage.

Hope, T. (2019) 'Social Science and the Governance of Crime: Crime Prevention Policy Making during the 1980s'. *Journal of Law and Society* 46(1): 141–68.

Hughes, G. (1998) *Understanding Crime Prevention*. Buckingham: Open University Press.

Hughes, G. and Edwards, A. (2011) 'Crime Prevention in Context' in N. Tilley (ed.) *Handbook of Crime Prevention and Community Safety*. Abingdon: Routledge.

Johnson, S., Guerette, R., and Bowers, K. (2012) 'Crime Displacement and Diffusion of Benefits' in B. Welsh and D. Farrington (eds) *The Oxford Handbook of Crime Prevention*. Oxford: Oxford University Press.

Kelly, L. (2012) 'Representing and Preventing Youth Crime and Disorder: Intended and Unintended Consequences of Targeted Youth Programmes in England'. *Youth Justice* 12(2): 101–17.

Lee, M. (2007) *Inventing 'Fear of Crime'*. Cullompton: Willan.

Lord, N., Campbell, L., and van Wingerde, K. (2019) 'Other People's Dirty Money: Professional Intermediaries, Market Dynamics and the Finances of White Collar, Corporate and Organized Crimes'. *British Journal of Criminology* 59: 1217–36.

Lösel, F. and Bender, D. (2012) 'Child Social Skills Training in the Prevention of Antisocial Development and Crime' in B. Welsh and D. Farrington (eds) *The Oxford Handbook of Crime Prevention*. Oxford: Oxford University Press.

Ludwig, J. and Burdick-Will, J. (2012) 'Poverty Deconcentration and the Prevention of Crime' in B. Welsh and D. Farrington (eds) *The Oxford Handbook of Crime Prevention*. Oxford: Oxford University Press.

Luiselli, J. et al. (2005) 'Whole-School Positive Behaviour Support: Effects on student discipline problems and academic performance'. *Educational Psychology* 25(2/3): 183–98.

Manning, M., Homel, R., and Smith, C. (2010) 'A Meta-Analysis of the Effects of Early Developmental Programs in At-risk Populations on Non-Health Outcomes in Adolescence'. *Children and Youth Services Review* 32: 506–19.

Marx, G. (2007) 'The Engineering of Social Control: Policing and Technology'. *Policing* 1(1): 46–56.

Matza, D. (1964) *Delinquency and Drift*. New York: Wiley.

McCord, J. (1978) 'A Thirty-Year Follow-Up of Treatment Effects'. *American Psychologist* (March): 284–9.

McCord, J. (1992) 'The Cambridge–Somerville Study: A Pioneering Longitudunal Experimental Study of Delinquency Prevention' in J. McCord and R. Tremblay (eds) *Preventing Antisocial Behavior: Interventions from Birth through Adolescence*. New York: Guilford Press.

Menichelli, F. (2020) 'Transforming the English model of community safety: From crime and disorder to the safeguarding of vulnerable people'. *Criminology & Criminal Justice* 20(1): 39–56.

Morgan, A. et al. (2015) *Effective Crime Prevention Interventions for Implementation by Local Government*. Canberra: Australian Institute of Criminology.

Morgan, J. (1991) *Safer Communities: The Local Delivery of Crime Prevention Through the Partnership Approach*. London: Home Office.

Morgan, L. (2013) 'Gated Communities: Institutionalizing Social Stratification'. *Geographical Bulletin* 54: 24–36.

O'Malley, P. (1992) 'Risk, Power and Crime Prevention'. *Economy and Society* 21(3): 252–75.

Petrosino, A., Petrosino, C., and Buehler, J. (2004) '"Scared Straight" and Other Juvenile Awareness Programmes for Preventing Delinquency'. *Campbell Systematic Review* 2.

Piquero, A. et al. (2008) 'Effects of Early Family/Parent Training on Antisocial Behavior & Delinquency'. *Campbell Systematic Review* 11.

Pitts, J. (1988) *The Politics of Juvenile Crime*. London: Sage.

Popper, K. (2002) *The Logic of Scientific Discovery*. Abingdon: Routledge.

Prior, D. and Paris, A. (2005) *Preventing Children's Involvement in Crime and Anti-Social Behaviour: A Literature Review*. Birmingham: University of Birmingham.

Putnam, R. (1995) 'Bowling alone: America's declining social capital'. *Journal of Democracy* 6: 65–7.

Repetto, T. (1976) 'Crime Prevention and the Displacement Phenomenon'. *Crime and Delinquency* 22: 166–77.

Reza, B. and Magill, C. (2006) *Race and the Criminal Justice System: An Overview to the Complete Statistics 2004–2005*. London: Home Office.

Rodger, J. (2008) 'The Criminalisation of Social Policy'. *Criminal Justice Matters* 74(1): 18–19.

Rose, N. (2000) 'Government and Control'. *British Journal of Criminology* 40: 321–39.

Sampson, R., Raudenbush, S., and Earls, F. (1997) 'Neighborhoods and Violent Crime: A Multilevel Study of Collective Efficacy'. *Science* 277(5328): 918–24.

Schweinhart, L. et al. (2005) *Lifetime Effects: The High/Scope Perry Preschool Study Through Age 40*. Ypsilanti: High/Scope Press.

Shain, F. (2011) *The New Folk Devils: Muslim Boys and Education*. Stoke-on-Trent: Trentham.

Sharma, D. and Scott, M. (2015) 'Nudge; Don't Judge: Using Nudge Theory to Deter Shoplifters', 11th European Academy of Design Conference, Paris, 22–4 April.

Sherman, L. et al. (1998) *Preventing Crime: What Works, What Doesn't, What's Promising*. Washington, DC: National Institute of Justice.

Sidebottom, A. et al. (2015) *Gating Alleys to Reduce Crime: A Meta-analysis and Realist Synthesis*. London: University College London. Available at: http://whatworks.college.police.uk/About/Documents/Alley_gating.pdf [Accessed 4 December 2020].

Simcox, R. (2019) 'The Groups Lining Up to Undermine UK's Successful Counter-Terror Strategy'. Washington, DC: The Heritage Foundation. Available at: www.heritage.org/terrorism/commentary/the-groups-lining-undermine-uks-successful-counter-terror-strategy [Accessed 4 December 2020].

Smith, M. and Clarke, R. (2012) 'Situational Crime Prevention: Classifying Techniques Using "Good Enough" Theory' in B. Welsh and D. Farrington (eds) *The Oxford Handbook of Crime Prevention*. Oxford: Oxford University Press.

Smith, R. (2015) 'Troubled, Troubling or Troublesome? Troubled Families and the Changing Shape of Youth Justice' in M. Wasik and S. Santatzoglou (eds) *The Management of Change in Criminal Justice*. Basingstoke: Palgrave Macmillan.

Squires, P. (2009) 'The knife crime "epidemic" and British politics'. *British Politics* 4: 127–57.

Squires, P. (2017) 'Community safety and crime prevention: a critical reassessment' in N. Tilley and A. Sidebottom (eds) *Handbook of Crime Prevention and Community Safety* (2nd edn). Abingdon: Routledge.

Sutherland, A. et al. (2005) *Role of Risk and Protective Factors*. London: Youth Justice Board.

Thaler, R. and Sunstein, C. (2008) *Nudge: Improving Decisions about Health, Wealth and Happiness*. New Haven, CT: Yale University Press.

Thomas, P. (2016) 'Youth, terrorism and education: Britain's Prevent Programme'. *International Journal of Lifelong Education* 35(2): 171–87.

Tilley, N. (1993) 'After Kirkholt—Theory, Method and Results of Replication Evaluations', Crime Prevention Unit Series Paper 47. London: Home Office.

Tilley, N. (2002) 'Crime Prevention in Britain, 1975–2010: Breaking Out, Breaking In and Breaking Down' in G. Hughes, E. McLaughlin, and J. Muncie (eds) *Crime Prevention and Community Safety: New Directions*. London: Sage.

Tilley, N. (2011) 'Introduction: Thinking Realistically About Crime Prevention' in N. Tilley (ed.) *Handbook of Crime Prevention and Community Safety*. Abingdon: Routledge.

Wacquant, L. (2008) *Urban Outcasts: A Comparative Sociology of Advanced Marginality*. Cambridge: Polity Press.

Wallin, E., Lindewald, B., and Andréasson, S. (2004) 'Institutionalization of a Community Action Program Targeting Licensed Premises in Stockholm, Sweden'. *Evaluation Review* 28(5): 396–419.

Weisburd, D., Farrington, D., and Gill, C. (2017) 'What Works in Crime Prevention and Rehabilitation: An Assessment of Systematic Reviews'. *Criminology & Public Policy* 16(2): 435–49.

Welsh, B. and Farrington, D. (2010) 'The Future of Crime Prevention: Developmental and Situational Strategies', Paper to National Institute of Justice, 2010. Available at: www.nij.gov/topics/crime/crime-prevention-working-group/documents/future-of-crime-prevention-research.pdf [Accessed 4 December 2020].

Welsh, B. and Farrington, D. (2012) 'Crime Prevention and Public Policy' in B. Welsh and D. Farrington (eds) *The Oxford Handbook of Crime Prevention*. Oxford: Oxford University Press.

Welsh, B. and Farrington, D. (eds) (2012) *The Oxford Handbook of Crime Prevention*. Oxford: Oxford University Press.

Welsh, B. and Pfeffer, R. (2013) 'Reclaiming crime prevention in an age of punishment: An American history'. *Puniushment & Society* 15(5): 534–53.

Welsh, B., Zimmerman, G., and Zane, S. (2017) 'The Centrality of Theory in Modern Day Crime Prevention: Developments, Challenges, and Opportunities'. *Justice Quarterly* 35(1): 139–61.

West, D.J. (1967) *The Young Offender*. Harmondsworth: Pelican.

White, W. and Carmody, D. (2018) 'Preventing Online Victimization: College Students' Views on Intervention and Prevention'. *Journal of Interpersonal Violence* 33(14): 2291–307.

Chapter 27

Anselin, L., Griffiths, E., and Tita, G. (2011) 'Crime Mapping and Hot Spot Analysis' in R. Wortley and L. Mazerolle (eds) *Environmental Criminology and Crime Analysis*. Abingdon: Routledge.

Armstrong, S. et al. (2013) *International Evidence Review of Conditional (Suspended) Sentences: FINAL REPORT*. Edinburgh: Scottish Centre for Crime & Justice, Research.

Baker, K. et al. (2005) *Further Development of ASSET*. London: Youth Justice Board.

Bandyopadhyay, S. (2012) *Acquisitive Crime: Imprisonment, Detection and Social Factors*. London: Civitas.

Beck, U. (1992) *Risk Society*. Sage: London.

Beck, U. and Willms, J. (2004) *Conversations with Ulrich Beck*. Cambridge: Polity Press.

Bowling, B. (1999) 'The Rise and Fall of New York Murder'. *British Journal of Criminology* 39(4): 531–53.

Bowling, B., Marks, A., and Murphy, C. (2008) 'Crime Control Technologies: Towards an Analytical Framework and Research Agenda' in R. Brownsword and K. Yeung (eds) *Regulating Technologies: Legal Futures, Regulatory Frames and Technological Fixes*. Oxford: Hart.

Braga, A. and Weisburd, D. (2015) 'Focused Deterrence and the Prevention of Violent Gun Injuries: Practice, Theoretical Principles, and Scientific Evidence'. *Annual Review of Public Health* 36: 55–68.

Braga, A., Hureau, D., and Papachristos, A. (2011) 'An Ex Post Facto Evaluation Framework for Place-Based Police Interventions'. *Evaluation Review* 35(6): 592–626.

Braga, A. et al. (2019) 'Hot spots policing and crime reduction: an update of an ongoing systematic review and meta-analysis'. *Journal of Experimental Criminology* 15: 289–311.

Brantingham, P. and Brantingham, P. (2011) 'Crime Pattern Theory' in R. Wortley and L. Mazerolle (eds) *Environmental Criminology and Crime Analysis*. Abingdon: Routledge.

Brooks, O. and Burman, M. (2017) 'Reporting rape: Victim perspectives on advocacy support in the criminal justice process'. *Criminology & Criminal Justice* 17(2): 209–25.

Brown, A. (2004) 'Anti-Social Behaviour, Crime Control and Social Control'. *Howard Journal* 43(2): 203–11.

Bullock, K. (2014) *Citizens, Community and Crime Control*. London: Palgrave Macmillan.
Burnett, R. and Roberts, C. (eds) (2004) *What Works in Probation and Youth Justice*. Cullompton: Willan.
Byrne, J. and Marx, G. (2011) 'Technological Innovations in Crime Prevention and Policing. A Review of the Research on Implementation and Impact'. *Cahiers Politiestudies Jaargang* 3(20): 17–40.
Carter, P. (2004) *Managing Offenders, Reducing Crime*. London: Strategy Unit.
Case, S. and Haines, K. (2009) *Understanding Youth Offending: Risk Factor Research, Policy and Practice*. Cullompton: Willan.
Clarke, R. (2012) 'Opportunity Makes the Thief. Really? And So What?'. *Crime Science* 1(3): 1–9.
Clevenger, S., Navarro, J., and Gilliam, M. (2018) 'Technology and the endless "cat and mouse" game: A review of the interpersonal cybervictimization literature'. *Sociology Compass* 12(12): e12639.
Cohen, S. (1985) *Visions of Social Control*. Cambridge: Polity Press.
Coleman, R., Sim, J., and Whyte, D. (2002) 'Power, Politics and Partnerships: The State of Crime Prevention on Merseyside' in G. Hughes and A. Edwards (eds) *Crime Control and Community*. Cullompton: Willan.
Cozens, P. (2011) 'Urban Planning and Environmental Criminology: Towards a New Perspective for Safer Cities'. *Planning Practice and Research* 26(4): 481–508.
Crawford, A. and Evans, K. (2017) 'Crime Prevention and Community Safety' in A. Liebling, S. Maruna, and L. McAra (eds) *The Oxford Handbook of Criminology* (6th edn). Oxford: Oxford University Press.
Crichlow, V. (2016) 'Will "broken windows policing" work in Trinidad and Tobago? A critical perspective on zero tolerance and community policing in a multi-ethnic society'. *Police Practice and Research* 17(6): 570–81.
Curran, F. (2019) 'The Law, Policy and Portrayal of Zero Tolerance School Discipline: Examining Prevalence and Characteristics Across Levels of Governance and School Districts'. *Educational Policy* 33(2): 319–49.
Deering, J. and Evans, J. (2018) *AssetPlus and Desistance-Informed Practice in a Welsh Youth Offending Service*. Cardiff: University of South Wales. Available at: https://pure.southwales.ac.uk/files/3025311/Asset_Plus_and_Desistance_Draft_Report.Final.pdf [Accessed 27 November 2020].
Ekblom, P. (2011) 'Designing Products Against Crime Theory' in R. Wortley and L. Mazerolle (eds) *Environmental Criminology and Crime Analysis*. Abingdon: Routledge.
Farmer, D. (1984) *Crime Control*. New York: Plenum Press.
Farrell, G. and Pease, K. (2011) 'Repeat Victimisation' in R. Wortley and L. Mazerolle (eds) *Environmental Criminology and Crime Analysis*. Abingdon: Routledge.
Farrell, G. et al. (2008) 'The Crime Drop and the Security Hypothesis'. *British Society of Criminology Newsletter* 62: 17–21.
Felson, M. (1995) 'Those Who Discourage Crime' in J. Eck and D. Weisburd (eds) *Crime and Place: Crime Prevention Studies*. New York: Willow Tree Press.
Felson, M. and Clarke, R. (1998) 'Opportunity Makes the Thief', Police Research Series Paper 98. London: Home Office.
Fraser, A., Ralphs, R., and Smithson, H. (2018) 'European Youth Gang Policy in Comparative Context'. *Children & Society* 32(2): 156–65.
Garland, D. (1990) *Punishment and Modern Society*. Oxford: Clarendon Press.
Garland, D. (2001) *The Culture of Control*. Oxford: Oxford University Press.
Geller, A., Fagan, J., and Tyler, T. (2018) 'Do the Ends justify the Means? Policing and Rights Tradeoffs in New York City', Columbia Public Law Research Paper No. 14-581.
Gemmell, J. (1996) 'The New Conditional Sentencing Regime'. *Criminal Law Quarterly* 39: 334–61.
Goldstein, H. (1979) 'Improving Policing: A Problem-Oriented Approach'. *Crime and Delinquency* 25: 236–58.
Grabosky, P. (1998) *Technology & Crime Control: Trends and Issues in Crime and Criminal Justice 78*. Canberra: Australian Institute of Criminology.
Grimwood, G. and Berman, G. (2012) 'Reducing Reoffending: The "What Works" Debate', Research Paper 12/71. London: House of Commons Library.
Hayward, K. (2007) 'Situational Crime Prevention and its Discontents: Rational Choice Theory versus the "Culture of Now"'. *Social Policy & Administration* 41(3): 232–50.
HM Inspector of Constabulary (2014) *Crime Recording: Making the Victim Count*. London: HMIC.
Holmberg, L. et al. (2020) 'Victims' rights: serving victims or the criminal justice system? An empirical study on victims of violent crime and their experiences with the Danish police'. *International Journal of Comparative and Applied Criminal Justice*. DOI: 10.1080/01924036.2020.1719525.
Home Office and Ministry of Justice (2015) *Integrated Offender Management: Key Principles*. London: Home Office.
Jackson, A. (2013) 'Admissibility of Fingerprints Taken on an Unauthorised Device'. *Journal of Criminal Law* 77: 376–9.
Jackson, J. and Bradford, B. (2009) 'Crime, policing and social order: on the expressive nature of public confidence in policing'. *British Journal of Sociology* 60(3): 493–521.
Joshi, J. and Gupta, K. (2016) 'Face Recognition Technology: A Review'. *IIJP Journal of Telecommunications* 8(1): 53–63.
Karn, J. (2013) *Policing and Crime Reduction: The Evidence and its Implications for Practice*. London: The Police Foundation.
Kennedy, L., Caplan, J., and Piza, E. (2018) *Risk-based policing: Evidence-based crime prevention with big data and spatial analytics*. Berkeley, CA: University of California Press.
Levitt, S. (1996) 'The Effect of Prison Population Size on Crime Rates: Evidence from Prison Overcrowding Litigation'. *Quarterly Journal of Economics* 111(2): 319–51.
Lewis, D.-M. (2014) 'The Risk Factor—(Re-)visiting Adult Offender Risk Assessments within Criminal Justice Practice'. *Risk Management* 16(2): 121–36.
Lipsey, M. and Cullen, F. (2007) 'The Effectiveness of Correctional Rehabilitation: A Review of Systematic Reviews'. *Annual Review of Law & Social Science* 3: 297–320.
Loader, I., Goold, B., and Thumala, A. (2014) 'The Moral Economy of Security'. *Theoretical Criminology* 18(4): 469–88.
Longstaff, A. et al. (2015) *Neighbourhood Policing: Past, Present and Future*. London: The Police Foundation.
Mackenzie, S. and Henry, A. (2009) *Community Policing: A Review of the Evidence*. Edinburgh: Scottish Government.
Merrington, S. (2004) 'Assessment Tools in Probation: Their Development and Potential' in R. Burnett and C. Roberts (eds) *What Works in Probation and Youth Justice*. Cullompton: Willan.
Merry, S. (1981) 'Defensible Space Undefended'. *Urban Affairs Quarterly* 16(4): 397–422.
Mews, A. et al. (2015) *The impact of short custodial sentences, community orders and suspended sentence orders on re-offending*. London: Ministry of Justice.
Ministry of Justice (2010) *Disabled People's Experiences of Targeted Violence and Hostility*. London: Ministry of Justice.
Ministry of Justice (2013) *Statistics on Race and the Criminal Justice System 2012*. London: Ministry of Justice.
Moriarty, L. (ed.) (2017) *Criminal Justice Technology in the 21st Century*. Springfield, IL: Charles C. Thomas.
Newburn, T. and Jones, T. (2007) 'Symbolizing Crime Control: Reflections on Zero Tolerance'. *Theoretical Criminology* 11(2): 221–43.
Newburn, T. and Reiner, R. (2007) 'Policing and the Police' in M. Maguire, R. Morgan, and R. Reiner (eds) *The Oxford Handbook of Criminology* (4th edn). Oxford: Oxford University Press.

Newman, O. (1972) *Defensible Space*. London: Architectural Press.

Ofer, U. (2011) 'Criminalizing the Classroom: The Rise of Aggressive Policing and Zero Tolerance in New York City Public Schools'. *New York Law School Law Review* 56: 1373–411.

O'Malley, P. (2010) *Crime and Risk*. London: Sage.

Packer, H. (1964) 'Two Models of the Criminal Process'. *University of Pennsylvania Law Review* 113(1): 1–68.

Piza, E. et al. (2019) 'CCTV surveillance for crime prevention'. *Criminology & Public Policy* 18(1): 135–59.

Ratcliffe, J. (2016) *Intelligence-Led Policing* (2nd edn). London: Routledge.

Reiner, R. (2000) *The Politics of the Police*. Oxford: Oxford University Press.

Reynald, D. (2010) 'Guardians on Guardianship: Factors Affecting the Willingness to Supervise, the Ability to Detect Potential Offenders, and the Willingness to Intervene'. *Journal of Research in Crime and Delinquency* 47(3): 356–90.

Roach, K. (1999) 'Four Models of the Criminal Process'. *Journal of Criminal Law and Criminology* 89(2): 671–716.

Roehl, J. (1998) 'Civil Remedies for Controlling Crime: The Role of Community Organizations'. *Crime Prevention Studies* 9: 241–59.

Scott, M. and Goldstein, H. (2005) *Shifting and Sharing Responsibility for Public Safety Problems: Response Guide No. 3*. New York: Centre for Problem-Oriented Policing.

Scott, M. et al. (2011) 'Problem-Oriented Policing and Environmental Criminology' in R. Wortley and L. Mazerolle (eds) *Environmental Criminology and Crime Analysis*. Abingdon: Routledge.

Sellers, B. and Arrigo, B. (2018) 'Virtue Jurisprudence and the Case of Zero-Tolerance Discipline in U.S. Public Education Policy'. *New Criminal Law Review* 21(4): 514–44.

Silverman, E., and Eterno, J. (2019). 'Advocate: CompStat's Innovation' in D. Weisburd and A. Braga (eds) *Police Innovation: Contrasting Perspectives*. Cambridge: Cambridge University Press.

Sin, C. et al. (2009) *Disabled People's Experiences of Targeted Violence and Hostility*. London: Office of Public Management.

Smith, R. (2006) 'Actuarialism and Early Intervention in Contemporary Youth Justice' in B. Goldson and J. Muncie (eds) *Youth Crime and Justice*. London: Sage.

Smith, R. (2014) *Youth Justice: Ideas, Policy and Practice*. London: Routledge.

Stemen, D. (2007) *Reconsidering Incarceration: New Directions for Reducing Crime*. New York: Vera Institute.

Stenson, K. (2002) 'Community Safety in Middle England' in G. Hughes and A. Edwards (eds) *Crime Control and Community*. Cullompton: Willan.

Stenson, K. (2009) 'The New Politics of Crime Control' in K. Stenson and R. Sullivan (eds) *Crime, Risk and Justice*. Cullompton: Willan.

Tarling, R. (1994) 'Editorial: The Effect of Imprisonment on Crime'. *Journal of the Royal Statistical Society. Series A* 157(2): 173–6.

The Sentencing Project (2013) *Shadow Report to the United Nations on Racial Disparities in the United States Criminal Justice System*. Washington, DC: The Sentencing Project. Available at: www.sentencingproject.org/publications/shadow-report-to-the-united-nations-human-rights-committee-regarding-racial-disparities-in-the-united-states-criminal-justice-system/ [Accessed 7 December 2020].

Tilley, N. (2002) 'The Rediscovery of Learning: Crime Prevention and Scientific Realism' in G. Hughes and A. Edwards (eds) *Crime Control and Community*. Cullompton: Willan.

Tilley, N. (2010) 'Whither Problem-Oriented Policing'. *Criminology & Public Policy* 9(1): 183–95.

Tilley, N. and Webb, J. (1994) *Burglary Reduction: Findings from Safer Cities Schemes*. London: Home Office.

Turley, C. et al. (2012) 'Delivering Neighbourhood Policing in Partnership', Research Report 61. London: Home Office.

Webster, C. (2015) '"Race", Youth Crime and Youth Justice' in B. Goldson and J. Muncie (eds) *Youth Crime & Justice* (2nd edn). London: Sage.

Weisburd, D. et al. (2010) 'Is Problem-Oriented Policing Effective in Reducing Crime and Disorder?'. *Criminology & Public Policy* 9(1): 139–72.

Weisburd, D. et al. (2019). 'Critic: Changing Everything so that Everything Can Remain the Same: CompStat and American Policing' in D. Weisburd and A. Braga (eds) *Police Innovation: Contrasting Perspectives*. Cambridge: Cambridge University Press.

Westmarland, N. et al. (2013) 'Protecting Women's Safety? The Use of Smartphone 'Apps' in Relation to Domestic and Sexual Violence', Research Briefing No. 12. Durham: Durham University School of Applied Social Sciences.

Wilson, E. and Hinks, S. (2011) *Assessing the Predictive Validity of the Asset Youth Risk Assessment Tool using the Juvenile Cohort Study (JCS)*. London: Ministry of Justice.

Wilson, J. and Kelling, G. (1982) 'Broken Windows'. *The Atlantic Monthly* 249(3): 29–38.

Wortley, R. (2011) 'Situational Precipitators of Crime' in R. Wortley and L. Mazerolle (eds) *Environmental Criminology and Crime Analysis*. Abingdon: Routledge.

Youth Justice Board/Ministry of Justice (2020) *Youth Justice Statistics 2018/19*. London: Ministry of Justice.

Zedner, L. (2006) 'Liquid Security: Managing the Market for Crime Control'. *Criminology and Criminal Justice* 6: 267–88.

Chapter 28

Aebi, M. and Tiago, M. (2018) *Prison Populations. Space 1*. Strasbourg: Université de Lausanne.

Allen, R. (2008) 'Changing Public Attitudes to Crime and Punishment—Building Confidence in Community Penalties'. *Probation Journal* 55(4): 389–400.

Almond, P. (2009) 'Understanding the Seriousness of Corporate Crime'. *Criminology and Criminal Justice* 9(2): 145–64.

Anderson, S. (2011) *The Social Care Needs of Short-Sentence Prisoners*. London: Revolving Doors Agency.

Armstrong, S. and Weaver, B. (2010) 'What Do the Punished Think of Punishment?', Research Report No. 04/2010. Glasgow: The Scottish Centre for Crime & Justice Research.

Ashworth, A. (2001) 'The decline of English sentencing and other stories' in M. Tonry and R. Frase (eds) *Sentencing and Sanctions in Western Countries*. New York: Oxford University Press.

Bandes, S. (2000) 'When Victims Seek Closure: Forgiveness, Vengeance and the Role of Government'. *Fordham Urban Law Journal XXVII*: 1599–606.

Banks, C. (2004) *Criminal Justice Ethics: Theory and Practice*. Thousand Oaks, CA: Sage.

Bateman, T. (2011) 'Child Imprisonment: Exploring "Injustice by Geography"'. *Prison Journal* 197: 10–14.

Bateman, T. (2017) *The State of Youth Justice 2017*. London: National Association for Youth Justice.

Beccaria, C. (1995) *On Crimes and Punishments and Other Writings*. Cambridge: Cambridge University Press.

Becker, G. (1968) 'Crime and Punishment: An Economic Approach'. *Journal of Political Economy* 76(2): 169–217.

Bentham, J. (2003 [1859]) *The Works of Jeremy Bentham*, Vol. 1.1. Chestnut Hill, MA: Adamant Media Corp.

Bronsteen, J., Buccafusco, C., and Masur, J. (2008) *Happiness and Punishment*. Chicago, IL: Chicago Law School.

Brownlee, I. (1998) *Community Punishment: A Critical Introduction*. London: Longman.

Carrier, N. (2010) 'Anglo-Saxon Penologies of the Punitive Turn'. *Champ Penal* VII: DOI: 10.4000/champpenal.7952.

Clarke, K. (2012) 'Ministerial Foreword' in Ministry of Justice, *Punishment and Reform: Effective Community Sentences*. London: Ministry of Justice.

Collica-Cox, K. and Sullivan, L. (2017) 'Why Retribution Matters: Progression not Regression'. *Theory in Action* 10(2): 41–57.

Duff, R. and Garland, D. (1994) 'Introduction: Thinking about Punishment' in R. Duff and D. Garland (eds) *A Reader on Punishment*. Oxford: Oxford University Press.

Edgar, K. (2010) *A Fair Response*. London: Prison Reform Trust.

Edwards, I. (2004) 'An Ambiguous Participant: The Crime Victim and Criminal Justice Decision-Making'. *British Journal of Criminology* 44: 967–82.

Esmaili, H. and Gans, J. (1999) 'Islamic Law Across Cultural Borders: The Involvement of Western Nationals in Saudi Murder Trials'. *Denver Journal of International Law and Policy* 28(2): 145–74.

Fletcher, G. (1999) 'The Place of Victims in the Theory of Retribution'. *Buffalo Criminal Law Review* 3(1): 51–63.

Foucault, M. (1979) *Discipline and Punish*. New York: Vintage Books.

Foucault, M. (1984) 'Complete and Austere Institutions' in P. Rabinow (ed.) *The Foucault Reader*. Harmondsworth: Penguin.

Friedman, D. (1979) 'Private Creation and Enforcement of Law: A Historical Case'. *Journal of Legal Studies* 8(2): 399–415.

Garland, D. (2011) 'The Problem of the Body in Modern State Punishment'. *Social Research* 78(3): 767–98.

Gauke, D. (2019) 'Beyond prison, redefining punishment', Speech, 18 February, Ministry of Justice. Available at: www.gov.uk/government/speeches/beyond-prison-redefining-punishment-david-gauke-speech [Accessed 7 December 2020].

Godfrey, B. and Lawrence, P. (2005) *Crime and Justice 1750–1950*. Cullompton: Willan.

Grayling, C. (2012) 'Foreword' in Ministry of Justice, *Punishment and Reform: Effective Community Sentences Government Response*. London: The Stationery Office.

Harrison, W. (1577) 'Description of Elizabethan England' in R. Holinshed et al. (eds) *Holinshed's Chronicles*. London: John Harrison.

Home Office (2014) *Anti-social Behaviour, Crime and Policing Act 2014: Reform of Anti-social Behaviour Powers: Statutory guidance for Frontline Professionals*. London: Home Office.

Hough, M., Jacobson, J., and Millie, A. (2003) *The Decision to Imprison: Sentencing and the Prison Population*. London: Prison Reform Trust.

Hough, M. et al. (2013) *Attitudes to sentencing and trust in justice: exploring trends from the crime survey for England and Wales*. London: Ministry of Justice.

Ignatieff, M. (1989) *A Just Measure of Pain*. Harmondsworth: Penguin.

Jacobson, J. and Kirby, A. (2012) *Public Attitudes to Youth Crime: Report on Focus Group Research*. London: Home Office.

Janssen, K. (2015) 'Public confidence in the Criminal Justice System—findings from the Crime Survey for England and Wales (2013/14)', Analytical Summary. London: Ministry of Justice. Available at: https://assets.publishing.service.gov.uk/government/uploads/system/uploads/attachment_data/file/449444/public-confidence.pdf [Accessed 7 December 2020].

Jennings, W. et al. (2016) 'Penal Populism and the Public Thermostat: Crime, Public Punitiveness, and Public Policy'. *Governance* 30(3): 463–81.

King, R. and Ward, R. (2015) 'Rethinking the Bloody Code in Eighteenth-Century Britain: Capital Punishment at the Centre and on the Periphery'. *Past and Present* 228(1): 159–205.

Kolber, A. (2009) 'The Subjective Experience of Punishment'. *Columbia Law Review* 109: 182–236.

Koritansky, P. (2012) *Thomas Aquinas and the Philosophy of Punishment*. Washington, DC: Catholic University of America Press.

Lammy, D. (2017) *The Lammy Review: An independent review into the treatment of, and outcomes for Black, Asian and Minority Ethnic individuals in the criminal justice system*. London, Ministry of Justice.

Lee, A. (2013) 'Public Wrongs and the Criminal Law'. *Criminal Law and Philosophy* 9: 155–70.

Materni, M. (2013) 'Criminal Punishment and the Pursuit of Justice'. *British Journal of American Legal Studies* 2(1): 263–304.

McLoughlin, E., Muncie, J., and Hughes, G. (2001) 'The Permanent Revolution: New Labour, New Public Management and the Modernization of Criminal Justice'. *Criminal Justice* 1(3): 301–18.

Ministry of Justice (2019) *Criminal Justice Statistics quarterly, England and Wales, April 2018 to March 2019*. London: Ministry of Justice. Available at: https://assets.publishing.service.gov.uk/government/uploads/system/uploads/attachment_data/file/825364/criminal-justice-statistics-quarterly-march-2019.pdf [Accessed 7 December 2020].

Moore, M. (1999) 'Victims and Retribution: A Reply to Professor Fletcher'. *Buffalo Criminal Law Review* 3(1): 65–89.

Morris, A. and Giller, H. (1987) *Understanding Juvenile Justice*. London: Croom Helm.

National Audit Office (2012) *Comparing International Criminal Justice Systems*. London: National Audit Office.

Naughton, M. (2005) 'Redefining Miscarriages of Justice'. *British Journal of Criminology* 45(2): 165–82.

Naughton, M. (2014) 'Criminologizing Wrongful Convictions'. *British Journal of Criminology* 54: 1148–66.

O'Malley (2009) 'Theorizing Fines'. *Punishment and Society* 11(1): 67–83.

Phillips, L. (2007) 'How Important is Punishment?', Speech to Howard League, 15 November.

Pratt, J. (2002) *Punishment and Civilisation*. London: Sage.

Prison Reform Trust (2013) *Prison: The Facts*. London: Prison Reform Trust.

Prison Reform Trust (2018) *Prison: The Facts*. London: Prison Reform Trust.

Roberts, J. and Hough, M. (2005) 'Sentencing Young Offenders: Public Opinion in England and Wales'. *Criminal Justice* 5(3): 211–32.

Social Exclusion Unit (2002) *Reducing Re-offending by Ex-Prisoners*. London: The Stationery Office.

Taylor, E., Clarke, R., and McArt, D. (2014) 'The Intensive Alternative to Custody: "Selling" Sentences and Satisfying Judicial Concerns'. *Probation Journal* 61(1): 44–59.

Thorsson, O. (2001) *The Sagas of Icelanders*. Harmondsworth: Penguin.

Tomlinson, M. (1981) 'Penal Servitude 1846–1865: A System in Evolution' in V. Bailey (ed.) *Policing and Punishment in Nineteenth Century Britain*. London: Croom Helm.

Uhrig, N. (2016) *Black, Asian and Minority Ethnic Disproportionality in the Criminal Justice System in England and Wales*. London: Ministry of Justice.

Vermunt, R. and Steensma, H. (2016) 'Procedural Justice' in S. Sabbagh and M. Schmitt (eds) *Handbook of Social Justice Theory and Research*. New York: Springer.

Waisel, D. (2007) 'Physician Participation in Capital Punishment'. *Mayo Clinic Proceedings* 82(9): 1073–80.

Webb, S. (2011) *Execution: A History of Capital Punishment in Britain*. Stroud: The History Press.

Wiener, M. (1990) *Reconstructing the Criminal: Culture, Law, and Policy in England 1830–1914*. Cambridge: Cambridge University Press.

Chapter 29

Bateman, T., Hazel, N., and Wright, T. (2013) *Resettlement of Young People Leaving Custody: Lessons from the Literature, Beyond Youth Custody*. London: Beyond Youth Custody. Available at: www.beyondyouthcustody.net/wp-content/uploads/Resettlement-of-

Young-People-Leaving-Custody-Lessons-from-the-literature.pdf [Accessed 7 December 2020].

Berghuis, M. (2018) 'Reentry Programs for Adult Male Offender Recidivism and Reintegration: A Systematic Review and Meta-Analysis'. *International Journal of Offender Therapy and Comparative Criminology* 62(14): 4655–76.

Bonta, J. et al. (2008) 'Exploring the Black Box of Community Supervision'. *Journal of Offender Rehabilitation* 47(3): 248–70.

Bonta, J. et al. (2011) 'An Experimental Demonstration of Training Probation Officers in Evidence-Based Community Supervision'. *Criminal Justice and Behavior* 38(11): 1127–47.

Cohen, S. (1985) *Visions of Social Control*. Cambridge: Polity Press.

Cullen, F. and Gendreau, P. (2000) 'Assessing Correctional Rehabilitation: Policy, Practice and Prospects' in L. Horney (ed.) *Criminal Justice 2000*, Vol. 3. Washington, DC: National Institute of Justice.

Durcan, G., Allan, J., and Hamilton, I. (2018) *From prison to work: A new frontier for Individual Placement and Support*. London: Centre for Mental Health.

Durnescu, I. (2011) Resettlement Research and Practices. An International Perspective. Utrecht: Confederation of European Probation. Available at Durnescu-CEP-Resettlement-research-and-practice-final.pdf (cep-probation.org) [Accessed 7 December 2020].

Duwe, G. and Johnson, B. (2013) 'Estimating the Benefits of a Faith-Based Correctional Program'. *International Journal of Criminology and Sociology* 2: 227–39.

Edgar, K., Aresti, A., and Cornish, N. (2012) *Out for Good: Taking Responsibility for Resettlement*. London: Prison Reform Trust.

Farrall, S. (2002) *Rethinking What Works with Offenders*. Cullompton: Willan.

Farrall, S. and McNeill, F. (2010), 'Desistance Research and Criminal Justice Social Work' in M. Herzog-Evans (ed.) *Transnational Criminology Manual*, Vol. III. Nijmegen: Wolf Legal Publishers. Available at: www.cep-probation.org/wp-content/uploads/2018/10/Farrall_McNeill_Transnational_Criminology_Manual.pdf.

Garland, D. (1985) *Histories of Punishment and Welfare*. Aldershot: Ashgate.

Gilbert, P. (2009) 'Moving beyond cognitive behaviour therapy'. *The Psychologist* 22: 400–3.

Gordon, M. (2010) 'The Failure of Prison and the Value of Treatment' in P. Priestly and M. Vanstone (eds) *Offenders or Citizens? Readings in Rehabilitation*. Cullompton: Willan.

Government of British Columbia (2012) *Revealing Research & Evaluation 6 (Fall)*.

Grimshaw, R. (2002) 'A Place to Call Your Own: Does Housing Need Make a Difference to Crime?'. *Criminal Justice Matters* 50(1): 8–9.

Grimwood, G. and Berman, G. (2012) 'Reducing Reoffending: The "What Works" Debate', Research Paper 12/71. London: House of Commons Library.

Hannah-Moffat, K. (2005) 'Criminogenic Needs and the Transformative Risk Subject'. *Punishment and Society* 7(1): 29–51.

Haqanee, Z., Peterson-Badali, M., and Skilling, T. (2015) 'Making "what works" work: Examining probation officers' experiences addressing the criminogenic needs of juvenile offenders'. *Journal of Offender Rehabilitation* 54(1): 37–5.

Harper, G. and Chitty, C. (2005) 'Executive Summary' in G. Harper and C. Chitty (eds) *The Impact of Corrections on Re-offending: A Review of 'what works'*. London: Home Office.

Hendrick, H. (2006) 'Histories of Youth Crime and Justice' in B. Goldson and J. Muncie (eds) *Youth Crime and Justice*. London: Sage.

HM Inspectorate of Prisons, HM Inspectorate of Probation, and Ofsted (2014) *Resettlement Provision for Adult Offenders: Accommodation and Education, Training and Employment*. London: HM Inspectorate of Prisons.

Hollin, C. (1999) 'Treatment Programs for Offenders: Meta-Analysis, "What Works", and Beyond'. *International Journal of Law and Psychiatry* 22(3–4): 361–72.

Holmes, T. (2010) 'Reforming Criminals' in P. Priestly and M. Vanstone (eds) *Offenders or Citizens? Readings in Rehabilitation*. Cullompton: Willan.

Ignatieff, M. (1978) *A Just Measure of Pain*. London: Penguin.

Johnson, B. and Jang, S. (2010) 'Crime and Religion: Assessing the Role of the Faith Factor' in R. Rosenfeld, K. Quinet, and C. Garcia (eds) *Contemporary Issues in Criminological Theory and Research: The Role of Social Institutions. Papers from the American Society of Criminology Conference*. Belmont: CENGAGE Learning.

Johnson, C. and Rex, S. (2002) 'Community Service: Rediscovering Reintegration' in D. Ward, J. Scott, and M. Lacey (eds) *Probation: Working for Justice* (2nd edn). Oxford: Oxford University Press.

Kelly, L. and Westmarland, N. (2015) *Domestic Violence Perpetrator Programmes: Steps Towards Change*. Durham: Durham University.

Leeson, C. (1914) *The Probation System*. London: P. S. King & Son.

Lewis, S. et al. (2003) *The Resettlement of Short-term Prisoners: An Evaluation of Seven Pathfinders*. London: Home Office.

Lipscombe, S. and Beard, J. (2014) *The Rehabilitation of Offenders Act 1974*. London: House of Commons Library.

Lipsey, M. (1995) 'What do We Learn from 400 Research Studies on the Effectiveness of Treatment with Juvenile Delinquents?' in J. McGuire (ed.) *What Works: Reducing Offending*. Chichester: Wiley.

Lipsey, M. (1999) 'Can Intervention Rehabilitate Serious Delinquents?'. *Annals of the American Academy of Political and Social Science* 564: 142–66.

Lipsey, M. and Cullen, F. (2007) 'The Effectiveness of Correctional Rehabilitation: A Review of Systematic Reviews'. *Annual Review of Law and Social Science* 3: 1–44.

Lipsey, M., Landenberger, N., and Wilson, S. (2007) 'Effects of Cognitive-Behavioural Programs for Criminal Offenders'. *Campbell Systematic Reviews* 6.

Losel, F. (2018) 'Evidence comes by replication, but needs differentiation: the reproducibility issue in science and its relevance for criminology'. *Journal of Experimental Criminology* 14: 257–78.

Maguire, M. (2007) 'The Resettlement of Ex-prisoners' in L. Gelsthorpe and R. Morgan (eds) *Handbook of Probation*. Cullompton: Willan.

Mannheim, H. (1946) *Criminal Justice and Social Reconstruction*. London: Routledge & Kegan Paul.

Martinson, R. (1974) 'What works? Questions and answers about prison reform'. *The Public Interest* 35: 22–54.

Martinson, R. (1979) 'New Findings, New Views: A Note of Caution Regarding Sentencing Reform'. *Hofstra Law Review* 7(2): 243–58.

May, T. (1991) *Probation: Policy, Politics and Practice*. Milton Keynes: Open University Press.

McCord, J. (1992) 'The Cambridge–Somerville Study: A Pioneering Longitudinal Experimental Study of Delinquency Prevention' in J. McCord and R. Tremblay (eds) *Preventing Antisocial Behavior: Interventions from Birth through Adolescence*. New York: Guilford Press.

McGuire, J. and Priestley, P. (1995) 'Reviewing "What Works": Past, Present and Future' in J. McGuire (ed.) *What Works: Reducing Offending*. Chichester: Wiley.

McNeill, F. (2005) 'Remembering Probation in Scotland'. *Probation Journal* 52(1): 23–38.

McNeill, F. (2009) *Towards Effective Practice in Offender Supervision*. Glasgow: Scottish Centre for Crime & Justice Research.

McNeill, F. (2012) 'Four Forms of "Offender" Rehabilitation: Towards an Interdisciplinary Perspective'. *Legal and Criminological Psychology* 2012: 1–19.

McNeill, F. (2014) 'Punishment as Rehabilitation' in G. Bruinsma and D. Weisburd (eds) *Encyclopedia of Criminology and Criminal Justice*. New York: Springer.

McNeill, F. and Weaver, B. (2010) *Changing Lives? Desistance Research and Offender Management*. Glasgow: Scottish Centre for Crime & Justice Research.

McWilliams, W. (1983) 'The Mission to the English Police Courts 1876–1936'. *Howard Journal* 22(1): 129–47.

Ministry of Justice (2010) *Breaking the Cycle: Effective Punishment, Rehabilitation and Sentencing of Offenders*, Cm 7972. London: Ministry of Justice.

Ministry of Justice (2013) *Transforming Rehabilitation: A Summary of Evidence on Reducing Reoffending*. London: Ministry of Justice.

Ministry of Justice (2014) *Guidance on the Rehabilitation of Offenders Act 1974*. London: Ministry of Justice.

Niven, S. and Olagundoye, J. (2002) 'Jobs and Homes: A Survey of Prisoners Nearing Release', Home Office Research Findings 173. London: Home Office.

Poulton, F. (2010) 'The Spiritual Factor' in P. Priestly and M. Vanstone (eds) *Offenders or Citizens? Readings in Rehabilitation*. Cullompton: Willan.

Purvis, M., Ward, T., and Willis, G. (2011) 'The Good Lives Model in Practice: Offence Pathways and Case Management'. *European Journal of Probation* 3(2): 4–26.

Raynor, P. (2003) 'Evidence-based Probation and its Critics'. *Probation Journal* 50(4): 334–45.

Raynor, P. (2004) 'The Probation Service "Pathfinders"'. *Criminal Justice* 4(3): 309–25.

Raynor, P. and Robinson, G. (2009) 'Why Help Offenders? Arguments for Rehabilitation as a Penal Strategy'. *European Journal of Probation* 1(1): 3–20.

Robinson, G. (2008) 'Late-modern Rehabilitation'. *Punishment & Society* 10(4): 429–45.

Robinson, G. and Crow, I. (2009) *Offender Rehabilitation: Theory, Research and Practice*. London: Sage.

Ross, E., Polascheck, D., and Ward, T. (2008) 'The therapeutic alliance: A theoretical revision for offender rehabilitation'. *Aggression and Violent Behavior* 13(6): 462–80.

Saleilles, R. (2010) 'The Individualization of Punishment' in P. Priestley and M. Vanstone (eds) *Offenders or Citizens?* Cullompton: Willan.

Sapouna, M., Bisset, C., and Conlong, A-M. (2011) *What Works to Reduce Reoffending: A Summary of the Evidence*. Edinburgh: Scottish Government.

Sherman, L. et al. (1998) *Preventing Crime: What Works, What Doesn't, What's Promising*. Washington, DC: US Department of Justice.

Stewart, D. (2008) 'The problems and needs of newly sentenced prisoners: results from a national survey', Ministry of Justice Research Series 16/08. London: Ministry of Justice.

Vanstone, M. (2004) 'Mission Control: The Origins of a Humanitarian Service'. *Probation Journal* 51: 34–47.

Viglione, J. (2019) 'The Risk-Need-Responsivity Model: How Do Probation Officers Implement the Principles of Effective Intervention?'. *Criminal Justice and Behavior* 46(5): 655–73.

Volokh, A. (2011) 'Do Faith-Based Prisons Work?'. *Alabama Law Review* 63(1): 43–95.

Ward, T. and Gannon, T. (2006) 'Rehabilitation, Etiology and Self-Regulation: The Comprehensive Good Lives Model of Treatment for Sexual Offenders'. *Aggression and Violent Behaviour* 11: 77–94.

Ward, T. and Maruna, S. (2007) *Rehabilitation*. Abingdon: Routledge.

Webster, R. et al. (2001) *Building Bridges to Employment for Prisoners*. London: Home Office.

Weiss, C. et al. (2008) 'The fairy godmother–and her warts: Making the dream of evidence-based policy come true'. *American Journal of Evaluation* 29(1): 29–47.

Werb, D. et al. (2016) 'The Effectiveness of Compulsory Drug Treatment: A Systematic Review'. *International Journal of Drug Policy* 28: 1–9.

Western, B. et al. (2015) 'Stress and Hardship after Prison'. *American Journal of Sociology* 120(5): 1512–47.

Wikstrom, P.-O. and Treiber, K. (2008) *Offending Behaviour Programmes*. London: Youth Justice Board.

Wong, K. (2019) 'If reoffending is not the only outcome, what are the alternatives?', Academic Insights, 2019/07, HM Inspectorate of Probation. Available at www.justiceinspectorates.gov.uk/hmiprobation/wp-content/uploads/sites/5/2019/11/Academic-Insights-Wong.pdf [Accessed 7 December 2020].

Wylie, L. and Griffin, H. (2013) 'G-map's Application of the Good Lives Model to Adolescent Males Who Sexually Harm: A Case Study'. *Journal of Sexual Aggression* 19(3): 345–56.

Zane, S., Welsh, B., and Zimmerman, G. (2015) 'Examining the Iatrogenic Effects of the Cambridge–Somerville Youth Study: Existing Explanations and New Appraisals'. *British Journal of Criminology*. DOI: 10.1093/bjc/azv033.

Chapter 30

Ahmed, E. and Braithwaite, J. (2011) 'Shame, Pride and Workplace Bullying' in S. Karstedt, I. Loader, and H. Strang (eds) *Emotions, Crime and Justice*. Oxford: Hart.

Allen, R. (2017) *Less is more—the case for dealing with offences out of court*. London: Transform Justice.

Austin, J. and Krisberg, B. (2002) 'Wider, Stronger and Different Nets: The Dialectics of Criminal Justice Reform' in J. Muncie, G. Hughes, and E. McLaughlin (eds) *Youth Justice: Critical Readings*. London: Sage.

Barnes, B. (2013) 'An Overview of Restorative Justice Programs'. *Alaska Journal of Dispute Resolution* 1: 101–20.

Bateman, T. (2015) 'Trends in Detected Youth Crime and Contemporary State Responses' in B. Goldson and J. Muncie (eds) *Youth Crime & Justice* (2nd edn). London: Sage.

Bell, A., Hodgson, M., and Pragnell, S. (1999) 'Diverting Children and Young People from Crime and the Criminal Justice System' in B. Goldson (ed.) *Youth Justice: Contemporary Policy and Practice*. Aldershot: Ashgate.

Bennett, C. (2006) 'Taking the Sincerity Out of Saying Sorry: Restorative Justice as Ritual'. *Journal of Applied Philosophy* 23(2): 127–43.

Blagg, H. (1985) 'Reparation and Justice for Juveniles'. *British Journal of Criminology* 25: 267–79.

Blagg, H. et al. (1986) *The Final Report on the Juvenile Liaison Bureau Corby*. Lancaster: University of Lancaster.

Bowling, B. and Phillips, C. (2003) 'Policing Ethnic Minority Communities' in T. Newburn (ed.) *Handbook of Policing*. Cullompton: Willan.

Boyes-Watson, C. (2000) 'Reflections on the Purist and Maximalist Models of Restorative Justice'. *Contemporary Justice Review* 3(4): 441–50.

Braithwaite, J. (1989) *Crime, Shame and Reintegration*. Cambridge: Cambridge University Press.

Braithwaite, J. (1998) 'Restorative Justice' in M. Tonry (ed.) *Handbook of Crime & Punishment*. Oxford: Oxford University Press.

Braithwaite, J. (2004) 'The Evolution of Restorative Justice' in UNAFEI (ed.) *Annual Report for 2003 and Resource Material Series No. 63*. Tokyo: UNAFEI.

Brehm, H., Uggen, C., and Gasanabo, J-D. (2014) 'Genocide, Justice, and Rwanda's Gacaca Courts'. *Journal of Contemporary Criminal Justice* 30(3): 333–52.

Campbell, C. et al. (2006) *Evaluation of the Northern Ireland Youth Conference Service*. Belfast: Northern Ireland Office.

Centre for Mental Health, Rethink, and the Royal College of Psychiatrists (2010) *Diversion: The Business Case for Action*. London: Centre for Mental Health.

Christie, N. (1977) 'Conflicts as Property'. *British Journal of Criminology* 17(1): 1–15.

Clamp, K. and Doak, J. (2012) 'More than Words: Restorative Justice Concepts in Transitional Justice Settings'. *International Criminal Law Review* 12: 339–60.

Cohen, S. (1985) *Visions of Social Control*. Cambridge: Polity Press.

Crawford, A. and Newburn, T. (2003) *Youth Offending and Restorative Justice*. Cullompton: Willan.

Daly, K. (2002) 'Restorative Justice: The Real Story'. *Punishment & Society* 4(1): 55–79.

Davis, G., Boucherat, J., and Watson, D. (1989) 'Pre-Court Decision-Making in Juvenile Justice'. *British Journal of Criminology* 29(3): 219–35.

Dignan, J. (1990) *Repairing the Damage*. Sheffield: University of Sheffield.

Flanagan, R. (2007) *The Review of Policing: Interim Report*. Surbiton: The Police Federation.

Gabbay, Z. (2005) 'Justifying Restorative Justice: A Theoretical Justification for the Use of Restorative Practices'. *Journal of Dispute Resolution* 2005(2): 349–97.

Gavrielides, T. (2017) *Restorative Justice: Ideals and Realities*. Abingdon: Routledge.

Graef, R. (2000) *Why Restorative Justice?* London: Calouste Gulbenkian Foundation.

Haines, A. et al. (2012) *Evaluation of the Youth Justice Liaison and Diversion (YJLD) Pilot Scheme*. Liverpool: University of Liverpool.

Haines, K. et al. (2013) 'The Swansea Bureau: A model of diversion from the Youth Justice System'. *International Journal of Law, Crime and Justice* 41(2): 167–87.

Hamilton, C. (2011) *Guidance for Legislative Reform on Juvenile Justice*. New York: Unicef.

Harris, N. and Maruna, S. (2006) 'Shame, Shaming and Restorative Justice' in D. Sullivan and L. Tifft (eds) *Handbook of Restorative Justice: A Global Perspective*. Abingdon: Routledge.

Her Majesty's Inspectorate of Probation (2016) *Referral orders—do they achieve their potential?* Manchester: HMIP.

Hough, M. et al. (2013) *Attitudes to Sentencing and Trust in Justice: Exploring Trends from the Crime Survey for England and Wales*. London: Ministry of Justice.

House of Commons Justice Committee (2009) *Cutting Crime: The Case for Justice Reinvestment*. London: The Stationery Office.

House of Commons Justice Committee (2013) *Youth Justice*. London: The Stationery Office.

Hughes, G., Pilkington, A., and Leisten, R. (1998) 'Diversion in a Culture of Severity'. *Howard Journal* 37(1): 16–33.

Jacobson, J. and Kirby, A. (2012) *Public Attitudes to Youth Crime: Report on Focus Group Research*. London: Home Office.

Johnstone, G. (2002) *Restorative Justice: Ideas, Values, Debates*. Cullompton: Willan.

Johnstone, G. (2011) *Restorative Justice: Ideas, Values, Debates* (2nd edn). Abingdon: Routledge.

Kretschmar, J. et al. (2016) 'Diverting Juvenile Justice-Involved Youth with Behavioral Health Issues from Detention: Preliminary Findings from Ohio's Behavioral Health Juvenile Justice (BHJJ) Initiative'. *Criminal Justice Policy Review* 27(3): 1–24.

Lacey, L. (2012) 'Youth Justice in England and Wales: Exploring Young Offenders' Perceptions of Restorative and Procedural Justice in the Referral Order Process'. PhD thesis, London School of Economics.

Lammy, D. (2017) *The Lammy Review: An independent review into the treatment of, and outcomes for Black, Asian and Minority Ethnic individuals in the criminal justice system*. London: Ministry of Justice.

Larsen, J. (2014) *Restorative Justice in the Australian Criminal Justice System*. Canberra: Australian Institute of Criminology.

Lemert, E. (1967) *Human Deviance, Social Problems, and Social Control*. Englewood Cliffs, NJ: Prentice Hall.

Maruna, S. et al. (2007) *Youth Conferencing as Shame Management: Results of a Long-term Follow-Up Study*. Belfast: ARCS.

Matrix Evidence (2009) *Economic Analysis of Interventions for Young Adult Offenders*. London: Barrow Cadbury Trust.

Mays, J. (1965) 'The Liverpool Police Juvenile Liaison Officer Scheme'. *The Sociological Review* Monograph No. 9: 185–200.

McAra, L. and McVie, S. (2007) 'Youth Justice? The Impact of System Contact on Patterns of Desistance from Offending'. *European Journal of Criminology* 4(3): 315–45.

Menkel-Meadow, C. (2007) 'Restorative Justice: What Is It and Does It Work?'. *Annual Review of Law and Social Science* 3: 10.1–10.27.

Mills, H. (2011) 'The "Alternative to Custody" Myth'. *Criminal Justice Matters* 83(1): 34–6.

Ministry of Justice (2010) *Breaking the Cycle: Effective Punishment, Rehabilitation and Sentencing of Offenders*. London: Ministry of Justice.

Ministry of Justice (2018) *Referral Order Guidance*. London: Ministry of Justice.

Mongold, J. and Edwards, B. (2014) 'Reintegrative Shaming: Theory into Practice'. *Journal of Theoretical & Philosophical Criminology* 6(3): 205–12.

Morgan, P. (1981) 'The Children's Act: Sacrificing justice to children's needs?' in C. Brewer et al. (eds) *Criminal Welfare on Trial*. London: Social Affairs Unit.

Morris, A. et al. (1980) *Justice for Children*. London: Macmillan.

Northern Ireland Office (2008) *Alternatives to Prosecution: A Discussion Paper*. Belfast: Northern Ireland Office.

O'Mahony, D. and Doak, J. (2017) *Reimagining Restorative Justice*. London: Bloomsbury.

Pratt, J. (1989) 'Corporatism: The Third Model of Juvenile Justice'. *British Journal of Criminology* 29: 236–54.

Restorative Justice Consortium (2006) *The Positive Effect of Restorative Justice on Re-offending*. London: Restorative Justice Consortium.

Rix, A. et al. (2011) *Youth Restorative Disposal Process Evaluation*. London: Youth Justice Board.

Robinson, G. and Shapland, J. (2008) 'Reducing Recidivism: A Task for Restorative Justice?'. *British Journal of Criminology* 48(3): 337–58.

Rutherford. A. (1992) *Growing out of Crime* (2nd edn). Winchester, Waterside Press.

Schiff, M. (2003) 'Models, Challenges and the Promise of Restorative Conferencing Strategies' in A. von Hirsch et al. (eds) *Restorative Justice and Criminal Justice: Competing or Reconcilable Paradigms?* Oxford: Hart.

Schur, E. (1973) *Radical Non-Intervention: Re-thinking the Delinquency Problem*. Englewood Cliffs, NJ: Prentice Hall.

Scottish Government (2019) *Restorative Justice Action Plan*. Edinburgh: Scottish Government.

Shapland, J. et al. (2007) *Restorative Justice: The Views of Victims and Offenders*. London: Ministry of Justice.

Smith, R. (2010) 'Children's Rights and Youth Justice: 20 Years of No Progress'. *Child Care in Practice* 16(1): 3–17.

Smith, R. (2011a) 'Developing Restorative Practice: Contemporary Lessons from an English Juvenile Diversion Project of the 1980s'. *Contemporary Justice Review* 14(4): 425–38.

Smith, R. (2011b) *Doing Justice to Young People*. Cullompton: Willan.

Smith, R. (2014a) *Youth Justice: Ideas, Policy, Practice*. Abingdon: Routledge.

Smith, R. (2014b) 'Re-inventing Diversion'. *Youth Justice* 14(2): 109–21.

Smith, R. (2018) *Diversion in Youth Justice: What Can We Learn from Historical and Contemporary Practice?* Abingdon: Routledge.

Smith, R. and Gray, P. (2019) 'The changing shape of youth justice: Models of practice'. *Criminology & Criminal Justice* 19(5) 554–71.

Smyth, P. (2011) 'Diverting Young Offenders from Crime in Ireland: The Need for More Checks and Balances on the Exercise of Police Discretion'. *Crime Law and Social Change* 55: 153–66.

Strang, H. et al. (2013) 'Restorative Justice Conferencing (RJC) Using Face-to-Face Meetings of Offenders and Victims: Effects on Offender Recidivism and Victim Satisfaction. A Systematic Review'. *Campbell Systematic Reviews* 2013: 10.

Sutherland, A. et al. (2017) *An analysis of trends in first time entrants to the youth justice system*. London: Ministry of Justice.

Suzuki, T. and Wood, W. (2018) 'Is restorative justice conferencing appropriate for youth offenders?'. *Criminology and Criminal Justice* 18(4): 250–67.

Szmania, S. and Mangis, D. (2005) 'Finding the Right Time and Place: A Case Study Comparison of the Expression of Offender Remorse in Traditional Justice and Restorative Justice Contexts'. *Marquette Law Review* 89: 335–58.

Taylor, C. (2016) *Review of the Youth Justice System in England and Wales*. London: Ministry of Justice.

Thorpe, D. et al. (1980) *Out of Care: The Community Support of Juvenile Offenders*. London: George Allen & Unwin.

Umbreit, M. (1989) 'Crime Victims Seeking Fairness, Not Revenge: Toward Restorative Justice'. *Federal Probation September*: 52–7.

Victim Support (2012) *Out in the Open: What Victims Really Think About Community Sentencing*. London: Victim Support.

Walgrave, L. (2003) 'Imposing Restoration instead of Inflicting Pain' in A. von Hirsch et al. (eds) *Restorative Justice: Competing or Reconcilable Paradigms?* Oxford: Hart.

Wilson, H. and Hoge, R. (2013) 'The Effect of Youth Diversion Programs on Recidivism'. *Criminal Justice and Behaviour* 40(5): 497–518.

Wong, K., Ellingworth, D., and Meadows, L. (2016) *Local Justice Reinvestment Pilot: Final process evaluation report*. London: Ministry of Justice.

Wood, W. (2015) 'Why Restorative Justice Will Not Reduce Incarceration'. *British Journal of Criminology*. DOI: 10.1093/bjc/azu/108.

Youth Justice Board (2020) *Youth Justice Statistics 2018–19*. London: Youth Justice Board.

Zehr, H. (2003) *The Little Book of Restorative Justice* (2nd edn). Intercourse, PA: Good Books.

Zimring, F. (2000) 'The Common Thread: Diversion in Juvenile Justice'. *California Law Review* 88(6): 2481–95.

Chapter 31

Althusser, L. (1971) *Lenin and Philosophy and Other Essays*. London: Verso.

Barton, A. et al. (2007) 'Conclusion: Expanding the Criminological Imagination' in A. Barton et al. (eds) *Expanding the Criminological Imagination*. Cullompton: Willan.

Bazemore, G. (1997) 'Conferences, Circles, Boards, and Mediations: The "New Wave" of Community Justice Decisionmaking'. *Federal Probation* 61(2): 25–37.

Beck, U. (1992) *Risk Society*. London: Sage.

Becker, H. (1967) 'Whose Side Are We On?'. *Social Problems* 14(3): 239–47.

Bianchi, H. (1994) 'Abolition: Assensus and Sanctuary' in A. Duff and D. Garland (eds) *A Reader on Punishment*. Oxford: Oxford University Press.

Blagg, H. (2009) *Evaluation of the Red Dust Role Models*. Victoria: Red Dust Role Models.

Blomberg, T. and Hay, C. (2007) '*Visions of Social Control* revisited' in D. Downes et al. (eds) *Crime, Social Control and Human Rights*. Cullompton: Willan.

Bowling, B. and Phillips, C. (2007) 'Ethnicities, Racism, Crime and Criminal Justice' in M. Maguire, R. Morgan, and R. Reiner (eds) *The Oxford Handbook of Criminology* (4th edn). Oxford: Oxford University Press.

Bruce, J. (2007) 'The Role of Structural Factors Underlying Incidences of Extreme Opportunism in Financial Markets'. PhD thesis, University of South Africa.

Carson, E. (2014) 'Prisoners in 2013', Bureau of Justice Statistics Bulletin, September. Washington, DC: US Department of Justice.

Chambliss, W. (1976) 'The State and Criminal Law' in W. Chambliss and M. Mankoff (eds) *Whose Law, What Order?* New York: Wiley.

Chantrill, P. (1998) 'The Kowanyama Aboriginal Community Justice Group and the Struggle for Legal Pluralism in Australia'. *Journal of Legal Pluralism* 40: 23–60.

Chapman, T. (2012) 'The Problem of Community in a Justice System in Transition: The Case of Community Restorative Justice in Northern Ireland'. *International Criminal Law Review* 12(3): 573–87.

Cohen, S. (1985) *Visions of Social Control*. Cambridge: Polity Press.

Cullis, J. et al. (2015) 'Do Poachers Make Harsh Gamekeepers? Attitudes to Tax Evasion and to Benefit Fraud'. *Journal of Behavioral and Experimental Economics* 58 (October): 124–31.

Edwards, T. (2015) 'Criminal Failure and "The Chilling Effect": A Short History of the Bhopal Criminal Prosecutions'. *Social Justice* 41(1–2): 53–79.

Foucault, M. (1977) *Discipline and Punish: The Birth of the Prison*. Harmondsworth: Penguin.

Gegout, C. (2013) 'The International Criminal Court: limits, potential and conditions for the promotion of justice and peace'. *Third World Quarterly* 34(5): 800–18.

Gibson, J. (2005) 'The Truth about Truth and Reconciliation in South Africa'. *International Political Science Review* 26(4): 341–61.

Gibson, J. (2009) 'On Legitimacy Theory and the Effectiveness of Truth Commissions'. *Law and Contemporary Problems* (Spring): 123–41.

Gilbert, M. and Settles, T. (2007) 'The Next Step: Indigenous Development of Neighbourhood-Restorative Community Justice'. *Criminal Justice Review* 32(1): 5–25.

Gramsci (1971) *Selections from Prison Notebooks*. London: Lawrence & Wishart.

Greener, I. (2006) 'Nick Leeson and the Collapse of Barings Bank: Socio-Technical Networks and the "Rogue Trader"'. *Organization* 13(3): 421–41.

Hopkins, K. (2015) 'Associations Between Police-Recorded Ethnic Background and Being Sentenced to Prison in England and Wales'. London: Ministry of Justice Analytical Services. Available at: www.gov.uk/government/uploads/system/uploads/attachment_data/file/479874/analysis-of-ethnicity-and-custodial-sentences.pdf [Accessed 8 December 2020].

Hoyle, C. and Zedner, L. (2007) 'Victims, Victimization and Criminal Justice' in M. Maguire, R. Morgan, and R. Reiner (eds) *The Oxford Handbook of Criminology* (4th edn). Oxford: Oxford University Press.

Hughes, J. (2015) 'Reconstruction without Reconciliation: Is Northern Ireland a "Model"?' in B. Kissane (ed.) *After Civil War: Division, Reconstruction, and Reconciliation in Contemporary Europe*. Philadelphia, PA: University of Pennsylvania Press.

Irwin-Rogers, K. (2018) 'Racism and Racial Discrimination in the Criminal Justice System: Exploring the views of men serving sentences of imprisonment'. *Justice, Power, Resistance* 2(2): 243–66.

Jefferson, T. (2015) 'The 2011 English Riots: A Contextualised, Dynamic, Grounded Explanation'. *Contention* 2(2): 5–22.

Jones, D. (2012) 'Conditions for Sustainable Decarceration Policies for Young Offenders'. PhD thesis, London School of Economics.

Karp, D. and Clear, T. (2000) 'Community Justice: A Conceptual Framework' in C. Friel (ed.) *Criminal Justice 2000*, Vol. 2. Washington, DC: US Department of Justice.

Keith, B. (2006) *Report of the Zahid Mubarek Inquiry*, Vol. 1. London: The Stationery Office.

Krisberg, B. and Austin, J. (1993) *Reinventing Juvenile Justice*. Newbury Park, CA: Sage.

Ku, J. and Nzelibe, J. (2006) 'Do International Criminal Tribunals Deter or Exacerbate Humanitarian Atrocities?'. *Washington University Law Review* 84(4): 777–833.

Lamble, S. (2013) 'The Quiet Dangers of Civilized Rage: Surveying the Punitive Aftermath of England's 2011 Riots'. *South Atlantic Quarterly* 112(3): 577–85.

Lammy, D. (2017) *The Lammy Review: An independent review into the treatment of, and outcomes for Black, Asian and Minority Ethnic individuals in the criminal justice system*. London: Ministry of Justice.

Lea, J. (1999) 'Social Crime Revisited'. *Theoretical Criminology* 3(3): 307–25.

Lea, J. (2002) *Crime and Modernity*. London: Sage.

Lea, J. (2010) 'Left Realism, community and state-building'. *Crime, Law and Social Change* 54(2): 141–58.

Lucas, G. (2011) '"New Rules for New Wars" International Law and Just War Doctrine for Irregular War'. *Case Western Reserve Journal of International Law* 43(3): 677–705.

Macpherson, W. (1999) *The Stephen Lawrence Inquiry*, Cm 4262-1. London: The Stationery Office.

Mair, G. and Millings, M. (2011) *Doing Justice Locally: The North Liverpool Community Justice Centre*. London: Centre for Crime and Justice Studies.

Mathiesen, T. (1974) *The Politics of Abolition*. London: Martin Robertson.

Mathiesen, T. (2008) 'The Abolitionist Stance'. *Journal of Prisoners on Prisons* 17(2): 58–63.

May, T., Gyateng, T., and Hough, M. (2010) *Differential Treatment in the Youth Justice System, Research Report 50*. London: Equality and Human Rights Commission.

McEvoy, K. and Mika, H. (2002) 'Restorative Justice and the Critique of Informalism in Northern Ireland'. *British Journal of Criminology* 42(3): 534–62.

McGrattan, C. (2012) 'Working Through the Past in Bosnia and Northern Ireland: Truth, Reconciliation and the Constraints of Consociationalism'. *Journal on Ethnopolitics and Minority Issues in Europe* 11(4): 103–26.

McLeod, A, (2015) 'Prison Abolition and Grounded Justice'. *UCLA Law Review* 62: 1156–239.

Mika, H. (2006) *Community-based Restorative Justice in Northern Ireland*. Belfast: Institute of Criminology & Criminal Justice, School of Law, Queen's University Belfast.

Ministry of Justice (2013) *Statistics on Race and the Criminal Justice System 2012*. London: Ministry of Justice.

Nagy, R. (2013) 'The Scope and Bounds of Transitional Justice and the Canadian Truth and Reconciliation Commission'. *International Journal of Transitional Justice* 7: 52–73.

Nurse, A. (2014) 'Critical Perspectives on Green Criminology: An Introduction' in A. Nurse (ed.) *Critical Perspectives on Green Criminology*. Internet Journal of Criminology. Available at: www.internetjournalofcriminology.com/peer-reviewed-edited-collections.

O'Brien, M. and Penna, S. (2007) 'Critical Criminology: Continuity and Change'. *Criminal Justice Review* 32(3): 246–55.

O'Shea, A. (2008) 'Truth and Reconciliation Commissions' in *The Max Planck Encyclopedia of Public International Law*. Oxford: Oxford University Press.

Pavlich, G. (1999) 'Criticism and Criminology: In Search of Legitimacy'. *Theoretical Criminology* 3(1): 29–51.

Pearce, F. (1977) *The Crimes of the Powerful*. London: Pluto Press.

Pearlman, S. (2015) 'Human Rights Violations at Guantánamo Bay: How the United States Has Avoided Enforcement of International Norms'. *Seattle University Law Review* 38: 1109.

Penrose, M. (1999) 'Lest We Fail: The Importance of Enforcement in International Criminal Law'. *American University International Law Review* 15(2): 320–94.

Pettit, B. and Western, B. (2004) 'Mass Imprisonment and the Life Course: Race and Class Inequality in U.S. Incarceration'. *American Sociological Review* 69: 151–69.

Phillips, C. and Bowling, B. (2017) 'Ethnicities, racism, crime and criminal justice' in A. Liebling, S. Maruna and L. McAra (eds) *The Oxford Handbook of Criminology* (6th edn). Oxford: Oxford University Press.

Prison Reform Trust (2014) 'Prison: The Facts—Bromley Briefings', Summer. London: Prison Reform Trust.

Prison Reform Trust (2017) 'Bromley Briefings Prison Factfile', Autumn 2017. London: Prison Reform Trust.

Quinney, R. (1970) *The Social Reality of Crime*. Boston, MA: Little, Brown.

Quinney, R. (1977) *State, Class, Crime*. New York: McKay.

Roberts, R. (2015) 'Racism and Criminal Justice'. *Criminal Justice Matters* 101(1): 18–20.

Rock, P. (2007) 'Sociological Theories of Crime' in M. Maguire, R. Morgan, and R. Reiner (eds) *The Oxford Handbook of Criminology* (4th edn). Oxford: Oxford University Press.

Rothman, D. (1985) 'Social Control: The Uses and Abuses of the Concept in the History of Incarceration' in S. Cohen and A. Scull (eds) *Social Control and the State*. Oxford: Blackwell.

Ryan, N. et al. (2006) 'Engaging Indigenous Communities: Towards a Policy Framework for Indigenous Community Justice Programs'. *Social Policy & Administration* 40(3): 304–21.

Scarman, L. (1982) *The Scarman Report*. Harmondsworth: Penguin.

Scott, D. (2013) 'Why Prison? Posing the Question' in D. Scott (ed.) *Why Prison?* Cambridge: Cambridge University Press.

Scraton, P. (2002) 'Defining "Power" and Challenging "Knowledge": Critical Analysis as Resistance in the UK' in K. Carrington and R. Hogg (eds) *Critical Criminology: Issues, Debates, Challenges*. Cullompton: Willan.

Shiner, M. et al. (2015) *The Colour of Injustice: 'Race', drugs and law enforcement*. London: Stopwatch.

Shiner, M. et al. (2018) *The colour of injustice: 'race', drugs and law enforcement in England and Wales*. London: StopWatch.

Sim, J. (2009) *Punishment and Prisons: Power and the Carceral State*. Sage: London.

Sim, J. (2012) '"Shock and Awe": judicial responses to the riots'. *Criminal Justice Matters* 89(1): 26–7.

Skaar, E. (2013) 'Reconciliation in a Transitional Justice Perspective'. *Transitional Justice Review* 1(10): 1–50.

Slapper, G. and Tombs, S. (1999) *Corporate Crime*. Harlow: Pearson Educational.

Smith, D. (2009) 'Criminology, Contemporary Society and Race Issues' in H. Bhui (ed.) *Race & Criminal Justice*. London: Sage.

Smith, R. and Fleming, J. (2011) *Welfare + rights: UR Boss Legal Service*. London: Howard League.

Stolzenberg, L., D'Alessio, S., and Eitle, D. (2013) 'Race and Cumulative Discrimination in the Prosecution of Criminal Defendants'. *Race and Justice* 3(4): 275–99.

Sturge, G. (2019) 'UK Prison Population Statistics', Briefing Paper No. CBP-04334. London: House of Commons Library

Sykes, G. (1974) 'The Rise of Critical Criminology'. *Journal of Criminal Law and Criminology* 65(2): 206–13.

Tavernier, P. (1997) 'L'Expérience des Tribunaux Pénaux Internationaux pour l'Ex-Yougoslavie et pour le Rwanda'. *Revue International de la Croix-Rouge* 79(828): 647–63.

Taylor, I., Walton, P., and Young, J. (1973) *The New Criminology*. London: Routledge & Kegan Paul.

Taylor, I., Walton, P., and Young, J. (eds) (1975) *Critical Criminology*. London: Routledge & Kegan Paul.

Tombs, S. and Whyte, D. (2009) 'The State and Corporate Crime' in R. Coleman et al. (eds) *State Power Crime*. London: Sage.

Tombs, S. and Whyte, D. (2015) *The Corporate Criminal: Why Corporations Must Be Abolished*. Abingdon: Routledge.

Vora, J. and Vora, E. (2004) 'The Effectiveness of South Africa's Truth and Reconciliation Commission'. *Journal of Black Studies* 34(3): 301–22.

Walker, N. (1974) 'Lost Causes in Criminology' in R. Hood (ed.) *Crime, Criminology and Public Policy: Essays in Honour of Sir Leon Radzinowicz*. London: Heinemann.

Walklate, S. (2004) *Gender, Crime and Criminal Justice* (2nd edn). Cullompton: Willan.

Weaver, B. (2011) 'Co-Producing Community Justice: The Transformative Potential of Personalisation for Penal Sanctions'. *British Journal of Social Work* 41: 1038–57.

Williams, K., Papadopoulou, V., and Booth, N. (2012) *Prisoners' Childhood and Family Backgrounds*. Ministry of Justice Research Series 4/12. London: Ministry of Justice.

Wilson, R., Huculak, B., and McWhinnie, A. (2002) 'Restorative Justice Innovations in Canada'. *Behavioral Sciences and the Law* 20: 363–80.

Wilson, S. (2001) 'The Myth of Restorative Justice: Truth, Reconciliation and the Ethics of Amnesty'. *South African Journal of Human Rights* 17: 531–62.

Yarrow, S. (2005) *The Experiences of Young Black Men as Victims of Crime*. London: Criminal Justice System Race Unit.

Young, J. (1986) 'The Failure of Criminology: The Need for a Radical Realism' in R. Matthews and J. Young (eds) *Confronting Crime*. London: Sage.

Young, L. (2014) *Improving Outcomes for Young Black and/or Muslim Men in the Criminal Justice System* (The Young Review). London: Barrow Cadbury Trust.

Youth Justice Board (2018) *Youth Justice Statistics 2016/17 England and Wales*. London: Ministry of Justice.

Chapter 32

Amrine, M. and Sanford, F. (1956) 'In the Matter of Juries, Democracy, Science, Truth, Senators and Bugs'. *American Psychologist* 1(1): 54–60.

Braun, V. and Clarke, V. (2006) 'Using thematic analysis in psychology'. *Qualitative Research in Psychology* 3: 77–101.

British Society of Criminology (2015) 'Statement of Ethics for Researchers in the Field of Criminology'. Available at: www.britsoccrim.org/ethics.

Brown, M. and Carrabine, E. (eds) (2017) *Routledge International Handbook of Visual Criminology*. Abingdon: Routledge.

Calvey, D. (2013) 'Covert Ethnography in Criminology: A Submerged yet Creative Tradition'. *Current Issues in Criminal Justice* 25(1): 541–50.

Calvey, D. (2017) *Covert Research: The Art, Politics and Ethics of Undercover Fieldwork*. London: Sage.

Cape, E. (2010) 'Adversarialism "Lite": Developments in Criminal Procedure and Evidence under New Labour'. *Criminal Justice Matters* 79(1): 25–7.

Cavan, S. (1977) 'Investigative Social Research: Individual and Team Field Research. Jack D. Douglas'. *American Journal of Sociology* 83(3): 809–11.

Chamberlain, J. M. (2013) *Understanding Criminological Research: A Guide to Data Analysis*. London: Sage.

Clark, T., Foster, L., and Bryman, A. (2019) *How to do your Social Research Project or Dissertation*. Oxford: Oxford University Press.

Clark, T. et al. (2021) *Bryman's Social Research Methods* (6th edn). Oxford: Oxford University Press.

Devlin, P. (1956) *Trial By Jury*. London: Stevens & Sons.

Finch, E. and Fafinski, S. (2019) *Criminology Skills* (3rd edn). Oxford: Oxford University Press.

Fitzgibbon, W. and Healy, D. (2019) 'Lives and spaces: Photovoice and offender supervision in Ireland and England'. *Criminology & Criminal Justice* 19(1): 3–25.

Foster, J. (1995) 'Informal Social Control and Community Crime Prevention'. *British Journal of Criminology* 35(4): 563–83.

Glaser, B. and Strauss, A. (1967) *The Discovery of Grounded Theory: Strategies for Qualitative Research*. Chicago, IL: Aldine.

Heap, V. and Waters, J. (2019) *Mixed Methods in Criminology*. London: Routledge.

Hey, J. D. (1998) 'Experimental economics and deception: A comment'. *Journal of Economic Psychology* 19: 397–401.

Holdaway, S. (1982) '"An Inside Job": a case study of covert research on the police' in M. Bulmer (ed.) *Social Research Ethics: An Examination of the Merits of Covert Participant Observation*. London: Macmillan.

Hood, R. (2002) 'Criminology and Penal Policy: The Vital Role of Empirical Research' in A. Bottoms and M. Tonry (eds) *Ideology, Crime and Criminal Justice*. Cullompton: Willan.

Humphreys, L. (1970) *Tearoom Trade*. Chicago, IL: Aldine.

Jones, P. and Wardle, C. (2008) '"No Emotion, No Sympathy": The Visual Construction of Maxine Carr'. *Crime, Media, Culture* 4(1): 53–71.

Kirby, S., Francis, B., and O'Flaherty, R. (2014) 'Can the FIFA World Cup Football tournament be associated with an increase in domestic abuse?'. *Journal of Research in Crime and Delinquency* 51(3): 259–76.

McCarthy, B. R., McCarthy, B. J., and Pealer, J. A. (2020) 'Ethics in Criminal Justice Research' in M. C. Bracewell et al. (eds) *Justice, Crime, and Ethics* (10th edn). Abingdon: Routledge.

Milgram, S. (1974) *Obedience to Authority: An Experimental View*. New York: Harper & Row.

Packer, H. L. (1964) 'Two Models of the Criminal Process'. *University of Pennsylvania Law Review* 113: 1–68.

Pearl, J. and Mackenzie, D. (2018) *The Book of Why: The New Science of Cause and Effect*. New York: Basic Books.

Pearson, G. (2009) 'The Researcher as Hooligan: Where Participant Observation Means Breaking the Law'. *International Journal of Social Research Methodology* 12: 243–55.

Rock, P. (2017) 'The Foundations of Sociological Theories of Crime' in A. Liebling, S. Maruna, and L. McAra (eds) *The Oxford Handbook of Criminology* (6th edn). Oxford: Oxford University Press.

Stevens, A. (2020) 'Access denied: Research on sex in prison and the subjugation of "deviant knowledge"'. *Criminology & Criminal Justice* 20(4): 451–70.

Stratton, G. (2015) 'Transforming the Central Park jogger into the Central Park Five: Shifting narratives of innocence and changing media discourse in the attack on the Central Park jogger, 1989–2014'. *Crime Media Culture* 11(3): 281–97.

The Boyer Commission on Educating Undergraduates in the Research University (1998) *Reinventing Undergraduate Education: A Blueprint for America's Research University*. Stony Brook, NY: State University of New York at Stony Brook.

The International Visual Sociology Association (nd) *Code of Research Ethics*. Available at: https://visualsociology.org/about/ethics-and-guidelines.html.

Tuomi, I. (2013) 'Open Educational Resources and the Transformation of Education'. *European Journal of Education* 48(1): 58–78.

Vohryzek-Bolden, M. (1997) 'Ethical Dilemmas Confronting Criminological Researchers'. *Journal of Crime and Justice* 20(2): 121–38.

Zimbardo, P. (1973) 'On the Ethics of Intervention in Human Psychological Research: With Special Reference to the Stanford Prison Study'. *Cognition* 22: 243–6.

Chapter 33

Balta, M., Coughlan, J., and Hobson, P. (2012) 'Motivations and Barriers in Undergraduate Students' Decisions to Enroll in Placement Courses in the UK'. *Journal of International Education Research* 8(4): 399–413.

Bowes, L. and Harvey, L. (2000) *The Impact of Sandwich Education on the Activities of Graduates Six Months Post-Graduation*. London: National Centre for Work Experience and the Centre for Research into Quality.

Chase, R. (2015) *Peers Inc: How People and Platforms are Inventing the Collaborative Economy and Rein-venting Capitalism*. London: Headline Publishing.

Cole, D. and Tibby, M. (2013) 'Defining and Developing your Approach to Employability: A Framework for Higher Education Institutions'. Available at: www.heacademy.ac.uk/sites/default/files/resources/Employability_framework.pdf.

Gibbs G (1988) *Learning by Doing: A guide to teaching and learning methods*. Oxford: Further Education Unit, Oxford Polytechnic.

Gubler, M., Arnold, J., and Coombs, C. (2013) 'Reassessing the protean career concept: Empirical findings, conceptual components, and measurement'. *Journal of Organizational Behavior* 35(S1): S23–40.

Hall, D. (1976) *Careers in Organizations*. Pacific Palisades, CA: Goodyear.

Hall, D. (1996) 'Protean Careers of the 21st Century'. *Academy of Management Executive* 10(4): 8–16.

Higher Education Careers Services Unit and the Association of Graduate Careers Advisory Services (2018) 'What Do Graduates Do?'. Available at: https://luminate.prospects.ac.uk/what-do-graduates-do.

High Fliers (2020) 'The Graduate Market in 2020'. Available at: www.highfliers.co.uk/download/2020/graduate_market/GM20Report.pdf.

Kolb, D. (1984) *Experiential Learning: Experience as the Source of Learning and Development*. Englewood Cliffs, NJ: Prentice Hall.

Law, B. and Watts, A. (1977) *Schools, Careers and Community*. London: Church Information Office.

Maguire, M., Williams, K., and Corcoran, M. (2019) '"Penal Drift" and the Voluntary Sector'. *Howard Journal of Crime and Justice* 58(3): 430–49.

Mandilaras, A. (2004) 'Industrial Placement and Degree Performance: Evidence from a British Higher Institution'. *International Review of Economics Education* 3(1): 39–51.

Pegg, A. et al. (2012) *Pedagogy for employability*. York: The Higher Education Academy. Available at www.advance-he.ac.uk/knowledge-hub/pedagogy-employability-2012.

Römgens, I., Scoupe, R., and Beausaert, S. (2020) 'Unraveling the concept of employability, bringing together research on employability in higher education and the workplace'. *Studies in Higher Education* 45(12): 2588–603.

INDEX

Aas, Katja Franko 376–80, 387, 394, 410, 429, 436
ABC (Always Be Critical) approach 18–19, 22
abolitionism 931–2, 947–51, 954
   grounds 948–9
   imprisonment 931, 946–51
   individualised concepts of guilt 931, 948
   Massachusetts experiment 949
   morally wrong, punishment as 949
   Radical Alternatives to Prison (RAP) 949–50
   responsibilising interventions 947
   victims, interests of 194, 932
   working, punishment as not 948–9
academia
   academic writing clinics 20
   employability and careers 1016–17
   interdisciplinary meeting point 8–9
   literature, reviewing 13, 969–71
   race and ethnicities 279
accommodation and rehabilitation 865, 880, 882, 888, 891
accountability
   abolitionism 947
   critical perspectives on punishment 931–2
   judicial independence 697, 699
   police 720, 721, 722
   prevention of crime 779
   privileged and powerful, crimes of 931
   retribution 840
   rule of law 695, 697
   social harm 593, 595
administrative criminology 952
adversarial justice 710–13, 729 *see also* adversarial-lite
   alternatives to punishment 922–5
   beyond reasonable doubt 84, 710
   Criminal Procedure Rules 710, 711
   cross-examination 710, 712–13, 715
   Crown Prosecution Service (CPS) 725–6
   disclosure of evidence 710, 732
   due process 752
   evidence 84–5
   financial resources 712
   inquisitorial approach 86–7, 713
   miscarriages of justice 86–7
   police 754–5
   presumption of innocence 710, 711
   principles 710–13, 715
   social harm 600, 610
   Transforming Summary Justice (TSJ) initiative 764
   truth 84–5, 710
   witnesses 85, 710, 711, 712–13
adversarial-lite 710, 744, 751–4
   cannabis and khat warnings 753–4
   community resolution 752–4
   conditional cautions 752–3
   Fixed Penalty Notices (FPNs) 753
   imprisonment, increase in 752, 754
   out-of-court disposals 752
   penal populism 752, 754
   Penalty Notices for Disorder (PNDs) 753–4
   policy 710, 744, 751–4
   statistics 752
age
   criminal responsibility, of 242, 243, 259–60, 459, 596, 702, 704
   neutralisation and drift 547, 549
agency 80, 242, 245, 249–50, 332
Agnew, Robert 249, 251
Agnew, Stuart 962–3
alcohol and drug treatment 875
alternatives to punishment 895–927 *see also* abolitionism; diversion; restorative justice
   adversarial justice 906
   alternatives as punishment 922–5
   community, involvement of 897, 898, 920
   consensus, lack of 921–2
   conventional assumptions, challenging 898
   court procedures, reform of 899
   delivering alternatives 906–16
   deterrence 919, 921
   due process 906, 923
   families, involvement of 897
   guilt 897, 906, 921, 923
   historical background 896
   implications of alternatives 919–21
   inclusion 899
   indigenous communities, problem-solving traditions from 900, 925
   individualised rights and responsibilities 906
   just deserts 897, 919
   limitations 921–5
   meaning and impact 917–25
   mitigation 906
   negotiated outcomes 900, 907
   offence resolution 897, 898–900
   old versus new justice 896–900
   perceptions and subjective feelings, weight given to 900
   practical implications of a resolution approach 898–9
   problem-solving approaches 896, 898–900, 925
   responsibility, acceptance of 900, 921–3
   sentencing
      purposes of 897
      tariff 906–7, 919–20
   temporal frame 898
   trust 899
   victims
      involvement 897, 899–900, 923–4
      priorities 898
amnesties 943–4
androcentrism
   criminology as androcentric 11
   feminism 325, 326, 336, 337, 340
   integrated theories of crime 651–3, 665
   race and ethnicities 279
   sociobiological theories 652–3
   subjectivity 102, 104
   youth offenders 242
animals 44, 188, 346–51
anomie
   culture 539–40, 545
   functionalism 529, 531–4, 555
   juvenile delinquency 542
   left realism 632
   neutralisation and drift 547
antisemitism 229, 230
antisocial behaviour (ASB)
   biosocial theory 652
   civil law/criminal law distinction 729–31
   community policing 815
   Criminal Behaviour Orders (CBOs) 731
   crime control 803, 808, 827
   defensible space 809
   definition 565
   harassment 154, 220–1
   police 811
   prescription drugs, treatment through 563–4
   prevention of crime 772, 774, 779, 783, 791–3, 796–9
   social construction 565
   social exclusion 552
   standard of proof 827
   subcultural theories 541–2
   young offenders 238, 244, 247, 250, 774
   zero tolerance 808, 813, 827
apologies 752, 901, 904, 911, 915, 920
Aquinas, Thomas 838
Arest, Andreas 584. 585–6
Aristotle 74–5, 80–1, 89

INDEX

artefactual risk factor theories 106–7, 246, 674, 677, 679
asbestos, industrial legacy of 594, 595
assessments 13–17
assisted dying 34, 529–30
attitudes to crime 137
attrition 133, 313
Auletta, Ken 551
austerity measures 593–4, 600, 642, 912
Australia
    environment courts, proposals for special 370
    fines 849
    indigenous communities 901
    Kowanyama, Queensland, establishment of a community justice programme in 947
    restorative justice 918

Bailey, Hannah 1003
Baker, David 201–2, 965
Bandura, Albert 503, 509, 511, 678
Barlow, Charlotte 750–1
barristers 1014–15
Barritt, Vickie 1018
Beccaria, Cesare 68, 89, 454–6, 850
Beck, Ulrich 820, 937
Becker, Howard 31, 256, 299, 567, 569, 586, 952
behavioural psychology 494, 504, 508
benefit fraud 942
Bentham, Jeremy 454, 455–6, 809, 849, 855–6
Berlin, Isaiah 36, 75
Better Case Management (BCM) initiative 764
Bhopal disaster 931, 953
Bianchi, Herman 948–9
bifurcation of criminology 648, 936, 937
biocentrism 367, 371
biological positivism 10, 476–9, 485–94, 648–50, 655
    born criminals 477, 481–2, 490, 493
    brain structure and function 485–8, 493
    central nervous system (CNS) 485
    chemical and biochemical influences 488–90, 493
    critical criminology 563
    data, collection of 481–2
    drugs or undergo operations, requirement to take 482
    early positivism 476, 516
    eugenics 482
    evolutionary psychology 492–3
    free will 478
    genetic factors 477, 480–2, 490–3
    pathological behaviour 479
    peripheral nervous system (PNS) 485
    personality types 482, 491
    physical appearance/facial features 480–3
    punishment 477–82, 491, 493, 516
    race and criminality 478–9
    science 481–2, 485–94, 509
    somatotyping (body types) 482
    sterilisation 482
    surveys 678
    testing 479
    treatment programmes 482
biology *see also* biological positivism
    artefactual risk factor theories 657–8
    biopsychological factors 651–2
    biopsychosocial explanations 657, 659
    feminism 580
    learning theories 525
    positivism 516–17
    sociobiological theories 648, 650–3, 655
biopiracy 349–50
bioprospecting 349–50
biosocial theory 650–2
Biondi, Karina 403
Black Lives Matter (BLM) movement 286, 297–8
    Commission on Race and Ethnic Disparities 298
    critical race theory 303
    decolonisation 380
    hate crime 212–13, 226–8
    institutional racism 723
    media 304
    music 179
    positivism 478
    protests 62, 201, 274, 277, 296
    race-switching exercises 302
    recognition, harms of 608
    repeat victimisation 202
    state racism 228, 578
    statistics 282
    stop and search 289
    young offenders 255–6, 258, 265
Blair, Tony 635, 656, 698, 940–1
Blake, Mark 278–9
blame 193, 476, 624
blocking devices 823
blogs 13–14, 15–16, 986
Bolsonaro, Jair 398–9
Bonger, Willem 567, 574–5
born criminals 477, 481–2, 490, 493
Bowling, Benjamin 201, 280, 293–5, 410–11, 722, 823, 933–4
Box, Steven 48, 526, 544–5, 547, 602
brain structure and function 485–8, 493
Braithwaite, John 908–9, 914, 925
Brantingham, Paul J 780–3, 785
Bratton, William 626, 813–14
Brazilian justice 396–403, 415, 424–5, 427
Brexit
    animals 371
    European Convention on Human Rights (EHRC) 47
    hate crime 281–2
    judicial independence 699, 700
    migrants, representations of 165
    national identity 533–4
    race and ethnicities 217, 227–8, 277, 281–2
    religious identity, hate crime based on 230
British Crime Survey (BCS) 125, 137, 139, 141, 188, 198, 216
broken windows theory 385, 626, 805
Bulger, James, murder of 258, 259
burden of proof 703, 710
Burgess, Ernest 536
Bush, George W 422–3, 812–13, 940–1
butterfly effect 686–7

Cain, Maureen 326, 335, 388, 394–5
Canada
    banishment 903
    circle courts 900, 901, 946
    Indian residential school system imposed on indigenous people 945
    indigenous communities 900, 901, 903, 945
    Truth and Reconciliation Commission 945
cannabis and khat warnings 753–4
capital punishment *see* death penalty
careers *see* employability and careers
Caribbean, feminism in the 394
Carrington, Kerry 335, 376, 380, 388, 415, 541–5
Case, Steve 101, 106–7, 116, 672, 676–7, 683–4, 822
causes of crime 669–89
    ABC (Always Be Critical) approach 670, 673–5, 677
    artefactual risk factor theories 674, 677, 679
    black box metaphor 681–3, 685
    change model, theory of 685–6, 687
    chaos theory/complex systems science 672, 686–7
    correlation 129, 476, 477, 677–80
    crime, concept of 670, 673
    culture of causality in explanatory theory 673, 674
    dark figure of explanation in criminology 682
    defining causes 671–4
    desistance from crime 674, 680, 683–4
    diversification 674
    empirical research 672, 674, 677, 680
    explanatory theory 673, 674, 687
    identifying causes, explaining crime by 679–80
    indicative factors 670
    influential factors 670
    innovative evaluation methods 683–5, 687
    interactive factors 670
    interpretivism 671–3
    left realism 632, 634
    neighbourhood and delinquency, causal link between 536
    operationalising the causes of crime 674
    positivism 451–2, 476, 670–4, 679, 685–7
    prevention of crime 670, 770–1
    proxy causes 682
    rational choice theory 674
    realism 621–2, 682, 684–5
    realistic evaluation approach 684–5
    rehabilitation 670
    research 674–9

responding to crime 680–6
scientific experiments, control in 674–7
social construction 673–4, 679–80
specialisation 674
subjectivity 674, 677, 679, 687
supposition 672, 674, 677, 679, 682–3, 687
survey research 672, 677–80
temporal precedence of criminogenic factors 679
what works 680–5
cautions 752–3, 907, 911–12, 921, 923
censuses 127–8
change model, theory of 685–6, 687
chaos theory/complex systems science 672, 686–7
charity work 1017–18
chemical castration 824
Chibnall's imperatives on social media 156
Chicago Area Project (CAP) 539
Chicago School 385, 388, 523, 536–9
children *see also* education and schools; youth offending and youth justice
    age of criminal responsibility 242, 243, 259-60, 459, 596, 702, 704
    care, in
      race and ethnicities 293, 298, 302
      sexual exploitation 774–5
    childhood, concept of 238–43
    Crime Survey for England and Wales (CSEW) 139
    criminalisation 923
    definition 239
    diversion 898, 923
    doli incapax 704
    gangs 287
    history, childhood in 238–40
    imprisonment 568–9, 579
    labelling 572
    media 152
    police 287
    pornography 412
    stop and search 287
    UN Convention on the Rights of the Child 1989 239, 259
    victimisation 580, 581
    victimology 199
    working with children or vulnerable adults 867
Christchurch mass shooting 158, 173
Christie, Nils 190–2, 205, 395, 602, 899–900, 908, 920
civil law/criminal law distinction 729–31
civil rights movements 212–13, 231, 567
Clamp, Kerry 902, 908
Clare's Law 315
Clarke, Kenneth 551, 749, 853, 901
Clarke, Ronald V 462–5, 796, 829
class
    chav, use of word 629–30
    consumerism 630–1
    critical perspectives on punishment 935
    differential association theories 523–4
    differential opportunity 545, 546–7
    feminism 332, 334, 336–9

    gender 318
    left realism 621, 632
    neutralisation and drift 547
    new underclass 552
    power control theory 654
    right realism 623, 641
    social control 936
    social disorganisation theories 536
    social exclusion 550–5
    sociological positivism 522, 523–6
    subcultural theories 540, 542, 544
    underclass 385, 388, 550–5, 623, 626–31, 849
classical criminology 10, 453–60, 469, 648–50
    18th century 451, 453
    actus reus 458
    blame 476
    causes of crime 674
    conditioning 500–2
    critical criminology 563, 586
    culpability 459, 460
    death penalty 455–6
    definition 451
    deterrence 455–6, 458
    Enlightenment 453, 457–9
    feudalism 457
    free will 99, 453–4, 459, 460, 478
    impulsive behaviour 460
    influence 457–60
    just and fair process 455
    labelling 572
    learning 476
    limitations 458–60, 470
    mens rea 458
    mental capacity 455–6, 459
    modern justice, impact on 457–8
    neo-classicism 460–70, 649–50
    power 453, 460
    proportionality 451
    punishment 451, 453–6, 458–60, 476, 478
    rational choice theory 451, 453–6, 459, 460, 461, 464–5
    retribution 455
    right realism 470, 649
    routine activity theory 461
    sentencing 458
    situational crime prevention 461, 476
    social contract 454
    supposition 99
    timing 459–60
    utilitarianism 455
classification of crimes
    either way offences 291, 701, 725, 730
    indictable offences 291–2, 700, 730–1, 854, 856
    summary offences 133, 700–1, 730, 764
Clear, Todd R 946–7
climate change 347–8, 350–1, 355, 363
Cloward, Richard A 250–1, 545–8, 679
Code of Ur-Nammu 694, 713
coercive control 315, 316, 319
cognition 500, 504–8

cognitive behavioural therapy (CBT) 506, 508, 869–70, 877–8, 881
Cohen, Albert 530–1, 542–5, 547–8
Cohen, Lawrence E 466
Cohen, Stanley 150, 151–2, 163, 252, 256, 385, 394–5, 411, 466, 573, 827, 888, 899–900, 937
Coleman, Alison 468–9
Coleman, Roy 29, 777–9
Colombia, drug trafficking in 417, 426–7
colonialism
    decolonisation 379–81
    postcolonialism 381
    power 66
    race and ethnicities 275–7, 303
    slavery 398–9
    transnational criminology 411, 415
communication and literacy 1005–6
communitarianism 81–3, 89–91
community disposals
    adversarial-lite 752–4
    Community Payback 714, 761, 847–8, 868
    Community Remedy 841
    community service paradigm 714
    Community Trigger 841
    conditions 733, 847–8
    critical perspectives on punishment 932, 945–7
    deterrence 830, 848
    diversion 904
    indigenous communities 946–7
    probation services 720, 732–5, 763
    public opinion 858
    rehabilitation 868, 873, 875, 848
    restorative justice 848, 915
    retribution 747–8, 853–4
    unpaid work requirements 847–8
    visibility 848
community engagement
    alternatives to punishment 897, 898, 920
    community-based partnerships and programmes 776, 779
    crime control 803, 817–18
    local politics of crime, case study on 777–8
    policing 762–3, 803, 814–15
    prevention of crime 777–9, 799
    restorative justice 903, 908, 932
    zero tolerance 813
community practices 756–61, 763–4
Community Rehabilitation Companies (CRCs) 733, 734, 873
comparative criminology 381–407
    archetypical cases 383
    Brazilian justice 396–403
    cities, emergence of global 385
    convergences 381–2, 384–93, 404
    critical race theory 384
    culture 382, 396–403
    definition 378
    demographic changes 384–5, 387
    deviant cases 384
    divergences 381–2, 393–403, 404
    Global North 380

comparative criminology (*Cont.*)
   Global South 380, 384
   globalisation 378–9, 383–4, 394
   interconnection 410
   interpretivism (cultural relativism/differences) 381, 383–4, 393–403
   Latin America 381–2, 396–403
   meta-analysis 382
   Nordic and Norwegian justice 393, 395–6, 397
   Norway, prison in 393, 395–6
   orientalism 395–6
   positivism 382–93
   prison 381, 393, 395–6
   probation service 385
   prototypical cases 383
   punitiveness and public protection 385, 388–93
   rehabilitation 384
   representative cases 383
   retribution 385
   sentencing 381
   sociological positivism 381
   strain theory 384–5, 388
   street crime 385, 387–8
   transnational criminology 412, 415
   urban violence 385–8
   war/crime distinction 415
compensation orders 752, 848
complex systems science/chaos theory 672, 686–7
computers *see* information technology; social media
confession evidence 754–8
consent to harm 40–1, 50
constitutions
   unwritten constitution of UK 694–5
   written constitutions 694
constructivism 249, 264, 663–4
control *see* crime control
convict criminology
   British Convict Criminology (BCC) 584
   critical criminology 97, 576, 583–6
   prisoners, voices of 584, 586
   spoiled identity 585–6
   stigma 584, 585–6
   truth 583–4
   United States 583–4, 586
Copson, Lynne 283, 595, 613–15
copyright 993, 995
Cornish, Derek B 462–5, 796
corporations
   deviance 953
   diversion 922–3
   general theory of crime (self-control theory) 654
   green technology 348–50, 354, 369–70
   Grenfell Tower disaster 840, 953
   labelling theory 953
   multinationals 368, 377, 412, 417, 419, 430–2
   negligence 930, 931
   recklessness 931
   regulatory regimes 953

   right realism 641
   social harm 598–601, 612
   sociological positivism 516, 526
   state crime 577
   transnational criminology 378, 412, 415–17
   war/crime distinction 415
corrective justice 74
correlation and causation 129, 476, 477, 677–80
costs
   crime control 822
   diversion 905, 918–19
   neo-classical criminology 462
   observations (researching by watching) 116
   restorative justice 918–19
county lines 242
courts 720, 729–32
   backlogs 731
   challenges for the courts 731–2
   citations 730
   civil law/criminal law distinction 729–31
   County Court 729
   Criminal Defence Direct (CDD) Services 731–2
   Crown Court 729–30
   diversity 732
   due process 732
   duty solicitors, shortage of 731–2
   either way offences 730
   environment courts, proposals for special 370
   family law 729–30
   funding, reduction in 731–2
   hierarchy of courts 700
   High Court 729
   HM Courts and Tribunals Service (HMCTS) 729, 731
   indictable offences 730
   Magistrates' Court 729–30
   practices 755–6
   private law 729–31
   public law 729–31
   role of the courts 730–1
   sentencing 730–1
   summary offences 730
   Transforming Summary Justice (TSJ) initiative 764
   virtual courts 88–9
Covid-19
   adversarial-lite 752
   Chinese people, crimes against 228–9
   crime control 51
   Crime Survey for England and Wales (CSEW) 137
   digitisation 745–6
   domestic violence 311–13
   employability and careers 1012
   fairness 46
   freedom, restrictions on 415, 416
   green criminology 365–6, 371
   imprisonment 739
   LGBT+/sexual orientation 226

   Nightingale courts 88
   police 722
   race and ethnicities 62, 228–9, 277, 281, 282–3, 289, 296, 832
   stop and search 289
   statistics 130
   transnational criminology 415, 416
   virtual courts 88
   war/crime distinction 415, 416
   young offenders 255–6, 265, 268
CPS *see* Crown Prosecution Service (CPS)
Crawford, Adam 632, 775, 781–3, 785–90, 797, 828–9, 910, 919–20
crime, concept of a
   causes of crime 670, 673
   crime control 823
   LGBT+/sexual orientation 596
   realism 640
   social harm 596–8, 610, 612–14
crime control 51, 66–8, 70–3, 803–35
   achieves, what crime control 822–7
   agencies and interests, role of other 803, 816–20
   antisocial behaviour 803, 808, 827
   capacity to impose effective and efficient measures 823
   classical criminology 451
   community policing 803
   community, role of the 803, 817–18
   complexity and unpredictability 826
   corrections 808, 810
   costs and benefits 822
   crime prevention 803
   defensible space 808–9, 817
   definition 804–8
   designing out crime 809, 817, 821, 828–9, 831
   detected and apprehending offenders 808
   deterrence 803, 808, 810, 812, 829–30
   direct control of disorder in progress 808
   due process 701, 805–8
   effectiveness 823, 831
   efficiency 806–7, 823, 831
   fairness 806
   fear of crime 809, 825, 831
   identification issues 833
   identified offender types 810, 823, 877
   imprisonment 810, 819–20, 831
   incapacitating offenders 808, 810–11
   inconvenience versus safety 825
   individual rights or stopping crime, protecting 806–7
   integrated offender management 831
   interests served by crime control 825–6
   intelligence-led policing 803
   judiciary 803, 819–20
   left realism 632, 634, 637
   limitations 831–3
   management of offenders 831–2
   managing and regulating the environment 809
   minimising harm 808
   miscarriages of justice 832–3
   moral challenges 832–3

neutralisation and drift 550
objectives 808–11
objects and technologies 820–2, 823
operating principles 808
planning out crime 817–18
police 803, 805, 807, 811–16, 818, 826, 831–2
predictive tools 803, 820–2
pre-emptive action 804, 808, 809, 816–17
prevention of crime 808, 809, 820–2
private security providers 803, 818–19
proactive approach 803, 818
racism and ethnicities 832–3
rationality of offenders 822
reactive, as 805
realism 640
rehabilitation 831, 866, 881
reoffending, minimising the risk of 821–2
repeat victimisation 821
retribution 803, 831
risk assessment 803, 810, 822, 831
risk management 803, 820–1, 822–3
rule of law 805, 818–19
scientific criminology 820, 822–3
securitisation of environment 816–17
social harm 596, 600–2
social inequalities 833
suppositions 823
surveillance 803, 823, 826
target hardening 803–4, 808–9, 817, 823, 831
technologies 820–2, 823–6
victimisation studies 825–6
works, whether crime control 828–30
zero tolerance 803, 808, 823, 827
crime, definition of 27–53
control, types of 51
criminalisation 44–5, 50–1
deviance 32–6
European Convention on Human Rights (EHRC) 47–8
harm principle 36–46, 50–1
limitations of the criminal law 49
need for criminal law 48–50
other ways to decide whether an action should be a crime 44–7
science 7, 8, 10
social construct, crime as a 27–32, 51
values and regulations, deciding on crimes using 45–7
crime pattern theory (CPT) 783, 784, 821
crime prevention 769–801 *see also* situational crime prevention
accountability 779
adaptation 795
antisocial behaviour 772, 774, 779, 783, 791–3, 796–9
Brantingham and Faust's model 780–3, 785
causes of crime, finding out the 670, 770–1
CCTV 777–8, 797
challenges in crime prevention 774–5
children from care at risk of sexual exploitation 773
choices of which crimes to prevent 770, 772, 776–8
communities at risk 786, 790
community-based partnerships and programmes 776, 779
consequences 794–7
Crawford's level of intervention 785–90
Crime and Disorder Act 1998 772, 781, 819
crime control 803, 808, 809, 820–2
criminalisation of social policy 780
crimogenic environments (risky situations) 773, 774
deflection and rational choice theory 796–7
definition 770–7
deradicalisation 776
deterrence 770, 787–8, 795
developmental crime prevention 788, 790–1, 794
dispersal orders 797–8
displacement 795–7
diversion 787, 788
early prevention programmes 792
education and schools 771, 781, 788–9
emergence and development of crime prevention 775–6
escalation 794–5
evidence-based approaches 798
fear of crime 771, 772, 773, 780
flexibility 779
focus of crime prevention 773–4
funding, reduction in 799
implementation of measures 790–1
judiciary 819
key developments 772
limitations 797–9
local initiatives 781–2
local politics of crime, case study on 777–8
Morgan Report 772, 776
objects of prevention 776
opportunist crime 775, 782, 783
perspectives on crime prevention 776–9
police 775, 781
policy and practice, frameworks for 779–90
potential offenders (risky people) 773–4, 786, 787, 789
potential victims 786, 789–90
poverty deconcentration 791
primary prevention 780, 786
priorities 770, 772, 776–9
quick fixes 797
race and ethnicity 799
radicalisation and deradicalisation 780, 782, 783, 799
rational choice theory 796–7
rehabilitation 770, 776
reoffending, risk of 821–2
replication 798
resources 772, 776, 778–9
responsibility for prevention 798–9
risk factors 791
risk management 771, 776
risky behaviour, targeting 792–3
Safer Cities programme 772, 776
Safer Schools Partnership (SSP) initiative 781
schools, targeting 788–9
science of prevention 798
secondary prevention 780–1, 786
social crime prevention 634, 791
social harms 774
social media 179
strategies 771–3, 776–7, 782–3, 788–9
success criteria 792–4
surveillance 783, 785, 797
target hardening 782, 785, 789
tertiary prevention 780–1, 786
theories 776
transferability 798
Troubled Families programme 776, 783
vulnerable groups or communities (at risk people) 773
welfare-led interventions 775, 776
what works 798
work, whether preventive measures 793–4
young offenders 260, 788–9, 799
zero tolerance 779, 796
crime scripts 465–6
Crime Survey for England and Wales (CSEW) 112, 136–42
accuracy 125–7
attitudes to crime 137
British Crime Survey (BCS) 125, 137, 139, 141, 188, 198, 216
children, views of 139
chronic victims, reporting on 141–2
comparability 127, 140
computer misuse 127
Covid-19 137
credibility 140
dark figure of crime 136–7, 217–18, 232
data collection 975
disablist hate crime 220
domestic violence 311–12
fraud 127
gender identity 140
generation of statistics 137–40
hate crime 216, 217–18, 232,
imprisonment, increase in 752
interviews 137, 140, 141
LGBT+/sexual orientation 225
limitations 140–2
online behaviour, inclusion of 140
police-recorded crime statistics 136, 140
politics 140–1
race and ethnicities 281
representative samples 137
samples 139
strengths 140
UK Statistics Authority 140
victimisation 137, 140–2
victimology 188, 195, 198–9, 201
vulnerable people, exclusion of 139, 141
which crimes are included 139–41
who is included 139, 141

Criminal Cases Review Commission (CCRC) 857
criminal justice institutions *see* institutions
criminal justice policies 744–54, 762–3 *see also* penal populism; zero tolerance policies
    adversarial-lite 710, 744, 751–4
    communism, collapse of 747
    development 744–5
    digitisation 745–6
    efficiency 745–6, 763–4
    executive, constitutional policy of 745
    implementation stage 744
    left realism 634–7, 642
    legislature, validation of 745
    McJustice 763–4
    modernisation 745
    origins and influences 744–6
    police 721, 722, 816
    prevention of crime 779–80
    public opinion 747–51
    regions 744
    retribution 852–5
    separation of powers 745, 746
    shared values 745
    Single Justice Procedure (SJP) 764
    time periods 747
    Transforming Summary Justice (TSJ) initiative 764
    victimology 196–8
criminal justice principles 693–717, 754–63 *see also* adversarial justice; rule of law ABC (Always Be Critical) approach 694
    Acts of Parliament 694
    adversarial justice 710–13, 715
    community practices 756–61, 763–4
    courtroom practices 755–6
    ignored or re-shaped, principles as being 744
    penal codes 694
    policing practices 754–5
    precedent 694–5
    principles, definition of 445
    restorative justice 713–14, 715
    retaliation 694
    unwritten constitution of UK 694–5
criminalisation 40–5, 75
    bifurcation process 936
    cannabis 33–4
    consent to harm 40
    crime, definition of 44–5, 50–1
    decriminalisation 565–6, 866
    deviance 32–3, 36
    drug use 41, 43
    harm principle 40–4
    historical background 223–4
    over-criminalisation 41, 42, 44
    powerful groups 50, 566
    race and ethnicities 276, 287, 291, 295, 934, 939
    riots of 2011 938
    social control 936
    social policy 780
    sociobiological theories 652
    values 45–7
    young offenders 255, 259
criminological theory 451–2
criminology, meaning of 1–10
critical criminology 48–9, 451, 561–89, 648 *see also* critical race theory (CRT); Marxist-inspired critical theories
    classicism 563, 586
    convict criminology 97, 576, 583–6
    critical, meaning of 563–4
    cultural criminology 563, 576, 582–3, 586
    definition 452
    discrimination and inequality 452, 563
    diversity of theories 576–86
    early positivism 572, 580
    feminism 562, 576, 579–81, 586
    gender 562
    green criminology 346, 349, 562
    labelling 562, 566–72, 586
    left realism 620, 621, 631, 637–8, 952
    Marxist-inspired critical theories 562, 572–6
    new criminology 586
    oppression 563
    positivism 563–4, 572, 580
    poverty 563
    power 452, 562, 564–6, 576–7
    race and ethnicity 562–3, 586
    realism 595, 620–1
    science 563–4, 586
    social construction 452
    social exclusion 555
    social harm 592, 595–602, 613
    state crime 561, 576, 577–9, 586
    statistics 132, 142
    subjectivity 100
    transnational criminology 415–17, 437
    treatment as control 564
    victimology 194–5
    young offenders 255
critical perspectives on punishment 929–55 *see also* abolitionism
    accountability 931–2
    bifurcation process 936, 937
    capitalism 953–4
    class 935
    community justice 932, 945–7
    corporations 930, 931, 953
    definition 930–2
    discriminatory practice not involving race 935–6
    dominance 930
    drama to routine, shift of punishment from 936–7
    face value, taking crime at 952–3
    fairness 930–1, 933
    green criminology 931
    hegemony 937–8
    human rights 930–1
    ideology 930
    imprisonment 935
    left realism 952–3
    legitimacy 930, 936–8, 953
    limitations 951–4
    Northern Ireland, resolving conflict in 944–5
    political resistance to oppression 952
    privileged and powerful, crimes of 930–1, 938–42, 952
    procedural justice 933
    race and ethnicity 930, 933–5, 939
    radical criminology 952–3
    real, crime as 952
    restorative justice 932
    riots of 2011 938
    risk management 937
    romanticising crime 952
    routine from drama, shift of punishment to 936–7
    social control theory 930, 935–8
    social justice 932
    solutions 942–51
    symbolism 930, 936
    systematic injustices 930
    tax fraud 930, 931
    transformative justice 932
    transitional justice 944–5
    truth and reconciliation 942–5
    unjust punishment 933–6
    youth justice system 930, 935
critical race theory (CRT) 299–303, 304
    aims 300
    application to ethnicity and crime in UK 301–2
    comparative criminology 384
    criticisms 300–1
    culture 300
    essentialism 300
    identity politics 300–1
    institutionalised racism 299
    intersectionality 300
    labelling 299
    microaggressions 301
    positivism 299
    power structures 300
    radical feminism 300
    social construction 300, 302
    United States 275, 299–302
cross-border criminology *see* transnational criminology
Crown Prosecution Service (CPS) 720, 724–9
    administrators 725
    adversarial justice 725–6
    advocacy 725
    annual reports 726–7
    Attorney-General (AG) 724
    careers 1014–15
    challenges for the CPS 725–9
    charging decisions 724–5
    Chief Crown Prosecutors 724
    Code for Crown Prosecutors 725, 726
    conviction rate 725
    CPS Direct 724–5, 764
    Crown Prosecutors, role of 725
    decisions to prosecute
        public interest test 725, 728

reasonable prospect of conviction 725
standard of proof 725
Denman Review 728–9
Director of Public Prosecutions (DPP) 724
disclosure 725–6
diversity 728–9
efficiency and funding 726–7
geographical areas 724
institutional racism 728–9
out-of-court disposals 752
paralegals 725
police 724–5, 728
private sector 728
prosecuting bodies 724
race and ethnicities 290–1, 298, 728–9
separation of powers 724, 728
victims 724
CRT *see* critical race theory (CRT)
cuckooing and mate crime 222
culpability/fault 459, 460, 703, 865
cultural criminology 10–11, 81, 539–55 *see also* subcultural theories
anomie 539–40
communitarianism 81–2
comparative criminology 382
critical criminology 563, 576, 582–3, 586
critical race theory (CRT) 300
cross-cultural comparisons 11
definition 539, 582
deviance 32–3
ethnomethodology 582, 583
evolutionary psychology 492
feminism 327–8, 331, 337
gangs 251–2, 253
gender 324, 326
globalisation 377, 381
green criminology 347
hate crime 212, 214
interactionism 582
justice, definition of 62–4
left realism 634
male privilege 331
masculinities 324
media 149
multiculturalism 82, 276–8, 285
occidentalism 394
phenomenology 582
police 68, 722
positivism 582
race and ethnicities 275, 277–8, 293
relativism 396–403
retribution 839
social construction 28, 31, 62
social disorganization theory 536–40
social exclusion 553
social harm 603, 606, 607–8
social structural theories 539–45
strain theory 539–40
urban violence 385
young offenders 240–1, 244–5, 250–4, 258
Cummings, Dominic 46, 178
curfews 803, 810
Currie, Elliot 82

custodial sentences *see* imprisonment
cybercrime
drug trafficking 432–3
media 149, 174–5, 179
rational choice theory 465
transnational criminology 417, 419, 432–5
victimology 203–4
cybersecurity 419, 432–5

Darke, Sacha 386, 392, 397, 400–3
data analysis 449, 977–80 *see also* secondary data analysis
data collection 975–80
analysing data 449, 977–80
biological positivism 481–2
discourse analysis 979
grounded theory analysis 980
narrative analysis 979–80
positivism 477, 481–2
primary data 975–6
qualitative methods 976–7, 979–80
quantitative methods 976–8
race and ethnicities 279–80
secondary data 975–6
SPSS software 977–9
thematic analysis 980
data protection 990
Davis, Kingsley 531, 534
death penalty
abolition 846, 847, 851
Bloody Code 846
classical criminology 455–6
juries' unwillingness to convict 846
miscarriages of justice 703, 855
public executions 846
public opinion 859
race and ethnicities 482–3
retribution 844, 845–7, 850–2, 855, 859
United States
due process 703
miscarriages of justice 703
race and ethnicities 482–3
retribution 851–2
Deepwater Horizon 356–7
defensible space 808–9, 817
antisocial behaviour 809
communal areas 809
design of living environment 809, 817
situational crime prevention 468–9
delinquency *see* juvenile delinquency
descriptive models of criminal justice 64–6, 450
deserts *see* **just deserts**
designing out crime 828–9
defensible space 809, 817
environmental criminology 817
housing standards 564
opportunism 828–9
predictive tools 821
rational choice theory 828
remote causes 828
situational crime prevention 467, 817, 828–9
target hardening 831

desistance
causes of crime 674, 680, 683–4
definition 683–4
diversion 904, 917–18
labelling theory 904
rehabilitation 683–4, 866, 877, 879–80, 885–6, 888–91
detention *see* imprisonment
deterrence
abolitionism 948
alternatives to punishment 919, 921
benefit fraud 787–8
classical criminology 455–6, 458
community disposal 830, 848
crime control 803, 808, 810, 812, 829–30
fines 848
focused deterrence 812
gun crime 830
imprisonment 829–30, 846
individual-level deterrence 830
labelling 572
over-deterrence 795
police 812, 831
population-level deterrence 829–30
prevention of crime 770, 787–8, 795
public protection 389
realism 622–4
rehabilitation 829–30, 881
retribution 843–4, 846, 848, 852–3
Scared Straight programme 787–8
sentencing 458, 819, 830
targeted deterrence 830
war crimes 940
young offenders 787–8, 830
developmental criminology 788, 791, 794
deviance 32–6
corporate crime 953
crime, definition of 32–6
criminalisation 32–3, 36
culture 32–3
double deviance thesis and gender 320–1, 322–3, 327
eco-warriors 35
fully social theory of crime and deviance 575–6
healthy, deviance as 33–5
media 149
primary deviance 568–9
secondary deviance 568–9
smoking 35
social control 33, 679
social rules and norms 32–3, 35
stigma 568–9
subcultures 33, 35, 542
theories 32
young offenders 250–2, 256–8
Devlin, Patrick 38
differential association theories 517, 523–7
class 523–4
company expectations 524
differential opportunity 547
learning theory 523–7
media 527
mentoring services 527

differential association theories (Cont.)
  motives and drives 525–6
  pathology 525
  peer groups 525–6
  power structures 525
  prosocial behaviour 527
  reintegrative shaming 526–7
  social distribution of crime 523
  sociological positivism 523–7
  street crime 525
  subcultural theories 542
  urban violence 385
  white-collar crime 523, 525–6
differential opportunity 545–7
Director of Public Prosecutions (DPP) 724
disabilities, persons with see also disablist hate crime
  additional learning support 19
  feminism 339
  victimology 198
disablist hate crime 212–13, 218, 219–23
  cognitive issues 219
  cuckooing and mate crime 222
  definition 219
  extent of hate crime 220–1
  harassment 220–1
  intellectual disabilities 220–2
  medical model 219
  mental health 220–2
  nature and dynamics 221–2
  physical issues 219
  police 219
  social model 219
  statistics 218
  violent crime 220–2
discrimination and inequality see also feminist criminology; hate crime; race and ethnicities
  critical criminology 452, 563
  critical perspectives on punishment 935–6
  environmental resources, access to 357
  imprisonment 935
  Index of Multiple Deprivation 603–4
  indigenous communities 901
  philosophical ideas of justice 74, 75, 76–8, 80
  positive discrimination 79
  social exclusion 552
  social harm 603–14
  social inequalities 826, 833
  state crime 578
  structural inequalities 620–1
dissertations 13
distributive justice 74
diversion 904–6 see also youth offending and diversion
  adverse impacts of justice system, as minimising 904
  agency interests 922–3
  alternatives as punishment 922–3
  apologies 904
  austerity measures 912
  community service 904

corporate interests 922–3
cost-effectiveness 905, 918–19
Crime and Disorder Act 1998 911
custody, as an alternative to 906
decarceration movement 906
delivering diversion 911–16
desistance 904, 917–18
due process 896
economically useful, as 898
green criminology 349
Intermediate Treatment (IT) 788
Juvenile Liaison Officer scheme in Liverpool 911, 923
labelling theory 896, 898, 904, 918, 920
mental health 918–19
minimum intervention 904
multi-agency process 912
negotiated justice 896
neoliberal state, withdrawal from 925
net-widening 922–3
non-criminal disposals (NCDs) 917
normalisation 904
objectives 905
offence resolution 897, 898, 906
police 911–12
practice, diversion in 911–14
pragmatic compromises 921
prevention of crime 787, 788
probation service 732
problem-solving approaches 896
radical non-intervention 896, 912
reduction in use 921
rehabilitation 866, 904
reintegration 905
reoffending rates 917
reparations 904, 912
reprimands and final warnings 911
responsibility
  acceptance 897, 905
  being held responsible versus taking responsibility 897
restorative justice 896, 904–5, 911–12, 915
sentencing tariff 907, 920
social inclusion 904
socially useful, as 898
spending cuts 921
structural issues 925
victims, marginalisation of 923–4
violent offences 921
young offenders 265–6, 788
diversity 276–8, 285, 699, 723–4, 728–9, 732–3
Dobash, Rebecca 313, 326, 331, 335
Dobash, Russell 313, 326, 331, 335
domestic violence
  abuse, definition to include 46
  caseworkers 1013
  Covid-19 311–13
  Crime Survey for England and Wales (CSEW) 311–12
  discretion 313
  draft Domestic Abuse Bill 315

emotional abuse 315
England football team, fortunes of 960–1
feminism 331, 332, 335, 339, 580–1, 967
gender 310–15
homicide 311
interpretivism 395
intersectionality 339
leniency 312–13
myths 313–14
offenders, women as 315–16, 319
patriarchy 331, 332
police 310–13, 340
programmes, lack of 890
rehabilitation 889–90
research 967
restorative justice 923–4, 925
statistics 310–13
dopamine 487–8
DOTS (Decision learning, Opportunity awareness, Transition learning, and Self-awareness) 1019–20
double jeopardy 702, 704–5, 707, 715, 755–6
Downes, David 8, 381–2, 391, 395, 631
drift see neutralisation and drift
drug offences
  cannabis
    decriminalisation 33–4
    harm principle 42
    medical use 29
    warnings 753–4
  cocaine trail 396, 398, 415, 426, 436
  county lines 242
  criminalisation 41, 43, 412, 414
  Drug Testing and Treatment Orders 875
  expensive addictions, drug users with 773
  harm principle 41–3, 50
  khat warnings 753–4
  Latin America 396, 398, 400, 416, 424–7
  LEAP (Law Enforcement against Prohibition) 424–5
  organised crime 416–18, 423–7, 432, 435–6
  perverse effects 795
  prohibition, effects of 424–5
  race and ethnicities 291–3
  rehabilitation 883, 887
  state and organised crime, cooperation between 418
  statistics 136
  transnational criminology 416–19, 423–7
  war on drugs 419, 423–7
Du Bois, WEB 276–7
due process 66, 68–74, 701–6, 715, 732
  adversarial justice 752
  alternatives to punishment 906, 923
  appeals 702
  Blackstone ratio 702, 705
  confessions 754
  crime control 701, 805–8
  criminal responsibility 702, 704
  diversion 896
  double jeopardy 702, 704–5, 715, 755–6
  fair procedure 701–2
  fundamental principles, reshaping 702–3

illegally-obtained evidence 808
judicial independence 701, 706
jurisdiction 702
miscarriages of justice 702, 703, 754–6
open justice 701, 705–6
police 754–5
presumption of innocence 702, 703–4, 715
reoffending, risk of 821
restorative justice 896, 921
retrospectivity 704
sentencing 752
separation of powers 701
technicalities 705
young offenders 263–4
Duff, Anthony 75, 83–4, 90
Duggan, Marian 967
Duggan, Mark, shooting of 61–2, 938
dumping of toxic, hazardous waste by transnational corporations into Africa and Asia 412, 417, 419, 430–2
Durkheim, Émile 33, 65, 89, 522, 527–34, 536

E3 (effective, engaged, and employable) students 17–18, 22
Eck, John 793–4
Edinburgh integrated pathways theory 662, 663–4
education and schools
 bullying 793
 compulsory education 239
 Education and Health Care Plans (EHCPs), appeals concerning 594, 595
 institutional racism 813
 needs, failure to meet 594, 595
 prevention of crime 771, 781, 788–9
 Safer Schools Partnership (SSP) initiative 781
 situational crime prevention 788–9
Edwards, Adam 779
Edwards, Ian 841–3
either way offences 291, 701, 725, 730
El Chapo (Guzmán, Joaquín) 425–7, 436
emotional or psychological harm 36, 603, 606, 607, 609
empirical research
 causes of crime 672, 674, 677, 680
 definition 98
 feminism 334–5, 336
 race and ethnicities 280
 right realism 624
 social control theories 653
 study 108
 surveys 677, 680
 validity 448
 what works 680
 young offenders 245
employability and careers 1001–22
 academia and research 1016–17
 boosting employability 1007–10
 business and customer awareness 1005
 charity work 1017–18
 communication and literacy 1005–6

Covid-19 1012
DOTS (Decision learning, Opportunity awareness, Transition learning, and Self-awareness) 1019–20
E3 (effective, engaged, and employable) students 17–18, 22
entrepreneurship and enterprise 1006–7
freelancing 1013
general points about workplace 1012–13
Gibbs' cycle of reflection 1002, 1004
Higher Education Achievement Report (HEAR) 1011
hybrid discipline, criminology as 1013
information technology 1006
internship 1008–9
journeying into careers 1011
key skills 1006
legal profession 1014–15
meaningful work 1019
numeracy 1006
part-time work 1009
Pedagogy for Employability report (Higher Education Academy Report) 1004
placements 1008–10
police 968, 1013–15
politics of crime 1013
positive, can-do attitudes 1004–5
postgraduate courses 1017–18
prisons, work in 1016
probation 968, 1015–16
problem-solving 1006
protean careers 1012
RARE (reflect, assess, react and evaluate) employability framework, producing your 1010–11, 1020
reflective learning 1002–4, 1019–21
self-employment 1013
social media 1018, 1020
specific criminology points about workplace 1013
support 20
tech-based industry 1012–13
types of career 1013–18
voluntary work 1009
what employers are looking for 1004–7
work-based assessments 15–16
work-based learning (WBL) 1002, 1007–10
work shadowing 1009
Youth Offending Teams (YOTs) 1015–16
employment and rehabilitation 867, 881, 882–5, 889, 891
endangered species 346, 349
Engels, Friedrich 550–1
enhanced pathways risk factor theories 648, 656, 660–4
Enlightenment 453, 457–9, 476
entrapment 158
entrepreneurship and enterprise 1006–7
environmental criminology see green criminology
epigenetics 493
epistemology 98–9, 106–9, 112, 117, 310, 324, 334–7, 340

Erikson, Kai 241, 530–1, 534
escalation 674, 794–5
essay-writing skills, applying 964–5
ethnicities see race and ethnicities
Etzioni, Amitai 74, 81–2
eugenics 482, 564
European Convention on Human Rights (EHRC)
 Brexit 47
 crime, definition of 47–8
 emergencies, derogation in times of 414
 European Court of Human Rights (ECtHR) 700–1, 707, 708–9
 fair hearing, right to a 415
 freedom of expression 231
 Human Rights Act 1998 707, 708–9
 judicial independence 700–1
 lawful chastisement 47
 liberty and security, right to 415
 Northern Ireland, torture of terrorist suspects in 577–8
 private and family life, right to respect for 47
 terrorism 414–15
 torture and inhuman or degrading treatment 47
 war/crime distinction 414–15
European Union 197, 205, 695, 707, 708 see also Brexit
Evans, Karen 828–9
evidence see also witnesses
 adversarial justice 84–5
 confessions 754–8
 evidence-based approaches 263–4, 794, 798
 illegally obtained evidence 808
 inquisitorial systems 86
 police 814
 young offenders 263–4
evolutionary psychology 492–3
exams 13
exceptionalism 395–6, 397
exclusion see social exclusion
experimental criminology 110–11, 680–2
explanatory theory 673, 674, 687
expressive justice 389
Extinction Rebellion 347
Eysenck, Hans 499–500, 678

facial features 480–3
facial recognition technology 823, 824
fairness
 adversarial justice 710
 classical criminology 455
 Covid-19 46
 crime control 806
 critical perspectives on punishment 930–1, 933
 due process 701–2
 fair hearing, right to a 415, 707–8, 756
 philosophical ideas of justice 75, 77–8, 81
 public opinion 858
 rehabilitation 891
 retribution 840–1, 843, 845, 855, 858–60

families
- alternatives to punishment, involvement in 897
- dysfunctional families 551–2
- Family Group Conferencing, Maori tradition of 901, 946
- family law 729–30
- genetic factors 477, 479, 481–2, 490–3
- learning theories 500
- male domination 331
- social disorganisation theories 538
- Troubled Families programme 791
- young offenders 247

Farrington, David 110, 246–7, 659, 678, 793
fault/culpability 459, 460, 703, 865
Faust, Frederic L 780–3, 785
fear of crime
- crime control 809, 825, 831
- feminism 952
- left realism 632
- media 149–50, 165
- prevention of crime 771, 772, 773, 780
- subjectivity 104
- victimology 198–9

Feinberg, Joel 36, 38–41
fellow students and student-staff committees 20–1
Felson, Marcus 466–7
feminist criminology 324–40
- additional feminist perspectives 339–40
- agency 332
- androcentrism 325, 326, 336, 337, 340
- backlash against feminism 582
- binary concept, gender as a 325, 326
- biology 580
- capitalism 332–4
- children, victimisation of 580, 581
- civil rights movements 325, 328–9
- class 332, 334, 336–9
- criminal justice system 340
- critical criminology 562, 576, 579–81, 586
- culture 327–8, 331, 337
- definition 324
- disabilities, women with 339
- domestic violence 331, 332, 335, 339, 580–1, 597
- double deviance thesis 327
- economic marginality 333
- empiricism 334–5, 336
- epistemology 310, 324, 334–7, 340
- essentialism 326
- family life, male dominance as feature of 331
- female offenders 325, 326, 329–31, 332–4, 336, 339
- femicide 326
- gangs 330
- gender norms, people who do not conform to 339
- gendered crimes 580–2
- glass ceiling 331
- hate crime 339
- intersectionality 325, 334, 336, 338–9, 580, 582
- liberal feminist theory 327–31, 335
- male offending 323, 329, 339, 340
- male privilege 331
- malestream criminology 340
- Marxism feminist theory 332–4
- masculinities 323
- media 328
- #MeToo movement 325
- misogyny as a hate crime 580
- myths 337
- newer perspectives 337–40
- ontology 335
- origins 324–5
- patriarchy 326, 328, 331, 334, 339
- pay gap 333
- police 340
- positivism 329, 580
- postmodern feminism 336–7
- power 336–7
- principles 325–7
- race and ethnicity 336–7, 338–9
- radical feminist theory 313, 331–2, 333–4, 335
- rape 331
- rational choice theory 329, 334
- relativism 337
- scientific methods 334–6
- second wave feminism 580
- sexual violence 580–1
- slavery 324–5
- social construction 325, 337, 339
- social media 325
- socialisation 327
- socialist feminist theory 333, 334, 638
- standpoint feminism 335–6
- statistics 325, 326–9
- stereotyping 325
- suffrage 580
- theories 325, 327–34
- third wave feminism 580
- transgender women 331, 332
- United States 324–5, 582
- victimisation 325, 326, 329–32, 334, 339, 340, 580, 967
- victimology 195, 207
- violent crime 329
- waves of feminism 324–5, 580

feudalism 457
fiction and entertainment 167–75, 179–80
films and TV 169–71, 173
financial harm 603, 606, 607, 609
fines 848–9, 855, 858–9
Floyd, George, killing of 57, 62, 179, 182, 226–7, 274, 282, 286–7, 289, 297, 478, 540, 563, 578, 723
focus groups 111, 112, 976
folk devils and moral panic 150–2, 163, 167, 259, 276, 540
football 278–9
Foucault, Michel 845, 846, 849–51, 936–7
France
- classical criminology 457
- French Revolution 747

fraud
- benefit fraud 942
- Crime Survey for England and Wales (CSEW) 127
- cybercrime 174, 179
- tax 930, 931, 942

free will
- causes of crime 674
- classical criminology 99, 453–4, 459, 460, 478
- differential association theories 526
- neutralisation and drift 547, 549
- positivism 477, 480, 526
- social harm 597
- sociobiological theories 652

freedom of expression 231
freelancing 1013
Freud, Sigmund 494–8, 678, 869–70
Fry, Elizabeth 868–9
functionalism 527–34, 555

Galop 225–6
Galton, Francis 482–4, 490
gaming 172, 174, 180
gangs
- children 287
- culture 251–2, 253
- definition 450
- differential opportunity 545
- feminism 330
- juvenile delinquency 541–4
- neutralisation and drift 547
- prison, conditions in 402
- race and ethnicities 287, 298, 301
- social media 176, 177–8, 179
- subcultural theories 541–2, 544

Garland, David 215, 256, 389, 460, 776, 799, 820, 827, 831, 833, 851–2, 871
gender 309–24, 340 *see also* androcentrism; feminist criminology
- binary concept, gender as a 325, 326
- chivalry thesis 320–1, 322, 323
- class 318
- coercive control 315, 316, 319
- criminal justice system 320–3
- critical criminology 562
- culture 324, 326
- determinism 317
- domestic violence 310–15, 319
- double deviance thesis/evil women hypothesis 320–1, 322–3
- hate crime 214, 215–16
- historical explanations of female offending 317–18
- homogenous communities 82
- intersectionality 310
- labelling 571
- left realism 632, 638
- masculinities 310, 323–4
- male victims 315
- media and female offenders 152, 153
- men as offenders 323
- misogyny 214, 215–16
- myths 315, 341

norms, people who do not conform to 339
paternalism 322
patriarchy 318
police 723
positivism 317
race and ethnicities 216, 318
rational choice theory 318–19
rehabilitation 321
sentencing 319–23
sex/gender 213
social constructs 318, 323
socialisation 311
statistics 218, 310–15, 318–20
stereotyping 316–17, 318, 322
subcultural theories 545
transgender identity 212–13, 218, 310
victim-blaming 313, 314–15
victimisation 314–16
victims, women as 310–15
women as offenders 315–23
   chivalry thesis 320–1, 322, 323
   double deviance thesis/evil women hypothesis 320–1, 322–3
   historical explanations 317–18
   imprisonment 735
   modern explanations 318–20
   nature and extent 317
   United States 320
young offenders 244
genetic factors 479–82, 490–3
born criminals 477, 481–2, 490, 493
adoption studies 477, 481–2, 490–3
determinism 491
epigenetics 493
evolutionary psychology 492–3
family studies 490
genome-wide association studies (GWAS) 491
innate dispositions of criminals 624, 625
nature and nurture 242, 244, 651
physical appearance 480–1
positivism 477, 479, 480–1, 516, 563–4
psychological positivism 499
right realism 623
social construction 491
twin studies 490–2
young offenders 244
geography, justice by 856
Gibbons, Amy 978–9
Gibbs' cycle of reflection 1002, 1004
global criminology 127, 379–81 *see also* comparative criminology; transnational criminology
global financial crisis 2008 581
globalisation 376–81, 383–4
colonialism 378, 381
communitarianism 81
critical criminology 378
culture 377, 381
definition 377–8
emergence of global criminology 378–9
Global North 377–8
Global South 377–8
human rights 377

information technology 377
integrated risk factor theories 655
international trade 377
interpretivism 394
justice 376–81
multinationals 377
transnational criminology 378–9, 410–11, 413, 430, 437
Good Lives Model (GLM) 877, 878–9, 884
Gottfredson, Michael 654, 655
Grabosky, Peter 794–5, 823
Gramsci, Antonio 937–8
Grayling, Chris 749, 847, 853–4, 912
green criminology 345–73
ABC (Always Be Critical) approach 346
access to justice 358
air pollution 348, 358, 364–8
animals 346–51
   Brexit 371
   cruelty 349
   endangered species 346, 349
   enforcement 348–9
   sentience 347
   species justice 357, 360, 366
   wildlife crime 348–9, 357, 363, 368, 371
anthropocentrism 358, 367
biocentrism 367, 371
biopiracy 349–50
bioprospecting 349–50
capitalism 354
Christianity 346
climate change 347–8, 350–1, 355, 363
context and origins 346–8
corporations 348–50, 354, 363, 368–70
courts, proposal for special environmental 370
Covid-19 365–6, 371
crimes or harms 362–6
critical criminology 346, 349, 562
critical perspectives on punishment 931
culture 347
definition 346–52
designing out crime 817
discrimination in access to environmental resources 357
diversion 349
ecocentrism 351, 360, 371
ecocide 42, 351, 357, 360–2
ecological jurisprudence 360–1
ecological justice 357, 360–1, 366
economics 353–5
endangered species 346, 349
enforcement 348–9
environmental harm 346–73
environmental justice 357–60, 366
Gaia hypothesis 347
Global North 349–50, 352–3
Global South 348–9, 357, 371
harm principle 42–3
indigenous people 347, 348–50, 358
market society 352–7
natural resources, exploitation of 349–50, 354
organised crime 348–9

policing green crimes 366–70
politics 349, 368
pollution 348, 352, 355–8, 363–9
punishment 349
race and ethnicity 358
rational choice theory 357
regulation 367–9
relative deprivation concept 357
response to environmental offending, types of 367–70
restorative justice 349
retribution 366–7
scope 348–52
social action approach 367
social harm 346, 606
social justice 357
socio-legal approach 367
species justice 357, 360
State, role of the 349
trafficking wildlife 348–9, 357, 371
transnational crimes 350
United States
   Environmental Protection Agency (EPA) 368–9
   pipeline construction 358–60
veganism 347
victimisation 362, 368
victimology 189
water 351–2
wildlife crime 348–9, 357, 363, 368, 371
wood 352–4, 367–8
zemiology 363
Green, Penny 416–19, 424
Grenfell Tower disaster
corporate crime 840, 953
race and ethnicities 282–3, 296, 298
social harm 592, 603–8
Groves, W Byron 538
Gualinga, Nina 349
guilt 897, 906–7, 909, 921, 923, 931, 948
gun crime 830

Haines, Kevin 822, 913
Hall, Edward 220–2
Hall, Steve 630, 639–40, 641
Hall, Stuart 168, 258, 276, 295, 614
Hamilton, Jaime 711–12, 731, 764
harassment 154, 220–1
Harbison, John 133–4
harm principle 36–46, 50–1 *see also* social harm
animal cruelty 44
consent 40–1, 50
criminalisation 40–4
drug use 41–3, 50
emotional or psychological harm 36
environmental/ecological harm 42–3
harm, meaning of 36–8
hate speech 39–40
indirect harm 41–4
limits 44
moral issues 38–41
non-humans 41–4
offence and anxiety, acts causing 38–41

harm principle (*Cont.*)
  omissions 36
  paternalism (nanny state) 41
  pollution 46
  remote harm 40
  self, harm to 41
Hart, HLA 75–6, 459
hate crime 211–34
  aggravating offences 213
  Black Lives Matter (BLM) 212–13, 226–8
  Brexit 281–2
  civil rights movements 212–13, 231
  Crime Survey for England and Wales (CSEW) 216, 217–18, 232
  culture 212, 214
  cybercrime 174–5
  difference 212, 214–15, 217
  disability 212–13, 218, 219–23
  EU Framework Decision on Racist and Xenophobic Crime 213
  freedom of expression 231
  gender/misogyny 214, 215–16, 339, 580
  gender/sex 213
  group identity 214–15
  harm principle 39–40
  hate crime, definition of 213–17, 232
  hierarchy of identities 214
  hostility, definition of 213, 231
  identity politics 212–13
  intersectionality 215–16, 232
  Law Commission 213
  legislation 213–14
  LGBT+/sexual orientation 212–13, 218, 223–6, 967
  #MeToo movement 212–13
  othering 212, 214–15, 217
  police 213–14, 217
  politics 212, 216
  power 214
  prejudice 212–17, 232
  prevention of crime 774
  race and ethnicities 39–40, 47, 212–13, 216, 218, 227–9, 281–2
  rates of hate crime 217–18
  recording of hate crime 217–18
  religious identity 212–18, 229–32
  segregation 215
  sentencing 213, 217
  shared suffering 215
  social construction 212
  social hierarchy 215
  social justice movements 212
  social media 175
  statistics 217–18, 232, 281–2
  subculture 214
  surveys 217–18
  terrorism 281–2
  transgender identity 212–13, 218
  victim-centred definition 213–14
  victimology 199, 212, 214, 232
  vulnerability 215
  xenophobia 213
Hayward, Keith 629–30
Heap, Vicky 1009

Herrnstein, Richard 624, 651
Higgins, Polly 360–1
Hillyard, Paddy 577, 595–602, 606, 614
Hinton, Mercedes 381–2
Hirschi, Travis 653–5, 679
historical background
  alternatives to punishment 896
  childhood 238–40
  classical criminology 451, 453, 457–9
  criminalisation 223–4
  drama to routine, shift of punishment from 936–7
  Enlightenment 453, 457–9, 476
  female offending 317–18
  feudalism 457
  imprisonment 846–7
  Industrial Revolution 457
  probation service 871
  race and ethnicities 275–7, 304
  rehabilitation 868–70, 874–6
  retribution 837, 839, 845–7, 849–51, 855
  statistics 127–9
  transportation 845, 846
Hobbes, Thomas 625, 641
Hogarth, William 627, 629
Hood, Roger 291–2
hooks, bell 338
Hope, Tim 140–2
hotspots 812, 815, 821
Howard, Michael 13, 114, 747, 948
Howarth, Kate 915–16
human rights 66, 69–73 *see also* European Convention on Human Rights (EHRC); Human Rights Act 1998
  autonomy 48
  broader, non-legal rights 48
  children 239, 243
  critical perspectives on punishment 930–1
  globalisation 377
  humiliation or degrading treatment 48
  physical integrity 48
  police 807
  prison population 391
  privacy 48
  UN treaties 47, 239, 243
  young offenders 246
Human Rights Act 1998 707–9, 715
  absolute rights 707, 709
  balancing rights 707–8
  challenges of using rights 708–9
  derogation in times of war or national emergency 707–9
  European Convention on Human Rights (EHRC) 707
  European Court of Human Rights (ECtHR) 707, 708–9
  European Union 707, 708
  fair hearing, right to a 415, 707–8
  judicial review 707
  liberty, right to 707–8
  politicians, hostility of 708–9
  public authorities, definition of 707
  public interest 708

  qualified rights 708
  Remedial Orders 707
  retrospectivity 707
  rule of law 707–9, 715
  strong rights (special or limited rights) 707–8
  torture and inhuman or degrading treatment 707, 708–9
Hume, David 62
Hunter, Rob 915–16
hybrid discipline, criminology as 1013

the ideal victim 190–2
identity theft 174
Ignatieff, Michael 838, 851, 868–9
Immigration Removal Centres (IRCs) 736–7, 744
imprisonment 720, 735–9
  abolitionism 931, 946–51
  alternatives to custody 853–4
  book ban 749
  Brazilian justice 399–403
  careers 1016
  categories of prisoners 735
  children 568–9, 579
  community-based centres 320–1
  comparative criminology 390–3
  conditions 401–3, 738
  contempt of court 736
  convict criminology 583–6
  Covid-19 739
  crime control 810, 819–20, 831
  Crime Survey for England and Wales (CSEW) 752
  deaths in custody 294, 295, 296–7, 579
  decarceration movement 906
  deterrence 829–30, 846
  digitisation 749
  discrimination 935
  diversion 906
  films 170–1
  fines, failure to pay 849
  gangs 402
  gender 320–1, 735, 868–9
  geography, justice by 856
  green technology 349
  Guantánamo Bay 940
  hard labour 847, 850
  historical background 846–7
  HMP Barlinnie's Special Unit 735–6, 737, 738
  hulks 845, 846
  IAC (Intensive Alternatives to Custody) schemes 854
  Immigration Removal Centres (IRCs) 736–7, 744
  Incentives and Earned Privileges (IEP) scheme 294
  increase in population 731, 735–8, 752, 754, 763, 854–5, 930
  institutionalisation, effects of 839–40
  judiciary 819–20
  Latin America 399–403
  Learning Together model 749–51

length of sent4nces 859
licence, periods on 819–20
media representations 160, 170–1, 179
mental health 935
Mother and Baby Units 320
Mubarek Inquiry 294, 295, 296–8, 935
Muslims 934–5
Norway, prison in 393, 395–6, 397, 737
Open University courses, access to 749
overcrowding 401–2
Panopticon 456–7, 809, 849
penal populism 752, 849, 853
politicians 737–8
power 737
pre-trial detention 390–1, 940
preventive detention 625
prison-industrial complex 736
Prison Rules 735
Prison Service Orders 735
Prisoners' Education Trust 749–51
private sector 738–9
proportionality 855–6, 906
public opinion 749
public protection 390, 737
punitiveness 752, 754
race and ethnicities 284, 285, 291–4, 738, 856, 859, 935
Radical Alternatives to Prison (RAP) 949–50
rehabilitation 321, 735–6, 737, 749, 867–9, 876
reoffending 830, 859
restorative justice 906
retribution 845–9, 851, 853–5, 859
rise in prison population 390–1
rule of law 735–7
Safer Living Foundation 749
segregation units 294
serious criminal record, definition of 752, 754
short-term imprisonment 830–1
social exclusion 935
statistics 291–2, 856, 934–5
terrorism 293
voices of prisoners 584, 586
women 735, 868–9
young offenders 600, 735, 819
Young Review 293
impulsive behaviour 460
incapacitating offenders 808, 810–11, 821, 823–4
inclusion 635–6, 899, 904
independence *see* judicial independence
indictable offences 291–2, 700, 730–1, 854, 856
indigenous communities
Canada 901, 903, 945
banishment in Canada 903
biopiracy 349–50
circle courts in Canada 900, 901, 946
collective guilt and responsibility 947
discrimination 901
Family Group Conferencing, Maori tradition of 901, 946

green criminology 347, 348–50, 358
inclusion, principle of 946–7
Kowanyama, Queensland, establishment of a community justice programme in 947
occidentalism 394
patent systems 349–50
problem-solving traditions 900, 925
restorative justice 901–3
traditional knowledge 349
United States, pipeline construction in 358–60
Industrial Revolution 457
information technology/technologies *see also* cybercrime; social media; surveillance/CCTV
careers in tech-based industry 1012–13
chemical castration 824
crime control 820–2, 823–6
cybersecurity 419, 432–5
detection 823
digitisation 289–90, 745–6, 749
employability and careers 1006
facial recognition technology 823, 824
globalisation 377
green technology 349
imprisonment 749
incapacitation 823, 824
library and computing services 20
misuse 127
online behaviour 140
police 289–90
power 937
restraint 823, 825
SPSS software 977–9
transnational criminology 411
inquisitorial systems 84, 86–7, 713
institutional racism 294, 586, 961–2
critical criminology 934–5
critical race theory (CRT) 299
Crown Prosecution Service (CPS) 728–9
music 172
police 214, 227, 296, 723–4, 813, 832–3, 961–2
retribution 859
schools 813
social justice 60, 62
state crime 578
stop and search 832–3
institutions 719–41 *see also* courts; police; prisons
Crown Prosecution Service (CPS) 720, 724–9
Home Office 129, 720–1, 744–5
local government organisations 720
Ministry of Justice 129, 720, 744–5
philosophical ideas of justice 77–8
probation services and community sanctions 720, 732–5
integrated risk factor theories 648, 655–64
artefactual risk factor theories 246, 648, 654, 656–61, 662, 664
biosocial theory 652

enhanced pathways risk factor theories 648, 656, 660–4
globalisation 655
official statistics 656
predictors 652
psychosocial risk factors 656
Risk Factor Prevention Paradigm (RFPP) 656, 658–9, 662, 664
young males, crime as committed by 655
integrated theories of crime 647–67
androcentrism 651–3, 665
between schools 649–50
bifurcation of criminology 648
biological positivism 648–50, 655
biosocial theory 650–2
classicism 648–50
context 648–50
exclusivity of theories 649
gratification of basic crimes 655
hybrid theories 648, 655
labelling theory 649
multi-factor theories 648
positivism 648–55, 664–5
rational choice theory 650
realism 648
reductionism 655, 658, 665
social control theories 648, 653–5
sociobiological theories 648, 650–3, 655
study 648
subjectivity 648, 655
supposition 648, 665
within school 649–50
within theory 649–50
interdisciplinary meeting point 8–10
International Criminal Court (ICC) 47, 942
international student support 20
internships 12, 1008–9
interpretivist criminology 98–100
Brazilian justice 396–403
causes of crime 671–3
comparative criminology 381, 383–4, 393–403
criminological theory 451
definition 98, 452
enhanced pathways risk factor theories 656, 662
epistemology 106
observations (researching by watching) 114
positivism 98–9, 382–93
public protection 391–2
qualitative research 98–100, 452
radical criminology 100
study 114
subjectivity 103
surveys 113, 114
truth 452
intersectionality
critical race theory (CRT) 300
definition 338
domestic violence 339
feminism 325, 334, 336, 338–9, 580, 582
gender 310
hate crime 215–16, 232
race and ethnicities 216, 280

INDEX

Iraq, US invasion of 412, 418, 940–1
Irwin-Rogers, Keir 176, 177–8

Jeffery, C Ray 651
Jewkes's news structures 160–2
Johnson, Boris 178, 416, 966
Johnson, Shane 795–7
joint enterprise 293, 303
Joker film 173–4
judicial independence 697–701, 715, 720
   accountability 697, 699
   anonymity 699
   apolitical, judges as 698, 699
   appellate courts 700, 701
   appointments, political influence on 698
   courts of first instance 700–1
   diversity, lack of 699
   due process 701, 706
   European Court of Human Rights (ECtHR) 700–1
   government, disagreements with 699
   hierarchy of courts 700
   impossibility of independence 697, 698–9
   Judicial Appointments Commission 698
   jury, trial by 701
   open justice 706
   precedent 700–1
   responsibilities 700–1
   security of tenure 699
   separation of powers 697, 699
   Supreme Court 700–1
   World Justice Project Rule of Law Index 697
judicial review 707
judiciary *see also* judicial independence
   adversarial justice 84–5
   crime control 803, 819–20
   inquisitorial systems 86
   public opinion 749, 858
   sentencing 819–20
   separation of powers 749
   Single Justice Procedure (SJP) 764
   United States Supreme Court, appointments to 698
Jung, Carl 498–9
just deserts
   abolitionism 949
   alternatives to punishment 897, 919
   public opinion 858
   rehabilitation 887
   retribution 837, 839, 841, 853, 858
justice, concept of 55–93
   bad luck or injustice 59–60
   culture 62–4
   fairness 58, 91
   justice, definition of 55–64
   like cases alike, treating 89
   models of criminal justice 64–74
   philosophical ideas of justice 74–83, 87
   proportionality 89–90
   punishment 58, 64, 87, 89–91
   reasoning, importance of just 58–9
   rules, application of 57–8
   sentencing 58, 87, 89–90

social construct, justice as a 62
social justice 59–62, 89–90
systems of criminal justice 83–7
virtual courts 88–9
juvenile delinquency *see also* youth offending and youth justice
   gangs 541–4
   labelling 544–5
   neighbourhoods and delinquency, causal link between 536
   neutralisation and drift 547–8
   peer groups 545
   prevention of crime 775
   social disorganisation theories 536–9
   strain theory 545, 547
   subcultural theories 541–5

Kalica, Elton 392–3, 396
Karam, Maria Lucia 424–5
Kardava, Ketevan 159
Karn, Jacqui 812
Karp, David R 946
Kelling, George 625, 626, 805
Kelly, Liz 794
kettling 810
King, Michael 64, 66
knife crime
   Knife Crime Prevention Orders 827
   media campaigns 178–9
   zero tolerance 814
knowledge, how criminology produces 95–121
   ABC (always be critical) mindset 97–8, 108
   evolution of criminological theories 99–100
   interpretivism 98–100
   knowledge in criminology, definition of 98–9
   positivism 98–100
   practicality of research methods 99
   production of criminological knowledge 97–9
   realism/pragmatism 98–9
   reflexivity 108–9
   social construction 97–8, 100
   sources of knowledge 97
   study 96–7, 99–100, 107–19
   subjectivity 96, 99–105, 119
   supposition 96, 99, 105–7, 119
   survey methods 96
   theories 98–100
   validity of knowledge 89, 97–9
Kohlberg, Lawrence 504–6
Kony, Joseph 420, 422

labelling theory 566–72, 649
   1960s, radicalism in the 567–8
   children 572
   civil rights movements 567
   corporate crime 953
   critical criminology 562, 566–72, 586
   critical race theory (CRT) 299
   deterrence 572

developmental crime prevention 791
deviance, nature of 568–72
diversion 896, 898, 904, 918, 920
enhanced pathways risk factor theories 662
escalation 794
gender 571
juvenile delinquency 544–5
new criminology 575
non-intervention 572
pathological criminals 567
positivism 567, 572
power 566, 572
psychological impacts 569
race and ethnicities 283–4, 571
rehabilitation 881
revolutionalising criminological thought 567–8
social construction 571–2
social interactionism 569
sociological positivism 524–7
spoilt identity 569
state crime 577
stigma 568–9, 572
subcultural theories 544–5
young offenders 255–6
Lammy Report 255, 291–2, 298–9, 304–5, 698, 856, 935, 948
Latin America 379–82, 396–403, 412, 414
Laub, John 245, 247–9
Laven, Louisa 1016–17
Lawrence, Stephen, murder of 60–1, 214, 227, 287, 295–8, 578, 935
Lea, John 417, 621, 632, 634, 639, 932, 952
learning *see also* learning theories
   academic journals 21
   alternative learning materials 21
   critical analysis texts 21
   direct teaching methods 11–12
   distance learning 12
   edited texts 21
   independent learning 12
   indirect teaching methods 12–13
   methods of learning and teaching 11–13
   monographs (research-based books) 21
   reflection 105, 108–9
   resources 21–2
   textbooks 21
   virtual and/or distance learning 12
   Virtual Learning Environment (VLE) 21
   work-based learning (WBL) 12, 1002, 1007–10
learning theories 500–9
   classical conditioning 500–2
   cognition 504–8
   differential association theories 523–7
   life-course criminology 500
   operant conditioning 502
   positivism 500–9
   social learning theory 500, 503–4, 654
left realism 631–9
   1970s and 1980s 631
   administrative criminology 952
   anomie 632

causation 632, 634
class 621, 632
consumerism 634
contradictory theories, integrating 639
crime, concept of 639
crime control 632, 634, 637
critical criminology 620, 621, 631, 637–8, 952
cultural inclusion 634
effects of crime, lack of acknowledgment of 621
exclusive society, rise of the 622
fear of crime 632
feminism 952
gender 632, 638
idealism 631
inclusion 635–6
individualism 634
integrated theory, as 632
local communities, communication with 634
lower class 621, 632
marginalisation 634, 636
Marxist-influenced critical criminology 631, 952
moral panics 621
multi-agency partnerships 635–6
New Labour 623
over-prediction of crime 638
policy 634–7, 642
positivism 637
powerful groups, crime by 638
race and ethnicity 632, 638
relative deprivation 632–5, 639
restorative justice 637
right realism 622–3, 631–2, 642
riots 2011 642–3
situational crime prevention 634
social crime prevention 634
social exclusion 623, 635–6
social structures 632
square of crime 634–7
street crime 631, 632
structural exclusion 634
subcultural theories 632
ultra-realism 639–40
victim surveys 632, 634
legal profession, careers in the 1014–15
Lemert, Edwin 256, 567–8
Leveson, Brian 728
Levitas, Ruth 635–6
LGBT+/sexual orientation 223–6
age of consent 224
communitarianism 82
Covid-19 226
crime, concept of 596
Crime Survey for England and Wales (CSEW) 225
criminalisation, history of 223–4
extent of crime 224–5
gay marriage 29
hate crime 212–13, 218, 223–6, 967
homogenous communities 82
police 723

religion 224
statistics 218, 223, 224–6
surveys 224–6
transgender people 224–5
victimology 198–9
Zoombombing 226
liberty and security, right to 415, 707–8
library and computing services 20
life-course criminology 248–9, 482, 500
lifestyle theory 466
Lister, Stuart 797–8
literature 168–9, 175
live broadcasts of proceedings 706
Loader, Ian 747
Local Criminal Justice Partnerships 720
local government organisations 720
local politics of crime, case study on 777–8
Locke, John 453, 454
Lombroso, Cesare 275, 476, 480–4, 490, 494, 580, 649–50, 671, 678
Lovelock, James 347
Lynch, Leon-Nathan 288–9, 722
Lynch, Michael 347–8

McAra, Lesley 256, 904–5
McDougall, Eve 315, 316, 499, 575–6
McIntosh, Mary 573
McKay, Henry 385, 536–9
McNeill, Fergus 256, 865–6, 873–4, 879, 885–6, 888–9
Macpherson Report 60–1, 214, 227, 287, 289, 295–8, 578, 935
McVie, Susan 256, 904–5
Magna Carta 575
mapping crime 821
Martinson, Robert 69, 881, 885–7
Maruna, Shadd 683–4
Marxism *see also* Marxist-inspired critical theories
feminism 332–4
sociological tradition 389
Marxist-inspired critical theories 562, 567, 572–6
bourgeoisie 573–4
capitalism 573–4
classicism 575
critical criminology 562, 572–6
fully social theory of crime and deviance 575–6
left realism 631, 952
neo-Marxism 575
new criminology 574–5
positivism 575
poverty 574, 576
power 573–4
proletariat 573–4
mass shootings 158, 173–4
Massive Open Online Course (MOOCs) 986, 1007
Mathiesen, Thomas 390, 396, 948–51
Matthews, Roger 417, 630, 632, 639
Matza, David 249–50, 547–50, 567
May, Theresa 709, 813
Mayes, Alex 206

Mayhew, Henry 128–9, 551, 627, 847
Mead, George Herbert 569
media 11, 147–85
Black Lives Matter (BLM) movement 304
celebrities 158–9
censorship 180
children 152
civil unrest 176
comments sections 181
content analysis 152–3
convict criminology 583
copycat crimes 173
criminogenic, media as 149, 173–6
cultural criminology 149
cybercrime 149, 174–6, 179, 965
deviance 149
differential association theories 527
discourse analysis 152–3
effects on crime 173–80
entrapment 158
facilitating crime 174–6
fears and anxieties 149–50, 165
female offenders 152, 153
feminism 328
fiction and entertainment 167–72, 173
films and TV 169–71, 173
folk devils 150–2, 163, 167
framing 152
front page outrage 154
gaming 172, 174, 180
generating news 158
ideological factors 155
inspiration for crime 173–4
key concepts 150–2
knee jerk legislation 149–50
knife crime, campaign against 178–9
language, use of 152–3
learning theories 527
literature 168–9, 175
mass shootings 173–4
migrants, representation of 164–8
music 171–2, 179–80
newspaper headlines 103
newsworthiness 154–62
older and richer victims 154
othering 162
police 154
pornography 175
positive influence, media as a 176–80
prisons and prisoners, representations of 160, 170–1, 179
privileged status of offenders 158
public opinion 149–50, 163, 165, 181
publicity 158, 173, 178
qualitative data 152–3
quantitative data 152
race and ethnicities 275, 276–7, 304
realism 621
reliability 152, 182
religious identity 230
representation of crime 153–67
research 152–4
secondary data analysis 152

media (*Cont.*)
   sexual crime, over-concentration on 152, 154
   social control 149–50
   social groups, media representation of 162–7
   sociological criminology 152
   subcultures 583
   subjectivity 102–3, 152
   subversion 149
   trust 182
   validity 152
   values 155
   victims, photos of 159
   violent crime, over-concentration on 152, 154
   what shapes media coverage 154–62
   young offenders 151–2, 162–4, 256
   youth subcultures 151–2, 163, 165, 256
mediation schemes 713–14, 907, 920
medication
   chemical castration 824
   incapacitation 823, 824
   requirement for offenders to take medication 482, 824
medical model of criminal justice 66, 69, 70, 72–3
Mednick, Sarnoff 650–1
mental capacity
   classical criminology 455–6, 459
   cognitive disadvantage 623
   cognitive theories 494
   disablist hate crime 219, 220–2
   imprisonment 935
   young offenders 244
mental health
   disablist hate crime 220–2
   diversion 918–19
   rehabilitation 866, 880, 882, 885, 887, 891
   support 20
Merico, Marisa 392–3, 396
Merton, Robert K 251, 534–6, 542, 545, 547, 632, 679
Mexico, drug trafficking in 417, 425–7, 432–3, 436
migrants, media representation of 164–8
Milgram Experiment 990, 991
Mill, John Stuart 36–7, 41
miscarriages of justice
   adversarial justice 86–7, 755
   compensation 857
   confessions 754
   crime control 832–3
   Criminal Cases Review Commission (CCRC) 857
   death penalty 703, 855
   due process 702, 703, 754–6
   police 754–5, 759
   public confidence 757
   retribution 855, 856–7
mitigation 906
models of criminal justice 64–74
   bureaucratic model 64–5, 66, 389
   corrective justice 74

   crime control model 66–8, 70–3
   descriptive models 64–6
   distributive justice 74
   due process model 66, 68–9, 70–4
   medical model 66, 69, 70, 72–3
   normative models 64, 66–74
   power model 64, 65–6
   rights model 66, 69, 70–3
   stigmatisation or status passage model 64, 66, 89–90
   substantive justice 74
   terrorism 70
   victims' interests/rights model 70, 72–3
modern slavery 276, 281, 298
Mods and Rockers 151–2, 163, 165, 256–7, 540, 542
morality
   abolitionism 949
   communitarianism 82
   crime control 51, 832–3
   folk devils and moral panics 150–2, 163, 167, 259, 276, 540
   harm principle 38–41
   legal moralism 38
   left realism 621
   observations (researching by watching) 116
   race and ethnicities 276, 277
   rehabilitation 866, 868–9, 874
   religion 38
   research, ethics and legality in 989–96
   retribution 837, 843
   right realism 624
Moronfolu, Grace 291, 728–9
Mtitimila, Upile 1014–15
Mubarek Inquiry 294, 295, 296–8, 935
multi-agency processes 635–6, 912
multi-factor theories 648
Muncie, John 164, 255, 583, 642
Munk, Tine 203–4
Murray, Charles 551–2, 555, 624, 626–8, 643
music 171–2, 179–80
Muslims
   Brexit referendum 230
   framing 152
   imprisonment 934–5
   Islamophobia 215, 218, 229–30, 231–2
   media 150–1, 153, 230
   moral panics 230
   radicalisation 252, 782
   September 11, 2001, terrorist attacks on US 231, 232
   social media 153
   stereotyping 153
   terrorism 102–3, 151, 231, 232
   victims 841
   women 230
M Lai massacre 421

Nagy, Rosemary 944–5
narrative victimology 195–6
National Association for the Care and Resettlement of Offenders (NACRO) 876, 1017

natural justice 821, 843
natural resources, exploitation of 349–50, 354
nature and nurture 242, 244, 651
Naughton, Michael 857
negligence 930, 931
negotiations
   alternatives to punishment 896, 900, 907
   restorative justice 896, 908, 920
Neighbourhood Watch 811
Nelken, David 376, 382–3
neo-classical criminology 460–70
neoliberalism 377, 390–1, 623
neutralisation and drift 547–50
   age 547, 549
   desperation 547, 550
   exceptions and defences in rule-based cultures 548
   free will 547, 549
   injury, denial of 548–9
   responsibility, denial of 548, 550
   types of neutralisation 548–9
   victim, denial of 549
new criminology 574–5
New Zealand
   Christchurch mass shooting 158, 173
   Family Group Conferencing, Maori tradition of 901, 946
   restorative justice 83
Newburn, Tim 376, 393, 395, 398, 722, 812–13, 910, 919
Newgate Calendar 127–8
Newman, Oscar 468, 817
Newton, Isaac 453
Nield, Katie 365–6
Nordic and Norwegian justice 395–6, 397
   Denmark 397
   Finland 397
   Norway, prison in 393, 395–6, 397, 737
   Swedish prison system 396, 397
North East Prison After Care Service (NEPACS) 883
Northern Ireland
   amnesties 944
   community justice 945–6
   external interested parties, involvement of 944
   homophobic hate crime 967
   peace-building initiatives 920, 944
   restorative justice 920, 945
   torture of terrorist suspects 577–8
Nothing Works 69, 880, 881, 886–7
nudge theory 783
nudity in public 36, 37–9
Nuremberg International Military Tribunal (IMT) 939–40

Obama, Barack 422, 578, 703
objectivist ontology 671
observations (researching by watching) 114–16
   covert observation 114–16, 976–7
   Hawthorne effect 114
   native, going 115–16

non-participant observation 114–15, 976
overt observation 114, 976–7
participant observation 114, 976
privacy 116
occidentalism 394
Oduro-Syim, Kwabena 571
offence and anxiety, acts causing 38–41
Ohlin, Lloyd E 250–1, 545–8, 679
O'Malley, Pat 810, 849
omissions 196
ontology 335
open justice 701, 705–6, 752, 764
opportunity
differential opportunity 545–7
opportunism 775, 782, 783, 828–9
organisations, perpetrators as 189
organised crime
displacement 795–6
drug trafficking 416–18, 423–7, 432, 435–6
green criminology 348–9
mafia or cartel paradigm 435–6
people smuggling 429, 435–6
rules/norms 519–20
social media 179
state crime 418
transnational criminology 378, 411–12, 416–18
orientalism 395–6
Orwell, George 65
othering 162, 212, 214–15, 217, 256, 258, 567, 625–30
out-of-court disposals 752

Packer, Herbert 66, 805–6, 818, 984–5
pain, criminalisation and punishment as inflicting 596, 598–600, 601
Pakes, Francis 87, 376, 379, 381–4, 396, 402
Panopticon 456–7, 809, 849
Park, Robert Ezra 536
paternalism 41, 322, 872
pathology 452, 479, 480, 516–17, 525, 567, 650
patriarchy
domestic violence 331, 332
feminism 318, 326, 328, 334, 339
power 66, 566, 654
Pavlov, Ivan 500–1, 509
Pawson, Ray 681–2, 684–5
Paxman, Jeremy 114
Pease, Emma 750–1, 797
peer groups 104, 500, 525–6, 541–2, 545, 547
Pemberton, Simon 592, 606, 610, 612–13
penal codes 694
penal populism 744, 746–51
adversarial-lite 752, 754
Brazilian justice 399
definition 746–7
elites, contesting powers of self-interested 747
fines 849
imprisonment 752, 754, 849, 853
people, claims to speak for the 747
popular sovereignty 747

public opinion 749
punitiveness 746, 751, 754, 763
race and ethnicity 747
right realism 626, 747
sentencing 751
shared values 745
people in criminal justice 761–3
people smuggling 412, 427–30
Pereira, Mike 961–2
personality types 482, 491
Phillips, Coretta 933–4
philosophical ideas of justice 74–83
capacity to engage, increasing 80
choices and agency 80
communitarianism 81–3, 89–91
criminalisation 75
culture 81
difference principle 76–7
distributive justice 74
equality 74, 75, 76–8, 80
fairness 75, 77–8, 81
future generations 77
impartial spectators 79–80
institutions and systems 77–8
liberty 76–7, 79, 81
necessity 74–5
original position 76–8
pluralism 79
positive discrimination 79
poverty 81
punishment 75, 78, 80–1
restorative justice 83
self-interest 76, 78–81
sentencing 75
social contract 76–8
social justice 74, 75, 78–9, 82–3
social norms 78–9
social outcomes 79
theory of justice 75–6
well-being 79–80
Phoenix, Jo 329–30, 924
physical appearance 480–3
physical punishment 47, 845–6, 850–1
Pitts, John 250–1, 254–5, 678
placements 12, 1008–10
planning out crime 817–18
Poland, women's strike in 214
police 720–4 see also Black Lives Matter (BLM) movement; police and race; police-recorded crime statistics; stop and search and race
access to legal advice 754–5
accountability 720, 721, 722
adversarial justice 754–5
antisocial behaviour 811
Brazilian justice 398–9
broken windows 805
brutality 398–9, 723
careers 968, 1013–15
cautions 911
challenges 722–4
charging decisions 724–5
chief constables 721
civil liberties, restraints on 807

community policing 762–3, 803, 814–15
community resolution 752
comparative criminology 381
confession evidence 754–8
consent, policing by 722, 724
crime control 803, 805, 807, 811–16, 818, 826, 831–2
Crown Prosecution Service (CPS) 724–5, 728
culture 68, 722
deterrence 812, 831
disablist hate crime 219
discretion 899
diversion 911–12
diversity 723–4, 728
domestic violence units 340
due process 754–5
effectiveness 811
establishment of the police service 775
ethnographic research 722
evidence-based approach 814
feminism 340
focused deterrence 812
freedom of movement 816
funding 721, 722
governance structure 720
Greater Manchester, Mayor of 721
green criminology 366–70
hegemony 938
Home Office 721
hotspot policing 812, 815
immediate response 811
independence 721, 722
intelligence-led policing 132, 803, 814, 815–16
kettling 810
LGBTQ+ 723
media 154
Metropolitan Police 721
minor offences, discretion in relation to 899
miscarriages of justice 754–5, 759
monitoring 811
moral guardians, police as 816
National Police Chiefs' Council (NPCC) 721
neighbourhood policing 815–16
out-of-court disposals 752
partnerships 811
Police and Crime Commissioners (PCC) 720, 721
Police and Crime Panels 721
Police and Criminal Evidence Act 1984 (PACE) and codes safeguards 754–5, 757
practices 754–5
predictive tools 821
priorities and policies 721, 722, 816
privatisation 722–3, 728, 811
proactive policing 803, 807, 811, 814
problem-oriented policing 812, 815
protests and freedom of movement 816
race and ethnicities 933
realism 640

police (*Cont.*)
  religious identity, hate crimes based on 217
  risk management 812
  role of the police 722
  Safer Schools Partnership (SSP) initiative 781
  self-help 811
  Sexual Assault Referral Centres 340
  Sexual Offences Investigative Techniques (SOIT) Officer 340
  social media 150
  subcultural theories 540
  support of the public 722–3
  surveillance 811
  targets and performance indicators 721, 831
  training 578
  transnational criminology 414, 417–18
  victimology 201, 202, 965
  visibility (bobbies on the beat) 722–3
  volunteers 811
  women 723
  young offenders 253
  zero tolerance 624, 626, 631, 803, 812–14
police and race *see also* stop and search and race
  children 287
  community perceptions 814
  complaints 286–7
  consent, policing by 286
  deaths in police custody 287
  digital policing 289–90
  folk devils 276
  gangs 287
  hate crime 213–14, 217
  institutional racism 214, 227, 296, 723–4, 813, 832–3, 961–2
  IOPC 286, 289
  Macpherson Inquiry 60–1, 214, 227, 287, 289, 295–8, 578, 935
  moral guardians, police as 816
  negative views 104–5
  police-recorded crime 217
  public opinion 286, 933
  radical criminology 578
  research 961–2
  schools 813
  statistics 933
  stereotyping 934
  use of force 287, 289
police-recorded crime statistics 126–7, 130–6
  attrition 133
  categories of crime 131–2
  comparability 136
  complicity 134
  comprehensiveness 136
  Computer-Aided Despatch (CAD) 134
  counting rules 135
  Crime Survey for England and Wales (CSEW) 136, 140
  critical criminology 132
  domestic violence 310–11
  drug offences 136
  generated, how statistics are 133–5
  intelligence-led policing 132
  justice gap 133
  limitations 136
  mapping 132
  notifiable offences 133, 136
  ONS 135–6
  punishment 134
  purpose 132
  reasons for reporting crime 135
  relevance 136
  reliability 135–6
  sexual offences 135
  strengths of statistics 136
  summary offences 133
  targeting 132
  UK Statistics Authority code of practice 135
  under-reporting 133–4
  violent offences 135
  workload 136
policies *see* criminal justice policies
politics *see also* penal populism
  Crime Survey for England and Wales (CSEW) 140–1
  employability and careers 1013
  far right organisations, increase in support for 277, 641
  green criminology 349, 368
  hate crime 212, 216
  Human Rights Act 1998 708–9
  identity politics 169, 212–13, 300–1
  imprisonment 737–8
  leading questions to interrogate evasive politicians, using 114
  nationalism, rise of 227–8, 641
  oppression, resistance to 952
  power 566
  public opinion 747–51
  public perceptions, stakeholders influencing 9–10
  race and ethnicities 228–9
  realism 622–3
  religious identity, hate crimes based on 230
  retribution 849, 853
  sentencing 858
  social harm 603
  theories 448
  victims 843
  young offenders 799
  zero tolerance 813
pollution 348, 352, 355–8, 363–9
Ponting, Clive 85
popular criminology 167–8
populism *see* penal populism
pornography 175
Porter, Natasha 1016
positivism 648–55, 664–5 *see also* biological positivism; psychological positivism; sociological positivism
  artefactual risk factor theories 656–7, 679
  Black Lives Matter (BLM) movement 478
  causative links 451–2, 476, 670–4, 679, 685–7
  classical criminology 100, 480
  comparative criminology 382–4, 393–5
  correlation and causation 476, 477
  critical race theory (CRT) 299
  cultural criminology 582
  data collection 477
  definition 451
  descriptive nature of findings 452
  early positivism 329, 480–4, 485, 490, 494, 516, 572, 580
  enhanced pathways risk factor theories 662
  Enlightenment 476
  experimental criminology 680–1
  feminism 329, 580
  free will 477, 480
  gender 317
  genetic factors 477, 479, 480–1, 490, 516
  interpretivism 98–9, 382–4
  labelling 567, 572
  learning theories 500–9
  left realism 637
  Marxist-inspired critical theories 575
  observations (researching by watching) 114
  pathological behaviour 452, 479, 480, 516–17
  physical appearance 480–2
  proportionality 672
  psychological traits 516
  psychopaths 509–10
  punishment 451, 477, 478–80
  quantitative research 451
  race and ethnicities 275, 478–9
  rational choice theory 650
  realism 621–3
  rehabilitation 451, 477, 478–80
  science 476–7, 480–1
  sentencing 482
  social construction, crime as a 673
  social control 480, 510, 653
  sociobiological theories 648, 650–3
  study 107, 114
  survey research 672, 679
  testing 451
  urban violence 387
  value neutral research 451
  victimology 193–4, 195
  welfare-oriented approach 388
  what works 680–1, 685–6
  young offenders 244–7, 250, 258–9, 265, 267
postgraduate courses 1017–18
post-truth 640
poverty
  crime, definition of 48–9
  critical criminology 563
  deconcentration 791
  globalisation 413
  Marxist-inspired critical theories 574, 576
  morality 623, 627
  philosophical ideas of justice 81

punitiveness 388
social conflict theories 518
social exclusion 551–2, 555
social justice 59–60
social poverty 627
subcultural theories 542
urban violence 387–8
young offenders 247
power 64–6 *see also* privileged and powerful, crimes of
arbitrariness 453
classical criminology 453, 460
criminalisation and decriminalisation 565–6
critical criminology 452, 562, 564–6, 576–7
critical race theory (CRT) 300
differential association theories 525
evasion of criminalisation by powerful 566
feminism 336–7, 564
hate crime 214
imprisonment 737
labelling 566, 572
Marxist-inspired critical theories 573–4
masculinity 323
patriarchy 566
pluralism 564
political power 566
power control theory 653, 654
social construction 564–6
social harm 598–9, 601–3
sociological positivism 522–3
state crime 577
structural changes 565
surveys 113
technologies of power 937
theories 449
victimology 195, 207
Pratt, John 389, 396, 467, 747, 851, 922–3
precedent 700–1, 703
precipitation 192–3, 195
prediction 652, 660, 670, 803, 820–2
pre-emptive action 804, 808, 809, 816–17
presentations 14–15
presumption of innocence 67–8, 394–5, 702, 703–4, 710, 711, 715
prevention of crime *see* crime prevention
price of crime, accepting the 843–4
principles *see* criminal justice principles
prisons *see* imprisonment
privacy 48, 116, 991, 992–3
private and family life, right to respect for 47
privatisation
Crown Prosecution Service (CPS) 728
imprisonment 738–9
police 722–3, 728, 811
private security providers 803, 818–19
probation service 733, 734, 873
privileged and powerful, crimes of 46, 930–1, 938–42, 952
benefit fraud 942
criminalisation, evasion of 566

Ideological and Repressive State Apparatuses (ISAs and RSAs) 941
left realism 638
Nuremberg International Military Tribunal 939–40
rogue traders 942
state crimes 940–2
tax evasion or avoidance 942
Tokyo International Military Tribunal 939
transnational criminology 415–19
vested interests 941, 952
war crimes 939–40
wars, casualties of 939
white-collar crime 521–3, 525–6, 624, 654
probation services 720, 732–5, 761–2
actuarial models 822
advice, assist and befriend 871
Approved Premises 734–5
careers 968, 1015–16
caseload 733
casework approach 872
challenges for probation services 733–5
community orders 733, 763
Community Rehabilitation Companies (CRCs) 733, 734, 873
comparative criminology 385
correction, from care to 873
diversion 732
diversity 733
dynamic characteristics 822
historical background 871
local Probation Committees 872
National Association of Probation Officers 871
National Probation Service (NPS) 732–5
OASys (Offender Assessment System) 733
Offender Group Reconviction Stage (OGRS) 822
origins 871–3
paternalism 872
privatisation 733, 734, 873
probation, definition of 732
Probation Delivery Partners 733
public perception 734
race and ethnicities 294
rehabilitation 714, 732–3, 734–5, 871–3, 875
reorganisation 873
reports 733
risk assessment tools 733
role of probation services 733
Scottish model 872–3, 875
social work, link with 733, 872–3, 888
static characteristics 822
supervision 734
suspended sentence orders 733, 763
training 873, 888
welfare, marginalisation of 888
problem-solving approaches 812, 815, 896, 898–901, 925, 932, 1012
procedural justice 933 *see also* due process
proportionality
alternatives to punishment 897
biological positivism 480

classical criminology 451
fines 849
imprisonment 855–6, 906
justice, definition of 89–90
positivism 672
psychological positivism 480
public opinion 858
punishment 89–90, 451, 478
rehabilitation 887
restorative justice 921
retribution 839, 846, 849, 851, 855–6, 858
sentencing 458
young offenders 263–4, 856
prosecutions *see* Crown Prosecution Service (CPS)
prosocial behaviour 520–1, 527, 791
psychoanalysis 494–8
psychological harm 603, 606, 607–8
psychological positivism 10, 476–7, 494–500
behavioural psychology 494
cognitive theories 494
critical criminology 563
early positivism 476, 481, 516
extroversion 498–500
genetics 499
impulsiveness 499–500
introversion 498–500
neuroticism 498–500
proportionality 480
psychoanalysis 494–8
psychoticism 498–500
punishment 479, 516
rehabilitation 479
social factors 499–500
surveys 678
treatment 479
psychology *see also* psychological positivism
behavioural psychology 504, 508
biopsychological factors 651–2
definition 8
emotional or psychological harm 36
evolutionary psychology 492–3
labelling 569
positivism 516
predetermination 525
psychosocial risk factors 657–9, 662–4
psychosocial theories 679–80
rehabilitation 866, 869–70, 874–6
social control theories 653
sociobiological theories 650
subjectivity 101
young offenders 240–2
psychopaths 509–10
psychotism 498–500
public inquiries 294–9, 304
public opinion 747–51 *see also* Crime Survey for England and Wales (CSEW); surveys
book ban imposed on prisoners 749
community disposals 858
death penalty 859
democracy 747–8, 751
judiciary 749

public opinion (*Cont.*)
   media 149–50, 163, 165, 181
   miscarriages of justice 857
   open justice 706
   penal populism 749
   policies 747–51
   politicians 747–51
   public perceptions, stakeholders influencing 9–10
   race and ethnicities 276, 283–4, 286
   retribution 858–9
   rule of law 748
   sentencing 748–51
   social construct, crime as a 30–2
   young offenders 163, 858
public protection 385, 388–93, 714
punishment *see also* alternatives to punishment; critical perspectives on punishment; retribution; sentencing
   biological positivism 477–82, 491, 493, 516
   causes of crime 670
   classical criminology 451, 453–6, 458–60, 476, 478
   crime control 803
   crime, definition of 49–50
   culpability 459, 460
   drama to routine, shift of punishment from 936–7
   justice, definition of 58, 64, 87, 89–91
   neo-classical criminology 462
   philosophical ideas of justice 75, 78, 80–1
   physical punishment 47, 845–6, 850–1
   positivism 451, 477, 478–80, 516
   proportionality 89–90, 451, 478
   punitiveness 385, 388–93
   right realism 622, 623–4, 642
   right to punish 936
   social exclusion 551
   spectacle, punishment as a 936
   statistics 134
   timing 459–60
   transnational criminology 414
   victimisation 89
   young offenders 239–40
purposes of punishment *see* deterrence; just deserts; rehabilitation; retribution
   qualitative research
   comparative criminology 383
   data collection 976–7, 979–80
   interpretivism 98–100, 452
   interviews 112
   media 152–3
   secondary data analysis 116–17
   victimology 199

quantitative research 98–100, 115–17
   comparative criminology 383
   data collection 976–8
   interviews 112
   media 152
   positivism 451

race and ethnicities 212–13, 273–307 *see also* Black Lives Matter (BLM) movement; critical race theory (CRT); institutional racism; police and race; stop and search and race
   abolitionism 950
   academic scholarship 279
   addressing racial inequality 294–9
   aggravated offences 213, 227, 282
   biological positivism 478–9
   black and criminal, association between being 283–4, 296
   Brexit 217, 227–8, 277, 281–2
   care system 293, 298, 302
   children 287, 293
   colonialism 275–7, 303
   Commonwealth, migration from 276
   communities at risk 790
   Covid-19 62, 228–9, 277, 281, 282–3, 289, 296, 832
   crime control 832–3
   Crime Survey for England and Wales (CSEW) 281
   criminal justice system 283–304
   criminal records 293
   criminalisation 276, 287, 291, 295, 934, 939
   critical criminology 562–3, 586
   critical perspectives on punishment 930, 933–5
   Crown Prosecution Service (CPS) 290–1, 298, 728–9
   culture 275, 277–8, 293
   custodial remands 285, 292
   data, collecting 279–80
   Denman Review 728–9
   discretion 285–6, 293, 301–2
   drug offences 291–3
   empirical research 280
   ethnocentrism 11, 102, 104, 247, 250, 279, 394, 652, 665
   EU Framework Decision on Racist and Xenophobic Crime 213
   far right organisations, increase in support for 277
   feminism 336–7, 338–9
   folk devils 276
   gangs 287, 298, 301
   gender 216, 318
   green technology 358
   Grenfell Tower disaster 282–3, 296, 298
   group identity 228
   hate crime 39–40, 47, 212–13, 216, 218, 227–9, 281–2
   history of race issues in UK 275–7, 304
   homogenous communities 82
   hostility 227, 228
   imprisonment 738, 856, 859, 933–5
   increase in crime 227–8
   intersectionality 216, 280
   joint enterprise 293, 303
   knowledge 279–80
   labelling 283–4, 571
   Lammy Review 291, 298, 304
   left realism 632, 638
   legislation 276, 287
   Macpherson Inquiry 60–1, 287, 289, 295–8
   media 275, 276–7, 304
   migration, encouragement of 276
   modern slavery 276, 281, 298
   moral panics 276, 277
   multiculturalism/diversity 276–8, 285
   nationalist ideology 227–8
   offending 283–4
   over-representation in criminal justice system 283–6, 298, 299
   penal populism 747
   police 227, 274, 276, 286–90, 296, 723–4, 816, 832, 933
      Macpherson Inquiry 60–1, 287, 289, 295–8
      stop and search 285, 286–9, 295–6, 299, 301
      use of force 287, 289
   politicians 228–9
   positivism 275, 478–9
   prevention of crime 799
   prison 284, 285, 291–7, 935
   probation service 294
   proportionality 930
   prosecution 290–1, 298
   public inquiries 294–9, 304
   public opinion 276, 283–4, 286
   racial inequality in UK 275–9
   racial profiling 283, 288–9, 299
   reports 279, 299
   riots 578
   Scarman Inquiry 287, 295, 296
   sentencing 227, 291–3, 933–4
   September 11, 2001, terrorist attacks on US 228
   slavery 275–7, 281, 298
   social construction 275, 303
   social disorganisation theories 536–8
   social harm perspective 281–2
   social justice 60, 62
   socio-economic disadvantage 934
   statistics 218, 227–8, 275, 279–92, 933–4
   stereotyping 934
   stigmatisation 302
   structural racism 227, 277
   subcultural theories 540–1
   systemic racism 226–7, 282–3, 287, 294, 934
   theories 299–303
   United States, digital policing in 290
   victimisation 281–3, 291, 296
   victimology 198, 201
   white privilege 274, 276, 304
   xenophobia 213, 228
   young offenders 255, 258, 292–3, 298, 856
   zemiology 281–2
radical criminology 97, 952–3
   communitarianism 81, 82–3, 90–1
   feminism 313, 331–2, 333–4, 335
   interpretivism 100
   political resistance to oppression 952
   race and police 578

transnational criminology 414
victimology 195
young offenders 245
radicalisation
    deradicalisation 776, 780, 782, 783, 799
    young offenders 251, 252–4, 258
rape culture 193–4
rape myth acceptance (RMA) 193
rational choice theory 10, 462–6
    background factors 465
    bounded rationality 464, 796–7
    causes of crime 674
    classical criminology 451, 453–6, 459, 460, 461, 464–5
    crime scripts 465–6
    cybercrimes 465
    deflection 796–7
    designing out crime 828
    enhanced pathways risk factor theories 656
    event decisions 463–5
    feminism 329, 334
    gender 318–19
    green criminology 357
    involvement decisions 462–3
    neo-classical criminology 459, 460, 462
    opportunism 828
    positivism 650
    prevention of crime 796–7
    retribution 843, 851
    routine activity theory 466–7
    situational crime prevention 468, 783
    situational variables 465
    social control theories 653, 654
    university campuses 444
    witnesses 444
    young offenders 249
Rawls, John 74, 75–8, 80–1, 83, 89–90
Raymen, Tom 640–2
Raynor, Peter 884, 887
Reagan, Ronald 622, 624, 626, 813
realism 10–11, 98–9, 648 *see also* left realism; right realism
    causes of crime 621–2, 682, 684–5
    classicism 622
    context 620–3
    crime control 640
    critical criminology 620–1
    deterrence 622
    ideological basis of competition between political parties 622
    media 621
    observations (researching by watching) 114
    policing strategies 640
    political context 622–3
    populism 622
    rehabilitation 622
    social exclusion 639
    social harm 639
    social justice 621
    structural inequalities 620–1
    study 108, 114
    theoretical context 620–2

ultra-realism 620, 639–42
realistic theory 685–6
recidivism *see* reoffending
recklessness 931
recognition, harms of 603, 606, 607–9
reductionism
    integrated theories of crime 655, 658, 665
    positivism 245, 250, 672
    study 111
    subjectivity 101
    young offenders 245, 250, 263
referral orders 901, 906–7, 909, 921
reflection and learning 105, 108–9, 1002–4, 1019–21
reform of offenders 714, 847, 848, 852–3, 865–6, 868, 875, 882
rehabilitation of offenders 863–93
    abolitionism 948
    accommodation 865, 880, 882, 888, 891
    alcohol and drug treatment 875
    Approved Premises 734–5
    assumptions 864–5
    Breaking the Cycle 873
    causes of crime 670
    certainty, increase in 885–6
    changes for the better 864, 867, 881
    change in circumstances, positive effect of 864–5
    children or vulnerable adults, working with 867
    choose to commit crime, offenders do not 865
    cognitive behavioural therapy (CBT) 869–70, 877–8, 881
    community disposals 848, 868, 873, 875
    community purpose, change will serve offender's needs and serve a 865
    Community Rehabilitation Companies (CRCs) 733, 734, 873
    comparative criminology 384
    compulsory, as 876, 887–8
    contagion 881
    correctional approach 869, 876–7, 888
    counselling 865
    crime control 831, 866, 881
    decriminalisation of offenders 866
    definition 864–6
    desistance 683–4, 866, 877, 879–80, 885–6, 888–91
    deterrence 829–30, 881
    development of rehabilitation 870–3
    disclosure of convictions 864, 867
    diversion 866, 904
    domestic violence 889–90
    drugs 883, 887
    employment 867, 881, 882–5, 889, 891
    expressive rehabilitation 888
    faith and moral redemption 874
    families, lack of involvement of 891
    fines 848
    first, putting the offender 888–91
    formal rehabilitation 867–8
    gender 321
    Good Lives Model (GLM) 877, 878–9, 884

historical background 868–70, 874–6
homelessness 889
ideology 194
impact of rehabilitation 884–6
imprisonment 321, 735–6, 737, 749, 867–9, 876
individualization of punishment 870, 875
integrated approach 883
just deserts 887
labelling 881
legal or judicial rehabilitation 866, 874
limitations 886–91
managerial rehabilitation 888
marginalisation 873
material needs, meeting 870, 874, 876
medical model 888
mental health 866, 880, 882, 885, 887, 891
models and practices in delivery of services 876–80
moral rehabilitation 866, 868–9, 874
neo-classical criminology 460
normalisation of offenders 864–9
Nothing Works 69, 880, 881, 886–7
objects of rehabilitation 873–6
paradigm conflicts 865–6
Pathfinder resettlement initiative 884
positive individual-led change 866
positivism 451, 477, 478–80
prevention of crime 770, 776
probation service 714, 733, 734–5, 871–3, 875
psychological rehabilitation 866, 869–70, 874–6
purpose of rehabilitation 867–70
realism 621–2
reform 865–6, 868, 875, 882
rehabilitation period 867
reintegration 865–8, 874–7, 880, 882, 887–9
removal of conditions which stand in the way of reintegration 867
reparations 866
resettlement 865–6, 875–6, 884, 891
restoration to previous living conditions 864
retribution 848, 848, 852–3
rewarding bad behaviour 871
Risk, Need, Responsivity (RNR) 877, 878, 879, 885
risk of reoffending 876
scientific approaches 869, 872, 874
social capital 879–80
social exclusion 888
social rehabilitation 866, 868–9, 874–6, 880
soft on crime rhetoric 864
spent convictions 864, 866, 867
stigma 868, 888, 891
success, judging 880–4
support 867, 874, 888, 891
symbolism 864
Transforming Rehabilitation (TR) programme 732, 734–5, 761–2
transition, stress of 866

rehabilitation of offenders (Cont.)
   transnational criminology 413
   utilitarianism 873, 888
   welfare of offenders 888–91
   young offenders 246, 880–1

Reiner, Robert 68, 149–50, 153–4, 170, 816

reintegration
   communitarianism 82–3
   diversion 905
   rehabilitation 865–8, 874–7, 880, 882, 887–9
   restorative justice 908–9, 914
   shaming 526–7, 909, 914

religion *see also* Muslims; radicalisation; religious identity, hate crime based on
   aggravated offences 213
   blasphemy 596, 597
   Christianity and the environment 346
   hate crime 212–18, 229–32
   Islamophobia 782
   LGBT+/sexual orientation 224
   moral issues 38
   statistics 218
   victims 199, 841

religious identity, hate crime based on 212–18, 229–32
   aggravated offences 213
   antisemitism 229, 230
   media 230
   moral panics 230
   Muslims/Islamophobia 215, 218, 229–30, 231–2
   police 217
   politics 230
   prejudice 229–30
   September 11, 2001, terrorist attacks on US 229, 230, 232
   statistics 218
   terrorism 229–31, 232

Renwick, Dan 603–5

reoffending
   imprisonment 830
   rates 859, 917–18
   risk 821–2
   young offenders 830

reparations
   community resolution 752
   diversion 904, 912
   rehabilitation 866
   restorative justice 714, 901, 907, 920, 921
   sentencing 714

reprimands and final warnings 911

research *see also* data collection; empirical research; qualitative research; quantitative research; surveys; writing up research
   academic literature, reviewing 969–71
      finding relevant literature 969–70
      reading schedules, planning 970
      revision of research questions 970
      statements of purpose, creation of 969
      writing up findings 970–1
   applied research 107
   assessments 15
   causes of crime 674–9
   conducting criminological research 959–97
   creative research methods, using 964
   data analysis 977–80
   development of topics into research questions 968–9
   doing and manipulating, researching by 110–11
   domestic violence 967
   employability 968, 1016–17
   essay-writing skills, applying 964–5
   ethics and legality in research 989–96
   ethnographic research 722, 762
   innovations in research 118–19
   locally inspired topics 966–7
   media 152–4
   multiple and mixed research methods 118, 119
   new frontiers of crime, topics inspired by 966
   new ground, breaking 963
   observations (researching by watching) 114–16
   personally inspired topics 967–8
   planning properly 963
   planning research projects 987–9
   projects, what makes good student research 962–5
   reasons for research 393–5, 960–2
   strategy, choosing research 971–5
   topic, choosing research 965–9
   triangulation 964
   valid and reliable, making sure findings are 963–4
   value neutral research 451

resettlement 865–6, 875–6, 884, 891

responsibility
   abolitionism 947
   acceptance 897, 900, 905, 921–3
   age of criminal responsibility 242, 243, 259–60, 459, 596, 702, 704
   antisocial behaviour 827
   being held responsible versus taking responsibility 897
   developmental crime prevention 791
   diversion 897, 900, 905, 921–3
   due process 702, 704
   neutralisation and drift 548, 550
   prevention of crime 798–9
   restorative justice 908–9
   situational crime prevention 467
   young offenders 255

restorative justice 761, 763, 901–3, 932
   apologies 901, 911, 915, 920
   collaboration 896, 908
   communitarianism 83
   community disposals 752, 848, 915
   community engagement 903, 908, 932
   community service ideal 713
   compulsion, role of 910–11, 921
   conferences 713, 908–11, 914–15, 918, 922
   consultative mechanisms 901, 908
   cost-effectiveness 918–19
   custody, as an alternative to 906
   definition 713, 896, 915
   delivering restorative justice 907, 922
   diversion 896, 904–5, 911–12, 915
   domestic violence 923–4, 925
   due process 896, 921
   Family Group Conferencing, Maori tradition of 901
   fault-finding ideology, move away from 919
   green criminology 349
   guilt 907, 909, 921
   humanising offenders 918
   indigenous people 901–3
   instant justice 915
   international nature 901, 903
   interpretivism 395
   left realism 637
   legitimacy 903, 907
   mediation schemes 713–14, 907, 920
   negotiated justice 896, 908, 920
   Northern Ireland 920, 945
   offence resolution 898
   origins 901–3
   philosophical ideas of justice 83
   practice, restorative justice in 908–11
   pragmatic compromises 921
   principles 713–14, 715
   prioritised, whose interests should be 898
   problem-solving approaches 896, 901, 932
   process, dealing with crime as a 896
   punishment or custody, as an alternative to 906
   referral orders 901, 906–7, 909, 921
   reintegration 908–9, 914
   reparations 714, 901, 907, 920, 921
   Restorative Justice Consortium 917
   Restorative Justice Council 901, 902, 908
   Restorative Justice Weeks 901
   retribution 848, 853, 919, 921
   Rwandan gacaca courts 903
   shaming 908, 909, 914
   spending cuts 921
   stigma 909
   theoretical background 714
   truth and reconciliation 942–3
   victim, participation of the 714, 907, 920, 923–4
   victimisation 909–10
   victimology 197
   voluntarism 921
   written communications 713
   young offenders 901, 903, 909, 914–16, 921–2, 925

restraint 823, 825

retaliation 694

retribution 837–61

abolitionism 949
   alternatives to punishment 921
   civilisation 851
   classical criminology 455
   community disposals 847–8, 853–4, 858
   comparative criminology 385
   corporate crime 840

correctional approach 848, 851
crime control 803, 831
culture 839
death penalty 844, 845–6, 850–2, 855, 859
definition 837–40
deterrence 843–4, 846, 848, 852–3
effects of punishment 855–7
equivalent harm 839–40
fairness 840–1, 843, 845, 855, 858–60
fines 848–9, 855, 858–9
green criminology 366–7
historical background 837, 839, 845–7, 849–51, 855
imposed, how punishments are 844–9
imprisonment 845–7, 850–1, 853–5, 859
institutionalisation, effects of 839–40
intention 839, 840
just deserts 837, 839, 841, 853, 858
miscarriages of justice 855, 856–7
moral order 837, 843
natural justice 843
physical punishment 845–6, 850–1
policies, practices and consequences 852–5
politics 849, 853
price of crime, accepting the 843–4
proportionality 839, 846, 849, 851, 855–6, 858
public opinion 858–9
punitive turn 849
race and ethnicity 856, 859
rationality 843, 851
recklessness 839
rehabilitation and reform 847, 848, 852–3
restorative justice 848, 853, 919, 921
restitution 840–1
rule of law 840–1
sentencing 841–4, 853–4, 858–60
simple retribution 839–40
spectators 846, 850
state, involvement of the 842–3, 850
symbolism 843, 850, 852, 859
transportation 845, 846
unfair advantage 840
victims 194, 841–4
war crimes 940
young offenders 856, 858
retrospectivity 695, 704, 707
revenge porn 29, 179
right realism 623–31
  anti-intellectualism 623
  austerity measures 642
  biosocial theory 651–2
  blame and responsibility, role of 624
  broken windows thesis 626
  classical criminology 470, 623, 649
  cognitive disadvantage 623
  corporate crime 641
  crime control 624, 626, 630
  critical criminology 621
  genetics 623
  innate dispositions of criminals 624, 625
  indeterminate sentences 625
  left realism 622–3, 631–2, 642

lower class 623, 641
neo-classical criminology 470
neo-conservatism 623
othering 625–30
policy 621, 624–30, 642
positivism 621, 623
preventive detention 625
punishment 622, 623–4, 642
rehabilitation 621
riots 2011 642
rule of law 625
social exclusion 551
social order, fears about the 625–6
sociological positivism 620
stop and search and race 630–1
street crime, focus on 623–4
ultra-realism 639–40
underclass 623, 626–31, 641
urban violence 385
welfare ideal, decline of 624
white-collar crime 624, 631
zero tolerance policing 626, 630
riots of 2011
  criminalisation 938
  critical perspectives on punishment 938
  left realism 642–3
  racism and ethnicity 578
  right realism 642
  severe sentences 938
  social exclusion 551
  social justice 61
  subcultural theories 541
  Trouble Families programme 776
  water cannons 966
  zero tolerance 813
risk assessment
  AssetPlus 263–5, 781, 822
  crime control 803, 810, 822, 831
  OASys (Offender Assessment System) 733, 781
Risk Factor Prevention Paradigm (RFPP) 656, 658–9, 662, 664
  supposition 106–7
  young offenders 246–7, 259, 261, 264, 659, 681
risk factors
  artefactual risk factor theories 246, 648, 654, 656–62, 664, 674, 677, 679
  potential offenders (risky people) 773–4, 786, 787, 789
  prevention of crime 791
  young offenders 258, 261–3
risk management 771, 776, 803, 812, 820–1, 822–3
Risk, Need, Responsivity (RNR) 877, 878, 879, 885
Ritzer, George 763–4
Roach, Kent 826
Robinson, Gwen 887–8, 917–18
Rock, Paul 672, 972, 985
rogue traders 942
Rohingya in Myanmar 29, 577
Rousseau, Jean-Jacques 453, 641
routine activity theory 466–7, 469

absence of guardians requirement 466
classical criminology 461
lifestyle theory 466
motivated offender requirement 466–7
neo-classical criminology 460
rational choice theory 466–7
situational crime prevention 783–5
rule of law 695–709 *see also* due process; judicial independence
  accountability 695, 697
  adversarial justice 715
  Brazilian justice 399
  crime control 805, 818–19
  flexibility 715
  Glorious Revolution 695, 697
  Human Rights Act 1998 707–9, 715
  imprisonment 735–7
  just laws 695
  parliamentary sovereignty 695
  public opinion 748
  retribution 840–1
  retrospectivity 695
  right realism 625
  separation of powers 695, 697, 715, 720
  transparency/open government 695
  truth and reconciliation 944
  World Justice Project Rule of Law Index 695, 696, 697, 705
Runciman, Walter 551, 632
Rwandan gacaca courts 903

sado-masochism 40, 50
Safer Cities programme 772, 776, 817
Safer Living Foundation 749
Said, Edward 395
Sampson, Robert 245, 247–9, 538, 790
Sanders-McDonagh, Erin 215–17
Savile, Jimmy 158
schools *see* education and schools
Schwendinger, Herman 47–8
Schwendinger, Julia 47–8
science
  biological positivism 481–2, 485–94, 509
  causes of crime 674–7
  chaos theory/complex systems science 672, 686–7
  classical criminology 453
  crime control 820, 833–4
  critical criminology 563–4, 586
  feminism 334–6
  positivism 476–7, 480–1
  prevention of crime 791
  Scientific Methods Scale 681
  scientism 563–4
  study of crime 7–8
Scotland
  children's hearing system 872–3, 904
  Crown Office and Procurator Fiscal Service 724
  hanging, survivor of 855
  HMP Barlinnie's Special Unit 735–6, 737, 738
  Kilbrandon Report 872–3
  probation service 872–3, 875

Scotland (Cont.)
  radicalisation 782
  rehabilitation 904
  restorative justice 901
  welfare approach 873
Scott, David 762–3, 973
secondary data analysis 96, 107, 116–18, 152, 975–6
securitisation
  crime control 816–17
  cybersecurity 419, 432–5
  electronic security 390
  gated communities and secure compounds 783, 819
  private security providers 803, 818–19
  situational crime prevention 793
self-employment 1013
Sen, Amartya 74, 78–82, 89, 90
sentencing see also community disposals; death penalty; imprisonment
  aggravated offences 213
  classical criminology 458
  comparative criminology 381
  complexities 459
  deterrence 458, 819
  diversity 732
  domestic violence 889–90
  fines 848–9, 855, 858–9
  gender 319–23
  guidelines 89–90, 731
  hate crime 213, 217
  indeterminate sentences 625, 751
  judiciary 819–20
  just deserts 853
  justice, concept of 58, 87, 89–90
  lenient sentences 858
  like cases alike, treating 89
  magistrates' courts 730
  mandatory sentences 751
  open justice 752
  out-of-court disposals 752
  penal populism 751
  philosophical ideas of justice 75
  politics 751, 858
  positivism 482
  proportionality 458, 855
  public opinion 748–51
  public protection 714
  punitive shift 714
  purposes of sentencing 714, 897
  race and ethnicities 227, 291–3
  reduction of crime 714
  rehabilitation and reform of offenders 714
  reparations 714
  retribution 853–4, 859–60
  riots of 2011 938
  seriousness of
  social exclusion 714
  suspended sentences 733, 763, 830
  tariff 906–7, 919–20
  transportation 845, 846
  victims 841, 842
separation of powers 700–1
  checks and balances 697

Crown Prosecution Service (CPS) 724, 728
judicial independence 697, 699
policies 745, 746
public opinion 749
rule of law 695, 697, 715, 720
sex workers 40–1, 480
sexual orientation see LGBT+/sexual orientation
Shakespeare, Thomas 220–1
shaming 81–3, 526–7, 908, 909, 914
Shapland, Joanna 917–18
Sharif, Omar 252, 253, 723
Shaw, Clifford 385, 536–9
Sheldon, William 482, 490, 678
Sherman, Lawrence 681, 798, 884–5
Sitkin, Lea 166, 167–8
situational crime prevention 781, 783–5
  anonymous spaces, reducing the number of 468
  burglaries 784–5
  categories of place 793
  CCTV/surveillance 467–9, 793
  classical criminology 461, 476
  crime pattern theory (CPT) 783, 784
  crimogenic environments (risky situations) 774
  defensible space theory 468–9
  design of goods 467
  design of living environment 817, 828–9
  escape 469
  evidence-based approach 794
  Kirkholt Project 784–5, 798
  left realism 634
  locks, use of 467
  neo-classical criminology 460
  opportunity theories 783
  predictive techniques 820–1
  rational choice perspective (RCP) 783
  rational choice theory 468
  responsibility 467
  routine activity approach (RAA) 783–5
  Safer Cities programme 817
  schools, targeting 788–9
  shoplifting 110
  securitisation 390, 793
  social crime prevention, distinction from 786–7
  social media 784–5
  street closures 793
  street lighting 793
  surveillance 390
  target hardening 467–8, 782, 785–6, 808, 817
Skinner, BF 502, 509
Skipp, Hollie 978–9
slavery 275–7, 281, 298, 324–5, 398–9
Smart, Carol 317, 325–6, 328, 335–7, 340–1, 586
Smith, Adam 353–4
Smith, Roger 329–30, 640–2, 828, 889–90, 913
Snow, John 128
social bulimia, concept of 553, 555
social conflict theories 518, 527

social construction 11, 97–8, 100
  antisocial behaviour (ASB) 565
  cannabis, medical use of 29
  causes of crime 673–4, 679–80
  crime as a social construction 27–32, 673
  crime, definition of 27–32, 51
  critical criminology 452
  critical race theory (CRT) 300, 302
  culture 28, 31, 62
  desistance 684
  feminism 325, 337, 339
  gay marriage 29
  gender 318, 323, 571
  hate crime 212
  justice, concept of 62
  labelling 571–2
  power 564–5
  public opinion 30–2
  race and ethnicities 275, 303
  social harm 601
  state, influence of the 29–30
  statistics 125
  victimology 189, 190, 195
  young offenders 242–3, 245, 255–6, 258
social contract 76–8, 454
social control theory 648, 783, 930, 935–8
  21st century theories 653, 654–5
  antisocial behaviour 827
  conformity, lack of 679
  control balance theory 653, 654
  conventional behaviours and activities, involvement in 653
  deviance 33, 679
  differential coercion theory 653, 654
  informal social control, aged-graded 248
  media 149–50
  positivism 480, 510, 517
  power control theory 653, 654
  rational choice theory 653, 654
  social disorganisation theories 538, 679
  social learning theories 654
  sociobiological theories 653–5
  stereotyping 936
  technologies of power 937
  traditional control theories 653–4
social disorganisation theories 518, 536–9
  Chicago Area Project (CAP) 539
  Chicago School 536–9
  class 536
  concentric zone model 536–7
  culture 536–40
  family disruption 538
  juvenile delinquency 536–9
  natural areas 536–7
  race and ethnicity 536–8
  residential mobility 536, 538
  sociological positivism 518, 536–9
  structural factors 538
  transnational criminology 413
  urban violence 385
  young offenders 536–9
  zonal theory 536–9
social exclusion 550–5
  cultural inclusion 553

definition 635
dysfunctional families 551–2
imprisonment 935
left realism 623, 635–6
poverty 551–2, 555
realism 551, 639
rehabilitation 888
sentencing 714
slums 550
social bulimia, concept of 553, 555
Social Exclusion Unit 552–3
sociological positivism 550–5
statistics 555
stigma 551–2
underclass 550–5
welfare, dependency on 551–2
social factors 650–1
social harm 11, 591–617
   accountability 593, 595
   adversarial justice 600, 610
   asbestos, industrial legacy of 594, 595
   austerity measures, deaths and harm due to 593–4, 600
   autonomy 592, 595, 606, 613
   corporate criminality 598–601
   crime, concept of 48–9, 596–8, 610, 612–14
   crime control 596, 600–2
   critical criminology 592, 595–602, 613
   critique of approach 612–14
   cultural harm 603, 606, 607–8
   definition 592–5
   dignity, harm to 606
   economic harm 603, 606, 607, 609
   educational needs, failure to meet 594, 595
   emotional harm 603, 606, 607–8
   environmental harm 606
   excluding many serious harms, 'crime' as 596, 597–8
   financial harm 603, 606, 607, 609
   free will 597
   green criminology 346
   Grenfell Tower fire disaster 592, 603–8
   inequalities 603–14
   levels and dimensions of social harm 606–9
   liberal regimes 610–12
   myopic, constructing 'crime' through criminal law is 596, 598
   myth of 'crime', criminology as perpetuating the 596–7
   ontological reality, 'crime' as having no 596, 599
   pain, criminalisation and punishment as inflicting 596, 598–600, 601
   petty events, 'crime' consists of 596, 597–8
   physical harm 603, 607
   power 598–9, 601–3
   preventable harms 594–5, 774
   production of social harm 609–12
   psychological harm 603, 606, 607–8
   public policy 600
   race and ethnicities 281–2
   realism 639
   recognition, harms of 603, 606, 607–9
   reduction of social harm 609–12
   relational harms 606
   social construction 601
   social democratic regimes 610–12
   social injustice 600
   state crime 613
   systemic social issues 603
   theoretical principles 592
   typology of harm 606–7
   victimisation 595
   welfare systems 610–11
   zemiology 48, 300, 363, 592, 595, 599, 602, 610–14
social inclusion 635–6, 899, 904
social justice 59–62, 89–90
   critical criminology 932
   green criminology 357
   philosophical ideas of justice 74, 75, 78–9, 82–3
   realism 621
   social justice movements 212
   transgender women 332
social learning theory 500, 503–4, 654
social media
   big data 179
   Chibnall's imperatives 156
   citizen journalism 180–2
   click bait 159–60
   dark net 176, 177
   employability and careers 1018, 1020
   fake news 181
   feminism 325
   gang violence 176, 177–8, 179
   generational variations 157
   harassment 154
   hate crime 175
   immediacy 154, 156
   location information 179
   paedophile vigilantes 180
   positive influence, media as a 176–7
   prevention of crime and detection 179
   revenge porn 176
   sexting 176
   situational crime prevention 784–5
   statistics 130
   subjectivity 102
   titillation 159–60
   visual content, preference for 157–8
   young offenders 256
social movements 50, 212–13, 231, 325, 328–9, 567 see also Black Lives Matter (BLM) movement
social process/interaction theories 517, 523–7
social structural theories/structuralism 517–18, 527–55 see also subcultural theories
social workers 733, 872–3, 888
socialisation 311, 327, 520–3, 651
sociobiological theories 648, 650–3, 655
sociological positivism 10, 476, 481, 515–59
   background of offenders 516
   causes of crime 679
   class 522, 523–6
   comparative criminology 381
   corporations 516, 526
   differential association 523–7
   early positivism 516
   free will 526
   functionalism 527–34, 555
   government, decisions by 516
   influence on criminal behaviour 516–17
   key concepts in sociology 518–23
   labelling perspectives 517, 523
   learning theory 524–7
   neo-positivism 516
   peer groups 525–6
   power 522–3
   reintegrative shaming 526–7
   right realism 620
   rules/norms 519–20, 521
   social conflict theories 518, 527
   social control theories 517
   social disorganisation theories 518, 536–9
   social exclusion 550–5
   social process/interaction theories 517, 523–7
   social structural theories/structuralism 517–18, 527–55
   socialisation 520–3
   status and role 518–20, 521
   strain theory 518, 534–9, 555, 679
   subcultural theories 518, 539–55, 679
   surveys 679
   theories 517–18
   white-collar crime 521–2, 526
soft on crime 799, 853, 864
solicitors 1014
South Africa 920, 943–4
South, Nigel 361–2
Sparks, Richard 376, 393, 395, 747
spectators 846, 850
Spencer, David 1014–15
spoilt identity 569
standard of proof 725, 827
Stanford Prison Experiment 990
state crime
   bombing 431–2
   children, incarceration of 568–9, 579
   civilian population, targeting of 421
   corporate crime 415–17, 436, 577
   critical criminology 561, 576, 577–9, 586
   discrimination 578
   drug trafficking 418
   green criminology 349
   imprisonment without trial 940
   institutional racism 578
   insurgents 421–2
   labelling 577
   orders, following 577
   organised crime 418
   power 415–16, 577
   privileged and powerful, crimes of 940–2
   race and ethnicities 228, 578, 613
   terrorism 417, 419–24, 577–8
   transnational criminology 378, 412, 415–21
   use of force, excessive and unlawful 940

statistics 123–45 *see also* police-recorded crime statistics
  adversarial-lite 752
  artefactual risk factor theories 656, 660
  censuses 127–8
  correlation distinguished from causation 129
  Crime Survey for England and Wales (CSEW) 125–7, 136–42
  critical criminology 142
  development of national crime statistics 127–30
  disablist hate crime 218
  domestic violence 310–14
  exploring, explaining, and responding to crime 124
  feminism 325, 326–9
  first large-scale survey 128–9
  gender 310–15, 318–20
  global criminology 127
  hate crime 217–18, 232, 281–2
  historical development 127–9
  illegitimacy 129
  illiteracy 129
  imprisonment 291–2, 856, 934–5
  Information Age 129, 130
  integrated risk factor theories 656
  LGBT+/sexual orientation 218, 223, 224–6
  mass victimisation surveys 125–7
  Office for National Statistics (ONS) 129, 135–6, 140, 199, 217, 312
  positivism 664
  public health 127–8
  public policy 129
  purpose of statistics 123
  race and ethnicities 218, 227–8, 275, 279–92
  religious identity, hate crimes based on 218
  secondary data analysis 116–17
  social construct, crime as a 125
  social disorganisation theories 539
  social exclusion 555
  social harm 597, 599–601
  social media 130
  sociobiological theories 652–3
  source of statistics 123–5
  stop and search 288–9, 933
  UK Statistics Authority 140
  victimology 188, 198–201
  young offenders 163, 246
  zero tolerance 813
Stenson, Kevin 826, 831–2
stereotyping
  feminism 325
  gender 316–17, 318, 322
  the ideal victim 191–2
  Muslims 150–1, 153
  race and ethnicities 934
  secondary victims 190
  social control theory 936
  young offenders 258
sterilisation 482

stigma 64, 66, 89–90, 935
  convict criminology 584, 585–6
  developmental crime prevention 791
  deviance 568–9
  labelling 568–9, 572
  race and ethnicities 302
  radicalisation 782
  rehabilitation 868, 888, 891
  restorative justice 909
  social exclusion 551–2
  welfare cuts 569
  young offenders 256
stop and search and race
  adversarial contact, as 287
  arbitrariness 812
  Black Lives Matter (BLM) movement 289
  children 287
  Covid-19 289
  critical criminology 933–4
  critical race theory (CRT) 299, 301
  driving expensive cars 934
  effectiveness 812
  institutional racism 832–3
  labelling 571
  miscarriages of justice 755
  proportionality 285, 287, 289, 296
  public opinion 933
  racism 723
  reasonable grounds 812
  right realism 630–1
  riots 295
  statistics 288–9, 933
  sus law 287, 295
  victimology 201
strain theory
  comparative criminology 384–5, 388
  culture 539–40
  differential opportunity 545
  neutralisation and drift 547
  social control theories 653
  sociological positivism 518, 534–9, 555, 679
  transnational criminology 413
  welfare-oriented approach 388
Stray, Melanie 225–6
street crime
  comparative criminology 385, 387–8
  differential association theories 525
  left realism 631, 632
  male victims 315
  right realism 623–4
structuralism 517–18, 539–55
Strudwick, Kate 978–9
study 96–7, 99–100, 107–19
  applied research 107
  doing and manipulating, researching by 110–11
  epistemology 107–9
  experimental method 110–11
  innovations in research 118–19
  multiple and mixed research methods 118, 119, 976
  observations (researching by watching) 114–16

  positivism 107, 114
  realism/pragmatism 108, 114
  research as study 107–9
  secondary analysis 107, 116–18
  situational crime prevention 110
  subjectivity 107–9, 118
  supposition 107–9, 118
  surveys 111–14
studying criminology 5–23
  ABC (Always Be Critical) approach 18–19, 22
  assessments 13–17
  E3 (effective, engaged, and employable) students 17–18, 22
  goals 17–18
  learning and teaching methods 11–13
  learning resources 21–2
  people, organisations, and systems 11
  presentations 14–15
  resources 21
  support (travel partners) 19–21
  themes and issues 11
  theories 10–11
subcultural theories 540–55
adaptation, type of 545–6
  anomie 542, 545
  antisocial behaviour 541–2
  class 540, 542, 544–5, 546–7
  conflict subcultures 545, 546
  deviance 33, 35, 542
  differential association theory 542, 547
  differential opportunity 545–7
  edgework 582
  emotions 582, 583
  gangs 541–2, 544, 545
  hate crime 214
  injunctions 541
  juvenile delinquency 541–5
  labelling 544–5
  left realism 632
  malice 544
  mods and rockers 151–2, 163, 256–7, 540, 542
  negativistic, behaviour as 544
  neutralisation and drift 547–50
  non-utilitarian, delinquency as 544
  opportunities, lack of 542
  peer groups 541–2, 545
  punk 540–1, 542
  race and ethnicity 540–1
  retreatist subcultures 545, 546
  risk-taking 582
  Road Life and Bad Boys 541, 542
  social exclusion and underclass 550–5
  sociological positivism 518, 539–55, 679
  strain theory 545, 547
  subculture, definition of 540
  style 582–3
  urban violence 385
  women 545
  youth culture 151–2, 163, 165, 250–2, 256, 540–5, 582–3
subjectivity 96, 99–105
  causes of crime 674, 677, 679, 687

constructive nature 119
media representation 102–3, 152
secondary data analysis 116–17
sociobiological theories 652
study 107–9, 118
supposition 99, 106, 119
surveys 113
suicide 596 *see also* assisted dying
summary offences 133, 700–1, 730, 764
support (travel partners) 19–21
academic writing clinics 20
disability and additional learning support 19
employability support 20
fellow students and student-staff committees 20–1
international student support 20
library and computing services 20
mental health support 20
programme handbooks 21
programme travel partners 20–1
staff 20
student societies 20
university travel partners 19–20
Virtual Learning Environment (VLE) 21
supposition 96, 99, 105–7, 119, 648, 665
causes of crime 672, 674, 677, 679, 682–3, 687
crime control 823
study 107–9, 118
subjectivity 99, 106, 119
surveillance/CCTV
crime control 803, 823, 826
electronic surveillance 390
natural surveillance 783
police 811
prevention of crime 777–8, 783, 785, 789, 797
situational crime prevention 467–9, 793
surveys 111–14 *see also* Crime Survey for England and Wales (CSEW)
closed questions 112, 976
correlation and causation 677–80
demographics 680
European Social Survey 975
European Survey on Crime and Safety 975
focus groups 111, 112, 976
hate crime 217–18
International Crime Victims Survey 975
interpretivism 113, 114
interviews 111, 112–14
closed questions 112
epistemology 112–13
open questions 112
qualitative methods 112
quantitative methods 112
semi-structured interviews 112–13
structured interviews 112, 976
unstructured interviews 112, 976
LGBT+/sexual orientation 224–6
mixed surveys 113
open-ended questions 112, 976
positivism 672, 677–9

power 113
psychosocial bias 680
questionnaires 111–13, 976
social desirability bias 113
statistics 677–8
strengths and weaknesses 137–9
structured surveys 112–13
study 111–14
victims 188, 632, 634
survivor, use of term 190
suspended sentences 733, 830, 873
Sutherland, Edwin H 379, 482, 523–7, 535, 542, 545, 614
Sykes, Gresham 547–50, 952
symbolism 864, 930, 936
systems of criminal justice 83–7 *see also* adversarial justice; inquisitorial systems

tagging 810, 823
target hardening
burglaries 817
crime control 803–4, 808–9
designing out crime 831
prevention of crime 782, 785, 789
situational crime prevention 467–8, 782, 785–6, 808, 817
zero tolerance 823
tax
benefit fraud 942
evasion or avoidance 942
fraud 930, 931, 942
multinationals 566
Taylor, Ian 552, 575–6, 614
teaching and learning methods 11–13 *see also* work-based learning (WBL)
technicalities 705, 710
technologies *see* information technology/technologies
terrorism
bad luck or injustice 59
cybercrime 176
European Convention on Human Rights (EHRC) 414–15
Geneva Conventions 422–3
hate crime 281–2
illegal detention 422–3
imprisonment 293, 422–3
inhuman or degrading treatment 70
Muslims 151
Northern Ireland, torture in 577–8
open justice 706
radicalisation 782, 783
religious identity, hate crimes based on 229–31, 232
rendition programme of US 422
September 11, 2001, terrorist attacks on US 228–31, 232
state crime 415, 419, 577–8
torture, psychological and physical 422, 423
transnational criminology 417
war on terror 419–24
testosterone 488–90, 493

textbooks 21
Thakur, Shanti 900
Thatcher, Margaret 469, 622, 626, 698
theories 10, 192–6, 206–7, 444–50
therapeutic healing 948
Thompson, Beverley 297
Tilley, Nick 681–2, 684–5, 770–2, 774, 777, 779, 798, 815, 826
Tokyo International Military Tribunal (IMT) 939
Tombs, Steve 595–603, 606–7, 609, 953
torture and inhuman or degrading treatment 70, 707, 708–9
tough on crime 258, 260, 623, 749, 751, 813, 853, 889, 953
traditional knowledge 349
transformative justice 932
Transforming Summary Justice (TSJ) initiative 764
transgender identity 212–13, 218, 224–5, 310, 331, 332
transitional justice 944–5
transnational criminology 409–39
chemical weapons in Iraq, use by US of 412
child pornography 412
clothing industry 413–14
civil society 418, 436–7
cocaine trafficking across Central America to US 412, 414
colonialism 411, 415
comparative criminology 412, 415
corporate crime 378, 412, 415–17, 430–2, 436
Covid-19 415, 416
critical criminology 415–17, 437
critical issues 435–6
cybercrime 417, 419, 432–5
cybersecurity 419, 432–5
definition 378, 411–19
drug trafficking 416–19, 423–7, 432–3, 435–6
dumping of toxic, hazardous waste by transnational corporations into Africa and Asia 412, 417, 419, 430–2
globalisation 378–9, 410–11, 413, 430, 437
green criminology 350
information technology 411
key areas 419–35
key themes 412–19
mafia or cartel paradigm 435–6
militarization 415, 419, 423
national and international dimension 413–14
NGOs 418, 436–7
organised crime 378, 411–12, 416–18, 423–7, 432
people smuggling 412, 419, 427–30, 435–6
police 414, 417–18
powerful and crimes of the powerless, crimes of the 415–19
powerful offenders 417, 419
public/private distinction 417–19
punishment 414

transnational criminology (Cont.)
  radical criminology 414
  rehabilitation 413
  scope 411–12
  social disorganisation 413
  state crime 378, 412, 415–22, 431–2, 436
  strain theory 413
  terrorism 417
  war/crime distinction 414–16
  war on terror 419–24
  zero tolerance 413, 415
transportation 845, 846
triad of criminology 7, 8, 10, 965
Trump, Donald 228–9, 230, 303, 358, 416, 422–3, 563, 578, 698, 813
trust 68, 182
truth
  adversarial justice 84–5, 710
  convict criminology 583–4
  inquisitorial systems 86
  interpretivism 452
  post-truth 640
  truth and reconciliation 942–5
Turing, Alan 223

Ugelvik, Thomas 396–7, 403
underclass 385, 388, 550–5, 623, 626–31, 849
under-reporting of crime 135
United States
  Cambridge-Somerville project 775
  chemical castration 824
  chemical weapons in Iraq, use by US of 412
  civil rights movement 567
  class 935
  classical criminology 457
  convict criminology 583–4, 586
  Covid-19 and war analogies 416
  crime control 833
  critical race theory (CRT) 275, 299–302
  death penalty
    due process 703
    miscarriages of justice 703
    race and ethnicities 482–3
    retribution 851–2
  deterrence 389, 828–9
  diversion 917
  drugs, war on 427
  environmental justice 357
  Environmental Protection Agency (EPA) 368–9
  feminism 324–5, 582
  fines 849
  gender 320
  green criminology 358–60, 368–9
  Guantánamo Bay 940
  Head Start programme 792
  Hit Man manual 175
  illegally-obtained evidence 808
  imprisonment
    harsh penal policies 390
    population 930
    pre-trial detention, increase in 390–1
  indigenous people 358–60

institutional racism 578
Iraq, invasion of 412, 418, 940–1
judges of the Supreme Court, appointment of 698
miscarriages of justice 703
Muslims 231–2
neoliberalism 390–1
pipeline construction 358–60
police 312–13, 578
public protection 389–91
race and ethnicities
  class 935
  crime control 833
  digital policing 290
  institutional racism 578
  September 11, 2001, terrorist attacks on US 228
  slavery 227
realism 622
religious identity, hate crimes based on 229, 230, 232
September 11, 2001, terrorist attacks on US 228–231, 232
slavery 277
subcultural theories 542, 544
what works 680
young offenders
  Cambridge-Somerville project 775
  Massachusetts experiment 949
  zero tolerance policing in New York 626
unwritten constitution of UK 694–5
urban violence 385–8
utilitarianism 66–8, 79, 455, 805, 873, 888

values and regulations, deciding on crimes using 45–7
veil of ignorance 76–7, 90
victimisation
  children 580, 581
  crime control 825–6
  Crime Survey for England and Wales (CSEW) 137, 140–2
  feminism 325, 326, 329–32, 334, 339, 340, 580, 967
  gender 314–16
  green criminology 362, 368
  mass victimisation surveys 125–7
  predictive tools 821
  punishment 89
  race and inequalities 281–3, 291, 296
  repeat victimisation 104, 201–4, 821
  restorative justice 909–10
  social harm 595
  social inequalities 826
  urban violence 388
  surveys 125–7
  victimology 188
victimology 187–209
  abolitionist ideology 194
  blaming victims 193
  children 199
  concepts 192–8
  Crime Survey for England and Wales (CSEW) 188, 195, 198–9, 201

crimeless victims 189
criminal justice process 205–6
critical victimology 194–5
cybercrime 203–4
debates 192–8
direct victims 189–90
disability, persons with 198
ethnicity 198, 201
EU Directive on Victims' Rights 197, 205
fear of crime 198–9
feminist victimology 195, 207
green criminologists 189
hate crime 199, 212, 214, 232
hierarchy of victims 191, 195
the ideal victim 190–2
indirect/secondary victims 189–90, 196, 202, 206–7
journals 193
long-term effects 188
measuring victimisation 198–204
Megan's Law 200
narrative victimology 195–6
omissions 196
organisations, perpetrators as 189
participation and inclusion 188, 205
police 201, 202, 965
policy approaches 196–8
positivist victimology 193–4, 195
power 195, 207
precipitation 192–3, 195
public policy 188
radical victimology 195
rehabilitation ideology 194
religion 199
repeat victimisation 104, 201–4
restorative justice 197
retributive or criminal justice ideology 194
rights and needs of victims 188, 194, 197, 200, 205
Sarah's Law 200
sexual orientation 198–9
social construction 189, 190, 195
statistics 188, 198–201
structural issues 194–5
surveys 188
survivor, use of term 190
theories 192–6, 206–7
UN
  Declaration of Basic Principles 196–8, 201
  Victims' Rights Advocate 196–7
Victim Personal Statement (VPS) 205–6
Victim Support charity 200, 205–6
victimity, concept of 188, 189
victimless crimes 189
Victims' Charter 188
Victims' Code 197, 205–6
victims, definition of 188–92, 196, 201
witnesses
  special measures 206
  Witness Charter 205
younger people 198
victims *see also* victimisation; victimology

abolitionism 932
alternatives to punishment, involvement in 897, 899–900, 923–4
blaming victims 313, 314–15, 789
Community Remedy 841
Community Trigger 841
Crown Prosecution Service (CPS) 724
defendants, rights of 842–3
denial of victim 549
gender 310–15
Good Samaritan laws 159
marginalisation 923–4
police 826
politicians 843
prevention of crime 786, 789–90
religion 841
restorative justice 714, 907, 920, 923–4
retribution 841–4
sentencing, role in 841, 842
surveys 632, 634
Victim Personal Statements (VPSs) 205–6, 842–3
Victim Support 200, 205–6, 923, 1017
Victimised Actor Model 653
victims' interests/rights model 70, 72–3
women's groups and reclaim the night marches 789–90
visual assessments 16–17
Voltaire 453
volunteers 811, 1009
Von Hentig, Hans 192
vulnerable groups or communities (at risk people) 139, 141, 215, 773

Walton, Paul 575, 586, 614
war/crime distinction 414–15
war crimes 939–40
Ward, Tony 416–19, 424
Weberian sociology 64–5, 389
welfare dependency 551–2
welfare-oriented approach 388–9, 775, 776, 888–91
Wertham, Frederick 192
West, Donald 246–7
Westmarland, Nicole 889–90
what works 680–6, 798, 828–30
white-collar crime 521–3, 525–6, 624, 654
White, Rob 347, 351–2, 358
Whitehead, Henry 128
Whyte, David 597, 953
Wigmore, John Henry 712
wildlife crime 348–9, 357, 363, 368, 371
Wilson, James Q 623, 624–6, 630, 651, 805
Winlow, Simon 639–40, 641
witnesses
  adversarial justice 85, 710, 711, 712–13
  cognition 508
  inquisitorial systems 86
  rational choice theory 444
  special measures for vulnerable witnesses 206, 710
  Witness Charter 205
Wollstonecraft, Mary 580
women *see* feminist criminology; gender

work-based assessments 15–16
work-based learning (WBL) 12, 1002, 1007–10
work shadowing 1009
writing up research 980–7
  academic literature 970–1, 980
  cognitive ability 982
  criticality, level of 982–3
  disseminating your findings 986–7
    articles, writing 987
    blogs or video diaries 986
    community groups or organisations, involving 987
    conferences, present at 987
    open education resource (OER), building a 986–7
    wiki, building a 986
  feedback 983, 984
  learning from others 984
  referencing 984–6
    compiling a reference list 985–6
    direct quotes 984–5
    indirect references 985
  software tools 983
  structure and content 980–3
  style of writing 983–4
  tone right, getting the 983
  what if question 982–3
written assessments 13–14

xenophobia 213, 228

Yar, Majid 629–30
Yates, Sarah 1003
Young, Jock 380, 389, 391, 551–3, 555, 563, 573–5, 586, 614, 621–2, 631–2, 634–5, 952
Young Review 935
youth offending and diversion 265–6, 896, 898, 905, 914–15, 925
  abuse at young offender's centre 819
  Beijing Rules 904
  cautions 907, 911–12, 921, 923
  early intervention strategies 904
  international agreements 904
  Juvenile Liaison Officer scheme in Liverpool 911
  Northamptonshire model 912–13, 917–18, 922
  reprimands and final warnings 911
  Riyadh Guidelines 904
  Scotland 904
  Swansea Bureau Initiative 913–14, 917–18
  Tokyo Rules 904
  Youth Justice Liaison and Diversion (YJLD) services 912
  Youth Restorative Disposal 912
youth offending and youth justice 237–71
  see also youth offending and diversion
  adolescence 240–1, 245–50, 487
  adverse childhood experiences (ACEs) 916
  age of consent 242

age of criminal responsibility 242, 243, 259–60, 459, 596
agency 242, 245, 249–50
alternative activities 788–9
androcentricism 247, 250
antisocial behaviour 238, 244, 247, 250, 774
apologies 915
artefactual risk factor theories 246, 658–60
Asset 261, 658–9, 789
AssetPlus 263–5, 781, 822
Black Lives Matter (BLM) movement 255–6, 258, 265
Cambridge Study 246–9
Children First, Offenders Second (CFOS) 266–7
constructivism 249, 264
contextual explanations 250–9
county lines 242
Covid-19 255–6, 265, 268
criminalisation 255, 259, 923
criminogenic influences 258, 265
critical criminology 255
critical theories 245
culture 240–1, 244–5, 250–4, 258
demonisation 163, 164
developmental age 238
developmental crime prevention 788, 791
developmental explanations of childhood 240–2, 245–50
deviance 250–2, 256–8
due process 263–4
early intervention 260, 261
education, compulsory 239
emergence, concept of 245
empirical research 245
enhanced pathways risk factor theories 661–4
escalation 794
ethnocentrism 247, 250
evidence-based practice 263–4
family criminality 247
gang culture 251–2, 253
gender 244
genetics 244
geography, justice by 856
Gluecks' study 247–9
history, childhood in 238–40
human rights 246
hyperactivity-impulsivity-attention deficit 244, 247
imprisonment 600, 735, 787–8, 935
individualised explanations 243, 244–50, 259
informal social control, aged-graded 248
interventionism, increase in 246
KEEP (Key Elements of Effective Practice) 261
labelling theory 255–6
learning disabilities 935
life course theory 248–9
low intelligence 244
mainstream responses to youth offending 259–64

youth offending and youth justice (*Cont.*)
    maltreatment of children, effects of 487
    Massachusetts experiment 949
    media 151–2, 162–4, 256
    moral panics 259
    nature or nurture 242, 244
    non-normative events 245
    normative events 245
    Onset 262–3, 789
    othering 256, 258
    police 253
    politics 799
    poor parenting 247
    positive youth justice 266–7
    positivism 244–7, 250, 258–9, 265, 267
    poverty 247
    prevention of crime 260
    progressive approaches 264–7
    proportionality 263–4, 856
    psychological explanations of childhood 240–2
    public opinion 163, 858
    punishment 239–40
    race and ethnicities 255, 258, 292–3, 298, 856, 930
    radical theories 245
    radicalisation 251, 252–4, 258
    rational choice theory 249
    reduction of crime 246–7, 259, 260
    reductionism 245, 250, 263
    referral orders 901, 906–7, 909, 921
    rehabilitation 246, 880–1
    reoffending 830
    resources, lack of 265–6
    responsibilisation 255
    restorative justice 901, 903, 906–7, 909, 914–16, 921–2, 925
    retribution 856, 858
    risk factors 258, 261–3
        artefactual risk factor theories 246
        Risk Factor Prevention Paradigm (RFPP) 246–7, 259, 261, 264, 659, 681
        twelve domains 261
    risk-focused interventions 261–4
    risk, reduction of 260
    Scared Straight programme 787–8
    social construction 242–3, 245, 255–6, 258
    social disorganisation theories 536–9
    social media 256
    social structures and processes, role of 255–9
    special educational needs 935
    statistics 163, 246
    stereotyping 258
    stigmatisation 256
    strong continuity 248
    structural background factors 248
    subcultural theories 151–2, 163, 165, 250–2, 256, 540–5, 582–3
    systemic issues 600
    teenage brain 240
    twin studies 244
    UN Convention on the Rights of the Child 1989 239, 259
    us and them 238, 258
    Western Europe, ages of criminal responsibility in 243
    young person, definition of 239
    Youth Inclusion and Support Panels (YISPs) 262–3
    Youth Inclusion Programmes (YIPs) 262–3
    Youth Justice Board (YJB) 261, 263–4, 744
    youth offender panels 903, 909
    Youth Offending Teams (YOTs) 1015–16
    Youth Restorative Disposal (YRD) 915
youth offending teams (YOTs) 262

Zaccone, Orlando 400
Zander, Michael 68, 69, 87
Zedner, Lucia 42, 44, 818–19
zemiology
    crime, definition of 48
    green criminology 363
    race and ethnicities 281–2, 300
    social harm 592, 595, 599, 602, 610–14
zero tolerance policies
    antisocial behaviour 808, 827
    crime control 803, 808, 823, 827
    police 624, 626, 631, 803, 812–13
    prevention of crime 779, 796
    punitiveness 390
    right realism 624, 631
    sex workers 796
    transnational criminology 413, 415
zonal theory 536–9.